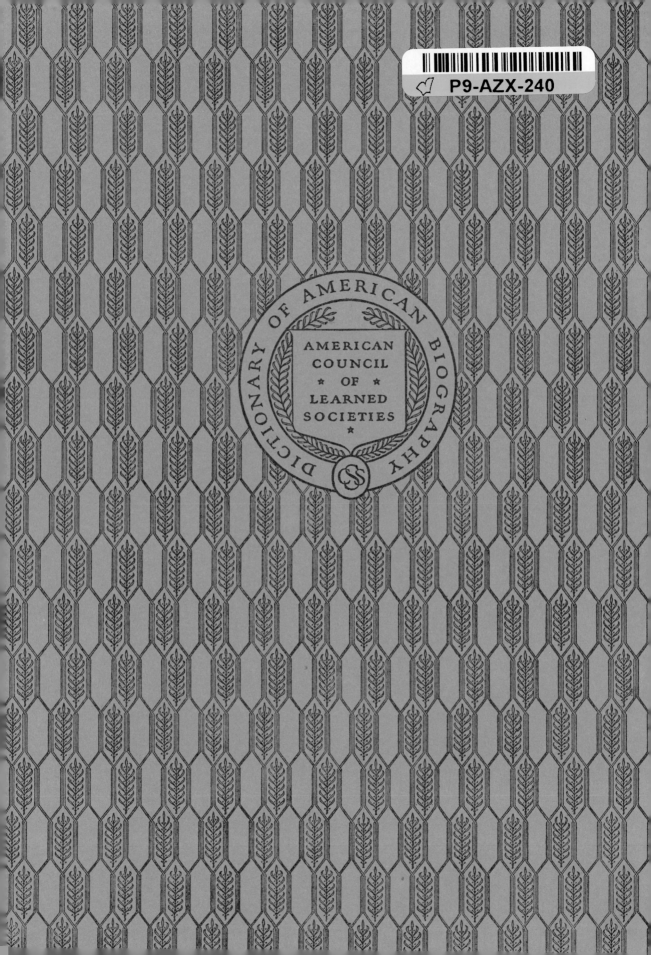

DICTIONARY OF AMERICAN BIOGRAPHY

AMERICAN
COUNCIL
★ OF ★
LEARNED
SOCIETIES
★

ACLS

DICTIONARY
OF AMERICAN BIOGRAPHY

PUBLISHED UNDER THE AUSPICES OF
THE AMERICAN COUNCIL OF LEARNED SOCIETIES

The American Council of Learned Societies, organized in 1919 for the purpose of advancing the study of the humanities and of the humanistic aspects of the social sciences, is a nonprofit federation comprising thirty-five national scholarly groups. The Council represents the humanities in the United States in the International Union of Academies, provides fellowships and grants-in-aid, supports research-and-planning conferences and symposia, and sponsors special projects and scholarly publications.

MEMBER ORGANIZATIONS

AMERICAN PHILOSOPHICAL SOCIETY, 1743
AMERICAN ACADEMY OF ARTS AND SCIENCES, 1780
AMERICAN ANTIQUARIAN SOCIETY, 1812
AMERICAN ORIENTAL SOCIETY, 1842
AMERICAN NUMISMATIC SOCIETY, 1858
AMERICAN PHILOLOGICAL ASSOCIATION, 1869
ARCHAEOLOGICAL INSTITUTE OF AMERICA, 1879
SOCIETY OF BIBLICAL LITERATURE, 1880
MODERN LANGUAGE ASSOCIATION OF AMERICA, 1883
AMERICAN HISTORICAL ASSOCIATION, 1884
AMERICAN ECONOMIC ASSOCIATION, 1885
AMERICAN FOLKLORE SOCIETY, 1888
AMERICAN DIALECT SOCIETY, 1889
ASSOCIATION OF AMERICAN LAW SCHOOLS, 1900
AMERICAN PHILOSOPHICAL ASSOCIATION, 1901
AMERICAN ANTHROPOLOGICAL ASSOCIATION, 1902
AMERICAN POLITICAL SCIENCE ASSOCIATION, 1903
BIBLIOGRAPHICAL SOCIETY OF AMERICA, 1904
ASSOCIATION OF AMERICAN GEOGRAPHERS, 1904
AMERICAN SOCIOLOGICAL ASSOCIATION, 1905
AMERICAN SOCIETY OF INTERNATIONAL LAW, 1906
ORGANIZATION OF AMERICAN HISTORIANS, 1907
COLLEGE ART ASSOCIATION OF AMERICA, 1912
HISTORY OF SCIENCE SOCIETY, 1924
LINGUISTIC SOCIETY OF AMERICA, 1924
MEDIAEVAL ACADEMY OF AMERICA, 1925
AMERICAN MUSICOLOGICAL SOCIETY, 1934
SOCIETY OF ARCHITECTURAL HISTORIANS, 1940
ECONOMIC HISTORY ASSOCIATION, 1940
ASSOCIATION FOR ASIAN STUDIES, 1941
AMERICAN SOCIETY FOR AESTHETICS, 1942
METAPHYSICAL SOCIETY OF AMERICA, 1950
AMERICAN STUDIES ASSOCIATION, 1950
RENAISSANCE SOCIETY OF AMERICA, 1954
SOCIETY FOR ETHNOMUSICOLOGY, 1955

DICTIONARY OF
American Biography

Supplement Three
1941–1945

Edward T. James, *Editor*

Philip M. Hosay, *Assistant Editor*
Marie Caskey, *Assistant Editor*
Philip De Vencentes, *Assistant Editor*

WITH AN INDEX GUIDE TO THE SUPPLEMENTS

Charles Scribner's Sons
NEW YORK

The preparation and publication of Supplement Three of the *DICTION-ARY OF AMERICAN BIOGRAPHY* has been made possible in part by the generosity of the New York Times Company. The preparation of the original twenty volumes of the Dictionary was made possible by the public-spirited action of the New York Times Company and its President, the late Adolph S. Ochs, in furnishing a subvention of more than $500,000. Entire responsibility for the contents of the Dictionary and its Supplements rests with the American Council of Learned Societies.

Printed in the United States of America
Library of Congress Catalog Card Number 44-41895
SBN 684-13199-4

American Council of Learned Societies Committee on the *Dictionary of American Biography*

Chairman, Walter Muir Whitehill

Alfred D. Chandler, Jr.   George W. Corner
Irving Dilliard   Wendell D. Garrett
Caryl P. Haskins   David McCord
Dumas Malone   Andrew Oliver

Frederick Burkhardt, *President, American Council of Learned Societies*

PREFACE

This volume is the third in a series of Supplements to the *Dictionary of American Biography* issued since the completion of the original set in 1936. Supplement Two carried the *Dictionary*'s coverage to the end of 1940. The present volume adds 573 significant figures who died during the succeeding five-year period, from the beginning of 1941 to the end of 1945. To facilitate locating a particular name, a consolidated list of the persons included in all three Supplements is appended to this volume.

The editors of Supplement Three have sought to meet the high scholarly and literary standards of the original work. The basis for inclusion remains the same: those listed are judged to have made a distinctive, not merely worthy, contribution to some aspect of American life. From a scrutiny of obituaries and necrologies covering the years 1941–45, the editorial staff assembled some 2,170 names for consideration. In choosing among them, the editors had the assistance of nearly 500 expert and uncompensated consultants, each of whom was sent a list of names in his field, which he was asked to rate on the basis of relative importance. These assessments gave the editors important guidance in making their final selection. As with earlier volumes, the writing of the biographical sketches was entrusted to a wide variety of contributors—475 in all—selected for their special knowledge of the person or his field of work. The dedicated and time-consuming effort of these contributors was often vastly out of proportion to the modest honorarium each received.

Like many similar enterprises, the *DAB* draws heavily on the goodwill of the scholarly community. Scores of local and specialized libraries have patiently answered inquiries and provided material to the contributors and editors. Students of reference librarianship at a group of library schools—Illinois, Wisconsin, Columbia, Carnegie (Pittsburgh), Emory, Louisiana State, the University of Wisconsin at

Preface

Milwaukee, and a special program at Brown—prepared biobibliographies on prospective *DAB* subjects that afforded helpful assistance to contributors and to the editorial staff. The *DAB* acknowledges its special obligation to Radcliffe College, which provided office space during the year 1968-69 and lent the assistance of its Hilles Library, and to Harvard University, which gave full and generous access to Widener Library and other libraries in the Harvard system, an indispensable resource in the editing and checking of articles.

The editors of Supplement Three have had the loyal support of many staff members. Research in connection with the gathering and weighing of names was done by Sheldon M. Stern, Margaret I. Porter, Helen L. Horowitz, and Helen R. Kessler. Editorial assistance of a high caliber was furnished by Lyle G. Boyd and, more briefly, by Paul Boyer and Janet W. James. The fundamentally important work of checking articles for accuracy was accomplished by two staff research associates, William F. Lichliter and Elizabeth F. Hoxie, together with a succession of part-time researchers, mostly graduate students at Harvard: J. Barry Bardo, George P. Birnbaum, Carl M. Brauer, Robert Jerrett III, Giora Kulka, Ernest Kurtz, Philip J. Lawrence, John O. C. Phillips, and Mitchell Zuckerman. Olivia A. Haehn and Karyn Fritzsche gave additional research assistance along with their secretarial duties. Elizabeth F. Hoxie and Alice Foster provided expert proofreading.

As with Supplement Two, the present volume is limited to persons who died in a given five-year period. From time to time names come to light that might well have been included in earlier volumes, and the editors hope eventually to be able to fill some of these gaps.

EDWARD T. JAMES

DICTIONARY
OF AMERICAN BIOGRAPHY

DICTIONARY OF

AMERICAN BIOGRAPHY

Adams — Young

ADAMS, HERBERT SAMUEL (Jan. 28, 1858–May 21, 1945), sculptor, was born in West Concord, Vt., the oldest of three children of Samuel Minot Adams, a native of that town, and Nancy Ann (Powers) Adams, whose birthplace was Croydon, N. H. His father, a machinist and patternmaker, soon moved the family to Fitchburg, Mass., where Herbert grew up. After education in local schools, he attended a technical school in Worcester, Mass., which later became the Worcester Polytechnic Institute, and the Massachusetts Normal Art School in Boston. In 1885 he went to Paris for a five-year stay, where he studied with the sculptor Antonin Mercié, the creator of "Gloria Victis," and established his own studio. One of his first pieces was a commission from the Town of Fitchburg: a bronze fountain (1888) depicting two boys playing with turtles. In Paris he also did the earliest of his portrait busts of women, generally acknowledged to be his most notable works. The best of these, the marble bust of Adeline Valentine Pond of Boston (now in the collection of the Hispanic Society of America in New York City), was exhibited at the Paris Salon of 1888. Miss Pond had also been a student of sculpture at the Massachusetts Normal Art School and in Paris, and on June 27, 1889, she and Adams were married in Auburndale, Mass. She later won some distinction as an art critic and author of *The Spirit of American Sculpture* (1923). The couple had no children.

In 1890 Adams began teaching at Pratt Institute in Brooklyn, N. Y. He gave up this post in 1898 to devote himself to his rapidly increasing commissions. Maintaining a studio in Greenwich Village, he later established another among the colony of artists settled near Cornish, N. H., where he was a close associate of the sculptors Augustus Saint-Gaudens [*q.v.*] and Daniel Chester French [Supp. 1]. As he took his place among the leaders of his profession, Adams executed works in bronze, marble, and terra cotta, including low reliefs, high reliefs, and figures in the round. Among them were architectural garden pieces and commemorative and portrait work for both public and private patrons.

Adams's portrait sculptures of women continued to win wide critical acclaim. In a marked departure from the bland neoclassic style, his delicate modeling and sensitive use of ornament and costume gave an effect of softness and spontaneity and created a new ideal of feminine beauty. In later portrait busts he introduced the use of tinting and of other materials such as wood, metals, and semiprecious stones to provide color. "Jeunesse" (Metropolitan Museum of Art, New York City) is of rose marble, gumwood, and silver gilt, with accessories of topaz and turquoise. Other polychrome busts include those of Mrs. Stephen H. Olin, Miss Marguerite du Pont, and the actress Julia Marlowe in the costume she wore as Juliet. Adams's straight portrait busts, such as his bronze study of Will Rogers, in Oklahoma City, Okla., were also successful, though less outstanding.

Adams early became known also for his portrait statues, including the bronze William Ellery Channing in the Boston Public Garden; the seated William Cullen Bryant, in Bryant Park behind the New York Public Library; and the strongly modeled Joseph Henry, commissioned by the Library of Congress and showing the influence of Saint-Gaudens. For churches and public buildings he executed a number of bronze doors, beginning with those for the Library of Congress, left unfinished at the death of Olin L. Warner, for which he composed female figures representing Truth and Research. The figures for the doors of the American Academy of Arts and Letters in New York City symbolized the various arts, and Adams made much further use of such personification of abstract concepts, a mode of sculptural decoration then popular. His doors for St. Bartholomew's Church, also in New York, were surmounted by a marble tympanum portraying Madonna and Child with kneeling angels. Many church memorials which he designed included angels of high artistic distinction. Subjects midway between the ideal and the real are "Girl with Water-Lilies" (Clapp Gardens, Cleveland, Ohio) and "Nymph of the Fynmere" (Cooperstown, N. Y.). Adams was also known for his incidental renderings of fruit and flowers, which gave freshness and sympathy to the larger works they ornamented.

His architectural sculpture includes a number of marble and bronze figures designed for courthouses and other public buildings. In the McMillan Fountain, Washington, D. C., in his war memorials for Winchester and Fitchburg, Mass., and in the figure of "Michigan," set against a lofty marble pylon in the Vicksburg (Miss.) Military Park, the elegant and vernacular traditions tend to merge, showing his gifts as an interpreter of the American dream.

Adams's career reached its peak about 1910. He continued to receive many commissions, but the advance of modern art gradually diminished his standing, though not the respect and affection which he evoked as a person. He figures in many memoirs of members of the Cornish colony, including that of Mrs. Daniel Chester French, who spoke of the simplicity and charm of the Adamses' home there, showing "no effort, no expense, no display." Adams was a founder (1893) of the National Sculpture Society and three times its president. Active in its affairs to the end of his life, he saw it gradually lose ground to the proponents of abstract art. Both at its meetings and individually he gave generous encouragement and counsel to younger sculptors, and the society now awards a Herbert Adams Memorial Medal as one of its highest honors. Adams was also president (1917–20) and an Academician of the National Academy of Design, a member of the American Academy of Arts and Letters, and the sculptor member

of the federal Commission of the Fine Arts. Yale University and Tufts College awarded him honorary degrees. He died in 1945, at the age of eighty-seven, in Doctors Hospital, New York City.

[Biographical material about Adams is slight; see *Nat. Cyc. Am. Biog.,* XIII, 510–11; *Who Was Who in America,* vol. II (1950); *N. Y. Times,* May 22, 1945. On his family, see Andrew N. Adams, *A Genealogical Hist. of Henry Adams of Braintree and His Descendants* (1898), pp. 1041, 1083; this gives his birth date as Jan. 25, but his birth certificate (Town of Concord, Vt.) confirms Jan. 28. The Art Dept. of the N.Y. Public Lib. has folios bequeathed by Adams's widow and scrapbooks. For comments on his sculpture, see: Lorado Taft, *Hist. of Am. Sculpture* (1903); Charles H. Caffin, *Am. Masters of Sculpture* (1903); Pan American Union, *Bull.,* July 1917; Ernest Peixotto in *Am. Mag. of Art,* May 1921; Beatrice G. Proske, *Brookgreen Gardens Sculpture* (1943); Wheeler Williams in *Nat. Sculpture Rev.,* Fall 1963; Wayne Craven, *Sculpture in America* (1968). For a personal impression, see Mary French, *Memories of a Sculptor's Wife* (1928).]

WILLIAM SENER RUSK

ADE, GEORGE (Feb. 9, 1866–May 16, 1944), author and playwright, was born in Kentland, Ind., the sixth of seven children and youngest of three sons. His father, John Ade, had migrated with his family in 1840 from Lewes, England, to Cheviot, Ohio. His mother, Adaline (Bush) Ade, was a native Ohioan of Scotch-Irish ancestry. At the time of George's birth his father was cashier in a local bank. Attending the Kentland village schools and working during the summers on a farm, young George developed a reputation as an absentminded dreamer with an appetite for reading but with little aptitude for farming. He rejected the influence of both his mother's Methodist faith and his father's affiliation with the Campbellite Church. In 1881, when he was fifteen, a local newspaper published one of his high school essays, his first appearance in print.

Two years later Ade entered Purdue University, the newly established agricultural school at nearby Lafayette. His father expected him to acquire a useful vocation in agriculture or the mechanical arts, but college only strengthened Ade's literary inclinations. Although he received a Bachelor of Science degree, he dodged mathematics and science as much as possible and excelled in English composition and literature. A thoughtful but popular student, he was president both of his fraternity, Sigma Chi, and of the literary society. He also frequented the Grand Opera House in Lafayette, where he took undifferentiated delight in the dramas, light operas, comedies, and minstrel shows performed by touring companies.

After finishing college Ade briefly studied law and had indifferent success as a reporter for Lafayette newspapers and as an advertising writer for a patent medicine firm. In 1890, on the advice of John T. McCutcheon, a Purdue friend who became a noted political cartoonist, Ade moved to Chicago and secured a job as a reporter for the Chicago *Morning News*. His quick wit, his enthusiasm for the Chicago scene, his eye for odd and amusing incidents, and his ability to find interest and significance in ordinary people and events—"shop-girls and stray dogs and cable-car conductors"—soon made him a leading reporter on the *Morning News* (later the *News-Record*, and then the *Record*). When the Columbian Exposition opened in Chicago in 1893, Ade was given the freedom to develop his own material in a column entitled "All Roads Lead to the World's Fair." His success with vignettes of people and incidents at the fair led to the establishment of his permanent daily column, "Stories of the Streets and of the Town." Illustrated by McCutcheon, the stories were so popular that the *Record* collected and sold them in paperback form. In 1896 Ade published his first book, *Artie*, composed of loosely related sketches concerning Artie Blanchard, a slangy, good-hearted office worker whose adventures had appeared intermittently in Ade's column. Two similar collections followed, centering about the characters of *Pink Marsh*, a Negro bootblack (1897), and *Doc' Horne* (1899).

In 1897, feeling "the necessity of concocting something different," Ade set out to develop a new form of sketch that would use current idioms and catch phrases, "because they were the salt needed for the proper savoring." Appearing in the *Record* on Sept. 17, "The Fable of Sister Mae, Who Did as Well as Could Be Expected" (as it was later titled) was the first of his celebrated "fables in slang." Encouraged by readers, friends, and an alert publishing house, Ade wrote a number of such pieces for his column in the *Record*; a collection, *Fables in Slang*, appeared in 1899. The book was an enormous success, selling 69,000 copies in the first year. Readers and critics alike were delighted by the character types impaled on a single phrase in this and subsequent volumes—the Martyr Who Liked the Job; the Music Teacher who came twice each week to bridge the awful chasm between Dorothy and Chopin; the Boarder who belonged to a Social Purity Club that had a Yell; Conventional Young Men, of the Kind that you see wearing Spring Overcoats in the Clothing Advertisements. Ade's audience also enjoyed the satirical deflation of country ignorance and city pretensions; the language, a mélange of contemporary colloquial expressions and clichés leavened by Ade's ability to twist new colloquialisms out of old and to create remarkable vernacular metaphors whose

imaginative brilliance was often masked by their homely rhetoric; a style of capitalization that provided an overwash of irony; and capstone morals that parodied the sober pomposity of the tales in McGuffey's *Readers*. Syndication of the fables soon followed, as did other collections in book form, including *More Fables* (1900), *Forty Modern Fables* (1901), *The Girl Proposition* (1902), and *People You Know* (1903).

Ade left the *Record* in 1900 and for a decade devoted his energies to writing for the stage. He produced a series of hits in both musical comedy (*The Sultan of Sulu*, 1902; *The Sho-Gun*, 1904) and dramatic comedy (*The County Chairman*, 1903; *The College Widow*, 1904, his best-known play; *Just Out of College*, 1905; *Father and the Boys*, 1908; and others). *The County Chairman*, said Ade, "contains no mystery, sex, crime, or triangular complications. It deals with neighborhood factions and local political feuds in a decidedly one-horse town." *The College Widow* also dealt with small-town life and introduced a new subject—collegiate adventures—to the American stage. Both plays well represent Ade's characteristic Horatian satire: genial, witty, sympathetic. Both were enthusiastically received and had extensive New York runs followed by long-lived road company productions. Ade's royalties occasionally amounted to $5,000 a week.

He invested much of the income from his writings in farmland in his native Newton County, Ind., including a 400-acre country estate, Hazelden, near Brook, where he settled permanently in 1904. Never having married, he spent the later years of his life in extensive foreign travel, in entertaining his many friends at Hazelden, and in social, political, and philanthropic activities. He served as a delegate to the Republican National Convention in 1908, trustee of Purdue University (1908–15), chief national officer of Sigma Chi, and director of publicity for the Indiana State Council of Defense during World War I. One of his last books, *The Old-Time Saloon* (1931), expressed his opposition to prohibition. All told, his works total more than three dozen books (most of them collections of short pieces), over a dozen plays, and at least 2,500 periodical pieces. Ade suffered a cerebral hemorrhage in June 1943 and died nearly a year later in Brook, Ind. He was buried in the family plot at Fairlawn Cemetery in nearby Kentland.

Though Ade enjoyed considerable contemporary fame (in 1908 he was elected to membership in the National Institute of Arts and Letters), his reputation declined sharply after World War I—perhaps because he had followed too closely the moral of one of his own fables: "Give the

People what they Think they want." He admittedly dealt in minor forms, and he lacked the sense of tragedy that gives depth to the humor of Mark Twain, whom he greatly admired. He was, for the most part, a satirist of the surface who attacked foibles rather than evils. But though his targets were small he hit them with precision. Such plays as *The College Widow* raised the standards of dramatic comedy in Ade's day and are still revived by amateur companies. Many of the stories which sprang from his journalism have not only retained their vitality but have become a significant social record of the age, and the fables are rediscovered with delight by every generation.

[Ade wrote a series of reminiscences published in *Cosmopolitan* and *Hearst's International,* especially vols. LXXVIII–LXXXII (1925–27) of the latter after it absorbed *Cosmopolitan;* and he contributed a brief autobiographical sketch to Stanley J. Kunitz, ed., *Authors Today and Yesterday* (1933). The only biography is Fred C. Kelly, *George Ade: Warmhearted Satirist* (1947). Kelly also edited *The Permanent Ade* (1947). See in addition William Dean Howells, "Certain of the Chicago School of Fiction," *North Am. Rev.,* May 1903, and "Editor's Easy Chair," *Harper's Monthly Mag.,* Feb. 1917; H. L. Mencken, *Prejudices: First Series* (1919); Thomas L. Masson, *Our Am. Humorists* (1922); Carl Van Doren, "Old Wisdom in a New Tongue," *Century Mag.,* Jan. 1923; Franklin J. Meine's introduction to his excellent edition of Ade's *Stories of the Streets and of the Town* (1941); obituary in *N. Y. Times,* May 17, 1944; Lowell Matson, "Ade—Who Needed None," *Literary Rev.,* Autumn 1961; Lee Coyle, *George Ade* (1964). Ade's place of death, given incorrectly in the *N. Y. Times* obituary, was confirmed by his death certificate (Ind. State Board of Health) and by Helen Thompson, Librarian, Brook-Iroquois Township Public Lib., Brook, Ind. Ade's writings are described in Dorothy R. Russo's definitive *Bibliog. of George Ade* (1947). His MSS., library, and papers were bequeathed to Purdue Univ.]
HAROLD H. KOLB, JR.

ADIE, DAVID CRAIG (Sept. 3, 1888–Feb. 23, 1943), social worker, was born in Hamilton, Scotland, the youngest of four children of Lawrence and Madeline (Cooper) Adie. His father was a railway passenger agent, and the family's resources were meager. Trained as a bookbinder in his youth, David Adie later became a labor organizer and joined the Independent Labour Party. Although he lacked a formal education, he read a good deal on his own, especially about America, and in 1913, after a brief stay in Canada, he emigrated to the United States. He settled in Minneapolis, Minn., where he found work in 1914 as assistant secretary of the Minneapolis Civic and Commerce Association, responsible for cultivating good relations between business interests and trade unions. On July 31, 1916, he married Ann Herr of Minneapolis, by whom he had one daughter, Jean Cooper.

When the United States entered World War I, Adie became an adviser to the Minnesota Public Safety Commission, which was responsible for the recruitment and placement of workers in factories. He also directed the reorganization of the state employment service, which regulated farm labor. An appointment as associate secretary of the War Labor Policies Board in 1918, a year before he became a citizen, took him to Washington, D. C., where he developed his skills as a labor arbitrator. After the war, in 1919, he became the impartial chairman of the arbitration board for the men's and boys' clothing industry in New York City, with responsibility for settling industrial disputes in some 2,000 factories employing about 70,000 workers. Adie then served briefly, from 1921 to 1922, as campaign manager of the American City Bureau in New York, which encouraged chambers of commerce to participate in civic and social service activities.

His work with this organization stimulated his interest in social work, and in 1921 he became the general secretary of the Charity Organization Society of Buffalo, N. Y., the oldest group of its kind in the nation. Under his leadership the Society's focus shifted from community social work to family welfare and casework. Convinced that welfare had become a science requiring the services of highly trained personnel, Adie helped establish a school of social work at the University of Buffalo and lectured there. He also was one of the founders of the Buffalo Council of Social Agencies, which acted as a coordinating center for about seventy-five local charities, and served as its first executive secretary.

Late in 1929 Adie was appointed by Gov. Franklin D. Roosevelt to the New York State Social Welfare Board. Three years later the board elected him State Commissioner of Social Welfare. In this capacity Adie appointed the heads of the city and county welfare districts, supervised their activities, enforced the public welfare law, and administered institutional and hospital care for delinquent children and the disabled, as well as public assistance programs for the aged, the blind, veterans, and dependent children and mothers. He was also an ex-officio member of the Temporary Emergency Relief Administration, which had been established in 1931 as a depression agency to provide public assistance to the unemployed through home and work relief. In 1937, after the federal Works Progress Administration had largely supplanted the state's work relief program, the TERA was disbanded and Adie assumed responsibility for its home relief operations.

By this time he had come to believe that permanent public assistance and social insurance programs were necessary to compensate for the inability of the economic system to provide everyone with the means of self-support. He felt that the resurgence of the economy at the end of the decade would create new job opportunities, but he nevertheless warned that aid to the blind, the aged, and other groups of unemployables would continue to increase. Convinced that unemployment was a national problem, he favored the broadening of federal social insurance, the implementation of state and federal rehabilitation services, and the creation of a federal welfare program which, through grants-in-aid to the states, would establish nationwide standards of eligibility and minimum and maximum allowances.

Adie was a compassionate individual who had deep insight into others and an ability to identify with the oppressed. Deeply religious, he had been a Methodist lay preacher in Scotland, but later became a Unitarian. In his speech he always retained the Scottish burr. Adie died at the age of fifty-four of peritonitis following surgery for a duodenal ulcer at the Albany (N. Y.) Hospital. His body was cremated at the Earl Crematorium in Troy, N. Y.

[David C. Adie, "Responsibility of the State in the Supervision of Public Welfare Programs," *Social Service Rev.*, Dec. 1939; Charity Organization Soc. of Buffalo, *Fifty Years of Family Social Work* (1927); N. Y. State Dept. of Social Welfare, *Democracy Cares: The Story Behind Public Assistance in N. Y. State* (1941); Emma O. Lundberg, "Pathfinders of the Middle Years," *Social Service Rev.*, Mar. 1947, pp. 31–34; unpublished paper on Adie by Arthur W. Lockner, Jr. (1958); obituaries in *Survey Midmonthly,* Mar. 1943, and *N. Y. Times,* Feb. 24, 1943.]

DAVID M. SCHNEIDER

ALFORD, LEON PRATT (Jan. 3, 1877– Jan. 2, 1942), publicist of industrial management, was born in Simsbury, Conn., the youngest of five children (four boys and one girl) of Emerson and Sarah Merriam (Pratt) Alford. His father, who had earlier been one of Connecticut's pioneer tobacco growers, was superintendent of the Collins Axe Company; he later (1886–87) served in the state legislature. Young Alford was educated at the Plainville (Conn.) high school and the Worcester (Mass.) Polytechnic Institute, where he received the B.S. degree in electrical engineering in 1896. He then joined the McKay Metallic Fastening Association in Winchester, Mass., which in 1902 became part of the United Shoe Machinery Company. Alford rose rapidly from assistant machine shop foreman to production superintendent, and when in 1902 the United Shoe Machinery Company built a new plant in Beverly, Mass.—at the time the world's largest reinforced concrete factory building—he assisted in its design and in the installation of its machinery. Over the next few years,

while working in the new plant, Alford completed a thesis entitled "Power Problems in Connection with the Development of Plans for a Manufacturing Plant," for which in 1905 he received the M.E. degree from Worcester Polytechnic. The following year he was promoted to head of United Shoe's mechanical engineering department.

Alford moved to New York City in 1907 to become associate editor of the *American Machinist,* a prestigious machinery and manufacturing journal to which he had contributed articles. While in New York he also became active in the American Society for Mechanical Engineers (A.S.M.E.), and through it became acquainted with such pioneers in industrial management as Frederick W. Taylor and Henry L. Gantt [*qq.v.*]. Thereafter Alford devoted his life to publicizing the ideas and programs of this movement.

Alford's report of 1911, "The Present State of the Art of Industrial Management," constituted in effect the first endorsement of Taylor's approach by the A.S.M.E. In two later reports for that organization (1922, 1932) Alford summed up and analyzed developments of the preceding decades. As editor-in-chief, from 1911 to 1917, of the *American Machinist,* and then as editor of *Industrial Management* (1917–20), *Management Engineering* (1921–23), and *Manufacturing Industries* (1923–28), he provided a platform for ideas in industrial management. He himself wrote many articles interpreting the work of Taylor, Gantt, and others to a large audience of engineers; he published a biography of Gantt in 1934. At the 1926 meeting of the A.S.M.E., Alford read a widely praised paper in which he presented a codification of scientific management principles. This codification, later expanded and published as *Laws of Management Applied to Manufacturing* (1928), earned its author in 1927 the first Melville Gold Medal awarded by the A.S.M.E.; it was largely incorporated into his later text, *Principles of Industrial Management* (1940). In 1927 Alford helped organize the Institute of Management, a research group affiliated with the American Management Association, and later served as the Institute's president. He received the Gantt Medal of the A.S.M.E. in 1931.

As vice-president from 1922 to 1934 of the Ronald Press Company, Alford prepared some of the first handbooks in the management field, *Management's Handbook* (1924) and *Cost and Production Handbook* (1934). He was active in other groups, including the American Engineering Council and the Society for the Promotion of Engineering Education. He left Ronald Press in 1934 (though remaining on its board of directors) to head the manufacturing costs unit of the Federal Communications Commission. In 1937 he was appointed chairman of the department of industrial engineering at New York University, a position he retained until his death.

On Jan. 1, 1900, Alford had married Grace Agnes Hutchins of Templeton, Mass., by whom he had one child, Ralph Irving. He was affiliated with the Methodist Episcopal Church. He died of a heart ailment at the Flower and Fifth Avenue Hospital in New York City the day before his sixty-fifth birthday, and was buried at Avon, Conn. Though not himself a management consultant, Alford performed a useful service in documenting, publicizing, and organizing the ideas and achievements of the theorists and practitioners in the burgeoning field of industrial management.

[William J. Jaffe, *L. P. Alford and the Evolution of Modern Industrial Management* (1957), is the principal source. See also Lyndall Urwick, ed., *The Golden Book of Management* (1956), pp. 192–95; *Who Was Who in America*, vol. II (1950); *Nat. Cyc. Am. Biog.*, Current Vol. A, pp. 183–84; and obituaries in *N. Y. Times*, Jan. 3, 1942, and *Mechanical Engineering*, Feb. 1942. Alford's papers are at N. Y. Univ.]

MILTON J. NADWORNY

ALLEN, EDGAR (May 2, 1892–Mar. 3, 1943), physiologist and anatomist, was born in Canyon City, Colo., the fifth of nine children and second of four surviving sons of Asa and Edith (Day) Allen. Both parents were descended from English settlers in New England in the 1630's, though the Allens, as Loyalists during the American Revolution, had removed to Canada, where Edgar's father was born. A graduate of the New York Medical School, Asa Allen had moved west with his wife via Michigan and Wisconsin; for a time he practiced in the gold-rush town of Cripple Creek, Colo. In 1900 he moved back east to Providence, R. I., where Edgar grew up. The family was not prosperous. When Edgar was in his early teens his father died, his mother found work as a librarian, and he and his brothers (one of whom, Richard Day Allen, became a leader in the vocational education movement) worked at odd jobs while attending high school in Pawtucket and Cranston, R. I. Edgar then entered Brown University, where he earned his way by waiting on table, tending furnaces, reading electric or gas meters, and teaching swimming. He also learned to sail in Narragansett Bay and Long Island Sound and acquired a love for the sea that continued throughout his life.

After receiving the Ph.B. degree from Brown in 1915, Allen entered the graduate school there to study biology and embryology, receiving the M.A. in 1916. His studies were interrupted by World War I, in which he served in France with a mobile unit of the Sanitary Corps. In 1919 he became an instructor in anatomy at Washington University, St. Louis, Mo. There he carried out research for his doctoral thesis, "The Oestrous Cycle of the Mouse," receiving his Ph.D. from Brown in 1921. These studies stimulated his interest in the physiology of reproduction and the sources of the ovarian hormones that induce the changes occurring during the estrous cycle. Working in close collaboration with the biochemist Edward A. Doisy, he was able to extract from ovarian follicles a cell-free material that produced the vaginal and uterine growth characteristic of that occurring during estrus. This finding, first reported in the spring of 1923 at a meeting of anatomists in Chicago, started a course of research that occupied both Allen and Doisy for many years.

In 1923 Allen was appointed professor of anatomy and chairman of the department in the medical school of the University of Missouri at Columbia, and in 1930 he became dean of the school and director of the University Hospitals. During this period he continued research on ovarian physiology and endocrinology with Doisy, who purified and subsequently chemically identified one of the female sex hormones, estradiol. Allen also collaborated with others, especially J. P. Pratt, chief gynecologist at the Henry Ford Hospital in Detroit, in studies of ova, ovarian function, and ovulation in women, work that culminated in their securing the first living ova from the human oviduct. Allen also established a colony of rhesus monkeys so that he could study ovarian function and regulation in primates.

In 1933 Allen left the University of Missouri to become professor of anatomy at the Yale University medical school. There he established laboratories to continue his studies on the endocrine aspects of reproduction, and also developed an intense interest in the relation of sex hormones to cancer. The action of the ovarian follicular hormones in stimulating growth especially interested him. His tremendous enthusiasm and energy attracted investigators, young and old, to work with him, and also attracted funds to support his researches.

Allen's publications, alone and with collaborators, number nearly 150 papers and books. While at Missouri he edited and wrote a chapter for the first edition of *Sex and Internal Secretions* (1932), a collection of contributions by endocrinologists and biologists. His papers dealt with the influence of estrogens in producing mammary and uterine cancer, with estrogen-withdrawal uterine bleeding in monkeys, with the application of colchicine to the study of growth processes, and with the mammalian egg and its development. Allen was president of the American Society for the Study of Internal Secretions (1941–42), which later became the Endocrine Society, and, at the time of his death, of the American Association of Anatomists. He received honorary degrees from Brown and Washington universities and was enrolled in the Legion of Honor in Paris in 1937. He was awarded the Baly Medal of the Royal College of Physicians in London in 1941.

On July 28, 1918, in Providence, R. I., Allen had married Marion Robins Pfeiffer, a student at Pembroke, the women's college of Brown. Their two daughters were Frances Isabelle and Marjorie Eleanor. The proximity of New Haven to Long Island Sound allowed Allen to enjoy the pleasures of sailing. Ruddy-faced, full of enthusiasm and drive, Allen had become white-haired at an early age, but he never tired of challenging the winds and tides. In 1934 he suffered a severe coronary occlusion, but after his recovery continued to work. At the beginning of World War II he joined the Coast Guard Auxiliary, and while on patrol he died of a heart attack, at the age of fifty. He was cremated, and the ashes scattered at sea.

[The fullest biographical account is in William C. Young, ed., *Sex and Internal Secretions*, vol. I (3rd ed., 1961), pp. xiii–xix. See also obituary by George W. Corner, C. H. Danforth, and L. S. Stone in *Anatomical Record*, Aug. 1943; and W. U. Gardner in *Science*, Apr. 23, 1943, and in *Yale Jour. of Biology and Medicine*, Mar. 1943. For a bibliography of Allen's publications see *ibid.*, Oct. 1944. Family information from Eleanor Allen (Mrs. George T.) Welch, a sister, and Frances Allen (Mrs. Garland J.) Marrs, a daughter.]

W. U. GARDNER

ALLEN, EDWARD TYSON (Dec. 26, 1875–May 27, 1942), forester, was born in New Haven, Conn., the youngest of the three sons of Oscar Dana Allen and Fidelia Roberts (Totman) Allen. His father, whose family had deep roots in New England, was professor of metallurgy and of analytical chemistry at Yale. Edward attended public schools until the age of thirteen. Thereafter he was tutored by his father, from whom he received an excellent education in the natural sciences, especially botany. When Oscar Allen retired in 1884, the family moved to southern California and, in 1888, to the state of Washington, where they took up a wilderness homestead near Mount Rainier. It was here that young Allen learned his forest lore.

In 1898, after a year as a reporter for the *Tacoma Ledger*, Allen was appointed forest ranger for the national forest reserves in the Pacific Northwest. The following year he joined the Bureau of Forestry—later renamed the Forest Service—in the United States Department of Agriculture and began a close association with the head of the bureau, Gifford Pinchot. As one of Pinchot's elite group of "boundary boys" in 1903–04, Allen helped determine national forest boundaries in vast regions of the West. He was appointed California State Forester in 1905 on Pinchot's recommendation, becoming one of the first persons in the nation to hold such a position. In 1906 he returned to the Forest Service and over the next three years was an inspector and district forester in charge of the national forests in Oregon, Washington, and Alaska. He drew up the first contract for the sale of standing timber in the national forests, a document that became a model for future timber contracts, and wrote the first authoritative manual on the administration of the national forest reserves.

Allen left public service in 1909 to become forester and manager of the Western Forestry and Conservation Association, an organization that he had helped to found. Composed chiefly of private forest-fire patrol associations in Idaho, Montana, Oregon, Washington, and California, it became one of the most dynamic private forestry groups in the West. Except for brief service during World War I as a member of the lumber committee of the Council of National Defense, which had jurisdiction over the purchase of lumber for war uses, Allen remained with the association until his retirement in 1932. He frequently acted as a mediator between the federal government and the lumber industry in disputes over excess profits taxes and governmental regulation of forest practices, and he acquired expert knowledge in forest economics and taxation. A strong advocate of the policy of "cooperation" in national forestry, Allen believed that timber owners could be educated to the advantages of scientific forestry and would adopt sound management practices out of a sense of enlightened self-interest. In this he differed from Pinchot, especially during the 1920's, opposing his old friend's proposed plan for compulsory regulation of timber cutting. Allen supported the efforts of William B. Greeley, head of the Forest Service from 1920 to 1928, to implement cooperative forestry policies. An accomplished publicist and lobbyist, Allen also helped draft the Clarke-McNary Act of 1924, which had a major influence on national forest policies in succeeding years. The act authorized cooperative federal-state programs in fire protection, in reforestation of denuded lands, in the encouragement of farm forestry, and in the purchase of cutover timber lands for inclusion in the national forests.

In his long career Allen participated in almost every aspect of forestry. He was one of the pioneers of federal and state forestry programs. He was a charter member (1900) of the Society of American Foresters and, at various times, a consultant to the Department of Agriculture, the Treasury Department, the Federal Trade Commission, and the Department of the Interior. He was for many years one of the chief spokesmen for the National Lumber Manufacturers' Association, serving both on its board of directors and as its counsel. He was a member of the National Forestry Program Committee. He published numerous articles in popular magazines and trade journals and was an expert on the life cycle of the Western hemlock. He also drafted a number of state forestry codes.

On Oct. 20, 1902, Allen married Matilda Price Riley of Norbeck, Md., who wrote fiction under the pseudonym "Maryland Allen." They had two daughters, Olmsted Tyson and Barbara. After the death of his first wife in 1927, he married on Feb. 18, 1928, Mildred Grudolf-Smith. Allen died of cancer at the age of sixty-six in Portland, Oreg., where he had made his home.

[There is correspondence by Allen in the following collections: Western Forestry and Conservation Assoc. records (Oreg. Hist. Soc.), Nat. Forestry Program Committee records (Cornell Univ.), Forest Service records (Nat. Archives), Gifford Pinchot Papers (Lib. of Cong.), William B. Greeley Papers (Univ. of Oreg.), and George C. Pardee Papers (Bancroft Lib., Univ. of Calif.). The best biographical sketches are in C. Raymond Clar, *Calif. Government and Forestry* (1959), pp. 247–49 (photograph on p. 233), and *Nat. Cyc. Am. Biog.*, XVIII, 27. Also useful is *Who Was Who in America*, vol. III (1960). There is information about Allen in: Gifford Pinchot, *Breaking New Ground* (1947); William B. Greeley, *Forests and Men* (1951); and George T. Morgan, *William B. Greeley* (1961). A Ph.D. dissertation by Lawrence Rakestraw, "A Hist. of Forest Conservation in the Pacific Northwest" (Univ. of Wash., 1955), places Allen in the context of local and state politics. The following articles provide insight into Allen's career as a forester: George T. Morgan, "The Fight against Fire: Development of Cooperative Forestry in the Pacific Northwest," *Idaho Yesterdays*, Winter 1962; Ralph S. Hosmer, "The Nat. Forestry Program Committee, 1919–1928," *Jour. of Forestry*, Sept. 1947; Shirley W. Allen, "We Present E. T. Allen," *Jour. of Forestry*, Mar. 1945; and "Interesting Westerners," *Sunset*, Sept. 1916 (with photograph). Among Allen's own articles, two are particularly revealing: "Method of Forestry Campaigning," *Am. Forestry*, Oct. 1912; and "Men, Trees and an Idea: The Genesis of a Great Fire Protective Plan," *Am. Forests and Forest Life*, Sept. 1926. His obituary appears in the *Portland Oregonian*, May 28, 1942.]

DONALD C. SWAIN

ALLEN, GLOVER MORRILL (Feb. 8, 1879–Feb. 15, 1942), naturalist, was born in Walpole, N. H., the second of three children and only son of the Rev. Nathaniel Glover Allen by his second wife, Harriet Ann Schouler. Both parents were natives of Massachusetts. The father,

himself the son of a minister, was a graduate of Harvard and the General Theological Seminary (Episcopal) in New York City. Already sixty-eight when his son was born, he died ten years later. On his mother's side, Allen was descended from James Scouler [*sic*], a calico printer who emigrated from Scotland in 1815; both his grandfather, William Schouler, journalist and public official, and an uncle, James Schouler, lawyer and historian [*qq.v.*], were prominent figures in Massachusetts.

Glover Allen grew up in Newton, Mass., where the family lived after his father's retirement in 1885. As a youth he spent much time observing the wildlife there and in the White Mountains, especially near Intervale, N. H., where his uncle James Schouler had a summer place. His ability as a naturalist was early apparent. The first of a number of accounts he wrote of local birds was published when he was only eleven, and while he was still in the Newton high school he prepared a well-documented collection of specimens of local mammals.

In 1901 Allen graduated magna cum laude from Harvard, where, in addition to the usual languages, he had learned Russian and in his spare time taught himself Danish. That same year he was appointed secretary and librarian of the Boston Society of Natural History. Continuing his studies, he received a Ph.D. in biology at Harvard in 1904 (with a thesis on "The Heredity of Coat Color in Mice") and went on to postdoctoral studies in forestry at the university and at the Harvard Engineering Camp on Squam Lake, N. H. Finding forestry less congenial than zoology, in September 1907 he applied successfully to Samuel Henshaw, director of the Museum of Comparative Zoology at Harvard, for a part-time job there.

By inclination both naturalist and scholar, Allen divided his time over the next two decades between his posts at Harvard and the Boston Society of Natural History. At the museum he had virtual charge, from 1907, of the mammal collections, although it was not until 1925 that he was formally appointed curator. For more than twenty years he took care of the department almost single-handed. The collections grew to be among the most representative and usefully organized of any in the world, largely because their orderly arrangement was an expression of his careful taxonomic judgment.

As librarian of the Boston Society of Natural History, a post which he held until 1928, Allen's knowledge of the literature and the ease with which he read many European languages enabled him to contribute much to the research of others. Because of these abilities, together with his precise command of English, his editorial work for the society set a high standard for the publications under his care. To these and other journals he regularly contributed perceptive reviews of current papers on birds and mammals. His competence in both fields is well attested by the fact that in 1936, at the height of his career as a mammalogist, he was made editor of the *Auk*, the journal of the American Ornithologists' Union. His scientific writings were "models of directness, clarity, and accuracy" (Clark, p. 266).

In 1924 Allen was appointed lecturer in zoology at Harvard. He gave two half-courses yearly on the natural history of birds and mammals; becoming an associate professor of zoology in 1928, he was appointed professor in 1938. Although classroom instruction held little interest for him, his great store of knowledge and his patience exerted a lasting influence on individual students at a time when the study of mammalogy was expanding in the United States.

Allen had a retentive memory which, coupled with remarkably accurate powers of observation and a precise ear, contributed much to his abilities both as a field naturalist and as a taxonomist. He made collecting trips to the Bahamas (1903), Labrador (1906), East Africa (1909), the British West Indies (1910), again to various parts of Africa (1912, 1926), Brazil (1929), and Australia (1931). These trips were usually not undertaken to further specific research projects, but the observations and material collected stimulated future work. Thus his *A Checklist of African Mammals* (1939) grew out of earlier regional studies in the Sudan, East Africa, and Liberia. His *The Whalebone Whales of New England* (1916), though it originated in field observations, not only provides a very thorough description of the morphological characteristics and known behavior of the species but also gives a carefully documented list of sightings and strandings. Of his most important works, *The Mammals of China and Mongolia* (2 vols., 1938–40) is noteworthy both for the excellence of the systematic treatment and for the careful historical account of studies of the area. His *Bats* (1939) remains the most detailed, accurate, and thoroughly readable general account available. His publications also include papers dealing with genetics, fossil mammals, and comparative anatomy.

Although shy and somewhat retiring, Allen took an active part in a number of professional organizations. A member of the Nuttall Ornithological Club, he served as president from 1919 to 1942. He was a charter member (1919) of the American Society of Mammalogists, and later became its president (1927–29); and in 1921 he

was made a fellow of the American Ornithologists' Union.

Allen was married on June 26, 1911, to Sarah Moody Cushing of Newburyport, Mass.; their only child was Elizabeth Cushing. He died in Cambridge of a coronary attack at the age of sixty-three and was buried there in Mount Auburn Cemetery.

[For family background see Allen H. Bent, *Walter Allen of Newbury, Mass., 1640, and Some of His Descendants* (1896). The following obituary articles give good accounts of the facets of Allen's personality as seen by a variety of his associates and include details of his field trips: Winsor Marrett Tyler in the *Auk*, Apr. 1943; Austin H. Clark in *Science*, Mar. 13, 1942; separate accounts by Thomas Barbour, Barbara Lawrence, William E. Schevill, Sherwood L. Washburn, and Mary B. Cobb in *Jour. of Mammalogy*, Aug. 17, 1943. Allen's journals of his field trips and his correspondence with professional colleagues are in the archives of the Museum of Comparative Zoology at Harvard. Other information from *Reports* of Harvard College Class of 1901; *Annual Reports* of the Museum of Comparative Zoology; and Allen's death record (Mass. Registrar of Vital Statistics). A full, annotated bibliography of his published works, by Barbara Lawrence, was published in New England Zoological Club, *Proc.*, XXIV (1947), 1–81.]

BARBARA LAWRENCE

AMERINGER, OSCAR (Aug. 4, 1870–Nov. 5, 1943), labor organizer and editor, Socialist pamphleteer, was born at Achstetten, near Ulm, in the German kingdom of Württemberg. His father, August Ameringer (pronounced with a hard "g" and with the accent on the first syllable), was a talented musician and a master cabinetmaker; his mother, whose maiden name was Hoffman, came of the Swabian Oberland peasantry. Oscar had a brother and a sister, both older. When he was six the family settled in Laupheim. An "unruly boy," he attended the local Catholic school, but the rigid discipline made him "miserable," and after seven years he left to become an apprentice in his father's shop. He also pursued interests in music and art. To avoid military service, he immigrated to the United States before his sixteenth birthday.

Living at first in Cincinnati, where his brother had settled, Ameringer found work in a furniture factory, but was fired when he became an organizer for the Knights of Labor. For a time he played the cornet in a traveling band. After a jobless winter (1887–88), during which he began a program of self-education in the Cincinnati Public Library, he successfully took up portrait painting in nearby towns. In 1890, shortly after becoming an American citizen, he returned to Germany to visit his mother and went on to study art at Munich, where he stayed for five years. He came back in 1896 in time to pick up a job in the Canton, Ohio, band that aided McKinley's "front porch" campaign, and then tramped over the Middle West and into Texas, teaching music and directing bands. His wanderings came to a temporary halt when he married Lulu Wood of Mount Sterling, Ohio, and settled in Columbus, where he worked for a time as a life insurance salesman. Influenced by the writings of Edward Bellamy and Henry George [*qq.v.*], and perhaps even more by the "muckraking" journalists, Ameringer ran in 1903 for the state legislature as a single-taxer and for mayor of Columbus as a Socialist. That same year he launched a newspaper, the *Labor World,* in which he favored industrial unions and denounced the American Federation of Labor and its "high priest," Samuel Gompers [*q.v.*].

When the *Labor World* folded, Ameringer moved on in 1907 to Oklahoma, attracted by rising Socialist sentiment among laborers and tenant farmers in the Southwest. Thereafter Oklahoma City remained his home base. As a field organizer for the Socialist party, he spoke at schoolhouse meetings and Socialist encampments, entertaining as well as instructing his audiences. He began writing Socialist pamphlets; one of the most popular was *The Life and Deeds of Uncle Sam: A History for Big Children* (1912). Around this time he launched a newspaper, the *Industrial Democrat,* and, when this failed, the *Oklahoma Pioneer.* He also organized the Oklahoma Tenant Farmers Union.

Invited in 1910 to Milwaukee to assist in the Congressional campaigns of Victor Berger [Supp. 1] and other Socialists, Ameringer, with his knowledge of the German language and of the farmer's problems, effectively reduced the normally large Republican vote in Waukesha County and thereby helped Berger win election. His reward was appointment first as state and then as Milwaukee County organizer of the Socialist party. While in Milwaukee he also edited the *Voice of the People,* a campaign sheet which was revived periodically, and wrote editorials for the party organ, the *Milwaukee Leader.* Back home, he established the *Oklahoma Leader* in 1914. That year he ran on the Socialist ticket for mayor of Oklahoma City and came close to winning. Like many other Socialists, he opposed American involvement in World War I, and when the *Milwaukee Leader* was one of several radical journals whose mailing privileges were revoked, he went to Milwaukee and helped raise money to keep it alive. In 1918 he was the unsuccessful Socialist candidate for Congress from Milwaukee. He was indicted for obstructing military service but was not brought to trial.

After the war Ameringer returned to Oklahoma, where he and his trouble-beset *Oklahoma Leader* helped form the Farmer-Labor Reconstruction League, a coalition of progressives, Socialists, and farmer and labor organizations modeled on North Dakota's Non-Partisan League. Capturing the Democratic primaries, the group in 1922 elected Jack C. Walton, former mayor of Oklahoma City and member of a railroad union, to the governorship, but his impeachment the next year in an aura of scandal seriously jeopardized Ameringer's newspaper. Aid came, however, from Illinois members of the United Mine Workers, whose newspaper, the *Illinois Miner,* he edited and published at his plant in Oklahoma City from 1922 to 1931. For it he wrote a vigorous, earthy, frequently humorous column under the pseudonym "Adam Coaldigger." His own paper, renamed in 1931 the *American Guardian,* became widely known in workingmen's circles.

During the economic depression of the 1930's Ameringer wrote so vividly about the anomaly of poverty and hunger in the midst of plenty that he was called upon to testify before a subcommittee of the House Labor Committee investigating unemployment (February 1932). His readable autobiography, *If You Don't Weaken* (1940), brought him a new audience. The book included his definition of politics as "the art by which politicians obtain campaign contributions from the rich and votes from the poor on the pretext of protecting each from the other" (p. 393). Ameringer's first marriage ended in divorce, and in 1930 he married Freda Hogan, daughter of an Arkansas Socialist. Though born a Roman Catholic, Ameringer became a member of the Unitarian Church. Following a prolonged illness that included a liver ailment, he died in the Polyclinic Hospital in Oklahoma City of a cerebral thrombosis at the age of seventy-three. He was buried in Fairlawn Cemetery, Oklahoma City. His three sons by his first marriage, Siegfried, Irving, and Carl, and his daughter by the second, Susan, all survived him.

Ameringer's special strength was his ability, as speaker and writer, to put a broadly Socialist message into witty, pithy, down-to-earth prose. He was remembered as the "Mark Twain of Labor" and the "Workers' Will Rogers." Carl Sandburg found in Adam Coaldigger's fables "the art of Aesop," their author holding "a supreme position in the American labor movement as a man of laughter, wit and satire."

[Ameringer's autobiography is the principal source, though it is not always reliable in detail. Other sources: McAlister Coleman, *Men and Coal* (1943); Donald D. Egbert and Stow Persons, eds., *Socialism and Am. Life* (1952); David A. Shannon, ed., *The Great Depression* (1960), which reprints extracts from Ameringer's testimony before the Congressional subcommittee; *Dict. Wis. Biog.* (1960); H. L. Meredith, "Oscar Ameringer and the Concept of Agrarian Socialism," *Chronicles of Okla.,* Spring 1967; Gilbert C. Fite, "Okla.'s Reconstruction League," *Jour. of Southern Hist.,* Nov. 1947; "Americans We Like," *Nation,* Jan. 18, 1928; *Common Sense,* Mar. 1940; John Chamberlain, "Debsian-Populist," *Saturday Rev. of Literature,* June 1, 1940; Milton Mayer in *Progressive,* Nov. 15, 1943; *Time,* Nov. 15, 1943; newspapers generally at time of death, especially *N. Y. Times, Milwaukee Jour., Milwaukee Sentinel,* and *Daily Oklahoman,* Nov. 7, 1943; *Okla. Union Farmer,* Nov. 15, 1943; death record from Okla. State Dept. of Health; personal acquaintance. A biobibliography compiled by Ann S. Green at the Univ. of Wis. Lib. School was helpful. Mrs. Siegfried Ameringer, Okla. City, provided family information.]

IRVING DILLIARD

AMES, JOSEPH SWEETMAN (July 3, 1864–June 24, 1943), physicist, university president, and government research administrator, was born in Manchester, Vt., the only child of George Lapham Ames and Elizabeth Laura (Bacon) Ames, whose families had migrated from England in the seventeenth century. His father, a physician and amateur naturalist, died in 1869, after moving his family to Niles, Mich. In 1872 Joseph entered the Shattuck School, an Episcopal institution in Faribault, Minn. Two years later, his mother married the school's rector, James Dobbin, by whom she had a second son. Excelling at Shattuck, Joseph Ames aspired to be a teacher of mathematics. At the new Johns Hopkins University, which he entered in 1883, his interests turned to physics, and after graduating in 1886 he worked for a time in Hermann von Helmholtz's laboratory in Berlin. In 1887 he returned to Hopkins to pursue spectrographic research, in which Henry A. Rowland [*q.v.*] had made the university preeminent. Beginning as a junior faculty member before receiving his Ph.D. in 1890, Ames continued to teach at the university, where he became a professor in 1898.

An ambitious and self-assertive young man, he "liked to have a finger in every pie," perhaps because he feared his stammer (which in later years he largely overcame) might make people underrate him. Since administration bored Rowland, Ames took over many organizational chores, and to complement Rowland's experimental genius, Ames emphasized library research and exposition. He gained a reputation for thorough and up-to-date knowledge of the whole range of physics and for the clarity and comprehensiveness of his lectures, which he presented with severe formality. He was author or editor of ten books (some with collaborators). These were all textbooks or historical compilations of the work of others; *The Constitution of Matter* (1913) comprised a series of lectures at Northwestern University. Except for reports of his spectro-

scopic experiments of the 1890's, his articles tended to be critical, historical, or explicatory. They dealt chiefly with relativity, wireless telegraphy, and aeronautics. He also wrote definitions in physics and aeronautics for the second edition of *Webster's New International Dictionary.*

On Rowland's death in 1901 Ames became director of the physical laboratory at Johns Hopkins, but his administrative talents made him influential throughout the university. In 1915 he became secretary of the academic council; in 1924, dean of the college faculty, a post where he proved warmly interested in undergraduates; and in 1926—without dropping the deanship—provost, a post which involved him in budgetary matters and in duties as acting president. At this point he announced that physics was changing too rapidly for him and that he would teach no more. He thereupon distributed his physical library among his students in a gesture characteristic of his concern for them.

In 1929, finding the choice of a president difficult, the Hopkins trustees turned to the sixty-four-year-old Ames as a dependable insider. The new president, who refused a formal inaugural, found himself leading the university through the worst of the Great Depression, years recalled by Hopkins officials as "cliff-hanging." The university under President Frank J. Goodnow [Supp. 2] had undertaken several projects, but the depression made it impossible to secure the necessary funds. Goodnow's "New Plan," which envisaged a university offering neither the first two years of college work nor the bachelor's degree, survived only in a highly attenuated form. Ames did, however, direct a general recasting of the undergraduate curriculum with emphasis on comprehensive examinations rather than course credits. Another reform that gave Ames satisfaction was the elimination of alumni control over athletic coaches, which allowed new attention to intramural sports.

For lack of funds the university's Institute of Law was forced to close in 1933, but the Walter Hines Page School of International Relations, which opened in 1930, managed to survive. Ames resisted pressures from academic purists to abolish the "sideshows"—the college for teachers and the summer school. With deficits mounting, 1933 brought a 10 percent faculty salary cut and a halt to major appointments. Throughout these difficulties, Ames proclaimed and preserved the Hopkins tradition, a unique blend of research, smallness, and informality.

Widely acquainted, Ames attended international scientific conferences, helped found (1899) the American Physical Society, of which he was president in 1919–20, and became in 1909 a member of the National Academy of Sciences. He was thus an appropriate leader for the National Research Council's mission to England and France in the spring of 1917 to assess the scientific needs of the war effort. Although remaining on the N.R.C. and serving as chairman of its Division of Physical Sciences, 1922–25, Ames was more intimately concerned with the National Advisory Committee for Aeronautics (forerunner of the National Aeronautics and Space Administration), of which he was a member from its establishment by Congress in 1915. Not simply "advisory," the N.A.C.A. was one of the government's most vigorous civilian scientific agencies. Atypically resilient after World War I, it continued to administer its own research program at Langley Field in Virginia and pioneered in research contracts with universities. Much of the N.A.C.A.'s achievement was ascribable to Ames, who was chairman of its executive committee, 1919–36, and chairman of the full committee, 1927–39. Serving without pay, he gave its work meticulous care, frequently visiting the main laboratory, instituting new lines of research, heading the annual conference with aircraft industry engineers, and presenting the agency's work to the public and to Congressional committees. The wind tunnel at Langley Field was among his special interests. Ames was honored in 1935 by the Langley Gold Medal of the Smithsonian Institution, awarded for his role in the "surpassing improvement of the performance, efficiency, and safety of American aircraft resulting from fundamental scientific research" under N.A.C.A. auspices. In 1939 the N.A.C.A. laboratory at Moffett Field in California was named for him.

Although his rotundity, baldness, and round spectacles gave him a benign, grandfatherly appearance, Ames was blunt and undiplomatic in manner. He himself spoke of his "set ways and self-confidence—not to say, stubbornness." He made biting public attacks on prohibition, Sunday closing laws, and teachers' oath laws. In the election of 1930 he headed the "Ritchie Citizenship League," supporting Democratic Gov. Albert C. Ritchie [Supp. 2]. Appointed to the Baltimore school board in 1932, Ames declared his intention to concentrate on the issues of cost and "gladiatorial" athletics. He relished sociability and for twenty years was president of the Baltimore Country Club. On Sept. 14, 1899, he married Mrs. Mary Boykin (Williams) Harrison, a widow with three grown children. This childless marriage was by all accounts an unusually happy one. Mrs. Ames died in 1931.

Ames admitted that he was thoroughly worn out at the end of his Hopkins presidency in 1935. He had little opportunity to enjoy retirement, for a stroke in May 1936 left him partially paralyzed. Although for a time N.A.C.A. meetings were held in his home, his health steadily worsened, and he resigned from the agency in 1939. He died four years later in Baltimore. His funeral took place at Mt. Calvary Protestant Episcopal Church, where he had long been a vestryman, and he was buried in St. Thomas Churchyard, Garrison Forest, Md. Dedicated to university ideals of research, Ames made his most significant contribution not in any investigations of his own or in his presidency of Johns Hopkins, but in building bridges between the scientific estates of the universities and the government and between pure and applied research.

[Henry Crew's memoir in Nat. Acad. Sci., *Biog. Memoirs*, vol. XXIII (1945), is the best available analysis of Ames's achievement in physics and includes a partial list of his publications. The obituary by N. Ernest Dorsey in *Am. Jour. of Physics*, June 1944, is valuable for its attention to his early years and for its psychological insight. George Boas, in *Word Study*, Oct. 1939, gives an intimate view by a nonphysicist colleague. For two major institutional contexts, see, besides annual reports of Johns Hopkins Univ. and the N.A.C.A., John C. French, *A Hist. of the Univ. Founded by Johns Hopkins* (1946), and George W. Gray, *Frontiers of Flight: The Story of NACA Research* (1948). Also helpful is A. Hunter Dupree, *Science in the Federal Government* (1957). Other sources consulted include scattered Ames letters in the Johns Hopkins Univ. Lib., clippings on his presidential years in the university's Alumni Records Office, and interviews and correspondence with former associates of Ames.]

HUGH HAWKINS

ANDERSON, SHERWOOD (Sept. 13, 1876–Mar. 8, 1941), author, was born in Camden, Ohio, the second son and third of seven children of Irwin McClain Anderson, a harnessmaker, and Emma Jane (Smith) Anderson. His middle name, which he never used, was Berton. His paternal great-grandparents, probably Scotch-Irish, had migrated in 1807 from Cumberland County, Pa., to a farm near West Union, Ohio, on which Anderson's grandfather and father grew up. His maternal grandmother had come to Ohio from Germany as a young girl. Irwin Anderson, a Union veteran of the Civil War, was a restless extrovert who preferred telling war tales and drinking to steady work. Leaving Camden in 1877, he moved his family in succession to Independence (now Butler) and Caledonia, and in 1884 to Clyde, in north central Ohio, where he worked improvidently at his trade and then as a house painter; his wife took in washing to supplement the family income. Karl, the oldest son, who was to become a painter, left to study art in Chicago; but Sherwood remained and helped support the family by a succession of jobs while completing, as an average student, grammar school and nine months of high school. Although his mother and sister were Presbyterians, he had little interest in formal religion.

During his childhood in Clyde, Anderson unconsciously absorbed impressions of small-town life that subsequently provided him with fictional material. Known to the town as "Jobby" for his scurrying, enterprising ways, he felt keenly the stigma of being the son of "a well known no-account" and wanted desperately to make money, to become respectable; yet he had other periods of dreaminess and of concentrated but undirected reading. He was later to believe that some of his storytelling gift came from his father, whom he disliked, but that his meek, hardworking mother, whom he loved, "first awoke in [him] the hunger to see beneath the surface of lives." After her death, in 1895, the family began to break up. Anderson worked in a Clyde bicycle factory and in 1896 went to Chicago, where he labored in a produce warehouse and studied arithmetic in night school. During the Spanish-American War he joined the National Guard and was stationed for four months in Cuba. He obtained a final year of schooling in 1899–1900 at Wittenberg Academy in Springfield, Ohio. The lively intellectual community of the Springfield boardinghouse where he lived with his brother Karl and other artists, teachers, and writers probably aroused his interest in becoming a writer.

For the time being, however, he was bent on business success, and in June 1900 he returned to Chicago and shortly became an expert copywriter with an advertising agency. His articles in two trade journals extolling the American businessman attracted much favorable attention. On May 16, 1904, he married Cornelia Pratt Lane, the cultivated daughter of a Toledo businessman. They had three children: Robert Lane, John Sherwood, and a daughter, Marion. In September 1906 the couple moved to Cleveland, where Anderson became president of United Factories, a mail-order firm. After financial reverses, they settled a year later in nearby Elyria, where he built up a mail-order paint business. Outwardly successful and conventional, Anderson inwardly became disturbed by the "slickness" of business practices, by developing tensions with his wife, and eventually by financial worries. He began writing fiction about 1909, partly as self-therapy, partly as a tentative career interest. On Nov. 28, 1912, overworked and under deep psychological stress, he walked out of his office in what he later claimed to be a conscious rejection of business; actually he had suffered a mental breakdown resulting in temporary amnesia. Recover-

ing, he left for Chicago in February 1913 and resumed his advertising work. Although he was to continue in advertising, off and on, until his final break in 1922, he resented his dependency on the world of business, which he later characterized as a universal network of prostitution.

The literary and artistic excitement of the current "Chicago Renaissance" encouraged Anderson to continue writing. Two apprentice-work novels composed in Elyria were published, the first through the efforts of Floyd Dell and Theodore Dreiser [Supp. 3]: *Windy McPherson's Son* (1916), the autobiographical story of a man's rise in and rejection of business, and *Marching Men* (1917), a labor novel. *Mid-American Chants* (1918) collected the free-verse poems he wrote after meeting the New York critics Waldo Frank, Van Wyck Brooks, and Paul Rosenfeld, who admired his work. In 1919 the pioneering publisher B. W. Huebsch issued *Winesburg, Ohio,* Anderson's masterpiece. Attacked by some critics for "sordidness" and "preoccupation with sex," these brooding Midwest tales, "plotless" but carefully formed, showed their author's sympathetic insight into the thwarted lives of ordinary people. Many of the small-town characters in this subtly organized work of art have been turned by psychic isolation into "grotesques"; yet it is largely from the grotesques themselves that George Willard, the youthful protagonist, learns self-understanding, emotional maturity, and the responsibilities of the writer. During the 1920's *Winesburg, Ohio* was often considered representative of the contemporary "Revolt from the Village," but it is now recognized as being instead a profound expression of human community and love.

Anderson's first marriage had ended in divorce on July 27, 1916, and on July 31, at Chateaugay, N. Y., he married Tennessee Claflin Mitchell, a music teacher widely acquainted in Chicago's artistic Bohemia. Soon these two independent temperaments began clashing; and Anderson, increasingly restive at having to support himself by advertising work, lived briefly in New York City in 1918 and, in 1920 (to escape the Chicago winter), in Fairhope, Ala. In these places he wrote his best novel, *Poor White* (1920), a picture of the destruction of an Ohio town's sense of community by industrialism.

Creatively, the period from 1916 to 1925 was Anderson's richest. Some of his finest stories were collected in *The Triumph of the Egg* (1921), including "I Want to Know Why" and the sadly comic "The Egg," and in *Horses and Men* (1923), including "The Man Who Became a Woman." Many of these tales and the minor novel *Many Marriages* (1923) manifested his dislike of sexual repression and middle-class conventionality, his opposition to business success and a machine civilization, and his conviction, reflected in his narrative technique, that life is essentially a series of intensely felt moments. *A Story Teller's Story* (1924), a fanciful autobiography, memorably described his life as representative of the artist in America. This period closed with *Dark Laughter* (1925), another study of walled-in personalities and his only financially successful novel. Anderson was highly regarded by writers like Dreiser and Hart Crane [Supp. 1]. A growing critical recognition was marked by his receiving in 1921 the first *Dial* award for his contribution to American writing.

In the spring and summer of 1921 Paul Rosenfeld paid Anderson's and his wife's expenses to France and England. Anderson was delighted with Paris and with meeting James Joyce and Gertrude Stein. Reading Gertrude Stein's work had, he felt, released a poetic second self within him—though equally important literary influences had been Turgenev, the English novelist George Borrow, George Moore, Mark Twain, and the King James Bible. In 1922 he left his second wife and lived first in New Orleans and then in New York City, where he met Elizabeth Norman Prall, manager of a bookstore. Early in 1923 he began residence in Reno, Nev.; and on Apr. 4, 1924, he divorced Tennessee, marrying Elizabeth Prall in Martinez, Calif., the following day and shortly thereafter returning to New Orleans with her. Just as he had encouraged Ernest Hemingway during their brief acquaintance in Chicago in 1921, so now he befriended William Faulkner and encouraged him to write about his own Mississippi county. Disliking the heat of New Orleans, the Andersons purchased a farm in the Virginia mountains near Marion and in the summer of 1926 built there a fieldstone house, "Ripshin," which was to be Anderson's usual summer residence for the rest of his life.

Horace Liveright [Supp. 1], publisher of *Dark Laughter,* was now paying Anderson $100 a week in return for one publishable volume a year. Under pressure to produce and in conflict with his gentle, more conventional third wife, he found writing difficult. *Sherwood Anderson's Notebook* (1926), a collection of previously published sketches and articles; *Tar: A Midwest Childhood* (1926); and *A New Testament* (1927) were of poor quality, and his stature among fellow writers was declining. Anderson's brief second trip to Paris in the winter of 1926–27 was marred by his illness and recurring depression. Having canceled his financial arrangement with Liveright, he found a pa-

tron in Burton Emmett, a wealthy advertising executive, and, subsequently, in Emmett's widow, who helped support Anderson well into the 1930's. In November 1927, with funds from Emmett, he bought two weekly Marion newspapers and began a country editor's life. Selections from his newspaper writings did make up *Hello Towns!* (1929); yet his depression soon returned. After Elizabeth left him late in 1928 (he was to divorce her in February 1932), he turned the newspapers over to his son Robert early in 1929 and began reporting on the life of Southern mill workers. His articles on the defeat of men, but not of women, by the Machine Age were collected in *Perhaps Women* (1931), and he finally completed an uneven novel, *Beyond Desire* (1932), partly based on the Southern textile strikes of 1929–30. This new interest in Southern working conditions was encouraged by Eleanor Gladys Copenhaver, a Marion girl nearly twenty years his junior who was industrial secretary of the national Y.W.C.A. They were married at Marion on July 6, 1933.

Briefly attracted to Communism, Anderson had attended a World's Congress against War in Amsterdam in August 1932, and through the 1930's he occasionally supported left-wing causes; but his admiration for Communist opposition to socioeconomic injustice was offset by his skepticism toward all ideologies and his gift for intuitive understanding of individuals. A final excellent collection of stories, *Death in the Woods* (1933), sold few copies because of Liveright's bankruptcy. To support himself, Anderson traveled about the United States as a journalist during the mid-1930's sensitively observing depression life; his articles written at this time were collected in *Puzzled America* (1935). *No Swank* (1934) brought together sketches of acquaintances; and his last novel, *Kit Brandon* (1936), told the story of a Southern mountain girl turned bootlegger. Dramatic versions of his tales were printed in *Plays: Winesburg and Others* (1937). Despite continued wanderings and occasional appearances at writers' conferences, he maintained his roots in Marion, and he celebrated small-town life in the sketches of *Home Town* (1940).

While preparing his autobiography, published posthumously as *Sherwood Anderson's Memoirs* (1942), Anderson embarked on an unofficial goodwill tour of South America with his wife. Sailing from New York in late February 1941, he fell ill when a piece of toothpick he had swallowed at a farewell party perforated his intestine. He was taken ashore in the Panama Canal Zone and underwent surgery at the Colón (Panama) Hospital, but died there of an intestinal obstruction and peritonitis at the age of sixty-four. His body was returned to Marion, Va., for burial in Round Hill Cemetery.

Anderson's work is uneven in quality, but his best tales, despite their apparent simplicity, are highly skilled in narrative art, and sympathetically uncover the buried psychological life of average Americans. His stories, more than his novels, were important in the Modernist movement for breaking down formula approaches to writing and for influencing subsequent generations of American novelists and story writers.

[Of greatest value for Anderson's life as a writer are the letters, documents, and memorabilia in the Sherwood Anderson Collection, Newberry Lib., Chicago. A selection of 401 letters is printed in Howard Mumford Jones and Walter B. Rideout, eds., *Letters of Sherwood Anderson* (1953). Additional details have come from the reminiscences of Karl Anderson, taped by Mrs. David L. Poor, and from interviews with Elizabeth Prall Anderson and Eleanor Copenhaver Anderson. Basic research on Anderson's life from 1876 to 1913 has been outstandingly done by William A. Sutton in his "Sherwood Anderson's Formative Years (1876–1913)" (Ph.D. dissertation, Ohio State Univ., 1943), parts of which have been published in the *Northwest Ohio Quart.*, July 1947, Jan. 1948, Winter 1949–50, and Summer 1950, and in Sutton's *Exit to Elsinore* (Ball State Monograph No. 7, Ball State Univ., 1967). See also Sutton's article on Tennessee Mitchell Anderson in *Ball State Univ. Forum*, Spring 1966. Useful information on Anderson's paternal ancestry is in Nelson W. Evans and Emmons B. Stivers, *A Hist. of Adams County, Ohio* (1900), pp. 354, 356–58, 504–05, 677–78. The files of the *Clyde* (Ohio) *Enterprise* and the *Smyth County News* (Marion, Va.) have provided material on Anderson's life in these two communities. Official county records have established the dates of Anderson's birth and of his marriages and divorces. The best factual biography is James Schevill, *Sherwood Anderson: His Life and Work* (1951); see also Irving Howe, *Sherwood Anderson* (1951). *Sherwood Anderson's Memoirs* (1942; critical edition, ed. by Ray L. White, 1969) gives fruitful biographical leads, but its details cannot be accepted uncritically. Paul P. Appel, ed., *Homage to Sherwood Anderson* (1970), is a collection of critical essays. For other references, see Eugene P. Sheehy and Kenneth A. Lohf, *Sherwood Anderson: A Bibliog.* (1960).]

WALTER B. RIDEOUT

ANDREWS, CHARLES McLEAN (Feb. 22, 1863–Sept. 9, 1943), historian, was born in Wethersfield, Conn., the oldest of three children and only son of Elizabeth Byrne (Williams) Andrews and William Watson Andrews [*q.v.*], who also had two sons and a daughter by a previous marriage. William Andrews and his brother Samuel James [*q.v.*] were leaders of the Catholic Apostolic Church, an evangelical group of English origins; a third brother, Israel Ward Andrews [*q.v.*], was president of Marietta College in Ohio. Since Charles's father traveled and lectured widely in behalf of his chosen sect, most of the responsibility for running the household, on a modest income, fell on Mrs. Andrews. The home atmosphere was one of happy, active piety,

and the children attended both Catholic Apostolic and Congregational services.

Charles was late in acquiring an interest in scholarship. He was an undistinguished student at the Hartford (Conn.) high school. After entering Trinity College in Hartford, he planned to drop out to go into business, but at his mother's insistence remained to graduate in 1884. For the next two years he was principal of a small high school in West Hartford. Discovering there that he liked to teach, he began graduate work at Johns Hopkins University, where his studies were largely financed by a maternal aunt, the wife of the Rev. Charles McLean, after whom he had been named.

The most influential of his teachers at Hopkins was Herbert Baxter Adams [*q.v.*], from whom he gained a lasting respect for the study of institutions as a key to historical understanding; but it was Frederick William Maitland, the English historian, whom Andrews later called "my master." He took Maitland and Leopold von Ranke, with his "scientific" history, as his guides in scholarship. Andrews received the Ph.D. in 1889; his dissertation, *The River Towns of Connecticut*, a study of the settlement of Wethersfield, Hartford, and Windsor, was published that year. In the fall of 1889 he joined the faculty of Bryn Mawr College, where he was a popular teacher. He married Evangeline Holcombe Walker, a recent graduate of Bryn Mawr, on June 19, 1895; they had two children: Ethel Walker (who married John Marshall Harlan, later a justice of the United States Supreme Court) and John Williams.

Although he published several articles on early American history, Andrews was not yet ready to concentrate in that field. A study of the English manorial system, textbooks on the history of modern Europe and England, and a popular history of contemporary Europe, Asia, and Africa gave him an unusual breadth of historical perspective. In the summer of 1893 he visited England, in part on a mission for the Historical Society of Pennsylvania to examine archival materials in London relating to Pennsylvania. This and later visits established his lifelong conviction that the American colonies could be correctly understood only if they were recognized for what they were at the time, that is, ongoing colonies of the English mother country, rather than as embryonic states of a future independent nation. He made his first emphatic public statement of this view, which was then unorthodox, in a paper read before the American Historical Association in 1898. When the Carnegie Institution of Washington, under the leadership of J. Franklin

Jameson [Supp. 2], sponsored a series of guides to documents pertaining to American history in foreign repositories, Jameson asked Andrews to undertake the volumes on English archives for the period before 1783. The resultant three volumes (1908–14), prepared with Frances G. Davenport, Andrews later regarded as his most important and lasting historical contribution.

Andrews was called in 1907 to Johns Hopkins, where for three years he held the chair formerly occupied by his old mentor, Adams. In 1910 he was appointed Farnam Professor at Yale, where he taught until his retirement in 1931. As at Hopkins, he worked almost exclusively with graduate students. He was a highly successful teacher of young scholars, stimulating their interest, encouraging independence, helping them with their personal concerns, and setting an example of the highest standard of thoroughness and intellectual integrity.

With the aid of his wife, who sought to free him completely from distracting cares, Andrews devoted nearly all his time to scholarly work and teaching. This tendency to seclusion was reinforced by increasing deafness, which as early as 1905 required the use of a hearing aid. Most of his writings after 1904 were concerned with early American history, particularly the formal structures of government and public life; social and cultural history, and party politics, held less interest for him. Probably the most important book of his teaching years was *The Colonial Background of the American Revolution* (1924), which consists of four essays addressed primarily to fellow historians and writers of textbooks. Andrews urged them to put aside ancient prejudices and long-standing traditions of British tyranny and to view the Revolution objectively as the result of an extended period of social, political, and economic development of the colonies, of an understandable though short-sighted and too rigid British colonial policy, and of the inevitable clash between these two. Although such an interpretation was not wholly new in 1924, Andrews's book was its most effective presentation. In the following year he served as president of the American Historical Association.

Upon retiring from Yale, Andrews engaged in systematic work on his long-planned major project. The first three volumes of *The Colonial Period of American History* (1934–37) traced the history of English settlement in the New World. A fourth volume (1938) examined in detail England's commercial and colonial policy. He planned three more volumes on the development of the colonies during the eighteenth century, but serious illness intervened and he never

regained the necessary strength. The appearance in quick succession of Andrews's four substantial volumes brought him wide acclaim. The first won the Pulitzer Prize in history in 1935, and two years later the National Institute of Arts and Letters awarded him its gold medal. In addition to an earlier honorary degree from Trinity, the 1930's saw similar honors from Lehigh, Yale, Harvard, and Johns Hopkins. Andrews died at the age of eighty in New Haven, Conn., and was buried in Cedar Hill Cemetery, Hartford.

[A collection of Andrews's papers is in the Yale Univ. Lib.; this includes extensive correspondence, brief reminiscences of his life to 1880, and a 34-page biographical sketch by his sister. A. S. Eisenstadt, *Charles McLean Andrews* (1956), is a full-scale interpretive biography. A shorter treatment of his scholarly career by Leonard W. Labaree is in the *William and Mary Quart.*, Jan. 1944; appended to it is a bibliography of Andrews's writings compiled by George Wilson Pierson. On his father, see Samuel J. Andrews, *William Watson Andrews: A Religious Biog.* (1900), and Plato E. Shaw, *The Catholic Apostolic Church* (1946).]

LEONARD W. LABAREE

ANDREWS, FRANK MAXWELL (Feb. 3, 1884–May 3, 1943), Army Air Corps officer, was born in Nashville, Tenn., the oldest of four children of James David and Louise Adeline (Maxwell) Andrews, and a descendant of Thomas Andrews, who came to Virginia from London about 1700. Frank's paternal grandfather was a Methodist minister in Tennessee, and the family remained in that faith. His father, a newspaper reporter, later became business manager of the *Nashville Banner* and a prominent real estate dealer. Frank graduated from Montgomery Bell Academy in Nashville in 1901 and the following year entered the United States Military Academy, from which he graduated in 1906. Commissioned a second lieutenant in the cavalry, he spent the next eleven years with cavalry units at bases in the West, Hawaii, and the Philippines. On Dec. 14, 1914, he married Jeannette Allen, daughter of Major General Henry T. Allen. They had three children: Josephine, Allen, and Jean.

In August 1917 Andrews was assigned to the Signal Corps for duty with the Air Section (soon to be known as the Air Service) in Washington, D. C. After flight training (April–July 1918) at Rockwell Field, San Diego, Calif., he was placed in command of Carlstrom and Dorr fields at Arcadia, Fla. Andrews, then a lieutenant colonel, had hoped for a combat assignment in France, but in October 1918 he was named supervisor of the Southeastern Air Service District with headquarters at Montgomery, Ala. He returned to Washington in March 1919 to become chief of the inspection division and a member of the advisory board in the office of the Chief of the Air Service.

In March 1920 he was assigned to the War Plans Division of the General Staff, a position he held until August. Late that summer he was ordered to Germany as Air Service officer of the American Army of Occupation; he assumed duties in the civil affairs area in June 1922.

Soon after returning from Germany in the spring of 1923, Andrews was assigned to Kelly Field, Texas, as post executive officer. He became commanding officer of the 10th School Group in July 1925 and a short time later assumed duties as commandant of the Advanced Flying School at Kelly. He held this important post until June 1927, when he moved into a new phase of his career, preparation for command. Andrews spent much of the six-year period from June 1927 to June 1933 in the army's various advanced schools: the Air Corps Tactical School at Langley Field, Va. (1927–28), the Command and General Staff School at Fort Leavenworth, Kans. (1928–29), and the Army War College in Washington (1932–33). Between the last two assignments he served for three years in the office of the chief of the Air Corps in Washington, D. C.

In the summer of 1933 Andrews was given command of the 1st Pursuit Group, then based at Selfridge Field, Mich. He enjoyed this assignment immensely, for it enabled him to spend more time in the cockpit, and in the mid-1930's he established several speed and long-distance records. When a few years later he was urged by friends to give up solo flying, he is reported to have said, "I don't want to be one of those generals who die in bed." More than a daring pilot, Andrews was a student of technique and one of the pioneers in instrument flying in a day when this was anathema to most "old timers."

Andrews was reassigned in the autumn of 1934 to Washington, D. C., where he worked with the Operations and Training Branch of the War Department General Staff during the final phases of the reorganization of the Air Corps. He was a strong supporter of the General Headquarters (GHQ) Air Force plan, which called for a central striking force under the top command of the army, and when that organization became a reality on Mar. 1, 1935, he was promoted to brigadier general (temporary) and placed in command; in December 1935 he was made temporary major general.

The idea of an "air force" separate from the support aviation assigned to army units had been urged on the War Department by Major General Mason M. Patrick [Supp. 3] during his tour of duty as chief of the Air Corps in the mid-1920's. It was not, however, until the emergence of the heavy bomber, represented by the B-9 and B-10

in the early 1930's, that the centralized strike force idea had any impact on the General Staff. Although some problems of conflicting responsibility remained (supply and training were still under the chief of the Air Corps, Major General Oscar Westover), the GHQ Air Force created in 1935 concentrated under one command aviation units previously under the scattered control of nine corps area commanders.

As GHQ Air Force Commander, the rugged, soft-spoken, silver-haired Andrews was able to whip the army's scattered and underequipped combat squadrons into a small but efficient fighting force. A firm believer in air power as an offensive weapon, he agitated constantly for more heavy, long-range bombers. The B-17 Flying Fortress was available after 1935, but the United States was still troubled by the economic depression, and the General Staff was not entirely convinced of air power effectiveness. When, after completing his tour of duty in February 1939 and reverting to his permanent rank of colonel, Andrews was ordered to the relatively minor post of air officer of the VIII Corps area, many air officers were convinced he was being punished for his aggressive campaign.

That fall, soon after Gen. George C. Marshall was appointed chief of staff of the army, Andrews returned to the General Staff as Assistant Chief of Staff for Training and Operations. On Nov. 14, 1940, he was named, on the personal recommendation of President Franklin Roosevelt, to command the Panama Canal Air Force; in September 1941 he was promoted to lieutenant general and his command responsibilities were expanded to include the Caribbean Defense Command. With the allied invasion of North Africa in November 1942, Andrews was sent to take command of United States forces in the Middle East. He was given command of all American forces in the European Theatre of Operations on Feb. 5, 1943, replacing Gen. Dwight D. Eisenhower, who had become Supreme Allied Commander in North Africa. That May, General Andrews was killed when the B-24 Liberator in which he was traveling attempted a low-visibility landing at Iceland and crashed into a hillside. He was buried in the American section of the Icelandic Civilian Cemetery at Reykjavik. In 1949 Andrews Air Force Base in Maryland was named in his honor.

[Alfred Goldberg, ed. *A Hist. of the U. S. Air Force, 1907–1957* (1957); Wesley Frank Craven and James Lea Cate, eds., *The Army Air Forces in World War II*, vol. I (1948); U. S. Air Force Hist. Studies: *The Development of the Heavy Bomber, 1918–1944* (1951), *Organization of Military Aeronautics, 1935–1945* (1946), and *Development of Air Doctrine in the*

Army Air Arm, 1917–1941 (1953); Frank M. Andrews, "Modern Air Power," *Vital Speeches,* Feb. 15, 1939; *Time,* Feb. 15, 1943, pp. 62, 64; *Who Was Who in America,* vol. II (1950); *Current Biog.,* 1942; *Nat. Cyc. Am. Biog.,* XXXII, 11; obituaries in *Time,* May 17, 1943, p. 67, and *N. Y. Times,* May 5, 7, 1943. Information about Andrews's father from obituary in *Nashville Banner,* Mar. 4, 1937 (courtesy of Public Lib. of Nashville and Davidson County). The Andrews Papers are in the Lib. of Cong. Other documents and photographs concerning Andrews are in the Nat. Archives, Washington, D. C.; Air Force Museum, Wright-Patterson Air Force Base, Ohio; and Air Force Photo File in the Pentagon, Washington.]

JAMES J. HUDSON

ANDREWS, JOHN BERTRAM (Aug. 2, 1880–Jan. 4, 1943), economist, social reformer, and labor expert, was born in South Wayne, Lafayette County, Wis., the youngest of four children (two girls and two boys) of Philo Edmund and Sara Jane (Maddrell) Andrews. His father, born in Illinois to parents who had migrated from New York and Massachusetts, had moved in 1852 to Wisconsin, where he taught school before settling on a farm. John's mother, whose parents had come from England and Pennsylvania, was a native of Wisconsin. The boy grew up on the family farm and at fifteen joined the Freewill Baptist Church, in which his father was active. He was educated at local schools, at Warren Academy, where he excelled in oratory, and at the University of Wisconsin, from which he received the B.A. degree in 1904. The following year he took an M.A. in economics at Dartmouth. Returning to Wisconsin for further graduate work under Prof. John R. Commons [Supp. 3], he earned the Ph.D. in history and economics in 1908. Andrews remained a devoted disciple of Commons and collaborated with him on several books, including *Principles of Labor Legislation* (1916), which became a standard text.

In December 1908 Commons secured Andrews an appointment as executive secretary of the new American Association for Labor Legislation, which Commons, Richard T. Ely [Supp. 3], and others had established to transform the social welfare proposals of labor experts into progressive legislation. As assistant secretary Commons selected another former student, Irene Osgood. She and Andrews were married on Aug. 8, 1910; they had one child, John Osgood. Under Andrews's direction, the Association worked for new or improved laws to provide compensation for industrial accidents, promote industrial safety, and institute unemployment, old age, and health insurance. A report on phosphorus poisoning in the match industry that Andrews prepared in 1908 for the United States Bureau of Labor launched the American industrial hygiene movement. The report broadened the definition of industrial accidents to include occupational disease and led in 1912 to federal legislation prohibiting the use of poisonous white phosphorus in matches. To publicize the Association's views, Andrews in 1911 founded the *American Labor Legislation Review;* he continued to edit it until his death, when it ceased publication.

Andrews did his most significant work in the social insurance movement. He took the lead in this field in 1912, when he appointed a commission to investigate the feasibility of health and unemployment insurance. The commission's report (1915) recommended compulsory health insurance, to be modeled on the programs then operating in Germany and England and to be financed by contributions from employer, employee, and the government. Designed to include all wage earners below a stipulated income level, the proposed legislation called for medical and cash benefits, to be distributed through local mutual funds. The American Association for Labor Legislation secured the introduction of its model bill in the California and New York legislatures. The bill came under immediate attack from physicians, fearful of government interference, and from some labor leaders, similarly fearful of state action in the welfare field and convinced that the physical examinations given under a health program would be used to dismiss workers active in unionization. Yet the most vigorous opposition came from employers, private insurance companies, and (in California) Christian Scientists. A wartime campaign branding health insurance as socialistic, immoral, and pro-German ultimately sent the bill to defeat in both states.

In the wake of this bitter fight Andrews increasingly shied away from European models for a social insurance program. Instead he developed, with Commons, an American approach that emphasized voluntarism rather than government control. His old-age program called for voluntary pension plans, and he geared his unemployment program not to the payment of benefits to the out-of-work but to the prevention of unemployment through employment exchanges, public works programs, production planning, market analysis, part-time employment, and the development of a slack-season trade. Andrews also proposed industrial training, restrictions on child labor, insurance for unemployables, and new immigration policies. The most distinctive part of his plan was a measure, originally devised by Commons, that would require each employer to set aside funds in individual company reserves. He reasoned that a natural reluctance to part with money in the fund would provide incentive for the employer to regularize employment.

Because his voluntaristic approach accorded

with American ideals of individualism and private enterprise, Andrews had considerable influence on private and state social insurance programs, and later on federal legislation. In 1919 he was the United States delegate to the International Labor Conference in Geneva, and two years later he participated in President Harding's Unemployment Conference. As a lecturer on labor legislation at Columbia for many years, he worked closely with Joseph P. Chamberlain, draftsman of numerous social welfare laws proposed initially by Andrews. The main features of his unemployment program were enacted into law in Wisconsin in 1932.

In New York, however, Andrews met considerable opposition from Abraham Epstein [Supp. 3], who along with Isaac Rubinow [Supp. 2] and other welfare advocates favored government-controlled social insurance programs. After a protracted battle between the competing factions, the New York legislature in 1935 decided in favor of a pooled-fund unemployment insurance plan (as against the individual reserves envisaged in the Andrews plan)—the first state in the nation to adopt such a program. Partly in deference to his critics, and partly because of the long controversy in New York, Andrews moved more cautiously on the national scene. In 1930 he drew up a model federal unemployment bill, based on the "American plan," which gave the states considerable latitude in enacting either the individual-reserve fund or pooled-fund schemes. The bill won the support of Senator Robert F. Wagner, one of the foremost advocates of labor legislation, and, with few major revisions, became part of the Social Security Act of 1935.

Andrews belonged to a generation of social scientists and specialists who translated the theories of the classroom into the laws and administrative regulations of local, state, and federal governments. A dignified and handsome man, he had considerable tact and impressed listeners with his earnestness. He died at the age of sixty-two at the Post-Graduate Hospital in New York City following an operation, and was buried in Ferncliff Cemetery, Hartsdale, N. Y. Along with Isaac Rubinow and Abraham Epstein, he was one of the major figures in the formative years of the American social insurance movement, as well as a noteworthy pioneer in American labor legislation.

[The John B. Andrews Papers at Cornell Univ. provide a detailed view of his manifold activities. The papers of the Survey Associates at the Univ. of Minn. contain several folders of Andrews correspondence. For brief published accounts, see obituaries in *N. Y. Times*, Jan. 5, 1943, and *Internat. Labor Organization*, vol. XLVII (1943); and *Who Was Who in America*, vol. II (1950). Family background can be traced through: microfilms of county census records at the State Hist. Soc. of Wis. for 1880 and 1890; the *Wis. State Jour.* (Madison), Nov. 9, 1930; and the *South Wayne* (Wis.) *Homestead*, Jan. 28, 1943. General treatments touching on the career of Andrews include Clarke A. Chambers, *Seedtime of Reform* (1963); Roy Lubove, *The Struggle for Social Security, 1900–1935* (1968); and Daniel Nelson, *Unemployment Insurance* (1969).]

GERALD D. NASH

ANNENBERG, MOSES LOUIS (Feb. 11, 1878–July 20, 1942), newspaper publisher and racing-news entrepreneur, was born in tiny Kalwischen, East Prussia, later part of the Soviet Union. He was one of eight children and the youngest of three sons of Jewish parents, Tobias and Sarah (Greenberg) Annenberg. In 1882 the father, a farmer and storekeeper, emigrated to the United States, and by 1885 the entire family had joined him in Chicago. Their way up from poverty was hard. Tobias Annenberg started a junk business but never achieved any degree of wealth. His sons went to work after only brief schooling, Moses in his father's business and then as a Western Union messenger, as a starter for a livery stable, and as a bartender. On Aug. 20, 1899, he married Sadie Cecilia Friedman, daughter of a Chicago merchant. They had nine children: Diana, Esther, Pearl, Janet, Enid, Walter Herbert, Leah, Evelyn, and Harriet.

William Randolph Hearst's arrival in Chicago drew two of the Annenbergs into his orbit. Hearst's new *Evening American* hired Annenberg's brother Max as a circulation manager, and in 1900 Max in turn hired Moe (as he was known) as a "40-mile road man" soliciting subscriptions. Moe rose fast. In 1904, when Hearst started a morning paper, the *Examiner*, he became circulation manager and took charge of the battle to capture choice street-sale positions from established papers—a competition that later broke into murderous gang warfare. The circulation war and his brother Max's deeper involvement in it dogged Moe's reputation ever after.

Before open fighting began, however, Moe had quarreled with his brother and had moved, about 1907, to Milwaukee, Wis. Pawning his young wife's jewelry to raise the initial $1,500, he started an agency to distribute all the Chicago papers. The business expanded gradually; in a dozen years he set up similar agencies in twenty cities. His first substantial money came from a promotion scheme suggested by his wife (a newspaper coupon offer of teaspoons decorated with state seals), and he was able to invest in such Milwaukee real estate ventures as automobile garages and inexpensive apartments. His career moved upward again in 1917 when Arthur Brisbane [Supp. 2], Hearst's premier editorialist, bought three Milwaukee papers and merged them into the *Wisconsin News*. He made Annenberg publisher; the new publisher promptly tripled the circulation to 80,000. When Brisbane sold the paper to Hearst (as was the custom in the Hearst organization), Annenberg remained as publisher for a year before Hearst called him to New York in 1920.

Annenberg thus attained the summit of the Hearst organization just twenty years after his humble start. The publisher made him circulation director for all Hearst newspapers and magazines and a member of his executive council. His salary was $50,000, but he was already making more from his own properties, which Hearst permitted him to keep. When Hearst covertly founded the *New York Mirror* in 1924, Annenberg became its president and publisher.

By 1926, Annenberg's personal enterprises were so substantial that he resigned from the Hearst organization. Among his holdings was the *Daily Racing Form*, which he had bought in 1922 with two associates. Later he added other horse-racing papers, notably the *New York Morning Telegraph*. In 1927 Annenberg pursued even larger returns by working his way into the racing wire services, which supplied instant information on racing results to subscribers—mostly illegal betting sites. He bought a half interest in the General News Bureau, based in Chicago, and acquired a partner named John L. Lynch.

Annenberg devoted the next seven years to driving out first the competition, then his own partners. About 1930 he absorbed the three major competing services and established a near monopoly of information transmitted from twenty-nine American racetracks to possibly 15,000 bookmaking establishments. To get rid of his partner Lynch, he started a rival bureau called Nation-Wide News Service, Inc. By manipulating the prices and services of both bureaus, Annenberg forced Lynch to sell out; the old General News Bureau was then discontinued and Nation-Wide took over. By similar means, Annenberg drove his partners out of the *Daily Racing Form*. He established a dominance not only in racing newspapers but in the miscellaneous publications, such as scratch sheets, used by bettors.

While the country struggled in the Great Depression, Annenberg prospered. The government estimated his income for the single year 1936 at more than $2,300,000; it also estimated that his net worth rose from just under $8,000,000 in 1930 to $19,500,000 in 1938. He divided his holdings into sixty-five or more corporate entities, controlled through holding companies—notably the Cecilia Company, named for his wife and held entirely by Annenberg family members.

Annenberg reentered general newspaper publishing in 1934 with the founding of the *Miami Tribune*. With his experienced touch it soon reached a circulation of 100,000. It also became involved in a dispute with Miami's mayor, E. G. Sewell, over the mayor's antigambling campaign. Before the fight ended, the *Tribune* had driven the mayor out of office. Annenberg abruptly sold the paper in 1937 in exchange for $500,000 and a daily in Ohio; the *Tribune's* city administration was swept out by Miami voters the next year.

Even before leaving Miami, Annenberg had staked his claim to journalistic respectability in Philadelphia. There, in August 1936, he bought the 107-year-old *Inquirer*. The price was said to have been $15,000,000; later court testimony set it at $6,750,000. The paper, declining in circulation, soon reversed itself under Annenberg's stimuli—a bounteous increase in comic strips, a sensational picture magazine, and the publisher's detailed attention to distribution. In two years daily circulation rose 23 percent to 345,000; the Sunday paper rose 55 percent to 1,036,000.

Annenberg used the *Inquirer* to jump into state politics on the side of the Republican organization of Joseph N. Pew, Jr. His chief newspaper competitor in Philadelphia, J. David Stern of the *Record,* was also his political antagonist, Stern being one of the few publishers close to the New Deal. Annenberg had supported Roosevelt in 1932 and 1936, but in a long editorial on June 30, 1937, he broke with the administration to pursue the double goal of political and business victory. In 1938 the *Inquirer* endorsed Superior Court Judge Arthur H. James to succeed Gov. George H. Earle, a Democrat known for his "little New Deal" program. Annenberg himself had become a major campaign issue. Senator Joseph F. Guffey assailed him in a statewide address, and Secretary of the Interior Harold L. Ickes came to Philadelphia to denounce him as "the scourge of two cities." A flurry of libel suits followed, all of them dropped after the Republican victory in November.

Annenberg's political emergence coincided with the first signs of official action against his racing-news monopoly. During the campaign, Governor Earle had inspired a state investigation that resulted in a Pennsylvania Public Utilities Commission order to three telephone companies to stop service to Annenberg's racetrack circuits. Annenberg responded by moving his facilities across state lines. More serious was his trouble with the federal government. On Apr. 25, 1939, Attorney General Frank Murphy announced that the findings of a three-year investigation of Annenberg's income taxes would be placed before Chicago grand juries. In August 1939 the grand juries produced two sets of indictments, one dealing with tax evasion, the other with the track-information monopoly. Annenberg was indicted for evading $3,258,809 in federal income taxes from 1932 through 1936; penalties and interest brought the total owed to more than $5,500,000. Annenberg's son, Walter, was indicted at the same time for aiding evasion. The second group of indictments charged that the Annenberg services had used the mails for an illegal lottery by distributing coded sheets that identified the horses. Only weeks later, federal pressure brought the collapse of the wire-service system: the American Telephone and Telegraph Company, Western Union, and Illinois Bell Telephone agreed to end service on their leased facilities, and Annenberg dissolved Nation-Wide at once.

Even with his wire-service business closed, Annenberg was unable to strike a bargain with the government. Although he maintained that he owed much less than the government claimed, he pleaded guilty on Apr. 23, 1940, to one charge of tax evasion—that for 1936. In June he signed an agreement with the Treasury to pay nearly $10,000,000 to cover all claims dating back to 1923. If he had hoped to avoid prison with this step, he was disappointed; he received a sentence of three years, and was sent to the Northeastern Federal Penitentiary at Lewisburg, Pa., on July 23, 1940. The other charges against him and his associates, including his son, were dropped or reversed.

Before entering the penitentiary, Annenberg had told an interviewer: "I am physically broken." During his sentence his health deteriorated. The Department of Justice, after turning down two parole applications in 1941, abruptly released him in June 1942. He died that July of a brain tumor at Rochester, Minn., where he had gone for treatment at the Mayo Clinic. His funeral, attended by Governor James, was held in Philadelphia, and burial took place in Mount Sinai Cemetery, Frankford, Pa. He was survived by his wife and eight of his children; Mrs. Annenberg engaged in widespread philanthropy before her death in 1965.

Those who knew Annenberg have paid scant tribute to his personal graces; he was parsimonious, harsh, boastful, and unscrupulous. His *Inquirer,* a circulation success, is remembered as a paper governed too often by his gross tastes and partiality. Yet even an enemy like J. David Stern of the *Record* conceded his courage and his executive ability. Walter Annenberg later blamed Stern for his father's misfortunes; Stern himself blamed James Cox, Democratic politician and a competi-

tor of Annenberg's in Miami. Still, Annenberg must be said to have brought about his own downfall, for he was fated to try to destroy, rather than merely outdo, his rivals; his fierce methods invited retaliation.

Annenberg's properties remained substantial even after the loss of the racing-wire services. Reorganized into Triangle Publications, they comprised a value of nearly $8,000,000 in stock. Continuing under Walter Annenberg's direction, they reached an estimated worth of $136,000,000 before the sale of the Philadelphia newspapers in 1969, when Walter Annenberg became United States ambassador to Britain. In Senate hearings on his appointment, he said that he had found his father's fate an inspiration, for "a tragedy of that magnitude will either destroy you or inspire you."

[The only extended account of Annenberg's career is John T. Flynn's series, "Smart Money," *Collier's,* Jan. 13, 20, 27, Feb. 3, 1940; part of the information evidently came from Annenberg personally. Gaeton Fonzi, *Annenberg: A Biog. of Power* (1970), a study of Walter H. Annenberg, draws heavily on Flynn for an account of Moses L. Annenberg's life. An authorized summary of Annenberg's activities appears in the *Phila. Inquirer* promotional book, *A Great Newspaper Is Re-Born* (1939), which also includes a photographic portrait. Annenberg is discussed in J. David Stern, *Memoirs of a Maverick Publisher* (1962), and Emile Gauvreau, *My Last Million Readers* (1941). Further information can be gleaned in George Seldes, *Lords of the Press* (1938); Virgil W. Peterson, *Barbarians in Our Midst* (1952); and Ferdinand Lundberg's wildly inaccurate *Imperial Hearst* (1936). (Other Hearst biographies have little information on Annenberg.) The writer is indebted to the Journalism Lib., Columbia Univ., for use of its extensive clipping file on Annenberg, to Charlotte Curtis of the *N. Y. Times* for her memorandum on Annenberg's Milwaukee years, and to Sam Rothstein for preliminary research on Annenberg biographical data. Obituaries appear in the *N. Y. Times* and *N. Y. Herald Tribune* of July 21, 1942. Annenberg's death record (Minn. State Board of Health) gives his year of birth as 1877; other sources agree on 1878.]

JAMES BOYLAN

ARMSTRONG, EDWARD COOKE (Aug. 24, 1871–Mar. 5, 1944), Romance philologist, was born in Winchester, Va., the third son and youngest of five children of James Edward Armstrong, a Methodist minister, and Margaret (Hickman) Armstrong. He was of Scotch-Irish descent. Although he grew up under the difficult economic conditions of Virginia after the Civil War, his parents enabled him to prepare for college at the State Normal School in Shepherdstown, W. Va., and at the Middleburg (Va.) Academy. He entered Randolph-Macon men's college at Ashland, Va., in 1887 and graduated with the A.B. degree in 1890, when not quite nineteen. In 1893, after two years as an instructor at Southwestern University, Georgetown, Texas, he entered the Johns Hopkins University as a graduate student in Romance languages. His doctoral dissertation was a critical edition of an Old French poem, "Le Chevalier à l'Épée," and he received his Ph.D. in 1897. On June 8, 1905, Armstrong married Emerline Mason Holbrook of an established Boston family. They had one son, Percy Holbrook.

For twenty years, from 1897 to 1917, Armstrong taught at Johns Hopkins, rising gradually through the academic ranks until he succeeded A. Marshall Elliott [q.v.] as chairman of the department of Romance languages after the latter's death in 1910. Armstrong's enduring respect for Elliott, under whom he had taken his doctorate, imbued him with the ambition to carry on and expand Elliott's pioneering work in the United States in training Romance scholars. As an assisting editor, contributor, and, from 1911 to 1915, co-editor of *Modern Language Notes* (which Elliott had founded), Armstrong wrote for this scholarly journal several articles and more than forty reviews and notices. He also began (1914), and edited for some years, the *Elliott Monographs* as a medium of scholarly publication in tribute to his predecessor. As an editor of *Modern Language Notes*, he regularly checked every detail of the articles submitted to him and aided the authors with constructive suggestions. His students, too, learned from him an enduring lesson in accuracy of content, exactness and brevity of language, sound reasoning, and freedom from preconceived judgments. He made every effort to place his students and other scholars of his acquaintance in the exact type of position for which he believed them to be best fitted; a number had distinguished careers in fields they had not originally contemplated.

In 1917 Armstrong resigned from Johns Hopkins to accept a post as professor of French language at Princeton University. There he organized a group of scholars to undertake a study of the Alexander corpus—Old French poems of the twelfth and thirteenth centuries dealing with Alexander the Great. The project, "one of the few large Romance enterprises that have been fathered in America" (Lancaster, p. 296), had resulted, by the time of his death, in fourteen volumes.

Although his own field was Old French language and literature, Armstrong had "a sound respect for honest, precise labor" in any period (Malkiel, p. 143). Under his editorship, for example, the first four numbers of the *Elliott Monographs* were devoted to the novelist Flaubert; others dealt with aspects of modern French literature. Of his more distinguished students, H. Carrington Lancaster was noted for his work on seventeenth-century literature and E. Preston

Dargan for his studies of the French eighteenth century and of Anatole France.

Armstrong took a leading part in the work of the Modern Language Association of America, of which he was president in 1918–19. As such he helped found the American Council of Learned Societies in 1919 and was its secretary-treasurer, 1925–29, and chairman, 1929–35. In the judgment of the Council's executive officer, Waldo G. Leland, "His part in shaping its course and determining its policies cannot be overestimated." Armstrong had "an intuitive understanding of persons and situations, as well as a keen and practical sagacity" (Leland, p. 33). He was also friendly and warmhearted, although firm and uncompromising in the high standards he demanded of himself and inspired in others. Among the honors that came to him were doctoral degrees from Oberlin College and the universities of Chicago, Paris, and Berlin. He was a fellow of the Mediaeval Academy of America and a member of the American Philosophical Society. For his postwar services as dean of American students at the University of Bordeaux (1919) and his other achievements he was decorated with the Legion of Honor by the government of France.

Armstrong retired from teaching at Princeton in 1939 as he approached the age of sixty-eight, but continued his own research ardently and, in spite of gradually failing health during the last year and a half of his life, uncomplainingly. During these final months, says Gilbert Chinard, Armstrong read and reread Montaigne's famous chapter "Of Experience," with its appropriate line, "There is no desire more natural than the desire of knowledge." He died of uremia at his home in Princeton and was buried in the Holbrook family plot in Brattleboro, Vt.

[Armstrong's publications include: *Syntax of the French Verb* (1909, with later editions in 1915 and 1927); *The French Metrical Versions of Barlaam and Josaphat* (1922); and *The Authorship of the Vengement Alixandre and of the Venjance Alixandre* (1926). Biographical references: Frederick A. Virkus, *A Compendium of Am. Genealogy*, IV (1930), 33–34; *Vita* appended to Armstrong's published doctoral dissertation (1900), p. 73; *Who Was Who in America*, vol. II (1950); *N. Y. Times*, Mar. 6, 1944; H. C. Lancaster in *Modern Language Notes*, Apr. 1944, p. 296; Waldo G. Leland in Am. Council of Learned Soc., *Bull.*, no. 38 (1945), pp. 33–34; Gilbert Chinard in Am. Philosophical Soc., *Year Book*, 1944; Alfred Foulet in *Romania*, LXVIII (1944–45), 394–95; Yakov Malkiel in *Romance Philology*, Feb. 1957. Professor Foulet, who knew Armstrong well, provided important information.]

GEORGE R. HAVENS

ARTHUR, JOSEPH CHARLES (Jan. 11, 1850–Apr. 30, 1942), botanist, was born in Lowville, N. Y., the first of two children and only son of Charles and Ann (Allen) Arthur. He was christened Charles Joseph but later reversed the names. His father, a farmer, was descended from an English immigrant who settled in Groton, Conn., about 1745; his mother was a native of Canada. When the boy was six years old, the family moved west and, after a brief stay near Sterling, Ill., settled on a farm in Floyd County, near Charles City, Iowa. Here, surrounded by the largely virgin prairie, Arthur developed the interest in plants that persisted throughout his life. He remembered his boyhood as "tranquil" and "wholesome . . . as free and unfettered as the boundless prairies." He early showed his independence by becoming skilled at needlework and avoiding the more strenuous boys' games such as touch-the-goal. The family were devout Methodists, but in adult life Arthur was affiliated with the Presbyterian Church.

After attending country schools and the Charles City high school, Arthur enrolled in 1869 with the first class at the newly established Iowa State College at Ames. Here his interest in botany was greatly stimulated by the instruction and the personal friendship of Prof. Charles E. Bessey [q.v.]. He received the B.S. degree in 1872 and in the same year published his first paper, on the double flowers in *Ranunculus rhomboideus*. Since no positions were available in the field of botany, he taught in country schools for several winters and then returned to Iowa State, receiving the M.S. degree in 1877 with a thesis on the anatomy of the wild cucumber vine. After a semester of study at Johns Hopkins University and a summer term at Harvard, where he worked with the mycologist William G. Farlow [q.v.], Arthur held instructorships at the universities of Wisconsin (1879–81) and Minnesota (1882). In 1884 he was named botanist at the newly founded Agricultural Experiment Station at Geneva, N.Y., and at the same time began to carry out research at Cornell University in plant pathology and mycology, for which he received the Sc.D. degree in 1886.

The following year Arthur moved to Purdue University in Lafayette, Ind., where he founded and for many years headed the department of botany and plant pathology. He instituted laboratory instruction in plant physiology and built up an important herbarium, later known as the Arthur Herbarium. His major contribution as a researcher was to mycology, and specifically to an understanding of the life cycles, geographical distribution, and classification of the rust fungi (order Uredinales) of North America. During his years at Purdue, the university became recognized throughout the world as a leading center of research in this field.

Arthur's interest in the life histories of rust fungi led him to propose a new system of classification based on variations in the life cycle. Although this system did not gain acceptance and he later abandoned it, the underlying concepts were important and served to emphasize the phylogenetic significance of the various types of life cycles. His ideas concerning nomenclature were unorthodox, and his continued adherence to them caused much confusion in the names of many species, some of which remains today. But these are relatively insignificant lapses in an otherwise remarkably productive career.

One of the most influential botanists of his era, Arthur carried out work on pear blight, cereal smuts, diseases of sugar beets, and potato scab that was of both scientific and economic importance. His research was instrumental in developing the liaison between the morphology of fungi and their physical characteristics. His pioneer contributions to knowledge of the rust fungi of North America remain unsurpassed, and many other advances were made by men trained by or associated with him. Obviously, the period in which he lived was a factor in his career. The vegetation of the continent was poorly known and the fungi more poorly still. Arthur chose to devote much of his life to a single order of important parasitic fungi, and did so with rare persistence, publishing 149 papers on the Uredinales between 1883 and 1936. Although he retired in 1915, retirement did not mean inactivity. *The Plant Rusts* (written with collaborators) was published fourteen years later, and his *Manual of the Rusts in United States and Canada* (1934) appeared when he was eighty-four.

Arthur was president of the Indiana Academy of Science (1893), the Botanical Society of America (1902, 1919), and the American Phytopathological Society (1933). He served the American Association for the Advancement of Science as secretary of Section F (1886) and assistant general secretary (1887). He was elected to membership in the American Philosophical Society and the American Academy of Arts and Sciences. He made many trips to Europe and took part in the International Botanical Congresses held in Vienna (1905), Brussels (1910), and Cambridge (1930). A courteous, almost a courtly, gentleman of small stature but great dignity, he remained remarkably open-minded and tolerant of the opinions, scientific and otherwise, of his associates. On June 12, 1901, he had married Emily Stiles Potter, member of a pioneer family of Lafayette, Ind., who died in 1935. There were no children. Arthur died at Brook, Ind., in his ninety-third year, of congestive heart failure and was buried in Springvale Cemetery in Lafayette.

[Frank D. Kern's memoir in *Phytopathology*, Oct. 1942 (with photograph and bibliography), is the most comprehensive biography. Other sources: Arthur's autobiographical essay, "Why a Botanist," and his "The Purdue Herbarium" (unpublished typescripts in Dept. of Botany and Plant Pathology at Purdue); G. B. Cummins and Ralph M. Caldwell in *Chronica Botanica*, Dec. 1942; E. B. Mains in *Mycologia*, Nov.–Dec. 1942; Raymond E. Girton, "The Teaching of Plant Physiology at Purdue in the Nineteenth Century," Ind. Acad. of Sci., *Proc.*, LXVII (1957), 260–64; J. W. Baxter and F. D. Kern, "Hist. of the Arthur Herbarium at Purdue Univ.," *ibid.*, LXXI (1961), 228–32; death record from Ind. State Board of Health; personal acquaintance, 1930–42. An oil portrait of Arthur by Robert W. Grafton, painted in 1931, is in the Dept. of Botany and Plant Pathology at Purdue.]
GEORGE B. CUMMINS

BACHE, JULES SEMON (Nov. 9, 1861–Mar. 24, 1944), financier and art collector, was born in New York City, the eldest son among the six children of Semon and Elizabeth (Van Praag) Bache. His father, a native of Fürth, Bavaria, had emigrated to the United States in the 1840's and founded what was to become one of the country's leading firms dealing in quality mirrors and glass fabrication. Jules Bache was educated at Charlier Institute in New York City and in Frankfurt, Germany, and supplemented his studies in Europe by extensive travel. Upon his return to the United States, he entered his father's firm as a submanager, but left in 1880 to become a cashier in his uncle's New York brokerage house of Leopold Cahn & Company. He was promoted to treasurer in 1881, admitted to partnership in 1886, and became head of the firm in 1892, at which time its name was changed to J. S. Bache & Company.

Shortly after Bache had become a partner in Leopold Cahn & Company, the governing committee of the New York Stock Exchange suspended the firm from trading for one year for splitting commissions. In 1893 J. S. Bache & Company was tried on a similar charge, and although the committee delivered a verdict of "not proven," Bache sold his seat on the exchange. Yet the firm prospered. It financed numerous large enterprises, handling the reorganization of the American Spirits Manufacturing Company (1895), the Glucose Sugar Refining Company (1897), the Distilling and Cattle Feeding Company (1905), popularly known as the "Whiskey Trust," and the Cosmopolitan Fire Insurance Company (1906). At the same time Bache expanded rapidly into the branch brokerage business. An innovative banker, he was notably successful in tapping the middle-class market. By 1905, with branch offices in Albany, Troy, Philadelphia, Rochester, Newark, Montreal, and Liverpool, England, J. S. Bache & Company had one of the most extensive private wire systems in the United States. It several times handled more than 200,000 shares in a single day. Continuing to expand after World War I, by 1945 it had thirty-seven branches and more than 800 employees. Among his other business activities, Bache was especially active in the Chrysler Corporation, of which he was a vice-president from 1929 to 1943, and in Dome Mines, Ltd., of which he was president from 1918 to 1943 and chairman of the board from 1943 until his death.

Bache's career as an art collector paralleled his success on Wall Street. It began largely through the influence of two friends—the investment bankers Philip Lehman and George Blumenthal—who were then forming their own collections. Bache started with decorative arts, but though his collection eventually included excellent examples of medieval enamels, early English and French silver, French eighteenth-century furniture, and sculpture, he turned his main interest to painting. Between 1919 and 1929 he acquired one of the greatest collections of old masters ever formed in this country. The initial purchases were Rembrandt's "Young Man in a Red Cloak" and "Le Billet Doux" by Jean Fragonard. In 1924 he acquired Van Dyck's magnificent "Portrait of the Artist," but the source of the purchase was perhaps more significant than the object, for with this transaction Bache entered into a relationship, both personal and commercial, with one of history's great art dealers, Joseph Duveen. Of his later acquisitions, which included works by Bellini, Botticelli, Crivelli, Raphael, Titian, Holbein, Hals, Vermeer, Goya, Velasquez, Watteau, Gainsborough, and Reynolds, some three-fourths were purchased from Duveen, and Bache freely acknowledged the dealer as his mentor.

As Bache grew older, he became concerned about the possible dispersal of his paintings. Tentative negotiations in 1936 with the Metropolitan Museum of Art foundered on his insistence that the collection be kept intact in contiguous galleries and labeled as the Jules Bache Collection; and the next year he set up a museum in his own home. The Metropolitan Museum, however, ultimately agreed to his terms and five years after Bache's death came into formal possession of his collection—fifty-four paintings, twenty pieces of sculpture, nine enamels, five pieces of furniture, eighteen pieces of silver, two tapestries, and four porcelains.

A man of definite opinions and quick decisions, tending to abruptness in his youth but mellowing with age, Jules Bache had an engaging personality, a zest for life, and a distinguished appearance. On May 23, 1892, he married Florence Rosalee Scheftel, daughter of a wealthy leather merchant of New York City. They had two daughters, Hazel Joy and Kathryn King. His wife divorced him in Paris on Aug. 11, 1925, for desertion. Bache was a delegate to the Republican National Convention in 1920. Although of Jewish descent, he was an Episcopalian in religion. He died in Palm Beach, Fla., at the age of eighty-two of chronic nephritis and was buried in Woodlawn Cemetery, New York City. He left not only an important art collection but a flourishing firm which, two decades later, had become the second largest stock brokerage house in the United States.

[Biographical material about Bache is limited: *Nat. Cyc. Am. Biog.*, XXXIV, 349–50; obituary in *N. Y. Times*, Mar. 24, 1944; *Who Was Who in America*, vol. II (1950); *Universal Jewish Encyc.*, II, 20–21; death record, from Fla. Bureau of Vital Statistics. There are frequent references to Bache in the *N. Y. Times*, 1891–1944 (see Index). On his business career, see: Mitchell C. Harrison, comp., *N. Y. State's Prominent and Progressive Men*, II (1900), 3–4; and articles on Bache & Co. in *Bankers' Mag.*, Aug. 1905, and the *Ticker*, Feb. 1908. On his art collection: records in the Metropolitan Museum of Art Archives (not open to the public); *A Catalogue of Paintings in the Bache Collection* (1929, rev. ed., 1944); illustrated description of Bache's private museum in *N. Y. Herald Tribune*, Nov. 16, 1937; Harry B. Wehle, "The Bache Collection on Loan," *Metropolitan Museum of Art Bull.*, June 1943; Francis Henry Taylor, "Masterpieces of the Bache Collection," *N. Y. Times Mag.*, June 20, 1943. A head by the sculptor Jo Davidson is at the Metropolitan Museum of Art.]

JOHN BUCHANAN

BAEKELAND, LEO HENDRIK (Nov. 14, 1863–Feb. 23, 1944), industrial chemist, inventor of Velox paper for photographic prints and of the synthetic plastic Bakelite, was born in St. Martens-Latem, Belgium, a village near Ghent. His father, Karel Lodewyk Baekeland, was an illiterate shoe repairman; his mother, Rosalia (Merchie) Baekeland, had worked as a maid before her marriage. A sister thirteen years younger than Leo was the only other child. The father would have been content to see his son follow in his footsteps, and when Leo was thirteen he was apprenticed to a shoemaker. The experience was an unhappy one, since the boy was a bookish lad with a highly imaginative mind. His mother, ambitious for him to rise out of the pattern of family poverty, encouraged him to attend the Athénée Royal, the government high school, where he excelled in scientific courses. He also enrolled for evening vocational classes at the École Industrielle de Gand, at the same time helping to finance his education by working in an apothecary shop. One of his teachers, Jules Marel, encouraged the youth to continue his education, and with the aid of a scholarship from the city government he enrolled in the University of Ghent as a chemistry student. He quickly attracted the attention of Prof. Theodore Swarts, distinguished student of fluorine chemistry, who made Baekeland his *préparateur*. He completed his bachelor's degree in two years; his doctorate of science, maxima cum laude, in two more. The degree was conferred in July 1884, several months before his twenty-first birthday.

Following his graduation, Baekeland became an assistant in chemistry at the nearby École Normale in Bruges, where Professor Swarts was also head of natural sciences. In 1887 he submitted an essay, "On the Phenomenon of Dissociation," to a competition for recent graduates of the four Belgian universities. This won him a gold medal and a sum of money for foreign study. He did not use the money immediately, however, since he was given a professorship in chemistry and physics at the Bruges normal school, an unusual appointment for so young a man. The next year an offer of an assistant professorship in chemistry drew him back to the University of Ghent. A further attraction was Céline Swarts, daughter of his professor and superior, to whom he was married on Aug. 8, 1889. They had three children: Jenny (who died in childhood), George Washington, and Nina.

Although Baekeland had been rising rapidly on the academic ladder and in 1886 had published a research paper on the influence of light on the oxidation of chloracetic acid, he questioned whether his future really lay in the academic life. He had developed an interest in photography, but was disturbed by the tediousness of the art as it was then carried out and with the inconsistent performance of commercial photographic plates. In 1887 he obtained a Belgian patent on a dry plate which carried its own developer in an inactive form. In association with Jules Guequier, a fellow faculty member at Ghent, he formed a company, Baekeland et Cie., to produce and market the plate, with Guequier's family providing the capital. The venture, however, was a fiasco. Capital was inadequate to see the company through the early period while developmental problems were being solved, and the time spent on company problems caused Professor Swarts to complain about Baekeland's academic performance. Immediately after his marriage, Baekeland abandoned the foundering company, drew his stipend for foreign study, and began visiting universities in other lands, hoping to find a position where he could combine academic contacts with industrial research. After a brief stay at the University of Edinburgh, his quest brought him across the

Atlantic to New York City. There Prof. Charles Frederick Chandler of Columbia persuaded him to remain in the United States and, in 1891, secured him a position as chemist for the New York firm of E. and H. T. Anthony, producers of dry plates and print papers for the photographic trade.

After two years with the Anthony company Baekeland left to become an independent consultant. This was an exceedingly difficult period in his life. He had sent his wife back to Belgium in 1890 for the birth of their first child, then left her stranded there for several years while he pursued ideas for a variety of inventions. A serious illness and mounting debts prompted him to concentrate his efforts upon a single invention with commercial possibilities: a photographic print paper that could be developed by artificial light. Since prints were then made by sunlight, which varied in intensity, quality was difficult to control. Baekeland's "gaslight paper," to which he gave the trade name Velox, utilized silver chloride, a less sensitive and slower developing silver salt than the more widely used silver bromide; development could be carried out by placing the negative and print paper close to a standard source of artificial light and working in illuminated quarters. To produce and market the new paper Baekeland formed the Nepera Chemical Company, in Yonkers, N. Y., in 1893. Leonard Jacobi, a scrap-metal dealer from San Francisco, provided the capital and proved a patient and understanding partner while production problems were being resolved.

As finally perfected, Velox paper was simple to produce, had a good shelf life, was easy to use, and gave prints with good contrast and resistance to fading; it was particularly acceptable in this period when photography was becoming popular among amateurs. By the end of 1896 it was obvious that the operation would be a profitable one. Three years later, when the Nepera firm was expanding its plant to keep pace with the rising volume of business, Baekeland accepted an offer —reportedly $750,000—from George Eastman [Supp. 1] and sold his firm to the Eastman Kodak Company.

Now that his investigations had placed a profitable product on the market, Baekeland lost his zest for business. Setting up a laboratory in a barnlike outbuilding of the estate he had acquired in Yonkers, he worked on other problems that interested him, particularly the electrolysis of common salt and the production of synthetic resins. His electrochemical ideas had lain dormant for many years, and to bring his knowledge up to date he spent the winter of 1900–01 in Ger-

many at the electrochemical laboratory of the Technological Institute of Charlottenburg. Electrochemical industries had developed rapidly during the 1890's but were still plagued by many technical problems. When Elon H. Hooker [Supp. 2] and his brothers became interested in the electrolytic cell patented by Clinton P. Townsend in 1902, they hired Baekeland as a consultant. The Townsend cell, designed for the production of sodium hydroxide and chlorine by the electrolysis of brine, differed from earlier commercial cells in that it contained a diaphragm to prevent mixing of the chlorine and alkali. At a pilot plant in Brooklyn, the carbon anodes deteriorated after two months' operation, but Townsend and Baekeland found that by changing to saturated brine this could be avoided. Baekeland also designed a sturdy diaphragm composed of woven asbestos cloth impregnated with colloidal iron oxide, and a method for resaturating electrolyzed brine. These contributions were embodied in the full-scale and successful plant which began operation at Niagara Falls in 1905 and became the Hooker Electrochemical Company.

During this same period Baekeland was also busy with his work on phenolic resins. The research of Adolf von Baeyer a quarter-century earlier in Germany had revealed the formation of inert, thick, dark products when phenol reacted with aldehydes, but since organic chemists of the day were interested primarily in compounds which crystallized in pure form, these amorphous mixtures were generally ignored. In 1891 W. Kleeberg studied the reaction of phenol with formaldehyde, but the resinous products still appeared unpromising. In the meantime, several plastic materials, particularly Celluloid, derived from nitrated cellulose and camphor, and Galilith, derived from casein and formaldehyde, received limited commercial acceptance.

Beginning his work in 1902, Baekeland undertook a careful study of the earlier reports of the reaction of phenol and formaldehyde and initiated further experiments in his own laboratory. By 1907 he was able to control the reaction in order to produce a good thermosetting resin (one which, when heated, becomes permanently solid, in contrast to thermoplastic resins like Celluloid and Galilith which soften upon subsequent exposure to heat). He found he could control the nature of the final product through use of pressure. By employing ammonia it was possible to slow down the reaction, making it possible through cooling to stop the reaction at intermediate stages. The resin, christened "Bakelite," was an electrical insulator, inert to heat, and resistant to most chemicals. While still in the plastic state, it could be molded into articles of intricate shape, then set in the desired form by heating. Its only major shortcoming was brittleness.

Bakelite was an almost instant success in the electrical industry, where it was adaptable to a multiplicity of uses. When Baekeland presented his first public report on the product before the New York Section of the American Chemical Society in February 1909, he had already explored the applicability of Bakelite in forty industries. Though he would have preferred to license his patents, Baekeland found it necessary to become involved himself in commercial production and distribution. In 1910 he organized the General Bakelite Company, in which he held a controlling interest; the firm of Roessler and Hasslacher, chemical importers, held the remaining stock and provided the factory (in Perth Amboy, N. J.) and an office in New York City. A steadily increasing market made continuous plant expansion necessary. Although several competitors arose, Baekeland was generally successful in defending his patents. His two principal competitors, Condensite Corporation of America and Redmanol Chemical Products Company, were absorbed into what had become the Bakelite Corporation in 1924. Baekeland as president was a dominant figure in the corporation's management.

An active participant in professional societies, Baekeland appeared to be most comfortable with chemical cronies. He was one of the founders of the Chemists' Club in New York City and served as its president in 1904 and as president of the American Chemical Society in 1924. He was also president of the Electrochemical Society (1909) and the American Institute of Chemical Engineers (1912). His many honors include the Nichols Medal of the American Chemical Society, the William Perkin Medal for industrial chemical research, the John Scott Medal of the Franklin Institute, and election to the National Academy of Sciences (1936).

Baekeland's concentration on invention and business made for rather indifferent relations with his family. His wife served as his secretary and confidante during the years when his principal inventions were being developed, but in later years she spent much time with children and grandchildren at a place in the Adirondacks while her husband lived in New York City or at the winter home in Coconut Grove, Fla., that he had acquired in the mid-1920's. He was disappointed that his son showed little interest in chemistry or in the Bakelite Corporation. The corporation was sold to Union Carbide and Carbon Corporation in 1939. Baekeland's last years were spent mostly in Florida, where he became a recluse; during this period his mind failed. He died of a coronary thrombosis at the age of eighty at a sanatorium in Beacon, N. Y., and was buried in Yonkers.

[There are unorganized personal papers in the possession of Baekeland's granddaughter Celine Baekeland Karraker, Redding Ridge, Conn. Prof. Jan Gillis, former rector of the Univ. of Ghent, has published a collection of documents and other biographical material: *Dr. L. H. Baekeland: Verzamelde Oorspronkelijke Documenten* (Brussels, 1965). Charles F. Kettering's memoir in Nat. Acad. Sci., *Biog. Memoirs*, vol. XXIV (1947), contains a full list of honors received by Baekeland and a bibliography of his published works. There is substantial biographical material in A. R. Matthis, *Leo H. Baekeland: Professeur, Docteur ès Sciences, Chemiste, Inventeur et Grand Industriel* (Brussels, 1948); and in John K. Mumford, *The Story of Bakelite* (1924). Short biographical sketches include: Wallace P. Cohoe in *Chemical and Engineering News*, Feb. 10, 1945; Jan Gillis in *Jour. of Chemical Education*, Apr. 1964; L. V. Redman in *Industrial and Engineering Chemistry*, Nov. 1928; Williams Haynes in Eduard Farber, ed., *Great Chemists* (1961); James Kendall. "Leo H. Baekeland and the Development of Phenolic Plastics," *Chemistry and Industry*, Jan. 29, 1949; and C. E. K. Mees, "Leo Hendrik Baekeland and Photographic Printing Papers," *ibid.*, Sept. 10, 1955. Death record from N. Y. State Dept. of Health.]

AARON J. IHDE

BAKER, SARA JOSEPHINE (Nov. 15, 1873–Feb. 21, 1945), physician and public health administrator, was born in Poughkeepsie, N. Y., the third daughter and third of four children of Orlando Daniel Mosher Baker, a prosperous attorney of Quaker ancestry, and Jenny Harwood (Brown) Baker, of colonial New England descent. She received her early education at local private schools and, to please her father, who had hoped for a son, became proficient in sports and games. When she was about ten she suffered a knee injury and for the next two years walked on crutches. She prepared to enter Vassar College, where her mother had been one of the first students, but was forced to give up the plan in 1890 when her father's death left the family in financial straits. Realizing that she must find a way to support her mother and surviving sister, she decided to use the family's small remaining capital to study medicine, perhaps because of her admiration for the physicians who had cared for her at the time of her accident. The opposition she encountered as a woman only strengthened her resolve, and in 1894, after a year spent in mastering the prerequisite scientific background, she entered the Woman's Medical College of the New York Infirmary for Women and Children, then under the direction of Dr. Emily Blackwell.

After graduating in 1898, Dr. Baker served a year's internship in the New England Hospital for Women and Children in Boston and then returned to New York City to begin general practice. Her income during the first year, derived almost entirely from obstetrical cases in a poor West Side neighborhood, was only $185. To supplement it, she persuaded a life insurance company to make her a medical examiner for female applicants for policies who wished a woman doctor. In 1901, after passing a civil service examination, she secured an appointment as a medical inspector in the city health department and spent five hours a week finding and reporting cases of contagious disease among schoolchildren. She soon discovered that the inspection system was a political structure with little relevance for disease control and planned to resign, but when in 1902 a reform administration took over the city government and reorganized the health department, she accepted a summer job visiting tenements in the Hell's Kitchen district to locate and care for babies with diarrheal diseases. In an epidemic of dysentery that summer some 1,500 infants were dying in the city each week, and Dr. Baker gained an intimate knowledge of the medical problems resulting from poverty and ignorance.

In the next few years, during which she was made an assistant to the commissioner of health, she carried out a variety of assignments and gradually evolved the idea that motivated the rest of her life: that the control of childhood disease should be a problem of prevention rather than cure. In the summer of 1908 she was allowed to test her plan for reducing infant mortality. Working in the congested slums of the Lower East Side with a staff of thirty nurses, she obtained each day from the registrar of records the name of every newborn child in the district. One of the nurses promptly visited the mother and taught her what to do to keep the baby well—breast feeding, efficient ventilation, frequent bathing, thin summer clothing, out-of-door airing wherever possible. These methods, commonplace today, were at that time completely new to the poor as well as to public health officials. When the demonstration program had been completed, the record showed 1,200 fewer deaths for that district than in the previous summer. Her success led to the creation that August of a Division (later Bureau) of Child Hygiene within the New York City Health Department, with Josephine Baker as its chief—the first official agency set up by any modern government to deal with the medical problems of infancy and childhood. By 1918, the infant death rate in the city had fallen from 144 to 88 per 1,000 live births.

Under Dr. Baker's leadership the Division of Child Hygiene implemented other programs designed to give babies a healthy start in life. The licensing system for midwives, who flourished among the immigrant populations, was put under

strict control and the standards raised. In 1911 a free six-month training course for midwives was established at the city's Bellevue Hospital, and new applicants for licenses were required to present a certificate from this or similar schools in Europe. New legislation required midwives to use silver nitrate drops in the eyes of all infants they delivered, to prevent blindness. To reduce the mortality rate in foundling institutions, which was much higher than in even the poorest homes, Dr. Baker stressed the value of the foster mother system, being one of the first to recognize the dangers of maternal deprivation. Recognizing that the "little mother," the small girl in a poor family who must take care of the next youngest child while their mother worked, was a vital factor in infant health, she organized Little Mothers' Leagues among schoolgirls; they were given practical instruction in child care and served as missionaries of the new health gospel in the tenements and slums. Later, in 1917, she gave additional impetus to the school lunch movement, estimating that 21 percent of the children in the New York public schools were undernourished. Working toward the same goal, child health, she organized the first Federation of Children's Agencies in New York City.

Dr. Baker was consulted by numerous governmental agencies that wished to set up units for child hygiene. She took an active part in the work of the federal Children's Bureau from the time it was established in 1912 until her death, serving for sixteen years as a consultant on its staff. She was one of the founders of the Association for Study and Prevention of Infant Mortality (1909, later the American Child Health Association) and was its president in 1917–18. She had promised herself to retire when all the states in the country had organized a bureau of child hygiene, and when this occurred, in 1923, she kept her word. Infant mortality in New York City had then dropped to 66 per 1,000.

Josephine Baker was the first woman to receive the degree of Doctor of Public Health from the University and Bellevue Hospital Medical College of New York University (1917) and the first to be named by the League of Nations to represent the United States on its health commission. She served as president of the American Medical Women's Association in 1935–36. She was known for the warmth of her personality and her strong sense of humor. In religion she was a Unitarian. Dr. Baker spent her last years at Trevenna Farm, her home in Bellemead, N. J.; at the time of her death she was a member of the New Jersey State Board of Health and of the board of directors of the New Jersey State Reformatory for Women at Clinton. She died of cancer at New York Hospital, New York City, at the age of seventy-one and was buried in the Poughkeepsie Rural Cemetery.

[Dr. Baker's autobiography, *Fighting for Life* (1939); obituary in *Medical Woman's Jour.*, May 1945; tributes in *Women in Medicine*, July 1945. Photographs of Dr. Baker are reproduced in each of the above and in *Nat. Cyc. Am. Biog.*, XXXVI, 91–92. See also *A Bureau of Child Hygiene* (Bureau of Municipal Research, N. Y. City, 1908).]

GEORGE ROSEN

BALL, FRANK CLAYTON (Nov. 24, 1857–Mar. 19, 1943), industrialist and philanthropist, was born in Greensburg, Trumbull County, Ohio, the fourth son and fifth of eight children of Lucius Styles Ball, a farmer, and Maria Polly (Bingham) Ball. Both parents were natives of Canada, although Lucius Ball was descended from Edward Ball, who migrated from England to Branford, Conn., in 1640. When Frank was six, his parents moved to a farm on Grand Island in the Niagara River, going from there to Tonawanda, N. Y., in 1865 and, three years later, to a small farm near Canandaigua, N. Y. Frank's mother had been a schoolteacher, and the parents' great regard for education, as a means of instilling "right ideals and true Christian principles," led them to send Frank and his brothers to Canandaigua Academy when they finished the public schools.

After their father's death, in 1878, an uncle in Buffalo undertook to launch Frank and his older brother Edmund Burke on a business career. In 1880, after several false starts, they bought a small business manufacturing wood-jacketed tin cans in which oils and varnishes were shipped. In keeping with their mother's wishes, the two oldest brothers, Lucius Lorenzo and William Charles, and the youngest, George Alexander, joined Frank and Ed in Buffalo in what was now called the Ball Brothers Company, with Frank as president.

The firm prospered through constant improvements in methods of manufacture, aggressive salesmanship, and alertness in meeting the demand for new products. When kerosene emerged as an illuminating fuel, a large metal tank fitted with a pump was produced for dispensing it in grocery stores. This was followed by the manufacture of a one-gallon metal kerosene can for family use, which in turn was replaced by a more popular glass oil jar. By 1882 Ball Brothers was producing its own glass containers, and three years later, after discovering that the patent covering the "Mason Improved Fruit Jar" had recently expired, the company began producing glass fruit jars and caps.

Coal used as fuel constituted much of the expense in glass making, and Ball and his brothers noted with interest the industrial boom based on gas as a cheap fuel which followed the discovery of natural gas in the oil-field areas of Ohio and Indiana. After visiting several towns in the area, they negotiated an offer from Muncie, Ind., of a seven-acre factory site, a free gas well nearby, and $5,000 for relocation expenses, and in 1887 they built a new factory there. With the move to Muncie the partnership was converted into a corporation. Frank continued as president, with Edmund as vice-president and general manager, William as secretary, George as treasurer, and Lucius (who had become a physician) as a director.

Through inventions of their own and the purchase of exclusive rights to use those of others, Ball Brothers enjoyed a phenomenal growth. By the mid-1920's the annual output of the Ball Mason jar had grown from 25,000 gross in 1888 to more than a million gross, with an annual income of more than $10,000,000. The company had built several factories elsewhere, was making its own zinc jar caps and cardboard shipping cartons, and would soon produce rubber jar rings.

During the Great Depression of the 1930's, sales of glass fruit jars, instead of falling, increased, and with them company profits. A "general understanding" of 1933 severely restricting the production of two major competitors was a factor in the company's dominant position in the glass jar industry, as Frank Ball admitted at a Congressional hearing in 1938. Four years later a federal court ruled that the Ball Brothers Company and seven other concerns had used patent rights and the Glass Container Association to establish a "trust" and took steps to bring such operations to an end.

Though Ball remained president of the family firm until his death in 1943, the brothers worked closely together, both in business and in their philanthropies. Their benefactions, which totaled more than $7,000,000, centered in their city and state. Their practice was to make each gift contingent upon a similar or larger contribution by the public. They gave some $2,000,000 for the Ball Memorial Hospital in Muncie and $500,000 to the James Whitcomb Riley Hospital for Children in Indianapolis. Donations to the Y.M.C.A., Y.W.C.A., and various churches came to another million dollars. Besides smaller gifts to Indiana University and several colleges (including Hillsdale in Michigan and Keuka in New York), they took a particular interest in the Muncie Normal School, which, aided by their benefactions (ultimately $2,000,000), became the Indiana State

Normal School in 1918, Ball State Teachers College in 1929, and in 1965 Ball State University.

Ball was married on Nov. 1, 1893, to Elizabeth Wolfe Brady of Muncie. They had five children: Edmund Arthur, Lucina (Lucy), Margaret Elizabeth, Frank Elliott, and Rosemary Wright. An active Mason, Ball supported the Republican party, served his church as Sunday school superintendent (originally a Universalist, he became a Presbyterian), traveled extensively abroad, and collected masterpieces of art which later were given to Ball State University. He was a director of the Federal Reserve Bank of Chicago, 1920–36. He died in Muncie at the age of eighty-five of a cerebral hemorrhage and was buried at Beach Grove Cemetery, Muncie.

Perhaps the most perceptive evaluation of Ball and his brothers appears in *Middletown in Transition,* part of the well-known study of Muncie by the sociologists Robert S. and Helen M. Lynd. Writing in 1936 of Frank and his brother George, the Lynds described them as "alert, capable, democratic, Christian gentlemen . . . men who never have spared themselves in business or civic affairs. . . . In their conscientious and utterly unhypocritical combination of high profits, great philanthropy, and a low wage scale, they embody the hard-headed ethos of Protestant capitalism with its identification of Christianity with the doctrine of the goodness to all concerned of unrestricted business enterprise. In their modesty and personal rectitude, combined with their rise from comparative poverty to great wealth, they fit perfectly the American success dream" (pp. 75–76).

[*Memoirs of Frank Clayton Ball* (privately printed, 1937); Edmund F. Ball, *From Fruit Jars to Satellites* (Newcomen Soc. address, 1960), on Ball Brothers; Robert S. and Helen M. Lynd, *Middletown* (1929) and *Middletown in Transition* (1937); Glenn White, *The Ball State Story* (1967); *Who Was Who in America*, vol. II (1950); *Nat. Cyc. Am. Biog.*, Current Vol. A, pp. 202–03; *N. Y. Times*, Dec. 16, 1938, Aug. 26, 1942, Mar. 20, 1943; *Muncie Evening Press*, June 3, 1941, Mar. 19, 1943, Apr. 1, 1965; *Muncie Morning Star*, Mar. 19, 20, Apr. 7, 1943; death record from Ind. State Board of Health.]

LESTER F. SCHMIDT

BAMBERGER, LOUIS (May 15, 1855–Mar. 11, 1944), merchant and philanthropist, was born in Baltimore, Md., one of five children and the younger of two sons of Elkan and Theresa (Hutzler) Bamberger. Both parents were German Jews of Bavarian origin. Elkan Bamberger, who was engaged in the wholesale notions business, had come to the United States in 1823 from a town near Nuremburg; his wife was born in Frederick, Md. Louis attended Baltimore public schools until the age of fourteen, when he went to work as a clerk and errand boy in the dry goods store,

Hutzler Brothers, owned by his maternal uncles. He joined his father's business in 1871 and a few years later, when the elder Bamberger retired, Louis and his brother Julius purchased the firm. In 1887 Louis Bamberger moved to New York City to work as a buyer for a San Francisco wholesale house while looking for a chance to establish his own business. The opportunity came in December 1892, when he purchased Hill and Cragg, a bankrupt dry goods house in Newark, N. J. After selling the stock, he organized the firm of L. Bamberger and Company, taking as partners Louis Frank and Felix Fuld. When Frank died in 1910, the two remaining partners bought out his interest. Fuld, who married Bamberger's sister Carrie in 1913, was associated with the company for thirty-six years.

Opening in February 1893, L. Bamberger and Company grew into New Jersey's largest retail business and one of the nation's largest department stores. Under Bamberger's direction the store pioneered in modern retailing techniques. From the beginning it operated on a satisfaction-guaranteed policy, and it was among the first stores to provide such conveniences as a restaurant and customer parking. In 1922 Bamberger established one of the pioneer commercial radio stations—WOR—known as the "Bamberger Broadcasting Company." Originally located on the top floor of the Newark store, it was soon shifted to Kearny, N. J., where its 5,000-watt transmitter made it one of the largest and most popular stations in the country. The store also published *Charm Magazine,* beginning in 1924. Always interested in the welfare of his employees, Bamberger provided a fully staffed educational department for their benefit, and when the first public financing of the company was instituted in 1927, employees were given the opportunity to purchase stock on a two-year installment plan. In 1929, after Felix Fuld's death, Bamberger and Carrie Fuld sold the department store to R. H. Macy and Company of New York for $25,000,000, and shortly afterward distributed $1,000,000 among nearly 240 employees with fifteen or more years of service. Bamberger continued to serve as chairman of the board of directors until 1939.

Bamberger's interest in philanthropy grew with the years. He made extensive donations of the conventional kind to a variety of civic, cultural, and humanitarian organizations in the Newark area. In response to the efforts of John Cotton Dana [*q.v.*] to establish an imaginative new museum in the city of Newark, Bamberger gave $650,000 in 1923 and 1924 to construct a building for the Newark Museum, and he contributed liberally to its permanent collection. He was also a friend and patron of Jewish organizations and gave generously to groups raising relief funds for Jews in Germany and Palestine.

Outstanding among Bamberger's benefactions was his endowment of the Institute for Advanced Study. Through the philanthropist Abraham Flexner, Bamberger and his sister Mrs. Fuld became interested in the creation of a new type of educational institution in the United States, an institution dedicated primarily to advanced research. In 1930 they gave $5,000,000 to found the Institute for Advanced Study on the condition that Flexner would organize and direct it. The site chosen was the town of Princeton, in accordance with Bamberger's wish that it be in New Jersey. The first unit, a school of mathematics distinguished by the presence of Albert Einstein, opened in 1933; a school of historical studies was added later. Here established scholars, given temporary or long-standing appointments, were free to pursue creative research. Bamberger served as president of the board of trustees until 1934, when he became a life trustee, and at his death he left the institute the greater part of his fortune. In all, he and his sister gave the institute approximately $18,000,000.

A short, slight man, Bamberger possessed quiet and cultured tastes. An enthusiastic collector of art, antiquities, and Americana, he left collections to the Newark Museum and the New Jersey Historical Society. Unusually modest, he carefully avoided personal publicity. His philanthropy was governed by the same careful consideration that marked his business life. His advice to Flexner on the organization of the Institute for Advanced Study was characteristic. "I am perfectly satisfied in mind, and I do not care that you do anything during my lifetime," he said. "We only want it to be right when we do it" (*I Remember*, p. 361). Bamberger never married. He died in his sleep of heart failure at his home in South Orange, N. J., at the age of eighty-eight. His body was cremated.

[Obituaries in the *N. Y. Times*, Mar. 12, 1944, *Newark Star-Ledger*, Mar. 12, and *South Orange Record*, Mar. 16; *New Jersey's First Citizen's and State Guide*, vol. II (1919); *New Jersey: A Hist.*, vol. V (1930); files in the N. J. Room, Newark Public Lib. Abraham Flexner's *I Remember* (1940) briefly discusses the endowment for the Inst. for Advanced Study. See also Flexner's "Louis Bamberger and Mrs. Felix Fuld," Am. Jewish Hist. Soc., *Publications*, no. 37 (1947), pp. 455–57; the Newark Museum's *Louis Bamberger: A Record of His Benefactions to His Community and His Country* (1934); *N. Y. Times*, Jan. 21, 1923, Mar. 13, 1924 (on his gifts to the Museum); and the article on Carrie Bamberger Fuld in *Notable Am. Women*. Mrs. August S. Bing, a grandniece, provided family information; death certificate from South Orange Dept. of Public Health. Pictures

of Bamberger can be found with the obituaries cited above and in the *Nat. Cyc. Am. Biog.*, XXXIII, 349; a portrait is in the Newark Museum.]

ROBERT J. FRIDLINGTON

BANCROFT, FREDERIC (Oct. 30, 1860– Feb. 22, 1945), historian and philanthropist, was born in Galesburg, Ill., to Catherine (Blair) and Addison Newton Bancroft; of their seven children, only he, an older brother, and a sister survived infancy. His mother's family had migrated from northern Ireland in the mid-eighteenth century. His father, who conducted a flourishing retail business, was related to the well-known New England Bancrofts. Frederic's education was the best that the West afforded, for the leading citizens of Galesburg were as attentive to education as their New England forebears whose institutions they copied. After attending the local Knox Academy, he enrolled in Knox College, in Galesburg. At the end of three years he transferred to Amherst College, where he graduated in 1882. Recognizing that his deepest interest was in scholarship, Bancroft enrolled for graduate study in Columbia University's School of Political Science, then only two years old. His doctoral dissertation, *A Sketch of the Negro in Politics* (1885), reflected his interest in the history of the South, a subject which remained his scholarly preoccupation for the remainder of his life. Soon after receiving his Ph.D. in 1885, he went abroad for further study at the University of Berlin.

Upon returning from his European sojourn in 1888, Bancroft accepted an appointment as librarian of the Department of State, largely because of the opportunity the position offered for research in its records and manuscripts. Although dismissed four years later by Secretary of State James G. Blaine [*q.v.*], who wished the position "for one of his pets," Bancroft decided to remain in the capital city. It was his home for the next fifty-three years. Although he gave occasional lectures at Columbia and other universities, Bancroft held no further jobs. Instead, with the financial support of his brother Edgar Addison Bancroft, a successful railroad attorney and corporation executive, he pursued an unhampered career of research and writing.

In the decades before World War I, Bancroft wrote a two-volume *Life of William H. Seward* (1900) and, with William A. Dunning [*q.v.*] of Columbia, contributed an extended sketch of the political career of Carl Schurz [*q.v.*] to the third volume (1908) of Schurz's *Reminiscences*. He also edited a six-volume edition of Schurz's *Speeches, Correspondence and Political Papers* (1913). Of all the public figures, political and literary, with whom he was acquainted, it was his friendship with Schurz that gave him greatest satisfaction. These writings were but a fragment of what Bancroft initially expected to accomplish. His most ambitious project, begun in 1903, was a history of the South. His painstaking and thorough research gained him recognition as one of the foremost authorities in the country on the antebellum South and the Civil War, but not until almost three decades later did he publish a book on either subject, and then only chapters of his proposed history—*Calhoun and the South Carolina Nullification Movement* (1928) and *Slave Trading in the Old South* (1931). Though the latter is an exemplary piece of scholarship and was for years the definitive work on the subject, Bancroft's contribution to history was, on balance, modest.

During the decades after World War I, Bancroft's historical work was subordinated to travel and, after his brother's death in 1925, to care of the estate he inherited. Largely through the influence of Allan Nevins, a professor of history at Columbia University and since the early 1930's a warm personal friend, Bancroft, who never married, decided to leave his estate to Columbia. He died in Washington in 1945 of congestive heart failure and was buried in Galesburg. By his wishes, his bequest, which came to nearly $2,000,000, has been used for the purchase of books on American history and for the annual award of prizes in American history and American biography.

[Bancroft's papers are in the Columbia Univ. Lib. These were the basis for Jacob E. Cooke's *Frederic Bancroft: Historian* (1957), which includes three previously unpublished essays by Bancroft on "The Colonization of Am. Negroes, 1801–1865." A brief and appreciative biographical sketch of Bancroft (anonymous, but written by William A. Dunning) appeared in the *Critic*, May 1900; and an obituary was published in the *Am. Hist. Rev.*, Apr. 1945.]

JACOB E. COOKE

BARBOUR, HENRY GRAY (Mar. 28, 1886–Sept. 23, 1943), pharmacologist, was born in Hartford, Conn., the first son and third of four children. His father, the Rev. John Humphrey Barbour, an Episcopal minister, was librarian of Trinity College in Hartford and, from 1889, professor of New Testament literature and interpretation at Berkeley Divinity School, New Haven, Conn. Through his father Barbour was descended from Peter Brown, a *Mayflower* settler of 1620, and Thomas Barbour, who came to America in 1635. His mother, Annie (Gray) Barbour, traced her descent from Samuel Gray, who came from Dorsetshire to Boston in the late seventeenth century.

Barbour attended the Hartford high school, received the A.B. degree from Trinity College in 1906, and graduated, M.D., from the medical school of the Johns Hopkins University in 1910. He remained there for a year after graduation, working with the pharmacologist John J. Abel [Supp. 2]. The year 1911–12 he spent in Europe, studying in Freiburg, Vienna (with Hans Horst Meyer), and London. In 1912 he became assistant professor of pharmacology and toxicology at Yale University, a post he left in 1921 to become professor of pharmacology at McGill University in Montreal. From 1923 to 1931 he was professor of physiology and pharmacology at the University of Louisville. He returned to New Haven in 1931 as associate professor of pharmacology and toxicology at Yale, and in 1937 became a research associate, attaining professorial rank in 1940.

Closest to Barbour's heart was his study of heat regulation in the animal body. Between 1912 and 1944 he published some 160 papers dealing with his researches in this field. He explored the physiology of heat production and heat loss, the regulation of body temperature by the central and peripheral nervous systems and by hormones, the production and relief of fever and hypothermia by drugs and toxins. He is particularly remembered for his many demonstrations of water exchange in the animal body and its importance for the control of temperature. For this study he developed (with the physiologist William F. Hamilton) the falling-drop method for measuring the specific gravity of fluids; the instrument devised for this purpose was still in demand from its manufacturer forty years later and underwent further refinement for the study of heavy water (deuterium oxide). Barbour concluded that the animal body regulates body temperature more closely than it does the osmotic pressure of its fluids. Perhaps his favorite demonstration was that antipyretic drugs such as aspirin lower body temperature only if it is higher than normal, a phenomenon still unexplained. He applied his study of water exchange and other metabolic processes to the physiology of addiction to and withdrawal from morphine, and to the physiology of general anesthesia. After heavy water became available in 1932, Barbour's research into its biological properties was embodied in eighteen papers. He published a textbook, *Experimental Pharmacology and Toxicology,* in 1932.

Barbour was not considered brilliant in formal lectures to large classes, or in the administration of departmental affairs. His strength lay in his ability to communicate, to students working closely with him, his enthusiasm for the experimental exploration of the unknown. While at

Louisville he introduced a program of research scholarships for medical students, and many of his publications arose from the resulting collaborations. Although some of these students later confessed that their original motivation had been financial, several went on to careers in academic medicine and research. Such students and his younger colleagues recalled Henry Barbour as an enthusiastic, painstaking investigator and author, and one with a warm interest in them and in their careers.

On Sept. 15, 1906, Barbour married Lilla Millard Chittenden, daughter of Russell H. Chittenden [Supp. 3], professor of physiological chemistry at Yale. Their children were Henry Chittenden, Dorothy Gray, and Russell Chittenden. Like his father, Barbour was an Episcopalian. He died in New Haven, Conn., at the age of fifty-seven, of acute pulmonary edema and hypertensive heart disease, and was buried there in Evergreen Cemetery.

[Obituary articles in *Science*, Nov. 19, 1943 (by William T. Salter), and *Jour. Am. Medic. Assoc.*, Oct. 23, 1943; personal communication from Dorothy Gray (Mrs. Jerald B.) Slavich. The Historical Lib. of the Yale Univ. School of Medicine has a mimeographed summary of Barbour's scientific publications, 1911–36. See also Yale Univ. School of Medicine, *Publications from the Laboratory of Pharmacology, July 1931–July 1941* (1941).]

PETER K. KNOEFEL

BARRÈRE, GEORGES (Oct. 31, 1876–June 14, 1944), flutist and conductor, was born in Bordeaux, France, the second of three sons of Gabriel François and Marie Périne (Courtet) Barrère. Neither parent was musical, the father being a furniture maker of moderate means. The family moved to Paris when the boys were young. As a member of a fife and drum corps young Georges played several instruments before deciding on the flute. In 1890 he entered the national Conservatoire de Musique. Enrolled as an auditor because of his youth, he proved a mediocre student under Henri Altès, but after transferring to Claude Paul Taffanel in flute and to Raoul Pugno and Xavier Leroux in harmony, he excelled and won first prize in 1895. After supporting himself by odd jobs and serving a year in the army, Barrère found ample scope for his art by teaching privately, playing in the Schola Cantorum under Vincent d'Indy (1899–1905), in the Colonne Orchestra (1900–05), and at the Paris Opéra. A young man of immense vitality and gregarious habits, he founded in 1895 the Société Moderne d'Instruments à Vent, which brought out more than a hundred new compositions for the flute as well as reviving music from the seventeenth and eighteenth centuries. The

Société was later subsidized by the Ministry of Arts.

Barrère was well established in Paris when Walter Damrosch invited him to become first flute in the New York Symphony Orchestra. He arrived in America on May 13, 1905. Objections of the musicians' union were overcome only after Damrosch featured his new soloist so often that his superiority was proven. In addition to his orchestral duties, Barrère soon organized several chamber music groups: the New York Symphony Wind Instruments Club in 1906, the Barrère Ensemble, comprising flute, oboe, clarinet, bassoon, and horn, in 1910, and the Trio Lutèce in 1913. With the addition of strings, trumpet, and drums (as required) in 1914, the Ensemble became the Barrère Little Symphony. Aided by an enterprising agent, these groups found wide acceptance throughout the nation; a typical season offered as many as 167 concerts. America had known chamber music for seventy-five years, mostly that of the string quartet; but music by Haydn, Mozart, and Beethoven involving woodwind instruments was not often heard, and to these Barrère added the newer Impressionists then gaining favor in France.

Slender, trimly built, and precise of manner, sporting a beard and appearing as the epitome of the genus Frenchman, Barrère soon found that audiences enjoyed his unique way with the English language, and he ever after combined performance with beguiling talks to his audiences. The Little Symphony was in demand by visiting artists, such as Isadora Duncan [*q.v.*], Adolf Bolm's Russian dancers, the Pavley-Oukrainsky dancers, and several enterprising singers. Whatever the occasion, Georges Barrère retained his identity as a special attraction, and the flute acquired new popularity as a concert instrument.

Barrère remained with the New York Symphony, except for one season (1918), until its merger with the New York Philharmonic in 1928, and then continued with that organization. Other regular engagements included the Worcester Music Festival under Albert Stoessel [Supp. 3] and, for twenty years, assistant conductorship of the Chautauqua Symphony. He taught at the Institute of Musical Art from 1905 to 1930 and thereafter at the Juilliard School. He edited several works for flute and keyboard by Bach and Handel and a Nocturne for flute and orchestra by the American composer Charles T. Griffes [*q.v.*]. Barrère became a naturalized American citizen in 1937.

A first marriage in France to Michelette Buran was terminated by divorce in 1916; there were two sons, Claude and Gabriel Paul. On July 6,

1917, he married Cécile Élise Allombert, by whom he had a son, Jean Clement. Georges Barrère died in 1944 of encephalomalacia at a Kingston, N. Y., hospital near his summer home in Woodstock. He was buried in Woodstock. A man of unusual wit and Gallic charm, Barrère, together with Georges Laurent of Boston and William Kincaid of Philadelphia, set a new standard for fine flute playing in America, cultivating and popularizing through several chamber ensembles an art form largely unknown or infrequently performed.

[*Georges Barrère* (privately printed autobiographical monograph, 1928); obituaries in *N. Y. Times* and *N. Y. Herald Tribune,* June 15, 1944; death record from N. Y. State Dept. of Health.]

H. EARLE JOHNSON

BARRYMORE, JOHN (Feb. 15, 1882–May 29, 1942), actor, christened John Sidney Blythe Barrymore, was the youngest of the three children of theatrical parents, Maurice and Georgiana (Drew) Barrymore [*qq.v.*]. Like his brother, Lionel, and sister, Ethel, John was born in the Philadelphia home of his maternal grandmother, Mrs. John Drew, Sr. [Louisa Lane Drew, *q.v.*], and inherited not only an illustrious name in theatrical history but an acting heritage that reached back four generations. Because their work often took the parents away from home, the children grew up under the stern but loving care of their grandmother. As the manager of the Arch Street Theatre, Mrs. Drew allowed her grandchildren to watch from one of the boxes at Saturday matinees on those rare occasions when their father played there. Otherwise the theatre served only as background for their lives, and all three saw a different future for themselves. "We became actors," said Ethel, "not because we wanted to go on the stage, but because it was the thing we could do best." When John Barrymore made his professional debut at the age of twenty-one, he acted from necessity rather than desire.

His mother was a Catholic convert, and John's formal education began at a school attached to the Academy of Notre Dame in Rittenhouse Square, Philadelphia. Three years later he entered the Georgetown (D. C.) Academy, but was expelled—so the story goes—after being caught with some older boys on a visit to a brothel. He then joined Lionel at Seton Hall Academy in East Orange, N.J. Their mother had died when John was eleven, and on Mrs. Drew's death, four years later, he was sent to England to continue his education. Enrolling at King's College, Wimbledon, he made his mark chiefly on the rugby field and on the romantic hearts of susceptible young women. The next year he spent at the Slade School of Art in London, where the manner of Aubrey Beardsley set the tone. He enjoyed the freedom of metropolitan life, but had to be rescued by his sister from the brink of a scandal that involved a married woman of title and an angry husband. Back in New York, Barrymore let his father pay a year's tuition at the Art Students' League but attended only one class, putting himself instead under the tutelage of the painter George Bridgman. At this point Barrymore's bizarre formal education ended. He enjoyed the carefree life of newspapermen, and despite his penniless state he joined their bohemian antics, occasionally selling a picture or doing a theatrical poster.

Turning to the theatre, he made his first professional appearance in Chicago on Oct. 31, 1903, in Hermann Sudermann's *Magda,* playing Max, a role Lionel Barrymore had done several years before. John Barrymore's New York debut on Dec. 28, 1903, in Clyde Fitch's *Glad of It,* led William Collier to cast him in *The Dictator.* Traveling with Collier for several years on a tour that led to San Francisco and Australia, he thoroughly learned his craft. On Sept. 4, 1909, at New York's Gaiety Theatre, he appeared in the title role as Nathaniel Duncan in *The Fortune Hunter,* and in the next five years the handsome young actor became a feminine idol. On Sept. 1, 1910, he married nineteen-year-old Katherine Corri Harris, a member of a socially prominent New York family. Separation while Barrymore toured and personal incompatibility led to repeated quarrels, and his wife obtained a divorce in December 1917.

Meanwhile Barrymore had made a decisive turn in his career through the influence of Edward Sheldon, a young playwright with whom he had formed a close and stabilizing friendship during a visit to Italy in 1914. At Sheldon's urging, Barrymore began to undertake dramatic roles and played William Falder, the tragic bank clerk in Galsworthy's *Justice,* for a successful season in 1916. Sheldon then engineered his friend's first romantic lead, in the title role of *Peter Ibbetson* (April 1917), rewriting portions of the play, helping to raise production money, and inducing Lionel to return to the stage as Colonel Ibbetson. John Barrymore's performance turned a sentimental love story into a memorable theatrical event that ended only because the star tired of his part. This impatience with the endless repetition of a role was to become a controlling factor in his career.

He nevertheless remained a serious dramatic actor and soon reached the full measure of his art in Shakespearean tragedy. After playing widely differing character roles in Tolstoy's *Redemption* (1918) and in Sheldon's adaptation of an Italian play, *The Jest* (1919), he opened at Arthur Hopkins's Plymouth Theatre on Mar. 6, 1920, in *Richard III,* in a production designed by Robert Edmond Jones and adapted by Sheldon. Aware that his voice did not suit Elizabethan verse, he engaged an elocution teacher, Margaret Carrington, who gave him six weeks of intensive training. His armor and sword were authentic copies of originals verified through the British Museum. By turning his right foot inward he walked with a crippled gait in a convincing portrait of the deformed and lame Gloucester. For the first time, he claimed, he felt he was the character he portrayed, even dreaming of himself as Richard. The critic Alexander Woollcott [Supp. 3] summed up the result as genius. The public's response matched this critical praise, but after twenty-seven performances the play closed when Barrymore collapsed. In addition to his strenuous preparation for the role and the performance itself, in which he did an acrobatic fall in the heavy armor, he had been making a motion picture and experiencing the turbulence of a new romance; the result was complete exhaustion.

Some weeks spent in recovery at a rest home followed. On Aug. 5, 1920, he married the poet Blanche (Oelrichs) Thomas, better known to her public by the pen name "Michael Strange." Settling in a small house in White Plains, N. Y., which he and his wife altered extensively and filled with period furniture, he cultivated the role of country gentleman. Their daughter, originally named Joan Strange Blythe but christened Diana, was born the following March. In April, joined by Ethel Barrymore, John opened in New York in *Clair de Lune,* a poetic drama composed by his wife that survived sixty-four performances only because of the glamor of the principals' names. Even before their marriage, however, the couple had quarreled repeatedly; after the play closed they sailed together for Europe but returned separately and thereafter lived together only briefly until their divorce in 1928.

John Barrymore gave his most memorable theatrical performance in *Hamlet,* which opened in New York on Nov. 16, 1922. For the producer Arthur Hopkins, Robert Edmond Jones again designed the scenery, using a massive flight of steps for the major playing area, building an apron stage over the orchestra pit, and replacing the customary footlights with spots above the balcony. This majestic set did justice to the intensity and grandeur of Barrymore's interpretation of the soul-torn prince. Stressing an incestuous relationship between the prince and his mother, Barrymore's *Hamlet* had strong Freudian overtones. Clarity and intelligence marked his performance. "There never has been such a great actor at any time, there never has been such shattering beauty in art," Robert Edmond Jones exclaimed. Barrymore's classic portrait of Hamlet as the pensive prince has become a staple of theatrical tradition.

Even though the house was sold out for weeks ahead, Barrymore closed the play in February 1923, after 101 performances, to sail for Europe. He played *Hamlet* again in New York for three weeks in November and then on tour for several weeks more. In the face of obstinate resistance, he finally obtained a theatre for a London presentation, investing $25,000 of his own money to rent the Haymarket, where he opened Feb. 19, 1925. Despite a caustic letter from Bernard Shaw complaining about Barrymore's surgery on Shakespeare, his performance captured British audiences, and the play ran for twelve weeks. The curtain then fell on Barrymore's stage career for fourteen years.

While becoming one of the most versatile and striking actors on the American stage, Barrymore had also taken a prominent place on the motion picture screen. His first movie appearance occurred in 1912 in *The Dictator,* filmed by Famous Players. He made fourteen more pictures, most of them for the same company, in the next nine years. Only in *Dr. Jekyll and Mr. Hyde* (1920), filmed during the preparation and playing of *Richard III,* did he find real scope for his acting talents. In 1925 he signed a contract with Warner Brothers for three "photoplays," each to pay him $76,250 for seven weeks' work with overtime at an additional 10 percent. This high salary marked Barrymore's emergence as a major figure on the screen and anticipated the princely sums he would receive later. *The Sea Beast* (1926), a version of *Moby Dick,* and *Don Juan* (1926), in which Barrymore played both the lover and his father, were memorable chiefly for the passion with which the hero embraced the actresses Dolores Costello and Mary Astor. The advent of talking films, which blighted the careers of stars like Douglas Fairbanks [Supp. 2] and John Gilbert [Supp. 2], only added to Barrymore's renown. By the time he joined Lionel at Metro-Goldwyn-Mayer studios in 1932, he was receiving $150,000 a picture. Here he made his most memorable films, including *Grand Hotel* (1932), *Rasputin and the Empress* (1932), with Lionel and Ethel, *Reunion in Vienna* (1933), and *Dinner at Eight* (1933). Whether he played bizarre character roles, as in *Svengali* (1931) and *Topaze* (1933), or handsome heroes like the

Russian prince and Garbo's lover, he served his public with his display of "the great profile." The legend of Barrymore grew, even while his health and art declined.

His third marriage, on Nov. 24, 1928, to the film star Dolores Costello, gave that legend a new dimension. Buying the three-and-a-half-acre estate of the director King Vidor in Beverly Hills, Calif., he added land and buildings until he had fifty-five rooms, in addition to a projection room, six swimming pools, dressing rooms, a rathskeller, a skeet range, a bowling green, several fountains, and a totem pole. Barrymore's growing thirst for the bizarre led him to acquire rare birds, a pet monkey, costly first editions, and a specially designed yacht manned by a full crew. His children by this marriage were Dolores Ethel Mae and John Blythe Barrymore, Jr.

But this real-life version of unreality could not last. Passionately in love with his wife, Barrymore was swept by insane jealousy and was subject to heights of rage and extravagances of compassion. His violent feelings often led him to excessive drinking, and alcohol brought on fits of violence. On Oct. 30, 1933, while filming a sequence for *Counsellor-at-Law,* he experienced a first lapse of memory, a symptom that grew to haunt and darken the remainder of his life, remembering as he did how such a lapse had culminated in his father's breakdown and final insanity. His first serious illness had occurred in 1930 when he suffered a severe gastric hemorrhage. He then developed headaches and a liver ailment. Physicians attributed his lapses of memory to brain damage from the excessive use of alcohol. Even during his illness Barrymore continued making pictures, one of his most successful, *Twentieth Century,* being filmed in 1934. Throughout these years he underwent numerous treatments and became a pawn in a struggle between his wife and his manager, Henry Hotchener, who had begun to look after his affairs in 1926. The Barrymores separated when he sailed to work in London and were divorced in October 1935.

Returning to New York and ill once more, Barrymore attracted a new admirer in Elaine Jacobs, who came to the hospital to interview him for her journalism studies at Hunter College. Now calling herself Elaine Barrie, she became his fourth wife on Nov. 8, 1936. In February 1937 she filed suit for divorce, but the couple were reconciled the following year. Deeply in debt, Barrymore made several movies to relieve some of the financial burden and also did radio broadcasts. In March 1939 he returned to the stage in *My Dear Children,* a trivial comedy in which he played an aging actor. By the time the troupe reached Chicago he had developed a spontaneous performance in which his failure to remember his lines freed him to caper to the audience's delight. After thirty-four gay weeks the play moved on to New York, where, despite a stay in Mount Sinai Hospital, he performed for four months. He struggled on, returning in the summer of 1940 to Hollywood, where he made several movies and appeared on Rudy Vallee's radio program. In the fall his wife divorced him. Bad health and bankruptcy haunted him, yet he worked to meet his debts. But the hill loomed too high for this modern Sisyphus. On May 19, 1942, he collapsed at a rehearsal, suffering from bronchial pneumonia. In the Hollywood Hospital his kidneys and circulation began to fail, and he died ten days later. Taken back into the Catholic Church on his deathbed, he was buried in Calvary Cemetery in Hollywood.

[The best biography is Gene Fowler's *Good Night, Sweet Prince* (1944), but it is marred by the author's affection and admiration for his subject. Alma Power-Waters, *John Barrymore: The Legend and the Man* (1941), is often inaccurate and partakes excessively of press-agentry. Barrymore's autobiographical *Confessions of an Actor* (1926) was ghostwritten by Karl Schmidt. Hollis Alpert's *The Barrymores* (1964) covers the lives of all members of the family in detail. The Theatre Collection of the N. Y. Public Lib. at Lincoln Center contains several scrapbooks of newspaper clippings, a number of magazine articles, and much photographic material; other material is at the Harvard Theatre Collection. See also Eric W. Barnes's biography of Edward Sheldon, *The Man Who Lived Twice* (1956), for its chapter on Barrymore's friendship with Sheldon; and the autobiographies of Ethel Barrymore (*Memories,* 1955), Lionel Barrymore (*We Barrymores,* 1951), Diana Barrymore (*Too Much, Too Soon,* 1957), and Michael Strange (*Who Tells Me True,* 1940). Blanche Yurka's autobiography, *Bohemian Girl* (1970), has a chapter on Barrymore's *Hamlet* (in which she played Gertrude); Brooks Atkinson has an excellent chapter on the Barrymores in his *Broadway* (1970).]

H. L. KLEINFIELD

BARTON, GEORGE AARON (Nov. 12, 1859–June 28, 1942), orientalist and biblical scholar, was born at East Farnham, Quebec, Canada, the third son and fifth of six children of Daniel and Mary Stevens (Bull) Barton, both devout Quakers. His father, a descendant of Roger Barton, who is believed to have come from Barton Manor, England, to Manhattan Island about 1641, was a farmer and the village blacksmith. Young Barton attended Oakwood Seminary, a Quaker boarding school at Poughkeepsie, N. Y. In 1879 he became an acknowledged minister of the Society of Friends. He completed his undergraduate education at Haverford College in Pennsylvania, receiving the A.B. degree in 1882. After a year in the insurance business in Boston, he became an instructor in mathematics and the classics at the Friends School in Providence, R. I. (1884–89). He then began graduate work at Harvard, where he studied under such eminent linguists and biblical scholars as Crawford H. Toy and Joseph H. Thayer [*qq.v.*] and in 1891 received the first Ph.D. awarded by Harvard in Semitics, with a thesis on "The Semitic Ishtar Cult."

In 1891 Barton was appointed professor of biblical literature and Semitic languages at Bryn Mawr College, a post he held for thirty years. On leave of absence in 1902–03, he spent the year in Palestine, where as director of the recently formed American School of Oriental Research in Jerusalem he worked with local archaeologists in field studies and excavation. In 1922 he left Bryn Mawr for the University of Pennsylvania, where he succeeded Morris Jastrow [*q.v.*] as professor of Semitic languages and the history of religion and remained until his retirement in 1932. From 1921 to 1934 he was the official director of the American School of Oriental Research in Baghdad.

Beginning in 1921, Barton also taught at the Divinity School of the Protestant Episcopal Church in Philadelphia as professor of New Testament literature. Here, and at the University of Pennsylvania, his principal colleague was his close friend James Alan Montgomery, a Semitist of equal distinction. The presence of these two scholars made Philadelphia a preeminent center of oriental and biblical studies. Through Montgomery, Barton in 1919 joined the Episcopal Church and was ordained to its priesthood, having left the Society of Friends the previous year because his strong feelings about German "brutality" in World War I made him unable to accept the Quaker opposition to war. He retired from the Divinity School faculty in 1937, at the age of seventy-seven.

Barton began his scholarly work at a time when biblical science was first being illuminated by the new discoveries in Near Eastern archaeology His imagination kindled, he devoted his life not only to biblical scholarship, but also to studying the religions and social structures of the ancient Near Eastern civilizations as revealed by Hebrew, Greek, Egyptian, and Babylonian records. His textbook, *Archaeology and the Bible* (1916), went through seven editions before his death and long remained standard in its field. His major contribution to scholarly literature was *A Sketch of Semitic Origins* (1902), which he eventually replaced with an altogether new work, *Semitic and Hamitic Origins* (1934). The integrity of Barton's scholarship is suggested by a sentence from the last book in which he confessed that he had "abandoned most of the important theories which he advocated thirty years ago" and acknowledged that even his latest views were only provisional. His exhaustive commentary on the book of Ecclesiastes (1908) in the International Critical Commentary series is a work of permanent value. The breadth of Barton's learning was of a type hardly possible in the more specialized age that followed. An expert in cuneiform epigraphy of both the Sumerian and Akkadian epochs, he produced a book, *The Origin and Development of Babylonian Writing* (1913), that remained the authoritative work on the subject for more than thirty years. When nearly seventy, he entered enthusiastically into the new field of Hittite studies. He was nevertheless no cloistered specialist, but found time to produce a number of popular and semipopular works on religious subjects, including a biography of Jesus (1922) and a treatise on the *Religions of the World* (1917). The range of his interests is indicated by his service as president of both the Society of Biblical Literature and Exegesis (1913–14) and the American Oriental Society (1916–17).

Barton became a naturalized citizen of the United States in 1900. He was twice married: on June 26, 1884, to Caroline Brewer Danforth, originally of Boston, who died in 1930; and on June 6, 1931, to Katherine Blye Hagy of New York. He and his first wife adopted a daughter, Rhoda Caroline. After his retirement Barton made his winter home in Coconut Grove, Fla., and his summer home at Weston, Mass. He died in Weston of a cerebral hemorrhage at the age of eighty-two and was buried in Mount Auburn Cemetery, Cambridge, Mass.

[MS. autobiography by Barton, "The Bookworm" (Archives of Univ. of Pa.) ; Barton's *A Year's Wandering in Bible Lands* (1904) and "The Confession of a Quaker," *Outlook*, Feb. 6, 1918 (on his wartime stand) ; Morris Jastrow, Jr., et al., "Prof. George Barton: An Appreciation," *Bryn Mawr Alumnae Quart.*, Nov. 1919 (with bibliography) ; obituaries by James A. Montgomery in Am. Philosophical Soc., *Year Book*, 1942, and, more briefly, in *Am. Jour. of Archaeology*, Oct.–Dec. 1942 ; E. A. Speiser et al. in *Bull. of Am. Schools of Oriental Research*, Oct. 1942 ; *Nat. Cyc. Am. Biog.*, Current Vol. D, pp. 441–42 ; *Stowe's Clerical Directory of the Protestant Episcopal Church*, 1941 ; information from Mrs. Barton ; death record from Mass. Registrar of Vital Statistics.]
ROBERT C. DENTAN

BASCOM, FLORENCE (July 14, 1862–June 18, 1945), geologist, was born in Williamstown, Mass., the youngest of the three surviving children (two daughters and a son) of John Bascom [*q.v.*], philosopher and college president, and Emma (Curtiss) Bascom, a former schoolteacher. Both parents were of seventeenth-century New England stock. John Bascom's intellectuality and fair-mindedness and the reform interests of both parents—temperance and woman suffrage—deeply influenced the intelligent and earnest young girl. In 1874, when she was twelve, her father left the Williams College faculty to accept the presidency of the University of Wisconsin.

Enrolling at the university when she was sixteen, Florence studied hard and ranged widely in her courses, graduating in 1882 with both the A.B. and B.L. degrees. As she continued her studies at Wisconsin, her interests turned increasingly to geology, under the influence of Prof. Charles R. Van Hise [q.v.], a great teacher and the leading structural geologist of his time. Roland D. Irving [q.v.], also on the Wisconsin faculty, greatly encouraged her; she received a B.S. degree in 1884 and an A.M. degree in 1887.

For two years (1889–91) Miss Bascom taught natural science at Rockford Seminary in Illinois. At about this time the new science of petrography, which originated in Germany, was brought to the United States by George Huntington Williams [q.v.] of Johns Hopkins University, then the leading graduate school in America. Miss Bascom's truly pioneering career now began. Although field geology was a highly unusual occupation for a lady in those Victorian times, she embarked upon it, and under Williams began to study the complicated terrain of the Piedmont area of Maryland, and later of Pennsylvania. For her doctoral dissertation she undertook to unravel the pre-Cambrian rocks of South Mountain along the Maryland-Pennsylvania line. By field and microscopic study, she showed that these formations were ancient lava flows. She received her Ph.D. from Johns Hopkins in 1893—the first woman to win this degree at Hopkins, and the first in America to earn a doctorate in geology.

For the next two years Miss Bascom was an instructor and associate professor of geology at Ohio State University. She moved in 1895 to Bryn Mawr College, which under President M. Carey Thomas [Supp. 1] included a strong group of feminists intent on establishing the intellectual position of women. Miss Bascom's prestige as a research scientist probably brought her to Bryn Mawr's attention, but it seems that there was no intention on the college's part to establish a fully organized geology department; the subject was not considered one of wide appeal to women. But Florence Bascom had other ideas. Her small allotment of space grew, and her single course expanded into a full major; in 1903 a second faculty member was added. She secured the Theodore D. Rand collection of mineral and rock specimens for Bryn Mawr, and successfully staved off President Thomas's attempt to reduce the geology program to a nonmajor elective. She was promoted to the rank of professor in 1906. Miss Bascom was soon sought out by graduate students, and several of those she trained became leaders in American geology. Indeed, until the mid-1930's a majority of American women geologists came from Bryn Mawr.

In 1896 Miss Bascom had pioneered again by becoming the first woman assistant on the United States Geological Survey. She was assigned to work on the intricate, highly metamorphosed rocks of southeastern Pennsylvania and northern Delaware. In an incredibly short time she brought out the Survey's Philadelphia Folio and Trenton Folio (both in 1909). This large area was surveyed, mostly in the summers, by foot, horseback, and buggy. She worked from dawn until dark, and insisted on the same routine for her students, both graduate and undergraduate. Her later Elkton-Wilmington Folio (1920) and her bulletins on the Quakertown-Doylestown and Honeybrook-Phoenixville districts (1931 and 1938) completed the areal survey of the region.

The foremost woman geologist of her time, Florence Bascom became the authority on the crystalline rocks of the so-called Piedmont province from the Susquehanna River to Trenton, N. J. By an agreement with the Maryland geologists, she used the term Baltimore gneiss for the basement complex of rocks, and her designation of the Wissahickon gneiss (schist), from the excellent exposures along Wissahickon Creek in Philadelphia, was adopted for that widespread formation far to the south into Virginia. She also had a keen interest in geomorphology and crystallography. She studied the streams and erosional surfaces of the Piedmont region and the origin of the surficial gravels, giving the name Bryn Mawr gravel to the deposits on the uppermost surface. In 1907 she spent a year studying in the laboratory of Victor Goldschmidt at Heidelberg. One result of this interest was the development of the two-circle contact goniometer for instruction in crystallography.

Florence Bascom became a legend: at Bryn Mawr, among geologists, and to the people of the countryside where she worked. A handsome, stylishly dressed woman, she impressed everyone with her physical vigor and her uncompromising moral and intellectual standards. She was the first woman to be elected a fellow of the Geological Society of America (1894); she became a councilor in 1924, and in 1930 vice-president, the only woman to hold these offices. Beginning in the first edition (1906), her name in *American Men of Science* was starred to designate that she ranked among the one hundred top geologists of her day.

Miss Bascom retired from her teaching at Bryn Mawr in 1928, but continued her work on the United States Geological Survey for another decade. She never married. Failing health caused her to retire, and she returned to live in the New England area she loved. She died in Northampton, Mass., in 1945 of a cerebral hemorrhage and was buried in the Williams College Cemetery.

[Memorial in *Am. Mineralogist,* Mar.–Apr. 1946, with a bibliography of Miss Bascom's publications; obituaries in *Science,* Sept. 28, 1945, and *Bryn Mawr Alumnae Bull.,* Nov. 1945; biographical sketch in Reuben G. Thwaites, ed., *The Univ. of Wis.* (1900), p. 360; *Am. Men of Sci.* (7th ed., 1944); *Who Was Who in America,* vol. II (1950); Cornelia Meigs, *What Makes a College?* (1956); death record from Mass. Registrar of Vital Statistics. See also sketch by Carroll S. Rosenberg in *Notable Am. Women,* I, 108–10.]

EDWARD H. WATSON

BATES, BLANCHE (Aug. 5?, 1873–Dec. 25, 1941), actress, was born in Portland, Oreg., the older of two daughters of theatrical parents. Her father, Francis Marion Bates, was originally from Baltimore; her mother, Eliza (Wren) Bates, from Buffalo, N. Y. After acting in the East, they had eventually settled in San Francisco, where Bates managed a stock company. The year after her birth Blanche's parents went to Australia, where for five years they won great acclaim as touring stars. Bates, however, was murdered in Melbourne by an unknown assailant on June 27, 1879. Mrs. Bates returned to San Francisco and continued acting to support her family.

Blanche's formal education ended with her graduation, in May 1889, from the Boys' High School in San Francisco—the first girl to graduate there. Her marriage the following year to an army lieutenant, Milton F. Davis, was unsuccessful, and the couple soon parted. After teaching kindergarten for four years, she turned to the stage, joining the company of L. R. Stockwell in 1893. She made her debut in *This Picture and That,* a one-act play by Brander Matthews [q.v.] (Stockwell Theatre, San Francisco, Aug. 21). When the company failed, she sought roles in New York City. Finding no opportunity there, she joined T. Daniel Frawley, an actor whom she had known in San Francisco, in a company bound for Denver in the autumn of 1894. Soon after, Frawley became a manager and took half the troupe on tour in Salt Lake City and Portland. He eventually leased the Columbia Theatre in San Francisco, where Blanche Bates appeared in the opening performance on May 13, 1895, in *Sweet Lavender* by Sir Arthur Wing Pinero. She remained with Frawley's company, which

toured in the West and Hawaii, until early 1898.

Increasingly ambitious, she left provincial touring to go again to New York, where, that spring, Augustin Daly [q.v.] hired her for his Shakespearean revivals. She played romantic secondary roles both in New York and on tour. On leave of absence from Daly's, she returned to the Baldwin Theatre in San Francisco to act in repertory; she created a minor sensation as Nora in *A Doll's House* on Nov. 6, 1898. Back with Daly, her next role was Countess Charkoff, an adventuress, in *The Great Ruby* (Feb. 9, 1899), but she quarreled with him over the selection of gowns and resigned after one performance.

The first step on the ladder to stardom came for Blanche Bates when David Belasco [Supp. 1] gave her the role of Cho-Cho-San in *Madame Butterfly,* his one-act play based on a short story by John Luther Long [q.v.] (Herald Square Theatre, Mar. 5, 1900). She attracted such attention as Madame Butterfly that there was a ready audience to see her as Cigarette in *Under Two Flags,* a part which required more endurance than depth of characterization (Garden Theatre, Feb. 5, 1901). So popular was her Yo-San in *The Darling of the Gods,* by Belasco and Long (Belasco Theatre, Dec. 3, 1902), that it ran for three years. Surcease from the exhaustion of this role came in Chicago in 1904, when she played Hedda in *Hedda Gabler* and Katharine in *The Taming of the Shrew.*

According to many observers, Blanche Bates gave her greatest performance as The Girl in *The Girl of the Golden West* (Belasco Theatre, Nov. 14, 1905), in which she received high praise for her hearty Western vitality. After three long years as The Girl, she demanded that Belasco cast her in a modern role, and with some reluctance he starred her in *The Fighting Hope* (Stuyvesant Theatre, Sept. 22, 1908), a meretricious play which, however, ran for two years. Her last appearance for Belasco was in *Nobody's Widow* by Avery Hopwood [q.v.] (Hudson Theatre, Nov. 15, 1910). William Winter [q.v.], sage of American critics, took her severely to task for perverting her talent in "twaddle and indelicacy" (*Wallet of Time,* II, 245).

On Nov. 28, 1912, she married George Creel, a Denver journalist later famous as head of the Committee on Public Information during the First World War; they had two children, Frances Virginia and George Bates. Her final break with Belasco came the following month, after which she was associated with Charles Frohman [q.v.], but with no great distinction. During the war years she acted in propaganda skits and plays. She then sought roles of deeper significance, but the only one which came close to her high standards was that of Nancy Fair in *The Famous Mrs. Fair* by James Forbes (Henry Miller Theatre, Dec. 22, 1919). She retired from the stage in 1926, but appeared briefly once more in New York as Lena Surrege in *The Lake* (Martin Beck Theatre, Dec. 26, 1933). She died of a cerebral thrombosis at her San Francisco home on Christmas Day 1941, at the age of sixty-eight. Following cremation, her ashes were placed in Mount Olivet Memorial Park in nearby Colma.

Blanche Bates was an attractive, vivacious woman, with expressive eyes and mobile features. She was noted for her spontaneity, humor, and great stamina, and for these reasons her best creation was probably The Girl. During her long career, she gave evidence of artistic ability, particularly when she played Ibsen or Shakespeare. Her limitations were those forced upon her by the near stereotypes with which Belasco so often peopled his spectaculars.

[An incomplete autobiography, containing some ambiguities on her early life and career, published in the *Sacramento* (Calif.) *Bee*, May 16, 23, 30, June 6, 13, 1942; William Winter, *The Wallet of Time* (1913) and *The Life of David Belasco* (1918); Craig Timberlake, *The Bishop of Broadway: David Belasco* (1954); Marvin Felheim, *The Theatre of Augustin Daly* (1956); Edmond M. Gagey, *The San Francisco Stage* (1950); Constance Rourke, *Troupers of the Gold Coast* (1928); Arthur H. Quinn, *A Hist. of the Am. Drama from the Civil War to the Present Day* (1936); Walter Brown and E. De Roy Koch, eds., *Who's Who on the Stage* (1908); John B. Clapp and Edwin F. Edgett, *Plays of the Present* (1902); John Chapman and Garrison P. Sherwood, eds., *The Best Plays of 1894–1899* (1955), and other volumes in the Burns Mantle *Best Plays* series; *Sydney Morning Herald*, June 30, July 7, 10, 14, 17, 19, 21, 23, 1879, Nov. 16, 1883, for information concerning the Bates murder; *San Francisco Call*, Aug. 21, 22, 1893; *San Francisco Chronicle*, Nov. 19, 26, 1893, Dec. 26, 1941; *N. Y. Times*, Feb. 10, 12, 26, 1899, Nov. 29, 1912, Dec. 26, 1941; *N. Y. Sun*, Sept. 23, 1908; clippings and programs in the Samuel Stark Collection, Stanford Theatre Collection. See also article by H. L. Kleinfield in *Notable Am. Women*, I, 113–14. Blanche Bates's birthday, usually given as Aug. 25, appears on her death certificate (Calif. Dept. of Public Health, under "Creel") as Aug. 5.]

NORMAN PHILBRICK

BAUSCH, EDWARD (Sept. 26, 1854–July 30, 1944), industrialist and inventor, was born at Rochester, N. Y., the first of six children of German Lutheran parents, John Jacob and Barbara (Zimmerman) Bausch. His father, a migrant in 1849 from Suessen, Württemberg, where he had served an apprenticeship to his elder brother, an optician, had opened an optical shop at Rochester in 1853. Starting as a distributor of his brother's products, John Jacob Bausch soon began to carve horn-rim spectacle frames and to grind lenses himself. In 1866, with Henry Lomb as a partner, he formed the Vulcanite Optical Instrument Company and acquired an exclusive franchise to make optical instruments from hard rubber. Young Edward Bausch attended the Rochester Realschule and Rochester High School and worked after school at the shop. One job was to rush the heated sheets of vulcanite from his mother's cookstove to his father's newly improvised hand press in an expanded shop opened nearby. In order to fit himself for the business, Edward won a scholarship in engineering at Cornell University, where he studied from 1871 until 1874, when he returned to assist in the layout of the new factory of the Bausch & Lomb Optical Company.

With the opening of the new building, Edward Bausch focused his attention on the design and production of the company's first microscopes. Under the tutelage of Ernest Gundlach, a skilled optician recently arrived from Germany, he built several microscopes in time to exhibit them at the Centennial Exposition in Philadelphia in 1876. As the company's representative in charge of that exhibit for three months, Bausch eagerly examined the machine tools and other new products of American and foreign production and met numerous scientists who were interested in optical equipment. He returned to Rochester determined to produce quality instruments in sufficient quantity to permit their sale at moderate prices. With several of his new scientific friends he became a charter member of the American Society of Microscopists (later the American Microscopical Society), formed in 1878. On Oct. 31 of that year he married Matilda G. Morrell of Syracuse; they had no children. On his honeymoon trip to Boston he visited Dr. Oliver Wendell Holmes [*q.v.*], whose enthusiastic endorsement of the Bausch & Lomb microscope had made that city the company's best market.

While in Boston, Bausch received a franchise to manufacture some of the objectives and other optical instruments designed by Robert B. Tolles and Alvan G. Clark [*q.v.*], the leading lens makers in the country, and on his return he visited and made a similar arrangement with the aging Charles A. Spencer, America's pioneer microscopist, in nearby Geneva, and persuaded Spencer's son Clarence to join the Rochester firm as an instrument maker. Bausch secured his first patent in 1882 on a Trichinoscope, a microscope designed for use in detecting contaminated meat. The next year he patented a microscope illuminator, and a year later a binocular microscope.

As one of the founders in January 1879 of the Rochester Microscopical Society, Bausch played an active role in its transformation two years later into the Rochester Academy of Science and participated in its programs and exhibits. The Microscopical Section remained the Academy's most active branch. With sixty members, each equipped with his own microscope, it was ready in 1884 to entertain the seventh annual convention of the American Society of Microscopists, which met in Rochester. Bausch seized this occasion to lead the visiting scientists, including two members of the Royal Microscopical Society of London, on a tour of his optical factory. In order to promote a more effective use of the microscope by amateurs as well as by scientists, he published in 1885 the first edition of his 96-page book, *The Manipulations of the Microscope*.

Although his work in microscopy continued, Bausch's interests were already shifting into the field of photography. He had assumed charge of the production of photographic lenses at the plant in 1883, and this new responsibility brought him into collaboration with another ingenious Rochesterian, George Eastman [Supp. 1]. Bausch probably supplied the lens but not the shutter used in the first Kodak, which Eastman patented in 1888. Three years later Bausch patented the iris diaphragm shutter, developed to supply Eastman's needs, and the Kodak manufacturer continued until 1912 to rely heavily on Bausch & Lomb for lenses and shutters for his expanding output.

When Bausch made his first trip to Europe in 1888, he visited all the principal optical centers and developed friendly relations with several microscopists in England and France, as well as with Roderich Zeiss and Prof. Ernst Abbe at Jena in Germany. He quickly recognized the scholarly leadership which that center enjoyed, and on later trips to Jena in 1890 and 1893 he negotiated working agreements with the Zeiss Optical Company which granted Bausch & Lomb the exclusive franchise in the American markets for the manufacture of its anastigmatic lenses, binoculars, and range finders. To strengthen the company's productive capacity, particularly in the instrument field, Bausch negotiated an alliance with Saegmuller & Company of Washington, D. C., which resulted in its absorption by Bausch & Lomb in 1905.

Three other Bausch brothers had early joined the family firm: Henry, John, and William. The youngest, William (1861–1944), affable and gregarious, developed a cordial relationship between the company's management and its expanding force of workmen. William Bausch also directed the company's optical glass plant, started experimentally in 1912 and brought into operation in 1915 in time to supply the needs of America and its allies in World War I. His ability to harmonize the joint efforts of the scientists as-

signed to the company by the National Defense Council and the Geophysical Laboratory of the Carnegie Institution with the local production force soon boosted output from 2,000 pounds a month to 2,000 pounds a day and won praise for Bausch & Lomb.

For more than half a century Edward Bausch was the firm's responsible head. He became vice-president in 1899 and on the death of his father in 1926 succeeded to the presidency, a post he held until 1935, when he became chairman of the board. Though he continued to explore new fields of development and took out some additional patents, his major contribution was in industrial management. The administrative skills he displayed prompted his election as an officer and director of four Rochester banks and five local industries. He also served as an officer and director of three local charities and of the Bureau of Municipal Research. A local benefactor, he provided, with other members of the Bausch and Lomb families, for the erection (1930) of the John Jacob Bausch and Henry Lomb Memorial building at the new river campus of the University of Rochester. He was so impressed by the scientific displays of the Deutsches Museum in Munich, which he visited on frequent trips to Germany, that he gave a site adjoining his home on East Avenue and a fund for the erection of the Rochester Museum of Arts and Sciences, completed in 1942. Two years later, at the age of eighty-nine, Bausch died in Rochester of bronchopneumonia. He was buried in Mount Hope Cemetery, Rochester.

[M. Herbert Eisenhart, "After Ninety-nine Years," *Balco News* (Bausch & Lomb magazine), May 1948; interview with Bausch by Harold A. Nichols in Rochester *Democrat & Chronicle*, Sunday Mag. Section, Sept. 27, 1942; Edward Bausch, "Early Am. Microscope Makers and Their Work" (typescript of paper delivered before Optical Soc. of America, May 1931, Rochester Public Lib.); William F. Peck, *Hist. of Rochester and Monroe County* (1908), II, 1324–25; *Rochester Times Union*, Jan. 24, 1933, July 31, 1944, Sept. 4, 1945; *N. Y. Times*, July 31, 1944; *Who Was Who in America*, vols. I (1942), on John Jacob Bausch, and II (1950), on Edward and William Bausch; J. W. Forrest, "The Bausch & Lomb Engineering Hist." (typescript, courtesy of Bausch & Lomb Optical Co.).]

BLAKE McKELVEY

BEACH, AMY MARCY CHENEY (Sept. 5, 1867–Dec. 27, 1944), composer and pianist, known professionally as Mrs. H. H. A. Beach, was born in Henniker, N. H., of old New England stock, the only child of Charles Abbott Cheney, a paper manufacturer, and Clara Imogene (Marcy) Cheney, a gifted amateur pianist and singer. The family moved to Boston in 1871.

Amy's remarkable musical abilities were evident from early childhood. By the age of two she was able to sing a large number of songs, and at four she started to learn the keyboard and to compose simple melodies. At six she began formal piano study, with her mother as teacher, and at seven gave her first recital, which included some of her own waltzes. She received her primary and secondary education at W. L. Whittemore's private school in Boston, giving particular attention to French and German. Her parents considered but abandoned the idea of taking her to Europe for study, and she continued her musical training in Boston, studying piano for six years (1876–82) with (Johann) Ernst Perabo [*q.v.*] and harmony (1881–82) with Prof. Junius W. Hill of Wellesley College. After further coaching with Carl Baermann [*q.v.*], she made her professional debut on Oct. 24, 1883, at the age of sixteen, in a concert at the Boston Music Hall, where she performed the G Minor Piano Concerto of Ignaz Moscheles with an orchestra conducted by Adolph Neuendorff [*q.v.*], as well as Chopin's Rondo in E-flat. Other recitals followed, evoking both popular and critical approval, and she made her first appearance with the Boston Symphony Orchestra on Mar. 28, 1885, playing the Chopin F Minor Concerto under the direction of Wilhelm Gericke [*q.v.*].

On Dec. 2, 1885, at the age of eighteen, Miss Cheney was married to Henry Harris Aubrey Beach, a widower many years older than she; they had no children. Her husband, a distinguished surgeon and an amateur musician, took a strong interest in his wife's career, saw to it that she was not disturbed by household problems, arranged for her to meet visiting musical celebrities, and encouraged her to concentrate on composing rather than public performance. Since her brief study with Hill constituted her only training in musical theory, she began a course of intensive study to teach herself composition and orchestration, although she continued to make occasional appearances with the Boston Symphony and at charitable performances.

During the next two decades Mrs. Beach produced a number of songs: musical settings for verses by French, German, and British poets, including those of Shakespeare, Burns, and Browning. Her setting for Browning's "The Year's at the Spring" became one of the most popular and was often included in the programs of the soprano Emma Eames. Mrs. Beach's first major work, a Mass in E-flat, was initially performed in 1892 by the Handel and Haydn Society of Boston and won high praise. Other compositions of this period include the *Gaelic* Symphony, first performed in 1896 by the Boston Symphony

Orchestra under Emil Paur; a Piano Concerto in C-sharp Minor, first performed by the Boston Symphony in 1900; and a Quintet for Piano and Strings (1908).

After the death of her husband (June 28, 1910), Mrs. Beach made her first visit to Europe, where she stayed for four years. Now resuming concert appearances, she gave many performances, chiefly of her own works, in Berlin, Leipzig, and other German cities, and was acclaimed both as a performer and as a composer. She returned to the United States in 1914, and for some twenty-five years continued her musical career. A devout Episcopalian, she wrote much church music, including a "Te Deum" (1922) and a communion service (1928). Her cantata "Canticle of the Sun," composed in 1925, was first performed at the Worcester (Mass.) Music Festival in 1931, under Albert Stoessel [Supp. 3]. During these later years she made her home in New York City and spent her summers at Centerville, Mass., on Cape Cod, and at the MacDowell Colony in Peterborough, N. H., where in 1938 she finished one of her last works, a Trio for Piano, Violin, and Cello.

Of the more than 150 works Mrs. Beach produced, nearly all were published. Her musical vocabulary was that of the late nineteenth-century romantic composers, and her style of expression changed very little in the more than fifty years that elapsed between the writing of her first works and the composing of her final song, "Though I Take the Wings of the Morning." Her use of chromaticisms often created complexities of performance not justified by the results. Nevertheless, her melodic ideas often soared; her harmonic sense was always sound and sometimes contrapuntal in the chromatic moves between progressions. She could turn out rousing polyphonic textures, all the more impressive because they were inserted into her compositions with caution and conviction. Her understanding of the human voice allowed her to create vocal works that appealed equally to singers and to audiences.

As a musician Mrs. Beach is properly classed with the New England group of composers, along with such figures as Edward MacDowell, Horatio Parker [*qq.v.*], and Geroge Chadwick [Supp. 1]. She was the first American to gain international recognition as a composer without studying abroad. She is all the more noteworthy as an eminent creative artist in a field that women rarely entered. No composer of her sex achieved greater renown and few composers of the period enjoyed greater esteem. Mrs. Beach died of heart disease at the age of seventy-seven at her home in New York City. Her ashes were placed in her husband's vault in Forest Hills Cemetery, Boston.

[Diaries, letters, press books, etc., of Mrs. Beach, in the author's possession; Charles H. Pope, *The Cheney Genealogy* (1897), pp. 547–48; Louis C. Elson in the *Musician,* July 1905; Percy Goetschius, *Mrs. H. H. A. Beach* (1906), chiefly a collection of critical notices and reviews; John Tasker Howard, *Our Am. Music* (1931), pp. 344–47; Burnett C. Tuthill in *Musical Quart.,* July 1940.]

WALTER S. JENKINS

BEACH, MRS. H. H. A. See BEACH, AMY MARCY CHENEY.

BEALE, JOSEPH HENRY (Oct. 12, 1861– Jan. 20, 1943), professor of law, was born in Dorchester, Mass. (later part of Boston), the oldest of the five children of Joseph Henry Beale and Frances Elizabeth (Messinger) Beale. His father, a descendant of Benjamin Beale (or Bale) who came from England to Dorchester in the seventeenth century, was engaged in a reasonably prosperous mattress business in New York and Boston. Young Joseph attended Chauncy Hall School in Boston and Harvard College, where he graduated in 1882. After a year as a master in St. Paul's School in Concord, N. H., he returned to Harvard for graduate study in the classics and history. In the fall of 1884 he entered the Harvard Law School, where he was one of the founders of the *Harvard Law Review*. At graduation, in 1887, he refused an offer to be law secretary for a year to Justice Horace Gray [*q.v.*] of the United States Supreme Court and instead opened a law office in Boston. On Dec. 23, 1891, he married Elizabeth Chadwick Day, daughter of Probate Judge Joseph M. Day of Barnstable County, Mass. They had three children: Elizabeth Chadwick, Joseph Henry (who died at the age of two), and Alice.

Beale's career teaching law began in 1890 when he gave six lectures on "Damages" (a subject on which he had recently helped edit the standard text) at the Harvard Law School. They were notably successful, and Harvard appointed him instructor in criminal law for the academic year 1891–92. He remained on the faculty until his retirement in 1938. A popular and skillful teacher, Beale was a brilliant dialectical fencer in the classroom, one who delighted in exploring every legal ramification of a case. For him the law was not a sociological phenomenon but a fascinating logical structure, discernible by anyone who could think aright.

Beale taught an amazing number of subjects. At various times in his career he gave an introductory course in jurisprudence, called "Principles of Legal Liability," as well as courses in the law of common carriers, of municipal corporations, of federal taxation, of torts, and of corporations. A course which Beale made a conspicuous feature of the third-year curriculum was "Conflict of Laws," concerning the rules governing private contractual relationships between citizens of different nations. Throughout his career Beale maintained that the legality of a contract can be determined only by the laws of the place where the contract was made. In his unyielding defense of this "territorial" principle, he often found himself in conflict with less dogmatic legal scholars.

Besides teaching, Beale wrote numerous articles for law reviews and twenty-seven books. Among these were a long series of volumes of edited cases for student use: *The Law of Foreign Corporations* (1904); his translation (1914) of a Latin treatise on the conflict of laws written by Bartolus of Sassoferrato (1314–1357); *A Bibliography of Early English Law Books* (1926); and the monumental three-volume *A Treatise on the Conflict of Laws* (1935).

Beale's labors were not limited to Harvard. In 1902 when President William Rainey Harper [*q.v.*] of the University of Chicago planned a law school, he asked Harvard for the loan of a professor. On two years' leave, Beale undertook the deanship of law at Chicago, recruited a faculty, and so founded that distinguished school. He participated in the organization of the American Law Institute and was reporter of its *Restatement of the Law of Conflict of Laws* (1934). He was a founder of the American Legal History Society in 1933 and its first president. For forty years he was a vestryman of Christ Church (Episcopal) in Cambridge, Mass., and for twelve years its senior warden. Six colleges and universities gave him honorary degrees, from Chicago and Wisconsin in 1904 to Cambridge University (1921), Harvard (1927), Boston College (1932), and Michigan (1933).

Short and rotund, Beale was vigorous and buoyant in person and a companionable friend. Like many other lawyers, he tried spare-time farming; for a time he raised dairy cattle in Waltham but gave up the enterprise when dairying became a regulated business. He died in Cambridge in his eighty-second year of arteriosclerotic heart disease and was buried in Forest Hills Cemetery, Boston.

[Memorials of Beale by five of his colleagues in *Harvard Law Rev.,* Mar. 1943; biographical sketch in *Harvard Legal Essays, Written in Honor of . . . Joseph Henry Beale and Samuel Williston* (1934); *Who Was Who in America,* vol. II (1950); information from Beale's daughter, Mrs. Basil Duke Edwards of Barnstable, Mass., and his grandson, Joseph Henry Beale Edwards, of the Boston bar. The best portrait of Professor Beale is that painted by Charles S. Hopkinson of Boston; it hangs in the Treasure Room of the Harvard Law School.]

ARTHUR E. SUTHERLAND

BEARD, DANIEL CARTER (June 21, 1850 –June 11, 1941), illustrator, author, and youth leader, was born in Cincinnati, Ohio, the youngest of four sons and fourth of six children of Mary Caroline (Carter) and James Henry Beard [q.v.]. His father was a professional painter, and two of Daniel's brothers, James Carter and Thomas Francis Beard [qq.v.], became illustrators. An imaginative, inventive boy, interested in camping and wildlife, Dan was educated at local schools. His application to the United States Naval Academy was rejected, and he then enrolled at Worrall's Academy in Covington, Ky., where he studied civil engineering. After graduating in 1869 with honors, he worked for the city engineer of Cincinnati on surveying projects until 1874, when he joined the Sanborn Map and Publishing Company of New York. For the next four years Beard traveled throughout the eastern United States diligently preparing maps for insurance companies. As a diversion on his travels he sketched scenes of nature and society which received praise from his father and brothers. Loneliness, occupational frustration, and family urgings finally induced him to abandon surveying in favor of illustrating, and in 1878 he rejoined the other Beards, who now lived in New York City. There he studied for four years in night classes at the Art Students' League while doing hack work in commercial design.

He soon began receiving magazine commissions. The juvenile monthly *St. Nicholas* published several of his wildlife sketches and in January 1880 featured his illustrated article "Snow-Ball Warfare." Popular interest prompted additional articles on activities for children, and two years later these were collected in *What to Do and How to Do It: The American Boy's Handy Book.* The volume quickly became a juvenile classic, and was followed by fifteen additional handicraft books over the next half-century.

Other illustrations for general magazines displayed a penchant for puckish, yet trenchant, satire that earned Beard a commission from Mark Twain [q.v.] to illustrate his novel *A Connecticut Yankee in King Arthur's Court* (1889). Beard's striking, often allegorical drawings, sharply critical of government, business, society, and religion, delighted Twain and most critics but outraged conservatives and caused some publishers to blacklist him; subsequent editions of *A Connecticut Yankee* contained only a handful of the original drawings. Some commentators remarked that the artist had made a single-tax tract of the book. Beard was indeed attracted by the blend of morality, individualism, and patriotism that characterized the single-tax movement;

he campaigned actively for the principles of his friend Henry George [q.v.] and even wrote a novel embodying them, *Moonblight* (1892). Beard's work for Twain, which included later novels as well, placed him among the leading American illustrators of his day.

To his active career of illustration, reform, outdoor sports, and New York club life, Beard in 1905 added the editorship of *Recreation,* a sportsmen's monthly, which under his direction took up the battle for wildlife conservation. To increase the magazine's circulation he organized the Sons of Daniel Boone, a boys' society dedicated to conservation, the outdoor life, and the pioneer spirit. He left *Recreation* in 1906 and affiliated his boys' group with another magazine, the *Woman's Home Companion.* Two years later he severed ties with both the *Companion* and the Sons of Daniel Boone, charging that the magazine staff was interfering with his youth organization. Beard then joined *Pictorial Review* and founded the Boy Pioneers of America (1909). This new society, like the earlier one, was an institutional effort to remedy what Beard saw as the decadent state of urban youth. In his early juvenile books he had emphasized the value of handicrafts for character development; by the mid-1890's he was arguing that the continuation of America's unique civilization depended upon this kind of training, which, while improving coordination, transmitted the traditions of the American pioneer.

Beard's youth programs had some influence on the formation of the Boy Scout movement in England in 1908 by Sir Robert Baden-Powell. This in turn inspired the consolidation of Beard's and other boys' societies (including the Woodcraft Indians of Ernest Thompson Seton) into the Boy Scouts of America in 1910. Although Beard did not initiate the consolidation, he was a charter member of the executive committee of the new organization and for the next three decades one of the three national Scout commissioners. He also designed the Scout hat, shirt, and neckerchief, planned both for utility and as symbols of the American frontiersman. A strenuous advocate of voluntary, rather than professional, adult leadership, Beard unsuccessfully opposed the increasing dominance of the Boy Scouts by the executive secretary, James E. West, and his national headquarters staff, who, he felt, were substituting a philosophy of social adjustment for a commitment to social reform, were regarding outdoor activities as attractive time fillers rather than vital correctives for a corrupt society, and were concentrating on bureaucratic efficiency rather than idealistic fellowship within the program.

In later life his venerable but spry figure and homey personality made "Uncle Dan" an American folk hero, widely known through his monthly column in the scout magazine *Boys' Life,* his boys' camp in Pennsylvania, his buckskin-suited public appearances, and his extensive correspondence with boys and with youth leaders. On Aug. 15, 1894, Beard had married Beatrice Alice Jackson, a member of a prominent Long Island family. She provided a steadying influence in his multifarious activities and prompted his conversion from the Swedenborgian Church to the Society of Friends. They had two children, Barbara and Daniel Bartlett. Ten days before his ninety-first birthday, Beard died of myocarditis at Brooklands, his estate in Suffern, N. Y. He was buried in the Brick Church Cemetery near his home.

[Beard's autobiography, *Hardly a Man Is Now Alive* (1939), provides an anecdotal treatment of his early life; this is closely followed by the only substantial published biography, Cyril Clemens and Carroll Sibley, *Uncle Dan* (1938). See also Allan R. Whitmore, "Beard, Boys, and Buckskins: Daniel Carter Beard and the Preservation of the Am. Pioneer Tradition" (Ph.D. dissertation, Northwestern Univ., 1970). A substantial collection of Beard's papers is in the Lib. of Cong. Useful brief accounts of Beard include: his autobiographical article, "The Scout—Boy and Man," *Mentor,* Aug. 1927; S. J. Woolf in *N. Y. Times Mag.,* June 16, 1940; Harry A. Stewart in *American Mag.,* May 1924; *N. Y. Times,* June 12, 13, 1941. Beard's satirical art is analyzed by B. O. Flower in the *Arena,* July 1904; Henry Irving Dodge in the *New Voice,* July 22, 1899; and Arthur N. Jervis in *Quart. Illustrator,* Oct.–Dec. 1893. Death record from N. Y. State Dept. of Health.]

ALLAN R. WHITMORE

BEAUX, CECILIA (May 1, 1855–Sept. 17, 1942), portrait painter, was born in Philadelphia, Pa., the second of two daughters who survived infancy. Her father, Jean Adolphe Beaux, a native of Nîmes, France, and a staunch Protestant, had come to Philadelphia at the age of thirty-eight to try to establish a silk factory. Her mother, Cecilia Kent (Leavitt) Beaux, was a New Yorker of colonial New England descent who had gone to Philadelphia as a governess after her father failed in business. She died a few days after the daughter's birth, and Jean Beaux soon returned to France, leaving the two girls to be reared by their maternal grandmother and their Aunt Eliza Leavitt, a gifted musician. The family was supported by a Quaker uncle, William Biddle, and provided with a rich background in literature, music, and art.

Save for two years in a Philadelphia finishing school, Cecilia Beaux was educated at home by her aunt. She early displayed marked talent in drawing, and at sixteen began a year's instruction at the studio of her cousin Catharine Drinker

[Catharine Ann Janvier, *q.v.*], whose brother Henry Sturgis Drinker married Aimée Ernesta Beaux, Cecilia's older sister. She also received some early knowledge of art from paintings in the Pennsylvania Academy of the Fine Arts and the Gibson Collection in Philadelphia. The latter she found particularly moving; in her autobiography she wrote that she felt "almost holy ecstasy" at the sight of a head by the popular French painter Thomas Couture, "vividly remembered" a Gustave Courbet tree, was "thrilled" by the dashing manner of the Italian portraitist Giovanni Boldini, and found the equally brilliant style of the Spaniard Carbo Fortuny "magical." It was to the work of these last two that her own later showed considerable affinity. Cecilia Beaux received further professional instruction from William Sartain [*q.v.*]. She admired Philadelphia's greatest painter of that period, Thomas Eakins [*q.v.*], and would have studied with him at the Pennsylvania Academy of the Fine Arts but for her Uncle Will, who opposed the life class and its "rabble of untidy art students" (Bowen, p. 163); she afterward thought it perhaps fortunate that she had not been exposed to Eakins's overpowering influence. To help support herself during these years she taught art at a private school and to a few individual pupils.

Miss Beaux's first important painting was a portrait of her sister and son Henry, done in 1883–84. Exhibited the following year at the Pennsylvania Academy, it won the Mary Smith Prize, and in 1886 it was exhibited in the Paris Salon (as "Les Derniers Jours d'Enfance"), a signal honor for a beginner. These tokens of recognition encouraged her to undertake further study abroad, and early in 1888 she went to Paris, where she worked at the Académie Julian, receiving instruction from such established artists as Joseph Robert-Fleury, Benjamin Constant, Adolphe Bouguereau, Charles Lazar, Gustave Courtois, and Pascal Dagnan-Bouveret. Whether because of this diversity of example, or because of willful independence, none of these teachers exerted any appreciable influence upon her. She traveled in France, visited Italy and England, and after nearly two years returned to the United States to begin in earnest her successful career, at first in Philadelphia and then, from 1900, in New York City.

Her work brought her numerous honors, many of them made the more impressive by their being accorded a woman. She received, in all, four Smith prizes from the Pennsylvania Academy, which also gave her a Gold Medal of Honor (1898) and the Temple Gold Medal (1900). In 1893 she was elected a member of the Society of American Artists and received a gold medal from the Philadelphia Art Club and the Dodge Prize of the National Academy of Design, which made her an Associate in 1894 and an Academician in 1902. She received gold medals also from the Carnegie Institute (1899), the Paris Exposition (1900), the Pan American Exposition in Buffalo (1901), the Louisiana Purchase Exposition in St. Louis (1904), the National Academy (1913), the Art Institute of Chicago (1921), and the American Academy of Arts and Letters (1926); she was elected a member of the American Academy in 1933. She received honorary degrees from the University of Pennsylvania (1908) and Yale (1912). Perhaps the crest of her career came when six of her portraits were accepted by the 1896 Paris Salon, which did her the further honor of hanging them as a group. In this year she was also made an Associée of the Société Nationale des Beaux Arts. As these honors suggest, she was highly esteemed by her colleagues, and was a much sought-after portraitist. Among her famous sitters were Mrs. Theodore Roosevelt and her daughter Ethel (1901–02) and, after World War I, Cardinal Mercier of Belgium, Premier Clemenceau of France, and the British admiral David Beatty (all in the National Collection of Fine Arts, Smithsonian Institution, Washington, D. C.).

Cecilia Beaux's painting style has the breadth and fluency—but not quite the same brilliance—as that of her acquaintance and contemporary, John Singer Sargent. It gives the appearance of rapidity, though in fact she was a slow worker. In a talk delivered at Simmons College in 1907, she described her purpose as the achievement of an "abstraction of reality" through the elimination of inessentials. She disapproved of portraiture that was merely "reproductive," believing that "imaginative insight" and "design" were the fundamental ingredients of a successful portrait.

In 1910 her friend Leila Mechlin wrote, "Miss Beaux is one of those painters who seem to have arrived almost abruptly on a plane of exceptional accomplishment beyond which comparatively little advance is made except in matters of facility. . . ." The statement was intended as a compliment, but it also points to a sameness and repetitiousness in Cecilia Beaux's mature art which is its major defect, although a virtue and necessity in a successful portrait painter. On the whole, her most pleasing pictures are informal ones of her family and friends, such as "Man with a Cat" or "At Home" (1902, National Collection of Fine Arts), of her brother-in-law Henry Sturgis Drinker; "Child with Nurse" (1894) and "Ernesta" (1914, Metropolitan Museum of

Art), portraying her niece Ernesta Drinker; "Richard Watson Gilder" (1902–03)—a close friend—and "The Dancing Lesson" (1899–1900, Art Institute of Chicago) and "After the Meeting" (1914, Toledo Museum of Art), paintings of Gilder's daughters.

During a visit to Paris in the summer of 1924 Cecilia Beaux fell and broke her hip. The accident left her a semi-invalid, and she did little more painting. She died in 1942 of a coronary thrombosis at "Green Alley," her summer home at Gloucester, Mass., at the age of eighty-seven. Burial was in Philadelphia's West Laurel Hill Cemetery. She had never married.

[Although Cecilia Beaux was frequently the subject of periodical articles and is often mentioned in surveys of American art, the most useful sources are her autobiography, *Background with Figures* (1930); the autobiography of her niece Catherine Drinker Bowen, *Family Portrait* (1970); Henry S. Drinker, *The Paintings and Drawings of Cecilia Beaux* (1955); and the sketch in *Nat. Cyc. Am. Biog.*, XL, 507–08. See also Thornton Oakley's appreciation, *Cecilia Beaux* (1943); Leila Mechlin, "The Art of Cecilia Beaux," *Internat. Studio*, July 1910; and the article on Miss Beaux in *Notable Am. Women*.]

NICOLAI CIKOVSKY, JR.

BECKER, CARL LOTUS (Sept. 7, 1873– Apr. 10, 1945), historian, was born on a farm in Black Hawk County, Iowa. Christened Lotus Carl, he was the second of four children and only son of Charles DeWitt Becker and Almeda (Sarvay) Becker. His father's German and Dutch ancestors had come to New York in the eighteenth century; his mother was of English and Irish descent. Charles Becker had served for three years in the Union Army during the Civil War before migrating with his wife from upstate New York to Iowa. There he acquired, over a period of time, 240 acres of prime farm land and became successful enough to retire in 1884 to nearby Waterloo. The Beckers were Republican in politics and Methodist in religion; and although Carl would subsequently break away from his family on both counts, there is no evidence of any major rupture in personal relations. Indeed, the style of their life—socially conventional, modestly comfortable, with moderation in thought and action—was one he always retained.

Carl Becker graduated from the West Side High School in Waterloo in 1892 and attended Cornell College in Mount Vernon, Iowa, for one year before transferring to the University of Wisconsin in Madison. At Wisconsin he read William Dean Howells and Henry James and toyed with the idea of becoming a writer. Influenced, however, by two of his teachers, Frederick Jackson Turner [q.v.] and Charles Homer Haskins [Supp. 2], he decided to become a writer of history, and when he graduated in 1896 he received honors for his senior thesis in that field. After two years of graduate work at Wisconsin, Becker went in 1898 to Columbia University, where he studied for one year under James Harvey Robinson [Supp. 2] and Herbert L. Osgood [*q.v.*]. He then taught at Pennsylvania State College (two years) and Dartmouth College (one year) before going to the University of Kansas at Lawrence in 1902. On June 16, 1901, he married Maude Hepworth Ranney, a widow several years his senior, whom he had known in New York City; they had a son, Frederick DeWitt.

Becker arrived at Kansas as an assistant professor without a Ph.D., and it was not until 1907 that he received his doctorate from the University of Wisconsin and his first promotion at Kansas. While acquiring a steadily growing reputation in his profession—and despite evidence of some unhappiness at Kansas—Becker remained there until 1916, when he left for the University of Minnesota. In 1917 he joined the history department at Cornell University in Ithaca, N. Y. He continued to teach at Cornell until his retirement in 1941, and there is abundant evidence that he found his colleagues and students, especially the graduate students, to his liking.

Despite his shyness and reserve, Becker became a popular and even legendary figure at Cornell. His undergraduate course in modern European history had a large enrollment. Becker guided a number of graduate students destined to make significant contributions to the historical profession—Leo Gershoy, Louis Gottschalk, Robert Palmer, and Harold T. Parker—but his reputation rests mainly on his publications. Although most of his writings were in American history, his teaching and his most famous book, *The Heavenly City of the Eighteenth Century Philosophers* (1932), were in European history.

Becker's *The History of Political Parties in the Province of New York* (1909), originally his Ph.D. dissertation, was a pioneering work which anticipated in its methodology and conclusions the researches in this field of Arthur M. Schlesinger and others. Its emphasis was upon the importance of property distinctions in the democratization of politics in New York. Of all the "economic interpretations" of American history, this book seems best to have survived the tests of time and criticism. His next major book, *The Eve of the Revolution* (1918), showed his ability to apply to history literary skills of a high order, as well as to provide convincing insights into the revolutionary psychology.

Becker's most abiding interest lay in the his-

tory of ideas, especially of those ideas which had helped bring about the American and French revolutions of the eighteenth century. While he sometimes utilized a qualified version of the economic interpretation of social and political history, he never took seriously the economic interpretation of the history of ideas. His *The Declaration of Independence* (1922) contains a superb exegesis and historical analysis of that document. *The Heavenly City of the Eighteenth Century Philosophers* sought not merely to examine the ideas of the philosophes—their belief in progress and human perfectibility—but also to underline the quasi-religious intensity evident in their psychological makeup.

Becker usually remained detached from public affairs, but he was greatly concerned with the problems posed by World War I, the Great Depression, and World War II and with the need for seeing such events in a proper historical perspective. In practice he supported American participation in both wars and Roosevelt's efforts to cope with the depression, but in theory he was perplexed over how to reconcile the need for "progressive" legislation and greater social control of economic activity with the traditions of individual liberty of which he was the historian. Becker had actively supported Woodrow Wilson during the first World War, and his disillusionment over the Peace of Versailles was especially intense. It should also be noted that many of Becker's historian friends were "New Historians" and as such more involved than he ordinarily was in the discussion of contemporary problems and more convinced than he that the study of history could contribute directly to curing the ills of society. It is against the background of this liberal, progressive "climate of opinion" (one of Becker's favorite phrases) and of his personal concern with the possible uses and abuses of history that one can best understand Becker's views on historiography and his famous espousal of "historical relativism," in his presidential address before the American Historical Association ("Everyman His Own Historian," *American Historical Review,* January 1932) and elsewhere.

Becker's "historical relativism" was aimed at exposing what he regarded as the limits of historical knowledge. His position contains two distinct theses, although he himself did not always distinguish between them: first, that the historian must employ principles of selection in organizing and interpreting historical data, and second, that these principles necessarily reflect the interests and values of the society in which the historian lives. While it now seems obvious that one could accept the first thesis without accepting the second, Becker thought not. He also had amazingly little to say about the kind of necessity or the nature of the interests and values involved in the second thesis. Moreover, he seemed genuinely puzzled when friends and critics accused him of having cut the ground from under the possibility of historical objectivity. Becker's explorations of "relativism," "detachment," "objectivity," and "fact" must, however, be regarded as pioneering efforts, the results of which were often unsatisfactory even to Becker himself. Still, by force of example, he convinced some of his contemporaries and successors to take a fresh look at the history of history and the logic of historical explanation.

In the 1940's, following an operation that relieved him from the gastric ulcers which had shadowed much of his adult life, Becker, who had a sizable readership outside the profession through reviews, textbooks, and essays, now became increasingly known to a more general audience through works such as *How New Will the Better World Be?* (1944) and *Freedom and Responsibility in the American Way of Life* (1945). After his retirement, he taught for a term at Smith College in 1942, but his remaining years were spent at home in Ithaca, N. Y., where he was finally free to devote all his time to writing. He died there of uremia in 1945. Following cremation, his ashes were buried in Pleasant Grove Cemetery, Ithaca.

[Burleigh T. Wilkins, *Carl Becker: A Biog. Study in Am. Intellectual Hist.* (1961), includes a bibliography of works by and about Becker and a photograph of him. The work draws extensively on Becker's papers in the Collection of Regional Hist. and Univ. Archives at Cornell; there is useful information also in the George Lincoln Burr and Charles Hull papers there. Cushing Strout, *The Pragmatic Revolt in Am. Hist.: Carl Becker and Charles Beard* (1958), discusses Becker's political and historiographical views. Charlotte Watkins Smith, *Carl Becker: On Hist. & the Climate of Opinion* (1956), explores his theory and practice of historical writing. Robert E. Brown, *Carl Becker on Hist. and the Am. Revolution* (1970), is a recent critique. George Sabine's preface to the 1955 edition of Becker's *Freedom and Responsibility in the Am. Way of Life* is still a useful account of some of Becker's philosophical dilemmas.]
BURLEIGH TAYLOR WILKINS

BECKET, FREDERICK MARK (Jan. 11, 1875–Dec. 1, 1942), metallurgist, was born in Montreal, Canada, to Anne (Wilson) and Robert Anderson Becket. His father, whose family came from Ayrshire, Scotland, was president of the City Ice Company of Montreal and a prominent member of its Erskine Presbyterian Church. His mother, of northern Irish descent, bore her husband twelve children, of whom only five (four boys and a girl) survived to adulthood; of these Frederick was the next to youngest. He attended local schools, learned to play the piano with considerable skill, developed a strong baritone voice, and became expert at rugby and hockey (in later years he played with New York City amateur teams). He was athletic in build, distinguished in appearance, and a good scholar. He achieved honors in thermodynamics in his senior year at McGill University, from which he graduated in 1895 with the degree of bachelor of applied science in electrical engineering.

Seeking a future in electrical work, Becket came to the United States and took a job with Westinghouse Electric and Manufacturing Company in East Pittsburgh, Pa. In 1896 he joined the Acker Process Company of Jersey City, N. J., where he came in contact with high-temperature electrochemistry. Eager to get into this field, but recognizing his need for more fundamental knowledge about it, he enrolled in the graduate school of Columbia University. In 1899 he received a master's degree in physical chemistry and was transferred to Acker's new plant in Niagara Falls, N. Y., as its chief electrician. The next year brought Becket both joy and tragedy. In 1900 he married Frances Kirby of New York City and three months later saw his twenty-two-year-old bride die of a ruptured appendix. With anguished thoughts making sleep difficult, he returned to Columbia to plunge into advanced study in chemistry with Prof. Charles F. Chandler and in metallurgy with Henry M. Howe [*qq.v.*].

Becket returned in 1902 to Niagara Falls, where he first took a job with the Ampere Electrochemical Company. A year later he struck out on his own, helping to organize the Niagara Research Laboratories, Inc., for electrometallurgical research. His associates and stockholders, however, became impatient for profitable results and drifted away, leaving Becket to handle the experimental, development, and sales efforts. In what he later called "one of the most valuable and interesting experiences of my lifetime," he worked out the technique of producing low-carbon ferroalloys and alloying metals by reducing ores in an electric furnace with silicon instead of carbon—the silicon reduction process. Such alloys had earlier been made by using aluminum instead of silicon, but that method had proved unsuitable to large-scale production. Becket's innovation laid the groundwork for the production of low-carbon ferrochrome and stainless steels. Beyond using silicon as a reductor, he also successfully experimented with the production of silicon alloys, which were eventually used with aluminum alloys in the manufacture of airplanes.

In 1906 Becket joined the newly formed Electro Metallurgical Company, a predecessor of

Union Carbide Corporation, which also acquired his patents and his laboratory. Here he became chief metallurgist and in 1907 began commercial production of ferrosilicon and low-carbon ferrochrome. By 1910 he had set up an experimental laboratory; extending the scope of his earlier work, he produced results which made possible the production of the ferrozirconium and ferrovanadium, alloys used in the production of armor plate during the last days of World War I. Becket was naturalized as a United States citizen in 1918. With the incorporation of Union Carbide, he became successively chief metallurgist and vice-president of the parent company and, in 1927, president of Union Carbide and Carbon Research Laboratories in Long Island City. Here he continued to do experimental work, with more than 120 patents issued in his name. His major achievements of this period, however, were in inspiring and developing the men who would further advance metallurgy and create the metals that would eventually take man to the moon and back.

In his work Becket displayed a keen intellect, a remarkable memory, great thoroughness, and an infinite capacity for detail. In person he had broad interests, high ethical standards, and a quiet, gentlemanly charm. On Oct. 8, 1908, Becket married Geraldine McBride of Niagara Falls; they had two daughters, Ethelwynn and Ruth. Becket's later years brought him honorary degrees from Columbia (1929) and McGill (1934) and the award of the Perkin (1924), Acheson (1937), Howe (1938), and Cresson (1940) medals. He served as president of the Electrochemical Society (1925–26) and the American Institute of Mining and Metallurgical Engineers (1933). He retired in 1940 and died two years later in Roosevelt Hospital, New York City. His remains were cremated. In 1956 the Electrochemical Society, on a grant from Union Carbide, established a scholarship in high-temperature electric furnace work in his name.

[Information from archives of Columbia Univ., McGill Univ., and Union Carbide Corp.; recollections of associates and relatives; biographical sketch in *Metal Progress*, Sept. 1935; obituaries in Electrochemical Soc., *Transactions*, LXXXII (1942), 34–36, and *Mining and Metallurgy*, Jan. 1943; articles on Union Carbide and Carbon Corp. in *Fortune*, June and July 1941; *Who Was Who in America*, vol. II (1950); *Niagara Falls Gazette*, Sept. 10, 1900 (first wife's death), Oct. 8, 1908 (second marriage), and Jan. 4, 1956 (award tribute); obituary in *N. Y. Herald Tribune*, Dec. 2, 1942.]

AUGUSTUS B. KINZEL
MARION MERRILL

BEDAUX, CHARLES EUGENE (Oct. 11, 1886–Feb. 18, 1944), efficiency expert, fascist collaborator, was born in Charenton-le-Pont, France, a suburb of Paris, a younger son of Charles Emile Bedaux, a draftsman, and Marie Eulalie (Plotkin) Bedaux. His two brothers reportedly went into civil engineering (a sister became a dressmaker); but Charles, restless and ambitious, left France in 1906 at the age of nineteen to seek his fortune in America. He worked as a sandhog under the East River in New York City, as a Berlitz teacher of French in St. Louis, and as management consultant in Grand Rapids, Mich., where he became a naturalized citizen in 1917. His first marriage, to Blanche Allen of St. Louis, ended in divorce; his second wife was Fern Lombard of Grand Rapids. By his first wife he had a son, Charles Emile, born in 1909.

Bedaux capitalized on the national interest in efficiency by devising his own system of management to rival that of Frederick W. Taylor [*q.v.*]. He opened an office in Cleveland in 1918 and, with the rapid growth of his business, moved to New York City in 1920. The popularity of the "Bedaux system" rested on its ability to produce dramatic increases in labor productivity quickly and cheaply. It was a simple system which did not, like Taylor's, involve a major restructuring of management. Rather, the Bedaux system placed virtually the entire burden for increased efficiency on labor. Taylor, by using the stopwatch, had shown how to determine the time required for any operation, but he had had to add an arbitrary allowance for necessary rest. Bedaux claimed to have discovered a method by which he could calculate the exact amount of rest required for any given task. By combining work and rest in the correct proportions, Bedaux could formulate a common measure for all human labor, which he called the Bedaux unit or "B," equal to the amount of work that should be performed in one minute. Such a standard unit of labor offered many advantages. It permitted comparisons of the relative efficiency of men, departments, and plants regardless of the type of work being done. It was the basis for an incentive system of wage payments. The worker received extra pay for work in excess of 60 "B" units per hour. Bedaux claimed that his system increased the average output per worker by one-third.

A brilliant opportunist with a gift for salesmanship, Bedaux enjoyed a remarkable success. By 1931 he had ten offices around the world employing over two hundred engineers. His system was adopted by more than six hundred firms employing over 325,000 workers, including some of the world's largest corporations. Bedaux was able to live in France in opulent luxury, leaving day-to-day operations to subordinates. The Bedaux system, however, declined in popularity in the 1930's owing to opposition from organized labor. An investigation sponsored by the American Federation of Labor concluded that beneath its pseudoscientific jargon the Bedaux system was simply a "speed-up." The report held that the production standards were arbitrary and frequently too high and that other elements of good management were neglected.

Wealth and success did not satisfy Bedaux's Napoleonic ambitions. He wanted to be accepted by the great and to play a role in large affairs. In 1937 he achieved international fame when the Duke of Windsor (the recent King Edward VIII of England) married the American divorcée Wallis Warfield Simpson at his château in France. Though Bedaux offered his hospitality without having previously met either the Duke or Mrs. Simpson, a friendship blossomed. Drawing upon contacts already formed with the Nazi elite, Bedaux arranged a German tour for the Duke, who was interested in labor conditions in various countries. Bedaux attempted to follow up this success by sponsoring a tour of the United States by the Windsors. The visit, however, had to be canceled because of the protests of American labor leaders against Bedaux and his system. This fiasco alienated Bedaux from the United States and encouraged his developing fascist sympathies.

After the fall of France in 1940, Bedaux became an economic adviser to both the Nazi rulers of France and the Vichy government. His most ambitious scheme was for a peanut oil pipeline and railroad across the Sahara by means of which he hoped to ease the shortage of edible oils in occupied Europe. While in Algeria to begin this project, he was captured by the Allies when they invaded North Africa in November 1942. Bedaux was returned to the United States, where he was held in custody by immigration authorities in Miami, Fla. In February 1944 it was determined that he was still an American citizen and that a grand jury should consider whether he should be indicted for treason and for communicating with the enemy. Still held in Miami, Bedaux then committed suicide by an overdose of sleeping pills. After Christian Science services in Boston, he was buried in Mount Auburn Cemetery, Cambridge, Mass.

[Charles E. Bedaux, *The Bedaux Efficiency Course for Industrial Application* (1917), a 324-page book published in Grand Rapids, Mich., by the Bedaux Industrial Inst., gives illuminating insight into Bedaux's ideas just before he devised the Bedaux unit, showing clearly his indebtedness to Frederick W. Taylor, Harrington Emerson, and other management pioneers. A later pamphlet, *Bedaux Labor Measurement* (Charles E. Bedaux Co., 1933), possibly by Bedaux himself, and Lester C. Morrow, "The Bedaux Principle of

Human Power Measurement," *Am. Machinist*, Feb. 16, 1922, present the Bedaux system in its mature form. For critiques of the system by industrial engineers, see Harlow S. Person in *New Republic*, Nov. 24, 1937, and especially "A.F.L. Report on the Bedaux System," *Am. Federationist*, Sept. 1935, unsigned but written by Geoffrey C. Brown. See also Spencer Miller, Jr., "Labor's Attitude Toward Time and Motion Study," *Mechanical Engineering*, Apr. 1938. On Bedaux's life, Janet Flanner, "Annals of Collaboration, Equivalism," *New Yorker*, Sept. 22, Oct. 6, 13, 1945, is an illuminating study, though inaccurate on the Bedaux system and on some biographical details. Of greater accuracy are the obituary and other articles in the *N. Y. Times*, Feb. 20, 1944. For earlier news coverage see the *Times* Index. Birth date, names of parents, and father's occupation from Bedaux's birth record (Mairie de Charenton-le-Pont). Photographs of Bedaux and comments on his circle are found in *Time*, Nov. 8, 15, 1937, and *Newsweek*, Nov. 15, 1937. Biographical references compiled by Susan Henkel, Univ. of Wis. Lib. School, were helpful.]

EDWIN LAYTON

BEERS, CLIFFORD WHITTINGHAM (Mar. 30, 1876–July 9, 1943), founder of the mental hygiene movement, who based his campaign on his own experience with mental illness, was born in New Haven, Conn., where his father, Robert Anthony Beers, a native of New York state, earned a modest living in the produce business. His mother, Ida (Cooke) Beers, was born in Savannah, Ga. Clifford was the fifth of six sons (one of whom died in infancy). To his knowledge none of his ancestors, who were English, or their American descendants suffered from mental disorder, though there was much eccentricity on his mother's side. Information about his childhood is sparse. His mother appears to have been emotionally withdrawn, his father gentle and somewhat ineffective; he was evidently left to the special care of an aunt. In 1894, after attending local public schools, he entered Yale University's Sheffield Scientific School. That year his next oldest brother was fatally stricken by what was thought to be epilepsy. Fear of a similar fate obsessed Beers before and after his graduation, Ph.B., in 1897. A few years later, while working for a New York City business firm, he suffered a mental breakdown and tried to commit suicide. From August 1900 to September 1903 he spent most of his time in three Connecticut mental hospitals—Stamford Hall, the Hartford Retreat (later called the Institute of Living), and the Connecticut State Hospital at Middletown—before he was pronounced improved and was released.

The indignities and actual violence which Beers and other patients endured at the hands of attendants in these institutions determined him to formulate plans for their reform. After his release he returned to the business world, intending to establish himself financially and socially before embarking on the career of reformer, but he became impatient and then excited and late in 1904 was persuaded to commit himself again to the Hartford Retreat, where he stayed for most of January 1905. Shortly thereafter he wrote *A Mind That Found Itself,* a vivid account of his illness and an exposition of his program to transform mental hospitals from essentially custodial institutions into therapeutic ones. Published in 1908, the book created a sensation. It received wide acclaim in the general and scientific press and stimulated hundreds of persons to write to Beers of its profound effect upon them.

Convinced that his book alone would not impel reform, Beers turned to organizational work, for which he proved singularly gifted. With the advice of the psychiatrist Adolf Meyer and the support of Dr. William H. Welch [*q.v.*] of Johns Hopkins, the philosopher William James [*q.v.*], and other prominent men, Beers established the Connecticut Society for Mental Hygiene in 1908 as a demonstration project. Its purposes were both preventive and remedial: to work for the prevention of mental disorders and defects and to raise standards of care for the mentally ill. The Connecticut example inspired the formation of similar organizations throughout the United States and Canada, and in February 1909 Beers founded the National Committee for Mental Hygiene, with headquarters in New York City, to initiate and coordinate reform on a national scale. His wife, Clara Louise Jepson of New Haven, a childhood friend whom he married on June 27, 1912, helped him in his work. Intense, clever, talkative, witty, dark eyes flashing out of a swarthy face, he was able to persuade wealthy persons to contribute hundreds of thousands of dollars to the National Committee. These funds, together with millions in foundation grants and the talents of the outstanding executives and experts whom the indefatigable Beers recruited, enabled the committee to achieve and maintain for several decades undisputed leadership and influence in practically every aspect of the mental health field, including popular and professional education, research, and treatment.

Beers's domineering, compulsive personality, however, created difficulties. As secretary of the National Committee and of a number of other organizations that he set up, he insisted on the right to oversee their activities, a demand that brought him into conflict with the committee's medical chiefs. In 1922, frustrated by this opposition, he decided to shift his main effort to international work. He originated the idea of the First International Congress for Mental Hygiene, for which he raised the money. Held in Washington, D. C., in May 1930, the meeting was attended by some 3,500 representatives from fifty-three nations and resulted in the formation of the International Committee for Mental Hygiene. During numerous trips abroad Beers enjoyed recognition everywhere as the founder and leader of the modern mental hygiene movement. He received many honors, some of which he actively sought, he said, for the prestige they reflected upon his cause; among the latter was the French government's naming him a chevalier of the Legion of Honor.

Meanwhile Beers had continued as secretary of the National Committee for Mental Hygiene. By 1934, however, glaucoma and arteriosclerosis forced him to reduce his workload. A few years later the committee had to curtail its programs because of a shrinkage of funds. Called upon to resume fund raising, for which he feared he no longer had the energy or self-confidence, Beers became depressed and suspicious and finally committed himself in June 1939 to Butler Hospital, Providence, R. I. He died there a few years later of bronchial pneumonia, some months after suffering a cerebral thrombosis, and was buried in Evergreen Cemetery, New Haven. He was survived by his wife; they had had no children for fear of transmitting a susceptibility to the mental illness that had struck Beers and by 1912 his younger brother. (His two remaining brothers later committed suicide in mental hospitals.) Beers was an Episcopalian in religion and a Republican in politics but showed limited interest in anything outside the "cause," for which he made substantial financial sacrifices. Only when he was almost sixty did he take up a hobby, oil painting.

In the large scope of his efforts Beers modeled himself after the industrial tycoons of the day, whom he greatly admired. He succeeded in virtually monopolizing the mental hygiene field for the organizations he founded, in extending his work on an international scale, and in educating a wide public. Unlike Dorothea Dix [*q.v.*], with whom he is best compared, Beers could collaborate with others, despite his tendency to dominate. Indeed, his accomplishments outlasted those of Miss Dix, for he was able to enlist some of the most talented men of his day in a movement that survived the death of its originator. His book continued to find readers; it was still in print in 1960, having appeared in five editions and thirty-five printings and in several foreign translations.

[The principal MS. source for a study of Beers and the organizations he founded is the extensive collection of papers held by the Nat. Foundation for Mental Hygiene, N. Y. City (established by Beers in 1928); this includes drafts of his book, articles, speeches, and letters received, as well as copies of virtually every letter Beers wrote from 1902 to his death. The most useful published sources are: *A Mind That Found Itself,* the successive editions and printings of which contain revised accounts of the mental hygiene movement; a collection of about 500 tributes to Beers, *Twenty-five Years After: Sidelights on the Mental Hygiene Movement and Its Founder,* ed. by Wilbur L. Cross (1934); and Albert Deutsch, *The Mentally Ill in America* (2nd ed., revised, 1949), chap. xv. The standard encyclopedias and directories contain material on Beers, among them the *Nat. Cyc. Am. Biog.,* XXXIV, 140–41. See also Robin McKown, *Pioneers in Mental Health* (1961); memorial articles in *Mental Hygiene,* Apr. 1944, and *Am. Jour. of Psychiatry,* Apr. 1944; and obituaries in *N. Y. Times* and *N. Y. Herald Tribune,* July 10, 1943. Some of the best sketches of Beers's activities and personality are in unpublished papers in the files of the Nat. Foundation for Mental Hygiene.]

NORMAN DAIN

BEHRENDT, WALTER CURT (Dec. 16, 1884–Apr. 26, 1945), architect and regional planner, was born in Metz, Lorraine, the only son and elder of two children. His parents, Alfred and Henriette (Ohm) Behrendt, both of western German origin, lived successively in Metz, Mainz, Wiesbaden, and Braunschweig before Alfred Behrendt assumed his final post, as director of the Reichsbank in Hannover. Though not rich, Behrendt's parents were always in comfortable circumstances.

After attending various humanistic Gymnasiums, Behrendt entered the Technische Hochschule in Charlottenburg and completed his engineering studies at the Technische Hochschule in Dresden, from 1907 to 1911, when he received the degree of Doctor of Engineering. From the outset his prime interest was architecture rather than structural engineering; and his doctor's thesis, on the uniform façade as a spatial element in city planning, embraced the two main fields he cultivated both as civil administrator and as scholar. It was in fact as architect that he served in the Prussian Ministry of Public Works, from 1912 to 1916. On Apr. 15, 1913, he married Lydia Hoffmann, an active concert pianist of distinction; they had no children.

Though disrespectful of Germany's militarist traditions, Behrendt exemplified both Prussian discipline and the Prussian sense of duty at their exacting best. Between 1916 and 1918 he served in the German army as a private, and he retained to the end, in other fields besides war, his pride and self-confidence as a "front-line fighter" and an expert marksman. After demobilization, he served in the Prussian Ministry of Public Health as housing and city planning adviser until 1927, when he became technical adviser to the Minister of Finance, Department of Public Buildings. In the first post, he was in charge of the technical and financial aspects of Germany's housing program in the 1920's and helped develop the high standard that made Germany, after England, the leader in this field. Similarly, in the design of new public buildings he threw off the incubus of ponderous official architecture and encouraged a more direct expression of modern functions and needs. Berlin, where he lived, was then the chief experimental center of the modern movement in architecture.

Since many of the new public housing developments were set in the heavy industry areas, Behrendt became concerned with the problems of regional planning; and he served as a consultant in the development of the Ruhr Valley industrial region, the Middle German soft-coal region around Halle and Merseburg, and the greater Hamburg region. (During World War II—though painfully anticipating the destruction to his native land—he placed his detailed maps of these areas at the disposal of the military forces of his adopted country.) Through Behrendt's personal contact with Charles Harris Whitaker [Supp. 2], editor of the *Journal of the American Institute of Architects,* as well as through the articles on German housing and regional planning he contributed to that journal, he exerted a positive influence on American thought in these fields, notably in the work of Henry Wright [Supp. 2] and Clarence S. Stein.

Behrendt's career as architectural historian and critic paralleled his work as administrator. As architectural editor and regular critic of the *Frankfurter Zeitung* and as editor of *Die Form* (1925–27), he was a sympathetic yet always discriminating advocate of the new movement in architecture and decoration which was promoted by the Deutscher Verbund and by both Henry van de Velde's Weimar School and Walter Gropius's Bauhaus. This same point of view was expressed in his many architectural articles. It was developed in his book *Der Kampf über den Stil in Architektur und Kunstgewerbe* ("The Struggle over Style in Architecture and the Crafts," 1920) and reaffirmed and restated in *Der Sieg des Neuen Baustils* ("The Victory of the New Building Style," 1927).

Germany's takeover by Nazism ended Behrendt's official career, for though his parents had espoused Protestantism, they were Jewish in origin. Fortunately his first visit to the United States in 1925 had given him a circle of helpful American friends, and when he left Germany in 1934 it was to become a visiting lecturer at Dartmouth College in Hanover, N. H. By temperament both he and his wife felt at home in America and played an animated part in the community —Mrs. Behrendt taught music and gave many brilliant piano concerts in Hanover. Behrendt's teaching at Dartmouth was interrupted by four somewhat strained and abortive years as technical director of the Buffalo (N. Y.) City Planning Association, beginning in 1937, but he returned as professor of city planning and housing in 1941. That year he became a full-fledged American citizen and built a handsome redwood home at Norwich, Vt., on a bluff above the White River, the first indigenous modern house in that region. Behrendt's Dartmouth career brought his entire life to a fruitful consummation by disclosing his strong vocation as a teacher, one who imbued his students with his own vivid humanity, moral responsibility, and scholarly zeal. More permanently, it gave him the opportunity to integrate his learning and his administrative experience in a masterly book, remarkable for both its range and its incisive judgments: *Modern Building: Its Nature, Problems, and Forms* (1937). Not as widely known as Nikolaus Pevsner's *Pioneers of the Modern Movement* (1936), nor as exhaustive as Siegfried Giedion's *Space, Time, and Architecture* (1941), Behrendt's *Modern Building* nevertheless remains probably the best critical and historical summation of the modern (postrevivalist, posteclectic) movement in architecture.

Wartime teaching pressures, plus the inner tensions of a sensitive personality full of timely forebodings about the human future, helped bring on a series of heart attacks that resulted in Walter Curt Behrendt's death at the age of sixty at his home in Norwich. He was buried in Hillside Cemetery there, a site that, like his home, commanded the stretch of river landscape he admired and loved.

[Biographical summary, prepared by Behrendt (*c.* 1941), in files of Dartmouth College; personal conversation and correspondence, 1925–45; information from Mrs. Lydia Hoffmann Behrendt.]
                                        LEWIS MUMFORD

BENCHLEY, ROBERT CHARLES (Sept. 15, 1889–Nov. 21, 1945), humorist, drama critic, film actor and writer, was born in Worcester, Mass., the younger of the two sons of Maria Jane (Moran) Benchley, whose father was a native of Protestant Northern Ireland, and Charles Henry Benchley, who came of an established and prominent New England family. Robert's paternal grandfather, an early supporter of the Republican party, served as lieutenant governor of Massachusetts. Charles Benchley held the more modest post of mayor's clerk in Worcester for thirty years. After Charles's first son, Edmund Nathaniel—thirteen years older than Robert—was killed in the Spanish-American War in 1898, young Robert received not only the concentrated affection of his mother but the dedicated attention of his late brother's fiancée, Lillian Duryea. In 1907

Miss Duryea sent him to Phillips Exeter Academy for his last year of high school and then on to Harvard.

Already evident at Exeter was the comic and dramatic talent that later generated Benchley's reputation. At Harvard, he was in great demand to play comic roles in amateur productions and to speak at dinners, where he alternated parodies of politicians with mock travelogues. In his senior year he was elected to the Signet Society, a literary club, to the Hasty Pudding, a social club renowned for its annual dramatic burlesque, and to the presidency of the *Lampoon,* the college humor magazine. He had few scholastic difficulties, except for an international law course, which he climaxed, it is said, by discussing the main issue of the final examination, a fisheries dispute, from the point of view of the fish. His failure in the course kept him from graduating with the class of 1912, and he received his A.B. the following year. On June 6, 1914, in Worcester, he married Gertrude Darling, a childhood schoolmate. They had two sons, Nathaniel Goddard and Robert.

Between 1912 and 1916 Benchley plodded through a succession of tedious jobs in Boston and New York, including secretarial work, public relations, and reporting. What little of his writing he was able to sell—his first humorous piece appeared in *Vanity Fair* in October 1914—he considered trivial. Routine assignments as a *New York Tribune* reporter early in 1916 further discouraged him, until Franklin P. Adams made him associate editor of the paper's Sunday magazine, for which he wrote weekly features such as "Do Jelly Fish Suffer Embarrassment?" Discharged by the *Tribune* in May 1917, principally for not conforming to its interventionist tone, he worked brief terms in the next two years as a producer's press agent, as publicity secretary to the federal Aircraft Board, back on the *Tribune* as editor of the *Graphic,* its Sunday pictorial supplement, and as a publicity agent for the Liberty Loan drive.

In May 1919 Benchley became managing editor of *Vanity Fair,* where he found congenial colleagues in Robert E. Sherwood and Dorothy Parker. The trio's irreverent wit and editorial independence irritated the top management; and when in January 1920 Miss Parker was dismissed for her candid theatrical reviews, Benchley and Sherwood resigned. From a small free-lance office shared with Miss Parker, Benchley then began writing a regular column for the New York *World,* "Books and Other Things," which ran for about a year. His first collection of humorous articles, *Of All Things,* appeared in 1921. In the spring of 1920 he was hired as drama critic by the humor magazine *Life,* a position he held until 1929. (During 1924 he dropped the use of his middle name.) His first contribution to the *New Yorker* appeared in December 1925 and by 1927 had developed into a regular feature, "The Wayward Press," in which he commented on current events under the pseudonym "Guy Fawkes." In 1929 he became drama critic for the *New Yorker,* where he stayed until 1940. For three years (1933–36) he also wrote a column of casual wit for King Features Syndicate.

Ten collections of Benchley's writings were published between 1921 and 1938. His book and drama reviews reflect the outlook of the educated everyman—sensible and rarely avant-garde. In his humorous pieces Benchley wrote as the absentminded but good-hearted Little Man, often frustrated but basically firm in his integrity and right reason. Benchley's writing seldom achieved the scope and savage irony of major American humorists like James Thurber and Ring Lardner [Supp. 1]; rather, it recalls the *Spectator's* eighteenth-century moderation, distinguished but also limited by its polite Addisonian good sense.

Benchley's career as critic and humorist was paralleled by his role as a popular comedian of stage, screen, and radio. In 1922 the "Vicious Circle" of wits whom he regularly joined for lunch at the Hotel Algonquin's "Round Table" produced an amateur revue in which he delivered a monologue, "The Treasurer's Report." Originally written in a taxi on the way to the first rehearsal, the skit was soon earning him money and fame. He gave it in Irving Berlin's *Music Box Revue* of 1923 and then on the Keith vaudeville circuit, and finally used it as his first motion picture short in 1928. During that same year he filmed another monologue, *The Sex Life of the Polyp.* In 1932 he wrote and acted a brief role in a full-length film, *Sport Parade.* After 1936, when his *How to Sleep* won the Motion Picture Academy's award for the best short film, he began a sequence of "how to" pictures. Between 1928 and 1945 he made nearly fifty shorts, appeared in a number of feature-length pictures, and collaborated on the scripts of many more. He entered radio in 1938 when he became master of ceremonies of the Old Gold program, which shortly afterward rose to sixth place in a national popularity poll.

Benchley's affability and generosity won him staunch friends. Strictly reared as a Congregationalist, throughout his life he gave time to various social welfare projects and controversial causes; he made extraordinary efforts, for instance, on behalf of Nicola Sacco and Bartolomeo Vanzetti [*qq.v.*]. He had no high regard for his talents as a humorist except as an easy means to income, but never found time for the "serious" writing he had always hoped to produce. According to his son, what he resented "was being considered a professional funny man, and as such not being taken seriously." In 1943 he announced that since few humorists remain funny after the age of fifty, he would write no more. He died in New York City in 1945 of a cerebral hemorrhage. His ashes were buried in Prospect Hill Cemetery, Nantucket, Mass.

[The major source on Benchley's life is Nathaniel Benchley's personal but generally reliable biography, *Robert Benchley* (1955). Both of Norris W. Yates's studies, *Robert Benchley* (1968) and "Robert Benchley's Normal Bumbler," in *The Am. Humorist* (1964), are biographically informative and critically astute. The most recent biography is Babette Rosmond's anecdotal *Robert Benchley: His Life and Good Times* (1970). Benchley's film career is reflected in the photographs and quotations of *The "Reel" Benchley* (1950) and in the academic assessment of Robert W. Redding's Ph.D. dissertation, "A Humorist in Hollywood: Robert Benchley and His Comedy Films" (Univ. of N. Mex., 1968). Three excellent brief commentaries on his writing and personality are: James Thurber in the *N. Y. Times Book Rev.,* Sept. 18, 1949; the obituary in the *New Yorker,* Dec. 1, 1945; and Robert E. Sherwood's foreword to Nathaniel Benchley's biography. *Current Biog.,* 1941, has an incidentally useful article. Nathaniel Benchley's *The Benchley Roundup* (1954) contains selections from his father's earlier volumes; Gertrude Benchley's *Chips Off the Old Benchley* (1949) compiles material previously uncollected.]

RONALD B. NEWMAN

BENDIX, VINCENT (Aug. 12, 1881–Mar. 27, 1945), inventor and industrialist, was born in Moline, Ill., the first child of John and Alma (Danielson) Bendix. His father, of Swedish descent, was minister of the Swedish Methodist Episcopal Church in Moline. Early in Bendix's childhood the family moved to Chicago, where, at thirteen, he designed a chainless bicycle. Though his father wished him to prepare for college, he left home at sixteen and went to New York City to pursue his interest in mechanical invention, supporting himself by such jobs as elevator operator and stenographer in a law office. He designed and supervised the building of an experimental motorcycle in which he reputedly interested Glenn H. Curtiss [Supp. 1], the aviation pioneer. Bendix acquired information and experience in mechanical technology as circumstances permitted, but there is no record of formal education in this field. He returned to Chicago about 1907.

Employed for a time as sales manager of the Holmsman Automobile Company in Chicago, Bendix became fascinated by the potential of the automobile. In 1908 he built and sold a few vehicles under his own name and thus gained insight into the inadequacies of the early motorcar. Realizing that hand cranking retarded its acceptance and that the first electric starting motors performed poorly, he concentrated, with what proved to be typical foresight, upon the development of a transmission device providing a dependable link between the starting motor and the car's engine. On Nov. 10, 1914, he was issued his first two patents on a "starter for engines." A year earlier he had found a manufacturer, the Eclipse Machine Company of Chicago, capable of making the triple-thread screw needed for the starter. In the year his patents were issued he licensed this company to manufacture the Bendix starter drive, the first being installed on Chevrolet's "Baby Grand" touring car. By 1919, production had soared to 1,500,000.

He also saw the opportunity to improve upon the early automobile brake. In France in 1923 at an automobile show, the restless, enthusiastic, incisive Bendix met the reserved, studious Henri Perrot, an outstanding French automobile engineer. Perrot had licensed General Motors in America to manufacture a linkage system for four-wheel brakes; he had also patented an internal-expanding brake shoe. At the time most automobiles had only simple two-wheel band brakes. Bendix seized the opportunity to acquire exclusive license to the Perrot brake shoe as well as Perrot's interest in the brake-linkage license granted General Motors. To manufacture the brake, he established the Bendix Brake Company in South Bend, Ind., and to finance expansion he formed the Bendix Corporation on Dec. 18, 1924. Production increased from 650,000 brakes in 1926 to 3,600,000 in 1928.

By 1924 the essence of Bendix's genius had emerged. He was an inventor—he acquired more than 150 patents, mostly on the brake and the starter—but his primary endeavor and success, to use his own words, was "the development and world-wide acceptance of some mechanical devices." He identified inadequacies in expanding technological systems, such as the automobile, and sought improvements either through his own inventions or through licenses on the patents of others. Through these he acquired a near monopoly of critical components. His interest and his drive extended beyond invention and development to the organization and financing of manufacturing. As the technology with which he associated expanded, he and his companies grew apace. Because he did not invent or manufacture a complete system or a consumer product, however, his crucial role in the history of technology and industry was obscured.

Bendix did not fundamentally change his style after his initial success with the starter drive

and the brake, but he played his role on a larger stage. During the "Lindbergh Boom" of 1927–29, he entered the aviation industry, on Apr. 13, 1929, changing the name of the Bendix Corporation to the Bendix Aviation Corporation and acquiring control of companies manufacturing aircraft components. Only 8 percent of the new corporation's sales were aviation products, but ownership of the Scintilla Magneto Company, producer of magnetos for aircraft; of the Pioneer Instrument Company, developer and maker of critical instruments for aerial guidance and control; of the Delco Aviation Corporation, manufacturer of electrical equipment for aviation; of the Eclipse Aviation Corporation, producer of aviation starters and generators; and of other aviation manufacturers deeply involved Bendix and the corporation, through its patents and its manufacturing facilities, in the expanding industry.

General Motors, for $15,000,000 cash and other considerations, had purchased one-quarter of the Bendix Aviation Corporation at the time of its founding. After the depression, in 1937, generally unsatisfactory conditions in the Bendix corporation led General Motors to install two members on its board of directors. Although Vincent Bendix remained president until Feb. 24, 1942, and was then briefly chairman of the board (until Mar. 18), his importance in the affairs of the corporation diminished. The corporation was reorganized from a form of holding company to an operating company, and managers and engineers from Bendix subsidiaries contributed to the creation of a research-and-development-based, highly diversified corporation that expanded dramatically during World War II.

During the 1920's Bendix invested heavily in Chicago real estate. His purchases included the luxurious home of Potter Palmer [q.v.] on Chicago's Lake Shore Drive, which he hung with Rembrandts and other works of art and called the Bendix Galleries. In 1929 he contributed $130,000 for an archaeological expedition to Tibet and other Asiatic countries under the direction of the Swedish explorer Sven Hedin; an object of the expedition was to purchase and bring back a complete Lama temple, to be erected in Stockholm, for which he gave $65,000. He was decorated by the Swedish king in September 1929. Bendix had a "dazzling" copy of the golden pavilion of Jehol in Manchuria erected at the Chicago World's Fair in 1933 and again at the New York World's Fair in 1939. By the 1930's he had become widely known to the public as an industrialist whose multimillion-dollar corporation made "at least one part of every automobile (starters, four-wheel brakes, air brakes, carburetors, air horns)," and also complex and vital parts for exciting new aircraft. The Society of Automotive Engineers elected him president in 1931. Bendix established the famous Transcontinental Air Race and donated the coveted Bendix Trophy. By 1938 he had organized the Bendix Home Appliances Corporation, which produced an automatic washing machine that became widely used.

On June 7, 1939, Vincent Bendix suffered "the biggest blow of my life" when declared an involuntary bankrupt after holders of Chicago real estate bonds he had guaranteed brought suit. Bendix listed assets of about two million dollars and liabilities of fourteen million. The Bendix Aviation Corporation was not involved, but Bendix resigned as president and chairman in order to be "free to devote my time to the field of development, unrestrained by executive demands." At the time of his death, at sixty-three, in New York City of coronary thrombosis, Bendix Helicopters, Inc., which he had formed in June 1944, was developing a four-passenger helicopter for mass production after the war. Bendix had married Elizabeth Channon on Apr. 6, 1922; she divorced him in July 1932. They had no children.

[*Bendix Technical Jour.*, Spring 1968; obituaries in *N. Y. Times* and *Chicago Tribune*, Mar. 28, 1945; *Scientific American*, May 1938, p. 259 (with portrait); *Soc. of Automotive Engineers Jour.*, Feb. 1931; May 1945; *N. Y. Times*, July 11, 1929, July 27, 1932, June 9, July 25, 1939, Mar. 21, 24, 1942; John T. Flynn, "Have You the Courage to Make Money?" *American Mag.*, June 1932; *Time*, Apr. 26, 1937, pp. 45–47, June 5, 1939, p. 73; *Moody's Manual of Investments*, 1931; *Poor's: Industrial Section*, 1925; information from Mrs. Marie Hoscheid, Moline Public Lib. Bendix's birth date, sometimes given as 1882, is confirmed by the *Moline Rev.-Dispatch*, Aug. 19, 1881.]

THOMAS PARKE HUGHES

BENÉT, STEPHEN VINCENT (July 22, 1898–Mar. 13, 1943), poet, novelist, and short story writer, was the second son and the youngest of three children of James Walker Benét and Frances Neill (Rose) Benét. His birthplace was Bethlehem, Pa., where his father, an army ordnance officer, was stationed at the Bethlehem Iron Works; his ancestral roots were in Florida, his great-great-grandfather Esteban Benét having come to St. Augustine from the Spanish island of Minorca about 1785. The family had a strong military tradition. Both Stephen's father and his paternal grandfather, after whom he was named, were West Point graduates; the elder Stephen Vincent Benét, though born in Florida, served in the Union Army during the Civil War and later became chief of army ordnance (1874–91). An uncle who settled in France, Laurence Vin-

cent Benét, became an official of La Société Hotchkiss et Cie., international munitions makers. Yet the Benét household was a literary one, and both Stephen's sister, Laura, and his brother, William Rose, became well-known authors in their own right. His father he later remembered as "the finest critic of poetry" he had ever known, and one who had taught him "many things about the writing of English verse, and tolerance, and independence and curiosity of mind."

Benét spent his childhood years at the Watervliet Arsenal in upper New York and the Benicia Arsenal in California. When he was three, scarlet fever weakened his eyesight, a condition that later frustrated his ambition to follow his father to West Point. He began his education at home while in Benicia, took correspondence courses under the Calvert System, and, when twelve, spent a year at the Hitchcock Military Academy at Jacinto, Calif., an unhappy experience which he described in his first novel, *The Beginning of Wisdom* (1921). In 1911 his father's command shifted to the Augusta Arsenal in Georgia, and Benét studied for four years at the nearby Summerville Academy. Following the example of his brother and sister, he had already begun to write verse; by 1913 he had published poems in *St. Nicholas* magazine, and his first slim collection, *Five Men and Pompey* (published at his brother William's expense), appeared in 1915, shortly after his graduation from the academy.

Benét entered Yale College in 1915. Although his academic record there was indifferent, he was elected chairman of the *Yale Literary Magazine* and was considered a prodigy for his fluent production of poetry, which won several prizes. He published his second and third volumes of verse, *The Drug-Shop* (1917) and *Young Adventure* (1918), while still an undergraduate. In the spring of 1918 Benét interrupted his schooling, determined to contribute to the war effort. By memorizing the official eye chart, he passed the army physical examination, but the deception was soon discovered. After a tedious clerical assignment in the State Department, he became a cryptographer for the military intelligence. He left Washington six weeks after the Armistice and finished his undergraduate work in June 1919. That fall he entered the Yale graduate school on a fellowship. In a literary workshop taught by Henry Seidel Canby he began his first novel, at the same time publishing his first short stories, in *Munsey's* and *Smart Set*. His manuscript of verse, submitted in lieu of the regular master's thesis, not only brought him the degree but, when published as *Heavens and Earth*

(1920), won him the Poetry Society of America award in 1921, which he shared with Carl Sandburg.

Going abroad on a Yale traveling fellowship, Benét enrolled at the Sorbonne in the fall of 1920. In Paris he fell in love with Rosemary Carr of Chicago. They were married in her home city on Nov. 26, 1921, and returned to Paris for their honeymoon. It was a happy marriage, to which were born three children: Stephanie Jane in 1924, Thomas Carr in 1926, and Rachel Carr in 1931. Meanwhile Benét published two more novels, *Young People's Pride* (1922) and *Jean Huguenot* (1923), the latter about an eccentric Southern belle. With Carl Brandt as his agent, he now concentrated on formula short stories for popular magazines, stories which remained a financial mainstay for the rest of his career. He continued to write verse, however, and in 1925 brought out, to considerable critical applause, a selection entitled *Tiger Joy*.

His next book, *Spanish Bayonet* (1926), a romantic historical novel set in colonial Florida, failed to place as a magazine serial because Benét refused to change the unhappy ending, but he had the satisfaction of having handled the narrative with the artistic conscience he usually reserved for his poetry. Increasingly unhappy with the popular fiction that Brandt was marketing for him, he began to experiment with American materials set in the past, often leavening them with fantasy to achieve the romantic and colorful quality of folklore. One of his first successful tales in this vein was "The Sobbin' Women" (*Country Gentleman,* May 1926). In 1926 four tales were cited in the honor rolls of both the O'Brien and the O. Henry anthologies of the year's best stories, and several, including "The Devil and Daniel Webster" and "Johnny Pye and the Fool-Killer," were subsequently published in special limited editions.

Meanwhile, a Guggenheim Fellowship in 1926 enabled Benét to take his family to France, where he worked on an epic poem about the American Civil War. *John Brown's Body* (1928), a Book-of-the-Month Club selection, became an immediate best seller and was awarded the Pulitzer Prize for poetry in 1929. Despite its popular acclaim, the poem was given only qualified praise by serious literary critics. Harriet Monroe [Supp. 2] dubbed it "a cinema epic" (*Poetry,* November 1928), and Newton Arvin wrote, "All the virtues of readability, romantic charm, reminiscent pathos, it has in abundance; the higher virtues that one might exact of such a performance, it very definitely lacks" (*New York Herald Tribune* book section, Aug. 12, 1928). Nevertheless,

Benét's reputation as a leading American poet had been established, and his status was consolidated by election to the National Institute of Arts and Letters in 1929 and to its inner circle, the American Academy of Arts and Letters, in 1938.

Benét had won financial success only to lose it in the stock market crash of 1929, which took most of his invested royalties. Prodded by Brandt, he went to Hollywood in 1929 to write the screenplay for D. W. Griffith's film *Abraham Lincoln,* for which he was paid $12,000. He disliked Hollywood and returned to grinding out popular short stories at reduced fees. From time to time he engaged in literary journalism for publications as varied as *Fortune* and the *New York Herald Tribune*'s book section. He accepted the editorship of the Yale Younger Poet Series, which annually published the work of an unknown poet, and became co-editor of the Rivers of America Series for Farrar and Rinehart. In collaboration with his wife, he brought out *A Book of Americans* (1933), a volume of light verse about famous historical characters. Benét's last novel, *James Shore's Daughter,* a comment on the American rich, appeared in 1934. He still found time for poetry and published *Burning City* (1936), in which he expressed the stresses of a "decade of tension." In 1937 he wrote the libretto for Douglas Moore's radio operetta *The Headless Horseman,* and he adapted his own memorable story "The Devil and Daniel Webster" both to an opera (1938), in collaboration with Moore, and to a film, *All That Money Can Buy* (1941). But his incessant labor took its toll; he suffered a nervous breakdown in 1939, his condition complicated by severe arthritis.

Benét had long abhorred totalitarianism, and at the outbreak of World War II he turned to writing propaganda against the Axis powers, justifying it as both an art and a necessary task. This work included *Dear Adolf* (1942) and radio scripts collected as *We Stand United* (1945). Early in 1943 he obliged the Office of War Information with *America,* a brief history that was published in 1945 and distributed wholesale throughout liberated Europe and Asia. Soon after writing it Benét died of a heart seizure at his home in New York City at the age of forty-four. He was buried in the Stonington (Conn.) Cemetery near his summer home. In a eulogy the poet Archibald MacLeish, a friend since their student days at Yale, praised Benét as a man "altogether without envy or vanity," who never "tried to present himself as anything but what he was." A long fragment of an epic poem about the American westward movement on which

Benét had been working for fifteen years was posthumously published in 1943 as *Western Star;* like *John Brown's Body,* it was chosen by the Book-of-the-Month Club and won a Pulitzer Prize.

[Charles A. Fenton, *Stephen Vincent Benét* (1958), is the best study. See also Parry Stroud, *Stephen Vincent Benét* (1962); George Abbe, *Stephen Vincent Benét on Writing* (1964); and Charles A. Fenton, ed., *Selected Letters of Stephen Vincent Benét* (1960). Many of Benét's letters and MSS. are in the Yale Collection of Am. Literature; others in family or private hands. Listings of Benét's works and of biographical and critical data may be found in Gladys Louise Maddocks, "Stephen Vincent Benét: A Bibliog.," *Bull. of Bibliog. and Dramatic Index,* Sept.–Dec. 1951, Jan.–Apr. 1952; Francis Cheney, "Stephen Vincent Benét," in Allen Tate, ed., *Sixty Am. Poets, 1896–1944* (1945); Robert E. Spiller et al., *Literary Hist. of the U. S.,* Bibliog. Vol. (1948), pp. 403–04; and Stroud, above, pp. 165–68. Of special interest is the memoir by his brother William Rose Benét in *Saturday Rev. of Literature,* Nov. 15, 1941. On his ancestry, see Frederick A. Virkus, ed., *The Abridged Compendium of Am. Genealogy,* I (1925), 299.]
THURMAN WILKINS

BENNETT, RICHARD (May 21, 1870–Oct. 22, 1944), actor, was born in Deacons Mills, Cass County, Ind., the older of two children and only son of George Washington and Eliza Leonora (Hoffman) Bennett. Like his pioneer forebears who had migrated to Indiana from New Jersey, George Bennett owned and operated a sawmill and served as a lay evangelical preacher; he was later sheriff of Howard County, Ind. Young Richard — christened Clarence Charles William Henry Richard — attended schools in Kokomo and Logansport, Ind. He acted in church and school theatricals as a boy; his mother encouraged his stage aspirations, but his father wanted him to enter the lumber business. Instead, Bennett left home and worked at a wide variety of odd jobs and occupations that included professional boxing, working aboard a Great Lakes steamer, and traveling with a medicine show. His quick temper and ready resort to fists made it necessary for him to keep moving.

After joining a tent show and then a minstrel troupe, Bennett attracted the attention of Joe Coyne, an English actor touring with *The Limited Mail,* who gave Bennett a job with the company. He made his professional debut in that melodrama at the Standard Theatre in Chicago on May 10, 1891, and soon graduated to the juvenile lead, Tombstone Jake. Near the end of the tour he appeared at Niblo's Garden in New York. Other road engagements followed, mostly in the Midwest, including two under the management of Gustave Frohman. In 1897 Gustave's brother Charles [q.v.] hired Bennett for the juvenile lead in *The Proper Caper,* which brought him again

to New York. This marked the beginning of Bennett's long but not exclusive association with Charles Frohman, under whose tutelage he developed into a matinee idol in a series of hits.

In 1905 he was graduated to more cerebral drama with the part of Hector Malone, opposite Clara Bloodgood, in Bernard Shaw's *Man and Superman.* Then came the role of Jefferson Ryder, the young hero of Charles Klein's *The Lion and the Mouse* (1905); when the play was taken overseas in 1906, Bennett made his London debut at the Duke of York's Theatre. Two years later Frohman selected him to play John Shand opposite Maude Adams in Sir James Barrie's *What Every Woman Knows* (Empire Theatre, New York, Dec. 23, 1908).

In 1913 Bennett undertook a daring venture. He had acquired the rights to *Damaged Goods,* Eugene Brieux's devastating study of the devastating social effects of hereditary syphilis. Despite many difficulties, he secured the endorsement of civic and health groups and managed to have it produced, first at special matinees, then for a regular run. He starred in the play, which had a successful tour, and later in a cinematic version. He also addressed clubs, church groups, and theatre audiences, scoring the hypocrisy that veiled the subject and advocating compulsory use of the Wassermann test in the issuance of marriage licenses. A subsequent Brieux play, *Maternity* (1915), a plea for legalized abortion, was not successful, but Bennett's role in it indicated his commitment to unpopular social causes.

Though Bennett occasionally returned to melodrama, he was becoming recognized as a leading actor in the artistic and realistic revolution in American drama after World War I. In February 1920 he was largely instrumental in persuading John D. Williams to put on Eugene O'Neill's first long play, *Beyond the Horizon,* in special matinees. Bennett was acclaimed as the poetical, tubercular hero, and the play won a regular engagement and the season's Pulitzer Prize. In other notable performances he played Andrew Lane in *The Hero* (1921), "He" in the Theatre Guild's production of Leonid Andreyev's *He Who Gets Slapped* (1922), and Tony in *They Knew What They Wanted* (1924), by Sidney Howard [Supp. 2], a paean to the new postwar morality.

For a time Bennett transferred most of his theatrical activities to the West Coast and to Hollywood, but he returned to Broadway in 1935 to take the role of Judge Gaunt in *Winterset,* Maxwell Anderson's poetical sequel to the Sacco-Vanzetti case. In 1938 he went into rehearsal as Gramp in *On Borrowed Time,* but was forced to withdraw before the New York opening because of memory blocks. Bennett subsequently took part in the founding of Bucks County Playhouse in New Hope, Pa., at which he directed several plays and gave readings.

Richard Bennett's personal life, meanwhile, almost rivaled his theatrical career in making the news. His first marriage, to Grena Heller in San Francisco in 1901, ended in divorce after two years. (Grena Bennett went on to become music critic for the *New York Journal-American* for over forty years.) On Nov. 8, 1903, he married Mabel Morrison, known on the stage as Adrienne Morrison (they had performed together in 1900). This second marriage, graced by the birth of three daughters—Constance Campbell, Barbara Jane, and Joan Geraldine—was considered ideally successful for twenty years. But a separation in 1923 was followed two years later by divorce. Unhappiness over the divorce led to the beginning of the heavy drinking that sometimes made Bennett's later work uneven. On July 11, 1927, he married an actress who had appeared in his stock company, Mrs. Aimee (Raisch) Hastings of San Francisco. They separated in 1934 and were divorced in 1937.

Two of Bennett's daughters achieved stardom in motion pictures, and he himself, besides acting in some 150 plays, appeared in occasional silent and sound films, among them *Arrowsmith* (1931) and Orson Welles's *The Magnificent Ambersons* (1942) and *Journey into Fear* (1943). Bennett was residing in Los Angeles when he contracted his final illness, arteriosclerotic heart disease, which led to his death from pulmonary edema in the Good Samaritan Hospital there in 1944. After funeral services in All Saints Episcopal Church, Beverly Hills, Calif., he was buried in the Morrison family plot in Old Lyme, Conn.

Richard Bennett was a handsome, aggressive, and dynamic actor brought up in the nineteenth-century tradition of stars and touring companies. From the start he was an honest and conscientious performer. According to the critic Elinor L. Hughes (*Boston Herald*, Sept. 15, 1925), he would learn all the other roles in a play before memorizing his lines, thus gradually arriving at his own interpretation. As he grew older, he developed from matinee idol to consummate character actor. Eugene O'Neill, at first irritated by Bennett's extensive cutting and rewriting of lines in *Beyond the Horizon,* soon admitted that "Bennett is really a liberal education" and that the experience had made him a better playwright (quoted in Sheaffer, pp. 476–77). On stage Bennett was famous for his curtain speeches and for his biting ad libs, usually directed at late arrivals or noisy audiences. Despite his antics, he was

serious about his art. At the time when American drama began to emerge from the inane escapism of Broadway, Richard Bennett was on the scene and ready to take part.

[Joan Bennett and Lois Kibbee, *The Bennett Playbill* (1970), gives the fullest biographical account of Richard Bennett. Information supplied by the Ind. State Lib., Indianapolis, from census schedules of 1870 and 1880 and other sources, supports the birth year, place of birth, and original first name of Bennett as given above. His death certificate also gives his birth year as 1870. Some facts about Bennett's early life appear in Ada Patterson, "Richard Bennett—An Actor to Be Reckoned With," *Theatre Mag.*, Feb. 1909, and in clippings in the Logansport (Ind.) Public Lib. For his stage performances, see John Parker, *Who's Who in the Theatre* (9th ed., 1939), as well as the statistical summaries in the *Best Plays* series, ed. by John Chapman, Garrison P. Sherwood, and Burns Mantle. There are occasional references in Arthur and Barbara Gelb, *O'Neill* (1962); Louis Sheaffer, *O'Neill: Son and Playwright* (1968); and Lawrence Langner, *The Magic Curtain* (1951). Besides numerous clippings in the Harvard Theatre Collection, see obituary in the *N. Y. Times*, Oct. 23, 1944, as well as the obituaries of Grena Bennett, Adrienne Morrison, and Barbara and Constance Bennett.]

EDMOND M. GAGEY

BENT, SILAS (May 9, 1882–July 30, 1945), journalist, critic of the American press, was born in Millersburg, Ky., where his father, James McClelland Bent, was a Baptist clergyman. His mother, Sallie (Burnam) Bent, was a Kentuckian; his father, born in St. Louis, Mo., was descended from John Bent, an Englishman who settled in Sudbury, Mass., in 1638. Among his forebears was Silas Bent (1820–1887) [*q.v.*], naval officer and oceanographer. Young Silas was the fourth among five children and the younger of two sons. Growing up in Kentucky, he was educated in public schools and at Ogden College in Bowling Green, from which he was graduated in 1902.

In that year he began his newspaper career in Louisville as a reporter on the *Herald* and the *Times.* Two years later he went to St. Louis, where he worked for the *Post-Dispatch* and, for a lesser period, the *Republic.* During the academic year 1908–09 he taught in the new school of journalism at the University of Missouri. Returning to the *Post-Dispatch,* Bent was assistant city editor until 1912, when he went to Chicago to handle publicity for the National Citizens' League, whose "sound banking" campaign contributed to Congressional passage of the Federal Reserve Act of 1913. For a short time he was on the *Chicago Evening American.* He moved in 1914 to New York and worked successively for the *Herald,* the *Tribune,* the *World,* and the *Times.* On the *Times,* he was a member of the Sunday magazine staff, 1918–20.

After directing newspaper and magazine publicity for the Democratic National Committee in the election year of 1920, Bent served as associate editor of *Nation's Business* in Washington through 1922. Concluding now that "legislation and national elections are swayed by the drive of publicity agencies upon the press," he turned to a career of free-lance writing and lecturing that was to make him a foremost critic of the policies and practices of the American press. Over the next two decades he wrote dozens of articles, largely critical and revelatory, for such magazines as the *Atlantic, Collier's, Outlook,* the *Nation,* and the *New Republic,* as well as nine books. His first book, originally a series of lectures at the New School for Social Research in New York, was the much-discussed *Ballyhoo: The Voice of the Press* (1927). In it he shared with his readers debunking descriptions of many newspaper practices that editors and publishers had generally kept to themselves. Though he scourged the rising tabloids, it was the "standard-sized, respectable, substantial press" that he bore into hardest. He showed how esteemed dailies trespassed on proper privacy, sensationalized murders and trials, and while exploiting "illicit love" avoided recognition of the scientific aspects of sex. He urged editors to be political but not partisan, to be less timid in making improvements, to engage in research and more thorough investigations, to print more and better foreign news, to recognize that the price of distortion was loss of the reader's confidence, and to protect serious news from being overwhelmed by trivia. He was in the forefront in warning editors to be on guard lest they lose a major aspect of the news function to radio, which he regarded as even more controllable and hence more dangerous.

Bent's main criticism was that under pressure of profit-motivated advertisers, publishers consolidated newspapers as properties and in the process produced "big industry" journalism, managed by editors who, seeking to be as inoffensive as possible, expressed fewer and fewer convictions. These trends, he held, failed to provide readers with the factual information and the editorial illumination required in a self-governing democracy. To show how courageously earlier editors had discharged their trust, Bent wrote *Newspaper Crusaders: A Neglected Story* (1939). Among his other books were a newspaper novel, *Buchanan of the Press* (1932), set in St. Louis and somewhat autobiographical, and two biographies, *Justice Oliver Wendell Holmes* (1932) and *Old Rough and Ready: The Life and Times of Zachary Taylor* (1946), the latter in collaboration with a cousin, Silas Bent McKinley.

During his free-lance years Bent made his home in Old Greenwich, Conn. His health weakened by excessive drinking, he died in the Stam-

ford (Conn.) Hospital of bronchopneumonia at the age of sixty-three. His wife, Elizabeth Chism Sims of Bowling Green, Ky., whom he had married on Oct. 3, 1916, survived him; they had no children. He was buried in Fairview Cemetery, Bowling Green. A leading historian of journalism (Mott, pp. 728–29) ranked Bent's *Ballyhoo* with Upton Sinclair's *The Brass Check* as a critical appraisal of the American press. With experience on Pulitzer, Hearst, and Ochs newspapers, in magazine editing, in political and economic public relations, and in education for journalism, Bent possessed credentials as an observer and critic of the press that could not be denied.

[Bent outlined his career in *Ballyhoo.* Facts about the family are from Allen H. Bent, *The Bent Family in America* (1900). See also *Who Was Who in America,* vol. II (1950); *Nat. Cyc. Am. Biog.,* XXXIV, 82; *Editor & Publisher,* Aug. 4, 1945; *N. Y. Times,* July 31, 1945; *St. Louis Post-Dispatch,* Oct. 4, 1932, July 31, 1945; and references to Bent in Frank L. Mott, *Am. Journalism* (1941); Simon M. Bessie, *Jazz Journalism: The Story of the Tabloid Newspaper* (1938); and George L. Bird and Frederic E. Merwin, *The Newspaper and Society* (1942). Particular information was supplied by Marguerite Roberts, Ferguson Lib., Stamford, Conn.; the Town Clerk of Stamford (death record); and Julia Neal, Ky. Lib. and Museum, Bowling Green, Ky. Linda W. Hausman lists many of Bent's magazine articles in her "Criticism of the Press in U. S. Periodicals, 1900–1939," *Journalism Monographs,* no. 4 (1967). His major books are annotated in Ralph E. McCoy, *Freedom of the Press* (1968).]
IRVING DILLIARD

BERGMANN, MAX (Feb. 12, 1886–Nov. 7, 1944), biochemist, was born in Fürth, Germany, the fifth son and seventh of nine children of Solomon and Rosalie (Stettauer) Bergmann. His father, a prosperous coal merchant, came of a Jewish family that had lived in the town for many generations. After completing his secondary schooling in Fürth, Bergmann took his first degree in 1907 at the University of Munich. He had originally been attracted to botany, but when he realized that many botanical problems could be solved only by the methods of organic chemistry, he enrolled in the chemical department of the University of Berlin, then headed by Emil Fischer. Working under Ignaz Bloch, Bergmann took the Ph.D. degree in 1911 with a dissertation on acyl polysulfides and thereupon became an assistant to Fischer.

During World War I, Bergmann was exempted from military service because of his position with Fischer and was closely associated with his chief's research on amino acids, carbohydrates, and tannins. After Fischer's death in 1919 Bergmann was appointed (in 1920) privatdozent in the University of Berlin and assistant director and head of the department of chemistry of the Kaiser

Wilhelm Institute for Textile Research. In 1921 he became director of the newly established Kaiser Wilhelm Institute for Leather Research in Dresden and received the title of professor in the Technische Hochschule of that city. Since the institute was partly supported by the leather industry, Bergmann was obliged to conduct research on chemical problems of technical interest (such as tanning) and to spend much time in consultation with leather manufacturers. He was president of the International Society of Leather Chemists, 1928–33. With Hitler's rise to power in Germany in 1933, Bergmann came to the United States. He was made an associate member of the Rockefeller Institute for Medical Research in New York City in 1934; three years later he became a full member, a position he held until his death.

Bergmann's scientific work before and after coming to the United States shows considerable continuity. The results of his research, and of that done under his direction, were published in some 350 articles in chemical and biochemical periodicals during the period 1913–46. In his association with Fischer, Bergmann made several basic contributions to carbohydrate, lipid, and amino acid chemistry, among them the elucidation of the structure of glucal and the development of new methods for the preparation of *alpha*-monoglycerides. While at Dresden he created one of the leading laboratories in the field of protein chemistry and attracted numerous young chemists from other countries (including the United States). One of these was Leonidas Zervas, who was associated with Bergmann during the years 1926–33 and joined him in the United States for two years (1935–37) before returning to his native Greece. Bergmann, Zervas, and their associates made numerous contributions to the chemistry of amino acids and peptides. Among them were studies on the mechanism of the racemization of amino acids, on the use of oxazolones for the synthesis of peptides, and on the transfer of the amidine group of arginine to glycine, a process later shown to occur in biological systems. In 1932 Bergmann and Zervas devised a new method for the synthesis of peptides, the "carbobenzoxy" method, which marked a new era in protein chemistry. Their method opened an easy route to large numbers of peptides—those containing optically active amino acids with reactive side chains—which had hitherto been difficult or impossible to prepare. Although many improvements in the methods of peptide synthesis were made by subsequent workers, especially after World War II, the fundamental importance of the pioneer work of Bergmann and Zervas is firmly established.

At the Rockefeller Institute, Bergmann directed the work of his laboratory along two lines. The first of these involved applying the carbobenzoxy method to the synthesis of peptides for possible use as substrates for proteolytic (protein-splitting) enzymes (such as pepsin). This work, largely pursued by Joseph S. Fruton, led in 1936–39 to the discovery of the first synthetic peptide substrates for these enzymes, thus opening the way for the study of their specificity of action. The second line of work, an approach to the unsolved problems of protein structure, was directed to the development of new methods for the quantitative analysis of the amino acid composition of proteins. With Carl Niemann, Bergmann in 1938 proposed that the arrangement of amino acids in a protein chain was periodic in nature; although this theory was later shown to be an oversimplification, it stimulated great experimental activity in the protein field. In Bergmann's laboratory, Stanford Moore and William H. Stein began work that later led them to solve the problem of the accurate quantitative determination of the amino acid composition of proteins. These researches were suspended after 1941, when Bergmann's laboratory turned its attention to the chemistry of war gases, a project under the auspices of the Office of Scientific Research and Development.

Bergmann was first married in 1912, to Emmy Miriam Grunwald, and had two children, Esther Maria and Peter Gabriel; the son became a theoretical physicist. The marriage ended in divorce, and on Mar. 20, 1926, Bergmann married Martha Suter; there were no children. In 1944, at the age of fifty-eight, he died of cancer at the Mount Sinai Hospital in New York City. He was buried at Ferncliff Cemetery, Hartsdale, N. Y.

[Obituaries by Hans T. Clarke in *Science,* Aug. 17, 1945, and C. R. Harington in *Jour. of the Chemical Soc.* (London), Oct. 1945; family data from Prof. Peter G. Bergmann, Syracuse Univ.]

JOSEPH S. FRUTON

BERRY, EDWARD WILBER (Feb. 10, 1875–Sept. 20, 1945), paleobotanist and educator, was born in Newark, N. J., the first of three children and elder son of Abijah Conger Berry and Anna (Wilber) Berry and a descendant of Henry Berry, who migrated from England to northern New Jersey before 1747. His father was working as a clerk when Edward was born. In later years he was a partner in a grocery and a salesman. Edward Berry was evidently a precocious youth: as a teenager he collected fossils in the Raritan Bay region, taught himself French and German, and, after two years at the Passaic (N. J.) high school, graduated at age fifteen. From 1890 to 1897 he worked as office boy and then as traveling salesman for a New York cotton goods outlet. During this period, influenced by the work of Jacob A. Riis [*q.v.*], he and two other young men started a successful movement to found a social settlement in Passaic. Berry next joined the *Passaic Daily News,* where over an eight-year period he was variously business manager, managing editor, president, and treasurer.

Meanwhile he was actively pursuing an interest in geology and botany. While with the *Daily News* he published an influential series of articles in scientific journals on New Jersey paleobotanical systematics. He joined the Torrey Botanical Club in New York, and in 1901 he received the Walker Prize of the Boston Society of Natural History for a paper on the forms and ancestry of the tulip tree. When in 1905 William Bullock Clark [*q.v.*], chairman of the geology department at the Johns Hopkins University and Maryland state geologist, whom he had met through the Torrey Club, urged him to help in the preparation of reports on Maryland's Cretaceous flora for the state geological survey, Berry resigned his newspaper post to resume his education.

Although he spent 1905–06 as a special student and 1906–08 as assistant to Clark in geology, he never took a degree at Johns Hopkins. (His only academic degree was an honorary Sc.D. from Lehigh in 1930.) Lack of college credentials, however, did not hinder Berry from advancing rapidly at Hopkins, from instructor (1907–10) to associate (1910–13), associate professor (1913–17), and professor (1917–42). He also served as dean of the college of arts and sciences (1929–42) and provost of the university (1935–42). As the careers of John Wesley Powell and William John McGee [*qq.v.*] also indicate, college degrees were largely irrelevant in appointments to the United States Geological Survey; thus Berry became a geologist (1910–17) and senior geologist (1917–42) on the Survey. He also served as assistant state geologist of Maryland (1917–42). The crisp style of his scientific writing and the rapid appearance of his articles reflected his journalistic background, which also prepared Berry for the editorial posts he held with the *Pan American Geologist, Botanical Abstracts, Biological Abstracts,* and the *American Journal of Science.*

Berry's success as a scientist despite his lack of a degree made him skeptical of pompous and irrelevant elements in college teaching and administration; he had a habit of calling bunk just that, and his forthrightness earned him animosity in some quarters. During the late 1920's and early '30's Berry aided in the revision of the Johns Hopkins curriculum away from majors and

requirements toward field examinations. Despite his distrust of the disciple system, he trained some noted paleontologists, including his own sons, Edward Willard Berry and Charles Thompson Berry, children of his marriage (Apr. 12, 1898) to Mary Willard, daughter of the Passaic postmaster, William Alpheus Willard.

Although his scientific work demonstrated Berry's competence in the emerging field of paleoecology, he concentrated on taxonomic paleobotany. His monographs on Cretaceous formations in Maryland and his *Lower Eocene Floras of Southeastern North America* (1916) greatly clarified classification of the ancient plants of the region, but some of his work has since been replaced by better schemes. He pioneered in the paleobotany of South America, leading the Williams expedition to the Andes in 1919 and collecting in Peru and Ecuador in 1927 and Venezuela in 1933. He published continually on South American paleontology until his death. Berry's textbooks, *Tree Ancestors* (1923) and *Paleontology* (1929), were well received by the profession. He was president of the Paleontological Society of America in 1924 and of the Geological Society of America in 1945. Among other honors that came to him were the Mary Clark Thompson Medal (1942) of the National Academy of Sciences, of which he had been elected a member in 1922. Reared as a Presbyterian, Berry later became a Congregationalist. He died of a coronary thrombosis at the age of seventy while visiting his son Charles in Stonington, Conn. His remains were cremated.

[Lloyd W. Stephenson's memorial in Geological Soc. of America, *Proc.,* 1945, provides the most reliable data and fullest published bibliography, plus a photograph and a portrait. See also *N. Y. Times* obituary, Sept. 21, 1945; John B. Reeside, Jr., in *Science,* Nov. 16, 1945; George Gaylord Simpson in Am. Philosophical Soc., *Year Book,* 1945; and *Nat. Cyc. Am. Biog.,* XXXIII, 491. An unpublished bio-bibliography by Robert C. Bellinger, prepared at the Univ. of Wis. Lib. School, was helpful. Johns Hopkins Univ. *Reports of the President, Annual Registers,* and *Catalogues* resolve conflicts among authorities on dates of Berry's scholarly posts. City directory listings of Berry's father, 1875–88, were supplied by the N. J. Reference Division, Public Lib. of Newark, N. J.; death record from Conn. Dept. of Health.]
MICHELE L. ALDRICH

BERRY, MARTHA McCHESNEY (Oct. 7, 1866–Feb. 27, 1942), educator, was born at Oak Hill plantation near Rome, Ga., the second of the six daughters and of the eight children of Thomas and Frances (Rhea) Berry. Of English-Irish lineage, the Berrys had reached Georgia by way of Virginia and Tennessee; the Rheas were Alabama cotton planters. Thomas Berry, a veteran of the Civil War, made a quick economic recovery during Reconstruction with the backing of Northern friends and became a wealthy planter and cotton broker. His children had private tutors and enjoyed European travel, and Martha also attended the fashionable Edgeworth School in Baltimore in 1882–83. She was especially close to her father, and his illness caused her to take a more active role in his business, bringing her into contact with the mountain people among his clients. With his death in 1887, Martha and her mother, an energetic, conventional woman, took over operation of the estate.

An attractive girl of small stature, fair skin, gray eyes, and black hair, Martha Berry was expected to marry well. One Sunday afternoon in the 1890's, however, while in an old playhouse on the plantation, she was startled by the appearance of three mountain children. A devout Episcopalian, who highly valued religious instruction, she invited them in and entertained them with Bible stories. On succeeding Sundays they brought others until more than forty were in attendance. In need of more space and wishing to spare the children their long walk, she shifted her base to a dilapidated church at Possum Trot, some eight miles from the plantation. Soon she again faced overflow crowds and with the aid of her sister Frances opened three other Sunday schools.

By the time she was thirty, her interest had turned into "a determined resolution to devote my entire time and means" to teaching the highland children "a way to help themselves." Breaking her long-standing engagement to an unsympathetic Virginia aristocrat, she opened a "day school" in a rough, one-room building that she erected on land inherited from her father adjacent to the plantation. As before, she was soon overwhelmed by potential students and established branches in the old buildings used formerly for her Sunday schools, securing two teachers from the county school board to assist her. She herself furnished the salary for one teacher, supplemented the pay of two others, and contributed all the supplies, as well as her own services.

Bad roads and weather kept many students away, however, and others reverted to apathy during the six months of vacation. She decided, therefore, to open a year-round boarding and manual labor school for boys fourteen and older. They could pay their way, she believed, by working for the school two hours a day in addition to the time spent in craft work and study. She thus became one of the first educators to set up a work-study plan. The Boys' Industrial School (later renamed Mount Berry School for Boys) opened on Jan. 13, 1902, with five students and two teachers. Once again, as applications poured

in from Georgia and adjoining states, the demand was greater than she could meet from her own resources. She turned her considerable charm and family connections to good account, persuading prominent Georgians like Hoke Smith [q.v.] to aid the school. She also began attending teachers' institutes. Attentive to the least detail and warmly responsive to the needs of each student, Miss Berry made the school flourish. By 1912 Georgia had established eleven district agricultural and mechanical schools modeled upon hers, and other states were soon to follow.

Before long, Miss Berry was making frequent trips north to seek funds from philanthropists. A master tactician, she achieved phenomenal success, enlisting such individuals as Robert C. Ogden, Andrew Carnegie [qq.v.], Theodore Roosevelt, and Henry Ford. When these men visited the school, her carefully prepared tours, with a great show of pretty rusticity, never failed of their desired effect. Ford especially grew interested and over the years was to give nearly four million dollars in buildings and equipment. The increasing gifts simply meant that Miss Berry accepted more students.

She soon realized that her boys were not returning to the mountains with their skills and decided the problem was a lack of suitable wives in their old homes. Against the advice of her board, she opened a school for girls on the same work-study basis in November 1909. Ever dissatisfied with her progress, she expanded her facilities as rapidly as possible: a grammar school was established in 1916 and in 1926 a junior college that four years later became a senior college.

Through the years, the "Berry way" of self-help, plain living, and close ties to the native culture remained unchanged. The curriculum included all forms of manual training necessary for rural living, as well as the usual academic subjects. In accordance with the prejudices and customs of the students' parents, the nondenominational religious services were kept very plain, and the social behavior of the students, especially girls, was strictly regulated. By 1929 the schools had graduated 7,000 students and had an average enrollment of 1,000 and a waiting list of 3,000.

Local and national honors were showered upon Martha Berry. In 1924 the state legislature gave her the "Distinguished Citizen of Georgia" award, and she was later appointed to the board of regents of the University of Georgia and to the state planning commission. In 1925 she received the Theodore Roosevelt Memorial Medal for Distinguished Service, and in 1931 the readers of

Good Housekeeping voted her one of the twelve greatest living American women. Some eight colleges and universities gave her honorary degrees. She died in an Atlanta, Ga., hospital at the age of seventy-five of cirrhosis of the liver and was buried beside Mount Berry Chapel on the school grounds.

[Harnett T. Kane and Inez Henry, *Miracle in the Mountains* (1965), a biography of Miss Berry, is the fullest source; information was also furnished by Robert L. Lattimore, Executive Assistant to the President, Berry College. Short sketches are in *Nat. Cyc. Am. Biog.*, Current Vol. C, p. 49; Durward Howes, ed., *Am. Women*, 1939–40; *Who Was Who in America*, vol. II (1950); and *N. Y. Times*, Feb. 27, 1942. There are numerous articles concerning Miss Berry; among the best are: John L. Matthews, "The Sunday Lady of 'Possum Trot,'" *Everybody's*, Dec. 1908; Katherine Glover, "Working for an Education in a Southern School," *Craftsman*, Mar. 1909; John C. Reese in *American Mag.*, Dec. 1910; Mary B. Mullett, "21 Years of Begging—for Other People," *ibid.*, Apr. 1923; Albert Shaw in *Am. Rev. of Revs.*, June 1925; Alice Booth in *Good Housekeeping*, Aug. 1931; "A Distinguished Citizen of Ga.," *School and Society*, Sept. 5, 1931; *Newsweek*, Apr. 22, 1940, pp. 37–38. Samples of her own writing are: "A School in the Woods," *Outlook*, Aug. 6, 1904; "The Growth of the Berry School Idea," *Survey*, Dec. 16, 1911; and her "Address" in Nat. Education Assoc., *Proc.*, 1929. Death record from Ga. Dept. of Public Health.]
JOHN S. EZELL

BESTOR, ARTHUR EUGENE (May 19, 1879–Feb. 3, 1944), educator, was born in Dixon, Ill., the first of two children and only son of Orson Porter Bestor and Laura Ellen (Moore) Bestor. Both parents came of old New England stock. His father, a native of Connecticut, had fought with an Illinois regiment during the Civil War; he afterward graduated from Brown University and became a Baptist minister, in which capacity he served churches in Illinois and Wisconsin. Arthur Bestor received his education at the Wayland Academy in Beaver Dam, Wis., and at the University of Chicago, from which he graduated, Phi Beta Kappa, in 1901. After teaching history and political science for two years at Franklin College in Indiana, he returned to the university to begin graduate work in history. He did not complete a Ph.D., but from 1904 to 1912 he was a lecturer on political science in the university's extension division.

After 1905 Bestor's consuming interest was the Chautauqua movement, founded in 1874 at Fair Point (later Chautauqua), N. Y., by Lewis Miller and John Heyl Vincent [*qq.v.*]. Bestor had first become acquainted with the movement through his father, who had organized several local adult education reading groups as part of the Chautauqua Literary and Scientific Circle. At the University of Chicago, Bestor was influenced by George E. Vincent [Supp. 3], a sociology professor who was also principal of instruction at the Chautauqua Institution (of which he later became president) and by William Rainey Harper [*q.v.*], the university's first president, who had been principal of Chautauqua's college of liberal arts. Through Vincent, Bestor was appointed assistant director of the Chautauqua Institution in the summer of 1905. Two years later he became director, in which position he had charge of all business matters and assisted in educational activities, and in 1915 he succeeded Vincent as president. As such, Bestor was responsible for the educational and administrative policies of all branches of the Chautauqua Institution, including the summer assembly, summer schools, home reading courses, and the physical plant at Chautauqua Lake.

Under Bestor's direction, Chautauqua participated fully in the American effort during World War I. It played host both to the Speakers' Training Camp for Patriotic Service, which trained persons to propagandize the war cause, and to the National Service School, where young women learned how to rehabilitate disabled war veterans. Bestor himself was secretary of the National Security League's Committee on Patriotism through Education and, later, chairman of the Y.M.C.A.'s War Council of the Platform Guild and its War Board Committee on Lectures and Entertainment in Training Camps. He also served at the invitation of Herbert Hoover as director of the lecturers' and speakers' division of the United States Food Administration, and in September 1917 was appointed by President Wilson as director of the speakers' division of the Committee on Public Information. For the latter he toured the United States, lecturing on "America and the Great War" and "The War and the Making of Public Opinion."

After the war, faced with competition from motion pictures, radio, and the automobile, as well as from universities and colleges that had adopted Chautauqualike programs of summer schools and extension courses, Bestor moved to expand the facilities and activities of the organization's home base. To ensure Chautauqua's survival as an educational institution, he encouraged specialization in three types of instruction: professional study for teachers, advanced musical training, and general cultural courses. His efforts to maintain academic respectability were further realized when in 1923 New York University agreed to accept courses taken at Chautauqua for degree credit.

At the same time, Bestor undertook an extensive building program and broadened the range of cultural activities at the Institution. In 1919 the New York Symphony made an extended appearance at Chautauqua, and thereafter it played a regular six-week engagement, after 1923 under the direction of Albert Stoessel [Supp. 3], who was also Chautauqua's musical director. The Rochester Opera Company brought opera to Chautauqua in 1926, and in 1929 the Chautauqua Opera Company was founded. The following year a repertory theatre, at which the Cleveland Playhouse gave a regular season, was established. Such cultural activities were an important adjunct to the Institution's attractions as a center of learning and outdoor recreation. Music, which had been clearly subordinate to other activities before World War I, eventually came to dominate the program at Chautauqua.

Though Bestor's program was largely responsible for Chautauqua's successful adjustment to a new era, it created a sizable debt which brought the Institution perilously close to disaster; unable to pay the interest on the debt, it went into receivership at the end of 1933. A group of loyal Chautauquans, acting independently, immediately formed the Chautauqua Reorganization Corporation, which managed to raise enough money by 1936 to clear away the debt. Thereafter Chautauqua's financial affairs were entrusted to the Chautauqua Foundation, Inc., an independent corporation established in 1937.

Bestor's contemporaries described his speeches as constructive, penetrating, and prophetic. In the judgment of his longtime friend Harry Overstreet, he was "no soft sentimentalist, no vague utopian. He was a realistic idealist who loved people and worked tirelessly and joyously for their good." Apart from Chautauqua, Bestor served the cause of adult education in numerous other capacities. He was a trustee of the League for Political Education and chairman of the board of trustees of its successor (1937), Town Hall, Inc. He served on the executive board of the American Association for Adult Education, was the American representative on the council of the World Association for Adult Education, and was a member of the advisory committee on emergency education to the United States Commissioner of Education. Bestor traveled extensively in the Near East and was a director of the American Schools in Sofia, Bulgaria, chairman of the board of trustees of Near East Relief, and a trustee of the Near East Foundation.

On Mar. 24, 1905, Bestor married Jeanette Louise Lemon of Bedford, Ind. They had four children: Arthur Eugene, Mary Frances, Jeanette Elizabeth (who died in infancy), and Charles Lemon. Stricken with encephalomyelitis in January 1944, Bestor entered St. Luke's Hospital in New York City but was transferred to the New York City Neurological Institute, where he died at the age of sixty-four. After funeral services at the Riverside Church in New York and at the Smith Memorial Library in Chautauqua, he was buried in the Chautauqua Cemetery.

[The most thorough treatment of Bestor is to be found in the MS. history of the Chautauqua movement by the late Prof. Harrison J. Thornton of the Univ. of Iowa. Additional information can be gleaned from letters and published writings of Bestor deposited in the Archive Collection of the Univ. of Iowa. Other biographical information is available in a memorial edition of the *Chautauquan Daily Supplement*, Aug. 4, 1944. See also: articles about Bestor and Chautauqua in *Independent*, Aug. 16, 1915, and *Rev. of Revs.*, July 1924; *Nat. Cyc. Am. Biog.*, XXXIII, 507–08; *Who Was Who in America*, vol. II (1950); Arthur E. Bestor, Jr., *Chautauqua Publications* (1934), which includes a historical sketch of Chautauqua; Jesse L. Hurlbut, *The Story of Chautauqua* (1921); and Rebecca Richmond, *Chautauqua* (1943).]

ROBERT L. UTLAUT

BETTMAN, ALFRED (Aug. 26, 1873–Jan. 21, 1945), lawyer and city planner, was born in Cincinnati, Ohio, the first of four sons of Louis and Rebecca (Bloom) Bettman. His youngest brother, Gilbert, became attorney general of Ohio and a justice of the Ohio supreme court. Both parents were Jewish: the father, a clothing manufacturer, had emigrated from Germany; the mother, daughter of an emigrant from Alsace, was born in Cincinnati. After graduating from the local Hughes High School, Bettman continued his education at Harvard, receiving the A.B. degree in 1894 and the LL.B. in 1898. He returned to Cincinnati, his lifelong home, and on June 20, 1904, married Lillian Wyler; there were no children.

A successful lawyer, Bettman served as assistant prosecuting attorney of Hamilton County, 1909–11, and as Cincinnati city solicitor, 1912–13. During World War I he was appointed special assistant to the Attorney General of the United States, working in the War Emergency Division of the Justice Department. Though responsible in this position for the drafting of many wartime restraints, notably those dealing with aliens, he was deeply concerned with the protection of personal liberties and was outspoken in his denunciation of the "Red Raids" of A. Mitchell Palmer [Supp. 2]. Bettman was also concerned with improving the efficiency of criminal prosecution agencies, in order to benefit both the accused and society. In 1921, for the Cleveland Foundation Crime Survey, he pioneered in the use of "Mortality Tables," which traced individual cases from arrest to final disposition. By showing how frequently prosecution failed at the pretrial stage, the tables exposed the lax and often corrupt administration of criminal law. Bettman made a similar study in 1930 for the National Commission of

Law Observance, and his methodology was widely adopted in the reform of criminal administration.

From his success as a lawyer Bettman moved to greater prominence in another field, city planning. The leaders of the American planning movement, a coalition of landscape architects, housing reformers, and community workers, early recognized the need for legal and institutional weapons in their battle and turned to lawyers for aid. Bettman had first become interested in planning while serving as city solicitor, and in 1917 he joined the United City Planning Committee. That year the committee successfully lobbied for an enabling act, drafted by Bettman, which allowed cities in Ohio to create planning boards. Bettman was chiefly responsible for another Ohio statute which in 1923 gave cities with master plans the right to regulate subdivisions within three miles of their boundaries. Appointed to the advisory committee on housing and zoning of the United States Department of Commerce, Bettman, along with Edward M. Bassett, the younger Frederick Law Olmsted, and others, helped prepare its influential Standard State Zoning Enabling Act of 1924, which encouraged the establishment of zoning commissions, and its Standard City Enabling Act of 1927, which suggested that the powers of zoning be transferred to city planning commissions and emphasized the need for a closer relationship between long-range planning and zoning.

Of more importance, however, was Bettman's role in upholding the constitutionality of zoning. When a federal district court declared a zoning ordinance unconstitutional, in the case of *Village of Euclid* v. *Ambler Realty Company,* Bettman volunteered to prepare a brief as amicus curiae when the case went before the Supreme Court in 1926. His argument that a zoning ordinance which barred the conversion of residential property to commercial and industrial use was an extension of the common law doctrine of public nuisance, rather than an exercise of the power of eminent domain, helped persuade the Court to declare zoning a legitimate expression of the police power, a decision that paved the way for the widespread adoption of land-use regulation.

Though the resulting zoning ordinances served mainly to enhance property values and protect the homogeneity of respectable suburbs, Bettman always stressed that zoning should be used as a constructive instrument in the implementation of a comprehensive plan. He participated in almost every phase of planning and at all levels of government; he became chairman of the Cincinnati Planning Commission in 1930 and of the Ohio Valley Regional Planning Commission in 1936,

served on the board of directors of the American City Planning Institute, and was president of the National Conference on City Planning (1932) and first president of the American Society of Planning Officials (1934). He also served in 1937 as the United States representative on the executive committee of the International Congress for Housing and Town Planning, and he spent many of his summers at the Town and Country Planning summer school in England. Bettman envisioned official planning agencies as largely research and advisory organizations, detached from the administrative and legislative spheres of government. Their major task was the preparation of an advisory master plan, which would coordinate and adjust the various interests of the community. Despite this somewhat static view of the public planning function, however, Bettman was himself flexible, undogmatic, and action-oriented. In the 1930's, for example, he helped develop the legal rationale for public housing, and at the time of his death he was preparing legislation for postwar urban redevelopment.

Few persons contributed more than Bettman to developing the legal and legislative foundations of American planning in the twentieth century. He was a member of the City Planning Committee of President Hoover's Conference on Home Building and Home Ownership (1931), legal consultant to the TVA, regional chairman of the National Resources Planning Board, and, for many years, counsel to the National Capital Park and Planning Commission, Washington, D. C. Patient, tolerant, vigorous of mind, and with a self-deprecating humor, Bettman never allowed his involvement in preparing legislation to hide his enduring concern for the individual citizen. In 1945, while returning to Cincinnati by train from Washington, D. C., he died of heart failure at Altoona, Pa. He was buried in the United Jewish Cemetery, Cincinnati.

[A good sample of Bettman's many published articles, including his most important court briefs, appears in his *City and Regional Planning Papers* (Arthur C. Comey, ed., 1946), which also includes a good biographical sketch of Bettman by John Lord O'Brian and an extensive bibliography. Another convenient source for tracing Bettman's views is the *Proc.* of the Nat. Conference on City Planning during the 1920's and '30's. For general surveys of the planning field by Bettman, see his article "City Planning Legislation" in John Nolen, ed., *City Planning* (2nd ed., 1929); and Edward M. Bassett, Frank B. Williams, Alfred Bettman, and Robert Whitten, *Model Laws for Planning Cities, Counties, and States* (1935). Mel Scott's comprehensive *Am. City Planning since 1890* (1969) includes details about Bettman's work. See also: *Class Reports* of Harvard College Class of 1894; *Who Was Who in America*, vol. II (1950); and obituaries in *Cincinnati Enquirer,* Jan. 22, 1945, *N. Y. Times,* Jan. 23, 1945, Am. Soc. of Planning Officials, *Newsletter,* Feb. 1945, *Jour. of Housing,* Feb. 1945, *Planning and*

Civic Comment, Jan. 1945, and *Jour. of the Am. Inst. of Planners,* Oct.-Dec. 1945. Bettman's sister-in-law, Mrs. Gilbert Bettman, provided biographical information.]

ROY LUBOVE

BEVAN, ARTHUR DEAN (Aug. 9, 1861–June 10, 1943), surgeon, was born in Chicago, Ill., to Thomas Bevan, a physician, and Sarah Elizabeth (Ramsey) Bevan, both originally from Ohio. Bevan attended high school in Chicago, spent a year (1878–79) at the Sheffield Scientific School of Yale University, and in 1883 received his M.D. degree from Rush Medical College in Chicago. He spent the next four years in the federal Marine Hospital Service, during the last year serving also as professor of anatomy at the University of Oregon Medical School in Portland. Bevan returned to Rush in 1887 as professor of anatomy (1887–99) and continued the affiliation for the rest of his professional life, becoming professor of surgical anatomy and associate professor of surgery in 1899 and professor and chairman of the department of surgery in 1902. After his retirement in 1934 he became a member of the board of trustees of Rush.

In addition to his teaching duties, Bevan carried on a successful private practice. He was a member of the surgical staff of the Presbyterian Hospital (1892–1943), serving as surgeon-in-chief, 1894–1934. A Presbyterian himself, in 1929 he donated $1,000,000 to the hospital's expansion program. Bevan specialized in surgery of the stomach and tumors of the breast, and for a long time his name was associated with an operation for hydrocele of the testis. He developed a number of surgical procedures, such as the "hockey-stick" incision for gallbladder operations to avoid severing important nerves, and in 1923 he performed the first operations in which ethylene-oxygen was used clinically as an anesthetic. Bevan contributed actively to the surgical literature and with his associate, Dean Lewis [Supp. 3], who made the translation from the German, he edited Erich Lexer's famous textbook, which appeared as *General Surgery* (1908) and became widely known as "Lexer-Bevan."

Although Bevan made no major contribution to the development of surgical science, he had an important influence on the course of medical education in the United States. A forceful, fearless man, hard driving, disdainful of personal attack and criticism, he devoted great effort to improving the standards for the training of surgeons and the medical profession in general. He served as chairman of the American Medical Association's original committee on medical education in 1902, which two years later became the Council on Medical Education, with Bevan again as chairman, a position he held until 1916, and again from 1920 to 1928. The committee had been formed to deal with the problem of the large number of proprietary and other largely inadequate schools that were then allowed to grant the M.D. degree. Bevan's vigorous campaign to raise the level of medical education led directly to the far-reaching and influential report of Abraham Flexner on this subject, commissioned by the Carnegie Foundation for the Advancement of Teaching and published in 1910. This long-continued activity of Bevan's must be considered his most significant contribution.

Bevan served as president of the American Medical Association in 1918–19. He was a founder (1913) and member of the first board of governors of the American College of Surgeons and served as president of the Chicago Medical Society (1898), the Inter-State Postgraduate Medical Association (1931), and the American Surgical Association (1932). During World War I he was director of surgery in the army surgeon general's office in Washington. A man of strong opinions, Bevan was an outspoken advocate of prohibition. He enjoyed fishing, shooting, and playing golf. On Feb. 3, 1896, he married Anna Laura Barber of Akron, Ohio. They had no children. Bevan died at the age of eighty-one, of acute myocardial failure, at his summer home in Lake Forest, Ill., and was buried in Lake Forest Cemetery.

[Obituaries in *Jour. Am. Medic. Assoc.,* June 19, 1943, Inst. of Medicine of Chicago, *Proc.,* vol. XIV (1943), and *Chicago Tribune,* June 11, 1943; Yale Univ., *Obituary Record of Graduates,* 1942–43; *Who Was Who in America,* vol. II (1950); death record from Ill. Dept. of Public Health.]

MARK M. RAVITCH

BEVIER, ISABEL (Nov. 14, 1860–Mar. 17, 1942), home economist, was born on a farm near Plymouth, Ohio, the fifth daughter and youngest child of Caleb and Cornelia (Brinkerhoff) Bevier, seven of whose nine children survived childhood. Her paternal ancestor, a Huguenot patentee of New Paltz, N. Y., had come from the Rhenish Palatinate in 1675; her Brinkerhoff forebears had emigrated from Holland to New Amsterdam in 1638; and the two families had several times intermarried. Her maternal grandfather, Henry Roelifsen Brinkerhoff (1787–1844), served in the New York state legislature and as senior general of the state militia before moving to Ohio in 1838; Roeliff Brinkerhoff [*q.v.*] was a first cousin of Isabel's mother.

Isabel attended the Plymouth high school for two years and Wooster (Ohio) Preparatory

67

School, meanwhile teaching country school for three summers. She then entered the College of Wooster, where she excelled in languages and literature and became the first state chairman of the Young Women's Christian Association. Following her graduation in 1885 with the Ph.B. degree, she spent two years as principal of the Shelby (Ohio) high school, taught mathematics and Latin for a year at the Mount Vernon (Ohio) high school, and in 1888 received a Ph.M. degree at Wooster.

That same year she suffered a severe blow with the death of her fiancé, an event which affected her intellectual interests permanently. To be near her former college roommate, then living in Pittsburgh, she accepted a position teaching science at Pennsylvania College for Women in that city, although, as she later wrote, this was a subject "about which I knew very little." To prepare for the post, she applied for instruction in chemistry at the Case School of Applied Science in Cleveland, Ohio. The first woman to be admitted, she worked there in the summers of 1888 and 1889 under the chemist Albert W. Smith, the first of several mentors who shaped her career. During her nine years at the Pennsylvania college she taught geology, physics, and botany, in addition to chemistry. She acquired further summer training by studying food chemistry at Harvard (1891) and by working as a chemist at the World's Columbian Exposition (1893) and in the laboratory of the agricultural chemist Wilbur O. Atwater [q.v.] at Wesleyan University. Under Atwater's direction she made nutritional studies in Pittsburgh and in Hampton, Va. (1898).

Miss Bevier disliked life in a women's college and resigned in 1897. After briefly studying organic chemistry at Western Reserve University, she went to the Massachusetts Institute of Technology to work in food chemistry under Ellen H. Richards [q.v.]. In 1898 she reluctantly accepted a post as professor of chemistry at another women's institution, Lake Erie College at Painesville, Ohio, but resigned after two years to become professor of household science at the University of Illinois.

Miss Bevier had been personally selected by President Andrew S. Draper [q.v.] to revive the university's home economics department. To build the kind of department he envisaged, he urged her to incorporate anything in the university curriculum she thought appropriate. Working closely with him and with Dean Eugene Davenport [Supp. 3] of the College of Agriculture, she eventually built a department that was highly respected locally and gained national prominence. Her goal was not to teach the mechanics of cooking and sewing, but to offer young women training in the chemical principles involved in nutrition and sanitation, to inculcate standards of taste in household furnishing and decorating, and to implant a sense of civic responsibility, all as part of a liberal education. She insisted on entrance requirements that met those of other departments in the university and made chemistry a prerequisite.

Tall and sturdily built, Miss Bevier was a vigorous leader. Though her talk was lightened by humor, she was forthright to the point of bluntness, sometimes showing impatience with what she considered superficialities. Her determination not to accept students who lacked the usual college entrance qualifications and her adoption of a scientific rather than a narrowly utilitarian approach to household economy evoked criticism from the women of the Illinois Farmers' Institute, and her rejection of a proposed advisory committee of Farmers' Institute women brought her into sharp conflict with that body. Fearful of alienating so influential a group, Dean Davenport advised Miss Bevier to resign, but she stood her ground and on her return from a year's leave of absence (1910–11) found herself vindicated. Following the establishment of extension courses in agriculture and home economics under the Smith-Lever Act, she was put in charge of the Illinois women's section (1914).

Miss Bevier served as a vice-chairman of the Lake Placid Conference on Home Economics, forerunner of the American Home Economics Association, of which she became vice-president on its founding in 1908, president (1910–12), and a member of the editorial board of its Journal of Home Economics (1909–12). She was the first chairman of the home economics section of the Association of Land Grant Colleges and Universities (1917–19). During World War I she was chairman of the Illinois committee for the conservation of food under the Council of National Defense and spent two months in the national office of the Food Administrator, where she helped prepare five bulletins on food. In 1918 she became a member of the first subcommittee on food and nutrition under the National Research Council. Her publications include many articles and several books, among them two laboratory manuals, Food and Nutrition (with Susannah Usher, 1906 and later editions) and Selection and Preparation of Food (with Anna R. Van Meter, 1907); The House: Its Plan, Decoration and Care (1907); and Home Economics in Education (1924). She also lectured widely.

Though a woman of great vitality and serenity, Isabel Bevier felt too tired at the age of sixty to face an impending departmental building program and resigned in 1921. She spent the next two years as chairman of the home economics department at the University of California at Los Angeles and, in 1925, a semester at the University of Arizona before returning to the University of Illinois in 1928 to join the staff of the extension service. After her second retirement, in 1930, she made her fourth trip to Europe, travel being one of her chief pleasures. Iowa State College had conferred on her a D.Sc. degree in 1920; her alma mater followed suit in 1936, and she became a fellow of the American Association for the Advancement of Science. A Presbyterian and a Republican, she was also a member of the League of Women Voters. In her last years she continued to live in Urbana, Ill., and she died at her home there of chronic myocarditis at the age of eighty-one. She was buried in Greenlawn Cemetery, Plymouth, Ohio.

[Good autobiographical accounts are: "How I Came to Take up Home Economics Work," *Home Economist and Am. Food Jour.*, May 1928 (a photograph of Miss Bevier appears on the cover); and "Recollections and Impressions of the Beginnings of the Dept. of Home Economics at the Univ. of Ill.," *Jour. of Home Economics*, May 1940. Much of this material is also to be found in (Juliet) Lita Bane's uncritical biography, *The Story of Isabel Bevier* (1955), which also contains excerpts from Miss Bevier's writings. See also obituaries by Lita Bane and Anna R. Van Meter in *Jour. of Home Economics*, June 1942. Eugene Davenport, "Home Economics at Illinois," *ibid.*, Aug. 1921, contains an excellent biographical account. Extensive MS. material concerning Miss Bevier may be found in the Dept. of Home Economics in Bevier Hall at the Univ. of Ill., including a 50-page autobiography, and in the papers of Presidents Andrew S. Draper and Edmund J. James in the Univ. Archives. The Bane biography reproduces the somewhat idealized portrait of Miss Bevier by Louis Betts that was painted for Bevier Hall. Although her death certificate gives her year of birth as 1859, other sources agree on 1860.]

MARY TOLFORD WILSON

BIRCH, REGINALD BATHURST (May 2, 1856–June 17, 1943), artist and illustrator, was born in London, England, the son of William Alexander Birch, an officer in the British army, and Isabella (Hoggins) Birch. When Reginald was five, his father went to India as manager of a river navigation company in Bombay, and the boy was sent to stay in the family of his paternal grandfather on the Isle of Jersey. He attended a local school and then entered St. Leonard's School for Boys at Hastings. In 1870 he moved with his parents to San Francisco, Calif.; he later became a naturalized citizen. In San Francisco he is said to have first exercised his drawing talent in helping his father prepare theatrical posters by incising the wooden blocks from which they were printed. Birch's abilities attracted the attention of the painter Toby E. Rosenthal [q.v.], who invited

him to work in his studio and encouraged him to obtain further training. Birch went abroad in 1873 and remained for eight years, studying art at the Royal Academy in Munich and later producing drawings for publications in Vienna, Paris, and Rome. Returning to the United States in 1881, he settled in New York City. He easily obtained commissions and began producing pen-and-ink drawings for stories and poems appearing in such magazines as *St. Nicholas*, the *Century*, *Harper's*, *Life*, and the *Youth's Companion*.

At the age of thirty Birch achieved his first popular success, which he never later surpassed, by his illustrations for the novel *Little Lord Fauntleroy* (1886) by Frances Hodgson Burnett [q.v.]. His depiction of the youthful hero, wearing long golden curls and clad in a black velvet suit with lace collar, patterned after the costumes of page boys in the court of Queen Victoria, so appealed to American mothers of the period that many sought to force their rebellious sons into similar garb. Birch was never allowed to forget his Fauntleroy and came to speak of him as "my Nemesis." For a time he was one of the leading magazine illustrators in New York and provided drawings for a dozen or more books, mostly for children, including Mrs. Burnett's *Sara Crewe* (1888). His drawings, deft and good-humored, somewhat resembled in style those of Charles Dana Gibson [Supp. 3], and he became known as "the children's Gibson."

With changing artistic fashions, the popularity of Birch's work declined, and after 1914 he received fewer commissions. A bon vivant, fond of wine and good food, he had never accumulated money, and in the early 1930's he was living in poverty, in a fifth-floor walkup apartment. Birch emerged from obscurity in the spring of 1933 when, at the age of seventy-six, he was asked to make the drawings for Louis Untermeyer's *The Last Pirate*, a collection of tales from the Gilbert and Sullivan operas. His popularity revived, and during the next eight years, until failing eyesight forced him to stop work, he illustrated some twenty books. An anthology of many of the stories and poems he had illustrated was published by Harcourt, Brace and Company in 1939 as *Reginald Birch—His Book*.

Birch was twice married and had a son, Rodney Bathurst, and a daughter. He was a founding member of the Society of Illustrators in New York. Kindly and urbane, always well dressed, Birch was a gentleman of the old school. He spent his last two years at the Home for Incurables in the Bronx, where he died at the age of eighty-seven of congestive heart failure. He was buried at Woodlawn Cemetery, New York City.

[*Biog. Sketches of Am. Artists* (5th ed., 1924); *Nat. Cyc. Am. Biog.*, XI, 307; *Who Was Who in America*, vol. II (1950); newspaper stories and interviews in the 1930's, such as *N. Y. Herald Tribune*, Mar. 19, 1933, *N. Y. World-Telegram*, Apr. 10, 1934, and *N. Y. Times*, Magazine Section, May 6, 1934; Birch's reminiscences in *Publishers' Weekly*, Oct. 19, 1935; *N. Y. Times* obituary, June 18, 1943, and editorial, June 19; Elisabeth B. Hamilton in *Horn Book*, Jan.-Feb. 1944; Walt Reed, *The Illustrator in America* (1966); death record from N. Y. City Dept. of Health. Theodore Bolton, *Am. Book Illustrators* (1938), lists his book work through 1937.]

WALT REED

BIRKHOFF, GEORGE DAVID (Mar. 21, 1884–Nov. 12, 1944), mathematician, was born in Overisel, near Holland, Mich., the oldest of the six children of David Birkhoff, a physician recently graduated from Rush Medical College in Chicago, and his wife, Jane (or Jennie) Gertrude Droppers. Both parents were of Dutch extraction, the mother native-born, the father having come to America as a boy. The family attended the Dutch Reformed Church.

George Birkhoff grew up chiefly in Chicago, to which the family moved when he was two. After earlier study (1896–1902) at Lewis Institute, he entered the University of Chicago, but transferred after a year to Harvard, where he received the bachelor's degree in 1905 and the master's in 1906. While still an undergraduate, in 1904, he published his first mathematical paper, "On the Integral Divisors of a^n-b^n," written jointly with another fledgling mathematician, Harry S. Vandiver, with whom he had been in correspondence about mathematical questions since 1901. Birkhoff was influenced at Harvard by Prof. Maxime Bôcher [*q.v.*], and though he returned to Chicago for his doctorate, working under the guidance of E. H. Moore [Supp. 1], he chose as his subject one close to Bôcher's principal interests. His dissertation dealt in a revealingly powerful way with the boundary value and expansion problems for ordinary differential equations of arbitrary order and earned him the Ph.D. summa cum laude in 1907.

Birkhoff spent the next two years as an instructor in mathematics at the University of Wisconsin. While there, on Sept. 2, 1908, he married Margaret Elizabeth Grafius of Chicago, known to their friends of later years as Marjorie. They had three children: Barbara, Garrett, and Rodney. Attendance at lectures given at Wisconsin by Prof. E. B. Van Vleck [Supp. 3] inspired Birkhoff with a lasting interest in linear difference equations. In 1909 he accepted a call to Princeton as preceptor. His three years there, during which he rose to professor, were scientifically fruitful. At first he continued working on difference equations, but he soon developed a new interest in dynamical systems and associated problems in the theory of differential equations. Strongly stimulated by Henri Poincaré's brilliant and profound papers, he made this his major scientific field and quickly won recognition in it as a master. In 1912 he was challenged by the appearance of one of Poincaré's last mathematical papers to attack a geometrical problem that had defied the great French mathematician. This problem was no mere curiosity but had an important bearing on the presence of periodic orbits in a dynamical system. Within months the young Birkhoff had scored a spectacular triumph by succeeding where the master had failed. When his solution was published early in 1913, it was received with worldwide acclaim.

Meanwhile, in 1912, Birkhoff had moved to Harvard, which was to remain his academic home for the rest of his life. There he reached the full development of his creative powers. Along with a series of brilliant papers on differential and difference equations, he published one on "The Restricted Problem of Three Bodies" (1915), which won him the Querini-Stampalia Prize of the Royal Venice Institute of Science, and his great memoir on "Dynamical Systems with Two Degrees of Freedom" (1917), which received the Bôcher Prize of the American Mathematical Society. His book *Dynamical Systems* (1927) was based on lectures delivered by invitation before the society. Still later, in 1935, his "Nouvelles Recherches sur les Systèmes Dynamiques" was crowned by the Pontifical Academy of Sciences (and published in its *Memoriae*). Of all the profound and beautiful results obtained by Birkhoff, however, his celebrated ergodic theorem of 1931 was probably the most influential and the most fruitful in fundamental consequences, not so much perhaps in dynamics itself as in probability theory, group theory, and functional analysis.

The ergodic theorem resolved in principle a problem of gas theory and statistical mechanics that had baffled theoretical physicists for half a century. For a number of years Birkhoff had realized the importance of invariant measures for the study of dynamical systems and had himself exploited them, as in his solution of Poincaré's geometrical problem. Poincaré had pointed out the significance of such measures for recurrence properties of dynamical motions, but it was John von Neumann who first showed their direct bearing on ergodicity and established a weak form of the ergodic theorem. Stimulated by hearing von Neumann lecture on this discovery, Birkhoff sought for a stronger version, and after a few days of concentrated effort invented methods that were crowned with success. Birkhoff's ergodic theorem was immediately recognized by mathematicians as the key to future developments in the field. Another somewhat earlier paper, written in collaboration with his colleague Oliver Kellogg, made a simple but highly original application of topological methods to the solution of functional equations.

Birkhoff's interest in classical dynamics brought him into increasingly close contacts with broader aspects of theoretical physics. In the early 1920's he gave much thought to the theory of relativity, a subject about which he eventually wrote two books. At about the same time he guided the doctoral dissertation of Carl Garabedian on some problems of elasticity. Later, when quantum theory had become a dominant interest of theoretical physicists, Birkhoff developed his own approach in a number of addresses and papers. His theory did not win general acceptance, however, nor was it developed far enough to have the scope required for the applications most in demand at the time.

From his student days Birkhoff had been intrigued by the quantitative bases proposed for canons of beauty ever since Grecian times. In the 1920's and '30's he set himself to work in earnest on this aesthetic problem. After many years of experimentation he published *Aesthetic Measure* (1933), in which he sought to analyze and appraise by means of an evaluative formula the elements of order and diversity that constitute the formal structures of musical compositions, art objects, and poetry. In a somewhat similar spirit Birkhoff also wrote a paper on ethics that appeared in the *Rice Journal*.

Birkhoff was not a polished lecturer—indeed he not infrequently came to class quite unprepared and occasionally failed to carry through proofs he had started—but he was a great teacher. He had a special gift for bringing out the creative talents of the more able students and forming them by the example he gave them daily of a first-class mathematical mind at work. His teaching bore fruit in many ways, as evidenced by the long list of doctoral dissertations prepared under his guidance and by the unusually large number of his former students—six in all—who became members of the National Academy of Sciences. In person Birkhoff had great natural charm and engaging frankness in expressing his judgments. His opinions were not rigidly held, and in the long run they were tempered both by his innate kindliness and by his essentially judicial approach.

Birkhoff had gradually become one of the most influential men in American mathematical circles, along with Oswald Veblen, Luther P. Eisenhart,

Griffith C. Evans, and Roland G. D. Richardson. First among equals because of his preeminence in research, he was often called upon to represent mathematics in wider scientific circles as well. Thus he played an important part in channeling American support to the mathematical institutes created at Göttingen and Paris after the First World War. He received many honors during his lifetime. He was elected to membership in the National Academy of Sciences (1918), the American Philosophical Society, and the American Academy of Arts and Sciences, as well as to the presidencies of the American Mathematical Society (1925) and of the American Association for the Advancement of Science (1937). He was a foreign member of the Académie des Sciences de Paris, the Accademia dei Lincei, and the Pontifical Academy. He received honorary doctorates from many universities at home and abroad: Athens, Brown, Buenos Aires, Chicago, Harvard, Illinois Institute of Technology, Lima, Paris, Pennsylvania, Poitiers, St. Andrews, Santiago, and Sophia. Such recognition was for him not a mere academic honor but an opportunity to enter more broadly into the fellowship of science and scholarship. Indeed, from the 1920's he and his wife took increasing pleasure in the many new friendships they were able to form with mathematicians in other parts of the world, friendships that frequent visits to Europe and trips to South America and the Orient enabled them to maintain and extend.

Birkhoff died of a coronary attack at the age of sixty at his home in Cambridge, Mass. He was buried in Mount Auburn Cemetery, Cambridge. His son Garrett also became professor of mathematics at Harvard.

[Birkhoff's *Collected Works* were published in three volumes by the Am. Mathematical Soc. (1950); each volume contains a photograph of Birkhoff. Biographical accounts include: Marston Morse in Am. Mathematical Soc., *Bull.,* May 1946; R. E. Langer in Am. Mathematical Soc., *Transactions,* July 1946; Oswald Veblen in Am. Philosophical Soc., *Year Book,* 1946; H. S. Vandiver in *Jour. of Mathematical Analysis and Applications,* Oct. 1963; D. D. Kosambi in *Mathematics Student,* Sept. 1944; E. T. Whittaker in *Jour. of London Mathematical Soc.,* Apr. 1945.]

MARSHALL H. STONE

BISHOP, JOHN PEALE (May 21, 1892– Apr. 4, 1944), author, was born in Charles Town, Jefferson County, W. Va., the first of two children and only son of Jonathan Peale Bishop, a physician, and Margaret Miller (Cochran) Bishop. His mother's family, descended from early eighteenth-century settlers in Virginia, had moved westward to the Shenandoah Valley, where the original Scottish strains had become mixed with English, Scotch-Irish, and German elements. His father, born in Connecticut, had grown up in Charles Town. Conscious and proud of his mother's Virginia forebears, Bishop thought of himself as a Southerner, yet with a particular point of view that was at least partly formed by being the son of a New England-born father and a product of the Border South.

His father died when Bishop was nine, and his mother remarried a few years later. The youth was reared in a family of genteel professional people and attended high school in nearby Hagerstown, Md. From his father he had acquired a strong interest in bird-watching and in painting; until he was seventeen he intended to become an artist, but a temporary failure of eyesight, possibly emotional in origin, forced him to give up the plan. During the many months when he had to be read to, he developed a strong love for poetry, and after his recovery he began writing verse; his first published poem, "To a Woodland Pool," appeared in *Harper's Weekly* of Sept. 28, 1912.

Bishop studied briefly at the Mercersburg (Pa.) Academy and then, several years older than his classmates, entered Princeton in the fall of 1913. He started publishing his poetry in the undergraduate *Nassau Literary Magazine,* and soon attracted attention by his mastery of verse technique and by his poise and self-possession. Among fellow students who later gained distinction were the critic Edmund Wilson and the novelist F. Scott Fitzgerald [Supp. 2], who used Bishop as his model for Tom D'Invilliers in *This Side of Paradise.* Bishop graduated with the Litt.B. degree in 1917, the year in which he published his first book of verse, *Green Fruit.* A few months later he was commissioned a lieutenant in the army; although he saw no combat, he served in Europe until 1919. After his return he worked for *Vanity Fair* magazine, where he became managing editor (1920–22). In 1922, with Wilson, he published *The Undertaker's Garland,* a collection of verse and prose.

Bishop was married on June 17, 1922, to Margaret Grosvenor Hutchins in New York City. He and his wife spent the next two years in Europe, and then, after an interim in New York City, settled in France at Orgeval, outside Paris. There their three sons—Jonathan Peale and the twins Robert Grosvenor and Christopher—were born. During these years in Europe, Bishop became acquainted with expatriate writers such as Ezra Pound, E. E. Cummings, and Ernest Hemingway and formed lifelong friendships with the poet Archibald MacLeish and the critic Allen Tate. Of this period in Bishop's life Tate has written: "More dependent upon a sympathetic literary society than most writers, he seemed . . . remote

and without concentration, except at intervals when he produced, in a burst of energy, a group of poems or an occasional story." He nevertheless completed a novel, "The Huntsmen Are Up in America" (never published), and a collection of stories, *Many Thousands Gone* (1931).

The Bishops returned to the United States in the autumn of 1933. After a few months in Westport, Conn., they moved on to New Orleans, and for the next few years lived alternately in Connecticut and in Louisiana. In 1937 they built a house at South Chatham, Mass., on Cape Cod, which thereafter remained their home. In 1933 Bishop published a collection of his poems, *Now With His Love,* and in 1935 a novel, *Act of Darkness,* and more poems, *Minute Particulars.* During this later period of his life (1933–40) he also wrote his finest criticism, essays, and reviews of poetry, among them "The South and Tradition," "Homage to Hemingway," "The Discipline of Poetry," "The Sorrows of Thomas Wolfe," and "Poetry and Painting." He reviewed work by Pound, W. H. Auden, Mark Van Doren, and others. His *Selected Poems* were published in 1941.

Bishop's contribution to American poetry was uneven—eclectic certainly, and sometimes imitative, particularly in his earlier published verses. Despite assertations by some contemporaries that he owed his reputation to the exaggerated claims of influential and uncritical friends, Tate, Wilson, and subsequent critics have emphasized the poetic craft discernible in Bishop's more successful pieces. Of his indebtedness to other poets—among them Eliot, Pound, and Valéry—Wilson, a close friend but no less a demanding critic, found these "no more important than catchphrases and intonations picked up in conversation that do not affect one's opinions or the quality of one's personality." Wilson further commented that Bishop "had never exploited his gifts or abused them in any way." These gifts were his lyricism and mastery of language, controlled by a commitment to disciplined artistry, as evidenced most clearly in poems like "Speaking of Poetry" and "The Hours," his elegy for Fitzgerald. In his other poems, several of which are excellent, he fused a vigorous sensuality with a deft and subtle diction. It is in isolated pieces, however, rather than a larger body of poems, that Bishop approaches greatness.

Although he was not a great poet, he was a critic of conscience and an able, though flawed, writer of fiction. The bulk of this writing, as well as his poetry, was an extension, elaboration, and repetition of one central idea: the need for, and the consequences of the lack of, tradition, a lack he felt particularly in the affairs of modern man. The search for tradition—that usable past that would have unified and made coherent an otherwise fragmentary and chaotic existence—led him to explore the role of myth; this, he believed, was the force that would regenerate the consciousness which had been buried under science and technology. In substance, myth and tradition were the heart of civilization, and in their recovery was the key to humane survival. Almost all of Bishop's work, a minor but finely realized achievement, was the record of his own attempts to rediscover and hold fast to that essential key.

During his final years, Bishop suffered frequent periods of ill health. He died of heart disease in the Cape Cod Hospital at Hyannis, Mass., in 1944, at the age of fifty-one, and was buried in the cemetery in East Harwich, Mass.

[The essential sources are Allen Tate's "Personal Memoir," in his edition of *The Collected Poems of John Peale Bishop* (1948, with frontispiece photograph of Bishop by Carl Van Vechten); *The Collected Essays of John Peale Bishop*, ed. with an introduction by Edmund Wilson (1948); Bishop's papers, on deposit in the Princeton Univ. Lib.; and information from Prof. Jonathan Peale Bishop, Cornell Univ. See also *Selected Poems of John Peale Bishop*, ed. by Allen Tate (1960); Robert L. White, *John Peale Bishop* (1966); William Arrowsmith, "An Artist's Estate," *Hudson Rev.*, Spring 1949; Joseph Frank, "The Achievement of John Peale Bishop," *Minnesota Rev.*, Spring 1962; Stanley Edgar Hyman, "Notes on the Organic Unity of John Peale Bishop," *Accent*, Winter 1949; and J. Max Patrick and Robert W. Stallman, "John Peale Bishop: A Checklist," *Princeton Univ. Lib. Chronicle*, Feb. 1946, an issue devoted to Bishop. Unpublished studies include Jesse Bier, "A Critical Biog. of John Peale Bishop" (Ph.D. thesis, Princeton, 1956); and Stephen C. Moore, "Variations on a Theme: The Poetry and Criticism of John Peale Bishop" (Ph.D. dissertation, Univ. of Mich., 1963). Death record from Mass. Registrar of Vital Statistics.]
STEPHEN C. MOORE

BITZER, GEORGE WILLIAM (Apr. 21, 1872–Apr. 29, 1944), pioneer motion picture cameraman, associate of D. W. Griffith, was born in the Roxbury section of Boston, Mass., to German immigrant parents, Johann Martin and Anne Marie (Schmidt) Bitzer. He was their second child and first of two sons. They baptized him Johann Gottlieb Wilhelm (recorded on his birth record as John William), but he adopted George William as his formal name, and throughout his career was known by his initials, G. W., or the nickname "Billy." Bitzer's father worked as a blacksmith and harnessmaker. Little is known about the boy's early life and education. At some point before his mid-twenties he moved to New York City, attended night classes at Cooper Union, and went to work as an electrician.

In 1896 Bitzer joined the newly formed American Mutoscope and Biograph Company, a pioneer motion picture firm which produced films and manufactured cameras, projecting equipment, and flip-card viewing machines. He ran the camera when the company filmed presidential candidate William McKinley on the lawn of his home in Canton, Ohio, and was the projectionist at the first New York showing of Biograph motion pictures on Oct. 12, 1896. In November 1899 Bitzer set up the lighting for the first successful artificially lighted indoor film, a record of the boxing match between Jim Jeffries and Tom Sharkey. After 1900 he became the principal cameraman at the Biograph studios, photographing films both for projection and for showing in the Mutoscope flip-card viewers.

The collaboration between Bitzer and D. W. Griffith, the most famous director-cameraman team in the history of American motion pictures, began in 1908 when Griffith gave up his acting career to become a director at Biograph. Over the next five years they made more than 300 one- and two-reel films together, culminating their Biograph careers with a four-reel epic, *Judith of Bethulia*, filmed in 1913 but not released until 1914. Leaving Biograph in 1913, they collaborated on the masterworks *The Birth of a Nation* (1915) and *Intolerance* (1916), the films which conveyed the mythic and moral possibilities of motion pictures to the American middle-class audience and firmly established movies as an American art and entertainment medium.

Commentators over the years have tried to separate the distinctive contributions of each man. Some have claimed that Griffith's reputation rests chiefly on Bitzer's technical skill, while others, more often, have asserted that Bitzer only reluctantly went along with Griffith's creative innovations. The recent availability of the Library of Congress paper-print collection of pre-1912 American films now makes it apparent that many technical innovations once attributed to Griffith, such as close-ups and special lighting techniques, were developed prior to 1908, partly in films photographed by Bitzer. Such findings take nothing away from Griffith's greatness, which lies in his imagination, his artistic seriousness, and his skill in visual composition and in creating atmosphere and dramatic tension. In Bitzer, Griffith found a brilliant technician who could realize his imaginative creations on film. Bitzer's chief contribution to motion picture technique was the development of the "iris," a process of shading out portions of the rectangular motion picture frame to focus attention and fade in or out of a scene, a process used most extensively in *The Birth of a Nation* and *Intolerance*.

During the 1920's relations between Bitzer

and Griffith became strained when the director brought in younger cameramen to work alongside his old associate. Bitzer last worked for Griffith on *Lady of the Pavements* (1929). In 1926 he founded a union, the International Photographers of the Motion Picture Industry, in New York. When a local of the union was set up in Hollywood in 1929, Bitzer was blacklisted by the motion picture industry. During the depression he was employed by the federal Works Progress Administration in a project preparing film strips and recorded lectures. He was living at the Motion Picture Country Home in 1944 when he suffered a fatal heart attack in Los Angeles. He was buried in Cedar Grove Cemetery, Flushing, N. Y.

Bitzer was a short, stocky man who wore a rumpled hat as he worked behind a motion picture camera. In middle age he became a convert from Lutheranism to Roman Catholicism. He entered into a common-law marriage with Elinore Farrell for some twenty years. After that relationship was dissolved, he married Ethel Boddy on Apr. 5, 1923. His widow and their son, Eden Griffith Joseph Bitzer, survived him.

[Several photographs of Bitzer at work appear in Kevin Brownlow, *The Parade's Gone By* (1968). Material pertaining to Bitzer is in the D. W. Griffith Archives, Museum of Modern Art, N. Y. Gordon Hendricks, *Beginnings of the Biograph* (1964), documents the early history of the company and prints portions of a Bitzer memoir. Kemp Niver, *The First Twenty Years* (1968), is especially valuable for its information on Bitzer's films before 1908. Lillian Gish, *The Movies, Mr. Griffith, and Me* (1969), discusses Bitzer's relations with Griffith. A detailed account of Bitzer's development of the "iris" technique is in Iris Barry, *D. W. Griffith, Am. Film Master* (1940). Bitzer's union activities are mentioned in Philip Sterling, "Billy Bitzer, Ace Cameraman," *New Theatre and Film*, Apr. 1937. Additional information was provided by Mrs. Ethel Bitzer.]

ROBERT SKLAR

BLACKFAN, KENNETH DANIEL (Sept. 9, 1883–Nov. 29, 1941), pediatrician, was born in Cambridge, N. Y., the oldest of three children of Harry Smith Blackfan and his wife, Estella Chase. Both his father and his grandfather were physicians, descended from early colonists of Pennsylvania. Young Blackfan graduated from the local high school in 1901 and then entered the Albany (N. Y.) Medical College, receiving the M.D. degree in 1905.

As a third-year medical student Blackfan came under the influence of Richard Mills Pearce [q.v.], the newly appointed professor of pathology and bacteriology, who took him into his laboratory the following summer and aroused in him an enthusiasm for exploring the frontiers of scientific medicine. After graduation Blackfan remained for a year as Pearce's assistant and then returned to Cambridge to take up general practice with his father. Frequent visits and discussions with Pearce, a summer resident at nearby Dorset, Vt., finally persuaded Blackfan in 1909 to leave general practice and seek special training. Having become interested in work with children, he went to Philadelphia, armed with letters from Pearce to two outstanding pediatricians and teachers, David L. Edsall [Supp. 3] and Samuel M. Hamill, and through their influence was appointed resident-in-charge under Hamill at the St. Vincent de Paul Foundling Hospital.

In the next two years Blackfan acquired a reputation as an outstanding student of pediatrics, and in 1911 he accepted a residency under John Howland [q.v.], professor of pediatrics in the medical school of Washington University in St. Louis, Mo. A year later, when Howland was appointed head of the department of pediatrics at the Johns Hopkins Medical School and Hospital, Blackfan joined him in Baltimore as his resident physician at the hospital's Harriet Lane Home, a recently built unit for infants and children. The appointment at that time was a long-term assistantship to the chief of pediatrics, with great responsibilities for the care of patients and the teaching of students and house officers, as well as for dealing with any problems that developed. Kenneth Blackfan was ideally suited for this multifaceted position. Children and parents adored him, and nurses and young doctors respected him. He was never impatient or inattentive with students, never raised his voice, and was always logical. He advocated close cooperation between the physician and the laboratory staff, and insisted that each child should be cared for as an individual whose needs should come before the demands of hospital and teaching routine.

Blackfan remained in Baltimore for eight years, becoming instructor in pediatrics at the Johns Hopkins Medical School (1913–17), associate (1917–19), and associate professor (1919–20). In the group of outstanding young pediatricians then at Hopkins, he was recognized as the leading clinician and teacher. He made important contributions to the treatment of diarrhea in infants and introduced (1918) the intraperitoneal injection of salt solution to replace lost fluid. He also carried out research on the recognition, treatment, and complications of meningococcus meningitis in children, and made a classical study of hydrocephalus with Walter E. Dandy, the famous Johns Hopkins brain surgeon. During the latter years of World War I, when most of the staff were in the armed forces, Blackfan also carried most of the burden of patient care and departmental management. He held a commission as lieutenant but was kept from active service by long-standing trifacial neuralgia, a painful affliction which he withstood with silent fortitude through the years.

Blackfan left Baltimore in 1920 to accept an appointment as professor of pediatrics and chief of the Children's Hospital at the University of Cincinnati. Three years later he moved to the Harvard Medical School to become Thomas Morgan Rotch Professor of Pediatrics and physician-in-chief at the Boston Children's Hospital. Here he found full scope for his talents as administrator, diplomat, physician, and teacher. He promoted closer cooperation between his pediatric department and the hospital's two other independent services, general surgery and orthopedic surgery, and won the support of qualified local pediatricians by inviting them to accept teaching and service positions in the hospital. He established closer relations with the Boston Lying-In Hospital, to provide better care for infants ailing at birth, and organized a number of special clinics for the treatment of children suffering from heart abnormalities and from such illnesses as diabetes, rheumatic fever, and celiac disease. He emphasized the importance of bacteriological and immunological research in treating the diseases of children and, with the financial help of the medical school, developed a notable research laboratory under the active leadership of James L. Gamble, an old friend from Johns Hopkins. In his own research Blackfan made important contributions to hematology and with a collaborator described a previously undefined blood abnormality, "hypoplastic anemia," in which the red cells alone fail to regenerate. Under Blackfan's leadership, the Children's Hospital of Boston and the department of pediatrics at Harvard Medical School achieved and maintained a preeminent place in the care of children, in research, and in the training of pediatric practitioners and teachers.

On Aug. 15, 1920, Blackfan had married Lulie Henry (Anderson) Bridges of Louisville, Ky., a widow with one son, Turner Anderson; Blackfan himself had no children. He was a Presbyterian in religion. Blackfan served as president of the American Pediatric Society in 1937–38. In the later years of his life his health declined, and after an operation for hyperplastic disease in the spring of 1941, he took a sabbatical year and started south, planning to spend the winter. Visiting in Louisville on the way, he died, at the age of fifty-eight, of a malignant brain tumor. He was buried in Woodlands Cemetery, Cambridge, N. Y.

Slight of build, gentle and soft-spoken, modest but firm, Blackfan rose in a dozen years from country practitioner to head of an outstanding department of pediatrics. Known as a skilled teacher,

an able organizer, an astute clinician, and a devoted physician to children, he had pursued two principal goals: to improve the health of children, and to build up the department entrusted to him.

[James L. Gamble et al., *Addresses Delivered at the Memorial Exercises at the Children's Hospital, Feb. 27, 1942, for Kenneth D. Blackfan* (Supp. to *Harvard Medical Alumni Bull.*, Apr. 1942); James L. Wilson in Borden S. Veeder, ed., *Pediatric Profiles* (1957); Harold K. Faber and Rustin McIntosh, *Hist. of the Am. Pediatric Soc.* (1966). See also: *Nat. Cyc. Am. Biog.*, XXXII, 162–63; and obituaries in *Am. Jour. of Diseases of Children*, Jan. 1942; *Jour. of Pediatrics*, Jan. 1942; Assoc. of Am. Physicians, *Transactions*, LVII (1942), 7–9; and *Jour. Am. Medic. Assoc.*, Dec. 13, 1941.]

LOUIS K. DIAMOND

BLACKTON, JAMES STUART (Jan. 5, 1875–Aug. 13, 1941), motion picture pioneer, known as J. Stuart Blackton, was born in Sheffield, England, the only child of Henry and Jessie (Stuart) Blackton. His father, a carriage maker, soon deserted the family; his mother remarried and had a second son. Reared as an Anglican, young Blackton attended Eton House Collegiate School. In 1886 he came with his family to the United States. For several years he worked as a carpenter, until his artistic talent brought him other jobs. He also took night classes at the City College of New York.

In 1896, while employed as a reporter and illustrator by the New York *World*, Blackton was sent to interview the inventor Thomas Alva Edison [Supp. 1], soon after the first public showing of motion pictures by means of Edison's new projector. Edison, whose studio was turning out short films for the new medium, photographed the young reporter drawing "lightning sketches" with chalk in a kind of performance that Blackton had been giving to clubs and other audiences in company with Ronald Reader, a "prestidigitateur," and Albert E. Smith, an "illusionist." Soon afterward Blackton and Smith purchased a Projecting Kinetoscope from Edison and began to exhibit motion pictures. Smith then transformed the projector into a camera, and the two young men began to make their own films.

Their first "posed" film, as Smith described it in his diary, was *The Burglar on the Roof*, produced in 1897, with Blackton as the burglar. This, like the other pictures of their first few years, lasted only one minute. It was designed to take advantage of their studio, the open roof of a building on Nassau Street in New York. Another important early film of Blackton and Smith was *Tearing Down the Spanish Flag*, made in 1898 during the Spanish-American War. Blackton once described the filming: "It was taken in a 10-by-12 studio room, the background a building next door. We had a flag pole and two 18-inch flags. Smith operated the machine and I . . . grabbed the Spanish flag and tore it down from the pole and pulled the Stars and Stripes to the top of the flag pole. That was our very first dramatic picture and it is surprising how much dramatic effect it created. . . . The people went wild" (quoted in Jacobs, p. 11). Not content to manufacture war news in the studio, Blackton and Smith went to Cuba to photograph the war at first hand. The close-up shots that Blackton made for their newsreels antedate by some ten years D. W. Griffith's development of the close-up as a standard element of the dramatic film.

When Blackton and Smith began to make films, they called their enterprise the Vitagraph Company of America. In 1900 they incorporated the company, with William T. ("Pop") Rock as a third shareholder. Blackton was vice-president and the artistic leader of Vitagraph. Originally one of the industry's leading directors as well as a cameraman, as Vitagraph grew he began to relinquish the direction of some of his films to others and developed the position of supervisor (or "producer," in the later language of the industry), in which he could guide the course of several films simultaneously. His *The Haunted Hotel* (1906) is said to have been the first film employing single-frame animation, a kind of trick photography (Spottiswoode, pp. 121–22). He is also reported to have made the first animated cartoon for theatrical projection and to have been the first to use dialogue in subtitles (Macgowan, pp. 118, 271). In 1909 Blackton produced the first films of feature length, *Les Miserables* in four reels and *The Life of Moses* in five; these were not shown as single features, however, but in installments, at the rate of one reel a week. Before America's entry into the First World War, Blackton made several films to advocate American preparedness, the most publicized being *The Battle Cry of Peace* (1915). Most of the early films of the Vitagraph Company were made in Brooklyn, where in 1903 Blackton, Smith, and Rock located its first studio. In 1911 they established a studio in Hollywood as well, though Blackton remained in the East at this time. Fond of boating, he became commodore of the Atlantic Yacht Club (1912–17) and adopted the title in his business life.

As a leader in the early film industry, Blackton, with members of six other companies, helped organize in 1908–09 the Motion Picture Patents Company, a trust of the holders of patents on equipment used in the making and projection of films. In 1910 he founded *Motion Picture Magazine,* the first magazine designed for film fans;

though it was initially conceived as a means of publicizing Vitagraph pictures, popular enthusiasm soon forced it to broaden its scope. He was the first president of the Motion Picture Board of Trade of America, organized in 1915.

Blackton resigned from Vitagraph in 1917 to accept a contract as producer and director with the Famous Players-Lasky Corporation. This arrangement lasted only briefly, however, and he next went to his native England to produce films, among them *The Glorious Adventure* (1921) and *The Virgin Queen* (1923). The first was among the earliest feature films to be photographed in color. In 1923 Blackton returned to Vitagraph, which was then operating chiefly in Hollywood, as a producer; he remained with the company until it was sold to Warner Brothers in 1925.

Blackton was married four times: in 1897 to Isabelle Mabel MacArthur, by whom he had two children, James Stuart and Marian Constance; in 1908, following a divorce, to the actress Paula Dean (Pauline Hillburn), by whom he had two children, Violet Virginia and Charles Stuart; on Jan. 31, 1931, two years after his second wife's death, to Dr. Helen R. Stahle, a Los Angeles orthodontist, who died in 1933; and, on Oct. 17, 1936, to Mrs. Evangeline Russell de Rippeteau, a film actress known professionally as Evangeline Russell.

Blackton prospered with the rise of Vitagraph, but lost his fortune in ill-advised real estate and other investments and was declared bankrupt in 1931. During the depression he was appointed the director of a federal relief film project in Hollywood. He died in Los Angeles in 1941, of injuries received in an automobile accident; following cremation, his ashes were placed in a crypt in Forest Lawn Memorial Park, Glendale, Calif. Although less important as a creative figure than D. W. Griffith or Edwin S. Porter [Supp. 3], Blackton contributed significantly to the growth of motion pictures as both art and industry.

[Albert E. Smith with Phil A. Koury, *Two Reels and a Crank* (1952), reminiscences of one of the founders of Vitagraph; Lewis Jacobs, *The Rise of the Am. Film* (1939); Terry Ramsaye, *A Million and One Nights* (2 vols., 1926), a lively history of motion pictures to 1925; Kevin Brownlow, *The Parade's Gone By* (1968), an illuminating study of the aesthetics of the silent film, principally in the U. S.; Kenneth Macgowan, *Behind the Screen* (1965), which treats all aspects of motion pictures from primitive devices before film to the wide-screen techniques of the post-World War II years; Raymond Spottiswoode, *Film and Its Techniques* (1951); references to Blackton in *N. Y. Times*, Feb. 1, 1931 (sec. 2), Oct. 18, 1936 (sec. 6), and obituary, Aug. 14, 1941; information from Marian Blackton (Mrs. Larry) Trimble, Beverly Hills, Calif.]

MALCOLM GOLDSTEIN

BLAKELEY, GEORGE HENRY (Apr. 19, 1865–Dec. 25, 1942), structural steel engineer, was born on a farm between Hanover and Livingston, N. J.; his parents were Joseph H. and Mary Ann (Gibson) Blakeley. He attended Rutgers College, graduating from the scientific department in 1884 with a B.S. degree, and then entered the engineering profession. His career followed an established pattern of apprenticeship training. After three years with a survey crew, he advanced to chief draftsman of the Riverside Bridge and Iron Works in Paterson, N. J., where he specialized in the structural design of bridges and buildings. In 1888 the Erie Railroad acquired his services, and two years later he became chief engineer of the Passaic Rolling Mill Company. For that company he designed and supervised the construction of the 155th Street Bridge over the Harlem River in New York City, the heaviest swing span thus far built and the first to have both a double drum and a double ring of bearing wheels. A sign of his rising professional status was his marriage on Apr. 12, 1893, to Grace Delia Bogart, daughter of Gilbert D. Bogart, a leading promoter of the growth and development of Passaic, N. J. They had one son, George Bogart.

During the 1890's architects and engineers began to apply the framing principles of bridge building to commercial architecture, and Blakeley contributed to this transition by publishing in 1900 the first of three handbooks he wrote on the uses of structural steel. While making a survey for the Passaic Rolling Mill of the different methods for processing steel, Blakeley became acquainted with Henry Grey, an American engineer who had designed a mill for rolling steel beams with wide flanges. Blakeley sought to interest the Passaic Rolling Company in adopting Grey's innovations, but without success, and Grey built an experimental mill in Germany. In 1906, after Charles M. Schwab [Supp. 2] had acquired the old Bethlehem Iron Company and the American rights to the Grey process, he hired George Blakeley as a structural engineer and two years later placed him in charge of promoting the use of the new steel sections. The thin-web, wide-flange girders, beams, and H-columns (later called Bethlehem sections) contained less than 11 percent of the steel used in traditional steel members, and engineers and architects were at first reluctant to employ them in public buildings. Blakeley is credited with the successful introduction of these structural members, which have since become standard shapes for steel design. They were first used in the Spencer Optical Company factory near Boston and in the Field Museum of Natural History in Chicago (completed in 1918); subsequently, because of their wide acceptance, Bethlehem Steel Company became one of the largest producers of commercial steel.

Blakeley was well rewarded for his contributions. In 1916 he became president of the new Bethlehem Steel Bridge Corporation, a post he retained until this Bethlehem subsidiary was dissolved in 1923. He was made vice-president of Bethlehem Steel Company in 1927, and when Bethlehem acquired the McClintic-Marshall Company, he became its president (1931–35). As such, he was the administrator of an annual fabrication capacity of 700,000 tons, one-sixth of the nation's total steel production capacity.

A Republican, an Episcopalian, and an art collector, Blakeley was known for his Lincolnesque humor. Rutgers University appointed him a lifetime trustee in 1919 and awarded him an honorary D.Sc. degree in 1924. He died at the age of seventy-seven at the home of his son in Newport, R. I., and was buried in Nisky Hill Cemetery, Bethlehem, Pa.

[George H. Blakeley, *A Manual of Useful Information and Tables Appertaining to the Use of Structural Steel as Manufactured by the Passaic Rolling Mill Co.* (1900), *Dimensions, Weights and Properties of Special and Standard Structural Steel Shapes Manufactured by Bethlehem Steel Co.* (1907), and *Catalogue of Bethlehem Structural Shapes* (1911); memoir by W. A. Hazard in Am. Soc. of Civil Engineers, *Transactions*, CVIII (1943), 1560–61; sketch of Blakeley in *Steel*, Feb. 12, 1931, pp. 291–92; obituary in *N. Y. Herald Tribune*, Dec. 25, 1942; *Who Was Who in America*, vol. II (1950).]

RAYMOND H. MERRITT

BLEASE, COLEMAN LIVINGSTON (Oct. 8, 1868–Jan. 19, 1942), governor of South Carolina and United States Senator, was born on his father's farm near Newberry Courthouse, S. C., the second son and sixth of eight children of Mary Ann (Livingston) and Henry Horatio Blease; he had five younger half brothers and sisters by his father's second marriage. Henry Blease, son of an emigrant from Liverpool, England, subsequently became a successful hotel and livery stable proprietor in the town of Newberry. The boy attended schools in Newberry and went on in 1879 to Newberry College, where he took preparatory classes and completed the junior year of the collegiate course. In 1887 he entered the law school of South Carolina College; he was expelled the following year for plagiarism in an essay contest. Following an unsuccessful candidacy for the state legislature in 1888, Blease enrolled at Georgetown University, received the bachelor of laws degree in 1889, and began a successful practice in Newberry and nearby Saluda. Reared in the convivial atmosphere of his father's hotel, he early acquired an ingratiating manner and a self-confident air.

In 1890 a political revolution led by Benjamin R. ("Pitchfork Ben") Tillman [q.v.] swept over South Carolina, and Blease, who was elected to the house of representatives from Newberry County in 1890 and 1892, became a Tillmanite floor leader. He was defeated in 1894 and 1896, but returned for a third two-year term in 1898. Following two unsuccessful campaigns for lieutenant governor (1900, 1902), Blease was elected by his Newberry constituents in 1904 to a four-year term in the state senate. This success encouraged him to run for governor, and after twice failing (1906, 1908), he was victorious in 1910, campaigning as the champion of the poor white farmer and the textile worker.

Blease's administration was wracked by political controversy. He issued an unprecedented number of vetoes, revoked the commissions of 6,000 notaries public, dissolved the state militia, and issued 1,743 paroles and pardons to inmates of state penal institutions. Although the bitter factionalism he engendered brought social reform to a virtual standstill, Blease did render constructive service in his successful efforts to obtain state support for the Medical College of South Carolina, in establishing a state tuberculosis sanatorium, and in abolishing an unsanitary textile mill in the state penitentiary.

Blease, however, was essentially a demagogue who fostered class and race antagonisms but ignored the real problems of poverty. His opposition to child labor laws, factory inspection, and compulsory school attendance mattered little to the mill workers and sharecroppers who formed the hard core of his political strength. They delighted in his attacks upon newspapers, corporations, aristocrats, and Negroes, whom he called "baboons and apes" (Simkins, p. 490). Flattered by the personal recognition he gave them, his working-class supporters helped him win a second term in 1912 despite the combined opposition of press, clergy, corporations, educators, and even Senator Tillman, who was alarmed by Blease's executive irresponsibility. When Blease ran for the United States Senate in 1914, a temporary reaction against "Bleaseism" brought about his decisive defeat by Ellison D. Smith [Supp. 3]. Two years later he lost the governorship by less than 5,000 votes, and many Bleaseites were elected to the legislature. Blease's vociferous attacks against Woodrow Wilson and United States participation in World War I brought his fortunes to a low ebb in 1918, when he lost all but three counties in a Senate race.

In the 1920's the political warhorse returned to the campaigns as a "new Blease," more dignified in manner and less vituperative in speech. Though unsuccessful in the gubernatorial contest of 1922, he won a seat in the United States Senate in 1924, defeating James F. Byrnes by a narrow margin. As a Senator, Blease was hostile to the League of Nations and the World Court, opposed the McNary-Haugen farm program, and delivered long harangues in defense of lynching and Southern womanhood. His Senate career was exhibitionist rather than distinguished, and in 1930 he was defeated for reelection in a second close contest with Byrnes. Although his influence now languished, the inveterate campaigner continued to win substantial support in his unsuccessful bids for the Senate in 1932 and for the governorship in 1934 and 1938.

Cole ("Coley") L. Blease was a product of the agrarian upheaval that convulsed South Carolina in the 1890's. An intelligent and personally attractive man, he used his talents to become the most thoroughgoing demagogue in South Carolina history. Where Tillman developed a constructive reform program, Blease merely led an incoherent protest that "never rose above partisan politics" (Burnside, p. 42). Blease was a Methodist and was active in a number of fraternal organizations, including the Odd Fellows, Red Men, and Moose. He was twice married: on Feb. 13, 1890, to Lillie B. Summers; and in 1939, five years after his first wife's death, to Mrs. Caroline Floyd, from whom he separated a year later. He resided in Columbia, S. C., from 1915 until his death, which followed an abdominal operation at the Providence Hospital there. He was buried in Rosemont Cemetery, Newberry.

[The Blease Papers at the S. C. State Archives, Columbia, consist of his correspondence as governor; there is apparently no collection of his private papers. The most comprehensive study of Blease is Ronald D. Burnside, "The Governorship of Coleman Livingston Blease of S. C." (Ph.D. dissertation, Ind. Univ., 1963); see also Kenneth W. Mixon, "The Senatorial Career of Coleman Livingston Blease, 1925–31" (master's essay, Univ. of S. C., 1970). There are valuable references to Blease in Robert M. Burts, "The Public Career of Richard I. Manning" (Ph.D. dissertation, Vanderbilt Univ., 1957), and a good chapter on Blease in Francis B. Simkins, Pitchfork Ben Tillman (1944). See also: Daniel W. Hollis, "Samuel Chiles Mitchell, Social Reformer in Blease's S. C.," S. C. Hist. Mag., Jan. 1969; James C. Derieux, "Crawling toward the Promised Land," Survey, Apr. 29, 1922; Rupert Vance, "Rebels and Agrarians All," Southern Rev., Summer 1938. For certain aspects of Blease's Senate career, see Blease's Weekly (Anderson, S. C.), 1925–26, and O. L. Warr, "Mr. Blease of S. C.," Am. Mercury, Jan. 1929. Blease's many political campaigns can be traced in Frank E. Jordan, The Primary State: A Hist. of the Democratic Party in S. C. (1967). See also obituary in Charleston News and Courier, Jan. 20, 1942. There is an excellent photograph of Blease as governor and a biographical sketch in David D. Wallace, Hist. of S. C., vol. IV (1934).]

DANIEL WALKER HOLLIS

BLICHFELDT, HANS FREDERIK (Jan. 9, 1873–Nov. 16, 1945), mathematician, was born in the small village of Iller in Grønbaek Sogn, Denmark, a dozen miles northeast of Silkeborg in Jutland. He was the younger of the two sons and third of the four children of Erhard Christoffer Laurentius Blichfeldt and his wife, Nielsine Maria Schøler, who also had one son by her first marriage. His father and his immediate ancestors were farmers, but earlier Blichfeldts included ministers and bishops, and among his mother's forebears were many scholars and teachers. In 1881 the family moved to Copenhagen, where they lived "very frugally." Before Blichfeldt emigrated to the United States in 1888, with his father and his older half brother, he had passed, with high honors, the general preliminary state examination conducted at the University of Copenhagen. In his early school career he had consistently excelled in mathematics, and by the time he took this examination, at the age of fifteen, he had discovered by himself the solutions of the general polynomial equations of third and fourth degrees—a remarkable performance for a schoolboy.

In his first four years in the United States, Blichfeldt "worked with my hands doing everything, East and West the country across," but particularly in the lumber industry of the Pacific Northwest. Then for two years, 1892–94, he was a draftsman for the engineering department of the city and county of Whatcom, Wash., where his unusual mathematical talent began to come to the attention of his employers and fellow workers. Although he had not pursued a formal high school education in the United States, in 1894 he was persuaded to apply for admission to the recently opened Stanford University. The country superintendent of schools, in a letter supporting his application, described him as "about 21, of most exemplary physique and morals, evidently cultured in his native tongue and fairly proficient in English. He is a real genius in mathematics—working intuitively to all appearance, abstruse integral calculus problems" (J. M. Hitt to President Jordan, May 14, 1894, Stanford University Archives). The free elective system, somewhat similar to Harvard's, that Stanford then followed was particularly well adapted to a young man of great mathematical ability and originality. Admitted as a special student, Blichfeldt received his A.B. degree in mathematics in 1896 and the A.M. in 1897.

Like many aspiring young mathematicians of his day, Blichfeldt determined to go to Germany and study at the University of Leipzig under Sophus Lie. Borrowing the necessary funds, he spent a year (1897–98) working with Lie, mastering the "Lie Theory" of continuous groups, and writing his doctoral dissertation, "On a Certain Class of Groups of Transformation in Space of Three Dimensions" (*American Journal of Mathematics*, April 1900), for which he received the Ph.D. summa cum laude in 1898. He then returned to Stanford, where he taught for the next forty years, from 1913 as professor.

While Blichfeldt was not a prolific writer—he sometimes lost interest in writing up a problem for publication once he had reasoned it through—he made important contributions, particularly in the theory of groups and in the geometry of numbers. Advancing over the work of mathematicians of such high standing as Felix Klein and Camille Jordan, he was able to solve the difficult problem of finding all finite collineation groups in four variables. His determination of precise limits for minima of definite quadratic forms in six, seven, and eight variables will remain a great achievement. In addition to some two dozen research papers of importance, he was the author of "Finite Groups of Linear Homogeneous Transformations" (Part 2 of *Theory and Application of Finite Groups,* by G. A. Miller, H. F. Blichfeldt, and L. E. Dickson, 1916) and *Finite Collineation Groups* (1917). He served as vicepresident of the American Mathematical Society in 1912 and represented the United States officially at two international mathematical congresses. In 1920 he was elected a member of the National Academy of Sciences, and in 1924–27 he served as a member of the National Research Council.

Blichfeldt never married, but family ties were strong, and he was in close touch with relatives both in Denmark and in the United States. His father lived with him for many years in Palo Alto.

Blichfeldt was particularly interested in the international exchange of ideas; he was influential in bringing such prominent European mathematicians as Harald Bohr, Edmund Landau, George Polya, and Gabor Szegö to Stanford as visiting lecturers or professors, an unusual undertaking during the depression decade of the 1930's.

A modest and unassuming man of quiet and friendly manner, Blichfeldt as a young man enjoyed bicycling, hiking, and swimming. Traveling was a favorite pursuit, particularly motoring. Such activities were restricted in his middle age and later years by angina. He died in the Palo Alto (Calif.) Hospital in 1945, seven years after his retirement, following an operation for cancer, and was buried in Alta Mesa Cemetery, Palo Alto.

[The principal secondary sources—E. T. Bell in Nat. Acad. Sci., *Biog. Memoirs*, vol. XXVI (1951), and L. E. Dickson in Am. Mathematical Soc., *Bull.*, Sept. 1947—were supplemented by information from records in the Registrar's Office and Archives of Stanford Univ.; correspondence with a cousin of Blichfeldt, Mr. G. L. Scholer of Alamo, Calif.; Blichfeldt's death record; and long personal acquaintance. The Bell and Dickson articles each include a bibliography of Blichfeldt's mathematical publications; Bell reproduces a good photograph of Blichfeldt as a young man. See also *Who Was Who in America*, vol. II (1950).]

HAROLD M. BACON

BLOCK, PAUL (Nov. 2, 1877–June 22, 1941), newspaper publisher and advertising executive, was born in Elmira, N. Y., the second son and third of five children of Jewish parents, John and Mary (Phillips) Bloch (later changed to Block). City directories of 1893 and 1894 list his father as a dealer in rags. Paul attended Elmira public schools and in 1893, at fifteen, became an advertising solicitor for the *Elmira Sunday Telegram*. Two years later he went to work for A. Frank Richardson, a publishers' representative, in New York City. In 1897 he formed Paul Block, Inc. (after 1908, Paul Block & Associates, Inc.), as a national agency to solicit advertising for daily newspapers, building it into one of the larger firms of its kind. At his death the company represented sixteen newspapers.

From advertising, Block moved into newspaper publishing. Beginning in 1916 he held varying degrees of ownership or control over thirteen newspapers for the periods indicated: the *Newark Star-Eagle* (1916–39), *New York Evening Mail* (1918–21), *Brooklyn Standard-Union* (1928–32), *Los Angeles Express* (1931), *Detroit Journal* (1917–22), *Duluth* (Minn.) *Herald* (1921–36), *Duluth News-Tribune* (1929–36), *Memphis News-Scimitar* (1921–26), *Lancaster* (Pa.) *New Era* (1923–28), *Milwaukee Sentinel* (1929–37), *Toledo Blade* (from 1926), *Toledo Times* (from 1930), and *Pittsburgh Post-Gazette* (from 1927). The Block group reached its peak size in 1931 with nine papers. He bought some when they were in or near bankruptcy and disposed of most during the Great Depression. At death, he retained only the *Toledo Blade, Toledo Times,* and *Pittsburgh Post-Gazette.*

Block was the only newspaper publisher closely associated with William Randolph Hearst. Friends for years, they entered a ten-year partnership in Pittsburgh in 1927. With $8,000,000 from the Hearst treasury, they bought four of the five Pittsburgh newspapers and consolidated them into two, Block's *Post-Gazette* and Hearst's *Sun-Telegraph.* Block became sole owner of the *Post-Gazette* when he bought Hearst's sizable

interest in 1937; at the same time, he returned to Hearst the unprofitable *Milwaukee Sentinel,* on which he had had a ten-year lease dating from 1929. In February 1931 Block bought the *Los Angeles Express,* which he sold to Hearst before the year was out, becoming a director of Hearst's merged *Herald-Express.* In addition, Paul Block & Associates represented some of the Hearst newspapers (seven in 1937).

Unlike the Scripps-Howard and Hearst newspapers, the Block group operated without central editorial direction. Block determined editorial policy on national issues, but allowed his editors much latitude otherwise. A man of strong convictions in public affairs, he sometimes wrote signed, page-one editorials in the style and typography of Arthur Brisbane [Supp. 2] of the Hearst group and gave them wider circulation as paid advertisements in newspapers in other cities. Preferring progressive but not sensational newspapers, he furnished his journals with an array of news and feature services. Under assignment from Block in 1937, Raymond Sprigle of the *Pittsburgh Post-Gazette* exposed the former Ku Klux Klan association of Hugo L. Black, whom President Roosevelt had nominated for the Supreme Court; the story won Sprigle a Pulitzer Prize.

Block was a strong Republican in national politics, but at the same time was a close friend and supporter of Mayor James J. Walker of New York City, a Democrat. The Hofstadter Committee, investigating Walker's conduct in office, heard testimony in 1932 that Walker had received $246,692 from a joint brokerage account with Block in which Walker had invested nothing, and that Block had been interested in a company that was seeking to sell tile to contractors building subways for the city.

Block was described late in life as a short, bald man with a fringe of gray hair and a sallow complexion. Two clues to the inner man might be his admiration for Napoleon, which he shared with some other builders of business empires, and his extraordinary emphasis on friendship. Time and again he stressed the importance of this quality, and he gave the name "Friendship" to both his private railroad car (in which he made three or four transcontinental trips a year) and his home in Port Chester, N. Y.

Nothing in the record indicates that Block shared the creative editorial impulse of Scripps, Hearst, or Pulitzer. In the words of a contemporary, he brought to chain journalism "the genius for advertising, the business office flair" (*World's Work,* February 1932, p. 68). It is perhaps fair to say that he was among the more efficient and ambitious of those publishers who ushered in the business-office age of American newspapers after World War I, and that—influenced perhaps by Frank Munsey [*q.v.*]—he early recognized, capitalized on, and accelerated the trend toward newspaper consolidation.

On Dec. 18, 1907, Block married Dina Wallach of New York City, by whom he had two children, Paul and William Karl. He died in his apartment in the Waldorf-Astoria Towers, New York City, at the age of sixty-three and was buried in Kensico Cemetery, Valhalla, N. Y.

[Block has not attracted the serious attention of historians of journalism; hence, one must rely on a voluminous yet inadequate periodical literature. Published summaries of his life appeared as obituaries in the *N. Y. Times, Pittsburgh Post-Gazette, Toledo Times,* and *Toledo Blade,* all of June 23, 1941, and *Editor & Publisher,* June 28, 1941. Much of his career is traceable through numerous reports in the *N. Y. Times* (see Index). Some insight into his methods is to be obtained from the anonymous "Journalism à la A & P," *World's Work,* Feb. 1932, a sympathetic discussion of chain or group newspaper management. A brief and complimentary account of Block's approach to journalism in Pittsburgh appears in J. Cutler Andrews, *Pittsburgh's Post-Gazette* (1936), pp. 301–02. George Seldes's acid evaluation in *Lords of the Press* (1938), pp. 65–70, makes no attempt at judicious balance. *Time* twice provided illuminating bits: Sept. 27, 1937, pp. 48–49, and Apr. 4, 1938, p. 55. The Steele Memorial Lib., Elmira, provided city directory listings for 1893–94. Only passing references appear in the principal histories of journalism—Edwin Emery, *The Press and America* (1954), and Frank Luther Mott, *Am. Journalism* (rev. ed., 1950) —as well as in Harold Ickes, *America's House of Lords* (1939).]

OLIVER KNIGHT

BOAS, FRANZ (July 9, 1858–Dec. 21, 1942), the leading American anthropologist of the first half of the twentieth century, was born in Minden, Westphalia, the third of six children of Meier and Sophie (Meyer) Boas and their first son. Both parental families can be traced back into the eighteenth century, and their histories reflect the experience of many German Jews in this period. By the time of Boas's birth his father, a prosperous merchant, retained only "an emotional affection for the ceremonial of his parental home," and Boas was born free of what he was later inclined to call "the shackles of dogma." His mother was a friend of Carl Schurz and a sister-in-law of Dr. Abraham Jacobi [*qq.v.*], and Boas later recalled that his thinking was molded in a home "in which the ideals of the Revolution of 1848 were a living force."

At the Froebel kindergarten which she had founded in 1854, Sophie Boas shared with her son her own devotion to science, encouraging from an early age his interest in natural history. Throughout his youth, both at school and during several extended periods of illness, Boas pursued various lines of nature study. As his Gymnasium

career progressed, his interests shifted from descriptive to comparative studies, and later from natural history to physics and mathematics. During the same period they broadened to include literature (he "devoured" Schiller and "immersed" himself in Goethe), history (he preferred "culture history" to that of "single men"), and music (he early acquired a competence at the piano which he maintained all his life). In his last year of Gymnasium, Boas planned, in deference to his father's wishes, to abandon natural science to enter the more "practical" study of medicine. However, with support from his Uncle Jacobi, he succeeded finally in winning his father's acquiescence to a university career in natural science and mathematics.

From 1877 to 1881 Boas studied successively at Heidelberg, Bonn, and Kiel. Like many German students, he drank and dueled and was several times briefly imprisoned for student pranks. His particular position in German culture, however, gave a special twist to the archetypical pattern: the dueling scars he bore through life were the by-product of recurring anti-Semitic insults which he refused to let pass unanswered. The same passionate element in his personality was also embodied in his intellectual pursuits. He later described his university studies as a "compromise" between the purely "intellectual" impulse which led him first to physics and "an intensive, emotional interest in the phenomena of the world" which led him to shift gradually toward the study of geography. Simultaneously, Boas went through an intellectual reorientation which helped define the terms of his whole anthropological career. His "materialistic" world view had already been called into question by his elder sister Toni, with whom he had an extremely close relationship during adolescence. His work at Bonn and Kiel under Theobald Fischer, a follower of the historical geographer Karl Ritter, led Boas toward a holistic, affective understanding of the relationship of man and the natural world. His doctoral dissertation on the color of sea water (*Beiträge zur Erkenntnis der Farbe des Wassers,* 1881) depended at crucial points on his own subjective judgment as experimenter, and the methodological problems involved led him toward epistemology on the one hand and the psychophysics of Gustav Fechner and Wilhelm Wundt on the other. During his last semesters at Kiel he was in close contact with the neo-Kantian philosopher Benno Erdmann; in the two years immediately after his doctorate he wrote a number of papers in psychophysics (e.g., "Uber die Grundaufgabe der Psychophysik," *Pflüger's Archiv,* XXVIII, 1882, pp. 566-76). In this context, Boas came to recognize "domains of our experience" where the quantitative, mechanistic assumptions of the physicist were not applicable, and to develop a program of research on the interrelationship of "the objective and the subjective worlds" which was to lead him eventually from physics to anthropology.

Germinating during a year of military service, this program began to take more definite shape during the winter of 1882–83, which Boas spent in Berlin (where he came in contact with Rudolf Virchow and Adolf Bastian, who were respectively Germany's leading physical and leading cultural anthropologist). Boas proposed to study the "reaction of the human mind to natural environment" by investigating the interrelationship of migration routes, native geographical knowledge, and actual physical geography among the Eskimo. In June 1883 Boas sailed for Baffin Land, where he spent more than a year in the region near Cumberland Sound, carrying on geographic and ethnographic researches. Life among the Eskimo had a profound effect on Boas. He already had felt alienated from a Germany which seemed to have abandoned the "ideals of 1848" for crass materialism, which was even then embarking on a policy of imperialism, and in which rising anti-Semitism threatened to bar him from an academic career. In this context, Boas felt strongly the appeal of a life in which one shared raw seal liver as one shared deprivation and cold, in which the rule of tradition was accepted without hypocritical pretense to superior rationality. On the one hand, Boas left Baffin Land with a profound conviction of the "relativity" of the idea of a "'cultured' individual." On the other, his scholarly interest shifted from migration routes to "the desire to understand what determines the behavior of human beings," and especially toward the problem of the "psychological origin of the implicit belief in the authority of tradition."

On his way back from Baffin Land, Boas spent the winter of 1884–85 in the United States, where he investigated job possibilities. Returning to Germany under pressure from his parents and from his mentor Fischer, Boas spent the next year working under Bastian at the Royal Ethnographic Museum in Berlin. There he waited through the long-drawn-out process of "habilitation" as privatdocent at the University of Berlin, for which he offered as thesis the geographical results of his Baffin Land researches. It was apparently here, under the influence of Bastian and Virchow, and while he was writing up the ethnographic results of his trip (*The Central Eskimo*, 1888), that Boas came finally to reject geographical determinism and to develop his characteristic

anthropological viewpoint. At the same time, he developed plans for a second trip into the field, this one to the area which was to be the focus of his anthropological interests for the rest of his life: the Indians of the Northwest Coast of Canada. Although he finally qualified as docent in physical geography in the late spring of 1886, Boas had barely given his inaugural lecture before he was off to America.

As it turned out, his departure was permanent. After a three-month stay in the Northwest, during which he made a general ethnographic reconnaissance of the area, Boas went to New York, where he accepted a position as geographical editor of *Science* magazine and, on Mar. 10, 1887, married Marie A. E. Krackowizer, an Austrian emigrant whom he had met five years before when she was on vacation in Germany. The next decade was a long and difficult struggle to establish himself professionally in a new country and in a discipline which was itself not yet firmly established, either intellectually or institutionally, and with whose dominant figures Boas found himself frequently at odds. Boas clearly saw that struggle as moving along three interrelated lines: theoretical reorientation; the development of empirical research; and the creation and control of institutional forms.

During the spring of 1887 he made two important statements of his basic scientific viewpoint. The first ("The Study of Geography," *Science*, Feb. 11, 1887) made explicit the never fully resolved epistemological tensions involved in his movement from physics to geography. Following the characteristic German distinction between the *Natur-* and the *Geisteswissenschaften,* Boas argued that there were two equally valid approaches to scientific "truth": the "physical" method, which by comparison of isolated facts sought to derive general laws; and the "historical" method, which involved an intuitive, empathetic attempt to "understand" the individual phenomenon for its own sake. In the second statement ("The Occurrence of Similar Inventions in Areas Widely Apart," *ibid.*, May 20, 1887), Boas confronted certain basic assumptions of the dominant evolutionary viewpoint in American cultural anthropology, and in effect subordinated the "physical" to the "historical" method as far as anthropology was concerned. He maintained that in order to define categories of human phenomena whose "similarity" was not the product of a priori assumption, one must transcend the viewpoint of the observer, get behind appearances, and untangle the historical complexity of the processes which affect human life. Only on this basis could comparative study lead to the formulation of true "laws" of cultural development.

Late in 1887, Boas agreed to undertake field work on the Northwest Coast under the auspices of a committee of the British Association for the Advancement of Science chaired by the leading British anthropologist E. B. Tylor and supervised in Canada by the American ethnologist Horatio Hale [*q.v.*]. During the next seven years Boas carried out five field trips. Under the broad mandate of the committee he collected data on the physical, linguistic, and cultural characteristics of a large number of Northwest Coast tribes, in the process accomplishing his "self-professionalization" in each of these major areas of anthropological inquiry. His primary focus, however, was on the Kwakiutl of Vancouver Island, and his primary interest was in the collection of accurate folktale texts which would serve as the basis for linguistic analysis and historical reconstruction. Although Boas found the relationship with Hale a difficult one, his connection with the British committee helped establish for him a position largely independent of the power structure of American anthropology, which centered in the federal Bureau of Ethnology, under John Wesley Powell [*q.v.*].

From one point of view, Boas's early career may be regarded as a series of efforts to con-solidate this independent position, while at the same time seeking to establish connections with the Bureau. In the fall of 1887 he tried unsuccessfully to organize an ethnological society in New York. Early the next year he established a lifelong tie to the Boston-based American Folklore Society (whose *Journal* he edited from 1908 to 1925). In the fall of 1889 he became a docent in anthropology at Clark University, then headed by G. Stanley Hall [*q.v.*], and there in 1892 produced the first American Ph.D. in anthropology. Boas's job at Clark ended with the financial crisis and faculty revolt of that same year. In the meantime, however, he had come in contact with Frederic Ward Putnam [*q.v.*], who was in charge of anthropology at Harvard, and who supervised the anthropological work of the World's Columbian Exposition. Boas spent the next two years as Putnam's chief assistant in Chicago, but his hopes for a permanent position there at the newly founded Field Museum were frustrated by what Boas regarded as the machinations of members of the Bureau of Ethnology. It was only after more than a year of unemployment that Boas succeeded in establishing what was to become a permanent institutional affiliation. In December 1895 he again joined Putnam as assistant curator of the department of anthropology at the American Museum of Natural History in New York, and early the following year he also accepted a position as lecturer in physical anthropology at Columbia University, where his Uncle Jacobi had for some years been exerting influence on his behalf.

From this institutional position in New York, which was strengthened in 1899 by promotion at Columbia to a full professorship, Boas embarked on an ambitious and in the long run successful attempt to redefine in his own terms the profession of anthropology in this country. His researches on the distribution of folklore elements, employing a quasi-statistical method derived in 1888 from E. B. Tylor, had eventuated by 1896 in a fully elaborated critique of the comparative method of anthropology (*Science,* Dec. 18, 1896; cf. *Indianische Sagen von der Nord-Pacifischen Küste Amerikas,* 1895). In addition to his reports for the British Association for the Advancement of Science, his field work had produced *The Social Organization and the Secret Societies of the Kwakiutl Indians* (1897), the first of a long series of ethnographic volumes on that tribe (which was supplemented by the work of George Hunt, a half-breed whom Boas trained and supervised as ethnographer). In 1897, with the financial support of Morris K. Jesup [*q.v.*], president of the American Museum of Natural History, Boas conceived and directed a long-run program of field research to investigate the historical relations of the aboriginal tribes of Northwestern America and the Asian continent (*Publications of the Jesup North Pacific Expedition,* 1898–1930). Simultaneously, his relations with the Bureau of Ethnology entered their best period, and he in effect assumed charge of the Bureau's linguistic research—a role which in 1901 was formalized by his appointment as honorary philologist. The same year saw the first of a long series of Ph.D.'s to emerge from his seminars at Columbia, as well as his promotion to a full curatorship at the American Museum. As Boas noted in a letter that May, all these activities were part of a master plan for the development of a professional anthropology based on the cooperation of museum and university in training researchers, and of philanthropy and government in a global program of research. To achieve this goal, Boas felt it was important that he retain "a certain amount of control" over the profession, even if the burden of administrative work made it difficult for him to pursue his own scientific research.

Boas was in fact to face several important setbacks over the next few years. After revitalizing the American Ethnological Society of New York and figuring prominently in the reorganization of the *American Anthropologist* in 1898, he played a major role in the founding of the American Anthropological Association in 1902. However, his attempt to limit its membership to a small group of professionals was defeated by the Washington anthropologists. The same year, a change in personnel and a general financial retrenchment in the Bureau of Ethnology considerably curtailed his effective control of anthropological research, under circumstances which in 1909 eventuated in an acrimonious dispute with the secretary of the Smithsonian Institution and the failure to offer Boas the then vacant position of chief of the Bureau. In 1905 Boas resigned from the American Museum of Natural History in a bitter dispute over what he regarded as the subordination of the Museum's research to public entertainment. But if these years were a period of retrenchment in his broader goals for American anthropology, they were also a period of intense scientific activity, which reached fruition in 1911 in the publication of three works which epitomized his contribution to each of the major areas of his anthropological interest.

The first of these was the initial volume of the *Handbook of American Indian Languages,* a decade-long cooperative effort which dragged along to completion after the Bureau cutback. Most of the contributors were Boas-trained, and all accepted the plan of analysis whose assumptions he elaborated in a lengthy introduction and embodied in his own contributions. Briefly, Boas's approach to language was based on the assumption that grammatical categories were unconscious classifications of an infinitely varied human experience which were historically conditioned and specific to each language. One could not analyze the Eskimo tongue in terms of traditional Indo-European categories: one must seek rather to present its "essential traits" as they would "naturally develop if an Eskimo, without any knowledge of any other language, should present the essential notions of his own grammar." Similarly, one could not place existing languages in any implicitly evaluative evolutionary framework. Every language was the product of a particular cultural experience and fully adequate to the needs thereof. It was this systematically relativistic viewpoint which was to serve as charter for the subsequent development of descriptive linguistics in this country—to which Boas was to contribute greatly as founder and editor of the *International Journal of American Linguistics* from 1917 to 1939.

The same relativistic critical stance toward the formal categories of traditional scholarship is evident in Boas's second major work of 1911, his report for the United States Immigration Commission on *Changes in Bodily Form of Descen-dants of Immigrants.* Using biometric techniques influenced by the work of Sir Francis Galton, Boas had from the early 1890's carried on a series of investigations which emphasized the interaction of environment and heredity in the growth process (e.g., *Statistics of Growth,* 1905). Building on these, the study he undertook in 1907 of 18,000 immigrants showed that the head forms of children born in the United States differed significantly from those of their parents. Boas thus challenged the dominant tradition in physical anthropology, which based its differentiation of human races on the assumption that head form was relatively impervious to environmental influences. Similarly, where other scholars tended to subsume the considerable variation of observed measurements into statically conceived "types," Boas emphasized the overlapping nature of all distributions of physical measurements, and thus the arbitrary character of many traditional racial distinctions.

The third and most important work of 1911 was *The Mind of Primitive Man* (2nd ed., 1938), which drew on various writings of the previous seventeen years to confront the widely current stereotype of the mentally inferior and dark-skinned savage. Although it was offered in the form of a critique of prevailing assumptions about the correlation of racial mental ability and cultural achievement, this volume was in fact a charter for the modern notion of the cultural determination of behavior, and for the modern anthropological concept of culture—which, in contrast to the humanistic notion of the "cultured man," or the evolutionary conception of the "stages" of a single human culture, is characteristically pluralistic and relativistic.

Boas was to make a total of eight more trips to the field (the last at the age of seventy-two), and almost every year until his death saw the publication of one or more pieces of scholarly work (e.g., *Tsimshian Mythology,* 1916; *Ethnology of the Kwakiutl,* 1921; *Primitive Art,* 1927; *The Religion of the Kwakiutl,* 1930; *General Anthropology,* 1938). However, the last thirty years of his life are best viewed in terms of his institutional and pedagogical activities, his public role as advocate of the anthropological viewpoint, and a series of political issues relating to his own somewhat ambiguous cultural identity (although he had become an American citizen in 1891, he remained in a deep sense culturally German and made more than a dozen trips back after his emigration).

In each of these respects the second decade of the century was one of considerable pain and frustration. Between 1910 and 1912 Boas was in

Mexico at the short-lived International School of American Archeology and Ethnology, which he had helped to found, and at which he did his only important archeological work. In 1914 surgical removal of a cancer left one side of his face permanently paralyzed. The outbreak of war that year was even more profoundly painful for him, and he was outspoken in his opposition to American entry. Indeed, he felt so strongly on the matter that for a brief period he joined the Socialist party, despite the fact that his political views were basically liberal rather than radical (he voted for McKinley in 1896, Hughes in 1916, La Follette in 1924, Roosevelt in 1940). In 1919 he publicly accused four unnamed anthropologists of prostituting their scientific integrity by spying for the United States government in Mexico. As a result, the dominance which he and his students had fought to maintain in the American Anthropological Association since 1911 was momentarily broken, and Boas, who had been president from 1907 to 1909, was censured and almost expelled. Within a few years, however, the weight of his pedagogical influence had reasserted itself, and for the next two decades or more, Boas and his students dominated American anthropology both institutionally and intellectually.

To mobilize support for the rebuilding of German intellectual life after the war, Boas was extremely active from 1920 to 1928 in the Emergency Society for German and Austrian Science and Art. With the rise of Nazism, however, his relationship to Germany underwent a further evolution, and the last decade of his life was a period of intense scientific and political activity in the struggle against racism and for intellectual liberty, both in Germany and the United States. From about 1900, Boas had devoted an ever-increasing portion of his energy to an attempt to modify public attitudes on issues of race (e.g., "The Negro and the Demands of Modern Life," *Charities*, Oct. 7, 1905; *Anthropology and Modern Life*, 1928). From the mid-1920's, he was instrumental in stimulating a wide range of research in this area by his students and others. After 1933 the pace of these activities heightened, despite his age and recurrent illness (he had suffered a serious heart ailment in 1931). Working first through the American Jewish Committee and later as chairman of the American Committee for Democracy and Intellectual Freedom, he planned and supervised research, wrote pamphlets, and organized statements and petitions of scientists attacking racism and intolerance. These activities continued without letup for six years after his retirement to an emeritus professorship in 1936. Indeed, his sudden death (of coronary heart disease) in the middle of his eighty-fifth year came as he was offering after-luncheon remarks to colleagues at the Columbia Faculty Club on the problem of racism.

Boas was survived by only three of his six children—Helene Marie, Ernst Philip, and (Marie) Franziska. Hedwig had died in infancy, and in the 1920's Gertrud had died of polio and Heinrich in a railway accident; Mrs. Boas had died in 1929 when struck by an automobile. The honors that came to Boas are too numerous to list. President of the International Congress of Americanists in 1928 and of the American Association for the Advancement of Science in 1931, he was a member of all the national honor societies in science, as well as honorary or corresponding member of at least twenty-five foreign scientific societies.

Physically, Boas was not a large man. But his wiry body and aquiline head embodied a powerful intellect and a spartan character, which were impelled to intense activity by the "ice-cold flame of the passion for seeking the truth for truth's sake." His critical faculties were as unsparing as his rather stern friendship was unswerving, although he softened a bit in relation to the women students who called him "Papa Franz." If some of his male students experienced episodes of alienation from him, and some of his students were at times confused by his unaccommodating teaching methods, yet there is no denying that his influence on them was great. Indeed, the general course of American anthropology until after 1940 may be seen as the working out of various aspects of Boas's own thinking. Until about 1920 the major preoccupation was the critique of evolutionism; the 1920's saw the dominance of diffusionary studies of culture areas; the 1930's, of studies of acculturation, culture patterns, and of culture and personality—all of which may be interpreted as deriving directly from Boas.

In the 1950's and 1960's, Boas came under sharp criticism from anthropologists who were concerned with the systematic study of social structure, or who turned once again to the study of the evolution of human culture in a deterministic framework. More generally, there was a widespread feeling that his anthropological contribution was negative rather than constructive, and there is no doubt that, as he conceived them, the methods of history and of science tended to be mutually inhibitive and to discourage generalization. But if Boas was not a system builder, his positive contribution was not limited to his "five-foot shelf" of data on the Kwakiutl. It went beyond his role in training several generations of anthropologists, or in the establishment of institutions and of professional standards. For implicit in his critique of nineteenth-century evolutionary assumptions was a different paradigm for the study of man, one which saw all human differences as the product of the varied cultures in which men were born and reared. From the late 1920's on, this orientation was fundamental to all of American social science, and in the third quarter of the twentieth century it was part of the intellectual baggage of a large proportion of educated Americans.

[The basic source is the Boas Papers in the Am. Philosophical Soc., Philadelphia, which consists of over 60,000 items. Diaries and a number of letters relating to his field work on the Northwest Coast were compiled by Ronald Rohner as *The Ethnography of Franz Boas* (1969), which also reproduces a number of photographs. Other letters are included in Margaret Mead, *An Anthropologist at Work* (1959). Boas published a selection of his scientific papers as *Race, Language and Culture* (1940); a selection of his public essays and addresses was published posthumously as *Race and Democratic Society* (1945). Biographical sources include the essays in two *Memoirs* of the Am. Anthropological Assoc.: no. 61 (1943), which contains a complete bibliography, and no. 89 (1959), edited by Walter Goldschmidt and entitled *The Anthropology of Franz Boas*; the memorial number of the *Jour. of Am. Folklore*, Jan. 1944; and Robert H. Lowie's memoir in Nat. Acad. Sci., *Biog. Memoirs*, vol. XXIV (1947). See also Melville Herskovits, *Franz Boas* (1953); George W. Stocking, Jr., *Race, Culture and Evolution* (1968); and, for a critical view, Marvin Harris, *The Rise of Anthropological Theory* (1968).]

GEORGE W. STOCKING, JR.

BOLZA, OSKAR (May 12, 1857–July 5, 1942), mathematician, was born in Bergzabern in the Palatinate of the Rhine, the oldest of four children of Moritz and Luise (Koenig) Bolza. His maternal grandfather was Friedrich Koenig, whose fortune derived from the development and manufacture of a rapid printing press. His father was in the judicial service, and during Bolza's early life the family moved from place to place in southern Germany until 1873, when they settled at Freiburg im Breisgau. It was hoped that Bolza would enter the family printing press factory, and to this end he studied for a time at a Gewerbeakademie while enrolled at the University of Berlin. His scholarly bent, however, won out. At first interested in languages and comparative philology, he was soon drawn to science. He initially tried physics, but experimental work did not attract him and in 1878 he decided to concentrate on mathematics.

Bolza spent the years 1878–81 in mathematical study under Elwin B. Christoffel and Theodor Reye at Strassburg, Hermann A. Schwarz at Göttingen, and particularly Karl Weierstrass at the University of Berlin. Undoubtedly, the fact that he was a student in the famous 1879 course of Weierstrass on the calculus of variations exerted a strong influence on the formation of

Bolza's mathematical interests, although some twenty years elapsed before he began active research in this field, for which he was to gain world renown. After preparing for and passing the Staatsexamen and completing a year of practical teaching in the Gymnasium at Freiburg, Bolza in 1883 returned to mathematical study and undertook a doctoral dissertation on the determination of hyperelliptic integrals which are reducible to elliptic integrals by a transformation of the third degree. He obtained a solution to his problem in 1885, but was anticipated by a more elegant one published by Edouard Goursat in the *Comptes Rendus*. Bolsa then turned to the corresponding problem for transformations of the fourth degree. His solution, and subsequent development of the work, formed the basis for his doctoral dissertation, under Felix Klein, and he received his degree from the University of Göttingen in June 1886.

As a student in Berlin, Bolza had made two intimate friends, the mathematician Heinrich Maschke [*q.v.*] and the physicist Franz Schulze-Berge. Schulze-Berge migrated to the United States in 1887, and his experience stimulated Bolza to follow a year later. Bolza secured a post as reader in mathematics at Johns Hopkins University in January 1889, and in October was appointed associate in mathematics at Clark University. In 1892 he was invited to join the faculty of the newly established University of Chicago, where he began teaching in January 1893. He persuaded Eliakim H. Moore [Supp. 1], the head of the department of mathematics, to secure an appointment for his friend Maschke as well. The three—Moore, Bolza, and Maschke—provided great strength for the department, and the Chicago graduate school of mathematics became at once one of the leaders in this country.

In the years following, Bolza took an active part in the International Mathematical Congress held at the Chicago World's Fair of 1893, in the colloquium lectures given afterward by Klein at Northwestern University, and in the transformation (1894) of the New York Mathematical Society into the American Mathematical Society, which he served as vice-president in 1903–04. At its third colloquium, in Ithaca in August 1901, he presented a series of lectures on the calculus of variations which were published in book form in 1904. Thereafter Bolza's primary mathematical interests centered in this subject. In 1908–09 he published a much enlarged treatise, *Vorlesungen über Variationsrechnung*, which sixty years later remained a classic in its field. During his years at Chicago nine students wrote doctoral dissertations under Bolza's guidance: three in the area of hyperelliptic integrals, one on singularities of algebraic curves, and five on variational theory. Of the last group, one was Gilbert A. Bliss (1900), who was a member of the mathematics faculty of the University of Chicago from 1908 to 1941, and who deserves major credit for the continuation of a strong school in the calculus of variations.

Through the years Bolza made many trips back to Freiburg, where his mother continued to live after the death of his father in 1891. There, on Dec. 27, 1898, he married an old acquaintance, Anna Neckel; they had no children. Maschke died in 1908, and two years later Bolza decided to return to Freiburg; before he left, the University of Chicago conferred on him the title of "Nonresident Professor of Mathematics," which he held until his death. For several years Bolza continued his mathematical lectures and research, as an honorary professor at the University of Freiburg. He returned to the United States for the last time in 1913 and lectured during the summer at the University of Chicago on function theory and integral equations. One of his students, William V. Lovitt, later published, with Bolza's permission, the notes he had taken on these lectures as *Linear Integral Equations* (1924).

The First World War put an end to Bolza's mathematical research. He continued to lecture until 1926, and again from 1929 to 1933, but from 1917 onward his principal interests were religious psychology and languages, particularly Sanskrit. In 1930 he published *Glaubenslose Religion* ("Religion without Belief"), under the pseudonym F. N. Marneck, and in 1938 a short monograph, *Meister Eckehart als Mystiker,* a study of a fourteenth-century German Dominican friar and mystic. The death of his wife in 1941 was a severe blow, and after a year of progressively failing health, Bolza died in Freiburg at the age of eighty-five.

Of Bolza's many contributions to the calculus of variations, two papers published in 1913 and 1914 have had material influence on the later development of the subject. In these he formulated a new and very general variational problem, now known as "the problem of Bolza," which included as special instances most of the simple integral problems that had been studied previously. The second paper in particular has direct significance for modern mathematical control theory, as it gives the earliest comprehensive treatment of the first variation for a simple integral problem involving inequality restraints, in nature either point restraints or differential inequalities.

[Bolza's autobiography, *Aus Meinem Leben* (privately printed, 1936); memoirs by Gilbert A. Bliss in Am. Mathematical Soc., *Bull.,* July 1944, and by Lothar Heffter in *Jahresbericht der Deutschen Mathematiker Vereinigung,* LIII (1943), 1–13—detailed discussions of Bolza's mathematical contributions, each with a bibliography (the Heffter article also includes a small picture of Bolza). See also obituary by Bliss in *Science,* Jan. 29, 1943; David E. Smith and Jekuthiel Ginsburg, *A Hist. of Mathematics in America before 1900* (1934); *Wer Ist's,* 1909 and later editions.]

W. T. REID

BORGLUM, JOHN GUTZON DE LA MOTHE (Mar. 25, 1867–Mar. 6, 1941), painter and sculptor, known as Gutzon Borglum, was born near Bear Lake, Idaho Territory, the first child of Cristine (Michelson) and James de la Mothe Borglum. His parents were Mormon converts who had come to the United States from Denmark in the early 1860's and had gone west with a wagon train. The elder Borglum worked for a time as a wood-carver, although before leaving Denmark he had nearly completed medical studies. The family moved in 1868 to Ogden, Utah, where a second son, Solon Hannibal Borglum [*q.v.*], was born. Mrs. Borglum apparently died or left the family, and James Borglum married her sister, Ida Michelson, by whom he had four more boys and three girls. In 1874 he moved on with his family to St. Louis, Mo., where he received an M.D. degree from the St. Louis Homeopathic Medical College; he then established a practice, first in Fremont, Nebr., and later in Omaha. Having left the Mormon Church, for a time he embraced Catholicism.

Gutzon finished primary school in Fremont and was then sent to St. Mary's College, a Jesuit boarding school in Xavier, Kans., where he completed his high school studies. His instructors were impressed with his talent for drawing but encouraged him to portray religious scenes rather than the subjects he found more congenial—cowboys, Indians, and horses. A classmate also awakened his interest in Italian painting and sculpture, and he determined to become an artist. After leaving St. Mary's, Borglum moved with his family to California in 1884. He apprenticed himself for six months to a Los Angeles engraver and lithographer, tried his hand at fresco painting, and then studied under Virgil Williams of the San Francisco Art Association. In San Francisco he also met William Keith [*q.v.*], known as the "Grand Old Man of California painting," whose landscapes fixed in Borglum an abiding inclination toward the dramatic and romantic in art.

During his early days in California, Borglum, working chiefly at painting, received the patronage of Jessie Benton Frémont, whose husband,

Gen. John C. Frémont [*qq.v.*], sat to him for a portrait in 1888, and who sent many visitors to his studio. In 1889 Borglum married Mrs. Elizabeth Putnam, an art teacher some twenty years his senior. When he determined to go to France for further study, Mrs. Frémont helped arrange for an exhibition of his paintings in Omaha, the sales from which provided the necessary funds. Borglum arrived in Paris in 1890. During his year there he studied at the Académie Julian and at the École des Beaux-Arts and formed a lasting friendship with Auguste Rodin, whom he came to venerate as one of the world's great sculptors. At the Paris Salon in 1891 Borglum exhibited a painting of a mare and new-born colt threatened by wolves, and the New Salon that year accepted one of his sculptures, "Death of the Chief," a bronze representing a horse with head bent over the body of its dead Indian master, which won him membership in the Société Nationale des Beaux-Arts.

The Borglums then went to Spain, where Gutzon spent more than a year in sketching and painting and, with the aid of introductions from Mrs. Frémont, delved into the early history of California and its Franciscan missions in the Spanish archives. On returning to California in 1893, he joined in the efforts of Charles F. Lummis [*q.v.*] for the preservation of the missions, and engaged in his first public controversy, opposing advocates of modern restoration of the ruined buildings.

In the next three years Borglum lived and worked in Sierra Madre, Calif., joined by his brother Solon, who had developed a strong interest in sculpting. Gutzon departed for England in 1896, believing that conditions there were more favorable for an artist. His paintings were exhibited at Buckingham Palace, and he was admitted to the Royal Society of British Artists, but popular recognition was slow. A commission to execute murals at the Queen's Hotel in Leeds was his first considerable success, and he gained some reputation for his portraits and busts, especially of children. During these years Borglum and his wife lived apart much of the time, increasingly alienated by the difference in their ages and by his lavish style of living and indifference to debt; Mrs. Borglum consented to a divorce in 1908.

Borglum returned to the United States in 1901 and established a studio in New York City. Thereafter he virtually abandoned painting for sculpture. For the St. Louis Exposition in 1904 he prepared the "Mares of Diomedes," a half-circle of seven stampeding wild horses, the leader ridden by an outlaw or Indian clinging to

his mount. The group won a gold medal and was purchased by a wealthy benefactor for the Metropolitan Museum of Art in New York. He also exhibited at St. Louis a strongly modeled statuette of John Ruskin. In 1905 Borglum was commissioned to make figures of angels and of the Twelve Apostles for the Cathedral of St. John the Divine in New York. Other important works of this period were the large marble head of Lincoln that in 1908 came to rest in the rotunda of the Capitol in Washington, the impressive equestrian bronze of Gen. Philip Sheridan [*q.v.*], set up in Sheridan Circle in Washington (1908), and the seated Lincoln in Newark, N. J. (1910). On May 19, 1909, he married Mary Williams Montgomery of New York City, a Wellesley graduate with a Ph.D. from the University of Berlin, whom he had met on shipboard in 1901. They settled on a country estate which Borglum purchased near Stamford, Conn., and named "Borgland." A son born in 1910 did not survive, but the couple had two other children, James Lincoln de la Mothe and Mary Ellis.

By 1915 Borglum's reputation as a sculptor was firmly established. In that year a group of Southerners invited him to carve a large head of Gen. Robert E. Lee [*q.v.*] at the base of Stone Mountain, an enormous granite dome a few miles northeast of Atlanta, Ga. After studying the site, he proposed instead a colossal Confederate memorial: a carved procession of riding and marching Confederate soldiers, extending a quarter of a mile across the sheer face of the mountain, grouped around the central figures of Lee, Jefferson Davis, and Stonewall Jackson [*qq.v.*] on horseback. Actual work on cutting the stone began in 1916 and required Borglum to devise new techniques to solve the difficult engineering problems, but after long interruptions, notably that occasioned by World War I, the first finished part, the twenty-foot-high head of Lee, was unveiled in January 1924. Shortly thereafter serious disagreements developed between the sculptor and the association organized to finance the memorial. Borglum was accused of spending money carelessly and giving too much time to other projects, while he in turn accused the committee of mismanagement of the funds and unwarranted interference with the execution of the memorial. He was discharged in February 1925, immediately destroyed his models to prevent their being used by a successor, and was then forced to flee the state to avoid arrest on a charge of malicious mischief. Though he hoped for some years to return to the project and carry out his original design, no satisfactory arrangement was ever worked out. Eventually the head of Lee was blasted away to accommodate the plans of another sculptor.

The Stone Mountain project had brought Borglum fame as a hewer of mountains, and in 1924 the state historian of South Dakota, Doane Robinson, invited him to visit the Black Hills to consider initiating a similar venture there. After a thorough investigation of the terrain, Borglum selected the granite face of Mount Rushmore as the site of what he conceived as a "shrine of democracy." As in Georgia, the problem of financing such an undertaking was perplexing, and there were several setbacks until Congress was prevailed upon in 1929 to authorize funds. Actual work at the mountain began in 1927, and the shrine remained Borglum's chief preoccupation for the rest of his life. Using dynamite as a method of gross stone removal and the engineering devices he had employed at Stone Mountain, he began the carving with the help of a large crew of workmen; the head of George Washington, sixty feet high and visible for a distance of more than sixty miles, was unveiled in an elaborate ceremony on July 4, 1930. During the next decade Borglum continued work on the busts of Jefferson, Lincoln, and Theodore Roosevelt, his favorite heroes, but progress was marred by continual conflicts between Borglum and the National Park Service, which had been given jurisdiction over Mount Rushmore. Domineering and wholly dedicated to executing his design, Borglum resented regulations that he regarded as interference with his art, while the Park Service found him uncooperative and impractical about money. Nevertheless, the work continued, and before his death he managed to bring all the figures to virtual completion.

Borglum's other important sculpture includes: the John W. Mackay statue (1906) at the University of Nevada; the Altgeld Memorial (1915) and a Sheridan statue (1924) in Chicago; the Trudeau Memorial (1917) at Saranac Lake, N. Y.; the Aycock Memorial (1924) in Raleigh, N. C.; the Wars of America Memorial at Newark, N. J. (1927); the North Carolina War Memorial (1929) on the battlefield of Gettysburg; the William Jennings Bryan Memorial in Rock Creek Cemetery, Washington, D. C. (1932, later sent on loan to the town of Salem, Ill., Bryan's birthplace); the statue of Thomas Paine (1937) in Paris; the Woodrow Wilson Memorial (1939) in Poznan, Poland (destroyed by the Nazis during World War II); and the Trail Drivers Memorial (1940) in San Antonio, Texas, where Borglum maintained a studio for a number of years after 1925.

In appearance Borglum was short and bald, with dark eyes, broad shoulders, and a bristling moustache. His speech was rapid and intense. A man of strong opinions, combative and outspoken, he made good newspaper copy and welcomed publicity; he became much more of a public figure than most artists. As a citizen he was deeply patriotic and believed it his duty to involve himself in any question relating to the public welfare. In Connecticut he took an active part in local affairs; he organized a bus company to improve transportation for farm people around Stamford and served for two years in the state legislature. He campaigned for Theodore Roosevelt and the Progressive party in 1912 and 1916, but afterward, disillusioned, returned to the Republican fold and to a more or less conservative political philosophy.

Aviation was one of Borglum's strong interests. He belonged to the Aero Club of America and was a friend of Samuel P. Langley [q.v.], who had narrowly missed receiving credit as the inventor of the airplane; Borglum himself tried his hand at designing a plane and a new type of propeller. During World War I he became concerned by the slow production of aircraft and, with President Wilson's permission, undertook an unofficial investigation of the industry at his own expense, finding what he believed to be evidence that many builders were inefficient, corrupt, and profiteering. When his report was ignored by government authorities he took his case to the newspapers, an action that led to a break with Wilson.

Always an enthusiastic joiner, Borglum was a 32nd degree Mason and a member of the Salmagundi Club of New York, the Architectural League of New York, and the Association of American Painters and Sculptors. Through the New York Parks Association he sought to keep the city parks free from exploitation. A vigorous participant in sports, he served on the New York Boxing Commission and was president of the International Sporting Club in 1921.

Early in March 1941, Borglum entered a Chicago hospital for a minor operation, and died there of a coronary occlusion a few days before his seventy-fourth birthday. He was buried at Forest Lawn Memorial Park, Glendale, Calif. His son Lincoln, who had served as his assistant for several years, finished the work at Mount Rushmore a few months later.

[The Lib. of Cong. has a collection of Borglum's papers; other materials are in family hands. There are two biographies: Robert J. Casey and Mary Borglum, *Give the Man Room: The Story of Gutzon Borglum* (1952), and the more carefully researched Willadene Price, *Gutzon Borglum: Artist and Patriot* (1961). Gerald W. Johnson, *The Undefeated* (1927), tells the story of the Stone Mountain fiasco. The story of Mount Rushmore is reconstructed in Robert J. Dean, *Living Granite: The Story of Borglum and the Mount Rushmore Memorial* (1949), and Gilbert C. Fite, *Mount Rushmore* (1952), the latter a highly meticulous and detailed account with a comprehensive bibliography. Certain family details were supplied by Lincoln Borglum, including a confirmation of the correct name of the mother of Gutzon and Solon Borglum (incorrectly given in the *DAB* article on Solon Borglum and in Gutzon's later *Who's Who* entries). Death record from Ill. Dept. of Public Health.]

THURMAN WILKINS

BOSTWICK, ARTHUR ELMORE (Mar. 8, 1860–Feb. 13, 1942), librarian, was born in Litchfield, Conn., to David Elmore Bostwick, a physician, and Adelaide (McKinley) Bostwick. He was apparently an only child. His father, a direct descendant of Arthur Bosticke, who emigrated from England before 1639 and settled in Stratford, Conn., died when Arthur was twelve years old. His mother, determined that the boy should not want for a full education, supplemented her means by taking in lodgers, renting her house in summer, playing the organ in a local church, and teaching music. Having attended Litchfield Institute, Arthur went on to Yale. He earned a B.A. (1881), while finding time in his senior year to be an editor of the *Yale Daily News,* organist of the Berkeley Association, and Class Day historian.

Bostwick came to library work only after careers in science and publishing. Following his graduation he stayed on at Yale to take a Ph.D. in physics (1883), studying in part under the younger Josiah Willard Gibbs [*q.v.*]. Disappointed in his hope for a permanent appointment at Yale, and having received several noncollege offers, he chose an instructorship in physical science at the Montclair (N. J.) high school. After two years (1884–86), fully convinced that teaching "a lot of kids" (Bostwick, p. 95) was not for him, Bostwick embarked on editorial work, at double his Montclair salary, by joining the staff of *Appletons' Cyclopaedia of American Biography,* with which he remained until 1888. Literary work for Henry Holt & Company followed, mainly the *Young Folks' Cyclopedia of Games and Sports* (1890), most of which he wrote himself, although his cousin John D. Champlin [*q.v.*] was joint author. Successively Bostwick became assistant editor of *Forum* magazine (1890–92); associate editor (1892–94) of *A Standard Dictionary of the English Language,* undertaken by Isaac K. Funk [*q.v.*] and Adam W. Wagnalls upon the expiration of the copyright of Webster's classic; and scientific editor of the Funk-founded *Literary Digest,* a position he was to occupy for more than forty years (1891–1933).

In 1895 he entered the world of librarianship, beginning at the top as librarian of the New York Free Circulating Library, which boasted William W. Appleton [*q.v.*], the publisher, as a founder and chairman of the library committee. Untried in the field, Bostwick quickly displayed an administrative talent which complemented that love of books he was always to consider an important qualification for library service. Although a scholar, he did not share the general view of many men of the time, like John Shaw Billings [*q.v.*], that libraries were primarily for reference use. He saw them as instruments of popular education. Under his direction the widely scattered branch libraries, in which he instituted an open-shelf policy, developed impressively. In 1899 he accepted the librarianship of the Brooklyn Public Library, recently taken over by the city. He successfully promoted the branch system with open shelves as well as a traveling library, started a children's collection, launched an apprenticeship program, and boosted annual book circulation from about 183,500 to more than a million. But struggles with civil service red tape made him happy to rid himself of "the Brooklyn incubus" (*ibid.,* p. 181) by returning on Feb. 1, 1901, to his former position with the Free Circulating Library, which was about to be merged with the Astor and Lenox libraries to create the New York Public Library.

As chief of the circulation department of the new library, whose expansion was aided by a $5,200,000 gift for library buildings from Andrew Carnegie [*q.v.*], Bostwick supervised the opening of as many as ten new branches at one time, began children's rooms and a training class, initiated cooperation with the public schools, and provided foreign language books for the swelling immigrant population, whose reading needs he met with rare understanding. By 1909 he was overseeing the largest circulation library in the world, with forty-one branches and an annual circulation of more than 6,500,000 volumes. Tall, stately, and reserved (he looked, Keith Kerman later reported, "as if he would send in a riot call if anyone presumed to slap him on the back"), Bostwick carried himself with an undeniable air of authority. His professional stature was further increased by his election as president of the American Library Association (1907–08) and by the appearance of his first book, which William Appleton suggested he undertake in 1908: *The American Public Library* (1910). A unique general treatise that combined a history of the subject with procedures for librarians, it went through four editions by 1929.

In 1909, weary of constant trials with Billings,

the New York Public Library's director, who was out of sympathy with the circulation department, Bostwick accepted an offer to head the St. Louis Public Library. With his fine administrative and organizational ability, his flair for experiment, his liberal views (he refused to stop the circulation of German books during World War I), and his experienced community-mindedness, he made it a leading educational institution of the city while raising its rank among national libraries. Upon his retirement in 1938 the trustees, in reviewing his achievements, cited among other facts the growth of branches from four to nineteen and of annual circulation from about one million to more than three million volumes. "A transplanted Easterner," as he himself phrased it, Bostwick so came to love St. Louis that he made it his permanent home.

During his years as a practicing librarian, Bostwick poured forth a stream of lucid articles on literature, library economy, and the sciences, physical, political, and social. He also edited series such as the Classics of American Librarianship (10 vols., 1914–33) and *Doubleday's Encyclopedia* (10 vols., 1931–41), delivered lectures, advised on library problems, and preserved a sense of humor. He served actively in several societies like the League of Nations Non-Partisan Association. Bostwick was widely respected for the broad range of his learning—he read French, German, Italian, and Spanish—as well as for the wisdom and sense of proportion he brought to the subjects he essayed. In 1925, invited by the Chinese Association for the Advancement of Education, he visited China to inspect her libraries and recommended the use of part of the Boxer indemnity payment for the improvement and extension of China's public libraries. Fond of music, travel, and parties, he indulged in bedtime reading of detective stories and was one of the first Perry Mason fans. He was an Episcopalian in religion and a Republican in politics. Bostwick died in his eighty-second year of a heart ailment (auricular fibrillation) in Oak Grove, Mo.; his ashes were buried in New East Cemetery, Litchfield, Conn. On June 23, 1885, at Carmel, N. Y., he had married Lucy Sawyer, who died in 1930. Of their three children—Andrew Linn, Esther, and Elmore McNeill—only the last survived him.

[A few Bostwick letters, chiefly to Richard Rogers Bowker, are in the Manuscript Division of the N. Y. Public Lib. A bibliography of his writings by J. A. Boromé is in the *Bull. of Bibliog.*, Jan.–Apr. 1944. Bostwick's autobiography, *A Life with Men and Books* (1939), is of interest. See also obituaries in *N. Y. Times* and *N. Y. Herald Tribune*, Feb. 14, 1942; *Who Was Who in America*, vol. II (1950); Yale Univ., *Obituary Record of Graduates*, 1941–42; Margery Doud's essay in Emily M. Danton, ed., *Pioneering

Leaders in Librarianship* (1953), and her fuller "Recollections" in *Wilson Lib. Bull.*, June 1953, reprinted in John D. Marshall, ed., *Am. Lib. Hist. Reader* (1961); *Nat. Cyc. Am. Biog.*, XIV, 339; James I. Wyer in *Lib. Jour.*, Mar. 1, 1942; Anne Carroll Moore in *Am. Lib. Assoc. Bull.*, Mar. 1942; Brooklyn Public Lib., *Annual Reports*, 1899–1901; St. Louis Public Lib., *Annual Report*, 1937–38; *Resolution of the Board of Directors of the St. Louis Public Lib., Mar. 6, 1942* (1942); Keith Kerman, "Interesting St. Louisans," *St. Louis Post-Dispatch*, May 25, 1930; Charles H. Compton, *Twenty-Five Crucial Years of the St. Louis Public Lib.* (1953). A portrait from a photograph taken about 1900 is in Harry M. Lydenberg, *Hist. of the N. Y. Public Lib.* (1923), and a photograph taken in 1938 serves as the frontispiece to Bostwick's autobiography.]

JOSEPH A. BOROME

BOVARD, OLIVER KIRBY (May 27, 1872–Nov. 3, 1945), newspaper editor, was born in or near Jacksonville, Ill., the first of two sons and second among five surviving children of Charles Wyrick Bovard and Hester (Bunn) Bovard. His mother was descended from English-Irish Presbyterians; his father's forebears, of French Huguenot ancestry, had come from Northern Ireland to Hannastown, Pa., before 1783. A printer and a native of East Liverpool, Ohio, Charles Bovard lived in a succession of central Illinois towns before settling in St. Louis by 1880. There he worked on several newspapers, among them the *Post-Dispatch*—owned by Joseph Pulitzer [q.v.]—of which he became telegraph editor in 1891.

Young Bovard left public school at fourteen and worked as a clerk in a number of St. Louis offices, including that of the *Post-Dispatch;* but he disliked clerking and determined to become a newspaperman. His interest in the currently popular sport of bicycling led to a job on the *St. Louis Star* in 1896 as general reporter and bicycle editor. Two years later, when the *Star* failed to print his disclosure of bribery in connection with a street railway franchise, Bovard took it to the *Post-Dispatch*, which published it and hired the young reporter.

Rising rapidly, Bovard became city editor in 1900. He quickly improved the quality of local reporting, initiated crusades against traction and utility frauds, and supported the efforts of such city reformers as Joseph W. Folk [q.v.]. A courageous and hardworking editor, Bovard in later years could seem aloof, imperious, and even severely abrupt, but his newsgathering abilities were always highly regarded. In 1908 he became acting managing editor, and the following year he was summoned by Pulitzer to work on the New York *World*. After ten months, however, he gave up a chance to become assistant managing editor of the *World* and chose to return to the *Post-Dispatch* as permanent managing editor.

A believer in the "one-man" school of journalism, Bovard consolidated his control over all news departments. He broadened national and international news coverage and, distrusting the wire services, established his own Washington bureau in 1918. That year his insistence on accuracy gave him what he regarded as his proudest moment in journalism: his refusal to print the false first report of the World War I armistice because his analysis of other news dispatches made him doubt its veracity. During the 1920's Bovard developed and stood behind a brilliant team of reporters, including Raymond P. Brandt, Richard L. Stokes, and four future Pulitzer Prize winners: Charles G. Ross, Marquis W. Childs, John T. Rogers, and Paul Y. Anderson [Supp. 2]. These avid correspondents dug into the Teapot Dome oil leases, solved notable local crimes, revealed illegal associations between utility executives and public officials, exposed voting corruption, and even helped unseat a federal judge, George W. English, in Illinois. Bovard worked closely with two successive editors of the *Post-Dispatch*'s editorial page, George Sibley Johns (1857–1941) and Clark McAdams [Supp. 1], on the Sacco-Vanzetti and other important cases.

After the onset of the Great Depression, Bovard had his staff probe its causes and consider possible remedies. He looked to Franklin D. Roosevelt in 1932 to restore the nation's economic health, but as the New Deal progressed, Bovard came to believe that it did not go far enough. The chief problem of American society, he concluded, was the unequal distribution of wealth. To remedy this, he advocated a reduction of the tariff and public ownership of natural resources, banks, public utilities, and railroads, even though this might require amending the Constitution. Rejecting Communism as authoritarian, he sought a middle ground, similar to the Swedish system, between capitalism and pure socialism and urged that the press educate the people to the value of such a system.

Bovard's philosophy brought him into conflict with Joseph Pulitzer, Jr. (1885–1955), who as editor and publisher increased his direction of the *Post-Dispatch* in the 1930's. A political moderate, Pulitzer disliked the reflection of Bovard's individual views in the *Post-Dispatch* and would not let the paper support the program of nationalization Bovard proposed. On July 29, 1938, citing "irreconcilable differences" with Pulitzer over the management of the *Post-Dispatch,* Bovard resigned as managing editor.

Declining invitations to news or writing positions elsewhere, he retired to Windridge Farm, his estate near Clayton, Mo. Now he found time for the hunting and fishing he had always enjoyed. Tall, erect, and handsome, he had married

Suzanne Thompson of San Antonio, Texas, on June 16, 1902; they had no children. He died of cancer in a St. Louis hospital and after Episcopal rites was buried at Bellefontaine Cemetery, St. Louis. Avoiding the limelight, Bovard had remained almost unknown in St. Louis, although he was a major influence in the community's life for more than thirty years. When he retired, his reputed salary of $75,000 made him probably the highest paid of managing editors; undoubtedly he was among the most highly esteemed by his craft. O.K.B., as he invariably signed himself, had never bothered to fill out the form for inclusion in *Who's Who in America,* but by his relentless investigative reporting he had written an unduplicated chapter in the history of crusading daily journalism.

[James W. Markham, *Bovard of the Post-Dispatch* (1954), is generally reliable, though it provoked thirty-four staff members to testify that they had found Bovard a "fine, fair, appreciative human being" and not the "cold, hard overlord" depicted by Markham (*St. Louis Post-Dispatch,* Nov. 14, 1954). Other sources: articles on Bovard by Paul Y. Anderson, in *St. Louis Star-Times,* Aug. 1, 1938, and by Irving Dilliard, in Louis M. Lyons, ed., *Reporting the News* (1965); obituaries in the press generally, especially St. Louis papers and *N. Y. Times; Editor & Publisher,* Nov. 10, 1945; author's personal knowledge; information from Mrs. Bovard. Valuable assistance was also provided by Bishop William Scarlett of Castine, Maine, and Roy T. King of St. Louis. See also: William A. Swanberg, *Pulitzer* (1967); *The Story of the Post-Dispatch* (booklet, 1968); Orrick Johns, *Time of Our Lives* (1937); Oswald Garrison Villard, *The Disappearing Daily* (1944); and Edwin Emery and Henry L. Smith, *The Press and America* (1954).]

IRVING DILLIARD

BOYD, HARRIET ANN. See HAWES, HARRIET ANN BOYD.

BOYD, JAMES (July 2, 1888–Feb. 25, 1944), novelist, was born in Harrisburg, Pa., the first of two sons and eldest of the four children of Eleanor Gilmore (Herr) and John Yeomans Boyd. The families of both parents had lived in Pennsylvania for several generations. Boyd's father, a socially prominent businessman and Presbyterian churchman, was heir to the wealth amassed by his father in the coal and iron business.

James Boyd attended the Hill School in Pottstown, Pa. (1901–06), graduated from Princeton (1910), and spent two years in England studying literature at Trinity College, Cambridge, before joining the faculty of the Harrisburg (Pa.) Academy in 1912 as a teacher of English and French. Illness repeatedly interrupted his teaching and forced him to abandon it altogether by 1914. A long convalescence was followed by brief employment on the editorial staff of *Country Life in America* during the fall of 1916 and several months' volunteer work with the Red Cross. He joined the army's Ambulance Service in August 1917 as a second lieutenant and took part in the St. Mihiel and Meuse-Argonne campaigns.

After his discharge, in July 1919, Boyd decided to become a writer. He had written stories, poetry, and plays intermittently since his early teens but had published nothing outside of school or college magazines, except for a few news stories, minor articles, and cartoons during his stints on the staffs of the *Harrisburg Patriot* in 1910 and *Country Life* in 1916. His family owned a farm in the Sandhills region of North Carolina near Southern Pines, and it was there that he settled. The move, although dictated partly by the need for a quiet place to work and a more salubrious climate, was prompted essentially by a strong personal attachment to the area developed during childhood vacations and a residence of more than two years following his illness in 1912. The region was to provide him with materials for much of his writing during the next twenty-five years.

Boyd's first stories and articles were quickly accepted for publication, and over the next fifteen years they appeared regularly in such magazines as *Scribner's,* the *Century, Harper's Monthly,* and the *American Mercury.* Boyd soon turned his attention, however, to the historical novels that were to consume most of his creative energy and upon which his literary reputation chiefly rests. His *Drums* (1925) was acclaimed as the best novel ever written about the American Revolution. Four others followed: *Marching On* (1927), a novel of the Civil War; *Long Hunt* (1930), about the hunters on the trans-Appalachian frontier during the late eighteenth century; *Roll River* (1935), a partly autobiographical novel about a Pennsylvania industrial family at the turn of the twentieth century; and *Bitter Creek* (1939), set in the Wyoming cattle country of the 1890's. The novels, especially *Drums* and *Roll River,* were enthusiastically received by both critics and the reading public; they are recognized as major steps in the development of the historical novel as a genre, carrying it beyond the older historical romance by means of greater historical accuracy, psychological and sociological awareness, moral and aesthetic sensitivity, and formal control. Boyd was elected to the National Institute of Arts and Letters in 1937 and the Society of American Historians in 1939.

In 1940 Boyd organized and served as national chairman of the Free Company of Players, a group of American writers concerned about the jingoistic and antidemocratic attitudes and behavior that were beginning to manifest themselves in American life as a result of the war in Europe. The group, which included Orson Welles,

Archibald MacLeish, Paul Green, William Saroyan, Stephen Vincent Benét [Supp. 3], Sherwood Anderson [Supp. 3], and others, produced and broadcast a series of original radio plays early in 1941. Their clear defense of freedom of speech, of assembly, and of the press during a period of national emergency incurred the wrath of conservative interests, and the Hearst press (then embroiled in a controversy of its own with Orson Welles over his film *Citizen Kane*) unsuccessfully sought to stop the Free Company series. In 1941 Boyd bought and became editor of the *Southern Pines Pilot,* which he transformed from a conservative, nearly defunct country weekly into a progressive regional newspaper.

On Dec. 15, 1917, Boyd married Katharine Lamont, daughter of Daniel Scott Lamont [*q.v.*], Secretary of War in the second Cleveland administration. They had three children: James, Daniel Lamont, and Nancy. Boyd had grace, vitality, and an effervescent wit. Fond of fox hunting, he was founder and master of the Moore County Hounds. Early in 1944, while attending a seminar at Princeton University, Boyd suffered a fatal cerebral attack at the age of fifty-five. His ashes were returned to Southern Pines for burial. His *Eighteen Poems,* written toward the end of his life, appeared a few months later.

[Boyd correspondence and MSS. in the Princeton Univ. Lib. and the Southern Hist. Collection of the Univ. of N. C.; interviews and correspondence with Katharine Lamont Boyd and Jackson Herr Boyd; John W. Jordan, *Encyc. of Pa. Biog.* (1914), I, 60–62, and III, 1068 (on Boyd's father); James Boyd, *Old Pines and Other Stories* (1952) and (ed.) *The Free Company Presents* (1941); *Princeton Univ. Lib. Chronicle,* Feb. 1945, pp. 55–81 (includes bibliography and photograph); David E. Whisnant, *James Boyd* (1972).]

DAVID E. WHISNANT

BRAND, MAX. See FAUST, FREDERICK SHILLER.

BRANDEIS, LOUIS DEMBITZ (Nov. 13, 1856–Oct. 5, 1941), lawyer, justice of the United States Supreme Court, was born in Louisville, Ky., the youngest of four children and the second son of Adolph and Frederika (Dembitz) Brandeis. The parents, both of whom came of old and cultivated Jewish families in Prague, had immigrated to the United States with the "pilgrims of 1848" afer the failure of the revolutionary liberal movements in central Europe. Settling first in Madison, Ind., where a business venture failed, the parents shortly moved across the river to Louisville. There the father established a grain and produce business which prospered until the depression of the early 1870's.

Louis attended public school in Louisville,

graduating from high school at fifteen as a gold medalist. At home he was encouraged to cultivate his intellectual and aesthetic bent, participating in the liberal German culture of books and music. He admired especially a scholarly uncle, Lewis Dembitz, a lawyer and early Zionist, in whose honor Louis changed his middle name from David to Dembitz. In 1872, upon the dissolution of the family business, he accompanied his parents on an extended visit to Europe, spending the years 1873–75 at the Annen Realschule in Dresden. He remained grateful for the intellectual development that he experienced there (learning, as he recalled later, how to generate new ideas by reflecting intensely on your materials), but he was glad to leave the unduly repressive atmosphere of the place for the freer air of Louisville.

Shortly after his return he entered the Harvard Law School in September 1875, and quickly established himself as an outstanding student. Supported by a loan from his brother and earnings from tutoring, he entered avidly into the dialectics of the case system of instruction, inaugurated by Christopher C. Langdell [q.v.] in 1870, and with his keen, subtle mind, gentle manners, and attractive dark features set off by deep-set blue-gray eyes, he found a ready welcome in the wider academic community of Cambridge. Through Prof. Nathaniel S. Shaler [q.v.], the naturalist and a fellow Kentuckian, he met the leading figures at Harvard, and in the law school he came under the influence of James Bradley Thayer [q.v.], professor of constitutional law, whose doctrine of judicial self-restraint in the review of acts of the legislature became a powerful theme in Brandeis's concept of the judicial office. Completing his legal studies with an academic record unsurpassed in the subsequent history of the school, Brandeis received his law degree in 1877. He spent the next year in graduate work at Harvard. The years at Harvard, he later remarked, "were among the happiest of my life. I worked! For me the world's center was Cambridge."

Notwithstanding this attachment, in 1878 Brandeis began the practice of law in St. Louis, the home of his sister Fannie and her husband, Charles Nagel, who later became a member of President Taft's cabinet. Brandeis joined the office of James Taussig, an uncle of the Harvard economist Frank W. Taussig [Supp. 2], but remained only nine months. Neither physically nor spiritually did he find the St. Louis of that day congenial; he suffered recurrently from malaria, and he missed the stimulating friendships of Cambridge and Boston. When his law school classmate Samuel D. Warren, Jr., proposed a partner-ship in Boston, he agreed to the venture, and the firm of Warren & Brandeis was established in 1879. Warren's family were proper and affluent Bostonians, and the association brought many social and professional relationships to Brandeis, perhaps the most enduring being an acquaintance with Oliver Wendell Holmes, Jr. [Supp. 1], the later Supreme Court justice. During his first two years of practice, Brandeis served as a part-time law clerk to Chief Justice Horace Gray [q.v.] of the Supreme Judicial Court of Massachusetts, shortly to be appointed to the United States Supreme Court. This was a mutually rewarding experience; Gray described the young Brandeis as "the most ingenious and most original lawyer I ever met."

The legal practice grew, important business clients sought out Brandeis for advice, and by 1890, at the age of thirty-four, he was earning approximately $50,000 a year. He found time to indulge other interests as well; fond of sailing and riding, he joined the Union Boat Club and was an organizer of the Dedham Polo Club (though in later years he described himself apologetically as a "supernumerary" on the polo field). He was attracted to a career in teaching, but after a year as an instructor at Harvard in the law of evidence (1882–83), he declined an offer of an assistant professorship in order to gain further experience in litigation and counseling. He was active, however, on behalf of the Harvard Law School, organizing a national association of alumni in 1886 and serving as its first secretary, and in 1891 becoming the first treasurer of the recently formed *Harvard Law Review*. He had earlier secured a gift of $90,000 for a professorship at the school with the stipulation that Holmes was to be its first incumbent, a position shortly terminated by Holmes's appointment to the Massachusetts bench.

Financial independence enabled Brandeis to devote himself to public causes, under an arrangement whereby he recompensed his law firm for the time that would otherwise have been devoted to remunerative clients. The impulses that impelled him in this direction were partly to be found in external events. Retrospectively, he attributed the turning point to the explosive violence in 1892 at the steel plants in Homestead, Pa., where, as he was to describe it, "organized capital hired a private army to shoot at organized labor for resisting an arbitrary cut in wages." At this time he was preparing a course of lectures on business law, to be given at the Massachusetts Institute of Technology. The shock of the Homestead affair caused him to discard his notes and begin again "from new angles. Those talks at

Tech marked an epoch in my own career." Earlier, in the 1880's, he had learned something of labor conditions from friends in Boston who were union organizers, and he was moved by the writings of Henry George and Henry Demarest Lloyd [*qq.v.*]. But in the end the influence of tractarians upon him was probably due to an innate affinity. As other men found enjoyment in hobbies such as art collecting or sports, he found his greatest satisfaction in trying to find remedies for social ills. There was a good deal of the puritan about him, in his sense of stewardship, self-discipline, and personal responsibility. "Responsibility," he insisted, "is the great developer of men." He used the term in the double sense of sharing in the making of decisions and being answerable for their outcome; responsibility was a necessary condition of spiritual freedom. To foster these traditional values in a time of burgeoning corporate enterprise and expanding bureaucracy was a daunting mission taken up by publicists, preachers, and social reformers; Brandeis brought to the undertaking the special gifts of an uncommon common-law lawyer, resourceful in translating parochial controversies into universal moral terms, and in turn devising ways of transforming moral values into the framework of legal and political institutions.

Viewed in this light, his achievements at the bar, though highly diverse in their subject matter, display a striking and distinctive harmony of theme. One of the earliest was a path-breaking article he published with his partner, Warren, in the *Harvard Law Review* of Dec. 15, 1890, on "The Right to Privacy." The outgrowth of certain offensive publicity concerning the social activities of Warren's family, it adumbrated a new legal concept that has had lasting influence. Building on diverse analogies in the law of defamation, of literary property, and of eavesdropping, Brandeis argued that the central, if unarticulated, interest protected in these fields was an interest in personal integrity, "the right to be let alone," that ought to be secured against invasion except for some compelling reason of public welfare.

Of broader immediate impact was the Public Franchise League which Brandeis helped found in Boston in 1900. For several years he was its moving force in resisting long-term exclusive franchises for the Boston Elevated Railway Company and other public utilities. As unpaid counsel for the League and the State Board of Trade, he addressed himself to the problem of rates and service in the gas industry in Boston. He successfully urged adoption (1906) of the London sliding-scale plan, under which dividends might be increased as rates were reduced. The great merit of the plan, in his view, was that it offered a built-in incentive to economy and fair rates, without reliance on bureaucratic regulation or public ownership. Regulation was too likely to be inefficient, and public ownership too likely to create new outlets for corruption. Politically he was able to appeal to the self-interest of the industry in averting more drastic measures. Whether his espousal of measures like the sliding scale marked him as a conservative, progressive, or radical was of no moment to him, though in later years he said that he had always considered himself a conservative. He regarded as doctrinaire those proposals of reform that neglected to assess the capacities, limitations, and accountability of men.

As unpaid counsel for life insurance policyholders, Brandeis investigated the economic inefficiencies and wastes involved in industrial life insurance, and in consequence devised a plan of savings-bank insurance for the workingman, whereby limited amounts of life insurance could be purchased over the counter at economical rates through the facilities of the banks. The plan, which Brandeis regarded as his most significant achievement, was successfully adopted in Massachusetts (1907), New York, and Connecticut. It served at once as a means of security for the wage earner, an incentive to thrift, a demonstration that an important financial enterprise could be conducted without external trappings and concentrated power, and a yardstick for the old-line companies.

Again without a fee, Brandeis represented certain stockholders of the Boston & Maine Railroad in an attack on a merger with the New Haven (achieved in 1909) which gave the latter a monopoly for a time on transportation in New England. Drawing on this and other encounters with business monopoly and with the interlocking financial interests that created and controlled it, and relying also on the disclosures of the Pujo Committee investigations of 1912–13, Brandeis published a series of articles in *Harper's Weekly* (1913–14) entitled "Breaking the Money Trust," which were later collected as *Other People's Money, and How the Bankers Use It* (1914). The volume furnished documentation and analysis for the Progressive movement; Senator Robert M. La Follette [*q.v.*] called it "epoch-making," and it was given new vitality in the early New Deal legislation (1933–35) for the protection of investors and consumers, requiring full disclosure in the sale of securities, separation of investment from commercial banking, and simplification of public utility holding company systems.

In 1910 Brandeis came into sharp collision with the Taft administration, in an investigation of its practices concerning the conservation of mineral lands in Alaska. A young employee in the Interior Department, Louis R. Glavis, charged collusion between departmental officials and the Guggenheim interests in opening those lands for sale. Rebuffed by the Secretary of the Interior, Richard A. Ballinger [*q.v.*], but encouraged by Gifford Pinchot, an ardent conservationist, Glavis took his case to President Taft, who after consultation with Attorney General George W. Wickersham [Supp. 2] exonerated Ballinger and ordered the discharge of Glavis. When *Collier's Weekly,* under the editorship of Brandeis's friend Norman Hapgood [Supp. 2], published Glavis's charges, a joint investigating committee of Congress was created to inquire into the affair. Brandeis was retained by Hapgood to represent Glavis. The extensive hearings took a turn highly embarrassing to Taft and the Republican majority on the committee when Brandeis was able to show that an elaborate opinion from Wickersham, on which Taft's decision purported to rest, in fact had been drafted subsequently and predated. Although in the end the President's action was supported by a vote of the committee on party lines, Ballinger resigned shortly thereafter and his successor promulgated policies for the conservation of Alaskan resources substantially in accord with recommendations formulated by Brandeis. Conservation of resources, however, was for him only one of the great themes of the inquiry; in his closing argument he recurred to his basic preoccupation: "We are not dealing here with a question of the conservation of natural resources merely; it is the conservation and development of the individual. . . . With this great government building up, . . . the one thing we need is men in subordinate places who will think for themselves and who will think and act in full recognition of the obligations as a part of the governing body . . ." (Mason, p. 281).

Brandeis's most important contribution as an advocate in constitutional litigation was what came to be known as the "Brandeis brief." Representing the state of Oregon in defense of its statute setting a maximum of ten hours of labor a day for women, he devoted three pages of his brief before the Supreme Court to the applicable principles of law and over a hundred pages to the facts concerning the effects of excessive hours on health, the experience of other countries, and opinions of experts on the subject. It was a form of argumentation new to the Supreme Court, and it was successful, eliciting the unusual tribute of a mention of the advocate by name in the Court's opinion (*Muller v. Oregon,* 208 U.S. 412 [1908]).

In the field of labor relations Brandeis put his emphasis on regularity of employment and a sharing of responsibility between management and workers; political democracy, he insisted, was incomplete without industrial democracy. The closed shop he opposed as he did other forms of monopoly. These convictions determined his course when he was called upon by both sides to mediate a strike in the New York garment industry in 1910. After protracted negotiations, he secured the agreement of the parties to a so-called protocol under which continuing joint boards would fix working conditions and settle grievances. A preferential union shop was established, whereby union standards would prevail and management would give preference to union men in hiring employees but without dictation by the union in selecting among union applicants. Brandeis agreed to serve as impartial chairman of the joint board of arbitration. Increasing militancy of the unions, however, and a corresponding rigidity on the part of the employers, placed insuperable strains on the protocol, and in 1916 it was abandoned.

His mediation in the garment workers' strike was one of two events that led Brandeis, in middle life, to a rediscovery of his Jewish origins and an active dedication to Zionism. His own upbringing had not been marked by Jewish observances, and in Boston he moved in secular professional and social circles and was absorbed in secular causes. But the experience of working with employers and employees who were first- or second-generation Jewish immigrants and discovering their exceptional intellectual and moral qualities awakened him to a new interest in his heritage. The other crucial event was a meeting in 1912 with Jacob de Haas [Supp. 2], who had been secretary in London to Theodor Herzl, the founder of modern Zionism. De Haas, who was familiar with the work of Brandeis's uncle, Lewis Dembitz, undertook to educate Brandeis in the history and aims of the movement, and Brandeis became an avid student, absorbing books on the subject as eagerly as de Haas could provide them. Brandeis saw in Zionism an opportunity to demonstrate how simple men, fortified by shared ideals, zeal, and courage, could establish a just and democratic commonwealth even against the greatest physical odds.

Once he was committed, his rise to leadership in the movement came quickly. When, on the outbreak of the war in 1914, the headquarters of the World Zionist Organization were moved to the United States, Brandeis was chosen as chairman of the operating committee. Through his friendship with President Wilson he was able to gain important support for the Balfour Declaration of 1917, pledging the creation of a national homeland for the Jewish people in Palestine, and later for a British mandate with adequate boundaries. He visited Palestine in 1919. In the following year occurred a rift between himself and Dr. Chaim Weizmann, the leader of European Zionism, over issues of structural organization and financial planning. In 1921 the breach was extended to the American side; Brandeis's insistence on financial autonomy for the American group alienated many supporters of Weizmann, especially among those of eastern European origin, and Brandeis withdrew from any position of responsibility, though not from the organization itself. He was joined by his principal supporters, including Rabbi Stephen S. Wise, Judge Julian W. Mack [Supp. 3], and Felix Frankfurter. His ardent support of the cause, however, did not abate. He was instrumental in the formation of the Palestine Economic Corporation for projects that could become self-supporting and the Palestine Endowment Fund for philanthropic programs. After he became a member of the Supreme Court, the cause of Zionism was the one extrajudicial interest that he permitted himself to pursue.

Brandeis's immersion in public causes was abetted by his wife, Alice Goldmark, his second cousin, whom he married on Mar. 23, 1891, in a ceremony performed by her brother-in-law Felix Adler [Supp. 1], the founder of the Ethical Culture Society. She was a daughter of Joseph Goldmark, physician and manufacturer, who became an exile after taking part in the revolutionary Austrian uprising of 1848, and a sister of Henry Goldmark [Supp. 3], civil engineer, and of the social reformers Josephine and Pauline Goldmark. There were two daughters of the marriage, Susan and Elizabeth. By common design the family lived frugally, although at the age of fifty Brandeis had become a millionaire. They spent summer vacations in a modest cottage at Chatham, on Cape Cod; always an intense worker, Brandeis was one of those who believe that a year's labor can be performed in eleven months but not in twelve.

In politics Brandeis was an independent. He bolted the Republican party to support Cleveland in 1884, but reverted to the Republicans to vote for Taft in 1908. For a time he was an enthusiastic progressive, speaking in the Middle West in early 1912 for the nomination of La Follette by the Republicans, but after the party split he gave his support to Woodrow Wilson in

preference to Theodore Roosevelt, the Progressive candidate. The position of the nominees on the issue of economic power was decisive for Brandeis: Roosevelt stood for the regulation of the monopolies, differentiating between good trusts and bad, while Wilson rejected the distinction and urged the regulation of competition in the interest of forestalling monopolies. A memorable meeting between Wilson and Brandeis took place on Aug. 28, 1912, in Sea Girt, N. J., at which Brandeis was able to fill out the nominee's general philosophic position with the specifics of experience and new directions. Brandeis campaigned for Wilson in a number of Eastern states, though he felt more appropriately cast in the role of adviser than political orator. Thenceforth a relationship of intimacy and mutual respect developed, and after Wilson's election there was reason to expect that Brandeis would be named to the cabinet as Attorney General or Secretary of Commerce. The President-elect did make detailed inquiries to that end, but apparently was dissuaded by hostile judgments of Brandeis as a dangerous radical who would be a divisive element in the administration.

Although without office, Brandeis was an influential adviser in the early years of the Wilson administration. When a sharp conflict arose within Democratic ranks in 1913 over the structure and control of the proposed Federal Reserve banking system, Wilson called on him for guidance. Brandeis gave strong support to the position of William Jennings Bryan [q.v.] and the progressives: that the system must be under the ultimate control of the government and not the banking community, and that its circulating notes must be obligations of the United States. The opposition, led by Senator Carter Glass, yielded, and the law as enacted reflected Brandeis's counsel.

In 1913–14 he applied himself, with his friend George Rublee, to the drafting of a bill for the enforcement of antitrust policy, with special emphasis on enjoining unfair and destructive trade practices (competition that kills, he called them) that were often a prelude to monopoly. When the bill was introduced by Congressman Raymond B. Stevens, Wilson gave it his strong support, and it became the Federal Trade Commission Act of 1914. The Commission itself turned out to be a disappointment to Brandeis, owing to its concentration on giving friendly advice to business and investigating what seemed relatively unimportant forms of unfair marketing, to the neglect of the protection of small competitors against predatory practices of dominant firms.

When a vacancy arose on the Supreme Court

owing to the death of Justice Joseph R. Lamar [*q.v.*], Wilson on Jan. 28, 1916, nominated Brandeis for the place. He was one of only three or four nominees in the history of the Court who had held no public office. For four months there was bitter controversy over the nomination in the Senate Judiciary Committee and in the country. Brandeis himself did not appear before the committee; not until 1939 was the practice of inviting a nominee instituted. His interests were represented by Edward F. McClennen, his partner, and George W. Anderson, United States Attorney in Boston, serving in effect as his counsel. Seven former presidents of the American Bar Association, including Elihu Root [Supp. 2] and William H. Taft, urged rejection. Much of the opposition was based ostensibly on the nominee's supposed lack of judicial temperament, though ironically some of the most impassioned critics complained that Brandeis had compromised his clients' interests to obtain results that would satisfy his own sense of right. Brandeis himself ascribed the opposition to the fact that he was a Jew, the first to be nominated to the Court, and to the impression that he was a radical. He had, in any event, offended some powerful financial and industrial interests over the course of the years, and these were arrayed against him. Wilson stood firm, and finally the nomination was reported favorably on party lines by the Judiciary Committee and was confirmed by the Senate on June 1, 1916, by a vote of 47 to 22. His radicalism was in truth an uncommon call to pursue seriously those values that society professed to cherish. His political and social philosophy was concisely expressed in a letter to Robert W. Bruere in 1922: "Refuse to accept as inevitable any evil in business (e.g., irregularity of employment). Refuse to tolerate any immoral practice (e.g., espionage). But do not believe that you can find a universal remedy for evil conditions or immoral practices in effecting a fundamental change in society (as by State Socialism). . . . Seek for betterment within the broad lines of existing institutions. . . . The great developer is responsibility. Hence no remedy can be hopeful which does not devolve upon the workers' participation in, responsibility for, the conduct of business. . . . [Democracy] demands continuous sacrifice by the individual and more exigent obedience to the moral law than any other form of government . . ." (Mason, p. 585).

On the Court, Brandeis was generally aligned with Justice Holmes, frequently in dissent, in support of the validity of state or federal social and economic legislation. But while Holmes delivered incisive, philosophic opinions reflecting a skeptical tolerance, Brandeis wrote massive, closely textured expositions of the problems and the legislative solutions, aiming to instruct no less than to persuade. His opinions on valuation and depreciation of public utility properties, relating accounting practices to public policy, have served as guidelines for regulatory agencies (*Missouri ex rel. Southwestern Bell Telephone Company* v. *Public Service Commission,* 262 U.S. 276, 289 [1923], dissent; *United Railways* v. *West,* 280 U.S. 234, 255 [1930], dissent). His opinion supporting graduated taxes on chain-store enterprises furnished an opportunity to state the case against giantism in business and in favor of cooperatives as an alternative (*Liggett Company* v. *Lee,* 288 U.S. 517, 541 [1933], dissent).

These were labors of love, since his philosophy of latitude for social experimentation and judicial self-restraint coincided in result with legislative solutions that he approved. Where the legislation or other governmental action was less appealing, he nevertheless followed his creed of self-restraint, placing process and structure above personal economic and social views. Thus in voting to uphold a law requiring certificates of convenience and necessity to enter the ice business, which he considered an ill-advised restriction on competition, he spoke of the dangers involved when judges sought to arrest the process of experimentation, as promising for the social sciences as it was fruitful for the natural sciences (*New State Ice Company* v. *Liebmann,* 285 U.S. 262, 280 [1932], dissent). When Congress limited the president's removal power over executive appointees, as it had been exercised by President Wilson, he did not hesitate to write one of his most powerful opinions in vindication of Congress and against the chief executive who had appointed him (*Myers* v. *United States,* 272 U.S. 52, 240 [1926], dissent). In a series of cases involving the duty of a state court to give full faith and credit to the judgments of other states, he took positions rejecting, literally, the claims of a widow, an orphan, and a workingman (*John Hancock Mutual Life Insurance Company* v. *Yates,* 299 U.S. 178 [1936]; *Yarborough* v. *Yarborough,* 290 U.S. 202 [1933]; *Bradford Electric Light Company* v. *Clapper,* 284 U.S. 221 [1931]).

As these cases suggest, those who saw Brandeis as a sentimental reformer were no less mistaken than those who regarded him as a dangerous radical. Judges, he believed, were fallible like other men. He liked to quote from Goethe: "Care is taken that the trees do not scrape the skies," and "Self-limitation is the first mark of the master." He took a restrictive view of the standing of litigants to challenge the constitutional validity of legislation and applied this canon even when a majority of the Court reached a decision on the constitutional merits that was congenial to him; thus he insisted that the stockholders' suit in which the Tennessee Valley Authority was upheld should not have been decided at all (*Ashwander* v. *TVA,* 297 U.S. 288, 341 [1936]). In the important case of *Erie Railroad Company* v. *Tompkins* he wrote the Court's opinion holding that the federal courts were not free to declare common-law rules different from those of the state in which a case arose; the decision overruled a practice of almost a century (304 U.S. 64 [1938]). Believing that the limits of capacity in even the best of men are soon reached, he distrusted centralization of governmental power equally with bigness in industry, valued the federal system as a means for the sharing of power and responsibility, and so was disposed to sustain the authority of the states until Congress had unmistakably preempted the field (e.g., *New York Central Railroad Company* v. *Winfield,* 244 U.S. 147, 154 [1917], dissent).

In one area—liberty of speech, press, and assembly—Brandeis was vigilant to strike down state or federal controls unless they were justified by a clear and present danger of serious public harm. One of his two most eloquent opinions restated the faith of the framers of the Constitution in an open society: "They recognized the risks to which all human institutions are subject. But they knew that order cannot be secured merely through fear of punishment for its infraction; that it is hazardous to discourage thought, hope and imagination; that fear breeds repression; that repression breeds hate; that hate menaces stable government; that the path of safety lies in the opportunity to discuss freely supposed grievances and proposed remedies; and that the fitting remedy for evil counsels is good ones" (*Whitney* v. *California,* 274 U.S. 357, 372 [1927], concurrence and dissent). Of matching eloquence is his opinion condemning wiretapping by federal officers in violation of state law: "Our Government is the potent, the omnipresent teacher. For good or for ill, it teaches the whole people by its example. Crime is contagious. . . . To declare that in the administration of the criminal law the end justifies the means—to declare that the Government may commit crimes in order to secure the conviction of a private criminal— would bring terrible retribution" (*Olmstead* v. *United States,* 277 U.S. 438, 471 [1928], dissent). The dissents in these cases, like his dissenting views generally, later became the law of the land.

Brandeis had a single-minded devotion to the Court as an institution and to the demands of the office. He made no public speeches, wrote no articles, and even declined to accept honorary degrees. He and his wife avoided the social activities of the capital, but maintained contact with members of the Washington community through regular weekly teas. The guest lists, unencumbered by protocol, brought together young and old, famous and obscure, who were generally subjected to searching questioning about their fields of expertise and in turn were likely to come away, if only by virtue of the questions themselves, with a clearer and heightened sense of their mission.

Brandeis's absorption in the work of the Court and his anxiety for its quality contributed to amicable relations with his colleagues, even those whose constitutional outlook differed sharply from his own. His judicial opinions were addressed to problems, not to personalities, and in their austere style and massive force they were calculated to overwhelm rather than to wound. So anxious was he that the Court's authority should derive from the intrinsic persuasiveness of its opinions and not from the symbols of power that he opposed the construction of a building for the Court, and after the marble edifice was completed in 1935 he steadfastly refused to occupy his chambers in it, continuing to use his study at home. Not wishing to share the confidences of the office beyond the assistance of a law clerk, he employed no secretarial help, managed his correspondence and wrote his opinions in longhand, and used the Court's printer to provide copies of successive drafts, sometimes running to dozens and scores of revisions. The qualities he brought to the deliberations of the Court were recognized by his colleagues. William H. Taft, his old antagonist, who became chief justice in 1921, said after two years of service together, "I have come to like Brandeis very much indeed." Chief Justice Charles Evans Hughes, who succeeded to the office in 1930, wrote of him that he was "the master of both microscope and telescope. Nothing of importance, however minute, escapes his microscopic examination of every problem, and, through his powerful telescopic lens, his mental vision embraces distant scenes ranging far beyond the familiar worlds of conventional thinking" (317 U.S. xxxv).

Brandeis was an admirer of Franklin D. Roosevelt but not an uncritical enthusiast of the New Deal. Its first phase, that of economic recovery, embodied measures that in his view relied excessively on centralized planning and the raising of prices. He joined in the decision holding the National Industrial Recovery Act unconstitutional (*A.L.A. Schechter Poultry Corporation* v.

United States, 295 U.S. 495 [1935]), but despite his distaste for the Agricultural Adjustment Act, he could not conscientiously find it invalid as an exercise of the spending power, and dissented, with Justices Harlan F. Stone and Benjamin N. Cardozo [Supp. 2], from the decision overturning it (*United States* v. *Butler*, 297 U.S. 1 [1936]). The second phase of the New Deal, directed to more far-reaching economic reform, was more congenial to him, and indeed a number of the legislative measures reflected his philosophy, as it had been absorbed by disciples such as Felix Frankfurter and a generation of law school graduates. The legislative program establishing minimum wages and unemployment insurance, guaranteeing collective bargaining, regulating securities issues and the stock exchange, requiring the reorganization of holding companies, and setting up the Tennessee Valley Authority, which served as a yardstick for electric utilities, was denounced by some as excessive governmental intermeddling and deprecated by others as temporizing with a system that needed basic transformation, but for Brandeis it represented the kind of reform that was manageable and liberating.

President Roosevelt's plan in 1937 to enlarge the Supreme Court, when his legislative program was in jeopardy of judicial death sentence, was a painful experience for Brandeis. Strongly as he disapproved most of the judicial vetoes of the period, he was even more concerned for the independence of the judiciary. Although he scrupulously refrained from any public utterance on the subject and rejected an invitation from Senator Burton K. Wheeler to give the Judiciary Committee the benefit of his views, he did suggest to Wheeler that he approach Chief Justice Hughes. This was done, and resulted in a letter from Hughes refuting charges that the Court required additional members to keep abreast of its business. The letter, which Hughes stated had the concurrence of the two senior Justices, Brandeis and Willis Van Devanter [Supp. 3], made an impact beyond its precise terms and contributed importantly to the defeat of the bill.

On Feb. 13, 1939, having concluded that he was unable to function at his regular pitch, Brandeis retired from active duty. He continued to live in Washington and to spend the summers in Chatham. He suffered a heart attack in the fall of 1941 and died a few days later in a Washington hospital. His ashes were interred beneath the law school at the University of Louisville, an institution in which he had taken a strong personal interest. Brandeis's distinctive eminence in the history of American law rests on an extraor-

dinary fusion of prophetic vision, moral intensity, and grasp of practical affairs.

[Brandeis's correspondence and personal papers are at the Univ. of Louisville. His working papers on the Court are at the Harvard Law School. His public papers are in process of collection at the Goldfarb Lib., Brandeis Univ. A multivolume edition of the *Letters of Louis D. Brandeis* is in process, ed. by Melvin I. Urofsky and David W. Levy (1971–   ). Other published writings by Brandeis include: *Business—A Profession* (1914), a collection of addresses; Alfred Lief, ed., *The Social and Economic Views of Mr. Justice Brandeis* (1930); Osmond K. Fraenkel, ed., *The Curse of Bigness: Miscellaneous Papers* (1934); and *Brandeis on Zionism: A Collection of Addresses and Statements* (1942). Alexander M. Bickel, *The Unpublished Opinions of Mr. Justice Brandeis* (1957), is an account, with text, of judicial opinions prepared but not delivered, illuminating the process of decision-making in the Court. Alpheus T. Mason, *Brandeis: A Free Man's Life* (1946), is the authorized biography. Earlier accounts include Alfred Lief, *Brandeis* (1936); Jacob de Haas, *Louis D. Brandeis: A Biog. Sketch, with Special Reference to His Contributions to Jewish and Zionist Hist.* (1929); and A. T. Mason, *Brandeis: Lawyer and Judge in the Modern State* (1933). More specialized studies are A. T. Mason, *The Brandeis Way: A Case Study in the Workings of Democracy* (1938), a narrative of the adoption of the savings-bank life insurance plan in Massachusetts; Samuel J. Konefsky, *The Legacy of Holmes and Brandeis* (1956); Melvin I. Urofsky, *A Mind of One Piece: Brandeis and Am. Reform* (1971); Felix Frankfurter, ed., *Mr. Justice Brandeis* (1932); Paul A. Freund, "Mr. Justice Brandeis: A Centennial Memoir," *Harvard Law Rev.*, Mar. 1957; and P. A. Freund, "Mr. Justice Brandeis," in *Mr. Justice*, ed. by Allison Dunham and Philip B. Kurland (1956). The political setting for his early efforts at reform in Massachusetts is explored in Richard M. Abrams, *Conservatism in a Progressive Era: Mass. Politics, 1900–1912* (1964). Relations with Wilson are described in Arthur S. Link's biography of Wilson. The struggle over confirmation is recounted in A. L. Todd, *Justice on Trial* (1964). Memorial proceedings in Supreme Court are printed in *U. S. Reports*, 317: ix–xlix (1942). Appreciations relating to the Zionist phase are contained in the *New Palestine*, Nov. 14, 1941. Newspaper comments at his death are collected in Irving Dilliard, ed., *Mr. Justice Brandeis, Great American* (1941). A Brandeis bibliography compiled by Roy M. Mersky was published in 1958 by the Yale Law School.]

PAUL A. FREUND

BRENNEMANN, JOSEPH (Sept. 25, 1872–July 2, 1944), pediatrician, was born near Peru, Ill., the second of at least five sons of Joseph and Mary (Schaefer) Brennemann. His father had come to the United States from Germany; his mother was born in Ohio of German parents. Growing up on his father's farm, Brennemann was educated in country schools and at the University of Michigan, from which he graduated with the Ph.B. degree in 1895. After teaching school for a year, he enrolled in the medical school of Northwestern University, but interrupted his studies to be with a sick brother in Texas, where he again taught school. He spent his third year of medical study at Gross Medical College in Denver, Colo., and then returned to Northwestern, receiving the M.D. degree in 1900.

On Jan. 2, 1903, he married Bessie Darling Daniels of Chicago. They had three daughters: Mary Elizabeth, Barbara, and Deborah Ann.

After two years as an intern at St. Luke's Hospital in Chicago, Brennemann established a general practice on Chicago's South Side, where he associated himself with a number of charitable medical clinics. By 1910 he had decided to make pediatrics his specialty, and that year he went for postgraduate training to Germany and Austria. On his return to Chicago he became attending physician to the pediatric departments of St. Luke's Hospital and the Wesley Memorial Hospital. Always greatly interested in dispensary work, in 1915 he also became attending physician in the outpatient department of the Northwestern Dispensary. Along with his private practice and hospital appointments, Brennemann taught pediatrics to junior medical students at Northwestern, where he served on the medical faculty as instructor (1903), clinical assistant (1904), associate (1907), assistant professor (1908), and associate professor (1918).

In 1921 Frank Billings [Supp. 1], dean of Rush Medical College of the University of Chicago, selected Brennemann for the post of chief of staff at the Children's Memorial Hospital of Chicago, and Brennemann, overcoming self-doubt, accepted. At the same time he became professor of pediatrics at Rush and at the University of Chicago School of Medicine. Since these posts brought no income, he continued his pediatric practice until 1930, when he was given a full-time salaried appointment.

Brennemann was a popular teacher. He spoke clearly, simply, and philosophically, conveying dramatically the highlights of pediatric practice. Active in the Section on Pediatrics of the American Medical Association and in the American Pediatric Society (of which he was president in 1929–30), he contributed many papers at their meetings and elsewhere. Among the more important were "A Contribution to Our Knowledge of the Etiology and Nature of Hard Curds in Infants' Stools" (*American Journal of Diseases of Children,* May 1911), which settled a long-standing controversy on the subject among physicians, and "Rheumatism in Children" (*Illinois Medical Journal,* July 1914), a major contribution to the subject of rheumatism and rheumatic heart disease. Perhaps his greatest achievement was his work as editor of *The Practice of Pediatrics* (1936), published in four loose-leaf volumes to permit continuous revision. He wrote many sections himself, solicited the others from a variety of contributors, and edited them painstakingly.

Brennemann combined gentleness of manner with a fine sense of humor that endeared him to children and parents, as well as to medical students and colleagues. He was an avid reader with broad intellectual curiosity and was noted for his independence of thought. In the practice of pediatrics he exerted a leavening influence for conservatism, urging a common-sense approach, a wariness of faddism, and a greater reliance on the child's natural defenses against infection.

Brennemann retired from the Children's Memorial Hospital and the University of Chicago in 1941. He spent the next two years as chief of staff at the Children's Hospital of Los Angeles and as professor and head of the department of pediatrics at the University of Southern California. Although he then retired to his country home in Reading, Vt., he remained active, serving as visiting pediatrician to the Milwaukee Children's Hospital during the month of April 1944. That July, back in Reading, he died suddenly of a heart attack at the age of seventy-one. A clinician to the last, he was studying his own electrocardiogram with his attending physician at the moment of death.

[Other significant papers by Brennemann include "The Out-patient Service of a Children's Hospital," *Archives of Pediatrics,* Apr. 1928; and his presidential address, "Vis Medicatrix Naturae in Pediatrics," Am. Pediatric Soc., *Transactions,* vol. XLII (1930). Biographical sources: obituary in *Am. Jour. of Diseases of Children,* Sept. 1944, by Stanley Gibson, who also wrote a biographical sketch in Borden S. Veeder, ed., *Pediatric Profiles* (1957); obituary by C. Anderson Aldrich in Inst. of Medicine of Chicago, *Proc.,* Oct. 15, 1944; sketch in *Semi-Centennial Vol. of the Am. Pediatric Soc., 1888–1938* (1938), p. 95; references in Harold K. Faber and Rustin McIntosh, *Hist. of the Am. Pediatric Soc.* (1966). Family information from 1880 census, La Salle County, Town of Eden (courtesy of Ill. State Archives). Brennemann's papers are at the John Crerar Lib., Chicago, in the Clifford G. Grulee Collection on Pediatrics.]

SAMUEL X. RADBILL

BRIGGS, LLOYD VERNON (Aug. 13, 1863–Feb. 28, 1941), psychiatrist, was born in Boston, Mass., the youngest of three children and only son of Lloyd Briggs, a stockbroker, and Sarah Elizabeth Elmes (Kent) Briggs. He was descended from settlers of the Massachusetts Bay and Plymouth colonies. Both his paternal and maternal grandfathers were well-known shipbuilders, and Briggs always retained close ties with the ancestral shipbuilding town of Hanover, Mass., on the North River. He attended Hanover Academy, the Boston Latin School, and Chauncy Hall School in Boston and at the age of fifteen passed the entrance examinations for the Harvard Medical School. Refused matriculation because of his youth, he secured admission to the lectures through the influence of his physician, Henry I. Bowditch [*q.v.*].

Two years later, having contracted tuberculosis, Briggs left school for a voyage to the Sandwich (Hawaiian) Islands. Upon his arrival in Honolulu in December 1880, he encountered a smallpox epidemic, qualified as vaccinating officer for the board of health, and inoculated more than a thousand persons in the first three weeks of January. A recurrence of tuberculosis caused him to return to the United States, and over the next twelve years he lived for a time in California, worked intermittently for his father and as a bank clerk, and acted as traveling companion to the ailing son of the Boston psychiatrist Walter Channing. When his health permitted, Briggs attempted to complete his medical training, attending both Tufts and Dartmouth for one year; he finally received his M.D. degree from the Medical College of Virginia in 1899.

Briggs returned to Boston to practice psychiatry and became associated with Channing's Brookline sanatorium, but he was soon at odds with his colleague over "irregularities" there. He spent the next five years in private practice and as physician to the mental department of the Boston Dispensary. In 1905 he left for Europe, where he studied insanity under Emil Kraepelin in Vienna and under Carl Jung in Switzerland.

After returning to Boston in 1906, Briggs, who had independent means, devoted the rest of his life to improving the treatment of the insane and the delinquent. His vigorous advocacy of state responsibility for maintaining scientific and humanitarian standards within both public and private institutions brought him into conflict with some physicians, and in the period 1910–13 he attracted wide notice. He was largely responsible for legislation passed in 1910 and 1911 to establish a centralized authority over the thirteen Massachusetts institutions for the mentally defective. In 1911 and 1912 he was nominated by the governor of Massachusetts for membership on the State Board of Insanity, but failed to win confirmation from the governor's council (an elective body). His opponents, accusing him of political scheming, denied his charges of abuses in the commitment of patients, of excessive use of physical restraints, and of inadequate nursing and medical services. Supported by a large number of prominent physicians, Briggs was elected chief of the medical staff of the Boston Dispensary in 1913, and shortly thereafter was seated on the State Board of Insanity.

The Board was reorganized in 1914 as a three-man paid commission and, under laws previously enacted, exercised more rigorous supervision of all institutions for the insane. As secretary to the Board, Briggs consulted such international authorities as Adolf Meyer, who had earlier been pathologist at the Worcester (Mass.) State Hospital. New procedures were instituted: the hospitals were opened regularly to the families and friends of patients; outpatient departments were established to provide aftercare; steps were taken to ensure that hospital medical supervisors assumed responsibility for treatment and restraint; better food, more adequately trained attendants, and better working conditions for attendants were provided; and occupational therapy and social work were introduced.

Briggs believed that mental illness must be studied in the same scientific manner as physical disease, and he urged the appointment of research pathologists at each institution. Eventually his efforts led to the establishment, in 1912, of the Boston Psychopathic Hospital and to the creation, in 1916, of a state Department of Mental Diseases, directed by a full-time professional psychiatrist. This later became the Massachusetts Department of Mental Health, with a Division of Mental Hygiene. Briggs also sponsored the Massachusetts law, passed in 1921, which required a psychological evaluation, before court trial, of persons indicted for capital crimes; the burden of assessing the mental responsibility of the accused was placed with the Department of Mental Diseases. Considered a pioneering model of enlightened penal reform, the "Briggs Law" was copied in other states.

Meanwhile, in 1917, Briggs had given up his practice for army service in World War I. At Camp Devens, Mass., he organized psychiatric screening procedures for army inductees. While stationed in France the next year as a major in the American Expeditionary Forces, he established neuropsychiatric services for victims of shell shock. He retained a reserve commission as lieutenant colonel after the war, serving as consultant to the army and to the Veterans' Bureau.

Briggs did not resume private practice after the war, but he maintained a heavy schedule, working from early morning until past midnight, although he suffered from angina pectoris in his later years. A voluminous writer, he produced a number of privately printed volumes dealing with his youthful travel experiences and with family history and genealogy, as well as books concerned with mental illness, such as *The Manner of Man That Kills* (1921) and *History of the Boston Psychopathic Hospital* (1922). He served on the National Committee on Prisons and Prison Reform and was a member of numerous professional organizations, including the

American Psychiatric Association, the American Institute of Criminal Law and Criminology, and the New England Society of Psychiatry (president, 1935).

On June 1, 1905, Briggs had married Mary Tileston Cabot. Their only child was Lloyd Cabot. His last published work, which appeared two months before his death, was an argument against capital punishment as a deterrent to crime. Often engaged in public debate, Briggs had sharp critics and staunch friends in Boston's political, medical, and academic circles. His friends warmly remembered his slight, goateed figure as he testified at legislative hearings or presided over the hospitable dinner table at his Beacon Street home. Briggs died at the age of seventy-seven of a coronary thrombosis while spending the winter in Tucson, Ariz. A lifelong Episcopalian, he was buried in the family plot at Hanover Center, Mass.

[Biographical material was gathered from: correspondence and conversations with Dr. Lloyd Cabot Briggs; *Who Was Who in America*, vol. I (1942); obituaries in the *N. Y. Times*, Mar. 1, 1941, *Jour. of Nervous and Mental Disease*, Dec. 1941, and *New England Jour. of Medicine*, May 1, 1941; L. Vernon Briggs, *Hist. and Genealogy of the Cabot Family, 1475–1927*, vol. II (1927). Briggs described his early life in three privately published volumes based on his journals: *Around Cape Horn to Honolulu in the Bark "Amy Turner," 1880* (1926); *Experiences of a Medical Student in Honolulu on the Island Oahu, 1881* (1926); and *Calif. and the West, 1881 and Later* (1931). He describes at great length his efforts to reform the State Board of Insanity and the conspiracy he believed was organized against him in *A Victory for Progress in Mental Medicine: Defeat of Reactionaries—The Hist. of an Intrigue* (1924); *Occupation as a Substitute for Restraint in the Treatment of the Mentally Ill: A Hist. of the Passage of Two Bills Through the Mass. Legislature* (1923); *Fifteen Months' Service on the Old Supervisory State Board of Insanity in Mass.* (1928); and *Two Years' Service on the Reorganized State Board of Insanity in Mass.* (1930). For a less partisan description of the conditions see Gerald N. Grob, *The State and the Mentally Ill: A Hist. of the Worcester State Hospital in Mass., 1830–1920* (1966). For an evaluation of the importance of the "Briggs Law," see S. Sheldon Glueck, *Mental Disorder and the Criminal Law: A Study in Medico-Sociological Jurisprudence* (1925). For a brief analysis of psychiatric theory contemporary with Dr. Briggs, see John C. Burnham, "Psychiatry, Psychology and the Progressive Movement," *Am. Quart.*, Winter 1960.]

BARBARA GUTMANN ROSENKRANTZ

BRINKLEY, JOHN RICHARD (July 8, 1885–May 26, 1942), medical charlatan, was born in Jackson County, N. C., between the Blue Ridge mountains and the Great Smokies, the only child of John Richard Brinkley, a country physician, and his fifth wife, Candace (Burnett) Brinkley. He was originally named John Romulus, but on the occasion of his Methodist baptism, or later, his middle name was changed to Richard. Orphaned at the age of ten, Brinkley was reared by an aunt and had a haphazard elementary school education. In 1907 or early 1908 he married Sally Wike, daughter of a local farmer, by whom he had three daughters: Wanda, Maxine, and Beryl. The couple were divorced in 1913, and on Aug. 23 of that year Brinkley married Minnie Telitha Jones of Memphis, Tenn.; they had one child, John Richard.

During his first marriage, Brinkley seems to have led a nomadic life that took him to various Southern towns as a railroad telegraph operator and then to Chicago, where he attended Bennett Medical College, an eclectic institution, but did not complete the course. Between 1913 and 1916 he practiced medicine in Arkansas on an "undergraduate license" and acquired (1915) a diploma from the Eclectic Medical University of Kansas City, a school which figured prominently in the diploma-mill scandals of 1922. He later obtained a fraudulent certificate from the National University of Arts and Sciences in St. Louis, as well as a diploma in medicine and surgery from the Royal University of Pavia in Italy. Admitted to practice in Arkansas, Brinkley, through reciprocal arrangements then in effect, obtained licensure in several other states, including Kansas, where he settled in the hamlet of Milford. There, in 1917, he began to transplant the gonads of goats into aging farmers. His operation, which promised sexual rejuvenation, was so successful, at least financially, that he was soon able to build a hospital, and his fees soared to $750, $1,000, and $1,500.

About 1922 Brinkley went to Los Angeles to operate on Harry Chandler [Supp. 3], a prominent real estate developer and publisher of the *Los Angeles Times*. Impressed by Chandler's new radio station, KHJ, and with a substantial fee in his pocket, Brinkley returned home and in 1923 founded KFKB, the first radio station in Kansas. A pioneer in the use of radio advertising, he gave a broadcast talk every night except Sunday on glandular troubles and "male weakness," and conducted a "medical question-box" series, through which he diagnosed the ailments of his listeners and developed a thriving mail-order drug business. Between medical programs, KFKB offered country music, market news, fundamentalist theology, and, as a public service feature, the College of the Air, which offered courses for credit from Kansas State College in Manhattan. In 1930 KFKB was selected in a contest sponsored by *Radio Digest* as the most popular station in the United States. The station's income ranged from $5,000 to $7,000 a week, supplemented by another $5,000 from an arrangement under which Brinkley sold secret remedies obtainable only from Brinkley-affiliated druggists.

Brinkley bolstered his position by giving free time over KFKB to prominent political figures in the state, but he soon ran into determined opposition from organized medicine. In April 1930 the Kansas Medical Society, spurred on by the American Medical Association and by a series of exposés in the *Kansas City Star,* filed a complaint charging him with addiction to alcohol, malpractice, and unprofessional conduct. In June the Federal Radio Commission, in an important decision that established its right to decide on the basis of past program content whether a radio station served the public interest, rejected KFKB's application for renewal of its license. That September, after extended hearings, the state medical board of Kansas revoked Brinkley's license to practice medicine on the grounds that the transplantation of goat glands into humans was biologically worthless.

Seeking to defend his reputation and protect his business interests, Brinkley announced his candidacy for governor of Kansas as an independent. Although it was too late to have his name printed on the ballot, he conducted a vigorous campaign, promising free schoolbooks, old-age assistance, a just tax structure, free medical clinics, and new roads, and played on religious themes to enhance his image as a messiah. Drawing support chiefly from central Kansas, an area that previously had been the backbone of the Populist movement, he polled a write-in vote of nearly 30 percent. It was widely conceded that if his name had been on the ballot Brinkley would have won the election. He tried again, though with less success, in 1932 and 1934.

Meanwhile, under an accommodation with the Mexican government, Brinkley had built a powerful transmitter, XER, at Villa Acuña, Coahuila, across the Rio Grande from Del Rio, Texas. From Milford, or from his hotel room in Del Rio, Brinkley advertised for patients by remote-control radio, while the mighty wave of XER (later XERA) washed over the whole of the United States with enough power left over, as a writer in the *Chicago Daily News* phrased it, "to light the street lights in Calgary." In 1933 Brinkley shifted all of his movable property, including his diamonds and $80,000 in cash, to Del Rio, where he deemphasized the gland graft and turned his attention to the prostate gland.

At Del Rio he continued to prosper, handling somewhere in the neighborhood of 16,000 patients over the next four and a quarter years and earning between eight and twelve million dollars. Frankly delighting in his material success, he accumulated about a dozen Cadillacs (on one of which the name "Dr. Brinkley" appeared in thirteen places), several oil properties, three large yachts, a Lockheed Electra airplane, a ranch in Texas, a goat farm in Oklahoma, and a 6,500-acre estate in North Carolina. He also built a branch hospital for the treatment of rectal diseases, situated in an orange and grapefruit grove in San Juan, Texas.

As the 1930's drew to a close, however, Brinkley suffered a series of reverses. These began with two critical articles in *Hygeia,* a publication of the American Medical Association, written by its editor, Morris Fishbein. With wounded pride, and claiming that his annual income had dropped to "about $810,000," Brinkley filed suit for libel, but a jury decided in 1939 that he had been correctly characterized as a quack, and the verdict was sustained on appeal. By that time Brinkley had been forced by a cut-rate competitor in Del Rio, who duplicated his prostate specialty, to relocate in Little Rock, Ark. He established two hospitals there, but hardly had time to capitalize on them. Plagued by malpractice suits totaling more than a million dollars and a government claim for $200,000 in back income taxes, Brinkley transferred his assets to others, including his second wife and their son. He then filed a petition in bankruptcy at Del Rio, subject, however, to the generous exemptions allowed under the Texas constitution. Finally, in the spring of 1941, Mexico, pressed by the United States to reallocate the wavelength assignments under the North American Regional Broadcasting Agreement of 1937, closed down XERA, and the voice of the radio physician was stilled forever. Although Brinkley successfully salvaged a large part of his fortune, his career in medicine had come to an end.

"Dr. Brinkley" was an artist in the manipulation of men, a Kansas Cagliostro, bold and imaginative in pushing his career in irregular medicine. In appearance he was blond and rotund, with shrewd blue eyes, reddish-brown moustache, neat goatee, and a retreating hairline. Emerging from obscurity with an insatiable yearning for power and place, he made a fortune by mingling a popular interest in the glands of internal secretion with the ancient symbolism of the billy goat and became — inadvertently — a shaper of broadcasting techniques and the evolution of radio law. Following the emergency amputation of a leg because of a blood clot, Brinkley died in San Antonio, Texas, in 1942, of heart disease and complications arising from the amputation. He was buried at Forest Hill Cemetery, Memphis, Tenn.

[Gerald Carson, *The Roguish World of Doctor Brinkley* (1960); Clement Wood, *The Life of a Man* (1934), a biased and unreliable treatment of Brinkley's career up to the date of publication, written on order, but the only source for certain details of Brinkley's early life; Ansel Harlan Resler, "The Impact of John R. Brinkley on Broadcasting in the U. S." (Ph.D. dissertation, Northwestern Univ., 1958); Don B. Schlecta, "Dr. John R. Brinkley: A Kans. Phenomenon" (master's thesis, Kans. State College, Hays, 1952); Thomas W. Schruben, *Kansas in Turmoil, 1930–1936* (1969), on his gubernatorial campaign; Thomas N. Bonner, *The Kans. Doctor—A Century of Pioneering* (1959), pp. 207–21; Eric Barnouw, *A Tower in Babel: A Hist. of Broadcasting in the U. S. to 1933* (1966); U. S. District Court for the Western District of Texas, Del Rio Division, "In the Matter of John R. Brinkley, Bankrupt Case No. 130"; interviews with persons who knew Brinkley. Promotional literature issued by Brinkley and reports of court cases, as well as a large collection of periodical and newspaper clippings, including extensive coverage in the *Kans. City Star* and *Times,* may be found in the files of the Bureau of Investigation, Am. Medic. Assoc. Substantial holdings also exist at the Kans. State Hist. Soc. A good short account is that of Jack D. Walker in *Jour. of the Kans. Medic. Soc.,* Dec. 1956.]

GERALD CARSON

BRISTOW, JOSEPH LITTLE (July 22, 1861–July 14, 1944), Senator from Kansas, was born near Hazel Green, Wolfe County, Ky., the younger of two children and only son of William Bristow, a circuit-riding Methodist minister, and Savannah (Little) Bristow. His father's forebears had emigrated from Bristol, England, to Virginia in the 1680's; a later generation had moved to Kentucky. Joseph's mother died in 1868, and the boy went to live on the Kentucky farm of his paternal grandfather, also a Methodist minister. In 1873 he joined his father (who had remarried) in Kansas, but he returned to Kentucky in 1876. On Nov. 12, 1879, at eighteen, he married Margaret Hester Hendrix of Flemingsburg, Ky. Of their five children—William H., Bertha May, Joseph Quayle, Frank Baker, and Edwin McKinley—the first two died in infancy.

With his bride, Bristow rejoined his father at Howard City, Kans., late in 1879, and after a year of farming entered Baker University in Baldwin, Kans., from which he graduated in 1886. That year he was elected to the first of two terms (1886–90) as clerk of the district court of Douglas County, during which time he read law. In 1890 he bought the first of a series of Kansas newspapers he was to own throughout his political career. In 1903 he became co-owner of the *Salina Evening Journal,* of which he was sole owner from 1907 to 1925. An ardent anti-Populist in a time of agrarian unrest, Bristow helped form the Kansas Republican League of 1892 and the Kansas Day Club, activities which caught the attention of the state G.O.P. leader, Cyrus Leland, Jr. He was defeated in his bid for a Congressional nomination in 1894, but served as secretary of the Republican state central committee and then as private secretary to Gov. Edmund N. Morrill [*q.v.*] from 1895 to 1897.

A sound-money Republican, Bristow supported William McKinley in 1896 and was rewarded with the office of Fourth Assistant Postmaster General, an influential position in the distribution of patronage. During the American occupation of Cuba he succeeded in reducing corruption in the island's postal system. A similar attempt in the United States, however, implicated several prominent Republican legislators, and President Theodore Roosevelt, under political pressure, forced Bristow to resign in January 1905. To make amends, Roosevelt appointed the Kansan special commissioner to the Panama Canal project to look into the management and policies of the Panama Railroad Company.

As an editor in the 1890's Bristow had shown progressive tendencies, and in 1906, when his faction in the splintered Kansas Republican party failed to support his Senatorial candidacy, he joined the antirailroad movement led by Walter R. Stubbs [Supp. 1]. Bristow and other progressives urged that Kansas adopt a direct Senatorial primary, a measure which finally passed in 1908. That year, in his second try for a Senate seat, Bristow's campaign was managed by William Allen White [Supp. 3], editor of the *Emporia Gazette.* Bristow defeated his former ally Chester I. Long in the primary and was elected to the Senate by the state legislature in January 1909.

Tall and ungainly, Bristow did not fit the prevailing image of Senatorial dignity. His voice was rasping and his English unpolished, but he was a commanding speaker of great earnestness and an uncompromising fighter on the floor. He based his arguments on fact and, according to one writer, "cared nothing for 'senatorial courtesy' or feelings" (Bowers, p. 331). In the Senate, Bristow allied himself with the Insurgents, led by Robert M. La Follette [*q.v.*], in opposing much of President Taft's program. He worked against the original Mann-Elkins railroad regulation bill of 1910 because he feared the proposed commerce court would weaken the Interstate Commerce Commission. Like other Insurgents, he also opposed the Payne-Aldrich Tariff. Bristow's most important legislative contribution was his authorship of the resolution which, with some modification, became the Seventeenth Amendment to the Constitution, providing for direct election of Senators. But several other progressive measures he introduced, including an amendment for woman suffrage, were unsuccessful.

Because of their close Senate relationship, Bristow initially supported La Follette for the Republican presidential nomination in 1912 and was among the last of the progressive Republicans to shift to Roosevelt. After the Republican split, he backed Roosevelt but refused to join the Progressive party, believing it would fail. This decision cost Bristow the support of Kansas Progressives when he ran for the Senate in 1914. The Progressives nominated a candidate of their own, Victor Murdock [Supp. 3]. In the Republican primary, Bristow was narrowly defeated by Charles Curtis [Supp. 2], who was elected to the Senate in November.

Late in 1914 Gov. Arthur Capper appointed Bristow to the Kansas Public Utilities Commission. He resigned in 1918 to attempt a Senate comeback, but was badly beaten in the primary by Capper, who was subsequently elected. After this defeat, Bristow moved to Virginia to develop and enlarge property he had purchased there. Though he often spoke of returning to Kansas, he spent the remainder of his life at his estate, Ossian Hall, in Fairfax County near Annandale. He died there of a heart attack and was buried in the family plot at Gypsum Hill Cemetery, Salina, Kans.

[The Joseph L. Bristow Papers are at the Kans. State Hist. Soc., Topeka. Autobiographical accounts include: *Fraud and Politics at the Turn of the Century: McKinley and His Administration as Seen by His Principal Patronage Dispenser and Investigator* (ed. by Joseph Q. and Frank B. Bristow, 1952), and an article in the *Saturday Evening Post,* Sept. 30, 1911. Biographical assessments are: A. Bower Sageser, *Joseph L. Bristow: Kans. Progressive* (1968); William H. Mitchell, "Joseph L. Bristow, Kans. Insurgent in the U. S. Senate" (M.A. thesis, Univ. of Kans., 1952); and articles in: *Outlook,* Nov. 21, 1908, Mar. 30, 1912; *American Mag.,* Oct. 1909; and *Rev. of Revs.,* Jan. 1904. Useful references to Bristow can be found in: *The Autobiog. of William Allen White* (1946); Walter Johnson, *William Allen White's America* (1947); James Holt, *Congressional Insurgents and the Party System, 1909–1916* (1967); Kenneth W. Hechler, *Insurgency* (1940); and Claude G. Bowers, *Beveridge and the Progressive Era* (1932).]
ROBERT SHERMAN LA FORTE

BRÖDEL, MAX (June 8, 1870–Oct. 26, 1941), medical illustrator and anatomist, was born in Leipzig, Germany, the second of three children and only son of Louis Brödel, a manager in the Steinweg piano works, and Henrietta (Frenzel) Brödel. Max Brödel was reared in the Evangelical Lutheran Church. He attended local public schools, spent a year (1884–85) at the Technical High School, studied at the Leipzig Academy of Fine Arts (1885–90), and served for two years (1890–92) in the German army.

To earn money during his years at the academy Brödel obtained part-time jobs drawing illustrations for the medical research being carried out at the University of Leipzig. While working for the physiologist Karl Ludwig, he met two mem-

bers of the Johns Hopkins Medical School faculty, the anatomist Franklin P. Mall and the pathologist William H. Welch [qq.v.]. Mall, impressed with Brödel's skill at portraying clinical material, was instrumental in bringing him to the United States, in January 1894, to make drawings of operative procedures and pathological specimens for the Hopkins gynecologist Howard A. Kelly [Supp. 3].

At Johns Hopkins, Brödel, feeling handicapped by his lack of medical knowledge, studied anatomy and physiology and learned to make his own dissections. His clear and informative illustrations for Kelly's *Operative Gynecology* (1898) and Thomas S. Cullen's *Cancer of the Uterus* (1900) brought him recognition as the foremost medical artist in the United States. In 1909 he was appointed an honorary member of the Medical and Chirurgical Faculty of Maryland, the only non-physician ever to receive such a privilege. In 1911, through the efforts of Dr. Cullen and with the financial support of the Baltimore philanthropist Henry Walters [q.v.], a "Department of Art as Applied to Medicine" was established at Johns Hopkins. Brödel was appointed director, with the rank of associate professor; in the years until his retirement in 1940 the department trained some 200 medical artists from throughout the United States and Canada.

When Brödel began his career, most medical publications were illustrated by relatively poor drawings made by draftsmen who lacked training in either medicine or art. Brödel based his work on close attention to anatomic detail. He insisted on seeing for himself the organ or process to be shown and gaining a thorough understanding of the clinical phenomena involved. "A clear and vivid [mental] picture," he wrote, "always must precede the actual picture on paper. The planning of the picture, therefore, is the all-important thing, not the execution." The resulting drawings constituted a positive addition to medical knowledge. To elucidate a problem he sometimes carried out laboratory research of his own. A serious infection of his left arm and hand, received in 1899 when he was dissecting autopsied material, resulted in damage to the ulnar nerve. He used the misfortune to discover more about the anatomy involved; in a set of meticulous drawings he mapped the areas of numbness in his arms and traced the later recovery of sensation. In another investigation, to determine the blood supply of the kidney, he delineated an area relatively free of blood vessels and suggested that in operations for kidney stone the incision be made along this line (now known as Brödel's line). He also devised a suture to repair a prolapsed kidney (now known as Brödel's suture).

During summer vacations at Ahmic Lake in Ontario Brödel relaxed by hunting, fishing, collecting fungi, and painting landscapes. His nonmedical sketching included the design of bookplates for several of his friends and a famous cartoon, "The St. John's Hopkins Hospital," showing William Osler [q.v.], wearing halo and wings, rising above the Johns Hopkins Hospital dome while various germs flee below. Brödel had a warm personality that brought him many friends. With the author Henry L. Mencken, he was a founder (1910) and a leading figure of Baltimore's Saturday Night Club. Perhaps Brödel's chief pleasure, aside from medical illustration, was playing the piano. An accomplished performer, he had begun studying at the age of six, and music, particularly that of Beethoven, remained a lifelong passion.

On Dec. 31, 1902, Brödel married Ruth Marian Huntington of Sandusky, Ohio, a biomedical artist who shared his delight in music. Their four children were Elizabeth, who served for many years as illustrator in the department of obstetrics and gynecology at Cornell Medical College; Ruth (who died young); Carl; and Elsa. Brödel died in Baltimore at the age of seventy of metastatic cancer of the pancreas, a few days after an operation. He had revolutionized medical illustration and had also taught a group of leading artists who have continued his work.

[Thomas S. Cullen, "Max Brödel," Medic. Lib. Assoc., Bull., Jan. 1945; Max Brödel, "Medical Illustration," Jour. Am. Medic. Assoc., Aug. 30, 1941; V. A. McKusick, "Brödel's Ulnar Palsy, with Unpublished Brödel Sketches," Bull. of the Hist. of Medicine, Sept.–Oct. 1949; Judith Robinson, Tom Cullen of Baltimore (1949); editorial in Baltimore Sun, Oct. 28, 1941; Ruth Huntington Brödel, "Notes on Max Brödel" (MS), supplied by his daughter Elizabeth H. Brödel. An extensive collection of photographs and portraits of Brödel, as well as originals of his work, is deposited in the Dept. of Art as Applied to Medicine of the Johns Hopkins Univ. School of Medicine. An oil portrait by Thomas Corner is reproduced in Jour. Am. Medic. Assoc., Mar. 12, 1938.]
VICTOR A. MCKUSICK

BROOKHART, SMITH WILDMAN (Feb. 2, 1869–Nov. 15, 1944), Senator from Iowa, was born in a log cabin near Arbela in Scotland County, Mo., the eldest of ten children (six boys and four girls) of Abram Colar Brookhart and Cynthia (Wildman) Brookhart. His father, a farmer of German-Swiss ancestry, was a native of Ohio; his mother, of Indiana. During Smith's childhood the family moved briefly to Minnesota and then in 1879 to Iowa. Smith was educated at country schools, at the Bloomfield (Iowa) high school, and at Southern Iowa Normal and Scientific Institute in Bloomfield, where he graduated

in 1889. While teaching school in Keosauqua, Iowa, he read law in local law offices. He was admitted to the bar in 1892 and went into practice in Washington Township, later forming a partnership with two of his brothers. During these years he also maintained a farm and entered into several local business ventures. He was a Methodist in religion. On June 22, 1897, he married Jennie Hearn of Keosauqua, by whom he had seven children: Samuel Colar (who died in infancy), Charles Edward, John Robert, Smith Wildman, Florence Hearn, Edith Alma, and Joseph Warren.

Brookhart's initiation into politics came in 1895 when he was appointed attorney for Washington County, a position he held until 1901. A vigorous opponent of railroads, corporate interests, and Eastern financiers, he aligned himself with the Republican party's progressive wing, led by Gov. Albert B. Cummins [q.v.], and was subsequently appointed to Cummins's staff. Having developed an impressive style of stump oratory, Brookhart made an unsuccessful bid for a Congressional nomination in 1910, after which he bought an interest in the *Washington County Press* and used its editorial columns to continue his populistic attacks on the railroads. He was appointed chairman of the Iowa Republican state convention in 1912 but chose to support Theodore Roosevelt and the Progressive party. Brookhart had joined the Iowa National Guard in 1894, had served in the Spanish-American War, and had become an expert marksman; during World War I he was chief instructor in small-arms marksmanship at two army camps, rising to the rank of lieutenant colonel.

After returning to civilian life, Brookhart in 1920 found himself in conflict with his mentor, Cummins, over the Esch-Cummins Transportation Act, which directed that railroad properties taken over by the government during World War I be returned to private control. In that year he challenged Cummins for the Republican Senatorial nomination. He was unsuccessful, but his strong performance and the onset of an agricultural depression made him a leading contender to fill the two-year unexpired term of Senator William S. Kenyon [Supp. 1], who resigned in 1922 to accept a federal judgeship. Despite opposition from the party organization, Brookhart won the primary and the general election with the backing of farmers and organized labor. He was elected to a full term in 1924, but by a very narrow margin, having lost considerable support by his public attacks on President Coolidge, his characterization of vice-presidential candidate Charles G. Dawes as a "plutogogue," and his undisguised enthusiasm for the Progressive presidential candidate, Senator Robert M. La Follette [*q.v.*]. Brookhart's Democratic opponent, Daniel F. Steck, abetted by the state Republican committee, contested the election results, and the Senate, after a prolonged investigation, voted to seat Steck. Undaunted, Brookhart defeated Cummins in the 1926 primary, and went on to win a decisive victory over the Democratic candidate.

In the Senate, Brookhart spoke out for the interests of the "common people" who had provided his electoral support. He aligned himself with the farm bloc and with the Republican insurgents, although his proposals and his sometimes inflamed rhetoric often made him seem more radical than his associates. Along with men like Henrik Shipstead, Lynn Frazier, and George W. Norris [Supp. 3], he was one of that group of Senators who came to be dubbed "Sons of the Wild Jackass." Brookhart quickly established a reputation as a caustic critic of Republican policies. An opponent of the administration's farm program, he supported an early version of the McNary-Haugen Bill and even urged the creation of a $1,500,000,000 federal fund to buy up the entire exportable surplus. He further embarrassed his party by opposing the tax policies of Andrew Mellon [Supp. 2] and by introducing measures to include representatives of agriculture and labor on the Federal Reserve Board, to abolish the gold standard, for federal control of stock speculation, and for government ownership of railroads and toll bridges. He also filibustered against the ship subsidy bill of 1923 and opposed the foreign debt settlement and the World Court. Although an avowed pacifist, he was a staunch friend of veterans and led the successful fight to override Coolidge's 1924 veto of the soldiers' bonus.

A square-jawed, muscular man who usually dressed in shapeless sack suits, Brookhart was, according to one observer, a combination of a "county seat lawyer, rural pedagogue, parlor Radical and Granger political philosopher" (Cook, p. 180). In his speeches he combined a barrage of statistical fact with a simplistic conspiracy theory of history. Farmers and workers were grievously mulcted by "predatory blocs" and by the "non-partisan league of Wall Street"; the Federal Reserve Board had deliberately chosen to deflate agriculture in a secret meeting on May 18, 1920; and agriculture's growth lagged behind the rest of the economy. A rigid teetotaler, Brookhart also felt the Eighteenth Amendment was being subverted by "High Finance." Stemming from such beliefs was his desire to create a new economic order. "Competitive economics," he argued, had proven "a stupendous and disastrous failure." As an alternative he proposed producers' and consumers' cooperatives, based on the Rochdale plan developed in Great Britain. Brookhart, who had traveled to the Soviet Union after his first election to the Senate, also praised that government's efforts to establish a cooperative economy.

In 1928, reversing his usual political posture, Brookhart campaigned extensively for Herbert Hoover, whose record as food administrator and in support of prohibition impressed him. He soon split with the new administration, however, over its farm program and returned to the familiar role of opposition. His political career ended with his defeat in the 1932 primary. He served as foreign trade adviser in the Agricultural Adjustment Administration from 1933 to 1935, ran unsuccessfully for the Senatorial nomination in 1936, and resumed his law practice in Washington, D. C., until 1943, when he retired to the home of a daughter at Prescott, Ariz. He died of cardiac disease at the age of seventy-five in the Veterans' Hospital in Whipple, Ariz., and was buried in Elm Grove Cemetery, Washington, Iowa.

[A small collection of Brookhart's papers is in the Iowa State Dept. of Hist. and Archives, Des Moines, Iowa. Published accounts include: Jerry A. Neprash, *The Brookhart Campaigns in Iowa, 1920–1926* (1932); Reinhard H. Luthin in *Agricultural Hist.*, Oct. 1951; Ray Tucker and Frederick R. Barkley, *Sons of the Wild Jackass* (1932); Louis H. Cook in *North Am. Rev.*, Feb. 1931; N. Y. *Times* obituary, Nov. 16, 1944; *Biog. Directory Am. Cong.* (1961). On his family background, see Howard A. Burrell, *Hist. of Washington County, Iowa* (1909).]

ALBERT U. ROMASCO

BROWN, CARLETON (July 15, 1869–June 25, 1941), philologist and professor of English, was born in Oberlin, Ohio, the elder of the two sons of Justus Newton Brown and Hattie Augusta (Sparhawk) Brown, both natives of Ohio. His middle name, which he early discarded, was Fairchild. His father, whose first American ancestor, Charles Brown, had emigrated from England to Rowley, Mass., about 1648, was a graduate of Oberlin College and, in 1871, of its theological seminary. During his son's childhood he held Congregational pastorates in Talladega, Ala. (1874–75), Wilton, N. H. (1876–78), Charlotte, Mich. (1878–81), and Owatonna, Minn. (1881–89). Carleton attended Pillsbury Academy in Owatonna, a Baptist preparatory school, and Carleton College in Northfield, Minn., where he received the B.A. degree in 1888. After working on two small-town newspapers (he was part-owner of one, the biweekly *Salida* [Colo.] *Mail*), he attended the Andover (Mass.) Theological Seminary (1890–93) and in 1894 was ordained a Unitarian minister. He served at St. Cloud,

Minn. (1894–97), and at Helena, Mont. (1897–1900), but in 1900 gave up the ministry for graduate study in English at Harvard. He received the Ph.D. degree in 1903 with a thesis on the English grammar schools before the Reformation.

Brown began his teaching career at Harvard, staying on as an instructor until 1905, when he moved to the English department at Bryn Mawr College. There he became associate professor in 1907 and professor in 1910. He spent four years (1916–20) at the University of Minnesota and, after a year at Oxford, England, returned to Bryn Mawr (1921–27). He then went to New York University, where he remained until his retirement in 1939 (at which time he was awarded an honorary LL.D.). The move to New York University had been spurred by its support of the Modern Language Association, of which Brown was secretary.

Primarily a medievalist, "a scholar's scholar," Carleton Brown devoted his principal research to Middle English manuscripts and their treatment of religious themes. His first book was *A Study of the Miracle of Our Lady Told by Chaucer's Prioress* (1910). Later came *A Register of Middle English Religious and Didactic Verse* (2 vols., 1916–20), afterward revised and expanded, in collaboration with Prof. Rossell Hope Robbins, as *The Index of Middle English Verse* (1943), a work that listed some four thousand manuscripts, secular as well as religious. Brown compiled anthologies of thirteenth-, fourteenth-, and fifteenth-century lyrics (1932, 1924, and 1939 respectively). In addition he edited several lesser texts: *Venus and Adonis* (1911); *Poems by Sir John Salusbury and Robert Chester* (1914), for the Early English Text Society; *The Stonyhurst Pageants* (1920) ; and *The Pardoner's Tale* (1935). Beginning in 1903 he regularly contributed articles and reviews, mainly on Chaucer and newly discovered texts, to journals such as *Modern Language Notes, Modern Philology,* and *PMLA (Publications of the Modern Language Association)*. He was honored by election as a fellow of the Mediaeval Academy of America and of the American Academy of Arts and Sciences.

A second major interest was the Modern Language Association of America, which Brown served as secretary from 1920 to 1934. Under his aegis, the Central Division was reunited with the parent body, the meager capital funds increased eightfold, and the membership more than doubled. He enlarged the association's journal, *PMLA,* and launched new publishing projects, notably the New Shakespeare Variorum Series and the *Middle English Dictionary.* As secretary, Brown was himself editor of *PMLA,* a sensitive post which

enhanced his reputation among the productive scholars of America. Upon his resignation as secretary in 1934, the association resolved that it owed to Brown more than to anyone else its "immense increases in resources, service, and prestige." He was elected president in 1936. His half-time commitment to the Modern Language Association while at New York University somewhat limited his guidance of graduate students, but both there and at Bryn Mawr he encouraged the highest scholarly standards, and many of the dissertations written by his students are still consulted.

Brown was a courteous man with strong convictions. Sometimes intransigent with department colleagues and with other scholars, he could at other times display great diplomatic skill. Though portly, he was physically strong, refusing to wear an overcoat in winter and capable, at seventy, of rowing for several hours under a hot sun. His comfortable but unostentatious house stood in a pleasant wooded section of Upper Montclair, N. J., which afforded a few trails where Brown could take his daily constitutional. He was ethically rigid, and sometimes out of sympathy with the changing attitudes of younger people, but his innate modesty is shown by his humility in realizing only belatedly that the volume ceremoniously presented to him in 1940 was not a gift for his library but a festschrift, a tribute from America's most distinguished medievalists.

Carleton Brown was first married to Emily Laura Truesdell of Owatonna, Minn., on June 7, 1893; their three children were Margery Lorraine, Wendell Edwards (who died in infancy), and Truesdell Sparhawk. After Emily's death in 1917, he married on Aug. 13, 1918, (Elizabeth) Beatrice Daw of Athens, Pa., a young Bryn Mawr-trained medievalist nineteen years his junior. Their three children were Emily Parker Lawless, Beatrice Carleton (who died in childhood), and Carleton Justus. Carleton Brown died at the age of seventy-one at Mountainside Hospital, Glen Ridge, N. J., of pulmonary edema owing to cardiac failure. After Unitarian services, he was cremated at Rosehill Crematory, Linden, N. J., and the ashes were interred at Owatonna, Minn.

[An appreciation of Brown by Percy W. Long appears in the *Essays and Studies in Honor of Carleton Brown* (1940). The Dec. 1935 issue of *PMLA* includes an appreciation and a bibliography of his writings. (Both items reproduce photographs of Brown.) The biographical sketch in *Nat. Cyc. Am. Biog.,* XXXI, 244–45, includes genealogical details and an accurate evaluation. Other information from: *Congregational Year-Book,* 1925, p. 49, and Oberlin College Archives (on his father) ; Harvard Univ. Archives (on his middle name) ; N. J. State Dept. of Health (death record); *N. Y. Times,* June 26, 1941 (obituary); and close personal association.]

ROSSELL HOPE ROBBINS

BROWN, WILLIAM ADAMS (Dec. 29, 1865–Dec. 15, 1943), Presbyterian minister, liberal theologian, and leader in the ecumenical movement, was born in New York City, the eldest of the three sons and three daughters of John Crosby Brown and Mary Elizabeth (Adams) Brown. His paternal great-grandfather was Alexander Brown (1764–1834) [*q.v.*], a Baltimore merchant and banker born in northern Ireland. His grandfather, James Brown (1791–1877) [*q.v.*], founded the Wall Street banking firm of Brown Brothers & Company, of which his father later became head. His maternal grandfather, William Adams [*q.v.*], was pastor of New York's Madison Square Presbyterian Church. Both families had important connections with Union Theological Seminary; James Brown and William Adams had been key figures in its founding, and John Crosby Brown was for many years a member of its board of directors.

In this large, close-knit circle, William was reared in an atmosphere of wealth and warm spiritual conviction. The two families shared a summer retreat in New Jersey, where they extended hospitality to tenement dwellers from the city, thus giving Brown a taste of charitable work. He attended St. Paul's School, Concord, N. H., spent a year studying art and music in Vienna, and then entered Yale, where he specialized in the classics and economics. Upon graduation in 1886, he returned for a year of further study in economics (he received an M.A. in 1888). Like many Yale men of the time he was deeply influenced by Prof. William Graham Sumner [*q.v.*]. In 1887 he entered Union Theological Seminary, where he particularly enjoyed studying biblical interpretation under Charles A. Briggs [*q.v.*]; he also took a philosophy seminar at Columbia under Nicholas Murray Butler. On graduation from Union (1890), he was awarded a fellowship for study abroad and spent two years at the University of Berlin. There he fell under the influence of Adolf Harnack, who became a lifelong friend and gave Brown (as he later wrote) "what I most needed at the time, the vision of what a teacher of religion should be—a man of conviction, disciplined by knowledge and tempered with sympathy." It was Harnack's strongly ethical focus—the theological legacy of Albrecht Ritschl—and his striving for a living faith that most attracted Brown. While in Berlin, Brown attended Socialist rallies and observed city mission work, and he visited Toynbee Hall in Lon-

don. On Mar. 30, 1892, he married Helen Gilman Noyes, by whom he had three sons— John Crosby, William Adams, Winthrop Gilman —and a daughter, Helen, who died in her teens.

On his return from Germany, Brown began a long teaching career at Union Theological Seminary and in January 1893 was ordained as a Presbyterian minister. He became professor of systematic theology at Union (1898–1930) and then research professor in applied Christianity (1930–36)—an apt title since his entire ministry was intensely activist. A Cleveland Democrat from his college days, Brown worked in the 1904 anti-Tammany campaign led by Charles H. Parkhurst [*q.v.*] and as a member of the Committee of Fourteen fought against commercialized vice. He was one of the group of alumni of Union Theological Seminary who in 1895 founded Union Settlement in New York City. His involvement in urban problems contributed to his selection in 1909 as chairman of the Home Missions Committee of the Presbytery of New York and his election a year later to the Board of Home Missions of the Presbyterian Church in the U.S.A. In this capacity he assisted Charles Stelzle [Supp. 3] in founding Labor Temple in New York and defended the right of radicals to speak there. Brown's conviction that the church must work actively as a social institution "if wrongs are to be righted and progress made possible" was reinforced by his 1916 tour of missions in Latin America and the Far East, and by his service as executive secretary of the General War-Time Commission of the Churches (organized by the Federal Council of the Churches of Christ in America) during the First World War. In 1920 he became the chairman of the Federal Council's Department of Research and Education.

A liberal and modernist in theology, Brown had two great concerns: discerning and teaching "the essence of Christianity," and the promotion of church unity, an ideal he had absorbed from both Briggs and Harnack. In his early career he was surrounded by the theological controversy generated by the impact of modern scientific thought, as reflected in the accusations of heresy lodged against Briggs and Arthur Cushman McGiffert [Supp. 1]. These instances combined with Brown's irenic temperament and his practical experience to strengthen his desire for an end to ecclesiastical disputes. Church unity he regarded as both a spiritual necessity and an indispensable precondition of effective church work, especially in bringing classes, nations, and races together in fellowship. He was a leader in the American delegation to the Universal Christian Conference (later Council) on Life and Work, held in Stockholm in 1925, and worked with Charles H. Brent [Supp. 1] in planning the World Conference on Faith and Order which met at Lausanne in 1927. When the two conferences met again in 1937, in Britain, Brown helped achieve a working relationship between them, a movement which culminated in the organization of the World Council of Churches (1938). Mrs. Brown shared her husband's zeal for ecumenism and served with distinction in various organizations devoted to this cause.

Second only to his concern for ecumenism was Brown's interest in higher education. From 1917 to 1934 he was a member of the Yale Corporation (the university's governing body), where he took a leading role in improving the quality of teaching and in better coordinating the various divisions of the university; he was acting provost of Yale in 1919–20. Brown was the first chairman (1924) of the Department of Research and Education of the Federal Council of Churches and president of the Religious Education Association, 1928–31. He was one of the founders and the first president of the American Theological Society, composed of teachers of theology. He led, as well, in the work of many other church-related educational projects, including the first major survey of American theological education; he wrote the summarizing volume of its report, *The Education of American Ministers* (4 vols., 1934).

In the midst of other labors, Brown took the degree of Ph.D., in absentia, from Yale in 1901. His doctoral thesis was the basis of *The Essence of Christianity* (1902), the first of his fifteen books. His focus remained Christocentric throughout, but he became progressively attached to the idea that a church made truly Christian could Christianize society. Thus he broadened the academic focus of his first book and of his *Christian Theology in Outline* (1906) to the more popular appeal of *Is Christianity Practicable?* (1916) and *Beliefs That Matter* (1928) —titles that reflect his indebtedness to the pragmatism of William James [q.v.]. These works confirm his early search for "a theology which could be preached as a gospel." The best summary of his mature thought, revealing both his ecumenical commitment and the evolution of his understanding of doctrine and the church, is *The Church: Catholic and Protestant* (1935).

At Union, Brown won more respect for his humanity than for his pedagogy. His outside commitments caused frequent absences from the seminary, but these were accepted by students and colleagues, who valued his patience, kindliness, and amiability. He had a lifelong interest in art and music and was an avid gardener. At his summer home in Seal Harbor, Maine, he enjoyed vigorous outdoor sports. Brown died in New York City in 1943 after an attack of pneumonia and was buried in Greenwood Cemetery, Brooklyn.

[Brown's autobiography, *A Teacher and His Times* (1940), covers both the personal and the professional aspects of his life; see also his "Seeking Beliefs That Matter" in Vergilius Ferm, ed., *Contemporary Am. Theology: Theological Autobiogs.*, 2nd series (1933). Samuel McCrea Cavert and Henry P. Van Dusen, eds., *The Church through Half a Century: Essays in Honor of William Adams Brown* (1936), includes an extended biographical essay, an analysis of Brown's contributions to the literature of religion, and a list of his writings down to 1936. See also *Who Was Who in America*, vol. II (1950); and Henry Sloane Coffin, *A Half Century of Union Theological Seminary* (1954).]

SAMUEL McCREA CAVERT

BRUCE, EDWARD BRIGHT (Apr. 13, 1879–Jan. 26, 1943), painter, lawyer, businessman, federal art administrator, was born in Dover Plains, N. Y., the second of three sons of James M. and Mary (Bright) Bruce. His mother wrote children's stories; his father, of Scottish descent, was a Baptist minister in Yonkers, N. Y. Young Bruce attended public and private schools in Yonkers and New York City. From earliest boyhood he hoped to become a painter, and at the age of fourteen he began drawing and outdoor sketching under the guidance of Arthur Parton [q.v.] and Francis J. Murphy. As he acquired technical skill, however, he found that he had nothing important to express, and gave up the idea of painting as a career. Influenced also by the desire to assist his family's precarious finances, he entered Columbia University—where he was a notable football player—and after receiving the A.B. degree in 1901, went on to the Columbia Law School, from which he graduated with honors in 1904. He began practice with the firm later headed by Paul D. Cravath [Supp. 2], but after three years moved to Manila as attorney for the American Philippine Railroad Company. The next year he formed his own law firm in Manila and became part owner of the *Manila Times*. On Nov. 29, 1909, in Yokohama, Japan, he married Margaret Stow of Santa Barbara, Calif. They had no children.

For the next ten years Bruce was involved in various business ventures, after 1911 in China, where as president of the Pacific Development Company he sought to promote Oriental trade. During this time he collected Chinese paintings and curios and learned a deep appreciation of their serenity, dignity, and rhythm. He began to look at nature anew, and resumed painting, finding that he now had something to say. In 1919 he and his wife returned to New York City. As Oriental trade began to encounter difficulties, Bruce turned more and more to artistic work; in 1921 the Bourgeois Gallery showed three of his paintings in a group exhibition, and the critic Henry McBride gave them an enthusiastic review.

The Pacific Development Company failed in 1922, and although Bruce received a number of lucrative offers in business and banking, he decided at this point to become a professional painter. Moving to Anticoli Corrado, Italy, he began serious work under the guidance of his friend Maurice Sterne, concentrating particularly on landscapes. He burned his first year's production but later had shows at Scott and Fowles (1925) and at the New Gallery (1927) in which every picture was sold. He bought a villa in Settignano, near Florence; lived, traveled, and painted in Italy and France; exhibited successfully in Paris, selling a landscape to the Luxembourg Museum; and returned to New York just after the stock market crash of 1929.

Contemporaries such as Leo Stein, who compared him to Matisse, recognized Bruce as an important painter. His landscapes were distinguished by his unique ability to perceive nature within the spatial framework of a picture, by simplicity of composition and execution, and by individual rhythms that grew naturally from the conception. (He produced very few portraits and only one mural, a view of San Francisco and the bay for the board room of the city's stock exchange.)

In 1930–31 Bruce lived and painted in Oregon and California. While visiting San Francisco, he was persuaded to become a lobbyist for the Manila Chamber of Commerce, to help promote Philippine independence, and in 1932 he moved to Washington, D. C. His acquaintance with Senator Key Pittman [Supp. 2] of Nevada, chairman of the Foreign Affairs Committee, led to his appointment as silver expert for the United States delegation to the London Economic Conference (1933). Increasingly involved in politics, Bruce kept open house for a stimulating company of politicians, administrators, experts, businessmen, journalists, and artists. In these years of depression and unemployment he was well informed about the innovative proposals of the New Deal, and when the Civil Works Administration was set up he was asked to organize an emergency program to give employment to artists, using CWA funds under the Treasury Department. Established as a temporary measure in December 1933, this first government-supported art project in the United States employed some 3,750 artists before it came to a close the following June. It was succeeded by two new programs, one in which artists were given jobs on the basis of need, and another (later the Treasury Department's Section of Fine Arts), which Bruce directed, in which artists chosen through anonymous competitions were commissioned to execute murals and sculpture for federal buildings such as post offices and courthouses. Vigorous and full of enthusiasm, with great personal charm and humor that could deliver a critical wallop in a joke, Bruce was uniquely the right man to create and administer this small but important experiment in government encouragement of the arts.

Perhaps owing to the great pressure of work, Bruce suffered a stroke in 1935, which partially paralyzed his left side. He recovered sufficiently to direct the Section of Fine Arts and to paint with a new interest and eye for color. He received a number of honors: the Columbia University medal for excellence (1937); a Doctor of Arts degree from Harvard (1938); and the Friedsam Gold Medal of the Architectural League (1938). In 1940 he was appointed to the federal Commission of Fine Arts by President Roosevelt. Early in 1943, while on a winter vacation, Bruce suffered a third stroke and died, at the age of sixty-three, in the hospital at Hollywood, Fla. His ashes were buried in the Santa Barbara (Calif.) Cemetery.

[On Bruce's painting, see his article, "What I Am Trying to Do," *Creative Art,* Nov. 1928, and appreciation in same issue by Leo Stein; Edwina Spencer, "Edward Bruce," *ibid.,* Feb. 1933, with a useful bibliography of other critical references; and Olin Dows in *Mag. of Art,* Jan. 1937. On his government work, see Olin Dows, "The New Deal's Treasury Art Programs," *Arts in Society,* vol. II, no. 4 (1963); Erica Beckh, "Government Art in the Roosevelt Era," *Art Jour.,* Fall 1960; and, for a comprehensive bibliography, Francis V. O'Connor, *Federal Support for the Visual Arts* (1969). See also obituaries in *Art Digest,* Feb. 1, 1943, and *Mag. of Art,* Feb. 1943. Mrs. Edward Bruce and Miss Maria Ealand provided information. There are papers of Edward Bruce in the Archives of Am. Art, Smithsonian Institution, Washington, D. C., and, on his art programs, in the Nat. Archives.]

OLIN DOWS

BRUSH, GEORGE DE FOREST (Sept. 28, 1855–Apr. 24, 1941), painter, was born in Shelbyville, Tenn., the second of three children and younger of two sons. His father, Alfred Clark Brush, had moved west from Connecticut to work in a sawmill in Ohio. There he married Nancy Douglas, whose forebears had left southern New England after the decline of the whaling industry. A restless man, the elder Brush moved on from Ohio to Tennessee, where he practiced dentistry, and, about 1855, back to Connecticut. Young Brush grew up chiefly in Danbury, Conn., where his father engaged in hat manufacturing.

Brush's mother was an amateur painter, and when the boy showed an inclination for drawing, he was encouraged and given rudimentary instruction at home. At sixteen he enrolled in the National Academy of Design in New York, under Prof. Lemuel E. Wilmarth [q.v.]. Three years later, in 1874, Brush entered the École des Beaux Arts in Paris, where, along with Abbott H. Thayer, J. Alden Weir [qq.v.], and other young Americans, he was a pupil of the famous academician Jean Léon Gérôme. Gérôme's style was one of infinite smoothness, where forms carefully drawn and modeled were brought to "a high French polish" with no visible brush strokes. This discipline suited Brush's thoroughgoing nature, and during his Paris years he seems to have set himself firmly against all rebellion, both in art and in personal conduct.

Brush returned from Europe in 1880. The following year he accompanied his brother on a trip to Wyoming and spent several years there and in Montana, traveling and sketching. He lived with various Indian tribes and developed a sympathy with their cultures and traditions and a concern over the rapid encroachment of white civilization. His paintings of Shoshones, Crows, and Arapahos brought him his first success. These Indian subjects were well composed, low keyed but rich in color, and meticulously painted in the approved Gérôme salon manner, but they did not portray the raw truth of a George Catlin [q.v.]. Rather, they were romantic tableaux composed much in the lyric vein of Longfellow's "Hiawatha." In "The Silence Broken," amid the hushed solitude of nature a startled Indian in a canoe looks up at the sudden call of a great white bird overhead; in "Mourning Her Brave," a squaw stands by her dead mate in the snow.

Upon his return from the West, Brush set up a studio in New York City and, in 1885, became an instructor in portrait and figure painting at the Art Students' League, where he taught, with some interruptions, until 1898. One of his pupils was Mary ("Mittie") Taylor Whelpley of Hastings, N. Y.; since her family opposed the match, they eloped and were married on Jan. 11, 1886. Their eight children were Alfred (who died in infancy), Gerome, Nancy, Tribbie, Georgia, Mary, Jane, and Thea. Gerome Brush had a modest success as a painter and sculptor, and Nancy and Mary became portrait painters. A peripatetic family, the Brushes spent frequent sojourns in Europe between 1898 and 1914, es-

pecially at Florence, Italy. They often summered in New Hampshire, where Brush bought a farm at Dublin in 1901.

Although Brush's poetic Indian canvases brought him recognition, they had a limited sale; and about 1890, to support his growing family, he shifted to other themes. Along with some portrait commissions, he began painting "mother and child" groups, semiclassical in nature, for which his wife and children served as models. These brought him a wide audience and financial success. The circular "Mother and Child" in the Boston Museum of Fine Arts (purchased in 1895 for $7,000) is one of the most celebrated and possibly the finest. Mrs. Brush is shown in profile holding one of her infants, who smiles out at the viewer from under a halo of blond curls. The contrast between the sweet-sad heavy-lidded mother and the "baby triumphant," its pink cheeks and translucent flesh tones set against the darker tones of the canvas, made it a popular favorite for many years. An earlier picture in this series, "At the Fountain," sold in 1920 for $18,000.

Brush had been elected to the Society of American Artists in 1882. He was made an Associate of the National Academy of Design in 1888—the year in which he won its First Hallgarten Prize—and an Academician in 1908. Other honors that came to him included gold medals from the Pan American and Louisiana Purchase expositions (1901 and 1904) and an honorary degree from Yale (1923). A charter member of the National Institute of Arts and Letters (1898), he was elected to its inner group, the American Academy of Arts and Letters, in 1910.

By nature Brush was a somewhat solitary man, a hard worker and a perfectionist, who lived close to his family. He was the refined late-nineteenth-century gentleman, a Christian though not a church member, proud, resistant to change, dedicated to "seeing beautifully," an enemy of "degenerate" elements in art (which he detected, for example, in the work of the French sculptor Rodin), and a believer in nobility and idealism as prime themes of painting. Like his friend Abbott Thayer, Brush was relatively untouched by the influence of the French Impressionists. Instead, in his later work, he preferred the serenity of fifteenth-century Italian painting and the lessons of that earlier teacher and writer, Cennino Cennini. Brush spent most of his later years in Dublin, N. H. He died at the age of eighty-five, of bronchopneumonia, in Hanover, N. H., and was buried in the Dublin Town Cemetery. Historically, George de Forest Brush defines the end of an era in which aesthetically concerned artists and architects, from William Morris to Richard Morris Hunt [q.v.], had attempted to restore and define the present in terms of the best of the past.

[Nancy Douglas Bowditch, *George de Forest Brush* (1970), a memoir by his daughter; George de Forest Brush, "An Artist among the Indians," *Century,* May 1885; Harold McCracken, *Portrait of the Old West* (1952), pp. 172–76; *Nat. Cyc. Am. Biog.,* XIII, 578–79; obituaries in *Art Digest,* May 1, 1941, *N. Y. Herald Tribune* and *N. Y. Times,* Apr. 25, 1941, and editorial, *ibid.,* Apr. 28; family information from Mrs. Bowditch; death record from Town Clerk, Hanover, N. H. For earlier evaluations of Brush, see Charles Caffin, *Am. Masters of Painting* (1901); Sadakichi Hartmann, *A Hist. of Am. Art,* vol. I (1902); Royal Cortissoz, *Am. Artists* (1923); Minna C. Smith in *Internat. Studio,* Apr. 1908; Lula Merrick, *ibid.,* Dec. 1922 (on his Indian paintings).]
WILLIAM M. JEWELL

BRYAN, CHARLES WAYLAND (Feb. 10, 1867–Mar. 4, 1945), governor of Nebraska and political adviser to his older brother William Jennings Bryan [q.v.], was born in Salem, Ill. He was the third son and seventh of eight children of Silas Lillard Bryan, Illinois state senator and circuit judge, and Mariah Elizabeth (Jennings) Bryan. After attending the Salem public schools and Whipple Academy in Jacksonville, Ill. (1883–84), Charles entered the University of Chicago (1885), but left before the end of his first year. In 1891 he followed his brother William to Nebraska. There he worked in Lincoln as a salesman and secretary of the Purity Extract Company and later in Omaha as a broker for an Eastern manufacturing firm. On Nov. 29, 1892, he married Bessie Louise Brokaw of Salem. They had three children: Silas Millard, Virginia, and Mary Louise.

Charles Bryan's political career began in 1896 when he agreed to handle the voluminous correspondence relating to his brother William's presidential campaign. This was the beginning of a long partnership. A hard and systematic worker with an encyclopedic memory for names and faces, Charles efficiently managed William's finances, scheduled his speaking engagements, kept an extensive card file on his political associates, and helped formulate his campaign strategy. For twenty-two years (1901–23) Charles ran his brother's journal, the *Commoner,* serving after 1914 as both associate editor and publisher.

Charles Bryan was regarded by many as more politically astute than his brother. He first sought office on his own in 1915 while William was serving as Secretary of State in the Wilson cabinet. Elected in that year to the Lincoln city commission, he was chosen mayor (1915–17) by his fellow commissioners and soon launched a campaign for municipal ownership of public utilities, expanded welfare programs, aid to the un-employed, and free legal services for the poor. To lower prices of consumer goods, he also proposed establishing public corporations to compete against utility companies, clothing manufacturers, and food processors. In 1916 and 1918 he made unsuccessful bids for the gubernatorial nomination, after which he was again elected to the Lincoln city commission and served as superintendent of streets and public improvements (1921–23). Although he won more votes than any other commissioner, he this time failed of election as mayor, having created enemies by his "radical" attacks on the conservative state government and wartime profiteers.

In 1922, after effecting a brief truce with Senator Gilbert M. Hitchcock [Supp. 1], the Bryans' perennial rival for control of the Nebraska Democratic party, Charles Bryan was elected governor, despite a statewide Republican tide. A Republican-dominated legislature, however, blocked most of the measures he advocated, including a state income tax, a reduced budget, and a rural credits program. He declined renomination in 1924 in order to become a candidate for the presidency. The Democratic national convention, deadlocked between William G. McAdoo [Supp. 3] and Alfred E. Smith [Supp. 3], finally chose the conservative John W. Davis. Although both Bryan brothers had opposed Davis, Charles accepted the vice-presidential nomination, which was offered to conciliate the Bryan wing of the party. A familiar national figure in the black silk skull cap he wore to protect his light-sensitive bald head, he campaigned vigorously, but failed to carry even his own state.

Two additional defeats for the gubernatorial nomination (1926, 1928) left him undaunted, and he subsequently won the governorship in 1930 and 1932. Working hard to solve the problems of the depression, he supported old age assistance, laws protecting bank depositors, and tariff reductions on manufactured goods. After unsuccessfully seeking nomination for the United States Senate in 1934, he served again as mayor of Lincoln (1935–37), only to be defeated in his final years as an aspirant for the governorship (1938, 1942) and Congress (1940). He died of cancer at his home in Lincoln at the age of seventy-eight and was buried in Wyuka Cemetery, Lincoln.

More of a businessman than William, Charles Bryan prized administrative efficiency and tried to reduce government expenditures. He lacked his brother's tact in dealing with political opponents, and he was not religiously motivated; he was never a church member as an adult. Yet he was a staunch supporter of prohibition and at one time headed the Nebraska Dry Federation.

Like his brother, he was basically an agrarian reformer.

[Larry G. Osnes, "Charles W. Bryan: 'His Brother's Keeper,'" *Nebr. Hist.*, Spring 1967 (the same author is at work on a full-scale biography); John G. W. Lewis, ed., *Messages and Proclamations of the Governors of Nebr., 1854–1941*, vols. III and IV (1942); Albert Shaw, "Nine Governors of the Middle West," *Am. Rev. of Revs.*, Mar. 1923; Chester H. Rowell, "Brookhart, Howell, and 'Brother Charley' Bryan," *World's Work*, Sept. 1923; articles on Bryan in *Am. Rev. of Revs.*, Oct. 1924, and *World's Work*, Sept. 1924 (an issue that also includes William Jennings Bryan's "My Brother Charles"); James C. Olson, *Hist. of Nebr.* (1955). There are useful references to Bryan in the biographies of his brother by Paul W. Glad, Paolo E. Coletta, Lawrence W. Levine, Charles M. Wilson, and Louis W. Koenig. There are papers of Charles and William Bryan at the Nebr. State Hist. Soc.; a collection of Charles's correspondence with his brother is still in family hands. Death record from Nebr. State Dept. of Health.]

PAOLO E. COLETTA

BRYAN, JOHN STEWART (Oct. 23, 1871–Oct. 16, 1944), Virginia newspaper publisher and college president, was born at Brook Hill, the estate of his maternal grandfather on the outskirts of Richmond. He was the eldest of the five sons of Joseph and Isobel Lamont (Stewart) Bryan. His mother was the daughter of a Scottish immigrant who had prospered in business; his father was descended from a late-seventeenth-century English settler in South Carolina. After serving during the Civil War with Mosby's Rangers, the elder Bryan practiced law and, in the Reconstruction era, recouped his fortunes in railroads, mining, and real estate. In 1887 he acquired the *Richmond Times* and in 1896 the evening *Leader*.

John Stewart Bryan grew up at Brook Hill and later resided at Laburnum, the Bryan estate near Richmond. He was reared in an atmosphere of gracious living, strong Episcopal faith, and close family ties, especially with his father. A tall, frail youngster, with eyesight handicapped by a boyhood accident, he attended private schools in Richmond and the Episcopal High School in Alexandria, Va., before entering the University of Virginia, where he graduated with both the A.B. and A.M. degrees in 1893. He returned to his alma mater a year later to study law but transferred to the Harvard Law School and received his LL.B. degree in 1897.

After briefly practicing law in New York City and Richmond, Bryan in 1900 joined his father in the management of his newspapers. Three years later the Bryans transferred control of the *Leader* to the Williams family (which owned the evening *News*) in exchange for their morning paper, the *Dispatch*, the two morning papers being merged as the *Times-Dispatch* and the evening papers as the *News Leader*. Bryan suc-ceeded his father as president of the company in 1907, and Joseph Bryan died the following year. Shortly before his death he had reacquired the *News Leader*, and most of the young publisher's time was devoted to writing editorials and managing that paper; he sold the morning *Times-Dispatch* in 1914.

In managing the *News Leader*, Bryan was especially fortunate in his choice of editor. In 1915 he appointed to this post Douglas Southall Freeman, who had joined the staff in 1912 as an editorial writer. Over the next three decades, although chiefly concerned with the dissemination of accurate information on public issues, Bryan and his distinguished editor ensured the paper's continuance as a moderately progressive force in Virginia life. Over the years the *News Leader* supported such political reforms as the direct primary and a simplified ballot, opposed prohibition, and ardently defended tax reform and better public schools. Bryan was one of the founders (1904) of the Cooperative Education Association of Virginia, which sparked the movement for strengthening public education in the state. On international issues, the *News Leader* advocated American involvement in World War I and enthusiastically endorsed Wilson's peace program and American participation in the League of Nations. Both Freeman and Virginius Dabney, the editor from 1922 of the *Times-Dispatch* (which Bryan repurchased in 1940), were indelibly influenced by the publisher's political philosophy.

Although never seeking political office, Bryan was a dedicated public servant. He held a number of community posts; he was chairman of the Richmond Public Library board, a founder of the Virginia Museum of Fine Arts, and president of the Virginia Historical Society. A prominent Episcopal layman, Bryan frequently attended the church's conventions and sat on its National Council (1919–28). He was a delegate to several Democratic national conventions. During World War I he served on the war council of the Y.M.C.A., a post that took him to the Paris Peace Conference. He was president of the American Newspaper Publishers Association, 1926–28.

The climax of Bryan's career was the presidency of the College of William and Mary. His formal connection with that venerable institution began with his appointment to the board of visitors in 1926; he was soon made vice-rector. With the failing health of President Julian A. C. Chandler [Supp. 1], Bryan was drawn more and more into the affairs of the college, an involvement which led to deepening affection for the institution, appreciation of its potential, and confidence in its future. Upon Chandler's death in May 1934, Bryan was asked to accept the presidency. Friends and family urged him to decline, fearful that his strength, at sixty-two, would be overtaxed, but he accepted with the understanding that he could not devote all his time or very many years to the office.

He envisioned William and Mary as a great liberal arts college with ample private endowment to pursue its destiny, but despite his efforts, large gifts were not forthcoming. With strong state support and some private funds, he pressed toward his goals by adding young teacher-scholars to the faculty and by improving the quality of the student body through a more selective admissions policy. The faculty was encouraged to develop its organization, revise the curriculum, and participate in the formulation of college policy. A man of generous spirit and a gifted conversationalist, Bryan made perhaps his greatest contribution to William and Mary through the impact of his personality, which infused both faculty and students with confidence in his aims and enthusiasm for bearing their share of the effort. He retired in 1942, confident that the college was committed to excellence.

Bryan married Anne Eliza Tennant of Petersburg, Va., daughter of a tobacco manufacturer, on June 4, 1903. Their children were: Amanda Stewart, David Tennant, and John Stewart. He died in Richmond in 1944, a week before his seventy-fourth birthday, of a cerebral hemorrhage, and was buried at Emmanuel Church near his birthplace.

[Douglas S. Freeman, "John Stewart Bryan," a book-length MS. at the Va. Hist. Soc., Richmond, which also has a collection of Bryan's papers (others remain in family possession); Minutes of the Board of Visitors and Minutes of the Faculty, College of William and Mary; Bryan's privately printed biography of his father, *Joseph Bryan* (1935); obituary by Douglas Freeman in *Va. Mag. of Hist. and Biog.,* Jan. 1945; obituaries in *William and Mary Alumni Gazette,* Dec. 1944, and *Va. Gazette* (Williamsburg), Oct. 20, 1944; *Nat. Cyc. Am. Biog.,* XXXIV, 25–26; *Who Was Who in America,* vol. II (1950); Allen W. Moger, *Virginia: Bourbonism to Byrd, 1870–1925* (1968); death record from Va. Dept. of Health. A portrait of Bryan hangs at the College of William and Mary.]

HAROLD L. FOWLER

BUCKNER, EMORY ROY (Aug. 7, 1877–Mar. 11, 1941), lawyer, was born in Pottawattamie County, Iowa, the eldest of three sons of James Monroe Dysant Buckner and Sarah Addie (Ellis) Buckner. The family lived on the farm of his paternal grandfather. His father worked as a schoolteacher, then as an itinerant preacher, becoming pastor of a rural Methodist church at

Hebron, Nebr., when Emory was six. While in school young Buckner spent one summer at a business college in Lincoln studying shorthand and another, after completing high school, at a teachers' institute. He then taught school, at first near Hebron and afterward in Guthrie, Oklahoma Territory, where the family moved in 1894.

In Oklahoma Buckner first came in contact with the law when he worked for three years as a court stenographer. In 1900 he left this job to enroll, at the age of twenty-three, at the University of Nebraska. With him went a former fellow teacher at Guthrie, Wilhelmina Kathryn Keach; they were married in the spring of their freshman year, on Apr. 4, 1901. They had three children: Ruth Farlow, Elizabeth, and Jean. At Nebraska, where Buckner was a Phi Beta Kappa student and an active campus figure, he was befriended by Roscoe Pound, the new dean of the law school, who recommended him to the Harvard Law School and helped raise the money to send him there, after his graduation in 1904. Despite the burden of supporting a wife and (in his last year) a child, Buckner ranked third in his Harvard class of about 190 when he graduated, LL.B., in 1907. Most important, he made lifelong friends, notably Felix Frankfurter, a student a year ahead of him.

On leaving Harvard, Buckner took a job in New York with the firm of Cravath, Henderson & de Gersdorff, but after only a few months he joined the staff of bright young assistants (including Frankfurter) which Henry L. Stimson had assembled to reform the United States Attorney's office in that city. He worked on one major case: the customs frauds of the American Sugar Refining Company, which the Stimson team prosecuted with great success. In 1910 an anti-Tammany district attorney, Charles Whitman, took office in New York County and hired Buckner away from the federal attorney's office. Two and a half years later, in the aftermath of the murder of a small-time gambler (Herman Rosenthal) who had offered to give evidence of corruption in the city's vice squad, Buckner was appointed counsel to a new aldermanic committee to investigate the New York Police Department. This job required his leaving public employment, and in the fall of 1912 he formed a law partnership with a former classmate, Silas W. Howland. The aldermanic investigation had its sensational moments, but most of its eighty public sessions were devoted to what Buckner called "hard steady plugging on fundamental questions of police administration." The final recommendations of the committee, published in 1913, produced less immediate result than Buckner had hoped, but within a decade nearly all the recommended reforms had been adopted.

Shortly after the investigation Buckner and Howland joined forces with two other young lawyers, Elihu Root, Jr., and Grenville Clark, to form a partnership that became one of the largest and most successful law offices in New York. Buckner's skill in planning and conducting trials attracted substantial clients, and he was an expert on internal organization; in large part he established what became the traditional pattern of the big Wall Street firm. Since the police investigation, Buckner had intervened only once in political life, when he managed the unsuccessful reelection campaign of Mayor John Purroy Mitchel [q.v.] in 1917. But in 1925 the Coolidge administration, fending off charges of corruption in the Justice Department, needed a nonpolitical United States Attorney in the Southern District of New York. Buckner accepted the post with a guarantee that he would be independent of Washington in handling the monstrous enforcement problems arising from prohibition and in choosing his staff.

The next two years marked the height of Buckner's public influence. Although he hated and indeed had violated the prohibition law, he took the pledge on accepting government office and insisted that everyone who worked for him do likewise. Virtually abandoning the hopeless piecemeal prosecution of some 75,000 prohibition offenders arrested in New York each year, Buckner instead sought to padlock the clubs, restaurants, and stores where alcohol was available. For a wild if brief period in 1925 it seemed possible that his tactics would dry up the city. But the countertide was too strong, and after a year Buckner turned his attention elsewhere. His most significant case was the prosecution of former Attorney General Harry M. Daugherty [Supp. 3] and former Alien Property Custodian Thomas W. Miller on charges of "conspiring to defraud the government of their best services"—i.e., taking bribes, a crime that could not be charged directly because of the statute of limitations. A first trial late in 1926 ended in a divided jury; in the second trial, Miller was convicted and Daugherty saved only by the recalcitrance of a single juror.

Buckner was not yet fifty when he resigned from the office of United States Attorney in 1927. Probably his most important subsequent case was the successful prosecution of Queens Borough President Maurice E. Connolly (a Democrat) for his part in sewer construction frauds. Buckner conducted the trial under special appointment from Gov. Alfred E. Smith [Supp. 3], a re-markable honor for a Republican to receive while Smith was running for president. Early in 1932 Buckner suffered the first of a series of strokes; he lived for nine more years, and continued to participate daily in the work of his firm, but he never again argued a case in court. A final stroke, at his New York home, ended his life in 1941.

Felix Frankfurter remembered Buckner as "zestful" and "companionable," a man who combined civic zeal with a tolerance for "the foibles and even the laxities of others" (letter to *New York Times,* Mar. 14, 1941). Though he enjoyed an eminent career at the bar, Buckner was best remembered for his extraordinary kindness to young lawyers. His door was always open to job-hunting law students, and if he could not hire them himself he was fertile with suggestions and introductions to possible employers. He kept up with nearly all the men who had ever worked for him, encouraging them and recommending them for more important positions. And he had a superb eye for talent: among those he aided were one future Supreme Court Justice (John M. Harlan) and four future judges on federal courts of appeals, as well as men who became ambassadors, Congressmen, and deans of major law schools.

[Martin Mayer, *Emory Buckner* (1968), is the only biography. A profile by Alva Johnston was published in the *New Yorker,* Mar. 12 and 19, 1932, under the title "Courtroom Warrior"; a pleasant youthful tribute called "The Investigator of the N. Y. Police" (by Felix Frankfurter, though unsigned) appeared in the *Outlook,* Sept. 28, 1912. Buckner's activities were extensively described in N. Y. City newspapers from Sept. 1912 through June 1913, and throughout his incumbency as U. S. Attorney, from Apr. 1925 through Mar. 1927. The considerable correspondence between Buckner and Frankfurter is on deposit at the library of the Harvard Law School, which also contains significant letters between Buckner and both Roscoe Pound and Learned Hand.]

MARTIN MAYER

BUCKNER, SIMON BOLIVAR (July 18, 1886–June 18, 1945), army officer, was born at the family home, Glen Lily, near Munfordville, Ky., the only child of Simon Bolivar Buckner [q.v.], West Point graduate and Confederate general, and his second wife, Delia Hayes Claiborne of Richmond, Va. His father, who was sixty-three when young Buckner was born, was afterward governor of Kentucky, 1887–91, and vice-presidential nominee on the "Gold Democrat" ticket in 1896. The boy was sent at the age of sixteen to the Virginia Military Institute and two years later received an appointment to West Point. Graduating in February 1908, he was commissioned a second lieutenant of infantry. His early assignments followed the customary pattern, including tours of duty in the Philippines and on the Mexican border. Much to his disappointment, he spent the World War I period in the United States. An early aviation enthusiast, he was detailed to the Aviation Section of the Signal Corps in 1917, held various training commands, and was then assigned to the Air Service operations section in Washington.

Like many army officers, Buckner spent a good part of the interwar years at school, as both student and teacher. For four years, 1919–23, he was at West Point teaching tactics to the cadets. The next two years he spent as a student first at the Infantry School at Fort Benning and then at the Command and General Staff School at Fort Leavenworth, where he served an additional three years as instructor. Then came four years at the Army War College in Washington, first as a student (1928–29) and then as executive officer. In 1932, as a lieutenant colonel, he returned to West Point as instructor (1932–33) and commandant of cadets (1933–36).

With this preparation, Buckner moved rapidly through a succession of command assignments, earning his colonel's eagles in January 1937. His first major independent command came in July 1940, when he was ordered to Alaska to organize the defense of that area against a threatening enemy across the Pacific. Within three months he was a brigadier general; he was promoted to major general in August 1941 in recognition of his achievement in building a viable Alaskan Defense Command. In this assignment, where he was under the navy's operational control, Buckner demonstrated an ability to work harmoniously with his sister service that was undoubtedly a factor in his subsequent assignment.

The Alaskan theatre first came under attack in June 1942, when the Japanese, as part of their Midway assault, sent a strong naval task force against Dutch Harbor. Army and navy planes attacked the approaching Japanese and drove them back with heavy losses, but not before they had succeeded in landing troops on Attu and Kiska in the Aleutians. The next year witnessed a series of moves by the Americans to drive the enemy from these bases, culminating in the capture of Attu in May 1943 and the reoccupation of Kiska. For his role in these operations, Buckner was promoted to lieutenant general and received the Distinguished Service Medal.

In June 1944 Buckner was ordered to the Central Pacific as commander-designate of the new Tenth Army to prepare for the projected invasion of Okinawa. Here his ability to get along with the other services proved invaluable. Adm. Richmond Kelly Turner, commander of the Joint Expeditionary Force for Okinawa and not

one to give praise lightly, later wrote that Buckner "enjoyed the complete confidence and devotion not only of his own Army troops, but also of the Marine Corps divisions and Navy land contingents which formed parts of the Tenth Army, and also of the naval and air forces operating in [its] support. . . ." The attack on Okinawa began with a landing on Apr. 1, 1945, the largest amphibious operation of the Pacific war. In two and a half months of bitter fighting the Tenth Army succeeded in pushing the desperate Japanese defenders back to the southwest tip of the island. It was there, on the afternoon of June 18, only a few days before the end of the campaign, that General Buckner met his death. While watching the progress of the battle from a forward observation position, he was struck in the chest by a piece of coral dislodged by a Japanese shell and died almost immediately. He was buried on Okinawa, but four years later his body was transferred to the Frankfort (Ky.) Cemetery, next to his father's grave.

Physically, Buckner was a tall man, powerfully built, with clear blue eyes, ruddy complexion, and brown hair that turned almost snow-white in later years. A stern disciplinarian and an exacting drillmaster, he demanded the most of his men but was always solicitous for their welfare and had a reputation for fair dealing. He had a boyish quality and an easy sense of humor that made him a popular figure in social gatherings. But he preferred hunting and fishing and the outdoor life to the social amenities. He learned to love Alaska during his years there and purchased property at Anchorage, planning to live there after the war. On Dec. 30, 1916, he had married Adele Blanc, daughter of a prominent New Orleans physician. They had three children: Simon Bolivar III, Mary Blanc, and William Claiborne. The elder son served in World War II, working his way up through the ranks to captain; the younger graduated from West Point in 1948.

[Roy E. Appleman et al., *Okinawa: The Last Battle* (1948), and Stetson Conn et al., *Guarding the U. S. and Its Outposts* (1964), two volumes in the U. S. Army in World War II series; George W. Cullum, *Biog. Register of the Officers and Graduates of the U. S. Military Academy,* Supp., vol. VIII, 1930–40, and vol. IX, 1940–50; Arndt M. Stickles, *Simon Bolivar Buckner* (1940), a biography of Buckner's father; *Who Was Who in America,* vol. II (1950); *Nat. Cyc. Am. Biog.,* XXXVII, 34–35; *Assembly* (Assoc. of West Point Graduates), July 1946; *N. Y. Times,* June 19, 1945.]

Louis Morton

BURNHAM, WILLIAM HENRY (Dec. 3, 1855–June 25, 1941), educational psychologist and mental hygienist, was born in Dunbarton, N. H., the youngest of seven children, four boys and three girls, of Samuel and Hannah (Dane) Burnham. His father, a descendant of Deacon John Burnham of Norwich, England, who emigrated to Ipswich, Mass., in 1635, was a farmer and proprietor of the general store in Dunbarton. For generations the Burnhams had been staunch Congregationalists. William received his elementary education in a rural school and his secondary education at the Manchester (N. H.) high school, from which he graduated in 1875. To qualify for admission to Harvard, he studied independently for the next three years while teaching in rural New Hampshire schools. He entered Harvard in 1878 and received the A.B. degree in 1882. After teaching briefly at Wittenberg College, Springfield, Ohio (1882–83), and the State Normal School at Potsdam, N. Y. (1883–85), he began graduate study at Johns Hopkins University under the psychologist G. Stanley Hall [*q.v.*], receiving his Ph.D. in 1888.

After two years as an instructor at Johns Hopkins, Burnham joined the original faculty of Clark University in Worcester, Mass., where his former mentor, Hall, was inaugurating a child-study program which was to make Clark nationally recognized as a pedagogical center. Beginning as a docent in pedagogy, Burnham became an instructor in 1892, assistant professor in 1900, and in 1906 professor of pedagogy and chairman of the department of pedagogy and school hygiene, a post he held until his retirement in 1926. Through his teaching of graduate students in psychology and education and through his published writings, Burnham for a time ranked in influence with his two eminent colleagues, Hall and Edmund C. Sanford [*q.v.*].

Burnham wrote more than two hundred papers on various facets of child study, the mental health of the schoolchild, and the development of the science of education. Like G. Stanley Hall, he followed extensive, rather than intensive, methods in his research, seeking to identify all significant aspects of the subject under investigation. Like Hall, too, he did not make a sharp distinction between somatic and mental health. His lectures were read from polished manuscripts, but for one reason or another he delayed sending many of them out for publication. It was only immediately preceding and during retirement that he produced his three books: *The Normal Mind* (1924), *Great Teachers and Mental Health* (1926), and *The Wholesome Personality* (1932).

While Burnham's ideas were considerably influenced in a direct way by Hall, particularly Hall's genetic orientation and his advocacy of a scientific, evolutionary approach to the study of child development, it is apparent that Burnham

was also receptive to the pervasive currents of Hegelian idealism, Darwinism, and pragmatism during his formative years. Like John Dewey, he stressed organism, environment, and adaptation. Burnham regarded the "supreme aim of education as the preservation and development of a wholesome personality in every child." The fundamental conditions of mental health, he stressed repeatedly, are integration and adjustment. The basic element of integration is within an infant at birth, and a normal course of personality development follows a sequence of integrations at higher and higher levels, at each stage reaching tentative solutions to problems, which reappear as problematical on a higher level. Thus for Burnham normal personality development was a continuing dialectic process. Education should mediate between an old habit (or conditioned response) that has failed or become inadequate and a new adaptation to the conditions of life which becomes a new habit.

Burnham was not a rigorous researcher, but his ideas were in the mainstream of the child development movement, and he was recognized as a leader in the fields of mental hygiene and child development. He was primarily a synthesizer whose writings were directed at teachers and school administrators rather than a mass audience. Burnham's application to educational psychology of the concept of the conditioned reflex is one of his important contributions.

Though Burnham's writings are informative rather than prescriptive, leaving practical applications of theory to his reader, he himself took some part in the organized mental hygiene movement. He was one of the founders of the Massachusetts State Society for Mental Hygiene and its president, 1916–20, and from 1917 until his death he was a member of the National Committee for Mental Hygiene. A quiet man, with a "sly, penetrating, subtle humor" that was evident in his lectures, Burnham never married. He continued to live in Worcester during his retirement, spending his summers in his birthplace, Dunbarton. For some years before his death he suffered from arteriosclerosis; the immediate cause of his death was pneumonia. He died in Dunbarton and was buried there.

[Two newspaper articles at the time of Burnham's retirement, in the *Worcester Telegram* of May 27 and June 13, 1926, together with the obituary in the *Worcester Gazette,* June 25, 1941, provide a rather full account of his life. See also obituaries in *Am. Jour. of Psychology,* Oct. 1941, and *Mental Hygiene,* Oct. 1941. Genealogical information from N. H. Hist. Soc., Concord; death record from Town Clerk, Dunbarton, N. H. A life-size bust of Burnham is in Atwood Hall at Clark Univ.; the Town of Dunbarton possesses a copy.]

BERNARD G. DeWULF

CABLE, FRANK TAYLOR (June 19, 1863–May 21, 1945), electrical engineer, active in the development and construction of submarines, was born in New Milford, Conn., the son of Abijah and Olive Lavinia (Taylor) Cable. After attending public schools and, for one year, Claverack College in Hudson, N. Y., Cable worked on his father's dairy farm until, at the age of twenty-five, he secured a position as a mechanic with the Gas Engine and Power Company in Morris Heights, N. Y. He next moved to Philadelphia, where during the day he worked as a technician at the Electro-Dynamic Company and at night studied electrical engineering at the Franklin Institute and at Drexel Institute of Technology. On May 29, 1892, he married Nettie Alice Hungerford of Sherman, Conn. There were no children.

Cable became involved in the early development of the submarine when in the autumn of 1897 he was sent by the Electro-Dynamic Company to Perth Amboy, N. J., to salvage a dynamo aboard the *Holland VI*. Designed by John P. Holland [*q.v.*] and launched in Elizabethport, N. J., the craft, as yet untried, had sunk at the dockside because of the carelessness of a workman. By reversing the current in the armatures to generate heat internally, Cable dried out the wiring and saved the Holland Torpedo Boat Company the expense and delay of having to remove the motor. Holland was impressed by the ingenuity of the young electrician and a few months later appointed him chief electrician aboard the *Holland VI*. In 1899 Cable took on the additional responsibility of trial captain, and the following year he skillfully commanded the *Holland VI* in a series of decisive trials on the Potomac River before a board of naval officers which resulted in its purchase as the navy's first submarine.

Cable moved in 1901 to Groton, Conn. (near New London), as superintendent of construction and operation of submarines for the Electric Boat Company, formed two years earlier by a merger of the Holland Torpedo Boat Company with the Electric Launch Company and the Electro-Dynamic Company. In 1902, after seeing the *Adder* or A-class boats through their preacceptance trials, he went to England to train the crew of the Holland-type British *A-1*. After his return he commanded the Electric Boat Company's *Fulton* in trials off Newport, competing against the *Protector,* designed by Simon Lake [Supp. 3]. The *Fulton* was sold to Russia during the Russo-Japanese War, and Cable went to Kronstadt to reassemble the dismantled vessel there and prepare it for shipment by flatcar on the Trans-Siberian Railway to Vladivostok. Soon afterward he delivered five A-boats to Russia's adversary,

Japan, supervised their assembly, and trained their crews. Two years later, in 1907, Cable became commander of the *Octopus* (later the *C-1*), which had been built by the Bethlehem Steel Company at the Fore River Yard in Quincy, Mass., and set new records for surface speed and hours submerged. This strenuous testing program no doubt contributed to the nervous breakdown which Cable suffered in May 1907; thereafter he devoted his energies increasingly to administrative matters.

Although he had come late to the group of men surrounding John P. Holland, Cable played a key role in the corporate maneuvers that stimulated the development of the modern submarine. The advantages of diesel (as against gasoline) engines for surface propulsion had become apparent. Cable urged the Electric Boat Company to undertake the manufacture of diesel engines, and when the company declined, he and Lawrence Y. Spear, a former naval constructor, in 1910 organized the New London Ship and Engine Company at Groton and obtained a license to build the M.A.N. (Maschinenfabrik Augsburg-Nürnberg) diesel; it was first used in twelve H-boats. The New London Company became a subsidiary of the Electric Boat Company in 1911, and Cable eventually rose to the position of manager of the parent firm. In this capacity he guided the Groton yard through World War I, witnessed the launching of twenty-five submarines (1924–41), and supervised the introduction of welded hulls.

Although Cable had known little of underwater craft when he first joined Holland, he learned quickly, and he received patents on a number of submarine devices, including a clinometer (1900) to measure the angle of descent. His book, *The Birth and Development of the American Submarine* (1924), gives a detailed personal account of early submarine history. Cable belonged to a number of professional organizations and was a member of the Congregational Church. He died in the Lawrence Memorial Hospital of New London at the age of eighty-one of kidney disease, and was buried in the Gaylord Cemetery at New Milford.

[Cable's *Birth and Development of the American Submarine* (which contains an excellent portrait) and his articles "The Submarine Torpedo Boat *Holland*," U. S. Naval Inst., *Proc.*, Feb. 1943, and "The Strange Cruise of the *Octopus*," *Cosmopolitan*, Aug. 1907; Cable's "Notebooks" of newspaper clippings, 1901–11, and other important Cable memorabilia at the Submarine Lib., U. S. Naval Submarine Base, New London, Conn.; Richard K. Morris, *John P. Holland: Inventor of the Modern Submarine* (1966); John Niven et al., eds., *Dynamic America* (1960), a well-written, documented history of the companies with which Cable was associated; *Nat. Cyc. Am. Biog.*, XXXIV, 164–65; death record from Town Clerk, New London.]

RICHARD KNOWLES MORRIS

CABOT, HUGH (Aug. 11, 1872–Aug. 14, 1945), surgeon, medical educator, medical reformer, was born at Beverly Farms, Mass., the summer home of his parents, James Elliot and Elizabeth (Dwight) Cabot of Brookline, Mass. He was one of twin boys, the last of seven surviving children, all sons. His father, a graduate of the Harvard Law School, briefly practiced law and architecture, but mainly devoted himself to his interests in natural history and philosophy; he was a friend and literary executor of Ralph Waldo Emerson [q.v.]. Mrs. Cabot, a cousin of President Charles W. Eliot [q.v.] of Harvard, added her considerable talent for music to the childhood curriculum her husband prescribed for their sons. Growing up in a Unitarian household and in a strongly humanitarian environment, all seven boys emerged as highly individualistic, productive adults, usually combining idealism with their practical endeavors in their respective professions. One brother, Richard Clarke Cabot [Supp. 2], preceded Hugh in entering medicine. Philip, Hugh's twin, was a successful public utility executive who became a philosopher of business and lectured at the Harvard School of Business Administration from 1924 until his death in 1941, blending his professional expertise with ethical fervor. Both twins were bluff, hard-working, and incisive.

Hugh Cabot attended the Roxbury (Mass.) Latin School and received the A.B. degree from Harvard in 1894 and the M.D. from the Harvard Medical School in 1898. After a year's surgical internship at the Massachusetts General Hospital, he entered practice with his cousin Arthur Tracy Cabot [q.v.] and from him acquired an interest in genitourinary surgery. Hugh Cabot organized a department in that field at the Massachusetts General Hospital in 1910. In that same year he began teaching at the Harvard Medical School, as instructor (1910–13), assistant professor (1913–18), and professor (1918–19) of genitourinary surgery. He accepted as natural obligations, along with his private practice, both teaching and charitable duties, the latter in the outpatient department of the Massachusetts General Hospital and at the Boston Dispensary. On Sept. 22, 1902, he married Mary Anderson Boit of Brookline. They had four children: Hugh, Mary Anderson, John Boit, and Arthur Tracy.

From the beginning of his professional career, Cabot felt "oppressed" by a "conflict of duties": the need to support himself and his family by his practice, and the moral obligation to teach and to provide medical care to the indigent. This common predicament, he became convinced, constituted the most serious flaw in the American medical system. World War I offered Cabot a temporary escape from this dilemma. In the spring of 1916 he helped recruit a "surgical unit" of fifty-seven doctors and nurses sent by Harvard to aid the British forces in France, where he served for three months. He returned to France in February 1917 as chief surgeon of General Hospital No. 22 at Camiers, and in October became the hospital's commanding officer (with temporary rank as lieutenant colonel in the Royal Army Medical Corps), a post he held until January 1919.

Soon after his return to the United States, Cabot was appointed professor and director of surgery at the University of Michigan Medical School; he assumed his new duties in January 1920. Enjoying the "undivided allegiance" assured by his full-time position, Cabot implemented reforms in medical education and hospital organization, many of them initiated by Victor C. Vaughan [q.v.], whom he succeeded as dean in 1921. To integrate and humanize the medical curriculum, he introduced comprehensive examinations and substantial reductions in lecture and laboratory hours required for some courses. To obviate conflict of interest in the faculty, he placed members on a modified full-time basis, entirely forbidding private practice; each man's salary, however, was supplemented in a manner roughly commensurate with his care of patients, who, if they could afford to pay, were charged on a sliding scale at University Hospital, a state-owned institution opened in 1925. To ensure academic autonomy, Cabot and the university's president, Clarence Cook Little, refused legislative appropriations contingent on the hiring of homeopathic faculty members.

Each reform effort met some opposition. A skilled diplomat might have survived; Cabot, whose unwillingness to bend with the wind was well known, was not a diplomat. He was short and solid in stature, and his typical stance—erect, with feet solidly planted apart—and the direct gaze from his austere countenance bespoke his uncompromising determination. The academic community divided into his staunch supporters and bitter enemies. Seizing upon one instance of his "autocracy" (his desire, shared by a majority of the surgical faculty, to create an anesthesiology department headed by a specialist), several disgruntled faculty members joined forces with the Board of Regents, where homeopathic interests were represented, to demand his resignation. Cabot refused, and on Feb. 7, 1930, was "relieved" as dean. Shortly after his dismissal, he accepted an invitation from his friend William James Mayo [Supp. 2] to become consulting surgeon at the Mayo Clinic and professor of surgery at the University of Minnesota Graduate School of Medicine. There for the next nine years he gloried in the successful operation of the "full-time" idea he had advocated and of group practice.

Cabot was a gifted clinician and a stimulating teacher. In a period when asepsis and relatively safe anesthesia had removed much of the risk from surgery, he emphasized the psychological factors in illness and urged an "abiding scepticism" in considering surgical intervention. Through the Association of American Medical Colleges, of which he was president in 1925 and 1926, and as a member of the Commission on Medical Education, he pressed educators to include in premedical work such behavioral studies as anthropology and psychology, and to introduce clinical experience earlier in the curriculum, lest students too long in laboratories and lectures view their first patients chiefly as experimental animals. Teachers in medical school, he firmly believed, should be clinicians, not merely researchers.

Cabot retired from his Minnesota posts in 1939 and returned to Boston to resume practice and devote himself to furthering medical reforms. Many of his ideas were far in advance of their time. He advocated sex education in the schools; federal medical licensure to supersede the inequitable standards of the state boards; an "open hospital" policy for all licensed physicians; the sale of drugs under generic rather than trade names; effective measures against fee splitting in all its forms; and expansion and specialization of nursing education.

It was primarily Cabot's attacks on the "antiquated fee system" that branded him a heresiarch in the eyes of orthodox medicine. Cabot became convinced that if all Americans were to receive the superb care modern knowledge and technology made possible, the federal government must assume the burden of medical school and hospital deficits and underwrite medical care for the indigent. To implement these convictions, he joined forces in the spring of 1937 with similarly concerned associates serving with him on the Medical Advisory Committee of the American Foundation. This group drafted "Principles and Proposals" which, although rejected by the American Medical Association at its convention in June and attacked editorially in its *Journal* (Oct. 16, 1937), received a hearing from President Roosevelt, wide attention in the lay and more liberal medical press, and considerable support within the profession. The 430 signatories whose names were listed as the "Committee of Physicians for the Improvement of Medical Care" (*New York Times*, Nov. 7, 1937) included many of the most distinguished figures in American medicine. Their open dissent from the position of organized medicine contributed to the atmosphere of imminent reform pervading the National Health Conference in which Dr. Cabot participated in July 1938.

He also took part in the first federal action against organized medicine under the Sherman Anti-Trust Law. In October 1938 Cabot testified for the government in its indictment of the American Medical Association and the District of Columbia Medical Society on charges that their actions against the Group Health Association of Washington constituted unlawful restraint of trade. Physicians participating in this cooperative, organized in 1937 to serve low-income federal employees, had found themselves barred from Medical Society membership and denied private hospital privileges. On appeal, the United States Supreme Court unanimously upheld the guilty verdict, breaking a path for similar prepayment plans elsewhere—among them Health Service, Inc., organized in 1939 by Cabot and a group of prominent Boston laymen and physicians, and the Associated Hospital Service Corporation (the "Blue Cross"), in which many Boston doctors collaborated on a nonprofit basis.

Among the professional honors Cabot especially prized were his election as a fellow of the American Surgical Association (1924); an LL.D. awarded by Queen's University, Belfast, Ireland, in 1925; and honorary fellowship in the Royal Society of Medicine (London). He was one of the founders of the American Board of Urology and a charter member of the American College of Surgeons. He served as president of the American Urological Association (1911) and the American Association of Genito-Urinary Surgeons (1914). His major publication in his specialty was *Modern Urology* (1918 and later editions). A Republican, a Unitarian, and, according to his Harvard colleague Walter B. Cannon [Supp. 3], "a Bostonian of the Bostonians," Cabot in 1941 became Massachusetts chairman of the committee for Russian War Relief. Overcoming initial local hostility, he organized effective committees throughout the state and envisioned a comparable postwar organization to serve as the cornerstone of permanent peace.

Cabot's first wife died in 1936, and on Oct. 8, 1938, he married Mrs. Elizabeth (Cole) Amory of Hingham, Mass. He died of a coronary attack shortly after his seventy-third birthday while sailing with his wife near their summer home in Ellsworth, Maine. He was buried at Walnut Hill Cemetery in Brookline.

[L. Vernon Briggs, *Hist. and Genealogy of the Cabot Family,* vol. II (1927), contains information about James Elliot Cabot (pp. 693–96) and brief accounts of the lives of each of his seven sons (pp. 757–64). There is a privately printed collection of *Letters of Elizabeth Cabot* (2 vols., 1905), and the Schlesinger Lib. at Radcliffe College has a collection of pertinent Cabot family papers. The most nearly complete list of Cabot's professional publications through 1936 (159 entries) is in *Physicians of the Mayo Clinic and the Mayo Foundation* (1937), together with a brief biographical article and a photograph. Besides *The Doctor's Bill* (1935) and *The Patient's Dilemma: The Quest for Medical Security in America* (1940)—both with useful prefaces— good examples of Cabot's publications intended to inform laymen are his candid presentation of the problem of venereal disease, "The Responsibility of the Community," *Collier's,* Nov. 1, 1913; "Give the Patient a Break," *American Mag.,* Apr. 1940; "The Lesson of the Rejectees," *Survey Graphic,* Mar. 1942, using draft statistics to show that current methods of practice had failed to produce a fit population. His writings on nursing include *Surgical Nursing* (with Mary Dodd Giles, 1931 and later editions); "The Future of Nursing Education," *Modern Hospital,* Feb. 1943; and "The Place of Nursing in Health Service," *Public Health Nursing,* Apr. 1943. Cabot served as co-editor with his brother Richard, from 1923 to 1926, of the Cabot Case Records, published in the *Boston Medic. and Surgical Jour.* (see Oct. 28, 1926, p. 870). Of many obituaries, all appearing in 1945, the most useful are: *N. Y. Times,* Aug. 16; *Jour. Am. Medic. Assoc.,* Aug. 25; *Lancet,* Sept. 8 and Sept. 15; *Survey Graphic,* Sept.; *New England Jour. of Medicine,* Dec. 6; and, by Walter B. Cannon, *Am. Rev. of Soviet Medicine,* Oct. Useful personal memoirs are by Frederick Pilcher in Calgary Associate Clinic, *Hist. Bull.,* Nov. 1946; and by Frederick A. Coller in *Annals of Surgery,* Dec. 1946. Cabot is included in various standard reference works, among them *Am. Men of Sci.* (3rd through 7th eds.) and the *Nat. Cyc. Am. Biog.,* XXXV, 547, which includes a portrait. On the Harvard Surgical Unit, see Cabot's accounts in *Harvard Graduates' Mag.,* Mar. 1917 and Dec. 1919; *N. Y. Times,* May 21, 1916, Jan. 31, 1919; and the recollections in *Harvard Unit B. E. F. Assoc. Newsletter,* Feb. 1946. The Mich. Hist. Collections, Univ. of Mich., has material concerning Cabot's tenure there. Additional information is in the *N. Y. Times,* Feb. 8, 9, 11, 1930. For press coverage of Cabot's reform efforts, see detailed articles (under "Medicine") in *Time,* Nov. 15, 1937, Aug. 1, 1938, and Dec. 18, 1939; *N. Y. Times,* Oct. 25, 1937 (editorial), Nov. 7, 1937, May 5, July 19, 24, Oct. 18, 1938, Mar. 26, Apr. 16, Oct. 17, 1939 and Aug. 6, 1941. Personal information was supplied by William F. Braasch, Norman Capener, Virgil S. Counseller, John L. Emmett, Reed Miller Nesbit, John Raaf, Henry King Ransom, Sir Herbert Seddon, and Waltman Walters. Death record from Maine Office of Vital Statistics.]
PATRICIA SPAIN WARD

CALDER, ALEXANDER STIRLING (Jan. 11, 1870–Jan. 7, 1945), sculptor, known as A. Stirling Calder, was born in Philadelphia, Pa., the oldest of six children—all of them boys—of Alexander Milne Calder and Margaret (Stirling) Calder. Both parents were natives of Scotland. The elder Calder, a stonecutter who turned to sculpture, worked on the Albert Memorial in London and then continued his career with great success in Philadelphia. His most noted works are the equestrian statue of Gen. George G. Meade [*q.v.*] in Fairmount Park (1887) and the colossal bronze statue of William Penn [*q.v.*] on the dome of the City Hall (1894). He worked for some twenty years on the decoration of the City Hall, producing many allegorical figures for other parts of the exterior as well.

His son Stirling attended Philadelphia public schools. As a youth he was greatly drawn to the theatre and also dreamed of a military career, but in 1886 he "drifted" into sculpture by enrolling in the Pennsylvania Academy of the Fine Arts. There he studied under the realist painters Thomas Eakins and Thomas Anshutz [*qq.v.*]. In 1890 Calder went to Paris, where he studied at the Académie Julian for a year with Henri Chapu and then at the École des Beaux Arts with Alexandre Falguière. Both were among the most talented French academic sculptors of the period. In addition to their part in the monumental sculptures then proliferating throughout Paris, both were impressive naturalistic portraitists, and although Calder was to become associated principally with large architectural sculptural commissions, he always maintained an interest in informal, realistic portraiture and the sensuous rendition of the nude in the tradition of Falguière. Returning to Philadelphia in 1892, Calder became an assistant instructor in modeling at the Pennsylvania Academy of the Fine Arts and established his own studio. In 1893 he received the gold medal of the Philadelphia Art Club and the following year won a competition to execute a portrait bust of the eminent surgeon Samuel D. Gross [*q.v.*].

The money from this first commission enabled Calder to marry, and on Feb. 22, 1895, Nanette Lederer of Milwaukee, Wis., a talented painter who had been a fellow student at the Pennsylvania Academy, became his wife. The couple spent the years 1895–97 in Paris. They had two children, Margaret and Alexander; the son became one of the major sculptors of the twentieth century. After returning to Philadelphia, Stirling Calder worked for some years at portraits and figure studies, continued to teach at the Pennsylvania Academy, and acted briefly (1905) as curator of sculpture for the Pennsylvania Museum. His long service on art committees and organizations began in 1904 when he was appointed to the advisory committee for sculpture of the St. Louis Exposition. One of his most attractive works of this early period, suggesting the artist's cultural roots in nature, is the portrait of his four-year-old son ("The Man Cub," 1901; bronze cast, Pennsylvania Academy of the Fine Arts). The most important of his early larger sculptures are the "Sun Dial" in Fairmount Park, Philadelphia (1903), and the granite "Sewell Cross" (1905), for the grave of Gen. William Joyce Sewell [q.v.] in Harleigh Cemetery, Camden, N. J., for which he was awarded the Walter Lippincott Prize.

Because of failing health Calder went to live in a ranch sanatorium at Oracle, Ariz., early in 1905 and for more than a year did no work. The family then moved to Pasadena, Calif., where he again opened a studio. In 1909 his statue of the Oregon pioneer Marcus Whitman [q.v.] won the grand prize at the Alaska-Yukon-Pacific Exposition held in Seattle. A sojourn in New York followed (1910–13), during which Calder lived at first in Croton-on-Hudson and then in Spuyten Duyvil and taught at the Art Students' League and at the National Academy of Design. During this period he created one of his first major sculptures, the Henry Charles Lea Memorial (1912) for Laurel Hill Cemetery, Philadelphia, an architectural-sculptural work of bronze and marble.

Moving again to California (1913–15), Calder was acting director of sculpture for the Panama-Pacific International Exposition at San Francisco (1915). For this he created the "Fountain of Energy," a globe surrounded by the four oceans and surmounted by a titanic rider on a horse, with the figures of Fame and Glory on his shoulders. This won the exposition's Designer's Medal. He also composed other monumental works for the fair and exhibited individual sculptures, including a portrait of his son, "The Laughing Boy." In 1916, after his return to New York, many monumental commissions came his way. The Depew Memorial Fountain in University Square, Indianapolis (1917), erected in collaboration with the sculptor Karl Bitter and the architect Henry Bacon [qq.v.], is one of the most elaborate. Calder's crowning figure, a dancing nymph with cymbals, reflects the tone of exciting, sensuous movement which he shared with Falguière.

Although Calder had not exhibited in the great Armory Show of 1913, he was in complete sympathy with its purpose of bringing together the new European and American art, and another major commission, the statue of George Washington, flanked by allegorical figures of Wisdom and Justice, on the arch at Washington Square, New York City (1918), suggests the effect of the new influence. The full-length Washington is clearly based on Houdon's statue in the Virginia state capitol, but the flattened, somewhat stylized accessory figures are reminiscent of the reliefs by Émile Antoine Bourdelle for the Théâtre des Champs Élysées—pseudomodern with overtones of cubism. More characteristic of Stirling Calder's

particular qualities are "Our Lady and the Holy Child," executed for St. Mary's Church, Detroit (1924), and "St. George of Princeton," for Walter L. Foulke Memorial Dormitory at Princeton University (1924), in which the complicated sculpture group is tightly organized with the architectural frame. The bronze and granite Shakespeare Memorial, "Hamlet and the Fool" (1932), in Logan Circle, Philadelphia, is another reminder of Calder's fundamental realistic training with Eakins and Anshutz.

Two very different works climaxed Calder's career and remain perhaps his most original contributions to American monumental sculpture. The "Swann Memorial: The Fountain of the Three Rivers" (1924), in the Logan Circle of the Parkway, Philadelphia, is a gigantic fountain in which three colossal bronze figures, symbolizing the three rivers of Philadelphia, are wholly integrated with architectural frame and fountain design. The highly individual memorial to Leif Ericsson in Reykjavik, Iceland (1931), for which Calder won a national competition, was presented to the people of Iceland by the United States to honor the one-thousandth anniversary of the establishment of the Icelandic parliament. The bronze sculpture, on a huge triangular base of red Texas granite, suggests the Viking at the prow of his ship at the moment of his discovery of the New World.

In addition to his monumental sculptures, Calder made many informal studies of the nude —small clay or plaster figures, which were sometimes cast in bronze. Such works as "Stooping Woman" (1919), "The Last Dryad" (1921), and "Scratching Her Heel" (c. 1920, Metropolitan Museum of Art) combine a classical tradition with realistic observation. (Although the sculptures of Stirling Calder and his son, Alexander, are diametrically opposed in concept and style, there was always a close relationship between the two men. Faced with the son's cutout metal mobiles, the father was polite but suggested that he preferred bronze for its tactile virtues. The informal bronze nude sketches illustrate his point.)

Calder's accomplishment as a portraitist is also evident in his sculptures of children and of his friends, among them artists of the "Ashcan School" such as Robert Henri and George Bellows [qq.v.]. The Henri is an elegant, romantic presentation; the Bellows, which shows the painter as a half-nude, muscular prizefighter, could be a symbol of the new realism which began the modern revolution in American painting. Two other portraits that illustrate the range of Calder's ability and imaginative power are the study for a monument to Walt Whitman, a free, romantic interpretation that catches the essential quality of the poet, and a profile self-portrait in low relief, highly abstract in the modeling of the figure and treatment of the artist's working clothes and beautifully sensitive in the sharp modeling of the head and hands.

Six feet tall and spare, with hair that whitened early in life, A. Stirling Calder was a distinguished figure. His daughter describes him as "introspective" and "moody"; he was well read and "loved to discuss philosophy and psychology." Calder was absorbed in his work and took little interest in social life or public appearances. He remained active until well into his seventies; his last completed sculpture, a monumental head of Winston Churchill, was shown in the spring of 1944 at the Grand Central Galleries in New York. He died in 1945, a few days before his seventy-fifth birthday, in St. Luke's Hospital, New York City, and was buried at West Laurel Hill Cemetery near Philadelphia.

[Published biographical material on Calder is limited chiefly to the sketches in *Who Was Who in America*, vol. II (1950), and *Nat. Cyc. Am. Biog.*, XXXIV, 237–38. The *Index of Twentieth Century Artists*, May 1935, lists his awards and exhibitions and museums holding his work and has a bibliography of critical articles and other references. Nanette Calder edited a privately printed volume, *Thoughts of A. Stirling Calder on Art and Life* (1947). Alexander Calder, *An Autobiog. with Pictures* (1966), contains many references to his father. Helpful family information was provided by Mrs. Margaret Calder Hayes, who is preparing a full-length study of the Calder family based on letters, photographs, and other family documents.]

H. HARVARD ARNASON

CALHOUN, PATRICK (Mar. 21, 1856–June 16, 1943), lawyer and financier, was born near Pendleton, S. C., at Fort Hill, the plantation home of his illustrious grandfather, John C. Calhoun [q.v.]. He was the fifth son and youngest of six children of Andrew Pickens Calhoun and his second wife, Margaret Maria (Green) Calhoun, whose father, Duff Green [q.v.], had been a political supporter of John C. Calhoun. A wealthy cotton planter, Andrew Calhoun was financially ruined by the Confederacy's defeat and died in 1865.

Young Patrick acquired most of his early education at country schools near Fort Hill. In 1871 he rode horseback to Dalton, Ga., to study law with his grandfather Duff Green. He was admitted to the Georgia bar at nineteen, but in 1876 he moved to St. Louis. Gaining admittance to the Missouri bar that same year, he opened a general practice, but his health failed a short time later, forcing him to retire temporarily to the Arkansas plantation of his older brother John Caldwell Calhoun. Around 1878 he settled in

Atlanta, Ga., to resume his legal career. By specializing in corporate law he quickly acquired a lucrative practice and a wide circle of business contacts. On Nov. 4, 1885, Pat Calhoun (as he signed his name throughout his life) married Sarah Porter Williams, who bore him eight children: Martha Margaret, Margaret Green, Patrick, George Williams, John Caldwell, Andrew Pickens, Mildred Washington, and Sarah Williams.

Calhoun was senior partner in the firm of Calhoun, King & Spalding from 1887 to 1894, but his energy and ambition led him into a wide range of business interests as well. He organized the Calhoun Land Company to raise cotton in the Mississippi Valley and acquired extensive properties in Georgia, South Carolina, and Texas. His other enterprises included oil, railroads, manufacturing, and mining. Between 1887 and 1893 he was a member of the syndicate controlling the Richmond Terminal, a holding company for several railroad properties. During that period his firm served as general counsel for the Terminal and two of its subsidiary roads, the Central of Georgia and the Richmond & Danville. Calhoun himself had a large financial interest in all three of these companies. In 1892 he resigned as their counsel and was ousted from the boards of the Terminal and the Central during a struggle for control. Two years later he acted for J. P. Morgan & Company in buying the now bankrupt Richmond Terminal and consolidating it into the Southern Railway system.

A tall, portly man with an air of sternness, Calhoun could be aggressive to the point of arrogance. To stabilize his own sometimes erratic judgment, he often relied upon the counsel of his brother John, a frequent business associate. A hot temper at times made him reckless of consequences. Once in 1889, when he was called a liar by a Georgia legislator during a committee hearing on a railroad consolidation bill, Calhoun challenged his adversary to a duel, which was held in Alabama to evade the Georgia antidueling law. The exchange was bloodless and the opponents parted as friends. On social occasions, Calhoun had a gracious charm and sharp wit that made him a favorite. He was devoted to his extensive family.

Calhoun's railroad ventures had brought him into Wall Street circles, and about 1894 he turned his full attention to business enterprises, giving up the practice of law and leaving the South. He developed and reorganized street railway properties in Pittsburgh, Baltimore, and St. Louis. After living briefly in New York City, he moved around 1896 to Cleveland and developed a section of Cleveland Heights known as Euclid Heights, where he later built a magnificent residence.

After the turn of the century, Calhoun entered the business life of San Francisco, where he helped amalgamate the street railways into the United Railroads of San Francisco, of which he became president in 1906. Despite opposition from the press and from prominent citizens, who preferred underground electrical conduits, Calhoun urged the construction of an overhead trolley network, and the United Railroads gave political boss Abraham Ruef [Supp. 2] $200,000 to help secure approval for the plan from the city's board of supervisors. In May 1907, after an investigation of his activities spurred by Fremont Older [Supp. 1], editor of the *San Francisco Bulletin*, Ruef admitted distributing this money to city officials, a confession which led to the indictment of Calhoun and other United Railroads executives for bribery. Calhoun's trial in 1909 resulted in a hung jury, and before a second trial could be held, an appellate court dismissed the case in August 1911.

By this time, Calhoun's position had become tenuous. He claimed to have lost $2,500,000 in the San Francisco earthquake and fire of 1906, in addition to the heavy legal expenses arising from his trial. In a bitter 1907 transit strike, he broke the power of the carmen's union only by importing strikebreakers and thus provoking a bloody riot. Now, in 1912, an investigation by the California Railroad Commission revealed that the United Railroads had authorized Calhoun to invest company funds without restrictions. The company's books had mysteriously disappeared, but testimony showed that Calhoun had invested and lost about $890,000 in the Solano Irrigated Farms Company, one of his private ventures; another $207,000 was unaccounted for. Lacking firm evidence, the commission could not indict, but the New York bankers who had helped finance the United Railroads, outraged at these losses, forced Calhoun to resign the presidency in the summer of 1913.

His career tarnished and his fortune dissipated, Calhoun largely retired from active business after this time. He made several heavy investments in real estate, but all of them failed. He drifted to New York in search of new opportunities, only to suffer humiliation there in 1916 when he was sued for unpaid office rent; at the hearing he testified that he was virtually penniless and that for the past two years the family had been living on his wife's funds. He is said to have become involved subsequently in the development of California oil fields, but little is known about his later business affairs. Calhoun died in Pasadena, Calif., at the age of eighty-seven of injuries received when he was struck by an automobile. He was buried on the family plantation where he had been born.

[A. S. Salley, Jr., "The Calhoun Family of S. C.," *S. C. Hist. and Genealogical Mag.*, Apr. and July 1906; *N. Y. Times*, Aug. 27, 1916, and obituary, June 18, 1943; *Atlanta Jour.*, June 17, 1943; *Nat. Cyc. Am. Biog.*, XXXIV, 231; *Men of America: A Biog. Dict. of Contemporaries* (1908); *Who Was Who in America*, vol. II (1950). On Calhoun and the San Francisco graft prosecutions, see Walton Bean, *Boss Ruef's San Francisco* (1952), and Lately Thomas, *A Debonair Scoundrel* (1962). On his duel, see *Atlanta Constitution*, Aug. 11, 1889, and George M. Battey, Jr., *A Hist. of Rome and Floyd County*, I (1922), 325–42. Other aspects of Calhoun's career are touched on in Maury Klein, *The Great Richmond Terminal* (1970), and William G. Rose, *Cleveland* (1950).]

MAURY KLEIN

CALKINS, GARY NATHAN (Jan. 18, 1869–Jan. 4, 1943), zoologist, was born in Valparaiso, Ind., the third of four sons of John Wesley Calkins, a retail merchant, originally from New York state, and Emma Frisbie (Smith) Calkins, who came from Ohio. Little is known of his life before his enrollment at the Massachusetts Institute of Technology in 1886. There Prof. William T. Sedgwick [*q.v.*] aroused in Calkins an enthusiastic and enduring interest in biology. After graduating from M.I.T. with the S.B. degree in 1890, he stayed on for three years as lecturer in biology and at the same time served as assistant biologist to the Massachusetts State Board of Health, testing local water supplies.

In the fall of 1893 Calkins began graduate work in zoology at Columbia University, where he studied under Edmund B. Wilson [Supp. 2] and received the Ph.D. degree in 1898. While still a graduate student, in 1894, he was appointed a tutor in zoology at Columbia, the beginning of a lifelong membership in the department. He advanced to instructor (1899), adjunct professor (1903), and professor (1904), and in 1907 he was named professor of protozoology (the biology of the lowest group of animal organisms, the protozoa). This was the first such appointment in the United States, and his was the first course in protozoology to be offered in any American university.

Calkins also began in 1893 a long association with the Marine Biological Laboratory at Woods Hole, Mass. Each summer for twenty-two years he gave an intensive six weeks' graduate course in protozoology covering essentially the same material included in his semester's course at Columbia. The rich abundance of protozoan species found in the fresh, salt, and brackish waters in and near Woods Hole contributed to the popularity of this course, but far more important was

Calkins's reputation as a brilliantly clear lecturer with a comprehensive grasp of his field.

Save for an early (1895) paper on the spermatogenesis of the earthworm *Lumbricus*, Calkins devoted almost his entire professional life to the study of the protozoa, investigating their cytology, physiology, and life histories, particularly those of the free-living ciliated forms. At a time when most biologists thought of the protozoa as merely an aberrant group of primitive forms, so low on the evolutionary scale that their study could add very little to the understanding of life processes, Calkins regarded the free-living protozoa as cells having essentially the same physiological and genetic characteristics as those found in cells of more complex organisms and hence, because of their ready accessibility and easy handling, a valuable group for the study of many general biological problems. His methodical and detailed studies of the protozoa examined their reactions to environmental changes and to chemicals, their regenerative powers at various phases in the cycle of cell division, and the role of the macronucleus and micronucleus in development.

Calkins is particularly noted for his studies of the life cycle of *Uroleptus mobilis*, which he likened in essential ways to the life cycle of a higher form, with periods of youth, maturity, and senescence. A line of this protozoon could be saved from death only by permitting it to go through the nuclear reorganization that occurs during encystment or during conjugation; thus a new line was started, with renewed vitality, to pass through the same three phases of the life cycle as had its parent line. The primary cause of this rejuvenescence, Calkins concluded, was the absorption into the cytoplasm of products from the old macronucleus as it disintegrated, products that are useful in the cell's metabolic activities. In this process of reorganization a new macronucleus was formed, "supplied from that most essential morphological element of the fundamental organization, the micronucleus."

The leading protozoologist of his generation, Calkins trained a large number of graduate students. Among these was Lorande L. Woodruff, who had a long and productive career of teaching and research at Yale. Calkins had great technical skill as a researcher. He developed and taught his students delicate cutting techniques (without the help of microdissection apparatus) and methods of embedding a few or even single animals for sectioning. Calkins was the author of some one hundred papers and books; the latter include *The Protozoa* (1901), the first authoritative volume on the subject published in the United States and one of the first in English,

and *The Biology of the Protozoa* (1926). He was elected to membership in the National Academy of Sciences (1919) and to the presidency of the Society of Experimental Biology and Medicine (1919–21). An early interest in the causes of cancer, which he thought might be associated with unicellular organisms, led to his presidency of the American Association for Cancer Research in 1913–14. In 1929 he received an honorary doctorate from Columbia.

Calkins was first married, on June 28, 1894, to Anne Marshall Smith of Cambridge, Mass. On Nov. 29, 1909, after her death, he married Helen Richards (Williston) Colton. By his second wife he had two children, Gary Nathan and Samuel Williston; Calkins also treated as his own son his second wife's child by her first marriage, Henry Seymour Colton. Calkins retired from his Columbia professorship in 1939. He died of pneumonia at his home in Scarsdale, N. Y., shortly before his seventy-fourth birthday and was buried in the churchyard of the Church of the Messiah (Episcopal) in Woods Hole, Mass.

[Gary N. Calkins, "Factors Controlling Longevity in Protozoan Protoplasm," *Biological Bull.*, Oct. 1934; memorial by Lorande L. Woodruff, *ibid.*, Aug.–Dec. 1944; D. H. Wenrich, "Some Am. Pioneers in Protozoology," *Jour. of Protozoology*, Feb. 1956; Reginald D. Manwell, *Introduction to Protozoology* (1961), pp. 597–98 (with photograph); *Nat. Cyc. Am. Biog.*, XXXIII, 50–51; *Am. Men of Sci.* (6th ed., 1938); *Who Was Who in America*, vol. II (1950); personal acquaintance; information from 1870 census listing of the Calkins family (courtesy of Ind. State Lib.) and from G. Nathan Calkins, Washington, D. C.]

MARY L. AUSTIN

CAMPBELL, CHARLES MACFIE (Sept. 8, 1876–Aug. 7, 1943), psychiatrist, was born in Edinburgh, Scotland, the son of Daniel Campbell, a banker, and Eliza (McLaren) Campbell. After preparing at George Watson College, he enrolled at Edinburgh University and in 1897 received the M.A. degree, with first class honors in philosophy. He then entered the medical college of the university, from which he received the M.B. and Ch.B. degrees summa cum laude in 1902. His interest having turned to psychiatry, he spent a year in France and Germany, where he obtained basic training in clinical neurology under Pierre Marie and Joseph Babinski at the Hospice de Bicêtre and in histopathology under Franz Nissl at Heidelberg. A year's residency at the Royal Infirmary in Edinburgh followed, during which he worked under Alexander Bruce.

Bruce had already sent one young physician to the United States to work with the eminent psychiatrist Adolf Meyer, and in 1904 Campbell followed suit. Meyer was then director of the Pathological Institute (later the Psychiatric Institute) of the New York State Hospitals for the Insane, located on Ward's Island in New York City. Joining the Institute staff, Campbell served there until 1911, save for a year (1907–08) back in Scotland on the psychiatric staff of the Royal Edinburgh Hospital. In 1911 he received the M.D. degree from Edinburgh with a thesis on "Focal Symptoms in General Paralysis." That same year he became assistant physician at Bloomingdale Hospital, White Plains, N. Y., serving also as instructor in psychopathology at the Cornell University Medical School. Two years later Meyer called Campbell to Baltimore to serve under him as associate director of the new Phipps Psychiatric Clinic at the Johns Hopkins Hospital; Campbell also became assistant professor of psychiatry at the Johns Hopkins Medical School. In 1920 he moved to Boston to succeed Elmer E. Southard [q.v.] as professor of psychiatry at the Harvard Medical School and medical director of the Boston Psychopathic Hospital, positions that he held for the rest of his life.

Although Campbell's early studies related to neurology and neuropathology, his interests later concentrated on emotional and personality problems. A brilliant teacher, he was primarily a clinician rather than a theorist, and in his work with students he emphasized the importance of obtaining a full knowledge of the patient and his circumstances. During his years at Johns Hopkins he developed what was probably his chief contribution to the understanding of emotional disorders, the view that mental illness was not an entity but the product of maladjustment to a total life situation, a conclusion he presented in his paper "On the Mechanism of Some Cases of Manic-Depressive Excitement" (*Medical Record*, Apr. 11, 1914). He was thoroughly acquainted with the writings of Freud and Adler and had studied briefly under Jung, but he adhered to no one school of psychiatric thought and urged the selection of valuable concepts from each. Although he could not be considered a follower of Meyer's psychobiological views, Campbell was one of the first to recognize the role of emotional conflict in producing physical symptoms. In his book *A Present-Day Conception of Mental Disorders* (1924) he set forth his conviction that some cases of chronic invalidism were "disorders of personal adaptation masquerading as physical ailments." An early proponent of the mental health movement, he urged that each community should provide centers for the diagnosis and treatment of emotional disorders, just as it provided for the treatment of disease. He spent much time in studying the problem of schizophrenia, work that was still incomplete at the time of his death.

Perhaps Campbell's most important achievement was the training he offered. With a sparkling wit, a passion for clear statement, and an intolerance of careless work, he sometimes gave offense, but he was unfailingly helpful to students in trouble, and young physicians from all over the world came to him as psychiatric residents. Each morning, with medical students and residents, he made ward rounds, wearing his white coat, armed with ophthalmoscope, reflex hammer, and stethoscope; he insisted on a thorough physical and neurological examination of the patient as well as a mental examination.

On June 3, 1908, Campbell married Jessie Deans Rankin of Scotland, also a physician, who predeceased him. Their children were Annie McNicol, Edith Storer, Charles Macfie, and Katherine Rankin. Campbell became a United States citizen in 1918. He served as president of the American Psychopathological Association (1918) and of the American Psychiatric Association (1937), and was a member of many other societies, including the American Neurological Association and the History of Science Society. In addition to numerous papers dealing with mental health, Campbell published five books, including *Human Personality and the Environment* (1934), which dealt with the problem of child delinquency, and *Destiny and Disease in Mental Disorders* (1935). C. Macfie Campbell, as he was known, died in Cambridge of a coronary occlusion a few weeks before the scheduled date of his retirement; his remains were cremated.

[Obituaries in *Archives of Neurology and Psychiatry,* Dec. 1943, *Jour. of Nervous and Mental Disease,* Nov. 1943, *Mental Hygiene,* Oct. 1943, *Am. Jour. of Psychiatry,* Sept. 1943, *Jour. Am. Medic. Assoc.,* Aug. 21, 1943, and *Lancet,* Sept. 4, 1943; *Who Was Who in America,* vol. II (1950); Alfred Lief, *The Commonsense Psychiatry of Dr. Adolf Meyer* (1948); death record from Mass. Registrar of Vital Statistics; personal recollection.]

HARRY C. SOLOMON

CANDLER, WARREN AKIN (Aug. 23, 1857–Sept. 25, 1941), Methodist clergyman and college president, was born near Villa Rica in Carroll County, Ga., the youngest of seven sons and tenth of the eleven children of Samuel Charles and Martha (Beall) Candler. He was a brother of Asa G. Candler [q.v.], founder of the Coca-Cola Company and a noted philanthropist. His father, a successful farmer and local merchant, was of English, Irish, and Italian ancestry; his mother was of Scottish descent. After local schooling, Warren entered Emory College, a Methodist institution in Oxford, Ga. He graduated with first honors in 1875 and, though not yet eighteen, was licensed to preach; nine months later he was admitted to the North Georgia Conference of the Methodist Episcopal Church, South.

An important influence upon the young pastor was Atticus Green Haygood [*q.v.*], Methodist minister and president of Emory College, with whom Candler boarded during his first two years of preaching. Serving in various pastorates in Georgia, Candler soon became a dynamic and highly successful revival preacher. Short, stout, and square-jawed, with a pugnacious air, he practiced a strenuous, emotional evangelism that brought mass conversions. A leader of the "New Puritanism" that swept the South in the 1880's, he emphasized the old doctrines and the inspiration of the Bible. His sermons were hard-driving attacks on individual indulgences, all of which he judged as sinful; he made little distinction between play reading, theatre- and moviegoing, dancing, drinking, gambling, and even playing or watching baseball games. A shrewd manipulator, able to speak on any topic with little preparation, he loved the limelight and enjoyed his platform successes.

In 1886 Candler became assistant editor of the Nashville *Christian Advocate,* official organ of the Southern Methodist Church. Two years later he was chosen president of Emory College, where over the next ten years he built a reputation for sound management. He increased the endowment and raised faculty salaries, arranged for the construction of a new library building, banned intercollegiate sports, lengthened the programs leading to the bachelor's degree to a full four years, and added a department of theology and two academic chairs (mathematics; history and political economy). He also upgraded the law school, persuading the state legislature to recognize its graduates as equal to law graduates of the University of Georgia.

In 1898 Candler was elected a bishop of the Methodist Episcopal Church, South, a position he held until he reached the age of compulsory retirement in 1934. Like the church's other bishops, he was an itinerant general superintendent; he continued to live in Georgia and traveled frequently to supervise conferences as far away as Denver. He was a defender of a strong, even autocratic, episcopacy in the tradition of George Foster Pierce [*q.v.*], but he had a large following among Methodist laymen; his outspoken defense of orthodoxy and his prominence led many to regard him as the leading bishop of his church. Active in foreign missionary work, in 1898 Candler made the first of twenty trips to Cuba, where he tried to build a strong native ministry. From 1903 to 1910 he had episcopal responsibility for Mexico; and in 1906 he supervised the mission work in the Orient, particularly the Korean mission, in which he had long been interested.

As a trustee of the Southern Methodist-founded Vanderbilt University in Nashville, Tenn., Candler strenuously opposed the weakening of denominational control that took place during the administration of Chancellor James H. Kirkland [Supp. 2], particularly the appointment of non-Methodists as professors and deans. The dispute was exacerbated in 1913 when Andrew Carnegie [*q.v.*] offered Vanderbilt a million dollars for its medical school on the condition that the school's seven-man governing board include the chancellor and three men connected with the best medical schools in the country. Candler decried Carnegie as an "agnostic steel-monger" and charged that the Carnegie and Rockefeller boards sought "to dominate the education of the United States." Meanwhile, in 1910, the Methodist General Conference initiated a lawsuit against Vanderbilt, claiming the right to elect the trustees and to veto any action taken by them. Both claims were denied in 1914 by the Tennessee supreme court in a decision that Candler labeled "a judicial theft."

Having lost Vanderbilt, the Southern Methodist Church, under Candler's leadership, voted to take over Southern Methodist University in Dallas from the Texas conference and to establish a new university at Atlanta. The latter was given the name Emory University and absorbed the earlier Emory College. To create the new university, Candler enlisted the support of his brother Asa, who gave an initial million dollars and subsequently six million more. The institution was on a sound financial basis under the administration of the two brothers: the Bishop served as chancellor (1914–19, 1920–22) and Asa as the first chairman of the board of trustees. They were also instrumental in building in Atlanta the Wesley Memorial Hospital, which later became a part of Emory University.

Although he often criticized the South, Candler had a deep loyalty to his section and disliked outside intervention and criticism. When John D. Rockefeller [Supp. 2] offered money to help combat hookworm in the South, Candler condemned the act as "singling out the South for all sorts of reform." The same regional loyalty led him to oppose the various moves for reunification of Northern and Southern Methodism. When his denomination's General Conference of 1924 adopted a plan of unification, Candler played a major role in defeating its ratification in the annual conferences. Not until 1939 was the union of the two churches (along with the much smaller Methodist Protestant Church) effected; although he did not then approve of it, Candler urged would-be seceders to remain within the national body.

Believing that Negroes should be educated, under Southern auspices, to become useful members of Southern society, Candler helped found, in 1884, Paine College in Augusta, Ga., and served for twenty-five years on its board of trustees. Candler was a lifelong prohibitionist. He nevertheless opposed the Woman's Christian Temperance Union because of its support of woman suffrage, and during the 1928 presidential campaign he firmly resisted appeals to speak out against Alfred E. Smith [Supp. 3], asserting that the church should remain aloof from politics.

On Nov. 21, 1877, Candler married Sarah Antoinette Curtright. They had five children: Annie Florence, John Curtright, Warren Akin, Emory, and Samuel Charles. Candler died at the age of eighty-four at his home in Atlanta of bronchopneumonia, and was buried in nearby Oxford. A college in Havana, Cuba, the school of theology at Emory, and a hospital in Savannah, Ga., all bear his name.

Bishop Candler has become something of a legend in Georgia Methodism. In addition to his platform achievement, he was a versatile and productive writer; but he was not a scholar, and little of his massive publication now has value. A master of humor, irony, sarcasm, and invective, he was also dictatorial, abrupt, intolerant, unwilling to compromise, and wholly lacking in a capacity for self-criticism. Yet his followers were legion, forgiving his shortcomings in the face of his achievement, much of which was made possible by the munificent generosity of his millionaire brother.

[Alfred M. Pierce, *Giant against the Sky: The Life of Bishop Warren Akin Candler* (1949), a somewhat laudatory biography. See also: Harold W. Mann, *Atticus Green Haygood* (1965); Charles H. Candler, *Asa Griggs Candler* (1950); Henry M. Bullock, *A Hist. of Emory Univ.* (1936); Thomas H. English, *Emory Univ., 1915–1965* (1966); Edwin Mims, *Chancellor Kirkland of Vanderbilt* (1940) and *Hist. of Vanderbilt Univ.* (1946). Candler carried on an enormous correspondence for many years, averaging three or four dozen letters daily; his papers, containing some 30,000 items, are in the Asa Griggs Candler Lib. of Emory Univ.]

WALTER B. POSEY

CANNON, ANNIE JUMP (Dec. 11, 1863–Apr. 13, 1941), astronomer, was born in Dover, Del., the eldest of three children of Wilson Lee Cannon, a well-to-do shipbuilder and farm owner, and his second wife, Mary Elizabeth Jump. The family included four children by Cannon's first marriage. As a girl, Annie learned the constellations from her mother, who had picked up some knowledge of astronomy at a Quaker school near Philadelphia. One of her childhood delights was to watch the rainbow-colored images formed when sunlight struck the prisms on a family candelabrum. This love of stars and spectra was to continue throughout her life.

Her formal education began in local schools,

including the Wilmington Conference Academy (Methodist), from which she graduated in 1880. Because of her eagerness for further knowledge, her father allowed her to enter Wellesley College in Massachusetts. There she studied with Sarah Frances Whiting, professor of physics and astronomy, and pursued an interest in spectroscopy. For a decade after her graduation from Wellesley in 1884, Miss Cannon lived at home in Dover. During this period she visited Italy and Spain to view a solar eclipse; always an ardent photographer, she carried with her one of the earliest box cameras with roll film, a Kamerette. In 1894, following the death of her mother, she returned to Wellesley, where she assisted Professor Whiting in the teaching of physics and took part in one of the first experiments carried out in the United States to confirm Roentgen's discovery of X-rays. The following year, after correspondence with Edward C. Pickering [q.v.], director of the Harvard College Observatory, she enrolled in Radcliffe College as a special student in astronomy.

In 1896 Pickering brought Miss Cannon to the staff of the Harvard Observatory, where, by her own preference, she began the study of variable stars and stellar spectra. Her first major publication, "Classification of 1122 Bright Southern Stars" (*Annals* of the Harvard College Observatory, vol. XXVIII, part 2, 1901), was a catalogue of spectra photographed at Harvard's station at Arequipa, Peru, and embodied a modified version of the early classification system used at Harvard by Williamina P. Fleming [q.v.] and the more complex one devised by Antonia C. Maury. Using the types of spectra that Mrs. Fleming had distinguished by the letters A, B, C, etc., Miss Cannon rearranged them to conform to Miss Maury's sequence of types I, II, III, etc., which was based on order of descending stellar temperature. Miss Cannon's system represented a sequence of continuous change from the very hot white and blue stars of types O and B, which showed many helium lines, through the less hot stars of types A, F, G, and K, to the very red stars of type M, which were cool enough so that compounds of chemical elements, such as titanium and carbon oxides, could exist in their atmospheres. Subdivisions of these classes were indicated by arabic numerals. Since the spectra of some stars did not fit in any of these categories, she listed them as "peculiar," and in copious notes provided a detailed description. In 1910 Miss Cannon's scheme was adopted as the official classification system at all observatories, and with later modifications this "Harvard System" has continued in use.

In 1911, promoted from her initial rank of

assistant to curator of astronomical photographs, Miss Cannon began work on one of the greatest compilations of astronomical information ever achieved by one person, the Henry Draper Catalogue of stellar spectra. This was published by the Harvard Observatory (as vols. XCI–XCIX of its *Annals*) between the years 1918 and 1924, and lists the spectral types of 225,300 stars, all those brighter than ninth magnitude. The catalogue also gives their positions and visual and photographic magnitudes, with notes on the peculiarities of individual stars. When the Henry Draper Catalogue was finished, Miss Cannon began work on an extension (*ibid.*, vols. C and CXII, 1925 and 1949), classifying fainter stars in selected regions of the sky, especially in the rich Milky Way areas in Cygnus, Sagittarius, and Carina, and in the Large Magellanic Cloud. During her lifetime she classified the spectra of some 400,000 stars.

Miss Cannon's interest in variable stars led her in 1903 to prepare a provisional catalogue listing the 1,227 variables known at that time (*ibid.*, vol. XLVIII, no. 3), and in 1907 she published a "Second Catalogue of Variable Stars" (*ibid.*, vol. LV, part 1), which included accurate positions, ranges of magnitude, periods, and spectral types of about 2,000 stars, together with detailed notes on their peculiarities. In the course of her study of photographic plates, she discovered five novae and over 300 variables, many of them from their characteristic spectra. She kept a card catalogue of references to all published and much unpublished information about known and suspected variable stars.

Miss Cannon was happy in her work and warm in her relationships with other people. Travel and attendance at astronomical meetings gave her much pleasure, and she took part in all meetings of the International Astronomical Union except the first one, held at Rome in 1922 when she was working at the Harvard Observatory station in Peru. No meeting of the American Astronomical Society was considered complete without her presence. Star Cottage, her home in Cambridge, Mass., was a mecca for astronomers from all parts of the world. She was especially fond of children, for whom she regularly gave parties.

Miss Cannon received many honors during her lifetime. Among them were election to the American Philosophical Society (1925)—one of its few women members—and as an honorary member of the Royal Astronomical Society (1914), and honorary degrees from the University of Delaware, the University of Groningen in Holland, Wellesley, Oxford University, where in 1925 she was the first woman to be honored with a doctorate of science, Oglethorpe University, and Mount Holyoke College. She was the first woman to receive the Henry Draper Gold Medal of the National Academy of Sciences, which was awarded in 1931 for her investigations in astrophysics, and also the first woman to be elected an officer of the American Astronomical Society (treasurer, 1912–19). In 1938 Miss Cannon was appointed William Cranch Bond Astronomer at Harvard University, a position she held until her retirement in September 1940. She died the following spring, of heart disease, at her home in Cambridge, Mass. Originally a Methodist, in New England she had become a Congregationalist. She was buried in the old family plot in Lakeside Cemetery, Dover, Del.

[The principal sources are Miss Cannon's papers and writings, and personal knowledge of the author. For published material see: Edna Yost, *Women in Science* (1943), chap. ii; "Women Astronomers at Harvard," *Harvard Alumni Bull.*, Jan. 13, 1927; Anne P. McKenney, "What Women Have Done for Astronomy in the U. S.," *Popular Astronomy*, Mar. 1904; obituaries, *ibid.*, Aug. 1941 (by Leon Campbell), Am. Philosophical Soc., *Year Book*, 1941 (by Harlow Shapley), *Science*, May 9, 1941 (by Cecilia Payne Gaposchkin), and *N. Y. Times*, Apr. 14, 1941, with editorial, Apr. 15. On her work at Wellesley, see Miss Cannon's memoir of Sarah Frances Whiting in *Popular Astronomy*, Dec. 1927. See also sketch by Dorrit Hoffleit in *Notable Am. Women*.]

MARGARET W. MAYALL

CANNON, JAMES (Nov. 13, 1864–Sept. 6, 1944), Southern Methodist clergyman, educator, and temperance reformer, was born in Salisbury, Md., the second son and fifth and youngest child of James and Lydia Robertson (Primrose) Cannon. His parents, dedicated Methodists of Scottish descent, were natives of Sussex County, Del. An uncle, William Cannon [*q.v.*], was a Civil War governor of Delaware, but the war forced Cannon's father, a Southern partisan, to move to Maryland. Settling in Salisbury, he prospered as a merchant, reared his children in comfort, and provided a family life in which religion and the church were central.

In 1881 young Cannon entered Randolph-Macon College and began his lifelong association with the state of Virginia. He had intended to become a lawyer, but after a religious conversion decided to enter the ministry. After graduating from Randolph-Macon (A.B. 1884), he attended Princeton Theological Seminary, where he was awarded a B.D. degree in 1888; in 1890 he received an M.A. from the College of New Jersey (later Princeton University). Cannon married Lura Virginia Bennett, daughter of William Wallace Bennett, former president of Randolph-Macon, on Aug. 1, 1888. Of their nine children, seven survived: Lura Lee, Virginia, James, Wallace Bennett, Richard Mason, David Primrose, and Edward Lee.

In November 1888 Cannon entered the Virginia Conference, Methodist Episcopal Church, South, and was assigned to the Charlotte circuit. After serving several pastorates, he became principal (1894–1911, 1914–18) of the Blackstone (Va.) Female Institute, which he developed into a flourishing college. Short and slight, bearded, and wearing gold-rimmed spectacles, Cannon was innocuous in appearance, but his keen mind, strong will, and combative temperament embroiled him in controversy from the outset. He challenged the established leadership of the Conference and proved himself a formidable antagonist; as a delegate to the General Conference of 1902 in Dallas, Texas, he first attracted the attention of the church at large. His influence broadened in 1904 when he became editor of the *Baltimore and Richmond Christian Advocate,* newspaper of the Virginia Conference. Despite continuing quarrels, including his leadership in a prolonged and successful battle to strengthen denominational control of Randolph-Macon College, he was recognized by 1909 as the dominant figure in the Virginia Conference. Two years later he was chosen as the first superintendent of Junaluska, the Methodist Southern Assembly near Waynesville, N. C., which he built and developed as a summer meeting place and recreation center for the church's mission and education boards and for Methodist families.

The General Conference of 1918 elected Cannon a bishop, an event which widened his responsibilities to include supervision of mission fields in Mexico, Cuba, Brazil, and the Congo. These episcopal duties, together with work for the Near East Relief and the World League against Alcoholism and attendance at various international gatherings, required extensive travel abroad. Meanwhile, he shouldered numerous burdens at home, including an active role in the Federal Council of Churches from the time of its founding in 1908. During the 1920's he was one of the Southern leaders in the movement for Methodist unification.

Although a prominent churchman, Cannon was best known as a temperance reformer. The influence of his mother, Methodist teachings, and experience with the victims of intemperance had instilled in him a hatred of the liquor traffic, and he became the driving spirit behind the Virginia Anti-Saloon League. In 1910 he founded a dry daily newspaper, the *Richmond Virginian;* four years later, after forcing the wet Democratic organization to permit a state referendum on prohibition, he led the drys to an overwhelming victory.

Meanwhile, the national Anti-Saloon League

had selected Cannon as chairman of its legislative committee, and he became the most effective of its lobbyists in Washington during the Wilson administration, when the League led the drive which culminated in the Eighteenth Amendment. During the 1920's he was increasingly powerful as a leader of both the Anti-Saloon League and the Southern Methodist Church. His political influence reached its peak during the presidential election of 1928. Refusing to support Alfred E. Smith [Supp. 3], a wet and a Roman Catholic, Cannon organized the Anti-Smith Democrats. His vigorous campaign helped swing five Southern states, including Virginia, into the Republican column on election day.

Cannon's triumph in 1928 was short-lived. The following summer powerful enemies, including the Hearst press and Senator Carter Glass of Virginia, initiated various charges against him. These included stock-market gambling, misusing campaign funds, hoarding flour during World War I, and, after his marriage on July 15, 1930, to Mrs. Helen Hawley McCallum, his former secretary (Lura Cannon had died in 1928), adultery. Five sensational years of Congressional hearings, church investigations, and legal battles followed. Cannon was officially cleared of wrongdoing, but the scandals bitterly divided his church and undermined his influence. Many continued to believe him guilty, either as charged or of improper conduct.

For three decades Cannon was a relentless and effective crusader for both prohibition and the church. As a leader he demonstrated a prodigious capacity for sustained work, extraordinary calm under pressure, and a tough-minded adherence to fact and logic rather than sentiment. Some found him ruthless; he was feared and respected, but rarely loved. Although conservative in theology, Cannon was often reformist on social questions. For him, as for many of his generation, prohibition was a progressive step toward human betterment, and his pragmatic approach to politics enabled him to secure its success. With repeal, however, he faded quickly from public view, and he retired in 1938. He died of a cerebral hemorrhage in Chicago, where he had gone to attend a meeting of the Anti-Saloon League, and was buried in Hollywood Cemetery, Richmond, Va.

[The best biographical account is Richard L. Watson, Jr.'s editorial introduction to Cannon's autobiography, *Bishop Cannon's Own Story* (1955); the autobiography itself is informative, but except for Cannon's activities as bishop, it terminates in the middle of the campaign of 1928. A perceptive early appraisal of Cannon appears in John J. Lafferty, ed., *Sketches and Portraits of the Va. Conference* (1901), pp. 446–49. The obituary by J. W. Moore in the *Va. Conference Annual*, 1944, pp. 140–43, is revealing.

Virginius Dabney's biography, *Dry Messiah: The Life of Bishop Cannon* (1949), though well written, is extremely hostile and somewhat outdated. For recent studies, see Robert A. Hohner, "Prohibition Comes to Va.: The Referendum of 1914," *Va. Mag. of Hist. and Biog.*, Oct. 1967, and "Bishop Cannon's Apprenticeship in Temperance Politics, 1901–1918," *Jour. of Southern Hist.*, Feb. 1968. Cannon's papers are in the Duke Univ. Lib. Other materials about him are in the Virginius Dabney Papers, Collins Denny Papers, and Carter Glass Papers, all in the Univ. of Va. Lib.; the Henry D. Flood Papers, Lib. of Cong.; the Ernest H. Cherrington Papers, Temperance Education Foundation, Westerville, Ohio; and the Frederick DeLand Leete Episcopal Papers, Bridwell Lib., Southern Methodist Univ. For good photographs of Cannon, see: (as a young clergyman) Jack Temple Kirby, *Westmoreland Davis: Va. Planter-Politician, 1859–1942* (1968), facing p. 117; (at mid-career) Dabney, facing p. 178; and (as bishop) *Bishop Cannon's Own Story*, frontispiece.]

ROBERT A. HOHNER

CANNON, WALTER BRADFORD (Oct. 19, 1871–Oct. 1, 1945), physiologist, born in Prairie du Chien, Wis., was the only son and eldest of four children of Colbert Hanchett Cannon and his wife, (Sarah) Wilma Denio. His American forebear on his father's side was Samuel Carnahan (later Cannon), a Scotch-Irish settler of 1718 in Massachusetts, some of whose descendants moved west to Ohio and thence to Wisconsin. His mother's family derived their name from Jacques de Noyon, a French Canadian coureur des bois who had come to Deerfield, Mass., about 1700 and married a local girl; a later branch of the family made its way from Vermont to New York state to frontier Minnesota. Colbert Cannon, unable to fulfill his childhood ambition to become a doctor, was a successful railroad official who read medical books avidly and practiced in the evening upon his neighbors. His wife, a former high school teacher, died when her son was ten.

The boy attended public schools in Milwaukee and St. Paul. On the father's suspicion that he had been idling, he was taken out of school between the ages of fourteen and sixteen and put to work. By the time he graduated from the St. Paul high school at nineteen, he had been bitten by Darwin's bulldog T. H. Huxley and shaken by the implications of Darwinism for religion. His favorite high school teacher successfully took it upon herself to get him a scholarship to Harvard.

The teachers in Harvard College who left a decisive mark upon him were the biologists Charles B. Davenport [Supp. 3] and George H. Parker. Cannon served as student assistant to Parker, a zoologist, for two years and did his first piece of research with Davenport on the phototaxis (orientation with respect to light) of minute swimming organisms. He graduated from Harvard College summa cum laude in 1896 and

received a master's degree in 1897 for his research with Davenport.

Meanwhile, he had enrolled in the Harvard Medical School. Henry Pickering Bowditch [q.v.], the founder in 1871 of the first physiological laboratory in the United States, soon interested Cannon in physiology. Cannon as a medical student also gave in Harvard College the course that he had assisted in as an undergraduate. On graduation from the Harvard Medical School in 1900 he had his choice between instructorships in zoology in the college or in physiology in the medical school. He chose physiology. Within six years of taking his M.D., Cannon was Bowditch's successor as George Higginson Professor of Physiology (1906–42).

When Cannon entered medical school in 1896, Roentgen's discovery of X rays in the previous year was still fresh. Bowditch encouraged Cannon to observe on a fluorescent screen the X-ray shadows from a metal ball swallowed by a goose. By the end of his freshman year, Cannon had made a permanent mark on the history of medicine by filling the greatest single gap in X-ray technique—the impossibility of obtaining satisfactory pictures from the soft organs of the alimentary canal. Cannon solved the problem by feeding the patient a meal mixed with bismuth subnitrate or barium sulphate, both opaque to X rays. In his initial publications of 1897, he neglected to mention barium, which eventually replaced bismuth as the agent of choice. The basic technique was soon employed in every modern hospital in the world to diagnose gastric and duodenal ulcers and tumors of the digestive tract.

For the history of science, the importance of this discovery lay in opening up new investigations of the physiology of digestion, a theme that occupied Cannon uninterruptedly from 1897 to 1911. For the first time an investigator was able to "see" food enter the stomach and follow its entire history there. Cannon demonstrated a steady rhythm of peristaltic waves by which food was churned and moved along through the stomach.

Cannon suspected that the cause of hunger was powerful contractions of the empty stomach. In 1911 his loyal student A. L. Washburn trained himself to tolerate a rubber tube in his esophagus leading to a small balloon just inside the stomach. If the balloon was moderately inflated with air and connected with a pressure gauge, Washburn found that whenever he was feeling hungry, and only then, heavy stomach contractions pressing upon the balloon were invariably recorded on the gauge.

Cannon eventually built this classic experiment into his famous theory of the "local" causes of hunger and thirst—stomach contractions and dryness of the mouth respectively. The upshot of subsequent researches has been to demonstrate that Cannon's theory is inadequate as a *comprehensive* explanation of hunger and thirst. No reservations on this score can diminish Cannon's achievement in working out a definitive picture of *The Mechanical Factors of Digestion* (1911), which entitle him to rank among the handful of great contributors to the physiology of digestion.

As early as 1897, Cannon had been surprised to observe that the peristaltic waves of the stomach in digestion would sometimes cease abruptly. He soon discovered that the animals in question were frightened or otherwise disturbed. There was already a considerable literature on psychic factors in digestion, but Cannon began very slowly to confront the nature of emotion in general. From 1911 to 1917 he concentrated on the experiments that made him the first investigator to focus persistently upon the physiology of emotions.

The special twist that Cannon gave to the topic was to effect a link with an entirely different line of researches. The discovery of adrenaline had touched off a successful quest for other physiologically active internal secretions and the enunciation of a general concept of "hormones." It was far from evident that any of the hormones had widespread effects upon the body as a whole. But the young English physiologist Thomas Renton Elliott published between 1904 and 1913 a series of papers in which he emphasized the striking similarity between many of the known effects of adrenaline and those produced by stimulating the sympathetic nerves ("involuntary" nerves acting upon the viscera among other organs). Elliott tentatively conjectured in print (more vigorously in conversation) that adrenaline might actually be involved in the transmission of sympathetic nerve impulses—a daring hypothesis of a chemical neurotransmitter in a period when neurotransmission was almost universally supposed to be a purely electrical phenomenon.

Only two major investigators took Elliott's publications as seriously as they merited, the young English pharmacologist Henry H. Dale and Walter B. Cannon. Many of the visceral processes studied by Cannon for their bearing upon digestion were under the control of sympathetic nerves, but the physiological reverberations in an emotionally disturbed animal often persisted long after the neurally transmitted stimulus had dis-

appeared. Cannon began to suspect that adrenaline directly liberated from the adrenal medulla might be the factor responsible for this prolongation. By this line of hypothesizing, Cannon became the first to bring hormone research to bear upon the physiology of emotions—a theme of which Elliott had nothing to say.

Cannon soon assembled evidence from his own laboratory that adrenaline helped to divert blood from the organs of the abdomen to the heart, lungs, central nervous system, and limbs; helped to remedy muscular fatigue; hastened the coagulation of blood; and cooperated with sympathetic nerves in bringing sugar stored in the liver back into the bloodstream. He ended by postulating a "sympathico-adrenal system" charged with enacting the physiology of strong emotions.

The other main import of his celebrated book *Bodily Changes in Pain, Hunger, Fear and Rage* (1915) was an effort, in the words of his subtitle, to explain "the function of emotional excitement." He argued that the bodily changes presided over by the sympathico-adrenal system were preparations for flight or fight. Sugar flooding from the liver into the blood would supply extra energy; steps to combat muscular fatigue were essential for fighting or running away; blood was shifted from the abdomen, where digestion could safely be halted till the crisis was over, to the heart, lungs, and limbs because these would bear the brunt of extraordinary exertions. In short, the terrified or furious organism was flung into an emergency mobilization of its total resources, keyed up to the "violent display of energy" required to flee from a peril or beat it down. If the defenses of the body were breached by a wound, bloodclotting would be more rapid than usual. This "emergency" theory of the physiology of emotions has dominated all subsequent discussions of the topic.

From theoretical discussions of flight or fight, Cannon was abruptly plunged into the real thing as a member of the Harvard Hospital Unit that left for France in May 1917. After the arrival of the American Expeditionary Force, he became director of a laboratory for research on shock and other medical problems at Dijon.

Cannon's first order of business after the war was to defend his reputation from a frontal assault upon the validity of everything he had to say about the release of adrenaline in emotional stress. Two well-regarded investigators at Western Reserve University, George N. Stewart [*q.v.*] and J. M. Rogoff, had published in 1917 a severe critique of Cannon's experimental technique and the alleged fallacies arising from it. He had tested for adrenaline by catheterizing the adrenal veins, and found that the adrenaline content of the blood withdrawn in times of stress went up sharply. But Stewart and Rogoff claimed that this demonstrated nothing about adrenal secretion in the intact organism. They argued that the rate of blood flow was slowed down by removing it from the body and that the concentration of adrenaline appeared to rise only because it was less diluted by a slowly moving bloodstream. In fact, they said, adrenal secretion was constant and steady and bore no relationship whatever to the emergency mobilization envisioned by Cannon.

In a brilliant communication of 1919, Cannon finessed the entire criticism by describing his preparation of a "denervated" heart, completely severed from the central nervous system (including the sympathetic nerves). In the absence of cardiac nerves, the heart itself served as an "indicator" of any substances circulating in the bloodstream that accelerated or slowed its beat. No blood had to be withdrawn for testing. With this new anatomical preparation, Cannon demonstrated that any stimulation of the remaining sympathetic nerves while the adrenal glands were intact led to a promptly accelerated heartbeat.

When the adrenal glands were also denervated, stimulation of the sympathetic system could still produce an accelerated heartbeat. Cannon and his collaborator J. E. Uridil were able to prove in 1921 that stimulation of the sympathetic nerves of the liver was involved. What was even more extraordinary, they discovered that when the heart, adrenals, *and* liver were all denervated, any form of excitement still produced acceleration, though in lesser amount and only after three minutes' delay. Cannon and his associates eventually found that acceleration could only be abolished completely by removing the entire sympathetic system. There was obviously a "mysterious factor" at work, somehow correlated with the distribution of functioning sympathetic nerves.

Cannon was hot on the trail of one of the greatest discoveries in twentieth-century physiology—the demonstration of a chemical transmitter of nerve impulses. The Austrian pharmacologist Otto Loewi showed, also in 1921, that if two frog hearts were isolated, one denervated and the other not, neural stimulation of the innervated heart would liberate a substance capable of producing the identical effect upon the denervated organ—accelerating the beat of the latter if the sympathetic nerve of the former had been stimulated, reducing the beat if the vagus (parasympathetic) nerve had been stimulated. Loewi privately thought that the accelerating substance was adren-

aline, but he was highly circumspect about this and used the neutral term "sympathetic substance" in print. His famous experiments of 1921, establishing the existence of two antagonistic transmitters, set Loewi on the high road to a Nobel Prize. Cannon might well have accompanied him if he had chosen to devote the 1920's single-mindedly to tracking down his own "mysterious factor."

The main reason that Cannon later gave for deciding against this was another opportunity for research arising out of the identical experiments that led him to the "mysterious factor." Once he had performed a total sympathectomy, surgical removal of the sympathetic system, to knock this factor out, Cannon saw himself as confronted with "a new type of organism that had been produced in the world, a well-developed mammal quite deprived of supposedly necessary sympathetic nerves." The functions and trigger points of the autonomic or "involuntary" division of the nervous system, of which the sympathetic nerves are a part, became Cannon's principal research problem of the 1920's.

Functionally speaking, the obverse of sympathectomy was decortication or decerebration—leaving the autonomic system intact and seeing how much of the brain could be removed (or disconnected) at progressively lower and evolutionarily more primitive levels before the autonomic system ceased to produce the effects attributed to it. Cannon and his associate S. W. Britton reported in 1925 that decorticated cats on recovering from anesthesia displayed intense fury *spontaneously*—what Cannon called "sham rage." In 1928 Cannon's collaborator Philip Bard found a "center" for rage, a very small portion of the hypothalamus that was still capable of producing "sham rage" when the cortex and much of the brain stem had been removed. Conversely, when this portion of the hypothalamus was extirpated, the capacity for rage was abolished.

Cannon was now prepared to issue a second edition of *Bodily Changes* (1929) containing his mature reflections on the physiology of emotions. A major new ingredient in the revised edition was Cannon's response to the criticism that he had gravely exaggerated the utility of strong emotional excitement in modern man. His critics argued that the physiological responses to stress illuminated by Cannon himself often produced injurious or even fatal results—literally consumed the person that harbored them. Cannon replied that he had never denied that normal processes could become pathological. In a new chapter on "Emotional Derangement of Bodily Functions," Cannon became one of the chief forerunners of psychosomatic medicine. Digestion and nutrition, he said, could suffer disastrously from the phenomenon that attracted his attention to the physiology of emotions in the first place, the cessation of mechanical and chemical processes in the alimentary canal in times of excitement. Blood pressure could be permanently driven up by repeated exposure to emotionally loaded situations.

Despite his increasing emphasis upon pathological conditions, Cannon's ultimate conclusion from his researches of the 1920's was overwhelmingly positive—that higher organisms incorporated an extraordinary assemblage of self-regulatory mechanisms conferring a dynamically achieved stability under all but the gravest external perils. In his most famous intellectual construction, Cannon coined in 1926 the term "homeostasis" for the tendency toward physiological stability. He published a full-scale account of homeostasis in *The Wisdom of the Body* of 1932. The main source of the new concept lay in Cannon's own topics of research, but the principal crystallizing agency was his encounter with the thought of the French physiologist Claude Bernard. With the single exception of evolution through natural selection, homeostasis has proved to be the most influential of all integrating concepts in biology.

When Cannon finally returned to the question of chemical neurotransmission in 1930, the two main investigators in the field were Otto Loewi and Henry Dale. Research was still largely oriented about Loewi's discovery of two substances acting oppositely upon the heart—Vagusstoff (vagus substance) slowing it down, Sympathicusstoff (sympathetic substance) accelerating it. Dale in the early 1930's was about to identfy the vagus substance as acetylcholine.

There were good reasons to suspect, with T. R. Elliott earlier in the century, that the sympathetic transmitter might be adrenaline. Adrenaline was secreted by the adrenal medulla, and there were morphological grounds for regarding the adrenal medulla as modified nerve tissue of the sympathetic system. More patently, adrenaline, like the sympathetic substance, was a cardiac accelerator. But as Dale had demonstrated in 1910, there were chemical homologues (near relatives) of adrenaline that had the same general effects as adrenaline itself—in Dale's coinage "sympathomimetic" properties.

With the Belgian Z. M. Bacq in 1931 and the Mexican Arturo Rosenblueth in 1932, Cannon showed that organs could be "sensitized" through denervation *or* the administration of small quantities of cocaine (ineffective in themselves), so that the organs in question became hypersensitive

to the substance released by stimulating sympathetic nerves anywhere in the body. As Loewi and a collaborator had shown in 1907 that cocaine was adrenaline-sensitizing, Cannon's findings tended to confirm Elliott's hypothesis. But Cannon and Rosenblueth in a major communication of 1933 concluded that sympathetic nerve stimulation did *not* always produce the same qualitative results as the administration or physiological release of adrenaline. Their solution to this riddle was their famous theory of the two "sympathins." In their terminology, adrenaline was merely a "mediator" of sympathetic impulses. The end result of transmitting the impulse was produced by the combination of the mediator with receptor substances in the organ or fiber that was being acted upon. The two basic combinations were "sympathin E" for excitatory effects and "sympathin I" for inhibitory.

Cannon's skepticism about the probable role of adrenaline took the very mild form of reducing it from the status of an essential and sufficient cause to that of an essential but insufficient mediator. Even this represented a significant dissent from the rapidly gathering consensus in the early 1930's that adrenaline had now been pinned down as the sympathetic substance. Otto Loewi was finally prepared in 1936 to announce publicly his adherence to this view.

Loewi was wrong. He himself in 1936 and Cannon and Kalman Lissák in 1939 pioneered in the preparation of sympathomimetic extracts from sympathetic nerves and a variety of organs innervated by them; and Cannon and Lissák sealed the argument by demonstrating that after the sympathetic nerves to an organ degenerated, the sympathomimetic activity of extracts from it virtually disappeared. The extracts that were active could be tested with the precision required to differentiate the effects of adrenaline from those of its homologues. Partly by this means the Swedish investigator Ulf von Euler in the years from 1945 to 1951 succeeded in demonstrating that the true neurotransmitter that Cannon had been looking for was noradrenaline—a discovery rewarded by a Nobel Prize in 1970.

With the arguable exception of the theory of the two sympathins, the part of Cannon's work that bore up least well under the scrutiny of the following generation was the importance that he attached to the adrenal component in a "sympathico-adrenal system." By "adrenal" he meant the adrenal medulla, the source of adrenaline. It has become increasingly clear that the absence of the adrenal medulla does not endanger life; and that Cannon tended to exaggerate the importance of adrenaline as an agent of physiological mobilization in emotion-fraught situations. Animals whose adrenal medulla has been extirpated are not severely handicapped in emergency situations outside the laboratory.

Apart from his role in the history of physiology, Cannon proved to be one of the few American scientists to leave a significant mark upon fields of science other than his own. He concluded *The Wisdom of the Body* with an epilogue on "Relations of Biological and Social Homeostasis." His theme was the need for a "comparative study of stabilizing processes" in the individual and the social organisms. Doctrines of homeostasis actually came to play a role in sociology, as a corollary to the influence exerted by Cannon's Harvard contemporary Lawrence J. Henderson [Supp. 3].

Another area in which the name and concept of homeostasis reverberated out of Cannon's control was in the new science unveiled by Norbert Wiener in his book of 1948, *Cybernetics, or Control and Communication in the Animal and the Machine*. Cannon's favorite collaborator in the last fifteen years of his life, Arturo Rosenblueth, called Wiener's attention to the fact that Cannon had long been grappling in the doctrine of homeostasis with the empirical consequences of negative feedback in the animal body.

In 1930 Cannon visited the leading younger physiologist of Spain, Juan Negrín, and through him met many university people who were talking of the need for a republic. When the Civil War came and Negrín eventually became prime minister, Cannon wholeheartedly embraced the Republican cause. His main contribution to the Spanish Loyalists consisted in serving for two years as the impeccably non-Communist national chairman of the Medical Bureau to Aid Spanish Democracy.

Cannon married on June 25, 1901, Cornelia James (Radcliffe 1899), whom he had known in high school. She became a novelist. They had a son, Bradford, himself a medical man, followed by four daughters: Wilma Denio, Linda, Marian, and Helen. Apart from canoeing or tramping in the woods in New Hampshire or Vermont with his perennially vigorous wife or friends on the Harvard faculty, Cannon let off steam by building furniture, modeling in clay, gardening, and reading about Lincoln.

Cannon suffered from severe allergies for the last twenty-five years of his life. At the end of the 1930's he discovered that he also had leukemia—probably a legacy from his early work with X rays—of which he died at his farmhouse near Franklin, N. H., in 1945, at the age of seventy-four. His ashes were scattered over the farm. He was nominated for a Nobel Prize in 1920 for his work on digestion, but his claim was ruled out as "too old." In 1934, 1935, and 1936 he was adjudged "prizeworthy" by the appropriate Nobel jurors but was not given a prize. He was president of the American Association for the Advancement of Science in 1939.

[Cannon's manuscript diary, Countway Lib., Harvard Medic. School; Cannon's autobiographical *The Way of an Investigator: A Scientist's Experiences in Medical Research* (1945); interview with Wilma Cannon Fairbank (daughter); scientific memoir, with complete bibliography of Cannon's publications, by Sir Henry Dale in *Obituary Notices of Fellows of the Royal Soc.*, May 1947; retrospective estimate by J. A. Herd, "The Physiology of Strong Emotions: Cannon's Scientific Legacy Re-examined," *Physiologist*, Feb. 1972; Joseph C. Aub and Ruth K. Hapgood, *Pioneer in Modern Medicine: David Linn Edsall* (1970), with information on Cannon's career at Harvard Medical School. For a personal impression, see the obituary by Cecil K. Drinker in *Science*, Nov. 9, 1945. A bibliography of Cannon's publications up to 1931 is included in *Walter Bradford Cannon: Exercises Celebrating Twenty-five Years as George Higginson Prof. of Physiology* (1932).]

DONALD FLEMING

CARLISLE, FLOYD LESLIE (Mar. 5, 1881–Nov. 9, 1942), financier and public utility executive, was born in Watertown, N. Y., the youngest of four sons of William Sylvanus and Catherine Rose (Burdick) Carlisle. Both parents were natives of Jefferson County, N. Y., the Carlisles having moved there about 1820 after several generations in New Jersey. Floyd's father, an expert mechanic in the local Davis Sewing Machine Company, stayed with the company when it moved to Dayton, Ohio, and Floyd attended public schools in both Watertown and Dayton. He graduated from Cornell University in 1903, having been president of his sophomore and senior classes and president of the university debating team. He then read law with an uncle and was admitted to the New York bar in 1905. Carlisle began practice in partnership with a brother, but soon moved into various business ventures. In 1910 he merged two Watertown banks to form the Northern New York Trust Company and became its president, a post he held until 1922. In 1916 he organized a syndicate of local businessmen which purchased the St. Regis Paper Company, of which he was president from 1916 to 1934.

Association with the paper industry led to an interest in public utilities. St. Regis utilized waterpower in its operations, and Carlisle, partly on his own and partly on behalf of the company, began acquiring waterpower sites and small electric companies. In 1920 these holdings were consolidated as Northern New York Utilities Company, and subsequently the company began a rapid program of expansion. To profit from financing this expansion, Carlisle formed his own investment banking house, F. L. Carlisle and Company. For a time he was associated with the maverick utility financier Howard Hopson, but after 1927, when the banking house headed by the younger J. P. Morgan [Supp. 3] launched an ambitious scheme to monopolize the financing of the entire electric utility industry, Carlisle broke with Hopson and joined forces with Morgan. His own holdings were merged with others in 1929 to form Niagara Hudson Power Company, of which he became board chairman, and interconnection of the huge waterpower resources at Niagara Falls with the great markets in New York City was begun.

In addition, Carlisle was made chairman of the board of the Consolidated Gas Company, which held together a sprawling network of electric utility companies in and around New York City. Over the course of a few years, Carlisle supervised the corporate reorganization of these several companies as Consolidated Edison. Between them, Niagara Hudson and Consolidated Edison controlled about three-quarters of the electric supply of the state. As a part of Morgan's larger plans, Carlisle was also made a director of various holding companies in the Morgan group, including Columbia Gas and Electric, United Gas Improvement, and the super-holding company, the United Corporation.

During the depression of the 1930's utility holding companies fell into disrepute and came under political attack, largely because of the failure of several of them and the indictment of a number of utility executives, including Hopson, Samuel Insull [Supp. 2], and W. B. Foshay. Executives in the Morgan group sought to cover their own shortcomings by joining the attack and attempting to see to it that only "bad" holding companies—that is, those outside Morgan's control—were punished. Accordingly, Carlisle struck the stance of a reformer, advised the New Deal in its crusade against the power industry, and was instrumental in the organization of the Edison Electric Institute (1933), whose avowed purpose was to purge the industry of evils and reform it from within. The effort was futile, for holding companies were given the "death sentence" by a federal act of 1935 and the concentrated power of the House of Morgan was broken by banking acts of the period.

In his declining years Carlisle resigned many of his corporate directorships and devoted himself increasingly to civic and educational work and to his interests as a sportsman. Like many others in the paper industry, he was interested in conservation and forestry, and he was one of the sponsors of the school of forestry at St. Lawrence Uni-

versity. He was also a trustee of Cornell University. An ardent yachtsman, he raced his M-class sloop *Avatar* in Long Island regattas and won many cups. He listed himself as a Democrat in politics and an Episcopalian in religion. Carlisle was stricken with a coronary embolism in October 1942, at the age of sixty-one, and died soon afterward at his home in Locust Valley, Long Island. He was buried in the family plot in Brookside Cemetery, Watertown. He was survived by his wife, Edna May Rogers, whom he had married on Nov. 21, 1912, and by their four children: John William, Adele, Floyd Leslie, and Catherine Carlisle.

[Carlisle's life is sketched in the *N. Y. Times,* Nov. 10, 1942, and *Electrical World,* Nov. 14, 1942. See also *Nat. Cyc. Am. Biog.,* XXXI, 391; *Who Was Who in America,* vol. II (1950). Family data from Rensselaer A. Oakes, *Genealogical and Family Hist. of the County of Jefferson, N. Y.* (1905), pp. 149–52, and from Flower Memorial Library, Watertown, N. Y. Information about Carlisle's business career is available in the records and libraries of St. Regis Paper Co., Consolidated Edison, and the Edison Electric Inst., and in the Federal Trade Commission report, *Utility Corporations,* (96 parts, 1928–37); part 72-A, the Summary Report, provides the point of departure for the use of the set.]

FORREST MCDONALD

CARR, WILBUR JOHN (Oct. 31, 1870–June 26, 1942), State Department official, was born near Taylorsville, Ohio, the elder of the two sons of Edward Livingston Carr, whose forebears had lived in Ohio since early in the century, and Catherine (Fender) Carr, of Virginia background. He grew up on his father's farm. He was named John Wilbur, but as a young man reversed his given names out of admiration for Wilbur R. Smith, the president of the Commercial College of the University of Kentucky, from which he graduated in 1889. After further commercial training in Oswego, N. Y., and an interval (1890–92) as secretary of the Peekskill (N. Y.) Military Academy, Carr entered the State Department as a clerk on June 1, 1892, commencing his labors that morning by addressing envelopes. Initially anticipating a career in the law rather than in government, he also attended Georgetown University, from which he received an LL.B. degree in 1894, and Columbian University (later George Washington University), which granted him an LL.M. in 1899.

Carr was transferred to the State Department's Consular Bureau as a clerk in 1897. At the outset he found the work a bore, remarking in his diary that it was "dwarfing to the mind." He persevered, however, and in 1902 became chief of the bureau, in charge of approximately three hundred consular posts. As early as 1894 he had helped draft a bill for the reform of the diplomatic and consular services, and as bureau chief he was largely instrumental in achieving two notable administrative reforms: the Lodge Act of April 1906, which placed the Consular Service on a regular salaried basis and thus rid it of the abuses connected with the old system whereby consuls kept all or part of their fees; and President Roosevelt's executive order of June 27, 1906, removing the service from politics by placing appointments and promotions on an examination basis. Now presiding over what was almost a new system, Carr worked tirelessly to introduce professional, nonpartisan standards. He was made chief clerk of the State Department in 1907, with responsibility for the Consular Service, of which he was formally made director in 1909. His effort to implement a merit system was a fragile undertaking, fraught with hazards. Particularly trying was the determination of William Jennings Bryan [q.v.], as Secretary of State, to bring "needy Democrats" into the department. Under Bryan's successor Robert Lansing [q.v.], however, the harassed Carr regained his authority.

Carr was the central figure in the drafting of the Rogers Act of 1924, which combined the consular and diplomatic services. In that year he became head of the newly created Foreign Service with the title of Assistant Secretary of State. All his considerable tact was needed to overcome the bitterness generated within the department by the Rogers Act, particularly among diplomats who opposed being linked with the consular personnel. In the later 1920's, officers of the old Diplomatic Service made a determined effort to relegate former Consular Service personnel to second-class status, but Carr managed to override the challenge. His strength lay in the universal recognition of his selfless dedication to the Foreign Service, many of whose members he knew personally. These same qualities gave weight to his frequent testimony at Congressional hearings on the department's budgetary requests.

Continuing in office by special presidential dispensation beyond the statutory retirement age of sixty-five, Carr retained his post until July 1937, when he relinquished it to his successor, George S. Messersmith, and became American minister to Czechoslovakia, a position he occupied until shortly after the Nazi take-over in March 1939. A colleague in Prague in these years, George F. Kennan, later appreciatively recalled Carr's "imperturbable patience, . . . studied softness of speech, and . . . transparent integrity" (Memoirs, p. 89). He was accompanied abroad by his second wife, Edith Adèle Koon, daughter of a Michigan lawyer, whom he had married on Jan. 20, 1917. His first wife, Mary Eugenia Crane, whom he had married on Nov. 3, 1897, died in 1911 after a long illness. There were no children by either marriage. Carr died in 1942 at the Johns Hopkins Hospital in Baltimore, Md., while being treated for chronic asthmatic bronchitis.

Wilbur Carr's long tenure in the State Department lends a striking continuity to its history; he was the last in a line of three administrators whose service spanned more than a century: William Hunter, who entered the department in 1829 and died in office in 1886; Alvey A. Adee [q.v.], who came in 1874 and stayed until his death in 1924; and Carr himself, who served for forty-five years, from 1892 to 1937. In some respects, Carr did not measure up to what might seem the minimal requirements of the responsible posts which he held. He had almost no experience with the actual making of foreign policy or the business of diplomacy; indeed, he did not go abroad until 1916. Balancing this, however, are his unquestioned personal qualities of industry, honesty, and tact, and an intense commitment to professionalism at a time when the impulses of American politics favored the spoilsmen. A transitional figure in the State Department's administrative development, he helped in important ways to lay the groundwork for the organic Foreign Service Act passed in 1946, four years after his death.

[Katharine Crane, *Mr. Carr of State* (1960), a somewhat adulatory biography; Warren F. Ilchman, *Professional Diplomacy in the U. S., 1779–1939* (1961); and references to Carr in Waldo H. Heinrichs, Jr., *Am. Ambassador: Joseph C. Grew and the Development of the U. S. Diplomatic Tradition* (1966), and George F. Kennan, *Memoirs, 1925–1950* (1967). Carr's papers, some 5,000 items including correspondence and diaries, are in the Lib. of Cong.]

ROBERT H. FERRELL

CARREL, ALEXIS (June 28, 1873–Nov. 5, 1944), surgeon and experimental biologist, was born at Sainte-Foy-lès-Lyon, a suburb of Lyons, France. He was the eldest of three children, two sons and a daughter, of Alexis Carrel-Billiard, a textile manufacturer, and his wife, Anne-Marie Ricard. Both parents belonged to well-placed bourgeois Roman Catholic families. When the boy was five years old, his father died. By family usage the elder son, dropping his baptismal names, Marie Joseph Auguste, was known, after the father, simply as Alexis Carrel. He attended a Jesuit day school and college (St. Joseph), where he made a good but not distinguished record. An uncle interested him in chemical experiments, and he evinced early interest in biology by dissecting birds.

After taking the first of his two baccalaureates (in letters at Lyons, 1890, and in science at Dijon, 1891), Carrel began medical studies at the University of Lyons, where from 1899 to 1902 he held the title of prosector. During his years as a medical student he was also extern or intern in various hospitals in Lyons, with one year as army surgeon with the Alpine Chasseurs. In 1898, attached to the laboratory of the famous anatomist Leo Testut, he demonstrated great technical facility in dissection and operative surgery. To his legal qualifications for medical practice, the University of Lyons in 1900 added the formal M.D. degree.

Carrel was first interested in surgery of the blood vessels by the death of President Carnot of France in 1894, caused by hemorrhage from a major artery cut by an assassin's bullet. At that period surgeons had no practical means of repairing such injuries, although a few pioneers (one of Carrel's teachers, Mathieu Jaboulay, among them) had made experiments on suturing the walls of blood vessels. Three major obstacles presented themselves: first, the mechanical difficulty of stitching relatively small and thin-walled structures; second, the necessity to avoid clotting of the blood within the vessel on sutures or raw tissues; and third, the risk of bacterial infection, especially dangerous in operations so close to the bloodstream. It is said that Carrel prepared himself for the difficult task of suturing blood vessels by taking lessons in embroidery. Using exceptionally fine needles and fine silk thread, handled with extraordinary dexterity, he lessened the risk of blood-clotting by an ingenious device. Turning back the ends of the cut vessels like cuffs, he stitched them so that the only surface exposed to the circulatory blood was the smooth lining of the vessel. He further avoided clotting by coating his instruments and threads with paraffin jelly, and avoided infection by the most scrupulous aseptic technique. Thus he succeeded not only in suturing wounds of arteries and veins, but also in restoring the flow of blood through completely severed vessels. This brilliant achievement was first reported in 1902.

Now approaching his thirtieth year, Carrel was a short, stocky man of great energy and self confidence, but with simple manners and abstemious habits. Shyness made him seem somewhat stiff, even rigid, in social contacts. He was outspokenly critical of hampering traditions and political maneuvering, which he thought characteristic of the Lyons medical faculty. As a young intellectual, he had begun to discard the more literal beliefs of his Church, but a poignant experience at this time—an apparently miraculous cure witnessed at Lourdes—confirmed his acceptance of supranatural phenomena as extending, not contradicting, the findings of natural science. An article thus describing what he had observed at Lourdes was criticized at Lyons by skeptics as merely credulous, by churchmen as too coldly scientific. The affair intensified the local opposition to Carrel's hoped-for university career which he had in part brought upon himself by his intellectual independence and critical attitude. Discouraged, he left Lyons for a winter of study in Paris, and in May 1904 went to Canada with a vague idea of becoming a rancher. On second thoughts he went on to the United States and accepted guest privileges in the department of physiology of the University of Chicago, where he remained from 1904 to 1906.

Resuming his experiments on blood-vessel surgery in an ever bolder and more imaginative way, Carrel was soon able to perform unheard-of feats, such as the replacement of a dog's kidney with one from another dog. His articles and lectures on this work soon led to an appointment at the young Rockefeller Institute for Medical Research in New York City, where he remained for three decades, from 1906 to the end of his scientific career in 1938. Continuing success in surgical experimentation, facilitated by the superior equipment and services of the Institute, was internationally recognized by the award of the Nobel Prize for 1912 in medicine and physiology. Upon the foundations laid by Carrel in these years rest all subsequent advances in surgery of the blood vessels and the heart and the transplantation of organs. On Dec. 26, 1913, Carrel married, in Brittany, Anne (de la Motte) de Meyrie, a devout Roman Catholic, widowed, with one son. Trained in nursing and surgical procedures, she encouraged his researches and philosophical speculations, and often assisted in his experiments. No children were born of this marriage.

Carrel's success in the experimental replacement of organs led him to think that human tissues and even whole organs might be cultivated artificially to be substituted for diseased parts of the body. Having learned in 1908 that Ross G. Harrison, anatomist at Yale, had grown frog's nerve cells outside the body, he sent an assistant to observe Harrison's methods. Carrel, adding to these by his own ingenuity, exceptional manual skill, and perfect command of asepsis, created a whole new art of tissue culture, applicable to the tissues of warm-blooded animals, including man. Stung by the incredulity of a French biologist about his earliest cultures, Carrel proved his case by consummate scientific enterprise. Taking a bit of tissue from the heart of a chick embryo, he and his assistants kept its cells alive and reproducing themselves continually through successive transfers to fresh nutrient medium. Intense public interest made the chicken heart culture world famous. This strain of connective-tissue cells, maintained for thirty-four years, in fact outlived Carrel himself. Although the art of tissue culture never attained the practical ends for which Carrel developed it, in his laboratory and many others it has contributed greatly to the study of normal cell life and of malignant growths, and more recently to the understanding of viruses and the preparation of vaccines.

With the outbreak of the First World War, Carrel, recalled to service with the French army, conducted a special hospital near the front lines for the study and prompt treatment of severely infected wounds. With the support of the Rockefeller Foundation and the collaboration of a biochemist, Henry B. Dakin, he developed an elaborate method of surgical cleansing of wounds followed by continuous irrigation with a special antiseptic solution. Too complicated for widespread use, the Carrel-Dakin method did not take hold in civilian surgery and has been completely superseded by antibiotic drugs.

After the war, Carrel, again at the Rockefeller Institute, launched a large-scale investigation of the cause of cancer, which he attributed to the artificiality of modern diets. The study, concealed from fellow scientists, conducted without adequate controls, and disregarding other possible causes of cancer, came to naught. This episode is sufficient evidence that Carrel was not a profound analyst but rather a superb scientist, advancing the progress of biology and surgery much as Thomas A. Edison [Supp. 1] advanced the practical use of electricity.

About 1930 Carrel, never hesitating to aim at far-distant goals, returned to the cultivation of whole organs in the laboratory. For several years thereafter he had an equally venturesome ally. The celebrated aviator Charles A. Lindbergh came to his aid by ingeniously designing a sterilizable glass pump for circulating nutrient fluid through an excised organ in a moist chamber. Carrel, with his expert staff, conquered the inherent physiological and chemical difficulties of the project sufficiently to keep certain animal organs alive for some days or weeks, but not long enough for any practical application in surgery. The experiments, however, were useful to subsequent workers in the development of heart-lung machines and other technical aids to vascular surgery and physiology.

In New York Carrel and his wife lived unostentatiously, limiting their social life to a narrow circle of friends. At the Rockefeller Institute he combined courteous aloofness from colleagues with a degree of self-dramatization, as when he conspicuously wore his white surgeon's cap at staff luncheons, or brought to the dining hall some especially distinguished visitor. With a small group of thoughtful intellectuals in the city, he indulged freely in speculations about the nature of man and man's hope for the future. They encouraged him to publish his book *Man, the Unknown* (1935), which attracted worldwide attention. Attempting to explain to lay readers what science teaches about the human body and mind, Carrel optimistically asserted that through scientific enlightenment mankind may improve the race, banish disease, prolong life, and reach new spiritual heights. But such achievements, he declared, could only be made by an intellectual, spiritual-minded aristocracy whose leadership the masses would accept.

About this time Carrel's work in the laboratory was drawing to a close. With the retirement in 1935 of Simon Flexner, director of the Rockefeller Institute, Carrel lost a leader who had encouraged his successes and understood his temperament. Although he made close personal friends and retained the intense loyalty of young scientists and technicians who worked with him, his reserve had not endeared him to senior colleagues, and the Institute's administration was somewhat disturbed by his philosophical writings, which many scientists thought were overspeculative. In 1938, when he reached the statutory age of retirement, neither Carrel nor the new director proposed that he continue his laboratory work at the Institute.

Carrel was at loose ends until the outbreak of World War II, which aroused his patriotism as a Frenchman (he had never become an American citizen) and awoke new dreams of serving mankind through his native land. Believing that Hitler, whose victory he expected, intended to reduce the population of France, Carrel thought that this dire plan could be offset by scientific methods of nutrition, public health, and genetics. Against official American advice, he went to Spain and thence to France, after the fall of Paris, as a member of a mission to investigate the nutritional needs of children in wartime, and remained in Paris under the German occupation. Declining Marshal Henri Pétain's offer of the ministry of health in the Vichy government, with visionary zeal he planned an Institute for the Study of Human Problems which should guide the postwar recovery and future development of France along the biological and philosophical lines expounded in *Man, the Unknown*. For this scheme he secured from the Vichy government a national charter and a large subvention and brought together in Paris a group of mostly young biologists, physicians, lawyers, and engineers who busied themselves with studies in nutrition, economics, and political science.

Carrel never concealed his distrust of French parliamentary democracy nor his low opinion of prewar politicians, to whom he ascribed the military debacle. Because of these opinions, and because he had accepted the Vichy government's support and had negotiated on behalf of his Institute with the German military command in Paris, he was reputed to be a collaborationist, with all the obloquy attached to that term. It is now clear that Carrel was at heart not disloyal either to France or to the America that had so long adopted him, but sought only the welfare of France according to his own conscience. Nevertheless, immediately after the Allied reoccupation, the new French government on Aug. 21, 1944, suspended him from the direction of his Institute and his arrest was expected.

By this time, however, Carrel was seriously ill with heart failure aggravated by the deprivations of life in wartime Paris. In his last days he was attended by several friendly French and American physicians and nursed by Mme. Carrel. Though not for many years a practicing Catholic, he received the last rites of the Church. After his death, in Paris, his body was interred in the little chapel of St. Yves near his home on the island of St. Gildas, Côtes-du-Nord. His Institute was officially disbanded. Carrel's achievement as a scientist is well summed up by his own words, "Je suis un créateur des techniques"—a creator of methods soundly based on scientific knowledge and executed with prodigious skill, incalculably useful to modern medicine and biology.

[Robert Soupault, *Alexis Carrel, 1873–1944* (in French; Paris, 1951); obituary notices in *N. Y. Times*, Nov. 6, 1944, and Am. Philosophical Soc., *Year Book*, 1944 (by Simon Flexner). See also George W. Corner, *Hist. of the Rockefeller Inst.*, 1901–1953 (1965); Albert H. Ebeling, "Dr. Carrel's Immortal Chicken Heart," *Sci. American*, Jan. 1942; Charles A. Lindbergh's introduction to Carrel's posthumous *Voyage to Lourdes* (1950) and Mme. Carrel's introduction to Carrel's *Reflections on Life* (1952); Joseph T. Durkin, *Hope for Our Time: Alexis Carrel on Man and Society* (1965). Carrel's writings also include, besides numerous articles in technical and popular journals, *The Treatment of Infected Wounds* (with Georges Dehelly, 1917); *The Culture of Organs* (with Charles A. Lindbergh, 1938); *La Prière* (1944; translated as *Prayer*, 1948); and *Jour après Jour* (posthumous selections from his journals and notebooks, 1956). The following personal friends have provided information: Adolf A. Berle, Charles A. Lindbergh, Peyton Rous, Ralph W. G. Wyckoff. Carrel's papers, and a great collection of his scientific materials, are in the library of Georgetown Univ., Washington, D. C.]

GEORGE W. CORNER

CARTER, BOAKE (Sept. 28, 1898–Nov. 16, 1944), journalist and radio commentator, christened Harold Thomas Henry Carter, was born in Baku, Russia, the son of Thomas Carter, a British oilman and consular agent at Baku, and Edith (Harwood-Yarred) Carter, of Irish birth; they also had a daughter, Sheelah. The boy was brought to England by his parents at the age of five. After preparatory schooling at Tunbridge Wells, he enrolled at Christ College, Cambridge University, where he took an active part in sports and served as a reporter on the *Cantabrian*. During World War I he attended a Royal Air Force training school in Scotland. After a period of study at the Slade School of Art in London and some work for the London *Daily Mail*, he went to the United States in 1920 and for several years wandered through the Southwest, Mexico, and Central America, working in the oil fields and writing for newspapers. He then moved to Philadelphia, where his parents had settled after the war, and became rewrite man, copyreader, and assistant city editor on the *Philadelphia Daily News*. He took out American citizenship in 1933.

Carter got his start in radio in 1930, when he was asked to describe a local rugby match over a Philadelphia radio station, WCAU; he later broadcast a simulated description of the Cambridge-Oxford boat race. Encouraged by his success, he took a month's leave from his newspaper job and tried to sell a program as news commentator but, failing to find a sponsor, returned to the *Daily News*. At about this time, on the advice of the station director, he adopted the first name Boake, common in his mother's family, as more distinctive for broadcasting purposes. The next year he began to give regular news broadcasts for his paper. Only five feet six inches tall, red-haired and wearing a trim moustache, he retained his British mannerisms and accent; his deep baritone voice made him an impressive commentator, and he soon gained a commercial sponsor.

Carter first achieved national fame in 1932, when the Columbia Broadcasting System engaged him to make daily reports and comments on the Lindbergh kidnapping case. Speaking from studios in Trenton, N. J., he was assisted by two network reporters who collected the material. Carter later covered the trial of the accused kidnapper, Bruno Richard Hauptmann, for the network, but instead of merely giving factual reports, he editorialized freely and infused his accounts with drama and emotion. His sensationalism caused CBS to discharge him, but public protest forced his reinstatement.

In January 1933 Carter signed a contract with

the Philco Corporation to give a fifteen-minute news broadcast under their sponsorship five nights weekly over the CBS network at a salary of $50,000 a year. He soon became the most popular commentator on the air. Stressing interpretation rather than factual narration of the news, speaking vividly and dramatically, he had a nightly audience estimated at more than ten million; he ended each broadcast with his familiar sign-off, "Cheerio." Carter prepared his own 2,000-word script for each program. He subscribed to a radio news service and obtained material from two teletype machines installed in his home at Torresdale, near Philadelphia, and from telephone conversations with a full-time representative in Washington, D. C. In addition to his radio work, Carter wrote several books, including *Black Shirt, Black Skin* (1935), *I Talk as I Like* (1937), and *Why Meddle in Europe?* (1939). In 1937 he also began writing a syndicated news column, "But—," which eventually appeared in some sixty daily papers.

Carter thrived on controversy, and preferred argument to neutrality. Since frequent targets of his acerbic criticism were the Roosevelt administration, labor unions, and naval policy, he made many enemies. He greatly admired the columnist Westbrook Pegler and from time to time conferred with Father Charles E. Coughlin—both archcritics of the New Deal. By the end of the 1930's angry reactions from labor and other groups he had attacked, together with accusations of fascist sympathies, had undermined Carter's popularity. Philco failed to renew his contract in January 1938, and though he soon acquired a new sponsor, General Foods Corporation, this contract was canceled in December 1938, largely because union members threatened to boycott the firm's products. Carter charged that the Roosevelt administration was persecuting him, but other factors probably were more important in his gradual eclipse. The open commercialism accompanying his broadcasts was out of key with the growing tension preceding World War II. By contrast, Raymond Gram Swing, a commentator whose popularity was rising, refused to read any commercials, even after a pause to separate news from advertising. Listeners were coming to prefer a straight account of events to a dramatized interpretation. In September 1939 Carter became a commentator for the Mutual Broadcasting System, but he never regained his old popularity.

In 1942, workers on the *New York Mirror,* which carried his column, charged Carter with being implicated in anti-Semitism and enemy propaganda, although the *Jewish Daily Forward* protested the charge. In self-defense, Carter

pointed out that he had recently joined a religious group based on Jewish practices and called by its founder, David Horowitz, the "Biblical Hebrew" movement. Carter devoted much of the energies of his final years to this group, which shared the "Anglo-Israel" doctrine that the Anglo-Saxon-Celtic races were in fact the lost tribes of Israel, and which sponsored the publication of a new translation of the Bible by a Palestinian mystic, Moses Guibbory.

Carter had married Beatrice Olive Richter, assistant society editor of the *Philadelphia Bulletin,* in 1924. Their two children were Gwladys Sheleagh Boake and Michael Boake. He and his wife were divorced on Nov. 7, 1941, and in August 1944, after he had moved to California, he married Paula Nicoll. He died a few months later, apparently of a cerebral hemorrhage, at the Presbyterian Hospital in Hollywood. A Los Angeles rabbi conducted the funeral service, and Carter was buried at the Home of Peace Mausoleum in Los Angeles. Combining a professional newspaper background with a frequently exaggerated rhetorical style, Boake Carter had helped shape the role of the news commentator, an enduring tradition in radio and television.

[The best accounts are A. J. Liebling, "Boake Carter," *Scribner's Mag.,* Aug. 1938; and *Current Biog.,* 1942. See also: *Who Was Who in America,* vol. II (1950); Erik Barnouw, *A Hist. of Broadcasting in the U. S.,* vol. II (1968); Stanley High, "Not-So-Free Air," *Saturday Evening Post,* Feb. 11, 1939, pp. 76–77; *Literary Digest,* Apr. 17, 1937, p. 30; *Newsweek,* Apr. 6, 1935, p. 33, July 18, 1936, p. 26, Aug. 24, 1942, p. 66; *Time,* Apr. 13, 1936, pp. 55–56, Aug. 22, 1938, p. 33, Oct. 28, 1940, p. 47, Aug. 24, 1942, pp. 44, 46; *N. Y. Times,* Nov. 8, 1941 (divorce), Nov. 17, 1944 (obituary); *Los Angeles Times,* Nov. 17, 20 (funeral), 1944. For details of Carter's involvement in the "Biblical Hebrew" movement (officially "The Society of the Bible in the Hands of Its Creator, Inc.") see David Horowitz, *Thirty-Three Candles* (1949); and Stewart Robb and Linda Folkard, *Strange Death of Boake Carter and Other Mysterious Matters* (pamphlet, 1946; in N. Y. Public Lib.). For Carter's radio style, hear "Hist. of Broadcasting: 1920–1950" (Folkways record 9171).]

MEYER WEINBERG

CARVALHO, SOLOMON SOLIS (Jan. 16, 1856–Apr. 12, 1942), newspaper executive, was born in Baltimore, Md., the youngest of four children (a daughter and three sons) of Sarah (Solis) and Solomon Nunes Carvalho (pronounced Car-VAI-yo). Both parents were of Sephardic Jewish descent. The father, born in Charleston, S. C., was a painter and photographer who accompanied John C. Frémont [*q.v.*] on the fifth of his Western expeditions.

Carvalho grew up chiefly in New York City, to which the family moved shortly before or during the Civil War. After receiving his A.B. from the City College of New York in 1877, he went to work as a reporter for the City News Association, studying law on the side. Admitted to the bar a few years later, he never practiced, but his legal studies served him in good stead. Presently he won a place on the New York *Sun* of Charles A. Dana [*q.v.*], where his sleuthing on murder and suicide stories led to broader editorial responsibilities. Shortly after the appearance of the *Evening Sun* in 1887, Joseph Pulitzer [*q.v.*] hired Carvalho to assist in launching the *Evening World.* His rise was rapid from then on. In 1892 Pulitzer summoned him to Paris, grilled him during a long carriage ride in the Bois de Boulogne, and sent him back to the *World,* then by far the largest newspaper enterprise in the country, with "absolute power over all expenditure in every department." This power "S. S.," as he signed himself, wielded shrewdly until the advent of William Randolph Hearst's *Journal* in 1895. To crush the one-cent newcomer, Pulitzer cut the *World* to that price at Carvalho's urging—a move that hurt the paper without visible effect on its rival. During the difficult rate negotiations with advertisers that followed, Pulitzer curtailed Carvalho's authority. Bitterly offended, S. S. at once went over to Hearst.

Within the Hearst organization, Carvalho came to be known as "Richelieu," an accurate reflection both of his role and of his sharp-featured, almost saturnine, appearance, heightened by a Richelieu goatee and a pronounced limp. (A short left leg, probably the result of a club foot, caused him to stump about with a cane.) When Hearst decided in the summer of 1899 to start a daily in Chicago in time for the 1900 presidential campaign, it was Carvalho who attended to the details. He engineered the Hearst invasion of Boston in 1903, and later invasions of other cities. He was credited with devising the bewilderingly complex corporate structure of the Hearst publications as a means of dodging libel suits. "Carvalho . . . really has charge of everything of importance in this institution, as you know," Arthur Brisbane [Supp. 2], who had followed him from the *Sun* to the *World* and thence to Hearst, wrote to a friend.

For a time his domain extended to managing Hearst's personal finances. Pulitzer, sensing that the willingness of Mrs. Phoebe Apperson Hearst [*q.v.*] to support her profligate son's ventures was related to her confidence in this canny manager, sought to win him back. In August 1902 an emissary armed with an offer worth $50,000 a year (and spurred by Pulitzer's promise of a year's pay if he succeeded) got to Carvalho, only to find him so enthusiastic about Hearst's political and journalistic hopes that the proposal could not even be put to him. "I do not want any personal

glory," a Pulitzer spy quoted S. S. as saying a little later, "but I do like the sense of power and authority as general manager, . . . having that man's absolute trust, and knowing that in most details my opinions will prevail."

As surrogate for Pulitzer and then for Hearst, Carvalho signaled the rise of the professional in newspaper management. His knowledge of the pressroom, of advertising, circulation, libel law, newsprint procurement, and in particular his ceaseless quest for talented personnel made him, to Pulitzer, "worth any three men I have." Illustrative of his prescience were private judgments, expressed long before they were apparent to others, that Pulitzer's sons would not be up to continuing the *World,* and that both titans of New York journalism might be eclipsed, one day, by the *Times* of Adolph Ochs [*q.v.*]. Hearst flattered S. S. with social attentions and such favors as a $25,000 bonus in 1902, an expense-paid trip to Europe in 1903, a Stearns automobile, and valuable antiques. Carvalho responded with a dedication that amounted to self-abnegation. Regarded by rivals as crafty, even Machiavellian, he took care to remain in the shadows, once smashing the camera of a newsman who had snapped his picture. Zealous in managing Hearst's affairs, he told a friend he was "the poorest possible manager of my own," having neglected them from his *World* days on.

Carvalho abruptly retired as general manager of the Hearst publications in November 1917, with no hint of discord. Others said later that he had quit because of a series of pro-German editorials in the Hearst papers. He nonetheless continued as a highly paid consultant of the organization for all his remaining years, presiding for many of them as chairman of its executive council. With his wife, Helen Cusack, whom he had married in May 1895 when she was a *World* reporter known as Nell Nelson, and his two daughters, Helen and Sarah, Carvalho passed many of his pleasantest hours on a farm in Metuchen, N. J., where he raised horses. This property, and a vast collection of Chinese porcelain accumulated by him over the years and worth many thousands, he disposed of at a fraction of their value; and the man who perhaps did more than anyone save Hearst himself to build the first great publishing empire left little when he died of arteriosclerosis at his home in Plainfield, N. J., in 1942. His body was cremated.

[Much of the information and all of the quotations in this sketch are drawn from the Pulitzer Papers, in the Lib. of Cong. and at Columbia Univ. The N. Y. *Evening Post,* Nov. 3, 1906, has an article on Carvalho. Other sources: Moses Koenigsberg, *King News* (1941); John K. Winkler, *William Randolph Hearst*

(1955); Don Seitz, *Joseph Pulitzer* (1924); *Editor & Publisher*, Dec. 8, 1917, Apr. 18, 1942. On his father see Bertram W. Korn, ed., *Incidents of Travel and Adventure in the Far West*, by Solomon N. Carvalho (1954); and George C. Croce and David H. Wallace, The *N.-Y. Hist. Soc.'s Dict. of Artists in America, 1564–1860* (1957). Mrs. Frank Crehore, Carvalho's daughter, provided helpful information.]
                                    LOUIS M. STARR

CARVER, GEORGE WASHINGTON (c. 1861–Jan. 5, 1943), agricultural chemist, educator, and botanist, was born on a farm near Diamond Grove, Mo., the second son and youngest of three children of Negro slave parents. When he was an infant his father was killed in an accident. Shortly thereafter George, his mother, and a sister were stolen and carried into Arkansas by raiders. His mother and sister disappeared, but a "bushwhacker" brought the boy back to his owner, Moses Carver, in exchange for a racehorse valued at $300. Frail and sickly as a child, George was cared for by Carver's wife and took the family name as his own. He performed various household tasks, obtained some rudiments of an education, and at an early age displayed keen interest in plants. At about the age of fourteen he left the Carver family to acquire formal education not then available to his race within the Diamond Grove community. Over the next few years he worked at odd jobs and attended grade schools in Neosho, Mo., and Fort Scott, Paola, and Olathe, Kans.; in Olathe he went to the Presbyterian church, the beginning of a lifelong affiliation. He received his high school training in Minneapolis, Kans., and there took the middle name "Washington" to distinguish himself from another George Carver. As he grew older he displayed skill in cooking, knitting, and crocheting, learned to do laundry work, became adept in growing plants, and developed talent for music and painting.

In 1885 Carver because of his race was refused admission to Highland College in northeast Kansas. He next became a homesteader near Beeler, Kans., where for nearly two years he attempted to farm, but he eventually found the blizzards and burning sun of the Kansas plains too unfriendly to his small agricultural enterprise. After mortgaging his homestead in 1888, he moved to Winterset, Iowa. Here he was encouraged by a friendly white family to make another effort to attend college. Taking their advice, he sought and won admission to Simpson College at Indianola, Iowa, in September 1890. He supported himself by doing laundry work and gave serious thought to a career as an artist. Four of his paintings of flowers were included in an Iowa art exhibit in 1892, and one was sent on the next summer to the World's Columbian Exposi-

tion in Chicago. This interest continued, and in later years Carver painted a great number of pictures in various media. While at Simpson College, however, he was persuaded to study agriculture as a pursuit promising greater economic reward than art. Accordingly, in 1891 he transferred to the Iowa State College of Agriculture at Ames, where he received the degrees of B.S. (1894) and M.S. (1896). His study at Ames brought him in touch with three future United States Secretaries of Agriculture. Two of them—James Wilson (then director of the Iowa agricultural experiment station) and Henry C. Wallace (then an assistant professor of agriculture) [*qq.v.*]—exerted important influence on Carver's thinking concerning basic agricultural problems, and the third, the six-year-old Henry A. Wallace, was initiated by Carver into the mysteries of plant fertilization. For two years Carver was a faculty assistant to the eminent botanist Louis H. Pammell [*q.v.*] and had charge of the college greenhouse, where he conducted experiments in cross-fertilization and propagation of plants that prompted Wilson to praise him as the ablest student in this work at the college.

Soon after the completion of his graduate study in 1896, Carver relinquished his post at Iowa State to accept an invitation from Booker T. Washington [*q.v.*] to go to Tuskegee Institute in Alabama as director of agricultural work, a position that was soon broadened to include direction of the school's agricultural experiment station. Here during forty-seven years Carver taught and experimented and became a legend. Small in stature, high-pitched in voice, and eccentric in habits and tastes, he acquired a strong image of unorthodoxy. These traits, combined with a deep reliance on religion, an abiding commitment to the promotion of human welfare, disregard of conventional pleasures, and utter lack of interest in monetary rewards, gave substance to the legend. His complete dedication to work apparently barred consideration of marriage, although for a short period he seemed to be deeply interested in the companionship of a teacher at the Institute.

The early years of Carver's work at Tuskegee included not only teaching but also playing the piano in concerts to raise funds for the school. These years were most notable, however, for his conducting of conferences and institutes at Tuskegee for Negro farmers to teach them better agricultural methods and the value of a balanced diet. He led in the inauguration of farm demonstration work, with its training of Negro agricultural extension agents. A "movable school of agriculture," financed by the philanthropist Morris K. Jesup [*q.v.*] of New York, carried equipment in a wagon to the homes of rural

Negroes. In a few years the "school" also provided demonstrations in home economics. The idea of the mobile school was adopted in educational programs for disadvantaged rural dwellers in several foreign countries and was considered by Carver to be one of his most important contributions to agricultural education.

His work with Southern farmers soon convinced him that their adversities were caused mainly by lack of crop diversification, insufficient knowledge of soil conservation and plant protection, and inadequate utilization of farm products and by-products. His concern about these conditions led to experiments, discoveries, and recommendations that brought him international acclaim. In talks to students and farmers and in voluminous correspondence he urged the planting of peanuts, sweet potatoes, cowpeas, and other neglected crops in place of cotton, which produced soil exhaustion and was increasingly prey to the boll weevil. At the same time he conducted investigations into diseases of peanuts and other Southern crops, and methods of preserving such crops through dehydration. This work generally was in advance of systematic studies of the United States Department of Agriculture. National attention was focused on Carver in 1921 when he presented testimony for peanut growers in hearings on the Fordney-McCumber tariff bill before the House Ways and Means Committee.

The development of peanuts and sweet potatoes from noncommercial crops to leading crops in the South during Carver's career was attributed to his demonstration of their possibilities. In a laboratory at Tuskegee, equipped largely with improvised equipment garnered from trash piles, he began about 1915 to develop special exhibits of peanut products that eventually included some 325 items, ranging from beverages, mixed pickles, and meal to wood fillers, ink, and synthetic rubber. Peanut growers in their trade magazine, the *Peanut World* (May 1921), called Carver a "miracle worker" and an "incomparable genius to whose tireless energies and inquisitive mind" the nation owed much in the development of the peanut industry. His products of the sweet potato numbered 118; also among his exhibits were seventy-five products from the pecan and many from soybeans, cotton, cowpeas, and wild plums. Some of these products offered immediate possibilities for commercial use. A great number, however, were significant chiefly as curiosities and as proof of the ability of a Negro mind. None of these discoveries were patented, since Carver wanted them to be available for the widest possible use. Patent Office records indicate that the only patent he ever obtained was one granted in 1925 for a

process of producing pigments from clay and iron, one of his several discoveries that suggested new uses for the abundant clay resources of the South.

Carver's varied discoveries brought him numerous honors. As early as 1916 the Royal Society of Arts in London elected him a fellow, apparently on the recommendation of Sir Harry H. Johnston, the famous naturalist, who praised the Tuskegee professor's knowledge of plant distribution in North and South America. For distinguished work in agricultural chemistry he was awarded the Spingarn Medal by the National Association for the Advancement of Colored People in 1923. Simpson College in 1928 and the University of Rochester in 1941 conferred on him the D.Sc. degree, and he received awards from the Theodore Roosevelt Memorial Association (1939) and the International Federation of Architects, Engineers, Chemists, and Technicians (1940). Accompanying these honors were lucrative offers for employment or consultation in the research laboratories of Thomas A. Edison [Supp. 1] and several industrialists. Such offers Carver promptly declined, citing his unwillingness to leave Tuskegee and his indifference to monetary rewards. He even rejected salary increases at Tuskegee, and did not seem to realize that acceptance of some financial recognition could have brought more resources to promote his investigations and educational work.

In spite of fame and honor, Carver did not escape the discrimination and insults widely suffered by the American Negro. His work at Tuskegee, which was of benefit to whites as well as blacks, was circumscribed by the segregation laws of Alabama. Travel, lodging, and eating facilities in the North and South were usually restricted for him. His endurance of these racial indignities without protest or abatement of zeal for service to all was in the tradition of the Tuskegee spirit of patience in race relations, and it doubtless accounted for the praise given by many white religious and civic groups.

Most of Carver's work was performed apart from the mainstream of scientific research. He did not participate in professional meetings of chemists and botanists or publish papers describing his discoveries in standard journals of scientific research. U. S. Department of Agriculture scientists seemed reluctant to appraise his chemical work and seldom mentioned it in their publications. Carver himself, moreover, seemed to put a cloak of obscurity over his discoveries when he gave the impression that they were based upon divine inspiration and revelation. His numerous experiment station bulletins were directed to farmers and housewives, not to scientists. He did, however, receive recognition from the Department of Agriculture for his work in collecting mycological specimens, some of them considered unusually rare, when in 1935 he was appointed a collaborator in the Mycology and Plant Disease Survey of the Bureau of Plant Industry.

Living on past eighty, Carver died from anemia at Tuskegee early in 1943. With tributes from leaders at home and abroad, he was buried on the campus beside Booker T. Washington. He left his entire estate, amounting to some $60,000, to a research foundation at Tuskegee, organized in 1940 and bearing his name, which sought to provide opportunity for advanced study by Negro youths in botany, chemistry, and agronomy. He was subsequently honored by a United States postage stamp and by the establishment of the George Washington Carver National Monument on the site near Diamond Grove, Mo., where he had spent his early childhood. His career was remarkable for its dedication to teaching and inquiry solely for humanitarian purposes, and probably most notable as an example of exceptional personal triumph over great obstacles.

[The most useful biographies, evidencing considerable use of basic primary sources, are Lawrence Elliott, *George Washington Carver: The Man Who Overcame* (1966), and Rackham Holt, *George Washington Carver* (1943); the latter work contains several good photographs of Carver. Other informative biographies are Arna W. Bontemps, *The Story of George Washington Carver* (1954), and Shirley Graham and G. D. Lipscomb, *Dr. George Washington Carver, Scientist* (1944). Highlights of Carver's work are presented in the report of Congressional hearings on the George Washington Carver Nat. Monument, Feb. 5, 1943; see also *N. Y. Times* obituary, Jan. 6, 1943. Carver's recommendations concerning methods of crop cultivation and utilization, descriptions of fungi, and views on varied agricultural matters are set forth mainly in some 44 bulletins issued by the Tuskegee Experiment Station (1898–1943). Personal papers of Carver (including reproductions of letters found in the Nat. Archives, Washington, D. C.) are among holdings of the Dept. of Records and Research at Tuskegee Inst. The George Washington Carver Nat. Monument includes a statue of Carver as a boy and a museum displaying many of his agricultural products and memorabilia.]

HAROLD T. PINKETT

CASH, WILBUR JOSEPH (May 2, 1900–July 1, 1941), author and journalist, was born in Gaffney, S. C., the eldest of four children (three boys and one girl) of John William and Nannie Lutitia (Hamrick) Cash. He was christened Joseph Wilbur but disliked his given names and used the initials only, reversing the order. His ancestry was Ulster Scotch on the Cash side, a mixture of that plus German on the Hamrick side, both strains American since the eighteenth century. His parents were plain up-country Southerners and devout Baptists. Cash attended public school in Gaffney, where his father operated the company store of a cotton mill, and,

beginning in 1912, the Baptist-supported Boiling Springs (N. C.) High School. Living next door to his maternal grandfather, who had been the first mayor of Boiling Springs, the boy grew up in an atmosphere of paternalistic white supremacy, but with a lifelong feeling for the country life of the South and its people.

An avaricious reader, Cash blossomed as a student during his last year in high school and gave the commencement address in April 1917. After a year of drifting between jobs, he entered Wofford College (Methodist) in Spartanburg, S. C., and completed the freshman year in 1919. There followed an unhappy semester at Valparaiso University in northern Indiana. Early in 1920 he enrolled at the Baptist-supported Wake Forest College in North Carolina. There, "Sleepy" Cash became a Young Turk, contributing pieces to student publications, indulging a certain bohemianism, admiring the iconoclastic H. L. Mencken, defending Wake Forest against the Fundamentalists, and generally rebelling against the set of values he had inherited from his parents. He graduated in 1922.

Uncertain about a career, and already beset by symptoms of endocrine disorders, Cash attended the college's law school for a year. Then two years of teaching at Georgetown College in Kentucky and at the Hendersonville (N. C.) School for Boys cured him of any love of pedagogy. Turning to journalism, he worked briefly for the *Chicago Post* and in 1926 joined the staff of the *Charlotte* (N. C.) *News*. He spent the summer and fall of 1927 on a bicycle tour abroad, which gave him the consuming interest in Europe later reflected in his editorials. The next summer his health broke down and he had to return to Boiling Springs. To support himself at home, Cash became editor of a short-lived semiweekly, the *Cleveland* (County) *Press* in nearby Shelby, in which he pilloried the anti-Catholicism of his neighbors during the fiery Smith-Hoover presidential campaign of 1928.

In July 1929 Cash contributed the first of many pieces to H. L. Mencken's *American Mercury:* "Jehovah of the Tar Heels," an exposé of United States Senator Furnifold M. Simmons [Supp. 2], patron of North Carolina's anti-Al Smith Democrats. A second article in October 1929, "The Mind of the South," was a brilliant piece of analysis that commended Cash to the publishing firm of Alfred A. Knopf, publisher also of the *Mercury.* The bitter depression years that followed saw Cash trying against odds to make a living as a free-lance writer in Cleveland County, applying unsuccessfully for foundation grants, and fighting uncertain health and poverty while he began the book that was to be his chief achievement. In October 1937, short of funds, he rejoined the *Charlotte News* as a full-time editorialist.

Cash devoted his editorials to the totalitarian evil he discerned overseas, and his Sunday book-page column largely to the South's malaise, but he was unable to bring his manuscript to completion before July 1940. He and his longtime fiancée, Mrs. Mary Ross Northrop of Charlotte, having agreed that they would be married on completion of the manuscript, were wed (he for the first time) on Christmas Day, 1940. *The Mind of the South* was published in February 1941, to almost unanimous critical acclaim, and the book instantly won him nationwide recognition. He received a Guggenheim Fellowship, and, since Europe was at war, arranged to spend his fellowship year in Mexico writing a novel about the cotton-mill South. Weak with dizziness and dysentery from the time of his arrival in Mexico City, on the night of June 30 he became irrational, suffering from the terrible delusion that Nazis were planning to kill him. He fled the next day while his wife was seeking help and was found dead in the Hotel Reforma hanged by his necktie. His cremated remains were returned to Shelby for burial in Sunset Cemetery.

W. J. Cash is remembered as the author of *The Mind of the South,* a brilliant intellectual tour de force and the product of a lifelong effort to understand his homeland. The book was not a history of the South but an analysis of the "sentiments, prejudices, standards and values" common to "every group of white people in the South" which gave that region its distinctive character. Exposing the falsity of those historic myths, the "aristocratic" Old South and the "progressive" New South, Cash described the emotional crises that had led to their origin and survival. He traced the interrelationships of religion, race, rhetoric, romanticism, leisure, and the cult of Southern womanhood; and the patterns formed by demagoguery, violence, paternalism, and evangelism. He found the Southern mind largely shaped by the agricultural conditions of its past and in 1940 believed it to be moving backward, rather than forward into the present, though he foresaw that the South would soon have to prove a greater "capacity for adjustment" than it had yet shown. He could not foresee that his book would aid in that adjustment, helping prepare the way for the revolutionary turn in Southern race relations that began in the mid-1950's.

[Joseph L. Morrison, *W. J. Cash: Southern Prophet* (1967), is the only biographical study; see also the same author's articles about Cash in the *Va. Quart. Rev.*, Spring 1965, *Journalism Quart.*, Winter 1967, and *N. C. Hist. Rev.*, Winter 1970. Other writings about W. J. Cash are all analyses of his book; the best of these is Edwin M. Yoder, "W. J. Cash after a Quarter Century," in Willie Morris, ed., *The South Today* (1965).]

JOSEPH L. MORRISON

CATTELL, JAMES McKEEN (May 25, 1860–Jan. 20, 1944), psychologist and science editor, was born in Easton, Pa., and reared in a family of some distinction and means. His father, William Cassady Cattell [*q.v.*], a Presbyterian minister, was president of Lafayette College in Easton. An uncle, Alexander Gilmore Cattell [*q.v.*], was a successful financier and United States Senator from New Jersey. James's mother, Elizabeth (McKeen) Cattell, was the daughter of James McKeen, a Presbyterian born in northern Ireland who became a prominent Easton manufacturer and merchant and left his daughter part of a substantial fortune.

The Cattells' homelife was warm and close and was intimately involved with the Lafayette College community. William Cattell, a man of great social gifts, was a successful money raiser and administrator who also fostered a progressive spirit on the campus in which scientific studies flourished. As the elder of the president's two children (the younger, Henry Ware Cattell, became a pathologist and medical editor), James was tutored by professors at the college and read widely on his own. He was interested in both literature and mathematics, and was an avid player of sports and games. This enthusiasm for games, he believed, was the source of his later interest in measuring individual differences ("Autobiography," p. 634). Entering Lafayette at sixteen, he graduated at twenty, attaining first rank in his class "without much effort" (*ibid.*). Cattell thought highly of his own intellectual powers and sometimes belligerently challenged his mentors. He claimed as his chief influence at Lafayette, not his father, but Francis Andrew March (1825–1911) [*q.v.*], a distinguished philologist who was the recognized intellectual leader of the college. This separation of roles between the entrepreneurial Cattell senior and the intellectual March may have helped shape the duality of Cattell's career and his views of university administration.

After graduating in 1880, Cattell went to Germany to study philosophy and spent two years with Wilhelm Wundt at Leipzig and Hermann Lotze at Göttingen, both of whom roused his interest in scientific psychology. With an essay on Lotze, Cattell won a fellowship to Johns Hopkins University and entered in October 1882. By midwinter he had decided to abandon philosophy for psychology and had planned the first of his experiments on the time of simple mental processes. When his fellowship was not renewed, he left in October 1883 to take his degree with Wundt. There were some early difficulties between them, but Wundt came to treat Cattell with the respect due an independent scholar, and they became friendly. In 1885–86 Cattell served as Wundt's first assistant in charge of the laboratory, and in 1886 he won his doctorate.

The series of experiments from which Cattell drew his dissertation centered on the reaction-time experiment, then the chief occupation of the Leipzig laboratory. Cattell saw the possibility of varying the method and applying it to a number of basic problems, and he produced seminal studies in reading, perception, and association. He slanted these experiments away from the introspective reports of the subjects, and their similarity, toward the quantitative measurement of responses and their range of differences. Cattell also observed artificialities in the experimental situation Wundt had set up, and in his own work he established a new standard of accuracy in method and elegance in design.

Beginning in 1885, when Cattell began to publish his work, he often went to England. Through George Croom Robertson, editor of *Mind,* he met the notable English scientists in his field, and in the fall of 1886 he decided to study further at St. John's College, Cambridge. Here he extended his experiments on association, set up a small laboratory, and lectured on experimental psychology. Treated as an equal by the best minds in his field, he talked often with Francis Galton, James Ward, and Alexander Bain. The importance they granted the evolutionary viewpoint, as well as the statistical methods of Galton, clarified Cattell's ideas and greatly influenced his subsequent work. Cattell enjoyed the constant social and intellectual intercourse he found in England, discovering that he had some of his father's talent with people. He was also impressed by the benefits to science which accrued from this contact and the well-centralized web of organization which sustained it.

Cattell's student years in Baltimore, Germany, and England—the period of his greatest originality and productivity in psychology—were laced with inner complaint. Cattell confided only to his private journal his recurrent feelings of depression, his frequent need of hallucinogenic drugs, and his underlying philosophic stance as a "sceptic and mystic." Delaying the time when he would settle down to a definite career, he cultivated the self-image of one who, unlike his own father, would "struggle and suffer" and "fight one's way through life." Cattell declared his life

"set straight" in 1887 when he became engaged to Josephine Owen, the daughter of a retired English merchant, who was studying in Leipzig. They were married on Dec. 11, 1888, in England, as he prepared to return to an academic career in America.

Cattell had taught at Bryn Mawr in 1887, and in the spring of 1888 had lectured for a term at the University of Pennsylvania; in January 1889 he returned permanently, receiving at the University of Pennsylvania the first American professorship wholly in psychology. Here Cattell did a series of experiments in psychophysics in which he changed the focus of the topic from the measurement of consciousness to that of behavior. In 1890 he first called attention to the need to make mental tests on large numbers of individuals, in order to get accurate measures of the constancy of certain mental processes and also to provide the individual with a gauge of his aptitudes and capacities. When he became professor of psychology at Columbia University in 1891, Cattell extended this work. His tests of elementary capacities of discrimination and perception, however, were shown not to measure general performance, so that the testing movement actually developed on different models.

In the two decades after 1895, Cattell made several other experimental contributions, the most important being the "order of merit" method, a form of rating scale developed in 1902 and used in arranging judgments of value in psychophysics and aesthetics. He later extended it to other fields where no objective scale existed, such as the ranking of scientists. Cattell also directed the work of such students as Edward L. Thorndike, Robert S. Woodworth, and Frederick L. Wells. During his years at Columbia he trained more future members of the American Psychological Association than were trained at any other institution.

Through his research and teaching, Cattell was a leading influence in making American psychology an experimental science, greatly occupied with method, quantification of data, and the statistical treatment of results. Under the stimulus of Galton's work, he led the American reorientation of Wundt's psychology of the generalized mind into a study of the range of behavior of individuals and groups under varying conditions. Cattell's chief failing, one shared by many scientific psychologists of his generation, was his blindness to those principles which characterize the organism functioning as a whole. This failure prevented him from extending his initial insights into association phenomena, mental testing, and the rating scale method, and limited the range of his psychological viewpoint. Cattell's lectures,

Wells reported, "hardly added to one's self-understanding in any important way." Still, the methods he pioneered proved to be an opening through which concern with the larger functioning of people entered scientific psychology. Cattell urged, moreover, that psychology deal with the problems of real life. Next to method, his chief interest was the practical application of his results, and he early supported practicing psychologists in their desire to make psychology a profession as well as a science.

His overriding concern with methods and applications allowed Cattell to take a nondoctrinaire position in his organizational work in psychology. In 1894 he founded, with James Mark Baldwin [Supp. 1], the *Psychological Review* as a journal which would· represent the full range of work being done in American psychology, theoretical as well as experimental. In his role as editor and owner until 1903, as a founder (1892) and president (1895) of the American Psychological Association, and as the psychologist second only to William James [*q.v.*] in the esteem of his colleagues, Cattell exercised a moderating influence on his profession, recognizing the value of many viewpoints in psychological work and salving many sectarian animosities.

The vision which allowed him to play this role also came from his wide contact with American science. In 1894 Cattell purchased the weekly magazine *Science* and deftly obtained the cooperation of eminent men in many fields to make the journal a central organ of news and opinion for American science. He became active in the affairs of the American Association for the Advancement of Science and in 1900 persuaded it to make *Science* its official organ, available to all members. This arrangement increased dramatically both the membership of the association and the circulation of *Science*. In 1901 Cattell became the first psychologist elected to the National Academy of Sciences, and he held many other honorific posts, including the presidency of the American Association for the Advancement of Science in 1924. He extended his owner-editorship to *Popular Science Monthly* in 1900 (renamed *Scientific Monthly* in 1915); *American Men of Science,* the biographical directory which he founded in 1906; the *American Naturalist* in 1907; *School and Society* (which he founded) in 1915; and *Leaders in Education,* another biographical directory, in 1932. After 1895 Cattell's interest in his publications and in the broad field of science began to eclipse his psychological work; though he continued to teach, by 1905 he had ceased to work as a research psychologist.

Cattell turned his wide organizational experience to account by formulating a sophisticated view of sciences as "developing organisms" which arise from the "individual experience" of each scientist "by a kind of natural selection" ("The Conceptions and Methods of Psychology," *Popular Science Monthly,* December 1904), and he began to study American scientists themselves. It was partly to obtain a homogeneous group for study that he compiled his *American Men of Science* and developed the "order of merit" method of rating. In the first and later editions of *American Men· of Science,* Cattell analyzed the origins and distribution of his scientists, often suggesting answers to important historical and eugenic issues. Though only occasionally appreciated by later scholars, this work forms the basis of a sociology of science in America.

Cattell also used his position as an editor and organizer to attempt a radical reform of the American scientific community. Inspired by his British experience, his high scientific ideals, the democratic socialism he had espoused since his student days in Europe, and a passionate belief in the right of people to control their own affairs—a belief widely held in the Progressive era—Cattell decried the dependency of scientists on university presidents, the government, the philanthropy of wealthy men, and, increasingly, on an amalgam of these powers in the form of philanthropic foundations. Though himself a member of the scientific establishment, he deliberately violated the accepted code of conduct by which affairs were handled beyond public view and used the influential medium of *Science* to urge his views with shrewd insight and acerbic wit.

Cattell's reform efforts went in two principal directions: the first, an attempt to make the American Association for the Advancement of Science, rather than the oligarchic National Academy of Sciences, the chief voice of American science. Cattell succeeded in modernizing the A.A.A.S. and increasing its membership, but it never received the recognition by the government or the support of the scientific rank and file he had hoped for. The first central power to emerge in American science in the twentieth century, the National Research Council, grew instead under the wing of the Academy and represented the institutional powers in science rather than the body of American scientists as individuals.

Cattell's second major effort was the movement to supplant the increasing power of the university president with faculty control. The university, he argued, should be run by an enlarged quasi-public body of trustees and by the faculty, who would control their own appointments and funds. The presidency should be divided into two positions: the chancellor, elected by the trustees, to function outside the university in a ceremonial and promotional capacity; and the rector, elected by the faculty to act as their chief within the university. The students, he remarked parenthetically, should have complete control of their own affairs. Although a sizable minority of academics agreed with Cattell's scheme of reform in the abstract and many admired his courage in advocating it, few were sufficiently concerned about the issue to neglect or threaten their professional work on its behalf. They did support Cattell's more moderate proposals, such as an American Association of University Professors, which he helped found in 1915.

The chief focus of Cattell's campaign was Columbia University, where President Nicholas Murray Butler carried to extreme lengths the tendencies toward centralization of university administration that were present throughout America. With little faculty support for his blunt attack on Butler's policies, Cattell became increasingly bitter, characterizing Butler as an "autocrat" who used "department store methods" of administration, and likening professors to "domestic servants." In the fall of 1917 Cattell finally lost the support of his faculty colleagues by his persistence and his manner of speaking and was thus thrown open to attack by Butler and the Columbia trustees, who had been trying for some time to remove him. That October, Cattell was fired by the trustees for having petitioned several Congressmen to send conscripts to Europe only with their consent, and for having written his petition on stationery bearing his Columbia address. His dismissal, part of a long series of incursions on academic freedom at Columbia, occasioned the resignation of the historian Charles A. Beard and became the most celebrated academic freedom case of the war.

After his dismissal Cattell continued his reform efforts for a time, but devoted most of his remaining energies to his publications and the A.A.A.S., all of which he controlled until very close to his death. Retaining the respect of his fellow psychologists, he was named president of the ninth International Congress of Psychology held in New Haven in 1929. In this period he rejected the work of William McDougall [Supp. 2] and Sigmund Freud as outside the pale of respectable science. In 1921, with his personal funds, he led in founding the Psychological Corporation to promote research.

Cattell declared that the two most important concerns in life were the pursuit of science and the rearing of children, and he devoted much attention to his family of seven: Eleth, McKeen, Psyche, Owen, Quinta, Ware, and Jaques. Believing the home a better tutor than the school, Cattell and his wife educated all their children until college age at their home on top of Fort Defiance Hill in Garrison, N. Y., forty miles north of New York City. His wife, and eventually his children, shared substantially in his editorial labors. Cattell died at the age of eighty-three in Lancaster, Pa., his publishing headquarters, of arteriosclerotic-hypertensive heart disease. His cremated remains were buried in the Easton (Pa.) Cemetery.

[The principal source for Cattell's life to 1888 is the Cattell Papers at the Lib. of Cong.; the letters to his family give an extended account of his activities, and his "Journal" (1880–87) is the only record of his inner thoughts and difficulties. The papers also contain a typescript "Autobiog.," which has been published by Michael M. Sokal in *Am. Psychologist,* July 1971, and a published *Memoir of William Cassady Cattell* (1899), the best portrayal of his father. The professional correspondence in the papers deals largely with Cattell's editorial duties and only occasionally illumines his career. The most valuable accounts of Cattell's professional career are: obituaries or memoirs in *Psychological Rev.,* July 1944 (by Robert S. Woodworth), *Am. Jour. of Psychology,* Apr. 1944 (by Frederick L. Wells), Nat. Acad. Sci., *Biog. Memoirs,* vol. XXV (1949; by Walter B. Pillsbury), and *Science,* Feb. 25, 1944; *The Psychological Researches of James McKeen Cattell: A Review by Some of His Pupils* (1914); Gardner Murphy, *Hist. Introduction to Modern Psychology* (1950), pp. 160–65, 351–53; and a doctoral dissertation by Michael M. Sokal, "The Education and Psychological Career of James McKeen Cattell, 1860–1902" (Case Western Reserve Univ., 1972). Albert T. Poffenberger, ed., *James McKeen Cattell, Man of Science* (2 vols., 1947), reprints the Woodworth and Wells obituaries, contains a nearly complete bibliography of Cattell's publications, and reprints most of his important writings on psychology, science, and reform, including his principal work on academic reform, *University Control* (1913). See also his *Carnegie Pensions* (1919). On Cattell's reform efforts and dismissal, see his "What the Trustees of Columbia Univ. Have Done" (privately printed for the Am. Assoc. of Univ. Professors) and "Memories of My Last Days at Columbia" (privately printed for members of the Faculty Club), both in the Cattell Papers; Walter P. Metzger, "Origins of the Association," *Bull.* of the Am. Assoc. of Univ. Professors, June 1965; Carol Gruber, "Mars and Minerva: World War I and the Am. Academic Man" (Ph.D. dissertation, Columbia Univ., 1968), chap. iv; *N. Y. Times,* June 21, 22, July 13, Oct. 2, 1917; and the correspondence with President Butler in the Cattell Papers. Variant spellings exist for the middle name of Cattell's father, but "Cassady" seems the best supported.]

DOROTHY ROSS

CHAFFEE, ADNA ROMANZA (Sept. 23, 1884–Aug. 22, 1941), army officer, was born in Junction City, Kans., the third of four children and only son of Adna Romanza Chaffee [*q.v.*] and his second wife, Annie Frances (Rockwell) Chaffee. The elder Chaffee, a cavalry officer who had first enlisted in the army during the Civil War, held important commands in the Spanish-American War and the Boxer Rebellion and served as the army's Chief of Staff (1904–06).

He saw to it that his son was taught to ride as soon as he was able to sit on a horse. The boy attended local public schools in the Southwest, as the family moved from one army post to another, and at the age of fourteen was sent to St. Luke's School for Boys at Wayne, Pa. In 1902 he entered the United States Military Academy at West Point. Upon graduating in 1906, he was commissioned and assigned to the 15th Cavalry, with which he served in Cuba. For two years (1907–09) he attended the Mounted Service School at Fort Riley, Kans. (1907–09). While there, on Dec. 15, 1908, he married Ethel Warren Huff of Columbus, Ga. They had one son, also named Adna Romanza.

Chaffee's skill as a horseman led to his assignment to the Army War College Detachment. He took part in mounted competitions at home and abroad and was sent to the cavalry school of the French army at Saumur, where he graduated in 1912. Back home, he served as an instructor at the Mounted Service School (1912–13) and then with the cavalry in the Philippines (1914–16), after which he was appointed an instructor at West Point (1916–17). When the United States entered World War I, Chaffee, now a major, went overseas with the 81st Division. He served as a student and instructor at the A.E.F. General Staff College at Langres, France, and saw action with the 81st Division and the IV, III, and VII Corps; he was promoted to colonel and awarded the Distinguished Service Medal and the Victory Medal with four Battle Clasps.

Upon his return to the United States in 1919, Chaffee reverted to his permanent grade of captain, but was soon promoted to major. Duty as an instructor at the Fort Leavenworth School of the Line (1919–20) was followed by important command positions, general staff assignments, and graduation from the Army War College in 1925. He commanded a squadron at Fort Myer, Va., for two years, and then was detailed to the G-3 Division (Operations and Training), War Department General Staff, where he served for four years and was promoted to lieutenant colonel.

Chaffee's historical importance lies in his leadership in the development of an American armored force. He had witnessed the use of tanks in World War I, and during the 1920's he came increasingly to believe that the cavalry's function of providing mobility on the battlefield would have to be performed by armored, motorpowered vehicles. When in 1927 Secretary of War Dwight F. Davis [Supp. 3], impressed by British tests along these lines, asked the General Staff to organize an experimental mechanized force, supervisory responsibility fell to Chaffee.

The resulting report, based largely on Chaffee's ideas, urged the development of a separate striking force, independent of both cavalry and infantry, to be made up of tanks, motorized infantry, and motorized guns. Chaffee's recommendations met much opposition within the army and stirred interbranch rivalries, but in 1930 an experimental mechanized unit was organized at Fort Eustis, Va. To head it Chaffee secured Col. Daniel Van Voorhis, who soon became wholeheartedly committed to the new concept. When a War Department restudy in 1931 threatened the disbanding of this force and the possible elimination of the cavalry as well, Chaffee attempted to save them both by proposing that the mechanized force be attached to the cavalry. This suggestion was sharply criticized by some influential cavalry officers, who feared that it would mean the end of the horse cavalry.

The War Department's final report directed every branch of the army to develop its own mechanized program. The Fort Eustis unit, as Chaffee had proposed, was turned over to the cavalry, and in June 1931 he was made the detachment's executive officer. Late the same year he accompanied cavalry elements to Camp Knox (later Fort Knox), Ky., where he worked doggedly to create a permanent post and then the nucleus of a mechanized force in the 1st Cavalry (Mechanized) Regiment. Taking part in the 1934 spring maneuvers at Fort Riley, Kans., Chaffee's unit demonstrated the superior speed and mobility of a mechanized force over horse cavalry, thus supporting Chaffee's argument that they must be used separately. In July 1934 Chaffee returned to the War Department General Staff as chief of the budget and legislative planning branch. In this key assignment he worked to expand the mechanized cavalry. On Nov. 1, 1938 —promoted to brigadier general—he was given command of the 7th Cavalry Brigade (Mechanized).

Further maneuvers, in 1939 and in May 1940, again showed the effectiveness of Chaffee's mechanized command, but his performance was overshadowed by the stunning success of German mechanized Panzer divisions in the "blitzkrieg" phase of World War II. On July 10, 1940, the army at last authorized an Armored Force, "for purposes of service test," with Chaffee as chief. By October he had set up two armored divisions and had been promoted to major general.

But long hours of labor over a prolonged period of time had wasted away Chaffee's tall, lean body. For much of the last year of his life he was hospitalized. He died of cancer in Massachusetts General Hospital, Boston, in August 1941 at the age of fifty-six. Earlier an Episcopalian, he was apparently a Christian Scientist at the time of his death. He was buried in Arlington National Cemetery beside his father.

[George W. Cullum, *Biog. Register of Officers and Graduates of the U. S. Military Acad.*, vols. V–VIII (1910–40); Kenneth Hechler et al., "The Armored Force, Command and Center" (MS., Hist. Section, Army Ground Forces, 1946); Mildred H. Gillie, *Forging the Thunderbolt: A Hist. of the Development of the Armored Force* (1947), which is also to a considerable extent a biography of Chaffee; Timothy K. Nenninger, "The Development of Am. Armor, 1917–1940" (M.S. thesis, Univ. of Wis., 1968); Paul M. Robinett, "Ground Force Mobility," *Military Rev.*, Mar. 1953; Arch Whitehouse, *Tank* (1960); William H. Chaffee, *The Chaffee Genealogy* (1909), pp. 428–36; *Who Was Who in America*, vol. I (1942), which gives Chaffee's religion as Episcopalian; *Nat. Cyc. Am. Biog.*, XXX, 7–8, which says he was a Christian Scientist; *Time*, Aug. 18, 1941, p. 35; obituary in West Point *Assembly*, Apr. 1942.]

PAUL M. ROBINETT

CHAMBERLAIN, CHARLES JOSEPH (Feb. 23, 1863–Jan. 5, 1943), botanist, was born on a farm near Sullivan, Ohio, the elder of two sons of Esdell W. and Mary (Spencer) Chamberlain, both native Ohioans. His father, who served in the Civil War as an infantryman, not only farmed but also invented and manufactured farm machinery such as horsepowered hay rakes and cider mills and ran a sawmill and a cheesebox factory. Music was the family's avocation, and Charles joined the local cornet band at the age of thirteen. He was educated in a one-room rural school. To give the sons better educational opportunities, the family moved in 1881 to Oberlin, Ohio, where the father managed a farm mutual insurance company. Charles found his earlier schooling insufficient for entering the Oberlin Conservatory of Music or even the local high school, but made up his scholastic deficiencies within a few months and completed the three-year high school course in two years. After another year spent in the senior preparatory department of Oberlin College, he entered the college itself, receiving the A.B. degree in 1888 at twenty-five.

As an undergraduate Chamberlain was attracted to botany by the teaching of Prof. Albert Allen Wright. During the five years after his graduation he taught school and, from 1889 to 1893, was principal of the high school at Crookston, Minn., but he returned to Oberlin during the summers to carry out histological studies in Wright's laboratory, work for which Oberlin awarded him the A.M. degree in 1894. Imbued with a strong desire to continue the study of botany and fired by the educational zeal of President William Rainey Harper [q.v.] of the University of Chicago, Chamberlain in the fall of 1893 enrolled there as a graduate student. Since no botany courses were available, he was persuaded to complete a "minor" in animal histology, cytology, and related vertebrate courses. The techniques he learned from his study of animal tissues, such as the use of staining, he later adapted to the study of plant tissues. In his second year at the university, John M. Coulter [q.v.], then president of Lake Forest University, was persuaded by Harper to commute to Chicago on Saturdays to teach botanically inclined graduate students. In 1895 Coulter became chairman of the new department of botany, and Chamberlain was placed in charge of the laboratory; he received the department's first Ph.D. in 1897.

Except for the year 1900–01, which he spent in postdoctoral research with Prof. Eduard Strasburger in Bonn, Germany, Chamberlain was intimately associated with the evolution of the Chicago department, progressing from assistant and associate in botany (1897–1901) through successive academic ranks to professor (1915–29). In his early years on the faculty he published his own researches on lower vascular plants, collaborated with colleagues on numerous morphological investigations, and with his mentor, Coulter, wrote *Morphology of Spermatophytes, Part 1: Gymnosperms* (1901), which was widely used in its expanded form, *Morphology of Gymnosperms* (1910). A companion volume on flowering plants appeared in 1903. Chamberlain's knowledge and skill in preparing and sectioning organisms for research and teaching became embodied in his *Methods in Plant Histology*, issued in five editions from 1901 to 1932.

Chamberlain's major area of research was the cycad genera, plants intermediate in appearance between tree ferns and palms. His study of the embryo development in *Zamia*, in collaboration with Coulter (1903), had shown him how little was known concerning the life histories, distribution, ecology, and diversity of cycads and other primitive seed plants. While in Germany he had learned the approximate location in Mexico of isolated stands of these palmlike, cone-bearing plants, and in 1904 he was able to visit that country, where he penetrated isolated plantations and jungles beyond Jalapa. His scientific zeal and personal charm appealed to the governor of Vera Cruz, who offered him a locomotive and other facilities for field excursions and collecting trips; friends of the governor also sent specimens to Chicago which yielded information on critical stages in plant development. These collections furnished the raw material for dissertations by the growing number of graduate students at Chicago. Between 1906 and 1910 Chamberlain made three additional visits to Mexico.

An extended trip, in 1911–12, to study and collect the cycads of Fiji, New Zealand, Australia, and South Africa and two Cuban tours (1914, 1922) to investigate the monotypic *Microcycas* further established Chamberlain as the undisputed leader in his field. He brought back to Chicago an assemblage of living plants which became the basis of the most representative collection of cycads in the world; from it, plants have been distributed to conservatories in Chicago and in many states. He had planned a monograph on the cycads, but his taxonomic efforts began too late to allow him to complete a comprehensive systematic treatment, and World War II prevented his return to localities in which the ecology and distribution of cycads could be studied more intensively. With help from his friend Dr. Shigéo Yamanouchi, a Japanese botanist who had studied at Chicago, he attempted to hybridize cycads, but results were equivocal and the slow growth of cycads precluded repetition of this effort.

Chamberlain contributed significantly to the spectacular rise of botanical science at the University of Chicago. His graduates have occupied important educational posts on several continents and have perpetuated his enthusiasm and intellectual integrity. One historian of science has called Chamberlain's books "keystones in the arch of morphological literature." His correspondence with plantsmen on all continents was extensive. A member of a dozen scientific societies in Europe and the United States, he served as vice-president of the American Association for the Advancement of Science in 1923 and as president of the Botanical Society of America in 1931.

Chamberlain's early love for music continued throughout his life. In Chicago he directed the choir of the Woodlawn Baptist Church for ten years and sang tenor in the Apollo Club for thirty-five. During World War I he and a faculty colleague became expert riflemen and instructed infantry recruits at Fort Sheridan. He retired as professor emeritus in 1929. Chamberlain was twice married: on July 30, 1888, to Mary E. Life, by whom he had a daughter, Mabel; and, following his first wife's death (1931), to Martha Stanley Lathrop, an organist, on Oct. 30, 1938. He died at his home in Chicago in 1943 of cancer and a weakened heart and was buried in Oberlin, Ohio.

[Chamberlain's *The Living Cycads* (1919) includes an account of his botanical trips. The Univ. of Chicago Lib. has a MS. autobiography by Chamberlain and other unpublished biographical material. Published references include: J. T. Buchholz in *Botanical Gazette*, Mar. 1943 (with portrait); *Am. Men of Sci.*, 1st ed. (1906) through 6th (1938); *Who Was Who in America*, vol. II (1950). Other information from personal acquaintance, 1929–42, and from Mrs. Martha Chamberlain. Mounted herbarium specimens of cycads, annotated by Chamberlain, are deposited in the Field Museum of Natural Hist., Chicago. An oil portrait by Edmund Giesbert and a bronze bust by Fred M. Torrey are at the Univ. of Chicago.]

PAUL D. VOTH

CHANDLER, HARRY (May 17, 1864–Sept. 23, 1944), Los Angeles newspaper publisher, civic leader, and real estate developer, was born in Landaff, N. H., the eldest of four children (three boys and one girl) of Moses Knight Chandler, a farmer, and Emma Jane (Little) Chandler. He was a descendant of William Chandler, who emigrated from England and settled in Roxbury, Mass., about 1637. After attending the district school in Lisbon, N. H., Harry Chandler went to Hanover, N. H., in the fall of 1882 planning to enter Dartmouth College, but a severe lung illness (reportedly contracted by diving on a dare into an ice-covered starch vat) kept him from matriculating, and his family sent him to Southern California to recover. Living in a tent in the San Fernando Valley near Los Angeles, he broke horses and harvested fruit for farmers in return for a share of their crops, which he then sold to threshing crews on the vast Van Nuys ranch. After accumulating several thousand dollars in this manner, he returned home in 1884 to resume his education, but the immediate recurrence of his illness again drove him to California.

In 1885, now twenty-one years old, Chandler began his newspaper career as a clerk in the circulation department of the *Los Angeles Times*, owned by Gen. Harrison Gray Otis [*q.v.*]. On Feb. 6, 1888, he married Magdalena Schlador; they had two daughters, Franceska and Alice May. Chandler soon purchased several newspaper routes and began handling his own delivery and collections (newspapers at that time being commonly distributed by independent contractors); he also began buying stock in the *Times*. Chandler's wife died in 1892, and two years later, on June 5, 1894, he married Marian Otis, daughter of General Otis. They had six children: Constance, Ruth, Norman, Harrison Gray, Helen, and Philip. Shortly after his second marriage, Chandler was appointed business manager of the *Times*.

Chandler early became involved in a number of speculative real estate ventures in Southern California and in Mexico. His newspaper provided him with valuable contacts, and around 1899, on the advice of a friend, he and a group of Southern California investors bought up land in the Colorado River desert above and below the Mexican border. In 1902 they formed two corporations, the California-Mexico Land and Cattle Company, which managed their lands in California's Imperial Valley (1,000 acres), and the Colorado River Land Company, a Mexican subsidiary that controlled the group's holdings south of the border. The second company became the more important as, over the next fourteen years, it acquired more than 800,000 acres of land in the Mexicali Valley and the Colorado delta. By 1931 the Colorado River company had spent $12,000,000 in developing the region, most of which was leased to tenant farmers engaged in the raising of cotton; it built canals and ditches, constructed roads and levees, and leveled extensive portions of the land. The company also had interests in other ventures, including banks, a canal company, and a cotton gin. Despite declining cotton prices during the 1930's and the expropriation of much of its land by the Mexican government, the company realized considerable income from its holdings.

Other ventures in which Chandler played a part included the formation of a syndicate in 1912 to buy the 286,000-acre Tejon Ranch in Los Angeles and Kern counties, on which some 20,000 cattle and horses were grazed. He himself purchased a 340,000-acre tract in New Mexico and Colorado which he used for both cattle raising and hunting. But the real estate developments which won Chandler the title of "California's landlord" were those in and around Los Angeles. Many were undertaken in partnership with Moses Hazeltine Sherman, a former schoolteacher and banker in Phoenix, Ariz., who had moved in 1889 to Los Angeles and had become a street-railway developer. In 1903 Chandler helped sell lots in Hollywood along the route of Sherman's rapid transit lines, eventually realizing a 60 percent profit.

A major factor in the expansion of the Los Angeles area was the provision of an adequate water supply. Most observers credit Chandler with being the prime force behind the *Times*'s successful campaign in the early 1900's to bring the water resources of the Owens Valley in the Sierras to Los Angeles. City Superintendent William Mulholland, backed by the city water board, of which Sherman was a member, mounted a campaign which successfully floated two municipal bond issues (1905, 1907) totaling $24,500,000, acquired Owens Valley land over the opposition of many local residents, and constructed an aqueduct which ran 233 miles from the Sierras to the upper end of the San Fernando Valley, north of Los Angeles. The aqueduct was completed in 1913.

Chandler had extensive interests in the San Fernando Valley. He, Sherman, General Otis, H.

J. Whitley, and others had formed a syndicate, the Suburban Homes Company, which purchased the Porter Ranch in 1905 and most of the holdings of the Van Nuys and Lankershim families in 1909 for about $2,500,000. They subdivided the 60,000 acres into residential and industrial property (serviced by the new water supply) which sold for $17,000,000 over a seven-year period. The 22-mile-long paved highway they built— Sherman Way—connecting the development with Los Angeles is said to have inspired the county to vote a bond issue for paved roads, the first issue for that purpose in the United States. Most of the San Fernando Valley was annexed to the city of Los Angeles in 1915.

In the mid-1930's Chandler organized a syndicate which purchased the estate of E. J. "Lucky" Baldwin, including portions of the old Ranchos Santa Anita and La Cienega, and subdivided the land into tracts in Arcadia, San Gabriel, and Baldwin Hills. With other holdings near the Santa Anita racetrack (for which he had helped obtain financing), he had become one of Los Angeles County's major landholders.

Meanwhile Chandler had risen rapidly on the *Times*. He was named assistant manager in 1898, and when General Otis later that year entered military service in the Spanish-American War, Chandler ran the paper. Thereafter he assumed increasing responsibility. He helped determine editorial policy, including the *Times*'s campaign for the construction of a man-made harbor in the San Pedro-Wilmington area of Los Angeles County and the annexing of this area to the city. San Pedro soon became one of the leading ports on the West Coast.

Upon the death of Otis in 1917, Chandler succeeded him as president and publisher of the *Los Angeles Times*. He expanded the paper, particularly its advertising pages. In 1921, 1922, and 1923 the *Times* led all other American newspapers in both volume of advertising and amount of classified advertising; as late as 1940 it was still third in total advertising and first in classified. Chandler added a rotogravure section and the *Times* Sunday Magazine. A farm and garden supplement evolved by 1940 into the more general Home Magazine. The *Times* was also the first newspaper in the nation to inaugurate a motion picture page. The paper made increasing use of large photographs, and Chandler was one of the founders of Press Wireless. In 1930–31 he served as president of the American Newspaper Publishers Association. In 1936, a year after moving to new headquarters, the *Times* streamlined its makeup, inaugurating a typography which won the Ayer Cup for excellence. By 1944 the newspaper had a circulation of 320,000 daily and 615,000 Sunday copies.

Perhaps Chandler's most important journalistic achievement was his use of the press to boost the qualities of Southern California. His father-in-law had formed the Los Angeles Chamber of Commerce in 1888, and Chandler helped plan the first of the promotional "Midwinter" editions of the *Times* which were sent annually to persons in the central states. Thousands of Midwesterners, wrote one observer, "amid bitter cold and high snowdrifts, eagerly absorbed the contents of these alluring pages and resolved someday to make California their home" (Ford, pp. 35–36). The *Times* seldom printed anything negative about Los Angeles, but frequently mentioned the rain, hail, tornadoes, dust, and snowstorms of Eastern weather. In 1921, the year Chandler organized the All-Year Club of Southern California to promote summer tourism, the city's Realty Board voted him "Los Angeles' Most Useful Citizen."

Chandler inherited from Otis a strong antipathy for organized labor. During the 1890's and early 1900's the *Times* engaged in a continual struggle, particularly with the typographers, to prevent the unionization of its plant. Partly as a result, the paper also campaigned for the open shop in all major industries in Southern California. Chandler helped organize the antiunion Merchants and Manufacturers Association, which for thirty years determined the economic and political policies championed by the city's business interests.

Shortly after 1 a.m. on Oct. 1, 1910, the *Times* building was blown up by a bomb tied to a gas main beneath the floor under Chandler's desk. Although he had already left the building, twenty employees, including his secretary, were killed. Chandler immediately denounced the bombing as the work of unionists, and the case drew national attention. In succeeding months, three union officials, including John J. McNamara, secretary-treasurer of the International Iron Workers, and his brother James, were arrested and charged with the crime. There followed a long series of negotiations in which defense attorney Clarence Darrow [Supp. 2] tried to save the lives of his clients by allowing them to confess and plead guilty. Chandler agreed to the arrangement since he realized the execution of the McNamaras might make them labor martyrs. Although details of the affair remain obscure, it seems clear that the McNamara confession prevented a Socialist from being elected mayor of Los Angeles, damaged the credibility of national union leaders, and helped preserve the open shop in Southern California.

One element in Chandler's success in avoiding unionization of the *Times* was the benevolent employment practices he followed. He paid higher wages than going union rates, seldom discharged loyal employees, and rewarded seniority. The *Times* was the first newspaper in the country to establish a personnel department and one of the first to adopt a forty-hour work week; and in the early 1920's the paper established a group insurance plan paid for by the company.

Chandler disliked public appearances and speechmaking and many times refused to run for office, but he devoted much of his time to political affairs. For many years he was the acknowledged leader of Southern California's conservative Republicans. Many political candidates were chosen in his office; he was sometimes called the "Governor of Southern California." Chandler's sincere, homespun manner made him few personal enemies, but he did have political opponents. A strong lifelong antipathy existed between Chandler and Hiram Johnson [Supp. 3], leader of the progressive wing of the state's Republican party. Some observers believe that their feud contributed to Charles Evans Hughes's loss of California, and thus of the presidential race, in 1916. Chandler opposed Woodrow Wilson, but supported the League of Nations. Other political foes included Upton Sinclair, who muckraked the *Times* and was in turn harshly attacked by Chandler when Sinclair ran for governor in 1934; Democratic governor Culbert Olson (1939–43); and Fletcher Bowron, mayor of Los Angeles (1938–53). Chandler was frequently criticized by other city newspapers, particularly the *Express,* the *Daily News,* and those owned by William Randolph Hearst. But during the depression he won Hearst's gratitude by assuming the mortgage on his estate at San Simeon.

The 1920's were Chandler's happiest years, for he was an acquaintance of both Warren Harding and Calvin Coolidge and a close friend of Herbert Hoover. Chandler promoted good will with Mexico and frequently played host to Mexican government officials; he is credited with persuading Harding to extend diplomatic recognition to the Obregón regime in 1923. The *Times* opposed the building of Boulder Dam on the Colorado River and consistently fought any measures providing for public ownership of utilities or transportation. Chandler turned down a number of federal appointments but accepted Hoover's nomination in late 1929 to the National Business Survey Conference, a group of twenty business leaders appointed to examine the emergency economic situation caused by the stock market crash. During the 1930's Chandler was a constant critic of the New Deal. In 1936 the *Times* praised Los Angeles police for turning away unemployed migrants at the California border.

Chandler pioneered in many of his city's commercial and cultural developments. He campaigned vigorously for the establishment of a Union railway station and a historical plaza at Olvera Street, which became civic landmarks. In 1922 he helped organize a $30,000,000 steamship company to purchase the government's Pacific shipping fleet, as well as the Central Investment Corporation which built the prestigious Biltmore Hotel. That year, too, he began the area's first commercial radio station, KHJ, which he sold in 1929 after an open-shop dispute. To prevent San Francisco from becoming the coastal airmail center, he organized Western Air Lines, the nation's oldest carrier, which won its first airmail contract in 1925. He also helped Donald Douglas attract capital to Southern California's fledgling aircraft industry. Chandler was instrumental in obtaining the financial backing to convert Throop College of Technology in Pasadena into the California Institute of Technology, of which he was a trustee from 1919 to 1943. For some years he was also a trustee of Stanford University.

At six feet two, Chandler was a big man, and many stories were told of his prowess in delivering papers, tussling with unionists, or pitching hay on one of his many ranches. A Congregationalist in religion, he abstained from alcohol, lived frugally, and commuted by foot whenever possible. His favorite charity was the Salvation Army. He was an indefatigable worker and forthright in his editorial positions. For his comments on the court decisions in certain labor cases still in process of appeal, he was found guilty in 1938 on two counts of contempt of court. His conviction was overturned by the United States Supreme Court in 1941—a landmark decision for freedom of the press. For their role in the decision, Chandler and the *Times* won their first Pulitzer Prize.

By the early 1940's three of Chandler's children had become active in various departments of the *Times*. He relinquished his position as president and publisher to his son Norman in 1941, but remained active as chairman of the board of the Times-Mirror Company. Three years later, at the age of eighty, he died of a coronary thrombosis in Good Samaritan Hospital, Los Angeles. He was buried in Hollywood Cemetery.

[There is no good biographical account of Chandler. Information about his many activities has been pieced together from a variety of sources ranging from the scholarly to the muckraking and including the following: Morrow Mayo, *Los Angeles* (1933); Remi Nad-

eau, *Los Angeles: From Mission to Modern City* (1960) and *The Water Seekers* (1950); Robert M. Fogelson, *The Fragmented Metropolis: Los Angeles, 1850–1930* (1967); Boyle Workman, *The City That Grew* (1935); Noel J. Stowe, ed., "Pioneering Land Development in the Californias," *Calif. Hist. Soc. Quart.*, Mar., June, Sept. 1968, an interview with the son of one of Chandler's associates in the Mexican and other land ventures; Lowell L. Blaisdell, "Harry Chandler and Mexican Border Intrigue, 1914–1917," *Pacific Hist. Rev.*, Nov. 1966; Anthony Cifarelli, "The Owens River Aqueduct and the *Los Angeles Times*" (M.S. thesis, Univ. of Calif., Los Angeles, 1969); Edward Ainsworth, *Memories in the City of Dreams: A Tribute to Harry Chandler* (1959) and *Hist. of the Los Angeles Times* (1948); Harris Newmark, *Sixty Years in Southern Calif., 1853–1913* (3rd ed., 1930); William R. Spaulding, *Hist. and Reminiscences, Los Angeles City and County*, vol. I (n.d.); John Anson Ford, *Thirty Explosive Years in Los Angeles County* (1961); William Bonelli, *Billion Dollar Blackjack* (1954), overtly hostile to Chandler; Louis Adamic, *Dynamite* (1931); George Seldes, *Lords of the Press* (1938); Sidney Kobre, *Modern Am. Journalism* (1959); Edwin Emery, *The Press and America* (2nd ed., 1962); *Editor & Publisher Year Book*, 1921; Frank J. Taylor, "It Costs $1,000 to Have Lunch with Harry Chandler," *Saturday Evening Post*, Dec. 16, 1939; Chandler's comments on the 1936 campaign in *Rev. of Revs.*, Mar. 1936; "Midas of Calif.," *Newsweek*, Oct. 2, 1944; "The Press: Third Perch," *Time*, July 15, 1935; *Who Was Who in America*, vol. II (1950); *Nat. Cyc. Am. Biog.*, XL, 498; *Los Angeles Record*, Mar. 4–7, 1924, Nov. 24, 1925; *Los Angeles Examiner*, July 11, 1926, Sept. 24–26, 1944; *Editor & Publisher*, Sept. 30, 1944; articles from the *Los Angeles Times* and *Among Ourselves*, a house organ, in the *Times* library; interview with Norman Chandler; *Dartmouth Alumni Mag.*, Dec. 1944, p. 64; father's occupation from Town Clerk, Landaff, N. H.]

GLENN S. DUMKE
JUDSON A. GRENIER

CHAPIN, CHARLES VALUE (Jan. 17, 1856–Jan. 31, 1941), public health officer and epidemiologist, was born and spent his life in Providence, R. I. His father, Joshua Bicknell Chapin, who came from an old New England family, was successively a physician, druggist, photographer, and state Commissioner of Education. His mother, Jane Catherine Louise (Value) Chapin, daughter of a refugee from the French Revolution, painted portraits and occasionally taught painting to supplement the family income. Charles was the second of their three children and the only son. He attended the Mowry and Goff School in Providence and Brown University, where he graduated, B.A., in 1876. Chapin was introduced to medicine by preceptors: his father and Dr. George D. Wilcox, a Providence homeopath. His medical training continued with a year at the College of Physicians and Surgeons of New York, followed by a year at the Bellevue Hospital Medical College, where he studied pathology under William H. Welch [q.v.] and received his M.D. degree in 1879. He interned at Bellevue Hospital under such physicians as Abraham Jacobi, Edward G. Janeway, and the elder Austin Flint [qq.v.].

After beginning private practice in Providence in 1880, Chapin also served for a few years as part-time pathologist at the Rhode Island Hospital and did medical charity work for the Providence Dispensary. He was on the faculty of Brown University between 1882 and 1895 as part-time professor of physiology. On May 6, 1886, he married Anna Augusta Balch of Providence; they had one child, Howard Millar Chapin, later librarian of the Rhode Island Historical Society.

Admittedly lacking a comforting bedside manner with patients, and impatient with the routine of private practice, Chapin in 1884 welcomed appointment as Superintendent of Health of Providence, the beginning of a career that was to make him internationally known. He remained in the position forty-eight years, adding in 1888 the duties of city registrar; statisticians and epidemiologists agreed that the data he compiled were unsurpassed by those of any other American city for accuracy and completeness. Chapin was one of the earliest American health officers to apply the techniques and findings of bacteriology to sanitary science. With Gardner T. Swarts he established, in 1888, the first municipal bacteriological laboratory in the United States. There, among more routine work, they performed pioneer tests of mechanical water filters and examinations of disinfectants. Adopting diagnostic methods developed elsewhere in the 1890's, Chapin made bacteriological analysis the practical basis of the fight to control diseases like diphtheria, though he subsequently found that he had to make some compromises between the scientific application of these methods and the realities of social conditions.

Contemporaries regarded Chapin as an iconoclast because he vigorously attacked outmoded medical and sanitary theories: among them, the idea that filth caused disease, that diseases were indiscriminately transmitted through the air, and that disinfection was a cure-all for sanitary evils. To replace theory, he conducted painstaking field studies and statistical analyses of the incidence of common infectious diseases and synthesized this knowledge with the pertinent findings of the extensive laboratory research of the day. He concluded that the ordinary infectious diseases of temperate climates were spread principally through contact between persons. Conversely, in the absence of sera or vaccines, he believed the most effective means of preventing such spreading were the control of carriers of disease who were themselves well, and strict observance of the precautions of personal cleanliness. He announced these findings in his famous book of 1910, *The*

Sources and Modes of Infection. In the new Providence City Hospital which he secured in 1910—an isolation hospital for patients with infectious disease—aseptic nursing principles were successfully applied, and the hospital became a model for similar institutions across the United States.

Chapin's ideas formed much of the scientific underpinning of the "new public health." An effective speaker and productive writer, he was among the foremost of those who, early in the twentieth century, shaped this broadened concept of community health, which carried public health work beyond environmental sanitation and the control of a few infectious diseases to a wide variety of preventive and curative services focusing on the individual. These services, carried out by lay health organizations as well as by official bodies, included such innovations as the antituberculosis campaign, the infant hygiene movement, inspection and care of schoolchildren, and public medical attention for the sick poor. Chapin also contributed much to the practical administration of public health work at all levels in the United States. His insistence, for example, that health officers rate (on a numerical scale) the importance of the various segments of their work and turn over to other agencies those activities, such as garbage collection, which had only a minor or indirect relation to health prompted many health officers to reappraise their functions, and his *Report on State Public Health Work* (1916), based on his comprehensive survey, exerted considerable influence. Chapin served as president of the American Public Health Association (1926–27) and as the first president (1927) of the American Epidemiological Society.

Personally modest, physically frail, and intellectually honest and plainspoken, Chapin had a high sense of duty to his community. His few leisure-time activities—sailing, reading mystery stories, and the pursuit of genealogy and studies of Rhode Island history—were all carried on with his family. He retired in 1932, at the age of seventy-six, and died nine years later in Providence of general arteriosclerosis. After funeral services at the Central Congregational Church, of which he had long been a member, he was buried in Swan Point Cemetery, Providence.

Charles Chapin was one of a brilliant group of American public health leaders—including Hermann M. Biggs, William T. Sedgwick, Victor C. Vaughan [*qq.v.*], and Theobald Smith [Supp. 1], as well as William H. Welch—whose generation had remarkable success in reducing human disease and extending life expectancy. He made distinctive contributions to this achievement, both in theory and in methodology. In the process he, probably more than anyone else, brought about a change in the image of the American health officer from that of political hack and chaser of smells to that of professional scientist.

[Collections of Chapin's papers exist in the R. I. Medic. Soc. Lib., the Brown Univ. Lib., and the R. I. Hist. Soc. Chapin also wrote a large compendium, *Municipal Sanitation in the U. S.* (1901). The *Papers of Charles V. Chapin, M.D.* (1934), ed. by Clarence L. Scamman, contains a short biographical account and a good bibliography. The only full-length study is James H. Cassedy, *Charles V. Chapin and the Public Health Movement* (1962), which includes a bibliography. Among professional appreciations are those by Wade H. Frost, "The Familial Aggregation of Infectious Diseases," *Am. Jour. of Public Health,* Jan. 1938; George E. Vincent in *R. I. Medic. Jour.,* Mar. 1927; and Charles-Edward A. Winslow, *The Conquest of Epidemic Disease* (1943), chap. xviii.]
JAMES H. CASSEDY

CHAPIN, HENRY DWIGHT (Feb. 4, 1857–June 27, 1942), pediatrician and social reformer, was born in Steubenville, Ohio, the second of five sons of Henry Barton Chapin and Harriet Ann (Smith) Chapin. Of New England Puritan stock, he was descended from Deacon Samuel Chapin, who emigrated from England around 1640 and settled in Springfield, Mass. His father, born in Rochester, N. Y., and a graduate of Yale, was a Presbyterian minister. Young Chapin grew up chiefly in Trenton, N. J., where his father held a pastorate from 1858 to 1866, and in New York City, where he attended the Chapin Collegiate School for Boys, of which his father was principal from 1867 to 1903.

In 1877, with a B.S. from the College of New Jersey (later Princeton University), Chapin began the study of medicine, probably spending much of the next two years with Dr. Stephen Smith [*q.v.*], his preceptor. He entered the College of Physicians and Surgeons in New York in 1879, completed the two brief lecture terms then required, and received the M.D. degree in 1881. After serving internships, it is said, at Bellevue Hospital and at the leper colony on Ward's Island in New York Harbor, he entered practice in 1884.

In 1885 Chapin began teaching a course in the diseases of children at the New York Post-Graduate Medical School and Hospital, and the next year was appointed professor in that subject both at the Post-Graduate School and at the Woman's Medical College of the New York Infirmary for Women and Children. Though he held the second post only until 1890, he retained the first until his retirement in 1920. At the hospital he was, at various times, director of diseases of children, supervising physician of the Babies'

Ward, and a member of the board of directors. Using ward rounds, discussion, and the case method, Chapin attained a reputation for excellence as a teacher.

His experience at the Post-Graduate Hospital with patients from the densely populated tenements of the Lower East Side alerted him to the special problems of nutrition and health among the children of the poor. In 1890 he launched a hospital social service at the Babies' Ward—one of the pioneer efforts of this kind—at first using volunteers experienced in social work and then, a few years later, employing trained nurses, who visited former patients, helping to implement the doctor's instructions (translated into German or Italian where necessary), and reported on home conditions that might affect medical treatment.

In one of his earliest papers on social problems, Chapin stated his conviction that "Economic laws are really . . . the outcome of physiological laws and conditions," and that society should therefore "strive to atone for its fearful inequalities, not by division and almsgiving, but by strengthening the weak for more successful effort" ("Social and Physiological Inequality," *Popular Science Monthly,* April 1887). Essential to this aim was proper early nourishment. He emphasized the importance of milk, not only for its nutritive value but also because he believed it played a significant role in the development of the digestive system. He therefore advocated that premature and sickly babies, if they could not be breast-fed, should be given a mixture that approximated as closely as possible the chemical constitution of maternal milk. When his experiments convinced him that no combination of ingredients could precisely duplicate these qualities, he established, in 1921, one of the early citywide breast-milk collection stations, conducted under the auspices of the Children's Welfare Federation of New York. Out of this same zeal for proper early nourishment evolved several of Chapin's most significant contributions to infant metabolism and nutrition, including recognition of the inability of infants to digest protein, and of the intestinal origin of acidosis. His technical writings include *The Theory and Practice of Infant Feeding* (1902) and *Diseases of Infants and Children* (1909), with Godfrey R. Pisek, which went through eight editions.

A major concern of Chapin's life was the welfare of neglected infants and children. His work in various hospitals in the New York area convinced him that prolonged institutionalization of children was harmful, often fatal, and he campaigned vigorously to support his views. Abraham Jacobi [*q.v.*] had earlier recognized the disease of "hospitalism"—the near-100 percent mortality among young patients detained on the wards indefinitely after recovery from acute illness—and had lost his staff position by advocating boarding out instead. Unlike the fiery Jacobi, Chapin gained acceptance for the idea of foster homes. In 1902 he founded the Speedwell Society, an organization that placed young inmates of hospitals and settlement houses in private homes, initially in Morristown, N. J. Contributions to the society provided milk, board, clothing, and "extras" for the children and paid the salaries of a physician and nurse who regularly visited each participating household. This system afforded a temporary family environment for more than 800 young convalescents in its first eight years, and, with additional units in Yonkers, New Rochelle, towns on Long Island, and other healthful areas outside New York City, by 1940 had cared for some 20,000 children.

On June 1, 1907, at the age of fifty, Chapin married Alice Delafield, the daughter of an Episcopal clergyman. To their disappointment, they had no children, but they devoted themselves to the welfare of foundlings. In 1910 they took in a baby girl abandoned in Central Park, the first of ninety-eight such infants to be nurtured in their home before being given to adoptive parents. This care of foundlings soon developed into the Alice Chapin Nursery, which in 1943 merged into the Spence-Chapin Adoption Service. All told, Chapin and his wife arranged 1,700 adoptions and indirectly found homes for some 2,000 other children, in addition to the British babies placed in American homes through Chapin's work as a member of the British-American Adoption Commission after World War I.

Always seeking ways to better the human condition, Chapin read widely among contemporary social philosophers, being deeply influenced by Herbert Spencer and John Fiske [q.v.], and by his own friend and classmate, Henry Fairfield Osborn [Supp. 1]. Chapin advocated limited eugenics, particularly by quarantine of the feeble-minded; but he believed that the prolonged period of infancy and growth in human beings made their heredity more malleable than that of lower animals, an optimistic philosophy he expressed most fully in Vital Questions (1905), Health First: The Fine Art of Living (1917), and Heredity and Child Culture (1922). His interest in education impelled him to cooperate in improving the public schools, and in 1895 he served on the advisory council of the Public Education Association of New York City, together with Felix Adler [q.v.] and five other reform-minded citizens led by Nicholas Murray Butler of Columbia.

Chapin was a charter member of the American Pediatric Society and its president, 1910–11; chairman of the pediatric sections of the American Medical Association (1912–13) and of the New York Academy of Medicine (1913); and president of the Hospital Social Service Association of New York (1921). He was active in the Working Woman's Protective Union, the Havens Relief Society, the Life Saving Benevolent Association, and the Children's Welfare Federation. He remained a Presbyterian and in politics was a Republican.

Although his bright eyes, erect carriage, and springy step long gave Chapin the appearance of a young man whose thick hair was prematurely white, severe arteriosclerosis forced his gradual retirement in the late 1920's. By 1931 he had given up his New York City office, and he eventually surrendered even the pleasures of his beloved Century Club which, together with travel, vintage wines, and playing the violin, constituted the major indulgences allowed by the puritan conscience that dictated a life of service. In 1933 he was awarded the Columbia University Medal for "outstanding contributions to problems relating to the care of children and as a pioneer in hospital social service." He died at his home in Bronxville, N. Y., having suffered from chronic myocarditis for three years, and was buried in Kensico Cemetery, Valhalla, N. Y.

[The best general biographical sources are: Marshall C. Pease in Borden S. Veeder, ed., Pediatric Profiles (1957), which pictures Chapin well but is sometimes inaccurate in detail; Nat. Cyc. Am. Biog., XXXI, 439–41; and obituaries in N. Y. Times, June 28, 1942, and Am. Jour. of Diseases of Children, Sept. 1942. See also biographical sketch in Semi-Centennial Vol. of the Am. Pediatric Soc. (1938), p. 11; Am. Men of Sci. (6th ed., 1938); and Who Was Who in America, vol. II (1950). On his father, see ibid., vol. I (1942); and on the family background, Gilbert W. Chapin, The Chapin Book of Genealogical Data (2 vols., 1924). For Dr. Stephen Smith as Chapin's preceptor, see Chapin's Heredity and Child Culture (1922), pp. 212–13. Dates of his various positions were obtained from medical directories and from affiliations listed in his publications. Chapin's death record (N. Y. State Dept. of Health) confirms the date of his death. Chapin's writings include: reports of his hospital social service in Forum, Mar. 1894, Archives of Pediatrics, Apr. 1905, and Medical Record, Mar. 3, 1917 (see also Jour. Am. Medic. Assoc., July 23, 1921, pp. 279–82); an account of the area and people he served in "A Little Journey with Theodore Roosevelt," Outlook, Oct. 22, 1924; articles on schools and school reform in Forum, May 1895, North Am. Rev., Jan. 1896, and Outlook, Dec. 24, 1898 (see also Sol Cohen, Progressives and Urban School Reform: The Public Education Assoc. of N. Y. City, 1895–1954, 1964); "Milk—A Remarkable Food," North Am. Rev., May 17, 1907; "We Can Have a New World in Two Generations," Ladies' Home Jour., Nov. 1922; articles on the Speedwell plan in Survey, Oct. 26, 1918, and Jan. 15, 1926, and on adoption in American Mag., Nov. 1919, and Rev. of Revs., Aug. 1928. The N. Y. Times obituary of Chapin's wife, Feb. 21, 1964, contains information about their joint adoption efforts.]

PATRICIA SPAIN WARD

CHAPMAN, FRANK MICHLER (June 12, 1864–Nov. 15, 1945), ornithologist, was born in Englewood Township (later West Englewood), N. J., the younger of two children and only son of Lebbeus and Mary Augusta (Parkhurst) Chapman, both of English ancestry. His father, a Wall Street lawyer, gentleman farmer, and civic leader, was descended from Robert Chapman, one of the settlers of Saybrook, Conn., in 1635. His mother was known for her flower gardens and love of music. Growing up in the New Jersey countryside, Chapman became familiar with wildlife and developed a special interest in birds. He continued to live on the family farm until suburban encroachments in 1905 drove him first to Englewood and then to New York City, his home until his death.

Chapman's ten years at Englewood Academy (interrupted by a term at a school in Baltimore, where the family stayed following his father's death in 1876) comprised his only formal education. He graduated in 1880, and then took a job in the collection department of the American Exchange Bank of New York City. Despite advancement, he found the work dull and spent his free time in hunting or field study. He also made the acquaintance of other bird lovers and studied the works of John Burroughs, Alexander Wilson, Elliott Coues [*qq.v.*], and others. In the spring of 1884 he undertook his first systematic ornithological survey, observing and recording bird migrations and collecting specimens for the recently organized American Ornithologists' Union. His report received high praise, which strengthened his determination to become an ornithologist; his growing contacts with naturalists of the Linnaean Society, the first Audubon Society, and the American Ornithologists' Union (of which he was elected an associate member in 1885 and a fellow in 1888) confirmed his resolve.

Resigning from the bank in 1886, Chapman went to Gainesville, Fla., to conduct his first intensive study in the field. Upon returning home the following summer, he took his notes and specimens to the American Museum of Natural History in New York to obtain help in identification. His enthusiasm for the work brought him a part-time job there, cataloguing his own and other collections. He became a regular staff member in 1888 when he was made an assistant to Joel A. Allen, head of the department of mammalogy and ornithology. Chapman retained his connection with the museum for the rest of his professional life, becoming associate curator in the department in 1901, curator of birds in 1908, and in 1920 chairman of the newly created department of birds, a post he held until his retirement in 1942.

Chapman instituted a number of innovations during his first decade at the museum. His early duties, identifying and cataloguing the specimens in the bird collections, gave him a comprehensive education in ornithological taxonomy. To make the exhibits more interesting to the public, he regrouped the specimens in separate displays of the birds to be found near New York City and in other geographical areas. He broadened his knowledge by a series of winter field trips to Florida, the Caribbean islands, Mexico, and Central and South America, which added to the museum's collections and provided material for a number of technical papers and books.

During this period Chapman helped develop still photography as a tool of bird study, an effort reflected in his *Bird Studies with a Camera* (1900) and *Camps and Cruises of an Ornithologist* (1908). He also began experimenting in 1907 with motion pictures. Both forms of photography proved useful in the popular lectures he had begun to give at the museum and in the schools. Further to stimulate public interest and concern, in 1899 Chapman founded and for thirty-six years edited the popular magazine *Bird-Lore,* "for the study and protection of birds." He took an active part in the campaign against the millinery trade that was destroying birds by the million for skins and plumes to use on women's hats, and throughout his life he continued to work for the conservation of birdlife, the enactment of protective laws, and the creation of bird sanctuaries. Never before had a professional ornithologist devoted so much time and effort to public education.

During his second decade at the American Museum, Chapman made further improvements in the public exhibits. His major innovation was the "habitat group"—mounted birds shown in natural attitudes in a lifelike reproduction of their actual habitat against an expertly painted background. The groups were so successful that the museum asked him to furnish an entire hall with habitat groups of North American birds and animals. These set a world standard for museum displays.

Traveling widely in search of habitat settings, Chapman gave increasing attention to the problem of life zones: the marked differences in bird populations in different geographical areas. He was particularly interested in the life zones in the Andes mountains of South America, and in his many exploring and collecting trips determined that the boundaries there were fixed primarily by altitude. On his South American expeditions he also discovered many new species, which provided subjects for the splendid talents of his friend Louis Agassiz Fuertes, the bird painter. After the United States entered World War I, Chapman's familiarity with the South American peoples led to his appointment with the Red Cross (1917–19) as director of its publications bureau and later as a special commissioner to Latin America.

Chapman possessed unusual skill in writing. In addition to his many technical papers, he wrote popular articles that appeared frequently in *Bird-Lore,* and in such magazines as *Popular Science Monthly,* the *National Geographic,* and the *Century.* Of his eighteen books, some of the more important are: *Handbook of Birds of Eastern North America* (1895), *The Warblers of North America* (1907), *The Distribution of Bird-Life in Colombia* (1917), and *The Distribution of Bird-Life in Ecuador* (1926). His autobiographical works include *My Tropical Air Castle* (1929) and *Autobiography of a Bird-Lover* (1933). His last book, *Life in an Air Castle* (1938), was written at his winter retreat on the island of Barro Colorado in Gatun Lake, Panama Canal Zone, and was an appropriate culmination to his career. In no other book does he express such a degree of serenity, and in no other does he write so well. The last chapter, "The Big Almendro," exhibits to the full the vital enthusiasm, humorous empathy, and devotion to scientific inquiry which Chapman brought to his long study of nature, and which made him in the early decades of the twentieth century her best-known professional champion.

Chapman was the first recipient (1912) of the medal of the Linnaean Society of New York (which he also served as president), and of the Elliot Medal (1917) of the National Academy of Sciences, which elected him to membership in 1921. His other honors include the Roosevelt Medal "for distinguished service" (1928), the John Burroughs Medal for nature writing (1929), and the Brewster Medal (1933) of the American Ornithologists' Union, of which he was president in 1911.

On Feb. 24, 1898, Chapman married Fannie (Bates) Embury, a widow with four children, who served as an expert assistant to her husband on his many collecting expeditions. The marriage produced one son, Frank Michler, who became a concert singer. Chapman throughout his career enjoyed the affection and respect of his associates, even though they recognized his basic shyness, his idiosyncrasies, his minor prejudices. A Presbyterian, a staunch Republican (although he followed his admired friend Roosevelt into the

Bull Moose camp), Chapman was also an unabashed Anglophile, seeing great hope in the English-Speaking Union and admiring the works of empire, British or American. He was below average height, but trim and endowed with notable inner strength, as the wide-ranging explorations, intellectual accomplishments, and public activities of his long life attest. He died in New York City in his eighty-second year, of uremic poisoning, and was buried at Brookside Cemetery, Englewood, N. J.

[The Dept. of Ornithology of the Am. Museum of Natural Hist., N. Y. City, has many of Chapman's notebooks, as well as some correspondence and book MSS. Another primary source is Elizabeth S. Austin's edition of certain journals and letters: *Frank M. Chapman in Fla.* (1967), useful for information and insight into his personality and augmenting the *Autobiog.* Additional popular books by Chapman are *The Travels of Birds* (1916), *Our Winter Birds* (1918), and *What Bird Is That?* (1920). A nearly complete listing of his publications accompanies the memoir by William K. Gregory in Nat. Acad. Sci., *Biog. Memoirs,* vol. XXV (1948); see also Austin (above), pp. 177–87. No full biography exists. Perceptive accounts by associates are those of Robert Cushman Murphy in the *Auk,* July 1950, and Ludlow Griscom in *Audubon Mag.,* Jan.–Feb. 1946 (both with portraits); interesting notes and photographs appear in Robert S. Lemmon's memoir in *Audubon Mag.,* Nov.–Dec. 1953. There are sections dealing with Chapman in Henry C. Tracy, *Am. Naturists* (1930); Donald C. Peattie, *A Gathering of Birds* (1939); Geoffrey T. Hellman, *How to Disappear for an Hour* (1947); and Victor W. von Hagen, *The Green World of the Naturalists* (1948). Hellman gives further Chapman anecdotes in his *Bankers, Bones & Beetles: The First Century of the Am. Museum of Natural Hist.* (1968). See also: *Who's Who in America,* various issues, 1899–1947; *Am. Men of Sci.* (1st through 7th eds.); *Nat. Cyc. Am. Biog.,* XXXVI, 23; and obituaries in *N. Y. Times* and *N. Y. Herald Tribune,* Nov. 17, 1945, and, for Mrs. Chapman, *N. Y. Times,* Sept. 23, 1944.]

ROBERT H. WELKER

CHITTENDEN, RUSSELL HENRY (Feb. 18, 1856–Dec. 26, 1943), biochemist, was born in New Haven, Conn., the only child of Horace Horatio and Emily Eliza (Doane) Chittenden. His father, a superintendent in a clothing factory, was descended from an old Connecticut family, the first member having migrated from Kent, England, in 1639. Russell attended local public and private schools and, since his family was of modest means, earned part of his expenses by factory work, gardening, and tutoring. He had hoped for a career in medicine, but, learning that he lacked adequate training in science, he enrolled in the Sheffield Scientific School at Yale, where he concentrated in chemistry. After his first year he was appointed a laboratory assistant, and in 1875 he graduated with the Ph.B. degree. His senior thesis (which reported his research on the chemical composition of mollusks) was published in condensed form in the *American Journal of*

Science in 1875 and in German translation in Liebig's *Annalen der Chemie.*

During his senior year Chittenden had been given responsibility for a newly created laboratory course in physiological chemistry (or biochemistry, as the field later became known), the first such course in America. This he continued to teach after graduation. In 1878 he went to Germany for a year, planning to study physiological chemistry in the Strassburg laboratory of the famous Felix Hoppe-Seyler, but, disappointed with the antiquated and overcrowded facilities he found on his arrival there, he moved to Heidelberg, where he was accepted in the laboratory of the physiologist Wilhelm (Willy) Kühne. There he attended Robert Bunsen's lectures on chemistry, took courses in anatomy and pathology, carried out physiological research, and for a time served as Kühne's assistant in lecture demonstrations.

Upon his return to Yale, Chittenden, while continuing to teach, completed the requirements for the Ph.D., which was granted in 1880. In 1882 he was appointed to the newly founded professorship of physiological chemistry in the Sheffield Scientific School. He rapidly built up the laboratory for instruction in this field, which was pursued by graduate students in chemistry as well as by medical students. By the mid-1890's as many as two hundred students were enrolled in Chittenden's lecture course, and by 1900 eleven students, including Lafayette B. Mendel [Supp. 1] and Yandell Henderson [Supp. 3], had earned the Ph.D. in his laboratory.

Chittenden's principal research up to 1890 dealt with the chemical nature of proteins. His earliest studies were made in collaboration with Kühne; the two discussed their work by correspondence and published their findings, jointly signed, in German and American scientific journals. An enormous amount of work was done on enzymatic splitting of proteins and analysis of fragments. Unfortunately, protein chemistry was then still in a very rudimentary state, and the work had little lasting importance; it did, however, contribute to an eventual understanding of the complexity of protein molecules. Parallel with the early protein work were studies on the enzymatic digestion of starch, particularly the role of acid and alkaline conditions in enzyme action. Of some interest also was Chittenden's isolation of papain, a protein-splitting enzyme obtained from pineapple.

Through his work on enzymes Chittenden had developed an interest in the general problem of nutrition, which led to some of his most important research, that on the protein requirements of man. At the beginning of the twentieth century, most experts in human nutrition advocated a diet high in caloric value and containing ample protein; the German chemist Carl von Voit recommended 118 grams of protein daily. In 1902 Chittenden learned of the dietary theories of Horace Fletcher [*q.v.*], a wealthy American businessman who, in his books and health lectures, advocated lengthy chewing of food. Chittenden invited him to New Haven, where Fletcher cooperated in physical fitness and physiological tests. Quickly discounting the mastication theory, Chittenden was nonetheless impressed with Fletcher's low-calorie diet, particularly the small amount of protein. With substantial financial aid from Fletcher and from the Carnegie Institution, the National Academy of Sciences, and private sources, Chittenden embarked upon extensive studies of low-protein diets, utilizing army volunteers and Yale athletes as subjects. He himself lowered his daily protein intake to about forty grams and claimed he was improved in health. His volunteers were maintained in good physical condition on 2,600 calories and fifty grams of protein per day. The results were presented in Chittenden's *Physiological Economy in Nutrition* (1904).

Chittenden's enthusiasm for a low-protein diet was viewed skeptically in many quarters, particularly by British and German authorities. To answer their criticisms, he undertook studies on dogs, which supported his conviction that such a diet had no ill effects, even in carnivorous animals. A critical analysis throws considerable doubt on the soundness of his conclusions, since the animals showed a deterioration in health following an extended time on the diet, and since he reported results on only six of the twenty animals under study. Animal feeding studies in other laboratories were beginning to reveal that proteins varied in nutritional composition and that the problem was more complicated than Chittenden had supposed. He defended his position in his book *The Nutrition of Man* (1907), and retained his enthusiasm for the low-protein diet during the rest of his life. Although nutrition experts eventually abandoned the high protein requirement set by Voit, they did not adopt the low figure supported by Chittenden.

In 1898 Chittenden was made director of the Sheffield Scientific School at Yale, and in 1904 he became treasurer as well, an office of considerable financial responsibility. Thereafter he carried out relatively little research of his own, although he continued to direct the work of others; and though he taught lecture courses until 1916, the direction of the laboratory fell to his pupil Mendel. During his twenty-four years as director, Chittenden greatly expanded both the faculty and the physical facilities of the Sheffield School, as an entity largely independent of Yale College. The two schools became "rival baronies," and in the resulting struggle for power, Chittenden's "aggressive and obstinate determination" (Henderson, p. 378) earned him the name of "little Napoleon." Budgetary problems, however, combined with dissatisfaction over the Sheffield School's lack of coordination with the college and the graduate school, brought a reorganization of the university after World War I, and when Chittenden retired in 1922, the school was effectively discontinued. Most of its courses were substantially integrated with those of the college, although the biochemistry courses that Chittenden had established were moved to the medical school.

Chittenden's position as dean of American biochemistry brought him a variety of responsibilities beyond the campus. He had early done work of some importance in toxicology, and this led to his appointment to the "Committee of Fifty," set up in 1893—in reaction against the campaign of the Woman's Christian Temperance Union for "scientific temperance instruction" in the schools [see Mary Hannah Hanchett Hunt]—to investigate the effects of alcohol on the human body. The results of his experiments, which showed that many of the harmful effects ascribed to alcohol were not confirmed in the laboratory, were incorporated in *Physiological Aspects of the Liquor Problem,* a two-volume work published by the committee in 1903. In 1908 Chittenden was made a member of the Referee Board of Consulting Scientific Experts appointed by Secretary of Agriculture James Wilson [*q.v.*] to help resolve differences of opinion between Harvey W. Wiley [*q.v.*], who had charge of enforcing the Pure Food and Drug Act of 1906, and members of the food industry, who wished to continue the use of preservatives and other food additives. After careful experiments with human volunteers, the board decided that small amounts of benzoates, sulfites, aluminum, and saccharin were without harm, but that copper salts had adverse effects. There was considerable public dissatisfaction with the conclusions of the Referee Board, and in 1915 it was quietly discontinued. During World War I, Chittenden served on the executive committee of the National Research Council. He was also called upon, along with Graham Lusk [Supp. 1], to represent the United States on an Inter-Allied Scientific Food Commission, which met in Europe early in 1918 to discuss minimum food requirements for the allied nations.

As one of the founders of the science of bio-

chemistry in America, Chittenden helped organize the American Society of Biological Chemists in 1906 and served as its first president. He was president of the American Physiological Society from 1895 to 1904. Five universities, including Yale, honored him with doctoral degrees, and he was elected to the National Academy of Sciences in 1890, at the early age of thirty-four.

Chittenden was a short, thin man (little more than five feet tall) with dark, penetrating eyes and a pointed black beard which turned gray only in his last years. Always neatly dressed, he gave an impression of self-confidence coupled with a reserve which prevented even close associates from becoming familiar with him. He worked very hard and expected hard work from his students and associates. An inspired teacher rather than a great experimenter, he was able to engender enthusiasm for his subject, and his laboratory supplied virtually a whole generation of biochemists in American institutions.

Chittenden was married to Gertrude Louise Baldwin on June 20, 1877. Their children were Edith Russell, Alfred Knight, and Lilla Millard (who married the Yale pharmacologist and physiologist Henry Gray Barbour [Supp. 3]). Mrs. Chittenden died in 1922, the year that her husband retired from active faculty duties. His remaining years were occupied primarily with historical writings, leading to his *History of the Sheffield Scientific School of Yale University, 1846–1922* (2 vols., 1928), *The Development of Physiological Chemistry in the United States* (1930), and *The First Twenty-five Years of the American Society of Biological Chemists* (1945). In his last years Chittenden suffered from arteriosclerotic heart disease. He died in the New Haven Hospital of bronchopneumonia at the age of eighty-seven and was buried in Evergreen Cemetery, New Haven.

[The Yale Univ. Lib. has several boxes of Chittenden's papers, including a MS. autobiography, "Sixty Years of Service in Science." There is also much autobiographical material in his books mentioned above. Hubert B. Vickery is the author of an excellent short biography in Nat. Acad. Sci., *Biog. Memoirs,* vol. XXIV (1947), which also carries an almost complete bibliography of Chittenden's published works. There are lengthy obituaries by Howard B. Lewis in *Jour. of Biological Chemistry,* May 1944, G. R. Cowgill in *Jour. of Nutrition,* July 1944, and Yandell Henderson in Am. Philosophical Soc., *Year Book,* 1943; and a short sketch by Graham Lusk in *Industrial and Engineering Chemistry,* Jan. 1929. See also George W. Pierson, *Yale: College and University, 1871–1937* (2 vols., 1952–55); and Virginia M. Schelar, "Protein Digestion, the Protein Requirement in Nutrition, and Food Additives: The Contribution of Russell H. Chittenden" (Ph.D. thesis, Univ. of Wis., 1969). Death record from Conn. State Dept. of Health.]

AARON J. IHDE

CHRISTIE, JOHN WALTER (May 6, 1865–Jan. 11, 1944), inventor and tank designer, was born in River Edge, N. J., the first son and second of four children of Jacob and Eliza (Van Houten) Christie. Both parents were of Dutch stock. Little is known of Christie's early life. At the age of sixteen he went to work in New York City at the Delamater Iron Works of Cornelius H. Delamater [q.v.], which had built the engines for the famous Civil War ironclad the *Monitor,* and in 1881 was completing the first successful submarine of John P. Holland [q.v.]. While working, Christie attended evening classes at Cooper Union. He later became a consulting engineer for several steamship lines, including Ward Lines, with which he was connected at the time of the Spanish-American War. After the war he developed and patented a ring-turning lathe which provided a stronger turret track for naval guns.

Soon after the turn of the century Christie entered the youthful automotive field. As was common at that period, he built cars of his own design and tested them in automobile races. In 1904 he began promoting a front-wheel-drive car he had designed. Over the next six years, operating in the same racing circles as Louis Chevrolet, Barney Oldfield, and other notables, Christie competed for the Vanderbilt Cup and the French Grand Prix and drove on American speedways at Daytona, Indianapolis, and elsewhere. During the same period he also invented and marketed a unique steam-engine piston-packing ring which was used for years in ferryboat engines. In 1912 Christie began to manufacture wheeled tractors to pull steam pumpers and other types of fire-fighting equipment; his sales to the New York City fire department amounted to nearly 200.

When this business declined, Christie in 1916 entered the field of military ordnance. During the border disputes with Mexico he introduced a four-wheel-drive truck designed to operate in the rugged terrain of the border area. The Army Ordnance Department that year contracted with Christie's Front Drive Motor Company for one of his motor carriages as the base for a self-propelled three-inch antiaircraft gun.

Christie took an active part in the development of tanks and other armored vehicles during and after World War I. Between 1916 and 1924 he built fifteen such vehicles for the army. His most important innovation was the convertible principle, which permitted the vehicles to travel either with or without tracks by utilizing a single suspension system and larger rubber-tired wheels; this revolutionary feature reduced the problems of short track life and eliminated the need for tank carriers. Nevertheless, none of Christie's armored vehicles was judged successful enough to be regularly adopted by the army. Turning to amphibious armaments, he produced an amphibious gun carriage which was successfully demonstrated on the Hudson and Potomac rivers in 1922 and 1923. This evolved into the first American-built tracked landing vehicle; but tests off Puerto Rico in 1924 found the vehicle unsatisfactory, the military rejected it, and the plans were sold to the Japanese government.

Late in 1928 Christie introduced a convertible tank chassis, the M 1928, which marked a milestone in tank design. The most notable feature was a new independent suspension system which permitted the tank to remain more nearly level when passing over obstacles or rough terrain, thus providing a more stable gun platform. The Christie suspension system also greatly enhanced the vehicle's speed, enabling the M 1928 to achieve 42 miles an hour with its tracked tread as against 18 miles an hour for existing army tanks. The army purchased seven Christie tanks from the inventor's Wheel Track Layer Corporation of Linden, N. J., in 1931, and subsequently purchased five Christie-type tanks from the American LaFrance Company. Under a patent contract with Christie, the Ordnance Department also built approximately twenty Christie-type vehicles at its Rock Island Arsenal. By 1939, however, the army had dropped the Christie system, with its long vertical helicoid springs positioned between two metal plates, in favor of the less expensive and commercially available vertical volute spring suspension system.

Christie's lack of success with the Army Ordnance Department stemmed in part from his personality. He was a rugged individualist with stubborn and impetuous qualities scarcely conducive to harmonious relations with the army officials with whom he dealt. Moreover, his tank ideas, the product of empirical application, did not conform well to contemporary military specifications, at a time when the new scientific management approach was being applied to arms development.

Christie's tank designs found greater acceptance outside the United States. Soviet observers, impressed by the demonstration of the M 1928, purchased two Christie tank chassis in 1930 and two years later purchased the turretless M 1932 "Flying Tank," a lightweight model designed by Christie to be fastened to the underside of an airplane and airlifted to the battle zone. The Christie tanks were the beginning of the Soviet BT series which evolved into one of the most effective tanks of World War II, the T-34. Impressed with the Soviet use of the Christie system, the British purchased from the American tank designer in October 1936 a 1930–31 model; the result was a long series of Christie-type cruiser tanks which effectively served the British army during the war.

Christie had consistently put his earnings into further developments of his inventions. At the time of his death, in the midst of World War II, he was penniless and bitter. He died in Falls Church, Va., of chronic myocarditis, at the age of seventy-eight and was buried in South Hackensack, N. J. Christie had married Elizabeth Law on Oct. 14, 1897. He was survived by his second wife, Jeanette D. Bennington, whom he had married in 1940, and a son, John Edward, adopted in 1920.

[Manuscript sources dealing with Christie's relationship with the military are at the Nat. Archives, Washington, D. C. (in the Chief of Arms Records), and at the Washington Nat. Record Center, Suitland, Md. (Chief of Ordnance General Correspondence Files). Both sources served as the bases for the author's "Rejection of Christie's Armored Fighting Vehicles" (M.A. thesis, Univ. of Cincinnati, 1970). There is a fair amount of published material dealing with Christie's career. The most reliable accounts are Ralph E. Jones et al., *The Fighting Tanks since 1916* (1933), which covers the design aspects of Christie's vehicles; and Arthur L. Homan and Keith Marvin, "Not Without Honor: An Account of the Life and Times of John Walter Christie," *Antique Automobile*, May, July 1965. See also *N. Y. Times* obituary, Jan. 12, 1944.]

GEORGE F. HOFMANN

CLAPPER, RAYMOND LEWIS (May 30, 1892–Feb. 1, 1944), newspaper columnist, was born on a farm in Linn County, Kans., near La Cygne, the only child of Julia (Crowe) and John William Clapper. He disliked his middle name and did not use it. His father, of Pennsylvania German ancestry, had ventured from Pennsylvania via Indiana to Kansas, where he married a local girl. John Clapper's small acreage proved unrewarding, and soon after Raymond's birth he moved his family to the Armourdale packinghouse section of Kansas City, Kans., where he worked in a soap factory. The enterprising boy grew up in an unlettered, intensely religious atmosphere, kindly but narrow, that included faithful attendance at Baptist services. By the age of eleven he was delivering groceries and peddling papers. An avid reader who organized an extensive file of clippings, he was drawn by his admiration for the Kansas editor William Allen White [Supp. 3] to the local print shop as its "devil," moved up to apprentice, and became a union journeyman. At seventeen he entered high school, but he did not complete the course.

On Mar. 31, 1913, Clapper married Olive Vincent Ewing. That autumn the bride and groom walked to Lawrence and enrolled in the University of Kansas. While his wife taught piano, Clapper worked at odd jobs, edited the college paper, and sent campus news to the *Kansas City Star*. In 1916, after three years in college and a brief stint on the *Star*, he joined the United Press in Chicago, where he and his wife lived at the Chicago settlement of Graham Taylor [Supp. 2].

Clapper's employment with the United Press took him in fast succession to Milwaukee, St. Paul, New York, and finally Washington. His first national news scoop came during the Republican National Convention of 1920 when Senator Charles Curtis [Supp. 2] emerged from the celebrated "smoke-filled room" and told his fellow Kansan that the party leaders were going to try to swing the nomination to Harding. Clapper soaked up national politics as night manager and chief political writer for the United Press in Washington (1923–28) and as bureau manager (1929–33). He also covered the Scopes "evolution" trial in 1925 and the London naval conference of 1930. Outraged by nepotism, graft, and waste of public funds, he gathered instances in a book, *Racketeering in Washington* (1933).

Clapper had thick, tousled hair, a beaklike nose, and gray, circled eyes. His head jutted forward from his shortish, slightly stooped body, visually suggesting his inquiring way of life. In September 1934, a year after he had left the United Press to join the *Washington Post*, he began a daily interpretive column, "Between You and Me." The feature caught on, and in December he accepted a proposal to write a similar column for the Scripps-Howard chain. Nine years later he was appearing in 176 papers and had an estimated ten million readers. He also wrote magazine articles, took up platform speaking, and entered into lucrative contracts for radio broadcasting, especially on the Mutual network. A political independent and an admirer of Emerson, he called himself a progressive Republican and "seventy-five percent New Dealer," supporting Roosevelt's attack on the economic collapse but opposing a third presidential term. His column, however, was widely respected for its fairness and objectivity. In 1939 he was elected president of the Gridiron Club, composed of Washington colleagues.

Regretting that he had resisted the urge to enlist during World War I, Clapper conscientiously followed the events leading toward World War II. At first an isolationist, he felt after Munich that conflict, with American involvement, was probably inevitable and after the fall of France took the interventionist side. He called Pearl Harbor "the result of our folly" in abandoning the Pacific to Japan. Becoming a traveling war correspondent, he reported the attack on Sicily and the bombing of Rome and late in 1943 headed into the South Pacific to write from New Britain, New Guinea, and Guadalcanal. During the invasion of the Marshall Islands, while he was reporting the devastation of the airfield at Eniwetok, his plane hit another American bomber and crashed in flames in the Eniwetok lagoon, killing all on board. His friends established the Raymond Clapper Memorial Association with an annual award to a Washington correspondent whose writings "have most perfectly embodied the ideals of fair and painstaking reporting and sound craftsmanship that marked Mr. Clapper's work." The first recipient was Clapper's fellow war correspondent Ernie Pyle [Supp. 3]. Olive Clapper, a lecturer and author, survived him with their daughter, Janet Ewing, and son, William Raymond (known as Peter). Mrs. Clapper edited a collection of her husband's later work, *Watching the World* (1944), which reflected his purpose of writing for the "milkman in Omaha" and his basic conviction that a newspaper correspondent "should be careful not to overestimate the information of the readers or to underestimate their intelligence."

[Mrs. Clapper wrote a detailed biographical sketch of her husband for *Watching the World,* which contains an introduction by Ernie Pyle and many photographs. See also: *Current Biog.,* 1940; Charles Fisher, *The Columnists* (1944); Leo C. Rosten, *The Washington Correspondents* (1937); Otto Fuerbringer, "Average Man's Columnist," *Saturday Evening Post,* Nov. 6, 1943, reprinted in John E. Drewry, ed., *More Post Biographies* (1947); Thomas L. Stokes and Dick Fitzpatrick, "A Reporter—First, Last and Always," *Quill,* Mar.–Apr. 1944; *Editor & Publisher,* Feb. 1944; newspapers generally following his death, especially the *N. Y. Times, N. Y. World-Telegram,* and *Kansas City Star.* Date of death and certain other facts from Mrs. Clapper and others through personal acquaintance. Clapper's papers are in the Lib. of Cong.]

IRVING DILLIARD

CLARKE, JOHN HESSIN (Sept. 18, 1857–Mar. 22, 1945), lawyer, progressive politician, and associate justice of the United States Supreme Court, was born in New Lisbon (later Lisbon), Ohio, the youngest of the three children and only son of John and Melissa (Hessin) Clarke. His ancestry was Protestant Irish, both his maternal grandfather and his father having emigrated from the north of Ireland. His father, a lawyer, sometime prosecuting attorney and judge, and vestryman of the Episcopal church, was one of the respected men of the community. He encouraged in his son a lifelong habit of reading, an interest in the law, and a sense of civic responsibility. Clarke was educated in the local elementary and high schools and attended Western Reserve College (then located in Hudson, Ohio), from which he

graduated in 1877. Continuing under his father's guidance the study of law he had begun as a senior, he passed the Ohio bar examinations cum laude in the fall of 1878. After two years of practice in New Lisbon, he moved to the larger arena of Youngstown, Ohio.

In Youngstown, Clarke rapidly became known as an outstanding trial lawyer in the area of corporation law, but his interests led him in many directions. He labored hard for the public library, lectured on Shakespeare and other poets, and became a part owner of the *Youngstown Vindicator,* for which he wrote editorials and an occasional column. He early entered local politics, choosing the Democratic party not only because of inherited allegiance but also because he shared the beliefs of its liberal wing in honest government, low tariffs, and civil service reform. His political rise was interrupted, however, in 1896 when he left the party to join the Gold Democrats in opposing Bryan and free silver. The next year he accepted a call to Cleveland, Ohio, to become a partner in the law office of Samuel E. Williamson and William E. Cushing. As trial lawyer for the firm, and later as general counsel of the Nickel Plate Railroad and regional counsel for the Erie Railroad and the Pullman Company, he became a specialist in all aspects of railroad law.

The debate over imperialism brought Clarke back into politics in 1900, this time as an anti-imperialist supporter of Bryan, and he soon joined the circle of Tom L. Johnson [*q.v.*], Cleveland's brilliant Democratic reform mayor (1901–09). Broadening his outlook, Clarke shared the faith of these progressive Democrats in reforms to democratize government, to eliminate the abuses of bossism and big business, and to aid labor. He found nothing incompatible in serving both the legitimate interests of the railroads he represented and the cause of progressivism; as he was to repeat many times, he voted his conscience, not his pocketbook. His intellectual honesty and courage in pursuing his convictions, his oratorical skill, and his commanding presence enhanced his political stature. In 1903 he was the Democratic nominee for United States Senator but was defeated in a Republican landslide. Drifting temporarily from the Johnson reformers, he supported the able but conservative Democratic governor Judson Harmon in 1908 and 1910. By 1913, having retired from his law practice, he was reunited with the Johnsonian Democrats through the help of Newton D. Baker [Supp. 2], successor to the now deceased Cleveland mayor, and he received their endorsement for the Senatorial race of 1914. That July, however, rather than face a hard fight in both the primary and the general elections,

Clarke accepted an appointment as judge of the federal district court of the Northern District of Ohio. Two years later President Wilson elevated him to the United States Supreme Court.

In his six years on the Supreme bench, Clarke wrote 129 opinions and 23 dissents. His fellow justices, with the exception of James C. McReynolds, liked and respected him. Clarke's decisions reflect his inborn humanitarianism, his acquired progressive beliefs, and his emotional dislike of violent change or extreme radicalism. He supported a broad extension of national and state power over the economy to aid labor, on the one hand, and to curb business malpractices and to prosecute the trusts, on the other. His opinion in *United States* v. *Reading Company* (253 U.S. 26 [1920]) revived the strong antitrust tradition of the Northern Securities (1904) and Union Pacific (1912) cases and served as a basic precedent for antitrust actions under the New Deal. His position on civil liberties was ambivalent. He took a liberal stance in protecting the rights of individuals against encroachment by overzealous public officials and in upholding the right of persons to a fair trial, as is borne out in his dissent in *Schaefer* v. *United States* (251 U.S. 466, 495 [1920]). But he held to a conservative stance in supporting the suppression of speech which had a tendency to subvert the established order or to impede America's military effort in the First World War. His opinion in the Abrams case (250 U.S. 616 [1919])—from which Brandeis and Holmes dissented—is the best-known example.

Never marrying, Clarke lived during his Youngstown years with his two sisters, to whom he always remained close. Their deaths of heart failure, one year apart, brought on a severe mental depression, and this, combined with fears for his own health, caused him to resign from the Supreme Court in September 1922 at the age of sixty-five. Within six weeks, however, he was able to shake off his melancholia by becoming immersed in a cause which deeply concerned him but in which he could not participate from the bench, namely, America's entry into the League of Nations. In the fall of 1922 he was persuaded to head the new committee which that December became the League of Nations Non-Partisan Association. As its president for five years he spoke and wrote for the "Great Cause," contributed financially to its support, and gave his own services without pay.

In 1931, troubled by respiratory ailments, Clarke moved to San Diego, Calif., where he remained for the rest of his life. He did what he could by his pen and purse to promote the candidacy of his most devoted friend, Newton D. Baker, for

the Democratic nomination for president in 1932. On Mar. 22, 1937, Clarke emerged from retirement to make a nationwide radio address supporting the constitutionality of the so-called "court-packing" bill of President Franklin D. Roosevelt, whose New Deal program he much admired. Although reluctant to see the two-term tradition broken, he continued to vote for Roosevelt in 1940 and again in 1944 because he agreed with the President's prewar and wartime policies. Clarke died in San Diego of a heart attack before the war ended; his body was cremated and buried in the Lisbon (Ohio) Cemetery. Although naturally religious and feeling a kinship with the Unitarians, he had shied away from any formal church affiliation. He left two major bequests: one of $100,000 to the public library in Youngstown, the other of about $1,500,000 (the residue of his estate) to Adelbert College, the undergraduate unit for men of Western Reserve University in Cleveland, which he had served as a trustee. Clarke's career had been a testament to the power of the American liberal tradition and the proposition that the man of business and politics can live by such ideals and have his reward.

[Primary sources: Clarke Papers, Western Reserve Univ. Lib.; Newton D. Baker Papers, Lib. of Cong., 1921–37; files of *Youngstown Vindicator* and of *Cleveland Plain Dealer* after 1897; publications of the League of Nations Non-Partisan Assoc., 1922–27, supplemented by the *N. Y. Times*. Secondary sources: David M. Levitan, "The Jurisprudence of Mr. Justice Clarke," *Miami Law Quart.*, Dec. 1952; Carl Wittke, "Mr. Justice Clarke in Retirement," *Western Reserve Law Rev.*, June 1949; Hoyt Landon Warner, *The Life of Mr. Justice Clarke* (1959).]

HOYT LANDON WARNER

CLEMENTS, FREDERIC EDWARD (Sept. 16, 1874–July 26, 1945), botanist and pioneer ecologist, was born in Lincoln, Nebr., the oldest of three children and only son of Ephraim George Clements by his first wife, Mary Angeline Scoggin. His father, son of an immigrant from Somerset, England, had left Marcellus, N. Y., his birthplace, to settle in Lincoln, where he maintained a photographer's studio. Growing up in the prairie province of the Great Plains, Frederic Clements entered the University of Nebraska at the age of sixteen, graduated, B.Sc., in 1894, and stayed on for graduate study in botany (M.A. 1896, Ph.D. 1898). On May 30, 1899, he married Edith Gertrude Schwartz, a recent alumna of the university, who took a Ph.D. in botany in 1904. They had no children.

At the University of Nebraska, Clements encountered some remarkable young people, including the future author Willa Cather, the future economist Alvin Johnson, and Roscoe Pound, later a renowned legal scholar and dean of the Harvard Law School but at this time a botanist. Present, too, was one of the great American teachers of botany, Charles E. Bessey [*q.v.*], who had developed good laboratory instruction and a superb library. Here in 1895 American plant geography began as Pound read Oscar Drude's *Handbuch der Pflanzengeographie* (1890) and went on to the close collaboration in field work with Clements that produced a classic pioneer study, *The Phytogeography of Nebraska* (1898).

For ten years, beginning in 1897, Clements taught botany at Nebraska, becoming full professor in 1905. He left in 1907 to head the botany department at the University of Minnesota. In 1917 he gave up teaching to become a research associate of the Carnegie Institution of Washington, working in Tucson, Ariz., until 1925, when he transferred to the Institution's Coastal Laboratory at Santa Barbara, Calif. Throughout this time his summers were spent at its Alpine Laboratory (which he founded) on Pikes Peak in Colorado.

At the time Clements began his career, America had long lagged behind Europe in the science of botany, save for the systematic study of flowering plants. With extraordinary zeal Clements attempted to tackle such diverse fields as the enormous group of fungi and, less propitiously, plant physiology, which was then taking shape under Charles R. Barnes [*q.v.*] at Chicago. Barnes's scathing review of Clements's small volume *Plant Physiology and Ecology* (1907) was undoubtedly a cause of lingering and unfair prejudice against Clements among some members of the profession. Added to this handicap was an impression Clements gave of aloofness, even coldness; this stemmed from his rigorous regimen of work and diet, enforced by a long-standing case of diabetes in a day before the discovery of insulin. Only by this means and through the constant devotion and assistance of his wife was Clements able to accomplish his monumental work in ecology.

Clements was one of the first, along with Henry C. Cowles [Supp. 2] at the University of Chicago, to appreciate the scientific importance of ecology—the study of life and environment—at a time when this study was looked on more or less tolerantly as a superficial emphasis on the obvious. He began on his own to master a range of languages, including Polish, although he had only a background of high school Latin. His motive was not only to acquire a key to foreign literature; he was convinced that the nascent field of ecology needed a precise terminology, which he proceeded to coin. This Clementsian system was at first resented, but much of it re-

mains basic. In 1916 appeared his great book *Plant Succession: An Analysis of the Development of Vegetation,* a work of profound scholarship enriched by his years of studying the development of plant communities in the field. Its essential thesis is that plant life has a tendency to occupy any available habitat, beginning with species that can endure the maximum impact of raw physical environment, and gradually moving toward a condition of relative equilibrium through a succession of species made possible as the community exerts increasing control of conditions. This idea was not original with Clements, as he takes pains to show by an impressive analysis of the historical literature. What he did was to formalize the concept, invest it with technical terms and a philosophical sweep, and enrich it with his own fund of field observations. Though supplemented and refined in later studies, *Plant Succession* remains the fundamental statement of the "Clementsian system."

In 1939 Clements collaborated with Victor E. Shelford, who had applied Cowles's methods of plant community study to animal communities, in writing a book on *Bio-ecology* to include both types of organisms. This greatly expanded the community concept. Clements had also developed improved methods for vegetation analysis especially suitable to grasslands. In the aftermath of the depression and drought of the 1930's, the severest effects of which were seen in the grassland region, he became a valued consultant in applied ecology as it concerned restoration of Western lands and land use policy in general. By thus including the effects of man on the land Clements helped round out the concept of ecology to apply to all forms of life in their relation to environment.

Meanwhile, both ecology and its sister science genetics were much concerned with the problem of variation. Mrs. Clements's doctoral thesis dealt with anatomical changes in leaves caused by environment, and Clements himself was deeply interested in the plasticity of plants under different conditions. This led him to the use of experimental transplants, moving plants into various environments and observing their structural responses. The botanist Stanley A. Cain, though disagreeing with these "Neo-Lamarckian concepts," hailed Clements as "a great ecologist of profound learning" (*Foundations of Plant Geography,* 1944).

Other botanists have found fault with aspects of Clements's theory of vegetation, particularly his concept that plant formation (the vegetation of a given area) is itself a living organism subject to growth, maturity, and decay; or what some regarded as his undue stress on climate at the expense of other factors in determining types of vegetation. The great British ecologist A. G. Tansley, himself among the early critics of Clementsian terminology, nonetheless concluded that Clements was "by far the greatest individual creator of the modern science of vegetation." A distinguished student of African ecology, John Phillips, has attested to the influence of Clements on that continent.

In physical appearance Frederic Clements was slender, erect, and active, in speech quick and cogent. Roscoe Pound remembered him as "thoroughly conscientious, possessed of high ideals, and devoutly religious," though not, apparently, in any formal sense, for he was not a churchgoer. He died in a Santa Barbara hospital at the age of seventy of uremia owing to nephrosclerosis. Following cremation, his ashes were returned to Lincoln, Nebr., for burial in the family plot.

[Obituaries and recollections of Clements by H. L. Shantz in *Ecology*, Oct. 1945, by A. G. Tansley in *Jour. of Ecology*, Feb. 1947, and by Raymond J. Pool, Roscoe Pound, and John Phillips in *Ecology*, Apr. 1954; personal communications from K. Forward, R. H. Moore, A. D. Stoesz, and L. D. Clements of Lincoln, Nebr., Mrs. Francis M. Smith of La Jolla, Calif., and Mrs. Clements; P. B. Sears, "Some Notes on the Ecology of Ecologists," *Sci. Monthly*, July 1956; death record from Calif. Bureau of Vital Statistics. Edith G. Clements, *Adventures in Ecology* (1960), deals with the lighter side of the couple's botanical travels. A collection of Clements's papers is at the Archives of Contemporary Hist. of the Univ. of Wyo.]

PAUL B. SEARS

COBB, IRVIN SHREWSBURY (June 23, 1876–Mar. 10, 1944), newspaperman, author, and humorist, was born in Paducah, Ky., the second of four children and elder of two sons of Joshua Clark Cobb and Manie (Saunders) Cobb. Both parents were descended from early settlers of Kentucky, his father's forebears having moved there from Vermont, his mother's from Virginia. Joshua Cobb had served in the Confederate Army. After the Civil War, with slight success, he engaged in the tobacco trade, conducted a steamboat business, and managed a river supply store in Paducah. The boy grew up in the large house of his maternal grandfather, Dr. Reuben Saunders. Another prominent figure of the town was Judge William Sutton Bishop, on whose front porch steps young Irvin would sit of an evening, listening to the talk of "elder statesmen, bragsters and gifted prevaricators" that laid an authentic basis for the regional characterizations in his later writings.

After elementary education in public and private schools, supplemented by appreciative reading of both the classics and dime novels, Irvin entered William A. Cade's academy in nearby Arcadia. He had hoped to study law, but when he was sixteen his grandfather died; his father was sunk in alcoholism, and the youth had to leave school to support the family. Given a job as a reporter on the *Paducah Daily News,* he became managing editor only three years later, at the same time serving as a correspondent for several large city newspapers, including the *Chicago Tribune.* In 1898 he worked briefly on the *Cincinnati Post,* and then on the *Louisville Evening Post,* for which he wrote political accounts and produced a humor column called "Sour Mash." He returned to Paducah in 1901 as managing editor of a new paper, the *Daily Democrat,* which soon merged with the *News.* Meanwhile, on June 12, 1900, he had married Laura Spencer Baker of Savannah, Ga., whom he had met when she visited a school friend in Paducah. They had one child, Elisabeth.

In August 1904, at the age of twenty-eight, Cobb went to New York City, where he managed to get on the *Evening Sun* just before his money ran out. His first major assignment was the Russo-Japanese peace conference in 1905. Avoiding routine matters, he developed a widely popular syndicated daily feature, "Making Peace at Portsmouth," whose brightness and novelty attracted attention in newspaper circles, and though he was not yet thirty, he was invited to join the *Evening* and *Sunday World* of Joseph Pulitzer [*q.v.*] as staff humorist. On the *World,* over the next six years, he produced a daily column, "Through Funny Glasses," prepared a page of humor for the Sunday color section, wrote the popular "Hotel Clerk" series, and composed humorous material for the McClure syndicate. The high point of this period was his coverage of the trial of Harry K. Thaw in 1907 for the murder of Stanford White [*q.v.*], about which he wrote some 600,000 words. In 1911 Cobb quit newspaper work to become a staff contributor to the *Saturday Evening Post;* he left the *Post* in 1922 to take a similar position on *Cosmopolitan* magazine, where he remained until 1932.

With the outbreak of World War I in August 1914, the *Saturday Evening Post* sent Cobb to Europe, where he was one of the earliest American correspondents to arrive. He traveled through France and Belgium and behind the lines in Germany. In early September he was one of five correspondents on the German side of the lines who wired a statement expressing skepticism about the much-rumored German atrocities against Belgian noncombatants. He returned to New York in 1915, but in 1917, after the United States entered the war, was again sent to the battlefronts, where he caught human interest details overlooked by most writers. Portly, homely, and always ready for a laugh, Cobb had gifts as a raconteur that made him welcome at every headquarters. His war experiences and impressions were collected in three books: *Paths of Glory* (1915), *"Speaking of Prussians—"* (1917), and *The Glory of the Coming* (1918).

Meanwhile the star reporter and war correspondent had become probably the most widely read short story writer of his time. "The Escape of Mr. Trimm," published in the *Saturday Evening Post* of Nov. 27, 1909, was followed by a stream of stories, often set in western Kentucky but not exclusively Southern in background, and published in the *Post*, the *Cosmopolitan*, and other magazines. His first collection of regional tales was *Back Home* (1912), which introduced Judge Priest, a gentle yet exceedingly sharp old Confederate veteran, fond of mint juleps but fonder of aiding innocents in trouble. The character became a favorite of magazine readers and appeared in several later volumes, including *J. Poindexter, Colored* (1922), which featured the judge's remarkable servant. Other collections of stories included *Local Color* (1916), *Sundry Accounts* (1922), *Red Likker* (1929), and *Faith, Hope and Charity* (1934). *Goin' on Fourteen* (1924) presented cross sections from a year in the life of a growing boy; *Alias Ben Alibi* (1925) recounted the exploits of a legendary city editor in New York; and *All Aboard* (1928) spun a romantic saga of the Tennessee River. Cobb related his own newspaper experiences in *Stickfuls* (1923). His story "Snake Doctor," published in *Cosmopolitan* in 1923, was awarded the $500 gold prize of the O. Henry Memorial Committee of the Society of Arts and Sciences. Cobb's books of humor attracted perhaps an even larger audience. One of the most amusing was *"Speaking of Operations—"* (1915), which sold more than 100,000 copies in its first year.

In his early New York days Cobb had also tried writing for the stage, beginning with the musical comedy *Funabashi* (1908), and his yen for the theatre accounted in part for his success as an after-dinner speaker and Chautauqua lecturer. He took severe losses in the stock market crash of 1929 and thereafter wrote few stories. In 1934, at the age of fifty-eight, he moved to Hollywood and entered the motion picture industry, both as a script writer and as an actor. His most notable role was the riverboat captain in *Steamboat Round the Bend* (1935), with Will Rogers [Supp. 1], who had earlier played a movie version of Judge Priest.

Cobb was a favorite subject for caricaturists, who scarcely needed to exaggerate his jutting eyebrows, heavy jowls, and triple chin, plus the jaunty cigar that was his trademark. The French government made him a chevalier in the Legion of Honor, and he received honorary degrees from the University of Georgia (1918), Dartmouth College (1919), and the University of Kentucky (1942). In politics he was a staunch Democrat of increasing conservatism. Cobb was sometimes irritable and hot-tempered, but was known for his generosity to those in want. He was a devotee of good living who took little exercise, although he liked fishing and hunting. In his early sixties his health declined, and in the autumn of 1943 he moved back to New York City. Ill of "dropsy," he died in his hotel apartment a few months later. He left explicit instructions that his funeral should be "kept cheerful," that it should include no religious service except, in deference to his Presbyterian mother, the reading of the Twenty-third Psalm, and that after cremation his ashes should be placed in Oak Grove Cemetery, Paducah, at the roots of a dogwood tree.

[Cobb's autobiographical *Stickfuls* and *Exit Laughing* (1941); Fred G. Neuman, *Irvin S. Cobb: His Life and Letters* (1938), with an introduction by O. O. McIntyre; Elisabeth Cobb, *My Wayward Parent* (1945); *Who Was Who in America*, vol. II (1950); and newspapers generally at the time of his death, especially the *Paducah Sun-Democrat*, Mar. 8, 10, 1944 (also a later review of his career, July 27, 1956). See also: *Lib. of Southern Literature*, vol. XVII, Supp. 1 (1923), pp. 159–65; Stanley J. Kunitz and Howard Haycraft, eds., *Twentieth Century Authors* (1942) and First Supp. (1955); and references to Cobb in Frank L. Mott, *Am. Journalism* (1941); Emmet Crozier, *Am. Reporters on the Western Front, 1914–18* (1959); and Edwin Emery, *The Press and America* (1954). For a dissenting judgment on Cobb's merits as a humorist, see H. L. Mencken, *Prejudices: First Series* (1920), pp. 97–104. The *N. Y. Times Index* contains scores of citations during Cobb's active years. Loula N. Cantrell of the Emory Univ. School of Librarianship provided an extensive and helpful compilation of sources; E. J. Paxton, Jr., of Paducah gave generous assistance. An oil portrait of Cobb by James Montgomery Flagg was hung in the lobby of the Irvin Cobb Hotel, Paducah, at its opening in 1929.]

IRVING DILLIARD

COGHILL, GEORGE ELLETT (Mar. 17, 1872–July 23, 1941), biologist and anatomist, was born in Beaucoup Township, Washington County, Ill., the fourth son and fifth of seven children of John Waller Coghill and Elizabeth (Tucker) Coghill. The families of both parents had come to Illinois in the 1830's, the Coghills from Virginia, the Tuckers from Pennsylvania. George spent his boyhood on his father's farm near Roseville, Ill., under a regime that demanded hard work and strict discipline. Though not wealthy, his father, a sometime businessman and teacher as well as farmer, managed to send all the sons to college.

After studying for two years at Shurtleff College, Alton, Ill., Coghill decided to enter the ministry and transferred to Brown University, where he received the A.B. degree in 1896. He then attended the Southern Baptist Theological Seminary in Louisville, Ky., but withdrew after six months, unable to reconcile his independent views with the dogmatism of the seminary. In poor physical and mental health as a result of this crisis, he went to New Mexico to recuperate and try to resolve his conflicts. After some months he concluded that psychological problems must have an origin in a biological situation, and that a knowledge of the physical mechanism of the nervous system would offer the best approach toward understanding the reactions of the human mind. At this time he met Clarence L. Herrick, then president of the new Territorial University of New Mexico. With his encouragement, Coghill in 1897 entered the graduate school of the university to study biology, and after receiving the M.S. degree in 1899 was appointed assistant professor. He returned to Brown University in 1900 and received the Ph.D. in zoology in 1902. On Sept. 13, 1900, at the beginning of his graduate studies at Brown, Coghill married Muriel Anderson, whom he had met in New Mexico. They had five children: Robert DeWolf, James Tucker, Louis Waller, Muriel, and Benjamin Anderson.

During the first decade after completing his doctorate, Coghill taught at Pacific University, Forest Grove, Oreg. (1902–06), Willamette University, Salem, Oreg. (1906–07), and Denison University, Granville, Ohio (1907–13). His research at this time was hampered by inadequate laboratory facilities, a heavy teaching load, and relative isolation from scientists with interests close to his. In 1913 he moved to the medical school of the University of Kansas, where he found better laboratory facilities and wider scientific contacts. Here he taught histology and human anatomy, becoming chairman of the department of anatomy in 1918.

During his years at Kansas, Coghill published the first five of twelve papers which are at the center of his scientific contribution. In these "Correlated Anatomical and Physiological Studies of the Growth of the Nervous System of Amphibia," published between 1914 and 1936 in the *Journal of Comparative Neurology,* Coghill reported the results of his long-range program of extremely laborious and largely single-handed research. He had chosen the salamander *Amblystoma tigrinum* (the subject of his doctoral thesis) as the chief experimental animal because it produced a large number of embryos, was easy to care for and study, and could tolerate a wide range of laboratory treatments. Since he believed that the ner-

vous system could be understood only in terms of its function—stimulating the performance of actual bodily work—he went beyond the conventional approach, which focused on anatomical changes in the developing nervous system, and correlated these changes with altered patterns of bodily movement. He was able to define a number of well-marked physiological stages, from the premotile phase through the swimming stage to the adultlike walking after the limbs had developed—a system that was analogous to but only roughly parallel with a more detailed morphological staging delineated during these same years by the embryologist Ross G. Harrison.

The "Correlated Studies" (and Coghill's other research reports) give the experimental evidence for his challenge to the then prevalent theory of the role played by reflexes in behavior: that simple local reflexes, a movement of a part of the body after the stimulation of sense organs, are the ontogenetically earliest form of movement, and that complex behavior develops as a coordination of such simple reflexes. Coghill found, instead, that movements involving the whole body occur before the sense organs develop, and independently of sensory stimulus; that from the beginning the organism exhibits a "total pattern" of behavior with a high degree of autonomy from the stimulating environment; and that this pattern of "maturation" and autonomy describes the organism's development better than does the theory of increasingly complex reflex responses. His research was also of significance to psychologists and other students of learning processes, since it indicated that behavior was not determined solely by the environment and outside events, but was also internally activated by the individual nervous system.

In 1925 Coghill left Kansas for Philadelphia, to become a member of and professor of comparative anatomy at the Wistar Institute of Anatomy and Biology, where he spent the next decade. He continued to issue the "Studies" and achieved rather belated recognition. He served as managing editor of the *Journal of Comparative Neurology* from 1927 through 1933 and as president of the American Association of Anatomists, 1932–34. In 1928 he delivered three lectures on anatomy and the problem of behavior at University College, London. He was awarded the Elliot Medal of the National Academy of Sciences in 1934 and was elected to membership in the Academy the next year.

Coghill, however, was increasingly frustrated in his expectation of a life of unhindered research at the Wistar Institute. During the first year he had been encouraged to expand the *Amblystoma* work as a part of what he envisioned as a broad collaborative program of research on embryogenesis and growth. Later it became apparent that his project was to be severely restricted. He and the director of the Institute, Milton J. Greenman, were temperamentally at odds, and the two also came into sharp conflict over the Institute's aims. The laboratory facilities Coghill hoped for never materialized, and he met increasing obstruction in his efforts to continue his research. His health began to fail, and in 1934 he suffered a heart attack, from which he made a partial recovery. Late in 1935, while on vacation hoping to regain full strength, he was summarily dismissed, even though his position at the Institute had been tenured.

Coghill retired to a farm near Gainesville, Fla., where he built a small laboratory and continued his research and writing as his health allowed. He died there of a heart attack in 1941, at the age of sixty-nine.

[Coghill's lectures in London were published as *Anatomy and the Problem of Behavior* (1929). C. Judson Herrick, *George Ellett Coghill, Naturalist and Philosopher* (1949), supersedes the same author's memoir in Nat. Acad. Sci., *Biog. Memoirs,* vol. XXII (1943); written by a scientist who was close to Coghill personally and to his scientific interests, it includes an extensive discussion of his ideas, as well as a photograph and a complete bibliography of his writings. See also obituaries in *Anatomical Record,* May 25, 1942 (by Herrick and D. S. Pankrantz), *Jour. of Comparative Neurology,* Oct. 15, 1941, and *Science,* Aug. 29, 1941.]

                                        PETER AMACHER

COHAN, GEORGE MICHAEL (July 3, 1878–Nov. 5, 1942), actor, playwright, composer, lyricist, and producer, was the youngest of three children and only son of Jeremiah John Cohan and Helen Frances (Costigan) Cohan. He was born in Providence, R. I., and baptized in the Catholic faith of his parents. His paternal grandfather, Michael Keohane, a tailor, had come to Massachusetts from County Cork, Ireland, and in the New World had simplified the spelling of the family name. Jerry Cohan, born in Boston, rejected a career as a harnessmaker to become a traveling vaudevillian. When he married Nellie Costigan of Providence, she became his theatrical partner. Their first daughter died in infancy, but Josephine, later a talented dancer, and George early joined their parents on the stage.

George M. Cohan thus grew up on the theatrical byways of America. The only classrooms he ever saw were in two Providence elementary schools, and his formal education terminated when he was eight. His only stopping places were with relatives in Providence and summer vacations in North Brookfield, Mass. As a baby he was carried onstage in a sketch written by his father. At the age of eight he played the violin in the orchestra for a road show called *Daniel Boone on the Trail.* The next year he made his speaking debut in Haverstraw, N. Y. Soon, as one of "The Four Cohans," he was appearing regularly in his father's sketches as well as performing solo songs, dances, and recitations. He achieved his greatest boyhood success at thirteen as the winning brat Henry Peck in *Peck's Bad Boy,* a cocky, confident character he closely resembled. Always, as he said, "a little guy," with piercing eyes, a shrewd grin, and a jutting Irish chin, he developed a versatile set of talents. He wrote his first play, a melodrama, when he was eleven and published his first song ("Why Did Nellie Leave Her Home?") when he was sixteen.

The Four Cohans crossed and recrossed America in the last decade of the nineteenth century, a time when the American theatre was a polyglot of touring Shakespeare, melodrama, and minstrel shows. During these years George contrived his peculiar song-and-dance style which was to become a popular feature of many of his later Broadway successes. He often strutted across the stage, his head thrust forward, singing and talking out of the corner of his mouth. During these years, too, he initiated his famous closing address to the audience: "My mother thanks you, my father thanks you, my sister thanks you, and I thank you." In moments of bitterness which marked the last twenty years of his life, Cohan fondly remembered these early days with his beloved family.

By the turn of the century, the Four Cohans had attained top money and top billing in vaudeville and were playing the more prestigious theatres in Chicago and New York. George, who had succeeded his father as sketch writer, also managed business affairs. In July 1899 he married Ethelia Fowler, a singer and comedienne known on the stage as Ethel Levey; in 1900 their only child, Georgette, was born. That same year the Four Cohans signed an agreement with the producer Louis C. Behman to tour under his management, with the understanding that he would produce George's first full-length musical comedy the following season. Thus on Feb. 25, 1901, the Cohans and Ethel Levey, who had joined their act, opened in New York in *The Governor's Son,* written, composed, and directed by George. Critical response was disappointing, and although the musical subsequently toured successfully, it closed after thirty-two performances. George's next attempt, *Running for Office,* met the same fate.

Undaunted, Cohan in 1904 formed a producing partnership with Sam H. Harris [Supp. 3]. Until it was dissolved in 1920, the firm presented many notable hits. Their first was *Little Johnny Jones,* Cohan's musical about an American jockey accused of throwing the English Derby, and starring the author and his family (minus Josephine, who had married the actor Fred Niblo). Completely American and brimming with a national pride which mirrored the mood of the country, it was a showcase for Cohan's eccentric song-and-dance routine. Its theatrical style, calling for "Speed! Speed! And lots of it!" was new, deriving from Cohan's background in vaudeville; his loud, exuberant showmanship, so different from European operetta, would become one of the hallmarks of American musical comedy. When *Little Johnny Jones* opened in New York on Nov. 7, 1904, the critics were once again lukewarm, despite two popular songs which became American "standards"—"Give My Regards to Broadway" and "Yankee Doodle Boy." They termed the show "brash," "naive," "optimistic," "jaunty," and "flag-waving." But Cohan's confidence remained undimmed, and during the successful tour of *Little Johnny Jones* he rewrote the script; when it reopened in New York on May 8, 1905, it was enthusiastically received.

A series of musicals followed which continued to express Cohan's love of America. Among them were *Forty-five Minutes from Broadway* (1906), written for the actress Fay Templeton and containing two enduring songs, the title song and "Mary Is a Grand Old Name"; *George Washington, Jr.* (1906), in which Cohan sang "You're a Grand Old Flag"; *Fifty Miles from Boston* (1908); *The Yankee Prince* (1908); *The Man Who Owns Broadway* (1909); and *The Little Millionaire* (1911). These shows all featured brisk, tuneful songs mixed into plots which combined comedy and melodrama.

Mellowing with the years, Cohan became a familiar and beloved figure on Broadway and at the baseball parks, where he often went to watch his favorite sport. In 1907 Ethel Levey divorced him, and on June 29 of the same year he married Agnes Nolan of Brookline, Mass., who had appeared in the chorus of *Little Johnny Jones.* They had three children: Mary Agnes, Helen Frances, and George Michael.

Despite his popularity as an actor and composer, Cohan passionately wanted to win recognition as a playwright. His nonmusical plays included *Popularity* (1906), a failure which he turned into a musical success three years later as *The Man Who Owns Broadway;* the comedy *Get-Rich-Quick Wallingford* (1910), which scored with critics and public (in February 1911 it was moved to the new George M. Cohan Theatre in Times Square); *Broadway Jones* (1912), in which Cohan appeared in his first "straight" part on Broadway; *Seven Keys to Baldpate* (1913), a mystery farce written in ten days and considered by the critics his best effort; and *The Tavern* (1920), a lively parody of popular thrillers. Although all are minor works of the American stage, Cohan in 1911 was welcomed into the playwrights' ranks at dinners given by both the Friars Club and the Society of American Dramatists and Composers.

In 1919, however, Cohan's stand in the strike of the Actors' Equity Association, a union formed to combat the Producing Managers' Association, ruined some of his lifelong friendships. As both an actor and a producer, he was in the center of the dispute. He was a man of great personal generosity, but he stood with the managers against Equity and the "closed shop," which he repeatedly called dangerous to actors. The strike, which lasted a month, ended in victory for Equity, and Cohan took it as a personal humiliation. He dissolved his partnership with Harris and vowed to withdraw from show business. He soon relented and continued to write, produce, and act—as in *The Song and Dance Man* in 1923—but without his former success, and he increasingly lost touch with the heartbeat of the theatre. His bitterness against Equity persisted. It is therefore something of an irony that in his last years he won repute not as a producer or a playwright but as an actor of skill and maturity, and in plays not of his own authorship; as the kindly father and newspaper editor in Eugene O'Neill's sentimental comedy *Ah, Wilderness!* (presented by the Theatre Guild in 1933) and as President Franklin D. Roosevelt in *I'd Rather Be Right* (1937), by George S. Kaufman and Moss Hart, with music and lyrics by Richard Rodgers and Lorenz Hart [Supp. 3].

Cohan's theatrical career was marked by an ardent and showy patriotism perhaps ingrained by his father, who had initiated the story that George had been born on the fourth, not the third, of July. One of his greatest outbursts of national feeling, inspired by America's declaration of war in 1917, resulted in his most popular song, "Over There," which sold a million and half copies. For "Over There" Congress awarded him a gold medal, which President Roosevelt presented in 1940.

Besides his many stage appearances, George M. Cohan wrote some forty plays, collaborated in as many others, had a part in the production of about 150 more, and composed more than 500 songs (Ewen, p. 44). Called one of "the two most important figures of the American musical stage during the first decade of the twentieth century" (Green, p. 25), the "Yankee Doodle Boy" spent his last years convinced that the American theatre no longer had any need of him. He died at his New York City home at the age of sixty-four, never having fully recovered from an intestinal operation the year before. Following services in St. Patrick's Cathedral, he was buried in the family mausoleum in Woodlawn Cemetery, the Bronx. A statue of George M. Cohan stands in Times Square overlooking the Broadway that he loved and, during the years of its early growth, powerfully symbolized.

[Ward Morehouse, *George M. Cohan* (1943), is a warmly admiring biography, reasonably well researched; it gives a full and discriminating account of his theatrical career but covers his personal life with less depth. Cohan's autobiography, *Twenty Years on Broadway* (1924), conveys well his style in life and onstage. Good analyses of Cohan's impact on American musical comedy are found in Stanley Green, *The World of Musical Comedy* (rev. ed., 1968), and David Ewen, *Complete Book of the Am. Musical Theatre* (1958); see also Ewen's *Popular Am. Composers* (1962). For the Equity strike, see Alfred Harding, *The Revolt of the Actors* (1929), and Brooks Atkinson, *Broadway* (1970). Both the Harvard Theatre Collection and the Theatre Collection of the N. Y. Public Lib. at Lincoln Center contain a wealth of clippings; Harvard also has typescripts and hand-copied musical scores of several early Cohan hits, including *Forty-five Minutes from Broadway* and *The Yankee Prince*. The Harvard collection includes a good photograph of Cohan as a debonair young showman; the N. Y. Public Lib., an excellent photograph (by Carl Van Vechten) of Cohan in his last decade.]
GEORGE PHILIP BIRNBAUM

COIT, STANTON (Aug. 11, 1857–Feb. 15, 1944), Ethical Culture leader and founder of America's first social settlement, was born in Columbus, Ohio; he was the fourth of seven children, but only he and two sisters lived to maturity. His father, Harvey Coit, a well-to-do dry goods merchant, was a native of Norwich, Mass., and a descendant of John Coit, who emigrated from England to America around 1630. His mother, Elizabeth (Greer) Coit, was born in Ohio; she had abandoned her orthodox Episcopal faith to become an ardent Spiritualist, and was a major influence in Coit's life.

Coit graduated in 1879 from Amherst College, and after remaining for two years as tutor in English literature, moved on to New York City. There he attended Columbia University, lived in the slums, and worked with Felix Adler [Supp. 1], founder of the Society for Ethical Culture. His own Emersonian bent and Adler's influence took Coit to Germany in 1883 to study Kant and idealist philosophy under Georg von Gizycki (a later co-worker in the Ethical movement). Coit received a Ph.D. from the University of Berlin in 1885, and following three months at Toynbee Hall, the pioneer social settlement in London,

resumed his work with Adler in New York.

In 1886 Coit moved to the Lower East Side, purchased a building at 146 Forsyth Street, between Rivington and Delancey streets, and there established what he called a "Neighborhood Guild"—the beginnings of the first social settlement in America. By organizing the working classes into "guilds," each of which was to contain about a hundred families, Coit hoped to regenerate the slums and thereby provide a base for civic reform. Unlike many middle-class socialists and reformers of his day, he had complete faith in the ability of the workingman to run his own affairs; leadership for activities sponsored by the guild was to arise directly out of the community. In this respect he distinguished his enterprise from Toynbee Hall and other English settlements. Joined at the Neighborhood Guild by other reformers, ministers, and labor leaders, Coit organized lectures, a kindergarten, theatricals, gymnasiums, and clubs, where boys and girls read books and took lessons in such subjects as wood carving and elocution.

At the same time Coit proselytized heavily for Adler's Ethical Culture Society, so successfully, in fact, that he was offered the major Ethical ministry in Britain, succeeding Moncure D. Conway [q.v.], at South Place Chapel, Finsbury, London. When he left New York in 1888, the Neighborhood Guild almost collapsed; it was reorganized in 1891 as the University Settlement by two of its original leaders, Charles B. Stover and Edward King. Shortly afterward John Lovejoy Elliott [Supp. 3], another member of the Ethical Culture Society, established the Hudson Guild, which incorporated some of Coit's ideas. But Coit had little influence on the American settlement movement after 1888; except for occasional visits, he spent the rest of his long life in England.

In England, Coit at first devoted himself to establishing Neighborhood Guilds, starting with one in London at Kentish Town. The idea took rapid root, and within three years he had five clubs, a circulating library, adult education classes, a choral and dance group, free Sunday concerts, and other activities. During the 1890's Coit turned increasingly to Ethical work, in part because of his success at South Place Chapel, where during his three-year tenure his popular lectures doubled membership. He created and led the West London Ethical Society (1894), the Union of Ethical Societies (1895), and the Moral Instruction League (1897), whose fight to secularize moral education in public schools he headed. He also edited the *Ethical World,* helped establish the *International Journal of Ethics,* and organized the International Foundation for Moral and Religious Leadership, which recruited and trained Ethical leaders.

Yet Coit was an idiosyncratic figure. A nervous extrovert with an excitable disposition and a flair for the dramatic, he developed his own personal synthesis of Emerson, Coleridge, Kant, the natural sciences, and socialism. He caused considerable consternation among his colleagues when, in 1909, he established an Ethical Church in the London suburb of Bayswater. When this seemed unsuccessful, he challenged the Church of England to remake itself along Ethical lines. Both ventures met opposition from those in the Ethical movement who regarded all churches as anathema. His Ethical Church did succeed as a reform center, attracting men like Bernard Shaw, Edward Carpenter, Walter Crane, Graham Wallas, L. T. Hobhouse, and J. A. Hobson. But his effort to create an Ethical liturgy and ritual failed to attract attention. He then turned to the study of the psychology of religion and suggested detailed formal changes that the Church of England should make. Hoping that God-worship could somehow be psychologically transferred to humanistic worship of communal moral ideals, he devised an apparatus of theoretical and psychological assumptions to supplant the Church's age-old myths and historic traditions. Influenced by Sir John Seeley's *Natural Religion,* Coit eventually came to believe that each nation (even the United States) needed its own national church. This took him far from the American Ethical-humanist camp; indeed, Adler regarded him as the enfant terrible of the Ethical movement.

Although in later life Coit moved away from practical social reforms and concerned himself with such matters as making a three-volume translation of Nicolai Hartmann's treatise, *Ethik* (1932), his ethical socialism never dimmed. He had been an active Fabian, he stood unsuccessfully as a Labour candidate for Wakefield in the 1906 election, and he lectured throughout England for the Labour Church at the turn of the century. On Dec. 21, 1898, he married a liberal German refugee, Mrs. Fanny Adela Wetzler, who encouraged him also in feminist work. They had three daughters: Adela I., Gwendolen E., and Virginia. Coit died at the age of eighty-six at Birling Gap, near Eastbourne, Sussex, England. Funeral services were held at Golders Green Crematorium. He is remembered as the pioneer in the American settlement movement and as the leader of the English Ethical movement at its time of greatest growth (1891–1914).

[Coit's writings include: *Neighborhood Guilds* (1892), *National Idealism and a State Church* (1907),

National Idealism and the Book of Common Prayer (1908), *The Soul of America* (1914), and *Two Responsive Services: In the Form and Spirit of the Litany and Ten Commandments for Use in Families, Schools and Churches* (1911), an example of his attempt to create a new ritual. The best single source on Coit is H. J. Blackham, ed., *Stanton Coit* (1948), which also gives selections from his works. Some of his letters are to be found in the Henry Demarest Lloyd Papers, Wis. State Hist. Soc., Madison. Other material is at the library of the Am. Ethical Union, N. Y. City. See also Howard B. Radest, *Toward Common Ground: The Story of the Ethical Societies in the U. S.* (1969); Allen F. Davis, *Spearheads for Reform: The Social Settlements and the Progressive Movement, 1890–1914* (1967); Amherst College Biog. Record, 1951; obituary in London *Times,* Feb. 16, 1944. Information on Coit's family from *Nat. Cyc. Am. Biog.,* XI, 573 (on his father), and the State Lib. of Ohio.]

PETER D'A. JONES

COMMONS, JOHN ROGERS (Oct. 13, 1862–May 11, 1945), economist, was born in Hollansburg in southwestern Ohio close to the Indiana border, the eldest of the three surviving children (two sons and a daughter) of John and Clarissa (Rogers) Commons. Both parents were ardent abolitionists. The father, a "studious reader" but a poor provider, came of North Carolina Quaker stock removed to Indiana; in later years he embraced in turn the doctrines of Herbert Spencer, Spiritualism, and Christian Science, a philosophical hegira which gave his son valuable insights into the relationship between experience and dogma. Commons's mother, a gifted and determined woman, was a devout Presbyterian of New England antecedents, a graduate of Oberlin College, and a former schoolteacher. When Commons was a small boy the family moved to Union City, Ind., where his father, earlier a harnessmaker, turned to journalism, editing newspapers there and in nearby Winchester. Young John graduated from the Winchester high school and in 1882, at his mother's urging, entered Oberlin; to support her children's education she moved to Oberlin and operated a student boardinghouse. Commons had to spend a year in Oberlin's "preparatory program," and he suffered the first of a succession of what he called "nervous breakdowns" in 1885–86, but he eventually received his A.B. degree in 1888. That fall, with the aid of borrowed funds and an introduction from one of his professors at Oberlin, he entered Johns Hopkins University to study with the economist Richard T. Ely [Supp. 3].

He left in 1890 without completing a Ph.D. to take an instructorship in economics at Wesleyan University in Middletown, Conn. On Dec. 25 of that year he married Ella Brown Downey of Akron, Ohio, an Oberlin classmate. They had five children, of whom only two, John Alvin and Rachel Sutherland, survived early childhood. When his Wesleyan instructorship was terminated after one year Commons returned to Oberlin to teach, again only for a year. Subsequent appointments at Indiana University (1892–95) and Syracuse University (1895–99) ended under a cloud, as administrators and trustees became alarmed by his growing reputation for radicalism. Turning to free-lance work, Commons and several associates organized a research bureau in New York City which for a time in 1899–1900 compiled a weekly index of wholesale prices for the Democratic National Campaign Committee. When, however, these statistics failed to supply the desired ammunition against the McKinley administration, the project ended. There followed a more satisfying interlude as Commons prepared a report on immigration for the United States Industrial Commission and served (1902–04) as assistant to Ralph M. Easley [Supp. 2], secretary of the National Civic Federation.

These years, for all their vicissitudes, were crucial to Commons's intellectual development. A self-conscious Midwesterner, he was proud of the traits he liked to associate with the Old Northwest: personal liberty, equality, resistance to arbitrary rule, and a suspicion of theorists not in touch with hard fact. Although he never became a minister as his mother would have liked—she had named him for a Protestant minister, John Rogers, martyred in England in the sixteenth century—he tried as a young man to reconcile Presbyterianism and social science. In 1893 he helped organize the American Institute of Christian Sociology, and a year later he published *Social Reform and the Church*. This formal involvement did not long survive his mother's death in 1892, but the structure of Midwestern Presbyterianism continued to shape Commons's belief that an educated elite was necessary to guide the masses through inevitable conflict toward social harmony. Presbyterianism also shaped his attitudes about man's fundamental character. Reared on God and sin, and realizing his own capacity for violence (as a child he once deliberately killed a dog in the presence of awed playmates), Commons considered conflict a natural human condition.

These formative influences prepared him for the ideas of Ely and other young American economists who, influenced by members of the German historical school like Gustav Schmoller, Adolph Wagner, and Ludwig J. Brentano, rejected the deductive rigidity of the classical school of economics. For them, economics could be understood only within the context of a nation's cultural development, institutional changes, and government policy, all of which, they maintained, had to be studied empirically through direct observation and interviews. These young Americans encouraged scholarly and technical discussions of economic and social problems; they hoped to exert a guiding hand on government and public opinion and foster harmony among clashing industrial groups. Through Ely, Commons was also exposed to the "Austrian School," with its emphasis on marginal utility (a concept which defines value in terms of demand rather than in terms of production cost) and to Prussian accomplishments in state efficiency and bureaucracy. Other influences touched him. He took seriously Karl Marx and Henry George [q.v.], but rejected their general conclusions. He drew on Hector Dennis of the University of Brussels, who wrote about labor councils. Finally, instead of Christian love as the resolver of conflict, he came to depend on the rationality of modern pagans like David Hume and Adam Smith in the eighteenth century and Charles Peirce and William James [qq.v.] in his own time.

Bringing such diverse intellectual perspectives to his teaching and writing, Commons soon became a controversial figure. A leader, along with Thorstein Veblen [q.v.] and Wesley C. Mitchell, of the emerging "institutional" economics, he ranged broadly in his classes over questions of socialism, the family, pauperism, charity, prisons, and the state. His own early works included the heterodox and poorly received *The Distribution of Wealth* (1893), *Proportional Representation* (1896), and a series of scholarly and popular articles on currency, labor, and municipal reform. In such works as his *Races and Immigrants in America* (1907) he revealed a special interest in behavioral variations among industrial groups, seeking to isolate what he called "racial" characteristics and then evaluate their effect upon the organizational life of trade unions or entire sectors of the economy. He attributed such traits to Italians, Jews, and Eastern Europeans; dogmatically postulated "superior" and "inferior" races; and characterized blacks as incapable of the "highest American civilization." But, uncritical and presumptuous as these speculations were, they did spring from a desire to examine empirically the social context of economic institutions and practices.

Commons returned to academia in 1904 when Professor Ely called him to the department of political economy at the University of Wisconsin. Here he was to remain until his retirement in 1932. Coming to a state dominated by a progressive governor, Robert M. La Follette [q.v.], Commons found an ideal environment for combining his scholarly pursuits with his interest in practical reform. With the aid of a loyal band of students, he drafted Wisconsin's civil service law (1905), its public utility law (1907), and its workmen's compensation act (1911)—the first in the nation to withstand constitutional challenge. He also framed legislation against exploitation by "loan sharks," helped initiate the first multi-language public employment office in the country, and advised La Follette on questions of railroad regulation and taxation. On the municipal level, he organized and directed (1911–13) a Bureau of Economy and Efficiency for Milwaukee's Socialist mayor. The achievement in which Commons took greatest pride was his role in the creation of the Wisconsin Industrial Commission, set up in 1911 to administer the state's various labor laws. (He himself was a member for its first two years.) The Commission's key feature was the procedure by which experts and representatives of conflicting economic interests together examined issues and then recommended codes which the Commission could impose on all employers. To facilitate acceptance, the Commission usually persuaded some model employers to try an innovation, which was then promulgated generally. Time and again, Commons and his students cited the Industrial Commission as a model for the handling of labor relations in a modern industrial society.

On the national level, Commons was one of the founders, with Ely and others, of the American Association for Labor Legislation (1906). He served from 1913 to 1915 on the United States Commission on Industrial Relations, appointed by President Woodrow Wilson to investigate the causes of labor unrest. He was also associated with the Russell Sage Foundation's famed "Pittsburgh Survey" (1906–07) and served on the editorial staff of *Survey Magazine,* which grew from it. Commons strongly supported America's role in World War I, endorsed Milwaukee's "Americanization" efforts, and urged employers to force their foreign-born workers to learn English, in part to reduce the threat of radicalism. One consequence of his jingoism was a break with Senator La Follette, who opposed the war and the domestic repression associated with it.

The decade of the 1920's brought an intensification of Commons's role in the shaping of public policy. In 1923 he helped represent four Western states before the Federal Trade Commission in opposition to the regional price discrimination of the United States Steel Company. Indeed, he frequently testified before legislative committees of all kinds, and for a time was something of an unofficial economic adviser to the House Committee on Banking and Currency. Along with his former student John B. Andrews

[Supp. 3], Commons argued that the goal of social insurance legislation should be the prevention of economic hardship rather than the maintenance or redistribution of income. Thus in the case of unemployment insurance, he urged that each employer be required to set aside his own reserve fund, on the assumption that, rather than see it depleted, he would conduct his business in such a way as to keep employment as high as possible. This concept found general expression in the unemployment provisions of the federal Social Security Act of 1935. Many of the programs which Commons and his students helped draft for Wisconsin also served as models for New Deal measures. A compulsive worker whose day began at 4 a.m., Commons also found time to serve for twelve years (1923–35) as president of the National Consumers' League.

At the same time, his scholarly reputation had been steadily growing. Since joining the Wisconsin faculty in 1904 he had become one of the most influential figures in the study of American trade unionism. In that year he had taken over Ely's project for collecting documents about labor history, and he and his students unearthed a wealth of printed and manuscript material. Drawing on this material, Commons was the principal editor of the ten-volume *A Documentary History of American Industrial Society* (1910–11), a pioneering work which provided a descriptive picture of American labor and industrial history comparable to that which Sidney and Beatrice Webb had achieved in their studies of the United Kingdom. But Commons wished also to create a conceptual framework for the documents and, in particular, to do so without invoking Hegelian dialectics or Marxian materialism. Utilizing the "stage" analysis of economic development, he focused on the transitional period between the primitive guild and the merchant-capitalist stages, concluding that in an age of improved production and transportation, the ability of a union to influence its members' employment depended on its success in regularizing and controlling trade conditions in their product's particular market area. Basic to all industries was "the historical extension of markets." This, together with the concept that the merchant, through the "price bargain" he struck, was the guiding force in industrial evolution, remained central in the writings of Commons and his students, which came to constitute the "Wisconsin School" of labor history.

That school reached its classic expression in the *History of Labor in the United States,* of which two volumes were published under Commons's editorial hand in 1918 and two more in 1935 by a group of his students—Don D. Lescohier, Elizabeth Brandeis, Selig Perlman, and Philip Taft. The main function of the *History,* of course, was to provide information about the past of trade unionism, but it served other functions as well. It supplied knowledge about protective labor legislation and other aspects of industrial relations important in the life of the American worker, such as personnel management and public employment offices. It argued forcefully, if not persuasively, that the trade unionism of Commons's good friend Samuel Gompers [*q.v.*], rooted in the concept of loosely federated, craft-oriented national unions, was the logical and natural result of American history; conversely, the *History* argued that challengers to this pattern, including citywide federations or movements based on socialism or other anticapitalist or radical ideologies, posed a threat to the trade union movement and therefore to the American worker. This monumental work also reflected Commons's conviction that labor history must be viewed as an integral part of a larger economic philosophy. As he said in his posthumously published volume, *The Economics of Collective Action* (1950), "I have never been able to think of the various social sciences as separate fields of history, political science, law, economics, ethics, and administration." What he had sought, he added, in a revealing comment upon the whole thrust of his professional life, was "some way of working through the whole complex of problems that grow out of this fundamental struggle" to make a living (p. 118).

Despite the great volume of his work in economics, Commons published only two clearly "theoretical" works, *Legal Foundations of Capitalism* (1924) and *Institutional Economics* (1934), although the ideas for both had been germinating for many years. Through these works he hoped to construct a useful theory of value. Unlike the classical economists, who saw disembodied economic forces moving inexorably by their own rules and working principally on individuals, Commons saw the economic process as one of the clash and conflict of institutions, such as corporations, trade unions, and governments. But institutions were more than physical entities; they had legal and moral dimensions as well. An institution, said Commons, was "collective action in control, liberation, and expansion of individual action."

Economic competition, he believed, arose out of a condition common to all societies: the necessity to protect property rights to scarce resources. Since resources are scarce, their value, allocation, and use are determined by complex exchange transactions which inevitably produce competition among the participants to achieve the most favorable terms of agreement. Transactions, which Commons considered the fundamental units of economic activity, were of three types: bargaining transactions, which occurred between parties of relatively equal status, and rationing and managerial transactions, which grew out of a superior-inferior relationship. With the rise of powerful monopolies in the United States, Commons feared that bargaining transactions would soon disappear.

Viewed historically, Commons knew, property involved more than tangible objects. A craftsman's labor, a firm's "good will," the expectation of future profit, were all types of intangible property over which rights could be exercised. Furthermore, as he wrote, "'property' cannot be defined except by defining all the activities which individuals and the community are at liberty or required to do or not to do, with reference to the object claimed as property" (*Institutional Economics,* p. 74). Collective action thus meant more than just the activities of organizations. It encompassed the entire range of social customs, laws, and, most especially, court decisions, through which the rights of property were exercised, expanded, or curtailed. Such "working rules" were not, however, fixed in natural law, but changed with time and place as custom and law changed.

Besides law and custom, ethics was an important philosophical companion to economics. Unlike his fellow institutionalist Thorstein Veblen, Commons refused to apply the biological principles of Darwinism to human economic behavior. Man had a will, he argued, and could adapt his environment and institutions to suit it. But if man is responsible for his own economic actions, he is also responsible for their effects. Thus while man possessed the power to exercise property rights—including the all-important right to withhold his property from the market—he also had the moral obligation to exercise it in a "reasonable" manner. Because of the ever-present possibility of conflict between parties to a transaction, ethics demanded that in every case an appeal to higher authority be permitted. "Where there is no remedy," he wrote, "there is no right." The final authority, according to Commons, rested with the courts, which alone, in cases of doubt, could determine the "reasonableness" of the use of property rights. It is not surprising that Commons saw the United States Supreme Court as the nation's "supreme faculty of political economy."

Commons had a deep faith in the ability of the courts to attenuate, if not to prevent, group conflicts. Courts, in fact, were the keystone of Commons's economic analysis; besides their contemporary importance, they were the unifying thread which passed through the various stages of capitalist history. In *Legal Foundations* he traced the central historical role of the English courts in molding the pattern of legal opinion to conform to changing economic relationships. By accommodating legal reality to custom, the courts had helped ease the transition from a feudal to a capitalist economy. And as the English courts had aided the rise of "merchant customs," Commons hoped that American courts would facilitate the acceptance of customs of the laboring class, including minimum wages, maximum hours, and improved conditions of labor.

Commons's final years were marked by personal difficulties and tragedy. The death of his wife in 1928 was followed two years later by the apparent suicide of his daughter. Shortly thereafter his son disappeared without a trace and did not return home until 1944. In 1934 his sister Anna, who had made her home with him following his wife's death, was killed in an automobile accident. His final years were spent in a trailer court in Fort Lauderdale, Fla. He died of myocarditis in 1945, at the age of eighty-two, while on a visit to Raleigh, N. C. Through all these vicissitudes, his scholarly productivity remained almost undiminished; a mere bibliographic listing of his books, articles, edited works, reviews, and fugitive writings totals more than thirty printed pages.

A small, slight man with piercing eyes, furrowed brow, and a large shock of unruly hair, Commons was modest and retiring in manner, yet never intimidated by intellectual challenges or public service responsibilities. Teaching did not come easily for him, but when at last he found a congenial classroom style—that of informally and somewhat unsystematically unfolding his ideas—he was able to establish warm relations with many of his students. His stature as an economist among his contemporaries is suggested by his election as president of the American Economic Association for 1918. But it was perhaps in the sphere of practical politics that he made his most memorable contribution. By converting into workable public policy sweeping reforms designed to make the industrial and political order more rational and more humane, Commons helped preserve and shape the economic order of the republic about which he felt so strongly.

[Commons's autobiography, *Myself* (1934); Lafayette G. Harter, *John R. Commons: His Assault on Laissez-Faire* (1962); memorial resolution by Selig Perlman, John M. Gaus, and Kenneth H. Parsons in Univ. of Wis. Faculty Minutes, Oct. 1, 1945; obituary by Selig Perlman in *Am. Economic Rev.,* Sept. 1945; Kenneth H. Parsons, "John R. Commons' Point of View," *Jour. of Land and Public Utility Economics,* Aug. 1942 (reprinted in Commons's *The Economics of Social Action*); Neil W. Chamberlain, "The Institutional Economics of John R. Commons," in Joseph Dorfman et al., *Institutional Economics* (1963); Joseph Dorfman, *The Economic Mind in Am. Civilization,* vols. III and IV (1949–59). See also Wesley C. Mitchell, "Commons on the Legal Foundations of Capitalism," *Am. Economic Rev.,* June 1924; Ben B. Seligman, *Main Currents in Modern Economics* (1962); Harlan L. McCracken, *Keynesian Economics in the Stream of Economic Thought* (1961). Commons's *The Economics of Collective Action* includes a bibliography of his writings.]

GERD KORMAN

CONBOY, MARTIN (Aug. 28, 1878–Mar. 5, 1944), lawyer, was born in New York City, the second son and second of three children (the oldest of whom died in infancy) of Martin and Bridget (Harlow) Conboy. Both parents were natives of County Roscommon, Ireland. Conboy's father, a Civil War veteran who had won the Congressional Medal of Honor, worked for a time as a government clerk and later as a member of the police department of Washington, D. C. Conboy attended Gonzaga College in Washington (A.B. 1898, A.M. 1899) while taking night school law courses at Georgetown University (LL.B. 1898, LL.M. 1899). He returned to New York in 1900 and worked as a law clerk before being admitted to the New York bar in 1903.

Although Conboy was somewhat humorless and literal in his approach to the law, his thoroughness early gained the respect of his colleagues. In 1905 he became a member of the firm of Griggs, Baldwin & Baldwin, of which John W. Griggs [q.v.], a former governor of New Jersey and United States Attorney General, was the senior partner. He remained with the firm until 1929. During World War I, as director of selective service for New York City, Conboy supervised the registration of almost 1,500,000 men; by effectively publicizing the efficiency of his office, he greatly enhanced his stature in legal circles and in local affairs.

Conboy was long active in the Catholic Church, and by the early 1920's he had become one of the leading Catholic laymen in New York City, serving as president of the Catholic Club, 1922–27, and receiving numerous honors from the Holy See, including the designation as knight commander of the Order of St. Gregory the Great in 1926. His Catholicism deeply colored his approach to public issues; he often insisted that government must be based upon the morality of the Church. In the aftermath of World War I, as counsel to the judiciary committee of the New

York State Assembly, Conboy prosecuted five Socialist assemblymen who were eventually expelled from the legislature. He argued that the defendants posed a threat not only to property rights and the constitution, but also to the family and the church, and to laws prohibiting the dissemination of birth control information through the mails. Two years later he sought court action in an attempt to have the novel *Ulysses* and the film *Ecstasy*—which he viewed at a special screening—banned as obscene. He then lobbied in the legislature for a "clean book" bill to counter liberalizing court decisions on censorship. Within the legal profession, he led the attack on the Eighteenth Amendment, which he called the work of "religious bigots and narrow-minded reformers" (*New York Times*, Apr. 3, 1922). Conboy supported the presidential bid of Alfred E. Smith [Supp. 3] in 1924 and bitterly attacked the Democratic convention for refusing to condemn the Ku Klux Klan by name. He backed Smith again in 1928.

An independent Democrat, Conboy sought for many years to remove judicial nominations from politics, proposing instead to base selection on professional qualifications as determined by the bar associations. His stand brought him into occasional sharp conflict with Tammany, and in 1929 he was seriously considered as a "fusion" candidate for mayor against James J. Walker. Conboy later worked closely with Gov. Franklin D. Roosevelt, at first as chairman of the governor's advisory committee on narcotics and then in 1932 as special adviser in the investigation of the affairs of Mayor Walker, a politically delicate case which culminated in the mayor's resignation.

After Roosevelt became president, Conboy praised his leadership and defended the New Deal as both constitutional and in accord with papal encyclicals. Roosevelt frequently conferred with Conboy on patronage matters, and in 1933 appointed him United States Attorney for the southern district of New York. In that capacity Conboy won test cases involving the New Deal's laws against gold hoarding and certain provisions of the National Industrial Recovery Act. He resigned after seventeen months to return to his lucrative private practice. In 1929 he had joined a firm which now became Conboy, Hewitt, O'Brien & Boardman. In the years that followed, Conboy handled some of New York's most sensational cases, serving as a special prosecutor in the income-tax case against Arthur (Dutch Schultz) Flegenheimer [Supp. 1] and as counsel for Charles (Lucky) Luciano, George E. Browne, and Michael J. Beirne. At the same time he

maintained friendly relations with the Roosevelt administration, and in 1936 he won for the government a decision before the Supreme Court upholding the federal arms embargo. Later he grew more critical of Roosevelt, charging that the administration had become coercive and personalized. His belief that only strict neutrality could keep the United States out of war, as well as his Catholicism, drove him into further opposition when he feared that the United States might send arms to the Spanish Republic. He nevertheless returned to government service in 1940 and 1941, serving as coordinating adviser to the New York State Director of Selective Service.

On July 31, 1912, Conboy married Bertha Letitia Mason of McLean, N. Y.; they had four children: Roger (who died in 1918), Catherine, Constance, and Marion. In the summer of 1943 he underwent a gall bladder operation. He died while hospitalized again the following winter at the New York Hospital, New York City. He was buried in Gate of Heaven Cemetery, Westchester County, N. Y.

[Conboy's writings include: "What We Found Out about People in the Draft," *American Mag.*, May 1919; "Can a Catholic Be President?" *Forum*, July 1924; "Rum, Romanism, and Rebellion," *ibid.*, June 1928, pp. 950–52; "Trial Experiences," *Georgetown Law Jour.*, May 1931; "Federal Criminal Law," in Alison Reppy, ed., *Law: A Century of Progress* (1937), I, 295–346; letter on the embargo of arms to Spain in *Internat. Conciliation*, Mar. 1939. Biographical sources: various references in *N. Y. Times*, especially Nov. 26, 1933 (p. 1), Mar. 6, 9, 1944; obituaries in Assoc. of the Bar of the City of N. Y., *Year Book*, 1944, and *Catholic World*, Apr. 1944; *Nat. Cyc. Am. Biog.*, XXXIII, 128 (portrait opposite); *Who Was Who in America*, vol. II (1950). Family data from Conboy's sister, Miss Mary Conboy.]

EDWARD PURCELL

CONE, HUTCHINSON INGHAM (Apr. 26, 1871–Feb. 12, 1941), naval officer, shipping executive, was the first of four children (three boys and a girl) of Daniel Newnan Cone and Annette (Ingraham) Cone, and a descendant of William Cone, a Georgian who had fought under Gen. Francis Marion [*q.v.*] during the American Revolution. His father, a native of Florida, served in the Confederate Army during the Civil War and in 1885–86 was a member of the Florida legislature. His mother, born in Wappingers Falls, N. Y., was reared in Savannah, Ga. Hutchinson Cone was born in Brooklyn, N. Y., but grew up in Florida. After graduating in 1889 from East Florida Military and Agricultural College at Lake City, he briefly taught school and then entered the United States Naval Academy. He studied engineering, was elected vice-president of his class, and graduated in 1894, forty-second in the class of forty-seven.

Following two years of sea duty on the North Atlantic Station, Cone received his commission as assistant engineer. He served for the next five years on the Asiatic Station and on ships of the Pacific Fleet, including the U.S.S. *Baltimore* during the battle of Manila Bay; he was commissioned an ensign in 1899. After training at the Naval Torpedo Station, he won his first command, the torpedo boat *Dale,* in 1903. Four years later he commanded the Second Torpedo Flotilla in a difficult passage from Norfolk, Va., to San Francisco, Calif., via the Straits of Magellan. Promoted to lieutenant commander in 1908, he was appointed fleet engineer for the Atlantic Fleet on its famous cruise around the world, a feat largely made possible by the efficient system he organized for continuous inspection and maintenance of machinery and power plants of ships at sea.

The success of this mission led President Theodore Roosevelt to name Cone in May 1909 to a four-year term as chief of the navy's Bureau of Engineering, with the temporary rank of rear admiral—an unprecedented appointment for one of his age (thirty-eight) and rank. During his tenure Cone did much to modernize the navy's engineering practices. He presided over the installation of steam turbines, began the changeover from coal- to oil-burning equipment, and initiated investigations which led to the adoption of electric drive. In 1913, gracefully accepting the reversion to his regular rank of lieutenant commander, he became executive officer (second in command) of the battleship *Utah;* he was temporarily in command during the occupation of Vera Cruz in 1914. This assignment was followed by two years (1915–17) as marine superintendent of the Panama Canal.

Soon after the United States entered World War I, Vice Admiral William S. Sims [Supp. 2], commander of naval forces operating in Europe, put Cone in charge of the United States Naval Aviation Forces, Foreign Service, with headquarters in Paris. Chiefly concerned with protecting convoys, Cone supervised the construction of air bases in the British Isles, France, and Italy, from which numerous attacks were launched on cruising submarines and submarine bases. Though he initially employed seaplanes for patrol and bombing, he became convinced that they were less effective than land aircraft and unsuccessfully sought replacements. Cone's problems with the Navy Department were considerable (not the least was obtaining aircraft and spare parts), but he brought the naval air force to a high level of operating efficiency. His war service ended abruptly in September 1918 when the merchant ship on which he was en route from Queenstown, Ireland, to London was sunk by a German submarine. Cone was severely injured by a torpedo explosion, and after lengthy hospitalization and several postwar assignments, he was retired in 1922 with the rank of rear admiral.

Cone's attention in his later years centered on the American merchant marine. Under appointment by President Coolidge, he served as vice-president and general manager of the United States Shipping Board Emergency Fleet Corporation (1924–26); as trustee and later vice-president of its successor, the Merchant Fleet Corporation (1928–35); and as commissioner and chairman of the United States Shipping Board (1928–33). In these positions he spoke out vigorously for an expanded merchant marine, which he termed the nation's second line of defense, and secured appropriations for a program of engineering development that stimulated research into diesel engine propulsion and new methods of shipbuilding. Cone interrupted his government service from 1926 to 1928 to take a position as vice-president and treasurer of the Daniel Guggenheim Fund for the Promotion of Aeronautics. He left the government permanently in 1935 because of a dispute with the Department of Commerce about changes in the administration of the Merchant Marine Act of 1928. In 1937 he became chairman of the board of directors of Moore-McCormack Lines, Inc.

Cone was warmly regarded by associates and respected for his administrative abilities and engineering knowledge; he received many decorations. After 1922 he made his home in Washington, D. C. He was married on Oct. 16, 1900, to Patty Selden, by whom he had two children, Elizabeth and Hutchinson; she died in 1922. On Dec. 17, 1930, he married Julia Mattis. Cone died of a heart ailment at Orlando, Fla., and was buried in Arlington National Cemetery. One of the more notable reformers in American naval history, he had played an important part in the development of the modern navy.

[The best accounts of Cone's career are the obituaries in the *Transactions* of the Soc. of Naval Architects and Marine Engineers, XLIX (1941), 404–09, and of the Am. Soc. of Mechanical Engineers, XIII (1945), pp. RI–53–54. For family background see William W. Cone, *Some Account of the Cone Family in America* (1903). A detailed account of Cone's World War I aviation activities is in Clifford L. Lord, *Hist. of Naval Aviation, 1908–1939* (4 vols., mimeographed, Office of Naval Hist., Washington, D. C.). Cone's official correspondence is in the Navy Records, Nat. Archives. A photograph of Cone and references to him are in Elting E. Morison, *Adm. Sims and the Modern Am. Navy* (1942); and Sims mentions Cone in his book *The Victory at Sea* (1921).]
RAYMOND G. O'CONNOR

CONNICK, CHARLES JAY (Sept. 27, 1875–Dec. 28, 1945), artist in stained glass, was born at Springboro, Pa., the son of George Herbert and Mina Mirilla (Trainer) Connick, both natives of Pennsylvania. He was one of eleven children, but only he, two sisters, and a brother survived early childhood. When Charles was seven his father became advertising manager of a farm journal and moved his family to Pittsburgh. He was not a good provider, however, and Charles had to leave high school to go to work. A teacher in the Methodist Sunday school he attended interested him in music and art, and at eighteen he became an apprentice-illustrator on the *Pittsburgh Press*. While covering a sports event he met J. Horace Rudy, a stained glass artist, who asked him back to his studio. As gas jets were lighted, the jumble of glass on the artist's workbench created a fleeting glory of broken prismatic color that changed the course of Connick's life.

In 1894 he became an apprentice in the shop of Rudy Brothers and began (as he later recalled) "to learn the processes whereby the dusky jewels of my first night's fairyland were changed to become quite ordinary affairs that satisfied customers and produced daily bread." The heavy opalescent glass of the time, arranged to simulate static pictures, completely lacked "the vibration of color in a constantly changing light" that had enthralled Connick in the unset pieces of glass lying on Rudy's bench. His rebellion against the accepted style of the 1890's led him to study N. H. J. Westlake's *History of Design in Painted Glass* and to experiment in the revival of medieval techniques. Horace Rudy, at heart an artist rather than a businessman, encouraged Connick's investigations and got him opportunities to work in other shops in Pittsburgh, New York, and Boston. Connick studied life drawing in night classes in Pittsburgh from 1895 to 1900, when he moved permanently to Boston. While working as a designer, he continued his studies from 1900 to 1909 at the Boston Art Club and the Copley Society.

In 1902 Connick's design for a rose window in the baptistry of St. James Church, Roxbury, Mass., gained him the friendship of the architect Ralph Adams Cram [Supp. 3] and marked the beginning of a close collaboration that continued for forty years. Two other events of this period contributed to the evolution of his craft. In 1909 five clerestory windows arrived for the Church of the Advent in Boston, made in England by Christopher W. Whall. When uncrated they seemed unimpressive, "all slopped over with paint," yet when they were installed, Connick

saw in them "a lovely low-toned vibration" that recalled his initial vision fifteen years before in Pittsburgh. Having learned from this experience "how tiny spots of light through these areas of dirty paint had, in distance, illuminated entire windows," he became a convert to Whall, whose *Stained Glass Work: A Textbook for Students and Workers in Glass* (1905) he studied with care. Even more significant was his first visit to England and France in 1910, when he fell under the spell of the windows of Chartres.

Connick set up a studio of his own in Boston in 1913. Here he created innumerable windows for the churches of Cram and Ferguson, Maginnis and Walsh, and other ecclesiastical architects. Affecting national taste as much as any single artist can be said to have done so, Connick substituted for opaque and opalescent glass the medieval practice in which color is transparent, and in which, through painting insignificant in itself, that transparent color is focused to create, with changes of light, a vibrating pattern of a peculiar and vivid beauty. Although his technique was inspired by the twelfth and thirteenth centuries, his designs and subjects were by no means completely medieval or ecclesiastical. He was quite as happy to portray Emily Dickinson or Abigail Adams as an early Christian martyr. His windows were installed throughout the United States. They are to be seen in the Cathedral of St. John the Divine, St. Patrick's Cathedral, and the church of St. Vincent Ferrer in New York City; in Cram's Princeton University Chapel (where they interpreted the works of Malory, Dante, Milton, and Bunyan); in the Fourth Presbyterian Church and St. Chrysostom's Church in Chicago; in several churches in Minneapolis and St. Paul; and in Grace Cathedral in San Francisco. Of his work in and around Boston, St. John's, Beverly Farms, Mass., is a fine example of his treatment of a small parish church in a consistent design. Probably his happiest "playground for the sun" was the Heinz Memorial Chapel at the University of Pittsburgh. There, in the city where he had his first vision of color in light, he was able to develop a great symphonic series of windows to control the vibrant light and color of a lofty interior, largely enclosed in glass.

Connick married Mabel Rebecca Coombs of Colrain, Mass., on July 20, 1920; there were no children. He and his wife made numerous trips to England and France to study stained glass. The fruits of their travels are combined, with reflections on his craft, in a remarkable folio, *Adventures in Light and Color: An Introduction to the Stained Glass Craft* (1937). Connick's learning, whimsicality, and wit shine brilliantly through this compendious work, which is dedicated to Ralph Adams Cram. Like Cram he lived with his art; he preached stained glass and fought for it, for he loved color in light with a Franciscan simplicity and intensity. He received a gold medal at the Panama Pacific International Exposition in 1915, the Logan Medal of the Art Institute of Chicago in 1917, and the craftsmanship gold medal of the American Institute of Architects in 1925. Princeton gave him an honorary degree in 1932, and Boston University in 1938. He was an honorary member of the American Institute of Architects, president of the Stained Glass Association of America, 1931–39, and a fellow of the American Academy of Arts and Sciences.

Connick died of cancer in Boston at the age of seventy. After services in the Swedenborgian church which he had attended, he was buried in the Newton (Mass.) Cemetery. He had often said that his windows should be signed by many names, for the men and women who worked with him were like an extension of his spirit, as well as of his hands and brain. It is not surprising that a quarter of a century after his death the Charles J. Connick Associates were still making glass at the Harcourt Street studio in Boston he had established in 1913.

[Connick's book, and the tributes to him in *Stained Glass*, Spring 1946, are the best sources. Other information from: *Nat. Cyc. Am. Biog.*, Current Vol. E, p. 386; *Who Was Who in America*, vol. II (1950); biographical references compiled by Carl H. Mengert, Univ. of Wis. Lib. School; and Connick's death record. Personal details were provided by Orin E. Skinner of the Charles J. Connick Associates and Robert P. Walsh of Maginnis & Walsh & Kennedy. The Christopher Whall windows are illustrated in *Parish of the Advent, Gifts and Memorials* (1911), pp. xxv–xxvi.]
WALTER MUIR WHITEHILL

CONRAD, FRANK (May 4, 1874–Dec. 11, 1941), electrical and radio engineer, was born in Pittsburgh, Pa., the son of Herbert Michael Conrad, a railroad mechanic, and Sadie (Cassidy) Conrad. Already skilled in the use of tools, Frank left school after completing the seventh grade and, at sixteen, was apprenticed as a bench hand at the original electrical manufacturing plant of George Westinghouse [*q.v.*] in Pittsburgh.

Conrad's extraordinary mechanical aptitude and inventiveness soon became apparent. After making improvements on the feeding mechanism for arc lamps, he was transferred to the test department of the Westinghouse company, and in 1897 he made his first important engineering innovation, the "round-type" electric meter, prototype of the modern watt-hour meter still in wide use. This success led to his appointment in 1904 as general engineer for special development, in which capacity he systematically redesigned all

switchboards, meters, and rheostats in general use. Beginning about 1910, Conrad became responsible for developing a complete automobile electrical system. Many features of later automotive wiring practice, such as push-button remote starter control, automatic cutoff for the starting motor, and voltage-regulated generators, were included in his original design.

Outside professional circles, Conrad's fame derived mainly from his pioneering efforts in radio broadcasting, which earned him a reputation as "Father of American Radio." He became interested in radiotelegraphy in 1912, when a bet that his watch could keep better time than a colleague's motivated him to build an amateur home receiver and monitor the official navy time signals. After the outbreak of World War I, Conrad conducted radio research at Westinghouse, at first for the British government and later for the army Signal Corps, working with Westinghouse vice-president Harry Phillips Davis. For this purpose, Conrad built transmitting and receiving stations at his home and at the company's East Pittsburgh plant. He developed the only reliable airplane radio to be widely employed in the war.

Conrad continued his radio experiments after the war, and late in 1919 he began broadcasts of recorded music from his home station, 8XK, in Wilkinsburg, Pa. The enthusiastic response of fellow amateur operators led him to institute regular programs in the summer of 1920. He transmitted the first "commercially sponsored" broadcast when a local music store from which he borrowed records asked to be acknowledged on the air. That September a Pittsburgh department store began to advertise "amateur wireless sets" which would receive Conrad's programs. Their popularity impressed Davis with the commercial possibilities of radio broadcasting, both for mass communication and to create a market for receiving sets. The result was that Davis and Conrad established Westinghouse's pioneer commercial radio station, KDKA in Pittsburgh, presenting their first regular broadcast on Nov. 2, 1920 —a report of Harding's landslide victory over Cox in the presidential election. KDKA stressed diversified programming and over the next year initiated the broadcasting of church services, sports events, news, and market and farm reports.

Conrad's technological innovations earned him a promotion to assistant chief engineer of the Westinghouse company in 1921, a post he held until his death. Placed in charge of all radio work, he contributed to the commercial development of shortwaves, then largely confined to amateur use, and demonstrated their usefulness in sending signals over long distances. KDKA erected a shortwave antenna in the fall of 1923; at an international conference in London the next year, Conrad astonished fellow delegates by picking up news from Pittsburgh on a small set with a curtain-rod antenna in his hotel room. Conrad later investigated ultra-high-frequency transmission and developed radio equipment for Westinghouse. Altogether, he was granted over two hundred patents for his ideas, many of them outside the radio field; among them were designs for circuit breakers, electric clocks, home refrigerators, mercury vapor rectifiers, electrical measuring instruments, and lightning arrestors.

Conrad's achievements were widely recognized. He received the coveted Liebmann Prize of the Institute of Radio Engineers in 1925 and two years later was elected the group's vice-president. The American Institute of Electrical Engineers bestowed on him its Edison Medal (1931) and Lamme Medal (1936), and the University of Pittsburgh granted him an honorary doctorate of science in 1928. Conrad remained professionally active until his death and enjoyed hobbies of gardening and astronomy at his Wilkinsburg home. In 1941, while traveling to Florida, he suffered a coronary thrombosis and died in Miami at the age of sixty-seven. He was survived by his wife, Flora Elizabeth Selheimer of Wilkinsburg, whom he had married on June 18, 1902, and their three children: Francis Herbert, Crawford Joseph, and Jane Louise (Mrs. George Edwin Durham). In 1953 Conrad became the fourth man elected to the Radio Hall of Fame, following Thomas A. Edison [Supp. 1], Guglielmo Marconi, and Reginald A. Fessenden [Supp. 1].

[Obituaries in *Electrical Engineering*, Jan. 1942, Inst. of Radio Engineers, *Proc.*, Feb. 1942, p. 109, and *N. Y. Times,* Dec. 12, 1941; *Nat. Cyc. Am. Biog.,* XXXV, 178–79. For accounts of Conrad's role in the development of radio broadcasting, see Gleason L. Archer, *Hist. of Radio to 1926* (1938); Eric Barnouw, *A Tower in Babel: A Hist. of Broadcasting in the U. S.,* vol. I (1966); Lloyd Morris, *Not So Long Ago* (1949); W. Rupert Maclaurin and R. Joyce Harmon, *Invention and Innovation in the Radio Industry* (1949); and E. P. J. Shurick, *The First Quarter-Century of Radio Broadcasting* (1946).]

CHARLES SÜSSKIND

COOK, WALTER WHEELER (June 4, 1873–Nov. 7, 1943), law teacher and scholar, was one of the chief formulators of the school of jurisprudential thought known as legal realism, a philosophy closely related to sociological jurisprudence. The second of three children and younger son, Cook grew up with an understanding of science and an addiction to rigorous thought. His father, Ezekiel Hanson Cook, born in Maine of early Pilgrim stock and a graduate of Bowdoin College, was a teacher of mathematics and a school

principal. His mother, Clara Wing (Coburn) Cook, also from an early American family, taught French and worked closely with her husband in the schools he headed. One of these, the public high school in Columbus, Ohio, where Walter was born, had an instructional program that was radical for its time and admitted Negro students on a basis of full equality. Walter Wheeler Cook attended public schools in Columbus and two of the schools his father successively headed: the State Normal and Preparatory Training School in Potsdam, N. Y., and the Rutgers College Preparatory School. He began his undergraduate work at Rutgers, but transferred after a year to Columbia College, from which he received his A.B. degree in 1894.

Having won prizes in mechanics and physics as an undergraduate, Cook became an assistant in mathematics at Columbia and continued to study mathematical physics there and, for two years (1895–97), in Germany, under a John Lyndall Fellowship awarded by Columbia. While abroad, however, he abandoned his study of physics, because of a belief then current that the discipline was a closed one which did not lend itself to further imaginative contributions, and upon his return to Columbia he took up the study of law and political science. He received the A.M. degree in 1899 and the LL.M. degree in 1901. In the latter year Cook became an instructor in jurisprudence and political science at the University of Nebraska, where he served with Roscoe Pound, the chief American proponent of sociological jurisprudence. He remained there until 1904, having become professor of law after two years. He then became professor of law at, successively, the University of Missouri (1904–06), University of Wisconsin (1906–10), University of Chicago (1910–16), Yale (1916–19), Columbia (1919–22), and again Yale (1922–28).

Meanwhile, in published articles commencing in the second decade of the century, Cook had been helping to shape the philosophy of legal realism. This philosophy, which drew heavily on the pioneering thought of Oliver Wendell Holmes, Jr. [Supp. 1], stresses the importance, in the growth and application of law, of social data and of the complexities of individual fact situations, as distinguished from the extrapolation of legal doctrine. Accordingly, a central task of legal statesmanship is continuously to ascertain and act upon relevant facts in developing and criticizing legal doctrines in relation to societal goals. Cook's part in the evolution of this view was his emphasis on the importance of modern scientific method for the fact-gathering and evaluating process and his insistence on the tentativeness of scientific and therefore of legal generalizations. He also stressed the importance of rigorous logical processes in the analysis and application of legal rules, and in this respect carried forward, as did Albert Kocourek at Northwestern University, the thought of Wesley Newcomb Hohfeld [*q.v.*], whose tenure at Yale overlapped Cook's by two years. By bringing these ideas and methods to bear in several volumes of teaching material and numerous articles on specific topics in professional journals, in addition to his more theoretical writings, Cook made important contributions in the particular areas of conflict of laws, procedure, and equity.

At both Columbia and Yale, Cook was in close touch with other legal scholars and educators, including Underhill Moore at Columbia and Karl N. Llewellyn at Yale, whose thought paralleled his and who engaged in conscious efforts to reform American legal education and research. Among those at Columbia were Herman Oliphant [Supp. 2], Hessel E. Yntema, and the economist Leon C. Marshall; in 1928 these three became, with Cook, the original faculty of a new Institute of Law at the Johns Hopkins University. As visiting professor there from 1926 to 1928, Cook had aided in formulating plans for the institute. The university had no law school; the functions of the new unit were to engage in legal research and to train a small number of scholars in research methods. The institute published pathbreaking statistical studies of trial-court proceedings, but was discontinued in 1933 because of the impact of the depression.

Cook's teaching, emphatic and colorful, was highly effective. In the classroom and in discussion he delighted in exposing weaknesses in the thought of those with whom he disagreed. His radical theories placed him naturally in opposition to conservative university administrations and to traditionalists in law schools and the legal profession, whose views and policies he sought to displace. Hence antagonism developed between him and some of those under whom he worked. Cook urged his ideas with single-minded intensity, orally and in writing, on every possible occasion, often conveying them to judges and other leading professional figures for comment. An expressive, though somewhat enigmatic, response is that in a passage in a 1928 letter from Mr. Justice Holmes to Cook, which says, "I hope that I may live to read your prospective book even though the perusal should crush me. I always am glad of anything that brings a letter from you." Yet Cook was not instinctively outgoing. Some who knew him best detected a basic shyness which limited his close associations and may have generated a compensating self-regard

and aggressiveness. He was, nevertheless, unfailingly courteous in his correspondence and published writings, and his personal and family relations were warm. He had a strong faith in freedom, discussion, and democratic processes, especially within the academic profession.

In 1934–35, following the termination of the Institute of Law at Johns Hopkins, Cook served as the salaried general secretary of the American Association of University Professors, of which he had been a charter member and president, 1931–33. He had earlier been president of the Association of American Law Schools, in 1915–16, and of the national law school honor society, the Order of the Coif, 1926–29. In 1935 he returned to teaching at Northwestern University, where he remained as professor of law until his retirement in 1943. He died that fall of a heart ailment at the age of seventy, in a hospital in Tupper Lake, N. Y., near his summer home. On Nov. 14, 1899, Cook had married Helen Newman of Washington, D. C. They had four daughters: Helen Coburn, Dorothy Newman, Edith Newman, and Mary Newman. On Sept. 23, 1931, following his first wife's death, he married Elizabeth Stabler Iddings of Baltimore, who survived him. His contribution to legal realism was an enduring and pervasive influence on legal thought, for this jurisprudential school affected legal education and the philosophy of judges and lawyers in the United States to an increasing extent during the middle decades of the twentieth century and, later, elsewhere in the world.

[This sketch is based on interviews with members of Cook's family, associates, and friends; on published writings by and about him and the Johns Hopkins Inst. of Law; and on a study of a significant collection of his MSS. and correspondence in the possession of his widow, Elizabeth I. Cook. For additional information see memorials in Assoc. of Am. Law Schools, *Handbook,* 1943, pp. 225–28, and in *Ill. Law Rev.,* Mar.–Apr. 1944, by Charles E. Clarke, Homer F. Carey, and Hessel E. Yntema (with portrait); and *Who Was Who in America,* vol. II (1950). On the Johns Hopkins Inst., see Frederick K. Beutel, *Some Potentialities of Experimental Jurisprudence as a New Branch of Social Science* (1957), pp. 105–13. On his father, see *Nat. Cyc. Am. Biog.,* XIII, 579–80; and *Obituary Record of the Graduates of Bowdoin College . . . for the Decade Ending 1 June 1909* (1911). See also the following works by Cook: *My Philosophy of Law: Credos of Sixteen Am. Scholars* (1941), pp. 49–66 (with portrait and bibliography); *Cases and Materials on Equity* (3rd ed., 1940); *Logical and Legal Bases of the Conflict of Laws* (1942), new and reprinted essays; "Improvement of Legal Education and of Standards for Admission to the Bar," *Am. Law School Rev.,* Fall 1917; "The Alienability of Choses in Action: A Reply to Prof. Williston," *Harvard Law Rev.,* Mar. 1917; "Privileges of Labor Unions in the Struggle for Life," *Yale Law Jour.,* Apr. 1918; "Hohfeld's Contribution to the Science of Law," *ibid.,* June 1919; "Scientific Method and the Law," *Jour. Am. Bar Assoc.,* June 1927; "Law and the Modern Mind—A Symposium," *Columbia Law Rev.,* Jan. 1931;

"Oliver Wendell Holmes, Scientist," *Jour. Am. Bar Assoc.*, Apr. 1935; "Eugenics or Euthenics," *Ill. Law Rev.*, Jan.–Feb. 1943; review of Beale, *Treatise on the Conflict of Laws*, in *Columbia Law Rev.*, Nov. 1935.]

RALPH F. FUCHS

COOK, WILL MARION (Jan. 27, 1869–July 19, 1944), musician and composer, was born in Washington, D. C., the second of three sons of John Hartwell Cook and Marion Isabel (Lewis) Cook. Both parents came from free Negro families. John Cook, born in Richmond, Va., had grown up in Detroit, Mich.; his wife, in Chattanooga, Tenn. Both were graduates of Oberlin College. Soon after their marriage they settled in Washington, D. C., where Cook became chief clerk in the Freedmen's Bureau (1867–72), graduated from the law department of Howard University in 1871, and was the first Negro to practice law in Washington. He later taught law at Howard and served as both trustee and dean.

Young Cook was christened Will Mercer, in honor of a close family friend, John Mercer Langston [q.v.]. The elder Cook died when Will was ten, but his mother taught sewing at Howard University and kept the family a step above genteel poverty. Will early showed talent for music. In 1884, at fifteen, he entered the Oberlin Conservatory of Music, where he remained for four years and became a proficient violinist. The proceeds of a benefit concert organized in Washington by a group of family friends, including Langston and Frederick Douglass [q.v.], enabled Cook to begin European study in 1889. He spent the next three years in Berlin, studying violin under Josef Joachim and music theory at the Hochschule. In 1894–95 he attended the National Conservatory of Music in New York, then headed by the composer Anton Dvořák, under whom he studied briefly.

Cook soon realized that race prejudice severely limited his chances for success as a classical composer, and he began to think of using his musical training to write in the Negro idiom for a popular audience. In the mid-1890's the minstrel show with its plantation stereotypes was giving way in popular favor to ragtime music and "coon songs." Blacks portrayed in coon songs were no less stereotyped, but they appeared in a contemporary setting which allowed some subtly realistic expression of black pathos and philosophy. Cook believed that he could adapt these musical forms successfully to Broadway in an all-Negro show. In New York he had met the team of Bert Williams [q.v.] and George Walker, black entertainers then just breaking into big-time vaudeville, who had made the cakewalk a national craze. Inspired by their act, he went home to Washington, and there, enlisting the help of Paul Laurence Dunbar [q.v.] on the libretto, he composed the music and lyrics for a short musical comedy, *Clorindy: The Origin of the Cake-Walk*. In an autobiographical fragment (*Theatre Arts*, September 1947) Cook records that when his mother heard the words to one of his songs, "Who Dat Say Chicken in Dis Crowd?" she exclaimed, "Oh, Will! Will! I've sent you all over the world to study and become a great musician, and you return such a *nigger*!" He adds the comment that she wanted him to write like a white man.

Back in New York, Cook persuaded the comedian Ernest Hogan and twenty-five other black singers and dancers to rehearse *Clorindy*. He finally won an audition with the manager of the Casino Theatre Roof Garden and was booked. At the close of the first performance, conducted by Cook on a summer night in 1898, the audience stood and cheered for ten minutes. Considered by James Weldon Johnson [Supp. 2] "the first demonstration of the possibilities of syncopated Negro music," *Clorindy* ran for several months. From it came Cook's first published song, "Dark Town Is Out To-night," which appeared under the pseudonym "Will Marion" in 1899; he subsequently used the name Will Marion Cook.

Over the next ten years Cook created much of the music for a series of black musicals featuring Williams and Walker. *In Dahomey* (1903), with lyrics by Dunbar, made Negro theatrical history by opening at the New York Theatre in Times Square, the center of theatredom. The show traveled to Europe in 1903, gave a command performance at Buckingham Palace, and made the cakewalk a fad in England and France. Other hits for Williams and Walker followed, such as *Abyssinia* (1906) and *Bandana Land* (1908). In 1906 Cook helped organize a ragtime band, the Memphis Students, with which he toured both Europe and America.

After about 1909, Cook's career as a Broadway composer languished. George Walker died, and Bert Williams joined Ziegfeld's *Follies*. Ragtime gave way to the blues and jazz. Cook's perfectionism and his acerbic, frequently volatile personality made him a difficult man to get along with, and he had little patience with the "Uncle-Tomming" often needed to succeed on white-dominated Broadway. He composed fragments of an opera, "St. Louis Woman," based on the Afro-American past, but never completed it, for financial necessity kept him working on popular songs and musicals. For a time he organized and conducted the New York Syncopated Orchestra, which he took to Europe in 1919, thus helping to introduce American jazz to European audiences. A number of Cook's musicians stayed on in Europe, the most famous being the jazz clarinetist and saxophonist Sidney Bechet. Despite his lack of outward success, Cook continued to offer a helping hand to younger musicians, including Luckey Roberts, James P. Johnson, Ethel Waters, Harold Arlen, and Duke Ellington. He gave Ellington a course in music so concentrated that Ellington, who had never received formal musical training, called Cook his private conservatory and acknowledged his "brief, but . . . strong influence" in the 1920's (*New Yorker,* July 8, 1944, p. 29).

Cook will be remembered for many popular songs, such as "Mandy Lou," "Swing Along Children," "The Rain Song," "Red, Red Rose," "That's How the Cake-Walk's Done," and "A Little Bit of Heaven Called Home," and for his best-known choral work, "Exhortation." In 1899 he married Abbie Mitchell, a singer-dancer in *Clorindy.* They had a daughter, Marion, and a son, Mercer, who became professor of romance languages at Howard University and later American ambassador to the Niger Republic. After their divorce in 1906, Abbie Mitchell went on to a successful career as an actress and singer. Cook died of cancer in New York City at the age of seventy-five and was buried in Woodlawn Cemetery, Washington, D. C.

[Will Marion Cook's autobiographical "Clorindy, the Origin of the Cakewalk," *Theatre Arts,* Sept. 1947; *The ASCAP Biog. Dict. of Composers, Authors and Publishers* (3rd ed., 1966); obituary in *Jour. of Negro Hist.,* Oct. 1944; Mercer Cook, "Will Marion Cook: He Helped Them All," *Crisis,* Oct. 1944; references to Cook in James Weldon Johnson, *Black Manhattan* (1930); Edith Isaacs, *The Negro in the Am. Theatre* (1947), pp. 32, 38, 46–48, 136–38; Rudi Blesh and Harriet Janis, *They All Played Ragtime* (1950); Lofton Mitchell, *Black Drama* (1967); and Ann Charters, *Nobody: The Story of Bert Williams* (1970). On Cook's parents, see "The Cook Family in Hist.," *Negro Hist. Bull.,* June 1946; alumni records of Oberlin College; *Semi-Centennial Register of the Officers and Alumni of Oberlin College, 1833–1883* (1883), pp. 106 and 113; *Howard Univ. Catalogue, 1868–69 to 1870–71;* and Walter Dyson, *Howard Univ.* (1941). A small collection of MSS., including fragments of an autobiography, is in the possession of Mercer Cook, who also supplied much personal information concerning his father.]

EUGENE LEVY

COOLEY, MORTIMER ELWYN (Mar. 28, 1855–Aug. 25, 1944), engineering educator and public utilities expert, was born near Canandaigua, N. Y., the fourth son and fifth of eight children of Albert Blake Cooley and Achsah Bennett (Griswold) Cooley, and a younger brother of Lyman Edgar Cooley [*q.v.*], who became a prominent hydraulic engineer. Like his distant cousin Thomas McIntyre Cooley [*q.v.*], he was descended from Benjamin Cooley, who settled in Springfield, Mass., in 1643. Reared on his father's moderately prosperous farm, Cooley received his early education at a local district school and at the Canandaigua Academy for Men. He then devoted one year to schoolteaching before entering the United States Naval Academy in 1874. There he studied steam engineering and graduated in 1878 as an engineer cadet. After advancing in 1880 to assistant engineer (ensign), he was ordered the following year to the University of Michigan as professor of steam engineering and iron shipbuilding.

Cooley responded well to academic life. He resigned from the navy in 1885 and, except for a brief tour of volunteer naval duty during the Spanish-American War, spent the rest of his career at Michigan. Bold and self-assured, he soon had mechanical engineering established as a specialized field at the university. He was a strong advocate of a broad liberal education for engineers. As dean after 1904, he made the school of engineering one of the most important in the university.

Cooley's career as a public utilities expert began in 1899 when the reform mayor of Detroit, Hazen S. Pingree [*q.v.*], asked him to appraise the properties of the Detroit Street Railways. The next year Pingree, who had become governor of Michigan, commissioned Cooley to organize a systematic, statewide evaluation of railroad properties, the first of its kind. Although not a railroad expert, Cooley developed standardized and rationalized procedures for evaluating public utilities. Instead of having a few bookkeepers inspect company records, he hired seventy-five engineers and sent them into the field to inspect the properties in person. The resulting survey was so well documented that it withstood all assaults by angry railroad executives and became the model for later utilities surveys. In 1902 Cooley made a similar survey for the colony of Newfoundland, and thereafter, because of his precise methods and his unimpeachable integrity, he was in considerable demand. He undertook surveys for Minneapolis, Milwaukee, Cleveland, St. Louis, Boston, New York City, Buffalo, and Washington, D. C., and from 1910 to 1921 was in charge of appraising hydro- and steam-electric properties and railroads for the Michigan Railroad Commission. His appraisal work received criticism, however, when in 1917 his delegation of too much authority to subordinates resulted in evaluating the St. Joseph Power Company at $250,000, though it was afterward found to be worth only $34,000. Cooley was also criticized in 1915 by a reform-minded engineer, Morris L. Cooke, as being too closely allied with big business.

Active in professional organizations, Cooley was president of the American Society of Mechanical Engineers (1919) and of the Society for the Promotion of Engineering Education (1920–21), a director of the American Society of Civil Engineers (1913–16), and a vice-president of Section D of the American Association for the Advancement of Science (1898). Cooley also served on government commissions and boards, such as the commission on awards of the Pan-American Exposition in Buffalo (1901), the Joint Postal Commission Advisory Board (1920–23), and the Block Signal and Train Control Board of the Interstate Commerce Commission (1907–12).

In 1922 he succeeded Herbert Hoover as president of the recently formed American Engineering Council and, like the founders, worked to make the organization a master research and policy-producing body for the American engineering profession. The council, however, lost support after publishing some controversial studies of waste and inefficiency in American industry, which included recommending the abolition of the twelve-hour day in steel and similar industries. Cooley resigned in 1924, ostensibly because he could not handle the job along with his duties at Michigan.

That year he was persuaded to run for the United States Senate on the Democratic ticket against the popular James Couzens [Supp. 2]. Though he had no hopes of winning, his campaign, based upon appeals for conservation and efficiency of resource use, drew considerable attention. Cooley retired in 1928 as dean of engineering. He was called back into public service in 1933 as state engineer for the Public Works Administration.

On Dec. 25, 1879, Cooley had married Caroline Elizabeth Moseley of Fairport, N. Y. They had four children: Lucy Alliance, Hollis Moseley, Anna Elizabeth, and Margaret Achsah. Cooley had a forceful personality and a mock gruff manner, yet generated great affection and respect among students, colleagues, politicians, and businessmen. He was an avid collector of Oriental rugs. After a prolonged illness, he died of cancer at the University of Michigan Hospital in Ann Arbor at the age of eighty-nine. He was buried in Woodland Cemetery, Canandaigua, N. Y.

[The most available source of information is Cooley's autobiography (with Vivien B. Keatley), *Scientific Blacksmith* (1947). Anyone seriously interested in his career, however, should consult his papers at the Mich. Hist. Collections, Univ. of Mich.; there are also letters of Cooley in the papers of other university faculty members there. Cooley himself published *The Cooley Genealogy* (1941). See also Melvin G. Holli and C. David Tompkins, "Mortimer E. Cooley: Technocrat as Politician," *Mich. Hist.*, Summer 1968; Kenneth E. Trombley, *The Life and Times of a Happy Liberal* (1954), a biography of Morris L. Cooke; and obituaries in *N. Y. Times*, Aug. 26, 1944, *Civil Engineering*, Oct. 1944, and *Mechanical Engineering*, Oct. 1944. Death record from Mich. Dept. of Public Health. There are good portraits of Cooley at the Univ. of Mich. and the Mich. Hist. Collections.]
MONTE A. CALVERT

COOLEY, THOMAS BENTON (June 23, 1871–Oct. 13, 1945), pediatrician, was born in Ann Arbor, Mich., the youngest of the four sons and two daughters of Thomas McIntyre Cooley [q.v.] and Mary Elizabeth (Horton) Cooley, and a younger brother of the sociologist Charles Horton Cooley. His father served as a justice of the supreme court of Michigan, first dean of the law school of the University of Michigan, and as the first chairman of the Interstate Commerce Commission. Young Cooley graduated from both the literary department and the medical school of the University of Michigan, receiving an A.B. degree in 1891 and an M.D. degree in 1895. After an internship at the Boston City Hospital (1895–97), he returned to the University of Michigan in 1897 as instructor in hygiene and physiological chemistry at the medical school.

Although pediatrics had not then become a recognized branch of medicine, Cooley developed a strong interest in the diseases of children and in 1901 went to Germany for a year's study, after which he spent an eighteen months' residency at the Boston City Hospital working with contagious diseases. In 1903 he returned to Michigan as assistant professor of hygiene at the medical school, but left after two years to open a private practice in pediatrics in Detroit, which thereafter remained his home. In Detroit, Cooley took an active part in the campaign to reduce the high death rate among infants suffering from diarrheal diseases, served as medical director of the Babies' Milk Fund, and helped establish medical inspections in the local schools. He was probably the city's first pediatrician in the modern sense—perhaps the first in the state—and certainly the foremost one for many years.

During World War I, Cooley served as a major with the American Red Cross in France (1918–19). As assistant chief of its children's bureau, he organized children's clinics, a training school for orphans and refugee children, and an adoption agency, work for which he was awarded the cross of the Legion of Honor in 1924. Back in Detroit, he was appointed chief of the pediatric service and chairman of the staff of the Children's Hospital of Michigan in 1921 and, in 1936, professor of pediatrics at Wayne University College of Medicine. He played a major role in the development of the Children's Hospital, urging the establishment of a salaried, full-time medical staff, as well as greater cooperation among the independent pediatric services and attention to fundamental clinical research. His lack of interest in administrative problems, however, as well as conflicts generated by his rather austere personality, prevented the establishment of the pediatric research center under the joint auspices of the hospital and the medical school which he had envisioned.

Cooley's own interests lay less in the individual patient than in the etiology of the disease. He centered his research in hematology and the anemias of childhood. Though he made a number of contributions to pediatric literature, the most important was his identification of the familial anemia that bears his name—Cooley's anemia, also known as thalassemia or Mediterranean anemia, because it was at first thought to occur only in families of Mediterranean stock. The disease, whose victims rarely survive childhood, was first described by Cooley in 1925. He suspected its hereditary nature and was delighted when later work by others demonstrated its genetic origin and mode of inheritance. He was similarly interested in sickle-cell anemia, a heritable disorder at first supposed to occur only in children of African descent, and was the first to find and report it in a child of white ancestry. He strongly urged the importance of genetics in medical education as a means toward identifying hereditary factors in other diseases.

Cooley was one of the founders of the American Academy of Pediatrics and served as its president in 1934–35. He also was president of the American Pediatric Society (1940–41). In 1940, the year before his retirement, he received an honorary Sc.D. from the University of Michigan.

In the judgment of one observer (Wolf W. Zuelzer), Cooley was "that unusual phenomenon, a pure intellectual strayed into medicine." A highly private, self-contained man, he wrote clearly and concisely, knew modern as well as the classical languages, and took great pleasure in music and painting. Although concerned with improving the pediatric training offered by the medical schools and the teaching hospitals, he stressed the importance of a liberal education in the humanities, warning that without it physicians would eventually become merely a group of technicians. He was a Congregationalist in religion. On Dec. 21, 1903, Cooley married Abigail Hubbard of Ashtabula, Ohio. Their two children were Emily Holland and Thomas McIntyre. He spent his summers at his cottage in Sorrento, Maine, where he enjoyed golf and boating. He became seriously ill in the summer

of 1945 and died that fall of hypertensive heart disease in the Eastern Maine General Hospital in Bangor, at the age of seventy-four.

[Wolf W. Zuelzer in Borden S. Veeder, ed., *Pediatric Profiles* (1957); obituaries in *Am. Jour. of Diseases of Children*, Jan. 1946, *Detroit Medic. News*, Nov. 19, 1945, and *Jour. Am. Medic. Assoc.*, Nov. 24, 1945; *Semi-Centennial Vol. of the Am. Pediatric Soc.* (1938), p. 111; *Nat. Cyc. Am. Biog.*, XXXIII, 93–94; *Who Was Who in America*, vol. II (1950); Mortimer E. Cooley, *The Cooley Genealogy* (1941). See also Cooley's papers "A Series of Cases of Splenomegaly in Children, with Anemia and Peculiar Bone Changes" (with Pearl Lee), *Am. Pediatric Soc.. Transactions*, 1925; and "Anemia in Children" (with E. R. Witwer and Pearl Lee), *Am. Jour. of Diseases of Children*, Aug. 1927.]

THOMAS E. CONE, JR.

CORIAT, ISADOR HENRY (Dec. 10, 1875– May 26, 1943), neurologist and psychoanalyst, was born in Philadelphia, Pa., the son of Harry and Clara (Einstein) Coriat. His father, born Hyram Curiat, was a Jewish immigrant from Morocco; his mother was a native Philadelphian. The family moved about 1879 to Boston, where the elder Coriat started out as peddler and eventually became a cigar manufacturer. Isador attended Boston public schools. After receiving his M.D. degree from Tufts Medical College in 1900, he worked for five years as assistant physician at the Worcester (Mass.) State Hospital, where psychiatry was being transformed by Adolf Meyer.

Thereafter Coriat lived in Boston, working at first as a neurologist. He served in that capacity on the staff of the City Hospital until 1919 and at Mount Sinai Hospital until 1914, meanwhile engaging in private practice. As a student Coriat had been co-author of *A Laboratory Manual of Physiological and Clinical Chemistry and Toxicology* (1898), and at Worcester he had investigated the chemistry and physiology of the nervous system. He soon became interested in the role of the mind in causing and curing functional nervous disorders. In Boston, then the center of interest in psychopathology and psychotherapy, he was particularly influenced by the distinguished neurologist Morton Prince [*q.v.*], with whom he worked at Boston City Hospital. Prince, an adherent of the French psychopathologist Pierre Janet, was the leading American student of the "subconscious"; he investigated multiple personalities and other dissociated mental states, as well as hypnosis. Coriat joined other physicians and psychologists, including William James [*q.v.*], who met at Prince's home to discuss these phenomena. He also became medical consultant to the Emmanuel Movement, a program of religious healing within the Episcopal Church that was sharply criticized by many physicians; with Elwood Worcester [Supp. 2] and Samuel McComb, the movement's ministers, he wrote *Religion and Medicine* (1908).

Between 1906 and 1908 Coriat became acquainted with the work of Sigmund Freud through the writings of A. A. Brill and James Jackson Putnam [*q.v.*], a Boston neurologist and the most prominent American convert to psychoanalyis. He later recalled that he initially considered Freud's theories on infantile sexuality and free association in dream analysis "nonsensical." Although he was impressed by Freud's lectures at Clark University in 1909, he still at that time viewed psychoanalysis as one of several valid therapies. Yet he was convinced that every mental symptom had a cause, and found psychoanalysis increasingly useful in connecting hysterical symptoms to repressed childhood experiences, often of a sexual nature. In 1913 Coriat publicly disagreed with Janet and announced his belief in the "complete validity" of psychoanalytic theory; the next year he joined the psychoanalytic study group which met at Putnam's home. After Putnam's death in 1918, Coriat was one of the few analysts in Boston, and the only one considered orthodox. Even then, however, he seemed broadly inclusive; he allowed his popular book *Abnormal Psychology* to be reprinted without a thoroughgoing psychoanalytic revision, and as late as 1920 he referred to Alfred Adler as "one of the greatest thinkers of the Freudian school."

Coriat's most important contribution was to keep psychoanalysis alive in Boston and to assist in establishing it on a professional basis. During the 1920's he held informal seminars with younger analysts, most of whom had been trained in Europe. He also took the lead in organizing the Boston Psychoanalytic Society in 1930, serving as its president in 1930–32 and 1941–42. In 1935 he helped found the Boston Psychoanalytic Institute, a training institute which he served as instructor, training analyst, and trustee. He was president of the American Psychoanalytic Association in 1924–25 and 1936–37.

Coriat was a prolific if not highly original writer. He had broad interests, and published numerous articles on anthropology, literature, history, and myth, as well as on purely clinical topics. Several of his books were intended for popular audiences: *Abnormal Psychology* (1910), *The Hysteria of Lady Macbeth* (1912), *The Meaning of Dreams* (1915), *What Is Psychoanalysis?* (1917), and *Repressed Emotions* (1920). Except for the first, these were written from a psychoanalytic viewpoint in an effort to popularize the new medical field. Like other early American analysts, Coriat tried to make psychoanalysis

palatable to the public by deemphasizing sexuality and explaining that "'sexual' has the same broad meaning as the word 'love.'" He believed psychoanalysis could help individuals sublimate infantile tendencies into useful intellectual and artistic pursuits, and especially praised the healing properties of religion. His most original and influential work was *Stammering: A Psychoanalytic Interpretation,* published in 1928 after more than a decade of research. He viewed stammering as an "oral neurosis" in which the sufferer protected himself against betrayal of his infantile sadistic tendencies.

Coriat worked easily with others and was considered by his colleagues a genial and sincere friend. He remained a tenacious advocate of psychoanalysis, subordinating personal predilections to the interests of the movement. His happy marriage, on Feb. 1, 1904, to Etta Dann, daughter of a Boston rabbi, ended with her death thirty years later. There were no children. Coriat died in Boston of a coronary thrombosis in 1943; his remains were cremated at Forest Hills Crematory, Boston. He is remembered as one of the early American Freudians.

[Isador H. Coriat, "Some Personal Reminiscences of Psychoanalysis in Boston," *Psychoanalytic Rev.,* Jan. 1945; *Nat. Cyc. Am. Biog.,* XXXII, 190–91 (with picture, facing p. 190); obituaries in *Psychoanalytic Rev.,* Oct. 1943 (by George B. Wilbur), and *Psychoanalytic Quart.,* July 1943 (by A. A. Brill); Ives Hendrick, ed., *The Birth of an Institute: Twenty-Fifth Anniversary, the Boston Psychoanalytic Inst.* (1961); Nathan G. Hale, Jr., "The Origins and Foundations of the Psychoanalytic Movement in America, 1909–14" (Ph.D. dissertation, Univ. of Calif., Berkeley, 1965), pp. 445–48; information from Drs. M. Ralph Kaufman, Ives Hendrick, and John M. Murray. The Coriat Papers, in the Countway Lib., Harvard Medical School, include newspaper clippings on the Emmanuel Movement, reviews of Coriat's books, teaching and reading notes, and papers on medical history. For a bibliography of his writings, see Alexander Grinstein, *The Index of Psychoanalytic Writings,* I (1956), 340–44. Information on Harry Coriat from *Phila. City Directory,* 1872–75, and *Boston Directory,* 1879–95, and from John Daly, Archival Examiner of Phila.]

BARBARA SICHERMAN

COUCH, HARVEY CROWLEY (Aug. 21, 1877–July 30, 1941), public utility promoter, was born in Calhoun, Ark., one of six children and the eldest son of Thomas Gratham Couch, a farmer and Methodist preacher, and Manie (Heard) Couch. The families of both parents had moved west from Georgia, where his mother was born. After attending a one-room schoolhouse in Calhoun and the Southwestern Academy in nearby Magnolia, Couch worked briefly as a clerk in a local drugstore. He then, in 1897, took a job as mail clerk on the Cotton Belt Railroad. In this capacity he met many small-town businessmen and politicians, making friendships which in time he put to profitable use. He conceived a plan of building a number of interconnected telephone exchanges along the railroad line, and in 1903, with about $150 of borrowed capital and credit from equipment manufacturers, he installed his first exchange in Bienville, La. He resigned his railroad job in 1905. Obtaining franchises from town councils and raising capital locally by selling bonds, he steadily built his network until, in 1910, he was operating fifty exchanges over 1,500 miles of lines. The following year he sold his properties to the Bell system for upwards of a million dollars.

Couch was already hatching a grander scheme. In the wake of the successful harnessing of Niagara Falls for electric power in 1904, enterprising promoters the nation over dreamed of growing rich in the hydroelectric power business, and near Couch's base of operations, on the Ouachita River, were several good dam sites. There was no industrial market for power in the area, but Samuel Insull [Supp. 2] was just then completing his much-publicized Lake County Experiment in northern Illinois, demonstrating the economic feasibility of interconnecting small towns and farms into integrated electric systems, and Couch determined to build such a system in Arkansas.

After acquiring electric and water properties in Arkadelphia, Ark., and initiating negotiations for the purchase of a power plant in nearby Magnolia, Couch in 1913 organized the Arkansas Power Company, which the following year was reorganized as the Arkansas Light & Power Company. The methods he employed in expanding this enterprise were typical of those of other utility promoters during the period. He obtained franchises through his growing political influence, and built markets by promoting and attracting industry. He raised capital through local banks and private subscriptions (his greatest natural gifts being personal charm and ability as a salesman), reviving a "booster" spirit that had been more or less defunct in the area since the days of the early railroad promoters. When his ventures outgrew such methods, he established financial connections in New York and sold bonds through investment banking houses. In one respect Couch was particularly imaginative. The demand for electricity was highly seasonal, being heavy during the long nights of the winter months and almost nonexistent during the other three seasons. Couch created a summer demand by promoting the use of electric power for irrigation in the Arkansas and Louisiana rice fields and a fall demand by persuading cotton gin owners to electrify their

operations; in both cases he induced equipment manufacturers to provide the consumers with easy credit for their conversion to electricity.

As Federal Fuel Administrator of Arkansas during World War I, Couch saw to it that Arkansas Light & Power did not suffer for lack of coal. Sorely needing legally authorized rate increases to compensate for wartime inflation, he induced the Arkansas legislature in 1919 to establish a state utility commission, replacing local regulation; the commission authorized a general round of rate increases before being abolished in 1921 because of adverse public opinion. By 1925, following the completion of the Remmel Dam on the Ouachita River, the construction of a steam-electric plant at Sterlington, La., and the purchase of several plants in Mississippi, Couch operated an extensive, integrated electric system that served most of Arkansas and much of northern Louisiana and western Mississippi.

That same year Couch sold his enterprises to the Electric Bond and Share Company, a gigantic holding company directed by Sidney Z. Mitchell [Supp. 3]. He continued to preside over the company he had created (now called Arkansas Power & Light) and, having established favorable connections with New York investment bankers and stockbrokers, regularly participated in lucrative financial syndicates. Because he was one of the few big businessmen who happened also to be an influential Democrat, his value to his Eastern friends increased with the election of President Franklin D. Roosevelt in 1932. His prominence had already led President Hoover that year to appoint him a director of the Reconstruction Finance Commission, and Roosevelt persuaded him to retain the post until 1934. With Eastern money, Couch ventured often into railroad reorganization and expansion, as well as other business deals, and in 1937 he acquired a controlling interest in the Kansas City Southern Railway.

Although he became a personal friend of Roosevelt, Couch's political connections did little to help the depressed state of the power industry in the 1930's. He was unable to obtain an RFC loan to extend electric service to farmers, and his company, like virtually all others, was forced to cut its rates several times during the decade. After the Rural Electrification Administration was set up in 1936, Arkansas Power & Light (like other utilities) first sought federal funds for rural electrification. When, however, it became clear that federal money would be used only to underwrite farmer-owned electric cooperatives, Couch attempted, with a large measure of success, to acquire such cooperatives as wholesale customers.

In certain respects he contributed a great deal to the progress of rural electrification. At his instigation two of his engineers developed the "Pittman line," halving the cost of rural power lines, and Couch worked out a plan whereby depression-ridden farmers contributed their labor instead of money toward the cost of farm extension lines. Both innovations hastened the spread of electric service to Southern farmers.

On Oct. 4, 1904, Couch had married Jessie Johnson of Athens, La. They had five children: Johnson Olin, Harvey Crowley, Kirke, Catherine, and William Thomas. Though not especially noted for his philanthropy, Couch was widely heralded for service to his state and generally regarded as the businessman who contributed most to its economic development. In 1940 he attended the Democratic National Convention and warmly supported Franklin Roosevelt's bid for a third term, but he opposed the left wing of the party and was among those who unsuccessfully fought the vice-presidential nomination of Henry A. Wallace. It was generally supposed that the strain and disappointment of the 1940 convention contributed to the failure of his health. A year later, at the age of sixty-three, Couch died of a heart attack at Couchwood, his summer home near Hot Springs, Ark. He was buried in Pine Bluff, Ark., where he had long made his home.

[Winston P. Wilson, *Harvey Couch: The Master Builder* (1947); John Clark, "A Hist. of Ark. Power & Light Co." (doctoral thesis, Harvard Graduate School of Business Administration, 1960); Federal Trade Commission report, *Utility Corporations* (96 parts, 1928–37); *N. Y. Times* obituary, July 31, 1941; David Y. Thomas, ed., *Arkansas and Its People,* III (1930), 310–12.]

FORREST McDONALD

CRAIG, MALIN (Aug. 5, 1875–July 25, 1945), army officer, was born in St. Joseph, Mo., the first of three children of Louis Aleck and Georgie (Malin) Craig. The family had a strong military tradition. Malin's grandfather James Craig, lawyer, Congressman from Missouri (1857–61), and president of the Hannibal and St. Joseph Railroad, had been a brigadier general in the Union Army during the Civil War. His father, a West Point graduate, became a career officer in the cavalry. His mother was the daughter of an army officer, and his brother, Louis Aleck Craig, Jr., also followed a notable career in the army.

Malin Craig grew up on small military posts in Kansas, Arizona, and New Mexico. He attended local schools and spent three-and-a-half years at Georgetown School and College in Washington, D. C., before entering West Point in 1894. Excelling in athletics and military science, he graduated in 1898 in time to join the Spanish-American War, participating with the 6th Cavalry in the Santiago Campaign. With the same unit, he served in the China Relief Expedition during the Boxer Rebellion (1900) and in the Philippines (1900–02), where he participated in a number of engagements and was aide-de-camp to Brigadier General J. Franklin Bell [Supp. 1] during the Philippine insurrection. On Apr. 29, 1901, in Manila, he married Genevieve Woodruff, daughter of Brigadier General Charles A. Woodruff; they had one child, a son, Malin.

Over the next sixteen years Craig held a variety of posts as he advanced in rank and responsibility. He graduated from the line and staff schools at Fort Leavenworth (1904 and 1905) and attended the Army War College in 1909–10. Relief duty in San Francisco following the earthquake and fire of 1906 prefigured his later notable work as director of relief during the Mississippi River flood of 1927 and in Venezuela after a severe earthquake in 1929. For six months in 1915 Craig rejoined Bell, now major general, as chief of staff of the 2nd Division, mobilized in Texas for possible hostilities with Mexico.

When the United States entered World War I, Craig, promoted to lieutenant colonel, was made chief of staff of the 41st Division, commanded by Major General Hunter Liggett [Supp. 1]. He remained with Liggett when the latter took command of the American I Army Corps in January 1918. Craig contributed significantly to the Corps's successful record in the Champagne-Marne battle (where, as Liggett later wrote, "the staff functioned without a hitch . . . mainly due to the ability and energy of Malin Craig"), the Second Battle of the Marne, the St.-Mihiel operation, and the Meuse-Argonne offensive, in which a change of plans suggested by Craig accomplished the relief of the "Lost Battalion." He was made brigadier general in June 1918 and had been recommended by Gen. John J. Pershing for promotion to major general when the war ended. After the Armistice he became chief of staff of the Third Army, which occupied the American sector on the Rhine.

Upon his return to the United States in August 1919, Craig reverted to his permanent rank of major. Duty as director of the Army War College (then for a brief time renamed the General Staff College) in 1919–20 and as commander of the District of Arizona (1920–21) followed, with promotions to colonel (June 1920) and brigadier general (April 1921). As commandant of the Cavalry School at Fort Riley, Kans. (1921–23), Craig improved the school and restored confidence in the cavalry's effectiveness. After commanding the Coast Artillery District of Manila and Subic Bay in the Philippines (1923–24), he was promoted to major general and chief of cavalry. Two years later, as major general of the line, he was detailed to the War Department General Staff as assistant chief of staff, with responsibility for operations and training.

Successive appointments placed Craig in command of the IV Corps Area, with headquarters at Atlanta, Ga. (1927); of the Panama Canal Division and Department (1927–30); and of the IX Corps Area, based at San Francisco (1930–35), and the Fourth Army (1933–35). During this period he participated in exercises (1931) with the United States Fleet to test regulations for joint action in the defense of Hawaii. Craig also administered the Civilian Conservation Corps in his area, handling with marked efficiency a contingent that eventually outnumbered the entire army. His duty in San Francisco came to an end in February 1935 when he was designated commandant of the Army War College.

In October of that year President Roosevelt appointed Craig Chief of Staff of the army, succeeding Gen. Douglas MacArthur. Heading the army in a time of international unrest, Craig carried out an ambitious program of modernization. He was especially disturbed by the General Staff's highly theoretical approach to planning, and after conducting a study that showed existing mobilization plans lacking in realism, he ordered a new Protective Mobilization plan that would set attainable goals. Convinced that the army's weapons were so inadequate in supply and so obsolete in design as to render it virtually unable to fight, he moved to replace the old Springfield infantry rifle with the Garand semiautomatic, and ordered antiaircraft guns of the Swedish Bofors 40 design. Under his direction antitank guns were developed and new tanks designed. He introduced tank regiments, supported improvements in signal communications which eventually led to the breaking of Japanese codes, reorganized the intelligence service, held special field exercises to acquaint infantry and cavalry with modern war techniques, and encouraged experimentation with the triangular division, which though smaller than the standard square division was more mobile and lent itself to use either as a mass or as three separate infantry-artillery combat teams. He chose able subordinates, among them Gens. George C. Marshall and Henry H. Arnold. Assisted by his tact in dealing with the administration and with Congress, Craig gained an increase in troop strength from 138,000 to nearly 190,000. When he relinquished his post in August 1939 at the mandatory retirement age of sixty-four, he

had given the army the capacity for directed expansion during World War II.

Craig was a natural leader, respected by superiors and subordinates alike. His quiet manner and somewhat austere appearance masked a lively sense of humor and a flair for picturesque language, as well as a tolerance for individual differences and an inner spiritual conviction. He was a Roman Catholic in religion. Hardworking, sound in judgment, he had foresight and a keen perception of character and ability. Craig shrank from publicity and was little known to the general public. Over the course of his career, however, he received a number of honors, including the Distinguished Service Medal with two Oak Leaf Clusters, several honorary degrees, and decorations from a number of foreign governments.

Following his retirement, Craig was appointed to the board of directors of the Columbia Broadcasting System, a post from which he resigned in 1942. He was recalled to active duty in September 1941 to serve as chairman of the Secretary of War's Personnel Board, which supervised officer promotions and military commissions to civilians. For some time Craig had suffered from severe arteriosclerosis. A cerebral thrombosis took him in 1944 to Walter Reed General Hospital in Washington, D. C., where he died fourteen months later of a coronary thrombosis. By his own request, he was buried in Arlington National Cemetery without military honors.

[War Dept. records; unpublished studies in the Office of the Chief of Military Hist.; George W. Cullum, *Biog. Register of the Officers and Graduates of the U. S. Military Acad.*, vols. III–IX (1891–1950); P. M. Robinett and H. V. Canan, "The Military Career of James Craig" (MS., 1968, State Hist. Soc. of Mo., Columbia); *Who Was Who in America*, vol. II (1950); obituaries in *N. Y. Times* and *Washington Times-Herald*, July 26, 1945; death record from D. C. Dept. of Public Health; genealogical information from Malin Craig, Jr. On Craig's work as Chief of Staff, see his published *Annual Reports*, 1936–39; Mark S. Watson, *Chief of Staff: Prewar Plans and Preparations* (1950); Marvin A. Kreidberg and Merton G. Henry, *Hist. of Military Mobilization in the U.S. Army, 1775–1945* (1955), pp. 455–553; and Russell F. Weigley, *Hist. of the U. S. Army* (1967).]

PAUL M. ROBINETT

CRAM, RALPH ADAMS (Dec. 16, 1863–Sept. 22, 1942), architect, was born in Hampton Falls, N. H., the eldest of three children of William Augustine and Sarah Elizabeth (Blake) Cram. His mother was the daughter of Ira Blake, "Squire" of Kensington, N. H. His father, a conscientious objector during the Civil War, became a Unitarian minister in 1868. After holding pastorates in Augusta, Maine (1869–72), and Westford, Mass. (1872–76), he sacrificed his career to return to the family farm in Hampton Falls to look after his aging parents, where he consoled himself with the writings of Emerson, Ruskin, Matthew Arnold, and the German philosophers. Ralph Cram attended school in Augusta and Westford; when he finished high school in Exeter, N. H., in 1880 there was no money for college. A book on house building by the British architect Charles J. Richardson, given him by his parents on his fifteenth birthday in 1878, had led him to construct models of houses and cities, and he now accepted his father's suggestion that he study architecture.

On New Year's Day, 1881, Cram went to Boston and, through the helpfulness of William R. Ware [q.v.], found a place in the recently established office of the architects Arthur Rotch [q.v.] and George T. Tilden, in which he remained for the next five years. He took full advantage of the artistic and literary opportunities of the city. He reveled in Wagner operas produced by Theodore Thomas [q.v.] and in pre-Raphaelite art shown at the Museum of Fine Arts, became a friend of Louise Imogen Guiney [q.v.] and the young Bernard Berenson, and wrote for the *Boston Evening Transcript*. In 1886, with $500 that he had won in a competition for the design of the Suffolk County Court House, he made his first trip to Europe, where he attended the Wagner Festival at Bayreuth and visited England, France, and Italy. On returning to Boston, he abandoned architecture for journalism and became an art critic for the *Transcript,* until a quarrel with the editor ended that career. After a precarious period of odd jobs, he got back to Europe in 1888 as tutor to a friend's stepson. During his eight-month stay, a Christmas Eve midnight mass at San Luigi dei Francesi in Rome gave him a new vision of the world, which was reinforced by three months in Palermo and Monreale with T. Henry Randall, an architectural student from Baltimore. A visit to Venice clinched his decision to get back into architecture.

Returning to Boston, Cram won a second prize of $1,300 for a deplorable entry in a competition for an addition to the Massachusetts State House, paid off his debts, and in 1890 formed a partnership with Charles Francis Wentworth. Although their earliest commissions were for (imitation) half-timbered domestic architecture, the firm soon began to specialize in the design of churches. The Christmas Eve mass in Rome had given Cram a vision of the Catholic tradition. As he hated the Renaissance and Reformation with equal fervor, much of post-Tridentine Roman Catholicism repelled him as strongly as the thought and art of Protestantism, but he found a haven in the Anglo-Catholic wing of the Episcopal Church. Soon after returning to Boston, he sought out the Cowley Fathers at their Mission Church of St. John the Evangelist, where, after instruction by the Rev. Arthur C. A. Hall [q.v.], later bishop of Vermont, he was baptized and confirmed. Thus he set his sights on an ideal (and largely imaginary) vision of pre-Reformation England, as a guide not only to architecture but to religious and social life.

Cram stoutly believed that Gothic, "which had been the perfect expression of Northern and Western Christianity for five centuries, and belonged to us, if we claimed it, by right of descent, had not suffered a natural death at the beginning of the sixteenth century, but had been most untimely cut off by the synchronizing of the Classical Renaissance and the Protestant Revolution." To him the obvious inference was that he should "take up English Gothic at the point where it was cut off during the reign of Henry VIII and go on from that point, developing the style England had made her own, and along what might be assumed to be logical lines, with due regard to the changing conditions of contemporary culture" (*My Life in Architecture,* pp. 72, 73). An ally in carrying out this vision soon appeared in the person of Bertram Grosvenor Goodhue [q.v.], then just twenty-one, who had won a competition for a cathedral in Dallas and needed to associate himself with a "going concern" to carry out the project. Cram took him on as a draftsman in 1890; in 1895 the firm became Cram, Wentworth & Goodhue. Although the Dallas cathedral was never built, Goodhue was an invaluable ally in the designing of All Saints', Ashmont (Boston), in 1892 and in a series of Episcopal parish churches that followed. A dozen years after Goodhue's premature death in 1924, Cram wrote of him: "From a professional point of view he was my *alter ego* and I like to think that I was his. What ability I had stopped short at one very definite point. I could see any architectural problem in its mass, proportion, composition, and articulation, and visualize it in three dimensions even before I set pencil to paper. I had also the faculty of planning, and I generally blocked out all our designs at quarter-scale. There my ability ceased. I had neither the power nor the patience to work out any sort of decorative detail. At this point Bertram entered the equation, to go on without a break to the completion of the work" (*ibid.,* pp. 77–78). When Wentworth died prematurely in 1899, Frank W. Ferguson joined the firm, which then became Cram, Goodhue & Ferguson.

The energies of Cram and Goodhue extended beyond architecture into a vision of a hopeful twentieth century, inspired by a compound of pre-Raphaelitism, William Morris socialism, Wagner, and a passion for the improvement of arts and crafts. Cram was involved in the organization of genial "brotherhoods" such as the "Pewter Mugs," the "Visionists," and the "Procrastinatorium," and he collaborated in the short-lived (1892) periodical the *Knight Errant,* to which Miss Guiney, Bliss Carman, Richard Hovey [*q.v.*], Ernest F. Fenollosa [*q.v.*], Berenson, and Charles Eliot Norton [*q.v.*] contributed. In 1893 Cram completed *Excalibur, An Arthurian Drama* (published in 1909) and wrote a very fin de siècle fantasy, *The Decadent: Being the Gospel of Inaction,* privately printed by Copeland and Day in Boston (1893), with decorations by Goodhue. In 1895 appeared Cram's *Black Spirits & White,* a series of antiquarian ghost stories that anticipated in date and mood those of Montague Rhodes James. In a more serious vein, Cram expounded with eloquence and conviction his Gothic vision, as in the essay "Meeting-houses or Churches," later reprinted in his *The Gothic Quest* (1907). Numerous articles written for the *Churchman* were subsequently collected in his *Church Building* (1901), which went through three editions. He published in 1898 a collotype album, *English Country Churches, One Hundred Views,* and in 1905 *The Ruined Abbeys of Great Britain.*

Hearing that the Japanese government was proposing to build new parliament houses in Tokyo, Cram and Goodhue produced a design, based on the indigenous architecture of the Ashikaga and Fujiwara periods but adapted to modern conditions; Goodhue did one of his most brilliant perspectives, and Cram went to Japan to promote the proposal. The Marquis Ito, then prime minister, was sufficiently impressed to include twenty thousand dollars in his budget for full preliminary designs; but his ministry fell, and the project ended. Out of the trip, however, came Cram's *Impressions of Japanese Architecture and the Allied Arts* (1905).

More substantial results came from the competition for the rebuilding of the United States Military Academy at West Point, which Cram, Goodhue & Ferguson won in 1903. The bold site on the Hudson River was singularly propitious for the exploitation of the firm's Gothic dreams. This commission required the establishment of a New York office, of which Goodhue took charge, Cram remaining in Boston. As neither partner wished to cede all rights in design, Goodhue took responsibility for the chapel and two of the cadet barracks, Cram for the post headquarters, riding hall, and power plant, while the other buildings were joint efforts. Although the buildings excited

admiration and gave great impetus to the spread of collegiate Gothic in the United States, the firm was, through the complications of government accounting, never completely paid for its services. Goodhue remained permanently in New York, for he and Cram were steadily "drawing apart in the matter of design—he along those vivid and original lines that finally culminated in his masterpiece, the State Capitol of Nebraska; I backward, if that is the word, to the various phases of Continental Gothic and away from the English Perpendicular of our earliest amatory experience. Steadily each pursued his own line until at last the two offices were practically independent" (*ibid.,* p. 114). St. Thomas's Church on Fifth Avenue, New York, was the last important project on which they worked together. Their partnership was dissolved in 1913; the firm continued to be known as Cram and Ferguson during the remainder of Cram's lifetime, although the year before Ferguson died—in 1926—Frank E. Cleveland, Chester N. Godfrey, and Alexander E. Hoyle became full members in it.

Cram was appointed supervising architect of Princeton University in 1909. During the twenty-two years he held that post, he achieved in Gothic style a consistency of construction that is rare in American universities. Cram and Ferguson were the architects of Campbell Hall, the Graduate College, and the chapel. In 1910 Cram was entrusted with the architectural design of the new Rice Institute at Houston, Texas, where he forsook Gothic in favor of a style involving Italian and Byzantine elements, with rich colors obtained from rose bricks and a profuse use of marbles and tiles. He was consulting architect for Bryn Mawr and Wellesley colleges and designed Georgian buildings for Wheaton, Williams, and Sweet Briar colleges and Phillips Exeter Academy, for, as he wrote in his autobiography (p. 238): "Having . . . no sympathy whatever with the abstract idea of an American Style that should be used for everything from a filling-station or cocktail bar to a graduate college or a cathedral, we have simply tried in every case to fit each . . . building to its tradition, purpose, and geographic place."

The extent and variety of Cram's churches can be seen in *The Work of Cram and Ferguson, Architects* (1929) and *American Church Building of Today* (edited by Cram, 1929). A singularly congenial task was the chapel of St. George's School, Newport, R. I. (1928), given by his close friend John Nicholas Brown. The most challenging and extended work in Cram's career was on the Cathedral of St. John the Divine in New York City, entrusted to him in 1912.

Twenty-five years earlier he had submitted two designs in a competition won by George Lewis Heins and C. Grant La Farge [Supp. 2] with a Romanesque plan. The choir, two ambulatory chapels, and the crossing (covered with a temporary tile dome) had been completed from this Romanesque plan when the cathedral authorities, having decided that they wished a Gothic building, turned to Cram. His solution of the problem was original and brilliant. The nave was completed in his lifetime, but the crossing and transepts remain unfinished. Although Cram's early church work was for Episcopal clients, he later designed various Roman Catholic and Protestant churches, but to his regret never had an opportunity to attempt a synagogue.

Cram married on Sept. 20, 1900, a Virginian, Elizabeth Carrington Read, daughter of Capt. Clement Carrington Read, C.S.A. They had three children: Mary Carrington, Ralph Wentworth, and Elizabeth Strudwick. In 1910 they bought a white farmhouse in Sudbury, Mass., which in recollection of Cram's Jacobite proclivities they named Whitehall. On the hillside there he built in 1914 St. Elizabeth's Chapel, a simple rubble structure of great charm, recalling the "first Romanesque" churches of Catalonia and Lombardy.

In 1914 Cram, although continuing his active architectural practice, accepted appointments as professor of architecture at the Massachusetts Institute of Technology and chairman of the Boston City Planning Board, posts that he held until 1921, when the pressure of private practice caused him to resign them both. The combination of the practice and teaching of architecture with an attempt to solve some of the physical problems of a growing city, while a great war was devastating parts of Europe he especially loved, led him to write a number of volumes of essays in which he offered Christian and Gothic suggestions about the solution of the world's problems. *The Ministry of Art* (1914), *Heart of Europe* (1915), *The Substance of Gothic* and *The Nemesis of Mediocrity* (1917), *The Great Thousand Years* (1918), *The Sins of the Fathers, Walled Towns,* and *Gold, Frankincense and Myrrh* (1919), *Towards the Great Peace* (1922) were all pleas for the unit of human scale, the passion of perfection, and the philosophy of sacramentalism, as substitutes for imperialism, the quantitative standard, and materialism.

In the 1920's Cram went to Spain and was swept off his feet by Sevilla cathedral and the Gothic churches of Catalonia. With John Nicholas Brown and Edward Kennard Rand [Supp. 3] he was instrumental in founding the Mediaeval

Academy of America in 1925, of which he was clerk (1926–33, 1936–41) and president (1933–36). In 1932 the Academy published his monograph *The Cathedral of Palma de Mallorca: An Architectural Study,* illustrated by the first accurate measured drawings of this great building. Although the twentieth century, to which Cram had looked forward with such hope, had proved to be as dismal as the nineteenth, he continued to build and write with undiminished fervor. He published *Convictions and Controversies* in 1935, the autobiographical *My Life in Architecture* in 1936, and *The End of Democracy* in 1937. He died in Boston of bronchopneumonia at the age of seventy-eight and was buried in his grounds at Whitehall in Sudbury.

For a New Englander, Cram was an unusually exuberant, imaginative, generous, and warm-hearted man, who regarded the arts as an integral part of life, and practiced what he preached. He was "scarcely less distinguished as an author than as an architect. Few men have been as consistent as he in the support of a central conviction" (Elisabeth M. Herlihy, ed., *Fifty Years of Boston,* 1932, p. 760). Not everyone agreed with Cram, but he received a fair share of honors, including honorary doctorates from Princeton (1910), Yale (1915), Notre Dame (1924), and Williams (1928), fellowship in the American Institute of Architects, American Academy of Arts and Sciences, Royal Society of Arts, and Royal Geographical Society, honorary membership in the Royal Institute of British Architects, and membership in the American Academy of Arts and Letters. Cram's work had a powerful influence upon American church architecture in the first four decades of the twentieth century. Although since his death both architecture and organized religion have moved in directions abhorrent to him, many of his ideas about man in his environment and the relation of the arts to life still carry conviction.

[Cram's own books, especially *My Life in Architecture,* are the principal source. See also Cram's volume on the firm's work, *Cram and Ferguson* (1931); Charles D. Maginnis's introduction to *The Work of Cram and Ferguson, Architects, Including Work by Cram, Goodhue, and Ferguson* (1929); and obituaries in the *Octagon,* Feb. 1943, and *Speculum,* July 1943.]

WALTER MUIR WHITEHILL

CRAVEN, FRANK (Aug. 24, 1875?–Sept. 1, 1945), actor, playwright, and director, christened John Francis Craven, was born, by most accounts, in Boston, Mass. His father, John T. Craven, and his mother, Ella (Mayer) Craven, both natives of New York state, were members of the famed Boston Theatre company, and he had a brother who was also an actor.

Frank Craven made the characteristic debut of a child of a theatrical family when at an early age he spoke a few lines in the melodrama *The Silver King* while clinging to his mother's skirts. During much of his childhood he trouped with his parents in many major cities—Philadelphia, Cleveland, Detroit, Boston—in the popular plays of the stock-company repertory, including *David Copperfield, A Celebrated Case,* and *Blow for Blow.* His mother educated him until he was about nine, when he was sent to a school in Plympton, Mass., where he stayed with friends while his parents were on tour. Later he attended a school in Reading, Mass., living on a farm and working in a sawmill and a tack factory until his late teens. Despite his early experience in the theatre, Frank had no desire to become an actor. His father wanted him to go into business; but after a short and unsuccessful experience as a mail clerk in a Boston insurance office, Craven returned to the stage, joining his father in Baltimore and playing the part of an old man in *The Silver King,* in which he had made his childhood debut.

He first appeared in New York in 1907 as Walter Marshall in *Artie.* It was not until after an apprenticeship of four years in minor parts, however, that he achieved a role that brought him his first personal success: the brash shipping clerk Jimmy Gilley in George Broadhurst's *Bought and Paid For,* produced in New York in 1911 by William A. Brady. Craven was not enthusiastic about the part. He had become more interested in writing for the theatre than in acting after contributing *The Curse of Cain's,* a show business skit, to a Lambs' Club "Gambol" in 1908, and he was earning as much as $200 a week for his sketches for vaudeville performers. But he had promised Broadhurst to appear in his play and could readily use the four or five weeks' salary, which was as long as he thought the play would last. Instead, it ran for 431 performances and was shown in San Francisco and in London. Craven provided the comic relief in this melodrama, and the audience, it is said, "simply hung on his lips, waiting for the next laugh." He had no faith in the glowing praise of his friends on opening night and was greatly surprised to find himself the star of a hit show.

During the run of *Bought and Paid For* Craven declined many offers for similar roles, still preferring writing to acting. But since producers would bring out his plays only if he promised to star in them, he appeared in his own *Too Many Cooks* (1914) and *This Way Out* (1917). In 1920 *The First Year,* produced by John Golden, with whom he was to be long associated, was, according to Burns Mantle, "the outstanding comedy success" of the season. Among the many other productions with which he was associated as actor, writer, or director were *The Nineteenth Hole* (1927), *That's Gratitude* (1930), and *Riddle Me This* (1932), as both author and actor; and *Whistling in the Dark* (1932) and *A Touch of Brimstone* (1935), as director. Beginning in 1929 Craven devoted much of his creative life to motion pictures, where he also functioned as actor, writer, and director. Among the many films in which he appeared were *State Fair* (1933), *City Limits* (1934), and *Miracles for Sale* (1939).

The special qualities of Frank Craven as a man and as an artist were best revealed to stage and screen audiences in the role which he himself called the "ideal Craven part"—that of the Stage Manager in Thornton Wilder's *Our Town,* produced by Jed Harris in 1938 and two years later made into a film in which Craven collaborated with the author on the scenario. In this role, which he liked because "it required no costume changes, no make-up or whiskers or anything to deceive the public," he embodied the homely virtues of small-town American life. Affable, genial, and humorous, he brought to the part, which was a combination of Chinese property man and Greek chorus, the same homespun qualities that had marked his earlier roles. A lifetime of trouping up and down the land had given him intimate knowledge of "homo Americanus." He once remarked: "I don't think there is a town of 5000 in this country that I have missed. It's too bad kids can't troupe like that nowadays. You met people, studied dialects, and it was good to get away from the narrow world of Broadway." His "pipe-in-mouth, hands-in-pocket informality" made him, as Bosley Crowther said of his screen interpretation of the Stage Manager, "the perfect New England Socrates—earnest, sincere, and profound."

Craven had married the actress Mary Blyth (divorced wife of the actor Arnold Daly) in Stamford, Conn., on May 8, 1914. They had a son, John, who appeared with his father in several plays, notably as George Gibbs in *Our Town.* Frank Craven died of a heart ailment in 1945 at his home in Beverly Hills, Calif., shortly after completing his last film, *Colonel Effingham.* Following Episcopal services, he was buried in the family plot in Kensico Cemetery, Valhalla, N. Y.

[Clippings in Theatre Collection, N. Y. Public Lib. at Lincoln Center, and in Harvard Theatre Collection, including obituaries in *N. Y. Times* and *N. Y. Herald Tribune,* Sept. 2, 1945; John Parker, ed., *Who's Who in the Theatre* (9th ed., 1939); *Enciclopedia dello Spettacolo,* III, 1691; "*Our Town*—from Stage to Screen," *Theatre Arts Monthly,* Nov. 1940; Eugene Tompkins, *The Hist. of the Boston Theatre, 1854-1901* (1908). Though Craven's birthplace is usually given as Boston, a 1914 interview (*N. Y. Tribune,* Apr. 12) indicates that he was actually born in Reading, Mass.; no birth record has been found in either city. His death record (Calif. Dept. of Public Health) gives his birth year as 1881, but other accounts suggest 1875.]

HELEN KRICH CHINOY

CRET, PAUL PHILIPPE (Oct. 23, 1876– Sept. 8, 1945), architect, was born at Lyons, France, the only child of Paul Adolphe and Anna Caroline (Durand) Cret. An uncle was an architect, and at fourteen Cret decided to follow that profession. He began the study of architecture in 1893 at the École des Beaux Arts of Lyons, but in 1896, after winning the Prix de Paris, transferred to the École des Beaux Arts of Paris, where between 1897 and 1903 he was enrolled in the Atelier Pascal. His brilliant record prompted the University of Pennsylvania to offer Cret a position as assistant professor of (architectural) design upon completion of his work for the diploma. Thus in the fall of 1903 he began an association that was to continue (after 1907 as professor of design) until his retirement in 1937. During that period architectural education in the United States came to be based largely on the precepts of the French École, with Cret as its most successful and respected exponent.

In his own architectural work, the commission that first won Cret wide professional acclaim was the headquarters building of the International Bureau of American Republics (later the Pan American Union) in Washington, D. C.; for this design, in association with Albert Kelsey, he took first place among ninety-seven entrants in a competition in 1907. In 1913 he won the commission for the Central Library Building at Indianapolis, again as the result of a competition, in this instance in association with the Philadelphia firm of Zantzinger, Borie & Medary. But before he could do more than make general studies for the plan and elevation, Cret was caught up in World War I. He was in France for the summer when the war broke out and hence reported for mobilization, serving at first in the Alpine Chasseurs and later as an officer interpreter attached to the American Expeditionary Forces.

In the aftermath of the war came an unprecedented demand for commemorative architecture, long a Beaux Arts concern. While still in uniform Cret was asked by Mrs. Theodore Roosevelt to design a memorial to her son Quentin at Chambéry, France (1919); and beginning in 1925 he served as architectural consultant to the American Battle Monuments Commission. His own designs for the monuments at Varennes and Fismes (both for the Pennsylvania Battle Monuments Commission, 1924), as well as those at Château-Thierry (1928), Bellicourt, Gibraltar (1930), and Waereghem, Belgium (1927), are usually considered among his best work, as is the

memorial at Providence, R. I. (1927), a well-proportioned column with a handsomely sculptured base.

Impatient with both the conservatism of the traditionalists and the pretensions of the self-styled moderns, Cret hoped to see American architecture evolve in the direction of a style that would have links with the past but would also be expressive of his own time—a kind of twentieth-century classicism based on good proportion, simplification, and a design that was the natural outgrowth of its structural system. With the possible exception of the Rodin Museum in Philadelphia (1928), designed in association with Jacques Gréber and perhaps for that reason the most "French" of his buildings, Cret's own search for such a modern American style was remarkably consistent. It may be followed in his major postwar commissions, beginning with the modified Renaissance of the Detroit Institute of Arts (1922, with Zantzinger, Borie & Medary) or the Barnes Foundation Gallery at Merion, Pa. (1923), and continuing through the massive and severely geometric Integrity Trust Company in Philadelphia (1923) to the more restrained urbanity of the Hartford County Building (1926, with Smith & Bassett) and the Folger Shakespeare Library in Washington, D. C. (1931, with Alexander Trowbridge as consulting architect). With the last two buildings also belongs much of Cret's work for the federal government: the courthouse at Fort Worth, Texas (1933), several post offices, and especially the Federal Reserve Bank in Philadelphia (1932) and the Federal Reserve Board Building in Washington, D. C. (1937), both of which are among his most successful and characteristic designs.

Cret helped plan the Century of Progress Exposition held at Chicago in 1933, as a member of its architectural commission. His particular contribution to this "festive stage setting"—to use his own words—was the Hall of Science, a windowless temporary building designed in the shape of a large U and devoid of any obvious reference to past styles.

Though in later years he had a number of partners, most of them former pupils, Cret's firm was known by his name alone as long as he lived, and he continued to take a close personal interest in what must have been as varied an architectural practice as any of its time. In fact, it was one of his major tenets that nothing which required careful detailing and good proportions was too insignificant for the architect's attention. Though known principally for its public structures, the firm also designed at least seven private residences; a central heating plant for Washington, D. C.

(1931); a power plant for Providence, R. I. (1940); three generating stations; the Pachyderm Building (1938) and the Service Building (1935) for the Philadelphia Zoo; and, after 1932 (in association with others), nearly a dozen of the new streamlined trains for as many different railroads. Cret also collaborated with engineers on the Bonneville Dam project on the Columbia River (1934) and on at least eight major bridges, the most important of which was the one over the Delaware River, now named for Benjamin Franklin (1922, with Ralph Modjeski [Supp. 2])—in its day the longest suspension bridge in the world. Universities for which he made planning studies include Wisconsin (1914, with W. P. Laird), Brown (1922), Pennsylvania (1925), and Texas (1930); for the last he also designed a number of buildings in association with Robert L. White. Throughout his career Cret was keenly interested in relationships among the arts, and sculpture played an important part in most of his designs.

His accomplishments as architect, planner, and teacher brought Cret recognition in many forms: the Philadelphia Award (1931); the medal of honor of the Architectural League of New York (1928); and, most important, the gold medal of the American Institute of Architects (1938), of which he was also a fellow. In 1940 Harvard awarded him an honorary degree, as had Brown and Pennsylvania earlier. He was elected to the National Academy of Design (1935) and the American Academy of Arts and Letters (1941).

Early in his career, on Aug. 29, 1905, Cret had married Marguerite Lahalle of Orleans, France; they had no children. In religion he was a Roman Catholic. His hearing had been impaired during the war, and in later years he was almost completely deaf, while an operation on his larynx left him unable to speak. Communicating by pencil and paper, he nevertheless continued his work and maintained his good humor until his death at sixty-eight, of a heart ailment, in a Philadelphia hospital. In his will he specified that nearly half of his estate of $200,000 was to go, after the death of his wife, to the University of Pennsylvania for its School of Architecture.

The artistic creed of Cret and others who believed that the past still had value for the present was challenged by the European architects who took up residence in the United States just prior to World War II and who sought to supplant the teaching of the French École with that of the German Bauhaus. It seems likely, however, that future historians may assign Cret a place nearer the mainstream of American architecture than some of his critics have supposed. If he was not

one of the truly "modern" architects of the twentieth century, at least his emphasis on rationality, restraint, clarity, and proportion prepared the stage for those who were.

[Among the fifty-odd articles and notices Cret wrote during a long professional career, those that offer the greatest insight, into his own views on architecture include: "The École des Beaux Arts: What Its Architectural Teaching Means," *Architectural Record*, May 1908; "Modern Architecture," chap. iv in *The Significance of the Fine Arts* (1923); "Memorials —Columns, Shafts, Cenotaphs and Tablets," *Architectural Forum*, Dec. 1926; "The Architect as Collaborator with the Engineer," *ibid.*, July 1928; "Ten Years of Modernism," *ibid.*, Aug. 1933; "The Hall of Science: A Century of Progress Exposition," *ibid.*, Oct. 1932; "The École des Beaux-Arts and Architectural Education," *Jour. of the Soc. of Architectural Historians*, Apr. 1941. Most of Cret's major buildings were published in one or more of the architectural periodicals of the period; see especially: "Am. Battle Monuments: France and Belgium," *Architectural Forum*, May 1932; Lancelot Sukert, "Folger Shakespeare Lib.," *Am. Architect*, Sept. 1932; Louis Skidmore, "The Hall of Science, A Century of Progress Exposition," *Architectural Forum*, Oct. 1932; "Federal Reserve Building, Washington, D. C.," *Am. Architect and Architecture*, Dec. 1937. Of the numerous tributes to Cret and articles about him, the following are the most helpful: George N. Allen in *Architectural Forum*, Apr. 1931; Kenneth Reid in *Pencil Points*, Oct. 1938; "Presentation of the Gold Medal to Paul Philippe Cret," *Octagon*, May 1938; John Harbeson in *Jour. of the A.I.A.*, Dec. 1945; Fiske Kimball in Am. Philosophical Soc., *Year Book*, 1945; "Paul P. Cret Number" of the *Federal Architect*, vol. XIV, no. 2 (1946); and John Harbeson, "Paul Cret and Architectural Competitions," *Jour. of the Soc. of Architectural Historians*, Dec. 1966. In 1967 Cret's former partners, who continued the firm after his death under the name of Harbeson, Hough, Livingston & Larson, deposited his papers and drawings in the Rare Book Room of the Van Pelt Lib. at the Univ. of Pa.]

GEORGE B. TATUM

CRILE, GEORGE WASHINGTON (Nov. 11, 1864–Jan. 7, 1943), surgeon, was born near Chili, Ohio, the fifth of eight children of Michael Crile, a prosperous farmer, and Margaret (Dietz) Crile. His father was of mixed Scotch-Irish and Dutch ancestry, his mother of Dutch background. Both families had settled in America before the Revolution and both had lived in Ohio for two generations. Crile attended district schools near his home and then worked as a teacher while studying at Northwestern Ohio Normal School (later Ohio Northern University), where he received the B.A. degree in 1884. Although both parents were English Lutherans, Crile, after reading Paine, Ingersoll, and Voltaire in his college years, became a lifelong atheist, devoted to the concept of intellectual freedom.

Entering the University of Wooster Medical Department (later absorbed by the Western Reserve University School of Medicine) in Cleveland in the spring of 1886, he received the M.D. degree in 1887 and served a year as an intern at University Hospital in Cleveland. His interest turned to the study of surgical shock when a close friend, a student assistant in the hospital, was injured in a streetcar accident and died in profound shock after the amputation of both legs.

Crile's subsequent career was characterized by ambition, industry, and an intense curiosity regarding the role of physiology and emotional factors in successful surgery, a relationship that at the time was not generally recognized. The years following his internship were occupied with establishing a busy practice; with animal experimentation into the nature of surgical shock; with teaching at the Wooster medical school (1889–1900); and with several trips for study in Europe, then almost a necessity for success in medicine. While abroad he worked (in 1895) with Britain's eminent neurosurgeon Victor Horsley on the problems of surgical shock, performing experiments to observe the effects of hemorrhage, anesthesia, and physical stresses such as traction on the peritoneum in the production of shock. Crile's first monograph, *An Experimental Research into Surgical Shock,* was awarded the Cartwright Prize by Columbia University in 1897 and was published two years later. Primarily a description of animal experiments, many of them crude by later standards although advanced for their day, the monograph represents an important pioneer attempt to delineate the causes, the nature, and the treatment of shock.

In 1900 Crile became clinical professor of surgery in the Western Reserve School of Medicine, and in 1911 professor of surgery. His research efforts during these years continued to focus on shock and related problems in surgery, and by 1914 he had published monographs on *Blood-Pressure in Surgery* (1903), on *Hemorrhage and Transfusion* (1909) and *Anemia and Resuscitation* (1914), and on anesthesia (*Anoci-Association,* 1914). Many of his conclusions were ahead of their time, and their importance was insufficiently appreciated. Crile saw the need for monitoring blood pressure in surgical patients and helped popularize the use of the Riva-Rocci sphygmomanometer (introduced into America by Harvey Cushing [Supp. 2]) for this purpose in 1901. Crile saw that the prevention of shock was of far greater importance than its treatment, and to this end he advocated atraumatic and bloodless surgery combined with safe anesthesia. Through animal experiments he demonstrated the importance of measuring the peripheral and central venous pressures and studied their relationship to cardiac output, hemorrhage,

and to replacement of blood volume. He learned that blood becomes acidotic in shock and suggested the use of bicarbonate solution to combat the condition. He devised and used clinically an ingenious "pressure suit" which was capable of restoring blood to the circulation by the application of external pressure. He also used epinephrine for the same purpose and recognized that the drug exerted its effect by constricting peripheral vessels.

Although Crile was an acute and accurate observer of the shock phenomenon, his theories of its cause were incorrect. He recognized the importance of avoiding loss of blood and the value of fluid therapy, but seemingly he did not perceive that fluid depletion, i.e., loss of blood or shift of other body fluids, is the chief etiologic agent of surgical shock. He postulated instead a "kinetic theory" based on changes which he believed to originate within the nervous system. Since untreated shock led to death, Crile went on to study methods for resuscitation of the dying. He successfully used saline solutions and epinephrine to treat patients seemingly *in extremis.* He soon came to realize that the brain imposed a time limit, and that if the brain was deprived of oxygen for more than a few minutes, all attempts at resuscitation were useless.

By 1903 Crile had realized that saline solutions were of limited benefit in the prevention and treatment of shock, and he was one of the first to use blood transfusions regularly in surgery. (In 1901 Karl Landsteiner [Supp. 3] had distinguished the four basic blood groups.) Initially he sutured the donor's artery painstakingly to the recipient's vein for transfusion (1905); later he devised a cannula to be used for this purpose. He recognized the dangers of overtransfusion, which he saw as "cardiac dilatation," and the risks of using incompatible blood, and by 1909 he had adopted methods for crossmatching blood. By 1914 he was able to state that "the ideal treatment for surgical shock [is] *the direct transfusion of blood."* By the end of World War I, Crile saw blood-banking techniques developed for military surgery, although two more decades were required before banked blood became available in civilian practice in this country.

Crile developed a "shockless" method of anesthesia ("anoci-association") by which he attempted to isolate the operative site from the nervous system, where he believed surgical shock to originate. Anoci-association made use of generous premedication with morphine and atropine, regional (procaine) block, and anesthesia by inhalation of nitrous oxide and oxygen administered by trained anesthetists. His "kinetic theory" of shock on which he based anoci-association was without foundation, but his methods were excellent and foreshadowed today's use of trained anesthetists and balanced anesthesia.

Crile's clinical experience was enormous, and he made many contributions to clinical surgery. He early became interested in surgery of the head, neck, and respiratory system and in 1892 performed what may have been the first successful total laryngectomy in this country. He recognized the need for complete excision of lymph nodes in cancer of the head and neck and devised a technique of radical dissection comparable to the radical operation of W. S. Halsted [q.v.] for carcinoma of the breast. Crile pioneered in surgery for goiter and was able to compile a very large series of successful operations (25,000 by 1936) on patients with hyperthyroidism. He also wrote extensively on other surgical diseases, such as cancer, peptic ulceration, and diseases of the biliary tract.

Military surgery interested Crile throughout his life. He served as an army surgeon in Cuba and Puerto Rico during the Spanish-American War, and during World War I he aided in the organization of the army's Medical Department. He was appointed director of clinical research for the American Expeditionary Forces, and while in France taught the need for whole blood transfusion, safe anesthesia, wide debridement, and adequate drainage for wounds. He also urged that the "moratorium wards" where soldiers were taken to die be redesignated "resuscitation wards," where soldiers would be given whole blood to resuscitate them instead of morphine to ease their deaths. He experimented with means of resuscitation even for apparently hopeless conditions. His methods were often imaginative, and included the administration of oxygen under pressure for gas casualties, epinephrine for patients in shock, and diluted sea water infusions to support victims of massive trauma.

On Feb. 7, 1900, Crile married Grace McBride of Cleveland, who actively shared and encouraged all of his interests. Their children were: Margaret, Elisabeth, George, Jr. ("Barney"), who also attained distinction as a surgeon, and Robert. Crile's chief interests outside of his profession were big-game hunting and horseback riding. He went on a number of safaris in Africa and made several family trips to the American West.

In 1924 Crile was sixty, the age of mandatory retirement from the surgical chair at Western Reserve, but retirement was unthinkable for a man of his energy. In 1921, with several colleagues, he had founded the Cleveland Clinic, where he subsequently acted as chief surgeon. His interest in research now included the comparative anatomy of the neuroendocrine system. He made trips to Florida, the Arctic, and Africa, where he collected some 4,000 species of animals for his dissections; the results appeared in his book, *Intelligence, Power and Personality* (1941). He became engrossed in a "radio-electric theory of life," and believed that the autonomic nervous system and the endocrine glands controlled energy release within the body, and that a number of disease states resulted from overproduction and release of energy. Unfortunately he projected his theories into clinical practice and attempted to cure such diverse conditions as hypertension, "neuro-circulatory asthenia," and epilepsy by "de-kineticizing" operations. These included adrenal gland denervations and removal of the celiac ganglion, a large nerve plexus deep within the abdomen. Crile performed many hundreds of these operations, probably with little real benefit to his patients. He also continued to operate during the later years of his life when age and its infirmities (including the loss of one eye and diminishing vision in the other) should clearly have disqualified him from active surgery. Despite these failings of his later years, Crile's place in American surgery is secure. His honors and accomplishments make an impressive list. He was a founder of the American College of Surgeons and served as its president (1916–17) and on its board of regents (1913–41). He became a consultant to the Air Force in 1941 and saw his pressure suit revived to prevent blackout in the fighter pilots of World War II. He also served as the president of the Cleveland Clinic from 1921 to 1940.

Crile remained active until a few weeks before his death. In 1941 he survived a plane crash in Florida, despite his age and in spite of serious injuries. During the last weeks of 1942 he developed bacterial endocarditis. He improved at first on penicillin (just then introduced) but succumbed to the disease in Cleveland early in 1943. His remains were cremated and the ashes were interred in the Highland Park Cemetery in Cleveland.

Crile was a man of great energy, imagination, curiosity, and organizational ability. His best work was done during the golden age of American surgery—roughly, from 1885 to 1915— when surgery evolved from a crude and chancy art to an applied scientific discipline. His greatest contributions were to surgical physiology, a field that has become of the highest importance to surgery during the decades since his death.

[The chief source of biographical information, with several excellent photographs, is *George Crile: An Autobiog.*, ed. by Grace Crile (2 vols., 1947). To this may be added obituary material from: the *Cleveland Clinic Quart.*, Apr. 1943; the *Bull.* of the Am. College of Surgeons, Feb. 1943; the *Annals of Surgery*, Apr. 1944 (by William E. Lower); and the Am. Philosophical Soc., *Year Book*, 1943 (by Evarts A. Graham). A contemporary popular evaluation of Crile's place in American surgery is to be found in his obituary in the *N. Y. Times*, Jan. 8, 1943. For Crile's role in popularizing the determination of blood pressure in surgery, see John F. Fulton, *Harvey Cushing: A Biog.* (1946). Crile's *Diseases Peculiar to Civilized Man* (1934) and *The Phenomena of Life: A Radio-Electric Interpretation* (1936) illustrate his later medical beliefs. Dr. George Crile, Jr., was most helpful in answering questions and commenting on this brief biography.]

A. SCOTT EARLE

CRISSINGER, DANIEL RICHARD (Dec. 10, 1860–July 12, 1942), Comptroller of the Currency and governor of the Federal Reserve Board, was born in Tully Township, Marion County, Ohio. The only child of John and Margaret (Ganshorn) Dunham Crissinger to survive infancy, he was descended from Henry Grissinger [*sic*], who emigrated in 1777 from Holland to Pennsylvania. Crissinger's mother, a native of Heidelberg, Germany, had earlier been widowed, and the family included two older half sisters. The elder Crissinger, a farmer, purchased in 1863 a country store in nearby Caledonia. Having acquired additional farm land and a lumber mill, he moved in 1883 to Marion. Young Crissinger was educated at a local one-room school, at Buchtel College (later the University of Akron), from which he graduated in 1885, and, after reading law briefly with Judge William Z. Davis, at the University of Cincinnati Law School (LL.B. 1886). Admitted to the bar in 1886, he returned to Marion, where he practiced for one year in partnership with Davis before winning office on the Democratic ticket: twice as prosecuting attorney (1888–93) and three times as city solicitor (1893–99). At the same time he built a highly respected law practice, acquired farm land, and developed a substantial stock-feeding business. In 1898 he became the attorney for the Marion Steam Shovel Company, the city's leading business firm.

An unsuccessful Democratic candidate for Congress in 1904 and 1906, Crissinger eventually became a Republican through his friendship with Warren G. Harding [*q.v.*], owner-editor of the *Marion Star*. He had known Harding since grade school, and the two were later drawn together by a common interest in civic improvement. They lived but a block apart, belonged to the Elks and Masons, met constantly at board of directors meetings, and played poker and billiards together. When Harding won the Republican presidential nomination in 1920, Crissinger headed the committee to entertain the city's out-of-town guests. On becoming president, Harding appointed his old friend Comptroller of the Currency, although Crissinger's only qualification was his presidency of a small bank in Marion. An able Comptroller, Crissinger extended branch banking within cities and sought to bring more state banks into the national banking system.

The appointment carried with it membership on the seven-man Federal Reserve Board, and on Jan. 12, 1923, Harding made Crissinger governor of the board, an office for which he was clearly unsuited. In the judgment of the economist Lester V. Chandler, Crissinger "knew almost nothing of economics and finance, learned little, [and] was incompetent as an administrator" (*Benjamin Strong*, p. 256). His inability to establish a good working relationship with the other members of the board created an atmosphere of internal bickering which disrupted routine work. Under his weak leadership, Benjamin Strong [*q.v.*] of the New York Federal Reserve Bank became more than ever the dominant figure in determining Federal Reserve policies.

Although Crissinger resigned in 1927 while under fire for forcing the Chicago Federal Reserve Bank against its wishes to lower its rediscount rates, he had apparently decided some months earlier to leave government service for a position with the F. H. Smith Company, a mortgage loan firm in Washington, D. C. As a director and chairman of the executive committee, Crissinger along with six other members of the firm was indicted by federal authorities in 1929 for using the mails to defraud, but the charges were dropped in 1932. Two years later Crissinger retired and returned to Marion.

On Apr. 18, 1880, Crissinger had married Ella Frances Scranton of Concord, Mich. They had two daughters, Donna Ruth and Beatrice Elizabeth. Bedridden after 1939, apparently from a weak heart, Crissinger died in Marion of pneumonia in 1942. A Universalist in religion, he was buried in the Marion Cemetery in an unmarked grave beside his parents.

[*N. Y. Times*, Jan. 21, 1923, sec. 8 (on his career), Jan. 23, 1923, Sept. 16, 1927, Dec. 11, 1929, Sept. 24, 1932, and obituary, July 14, 1942; *Marion Star*, Apr. 19, 1897, July 1, 1919, July 13, 1942; *Literary Digest*, July 30, 1927, p. 62, Oct. 15, 1927, p. 84 (with portrait); *Who's Who in the Nation's Capital*, 1934–35; *Nat. Cyc. Am. Biog.*, Current Vol. C, p. 244, and XLV, 318; *Who Was Who in America*, vol. II (1950); Francis Russell, *The Shadow of Blooming Grove* (1968); Ross Robertson, *The Comptroller and Bank Supervision* (1968); Lester V. Chandler, *Benjamin Strong: Central Banker* (1958); Benjamin M. Anderson, *Economics and the Public Welfare* (1949); Elmus R. Wicker, *Federal Reserve Monetary Policy* (1966);

C. S. Hamlin Papers and Diaries in Lib. of Cong.; Benjamin Strong Correspondence in N. Y. Federal Reserve Bank.]

DONALD L. KEMMERER

CROZIER, WILLIAM (Feb. 19, 1855–Nov. 10, 1942), army officer and inventor, was born in Carrollton, Ohio, the younger of two children and only son of Robert and Margaret (Atkinson) Crozier. The year after his son's birth, Robert Crozier moved from his native Ohio to Leavenworth, Kans., where he followed a prosperous career as lawyer, founder of a newspaper, bank cashier, chief justice of the Kansas supreme court, and, briefly, United States Senator (1873–74). William Crozier attended the Ann Arbor (Mich.) high school, planning to enter the engineering college at the University of Michigan, but instead accepted an appointment in 1872 to the United States Military Academy at West Point, where he graduated, fifth in his class, in 1876.

Commissioned as second lieutenant in the 4th Artillery, Crozier served in the campaigns against the Sioux and Bannock Indians before returning to West Point as assistant professor of mathematics in 1879. He was promoted to first lieutenant in 1881. In 1887 he joined the staff of the Chief of Ordnance in Washington, D. C., and there developed a professional interest in large-caliber guns and coastal defenses—an interest which was reflected in his appointment as inspector general of Atlantic and Gulf Coast defenses during the Spanish-American War and in his selection, while still a captain, as a delegate to the International Peace Conference at The Hague in 1899. Crozier served as inspector general of volunteers, with the temporary rank of major, between May and November 1898. In 1900 he was a staff officer in the field during the Philippine Insurrection and chief ordnance officer of the Peking relief expedition during the Boxer Rebellion.

President Theodore Roosevelt, acting on the recommendation of Secretary of War Elihu Root [Supp. 2], chose Crozier in 1901 as Chief of Ordnance, a position he was to hold (save for an interim, 1912–13, as president of the Army War College) for the next seventeen years—an unprecedentedly long tenure. With this appointment came the rank of brigadier general. Crozier undertook extensive reorganization of the manufacturing arsenals of the Ordnance Department with a view to increasing their efficiency and their ability to compete with private armaments manufacturers. He also reorganized the logistic work of the department, developing plans for the storage and rapid distribution of ordnance equipment to combat troops in the event of war. Extensive testing

and development work on automatic small-caliber weapons was also carried out. In these and other respects Crozier contributed substantially to American military preparedness on the eve of World War I.

Promoted to the rank of major general in October 1917, Crozier was appointed to the War Council by President Wilson and saw service in Europe on the Western and Italian fronts, inspecting military installations. As a member of the Supreme War Council, he and the British minister of munitions, Winston Churchill, cooperated in developing plans for the standardization and pooling of all ordnance equipment used by the Allied armies, including particularly the Anglo-American joint tank program. For his service during the war Crozier was decorated by the governments of France, Italy, and Poland. At the conclusion of hostilities, in 1918, he was appointed commander of the Northeastern Department of the army, with headquarters in Boston; he was retired at his own request on Jan. 1, 1919.

Crozier's reputation as an inventor rests largely on his development of a large-caliber wire-wrapped gun and (in collaboration with Gen. A. R. Buffington) of the Buffington-Crozier disappearing gun carriage (patented 1896), which was adopted as standard equipment for the coast defenses of the United States. Crozier was also the chief designer of most of the siege and seacoast gun carriages in use by the army before World War I. For his work in the improvement of military armament he was awarded an honorary Doctorate of Engineering by the University of Michigan in 1923 and the Army Ordnance Association's gold medal in 1931. In 1940 the Association established in his honor the Crozier Gold Medal, to be awarded for outstanding contributions to the progress of American ordnance.

Crozier spent the years between his retirement and his death largely in world travel. He died at his home in Washington, D. C., of bronchopneumonia and was buried in Arlington National Cemetery. He was survived by his wife, Mary Hoyt (Williams) Crozier, whom he had married on Oct. 31, 1913; they had no children. In religion he was an Episcopalian.

Respected in his own time primarily as an inventor and administrator, Crozier now appears more significant for his insight into the relationship between technology and military potential. His long career as Chief of Ordnance was distinguished by dedication to the concept of the Ordnance Department as an agent of scientific advance in arms manufacture and procurement. Crozier saw two essential roles for the publicly owned arsenals: they were to be pilot plants in advancing the technology of military production, and they were to set the standards of efficiency by which the bids submitted by private arms manufacturers could be appraised. This concept inevitably involved him in controversy, in view of the large sums of money involved in arms contracts, the small number of influential firms submitting bids, and the hostility of legislators to the idea of the government competing with private business. In his reorganization of work in the arsenals Crozier received assistance from Frederick W. Taylor [*q.v.*], the pioneer of "scientific management," and certain of Taylor's associates were employed to introduce improved methods at the arsenal in Watertown, Mass. This, however, was only one episode in Crozier's lifelong campaign to systematize military procurement. His contribution to American military preparedness before World War I was substantial; his innovations in defense procurement, though limited in their immediate impact, were creative efforts to deal with a problem that still awaits solution.

[William Crozier, *Ordnance and the World War: A Contribution to the Hist. of Am. Preparedness* (1920); George W. Cullum, *Biog. Register of the Officers and Graduates of the U. S. Military Acad.* (3rd ed., 1891); Ordnance Dept. Records, War Records Division, Army Section, Nat. Archives; *Annual Reports* of the Chief of Ordnance, 1891–1918; *Nat. Cyc. Am. Biog.*, XXXII, 329; obituaries in *Army Ordnance*, Jan.–Feb. 1943, and *N. Y. Times*, Nov. 11, 1942; Hugh G. J. Aitken, *Taylorism at Watertown Arsenal* (1960); Calvin D. Davis, *The U. S. and the First Hague Peace Conference* (1962); death record from D. C. Dept. of Public Health; information on Crozier's father from *Biog. Directory Am. Cong.* (1960) and from the Kans. State Hist. Soc.]
　　　　　　　　　　　　HUGH G. J. AITKEN

CUBBERLEY, ELLWOOD PATTERSON (June 6, 1868–Sept. 14, 1941), educator, symbolized the search for order in public education, the professionalization of teaching and administration, and the rise of education as a university study. Born in Antioch (later Andrews), Ind., he was the only child of Catherine (Biles) Cubberley, a Philadelphian who came of a Delaware Quaker family, and Edwin Blanchard Cubberley, a druggist, who was born in Licking County, Ohio, of English lineage. Ellwood worked in his father's drugstore, attended the local high school, and entered the college preparatory department of Purdue University. His parents hoped that he would study pharmacy and eventually run the family business.

In 1886, however, a talk by David Starr Jordan [*q.v.*], then president of Indiana University, on "The Value of Higher Education" gave Cubberley a vision of an exciting world of scholarship and service, of science and idealism, that made small-town life and the drugstore seem narrow and parochial. Like many other small-town or rural boys, he determined to enter this new frontier. He registered at Indiana University, where Jordan became his adviser and later employed him as an assistant in giving stereopticon slide lectures across the state. This relationship decisively shaped Cubberley's career, for Jordan recommended him for two positions and ultimately brought him to Stanford. At Indiana University, Cubberley majored in physics and received his A.B. in 1891 after taking a year out to teach in a one-room school.

Cubberley remained in Indiana for the next five years. After briefly teaching at a Baptist college in Ridgeville, he became professor of physical science at Vincennes University, where despite a heavy teaching load he found time to publish two papers in geology. In 1893, at the age of twenty-five, he became president of Vincennes, a post he occupied for the next three years. Meanwhile, on June 15, 1892, he married Helen Van Uxem, who had been a fellow student at Indiana University; they had no children.

In 1896 Cubberley accepted an offer to become superintendent of schools in San Diego, Calif. There he found himself the center of political controversy since several school board members had wanted to hire a local person. He was also disturbed to discover that the board itself, rather than the superintendent, actually controlled the school administration, through subcommittees that determined the hiring and firing of teachers, the choice of curriculum, and the management of finances. Aggressive and hardworking, Cubberley tried to convince the board that it should act as a legislature and leave the administration to him, and in his annual reports he urged the citizens to adopt new courses of study and new forms of school organization. The experience convinced him that school boards should be nonpolitical and that efficiency in education demanded that administrators have autonomy. In much of what Cubberley later wrote about school administration, he drew on this experience in San Diego; his descriptions of the qualities necessary for a successful superintendent were essentially a self-portrait.

In 1898 Cubberley decisively shaped his future when he accepted an appointment as assistant professor of education at Stanford University. Although he had had almost no training in the field, the scope of the task appealed to him, for he believed that the department should strive to raise the standards of California schools and to improve the qualifications of the teachers. This would, he realized, involve "Herculean labor," but hard work was second nature to Cubberley. He found that many people at Stanford disagreed with his exalted view of education. David Starr

Jordan (then president of Stanford) gave him three years to make the education department academically respectable or see it abolished.

Cubberley faced staggering obstacles. In his first year he was assigned to teach courses in which he was a novice: the theory and practice of teaching, the history of education, and school administration. He found that the scholarly literature of education was scanty: a few writings of European educational theorists; a few works in the slowly emerging field of psychology; and a handful of common-sense books by schoolmen—hardly the basis of a "scientific" body of knowledge. Thus he not only had to discover what it was he should be teaching, but had to convince his colleagues that it was worth teaching. He succeeded. Before his first year ended he had persuaded Jordan to retain the department of education. In 1906 he was made a full professor, and by 1917 his work had gained such renown that the trustees made his department a professional school and appointed Cubberley its dean.

In 1901 Cubberley went to Teachers College, Columbia, on a year's leave to earn an M.A. in school administration, taking about half his work in sociology and half in education. Two years later he returned to Columbia, then a mecca for aspiring schoolmen, where under a brilliant faculty that included Paul Monroe, John Dewey, and Edward Thorndike he received the Ph.D. in 1905, with a dissertation on *School Funds and Their Apportionment*. (Thorndike commented after Cubberley's doctoral oral that he was "a good man but not a good scholar.")

Cubberley's experience at Teachers College intensified his evangelical fervor for public education, his quest for "social efficiency," and his awe of science. In *Changing Conceptions of Education* (1909) he foreshadowed these themes, which became basic in his later writings. Education he regarded as social engineering, the schools as instruments of progress in conscious social evolution. Like Dewey, he looked back with nostalgia on a preindustrial America where experience in home and farm, in workshop and country village, provided an informal education. In an industrial age, by contrast, children needed to acquire skills and knowledge deliberately in the schools. Similarly, the moral guidance once given the young through home and church was now left largely to the public schools. "Each year the child is coming to belong more and more to the state," he wrote, "and less and less to the parent" (p. 63). Complicating the problem was the influx of vast numbers of immigrants from southeastern Europe whom he characterized as "Illiterate, docile, lacking in self-reliance and initiative, and not possessing the Anglo-Teutonic conceptions of law, order, and government" (p. 15). Negroes he also considered inferior. Cubberley did not flinch from these challenges, but argued that the schools must become a unifying influence. The curriculum must adjust to social and economic facts, give up the idea that all children are equal, and offer specialized educational facilities. The fate of the nation, he believed, depended on education, and the schools must teach children the principles of effective, honest government and a sense of moral and economic values.

Obviously a school system fit for such a task must itself be free from political influence. Hence Cubberley advocated nonpartisan school boards and officials appointed on merit. Teachers must be knowledgeable about the needs and problems of democracy, and school superintendents must work with the precision and efficiency of the industrialist. "Our schools are, in a sense, factories," Cubberley wrote in *Public School Administration* (1916), "in which the raw materials (children) are to be shaped and fashioned into products to meet the various demands of [twentieth-century] life" (p. 338). Cubberley's ideology was sometimes ambivalent or inconsistent. He praised democracy but sought to remove the control of the schools as far as possible from the people. Although he desired to give teachers professional status, he opposed granting them tenure or a strong voice in educational policies. Urging that education should become "scientific," he nonetheless spoke and wrote with evangelical rhetoric. Certain ethnic groups he regarded as inherently inferior, yet he believed that education might somehow improve them and save the republic. Skeptical of social reformers and panaceas in other domains, he still maintained a utopian faith in reform through education.

In his many publications—he was the author or co-author of nearly thirty books and reports and scores of articles—Cubberley largely followed the lines of argument advanced in *Changing Conceptions of Education*. His *Public Education in the United States* (1919) sold over 100,000 copies and, together with *The History of Education* (1920), profoundly influenced the writing of educational history in this country. He told the story of the public schools in evolutionary terms, probing the past for the roots of present-day institutions. Often he cast the narrative in the form dictated by his sources—usually the writings of school officials and reformers—and offered a clear-cut cast of good and bad actors. The result was a house history by and for schoolmen, a view from the inside, normally from the top down, presented as an inspiration and as a guide for practical action. Although it gave professionals a strong esprit de corps and sense of heritage and direction, it also narrowed the perspective on important policy questions that schoolmen would face in the twentieth century and presented an anachronistic picture of important historical developments.

As editor of the influential Houghton Mifflin Riverside textbooks in education, Cubberley helped define and develop the character of professional studies outside his own fields of history and administration. He edited nearly a hundred volumes, mostly empirical in approach, dealing with measurement, guidance, methodology, psychology, sociology, and administration in education. In other ways as well he became an elder statesman of education, serving on numerous school investigating commissions (he was a pioneer of the school survey movement) and on many local, state, and national committees. While carrying burdens of administration, writing, consulting, and teaching that would have staggered a less energetic man, he yet found time to amass a substantial fortune through investment of his royalties and honoraria. He and his wife left to the Stanford School of Education gifts exceeding $770,000.

Cubberley retired in 1933 and some eight years later died of a heart attack in Palo Alto, Calif. He was buried in nearby Alta Mesa Cemetery. Cubberley the man had been precise, positive in manner and opinions, phenomenally well organized and industrious, devoted to his wife and kindly to students and colleagues. During his half-century of work for public education in the United States, he had come to be identified with the cause he represented. He was both symbol and catalyst of the managerial and ideological transformation of the common school that took place during his lifetime.

[Jesse B. Sears and Adin D. Henderson have written a comprehensive biography, *Cubberley of Stanford and His Contribution to Am. Education* (1957); it includes full lists of writings by and about Cubberley up to 1957. The most important later appraisals of his work are: Lawrence Cremin, *The Wonderful World of Ellwood Patterson Cubberley* (1965); Bernard Bailyn, *Education in the Forming of Am. Society* (1960), pp. 3–15, 55–58, and Bailyn's "Education as a Discipline, Some Hist. Notes," in John Walton and James L. Kuethe, eds., *The Discipline of Education* (1963), chap. vi; William W. Brickman, "Revisionism and the Study of the Hist. of Education," *Hist. of Education Quart.*, Dec. 1964; and Raymond E. Callahan, *Education and the Cult of Efficiency* (1962), chap. viii. The Stanford Univ. Lib. has a number of Cubberley papers.]

DAVID B. TYACK

CURTIS, HEBER DOUST (June 27, 1872– Jan. 9, 1942), astronomer, was born in Muskegon, Mich., the elder of two children, both of them sons, of Orson Blair Curtis and Sarah Eliza (Doust) Curtis. His father, who traced his ancestry to a Connecticut settler of 1638, served in the Union Army during the Civil War. After the war he graduated from the University of Michigan and was successively a teacher, editor, and deputy collector of customs in Detroit. Heber Curtis's mother, born in England but reared in the United States, also taught school briefly.

The Curtises moved to Detroit when Heber was about seven, and the two boys were reared in a comfortable but strict Methodist household that forbade such amusements as dancing, cards, and the theatre, but encouraged the reading of good books. Heber attended the Detroit public schools and the University of Michigan, where he concentrated on the study of classical languages; he showed some mathematical ability but no interest in the natural sciences despite the outstanding position of astronomy at the university. After receiving the A.B. degree in 1892 and the A.M. in 1893, he taught Latin at the Detroit high school for six months and in 1894 accepted a position as teacher of classical languages at Napa College, a small Methodist institution not far from San Francisco. He was married on July 12, 1895, to Mary Deborah Rapier of Ann Arbor, Mich.; their four children were Margaret Evelyn, Rowen Doust, Alan Blair, and Baldwin Rapier.

The move to Napa College was a turning point in Curtis's career, for a small telescope at the college excited his interest, and he began on his own to study astronomy. Two years later, when Napa College merged with the University of the Pacific (then located in San Jose), he found an even better telescope, a 6-inch Clark refractor. He pursued his studies so successfully that at the end of a year he had completed the shift away from the classics and was appointed professor of mathematics and astronomy. In 1898 he supplemented his individual study with summer work at the Lick Observatory near San Jose.

Curtis spent the years 1900–02 on a Vanderbilt Fellowship in Astronomy at the University of Virginia. He joined the Lick Observatory expedition to Thomaston, Ga., to observe the solar eclipse in 1900, and his ingenuity and competence so impressed William Wallace Campbell [Supp. 2], the director, that he offered Curtis an assistantship at the observatory as soon as he received the Ph.D. at Virginia. This he did in 1902; he remained on the Lick staff until 1920. During the years 1906–10 he was in charge of the Lick Observatory station in Santiago, Chile, which had been established to determine the radial velocities of stars in southern latitudes. Upon his return he was placed in charge of the 36-inch Crossley reflector.

The next ten years were a period of remarkable scientific productivity for Curtis. From his youth he had been fascinated by machine tools and their use, and he now turned his mechanical ability to improving the Crossley so that it became one of the most efficient telescopes of its time. With this instrument he undertook an extensive program of photographing the nebulae, including those spiral objects whose nature was still in dispute. Curtis maintained that they were separate galactic systems beyond our own, reasoning that our own galaxy had a similar spiral structure. The starless regions of the Milky Way he interpreted as light-absorbing clouds of gas and dust rather than "holes" in space, and he suggested that the dark bands shown by some of the spiral nebulae indicated the presence of similar areas of obscuration. His discovery, with George W. Ritchey [Supp. 3], of novae in the spirals further convinced Curtis of their extragalactic nature. He estimated our galaxy to be about 30,000 light years in diameter and considered the spiral nebulae to be comparable objects.

The leading protagonist of the opposing view, the astronomer Harlow Shapley (then at Mount Wilson Observatory), derived a probable diameter of 300,000 light years for our galaxy. He believed the spiral nebulae were much smaller objects associated with our system of stars. The two men presented their views, by invitation, before the National Academy of Sciences in Washington in a famous debate in 1920, but the questions at issue could only be settled by further observations. Edwin P. Hubble's discovery in 1925 of Cepheid variable stars in the spiral nebulae definitely established their nature as separate galaxies. As of 1971, the prevailing estimate of our galaxy's diameter falls about midway between those of Curtis and Shapley.

In 1920 the observational phase of Curtis's nebular program terminated when he became director of the Allegheny Observatory of the University of Pittsburgh, succeeding Frank Schlesinger [Supp. 3]. Curtis, with his mechanical ingenuity, improved the observatory's equipment and taught in the university. In 1930 he moved to the University of Michigan as the director of its observatory, expecting that funds for a large reflecting telescope would become available through the generosity of the banker Thomas W. Lamont. The disc of 97½ inches aperture was successfully cast, but the economic depression prevented Lamont from financing the remainder of the project. Despite his disappointment and the lack of modern instrumentation, Curtis energetically developed the work of the Michigan observatory. He entered into a close cooperation with Robert R. McMath, industrial engineer and astronomer, who

in 1931 was co-donor of the McMath-Hulbert Observatory to the university.

Curtis's honors included election to the National Academy of Sciences (1919), to the American Philosophical Society (1920), and to the vice-presidency (for Section D, Astronomy) of the American Association for the Advancement of Science (1924). He never abandoned his earlier interest in languages. During his years in Chile he had learned Spanish; and on his journey to Sumatra in 1926, one of his eleven eclipse expeditions, he learned to speak Malay. His broad interests and gift for graceful expression made him an able public lecturer. He was a good companion, known for his spontaneous acts of thoughtfulness. Though he remained a Methodist, he was never a strict sectarian; he was interested in philosophy and in the relations between science and religion. He died of a coronary thrombosis at his home in Ann Arbor at the age of sixty-nine and was buried in Forest Lawn Memorial Park, Glendale, Calif.

[Curtis's most important publications are: three monographs on nebulae in vol. XIII (1918) of the *Publications* of the Lick Observatory; "The Scale of the Universe," his lecture debate with Harlow Shapley, in Nat. Research Council, *Bull.*, May 1921; and his "The Nebulae" in *Handbuch der Astrophysik,* V (1933), 774–936. Biographical sources: Robert G. Aitken in Nat. Acad. Sci., *Biog. Memoirs*, vol. XXII (1943); Robert R. McMath in Astronomical Soc. of the Pacific, *Publications*, Apr. 1942, and in Am. Philosophical Soc., *Year Book*, 1942; Dean B. McLaughlin in *Popular Astronomy*, Apr. 1942; *Who Was Who in America*, vol. I (1942); information from Mrs. Alexander Walters, a daughter; close personal friendship, 1916–20.]

C. D. SHANE

DABNEY, CHARLES WILLIAM (June 19, 1855–June 15, 1945), chemist, agriculturist, college president, was born in Hampden-Sydney, Va., to Margaretta Lavinia (Morrison) Dabney and Robert Lewis Dabney [q.v.]; he was the third of their six sons and the oldest of the three who lived to adulthood. His father was a prominent and conservative Presbyterian theologian in the South. Young Dabney attended Hampden-Sydney College, received the B.A. degree in 1873, and taught for a year in a nearby public school. He then enrolled in the graduate school of the University of Virginia, where for the next four years he studied the natural sciences. In 1877 he took a position as professor of sciences at Emory and Henry College, but left after a year to study chemistry in Germany at the universities of Berlin and Göttingen, receiving the Ph.D. from Göttingen in 1880.

Upon returning to the United States, Dabney was appointed state chemist and director of the North Carolina Agricultural Experiment Station. He initiated scientific investigations of soils, fertilizers, and crops, discovered new deposits of phosphate and tin, and promoted a state exposition that stimulated the industrial development of North Carolina. He also took the lead in a movement to establish a state school of the industrial, or practical, arts which brought about the founding in 1887 of the Agricultural and Mechanical College of North Carolina at Raleigh. He was one of the founders, in 1884, of the Association of Official Agricultural Chemists.

Dabney's strong interest in industrial education led to his appointment in 1887 as president of the University of Tennessee and director of its Agricultural Experiment Station. The university was at that time little more than a semimilitary academy with an enrollment of 125, but under Dabney's aggressive leadership it soon grew into a modern coeducational institution with more than 800 students. He relaxed rules requiring students to wear uniforms and attend drills, established academic standards for admission, replaced 80 percent of the faculty, and in 1893 opened the university to women. Emphasizing industrial education, he created a school of mechanical arts (later the machine design and drawing school), expanded course offerings in agriculture, and developed new curricula leading to degrees in civil, mechanical, mining, and electrical engineering, as well as in chemistry and metallurgy. He also added a teacher training school and a law department, both two-year programs.

Dabney took a leave from his duties at the University of Tennessee to serve for three years, beginning in 1894, as Assistant Secretary of the United States Department of Agriculture. He had sought the position partly for its prestige, but partly also because he feared that the new Secretary of Agriculture, Julius Sterling Morton [q.v.], would discontinue a federal funding program to land-grant colleges which had been authorized by the Hatch Act and the second Morrill Act. As Assistant Secretary, Dabney reorganized existing scientific divisions and created new ones, including dairy, agricultural soils, and agrostology divisions. Because the country's land-grant colleges offered little in the way of graduate training, he recommended that the department itself train scientists.

Dabney returned in 1897 to the University of Tennessee with a deeper conviction of the importance of scientific training to the industrial progress of the South. Realizing that the success of such training depended upon the quality of education at the elementary and secondary levels, he became active in the Conference for Education in the South, which had been established in 1898 by a group of Northern philanthropists and Southern educators. Though the Conference had been devoted mainly to Negro education, it soon broadened into a movement to promote universal education throughout the South. In 1901, at the urging of Dabney and others, the Conference created the Southern Education Board to generate popular support for free public education, and until 1903 Dabney directed the board's propaganda bureau, the "Bureau of Information and Advice on Legislation and School Organization." In 1902 he also organized, at the University of Tennessee, a summer school training program for teachers which developed into the highly successful Summer School of the South. Dabney's sharp criticism of educational facilities in the South, his insistence on greater public tax support for schools, and his active involvement in an organization which sought to improve Negro education aroused hostility in Tennessee, and when he was offered the presidency of the University of Cincinnati, at a substantial increase in salary, he accepted.

At the time of Dabney's arrival, in 1904, the University of Cincinnati was a small liberal arts college; for years its policies had been dictated by local politicians. Regarding the municipal university as another step toward the democratization of education, Dabney welcomed the prospect it offered of bringing a college education to those who could not otherwise afford one. Yet he accepted appointment as president only after Cincinnati's Republican political boss, George B. Cox [q.v.], assured him that he would not interfere in the school's internal affairs. Operating on the same assumptions that had guided his actions at Tennessee, Dabney sought to adapt the University of Cincinnati's educational policies to the needs of the community. He created a college for teachers (1905), started a graduate school (1906), organized a college of medicine (1909) which later took over a new city hospital, and established a number of new departments, among them home economics (1914), physical education (1916), and vocational education (1918). He also added a school of nursing to the medical college (1916), made the college of law an integral part of the university (1918), and established a separate college of engineering (1904), to which he named as dean Herman Schneider [Supp. 2], whose cooperative plan of technological education, alternating classroom and shop work, he supported. Under Dabney the student body increased by more than 3,000, eight new buildings were constructed, and the university's annual income rose from $130,909 to $855,000.

Dabney was an impressive figure, solidly built, broad-shouldered, square-jawed, with a ruddy complexion, dark eyes, and a wiry moustache;

his black hair in time became snow white (McGrane, p. 195). On Aug. 24, 1881, he married Mary Chilton Brent of Fayette County, Ky., by whom he had three daughters: Marguerite Lewis, Mary Moore, and Katharine Brent. After retiring in 1920, Dabney organized a firm of geologists and engineers in Houston, Texas. He also wrote an extensive historical survey, *Universal Education in the South* (2 vols., 1936), in which he recommended federal aid to education. Dabney died of a coronary thrombosis shortly before his ninetieth birthday, at Asheville, N. C., where he had stopped while traveling from Florida to Cincinnati. He was buried in Cincinnati.

[For Dabney's ideas about education, see, in addition to his *Universal Education in the South*, his monograph *Agricultural Education* (1900) and his articles "A Nat. Dept. of Science," *Science*, Jan. 15, 1897; "The Nat. University," *ibid.*, Mar. 5, 1897; and "The Municipal University," *School and Society*, Jan. 16, 1915. On his life and work, see Stanley J. Folmsbee, *Tenn. Establishes a State Univ.: First Years of the Univ. of Tenn.* (1961); James R. Montgomery, *The Volunteer State Forges Its Univ.: The Univ. of Tennessee, 1887–1919* (1966); A. Hunter Dupree, *Science in the Federal Government* (1957); Reginald C. McGrane, *The Univ. of Cincinnati* (1963); *Nat. Cyc. Am. Biog.*, Current Vol. E, p. 323; *Who Was Who in America*, vol. II (1950); obituaries in *School and Society*, June 23, 1945, and Assoc. of Official Agricultural Chemists, *Jour.*, Aug. 1945. Death record from N. C. Board of Health. An extensive collection of Dabney's papers, including an uncompleted MS. autobiography, is at the Southern Hist. Collection, Univ. of N. C. The Univ. of Tenn. Lib. has records of his presidency. The Nat. Archives has records covering his activities as Assistant Secretary of Agriculture and as director of the Tenn. Experiment Station.]

VIVIAN WISER

DALLIN, CYRUS EDWIN (Nov. 22, 1861–Nov. 14, 1944), sculptor, was born in the frontier settlement of Springville, Utah, where his parents, Thomas and Jane (Hamer) Dallin, had settled after emigrating from England; though not themselves Mormons, they had followed relatives who were. He was the eldest son and the second of eight children. Reared in a log cabin at the foot of the Wasatch Mountains, Cyrus often played with Indian boys from the nearby Ute encampments, visited their tents, and learned from them how to model little animals from the local clay. These friendships generated a deep respect for the Indian culture. Dallin's father, a farmer, worked during the winter in the nearby Tintic mining district, and at eighteen Cyrus secured a job there, seeking to earn money to enter the academy at Provo, Utah. From soft white clay excavated from the mines he modeled two portrait heads that excited local praise. Exhibited at a fair in Salt Lake City, they attracted the attention of two wealthy miners, who provided the money to send Dallin east to study. His association, on the train journey, with a delega-

tion of Crow Indians en route to Washington renewed his respect for the Indian character and his admiration for the Indian physique.

Arriving in Boston, Dallin in 1880 commenced an apprenticeship in the studio of Truman H. Bartlett, father of Paul Bartlett [q.v.], who was also to become a well-known sculptor. To support himself Dallin worked during the day in a terra-cotta factory. He made rapid progress in sculpture and by 1882 had opened his own studio in Boston, which he operated for the next six years. In 1885 his model won the competition for an equestrian statue of Paul Revere for the city of Boston, but funds were lacking to complete the project. (Not until 1940, more than fifty years later, was the statue finally enlarged, cast in bronze, and erected.) In May 1888 Dallin's life-size study of "The Indian Hunter" won the gold medal of the American Art Association in New York.

Realizing his need for further study, Dallin in 1888 went to Paris, where he worked in the atelier of the famous Henri Michel Chapu. He began by modeling several pieces inspired by classical subjects, but he retained his interest in the American Indian. During a Paris visit of the "Wild West" show of Buffalo Bill Cody [q.v.], Dallin used one of the troupe's Indian members as a model and drew on his own memories of a powwow between army officers and chiefs which he had witnessed to produce a small model of a mounted Indian, arm and spear upraised in a dignified plea for peace with the white man. At the Paris Salon of 1890, "The Signal of Peace" won an honorable mention. The full-scale work was exhibited at the World's Columbian Exposition in Chicago in 1893, where it won a bronze medal and brought fame to Dallin; it was subsequently placed in Chicago's Lincoln Park.

This was the first of Dallin's four great equestrian groups on Indian themes. The second, "The Medicine Man" (Fairmount Park, Philadelphia), which won a silver medal at the Paris Exposition of 1900, portrays a commanding prophet, perhaps warning his tribe against the deceit of the white invader. Next came "The Protest," representing the Indian's decision to fight for his rights, which was awarded a gold medal at the St. Louis Exposition of 1904 but never put into permanent material on a large scale. The final group represents the defeated Indian astride his pony, his face raised to heaven in supplication and his arms outstretched in prayer—"The Appeal to the Great Spirit" (Museum of Fine Arts, Boston).

Of Dallin's other Indian subjects, the best is his "Massasoit" (1921; Plymouth, Mass.). Interspersed with his Indian pieces were several monuments to the pioneer settlers of Utah. The earliest of these was made in 1895 for Salt Lake City (where he also made the figure of the Angel Moroni that tops the Mormon Temple); he later (1931) produced the "Pioneer Woman of Utah" (Springville, Utah), for which his mother posed. His "Anne Hutchinson" (State House, Boston) memorialized the Puritan religious dissenter. Among the many other productions of his studio were: "Sir Isaac Newton" (Library of Congress); "The Cavalryman" (Hanover, Pa.); "General Hancock" (Gettysburg, Pa.); "The Scout" (Kansas City, Mo.); Soldiers' Monument (Syracuse, N. Y.); "Indian Hunter" (Arlington, Mass.); and "Spirit of Life" (Brookline, Mass.).

After Dallin's return from Paris in 1890, he had established his studio in Boston, where he remained for the rest of his life except for intervals in Utah (1891–94), in Philadephia (1895–96), where he taught modeling at the Drexel Institute, and in Paris (1896-99), where he studied with Jean Dampt. For more than forty years Dallin taught sculpture at the Massachusetts Normal School of Art, retiring in 1942. On June 16, 1891, he had married Vittoria Colonna Murray of Boston. Their three sons were Edwin Bertram, Arthur Murray, and Lawrence. Dallin's work won high awards, and he was elected to the National Institute of Arts and Letters and to the Royal Society of Arts in London, among other honors. In religion he was a Unitarian. Archery and astronomy were his principal hobbies. He died of a coronary thrombosis at his home in Arlington Heights, Mass., shortly before his eighty-third birthday and was buried at Mount Pleasant Cemetery, Arlington.

The Chicago World's Fair of 1893, coinciding with the closing of the frontier, helped stir interest in the American West. Along with Hermon A. MacNeil, Cyrus Dallin was among the first sculptors to take the American Indian as his subject and one of the most successful in endowing his tragic hero with nobility and dignity.

[The two most useful biographical articles are those of William Howe Downes in *New England Mag.*, Oct. 1899, and E. Waldo Long in *World's Work*, Sept. 1927; see also William L. Stidger, *Human Side of Greatness* (1940). For critical comment, see Lorado Taft, *Hist. of Am. Sculpture* (1903), pp. 496–501, and Wayne Craven, *Sculpture in America* (1968), pp. 527–31. See also A. Seaton-Schmidt in *Internat. Studio*, Apr. 1916; M. Stannard May in *New England Mag.*, Nov. 1912; William Howe Downes in *Scribner's Mag.*, June 1915; Katherine Hodges in *Am. Mag. of Art*, Oct. 1924; *Who Was Who in America*, vol. II (1950); and obituaries in *N. Y. Times* and *Christian Science Monitor*, Nov. 15, 1944. Information about Dallin's parents was supplied by Mr. John James, Librarian, Utah Division of State Hist.; death record from Mass. Registrar of Vital Statistics.]

WAYNE CRAVEN

DANIELS, WINTHROP MORE (Sept. 30, 1867–Jan. 2, 1944), economist, member of the Interstate Commerce Commission, was born in Dayton, Ohio, the second son and second of four children. His father, Edwin Adams Daniels, who became a manufacturer of carriage wheels, and his mother, Mary (Kilburn) Daniels, were both descended from colonial Massachusetts families which had migrated to Ohio in the 1850's. Their son prepared at a private academy and entered the College of New Jersey (Princeton) with the class of 1888. Daniels was twice elected president of his class. His classmates remembered him as one of its "most brilliant members," and he had a reputation as a conversationalist and story teller. He took an active part in debating and undergraduate writing and at commencement delivered the valedictory oration. Of the Princeton influences Daniels found congenial, he later recalled the "historical spirit" and the "dictates of common sense" dominating all studies, and a "theistic metaphysics" opposed to "agnosticism, materialism, or idealism." Alexander Johnston [q.v.], professor of jurisprudence and political economy (whose textbook on American history Daniels was to revise and extend in 1897), he felt embodied these traits.

Upon graduation Daniels spent a year or two as intellectual handyman at a preparatory school near Princeton, while studying for an M.A. degree which he received from Princeton in 1890. He then enrolled in the University of Leipzig to study history and political economy. In 1891 he secured a position at Wesleyan University, and the following year one as assistant professor of political economy at Princeton, where his departmental "chief" was Woodrow Wilson. Besides a general course in economics, Daniels found himself teaching principles of public finance, which as an undergraduate course many economists then regarded as having dubious academic standing. He was appointed professor in 1895. For many years Daniels was a member of a group-conscious "Young Faculty," led by Wilson, who frequently voted together on college affairs. To research he preferred teaching undergraduates, a role in which he excelled; he also published a successful textbook, *The Elements of Public Finance* (1899). On Oct. 12, 1898, he married Joan Robertson, the daughter of a Connnecticut papermaker. The couple had one child, Robertson Balfour.

Though in the 1890's the village of Princeton was an isolated country town, New York City, the center of American publishing, was near at hand, and ambitious faculty members sought to become reviewers or editors. By 1903 Daniels had broken into the *Nation;* and soon in summer vacations he was serving on the editorial board of the *Nation* and the New York *Evening Post,* which were run as joint enterprises. He often reminded social "scientists," Cassandras, "fledgling reformers," and apostles of the Social Gospel that to their schemes there was an alternative program: "the full amplification of individual liberty, where the humblest citizen may sit 'under his own vine and fig-tree,' with no tax to pay to the tariff baron, with no graft to render to the politician, with no obeisance to make to the labor union, and with no enforced deference to his fellows who find their pleasure in mapping out the way to Utopia" (*Nation,* July 28, 1904, p. 69). In brief, Daniels's outlook was factual, individualistic, affirmative, moralistic, and elitist. He feared these traits made him something of a "Bourbon"; actually, his aversion to abstraction prevented him from being a complete apostle of laissez-faire.

In 1910 Woodrow Wilson entered New Jersey politics and won the governorship on a wave of reform. Daniels followed his leader, for Wilson in 1911 appointed him to the New Jersey Board of Public Utility Commissioners and, when he reached the White House, promoted his friend in 1914 to an unexpired term in the Interstate Commerce Commission. Only presidential pressure forced Daniels's nomination through the Senate. At issue were the principles he held about the correct basis for setting "just and reasonable" railroad rates. On the New Jersey Commission he had prepared its ruling on a complaint against gas rates in Passaic; the Commission ordered a reduction, but in ascertaining the proper rate base included such intangibles as "going concern value." This decision had affronted local reformers. On the national scene, it also antagonized the hard core of Republicans and Westerners in the Senate who, under the tutelage of Robert La Follette [*q.v.*], had contended through a long struggle for "enlightened" regulation that a physical valuation of railroad property was the correct base for determining rates.

Daniels came upon the ICC when that body was considering a petition from railroads in the Northeast and Midwest for an increase of 5 percent in freight rates, and at a time when Wilson, the "New Freedom" behind him, was turning an increasingly friendly ear to the needs of business. Louis D. Brandeis [Supp. 3] as special counsel to the ICC opposed the increase, repeating his plea of 1910 that the adoption of scientific management principles would ensure sufficient savings to meet the railroads' needs. The Commission's decision, in July, granted a 5 percent advance within the Midwestern states only. Daniels in his dissent explicitly dismissed the amount of Brandeis's savings as inadequate. Since 1906, he pointed out, the average rise in the world's price level had been between 30 and 50 percent; meanwhile railroad rates had stood still and the railroads' net income had declined. Fairness to the roads and to the community demanded a massive inflow of capital investments for modernization. Rates must be raised: "A living wage is as necessary for a railroad as for an individual." Within a few months a majority of the Commission fell into step, particularly after the outbreak of war in Europe, and in December the ICC granted the higher rates for the Northeast as well. Early in 1917 Wilson nominated Daniels for a full six-year term on the Commission. Again the irreconcilables in the Senate attacked Daniels as "reactionary"; they convinced fewer of their colleagues than in 1914. In accordance with custom, the Commission itself elected Daniels its chairman for the year 1918–19.

The added pressures of American mobilization compelled Wilson temporarily to nationalize the railroads at the end of 1917. In returning them to private ownership and operation after the war, the Transportation Act of 1920 introduced the novelty of permitting railroads to consolidate into a number of systems, including strong and weak roads, so that their rates would be as uniform as possible and thus more easily and more fairly regulated. In retrospect, Daniels preferred greater emphasis upon maintaining competition and the regulatory powers of the ICC.

Tired of the labors of his position, Daniels resigned from the ICC on July 1, 1923, six months before the expiration of his term, and accepted the Cuyler Professorship of Transportation in the Yale Graduate School. Although he published little in these years, he did deride the inconsistencies of the New Deal in a playful essay, and declared that an "Old Economist" like himself was now as much in exile as a "White Russian in Paris or New York." He retired from Yale in 1935. The next year he served as a trustee under the receivership of the New York, New Haven & Hartford Railroad, but a severe stroke in 1937 curtailed his activities. A Presbyterian in his Princeton days, Daniels in his later years was a member of the Congregational Church. He died of heart disease at his home in Saybrook, Conn., and was buried in Cypress Cemetery, Saybrook Point.

[Unpublished autobiographical sketch in the possession of Daniels's son; Daniels's *Recollections of Woodrow Wilson* (1944) and "The Passing of the Old Economist," *Harvard Business Rev.,* Apr. 1934; material provided by Princeton Univ. Archives; Ransom E. Noble, Jr., *N. J. Progressivism before Wilson* (1946); Henry W. Bragdon, *Woodrow Wilson: The Academic Years* (1967); Bliss Perry, *And Gladly Teach* (1935); Arthur S. Link, *Wilson*, vols. I and II (1947–56); I. L. Sharfman, *The Interstate Commerce Commission* (4 vols., 1931–37); K. Austin Kerr, *Am. Railroad Politics, 1914–1920* (1968); obituaries in *N. Y. Times,* Jan. 4, 1944, and *Princeton Alumni Weekly,* Jan. 28, 1944; death record from Town Clerk, Saybrook, Conn.]

EDWARD C. KIRKLAND

DAUGHERTY, HARRY MICAJAH (Jan. 26, 1860–Oct. 12, 1941), lawyer, politician, cabinet officer, was born in Washington Court House, Fayette County, Ohio, one of four sons of John Harry and Jane Amelia (Draper) Daugherty. His father, of Scotch-Irish descent, was a merchant tailor who had come to Washington Court House after spending his youth in Lancaster, Pa., and Zanesville, Ohio; his mother came of an old Virginia family. When Daugherty was four, his father and two of his brothers died in a diphtheria epidemic which also left him in a weakened condition. The frail youngster later worked at an assortment of jobs to supplement the family's meager income and to complete his local schooling. He then entered the University of Michigan law school and, after receiving the LL.B. degree in 1881, returned to Washington Court House, where he began the practice of law. On Sept. 3, 1884, he married Lucy Matilda Walker of Wellston, Ohio. They had two children, Emily Belle and Draper Mallie.

Too energetic and ambitious to limit himself to the law, Daugherty joined the Republican party in 1881. That summer he was a delegate from Union Township to the county judicial convention, and the following year he was elected township clerk. He next won a seat in the Ohio house of representatives—the highest elective office he ever attained. After serving two terms (1890–94), he unavailingly sought nominations for state attorney general (1895), Congressman (1892 and 1896), governor (1899), and United States Senator (1909). His calculating and combative nature, in addition to an unsavory reputation as a political lobbyist at the state capitol, contributed to his lack of success. More important, he forfeited the support of the party leaders. In 1892, when the Ohio legislature elected John Sherman United States Senator over Joseph Foraker [*qq.v.*], opponents accused Daugherty of switching his vote from Foraker to Sherman for seven $500 bills. Seven years later he alienated the contingent of Mark Hanna [*q.v.*]—after Foraker's, the second major faction of the Ohio party—by his unsuccessful bid for the gubernatorial nomination. Now on the political fringe, Daugherty combined in 1906 with Congressman Theodore Burton [Supp.

1] in an abortive insurgent attempt to overthrow the party organization controlled by Foraker and Hanna lieutenant Charles Dick. He then joined the camp of William Howard Taft, but found his Senatorial ambitions stifled when Burton won the nomination in 1909 and when President Taft failed of reelection in 1912. In a final attempt for elective office Daugherty suffered a humiliating defeat in the 1916 Senatorial primaries.

Though Daugherty failed to win the backing of the Ohio Republican party in his quest for public office, he utilized his organizational and oratorical skills to good effect as a party campaigner. In that capacity he served the Ohio party for almost forty years. He was active nationally in the presidential campaigns of William McKinley in 1896 and William Howard Taft in 1908 and 1912. As Taft's Ohio chairman in 1912, Daugherty purged the Republican party of its disloyal members and prevented Progressive party candidates from running on the Republican ticket. His actions caused considerable resentment among Progressives and liberal Republicans, who later blamed him for hindering a Republican-Progressive rapprochement. A born intriguer, Daugherty managed to hang on by impressing Republicans with his capacity to control a faction of the party. Accordingly, many political leaders, including Senator Warren G. Harding, sought his support after 1912.

Daugherty achieved national prominence when he backed Harding for the Republican presidential nomination in 1920. The Daugherty-Harding relationship was never the brotherly one that Daugherty later recalled. Only after 1911 had there been political accord, and even then serious differences arose. As late as 1918 the two were at odds when Daugherty tried to subvert Harding's attempt to reunite the Ohio Republicans under his leadership, and Harding regarded Daugherty with suspicion until he committed himself in 1919 to the Ohio Senator's presidential candidacy. Contrary to myth, Daugherty as Harding's political manager hindered almost as much as he helped; in the Ohio primary campaign of 1920, his divisive tactics alienated many Republicans who otherwise would have backed Harding. Harding's nomination resulted chiefly from his availability, his own efforts, and a deadlocked convention, but he nevertheless rewarded Daugherty by appointing him Attorney General.

The burly, thick-necked Daugherty, whose trademarks were a derby hat and diamond stickpin, shortly became a center of controversy. He failed to provide direction for the Department of Justice, which soon developed a reputation for inefficiency and ineptness. Handicapped by his political appointees, Daugherty was unsuccessful in supervising the important war fraud, prohibition, and antitrust litigations. He fared better, with Chief Justice Taft's help, in expanding the federal court structure, but undermined this accomplishment by his sweeping railroad strike injunction in 1922. The injunction, which prohibited officers of unions from in any way encouraging employees to leave their jobs, so embittered organized labor that an impeachment was attempted that same year. More damaging to Daugherty was the chicanery that was associated with his department. He himself appeared to have been illicitly involved in at least one transaction, that of accepting a bribe to return the American Metal Company, which had been confiscated as alien property by the federal government during World War I, to private hands. As a result, he was twice brought to court on a charge of defrauding the government, but because he had destroyed important financial records of the company, the grand jury investigations were inconclusive. He was dismissed by President Coolidge in April 1924 and spent the rest of his life trying to vindicate his career and create the myth that he had dominated Harding. In 1941, at the age of eighty-one, he died of a heart attack in Columbus, Ohio, his principal home since 1890. A Methodist in religion, he was buried in the family mausoleum at the Washington Court House Cemetery.

[James N. Giglio, "The Political Career of Harry M. Daugherty" (Ph.D. dissertation, Ohio State Univ., 1968); obituary in *N. Y. Times*, Oct. 13, 1941; *Columbus Citizen*, Sept. 21, 1941; autobiographical sketch, Daugherty to Ray Baker Harris, June 7, 1938 (Ray Baker Harris Deposit of Warren G. Harding material, Box 9/3, Ohio Hist. Soc.). See also *Nat. Cyc. Am. Biog.*, XXXIII, 124–25; and Daugherty's often unreliable *The Inside Story of the Harding Tragedy* (1932). The most useful manuscript sources on Daugherty are the William Howard Taft Papers, Lib. of Cong., and the Warren G. Harding Papers, Ohio Hist. Soc. Although Daugherty had willed his personal correspondence to his daughter Emily Rarey, he apparently destroyed it just before his death.]
JAMES N. GIGLIO

DAVENPORT, CHARLES BENEDICT (June 1, 1866–Feb. 8, 1944), biologist and eugenicist, was the youngest of five sons and eighth of the nine children of Amzi Benedict Davenport by his second wife, Jane Joralemon Dimon. The family home was in Brooklyn, N. Y., but he was born on the farm near Stamford, Conn., where the Davenports lived each year from May through November. His father, born near Stamford, had moved in 1836 to Brooklyn, where he established a private academy; he later went into the real estate business. Proud of his descent from John

Davenport [*q.v.*], the Puritan divine who was co-founder, in 1638, of the New Haven colony, he compiled the family genealogy. Charles's mother, a native of Brooklyn, was of English, Dutch, and Italian ancestry. Her inheritance from Teunis Joralemon, her maternal grandfather and a prominent Brooklyn merchant and civic leader, gave the family financial independence. One of Charles's brothers, William Edwards, became a Congregational minister and founded the Italian Settlement Society of Brooklyn; another, James, was a judge in New York; a sister, Frances Gardiner, became a historian. He also had two half brothers by his father's first marriage.

From his mother, who had a kindly and affectionate nature, Davenport acquired a love of natural history, and during summers on the farm he made the most of his opportunities to study wildlife. His early formal education was administered by his father, a Congregational deacon of strict religious views and a harsh disciplinarian. Getting his lessons in the intervals of endless chores in the real estate office or on the farm, the boy was not permitted to attend school until he was thirteen. His father then let him enter Brooklyn Polytechnic Institute on the condition that he take the engineering course. He completed the four high school years and three years at the college level, acquiring a thorough training in mathematics, and graduated in 1886 with a B.S. degree in civil engineering. Davenport stood first in his class and was editor-in-chief of the school newspaper and class orator, but his early isolation had already marked him with a sense of inferiority and a premature seriousness.

After graduation he left home and worked for nine months as a rodman on a railroad surveying crew in northern Michigan. During this time he learned Latin, passed his twenty-first birthday, and earned enough to wrench free from his father and to enter Harvard. There he studied zoology, receiving the A.B. in 1889, the Ph.D. in 1892, and then an appointment as instructor. On June 23, 1894, he married Anna Gertrude Crotty, a Radcliffe graduate student from Kansas, who became his only close counselor and collaborated with him on much of his work. They had two daughters, Millia Crotty and Jane Joralemon, and a son, Charles Benedict, who died in childhood of polio.

At Harvard, Davenport became a disciple of the anatomist Edward L. Mark, and with his strong mathematical background he soon established himself as one of the leaders in the field of biostatistics. His *Experimental Morphology* (2 vols., 1897–99) was essentially a plea to biologists to employ the quantitative and experimental methods of chemistry and physics. This was followed by *Statistical Methods with Special Reference to Biological Variation* (1899), in which he introduced American biologists to the biometrical investigations of the English biologist Karl Pearson, who, along with Francis Galton, attempted to utilize statistical methods in determining the laws of heredity. This was the first scientific reflection of Davenport's lifelong interest in heredity.

Ambitious for advancement, Davenport in 1898 became director of the summer biological laboratory which the Brooklyn Institute of Arts and Sciences maintained at Cold Spring Harbor, Long Island, a position he retained until 1923. His paper on "The Animal Ecology of the Cold Spring Harbor Sand Spit" (1903), which grew out of his work there, greatly influenced animal ecologists of the day. He left Harvard in 1899 to accept an assistant professorship at the University of Chicago, where he was promoted to associate professor in 1901.

Davenport was one of the earliest Americans to become aware of the rediscovery of Mendel's laws of heredity in 1900. He was at first doubtful of their general importance, but after the British geneticist William Bateson visited him in 1904, he became one of the first American proponents of the new theory. Breaking with Pearson, whose statistical methods merely described what Mendel's laws promised to explain, he now turned to genetics. In a vigorous two-year campaign he induced the Carnegie Institution of Washington to found a research institute in this field, the Station for Experimental Evolution, set up in 1904 at Cold Spring Harbor with Davenport as full-time director. He now had large funds and numerous research appointments at his disposal and soon became one of America's earliest "scientific influentials." He set his staff to work on a number of problems in cytology and breeding, and himself undertook breeding experiments with a wide variety of insects and animals. But Davenport soon diverted his efforts to human genetics. Beginning in 1907, he published a series of articles with his wife on the heredity of eye, skin, and hair color. In these studies he made several solid contributions, but his work now began to suffer from hasty and uncritical preparation. Although he worked intensely and wrote voluminously, he tended to reduce complex social and cultural phenomena to simple genetic terms, and he refused to seek or to accept advice and criticism.

From the beginning, genetic principles appealed to Davenport as a guide for social action, and he was an early supporter of the eugenics movement, which promised to elevate the human race through improvements in heredity. In 1910 he persuaded Mary Williamson Harriman, widow of the rail-

road magnate Edward H. Harriman [*q.v.*], to finance the establishment of a center for the study of eugenics under his direction next to the experimental station at Cold Spring Harbor. From this time, Davenport worked almost exclusively in the field of eugenics and human heredity. In his most important work, *Heredity in Relation to Eugenics* (1911), he set forth his conviction that all human characteristics, both physical and mental, were the products of immutable genes, and that traits appeared in succeeding generations in simple Mendelian ratios. He publicly promoted the eugenic program of urging the "fit" to reproduce and preventing the "unfit" from doing so, convinced that in this way "imbecility, poverty, disease, immorality" could be eliminated from society.

At the Eugenics Record Office (merged with the Station for Experimental Evolution in 1920 to form the Carnegie Institution's Department of Genetics), Davenport and Harry H. Laughlin [Supp. 3], whom he appointed as superintendent, trained field workers to gather family data at asylums, reformatories, and other institutions, to be used for studies of the inheritance of mental traits and social behavior. Believing that the dilution of Anglo-Saxon blood in the United States endangered democracy, Davenport supported immigration restriction and was an advocate of racial segregation. He energetically publicized his social views in writings and lectures, by his eminence and reputation giving them a scientific sanction in the eyes of many laymen.

Davenport was elected to the American Philosophical Society in 1907 and to the National Academy of Sciences in 1912. Though shy and uncomfortable in groups all his life, he was a member of many professional and civic organizations; he delighted in promotion, fund raising, and organization. As the administrator of three associated laboratories, he was a vigorous builder of plant and staff but was less successful in inspiring confidence and cooperation among his fellow workers. Nonetheless, his reputation, and the research opportunities offered by the laboratories, attracted many of the ablest young biologists of the day to Cold Spring Harbor and to the study of genetics.

As Davenport became absorbed with the eugenics movement, he drifted away from the mainstream of genetics. Before World War I, he was only one of many prominent geneticists who looked favorably upon eugenics; but by the late 1920's, when the movement had become racist and when inheritance was seen to be a much more complex process than had at one time been supposed, most reputable geneticists had become hostile toward it. By 1934, when Davenport finally retired, his continued participation had made him an anomaly. The Carnegie Institution withdrew the last of its support from the eugenics program at Cold Spring Harbor in 1940.

In retirement Davenport lived on at Cold Spring Harbor. He continued his research in human heredity and in ten years published forty-seven papers, one book, and a revision of another. Disturbed by the social philosophy of the New Deal, he organized a taxpayers' association to prevent what he regarded as encroachments by the growing welfare state. He died at Huntington, Long Island, at the age of seventy-seven, of pneumonia contracted while boiling the head of a beached killer whale in an open shed in midwinter in order to secure the skull for the Whaling Museum at Cold Spring Harbor, of which he was the founder and director. Although widely recognized as one of the leading biologists of his time, Davenport made few fundamental contributions to the field of genetics. His importance lies in his work as an administrator, organizer, and popularizer of science and as a leader in the eugenics movement.

[Davenport's papers, at the Am. Philosophical Soc., Philadelphia; E. Carleton MacDowell, "Charles Benedict Davenport, 1866–1944: A Study of Conflicting Influences," *Bios,* XVII (1946), 3–50, the most comprehensive biography; Oscar Riddle in Nat. Acad. Sci., *Biog. Memoirs,* vol. XXV (1949), good on his personality; Charles E. Rosenberg, "Charles Benedict Davenport and the Beginning of Human Genetics," *Bull. of the Hist. of Medicine,* May–June 1961. See also memoirs by G. H. Parker in Am. Philosophical Soc., *Year Book,* 1944, and by Morris Steggerda in *Am. Jour. of Physical Anthropology,* June 1944; Mark H. Haller, *Eugenics: Hereditarian Attitudes in Am. Thought* (1963); John Higham, *Strangers in the Land* (1955); and, on his family, Amzi Benedict Davenport, *A Supp. to the Hist. and Genealogy of the Davenport Family* (1876).]

KENNETH M. LUDMERER

DAVENPORT, EUGENE (June 20, 1856–Mar. 31, 1941), agricultural educator, was born on a farm near Woodland, Mich., the only child of Esther (Sutton) and George Martin Davenport. His father's ancestry was English and Dutch, his mother's Pennsylvania Dutch. The elder Davenport had grown up with little formal schooling near Ithaca, N. Y., and at eighteen had migrated with his family to northern Ohio. There he married the daughter of a family of spinners and weavers and abandoned his trade as a carpenter and joiner to become a farmer. In 1855 the couple removed to a tract of their own in the southern Michigan timberland, where Eugene was born in a log house.

This frontier environment and close association with his father in turning the hardwood forest into a farm strongly influenced Daven-

port's life. The boy's earliest recollections were of making maple sugar, and he became expert with the ax and crosscut saw. He attended the district school and a local private school, began teaching at eighteen, and graduated from nearby Michigan Agricultural College in 1878. For the next ten years he and his father operated the family farm. During this time Davenport taught in a neighboring private school, where he met Emma Jane Coats, whom he married on Nov. 2, 1881. They had two daughters, Dorothy and Margaret, of whom the first died shortly after birth. Davenport obtained a master of science degree from his alma mater in 1884. Returning there in 1888, he served for a year as assistant to Prof. William J. Beal [q.v.] and as assistant botanist of the experiment station, and from 1889 to 1891 as professor of agriculture and superintendent of the college farm.

He resigned in 1891 and went to Brazil, where he had been invited to establish and preside over an agricultural college at Piracicaba for a year, after which the state of São Paulo was to take it over. The undertaking, however, proved premature, and Davenport left Brazil in April 1892, returning by way of England in order to study the methods of scientific agriculture practiced at Rothamsted. Back home he resumed the life of a farmer at Woodland. In the fall of 1894 he agreed to become dean of the College of Agriculture at the University of Illinois.

Arriving in Urbana on Jan. 1, 1895, Davenport found the college in a neglected state. It had nine students and offered only a short winter course; and the recently installed president, Andrew S. Draper [q.v.], opposed agricultural education. Davenport was made professor of animal husbandry in March 1895, although Draper did not appoint instructors in agriculture proper and dairying until fifteen months later. Davenport's main battle was for funds, and to gain them he boldly went over the president's head to the farmers and politicians. He helped organize the Illinois Farmers' Institute, which in 1899 persuaded the legislature to appropriate money for an agricultural building and to see that the college received more revenue. The institute itself supplied scholarships; Davenport greatly enlarged the curriculum and appointed four new instructors; and enrollments dramatically increased.

Davenport had been appointed director of the Agricultural Experiment Station at the university in 1896, and to enlist support for it he cultivated the leaders of Illinois farm organizations. He had representatives of the producers' associations lobby for categorical appropriations for research in their special areas. His success assured the college and the station ample means, but he paid a heavy price for it. The advisory committees of prominent agriculturists he established were in a position to influence research policy and require immediate results. When they demanded the firing of the head of the household science department, Isabel Bevier [Supp. 3], Davenport sacrificed principle to expediency and asked for her resignation.

Well before the First World War, Davenport had firmly established the College of Agriculture and the Experiment Station among the leading institutions of their kind. Through extension services in agriculture and home economics he linked the state with the university. Davenport was much in demand as a public speaker. He issued many technical bulletins, wrote prolifically on farm problems and national affairs for periodicals, and published a textbook, *Principles of Breeding* (1907), and an abbreviated version, *Domesticated Animals and Plants* (1910). In *Education for Efficiency* (1909) he argued for including agriculture and home economics as integral parts of the public school system. During the First World War he advised the federal government on food policy. Davenport used his political allies to support the university's general needs, and from 1920 through 1922 he served as vice-president of the university as well as dean of the agricultural college.

Upon retiring in 1922, Davenport returned to Woodland. The deaths of his daughter (1930) and his wife (1935) saddened his later years. He spent his remaining days completing *Timberland Times* (1950), a charming memoir of pioneer days in Michigan, and writing a rambling autobiography, which was never published. Davenport died of nephritis at his Woodland home at the age of eighty-four; he was buried in Woodland Memorial Park.

A man of decided opinions, Davenport was a staunch Republican. Personally abstemious, he abhorred cigarettes and alcohol; at the Michigan ratification convention in 1933, he was the only delegate to oppose repeal of the Eighteenth Amendment. He believed in hard work, thrift, and self-reliance, and in the blessings of civil and religious liberty. He grew up favoring Universalist beliefs but became a Congregationalist. Rather short but imposing in physical appearance, he had a high forehead and trim whiskers that framed regular features. Although ambitious and self-willed, he could indirectly call out the best effort in others. His primary contribution was as an educator and entrepreneur of research in agriculture.

[The Univ. of Ill. Archives has extensive source material: the Davenport Papers (1857–1954), which touch on personal as well as professional affairs and include his MS. autobiography, "What One Life Has Seen"; the Agricultural Dean's Office Letterbooks, 1888–1911; Agricultural Dean's Office Subject File, 1895–1964; and Agricultural Experiment Station Letterbooks, 1901–04, 1907–12. A valuable guide to Davenport's extensive writings is "A Bibliog. of Writings Published and Unpublished by and about Eugene Davenport" (1954), compiled by Mrs. Ruth Warrick in consultation with Anna C. Glover, Davenport's secretary (copy in Univ. of Ill. Lib.). Among published accounts of Davenport, the best are T. J. Burrill in *Ill. Agriculturist*, June 1915; and obituaries in the *N. Y. Times*, Apr. 1, 1941, and *Science*, Aug. 1, 1941, the latter by his longtime colleague and friend, David Kinley. Other information from Prof. Elmer Roberts, a student and later colleague of Davenport. See also Winton U. Solberg, *The Univ. of Ill., 1867–1894: An Intellectual and Cultural Hist.* (1968), which describes the setting into which Davenport stepped at Urbana; and Richard G. Moores, *Fields of Rich Toil: The Development of the Univ. of Ill. College of Agriculture* (1970). Mr. Harry J. Cahalan is engaged in a critical study of Davenport's career. A portrait of Davenport by Sidney E. Dickinson hangs in the College of Agriculture.]

WINTON U. SOLBERG

DAVIS, DWIGHT FILLEY (July 5, 1879–Nov. 28, 1945), sportsman and public official, was born in St. Louis, Mo., the youngest of the three sons of John Tilden Davis and Maria Jeanette (Filley) Davis. His paternal grandfather, Samuel Craft Davis, had founded a wholesale dry goods house in St. Louis in 1835; his father was a successful merchant and banker. In keeping with the family's position of wealth and prominence, Davis was educated at Smith Academy in St. Louis and at Harvard, where he chiefly excelled as a tennis player. He was three times national doubles champion (1899–1901). In 1900, the year he graduated from college, he donated a trophy, the famous Davis Cup, as a symbol of international tennis supremacy.

Returning to St. Louis, Davis studied at the Washington University Law School, but though he received the LL.B. degree in 1903, he did not practice, nor did he follow his father into business. Instead, he became involved in local civic affairs, with a special interest in the development of recreational facilities. He served as a member of the board of the public library (1904–07), the board of control of the Museum of Fine Arts (1904–07, 1911–12), and the city government's house of delegates (1907–09) and board of freeholders (1909–11), and as chairman of the City Planning Commission (1911–15). As city park commissioner (1911–15) he greatly expanded local athletic facilities, developing public golf links, baseball grounds, and the first municipal tennis courts in the United States. His civic experience led to service on the executive committee of the National Municipal League (1908–12).

An advocate of military preparedness, Davis fought in France during World War I with the 5th Regiment of the Missouri National Guard, winning the Distinguished Service Cross for "extraordinary heroism in action." He returned home a war hero with the rank of lieutenant colonel, and in 1920 ran unsuccessfully for the Republican nomination to the United States Senate. Shortly afterward he was appointed by President Warren G. Harding as director of the War Finance Corporation.

In 1923 Davis was named Assistant Secretary of War, and as such defended his department against charges made by Col. William ("Billy") Mitchell [Supp. 2] of having neglected military aviation. Promoted in 1925 to Secretary of War, in succession to the ailing John W. Weeks [q.v.], Davis approved the findings of a presidential board, headed by Dwight W. Morrow [Supp. 1], which recommended court-martialing Mitchell but urged advances in both military and commercial aviation. Davis was responsible for the establishment of the Army Industrial College (1923), to educate officers in the problems of mobilizing industry in time of war, and for the army's first experiments with a mechanized force, under the guidance of Adna Romanza Chaffee [Supp. 3].

In 1929 President Herbert Hoover appointed Davis governor general of the Philippines. There he worked to improve economic conditions, building new roads and harbors, developing a school system, and initiating new banking laws. He resigned in 1932, presumably because of his wife's poor health, and devoted the next few years to traveling and to developing a Florida tung-oil plantation. Beginning in 1935, he also served on the board of trustees of the Brookings Institution, after 1937 as chairman. He returned to public life in 1942 when, despite his opposition to what he considered the "fascist" flirtations of the New Deal, he accepted appointment as director general of the Army Specialist Corps, which selected for commissions men with special skills who had failed the physical examination.

Distinguished in appearance, tall and kindly looking, Davis enjoyed prosperity and progressed in power while blending inconspicuously into the background of his times. On Nov. 15, 1905, he married Helen Brooks of Boston. They had four children: Dwight Filley, Alice Brooks, Cynthia, and Helen Brooks. Mrs. Davis died in 1932. On May 8, 1936, Davis married Pauline (Morton) Sabin, the widowed daughter of Paul Morton [q.v.]. Brought up as a Baptist, he remained in that denomination. He died of a heart attack at his home in Washington, D. C., and was buried in Arlington National Cemetery.

[Published biographical accounts include: obituaries in *N. Y. Times* and *Washington Post*, Nov. 29, 1945; *Who's Who in St. Louis*, 1928–29; Harvard College Class of 1900, *Fiftieth Anniversary Report* (1950); *Nat. Cyc. Am. Biog.*, Current Vol. A, pp. 10–11, and XL, 50–51. The Mo. Hist. Soc., St. Louis, has clipping files and the annual reports of the St. Louis Park Dept. The St. Louis Public Lib. has a 1907 speech by Davis, "Some Municipal Problems." Davis's War Dept. and Philippine Islands activities are reflected in contemporary periodical literature; see also his article in *Current Hist.*, Feb. 1926; and Russell F. Weigley, *Hist. of the U. S. Army* (1967), pp. 407, 410. On his father, see Walter B. Stevens, *St. Louis* (1909), III, 50–52. St. Louis friends of Davis, such as George Hagee, Clifford Greve, and Harry Gleick, provided valuable information. There is no collection of Davis's papers, but personal correspondence can be tracked down elsewhere, especially in the William Howard Taft Papers, Lib. of Cong.]

JERRY ISRAEL

DAVIS, NORMAN HEZEKIAH (Aug. 9, 1878–July 2, 1944), banker and diplomat, received his name from his birthplace, Normandy, a small town in middle Tennessee. He was one of seven children and the second of five sons of Maclin Hezekiah and Christina Lee (Shofner) Davis. His paternal ancestors had emigrated from Wales to Virginia and North Carolina in the 1740's. Davis spent most of his boyhood in Tullahoma, Tenn., where his father, previously the manager of a general store in Normandy, settled about 1884 and bought a sawmill, a distillery, and a farm. The boy attended local schools and the preparatory school of William R. Webb [q.v.] at nearby Bell Buckle, and in 1897 entered Vanderbilt University. The death of his father the following year forced him to leave college and help support the family, but after a severe attack of asthma, he spent a year in California as a student at Stanford (1899–1900). Meanwhile, in October 1898, he had married Mackie Paschall, a childhood friend. They had eight children: Maclin, Norman, Martha, Christine, Good, (John) Paschall, Mary, and Sarah.

Upon returning to Tennessee in 1900, Davis managed a farm and bought an interest in a local factory. He moved two years later to Cuba, both to improve his health and to take advantage of the island's expanding economy. In 1905, having learned Spanish and banking, he organized the Trust Company of Cuba, of which he soon became president. In this and other enterprises, over the next decade, he amassed a considerable fortune. He was convicted of fraud during this period for failing to disclose to a stockholder the profits of one of the companies of which he was an officer, but Davis always felt that he was morally innocent. After America's entry into World War I in 1917, he severed most of his business connections in Cuba, moved to New York City, and volunteered his services to the federal government.

A lifelong Democrat, Davis soon found a niche in the Treasury Department, and in mid-1918 he successfully negotiated a loan from neutral Spain. His Cuban experience had convinced him of the importance of international finance and made him confident that most international problems could be settled by a "business approach." Late in 1918 he was sent again to Europe as a Treasury assistant to Herbert Hoover in his negotiations on postwar relief policies, and in January 1919 Davis became financial adviser to the American commission at the Paris Peace Conference. He was also one of the three American members of the Reparations Commission and fought to prevent the imposition of an unrealistic war settlement upon Germany. An ardent Wilsonian and supporter of the League of Nations, Davis was made Assistant Secretary of the Treasury in charge of the Foreign Loan Bureau in October 1919. There he strongly opposed the cancellation of Allied war debts. Wilson, who described Davis as "too fine a man to let go from the public service," appointed him Under Secretary of State in June 1920. In this post, he helped establish the American policy of nonrecognition of the Soviet government, advocated a new Pan-Americanism to replace Dollar Diplomacy in Latin America, and worked to strengthen Anglo-American relations.

A quiet, deliberate man, patient and persuasive, Davis possessed a quick intellect and a lively sense of humor. His unaffected directness won him the confidence of the many public officials with whom he dealt, both in the United States and in Europe. Although the new Republican Secretary of State, Charles Evans Hughes, asked him to remain in the department, Davis was too committed a Democrat and too bitter over the defeat of the Versailles Treaty to accept.

A strong internationalist, Davis consistently urged American support of the League of Nations and the World Court and advocated the reduction of tariffs. In 1921 he helped organize the Council on Foreign Relations and became a frequent contributor to its publication, *Foreign Affairs*. He led a League commission in 1924 which settled a dispute over the Baltic port of Memel, and in the same year he became president of the Woodrow Wilson Foundation. He was chosen by President Coolidge as a delegate to the Geneva Economic Conference of 1927, and he served in a private capacity on the League's Financial Committee in 1931.

Davis's chief concern of the 1930's was the issue of disarmament. He had little hope that the Kellogg-Briand Pact of 1928 by itself would prevent war, and believed that arms reduction could

be achieved only through mutual security agreements. President Hoover appointed Davis a member of the American delegation to the General Disarmament Conference which convened in Geneva in 1932. When Franklin D. Roosevelt took office, he made Davis chairman of the delegation, with the rank of ambassador. At Davis's urging, Roosevelt authorized him to commit the United States, should a general plan of disarmament be adopted, to "consult" with other governments in case of a threat to the peace and possibly to refrain from interfering with League of Nations sanctions against an aggressor; but the conference never came close to agreement and lapsed in 1934. Davis led the American delegation to the second London Naval Conference (1935–36), which sought to achieve an agreement on naval limitation among the United States, Great Britain, France, and Japan; but Japan withdrew and the other powers reached only a minor accord. Davis also headed the delegation to the Nine-Power Treaty Conference of 1937 at Brussels, called to deal with a new Japanese attack on China. He is credited with drafting much of President Roosevelt's speech that October urging a "quarantine" of aggressor nations, an address that stirred strong isolationist reactions.

In 1938 Roosevelt appointed Davis as head of the American Red Cross. He held this post, along with the presidency of the International Red Cross, until his death. He continued to advise the President on foreign policy, and beginning in 1941 he became increasingly involved in postwar planning. Davis died of a cerebral hemorrhage in 1944, at the age of sixty-five, while vacationing at Hot Springs, Va. He was buried, after Episcopal services, in Alexandria, Va. Although little known to the general public, Davis was respected in government circles both as an executive agent who carried out American foreign policy and as a planner who helped shape it.

[Norman H. Davis Papers, Lib. of Cong.; Harold B. Whiteman, Jr., "Norman H. Davis and the Search for International Peace and Security, 1917–1944" (Ph.D. dissertation, Yale Univ., 1958); Thomas C. Irvin, "Norman H. Davis and the Quest for Arms Control, 1931–1938" (Ph.D. dissertation, Ohio State Univ., 1963); Margaret R. Appelbaum, "Norman H. Davis, Diplomat of the '30's" (senior thesis, Vassar College, 1964); Hill Turner in *Vanderbilt Alumnus*, July–Aug. 1944; J. M. Galloway in *Tenn. Hist. Quart.*, Summer 1968; *N. Y. Times* obituary, July 2, 1944. See also Cordell Hull, *Memoirs* (2 vols., 1948); Julius W. Pratt, *Cordell Hull* (2 vols., 1964) —vols. XII and XIII in The Am. Secretaries of State and Their Diplomacy, ed. by Samuel F. Bemis; Robert A. Divine, *The Illusion of Neutrality* (1962).]
HAROLD B. WHITEMAN, JR.

DE FOREST, ALFRED VICTOR (Apr. 7, 1888–Apr. 5, 1945), metallographer, expert in the field of metal testing and inspection, was born in New York City, the second of three children and the first son of Lockwood and Meta (Kemble) de Forest. He was a nephew of Robert Weeks de Forest [Supp. 1], New York lawyer and social welfare leader. Alfred's maternal grandmother had been a DuPont, and an uncle, Peter Kemble, who worked at the DuPont mills, lived with the family and maintained a workshop and darkroom, as did another uncle, Henry Wheeler de Forest, who lived nearby. These men gave Alfred his introduction to science and engineering. His father was a noted artist and interior decorator and an avid devotee of sailing.

Young Alfred in turn became a sailing enthusiast, and after graduating from the Middlesex School in 1907, he enrolled as a student of naval architecture at Massachusetts Institute of Technology, obtaining the S.B. degree in 1912. In 1913, after a brief term as draftsman for the New London Ship & Engine Company, he accepted a position as instructor in thermodynamics and graphics at Princeton University. There he met Donald P. Smith, professor of metallography and physical chemistry, through whose influence he acquired his deep and lifelong interest in those subjects. In the fall of 1915 he served as a metallographic laboratory assistant to William Campbell [Supp. 2] at Columbia University. From 1916 to 1918 he was employed by the Remington Arms Company in Bridgeport, Conn. Then in 1918 he moved to the American Chain Company, also in Bridgeport, as a research engineer.

For the next twelve years de Forest was actively engaged in experimental developments in welding and machine building and in applications of electrical and magnetic principles to inspection techniques. He became a pioneer in fatigue testing and in the invention of magnetic strain gauges and load-measuring devices, and was awarded a number of patents. He wrote papers for the American Society for Metals, the American Institute of Metallurgical Engineers, the Iron and Steel Institute, the American Society for Testing Materials, and the International Society for Testing Materials. In 1928 one of his many papers on magnetic inspection won him the Dudley Medal of the American Society for Testing Materials. Later honors included the Longstreth Medal of the Franklin Institute (1936) and the Sylvanus Albert Reed Award of the Institute of Aeronautical Science (1938).

When the depression of the 1930's dried up funds for research, de Forest turned to consulting as a full-time occupation, his clients including John Chatillon Sons in New York, Wyckoff Drawn Steel and Spay Chalfont companies in Pittsburgh, and the Walworth Company. The most significant development of his consulting period was the invention of a method of detecting, by magnetic means, defects or cracks in a piece of iron or steel caused in the process of forging or welding or by fatigue or wear. This led to the founding, in 1930, of the Magnaflux Corporation, which he headed as president.

In 1934, prompted by a concern for his son's undergraduate work at Harvard and for the entire nature of engineering education, de Forest accepted a position as a professor at Massachusetts Institute of Technology, upon the urging of Vannevar Bush, then a dean, and Jerome Hunsaker, head of the mechanical and aeronautical departments. "Of teaching I knew nothing and I was familiar with little of the content of mechanical engineering," he confessed, but the challenge of working with engineering students and the opportunity for close association with the M.I.T. faculty were too tempting to resist. It was a position perfectly suited to his fertile mind and dynamic personality, and he filled it with skill and imagination until his death.

To his students, Professor de Forest, partially crippled by a bout with polio, presented a striking appearance. His high, rounded forehead topped off by a wild mane of gray-white hair, his flashing blue eyes, and the permanent trace of a smile about his lips rightly suggested a man of wisdom who very much enjoyed life. His associates were continually amazed by the speed and precision of his mind and his boundless enthusiasm and energy. While at M.I.T. he joined with Prof. Arthur C. Ruge to found (1939) the Ruge-de Forest Company, and their partnership turned out significant inventions and ideas relating to the fields of inspection and testing. The most important of these involved the bonded wire strain gauge, which found critical application in the aircraft and shipbuilding industries in World War II.

On Aug. 22, 1912, at Bar Harbor, Maine, de Forest married Izette Taber of Philadelphia, a noted lay psychoanalyst and student of Freud and Sandor Ferenczi. They had two children, a son, Taber (1913), and a daughter, Judith Brasher (1915). De Forest's religious affiliation was with the Episcopal Church. In 1945, two days before his fifty-seventh birthday, he died of a heart attack at Marlborough, N. H., where he had a home; he was buried there in the family cemetery. He had exerted a major influence on the formation and development of the modern inspection and testing industries.

[The primary source of information was a detailed interview with de Forest's son, Taber de Forest, of

Marlborough, N. H., who made available family papers, including a brief MS. autobiography by his father. The family also has an oil painting of de Forest by Rosamund Burgess. Other sources: biographical sketch by Edward C. McDonald, Jr., in *Metal Progress,* Mar. 1944 (with photograph); Frank G. Tatnall, *Tatnall on Testing* (1966), which makes extensive reference to de Forest and his work; obituary in the M.I.T. *Technology Rev.,* May 1945; personal recollections of a professional associate, Mr. Albert Eplett, Orange, Conn.; and *Genealogy of the DuPont Family* (privately printed, 1958), Chart 15, which traces the Kemble and de Forest families. See also *N. Y. Times,* Apr. 6, 1945; *Who Was Who in America,* vol. II (1950); and *Nat. Cyc. Am. Biog.,* XXXV, 408–09.]

JAMES A. MULHOLLAND

DELAND, MARGARET (Feb. 23, 1857–Jan. 13, 1945), author, was born near Allegheny, Pa., the only child of Sample Campbell, a Pittsburgh clothing merchant, and his second wife, Margaretta Wade, daughter of an ordnance manufacturer whose English ancestors had been early settlers in Maryland. She was christened Margaretta Wade but later shortened the name to Margaret. Her father, who had two grown children by an earlier marriage, was a native of Kentucky. Her mother died at Margaret's birth, and she was placed in the household of her maternal aunt and uncle, Lois (Wade) and Benjamin Bakewell Campbell. (Her uncle, though of the same name, was not related to her father, who died when she was about four.) Reared as a daughter amid a colony of aunts, uncles, and cousins, she grew up on a plantation-like estate in Manchester, on the banks of the Ohio River near Allegheny. It was apparently an agreeable childhood despite religious training in a gloomy Calvinism "only faintly brightened by a stratum of Episcopalianism from my Wade grandparents."

A spirited girl, Maggie Campbell did not easily accept the rules of propriety laid down for young women of her day. At the age of sixteen, following a youthful love affair, she was sent to Pelham Priory, a boarding school near New Rochelle, N. Y., for "young females of good family connections." The school stressed religion and deportment, and she was once censured for the "indecorum" of running into the hall. This was the first of many indecorums of which Mrs. Deland would be accused, as, through works both of fiction and of charity—her two central occupations—she extended her reputation for daring and resolution from her family circle to a vastly larger audience.

She returned home from Pelham Priory at the end of a year, determined to live independent of family authority, and in 1875 she was allowed to go to New York City to study art and design at Cooper Union. The next year, by way of a competitive examination, she received an appointment as an assistant instructor of drawing and design at the Normal College of the City of New York (later Hunter College), where she taught for nearly four years.

During a summer holiday in Vermont in 1878 she met Lorin Fuller Deland, the junior member of a Boston printing firm, Deland and Son. They were married on May 12, 1880, at her uncle's house in Fairfield, Pa. Established in Boston, the Delands compromised their religious differences— he was a Unitarian, she a Presbyterian—by attending Episcopalian services at Trinity Church. Coming under the influence of its rector, Phillips Brooks [*q.v.*], and his ideals of community and social service, the couple adopted a cause which at that time was widely regarded as shocking: helping unmarried mothers. Themselves childless, the Delands took into their home both mothers and infants, in the belief that a fallen woman, if permitted to keep her child and allowed to become self-supporting, would be transformed, her life redeemed by the healing power of her infant's love. This theory was confirmed by considerable success among the some sixty girls whom they aided in this fashion over a period of four years.

To help make ends meet during these years, Mrs. Deland began painting china, which she sold to a Boston merchant, and also (at her husband's suggestion) sold verses to be used on Christmas cards, then coming into vogue. She had often written poems for her own pleasure, but her entrance into the literary world came about by chance when a friend, without her knowledge, took some of her poems to the editor of *Harper's Magazine,* which published them. Encouraged, she continued to write, and in 1886 Houghton, Mifflin & Company published a collection of her poems, *The Old Garden,* which had a good sale.

Urged by her husband to try her hand at fiction, Mrs. Deland had by this time begun writing a novel on a theme which had long preoccupied her: the consequences of fanatic Calvinism. *John Ward, Preacher* (1888) portrays a zealot who in carrying Calvinist dogma to its logical end is driven to sacrifice his beloved wife because she is unable to embrace the doctrine of reprobation. Conventionally written, the novel exhibits Mrs. Deland's skill in devising a complex plot to illustrate those doctrinal intricacies that she hoped to condemn. Among those readers in England and America who regarded it as an attack on religion, the book acquired the reputation of a scandalous work. Today it is little read and is chiefly of historical interest, as an example of the influence of Olive Schreiner's noted work of protest against religious intolerance, *The Story of an African Farm* (1883), and as a novel which used the genre of genteel domestic fiction to express dissent.

Two later novels in a similar vein, *The Awakening of Helena Richie* (1906) and *The Iron Woman* (1911), also received considerable réclame. Mrs. Deland's concern, however, was solely with the moral issues in personal relationships. In none of her work did she strike a note of social protest. She was opposed to woman suffrage, and those of her heroines who imbibed the social philosophy of the Progressive era were presented with a touch of caricature. Her code of ethics was likewise traditional (she refused, for instance, to countenance divorce). Her basic loyalty to the values of an earlier day is most apparent in her short stories about the orderly and sheltered world of "Old Chester," a Pennsylvania village patterned after the Manchester of her childhood, and its lovable Episcopalian shepherd, Dr. Lavendar. Collected in *Old Chester Tales* (1898), *Dr. Lavendar's People* (1903), and other volumes, these stories won Mrs. Deland a devoted following in the two decades before the First World War. Her autobiographical volumes, *If This Be I* (1935) and *Golden Yesterdays* (1941), still warrant attention as a record of the many transformations of American social history during the nearly eighty years of her adult life.

In 1917, the year when her husband died, Margaret Deland received an honorary degree from Rutgers University; she received similar honors from Tufts (1920), Bates (1920), and Bowdoin (1931). Elected to the National Institute of Arts and Letters in 1926, she was among the first women (after Julia Ward Howe [*q.v.*] in 1907) to receive that distinction. She died in 1945 of coronary heart disease at her home in the Hotel Sheraton in Boston and was buried in Forest Hills Cemetery. At her death the *New York Times* wondered that the writings of this "mildest and most serene of gentlewomen" should have stirred up "such bitter and hostile feelings." Twenty-five years after her death, she had almost disappeared from the standard studies of American literature, and it was necessary to recall from obscurity Mrs. Deland's modest but permanent contribution to the long history of resistance to intolerance and cruelty in America.

[Mrs. Deland's *If This Be I* and *Golden Yesterdays* are the principal sources. Short biographical entries are found in: *Nat. Cyc. Am. Biog.*, XXXIII, 506; Stanley J. Kunitz and Howard Haycraft, *Twentieth Century Authors* (1942); and *Who Was Who in America*, vol. II (1950). Small efforts of appraisal are given in Percy H. Boynton, *America in Contemporary Fiction* (1940), and in the *N. Y. Times* obituary, Jan. 14, 1945. The only recent scholarly estimate is that of J. C. Levenson in *Notable Am. Women*, I, 454–56.]

WILLIAM WASSERSTROM

DeLEE, JOSEPH BOLIVAR (Oct. 28, 1869–Apr. 2, 1942), obstetrician, was born at Cold Spring, N. Y., in the Hudson Valley, the fifth son and ninth of ten children of Morris and Dora (Tobias) DeLee. Both parents were Jewish immigrants from Poland; his father was the son of a French army surgeon who had settled there after Napoleon's defeat at Moscow. Joseph attended elementary school in Cold Spring and finished grammar school in New Haven, Conn., where his father had moved his dry goods business. After a brief residence in New York City, the family moved in 1885 to Chicago. Joseph graduated from the South Division High School in 1888 and, although his father had wished him to become a rabbi, entered the Chicago Medical College (later the Northwestern University Medical School), receiving the M.D. degree in 1891. Among his professors he was particularly influenced by W. W. Jaggard in obstetrics.

DeLee's eighteen months' internship at the Cook County (Ill.) Hospital gave him a close acquaintance with the low state of obstetrical care, and he determined to devote himself to the goal of raising both the standards and the standing of obstetrics as a medical specialty. He continued his training in Europe, studying maternity hospitals and home obstetrical services in Berlin, Vienna, and Paris, and in 1894 returned to Chicago. The next year he rented four rooms in a tenement basement and opened the Chicago Lying-in Dispensary, a maternity clinic which offered free prenatal care and obstetric service in the patient's home. He secured interns and senior medical students to assist in the work and in 1896 himself became chairman of the department of obstetrics and gynecology at Northwestern University Medical School, but the Dispensary remained an independent undertaking. A hospital was added in 1899, and in 1917 a new 100-bed building was erected. DeLee himself did most of the fund raising, initially from Chicago's Jewish community (although the Lying-in Hospital was never sectarian), after 1908 with the aid of a Women's Board headed by Janet Ayer (Mrs. Kellogg) Fairbank, a well-to-do Chicagoan.

DeLee's life was a crusade to prevent unnecessary death in childbirth. When he began, most babies among the working classes were delivered by midwives, and none of the abler medical students thought of specializing in such a field. Through teaching and writing DeLee sought to give medical students practical training in childbirth as well as careful instruction in pathological cases. As a teacher he was unsurpassed. Chiefly he taught by precept. He spoke to large groups of observers while delivering a patient; never stepping out of character, he remained the pedagogue as he walked through the corridors or even sat in his room to relax. His writings further spread his principles and techniques, beginning with his *Obstetrics for Nurses* (1904), which went through twelve editions in his lifetime, and culminating in his monumental *The Principles and Practices of Obstetrics* (1913), which he spent several years in writing and for which he supervised the making of nearly a thousand photographs and drawings. It became a standard text both in this country and abroad and went through repeated editions. DeLee pioneered in producing motion pictures as an aid to teaching. He completed sixteen in all, and his four-reel film on delivery by low cervical Caesarian section was the first such document to be made with sound. For nearly four decades (1904–41) DeLee edited the *Yearbook of Obstetrics*, and he contributed more than seventy-five papers to medical journals. He also lectured widely; he spoke and wrote authoritatively, lucidly, crisply, and with wit.

One of DeLee's fundamental principles, which he did much to establish, was his emphasis on strict asepsis during delivery. Another conviction, from which he never wavered, was that the best way to prevent and treat puerperal fever was to isolate all infected women in a separate structure, a feature he embodied in his hospital. He devised or improved many obstetrical instruments. He advocated the use of local infiltration anesthesia because it was the safest of all anesthetics. His favorite maxims, inscribed on the walls of his delivery rooms, were "Non vi sed arte" (Not with force but with art) and "Primum non nocere" (First do no harm). He proclaimed the value of a properly timed episiotomy, improved the technique of the low cervical Caesarian section, and introduced the "prophylactic forceps" operation. Many physicians who censured him for "radicalism" later became converts to his views.

In 1924 the University of Chicago began overtures to DeLee to affiliate the Lying-in Hospital with its medical school, offering to build a new hospital for his use. Though fearing a reduction in the community service aspects of the hospital and reluctant to give up his independence, DeLee eventually gave his consent. The affiliation became effective in 1929 (at which time he gave up his Northwestern University appointment for a comparable one at Chicago), and the new building opened its doors in 1931. The change proved a great personal disappointment, as he found himself increasingly subordinated within a medical school with a strong scientific emphasis. University rules compelled his retirement four years later at the age of sixty-five.

The move highlighted DeLee's chief weakness, his lack of a research orientation. A humanitarian and a superb craftsman in the obstetrical art, DeLee was empirical in method, clinical in approach. For the most part he trained clinicians who chose private practice. Their influence on the profession was thus limited, as compared to the students of John Whitridge Williams [*q.v.*] at Johns Hopkins, who came to fill professorial chairs in many medical schools.

An individualist, a perfectionist, a man of high ideals to which he selflessly devoted himself (and his personal means), DeLee could be stubborn and uncompromising in pursuit of those ideals. His lack of tact, especially when he encountered instances of careless obstetrical technique, sometimes involved him in personal controversy, as did some of his public statements. DeLee never married, avoided close friendships, and lived only for obstetrics. Tall and erect, he made a striking appearance with his intense dark eyes, white hair, and full moustache and pointed beard. He died at the age of seventy-two at his home in Chicago, of a coronary thrombosis. Before his death he had arranged for the continuation of his dispensary as the Chicago Maternity Center. The main building of the Lying-in Hospital and a professorship at the University of Chicago bear his name.

[Morris Fishbein and Sol Theron DeLee, *Joseph Bolivar DeLee: Crusading Obstetrician* (1949), a full-scale biography based on DeLee's personal papers; memoir and appraisal by M. Edward Davis in *Lying-in*, Jan.–Feb. 1968; biographical sketch in Leslie B. Arey, *Northwestern Univ. Medical School, 1859–1959* (1959). See also David J. Davis, ed., *Hist. of Medical Practice in Ill.*, vol. II (1955); Thomas N. Bonner, *Medicine in Chicago, 1850–1950* (1957); obituaries in *Am. Jour. of Obstetrics and Gynecology*, June 1942, *Western Jour. of Surgery, Obstetrics and Gynecology*, July 1942, *Jour. of Obstetrics and Gynecology of the British Empire*, Aug. 1942, and *Jour. Am. Medic. Assoc.*, Apr. 11, 1942; and *Chicago Tribune*, Apr. 3, Nov. 22, 1942. A portrait of DeLee by Sir William Orpen hangs in the lobby of the Lying-in Hospital.]

MORRIS FISHBEIN

DE LEEUW, ADOLPH LODEWYK (May 6, 1861–Dec. 5, 1942), engineer and machine designer, was born in Zwolle, the capital of Overijssel province in the Netherlands. He was the son of Andries De Leeuw, an accountant, and his second wife, Henriette de Jonghe. Because of poor health, the boy did not attend school until he was eleven years old, but at thirteen he passed the examination for a scholarship awarded by the government to the top twenty students in the country. Educated at private schools in Haarlem, at the Polytechnic in Delft, and at the University of Leyden, he received degrees in science and in mechanical and electrical engineering. He then taught mathematics and applied mechanics at the Lauer Institute in Arnhem and, while still in his mid-twenties, wrote two widely used books on algebra and geometry.

In 1890 De Leeuw emigrated to America. After working briefly in the Pennsylvania Railroad shops at Altoona, Pa., he was employed by a number of companies in New York and Ohio before being engaged by the Pond Machine Tool Company in Plainfield, N. J. He was transferred in 1897 to the Niles Tool Works in Hamilton, Ohio. There he met Katherine Caroline Bender, whom he married on June 15, 1898; they had two daughters, Adèle Louise and Cateau Wilhelmina. After a few years as chief engineer at Niles, where he was one of the pioneers in applying the electric motor to the operation of machine tools, De Leeuw opened his own office in Hamilton as a consulting engineer.

One of his clients was the Cincinnati Milling Machine Company. De Leeuw became chief engineer of the company in 1908 and two years later moved his family to Cincinnati. He laid out a new plant at Oakley and designed the efficient production line for which the company was long noted, but his main energies were devoted to a prolonged series of systematic experiments with the milling machine, a highly versatile machine tool which shapes metal to precise specifications by use of a rotary multiple-tooth cutter. De Leeuw focused particularly upon the relationship between the milling cutter and the machine itself, and the complex of stresses to which the cutting edges are subjected while in contact with the metal being acted upon. After establishing that the cutters then in use were not as strong as the machines which drove them, he undertook to correct this imbalance by redesigning them. The most distinctive feature of his new cutters was teeth much more widely spaced than before. Further investigation also established optimal design for rake angles of the teeth as well as their optimal steepness and staggering. De Leeuw's research, closely analogous to that of Frederick W. Taylor [q.v.] on single-point cutting tools, resulted in increasing both the speed with which milling machines could remove metal and the durability of the cutters. The new cutters, in turn, led to other innovations, including new cooling techniques to compensate for increased speed, and improvements in feed mechanisms, in speed control, in the transmission of power, and in unit construction. De Leeuw's designs were widely adopted throughout the machine tool industry and remain the major achievement of his career.

In 1914 De Leeuw accepted an appointment as chief engineer of the Singer Manufacturing Company and was placed in charge of its plants both in America and in Europe. During World War I he played a major part in converting them to wartime production. When the French awarded Singer the contract for manufacturing the recoil mechanism for their 75-millimeter artillery pieces, a mechanism never before produced in the United States, De Leeuw not only set up the necessary factories with remarkable speed but also designed a series of machines that performed the work automatically.

After the war, in 1919, he opened an independent consulting office in New York City. Numerous large firms retained him, primarily to solve problems of production control and management. In 1923, at the request of Stanley P. Goss, he designed a new line of automatic chucking machines; the two men joined in the formation of the Goss and De Leeuw Machine Company in New Britain, Conn., and De Leeuw served as vice-president and chief engineer of this firm until his death.

De Leeuw contributed many articles to technical and professional journals, and for a time was consulting editor to the *American Machinist*. A prolific inventor, he took out more than fifty patents, the most important of which concerned the milling machine. He died of a heart attack in Plainfield, N. J., at the age of eighty-one.

[Most of the biographical material concerning De Leeuw was provided by his daughters. An obituary appeared in the *N. Y. Times* on Dec. 6, 1942. A list of De Leeuw's patents and an unpublished MS. by Sol Einstein, "Forty Years of Milling Machine Development by the Cincinnati Milling Machine Co." (dated June 23, 1923), were made available by the company. For an authoritative treatment of De Leeuw's contributions to the development of the milling machine, see Robert S. Woodbury, *Hist. of the Milling Machine* (1960). De Leeuw published several books, including *Metal Cutting Tools: Their Principles, Action and Construction* (1922). He described his experimental work on the milling machine and milling cutters in two articles appearing in the *Transactions* of the Am. Soc. of Mechanical Engineers: "Efficiency Tests of Milling Machines and Milling Cutters," XXX (1908), 837–59, and "Milling Cutters and Their Efficiency," XXXIII (1911), 245–77.]

NATHAN ROSENBERG

DETT, ROBERT NATHANIEL (Oct. 11, 1882–Oct. 2, 1943), composer and choral conductor, was born in Drummondsville, Ontario, Canada, later part of the town of Niagara Falls. He was the third son and youngest of four children of Robert Tue Dett and Charlotte (Johnson) Dett, both of Afro-American descent. His mother, though born in Canada, came of a family that had lived near Washington, D. C. His father, a native of Reisterstown, Md., worked for a railroad and operated a small hotel in Niagara Falls. Both parents played the piano and sang.

Nathaniel displayed a precocious interest in poetry and music, and from his maternal grandmother he gained some familiarity with Negro folk songs. He learned to play the piano by ear and had his first formal lessons before he started school. After the family moved to the American side of Niagara Falls in 1893, he began lessons with an Austrian teacher and attracted attention by his ability to improvise. To earn money for his education he worked in the summers as a bellboy and unofficial house pianist at the Cataract Hotel. A concert given there by Fred Butler, a well-known black singer, inspired Dett to make music his career. During his high school years, at the Niagara Falls (Canada) Collegiate Institute, he studied (1901–03) with Oliver Willis Halsted, who operated a conservatory at Lockport, N. Y. His first published work, a piano piece, "After the Cake-Walk," appeared in 1900.

Upon graduating from the Collegiate Institute in 1903, Dett entered the Conservatory of Music at Oberlin College in Ohio, where he enrolled in a five-year course with a major in composition. To pay his way he worked part time; he also received financial assistance and encouragement from a Cleveland banker who had heard him play in Niagara Falls. At Oberlin, Dett studied piano with Howard Handel Carter and, during the fifth year, with George Carl Hastings; he studied theory with Arthur E. Heacox, organ with J. R. Frampton, and composition under George Whitfield Andrews. After graduating with the Bachelor of Music degree in 1908, he taught music at two Negro colleges, Lane College in Jackson, Tenn. (1908–11), and Lincoln Institute (later Lincoln University) in Jefferson City, Mo. (1911–13). During these first years in the South, Dett learned many new Negro folk songs and developed a deep respect for the intrinsic beauty of spirituals. He also received warm encouragement from Mme. E. Azalia Hackley, a talented black pianist and singer who devoted her life to aiding Negro musicians and stimulating interest in Negro music. Through her influence, Dett was appointed director of music at Hampton Institute in Virginia in 1913, a post he held for nearly two decades. On Dec. 27, 1916, he married Helen Elise Smith of New York City, who had been the first Negro graduate of the piano department of the Institute of Musical Art in New York. The Detts had two daughters: Helen and Josephine.

At Hampton Institute, Dett found a strong tradition of "plantation singing," group singing of Negro religious folk songs involving interaction between a "leader" and a chorus. Dett was to modify the role of these spirituals and to introduce new and broader forms and expression into Hampton's musical life. Studying the spirituals, he began to arrange them as hymns for four-part *a cappella* singing. He also drew upon the spirituals to compose anthems and oratorios for his Hampton choirs, whom he trained in classic choral works as well. He brought renowned visiting musicians to the institute for recitals and toured widely with his choirs.

"Listen to the Lambs" (1914), written originally for an eight-part chorus of unaccompanied voices, is the most popular and perhaps most characteristic example of Dett's use of the spiritual as the basis for a larger musical form. It was composed to give Negro people "something musically which would be peculiarly their own and yet which would bear comparison with the nationalistic utterances of other people's work in art forms." The work draws its main theme and words from the spiritual of the same name; its secondary theme is original but retains a simple folk style and uses the phrase "He shall feed his flock" from Isaiah. A variety of devices create excitement in the work: text against text in different voices; male and female vocal quality juxtaposed; steady versus syncopated rhythm; basses and tenors in countervailing stepwise ascents and descents; extreme and contrasting dynamic levels; humming accompaniment in low and moderate register to a lyrical melodic line in soprano; and relentless repetition in word and music of the phrase, "all-a-crying," creating great tension in the final climax. Later comparable anthems included "I'll Never Turn Back" (1917), "Gently Lord, O Gently Lead Us" (1924), "Let Us Cheer the Weary Traveler" (1933), and some nineteen others published between 1914 and 1941.

During his years at Hampton, Dett frequently spent summers in further musical study, at Columbia University, the American Conservatory of Music in Chicago, and Oberlin. In 1919 he took a year's leave to study at Harvard, where in 1920 he won the Bowdoin Prize for his essay "The Emancipation of Negro Music" and the Francis Boott Prize for the best composition in concerted vocal music, "Don't Be Weary, Traveler." In the summer of 1929 he studied with Nadia Boulanger at Fontainebleau. As a collector or transcriber, he prepared four volumes of Negro spirituals totaling seventy-one songs. His 1927 edition of *Religious Folk-Songs of the Negro as Sung at Hampton Institute* (the fourth of a series begun in 1874) contained 164 spirituals.

Dett's choral compositions and arrangements

were a major contribution to American music. In 1926 he conducted the Hampton Institute Choir in an *a cappella* concert at the Library of Congress under the sponsorship of the Elizabeth Sprague Coolidge Foundation. Other concerts were given in Carnegie Hall, New York (1928), Symphony Hall, Boston (1929), the Philadelphia Academy of Music (1929), and at the White House (1930). He took a forty-voice choir on a highly successful three-month European tour in the spring of 1930.

As a black composer Dett ranks with Harry T. Burleigh, Will Marion Cook [Supp. 3], and the Afro-English Samuel Coleridge-Taylor. Of the Americans, however, Dett was the most prolific and varied in the forms in which he worked. Except for "Juba Dance"—the fifth part of his "In the Bottoms Suite" (1913) and the most popular of all his piano compositions—his published piano works were not typically based on Afro-American folk idiom but fall rather into the late nineteenth-century romantic mode. However, his oratorio "Chariot Jubilee" (1921) was based on fragments of the spiritual "Swing Low, Sweet Chariot"; and his largest choral work, "The Ordering of Moses" (1937), an oratorio first performed in 1937 under the auspices of the Cincinnati Music Festival Association, draws its pervasive melodic idea from the spiritual "Go Down, Moses." The same year marked the first performance of Dett's "American Sampler," an orchestral work commissioned by the Columbia Broadcasting System, which used non-Negro themes.

There are indications that Dett did not get along well with the administration at Hampton, and in 1931 he was asked to leave. After a year of study at the Eastman School of Music at Rochester, N. Y., where he received the Mus.M. degree in 1932, he resigned from the Hampton faculty. For some years he remained in Rochester, teaching, lecturing, and composing; from 1937 to 1942 he was on the staff of Bennett College in Greensboro, N. C. Dett received honorary degrees from Howard University (1924) and Oberlin College (1926). He served for two terms as president of the National Association of Negro Musicians (1924–26), and received the Harmon Foundation Medal for creative achievement in music.

Early in 1943, during World War II, Dett became a musical adviser to the United Service Organizations (U.S.O.) and was assigned to duty in Battle Creek, Mich. He died there a few months later after a heart attack, and was buried in Fairview Cemetery at Niagara Falls, Ontario.

[Autobiographical interview in *Etude*, Feb. 1934; *Who's Who in Colored America*, 1941–44; John Tasker Howard, *Our Am. Music* (3rd ed., 1946); obituaries in *N. Y. Times*, Oct. 4, 1943, and *Jour. of Negro Hist.*, Oct. 1943.]

WALTER FISHER

DEVANEY, JOHN PATRICK (June 30, 1883–Sept. 21, 1941), Minnesota lawyer, jurist, and politician, was born in Lake Mills, Iowa, to Patrick and Ellen (La Velle) Devaney. His father, a farmer and mechanic who had come to the United States from Ireland in 1842, was a Confederate veteran of the Civil War. John Devaney attended the public schools of Lake Mills and the University of Minnesota, where he received an A.B. in 1905 and, after going on to the law school, the degrees of LL.B. (1907) and LL.M. (1908). Thereafter he practiced law in Minneapolis. Specializing in common carrier law, he became well known for his effective courtroom presentations. Much of his reputation stemmed from his successful advocacy of the damage claims of a group of northern Minnesota homesteaders whose farms had been destroyed by a forest fire in 1917.

In the late 1920's Devaney became active in state politics, supporting the successful gubernatorial campaign of his friend Floyd B. Olson [Supp. 2] in 1930. In August 1933 Olson appointed Devaney chief justice of the Minnesota Supreme Court to fill an unexpired term; the following year he was elected to a six-year term by a substantial majority. On the bench Devaney's tendency was to champion the individual against the larger economic interests, and he became known as a liberal jurist. In *Nelson* v. *McKenzie Hague Company* (1934) he dissented vigorously from a ruling which held that a construction firm under contract with the state was immune from private damage suits under the Minnesota private nuisance statute. In *Romain* v. *Twin City Fire Insurance Company* (1934) and in *Thompson* v. *Prudential Life Insurance Company of America* (1936) he rejected the claims of insurance companies trying to avoid payment to individuals on technical grounds. His concern for the individual extended less frequently to claims made against the state. In one of his more significant rulings, *Anderson* v. *Ueland* (1936), he denied the suit of a gardener for benefits under the Minnesota Workman's Compensation Act on the grounds that the act excluded domestic servants and that the gardener was involved in the maintenance of a private home.

Devaney's opinions also revealed concern over the rising rate of crime, as in *Vos* v. *Albany Mutual Fire Insurance Company* (1934), where he spoke out strongly against the threat of organized crime and denied the benefits of an insurance policy to a small "still" operator. During his tenure as chief justice, Devaney headed the Minnesota Crime Commission of 1934, which offered thirty-five suggestions for revising the state's criminal code, twenty-five of which were later enacted. Mostly alterations in trial and parole procedures, these recommendations show a concern for law and order and a desire for a more scientific approach to the legal process. Some were aimed at speeding cases through the courts, others toward more effective prosecution of crime; one, for example, advised that the judge or prosecutor be allowed to note a defendant's refusal to testify.

Devaney resigned as chief justice on Feb. 15, 1937, in order to take part in the formation of the National Lawyers Guild, of which he was chosen the first president. The Guild's purpose, as he explained it in the first issue of its *Quarterly* (December 1937), was to create "a liberal alternative" to the American Bar Association. Devaney soon took an active part in the Guild's campaign in support of President Roosevelt's court reorganization or "court-packing" bill. Testifying before the Senate Judiciary Committee, he offered a legal-realist critique of the Hughes Supreme Court, accusing it of fostering and hiding behind the "dangerous myth" of judicial impersonality. Shortly thereafter his name was rumored as a possible candidate for the Court.

After serving a one-year term as Guild president, and for a brief period as chairman of the Industry Committee of the Wages and Hours Division of the Department of Labor, Devaney returned to his Minneapolis law practice and became more active in Democratic party politics. In 1940 he was an active participant in the Roosevelt-Wallace campaign in Minnesota, after which he was chosen by the national chairman, Edward J. Flynn, to head a three-man committee to work out a fusion of the Minnesota Democrats with the Farmer-Labor party. As Flynn's personal representative, Devaney exerted a powerful influence on local politics. He was also appointed by Roosevelt to several emergency boards to settle labor disputes in the Northwest, one of which, in 1940, averted a strike of the 30,000 employees of the Railway Express Agency.

On Sept. 14, 1941, Devaney declared his candidacy for the United States Senate, but one week later, while conferring on party matters in Milwaukee, Wis., he suffered a stroke and died there. After Catholic funeral rites, he was buried in Minneapolis. His wife, Beatrice Langevin, whom he had married on Feb. 20, 1919, and their three children—Patrick, Beatrice, and Sheila—survived him.

[Devaney's judicial opinions are in *Minn. Reports*, vols. 189–199. More generally, see *Nat. Cyc. Am.* *Biog.*, XXXIII, 481–82; *Who's Who in America*, 1940–41; *Who's Who in Law*, 1937, p. 244; obituary in *N. Y. Times*, Sept. 22, 1941.]

PAUL L. MURPHY

DINWIDDIE, COURTENAY (Oct. 9, 1882–Sept. 13, 1943), social worker, was born in Alexandria, Va., the sixth son and last of the eight children of William and Emily Albertine (Bledsoe) Dinwiddie. His father, a native Virginian of Scottish colonial stock, was a Presbyterian minister and schoolteacher. His mother, although born in Illinois, had family roots in Kentucky and Virginia, for she was the daughter of Albert Taylor Bledsoe [q.v.], Assistant Secretary of War in the Confederate government. One of Courtenay's brothers, Albert Bledsoe Dinwiddie [Supp. 1], served as president of Tulane University; a sister, Emily, became a prominent social worker.

Dinwiddie attended his father's Brookland School for Boys in Greenwood, Va., and went on to Southwestern Presbyterian University (A.B. 1901) and the University of Virginia, where he took two years of graduate study. He then returned to Greenwood as manager of the family farm. Influenced perhaps by his sister, he decided to enter social work. His first position, as secretary to the president of the board of Bellevue and Allied Hospitals, New York City (1905–06), foreshadowed a lifelong interest in public health organization. In 1906–10 he served as executive secretary of the New York City Visiting Committee of the State Charities Aid Association. Dinwiddie married Susan Anderson Ellis of Clarksville, Tenn., on May 8, 1907. There were four children (of whom the first two died in childhood): Courtenay Lee, Hope, Jean, and Donal.

Dinwiddie left New York in 1910 to become secretary of the Duluth (Minn.) Associated Charities and superintendent of the city's Board of Public Welfare. In his next position, as superintendent of the Cincinnati Anti-Tuberculosis League, beginning in 1913, he was instrumental in the establishment of a citywide Public Health Federation. His views on health and welfare organization were greatly influenced by his executive experience with the Cincinnati Social Unit from 1917 to 1920. Focusing on health, the Social Unit marked an effort to increase the influence of the ordinary citizen in public affairs. The residents of the city's Mohawk-Brighton area were organized by occupations and residential blocks, and their cooperation was sought in devising a strategy for coping with neighborhood problems.

Beginning in the 1920's Dinwiddie focused his interests in community organization and health upon child welfare. He became the first executive secretary of the National Child Health Council, established in 1920 to coordinate the work of several national agencies. He then served from 1923 to 1925 as general executive of the American Child Health Association, formed by the merger of the American Child Hygiene Association and the Child Health Organization of America. Under his leadership the association developed a comprehensive program which included research, training of health personnel, public information, and community health organization. His most significant contribution to child welfare and health in this decade was made as director of the Commonwealth Fund's Child Health Demonstration Committee (1923–29). The committee sponsored four demonstrations (Fargo, N. Dak.; Athens and Clarke County, Ga.; Rutherford County, Tenn.; Marion County, Oreg.) in order to prove that a balanced public health program could be established in small communities.

In 1930 Dinwiddie became general secretary of the National Child Labor Committee, which he directed in a series of distinctive campaigns. During the early New Deal, the committee was instrumental in the struggle to include child labor provisions in the production codes of the National Recovery Administration. Following a futile campaign for ratification of the federal child labor amendment, the committee supported the successful drive to include child labor provisions in the Fair Labor Standards Act of 1938. Dinwiddie, who struggled unceasingly to prevent the weakening of child labor regulations during World War II, was particularly moved by the plight of the agricultural child worker. As chairman of the Emergency Committee for Food Production in 1943, he resisted Congressional efforts to dismantle the Farm Security Administration and thus the nation's battle against rural poverty. Later in the same year he was stricken with a heart attack while playing tennis, and died in New York City at the age of sixty. He was buried in Greenwood, Va.

Courtenay Dinwiddie's career testifies to the emergence of the professional community organizer in social work. Especially adept at managing projects which required the cooperation of diverse public and private agencies, he exemplified the role of the professional in initiating social change. At the same time, he placed unusual emphasis upon the need for local citizen participation in the formulation of programs. As secretary of the Cincinnati Social Unit experiment, he pioneered in the search for concrete techniques of neighborhood organization which would increase the citizen's civic role.

[The following publications by Courtenay Dinwiddie deal with his community organization, public health, and child welfare activities prior to the 1930's: "Co-operation and Co-ordination in Public Health Work in Cincinnati," Nat. Conference of Social Work, *Proc.,* 1920, pp. 191–94; "The Work Accomplished by the Social Unit Organization," *ibid.,* 1918, pp. 495–506; "The Nat. Child Health Council," *ibid.,* 1921, pp. 158–62; *Community Responsibility: A Review of the Cincinnati Social Unit Experiment* (N. Y. School of Social Work, 1921); "Progress in Child Health," Am. Child Health Assoc., *Transactions,* 1924, pp. 9–34; *Child Health and the Community: An Interpretation of Cooperative Effort in Public Health* (Commonwealth Fund, 1931). His many articles describing the work of the Nat. Child Labor Committee include: "Controlling Child Labor through Code Procedure," *Am. Federationist,* Jan. 1934; "Let Us End Child Labor," *Nat. Parent-Teacher,* Jan. 1935; "Child Labor in a Nation at War," *Social Service Rev.,* Dec. 1943; and, on rural poverty, two Nat. Child Labor Committee publications, *Child Laborers Today* (1939) and *How Good Is the Good Earth?* (1942). Biographical sources: obituaries in *N. Y. Times,* Sept. 14, 1943, *Social Service Rev.,* Dec. 1943, and *Survey Midmonthly,* Oct. 1943; *Who Was Who in America,* vol. II (1950); family information from Mrs. Lewis Littlepage Holladay and Mr. Donal Dinwiddie. A biographical source outline prepared by Eileen Gerling, Division of Librarianship, Emory Univ., was helpful.]

ROY LUBOVE

DITMARS, RAYMOND LEE (June 20, 1876–May 12, 1942), herpetologist, was born in Newark, N. J., the younger of two children and only son of John Van Harlingen Ditmars and Mary (Knaus) Ditmars. His mother, daughter of a firearms inspector at the Colt arms factory in Hartford, Conn., was descended from an old Pennsylvania family. His father, whose Dutch forebears (originally Van Ditmarsen) had obtained one of the early land grants on Long Island, was born on a plantation in Pensacola, Fla., and served in the Confederate Army during the Civil War. After the war he moved to Newark, N. J., where he prospered in the furniture business, and then, when his son was about six, to New York City.

Raymond Ditmars attended Miss Ransom's School for Boys and the Barnard Military Academy in New York but resisted his parents' wish that he go on to West Point. Already an enthusiastic amateur naturalist, he instead took a job (1893) as assistant in the entomological department of the American Museum of Natural History. Although he worked with insects, he was primarily interested in snakes and soon acquired a sizable collection through purchases from experts, amateurs, and circus snake charmers. Seeking a larger salary to maintain and expand his collection, Ditmars left the museum at the end of 1897 to work at first as stenographer for an optical instrument company and then as a reporter for the *New York Times.* A story he wrote on the New York Zoological Park, then being laid out in the Bronx, led in 1899 to his appointment as assistant curator of reptiles at the new facility, by the zoo's director, William Temple Hornaday [Supp. 2].

Here Ditmars remained for the rest of his life, eventually becoming curator of mammals as well as reptiles. On Feb. 4, 1903, he married Clara Elizabeth Hurd of New York City. She and their two daughters, Gladyce and Beatrice, often assisted him in his work. Early in his career Ditmars began to popularize his knowledge of snakes and other animals by lecturing to church groups, social clubs, students, and scientific societies. With a genial personality and a flair for theatrics, he embellished his lectures with a miniature animal act in which waltzing mice, a leaping jerboa, a lemur, and various snakes demonstrated to the audience their natural agility. A pioneer in nature photography, Ditmars as early as 1910 enlivened his lectures with motion pictures of animal behavior made in a makeshift studio at his Scarsdale, N. Y., home. He was perhaps best known, however, for the scores of articles and the several illustrated books through which he brought a wider knowledge of herpetology to the general public.

Despite his popular reputation as a leading authority on reptiles, Ditmars never won full acceptance in scientific circles. He published few papers based upon original research. Except for promoting the study of snake venoms, he did not participate in the rapid development of herpetology during the 1920's and 1930's, when new studies in classification, ecology, distribution, and life histories of reptiles appeared, and his later books were on general natural history. Yet his talent for presenting facts about reptiles in a careful and entertaining way, particularly in *The Reptile Book* (1907) and *Reptiles of the World* (1910)—for two decades almost the sole popular works of their kind—helped lay the groundwork for later advances in herpetology by recruiting new investigators. Ditmars received a gold medal in 1929 from the New York Zoological Society in recognition of thirty years of faithful service, and in 1930 he was awarded an honorary degree by Lincoln Memorial University, Harrogate, Tenn. His many years of lecturing had weakened his throat, and after a prolonged attack of bronchitis, he died of pneumonia at St. Luke's Hospital in New York City at the age of sixty-five.

[Ditmars wrote two accounts of his experiences, *Confessions of a Scientist* (1934) and *The Making of a Scientist* (1937). See also L. N. Wood, *Raymond L. Ditmars* (1944); obituaries in *Herpetologica,* July 15, 1942, pp. 81–82, and *Copeia,* July 10, 1942, p. 131; obituary and editorial in *N. Y. Times,* May 13, 1942; *Who Was Who in America,* vol. II (1950).]

CLIFFORD H. POPE

DODGE, RAYMOND (Feb. 20, 1871–Apr. 8, 1942), psychologist, was born in Woburn, Mass., the second of two sons of George Smith Dodge, a native of Vermont, and Anna (Pickering) Dodge. In later years he described himself as "defective in auditory and somewhat above the average in motor and kinaesthetic imagery," qualities which, he believed, accounted for his difficulties with linguistic pursuits and his success in mechanical invention and manipulation. Ten years younger than his brother, he was close to his father, an apothecary who took a Harvard M.D. in middle life but failed to establish a successful practice and instead became a Congregational minister. The son, although intrigued by his father's library of medical and philosophical books, found his greatest satisfaction in the workshop in the rear of the drugstore, where good tools were available; and there he probably first developed the interest and the skills which determined the direction of his later scientific achievement. His serious introduction to philosophy began as a freshman at Williams College, and his absorption in philosophical problems continued throughout his life. He received the A.B. degree at Williams in 1893.

Minimal family resources forced him to earn his own way at college and after graduation to accept employment as assistant librarian at Williams in order to finance a start on work for the doctorate. A combination of circumstances led him to the University of Halle to study under Benno Erdmann. His two years of study in Germany were years of dire poverty, which left scars on his social attitudes, but there were the compensations of stimulating associations and a devoted attachment to Erdmann that endured until the latter's death in 1921. It was during Dodge's early days at Halle that a need expressed by Erdmann in connection with study of the reading process led the young American to the explorations which resulted in the invention of the Erdmann-Dodge tachistoscope and marked his transition from philosophy to the emerging field of psychology. He was awarded the Ph.D. degree in 1896, and his dissertation, *Die Motorischen Wortvorstellungen,* was published that year.

Returning to the United States, Dodge married Henrietta C. Cutler of West Acton, Mass., on Aug. 18, 1897. They had no children. After a year of teaching at Ursinus College in Pennsylvania, he was in 1898 appointed to the faculty of Wesleyan University, Middletown, Conn. There he remained for twenty-six happy and productive years with only three interruptions: a sabbatical year in 1909–10, part of which he spent studying with the physicist-engineer Lucien Bull at the Marey Institute in Paris and part with the physiologist Max Verworn at Göttingen; a year (1913–14) as psychologist in a program studying the psychomotor effects of alcohol at the Nutrition Laboratory of the Carnegie Institution; and some months during 1918 as consultant to the navy on training matters. The instruments he devised for the training of gun pointers and for the detection of submarines were widely used.

In an article published in 1919, Dodge proposed the idea of a "College of Mental Engineering . . . for coordinating the available fragments of our science of the social mind for the practical solution of . . . pressing [postwar] social problems." Such were the objectives of the Institute of Psychology founded at Yale in 1924. Dodge devoted many months to assisting in its promotion and planning, and in 1924 he reluctantly severed his ties with Wesleyan and accepted appointment as professor of psychology at Yale. Dodge, Robert M. Yerkes, and Clark Wissler constituted the first directorate of the Institute, which five years later was broadened to include psychiatry and became the Institute of Human Relations. Dodge remained at Yale until his retirement in 1936, continuing his productivity despite the increasing disabilities of Parkinson's disease and serving as an invaluable source of ideas and guidance for the research of many colleagues and students. After retirement he lived in Tryon, N. C., where he died of pneumonia in 1942.

A rigidly objective scientist, Raymond Dodge was also a warm, human personality. Although he would contend that the thrill derived from the success of a new technique or from a new scientific discovery was unscientific, his glee at seeing the tachistoscope "work" and at viewing his first eye-movement record belied his contention. During his years at Wesleyan his advice was constantly sought by the administration and by his peers on the faculty. He was a popular teacher both in the undergraduate classroom and the graduate seminar. Students admired the clarity of his expositions and delighted in his humor and the irresistible chuckle which punctuated his sentences.

To a later generation Dodge's name is not well known, for he made no great contributions to psychological theory. It was as a genius in the devising of instrumental techniques for the experimental investigation of numerous processes in individual human behavior that he made the contributions that brought him many professional honors, including the presidency of the American Psychological Association (1916–17), chairman-

ship of the Division of Anthropology and Psychology of the National Research Council (1922–23), and election to the National Academy of Sciences (1924), at a time when membership in that august body of scientists was unusual for a psychologist. The invention of the Erdmann-Dodge tachistoscope and the ensuing experiments on reading, culminating in the pioneering and classic monograph by Dodge and Erdmann, *Psychologische Untersuchungen über das Lesen* (1898); the corneal reflection and concave mirror techniques for the photographic registration of eye movements, and the subsequent descriptive classification of the types of eye movements and their study under a variety of psychophysiological conditions; the rotating apparatus for the investigation of vestibular experience and ocular nystagmus; his wartime instruments for the navy—all remain landmarks in the annals of experimental psychology. His determination of the manner in which the eye moves in reading has been fundamental to later research in this field. Significant contributions to the development of theory lie in Dodge's "A Working Hypothesis for Inner Psychophysics," published in the *Psychological Review* in 1911; in his "Theories of Inhibition," appearing in the same journal in 1926; and in his book *Conditions and Consequences of Human Variability* (1931). It is the phenomenon of human variability that constitutes the theme which interrelates his many widely ranging research investigations and publications.

[Autobiographical sketch in Carl Murchison, ed., *A Hist. of Psychology in Autobiog.*, vol. I (1930); Walter R. Miles, ed., *Psychological Studies of Human Variability* (Dodge Commemorative Number, *Psychological Monographs*, no. 212, 1936); *Who Was Who in America*, vol. II (1950); personal association. See also Walter R. Miles in Nat. Acad. Sci., *Biog. Memoirs*, XXIX (1956), 65–115 (with bibliography); and obituary articles in *Am. Jour. of Psychology*, Oct. 1942 (by R. M. Yerkes), *Psychological Rev.*, Sept. 1942 (by R. S. Woodworth), and *Science*, May 8, 1942 (by Carl E. Seashore). Death record from N. C. State Board of Health.]

CARLETON F. SCOFIELD

DOW, ALEX (Apr. 12, 1862–Mar. 22, 1942), public utility executive, was born in Glasgow, Scotland, the elder of two children and only son of William and Jean (Keppy) Dow. His father, the son of a blacksmith, was an improvident businessman, but Dow's hardworking mother made the most of the family's meager resources. Young Alex left the Presbyterian parish school at the age of eleven and went to work as an office boy in his father's short-lived real estate firm. The following year he became a clerk for the North British Railway in Glasgow, where he also served as a volunteer linesman's helper and developed an early interest in electricity.

In 1880, following his mother's death, he moved to Liverpool and took a job with the Cunard Lines as a stenographer and later as a ticket seller. A brief trip in 1882 to New York City as assistant purser aboard a Cunard ship convinced him that new opportunities awaited him in America, and later that year he immigrated to Baltimore, where he worked for the Baltimore & Ohio Railroad, at first as an immigrant agent accompanying steerage passengers to Chicago and then in the railroad's telegraph department. Dow joined the Brush Electric Light Company in Baltimore in 1886 and three years later transferred to the company's Chicago branch as district engineer. His work in designing and supervising the installation of an arc lighting system for Chicago's South Park in preparation for the World's Fair of 1893 earned him a wide reputation.

Dow was called to Detroit in 1893 to design and supervise the construction of a city-owned electric plant, which Mayor Hazen S. Pingree [q.v.] hoped would end the disorder and corruption created by private competition for the municipal street lighting contract. Three years later, after completing the project, Dow became manager of the Edison Illuminating Company, one of several private electric companies then engaged in a bitter struggle for control of the Detroit market. Failing to effect a merger with his less solvent competitors, Dow further weakened them by reducing prices while maintaining quality service. When they fell into bankruptcy, he acquired their plants and brought them into a coordinated system. To ward off new competition, Dow declared his readiness to supply electricity, at a uniform price, to any part of the city, even areas where such service might be unprofitable. In 1903, to secure the capital needed for a new power plant, the firm was reorganized into the Detroit Edison Company. At first as vice-president and general manager, and from 1912 as president, Dow built the company into one of the largest in America; at the time of his retirement in 1940 its invested capital had grown to more than $340,000,000.

Despite his limited training, Dow sought to keep abreast of the latest advances in electrical technology. His early decision, for example, to generate electricity at sixty cycles, rather than the then conventional twenty-five used for direct-current transmission, indicated his faith in the long-range success of alternating current. He also lowered operating costs by installing (1907) in the company's new Delray generating plant a Type W Stirling boiler which increased the plant's firing efficiency. Other development insti-tuted under Dow included the automation of the system's substations, which converted generated current into the proper voltage for redistribution to consumers; the establishment of the "belt line," an integrated system of power transmission lines which reduced the necessity of constructing new power plants; and the installation of equipment permitting the production of high-temperature steam in order to increase the maximum limits of pressure in steam turbines. To keep Edison abreast of technological advances, Dow established in 1925 what was probably the first research department in the electric utility industry.

Dow's major contribution, however, was in the field of management and administration. A shrewd businessman himself, he early attracted new industry to Detroit by devising a differential rate formula. Since, as he reasoned, generating equipment had to be available whether customers were using power or not, large industries which operated around the clock should be given rate advantages for their use of current during off-peak hours. Dow also gained the confidence of the public in Edison's operations. Though he believed utilities should have monopoly status, he accepted the corollary of full public accountability. In the company's accounting practices he regularly anticipated new legal requirements set by city and state regulatory commissions. Dow also fought off attempts by holding companies to gain control of Edison for speculative purposes, and during the 1920's he avoided the questionable practices of many utility companies. Under his regime there were no stock bonuses, watered stock, splits, or acquisitions at inflated prices. Stock of only one class existed, and all bonds issued were under a single mortgage contract.

Dow was active in professional and civic organizations, serving as a director of the Edison Electric Institute, as a member of the Detroit Board of Water Commissioners, and, from 1932, as civilian chief of the War Department's Detroit Ordnance District. He lived in a large country home near Ann Arbor, Mich., and traveled extensively. He was a member of St. Andrew's Church (Episcopal) in Ann Arbor. Dow died of pneumonia at the University of Michigan Hospital in Ann Arbor, and was buried in Lorraine Park Cemetery, Baltimore, Md. He was survived by his wife, Vivienne Kinnersley of Baltimore, whom he had married on Apr. 24, 1889, and their four children: Dorothy, Margaret, George Lathrop, and James Douglas.

[For the business career of Alex Dow, see Raymond C. Miller, *Kilowatts at Work: A Hist. of the Detroit Edison Co.* (1957), which includes an extensive bibliography and a description of company archive holdings. For biographical appraisals, see Prentiss M. Brown, *Alex Dow* (Newcomen Soc., 1951), and *N. Y. Times,* Mar. 23, 1942. Family data were secured from a son, James Douglas Dow. Dow's more significant speeches and professional papers are in his *Some Public Service Papers, 1892–1927* (privately printed, 1927). Death record from Mich. Dept. of Public Health.]

RAYMOND C. MILLER

DREIER, MARGARET. See ROBINS, MARGARET DREIER.

DREISER, THEODORE (Aug. 27, 1871–Dec. 28, 1945), one of the perhaps half-dozen major novelists of the United States, was also the first major American writer whose background was totally outside the pale of Protestant, Anglo-Saxon, middle-class respectability. His father, John Paul Dreiser, was a German Catholic immigrant, a weaver whose drive and readiness to move to a better job led, at the end of some twenty-three years, to his becoming supervisor of a woolen mill of his own in Sullivan, Ind. A disastrous fire and then, in rebuilding, a serious injury turned his fortunes. For the rest of his life he was a bitter witness to that downward social mobility that usually goes unrecorded, and one sign of his bitterness was his sometimes blaming his failure on the "Yankee" chicanery of his partners in the mill. His animus was the obverse of that which, in the words of a genteel academic reviewer (Stuart P. Sherman [*q.v.*]), later identified the novelist scornfully as coming from the "'ethnic' element of our mixed population." Dreiser's mother, of Pennsylvania German descent, was also from outside the officially recognized mainstream. Her father, an Ohio farmer, kept up an active though indefinite Pietist tradition: Dreiser referred to him indifferently as Moravian, Mennonite, or Dunkard, but knew for sure that he had forbidden his daughter to marry a Catholic. At seventeen Sarah Maria Schänäb ran off and married John Dreiser anyhow, on New Year's Day of 1851.

The Dreisers moved to Fort Wayne, Ind., then Terre Haute, then Sullivan. They had retreated to Terre Haute with their eight surviving children when Theodore was born in August 1871, the next to last of five sons and of ten children whose lives were to be loosely but often strongly intertwined. The large family was by then sliding downhill. The father was frequently out of work, the mother took in roomers and did washing, the children learned early to pick up coal along the railroad tracks and knew what it meant to be sent home from school when they were shoeless in cold weather. In Theodore's first seven years they lived in five or six houses in Terre Haute, and then their moving began to cover a

wider area. In 1879 the family tried to make ends meet by splitting up. Theodore, with his mother and the younger children, lived in several Indiana towns and briefly in Chicago before they settled in Warsaw, Ind., in 1884. There he passed his early adolescence, a happy, painful formative period. At sixteen he left home and went to Chicago, where he hoped to make it on his own.

His German and Catholic background had less to do with keeping him outside the mainstream than poverty and its cultural handicaps. The fact of German descent made little difference to any of the family in their getting ahead or their falling behind economically or socially. One cultural effect on Dreiser was his anti-British prejudice, especially as it was stimulated by American anti-Germanism during two world wars. Another such effect was his anti-Semitism, which, though sufficiently accounted for by American nativism and the mutual hostility of ethnic groups, was partly a defensive response on behalf of Hitler's Germany. On its positive side, German descent was a cultural link that helped bind him in spontaneous friendship with H. L. Mencken. For Mencken the cultural attainments of the European middle class gave an ironic vantage on American pretensions, and over the years he often got Dreiser to commemorate this birthright with good beer and good food at Lüchow's famous restaurant in New York. But Dreiser, though he responded happily to Mencken's instruction, does not seem to have had a detailed command of his ancestral heritage. He was bilingual, to be sure: in *Dawn,* his memoir of early life, he recalls being taught in German and learning Gothic letters and noting the illustrations of homeland scenes in his German eclectic reader, but he deliberately makes little of his later exposure to the German classics. His German background, though its effects are hard to measure, was one side of his past that he never rejected.

On the other hand, he decidedly rejected Catholicism. His father's orthodoxy, a matter of rules and observances, seemed to deny pleasures for no understandable reason. John Dreiser's religion, like his other ineffectual assertions of authority, struck the son as being harsh, gloomy, and irrelevant. Yet the father had his way in having the children attend parochial schools, though they knew full well that the tuition money might be spent on pressing physical needs. What Theodore resented most about these schools was neither the cost nor even the terrors of the disciplinarian spirit that prevailed, but the vacuity of the studies —no history, no science, unlimited catechetical rote. This experience became the focus of his later strident anti-Catholicism. The 1884 move to Warsaw was memorable in that he and the other two youngest Dreisers were allowed at last to attend public schools. In one sense it was too late. When he was fifty he admitted, "Grammer was ever a mystery to me and I never mastered its rules." Yet his seventh-grade teacher, May Calvert, perceived in him a sensitivity and intelligence that she encouraged, and she passed him to the next grade with a reassuring "Grammar isn't everything." His high school teacher two years later, Mildred Fielding, also discerned his promise and urged him to "study and go on." In 1889 she was to seek him out in Chicago and, with her savings, send him to Indiana University for a crucial year of higher education. The sympathy and openness of the public schools gave Dreiser a sense of liberation from all that had been repressive in his life. But his experience of the open society was spasmodic at best, enough to sharpen his sense of what he had missed but not enough to give him confidence that he might master his world.

His experience of poverty, both as physical hardship and as social disability, was far more constant. He knew what it was to subsist on potatoes and fried mush and how it felt to be cold, and he took from childhood a lifelong dread of poverty and winter that he recognized as one of his deepest characteristics. His mother's taking in laundry and keeping house for roomers exposed him to harsh lessons in social class that came from schoolmates and neighbors. The fundamentally disorganizing effect of poverty on the family only began with the breakup of the single household for the sake of economy. It showed itself also in the casual departure of older sisters as they came to the age of pleasure and the distress of illegitimate pregnancy that brought them home to their mother. One sister, Emma, eloped with a man who worked in a high-class Chicago bar and was running off with the receipts; at Montreal he came to his senses and sent back most of the money, after which the couple went on to New York and anonymity. Though no such startling crime involved any of the Dreiser sons, two of them were at different times briefly jailed for stealing. Theodore himself learned to steal, and he would later shock the public by telling candidly how, when working as a collections agent in Chicago, he succumbed to the temptation to hold back funds. Even the family model of success was only marginally respectable. Paul Dresser, the older brother with the changed name that was supposed to be easier to remember, became a popular song-and-dance man and songwriter. He rescued the family at one of its worst moments by setting them up in Evansville, the town where he himself lived with Sallie Walker ("My Gal Sal"), a local madam. Theodore was eleven when a street-friend enlightened him on the facts of the case. At Warsaw five years later, though he relished the liberation of public schooling, he had to learn to live with the notoriety of his sister Sylvia's coming home pregnant and, when she was able to work again, leaving the baby with its grandmother. When Theodore left for Chicago, he was fleeing the small town as well as seeking his fortune in the city.

The tall, spindling youngster had too little strength and no taste at all for heavy unskilled work, and his first jobs did not last long. In time he found a place in a hardware warehouse that suited his capacities. It also appealed to his imagination in that it gave him a sense of relatedness to a larger, organized, important world. Here, as later, he had the knack of finding people who wanted to educate him; in this instance his older patron was a working-class autodidact and small-scale roué, who lectured him on philosophy and life and set him to reading history. He left the warehouse for his year at Indiana University, where he began to know his intellectual and personal powers as well as some of the limiting exclusions—from convivial fraternities and other costly social pleasures—that affected his life. He returned to petty white-collar jobs in Chicago, like real estate clerk and collections agent, which gave him wider and wider acquaintance with people all over the city. As he thought vaguely of becoming a writer, he identified himself with the enormous new-built metropolis, traditionless and daring to make new traditions. At twenty he became a reporter for the *Chicago Globe*. Straight reportage was never to be his strong point, but his observation and retentiveness and, in his feature writing, reflection on scenes of success and failure helped him rise as he went from one newspaper to another in Chicago, St. Louis, and elsewhere.

As escort to a group of award-winning teachers sent by the *St. Louis Republic* to the Chicago Fair of 1893, he met Sara Osborne White, a "pure sweet girl" from a prosperous, orderly, churchgoing family in Montgomery City, Mo. He fell in love with her and the middle-class home life she stood for, though five years of vacillation intervened before he married her on Dec. 28, 1898. In 1894, trying his luck in Ohio, he met Arthur Henry of the *Toledo Blade*. In a more serious sense he fell in love with him—"If he had been a girl I would have married him, of course. . . . Our dreams were practically identical. . . ." Henry, in 1899, turned Dreiser to fiction, challenged him to write a novel, encouraged and exhorted him past the points where he was blocked, drove, coaxed, edited, and altogether earned the dedication he got of *Sister Carrie*.

But before Dreiser attained either his domestic or his literary dreams, he had to complete his education as a journalist. Insofar as that education came from books, a Pittsburgh phase in 1894 was crucial. There, "for a period of four or five months," Dreiser "ate, slept, dreamed, lived" Balzac and conceived the imaginative richness of the modern city. A little later came his shattering encounter with Huxley, Tyndall, and Herbert Spencer, who not only destroyed his last traces of Catholic belief but dissolved all his assumptions about man and universe: "Up to this time there had been in me a blazing and unchecked desire to get on and the feeling that in doing so we did get somewhere; now in its place was the definite conviction that spiritually one got nowhere. . . ." Yet by the end of that year, he acted on his quickened ambition to get somewhere and, with $240 in savings, set off for New York. His practical education reached its climax there. He learned that a provincial newspaperman in the big city, when he got work at all, got poor assignments at bad space rates. While he was himself sinking towards destitution, he roomed with his sister Emma, who seemed even closer to going under. He helped her leave her ex-barkeeper lover, who had got to the point of not even looking for work.

In his own straits, despite flophouse and hockshop living, he was not beaten like that. Knowing his talent as a feature writer if not a newsman, he went to brother Paul with a proposition that his music firm publish a house magazine, and the idea was taken up. He edited *Ev'ry Month,* as he called it, for two years from its inception in 1895, printing songs, stories, and articles with wide appeal. He even provided Paul with a first stanza and chorus for the hit song "On the Banks of the Wabash." Although the magazine prospered, he broke away from the success he had sought as he would again thereafter. This time he stayed in the magazine world, writing for *Munsey's, Cosmopolitan, Success,* and others, and making a name with his interviews of tycoons and his sketches of the urban poor. He was soon making enough to get married on, and despite the fact that the emotion behind his commitment had long since begun to fade, he went through with it. If he overestimated his gift for domesticity, he was shrewder as an entrepreneur of his own writing. He knew himself to be a highly productive free lance, distinguished enough to make *Who's Who in America,* and he lost no time to compunctions when he was occasionally careless in taking over sources verbatim. He little guessed how deeply

he could commit himself to a noncommercial work or how intransigent he would prove in matters of artistic conscience. Then he wrote his novel.

Sister Carrie is the story of a small-town girl, her response to the great cities of Chicago and New York, her encounters with love and desire, and her rise past jilted lovers to theatrical success. Dreiser envisioned her world as it came to her, in the only terms he honestly knew, and he virtually left out the world as it was supposed to be. When he mentioned conventional standards of conduct, it was to show how little they affected the actual making of choices or the working out of consequences—in Carrie's casual acceptance of her first lover, for example, or her remaining unpunished by providence at the end. Although he drew upon incidents in his sisters' lives, he based the novel on his own inward dreams, historical understanding, and vivid recall of how the modern city strikes an individual sensibility. He portrayed as no one had before the immensity, isolation, and pathos of seemingly ordinary experience. What educated readers tended to see was the violation of taboos, but Frank Norris [*q.v.*], the great advocate of naturalism in American fiction, read the manuscript for Doubleday, Page & Company and immediately recognized a masterpiece. Norris's editorial judgment led to Dreiser's getting a contract, but when Frank Doubleday [Supp. 1] and his wife returned from Europe in September 1900, their disapproval almost stopped publication. Dreiser doggedly held the firm to its contract, but in fighting thus for his book he proved to have been naive. Except for Norris's getting copies to reviewers, there was no advertising or marketing effort, and virtual suppression was almost as effective as the real thing: only 456 copies were sold.

Although Dreiser's imaginative energies were at the flood—after finishing *Carrie* he had begun two other novels—he now faltered as he saw the great concentrated effort of his life come to nothing. The smashing blow was not only to the inner self: total royalties of only $68.40 for all that effort spelled an economic disaster also. Though he reverted to free-lance magazine writing, he suffered from fatigue and anxiety and he worked less and less easily. He and his wife separated and came together more than once, for economic as well as temperamental reasons. Over a period of three years he was gradually reduced again to the hunger and cold he had dreaded. This time he suffered also from psychic symptoms, like the felt presence of a Doppelgänger, and from the listlessness of spirit that he had imagined for Carrie's lover Hurstwood, whose long journey downhill to suicide he seemed to reenact. At the point of ultimate despondency, his resolve to end his life was turned aside by chance—first his encounter with a good-natured boatman at the river's edge and, a little later, discovery by brother Paul, who got him to a sanitarium where he could begin to recover. Though institutional society seemed to declare that he had no right to exist, he was not finally excluded from the bonds of men in general or the ties of blood. It is doubtful that unaided he could have renewed his will to live.

Dreiser came back from his struggle with poverty and battered spirits and made himself, even more than in the 1890's, a great success according to received commercial standards. He began with heavy physical labor on a railroad. After six months, feeling ready for intellectual exertion again, he took on a subeditor's duties in the features department of the *New York Daily News*. At just the time that Paul's fortunes began to collapse, his own began to rise. In 1904 he joined Street & Smith, the dime-novel house; as editor of *Smith's Magazine,* started the next year, he made a success that he could measure by the circulation of 125,000. Not long after Paul's death in 1906, which he took like a man whose mental health was secure, he moved from his "moderately comfortable and autocratic position" at *Smith's* to *Broadway Magazine,* and he proved to his new employers by quick and calculable results that he was well worth the jump in salary. He did not forget the past: he used his new affluence to back a second edition of *Sister Carrie* published by B. W. Dodge in 1907, and he had the satisfaction of finding favorable reviewers and a ready public.

But literature was not now Dreiser's life, business was. That same year he went to Butterick Publishing Company to run their three women's magazines, through which they purveyed fiction, uplift, fashion, and a desire for their sewing patterns to over a million American homemakers. At a time when two thousand dollars a year was a good middle-class salary. Dreiser began at five thousand. His personal drive, command of detail, quickness to invent and develop popular features, and close supervision of his large staff made him a big man at Butterick, as his twelfth-story office attested. As editor of *Delineator* he made his policy clear: "We like sentiment, we like humor, we like realism, but it must be tinged with sufficient idealism to make it all of a truly uplifting character." When he met Mencken, then ghostwriting a baby-care series for the magazine, he showed both playful and serious sides that his editorship concealed. But he really lived his role:

in 1909 he began secretly to edit the *Bohemian* as diversion from his main cares and he invited Mencken to contribute, but he warned his Baltimore friend that he wanted no "tainted fiction or cheap sex-struck articles." His official prudery, contrasted with his earlier fearlessness, was absurd. All the more so in that, recovering from his 1904 breakdown, he had confirmed his "varietist" taste in love and begun a career of sexual incidents that became a fixed pattern of his life. His Don Juan compulsion partly expressed a desire for conquest and demonstrated potency. (Once, later, when involved in a newspaper scandal, he claimed to be impotent, and, childless after so many affairs, he had reason to doubt his fertility.) It also expressed a desire for sentimental love talk, pet names, mothering. Dreiser's multiple life was simplified when a member of the Butterick staff, whose seventeen-year-old daughter he was feverishly paying court to, got him fired. Freed from the requirements of his position, he now separated definitely from his wife, even though he did not win the girl. As for Butterick, he felt no regrets since "the big work was done here."

Probability, in the guise of chance, had freed Dreiser from business and from marriage. He now put his gathered energies once more into the writing of novels. In a new surge of creativity he produced *Jennie Gerhardt* (1911), *The Financier* (1912), *The Titan* (1914), and *The "Genius"* (1915) but the speed with which he seemed to write was deceptive. *Jennie* had been begun in 1901 along with a narrative which was the germ of *An American Tragedy,* while at this time he conceived both *The Bulwark* and *The Stoic,* finished thirty years later and published posthumously. Even as he wrote these novels, he more than once put one aside to take up another. Their intertwined histories suggest that Dreiser tapped into stories that grew at their own pace rather than contriving stories to suit his conscious purposes. In this the artist differed from the literary businessman; he made up for what he lacked in craftsmanship by his respect for his materials. In *Jennie* he portrayed womanly devotion and endurance with an objectivity radically different from the enveloping pathos of *Carrie*. For the incidents of unsanctioned love and illegitimate birth he drew on more than his sisters' experience. Dreiser had begun the novel shortly after his father's death at the end of 1900, when he had just had his own first taste of great hopes come to nothing. As he explored the relation between daughter and father with sympathy for both, he evidently groped toward an understanding of his own past. He also rendered in detail the barriers that fell between his working-class heroine and her upper-middle-class lover, and thus broke through the American assumption that social class was nonexistent or inessential. Moreover, by ignoring English literary conventions as he did so, he underscored the novelty for American fiction and American self-awareness of his demonstration that social structure could make an irrevocable difference in individual lives. What kept the social novel in its large tragic context was that the human need for acceptance transcended historical conditions; the center of gravity lay in the need to endure what nature gives in the way of death and grief. For this ultimate Dreiserian quality the author was, it happened, dependent on outside guidance. When his friend Lillian Rosenthal read his draft with a happy ending and told him it was out of character, he knew she was right and set himself to redo the last part of the novel. In his way of groping after truth, he came more and more to depend on the help of friends, usually women.

The great exception was his next completed work, *The Financier,* still the best American novel of business and the businessman. Dreiser, with the pleasures of power and the emptiness of success still fresh in his mind, was surer of his conception than with Jennie, and for guidance he relied on his own energetic research into the life of his model, the street-railway magnate Charles Tyson Yerkes [*q.v.*]. The fictional Frank Cowperwood has the intelligence, will, and temperament to outlast the worst that chance can deal and still seize chance thereafter; his self-aggrandizement is heroic as well as frightening. The less interesting sequel, *The Titan,* details Cowperwood-Yerkes's stock and street-railway manipulations in Chicago and his long series of sexual conquests. Harper's, after having printed and advertised the novel, backed out of publishing it, and Dreiser had to find another publisher, as he now could do. *The "Genius,"* Dreiser's self-portrait as an artist, throws light on his relation to realistic painters and photographers, notably Everett Shinn and Alfred Stieglitz. What he had to say about the growth of artistic perception and the creative temperament was less immediately striking, however, than his candid record of marital incompatibility and varietist sexual life. The novelist's cause, he believed, was truth-telling even more than it was sexual liberation, and educated readers reacted accordingly. The *Nation*'s reviewer, Stuart Sherman, professed to believe that characters could not behave as Dreiser's did without feeling shame. A more telling attack came the next year when John S. Sumner of the New York Society for the Suppression of Vice,

holding the threat of prosecution over the publisher, got the book withdrawn.

Luckily 1916 was not like 1900. In the first place, Dreiser now had the stamina to weather the attacks and go on writing. The drying up of royalties and inability to sell his work to magazines had him several times at the edge of economic hardship, but he did not falter. Although, as W. A. Swanberg points out, one effect of censorship was that after *The "Genius,"* he did not produce another novel for ten years, he did write plays, poems, stories, memoirs, travel books, and philosophical reflections. Moreover, his survival no longer depended on inner strength only, for he no longer struggled alone. When Mencken generaled a campaign against the suppression of *The "Genius,"* he was able to enlist the support of Amy Lowell [*q.v.*], Edwin Arlington Robinson [Supp. 1], Sinclair Lewis, Sherwood Anderson [Supp. 3], Max Eastman, and many others. It was an exciting time when young writers could think that, with their arrival, the nation was coming of age. The young recognized Dreiser's rank as a novelist and his importance as a precursor and champion of liberation. Dreiser, in his midforties, was pleased with the recognition and accepted the role. With his then mistress, he kept a salon in Greenwich Village. He gave interviews —"Personally, my quarrel is with America's quarrel with original thought." In his play *The Hand of the Potter,* in which a mentally defective sex murderer questions personal responsibility— "I didn't make myself, did I?"—and in stories that explored such taboo subjects as marital incompatibility and prostitution, he deliberately set himself against conventional standards. Where once he had been naive, he now consciously played his part in "breaking the bonds of Puritanism."

Yet his best work of the period was *Twelve Men* (1919), which dated mostly from the time of his innocence and the breakdown and recovery after the suppression of *Sister Carrie.* In his need he had done these studies of other men, including his brother Paul, whose individual power to survive he could search out when he had little faith in his own sources of strength. For the revision of his old articles he owed much to the stylistic editing of his most discerning adviser-critic, Dorothy Dudley, and yet, with fifteen years gone by, he rushed much of the material through her hands. He was less interested in rewriting than in reaffirming the need to build on realities outside oneself. To the same end he was pursuing his study of science more systematically and coming to focus on psychology; friendships with A. A. Brill and Jacques Loeb [*q.v.*] date from this period. And family still counted for much. In

1919 he met Helen Patges Richardson, a second cousin on his mother's side, twenty-five years old and good-looking, and he entered into what was for him the most stable relationship of his life. Except for intervals when he was uneasy at being fettered or she could not bear his infidelities, Dreiser lived with her the rest of his life. (Refusal of divorce by Sara White Dreiser, who died in St. Louis in 1942, was his insurance against marriage.)

Unable to make progress on *The Bulwark,* he started work on *An American Tragedy.* As early as 1901, when he began a narrative called "The Rake," he had wanted to treat the fetters of sexual attachment as they interfered with movement up the pecuniary and social ranks and to trace the circumstances that could lead an ordinary man to the terrible act of murder. His own long engagement and restive marriage gave him insight into the chains a man might wish to break. And his imagining the artist's wife, in the semi-autobiographical *The "Genius,"* as dying in childbirth suggests how deeply he was involved with the theme. He made at least one more false start with the novel, however, for he needed the right subject matter as well as the right theme, something he could respect as independent of his personal invention. Having studied some fifteen actual cases, he settled on that of Chester Gillette, who in 1906 had killed his pregnant girl friend Grace Brown when the illicit relation threatened his getting ahead socially and economically in his small town in upstate New York. As Dreiser shaped the story to his conception, he could "feel it an honor to be permitted to even attempt to tell such a tale." In the telling, he did not simply follow the newspapers or the court records. His new working title, "Mirage," emphasized the illusions of acquisitiveness and desire that prompted his protagonist, Clyde Griffiths, to the enormity of his act. His final title emphasized his painstaking demonstration that the false values of American society were more responsible for the crime than was individual will.

Having written the novel which, except perhaps for *Huckleberry Finn,* made the most trenchant criticism of American society, ironically he had his first popular success. When it came out in 1925, it was not a best seller, but royalties, movie rights, and a percentage from the stage version made Dreiser comfortable and to spare. He bought a place in the country. He became a personage, a deliverer of opinions and a wearer of sporty clothes. He did not forget his old battles, however, and he went on to fight Paramount Pictures when they presented a script in which Clyde Griffiths came through, as he saw it, as "an un-sympathetic 'smart aleck' who cares only for one thing . . . a scheming, sex-starved 'drugstore cowboy.'" He won major changes, even though a good film of the novel was not made until *A Place in the Sun* (1951). In this new battle, moreover, he saw himself as taking the part of other writers less able to stand up against the Hollywood conversion of their work into a debased commercial product. He no longer conceived his cause as that of a virtually powerless individual struggling against desperate odds.

For the rest of his life Dreiser kept in mind the public, political implications of his role. When in 1927 he visited the Soviet Union with a group of specially invited writers, he went and, as he thought, returned an individualist. Although he pitied the "minute individual attempting to cope with so huge and difficult a thing as life," he did not then translate this feeling into a political motive. But the author of *An American Tragedy* was moved by the case of Tom Mooney [Supp. 3], the radical convicted of murder in the San Francisco Preparedness Day bombing of 1916, and by that of the Scottsboro boys, eight young Alabama blacks sentenced to death in 1931 for an alleged rape, and he joined the organized effort to attain justice for the victims of the law. Also, an automobile trip across the United States in 1930 made him an eyewitness to depression breadlines and widespread suffering. Remembering the Soviet model, he now saw social misery and radical inequality as historical conditions subject to change, not absolutes of the cosmic order. So in his sixtieth year he became chairman of the National Committee for the Defense of Political Prisoners, and for more than a decade he made himself available as a public supporter of Communist-sponsored causes. Sometimes he did noble work, as in helping break through the communications blackout which the coal mine operators imposed while violently suppressing unionization in Harlan County, Ky. (1931). In 1938, after conferring with Spanish Republican leaders in Barcelona, he conveyed to President Roosevelt a proposal to assist war victims on both sides and thus helped initiate American relief policy. But his activity as speaker and pamphleteer became more and more reflexive as he followed the tactical vagaries of pro-Communist politics, modified not by independent thought so much as by individual feelings. The triumph of reason over prejudice was sometimes precarious: "Hitler is not attacking the Jewish religion, or if so, I have heard no comment to that effect. . . . That one race of people should be compelled against its will and inclinations to associate with another is at least debatable; but that its opposition should lead to torture or cruel suffering for the race objected to, I cannot see" (1936; *Letters,* III, 765); "Please don't imagine because I say this that I have anything against the English people as such —the English rank and file—as set over against the English Lord and Ladies and financiers . . ." (1941; *ibid.,* 936). At his best he could recall his mother's poverty and wretchedness and simply declare himself to be "for a social system that can and will do better than that for its members— those who try, however humbly,—and more, *wish to learn how* to help themselves" (1943; *ibid.,* 982). When he finally joined the Communist party in 1945, the last year of his life, he considered his act an affirmation of internationalism, equality, and a reordered social system, not the undertaking of a discipline of power.

In his sixties, he continued his persistent study of science with a view to making a comprehensive naturalist philosophy of being. He never completed the task, but in science he got round his analytic deficiencies and reached fundamental affirmations more easily than in politics. He knew enough to be free from sentimental fear of the machine or of scientists, and he valued great scientific observation as "spying out the ways of this mystery of which we are a part." His own observations led to moments of vision in which he contemplated the creative force in the beauty of a flower, a snake. This spirit renewed his own creative powers, and in 1942 he resumed work on novels long set aside. He expressed his religious acceptance convincingly in the Quaker piety which informs *The Bulwark* (published posthumously in 1946), much less so in the concern with Yoga in *The Stoic* (published posthumously in 1947). The same mood affected his awareness of how much he depended on Helen, whom he married at last on June 13, 1944, more or less secretly, in Stevenson, Wash.

Dreiser had all but finished both late novels before he died of a heart attack in 1945, at the age of seventy-four, at his home in Hollywood, Calif. When he was buried at Forest Lawn Memorial Park, the speakers were the Rev. Allan Hunter, whose Congregational church Dreiser had attended, John Howard Lawson, the Hollywood writer who would soon be blacklisted for Communist affiliations, and the actor Charles Chaplin, who would soon be excluded from the United States for the same reason. Dreiser left his estate to Helen, requesting in his will that she pay certain amounts to the surviving members of his family and leave the residue to a Negro orphanage. His controversial career as a political figure for a time overshadowed his literary achievement. His art and his politics both derived

from a profound sensitivity to the inequalities of American life, just as his business career with Butterick and his insight into Yerkes-Cowperwood and Chester Gillette–Clyde Griffiths stand in different ways as warning against uncritical conformity to received values.

[Dreiser has been fortunate in his biographers. W. A. Swanberg, *Dreiser* (1965), is the most comprehensive factual account; some evident antipathies, especially for the political Dreiser, do not interfere with accuracy. F. O. Matthiessen, *Theodore Dreiser* (1951), is a model critical biography and remains the best overall literary study. The first literary and biographical study, still rewarding, is Dorothy Dudley, *Forgotten Frontiers: Dreiser and the Land of the Free* (1932); the author, Dreiser's friend from 1916 and a contributor of editorial help, records his significance for the generation that came of age during the First World War. Robert H. Elias, *Theodore Dreiser: Apostle of Nature* (1949), gives a sympathetic account of Dreiser's intellectual development, based on full research and on firsthand acquaintance dating from his student inquiries of 1937. Alfred Kazin and Charles Shapiro, eds., *The Stature of Theodore Dreiser* (1955), documents the changing literary reputation and offers a useful bibliography of reviews and comment. Ellen Moers, *Two Dreisers* (1969), focuses on the artistic and scientific resources that went into the making of *Sister Carrie* and *An American Tragedy* and shows how much new detail a fresh analysis can elicit from a wide range of materials. Primary materials center in the vast collection at the Univ. of Pa., which includes most of Dreiser's letters, MSS., and clipping files. Other relevant collections are at Ind. Univ., Cornell, Yale, Princeton (for the Mencken side), the N. Y. and Los Angeles public libraries, and elsewhere. Dreiser's autobiographical volumes are, in order of subject chronology, *Dawn* (1931), *Newspaper Days,* originally called *A Book About Myself* (1922), *A Traveler at Forty* (1913), and *A Hoosier Holiday* (1916). At the Univ. of Pa., the manuscript versions of *Dawn* and *Newspaper Days* give names undisguised by fictionalizing and otherwise vary in some details from the published text; also, the unfinished manuscript "An Amateur Laborer" covers the period of breakdown and recovery after *Sister Carrie.* Robert H. Elias, ed., *Letters of Theodore Dreiser* (3 vols., 1959), gives a valuable selection. Helen Dreiser, *My Life with Dreiser* (1951), is an indispensable record of personal history. It is complemented by the volumes of editor-collaborators: Louise Campbell, ed., *Letters to Louise* (1959), and Marguerite Tjader [Harris], *Theodore Dreiser: A New Dimension* (1965).]

J. C. LEVENSON

DU PONT, FRANCIS IRÉNÉE (Dec. 3, 1873–Mar. 16, 1942), chemist, inventor, stockbroker, was born at Hagley House near Wilmington, Del., the eldest of ten children of Elise Wigfall (Simons) and Francis Gurney du Pont, and a great-grandson of Eleuthère Irénée du Pont [*q.v.*], founder of E. I. du Pont de Nemours and Company. His father was works manager of the company's black powder mills on Brandywine Creek.

Francis at an early age constructed models of mills, waterwheels, and machinery, a talent fostered by his father, who made a workroom for him in their home. Educated by his parents, by tutors, and at Martin's Day School in Philadelphia, he entered the University of Pennsylvania in 1890, but soon withdrew because of an eye injury suffered in a laboratory accident. For the next two years he remained at home, studying with his father and private tutors. He then enrolled in the Sheffield Scientific School of Yale. There he experimented with the chemical components of smokeless powder, encouraged by his father, who was encountering problems in the production of this new type of explosive at the company's recently established plant in Carney's Point, N. J.

After graduating from Yale in 1895, du Pont went to work at Carney's Point, where he taught technicians who were inexperienced in chemistry how to make daily tests and analyses at various stages in the powder-making process. When in 1902 his cousins Alfred Irénée du Pont [Supp. 1], Thomas Coleman du Pont [Supp. 1], and Pierre Samuel du Pont acquired control of the Du Pont Company, Francis was made a member of the board of directors and superintendent of the Carney's Point plant. Within a year he left the plant to establish an experimental laboratory in a small converted cotton mill on Brandywine Creek. From this grew the Du Pont Company Experimental Station, which he directed until 1916.

Though an able administrator, du Pont preferred research, and his emphasis on research and development, in association with Charles Lee Reese [Supp. 2] and others, moved the Du Pont Company in the direction of diversification as a manufacturer of artificial leather, paints, lacquers, dyes, photographic film, plastics, chemicals, and improved explosives. He himself took out almost fifty patents from 1895 to 1915, principally in explosives chemistry and engineering. He early devised an improved nitrometer for measuring the amount of nitrogen in nitrocellulose (the base material of smokeless powder) that was quickly adopted by the rest of the industry. This was followed by a major advance in industrial chemistry, Francis du Pont's invention of a fixation process that converted inert nitrogen, an abundant component of air, into chemically active oxides that could be made into compounds having industrial uses. The process involved heating air to a high temperature by an electric arc, then rapidly, almost simultaneously, cooling it, after which the oxides were converted into nitric acid.

Du Pont also made the handling of nitrocellulose less hazardous by dehydrating it before adding the solvents that converted it into powder, and then worked out a method of recovering over 50 percent of the solvents for reuse. After improving a German catalytic process for the manufacture of sulfuric acid, he succeeded in making sulfuric acid readily absorb gaseous nitric acid, thereby creating the mixed acid essential for making nitrocellulose. He also developed a gravity liquid process for separating different types of mineral solids. Additional patents for an improved draftsman's triangle and for putting tips on shoelaces may have been born out of dissatisfaction and exasperation with these simple but essential everyday items.

Du Pont withdrew from the family firm in 1916, when his cousin Alfred I. du Pont, with whom he was aligned, failed to block the sale of T. Coleman du Pont's stock to a group headed by Pierre S. du Pont. With his brother Ernest, Francis du Pont then organized the Ball Grain Explosives Company, which made powder by a "wet mix" process, and in 1919 they established a second explosives company, the U. S. Flashless Powder Company. Du Pont then became absorbed in another firm that he had founded, the Delaware Chemical Engineering Company, which under his direction undertook a wide range of research and development in chemistry and engineering.

In 1931 he embarked upon a new business career when he purchased a seat on the New York Stock Exchange, initially to handle his own stock transactions and eliminate brokers' commissions. Thereafter he divided his time between Francis I. du Pont and Company in New York City, which became one of the country's leading brokerage firms, and the Delaware Chemical Engineering Company in Wilmington, where he made a number of improvements and inventions in the fields of petrochemicals and synthetic rubber. In 1936 he organized still another company, the Wilmington Chemical Corporation, for the development of a cheaper and simpler method (originated by an Austrian chemist, Fritz S. Rostter) of making plasticizers or extenders from petroleum wastes. By 1942 his patents numbered more than a hundred.

Widely read in political economy, du Pont was a supporter of the single-tax theory of Henry George [q.v.]; in 1900 he aided in founding the single-tax community of Arden near Wilmington. As an advocate of the direct ballot and the initiative and referendum, he ran unsuccessfully in 1912 on the Progressive ticket for mayor of Wilmington. He was a member of the Episcopal Church but a less active communicant than his father had been. Quiet and introspective, he sometimes appeared diffident and aloof. On Sept. 1, 1897, he had married Marianna Rhett of Charleston, S. C., by whom he had nine children: Emile Francis, Hubert Irénée, Elise, Francis, Edmond,

Alfred Rhett, Alexis Irénée, Marianna Rhett, and Marie Delphine. His wife tactfully tolerated his disregard for the social amenities when at times he disappeared from dinner parties, later to be found in his private cellar laboratory working on a solution that had come as a sudden inspiration. Du Pont died at the West Side Hospital in New York City at the age of sixty-eight from a blood infection, *streptococcus viridans*. He was buried in the du Pont family burial ground, a short distance from his birthplace.

[Papers of Francis I. du Pont are in the keeping of his sons Emile F. and Edmond du Pont, who provided recollections of their father. A brief account appears in *Francis Gurney du Pont: A Memoir*, ed. by Allan J. Henry (privately printed, 1951), I, 155–57. A lengthier sketch, which gives considerable attention to his achievements as inventor, is in H. Clay Reed and Marion B. Reed, eds., *Delaware: A Hist. of the First State* (1947), III, 545–46. Scattered references are to be found in William S. Dutton, *Du Pont: One Hundred and Forty Years* (1949); Marquis James, *Alfred I. du Pont: The Family Rebel* (1941); William H. A. Carr, *The du Ponts of Del.* (1964); and Charles E. Arnold, *My Remembrances of the Du Pont Experimental Station* (1947).]

NORMAN B. WILKINSON

EASTMAN, JOSEPH BARTLETT (June 26, 1882–Mar. 15, 1944), reformer and public administrator, was born in Katonah, N. Y., the only son and younger of two children of John Huse Eastman, a Presbyterian minister, and his wife, Lucy King, of Binghamton, N. Y. He was a direct descendant of Roger Eastman, a native of Langford, Wiltshire, England, who settled in Salisbury, Mass., in 1638. Young Eastman grew up in Katonah and, after 1895, in Pottsville, Pa., where he attended the local high school. He then spent a year (1899–1900) learning the Latin and Greek necessary for entrance into Amherst College (his father's alma mater), from which he graduated with a B.A. in 1904. That year a fellowship to work on the small staff of Robert A. Woods [*q.v.*] at the famed South End House in Boston launched him on his lifelong career as a public servant.

Like many American cities at the time, Boston was experiencing a vigorous reform movement. In 1900 several eminent lawyers and businessmen, including Louis D. Brandeis [Supp. 3], Edward A. Filene [Supp. 2], and George W. Anderson, had founded the Public Franchise League to serve as a "watchdog" over the municipal utilities. In 1905, when Brandeis sought a full-time secretary for the League, Woods suggested the twenty-three-year-old Eastman. For the next decade, Eastman for all practical purposes *was* the League, personally and sometimes single-handedly investigating proposed railway mergers, testifying before legislative committees on pending railway, gas, and electric rate changes, exposing stock frauds, and preparing bills for presentation to the state legislature. In 1906, at Brandeis's suggestion, he enrolled in the Boston University law school, but his duties at the League forced him to drop out the next year. For much of the time, Eastman worked for an uncertain salary that rarely reached $1,000 a year; sometimes he was forced to enclose in the League's Annual Report personal pleas for money from its putative sponsors.

In 1913, in part as a result of Eastman's efforts, Massachusetts established a state Public Service Commission. Two years later Eastman replaced George W. Anderson on the Commission when President Woodrow Wilson named Anderson United States District Attorney for Massachusetts. In 1917 Wilson elevated Anderson to the Interstate Commerce Commission. When, late in 1918, Anderson moved on to a federal judgeship, Eastman once more replaced him. On Jan. 24, 1919, when the Senate confirmed his appointment, Eastman became, at thirty-six, one of the youngest members to sit on the ICC; he was to remain with it for the rest of his life, serving twice as chairman.

Joseph Eastman's extraordinary contribution to public administration cannot be demonstrated readily by references to "landmark" decisions or innovations such as lend drama to legislative, executive, diplomatic, or judicial careers. Nevertheless, one may catch something of the man's uniqueness from his longevity in office in a sector of government notorious for short tenure. A believer in "scientific" efficiency in government, he eschewed politics and belonged to no party. Though appointed by a Democratic president, he gained reappointments from Harding, Hoover, and Franklin Roosevelt. Eastman's nondogmatic objectivity was almost universally acknowledged. Thus, for example, although most railroad managements had sharply disagreed with Eastman's position on vital issues, they accepted equally his reappointment by Harding in 1922 because they recognized his stern competence. Eastman's special place is perhaps best expressed by a somewhat offhand comment made in a critical study of the federal regulatory commissions written in 1962. "In the 1920's," writes Henry J. Friendly, "when the spirit of Commissioner Eastman was abroad throughout the land," students of government had "been taught to expect, or at least to hope" that the regulatory agencies could "combine the celerity of Mercury, the wisdom of Minerva, and the purity of Diana" (*The Federal Administrative Agencies: The Need for Better Definition of Standards*, 1962, p. vii).

Many of Eastman's most noteworthy specific efforts proved to be in losing causes. While still with the Massachusetts Public Service Commission, in 1916, he was the first clearly to formulate the "prudent investment" principle for determining "fair" rates for the regulated utilities companies. The federal Supreme Court in 1898 (in *Smyth* v. *Ames*) had ruled that no commission could fix rates that failed to permit a fair and reasonable return, but it neglected to declare whether the returns should be based on the value of a company as measured by capital actually invested or as measured by the physical assets of the company, to be gauged, in turn, by current potential replacement costs. Mindful of continuing inflationary pressures, the railroads favored the latter, but Eastman asserted that "capital honestly and prudently invested must, under normal conditions, be taken as the controlling factor." In *St. Louis and O'Fallon Railway Co.* v. *United States* (1929), however, the Supreme Court (with Justices Holmes, Stone, and Brandeis dissenting) overrruled Eastman's attempt to apply the principle to ICC decisions.

Shortly after World War I, during which the nation's railroad system was taken over by the federal Railroad Administration, Commissioner Eastman advised against returning the railroads to private management. Although he had little faith in public ownership per se, he believed the railroads were in a poor credit position at the time and therefore could not operate efficiently without government coordination. This placed him in direct opposition to railroad owners and management, who disingenuously charged the Railroad Administration with "ruining" the railroads. "As you know," he wrote to a friend in 1923, "more deliberate lies were told in regard to what happened during federal control than there have been upon almost any subject that I am acquainted with." His views on the subject also nettled the nation's shippers, with whom Eastman had usually been identified in the past. The shippers had come to distrust the Railroad Administration because during the war it had tended to adopt policies that originated with railroad managers, contrary to the trend of ICC policy over the previous decade. Moreover, businessmen generally, and especially in 1919–20, reacted emotionally to anything that suggested "socialism," and the fact that only organized labor gave support to public ownership—in the form of the Plumb Plan—helped foredoom Eastman's discerning advice. His "alliance" with labor interests was not enduring. Eastman found it necessary to oppose some of labor's demands on the grounds that the railroad industry was not strong enough to absorb them, and by the late 1920's much of organized labor had begun to treat him with suspicion.

On the other hand, his demonstrable expertise and judiciousness made him the perfect candidate for Federal Coordinator of Transportation when Congress acted in 1933 to bring some order to an industry damaged more than most by the Great Depression. Although he was not a lawyer, his ICC reports were extensively respected. As Chief Justice Harlan F. Stone remarked some years later, "When our court gets a case which involves a decision and order of the Interstate Commerce Commission, we always thumb it through first to see what Joe Eastman has said in his Opinion." Eastman's efforts as Federal Coordinator nevertheless failed. "He effected little coordination of the railroad groups," writes the episode's historian, "because they would not let him." In attempting to develop a policy to maximize the public interest, Eastman transgressed upon the special interests of railroad labor and railroad management, as well as upon certain jealously guarded prerogatives of other governmental agencies. When "both the carriers and the unions, . . . by treaty, made temporary peace with each other and then deserted the coordinator," he had no power base from which he could operate effectively. His formal powers lapsed when Congress declined to renew them in 1936.

In 1941 another national emergency produced a final call to Eastman to serve in the capacity of coordinator, this time as Director of Defense Transportation. His greater success in this special assignment probably resulted from his tacit recognition this time of the need to work with the principal spokesmen of interest groups most directly engaged in the transportation industry. Thus he came to rely heavily on railroad management leaders and on representatives of the major shippers' associations.

Eastman never married. He lived with his sister, Elizabeth Eastman, from 1919 until his death. He died in Emergency Hospital, Washington, D. C., of a coronary occlusion, after a brief illness. Although he professed no particular religious affiliation, funeral services were held at All Souls' Memorial Episcopal Church in Washington. He was buried in the family plot in Binghamton, N. Y. A final tribute by the *Washington Post* fairly summed up Joseph Eastman's achievement: "Here was a man who dignified the title 'bureaucrat.' "

[Claude M. Fuess, *Joseph B. Eastman: Servant of the People* (1952), a full-scale biography; G. Lloyd Wilson, ed., *Selected Papers and Addresses of Joseph B. Eastman, Director, Office of Defense Transportation* (1948); Earl Latham, *The Politics of Railroad Coordination, 1933–1936* (1959); I. L. Sharfman, *The Interstate Commerce Commission* (5 vols., 1931–37). Eastman's papers are at Amherst College. A bronze bust of Eastman is in the rotunda of the Interstate Commerce Commission Building.]

RICHARD M. ABRAMS

EDMUNDS, CHARLES WALLIS (Feb. 22, 1873–Mar. 1, 1941), pharmacologist, was born in Bridport, Dorset, England, the third of five sons and seventh of nine children of Thomas Hallett Edmunds and Caroline (Wallis) Edmunds. In 1883 the family emigrated to the United States and settled in Richmond, Ind., where the father, previously in the tannery business, operated a chair factory. Charles attended the University of Indiana for one year (1895–96) and then transferred to the University of Michigan, where he received the M.D. degree in 1901 and later (1904) the A.B. degree.

While serving his internship at the university's medical school, Edmunds attracted the attention of Arthur R. Cushny [q.v.], head of the department of materia medica and therapeutics, by his keen observations in a case of cardiac irregularity, a field in which Cushny was interested. As a result, Edmunds in 1902 was appointed an assistant in the department. When Cushny returned to England in 1905, Edmunds was promoted to lecturer, and in 1907 to professor; he remained with the department for the rest of his career. During his early teaching years he took postgraduate work with Rudolf Gottlieb and Hugo Magnus at the University of Heidelberg (1905) and with Cushny at University College, London (1907), and he spent the summer months of 1908 and 1909 at the Hygienic Laboratory (later the National Institute of Health) in Washington, D. C. In later years he was secretary of the medical school (1911–21) and assistant dean (1918–21). Quiet and tactful, Edmunds was an able administrator. He also enjoyed teaching and took a helpful personal interest in his associates.

Pharmacology was still a relatively new discipline in American medical schools when Edmunds began his career, the first such department having been set up at the University of Michigan in 1892 under John J. Abel [Supp. 2]. Edmunds grew with the science and made notable contributions to its development. His major concern was the establishment of drug standards and methods of bioassay for such drugs as digitalis and ergot, for which chemical assay methods were not available. He also worked at standardizing the potency of liver extracts and other substances used in treating pernicious anemia. For thirty years (1910–40) he served on the committee for revision of the United States Pharmacopeia; under his leadership official (U.S.P.) bioassay methods of standardization were intro-

duced. Edmunds went to Geneva in 1925 as a member of the international committee on drug standardization of the Health Committee of the League of Nations. He was for twenty years (1921–41) a member of the Council on Pharmacy and Chemistry of the American Medical Association, which then had considerable unofficial authority in the labeling and advertising of new drugs, and was chairman of its committee on grants to support research on therapeutic problems.

Among the subjects of Edmunds's laboratory research were the actions of botulinus and diphtheria toxins, autonomic drugs, and caffeine. Deeply interested in the problem of safe narcotics in medical practice, he investigated the role of chemical structure in the addictive properties of morphine and its derivatives, and was a member (1930–40) of the committee on drug addiction of the National Research Council. He also experimented in the intravenous use of dextrose in treating circulatory collapse in diphtheria, the subject of his Henry Russell lecture (1937) at the University of Michigan. In addition to his papers, he was co-author with Cushny of *A Laboratory Guide in Experimental Pharmacology* (1905), which went through at least three revisions, and with J. A. Gunn of Oxford, England, he made successive revisions of Cushny's *Textbook of Pharmacology and Therapeutics;* both textbook and manual did much to set the pattern of classroom instruction in the field of pharmacology.

Edmunds felt strongly that pharmacology should be maintained as a discipline separate from physiology and biochemistry in medical schools; to this end he used all the influence he could muster. Sensitive to conflicts of interest in science, he strongly supported a movement which for some time excluded pharmacologists employed by industry from membership in the Society for Pharmacology and Experimental Therapeutics. Edmunds was one of the eighteen founders of this society and served for three years (1921–23) as its president.

On Sept. 15, 1909, Edmunds married Lilian Virginia Kaminski. They had two children, Ann and Charles Wallis. An Episcopalian by upbringing and a staunch Republican, Edmunds appreciated good music and the theatre, and enjoyed gardening. Perhaps his greatest pleasure came from the painting of watercolors during summers on Monhegan Island off the Maine coast. He died suddenly of a coronary embolism shortly after his sixty-eighth birthday at his home in Ann Arbor, Mich., and was buried in Richmond, Ind.

[Obituaries in *Science*, Apr. 18, 1941 (by Nathan B. Eddy), and *Jour. Am. Medic. Assoc.*, Mar. 15, 1941; *Who Was Who in America*, vol. I (1942); K. K. Chen, ed., *The Am. Soc. for Pharmacology and Experimental Therapeutics, Inc.: The First Sixty Years, 1908–1969* (1969), p. 27; family information from Morrisson-Reeves Lib., Richmond, Ind., and from Edmunds's daughter, Mrs. Noyes L. Avery, Jr.]
RALPH G. SMITH

EDSALL, DAVID LINN (July 6, 1869– Aug. 12, 1945), physician and medical educator, was born in Hamburg, N. J., the sixth of the seven sons of Richard E. Edsall, the proprietor of a large general store and twice a state legislator, and Emma Everett (Linn) Edsall, whose family included a number of physicians. Both parents were descendants of early settlers in New Jersey and were chiefly of English ancestry, the first American Edsall having emigrated in 1648 from England to Boston and then moved on to New Amsterdam.

Edsall entered Princeton to study the classics, but the required courses in biology soon shifted his interests to the laboratory, and after receiving the A.B. degree in 1890 he followed his older brother Frank to the medical school of the University of Pennsylvania. He graduated, M.D., in 1893. After interning for a year at Mercy Hospital in Pittsburgh and studying in London, Graz, and Vienna (1894–95), he opened a practice in Pittsburgh. After six months, however, he returned to the University of Pennsylvania Medical School as an assistant. His work attracted the notice of the great teacher and clinician William Pepper [*q.v.*], who made Edsall his recording clerk and appointed him an associate in clinical medicine at the newly established Pepper Laboratory for Clinical Research.

Edsall's work in Pittsburgh had roused his curiosity about the relation between the illnesses suffered by the steelworkers and conditions in the mills, and his study abroad had convinced him of the value of laboratory research in the understanding of human disease. At the Pepper Laboratory he used the relatively new techniques of biological chemistry to make fundamental studies of nutritional diseases, metabolic abnormalities of children, and the effects of occupation on health. Between 1897 and 1910 he and his occasional collaborators produced more than seventy papers, which brought him a national reputation. In 1904 he published the first description of the disease later delineated as "heat cramps," sometimes called "Edsall's disease," a severe disorder (caused, so later research revealed, by salt depletion) that attacked workers after exposure to intense heat. He also studied the role of industrial conditions in producing chronic metallic poisoning.

Edsall thus became widely known as one of the few scientifically trained doctors of his day, men who sought to understand the physiological and biochemical processes of disease in order to find fundamental principles of treatment. In 1905 William Osler [*q.v.*] chose him as one of the twenty-four original members of the Interurban Clinical Club, a select group of leading physicians of Philadelphia, Boston, New York, and Baltimore. In 1907 Edsall was appointed professor of therapeutics and pharmacology at Pennsylvania, and in the same year he helped found the American Society for Clinical Investigation, whose members were known as the "Young Turks" because of their revolutionary approach to medicine. He also became president of the Philadelphia Pediatric Society (1908) and of the American Pediatric Society (1909).

The famous Flexner report, detailing the poor quality of much of the medical training offered in the United States, led to revolutionary changes in many of the medical schools. Edsall was deeply involved in these movements for change, in three different schools. Invited in 1909 to head the reforms projected at the Washington University School of Medicine in St. Louis, he formulated far-reaching proposals, and his influence was important in bringing such outstanding men as the pathologist Eugene L. Opie, the physiologist Joseph Erlanger, and the biological chemist Philip A. Shaffer to St. Louis. Edsall was finally persuaded, however, to stay at Pennsylvania, where a radical reorganization raised him to the top chair of professor of medicine in 1910. At first the university seemed ready to carry out his farseeing ideas on medical education, which included putting the clinical professors on a salaried basis and requiring them to give at least half time to teaching and research, but what had seemed to be unanimous support for these radical changes evaporated. Deeply disappointed, Edsall resigned in 1911 and went, after all, to Washington University as professor of preventive medicine. His close friend John Howland [*q.v.*] came as professor of pediatrics. Both Edsall and Howland, however, were rapidly disillusioned by lack of effective support from the administration for the development of their respective departments, and by the obstructive attitude of a few of their colleagues. With regret they decided to leave.

Thus in 1912 Edsall accepted an invitation to Boston as Jackson Professor of Clinical Medicine at the Harvard Medical School and head of the East Medical Service of the Massachusetts General Hospital. There he led a major development and expansion of research. He continued studies on nutrition, established an industrial disease clinic, and offered cooperation to manufacturers in determining and eliminating the causes of diseases related to occupational conditions. He had a genius for fostering the careers of promising young men who later became outstanding physicians; among them in those early days were James Gamble, J. Howard Means, Walter Palmer, and Paul Dudley White. In 1918 Edsall became dean of the Harvard Medical School. In 1922, through funds provided by the Rockefeller Foundation, Harvard's public health departments were amalgamated to form a separate School of Public Health, and as the full-time dean of both schools, Edsall resigned his hospital position and abandoned the practice of medicine.

The seventeen years of Edsall's deanship were a period of remarkable growth and scientific advance. Financial support for medical education and research increased manyfold. As chairs fell vacant and it became possible to support the departments on a modern basis, the school moved gradually (in the flexible Harvard style) toward a system in which teachers of the clinical courses devoted full time to their classes. The curriculum, always under revision, was drastically altered to allow students more freedom of choice and more independence. The new fourth-year general examination was designed to make students coordinate their knowledge. Edsall never lost sight of the fact that a school meant students and teachers, not buildings or systems. He assembled a great staff, bringing to the Harvard Medical School such leaders as Hans Zinsser [Supp. 2] in bacteriology, Alice Hamilton in industrial medicine (the first woman appointed to the faculty), Kenneth Blackfan [Supp. 3] in pediatrics, and Soma Weiss [Supp. 3] in medicine. Edsall also exerted a wide influence through the Association of American Medical Colleges. In 1927 he became a trustee of the Rockefeller Foundation, and his reports recommending that the foundation concentrate its medical education funds in support of the best and most promising researchers, and advocating a major shift to support of psychiatry, were of far-reaching importance. Under Rockefeller auspices in 1926 Edsall spent six very successful months in China, as an adviser on the future development of the department of medicine at the Peking Union Medical College. He retired as dean and Rockefeller trustee in 1935, but in the period preceding World War II took an active part in finding suitable positions for refugee European scientists.

Edsall was six feet four and generously proportioned, with a deep voice and a deliberate and dignified manner. His qualities of sound

judgment, patience, candor, and intellectual honesty were combined with the kind of courage that led him to say, "The best way to avoid a danger is to run plumb at it." He liked people and dealt easily with both patients and colleagues. He enjoyed detective stories, and found relaxation in hiking and mountain climbing. Brought up as an Episcopalian, he later became detached from the church.

On Dec. 22, 1899, Edsall married Margaret Harding Tileston of Boston. Their children were: John Tileston, who became professor of biological chemistry at Harvard; Richard Linn; and Geoffrey, who became professor of applied microbiology at the Harvard School of Public Health and head of the state public health laboratories. Edsall's first wife died in November 1912. In June 1915 he married Elizabeth Pendleton Kennedy; they were divorced in 1929. On May 3, 1930, he married Louisa Cabot Richardson, his assistant in the dean's office. Increasing heart insufficiency made Edsall an invalid in his last two years. He died of congestive heart failure in Cambridge, Mass., at the age of seventy-six; his ashes were buried near his summer home in Greensboro, Vt.

[Joseph C. Aub and Ruth K. Hapgood, *Pioneer in Modern Medicine: David Linn Edsall of Harvard* (1970), a full-scale biography, draws upon Edsall papers in the archives of the three medical schools where he taught, the archives of the Rockefeller Foundation, and the personal papers in the hands of his son John T. Edsall. See also, for Edsall's Philadelphia years, George W. Corner, *Two Centuries of Medicine: A Hist. of the School of Medicine, Univ. of Pa.* (1965); concerning Edsall at the Mass. Gen. Hospital, see James Howard Means, *Ward 4* (1958), and the following periodical references: Cecil K. Drinker in *Harvard Public Health Alumni Bull.*, Nov. 1945; C. Sidney Burwell in *Harvard Medical Alumni Bull.*, Oct. 1945; J. H. Means in *New England Jour. of Medicine*, Nov. 1, 1945; and a special issue, "Dr. Edsall and the Development of the School," *Harvard Medical Alumni Bull.*, Oct. 1935. On his father and his forebears, see James P. Snell, *The Hist. of Sussex and Warren Counties, N. J.* (1881), p. 344; and George E. McCracken, "Samuel Edsall of Reading, Berks, and Some Early Descendants," *N. Y. Genealogical and Biog. Record*, July 1958.]

JOSEPH C. AUB

EILSHEMIUS, LOUIS MICHEL (Feb. 4, 1864–Dec. 29, 1941), painter, was born on his family's estate, Laurel Hills Manor, in North Arlington, N. J., the sixth of seven surviving children and fourth of five sons of Henry Gustave and Cecilie Elise (Robert) Eilshemius. His father had crossed the Atlantic from Holland and had become a prosperous importer; he retired at the age of forty to spend a life of cultivated leisure at his country manor and at the family's winter home in New York City. His mother, a devout member of the French Evangelical Church, was of French-Swiss extraction, a cousin of the Swiss artist Leopold Robert. She herself made excellent academic drawings and nurtured her son's artistic tendencies. Eilshemius attended private schools in New York City and Geneva, Switzerland (1873), and the Handelschule in Dresden (1875–81), where he studied languages and began his elementary art training. Upon returning to America, he followed his father's wishes that he enter business and worked briefly as a bookkeeper for a wholesale house, then (1882) began the study of agriculture at Cornell University. He left after two years without completing a degree when his prodigious outpouring of poetry, drawings, and watercolors convinced his father that he was destined for a career in the arts.

From 1884 to 1886 Eilshemius studied at the Art Students' League in New York, but, disliking the formal instruction, came mainly under the influence of Robert C. Minor [q.v.]. His early work reflected the cool lyricism and hazy masses of Minor's Barbizon-influenced style and adapted in a personal way his teacher's selective approach to subject matter. Despite two years in Paris (1886–88) at the classical Académie Julian under Adolphe Bouguereau, these tendencies in Eilshemius's painting intensified as he became attracted to Corot's work and studied in Belgium with Minor's teacher, Gérard van Luppen. In 1887 one of Eilshemius's paintings was accepted at the National Academy of Design, and two were exhibited the following year. In 1890 and 1891 he was represented at the Pennsylvania Academy of the Fine Arts. No further showings followed, however, and when the attention and sales for which he had hoped failed to materialize, he simplified his name to "Elshemus," in a vain attempt to remove an obstacle to his success. (He resumed the original spelling about 1914.)

The death of his father in 1892 left Eilshemius with the means to maintain a studio in New York, live modestly, and travel widely. The years 1892–94 were spent sketching, painting, and writing poetry in Europe and North Africa. In 1901 and 1902 Eilshemius traveled to Samoa and the South Seas, as well as in the Southern United States and Europe; many of his finest paintings were done at this time. After 1895, privately printed volumes of his writings began to appear: more than a dozen volumes of poetry, two of short stories, a novel, and various essays and musical compositions. The recognition he sought still eluded him, and the continuing frustration took its toll. Bombarding newspapers with hundreds of letters and eccentric accounts of his greatness, he became known as the "Mahatma of Manhattan's Montparnasse" and the "Transcendental Eagle of the Arts."

Eilshemius's seemingly offhand, spontaneous, and simplified style was distrusted by fellow artists, critics, and the public alike, until in 1917 Marcel Duchamp called "Supplication" one of the two really important paintings shown at the Society of Independent Artists. Even this acclaim, and one-man shows at Duchamp's Société Anonyme (1920, 1924) and the Valentine Gallery (1926), failed to attract the public to Eilshemius's accumulating oeuvre. His last efforts were swiftly executed and qualitatively uneven "unpremeditated paintings"; although misunderstood at the time, they seem in retrospect almost to foreshadow some of the later avant-garde movements in American art. In 1921, at the age of fifty-seven, deeply discouraged, Eilshemius gave up painting for good. He was permanently paralyzed by an automobile accident in 1932. At about this time his work suddenly came into vogue. Between 1932 and 1941 he received more than twenty-five one-man exhibitions in New York, with enormous gallery sales and publicity. After over forty years, the art world had come to recognize, and a few enthusiasts to accept without reservation, the essentially romantic quality of his poetic landscapes, his melodramatically fierce canvases, and, particularly, his lyrical and magically disturbing nudes. But illness, shrinking income, and increasing irascibility confined Eilshemius to his home and prevented him from enjoying this final decade of success. In December 1941, having contracted pneumonia, Eilshemius was sent to Bellevue Hospital in New York City, where he died after twelve days. He was buried at Greenwood Cemetery in Brooklyn.

[No systematic assessment of the actual sources of Eilshemius's style or his influence on subsequent painters has yet been undertaken. Useful references include: William Schack, *And He Sat among the Ashes* (1939), a biography of Eilshemius written during his lifetime; Hugh Stix, *Masterpieces of Eilshemius* (1959), with bibliography; and Roy R. Neuberger, *The Neuberger Collection* (1968). Each contains numerous illustrations. See also *N. Y. Times* obituary, Dec. 30, 1941; and Henry McBride, "The Discovery of Louis Eilshemius," *The Arts*, Dec. 1926. Excellent likenesses of Eilshemius exist: a portrait by Milton Avery, reproduced in Hilton Kramer, *Milton Avery: Paintings, 1930–1956* (1962), and a photograph by Carl Van Vechten in the Schack biography. Paintings by Eilshemius are held by many major museums and collectors, especially the Whitney Museum of Am. Art, the Phillips Gallery in Washington, D. C., and the Roy R. Neuberger Collection.]

ROBERT BARTLETT HAAS

ELLIOTT, JOHN LOVEJOY (Dec. 2, 1868–Apr. 12, 1942), social worker and Ethical Culture leader, was born in the prairie town of Princeton, Ill., the first of the four sons of Elizabeth (Denham) and Isaac Hughes Elliott. His father, of Scotch-Irish descent, had graduated from the University of Michigan in 1861 before enlisting as a captain in the 33rd Illinois Regiment during the Civil War. He rose to the rank of brigadier general and, after the war, settled in his native Princeton, where he eked out a living as a struggling farmer and married a stepdaughter of the abolitionist Owen Lovejoy [q.v.]. From both parents young Elliott acquired a fierce independence of character and a passion for learning, and from Robert Ingersoll [q.v.], his father's friend and a regular guest in the Elliott home, he derived many of his social and religious views.

Elliott attended local schools and then worked his way through Cornell University in Ithaca, N. Y. Although his undergraduate record was generally undistinguished, he was popular with fellow students, who elected him president of his senior class. At Cornell he also came under the influence of Felix Adler [Supp. 1], who was several times invited to the university to speak on the Ethical Culture movement. Elliott graduated in 1892 and, after two years in Germany at the University of Halle, where he wrote a thesis on "Prisons as Reformatories" and earned a Ph.D. in philosophy, he became Adler's assistant and protégé in New York City. There he settled into a round of activities as teacher, lecturer, scholar, and organizer for the Society for Ethical Culture, activities that put him in daily contact with stimulating persons in the arts, society, and politics.

In New York he also moved among the disadvantaged, observing firsthand the desperate social conditions of the poor, especially the immigrant poor, in their dilapidated and noisome neighborhoods. As was the case with many young idealists of that generation, his conscience would not permit him to live sheltered from hardships suffered by others, and in 1895 he founded one of the great early settlement houses, the Hudson Guild, in the Chelsea district on the West Side of Manhattan, then a predominantly Irish neighborhood. The Guild's programs began modestly enough with boys' clubs and a kindergarten for the children of working mothers, but soon branched out to include a printshop for training children as apprentices, a cooperative store, an employment bureau for unskilled women, and a 500-acre New Jersey farm worked by Guild families. There were also free outdoor movies in the summer, sports, crafts, dramatic productions, music, domestic science classes, citizenship courses, health clinics, guided trips to libraries and museums, and summer camps. Elliott insisted upon the participation of the neighbors themselves in the governance of settlement house affairs. The chief purpose of the Hudson Guild, one that transcended all of the programs, was "to develop the

latent social power in the men and women, the boys and the girls." It was a method and a principle to which Elliott himself could not always adhere, for however deeply he was committed to democratic ways, to self-determination of persons and communities, he was by temperament impatient and, when frustrated, given to sudden, violent fits of temper. His friends and acquaintances, however, remembered most vividly the spontaneity and infectious quality of his laugh.

Though Elliott devoted himself to the Hudson Guild, he continued his duties at the Society for Ethical Culture, and in 1933, following Felix Adler's death, he became its senior leader. He taught classes in ethics, spoke before groups, and officiated at marriages and burials. Both aspects of his career led him naturally to the espousal of social reform: mothers' pensions, juvenile courts, and prison reform during the Progressive Era; relief, conservation, and old age and unemployment insurance during the New Deal. He was one of the chief founders of the American Civil Liberties Union (1920) and served actively on its board until his death. In 1938, moved by the plight of refugees escaping to America from tyranny in central Europe, he became the initiator and chairman of the Good Neighbor Committee, which labored into the war years to assist émigrés in finding jobs and in making places for themselves in their new communities. Loyal to his profession, Elliott served as president of the National Federation of Settlements, 1919–23, and later as head of the United Neighborhood Houses of New York. He was also a member of the State Committee on Education and the New York City Council of Social Agencies.

Elliott never married, perhaps, as his biographer suggests, because he could not find a woman quite the equal of his mother. A man of deep passions, he loved both contemplation and action. He was a naturally provocative and skilled teacher who was happiest when working with children. Administration was not his long suit; he chafed under the routine of having to keep Hudson Guild going. He died at the age of seventy-three in Mount Sinai Hospital, New York City; his ashes were buried in Mount Pleasant Cemetery, Hawthorne, N. Y.

[Tay Hohoff, *A Ministry to Man: The Life of John Lovejoy Elliott* (1959), a popular biography; and the chapter on Elliott in Howard B. Radest, *Toward Common Ground: The Story of the Ethical Societies in the U. S.* (1969), are the best sources. There are numerous articles by and about Elliott in the *Survey* and *Survey Graphic*, the *Proc.* of the Nat. Conference of Social Work, the *N. Y. Times*, and other periodicals. On his father, see H. C. Bradsby, ed., *Hist. of Bureau County* (1885), p. 513. Two folders of Elliott's correspondence, 1931–42, are in the papers of the Survey Associates; one folder, 1915–42, in the papers of the Nat. Federation of Settlements; and some scattered correspondence in the papers of the United Neighborhood Houses of N. Y.—all in the Social Welfare Hist. Archives Center, Univ. of Minn.]

CLARKE A. CHAMBERS

ELLIS, CARLETON (Sept. 20, 1876–Jan. 13, 1941), chemist and inventor, was born in Keene, N. H., to Marcus Ellis, a florist, and Catharine (Goodnow) Ellis. His paternal ancestor, Richard Ellis, had left England in 1632 and was one of the original settlers of Dedham, Mass. A camera which Carleton's father gave him on his eleventh birthday aroused the boy's interest in the chemical reactions involved in photography. After graduating from the Keene high school he entered the Massachusetts Institute of Technology, planning to become a research chemist; he received the B.S. degree in 1900 and stayed on for two more years as an instructor.

During his senior year at M.I.T., Ellis had conceived his first invention, a compound for removing paint and varnish. Lacking money to hire legal assistance, he studied patent law, prepared his own application, and was granted the patent. In 1902, with borrowed funds, he began manufacturing the compound in an old shed in Dedham, Mass. The receipt of his first big order, from the Pennsylvania Railroad for a carload lot, assured the success of the venture. Ellis joined forces with competitors in 1905 to form the Chadeloid Chemical Company, a patent holding and licensing company, which took over his patent and many others relating to paint and varnish removers and achieved financial success. His compound proved to be the most effective yet devised and came into worldwide use.

In 1907, with Nathaniel L. Foster, Ellis founded the Ellis-Foster Company to carry on research in industrial chemistry and to patent the results. With laboratories in both Montclair, N. J., and Key West, Fla., and a large staff of chemists and engineers, Ellis produced an average of more than two inventions each month during the next twenty-five years. His patented processes were incorporated into nearly every area of applied chemistry. In 1913 he patented a method for the hydrogenation of vegetable oils, a process that made possible the cheap production of an improved oleomargarine and became the basis for the margarine industry and for the production of other hydrogenated-oil shortenings.

Ellis's best-known research was that relating to petroleum; some 200 of his patents fall in this field. The most important of these inventions, in his own judgment, was the "tube and tank process" of cracking crude oil (1919), one of the half-dozen early cracking processes that proved commercially successful. The Standard Oil Company of New Jersey took over Ellis's invention, and by 1940 over forty billion gallons of gasoline had been produced through its use. During World War I, Ellis synthesized the commercially valuable isopropyl alcohol (later widely used as an automobile antifreeze) from the waste gases produced in the cracking of oil. He also invented a process for the preparation of acetone—then in wartime demand—by the catalytic oxidation of isopropyl alcohol, selling the patent rights to Standard Oil. With the aid of other research by Ellis, automobile manufacturers were able to increase the power of engines and gasoline refiners to achieve higher-octane gasolines.

The paint and varnish field continued to be of major concern to Ellis. Hoping to compound the perfect paint, he tried and rejected all the natural oils and resins and then turned to synthetic ones. In 1925 he produced the first durable lacquer for automobile paint, a combination of synthetic tung oil, soy beans, and synthetic resins that he had developed. These synthetic products saved the American paint industry from paralysis when the import of natural oils and resins from China was curtailed by the Sino-Japanese conflict. About 300 of Ellis's patents dealt with resins and resulted in hundreds of improvements in paints and lacquers.

Research on synthetic resins led Ellis into the field of plastics. Observing the development of a successful phenolic resin plastic by Leo Baekeland [Supp. 3], and noting European experiments with urea-formaldehyde resins, Ellis sensed that urea-formaldehyde would also become a molding material. The processes he developed and patented were the basis for the Unyte Corporation (1932), of which he was one-third owner; by 1935 his inventions in this field had gained him a large personal fortune. During his last years Ellis devoted himself to research on methods of producing vegetables and flowers grown in chemical solutions instead of in soil; his book *Soilless Growth of Plants* (1938) became a standard work on the subject.

Ellis was granted 753 United States patents, at the time of his death the third highest number granted to any individual. Among his last inventions were a fireproof coating for war planes to protect against incendiary bullets and an instant-drying ink for newspaper printing. His publications made basic contributions to the literature of industrial chemistry. Ellis's books include *The Hydrogenation of Oils* (1914); *Gasoline and Other Motor Fuels* (1921), with Joseph V. Meigs; *Synthetic Resins and Their Plastics*

(1923); *The Chemical Action of Ultraviolet Rays* (1925), with Alfred A. Wells; *The Chemistry of Petroleum Derivatives* (2 vols., 1934–37); *The Chemistry of Synthetic Resins* (2 vols., 1935); and *Printing Inks: Their Chemistry and Technology* (1940). He was a charter member of the Inventors' Guild and belonged to a number of professional organizations. His honors include the Edward Longstreth Medal of the Franklin Institute (1916).

Ellis married Birdella May Wood of Dayton, Ohio, on Nov. 28, 1901. They had four children: Eleanor Josephine, Marjorie Olive, Carleton, and Bertram. The family lived in Montclair, N. J., and had a summer home in Hyannis Port, Mass., and a winter home in Nassau, Bahama Islands. Ellis was a Congregationalist. During the last two years of his life he suffered from poor health, and a few months after his sixty-fourth birthday, while traveling to Nassau, he developed influenza. He died in the St. Francis Hospital at Miami Beach, Fla., and was buried in Montclair.

[*Nat. Cyc. Am. Biog.*, XXXII, 33–34; *Chemical Industries*, Apr. 1940, p. 488; *Industrial and Engineering Chemistry (News Edition)*, June 20, 1936; *Who Was Who in America*, vol. I (1942); *N. Y. Times*, Jan. 14, 1941. See also references to Ellis's work in Williams Haynes, *Am. Chemical Industry*, III (1945), 146–48, IV (1948), 392–93, and VI (1949), 399; and, on his role in the plastics industry, *Fortune*, Mar. 1936, pp. 69–75, 143–50.]

ALBERT B. COSTA

ELY, RICHARD THEODORE (Apr. 13, 1854–Oct. 4, 1943), economist and reformer, was born in Ripley, N. Y., the eldest of three children (two boys and a girl) of Ezra Sterling Ely, a self-educated civil engineer, and Harriet Gardner (Mason) Ely. Both parents came of New England stock. The father, descended from a partisan of Oliver Cromwell who had fled from England in the 1660's and settled in Connecticut, was a rigidly devout Presbyterian with a concern for equality and social reform. The mother, a former schoolteacher and an amateur artist, was an energetic and affectionate woman who tempered her husband's religious austerity. Shortly after Richard's birth, the family moved to a farm near Fredonia, N. Y. Young Ely attended local public schools and the Fredonia Academy, and in 1871 taught at a country school at nearby Mayville. In 1872 he entered Dartmouth College, but transferred after a year to Columbia, from which he received a B.A. degree in 1876.

A Columbia scholarship took him next to Germany to study philosophy at the University of Halle. There he met Simon N. Patten [*q.v.*], who introduced him to Prof. Johannes Conrad, an expert on agrarian economics and a member of the German historical school of economics. This school rejected the classicists' mechanistic and deductive approach with its fixed and individualistic concepts of property, wages, and economic law and instead viewed economic behavior as a matter of cultural patterns and governmental policy. Increasingly excited by economics, Ely soon moved to the University of Heidelberg, where he studied under Karl Knies, a leading historical economist, and received the Ph.D., summa cum laude in 1879. After an additional year of study at the universities of Geneva and Berlin, he returned to the United States. In 1881 he joined the faculty of Johns Hopkins University in Baltimore as a lecturer on political economy, and by 1887 rose to the rank of associate professor. Meanwhile, on a vacation trip to Virginia, he met Anna Morris Anderson, daughter of one of the state's "first families," and on June 25, 1884, they were married. They had four children: Richard Sterling, Josephine Anderson (who died in infancy), John Thomas Anderson, and Anna Mason.

At Johns Hopkins, Ely became a leader in the development of the "new economics," numbering among his students John R. Commons [Supp. 3], Edward A. Ross, and Woodrow Wilson. He cooperated with other young foes of the classical school in organizing the American Economic Association in 1885, then served as its secretary (1885–92) and eventually as its president (1900–01). Ely believed that the inductive methods of modern science would, if applied to economics, help rectify the errors of the classical school. Economic principles, he thought, were not governed by natural law and must be grounded in the real needs of society in a particular time and place; they must change as society changes. Rejecting the laissez-faire and self-interest arguments of the disciples of Herbert Spencer, he viewed society as an organic whole in which all the parts were interdependent. He scoffed at the notion that social regulation would lead to slavery, and argued that unfettered individualism was a threat to social cohesion. In Ely's opinion, the state, as the most important instrument of the social organism, should play a positive role in the economy. He envisioned the eventual advent, through evolutionary stages, of a cooperative commonwealth. For the meantime he advocated such reforms as factory regulation, recognition of the rights of labor unions, slum clearance, immigration restriction, and working-class savings banks.

In his approach to economics, Ely was a forerunner of such twentieth-century institutional economists as Thorstein Veblen, Wesley C. Mitchell, and his own protégé, Commons. Yet unlike most of these, Ely included religious and ethical convictions as integral parts of his social and economic outlook. Having abandoned the strict Presbyterianism of his father, he became an Episcopalian with a strongly social gospel outlook. He was a personal friend of almost every prominent social gospel minister and frequently addressed religious groups on social topics. He popularized the views of English Christian Socialists. He influenced many future clergymen through his lectures at the Chautauqua summer school. And with the Rev. William D. P. Bliss [*q.v.*] he helped form the Episcopal Church's Christian Social Union, serving as its first secretary (1891–94). Ely consistently urged the churches not to align themselves with the apostles of the status quo. "It is the mission of Christianity," he said, "to bring to pass here a kingdom of righteousness" (*The Social Aspects of Christianity*, 1889, p. 53). Indeed, Christianity provided the single unifying theme to Ely's work. In his view economic rules were flexible, but the Christian concept of "brotherhood" was an immutable part of man's nature.

During the 1880's Ely applied his economic and religious beliefs to the support of peaceful unionism, particularly that of the Knights of Labor. In *The Labor Movement in America* (1886) he attacked the classicists' axioms that labor was merely a commodity, subject to the laws of supply and demand, and that under the existing system unorganized workers were free and equal parties to a contract. Labor unions, he maintained, brought workingmen into a more equitable relationship with employers and thus helped close the growing rift between the two classes. They also served an educational and moral function, and in their emphasis on brotherhood they were a potential mainstay of social harmony.

Now much in demand as a writer and lecturer, Ely won a broad hearing for the new ethical economics. But his support of trade unions brought intense criticism from conservatives and genteel reformers alike, who often spoke through the pages of the *Nation* as edited by E. L. Godkin [*q.v.*]. Ely moved in 1892 to the University of Wisconsin as director of its new School of Economics, Political Science, and History. Two years later the *Nation* published a letter ostensibly written by Wisconsin's pugnacious state superintendent of education, Oliver E. Wells, charging that Ely had given advice to a strike organizer during a local labor dispute, and that he subtly taught socialism. After the celebrated hearing, the university regents vindicated him and grandly asserted the academic right of an untrammeled "winnowing and sifting" of truth. Their lofty rhetoric won him a place in the annals of academic freedom.

Actually, however, Ely had based his defense not on the right of academic freedom but on a denial of the charges. For Ely was by no means as radical as his critics assumed. With the decline of the Knights of Labor in 1886–87 he had lost faith in the inevitability of the cooperative commonwealth. Recurrent labor strife of the early 1890's seemed to him a serious threat to social harmony. By 1890 he called himself a "Progressive Conservative," and such socialism as he continued to advocate was most Fabian-like. Experience as a member of Baltimore (1885) and Maryland (1886) tax commissions had caused him more and more to think at the level of very specific reforms, of the "gas-and-water" variety. In *Socialism and Social Reform* (as his *Socialism: An Examination of Its Nature, Its Strength and Its Weakness, with Suggestions for Social Reform* was commonly called), published in 1894 just months before his academic freedom trial, he called for socialization of natural monopolies such as public utilities, telephones, railroads, and mineral deposits; but he declared that many activities of industrial life were best carried out under a system of competitive private ownership. And even his arguments for public ownership of monopolies included a conservative strain: disliking the disorder of strikes, Ely reasoned that where socialization made public employees of workers, labor and management would have to settle their disputes through orderly negotiation.

By temperament and ideology, Ely seemed unable to work with farmer-labor organizations. He felt more comfortable with the middle-class reformers and Christian Socialists to whom he addressed his writings. In 1894 he described himself as an "aristocrat rather than a democrat," and he believed that the working classes must accept the leadership of an elite of intellect and achievement. After the mid-1890's he did less popularizing of reform and returned to more "academic" activities.

Short, awkward, and often quarrelsome, Ely was always ambitious, and for a time at Wisconsin he proved an adroit practitioner of academic politics. He continued to have some interest in labor-related reform and in 1906 became the first president of the American Association for Labor Legislation. With the election in 1900 of Robert M. La Follette [*q.v.*] as governor of Wisconsin, the University of Wisconsin became an important ally of the state government in progressive advance. Along with many of his colleagues, Ely served as an informal adviser to La Follette in the development of the policies that were known as the "Wisconsin idea." But with the outbreak of World War I, Ely became an ardent supporter of preparedness and of American participation, and over these issues he broke with La Follette. Through organizations like the Loyalty League and the National League to Enforce Peace, he even helped wage a bitter campaign in 1918 to defeat La Follette's bid for reelection to the United States Senate.

Moreover, by this time Ely had again shifted his attention to a new set of ideas, ideas that eventually led to a break with many old friends and with the university that had been his base for a third of a century. As a student in Germany he had been exposed to discussions of governmental land policy, and in his tax commission work in Maryland he had studied the issue firsthand. Later, to augment his income, he had privately engaged in land speculation, so extensively that by 1914 he had organized five different realty companies with land as far afield as Canada and Washington state. In 1916 Ely read a paper before a section of the American Economic Association calling for a more sophisticated land economics. Ever the empire builder, he helped organize the American Association for Agricultural Legislation in 1917, and three years later his own Institute for Research in Land Economics (later renamed the Institute for Research in Land Economics and Public Utilities). He now developed a doctrine of rent or of "ripening costs" which justified private receipt of the increment when land appreciated in value as a result of socially induced changes. His doctrine angered single-taxers but pleased some business interests. Ely established close liaisons with the National Association of Real Estate Boards and leading public utility executives, who in turn helped finance his researches. Although the Institute published material not altogether to its sponsors' liking, on at least one occasion Ely revised a textbook to make it more palatable to public utility men (Rader, pp. 224–26).

In 1925, under attack from Senator La Follette and Wisconsin single-tax forces, Ely moved his Institute to Northwestern University in Evanston, Ill. In its new location, more advantageous for urban land studies, the Institute expanded its operations and began publishing the *Journal of Land & Public Utility Economics*. These activities even became the catalyst for Ely's remarriage (his first wife having died in 1923): on Aug. 8, 1931, at seventy-seven, he wed Margaret Hale Hahn, a thirty-two-year-old member of his staff and a former student, who bore him two more children, William Brewster and Mary Charlotte. But in the early 1930's support for the Institute ebbed. In 1932 Ely moved a reduced

operation to New York City, and later he retired to the town of his ancestors, Old Lyme, Conn. There, at the age of eighty-nine, he died of coronary arteriosclerosis. His ashes were interred at Forest Hill Cemetery, Madison, Wis.

Ely had helped spread anti-laissez-faire ideas among the more sophisticated reading public, but he had not been the man to implement those ideas. He was too frequently caught between his reform impulses and his desire for personal approval from middle-class intellectuals (see Rader, pp. 157–58). Furthermore, with his Bismarck-like views of authority and the state and his philosophical elitism, he did not speak fully in an American idiom. His relationship with the progressive movement of his day was, therefore, ambiguous. Yet Ely's reformism was not. He ceased to advocate gas-and-water socialism; but in his land economics he strongly emphasized that government should plan and develop land use, and he continued to advocate outright government ownership of various mineral, forest, and other lands. Indeed, in view of the industrialized economy's assault on man's environment, his call for intelligent land use may have been more prophetic than his labor reformism. In 1938, at eighty-four, he affirmed that he was "still fired by an ambition to 'set the world right,' just as my father before me" (*Ground Under Our Feet*, p. 250).

[The State Hist. Soc. of Wis. has a rich collection of Ely's papers (254 boxes), as well as papers of a number of his associates. The Ely Papers have been extensively used in Benjamin G. Rader's full and balanced biography, *The Academic Mind and Reform: The Influence of Richard T. Ely in Am. Life* (1966). Ely left a self-congratulatory but useful account of his own life in his *Ground Under Our Feet* (1938). His other numerous works include *The Past and Present of Political Economy* (1884); *Studies in the Evolution of an Industrial Society* (1903); *Property and Contract in Their Relations to the Distribution of Wealth* (2 vols., 1914); *Land Economics* (with George S. Wehrwein, 1928); and his popular elementary economics textbook, *Outlines of Economics* (1893 and later editions). Among his articles deserving special mention are "A Programme for Labor Reform" (with Seth Low), *Century*, Apr. 1890; "Fundamental Beliefs in My Social Philosophy," *Forum*, Oct. 1894; "Landed Property as an Economic Concept and as a Field of Research," *Am. Econ. Rev.*, Mar. 1917 (Suppl.); "Research in Land and Public Utility Economics," *Jour. of Land & Public Utility Economics*, Jan. 1925; and, to demonstrate how conservative Ely could be for certain audiences, "Robber Taxes," *Country Gentleman*, July 12, 1924. For interpretive synopses of Ely's ideas, see David W. Noble, *The Paradox of Progressive Thought* (1958); Sidney Fine, *Laissez Faire and the General-Welfare State: A Study of Conflict in Am. Thought, 1865–1901* (1956); Allan G. Gruchy, *Modern Economic Thought* (1947); and vols. III-V of Joseph Dorfman's *The Economic Mind in Am. Civilization* (1959). A useful work on the context of economic thought out of which Ely's ideas arose is Dorfman's essay in Dorfman et al., *Institutional Economics* (1963). Henry C. and Anne Dewees Taylor, *The Story of Agricultural Economics in the United States, 1840–1932* (1952), includes material on the evolution of

Ely's land economics. Hugh Hawkins, *Pioneer: A Hist. of the Johns Hopkins Univ., 1874–1889* (1960), and Merle Curti and Vernon Carstensen, *The Univ. of Wis.: A Hist., 1848–1925* (1949), describe the universities in which Ely worked, with frequent references to him. The primary documents of his academic freedom "trial" are among the records of the Univ. of Wis. Regents, in the Univ. Archives; Theron F. Schlabach has told the story, and summarized Ely's social outlook, in "An Aristocrat on Trial: The Case of Richard T. Ely," *Wis. Mag. of Hist.*, Winter 1963-64. Theodore Herfurth's booklet, *Sifting and Winnowing: A Chapter in the Hist. of Academic Freedom at the Univ. of Wis.* (1949), recounts the origin and history of the regents' bold statement. Genealogical information may be found in Moses S. Beach and William Ely, *The Ely Ancestry* (1902). Portraits of Ely are in the State Hist. Soc. of Wis.'s Iconographic Collection and in the Univ. of Wis. Archives.]

THERON F. SCHLABACH

EMMET, WILLIAM LE ROY (July 10, 1859–Sept. 26, 1941), electrical and mechanical engineer, was born on Travers Island near what is now New Rochelle, N. Y., the second of six sons and fourth of ten children of William Jenkins Emmet and Julia Colt (Pierson) Emmet. His great-grandfather was Thomas Addis Emmet (1764–1827) [*q.v.*], noted Irish patriot, whose brother Robert was the tragic hero of an ill-fated Irish uprising. His grandfather, also named Robert, was a noted lawyer and judge. His father operated a sugar business successfully during the Civil War, but its failure shortly after left the family in chronically straitened financial circumstances. Emmet later characterized his mother, the granddaughter of Jeremiah H. Pierson, Congressman from New Jersey and prominent Ramapo Valley mill operator, as a "beautiful" woman of "extraordinary intelligence and exalted ideals." The playwright Robert E. Sherwood was one of his nephews.

During a happy childhood in rural Westchester County, Emmet developed a lifelong fondness for nature, fishing, sports, and music. He was an indifferent student in three elementary schools. Financial stringency led him to apply to the United States Naval Academy, where, after first failing the admissions examination and taking work at the Maryland Agricultural College, he was admitted in 1876. He graduated fifty-fourth in a class of seventy-six in 1881. Naval retrenchment brought about his discharge in 1883, although he served during the Spanish-American War as navigator on a collier and during World War I as a member of the Naval Consulting Board.

Between 1883 and 1891 Emmet held various posts, the most important being with Frank J. Sprague [Supp. 1], pioneer in electric traction, for whom he did installing and troubleshooting on electric street railways in various cities. The job confirmed Emmet's interest in electrical en-

gineering. In 1891 he joined Samuel Insull [Supp. 2] and the Edison General Electric Company in Chicago. He moved the following year to the New York offices of the newly organized General Electric Company and in 1894 to its Schenectady plant, where he remained until retirement.

During his early years, Emmet was responsible for a variety of technical improvements in electrical apparatus. While working for Sprague he improved motors, patented a new trolley device, and contrived a superior insulating material of varnished cambric, a material he developed further in his years with General Electric. His interest in electric distribution problems led to a pioneering text, *Alternating Current Wiring and Distribution* (1894). With E. M. Hewlett he developed oil switches, essential for high-voltage work. For about a decade Emmet was responsible for G.E.'s participation in the epochal Niagara Falls power project; his converters, transmission lines, and generators contributed significantly to its success.

About 1899 Emmet turned his attention to steam turbines, particularly as a source of power for electric generators. Working with Charles G. Curtis, he was chiefly responsible for developing the first two generations of successful steam turbines which, in less than a decade, effectively eliminated reciprocating engines as prime movers in steam generating plants. Emmet also helped introduce mica tape insulation and improved cooling systems in generators which developed insulation breakdowns from high-speed high-temperature operation.

By 1909 the steam turbine had achieved such economies that Emmet began to campaign for turbine-generated electrical propulsion on ships. His initial installation on the 20,000-ton naval collier *Jupiter* proved more efficient than reciprocating engines and both more efficient and more reliable than geared turbine engines. During World War I, General Electric provided Emmet-designed geared turbines for some three hundred merchant ships and fifty destroyers and subsequently produced turbo-electric drives for the new battleship *New Mexico* and for the two battle cruisers that were ultimately converted into the aircraft carriers *Lexington* and *Saratoga*.

Emmet's later years were devoted to the mercury vapor turbine. Mercury with its high boiling point and other physical properties offered substantial theoretical promise as a thermodynamic fluid in very high temperature ranges, but the long and costly development of a practical device extended beyond Emmet's lifetime. Between 1928 and 1949 General Electric built eight mercury-steam generating plants, including developmental models. The designs were technically sound and economically efficient, but the development of very-high-pressure high-temperature steam turbines doomed the mercury-vapor engines to economic extinction.

In large degree self-taught, Emmet had a profound faith in experimentation. But he also respected and made good use of both theory and mathematics. Persistent and determined, he deeply believed the secret of engineering success to be close attention to detail. A thoroughgoing individualist who argued that creative ideas came from individuals, not committees, he nevertheless recognized the necessity for large organizations and won the confidence and support of his superiors in General Electric, who gave him substantial independence in his work. His achievements earned him election to the American Philosophical Society (1898) and the National Academy of Sciences (1921), two honorary degrees, and several important scientific medals, including the Edison Medal of the American Institute of Electrical Engineers (1919), the Elliott Cresson Medal of the Franklin Institute (1920), and the David W. Taylor Medal of the American Society of Naval Architects and Marine Engineers (1938).

Emmet never married; he lived successively with two of his brothers and a nephew. During his youth he was, he reports, a deeply religious Anglican, but in later years religion played little part in his life. He died at the age of eighty-two at his nephew's home in Erie, Pa. He was buried in Arlington National Cemetery.

[William Le Roy Emmet, *The Autobiog. of an Engineer* (2nd ed., 1940), is full, interesting, and candid and includes some interesting photographs. Willis R. Whitney's memoir in Nat. Acad. Sci., *Biog. Memoirs,* vol. XXII (1943), though written by an eminent scientist who knew and admired Emmet, is disappointingly insubstantial; it includes a partial list of Emmet's more than forty journal articles but none of his 122 patents. A better memoir by the same author is in the *Year Book* of the Am. Philosophical Soc. for 1941. See also: *Who Was Who in America,* vol. I (1942); *Am. Men of Sci.* (6th ed., 1938); *Nat. Cyc. Am. Biog.,* XXX, 96–97; obituary in *N. Y. Times,* Sept. 27, 1941; and, on his forebears, Thomas A. Emmet, *The Emmet Family* (1898). Other information from Registrar, U. S. Naval Acad., and C. E. Kilbourne, Gen. Electric Co. *Power Generation,* Mar. 1950, describes most of the mercury vapor steam generating plants put into service.]
KENDALL BIRR

ENGEL, CARL (July 21, 1883–May 6, 1944), musicologist and composer, was born in Paris, France, one of at least three children of German parents, Joseph C. and Gertrude (Seeger) Engel. He came of a musical family. One of his great-grandfathers, Joseph Kroll, founded Kroll's Etablissement, a Berlin concert garden

for summer opera, which Engel's grandfather J. C. Engel helped make internationally famous. Young Engel, a Catholic by upbringing, studied at humanistic Gymnasiums in Germany and attended classes at the universities of Strassburg and Munich, specializing in music, philosophy, and literature. He studied violin with Fabian Rehfeld (Berlin), piano with Lina Schmalhausen (Strassburg), and composition with Ludwig Thuille (Munich).

When Engel moved to the United States with his family in 1905, he had already begun to publish his compositions. He quickly became a part of the musical world of New York and in the first winter was given a performance of his song cycle, "Rubáiyát of a Persian Kitten," with text by Oliver Herford [Supp. 1]. In 1909 Engel went to Boston to discuss some of his compositions with Charles Martin Loeffler [Supp. 1] of the Boston Symphony, and remained to become adviser and editor on the staff of the Boston Music Company, founded in 1885 by the younger Gustave Schirmer. Over the next twelve years Engel directed the publishing policy of the firm and continued his own composing of piano, violin, and vocal works, which included "Perfumes," for the piano, and "Triptych," for violin and piano (1920). During these years he also began writing criticism and reviews for the *Atlantic Monthly* and the *Boston Transcript,* his wit and musical judgment attracting wide attention.

A thoroughly trained and highly gifted musician, Engel was called from Boston to the Library of Congress in Washington as chief of the Music Division, a position he held from Jan. 1, 1922, until June 30, 1934. As the brilliant successor to Oscar G. T. Sonneck [q.v.], he maintained the collections and service at the highest level. Believing that the library's function should be not only to collect music but also to make it heard, Engel encouraged Mrs. Elizabeth Sprague Coolidge in her organizing of the chamber music concerts given at the Freer Gallery of Art (1924) and in her later establishment (1925) of a permanent foundation to provide musical performances under the auspices of the Library of Congress. He also established (1929) the Friends of Music in the Library of Congress, through which he secured many gifts. Wishing to preserve the varied musical traditions of the country, he instituted (1928) the collection and recording of American folk songs and ballads, then a largely neglected field of scholarship. He worked tirelessly to promote the study of music in America, his effort to induce universities to add musicology courses to their curricula being particularly effective. His urbane annual reports set a new standard for serious reading made pleasurable.

In 1929 Engel succeeded Oscar Sonneck as editor of the *Musical Quarterly,* for which he wrote many scintillating articles. His "Views and Reviews" in this journal were brilliant, witty, and well reasoned; they were the despair of those whom he attacked, the glory of those whom he praised. His more formal articles for the magazine were equally expert, products of a master pen and a penetrating mind. From 1929 to 1932 Engel was given leave of absence from the Library of Congress to become president of the New York music publishing house of G. Schirmer, Inc. He was urged to take the presidency on a permanent basis, and though reluctant to leave the congenial scholarly setting of the Library of Congress, he ultimately accepted. He directed this important firm from 1934 until his death.

In addition to his writings in the *Musical Quarterly,* Engel issued two volumes of essays on musical topics, *Alla Breve* (1921) and *Discords Mingled* (1931), besides contributing to many musical and other journals. His administrative and literary responsibilities unfortunately left him little time for writing music. He was a thoroughly accomplished composer, whose works were more French than German in idiom and impressionistic in effect. Several piano solos and a number of songs, particularly settings for poems by Amy Lowell [*q.v.*]—with whom he had established a friendship early in his Boston stay—attest to his creative sensitivity.

In person Engel was extremely temperamental, calm and placid at one moment, at another fiery, exuberant, sarcastic, or bitter, but his warm heart and a fundamental sense of fairness endeared him to his colleagues. He was widely read in French, German, English, and American literature, and this broad cultural background widened his sympathies as a critic of music and musical trends. He was also helpful, understanding, and encouraging toward younger colleagues. Engel became an American citizen in 1917. On July 29, 1916, he married Abigail Josephine Carey of Boston; they had one daughter, Lisette. Among other distinctions, he was an organizer (1934) of the American Musicological Society and its president in 1937–38; a chevalier of the (French) Legion of Honor (1937); and the recipient of an honorary degree from Oberlin College (1934). Engel died at his home in New York City in 1944 at the age of sixty. His body was cremated and the ashes scattered.

[Gustave Reese, ed., *A Birthday Offering to (C. E.)* (1943), which includes articles on Engel by John Erskine, Harold Spivacke, Norman Peterkin, and Percy Lee Atherton and a selected list of his literary and musical works; Harold Bauer, "Carl Engel," and Gustave Reese, "A Postscript," in *Musical Quart.,* July 1944; Engel's reports as Chief of the Music Division, in Librarian of Cong., *Annual Reports;* obituary in *N. Y. Times,* May 7, 1944.]

EDWARD N. WATERS

ENO, WILLIAM PHELPS (June 3, 1858–Dec. 3, 1945), pioneer in traffic regulation, was born in New York City, the fifth son and youngest of nine children of Lucy Jane (Phelps) and Amos Richards Eno. He came of old New England stock, being a direct descendant of James Enno, who emigrated about 1648 from England to Windsor, Conn., and of William Phelps, one of the first settlers of Windsor. The conservationist Gifford Pinchot and his brother Amos Pinchot [Supp. 3] were Eno's nephews. His parents were both born in Simsbury, Conn., but later moved to New York City. There Amos Eno, a prominent banker and real estate developer, built the original Fifth Avenue Hotel.

During William's youth his family traveled extensively, and by the time he entered Yale in 1878 he had attended some fifteen schools in Europe and America. At the end of his junior year he contracted scarlet fever and withdrew from college. (In 1891, in response to a petition by his classmates, Yale awarded him the B.A. degree as of 1882.) Following a prolonged period of recuperation, he went to work in his father's realty office. His true interest lay elsewhere, however. In his early travels he had been appalled by the chaotic traffic conditions he saw everywhere but in London, where good sense and common courtesy governed the movement of vehicles. When his father died in 1898, leaving him an inheritance of a million dollars, Eno turned to the study of traffic.

Automobiles were then a rarity, but Eno anticipated their future importance and began devising traffic regulations which would serve the long-term needs of American cities. In 1902 he persuaded police authorities in New York City to implement the English block system, in which mounted officers regulated cross traffic at intersections. The following year he published *Rules for Driving,* a pamphlet which for the first time proposed a set of uniform laws for all vehicles, defining the word "vehicle" to include "equestrians and everything on wheels or runners, except street cars and baby carriages." His traffic code laid down basic rules for passing, turning, crossing, and stopping, as well as the use of hand signals and the right of way. The first comprehensive system of traffic regulation in the world, it was officially adopted in October 1903 by New York City. Eno also advocated signal towers, uniform street signs, safety islands for pedestrians, clearly marked crosswalks, special plans to relieve congestion in theatre and business districts, and clearly designated bus and streetcar stops. His most noted contribution, perhaps, was his system of one-way rotary traffic for multiple intersections, which was first put into effect in 1905 at Columbus Circle in New York and later, in 1907, at the Arc de Triomphe in Paris.

Eno attacked other traffic problems in Paris over a period of years beginning in 1909. By distributing copies of a primer entitled "Le Problème de la Circulation" among drivers and the police, and posting placards at stables, garages, and cab stands, he built up public support for a set of police regulations like those in New York and saw them go into effect in 1912. He frequently served as a consultant to municipalities in Asia and Latin America, as well as in the United States and Europe. In 1912 he became chairman of the automobile regulations committee of the National Civic Federation.

During World War I, in addition to serving as director of the Home Defense League of the District of Columbia (his home from 1902 to 1938), Eno headed the committee on transportation of war workers of the War Industries Board, in which capacity he directed the transportation of influenza victims to temporary hospitals. At the same time he devised a traffic code for the Allied forces in France (also used in North Africa during World War II) which facilitated convoy movements and permitted the rapid passage of ambulances. In 1921 he established at Saugatuck, Conn., the Eno Foundation for Highway Traffic Regulation, a nonprofit center for research in traffic engineering, highway design, and traffic enforcement. By publishing the results of this research, and thereby educating the public, Eno hoped to accelerate the pace of traffic reform, the slowness of which he attributed to unimaginative, inexperienced, and, at times, meddlesome public officials.

Through his foundation, which in 1933 became affiliated with Yale University, Eno published several technical books, including *Fundamentals of Highway Traffic Regulation* (1926), *Simplification of Highway Traffic* (1929), and *Uniformity in Highway Traffic Control* (1941). Yet his perspective was never purely technical. He early identified traffic reform with the broader fields of city planning and the reduction of pollution; and in the 1930's he waged a vigorous

antinoise campaign, the major result of which was a ban in Paris on the use of automobile horns. He opposed, however, the use of traffic lights, considering them too inflexible, and continued to prefer the use of policemen to direct traffic.

Eno's white moustache and Vandyke beard gave him an imposing appearance. He received several honors, including election as honorary president of the National Highway Traffic Association (1935) and as a fellow of the New York Academy of Sciences (1937). He was twice married: on Apr. 4, 1883, to Alice Rathbone, who died in 1911, and on Apr. 18, 1934, to Alberta (Averill) Paz, a widow; he had no children. In 1938 Eno moved to Saugatuck, Conn. He died of bronchopneumonia at the Norwalk (Conn.) General Hospital at the age of eighty-seven and was buried in Center Cemetery, Simsbury, Conn.

[Eno's *The Story of Highway Traffic Control, 1899–1939* (1939), a collection of his correspondence interspersed with personal recollections and observations (with portrait); Eno's report of his work in Paris in *Am. City*, Jan. 1914, pp. 41–42; Arno Dosch, "The Science of Street Traffic," *World's Work*, Feb. 1914; various references in *N. Y. Times*, 1914–45 (see Index); articles by and about Eno in the *Rider & Driver*, 1900–14; Henry L. Eno, *The Eno Family, N. Y. Branch* (1920), on his family background; Yale College Class of 1882, *Anniversary Records;* Yale Univ., *Obituary Record of Graduates*, 1945–46; *Who Was Who in America*, vol. II (1950); *Nat. Cyc. Am. Biog.*, XLVII, 613–14; obituaries in *N. Y. Times* and *N. Y. Herald Tribune*, Dec. 4, 1945, and *Traffic Engineering*, Dec. 1945; conversations with Profs. Kent Healy and Fred Hurd; biographical references compiled by Blanche L. Singer, Univ. of Wis. Lib. School.]

MARC ROSS

EPSTEIN, ABRAHAM (Apr. 20, 1892–May 2, 1942), pioneer in the American social insurance movement, was born in Luban, Russia, near Pinsk, the eldest of nine children of Jewish parents, Leon and Bessie (Levovitz) Epstein. His father was an innkeeper, and Epstein grew up in dire poverty. Driven by a burning desire for education, he attended local Hebrew schools and later traveled from village to village as a teacher to earn money for books. During these years he became acquainted with Marxist doctrines, and his early Hebrew education, so he later recalled, stimulated a humanitarian interest in social problems.

With few opportunities open to Jews in Russia, Epstein left in 1910 for the United States. For a year and a half he lived in New York City, attending night school and working at various factory and store jobs which provided only a meager living. A friend then found him a position teaching Hebrew in Pittsburgh, Pa. Soon after his arrival he passed a boys' school and stopped in to inquire about enrolling. It was the East Liberty Academy, an exclusive private school, but the headmaster, impressed by Epstein's earnestness and ability, admitted him and helped him with his studies. A tuition scholarship next enabled him to enter the University of Pittsburgh, from which he graduated in 1917 with the B.S. degree. That same year he became an American citizen. Epstein remained at the university for an additional year of graduate work in economics under Francis D. Tyson and conducted a detailed survey of the employment and housing conditions of Pittsburgh blacks. His report, *The Negro Migrant in Pittsburgh,* was published in 1918. It won him offers of fellowships from several universities, but he accepted instead a position as executive secretary and research director of the Pennsylvania Commission on Old Age Pensions.

This state agency, headed by the Socialist legislator James H. Maurer [Supp. 3], had been created the year before to investigate the problems of the aged and to draft proposed legislation. Save for a frustrating interim (1922–23) with the Fraternal Order of Eagles, a benevolent organization then also seeking pension legislation, Epstein remained with the Commission until 1927. He began by preparing a comprehensive report, based on visits to public almshouses and individual recipients of charity throughout the state. Despite the vigorous opposition of business groups, Epstein helped secure passage of a state-financed old-age pension program in 1923. The legislature, however, failed to appropriate the necessary funds; the pension act was declared unconstitutional in 1924; and when, three years later, the Pennsylvania lawmakers voted down a constitutional amendment that would have authorized such legislation, the state commission came to an end.

Epstein had meanwhile built up a substantial reputation as an expert on social insurance. He reached the general public through his pioneering books *Facing Old Age* (1922) and *The Challenge of the Aged* (1926), through magazine articles, and through frequent talks before labor unions and social welfare groups. Although the American Association for Labor Legislation, led by John B. Andrews [Supp. 3], had been active before World War I in the social insurance movement, Epstein felt its interest had lagged. Upon leaving the Pennsylvania commission in 1927, he therefore founded his own American Association for Old Age Security, with headquarters in New York City. He served as its executive secretary and guiding spirit until his death.

Supported by voluntary contributions, Epstein's association continued to press for old-age pension laws. Six states had such laws in 1928; by 1934, in considerable part through his efforts, the number had grown to twenty-five. Increasingly, however, a cleavage became apparent in the social insurance movement between followers of John B. Andrews and John R. Commons [Supp. 3] on the one hand and Epstein and his associates—including Isaac M. Rubinow [Supp. 2] and the economist Paul H. Douglas—on the other. The Andrews group favored private social insurance programs, run on an actuarial basis, and regarded them simply as means of preventing suffering and destitution. Epstein, drawing on his observations in Europe, believed firmly that such programs should be financed and controlled by the government, and that they should serve a broader social purpose, helping to redistribute wealth and maintain the underprivileged.

The two philosophies came into conflict when public attention, under the impact of depression, turned toward unemployment insurance. Wisconsin in 1932 adopted the "American plan" of Andrews, under which each employer was to maintain his own benefit fund. When a similar bill was introduced in the New York legislature, Epstein and his associates advanced their own "European plan" for a pooled, government-operated fund; after prolonged debate, their proposal was adopted in 1935. In the process, personal bitterness intensified between Andrews and Epstein, a man of strong and passionate convictions.

Having broadened his program to include health insurance as well as unemployment benefits, Epstein in 1933 changed the name of his organization to the American Association for Social Security. He publicized his ideas through a journal, *Social Security,* through lectures, and through testimony at Congressional hearings, and he gave courses at Brooklyn College and New York University. From 1934 to 1937 he served as United States representative on the social insurance committee of the International Labor Office of the League of Nations. Perhaps his greatest popular impact came from his widely read book *Insecurity: A Challenge for America* (1933). Nevertheless, his feud with Andrews had created enemies within reform circles, and despite his prominence, the Roosevelt administration did not consult Epstein when drafting the Social Security Act of 1935—a blow from which, so his friends assert, he never recovered. Epstein criticized the Social Security Act for failing to make provision for government contributions, for leaving control of unemployment compensation to the states, and for the large reserve fund it set up, which reduced purchasing power. Many of the changes he suggested were adopted in 1939 by Congress, which extended benefits to dependents, modified the reserve requirements, and increased benefits to low-income groups by determining payment on the basis of average, rather than lifetime, wages. The Social Security Board made Epstein a consulting economist, and at the time of his death he was busily preparing postwar plans for social security and reconversion.

Epstein was a small, frail man, just over five feet tall, with a balding head and a high-pitched voice. On Feb. 24, 1925, he had married Henriette Castex of Toulouse, France. They had one son, Pierre Leon. The wholehearted energy Epstein devoted to his work took its toll. After a year of heart trouble, he died of pneumonia at Polyclinic Hospital in New York City at the age of fifty. He was buried in Beth David Cemetery. Along with Andrews and Rubinow, he was one of the founding fathers of social security in the United States. His most important contribution had been to transmit European social insurance ideas and publicize them in the United States, and especially to dramatize the plight of the aged.

[The bulk of Epstein's papers are at Columbia Univ.; additional MS. materials are at Cornell Univ. Louis Leotta, Jr., "Abraham Epstein and the Movement for Social Security, 1920–1939" (Ph.D. dissertation, Columbia, 1965), is informative. A lengthy obituary is in *Social Security,* Sept.–Oct. 1942. See also biographical sketch by Paul Douglas in the 1968 edition of Epstein's *Insecurity;* obituary in *N. Y. Times,* May 3, 1942; and *Who Was Who in America,* vol. II (1950). Epstein is frequently discussed in the broad context of the social insurance movement in Clarke Chambers, *Seedtime of Reform* (1963); Roy Lubove, *The Struggle for Social Security, 1900–1935* (1968); and Daniel Nelson, *Unemployment Insurance: The Am. Experience, 1919–1935* (1969).]

GERALD D. NASH

ESCH, JOHN JACOB (Mar. 20, 1861–Apr. 27, 1941), Congressman and member of the Interstate Commerce Commission, was born near Norwalk, Monroe County, Wis., the second of five children, four boys and a girl, of Henry and Matilda (Menn) Esch. His father had emigrated from Westphalia, Germany, while still a youth; his mother was born of German parents in Missouri. Henry Esch was at various times a farmer, groceryman, and preacher of the Evangelical Association. Though beginning with little, the Esches attained moderate prosperity and passed on to their children strong religious convictions and thrifty habits.

John Esch grew up in Milwaukee, where the family moved in 1865, and after 1871 in Sparta, Wis. An excellent student, he attended the University of Wisconsin, where he was elected to Phi Beta Kappa and graduated in 1882. After an interlude as teacher and assistant principal of the

Sparta high school, he returned to the university and took a law degree in 1887. That same year he was admitted to the Wisconsin bar and began practice in La Crosse, Wis. On Dec. 24, 1889, he married Anna Herbst of Sparta, like himself of German parentage. The couple had nine children: Paul, Irene, Helen, Marie, Ruth, Anna, John, Mark, and Margaret. The family were staunch members of the First Congregational Church of La Crosse.

Esch soon became active in the Wisconsin State Guard and in Republican politics. He helped organize guard companies in both Sparta and La Crosse that later became part of the 3rd Regiment, Wisconsin National Guard; from 1894 to 1896 he served as judge advocate general with the rank of colonel. Esch was a delegate to the Republican state conventions of 1894 and 1896, serving in the latter year as chairman. In 1898 he won election to Congress from the 7th Wisconsin District, a position he held for twenty-two years.

Though not an intimate associate of Robert M. La Follette [*q.v.*], Esch had progressive leanings and was counted as friendly to the La Follette organization. In 1908 he sought a Senate seat but lost in the preferential primary to Isaac Stephenson [*q.v.*]. Esch served on the House Military Affairs and Public Lands committees, but made his major contributions as a member (from 1903) of the Committee on Interstate and Foreign Commerce. In 1905 he sponsored the Esch-Townsend Bill to give the Interstate Commerce Commission the power to fix maximum railroad rates. The measure passed the House but failed in the Senate. The Hepburn Act of the following year did grant the ICC authority to establish "just and reasonable" freight rates, but failed to lay down precise guidelines. Like most of his constituents, Esch strongly opposed American involvement in World War I. He supported the McLemore Resolution in 1916 warning Americans to stay off armed merchant ships and, with a majority of the Wisconsin delegation, voted against the declaration of war the following year.

As the ranking Republican, Esch became chairman of the powerful House Commerce Committee following his party's Congressional victory in 1918. He wrote and sponsored, with Senator Albert B. Cummins [*q.v.*] of Iowa, the Transportation Act of 1920, designed to return the nation's railroads to their private owners after the war, compensate them for the years of federal control, and provide for the possible future amalgamation of the railroads into a number of "systems." This measure, popularly called the Esch-Cummins Act, became law over the strenuous opposition of Senator La Follette, who argued that the compensation was excessive and would result in higher freight rates and consumer prices; instead, La Follette advocated that federal control be extended for two years. Charging that Esch had gone over to the reactionaries, La Follette and his allies in the Non-Partisan League brought about his defeat in the 1920 Republican primary, thus ending Esch's legislative career.

President Harding, again over La Follette's objections, appointed Esch to the Interstate Commerce Commission in 1921. During his seven-year term, Esch served as chairman in 1927. Although he was renominated in 1928, a group of Senators from Southern coal-producing states, who felt his ICC rulings had favored Pennsylvania shippers, successfully blocked his confirmation. Esch then resumed the practice of law, heading the Washington firm of Esch, Kerr, Taylor, and Shipe until 1938. He also served as president of the American Peace Society (1930–38). Upon his retirement he returned to La Crosse. He died there of heart disease at the age of eighty and was buried in Oak Grove Cemetery, La Crosse. A keenly intelligent and industrious man, Esch is remembered for his interest in railroad regulation and his co-authorship of the Transportation Act of 1920.

[Esch's papers are at the State Hist. Soc. of Wis. Other sources include: *Biog. Directory Am. Cong.* (1961); *Dict. Wis. Biog.* (1960); *Who Was Who in America*, vol. I (1942); *Nat. Cyc. Am. Biog.*, Current Vol. A, pp. 530–31; obituaries in *N. Y. Times* and *Wis. State Jour.* (Madison), Apr. 28, 1941. See also Alexander M. Thomson, *A Political Hist. of Wis.* (1900); and Herbert F. Margulies, *The Decline of the Progressive Movement in Wis., 1890–1920* (1968). For accounts of the Esch-Cummins Act, see I. Leo Sharfman, *The Am. Railroad Problem* (1921); and K. Austin Kerr, *Am. Railroad Politics* (1968). On Esch's family background, see Andrew J. Aikens and Lewis A. Proctor, eds., *Men of Progress: Wis.* (1897), p. 341; *Biog. Hist. of La Crosse, Trempealeau and Buffalo Counties, Wis.* (1892), p. 360. Death record from Wis. Dept. of Health and Social Services.]
                                    ROBERT S. MAXWELL

EWING, JAMES (Dec. 25, 1866–May 16, 1943), pathologist, was born in Pittsburgh, Pa., the second of three sons and third of five children of Thomas and Julia Rupert (Hufnagel) Ewing. His mother, of German descent and a native of Stockbridge, Mass., had graduated from Mount Holyoke Seminary and had taught school. His father, whom Ewing considered the dominant influence in his life, was of Scotch-Irish ancestry, a descendant of an earlier Thomas Ewing who served in the Pennsylvania Assembly in 1738–39. Active in the Presbyterian Church both as an elder and as a trustee of Western Theological Seminary in Pittsburgh, he had graduated from Jefferson College, taught school, and then

embarked upon a successful legal career, during which he was presiding judge of the second Pittsburgh Court of Common Pleas (1873–97).

In his youth James Ewing showed an interest in natural history. He attended public schools in Pittsburgh until 1880, when he developed osteomyelitis of the femur, which kept him bedridden for the next two years. His education was continued by private tutors, and though the infection left him with a permanent disability, he went on to college, where in spite of his lameness he enjoyed playing tennis. After receiving the B.A. degree in 1888 from Amherst, Ewing studied at the College of Physicians and Surgeons of Columbia University, from which he graduated in 1891. He then interned at the Roosevelt Hospital in New York, where in his first medical paper, written when the use of blood counting techniques was still in its infancy, he described the role of white blood cells in pneumonia.

For the next few years Ewing divided his time between private practice and teaching histology and clinical pathology at Columbia. His superior there was T. Mitchell Prudden [*q.v.*], to whom he credited his major conceptions in pathology. The many papers which Ewing published during this period include several on malaria, which he encountered while serving as a contract surgeon at nearby Camp Wikoff during the Spanish-American War.

In 1899 Ewing was appointed the first professor of pathology at Cornell University Medical College, the school's only full-time faculty member at the time. A prodigious worker and a forceful speaker, he had an important influence on the growth and development of the school during the thirty-two years of his tenure. On July 19, 1900, Ewing married Catherine Crane Halstead; their son, James Halstead, was born in 1902. The next year, during her second pregnancy, Mrs. Ewing died from toxemia and acute yellow atrophy of the liver. Ewing's research into the toxemias of pregnancy and related conditions clearly reflects his sense of loss. After his wife's death he became somewhat of a social recluse and moved to Westhampton, Long Island, where he reared his son. During the intermediate years of his life Ewing was afflicted with painful paroxysms of tic douloureux, a condition that eventually necessitated surgery, which left him with a partial facial anesthesia and corneal abnormalities.

Despite these hardships, Ewing persevered in his research, which came to center on malignancies. His study in this field had been stimulated by the Collis P. Huntington Fund for

Cancer Research, established at Cornell in 1902 by the widow of the railroad magnate Collis P. Huntington [*q.v.*]. By 1910 the work carried on under the fund had made Ewing the leading cancer pathologist in the city. He had become convinced, however, that the most fruitful approach would combine pathological research with clinical studies of cancer patients. A generous source of funds to procure the hospital needed for this purpose was found in James Douglas [*q.v.*], a mining engineer, originally trained in medicine, who had a deep interest in the therapeutic possibilities of radium. Douglas formed a corporation to develop American pitchblende deposits, and the money from this venture, in addition to other grants from Douglas, in 1914 financed the reorganization of the Memorial Hospital, an affiliate of Cornell Medical College, into a specialized institution for cancer treatment and research.

Under Ewing's influence the hospital, later known as the Memorial Hospital for Cancer and Allied Diseases, became the world leader in the clinical classification and diagnostic histology of tumors. Ewing was a founder of the tumor registry of the American College of Surgeons. He trained a large number of specialists in cancer research, and his many articles on irradiation as a mode of cancer therapy promoted the development of improved X-ray techniques. The hospital itself was an innovation that stimulated the founding elsewhere of similar institutions with a concentrated area of interest. Medicine also owes Ewing a debt for his determination to have oncology recognized as a medical subspecialty for the diagnosis and treatment of cancer.

In addition to more than 150 articles, Ewing in his early years published *Notes on Clinical Diagnosis* (1898) and *Clinical Pathology of the Blood* (1901), as well as portions of a textbook on legal medicine. His leading work was *Neoplastic Diseases* (1919), which for decades remained the standard text on tumors. As a reminder of his eminence in the diagnosis and treatment of neoplastic diseases, an infrequent malignancy of bone which he first described bears the eponym "Ewing's sarcoma."

Ewing was a founder and first president (1907–09) of the American Association for Cancer Research and a founder (1913) of the American Society for the Control of Cancer (later the American Cancer Society), which sought to educate both physicians and laymen in the importance of recognizing early signs of cancer. Most of the popular educational material distributed by the society came from his hand. In 1932 he relinquished his chair of pathology at Cornell to become medical director of Memorial Hospital, a

role he had unofficially filled for two decades. Ewing was a member of many professional organizations both in Europe and in the United States; he served as president of the American Society of Pathologists and Bacteriologists (1906) and the Society of Experimental Biology and Medicine (1912), and was elected to the National Academy of Sciences in 1935. He retired in 1939 at the age of seventy-three but remained active in research and teaching until his death four years later, at Memorial Hospital, from cancer of the urinary bladder. The James Ewing Hospital of New York, a city hospital for cancer patients, and the James Ewing Society dedicated to cancer research perpetuate his name.

[Abundant biographical material and personal letters are in the Lee Coombe Lib., Memorial Hospital for Cancer and Allied Diseases, N. Y. City. Published sources include: "Appreciation" by William H. Welch in *Annals of Surgery*, Jan. 1931; obituaries in *N. Y. Times*, May 17, 1943, *Jour. Am. Medic. Assoc.*, May 22, 1943, and *Archives of Pathology*, Sept. 1943; and memoir by James B. Murphy in Nat. Acad. Sci., *Biog. Memoirs*, vol. XXVI (1951). On his father, see obituary in *Legal Intelligencer* (Phila.), May 21, 1897.]

JEFFREY A. KAHN

FAIRFAX, BEATRICE. See MANNING, MARIE.

FALL, ALBERT BACON (Nov. 26, 1861– Nov. 30, 1944), lawyer, Senator from New Mexico, cabinet officer, was born in Frankfort, Ky. He was the eldest of three children (two boys and a girl) of Edmonia (Taylor) and Williamson Ware Robertson Fall, both schoolteachers. His paternal great-grandfather had emigrated in 1817 from Surrey, England, to Kentucky; his mother came of a prominent Kentucky family. When Albert's father joined the Confederate Army during the Civil War, the child went to live in Nashville, Tenn., with his grandfather Philip Slater Fall, a former Baptist minister who had become a leader in the Campbellite movement led by his close friend Alexander Campbell [*q.v.*]. From this scholarly grandfather the boy acquired the habit of reading omnivorously. At the age of eleven he took a job in a cotton mill. Although he attended schools taught by his father, he was largely self-educated.

After teaching school and reading law in his spare time, Fall moved west in 1881 in search of employment and a milder climate; throughout his life he was plagued by respiratory ailments. He worked as a cattle drover and as a cowboy cook before settling in Clarksville, Texas, where he sold insurance, operated a real estate agency, and, for a time, ran a small grocery store. On May 7, 1883, he married Emma Garland Morgan, whose father, Simpson H. Morgan, had been a representative from Texas to the Confederate Congress. They had four children: John Morgan, Alexina, Carolyn, and Jouett.

Soon after his marriage Fall set out on a prospecting trip through eight states of Mexico, finally locating at Nieves in the state of Zacatecas, where he worked in hard-rock mining operations. This was the beginning of a lifelong interest in Mexico and in Mexican mining. He returned to Clarksville in 1884. A later prospecting trip took him to the mountains of southern New Mexico Territory, and in 1887 he settled at Las Cruces. There he became a practicing attorney (1889) and had a rough-and-tumble political apprenticeship as a Democrat at a time when political rivalries often led to gunfights and the mysterious disappearance of opponents. He served as a member both of the territorial house (1890–92) and the territorial council (1892–93, 1896–97, 1902–04), as an associate justice of the New Mexico supreme court (1893–95), and twice, briefly, as territorial attorney general (1897, 1907). In 1910 he was a delegate to the New Mexico constitutional convention.

In his law practice, Fall, though always maintaining his voting residence in New Mexico, opened an office in El Paso, Texas, where he represented irrigation and development enterprises, mining companies, timber concerns, railroads, and other industrial interests. At the same time he increasingly devoted himself to mining promotion in northern Mexico. Small-scale ventures led to an involvement in some of the multimillion-dollar operations of William C. Greene [q.v.], from which he derived a modest fortune and several potentially valuable Mexican mining properties. Because of his strong sympathy for private enterprise, particularly in the exploitation of natural resources, Fall early gained the image of a "corporation man."

Although professing himself a Democrat as late as 1904, Fall for various reasons—not the least, his admiration for Theodore Roosevelt—had already begun a shift to the Republican party that became official in 1908, when he was a delegate to the national convention. When New Mexico achieved statehood in 1912, Fall became one of its first two United States Senators. In appearance somewhat like "Buffalo Bill" Cody [q.v.], bombastic and often cynical, Fall gained national attention as the most outspoken Senate advocate of forceful protection of American property rights in revolution-torn Mexico. In 1919 and 1920 he headed a Senate subcommittee which conducted a freewheeling investigation of Mexican affairs. He was a bitter critic of President Woodrow Wilson's Mexican policy and an opponent of the Treaty of Versailles, sometimes being classed among the irreconcilables.

Fall became a poker-playing crony of Warren G. Harding while the two served together on the Senate Foreign Relations Committee. When Harding became president in 1921, he wanted Fall for his Secretary of State, but upon being dissuaded by Republican leaders, appointed his friend instead as Secretary of the Interior. Less than three months after taking office, Harding and his Secretary of the Navy, Edwin Denby [q.v.], obligingly agreed to transfer control of naval oil lands to Secretary Fall. Several months later, in 1922, Fall stealthily negotiated drilling agreements with Harry F. Sinclair for the Teapot Dome Naval Oil Reserve in Wyoming and with Edward L. Doheny [Supp. 1], an old prospector friend, for a similar reserve at Elk Hills, Calif. Fall himself, as disclosed by later Senate investigations, received at least $404,000 and some blooded livestock from Sinclair and Doheny. Meanwhile, Fall's proposal to transfer the Forest Service from the Agriculture back to the Interior Department had roused conservationist opposition. Dissatisfied with public service generally and with what he felt was his insufficient role in administration councils, Fall retired from the cabinet in March 1923.

That October Senator Thomas J. Walsh [q.v.] began pressing the hearings that brought out into the open what became known as the Teapot Dome scandal. The notoriety given the affair in the 1924 and 1928 elections and the sensational criminal and civil court actions that followed the Senate investigation kept Fall and Teapot Dome in the headlines for nearly a decade. Fall's initial false testimony that he had borrowed from the newspaper publisher Edward B. McLean [Supp. 3] the $100,000 that Doheny later admitted sending him in a "little black bag" did much to discredit him. To a large extent, all the iniquity of the besmirched Harding administration was ascribed to Fall. The Teapot Dome and Elk Hills leases were canceled by the courts in 1927, and two years later Fall was found guilty of accepting a bribe. Doheny was acquitted of giving the same bribe that Fall had been found guilty of receiving. Sinclair served short prison sentences for contempt of Congress and jury shadowing, but otherwise he, too, went free.

In 1931, sixty-nine years old and suffering from a chronic heart ailment, pleurisy, and crippling arthritis, Fall left his home by ambulance to begin a one-year prison term, the first American cabinet officer ever convicted and imprisoned for a serious crime committed while in office. In his last years, broken in health, reputation, and finances, he was staunchly supported by his wife. He died of heart failure in 1944 at the Hotel Dieu hospital in El Paso, Texas, where he had lived since the loss of his Three Rivers, N. Mex., ranch in 1936. He was buried in Evergreen Cemetery, El Paso.

Although for many Fall came to epitomize the unfaithful public servant, he insisted to the end that his personal acquisitions from Sinclair and Doheny were legitimate loans and normal business transactions having no bearing on his official leasing policy. The drilling agreements with the two oil magnates, he maintained, had saved the Wyoming and California reserves from drainage through private wells on adjoining lands. His program had envisioned preservation of the oil for future use in above-ground storage tanks, as well as making it immediately available to the navy, whose high command was apprehensive of an attack by the Japanese in the Pacific. Later, the strategic role of Pearl Harbor in World War II convinced Fall that his thwarted efforts to build a great fuel depot there twenty years before had been vindicated.

[The main body of Fall papers, which relates mostly to his Senate and cabinet service, is in the Huntington Lib., San Marino, Calif. Other collections of his papers are held by the family and by the Univ. of N. Mex. Lib. Three articles by David H. Stratton draw heavily on these manuscript sources: "N. Mex. Machiavellian? The Story of Albert B. Fall," *Montana: The Mag. of Western Hist.*, Oct. 1957; "President Wilson's Smelling Committee," *Colo. Quart.*, Autumn 1956; "Behind Teapot Dome: Some Personal Insights," *Business Hist. Rev.*, Winter 1957. Fall's reminiscences about his early life (to about 1891), ed. with annotations by David H. Stratton, are found in *The Memoirs of Albert B. Fall* (Southwestern Studies, vol. IV, no. 3, Monograph 15, 1966). For descriptions of Fall's career in the Southwest, not always accurate in detail, see Charles L. Sonnichsen, *Tularosa: Last of the Frontier West* (1960), and William A. Keleher, *The Fabulous Frontier* (rev. ed., 1962). Three recent books give accounts of various aspects of the Teapot Dome scandal: Morris R. Werner and John Starr, *Teapot Dome* (1959); Burl Noggle, *Teapot Dome: Oil and Politics in the 1920's* (1962); and J. Leonard Bates, *The Origins of Teapot Dome: Progressives, Parties and Petroleum, 1909–1921* (1963).]

DAVID H. STRATTON

FARISH, WILLIAM STAMPS (Feb. 23, 1881–Nov. 29, 1942), oil company executive, was born in Mayersville, Miss., the son of William Stamps Farish and Katherine Maude (Power) Farish. His father, a lawyer, had come from Virginia, where the first Farish in America had settled after emigrating from England in 1730. Young Farish graduated from St. Thomas Hall in Holly Springs, Miss., and entered the University of Mississippi, where he took the law course, earning part of his expenses by teaching school. In 1900 he received the LL.B. degree, was admitted to the bar, and entered

practice at Clarksdale. The next year he went to Beaumont, Texas, to look after the oil interests of an English syndicate in which an uncle was an investor.

Like scores of other young men attracted to Texas by the discovery of oil at Spindletop in January 1901, Farish soon entered business for himself. His first venture, a partnership, ended in bankruptcy and the partner's death, but in promptly paying off the firm's debts, Farish established his credit. By 1904 he had joined another young man, Robert Lee Blaffer, in a new partnership. Beginning as contract driller and trader in oil-land leases, Blaffer & Farish soon went into the production of oil on its own. In 1905, in order to concentrate on the Humble oil field, the partners moved to Houston. They also entered into several other ventures, especially in the new oil fields of northern Texas. By 1916 Farish had become one of the leading independent oilmen in Texas.

Although successful as a producer of oil, Farish, like other independent oilmen in Texas, had run into serious trouble in 1915. Under the Texas system of selling their product to major companies under time contracts which specified the price the buyers would pay and the maximum amount they could be required to take, producers who had entered sales contracts early in 1915, when prices were declining sharply, had to sell well below the market prices, which rose dramatically late in the year. Farish then spearheaded the organization in 1916 of the Gulf Coast Oil Producers Association in order to bring about a concerted attack on the small producers' marketing problems. As the association's president, he tried to arrange to sell directly to refineries in the East in order to bypass the major companies in Texas, but he soon learned that the Eastern refiners required a steady supply in large volume. To meet this requirement Farish proposed that the producers pool their oil. Failing in this effort, he persuaded several other oil producers, with whom he had had close business and personal relations over the years, to merge their holdings in 1917 in a new corporation, Humble Oil & Refining Company.

The new company's immediate objective was to build a large producing business, and Farish, as a director and vice-president, had overall responsibilty for production. Humble expanded rapidly, but its growth potential soon exceeded its capital resources. To raise new capital, Farish negotiated an agreement with the president of Standard Oil Company (New Jersey), Walter C. Teagle, whom he had met while serving on the Petroleum Committee of the wartime Council of National Defense, and in 1919 Humble sold half of its enlarged capital stock to the Eastern company. Since its dismemberment in 1911 by decision of the United States Supreme Court, Standard Oil Company (New Jersey) had been trying to secure large domestic production of its own. Humble, for its part, gained from the affiliation not only funds for expansion and diversification but also a stable market for its production.

Farish was elected president of Humble Oil in 1922, and over the next decade he guided its growth from a loose aggregation of small producers, whose greatest asset was practical experience, into a complex and well-coordinated organization that relied heavily upon scientific research and utilized advanced engineering techniques. Although Farish continued to emphasize production, he also promoted diversification and integration, supporting the development of a large pipeline system and the building of several refineries, notably the large and progressive one at Baytown, Texas. At the same time Humble became a large purchaser of crude oil, daily posting in the fields where it purchased the prices it would pay for oil. Under Farish, the company also built outstanding research and operating organizations, notably in exploration and production. It thereby not only greatly improved its own search for new oil fields and its production; it also contributed to the advance of the industry's technology.

A farsighted executive, Farish early came to see the need for reform in the oil industry's producing practices and for change in the laws governing the production of oil and gas. Under the "Rule of Capture"—a legal principle that ascribed ownership of oil to anyone who gained possession of it through wells on land he owned or had leased—competing producers tapping a given field had every incentive to drain that field as rapidly as possible, with resultant waste and instability. As a director and president in 1926 of the American Petroleum Institute, Farish addressed local and national meetings of oilmen, calling for a program of reform in the producing industry's operations. At first he favored self-regulation. Representing the oil industry, he was chairman of the Committee of Nine set up in 1927 by the Federal Oil Conservation Board to study the industry's problems and explore ways to solve them. As research and experience contributed to a better understanding of oil and gas reservoirs, their petroleum content, and the natural forces affecting production, Farish came to support, as the most practical and equitable system of regulation, proration (dividing a field's

allowable production among its producers) under state laws in accordance with market demand as estimated by the Federal Bureau of Mines.

Farish left Humble Oil & Refining Company in 1933, with some reluctance, to become chairman of the board of directors of Standard Oil Company (New Jersey). He had served as a director of the company from 1927 and as the board's leading authority on new production concepts and methods and the domestic oil producing industry in general. In 1937 he was elected president, a position he retained until his death. He thus headed this large multinational concern in the early years of World War II. He was a member of the Petroleum Industry War Council, which assisted government agencies in providing the United States and its allies with oil products for war.

An omnivorous reader with a photographic memory, Farish had a broad grasp of the oil industry. His fairness, flexibility, and decisiveness won him the respect and loyalty of his associates, but his reserved manner and his uncompromising support of what he considered right sometimes irritated politicians and other outsiders. Tall and of a strong physique, he loved the outdoors and found recreation in hunting and riding. Farish was an Episcopalian in church affiliation. On June 1, 1911, he married Libbie Randon Rice of Houston. They had two children, William Stamps and Martha Botts. In 1942, at the age of sixty-one, he died in Millbrook, N. Y., of a heart attack, believed by those close to him to have been brought on by wartime strains and overwork. He was buried in Glenwood Cemetery, Houston.

[Henrietta M. Larson and Kenneth W. Porter, *Hist. of Humble Oil & Refining Co.* (1959); Henrietta M. Larson, Evelyn H. Knowlton, and Charles S. Popple, *Hist. of Standard Oil Co. (N. J.): New Horizons, 1927–1950* (1971); obituaries in *The Lamp,* Dec. 1942, and *N. Y. Times,* Nov. 30, 1942.]

HENRIETTA M. LARSON

FARRAND, MAX (Mar. 29, 1869–June 17, 1945), historian and library director, was born in Newark, N. J., the youngest of the four sons of Louise (Wilson) and Samuel Ashbel Farrand, and a brother of Livingston Farrand [Supp. 2]. After graduating in 1885 from Newark Academy, of which his father was headmaster, Max attended Princeton, from which he graduated in 1892. He majored in biology, but among his friends were students with strong literary interests, including the novelist Booth Tarkington, and after taking a course with Woodrow Wilson [q.v.], Farrand decided to pursue graduate study in history. He interrupted his graduate work at Princeton with brief periods of study at Heidelberg and Leipzig, where he became familiar with the scientific approach to history and developed a penchant for accuracy which he later applied to his editorial work. Having completed his Ph.D. in 1896, with a dissertation on *The Legislation of Congress for the Government of the Original Territories of the United States, 1789–1795* (1896), he accepted a position at Wesleyan University in Connecticut and there quickly rose to the rank of professor.

In 1901 David Starr Jordan [*q.v.*], president of Stanford University, persuaded Farrand to become head of the department of history at Stanford. But he soon found that administering a department was no easy matter, and he was disappointed when the offer of a professorship to Frederick Jackson Turner [*q.v.*] had to be postponed indefinitely following the 1906 earthquake, which destroyed many campus buildings. Farrand was also dissatisfied with Stanford's limited library resources, which he judged inadequate for historical research and graduate study. In 1905–06 he taught at Cornell as a visiting professor, and in 1908 he accepted an offer from Yale, where he remained until 1925. A demanding teacher and a forceful lecturer, he devoted much of his time at Yale to guiding students, particularly honors students and those who took his course on historical criticism. Farrand assumed additional responsibilities, beginning in 1919, as an administrator of the Commonwealth Fund, a philanthropic foundation, headed by Edward S. Harkness [Supp. 2], whose work included the granting of fellowships to bring visiting British scholars to American educational institutions. He served as the Fund's general director until 1921 and later (1925–27) as director of its division of education.

While at Yale, Farrand wrote two historical studies, *The Framing of the Constitution* (1913) and *Fathers of the Constitution* (1921), as well as a widely used textbook, *The Development of the United States from Colonies to a World Power* (1918). He published his best-known work in 1911, the three-volume *Records of the Federal Convention of 1787* (a supplementary volume appeared in 1937). Immediately recognized as a model of historical editing, this study made use of letters, diaries, and memoirs written by members of the convention to present a chronological account of the drafting of the federal Constitution.

During a visit to southern California in 1926, Farrand met the astronomer George E. Hale [Supp. 2], a trustee of the library and art gallery which the railroad executive Henry E. Hunting-

ton [*q.v.*] was setting up on his estate in San Marino, Calif. Farrand was invited to participate in the planning of the library and prepared an "operating program" which was approved by Huntington. In February 1927 he was appointed director of research. Backed by advice from fellow scholars, Farrand soon succeeded in transforming a wealthy collector's library into a leading research center for the study of Anglo-American civilization. With Hale's support, he persuaded Huntington to increase his initial endowment of $4,000,000 to an ultimate $10,500,-000, and thus was able to set up a research staff, to finance a program of fellowships for scholars, to equip the library with extensive reference and bibliographical aids, and to publish, under the library's imprint, the *Huntington Library Bulletin* (later *Quarterly*) and a stream of monographs. He continued as director of research until his retirement in 1941.

On Dec. 17, 1913, Farrand had married Beatrix Cadwalader Jones, a well-known landscape architect from a distinguished New York family. There were no children. Together they entertained staff members and visiting scholars in the director's house on the Huntington Library grounds. Farrand was president of the American Historical Association in 1940. He received honorary degrees from seven colleges and universities, including Michigan, California, and Princeton. An imposing, broad-shouldered, bespectacled figure, he was an enthusiastic golfer and freshwater fisherman. Farrand died of cancer at the age of seventy-six at his summer home at Reef Point, Bar Harbor, Maine. Following cremation, his ashes were scattered at Reef Point.

[The Max Farrand Papers, Henry E. Huntington Lib., are the most important source; other MS. materials at the library are in the Trustees Files, Biog. Files, and Frederick Jackson Turner Papers. A photograph of Farrand about 1935 and portions of the Turner-Farrand correspondence are published in Wilbur R. Jacobs, *The Historical World of Frederick Jackson Turner* (1968). On Farrand's directorship of the Huntington Lib., see its *Annual Reports, 1927–41*, especially 1940–41; Harold D. Carew in *Touring Topics*, Dec. 1929; Godfrey Davies, "The Huntington Lib. as a Research Center, 1925–1927," *Huntington Lib. Quart.*, May 1948; Ray A. Billington, "The Genesis of the Research Institution," *ibid.*, Aug. 1969; and John E. Pomfret, *The Henry E. Huntington Lib. and Art Gallery* (1969). See also *Who Was Who in America*, vol. II (1950); and obituaries in *Huntington Lib. Quart.*, Nov. 1945, Am. Philosophical Soc., *Year Book*, 1945 (by St. George L. Sioussat), *Am. Hist. Rev.*, Jan. 1946, and *N. Y. Times*, June 18, 1945. Death record from Town Clerk, Bar Harbor, Maine.]

WILBUR R. JACOBS

FARRELL, JAMES AUGUSTINE (Feb. 15, 1862–Mar. 28, 1943), steel executive, was born in New Haven, Conn., the first of four sons and second of six children of John Guy Farrell and

Catherine (Whalen) Farrell. His father, an Irish Catholic, had come to the United States in 1848 from Dublin. Following family tradition, he was by turns a merchant, sea captain, and shipowner, and James early acquired a lifelong love for sailing ships. When James was sixteen, his father was lost with one of his ships, and the boy had to leave school and go to work as a laborer in a steel wire mill in New Haven. Nine years later, in 1888, he moved to Pittsburgh, Pa., where he worked for the Pittsburgh Wire Company, again as a laborer. On June 11, 1889, he married Catherine McDermott, who bore him five children: John Joseph, Mary Theresa, Catherine, James Augustine, and Rosamond. Both sons became prominent in the shipping business as executives of the Farrell Lines.

Hoping to advance at the Pittsburgh Wire Company to salesman, Farrell studied at night both to improve his education and to learn every aspect of the wire-drawing trade. Although sources differ, it appears that the company made him a salesman about 1889, and within three years promoted him to sales manager with offices in New York City. Farrell's success was attributed to his thorough knowledge of customers' needs. Though an excellent conversationalist, he was a "teetotaler" and never entertained clients in saloons or clubs; but he gained a wide reputation for honesty and reliability. In 1893 he became general manager of Pittsburgh Wire, and during the business panic of that year he managed to keep his firm solvent by seeking out foreign markets, as yet a relatively untapped source.

Farrell's knowledge of foreign markets proved the key to his advancement. In 1899 Pittsburgh Wire merged with the American Steel and Wire Company of New Jersey, and he became head of foreign sales; when this company was in turn absorbed by the newly formed United States Steel Corporation in 1901, Farrell received a similar position in the parent organization. Two years later he was named president of the U. S. Steel Products Corporation, a subsidiary formed to coordinate all foreign sales. In eight years in that post, he tripled the company's export business, sharply cut the cost of foreign trade, and purchased a fleet of ships to transport the growing variety of steel products.

So successful was Farrell that in 1911 the banker J. P. Morgan and Elbert H. Gary [qq.v.], chairman of United States Steel, selected him to replace the retiring William E. Corey [Supp. 1] as president of the company. He held that office until 1932, during which time he increased steel output from 6,000,000 to 29,000,000 tons.

After the death of Judge Gary in 1927, the company's operations were divided, with Myron C. Taylor as director of financial affairs and Farrell as both head of operations and chief executive officer.

Farrell was a prodigious worker and a firm believer in the American success credo. "Every American boy," he once said, "by strict application can master the techniques of any business, and has the same chance to do the same thing that I have done." His testimony during the federal government's 1913 antitrust suit against U. S. Steel demonstrated his remarkable memory for details. An internationalist in foreign trade matters, Farrell was chairman of the foreign relations committee of the American Iron and Steel Institute from 1910 to 1932 and for many years chairman of the National Foreign Trade Council. He also served as honorary president of the Pan American Society and honorary vice-president of the Iron and Steel Institute of Great Britain. He was a member of two foreign orders of merit, and as a leading Catholic layman was twice decorated by the Vatican. In 1929 he was awarded the first Gary Memorial Medal for "meritorious service to the steel industry."

Despite his position, Farrell lived without ostentation and enjoyed privacy. His laboring background made him comfortable in the presence of workers, and he was sympathetic to their needs. He early advocated the adoption of workers' compensation benefits and pension funds and the improvement of working conditions. He apparently opposed trade unionism, however, and during the famous steel strike of 1919 refused to negotiate.

Farrell resigned his executive positions at U. S. Steel in 1932 but remained a member of the board of directors until his death. In his retirement he divided his time between New York City and Rockledge, his estate in South Norwalk, Conn., where he pursued the hobby of sailing, the only pastime he had ever enjoyed. He died of heart disease in New York City at the age of eighty-one and was buried at Gate of Heaven Cemetery, Hawthorne, N. Y.

[Amundel Cotler, *Authentic Hist. of the U. S. Steel Corp.* (1916) and *U. S. Steel: A Corp. with a Soul* (1921); Frank C. Harper, *Pittsburgh of Today* (4 vols., 1931); B. C. Forbes, *Men Who Are Making America* (1916), pp. 105–14; references to Farrell in *Fortune,* June 1931, p. 154, and Mar. 1936, pp. 157, 178; *Who Was Who in America,* vol. I (1942); *Nat. Cyc. Am. Biog.,* XXXII, 54–55; obituaries in *N. Y. Times,* Mar. 29, 1943, *Wall Street Jour.,* Mar. 29, 1943, and *Iron Age,* Apr. 1, 1943; family information from James A. Farrell, Jr. Though Farrell's birth year is sometimes given as 1863, family sources and his death record confirm 1862.]

S. K. STEVENS

FAUST, FREDERICK SHILLER (May 29, 1892–May 12, 1944), poet and popular author, better known as "Max Brand," was born in Seattle, Wash., the second child of Gilbert Leander Faust and his third wife, Elizabeth Uriel, respectively of German and Irish background. His mother died when Faust was eight. His father was a lawyer, land speculator, bank president, and lumber-mill owner in Seattle and in California before he, too, died when Frederick was thirteen. "My father," Faust once wrote, "was a passionate man with a good deal of brain but also with an unhappy talent for acting parts. . . . I loved him a great deal but I kept seeing through the sham . . ." (Richardson, p. 17). Thrown on his own at thirteen, Faust lived and worked on a succession of farms and ranches in central California and attended nineteen different public schools, each time with a "series of fist fights until I had found my place." "I grew up," he recalled, ". . . learning to withdraw from children of my age, thrown utterly into a world of books and daydreaming" (*Notebooks*, p. 15).

In 1911, after graduating from the Modesto (Calif.) high school, Faust entered the University of California at Berkeley. Although his major was social science, he was active in writing as the editor of the *Pelican,* a campus humor magazine, and on the staff of the *Occident* and the 1915 yearbook. He left the university in his senior year for disciplinary reasons. Over the next two years he worked briefly on a Honolulu newspaper, served short terms in the Canadian and American armies, contracted influenza, which left him with a weak heart, and tried to make a living by writing. Meanwhile, on May 29, 1917, he had married Dorothy Shillig. They had three children: Jane, John Frederick, and Judith Anne.

A large man with a zest for living and a driving appetite for work, Faust sold his first stories to *All-Story Weekly* and *Argosy* magazines in 1917 under the pseudonym "Max Brand." Two years later his first novel, *The Untamed,* launched him upon the career which eventually earned him the title "The King of the Pulp Writers." His novels and stories were so successful that he purchased the Villa Negli Ulivi in Florence, where he lived from 1926 to 1938. He then became a writer for Metro-Goldwyn-Mayer and Warner Brothers studios, adapting his own works for motion picture production (most notably the "Dr. Kildare" series) and working on scenarios for other movies. In 1944 he was appointed a war correspondent for *Harper's.* That May, at the age of fifty-one, he was killed in action in the assault on Santa Maria Infante, Italy. He was buried in the divisional cemetery.

With the possible exception of Gilbert Patten [Supp. 3], the creator of Frank Merriwell, Faust was the most prolific writer America has ever produced. He is estimated to have published more than 30,000,000 words during his lifetime, the equivalent of at least 400 full-length books; and he reportedly left 15 additional novels in manuscript. *The Untamed* (1919), *Destry Rides Again* (1930), *Singing Guns* (1938), *The Border Kid* (1941), and *Silvertip* (1942) are the most popular Westerns written under the "Max Brand" pseudonym, but Faust signed at least eighteen other pen names to his writing, including "George Challis," "Evan Evans," "George Owen Baxter," "David Manning," "Peter Henry Morland," "Frederick Frost," and "Walter C. Butler." He wrote historical romances (*The Naked Blade,* 1938), spy thrillers (*Secret Agent Number One,* 1936; *Spy Meets Spy,* 1937), and detective mysteries (*The Night Flower,* 1936; *Six Golden Angels,* 1937). The same fertile imagination overwhelmed Hollywood; he worked on the scripts of many different movies, including seven "Dr. Kildare" stories. Faust professed indifference to his pulp fiction, calling it "old melodramatic junk" and complaining that "money and prose and prose and money make a bad combination for a goal" (*Notebooks,* pp. 31, 45). Nevertheless, the pulps paid him handsomely—and in 1936 he confessed that he needed $70,000 a year "simply to keep my mouth and nose above water."

The writing of which he was most proud and which he took most seriously was his poetry. His first published work was *One of Cleopatra's Nights,* the Emily Chamberlain Cook Prize Poem for 1914, issued by the University of California Press. Later collections of poetry include *The Village Street and Other Poems* (1922) and *Dionysus in Hades* (1931). They depend on an enormous knowledge of classical and medieval legend and myth, a romantic poetic style, and a tightly controlled and formal sense of prosody. Indeed, there are ways in which Faust's pulp fiction closely resembled much of his poetry: it emphasized a lyric prose style, action and intricate plot development rather than realistic setting and characterization, and melodramatic (occasionally superhuman and bizarre) feats of daring.

[Robert Easton, *Max Brand* (1970), by Faust's son-in-law, is the prime source of information and contains the fullest bibliography of Faust's writings. See also Darrell C. Richardson, *Max Brand: The Man and His Work* (1952), which contains critical and biographical essays by various hands; John Schoolcraft, ed., *Notebooks and Poems of "Max Brand"* (1957); and *Nat. Cyc. Am. Biog.,* XXXIII, 203. The irregular periodical *Fabulous Faust Fanzine* (1948–) collects previously unpublished material by Faust and articles and appreciations by others. The Univ. of

HAMLIN HILL

FENNEMAN, NEVIN MELANCTHON (Dec. 26, 1865–July 4, 1945), geographer and geologist, was born in Lima, Ohio, to William Henry and Rebecca (Oldfather) Fenneman, both of German descent. His father, a minister of the Reformed Church in America, was the son of Johann Heinrich Vennemann of Brochterbeck, Westphalia, who emigrated to Cincinnati in 1840. The Oldfathers (originally Aultvater) had settled in the Shenandoah Valley in Virginia during the colonial period. The only son and third child in a family of four, Nevin was brought up in his father's parsonage in Lima, and then, as his father moved to new pastorates, in Waterloo, Ind., and Tiffin, Ohio. He graduated, A.B., from Heidelberg College in Tiffin in 1883, at the age of seventeen.

A descendant of Prussian schoolmasters, Fenneman followed his two older sisters into public school teaching. An interest in physical geography led him to spend the summer of 1890 in field work on the physical attributes of Wisconsin lakes, an experience which began a fruitful association with the geologists Thomas C. Chamberlin and Charles R. Van Hise [*qq.v.*]. Two years later Fenneman left a high school teaching post to become professor of physical sciences at Colorado State Normal School in Greeley. In 1895 he took the famous summer geology course of William Morris Davis [Supp. 1] at Harvard and began another lasting association. Fenneman resigned his post at Greeley in 1900 to study under Chamberlin and Rollin D. Salisbury [*q.v.*] at the University of Chicago, earning his A.M. degree the same year and his Ph.D. in geology in 1901. In January 1902 he became the first professor of geology at the University of Colorado, and in 1903 President Van Hise called him to the University of Wisconsin. He moved in 1907 to the University of Cincinnati to establish a department of geology and geography, and remained there for the rest of his life, continuing to teach even after he became professor emeritus of geology in 1937.

Fenneman's scholarly career yielded two major books and some fifty articles and geological survey monographs. Between 1901 and 1924 he was associated, for many summers, with the United States Geological Survey and at various times with the Wisconsin Geological and Natural History Survey (1900–02), the Illinois Geological Survey (1906–08), and the Ohio Geological Survey (1914–16). Research on the lakes of Wisconsin, the oil fields of Colorado and the Gulf Coast, the Yampa coal field of Colorado, the geology and physiography of the St. Louis quadrangle, and the Pleistocene and economic geology of the Cincinnati area established his early reputation as a geologist and gave him a varied field work background for his later books. Normally, however, his interest in landforms was less in the geological processes involved than in the application of physiographic generalizations to the analysis of specific regions. His paper "Physiographic Boundaries within the United States" (*Annals of the Association of American Geographers,* 1914) was the first attempt to define the precise boundary lines of a system of uniform subdivisions of the United States. Such subdivisions, he felt, would serve two purposes: "the discussion and explanation of the physical features of the country," and the creation of "a basis for the plotting and discussion of social, industrial, historical, and other data of distinctly human concern." A later paper, "Physiographic Divisions of the United States" (*ibid.,* 1916), and subsequent revisions published in 1921 and 1928 elaborated Fenneman's earlier map and named and defined a standard system of American landform regions.

Fenneman's major book, the *Physiography of Western United States,* appeared in 1931, in his sixty-sixth year; it was followed in 1938 by a similar volume on the Eastern United States. These ambitious works undertook to analyze and synthesize existing knowledge on the geomorphology of each of Fenneman's regions, both as an ordering of existing research and as a basis for future research and teaching. The books are classics of regional generalization, fairly representing differing viewpoints on the interpretation of geomorphologic phenomena. His other geographic work ranged from a survey of the natural and industrial resources of the Cincinnati region to responsibility for preparing scientific data on Africa as a member of "The Inquiry," the group of scholars assembled by Col. Edward M. House [Supp. 2] during World War I to assist President Wilson's objectives in the peace settlement. Fenneman had a lifelong interest in education, and several of his publications were shaped for a popular or pedagogic audience. Gruff and forbidding, in the eyes of trembling freshmen, behind his Vandyke beard, he was highly regarded by the better students and by his colleagues for his challenging standards of achievement in both intellectual and ethical terms and for his unfailing personal assistance.

Fenneman served as chairman of the Division of Geology and Geography of the National Research Council in 1922–23, and was vice-president of the American Association for the Advancement of Science and chairman of its geology section in 1923. A founder of the Association of American Geographers in 1904, he became its president for 1918. In his presidential address, "The Circumference of Geography" (*Geographical Review,* March 1919), Fenneman called upon geographers to make geography an integrating discipline, studying regions "in their entirety, their compositeness, their complexity, their interrelations of physical, economic, racial, historic, and other factors." By stressing what seemed to him the core of his science, namely regional geography, he introduced to American professional geographers what was to become the key concept of their discipline for the next generation. He was president of the Geological Society of America in 1935.

Fenneman was an active member of the Mount Auburn Presbyterian Church in Cincinnati and, among other civic organizations, a regular participant in the Literary Club of Cincinnati; writing essays was his one hobby. On Dec. 26, 1893, he had married Sarah Alice Glisan of Fredonia, N. Y., a fellow teacher at the Colorado State Normal School. She died in 1920, and they had no children. While hospitalized for a minor ailment, Fenneman died of pneumonia in Cincinnati at the age of seventy-nine.

[Obituaries in *Annals of the Assoc. of Am. Geographers,* Dec. 1945 (by John L. Rich), Geological Soc. of America, *Proc.,* 1945 (by Walter H. Bucher)— both with bibliographies of his publications—*Science,* Aug. 10, 1945 (by Raymond Walters), *Geographical Rev.,* Oct. 1945, and *N. Y. Times,* July 6, 1945; *Nat. Cyc. Am. Biog.,* Current Vol. D, p. 304. A portrait of Fenneman by Frank M. Myers is at the Univ. of Cincinnati.]

WILLIAM A. KOELSCH

FERGUSON, JAMES EDWARD (Aug. 31, 1871–Sept. 21, 1944), governor of Texas, was born near Salado, Bell County, Texas, the third son and fourth of five children who survived infancy. His parents, James Edward and Fannie (Fitzpatrick) Ferguson, were of Scotch-Irish descent and modest means. The father, a Methodist minister, farmer, and gristmill operator, died when Jim was four years old. The boy's formal education ended with the sixth grade in Salado public schools. At sixteen he left home for the Pacific Coast, where for two years he worked as an itinerant laborer, bellhop, roustabout, grape picker, teamster, and miner. He then returned to Texas and, after working on construction and railroad gangs, moved back to Bell County in 1895. There he farmed and studied law. He was admitted to the bar in 1897 and established a practice in Belton, the county seat. On Dec. 31, 1899, he married Miriam Amanda Wallace, daughter of a prosperous Bell County farmer. They had two daughters: Ouida Wallace and Ruby Dorrace.

Soon after his marriage, Ferguson moved to Temple, Texas, where he assisted in organizing the Temple State Bank in 1907. He also took an interest in local politics, though his activities were marked neither by uniform success nor by devotion to fixed principle. In 1902 he supported Congressman Robert L. Henry, a friend of Senator Joseph W. Bailey [Supp. 1] of Texas, in Henry's successful bid for reelection; in 1908, however, he fought in vain against Bailey's control of the Texas delegation to the national Democratic convention. In 1910 he endorsed a progressive candidate for governor, Attorney General Robert V. Davidson, but saw him lose; in 1912 he helped conservative Gov. Oscar B. Colquitt win reelection.

Though barely known outside Bell County, Ferguson jolted Democratic party leaders in 1914 by winning the gubernatorial primary and general election. In defeating a widely known ex-Congressman and progressive-prohibition spokesman, Thomas H. Ball, Ferguson unveiled a political style composed in equal parts of wit, slander, and sarcasm which made him immediately popular in the rural areas of the state. "Farmer Jim" further won the undying loyalty of white tenant farmers when he voiced their demands that the practice by landlords of charging a money bonus in addition to a percentage of the crops be outlawed and that rents be held to one-third of the grain and one-fourth of the cotton crops. His more basic political beliefs were reflected in promises to veto any legislation extending prohibition and to give the state a rest from the progressive reforms of the preceding decade. Once in office, Ferguson signed a bill which gave lip service to renter demands but which was unenforced at the time and was declared unconstitutional in 1921. He had more success in his fight against prohibition, woman suffrage, and laws regulating corporate wealth, but his most constructive achievements were laws improving rural education and compelling school attendance.

Ferguson won reelection easily in 1916, though charges were made late in the campaign that he had mishandled state funds and received generous loans from brewers. These charges were aired more fully when the legislature convened, but the session ended with the governor's power intact. Shortly after adjournment, Ferguson vetoed virtually the entire University of Texas appropriation because the board of regents had ignored his suggestions regarding the selection of a president and the dismissal of faculty members known to be hostile to him. His veto brought powerful alumni support to those already seeking his removal—prohibitionists, suffragists, progressives. Members of a legislative committee charged with locating a new agricultural college in west Texas next accused Ferguson of falsifying the report on the proposed site. On Aug. 1, 1917, the legislature reconvened to consider impeachment. Twenty-one charges were formally voted by the house of representatives, and the senate convicted the governor on ten. Five related to unlawful deposit of state funds in his Temple bank; two involved loans he had received, one from his bank in excess of legal limits and one from parties later identified as brewery officials in the amount of $156,000; and three charges concerned his interference in University of Texas affairs. The verdict of the senate removed Ferguson from office and declared him ineligible to hold any state office in the future.

Ferguson appealed the decision of the legislature to the electorate by announcing his candidacy for governor in 1918, but was badly defeated by William P. Hobby, the lieutenant governor who had succeeded him in 1917. He kept his name before the voters in 1920 as the presidential candidate of his own American party and in 1922 as an unsuccessful candidate for the United States Senate. When the Democratic party split over the Ku Klux Klan issue in 1924, he seized the opportunity to clear his name. Barred by the courts from running himself, he announced the gubernatorial candidacy of his wife (though in earlier years he had strongly opposed woman suffrage). The Fergusons campaigned against the Klan's secrecy, its Victorian moral code, and its prohibitionist views, but they "out-Klanned the Klan" on the issue of white supremacy and defeated the Klan candidate, Judge Felix Robertson.

Upon Mrs. Ferguson's election, her husband moved into an office adjacent to the governor's suite. In what was in effect his third administration, Ferguson attracted considerable attention for the excessive number of pardons his wife granted to persons convicted of violating the state liquor laws, and he drew charges of favoritism in the awarding of state highway construction contracts. The governor succeeded in having the legislature grant amnesty to her husband, though this action was rescinded the following year. She also succeeded in having an antimasking law adopted which furthered the demise of the Klan. The elimination of the Klan from politics, however, permitted the anti-Ferguson elements of the Democratic party to close ranks, and "Ma" Ferguson was defeated in 1926 and 1930.

The depression of the early 1930's once more created a crisis in party leadership favorable to the Fergusons, and in 1932 Mrs. Ferguson won the governorship for the second time. The repeal of prohibition and the issuance of relief bonds, along with the efficient conduct of the governor's office, made the last Ferguson administration the most successful and the one most free from partisan attack. "Fergusonism," however, was clearly on the wane after 1934, though Mrs. Ferguson made a token race for governor in 1940. Four years later James E. Ferguson died of a stroke in Austin, Texas. He was buried in the Texas State Cemetery in Austin. His wife survived him by seven years.

[No biography exists of James E. Ferguson, partly because there are no personal papers. Files of *Home and State,* the prohibition weekly published in Dallas in 1914, and *Ferguson Forum,* the governor's own publication in the 1920's, provide sharply contrasting views of the man. The best published accounts are by Ralph W. Steen: see his *Twentieth Century Texas* (1942), his contribution to Frank C. Adams, ed., *Texas Democracy* (4 vols., 1937), his "The Ferguson War on the Univ. of Texas," *Southwestern Social Sci. Quart.,* Mar. 1955, and his sketch of Ferguson in the *Handbook of Texas* (2 vols., 1952). Comparable in some respects are Seth S. McKay, *Texas Politics, 1906–1944* (1952); McKay and Odie B. Faulk, *Texas after Spindletop* (1965); and Reinhard H. Luthin, *Am. Demagogues—Twentieth Century* (1954). Charles C. Alexander, "Crusade for Conformity: The Ku Klux Klan in Texas, 1920–1930," Texas Gulf Coast Hist. Assoc., *Publication Series,* vol. VI (1962), is useful in understanding the gubernatorial campaign of 1924. Two doctoral dissertations describe conditions at the beginning and end of the Ferguson era in Texas: James A. Tinsley, "The Progressive Movement in Texas" (Univ. of Wis., 1954), and Lionel V. Patenaude, "The New Deal and Texas" (Univ. of Texas, 1953). Ouida Ferguson Nalle, *The Fergusons of Texas* (1946), is a daughter's uncritical account.]

JAMES A. TINSLEY

FERGUSON, JOHN CALVIN (Mar. 1, 1866–Aug. 3, 1945), missionary educator, public official in China, and connoisseur of Chinese art, was born near Belleville, Ontario, Canada, the third son and youngest of six children of John Ferguson, a Methodist minister of Scottish ancestry, and Catherine Matilda (Pomeroy) Ferguson. He studied for a time at Albert College in Belleville and then moved to Boston, Mass., where he served as associate pastor of the People's Church (1885–87) and attended Boston University. After receiving the A.B. degree in 1886 and studying in the theological school, he was ordained in the Methodist ministry. Missionaries in China were then developing Christian colleges to supplement lower schools established earlier, and Bishop Charles H. Fowler [*q.v.*] persuaded the gifted and energetic Ferguson to start a college in Nanking for the Methodist mission. On Aug. 4, 1887, before sailing for China, he married Mary Elizabeth Wilson of Rochester, N. Y., a minister's daughter. They had nine children: Luther Mitchel, Helen Matilda, Alice Mary, Florence Wilson, Charles John, Mary Esther, Robert Mason, Duncan Pomeroy, and Peter Blair.

Ferguson spent his first months in China at Chinkiang, making an intensive study of the language; with a background of training in Greek, Latin, and Hebrew, he learned rapidly. In 1888 he opened the new Nanking University as its first president, with a class of fifteen students who met in the living room of his home. During the next decade he designed a college curriculum, translated chemistry and mathematics texts into Chinese, and drew up plans and supervised the construction of buildings for the new institution, which soon became a notable center of Western education. Unlike many of his missionary contemporaries, he was also convinced that China had much to teach him and sought out the usually inaccessible scholar-officials who best embodied the virtues of Chinese culture. His command of the language, admiration for China, and respect for Chinese etiquette won him many friends. Tall and blue-eyed, with long, fair hair, flowing mustaches and bushy eyebrows, he was accepted in the courts and homes of the local mandarins and even of the viceroy. Officials sought his advice on matters concerning the West. In return he was allowed to see the bronzes, porcelains, and paintings hidden in the great compounds, and his passion for Chinese art began to stir.

One of the officials who came to admire Ferguson was Sheng Hsuan-huai, an entrepreneur and banker of doubtful reputation but tremendous power, who wished to found a technical institute in Shanghai. At his invitation Ferguson in 1897 left Nanking and the mission field to establish and become president of Nanyang College (later Chiaotung University). For the next several years Ferguson's career was linked with Sheng's multiple ventures. In 1899 Sheng helped him acquire a small Shanghai Chinese-language paper, *Sin Wan Pao,* which under a competent Chinese staff grew to be the largest daily in Shanghai and provided a comfortable income for Ferguson and his growing family. In 1902 Ferguson was appointed secretary of the new Ministry of Commerce; from 1903 to 1905 he served as chief secretary of the Imperial Chinese Railway Administration, which Sheng had run since 1896; and in 1911 he was made foreign secretary to the Ministry of Posts and Communications, of which Sheng was head. In this close formal relationship with the imperial regime, rare though not unknown for a foreigner, Ferguson was also often asked to carry out foreign missions for the Manchu government.

During these years Ferguson's capacity for rigorous self-discipline allowed him to continue other activities as well. An early riser, he read his New Testament, in Greek, before breakfast and dispatched a voluminous personal correspondence before turning to other matters. These included completing work for a Ph.D. degree awarded by Boston University in 1902 for a thesis on the Chinese examination system; editing the *Journal* of the North China branch of the Royal Asiatic Society (1902–11), to which he also contributed many articles; and serving as vice-president of the Red Cross Society of China (which Sheng founded in 1909). As chairman of the relief commission during the famine of 1910–11 Ferguson raised nearly a million dollars to help provide food for the starving. He was thus becoming that most admired of traditional Chinese figures, the scholar-official, prominent in public affairs, philanthropic, and steeped in a knowledge of Chinese culture. Although he never wore Chinese dress, for his seventieth birthday an artist drew a portrait of him wearing the robes of a scholar, for his Chinese friends thought of him in this role.

But traditional China was dying. Just after Ferguson moved to Peking in 1911, the October revolution ended two thousand years of imperial rule and ushered in an era of political chaos. Sheng fled to Japan, his power gone, and in 1914 Ferguson brought his family back to Newton, Mass., intending to retire. He returned to Peking in 1915, however, at the request of the new government and remained there until World War II. Installed in a great compound built for a grand councillor of the Ch'ing Dynasty, he continued to serve as government adviser and to oversee his thriving Shanghai newspaper, which he owned until 1929. He was a member of the Chinese delegation to the Washington Conference of 1921. From 1914 on, he published several articles warning against Japanese designs on China. A champion of China's independence and a critic of Western exploitation, he nevertheless did not espouse the growing revolutionary movement. He also continued to study and write about Chinese culture.

Ferguson's deepest love, however, was reserved for Chinese art. Throughout the years he had been acquiring a good selection of Chou bronzes, Han candlesticks, jade pens, rubbings, and fine paintings. In 1914 he mounted a special exhibition of his paintings for the Metropolitan Museum of Art in New York and produced a pamphlet on bronzes for the Smithsonian Institution. Thereafter he served as art buyer and consultant for the Metropolitan, the Freer Gallery, and other museums. He also published many articles and several books on art, including two monumental catalogues (in Chinese) on paintings and bronzes. The most charming of his books is the *Noted Porcelains of Successive Dynasties* (1931), an annotated reproduction of an important Ming collection. Ferguson printed it himself, as a labor of love, in collaboration with the superintendent of the famous Ching Te-kien pottery works. To reproduce the color paintings, the two men had paper handmade by a T'ang Dynasty formula and brought printing presses from Germany; they even cast their own type.

After the beginning of the war with Japan, Ferguson remained in his house with one daughter, working on a catalogue of rubbings. He was briefly interned in the British embassy, and was repatriated to the United States on the liner *Gripsholm* in December 1943. He was then seventy-seven. Less than two years later he died of arteriosclerotic heart disease in a sanatorium at Clifton Springs, N. Y., and was buried in the Newton (Mass.) Cemetery. His wife and three of their nine children had died before him.

Ferguson had succeeded in being both Western scholar and Chinese mandarin, a mediator between two cultures rather than an outstanding figure in any one field. He felt that China had given him a life full of adventure and romance, and he reciprocated by leaving his collection of art to Nanking University.

[Ferguson's other major writings are: *Outlines of Chinese Art* (1919); *Chinese Painting* (1927); *Survey of Chinese Art* (1939); *Catalogue of the Recorded Paintings of Successive Dynasties* (1934) and *Catalogue of the Recorded Bronzes of Successive Dynasties* (1939), both published in Chinese; and a lively, readable section on Chinese mythology in *The Mythology of All Races,* vol. VIII (1928), on China and Japan, ed. by John A. MacCulloch. The most comprehensive biographical account is in the *Nat. Cyc. Am. Biog.,* XXXIV, 208–10, which contains a picture of the elderly Ferguson (facing p. 209). A graceful tribute on Ferguson's seventy-fifth birthday by the Sinologist R. H. van Gulik can be found, along with a picture and bibliography of Ferguson's writings, in the journal *Monumenta Serica,* vol. VI (1941). Dr. Ferguson's daughters Miss Mary Esther Ferguson and Mrs. John C. Beaumont provided invaluable personal memories; they have papers, pictures, and miscellaneous memorabilia. Death record from N. Y. State Dept. of Health.]
SHIRLEY STONE GARRETT

FERREE, CLARENCE ERROL (Mar. 11, 1877–July 26, 1942), research scientist in psychology and physiological optics, was born in Sidney, Ohio, the third of four children and youngest son of Jeremiah Dixon Ferree, a prosperous farmer of Pennsylvania Huguenot descent, and Arvesta (Line) Ferree. Both parents were na-

tives of Shelby County, Ohio, and members of the Methodist Church. After teaching in a public secondary school for three years, young Ferree attended Ohio Wesleyan University, where he received the B.S. and A.M. degrees in 1900 and an M.S. in 1901. In 1902 he began graduate work in psychology at Cornell University. He spent the year 1905–06 as an instructor in physics and psychology at the University of Arizona, but returned to Cornell, where he received his Ph.D. under Edward B. Titchener [*q.v.*] in 1909.

Meanwhile, in 1907, Ferree had been appointed lecturer in experimental psychology at Bryn Mawr College. There he spent the next two decades of his career, becoming associate professor and director of the psychological laboratory (1912) and professor of psychology (1917). Among his first graduate students was Gertrude Rand (Oct. 29, 1886–June 30, 1970), a Cornell alumna (A.B. 1908) who received the Ph.D. degree at Bryn Mawr in 1911. The two continued a close scientific collaboration, published a number of papers together, and were married on Sept. 28, 1918; they had no children.

Ferree's early interests in psychology lay in the experimental study of conscious processes such as attention, hearing, and seeing. To attack these problems, he concentrated on the function of human vision and developed methods and instruments to measure, in a precise way, the eye's physiological response to visual stimuli. Thereafter his interests narrowed to physiological optics, the relation between vision and illumination and ophthalmology. In 1912 he served on a joint committee of the American Medical Association and the Illuminating Engineering Society to study lighting in relation to the welfare and hygiene of the eye. He was the first to demonstrate in the laboratory that the eye functions better in one system of illumination than in another.

With Gertrude Rand (who retained her maiden name in professional work) and the help of capable technical assistants, Ferree developed various optical apparatus, ophthalmological instruments, and glareless lighting appliances. He devised equipment for measuring the speed of ocular accommodation and convergence, visual acuity, light and color sense, visual fields and areas of impaired seeing, the visual effects of various spectral wavelengths, and visual reaction times and sensitivities. He and his wife also made contributions in the fields of industrial lighting, efficiency engineering, and direct-indirect (louvered) lighting fixtures. During World War I, at the request of the military forces, he undertook investigations of ocular fitness and individual differences in visual acuity at low illuminations, to aid in such tasks as selecting men for lookout duty on battleships.

Ferree left Bryn Mawr in 1928 to become director of the research laboratory in physiological optics at the Wilmer Ophthalmological Institute of the Johns Hopkins University Medical School and Hospital, where (in 1932) he was appointed adjunct professor of physiological optics. Gertrude Rand went with him to Johns Hopkins as associate professor in research ophthalmology (1928–32) and in physiological optics (1932–36). After failing health forced Ferree to retire in 1936, he continued work at his home in Baltimore, with his wife as his research associate.

Ferree was a member of various scientific organizations, including the American Psychological Association, the Illuminating Engineering Society, and the Optical Society of America. Known to his associates as an intensive worker and a man of "aggressive drives," he was also able in directing the work of others. With various collaborators, chiefly his wife, he published some 250 papers; some of those by Ferree and Rand were collected in *Studies in Physiological Optics* (2 vols., 1934). Although much of the apparatus Ferree devised has since been superseded, the basic principles of the Ferree-Rand visual fields perimeter are still considered highly significant and useful. He made lasting contributions as a pioneer in the standardized quantitative study of visual functions, stressed the development of precision equipment, and exemplified the interdisciplinary approach to ophthalmologic investigation.

Ferree died at his home in Baltimore in 1942, at the age of sixty-five, of a coronary occlusion. Gertrude Rand, who in Ferree's declining years seems to have been the stronger member of the team, continued her research—first as associate director of the physiological optics research laboratory at the Wilmer Institute (1928–36) and later at Columbia University's College of Physicians and Surgeons as research associate in ophthalmology on the Knapp Foundation (1943–57). She became known especially for her part in developing the Hardy-Rand-Rittler color plates, a recognized test for color deficiency and color blindness.

[The Friedenwald Lib. of the Wilmer Ophthalmological Inst. has a collection (in booklet form) of obituary reports, notes made by Ferree on the development of his work, and a bibliography of his writings. Published sources include: obituaries in *Am. Jour. of Psychology*, Jan. 1943 (by Forrest Lee Dimmick), the *Jour.* of the Optical Soc. of America, July 1943 (by Gertrude Rand), *Archives of Ophthalmology*, Apr. 1943 (by Le Grand H. Hardy), and the *Transactions* of the Illuminating Engineering Soc., Sept. 1942. See also *Who Was Who in America,* vol. II (1950); and, on Gertrude Rand, *Who's Who in America*, 1970–71. Other information from professional associates of

Ferree. On his father, see A. B. C. Hitchcock, *Hist. of Shelby County, Ohio* (1913), pp. 718–20. The Amos Memorial Public Lib., Sidney, Ohio, provided family data, including a census listing of 1880.]

                                                J. D. ANDREWS

FIELDS, LEWIS MAURICE. See WEBER, JOSEPH MORRIS.

FINNEY, JOHN MILLER TURPIN (June 20, 1863–May 30, 1942), surgeon, was born near Natchez, Miss., the younger of two sons of Ebenezer Dickey Finney, a Presbyterian minister and principal of a boys' school, and Annie Louise (Parker) Finney, a music teacher in a neighboring school for girls. His father's ancestors, Scotch-Irish Presbyterians, had come from Belfast in 1720 and settled in Chester County, Pa.; a branch of the family moved to Churchville, Md., where John's father was born. His mother was a New Englander whose forebears had migrated to Massachusetts early in the seventeenth century. She died when he was five months old, and for the next three years he was reared with the children of a family friend, Mrs. Stephen Turpin; in gratitude, his father added "Turpin" to the boy's name. At the end of the Civil War the elder Finney took his sons north, where they lived with relatives in Winchester, Ill., until 1871, when he established a household in Bel Air, Md.

From earliest boyhood John Finney had wished to study medicine. After attending local schools and the Bel Air Academy, he entered Princeton, where he excelled in sports, particularly football, and graduated in 1884. He then enrolled in the Harvard Medical School, but because of an attack of typhoid he was not able to complete the three-year course until 1888. He received the M.D. degree in 1889, after a term of service on the resident surgical staff of the Massachusetts General Hospital.

In May 1889 Finney secured an appointment in the surgical dispensary of the new Johns Hopkins Hospital in Baltimore. He thus joined a brilliant staff that was soon attracting the ablest graduates of American medical schools. In addition to acting as surgeon in the outpatient department, Finney worked in the laboratory of the pathologist William H. Welch [*q.v.*] and, in particular, served as anesthetist for William S. Halsted [*q.v.*], the chief of surgery, who stressed the use of aseptic techniques and was conducting the first surgical residency system in the United States. Finney's appointment carried no salary, however, and in 1890 he began private practice, while continuing his work in the dispensary and acting as head of the surgical service during Halsted's absences. The rules then prevailing at

Johns Hopkins did not allow him to use its facilities for his private patients, and at first he performed his surgical operations in the patients' homes. As his practice grew, he began using the Union Protestant Infirmary and was instrumental in modernizing and enlarging its facilities and in transforming it, in 1919, into the Union Memorial Hospital. Under his leadership a strong group of clinical surgeons was attracted to the staff.

On Apr. 20, 1892, Finney married Mary E. Gross of Harrisburg, Pa., a member of the first class graduating from the Johns Hopkins Training School for Nurses. Their four children were John Miller Train, Eben Dickey, George Gross, and Mary Elizabeth; the first and third sons became physicians. In 1893 Dr. Finney was appointed associate in surgery at both the Johns Hopkins Hospital and the Johns Hopkins University Medical School. He remained on the medical faculty until his retirement in 1933, becoming associate professor of surgery in 1898 and professor of clinical surgery in 1912. During these years he refused invitations to professorships in other institutions, including the University of Texas and the Harvard Medical School; he was also offered the presidency of Princeton after Woodrow Wilson resigned in 1910. Continuing on the staff of the Johns Hopkins Hospital, he headed its surgical clinic from 1899 to 1914 and for three years (1922–25) served as surgeon-in-chief, following the death of Dr. Halsted.

Finney's talent lay in clinical surgery. His abilities gained wide recognition, and celebrated patients sought his services. A general surgeon of the old school, he was skillful in all types of operation but gradually gave more and more attention to lesions of the stomach and intestines, and achieved particular renown in connection with gastric surgery. His pyloroplasty, an operation for the relief of duodenal ulcer, remains a standard procedure and, currently associated with division of the vagus nerve, has had a considerable resurgence in popularity. As a teacher Finney exerted a considerable influence on many of the men who were surgical residents during his years at Hopkins, but his particular interest was in the direct care of patients.

Finney was the first president (1913–16) of the American College of Surgeons. He was president also of many other organizations, including the American Surgical Association (1921) and the Society of Clinical Surgery. During World War I he was commissioned a major and in 1917 went overseas as director of the Johns Hopkins Unit, Base Hospital 18. While in France he was made chief consultant in surgery of the A.E.F. and rose to the rank of brigadier general. He was an honorary member of various foreign medical societies, including the Académie Royale de Médecine of Belgium and the Royal College of Surgeons of England. In 1932 he was awarded the Bigelow Medal of the Boston Surgical Society, and in 1937 he was honored by the establishment of the Finney-Howell Research Foundation for the Investigation of Cancer. He received honorary degrees from Tulane University (1935) and Harvard (1937).

Genial and courteous, a willing raconteur, Finney had a strong sense of right and wrong and was held in high esteem. He was deeply religious and served as an elder of the Presbyterian Church and as chairman of the Baltimore branch of the National Conference of Christians and Jews. He had a strong interest in education, was a life trustee of Princeton, and served as chairman of the board of trustees of the Gilman Country School for Boys in Baltimore and of the McDonogh School for Boys in McDonogh, Md. He was a leader in establishing Provident Hospital in Baltimore, where Negro physicians and nurses could carry on their work, and he served as chairman of the board of trustees of Lincoln University at Oxford, Pa. A few days before his seventy-ninth birthday, Finney died at his home in Baltimore of a coronary thrombosis. He was buried in the Presbyterian cemetery at Churchville, Md.

[Finney's autobiography, *A Surgeon's Life* (1940); obituaries in *Surgery, Gynecology and Obstetrics*, July 1942 (by William A. Fisher), and *Annals of Surgery*, Apr. 1944 (by John Staige Davis); Sir D'Arcy Power and W. R. Le Fanu, *Lives of the Fellows of the Royal College of Surgeons of England, 1930–1951* (1953), pp. 282–85; Loyal Davis, *Fellowship of Surgeons: A Hist. of the Am. College of Surgeons* (1960); information from Dr. George C. Finney and, on Finney's Johns Hopkins appointments, from Miss Janet B. Koudelka of the William A. Welch Medic. Lib., Johns Hopkins Univ.; death record from Baltimore City Health Dept.]

MARK M. RAVITCH

FISHER, CLARENCE STANLEY (Aug. 17, 1876–July 20, 1941), Near East archaeologist, was born in Philadelphia, Pa., the son of Frederick Theodore and Emily Margaret (Shewell) Fisher. His paternal grandfather had come to Pennsylvania from Württemberg in 1816; his father is listed in city directories as a mattressmaker. Clarence Fisher was educated in the public schools of Philadelphia until 1890 and graduated from Eastburn Academy in 1893. He attended the University of Pennsylvania, receiving the B.S. degree in architecture in 1897. He then worked for a year as an architect in the office of John L. Mauran in St. Louis, Mo.

Fisher's architectural interests were strongly classical—his graduation thesis had been a plan for a classical building of his own design—and in 1898 he turned to the study of ancient buildings as an archaeological architect for the University of Pennsylvania's Babylonian Expedition to the Sumerian city of Nippur. When the expedition ended in 1900 he worked for two years at the University Museum in Philadelphia, where its findings had been deposited. In 1903 the post of research fellow in Babylonian architecture at the University of Pennsylvania was created for him; he resigned it in 1905 to work independently. On Nov. 14, 1907, he married Florie M. Carswell, daughter of a Baptist minister in Philadelphia. They had one son, Clarence Stanley.

The archaeological work in Palestine for which Fisher is best known began in 1909, when he was a leading member of the Harvard University Expedition to Samaria, under the direction of George A. Reisner [Supp. 3]. The first major American investigation in Palestine, the expedition introduced a new era in the disciplines and techniques of archaeological research. In earlier work in Egypt, Reisner had pioneered in the stratigraphic excavating of complete areas of an ancient site. His work in Egypt was continuing, and much of the responsibility for the digging at Samaria fell to Fisher.

In the next thirty years, Fisher developed Reisner's methods as director of or adviser to successive American expeditions. His insistence upon the most careful kind of surveying and mapping—the drawing of exact architectural plans of every building and wall; recording the location of every object encountered, however small, including each fragment of pottery, so that an excavated level with all its contents could be restored on paper—profoundly affected the development of Palestinian archaeology. Fisher was to remain in the Near East, mostly in Jerusalem, for the rest of his life, with rare visits to and from his family in America. From 1914 to 1925 he held an appointment as chief archaeologist and Egyptologist of the University Museum in Philadelphia. He spent the war years working in Egypt for Near East Relief.

The fifteen years after World War I proved to be a golden age for archaeological work in Palestine and the other Near Eastern countries mandated to European governments, which encouraged the study of antiquities. Fisher was a shy, taciturn, high-strung person who did not work well in harness with others, and as a result he never remained throughout all the campaigns of any one excavation. For two years (1921–23), under the auspices of the University Museum, he directed the excavation of the citadel of Beth-shan, where he found the first anthropoid slipper-shaped coffin to be discovered in Palestine. On this site Fisher and his successors uncovered a series of Egyptian fortresses from the fourteenth to the twelfth centuries, as well as a sequence of strata going back into the fourth millennium. During the winters of these years Fisher served as architect for excavations in Egypt (at Giza, Girga, Thebes, and Memphis) directed by Reisner. In 1925 the Oriental Institute of the University of Chicago placed Fisher in charge of the excavation of the biblical town of Megiddo, but by 1928 and 1929 he had quit that position to direct the first two seasons of excavation at Beth-shemesh for Elihu Grant of Haverford College.

Fisher was appointed professor of archaeology at the American School of Oriental Research in Jerusalem in 1925. In the following years he served as adviser or architect to a series of cooperative investigations under the aegis of the school. One of these, the expedition of 1938 to Khirbet Tannur in Transjordan, was the last major work he was to complete.

Extensive excavation in Palestine came to an end with the onset of fighting between Arabs and Jews in 1936. Thereafter Fisher gave his full time to his professorship at the American School. He was a master of the art of teaching informally. His emphasis upon the importance of pottery, of exact pottery drawings and archaeological plans, was conveyed to all who came under his influence. For years he worked steadily on his monumental "Corpus of Palestinian Pottery," but death interrupted its completion; it was never published, and it has since been outmoded by subsequent advances in pottery dating.

In his last years Fisher was an active citizen of Jerusalem. During World War II he was perhaps the most influential and active member of the committee appointed by the British Mandatory Government to look after educational institutions that had been run by German and Italian nationals. He served also as the representative in Palestine of the Lutheran Church of America (his denomination) and as a member of the board of directors of the Jerusalem Y.M.C.A. and of the German (Schneller) Orphanage. Generous to a fault, quick in his sympathies for the underprivileged, he was the moving spirit, two years before his death, in the founding of the Dar el-Awlad, the Home for Children, in Jerusalem, where homeless basketboys from the Suq (Old City) found refuge, guidance, and instruction. He himself legally adopted a Christian Arab boy, whose name thenceforth was David Fisher. Clarence S. Fisher died at the age of sixty-four at Government Hospital in Jerusalem. He was buried in the Protestant Cemetery on Mount Zion, where his gravestone stands close by the grave of another famous archaeologist, Sir Flinders Petrie.

[Fisher's principal publications are: *Excavations at Nippur* (2 parts, 1905–06); *Harvard Excavations at Samaria,* with George A. Reisner and David G. Lyon (2 vols., 1924); *The Excavation of Armageddon* (1929); "Jerash-Gerasa 1930" (with Chester C. McCown) and "The Campaign at Jerash in Sept. and Oct. 1931," in Am. Schools of Oriental Research, *Annual,* 1929–30 (published 1931). Fisher's unpublished "Corpus of Palestinian Pottery" is in the custody of the Am. Schools of Oriental Research, with headquarters in Cambridge, Mass. Biographical sources: obituaries by Nelson Glueck in *Bull. Am. Schools of Oriental Research,* Oct. 1941, and *Biblical Archaeologist,* Sept. 1941; *Nat. Cyc. Am. Biog.,* XL, 286–87; and references to Fisher's work in: Chester C. McCown, *The Ladder of Progress in Palestine* (1943); William F. Albright, *The Archaeology of Palestine* (1949 and later editions); G. Ernest Wright, *The Bible and the Ancient Near East* (1961) and *Biblical Archaeology* (1962), and his "The Phenomenon of Am. Archaeology in the Near East," in James A. Sanders, ed., *Near Eastern Archaeology in the Twentieth Century* (1970). Information on Fisher's family background from Philadelphia city directories (courtesy of Free Lib. of Phila.) and from records of the Univ. of Pa.]

NELSON GLUECK

FISHER, FREDERIC JOHN (Jan. 2, 1878–July 14, 1941), automotive manufacturer, was born in Sandusky, Ohio, the eldest of the seven sons and four daughters of Lawrence and Margaret (Theisen) Fisher. His paternal grandfather, Andrew Fisher, had been a wagon and carriage builder in his native Germany; after arriving in the United States, he became a merchant in Peru, Ohio, where his son Lawrence was born in 1852. Lawrence settled in Norwalk, Ohio, opening a blacksmith and wheelwright shop there, and later moved to Sandusky, where he married. He eventually returned to Norwalk with a growing family. Frederic—or Fred, as he was called by most—attended a Catholic parochial school in Sandusky, finished the eighth grade, and at fourteen entered the family business. Under his father's tutelage he became an expert carriage maker.

In 1902 Fred went to Detroit, Mich., and took a job as a four-dollar-a-week draftsman for the C. R. Wilson Carriage Works, at that time the largest manufacturer of automobile bodies in the city. In these years Detroit was fast rising to its eminence as the principal center of motor vehicle production in the United States. In 1907 Fisher became superintendent of the Wilson shop. Meanwhile, he had been joined by his brothers. Five of them—Charles Thomas, Alfred Joseph, Lawrence Peter, William Andrew, and Edward Francis—would be associated with him in a variety of industrial and financial enterprises over a period of some thirty-five years. (The remaining brother, Howard Albert, had no part in these ventures.) Until his death, Fred was the acknowledged leader of the Fisher brothers, who constituted one of the most closely knit family groups in modern American business history.

In July 1908 Fred and his brother Charles organized the Fisher Body Company as a Michigan corporation with a capitalization of $50,000 and established a plant in Detroit. The other four brothers were brought into the firm, and an uncle, Andrew Fisher, served briefly as president until the brothers purchased his interest. The business flourished from the start. Fisher bodies were designed specifically for automobiles rather than as modifications of horse-drawn vehicles; consequently, they were sturdier and more shockproof than those made by competitors. Moreover, the Fishers grasped the possibilities of the closed car long before it became the standard type of passenger automobile. The order for 150 closed bodies that Cadillac placed with them in 1910 was the first volume order of its kind in the United States and led directly to the formation of the Fisher Closed Body Company in 1912. In the same year the brothers organized the Fisher Body Company of Canada, Ltd., at Walkerville, Ontario. Within four years the combined profits of the Detroit and Walkerville companies had increased almost fourfold to $1,390,592. In August 1916 the three firms were merged into the Fisher Body Corporation, a holding and operating company chartered in New York with a capitalization of $6,000,000. This amalgamation, with a total annual capacity of 370,000 units, made the Fisher facilities the largest of their type in the industry. The enterprise was financed principally through the reinvestment of profits.

In 1919 General Motors, pursuing an ambitious program of expanded vertical integration under William C. Durant, acquired a 60 percent interest in Fisher Body and agreed to buy practically all of its auto bodies from Fisher for ten years at a price of cost plus 17.6 percent. The acquisition cost General Motors $27,600,000 under an agreement whereby Fisher Body increased its 200,000 shares of common stock to 500,000 and sold the new issue to General Motors at $92 a share. The Fishers, however, retained managerial control of their firm. Immediately after the First World War they constructed at Cleveland, Ohio, a facility which ranked as the world's largest body factory until their Flint No. 1 body plant was erected in Michigan, and between 1922 and 1929 their company built or acquired some twenty factories in various parts of the country. Fred Fisher joined the executive committee of General Motors in 1922, and two years later was made a vice-president of the corporation and a member of its finance committee.

Of the many properties acquired by the often impulsive Durant before he was finally deposed as head of General Motors in 1920, the Fisher concern proved to be one of the most profitable. It yielded high returns in the postwar years, when American auto makers and motorists shifted their preference from the open touring car to the closed car. In 1919, 90 percent of the automobiles produced in the United States were open cars; in 1927, by contrast, 85 percent were closed cars. The Fisher company made $23,000,000 in 1923 on a volume of 417,000 bodies; in 1925 its net earnings on 575,000 units were equal to a return of 18.9 percent on a valuation of $143,000,000 in assets.

The Fishers introduced numerous improvements in body hardware and interior fittings, notably steel panels, the rubber weather strip for windshields, side window vents, and the Ternstedt window regulator. They pioneered in the development of steel body presses and steel-faced dies, and were the first to use lacquer instead of paint on auto bodies. Their Fleetwood custom division, acquired in 1925, became a byword for excellence in design and craftsmanship. The trademark "Body by Fisher," with its emblem of a Napoleonic coach in silhouette, became familiar to millions of motorists.

In 1926 the minority stockholders of the Fisher Body Corporation, consisting chiefly of the six brothers, sold their 40 percent interest to General Motors in exchange for G.M. common stock with a market value of $130,000,000. Fisher Body became a division of General Motors, and each of the six brothers was named to a post in the corporation or one of its subsidiaries. William was made president of Fisher Body, and Lawrence became head of the Cadillac division. Fred continued to serve as a vice-president of General Motors until his resignation in January 1934. Meanwhile, in 1927, the Fishers began construction of an office building in Detroit, the Fisher Building, designed by the architect Albert Kahn [Supp. 3]. By 1928 Fred's personal fortune was estimated at $50,000,000. The combined holdings of the brothers were later set at $500,000,000.

Seeking new investment outlets for their accumulated capital, the Fishers entered the stock market for the first time in 1926. Their operations were conducted through a family concern, Fisher & Company, of which Fred was chairman. In 1927-29, as the great bull market of the Coolidge era moved toward its climax, the Fishers' carefully planned and boldly executed maneuvers, frequently carried out together with the Wall Street operator Arthur W. Cutten, brought them a national reputation as shrewd speculators.

The market crash of 1929 wiped out their paper profits, and soon afterward the Fishers withdrew from large-scale trading.

Fred Fisher was a director of some twenty corporations, including North American Aviation, the Sperry Corporation, the National Bank of Detroit, and the Intercontinental Trust Company of Chicago. Shy and retiring, he was not prominent in public affairs, but with his brothers he contributed to the Republican party, giving $100,000 to the Hoover campaign in 1928. He made large philanthropic donations to Detroit educational and charitable organizations, and was a trustee of the Detroit Symphony Society and the Detroit Community Fund. A Catholic, he was a trustee of the University of Notre Dame and in 1929 was decorated by Pope Pius XI with the Order of Malta. In 1932 he contributed $25,000 to the Association against the Prohibition Amendment. Fisher had married Burtha Meyers on June 24, 1908. There were no children. He maintained a palatial home in Detroit, and his 226-foot yacht, *Nakhoda,* built in 1930 at a cost of $1,000,000, was among the most luxurious of that era. He died in 1941 of subacute bacterial endocarditis at the Henry Ford Hospital in Detroit. Burial was in Mount Olivet Cemetery, Detroit. All of his brothers survived him.

[There are useful summary accounts of the Fisher enterprises in Arthur Pound, *The Turning Wheel* (1934), and Lawrence H. Seltzer, *A Financial Hist. of the Am. Automobile Industry* (1928). Kenneth R. Baldwin, "The Custom Cadillac: The Fleetwood Story," *Classic Car,* Fall 1961, has some interesting details on Fisher body innovations. Biographical sources: *N. Y. Times,* July 15, 17, 1941; *Detroit News,* July 14, 17, 1941; *Detroit Free Press,* July 15, 1941 (includes good portrait); Alfred P. Sloan, Jr., *My Years with General Motors* (1964); Edward D. Kennedy, *The Automobile Industry* (1941); *Who Was Who in America,* vol. I (1942); family information; death record (Detroit Dept. of Health). Contemporary accounts of the Fishers as stock market operators are John T. Flynn, "Riders of the Whirlwind," *Collier's,* Jan. 19, 1929, and Earl Sparling, "Market Makers: Fred J. Fisher," undated clipping, *N. Y. Telegram,* 1929, in Automotive Hist. Collection, Detroit Public Lib.]

WILLIAM GREENLEAF

FISKE, BRADLEY ALLEN (June 13, 1854– Apr. 6, 1942), naval officer, was born in Lyons, N. Y., the eldest of four children of William Allen and Susan (Bradley) Fiske. His father, whose English forebear, William Fiske, had settled in Salem, Mass., in 1637, was an Episcopal minister. The family moved to Cleveland, Ohio, in 1860 and six years later to Cincinnati. After attending public schools, Fiske was appointed a cadet midshipman in the United States Naval Academy when he was barely sixteen. He graduated in 1874, the second in his class.

For the next twenty-five years, Fiske performed the generally unexciting duties that filled out the ordinary naval career of the period. Cruising along the coastal sea-lanes or sailing in the waters surrounding American naval stations in distant lands, he served as navigator, gunnery officer, or executive officer on small ships. He was, however, on the *Yorktown* in 1891 when that gunboat was sent to Valparaiso, Chile, after several American sailors had been killed in the streets by an angry mob; and two years later he was aboard the *San Francisco,* flagship of a squadron that put in at Rio de Janeiro to protect American merchant ships from revolutionary elements of the Brazilian navy. This was a memorable occasion because for the first time in years vessels of the navy cleared for action and fired warning shots across the bows of ships of another nation.

As navigator of the *Petrel* in 1898, Fiske saw more dangerous action in the battle of Manila. For his "conspicuous" and "heroic" conduct in standing in an exposed position to take the range of the Spanish ships with a stadimeter—one of his own inventions—he was commended by Adm. George Dewey [*q.v.*]. Following the peace with Spain he remained in the islands, serving on the *Monadnock* and the *Yorktown* and taking part in the frequent bombardment of shore installations during the subsequent Filipino insurrection. He rose more rapidly in the first decade of the new century, becoming captain, in turn, of the cruiser *Minneapolis,* the coast-defense monitor *Arkansas,* and the armored cruiser *Tennessee.* Promoted to rear admiral in 1911, he commanded various battleship divisions in the Atlantic Fleet before his final assignment to shore duty.

What gave Fiske his importance and distinction in the navy, however, was not so much the competent performance of his regular duties as his restless investigation of the new technology which, during his lifetime, was transforming the design of ships and ordnance as well as the nature of naval warfare. Without much formal training in engineering, but supported by a logical and inquiring mind, he educated himself during the long empty hours at sea in physics, optics, and especially in the growing field of electricity. Such preparations, coupled with his increasing curiosity about mechanical matters, enabled him to develop a series of significant inventions, including an electric ammunition hoist, wireless-controlled ships and torpedoes, the torpedo plane, a new kind of ship communication system, and electrically controlled gun turrets. Fiske's most important invention was the naval telescope sight which he devised in 1891, while on leave from the *Yorktown.* Initially condemned as useless by his commanding officer, Robley D. Evans [*q.v.*], within seven years it had become standard issue for all ships. Together with the stadimeter, his electric rangefinder, these instruments laid a solid foundation for a new kind of naval gunnery which, as has often been said, converted what had been an uncertain art into an exact science. The fact that so many of his inventions were met with resistance both by individual officers, cheerfully fixed within their customary routines, and by the naval bureaus, immobilized within ancient departmental practice, caused Fiske to turn his attention to changes in the system of naval education and the structure of naval organization. He formed a remarkable group of enlightened officers—Stephen B. Luce [*q.v.*], Henry Clay Taylor, William S. Sims [Supp. 2], Albert Lenoir Key, William F. Fullam—who in this period were fighting to raise the intellectual level of the service and to increase the amount of military energy, as opposed to the inertia of simple maintenance, that flowed through the directing offices of the Department. Less at home in political situations than the others, and without the sense of crusade that stirred in some of them, Fiske nevertheless was indispensable to the purposes they all sought because he supplied them with the technical improvements they could fight for.

Fiske's contribution to the reform of the navy was recognized by his appointment in 1913 as aide for operations, the chief military adviser to Secretary of the Navy. This capstone to his career brought him little but frustration because of his continuous differences with Secretary Josephus Daniels, a man of humane impulses but a provincial who misunderstood in almost every possible way what a navy was about. Fiske therefore resigned in 1915.

Shortly thereafter, in 1916, Bradley Fiske retired from active duty, as he was required by law to do at the age of sixty-two. He lived for the remaining quarter-century of his life most of the time in New York City, at the Hotel Commodore and later at the Waldorf-Astoria. He continued his intelligent interest in the naval service and wrote three useful books: *The Navy as a Fighting Machine* (1916); his illuminating autobiography, *From Midshipman to Rear Admiral* (1919); and *The Art of Fighting* (1920).

Whether on active duty or in retirement, Fiske was a civilized man, literate, humorous, liberal in spirit, and warm in sympathy, with an attractive elegance in person and manner. On Feb. 15, 1882, he married Josephine Harper, daughter of Joseph Wesley Harper of the New York publishing firm; they had one daughter, Caroline Harper.

Fiske died in New York City in 1942 and was buried in Arlington National Cemetery. He was one of the very small group of officers who had most to do with taking the navy from the timeless days of sail into the modern conditions of steel, steam, high explosives, and electricity.

[Bradley Fiske, *From Midshipman to Rear Admiral* (1919); Elting E. Morison, *Admiral Sims and the Modern Am. Navy* (1942); Bernard Brodie, *Sea Power in the Machine Age* (1941); *N. Y. Times*, Apr. 7, 1942. There is abundant Fiske material in the Navy Dept. records, Nat. Archives, Washington, D. C.]

ELTING E. MORISON

FISKE, HARRISON GREY (July 30, 1861–Sept. 2, 1942), theatrical journalist, producer, and director, was born in Harrison, N. Y., the second of three sons of Lyman Fiske, a prosperous hotel owner, and Jennie (Durfee) Fiske, both of seventeenth-century Massachusetts descent. The family moved to New York City during his boyhood, and he remained a confirmed New Yorker throughout his life. He received his early education from tutors and at a school run by Mrs. George C. Vandenhoff, Jr.; her husband, a retired English actor, gave Shakespearean readings which instilled in the boy an enduring love of Shakespeare. After attending Dr. Chapin's Collegiate Institute in New York City, Fiske traveled for a summer in Europe and then, in 1878, entered New York University.

He had first become enamored of the stage when as a small child he was taken to see a play at Barnum's Museum, and his father had later given him a toy theatre. As a boy he also had a printing press on which he got out his own monthly paper. During his teens he combined the two interests as dramatic critic for the *Jersey City Argus* and the *New York Star*, papers on which his family had influence, and while in college he began contributing to the *Dramatic Mirror*, a New York weekly. He left college after his freshman year to become a journalist. His father bought an interest in the *Dramatic Mirror* and made his son (then eighteen) the editor; young Fiske became sole owner in 1888.

Fiske's courageous editorial policy turned the *Dramatic Mirror* into the artistic and professional conscience of the American theatre. Distressed by the plight of out-of-work actors and by the laissez-faire practices of the American stage, Fiske in his paper battled successfully to establish the Actors' Fund, chartered in 1882—the first voluntary, large-scale social security measure for an always insecure profession. Another *Mirror* campaign sought the improvement of working conditions and the regulation of health hazards in theatres; Fiske disapproved, however, of attempts to organize an actors' union. He helped

secure passage of the Cummings Act of 1896 and subsequent laws to protect playwrights against literary piracy. In the theatrical world he consistently championed the creative artist against the profiteer.

After a prolonged infatuation with Fanny Davenport [*q.v.*], an actress almost ten years his senior, Fiske in 1886 began a leisurely courtship of a younger actress, Minnie Maddern [see Minnie Maddern Fiske, Supp. 1]. She divorced her first husband, and on Mar. 19, 1890, she and Fiske were married at Larchmont, N. Y. They had no children. The marriage, though unromantic in the conventional sense, proved of vital importance to the American theatre. Miss Maddern, daughter of itinerant actors, limited in formal education but possessing a practical knowledge of the theatre, and Fiske, the urbane, well-to-do gentleman with literary tastes and a passion for the drama, together were uniquely suited to the task of reforming and civilizing the American stage. Mrs. Fiske taught her husband the realities of the hazardous, day-to-day existence of the barnstorming troupe; he devoted himself to her career, encouraged her artistic growth, and helped shape her taste until she was considered one of the most intellectually progressive of actresses. In an interview with Alexander Woollcott [Supp. 3], Mrs. Fiske referred to her husband as her "artistic backbone."

The Fiskes spent twelve years fighting the theatrical trust known as the Syndicate, a combine of theatre managers formed in 1896 by Charles Frohman, Abraham L. Erlanger [*qq.v.*], Marc Klaw [Supp. 2], and Al Hayman of New York, and Samuel Nixon (Nirdlinger) and J. F. Zimmerman of Philadelphia. Their professed aim was to rationalize theatrical booking and eliminate wastefully competitive practices. In fact, the Syndicate attempted to create a nationwide monopoly so that no play could be booked and no actor employed without its consent. Using the customary pressure tactics of the age, they soon brought most independent managers, as well as most actors, within their power.

In the meantime, after several years' retirement, Mrs. Fiske had returned to the stage under her husband's management. Her first important role was that of Nora in Ibsen's *A Doll's House* (1894). For twenty years the American stage had ignored Ibsen, but the Fiskes also succeeded in producing *Hedda Gabler* (1903), *Rosmersholm* (1907), *Pillars of Society* (1910), and *Ghosts* (1927). Despite the Syndicate's growing control of the first-class theatres, they took most of their productions on tour and sometimes improvised stages in churches, vaudeville houses, and roller-skating rinks. *Rosmersholm*, thought to be a "heavy" play, made a considerable profit and interested even small-town audiences. Fiske's productions of Ibsen, carefully designed, staged, and directed, using first-rate actors in all parts but rejecting the star system, were typical of his revolutionary work in the American theatre.

Fiske continued to war against the Syndicate both as producer of his wife's independent ventures and in the pages of his *Dramatic Mirror*. He was finally able to lease the Manhattan Theatre from 1901 to 1906 and thus provide a New York stage for Mrs. Fiske. At great personal and financial sacrifice, the Fiskes held out against the Syndicate, and they excited considerable public distaste for its methods. By 1910 the Shubert Brothers had defeated the Syndicate by imitating them; the battle was over. But by that time the Syndicate had yielded to the Fiskes' independent policies and Mrs. Fiske was appearing under the auspices of Daniel Frohman.

Besides Ibsen's plays, the Fiskes' most successful productions during their lifelong collaboration included Lorimer Stoddard's dramatization of Thomas Hardy's *Tess of the D'Urbervilles* (first produced in 1897); Victorien Sardou's *Divorçons* (1896); *Becky Sharp* (1899), an adaptation by Langdon Mitchell [Supp. 1] of Thackeray's *Vanity Fair*; Mitchell's original play *The New York Idea* (1906); Herman Sudermann's *Magda* (1899); Edward Sheldon's *Salvation Nell* (1908); and *Mrs. Bumpstead-Leigh* (1911), by Harry James Smith [*q.v.*]. In their constant search for new American playwrights and in their work with Mitchell, Sheldon, Smith, and Moeller, the Fiskes had as salutary an effect on American dramatists as their productions of Ibsen had on the American playgoer. Later notable productions were Hatcher Hughes and Elmer Rice's *Wake Up, Jonathan* (1921), St. John Ervine's *Mary, Mary, Quite Contrary* (1923), Sheridan's *The Rivals* (1925), and Fred Ballard's *Ladies of the Jury* (1929).

In 1911 Fiske sold the *Dramatic Mirror* and turned increasingly to dramatic production. Among the other actors who appeared under his management, the two greatest were George Arliss and Otis Skinner [Supp. 3]. He also introduced the famous Yiddish tragedienne Bertha Kalich to the English-speaking stage. Fiske's most famous independent venture was his 1911 production of Edward Knoblauch's *Kismet*, in which Skinner created his most memorable role. *Kismet*, which ran for two years, was assembled with little regard for cost and, like other Fiske productions, was carefully cast and elegantly set in the taste of the times.

In 1914 Fiske's production of *Just Herself*, in which he attempted to make the Russian ballet dancer Lydia Lopokova into an actress, was a failure; it wiped out all profits from the preceding two years and sent him into bankruptcy and to the brink of suicide. His friends offered him help, but he preferred to work off his debts and to reduce his standard of living; a bon vivant, he had lived beyond his means for some years. After the Fiskes' production of *The Merry Wives of Windsor* toured successfully in 1928, they attempted *Much Ado About Nothing*, with disastrous results, driving Fiske for the second time into bankruptcy. He staged his last play (*Against the Wind*) in Chicago in 1931.

Fiske also wrote short stories and plays, but none achieved lasting fame. In later years the Fiskes, although remaining close friends and business partners, lived apart except for summers at their camp in the Adirondacks. Surviving his wife by ten years, Fiske died of a heart attack at the age of eighty-one in his New York apartment.

[Archie Binns, *Mrs. Fiske and the Am. Theatre* (1955), covers her husband's career as well, making use of Harrison Fiske's MS. autobiography. Other sources: Robinson Locke Scrapbooks, Theatre Collection, N. Y. Public Lib. at Lincoln Center (vols, 202, 210); files of N. Y. *Dramatic Mirror*, especially anniversary edition, Dec. 24, 1898; Paul Roten, "The Contributions of Harrison Grey Fiske to the Am. Theatre as Editor of the N. Y. *Dramatic Mirror*" (Ph.D. dissertation, Univ. of Mich., 1962); registrar's records, N. Y. Univ.; Alexander Woollcott, *Mrs. Fiske* (1917); *Nat. Cyc. Am. Biog.*, X, 252–53; *Who Was Who in America*, vol. II (1950); John Parker, ed., *Who's Who in the Theatre* (9th ed., 1939); obituaries in N. Y. *Times* and N. Y. *Herald Tribune*, Sept. 4, 1942. The papers of Harrison Grey Fiske and of Mrs. Fiske are in the Lib. of Cong.]

ROBERT J. DIERLAM

FLANNAGAN, JOHN BERNARD (Apr. 7, 1895–Jan. 6, 1942), sculptor, was born in Fargo, N. Dak., the eldest of three sons of Martin Flannagan, an itinerant police reporter, and Margaret (McDonald) Flannagan, a schoolteacher. The family's economic status was always critically low. When the boy was five his father died and his mother was forced to place her children in a Catholic orphanage while she took training for more remunerative work. Flannagan later said that he had been deserted, and this lifelong impression is reflected in his treatment of the mother theme in sculpture.

At nineteen he enrolled in the Minneapolis Institute of Arts, where he studied painting with Robert Koehler [*q.v.*] irregularly for three years. He later disdained his academic training. A contemporary has described him as a discontented Institute student, a taciturn and unsmiling youth who read Schopenhauer and Nietzsche. Between

1917 and 1921 Flannagan served in the merchant marine. The next year, out of work in New York, sleeping in subway cars and already an alcoholic in need of rehabilitation, he was brought to the attention of the painter Arthur B. Davies [q.v.], who humanely employed him as a laborer on his farm in Congers, N. Y. With Davies's encouragement, Flannagan began to paint again and to carve wood and in 1923 was able to exhibit works at the Montross Gallery in the distinguished company of Davies, William Glackens [Supp. 2], Walt Kuhn, Charles Sheeler, and Charles and Maurice Prendergast [q.v.].

Having moved on to New City, N. Y., and now encouraged by two other painters, Alexander Brooks and Henry Varnum Poor, Flannagan sometime in 1926 began to cut stone, the medium of most of his sculpture and the material in which his ideas were best expressed. His first one-man show, comprising nine works, was held in 1927 at the Weyhe Gallery. Here began an artist-and-patron association with Erhard Weyhe which lasted until 1938, when Flannagan received the support of Curt Valentin and the Buchholz Gallery. Living intermittently at Woodstock, N. Y., Flannagan in 1929 married Grace McCoy. Their only child, Moira, was born the next year at Connemara, County Galway, Ireland, where the sculptor had gone to carve stone in relative isolation and to identify himself more closely with his Irish heritage. Flannagan always cherished his Irish gifts as a raconteur and as a scoffer who saw life mostly "through the bottom of a glass." His caustic and self-mocking wit was evident in his conversation and in his letters and sometimes also in his sculpture, as for example in his "Tired Irishman," a recumbent pig.

It was during his first Irish sojourn that Flannagan experienced troubling hallucinations and other warnings of the breakdown which was to come in 1934. Although he returned to the United States in 1931, he was back in Ireland on a Guggenheim Fellowship from March 1932 to March 1933. The Irish period was productive of a very large number of stone works, but Flannagan came home to New York debilitated and in September 1934 voluntarily entered a mental hospital (Bloomingdale Hospital, White Plains, N. Y.). Approximately seven months of "enforced incarceration" left him bitter and convinced of his doom. Shortly after leaving Bloomingdale, Flannagan was divorced; on July 8, 1935, he married Margherita La Centra.

The remaining seven years of his career saw significant work in both stone and bronze, although during much of this time he was either ill or otherwise severely handicapped. He wore a leg cast for more than a year after a mishap with an automobile and subsequent operations in 1936. Most serious was the brain damage incurred when he was struck by an automobile in Washington Square, New York City, in March 1939. Four operations failed to alleviate the effects of the accident; partly blinded and suffering from poor coordination, he was forbidden to cut stone. Nonetheless, he continued to work even during his last year, one of almost constant pain and continuing struggle with alcoholism. Early in 1942 Flannagan committed suicide by turning on the gas in his New York City studio. He was buried in Calvary Cemetery, Long Island City, N. Y.

Flannagan's discovery of stone as a medium was virtually his discovery of sculpture. He used a *taille directe* method similar to Constantin Brancusi's, preferably upon relatively small field stones. Finding "an image in the rock," and acting as liberator of the form, he developed a theory of emergent imagery very close to the notions of the fourteenth-century German mystic Meister Eckhart and to those of early Buddhist sculptors. Readings in the works of Ananda Coomaraswamy, student of Far Eastern art, doubtless reinforced this view. Flannagan conceived generalized forms, doing as little actual carving as possible; thus, most of his stone works appear to be in a process of becoming.

The themes which he regarded as most important refer to birth or death and suggest a union of these opposites in one conception. For example, his "Triumph of the Egg, I" (1937) represents a chick only partly emergent from its egg but seemingly forever attached to the mother vehicle. It is noteworthy that the sculptor's original title for the piece was "Still Born Bird," and that it was carved after extensive psychiatric experience had made him more than ever aware of "a stirring impulse from the depth of the unconscious." Notions of a "wishful rebirth fantasy" possessed him, as did also "the timeless, changeless finality of death." Flannagan's total work is too large for an enumeration of significant pieces, but his last finished work and a projected one should be mentioned: he regarded them as the finales of "an evil existence." "Beginning" is a bronze depicting a nude female seated upon the ground with legs outspread and a newborn infant between them, the neonate represented in such a manner that its viability is doubtful. The planned but never begun work was a Pietà subject, on the drawing for which Flannagan wrote: "the perfect symbol of death, return to being a part of the Mother principle as we all shall be and be covered by Mother Earth."

Flannagan's reliance on the motivational force of the subconscious anticipates the spirit of the action painters of the 1940's and 1950's despite great stylistic differences. He has been recognized as a major figure in American art in the period between the two world wars, when many sculptors were devoted to the making of uninspired monuments. As one who sought by a relatively abstract approach to express quite abstract ideas, he stands almost entirely alone in his time.

[Margherita Flannagan, ed., *Letters of John B. Flannagan* (1942), with introduction by W. R. Valentiner; John B. Flannagan, "Image in the Rock," *Mag. of Art,* Mar. 1942 (a credo, the most valuable single expression of his philosophy); Dorothy C. Miller, ed., *The Sculpture of John B. Flannagan* (Museum of Modern Art, 1942), with introduction by Carl Zigrosser and a statement by the artist; private papers in the possession of Margherita La Centra Flannagan (now Montgomery); Joseph S. Bolt, "John Bernard Flannagan" (Ph.D. thesis, Harvard Univ., 1962). No really good photographs of Flannagan exist, although one is published in the *Letters.*]
JOSEPH SULLIVAN BOLT

FLEXNER, BERNARD (Feb. 24, 1865–May 3, 1945), lawyer, philanthropist, and Zionist leader, was born in Louisville, Ky., the fifth son and fifth of the nine children of Morris (originally Moritz) and Esther (Abraham) Flexner. His father, born in Neumark, Bohemia, in 1820, had lived for two decades in France before emigrating to New Orleans in 1853, and thence, the next year, to Louisville. His mother, born in the Rhineland, had emigrated to Louisville in 1855. The panic of 1873 ruined Morris Flexner's prosperous hat business and impoverished the large family. Before his death in 1882 he urged his children to avoid the commercial world and to seek professional careers. Bernard's education was slowed by eye trouble, which kept him in the shadow of his brilliant brothers Simon and Abraham. Simon, two years older than Bernard, later became a noted pathologist and the director of the Rockefeller Institute for Medical Research; Abraham, a year younger than Bernard, became a famous foundation executive and the first director of the Institute for Advanced Study at Princeton, N. J.

Bernard Flexner studied law at the University of Louisville (LL.B. 1898) and afterward at the University of Virginia. Admitted to the Kentucky bar in 1898, he soon gained a reputation not only for his legal capacity, but also for his public spirit. Particularly concerned with the plight of young lawbreakers, he became an early supporter of the juvenile court movement which was then sweeping the country. He wrote numerous articles on the subject for *Charities* (later the *Survey*) and from 1906 to 1911 was chairman of the Juvenile Court Board of Jefferson County (Louisville), in which post he helped draft the state's juvenile court law. Flexner hoped that the juvenile court would develop into a tribunal with broad power to deal not only with juvenile delinquency but also with the whole spectrum of family problems contributing to both dependency and delinquency; he felt it should have criminal jurisdiction over adults contributing to delinquency. He also urged the development of professional training for probation officers and social workers.

Flexner's legal skill led Martin Insull, brother of the utilities magnate Samuel Insull [Supp. 2], to engage him as counsel for the Insull utility properties in the Louisville area. In 1911, when these small companies were being consolidated into the Middle West Utilities Company, Martin Insull brought Flexner to Chicago as the company's first general counsel. Flexner prospered greatly in the new market for utility stocks and bonds, and in 1917 he moved to New York City as a counsel for Halsey, Stuart and Company, the chief outlet for Insull's bonds.

The move to New York was also prompted by Flexner's desire to give effective support to the Zionist cause. In July 1917 he had served on the American Red Cross Commission to Rumania, where he had been shocked not only by the oppression of eastern European Jewry, but also by personally experiencing discrimination. Becoming convinced that the Jews had to possess a legally recognized homeland in order to compete on equal terms with other peoples of the earth, he supported the Zionist Organization of America, then led by Louis D. Brandeis [Supp. 3], and served as counsel of the Zionist delegation to the Paris Peace Conference. In 1921 a bitter conflict within the Zionist Organization of America between supporters of Brandeis and supporters of Dr. Chaim Weizmann, president of the World Zionist Organization, over the future leadership and economic policies of Palestine ended in defeat of Brandeis's program, after which he and his followers, including Flexner, withdrew.

From New York, Flexner found other ways to aid both Palestine and Jewry. As chairman of the medical and sanitary committee of the American Jewish Joint Distribution Committee he worked tirelessly to aid Polish Jews suffering in the ruins of a war-ravaged Europe. More importantly, he persuaded Felix M. Warburg [Supp. 2] and other wealthy non-Zionist patrons of the Joint Distribution Committee to channel their Palestine funds into a new agency, the Palestine Economic Corporation, which was founded in 1925 with Flexner as president and

Warburg, Louis Marshall [*q.v.*], Herbert H. Lehman, and Robert Szold as its chief backers. The new corporation, a combination of the Palestine assets of the Joint Distribution Committee, the Palestine Cooperative Company, and the American Palestine Company, stimulated Palestinian development by lending money to artisans and businessmen and by financing a hydroelectric plant on the River Jordan, potash works on the shore of the Dead Sea, and home-building projects. Although not himself a magnetic leader, Flexner served as a catalyst between such disparate personalities as Brandeis and Warburg; he was chairman of the board of directors of the corporation from 1931 to 1944. In 1929 the World Zionist Organization, seeking further to enlist non-Zionists in the practical work of building up Palestine, set up a new body, the Jewish Agency for Palestine, designed to represent all sections of world Jewry. The Brandeis group at this time rejoined the movement, and Flexner became a member of the Agency in 1930.

In other causes, Flexner joined with Newton D. Baker [Supp. 2] and others in 1928 to publish the complete transcript of the Sacco-Vanzetti trial [see Nicola Sacco] and distribute it to libraries throughout the world. He gave generously to the University of Louisville and, in the names of his brother Abraham and his sister Mary, established lectureships at Vanderbilt University and Bryn Mawr College. When Hitler's rise to power drove many German Jews into exile in 1933, Flexner helped establish the Emergency Committee in Aid of Displaced German Scholars. In 1935 he was elected secretary of the Refugee Economic Corporation.

Despite his active public life, Bernard Flexner was a private man who kept his own counsel. Though he could, on occasion, be curt with his associates, his personal loyalty and integrity and his legal and business skill were highly valued by the more famous figures whose lives he touched. A bachelor, he spent his last years with his sister Mary in a Park Avenue apartment. He died of pneumonia at the age of eighty at the Columbia-Presbyterian Medical Center in New York City.

[Flexner's writings include: "The Juvenile Court as a Social Institution," *Survey*, Feb. 5, 1910; with Roger N. Baldwin, *Juvenile Courts and Probation* (1914); with Reuben Oppenheimer, *The Legal Aspect of the Juvenile Court* (U.S. Children's Bureau, Publication no. 99, 1922); with Oppenheimer and Katharine F. Lenroot, *The Child, the Family, and the Court* (U.S. Children's Bureau, Publication no. 193, 1929); *Mr. Justice Brandeis and the Univ. of Louisville* (1938). For family background see Abraham Flexner, *An Autobiog.* (1960). There is material on the Palestine Economic Corporation in the Am. Jewish Archives, Cincinnati. See also Joseph C. Hyman,

Twenty-Five Years of Am. Aid to Jews Overseas (1939); Boris D. Bogen, *Born a Jew* (1930); Rufus Learsi, *The Jews in America* (1954); *Who's Who in Am. Jewry*, 1938; *Universal Jewish Encyc.*, IV, 328; memorial by Charles C. Burlingham in Assoc. of the Bar of the City of N. Y., *Year Book*, 1946; obituaries in *N. Y. Times* and *N. Y. Herald Tribune*, May 4, 1945, and *New Palestine*, May 31, 1945. Certain other facts provided by Prof. Forrest McDonald, Wayne State Univ., biographer of Samuel Insull, and by Mr. Robert Szold, N. Y. City.]

ROBERT M. MENNEL

FLEXNER, JENNIE MAAS (Nov. 6, 1882– Nov. 17, 1944), librarian, was born in Louisville, Ky., the eldest of the five children (four daughters and one son) of Jacob Aaron and Rosa (Maas) Flexner. Her paternal grandparents, Moritz and Esther (Abraham) Flexner, orthodox Jews born in Bohemia and the Rhineland respectively, had come to the United States in the 1850's and settled in Louisville. Three of Jennie's uncles were to make outstanding contributions to American life: Abraham as educator and foundation administrator; Bernard [Supp. 3] in law and jurisprudence; and Simon as physician and scientist. Jennie's father, a druggist who did much to further his brothers' education, later studied medicine and became a practicing physician in Louisville.

Miss Flexner attended local schools. Since lack of money prevented her going to college she became a secretary (1903–04), but she found the work uncongenial and in 1905 joined the staff of the Free Public Library of Louisville. Recognizing the need for professional training, she spent a year (1908–09) at the library school of Western Reserve University, Cleveland, Ohio, and then returned to her Louisville post. In 1912 she became head of the circulation department, a position she held until 1928. During these years she served first as instructor in and later as supervisor of a training course for librarians.

At the beginning of the twentieth century the American public library was undergoing a transition from the passive role of custodian of books to the more active one of trying to bring book and reader together and thus serve as a means of popular education. During her years at the Louisville library, Miss Flexner developed the concept of a library service that could help guide a patron's reading according to his individual needs. She also urged the need for training black as well as white librarians, and was instrumental in establishing a branch library for Negroes, the first in the South. In 1926, at the request of the American Library Association, which was trying to fix standards and curricula for library schools, she took a leave of absence to study methods used in libraries of different sizes. The resulting book, *Circulation Work in Public Libraries* (1927), which emphasized the crucial function of the circulation librarian, for many years remained a basic text.

In 1928 Jennie Flexner was invited to join the staff of the New York Public Library to inaugurate a readers' advisory service which would help adults carry forward their postschool education through programs of systematic reading. She remained there for the rest of her life. Enthusiastic, generous, and friendly, she worked with both individuals and groups. She tried especially to reach foreign-born readers, members of minority groups, and those who sought "wider horizons of an occupational and personal sort." Some clients asked for help in locating an interest, others came hoping to find in books respite from personal problems and emotional stress.

As head of the Readers' Adviser's Office of the New York Public Library, Miss Flexner was particularly responsive to social crises. During the depression years of the early 1930's many of her clients were either unemployed men in search of vocational guidance and technical books or young people of college age who lacked the means for a formal education. As the public need for educational assistance began to exceed the budgetary capacity of a city in depression, Miss Flexner increased her work among groups and compiled book lists for mass distribution. She lectured, for example, to unemployed adults attending continuation schools and compiled bibliographies for use on radio programs such as "Town Meeting of the Air."

During the late 1930's Miss Flexner and her trained assistants gave increasing attention to the exiles coming to New York as refugees from European dictatorships. She was particularly concerned with the needs of displaced intellectuals, librarians, and physicians. Besides helping them find appropriate aid, she worked with the National Refugee Service to produce "Interpreting America," a book list designed to assist in their adjustment to life in the United States. During World War II, in cooperation with organizations such as the Book Mobilization Committee and the Y.M.C.A., she helped choose collections of books to be sent to the troops abroad and to German prison camps. Her long-standing interest in Negro problems continued, and in the early 1940's she began to give concentrated attention to filling the reading needs of Harlem residents in such areas as "housing, recreation, social work, women and their status, labor and unemployment, education, [and] crime."

Miss Flexner advised on the selection of books for hospitals, schools, welfare organizations, trade unions, political clubs, and government agencies.

Devoted to music, and a close friend of the harpsichordist Yella Pessl, she supported the concerts of recorded music given at the New York Public Library. She was a member of the Board of Education for Librarianship (1927–32) of the American Library Association, and served as secretary of the American Association for Adult Education and as president of the New York Library Club. In addition to numerous articles and books for librarians, she wrote for the layman *Making Books Work: A Guide to the Use of Libraries* (1943). Miss Flexner's work at the New York Public Library was cut short when she died of a heart ailment at her home in New York City at the age of sixty-two. She was buried at Adath Israel Cemetery in Louisville.

[Other books by Miss Flexner are *A Readers' Advisory Service* (with Sigrid A. Edge, 1934) and *Readers' Advisers at Work* (with Byron C. Hopkins, 1941). Biographical sources: sketch by Esther Johnston in Emily Miller Danton, ed., *Pioneering Leaders in Librarianship* (1953); Sigrid A. Edge in *Bull. of Bibliog.*, Jan.–Apr. 1940 (with photograph); obituaries in *Lib. Jour.*, Jan. 1, 1945, and *N. Y. Times*, Nov. 18, 1944; clippings, correspondence, and Miss Flexner's annual reports (MS.) in Office of Readers' Adviser, N. Y. Public Lib.; Abraham Flexner, *An Autobiog.* (1960), on the family background; information from Mrs. Hortense Flexner King (sister) and Mrs. Paul Lewinson (cousin).]

SIDNEY DITZION

FOKINE, MICHEL (Apr. 25, 1880–Aug. 22, 1942), dancer and choreographer, was born in St. Petersburg, Russia; he was christened Mikhail Mikhailovitch but later chose to use the French form of his name. His father, Mikhail Vasilievitch Fokine, was a prosperous middle-class merchant; his mother, Catherine (Kind) Fokina, came from Mannheim, Germany. Fokine was the last but one in a family of eighteen children, of whom only four boys and one girl survived infancy. Their mother imbued the children with her own love of the theatre: Michel's brother Vladimir became a well-known actor, and his brother Alexandre, who married the ballerina Alexandra Fedorova, founded the Troitsky Miniature Theatre.

As a child Michel showed such a love and aptitude for dancing that his sister persuaded their father to enter him in the Imperial Ballet School in St. Petersburg. He became a pupil there in 1889, mastering the classical ballet steps under such teachers as Platon Karsavin, Paul Gerdt, and Nicolas Legat. This sound technical foundation in the "old ballet" later served as an essential base for Fokine's dance innovations. An exceptionally intelligent boy, he also acquired a thorough knowledge of art and music, which helped provide later choreographic inspiration; he learned to play the piano and several stringed instruments and became proficient at painting in oils. In 1898 he graduated from the school and joined the Imperial Ballet as a dancer.

As a member of the company, Fokine attended the classes of Christian Johansson and in a few years acquired a considerable reputation for his strong technique and distinguished presence. He was a virile, handsome dancer and an excellent mime, with fiery eyes and hair that early began to thin and take the shape of an encircling Roman wreath. He was appointed to the teaching establishment at the Imperial Ballet School in 1904. In 1905 he married the talented ballerina Vera Antonova, who achieved renown as Fokina. She shared his creative work throughout his life, performing in his ballets and serving as his dancing partner. Their only son, Vitale, also became a dancer.

Fokine's sense of theatre and his study of arts other than the dance had opened his eyes to the shortcomings and absurdities of classical ballet as produced in St. Petersburg: the concentration of interest on the star ballerina, the repetition of formal dance steps that were often irrelevant to the theme to be expressed, costuming that imposed the short ballet tutu on the performers regardless of the country or historical epoch represented in the story, and a lack of harmony among dance movement, music, and stage setting. It became his aim from the beginning to eradicate these weaknesses. In his first ballet, *Acis and Galatea,* a school performance staged in 1905, Fokine tentatively put some of his ideas into practice. It was probably in 1907 that he created the famous solo dance *The Dying Swan,* with music by Saint-Saëns, for his colleague Anna Pavlova (Vera M. Krasovskaya, *Anna Pavlova,* 1964, pp. 19 ff.). In the same year, for a charity performance, he staged *Eunice* and the first version of *Chopiniana.* The success of these early efforts led to his first important ballet for the Maryinsky Theatre, *Le Pavillon d'Armide* (1907), and in 1908 he reworked *Chopiniana* into *Les Sylphides,* which remains one of the most popular and poetic of standard ballets.

Although Fokine was gradually establishing his ideas of artistically coherent dance productions in St. Petersburg, it was with the Russian Ballet managed by Sergei Diaghilev that he first developed them fully, setting the example which was to give the art of ballet a new direction. Diaghilev took a company to western Europe for the first time in the spring of 1909, with Fokine as its ballet master. In that historic season in Paris he produced the wild, barbaric Polovetsian dances from Borodin's *Prince Igor,* the Egyptian splendors of *Cleopatra,* and revivals of *Les Syl-*phides and *Le Pavillon d'Armide.* In addition to Fokine and Vera Fokina, the company included such stars as Tamara Karsavina, Pavlova, and Nijinsky. To the Paris audience the technical strength and vitality of the dancers and the artistic cohesion of the ballets came as a revelation, and the Diaghilev Ballet, although originally formed only for the tour, became a permanent feature of the European theatre until the death of Diaghilev in 1929. Fokine dominated the company as ballet master in its first and most productive period, producing, among other works, *Carnaval, Scheherazade,* and *The Firebird* in 1910, *Le Spectre de la Rose* and *Petrouchka* in 1911, *The Blue God Thamar* and *Daphnis and Chloë* in 1912, and *The Legend of Joseph* and *Le Coq d'Or* in 1914.

With these masterpieces Fokine laid the foundation of modern ballet. He reaffirmed the basic principles of classic choreography (though discarding some outmoded traditions) and added a new dimension. His ballets were produced in collaboration with such eminent musicians as Igor Stravinsky and Maurice Ravel and artists such as Alexandre Benois and Leon Bakst. With them, Fokine was able to realize his conception of ballet as a composite art in which, ideally, painting, music, and the dance are allied and no one component is given undue prominence. In a notable letter to the London *Times* in 1914, Fokine propounded his "five rules," which in essence expressed his conviction that all aspects of a ballet must be subordinated to the dramatic expression of its theme.

Fokine's association with the Diaghilev Ballet ended in 1914. During World War I he and his wife traveled widely giving concert performances. In 1918 they left Russia for the last time and the following year went to New York City to stage dances for some of the spectacular entertainments of the producer Morris Gest [Supp. 3]. Thereafter Fokine made his home in the United States; he became a citizen in 1932. During the 1920's he taught dancing and produced minor works such as *Le Rêve de la Marquise* (1921) and *Les Elfes* (1924), given at the Metropolitan Opera House. He also staged ballet acts at various theatres and nightclubs.

When Fokine and his wife arrived in the United States, they found almost no tradition of a ballet theatre. Their joint concert appearances (which continued until 1933), their teaching activities, and such events as their staging of Fokine ballets before an overflow audience in Lewisohn Stadium in New York had great influence in awakening American interest in ballet, an interest that grew to major proportions. Fokine admired such American dancers as Ruth St. Denis and Isadora Duncan [*q.v.*], but disliked the work of some other proponents of the modern dance, whom he considered ignorant dilettantes. He continued to give occasional productions in Europe, and in 1935 returned to Paris and resumed his connection with the mainstream of the Ballets Russes. The mantle of Diaghilev had passed to René Blum and Col. Wladimir de Basil, for both of whom Fokine staged important new ballets: *L'Epreuve d'Amour* and *Don Juan* for Blum in 1936, and *Cendrillon* (1938) and *Paganini* (1939) for de Basil. The last company with which he worked was Ballet Theater in the United States, for which he produced *Bluebeard* in 1941.

Fokine was in Mexico City during the summer of 1942, preparing for the production of *Helen of Troy*, when he was partially crippled by the development of a blood clot in his left leg. He returned to New York City and died a few days later, of pneumonia, at the West Side Hospital. After Russian Orthodox services, he was buried at Ferncliff Cemetery, Ardsley, N. Y.

Fokine's significance in the history of ballet cannot be overstated. While remaining true to its classical traditions, he was largely instrumental in raising ballet from a state of decadence and stagnation and making it a popular and vital theatre art. His biographer, Cyril Beaumont, sums up his career: "As a reformer, he is to the twentieth century what [Jean-Georges] Noverre was to the eighteenth, for he has exerted a profound and beneficial influence in every branch of the art of ballet."

[Fokine's memoirs were published posthumously under the title *Memoirs of a Ballet Master,* edited by Anatole Chujoy (1961). The standard study of Fokine's career, published before his work for de Basil and Blum, is Cyril W. Beaumont's *Michel Fokine & His Ballets* (1935). Details of Fokine's association with the Imperial Ballet School are to be found in M. Borisoglebsky, *Materiali po Istorii Russkovo Baleta* (Leningrad, 1938–39). Fokine also figures largely in the many works which have been written on the Diaghilev Ballet, notably Prince Peter Lieven's *The Birth of Ballets-Russes* (1936), Alexandre Benois's *Reminiscences of the Russian Ballet* (1941), Sergei L. Grigoriev's *The Diaghilev Ballet* (1953), and Cyril Beaumont's *The Diaghilev Ballet in London* (1940).]

IVOR GUEST

FORD, EDSEL BRYANT (Nov. 6, 1893– May 26, 1943), automobile manufacturer, was born in Detroit, Mich., the only child of Henry and Clara (Bryant) Ford. On his father's side he was of Irish and Dutch or Belgian descent; on his mother's, English. He attended the Detroit public schools through the grammar grades and then the Detroit University School, a private academy. Edsel Ford grew up with the auto-

mobile industry: his father's first successful automobile was tested in the year of his birth; the Ford Motor Company was organized when he was nine; and the popular Model T was introduced when he was fourteen. From young boyhood Edsel displayed a keen interest in these developments, often stopping on his way home from school to help in the office or visit the experimental room. His father early fitted out a workshop for him in the garage of the family residence in Detroit and in 1908 gave him a car of his own: a Model N, predecessor of the Model T. He began to work at the Ford plant in 1912, after a family trip to Europe, and spent time in all the chief departments of the company. He introduced his father to his gifted manual arts teacher at the University School, Clarence W. Avery, who soon joined the company and is generally given principal credit for the development of the moving assembly line.

Though interested in mechanics, Edsel Ford soon showed a marked bent for administration, and late in 1915, on the resignation of James Couzens [Supp. 2], he became, at twenty-two, the company secretary. Several years afterward he also assumed the post of treasurer. Though lacking Couzens's reputation and personal force, Edsel soon gave evidence of his own considerable talent. His testimony at the *Chicago Tribune* trial of 1919 (growing out of his father's suit against the newspaper for an editorial attack) revealed an exact and comprehensive knowledge of all Ford activities and an ability to discuss them clearly.

On Nov. 1, 1916, Edsel Ford married Eleanor Lowthian Clay, niece of Joseph L. Hudson, owner of the largest Detroit department store and a power in the Hudson Motor Car Company. Their first son, Henry Ford II, was born in 1917, followed by Benson (1919), Josephine (1923), and William Clay (1925). Resident for a time in Detroit, the family eventually established a home at Gaukler Pointe on Lake St. Clair, with a summer home at Seal Harbor, Maine, and a winter one at Hobe Sound, Fla.

From 1915 on, Edsel Ford took a leading role in all aspects of Ford Motor Company affairs. He helped introduce the Fordson tractor; watched over sales, advertising, and foreign operations; and, in 1917–18, assisted in managing the company's wartime production. On Dec. 31, 1918, after the resignation of his father, he was elected president of the company, an office he held until his death. It was his initiative which led to the family's purchase of the minority stock holdings in 1919, assuring complete family control of the corporation. During the 1920's, while his father was often involved with outside projects, Edsel coordinated the varied work of the firm and kept it operating efficiently. With his brother-in-law Ernest C. Kanzler he undertook an urgently needed program of modernization and expansion of Ford's existing branch factories and the construction of new ones. The entire program, costing $150,000,000, eventually provided thirty-six plants. He also took an active part in the acquisition of the Lincoln Motor Company in 1922. He was a devotee of aviation, and after the Stout Metal Airplane Company was absorbed by the Ford company in 1925, he encouraged the design of a trimotor plane and fostered an annual "Air Reliability Tour" to promote more dependable flying.

Edsel Ford had a particular flair for automobile styling, and was an early advocate of improvements in the Model T. In 1924, when his father, faced with rising competition, was at last ready to permit such changes, Edsel introduced improved brakes, balloon tires, all-steel bodies, enclosed cars, and a choice of colors instead of the standard black. He was intimately involved in the design and styling of the Model T's successor, the Model A (1927), and, after its rather brief career, of the V-8. He was also responsible for introducing the Lincoln-Zephyr (1936) and the Mercury (1939), medium-priced cars designed to meet the competition of General Motors and Chrysler. "He knows style—how a car ought to look," his father asserted, "and he has mechanical horse sense, too."

Though he bore the title of president, Edsel Ford recognized that his father was the real head of the company—a fact the elder Ford at times made painfully clear by canceling projects which he had apparently approved and upon which Edsel had made considerable progress. Though it cost him dearly in emotional strain, the son never questioned his father's right to determine policy. Through the early 1930's such interference (usually carried out by Henry Ford's executive assistant Ernest G. Liebold or by production chief Charles E. Sorensen) was only occasional. But with the emergence of Harry Bennett as Henry Ford's chosen deputy in the middle 1930's, Edsel began to encounter far more severe difficulties—as did many other Ford officials. As head of the Ford security force, Bennett used his great power in a generally disruptive way, harassing Edsel by bringing about the discharge or resignation of a succession of capable Ford officials. It was Bennett who guided Henry Ford's antiunion policy, and for some time Edsel's efforts to modify this policy met with no success. In April 1941, however, Edsel played an influential role in bringing about a generous settlement with the United Auto Workers—an achievement whose importance Bennett himself later acknowledged. In the early 1940's Edsel Ford experienced periods of profound discouragement as his aging father grew increasingly suspicious of those around him, including his own son, and leaned more and more heavily on Bennett. Declining company profits also contributed to his tension and frustration.

Despite the genuine and tragic conflicts that developed between him and his father, Edsel Ford remained a highly influential and widely respected figure in the Ford Motor Company. Before and during the Second World War he played an important part in increasing production and launching new undertakings. In 1940 he brought his two older sons into the company. His premature death at his home on Lake St. Clair in May 1943, at the age of forty-nine, came just as the company's war production was reaching its peak. The complex causes of death included stomach cancer and undulant fever, undoubtedly aggravated by exhaustion and nervous strain. Following Episcopal services at Christ Church chapel, Grosse Pointe, Mich., he was buried in Woodlawn Cemetery, Detroit. In September 1945, after an interval during which the elder Henry Ford nominally resumed leadership of the company, the presidency passed to Henry Ford II, whose first act was to dismiss Harry Bennett.

Slight of build, dark-complexioned like his mother's family, Edsel Ford was invariably courteous and considerate, but could at the same time be firm and plainspoken. Though he lacked his father's genius, he was a man of diligence, poise, and discrimination who, in the opinion of many Ford executives, would have succeeded in rejuvenating the Ford Motor Company had he lived. With his wife he shared an interest in the arts; they helped support the Detroit Symphony Orchestra and built up a large collection of paintings, including many modern canvases. Edsel encouraged the American artist Charles Sheeler to make a series of paintings of the Rouge River plant and was responsible for the commissioning of a Diego Rivera mural for the Detroit Institute of Arts. A mountain range in Antarctica bears his name, in commemoration of his support of Adm. Richard E. Byrd's expeditions there in 1928–30 and 1933–35. The Ford Foundation was established through his initiative in 1936, and his large fortune, after provision for his family, constituted its initial endowment.

[Edsel Ford's activities are covered in the history of the Ford Motor Co. by Allan Nevins and Frank Ernest Hill, *Ford* (3 vols., 1954–63). For other aspects of his career see Mira Wilkins and Frank Ernest Hill, *Am. Business Abroad: Ford on Six Continents* (1964), and William Greenleaf, *From These Beginnings: The Early Philanthropies of Henry and Edsel Ford, 1911–1936* (1964). Many items in the Ford Archives, Ford Motor Co., Dearborn, Mich., deal with Edsel Ford. Material about his life before and soon after his marriage can be found in the Fair Lane Papers (Accession 1 of the Ford Archives), and his full business correspondence in Accession 6 is revealing. Many tape-recorded reminiscences in the Archives deal somewhat with his work, character, and relationship to his father, among them those of Fred L. Black, Harold Hicks, and Laurence Sheldrick.]

FRANK ERNEST HILL

FORD, WORTHINGTON CHAUNCEY (Feb. 16, 1858–Mar. 7, 1941), historical editor and bibliographer, was born in Brooklyn, N. Y., the eldest son among the eight children of Gordon Lester Ford [*q.v.*], businessman and book collector, and Emily Ellsworth (Fowler) Ford. With his brother Paul Leicester Ford [*q.v.*] he shared a precocious interest in books and scholarship. Both sons were aided and encouraged by their father in editing and printing the eighty or more bibliographical and documentary compilations they issued over the imprint of the Historical Printing Club of Brooklyn from 1876 to 1899.

Worthington was sent to Brooklyn Polytechnic Institute and then enrolled in Columbia College with the class of 1879, where he shone in classical and economic studies; but his deafness caused him to withdraw before graduation, and he spent several years as cashier of an insurance company and as a writer on finance and political economy for the New York *Evening Post* and *Herald*. He was only twenty-one when he published his first book, a revised edition of *Wells' Natural Philosophy for the Use of Schools,* by David A. Wells [*q.v.*] (2 vols., 1879). His next, *The American Citizen's Manual* (2 vols., 1882–83), was more important: the first American textbook in civics worthy of the name, it was at once learned and illuminating on the complexities of the different state governments and displayed decidedly frank and progressive views in favor of civil service reform, railroad regulation, and unrestricted immigration, while opposing high tariffs.

These views were those of the Cleveland Democrats, and during Grover Cleveland's two presidential terms Ford held government appointments, first as chief of the Bureau of Statistics in the State Department, 1885–89, and later, with the same title, in the Treasury Department, 1893–98. His real contribution as a government servant, however, resulted from the circumstance that the State Department in the 1880's housed the most valuable assemblage of official and personal sources for early American history in existence. These included the records of the Continental Congress and the personal papers of Washington, Franklin, Hamilton, Jefferson, Madison, and Monroe, acquired by the nation at various times earlier in the century. This treasure trove cast its spell on Ford and submerged the statistician-economist in the historian-archivist-editor.

Ford projected a plan for publishing these bodies of historical material in scholarly editions at government expense. Secretary of State Thomas F. Bayard [*q.v.*] gave the plan official support, and President Cleveland recommended it in a message to Congress in 1888. But the project was hopelessly premature. Congress's indifference freed Ford to undertake negotiations with G. P. Putnam's Sons, which, with Ford performing his editorial work at the remarkable pace he maintained throughout life, published *The Writings of George Washington* in fourteen volumes between 1889 and 1893. Ford's brother Paul meanwhile undertook a comparable edition of Jefferson's *Writings,* and still other editions followed from other hands. Though by no means definitive, the Putnam editions, thanks to the Fords, set new standards for historical sources in typographical excellence, fidelity of text, and authoritative annotation.

In 1898 Worthington Ford moved to the Boston Public Library to become head of the department of documents and statistics newly established by its librarian, Herbert Putnam. Ford moved vigorously to develop services essentially anticipating those of a modern business reference library, but once again he was drawn to neglected historical riches, in this case the manuscripts that had accumulated over the years in the library without much notice. In 1899 he was given the added title of chief of the department of manuscripts, and for five years (1900–04) he issued a handsomely printed annual volume of *Historical Manuscripts in the Public Library of the City of Boston.*

In 1902 Herbert Putnam, now Librarian of Congress, summoned Ford to head the Library's comparatively new Division of Manuscripts. During his six-year tenure the division became the outstanding center of its kind in the country. With Putnam's support and the active intervention of President Theodore Roosevelt (see his Executive Order of Mar. 9, 1903), Ford gathered in from the State Department and other government agencies the records and other accumulations of historical material not needed for administrative purposes. Private owners were persuaded, and funds were found, to bring to the Library the papers of Presidents Jackson, Van Buren, Polk, Andrew Johnson, and Pierce, as well as those of other prominent American statesmen and intellectual and cultural leaders. Ford instituted effective procedures for processing these often massive bodies of manuscripts and making their contents known to scholars. He himself undertook the editing, for the Library, of the *Journals of the Continental Congress, 1774–1789,* completed a dozen (of the ultimate thirty-four) volumes, and left three more in or ready for the press.

Late in 1908 Ford moved to Boston to become director of research and publication at the Massachusetts Historical Society, with the title of editor. There he strove as if possessed by demonic force to make the vast unpublished resources of the Society available in print. In his twenty-year incumbency he prepared for the press no fewer than fifty substantial volumes of *Proceedings, Collections,* and special publications. Many of these were largely, and some were wholly, his own work, including his chief monument as a learned editor, William Bradford's *History of Plymouth Plantation* (2 vols., 1912), and such still standard bibliographies as *Broadsides, Ballads, &c. Printed in Massachusetts, 1639–1800* (1922). To the fifty volumes must be added the 261 publications of "Photostat Americana," which Ford initiated in 1914 by operating one of the first photostat machines himself.

Ford was continuously active in the affairs of the American Historical Association and served as its president in 1917. From 1916 to 1923 he was consulting librarian at the John Carter Brown Library in Providence, R. I., devoting one day a week to its affairs and supervising publication of four volumes of its new *Catalogue* covering a good part of its seventeenth-century Americana. He also gained access to the archives of the Adams family, the greatest assemblage of its kind in the nation but until Ford's advent virtually closed to inquirers. Earning the trust of the family, he became unofficial custodian of the collection and obtained permission to prepare an edition of the *Writings of John Quincy Adams,* of which seven volumes were published, 1913–17, before it became a wartime casualty. He also saw both Charles Francis Adams's *Autobiography* (1916) and the first trade edition of *The Education of Henry Adams* (1918) through the press, and edited a splendidly readable collection of transatlantic Adams correspondence, *A Cycle of Adams Letters, 1861–1865* (2 vols., 1920), as well as, late in his life, the *Letters of Henry Adams* (2 vols., 1930–38).

Amid such strenuous editorial and publishing activity, it is not surprising that faults of haste and carelessness sometimes crept in: mistakes in dating documents, assigning their authorship, and rendering their texts. The most serious instance was the first volume (1925) of the Massachusetts Historical Society's new series of *Winthrop Papers,* which had to be recalled, re-edited, and reprinted because of errors and inconsistencies that were pointed out by reviewers and by a special committee of the Society. Ford thereupon submitted his resignation, which took effect in 1929.

Later that year he went to Europe as director of "Project A" for the Library of Congress, to search out and reproduce materials for American history in foreign archives and libraries. To this was joined a more general roving mission as the Library's "European representative" for acquisitions and related matters. Budgetary restrictions brought both missions to an end by 1933, but Ford continued to live abroad. On Oct. 11, 1899, he had married Bettina Fillmore Quin of Washington, D. C.; they had two daughters, Crimora Chauncey and Emily Ellsworth. Mrs. Ford died in Paris in 1931. Ford's deafness had increased with age, but he continued to communicate through a lifelong habit of wide correspondence. His letters are marked by the same crisp, often sardonic, and always lucid style found in his published writings.

When the German army invaded France in June 1940, Ford left his home at Le Vésinet, near Paris, and, at the age of eighty-two, "rode the crest of the invasion wave into unoccupied France." Remaining there until February 1941, he made his way to Lisbon and obtained passage to New York on the American Export Line's *Excalibur.* He died on shipboard after a week at sea.

[Ford's personal papers form a large part of the immense collection of Ford family MSS. in the N. Y. Public Lib. Other MS. sources include the correspondence of Charles Francis Adams (1835–1915) in the Adams Papers, Fourth Generation, Mass. Hist. Soc.; Ford Papers and records of the Council in the same institution; administrative papers in the Boston Public Lib., Lib. of Cong., and John Carter Brown Lib.; and the Ford file in the Nat. Personnel Records Center, Nat. Archives and Records Service, St. Louis. Paul Z. DuBois's doctoral dissertation, "Paul Leicester Ford: An Am. Man of Letters" (Case Western Reserve Univ., 1968), is very helpful on family details and the brothers' joint ventures. The present writer's "Worthington Chauncey Ford, Editor," Mass. Hist. Soc., *Proc., 1971,* is the fullest published sketch to date and cites the principal printed sources.]

L. H. Butterfield

FOX, DIXON RYAN (Dec. 7, 1887–Jan. 30, 1945), historian and college president, was born in Potsdam, N. Y., the only child of Julia Anna (Dixon) and James Sylvester Fox. His paternal grandparents had emigrated from Tipperary, Ireland, to Morley, N. Y., in 1842. His father, a salesman for a Vermont marble and granite company, had given up Catholicism and become an active Mason; his mother was a Presbyterian. As the father's business often took him away from home, the chief responsibility for Dixon's upbringing fell on his mother, who loved art and music and placed a high value on education. Fox made a brilliant scholastic record at the Potsdam Normal School (1904–07) and then, at nineteen, began teaching at a school in Westchester County, N. Y. While there he enrolled in Columbia College, from which he graduated in 1911.

For a time Fox thought of a teaching career in political science, but he eventually turned to American social history. As a graduate student at Columbia, he studied under Herbert L. Osgood, William A. Dunning [qq.v.], and Charles A. Beard, receiving his Ph.D. in 1917. He was appointed to the Columbia faculty as an instructor in history in 1913 and remained for over two decades, from 1927 as professor. On June 7, 1915, he married Marian Stickney Osgood, daughter of Professor Osgood. They had two sons, Herbert Osgood and Harold Dixon.

Fox's contribution as a historian is only partially revealed in his published writings. Much of his time and energy went into editorial work, into his large and popular lecture courses, and into supervising the research of doctoral candidates. For one year (1927–28) he served as director of the American University Union in London, lecturing to large audiences in eighteen British universities and colleges. His genial wit on the public platform won him considerable renown, and he was a featured speaker at many professional meetings and college convocations.

Fox's doctoral dissertation, *The Decline of Aristocracy in the Politics of New York* (1919), described the social forces which he believed had brought about the gradual democratization of political processes in his native state. It also illustrated his conviction that the political scene, whatever its military conflicts and diplomatic intrigues, was shaped by powerful social and economic forces, which required careful study in the local incident if their general significance was to be understood. This thesis was implicit in much of his later writings, particularly *Caleb Heathcote, Gentleman Colonist* (1926), *Ideas in Motion* (1935), and *Yankees and Yorkers* (1940). Fox made his most important contribution to the understanding of American social history as coeditor, with Prof. Arthur M. Schlesinger of Harvard, of the thirteen-volume History of American Life series (1927–48), which sought to "free American history from its traditional servitude to party struggles, war and diplomacy,

and to show how it properly includes all the varied interests of the people."

In 1934 Fox was called to the presidency of Union College in Schenectady, N. Y. A highly successful fund raiser, he also infused great enthusiasm into the student body and faculty, and by his imaginative leadership did much to further his ideal of the small liberal arts college. He improved faculty salaries and the system of promotion, introduced apprenticeships in government work which gave qualified students a chance to match theory with practical experience, and, with the backing of the Carnegie Foundation, established the Mohawk Drama Festival, the first such collaboration between an American college and the professional theatre.

Fox also made an important contribution to the New York State Historical Association, a private historical agency, which he served as president from 1929 to his death. With the aid of highly competent directors, he transformed it from a small group of intelligent amateurs into one of the most vigorous and resourceful state historical societies in the nation. At its meetings he brought professional and amateur historians into fruitful cooperation. His influence was apparent in the association's many scholarly publications, including the ten-volume *History of the State of New York,* edited by Alexander C. Flick (1933–37).

To every activity in which he became interested, Fox brought fruitful ideas. He had the rare ability to persuade others of the importance of his own enthusiasms. His wit was always kindly and his humor never forced. He was more than six feet tall and slender in build, with hair that turned white before he was thirty, giving him a distinguished appearance. He was a hard worker, who never believed that he could exhaust his own strength. In 1945, while actively engaged in his administrative duties at Union College, he suffered a fatal heart attack and died in Schenectady at the age of fifty-seven. He was buried in Sleepy Hollow Cemetery, Tarrytown, N. Y.

[Dixon Ryan Fox Papers, Columbia Univ. Lib.; memoir by Julian P. Boyd in Am. Philosophical Soc., *Year Book,* 1946; chapter by John A. Krout in Clifford L. Lord, ed., *Keepers of the Past* (1965); biographical sketch by Robert V. Remini in 1965 reprint of Fox's *The Decline of Aristocracy in the Politics of N. Y.;* Charles N. Waldron, *The Union College I Remember* (1954), pp. 95–101; Walter M. Whitehill, *Independent Historical Societies* (1962), pp. 330–34; *Who Was Who in America,* vol. II (1950); *N. Y. Times,* Jan. 31, 1945; personal knowledge.]
JOHN A. KROUT

FRAME, ALICE SEYMOUR BROWNE (Oct. 29, 1878–Aug. 16, 1941), Congregational missionary and educator in China, was born in

Harpoot, Turkey, the eldest of three daughters and three sons of missionary parents, John Kittredge Browne and Leila (Kendall) Browne. Both parents were natives of Massachusetts; Browne was a graduate of Harvard and of Andover Theological Seminary. Alice's mother was her teacher during her early years in Turkey. She was then sent home to Massachusetts to study at the Cambridge Latin School before entering Mount Holyoke College, from which she graduated in 1900 with Phi Beta Kappa honors. In college she was active in the work of the Y.W.C.A. and popular with her classmates for her lively intelligence and charm.

Mount Holyoke was notable not only because it was a pioneer in the higher education of women, a veritable breeding ground of feminism, but also because it urged its graduates to take up missionary work as a career. Increasing numbers of unmarried American women missionaries, including Mount Holyoke graduates, had been sent abroad as teachers and doctors since the formation of women's mission boards shortly after the Civil War. Alice's mother had, in fact, received the call to missionary work while a student at Mount Holyoke and had left without graduating. The example of her parents and her college thus influenced Alice Browne to become a missionary educator, and the drama of the Boxer Rebellion, with its stories of missionary martyrdom and heroism, decided her to seek service in China.

Though slight and delicate in appearance, she had great reserves of physical strength and will. To prepare herself as a religious educator, she first attended Hartford Theological Seminary for three years and earned a B.D. degree (1903). She then worked for two years in the United States for the Woman's Board of Missions (Congregational) as secretary of young people's work. In 1905 she sailed for China, financed by contributions from Mount Holyoke students and alumnae, who were to provide her lifetime support. Her deep commitment to the career she had chosen soon became evident.

Alice Browne's first stop was Tungchow, a town near Peking that had become a missionary educational center. Within a year she had learned Mandarin well enough to do evangelistic work in country districts, and had also become principal of the Fu Yu Girls' School. Her fluency in the language was later considered remarkable. The variety of work and her professional independence made this a happy period in her career. Her administrative and intellectual reputation, however, soon propelled her out of Tungchow. A leading missionary goal had been higher education for Chinese women. Shortly before Alice Browne's

arrival in China, Luella Miner had organized the first women's college in the country, North China Union College for Women, in Peking. In search of competent teachers and administrators, Miss Miner invited Alice Browne to teach at the college for a year, not only as a prospective faculty member but as her possible successor as head of the college.

Miss Browne's engagement to Murray Scott Frame, a missionary she had met in Tungchow, disrupted this plan. After a furlough which she largely spent studying at Columbia University and Union Theological Seminary, they were married in Kyoto, Japan, on Oct. 10, 1913. The couple had three children: Frances Kendall (who died in infancy), Murray Scott (who died at birth), and Rosamond. In 1918 Frame died of typhus. Left with her infant daughter, Mrs. Frame set about to rebuild her life. By now her roots were in China, and soon after her husband's death she temporarily assumed leadership of the North China College for Women; after a brief furlough in the United States she became its official head in 1922.

The college had affiliated in 1920 with the all-male Yenching University, an interdenominational institution in Peking headed by John Leighton Stuart. Mrs. Frame's first major task was to oversee the construction of the women's college buildings at Yenching. Donations from Mrs. Russell Sage [Margaret Olivia Slocum Sage, q.v.] and Mrs. David B. Gamble, among others, provided for the erection of a full complement of administrative, classroom, and residential quarters, which were formally opened in September 1927. During these years Mrs. Frame's feminist convictions were thoroughly tested. Although her school became the largest Christian women's college in China, with an enrollment of more than two hundred women by 1930, girls were outnumbered by male students in the university two and a half to one. Alice Frame was determined that the identity, the financial resources, and the autonomy of the women's institution should not be swallowed up. It is not certain that she was the primary force behind the plan, later dropped, for a geographically separate women's college with a moat around it. But it is well remembered that she fought to get female faculty members promotions, that she kept control of the women's college funds, and that she was proof against both the charm and the occasional high-handedness of President Stuart. She was officially, and clearly, dean of Yenching Women's College, not the university's dean of women. According to Margaret Speer, her successor, Mrs. Frame was a "masterful woman." Her masterfulness invited criticism, especially from male students and faculty, but she succeeded in preserving much of the independence of her institution. A recent historian of Yenching, Prof. Philip West, credits her with setting a high standard for women students, thus helping to create the college's distinguished reputation in North China higher education.

The 1920's presented problems for Yenching, in common with other Christian colleges in China. The growth of nationalism, anti-Christian movements, the rise of new life styles for the young, and changing views about the curriculum all sent shock waves across the campus. Pressure grew to appoint Chinese as top administrators. A Chinese scholar, Wu Lei-ch'uan, was made chancellor of Yenching and began to press for a unified administration of the male and female colleges. Vulnerable not only as a foreigner but also as an administrator, Alice Frame came under attack and even personal threat, particularly by male students who found her a convenient target for their feelings of frustration and dissidence. In 1930 she asked to resign as soon as a Chinese woman could be found to replace her, and the next year she returned to Tungchow and to her work in the countryside, serving as secretary of religious education for the Congregational Church in North China. .

Mrs. Frame developed tuberculosis in 1932 and the following year went back to the United States, where, even while convalescing, she was still able to report that mountain climbing was a hobby and walking her favorite sport. In 1934 she again took up her work in China until, ill with cancer, she returned once more to the United States in 1940. She died in Newton, Mass., at the age of sixty-two. Her daughter Rosamond, like her mother a Mount Holyoke graduate and teacher in China, served as a field agent in China for the Office of Strategic Services in World War II.

[The writer acknowledges the help of Miss Margaret Bailey Speer and Prof. Philip West. A fuller treatment can be found in an article by Grace M. Boynton in *Notable Am. Women*, I, 658–60. See also Durward Howes, ed., *Am. Women*, 1937–38. Mrs. Frame's papers are in the archives of the Am. Board of Commissioners for Foreign Missions, Houghton Lib., Harvard Univ. On Yenching Univ., see Dwight Edwards, *Yenching Univ.* (1959); and Howard S. Galt, "Yenching Univ., Its Sources and Its Hist." (microfilm at United Board for Christian Higher Education in Asia, N. Y. City). A recent general study, Jessie G. Lutz, *China and the Christian Colleges: 1850–1950* (1971), provides useful background.]

SHIRLEY STONE GARRETT

FRASER, LEON (Nov. 27, 1889–Apr. 8, 1945), banker, was born in Boston, Mass., the only child of John Fraser, a Scottish immigrant, and Mary (Lovat) Fraser, who was partly of French-Canadian descent. His mother died at his

birth; his father turned the child over to a fellow Scot, Ronald E. Bonar, and then disappeared; according to report, he later went to the Klondike. Bonar and his wife, Susan (Dayton) Bonar, adopted the child. Although Fraser did not use his foster father's name, he seemed to hold his foster parents in deep affection. Bonar, who had a hat manufacturing plant in New York City, spent much time on the family farm in North Granville, N. Y., which Fraser always looked upon as his home. There he attended the village school, did farm chores, and became deeply attached to rural life.

After preparing at Trinity, an Episcopal school in New York City, Fraser attended Columbia College, where he took a particular interest in such extracurricular activities as the literary magazine (of which he was editor-in-chief), the undergraduate newspaper, and the varsity debating team (of which he was captain). He was graduated in 1910. The next five years he spent enrolled, often simultaneously, in various Columbia faculties: in the School of Law; in the newly founded School of Journalism, from which he received a B.Litt. degree in June 1913; and in the Graduate Faculties. He received an A.M. degree in June 1912, with a major in English and a minor in law, and a Ph.D. degree in June 1915, with a major in politics and minors in law and international law, presenting as his dissertation a study of "English Opinion of the American Constitution and Government (1783–1798)." Although he did not graduate from the law school, he was admitted to the New York bar in 1913.

While a graduate student at Columbia, Fraser also served on the editorial staff of the New York *World* (1913–14) and spoke on street corners for various political candidates. In 1915 he joined the Columbia faculty as a lecturer (later instructor) in public law, but his academic career came to an abrupt end. In April 1916, while Fraser (at the suggestion of Dean Frederick P. Keppel [Supp. 3] of Columbia) was giving speeches for the American Association for International Conciliation, a peace society headed by Columbia's president, Nicholas Murray Butler, he was reported by the newspapers as having said that anyone who went to the Plattsburgh military training camp was a "benighted fool." Fraser was called before a committee of the Columbia trustees, and though he denied making such a statement or holding such an opinion, the trustees next year recommended against his reappointment. The episode, a bitter blow to Fraser, was of great importance in shaping his future attitudes and career.

He had meanwhile enlisted in the army, in

which he rose from private to major and served in the Judge Advocate General's Department of the A.E.F. in France. Upon his return, in 1920, he served briefly in the Bureau of War Risk Insurance in Washington and, the next year, as executive officer and acting director of the federal Veterans' Bureau. He then joined the Paris staff of Coudert Brothers, an international law firm which specialized in counseling American banking and industrial companies on European loans and investments. On Oct. 21, 1922, in France, he married Margaret M. Maury of Washington, D. C. They had no children of their own but adopted an infant son, James Leon Fraser, in 1931.

Leaving Coudert Brothers, Fraser served from 1924 to 1927 as general counsel for the Dawes plan and as Paris representative of the office of the Agent General for Reparation Payments. Three years (1927–30) followed as the New York correspondent of the Boston legal firm of Ropes, Gray, Boyden and Perkins. In 1930 he returned to Paris at the invitation of Owen D. Young to serve as his legal and economic expert in connection with the drafting of the Young Plan and the charter of the Bank for International Settlements. When the B.I.S. was organized in 1930, Fraser was made director and alternate of the president, Gates W. McGarrah [Supp. 2]; he was president from 1933 to 1935. During these years Fraser promoted central bank cooperation, helped develop the standstill agreements with Germany, and participated in the granting of emergency credits to the Reichsbank and to central banks in Hungary, Austria, Yugoslavia, Danzig, and the United Kingdom. His ability at the B.I.S. to reconcile divergent points of view, to obtain the harmonious cooperation of directors representing many nationalities, and to enlist the loyalty of the staff greatly advanced the cause of international monetary cooperation.

Upon his return to the United States, Fraser joined the First National Bank of New York, at first as vice-president (1935–36) and then (from Jan. 1, 1937) as president. One of his associates has questioned whether this was the ideal position for Fraser, who was forced to devote himself to day-to-day pressing administrative concerns (though he did so with great effectiveness) rather than with broad international economic and political problems. He nonetheless emerged as a spokesman for the banking community, and in 1941 was elected for a three-year term as a director of the Federal Reserve Bank of New York.

In April 1945, at fifty-five, Fraser returned to his boyhood home of North Granville and took his own life. Although it came as a distinct surprise to his associates, this was not an impulsive act. In a farewell letter he explained that he had long suffered from a steadily increasing depression. Friends have commented on the loneliness of Fraser's life: his orphaned boyhood, his desolation at the death of his wife in 1942, his lack of close friends despite a highly gregarious nature. In an editorial comment the *New York Times* remarked that Fraser had never lost the wide-ranging curiosity he had shown as a reporter. His associates recalled his great capacity to absorb facts, to understand the inner workings of the financial system, and to form astute judgments, as well as his independence of thought, his flexibility of mind, and his refusal to accept the importance of business as overriding, or to be awed by wealth, power, or authority. After Episcopal services, he was buried in the Granville (N. Y.) Cemetery.

[Contemporary biographical sketches of Fraser appeared in the *American Mag.*, July 1933 (by John Janney); *Saturday Evening Post*, July 31, 1937 (by Henry F. Pringle); and *New Yorker*, Feb. 14 and 21, 1942 (by Matthew Josephson). See also *N. Y. Times*, Apr. 9, 10, and 11, 1945; *Who Was Who in America*, vol. II (1950); and Sheridan A. Logan's forthcoming history of the First National Bank. Information about Fraser's career at Columbia was supplied by the Registrar, the Secretary, the Columbiana Collection, and Prof. Arthur W. Macmahon. Helpful recollections and appraisals were received from associates of Fraser in his Paris years and at the First National Bank, including Winthrop W. Aldrich, Karl Blessing, W. Randolph Burgess, Dr. Antonio d'Aroma, Maurice Frère, Robert G. Fuller, Sheridan A. Logan, Alexander C. Nagle, Dr. Rudolf Pfenninger, Ivar Rooth, Dr. Hjalmar Schacht, and Allan Sproul.]

B. H. BECKHART

GALE, HENRY GORDON (Sept. 12, 1874–Nov. 16, 1942), physicist, was born in Aurora, Ill., the youngest in a family of three sons and two daughters. His father, Eli Holbrook Gale, a physician and a graduate of Middlebury College in Vermont, had gone west to Illinois after receiving his M.D. from the University of Pennsylvania and had married Adelaide Parker in Aurora. Little is known of Gale's childhood except that his mother died when he was six months old and that he lived during early childhood on the farm of his maternal grandparents.

His long academic career was spent entirely at the University of Chicago. He entered with its first class in 1892 and received the A.B. degree in 1896 and the Ph.D., summa cum laude, in 1899. For his doctoral thesis, on the refractive index of air at pressures up to nineteen atmospheres, he used an interferometer of his own invention. He joined the department of physics in 1899 as an assistant, advanced to instructor (1902) and, in due course, to professor (1916) and department chairman (1925). He also served the university as an undergraduate dean (1908–22), dean of the Ogden Graduate School of Science (1922–30), and, when the graduate college was separated into divisions, dean of the division of physical sciences (1931–40). Among Gale's lasting contributions was initiating the arrangement by which the University of Texas and the University of Chicago jointly founded the McDonald Observatory in western Texas in 1939. He also worked for the establishment of a department of meteorology at Chicago and formed the Institute of Meteorology in 1940.

As a researcher Gale worked mostly in collaboration with others, often leading scientists, his responsibility usually being the exacting and sometimes tedious technical aspect of the experiments. The noted astronomer George Ellery Hale [Supp. 2] invited Gale to Mount Wilson Observatory in 1906 and asked him to synthesize in the laboratory conditions that would produce the same spectroscopic effects as those produced by sunspots. The techniques he devised, with the collaboration of Hale and Walter S. Adams, were of great value to astrophysical and physical research. A fundamental tool was their temperature classification of spectral lines, used in analyzing the complex spectra of most of the elements. Gale also published a series of papers with Adams on the effect of pressure on the character and displacement of spectral lines of several elements.

Gale collaborated with Albert A. Michelson [q.v.] on two significant investigations. The first, the observation of tides in the solid earth, was made at the Yerkes Observatory of the University of Chicago. Gale had the responsibility for all of the observations and the photographic records. The findings, which his meticulous care made dependable, were that "the tides in the actual earth are 0.310 of what they would be if the earth were fluid" (Crew, p. 87). Their second set of experiments, for which Gale did the long and difficult labor of collecting data, sought to determine the effect of the earth on the time taken by light to complete a long circuit. For this purpose a light beam was divided into two parts and sent in opposite directions around a city block, in a twelve-inch evacuated pipe. Gale also raised to a higher level of accuracy the engine for ruling diffraction gratings, devised by Henry A. Rowland [q.v.] and earlier improved by Michelson.

Gale's most important scientific writing was as co-author, with Robert A. Millikan, of several textbooks. The most influential was *A First Course in Physics* (1906), designed for the beginner in high school or college, which sought to convey the method and history of physics and some appreciation of the social results that followed from new scientific theories. Used by a generation of students, it was followed by laboratory manuals and by *A First Course in Physics for Colleges* (1928) and *New Elementary Physics* (1936).

Gale was editor of the *Astrophysical Journal* (1912–40), president of the American Physical Society (1929–31), and vice-president of the American Association for the Advancement of Science (1934). Some quality of his personality is conveyed by his zeal as a football player in college despite his slight build, and by his enlistment in the army during World War I at the age of forty-two. On Jan. 5, 1901, he married Agnes Spofford Cook; they had one child, a daughter, Beatrice Gordon. Gale died of a coronary thrombosis in Billings Memorial Hospital, Chicago.

[The obituary by Henry Crew in *Astrophysical Jour.*, Mar. 1943, includes a good description of Gale's scientific achievements. *Henry Gordon Gale, 1874–1942; A Record of the Memorial Services Conducted by Members of the Faculty of the Univ. of Chicago* (privately printed, 1943) has useful information and a complete bibliography. Both items reproduce photographs of Gale. See also *Who Was Who in America*, vol. II (1950); *N. Y. Times*, Nov. 17, 1942; and, on their textbooks, *The Autobiog. of Robert A. Millikan* (1950).]

HAROLD I. SHARLIN

GANSO, EMIL (Apr. 14, 1895–Apr. 18, 1941), painter and printmaker, was born in Halberstadt, Germany, the youngest child in a large working-class family. His father, Wilhelm Ganso, had been a French soldier. Captured and imprisoned in Germany during the Franco-Prussian War, he remained in the Harz Mountains after his release, married a German girl, Johanna Niemand, and died in 1896, when Emil was just a year old.

As a boy, Ganso liked to draw with colored crayons, but the family was too poor to allow him to develop this interest, and he was apprenticed to a pastry cook and confectioner. A chance meeting with a man who had visited the United States gave him the idea of emigrating there. In 1912 he signed on as a journeyman pastry cook with a ship's crew and jumped ship after landing in Hoboken, N. J. Only seventeen, penniless, knowing no English, he found a job in a bakery and began to learn the language. After a year he visited New York City and its museums, and soon moved to Manhattan.

Working in a bakery by night, by day he began to draw and paint. His only formal training came during two months of free study in the life class of the National Academy School. He also learned from meeting other artists and probably was a frequent visitor to museums and galleries, since he rapidly gained a command of drawing techniques. His first prints were linoleum cuts and woodcuts. From the library he borrowed a book on etching and improvised the special equipment needed to print intaglio plates.

Ganso continued to support himself by working as a baker for more than ten years. During this period he acquired proficiency in pastel and oils as well as in the printmaking media of woodcut, etching, and lithography. In 1926 he took a collection of his work to the gallery of Erhard Weyhe, who gave him his first one-man show in that year and agreed to pay him an annual retainer. One of his paintings was shown at an exhibition of independent artists at the Waldorf, and his work appeared at the Whitney Studio Gallery. With such support, Ganso was able to give up baking and move into his own studio at 900 Sixth Avenue.

Early critics praised Ganso's naive and direct point of view. Soon after his first exhibit, however, he formed a friendship with Jules Pascin, an artist noted both for his sensuous figure studies and for his flamboyance and wit; Pascin exercised an important influence on Ganso, both as an artist and as a person. As Ganso's own art matured, this influence diminished, but he retained a preference for the nude and the still life as basic subjects. Later on, when he had taken a summer studio in the artists' colony at Woodstock, N. Y., he added landscape to his repertory.

In the judgment of Carl Zigrosser, Ganso was fundamentally "a stylist—that is to say, more concerned with how he said a thing than with what he said." His work evoked a world of vitality, beauty, and sensuous charm, always without sentimentality. His free and painterly approach to his printmaking and his enormous gift for vigorous drawing enlivened his art, and he exhibited great skill in devising new or improved technical processes. He was always a prodigious worker. In the decade 1931–41, besides his paintings and watercolors, he produced (and printed himself) more than fifty wood engravings, more than a hundred etchings and aquatints, and some one hundred lithographs. A Guggenheim Fellowship awarded in 1933 enabled him to travel to Europe to study graphic processes, especially lithography, as well as pigments and painting methods.

In 1939 Ganso was appointed artist-in-residence at Lawrence College in Appleton, Wis., and in September 1940 he began teaching at the University of Iowa, at Iowa City. He was an inspired teacher. His mastery of materials and techniques was thorough, and he had the ability to communicate the stages through which he passed in his work to achieve an effect. His background left him not at all doctrinaire or snobbish about art; he was, moreover, a gifted raconteur. Ganso died of a coronary thrombosis in 1941 at his home in Iowa City at the age of forty-six; his wife, Fanny, survived him. His remains were cremated.

[The only extended treatment of Ganso is in Carl Zigrosser, *The Artist in America* (1942), pp. 165–72; among the four reproductions of Ganso's work is his wood engraving self-portrait. See also Norman Kent in *Am. Artist*, Nov. 1944; *Who's Who in Am. Art*, 1940–41; *Time*, Mar. 30, 1936; *Art Digest*, May 1, 1941, p. 14. Ganso's death record (Iowa State Dept. of Health) is the source for his parents' names.]

ALAN M. FERN

GARFIELD, HARRY AUGUSTUS (Oct. 11, 1863–Dec. 12, 1942), lawyer, college president, and public official, was born in Hiram, Ohio, the first son of James Abram Garfield, the future president of the United States, and his wife, Lucretia Rudolph, daughter of one of Hiram's leading families. He was the second of their seven children (two girls and five boys) and the oldest to survive infancy. A brother, James Rudolph Garfield, became Secretary of the Interior in the cabinet of President Theodore Roosevelt.

At the time of Harry's birth his father was serving in the Civil War as chief of staff to Gen. William S. Rosecrans [*q.v.*]; he was seated in Congress when the boy was two months old, and from then until he became president in 1881 the family lived in both Washington and Ohio. Harry's early education was a mixture of public and private schooling and parental tutoring, ending with two years (1879–81) at St. Paul's School in Concord, N. H. He was accompanying his father to the twenty-fifth reunion of the President's Williams College class when Garfield was shot on July 2, 1881, by the assassin Charles J. Guiteau; when the President died on Sept. 19 young Harry had begun his freshman year at Williams. After graduating (B.A.) in 1885, he taught Latin and Roman history for a year at St. Paul's. He then studied at the Columbia University Law School (1886–87) and read law at All Souls College, Oxford, and in London at the Inns of Court (1887–88). On June 14, 1888, he married Belle Hartford Mason, a member of a wealthy Cleveland family and a distant cousin, who bore him four children: James, Mason, Lucretia, and Stanton.

Admitted to the Ohio bar on his return from England in 1888, Garfield opened a law partnership in Cleveland with his brother James. From 1892 to 1895 he also taught contracts at the law school of Western Reserve University. He organized a railroad and coal company that was sold at considerable profit to the Lake Shore and

Michigan Southern Railroad. The experience demonstrated his sound business sense as well as his integrity, fairness, and responsibility, but the degree to which enterprise devoured his time and energy made him fearful that a busy corporate practice would demand the sacrifice of what he called his "higher nature." Such fears must have informed his energetic and effective work as founder and president of the Cleveland Municipal Association, a good-government reform group which he headed from 1896 to 1899, when it defeated the city's Republican political boss. In 1903 Woodrow Wilson, then president of Princeton and seeking a man both experienced in politics and committed to the progressive vision of a better world, persuaded Garfield to fill the chair of politics at Princeton. He held this post from 1904 until 1908, when he accepted the presidency of Williams College.

Garfield was forty-four when he arrived at Williams, of medium stature, somewhat heavily built, with a roundish handsome face, dark hair, and brown eyes. His serenity, judicial turn of mind, and aristocratic bearing lent themselves most effectively to formal relationships, and most students and many faculty never made their way through the reserve and dignity to the essentially pleasant and friendly man within. A son described him as "emotionally conservative but intellectually liberal."

The Williams presidency enabled Garfield to preach, by word and example, the values of public service, good citizenship, and moral leadership which he, like Woodrow Wilson, regarded as essential to individual worth and effective democratic government. At a time when many, perhaps most, students regarded college primarily as a social experience, he was one of the administrators who with their faculties earnestly stressed the legitimacy of classroom learning. Beginning in 1911 he initiated a series of curricular reforms at Williams which brought the study of particular subject areas under the control of prerequisites and sequence, giving some encouragement to academic study of greater depth and quality. These tendencies were reinforced by a strengthened faculty, a rejection of professionalism in athletics, and the introduction of an honors degree program.

In the age of rising universities, Garfield kept Williams loyal to collegiate ideals. It grew, but slowly and without perceptible damage to its style, which was imbedded in Latin requirements for admission, daily compulsory chapel, and Greek-letter fraternities. Students were overwhelmingly recruited from Eastern boarding schools, faculty were presumably able to draw on resources other than their salaries in order to participate in the good life, and the college community was held together by afternoon tea rather than cocktail parties. Garfield himself presided over this scene with unchallenged power: he hired and he fired. For him Williams remained what it had always been—a community where candidates for responsible positions in the governing class reaffirmed and strengthened a commitment to certain qualities of character and behavior denoting a gentleman. He himself symbolized those qualities. During prohibition he denied his well-stocked cellar to himself and his guests, but he enjoyed drink honestly on his European trips. Once he appeared at a local fire at 2 a.m. impeccably groomed, even to a stickpin in his tie.

Though for the most part a Republican by preference, Garfield voted the Democratic ticket in 1912 and 1916 (as he would again in 1920 and 1936). He served Wilson as wartime Fuel Administrator from Aug. 23, 1917, to Dec. 19, 1919. Administering an agency of 18,000 men and women—most, like himself, unpaid volunteers—he gave effective and judicious attention to the needs of the nation, management, and labor, and succeeded in increasing bituminous coal production, stabilizing fuel prices, and reducing domestic consumption. His wartime association with Bernard Baruch led to the establishment in 1921 at Williams of the internationally known and widely copied Institute of Politics, a characteristic manifestation of Garfield's ideals and talents. Subsidized for its first three years by Baruch and later by others, the Institute brought to the campus each August several hundred men and women from universities and public life, at home and abroad, for lectures and discussions on international problems. Besides the quota of honorary degrees that normally comes to a college president, Garfield was elected president of the American Political Science Association in 1923.

In his long tenure at Williams, Garfield gave expression to the values and attitudes that were then thought to be synonymous with all that was best in American life. Complacency and a passivity toward student discontent with the Latin requirements and compulsory chapel characterized the last years of his presidency. He was succeeded in 1934 by Tyler Dennett, who in three stormy years awakened the Williams community to an awareness of an era that Garfield had sought to deny, to avoid, or at least to delay. In his retirement Garfield made his home in Washington, D. C. He died of cardiac decompensation at the age of seventy-nine while visiting in Williamstown and was buried in the Williams College Cemetery.

[The Harry A. Garfield Papers are among the Garfield Family Papers at the Lib. of Cong. and in the Williams College archives. Other sources: Lucretia Garfield Comer, *Harry Garfield's First Forty Years* (1965); Harry A. Garfield, *Lost Visions* (1944); E. Herbert Botsford, *Fifty Years at Williams*, vol. IV (1940); *The Institute of Politics at Williamstown, Mass.: Its First Decade* (1931); U. S. Fuel Administration, *Final Report*, by H. A. Garfield (1921); Williams College, *Obituary Record*, 1947; correspondence and interviews with associates of Garfield; death record from Mass. Registrar of Vital Statistics.]

FREDERICK RUDOLPH

GEHRIG, HENRY LOUIS (June 19, 1903–June 2, 1941), baseball player, better known as Lou Gehrig, was born in the Yorkville section of Manhattan in New York City. His father, Heinrich Gehrig, a native of Baden, Germany, was an ironworker by trade and worked variously as a tinsmith, mechanic, and janitor; his mother, Christina (Pack) Gehrig, born in Denmark, held jobs as a housekeeper and domestic. Lou was the only one of their children who survived infancy. Naturally shy, he seems to have been made more so by the anti-German hysteria that developed during World War I. A strapping, broad-shouldered boy, he spent long hours playing baseball and football on the sandlots and in the schoolyards of New York City. He attended the High School of Commerce, where he excelled at both sports. His prowess on the gridiron brought him to the attention of Buck O'Neill, the football coach at Columbia College, and through the intervention of an alumnus who had hired Mrs. Gehrig as a housekeeper for a fraternity at Columbia, Gehrig was persuaded to enroll there in 1921.

During his first year at Columbia, Gehrig was barred from participation in athletics because, apparently unaware of the rules governing college sports, he had played professional baseball with the Hartford team of the Eastern League. In 1922 he began playing on Columbia's baseball team. His spectacular performance attracted the notice of Paul Krichell, head scout for the New York Yankees, and in 1923, immediately after the close of the Columbia baseball season, Gehrig left college to join the Yankees.

After two years of seasoning at Hartford, Gehrig became a Yankee for good, entering a game as a pinch hitter on June 1, 1925, and becoming the starting first baseman on the following day. His fielding was at first undistinguished, and in the words of one biographer he was "something of a stumblebum." But he soon found his legs at first base. The flamboyant Yankee slugger Babe Ruth, whom Gehrig idolized, liked the young player and helped him improve his batting. In 1926, while Gehrig was still learning the fine points of hitting, manager Miller Huggins [*q.v.*] moved him to fourth place in the batting order, the important cleanup position. Within a year he and Ruth had become known as the "twins" and had begun to please fans with their friendly competition for home runs (a competition Gehrig never won).

Batting and throwing left-handed, standing six feet one inch tall and weighing about 200 pounds, Gehrig emerged as a national idol. His unaffected grin became as familiar to millions as the number "4" on his uniform that identified him as a member of the Yankees' "Murderers' Row" of sluggers. From 1925 to early 1939 Gehrig was in the lineup for every regular game the Yankees played—2,130 in a row. He hit 493 home runs, batted in 1,990 runs, and compiled a lifetime batting average of .340. From 1926 to 1937 he hit for an average of .300 or better in every season and drove home more than 150 runs in each of seven seasons. He was chosen "Most Valuable Player" in the American League in 1927, 1931, 1934, and 1936. In 1939 he was elected to baseball's Hall of Fame at Cooperstown, N. Y. On June 3, 1932, Gehrig performed a feat matched only twice before—and never by Ruth—when he struck four home runs in a single game, against the Philadelphia Athletics.

Gehrig's playing skill declined markedly in 1938, when he batted only .295 and hit only 29 home runs—his worst year since 1925. The decline continued during spring training the following year, and he played his last big-league game on Apr. 30, 1939, against the Washington Senators. He then asked to be benched, and early in June he entered the Mayo Clinic in Rochester, Minn., where tests showed that he was suffering from amyotrophic lateral sclerosis—a hardening of the spinal cord producing symptoms similar to those of infantile paralysis. The disease was progressive and had no known cure. Gehrig's quiet courage in accepting the end of his career as the "Iron Horse" and his gallantry in combating a fatal disease added to his stature as a popular hero. During the remainder of the season he served as a nonplaying captain of the Yankees, and on July 4 "Appreciation Day" ceremonies were held in his honor at the Yankee Stadium, attended by members of the great Yankee teams on which he had played and by more than 60,000 fans.

A diffident, reserved man, Gehrig was noted for his lack of temperament and for his kindness to rookie players. He centered his nonprofessional life around his parents, with whom he lived in

New Rochelle, N. Y., until 1933, when on Sept. 29 he married Eleanor Grace Twitchell of Chicago. They had no children. After the 1939 season he retired from baseball and accepted a post on the municipal Parole Commission tendered him by Mayor Fiorello H. La Guardia of New York City. Although Gehrig's health continued to deteriorate, he carried out his duties conscientiously, working with boys' clubs and helping to combat juvenile delinquency, until a month before his death. He died shortly before his thirty-eighth birthday at his home in the Riverdale section of the Bronx. After services at Christ Episcopal Church in Riverdale, his remains were cremated and the ashes buried in Kensico Cemetery, Valhalla, N. Y.

Unlike the high-living Babe Ruth, Gehrig led a relatively retiring and frugal existence. His estate was appraised at $171,251, all derived from baseball and from a motion picture based on his life. His fame owed much to the ample leisure many Americans enjoyed between the two World Wars and to the spread of radio broadcasting. At a time when the public increasingly found its heroes in the sports and entertainment worlds rather than in the arena of politics, "Columbia Lou"—as he was often called—represented the rags-to-riches saga in the Horatio Alger tradition. Although overshadowed by Ruth both as a player and as a public idol, Gehrig earned applause for his love of home, his dedicated effort to excel as a fielder, his physical durability, and the model of character he set for the youth of his day.

[Popular biographies of Gehrig by Stanley W. Carlson (1940), Richard Hubler (1941), Paul Gallico (1942), and Frank Graham (1942); *Who's Who in N. Y.*, 1938; *N. Y. Post*, June 3, 1941; *N. Y. Times*, July 5, 1939, June 3, 4, 1941, Sept. 16, 1941 (burial), Apr. 7, 1945 (estate), Aug. 19, 1946, and Mar. 13, 1954 (obituaries of his parents).]

HENRY F. GRAFF

GENTHE, ARNOLD (Jan. 8, 1869–Aug. 9, 1942), photographer, was born in Berlin, Germany, the first of three sons of Hermann and Louise (Zober) Genthe. His father, whose family was of Dutch origin, was a professor of Latin and Greek at the Graues Kloster (Gray Monastery) in Berlin. His mother's family, like his father's, was associated with education, and one of her cousins was the painter Adolf Menzel. During Arnold's boyhood his father's successive academic posts took the family to Frankfurt am Main, to Korbach in the province of Waldeck, and finally to Hamburg, where the elder Genthe founded and became the first president of the Wilhelm Gymnasium. After attending his father's school, Arnold wished to become a painter, but the family's straitened finances following his father's death in 1886 constrained him to prepare for an academic career. In 1888 he entered the University of Jena, where he studied classical philology, archaeology, and philosophy and received the Ph.D. in 1894. He then spent a year in Paris at the Sorbonne, where he took courses in French literature and the history of art.

In 1895 Genthe accepted the invitation of Baron Heinrich von Schroeder, a friend who had married a wealthy Californian, to come to San Francisco as tutor to his son. Genthe was fascinated by the city, and particularly by the large Chinese quarter. Wanting to make a visual record of it and finding his efforts at painting and sketching inadequate, he turned to photography. His unposed pictures, taken inconspicuously with a small, hand-held camera, not only showed aspects of life in Chinatown hitherto almost unknown but were revolutionary in their directness.

When his work as tutor ended in 1897, Genthe decided to remain in San Francisco and become a professional photographer. Expanding his technical knowledge through reading and membership in the California Camera Club, he began to experiment with portraiture. He opened a studio on Sutter Street in 1898 and sent announcements to the society friends and acquaintances he had made through his former employer. Success came quickly, for his softly focused, naturally posed photographs contrasted favorably with the formal studio portraits of the day. As the rich, the famous, and the beautiful came to Genthe's studio, his reputation grew. During these early years he photographed, among many others, the authors Frank Norris and Jack London [*qq.v.*], the actresses Sarah Bernhardt and Margaret Anglin, and the pianist Ignace Paderewski. Reproductions of his work appeared in the photographic journals, along with articles by Genthe describing his techniques and approaches to his craft. In 1899 he made the first of many visits to New Mexico, where he obtained notable photographs among the Hopi, Navajo, and Zuñi tribes.

After the San Francisco earthquake of Apr. 18, 1906, Genthe borrowed a camera (his own had been damaged) and roamed the city to record the devastation. During his absence his studio was dynamited to prevent the spread of the fire; only the Chinatown negatives, stored in a friend's vault, were saved. His pictures of the ruined city and its inhabitants constitute a unique record and compare with his Chinatown work in directness and force of imagery.

Genthe resumed his photographic work in a new studio, but in 1911, at the urging of friends, he moved to New York City, which remained his home for the rest of his life. His sitters continued to be noted personalities representing many aspects of American life and culture, and included Presidents Theodore Roosevelt, Taft, and Wilson. His portraits of John D. Rockefeller showed the man as a human being, not as a giant of business. His studies of the film actress Greta Garbo were said to have been important in furthering her career and set a standard for the portrayal of feminine beauty, of which he became known as a connoisseur. He had a strong interest in the performing arts, particularly the dance. He repeatedly photographed Isadora Duncan [q.v.] and her troupe over the years, often using a hand-held camera to capture the fleeting qualities of the dance movements. His studies record most of the major dancers and dance groups of the 1920's and '30's, including Ruth St. Denis and Ted Shawn, the Morgan Dancers, and Anna Pavlova. One of the first to become interested in color photography, Genthe exhibited his color work as early as 1911, and examples of it were published almost as soon as this was technically possible.

Tall, handsome, and charming, Genthe was a man of culture, a collector and connoisseur of Oriental art. He became an American citizen in 1918. Throughout his life he enjoyed travel. He visited Japan, Korea, Greece, and parts of Europe, North Africa, and Central America, and the photographs made on these trips were often used for an exhibition or in one of his many publications. Among his books are: *Pictures of Old Chinatown* (1908), with text by Will Irwin; *The Book of the Dance* (1916); *Impressions of Old New Orleans* (1926); and *Isadora Duncan: Twenty-four Studies* (1929). Genthe never married. He died of a coronary occlusion at the age of seventy-three while visiting friends in New Milford, Conn.; his remains were cremated.

Genthe was a major figure in the history of photography. He made full use of his craft and contributed significantly to its development, particularly in the area of documentary photography, as seen in his Chinatown and earthquake pictures and his studies of the dance.

[The Arnold Genthe Collection in the Lib. of Cong. includes his studio records, some 20,000 negatives, and many prints. For a description, see Paul Vanderbilt's article in the library's *Quart. Jour. of Current Acquisitions,* May 1951, which also gives information about Genthe's life and career and includes a bibliography. The most important personal source is Genthe's autobiography, *As I Remember* (1936), which includes reproductions of many of his photographs. A recent evaluation is Peter Pollack, *The Picture Hist. of Photography* (1958), chap. xxiv. See also *Nat. Cyc. Am. Biog.,* Current Vol. E, pp. 353–54. Death record from Conn. State Dept. of Health.]

JERALD C. MADDOX

GEST, MORRIS (Jan. 17, 1881–May 16, 1942), theatrical producer, was born Moses Gershonovitch in Koshedary, near Vilna, Russia. He was one of at least three sons and five children of Leon and Louisa (Miklishansky) Gershonovitch. Too intractable, perhaps, to get along with his father, a Talmudic scholar who manufactured soap and perfume, Morris was shipped off, at the age of twelve, to an uncle in Boston. As a boy he worked in his uncle's shop, sold newspapers, shined shoes, posted bills, and finally got a job in the library of the federal courthouse. He had some public schooling, but later credited his education chiefly to the Boston Public Library.

Stagestruck from the first time that he saw bright lights, Gest did not keep his courthouse job for long. He swept the stages of Boston theatres, appeared as a "wild man" in a local sideshow, working with a carnival in Maine, and managed properties for a troupe of Yiddish performers. In 1902 he ventured to New York City, where he was soon doing odd jobs for the producer Oscar Hammerstein [q.v.]. Recognizing the young man's enterprise, Hammerstein sent him to Europe to engage foreign acts for the Victoria Theatre. The European contacts he made at this time were to prove profitable in later years.

In 1905 Gest entered into partnership with F. Ray Comstock to form a theatrical producing firm that lasted for twenty-three years. Financial success did not come quickly, however, and only their operation of the candy concession at the Hippodrome Theatre kept them going until their first hit—George V. Hobart's play *Experience* (1914). Thereafter the partners pursued diverse interests. While Comstock presented intimate musical comedies at the Princess Theatre, frequently with music by Jerome Kern [Supp. 3], Gest indulged his passion for color and size by staging lavish spectacles, first at the Manhattan Opera House, which he operated from 1914 to 1920, and then at the huge, unwieldy Century Theatre, which he took over, at the invitation of the financier Otto H. Kahn [Supp. 1], in 1917. Among his productions at the first theatre were *The Wanderer* (1917), a Biblical pageant, and *Chu Chin Chow* (1917), a musical tale of the Orient. At the Century Theatre, his *Aphrodite* (1919) and *Mecca* (1920) were perhaps the largest and most elaborate presentations seen in New York up to that time. Though not highly profitable, they toured successfully.

But spectacle was not enough to satisfy Gest, who had acquired a taste for art as well as glitter. He had apparently had a hand in bringing the Ballet Russe to America in 1910, and in 1919 he persuaded the great Russian ballet master

Michel Fokine [Supp. 3] to come to the United States to stage the dancing scenes in *Aphrodite*. In succeeding years Gest imported other equally distinguished foreign artists. In 1922 he brought the *Chauve-Souris* revue of Nikita Baliev. The next year he sponsored the first American engagement of the Moscow Art Theatre of Konstantin Stanislavski. The group performed from 1923 through 1925 in a repertory of thirteen plays and provided America with a first-hand view of true ensemble acting by a great company. Several of its leading actors remained in the United States and became influential teachers of what was eventually to be termed the "Stanislavski System," profoundly influencing American acting technique. Gest also arranged the final American tour (1923–24) of the great Italian tragedienne Eleonora Duse. One of his largest, most costly, and most noted productions was *The Miracle* (1924), a religious pantomime staged by the German director Max Reinhardt with a cast of 600. Presented at the Century Theatre, whose interior the designer Norman Bel Geddes converted into a Gothic cathedral, it won critical acclaim and ran for 298 performances. Gest later presented it profitably on tour.

Morris Gest ended his partnership with Comstock in 1928 and became an independent producer. That year he sponsored Max Reinhardt's leading actor, Alexander Moissi, in productions of Ibsen's *Ghosts* and Tolstoi's *Redemption* staged by David Belasco [Supp. 1], whose daughter, Reina Victoria, Gest had married on June 1, 1909. In 1929 he brought from Germany the Freiburg Passion Play, but lost heavily on the engagement and the next year filed for bankruptcy. None of his productions of the 1930's, including *The Wonder Bar* (1931), an experimental musical starring Al Jolson, and a Chinese drama, *Lady Precious Stream* (1936)—his last Broadway production—equaled his earlier successes.

Gest produced several motion pictures, including *Hearts of the World* (1915), directed by D. W. Griffith, and *The Thief of Bagdad* (1924), starring Douglas Fairbanks [Supp. 2]. He ended his career on a note of showmanship with a midget village at the New York World's Fair of 1939. Three years later Gest entered the Midtown Hospital in New York City with pneumonia and died there of a heart attack at the age of sixty-one. He was buried in the Belasco family mausoleum in Linden Hill Cemetery, Maspeth, in Queens.

Absorbed in the theatre, Gest was, as he once admitted, a "complete egoist" (*Theatre Magazine,*

October 1922, p. 223). He and his wife had no children, but in 1922 he managed to bring his relatives from Russia to America. He dressed in a distinctive flowing Windsor tie and black artist's hat that were long familiar on Broadway. Always a showman, he nevertheless displayed a discriminating theatrical taste and an eagerness to promote the finest foreign talent, often with a surprising disregard for monetary success.

[The best biographical sources are obituaries in the *N. Y. Times,* May 17, 1942, and *Variety,* May 20, 1942; and the sketch in the *Nat. Cyc. Am. Biog.,* XXXVIII, 394–95. The last gives his parents' names as above; *Who's Who in Am. Jewry,* 1938–39, has his mother's name as Elizabeth. For an able appraisal of Gest, see Alexander Woollcott, *Enchanted Aisles* (1924). See also his own comments on his work in "Going Broke for Art's Sake," *Theatre Mag.,* Oct. 1922, and "Bringing Exotic Art to Broadway," *ibid.,* Mar. 1924. On *The Miracle,* see Oliver M. Sayler, ed., *Max Reinhardt and His Theatre* (1924), and Ernst Haeussermann, *Max Reinhardt's Theaterarbeit in Amerika* (1966).]

ALFRED G. BROOKS

GHENT, WILLIAM JAMES (Apr. 29, 1866–July 10, 1942), socialist and author, was born in Frankfort, Ind., the sixth of eight children and only son of Ira Keith Ghent and Mary Elizabeth (Palmer) Ghent. The families of both parents had moved to Indiana in the 1830's: the Palmers from Kentucky, the Ghents from Canada, where William's great-grandfather, a North Carolina Loyalist, had settled during the American Revolution. When William was two the family moved to Kansas and took out a homestead, but after six discouraging years they returned to Frankfort, where Ira Ghent opened a drugstore. William left public school at the age of thirteen for a job as printer's devil on a local newspaper, and soon became a skilled compositor. He joined the International Typographical Union, a membership he retained for over fifty years, and as a "tramp printer" traveled throughout the United States.

In the 1890's Ghent began to write on social and political topics and became active in reform groups. Describing himself as an independent socialist, he participated in the People's party campaign of 1892 in New York City by denouncing the influence of Daniel De Leon [*q.v.*] and the Socialist Labor party. Ghent's socialism resembled the gradualist, middle-class views of the Bellamyite Nationalists and American Fabians with whom he increasingly associated. In 1894 he helped found the Social Reform Club of New York City, an organization designed to bring workers and middle-class intellectuals together to "better the condition of the wage earner." He served briefly (1897–98) as editor of the *American Fabian,* until his support of the Spanish-

American War caused a furor in socialist circles. In 1899 he became literary manager of the campaigns of Samuel M. ("Golden Rule") Jones [Supp. 1] for reelection as mayor of Toledo and for the governorship of Ohio.

Ghent's first and most original book, *Our Benevolent Feudalism*, was published in 1902. Perceiving financial consolidation as the key trend in American society, he predicted the end of competition and the emergence of a police state in which the ruling industrial capitalists, the new lords of a reborn feudalism, would ensure social peace by bestowing economic security on the working masses. In *Mass and Class: A Survey of Social Divisions* (1904) he revealed a greater optimism, arguing, despite his general acceptance of Marxian economic analysis, that a collectivist commonwealth would eventually be achieved through democratic means. In the meantime, he declared, many "lawless" activities of labor were justified by intolerable economic conditions. His ingrained aversion to radicalism, however, soon caused him to abandon this view.

Ghent joined the growing Socialist party in 1904 and aligned himself with men like Morris Hillquit [*q.v.*] and Algernon Lee, editor of the *Worker*, in espousing political and educational activities and opposing labor violence. In 1906 he helped organize the Rand School of Social Science in New York City; he taught classes there, served as its secretary (1906–09), the only full-time administrative position, and as president (1909–11). On July 17, 1909, Ghent married Amy Louise Morrison of Wooster, Ohio, a member of the school's clerical staff. They had no children.

Ghent was an active and articulate expounder of socialism during these years. Although not a "street crowd pleaser," he was a popular speaker with middle-class audiences. In 1910, despite the opposition of the party's left wing, he endorsed New York State's workmen's compensation law. The following year he became secretary to Socialist Congressman Victor Berger [*q.v.*] and helped him frame an unsuccessful old age pension bill. At the 1912 Socialist convention Ghent sponsored an amendment to the party's constitution providing for the expulsion of anyone who advocated sabotage or violence, an amendment that was used the following year to oust William D. ("Big Bill") Haywood [*q.v.*] of the I.W.W. from the national executive committee.

Having contracted tuberculosis, Ghent moved in 1913 to Phoenix, Ariz., and the next year to Los Angeles, Calif., where he continued to lecture and write. He refused to join in the Socialist party's repudiation of World War I, and in 1916

he left the party. With other disaffected socialists, he later formed the prowar Social Democratic League.

During the 1920's Ghent became an aggressive opponent of both Marxism and Soviet Russia. Defending capitalism as a bulwark against bolshevism, he wrote articles for several conservative and ultranationalist journals; some of these were collected in his book *The Reds Bring Reaction* (1923). Ghent returned to New York City in 1924. Three years later he became an editor-writer (1927–28) on the staff of the *Dictionary of American Biography* in Washington, D. C. Then, and afterward as a contributor, he wrote a number of articles on figures of the frontier and the Old West, a field in which he had become interested while working as a reference librarian at the University of California in Los Angeles in 1922–23. During the last decade of his life he published three books on Western subjects. Ghent died at his Washington home of a coronary occlusion at the age of seventy-six. He was buried at Fort Lincoln Cemetery in Washington.

[Ghent Papers, Lib. of Cong. (also useful are the Morris Hillquit Papers, State Hist. Soc. of Wis., and the Victor Berger Papers, Milwaukee County Hist. Soc.); Harold S. Smith, "William James Ghent, Reformer and Historian" (doctoral dissertation, Univ. of Wis., 1957); Lawrence Goldman, "W. J. Ghent and the Left," *Studies on the Left*, Summer 1963; *Who Was Who in America*, vol. II (1950); obituary in *Sunday Star* (Washington), July 12, 1942; death record from D. C. Dept. of Public Health. Ghent's later books are *The Road to Oregon* (1929), *The Early Far West* (1931), and, with LeRoy R. Hafen, *Broken Hand: The Life Story of Thomas Fitzpatrick, Chief of the Mountain Men* (1931).]

HAROLD S. SMITH

GHERARDI, BANCROFT (Apr. 6, 1873–Aug. 14, 1941), telephone engineer and corporation executive, was born in San Francisco, Calif., the older of two sons of Bancroft and Anna Talbot (Rockwell) Gherardi. He was a grandson of Donato Gherardi, who came to the United States in the 1820's as a political refugee from Italy, taught Latin and Italian at the Round Hill School in Northampton, Mass., and married a sister of its director, the historian George Bancroft [*q.v.*]. The elder Bancroft Gherardi was a naval officer who served on the U.S.S. *Niagara* (which in 1858 laid the first Atlantic cable), participated in several Civil War engagements, and rose to the rank of rear admiral; his other son, Walter Rockwell Gherardi, also followed a naval career. Young Bancroft's schooling depended on where his father's naval duties took him. After receiving a B.S. degree from the Polytechnic Institute of Brooklyn in 1891, he proceeded to Cornell, where he was awarded the degrees of Mechanical Engineer in

1893 and Master of Mechanical Engineering in 1894.

Jobs were scarce in 1895, and Gherardi fortuitously entered telephony when, through a family friend, Bradley A. Fiske [Supp. 3], he found a job with the Metropolitan Telephone and Telegraph Company, predecessor of the New York Telephone Company. From 1895 to 1900 he did important work improving the efficiency of telephone cables, developing telephone transmission theory, and establishing engineering requirements for aerial cables and poles. In 1900 he headed the New York Telephone Company's newly organized traffic engineering department; the following year he became chief engineer of the New York and New Jersey Telephone Company, and in 1906 assistant chief engineer of both the New York Telephone Company and the New York and New Jersey firm. Despite expanding executive responsibilities he kept his hand in technical problems. He was particularly active in designing new telephone buildings and arranging their equipment. In 1902 he and John J. Carty [Supp. 1] engineered the first commercial application of the loading coils invented by Michael Pupin [Supp. 1].

In 1907 Gherardi moved to the American Telephone & Telegraph Company, first as equipment engineer and then in 1909 as engineer of plants. For the next several years he worked closely with Carty, Frank B. Jewett, Edwin H. Colpitts, and other members of the strong research and engineering team which A.T. & T. assembled in New York City. Gherardi was associated with numerous important telephone innovations, including the design and construction of long-distance underground cables, the development of transcontinental telephony, and the improvement of signaling methods on toll lines.

In 1918, when Carty went to France with the army, Gherardi rose to acting chief engineer of A.T. & T.; the following year he became chief engineer and in 1920 vice-president, positions he held until retirement in 1938. A full appraisal of Gherardi's career during these two decades awaits an administrative history of A.T. & T., but he was evidently an able administrator. A colleague who knew him well suggested that Gherardi possessed personal qualities helpful to an executive in a large and complex organization: a profound sense of order, an almost overpowering conscientiousness, decisiveness, an unerring ability to locate weak spots in proposals and men, and an intolerance of those who lacked clear thinking or a readiness to reach prompt decisions (Buckley, pp. 159, 172).

While Gherardi was chief engineer, major technological innovations within the Bell system (A.T. & T. and its affiliates) generally originated in the engineering department of the Western Electric Company; in 1925 this department was reorganized as the Bell Telephone Laboratories under the direction of Carty and Jewett. A.T. & T.'s engineering department, under Gherardi, then promoted these new ideas and instruments in the Bell system and assisted Bell companies with engineering and operating problems. Gherardi proved particularly adept at balancing the often conflicting claims of standardization and innovation within the Bell system's semiautonomous units. Probably Gherardi's most critical decision during these years was his recommendation in 1919 that Bell adopt dial-operated machine switching. A.T. & T. chose the panel type developed by Western Electric over the Strowger step-by-step system manufactured by Automatic Electric, although the latter method was made compatible with Bell equipment and was used in some situations. By Gherardi's retirement in 1938, 52 percent of the phones in the Bell system were dial.

During these years Gherardi also served on the boards of directors of several A.T. & T.-affiliated companies and on numerous engineering committees, published regular summaries of progress in telephone technology, and occasionally acted as a corporate spokesman. An ardent supporter of standardization, he served as president of the American Standards Association in 1931–32. President of the American Institute of Electrical Engineers in 1927–28 and recipient of the Edison Medal in 1932, he was elected to the National Academy of Sciences in 1933.

Gherardi married Mary Hornblower Butler, daughter of a Paterson, N. J., manufacturer, on June 15, 1898. The couple were childless but were close to the family of his brother Walter. An active Episcopalian and member of numerous clubs, Gherardi served as a trustee of both Cornell and the Polytechnic Institute of Brooklyn. He was a Republican with economic and political views characteristic of corporate executives of his time (e.g., *New York Times,* Jan. 12, 1933, p. 10). He died of a heart attack while vacationing in French River, Ontario, Canada, and was buried in Short Hills, N. J., his longtime residence. Though he fell short of the highest achievements in science, technology, and industrial organization individually, the sum of Gherardi's accomplishments rightfully brought him the highest honors of the engineering profession.

[Oliver E. Buckley in Nat. Acad. Sci., *Biog. Memoirs,* vol. XXX (1957), provides a good sketch by a man who knew Gherardi well. It includes a photograph and a complete list of Gherardi's five patents and his more than thirty publications. Also useful is Gano Dunn's sketch in *Electrical Engineering,* Feb. 1933. Other sources: obituary in *N. Y. Times,* Aug. 16, 1941; *Who's Who in America,* 1938–39; *Am. Men of Sci.* (6th ed., 1938); transcript of Gherardi's record, Polytechnic Inst. of Brooklyn; unpublished biographical data and reprints provided by Information Dept., Am. Telephone & Telegraph Co.]

KENDALL BIRR

GIBSON, CHARLES DANA (Sept. 14, 1867–Dec. 23, 1944), cartoonist and illustrator, was born in Roxbury, Mass., the second of three sons and second of the six children of Charles De Wolf Gibson and Josephine Elizabeth (Lovett) Gibson. His father, who was a salesman for the National Car Spring Company, a family firm, was descended from John Gibson who had settled in Cambridge, Mass., by 1638. His maternal grandfather was assistant secretary of state of Massachusetts for forty years, and his maternal great-grandfather, William Lovett of Boston, was a noted painter of miniatures.

Gibson grew up in modest circumstances. Early in his life the family left Boston and, after sojourns in Chicago and St. Louis, settled in Flushing, Long Island, when he was eight. His boyhood skill in cutting silhouettes prompted his family to apprentice him at thirteen to the sculptor Augustus Saint-Gaudens [*q.v.*]. Work in three dimensions did not prove congenial, however, and Gibson soon returned home to attend the Flushing high school. Upon graduating in 1884, with the encouragement of the illustrator Dan Beard [Supp. 3] he enrolled in the Art Students' League of New York, where he spent two years. His instructors at this time included Kenyon Cox, William Merritt Chase, and Thomas Eakins [*qq.v.*]. More than six feet tall and powerfully built, Gibson also gave time to sports, such as rowing, swimming, and weight lifting.

In 1886 Gibson sold his first drawing to John Ames Mitchell [*q.v.*], founder and publisher of the humor magazine *Life,* then barely three years old. In the next two years he contributed numerous drawings to *Life* and to two other comic magazines, *Puck* and *Tid-Bits.* Having achieved a moderate success, Gibson visited Europe in the summer of 1888. In London he called on George Du Maurier, the great cartoonist of the British periodical *Punch,* from whom his early fine-line technique clearly stemmed, and then went to Paris for a summer course at the Atelier Julian.

Upon his return to New York, Gibson began illustrating stories for *Harper's, Scribner's,* and the *Century.* With consistent emphasis on the upper middle classes, he portrayed noble men and elegant women of pure motives, unsullied by crass thoughts or petty cares. His sketches were in close accord with the aristocratic idealism ex-

pressed in the writings of his friend Richard Harding Davis [*q.v.*]; some of the best work of both resulted from their later collaboration as novelist and illustrator in *The Princess Aline* (1895) and *Soldiers of Fortune* (1897). Replete with authentic details of the period, Gibson's drawings reflect the manners, dress, and attitude toward life of the young generation that idolized Davis, Rudyard Kipling, and Robert Louis Stevenson.

For a mass readership Gibson became the official illustrator of life in smart society. With innate humor and a gently satirical understanding of human frailty, he depicted the foibles of the newly rich, graphically contrasting the natural American with ambitious society types struggling for position, money, or luxury. Several type characters, such as the distinguished Bishop and the celebrated Gibson Girl, were particularly his own.

With the Gibson Girl, who came to full development around 1890, he evoked a distinctive type of young woman and saw her acclaimed the American ideal. She had been foreshadowed in earlier work, but now a technique of fine lines, fastidious cross-hatching, and subtle shading brought to life a tall, radiant being with a clear, fearless gaze, delicately molded lips, and a slightly uptilted nose. Pictured on plates, glorified in song, portrayed on the stage, she became the symbol of the "Gay Nineties" and "Art Nouveau." The Gibson Girl played tennis and golf, rode horseback, swam, and bicycled, thus helping bring the athletic girl into vogue. Women looked to her to learn how to dress, stand, sit, walk, shake hands, eat, and enter vehicles. She remained their model until World War I.

In 1893 thirty-nine of Gibson's drawings were exhibited at the Chicago World's Fair. The next year Robert H. Russell published *Drawings, by Charles Dana Gibson,* a large folio of eighty-four pen-and-inks, which was followed during the next decade by a dozen similar volumes. In 1893 Gibson set up a studio in Paris for a year and explored the cafés and night life with James B. Eustis [*q.v.*], the American ambassador, or with Richard Harding Davis, who was making a grand tour abroad. Gibson's stay in Paris significantly affected his later work. He gradually moved away from the use of fine-line drawing in favor of fewer and bolder strokes. This new technique was evident in his creation of the downtrodden Mr. Pipp, taken abroad by his wife and daughters, whose portrayal captured the age of innocence of American travel in Europe.

In 1902 *Collier's* contracted with Gibson for a hundred double-page cartoons to be delivered over a period of four years. For these he was to be paid $100,000, the largest sum ever offered an illustrator for such a commission and an indication of the changes that advertising revenue and increasing circulation were making in magazine production. (Gibson actually fulfilled only half of the contract.) Deciding in 1905 to abandon pen and ink for oils, he gave up an estimated annual income of $65,000 and went abroad, where for three years he studied painting in Spain, France, and Italy. The financial panic of 1907, when a large part of his savings was wiped out with the failure of the Knickerbocker Trust Company, ended this experiment, and he returned to New York to work for *Life, Collier's,* and *Cosmopolitan.* After the sinking of the *Lusitania* in World War I, Gibson used his pen against Germany. He transformed the Gibson Girl into Miss Columbia, the most militant woman in the country, and bitterly caricatured the Kaiser. When the United States entered the war, Gibson at the request of George Creel, chairman of the Committee of Public Information, formed and directed a Division of Pictorial Publicity which produced posters and drawings to spur the war effort.

His energies during the 1920's were devoted to *Life.* Upon the death of John Ames Mitchell in 1918, Gibson headed a syndicate that bought the magazine, and in 1920 he became the owner and editor-in-chief. Lacking free time, and having little sympathy for the "flapper," who had become the new popular feminine model, Gibson did not do much drawing during the 1920's. He was too gentle and indecisive to make a successful editor, and *Life,* like the other humorous periodicals of its day, gradually deteriorated. Discouraged by the depression, by editorial difficulties, and by the lack of enthusiasm he brought to his drawing, Gibson in 1932 sold his entire interest in *Life.*

Thereafter he revived his old dream of painting and devoted most of his time to portraits and landscapes, working at his New York studio and on the Maine island (near Islesboro) where he spent his summers. He had been elected to the National Institute of Arts and Letters in 1898, and in 1921 he was elevated to its inner circle, the American Academy of Arts and Letters. The National Academy of Design made him a director in 1932 and during the 1934–35 season gave him a one-man show that was well received by the critics, though by this time his painting was too traditional to be considered very significant.

On Nov. 7, 1895, Gibson had married Irene Langhorne of Richmond, Va., a sister of Lady Astor and a frequent model for the Gibson Girl. Their two children were Irene and Langhorne.

Gibson continued to paint during his last years. He died of myocarditis at his home in New York City at the age of seventy-seven and was buried in Mount Auburn Cemetery, Cambridge, Mass.

[Fairfax Downey, *Portrait of an Era as Drawn by C. D. Gibson* (1936); J. M. Bulloch in the *Studio,* June 1896; Charles Belmont Davis in the *Critic,* Jan. 1899; *Collier's Weekly,* Nov. 29, 1902, pp. 8–9; Robert Grant, *ibid.,* Jan. 31, 1903; Robert M. Chambers, *ibid.,* Oct. 21, 1905; M. H. Spielmann in *Mag. of Art,* Nov. 1903; *Current Literature,* Dec. 1905, pp. 617–20; Perriton Maxwell in *Arts & Decoration,* May 1922; Mark Sullivan, *Our Times,* vol. I (1926); S. J. Woolf, "The Gibson Girl Is Still with Us," *N. Y. Times Mag.,* Sept. 20, 1942; Robert Koch, "Gibson Girl Revisited," *Art in America,* vol. LIII, no. 1 (1965). On his genealogy, see Mehitabel C. C. Wilson, *John Gibson of Cambridge, Mass., and His Descendants* (1900).]

WILLIAM F. LICHLITER

GIFFORD, SANFORD ROBINSON (Jan. 8, 1892–Feb. 25, 1944), ophthalmologist and microbiologist, was born in Omaha, Nebr., the eldest of four children of Harold Gifford, an ophthalmic surgeon, and Mary Louise (Millard) Gifford. His father, a graduate of Cornell University and the University of Michigan Medical School, was a native of Milwaukee, Wis.; his mother came of a pioneer Omaha family. Young Gifford was named after his great-uncle Sanford Robinson Gifford, 1823–1880 [*q.v.*], a well-known American painter of the Hudson River School. He attended the Omaha High School and Cornell University, where he majored in languages and literature and received the B.A. degree in 1913. While serving as an instructor in English at the University of Nebraska he decided on a medical career. After spending some months in mastering the prerequisite sciences, which he had avoided as an undergraduate, he entered the University of Nebraska College of Medicine in the fall of 1914 and graduated in 1918 with high honors. Shortly thereafter he went overseas with the university's medical unit and served as officer in charge of the army's bacteriology laboratory in Base Hospital 49 in Allery, France, and later in the army of occupation in Germany. He returned to Omaha upon his release from the service in 1919, completed a two-year internship in the Nebraska Lutheran Hospital, and then joined his father in his ophthalmological practice.

From the outset of his career Gifford showed a versatility of skills: in eye surgery, in acute clinical perception, in meticulous laboratory investigations, and in effective teaching. In 1919 he became an instructor in the University of Nebraska College of Medicine, and in 1924 he earned an M.A. degree and was promoted to assistant professor. Becoming interested in the problem of eye diseases caused by certain bacteria and fungi, Gifford studied during the year 1923–24 in the eye clinics and laboratories of Tübingen, Vienna, and the Royal London Ophthalmic Hospital (Moorfields) and spent much time with the two best-known ophthalmic bacteriologists of that day, Victor Morax in Paris and Theodor Axenfeld in Freiburg. By the end of 1929 he had published fifty-three scientific papers, eighteen of which dealt with bacteriological subjects. The most important of these involved the ocular diseases produced by the leptothrix, the fusiform bacillus, the fungus sporothrix, and viruses. Another research interest was the biochemistry of the eye, particularly the crystalline lens, on which he wrote a number of papers.

In 1929 Gifford was persuaded by his friend Irving S. Cutter, former dean of the University of Nebraska College of Medicine and now dean of the Northwestern University Medical School in Chicago, to come to that institution as professor and head of the reorganized department of ophthalmology. With characteristic skill and energy, Gifford expanded the ophthalmic clinic at Northwestern to include a postgraduate course and established new residency programs in ophthalmology at Passavant Memorial Hospital (1930), where he served as director of ophthalmology, and later (1941) at the Wesley Memorial Hospital, both affiliated with the Northwestern Medical School. After 1932 he was also on the staff of the Cook County Hospital. One pioneering feature of his teaching was the use of a large collection of Kodachrome slides, which he had prepared himself, of representative ocular diseases. Although Gifford had a large private practice and a heavy teaching schedule, he found his research of even greater interest and produced a steady flow of important papers, sometimes with collaborators, on biochemical and bacteriological aspects of eye disease, clinical and surgical procedures, and ophthalmic problems associated with a general physical condition such as diabetes or vascular disease. His bibliography contains some 150 titles, including *A Handbook of Ocular Therapeutics* (1932) and *A Textbook of Ophthalmology* (1938). He served as an associate editor of the *Archives of Ophthalmology* from 1928 onward and as a corresponding editor of the (German) *Klinische Monatsblätter für Augenheilkunde* from 1928 to 1940.

Gifford married Mary Alice Carter of Omaha on July 11, 1917. They had two children, Sanford Robinson and Carter. Gifford kept fit with highly competitive games of squash and tennis, was a much-sought-after companion, appreciated for his

eloquence and enthusiasm, and never abandoned his interest in music and English literature. When he appeared on a scientific program, his paper, in which scientific accuracy was enhanced by good writing and gentle wit, always attracted a large audience.

In February 1944, while treating a medical student who had an acute conjunctivitis, he was infected with the rare virus (pigeon) that was responsible; he died four days later of virus pneumonia in the Passavant Memorial Hospital in Chicago at the early age of fifty-two. He had recently bought a vacation home in Santa Barbara, Calif., and it was in the Santa Barbara Cemetery that his ashes were buried. In 1944 the ophthalmology section of the American Medical Association posthumously bestowed on him its highest honor, the Howe gold medal. A portrait by Edgar Miller, showing Gifford's characteristic quizzical and alert expression, hangs in a corridor of Passavant Hospital.

[Memorial issue of Northwestern Univ. Medic. School, *Quart. Bull.*, Fall 1944; obituaries in Am. Ophthalmological Soc., *Transactions*, 1944, *Archives of Ophthalmology*, Apr. 1944, *Am. Jour. of Ophthalmology*, May 1944, *Jour. Am. Medic. Assoc.*, Mar. 4, 1944, *Chicago Tribune* and *N. Y. Times*, Feb. 26, 1944; *Nat. Cyc. Am. Biog.*, XXII, 227 (on Gifford's father), and XXXII, 457; *Who Was Who in America*, vol. II (1950); information from members of the family, personal recollection, and notes and letters. Besides the painting mentioned above, a portrait bronze of Gifford by the sculptor Malvina Hoffman is in the possession of the family.]

DERRICK T. VAIL

GLASGOW, ELLEN ANDERSON GHOLSON (Apr. 22, 1873–Nov. 21, 1945), novelist, was born in Richmond, Va., the ninth of ten children and fifth of six daughters. Her father, Francis Thomas Glasgow, was a dour Presbyterian whose Scotch-Irish ancestors had settled in the Shenandoah Valley of Virginia in 1766; a graduate of Washington College (later Washington and Lee University), he was one of the managing directors of the Tredegar Iron Works in Richmond, which during the Civil War had supplied munitions and ordnance to the Confederate Army. Her mother, Anne Jane (Gholson) Glasgow, was an Episcopalian of long-established Tidewater Virginia stock. Thus Ellen Glasgow inherited both the Calvinistic passion for endurance and fortitude and the social graces and sensibility of an aristocratic tradition—conflicting attitudes reflected in much of her fiction.

Like her mother, whom she almost worshiped, Ellen was always in uncertain health and suffered frequent headaches, probably emotional in origin; her childhood nurse, commenting on her sensitive nerves, once remarked that she was "born without a skin." She attended private schools for a few months each year, but, because she disliked school and attendance often made her ill, she received little formal education. She acquired a thorough knowledge of English literature and history from her father's excellent library, and later, guided by George Walter McCormack, the husband of her sister Cary, she also read widely in political science, economics, sociology, and evolutionary theory. She succeeded in passing a comprehensive examination in political economy given her privately by a professor friend at the University of Virginia; as a woman she could not be admitted to that institution.

In 1889, at the age of sixteen, she had begun to develop deafness, a condition that persisted and worsened, although she did not lose her hearing completely until she was past thirty-five. She was no recluse, however; she made her debut at a St. Cecilia's Ball in Charleston, S. C., and was a popular "belle" at the Virginia Military Institute, the University of Virginia, and the summer resorts. She also spent a winter working at the city mission in Richmond, where she learned something of the problems of the poor. During her teens the family moved from her birthplace on East Cary Street to the gray-walled, gracious house at One West Main Street where she spent most of her life and did most of her writing.

At the age of seven she had resolved to become a writer, and had begun by making verses. At seventeen she had completed four hundred pages of a novel, which she later destroyed; at eighteen she began a new novel, but in her extreme grief at her mother's death, from typhoid fever in 1893, destroyed much of the manuscript. The loss of her mother, who had long suffered from melancholia, produced great emotional stress, particularly since Miss Glasgow strongly disliked her father and blamed him for her mother's depression. She returned to and completed the novel in 1895. Published anonymously in 1897 as *The Descendant,* and attributed by some reviewers to Harold Frederic [*q.v.*], it is the tragic story of the bastard son of a Virginia aristocrat father and a poor-white mother; an outcast in his own society, he goes to New York City and becomes a successful journalist and worker in reform movements. The book reflected Miss Glasgow's Fabian socialism and was for its time a radical work. In 1896, at the invitation of an older brother living in London, she made the first of what were to be many trips to Europe. Her second novel, *Phases of an Inferior Planet,* was published under her name in 1898. Also laid in New York City, it is the story of a rebellious scientist-philosopher.

Most of the year 1899 Miss Glasgow spent traveling in Europe and the Mediterranean countries. After her return that winter, while visiting in New York, she met and fell in love with a man whom she calls in her autobiography "Gerald B—" and whom she describes as older, a financier, and the married father of two sons; other evidence, however, suggests that he was a physician. When he died in 1905, she suffered severe emotional shock, but during the time that they were lovers she did her first important writing and found her true subject, the social history of Virginia, to be set forth in a series of novels. Her design was, she said later, to portray "the retreat of an agrarian culture before the conquests of an industrial revolution, and the slow and steady rise of the lower middle class." Her longtime friend James Branch Cabell later declared that her project of a social history was an after-the-fact idea that he gave her in 1928, but—whether consciously or not—she had embarked by the turn of the century on a fictional exploration of most of the historical movements, regions, and classes in Virginia in the period 1850 to 1939. The first of these novels was *The Voice of the People* (1900), which recounts the rise, between 1870 and 1898, of Nicholas Burr, a poor white, to the governorship of Virginia. It demonstrates in an early form her sympathy with the emerging middle class, her sense that the aristocratic tradition had outlived its usefulness and demanded meaningless sacrifices, and the ironic view through which she was able to see the strengths and weaknesses of both classes. She later said that the South needed "blood and irony," and *The Voice of the People* was the first of her books intended to supply both.

The second, *The Battle-Ground* (1902), was her "Civil War novel" and covered Virginia life between 1850 and 1865. *The Deliverance* (1904) was her first really good work. Taking place during the Reconstruction, it deals with the aristocratic Blakes, now dispossessed by their former overseer, yet struggling to preserve the old and find new ways of life. In 1902 she published her only volume of poetry, a mediocre small book, *The Freeman and Other Poems.*

Following "Gerald B—'s" death she wrote a bad novel based on her love affair and set in New York City, *The Wheel of Life* (1906), and another poor work, this time set in Virginia, *The Ancient Law* (1908). She continued to travel nearly every summer, was briefly engaged to a poet, helped start the woman suffrage movement in Virginia, and sorrowfully watched the long and painful illness of her sister Cary, who died in 1911. Cary's nurse, Anne Virginia Bennett, remained at One West Main Street as secretary, companion, and general manager for the remainder of Miss Glasgow's life.

Meanwhile her commitment to her craft and her "design" reasserted itself. *The Romance of a Plain Man* (1909) records the rise of Ben Starr from poverty to wealth and social acceptance in Richmond between 1875 and 1910. A companion study of the changing status of the common people, *The Miller of Old Church* (1911), laid in rural southside Virginia, deals with changes in the political and economic life of a "plain" farmer. *Virginia* (1913), an ironic portrait of an "ideal" Virginia lady of the 1880's, was the first of her novels to give promise of enduring. Its companion, *Life and Gabriella* (1916), deals with a "new woman," the action taking place partly in New York City, a locale that Miss Glasgow was never able to handle with distinction.

Ellen Glasgow spent the summer of 1914 in England, where she was well received by many literary figures, including Joseph Conrad and Thomas Hardy. The outbreak of the First World War depressed her deeply, and her emotional life was not made easier by a friendship, begun in 1915, with Henry W. Anderson, the "Harold S—" of her autobiography, a successful lawyer and Red Cross envoy to Rumania. They became engaged in 1917, but the engagement was broken in 1919, following several violent quarrels, after one of which she took an overdose of sleeping tablets. The relationship nevertheless continued throughout her life. During the height of this unhappy friendship, Miss Glasgow wrote two novels that were failures: *The Builders* (1919), a domestic melodrama with a substantial amount of polemical political commentary, and *One Man in His Time* (1922), a tragicomedy about a radical Virginia governor. In 1923 she published a collection of eight short stories, *The Shadowy Third, and Other Stories*. These and the five other stories she wrote, none of them truly distinguished, appear in the *Collected Stories of Ellen Glasgow* (edited by Richard K. Meeker, 1963).

In 1922 Miss Glasgow began *Barren Ground* (1925), generally considered one of her two best novels. A grim story of fortitude and persistence, demonstrating, she said, that "one may learn to live, one may even learn to live gallantly, without delight," it is the account of Dorinda Oakley's struggle with life and the soil. A rural novel, reminiscent of the works of Thomas Hardy, it recounts events that could happen, she declared, "wherever the spirit of fortitude has triumphed over the sense of futility." Her books had always found a responsive audience, and several of them had been best sellers, but *Barren Ground*

brought her critical acclaim and inaugurated her period of greatest accomplishment.

It was followed in 1926 by *The Romantic Comedians*, an almost perfectly constructed comedy of manners laid in Queenborough (Richmond) and centered around the marriage of an old man to a young wife. *They Stooped to Folly* (1929), another Queenborough comedy of manners, played amusing variations on the theme of the "ruined woman." In 1932 came *The Sheltered Life*, a tragicomedy of Queenborough, which ranks with *Barren Ground* as her finest work. A study of modern life viewed through the eyes of very young Jenny Blair and very old General Archbald, it deals with the changing mores of an aristocratic society under the impact of industrial and social change, and expresses her conviction that sheltering from the realities of life brings not safety but disaster. In "The Deep Past," the section in which General Archbald reviews his life, he realizes that he has always done what was expected of him but never what he wanted to do; this section is Miss Glasgow's finest piece of writing and a masterful treatment of time and memory.

Two other novels were published in her lifetime: *Vein of Iron* (1935), a grim picture of life in the Virginia mountains, which she called a "drama of mortal conflict with fate"; and *In This Our Life* (1941), a dark view of the decay of the quality of life in Queenborough, which shows, she said, "that character is an end in itself." *In This Our Life* was awarded the Pulitzer Prize, perhaps more as a recognition of its author's career than of its own merit. In the last years of her life honors were heaped upon Miss Glasgow. She received honorary degrees from the University of North Carolina (1930), the University of Richmond (1938), Duke University (1938), and the College of William and Mary (1939). In 1932 she was elected to the National Institute of Arts and Letters, and in 1938 to the American Academy of Arts and Letters, whose Howells Award she received in 1940.

She suffered a heart attack in 1939, and a second one in 1940, after which her life was very restricted. In 1943 she published a collection of essays prefatory to her novels, *A Certain Measure*, which defines her artistic ideals, states her concept of the novel, and makes a by-no-means-modest evaluation of her work. She died of a heart attack at her home in Richmond at the age of seventy-two and was buried in the Glasgow family section of the Hollywood Cemetery in Richmond.

During the last years of her life she worked on an autobiography to be published at the discretion of her literary executors after her death. It appeared in 1954 as *The Woman Within,* a remarkably frank picture of a morbidly sensitive woman and a committed artist. What will probably be the last of her publications, a short novel, *Beyond Defeat,* written as an epilogue to *In This Our Life,* was published in 1966.

To the world of her friends and social and literary acquaintances, Ellen Glasgow was a small, attractive, rather gay person, a little of the grande dame in her social relations. She was mistress over elaborate social gatherings at her home. In her fiction she celebrated a stoic fortitude toward the difficulties of life. But her autobiography reveals that she was actually a person of great sensitivity who underwent much physical and emotional suffering; one who from infancy experienced a "sense of doom"; and whose inner life contained little of either the gaiety or the fortitude with which she faced the world. Her revulsion from suffering is clear in her lifelong work with the Society for the Prevention of Cruelty to Animals.

The magnitude of the task Ellen Glasgow set herself as a social novelist is impressive, and the range of her knowledge of the varieties and qualities of life in Virginia was great. Yet her ultimate value as a writer of fiction rests on her witty and epigrammatic style and on the irony which is a pervasive quality in her best work; and that best work is, with the exception of *Barren Ground,* in the tradition of the novel of manners. Historically she is important as the first Southern voice raised in loving anger against the falseness and sentimentality of the accepted traditions of the region. Her great theme, whether handled comically or tragically, was the individual in conflict with society, and that theme served her well both in analyzing social structures and in mocking manners and pretensions. Although she fell short of the greatness to which she aspired, Ellen Glasgow was an artist of integrity, a social historian of impressive scope, and on several occasions a fine novelist.

[The best guide to information about Ellen Glasgow is William W. Kelly, *Ellen Glasgow: A Bibliog.* (1964). This lists her works, with information on their writing and publication, lists published portraits and materials about her life and works, and has a checklist of the holdings in the Ellen Glasgow Collection in the Alderman Lib. at the Univ. of Va., which is the largest and most important collection of her letters and MSS. No full-length biography exists, but *Letters of Ellen Glasgow,* ed. by Blair Rouse (1958), and her autobiography, *The Woman Within* (1954), are indispensable biographical sources. Long obituaries are in the *Richmond* (Va.) *Times-Dispatch,* Nov. 22, 1945, and the *N. Y. Times,* Nov. 22, 1945. Book-length studies of her work, with brief biographical information, are: Frederick P. W. McDowell, *Ellen Glasgow and the Ironic Art of Fiction* (1960);

Blair Rouse, *Ellen Glasgow* (1962); and Joan Foster Santas, *Ellen Glasgow's Am. Dream* (1965). Louis Auchincloss's Univ. of Minn. pamphlet, *Ellen Glasgow* (1964), although not always reliable on biographical data, is the finest single appreciation of her qualities as a novelist of manners. James Branch Cabell, *As I Remember It* (1955), questions her early conscious intention to write a social history. C. Hugh Holman, *Three Modes of Modern Southern Fiction: Ellen Glasgow, William Faulkner, Thomas Wolfe* (1966), examines her as an ironic novelist of manners. Maxwell Geismar, *Rebels and Ancestors* (1953), pp. 219–86, gives extended critical analysis of her novels.]

C. HUGH HOLMAN

GODDARD, ROBERT HUTCHINGS (Oct. 5, 1882–Aug. 10, 1945), rocket and space pioneer, was born in a Worcester, Mass., farmhouse to Nahum Danford Goddard and Fannie Louise (Hoyt) Goddard. Their first child and the only one to survive infancy, he was descended on both sides from seventeenth-century English immigrants. The family early moved to the Roxbury section of Boston, where his father was part owner of a small firm manufacturing machine knives, and where Robert grew up in comfortable circumstances. Physically frail, he fell behind in school and took to amusing himself with such imaginative projects as the synthesis of diamonds. Reading H. G. Wells's *The War of the Worlds* in 1898 touched off a lifelong interest in rocketry. On Oct. 19, 1899, he experienced an almost mystical vision of space flight, and forty years later he still remembered Oct. 19 as "Anniversary Day."

The Goddard family had returned to Worcester in 1898 for the sake of Mrs. Goddard, who had contracted tuberculosis. Robert graduated from Worcester's South High School in 1904, at the age of twenty-one. He completed a general science course at Worcester Polytechnic Institute in 1908 and the next year began doctoral studies in physics at Clark University in Worcester. His dissertation in 1911 was an early investigation of solid-state phenomena. Throughout his college years Goddard recorded a growing interest in space flight in his notebooks, where on Feb. 2, 1909, he envisaged a rocket employing liquid-hydrogen fuel and a liquid-oxygen oxidizer.

After an additional year at Clark, Goddard went to Princeton's Palmer Physical Laboratory on a research fellowship. There he devoted his evenings to the theory of rocket propulsion. Illness diagnosed as tuberculosis forced his return to Worcester in the spring of 1913, but he took advantage of his convalescence to convert his Princeton theories into patent applications. The resulting patents (No. 1,102,653 of July 7, 1914, and No. 1,103,503 of July 14, 1914) covered three broad claims basic to rocketry: (1) a combustion chamber and nozzle, (2) the feeding of successive portions of propellant, liquid or solid, into the combustion chamber, and (3) multiple rockets, each discarded in succession as its propellant became exhausted.

A part-time teaching position at Clark in 1914 provided time and facilities to back theoretical work with actual efficiency tests on ordinary powder rockets and on nozzle-equipped steel rockets. Costs soon exceeded Goddard's meager resources. In the fall of 1916 he solicited help from the Smithsonian Institution, which responded with a grant of $5,000. To support his application, Goddard had sent the Smithsonian a manuscript entitled "A Method of Reaching Extreme Altitudes," in which he proposed to develop a rocket to reach hitherto inaccessible regions of the upper atmosphere for meteorological and solar-physics measurements. This paper set forth the theory of rocket propulsion, showing that if the velocity of gas expulsion and the propellant-to-rocket ratio were increased significantly, a tremendous increase in altitude was possible, even escape from the earth's gravity. Although Goddard did not describe a working model, he reported his experiments with steel chambers and nozzles and outlined a breechblock cartridge mechanism for feeding the solid propellant.

Goddard's work under the Smithsonian grant was interrupted by the entry of the United States into World War I. As with so many university scientists, weapons development work preempted his time. Under a $20,000 Signal Corps allotment, he directed work on the military possibilities of rockets in the shops of the Mount Wilson Solar Observatory. This led just before the Armistice to a demonstration of a recoilless rocket light enough for infantry. Through Clarence N. Hickman, a Goddard associate, this was a direct ancestor of the bazooka of World War II.

Back at Clark, pressure from his department head and a sensational press report led Goddard to propose that the Smithsonian publish his 1916 manuscript. With minor revisions, including an added discussion of multistage rockets, *A Method of Reaching Extreme Altitudes* appeared in the *Smithsonian Miscellaneous Collections* for 1919. The sixty-nine-page monograph might have gone unnoticed had not the Smithsonian press release of Jan. 11, 1920, referred to Goddard's incidental suggestion that a sufficient amount of flash powder sent by rocket to the moon, if ignited on impact and observed by telescope, would prove escape from the earth's attraction. Newspapers throughout the country headlined the "moon rocket" theme, and Goddard became a brief sensation. The notoriety contributed to his distrust of publicity. At the same time, it impelled him to dispatch a clarifying confidential paper to the Smithsonian in which he foresaw automated spacecraft to photograph celestial bodies and manned landings on the planets. Oxygen/hydrogen and ion propulsion would provide the energy necessary to explore the solar system. Thus by 1920 Goddard had sketched out the potential of space flight. In Russia, Konstantin E. Tsiolkovskii (1857–1935) had published in 1903 an article on "The Investigation of Space by Reaction Devices," and in 1923 Hermann Oberth's *The Rocket into Interplanetary Space* would appear in Germany. Both men were Goddard's peers in vision, but Goddard alone had put his theories to experimental test.

Goddard became head of the department of physics at Clark in 1923. The next year, on June 21, he married Esther Christine Kisk, a spirited Worcester girl of Swedish descent who was working as a secretary in the president's office at Clark. There were no children, and Mrs. Goddard served as assistant and confidante in the years of experiment that lay ahead. Goddard was forty-two at his marriage, slight in stature and bald, with a close-cropped moustache. Among strangers he seemed quiet and reticent, but he was warm and witty with friends. Ingenious, persistent, and methodical in the laboratory, he sought relaxation in playing the piano and painting. For all his prosaic appearance, he was a dreamer with a strong sense of destiny.

In 1921 Goddard abandoned his solid-fuel cartridge mechanism and concentrated on demonstrating the feasibility of liquid-fuel rockets. With small grants from Clark and the Smithsonian, he developed a rocket motor to run on gasoline and liquid oxygen. Pumps caused some difficulty, and he turned to gas pressure to force fuel and oxidizer into the combustion chamber. On Mar. 16, 1926, he achieved the world's first flight of a liquid-fuel rocket near Auburn, Mass. The rocket, only 10 feet long and unsheathed, rose 41 feet and traveled laterally 184 feet during a flight of two and a half seconds. On July 17, 1929, a larger, more sophisticated model reached twice the 1926 altitude before crashing in flames 171 feet from the launching tower. By this time, considerable interest in rocketry had developed in both Germany and the Soviet Union, but the first German liquid-fuel rocket did not fly until 1931 and the first Soviet model not until sometime after 1932.

The noisy, fiery test of July 17 brought Goddard and his "moon rocket" to public attention once more. The commotion forced him to transfer tests to a secluded site at Fort Devens in Massachusetts. It also brought a visit from the noted aviator Charles A. Lindbergh, who, impressed by

Goddard's plans and competence, persuaded the philanthropist Daniel Guggenheim to provide an initial $50,000 for two years of work. Goddard now took leave from Clark and shifted his small staff to Roswell, N. Mex., where he set up his machine shop at a rented ranch property and erected his launching tower ten miles out in the mesquite. There he worked for a decade, except for 1932–34, when the depression and the death of Daniel forced the Guggenheims to retrench.

At Roswell, Goddard's first objective was reliable motor performance and flight stability. He proceeded systematically from static to flight tests, always careful to record experimental aims, equipment characteristics, results, and modifications for test in subsequent trials. He never neglected patent claims. Two 1932 patents reflect his first years at Roswell: No. 1,879,186, which covered curtain or film cooling, a method of protecting the thin walls of the combustion chamber with a spray of liquid fuel, and No. 1,879,187, which covered a stabilizing system consisting of gyroscopically controlled vanes located in the rocket exhaust. On Dec. 30, 1930, Goddard launched a fixed-vane rocket powered by a 5.75-inch-diameter motor which reached 2,000 feet. Automatic stabilization was the next step. Two flight tests with gyroscopically controlled vanes in the spring of 1932 were failures, but on Mar. 28, 1935, a rocket rose to 4,800 feet, traveled 13,000 feet along the ground, and attained a speed of 550 miles per hour. A similar rocket reached 7,500 feet on May 31.

From 1935 Goddard felt increasing pressure to achieve high-altitude flights. After disappointing tests with 10-inch motors, he turned to improved rockets powered by his 5.75-inch motor. On Mar. 26, 1937, a rocket featuring light tank construction reached between 8,000 and 9,000 feet. On July 28 a rocket with gimbal (movable tailpiece) steering did only slightly better than 2,000 feet. Goddard now concluded that pumps would have to replace pressurized-gas fuel systems. He developed high-speed, lightweight aluminum pumps driven by liquid-oxygen gas generators. These were incorporated in a new and larger rocket, almost 22 feet tall and 18 inches in diameter. A flight test in August 1940 brought an altitude of only 300 feet but demonstrated the pump principle.

While Goddard experimented in the desert at Roswell, the Germans moved beyond him. Drawing support from Wehrmacht interest in a weapon system not prohibited by the Versailles Treaty, German rocket engineers began work in 1931. Between 1939 and 1941 they launched some twenty rockets and attained altitudes of eight miles. The Germans had mounted a team effort; Goddard persisted as a lone engineer-experimenter supported by a handful of technicians. Goddard was reluctant to take others into his confidence, in part because he was convinced that his work was being copied abroad, but in larger part because he was a lone wolf by temperament. Lindbergh and the Guggenheims realized this and sought to draw him out. In response to suggestions from Lindbergh, he presented a paper, "Progress in the Development of Atmospheric Sounding Rockets," at the American Association for the Advancement of Science meetings in December 1935 and published a general report, *Liquid-Propellant Rocket Development,* in the *Smithsonian Miscellaneous Collections* in March 1936. Harry Guggenheim tried in vain to persuade Goddard to collaborate with the Guggenheim aeronautical research centers at New York University and the California Institute of Technology. Goddard was willing to subcontract the design of limited componentry, but he would not agree to conditions specifying collaboration and information exchange throughout the project.

In the spring of 1940 Guggenheim suggested that Goddard offer his services to the army and navy. Goddard tried to interest officials in the military applications of liquid-fuel rockets. No one wanted to develop them as long-range missiles, but in 1941 the navy asked him to produce a preliminary model of a liquid-fuel, variable-thrust, jet-assist takeoff unit for aircraft. In July 1942 the navy transferred Goddard and his staff to the Naval Engineering Experiment Station at Annapolis. There, an unsuccessful flight test led the navy to turn to the cheaper and more dependable solid-fuel units.

Goddard now sat on the sidelines. Military rocket development centered at the Jet Propulsion Laboratory at the California Institute of Technology. His own work was fragmentary, and Goddard, feeling in poor health, noticed that his voice was failing. In these circumstances, he turned to perfecting the record. He reviewed his notes and filed applications which added thirty-five patents to the forty-eight he already had. His wife, using additional papers he had prepared, applied successfully for 131 posthumous patents. In one "write-up," which he called "The Ultimate in Jet Propulsion," Goddard summarized his reflections on the whole range of space flight— ion engines, nuclear rockets, planetary landing techniques, weightlessness, and reentry.

In 1944 Goddard read press reports of the German vengeance weapons. The V-1 flying bomb, he concluded, was powered by an air-breathing resonance chamber of a type he had patented in 1934. The V-2, with thrust more than one hundred times that of his Roswell motors, vindicated his faith in liquid-fuel rockets. In March 1945, when he inspected a captured V-2, he found that except for size and the use of alcohol fuel rather than gasoline, the V-2 was virtually identical in components and layout to the rockets he had flown in New Mexico. Goddard believed the Germans had copied him. Actually, the Peenemünde rocketeers were astonished to learn after the war of the scope and detail of Goddard's work; the similarity reflected the phenomenon of multiple invention. Working independently, Goddard and the Germans had built their rockets the only way they could be built.

Goddard's health now declined rapidly. Surgery on June 19, 1945, revealed a malignant growth in his throat. On July 5 doctors performed a laryngectomy, and on Aug. 10 he died at the University of Maryland Hospital in Baltimore. He was buried at Hope Cemetery, not far from his Worcester home.

Goddard's 214 patents are the measure of his accomplishment. They so thoroughly posted the whole range of rocket technology that it was virtually impossible to construct a rocket without infringing on one or more of them. In 1960 the government settled an infringement claim filed by the Guggenheim Foundation and Mrs. Goddard for $1,000,000 and acquired rights to use the Goddard inventions in rockets, guided missiles, and space exploration.

Goddard played a transitional role in technological research and development. Unlike Tsiolkovskii and Oberth, he concentrated on the engineering, not merely the theory, of space flight. Soundly trained in physics, he remained nonetheless the Yankee tinkerer-inventor of a simpler age. The future lay with team efforts such as Theodore H. Von Kármán had organized at the Jet Propulsion Laboratory and the military services would soon set in motion. No one man could master the complex of technical specialties which rocket development demanded. Yet in a more fundamental sense Goddard failed to develop an operational rocket because he was ahead of his time. The United States in the 1930's was not ready to support rocket development, and not even so enterprising a promoter of big science as Ernest O. Lawrence, who built the first cyclotron, could have marshaled the necessary resources. In 1940 and 1941 American scientific and military leadership was thinking of weapons that would win the war. Events justified the priority they gave to nuclear arms. The *Time* notice of Goddard's death reflected the order of things. Appearing in the Aug. 20, 1945, issue (p. 77), which featured the atomic explosion over Nagasaki and the Smyth Report on atomic energy, it closed with Goddard's prediction that "a rocket . . . will some day successfully reach one of the planets."

[The voluminous Goddard papers at Clark Univ. in Worcester contain correspondence, notebooks, journals, scrapbooks, and memorabilia which document the inventor's life and work. A selection, edited by Esther C. Goddard and G. Edward Pendray, was published as *The Papers of Robert H. Goddard, 1898–1945* (3 vols., 1970). There is also a Goddard file at the Smithsonian Institution in Washington. Besides Goddard's two basic publications, mentioned in the text, his condensation of his experimental notes of 1929–41 was published posthumously as *Rocket Development: Liquid-Fuel Rocket Research, 1929–1941* (1948). His published *Papers*, above, include an autobiographical sketch. See also Goddard's note "That Moon-rocket Proposition," *Sci. American*, Feb. 26, 1921, and "A Letter from Dr. Goddard," *Am. Interplanetary Soc. Bull.*, June-July 1931. Other basic primary sources are Goddard's patents, a replica of his 1926 rocket and later models and components at the Smithsonian Nat. Air and Space Museum, Washington, D. C., and his launching tower, a replica of his workshop, motors, controls, experimental apparatus, drawings, and notes at the Goddard Rocket and Space Museum, Roswell, N. Mex. The best biography of Goddard is Milton Lehman, *This High Man* (1963), which is based on his papers and on extensive interviews. Wernher von Braun and Frederick I. Ordway III, *Hist. of Rocketry & Space Travel* (1966), is strong on Goddard's technical achievement. Bessie Z. Jones, *Lighthouse of the Skies: The Smithsonian Astrophysical Observatory, Background and Hist., 1846–1955* (1965), details Goddard's relationships with the Smithsonian Institution. Of several short biographical sketches, see Eugene M. Emme in *Airpower Historian*, Oct. 1960; and G. Edward Pendray in *Astronautics*, July 1937, in *Science*, Nov. 23, 1945, and in *The New Treasury of Science*, ed. by Harlow Shapley et al. (1965). See also Pendray's chapter, "Pioneer Rocket Development in the U. S.," in Eugene M. Emme, ed., *The Hist. of Rocket Technology: Essays on Research, Development, and Utility* (1964). For rocket work in Germany, see Walter R. Dornberger, "The German V-2," in *ibid.*; Wernher von Braun, "German Rocketry," and Hermann Oberth's autobiography in Arthur C. Clarke, ed., *The Coming of the Space Age* (1967); and Willy Ley, *Rockets, Missiles, and Men in Space* (1968). For work in the Soviet Union, see Tsiolkovskii's autobiography in Clarke; and A. A. Blagonravov et al., eds., *Soviet Rocketry: Some Contributions to Its Hist.* (1966). For rocket developments at the Calif. Inst. of Technology, see Frank Malina, "Origins and First Decade of the Jet Propulsion Laboratory," in Emme, above.]

OSCAR E. ANDERSON, JR.

GOETSCHIUS, PERCY (Aug. 30, 1853–Oct. 29, 1943), music theorist, was born in Paterson, N. J., the only son of John Henry Goetschius, a civil engineer, and Mary Ann (Berry) Goetschius. Of Swiss ancestry, he was descended from John Henry Goetschius [*q.v.*], a prominent Dutch Reformed clergyman in eighteenth-century America. Percy attended the local schools until he was twelve; then, because of poor health, he left to seek the benefits of outdoor life as a surveyor's assistant, and within a few years joined his father's engineering business. As a boy he had taught himself to play the piano and the flute. His interests were encouraged by one of his father's clients, the violinist Ureli C. Hill [*q.v.*], who gave him a copy of Bach's *Well-Tempered Clavichord* and arranged for him to attend public rehearsals of the Philharmonic Society of New York. These experiences made him determine on music as a career, and in his teens he served as organist and choir director at a local church.

In 1873, despite his father's strong opposition, Goetschius went to Germany to enter the Stuttgart Royal Conservatory, where he studied piano with Sigmund Lebert and Dionys Pruckner and composition and theory with Immanuel Faisst, who exercised a major influence on his development. During his student years Goetschius taught the English-language harmony classes, and after graduating in 1876 he became a member of the Stuttgart faculty, teaching harmony, composition, and music history. He also wrote for two Stuttgart newspapers, reviewing concerts for the *Schwäbischer Merkur* and operas for the *Neues Tageblatt,* and was a correspondent for German musical periodicals. In 1885 the King of Württemberg conferred on him the title of Royal Professor, an honor Goetschius always valued highly.

In 1890, after seventeen years in Germany, he returned to the United States to take the chair of musical theory, history, and advanced pianoforte at Syracuse University. He resigned two years later to join the faculty of the New England Conservatory of Music in Boston, as professor of harmony, counterpoint, composition, and music history. In spite of his great popularity as a teacher, his relations with the director of the Conservatory, Carl Faelten, were not happy, and in 1896 Goetschius resigned and set up his own private studio in Boston. In 1897 he added to his duties the post of organist and choir director of the First Parish Church in Brookline, Mass.

In 1905 Frank Damrosch [Supp. 2] selected Goetschius as head of the department of theory and composition of the newly formed Institute of Musical Art in New York City (later amalgamated with the Juilliard School of Music), where he remained until his retirement in 1925. His presence attracted hundreds of the country's most gifted musicians, and he thus exerted a wide influence upon musical composition and music education in the United States. Among the distinguished musicians who considered "Papa" Goetschius, as he was affectionately called, their musical father were the composers Daniel Gregory Mason, Wallingford Riegger, Theodore Chanler, Arthur Shepherd, Bernard Rogers, Samuel Gardner, Samuel Barlow, Ulric Cole, Henry Cowell, and Howard Hanson, and the theorists George Wedge, Howard Murphy, Donald Tweedy, and Edwin Stringham.

As a teacher Goetschius was a strict disciplinarian, and his "bespectacled visage," "intellectual brow," and "closely cropped beard" (Shepherd, p. 310) gave an initial impression of austerity. He possessed, however, a delightful sense of humor, and his gracefully phrased lectures and agile piano demonstrations of musical structure and harmony made him a skilled pedagogue. He took a deep and sympathetic interest in the aesthetic problems of his student composers. His musical gods were Bach, Mendelssohn, and Brahms. Although his musical knowledge was encyclopedic, he had little interest in "strict" counterpoint or the music of the seventeenth century. Nor did he approve of the direction taken by such composers as Ravel, Debussy, and Richard Strauss; and he described Wagner's harmonic technique as one of "wandering harmonies." Goetschius considered the major scale a "natural phenomenon" and warned his pupils against perverting it by extravagant or eccentric chords and tonal progressions.

Besides his work in the classroom, Goetschius wrote more than fifteen textbooks. The first, *The Material Used in Musical Composition,* was published in Stuttgart in 1882 for the English-speaking students of the Conservatory. Later reprinted in the United States, it has gone through at least twenty-six editions and has probably had greater influence on the teaching of music theory in the United States than any other single text. Only slightly less influential was his *The Theory and Practice of Tone-Relations* (1892), a somewhat simpler and more readable exposition of the Goetschius theories of harmonic and melodic relationship. Among his other books are the very popular *The Homophonic Forms of Musical Composition* (1898), *Lessons in Music Form* (1904), and *The Larger Forms of Musical Composition* (1915). Although Goetschius did some composing, particularly in his early years in Stuttgart, few of his works were published.

Goetschius married a former pupil, Marie C. C. Stéphany, of Metz, Germany, in 1889. They had a daughter and a son, Percy Berry, who became a physician. After Goetschius retired from the Institute of Musical Art in 1925, he settled in Manchester, N. H., where his son was in practice, and undertook the most important editorial work of his career, the mammoth Analytic Symphony Series. Published by the Oliver Ditson Company in forty-three volumes during the years 1925–31, the series comprises detailed analyses of symphonies, from Haydn to d'Indy and Sibelius, arranged for piano, two hands. (Bruckner and Mahler were omitted, as lacking in "structural consistency.") Living on to the age of ninety, Goetschius died of a cerebral hemorrhage at his home in Manchester. His ashes were placed in Harmony Grove Cemetery, Salem, N. H.

[Mother Catherine Agnes Carroll, R.S.C.J., "Percy Goetschius, Theorist and Teacher" (Ph.D. dissertation, Eastman School of Music, Univ. of Rochester, 1957); Arthur Shepherd, "'Papa' Goetschius in Retrospect," *Musical Quart.*, July 1944; *Nat. Cyc. Am. Biog.*, XIV, 258–59; J. T. H. Mize, ed., *Who Is Who in Music* (5th ed., 1951), p. 444; *Who Was Who in America*, vol. IV (1968); death record, N. H. Dept. of Health and Welfare.]

HOWARD HANSON

GOLDMARK, HENRY (June 15, 1857–Jan. 15, 1941), civil engineer, was born in New York City, the oldest of ten children. He was a brother of Josephine and Pauline Goldmark, leading social reformers, and a brother-in-law of Felix Adler [Supp. 1] and Louis D. Brandeis [Supp. 3]. His father, Joseph Goldmark, was an older half brother of the Austrian composer Carl Goldmark. Born in Vienna, Joseph Goldmark took a leading part in the revolution of 1848, served for a time as a liberal member of the Austro-Hungarian Reichstag, and then, in the wake of political repression, fled in 1851 to New York City. There he married Regina Wehle, a well-educated woman whose family had emigrated in 1849 from Prague to Madison, Ind., and later moved to New York. Although at first he practiced his profession of medicine, Joseph Goldmark soon perfected a method for producing fulminate of mercury, which he proceeded to manufacture, along with other explosives, in a factory in Brooklyn.

The family lived in a large home in a suburban part of Brooklyn, and Henry Goldmark received his early education at the local Collegiate and Polytechnic Institute. In 1874 he entered Harvard, where, in addition to taking courses in mathematics and sciences, he acquired a lifelong interest in literature. After graduating in 1878, he spent two years studying civil engineering at the Royal Polytechnic School in Hanover, Germany, and then returned to begin his professional career. His early work was chiefly in the construction of railroad bridges. He had field experience with the Erie Railroad, with the Texas and St. Louis Railroad (the Cotton Belt Route), as supervisor of a locating party in Texas, and with the West Shore Railroad of New York before turning, in 1884, to the study of metallurgy. Visiting a variety of metallurgical and structural plants, he developed a thorough knowledge of metals which he applied, over the next few years, in advising a number of railroads on the safety of their bridges and on how to reinforce them so as to accommodate increasingly heavy train loads.

Because of his familiarity with structural problems, Goldmark was hired in 1891 to assist in the design of several of the largest buildings at the World's Columbian Exposition in Chicago, including the famous Machinery Hall. His next important commissions were to design a steel dam for the Pioneer Electric Power Company of Ogden, Utah (1896), and, with George S. Morison [*q.v.*], the Connecticut Avenue viaduct, a concrete arch over Rock Creek Park in Washington, D. C. (1897). From 1897 to 1899 he was design engineer with the United States Board of Engineers on Deep Waterways, which was then completing a study on the feasibility of a ship canal from the Great Lakes to tidewater. He had been interested for some time in deepwater technology, having in 1891 written the report of a committee to investigate the failure of the South Ford Dam (American Society of Civil Engineers, *Transactions*, vol. XXIV, 1891). In 1899, while resident engineer for a railroad and highway bridge over the Missouri River at Atchison, Kans., he delivered a series of lectures, later printed by Cornell University, on the history of locks and lock gates for ship canals. His interest in waterways was at this time, however, clearly secondary to his structural work, and from 1902 to 1906 he designed and supervised the construction of several locomotive and car shops for the Canadian Pacific Railroad.

Goldmark's varied interests, together with his knowledge of deep-water technology, led in 1906 to his appointment as one of the design engineers of the Isthmian Canal Commission. He spent two years in Washington drawing up preliminary plans for the equipment of the Panama Canal locks, and then six years at Culebra in the Canal Zone supervising their installation. Goldmark's principal contribution to the historic project, of which Gen. George W. Goethals [*q.v.*] was chief engineer, was the design and installation of the lock gates and of the chain fenders, huge chains spanning the channel which when raised would protect the gates from possible damage by a drifting ship. He also designed valves and electrical equipment for the canal's operation, and movable caisson emergency dams.

When work on the Panama Canal had been completed, Goldmark moved in 1914 to New York City, where he opened an office as a consulting engineer. From 1914 to 1917, with General Goethals, he helped design the New Orleans Inner Navigation Canal connecting the Mississippi River with Lake Pontchartrain; he was chiefly responsible for the lock gates, valves, electrical machinery, and a new type of movable steel stop-log emergency dam. Shortly afterward he was appointed to the board of consulting engineers on the New York Barge Canal. In 1919, for the Japanese government, he designed the gates, valves, and electrical equipment for a new harbor at Chemulpko, Korea. Later work included investigations for a proposed hydroelectric project in South Carolina and for a tidal-electric project in Passamaquoddy Bay, Maine. Goldmark also served as chairman of the committee to pass on the plans for the United States Navy dirigible *Shenandoah* and the army's semirigid airship *RS-1*, and in 1927 he designed loading equipment for the Seatrain ships to carry railroad cars between Havana, Cuba, and the United States.

Goldmark retired in 1928 and settled in Nyack, N. Y. Active in professional organizations, he represented the American Society of Civil Engineers from 1923 to 1926 on the National Research Council. In 1898 the Society awarded him the Thomas Fitch Rowland Prize for a paper on the hydroelectric plant at Ogden, Utah. Goldmark was twice married: on Sept. 25, 1892, to Louise Condit Owens of Kansas City, Mo., who died in July 1897; and on June 8, 1899, in Detroit, Mich., to Mary Carter Tomkins of New York, the daughter of an Episcopal minister. He had two children by his second marriage, Elliott Regina and Henry. Goldmark died in Nyack at the age of eighty-three from injuries suffered when he was accidentally struck by a car. He was buried in Hartsdale, N. Y., the home of his sisters Josephine and Pauline.

[Memoir by Jacob Feld in Am. Soc. of Civil Engineers, *Transactions,* CVI (1941), 1588–93; autobiographical account in Harvard Class of 1878, *50th Anniversary Report* (1928); *Nat. Cyc. Am. Biog.,* XXXVIII, 297–98 (largely derived from the class report); *Who's Who in Engineering,* 1937; *N. Y. Times,* Jan. 16, 1941. For the family background, see Josephine Goldmark, *Pilgrims of '48* (1930).]
ALAN TRACHTENBERG

GOLDSTEIN, MAX AARON (Apr. 19, 1870–July 27, 1941), physician and educator of the deaf, was born in St. Louis, Mo., the oldest of four children of Jewish parents, William and Hulda (Loewenthal) Goldstein. His father, a native of Poland, had come to the United States in 1853 and settled in St. Louis, where he became a wholesale clothing merchant. The upper-middle-class family was devoted to the arts, particularly music. Max graduated from Central High School in St. Louis in 1888 and in 1892 received the M.D. degree from Missouri Medical College (later the Washington University School of Medicine). After a year's internship at the St. Louis City Hospital, he went to Europe for postgraduate study in otolaryngology in Berlin, Vienna, Strassburg, and London. He returned to St. Louis in

1895 and established a practice. From that year until 1912 he was also professor of otology in the Beaumont Medical College and its successor, the St. Louis University School of Medicine. In 1896 he founded and became editor of the *Laryngoscope,* a journal devoted to disorders of the ear, nose, and throat, which he continued to manage until his death.

During his study in Vienna, Goldstein had become interested in the problem of teaching deaf children to communicate. Educators of the deaf in the United States were still not agreed on the best method—sign language, manual spelling, oral means, or some combination of these. In his work at the St. Joseph School for the Deaf in St. Louis, particularly with children who had some residual hearing, Goldstein became convinced that the "acoustic method," the use of amplified sound, would facilitate learning to talk, and that the most effective approach lay in close collaboration between trained teachers, physicians, and scientists who understood the physical mechanisms involved in hearing and producing speech sounds. Securing the financial support of friends, in 1914 he opened his own school, the Central Institute for the Deaf, with four pupils and two women teachers in a tiny apartment above his medical office. Goldstein experimented with many means of auditory amplification and with the use of music for acoustic stimulation. As the institute grew, its goals broadened to include the training of teachers, outpatient clinics, and research in the hereditary, physiological, and psychological factors involved in defects of hearing and speech. The Central Institute, which in 1931 was affiliated with Washington University, by 1969 had a staff of nearly a hundred workers and had gained worldwide influence.

In 1917, in an effort to rally all those interested in the welfare of the deaf child to support the oral method, Goldstein established the Society of Progressive Oral Advocates; he was its president until 1939. Its special goals were to promote closer cooperation between teachers of the deaf and ear specialists and to standardize the methods used in state schools for the deaf. (Later renamed the National Forum on Deafness and Speech Pathology, this organization went out of existence in 1953.) In 1922 Goldstein founded *Oralism and Auralism,* a quarterly journal of deafness and speech disorders, which he edited until 1933. Goldstein had a contagious zest for demonstrating his methods before scientific and professional groups and young teachers in training, and an acerbic wit with which he rebuffed those who were skeptical of his lofty aims for the deaf. He constantly emphasized the need to marshal the resources of many sciences in the cause, and he tirelessly urged physicians, engineers, phoneticians, psychologists, and neurophysiologists to bring their distinctive knowledge to bear on the problem of deafness.

Goldstein served as president of the American Otological Society (1927–28), the American Laryngological, Rhinological, and Otological Society (1930–31), and, in 1937–38, the American Society for the Study of Disorders of Speech (later the American Speech and Hearing Association). He received an honorary LL.D. from Washington University in St. Louis in 1937. Throughout his life he took an active part in the city's civic affairs, particularly community enterprises in the arts. An accomplished pianist and an enthusiastic collector of prints and pre-Columbian art, he was president of the St. Louis Art League, 1917–19. He received the city's award for distinguished service in 1933.

Goldstein married Leonore Weiner on June 4, 1895; they had one daughter, Helen Ruth. In January 1941 Goldstein suffered a stroke, from which he recovered, but he died a few months later of coronary disease at his summer home in Frankfort, Mich. He was buried in Mount Sinai Cemetery, St. Louis.

[Goldstein was the author of two books, *Problems of the Deaf* (1933) and *The Acoustic Method for the Training of the Deaf and Hard-of-Hearing Child* (1939). The fullest biographical accounts are the obituaries in the *Laryngoscope,* July 1941, *Jour. of Speech Disorders,* Sept. 1943 (with a list of his publications), and *Volta Rev.,* Oct. 1941; and the sketch in the *Nat. Cyc. Am. Biog.,* XXXVII, 278–79. Other obituaries are in the *St. Louis Post-Dispatch* and *St. Louis Globe-Democrat,* July 28, 1941, *Annals of Otology, Rhinology and Laryngology,* Sept. 1941, and *Jour. Am. Medic. Assoc.,* Sept. 6, 1941. See also Max A. Goldstein, "The Soc. of Progressive Oral Advocates: Its Origin and Purpose," *Volta Rev.,* Sept. 1917; and Hugo F. Schunhoff, *The Teaching of Speech and by Speech in Public Residential Schools for the Deaf in the U. S., 1815–1955* (1957), pp. 46–49.]

S. RICHARD SILVERMAN

GOLDWATER, SIGISMUND SCHULZ (Feb. 7, 1873–Oct. 22, 1942), hospital and public health administrator, was born in New York City, the second son and fourth of the nine children of Henry and Mary (Tyroler) Goldwater. His father, of Jewish background, was a tobacconist and later a pharmacist. Sigismund attended New York public schools but left at the age of thirteen to go to work. At seventeen he became an editor of the *Cloak Journal,* a garment trades publication. While covering a strike for the paper, he became interested in the problems of labor and capital, and soon afterward resigned to study economics and sociology at the institute established by George Gunton [q.v.]. In 1894 he enrolled in the political science course at Columbia University and the following year went to Germany, where he studied social problems at the University of Leipzig. Returning to America with a deep commitment to social reform, he entered the University and Bellevue Hospital Medical College (the medical school of New York University), hoping to use medicine as a stepping-stone to a career in public health. He graduated in 1901 with the M.D. degree, interned at Mount Sinai Hospital in New York, and then, despite a brilliant record as a clinician, accepted appointment as assistant superintendent of Mount Sinai. Advancing to superintendent in 1903, he was one of the first medically trained hospital administrators in the United States.

Despite a growing trend toward specialization, Goldwater adhered to the concept of a general hospital, believing that institutions in which all branches of medicine were fully integrated provided the best care. In 1906 he established a social service department at Mount Sinai—the third such department in the country—and he actively aided in the founding of a dentistry department and in the reorganization of the hospital's medical education services. Convinced that the fundamental task of medicine was to preserve health rather than cure the sick, he encouraged the development of an extensive outpatient service. Goldwater also favored the pavilion-type over the single-unit hospital; he was convinced that its flexible structure would enable it to adapt more easily to the changing needs of the community.

In 1914 Goldwater was called by the reform mayor John Purroy Mitchel [q.v.] to the post of commissioner of health of New York City. In this position he began implementing a broad medical program which sought to establish minimum health and sanitary standards for everyone. As preventive health measures, he urged periodic physical examinations for the entire population, and he established a bureau of health education, the first of its kind to be affiliated with a public health agency. He also obtained a city ordinance that required patent medicine manufacturers either to list every ingredient on the label or to register their formulas with the department.

Goldwater resigned his city post in the fall of 1915 and returned to Mount Sinai Hospital, where he became director in 1917. As his reputation grew, he was frequently called upon as a consultant in hospital planning and construction. Altogether he advised nearly two hundred hospitals, including thirty-eight in New York and eighteen in Philadelphia. In 1924 he was appointed medical counselor of the federal Veterans' Bureau, and in 1927 he helped plan the reorganization of the British voluntary hospital system.

He also carried out major reforms at Charity Hospital in New Orleans, an institution that had long been plagued by political corruption. Goldwater resigned as director of Mount Sinai in 1928, but maintained his affiliation with the hospital and continued to be active as a consultant.

In 1934, when the city's health problems had been intensified by the growing severity of the depression, Goldwater accepted appointment as commissioner of hospitals of New York City. With the vigorous support of Mayor Fiorello La Guardia, he began a reorganization of the city's twenty-six municipal hospitals, most of which had suffered from years of neglect. He greatly increased their efficiency by insisting upon a high degree of autonomy for each hospital's staff, by bringing all lay personnel under the civil service merit system, and by establishing expert consulting boards in medicine, nursing, dentistry, and administration. He also succeeded in securing substantial funds from federal, state, and city governments, including a $7,000,000 municipal appropriation for the construction of a clinical research hospital devoted to the study of chronic diseases. Originally called Welfare Hospital, it was later renamed the Goldwater Memorial Hospital.

Goldwater resigned in 1940 to become president of the Associated Hospital Service, the city-wide "Blue Cross" hospital insurance organization. An advocate of the voluntary hospital system, he rejected compulsory health insurance plans and instead favored voluntary nonprofit prepayment hospital insurance, supplemented by government per-capita subsidies to general hospitals. He also encouraged the implementation of group medical practice. By coordinating the efforts of hospitals, physicians, and industrial and labor groups, he was able, under the auspices of the Associated Hospital Service, to organize Community Medical Care, which provided low-cost medical care in hospital wards to low-income families.

Goldwater was president of the American Hospital Association (1908), vice-president of the New York Academy of Medicine (1913), and president of the American Conference on Hospital Service (1924–26). Among his honors were degrees from Marquette University (1925) and New York University (1939) and the American Hospital Association's award of merit (1940). He was a member of the Society for Ethical Culture. On Feb. 8, 1904, he married Clara Aub, the daughter of a New York City merchant. They had three children: Janet Teres, Robert John, and Mary Margaret. Goldwater died of cancer at Mount Sinai Hospital at the age

of sixty-nine and was buried in Mount Pleasant Cemetery, Hawthorne, N. Y.

[The fullest account of Goldwater's career is in Joseph Hirsh and Beka Doherty, *The First Hundred Years of the Mount Sinai Hospital of N. Y.* (1952), pp. 137–48. The best obituaries are those in *Hospital Management*, Nov. 1942, *Jour. of Mount Sinai Hospital,* Jan.–Feb. 1943, and the *Modern Hospital*, Nov. 1942. See also Goldwater's article in *N. Y. Times*, May 10, 1914 (magazine section); *Nat. Cyc. Am. Biog.*, XXXI, 411–12; and obituaries in *Jour. Am. Medic. Assoc.*, Nov. 7, 1942, and N. Y. Acad. of Medicine, *Bull.*, Mar. 1943. Family information from Prof. Robert Goldwater, N. Y. Univ.]

JOHN DUFFY

GORRELL, EDGAR STALEY (Feb. 3, 1891–Mar. 5, 1945), military aviator, was born in Baltimore, Md., the son of Charles Edgar Gorrell, a carpenter and construction superintendent, and Pamelia Stevenson (Smith) Gorrell. He was educated at Baltimore City College (1904–07) and the United States Military Academy, from which he received a B.S. degree and an army commission (infantry) in 1912. While a cadet at West Point he was attracted to flying, and in 1915 he qualified as a military aviator at the Signal Corps flying school in Coronado, Calif. Assigned to the 1st Aero Squadron as a pilot, Gorrell accompanied it to Columbus, N. Mex., on Mar. 13, 1916, and participated in the American punitive expedition into Mexico. In September 1916 he was transferred on student status to the Massachusetts Institute of Technology, where he received an M.S. degree in aeronautical engineering the following spring. Shortly after United States entry into World War I and his promotion to captain, Gorrell was selected, on the basis of his training at M.I.T., to accompany the technical mission being sent to Europe under Major (later Col.) Raynal C. Bolling to secure information to be used in planning wartime aviation production in the United States.

Landing in Great Britain on June 26, 1917, the Bolling Mission obtained technical data from British air leaders; several of its members, including Gorrell, also visited France and Italy. Its report, sent to Washington in August, recommended that all United States manufacturing capability above what was required to provide planes for flight training and for the support of ground forces be committed to the production of a powerful American bombing force. Gorrell was next assigned to the Paris headquarters of the Air Service, American Expeditionary Forces (Lines of Communication), as director of its technical section, with the duty of initiating purchases "of every article necessary for the Air Service." Already attracted to Italian ideas about strategic bombing, Gorrell entered into a correspondence with the industrialist Count Caproni di Taliedo in October–November 1917 which seems to have reinforced his belief in the importance of strategic air power. This view he embodied in a paper prepared for the chief of the A.E.F. Air Service, "The American Proposal for Strategic Bombing" (Nov. 28, 1917). Possibly as a result, Gorrell was named chief of Strategical Aviation, Air Service, A.E.F. (Zone of Advance), on Dec. 3, 1917. Here he made detailed plans for the employment of an American bombing force, but the war ended before the planes were produced.

Despite the pioneering nature of Gorrell's early advocacy of strategic air power, his concepts about the employment of aviation turned markedly conservative after Jan. 21, 1918, when he was transferred to high staff duty, first as Air Officer, G-3 Division, General Staff, A.E.F., and later as Assistant Chief of Staff, Air Service, A.E.F. In the latter duty, he was promoted to the rank of colonel, becoming at the age of twenty-seven one of the youngest to hold the rank since the American Civil War. Following the Armistice, Gorrell headed a project at Tours, France, which was charged to evaluate American air combat experience and to prepare "an exhaustive record covering the narrative, statistical, technical, and tactical history of the Air Service." Two tentative Air Service manuals prepared under Gorrell's direction early in 1919 reported the lesson that "when the Infantry loses the Army loses. It is therefore the role of the Air Service, as well as that of other arms, to aid the chief combatant, the Infantry." Upon his return to Washington later that year, Gorrell threw himself into the fight of the War Department's General Staff to prevent the establishment of a separate air force coequal with the army and the navy, one of his published arguments being that aircraft were incapable of decisive action against a hostile army.

Gorrell resigned from the army on Mar. 19, 1920, and devoted the rest of his life to business. He was associated with two automobile manufacturing companies, first Nordyke & Marmon (1920–25) and then the Stutz Motor Car Company (1925–39), rising in the Stutz company to president and chairman of the board. In 1934 he served as a civilian member of the War Department Special Committee on the Army Air Corps (Baker Board) and agreed with the majority view against the establishment of a separate air force. In 1936 he was the founding president of the Air Transport Association of America, and as such was often called the "czar" of the commercial airlines. In this position he worked vigor-

ously to secure larger federal appropriations for civil airways and airports. He was a tireless speaker in the years 1938–41 on the need for an expanded American aircraft production industry as a first line of military preparedness, but he continued to insist that aviation should be integrated with the army and navy.

On Dec. 10, 1921, Gorrell married Ruth Maurice of New York City; their children were Mary and Edgar Staley. Shortly before his death he married Mrs. Mary Frances (O'Dowd) Weidman, on Feb. 22, 1945. In his later years he maintained a home in Lake Forest, Ill., and an office in Washington, D. C. He died in Washington of a heart ailment in 1945, at the age of fifty-four. As requested in his will, his body was cremated and the ashes scattered over the Military Academy at West Point by an Army Air Forces plane.

[The fullest account of Gorrell's career is the obituary in *Assembly* (the West Point alumni magazine), Oct. 1945; see also *Who Was Who in America*, vol. II (1950). His father's occupation is given in Baltimore city directories, 1891–1908, and confirmed by records of the U. S. Military Acad. His service in World War I and the paradox of his ideas on the employment of aviation are treated in Irving B. Holley, Jr., *Ideas and Weapons* (1953). The "Gorrell History" of the Air Service, A.E.F., now deposited in the Nat. Archives, consists of some 180 MS. volumes and is available on microfilm. The Air Force Hist. Division Archives, Maxwell Air Force Base, Ala., possesses copies of many of Gorrell's addresses of the 1938–41 period, as well as of his correspondence with Caproni. His strategic bombing paper is reproduced in the *Air Power Historian*, Apr. 1958. Gorrell's testimony before Congressional committees concerned with aviation matters during the 1920's and '30's is rich in autobiographical material, not all of which is accurate.]

ROBERT FRANK FUTRELL

GORTNER, ROSS AIKEN (Mar. 20, 1885– Sept. 30, 1942), biochemist, was born on a farm near O'Neill, Nebr., the third son and youngest of four children of Joseph Ross Gortner, a Methodist minister, and Louisa Elizabeth (Waters) Gortner. His father, whose German forebears had settled in Pennsylvania in the mid-eighteenth century, had moved west, first to Illinois and then in 1882 to Nebraska. There he took up a homestead while covering a sixty-mile circuit each week. In 1887 he enlisted as a missionary and took his family to Liberia. Early in 1888, when Ross was nearly three, his father died of "African fever" (probably malaria or yellow fever), and the mother and children returned to Nebraska. Gortner secured his early education under the handicap of frequent moves from one Nebraska town to another and the added responsibility, for several years, of caring for his invalid mother and doing all the housework.

In 1902 his mother settled in University Place,

near Lincoln, Nebr., where Gortner entered the preparatory and college departments of Nebraska Wesleyan University. In the next five years he completed a three-year preparatory course and a four-year college course, while caring again for his mother, whose illness had recurred; she died of pernicious anemia in 1905. At Nebraska Wesleyan Prof. Frederick J. Alway interested Gortner in chemistry; he earned his tuition by working as an assistant in that department, and by 1907, when he received the B.S. degree, he had published five papers with Alway. He then secured an assistantship at the University of Toronto, where he studied physical chemistry under W. Lash Miller, receiving the M.S. degree in 1908. From Toronto he moved to Columbia University, where his work in organic chemistry under Marston T. Bogert earned him the Ph.D. degree in 1909. The next five years (1909–14) he spent in research at the Carnegie Institution's Station for Experimental Evolution at Cold Spring Harbor, N. Y. Under the influence of the botanist James Arthur Harris [q.v.], with whom he formed a lifelong friendship, Gortner quickly recognized the role of physical chemistry in the understanding of biological problems and did pioneer work in the application of colloid chemistry to biology. Shifting his primary interest from organic to biological chemistry, he embarked on studies of melanin pigments in animals, the chemical changes associated with embryonic growth, and, in association with Harris, the physicochemical characteristics of saps isolated from plants.

In 1914 Gortner moved to the University of Minnesota as associate professor of soil chemistry in the College of Agriculture, where his former teacher Alway had recently been appointed professor. Two years later he was made associate professor of agricultural biochemistry; and the following year he became both professor and head of the division of agricultural biochemistry at the Minnesota Agricultural Experiment Station, a double appointment which he held for the rest of his life. Gortner first carried out research in the organic constituents of soil, but he later turned his attention to the nature of proteins, particularly as representatives of colloidal systems. He also made extensive investigations of the breakdown products of proteins during acid hydrolysis, and examined the characteristics of the sulfur-containing amino acid cystine in proteins. Work on the chemistry of flour led to elucidation of the nature of the various proteins present in the wheat grain. He also studied the chemistry of wood and the pulping process, and the role of water in living processes.

Gortner's work was characterized, not by a major theoretical contribution but by a steady series of factual advances leading to an improved understanding of plants and animals as chemical systems. He published more than 300 papers and books, whose titles attest to the broad-ranging nature of his mind and his concern for the influence of scientific discoveries on society as a whole. His textbook, *Outlines of Biochemistry* (1929), became a major treatise and was unique in its day for the emphasis given to proteins as part of a colloidal system. His George Fisher Baker Lectures at Cornell University (1935–36) were published as *Selected Topics in Colloid Chemistry* (1937).

Gortner's greatest influence was probably as a teacher, and his efforts went far beyond the formal classroom. He built up a large graduate program at Minnesota and personally directed the work of more than eighty candidates for advanced degrees. His enthusiasm, not only for biochemistry but for science as a whole, caused him to be widely sought as a lecturer and writer. A popular lecture, "Scientific Genealogy," embodied his view that a scientist gains immortality through the work of his students. Gortner was elected to the National Academy of Sciences in 1935 and was an active member of the American Chemical Society, serving as chairman of the biochemistry division in 1919 and of the colloid division in 1931. He was president of the American Society of Naturalists in 1932 and of Sigma Xi, the scientific honorary society, in 1942.

Gortner was married on Aug. 4, 1909, to Catherine Victoria Willis of Dorchester, Nebr. Their four children were Elora Catherine, Ross Aiken, Willis Alway, and Alice Louise. Both sons became biochemists. Mrs. Gortner died in 1930, and on Jan. 12, 1931, Gortner married Rachel Rude, who had been his secretary for many years. In the summer of 1938, while serving as a consultant to the Sugar Planters Experiment Station in Hawaii, he suffered a heart attack which was correctly diagnosed only after his return to Minnesota in the fall. Although he remained in poor health, he embarked on a study of sulfur metabolism in plants and continued his university duties with much of his usual enthusiasm, until hospitalized by severe heart attacks. He died at his home in St. Paul, Minn., in 1942, a few days before a planned testimonial dinner in his honor.

[Samuel C. Lind's memorial in Nat. Acad. Sci., *Biog. Memoirs*, vol. XXIII (1945), which carries a full bibliography of Gortner's publications; obituaries by Charles Albert Browne, in *Sci. Monthly*, Dec. 1942, and L. S. Palmer, in *Science*, Oct. 30, 1942. Some of Gortner's papers have been preserved in the Biochemistry Dept. of the Univ. of Minn.]
AARON J. IHDE

GRANGER, WALTER (Nov. 7, 1872–Sept. 6, 1941), paleontologist, was born in Middletown Springs, near Rutland, Vt., the oldest of five children of Charles H. Granger, an insurance agent, and Ada Byron (Haynes) Granger. His middle name, which he early discarded, was Willis. Through his father he was descended from Launcelot Granger, who came from England and settled in Newbury, Mass., in 1654. As a boy, Walter was deeply interested in the birds and mammals of the region. In 1890, after two years in the Rutland high school, he ended his formal education to accept a job, secured through a family friend, at the American Museum of Natural History in New York City.

Granger's first duties were janitorial, but his knowledge of taxidermy soon involved him in the preparation of study specimens of birds and mammals under the supervision of the ornithologist Frank M. Chapman [Supp. 3]. When in 1894 he was sent with an expedition to collect living specimens from the Badlands of South Dakota, an area abounding in fossil forms, he developed a strong interest in paleontology, and in 1896, on Chapman's advice, he transferred from the museum's department of birds and mammals to the department of vertebrate paleontology, which had recently been organized by Henry Fairfield Osborn [Supp. 1]. That year Granger served as field assistant to Jacob L. Wortman on an expedition to collect fossil mammals in the San Juan Basin of New Mexico. In 1897 he worked with the museum's crew collecting dinosaurs in Wyoming. The following summer they retrieved from the rich Bone Cabin quarry enough fossil bones to fill two freight cars, as well as the famed *Brontosaurus* skeleton found at Nine Mile quarry. Granger's second publication (1901), jointly with Henry Fairfield Osborn, was on sauropod dinosaur limb bones from the Nine Mile deposit.

During these years a fruitful friendship and collaboration had begun at the American Museum between Granger, William Diller Matthew [*q.v.*], and Albert (Bill) Thomson. Granger was an extrovert, a jolly companion welcome in any company, who became a great collector, field geologist, and stratigrapher. The more introverted Matthew, a Canadian citizen, was beginning a career as one of the most distinguished research scientists working in the United States. Thomson was a quiet, sensitive farm boy from South Dakota who became one of the most skilled field and laboratory technicians of his time. In 1903 Osborn assigned to Granger the American Museum's investigations of early mammals in North America. With some important interruptions, this campaign occupied much of the rest of Granger's life. With Thomson

as his technical assistant and Matthew as his senior in research he revolutionized knowledge of the Age of Mammals and laid the main basis for early Cenozoic faunal and stratigraphic studies in North America. Among Granger's important expeditions in this connection were those which studied the Eocene of Wyoming (1903–06, 1909–14, 1916), the Paleocene and Eocene of New Mexico (1912–14, 1916), the Eocene of Colorado (1916, 1918), and the Oligocene of South Dakota (1938–41).

Granger's work on other continents became better known than his work in the United States, though it was of no greater importance. In 1907 he went with Osborn to North Africa and made a large collection of early mammals from the Fayum region of Egypt. Most of his time between 1921 and 1931 was spent collecting fossil vertebrates and making stratigraphic studies in China and Mongolia. The fossils which Granger and his assistants, including Bill Thomson, unearthed in Mongolia, in the course of the American Museum's Central Asiatic Expeditions directed by Roy Chapman Andrews, became world famous. Granger served as second in command and chief paleontologist of these expeditions, which explored the Gobi Desert in a caravan of camels and trucks in 1922 and 1923, 1925, 1928, and 1930. The finding of dinosaur eggs (not, in fact, the first known) was most widely acclaimed, but this was of relatively little importance compared with the unexpected and stunning discovery of a long sequence of rich and bizarre faunas of fossil vertebrates, hitherto completely unknown, extending from dinosaurs early in the Age of Reptiles through a whole succession of faunas in the Age of Mammals up to our own time. The collections revealed literally hundreds of animals new to science and included, among many others, a whole growth series of frilled dinosaurs, the earliest known mammal skulls, the largest known land mammal (a rhinoceros, *Baluchitherium*), and shovel-tusked mastodons.

Preliminary descriptions of many of the Asiatic discoveries were published jointly by Granger and Matthew and, after Matthew's death in 1930, by Granger and William K. Gregory, another colleague at the American Museum. Even in the late 1960's, however, the study was not yet complete, and a third generation of paleontologists was still carrying out research on Granger's Asiatic discoveries.

A self-made scientist, Granger advanced to the rank of curator (equivalent to the university rank of full professor) in 1927. He published some seventy-five technical research papers, along with numerous notes, reviews, and popular articles. He was impatient of the routine of reports, and the actual words of his papers were sometimes written by a co-author, though with his active collaboration. His "Revision of the Eocene Horses" (1908), a model treatment, remained standard for several decades. His major publication was probably the memoir on the classic American Paleocene mammalian faunas on which he collaborated with Matthew, but he removed his name from the title page when he edited the work after Matthew's death.

On Apr. 7, 1904, Granger married a first cousin, Annie (Anna) Dean Granger of Brooklyn. They had no children. A highly social person, loved by his associates, he was active in a number of professional societies and clubs. His favorite was the Explorers Club of New York; he served as president in 1935–37 and was one of the few honorary members. Granger died in his sleep of a coronary thrombosis in Lusk, Wyo., while returning with Thomson to a field camp after attending a conference of the Society of Vertebrate Paleontology. His ashes were privately interred in Vermont.

[Field records and correspondence in the files of the Am. Museum of Natural Hist.; records and collections of the Simroe Foundation (Tucson, Ariz.); personal acquaintance; memoir of Granger by G. G. Simpson in Geological Soc. of America, *Proc.*, 1941, with portrait and bibliography. Numerous articles by Granger and others referring to his activities are in *Natural Hist.* magazine, especially 1921–40; see also the sketch by D. R. Barton, Mar. 1941. The series of collected papers, *Fossil Vertebrates in the Am. Museum of Natural Hist.*, especially vols. II–XIII (1903–37), list Granger's expeditions and describe many of his discoveries. Roy Chapman Andrews, *On the Trail of Ancient Man* (1926), includes a popular account of Granger's work in Mongolia through 1925. There are field photographs of Granger, Matthew, and Thomson in the 1890's and an illustrated summary of Granger's later explorations in Mongolia in E. H. Colbert, *Men and Dinosaurs* (1968). See also *Nat. Cyc. Am. Biog.*, XXXV, 405–06; and obituary by C. Forster-Cooper in *Nature*, Nov. 29, 1941. On his family see James N. Granger, *Launcelot Granger of Newbury, Mass., and Suffield, Conn.: A Genealogical Hist.* (1893), pp. 219, 358.]

GEORGE GAYLORD SIMPSON

GRAVES, DAVID BIBB (Apr. 1, 1873–Mar. 14, 1942), governor of Alabama, was born on a farm in Hope Hull, Montgomery County, Ala., the son of David and Mattie (Bibb) Graves. His father, a cotton planter and veteran of the Confederate Army, was descended from Thomas Graves, who in 1608 emigrated from England to Jamestown, Va., and later served in the first Virginia House of Burgesses. Graves's mother, of colonial Welsh ancestry, came of a family of some political prominence; she was a cousin of William Wyatt Bibb [*q.v.*] and his brother Thomas Bibb, both governors of Alabama. When David was a year old his father died, and he was

brought up by his paternal grandfather, Russell Graves, on an Alabama farm. He later lived with an uncle in Texas.

With roots in both states, Graves received his early education in the public schools in Texas and at the Starke University School in Montgomery, Ala., and in 1890 enrolled at the University of Alabama. Upon graduating in 1893 with a degree in civil engineering, he studied law for one year at the University of Texas, read law the following year in Montgomery, and then went to Yale, from which he received the LL.B. degree in 1896. He was admitted to the Texas bar in 1894 and the Alabama bar in 1897. Entering politics almost immediately, Graves in 1898 was elected to a four-year term in the Alabama legislature. In 1901 he was appointed city attorney of Montgomery, but his political advancement came chiefly through the national guard. Appointed aide-de-camp in 1897, with the rank of captain, he quickly rose to assistant adjutant general and then to adjutant general, a position he held from 1907 to 1911. In 1916 he helped organize the 1st Alabama Cavalry and, following Pancho Villa's forays into Texas and New Mexico, saw service on the Mexican border. That same year he was elected chairman of the Alabama state Democratic executive committee, in which capacity he sought to substitute a primary for the convention system of nomination.

When the United States entered World War I, Graves, now with the rank of colonel, went to France as commander of the 117th U. S. Field Artillery, which consisted of units of the former 1st Alabama Cavalry. He returned home in 1919 a war hero and organized the Alabama section of the American Legion, of which he was elected the first state chairman. With the support of World War veterans, he ran for the Democratic gubernatorial nomination in 1922 but was overwhelmed by William W. Brandon. Four years later, however, having been endorsed by the Ku Klux Klan, he was elected governor. A practical politician, Graves had built a large following on personal favors and friendships, rather than on ideological issues. By adeptly dealing with different interest groups, he drew support from both the northern part of the state, an area of small farmers, with a tradition of agrarian radicalism, and from the black belt, an area of many Negroes and large landowners who usually followed the conservative lead of corporate interests in Mobile and Birmingham.

Once in office Graves pursued a moderately progressive course, one that had been already inaugurated by Gov. Thomas E. Kilby (1919–23) and subsequently maintained by Brandon. He abolished the convict leasing system and, in keeping with a pledge made to the farmers, raised taxes on public utilities, railroads, and coal and iron companies. But he also accepted a tax on cigarettes and cigars, which was especially unpopular among the small farmers. The new revenue thus secured was used to expand educational and public health facilities, increase teachers' salaries and veterans' pensions, fund an ambitious road-building program, construct new bridges, and improve port facilities in Mobile. Though an admitted member of the Klan, Graves, in response to mounting criticism of Klan terrorism, refused to appoint Klansmen to state positions. Yet at the same time he was dilatory in publicly condemning the organization, and he made the prosecution of its members difficult by allocating too little money for the purpose.

Prevented by state law from serving two consecutive terms, Graves was not a candidate for governor in 1930, but in 1934 he again won election, campaigning on his previous record and as a New Dealer. He favored such reforms as the federal child labor amendment, unemployment insurance, and cooperation with the TVA, and he endorsed the referendum and recall. Prohibition emerged as a major issue in the campaign. His two opponents supported repeal, but Graves's astute political sense led him to oppose it, though he was not a dry by personal conviction. (The legislature in 1936 rejected his proposal for a referendum requiring a statewide majority for repeal and instead passed a county option law over his veto; but only one-third of the counties voted for repeal.)

To maintain his popularity among the farmers in northern Alabama and the working classes, Graves made good on his commitment to New Deal legislation, winning a reputation as one of the most progressive governors in the South. He continued to increase expenditures for public education, created a rural electrical authority, and established a labor department, a public welfare department, and a public works program to relieve unemployment. He supported Alabama's first old-age assistance law and successfully sought legislation exempting homesteads worth less than $2,000 from taxation. Yet Graves also cooperated with conservative elements in the state. With financial support from Birmingham industrial interests, who desired a reduction in transportation costs, he led a movement of Southern governors to change the existing railroad freight rate structure, claiming that equalization of class rate differentials between the South and the rest of the country would bring higher wages to Southern workers.

Near the close of Graves's second administration a Senate vacancy was created by the elevation of Hugo Black to the United States Supreme Court. Explaining that he did not want to give any of the prospective contenders an undue advantage in the 1938 elections, Graves filled the post by appointing his wife, Dixie (Bibb) Graves of Montgomery, a first cousin, whom he had married on Oct. 10, 1900. She served less than a year, voluntarily stepping down for Black's successor. Upon leaving the governorship, Graves, who liked to be called "The Little Colonel" and "Bibb the Builder," resumed the practice of law. He also served as a member of the National Advisory Committee on Agriculture and of the Interregional Highway Committee. A member of the Christian Church and a trustee of Bob Jones College, Graves received several honorary degrees from colleges in Alabama. While making plans to run again for governor, he died in Sarasota, Fla., of a coronary thrombosis at the age of sixty-eight. He was buried in Montgomery. His wife survived him; there were no children.

[There is no full-length biography of Graves, but there is a sketch in Thomas McA. Owen, *Hist. of Ala. and Dict. of Ala. Biog.*, III (1921), 693–94. Other sources include Albert B. Moore, *Hist. of Ala.* (1934); William E. Gilbert, "Bibb Graves as a Progressive, 1927–1930," *Ala. Rev.*, Jan. 1957; *Nat. Cyc. Am. Biog.*, XXXI, 13; *N. Y. Times*, Aug. 9, 1926, Mar. 15, 1942; *Ala. Hist. Quart.*, 1948 issue, pp. 63–64; Arnold S. Rice, *The Ku Klux Klan in Am. Politics* (1962); David M. Chalmers, *Hooded Americanism: The First Century of the Ku Klux Klan* (1965); James B. Sellers, *The Prohibition Movement in Ala., 1702–1943* (1943); Robert A. Lively, *The South in Action: A Sectional Crusade Against Freight Rate Discrimination* (1949); V. O. Key, Jr., *Southern Politics* (1949); and "Unofficial Observer," *Am. Messiahs* (1935). See also Lee Clark Cain, "Ala. Public School Progress under the Governorship of David Bibb Graves" (unpublished Ph.D. thesis, Univ. of Ala., 1962).]

PHILIP M. HOSAY

GREGORY, CLIFFORD VERNE (Oct. 20, 1883–Nov. 18, 1941), agricultural journalist and farm leader, was born near Burchinal, Cerro Gordo County, Iowa, the eldest of three children— two sons and an adopted daughter. His father, Elmer Olmstead Gregory, whose forebear Henry Gregory had emigrated from Scotland to Springfield, Mass., in 1633, was a native of New York state; he had lived in Illinois before settling in Iowa by 1878. Although he owned a substantial farm, he preferred to work as a carpenter or contractor, leaving much of the farm work to his sons. Gregory's mother, Millie E. (McFarlin) Gregory, a native of Michigan, had been a schoolteacher.

In 1906 Clifford Gregory began the study of animal husbandry at Iowa State College in Ames. There he also developed an interest in journalism and helped support himself by acting as a local correspondent of the *Mason City Globe-Gazette* and selling articles to *Country Life* magazine. He taught journalism during his junior and senior years, and after graduating in 1910 he stayed on for a further year as an instructor in journalism and bulletin editor for the Iowa Agricultural Experiment Station. On June 29, 1910, he married Edna Laura Springer of Revere, Minn. Their six children were Gwendolyn Ruth, Merrill Clifford, Howard Verne, Barbara, David Walter, and Shirley Ann.

Gregory moved to Chicago in 1911 to become editor of the *Prairie Farmer*. This struggling periodical, one of the oldest farm papers in the United States, had been bought a few years earlier by Burridge D. Butler, former publisher of the *Minneapolis Daily News*. Gregory soon reestablished the *Prairie Farmer*'s reputation as a major farm journal. He encouraged communications from farm people. His wit enlivened the paper's columns; he early inaugurated a regular feature, "The Song of the Lazy Farmer," which amused thousands of readers for a quarter of a century, and created characters such as Senator Hiram Cornborer and the homespun philosopher John Turnipseed, through whom he could express his ideas. Gregory urged a progressive, adaptive agriculture. He advocated better business methods, the use of limestone and rock phosphate to maintain soil fertility, and soybeans as a cash crop; he sponsored tractor demonstrations and urged the vaccination of calves to fight brucellosis. With his friend and former classmate Henry A. Wallace, he popularized cornhusking contests to glamorize an arduous Midwestern task, and in 1925 he began the program of Master Farmer awards, which soon became a national institution.

Gregory involved himself directly in efforts to develop greater cooperation among farmers. He gave strong support to the Illinois Agricultural Association when it was formed in 1916, became a vice-president in 1918, helped place the association on a sound financial basis, and urged that it emphasize economic services rather than agricultural education. He also participated in the organization of the American Farm Bureau Federation in 1919, and the next year worked in its study of the grain market and cooperative sales programs.

Gregory was a leader in the movement to mobilize Congressional support for the McNary-Haugen bills [see George N. Peek, Supp. 3]. He was mentioned as a possible choice for Secretary of Agriculture after the election of Franklin D. Roosevelt in 1932, but gave his full support to Henry Wallace, who received the appointment. Gregory endorsed the New Deal agricultural programs and helped write the Agricultural Adjust-

ment acts of 1933 and 1938; he served on the National Corn-Hog Committee of the first Agricultural Adjustment Administration, on the President's Commission on Rural Cooperatives (1936), on the Agricultural Priorities Division of the National Defense Council, and on the Agricultural Advisory Committee of the Department of Agriculture. He was also a director of the Federal Reserve Bank in Chicago. In 1937, after a long conflict with Butler over the *Prairie Farmer*'s finances and editorial policy, Gregory resigned to become associate publisher of *Wallaces' Farmer and Iowa Homestead* and of the *Wisconsin Agriculturalist*.

Five feet nine inches tall and prematurely bald, Gregory was a poised and humorous speaker. He was also a skilled mediator. He took pride in his efforts to promote farm organizations and in his ability to speak for the farmer in Washington. In 1940 he was awarded the Distinguished Service Medal of the American Farm Bureau Federation. He was president of the Agricultural History Society (1935–36) and also served as president of the board of education of the Chicago suburb of Wheaton, Ill., while living there. An active Methodist and a Mason, he found time for golf and other outdoor recreations. He died in 1941, at the age of fifty-eight, at the Iowa Methodist Hospital in Des Moines following an appendectomy. He was buried in the Wheaton Cemetery.

[James F. Evans, *Prairie Farmer and WLS: The Burridge D. Butler Years* (1969), a careful and judicious study, contains the most extended treatment of Gregory. References appear in a number of other studies of Midwestern agriculture or its leaders, most notably Christiana McFadyen Campbell, *The Farm Bureau* (1962). Informative obituaries and memorial notes or editorials appeared in *Des Moines Register*, Nov. 19, 20, 23, 1941, *Mason City Globe-Gazette*, Nov. 18, 1941, *Wallaces' Farmer and Iowa Homestead*, Nov. 29, 1941 (with picture), and *Prairie Farmer*, Nov. 29, 1941. See also *Nat. Cyc. Am. Biog.*, XXXI, 391–92; and *Who Was Who in America*, vol. II (1950). Walter T. Borg published a short biographical sketch and an extended listing of Gregory's publications in *Agricultural Hist.*, Apr. 1942. Family data from the U. S. census schedules for Cerro Gordo County, Iowa, 1870 and 1880; and from Mrs. Clifford V. Gregory and Howard B. Gregory. According to Evans, a collection of Gregory's correspondence during the *Prairie Farmer* years is in family hands.]

ALLAN G. BOGUE

GREGORY, MENAS SARKAS BOULGOURJIAN (July 14, 1872–Nov. 2, 1941), psychiatrist, was born in Marash, Turkey, of Armenian parents. His father died when he was two years old, and after his mother's remarriage he was shifted from relative to relative. In his youth he bore his stepfather's name of Boulgourjian. In 1894, the year when the great Armenian massacres began in Turkey, he received the A.B. degree from Central Turkey

College, an American mission school at Aintab. There his acquaintance with the medical missionary Fred D. Shepard [q.v.] roused an ambition to go to the United States to study medicine. Upon his arrival he joined a group of Armenians near Albany, N. Y., and in 1895 enrolled in the Albany Medical College. Forced to earn his own way, he worked in various laboratories and held summer jobs; during one, at the Binghamton State Hospital, he met the psychiatrist Smith Ely Jelliffe [Supp. 3], the beginning of a lifelong friendship. At the conclusion of his medical training he assumed the name Gregory, the Anglicized form of his father's surname, Krikorian.

Graduating in June 1898, Gregory practiced briefly in Troy, N. Y., before becoming an intern at Craig Colony for Epileptics in Sonyea, N. Y. He was then appointed junior assistant physician at Kings Park State Hospital, Long Island. In February 1902 he became assistant alienist in the psychopathic department of Bellevue Hospital in New York City and, two years later, chief alienist and director of the department. When, in 1921, a number of city hospitals were consolidated into one department, Gregory was appointed director of its psychopathic division.

One of Gregory's major interests was improving the psychiatric facilities at Bellevue Hospital and transforming them from a largely custodial role to one of treatment and rehabilitation. On trips abroad he studied the construction and management of European psychiatric hospitals, and at home he enlisted the influence of politicians as well as the medical profession. His efforts culminated in the erection of a new Bellevue Psychiatric Hospital, housing 600 patients, which was formally opened on Nov. 2, 1933. A year later, for reasons which have never been made clear—perhaps in part because of his close relations with Tammany politicians—Gregory was forced to resign his post under pressure from the new commissioner of hospitals, Sigismund S. Goldwater [Supp. 3], an appointee of the fusion reform administration. The city's leading psychiatrists met to protest Gregory's resignation, and the *American Journal of Psychiatry* denounced Goldwater's action in an acrimonious editorial.

An able clinician and teacher, Gregory was professor of mental diseases at the University and Bellevue Medical College (New York University) from 1918 to 1924, when the title was changed to professor of psychiatry; he became professor emeritus in 1937. He had earlier held faculty appointments at the College of Physicians and Surgeons and at the New York Post-

Graduate Hospital and Medical College. During World War I he served in the Army Medical Corps as a neuropsychiatrist. He often acted as an expert witness in legal proceedings, and in 1931 he was asked to form a psychiatric clinic at the Court of General Sessions, which in less than three years carried out more than 3,000 pre-sentencing psychiatric evaluations.

In his capacity as administrator and teacher Gregory introduced a number of European innovations in the field of psychiatry. Generations of students, residents, and colleagues learned from him about Kraepelinian classification and the importance of new dynamic concepts, particularly psychoanalysis; it was he, for example, who brought the brilliant analyst Paul Schilder from Vienna to Bellevue. For decades Gregory was among the most influential psychiatrists in shaping the development of his profession in America, not only in New York but, by means of his frequent attendance at professional meetings, throughout the country. Often consulted by his peers, he was elected president of the New York Psychiatric Society (1930–32) and the New York Society for Clinical Psychiatry (1925–27). Although he often abstracted foreign literature for American physicians, Gregory's own bibliography of articles is short. It reflects his interest in alcoholism (which he believed to be a defense against psychosis) and the relationship of general medicine to psychiatry. His open-mindedness and dynamic approach are suggested by his contention that physicians could learn much about the psychology of illness from nonmedical groups such as Christian Scientists.

In appearance, Gregory had "a beaming, infectious smile that would inspire a gayer outlook in his most depressed patients." Scarcely more than five feet tall, he was acutely sensitive about his height and once confided to Abraham A. Brill that he had never married for fear that his children would inherit his stature. His personal interests were golf and collecting medieval wood carvings. He died of a sudden heart attack at the age of sixty-nine while playing golf at the Lakeview Country Club at Tuckahoe, N. Y. In his will he left a bequest to endow a professorship and an annual lectureship at New York University.

[A. A. Brill and Smith Ely Jelliffe in *Jour. of Nervous and Mental Disease*, Feb. 1942; Louis Casamajor in *Archives of Neurology and Psychiatry*, Feb. 1942; Samuel Feigin in *Mental Hygiene*, Jan. 1942; Frederick W. Parsons in *Am. Jour. of Psychiatry*, Jan. 1942; *N. Y. Times*, Nov. 3, 1941; *Medical Violet* (N. Y. Univ. College of Medicine yearbook), 1942, p. 42; information from Alumni Assoc. Office, Albany Medical College. See also: *Boston Medic. and Surgical Jour.*, Aug. 16, 1906, pp. 182–83; *N. Y. Herald Tribune*, Nov. 3, 1933; *N. Y. Times*, June

27, 28, 30, 1934; *Am. Jour. of Psychiatry,* Nov. 1934 (editorial) and May 1942 (extract from will); Clarence P. Oberndorf, *A Hist. of Psychoanalysis in America* (1953), pp. 80–81.]

GUGGENHEIM, SIMON (Dec. 30, 1867–Nov. 2, 1941), business executive, United States Senator, philanthropist, was born in Philadelphia, Pa. He and his twin brother, Robert (who died in his ninth year), were the seventh and eighth of the eleven children of Meyer Guggenheim [*q.v.*] and Barbara (Myers) Guggenheim. Among Simon's five older brothers was Daniel Guggenheim [*q.v.*]. Their father, who had emigrated in 1847 from one of Switzerland's two small Jewish ghettos, had advanced rapidly, in Philadelphia, from peddler to manufacturer to commission merchant and then to importer of fine lace. By the time of Simon's birth he was wealthy, and during the next two decades he embarked on the mining and smelting ventures which, under the direction of his sons, were to amass the largest fortune ever made from mining—about $500,000,000 by 1920. Simon received his education in the public schools of Philadelphia and at the Pierce School of Business there, and then spent some time in Spain learning Spanish, a useful tool in his ore-scouting ventures for the family firm.

In 1888 he became chief ore buyer for M. Guggenheim's Sons and settled in Pueblo, Colo., moving to Denver in 1892. When, in 1901, the Guggenheims gained a controlling interest in the American Smelting and Refining Company, Simon became a member of the board of directors and was appointed the company's treasurer and Western representative. On Nov. 24, 1898, he married Olga Hirsch, daughter of a New York real estate operator. They had two sons: John Simon and George Denver.

Meanwhile Guggenheim had sought to bring a new dimension of influence to the family by entering Colorado politics. In 1896 he persuaded the Silver Republicans to nominate him for lieutenant governor, but his name was withdrawn when it was learned that at twenty-nine he was under the constitutional age for that post. Two years later the National People's Party, a coalition of Silver Republicans and moderate Populists, picked Guggenheim as their candidate for governor. But his brothers argued that his running as a free-silverite might damage the family's ties with Eastern sound-money conservatives; the Colorado press was hostile (it had recently portrayed him as an Eastern Jewish monopolist), and Simon, sensing that he could not win, withdrew before the election. His ambitions persisted, however, and in 1904 he opened a political office in Denver. Early in 1907 the Colorado legislature

elected him to the United States Senate as a Republican. Colorado newspapers charged that he had purchased his seat, but this was true only in the sense that his lavish donations to Republican party coffers had given him useful political leverage.

Guggenheim's record in the Senate was not especially distinguished. He spent much of his time promoting Colorado tourism, seeking federal projects for his state, and satisfying constituents' requests for favors. He endorsed the popular election of Senators, voted for the Payne-Aldrich Tariff, and supported the establishment of the Children's Bureau, but participated in an unsuccessful filibuster against the creation of the Department of Labor. On at least one occasion he sought to aid the family interests. The Guggenheims and J. P. Morgan [*q.v.*] in 1906 had formed a syndicate to mine copper in Alaska. To provide a ready source of fuel for its railroad, the syndicate illegally bought up individual land claims in Alaska's coal region, a transaction in which Richard Ballinger [*q.v.*], later President Taft's Secretary of the Interior, acted as counsel for the sellers. Gifford Pinchot, the director of the United States Forest Service, had consistently opposed corporate exploitation of public resources, and in January 1909 Guggenheim introduced a resolution, subsequently buried in committee, to investigate Pinchot's office. A few months later, when Pinchot learned of the syndicate's deal and of Ballinger's role in it, he used the information to attack the anticonservationist Secretary, thus setting off the celebrated Ballinger-Pinchot affair.

Guggenheim left the Senate in 1913, having previously declared that he would not seek another term. He then assumed three top executive positions in the New York headquarters of the family business. In 1919, when his brother Daniel retired, Simon succeeded him as president of the American Smelting and Refining Company, a position he held until his death.

In later life Guggenheim took an increasing interest in philanthropy. The early death of his older son in April 1922, following a mastoid operation, prompted the former Senator and his wife to establish the John Simon Guggenheim Memorial Foundation with an initial gift of $3,000,000. Planned in consultation with two former Rhodes scholars, President Frank Aydelotte of Swarthmore College and Henry Allen Moe (who became the foundation's first and longtime head), and incorporated in 1925, the foundation granted fellowships in arts, sciences, and humanities to young individuals of proven ability. The terms of the grants were flexible, and the recipients were never pressured to produce specific results. Guggenheim and his wife added $1,000,000 to the foundation in 1929 to establish Latin American Exchange Fellowships and several millions more by 1941, and in his will he named the foundation the residual legatee of his wealth. Over the years, Guggenheim fellowships have given thousands of scholars and artists a free year of study, research, and travel they might not otherwise have enjoyed.

Other Guggenheim gifts went to the Colorado School of Mines, the University of Colorado, Hebrew Union College in Cincinnati, the National Jewish Hospital in Denver, and Mount Sinai Hospital in New York City. All told, his benefactions came to $20,000,000. Although proud of his Jewish heritage, Simon Guggenheim adhered to no religious organization. He was a small man with heavy features and dark, deep-set, world-weary eyes. He died of pneumonia in Mount Sinai Hospital and was buried in Woodlawn Cemetery in New York City.

[Edwin P. Hoyt, Jr., *The Guggenheims and the Am. Dream* (1967); Milton Lomask, *Seed Money: The Guggenheim Story* (1964); Isaac F. Marcosson, *Metal Magic: The Story of the Am. Smelting and Refining Co.* (1949); Harvey O'Connor, *The Guggenheims: The Making of an Am. Dynasty* (1937); obituary in *N. Y. Times*, Nov 4, 1941; interviews with Ernest M. Lundell, Jr., Harry F. Guggenheim, Harold Loeb, Medley G. B. Whelpley, Bernard Baruch, and other friends and relatives. See also: Ellis Meredith, "The Senatorial Election in Colo.," *Arena*, Oct. 1907; Bernard Peach and Paschal Reeves, "John Simon Guggenheim Memorial Foundation," *South Atlantic Quart.*, Spring 1961; and, on the Morgan-Guggenheim syndicate and the Ballinger affair, James Penick, Jr., *Progressive Politics and Conservation: The Ballinger-Pinchot Affair* (1968). No Simon Guggenheim papers as such exist.]

MILTON LOMASK

GULICK, SIDNEY LEWIS (Apr. 10, 1860– Dec. 20, 1945), Congregational missionary to Japan, promoter of better American-Japanese relations and of international goodwill, was born at Ebon in the Marshall Islands, the third of seven children and first son of missionary parents, Luther Halsey Gulick (1828–1891) [*q.v.*] and Louisa (Lewis) Gulick. His grandfather Peter Johnson Gulick, a descendant of Hendrick and Geertruyt (Willekens) Gulick, who had emigrated from Holland to New Amsterdam in 1653, had come to the Sandwich Islands in 1827 as a missionary, and several of Sidney's uncles and cousins were active in mission work in Micronesia and in Asian countries. His childhood was spent primarily in Hawaii and in Europe, but when his father accepted an appointment in 1875 as representative of the American Bible Society in Japan and China, Sidney remained with his mother in California for schooling.

After taking his A.B. at Dartmouth in 1883, Gulick attended the Union Theological Seminary in New York City and in 1886 was ordained a Congregational minister. A short period of supply work at the Willoughby Avenue Mission in Brooklyn followed. He was then accepted by the American Board of Commissioners for Foreign Missions and in late 1887, after his marriage on Sept. 14 to Cara May Fisher, was sent to Japan. The Gulicks had five children: Susan Fisher, Luther Halsey, Leeds, Ethel, and Sidney Lewis.

For more than a decade Gulick worked in southern Japan in the provincial centers of Kumamoto and Matsuyama. His reputation as an author was first established by a thoughtful study of Japanese national character entitled *Evolution of the Japanese, Social and Psychic* (1903). He was appointed professor of theology at the Doshisha University in Kyoto in 1906, and in this post continued to do much writing in both English and Japanese, especially on evolution and other scientific subjects as related to Christianity. He served also as lecturer on comparative religion at Kyoto Imperial University. In the Association Concordia and the Peace Society of Japan he became associated with some of Japan's most progressive political leaders; he was also an organizer and vice-president of the American Peace Society of Japan. Through these organizations he became concerned with the issues of immigration and race relations that were arising between Americans and Japanese, particularly on the West Coast of the United States.

When Gulick returned home on furlough in June 1913, American Board missionaries in Japan urged him to present a memorial asking the Federal Council of the Churches of Christ in America to appoint a commission to study the problems of relations with Oriental races from the standpoint of Christian statesmanship. As a result of several months of firsthand study of the situation in California, Gulick prepared an authoritative book, *The American Japanese Problem* (1914), in which he proposed that any quota system for immigration restriction be racially nondiscriminatory. In 1914 he accepted the Federal Council's request that he enter its service as secretary of a new Commission on Relations with Japan. Early the next year he was sent with Shailer Mathews [Supp. 3], then president of the Council, as a "Christian embassy" to Japan; they spent several months consulting with Japanese leaders and making speeches throughout the country.

During the next two decades Gulick's tireless efforts in writing, speaking, and lobbying in

Washington made him one of the leading public figures concerned with Japanese-American relations. Inevitably he became involved in controversy; several times anti-Japanese elements charged that he was an agent in the pay of the Japanese. From 1921 to 1934 he was secretary of a National Committee on American-Japanese Relations headed first by Jacob Gould Schurman [Supp. 3] and then by George W. Wickersham [Supp. 2]. As secretary (1919–34) of the National Committee for Constructive Immigration Legislation, Gulick formulated proposals for national origins quotas that had a direct influence on subsequent legislation. Gulick recognized the practical necessity for limiting the numbers of Japanese immigrants, but wanted this done through a system that would give them full legal equality. The act of 1924 excluding Japanese entirely was, therefore, a great disappointment. Thereafter he worked for good relations directly between the peoples of the two countries through such means as the Federal Council's project for sending nearly 13,000 "doll messengers of good-will" to Japan.

Gulick's functions within the Federal Council's Commission on Relations with the Orient and its Commission on International Justice and Goodwill gradually involved him in a wider range of Asian problems. His trip abroad of 1922–23, which he described in *The Winning of the Far East* (1923), took him to China, Korea, and the Philippines as well as to Japan. From 1928 to 1930 he gave much time and energy to organization of China Famine Relief.

Although Gulick was recognized as the Federal Council's Asian specialist, his work for the churches was international in scope and ecumenical in spirit. He was present at the meeting in Constance, Germany, in early August 1914 at which the World Alliance for International Friendship through the Churches was formed just as war was breaking out, and he took the lead in organizing an American Council of the Alliance, an interest reflected also in his book *The Fight for Peace* (1915). From 1917 to 1920 he served as the Alliance's representative on the National Committee on the Churches and the Moral Aims of the War. He actively urged American ratification of the Treaty of Versailles embodying the League of Nations Covenant and, later, American adherence to the Permanent Court of International Justice. At the Universal Christian Conference on Life and Work held in Stockholm in the summer of 1925, Gulick was made secretary of a special commission on the church and race relations and formulated its report. He played a leading part during 1928 in collecting and presenting in Washington petitions from more than 185,000 members of some thirty denominations urging the ratification of the Kellogg-Briand Pact for the renunciation of war. Working in these endeavors with many of the clerical and lay leaders of his time, Gulick made distinctive contributions as organizer, drafter, and publicist. His talents were early recognized by honorary doctorates of divinity conferred by Dartmouth in 1905 and by Yale and Oberlin in 1914.

Gulick retired from his multiple duties in the Federal Council in mid-1934 and went to live in Honolulu. There he made a sociological study, *Mixing the Races in Hawaii* (1937). Much of his time in his last years was devoted to extensive studies of oriental philosophies and religions, parts of which were published posthumously in *The East and the West: A Study of Their Psychic and Cultural Characteristics* (1963). He died of cancer at Boise, Idaho, in 1945 while visiting a daughter there. His remains were cremated.

[Gulick's report letters to the Am. Board of Commissioners for Foreign Missions and some personal papers are deposited in the Houghton Lib., Harvard Univ. Family history is covered in detail by David E. Gulick, *Gulicks of the U. S. A.* (1961). The material on Gulick's work for the Federal Council of Churches to be found in its published reports and the *Federal Council Bull.* is illuminated by two works by Charles S. Macfarland: *Pioneers for Peace through Religion* (1946) and *Christian Unity in the Making* (1948). Gulick was the author of many books, pamphlets, and articles in addition to those mentioned above. Other sources: obituary in *N. Y. Times*, Dec. 24, 1945; personal information supplied by Prof. Edward Gulick of Wellesley College and Mr. and Mrs. John G. Barrow; death record from Idaho Dept. of Health.]

ROBERT S. SCHWANTES

GUNN, SELSKAR MICHAEL (May 25, 1883–Aug. 2, 1944), public health administrator, was born in London, England, one of four children of Michael Gunn, a theatrical manager, and Barbara Elizabeth (Johnston) Gunn. His unusual first name derived from a landmark in his ancestral Irish village of Wexford. Reared in England, Gunn attended Kensington Park College in London, 1896–1900. At the age of seventeen he came to the United States to study at the Massachusetts Institute of Technology, where he received the S.B. degree in biology in 1905. He later (1917) earned a certificate from the Harvard-Technology School for Health Officers. At M.I.T. he studied under William Thompson Sedgwick [*q.v.*], participating in the early public health investigations conducted at the Institute's Sanitary Research Laboratory and Sewage Experiment Station. Like many early students of sanitary science, Gunn began his career as a bacteriologist, working first at the Boston Bio-

Chemical Laboratory and then as assistant bacteriologist to the Iowa State Board of Health (1906–08).

Gunn's first experience with the broader problems of public health administration came when he accepted the position of health officer of Orange, N. J., in 1908. Disturbed by the number of tuberculosis cases that were never reported until after the patient died, he organized an unusual program for the detection of unidentified infection. Instead of relying on physicians' reports, he developed a cooperative campaign among the local branch of the National Tuberculosis Association, voluntary social work agencies, and the board of health. He joined with Dr. Charles V. Chapin [Supp. 3], health officer for Providence, R. I., in urging public health departments to make "scientific budgets," allocating their limited resources to the prevention of disease, rather than garbage collection and plumbing inspection.

Gunn returned to M.I.T. as an instructor in sanitary biology in 1910, retaining a particular interest in the organization of health services for cities. While he continued to teach until 1917 and was promoted to the rank of associate professor, he also found time to serve (1911) as sanitary consultant to the Milwaukee Bureau of Economy and Efficiency under the economist John R. Commons [Supp. 3]. Gunn's papers on milk, housing, communicable disease, and the organization of public health administration received national recognition.

Gunn was elected secretary of the American Public Health Association in 1912 and for the next five years served as managing editor and then editor of its *American Journal of Public Health*. At a time when the association was attempting to increase its membership and influence without sacrificing newly acquired professional standards, he succeeded in doubling the *Journal's* circulation. He was a member of the Massachusetts State Board of Labor and Industries, 1913–14, when it first undertook sanitary inspection of factories, and in 1915–16 was director of a pioneering Division of Hygiene in the reorganized Massachusetts Department of Health.

Gunn's energy, broad experience, and fluency in French led to his appointment, in the summer of 1917, as associate director of the Commission for the Prevention of Tuberculosis in France, sponsored jointly by the Rockefeller Foundation and the French government. The commission established a rural and an urban demonstration project, organized courses for French medical personnel, and, with the American Red Cross, equipped dispensaries throughout France. A survey of tuberculosis in the industrial cities of northern France, intended to augment existing public health services, was among the responsibilities assigned to Gunn. As the Foundation gradually turned over its program to French authorities, Gunn was sent in 1920 to Prague, as adviser to the new Czechoslovakian Ministry of Health. He returned to the Paris office of the Foundation in 1922, where he remained for the next ten years. Named associate regional director of the Rockefeller Foundation's International Health Division in 1925, he gave advice on the organization of health services throughout the continent. From 1927 to 1941 he was a vice-president of the Foundation.

Following a short visit to China in the summer of 1931, Gunn urged the Rockefeller Foundation to integrate its medical and public health services in that country with Chinese institutions, rather than establish enclaves of American scientific experts; the traditional, isolated, missionary approach, he felt, could stifle or disrupt native efforts to improve social and economic conditions. He put this policy into effect while personally guiding the Rockefeller Foundation's major commitment in China from 1932 to 1937. Although he recognized the political instability of the Nanking Kuomintang government, he pursued a program designed to lend authority to Chinese initiative in rural reconstruction, scientific and medical education, and public health.

With the outbreak of war in 1939, Gunn was again sent to France; he remained until six days before the Nazis overran Paris in 1940. Upon his return to the United States, the Rockefeller Foundation lent him to the National Health Council for a three-year survey of voluntary health agencies. He put this work aside for one year, in 1943, to direct the Office of Foreign Relief and Rehabilitation, predecessor to the United Nations Relief and Rehabilitation Administration.

Gunn's active career left him little time for writing. His reports to the Rockefeller Foundation, particularly on China, testify to his profound understanding of complex political and social issues and his imaginative adaptation of Western public health standards. His comprehensive study *Voluntary Health Agencies,* written with Philip S. Platt, was published posthumously in 1945. Versatile and fun-loving, Gunn also wrote a children's book, *The Doings of Dinkie* (1937). He was a Unitarian in religion. Gunn was married on Nov. 15, 1911, to Clara J. Coffin of East Orange, N. J., by whom he had a daughter, Barbara Mary (born 1916), his only child. Following a divorce (1930), he married the actress Carroll McComas in Shanghai on July 6, 1933.

He died of a coronary thrombosis at the age of sixty-one at his home in Newtown, Conn.

[Biographical material from *Who Was Who in America,* vol. II (1950); *N. Y. Times,* Aug. 3, 1944; *Nat. Cyc. Am. Biog.,* XXXIV, 319; *Technology Rev.* (Mass. Inst. of Technology), Jan. 1919, p. 47; and Rockefeller Foundation, *Annual Report,* 1944. Many of Gunn's early papers were reprinted in Mass. Inst. of Technology, *Contributions from the Sanitary Research Laboratory and Sewage Experiment Station,* 1905–14. On his work with the Rockefeller Foundation, see Raymond B. Fosdick, *The Story of the Rockefeller Foundation* (1952); "L'Oeuvre de la Commission Rockefeller pour la Lutte contre la Tuberculose," *Bull. de la Statistique Générale de la France,* Apr. 1922; Bernard L. Wyatt, *Rev. of the Work of the Medical Bureau of the Commission for the Prevention of Tuberculosis in France* (Paris, 1921), For a thorough evaluation of Gunn's important years in China, see James C. Thomson, Jr., *While China Faced West: Am. Reformers in Nationalist China, 1928–1937* (1969). Gunn's birth record (Gen. Register Office, London) gives his father's occupation.]
BARBARA GUTMANN ROSENKRANTZ

HANNA, EDWARD JOSEPH (July 21, 1860–July 10, 1944), Roman Catholic archbishop, was born in Rochester, N. Y., of Irish parents. His mother, Anne (Clark) Hanna, was a native of County Cavan. His father, Edward Hanna, had emigrated to the United States in 1837 from Newcastle, County Down, and settled in Rochester, where he soon prospered as a manufacturer of flour barrels. Edward was the first of their six children. He was educated in public and parochial schools and at the Rochester Free Academy, where he competed for honors with Walter Rauschenbusch [*q.v.*], the future Baptist theologian and proponent of the social gospel. Upon his graduation in 1879, having announced his intention to become a priest, Hanna was sent by Bishop Bernard McQuaid [*q.v.*] to Rome for his training. There he lived at the North American College and took courses at the Urban College of the Congregation of Propaganda. He was ordained in 1885, a year ahead of his class, and in 1886 received the D.D. degree.

Fluent in both Italian and Latin, Hanna stayed on in Rome for a year as a resident tutor at the North American College and a part-time faculty member at the Urban College before being recalled in 1887 by McQuaid. Back in Rochester, he was asked to minister to the new Italian immigrants working in the clothing industry; from this experience stemmed his later concern with social problems. He was also assigned to the preparatory seminary in Rochester as a teacher of classics. When St. Bernard's Seminary opened six years later, Hanna became its first professor of dogmatic theology, a position he occupied for the next nineteen years.

A progressive theologian who sought to relate Catholic doctrine to contemporary historical and critical thought, Hanna soon became embroiled in a painful controversy. In several articles published during the years 1905–07 he discussed such disputed points of doctrine as the completeness of Christ's human knowledge and the procedure for absolution of sins, examining them in the light of both tradition and historical development, and surveying heterodox arguments. In one of his essays (published in the Protestant *American Journal of Theology,* January 1906) he suggested that Catholic dogma had developed in stages, and that man's understanding of dogma was relative. Hanna did not, however, accept the position of the loosely organized Modernist movement within the Church, which held that the truth of dogma itself was relative. A Papal encyclical of 1907 condemned Modernism. That same summer Archbishop Patrick Riordan [*q.v.*] of San Francisco nominated Hanna as his coadjutor and successor. Vigorously endorsed by McQuaid, the appointment was about to receive the Vatican's approval when one of Hanna's colleagues at St. Bernard's Seminary sent a ringing protest to Rome challenging his orthodoxy. In spite of numerous testimonials in his favor, including Riordan's personal intervention, the Vatican declined to grant the promotion.

The Modernist controversy soon faded, and in 1912 the Vatican acceded to Riordan's request, though with the provision that Hanna be made auxiliary bishop, not coadjutor with right of succession. Upon Riordan's death in 1915, Hanna was nonetheless appointed archbishop of San Francisco, a post he held for twenty years. Under his administration, the Far West's largest Catholic archdiocese continued to grow. Forty-four parishes were added, thirty-four parochial schools, and eight high schools, and Hanna established two preparatory seminaries: St. Joseph's College to serve several Western and Pacific dioceses, and Maryknoll to train foreign missionaries.

Archbishop Hanna was one of the organizers of the National Catholic Welfare Council (later Conference), formed in 1919 by the American hierarchy to coordinate nationwide activities of the Church in the fields of education and social welfare, and to voice the stand of the Church on legislative questions. As chairman of its administrative committee until his retirement in 1935, Hanna was the executive head of the Conference, directing the work of John J. Burke [Supp. 2] as general secretary. Within California, Hanna took an active civic role. In 1913 he became a member, and in 1920, chairman, of the State Immigration and Housing Commission. As a member of the wage adjustment board of the building trades industry in San Francisco and chairman of the impartial wage board of San Francisco, he distinguished himself as a labor mediator, particularly by settling a building trades strike in 1921. During the depression he was a member of the National Citizens' Committee on Welfare and Relief Mobilization and chairman of the California State Committee on the Unemployed and of the State Emergency Committee. President Franklin D. Roosevelt appointed the archbishop chairman of the National Longshoremen's Arbitration Board in 1934.

Hanna's personality was exceptionally attractive. Students and colleagues found him unfailingly companionable, kindly, and considerate. In 1935, his health having begun to fail, he resigned his see. He retired to Rome, where he resided for the next nine years at the Villa San Francesco. Hanna died in Rome shortly before his eighty-fourth birthday; his remains were subsequently returned to San Francisco for interment in Holy Cross Cemetery. Among many honors, he had received in 1934 an honorary LL.D. from the University of California at Berkeley and in 1935 the American Hebrew Medal, presented annually to the person most eminent in promoting better understanding between Christians and Jews.

[Archives of the Congregation de Propaganda Fide, the Archdiocese of San Francisco, and the Diocese of Rochester; *Monitor* (San Francisco), Aug. 22, 1947; Robert F. McNamara in *Rochester Hist.*, Apr. 1963; obituary in *Catholic Action*, Aug. 1944; Thomas F. Millett in *New Catholic Encyc.*, VI, 914–15; personal information.]

JAMES P. GAFFEY

HANSON, JAMES CHRISTIAN MEIN-ICH (Mar. 13, 1864–Nov. 8, 1943), librarian, was born at Sørheim, a farm in the district of Nord-Aurdal in the Valdres valley of Norway. He was the second son and sixth of eight children of Gunnerius (or Gunnar) and Eleonore Adamine (Röberg) Hansen. His first name was originally Jens, but in America his playmates called him Jim, which was formalized as James, a change that he afterward regretted. The change in the spelling of his surname was gradual and inconsistent, but by 1897 he had adopted the invariable signature "J. C. M. Hanson." Hanson's father was a government official and a landowner, but the family was large and economic prospects in Norway poor. When Hans Röberg, a half brother of Hanson's mother who had settled in Decorah, Iowa, offered an education to one of the boys, nine-year-old Jens was chosen. He graduated, B.A., from Luther College in Decorah in 1882.

Two years at Concordia Seminary (Lutheran) in St. Louis, Mo., followed, but Hanson was not drawn to the ministry. Instead he moved to Chicago, where for four years he taught at a parochial school and an evening school for adult immigrants. In 1888 he enrolled as a graduate student in history at Cornell University in Ithaca, N. Y. Lack of money forced him to drop out after two years, and in 1890 he joined the staff of the recently organized Newberry Library in Chicago. Here he received basic training in librarianship under William Frederick Poole [*q.v.*] and his distinguished staff. In 1893 Hanson became head cataloguer at the University of Wisconsin Library.

Three years later, in September 1897, Hanson was called to the Library of Congress in Washington, D. C., as chief of its catalogue division. The library was about to move into its new building. Its catalogues were incomplete and not always accurate; the existing classification scheme was badly outgrown. Hanson undertook a complete bibliographic reorganization. This monumental task, begun during the brief administration of John Russell Young [*q.v.*] as Librarian of Congress and completed under his successor, Herbert Putnam, involved the devising of a new classification system for the library's 800,000 volumes and the creation of a new catalogue. Hanson always credited Charles Martel [Supp. 3], his assistant and successor, as the "chief architect" of the new classification, but the conception and the notation chosen were Hanson's. The new catalogue he decided to construct in card (rather than book) form; the size he chose for the cards has since become standard in libraries all over the world. The catalogue was to be arranged on the dictionary principle (specific entries in a single alphabetical sequence). In applying this principle to a collection of such unprecedented size and complexity, however, Hanson developed many expansions which became incorporated into the cataloguing rules. In the subject component of the catalogue, he introduced major modifications of the dictionary principle that are still evident in the widely used list of Library of Congress subject headings. When Herbert Putnam inaugurated the practice of printing and distributing copies of Library of Congress catalogue cards to other libraries, it was Hanson who planned their content and format to make them of maximum usefulness. The unprecedented standardization in cataloguing made possible by the availability of these cards virtually revolutionized the bibliographical organization of American libraries.

Hanson also provided vital leadership in the working out of a uniform code for library cataloguing. In 1900 the American Library Association set up a committee for this purpose, with

Hanson as chairman. Through extensive correspondence and discussion with other librarians he was successful in reconciling widely diverse views. In 1904, when the code was nearly complete, the committee was authorized to negotiate a joint code with the Library Association of Great Britain. Hanson's diplomacy, together with his wide knowledge of European as well as American library practices, brought agreement on an Anglo-American cataloguing code, published in 1908 as *Catalog Rules, Author and Title Entries*.

In 1910 Hanson moved to the University of Chicago as associate director of its libraries, which he reorganized to achieve bibliographical control in a highly decentralized system. When the Graduate Library School was established at the University of Chicago in 1928, he became a professor there. That same year he went to Italy, where he headed the team of American experts who assisted in the reorganization of the Vatican Library in Rome. After his return to Chicago, he taught until his retirement in 1934, when he went to live at his former summer home at Sister Bay, Wis.

Hanson has been described as a "blond giant," and his athletic prowess, particularly in baseball, was somewhat unusual for a librarian. His scholarship and erudition, including facility in sixteen languages, and the "bedrock" integrity of his character inspired respect; his kindliness, modesty, and generous spirit evoked the affection of his colleagues and students. Among the honors that came to him was appointment by the Crown of Norway as Commander of the Order of St. Olav, in 1928. On Nov. 26, 1892, Hanson married Sarah Nelson, who had been his pupil during his early years of teaching in Chicago. They had five children: Karl Burchard, Valborg Charlotte, Eleanore Bergliat, Thorfin Armand, and Harold Beck. Surviving his wife by seven years, Hanson died at Green Bay, Wis., in 1943 of peritonitis from a perforated duodenal ulcer. He was buried in the Lutheran cemetery at Ellison Bay, Wis.

[The two fullest published sources on Hanson are the Hanson "festschrift" number of the *Library Quart.*, Apr. 1934, which includes an authoritative biographical sketch by Pierce Butler, William Warner Bishop's "J. C. M. Hanson and Internat. Cataloging," and a bibliography of Hanson's publications up to that time; and Haynes McMullen's sketch in Emily Miller Danton, ed., *Pioneering Leaders in Librarianship* (1953). Hanson's publications after 1934 include a major work, *A Comparative Study of Cataloging Rules Based on the Anglo-American Code of 1908* (1939), and two articles that are frequently quoted: "Corporate Authorship Versus Title Entry," *Library Quart.*, Oct. 1935, and "Organization and Reorganization of Libraries," *ibid.*, July 1942. Collections of Hanson's papers are in the Luther College Lib., Decorah, Iowa, and the Univ. of Chicago Lib. The first collection includes a MS. autobiography; a copy is at the Univ. of Chicago. The Lib. of Cong. Archives include the reports of the Catalogue Dept. (Catalog Division after 1900) from 1897 to 1910 and other pertinent MS. materials. See also: obituary in *Library Jour.*, Dec. 1, 1943 (by Pierce Butler); the poignant personal tribute by J. Christian Bay in *Library Quart.*, Jan. 1944; *Nat. Cyc. Am. Biog.*, XXXIV, 131–32; *Who Was Who in America*, vol. II (1950); and Edith Scott, "J. C. M. Hanson and His Contribution to Twentieth-Century Cataloging" (Ph.D. dissertation, Univ. of Chicago, 1970).]

EDITH SCOTT

HANUS, PAUL HENRY (Mar. 14, 1855– Dec. 14, 1941), educator, was born at Hermsdorf unter dem Kynast, Upper Silesia, Prussia, the second son and youngest of three children of Gustav Hanus, owner of a small factory, and Ida (Aust) Hanus. After the death of her husband, Ida Hanus moved her family to Wisconsin in 1859 and married Robert George, a German-born mining engineer. Paul grew up chiefly in Mineral Point, Wis., with sojourns near Kingston, N. Y., and, during his teens, in Denver, Colo. He worked at various times as a druggist's apprentice, but his stepfather sympathized with his desire for more schooling and financed his studies first at the State Normal School at Platteville, Wis., and then at the University of Michigan. Energetic, ambitious, and a good student, Hanus found botany, zoology, geology, and mathematics the most exciting subjects. He received his B.S. degree in 1878.

Upon graduating, Hanus returned to Denver to teach in one of the city's high schools. The next year he became instructor in mathematics at the University of Colorado in Boulder, but left after a year and opened a drugstore in Denver. On Aug. 10, 1881, he married a former pupil, Charlotte Hoskins; they had one daughter, Winifred. That fall Hanus returned to the University of Colorado as professor of mathematics. He often spoke at teachers' institutes and by the mid-1880's discovered he was "much more interested in studying schools than . . . in studying mathematics." In 1886 he became the principal of a second high school in Denver, and in 1890, the first professor of pedagogy at the new Colorado State Normal School at Greeley.

As a trustee of the Unitarian church in Denver, Hanus had become acquainted with Samuel A. Eliot, its pastor, and had met his father, President Charles W. Eliot [q.v.] of Harvard. In 1891 Eliot called Hanus to Harvard to fill the university's first faculty position in the history and art of teaching. Eliot's purpose was not to establish education as a discipline within Harvard College, but rather to find an administrative coordinator for his current campaign to "reform and uplift"

American secondary education, and thereby bring more and better-prepared freshmen to Harvard. In addition, Eliot had agreed that Harvard should offer in-service courses for teachers in order to forestall the creation in Boston of a "high" normal school for training secondary teachers. The courses were not expected to interest regular Harvard students, nor was degree credit offered for them.

Hanus was relatively inexperienced in teaching education courses. The few other men who held university positions in education (or pedagogy) in 1891, like William H. Payne [q.v.] of Michigan, were steeped in the normal-school tradition and sought to deduce a "science of education" from the writings of the great educational philosophers of the past. Hanus, by contrast, was suspicious of deduction as a method and bored by history. His scientific and mathematical background had taught him the importance of exact data, of "facts" rather than "opinions." He began with somewhat conventional courses in the history of education, the "art of teaching," and the "theory of teaching." The theory course quickly revealed Hanus's commitment to the curriculum reforms Eliot advocated: a greater variety of subject offerings and the elimination of most requirements. From the beginning Hanus was supported by men like William James and Josiah Royce [qq.v.], but he met skepticism and even contempt from others on the faculty.

Throughout the 1890's Hanus participated in various phases of Harvard's school reform effort, and succeeded—over faculty opposition—in getting his courses accepted for regular credit. By 1900, however, his interests had begun to move in new directions. Turning away from teacher education as a primary activity, he concentrated instead on the training of school superintendents and on broader questions of educational policy. He now believed that the social aims of education took precedence over the cultural. The central social problem, in his view, was how schools could help adolescents adjust to the new industrial order. Believing that vocational identity and competence were the greatest needs of urban youths, Hanus became chairman of the Massachusetts Commission on Industrial Education in 1906 and advocated separate vocational schools untainted by academic biases. He also encouraged the vocational guidance movement in Boston and helped introduce instruction in that subject at Harvard in 1911.

Hanus's growing sense of his role as a professional educator—he founded the New England Association of College Teachers of Education and helped found the National Society of College Teachers of Education—reflected not only his concern for the social uses of education but also his preoccupation with the methods by which valid educational knowledge was produced. He argued that educators would never be respected as professionals unless their claims were based on incontrovertible data, and the effects of their methods were measurable in actual practice. Hanus was no psychologist, and hence could not participate in the research on learning and educational measurement which expanded so dramatically in the first decade of the century; his "moral equivalent" for such research was the school survey, an attempt to assess an entire school system's performance against the best available standards. He directed notable surveys of the New York City school system (1911–12) and of Hampton Institute, Hampton, Va. (1917–20).

The continuation of education courses at Harvard was assured in 1901 when Hanus was promoted from assistant professor to professor and thus given tenure, but he realized that his department had to grow rapidly to keep up with education departments elsewhere. In spite of the antagonism of A. Lawrence Lowell [Supp. 3], who succeeded Eliot in 1909, Hanus pressed for the creation of a separate professional faculty of education. His social and vocational emphases appealed to several wealthy businessmen who brought new funds to the department; and his friendship with Abraham Flexner of the General Education Board, forged during the New York and Hampton surveys, led eventually to the endowment of Harvard's Graduate School of Education in 1920. Hanus retired in 1921, embittered by Lowell's failure to make him honorary dean, thus recognizing him as the school's true founder.

Hanus had labored for three decades at Harvard, but Columbia and several other universities had larger and more powerful schools of education; he had published many books, but none had had the national impact of those of Ellwood Cubberley [Supp. 3], George Strayer, or other educators of his generation. Without a penetrating mind, a facile pen, or the personality skills to disarm suspicious Harvardians like Lowell, Hanus could not make the most of his opportunities; his main influence was extended through a small group of loyal students who became superintendents of schools. Hanus died of uremia in Cambridge in 1941, at the age of eighty-six. His remains were cremated and the ashes scattered. His life reveals the pattern by which a new profession was created faster than a reliable body of knowledge on which to base its claims.

[Hanus's papers are in the Harvard Univ. Archives. His major essays and speeches are collected in *Educational Aims and Educational Values* (1899), *A Modern School* (1904), *Beginnings in Industrial Education* (1908), and *School Administration and School Reports* (1920). The New York survey appeared in many volumes; Hanus's summary and interpretation is *School Efficiency: A Constructive Study Applied to N. Y. City* (1913). His most revealing book—an important document in American educational history— is his autobiography, *Adventuring in Education* (1937); it includes a photograph of him. Death record from Mass. Registrar of Vital Statistics. For a longer discussion of Hanus's role at Harvard, see Arthur G. Powell, "The Education of Educators at Harvard, 1891–1912," in Paul H. Buck, ed., *Social Sciences at Harvard, 1860–1920* (1965).]

ARTHUR G. POWELL

HAPGOOD, HUTCHINS (May 21, 1869– Nov. 18, 1944), newspaperman and author, was born in Chicago and reared in Alton, Ill. He was the second of the three sons and four children of Charles Hutchins Hapgood and Fanny Louise (Powers) Hapgood; Norman Hapgood [Supp. 2] was his older brother. Their father, a prosperous plow manufacturer and admirer of the freethinker Robert G. Ingersoll [q.v.], was a native of Petersham, Mass.; their mother, of New York City. Sensitive and introverted, Hutchins spent a year at the University of Michigan and then three years at Harvard, from which he graduated with honors in 1892. After a year and a half of world travel and casual study in Germany, he returned to Harvard, where he served for a year (1896–97) as assistant to Prof. George Pierce Baker [Supp. 1] and took an A.M. in 1897. That fall he became a reporter on the *New York Commercial Advertiser,* where his brother Norman was already employed. In June 1899 he married Neith Boyce, a journalist on the same paper. They had two sons, Boyce and Charles, followed by two daughters, Miriam and Beatrix.

As a staff member on the *Commercial Advertiser,* where city editor Lincoln Steffens [Supp. 2] had recruited a talented group of "personal journalists" to capture the drama and color of New York life, Hapgood wrote impressionistically of the varied and picturesque peoples of the city, including the "new immigrants" of the post-Civil War decades. In 1902 a selection of these articles appeared in book form as *The Spirit of the Ghetto.* In these vivid portraits of Jewish life on New York's Lower East Side (a life to which he had gained access through his friendship with Abraham Cahan, a fellow *Commercial Advertiser* reporter), Hapgood rejected both moralizing and stereotyping in favor of sharp and sensitive delineations of specific individuals. The work was illustrated by Jacob Epstein, then an unknown ghetto youth, who went on to a distinguished career as a sculptor.

The next several years brought a variety of activities and places of residence. Hapgood left the *Commercial Advertiser* in 1903 and, after several months in Italy, joined the *New York Morning Telegraph,* a paper specializing in sports news. About 1910, after an interval in Chicago as drama critic for the *Chicago Evening Post,* another stay in Italy, a year in Indianapolis as a salesman for a conserve company owned by his younger brother, William, and a stint as an editorial writer with Oswald Garrison Villard's New York *Evening Post,* he returned to the *New York Globe* (the old *Commercial Advertiser* under a new name), where he remained until 1914. His journalistic subjects were diverse: a "warm spring day, a French girl, a picture at Stieglitz's, an inspired bum in a saloon, a suffrage meeting, an interview with Bill Haywood, or a strike . . ." (*Victorian in the Modern World,* p. 285).

In this period Hapgood also produced *The Autobiography of a Thief* (1903), *The Spirit of Labor* (1907, in collaboration with Anton Johannsen, a radical workingman whom he had met in a bar), *An Anarchist Woman* (1909), and *Types from City Streets* (1910), another collection of newspaper vignettes. In 1912 he contributed an introduction to the *Prison Memoirs* of the anarchist Alexander Berkman [Supp. 2]. These books, as the titles suggest, drew heavily upon his friendships in radical and anarchist circles and reflected a desire to explain "the far-reaching revolutionary tendencies of the labor movement" (*ibid.,* p. 210). The Hapgoods lived at this time in Dobbs Ferry, N. Y., in a large house purchased for them by Hutchins Hapgood's father.

Increasingly, however, Hapgood's creative potential was dissipated. Involvement with artistic and bohemian circles, extended travels in Italy and France, and hours spent in romantic intrigues, late-night rambles, and barroom conversations with marginal people produced many rich friendships—with Josiah Flynt [see Josiah Flint Willard, Supp. 1], Emma Goldman [Supp. 2], Clarence Darrow [Supp. 2], Mabel Dodge, Bernard Berenson, Gertrude and Leo Stein— but little in the way of literary or journalistic accomplishment. Already in his forties, he was powerfully attracted by the youthful cultural revolt of the prewar years, with its emphasis on free, uninhibited self-expression. In 1915 he was one of the original Provincetown (Mass.) Players, thereby adding George Cram Cook [q.v.], Susan Glaspell, and Eugene O'Neill to his circle. He and his wife wrote and performed one of the group's early plays, *Enemies* (1916), a dialogue between a man and a woman. Meanwhile, politics and social movements touched him less and less. The turning inward occasioned by the death of his son Boyce in the influenza epidemic of 1918 merely accentuated a tendency already well under way. His anonymous *The Story of a Lover* (1919) expressed his intense, personal view of life and his mystic idealization of erotic experience.

Not steadily employed after 1914, Hutchins Hapgood found himself spiritually adrift following the First World War. In the conformist climate of the 1920's, it became clear that neither individual liberation nor working-class revolution could be counted upon to redeem American society as Hapgood had hoped. Though he could count numerous friends among old-time Progressives such as Lincoln Steffens and exemplars of the modern temper like Ernest Hemingway, their social and intellectual frames of reference provided him with neither new themes nor interested editors. In 1922 he sold the Dobbs Ferry house, and after two years in Europe the family divided its time between Provincetown, a summer place in Richmond, N. H., and Key West, Fla. Having speculated with his inheritance in the 1920's, Hapgood was left by the crash of 1929 "a man with many responsibilities, with a very small income that he was trying continually to augment by some spectacular literary success that never came" (*ibid.*, p. 538). Overshadowed all his life by his older brother, he was also outdistanced by Lincoln Steffens, whose *Autobiography* he sought to emulate with his own prolix *Victorian in the Modern World* (1939). Reviewers, weighing his memoirs in an era of social crisis, were generally gracious to the "unrepentant libertine" but tended to agree with his own harsh self-assessment: "I confess to having led a dissipated life, with women and drink—waste, waste, self-indulgence" (*ibid.*, p. 331). He died in Provincetown of a cerebral hemorrhage at the age of seventy-five; he was buried in the East Cemetery in Petersham, Mass. *The Spirit of the Ghetto* is Hutchins Hapgood's best-known book. In it, the group cohesion and sense of purpose of the community he was describing inspired an enduring portrait. His other combinations of art and journalism are also likely to serve students of the era and interest some readers.

[Hapgood's autobiography is a basic source. It is complemented by such memoirs as Mabel Dodge Luhan's *Movers and Shakers* (1936). See also: Moses Rischin's introduction to the John Harvard Library edition (1967) of Hapgood's *Spirit of the Ghetto,* which offers a specialized view of the author and his book; Hapgood's autobiographical sketch in Stanley J. Kunitz and Howard Haycraft, eds., *Twentieth Century Authors* (1942); *Who's Who in America,* various issues; and *N. Y. Times,* Nov. 19, 1944. Death record from Mass. Registrar of Vital Statistics. For Neith Boyce Hapgood, see Richard E. Banta, comp., *Ind. Authors and Their Books* (1949). Hapgood's papers are in the Yale Univ. Lib.]

LOUIS FILLER

HARDWICK, THOMAS WILLIAM (Dec. 9, 1872–Jan. 31, 1944), Congressman, Senator, governor of Georgia, was born in Thomasville, Ga., the younger of two sons of Robert William Hardwick, a planter, and Zemula Schley (Matthews) Hardwick. His father died when the boy was ten, and his mother moved to Tennille in Washington County, Ga., where his English forebears on both sides of the family had been pioneer settlers. He attended grammar school in Tennille and Gordon Institute in Barnesville, Ga., before graduating in 1892 from Mercer University. He then studied at the Lumpkin School of Law of the University of Georgia and, following graduation in 1893, established a practice in Sandersville, the seat of Washington County. From 1895 to 1897 he served as county prosecuting attorney.

Running as a conservative Democrat, opposed to the radical agrarianism of Thomas E. Watson [*q.v.*], Hardwick overcame stiff Populist opposition in 1898 to win a seat in the state house of representatives. There his support of railroad regulation and his pledge to disenfranchise the Negro laid the basis for an alliance with Watson, who in 1902 backed Hardwick in his successful bid for election to Congress. For the next eight years the two remained allies; in 1906, at the Democratic state convention, they overthrew the party's conservative faction and secured the nomination of a progressive, Hoke Smith [*q.v.*], for governor. In 1908, however, Watson, over Hardwick's objection, deserted Smith for the conservative Joseph M. Brown; and the alliance finally disintegrated in 1910 when Hardwick refused to appoint one of Watson's friends to a petty political office. Though Watson ran against him that year, Hardwick was returned to Congress, where, as a member of the House Rules Committee, he helped the Wilson administration enact the Clayton Anti-Trust Act, the Underwood Tariff, and the Federal Reserve Act.

With backing from Hoke Smith, Hardwick was elected in 1914 to complete the unexpired Senatorial term created by the death of Augustus O. Bacon [*q.v.*]. In the Senate, Hardwick became increasingly hostile to the Wilsonian program. He opposed the Keating-Owen Child

Labor Act and the Eighteenth Amendment. Though he voted, reluctantly, for the declaration of war in 1917, he considered the draft an attempt to "Prussianize" the country. He particularly objected to the extraordinary wartime powers granted to the president, and voted against the Food and Fuel Control Act, the Railroad Control Act, and the Espionage Act. When Hardwick sought reelection in 1918, President Wilson, in an open letter to Georgia voters, called him "a constant and active opponent of my administration." This letter contributed to Hardwick's overwhelming defeat by William J. Harris, an ardent Wilsonian and chairman of the Federal Trade Commission. During his final year in the Senate, Hardwick favored United States membership in the League of Nations but objected on constitutional grounds to participation in measures for collective security.

In 1920 Hardwick was elected governor of Georgia. His victory was based upon a new accord with Watson, whose disenchantment with Wilson, opposition to the League of Nations, and nativist views he shared. As governor, Hardwick established a state audit department, enacted the state's first gasoline tax, and recommended a graduated income tax in an effort to bolster Georgia's economy, which had sagged in the wake of the boll weevil's devastating destruction of cotton crops. Despite his nativist sympathies, Hardwick's abhorrence of violence brought him into conflict with a resurgent Ku Klux Klan. He publicly demanded that the Klan unmask, offered legal assistance to Klan victims, and recommended martial law to maintain order in areas where Klan terrorism prevailed. His attack upon the Klan brought about his defeat for reelection in 1922.

Hardwick made two unsuccessful bids to return to the Senate, running in 1922 against Walter F. George and in 1924 against William J. Harris. He placed third in the 1932 gubernatorial race, which was won by Eugene Talmadge. Between political campaigns Hardwick had resumed the practice of law in Washington, D. C., Atlanta, and Sandersville. He was twice married: on Apr. 25, 1894, to Maud Elizabeth Perkins, by whom he had a daughter, Mary; and in 1938, a year after the death of his first wife, to Sally Warren West. In religion, Hardwick was an Episcopalian. He died of a heart attack in Sandersville at the age of seventy-one and was buried there in the Old City Cemetery.

[The Thomas W. Hardwick Papers, in family hands, include his unfinished MS. "Recollections of Fifty Years," covering his career to 1914. Josephine Newsom Cummings used the papers for her M.A.

thesis, "Thomas William Hardwick" (Univ. of Ga., 1961). Alfred Edward Hicks, "Watson and Hardwick in Ga. Politics" (B.A. thesis, Trinity College, Hartford, 1967), is a detailed account of the alliances and antagonisms. See also C. Vann Woodward, *Tom Watson* (1938), and, for Hardwick's relations with Hoke Smith, Dewey W. Grantham, *Hoke Smith and the Politics of the New South* (1958). The Joseph M. Brown Collection (Univ. of Ga.) and the Joseph M. Brown Papers (Atlanta Hist. Soc.) bear on his relations with that political leader. Hardwick's opposition to Wilson's policies is treated in Arthur S. Link, *Wilson: The Struggle for Neutrality, 1914–1915* (1960), and Seward W. Livermore, *Politics Is Adjourned: Woodrow Wilson and the War Congress, 1916–1918* (1966); see also the *N. Y. Times,* July 26, 1917. His major gubernatorial recommendations are found in the appropriate volume of the *Ga. Governors' Addresses*. See also *Biog. Directory Am. Cong.* (1961); *Nat. Cyc. Am. Biog.,* Current Vol. B, pp. 296–97; *Atlanta Constitution,* Feb. 1, 2, 1944.]

WILLIAM M. GABARD

HARRINGTON, JOHN LYLE (Dec. 7, 1868–May 20, 1942), civil and mechanical engineer, bridge designer, was born in Lawrence, Kans., the second son and second of at least five children of Robert Charles and Angeline Virginia (Henry) Harrington. His father was a descendant of James Harrington, who emigrated from England in the latter part of the eighteenth century and settled in Binghamton, N. Y. Robert Harrington had served in the Civil War with an Illinois regiment before moving to Kansas, where he became a farmer and, for a time, a merchant near Lawrence. About 1877 the family moved to a new farm in neighboring Johnson County, near De Soto. Young Harrington early demonstrated the drive and initiative that were to characterize his career. Though his formal education in grade and secondary schools totaled no more than four years, he read widely and purposefully, and at twenty-two he was admitted to the University of Kansas by examination. He worked his way through college, yet managed to enjoy an active social life as a member of Sigma Nu fraternity and to do enough work in arts, science, and engineering to graduate in 1895 with honors and with three degrees: B.S., A.B., and C.E.

While in college Harrington had spent two summers working in the office of the noted bridge engineer John Alexander Low Waddell [Supp. 2] in Kansas City, Mo. During the twelve years after his graduation, in keeping with his habit of systematic self-education, he took a succession of jobs with bridge, steel, railroad, and construction firms in various parts of the country, staying only long enough at each to absorb the experience he felt was useful. (While with a Montreal company he earned the degrees of B.S. and M.S. from McGill University.) In 1907 he returned to Kansas City, where for the next thirty-five years he was a consulting engineer specializing in bridges: from 1907 to 1914 as a junior partner with Waddell, from 1914 to 1928 as senior partner with Ernest E. Howard and Louis R. Ash, and after 1928 as senior partner with Frank M. Cortelyou. To this work Harrington brought not only a thorough background in civil engineering, but also experience in mechanical engineering gained while employed by the C. W. Hunt Company in New York City from 1901 to 1905. From 1907 to 1932 he was involved in the design and usually also the construction of more than 225 bridges, including six across the Mississippi, four across the Missouri, and others across such major waterways as the Columbia, the Colorado, the Don in Russia, and the Yalu in Manchuria.

Nearly half of Harrington's bridges were movable types (vertical lift, bascule, and swing), for which sound mechanical engineering was vital, but his most important accomplishment was the development of the vertical lift bridge from the basic invention of J. A. L. Waddell. In this type of bridge an entire span is raised and lowered vertically by cables running over sheaves in towers at both ends. Counterweights in each tower exactly balance the moving bridge section, very much as in a counterweighted window. Waddell's South Halsted Street bridge in Chicago, built in 1893, had all the basic features of the type in its modern form. But Waddell was not a mechanical engineer and the bridge was not completely successful; no others were built until Harrington joined the partnership fourteen years later, bringing the mechanical engineering skill to develop Waddell's invention into a rational, well-integrated design. His success with the vertical lift bridge caused it to replace the bascule (or drawbridge) where wider channels were required for navigation. The achievement was unfortunately marred by a controversy between the two men which because of Harrington's inflexibility and Waddell's vanity left a legacy of bad feeling on both sides.

Harrington was dedicated to his profession. He was active in the American Society of Mechanical Engineers, serving as president in 1923, and from 1926 to 1932 he was a member of the American Engineering Council, an organization devoted to bringing the engineer's knowledge to the service of government. In the midst of his public service his reputation suffered a reverse. Finding himself in debt as the result of some land speculations, Harrington may have been tempted to spread himself too thin in the highway bridge construction boom of the later 1920's. By 1927 he was involved in the design or construction of more than thirty bridges at one time. Two accidents indicate that even Harrington's incredible drive and energy

were not sufficient for this task. In September 1927 one span of his bridge across the Mississippi at Louisiana, Mo., collapsed while under construction, with the loss of one life, owing to the failure of temporary timber props. In June 1928 his newly completed bridge across the Colorado at Blythe, Calif., failed when a flood damaged the piers on which the bridge rested. After this time he built few bridges, but his profession did not forget his outstanding earlier accomplishments. In 1930 he received an honorary doctorate in engineering from the Case School of Applied Science, and President Hoover appointed him in 1932 to the Engineers Advisory Board of the Reconstruction Finance Corporation.

Harrington had married Daisy June Orton of White Cloud, Kans., a graduate (in music) of the University of Kansas, on June 21, 1899. They had one son, Thomas Orton Harrington. Rather reserved, Harrington had few intimates. He was a Republican and a Presbyterian and was for many years a trustee of Robert College in Turkey. In 1937 he suffered a stroke; a third stroke in 1942 caused his death. He died in Kansas City and was buried there in Forest Hill Cemetery.

[The best published biographical accounts are the obituary by Frank M. Cortelyou et al. in Am. Soc. of Civil Engineers, *Transactions*, CVII (1942), 1768–72; the sketch (apparently autobiographical) in *Nat. Cyc. Am. Biog.*, Current Vol. A, pp. 459–60; and Neil M. Clark in *American Mag.*, Feb. 1925. Mr. Frank M. Cortelyou also provided important information (correspondence now in Western Hist. Manuscript Collection, Univ. of Mo.). See also: Am. Soc. of Mechanical Engineers, *Transactions*, XLV (1923), 1–2 (with photograph); *Who's Who in Engineering* (5th ed., 1941); obituary in *N. Y. Times*, May 21, 1942. Harrington's writings include: "Recent Developments in Bridge Superstructures," Engineers' Soc. of Western Pa., *Proc.*, Mar. 1939 (his own assessment of his work on the vertical lift bridge); his contributions to the volume he edited with J. A. L. Waddell, *Addresses to Engineering Students* (1911); and his presidential address to the Am. Soc. of Mechanical Engineers in its *Transactions*, XLV (1923), 257–69, which expresses his professional philosophy. Ernest E. Howard, "Vertical Lift Bridges" and "Discussion on Vertical Lift Bridges," Am. Soc. of Civil Engineers, *Transactions*, LXXXIV (1921), 580–695, includes an evaluation of Harrington's work. On his bridge failures, see *Engineering News-Record*, Sept. 29, 1927, pp. 523–24, and Oct. 31, 1929, pp. 683–84. The Kans. State Hist. Soc., Topeka, provided data from census listings of the Robert C. Harrington family, 1870–85.]
EDWIN LAYTON

HARRIS, SAM HENRY (Feb. 3, 1872–July 3, 1941), theatrical producer, was born on the Lower East Side of New York City, the son of Max Harris, who owned a tailor shop where the family lived, and his wife, Sara (or Lena) Lippman. Both parents were Jewish immigrants, the father from Poland, the mother from Germany. Sam quit school at an early age and tried his hand at a wide assortment of jobs including delivering hats, selling cough drops, acting as messenger for a telegraph company, and collecting commissions for supplying towels and soap to office buildings. Drawn to show business, by seventeen he had become a stagehand in Miner's Bowery Theatre. At the same time he inaugurated his lifelong interest in gambling and sports by promoting young prizefighters. When his second fighter, Terry McGovern, won the bantamweight championship of the world in September 1899, Harris joined with a booking agent, Samuel A. Scribner, to star McGovern in a successful burlesque, *The Gay Morning Glories*.

Harris next joined the producers Al (Albert H.) Woods and Patrick H. Sullivan in the new firm of Sullivan, Harris, and Woods, purveyors of 10-20-30-cent melodramas and burlesques. They brought some eight plays to the stage from 1900 to 1904, including *The Road to Ruin, The Bowery after Dark* (again starring McGovern), and—their biggest hit—*The Fatal Wedding*. The producing team broke up in 1904. In the spring of that year, at a picnic shortly after their first meeting, Sam Harris and George M. Cohan [Supp. 3] cemented with a handshake a notable partnership. Neither man had much money, but they had enthusiasm and a sense of showmanship. Their first production was Cohan's own musical, *Little Johnny Jones* (1904). In the chorus were two sisters from Brookline, Mass., Agnes and Alice Nolan. Cohan married Agnes in 1907. On Mar. 2, 1908, at Long Branch, N. J., Harris married Alice Nolan. (This was his second marriage, the first having ended in divorce in 1907.) Alice died in 1930, and on Mar. 19, 1939, Harris married Mrs. Kathleen ("China") Nolan Watson. He had no children by any of his marriages.

During their sixteen-year association Cohan and Harris produced more than fifty plays; in addition they owned theatres in several cities, had five companies on the road at one point, owned a music publishing firm, and even ran their own minstrel show. In 1920, the year after the Actors' Equity Association called its successful strike against the Producing Managers' Association, of which Harris was president, the famous partnership came to en end. Speculation as to the cause was rife. Perhaps the impulsive Cohan in his frustration actually intended to carry out the threat he had made time and again: if Equity won he would never produce another play. There was no animosity in the parting. The two men remained warm friends and even worked together later, joining finally to produce *Fulton of Oak Falls* in 1937.

After the split Harris began the most success-ful segment of his career. The roster of more than fifty plays he produced from 1920 until his death reads like a list of hits. It includes *Rain* (1922), starring Jeanne Eagels [q.v.]; *Cradle Snatchers* (1925), with Mary Boland, Edna May Oliver, and Humphrey Bogart; *The Jazz Singer* (1925), in which George Jessel portrayed a Jewish cantor's son who chose to sing in the theatre rather than the synagogue; *The Cocoanuts* (1925) and *Animal Crackers* (1928), musical comedies featuring the four Marx Brothers; *Dinner at Eight* (1932), a drama by George S. Kaufman and Edna Ferber; *As Thousands Cheer* (1933), a musical revue by Irving Berlin and Moss Hart with a cast headed by Marilyn Miller, Clifton Webb, Helen Broderick, and Ethel Waters; *Night Must Fall* (1936), a psychological melodrama; *Stage Door* (1936), a comedy by Kaufman and Ferber; *I'd Rather Be Right* (1937), starring Cohan; *The Man Who Came to Dinner* (1939), a comedy with Monty Woolley cast as Sheridan Whiteside, a "friendly cartoon" of Alexander Woollcott [Supp. 3]; and *Lady in the Dark* (1941), a musical play starring Gertrude Lawrence. Toward the end of Harris's career, George S. Kaufman and Moss Hart were his unofficial partners. In 1921 he built the Music Box Theatre with Irving Berlin and Joseph Schenck, and here many of his biggest hits were presented, including the *Music Box Revues*. Three of his productions won Pulitzer Prizes: Owen Davis's *Icebound* (1923); *Of Thee I Sing* (1932), a musical comedy with a score by George Gershwin [Supp. 2]; and Kaufman and Hart's comedy *You Can't Take It with You* (1937). His production of John Steinbeck's *Of Mice and Men* won the New York Drama Critics Circle award in 1938.

Harris formed a syndicate to buy the Lyceum Theatre in New York in 1940, although by that time he had sold most of his theatres to the Shuberts. Despite the loss of some two million dollars in the stock market crash of 1929, he was able to continue his work in the theatre during the depression and, indeed, to provide help for others—as vice-president of the Jewish Theatrical Guild, as a member of the Stage Relief Fund, as donor of scholarships to the Theatre Guild's school of acting, and as producer, in Palm Beach, Fla., of a number of benefits for underprivileged children. Sam Harris died of cancer in his apartment in the Ritz Tower Hotel in New York City at the age of sixty-nine and was buried in Woodlawn Cemetery in the Bronx.

As a man, Harris was quiet, generous, and honest—the "last of the handclasp managers," Cohan called him. As a producer, he preferred comedy to tragedy and liked musical shows best of all. He felt the playwright to be especially important, and with him selected the director and the designer and participated in casting. He never sat in on rehearsals until just before a production opened, and then he helped with final changes. All of this may have resulted, as Max Gordon suggests, in the public knowing that Harris's name on a show stood for "impeccable taste, shrewd showmanship, and something called, for lack of a better word, 'class.'"

[The largest collection of material concerning Sam H. Harris is in the Theatre Collection of the N. Y. Public Lib. at Lincoln Center, which has portfolios of clippings and photographs covering all of his career and a collection of programs. The Sam H. Harris Collection at the Princeton Univ. Lib. has 131 bound typescripts of plays produced by him (none of them annotated) and a few letters. Useful articles about Harris appeared in the N. Y. *Dramatic Mirror*, May 26, 1917, *American Mag.*, May 1922, and *Theatre Arts Monthly*, Oct. 1938; see also obituaries in *N. Y. Times*, *N. Y. Herald Tribune*, and *PM*, July 4, 1941. Most books dealing with the theatre of the last fifty years contain references to Harris; see especially Ward Morehouse, *George M. Cohan* (1943) and *Matinee Tomorrow* (1949), and Max Gordon, *Max Gordon Presents* (1963). Marriage record (to Alice Nolan) from N. J. State Dept. of Health. Harris's death certificate gives his parents' names as Marks Harris and Lena Lippman; other accounts have Max and Sara.]

JULIAN MATES

HARRISON, BYRON PATTON (Aug. 29, 1881–June 22, 1941), Congressman and Senator from Mississippi, the first of four children of Robert and Myra Anna (Patton) Harrison, was born at Crystal Springs, Copiah County, in southwest Mississippi. Through his father he was descended from the Virginia Harrisons and was distantly related to Presidents William Henry and Benjamin Harrison. Robert Harrison died before his eldest child had reached his seventh birthday, and the boy early had to help supplement the family income by hawking newspapers and driving a two-mule carryall. After attending public school, he enrolled in Mississippi State College for a brief period and in 1899–1900 attended Louisiana State University, where he gained recognition as a pitcher on the baseball team; for a time after leaving college, he played semiprofessional baseball in Mississippi. Later he taught school in Leakesville, Greene County, during which time he studied law and was admitted to the bar in 1902. He married Mary Edwina McInnis of Leakesville on Jan. 19, 1905. They had three children: Catherine, Mary Ann, and Byron Patton.

Harrison's political career began in 1906, when he was elected to the first of two terms as district attorney of the newly created second judicial district of Mississippi. Two years later he moved

to Gulfport, where he was chosen a delegate to the Democratic National Convention; and in 1910, now familiarly known as "Pat," he was elected to Congress from Mississippi's 6th district. He remained in the House for four terms and proved a loyal supporter of President Wilson. For more than a decade the Democratic party in Mississippi was split between factions headed by Senators John Sharp Williams and James K. Vardaman [*qq.v.*]. In 1918, with Vardaman's influence waning, Harrison, backed by Williams, made a direct challenge for Vardaman's Senate seat in the Democratic primary. Vardaman had opposed Wilson in both domestic and foreign measures and was branded by the President as one of "the little group of willful men" who had filibustered against the Armed Neutrality Bill. At the climax of the primary campaign, Wilson issued a public appeal to Mississippi voters to defeat Vardaman, an appeal generally credited as the decisive factor in Harrison's narrow victory.

As a freshman Senator, Harrison advocated America's entry into the League of Nations and, afterward, into the World Court. He gained national prominence during the Republican ascendancy of the 1920's by his skillful badgering of the executive branch for its failures and blunders, and soon won a place of leadership in Democratic councils. He was selected temporary chairman of the party's national convention of 1924, where he delivered the keynote address. Four years later he courageously campaigned for Alfred E. Smith [Supp. 3] in the presidential campaign when many Southern politicians feared to do so, and after the humiliating Democratic defeat, Harrison was one of the leaders who undertook the job of rebuilding the shattered party. In 1930, as in 1924, he was reelected without opposition. Although himself a conservative Southerner, he was an early supporter of the candidacy of Franklin D. Roosevelt. In the Democratic victory of 1932 the party won control of both houses of Congress, and Harrison, who had been the ranking Democrat on the powerful Finance Committee, moved to the chairmanship.

In this post Harrison demonstrated skill at pushing early New Deal legislation through Congress. When Vice-President John Nance Garner and majority leader Joseph T. Robinson [Supp. 2] had a piece of legislation they wanted to be sure would reach the floor, they routed it through the Finance Committee, whose membership had been largely selected by Harrison himself. Thus the National Industrial Recovery Act, the bill to legalize the sale of light wines and beer, and parts of the original Agricultural Adjustment

Act were virtually "horse-traded" through the Senate by Harrison. Because he was on good terms with all factions of his own party as well as with the Republicans, he had little trouble persuading his colleagues to follow his lead. Despite his private reservations, for example, he maneuvered the administration's undistributed corporate profits tax through a reluctant Senate in 1936. But Harrison's economic views remained closer to those of his friend and supporter Bernard Baruch than to those of F.D.R.; and in 1938, when the administration agreed to a slight reduction of the tax, Harrison echoed Baruch's demand for complete repeal, settling finally for rates much lower than the President had suggested. The tax was repealed the following year. By this time Harrison's formerly close relations with Roosevelt had become strained. After the death of Senator Robinson in July 1937, when Harrison and Senator Alben W. Barkley of Kentucky actively sought the post of majority leader, Roosevelt gave his support to the more liberal Barkley, thus assuring the Kentuckian's one-vote victory in the Democratic caucus.

Harrison did not openly break with the New Deal, but he was now free to follow his conscience in opposing many administration programs he would have had to endorse as Senate Democratic leader. Besides his stand on the profits tax, he was a leader of the filibuster which blocked an antilynching bill in 1938. He nonetheless refused to sign a bipartisan manifesto denouncing New Deal spending and interference with private enterprise in December 1937; he worked tirelessly for the reciprocal trade agreements program; and he supported Roosevelt's plan to reorganize the executive department in 1939. On the death of Senator Key Pittman [Supp. 2] and with the President's blessing, Harrison was elected president pro tempore of the Senate in January 1941. During that same year he was largely responsible for preventing a filibuster designed to block the Lend-Lease bill for military aid to Great Britain.

A tall and loose-jointed figure, bald and beak-nosed, Harrison was careless of dress but had an amiable disposition and courtly manner. In debate, his sallies were marked by good humor and witticisms that stung but left no scars, and he was widely popular both in and out of Congress. As much as he could, he avoided the social life of the capital. He had accumulated a fortune of about a half-million dollars in the 1920's through real estate speculation around Gulfport, but lost it in the depression of the 1930's.

In the winter of 1940–41 it was apparent to his colleagues that Harrison's health was failing.

In April he entered an Arkansas hospital suffering from fatigue. His illness took a new turn in mid-June when he underwent an emergency operation for an intestinal obstruction at Washington's Emergency Hospital, and he died six days later. After Methodist services in Gulfport, Miss., attended by Vice-President Henry A. Wallace, Secretary of the Treasury Henry Morgenthau, Jr., and a host of colleagues, he was buried in Evergreen Cemetery in Gulfport. Although he lacked the dynamic and intellectual qualities of a truly great political leader, Harrison was a skillful parliamentarian and a persuasive pleader. He was one of the most popular men ever to serve in public life in Mississippi.

[Miss. State Univ. has a small collection of Harrison's papers. There are letters to and from him in the following collections: John Sharp Williams Papers and Woodrow Wilson Papers, Lib. of Cong.; the John Joshua Coman Papers, Henrietta (Mitchell) Henry Papers, Dennis Murphree Papers, and Oscar Bomar Taylor Papers, all in the Miss. Dept. of Archives and Hist. at Jackson; and a few of his letters in the William Neyle Colquitt Papers, Duke Univ., and the Charles M. Hay Papers in the Western Hist. Manuscript Collection at the Univ. of Mo. There are vital data in: *Biog. Directory Am. Cong.* (1961); *Who Was Who in America*, vol. I (1942); and 77 Cong., 2 Sess., *Memorial Services . . . Byron Patton Harrison* (1944). For contemporary comment see *Newsweek*, May 11, 1935, p. 20, Dec. 13, 1937, p. 14; *Outlook*, Aug. 5, 1931, pp. 430–32; *Saturday Evening Post*, Apr. 21, 1923, p. 27. There are many data in various Mississippi newspapers, especially the *Jackson Clarion-Ledger*, May 18, 19, June 8, 1916, Aug. 2, 16, 24, 1917; *Vicksburg Post*, Aug. 25, 1917; *Vicksburg Herald*, various issues, June 1918; *Jackson Issue*, spring and summer 1918. For obituary and career analysis see *N. Y. Times*, June 23, 1941. See also William S. Coker, "Pat Harrison: The Formative Years," and "Pat Harrison—Strategy for Victory," *Jour. of Miss. Hist.*, Oct. 1963 and Nov. 1966; James T. Patterson, *Congressional Conservatism and the New Deal* (1967); Albert D. Kirwan, *Revolt of the Rednecks: Miss. Politics, 1876–1925* (1951); and Allan A. Michie and Frank Ryhlick, *Dixie Demagogues* (1939), a somewhat biased account.]

ALBERT D. KIRWAN

HARRISON, PAT. See HARRISON, BYRON PATTON.

HART, ALBERT BUSHNELL (July 1, 1854–June 16, 1943), historian, was born at Clarksville (now Clark), Mercer County, Pa., the third son and fourth of five children of Albert Gaillard (or Gailord) Hart, a physician, and Mary Crosby (Hornell) Hart. His father was a descendant of Stephen Hart of Ipswich, England, an early settler of Cambridge, Mass., whose great-grandson, Gad Hart, had moved from Connecticut to the Western Reserve section of Ohio in 1804. Gad's son Ambrose married Lovicy Bushnell of Hartland, Conn.; their son was the historian's father. On his mother's side he was fifth in descent from the Rev. Nils or Nicholas Hornell, a Swedish Lutheran minister who settled in

York, Pa., in 1763. The Harts were staunch Congregationalists. Dr. Hart, a graduate of Western Reserve College, moved across the border into Pennsylvania to begin his medical practice at Clarksville; there he also acquired a dam and gristmill and became an abolitionist, attending the 1848 Free Soil party convention. In 1860 he removed to Hartford, Trumbull County, Ohio, and in 1864 to Cleveland, where he became a prominent citizen. For three years during the Civil War he served as an army surgeon. The strong Union sentiment of that time remained with Albert Bushnell Hart all his life.

After public grade schooling and two years at the private Humiston's Cleveland Institute, Albert B. Hart entered the city's West High School and graduated with distinction in 1871. Following the lead of his older brother Hastings H. Hart [Supp. 1], later a social worker, he went to work as bookkeeper for a Cleveland firm. The turning point of his career came in 1873–74 when he traveled in the East and was fascinated by Boston and Cambridge. Encouraged by his high school teachers and pastor, he tried for Harvard and after a year's preparation passed the entrance examinations with honors in 1876. Although several years older than most of his Harvard classmates and of a different background, he made many friends, notably his fellow student Theodore Roosevelt, and contributed articles to the *Advocate,* the college literary journal, becoming its chief editor. He made Phi Beta Kappa, graduated summa cum laude, and was chosen by his classmates to deliver the Ivy Oration of 1880.

Hart studied history under Ephraim Emerton [Supp. 1] and Henry W. Torrey, but he found his greatest inspiration from a course on the history of the fine arts given by Charles Eliot Norton [*q.v.*], who in 1879 urged Hart to make history his profession. After spending one postgraduate year at Harvard, he proceeded to Europe, where at the University of Freiburg in Baden he took the famous seminar in American history of Hermann von Holst [*q.v.*] and received his Ph.D. in 1883. His dissertation, *The Coercive Powers of the Government of the United States of America* (1885), he later enlarged and published as *Introduction to the Study of Federal Government* (1891). He also spent several months in Paris, where he studied government and history at the École des Sciences Politiques.

Upon his return to Cambridge in search of a job, Hart's breezy manner and aggressive personality were viewed dubiously by some of the older Harvard historians; but President Charles W. Eliot [*q.v.*] wanted a "go-getter" to put American history on its academic feet and in 1883

appointed him an instructor. In his hands the general course for undergraduates on American political and constitutional history, known as History 13, became an institution, one that most undergraduates chose and which they always enjoyed, although it was not easy. His pupils included many who chose history for a career, besides many future Senators and governors and a future president, Franklin D. Roosevelt. His other courses included American diplomatic history and political theory.

Hart was a great lecturer and teacher, which President Eliot recognized by promoting him to assistant professor in 1887 and full professor ten years later. He organized his courses well, supplying students with an *Outline* (1884), followed by syllabi such as *Topics and References* (1893), and finally with a substantial *Manual of American History, Diplomacy and Government* (1908), stating which lecture came when, and giving ample references for general reading and special studies. His notes for History 13, which became more and more voluminous, were carried across the college yard from his office by a perspiring assistant and stacked on his desk in the lecture hall. Sometimes he lectured completely ad lib, more frequently he leafed through the notes, producing extracts to read aloud; and the students frequently rewarded his eloquence and wit by applause, which he relished.

The only German method that Hart used was the seminar for graduate students. This he conducted jointly with his colleague Edward Channing [Supp. 1] during the decade of the 1890's, after which they separated, but not before publishing the Channing and Hart *Guide to the Study of American History* (1896). This was enlarged to the Channing, Hart, and Turner *Guide* (1912) after Frederick J. Turner [*q.v.*] had joined the faculty and to the *Harvard Guide* (1954) by their successors. The early *Guides* had an immense influence throughout the United States at a period when the teaching and study of American history were rapidly expanding. Hart also wrote the biography *Salmon Portland Chase* (1899) in the American Statesmen series, *Essentials in American History* (1905), a popular textbook, and *American History Told by Contemporaries* (5 vols., 1897–1929). This last was a pioneer in the field of American history "readers," an excellent anthology of personal narratives, poetry, novels, etc. These books, in addition to the American Nation series (see below), gave Hart a national reputation; and after being an editor of the *American Historical Review* for fourteen years, he was elected president of the American Historical Association in 1909.

From that time on, Hart was often called "The Grand Old Man" of American history; to have been his pupil was enough recommendation for a young scholar to a university post. He had superb presence (the modest hirsute adornment of the college senior developing into a patriarchal full beard and flowing moustaches), a sonorous voice, and impressive diction, qualities which made him a favorite speaker for all manner of civic and patriotic occasions. He was a great "joiner," belonging to most of the historical societies of New England and many of the Middle West, and to the Loyal Order of the Moose.

As an editor of historical works, Hart was most significant. His first important editorial work was the Epochs of American History series, three volumes (1891–93), of which he wrote *Formation of the Union* and persuaded Prof. Woodrow Wilson of Princeton to write *Division and Reunion.* His greatest editorial accomplishment was the American Nation series (published in the years 1904–07), which in twenty-five chronological and topical volumes (followed by three supplementary ones) gave a comprehensive survey of the whole of American history. This superb series owed its unique value to the fact that it was written by the first generation of American professional historians. Several of the volumes, among them Hart's own *Slavery and Abolition,* broke new ground; and some have never been superseded. Hart was a tough, rigorous editor, blue-penciling texts liberally and enforcing deadlines. He had planned an American biographical dictionary, but amiably stood aside when the American Council of Learned Societies undertook to sponsor the *Dictionary of American Biography.* In later years he edited an excellent five-volume *Commonwealth History of Massachusetts* (1927–30).

In 1910, the year before government separated from history in the Harvard faculty structure, Hart succeeded A. Lawrence Lowell [Supp. 3] as Eaton Professor of Government. As such he carried on, giving popular courses and seminars on American government and diplomatic history, until his retirement in 1926. His eminence in this field led to his election as president of the American Political Science Association in 1912, and with Andrew C. McLaughlin he edited the *Cyclopaedia of American Government* (3 vols., 1914). He received honorary degrees from several American universities, and from the University of Geneva.

In the meantime, Hart had been writing many articles and short books, and delivering many lectures. For fifteen years (1910–19, 1926–32) he edited the *American Year Book,* and with Channing he started in 1892 the American History Leaflets, presenting important documents in compact form with scholarly introductions. He also edited a series of wall maps of American history; and the maps compiled for the American Nation series, at a time when there was no such thing as an American historical atlas, were later republished as *Harper's Atlas of American History* (1920). In a word, Hart was one of those rare scholars who had a genius for popularization.

Hart took an active role in politics and supported many good causes. He served on the Cambridge School Committee and became a useful member of the Massachusetts Constitutional Convention of 1917. As a delegate to the Republican national convention of 1912 he ardently supported the candidature of his friend Theodore Roosevelt, and with him seceded to form the Progressive party; in 1916 he sadly followed his leader back into the Republican fold. He traveled far and wide on his sabbaticals, on one occasion around the world, and on another, following the example of Frederick Law Olmsted [q.v.], through the backcountry of the South from Texas to North Carolina. These two journeys were described in letters to newspapers, some of which subsequently appeared as books: *The Obvious Orient* (1911) and *The Southern South* (1910). Hart's interest in Negro advancement (one of his pupils was W. E. B. DuBois) led to his being elected a trustee of Howard University.

Hart had married, on July 11, 1889, Mary Hurd Putnam of Manchester, N. H., who died in 1924. They had no children of their own but adopted twin boys, Albert Bushnell and Adrian Putnam. About the year 1935 Hart began to decline, and his last years were lonely and unhappy. His sons were a disappointment, and moved away. Most of his friends and contemporaries were dead. Students regarded him as a sort of Rip Van Winkle; he wandered aimlessly through the stacks of Harvard's Widener Library like a bearded ghost. Death (of myocarditis) came as a release in 1943, shortly before his eighty-ninth birthday. He died in the McLean Hospital, Belmont, Mass., and was buried, after Congregational services, in the Cambridge city cemetery.

As a historian, Hart belonged to the political and constitutional school, although he was friendly and hospitable to the rising generation of social historians. Brought up, like most American historians of the time, in the New England Federalist-Whig-Republican tradition, he nevertheless took an intense interest in the South and West, and believed ardently in the Jeffersonian heritage. As a prose writer he was clear and forceful, but hardly elegant; as an editor he was superb, pruning excrescences and altering phrases for the better. "At the end of fifty years," wrote Hart in his Harvard class report in 1930, "I have the satisfaction of believing that I was one of a group of young men who made history and government vital subjects for college and graduate school." That indeed was his greatest achievement —making American history, in particular, a respected academic subject, and providing the books, manuals, and printed sources so that it could be properly taught in any high school or college. He influenced for good the lives of countless men and women to whom he taught love of country, based on a sound knowledge of their country's past. He may be said to have been an educational counterpart to his friend Theodore Roosevelt in building the moral strength of American democracy.

[For biographical data see: memoir by Clifford K. Shipton in Am. Antiquarian Soc., *Proc.,* 1943, pp. 120–25; Lester J. Cappon, "Channing and Hart: Partners in Bibliog.," *New England Quart.,* Sept. 1956; tribute by S. E. Morison in Mass. Hist. Soc., *Proc.,* XLVI (1942), 434–38; and the more extensive memoir by the same author, *ibid.,* LXXVII (1966), 28–52; printed *Reports* of the Harvard Class of 1880; Hart's own chapter on "Government," and Emerton's on "History," in S. E. Morison, ed., *The Development of Harvard Univ., 1869–1929* (1930); faculty minute on his death in *Harvard Univ. Gazette,* Dec. 18, 1943. See also Elizabeth Donnan and Leo F. Stock, eds., *An Historian's World: Selections from the Correspondence of John Franklin Jameson* (1956); Alfred Andrews, *Genealogical Hist. of Deacon Stephen Hart and His Descendants* (1875); and Carol F. Baird, "Albert Bushnell Hart," in Paul H. Buck, ed., *Social Sciences at Harvard, 1860–1920* (1965). Miscellaneous clippings and family letters are in the Harvard Univ. Archives, but Hart's vast collection of correspondence was sold by his heirs to an autograph dealer and scattered. A MS. memoir of his father is in the Western Reserve Hist. Soc., Cleveland. No portrait of Hart was ever painted, but a bronze bust from life by Karl Skoog is in the Am. Swedish Hist. Museum, Phila. Photographs will be found in the Class of 1880 reports, and in Morison's *Development of Harvard Univ.,* cited above.]

SAMUEL ELIOT MORISON

HART, LORENZ MILTON (May 2, 1895– Nov. 22, 1943), musical comedy lyricist, was born in New York City, the elder of two sons of Max M. and Frieda (Isenberg) Hart. Of Jewish background, he traced his descent through his mother from the German poet Heinrich Heine. His father, a business promoter, was sufficiently prosperous to enable Lorenz, after preparation at two private schools, to spend two years (1914–16) at the School of Journalism of Columbia University. Reared in a worldly, bibulous home, temperamentally alienated from a rather coarse-grained father, indifferent to academic studies outside literature and drama, Hart was perhaps even more than Cole Porter the expressive bard of the urban generation which matured during the interwar years 1919–41. Much of his work—slick, breezy, and yet mordant, even morbid—reflects their tart disillusion. A bachelor living with his widowed mother, whom he once described as a "sweet, menacing old lady," he was a restless world traveler and, especially after his mother's death, an alcoholic who disappeared for weeks on end to escape a life periodically unbearable. But with all his moody unreliability he found his destiny as lyricist to his more stable friend Richard Rodgers.

Their lifetime collaboration began in 1918, when Hart was working for the Shuberts translating German plays and Rodgers was writing varsity shows at Columbia. The two contributed to the Broadway musical *Poor Little Ritz Girl* (1920), and by 1925 they had their own success on Broadway, *The Garrick Gaieties,* an intimate review sponsored by the Theatre Guild in revolt against huge, flossy "girlie" productions. Rodgers and Hart believed that monotony was killing the musical, that songwriters must integrate libretto, lyrics, and music. "Sentimental Me" (*Garrick Gaieties*), a parody of mawkish popular songs, appealed to the hard core of their market—people who were either genuinely urban upper-middle class, or who embraced the sophisticated, innovative New York music and the *New Yorker* magazine in order to avoid being like the "little old lady from Dubuque." The praise of Manhattan's "smart set"—Dorothy Parker, Robert Benchley [Supp. 3], Alexander Woollcott [Supp. 3]—enhanced the popularity of Rodgers and Hart's *Peggy Ann* (1926), a surrealistic Freudian study of an ambitious young career girl.

With personal growth, with changing times, Hart's range broadened and deepened. In the 1920's he was insouciant: "The Girl Friend" (*The Girl Friend,* 1926), "Manhattan" (*Garrick Gaieties*), "Thou Swell" (*A Connecticut Yankee,* 1927), "You Took Advantage of Me" (*Present Arms,* 1928). In the 1930's, while he developed his satirical vein (*I'd Rather Be Right,* 1937, was a take-off on politics), he was more sober, even somber, with an almost despairing melancholy. In "Little Girl Blue" (*Jumbo,* 1935) a woman—ironically, girl no longer—sings, "Sit there and count your fingers, . . . Old girl, you're through"; in "Spring Is Here . . . I Hear" (*I Married an Angel,* 1938), the caustic wordplay again evokes a depression-ridden urban world of unmarried adults in lonely, loveless rooms.

Not all was harsh: an etherealized tenderness, an almost desperate romanticism typical of the 1930's suffused "Have You Met Miss Jones?" and the title song from *I'd Rather Be Right,* "The Most Beautiful Girl in the World" and "My Romance" (both from *Jumbo*), "Where or When" (*Babes in Arms,* 1937), the title song from *I*

Married an Angel, and "Falling in Love with Love" (*The Boys from Syracuse,* 1938). *Syracuse,* based on *A Comedy of Errors,* was the pioneer adaptation of Shakespeare for musical comedy. If these songs were delicately oblique enough to suit a post-Victorian generation still afraid to pursue hedonism too far or at least too openly, sentimentality still did not eliminate realism: Hart fused the two in a poignant tribute to a homely lover, "My Funny Valentine" (*Babes in Arms*).

By 1940 Hart and Rodgers had decided that more of the naturalism of contemporary literature and drama must come to musical comedy. In collaborating with John O'Hara on an adaptation of his novel *Pal Joey,* they were somewhat in advance of a public reluctant to accept the possibility that nice-looking, lithe young white song-and-dance men could fornicate with and leech upon women. Joey did both. Most of the numbers were harshly witty. An older woman, despoiled by Joey, sings to the ingenue, "Take him, but don't ever let him take you." Received with mixed response, *Joey* was revived for enthusiastic audiences a decade later. Similar sarcasm pervaded *By Jupiter* (1942).

When wartime came, Hart was out of step with a patriotic public absorbed with traditional American values. The folksy *Oklahoma!*—that hearty slice of rural Americana conceived by Rodgers—held no interest for Hart, now immersed in cheap midtown Manhattan bars, and Rodgers turned for lyrics to Oscar Hammerstein II. Hart returned to collaboration with Rodgers on a 1943 revival of *A Connecticut Yankee.* On opening night, acting strangely, he slipped away and vanished for two days. Found ill in a hotel room, he was rushed to a New York City hospital, where he died three days later of pneumonia. He was buried in Mount Zion Cemetery, Maspeth, Queens. His brother Teddy, a musical comedy star, was his sole survivor.

A student of literature and an inveterate play-goer from childhood, Lorenz Hart contributed to musical comedies sharp, tasteful lyrics finely coordinated with rhythm and melody and with the plot, mood, and action of the play. Although lyrical fashions moved away from his pungent colloquialism with the banalities of the 1950's and the "hip" polemics of the 1960's, Hart brought into the mainstream of songwriting a conversational directness like Ernest Hemingway's which eliminated strained poetic diction and bathos. If much of his work seemed precious to a more earnest later generation, not so the biting criticism of urban life implied in "The Lady Is a Tramp" (*Babes in Arms*).

[For a list of Hart's work, see *The ASCAP Biog. Dict. of Composers, Authors and Publishers* (3rd ed., 1966). David Ewen, *Richard Rodgers* (1957), contains photographs and valuable insights on Hart. The best short biographies are: Richard Rodgers's introduction to *The Rodgers and Hart Song Book* (1951) and the *Rodgers and Hammerstein Fact Book* (1955); *Current Biog.,* 1940; Irwin Stambler, ed., *Encyc. of Popular Music* (1965), with portrait; Margaret Harriman, *Take Them up Tenderly* (1944); *Time,* Sept. 26, 1938, p. 35. See also obituaries in *N. Y. Times,* Nov. 23, 1943 (and editorial, Nov. 25), and *Variety,* Nov. 24, 1943.]

HUGHSON MOONEY

HARTLEY, MARSDEN (Jan. 4, 1877–Sept. 2, 1943), painter and poet, was born in Lewiston, Maine, the youngest of nine children and third son of Thomas and Eliza Jane (Horbury) Hartley. Both parents were natives of Staleybridge, Lancashire, England, and had emigrated in 1857. The father, a devout Episcopalian, worked sporadically as a cotton spinner and then as a theatre billposter. To help eke out the meager family income, the mother often worked as well. She died when Hartley was eight, leaving his childhood "vast with terror and surprise" (*Adventures,* p. 3). Thomas Hartley subsequently married another Staleybridge immigrant, Martha Marsden, whose maiden name the boy—christened Edmund—adopted.

Hartley quit school at fourteen to work in a shoe factory. His family, meanwhile, had moved to Cleveland, Ohio, where he joined them in 1892 and went to work as an office boy at a marble quarry. A childhood interest in art, seen in drawings he made at the age of thirteen for a local naturalist, developed into serious study on a scholarship at the Cleveland Art School, under Cullen Yates and Nina Waldeck. Hartley went to New York City in 1898, studying first at the school of William Merritt Chase [*q.v.*]; discouraged by the shallow academicism of Chase and his other teachers, F. Luis Mora and Frank Vincent DuMond, he switched to the National Academy of Design in 1900. Here and at the Art Students League he studied off and on until 1905 with George Maynard [*q.v.*], Edwin H. Blashfield [Supp. 2], and Edgar M. Ward.

Until 1911 Hartley alternated convivial New York winters with lonely summers in Maine, where he once lived in a deserted farmhouse on four dollars a week. Plagued by insecurities, in 1905 he suffered a profound depression during which he painted a series of pictures on suicidal themes. Three years later he was painting small, impressionistic mountain landscapes and, in 1909–10, black landscapes influenced by Albert Pinkham Ryder [*q.v.*]. The rapid succession of stylistic "periods" became characteristic of Hartley's painting through most of his life. Alfred Stieglitz launched Hartley's career in 1909 with his first one-man exhibition, which, though poorly received, gained him acceptance into the artistic vanguard of Stieglitz's "291" gallery—Alfred Maurer, John Marin, Arthur Dove, Max Weber, and others—and exposed him to modern European trends in art.

In 1912 Stieglitz and Arthur B. Davies [q.v.] raised money to send Hartley to Paris, where he frequented Gertrude Stein's studio. He abandoned personal realism for flat, decorative canvases, experimenting with Picasso's cubism and Matisse's Fauvism in darkly outlined still lifes and vibrantly colored collages. He moved on to Germany, where he spent the next three years. He met Wassily Kandinsky, exhibited with the "Blaue Reiter" group of expressionists in 1913, and had a one-man show at Graphic-Verlag (1915–16). In Berlin he also participated in the first autumn salon of "Der Sturm." Meanwhile, his paintings appeared in the Armory Show of 1913 in New York, and the next year a show at "291" reviewed his European work. His paintings were also hung in the New York Forum Exhibition of 1916. During this period Hartley produced some of his finest work, combining the emotional colors of expressionism with cubist fragmentation in abstract and semiabstract interpretations of movement. Until the depression, Hartley continued to travel regularly between the United States and Europe. He experimented with a variety of styles, ranging from German military studies to folk and peasant motifs on glass. In New Mexico during 1918–19 he painted mountain landscapes in a high-keyed expressionist style, and also worked in pastel.

After 1916 writing became a major outlet of his creative impulses and aesthetic ideals. He had experimented with poetry since his early days in New York and had begun some essays while in Germany, but it was not until a summer sojourn at Provincetown, Mass., that he began writing for publication. Stieglitz encouraged him, as did Hart Crane [Supp. 1], whose poetry influenced his own, and Sherwood Anderson [Supp. 3]. Hartley contributed to the *Dial, Poetry* magazine, and William Carlos Williams's *Contact*. His volume of essays, *Adventures in the Arts* (1921), and his *Twenty-five Poems* (1923), influenced by Emily Dickinson [q.v.] and imagism, reveal the stylistic and philosophic uncertainties which characterized his painting.

In 1921 an auction of his paintings, arranged by friends, netted $4,000 and enabled Hartley to travel to Venice, and then to Aix-en-Provence, where he worked from 1926 to 1928. There he abandoned expressionism for the severe discipline of Cézanne, renouncing imaginative painting to seek a new "formula" in nature "as an intellectual idea." With the depression he was forced to return, in 1930, to New York. The financial support he had received from Stieglitz and the diplomat William C. Bullitt now diminished. He lived in New York and New England, where he began his first "Dogtown" series (1931–36), evocative studies of the glacial boulders and deserted cellar holes on Cape Ann in Massachusetts. In 1932 he traveled to Mexico on a Guggenheim Fellowship, where he painted a series on Mount Popocatepetl, as well as various symbolic subjects. He returned to Berlin and Bavaria in 1933, and briefly visited Bermuda and Nova Scotia in 1935, but after 1936 returned to his native Maine, where he developed his distinctive style of "regionalism" and symbolism. Broad simplification in his seascapes, landscapes, and nature studies, rendered in flat masses enclosed within heavy contours, and in rich, glowing colors conveying strongly symbolic overtones, characterize his finest works. His "Mount Katahdin" series and other paintings reveal his love of mountains, which had a deep symbolic meaning for him as they did for Thoreau, whom he admired. In nature, then, he had found his theme—the tragic human condition.

After 1939 Hartley's work sold well and was exhibited often, especially at the Hudson Walker Gallery, the Paul Rosenberg Gallery, and the "American Place" gallery. Yet despite his success he withdrew increasingly from social life and contented himself with a studio in a hen coop in Corea, Maine. Hartley was a complex and contradictory figure. Afflicted with recurring bouts of melancholy and possessed of a notorious vanity, he remained a bachelor, and in his last years seemed to find roots in the simple life of rural Maine. This profound sense of place is fused with his theme of nature in some fine poems, collected in *Androscoggin* (1940) and *Sea Burial* (1941). A devout Episcopalian in earlier life, Hartley expressed no religious convictions as he grew older, despite the occasional appearance of religious symbols in his last paintings. He died of a heart ailment in Ellsworth, Maine, at the age of sixty-six. His ashes were scattered on the Androscoggin River. Over a lifetime he had produced more than nine hundred paintings.

[Hartley's books include *Adventures in the Arts: Informal Chapters on Painters, Vaudeville, and Poets* (1921) and the posthumous *Selected Poems* (1945). The only published biographical study is Elizabeth McCausland's monograph, *Marsden Hartley* (1952). Robert N. Burlingame, "Marsden Hartley: A Study of His Life and Creative Achievement" (Ph.D. dissertation, Brown Univ., 1953), deals in detail with

Hartley's life, with particular attention to his poetry, and includes an extensive bibliography. See also Herbert J. Seligman, "Marsden Hartley of Maine," *Down East*, Nov. 1956, Jan. 1957. Significant exhibition catalogues are: An American Place, *Marsden Hartley: Exhibition of Recent Paintings* (1937), and Museum of Modern Art, *Lyonel Feininger, Marsden Hartley* (1944). Among numerous periodical articles, important discussions, often with reproductions, include: Robert N. Burlingame in *New England Quart.*, Dec. 1958; Donald Gallup in *Mag. of Art*, Nov. 1948; Clement Greenberg, "Art," *Nation*, Dec. 30, 1944; Jerome Mellquist in *Commonweal*, Dec. 31, 1943, and *Perspectives, USA*, Summer 1953; Duncan Phillips in *Mag. of Art*, Mar. 1944; and Hudson D. Walker in *Kenyon Rev.*, Spring 1947. See also Paul Rosenfeld's *Port of N. Y.* (1924) and *Men Seen: 24 Modern Authors* (1925). An unpublished biobibliography by Susan Otis Thompson (1963) was helpful. Hartley's paintings appear in most major American galleries. His papers are at Yale Univ., with some material also at the Museum of Modern Art in N. Y. and the Archives of Am. Art at the Smithsonian Institution, Washington. A terra-cotta head of Hartley (1942) by Jacques Lipchitz is in the Metropolitan Museum of Art, N. Y.]

ALFRED V. FRANKENSTEIN

HARTMANN, CARL SADAKICHI (Nov. 8, 1867?–Nov. 21, 1944), author and art critic— once described by John Barrymore [Supp. 3] as "presumably sired by Mephistopheles out of Madame Butterfly"—was born in Nagasaki, Japan. His Japanese mother, Osadda, died shortly after his birth and his father, Oskar Hartmann, an attaché in the German consulate, sent Sadakichi and his elder brother to Hamburg, where he lived with an uncle and was baptized a Lutheran; at that time a birth date was arbitrarily selected. Sadakichi was closer to his uncle than to his father. The latter sent him in 1882 to Philadelphia, where, after a year at the Spring Garden Institute, he seems to have fended for himself. Having introduced himself to Walt Whitman [*q.v.*], he served the poet as factotum (1884–85) and then booked a seven-dollar passage to Europe, where for a time he was an apprentice in the "mad King" Ludwig's Royal Theatre. From Munich he went to Paris, where he became associated with the symbolist poet Mallarmé. Until 1923, when he settled somewhat permanently in southern California, he drifted among art centers, partly to satisfy his Faustian appetite for experiences, partly to find respite from asthmatic attacks.

Sadakichi's life was one of bohemian independence. In 1891 he took as his common-law wife Elizabeth Blanche Walsh, a nurse. By 1901 their family included five children—Atma Dorothy, Nurva, Paul Walter, Marion, and Edgar Allan— and about 1900 the poet Anne Throop bore him another child. A common-law union, begun a few years later, with the artist Lillian Bonham resulted in seven more children: Roderigo, Marigold, Wistaria, Tansy, Jonquil, Robert, and Aster.

Mythmongers emphasized Sadakichi's outlandishness, and he fostered the image with sharp insults and "grotesque, obscene, maniacal dances" (De Casseres, p. 398). In the decades before the First World War, Greenwich Villagers dubbed him "King of Bohemia." In 1893 he spent the Christmas holidays jailed in Boston for having "stabbed the religious consciousness of New England" with his play *Christ*, which called for nude scenes and an orgy in which a dance embodies the religious theme of the drama, that Christ's doctrine of universal spiritual love is a transmutation of youthful sensuous love. Sadakichi's demand for a stage manager who "will borrow freely from all the arts" illustrates his connection with the *symbolistes* and their principle of correspondences among the senses, as does a later essay, "In Perfume Land" (*Forum*, August 1913), in which he explores the theory of correspondent sensations and recounts his experiments with perfume "symphonies." *Christ* was only the first in a series of free-verse dramas; others were *Buddha* (1897), *The Last Thirty Days of Christ* (1920), *Confucius* (1923), *Moses* (1934), and an unpublished play about Mary Baker Eddy [*q.v.*]. The plays were printed at his own expense, as were his short story collections (1899, 1908, 1930) and most of his poetry: *Drifting Flowers of the Sea* (1906), *My Rubaiyat* (1913), and *Tanka and Haikai* (1915).

Sadakichi was never regularly employed, although from 1893 through 1907 he was a European correspondent for the S. S. McClure Syndicate, and from 1897 through 1903 he wrote for the New York *Staats-Zeitung*. He made three attempts at publishing art magazines, and he was a lecturer with the Carnegie Art Institute of Pittsburgh in 1907 and 1908. He worked as a book designer and writer in the Roycrofter colony of Elbert Hubbard [*q.v.*] from 1912 to 1914. In 1924 Douglas Fairbanks [Supp. 2] gave him a role in the film *The Thief of Bagdad*, but Sadakichi quit in the middle of production. Most of his intermittent income came from the more than 1,700 lectures which he gave in his lifetime, from the imperious panhandling to which he subjected his admirers in later years, and from his critical books and articles.

Sadakichi's critical writings convey none of the audacious posturing associated with other aspects of his life. He wrote four books on art, beginning with *Shakespeare in Art* (1900). His *Japanese Art* (1904) was published at a time when Japanese influences were a major cultural force; and although he apparently could not read Japanese, his exotic name and appearance, coupled with his very real talents, contributed toward making him one of America's few authorities on the art, fiction, and drama of Japan. The critical approach in his two-volume *A History of American Art* (1902, revised 1932) bridges two eras, for while he applies nineteenth-century terms to academic art, he applies modern standards for newer painters, including his favorite, Albert Pinkham Ryder [*q.v.*]. In *The Whistler Book* (1910) Sadakichi uses the life and work of James McNeill Whistler [*q.v.*] to anticipate twentieth-century problems in the art of painting: its relation to photography; the influences on painters of artificial light, industrialization, and primitive and oriental art; and the limitations of art for art's sake, which he feared might end in absolute "paucity of idea."

Later he dealt with similar problems in the aesthetics of dance ("Black Butterflies," *Forum*, February 1914). Allowing for the greater skill of ballet, he liked the independence of modern technique, for "the finest expression of dancing would be without music." Sadakichi also wrote several nature essays in the manner of his friend John Burroughs [*q.v.*], to accompany photographic illustrations. These, and other essays on the art of photography (some under the pseudonym "Sidney Allan"), express the view that snapshot photography had saved the art from continuing as false imitation of painting.

By the 1920's Sadakichi's influence had waned, and his commissioned writing was limited to reminiscences of notable friends. The world to which he belonged had expired in two world conflicts, and in the 1940's he was harassed by officials who suspected him of signaling to Japanese vessels, despite the fact that he had been an American citizen since Columbus Day, 1894. In his last years he lived on the Morongo Indian reservation, southeast of Los Angeles, in a little cabin he had built with funds provided by George Santayana, Ezra Pound, Booth Tarkington, and others. Poverty-ridden and obsessed with a desire for literary immortality, he would occasionally visit the Hollywood artist John Decker to drink, dance, promote loans, and trade insults with W. C. Fields, John Barrymore, and Gene Fowler. In 1944, fearful that Fowler had abandoned writing his life story, he began an autobiography. He died that fall, of a coronary thrombosis, in St. Petersburg, Fla., where he had gone to consult records in the home of his eldest daughter. He was buried in Royal Palms Cemetery, St. Petersburg.

[Extensive collections of papers are at the Univ. of Calif. at Riverside, the Univ. of Oreg., Yale Univ., and the Hist. Soc. of Pa. Gene Fowler's account of Sadakichi Hartmann, *Minutes of the Last Meeting* (1954), is entertaining but abounds in inaccuracies, some of which are corrected by Harry Lawton in a series in the *Riverside* (Calif.) *Enterprise*, Aug. 3–15, 1954. See also the *Sadakichi Hartmann Newsletter*,

1969– . Samuel Dickson's *San Francisco Is Your Home* (1947) tells of Sadakichi's life in the Bay Area. Contemporary sources include *Who's Who in America*, 1940–41; *N. Y. Times*, Nov. 23, 1944; Benjamin De Casseres, "Five Portraits in Galvanized Iron," *Am. Mercury*, Dec. 1926; "The Most Mysterious Personality in Am. Letters," *Current Opinion*, Aug. 1916. Additional minor works by Sadakichi are listed in the *Readers' Guide to Periodical Literature*, 1891–1938, and the Lib. of Cong. catalogue. Other information from correspondence with relatives. A variety of portraits of Sadakichi are to be found in Fowler and Lawton, above.]

FRED E. H. SCHROEDER

HATCHER, ROBERT ANTHONY (Feb. 6, 1868–Apr. 1, 1944), pharmacologist, was born in New Madrid, Mo., the fourth of five children and the only one to survive infancy. His father, Richard Hardaway Hatcher, a lawyer impoverished by the Civil War, was descended from William Hatcher, who came from England to Henrico County, Va., in 1635. His mother, Harriet Hinton (Marr) Hatcher, was of seventeenth-century Scottish ancestry.

Hatcher spent his boyhood in New Orleans, La., in the home of an uncle, Robert H. Marr, a justice of the Louisiana supreme court, and attended local schools. Drawn to pharmacy, he entered the Philadelphia College of Pharmacy and after graduating, Ph.G., in 1889 spent several years as a druggist in New Orleans. Since he wished to understand more about the physiological action of drugs, he enrolled in the medical college of Tulane University and received the M.D. degree in 1898. The next year, after a brief visit to Europe, he became professor of materia medica at the Cleveland School of Pharmacy and, a year or so later, demonstrator in pharmacology at the Western Reserve Medical School. The newly established pharmacology department at Western Reserve was headed by Torald H. Sollmann, a product of training abroad where the science of experimental pharmacology was thriving long before it gained a foothold in the United States. Hatcher's collaboration with Sollmann proved a stimulating one and resulted in their joint publication of *A Textbook of Materia Medica* (1904).

In 1904, at the age of thirty-six, Hatcher joined the staff of the Cornell University Medical College in New York City as instructor in pharmacology. He spent the rest of his active career at Cornell, becoming assistant professor in 1906 and professor and head of the department of pharmacology and materia medica in 1908 (the term "materia medica" was later dropped from his title). During the early period of his tenure at Cornell he was also called upon to inaugurate the teaching of pharmacology at Harvard and at the University of Chicago.

Hatcher took great pleasure in teaching. He encouraged student participation in the classroom, and in laboratory exercises laid stress on cultivating the powers of observation. He himself was a dedicated researcher in experimental pharmacology, which he regarded as the road to rational drug therapy in man. His basic principle was that of Thoreau: "No way of thinking or doing, however ancient, can be trusted without proof." His staff was small, and he had no interest in expansion. Among his assistants and associates were Cary Eggleston, who later became involved in clinical pharmacology and the practice of cardiology; Janet Travell, who after years in the laboratory also turned to clinical pharmacology and medical practice, and later became personal physician to President John F. Kennedy; Soma Weiss [Supp. 3]; and Harry Gold. These associates adopted Hatcher's approach to investigating the diverse behavior of drugs in man—absorption, distribution, elimination, bioassay—which developed into the present discipline of clinical pharmacology. Hatcher sometimes suggested to a student a subject for investigation, but he gave his staff complete freedom to define their own projects and pursue them experimentally. The stream of publications that flowed from his laboratory, together with the aloof formality of his appearance and manner, gave·Hatcher something of a legendary character.

Hatcher's investigations extended over a large field. A first-rate experimentalist, he carried out studies of strychnine, morphine, the cinchona alkaloids, and local anesthetics. He analyzed the reflex mechanism of emesis (vomiting) and the role of various drugs in producing it, subjects that had been neglected by physiologists. He is perhaps best known for his extensive investigations of the action of digitalis. By assaying biologically the action of crude and purified preparations, he helped define the Hatcher-Brody cat unit of digitalis leaf that made possible safe and routine use of the drug in heart disease.

Hatcher was one of the founders (1908) of the American Society for Pharmacology and Experimental Therapeutics and in 1934 was elected president. He was a member of the Council on Pharmacy and Chemistry of the American Medical Association from its founding in 1905 until 1943. His critical analysis of publications submitted by the pharmaceutical industry to buttress their claims for new therapeutic preparations was a strong force in shielding American medicine from the onslaughts of nostrums and quackery. In addition to his textbook and many papers, he published *The Pharmacopeia and the Physician* (1906), with Martin I. Wilbert, and *The Phar-*

macology of Useful Drugs (1915). From 1910 to 1935 he was a member of the committee of revision of the United States Pharmacopeia.

Hatcher's life style was unpretentious, thrifty, and rather bland, though close acquaintance suggested that he had by strict self-discipline overcome hedonistic leanings. A devout Presbyterian, he showed little interest in social activities but found his chief recreation in reading history, biography, and science. On Dec. 28, 1904, he married May Quinn Burton of Lewes, Del.; their only child, Robert Lee, became an economist. Hatcher retired from his Cornell professorship in 1935. In his last years he suffered from heart disease, and during his terminal illness he lay in bed enjoying Aristotle and Plato in Jowett's translation. He died at the age of seventy-six at his home in Flushing, N. Y., of a myocardial infarction, and was buried in the cemetery of the Presbyterian church in Lewes.

[*Am. Men of Sci.* (7th ed., 1944); information on Hatcher's early life from his son; Theodore Koppanyi in *Science*, May 26, 1944; personal acquaintance. See also *Jour. Am. Medic. Assoc.*, Apr. 8, July 29, 1944; and, on his ancestry, *Nat. Cyc. Am. Biog.*, XXXIII, 289–90.]

HARRY GOLD

HAWES, HARRIET ANN BOYD (Oct. 11, 1871–Mar. 31, 1945), archaeologist, was born in Boston, Mass., the only daughter and the youngest of five children of Alexander and Harriet Fay (Wheeler) Boyd. Her paternal grandfather had emigrated from Northern Ireland in 1816 and settled in Boston, where he established the family business of manufacturing harness, trunks, and leather hose for fire engines. This profitable enterprise was carried on by Alexander Boyd, who married into an old New England family. His wife died the year after Harriet's birth. Harriet was reared as a Unitarian but later became a convert to the Episcopal Church.

After graduation from Smith College in 1892, Miss Boyd taught ancient and modern languages as a tutor in North Carolina and at a school in Delaware. In 1896, wishing to prepare herself for college teaching, she entered the American School of Classical Studies in Athens. Her imagination had been fired by recent archaeological discoveries in Crete. Since there was evidently no opportunity for a female student to take part in the school's excavation program, she decided to use part of her grant as Agnes Hoppin Memorial Fellow to underwrite an excavation of her own, and went to Crete to look for a site.

In Crete she was encouraged and helped by the eminent English archaeologists Arthur J. Evans and David G. Hogarth. Fresh from her inspection of Evan's epoch-making excavation of the Palace of Minos at Knossos, Miss Boyd and Miss Jean Patten, a fellow Bostonian who was interested in Cretan plants, set out on muleback to explore the island. At Kavousi in eastern Crete, they discovered houses and tombs of the early Iron Age. The results of this brief excavation, published the following year in the *American Journal of Archaeology,* provided Miss Boyd with the material for her master's thesis at Smith (1901). More important, this initial campaign led to the subsequent discovery of Gournia, a Bronze Age town overlooking the Gulf of Mirabello, which remains the only well-preserved urban site of the Minoan age to have been uncovered in three-quarters of a century's work on Crete. There Miss Boyd excavated during the seasons of 1901, 1903, and 1904, under the sponsorship of the American Exploration Society of Philadelphia. The results of this and other lesser digs on the isthmus of Hierapetra were widely published, most fully in an illustrated folio volume, *Gournia, Vasiliki and Other Prehistoric Sites on the Isthmus of Hierapetra, Crete* (1908).

During the years 1900–06 Miss Boyd spent part of her time at Smith College, where she taught courses in archaeology, epigraphy, and modern Greek. In 1904 she gained permission from Cretan authorities to bring to the Free Museum of Science and Art in Philadelphia (later the University Museum) a selection of the finds made in her excavations. Subsequently some of these objects passed to the Metropolitan Museum of Art in New York as gifts from the American Exploration Society. As the first woman to have been responsible for the direction of an excavation and for the publication of its results, Miss Boyd won international fame. In recognition of her achievements, Smith College awarded her the honorary degree of L.H.D. in 1910.

On Mar. 3, 1906, Harriet Boyd was married, in New York, to Charles Henry Hawes, an English anthropologist she had met in Crete; their two children were Alexander Boyd and Mary Nesbit. For some years after her marriage Mrs. Hawes carried on her scholarly activity unofficially, bringing out *Gournia* and, in collaboration with her husband, *Crete, the Forerunner of Greece* (1909), a small volume for the general public. Hawes taught for a time at the University of Wisconsin, served as a professor at Dartmouth College (1910–17), and after the war became assistant director (1919–24) and then associate director (1924–34) of the Museum of Fine Arts in Boston. With the return to Boston, Mrs. Hawes resumed teaching, becoming lecturer

on ancient art at Wellesley College, a position which she held until 1936.

Harriet Hawes had a lifelong concern for political and social justice. As an undergraduate at Smith she had been stirred by reports on the Czarist penal colonies in Siberia, and had repeatedly walked from the college to nearby Florence, Mass., to talk with English cutlery workers bent on forming a union in order to achieve better working conditions. Her courage, her conviction that a rational international society was attainable, and her compassion for human suffering had led her to serve as a volunteer nurse in the Greco-Turkish War in 1897 and in a Florida camp during the Spanish-American War (1898). During World War I she returned to Greece to establish an emergency field hospital off Corfu to care for soldiers of the retreating Serbian army, and in 1917 she was instrumental in organizing and establishing the Smith College Relief Unit, the first such private group of women to serve in France, in the devastated region of Grécourt. While at Wellesley she was the object of a $100,000 lawsuit for her part in helping and advising the striking workers of a Cambridge shoe factory. She was an ardent New Dealer during the 1930's.

Mrs. Hawes's involvement with contemporary problems left little time, in later years, for scholarly activities, and the investigations she had begun of major monuments on the Athenian Akropolis, in particular the Erechtheion and the sculptures of the Parthenon, were never completed or published. Her importance as an archaeologist therefore rests on her work in Crete. The small number of undergraduates at Wellesley who knew her as a white-haired little lady with keen blue eyes, clad in timeless garments reflecting her lack of interest in the world of fashion, found her a memorable teacher. Her intense commitment to both the active and the contemplative life, to the present as well as to the past, gave a broad dimension to the study of antiquity, transmitting an awareness of humane values together with an acute sense of the excitement of scholarly activity. After their retirement, Mrs. Hawes and her husband lived in Washington, D. C. In 1945, a little more than a year after her husband's death, she died there of peritonitis. She was buried in Forest Hills Cemetery, Boston.

[The Harriet Boyd Hawes Papers in the Smith College Archives, an extensive collection including correspondence, journals, MSS., clippings, etc.; personal acquaintance; information supplied by Alexander Boyd Hawes. Published biographical material includes obituaries in *Wellesley Mag.,* June 1945, and *Smith Alumnae Quart.,* Aug. 1945; Harriet Boyd Hawes, "Memoirs of a Pioneer Excavator in Crete," *Archaeology,* Summer and Winter 1965; *A Land*

Called Crete (*Smith College Studies in Hist.,* vol. XLV, 1968), a symposium in memory of Mrs. Hawes; Louise Elliott Dalby, *"An Irrepressible Crew"*: *The Smith College Relief Unit* (Sophia Smith Collection, Smith College, 1968); and sketch in *Notable Am. Women.* Death record from D. C. Health Dept.]

PHYLLIS WILLIAMS LEHMANN

HAWLEY, WILLIS CHATMAN (May 5, 1864–July 24, 1941), educator, Congressman, was born near Monroe, Benton County, Oreg., the second of at least three children and the oldest son of Sewel Ransom Hawley and Emma Amelia (Noble) Hawley. Both parents had come to Oregon in the 1840's as the children of early settlers, Hawley's father from Ohio, his mother from Illinois. Hawley took pride in his pioneering background. Growing up as the son of a moderately successful farmer, he attended country schools and worked his way through Willamette University in Salem, Oreg., from which he graduated with a B.S. degree in 1884. On Aug. 19, 1885, he married Anna Martha Geisendorfer, daughter of an Albany, Oreg., farmer. They had two sons, Stuart Cecil and Kenneth Fabius, and a daughter, Iras Alma.

For two years after leaving college, Hawley served as principal of Umpqua Academy in Wilbur, Oreg. He then returned to Willamette University, where in 1888 he earned both an A.B. and an LL.B. Although he was subsequently (1893) admitted to the Oregon bar, he did not practice law extensively but instead followed a career in education. In 1888 he became president of the Oregon State Normal School at Drain. Three years later he received an A.M. from Willamette and joined its faculty as professor of mathematics. In 1893 he shifted to the chair of "political history, political economy, and political science" (soon changed to history, economics, and constitutional law), and that same year he became president of the university. He stepped down in 1902 to become vice-president and dean, but continued to teach until 1907. A popular campus figure, he seems to have had a close relationship with the students. He was also president of the Willamette Valley Chautauqua Association and an active Methodist.

During his years at Willamette University, Hawley was a frequent public lecturer. Although not particularly dynamic in personality, he was an impressive figure—over six feet tall and of sturdy physique—and a popular speaker. In 1906 he ran for Congress from Oregon's first district as a Republican. He was elected for what proved to be the first of thirteen terms. Hawley's party regularity and his quiet, unruffled manner were popular with his Congressional colleagues, and he achieved considerable influence in Republican councils, serving as chairman of the party's House caucus in the 69th and later Congresses. He gained a particular reputation as an expert in taxation and tariff matters. As a member of the House Ways and Means Committee, he wrote the agricultural schedule for the Fordney-McCumber Tariff of 1922.

Hawley reached the apex of his career in 1928 when he succeeded to the chairmanship of the powerful Ways and Means Committee, a post that brought him the only widespread attention he received outside Congress. Herbert Hoover had promised in the 1928 presidential campaign to revise the tariff, and this became an early item of business when Congress met in special session in April 1929. Hawley, a champion of the protective tariff, exercised firm control of the committee hearings and quickly maneuvered the administration bill through the committee and the House, which passed it on May 28, 1929. Senate opposition, however, to a companion bill sponsored by Senator Reed Smoot [Supp. 3] of Utah delayed final passage of the act until June 1930.

Originally conceived as a "reform" measure to aid American farmers by increasing the import duties on agricultural products, the law as finally passed raised the rates on a wide variety of goods to unprecedented levels. Many blamed the Smoot-Hawley Tariff for intensifying the depression of 1929, and it became an important issue in the 1932 elections. Despite his defense of the act, Hawley was defeated in the Republican primary of that year. He returned to the practice of law in Salem, Oreg., where he died of a cerebral hemorrhage in 1941. He was buried in Salem's City View Cemetery.

[Biographical material is slender. See *Biog. Directory Am. Cong.* (1961); Clayton F. Moore in *Tariff Rev.,* Apr. 1928; *Nat. Cyc. Am. Biog.,* XXXII, 352; *Who Was Who in America,* vol. I (1942); Joseph Gaston, *The Centennial Hist. of Oreg.* (1912), II, 553; *N. Y. Times* feature stories, Apr. 22, 1928 (sec. 10), and May 19, 1929 (sec. 10), and obituary, July 25, 1941; obituary in *Oreg. Statesman* (Salem), July 25, 1941. Family data from federal census of 1870 (courtesy of Oreg. State Lib., Salem). Robert M. Gatke, *Chronicles of Willamette* (1943), contains material on Hawley's academic career. For his tariff and tax views, see his "The New Tariff: A Defense," *Rev. of Revs.,* July 1930; and *Cong. Digest,* Mar., May 1932. Elmer E. Schattschneider, *Politics, Pressures, and the Tariff* (1935), provides details of how Hawley functioned as Ways and Means Committee chairman in drawing up the tariff bill.]

STANLEY D. SOLVICK

HAYES, JOHN WILLIAM (Dec. 26, 1854–Nov. 25, 1942), labor leader, was born in Philadelphia, Pa., the second of eight children and oldest son of Edward Hayes, a mason, and Mary (Galbraith) Hayes. Both parents were natives of Ireland. According to his own account, John

Hayes never attended school. He went west at about the age of seventeen, worked as a farmhand in Illinois, and then drifted into railroading, becoming a brakeman on the Dayton & Michigan and then on the Pennsylvania Railroad. That hazardous calling cost him his right arm in 1878, after which he learned telegraphy. He had joined the Knights of Labor in 1874, and in his new trade he was a delegate to the national telegraphers' convention of 1883 which called a strike for higher wages. Blacklisted after the strike failed, he opened a grocery store in New Brunswick, N. J., where his family had settled in the late 1860's. On July 25, 1882, he married a New Brunswick girl, Nellie A. Carlen. They apparently had no children.

On good terms with the influential Knights of Labor District Assembly 49 in New York City, Hayes was elected to the General Executive Board of the Knights in 1884. He soon became the chief ally and confidant of Terence V. Powderly [q.v.], General Master Workman of the Knights, and in 1888 was elevated to the post of General Secretary-Treasurer. His pince-nez and handlebar moustache of this period echoed those of Powderly. Hayes seems to have been an efficient administrator. Not an orator or a leader of men, he took naturally to wire-pulling. In 1888, working through Democratic party contacts in New Jersey, he came close to winning the federal Commissionership of Labor for Powderly (and, presumably, a job for himself). He was a delegate, with Powderly, to the Omaha convention of the Populist party in 1892; unmoved by visions of reform, he worked behind the scenes with free-silver interests seeking to nominate Judge Walter Q. Gresham [q.v.]. The next year, turning against his friend and patron, Hayes served as hatchet man for a coalition of New York socialists led by Daniel De Leon [q.v.] and Populist-minded agrarians led by James R. Sovereign of Iowa that ousted Powderly from his post as head of the Knights of Labor.

By 1893 the Knights had long since lost its dominant place in the American labor movement, giving way to the American Federation of Labor. Through its declining years Hayes remained in firm control, as General Secretary-Treasurer until 1902 and then as General Master Workman, until he closed down the organization's Washington headquarters in 1916. He continued to use his title, however, and to publish the *National Labor Digest,* which he recommended to employers during the Red Scare of 1919 as an antidote to Bolshevism.

His chief activity of later years was business promotion. As early as 1892 Powderly had noted that Hayes "seems to be possessed of the idea of acquiring riches." He developed the "Hayes process" for manufacturing illuminating gas from soft coal and by 1895 had secured its adoption in two cities. His most successful venture was the North Chesapeake Beach Land and Improvement Company, a real estate development at North Beach, Md., which he began in 1907. Living on to the age of eighty-seven, Hayes died at North Beach in 1942 of hypertensive cardiovascular disease. Following a requiem mass at St. Gabriel's Church in Washington, he was buried in Washington's Mount Olivet Cemetery.

John W. Hayes typified one aspect of the Knights of Labor, its lack of a strong working-class consciousness, as seen in the casual way in which its leaders often shifted over to business or professional roles. He failed, however, to share another important characteristic: the vein of idealism, the urge toward reform found in such leaders as Powderly, Ralph Beaumont, and Richard Trevellick [q.v.].

[The Hayes Papers, Catholic Univ. of America (56 boxes, c. 1885–1920), are about equally divided between his official correspondence with district and local assemblies and his personal affairs, mostly of the 1890's and later. For the years 1884–92 the best source is the voluminous Powderly Papers, also at Catholic Univ. Family data were secured from federal census schedules of 1870 and 1880 (courtesy of Mrs. Rebecca B. Colesar, Archives and Hist. Bureau, N. J. State Lib., Trenton); death record from Md. Division of Vital Records. Published sources: biographical sketch in *Jour. of the Knights of Labor,* Nov. 27, 1890; George E. McNeill, ed., *The Labor Movement* (1887), p. 608; and the sketch in a convention brochure, *22d Annual Session of the Gen. Assembly of the Knights of Labor* (1898), in the Powderly Papers (Box A1-186); T. V. Powderly, *The Path I Trod* (1940), pp. 347n, 366n; Norman J. Ware, *The Labor Movement in the U. S., 1860–1895* (1929); *Who's Who in the Nation's Capital,* 1938–39; obituary in *Washington Times-Herald,* Nov. 28, 1942 (courtesy of D. C. Public Lib.). The 1898 convention brochure, above, reproduces a photograph of Hayes.]

EDWARD T. JAMES

HAYES, MAX SEBASTIAN (May 25, 1866– Oct. 11, 1945), labor editor and socialist leader, was born on his father's farm near Havana, Huron County, Ohio. Christened Maximilian, he was the older of two sons of Joseph Maximilian Sebastian Hoize, a Swiss, and Elizabeth (Storer) Hoize, an Alsatian, who after coming to America changed their name to Hayes. The boy was educated at a rural school and at a grammar school in Fremont, Ohio, to which his parents moved in 1876. At the age of thirteen he entered a printing office as an apprentice. The family moved to Cleveland in 1883, and the following year Max went to work at the *Cleveland Press* and joined the International Typographical Union. He remained a member of his local the rest of his life and was its representative to the

Cleveland Central Labor Union from 1890 to 1939.

In 1891 Hayes founded, with Henry Long, a weekly labor newspaper, the *Cleveland Citizen*, which he edited from 1892 until 1939 as the official journal of the Central Labor Union—an unusually long life for a labor paper. Hayes was a socialist by conviction but, realizing that most workingmen opposed socialism, he lent his support at first to such movements as greenbackism, Populism, the single tax, and the eight-hour day. In 1896, however, he wrote in the *Citizen* that these reforms would not end wage slavery and urged workers to join "a class-conscious political party," take control of the government, and "establish a co-operative commonwealth." That year he joined the Socialist Labor party.

Throughout his career Hayes remained convinced that socialists should work within the established labor movement. In this he differed sharply from the leader of the Socialist Labor party, Daniel De Leon [*q.v.*]. Along with Morris Hillquit [Supp. 1] and others, Hayes broke with De Leon in 1900 to establish a dissident Socialist Labor party, which nominated Job Harriman for president and Hayes for vice-president. A coalition, however, with the Social Democratic party led by Eugene Debs [*q.v.*] brought about a substitute ticket of Debs and Harriman, and Hayes instead ran for Congress. The two groups merged a year later as the Socialist party, with Hayes a member of the national committee.

In accordance with his convictions, Hayes became active in the American Federation of Labor. Beginning in 1898, he was regularly a delegate to its annual conventions, at first representing the Cleveland Central Labor Union and thereafter (1902–37) the International Typographical Union. Hayes found his dual role as socialist and trade union leader difficult to maintain. On the one hand he sought to educate and convert the workers to socialism and to persuade the A.F. of L. to take independent political action and endorse socialist principles. On the other, he opposed excessive criticism of unions and any socialist attempts to take over unions or interfere in their internal affairs. Hayes never quite resolved this conflict, and his policies consequently wavered between introducing socialist resolutions and declaring them unnecessary; between stating that it did not matter who headed the A.F. of L. and contesting Samuel Gompers [*q.v.*] for the presidency in 1912; between criticizing the Federation and defending it. With other moderate socialists, Hayes strongly opposed the formation of the Industrial Workers of the World, both because of its anarchist and revolutionary tendencies and because of its antagonism to the A.F. of L., and he defended the Federation against the charge that it neglected the organization of unskilled workers and discouraged industrial unionism.

Hayes opposed America's involvement in the European war, which would benefit only "the business interests of a few speculators," but when war was declared he acquiesced as a loyal citizen. Yet he defended the socialists who were prosecuted for their opposition to the war. He also defended the Bolshevik revolution, and although he criticized the Soviet regime for making peace with Germany and establishing a "dictatorship," he continued to regard it as a workers' government which was making great progress. Throughout the 1920's he advocated American recognition of the Soviet government and the establishment of trade relations.

In 1919 the left wing of the Socialist party won control of the Cleveland section, and Hayes left the party. Still a proponent of independent political action, he presided over the convention in November 1919 that organized the National Labor party. The party merged in 1920 with the left wing of a middle-class progressive group, the Committee of 48, to form the Farmer-Labor party, which nominated Parley Christensen, a reform-minded lawyer, for president and Max Hayes for vice-president; they received some 300,000 votes that fall. Hayes represented the party at the Conference for Progressive Political Action, called in 1922 on the initiative of the railway unions, but withdrew when the Conference defeated his resolution for independent political action by farmers and workers.

During the 1930's Hayes became an ardent New Dealer. He blamed the depression on a lack of purchasing power, proposed the adoption of a thirty-hour work week, and urged the cooperation of business and organized labor to reduce suffering and prevent revolution. He served as a member of the Ohio State Adjustment Board of the National Recovery Administration. An advocate of public housing legislation, he was also a member of the Cleveland Metropolitan Housing Authority from its inception in 1933. He had been instrumental in forming the Consumers' League of Ohio in 1900, and he remained labor's representative in the organization until his death.

Hayes married Dora Schneider, a salesclerk, on Dec. 11, 1900. They had one daughter, Maxine Elizabeth. Hayes was baptized a Catholic and had once considered studying for the priesthood, but early became disillusioned, left the Church, and thereafter was a critic of the "church bosses." He was a member of the Masonic order and the Knights of Pythias. In 1939 he suffered a cerebral hemorrhage, which paralyzed his left side. Bedridden for the next six years, he died at the age of seventy-nine at his home in Shaker Heights, a suburb of Cleveland. He was buried in Cleveland's Lakeview Cemetery. For nearly three decades he had been the leading unionist in the socialist movement and the leading socialist in the A.F. of L.

[The *Cleveland Citizen*, 1891–1939, provides the most continuous and detailed record of Hayes's ideological development; the issue of Oct. 12, 1945, contains an obituary. Hayes's papers are at the Ohio Hist. Soc. in Columbus. Other sources are the *Proc.* of the Am. Federation of Labor, 1898–1927; the *Internat. Socialist Rev.* of Chicago, 1900–11, for which Hayes wrote a monthly review of labor news and several articles; and his testimony before the U. S. Commission on Industrial Relations, in its *Final Report and Testimony* (64 Cong., 1 Sess., Senate Doc. 415, 1916), II, 1557–65. For brief biographical summaries, see *Who Was Who in America*, vol. II (1950); and *Nat. Cyc. Am. Biog.*, XXXVII, 110. A number of books on the history of socialism and the labor movement are useful for background information as well as specific references to Hayes. The most important are Nathan Fine, *Labor and Farmer Parties in the U. S., 1828–1928* (1928); Philip S. Foner, *Hist. of the Labor Movement in the U. S.*, vols. II-IV (1955–65); Ray Ginger's biography of Debs, *The Bending Cross* (1949); Marc Karson, *Am. Labor Unions and Politics, 1900–1918* (1958); Ira Kipnis, *The Am. Socialist Movement, 1897–1912* (1952); Bernard Mandel, *Samuel Gompers* (1963); and Howard H. Quint, *The Forging of Am. Socialism* (1953). Helpful information was provided by Mr. and Mrs. Albert I. Davey, the daughter and son-in-law of Max Hayes, and by Mrs. Jean Tussey, all of Cleveland.]

BERNARD MANDEL

HECKSCHER, AUGUST (Aug. 26, 1848– Apr. 26, 1941), mine executive, real estate operator, philanthropist, was born in Hamburg, Germany, the only child of Johann Gustav Wilhelm Moritz Heckscher and Antoinette (Brautigam) Heckscher. His father, a noted lawyer and public official who served during the revolution of 1848 as Minister for Foreign Affairs in the provisional German government headed by Archduke John of Austria, hoped his son would join the bar, but August seemed intent upon becoming a merchant. Accordingly, he was sent to school in Switzerland and, after returning home, was apprenticed for three years to an exporting house in Hamburg.

In 1867, against his parents' wishes, he decided to emigrate to the United States, where he had relatives. Borrowing $500 in gold from his mother, he booked passage for New York City. There he rented a small room and set out to teach himself English. He joined the Mercantile Library on Astor Place and spent twelve to fifteen hours a day reading English books and practicing diction; within three months he could read and write the language well. He then called on his cousin Richard Heckscher, who, with other members of the family, owned some 20,000 acres of anthracite lands and a mining company in Schuylkill County, near Shenandoah, Pa. Although he was only nineteen years old and knew nothing of the industry, Heckscher was hired to help run the company. Two weeks later, when his cousin became ill, he took over complete management. His business training, his drive, and his good sense carried him through, and the mine prospered.

When in 1884 the Heckscher mine was sold to the Philadelphia & Reading Coal and Iron Company, Heckscher invested his share of the substantial profits in the Lehigh Zinc & Iron Company, which he had helped organize three years earlier at South Bethlehem, Pa. The competition of the powerful New Jersey Zinc & Iron Company forced the Heckscher concern to purchase land near that of its larger rival in Sussex County, N. J. When it opened a mine on the new land, it discovered the richest zinc deposits in the United States. New Jersey Zinc asserted title to the ore lands, and one of the most famous court cases in the history of jurisprudence resulted. Pouring all his energy and financial resources into the battle, Heckscher with his lawyers fought the case from court to court for ten years, winning eventual vindication. The Pennsylvania and New Jersey concerns merged shortly thereafter (1897), with Heckscher becoming general manager, a post he retained until 1904. Resigning that year, at age fifty-six, the tufty-bearded immigrant intended to retire. New York real estate, however, caught his interest, and he began a new and extremely successful career. He shrewdly acquired land and buildings in midtown Manhattan, particularly around 42nd Street. Within a few years he was one of the largest real estate operators in the city, accumulating many millions on his investments.

Heckscher had a sense of social obligation, and he began to donate much of his wealth to various good causes. Concerned with the plight of delinquent, homeless, and neglected children, in 1921 he established the Heckscher Foundation for Children. One of the foundation's first acts was to construct a five-story building on upper Fifth Avenue for the New York Society for the Prevention of Cruelty to Children, to serve as a neighborhood center and a home for children committed to the society by the courts. The building, which contained dormitories for several hundred children, an infirmary, classrooms, an 800-seat theatre, and a large indoor swimming pool, was the finest home and recreation facility of its kind in America; its total cost of

$4,000,000 made it the largest single charitable donation for the benefit of children in New York's history. Heckscher gave generously also for the establishment of day nurseries and dental clinics, and made funds available for parks and playgrounds in congested areas throughout New York City. In 1926 he became concerned with the city's crowded and disease-breeding tenements, which he sought to have torn down and replaced by modern, sanitary, fireproof structures. With the encouragement of Mayor James J. Walker, he developed several ambitious but unrealistic plans for this purpose, which achieved considerable publicity but soon lapsed into oblivion.

On Oct. 13, 1881, Heckscher had married Anna P. Atkins, daughter of a pioneer Pottsville, Pa., ironmaster, who bore him two children: Gustave Maurice and Antoinette. In 1924 his wife died and his son, who had lost heavily in the Florida land boom, was adjudged bankrupt. Heckscher became a victim of gout and rheumatism but through vigorous exercise, daily swimming, and a rigorous diet managed to regain his health. In July 1930 he married an associate in his child welfare work, Mrs. Virginia Henry Curtiss, the widow of Edwin Burr Curtiss, onetime president of A. G. Spalding & Brothers. In later life Heckscher was chairman of the board of Union Bag and Paper Corporation and an officer and director of many other companies, including several banks and real estate corporations. A devoted yachtsman, known as "Commodore" to his friends, he was also a collector of art. Living to the age of ninety-two, he died at his winter estate at Mountain Lake (near Lake Wales), Fla., of "malnutrition and anemia with arteriosclerosis." After Episcopal services, he was buried in Woodlawn Cemetery, New York City. His grandson and namesake became Commissioner of Parks in the administration of Mayor John V. Lindsay.

[For Heckscher's life, see the long obituary in the *N. Y. Times*, Apr. 27, 1941; sketch in B. C. Forbes, *Men Who Are Making America* (1916); *Who Was Who in America*, vol. I (1942); *Nat. Cyc. Am. Biog.*, XIV, 177–78; and interview by George Mortimer in *American Mag.*, Mar. 1923. For his philanthropic work, see *N. Y. Times*, May 12, 1921, June 5, 1921 (sec. 7), Aug. 29, 1922; *Literary Digest*, May 25, 1929, p. 28; *School and Society*, May 11, 1929, p. 605. For Heckscher's attempts to improve N. Y. City housing, see *Literary Digest*, Nov. 6, 1926, p. 13; and Roy Lubove, "I. N. Phelps Stokes," *Jour. of the Soc. of Architectural Historians*, May 1964, pp. 85–86. For photographs of Heckscher, see *N. Y. Times* obituary, above, and *World's Work*, Oct. 1922, p. 568. Other references: August Heckscher, "Life Begins at Eighty," *Am. Mercury*, Oct. 1939; *N. Y. Times*, May 1, 1941; and *Time*, May 5, 1941, p. 64. Death record from Fla. State Board of Health.]

WALTER I. TRATTNER

HENDERSON, LAWRENCE JOSEPH (June 3, 1878–Feb. 10, 1942), biochemist and physiologist, influential also as a sociologist and as a natural philosopher in the broad sense, was born in Lynn, Mass., the oldest child of Joseph Henderson, a commission merchant, and Mary Reed (Bosworth) Henderson. His father was a native of Salem, Mass. His mother, whose grandparents had moved west to Pittsburgh and thence to Ohio, where she was born, had met Joseph Henderson during a visit to relatives on the East Coast. A woman of marked ability and independence of character, she had been reared in a strongly Calvinistic family but became quite detached from organized religion. Lawrence grew up with two younger brothers; three other brothers, one a twin of Lawrence's, died in infancy. The family was prosperous in his early years, though less so after the depression of 1893, which affected Joseph Henderson's business severely. Of his upbringing Henderson later wrote: "I acquired in childhood and have preserved many of the standards of a respectable, old-fashioned Yankee, and perhaps still more a deep feeling that the pattern of behavior with which these sentiments correspond is the decent and respectable way to live."

As a boy Henderson attended the Salem, Mass., public schools, where he excelled in physics. He entered Harvard College in 1894, at the age of sixteen, and received the degree of A.B. magna cum laude in 1898. In science, he took a particularly active interest in physics and physical chemistry; as a result of an accidental observation in the laboratory he undertook a research problem under the guidance of Professor Theodore W. Richards [*q.v.*], the results of which were published in a German journal. Courses in philosophy and in French literature also roused his interest. At the end of his sophomore year he rigged up a primitive chemical laboratory and gave a six-week intensive course in elementary chemistry to his brother Harry, whose schoolwork had been delayed by illness for a year; he always considered this one of his most valuable experiences.

Wishing to learn biochemistry, Henderson entered the Harvard Medical School in 1898. There he worked with a great deal of independence, devoting only the barely necessary amount of time to some of the routine courses that did not interest him, living at the university in Cambridge, and associating chiefly with nonmedical friends. After receiving the M.D. degree cum laude in 1902, he made no attempt to practice medicine but went abroad for two years to work in the famous laboratory of Franz Hofmeister in

Strassburg. The research problem that he undertook there came to little, but he found the experience immensely valuable. He came to know well a group of young men—Franz Knoop, Gustav Embden, and Karl Spiro, among others—who were later to become leaders in German biochemistry, and he developed lines of independent thought that were to prove fruitful in later years. Life in Strassburg also sharpened his political awareness; in Alsace, which had passed from France to Germany after the war of 1870, no one could escape the tensions between the French and Germans. Within a few months Henderson had become an intense Francophile, and he acquired a lasting dislike and distrust of what he saw as German arrogance and aggressiveness. Politics aside, he found life in Europe delightful and journeyed there repeatedly throughout his life.

Henderson returned to the Harvard Medical School in 1904 as a lecturer in biological chemistry and began research in Richards's laboratory on the heats of combustion of organic molecules in relation to their structure. In the following year, he and his friend Carl L. Alsberg (later professor at Stanford) were appointed instructors. In 1910 Henderson moved back to Harvard College, where he taught for the rest of his life. His introductory course in biological chemistry—designed as a liberal arts course, not a preprofessional one—served as an intellectual stimulus to many students during the next quarter-century. Appointed a full professor in 1919, Henderson the next year established a laboratory of physical chemistry at the Harvard Medical School, but left its actual direction in the hands of a younger colleague, Edwin J. Cohn, who thereby started a distinguished career in protein chemistry.

During the years from 1907 to 1910 Henderson made his first major contribution to science. He was concerned with the balance between acids and bases in the animal organism, as measured by the hydrogen ion concentration, and the processes whereby the organism maintains itself nearly at the point of neutrality. He recognized that the hydrogen ion concentration of any medium is stabilized by the presence of a mixture of an acid with one of its salts, the two being present in nearly equivalent amounts. This phenomenon, known as buffer action, is fundamental for the stability of all living organisms. Henderson noted also that a mixture of carbonic acid and bicarbonates is particularly effective in maintaining the blood in a nearly neutral state. Although these principles were implicit in discoveries already made by physical chemists, Henderson was the first to formulate them explicitly and to demonstrate their immense importance for the living organism.

Carbonic acid is unique among acids, since its aqueous solutions are constantly undergoing exchange with the carbon dioxide of the atmosphere. This carbonic acid buffer system thus serves to stabilize the hydrogen ion concentration of the oceans and other natural waters, as well as that of living organisms. Henderson soon came to recognize the profound geochemical implications of these facts. He found similar significance in the extraordinary properties of water: its high melting point and boiling point, its high surface tension, the fact that ice is lighter than cold water and therefore floats, and many others. Thus water and carbon dioxide are uniquely fit to serve as the basis for life as we know it. Moreover, the properties of the three elements—carbon, hydrogen, and oxygen—which enter into the composition of water and carbon dioxide are also unique in permitting the formation of a vast variety of substances that serve as the basis for the structure and function of living organisms. Henderson formulated these ideas systematically, and in full detail, in his book *The Fitness of the Environment* (1913), which has profoundly influenced the thinking of biologists ever since.

In a later book, *The Order of Nature* (1917), he carried the inquiry further, stressing again the extraordinary properties of carbon, hydrogen, and oxygen, and the unique fitness of their compounds not only for life but for the promotion of variety in physico-chemical systems, for the meteorological cycle, and thus for the physical evolution of the earth. He concluded that these basic facts pointed clearly to a "teleological order" in the universe, although he explicitly disavowed any attempt to associate this order with notions of design or purpose in nature, and considered his views fully compatible with a mechanistic outlook on the problems of biology. His searching historical review, in this volume, of the problem of teleology as envisaged by philosophers and scientists from Aristotle onward bears witness to Henderson's remarkable breadth and depth of reading; for several years, beginning in 1908, he had regularly taken part in the philosophy seminar of Josiah Royce [*q.v.*].

Henderson's work on blood, which began about 1918, was his greatest contribution to biochemistry. When oxygen enters the blood, it tends to drive off carbon dioxide, and the converse effect also necessarily holds. This mutual interaction greatly increases the efficiency of blood for taking on oxygen and discharging carbon dioxide in the lungs. Accompanying these changes there is a flow of water and an exchange of chloride and bicarbonate ions between the blood plasma and the red cells that contain the oxygen-binding protein hemoglobin. All these processes, and others, are mutually dependent; a change in any one variable in the system induces changes in all the others. Influenced by J. Willard Gibbs [q.v.] and the French mathematician Maurice d'Ocagne, Henderson developed a quantitative method of describing these complex interrelations in the form of nomographic charts, from which the changes in all the variables resulting from a change in any one of them could easily be read off. The urgent need for better experimental data led to close informal collaboration with Donald D. Van Slyke at the Rockefeller Institute. Van Slyke was a superb experimenter, whereas Henderson was glad to leave the experimental work to others. Later Arlie V. Bock, D. Bruce Dill, and others came to work in the Fatigue Laboratory which Henderson had been instrumental in establishing at Harvard, and greatly extended the scope of the experimental work. In 1928 Henderson published his comprehensive book *Blood: A Study in General Physiology,* based on his Silliman Lectures at Yale. This set forth the principles of his approach, with a great array of experimental data concerning the blood of animals, and of man in health and disease. His treatment is also important in exemplifying a general approach that can in principle be applied to many other kinds of complex systems of interacting components.

In 1926 Henderson read Vilfredo Pareto's treatise on general sociology and recognized at once that Pareto's thinking about social systems was closely akin to his own analysis of blood as a system of mutually interacting components. He became convinced for the first time that there existed a fruitful way of thinking scientifically about society and human relations. Six years later he began with enthusiasm to conduct a seminar in the sociology department on Pareto, which attracted many gifted students; and in his last years he gave a course entitled "Concrete Sociology," still profoundly influenced by Pareto but increasingly bearing the stamp of Henderson's own thoughts and outlook.

Henderson had been instrumental in bringing George Elton Mayo, the British industrial sociologist, to the Harvard Business School, and their association aroused his deep interest in the human problems of industry and of the practice of medicine. Working with Dean Wallace Donham of the Business School, Henderson secured support from the Rockefeller Foundation for the establishment, in 1927, of a laboratory of human physiology, the Fatigue Laboratory, which sought to determine what chemical changes take place in the body to produce fatigue, and what circumstances—nutritional, atmospheric, and environmental—initiate the physiological changes. For the rest of his life Henderson maintained his office at the Harvard Business School, adjacent to the laboratory, where he was consulted almost daily on policy matters by several successive deans.

Henderson's active interest in the broader affairs of Harvard University took other forms. In 1911 he persuaded President A. Lawrence Lowell [Supp. 3] to let him give a course in the history of science, one of the earliest in an American university and one that he continued to teach for three decades. He was a leader in the founding, in 1933, of Harvard's Society of Fellows, which each year chooses a group of young men of outstanding promise and gives them a secure stipend, together with a maximum degree of freedom to develop along their own lines, for a period of three years or more. Henderson relished presiding over the weekly dinners of the Fellows; he keenly appreciated good food, good conversation, and good wine, of which he was a discriminating judge. The breadth of his interests is attested by his role in bringing to Harvard such distinguished scholars as the historian of science George Sarton, the philosopher Alfred North Whitehead, and the geographer Raoul Blanchard. His personal friendships ranged widely, including such diverse people as the poet Edwin Arlington Robinson [Supp. 1], the medievalist Henry Osborn Taylor [Supp. 3], and the author Bernard DeVoto.

On one of his frequent visits to Europe, Henderson was Harvard Exchange Professor at the Sorbonne in 1921; he later became a member of the French Legion of Honor. He received honorary degrees from the universities of Cambridge and Grenoble. From 1936 until the end of his life he was foreign secretary of the National Academy of Sciences, and did much to promote relations with the scientists of Western Europe, especially of Great Britain. He remained deeply attached to New England, and spent many summers at his camp on Lake Seymour at Morgan Center, Vt. On June 1, 1910, he had married Edith Lawrence Thayer, a sister-in-law of his former professor, T. W. Richards. They had one son, Lawrence Joseph. Henderson died in Massachusetts General Hospital, Boston, at the age of sixty-three, from a pulmonary embolism following an operation for cancer. He was buried in Mount Auburn Cemetery, Cambridge.

In the words of an associate, Dickinson Richards, Henderson was "a stoutish man of middle stature," with "light thinning red hair and a red beard, graying as the years moved on. His eyes were wide and very blue, his cheeks pink, his expression in repose a little surprised, in his earlier years even a little cherubic." His voice was high-pitched, perhaps as a result of a nearly fatal attack of diphtheria in childhood. He loved discussion and would often maintain his position with great force and sometimes with strong emotion. His mind and temperament were complex. Especially in his later years, he spoke often with intense distrust of "intellectuals," liberals, and uplifters, who he felt failed to understand the deep nonrational sentiments that are an essential foundation for a satisfactory and stable society; on occasion he could infuriate some of his hearers, who thought him cynical, or pedantic, or both. Yet he was also full of kindness and helpfulness, especially to the young; he recognized and encouraged talent in young men of the most diverse sorts who came to the Society of Fellows. He respected good workmanship, whether in a carpenter or a mathematical physicist. Henderson's analysis of the biological significance of the properties of matter, and his vision of organization and regulation in biological systems, have left an enduring imprint on the thinking of biologists. His influence as a sociologist, though harder to estimate, is certainly significant. In diverse ways he contributed to the development of Harvard University and to the broadening of the intellectual outlook of many younger people who came in contact with him.

[Besides the books mentioned above, Henderson published *Pareto's General Sociology: A Physiologist's Interpretation* (1935). Many of his papers, including his unpublished "Memories" (265 typewritten pages), are in the archives of the Harvard Business School or in the Harvard Univ. Archives in Widener Lib. There is a valuable memoir by Walter B. Cannon in Nat. Acad. Sci., *Biog. Memoirs*, vol. XXIII (1945), with a nearly complete bibliography. The most detailed study is J. L. Parascandola, "Lawrence J. Henderson and the Concept of Organized Systems" (Ph.D. dissertation, Univ. of Wis., 1968). Edward W. Forbes and John H. Finley, Jr., eds., *The Saturday Club: A Century Completed, 1920–1956* (1958), includes Crane Brinton's perceptive portrait of Henderson as a man. For other valuable articles on Henderson, see Ronald M. Ferry in *Science*, Mar. 27, 1942; memorial minute by Brinton, Ferry, Edwin B. Wilson, and Arlie V. Bock in *Harvard Univ. Gazette*, May 16, 1942; Dickinson W. Richards in the *Physiologist*, May 1958; J. H. Talbott in *Jour. Am. Medic. Assoc.*, Dec. 19, 1966; Jean Mayer in *Jour. of Nutrition*, Jan. 1968; D. Bruce Dill, "The Harvard Fatigue Laboratory," *Circulation Research*, Supp. I to vols. XX–XXI (Mar. 1967). Family information and suggestions from Robert G. Henderson and Lawrence J. Henderson, Jr. Birth and death records from Mass. Registrar of Vital Statistics. Two recent publications are: *L. J. Henderson on the Social System* (1970), a selection of Henderson's sociological writings ed. by Bernard Barber; and John Parascandola, "Organismic and Holistic Concepts in the Thought of L. J. Henderson," *Jour. of the Hist. of Biology*, Spring 1971 (with a note on the Henderson Papers).]

JOHN T. EDSALL

HENDERSON, YANDELL (Apr. 23, 1873– Feb. 18, 1944), physiologist and toxicologist, was born in Louisville, Ky., the older of the two sons of Isham Henderson and Sally Nielsen (Yandell) Henderson. His father, a lawyer and engineer, built the first canal around the falls of the Ohio near Louisville and was part owner of the *Louisville Journal*, 1849–68. His mother came of a Tennessee family with a strong medical tradition: his grandfather Lunsford Pitts Yandell [*q.v.*] had helped found a medical school in Louisville in 1837; his uncle David Wendel Yandell [*q.v.*] was medical director of the Confederate Department of the West and afterward president of the American Medical Association. Yandell Henderson attended Chenault's School in Louisville and entered Yale College in 1891. In 1895 he began graduate work at Yale, studying physiological chemistry under Russell H. Chittenden [Supp. 3], and in 1898 received his Ph.D. His first published paper, "A Chemico-Physiological Study of Certain Derivatives of the Proteids," written with Chittenden and his assistant Lafayette B. Mendel [*q.v.*], appeared in the *American Journal of Physiology* in 1899. Meanwhile, in 1898, Henderson, like other American chemists of the period, had gone to Germany to complete his education. At Marburg he studied under Albrecht Kossel and at Munich under Carl Voit.

Upon his return in 1900, Henderson became an instructor in the physiological laboratory of the Yale Medical School (advancing to assistant professor in 1903 and professor in 1911) and began research on the physiology of the circulation. The results of his experiments led him to question current theories of the action of the heart and, in turn, to investigate the physiological role of carbon dioxide in respiration. Theories of mammalian circulation at that time were based chiefly on studies of the frog, the favorite experimental animal since the days of William Harvey. Henderson—a leader in shifting laboratory instruction in physiology from the study of the frog to that of mammals—used dogs and cats as subjects and devised new instruments which revealed hitherto unrecognized and distinctive characteristics of the mammalian heartbeat. This work led him to challenge the accepted theory that the return of blood to the heart was produced by auricular contraction. Instead, he proposed the existence of a "venopressor mechanism" and characteristically tried to discover the nature of this mechanism by studies on animals in which an acutely low blood pressure (shock) had been produced by various means. To his surprise he found that increasing the rate of artificial respiration aggravated the circulatory failure. Since forced ventilation depletes the blood of carbon dioxide, he associated the loss with the accelerated fall in blood pressure. This observation became the basis for Henderson's famous "acapnia theory of shock," which he first set forth in the *British Medical Journal* of Dec. 22, 1906. This theory was received with incredulity, and, as Henderson admitted in his autobiographical *Adventures in Respiration* (p. 19), "it was doubtful whether I could have succeeded had not J. S. Haldane and his collaborators, at the most convenient moment for me (1905), published their epoch-making studies on the part that carbon dioxide plays in the normal control of respiration." In an address in 1909 ("Fatal Apnoea and the Shock Problem," Johns Hopkins Hospital, *Bulletin,* August 1910) he pointed out the role of severe pain in stimulating overventilation and described experiments in which an anesthetized animal was made to rebreathe a certain amount of its own expired air so as to maintain a proper level of carbon dioxide in the blood and thus prevent respiratory failure. This and later work led the way to the clinical use of a mixture of carbon dioxide and oxygen after anesthesia. The "acapnia" theory was eventually discarded, but not before its author had used it as the basis for his pioneer studies of ventilation, noxious gases, and resuscitation.

Henderson actively supported Haldane in his dispute with Joseph Barcroft over the important question of whether the lungs could actively secrete oxygen when the oxygen content of the air was decreased. To test the theory (eventually disproved by Barcroft), and to determine the mechanisms involved in man's adaptation to low atmospheric pressures, Henderson in 1911 joined Haldane and others in an Oxford-Yale expedition to Pikes Peak in Colorado. In a laboratory set up at some 14,000 feet they performed experiments whose results later became the basis for understanding the physiological disturbances suffered by aviators at high altitudes.

Henderson also undertook studies of ventilation for the United States Bureau of Mines. In 1920, in collaboration with Howard Wilcox Haggard, he determined standards of ventilation which were used in the design of the Holland Tunnel under the Hudson River and which became generally accepted for similar tunnels throughout the world. The two men also made a thorough investigation of the mechanism and treatment of poisoning by noxious gases—notably carbon monoxide—which was summarized by Henderson's most important book (written with Haggard), *Noxious Gases and the Principles of Respiration Influencing Their Action* (1927). In 1922 the Henderson-Haggard inhalator for use in asphyxia

became standard equipment for rescue squads and has had wide use in stimulating breathing in the newborn.

Henderson's demonstration of the effectiveness of carbon dioxide in the relief of anoxia led him into further disputes with biochemists over the relationship of anoxia to acidosis. Prof. Lawrence J. Henderson [Supp. 3] of Harvard had introduced into physiology the concept of an acid-base balance, according to which an excessive accumulation of carbon dioxide and other acids in the body must accompany asphyxiation, so that the administration of carbon dioxide in asphyxia would aggravate the condition. Yandell Henderson vigorously defended his own view and termed as "pseudo-acidosis" the condition described by L. J. Henderson. The chemical vagueness of this definition made it unacceptable to biochemists. Yandell Henderson, however, believed with Haldane in a complexity of the animal economy beyond the reach of contemporary physical science, as he stated at the beginning of his important paper on the "Physiological Regulation of the Acid-Base Balance of the Blood" (*Physiological Reviews,* April 1925) and throughout his *Adventures in Respiration* (1938).

During World War I, Henderson served as chief of the physiological section of the war-gas investigations conducted by the Bureau of Mines. He carried out research in methods of chemical warfare and improved the design of the gas masks worn by the Allied armies in France. As chairman of the medical research board of the Aviation Section of the army Signal Corps (1917–18), he organized a laboratory to test the highest altitude a particular individual could safely withstand.

When Henderson opposed the reorganization of Yale University in 1920, he was removed from his professorship at the medical school and (in 1921) appointed professor of applied physiology in the graduate school. With no teaching duties, he continued his investigation of respiration and circulation. He also undertook other assignments. Much dissatisfaction was felt at Yale at this time because many younger faculty members were underpaid and were expected to supplement their incomes by summer employment. Appointed to study the problem, Henderson produced (with Maurice R. Davie) a forthright document, *Incomes and Living Costs of a University Faculty* (1928), that made bold recommendations for improving the salary scale.

As a young man Henderson had shown some interest in public affairs. He was a delegate to the Progressive National Convention in 1912 and ran for Congress on that party's ticket in 1912 and 1914. During the 1920's he became concerned with the prohibition question. Regarding distilled liquors as dangerous and habit-forming narcotics, he proposed discouraging their use through high taxes, and his testimony before a Congressional committee was partly responsible for the limits set in the 1933 legislation that permitted the sale of beer containing 3.2 percent alcohol by weight.

Henderson married Mary Gardner Colby of Newton Center, Mass., on Apr. 2, 1903. Their children were Malcolm Colby and Sylvia Yandell. A member of many professional societies, Henderson was elected to the National Academy of Sciences in 1923 and to the American Philosophical Society in 1935. He became professor emeritus at Yale in 1938. In 1944, at the age of seventy, he died of cancer at Scripps Memorial Hospital, San Diego, Calif. His remains were cremated and the ashes buried in East Lawn Cemetery, Williamstown, Mass., the home of his son-in-law. Outspoken and tenacious of his opinions, Henderson often allowed his personality to exacerbate his scientific disputes, but his ideas, though not always right, provided a strong stimulus to continued research in a complex field.

[Henderson's autobiographical *Adventures in Respiration,* a defense of his physiological theories, which includes a bibliography of his publications; obituaries in Am. Philosophical Soc., *Year Book,* 1944 (by Howard W. Haggard), *Jour. of Industrial Hygiene and Toxicology,* May 1944 (by Cecil B. Drinker), and *Nature,* Mar. 11, 1944; *Nat. Cyc. Am. Biog.,* XXXVI, 25–26 (with photograph); *Who's Who in Ky.,* 1936; Yale Univ., *Obituary Record,* 1943–44; information from Prof. Malcolm C. Henderson, Berkeley, Calif.; death record from Calif. Dept. of Public Health. For Henderson's views on the liquor question, see his *A New Deal in Liquor* (1934). On his father, see Thomas D. Clark, *A Hist. of Ky.* (1937), pp. 343–44.]

C. N. H. LONG

HENRICI, ARTHUR TRAUTWEIN (Mar. 31, 1889–Apr. 23, 1943), bacteriologist and microbiologist, was born in Economy (later Ambridge), Pa., the youngest of five children, four of them boys, of Jacob Frederick and Viola (Irons) Henrici. Though his mother's family was Scottish, he was mostly of German descent. The Henricis, originally religious dissenters from the Piedmont province of Italy, had settled in the Rhenish Palatinate, from which Arthur's great-uncle, Jacob Henrici, led a family group in 1823 to the United States; there he joined the Harmony Society of George Rapp [*q.v.*], a communitarian settlement at Economy, of which he became the leader after Rapp's death. Arthur's father, however, was not a member of the Society, and the boy grew up in Pittsburgh, where his father was a bookseller and writer for newspapers and magazines and a member of the Unitarian Church.

Young Henrici attended public schools in Pitts-

burgh. As a boy, he was allowed to share in his father's hobby of microscopy and spent many hours observing bacteria. A high school biology course strengthened this interest, and in order to study bacteriology he entered the University of Pittsburgh Medical School. After graduating in 1911, first in his class, Henrici stayed on in Pittsburgh for another year and a half studying pathology and bacteriology at St. Francis Hospital. In the summer of 1913 he was appointed instructor in pathology and bacteriology at the University of Minnesota. There he remained for the rest of his career, moving up the academic ranks to become assistant professor in 1916, associate professor in 1920, and professor in 1925. His teaching was interrupted by wartime duty (1917–19) in the army medical corps, where he was involved in the production of typhoid vaccine and was later assigned as bacteriologist to a hospital near Vichy, France.

Henrici's primary scientific interests lay in the morphology and taxonomy of microorganisms and of certain "higher" forms such as yeasts and molds. At the International Botanical Congress of 1926 he presented a widely acclaimed paper at a symposium on bacterial variation, then a controversial subject. His first book, *Morphologic Variation and the Rate of Growth of Bacteria* (1928), established his reputation; it brought order into this then chaotic area of bacteriology and offered fresh points of view. Henrici showed conclusively that bacteria exhibit highly regular changes in size, structure, and form, which depend upon the phase of the life cycle as well as the culture conditions, and that the rigidity of the Cohn-Koch dogma had to be relaxed somewhat regarding the range of these changes in any given pure culture. The work required a great deal of painstaking microscopic observation and reveals Henrici's great skill in this area. His *Molds, Yeasts, and Actinomycetes* (1930) gave him deserved international renown. Henrici's third and last book, *The Biology of Bacteria* (1934)— widely used as a college text—accurately reflected his wide-ranging interest in bacteria as legitimate objects for study in their own right, entirely apart from their importance as economic or disease agents, an approach that marked the microbiologist as distinct from the bacteriologist. He also made notable contributions to knowledge of the ecology and taxonomy of fresh- and salt-water microorganisms, a project begun during vacations in the Minnesota lake region.

Henrici was elected president of the Society of American Bacteriologists (later the American Society for Microbiology) in 1939. He was also a member of the Society of Experimental Biology and Medicine, the Limnological Society of America, and the Mycological Society of America. He was a masterful lecturer and teacher, and his wide range of knowledge and interests established "Henrique," as his students and friends called him, as an always reliable source of information on esoteric subjects.

Henrici's hobbies were as wide-ranging as his scientific interests. Over the years they included photography, etching, music (he played the flute well enough to be in a chamber group composed of members of the Minneapolis Symphony Orchestra), rifle marksmanship, and the building of an early radio set, for which he obtained plans and tubes from the inventor Lee de Forest. He generally pursued each hobby only to the point where he had mastered it and achieved recognition, after which he turned to something else. Although Henrici was not a member of any particular church, he frequently attended Quaker meetings. As to political philosophy, he at first considered himself a socialist, but later supported the Democratic party and Roosevelt's New Deal.

On Aug. 7, 1913, Henrici married Blanche Ressler. Their three children were Carl Ressler, Ruth Elizabeth, and Hazel Jean. Henrici died at the University Hospital in Minneapolis of a coronary thrombosis at the early age of fifty-four; he was buried in Sunset Memorial Cemetery, Minneapolis. His work had a significant and permanent impact on microbiology, particularly enriching the fields of bacterial morphology and ecology.

[*Henrici: Recollections by Some Close Friends and Associates* (1960), a booklet of six informal essays prepared by the Henrici Soc. for Microbiologists; obituaries in *Jour. of Bacteriology*, Dec. 1943 (by Robert L. Starkey and Selman A. Waksman), *Science*, July 23, 1943 (by W. P. Larson), *Mycopathologia*, IV (1948), 120–23 (by Charles H. Drake), with bibliography of Henrici's publications, and *Jour. Am. Medic. Assoc.*, July 3, 1943; *Who Was Who in America*, vol. II (1950). Information on the family background from Mr. Max Henrici, Coraopolis, Pa., a brother, and from the Pa. Division, Carnegie Lib. of Pittsburgh.]

RAYMOND N. DOETSCH

HENRY, ALICE (Mar. 21, 1857–Feb. 14, 1943), labor leader, was born in Richmond, Victoria, Australia, a suburb of Melbourne. She was the oldest of three children of Margaret (Walker) Henry, a seamstress, and Charles Ferguson Henry, an accountant and a Swedenborgian in religion, who had married soon after they emigrated from Glasgow, Scotland, in 1852. Growing up in Melbourne, Alice attended common and private schools, received private instruction in literature and logic, and studied and did pupil teaching at the Educational Institute for Ladies. In 1884 she began writing newspaper pieces. Soon after-

ward she joined the staff of the *Australasian,* and thereafter worked upward on the journalistic ladder by turning out society notes, recipes, and features for this weekly and its affiliated daily, the Melbourne *Argus.* She became interested in reforms affecting the condition of workers, women, and handicapped children.

By the turn of the century, her parents having died some years before, Alice Henry had few ties in Australia and felt free to explore new countries overseas. In 1905, at the age of forty-eight, she sailed for England. For the next six months she studied workers' education, heard Bernard Shaw speak and the suffragist Christabel Pankhurst agitate. Then, at the urging of the many Americans she had met in her travels, she set out for the United States with a mere $150, hoping to find employment, and arrived in January 1906. Friends in reform circles arranged speaking and writing assignments. She shared the platform with such notables as Edwin Markham [Supp. 2] and Susan B. Anthony [*q.v.*], talking about wage boards and woman suffrage in Australia. Jane Addams [Supp. 1] summoned her to Hull House to help in a drive for the municipal vote for women in Chicago.

Alice Henry was then at "the height of her powers, a newspaperwoman of ability, a feminist, an ardent supporter of labor" (Dreier, p. 10). At the request of Margaret Dreier Robins [Supp. 3], president of the National Women's Trade Union League (founded in 1903), Alice Henry became secretary of the League's Chicago office. The monthly *Union Labor Advocate* provided rent-free desk space, and in 1908 Miss Henry was invited to start a women's section in this paper. In January 1911 the League launched its own monthly, *Life and Labor,* with Alice Henry as editor. Her opening editorial declared that the new publication would strive to "bring the working girl into fuller and larger relationship with life on all sides."

For four and one-half years she filled its pages with factual reports about working women, firsthand accounts of their strikes and their national and worldwide organizational activities. Her editorship reflects a turbulent time marked by such significant strikes involving women as the New York shirtwaist makers' and cloakmakers' strikes of 1909 and 1910 and the walkout of men's-wear workers in Chicago in 1910. The conduct and consequences of these conflicts were analyzed in detail in *Life and Labor;* so too, in 1911, were the causes of the Triangle Shirtwaist Company fire in New York City, which took 146 lives. These and other aspects of the cause of working women she set forth also in her two books, *The*

Trade Union Woman (1915) and *Women and the Labor Movement* (1923).

Alice Henry left her editorial post in June 1915 to take on lecturing and secretarial assignments for the League's educational department. From 1920 to 1922 she was director of its school to train working women in the art of effective union leadership. She was course lecturer at the first Bryn Mawr Summer School for Workers in 1921. She returned to Europe in 1924 to survey workers' education and then went on to Australia for a year's stay. Back in the United States, she moved because of illness to Santa Barbara, Calif., where she lived from 1928 to 1933. She never married. Returning to Australia in 1933, she died there ten years later in a Melbourne rest home.

Alice Henry's strength as a journalist lies in an intense concern with detail, whether she is describing a complex industrial process, commercial candy-dipping, proportional representation, fertilization of the fig, or special care of the handicapped. An associate (Pauline Newman of the International Ladies' Garment Workers' Union) remembered her as "white-haired and warm-hearted but always terribly serious about the cause of the working girl." Miss Henry depicted working women as an oppressed minority. To their liberation she brought single-minded dedication and journalistic skill at a time when their fights for voting rights and industrial rights coincided.

[*Memoirs of Alice Henry,* ed. by Nettie Palmer (mimeographed, Melbourne, 1944), which outlines events of her life and pays warm tribute to Australian and American colleagues; files of *Life and Labor,* Jan. 1910–June 1915 (a photograph of her is in the Dec. 1912 number); Mary E. Dreier's appreciative obituary in *Life and Labor Bull.,* Apr. 1943; Frederick D. Kershner, Jr., in *Notable Am. Women,* II, 183–84. Gladys Boone, *The Women's Trade Union Leagues in Great Britain and the U.S.A.* (1942), provides fuller background. Alice Henry's "Industrial Democracy," *Outlook,* Nov. 3, 1906, is a good example of her free-lance work. The *Am. Labor Year Book* (Rand School of Social Science), 1916, 1917–18, and 1919–20, contains her reports on the Women's Trade Union League.]

LEON STEIN

HERRIMAN, GEORGE JOSEPH (Aug. 22, 1880–Apr. 25, 1944), cartoonist, was born in New Orleans, La., the oldest child of George Joseph Herriman, a tailor, and Clara (Morel) Herriman. There were at least three other children, two daughters and a son. Articles published during Herriman's lifetime and apparently based on his own statements describe him as being of either French or Greek parentage and his father as, variously, "a Parisian tailor and amateur astronomer," a baker, and a barber. Herriman's death certificate lists his parents as natives of France; but it is clear from census and birth records that they were in fact natives of Louisiana, as were his grandparents on both sides. Herriman's birth certificate lists him as "colored"; the federal census for 1880 designated his parents as "mulatto."

Herriman in later life was extremely shy, almost a recluse. Accounts of his early life are vague and, probably, often apocryphal. At some time during his childhood the family moved to Los Angeles, where they presumably assumed a white identity. Somehow George learned to draw and paint, though there are indications that his father frowned upon this pursuit; he did not complete high school. There are stories of his unsuccess at this point, often with a wry turn. Thus there developed the tradition of young Herriman as a feckless, knockabout adolescent, fired from a bakery "for eating too many cream puffs," failing, out of meekness, as a fruit peddler, and stumbling about on the scaffolding in his brief, equally hapless stint as a house painter. At one point he apparently worked as a painter of shop windows. One of his sketches was published by the *Los Angeles Herald* in 1897, and the paper hired him at a salary of two dollars a week, some say as an office boy, others as a worker in the engraving plant. As early as 1901 he began publishing full-color Sunday cartoons, though he had not yet devised any comic strips. By November 1902 he was sufficiently well known to be included in a *Bookman* magazine survey of American comic artists. On July 7 of that year, in Los Angeles, he married Mabel Lillian Bridge, by whom he had one daughter, Mabel.

"Lariat Pete," Herriman's first strip, ran in the *San Francisco Chronicle* in 1903. Several years later Herriman "rode the rails to New York in search of fortune," and the sometime cartoonist found himself on Coney Island, where he painted canvases and billboards for sideshows and concession stands and, according to tradition, also worked as a barker for a snake act. At this time he sold a few cartoons to the old *Life* and *Judge,* and then landed a job with the New York *World* on the success of some grotesque billboards. He did political and sports cartoons for the *World* and developed several short-lived strips, including "Major Ozone, the Fresh Air Fiend," which ran in the *San Francisco Call* (1906). In 1907 or 1908 he was hired by the Hearst publications, for whom he drew "Mary" and other comic strips which failed to catch on. His first successful creation was "The Dingbat Family" (1910), whose housecat and its nemesis mouse became so popular that they soon appeared as a substrip below the Dingbats, becoming "Krazy Kat and Ignatz" in 1911. By 1913, as "Krazy Kat," Herriman's greatest and best-loved strip was well established, and it ran without interruption until his death.

Though never achieving the mass following of such strips as "Blondie," "Krazy Kat" enjoyed a wide and fanatically devoted readership that ranged from ordinary comics fans to President Wilson and the avant-garde. The romantic triangle of the Kat ("he of the indeterminate gender"), Ignatz Mouse, and Offissa Bull Pupp was played against scenery of arid Coconino County, a background in a constant state of transmogrification, and in the upper reaches of the atmosphere. The nexus of the strip was the unending and unresolved warfare of Ignatz, the truculent brick-tossing cynic, against Krazy, who loved the Mouse with whole-souled devotion, while the phlegmatic doughty Offissa Pupp, enamored of the Kat, strove to frustrate the Mouse's evil designs. Numerous other characters passed through the strip and engaged in tender or bizarre by-play, and there were excursions into allegory and myth, but the heart of the strip was its love story. Herriman's art was characterized by a seemingly artless yet masterfully executed technique. He used various unconventional devices, and expressed a desire for greater innovation in comic strip art. His full-color strips were considered brilliant. The language of the strips—at once grandiloquent and homely—was as unique as the art, with extravagant word plays which delighted initiates and baffled others. "Fey," "insane," and "metaphysical" were some of the terms used by enthusiasts to describe "Krazy Kat."

In 1921 the composer John Alden Carpenter created a jazz pantomime based on the strip, which was performed by the Chicago Opera Company before being presented in New York at a Town Hall Concert in 1922, with scenario, costumes, and moving backdrops by Herriman. Generally dismissed by critics, the production, and the strip that inspired it, were praised by Deems Taylor in *Vanity Fair.* A later performance in the *Greenwich Village Follies* prompted the critic Stark Young to write a fond tribute, in the *New Republic,* to the "tiny, diaphanous and crack-brained epic of love." Writing of the strip itself, Gilbert Seldes (*The Seven Lively Arts,* 1924) praised Herriman as a master of irony and pathos comparable to Dickens and Charlie Chaplin. The "spiritual force" and "frank frenzy" of "Krazy Kat" moved E. E. Cummings to celebrate the strip as a "meteoric burlesk melodrama" of the triumph of love, democracy, and individual integrity. Other critics and scholars have examined it in terms of surrealism and comic strip artistry, and even as a document of social and economic crisis.

Herriman himself regarded his creation in simple and deeply affectionate terms. A modest man with aspirations toward serious painting, an animal lover, and a dandy, he was greatly loved by a small circle of intimates. In 1923 Herriman began a new strip, "Stumble Inn," using characters from his earlier creations. He also illustrated a book by Don Marquis [Supp. 2], *Archy Does His Part* (1935). After the death of his wife around 1934, Herriman lived with his daughter. He died in their Los Angeles home at the age of sixty-three of nonalcoholic cirrhosis of the liver. Following services at the Little Church of the Flowers, Forest Lawn Memorial Park, his remains were cremated.

[Official records establish certain basic facts of Herriman's life: his birth record (New Orleans Health Dept.); federal census schedules of 1880; marriage record (County Recorder, Los Angeles County, Calif.); death record (Calif. Dept. of Public Health). Aside from the birth and census records, there are no known sources that are completely reliable on Herriman's early life. Variant accounts of his ancestry, his father's occupation, and his early career are found in the *New York Times* obituary, Apr. 27, 1944; *Time,* May 8, 1944, p. 94; clippings in the music collection of the Boston Public Lib.; a "Biographical Note" in the anthology, *Krazy Kat* (1946), which also contains the E. E. Cummings essay; Barbara Gelman's foreword to the new and greatly revised *Krazy Kat* anthology (1969), which reproduces some color strips; and *Vanity Fair,* Dec. 1930, p. 72. Information on his early strips and on the beginnings of "Krazy Kat" and discussion of Herriman's techniques can be found in Gelman; Stephen Becker, *Comic Art in America* (1959), pp. 344-50; Martin Sheridan, *Comics and Their Creators* (1942), pp. 64-65; and Gilbert Seldes, *The Seven Lively Arts* (1924). The John Alden Carpenter score of "Krazy Kat," a Jazz Pantomime (1922) is illustrated by Herriman and contains Carpenter's brief essay on the strip. Appreciations of "Krazy Kat" are in Seldes; Deems Taylor, "America's First Dramatic Composer," *Vanity Fair,* Apr. 1922; and Stark Young, "Krazy Kat," *New Republic,* Oct. 11, 1922. On Herriman's personality, see *Time* (above) and *Literary Digest,* Apr. 20, 1935, p. 25. There are good photographs of Herriman in the latter, and in Sheridan (above); *Bookman,* Nov. 1902, p. 266; and *Vanity Fair,* Mar. 1932, p. 27.]

MARIE CASKEY

HERSHEY, MILTON SNAVELY (Sept. 13, 1857–Oct. 13, 1945), chocolate manufacturer, philanthropist, was the only child of Henry H. and Fannie B. (Snavely) Hershey. His Swiss Mennonite forebears had settled in Lancaster County, Pa., in 1719, and Hershey was born in his great-grandfather's farmhouse in adjacent Dauphin County, in Derry Township on the site of the later Hershey, Pa. His father was a perennial optimist, moving from farm to farm and from city to city promoting petty enterprises, none of them successful; his mother, the daughter of a Mennonite bishop, was a stabilizing influence. Hershey attended seven schools in eight years, never going beyond the fourth grade level. At the age of fourteen he took his first job, as a printer's devil on a newspaper in Lancaster, Pa., but, bored and inefficient, was fired within the year. With his next position, however, as apprentice to a Lancaster confectioner, he found his life's work.

After completing a four-year apprenticeship, Hershey in 1876 went into business for himself in Philadelphia. Making candy by night and selling it by day, inadequately capitalized and fighting strong competition, he could not make his business pay; by 1882 he had worked himself into a state of exhaustion and had to give up. For a time he worked for a confectioner in Denver, where his roving father had located. Father and son next ran a candy business in Chicago, until the elder Hershey endorsed a friend's bad note. Young Hershey made another start in New York City, but after initial success the venture collapsed in 1886.

Back in Lancaster, Hershey scraped together enough money to begin afresh. In Denver he had discovered that fresh milk, properly used, could give candy a delicious flavor. The fresh-milk caramels he was making in Lancaster pleased an English importer, who gave him a large order, and a local banker, impressed by his determination, provided funds for the equipment and personnel needed to fill it. Success followed quickly; less than three years later Hershey was one of Lancaster's wealthiest citizens.

A highly innovative confectioner, Hershey personally concocted most of his candies. Throughout the 1890's his principal products were caramels, some of them flavored with chocolate which he bought from other manufacturers. In 1893, inspired by German chocolate-making machinery exhibited at the Chicago World's Fair, he decided to produce his own chocolate. Soon he was making not only caramels but a variety of chocolate cigars, miniature bicycles, and other novelties. Deciding to concentrate on chocolate, in 1900 he sold his caramel business for $1,000,000 to his chief rival, the American Caramel Company, and in 1903 began construction of a new factory in his native Derry Township, in the heart of the Pennsylvania Dutch dairy country. Through lengthy experimentation, he had perfected his formula for chocolate, and he now began mass-producing five-cent milk chocolate and almond milk chocolate bars—the foundation of his great success. Although he did no advertising ("quality," he believed, "is the best kind of advertising"), his sales grew rapidly: $622,000 in 1901; $5,000,000 in 1911; $20,000,000 in 1921; $30,000,000 in 1931; $55,000,000 in 1941. The firm was incorporated in 1927 as the Hershey Chocolate Corporation, but Hershey

remained the dominant figure as majority stockholder and chairman of the board.

Around his factory Hershey constructed a town, a self-sufficient community that came to include schools, churches, stores, a bank, an inn, golf courses, an amusement park, zoo, football field, and dancing pavilion, all Hershey-owned. He operated his community enterprises with enlightened self-interest. He insisted that the company store earn only a modest profit, and he rented houses to employees at low rates. In 1930, to provide employment during the depression, he launched a large building program that added to the town, over the next nine years, a community building, a 150-room hotel, a large new school, an office building, a sports arena, and a 17,000-seat football stadium. Pleasingly laid out, the town of Hershey came to resemble a college community more than an industrial center. Yet, unincorporated and without a mayor or municipal government, it remained entirely under Hershey's paternalistic control. Along with the amenities of his model town, Hershey's employees received only moderately good wages. Labor organization and labor strife first came to Hershey in 1937, when club-wielding dairy farmers routed a C.I.O. union's sit-down strike for a closed shop. Peace was soon restored, and three years later the Hershey plant was organized by an A.F. of L. union.

On May 25, 1898, at age forty, Hershey married Catherine Sweeney, a New York City shopgirl. In 1909 the childless couple decided to house and educate four orphaned boys, a venture which expanded to become a trade school for orphans. As the school grew, vocational training was gradually supplemented by business and college preparatory curricula. Hershey's wife died in 1915. Three years later he placed the bulk of his fortune, valued at $60,000,000, in trust for the Hershey Industrial School (later renamed the Milton Hershey School). So strong was the school's financial position that in 1963, nearly two decades after Hershey's death, it set aside $50,000,000 to build the Milton S. Hershey Medical Center at Hershey as the medical school of Pennsylvania State University.

In appearance, Hershey in his sixties was short, stout, and ruddy-faced, with a small gray moustache. In the judgment of *Fortune* magazine (January 1934, p. 80), he was "disinterested, sincere, [and] warm-hearted, with a genuine desire to do good to his neighbors." At the same time he had "the strong will, the ego, and the intellectual limitations of many another self-made man," and hence wanted to "do things for people rather than supply them with the money to do things for themselves." Hershey stepped down from his post as chairman of the board in 1944, shortly after his eighty-seventh birthday. He died a year later in the Hershey Hospital following a heart attack and was buried in Hershey Cemetery.

[Joseph R. Snavely, *An Intimate Story of Milton S. Hershey* (1957); Katherine B. Shippen and Paul A. W. Wallace, *Biog. of Milton S. Hershey* (1959); Samuel F. Hinkle, *Hershey* (1964); Hershey Chocolate Corp., *The Story of Hershey, the Chocolate Town* (1960); articles about Hershey or his town in: *Literary Digest*, Dec. 1, 1923; *Current Opinion*, Jan. 1924; *Forbes Mag.*, Mar. 1, 1929; *Fortune*, Jan. 1934; *Investor's Reader*, Sept. 6, 1967; *Business Week*, Apr. 17, 1937; *N. Y. Times*, Nov. 9, 10, 18, 1923, Oct. 14, 1945 (obituary). The Shippen-Wallace book contains photographs of Hershey at various stages of his life. A bronze statue of Hershey stands in the foyer of the Milton Hershey School.]

DAVID L. LEWIS

HERTZ, ALFRED (July 15, 1872–Apr. 17, 1942), orchestra conductor, was born in Frankfurt am Main, Germany, the younger of two sons of Jewish parents, Leo and Sara (Koenigswerther) Hertz. His father is said to have been a well-to-do merchant. Crippled in one foot by polio in infancy, Hertz began piano lessons at the age of six. At twelve he overrode his parents' wish that he study law and entered the Raff Conservatory of Music in Frankfurt, where his principal teacher was Hans von Bülow. After graduating at the age of nineteen, Hertz was appointed to the unpaid post of "Correpetitor," or assistant conductor, at the Opera House in Halle. The next year (1892) he became assistant conductor at the Hoftheater (Court Theatre) in Altenburg, Saxony, and in 1895 he was given his first full conductorship, at the Stadttheater (Municipal Opera House) in Elberfeld.

Hertz remained at Elberfeld for four years, and his career progressed rapidly. In 1899 he visited London at the request of Frederick Delius and conducted a concert of that composer's works, then little known. Just after signing a three-year contract as director of the Stadttheater in Breslau, Hertz received an offer from the Metropolitan Opera House in New York. When the Breslau contract expired in 1902, he came to the United States and was appointed permanent conductor of German opera at the Metropolitan—at twenty-nine, the youngest musician ever to hold that post. In the summer and fall of 1910 he also conducted several Wagner operas at Covent Garden in London. He was married on July 15, 1914, to Lilly Dorn (Lillian Kornblüh), a Viennese and an accomplished lieder singer. They had no children. Hertz became a United States citizen in 1917.

In 1915 Hertz visited San Francisco to conduct concerts at the Panama-Pacific Exposition and was asked to remain as conductor of the San Francisco Symphony Orchestra. Holding this post from that fall until his retirement in 1930, he built the orchestra into an institution of worldwide importance. Between seasons, he inaugurated (1922) and conducted the first four seasons of summer "Symphonies under the Stars" in the Hollywood Bowl at Los Angeles. After his retirement, Hertz remained active as guest conductor and he emerged from retirement briefly in 1938 to serve as supervisor of the Federal Music Project for Northern California. He was the first American conductor to give a regular series of symphony concerts on the radio (the Standard Symphony Hour, 1932–36), and the first to open his orchestra to women performers.

Hertz was best known as an interpreter of German music, and particularly of Richard Wagner. While at the Metropolitan, he conducted the first performance of *Parsifal* outside Bayreuth (Dec. 24, 1903), and he presented the American premiere of Richard Strauss's *Salome* (Jan 22, 1907). But he was also a champion of new works by European and American composers. At the Metropolitan he directed the world premieres of Humperdinck's *Koenigskinder* (Dec. 28, 1910), Horatio Parker's *Mona* (Mar. 14, 1912), and Walter Damrosch's *Cyrano de Bergerac* (Feb. 27, 1913), as well as the Metropolitan's first performance of Frederick Converse's *Pipe of Desire* (Mar. 18, 1910). Among the orchestral composers whom Hertz "discovered" was Roy Harris.

Hertz was known as a jovial raconteur who enjoyed performing burlesques of classical masterpieces. He composed a number of songs which his wife, who died in 1948, featured in recitals. In later years he made orchestral arrangements of classic songs. During the last five years of his life Hertz suffered from heart disease. He died of pneumonia in a San Francisco hospital at the age of sixty-nine. His remains were cremated at Home of Peace Cemetery. In 1950 a bequest of more than $400,000 from Hertz's estate was accepted by the University of California at Berkeley to establish an endowment fund for musical scholarships and to erect a campus music building, which was named for him.

[Hertz's autobiography, "Facing the Music," written in 1932 and published in the *San Francisco Chronicle*, May 10–July 14, 1942, is the principal source. See also: *Nat. Cyc. Am. Biog.*, Current Vol. E, pp. 500–01; *Who's Who in Am. Jewry*, 1938–39; David Ewen, ed., *Living Musicians* (1940); William H. Seltsam, *Metropolitan Opera Annals* (1947); *Who Was Who in America*, vol. II (1942); *N. Y. Times* obituary, Apr. 18, 1942. Death record from Calif. Dept. of Public Health.]

ALFRED V. FRANKENSTEIN

HIRSCH, ISAAC SETH (Dec. 3, 1880–Mar. 24, 1942), radiologist, known as I. Seth Hirsch, was born in New York City, one of the five sons and two daughters of Abram and Ida (Sable) Hirsch, orthodox Jews of Russian birth. Family circumstances appear to have been fairly good, since one brother was able to study law, and Seth attended the College of the City of New York (1895–98). He then entered the College of Physicians and Surgeons at Columbia University, where he received the M.D. degree in 1902. Following an internship at Beth Israel Hospital in New York City, he was attracted to research in bacteriology but, for economic reasons, chose to engage in the private practice of general medicine and pediatrics. Soon, however, he turned to radiology, and in 1910 he was appointed "X-ray photographer" at Bellevue Hospital, a post in which he continued (under various titles) until 1926. Hirsch fought determinedly for more space, better equipment, and trained personnel, and in spite of opposition from some municipal authorities succeeded in making the Bellevue X-ray department one of the finest in the country. In 1914 he was made professor of roentgenology in the New York Post-Graduate Medical School.

After wartime service in the army medical corps, Hirsch returned to his hospital duties. In 1920 he published his first textbook, *The Principles and Practice of Roentgenological Technique,* and in the same year he received a diploma in radiology from Cambridge University, England. A second book, *The Principles and Practice of Roentgen Therapy,* appeared in 1925. Before the opening of the new Beth Israel Hospital in 1928, Hirsch planned its X-ray department, of which he was the director until shortly before his death. In 1933 he became professor of radiology at the College of Medicine of New York University. During these years he carried out studies in the use of X-rays in recording heart sounds and studying the valvular actions that produced them. Neither his textbooks nor his threescore papers, however, blazed new trails in medicine; a well-educated and widely experienced radiologist, Hirsch was an organizer and expounder rather than an original investigator.

A former colleague has described Hirsch as "fast-moving, well-dressed, and articulate" with "an aristocratic appearance and a shock of white hair" and a personality that could be "antagonistically vibrant." Keenly intelligent, with an explosive temperament, he was sometimes bitingly critical of others, including his students, who, however, usually came to remember with affection his ability as a radiologist and skill and diligence as a teacher.

Throughout his professional life Hirsch maintained a private practice in radiology, the income from which enabled him to travel frequently in Europe and, while at home, to develop his considerable skills in sculpture, painting, and playwriting. He founded the New York Physicians Art Club and entered some of his own works at its annual exhibitions. In 1924 he married Lila Calhoun Hindsman of Fort Worth, Texas. They had no children. Hirsch died at Mount Sinai Hospital in New York, of cardiovascular disease, in his sixty-second year; although he himself was not religious, he was buried according to orthodox rites.

[Smith Ely Jelliffe, "I. Seth Hirsch, M.D.: An Appreciation," *Radiology,* July 1939; Henry K. Taylor, "Dr. I. Seth Hirsch—A Recollection," *Hebrew Medic. Jour.,* 1948, vol. I, pp. 147–43; obituaries in *Am. Jour. of Roentgenology,* May 1942, *Annals of Internal Medicine,* June 1942, *Jour. Am. Medic. Assoc.,* May 2, 1942, and *N. Y. Times,* Mar. 25, 1942; *Who's Who in America,* 1940–41; personal recollections of Dr. Henry K. Taylor; death record, N. Y. City Dept. of Health. A portrait of Dr. Hirsch by Nikol Schattenstein, presented to him in 1939 by colleagues, friends, and former students, is reproduced in the *Am. Jour. of Roentgenology,* above.]

PAUL C. HODGES

HITCHCOCK, THOMAS (Feb. 11, 1900– Apr. 19, 1944), sportsman and military aviator, known as Tommy Hitchcock, was born at Mon Repos, the winter home of his parents in Aiken, S. C. His paternal grandfather, Thomas Hitchcock, had been a financial writer and part owner of the New York *Sun,* but it was his father, also named Thomas (1860–1941), who set the family tradition. Himself a noted sportsman, he attended Oxford University (B.A., 1884), where he played polo against Cambridge. In the United States he helped popularize the game — which the younger James Gordon Bennett [*q.v.*] had introduced in 1871—becoming captain of the United States team in the first Anglo-American polo match in 1886 at Newport and a charter member of the United States Polo Association (1890). A steeplechase rider and early member of the Meadow Brook Club at Jericho, Long Island, the elder Hitchcock also bred horses, which he raced in Europe, founded a golf club, trained hunting dogs, and became an ardent huntsman. His wife, Louise Mary Eustis of Aiken, S. C., was a daughter of George Eustis [*q.v.*] and a granddaughter of William W. Corcoran [*q.v.*], founder of the Corcoran Art Gallery. Sharing her husband's enthusiasm for sports, she was one of the leading horsewomen and socialites of her day and founder of the Meadow Larks, which trained young polo players. Tommy was the third of the Hitchcocks' four children and the older of two sons.

Growing up at Mon Repos and at Broad Hollow, his parents' estate in Old Westbury, Long Island, he took to the saddle under their tutelage at the age of three. He trained in the Meadow Larks, competed at Narragansett Pier in 1913, and was a member of the junior and senior foursomes in 1916. When the United States entered World War I, Hitchcock, then a student at St. Paul's School in Concord, N. H., volunteered for military service but was rejected as too young. He then joined the Lafayette Escadrille, the group of American volunteers in the French aviation service. Shot in the thigh in March 1918 and forced to land in German-held territory, he was imprisoned at Lecheld. He escaped by jumping the train on which he was being transferred to another camp and, though contracting influenza, eventually made his way to France, where he joined the American Air Service. An eighteen-year-old lieutenant and holder of the Croix de Guerre for valor in downing three German planes, he came home in 1918 a hero.

Upon his return Hitchcock entered Harvard, and while a student there gained national recognition as a member of the United States Polo Association's championship teams of 1919, 1920, and 1921. During the postwar sports revival the game, which had been speeded up and technically improved by Harry Payne Whitney [q.v.], Devereux Milburn, and other players, received broad coverage from the metropolitan press, the rotogravure sections, and sophisticated journals like *Vanity Fair* and the *New Yorker*. Highly publicized international matches drew not only society notables but crowds of as many as 40,000 spectators. In 1921 the long-hitting, hard-driving Tommy Hitchcock led the United States foursome to victory over the British. Already a ten-goal player, he decided to dedicate himself to polo when he graduated from Harvard in 1922. He captained the Olympic team which lost to the Argentines in 1924, but led the Americans to victory over the English in 1927 and the Argentines in 1928. Recognized as probably the greatest player in the history of the game, he was elected in 1928 to the executive committee of the Polo Association.

Hitchcock continued to play in major polo contests during the 1930's, maintaining a ten-goal rating in all but two years before 1939. At the same time he served as a director of the United Electric Shovel Coal Corporation and, after 1932, was associated with the banking firm of Lehman Brothers. He became a partner in the Lehman firm in 1937 and gained some prominence in the development of American export airlines. An aviation enthusiast, he often flew his seaplane to work, landing in the harbor at the foot of Wall Street. On Dec. 15, 1928, he had married Margaret Mellon Laughlin, widow of Alexander Laughlin, Jr., and daughter of William Larimer Mellon of Pittsburgh. They had four children: Margaret, Louise, and the twins Thomas and William. Tall and strongly built, Hitchcock was a quiet person of deep reserve, with few intimate friends.

When the Japanese attacked Pearl Harbor in 1941, the veteran aviator volunteered and was commissioned a lieutenant colonel in the Army Air Corps. He was stationed in England, where he served as an assistant military attaché for air. In April 1944, while testing a P-51 Mustang, he died in an air crash near Salisbury at the age of forty-four.

[Newell Bent, *Am. Polo* (1929), pp. 374–76; Harry W. Smith, *Life and Sport in Aiken* (1935); Grantland Rice, *The Tumult and the Shouting* (1954); John A. Krout, *Annals of Am. Sport* (1929); William Patten, ed., *The Book of Sport* (1901); *Who's Who in Am. Sports,* 1928; files of *Polo Mag.; Time,* May 1, 1944, p. 71; *Harvard Alumni Bull.,* Apr. 29, 1944; *N. Y. Times,* Apr. 20, 21, 1944; London *Times,* Apr. 21, 1944. On his father, see *N. Y. Times,* Sept. 30, 1941; and *Nat. Cyc. Am. Biog.,* XXXVI, 297.]

JOHN R. BETTS

HODSON, WILLIAM (Apr. 25, 1891–Jan. 15, 1943), welfare administrator, was born in Minneapolis, Minn., to Anna (Redding) and William Hodson. Little is known of his background save that his father died when the boy was young, leaving his mother, "a woman of great character and intelligence," with the problem of family support. After earlier schooling, William attended the University of Minnesota, where he edited the college annual, learned the art of persuasive oratory on the debating team, won election to Phi Beta Kappa, and graduated in 1913.

Hodson next entered the Harvard Law School, but from the start displayed an interest also in social welfare. A volunteer in the school's legal aid bureau, he spent his summers working for the Associated Charities of Minneapolis. He received the LL.B. degree in 1916, served briefly as chief counsel of the Minneapolis Legal Aid Society, and in 1917 was appointed secretary and legal research investigator of the Minnesota Child Welfare Commission. In that post Hodson became the chief architect of a new children's code, enacted into law in thirty-nine separate bills during the legislative session of 1917. For the next four years, as director of the newly created Children's Bureau in the State Board of Control, Hodson gave substance to the form of the code and made Minnesota one of the leading states in the child welfare field. On May 4, 1918, in Minneapolis, he married Gertrude Prindle; their three children were Judith, William, and Jeremy.

Hodson moved in 1922 to New York City, where he joined the Russell Sage Foundation as director of its division of child welfare and (1924) of its department of social legislation. In 1925 he became director of the Welfare Council of New York City, a federation of private social service agencies. He left this post at the end of 1933 to become commissioner of welfare under Mayor Fiorello La Guardia. With a quarter of the city's population on the relief rolls during the Great Depression, Hodson set a standard of humane and efficient administration of relief funds that was to become a model for the nation. His first directive to welfare agents ordered that all clients be treated as though they were relatives, neighbors, and friends. At all times he proceeded from the premise that persons on relief were neither lazy nor dishonest, as was so often charged, but honest folk who wanted to work. Under his direction, too, the administration of welfare was brought under comprehensive civil service. During his nine years as commissioner he managed more than $1,300,000,000, yet there was never a financial scandal and never a charge of playing partisan politics.

Though an administrator of relief, Hodson was convinced that the dole was demoralizing both to the unfortunate clients and to society itself. As early as October 1931, in a widely publicized letter to President Hoover, he urged federal action to meet the unemployment crisis. That winter, when a Senate subcommittee held hearings on the problem, Hodson, along with Linton B. Swift, executive director of the Family Welfare Association of America, and Walter West, executive secretary of the American Association of Social Workers, helped mobilize the social workers who testified to the inadequacy of private and local relief—the first coordinated drive of professional social workers during the depression. Through leadership in the American Association of Social Workers (president, 1924–26), the National Conference of Social Work (president, 1934), and the American Public Welfare Association (president, 1940) Hodson labored to persuade the profession that it had to move beyond social service to social action—to provide more just procedures of welfare, to broaden security, and to open up new opportunities for disadvantaged groups and classes. He thus became one of the foremost proponents of work relief and public works, old-age pensions, unemployment insurance, elimination of the

means test, and a broad system of compulsory government health insurance.

Hodson had what one reporter called a "disarming gentleness." Unfailingly kind, he was also hard-headed and tough, and intolerant of inefficiency and callousness in others. Welfare and law were the blend of his personality and career. A pragmatist in the New Deal tradition, he nevertheless pushed beyond the essentially moderate programs of Franklin D. Roosevelt; his position on social measures was always substantially in advance of that of the main body of social workers. Early in 1943, while en route to a wartime relief mission in North Africa, he was killed in an airplane crash at Paramaribo, Dutch Guiana. At the time of his death he had been pressing for the broadening of social protection during the war and for a postwar government program to ensure full employment.

[Articles and speeches by Hodson, over the years of his active career, may be found in the *Survey, Survey Graphic, Social Service Rev.,* the *Proc.* of the Nat. Conference of Social Work, *Vital Speeches of the Day,* the *Annals of the Am. Acad. of Political and Social Sci.,* and *Commonweal.* There is no biography of Hodson, and little mention of him in general works on the history of social service or public welfare. Much of his career, however, can be reconstructed from news stories in the *N. Y. Times* (see Index). See also *Who Was Who in America,* vol. II (1950); *N. Y. Times,* Jan. 21, 22, 1943; and obituaries in *Survey Midmonthly,* Feb. 1943, and *Social Service Rev.,* Mar. 1943. Information about his background from "Memorial for William Hodson under the Auspices of the Hennepin County Bar Assoc., . . . Feb. 27, 1943" (typescript, Minneapolis Pub. Lib.). There is one folder of Hodson correspondence, covering the years 1930–42, in the papers of Survey Associates, located at the Social Welfare Hist. Archives Center, Univ. of Minn.]

CLARKE A. CHAMBERS

HOLT, ARTHUR ERASTUS (Nov. 23, 1876–Jan. 13, 1942), Congregational clergyman, specialist in social ethics, was born on his father's farm near Longmont, Colo. He was the eldest of three children of Asa Dutton Holt and Fanny (Merrill) Holt, upstate New Yorkers of New England descent who had joined the famous colony of Horace Greeley [*q.v.*] in the West. Asa Holt was a devout Presbyterian and a leader in organizing cooperative milling and irrigation facilities in the community.

While an undergraduate at Colorado College, Holt decided on a career of Christian service. After graduating in 1898, he enrolled at the Yale Divinity School but, finding it "stuffy," moved the next year to the new University of Chicago Divinity School, attracted by its vigorous spirit of inquiry. At Chicago, Holt worked particularly with Prof. Gerald Birney Smith [*q.v.*], under whom he completed his Ph.D. in 1904. His brief dissertation, *The Function of Christian Ethics* (1904), was a survey of earlier trends and also a statement of his own viewpoint. Influenced by the philosophy of John Dewey, Holt contended that the function of Christian ethics was to help men make choices pragmatically, rather than to prescribe absolute, authoritative codes of conduct, as both Catholic and Protestant ethical systems had tended to do.

During his final year at the University of Chicago, Holt had taken courses at McCormick Theological Seminary (Presbyterian), from which he received the B.D. degree in 1904. That year he was ordained in the Congregational ministry, and on Dec. 27 he married Grace Louise Bradshaw of Chicago. Their children were Frances Merrill, John Bradshaw, and Florence Eugenie. For the next fifteen years Holt served in a succession of parishes: Congregational churches in Pueblo, Colo. (1904–09), and Manhattan, Kans. (1909–16), and a Presbyterian church in Fort Worth, Texas (1916–19). His pastoral work was characterized by a strong ecumenicity, concern for the social services of the church, and continued interest in rural problems.

In 1919 Holt became secretary of the Congregational Education Society's Social Service Department and moved to its headquarters in Boston. The department sought to foster an awareness of social problems through books, pamphlets, study courses, and the like; Holt's writings for it, including two study guides, *Social Work in the Churches* (1922) and *Christian Fellowship and Modern Industry* (1923), were widely distributed. In 1924 Holt was called to the Chicago Theological Seminary (Congregational) to succeed Graham Taylor [Supp. 2] as professor of social ethics. Receiving a parallel appointment (1925) in the University of Chicago Divinity School (with which the seminary was affiliated), he also assumed responsibility for the university's doctoral program in social ethics. This dual appointment brought him into direct contact with the research-oriented social sciences; he held it for the rest of his life.

To his teaching Holt brought a contagious enthusiasm. He added to the seminary's curriculum an innovative course in "Social and Religious Research and Survey," into which he presently brought as co-instructor Samuel C. Kincheloe, a Disciples of Christ minister who had taken a doctorate in sociology at the University of Chicago. Within the Chicago community Holt conducted a variety of surveys—social analyses of individual churches and their membership, a community-wide survey of church distribution, studies of distressed dairy farmers and the city's unemployed. In 1929–30 he was sent by the Y.M.C.A. and the Y.W.C.A. to undertake a study of their work in India, Burma, and Ceylon.

Holt played his most important national role at the Congregational General Council of 1934 when he was the prime mover in the creation of the Congregational Council for Social Action. This major denominational agency was intended as a vehicle for cooperating with movements for social justice outside the churches. Holt was made chairman; but conservative opposition stirred up by a resolution adopted at the same General Council committing the church to work toward abolition of the profit system weakened his position, and he stepped down in 1936.

Holt's uniqueness among leaders in the Social Gospel movement derived from his predominant concern with rural life. He insisted that the greatest problem facing Americans was to establish a larger conception of justice that would include agrarian groups. Especially indicative of this lifelong emphasis were the articles he wrote for the *Christian Century* during the 1930's, numbering more than a score, in which he sympathetically interpreted current farmers' protests and the New Deal's farm program. Unfortunately, he never attained full rapport with urban America, and many of his writings were marked by biting criticisms of urban life, which he saw as controlled by the "trader classes," and by nostalgia for the primary, face-to-face relationships of the decentralized community.

In his books he combined the roles of religious sociologist and of prophet of social justice. *The Bible as a Community Book* (1920) interpreted the history of Israel as a struggle between rural, tribal values and the corruptions of increasing contact with urban trade centers, culminating in the message of the prophets and Jesus, which universalized the earlier values of family and tribe. Similarly, in *The Fate of the Family in the Modern World* (1936) he attributed to an individualism rooted in urbanization and industrialization the blame for family disintegration. In *This Nation Under God* (1939) and *Christian Roots of Democracy in America* (1941) he challenged Americans to fulfill the promise of a community of social justice in order to survive the threats of fascism and communism.

Early in 1942, a few months before his scheduled retirement, Holt died suddenly of a coronary thrombosis in his study in Chicago. His ashes were buried at Merom, Ind., the site of the Merom Institute for the study of rural problems which he had been instrumental in establishing in 1936 and to which he had sent his students for rural parish field work.

[Holt's personal papers, including engagement books, correspondence, and materials for his courses, are at the Chicago Theological Seminary. The most substantial work on him is Carlus O. Basinger, "Arthur E. Holt: The Man and His Social Ethics" (M.A. thesis, Univ. of Chicago Divinity School, 1945). A perceptive analysis by a colleague is contained in Arthur C. McGiffert, Jr., *No Ivory Tower: The Story of the Chicago Theological Seminary* (1965), pp. 186–98. For briefer mention, see: *Nat. Cyc. Am. Biog.*, XXI, 463–64; *Who Was Who in America*, vol. I (1942); interview with Holt in *Christian Century*, Mar. 29, 1933; and obituary in *N. Y. Times*, Jan. 14, 1942. See also Robert M. Miller, *Am. Protestantism and Social Issues, 1919–39* (1958).]

JACOB H. DORN

HOLT, WINIFRED (Nov. 17, 1870–June 14, 1945), worker for the blind, was born in New York City, the second daughter and fourth of seven children of the publisher Henry Holt [*q.v.*] and his first wife, Mary Florence West. Through her father she was descended from a mid-seventeenth-century settler of New Haven, Conn.; her mother, who died when Winifred was eight, was the daughter of a New York financier. Winifred Holt attended the Brearley School in New York but later attributed her real education to the conversation of the artists and writers who were entertained in the family home. She herself early developed a fine singing voice and talent for both the piano and sculpture. At the age of sixteen a "new and absorbing world" of "suffering humanity" opened up when her father took her to the Neighborhood Settlement House in the Bowery, where for some time she spent one afternoon each week working with members of a boys' club.

Because of prolonged ill health in her early twenties she was sent abroad with her younger sister, Edith, and settled in Florence, where her sculpture earned her admission to a studio. In 1897 she returned to New York and continued her study at the Art Students' League, but the pleasures of art and social life did not satisfy her, and continued poor health caused her to return to Florence in 1901. There her concern for the handicapped was revived; the illness of her maid revealed the lack of medical care for the poor, and a chance encounter with a group of blind boys, enjoying a concert through the use of unsold tickets provided by the government, roused her sympathy for those deprived of sight.

After returning to New York in 1903, Winifred and Edith Holt established a bureau to provide theatre and concert tickets for the blind in the home they shared with their brother Roland. Winifred's meetings with individual applicants soon convinced her that the blind were a neglected segment of society and that in general they led empty lives, without occupation or hope. She came to believe that their most important need

was employment, a way to become self-reliant and financially independent—a revolutionary view at a time when informed opinion agreed that unlimited charity was the only humane treatment. Thereafter, although she continued to work at her sculpture, studied with Augustus Saint-Gaudens [*q.v.*], and executed several notable portrait busts (including one of Helen Keller), Miss Holt devoted her life to improving opportunities for the blind.

One of her first steps was to travel to London in 1904 to study methods of training at the Royal Normal College and Academy of Music for the Blind, founded by Sir Francis Campbell, who was himself sightless. To appreciate the problems involved in learning, she wore a blindfold while carrying out the assignments. After her return, she and her sister Edith organized in November 1905 the New York Association for the Blind. Winifred Holt, who combined wit and charm with a commanding intellect and an iron will, displayed a masterful talent for fund raising and publicity, superb oratorical ability, and a mystical faith in her cause. After her sister's marriage in 1908, she carried on the crusade single-handed.

One of Miss Holt's objectives was teaching the public that much blindness could be prevented. Her lectures and writing, together with the work of Louisa Lee Schuyler [*q.v.*] and Dr. F. Park Lewis [Supp. 2], led to the organization (1915) of the National Committee (later Society) for the Prevention of Blindness, and helped secure the passage of laws requiring treatment of infants' eyes at birth with silver nitrate solution. Her second goal, in which she took an even stronger interest, was educating the blind to become useful and self-supporting members of society. Her home had quickly become a meeting place for the sightless, and there she set up classes in which they could learn remunerative skills, such as sewing, basket and broom making, rug weaving, piano tuning, and the operation of telephone switchboards. To obtain funds for expansion, she enlisted the aid of prominent people in public life, and in 1913, with help from the Russell Sage Foundation, the New York Association for the Blind was able to open "The Lighthouse," on East 59th Street, a social settlement for the sightless. Her pioneer work there won worldwide recognition, and in 1914 she received the gold medal of the National Institute of Social Sciences. That summer in London she addressed the International Conference on the Blind.

Miss Holt advocated a wide variety of academic, vocational, and athletic training for the sightless. She opposed segregating them in special classes in separate institutions and was able to prevail upon the New York City Board of Education to abandon this practice in the public schools. Having taught herself braille, she made a study of the various tactile prints then in use for the blind and was instrumental in having braille adopted in the city schools, again setting an influential precedent.

Upon the outbreak of World War I, Miss Holt offered her services to the Allies. She established Lighthouses in France at Bordeaux and Paris while acting as consultant on the rehabilitation of men blinded in war. The French Lighthouses achieved remarkable results in reeducating the blind of all backgrounds. Miss Holt's standards were high; the quality of the Lighthouses' knitted goods was such that the designer Worth utilized them to launch the fashion of knitted dresses. The French government recognized Miss Holt's services by making her a chevalier of the Legion of Honor. In 1919 she inaugurated the Italian Lighthouse at Rome, and was honored by the award of that nation's gold medal.

In Rome she met Rufus Graves Mather, an American expatriate engaged in research on Italian art and a member of the Italian Lighthouse board. They were married at the New York Lighthouse on Nov. 16, 1922, and for a number of years toured the world to initiate programs for the blind, visiting, in all, thirty-four countries. In 1937 they settled in Williamstown, Mass., where Mrs. Mather continued to supervise the expansion of the American Lighthouses. In 1945, in a ceremony at New York's Carnegie Hall, the Lighthouse workshop received the "E" Award of the army and navy for merit, a confirmation of her belief that the blind could compete with the sighted on an equal basis. Shortly afterward she became ill; she died that June of congestive heart failure at the House of Mercy in Pittsfield, Mass., at the age of seventy-four. After funeral services in St. John's Episcopal Church in Williamstown, her ashes were buried in Evergreen Cemetery, Morristown, N. J.

[The two most important sources for the life and work of Winifred Holt Mather are: Edith Holt Bloodgood and Rufus Graves Mather, eds., *First Lady of the Lighthouse* (1952), consisting of an unfinished autobiography, letters, and speeches; and the *Annual Reports* of the N. Y. Assoc. for the Blind. Winifred Holt acted as a special correspondent for the *N. Y. Times*, 1916–18; her articles give a fine picture of her work with the war blind. Her book *The Light Which Cannot Fail* (1922) contains interesting accounts of her experiences. Useful on her early work are a sketch in the *American Mag.*, Nov. 1910, pp. 37–41, and Irma Craft, "People of the Night," *Century Mag.*, July 1914. See also *Nat. Cyc. Am. Biog.*, XXXIV, 400–02; and *Notable Am. Women*, II, 209–10.]

LLOYD C. TAYLOR, JR.

HOUGHTON, ALANSON BIGELOW (Oct. 10, 1863–Sept. 16, 1941), glass manufacturer, Congressman, diplomat, was born in Cambridge, Mass., the second of five children and elder son of Amory and Ellen Ann (Bigelow) Houghton. Both parents were natives of Boston; his father's forebear, John Houghton, had come to Massachusetts from England about 1650. Alanson's grandfather Amory Houghton, Sr., who had operated a small glass factory in Massachusetts since 1851, moved the family in 1864 to Brooklyn, N. Y., where he and Amory, Jr., took control of the Brooklyn Flint Glass Company; in 1868 they moved to Corning, N. Y., and founded the Corning Flint Glass Company. This business failed and was sold in 1871, but Alanson's father stayed on as manager. Four years later he formed his own company, the Corning Glass Works, which specialized in the manufacture of railway signal glass, thermometer tubing, and pharmaceutical glass.

Alanson attended the Corning public schools, St. Paul's School in Concord, N. H., and Harvard College, where he graduated, A.B. magna cum laude, in 1886. Planning a scholarly career, he spent the next three years in Europe studying political economy at the universities of Göttingen, Berlin, and Paris. While abroad he completed an article on Italian finance for the *Quarterly Journal of Economics* (January and April 1889) and contributed background material for a chapter in James Bryce's *The American Commonwealth*.

In 1889, however, his father fell ill, and Houghton was called into the rapidly expanding family business. Starting out as a shipping clerk in order to learn the business from the ground up, he became vice-president for sales in 1903, president in 1910, and chairman of the board in 1918. During his presidency the Corning Glass Works trebled in size, a growth attributed in part to his salesmanship, to war contracts, and to the invention of heat-resistant Pyrex glass. Under Houghton the company also developed the first standardized railway signal glass and in 1908 established one of the first industrial research laboratories.

Houghton married Adelaide Louise Wellington of Corning on June 25, 1891, and the couple had five children: Eleanor Wickham, Amory, Quincy Wellington, Matilda, and Elizabeth. As the glass works flourished, the Houghton family increasingly came to dominate the civic and religious life of the community. Alanson served as president of the Corning board of education and of the Protestant Episcopal Board of Religious Education of Western New York. A generous contributor to the Republican party, he was a presidential elector in 1904 and 1916. In 1918 he was elected to the first of two terms in Congress. As a member of the House Foreign Affairs Committee and then of the Ways and Means Committee, he was considered a diligent and intelligent legislator.

Houghton resigned his seat in 1922 when President Harding selected him as America's first postwar ambassador to Germany. Houghton believed that a stable Europe, with a reintegrated, democratic Germany, was necessary both to ensure a future market for a growing American surplus and to check the potential threat of Soviet Russia. At a time when the war reparations issue was becoming inflamed, with the French taking a hard line, Houghton advocated a friendly attitude toward Germany, which he regarded as abiding faithfully by its treaty obligations. His cordial relations with the German people contributed to his effectiveness in persuading a reluctant Weimar government to accept the Dawes Plan in 1924.

Houghton's pro-German sympathies were resented by both the British and the French. Nevertheless, when Frank B. Kellogg [Supp. 2] was appointed Secretary of State in 1925, President Coolidge chose Houghton to replace him as ambassador to Great Britain; and despite initial misgivings, the British quickly found him to be a sincere friend. In the next few years, Houghton achieved some notoriety as an outspoken diplomat. In May 1925, in a warning clearly aimed at France, he declared that the United States would stop sending money to Europe if the powers continued to arm for war. Back in the United States in the spring of 1926, he told Coolidge that the Locarno agreements, which sought to establish a military and diplomatic balance in Europe, were in jeopardy; this pessimistic report sparked a heated debate in Congress and the press. In a speech at Harvard in June 1927 he called for new peace machinery including one-hundred-year nonaggression pacts which would be submitted to popular referenda, thus putting the issues of war and peace directly into the hands of the people. For the rest of his life Houghton was closely associated with peace causes and was a trustee and treasurer of the Carnegie Endowment for International Peace.

Houghton returned to the United States in 1928 to run for the Senate, but lost to his Democratic opponent, Dr. Royal S. Copeland [Supp. 2]. Although he resigned his ambassadorship the following year, he remained interested in politics. Along with his old friend Frank O. Lowden [Supp. 3] and President Nicholas Murray Butler of Columbia, he sought in 1931 to improve the

sagging image of the Republican party and thus prevent its defeat in 1932. During the 1930's he was active in educational and religious organizations and in 1934 was elected chairman of the board of directors of the Institute for Advanced Study at Princeton, N. J.

Dignified and somewhat reserved, Houghton had the respect of his employees and enjoyed a warm family life. He died of cardiac failure owing to arteriosclerosis at his summer home in South Dartmouth, Mass., in 1941 and was buried in Hope Cemetery Annex in Corning. Houghton was an uncommon industrial statesman who guided the Corning Glass Works to national prominence. As a public servant in the 1920's he was an articulate spokesman for that segment of the business community which saw a relationship between American security and prosperity and world peace.

[No scholarly study of Houghton exists, nor any collection of Houghton papers. The best biographical accounts are in Beckles Willson, *America's Ambassadors to England* (1928), and Arch Merrill, *Fame in Our Time* (1960), pp. 139–45. Also useful is the sketch in the *Nat. Cyc. Am. Biog.*, Current Vol. B, pp. 7–8. (Both the *Nat. Cyc.* and the Willson book include photographs of Houghton.) See also William T. Hutchinson, *Lowden of Ill.* (1957). Of contemporary magazine accounts, the best are Frederick L. Collins in *Woman's Home Companion*, Jan. 1926; James B. Morrow in *Nation's Business*, June 1922; and *Current Opinion*, Aug. 1922, pp. 193–95. The privately printed diary of Houghton's wife, Adelaide Houghton, *The London Years 1925–1929* (1963), adds little except for the rich section of photographs. Generally, anyone interested in Houghton must rely upon scattered references in the relevant volumes of the State Dept.'s *Papers Relating to the Foreign Relations of the U. S.* and the *N. Y. Times Index*. On the family, see John W. Houghton, *The Houghton Genealogy* (1912). Death record from Mass. Registrar of Vital Statistics.]

MELVIN SMALL

HOVEY, OTIS ELLIS (Apr. 9, 1864–Apr. 15, 1941), civil engineer and specialist in the design and construction of bridges, was born in East Hardwick, Vt., the oldest of four children of Jabez Wadsworth Hovey and Hannah Catherine (Montgomery) Hovey. His ancestors were among the early settlers of Massachusetts, having come from England to Ipswich about 1635. His father was a farmer, schoolteacher, and part-time surveyor. When in the early 1870's a railroad location survey party ran its line through his home town, Otis determined to study engineering.

From local schools, he went on to nearby Dartmouth College, graduating first from its Chandler Scientific School (B.S. 1885) and then from its Thayer School of Civil Engineering (C.E. 1889). Before entering Thayer he acquired field experience as a construction engineer with the Hoosac Tunnel and Wilmington (Vt.) Railroad and as a draftsman with the bridge department of an iron works in Delaware; in 1888 he was resident engineer on a large mill dam in Chicopee, Mass. Just before receiving his C.E. degree, Hovey accepted an instructorship in civil engineering at Washington University in St. Louis, Mo.

He left teaching a year later when the renowned bridge engineer George S. Morison [*q.v.*] asked him to assist in surveys of a proposed bridge over the Detroit River. Hovey's excellent performance on this project led Morison to place him in charge of the consulting firm's drafting room in Chicago. Here the young engineer participated in studies and designs for a wide variety of structures, including railroad viaducts at Memphis, Tenn., and St. Louis, Mo.; large bridges at Bellefontaine, Mo., Alton, Ill., and Leavenworth, Kans.; and, of particular interest to Hovey, the Chicago and Northern Pacific bascule bridge over the West Fork of the Chicago River (1895). He also made detailed designs and cost estimates for a proposed 3,200-foot-span suspension bridge across the Hudson River, almost forty years before the famous George Washington Bridge was erected.

In February 1896 Hovey joined the Union Bridge Company as engineer-in-charge of its Athens, Pa., office. When Union Bridge merged with several other small companies in 1900 to form the American Bridge Company (a subsidiary of United States Steel), Hovey became engineer of design at Pencoyd, Pa. His organizing and engineering ability proved invaluable to the new firm. In 1904 his office moved to New York City. He became assistant chief engineer in 1907 and consulting engineer in 1931.

During these years Hovey was involved in virtually every aspect of bridge building—from the concept and design through the fabrication and erection. His reputation became international, and as an expert in bridge construction he traveled to such far-flung places as South Africa and Turkey. His specialty, however, was large movable steel structures, principally bridges, but also dams. One of the more intricate aspects of "swing" bridges is their turntables; more than a quarter-century after his death three major types of pivots which he designed and patented were still called "O-center," "E-center," and "H-center," after Hovey's initials. Among his more difficult projects were the construction of the steel flood-regulation gates for the Panama Canal (1912) and the strengthening of New York's Williamsburg Suspension Bridge (1914). During his career with the American Bridge Company, Hovey wrote the first of his two major

works, *Movable Bridges* (2 vols., 1926–27), covering comprehensively both the superstructure and the machinery of these complicated structures. His writing was remarkable for its conciseness and clarity, and after his retirement, in 1934, at the age of seventy, he produced a second major work, *Steel Dams* (1935), for the American Institute of Steel Construction.

In his later years Hovey maintained a consulting practice and continued to serve as treasurer for the American Society of Civil Engineers, a position he had held since 1921. In 1937 his colleagues elected him to honorary membership in the society. In 1930 he was appointed to the board of the Engineering Foundation, a research foundation established by Ambrose Swasey [Supp. 2] in 1914; he became its director in 1937.

As an engineer for a large fabricating firm, Hovey received little public credit for his work, but this did not trouble him; he found his pleasure in doing a difficult job to his own satisfaction. A prodigious worker, orderly and systematic, he also had a serene and kindly nature that led him to take a particular interest in helping younger colleagues. Outside his profession, he served as a deacon in the Presbyterian Church, took much pleasure in music (he was an accomplished flutist), and was an amateur photographer. He died of cancer in New York City in 1941, soon after his seventy-seventh birthday, and was buried in the cemetery at Hartford, Vt., where he had a summer home. He was survived by his wife, Martha Wilson Owen, originally of Toledo, Ohio, whom he had married on Sept. 15, 1891, and their two children, Otis Wadsworth (a civil engineer) and Ellen Catherine.

[Memoir in Am. Soc. of Civil Engineers, *Transactions*, CVIII (1943), 1537–43; *Nat. Cyc. Am. Biog.*, XXXII, 471; records of Am. Soc. of Civil Engineers; information from Town Clerk, Hardwick, Vt., and from Otis W. Hovey.]

NEAL FITZSIMONS

HOWARD, LESLIE (Apr. 3, 1893–June 1, 1943), stage and screen actor and director, was born Leslie Howard Steiner (or Stainer), in London, England, the eldest of the three sons and two daughters of Ferdinand Steiner, a Hungarian-born British citizen, and Lilian (Blumberg) Steiner. His father, a stockbroker's clerk, had hoped to become a professional musician, and his mother was a gifted amateur in painting and singing. Shortly after Leslie's birth the family moved to Vienna for a stay of several years. Upon returning to England they settled in Upper Norwood, a London suburb.

Leslie disliked school but developed a special enthusiasm for writing. In his early teens he began turning out stories, plays, and short musical comedies and sold a number of thrillers to pulp magazines. To encourage him, his mother organized a neighborhood dramatic club where both she and her son often appeared in his plays. He entered Dulwich College but, at his father's insistence, left at the age of nineteen to earn a living as a bank clerk. World War I allowed him to break away from a detested career. He enlisted, was commissioned as a second lieutenant of cavalry in March 1915, and went to France in the spring of 1916, but in 1917 he was invalided home with shellshock and resigned his commission. His experience in the cavalry, where he first learned to ride, gave him a love of horses that later found expression in polo.

In 1916, before leaving for France, he had married Ruth Evelyn Martin, the daughter of a laundry manager of Colchester. Their two children were Ronald and Leslie Ruth. His wife proved to be a sustaining influence throughout the career to which he now turned. Unwilling to return to the bank, he determined to become an actor. He dropped his surname and, as Leslie Howard, made his first professional appearance in 1917, touring the provinces as Jerry in *Peg o' My Heart*. His London debut came on Feb. 14, 1918, in a small part in Sir Arthur Pinero's *The Freaks*. He became interested in the art of the film in 1920 and, with a young scenario editor, Adrian Brunel, formed Minerva Films, with Howard as managing director as well as leading actor. The company failed after producing three short comedies, distinguished by their avoidance of slapstick. Eventually he would appear in at least thirty-five stage productions and twenty-five motion pictures.

In the fall of 1920 the American theatrical producer Gilbert Miller brought Leslie Howard to the United States, where he made his debut in New York City in *Just Suppose* on Nov. 1. He continued to appear on the New York stage for several years, often as the juvenile lead in light comedies; in 1925 he played opposite Katharine Cornell in the romantic drama *The Green Hat*. A popular actor, he also received growing critical acclaim. In 1926 he began to alternate appearances in New York with others in London, although it took him some time to build a following in England; after his long stay in the United States, the English regarded him as "that American actor." Stardom came in March 1927, when he scored a great success in New York with Jeanne Eagels [*q.v.*] in *Her Cardboard Lover* (a part he played in London the following year with equal success, with Tallulah Bankhead). He solidified his reputation that October with a

brilliant performance in New York in John Galsworthy's drama *Escape*. Although Howard depended on acting as a means of livelihood, he never especially enjoyed it and became increasingly interested in directing and producing, serving with Gilbert Miller as co-producer of plays in which he often acted as well. He had never stopped writing, and during the 1920's he sold several light essays (generally about acting and the theatre) to such magazines as *Vanity Fair* and the *New Yorker*. In 1927 he directed and appeared in *Murray Hill*, a farce he had written over a period of several years. It opened to mixed reviews, and only one other of his many plays was produced.

During the 1920's American audiences were captivated by Howard's quiet, persuasive, and singularly English charm. Though generally a shy, home-loving man, he became a notable figure in the social, intellectual, and artistic circles of New York and Long Island. In the decade 1929–39 Howard appeared on Broadway as Peter Standish in John Balderston's *Berkeley Square* (1929); as Tom Collier in Philip Barry's *The Animal Kingdom* (1932), which Howard directed and co-produced with Gilbert Miller; as Alan Squier in Robert E. Sherwood's *The Petrified Forest* (1935); and as Hamlet (1936) in his own production of the play. Though his Hamlet evoked a generally unfavorable critical response, it was a thoughtful and serious interpretation and Howard believed in it; he took the play on tour throughout the United States, where it was especially well received by college students.

Howard's initial American film appearance in *Outward Bound* (1930) made him a major star. His roles in many delightful comedies and romances are easily forgotten, and his acting in *Romeo and Juliet* (1936) was often embarrassing, but there is a whole series of Howard performances that are genuinely memorable: those in *Of Human Bondage* (1934), *The Scarlet Pimpernel* (1935), the movie version of *The Petrified Forest* (1936), *Pygmalion* (1938, with Howard as co-director), and as Ashley Wilkes in *Gone with the Wind* (1939). To the millions in his stage and screen audiences in the United States and Great Britain, Howard came to typify the romantic intellectual, the "gentleman with guts." He stood for the attractive, thoughtful man of culture, the artist or the poet, threatened by the increasingly brutal and vicious world around him but fighting to the last for decency, gentility, civilization.

With the outbreak of World War II in 1939, Howard, still a British citizen, returned with his family to England to aid the war effort. He produced, directed, and sometimes appeared in a series of propaganda films designed for American audiences. Several were documentaries of the highest quality. *The First of the Few* (1941), for example, told the story of R. J. Mitchell, the designer of the Spitfire fighter plane, and the development of British air power. Although he had not been successful on radio in the United States, Howard made a series of weekly BBC broadcasts to North America, "Britain Speaks," as part of the propaganda effort.

In the spring of 1943, at the request of the British Council, Howard went as a goodwill ambassador to give a series of lectures in the neutral countries of Spain and Portugal. On the return flight from Lisbon his plane was shot down over the Bay of Biscay by German aircraft. His body was never recovered.

[Howard's daughter, Leslie Ruth Howard, has written a good biography, *A Quite Remarkable Father* (1959). See also: Adrian Brunel, *Nice Work: The Story of Thirty Years in British Film Production* (1949); Ian Colvin, *Flight 777* (1957), a book devoted to the "mystery" of Howard's final flight; sketch in *Dict. Nat. Biog.*, 1941–50; John Parker, ed., *Who's Who in the Theatre* (9th ed., 1939); *N. Y. Times*, June 4, 1943. The Theatre Collection of the N. Y. Public Lib. at Lincoln Center has a valuable file of clippings. On his film career, see Homer Dickens in *Films in Rev.*, Apr. 1959; *The Am. Movies Reference Book: The Sound Era* (1969). The personal memoir by C. A. Lejeune in the *N. Y. Times*, June 29, 1943, sec. 2, offers a shrewd estimate of Howard as symbol. Miss Howard's biography contains a good selection of photographs; others are in Daniel Blum, *Great Stars of the Am. Stage* (1952). Though Miss Howard gives the family name as "Stainer," on Howard's birth record (Gen. Register Office, London) it is "Steiner."]
WARREN I. SUSMAN

HOWELL, WILLIAM HENRY (Feb. 20, 1860–Feb. 6, 1945), physiologist, was born in Baltimore, Md., the fourth child in a family of four sons and one daughter. Both his parents, George Henry and Virginia Teresa (Magruder) Howell, were of southern Maryland stock; his father operated a plastering business. Howell attended the public schools of Baltimore, and while at the City College (a high school) at the age of fifteen served as laboratory assistant to the teacher of physics and chemistry, who allowed him to carry on experiments of his own. Three years later (1878), intending to study medicine, he applied to President Daniel C. Gilman [*q.v.*] of the Johns Hopkins University for immediate admission to college without finishing his high school course. His request was granted, and he received the A.B. degree in 1881.

Since the Johns Hopkins Medical School had not yet been opened, Howell enrolled as a doctoral candidate in biology under Henry Newell Martin [*q.v.*], while also attending classes in anatomy and clinical medicine at the medical school of

the University of Maryland. The influence, however, of Martin and association with the brilliant teachers and students at Johns Hopkins during these student days turned Howell to research in physiology instead of the study of medicine. Before taking his doctorate in 1884 he was already engaged in important studies of the physiology of the heart, at first in association with Martin but later independently. Among five papers of his own written at this time, one, on the relation of the output of the heart to body weight, appeared in the *Philosophical Transactions* of the Royal Society of London while he was still a graduate student. His doctoral dissertation dealt with coagulation of the blood. European investigators had differed, in studying the transformation of the fluid protein fibringen to the insoluble fibrin of the clot, as to whether this conversion requires the presence of another protein (globulin) as well as an active agent of then unknown nature (thrombin). By working with the blood of the terrapin, which does not contain globulin, Howell excluded the need of globulin in the clotting process.

Upon receiving his degree, Howell was appointed assistant professor of biology at Johns Hopkins and in 1888 was promoted to associate professor, teaching comparative anatomy and physiology. His students of this period, as of his later years, admired his calm, unassuming manner and absolute sincerity, as well as the remarkably clear and polished style of his lectures. Newell Martin was now failing in health, and Howell carried an increasing burden of departmental administration, acquiring useful experience for his subsequent career but delaying his progress in experimental research.

In 1889 Howell went to the University of Michigan as lecturer in physiology and histology in its medical school. A year later he was made professor of these subjects. It is said that his laboratory course in physiology was the first such course to be required for all students in any medical school in the United States. Resuming his research, he published among other contributions one describing the particles in red blood cells now known as Howell-Jolly bodies. Another and more important discovery of this period was that of the importance of inorganic salts in maintaining the beat of the heart. While at Ann Arbor he worked also, in association with G. Carl Huber [Supp. 1], later professor of anatomy there, on a study of the degeneration of peripheral nerve fibers after severance of a nerve, in which various details of the degeneration process, now familiar, were carefully described.

Howell's short stay of three years at Ann

Arbor was followed by another, still more brief, at Harvard Medical School as associate professor of physiology under Henry P. Bowditch [*q.v.*]. This was cut short in 1892 when President Gilman of Johns Hopkins offered Howell the chair of physiology in the new Johns Hopkins Medical School. He was the only one of the distinguished group of preclinical professors Gilman gathered to start the school, including F. P. Mall, William H. Welch [*qq.v.*], and John J. Abel [Supp. 2], who had not received his training partly in German universities. He spent the rest of his life in Baltimore, in constantly productive research, teaching, and administration.

Most of Howell's publications after 1892 deal with the physiology and pathology of the blood. In this field of research he became an internationally recognized authority, bringing to it not only broad biological experience but also command of the biochemical methods then available for working with the highly complex and little-understood ingredients of blood plasma, serum, and clots. In particular, he devoted much time and energy, after 1909, to the difficult problem of clotting, which he had begun to study while a graduate student. Although he did not reach a final solution of the way by which several ingredients of blood and tissue fluid combine to form a clot, his researches and hypotheses, published in a long series of contributions ended only by his death, were constantly stimulating to other workers in the field.

Notable among his discoveries were those establishing the role of phosphatides, especially cephalin, in the process of clotting. About 1916 Howell assigned to a medical student, Jay McLean, the project of extracting from heart and liver tissues certain substances, presumably phosphatides, which in crude form were known to facilitate clotting. Actually McLean's experiments yielded a substance that retards clotting. Following this clue, with another of his students, L. Emmett Holt, Jr., Howell by skillful chemical procedures secured a purified substance having powerful anticoagulant action. This substance he named "heparin" because he found it in large amounts in the liver. After further purification, heparin has become very useful in preventing clotting in blood transfusions and in operations upon blood vessels, and in limiting the extension of clots already existing in the blood vessels, as in coronary thrombosis and similar obstructions elsewhere.

Never closely confining himself to one field of research, Howell interspersed among his studies of the blood numerous investigations of other problems. One of these dealt with the pituitary gland; he was apparently the first to suggest (1897) that the two lobes of this gland are different in their endocrine function, the posterior lobe alone producing a substance (pituitrin) that causes contraction of blood vessels.

In the early 1890's physiological research and teaching in the United States had advanced sufficiently to call for a collaborative textbook. Howell was chosen to edit it and brought out in 1896 the first edition of *An American Text-book of Physiology* and in 1900 a second edition. Shortly thereafter he began to write his own *Text-book of Physiology for Medical Students and Physicians,* first published in 1905. The clarity, balance, and thorough coverage of this work won it the prompt and enduring approval of teachers and students in practically all the American medical schools. During Howell's lifetime it went through fourteen editions; after his death it was carried on by a group of younger physiologists.

The success of the textbook imposed upon its author the heavy burden of keeping it up to date by successive revisions as current progress demanded. This labor, carried out largely during summer vacations, did not prevent Howell from continuing his investigations while carrying on much of the teaching in his department. He was in the student laboratory at every triweekly session, and lectured regularly. His lectures, though delivered without notes, were so perfectly worded that they could have gone directly to the printer, so thorough and yet so effortlessly presented as almost to spare his hearers the need to wrestle mentally with the subject under discussion. They were accompanied, whenever possible, by faultless lecture-table experiments. In the laboratory the medical students found him a friendly, careful instructor, not so provocative intellectually, perhaps, as some of his less polished colleagues; but to older men who joined him in research or sought his advice on problems of their own he was a stimulating leader. Two who worked with him closely, Joseph Erlanger and George H. Whipple, received the Nobel Prize.

At the peak of his career as investigator, teacher, and author, Howell accepted in 1899 the deanship of the Johns Hopkins University School of Medicine as successor to William H. Welch. In his outwardly calm, unhurried way he conducted the dean's office to the satisfaction of faculty, colleagues, and students, while the school and its affiliated Johns Hopkins Hospital grew larger and more complicated. The added burdens, however, caused Howell chronic gastric difficulties which forced him to resign the deanship in

1911, while retaining his professorship and research activities. Portraits made at this time show the strain of overwork and ill health upon his kindly, thoughtful countenance.

Howell's executive services to the Johns Hopkins University were, however, by no means over. When the university's School of Hygiene and Public Health was organized in 1916, Welch, who headed it, appointed Howell assistant director and, the next year, professor of physiology (at which time he left the medical school). Howell effectively organized the teaching of physiology in the new school, different in many ways from that of the medical school. On Welch's retirement in 1925 he became its director, holding that post until his own retirement in 1931 at the age of seventy.

Howell was influential as scientist and leader of scientific affairs outside as well as within the university. He was a charter member of the American Physiological Society, a member of its council for twenty-two years, and its fourth president, serving for five terms (1905–09). In 1929 he was president of the first international congress of physiology held in the Americas. He was elected to the American Philosophical Society in 1903 and the National Academy of Sciences in 1905. Other honors included degrees from Michigan, Yale, and the University of Edinburgh. After his retirement from the Johns Hopkins School of Hygiene, Howell served for two years as an officer of the National Research Council, at first as chairman of the Division of Medical Research and later as chairman of the Council.

Howell married, on June 15, 1887, Anne Janet Tucker of Baltimore. They had three children: Janet Tucker, Roger, and Charlotte Teresa. The elder daughter, Janet Howell Clark, became professor of biophysics and dean of the college for women of the University of Rochester; Roger Howell became dean of the law school of the University of Maryland. Howell was an Episcopalian in religious affiliation. In his last years he devoted himself to continuing revision of his celebrated textbook and to research in a laboratory provided by the university. He died in Baltimore shortly before his eighty-fifth birthday of a coronary occlusion sustained in the laboratory.

[Joseph Erlanger, "William Henry Howell," in Nat. Acad. Sci., *Biog. Memoirs*, XXVI (1951), 153–80 (with portrait and complete bibliography); obituary in *Jour. Am. Medic. Assoc.*, Feb. 17, 1945; addresses at 60th anniversary of Dr. Howell's graduation from college in *Johns Hopkins Hospital Bull.*, Apr. 1941. A superb portrait in oil by Cecilia Beaux [Supp. 3] is owned by the Johns Hopkins Univ. School of Medicine.]

GEORGE W. CORNER

HRDLIČKA, ALEŠ (Mar. 29, 1869–Sept. 5, 1943), physical anthropologist, was born in Humpolec, Bohemia (later part of Czechoslovakia), the first of the five sons and two daughters of respected middle-class parents, Maximilian and Karolina (Wagner) Hrdlička. His father was a master cabinetmaker who owned his shop. Aleš attended local schools and received private tutoring in Latin and Greek from a Jesuit priest who was attracted by the boy's ability. He left high school in 1882, in his fourteenth year, to emigrate with his father to New York City, where the other members of the family later joined them.

In New York, Hrdlička's education was slowed by the need to learn English and to contribute to the family income. For six years he worked by day in a cigar factory and attended school at night. Then, in 1888, a serious attack of typhoid fever altered the course of his life. The attending physician, a trustee of the Eclectic Medical College in New York, became interested in Hrdlička and persuaded him to undertake the study of medicine at the college. Graduating at the head of his class in 1892, he started a practice in New York's East Side and at the same time, to broaden his medical background, began attending the New York Homeopathic Medical College, from which he graduated, again at the head of his class, in 1894. Shortly thereafter, he passed the Maryland State Medical Board (allopathic) examination, hoping to be able to join the staff of the Johns Hopkins Hospital in Baltimore, but he gave up this plan to accept the offer of a research internship in the new State Homeopathic Hospital for the Insane at Middletown, N. Y.

Hrdlička's lifelong interest in anthropology began here, when his autopsies and examinations of the patients suggested the possibility that physical characteristics and skeletal measurements might show systematic differences according to sex and the type of insanity. The results of these first studies attracted attention and brought Hrdlička an invitation to join the proposed Pathological Institute of the New York State Hospitals. To secure additional training, he went to Europe early in 1896 to study at various hospitals, and in Paris was influenced especially by the anthropologist Léon Manouvrier. Returning to New York in September, Hrdlička organized an extensive program with a number of assistants, planning to make detailed studies of some 40,000 mentally abnormal persons being cared for in state institutions. To obtain analogous material on normal persons, he established connections with George S. Huntington, professor of anatomy at the College of Physicians and Surgeons in

New York, who was making a collection of documented human skeletons from the dissecting rooms, and with the archaeologist Frederick W. Putnam [*q.v.*] of the American Museum of Natural History. Putnam was organizing expeditions to study Indians in various parts of North America and arranged for Hrdlička to accompany Carl Lumholtz on his last expedition (1898) to Mexico. Hrdlička's study convinced him that "normal" Mexican Indians showed marked differences in physical pattern from white populations. This experience, coupled with the financial collapse of the Pathological Institute, forced the abandonment of his project and turned him entirely in the direction of anthropology.

Further field work in Mexico and the American Southwest for the American Museum of Natural History brought Hrdlička to the attention of William H. Holmes [Supp. 1] of the Smithsonian Institution, who invited him to Washington to form a new Division of Physical Anthropology in the United States National Museum. This move, which occurred in 1903, began the most important phase of Hrdlička's career. Starting as an assistant curator, he became curator in 1910, a position he held until his retirement in 1942.

At the museum, Hrdlička devoted himself to assembling and studying human skeletal remains from all parts of the globe, many of them gathered during his own extensive travels. This skeletal collection—one of the world's largest—provided material for the greater part of Hrdlička's many scientific publications, which include catalogues of crania and monographs on the antiquity of man in America and on the most ancient skeletal remains of man in the Old World. Although he devoted less attention to the living, he published many reports on the normal range of physical variation among the white, black, and Indian elements of the American population. He regarded the Alaskan Eskimos and Indians as of particular importance in his study, and in the period 1926–38 he made yearly expeditions to the area, beginning in the north and ending in Kodiak and the Aleutian islands.

Possessing an extraordinary capacity for work, Hrdlička was a powerful force in establishing physical differences and skeletal measurements as tools for distinguishing races and determining the history of the human species. His great influence is indicated by his roles as founder (1918) and editor (1918–42) of the *American Journal of Physical Anthropology* and as founder (1930) and first president (1930–31) of the American Association of Physical Anthropologists. He gave much time also to general scientific organizations and to international congresses, and was made a

member of the American Philosophical Society (1918) and the National Academy of Sciences (1921). He received honorary Sc.D. degrees from the University of Prague (1922) and from the University of Brno (1927), and in 1927 was awarded the Huxley Memorial Medal of the Royal Anthropological Institute of Great Britain and Ireland. His most important books include *Early Man in South America* (1912), *Anthropometry* (1920), *The Old Americans* (1925), and *The Skeletal Remains of Early Man* (1930).

Hrdlička was noted for the tenacity of his views. He rejected all evidence for the antiquity of man in the Americas and steadfastly defended his conclusion that the Indians were relatively recent migrants from Asia, by way of the Bering Strait and Alaska. He was reluctant to accept the advent of new methods in anthropology. His rather scanty background in biology, biochemistry, and mathematics made him distrustful of modern genetic, physiological, and statistical approaches to problems of race differentiation, and as an editor he usually gave preference to papers based on anthropometry.

A man of commanding presence, although below medium height, he enhanced the effect by speaking with a marked foreign accent, wearing his hair fairly long, and dressing in an old-fashioned style. Conservative as well in some of his attitudes, he strongly opposed the entry of women into science, believing their place was in the home. Hrdlička was first married, in September 1896, to Marie Strickler Dieudonné, a young French woman he met in New York. This happy marriage ended with her death in 1918. In 1920 he married Mina Mansfield, of Czech descent. He had no children. Hrdlička died at his home of a heart attack, at the age of seventy-four. His ashes, together with those of his first wife, were placed in 1968 in the family plot in Rock Creek Cemetery, Washington.

[Memoir by Adolph H. Schultz in Nat. Acad. Sci., *Biog. Memoirs*, vol. XXIII (1945); T. D. Stewart in *Am. Jour. of Physical Anthropology*, Mar. 1940, and in Miloslav Rechcigl, Jr., ed., *The Czechoslovak Contribution to World Culture* (1964). See also: obituaries in *Am. Anthropologist*, Jan.–Mar. 1944 (by M. F. Ashley Montagu), *Science*, Sept. 17, 1943 (by Wilton M. Krogman), and *Am. Philosophical Soc., Year Book*, 1943 (by Clark Wissler); *Nat. Cyc. Am. Biog.*, Current Vol. C, pp. 90–92; Bernard Jaffe, *Outposts of Science* (1935), pp. 47–80.]

T. D. STEWART

HUNTER, ROBERT (Apr. 10, 1874–May 15, 1942), social worker, Socialist, and writer on social problems, was born in Terre Haute, Ind., the only child of William Robert and Caroline (Fouts) Hunter. He was christened Wiles Robert but as an adult dropped his first name. The son of a wealthy carriage manufacturer of Scottish descent, he was educated in the Terre Haute public schools, by private tutor, and at Indiana University, from which he received the B.A. degree in 1896.

Hunter was appalled by the unemployment and misery of the depression of 1893, particularly the suffering among workers laid off at his father's factory, and upon graduation decided to become a social worker. From 1896 to 1902 he served as organizing secretary of Chicago's Board of Charities, residing at the famous Hull House for the last three of those years. He also belonged to numerous social reform organizations. His first publication, *Tenement Conditions in Chicago* (1901), was a survey of working-class housing undertaken for one such group, the City Homes Association. Owing to the income he received from the family business, Hunter was able to travel widely. In the summer of 1899 he visited London's Toynbee Hall, the original urban settlement house, where he met European reformers and socialists.

Hunter left Chicago for New York City in 1902 to become head worker at the University Settlement on Rivington Street. He also became chairman of the Child Labor Committee, set up in 1902 by New York social workers, and directed its successful campaign for a statewide child labor law, enacted in 1903. His marriage, on May 23, 1903, to Caroline Margaretha Phelps Stokes, daughter of the New York civic leader Anson Phelps Stokes [*q.v.*] and a sister of Isaac Newton Phelps Stokes [Supp. 3], brought him additional wealth and a place among the city's social elite. Indeed, throughout his life Hunter remained the well-groomed, impeccably dressed gentleman, his entire demeanor conveying wealth and good breeding. Giving up his Rivington Street post in 1903, he thereafter held no regular position. He and his wife had four children: Robert, Phelps Stokes, Caroline Phelps, and Helen Louisa.

In 1904 Hunter published his most important book, *Poverty,* the first general statistical survey of America's poor. The work was perhaps naive by later sociological standards; Hunter employed racial stereotypes when describing immigrants and moralistic categories in portraying vagrants. He nevertheless proved by careful statistical investigation that most poor families suffered as a result of social forces beyond their control, not because of personal immorality or sloth. Contrary to the older American tradition, he further asserted that the working poor—"underpaid, underfed, underclothed, badly housed, and overworked" —were worse off than the dependent pauper, and

that improving their conditions was the best way to combat dependency. Hunter developed a typology of poverty and an analysis of the "culture of poverty" similar in many ways to that "originated" fifty-odd years later by Oscar Lewis and Michael Harrington.

Shortly after his marriage, Hunter had again visited Europe, renewing his acquaintance with Continental socialists and also making a pilgrimage to Tolstoy's estate in Russia. In 1905 he declared himself a socialist, and that September he was elected to the first executive board of the Intercollegiate Socialist Society. As he later explained it: "The aims, scholarship, and mental equipment of the . . . theoreticians of the socialist movement acted like a magnet to one seeking, as I was, a sovereign remedy for poverty" (*Revolution: Why, How, When?* 1940, p. 7). Hunter rose rapidly in the Socialist party, as befitted a young man of wealth, social position, and fame in a political organization eager to become "respectable" and "American." In 1908 he stood as Socialist candidate for the New York state assembly and in 1910 (having moved to Noroton, Conn.) for the governorship of Connecticut. At the same time he served on the party's national executive committee (1909–12) and represented American socialism at the 1907 convention of the Third International in Stuttgart and the 1910 meeting in Copenhagen. Within the American Socialist party Hunter allied with the faction that desired amicable relations with the American Federation of Labor, frowned upon the rhetoric of revolution and violence, looked askance at unlimited immigration, and scarcely differed from the more advanced wings of the Progressive movement. So antipathetic was he to violence and unrestrained radicalism that in 1914 he published *Violence and the Labor Movement,* a damning, if simpleminded, indictment of the Industrial Workers of the World, as well as of all other forms of anarchism and syndicalism. In it he paid tribute to the socialism of Marx and Engels, which, according to Hunter, stood "almost alone today faithful to democracy."

That same year, when European socialists proved impotent to forestall the violence of world war, Hunter's idealistic notions of socialism were so shattered that he left the party. More a romantic than a "scientific" socialist, he lacked substantial grounding in Marxist history, economics, and sociology; most of his rather rudimentary ideas seem to have been drawn from shallow socialist journalism and polemics. After his break with the party he drifted away from social work and reform. In 1918 he moved to California, living in Berkeley and lecturing in economics and English at the University of California (1918–22). He next resided at Pebble Beach (1926–29), a period during which he wrote *The Links* (1926), a book on golf-course design, and laid out several West Coast golf courses. He moved to Santa Barbara in 1930. During the last years of his life Hunter became an inveterate critic of President Franklin D. Roosevelt and the New Deal and an admirer of the right-wing Committee for Constitutional Government. In his book *Revolution* (1940) he totally rejected Marxism and asserted that revolutions result from conspiratorial activities, not objective social conditions, and that, despite the Great Depression, capitalism, especially the American variety, had abolished poverty and produced social harmony. After a prolonged illness, Hunter died of angina pectoris in 1942 at Montecito, Calif., near Santa Barbara; his remains were cremated. Though Hunter's later writings add little to his reputation, none can gainsay the brilliance and impact of *Poverty,* or his solid achievements as a social worker in Chicago and New York.

[Peter d'A. Jones's introduction to the 1965 paperback edition of Hunter's *Poverty* offers a clear and concise account of his life as well as an excellent analysis of the book itself. See also David A. Shannon, *The Socialist Party of America* (1955); Ira A. Kipnis, *The Am. Socialist Movement, 1897–1912* (1952); Jeremy Felt, *Hostages of Fortune: Child Labor Reform in N. Y. State* (1965); *Nat. Cyc. Am. Biog.,* XIV, 353–54, and XXXI, 16; *N. Y. Times,* May 17 (obituary) and 19 (editorial), 1942. Death record from Calif. Dept. of Public Health. Hunter's own writings are a major source; besides those already mentioned, see *Socialists at Work* (1908), a study of socialists and socialism in the various Western and Central European nations; *Why We Fail as Christians* (1919), a clear indication of his increasing conservatism; and *Labor in Politics* (1915), a political broadside.]

MELVYN DUBOFSKY

HYVERNAT, HENRI (June 30, 1858–May 29, 1941), orientalist, was born at St. Julien-en-Jarret, Loire, France. Christened Eugène Xavier Louis Henri Hyvernat, he was the fifth of nine children and youngest of four surviving sons of Claude and Léonide (Meyrieux) Hyvernat. His father was a mining engineer, who for three years after the revolution of 1848 had edited the *Gazette de Lyon;* his mother came of a family of mining engineers and artists. Both parents were devout Catholics, and at the age of nine Henri was sent to the Petit Séminaire de St. Jean, at Lyons, where he remained until he was eighteen. There he displayed a marked talent for languages, mastering Latin, Greek, and English, and developed a strong interest in geology and the cosmological questions raised by Darwinism.

After graduating from the seminary in 1876 (at which time he was also awarded a bachelor's

degree by the University of France in Lyons), Hyvernat spent a year at home and then became a candidate for the priesthood, studying at Sulpician seminaries in Issy (1877–79) and Paris (1879–82). At the Paris seminary, under the influence of the Abbé Fulcran Grégoire Vigouroux, he undertook to learn Hebrew, Syriac, and ancient Babylonian. He was ordained on June 3, 1882, and was appointed chaplain at the church of St. Louis des Français in Rome. While in Rome he obtained the degree of Doctor of Divinity (1882) from the Pontifical University and became acquainted with the leading orientalists then resident in Italy. In the next few years he wrote a series of three articles for the newspaper *Le Monde* (1883) on the Assyrian monuments of the Vatican, translated and edited a collection of Coptic texts, which he published as *Les Actes des Martyrs de l'Égypte* (1886–87), and an *Album de Paléographie Copte* (1888), and served, from 1885, both as professor of Assyriology and Egyptology at the Roman Seminary and as interpreter for Near Eastern languages in the Congregation for the Propagation of the Faith.

At this time churchmen in the United States were making plans to establish a Catholic university in Washington, D. C., and to enlist a faculty of scholars. Bishop John J. Keane [*q.v.*], who later became the first rector, in 1887 invited Hyvernat to become professor of Semitics in the new institution. Encouraged by Pope Leo XIII, he accepted the post and, in the time intervening before the university opened, went to the Near East with a mission from the French government to study cuneiform inscriptions in Armenia, in the region around Lake Van. The report, *Du Caucase au Golfe Persique* (prepared by Paul Müller-Simonis), was published in 1892.

Hyvernat arrived in Washington in November 1889 for the opening of the Catholic University of America, one of the four European scholars who formed its initial faculty. Six years later he founded the department of Semitic and Egyptian languages and literatures, over which he presided for the rest of his life. He was devoted to his work in archaeology and philology and for many years combined winters of teaching and writing with summers of research in Europe and in Egypt. In the *Revue Biblique* and elsewhere he published a number of articles on Coptic and Arabic versions of the Bible. In 1903 Hyvernat joined with Jean Baptiste Chabot and others to launch the Corpus Scriptorum Christianorum Orientalium, comprising edited texts of Arabic, Coptic, Ethiopic, and Syriac works with separately issued translations in Latin or a European language. This series was transferred in 1912 to the joint ownership of the Catholic universities of Louvain and of America, and at the time of his death some 120 volumes had been published. Hyvernat directed the Coptic section until 1930 and published the Coptic *Acta Martyrum* (4 parts, 1907–50); his pupil and later colleague Arthur Adolphe Vaschalde contributed largely to the Syriac section.

In Paris in the summer of 1910, Hyvernat learned that a dealer was offering for sale a collection of more than fifty Coptic manuscripts, found in the ruins of the Egyptian monastery of St. Michael of the Desert, near Hamuli in the Fayum oasis. The following year, when the collection was bought by the elder J. Pierpont Morgan [*q.v.*] for his library in New York, Hyvernat approached him and was commissioned to prepare a catalogue of the material and to track down scattered folios still in the hands of Egyptian dealers or in European libraries. Hyvernat also supervised the repair of the manuscripts, carried out in the workshops of the Vatican Library, and prepared a photographic edition, which because of the interruption of World War I was not completed until 1922. In 1919 Hyvernat issued a *Check List of Coptic Manuscripts in the Pierpont Morgan Library*. Because of a chronic hip ailment and recurring periods of poor health, he was unable to prepare the full catalogue he had planned, but he completed an abbreviated version for the Morgan Library in 1932. In his later years he turned over to the Catholic University of America his own collection of Syriac and Arabic manuscripts, as well as his library and his bibliographical files, and provided an endowment to establish the Institute of Christian Oriental Research as an adjunct to the department he had founded.

For his work as an orientalist, Hyvernat was made chevalier (1926) and officer (1938) of the Legion of Honor and a member of the American Academy of Arts and Sciences. He also received an honorary Litt.D. from the University of Michigan (1919). In 1939, the golden jubilee year of Catholic University, Pope Pius XI raised him to the rank of prothonotary apostolic. Hyvernat died of cancer at the Providence Hospital in Washington in his eighty-third year, and was buried in the Catholic University plot in Mount Olivet Cemetery, Washington.

[Theodore C. Petersen's memoir in the *Catholic World*, Sept. 1941, is the fullest account. (A longer version in typescript is at Catholic Univ. of America.) The same author's sketch in the *New Catholic Encyc.* includes a picture of Hyvernat. See also *Am. Catholic Who's Who*, 1940–44; and *Who Was Who in America*, vol. I (1942).]

PATRICK W. SKEHAN

IRWIN, ELISABETH ANTOINETTE (Aug. 29, 1880–Oct. 16, 1942), progressive educator, was born in Brooklyn, N. Y., to Josephine Augusta (Easton) and William Henry Irwin. She was the youngest of four children, of whom only she and a brother survived childhood. Her father, a grain merchant, was a descendant of William Irwin, a Scotch-Irish immigrant who settled in Dutchess County, N. Y., about 1714; her mother's Puritan forebear, Joseph Easton, had come from England to Massachusetts about 1633. Although Elisabeth was reared in comfortable material circumstances, she apparently had a rather bleak childhood. Of her father, she later wrote curtly that he "was a staunch Republican. His avocations were animals, horses and dogs, and reading." Eventually she broke with her family completely.

Elisabeth Irwin attended Packer Collegiate Institute in Brooklyn (1890–99) and then entered Smith College. After receiving an A.B. in 1903 she enlisted in the social settlement movement, becoming in 1904 a resident at the College Settlement on New York's Lower East Side, where she remained for a year. For several years (1905–09) she experimented with the carefree life, traveling with a friend about the East, peddling notions from a horse-drawn cart in the country around Danbury, Conn., and contributing free-lance articles on social issues to newspapers and to women's journals. She worked at the College Settlement again in 1909–10.

Miss Irwin then joined the staff of the Public Education Association of New York City in the capacity of "visiting teacher" (social worker) and psychologist. A citizen group founded in 1894 to work for the improvement of the public schools, the association was marshaling its considerable influence behind progressive education as an agency of social reform. In this movement Elisabeth Irwin was to take a leading part. For six years she worked with the Board of Education's department of ungraded classes, administering Binet intelligence tests to mentally defective schoolchildren. (She kept abreast of the latest developments in the field of social work by taking courses in the New York School of Philanthropy and at Columbia University, from which she received an M.A. in 1923.) In 1916, at Public School 64, she began a pioneer experiment in the identification and instruction of gifted children. This had led by 1921 to the classification of all the children in the school into homogeneous groups on the basis of "intelligence quotient" or I.Q.

In 1922, still under the aegis of the Public Education Association, Miss Irwin launched a new project, an experiment in revising the public school curriculum and teaching methods. The project, located initially in a public school on East 16th Street, was promptly christened "The Little Red School House." With a hundred first-graders as the initial experimental group, she deemphasized conventional academic subjects and skills and reorganized the curriculum around occupations and the arts, introducing play and group activities in a permissive classroom atmosphere. At its peak size, in 1931, the program involved only 267 children, but it gained an international reputation as one of the country's foremost examples of a progressive public school.

Miss Irwin had hoped to develop a curriculum and methods suitable for use throughout the public schools, and her experimental program continued for ten years as part of the city school system. It met strong opposition, however, from many politicians, from some school officials, and from immigrant parents who wished their children to receive a standard American education. An investigation in 1930–31 found that Miss Irwin's pupils were much less advanced than children in other public schools in such basic skills as arithmetic, reading, and spelling, and in 1932 the city withdrew its support. That fall, with the aid of a group of friends and Greenwich Village residents, Miss Irwin organized another Little Red School House, at 196 Bleecker Street, as a private, progressive elementary school; in 1941 she added a high school department (after her death renamed the Elisabeth Irwin High School).

Miss Irwin was a competent, determined, and resourceful administrator. Her independent Little Red School House, founded in the midst of the depression, became one of the best-known and most respected progressive schools in the country. Her achievement as a public school reformer, however, is more debatable. Even in its private phase, she continued to regard her school as a model of progressive methods suitable for general use in the public schools. She had never operated, however, under conventional public school conditions: as a public school experiment, the Little Red School House always received support from foundations and wealthy patrons; as a private school, its clientele had little in common with children in the ordinary public school.

Miss Irwin's work, more clearly than that of any other progressive educator, represents the efforts of progressives to transform the curricula and procedures of the public schools according to the principles of the contemporary mental hygiene movement. She assumed that the

social and emotional adjustment of children must be the overriding concern of the educator, that their intellectual development could be taken for granted. Apparently she did not consider the possibility that a laissez-faire policy regarding intellectual development would limit the social mobility of pupils who lacked a favorable cultural background.

Elisabeth Irwin was a short, stout, capable-looking woman with a fair complexion, blue eyes, and short-cropped white hair. Her face was plain but expressive of strength of character and intelligence. Indifferent to dress, uninhibited in speech, she possessed a lively wit and a shrewd common sense. Most of the leaders in the field of progressive education in New York City were her personal friends. She was a charter member of the Bureau of Educational Experiments and the Associated Experimental Schools, and a member of the Progressive Education Association, the Teachers Union, and the American Civil Liberties Union. She enjoyed the theatre and informal parties, but derived most of her pleasure from her work and her association with children. A militant feminist (and pacifist), she disparaged marriage but experimented with domesticity by legally adopting one child, Elizabeth H. Westwood, and helping rear at least three others. Miss Irwin lived for thirty years in Greenwich Village with the historian and biographer Katharine Anthony; the two also maintained a summer home in Gaylordsville, a section of New Milford, Conn. At home, Miss Irwin usually had a cat or two perched on her shoulders, a pair of Irish terriers at her feet. She died of cancer at New York Hospital in New York City after a lengthy illness. A simple Congregational funeral service preceded her burial in Gaylordsville.

[Miss Irwin published many articles on progressive education; her views are best summarized in *Fitting the School to the Child* (1924), written with Louis Marks. Biographical sources: obituaries in *N. Y. Times,* Oct. 17, 1942, *N. Y. Herald Tribune,* Oct. 17, 1942 (with photograph), the *Villager,* Oct. 22, 1942, *New Milford* (Conn.) *Times,* Oct. 22, 1942, *Danbury* (Conn.) *News-Times,* Oct. 22, 1942, and *Smith Alumnae Quart.,* Feb. 1943; *Who Was Who in America,* vol. II (1950); Lucy Sprague Mitchell, *Two Lives* (1953), pp. 413–22, and "A Tribute to a Pioneer," *Progressive Education,* Feb. 1943; clippings and photographs at the Little Red School House and in the possession of Mrs. Aida Anthony Whedon; information supplied by Mrs. Whedon, Mr. Howard Gresens, Mrs. Margarite Tarlau, and Mrs. Mabel Hawkins. For family information: Ralph S. Hosmer and Martha T. Fielder, *Genealogy of That Branch of the Irwin Family in N. Y. Founded in the Hudson River Valley by William Irwin, 1700–1787* (1938); and William S. Easton, *Descendants of Joseph Easton, Hartford, Conn., 1636–1899* (1899). On Miss Irwin's settlement period, see her articles in *Craftsman,* July 1907 and July 1908. For her early work in mental testing:

Truancy: A Study of the Mental, Physical and Social Factors of the Problem (Public Education Association of N. Y. City, 1915). For the experiment in the education of the gifted: Louise F. Specht, "Terman Class in Public School No. 64," *School and Society*, Mar. 29, 1919. For the Little Red School House experiment: Elisabeth Irwin, "Personal Education," *New Republic*, Nov. 12, 1924; "How Much Wood Can a Woodchuck Chuck if He Doesn't Chuck All Day," *Progressive Education*, Apr.–June 1928; Elisabeth Irwin, "The Teacher Steps Out," *Survey*, Dec. 15, 1929; and Sol Cohen, *Progressives and Urban School Reform* (1964). Agnes de Lima et al., *The Little Red School House* (1942), describes the school's post-1932 career.]

SOL COHEN

JACKSON, EDWARD (Mar. 30, 1856–Oct. 29, 1942), ophthalmologist and surgeon, was born in West Goshen, Chester County, Pa., the eldest of the three sons and one daughter of Emily (Hoopes) Jackson and Halliday Jackson, whose family also included a son by the father's first marriage. Halliday Jackson, a devout Quaker whose English forebears had migrated in 1725 from Ireland, was a writer and lecturer and had served as principal of the Friends' Institute in New York City (1849–54) before returning to Pennsylvania to teach. His son Edward attended Union College in Schenectady, N. Y., and received the degree of Civil Engineer in 1874. His decision to turn to medicine was made with a friend and fellow engineering student at Union, Joseph Price [*q.v.*], after a summer that included travel and working together on an Iowa farm.

Enrolling at the University of Pennsylvania, Jackson received the M.D. degree in 1878 and began general practice in West Chester, but his career was interrupted by an attack of diphtheria which caused a prolonged paralysis of his leg muscles and the focusing muscles of his eyes. During a lengthy convalescence, he became interested in defects of vision, read widely on the subject, and in 1884 moved to Philadelphia to practice ophthalmology, a field in which his early training in mathematics and engineering was of particular advantage. In 1885 and 1886 he published two important monographs on the use of the retinal shadow test, first described a decade earlier by Ferdinand L. J. Cuignet, to measure refractive errors of the eye; these were followed by a detailed study in 1895, *Skiascopy and Its Practical Application to the Study of Refraction*. Thereafter, his major scientific contributions were in the field of refraction. He was largely responsible for popularizing the use of the crossed cylinder for testing the amount and axis of astigmatism.

Jackson was appointed professor of ophthalmology at the Philadelphia Polyclinic and School of Graduates of Medicine in 1888 and surgeon to Wills Eye Hospital in 1890. Among his important contributions, in addition to his teaching and writing, was his help in establishing the Ophthalmic

Section of the College of Physicians of Philadelphia as a distinct entity (1890), in effect raising ophthalmology to the status of a separate specialty in medicine. He was also instrumental in securing higher standards of professional training, through the creation of the American Board for Ophthalmic Examinations (1916), which later became the American Board of Ophthalmology and was the forerunner of twenty such groups which today certify medical specialists. Convinced that medical skill depended on a knowledge of new developments, Jackson continually urged the need for broader professional education. To provide access to the foreign literature, he founded (1904) the *Ophthalmic Year Book,* a survey of articles from journals in all parts of the world. He served as its editor until 1917, and when necessary subsidized its publication.

On Oct. 9, 1878, Jackson married Jennie L. Price of West Chester. Their children were Ethel, Robert Price, Thomas Hoopes, Edward, Herbert Clifford, and Helen. In 1894 Mrs. Jackson developed tuberculosis and the family moved to Denver, Colo., where she died in 1896. Jackson returned to Philadelphia but after two years moved permanently to Denver. On June 2, 1898, he married Emily Churchman of that city; they had no children.

Jackson continued his professional activities in Denver. In 1899 he collaborated in the formation of the Denver (later Colorado) Ophthalmological Society, and in 1905 he was appointed professor of ophthalmology at the medical school of the University of Colorado, a post he held until his retirement in 1921. In 1915 he instituted a series of summer congresses for eye specialists, a plan of postgraduate education that has been widely emulated. In 1918 he became the first editor of the Third Series of the *American Journal of Ophthalmology,* a post he retained until 1927. For his work in the movement for the prevention of blindness he was awarded the Leslie Dana Gold Medal in 1925.

In Denver, Jackson joined the Unitarian Church, although in 1939 he also renewed his earlier membership in the Society of Friends. He enjoyed concert music and often visited art galleries and museums. For some years he was an enthusiastic supporter of the single-tax movement of Henry George [*q.v.*]. He led an abstemious life and made mountain climbing a major hobby. A tall, slender man with a preoccupied air, he regularly attended medical meetings and took an active part in the discussions until the end of his life. He died in Denver of a heart block at the age of eighty-six. His ashes were scattered over his own land in Hidden Valley, in Rocky Mountain National Park.

[Introduction by George E. de Schweinitz to *Contributions to Ophthalmic Science Dedicated to Dr. Edward Jackson* (1926); obituary articles in *Am. Jour. of Ophthalmology*, Jan. 1943 (by William H. Crisp; see also other recollections in same issue and reproductions of two oil portraits of Jackson) and Feb. 1943 (by Burton Chance), *Archives of Ophthalmology*, Jan. 1943 (by Arnold Knapp), *Bull. of the Am. College of Surgeons*, Feb. 1943 (by Harry S. Gradle), and *Jour. Am. Medic. Assoc.*, Nov. 7, 1942; William H. Crisp, "Edward Jackson's Place in the Hist. of Refraction," *Am. Jour. of Ophthalmology*, Jan. 1945; *Nat. Cyc. Am. Biog.*, XLII, 439; information from Jackson's grandsons, Edward J. Ramaley of Denver and David Ramaley of Boulder, Colo.]
FRANK W. NEWELL

JACKSON, ROBERT R. (Sept. 1, 1870–June 12, 1942), Negro political and civic leader, was born in Malta, Ill., but while still an infant moved with his parents to Chicago, where he spent the remainder of his life. His father, William Jackson, was a native of St. Catherines, Ontario, Canada; his mother, Sarah (Cooper) Jackson, of Hagerstown, Md. The family was poor, and at the age of nine Robert began work after school hours as a bootblack and newsboy. He left school in 1883 at the end of the eighth grade. Five years later, passing a civil service examination with a high score, he entered the postal service, where in nine years he advanced to the position of assistant superintendent of a Chicago postal station. During this period he also entered into a number of business ventures, and became active in local military, fraternal, and political affairs. He joined the Illinois national guard in 1888 as a drummer boy, and during the Spanish-American War was commissioned a major. (He subsequently saw service on the Mexican border and was a training camp instructor during World War I.) His principal business enterprise was a printing company which supplied constitutions and by-laws to black fraternal orders; its prosperity enabled Jackson to leave the postal service in 1909. He was a member of nearly every black lodge and civic club in the city.

Jackson became best known, however, as a political leader. "The Major," as he was commonly called, entered politics in the 1890's as a protégé of Edward Wright, Chicago's first successful Negro machine politician, and Jackson's entire political career was closely linked with the rise and fall of Wright's Republican organization, which dominated Negro politics in the city from the turn of the century until the 1930's. After 1915, Wright and Jackson were firmly allied with Mayor William Hale Thompson [Supp. 3], the flamboyant political boss who virtually ran Chicago politics for a decade and a half. Jackson was elected to the state legislature in 1912 and to the city council in 1918, at a time when thousands of Southern black migrants were crowding into Chicago in search of jobs and a greater measure of human dignity. Conditioned by their Southern experience to support the "party of Lincoln," the migrants formed the core of Jackson's electoral base.

As legislator and alderman, Jackson attempted to represent the interests of these constituents while at the same time giving vital political support to Wright and Thompson. During his three terms in the legislature (1913–19), he was instrumental in killing an anti-intermarriage bill and a bill that would have reduced employment opportunities for Negroes on the railroads. He also fought to curb the distribution of racist films and literature and secured a $50,000 appropriation for an Emancipation Golden Jubilee in 1913. On the city council, representing the Second Ward (later the Third Ward), Jackson sponsored a pure milk ordinance, an ordinance forbidding Ku Klux Klan parades in the city, and appropriations for schools, athletic fields, playgrounds, and parks in the black community. For a time, he served as Thompson's floor leader.

In his twenty-one years on the city council, Jackson weathered numerous electoral challenges from both within and outside the Thompson-Wright organization. In the 1930's, however, his political fortunes ebbed as the Republican Thompson machine was replaced by the Democratic Kelly-Nash machine and the majority of Negro voters, hit hard by the depression, shifted their allegiance to the Democratic party and Roosevelt's New Deal. Jackson attempted to make his peace with the new political order and for a while had the support of the Democratic leadership. But unlike his fellow black councilman William Dawson, he never became a Democrat, and he was defeated by a Democratic challenger in 1939. For the next two years he was the commissioner of the Negro American (Baseball) League; he had had a lifelong interest in baseball and was the owner of the Chicago Columbia Giants. When the league failed to rehire him he promptly organized the Negro Baseball League of America in 1942, but it did not last out the season. Jackson died that same year of cerebral apoplexy at the Provident Hospital in Chicago, and was buried in Chicago's Oakwood Cemetery. He was survived by his wife, Hattie Ball Lewis, and their one son, George.

Robert R. Jackson belonged to a generation of black politicians who attempted to build political organizations comparable to the finely tuned machines of the white immigrant political bosses. His primary concerns were patronage jobs and police protection for his constituents and practical improvements for the community he represented. He never questioned the political system within which he operated or thought in terms of long-range goals. His own rise from poverty to affluence and prestige, which he never tired of recalling, indicated to him that blacks could make the system work for them, and he sharply criticized those who failed to work hard, save money, and care for property. Reform-minded contemporaries frequently pointed to the limitations of this approach and questioned the value of the favors which Jackson and his colleagues won for their people. Clearly, Jackson's politics did little to meet the deep-seated problems of the urban black ghetto—the problems of poverty, discrimination, and alienation. Yet he saw no viable alternatives: the reform movements of his day usually ignored black people, and radical programs seemed to him utopian and impractical. Despite criticisms of his politics, few contemporaries attacked Jackson personally. Congenial and eager to please, he avoided the bitter personal fights waged by many of his political allies, and even his opponents admitted that he was honest and sincere. Faced with limited options, Jackson attempted, within the framework of his own value system, to alleviate, at least, the hardships of ghetto life.

[The outline of Robert R. Jackson's life can be found in obituaries in the *Chicago Defender*, June 20, 1942, and the *Chicago Sun*, June 14, 1942, and in a biographical sketch in the Chicago *Whip*, July 6, 1929; see also *Ill. Blue Book*, 1917–18, p. 132. His political career, particularly his relationship to the Thompson machine, is discussed in Harold Gosnell, *Negro Politicians* (1935), and in Allan H. Spear, *Black Chicago: The Making of a Negro Ghetto* (1967). The transcript of an interview with Jackson, July 27, 1938, can be found in the files of the Ill. Writers Project, Works Progress Administration, at the George Cleveland Hall branch, Chicago Public Lib. Jackson's death record (Ill. Dept. of Public Health) supplied data on his parents. His political and civic activities were reported regularly in the *Chicago Defender* (1905–42), the Chicago *Broad Ax* (1899–1931), and the Chicago *Whip* (1919–30). His work as a legislator and alderman can be traced in the Ill. Legislative Reference Bureau's *Legislative Digest*, 1913–19, and the *Jour. of Proc.* of the Chicago City Council, 1918–39. The conditions that led to Jackson's defeat in 1939 are discussed in Elmer Henderson, "A Study of the Basic Factors Involved in the Change in the Party Alignment of Negroes in Chicago, 1932–38" (master's thesis, Univ. of Chicago, 1939); and Rita Werner Gordon, "The Change in the Political Alignment of Chicago's Negroes during the New Deal," *Jour. of Am. Hist.*, Dec. 1969. On his baseball connections, see Robert W. Peterson, *Only the Ball Was White* (1970).]

ALLAN H. SPEAR

JACKSON, WILLIAM HENRY (Apr. 4, 1843–June 30, 1942), photographer and painter of the West, was born in Keeseville, N. Y., the eldest of the five sons and two daughters of George Hallock Jackson, of Irish descent, and Harriet Maria (Allen) Jackson, of English ancestry. Both parents were members of the Society of Friends. The father, a carriagemaker and blacksmith, moved frequently during William's childhood: to Columbus, Ga., Plattsburg and Peru, N. Y., Petersburg, Va., Philadelphia and, in 1853, to a large farm near Troy, N. Y. William received his early schooling at Peru, where he first began to draw and paint. His mother, a graduate of the Troy Female Seminary and a talented watercolorist, encouraged him, and her gift of *The American Drawing Book* by John G. Chapman [*q.v.*] helped him to teach himself. By painting window shades and show cards he was soon able to earn enough to buy materials. He finished his formal education at the age of fifteen, in Troy, and began work in the studio of Troy's leading photographer, C. C. Schoonmaker, as a piecework retoucher; in 1860 he moved to the employ of Frank Mowrey, a photographer in Rutland, Vt., where he retouched and tinted photographs.

In 1862 Jackson enlisted in the 12th Vermont Volunteers, but his military service in the Civil War was limited to guard duty in the Potomac area. During this time he began to keep a journal and make sketches of the scenes around him, a habit that he continued throughout his life. When his term of enlistment was over, he returned to his job in Rutland; in 1865 he became an artist with the leading photographer in Burlington, Vt., known only as F. Styles.

In the spring of 1866, after a quarrel with his fiancée had resulted in the breaking of their engagement, Jackson left Vermont for New York City and, with two friends, determined to seek his fortune in the silver mines of Montana. By pawning their possessions and taking odd jobs, the trio eventually reached St. Joseph, Mo., where they signed up as bullwhackers on an immigrant train of twenty-five covered wagons bound for Montana. In the arduous journey across the Nebraska and Dakota plains and the Rocky Mountains, Jackson continued to keep a diary and made pencil sketches of the landscape, the wagon train, the frontier settlements, and the Indians; in later life these would provide material for his paintings. After some three months he left the wagon train and made his way on foot to Salt Lake City. All but penniless, he was befriended by a Mormon farmer, for whom he worked until he had earned enough to join—this time as passenger—a wagon train bound for California. He arrived at Los Angeles at the end of January 1867. That spring he decided to return to the East and signed on to help drive a consignment of wild horses to the railhead at Cheyenne and take them on by train to Omaha.

In Omaha, Jackson took a job with a photographer. Two of his brothers joined him in 1868; the three bought a photographic studio and hired a portrait artist. Now free to take trips into the countryside, Jackson began what became the major work of his life: making a photographic record of the development of the West. The dry plate process had not yet been perfected and the collodion process then in use required that the glass plates be sensitized just before use and developed immediately afterward. Fitting up a horse-drawn wagon as laboratory and darkroom, Jackson traveled widely, photographing Indians, frontiersmen, and the construction of the transcontinental railroad. On Apr. 10, 1869, in Omaha, he married Mary Greer of Warren, Ohio. Shortly after the historic joining of the rails at Promontory Point that May, he received an order for ten thousand stereographic photographs of scenes along the railroad. He spent the summer in Wyoming and Utah and returned to Omaha "with just about the finest assortment of negatives that had yet come out of the West."

During this trip he had met Ferdinand V. Hayden [q.v.], director of the United States Geological and Geographical Survey of the Territories, and in 1870 Hayden invited Jackson to join the Survey as photographer. Each summer for the next eight years Jackson traveled with the Survey through almost unknown regions of the West. He was the first to photograph the extraordinary natural wonders of Yellowstone, and it was largely the evidence of his pictures that moved Congress in 1872 to preserve that region as the nation's first national park. With two mules to carry his processing equipment and his bulky camera—in later years he sometimes used plates as large as 20 x 24 inches—he climbed the Rockies and the Grand Tetons, explored Wyoming, Utah, and Colorado, and took the first pictures of the cliff dwellings of Mesa Verde. In 1871 he sold his Omaha studio and moved to Washington, D. C., where he spent the winters cataloguing and printing the negatives he had so arduously made. His wife died in 1872, following the birth of a daughter, who died soon afterward. On Oct. 4, 1873, in Cincinnati, Jackson married Emilie Painter, whom he had first met when her father was Indian agent on the Omaha Reservation. They had three children: Clarence, Louise, and Harriet.

When the Hayden Survey was discontinued in 1879, Jackson returned to settle in the West, opening a commercial studio in Denver, Colo., where he specialized in landscape photography. The railroads, once again his chief clients, wanted pictures for publicity purposes, and Jackson now traveled much of the time in a private car fully equipped as a darkroom. His business expanded, and in 1892 he formed with Walter F. Crosby, a wealthy amateur photographer, the W. H. Jackson Photograph and Publishing Company.

While visiting the World's Columbian Exposition at Chicago the next year, Jackson was enlisted to make photographs to illustrate the official report. This assignment led to his appointment as photographer to the World's Transportation Commission, a private group sponsored by Chicago's Field Museum to survey foreign railroad operations. On this mission Jackson embarked for London early in October 1894 and returned seventeen months later, having circled the globe. A high point of the trip was a midwinter journey of 3,000 miles by sledge, at subzero temperatures, to reach the eastern terminus of the Trans-Siberian railroad. A photograph supplied every week to *Harper's Weekly* supported his family during his absence.

In 1898, after merging his Denver business with the Detroit Publishing Company, Jackson moved to Detroit, where for some years he supervised the company's production of colored prints. After 1902 he largely gave up photographic expeditions in the field, but he continued active in business until 1924, when he retired at the age of eighty-one and moved to Washington. His second wife had died in 1918. Unwilling to remain idle, in 1929 Jackson became research secretary of the Oregon Trail Association, for which he painted some fifty watercolors recording the trail's history. At this time he went to live in New York City. In 1935, now in his nineties, Jackson accepted a commission from the National Park Service to execute murals depicting the early days of the geological surveys for the new Interior Department building in Washington. His lively autobiography, *Time Exposure,* was published in 1940.

Jackson's collection of over 40,000 negatives had been acquired by Henry Ford in 1936 for the Edison Institute, Dearborn, Mich. The collection was later divided between the Library of Congress in Washington and the Colorado Historical Society in Denver. Jackson's photographs, long appreciated for their value as ethnological, geological, and geographical documents, were first exhibited as works of art by the Museum of Modern Art, New York, in 1942. Retaining his extraordinary vigor to the end of his life, Jackson died in Midtown Hospital, New York City, at the age of ninety-nine of injuries resulting from a fall in his apartment. He was buried in Arlington, Va., at a site selected by the National Park Service. Several landmarks in Wyoming and California bear his name.

[Many of Jackson's diaries are in the N. Y. Pub. Lib. and the State Hist. Soc. of Colo. Those for 1866–

67 and 1873–74 have been published in LeRoy R. and Ann W. Hafen, eds., *The Diaries of William Henry Jackson* (1959). Extensive quotations from the 1878 diary are in the excellent article on Jackson by Fritiof Fryxell in the *Am. Annual of Photography, 1937.* Jackson's autobiography, *Time Exposure,* is a basic source. See also his *The Pioneer Photographer,* written in collaboration with Howard R. Driggs (1929). An extensive collection of his photographs was published, with a text by his son Clarence S. Jackson, as *Picture Maker of the Old West: William H. Jackson* (1947).]

BEAUMONT NEWHALL

JAMES, ARTHUR CURTISS (June 1, 1867– June 4, 1941), railroad financier and philanthropist, was the only child of Daniel Willis James [*q.v.*] and Ellen Stebbins (Curtiss) James. He was born in New York City into established mercantile-manufacturing wealth. His paternal grandfather, Daniel James, had been a founding partner of the house of Phelps, Dodge & Company in 1834. His father, who became one of the two directing partners in 1879, helped expand Phelps Dodge's manufacturing activities and initiate the firm's investments in Arizona copper mining and Western railroading. In the 1880's D. Willis James also invested in and became a director of the St. Paul, Minneapolis & Manitoba Railway, the immediate forerunner of the Great Northern Railway Company. As a member of its finance committee he worked closely with the road's president, James J. Hill [*q.v.*], the beginning of a long business relationship.

Arthur James attended the private Arnold School in New York City and graduated from Amherst College with an A.B. degree in 1889. After graduation he entered the Phelps Dodge firm. He became a partner in 1892, and by 1900, with his father's semiretirement, he had assumed a guiding role. At his father's death in 1907, James's inheritance made him the largest single stockholder of Phelps Dodge, which was incorporated the following year into a holding company. Yet James was essentially a finance capitalist, and although he served as a vice-president (1909–30) and director (1908–41) of the company, he left formal operations to others. His own business activities increasingly involved the financing of railroad systems.

Throughout the 1880's and 1890's, Phelps Dodge had actively built railroads to facilitate its mining interests in the Southwest. In 1901 the firm consolidated these lines into the El Paso & Southwestern Railroad, and James was named first vice-president. In this role, over the following years, he sought to give the line transcontinental status by extending it northward and linking it to the Chicago, Rock Island & Pacific, of which he also became a director. James had other substantial railroad interests, inherited from his father, in the Northern Pacific, the Great Northern, and the Chicago, Burlington & Quincy. Neither an owner-entrepreneur, in the manner of Hill, nor a professional manager of the type which came to dominate the modern integrated company, James participated as a counselor in strategic decisions by virtue of his investments, helping to establish—in the term coined by J. P. Morgan [*q.v.*]—a "community of interests" among corporations in which he had a substantial stake.

During the 1920's James shifted his attention to his interests in the Northern lines, in which he was one of the largest individual investors. He was elected to the board of the Great Northern in 1924. That same year he abandoned his efforts to extend the El Paso & Southwestern to California when the Southern Pacific, to prevent this competition, purchased the road through an exchange of securities. Although this transaction made James the largest shareholder of Southern Pacific, he sold his shares in 1926. At the same time, through a gradual accumulation of common stock, he acquired a controlling interest in the Western Pacific Railroad, of which he became chief executive officer. This road, which ran between San Francisco and Salt Lake City, also connected with Denver through its interest in the Denver & Rio Grande Western; thus the Burlington, which ran between Chicago and Denver (and of which James was a major stockholder), gained direct access to the West Coast. James also supported an extension of the Western Pacific into northern California, and by 1931 his line connected with the Great Northern, fulfilling Hill's goal of giving the Great Northern friendly access to San Francisco. With completion of these linkages, James held interests in over 40,000 miles of rails, far surpassing the empires of earlier railroad magnates. He also served, in the course of his career, as a director of many other railroads, banks, and manufacturing industries.

James was in addition an active philanthropist. Following a tradition established by his grandfather and father, he gave away without fanfare an estimated $20,000,000 during his lifetime. His will left about $25,000,000 to create the James Foundation, specifying that the income and, at the end of twenty-five years, the principal be distributed to the various institutions he had aided during his life—among them Union Theological Seminary in New York City, Amherst College, the Children's Aid Society of New York, Hampton Institute, the Metropolitan Museum of Art, the American Board of Commissioners for Foreign Missions, and his own First Presbyterian Church of New York. At its liquidation in 1965, the foundation had disbursed more than $144,000,000.

Yet James also enjoyed the indulgent life of the very wealthy. On Apr. 23, 1890, he had married Harriet Eddy Parsons of Northampton, Mass., a student at Smith College. The childless couple maintained lavish homes in New York City, Newport, and Miami, and a country place in Tarrytown, N. Y. An avid yachtsman, James frequently sailed his full-rigged bark to Europe, South America, and Africa, and once even around the world; he served as commodore of the prestigious New York Yacht Club in 1909–10. In an era when shaven faces were the vogue, he wore a full beard. A lifelong Republican, James nevertheless supported Alfred E. Smith [Supp. 3] for president in 1928 because of his strong aversion to prohibition, and he backed Franklin D. Roosevelt and the New Deal. Although one of the richest and most powerful men in America, James was not widely known. His social and business roles were quiet; his philanthropy bordered on secrecy. In failing health during his last years, he retired from the board of the Western Pacific in 1939 and relinquished most of his other business posts over the next two years. He died of pneumonia, a month after the death of his wife, at the Columbia-Presbyterian Medical Center in New York City, and was buried in Greenwood Cemetery, Brooklyn.

[James is credited with two publications: "Advantages of Hawaiian Annexation," *North Am. Rev.*, Dec. 1897, and, with Thomas C. McClary, "A Plea for Our Railroads," *Saturday Evening Post*, Jan. 16, 1932. For his relation to Phelps Dodge, see Robert Glass Cleland, *A Hist. of Phelps Dodge, 1834–1950* (1952). Helpful on his railroad activities are Vincent Guy Sanborn, "An Unknown Railroad Croesus," *Mag. of Wall Street*, Dec. 4, 1926; Frank J. Williams, "A New Railroad 'Giant,'" *Am. Rev. of Revs.*, Feb. 1927; and "Arthur Curtiss James Retires," *Railway Age*, Nov. 11, 1939. Illuminating obituaries are found in the *N. Y. Times* and *Wall Street Jour.* for June 5, 1941; see also *Amherst College Biog. Record*, 1951. James's name appears frequently in railroad sources of the 1920's and 1930's and with some frequency in acknowledgements of philanthropic contributions. An unpublished biographical outline by Adrienne M. Cameron, Univ. of Wis. Lib. School (June 1966), was helpful.]

WILLIAM O. WAGNON, JR.

JAMES, WILL RODERICK (June 6, 1892– Sept. 3, 1942), Western author and artist, was born at St. Nazaire de Acton, Quebec Province, Canada. His real name was Joseph Ernest Nephtali Dufault, and he was the second son and second of six children of Jean and Josephine Dufault, both French-speaking natives of Quebec Province. Shortly after his birth, the family moved to Montreal, where his father ran a small hotel and the boy attended a Catholic primary school. At the hotel James met old trappers whose stories probably suggested details which would later help form his sham autobiography, *Lone Cowboy*. According to his self-constructed

myth, he was born near Judith Gap, Mont., the son of a West Texas cattle drover and a beautiful Californian of Spanish and Scotch-Irish descent who died shortly after his birth and from whose supposed maiden name, Rodriguez, he derived his middle name. His father, he asserted, was killed by a locoed steer. Will had then been cared for by an itinerant French trapper named Jean Beaupré, or "Old Bopy," with whom he trapped along the Mackenzie and in the isolated Peace River country of Canada until 1906, when the old man disappeared, presumably drowned, leaving the boy on his own.

In reality James lived in Montreal until 1907, reading all he could find about the American West. He spent the next three years in the Canadian provinces of Saskatchewan and Alberta, learning English and the life of a cowhand. At eighteen he seems to have been arrested in connection with the fatal wounding of a drunken sheepherder. Shortly afterward he changed his name to C. W. Jackson, and then to W. R. or Will James. Now a wandering bronco rider, he drifted from Canada through Montana to southern Idaho, where he rounded up wild horses in 1911 and 1912. After moving to Nevada, he was convicted of cattle rustling and sentenced to the Nevada State Prison, where he served for nearly a year before winning parole in April 1916. After a brief interim as a stunt man in Western movies for the Thomas Ince Studios in Los Angeles—his tall, slim figure and rather sharp face were quite photogenic—he resumed his drifting life until May 1918, when he was inducted into the army. He served as a private for nine months.

James had been sketching Western subjects since early youth, and he now sought to become an artist in the style of Frederic Remington [q.v.] and Charles Russell. After recovering from a serious accident, when his bronco threw him headfirst against a railroad track, he briefly attended the California School of Fine Arts in San Francisco in 1919. The routine bored him, however, as did the artists' colony in Sausalito, where he lived for a time; and on the advice of the artist Maynard Dixon he gave up academic training to concentrate on developing his natural style. His first published sketch appeared in *Sunset Magazine* (January 1920), which began taking others each month. Feeling confident in his new career, he returned to Nevada and married Alice Conradt, the sister of a close friend, on July 7, 1920. He continued to sell occasional sketches while working as a stock watcher near Kingman, Ariz., and as a cowhand on the Springer CS Ranch in Cimarron, N. Mex. In 1921 he received a scholarship to the Yale Art School, but soon dropped out and, after a brief stay in New York, returned to Reno, Nev., in 1922.

His real success began when he tried writing and illustrating his own material. *Scribner's Magazine* published his first article, "Bucking Horses and Bucking-Horse Riders" (March 1923), and paid him $300. Stories and articles for *Scribner's,* the *Saturday Evening Post, Sunset,* and *Redbook* followed, and calendar companies and pulp magazines solicited his drawings. With savings from such work he bought a small parcel of land at Frankton, Nev., in Washoe Valley, where the Conradts built him a cabin.

Under the guidance of Maxwell Perkins, editor at Charles Scribner's Sons, James began to publish books in 1924. *Cowboys, North and South,* a collection of illustrated articles and probably his best nonfiction work, was followed by *The Drifting Cowboy* (1925), a series of short stories. In 1926 appeared his first and best novel, *Smoky,* the story of a cowboy and his horse. It enjoyed several printings, was translated into seven languages, and won the Newbery Award. The naturalist William Hornaday [Supp. 2] called it "one of the truly great horse stories in our language." Now a successful popular writer, James sold his Nevada property in 1927 and bought or leased 8,000 acres near Pryor, Mont., to form the Rocking R Ranch. Here, or from his winter quarters in San Francisco or Hollywood, he continued to turn out popular Western stories. His apocryphal autobiography, *Lone Cowboy* (1930), fooled even his wife and went unexposed until 1967; a choice of the Book-of-the-Month Club, it boosted James to the apex of his career.

From this point on he suffered a steady personal decline, precipitated by success, guilt over his concealed past, and a loss of inspiration. He drank too much and began to have trouble with his wife. His later work became melodramatic and merely rehashed or elaborated upon former plots. At its best, James's writing rang with authenticity in the Western idiom and reflected his own restlessness and nostalgic love of the rough, open West. At its worst, it was still pleasant reading. In 1934 James was committed to the Kimball Sanitarium in La Crescenta, Calif., for alcoholism. Alice ended their childless marriage with a legal separation in 1935, but they were never divorced. He died from "alcoholic complications" at Hollywood Presbyterian Hospital in 1942. Though born a Catholic, he had never regarded himself as a religious man. His remains were cremated and his ashes scattered over his Montana ranch.

[Other books by James include: *Cow Country* (1927), *Sand* (1929), *Big-Enough* (1931), *Sun Up* (1931), *All in the Day's Riding* (1933), *The Three Mustangeers* (1933), and *Horses I've Known* (1940). The one reliable biographical account is Anthony Amaral, *Will James: The Gilt-Edged Cowboy* (1967), which includes a bibliography. James is mentioned in: Maxwell Perkins, *Editor to Author* (1950), a selection of letters by Perkins; Alice P. Hackett, *Sixty Years of Best Sellers* (1956); and Douglas Branch, *The Cowboy and His Interpreters* (1926). James's papers, as of 1967, were in the possession of Eleanor Snook of Billings, Mont. The archives of Charles Scribner's Sons, at the Princeton Univ. Lib., contain a number of James's letters to his editors.]

THURMAN WILKINS

JASTROW, JOSEPH (Jan. 30, 1863–Jan. 8, 1944), psychologist, was born in Warsaw, Poland, one of the seven children of Bertha (Wolfsohn) and Marcus Jastrow and a younger brother of the Semitics scholar Morris Jastrow [*qq.v.*]. His father, a scholarly rabbi educated in German universities, was banished from Poland for supporting the patriot cause against Russian domination. In 1866, after several years in Germany, he accepted a call to Congregation Rodeph Shalom in Philadelphia, where he became a leader in American conservative Judaism.

Joseph Jastrow attended the University of Pennsylvania (A.B. 1882) and went on to the Johns Hopkins University, where he studied philosophy, came under the influence of C. S. Peirce and G. Stanley Hall [*qq.v.*], and developed an interest in the emerging science of psychology. In 1886 he received what was apparently the first Ph.D. degree in the United States specifically in psychology. Unable at this time to obtain a teaching position in the new field, he continued as honorary fellow at Hopkins until 1888, when he went to the University of Wisconsin as professor of experimental and comparative psychology. Some of the eighteen published papers of his Hopkins years he gathered into his first book, *Fact and Fable in Psychology* (1900).

At Wisconsin Jastrow established the third psychological laboratory in the United States. He guided research by his students and continued his own experimental interest in problems of sensation, perception, involuntary movement, association, and reasoning. His work with illusions included an original ambiguous rabbit-duck figure which found a place in many textbooks of general psychology. He also taught courses in philosophy, especially aesthetics, a subject in which he maintained a lifetime interest. His approach to psychology was broad and eclectic; he belonged to no "school" of psychology but found something to accept in them all. When the American Psychological Association was established in 1892 he became its first secretary, and in 1900 he was elected president.

At the Chicago World's Fair of 1893 Jastrow arranged the first public exhibit of psychological apparatus and set up a laboratory where for a small fee visitors could take a variety of tests: in sensory and sensory-motor tasks, sensitivity to pain, eye-hand coordination, visual acuity, color blindness, reaction time, and the like. The results of this large-scale testing program were carefully recorded but never processed or published. Jastrow's heavy teaching load, combined with his work for the World's Fair, resulted in a breakdown of health in 1894, which left his energy greatly curtailed, even after a year's leave for recuperation. He continued to teach until his retirement in 1927, although he has described his latter years as "full of anxiety and illness" (Murchison, *History of Psychology in Autobiography,* p. 151). Dissatisfaction with his salary (a request for an increase in 1907 was denied on the ground that he had turned away from research to popularization) and the feeling that he never obtained the recognition he deserved left him embittered. His books of this period include *The Subconscious* (1906), *The Qualities of Men* (1910), *Character and Temperament* (1915), and *The Psychology of Conviction* (1918).

After retirement Jastrow moved to New York City, where he taught at the New School for Social Research (1927–33) and at Columbia, gave frequent lectures to clubs and other groups, and developed a newspaper column, "Keeping Mentally Fit," which was published by the Philadelphia Public Ledger Syndicate from 1927 to about 1932. A volume of material collected from the column, published under the same title in 1928, proved highly popular. Eight more books of popular psychology followed before Jastrow's death. He also reached a wide public through a series of radio talks for the National Broadcasting Company from 1935 to 1938. His mission was to combat error and charlatanism and advance the cause of mental health.

Jastrow was short in stature, with carefully trimmed beard and moustache, and dignified and reserved in person. He was a collector of art objects, especially wood carvings. On Aug. 2, 1888, he had married Rachel Szold, daughter of a Baltimore rabbi and sister of Henrietta Szold [Supp. 3], the well-known Zionist leader. He shared his sister-in-law's interest in Zionism and woman suffrage, but did not retain the Jewish faith of his upbringing. Mrs. Jastrow died in 1926; they had no children of their own, and their adopted son, Benno, was killed in World War II. Jastrow died of a coronary occlusion in 1944 at the Austen Riggs Foundation in Stockbridge, Mass., and was buried in Baltimore, Md.

Jastrow began his career as an active member of the first generation of American experimental psychologists and seems to have had a genuine talent for research. He was basically a humanist in outlook, however, and after some years turned away from the laboratory to undertake the interpretation of psychological findings to a popular audience. In this he showed unusual talent.

[A short autobiography may be found in Carl Murchison, ed., *Hist. of Psychology in Autobiog.,* vol. I (1930). Clark L. Hull's obituary in the *Am. Jour. of Psychology,* Oct. 1944, is an objective and sympathetic appraisal. The obituary by W. B. Pillsbury in *Psychological Rev.,* Sept. 1944, contains a photograph. There are references to Jastrow in Merle E. Curti and Vernon R. Carstensen, *The Univ. of Wis.: A Hist., 1848–1925* (1949). A complete bibliography up to 1931 may be found in Carl Murchison, ed., *Psychological Register,* vol. III (1932). A few Jastrow letters and some notes and lecture materials now in the possession of Prof. S. B. Sells, Texas Christian Univ., are to be housed in the Archives of the Hist. of Psychology, Univ. of Akron. There are some letters also in the James McK. Cattell Papers in the Lib. of Cong. Personal recollections were provided by Profs. Sells, Frank Geldard (Princeton), and Horace M. Kallen. Death record from Mass. Registrar of Vital Statistics.]

MAX MEENES

JELLIFFE, SMITH ELY (Oct. 27, 1866–Sept. 25, 1945), neurologist, psychoanalyst, and medical editor, was born in New York City and grew up in Brooklyn. His father, William Munson Jelliffe, was a teacher and ultimately principal in the Brooklyn public schools; his mother, Susan Emma (Kitchell) Jelliffe, had also been a teacher. Jelliffe had a sister nine years his senior, who had a large hand in his upbringing, and a younger brother; two older brothers died in childhood.

Jelliffe's childhood was normal and active, and family legend has it that he was early renowned for his mental abilities. At the age of seventeen he underwent a "typical adolescent conversion" (as he later put it) to the Baptist Church. As a boy he had a strong interest in botany and natural history, but at his father's insistence he enrolled in the Brooklyn Polytechnic Institute to study civil engineering, graduating in 1886. In order to gratify his scientific interests and at the same time enter a profession that might make him more acceptable to his future wife's family, he enrolled in the College of Physicians and Surgeons in New York City, from which he received his M.D. in 1889. In later years, finding that academic preferment required additional degrees, he took an A.B. at Brooklyn Polytechnic in 1896 and, at Columbia, a Ph.D. in 1899 (with a thesis on the flora of Long Island) and an A.M. in 1900—a sequence possible then.

After a year's internship at St. Mary's Hospital, Brooklyn, and a *Wanderjahr* abroad financed by his mother's cousin Smith Ely, former mayor of New York (for whom he was named), Jelliffe began general practice in Brooklyn. Having a prodigious capacity for work, he turned his hand to a variety of activities to fill his time and augment his income. He taught night school, did part-time hospital pathological and clinical work, and acted as a Board of Health sanitary inspector. Like other young physicians of his time, he earned money by writing anonymous editorial material and book reviews for medical journals. His boyhood attraction to botany had developed into an interest in pharmacology, and in 1894 he was appointed instructor of pharmacognosy and materia medica (the composition and medical use of drugs derived from plants and animals) in the New York College of Pharmacy. The income enabled him to marry, on Dec. 20, 1894, his long-time fiancée, Helena Dewey Leeming of Brooklyn, and to move to New York City. They had five children: Sylvia Canfield, Winifred, Helena, Smith Ely, and William Leeming. Mrs. Jelliffe died in 1916, and on Dec. 20, 1917, Jelliffe married Bee Dobson, who later wrote under the name of Belinda Jelliffe.

Jelliffe's early signed publications dealt with botany and pharmacology, and from 1897 to 1901 he edited the *Journal of Pharmacology*, published by the New York College of Pharmacy. Meanwhile he had spent the summer of 1896 at the Binghamton (N. Y.) State Hospital, where he combined a country sojourn with earning a little money. There he met William Alanson White [Supp. 2], a staff member who was to become head of St. Elizabeths, the government hospital in Washington. Their friendship, which grew closer with the years, helped turn Jelliffe's attention to psychiatry. Although Jelliffe acted as an alienist in the courts—one of his major study trips to Europe was financed by his fee for testifying in the famous trial (1906) of Harry Thaw for the murder of the architect Stanford White [*q.v.*]—he was at first primarily a neurologist, specializing in outpatients rather than a hospital clientele. As such he was able easily to change his practice later to psychoanalysis.

Although Jelliffe gained fame as a specialist in nervous and mental diseases and was honored by foreign society memberships, he was not one of the profession's small elite. He held only relatively minor and unprestigious teaching and hospital posts. In 1907 he gave up teaching pharmacology and until 1913 was clinical professor of mental diseases in the ill-fated Fordham University medical school—the most substantial teaching post he ever held. While there he helped bring Carl G. Jung for a lecture series (1912) that precipitated the famous break between Jung and Freud. Jelliffe belonged to a large number of professional societies, attended meetings, and spoke often. But it is significant of his position in the profession that he was not elected president of the American Neurological Association until 1929–30. He felt himself, correctly, to be something of a maverick among conventional neurologists and psychiatrists.

Much of Jelliffe's maverick status derived from his embracing psychoanalysis—one of the first gentiles to do so—at a relatively early date (publicly announced in 1913). He was the most important prewar convert of his friend Abraham A. Brill. Jelliffe took up the practice of psychoanalysis and advocated the psychoanalytic viewpoint. Even within the movement, however, he remained a nonconformist and used analysis in his own way. For a long time he honored variant analysts almost as much as Freud (whom he did not meet until after World War I). From the beginning of his psychoanalytic practice he utilized lay analysts who worked under his supervision in his office. American analysts forced the psychoanalytic movement to operate within strictly medical channels, much to the disgust of Freud, but not until well into the 1920's did Jelliffe abandon the use of lay analysis and move closer to American orthodoxy. Always the physician, he ultimately became more "medical" than his psychiatric colleagues and earned the title of "Father of Psychosomatic Medicine" for his work on psychic determinants of organic pathology. It was particularly his coupling of Freudian dynamic mechanisms with ordinary physical disease processes that made him appear to the profession at large as an extremist amongst the Freudians.

Jelliffe had "no penchant or talent for teaching," and hence left no pupils closely identified with his viewpoint. His writing and speaking tended to be brilliant but unsystematic, his original ideas lost in a mountain of erudition, as he himself once observed. His greatest influence came through purveying the ideas of others. The translation with W. A. White of Paul C. Dubois's book on psychotherapy in 1906 (done primarily by Mrs. Jelliffe), for example, was a major event in crystallizing the psychotherapy movement in American medicine.

Although Jelliffe carried on a large and successful private practice, a continuing and important thread in his career was his editorial role. From 1900 to 1905 he served as editor of the weekly *Medical News,* and for the four following years as co-editor of its successor, the *New York Medical Journal*—one of the two or three leading medical journals of the country. Meanwhile, in 1899 he had begun editorial work on the *Journal of Nervous and Mental Disease,* a leading monthly in neurology and psychiatry, and in 1902 he became its owner and managing editor. For more than a decade and a half another neurologist, William G. Spiller, edited the original articles and Jelliffe the rest—editorials, book reviews (a large percentage of which throughout his forty-three years as editor came from his own pen), and summaries of foreign literature. The *Journal* was still close to the top position in its field when he retired as editor in 1945. The venture was always profitable, even after what appeared to him as the deliberate attempt of some old-line neurologists to draw patronage away by founding the *Archives of Neurology and Psychiatry* in 1919. Jelliffe believed that he had offended the neurology "establishment" by including a large amount of psychoanalytic material. In 1913 much of this material was taken out and placed in the new *Psychoanalytic Review* (the first English-language psychoanalytic periodical), edited jointly by Jelliffe (who was also publisher) and White, but Jelliffe soon reverted to carrying a substantial amount of psychoanalytic material in the *Journal.*

Unlike many editors, Jelliffe was extremely catholic in what he chose to include. The most technical histological or clinical contributions were printed next to literary or philosophical essays or reviews. For decades Jelliffe was acknowledged as unexcelled in America in his grasp of neurological literature. A monograph series sponsored by the *Journal* provided an outlet for papers that were unlikely to find commercial publishers; from 1907 to 1943, sixty-nine volumes appeared in the series, some of them in several editions. They were mostly translations, including obscure but important neurological works and the first English translations of the new psychoanalytic literature. Jelliffe's influence on American physicians was exerted chiefly through his editorial work and by the famous textbook, *Diseases of the Nervous System,* written with White, which went through six editions between 1915 and 1935.

In his maturity, Jelliffe was a tall, portly man of distinguished mien. Vigorous and energetic, he enjoyed swimming, tennis, eating, theatre-going, and the good life in general; and he was a superb and witty conversationalist. In his later years he suffered from Paget's disease, with resulting impairment of memory and increasing deafness. He died at his summer home at Huletts Landing, N. Y., on Lake George at the age of seventy-eight, of uremia caused by carcinoma of the prostate. He was buried in the family plot in Dresden Township, N. Y.

The interest in natural history with which Jelliffe began his career found expression not only in his work in pharmacology, but also in his holistic psychoanalysis, where he included the natural factors of both psyche and soma. As a Lamarckian, he included culture as part of the natural world. He was a humanist, interested in the individuality of his patients and the total human drama. His theoretical and speculative work was usually based on his mastery of the neurological-psychiatric literature.

[Useful autobiographical accounts by Jelliffe are: "Psychotherapy in Modern Medicine," *Long Island Medic. Jour.,* Mar. 1930; "Glimpses of a Freudian Odyssey," *Psychoanalytic Quart.,* 1933; and "The Editor Himself and His Adopted Child," *Jour. of Nervous and Mental Disease,* Apr. 1939. Obituaries are in the *Psychoanalytic Rev.,* Oct. 1948 (see especially those by Karl Menninger and George Devereux); *Jour. of Nervous and Mental Disease,* Sept. 1947; *Archives of Neurology and Psychiatry,* Oct. 1945; and *N. Y. Times,* Sept. 26, 1945. The major secondary accounts are *Nat. Cyc. Am. Biog.,* XXXIII, 360–61; and Nolan D. C. Lewis, in Franz Alexander, Samuel Eisenstein, and Martin Grotjahn, eds., *Psychoanalytic Pioneers* (1966). The two best bibliographies of Jelliffe's writings, which supplement each other, are in the *Jour. of Nervous and Mental Disease,* Sept. 1947; and in Alexander Grinstein, *The Index of Psychoanalytic Writings,* vol. II (1957). For background, see Clarence P. Oberndorf, *A Hist. of Psychoanalysis in America* (1953); John C. Burnham, *Psychoanalysis and Am. Medicine, 1894–1918* (1967); *Semi-Centennial Anniversary Vol. of the Am. Neurological Assoc.* (1924); and William A. White, *The Autobiog. of a Purpose* (1938). The bulk of the Jelliffe Papers were destroyed in a fire; some remaining fragments (including a birth certificate) are in the hands of the family and in the Menninger Foundation Lib. Fragments of his extensive correspondence exist in other collections, such as the Freud Archives.]

JOHN C. BURNHAM

JESSUP, WALTER ALBERT (Aug. 12, 1877–July 5, 1944), educator, university and foundation president, was born in Richmond, Ind., the only child of Albert Smiley Jessup and Anna (Goodrich) Jessup to survive infancy. His paternal forebears had come from Virginia before the War of 1812 as part of the great Quaker migration from the Carolinas and Virginia that made the Whitewater Valley of Indiana the "Jerusalem of Quakerism for all the Northwest." His grandfather, Levi Jessup, helped manage the Friends Boarding School which became Earlham College in 1859 and which his father attended. His mother, not a Quaker, came of a family that included merchants and politicians; a cousin, James Putnam Goodrich, served as governor of Indiana, 1917–21. Jessup's mother died when he was eleven. In 1890 his father married Gulia E. (Hunnicutt) Jones, a teacher and the widow of a Friends minister, who bore him a son and a daughter.

Growing up on his father's farm, Jessup attended a rural school and then the high school in Economy, Ind., graduating in 1895. He spent a year at Earlham College but withdrew to help his father on the farm and to teach in a nearby school. On June 28, 1898, he married Eleanor Hines of Noblesville, Ind.; they later adopted two children, Richard and Robert (Bob) Albert. Over the next decade Jessup rose from teacher to principal to superintendent of schools (Westfield Township, 1900–07; Madison, Ind., 1907–09). Meanwhile he earned a B.A. degree from Earlham in 1903 and an M.A. from Hanover (Ind.) College in 1908. In 1909 he enrolled in Teachers College, Columbia University, from which he received the Ph.D. in 1911.

Jessup returned to his home state as professor and dean of the school of education at Indiana University, but left a year later, in 1912, for an equivalent post at the State University of Iowa in Iowa City. Jessup was an active dean. Besides lecturing widely in Iowa and throughout the nation, he continued to work with Phi Delta Kappa, which he had helped transform, while at Teachers College, into a national educational honor society. He served on public school survey commissions, advised boards of education, and collaborated with Lotus Delta Coffman [Supp. 2] on several ventures, including a book, *The Supervision of Arithmetic* (1916). In 1916 he became president of the State University of Iowa.

The university, coeducational from its opening in 1855, had grown slowly and somewhat cautiously under Jessup's predecessors, who with only a few exceptions had been Protestant clergymen. In 1916 the College of Liberal Arts was the central core, with a modest graduate school and professional schools in law, medicine, engineering, and education. An earnest, hardworking, straightforward, forceful, but undramatic man, Jessup was remarkably successful in winning support for the improvement and enlargement of the university. In the words of an Iowa historian, Jessup had a "rare skill in public relations; he could make an acquaintance permanently on first meeting. He had a mental personnel sheet . . . of every state official and of other key people in all parts of the state" (Earle D. Ross, *The Land Grant Idea at Iowa State College,* 1958, p. 177). During his eighteen years as president the campus expanded from 42 to 324 acres, the faculty grew from 273 to nearly 500, the student body from 3,500 to almost 10,000, and a substantial building program was carried on. A division of physical education and schools of journalism, religion, the fine arts, and letters emerged within the College of Liberal Arts. In 1917 a compre-

hensive program for the study of all aspects of child development was launched. A Rockefeller grant in the early 1920's helped provide for a new medical school and a new general hospital; a children's hospital and a psychopathic hospital were also built.

The great expansion of the university inspired remarkably little opposition. A somewhat destructive rivalry with Iowa State College (later University) at Ames over the overlapping of courses of study continued and for a time intensified, but after Raymond M. Hughes became president of Iowa State in 1927, relations grew more amicable. Jessup faced two fairly substantial crises calmly. The first involved the suspension of Iowa from the Big Ten in 1929 for subsidizing athletes. The second grew out of an extended and flamboyant attack in 1930–31 by Verne Marshall, editor of the *Cedar Rapids Gazette,* who charged that Jessup and other university officials were guilty of financial, business, and other mismanagement. A legislative investigation yielded both majority and minority reports but found no clear evidence of wrongdoing. The Iowa college and university presidents elected Jessup president of their association the next year.

Jessup left Iowa in 1934 to become president of the Carnegie Foundation for the Advancement of Teaching, with headquarters in New York City. The depression had greatly curtailed the Foundation's income. Jessup is credited with obtaining additional funds from the Carnegie Corporation to meet the Foundation's commitments for teacher pensions. He also became a kind of counselor-at-large for American college and university presidents. His response to the changing educational scene can be glimpsed in his annual reports. Somewhat conservative by nature, Jessup viewed universities as agents of orderly and intelligent change but deplored innovation for its own sake. He was wary of "practical" education and feared graduate schools were becoming ineffective. During World War II he expressed concern that both support and control of scientific research were coming to be centered in Washington, and he deplored the growth of a system in which research and other grants were being made directly to individuals and departments in universities, thus making more difficult the university president's job of "keeping his institution on an even keel."

A compact man of average height, Jessup was thick-chested and square-jawed; he enjoyed golf, swimming, and fishing. He was a Methodist, a Mason, and a Republican. In 1941 he took on the additional duty of president of the Carnegie Corporation. He died in New York City four years later, at the age of sixty-six, of a sudden coronary thrombosis. His ashes were buried in Oakland Cemetery, Iowa City.

[The most substantial body of Jessup papers is in the Univ. of Iowa Archives. These include presidential correspondence, 1916–34, many unpublished addresses, personal papers, several memoirs dealing with his career, a preliminary bibliography of his writings and addresses by Ada M. Stoflat, and a compilation of biographical data by Rogene Hubbard. Frederick Gould Davies, "Hist. of the State Univ. of Iowa: The College of Liberal Arts, 1916–34" (doctoral dissertation, State Univ. of Iowa, 1947), treats aspects of Jessup's Iowa career in detail. The annual reports of the Carnegie Foundation for the Advancement of Teaching, 1934–44, and those of the Corporation, 1941–44, reflect Jessup's position on many educational matters. See also: Howard J. Savage, *Fruit of an Impulse: Forty-five Years of the Carnegie Foundation, 1905–1950* (1953); *Who Was Who in America*, vol. II (1950); *Nat. Cyc. Am. Biog.*, XXXVII, 294–95; obituary in *N. Y. Times*, July 8, 1944.]

VERNON CARSTENSEN

JOHNSON, ALEXANDER (Jan. 2, 1847–May 17, 1941), social worker, was born in Ashton-under-Lyne, Lancashire, England. He was the youngest of four children (two boys and two girls) of John Johnson, a devout Baptist and a prosperous merchant tailor with Chartist sympathies, and Amelia (Hill) Johnson. The boy was named William Alexander, and his family usually called him "Will," but he later dropped his first name. Although his formal education—in private schools, at the Mechanics' Institute, and at Owens (later Victoria) College, Manchester—included no training in welfare work, he early had a taste of the philanthropic life. His parents made their home something of a relief agency, dispensing food and money to the striking cotton spinners and weavers in the 1850's and to those suffering from hunger during the "cotton famine" of the 1860's. In 1869, partly because of these same economic conditions, Alexander Johnson immigrated to Canada and settled in Hamilton, where he worked in a tailoring factory. He lived with his employer, William Johnston, and, on June 6, 1872, married Johnston's daughter, Eliza Ann. They had seven children: Kathrine Dulcie, Herbert Spencer, William Amyas, John Hill, George Alexander, Margaret Marion, and Enid.

Shortly after his marriage Johnson moved to Chicago and then, around 1877, to Cincinnati, Ohio, where he worked in the manufacturing department of a clothing firm. In 1882 he volunteered as a "friendly visitor" to the poor for the Cincinnati Associated Charities, one of the many newly established private agencies which sought to centralize charitable work and place it on a "scientific" basis. Two years later he was promoted to general secretary and was made a paid member of the staff, thus embarking upon a career as a professional social worker. In keeping with the principles of the charity organization movement, Johnson persuaded a number of local charities to use his agency as a central investigating body before dispensing relief. He also established a wood yard, in which applicants for charity were given a work test, and developed fresh-air activities for mothers and children. In 1886 he was called to the Chicago Charity Organization Society, where he served for three years as general secretary.

Johnson moved into public welfare work in 1889 when he became secretary of the new Indiana State Board of Charities, established at a time when many states were bringing local public welfare activities under state control and were developing facilities for specialized needs. It was Johnson's responsibility to inspect state and county institutions. He devised a central registry for all institutional inmates and sought to have the mentally retarded, who comprised the largest group in almshouses, segregated by sex in asylums. Growing interest in mental retardation led to his appointment in 1893 as superintendent of the Indiana State School for the Feeble-minded at Fort Wayne. Here he operated on the assumption that the retarded should receive both permanent institutional care and training in a useful occupation. Johnson, who had hired his wife as assistant superintendent, managed to survive a state senate investigation in 1896–97 growing out of charges of nepotism, but he resigned in 1903, believing that his method of handling the retarded had lost the support of both the governor and the board of trustees.

Johnson moved in 1904 to New York City as associate director of the New York School of Philanthropy (later the Columbia University School of Social Work). Here he helped develop a curriculum for the study of social work and lectured on public institutions. In the same year he assumed the salaried post of secretary of the National Conference of Charities and Correction (later the National Conference of Social Welfare), the leading nationwide forum for public and private welfare workers. Johnson had long been active in the organization, having previously served as the unsalaried secretary (1890–93, 1900) and as president (1897). Increasing commitments to the National Conference forced his resignation in 1906 from the School of Philanthropy, though he continued to lecture there and at other schools of social work. A shrewd manager, Johnson placed the Conference on a secure financial footing, transformed it from a collection of individuals to a gathering of organizations, and helped arrange the program and speakers that brought it into the forefront of progressive social reform.

In 1912 Johnson moved to the Vineland (N. J.) Training School—of which his brother-in-law Edward R. Johnstone (who had added an "e" to the family name) was principal—as the director of its extension department. The school sought to promote occupational training for mental defectives, and the extension department had been recently founded to spread word of its work to groups in other parts of the country interested in establishing institutions similar to Vineland. When the department was moved to permanent headquarters in Philadelphia in 1915, Johnson took the post of field secretary. Stressing both the educability of mental defectives and the genetic cause of their problem, he waged a five-year campaign that succeeded in promoting forward-looking legislation and improved treatment of the retarded in more than thirty states.

From 1918 to 1922 Johnson worked for the American Red Cross, at first in the home service department dealing with the problems of soldiers and their families and later as a lecturer on the Red Cross in the Southern division. He retired in 1922, but for many years continued writing articles and serving as a consultant and an active member of the National Conference. In politics he was a Democrat, in religion a Unitarian. Johnson died at the home of his son Will in Aurora, Ill., at the age of ninety-four, of myocardial degeneration. He was buried in Crown Hill Cemetery, Indianapolis, Ind.

[Johnson's autobiography, *Adventures in Social Welfare* (1923), is a basic source, though it is weak on his life before entering social work and was written while much of his career still lay ahead of him. Also useful are his book *The Almshouse* (1911) and his addresses and articles in the *Proc.* of the Nat. Conference of Charities and Correction and in *Survey* magazine. Kathrine R. McCaffrey, "Founders of the Training School at Vineland, N. J." (Ed.D. dissertation, Teachers College, Columbia Univ., 1965), has important material on Johnson and his brother-in-law. See also: obituaries in *Social Service Rev.*, Sept. 1941, and *N. Y. Times*, May 18, 1941; *Who Was Who in America*, vol. I (1942); *Encyc. of Social Work* (15th issue, 1965); and references in Frank Bruno, *Trends in Social Work as Reflected in the Proc. of the Nat. Conference of Social Work, 1874–1946* (1948), and James Leiby, *Charity and Correction in N. J.* (1967). Death record from Ill. Dept. of Public Health. Mrs. Myron J. Sharp, Granby, Conn., provided family data. There are letters of Johnson in the Edward R. Johnstone Papers, Rutgers Univ.; and in the *Survey* Papers at the Social Welfare Hist. Archives Center, Univ. of Minn.]

HACE TISHLER

JOHNSON, DOUGLAS WILSON (Nov. 30, 1878–Feb. 24, 1944), geologist, geomorphologist, and geographer, was born in Parkersburg, W. Va., the second son and second of the four surviving children of Jennie Amanda (Wilson) and Isaac Hollenback Johnson. His father, whose forebears had moved from New Jersey to Virginia in 1750, had graduated from Marietta College in Ohio and had become a lawyer. He gave up his practice, however, to join with his wife, a woman of education and intellect, in the crusade for prohibition, founding and editing a temperance journal, the *Freeman*.

After graduating from the local high school and teaching for a few months in a country school at Long Reach, W. Va., Douglas Johnson entered Denison University at Granville, Ohio, where he took his first geology course under William G. Tight. He spent two years at Denison (1896–98) and then for reasons of health transferred to the University of New Mexico. There he came under the influence of the president, Clarence L. Herrick, who had earlier taught natural history at Denison. Working with Herrick on summer field trips for the Geological Survey of New Mexico, Johnson determined on a career in geology, and after receiving the B.S. degree in 1901 and teaching for a year at the Albuquerque (N. Mex.) high school, he entered Columbia University, where he studied under James F. Kemp [*q.v.*] and received the Ph.D. in 1903. He served as instructor and assistant professor of geology at the Massachusetts Institute of Technology (1903–07), moved to Harvard as associate professor (1907–12), and then went as associate professor to Columbia, where he spent the rest of his life, becoming professor in 1919. Outstanding as a teacher because of his clear exposition and his enthusiasm for his subject, in 1926 he established a graduate seminar in geomorphology that helped train a large number of professionals in this field.

At M.I.T. and at Harvard, Johnson came in close contact with William Morris Davis [Supp. I], founder and major exponent of the American school of geomorphology, who had introduced a special terminology to express his ideas of surface processes as stages in the orderly growth and development of land forms. Johnson became a firm follower of the Davisian approach, and it was his extensions of the method that brought him his greatest fame as a geomorphologist. After editing a series of Davis's papers (*Geographical Essays*, 1909), he turned to a study of the evolution of shorelines. His *Shore Processes and Shoreline Development* (1919) and *The New England-Acadian Shoreline* (1925), which became standard works, derived from observations made during extensive field trips in North America and in Europe. He proposed the idea of a life cycle in the development of shorelines and introduced a classification based largely on emergence or submergence of the coast. In *Stream Sculpture on the Atlantic Slope* (1931) he re-examined the geomorphic history of the northern Appalachians and the coastal plain, expanded Davis's earlier interpretation of their history, and proposed that the direction of the major streams flowing to the Atlantic resulted from the regional superposition of streams from a cover of sediments of the Cretaceous age on the general geologic structure of the area. His books also include *The Origin of Submarine Canyons* (1939) and *The Origin of the Carolina Bays* (1942).

With the beginning of World War I, Johnson became interested in the effect of topography on military operations. Commissioned a major in the army intelligence, he was sent to the chief European fronts to evaluate the strategic importance of land formation under the conditions of the war. Books resulting from these activities were *Topography and Strategy in the War* (1917) and *Battlefields of the World War* (1921). Johnson also served as chief of the important Division of Boundary Geography for the American delegation to the peace conference in Paris (1918–19) and as such had considerable influence on establishing the boundaries of postwar Europe.

In addition to publishing some ten books and more than 150 scientific papers, Johnson in 1938 founded the *Journal of Geomorphology*, an international periodical that ceased publication in 1942, a victim of World War II. Its volumes contain a sequence of twelve articles by Johnson on "The Scientific Method," in which he developed his views on the proper approach to geomorphic investigation.

Johnson belonged to a large number of scientific organizations, including the National Academy of Sciences (1932), the American Philosophical Society (1920), the Association of American Geographers (president, 1928), and the Geological Society of America (president, 1942). Among his honors were membership in nine foreign societies, the Jannsen Gold Medal of the Paris Geographical Society (1920), the Cullum Medal of the American Geographical Society (1935), and honorary degrees from Columbia and three French universities. He was a member of Riverside Church in New York. An outspoken conservative in politics, Johnson was active during the New Deal period in the National Committee to Uphold Constitutional Government, particularly in its opposition to President Roosevelt's plan to enlarge the Supreme Court.

On Aug. 11, 1903, Johnson married Alice Adkins of Granville, Ohio. Their five children all died within a few hours of birth. Although she had become totally blind before their marriage,

Mrs. Johnson usually accompanied her husband on his travels, and friends believed that it was his lifelong habit of describing for her the scenes of their journeys that helped make him a masterly interpreter of geographical details and relationships. A devoted husband, he shared with his wife a love of music and of romantic poetry. Close friends, too, found him warm and enthusiastic, but in most relations he maintained an air of dignified formality. He ordered his own life with rigid self-discipline. Systematic and logical by nature, he felt a close bond with France and enjoyed reading French literature. Alice Johnson died in 1938. On Sept. 8, 1943, Johnson married Mrs. Edith (Sanford) Caldwell. A few months later he died of a heart attack at his winter home in Sebring, Fla. He was buried in Maple Grove Cemetery, Granville, Ohio.

[Memorials by: Frank J. and Anna Z. Wright, in Geological Soc. of America, *Proc.*, 1944; Armin K. Lobeck, in Assoc. of Am. Geographers, *Annals*, Dec. 1944; Charles P. Berkey, in Am. Philosophical Soc., *Year Book*, 1944; and Walter H. Bucher, in Nat. Acad. Sci., *Biog. Memoirs*, vol. XXIV (1947). See also *Who Was Who in America*, vol. II (1950). Johnson deposited some biographical material with the Nat. Acad. Sci.; additional material is in the file of the Dept. of Geology, Columbia Univ.]

SHELDON JUDSON

JOHNSON, EDWARD AUSTIN (Nov. 23, 1860–July 24, 1944), Negro educator, lawyer, and politician, was born near Raleigh, N. C., one of eleven children of Columbus and Eliza A. (Smith) Johnson. Both parents were slaves. After receiving some early training from Nancy Walton, a free Negro who taught languages, Johnson continued his education at the Washington School in Raleigh, founded in 1866 by Northern philanthropists. He completed high school there and made plans to attend Oberlin College, but was persuaded instead to enroll at the newly established Atlanta University in Atlanta, Ga. Arriving in January 1879 with his savings of seventy-five dollars Johnson earned his expenses by teaching during the summers and by working as a barber.

After graduating in 1883, Johnson served as a teacher and principal, first of the Mitchell Street Public School in Atlanta (1883–85) and then of his alma mater, the Washington School (1885–91). While teaching, he studied law at Shaw University in Raleigh, and upon being awarded the LL.B. degree in 1891, he joined the faculty there. He became dean of the law school in 1893.

Because opportunities for Negroes to practice law were limited, Johnson became active in Republican politics. During the 1890's he served for two years on the Raleigh board of aldermen and for seven years as assistant to the United States

Attorney for the Eastern District of North Carolina. Johnson was also chairman of the Republican party in the 4th Congressional District and attended the national conventions of 1892, 1896, and 1900.

Although he was now well established economically, the early years of the twentieth century in the South saw the disenfranchisement of the Negro and the passage of "Jim Crow" laws, and in 1907, at the age of forty-seven, Johnson moved to New York City. He settled in the rising black community of Harlem, was soon admitted to the New York bar, and began practicing law. Resuming political activity, he served as a Republican committeeman in the 19th assembly district. In 1917, running with support from the United Civic League, a nonpartisan black political group, he was the first Negro to win election to the New York state legislature. As a member of the assembly he assisted in the enactment of a bill to create free state employment bureaus, and he introduced legislation to prevent discrimination in publicly supported hospitals. He also helped secure an amendment to the Levy Civil Rights Act of 1913 making it a misdemeanor to discriminate on the basis of race, color, or nationality in public employment or in such public facilities as hotels, common carriers, theatres, and other places of amusement.

Failing in his bid for a second term in 1918, Johnson resumed his law practice. He became blind in 1925. Despite this handicap, in 1928 he accepted (after two other black politicians had rejected it) the Republican nomination for Congress in the 21st Congressional District, the majority of whose voters were white Democrats. The popular Alfred E. Smith [Supp. 3] headed the Democratic ticket, and Johnson ran, as he later wrote, not because he felt he could win but to stir black voters to register.

In the course of his career, Johnson wrote several books dealing with the condition of Negroes in America. *A School History of the Negro Race in America from 1619 to 1890* (1891), which closely followed the self-help philosophy of Booker T. Washington [q.v.], sought to remedy the inadequate treatment of Negroes in schoolbooks, and emphasized the necessity of race pride. In 1904 he published *Light Ahead for the Negro,* a utopian novel in which his white protagonist, transported to "Phoenix," Ga., in the year 2006, discovers a society based on racial harmony and full economic opportunity for blacks. For the near future, however, the novel accurately predicted the mass northward migration of Negroes. In his last book, *Adam vs. Ape-Man in Ethiopia* (1931), Johnson claimed that black Ethiopians

were the first people to evolve, and that their civilization had flourished while white Europeans had "yet to emerge from the reindeer age and the ape-man type." The culture of the Egyptian empire, he maintained, derived originally from black men and declined only after the invasion of white "injustice and greed"; and he saw in this a warning for white, Christian America.

Johnson was one of the founders (1900) of the National Negro Business League and a member of the Harlem Board of Trade and Commerce. He was also active in the Congregational Church and the Y.M.C.A. On Feb. 22, 1894, he had married Lena Allen Kennedy, by whom he had one daughter, Adelaide. He died at the age of eighty-three at Sydenham Hospital in New York City, and was buried in Woodlawn Cemetery, New York. A nephew, Edward R. Dudley, later became prominent in Democratic politics, serving as borough president of Manhattan and justice of the state supreme court.

[Johnson also wrote a *Hist. of Negro Soldiers in the Spanish-Am. War* (1899). For biographical material, see his articles "A Student at Atlanta Univ.," *Phylon,* Second Quarter 1942, and "A Congressional Campaign," *Crisis,* Apr. 1929; Wilbur Young and A. J. Gary, "Biog. Sketches" (WPA Writers Program, 1939), microfilm in Schomburg Collection of N. Y. Public Lib.; "Life and Work of Edward A. Johnson," *Crisis,* Apr. 1933; John A. Morsell, "The Political Behavior of Negroes in N. Y. City" (Ph.D. dissertation, Columbia Univ., 1950), pp. 33–35; *Who's Who in Colored America,* 1941–44; obituaries in *N. Y. Times,* July 25, 1944, *N. Y. Herald Tribune,* July 26, 1944, *N. Y. Age,* July 29, 1944; and *N. Y. Amsterdam News,* July 29, 1944.]
EDWIN R. LEWINSON

JOHNSON, ELDRIDGE REEVES (Feb. 6, 1867–Nov. 14, 1945), inventor and business executive, was born in Wilmington, Del., the only child of Asa S. and Caroline (Reeves) Johnson, both of colonial American descent. He spent his boyhood in Dover, Del., where his father was a moderately prosperous building contractor. From an early age the boy displayed considerable mechanical ability. At sixteen, after his graduation from the Wesley Conference Academy in Dover, he went to Philadelphia, where he served an apprenticeship as a machinist with Jacob Lodge & Son. In addition, he took night classes in mechanical drawing at the Spring Garden Institute. Later, in 1888, he became manager of Andrew Scull's small machine shop in Camden, N. J. Within a year he resigned to go on a "sort of general scouting expedition through the West." In later life he observed that this trip, which lasted over a year, had been "a great education, as it lifted me out of mental ruts formed by a long apprenticeship and a narrow circle of acquaintances." Because Johnson thought that opportunities for advancement were more plentiful in the East, he returned to Philadelphia in 1891 and formed a partnership with Scull; he purchased his partner's interest in 1894.

For two years the work of repairing factory machines and building experimental models for inventors yielded Johnson little financial reward. Early in 1896, however, when a hand-propelled Gramophone was brought to his shop, his fortunes began to change. Although it sounded like "a partially educated parrot with a sore throat," Johnson became fascinated with this talking machine, which had been invented by Emile Berliner [Supp. 1] in 1887. Within a few months Johnson had developed a spring-driven motor and had secured a contract to supply the Berliner Gramophone Company with 200 of them. Continuing his experiments with talking machines and records, the following year he produced an improved sound box, developed jointly with Alfred Clark, and a better motor, which together formed the basis of Berliner's Improved Gramophone. By 1898 Johnson was manufacturing 600 complete Gramophones per week for the Berliner Company. Because of the conflicting claims to basic inventions that were then plaguing the phonograph industry and the complex litigation over patent infringement that for a time prevented Berliner from selling his own product, Johnson in 1900 decided to sell talking machines and records on his own. In October 1901 he founded and became president of the Victor Talking Machine Company, and in return for 40 percent of the common stock, acquired title to the Berliner patents.

Under the administration of Johnson, who had a substantial controlling interest, the Victor Company became a vast success. During its first two decades Victor was the leader of the American phonograph industry—in quality, artists, repertoire, advertising, and sales. This leadership was exemplified by the introduction in 1906 of the internal-horn Victrola, which revolutionized phonograph construction. Numerous other technical advancements by Johnson and his staff permitted Victor to produce disc machines and records of a generally higher quality than those of its competitors. Furthermore, by signing exclusive, long-term contracts with many of the best-known operatic, concert, and stage celebrities, Victor established the reputation of providing the best in recorded music. These factors, however, might not have ensured Victor's dominance of the industry without an effective advertising program. Through affiliations with foreign companies, the Victor trademark—a dog seated before a phonograph horn, his ear cocked to "His Master's Voice"—soon became famous throughout the world.

During the early 1920's Victor's creative role diminished. Although rival firms like Sonora and Brunswick were catering to a growing public taste for "period" cabinets with broad, flat tops, Johnson clung to the Victrola's traditional square, vaulted lid. The company was also slow to expand its recording repertoire of classical music, and obstinately disregarded the competitive potential of radio, leaving it to others to market radio-phonograph combinations. By mid-decade Victor's sales had declined to $20,000,000, a decrease of 60 percent in four years. In 1925, however, Victor agreed to incorporate the Radio Corporation of America's Radiola into its consoles, and later the same year introduced the Orthophonic Victrola, with a new sound system and electrically recorded discs. With these developments, the company's sales rebounded. At this opportune time, Johnson, who had been ill for several years, retired as president and sold his controlling stock interest to a banking syndicate for an estimated $15,000,000. Two years later Victor was merged with the Radio Corporation of America.

Among Johnson's varied interests were archaeology, yachting, fishing, and collecting prints, books, and manuscripts. He was an Episcopalian, a member of numerous clubs, and an active Republican. Among his substantial gifts to the University of Pennsylvania, which awarded him an honorary doctorate in 1928, was an $800,000 donation in 1927 for the establishment of the Eldridge R. Johnson Foundation for Research in Medical Physics.

On Oct. 5, 1897, Johnson married Elsie Reeves Fenimore. They had one son, Eldridge Reeves Fenimore Johnson. Johnson died of a heart attack at his home in Moorestown, N. J., at the age of seventy-eight. He was buried in West Laurel Hill Cemetery, Bala-Cynwyd, Pa. In the early twentieth century his inventive and executive talents had made the Victor Talking Machine Company a leading innovative force in the industry which brought music to all classes of homes.

[Johnson's papers are in the possession of the family and are not open for research. The Eldridge Reeves Johnson Memorial Collection, Del. State Museum, Dover, contains phonographs, records, and other memorabilia regarding Johnson and the talking machine industry. No published biography exists. *Eldridge Reeves Johnson: Industrial Pioneer* (36 pp., 1951) includes numerous illustrations, a list of patents issued to Johnson, and a brief, superficial account by Johnson of his business career. This account is also incorporated into Thomas F. Harkins, "His Master's Voice," *A Century of Service: Spring Garden Inst., 1850–1950* (1950). Other useful writings are: memoir by Detlev W. Bronk in Am. Philosophical Soc., *Year Book*, 1946; obituary in *N. Y. Times*, Nov. 15, 1945; Oliver Read and Walter L. Welch, *From Tin Foil to*

Stereo (1959); Roland Gelatt, *The Fabulous Phonograph* (1955); and Dane Yorke, "The Rise and Fall of the Phonograph," *Am. Mercury,* Sept. 1932. Some information was obtained from E. R. Fenimore Johnson.]

JOHN VEIL MILLER, JR.

JOHNSON, GEORGE (Feb. 22, 1889–June 5, 1944), Roman Catholic priest and educator, was born in Toledo, Ohio, the elder of the two children of Henry and Kathryn (McCarthy) Johnson. Both parents were natives of Toledo; his paternal grandparents had come from Holland, the McCarthys from Ireland. The elder Johnson was a meatcutter by trade but also worked as a police officer. When George was a boy his father deserted the family, leaving his mother in meager circumstances; later she ran a small variety store.

After attending local parochial schools and the preparatory department of St. John's University in Toledo, Johnson, a personable and industrious young man, obtained a scholarship to the college division of St. John's. He graduated in 1910 and, having developed an interest in making the Catholic Church more understandable to non-Catholics, decided to become a priest. Following two years at St. Bernard's Seminary in Rochester, N. Y., he was sent to the North American College in Rome, an honor accorded to only a few seminary students marked for leadership. Upon his ordination in 1914, he returned to Toledo and became personal secretary to Bishop Joseph Schrembs [Supp. 3]. In 1916 Johnson enrolled at the Catholic University of America, where he studied school administration and curriculum construction and received the Ph.D. in 1919. He then became superintendent of the Catholic schools of the Toledo diocese.

Two years later, however, Johnson was called back to Catholic University as associate professor of education. He remained there until his death and helped bring the school of education to national stature. Johnson was less a scholar than a propagandist, public relations man, and national spokesman for Catholic education. As director of the department of education of the National Catholic Welfare Conference (1928–44) and as secretary general of the National Catholic Educational Association (1929–44), he kept the bishops abreast of recent trends in public education and publicized Catholic views on educational reform and legislation. For twenty-three years he was also one of the editors of the *Catholic Educational Review,* and he often prepared the text of statements made by the American Catholic hierarchy on educational matters. Both President Hoover and President Roosevelt appointed him to national advisory committees on education.

Though trained along classical lines, Johnson was receptive to progressive concepts in education. He rejected the importance of teaching subject matter, and subscribed instead to the belief that Catholic education should involve the total integration of Catholic culture and American society. Committed to the theory that students learn best by doing, he favored supplementing traditional study and recitation assignments with group discussions, field trips, and projects. He also endorsed the use of objective tests and supported educational programs geared to the individual needs of each child. Johnson gave concrete expression to his ideas at the Campus School of the Catholic University, which he founded in 1935. Here he adapted the standard Catholic school curriculum, of which religion formed the core, to progressive teaching techniques. The classrooms were designed to facilitate group discussion, and students were encouraged to take part in planning a program of instruction.

In 1944, while delivering the commencement address at Trinity College in Washington, D. C., Johnson died of a heart attack at the age of fifty-five. He was buried in Mount Olivet Cemetery, Washington. At the time of his death he had been directing the preparation of curricula and textbooks for the nation's Catholic schools, a project sponsored by the Commission on American Citizenship of the American bishops.

[Memorial articles in *Catholic Educational Rev.,* Sept. 1944 and Apr. 1945; *Catholic School Jour.,* Apr. 1951, an issue devoted to a review of Catholic education, 1900–50; Nat. Catholic Educational Assoc., *Bull.,* Nov. 1936, Aug. 1944; obituary in *N. Y. Times,* June 6, 1944; editorial in Washington *Evening Star,* June 6, 1944; *Who Was Who in America,* vol. II (1950); information from a sister, Mrs. Frank Drobka of Washington, D. C., from Francis I. Nally of the Toledo *Catholic Chronicle,* and from a former teacher of Msgr. Johnson, the Rev. James Mertz, S.J.]

NEIL G. McCLUSKEY

JOHNSON, HIRAM WARREN (Sept. 2, 1866–Aug. 6, 1945), governor of California and United States Senator, was born in Sacramento, Calif., one of the five children and the younger of two sons of Grove Laurence and Annie Williamson (de Montfredy) Johnson. His father was of English stock, his mother of mixed English and French. Grove Johnson had come to California in 1863 from his native Syracuse, N. Y. He began a law practice in Sacramento in 1873 and four years later was elected to the state assembly as a Republican. He returned periodically to the assembly, serving as late as 1907–09. He also won election to Congress in 1894 but was defeated two years later. As a successful attorney and legislator, he became known as a defender of the interests of the Southern Pacific Railroad, whose pervasive political power in California was to become the chief issue in his son's early political campaigns.

After attending the public schools of Sacramento and working for two years in his father's law office, Hiram Johnson went on in 1884 to the University of California at Berkeley. He dropped out during his junior year, however, and for the next two years worked as a shorthand reporter and read law in his father's office. On Jan. 23, 1887, he married Minnie Lucretia McNeal, the daughter of a Sacramento contractor and politician. They had two sons: Hiram Warren and Archibald McNeal. Johnson was admitted to the California bar in 1888, and in partnership with his father and his brilliant elder brother, Albert M. Johnson, soon made a reputation as a skillful trial lawyer. Politics attracted him; he managed his father's successful campaign for Congress in 1894. In 1901, in public opposition to the elder Johnson, he supported a reform candidate for mayor of Sacramento and was appointed city attorney, winning something of a reputation for fighting political corruption and vice.

Meanwhile, the two Johnson brothers had become permanently estranged from their father over politics, a quarrel that in 1902 led them to establish a law firm in San Francisco. Practicing alone beginning in 1904, Hiram added to his reputation both as a trial lawyer and as a supporter of civic reform. He first achieved public notice as attorney for the aggrieved wife in a well-publicized and somewhat sensational bigamy case. In October 1906 he joined in the effort, led by Fremont Older [q.v.] and others, to rid San Francisco of political corruption and the dominance of the labor-affiliated political machine of Abraham Ruef [Supp. 2]. As an assistant district attorney, Johnson helped prepare and conduct the graft prosecutions, and when, in November 1908, the chief prosecutor, Francis J. Heney [Supp. 2], was shot and wounded, Johnson was the logical candidate to take his place.

The spectacular trial of Ruef and his associates, among whom were Patrick Calhoun [Supp. 3] and other San Francisco utility executives, made national headlines. Johnson's success in winning the conviction of Ruef brought him to prominence among the state reformers who in 1907 had founded the "Lincoln-Roosevelt Republican League" to free California from the control of the Southern Pacific Railroad. Public interest in him increased in January 1909 when, as representative of the Direct Primary League, he testified before a legislative committee and in so doing clashed directly and vocally with his father. By 1910 the Lincoln-Roosevelt League was ready to challenge the dominant group in the Republican party and asked Johnson to run for governor. Both Johnson and his strong-willed wife at first opposed the idea, but Mrs. Johnson soon changed her mind and helped persuade her husband to make the race. Aligned with Johnson under League auspices was a full slate of candidates for both houses of the legislature and other state offices.

Although the League's platform included many political and social reforms, Johnson centered his campaign around the slogan "Kick the Southern Pacific out of politics." In what was to become characteristic behavior, he quickly grew disillusioned with the political amateurs in the Lincoln-Roosevelt League and in effect conducted a personal campaign independent of organizational affiliation. He easily defeated the opposing candidates in the Republican primary and then, in a much closer contest, the nominee of the Democratic party, Theodore Bell. The reform ticket also won a majority of the legislative contests, ensuring control of the statehouse.

Photographs of the new governor reveal a man who did not change much physically for the next thirty-five years. His body was short and rather heavy. A round face and square chin were emphasized by a high collar. Though Johnson was a pleasant man in private, his public pictures, then as later, invariably showed him in the role of a prosecutor, somberly and determinedly dedicated to striking down evil. Plain in his personal habits, extremely jealous and even vain of his reputation, he was easily irritated and seldom forgave an opponent. Having few interests outside of politics and the law, he was not a cultured person. His chief amusement during his early maturity was seeing Western movies; in later years, it was playing dominoes. His speeches, though precise and well organized, were innocent of adornment or elegance, resting more upon moral and intuitive judgments than upon research and intellectual analysis. He sometimes pretended to deprecate his political skill, but he was, in fact, a consummate politician. He cultivated newspaper publishers and other opinion molders and counted many of them among his supporters.

Johnson was cautious in approaching a political commitment but was awesomely steadfast once such a commitment had been made. He soon left no doubt that he intended to legislate every item in the Lincoln-Roosevelt League's program. "Nearly every governmental problem that involves the health, the happiness, or the prosperity of the State," Johnson declared in his inaugural address on Jan. 3, 1911, "has arisen because some private interest has intervened . . . to exploit either the resources or the politics of the state. . . ." The reform majorities in both houses of the legislature responded strongly to his specific proposals; the program adopted by the 1911 legislature has scarcely been rivaled in the history of any state. An initiative, referendum, and recall measure, including a provision for the popular recall of judicial decisions, was passed and eventually approved by the voters. The primary law was amended to include an advisory vote for the selection of United States Senators. A short-ballot measure was accepted. A civil service system was adopted, and a state board of control established to act as a watchdog over all financial operations. (The board of control has remained a powerful organ in the appropriation and expenditure of state funds.) A conservation commission was also created, though in the early part of its career it was more concerned with the effective use of the state's natural resources than in saving them for the future. Since much of the criticism of the existing railroad machine had hinged on its connection with the liquor and vice traffic, a local-option law was passed that resulted in the disappearance of saloons from over four hundred towns and cities. Similar measures prohibited slot machines, racetrack gambling, and houses of prostitution. Some thirty-nine bills advocated by organized labor were passed in the 1911 session of the legislature, among them measures providing for workmen's compensation for industrial accidents, an eight-hour day for working women, and—over the bitter opposition of the state's agricultural interests—significant restrictions on child labor.

Of all the acts passed during the first Johnson administration, the Public Utilities Act probably excited the most public interest. Although the legislation covered all utilities, it was aimed particularly at the Southern Pacific Railroad, whose influence Johnson had promised to eradicate from state government. By this measure and later amendments, the long-dormant state railroad commission was given the power to establish rates, make physical evaluations of all the state utilities, regulate securities, and establish uniform standards of bookkeeping. When rounded out with the usual list of prohibited activities, the act created one of the most effective systems of railroad control then existing in the country.

Turning to the national political scene, Governor Johnson and his reform-minded advisers early made known their support for the effort to defeat President William Howard Taft and his conservative allies in Congress in the elections of 1912. A charter member of the National Progressive Republican League organized in January 1911, Johnson subsequently supported the announced candidacy of Senator Robert La Follette [q.v.] for the Republican presidential nomination. But along with most of the California progressives, Johnson preferred Theodore Roosevelt to La Follette, and long before Roosevelt's official announcement in March 1912, he had joined the inner circle of the ex-President's advisers. In the California presidential primary the Johnson forces easily defeated the Taft Republicans. At the turbulent 1912 Republican national convention in Chicago, Johnson played a role second only to that of Roosevelt in the unsuccessful effort to defeat Taft. Denouncing the Taft forces as "porch-climbing political burglars," Johnson twice led the California delegates out of the convention, and even before Taft's nomination all but two of the California delegates agreed to support a new party headed by Roosevelt. It was Johnson, as chairman of the new party's provisional national committee, who made the first official speech as the dissident Roosevelt delegates met at Chicago's Orchestra Hall following the close of the Republican convention, and a month later he was nominated as the Progressive party's vice-presidential candidate. During the ensuing campaign Johnson gave more than five hundred speeches in twenty-two states and even filled in for Roosevelt during the latter's convalescence after an assassination attempt in Milwaukee. But though the Progressives carried California by a small margin and far outpolled Taft nationally in both electoral and popular votes, victory went to the Democrat, Woodrow Wilson.

In 1913 the Progressives faced a dubious future in both the nation and California. Without either elected officials or patronage, the national party rapidly began to dissolve, and in California the unity that had once marked the original Lincoln-Roosevelt Republicans began to erode. One explanation lies in the very success of the League in enacting its original program. Compared to the 1911 legislative sessions, those of 1913 and 1915 were rather lackluster. The 1913 session did create state commissions on industrial welfare, industrial accidents, and immigration and housing, and it enacted the Governor's proposal to permit the cross-filing of political candidates on any or all of the party tickets in primary elections. Cross-filing served the immediate need of the reformers for a way to reenter the Republican party after their defection in 1912 and thus to continue their dominance in the state, but it gave California politics a special and confusing character that was to be perpetuated for the next forty years. The 1913 legislature also passed a law (aimed at Japanese immigrants) which prohibited aliens from owning land in the state. None of these measures except the alien land legislation inspired much enthusiasm, and the land law caused the Wilson administration much embarrassment with Japan and was criticized by many independent liberals who had previously supported Johnson. Personal and political rivalries also split the Johnson supporters. In 1914, when Francis Heney ignored Johnson's wishes and ran for the Senate, not only he, but also much of the Progressive state ticket, went down to defeat, while Johnson, again conducting a highly personal and nonpartisan campaign, was reelected to the governorship by a handsome margin. The bitterness arising from this election sharpened the divisions among Johnson's backers.

In 1916 Johnson was elected to the United States Senate. The move to Washington might have served to insulate him from the tensions of state politics, but his reluctance to turn over the governorship to an incumbent lieutenant governor whom he did not trust signaled a continuing close involvement in California politics which again inspired widespread criticism among many Progressives. One of the best known, and most censured, of Johnson's actions, though one for which he was not totally responsible, occurred during the 1916 campaign. Charles Evans Hughes, the Republican nominee for president, made fairly evident during a preprimary visit to California that he preferred the nomination of a regular Republican for Johnson's Senatorial seat. A few days later, when both men stopped at the same Long Beach hotel, the sensitive Johnson refused to call on Hughes, and the latter, unaware of Johnson's presence until a few moments before the Governor's departure, moved too slowly to establish communication. Johnson and his Progressives subsequently won a sweeping victory in the Republican primary and thus became responsible for managing the Hughes campaign, a job they undertook, according to one dispassionate observer, "with determination but without enthusiasm." In private, Johnson described Hughes as "a mysterious, stuffed prophet" and wrote: "I don't know any reason . . . why we should break our necks in this campaign. . . . I have made my choice for Hughes, but during the campaign, I am going my own way as usual" (Olin, pp. 122–23). Johnson won his Senate seat by a margin of 300,000 votes, but Hughes lost the state by less than 4,000 votes and thus the national election. Johnson and his reformers were promptly charged with party treason, a long-remembered indictment which further exacerbated the intraparty strife in California.

As a new Senator, Johnson was immediately confronted with President Wilson's call for a declaration of war against Germany. Although he sympathized with most of Senator La Follette's arguments against entering the war, he uneasily supported Wilson's war message and thereafter most of the administration's war bills. During the hostilities, however, Johnson remained a liberal critic of the administration, seeking to increase taxes on the rich and on war profiteers, to diminish the stringent provisions of the Espionage Act, and to soften the rigors of censorship. Before and after the armistice he remained disdainful of the "professional patriots" and quarreled repeatedly with his fellow Californian George Creel, head of the government's war propaganda effort, and with Attorney General A. Mitchell Palmer [Supp. 2].

Johnson's main criticisms, however, were directed against Wilson's foreign policy. He was violently opposed to the military intervention in Russia, and although at first intrigued with the idea of a league of nations, he subsequently became a leader of the "Irreconcilables" in Congress who opposed both the Treaty of Versailles and its incorporated plan for the League. Johnson's opposition to the peace was couched in both liberal and isolationist terms. He deplored the political settlement as undemocratic and contrary to Wilson's own principles of "open diplomacy" and "self-determination." For the most part ignoring the German provisions of the treaty, he directed his criticisms at the "rape of China" (the Shantung provision) and assailed the League as an instrument chiefly set up to preserve the "old dynastic empires of Britain, France, and Italy," and in particular the British Empire "with its seething millions of discontented people." Since in his view American security was in no danger, participation in the League would "qualify the nation's independence" and "impair its sovereignty" for no conceivable return. More important, Article X of the Covenant would, he contended, practically guarantee the use of American soldiers to stabilize Europe and "to act as riot police in every new nation's backyard." Although it was the inability of the "Reservationists" to agree, and not the opposition of the Irreconcilables, that was responsible for the Senate's refusal to ratify the treaty, Johnson always considered that his group's pressure on Senator Henry Cabot Lodge [q.v.] was a force in the final outcome.

Johnson's implacable opposition to the Versailles Treaty was responsible for yet another major schism among California progressives, for many of them were ardent supporters of the

League. During the 1920 "favorite son" contest for California's presidential delegates, Johnson, while winning the support of the Hearst papers, lost that of many of his former prominent backers who preferred the Wilsonian internationalist Herbert Hoover. But Johnson decisively won the California Republican contest against Hoover and picked up enough support outside his home state to poll 133 votes and win third place on the first four ballots at the Republican national convention. After Harding's convention victory, the possibility of Johnson's nomination for the vice-presidency was broached, but he refused in disgust, and thus lost the opportunity for the office he so much coveted.

Although his party was in power for twelve years after the 1920 election, Johnson was never sympathetic to its leadership and rarely with its policies. He voted for the Fordney-McCumber Tariff, but also supported the McNary-Haugen Bill and other farm measures opposed by the Republican regulars. After a futile campaign for the 1924 Republican presidential nomination, he spoke for La Follette's Progressive party candidacy during the election campaign; four years later he repeated his gesture of opposition to Hoover's nomination. His one important achievement in domestic affairs during the 1920's was in sponsoring, against the opposition of the private utility companies, the bill for a federal Boulder Dam (1928).

In foreign affairs Johnson was also usually at odds with the party leadership. On two occasions he was a leader in the successful opposition to presidential recommendations that the United States join the World Court. In 1930 he attacked the London Naval Pact supported by Hoover. Calling the tonnage limitation agreement "the wickedest act" since the attempt to enter the League, Johnson teamed with William Randolph Hearst and the naval establishment to oppose the limitation on capital-ship construction. Subsequently, he unsuccessfully opposed President Hoover's moratorium on the payment of war reparations and war debts. In 1934 he gained some solace by successfully sponsoring the Johnson Act, which prohibited loans to any foreign government in default on its war debt to the United States.

With the onset of the depression, Johnson increased his criticism of both the Hoover administration and the New York bankers whom he blamed for much of the economic distress. From 1930 on, he regularly joined the progressive Republicans and a majority of the Democrats in demanding more relief funds. Refusing offers of support from progressives who urged him to con-

test the renomination of Hoover, he advocated the election of Franklin D. Roosevelt and was repaid for his support by the offer of the Secretaryship of the Interior, which he refused. His name also appeared on the President's list of possible Supreme Court appointments. Encouraged by Roosevelt's friendship, Johnson willingly cooperated with the early New Deal, supporting most of the administration measures proposed during the "hundred days." But from 1934 on, events in California propelled him toward the conservative side of the political spectrum. The San Francisco general strike of 1934 he labeled "revolution," and Upton Sinclair's "End Poverty in California" campaign of the same year, "damned foolishness."

By 1936 Johnson's enthusiasm for the New Deal had so waned that he refused to take any part in the presidential contest. He was openly jubilant over the defeat of the administration's "court-packing" bill, and he opposed some of the New Deal social measures during Roosevelt's second administration. His real opposition to Roosevelt, however, stemmed largely from foreign policy concerns. In supporting the Neutrality Act of 1935, and in opposing Roosevelt's proposal to join the World Court, he fought to curb presidential options in foreign affairs, but his differences with the administration were muted until the President's "Quarantine Speech" of October 1937. Johnson considered the speech and Roosevelt's naval expansion bill of 1938 as "harbingers of war." Thereafter Johnson openly opposed virtually every point of the administration's foreign policy. He voted against the preparedness bills, including the Selective Service Act of 1940; he disapproved of Roosevelt's verbal efforts to moderate the actions of Hitler and Mussolini, and rigidly supported the diehard "isolationist" position during the six weeks' debate over deleting the arms embargo provisions from the Neutrality Act. After Hitler's invasion of Poland, Johnson argued that Germany would never conquer Europe and certainly would not attack the United States.

During the presidential contest of 1940 Johnson was a most unhappy man. He vehemently opposed a third Roosevelt term, but after the nomination of Wendell Willkie [Supp. 3] he was almost as displeased with the Republican ticket. The subsequent Roosevelt victory, the passage of the Lend-Lease Act, and the signing of the Atlantic Charter, all of which he denounced, increased his bitterness. After Pearl Harbor, although Johnson loyally supported the war effort, he maintained his dogged opposition to Roosevelt's foreign policy. He had started his Senatorial career opposed to "all foreign entanglements"; he ended it on the same note. On July 13, 1945, as the ranking minority member of the Senate Foreign Relations Committee, he cast the lone negative vote against reporting the charter of the United Nations to the floor of the Senate. And though because of illness he could not participate in the debates, his vote was paired against the charter, which won the chamber's approval by a count of 82–2. Johnson died that August of a cerebral thrombosis at the Bethesda (Md.) Naval Hospital. After nonsectarian services in the city hall of San Francisco, he was buried in Cypress Lawn Cemetery in that city.

Hiram Johnson always viewed politics in intensely personal terms, perhaps in part a consequence of the bitter family disputes occasioned by his own youthful commitment to political reform. He was often testy with associates even in the early days, and the acidulous and suspicious elements of his character grew with age. "When a man opposes Johnson," Senator William Borah [Supp. 2] once said, Johnson "hates him. He feels that the opposition is directed personally against him, not against the policy that separates them" (Olin, p. 97). By the end of his career a lonely negativism had become almost ingrained. When the new Senate Office Building was opened, Johnson alone among the Senators refused to move into the new quarters, continuing to maintain his office in the Capitol Building itself. But although his last years were not happy ones, attended as they were by failing health and by his increasingly isolated position on foreign policy, he had at least one monumental consolation: his reputation as an incorruptible independent was a priceless political asset, and throughout thirty-six years, during seven elections, two for the governorship and five for the Senate, the voters of California had never failed him.

[The extensive Johnson Papers are in the Bancroft Lib., Univ. of Calif., Berkeley. The papers of Chester H. Rowell, in the same institution, contain many Johnson letters, as do those of Meyer Lissner in the Borel Collection, Stanford Univ., and Edward A. Dickson, Special Collections Lib., Univ. of Calif., Los Angeles. George E. Mowry, *The Calif. Progressives* (1951), and Spencer C. Olin, Jr., *Calif. Prodigal Sons* (1968), cover the California phase of Johnson's career and contain extensive bibliographies. See also *N. Y. Times* obituary, Aug. 7, 1945; and Irving McKee, "The Background and Early Career of Hiram Warren Johnson, 1866–1910," *Pacific Hist. Rev.*, Feb. 1950.]

GEORGE E. MOWRY

JOHNSON, HUGH SAMUEL (Aug. 5, 1882–Apr. 15, 1942), army officer and government administrator, was born in Fort Scott, Kans., the oldest of three sons of Samuel and Elizabeth (Mead) Johnson (originally Johnston).

The Meads had come to Connecticut from England in the seventeenth century, the Johnstons from northern Ireland around 1812. As a struggling Illinois country lawyer, Samuel Johnston had dropped the "t" to avoid being confused with a Negro attorney of the same name. Variously a farmer, small-time land speculator, and postal clerk, he moved his family repeatedly in search of better fortune—from Illinois to Fort Scott, thence to other Kansas towns, and finally, in 1893, to the newly opened Cherokee Strip in Oklahoma Territory, where young Hugh grew up among gun-slinging frontiersmen and Indians. The boy early showed his sassy spirit; at the age of four he insisted, "Everybody in the world is a rink-stink but Hughie Johnson, and he's all right." In Alva, Okla., where his father prospered as postmaster and rancher, Hugh attended Oklahoma Northwestern Normal School, which awarded him a diploma in 1901. Meanwhile, in 1899, he had entered the United States Military Academy at West Point, from which he was graduated, B.S., in 1903.

For the next two decades Hugh Johnson served as a soldier in America's new empire. As a second lieutenant stationed near the Texas border with the 1st Cavalry, he married Helen Leslie Kilbourne, the sister of a West Point classmate, on Jan. 5, 1904; their only child, Kilbourne (who reverted to the spelling "Johnston"), later went to West Point. In 1906 the young lieutenant took on an awesome responsibility as acting quartermaster charged with caring for 17,000 victims of the San Francisco earthquake, the first of his experiences with economic mobilization. From 1907 to 1909 he served a tour of duty in the Philippines. When he returned, the army detailed him to be executive officer of Yosemite National Park in California (1910–12) and superintendent of Sequoia National Park (1911). By then he had begun to publish potboiling fiction, including two juveniles, *Williams of West Point* (1908) and *Williams on Service* (1910), as well as short stories about military life which appeared in national magazines.

Johnson's career as soldier-administrator took an important turn in 1914 when the War Department ordered him to begin a cram course at the University of California Law School. The lieutenant, who until then had lived the rootless, rowdy, sometimes irresponsible life of a Kipling border officer, applied himself so diligently that within eighteen months the university awarded him both an A.B. and a J.D. with honors. On the afternoon of his graduation in 1916, Johnson departed for Chihuahua, Mexico, to join Gen. John J. Pershing's punitive expedition in pursuit of Pancho Villa. Assigned to the commandant's staff as judge advocate, he quickly revealed the temperament that had led his men to call him "Tuffy" Johnson. Pershing commented: "When Johnson gets gruff, he really seems to devour you, bones and all. Even I, his superior officer, felt that way" (*Washington Post,* Apr. 16, 1942). That October he went to Washington as assistant to the law officer in the Bureau of Insular Affairs, in charge of the civil litigation of the overseas empire.

World War I rocketed Johnson to national prominence. As a newly appointed captain on the army's legal staff, he wrote the key sections of the Selective Service Act of 1917. Without authority, he boldly ordered 30,000,000 registration forms printed and distributed before the law was enacted. Two weeks after the passage of the act he was named major judge advocate in charge of directing the draft; for his energetic performance in this post he was awarded the Distinguished Service Medal. Johnson also represented the army on the War Industries Board, where he began his long association with Bernard Baruch, the head of the board, and played an important role in the war mobilization as chief of military purchase and supply. In these posts, he rose swiftly to lieutenant colonel and colonel, and at thirty-five became the youngest brigadier general since the Civil War. In the fall of 1918 he took command of the 8th ("Pathfinder") Division, but the war ended as he was about to embark for France. Heartsick at being denied the chance to lead troops into battle, General Johnson resigned from the army in February 1919.

Johnson passed the years of the Republican interregnum between Wilson and Roosevelt in business ventures with wartime associates, acquiring the expertise that would serve him in good stead in the next mobilization under the New Deal. In September 1919 he joined George N. Peek [Supp. 3] in the Moline Plow Company as assistant general manager and general counsel, the start, as Johnson later put it, of "seven years of unrelieved hell and disappointment—a seven years' fight to save a company doomed to destruction from the first day we saw it" (*The Blue Eagle,* p. 106). During these same years he aided Peek in developing the seminal ideas of the McNary-Haugen Bill for federal aid to agriculture. In the fall of 1927 he went to New York as an assistant to Bernard Baruch at a salary that eventually exceeded $100,000 a year. It was as a "Baruch man" that Johnson became a member of Franklin D. Roosevelt's "Brain Trust" in July 1932 and contributed speeches to F.D.R.'s first presidential campaign.

In 1933 President Roosevelt called on Johnson to administer the National Industrial Recovery Act, a law which the General had helped draft. Johnson carried out this new assignment with such demonic energy that he rivaled the President for national headlines. The indefatigable head of the National Recovery Administration (NRA) worked from sixteen to twenty hours a day and, at a time when air travel was still novel, flew 40,000 miles in an army Condor, organizing and haranguing parades and mass rallies to invest the cause with patriotic ardor. He supervised "codes," worked out in conjunction with employers and employees, for more than 500 industries, helped establish maximum hours and minimum wages as national policy, and made the "Blue Eagle" symbol of the NRA a household emblem.

Johnson's appearance and demeanor marked him as an unreconstructed horse soldier. Stocky, thick-necked, powerfully built, "Old Ironpants" had the jutting jaw, gravelly voice, and brusque manner of one accustomed to command. His open collar, uprolled sleeves, and rumpled trousers implied he was still in the field. But he stared at the world through improbable horn-rimmed glasses, and his ruddy complexion, deep pouches, and sagging paunch suggested dissipation. The columnist Raymond Clapper [Supp. 3] described him as "gruff and tough, with large round hard-blue eyes which can become as flinty as a banker's, a jaw that snaps with the impact of a sledge hammer." Yet this same truculent warrior wept over opera arias, nurtured rare plants, and had a sentimental and romantic perception of the world. Johnson, as Arthur M. Schlesinger, Jr., has written, "saw all life as melodrama slightly streaked with farce; he was forever rescuing the virtuous, foiling the villains." His cavalryman's language captivated the country. He gave currency to words like "chiseler" and "crack down," suggested that code evaders like Henry Ford would "get a sock right on the nose," and sneered at a writer "in whose veins there must flow something more than a trace of rodent blood."

Yet Johnson carried vituperation, like so much else in his life, to excess, and by 1934 he was becoming an embarrassment to the administration. He overextended himself, lost his temper too often, brawled with businessmen and labor leaders, cabinet officers and Senators, drank heavily, and, frequently ill or absent from his office, gave too much rein to "Robbie," his attractive, red-haired confidential secretary, Frances Robinson. Critics charged, not always fairly, that he impeded recovery, fostered monopoly, hurt small business, and substituted bluster for coherent policy. While some accused Johnson of being "a sheep in wolf's clothing," others, recalling that he had once jocularly identified himself with Mussolini, branded him a would-be dictator with a fondness for the corporate state. Secretary of Labor Frances Perkins recalled that Baruch had warned her: "I think he's a good number-three man, maybe a number-two man, but he's not a number-one man. He's dangerous and unstable. . . . I'm fond of him, but . . . Hugh needs a firm hand" (Perkins, pp. 200-01). By the summer of 1934 Roosevelt recognized that the General would have to go, and on Oct. 15 Johnson's tenure as NRA administrator ended. At a farewell conference, Johnson called NRA "as great a social advance as has occurred on this earth since a gaunt and dusty Jew in Palestine declared . . . a new principle in human relationship," quoted the final words of Madame Butterfly before she took her life, and wept copiously.

Johnson's subsequent career proved anticlimactic. In 1935 he turned in a three-month stint as Works Progress Administrator in New York City and in 1936 represented the Radio Corporation of America as labor counsel. But he spent most of his final years as a syndicated columnist for the Scripps-Howard chain and as a radio broadcaster. Johnson's column, at the outset pro-New Deal, gradually shifted to denunciation of the administration's "radical" inclinations. Credited with helping develop a boom for Wendell L. Willkie [Supp. 3] as the Republican presidential candidate, he became one of Willkie's most prominent supporters in 1940, but, predictably, found fault with the way the campaign was conducted. In a book published in 1941 he warned that the administration was *Hell-Bent for War*, but he was deeply wounded when Roosevelt turned down his application for renewal of his commission as brigadier general. He died of pneumonia the following April, at the age of fifty-nine, in his apartment at the Wardman Park Hotel in Washington, D. C. An Episcopalian of Anglo-Catholic leanings, he was buried with military honors in the National Cemetery at Arlington, Va., a fitting end for one who had contributed the perspective of a military mobilizer to the growth of the twentieth-century state.

[Johnson's autobiography, *The Blue Eagle from Egg to Earth* (1935) ; Matthew Josephson, "The General," *New Yorker*, Aug. 18, 25, Sept. 1, 1943 ; Jonathan Mitchell, "The Versatility of General Johnson," *Harper's*, Oct. 1934 ; Raymond Clapper, "Top Sergeants of the New Deal," *Rev. of Revs.*, Aug. 1933 ; Arthur M. Schlesinger, Jr., *The Age of Roosevelt* (3 vols., 1957–60) ; Frances Perkins, *The Roosevelt I Knew* (1946) ; "Unofficial Observer" (John Franklin Carter), *The New Dealers* (1934) ; Gilbert C. Fite, *George N. Peek and the Fight for Farm Parity* (1954) ; *Current Biog.*,

1940 ; *N. Y. Times*, Apr. 16, 1942 ; *Washington Post*, Apr. 16, 1942.]

WILLIAM E. LEUCHTENBURG

JONES, LEWIS RALPH (Dec. 5, 1864–Apr. 1, 1945), plant pathologist, was born in Brandon, Fond du Lac County, Wis., the third son and third of six children of David Jones, a successful farmer, and Lucy Jane (Knapp) Jones, who had taught school before her marriage. His father was a native of Wales, his mother of Vermont. Jones received his early education in Brandon and in 1883 entered nearby Ripon College, where he took a special interest in biology. Sympathetic teachers, then and earlier, aided his advancement, and in 1886 he transferred to the University of Michigan. To help finance his education he taught science for a year and a half at the Mount Morris (Ill.) Academy (1887–88). When he returned to Michigan, he gave up his plan for a medical career and chose to specialize in botany; he received the Ph.B. degree in 1889 and the Ph.D. in 1904, with a dissertation on the relationship of exoenzymes to bacterial diseases of plants. Meanwhile (1889) Jones had accepted a position as instructor at the University of Vermont and botanist at the Vermont Agricultural Experiment Station; he was made professor of botany in 1893. In 1910 he moved to the University of Wisconsin, where he became head of the newly organized department of plant pathology.

Jones began his career at a time when his specialty—plant pathology—was emerging as an offshoot of mycology, plant therapeutics, and bacteriology. Around mid-century Anton De Bary in Germany had worked on the causal relations between specific fungi and plant diseases, and in the 1880's Alexis Millardet in France had discovered the curative powers of Bordeaux mixture, a copper-based fungicide. At about the same time, Robert Koch of Berlin had developed a method of isolating bacterial cultures for laboratory study and had inspired the scientific world with his papers identifying the tubercle bacillus and the cholera microorganism. Largely because of De Bary's work, botanists of the time had a strong attachment to the idea that plant diseases were mycological in origin and were reluctant to accept bacteria as plant pathogens, although before 1880 Thomas J. Burrill [*q.v.*] in Illinois had gone far toward proving that a fire blight epidemic of pears in the Midwest was incited by bacteria. The issue was settled mainly by Erwin F. Smith [*q.v.*], of the United States Department of Agriculture, in his research and in his protracted controversy with Alfred Fischer of Germany. Once the early scientific excitement abated over the role of parasites—first fungi and then bacteria

—in causing plant diseases, plant pathologists centered their attention on the host plant itself and then on its total environment. Jones was always on the research frontier of each new development, and he has been credited with initiating interest in the environmental aspects of plant pathology.

While at Vermont, Jones pioneered in the use of Bordeaux mixture in the United States. He began what became a twenty-year experimental program of spraying various mixtures on different varieties of potatoes. His studies made possible a much greater control of potato diseases and a resulting increase in yield. His more than fifty publications on the subject include a classic paper on *Phytophthora infestans,* the fungus producing the late blight. For the Department of Agriculture he searched in Europe for disease-resistant potatoes. He also carried out fundamental studies on the bacterial soft rot of carrots and other vegetables. He encouraged the efforts of amateur botanists by organizing the Vermont Botanical Club, and helped create the Vermont Forestry Association. At Wisconsin, Jones concentrated on the development of disease-resistant plants. He also continued his investigation of the role of environmental factors in plant pathology, and his study of cabbage yellows, a Fusarium wilt disease, was one of the earliest to demonstrate the relationship between soil temperature and plant diseases. Although his work tended to focus on the diseases of economically important plants, the results were also contributions to basic science. Jones strongly believed in the value of research, and once wrote that its spirit "must not be restrained by the artificial bounds of professional or administrative classification."

The department of plant pathology at Wisconsin—the second one in the United States—granted some 150 doctoral degrees before Jones retired in 1935. He was a charter member and first president (1909) of the American Phytopathological Society and was the first editor (1911–14) of its journal, *Phytopathology.* He also served as president of the Botanical Society of America (1913); chairman (1922) of the division of biology and agriculture of the National Academy of Sciences (to which he was elected in 1920); honorary president of the Third International Congress of Microbiology (1939); and member of President Franklin Roosevelt's Science Advisory Board. He received several honorary degrees, including a D.Sc. from Cambridge University. A thin, handsome man who wore rimless glasses, Jones was an effective teacher, not because of any expositorial brilliance but because he emphasized the "doing" in scientific education. He enjoyed outdoor life and was an active member of the Congregational Church.

Jones was twice married: on June 24, 1890, to May I. Bennett, a Ripon classmate, who died in 1926; and on July 27, 1929, to Anna M. Clark, who had worked with him in Vermont on a study of sap flow in maples. He had no children. After retirement, Jones and his second wife often spent their winters in Florida and their summers in Brookfield, Vt. He died of a coronary thrombosis at the age of eighty in Orlando, Fla., and was buried in the family plot at Brandon, Wis.

[Two of Jones's articles on the state of his science are: "Problems and Progress in Plant Pathology," *Am. Jour. of Botany,* Mar. 1914, and "Securing Disease Resistant Plants," *Science,* Apr. 2, 1926. The most complete obituaries are: G. W. Keitt and F. V. Rand in *Phytopathology,* Jan. 1946; and J. C. Walker and A. J. Riker in Nat. Acad. Sci., *Biog. Memoirs,* vol. XXXI (1958). The latter contains a list of Jones's publications. For background information, see: Andrew D. Rogers, *Erwin Frink Smith* (1952); U. S. Dept. of Agriculture, *Yearbook of Agriculture,* 1953 ("Plant Diseases"); Erwin F. Smith, "Fifty Years of Pathology," Internat. Cong. of Plant Sciences, *Proc.,* 1926; Herbert H. Whetzel, *An Outline of the Hist. of Phytopathology* (1918); Paul F. Clark, *Pioneer Microbiologists of America* (1961); and Edward H. Beardsley, *Harry L. Russell and Agricultural Science in Wis.* (1969). For an overview of the history of agricultural science in government, see A. Hunter Dupree, *Science in the Federal Government* (1957). The potato project is described in B. F. Lutman, *Twenty Years' Spraying for Potato Diseases* (Vt. Agricultural Experiment Station, *Bull.* no. 159, May 1911). Census listing of 1870 from State Hist. Soc. of Wis.; death record from Fla. Bureau of Vital Statistics. Jones's papers are in the Univ. of Wis. Archives and in the Dept. of Botany, Univ. of Vt.]

MORGAN SHERWOOD

JUDAY, CHANCEY (May 5, 1871–Mar. 29, 1944), limnologist, was born near Millersburg, Ind., the fourteenth of fifteen children and youngest of nine sons of Baltzer and Elizabeth (Heltzel) Juday. His ancestors were English, and had lived in Maryland before 1789; his father was a native of Ohio, his mother of New York state. Growing up on his father's farm, Juday attended a country grade school, the Millersburg public school, and special summer schools, and obtained a county teacher's license in 1890. After two years at Indiana State Normal School in Terre Haute, he attended Indiana University, where he received the B.A. degree in 1896 and an M.A. in 1897. His zoology professor, the ichthyologist Carl H. Eigenmann [q.v.], had aroused his interest in lakes, and Juday did his first published research on the hydrography and plankton of Turkey Lake (now Lake Wawassee, Kosciusko County, Ind).

After two years of high school teaching at Evansville, Ind., he joined the Wisconsin Geological and Natural History Survey, in Madison, as a biologist. Shortly thereafter he contracted tuberculosis and went to Colorado to recuperate. For two years (1902–04) he was on the University of Colorado faculty, and in 1904–05 he was an instructor at the University of California, working on fish and plankton. He resumed his Wisconsin position in 1905, collaborating with Edward A. Birge, a pioneer limnologist and later president of the University of Wisconsin. From October 1907 to June 1908 Juday traveled in Europe, visiting freshwater biology laboratories. He studied semi-tropical lakes in Guatemala and El Salvador in February 1910. The next summer, working with Birge, he investigated the Finger Lakes of New York state. He was married that fall, on Sept. 6, 1910, to Magdalen Evans of Madison, who bore him three children: Chancey Evans, Mary Whetham, and Richard Evans.

Juday's responsibilities at Madison had been extended in 1908 to include teaching at the University of Wisconsin, where he offered courses in limnology and plankton organisms. His first extensive publication was on dissolved gases in lake waters (1911, with Birge; largely Juday's work); it was followed by another on the Finger Lakes (1914) and one on plankton of Wisconsin lakes (1922). He also published a study of the hydrography and morphometry of Wisconsin lakes (1914), as well as several papers on the biology of individual organisms he encountered.

About 1919 Juday and Birge shifted most of their field work from Lake Mendota to Green Lake, where they continued studies on biological productivity and light penetration. In 1925 they founded the Trout Lake Limnological Laboratory, in Vilas County, Wis., of which Juday served as director until his retirement in 1941. After becoming professor of limnology at the University of Wisconsin in 1931, Juday supervised the research of many doctoral candidates on the growth of freshwater fish and other limnological problems. His growing reputation attracted prominent American and European biologists to work at Madison and the Trout Lake laboratory; many local Wisconsin scientists also undertook cooperative lake studies with him.

Juday's continuing scientific objective was to determine the most significant factors influencing biological productivity in lakes. For this he collected prodigious amounts of data on the standing crops of plankton, bottom organisms, and aquatic plants, trying to correlate these with environmental conditions. Though he was only partially successful, no one in the early twentieth century did more to elucidate such relationships. The massive foundation of factual knowledge he accumulated greatly advanced the new science of limnology, and he trained many new workers in this field.

Juday was president of the American Microscopical Society (1923) and the Ecological Society of America (1927), and first president of the Limnological Society of America (1935–37). He served as secretary-treasurer (1922–30) and president (1937–39) of the Wisconsin Academy of Sciences, which published many of his papers. The Academy of Natural Sciences of Philadelphia awarded him the Leidy Medal in 1943; in 1950 the International Association of Limnology presented the Naumann Medal to the University of Wisconsin in recognition of his work and that of Birge.

Personally Juday was a gentle man, exceedingly modest about his own attainments, sincere and helpful to those seeking advice. He was slender, of average height, not very muscular, but able to hold his own in field work. He retired from his university post in 1941. Three years later he died of uremia in a Madison hospital and was buried in Forest Hill Cemetery, Madison.

[*Special Publication* No. 16 of the Limnology Soc. of America (1945), containing obituary notice by L. E. Noland and list of Juday's publications by A. D. Hasler; obituaries by Paul S. Welch, in *Ecology*, July 1944, with full-page portrait, and by A. S. Pearse in *Science*, June 23, 1944; long personal acquaintance; information from Mrs. Juday; death record from Wis. Dept. of Health and Social Services.]

LOWELL E. NOLAND

JUST, ERNEST EVERETT (Aug. 14, 1883–Oct. 27, 1941), zoologist, was born in Charleston, S. C., the first of three children of Charles Frazier Just and Mary (Matthews) Just, both of Negro ancestry. His father, a wharf builder, died when Ernest was four. His mother, a deeply religious woman with a concern for improving the status of her people, opened a school, where he received his early education. At the age of eleven he entered a public school for Negroes at Orangeburg, S. C., where he remained for six years. Having read in the *Christian Endeavor World* an article on the Kimball Union Academy at Meriden, N. H., he applied there for admission and entered in 1900, after working his way north on board a ship. He completed the four-year course in three and won a scholarship to Dartmouth College, Hanover, N. H., where he specialized in zoology, was elected to Phi Beta Kappa, and received the A.B. degree, magna cum laude, in 1907. He then became an instructor in biology at Howard University in Washington, D. C., where he remained a faculty member for the rest of his life. On June 26, 1912, he married Ethel Highwarden of Columbus, Ohio, a fellow teacher at Howard. Their three children were Margaret, Highwarden, and Marybelle.

Just began graduate training in the summer of 1909 at the Marine Biological Laboratory in Woods Hole, Mass. He was to return there, as a student and then as a member of the scientific community, nearly every summer for the next twenty years. As research assistant (1911–12) to Prof. Frank R. Lillie of the University of Chicago he studied the fertilization and early development of the eggs of sea urchins and marine worms, and published his first paper in 1912. Lillie helped him obtain funds from the National Research Council, which for some years supported Just's investigations at Woods Hole.

At Howard, Just was made professor and head of the department of zoology in 1912; from 1912 to 1920 he also served as professor of physiology in the medical school. Because of his record in research and his effective efforts to improve the quality of the medical training at Howard, he was chosen in 1915 as the first recipient of the Spingarn Medal of the National Association for the Advancement of Colored People, awarded annually for high achievement by a Negro. A year's leave of absence in 1915–16 enabled him to·complete his graduate study at the University of Chicago, where in 1916 he received the Ph.D. degree, magna cum laude.

A brilliant experimentalist whose command of French and German gave him full access to the literature, Just had an extraordinary understanding of the embryology of marine organisms, and his colleagues at Woods Hole frequently drew upon his advice and assistance. He developed new cytological and embryological techniques with which he studied the fertilization and physiology of the eggs of marine organisms, the process of cell division, the mechanism of water transfer in living cells, artificial parthenogenesis, the use of ultraviolet rays to change the number of chromosomes in the reproductive cell, and the changes in the development of the egg resulting from altered physical and chemical conditions. Through a combination of exact observation and experiment, Just arrived at the stimulating concept that the ectoplasm (cortex) of an animal egg cell is the prime factor in the initiation of development (fertilization), and through its interplay with cytoplasm is a causative factor in differentiation and in the building up of nuclear material. Thus, in this view, both differentiation and the action of the gene in heredity result from an interplay of ectoplasm and nucleus with the cytoplasm. Just's concept is of pioneer significance to contemporary investigations of the biochemical constitution and function of the cell surface and membranes in general.

Just set forth this concept in his *Biology of the Cell Surface* (1939). His other publications include some sixty papers, as well as a monograph, *Basic Methods for Experiments on Eggs of Marine Animals* (1939). He was a fellow of the American Association for the Advancement of Science, vice-president of the American Society of Zoologists (1930), and a member of a number of other scientific organizations. He also served as an editor of *Physiological Zoology,* the *Biological Bulletin, Protoplasma* (Berlin), and the *Journal of Morphology.*

In appearance Just was a tall, slender man of great dignity. Although his work commanded the respect of the most eminent biologists of his day, as a deeply sensitive human being he suffered severely from "the stigma that white Americans, scientists included, applied to Negroes" (Nabrit, p. 121). Howard University was generous with leaves of absence, and Just in his later years was able to obtain a series of research grants from the General Education Board, the Carnegie Corporation, the Rosenwald Foundation, and Julius Rosenwald. As a Negro, however, he was never invited to a post at an American university or research institute where he would have had a permanent laboratory and facilities commensurate with his abilities. By contrast, on trips abroad he was not only recognized as a scientist but warmly received as a person. As he grew older he became increasingly embittered and largely abandoned his earlier attempts to encourage black students to obtain advanced training, believing that their efforts, even if successful, would lead only to frustration. In the early 1930's he gave up teaching altogether and, supported by Rosenwald grants, went to Europe to live, working at the Kaiser Wilhelm Institute in Berlin and at laboratories in Italy, France, and Russia. His two books were published during this period. Just returned to the United States in 1941 and died of cancer a few months later in Washington, D. C., at the age of fifty-eight. He was buried there in Lincoln Cemetery.

[Profile by S. Milton Nabrit in *Phylon,* Second Quarter 1946; obituaries by Frank R. Lillie in *Science,* Jan. 2, 1942, and *Anatomical Record,* Feb. 25, 1942. See also sketches in Mary White Ovington, *Portraits in Color* (1927), *Crisis,* Feb. 1932, and *Opportunity,* Sept. 1942; and obituaries in *Jour. of Negro Hist.,* Jan. 1942, and *Jour. of Nervous and Mental Disease,* Feb. 1943.]

FRED D. MILLER

KAHN, ALBERT (Mar. 21, 1869–Dec. 8, 1942), architect, was born in Rhaunen, Westphalia, Germany, the eldest of six children of Joseph and Rosalie (Cohn) Kahn. He spent his childhood in the Grand Duchy of Luxembourg, where he was educated in the local schools. His father, a rabbi and teacher, immigrated around 1880 to Detroit, Mich., where he struggled to earn a living as a fruit peddler. Young Albert longed to become an artist, and was encouraged by a local sculptor, Julius Melchers (father of the painter Gari Melchers [q.v.]), who permitted him to attend his art school free of charge on Sunday mornings. Discovering that his pupil was partially color-blind Melchers suggested that he become an architect, and in 1885 secured a job for him as an office boy in the architectural office of Mason and Rice.

Kahn soon became a draftsman, learning much about architecture in the firm's excellent library. A scholarship from the *American Architect* in 1890 provided a year's study in Europe, where he traveled for several months with Henry Bacon [q.v.] and sketched monuments. On his return he went back to Mason and Rice, but left in 1896 to form a partnership with two fellow employees, George W. Nettleton and Alexander B. Trowbridge. With Nettleton, Kahn designed in 1898 a private library for the newspaper publisher James E. Scripps [q.v.], modeled after the chapter house of Westminster Abbey. The partnership dissolved after Trowbridge departed to become dean of the Cornell University College of Architecture and Nettleton died in 1900. After briefly collaborating with George D. Mason, Kahn began practice on his own in 1902.

One of his early independent works was the Engineering Building at the University of Michigan (1903). Its concrete construction made him aware of the shortcomings of the empirical method of reinforcement, and thereafter he employed a superior system of reinforced concrete which his brother Julius, a civil engineer, developed. To manufacture the principal component of this system, the Kahn bar (a main reinforcing bar with shear members rigidly attached), Julius organized the Trussed Concrete Steel Company in Youngstown, Ohio.

Another of Albert Kahn's early undertakings —remodeling the home of Henry B. Joy [Supp. 2], president of the Packard Motor Car Company—led to his first major commission, the design of the Packard factory in Detroit. After initially employing conventional mill construction, he utilized the Kahn bar in 1905 to construct the tenth unit of the Packard plant, one of the first concrete factory buildings in Detroit.

Responding to the demand for more factories created by the burgeoning automobile industry in Detroit, Kahn subsequently applied this new method of construction to the Chalmers, Hudson,

and Dodge plants. Of more importance was his Highland Park plant (1909–14) for the Ford Motor Company. Here Kahn designed a building to accommodate Henry Ford's concept of a complete factory under one roof, a concept radically different from previous factory designs in which separate buildings were provided for every process. Moreover, by combining extensive steel window sash, imported from England, with concrete construction, Kahn transformed the American factory from a dingy eyesore into a bright, cheerful place. A few years later Kahn designed for Ford a half-mile-long factory ("Building B") in which the manufacturing process could take place not only under one roof but on one floor. It had a steel frame, previously employed by Kahn in tall commercial structures (the Detroit Free Press Building, the Kresge Building), and the walls were an unbroken expanse of glass. This building, located on a vast tract of land in Dearborn, Mich., near the River Rouge, was but one component of the large, self-sufficient complex which Ford had determined to build. In the 1920's a steel mill, a glass plant, a power plant, port facilities, and additional manufacturing facilities were added to complete the River Rouge plant. Working closely with Ford and other clients, Kahn evolved a new functional industrial architecture to meet the extraordinary demands of the automobile industry.

Although closely related to his industrial architecture, Kahn's commercial architecture frequently departed from the utilitarian simplicity that distinguished his factory buildings. He believed that commercial buildings, as a prominent feature on the urban landscape, demanded more elaborate treatment. His eight-story Trussed Concrete Steel Company Building (1907), the first office building of concrete construction in Detroit, was faced with white brick piers and metal spandrels. He used white glazed terra-cotta on the exterior of the Grinnell Building (1908) and the Ford Sales Office (1910–13; later known as the Boulevard Building). The latter's clean-cut grid design and reduced wall surfaces call to mind the Carson Pirie Scott store of Louis Sullivan [q.v.] in Chicago. On a European vacation in 1912, Kahn discovered the rich, warm brickwork of the palaces in Siena and Bologna, which he soon applied to a series of functional buildings for the University of Michigan at Ann Arbor: the Hill Auditorium (1913), the Natural Science Building (1917), and the University Library (1919). He drew on the work of the German architects Alfred Messel and Joseph M. Olbrich to give the Detroit News Building (1915) massive stone piers and arcades, a design that satisfied George G. Booth, president of the *News*, who wanted a monumental external treatment. Kahn's admiration of the Italianate work of McKim, Mead & White was clearly reflected in his Detroit Athletic Club (1915), Detroit Trust Company (1915), and William L. Clements Library in Ann Arbor (1923). The residence he built for Goodloe Edgar (1915) in Grosse Pointe (one of the limited number of houses he designed as a special favor for major clients) followed the pattern established by Charles A. Platt [*q.v.*] in his Italianate residential work.

Kahn built many commercial structures in Detroit during the prosperous 1920's. The fifteen-story General Motors Building (1922) was one of the largest office buildings in the country. Though the details were Italian Renaissance, the four majestic projecting wings emphasized mass rather than detail. Following a trend established in New York City as a result of setback laws, his second Detroit Free Press Building (1925) and the Maccabees Building (1927) were composed of tower masses supported on lower stories. As Kahn became older, he relied more upon tradition, rejecting the experimental and bizarre tendencies of contemporary commercial architecture. His twenty-eight-story Fisher Building (1928), with its peaked Gothic roof, closely resembled the New York Life Insurance Company Building (1928) of Cass Gilbert [Supp. 1]; but Gilbert's fussy Gothic details were abandoned in favor of a more modern decorative treatment. Despite its conservatism, the Fisher Building won Kahn the silver medal of the Architectural League of New York in 1929.

Kahn's greatest achievements were in industrial architecture, and there he continued to make progress. By 1929 he had assembled a staff of 400, including 175 architects, who designed plants for all the major automobile manufacturers, in addition to other industrial concerns. At the request of the Russian government in 1928, Kahn participated in the industrialization program of the first Five-Year Plan, a project that involved building 521 factories in twenty-five cities at a cost of two billion dollars. Only a dozen of these factories were designed in Detroit; the rest were done in Moscow, where over a three-year period Kahn technicians trained 4,000 Soviet engineers.

Before building a plant, Kahn made a careful study of the flow of production. He also felt that it was important to assure pleasant working conditions by providing adequate heating, ventilation, and natural lighting. These architectural principles were best expressed in his 1928 Plymouth plant in Detroit. All on one level, it was a half mile long. Natural lighting was provided throughout by monitors. There were twelve and a half miles of conveyor systems, and the assembly line was the longest in the industry. Frequently an industrial building by Kahn reached a high aesthetic level by the sheer simplicity of its construction and the weightless transparency of its glass walls. Such a building was the De Soto press shop of the Chrysler Corporation in Detroit (1936), which consisted of a huge glass cage suspended from trusses. Another was the Chrysler Corporation's half-ton truck plant (1938), in which the monitors were hung below the roof level, instead of projecting above it, in order to provide better natural illumination. By 1937 Kahn's architectural firm, which designed over a thousand factories for Ford and 127 buildings for General Motors, was handling 19 percent of all architect-designed industrial buildings in America.

With the coming of World War II, Kahn directed his energy toward the war effort. He designed bases for the navy and, employing techniques that he had already perfected, laid out plants at key centers across the continent; his Chrysler tank arsenal (1941) near Detroit consisted of a high glass cage three blocks long. Many of his plants were constructed of concrete in order to save steel. The Ford Motor Company's Willow Run bomber plant (1941–43), covering seventy acres near Ypsilanti, Mich., was the giant of them all. For protection against air attack, Kahn eliminated glass areas and substituted artificial light for natural light. Here Henry Ford applied to airplane production the assembly-line method that he had developed in manufacturing automobiles.

After architecture, Kahn's two greatest interests were music and art. He was a patron of the Detroit Symphony Society, a collector of French Impressionist paintings, and for twenty years a member of the Arts Commission of the Detroit Institute of Arts. A man of staunch faith, he was a member of Temple Beth El. On Sept. 14, 1896, he had married Ernestine Krolik. They had four children: Lydia, Edgar Adolph, Ruth, and Rosalie. The strain of his war work took its toll upon Kahn, and he died in Detroit of a bronchial ailment at the age of seventy-three. He was buried in the White Chapel Memorial Cemetery, Troy, Mich.

Like most other architects of his generation, Kahn was an eclectic, but it was not as an eclectic that he excelled. He concentrated on the lowly factory, which had been shunned by other architects, and elevated it to one of the most significant architectural expressions of our times.

That contribution alone assures him an important place in the history of American architecture. It might be said that he did for the factory what Louis Sullivan did for the skyscraper and what Frank Lloyd Wright did for the private residence.

[George Nelson, *The Industrial Architecture of Albert Kahn, Inc.* (1939); Albert Kahn, Inc., *Industrial and Commercial Buildings* (1936); *Architectural Forum*, Aug. 1938, a special issue devoted to Kahn; W. Hawkins Ferry, *The Buildings of Detroit* (1968) and *The Legacy of Albert Kahn* (1970); Albert Kahn, "Architectural Trend," Md. Acad. of Sci., *Jour.*, Apr. 1931, and "Industrial Architecture," Mich. Soc. of Architects, *Weekly Bull.*, Dec. 27, 1939; Allan Nevins, *Ford* (3 vols., 1954–63); Clarence M. Burton, *The City of Detroit* (1922); Malcolm W. Bingay, *Detroit Is My Own Home Town* (1946); *Nat. Cyc. Am. Biog.*, XXXI, 264–65; Albert N. Marquis, *The Book of Detroiters* (1908); Detroit city directories; *Architectural Record*, Jan. 1943; Mich. Soc. of Architects, *Weekly Bull.*, Mar. 30, 1943. European sketches and personal correspondence of Kahn are owned by the family.]

W. HAWKINS FERRY

KAHN, GUSTAV GERSON (Nov. 6, 1886–Oct. 8, 1941), popular song lyricist, was born in Coblenz, Germany, to Jewish parents, Isaac and Theresa (Mayer) Kahn. His father, a cattle dealer, came to the United States when Gus was five and settled in Chicago. The boy attended public schools there and then supported himself by working as clerk in a hotel-supply firm and in a mail-order house. By this time writing song lyrics had become his principal diversion. The first to be published, "I Wish I Had a Girl" (1907)—with music by Grace Le Boy, his chief early collaborator—was sufficiently successful to encourage him to concentrate on song writing and preparing special material for vaudevillians. A significant development in his career came when he teamed up with the composer Egbert Van Alstyne, with whom he wrote his first two substantial hits, "Memories" (1915) and the still popular "Pretty Baby" (1916), the melody of the latter written by Van Alstyne in collaboration with the ragtime pianist Tony Jackson. These were followed by such successes as "Sailing Away on the Henry Clay" (1917) and "Your Eyes Have Told Me So" (1919). Meanwhile, on Aug. 18, 1915, he had married Grace Le Boy; they had two children, Donald and Irene.

Though Kahn continued to live in Chicago, he became very much a part of the New York musical scene of the 1920's. He contributed lyrics to the music of numerous Broadway composers, most notably Walter Donaldson. The first Donaldson-Kahn songs, "My Buddy" and "Carolina in the Morning," were both leading sellers in 1922. Others were "Beside a Babbling Brook" (1923), "Yes, Sir, That's My Baby" (1925), written for and popularized by Eddie Cantor, and "She's Wonderful" (1928). In 1928 the two wrote the score for *Whoopee,* a Broadway musical produced by Florenz Ziegfeld [*q.v.*] and starring Eddie Cantor, which introduced "Makin' Whoopee," "My Baby Just Cares for Me," and "Love Me or Leave Me." Another composer for whom Kahn wrote lyrics during the 1920's was Isham Jones, a collaboration that yielded "Swingin' Down the Lane" (1923) and, in 1924, "It Had to Be You," "The One I Love Belongs to Somebody Else," and "I'll See You in My Dreams."

After 1933 Kahn worked chiefly in Hollywood. He contributed lyrics for many motion pictures to music by Walter Donaldson, Jimmy McHugh, Sigmund Romberg, and others. Among his screen musicals were two Eddie Cantor vehicles, *Whoopee* (1930) and *Kid Millions* (1934), and two Nelson Eddy-Jeanette MacDonald features, *Naughty Marietta* (1935) and *Rose Marie* (1936).

Kahn was one of the most successful and prolific lyricists of his time. During a twenty-year period he averaged six song hits each year; the number of his published songs exceeds five hundred. Besides those already mentioned, he was responsible for the words to "Toot, Toot, Tootsie" (in collaboration with Ernie Erdman), which Al Jolson introduced in *Bombo* in 1922 and then made one of his specialties; "My Isle of Golden Dreams" (1919); "Ain't We Got Fun" (1921); "Nobody's Sweetheart" (1924); and "I Never Knew" (1925). His last song was also a hit: "You Stepped Out of a Dream," which Tony Martin introduced in the motion picture *The Ziegfeld Girl* in 1940. Gus Kahn died of a heart attack at his home in Beverly Hills, Calif., in 1941, at fifty-four. A decade later his career was romanticized in the motion picture *I'll See You in My Dreams* (1951).

Kahn had an ear for youthful speech and sought (as he put it in 1927) to "express colloquially something that every young person has tried to say—and somehow *can't*" (McEvoy, p. 137). Basically he was a functional lyricist who sought simplicity and directness of expression without falling back on clichés. He never used a two-syllable or three-syllable word when a one-syllable word would do, and he avoided virtuosity of rhyming, unusual figures of speech, and esoteric allusions. The simplicity of his vocabulary and style, however, did not conceal a remarkable skill for shaping verses that lent themselves readily and gracefully to singable tunes.

[*The ASCAP Biog. Dict. of Composers, Authors and Publishers* (3rd ed., 1966); Jack Burton, *The Blue Book of Tin Pan Alley* (1950); David Ewen, *Am. Popular Songs* (1966) and *New Complete Book of the*

Am. Musical Theater (1970); Sigmund Spaeth, *A Hist. of Popular Music in America* (1948); J. P. McEvoy, "Do You Know What Makes a Popular Song Popular?" (an interview with Kahn), *American Mag.*, June 1927; Irwin Stambler, *Encyc. of Popular Music* (1965); *Who's Who in Am. Jewry*, 1938–39; *N. Y. Times*, Oct. 9, 1941.]

DAVID EWEN

KEITH, ARTHUR (Sept. 30, 1864–Feb. 7, 1944), geologist, was born in St. Louis, Mo., one of two sons of Massachusetts parents, Harrison Alonzo Keith, a schoolteacher, and Mary Elizabeth (Richardson) Keith. His father was descended from the Rev. James Keith, who settled in Bridgewater, Mass., in 1662 as its first pastor; his mother's earliest American ancestor was Thomas Richardson, who came to Charlestown, Mass., in 1630. Both parents had graduated from Antioch College in Ohio in 1859. A few years after Arthur's birth, the family moved to Quincy, Mass., the birthplace of his father, who for many years was principal of the Quincy high school and afterward mayor.

After attending Quincy public schools and preparing for college at Adams Academy, Arthur Keith entered Harvard, where he excelled in athletics. He was also interested in sailing and designed yachts; in later life he attributed his remarkable physical endurance as a field geologist to this early training in outdoor sports. Keith graduated from Harvard, A.B., in 1885 and on the advice of Prof. Nathaniel Southgate Shaler [*q.v.*] decided to make geology his career. He studied for a year at Harvard's Lawrence Scientific School, receiving the A.M. degree in 1886, and spent another year in the Harvard "Graduate Department." For part of this time he also worked in the Boston area for the Massachusetts Topographical Survey.

In June 1887 Keith joined the United States Geological Survey. His first duty was with a field mapping party in the Appalachian area of Tennessee as assistant to the geologist Bailey Willis. That fall he moved to the Survey's headquarters in Washington, D. C., where he helped prepare the map in final form from the field notes. From 1888 to 1895 he was in charge of his own field party as assistant geologist; in 1895 he was promoted to the rank of geologist. Over the next two decades, alternating summer surveying trips with winter preparation of reports, Keith concentrated on the geological structure of the Appalachian Mountain chain. By 1906 he had compiled some fifteen folios for the *Geological Atlas of the United States,* comprising detailed maps and geological descriptions of more than 15,000 square miles of the mountain region from Maryland south to Tennessee and the Carolinas, one of the most structurally complex in the United States.

In 1906 Keith was placed in charge of the Geological Survey's mapping program for the entire United States. When in 1912 the work was subdivided into two parts, east and west of the 100th meridian, he continued to direct the eastern section. In 1921 he gave up this administrative work and returned to full-time research, now chiefly on the central and northern parts of the Appalachian Mountain system. After officially retiring in 1934, at the age of seventy, he continued to work in the field and extended his study of the Appalachians by expeditions to New England and into the Canadian province of Quebec.

Keith's quadrangle reports, maps, and short articles contained an immense amount of stratigraphic and structural data, the results of his field work. His primary interest was factual rather than theoretical, but from his field observations he did evolve a general theory on the origin of the Appalachians which he first advanced, with characteristic modesty, in his "Outlines of Appalachian Structure" (Geological Society of America, *Bulletin,* June 1923). Keith proposed that batholithic intrusions had furnished the heat and force required to form the mountain belt. The force of these intrusions, he reasoned, caused pressure from the Atlantic floor against the margin of the continent, resulting in deformation of the geosynclinal sediments to the west. One section of the paper was headed "Suboceanic spread"; nearly fifty years later, sea-floor spreading was a topic of current discussion in geological circles. In his presidential address to the Geological Society of America in 1927 ("Structural Symmetry in North America," *ibid.,* March 1928), Keith expanded his theory and applied it to the entire North American continent.

On several occasions Keith was called upon to assist in matters of public policy. A special report he prepared on the resources of the southern Appalachians and their conservation was used by Theodore Roosevelt in a message to Congress in 1902. During World War I he made a report on features of possible military importance along the northern boundary of New England, and in 1933, for the Tennessee Valley Authority, he examined the site of Norris Dam. He was elected to the National Academy of Sciences in 1928 and served as its treasurer from 1932 to 1940. During the years 1928–31 he was chairman of the Division of Geology and Geography of the National Research Council.

A scholarly New Englander who brought great diligence to his work, Keith set high standards for himself and expected the best from those who worked under him, yet at the same time was generous in his help. His work in the Appalachians places him in the front rank of field geologists. His theories, which he published only reluctantly, were based on the knowledge available at the time; it remains for history either to bear them out or to disprove them.

Keith made his home in Washington, D. C., with his mother until her death. He then married, on June 29, 1916, Elizabeth Marye Smith of Athens, Ohio, a graduate of the Washington College of Law, who usually accompanied him on field trips. They had no children. Keith was a Unitarian in religion. He died of cancer in a sanatorium at Silver Spring, Md., a few months before his eightieth birthday.

[Memoirs of Keith by Esper S. Larsen, Jr., in Geological Soc. of America, *Proc.*, 1944; by Chester R. Longwell in Nat. Acad. Sci., *Biog. Memoirs,* vol. XXIX (1956); and by Allyn C. Swinnerton in Am. Assoc. of Petroleum Geologists, *Bull.*, Oct. 1944 (each with portrait, and the first two with lists of his publications). See also: Keith's autobiographical statements in the published *Reports* of the Harvard College Class of 1885; *Am. Men of Sci.* (7th ed., 1944); *Who Was Who in America*, vol. II (1950). Death record from Md. Division of Vital Records. On his father, see obituary in *Boston Transcript,* June 8, 1911.]

MARJORIE HOOKER

KELLEY, EDGAR STILLMAN (Apr. 14, 1857–Nov. 12, 1944), composer, was born in Sparta, Wis., the older of two sons of Hiram Edgar Kelley, a merchant, afterward a newspaper editor and federal revenue officer, and Mary Clarinda (Bingham) Kelley. His father was a native of Connecticut, his mother of Vermont. On his father's side the boy was descended from William Kelley, a Rhode Islander who served in the Revolutionary War; on his mother's, from Thomas Bingham, an English settler in Connecticut in 1642.

Kelley began his musical education at the age of eight, when his mother, an accomplished musician, gave him his first piano lessons. Stimulated by hearing a concert by the Negro prodigy "Blind Tom" (Thomas Greene Bethune), he began serious study of the piano and during the period 1870–74 worked under Farwell W. Merriam. A visit to Chicago to hear performances by the pianist Anton Rubinstein and the violinist Henri Wieniawski, playing with the orchestra of Theodore Thomas [q.v.], strengthened Kelley's resolve to make music his career, and in 1874 he moved to that city and for two years studied piano with Napoleon Ledochowski, director of the Chicago Conservatory of Music, and harmony and counterpoint with Clarence Eddy [Supp. 2]. Wishing to perfect his musical skills in Germany, Kelley in 1876 enrolled as a student in the Stutt-

gart Conservatory, where his teachers were Max Seifriz (composition), Wilhelm Krüger (piano), and Friedrich Finck (organ); in 1878 he transferred to the conservatory of Wilhelm Speidel, with whom he studied piano.

After graduating from Speidel's conservatory in 1880, Kelley returned to the United States. He divided his time at first between the San Francisco area (1880–86, 1892–96) and New York City. During his early years in California he earned his living as a music teacher and church organist and intensified his efforts to compose. He first came to national attention on Aug. 3, 1883, when Theodore Thomas's orchestra performed his *Macbeth* overture in Chicago. Kelley's incidental music to the play was a factor in its successful San Francisco production in 1885. An interval as a light-opera conductor led to one of the biggest triumphs of his career: his *Puritania, or The Earl and the Maid of Salem,* with libretto by C. M. S. McLellan; produced by the Pauline Hall Opera Company, it opened in Boston on June 6, 1892, and ran for a hundred consecutive performances before going on tour. Kelley's "Aladdin" suite, based on his study of Chinese music in San Francisco, was first performed in that city on Feb. 9, 1894. He also composed the incidental music for William Young's dramatization of the Lew Wallace [q.v.] novel *Ben Hur,* first performed in New York City on Nov. 27, 1899, which remained a popular favorite for more than two decades.

While continuing his composing, Kelley held a variety of positions: music critic (*San Francisco Examiner,* 1893–95), teacher (New York College of Music, 1891–92; Yale, 1901–02), and lecturer (extension department of the University of the State of New York, 1896–1900). He returned to Germany in 1902 and for eight years taught piano and composition in Berlin, where his Piano Quintet (Opus 20) was first performed in December 1905.

On July 23, 1891, Kelley had married Jessie M. Gregg of San Francisco, one of his piano pupils and a talented musician; they had no children. In 1910 they left Berlin to accept positions at Western College for Women in Oxford, Ohio, where Mrs. Kelley served as director of music (1910–34) and Kelley became lecturer in music theory and holder of a fellowship in musical composition. The first such fellowship awarded to any composer in the United States, it enabled him to devote himself almost exclusively to creative work. In 1911 he accepted a concurrent appointment as head of the music theory department at the Cincinnati Conservatory of Music, where he usually spent one day a week teaching; he remained active in both positions until his retirement in 1934.

During this very productive period Kelley composed his Second or *New England* Symphony (first performed at Norfolk, Conn., June 13, 1913); an oratorio, *Pilgrim's Progress* (Cincinnati, May 10, 1918); and his "Alice in Wonderland" suite (Norfolk, Conn., June 5, 1919). His tone poem "The Pit and the Pendulum" was first performed at the May Festival in Cincinnati on May 9, 1925, and won the prize offered by the National Federation of Music Clubs for the best new American work for orchestra. His First Symphony, *Gulliver in Lilliput,* begun as early as 1893, was not completed until 1936 and was first presented in Cincinnati on Apr. 9, 1937; it was given a nationwide radio performance later that month by Walter Damrosch and the NBC Symphony Orchestra in honor of Kelley's eightieth birthday. Kelley was also the author of two books, *Chopin the Composer* (1913) and *Musical Instruments* (1925).

After 1934 Kelley made his home in New York City, though he paid occasional visits to Cincinnati. He received honorary degrees from Miami University (1916) and the University of Cincinnati (1917). He died in New York City at the age of eighty-seven.

Kelley was a composer of refinement and taste, with a bent for humor and the exotic. His compositions were mildly nationalistic in intent, though Teutonic in sound and technique; many were intended as musical representations of events in American history or tales by American writers such as Irving and Poe. He appears to have been strongly influenced by the music of Richard Strauss (of which he was a fervent admirer) and by Strauss's theories of program music. Kelley displayed great ingenuity in using music to suggest the sounds of battle, the galloping of horses, or the humorous spectacle of Gulliver falling asleep, but his work lacked the forward-looking elements found in such exceptional contemporaries as Igor Stravinsky and Charles Ives. Some of Kelley's scores achieved extraordinary popularity during his lifetime, and he was often considered the successor to Edward MacDowell [q.v.] as the leading American composer of his day. A quarter-century after his death, however, his music was all but unknown and appeared doomed to oblivion.

[The Kelley Papers are at Western College, Oxford, Ohio. Two doctoral dissertations offer the fullest account of his life and work: by Maurice R. King (Fla. State Univ., 1970) and by Leonard L. Rivenburg (Ohio State Univ., in progress). Published accounts of Kelley, mostly brief, include: William S. B. Mathews, *One Hundred Years of Music in America* (1889); Louis C. Elson, *The Hist. of Am.*

Music (1904); *Nat. Cyc. Am. Biog.,* XI, 388; W. Altmann in *Allgemeine Musik-Zeitung,* Mar. 27, 1908; Rupert Hughes, *Am. Composers* (1914); César Saerchinger, *Internat. Who's Who in Music* (1918); *Grove's Dict. of Music and Musicians* (3rd ed., 1927) and its *Am. Supp.* (1928); *N. Y. Times* obituary, Nov. 13, 1944; *Baker's Biog. Dict. of Musicians* (5th ed., 1958); and John Tasker Howard, *Our Am. Music* (4th ed., 1965). Family data from census schedules of 1860 and 1870 (courtesy of State Hist. Soc. of Wis.), which list him as Stillman E. Kelley.]

                                        IRVING LOWENS

KELLOGG, JOHN HARVEY (Feb. 26, 1852–Dec. 14, 1943), surgeon and health propagandist, originator of flaked cereals, was born in Tyrone Township, Livingston County, Mich., the first son and fourth of the eight children of John Preston Kellogg and Ann Janette (Stanley) Kellogg who survived infancy. His father, who also had five children by a previous marriage, had moved to the Michigan frontier in 1834 from Hadley, Mass., where the family had farmed for five generations. His second wife, a former schoolteacher, proved adept at managing money and also persuaded her husband to adopt superior farming methods. Kellogg was an abolitionist and a temperance advocate. He was a Baptist and then a Congregationalist before becoming, in 1852, a convert to the Seventh-day Adventist Church. Shortly thereafter the family moved to Jackson, Mich., and, when John Harvey was four, to Battle Creek, soon to become Adventist world headquarters. Here the senior Kellogg operated a small grocery store and broom factory.

Although John's upbringing was strict, and the religious atmosphere "sad and solemn," it was not unusually repressive. As a youth he spent more time in the broom factory than in school, but he compensated for a limited formal education by reading into the early morning hours. At the age of twelve he began learning the printing trade in the Adventist publishing house, and in the next four years progressed from printer's devil to editorial assistant. At this time Ellen G. White [q.v.], the leader of the church, was encouraging Seventh-day Adventists to accept many health reform principles as part of their religious duty. As John set type for her first articles on health, he decided to adopt the practices she advocated, including vegetarianism. Later he read extensively in the works of such health reformers as Sylvester Graham and Dio Lewis [qq.v.]. From these predecessors he gradually developed a system of preventive "natural" medicine which he promulgated vigorously for over sixty years.

A childhood ambition to become an educator led Kellogg at sixteen to spend a year teaching a rural school. Subsequently he finished his high school course at Battle Creek and in 1872 enrolled in the teacher training program at Michigan State Normal College in Ypsilanti. That same year church leaders sponsored him in a five-month course at Dr. Russell Trall's Hygeio-Therapeutic College in Florence Heights, N. J. Rejecting the Trall system, Kellogg turned to a career in orthodox medicine. After a year at the University of Michigan Medical School, he transferred to Bellevue Hospital Medical College in New York City, where he took his degree in 1875 with a thesis arguing that disease is a natural defense mechanism of the body.

While still a medical student, Kellogg became editor of the Adventist monthly the *Health Reformer*, whose name he changed in 1879 to *Good Health*. From then until his death, scarcely an issue appeared which did not contain several articles and editorials from his pen. In 1876 he became medical superintendent of the Western Health Reform Institute in Battle Creek, which the Adventists had founded ten years earlier in an effort to provide medical treatment emphasizing natural and rational remedies. Kellogg soon began a concerted campaign to publicize the Institute, which he renamed the Battle Creek Sanitarium, himself choosing the last word, which he defined as "a place where people learn to stay well."

At the Sanitarium, Kellogg applied his health teachings, which he called "biologic living" or "the Battle Creek Idea." He advocated total abstinence from alcoholic beverages, tea, coffee, chocolate, tobacco, and condiments. He favored discarding all meat and using milk, cheese, eggs, and refined sugars sparingly, if at all. Man's natural foods, Kellogg claimed, were nuts, fruits, legumes, and whole grains. These should be thoroughly chewed (for a time Horace Fletcher [q.v.] was associated with Kellogg) and eaten in moderation. Obesity was to be shunned as the plague. Kellogg was always suspicious of drugs. He maintained that the best medicine was a reformed diet, sensible clothing, correct posture, and a program of regular exercise and rest, with liberal exposure to fresh air and sunshine. He was also enthusiastic over the curative effects of a variety of water treatments. During the last third of his life Kellogg dressed completely in white. He insisted that this was for health purposes, but many believed it was a clever way of calling attention to himself and his ideas.

To a much larger degree than earlier health reformers, Kellogg attempted to construct a scientific foundation under his teachings. Partly to provide this foundation through surveying medical practices abroad, and partly also to perfect his skill in surgery, Kellogg made repeated trips to Europe, where he studied under prominent

medical men. His sharp mind and great manual dexterity allowed him to develop into a skilled surgeon. In the 1890's he set a record of 165 successive abdominal operations without a fatality. Part of his success may have been due to the antishock measures he insisted upon and a program of bed exercises which he originated to help prevent postoperative complications. In the course of his career Kellogg performed over 22,000 operations. He assigned all surgical fees to the Battle Creek Sanitarium, or similar institutions, for use in the treatment of charity cases or for health propaganda. He was elected to the American College of Surgeons in 1914.

For the first two decades of his health crusade, Kellogg enjoyed wide Adventist support, though his domineering and fault-finding manner was often reproved by Ellen White. She and other church leaders also expressed doubts about the wisdom of concentrating Adventist health and education facilities in Battle Creek, and urged Kellogg to curb his desire for ever-expanding programs. Kellogg, who needed little sleep, regularly worked sixteen or eighteen hours a day and gave generously of his time and money to these new projects; he expected the church to keep pace with his plans. These policy differences were exacerbated by his combative and suspicious temperament and by religious issues. His increasing emphasis on the nonsectarian and purely humanitarian nature of Adventist-sponsored projects, his theological departures, and his accusations of meddling against prominent Adventists produced deep divisions within the leadership. After several open clashes, Kellogg was excommunicated on Nov. 10, 1907, and subsequently waged battles with the church over control of the Sanitarium.

That institution prospered under Kellogg's direction. In the early decades of the twentieth century, hundreds of prominent Americans, from the financial wizard C. W. Barron to industrialists like John H. Patterson [qq.v.] and merchants like J. C. Penney, regularly came to Battle Creek to be rejuvenated through the Sanitarium program of diet, exercise, and hydrotherapy, and Kellogg, with his public relations skills, made their presence known. The Sanitarium's patients had multiplied to 1,200 by the 1920's, the period of its heyday. Even the sanguine Kellogg, however, opposed the new additions, including a fifteen-story tower, that the directors voted to build in 1927. The debt forced the Sanitarium into receivership when the depression cut down patronage, and it never recaptured its past prosperity.

Kellogg had established an experimental food laboratory at the Sanitarium in an effort to develop a wide variety of nutritious food products. There, in the early 1890's, he developed the first flaked cereal by feeding cooked wheat through a pair of rollers and scraping the flakes from the rollers with a bread knife. He enlisted the help of his younger brother, Will Keith, then serving as Sanitarium business manager, and they applied the process also to corn and rice. Will soon went on to make corn flakes the cornerstone of a multi-million-dollar prepared breakfast-food industry, following the promotional example of C. W. Post [q.v.], who, while a patient at the Sanitarium, saw the possibilities in an imitation coffee and a cereal patterned after an earlier Kellogg creation, Granola. Other products of Kellogg's food laboratory included a variety of imitation meats prepared from nuts and wheat gluten, various coffee substitutes, peanut butter, and an artificial milk made from soy beans. Strong policy differences with Will led to a split of the brothers' food manufacturing interests, and in a series of lawsuits Will secured the right to market his products under the Kellogg name. John established the rival Battle Creek Food Company, but it never achieved equal success.

A prolific author, Kellogg incorporated his health ideas into nearly fifty popular books and a host of technical papers. His early sex education manual, *Plain Facts about Sexual Life* (1877), sold over half a million copies in various editions, and *Rational Hydrotherapy* (1901) received wide acceptance in medical circles. Kellogg also lectured from coast to coast before large audiences. He spoke rapidly and convincingly and used a wealth of scientific data which awed most laymen. His propagandistic abilities were enlisted in the field of public health as a member of the Michigan State Board of Health (1879–91 and 1911–17).

On Feb. 22, 1879, Kellogg married Ella Ervilla Eaton of Alfred Center, N. Y. For over forty years she served as his chief literary assistant and collaborated in his food experiments, besides taking an active role in the national Woman's Christian Temperance Union. The couple had no children, but they reared forty-two foster children, a small fraction of whom were legally adopted.

With Adventist support, Kellogg in 1895 founded the American Medical Missionary College in Chicago to train doctors in "rational" medical techniques. Fifteen years later, following his expulsion from the Adventist Church, it merged with the University of Illinois Medical School. At the Battle Creek Sanitarium, Kellogg developed schools of nursing, physical education, and home economics. These were combined with a liberal arts program in 1923 to form Battle Creek College; during its fifteen-year existence

the doctor's earnings from his food creations provided the college's major support. In 1914 Kellogg created the Race Betterment Foundation, also endowed with Battle Creek Food Company stock, to promote his new interest in eugenics.

During his long life, Dr. Kellogg saw his cereal creations revolutionize the average American breakfast. His many and diverse activities helped focus public attention on the importance of diet, cleanliness, exercise, fresh air, and rest in maintaining health. He was planning new endeavors when, in December 1943, he suffered an acute attack of bronchitis. Pneumonia developed, and he died in Battle Creek at the age of ninety-one. He was buried in Oak Hill Cemetery, Battle Creek.

[Richard W. Schwarz, *John Harvey Kellogg, M.D.* (1970), is the fullest account of Kellogg's life and work. Significant obituaries are found in the *Battle Creek Enquirer and News,* Dec. 15, 1943, and the *Jour. Am. Medic. Assoc.,* Dec. 25, 1943. For his genealogy, see Timothy Hopkins, *The Kelloggs in the Old World and the New* (1903). Kellogg's basic ideas and activities can be traced in his voluminous writings, particularly in *Good Health* (1878–1944). The best summary of his health philosophy is his *How to Have Good Health through Biologic Living* (1932). Substantial Kellogg MS. collections are in the Mich. Hist. Collections, Univ. of Mich., and the Museum, Mich. State Univ., East Lansing. Popular accounts of Kellogg and his health crusade, accurate in spirit but not in detail, are found in Gerald Carson, *Cornflake Crusade* (1957), and Ronald M. Deutsch, *The Nuts among the Berries* (1961).]

RICHARD W. SCHWARZ

KELLY, HOWARD ATWOOD (Feb. 20, 1858–Jan. 12, 1943), gynecologist and surgeon, was born at Camden, N. J., to Henry Kuhl Kelly, a prosperous Philadelphia sugar broker, and his wife, Louisa Warner Hard, daughter of an Episcopal clergyman. Howard was the second of their six children, of whom the oldest—the only other boy—died in infancy. His father was descended from Thomas Kelly, a North of Ireland convert from Anglicanism to the Methodist Church, who settled in Philadelphia in the mid-eighteenth century. Through his maternal grandmother, Howard Kelly was a descendant of Michael Hillegas [q.v.], first Treasurer of the United States. Growing up in Philadelphia, Kelly developed an early interest in natural history through his nature-loving mother and a family friend, the entomologist John L. Le Conte [q.v.]. While attending Faires Classical Institute, he became a competent amateur naturalist under the guidance of Edward D. Cope [q.v.] of the Philadelphia Academy of Natural Sciences, of which the boy became a member at the age of seventeen. In these adolescent years he also evinced deeply evangelical religious feelings. It was a presage of his whole career that when he was twenty years old his mother gave him a handsome Bible and his father a microscope.

As an undergraduate at the University of Pennsylvania, Kelly not only made an all-around high record in both classical and scientific studies, but also continued his outdoor activities by going on long camping trips. He wished to become a naturalist but gave up the idea because of his father's objections and, after receiving his A.B. degree in 1877, entered the medical school of the University of Pennsylvania. In the last year of medical study, overwork and persistent insomnia brought a breakdown of health, and in February 1881, only two months before graduation, he left school to spend a year recuperating at a ranch in Colorado.

Returning to Philadelphia, Kelly was graduated in medicine in 1882 and became a resident physician at the Episcopal Hospital in Kensington, a populous North Philadelphia district. His devotion to the laboring classes of Kensington and a rapidly developing interest in gynecological surgery led him about 1884 to establish a special hospital that was later incorporated as the Kensington Hospital for Women. By this time the introduction of antiseptic surgery and advances in pathology and bacteriology had made possible the surgical treatment of abdominal and pelvic diseases in women. Kelly was particularly fitted for this specialty by his broad biological knowledge, his extraordinary manual dexterity, and the "affectionate consideration" with which he treated his patients. In 1886–89 he made several visits to Europe to observe gynecological work, especially in Germany. At home he began to attract professional attention through the skill and boldness of his operations. Following methods learned in Germany, he performed the first successful caesarian section in Philadelphia under antiseptic conditions; the operation had been abandoned fifty years before because of the risk of infection.

The University of Pennsylvania now began to think of adding Kelly to its medical faculty. William Osler [q.v.] was attracted to him through their mutual interest in the history of medicine and their love of old medical books. Largely through Osler's influence, Kelly in 1888 was appointed associate professor of obstetrics with the right of succession to the chair of gynecology. The next year, however, Osler went to Baltimore to the newly opened Johns Hopkins Hospital, and on his recommendation Kelly was called there as gynecologist-in-chief as well as professor of gynecology in the projected medical school of the Johns Hopkins University, which

opened in 1893, when Kelly was thirty-five years old.

Gathering around him able associates, Kelly made his clinic famous in this country and abroad. Visitors to his operating room found him the most skillful abdominal surgeon they had ever seen, combining extreme dexterity with speed and decisiveness. He and his staff based their diagnosis and treatment on the modern pathology of infectious disease and tumors. Kelly himself devised many instruments and procedures, including the "Kelly pad" for obstetrical and surgical tables (introduced in his Kensington days and now widely used), the bisection method for excising the densely adherent uterus, an ingenious method of catheterizing the ureters via the air-filled bladder, and numerous diagnostic procedures in urology.

As a teacher of medical students, Kelly preferred to offer clinical examinations and operating-room demonstrations, at which he was dramatically effective, but he also gave occasional informal talks. At least a score of men went out from his Johns Hopkins staff to become professors in leading medical schools. Alone or with colleagues, he wrote valuable handbooks on surgical and medical gynecology, abdominal surgery, and urology. To assure accurate and artistic illustration of these books he employed Max Brödel [Supp. 3], who became America's most distinguished medical illustrator; through Brödel and other artists Kelly greatly improved American standards of surgical illustration.

Kelly soon acquired a national reputation and an extensive private practice. In 1892 he took over a small private sanatorium near his home on Eutaw Place, Baltimore, which he developed into a large hospital and clinic. There at his own expense he experimented enthusiastically with new scientific aids to surgery. He had, for example, the first X-ray apparatus used in Baltimore for diagnostic purposes. About 1903, when the medical uses of radium became apparent, he was one of the first American physicians to employ it in treating cancer. After several purchases of radium from Europe, he personally invested a large sum in a project to extract radium from Colorado ore, which provided ample supplies for his own institution and others. In his last years as a surgeon he took a similar interest in the development of electrosurgery. He was president of the American Gynecological Society in 1912.

Kelly's importance in the early development of the Johns Hopkins Hospital and School of Medicine is commemorated by his inclusion, along with Osler, William H. Welch, and William S.

Halsted [*qq.v.*], in the famous group portrait "Four Doctors," painted by John Singer Sargent [*q.v.*] in 1905 (now in the Welch Medical Library at Johns Hopkins). Kelly's outside activities and the busy practice of his sanatorium, however, somewhat limited his participation in the school's affairs, and his religious evangelism set him a little apart from his associates, despite their respect and admiration for his surgical and organizational talents. He continued to hold his positions at the medical school and hospital until 1919. The school, after considerable debate, had adopted a policy that clinical professors must give full time to teaching and research, and Kelly, unwilling to give up his hospital and his private practice, chose to resign, at the age of sixty-one.

At his home near the Kelly Clinic he kept his extensive collections—mineralogical specimens, snakes living and preserved, natural history paintings—and a valuable library of old and rare books on early medicine and surgery, early Bibles and theological works, and books on herpetology, mycology, and lichenology. Well qualified for historical studies—he read Greek, Hebrew, Latin, and several modern languages—and aided by a succession of able secretary-librarians, he published many articles, chiefly biographical, on the history of medicine, and wrote or edited several books, of which the most important is the *Dictionary of American Medical Biography* (with Walter L. Burrage, 1928).

Dr. Kelly believed in standing on one's own feet in this world and getting to Heaven by Christian faith and good works. He charged high fees to wealthy patients but treated the poor for nothing, generously supported numerous public philanthropies and missionary enterprises, and unostentatiously carried on extensive private charities. He was a lay reader in the Episcopal Church and often preached in Baptist, Methodist, and Presbyterian pulpits. His religion gave him his answers to many problems of the day and made him a lifelong moral crusader. In 1895, as a watcher at the polls for the Baltimore Reform League, he was physically assaulted but paid the fine of one of his attackers. He actively worked for the repressive Sabbatarian program of the Lord's Day Alliance, cheerfully accepting the gibes of faculty colleagues. When, after a long civic campaign, Baltimore's houses of prostitution were closed, Dr. Kelly financially supported a home for women seeking rehabilitation. An ardent prohibitionist, he backed the Anti-Saloon League. In view of his great professional reputation, these religiously motivated reform interests drew much newspaper attention. The irreverent comments of Henry L. Mencken in the Baltimore *Sun* in particular greatly amused local readers and even Dr. Kelly himself, who often good-naturedly retorted in kind while proposing to pray for his witty antagonist.

On June 27, 1889, while in Germany, Kelly had married Laetitia Bredow, daughter of a physician of Stettin. They had nine children—Olga Elizabeth Bredow, Henry Kuhl, Esther Warner, Friederich Heyn, Howard Atwood, William Boulton, Margaret Kuhl, Edmund Bredow, and Laetitia Bredow—of whom only the youngest son became a physician. An expert canoeist and strong swimmer, Kelly long kept up his outdoor activities at his summer camp on Ahmic Lake in Ontario. His sturdy physique enabled him to continue his surgical work to the age of eighty. He died five years later at Union Memorial Hospital in Baltimore, of arteriosclerosis and uremia. His wife, who had been an invalid for several years, died a few hours afterward; they were buried in Woodlawn Cemetery, Baltimore.

[Audrey W. Davis, *Doctor Kelly of Hopkins* (1959), a biography by his longtime secretary-librarian; articles about Kelly in *Bull. of the Johns Hopkins Hospital*, XXX (1919), 287–93 (by Thomas S. Cullen, with portraits and a bibliography to 1919), LIII (1933), 65–109, and LXXIII (1943), 1–22 (by Curtis F. Burnam); George W. Corner, "Howard A. Kelly as a Medical Historian," *Bull. of the Hist. of Medicine,* July 1943 (with complete bibliography of his books and papers in medical history and biography); Willard E. Goodwin, "William Osler and Howard A. Kelly," *ibid.*, Dec. 1946.]

GEORGE W. CORNER

KEMMERER, EDWIN WALTER (June 29, 1875–Dec. 16, 1945), economist, was born in Scranton, Pa., the eldest of the six children of Martha Hanna (Courtright) and Lorenzo Dow Kemmerer. Both parents were of colonial stock; the father, a railroad yardmaster, was descended from Johannes Nicholas Kemmerer, who came to America from the German Palatinate in 1742. When Edwin was fifteen the family moved to nearby Factoryville, where he attended Keystone Academy. He then worked his way through Wesleyan University, where he specialized in economics, and upon graduation in 1899 won a fellowship to Cornell. After two years of graduate work under Prof. Jeremiah W. Jenks [*q.v.*], Kemmerer became an instructor in economics and history at Purdue University. On Dec. 24, 1901, he married Minnie Rachel Dickele of New Haven, Conn. They had two children, Donald Lorenzo and Ruth.

Kemmerer developed an early interest in monetary theory. His senior thesis as an undergraduate was a defense of the quantity theory of money, which finds a correlation between the money supply and general price levels; and in his doctoral dissertation, later published as *Money and Credit Instruments in Their Relation to General Prices* (1907), he devised statistical methods to support his arguments. Kemmerer was awarded the Ph.D. in 1903. That same year, on the recommendation of Professor Jenks, he was appointed financial adviser to the United States Philippine Commission. He drafted the Gold Standard Act under which the Philippine currency was reorganized, and from 1904 to 1906 he was chief of the Division of Currency of the islands' government. Upon returning to the United States in 1906, Kemmerer became assistant professor of political economy at Cornell. He advanced in 1909 to professor. In 1912 he moved to Princeton University, where he remained until his retirement in 1943.

In later writings Kemmerer further developed his theories of money and banking. In *Seasonal Variations in the Relative Demand for Money and Capital in the United States* (1910) he concluded that the American currency system was generally unresponsive to fluctuations in demand, and he thereafter worked vigorously for the establishment of a central banking system. When such a system was created in 1913, he wrote a popular book, *The A.B.C. of the Federal Reserve System* (1918), to increase public interest in its operations. Kemmerer codified most of his theories in 1935 in his textbook *Money: The Principles of Money and Their Exemplification in Outstanding Chapters of Monetary History.*

Kemmerer is best known for the series of missions he undertook as an adviser to underdeveloped countries on financial matters, missions which won him international renown as the "money doctor." In the summer of 1917 he served as counselor to the government of Mexico and in 1919 to Guatemala. Three years later he toured seven Latin American countries, where he made a favorable impression as a perceptive and intelligible analyst of their economic problems. Over the next decade he headed financial missions to Colombia (1923, 1930), Chile (1925), Poland (1926), Ecuador (1926–27), Bolivia (1927), China (1929), and Peru (1931), and was co-chairman of missions to South Africa (1924) and Turkey (1934). He served in 1924 as banking and monetary expert of the Dawes Commission on European reparations. Kemmerer's recommendations to underdeveloped countries followed a broadly uniform pattern, but with skillful adaptation to local conditions: exchange stabilization, usually with some form of the gold exchange standard; establishment of a central bank; regulation of commercial banks; tax simpli-

fication and a balanced budget; more modern government accounting and budgetary practices. It was a simple formula, but until the onslaught of the Great Depression it worked well. In the light of history, Kemmerer has been criticized for imposing a gold standard upon underdeveloped countries, but the main reason countries called upon him in the 1920's was that they suffered from politically managed currencies and wanted advice on how to stabilize exchange rates.

Kemmerer's trip to South America in 1922 had strengthened his view that inflation was the great monetary disease. The idea that the common man in particular had suffered from inflation was central to his approach, and in all countries he attempted to get labor's opinion on monetary problems. He found it difficult to adjust his thinking to the new economic conditions brought on by the depression. The gold standard had been swept away and deflation and unemployment had become the major problems, but Kemmerer continued to regard inflation as the prime danger. He spoke out against the monetary and fiscal policies of the Roosevelt administration, and as late as 1944 he suggested a postwar plan for the rehabilitation of the world monetary system under the gold standard.

Friendly and outgoing, Kemmerer had a wide circle of friends. His concern with the professional standing of the college teacher led him to take part in the founding of the American Association of University Professors in 1913. Among the honors that came to him were the presidency of the American Economic Association (1926) and degrees from universities in Ecuador and Bolivia, as well as from Occidental College, Oglethorpe University, Wesleyan, Rutgers, and Columbia. He died at the age of seventy in Princeton, N. J., following a heart attack, and was buried in the Princeton cemetery. His will left substantial bequests to Scranton-Keystone Junior College, Wesleyan, Cornell, and Princeton.

[Kemmerer Papers, in Manuscript Division of Princeton Univ. Lib.; reports of Kemmerer's missions in Internat. Finance Section of the same library; Christian Gauss, "The Education of Walter Kemmerer," *Saturday Evening Post*, Apr. 14, 1934; obituary in *Am. Economic Rev.*, Mar. 1946, pp. 219–21; Joseph Dorfman, *The Economic Mind in Am. Civilization*, vol. IV (1959); *Who Was Who in America*, vol. II (1950); Kemmerer Family Assoc., *Two Centuries of Kemmerer Family Hist.* (1929); personal acquaintance.]

FRANK W. FETTER

KENNEY, MARY. See O'SULLIVAN, MARY KENNEY.

KEPHART, JOHN WILLIAM (Nov. 12, 1872–Aug. 6, 1944), jurist, was born in Wilmore, Cambria County, Pa., the fourth son and fourth of five children of Samuel and Henrietta (Wolfe) Kephart and a descendant of John Kephart, who came in 1750 from the Upper Rhineland to Berks County, Pa. His father, a Civil War veteran, was an itinerant country storekeeper. He died in 1874, and three years later Kephart's mother, to further her children's education, placed them in the Soldiers Orphans School in McAllisterville, Pa.

After graduating in 1889 as valedictorian of his class, Kephart worked briefly as timekeeper with a construction gang and then as a telegrapher for the Pennsylvania Railroad. He enrolled in 1890 at Allegheny College, but lack of funds forced him to withdraw after two terms and return to the railroad. Impressed by his industry, interested officials in the company arranged a work schedule that permitted him to attend Dickinson Law School in Carlisle, Pa.; he graduated there in 1894.

Kephart opened a practice in Ebensburg, Cambria County, and was soon retained by the Pennsylvania Railroad as its county attorney. On Dec. 1, 1904, he married Florence May Evans, daughter of Alvin Evans, a local lawyer, bank president, and Republican Congressman. They had three children: Alvin Evans, Henrietta, and John William. In 1906 Kephart became Cambria County solicitor, a position he held for eight years. In 1913 he decided to seek election to the county court but, failing to win the endorsement of the local Republican party, ran instead as an independent candidate for the state superior court. He used the novel technique of sending a personal message by postcard to every registered voter in the state, and was elected to one of the two vacant seats, having finished second in a field of four. During his four years on the superior court, Kephart heard some three thousand cases and wrote four hundred opinions.

In 1918, this time with Republican support, Kephart won election to the Pennsylvania supreme court. Of the 1,100 opinions he wrote on this bench, a few became well known. His dissent in *Mahon* v. *Pennsylvania Coal Company* (274 Pa. 489 [1922]), on the limits of a state's power to appropriate private property, without compensation, under the police power, was adopted by the United States Supreme Court; it was subsequently cited as precedent to demonstrate that the due process clause of the Fourteenth Amendment imposes the same obligations on the states as the Fifth Amendment does on the federal government. Kephart wrote the basic decision allowing appeals from rulings of such state administrative agencies as the Public Service Commission, *In re Relief*

Electric Light, Heat, and Power Company's Petition (63 Pa. Super. 1 [1916]). He also wrote the leading Pennsylvania decision upholding the rights of peaceful picketing in labor disputes, *Jefferson and Indiana Coal Company* v. *Marks* (287 Pa. 171 [1926]), and extended the liability of employers under the Pennsylvania workmen's compensation act.

Kephart's proven abilities as a vote-getter led to Republican proposals that he run for the United States Senate in 1928 and 1940 and for governor in 1931, but he declined all such bids. In 1933 he came under criticism for allegedly purchasing stock through J. Pierpont Morgan [Supp. 3] at a price below the market. In what was widely regarded as a political move, Gov. Gifford Pinchot called for his resignation. Kephart remained on the court, and in 1936 became through seniority the chief justice. While in this position, he pushed through the state legislature a statute (1937) giving the court authority to prescribe by general rule the practice and procedure in civil actions of the state's trial courts.

After his retirement in 1940, Kephart practiced law with his sons (who later formed the leading Philadelphia firm of Stassen and Kephart) and served as special counsel to the Pennsylvania Railroad and to Denis Cardinal Dougherty, Roman Catholic archbishop of Philadelphia. (Kephart himself was a Lutheran.) He also participated in the campaign to nominate Wendell Willkie [Supp. 3] as Republican candidate for the presidency. An ardent horseman, he spent his summers in Montana, where he owned a ranch. He died at the age of seventy-one in his rooms in the Warwick Hotel in Philadelphia from second-degree burns suffered when he inadvertently scalded himself while taking a shower. He was buried in Lloyd's Cemetery, Ebensburg, Pa.

["Proc. in the Supreme Court of Pa. in Memory of Former Chief Justice John W. Kephart, Sept. 25, 1944" (350 Pa., xxiii–xxxii); W. H. Hitchler in *Dickinson Law Rev.*, Jan. 1945; *Martindale's Am. Law Directory*, 1914; *Who Was Who in America*, vol. II (1950); *Nat. Cyc. Am. Biog.*, XXXVII, 119 (with portrait); obituaries in *Pittsburgh Post-Gazette* and *N. Y. Times*, Aug. 7, 1944. For a recent view of Kephart's labor decisions, see *Pa. Law Encyc.* (1961), "Workmen's Compensation," sec. 3.]
EARL FINBAR MURPHY

KEPPEL, FREDERICK PAUL (July 2, 1875–Feb. 8, 1943), college dean, foundation executive, was born at Staten Island, N. Y., the first of two sons of Frederick and Frances Matilda (Vickery) Keppel. Both parents were natives of Ireland. His father came of an English Methodist family of Dutch extraction that had emigrated to Canada; moving to Utica, N. Y., and then to New York City, he became an art dealer, specializing in prints and engravings. Young Frederick grew up in a happy upper-middle-class family in Yonkers, N. Y., where he attended public schools. Since his father wished his sons to have some business experience before college, he worked for two years, after high school, in the stock room of the family firm. He entered Columbia University in 1894; an excellent student, involved in a wide variety of college activities, he received the A.B. degree in 1898.

Keppel's literary and philosophical bent led him next to an editorial position with the publishing firm of Harper & Brothers. Within two years, however, he was called back to Columbia as assistant secretary (1900–02) and then secretary (1902–10). In 1910 he became dean of Columbia College, at thirty-five the youngest ever named. Though he succeeded the legendary "Van Am"— John Howard Van Amringe [q.v.]—Keppel quickly left his mark on Columbia. His constant desire was to maintain a small college atmosphere in which a student's particular problems could be dealt with sympathetically and his individual potential fulfilled. To these ends, he was instrumental in creating a student advisory system; he successfully urged the appointment of a university physician; he encouraged student self-government; and he made continual efforts to recruit faculty who would be vital, enthusiastic, and approachable. His own "open door" policy of ready accessibility became known throughout the university and won the warm regard of the students.

When the United States entered World War I, Keppel took a leave of absence from Columbia to become a confidential clerk to Secretary of War Newton D. Baker [Supp. 2]. Within a year he was promoted to the newly created post of Third Assistant Secretary of War "in charge of all non-military matters concerning the lives of soldiers," a post in which he demonstrated a humane efficiency. On the termination of hostilities Keppel became vice-chairman and director of foreign relations for the American Red Cross (1919–20), and then the American delegate to the International Chamber of Commerce, with offices in Paris. In December 1922, soon after his return, he was appointed president of the Carnegie Corporation of New York, a foundation established in 1911 by Andrew Carnegie [q.v.] for the "advancement and diffusion of knowledge" and, until 1919, personally directed by Carnegie.

F.P.K., as Keppel became known within the Corporation, was superbly fitted by temperament and experience to guide its formative independent years. His strong sense of duty and his deep interest in people meant that he gave personal consideration to the many requests for aid that flowed in, receiving them with sympathetic friendliness yet able to form a quick intuitional judgment. His role, however, was never wholly passive. He believed that the Corporation should itself take the initiative in discovering new outlets for philanthropy. Imagination and creativity were his goals. Wary of bureaucratic rigidity, he placed great reliance on frequent consultation with outside groups, such as learned societies and professional organizations; and he maintained the Corporation's flexibility by avoiding long-term commitments and courageously halting grants when careful audits suggested diminishing returns. A longtime opponent of overspecialization in foundation giving, Keppel preferred to spread the resources widely and to encourage the unorthodox dissenter. At times this policy was wasteful, and it was often difficult to justify publicly; but occasionally it was dramatically successful. Among Keppel's "hunches" were grants which led to the discovery of insulin and to the writing of Gunnar Myrdal's report on the American Negro.

Certain areas of Carnegie Corporation giving reflected Keppel's personal interests. His basic hope was to foster "general education," by which he meant a process of learning which continued throughout life. The most daring expression of this impulse was his encouragement of the adult education movement. After an initial conference in 1924, the Carnegie Corporation was able to launch, two years later, the American Association for Adult Education, and through this new organization it channeled annual grants for studies and demonstrations. An equally novel field of philanthropic activity was the Corporation's encouragement of the fine arts. Doubtless influenced by his father, and aware of the growing importance of leisure in American life, Keppel was less concerned with training professional artists than in arousing a new appreciation of art among the general public through the sponsorship of exhibitions and museum art classes. He also established a special program of fellowships which financed the graduate training of nearly all the generation's outstanding teachers. Finally, Keppel fostered general education through the Corporation's continued interest in improving the quality and usefulness of American libraries. In particular he was largely responsible for the creation of the University of Chicago Graduate Library School.

Keppel was never oblivious of the social dangers in philanthropic giving. He sympathized with fears that the foundation might autocratically come to control learning and direct opinion, and he viewed the private endowment as a public trust whose officers were responsible to society. Since he believed that public confidence could only be based on public knowledge, he published annual reports which were noted for their lucid, searching commentaries. In addition, a steady stream of perceptive articles and books flowed from his pen. Two books, *The Foundation: Its Place in American Life* (1930) and *Philanthropy and Learning* (1936), were trail-blazing essays on the role of philanthropy in America.

Keppel married, on Jan. 31, 1906, Helen Tracy Brown, of New York City. They had five sons: Frederick Paul, Charles Tracy, David, Gordon, and Francis. The family eventually settled at Bally Vale, an attractive country home at Montrose, N. Y. Here Keppel liked to relax. He would fish and swim in adjacent waters, and plant trees to create pleasant vistas. Keppel was a member of a number of clubs; his favorite was the Century in New York, and when in the city he usually lunched there. Among his many honors were degrees from ten universities, including Columbia, Harvard, and St. Andrews (Scotland), and the French government's award of the Legion of Honor.

Keppel retired as president of the Carnegie Corporation in October 1941, but continued as a consultant, and again served the government, first as a member of the President's Committee on War Relief Agencies and then as a member of the State Department's Board of Appeals on Visa Cases. The latter had been set up to deal with the large number of refugees seeking to enter this country from a war-torn Europe. While returning to New York from a meeting of this board in Washington, he suffered a heart attack and died later the same day in New York City. After Episcopal services, he was buried at Montrose, N. Y.

[Besides his annual reports and his two books cited above, see Keppel's *The Arts in Am. Life* (with Robert L. Duffus, 1933), and his articles "Opportunities and Dangers of Educational Foundations," *School and Society*, Dec. 26, 1925; "The Adult Education Movement," *Current Hist.*, Jan. 1928; and "Responsibility of Endowments in the Promotion of Knowledge," Am. Philosophical Soc., *Proc.*, 1937. See also: Horace Coon, *Columbia: Colossus on the Hudson* (1947); Brenda Jubin, *Carnegie Corporation Program in the Arts, 1911–67* (1968). Biographical sources: David Keppel, *FPK* (privately printed, 1950), which describes his family background and youth; Harry J. Carman et al., *Appreciations of Frederick Paul Keppel* (1951), essays on various facets of his career; *N. Y. Times* obituary, Sept. 9, 1943, and editorial, Sept. 10; information from Charles Dollard (a later president of the Carnegie Corporation) and Francis Keppel. On Keppel's father, see *Nat. Cyc. Am. Biog.*, XXII, 386.]
JOSEPH C. KIGER

KERN, JEROME DAVID (Jan. 27, 1885–Nov. 11, 1945), composer of stage and motion picture musicals, was born in New York City,

the youngest of three surviving sons of Henry and Fannie (Kakeles) Kern. Like many early twentieth-century composers, he came of a "respectable" middle-class Jewish family strongly rooted in European culture. His father, born in Baden-Baden, Germany, and reared in New York City, was a successful businessman; his mother, an American of Bohemian ancestry, gave him his first piano lessons when he was five.

Growing up in New York and, after 1895, in Newark, N. J., where his father headed a merchandising firm, young Kern graduated from high school in 1902 and went on to study piano and harmony at the New York College of Music. He took additional academic training in Germany in 1903 and then worked on musical comedies in London for the American producer Charles Frohman [*q.v.*]. Kern returned to the United States in 1904 and continued his interest in musicals, which were then characterized by frou-frou Viennese pastiche or hurdy-gurdy leg shows. Seeking a foothold in the musical world, he became a successful song "plugger" for a leading publisher, T. B. Harms. Soon the neatly dressed youth of nineteen, peering "soberly through his eyeglasses like a college professor," began to arrange for Harms and Shapiro-Bernstein; before long he was writing songs for interpolation into stale musicals.

By 1911 Kern was working on his own shows. His first success was *The Girl from Utah* (1914), which included his song "They Didn't Believe Me." Highly polished and yet warmly melodic, his music was more than conventionally pretty, and distinctly superior to the standard product. At this juncture the producer F. Ray Comstock, prompted by literary agent Elisabeth Marbury [Supp. 1], hired Kern to supply the scores for a series of musical comedies for his small Princess Theatre. With Guy Bolton and P. G. Wodehouse as librettists, Kern turned away from the conventional costume extravaganza to write about modern people in believable situations, the songs forming a meaningful part of the action. The new technique, first perfected in *Very Good, Eddie* (1915), created a string of hits and a distinctively American form of musical comedy. Smooth ballads like "Babes in the Woods" (from *Very Good, Eddie*) and "Nesting Time in Flatbush" and "Till the Clouds Roll By" (both from *Oh, Boy!* 1917) impressed the young George Gershwin [Supp. 2] to the point of emulation.

Kern remained in or near the vanguard throughout his career. With *Show Boat* (1927) he not only brought something of a "blues" feeling into his melodies but also realized his aims for still greater maturity on the musical stage.

In addition to a masterly integration of music, lyrics, and book, *Show Boat* offered a social realism and emotional depth unique at that time. "Bill" and "Can't Help Lovin' Dat Man," sung by Helen Morgan [Supp. 3] as the mulatto Julie, helped popularize the black-tinged "torch song." "Ol' Man River," sung by Jules Bledsoe (and in the 1929 and 1936 film versions by Paul Robeson), presented for the first time in a major musical play a dignified, tragic black man, a stevedore "tired of livin' an' skeered of dyin'," rather than the conventional buffoon. P. G. Wodehouse adapted the book from the Edna Ferber novel, and Kern had also chosen a top lyricist, Oscar Hammerstein II. In the 1920's and early 1930's, the lyricist Otto Harbach frequently collaborated with Kern, and Kern and Hammerstein revived the successful partnership of *Show Boat* in the late 1930's. Kern generally picked collaborators who shared his belief that music should realistically fit mood and character, and challenged the commercially minded producers' formula of inane music, splashy production, and disjointed, inconsequential books. Widely recognized for his influence in raising the standards of the musical, he was a member of the Dramatists' Guild, the Authors' League, the French Société des Auteurs, and the highly selective National Institute of Arts and Letters, as well as the American Society of Composers, Authors, and Publishers.

Kern's talent was many-faceted. His predilection for romantic ballads did not rule out inventiveness in dance idioms; he was, for example, among the very first to write skillfully for the new foxtrot dance form. "Some Sort of Somebody" (in *Very Good, Eddie*) foreshadowed the development of deftly blended rhythmic and melodic intricacies in three of his songs for the movie *Swing Time* (1936): "Bojangles of Harlem" (a tribute to the black tap dancer Bill Robinson), "Never Gonna Dance," and "The Waltz in Swing Time." After thirty years of prolific output his tricky "Put Me to the Test" (from the 1944 film *Cover Girl*) far surpassed the stock bounces of the day. He could also be poignant, wistful, as in "The Way You Look Tonight" (*Swing Time*), the Academy Award song of 1936; "All the Things You Are" (*Very Warm for May*, 1939); "The Touch of Your Hand" and "Smoke Gets in Your Eyes" (*Roberta*, 1933).

Kern's musical tastes reflected the man—urbane, zestful, and yet in some ways refined to the point of primness. His hobby was collecting rare books. His musical intensity was tempered by polished craftsmanship, cerebral control. He was of, and wrote for, a generation more inhibited than the next. He did not let out all the stops;

his biographer describes his courtship as "a page from a stuffy Victorian novel" (Ewen, p. 45). His music, although often rhapsodic, seldom effloresced. Such restraint, later criticized as "a certain lack of boldness" (*New Yorker*, Nov. 12, 1955, p. 135), stemmed perhaps partially from the discipline of Judaism, with which he always identified although taking no part in formal religion.

Though close to popular taste, Kern did not cater to it but led it to new levels of discrimination. His favorite composers were Tchaikovsky, Wagner, and Irving Berlin. Handsomely rewarded by his public, he lived luxuriously in Beverly Hills, Calif., after 1939. He died in 1945, at sixty, of a cerebral hemorrhage while visiting New York City; his remains were cremated. Kern was survived by his wife, Eva Leale, a native of London whom he had married on Oct. 25, 1910, at Walton-on-Thames, England, and by their daughter, Elizabeth Jane.

At the time he began his career, Jerome Kern's native city was the heart of a music industry dominated by first-generation Americans who still tended to admire, and cater to a market which admired, songs of genteel European derivation. Kern carried something of his early environment and training into his music; but to whatever extent he was influenced by the "classics" and European light opera, he was an innovator who left popular music fresher than he found it. His influence on the best younger composers was immense. "You had to worship Kern," said Richard Rodgers (Green, p. 138).

[A list of Kern scores is found in *The ASCAP Biog. Dict. of Composers, Authors and Publishers* (3rd ed., 1966) and in David Ewen's biography, *The World of Jerome Kern* (1960), which also contains photographs. Valuable short biographies and articles are in: Irwin Stambler, ed., *Encyc. of Popular Music* (1965); Oscar Hammerstein's introduction to *The Jerome Kern Songbook* (1955); Stanley Green, *The World of Musical Comedy* (1960); Cecil Smith, *Musical Comedy in America* (1950); Irving Kolodin in *Saturday Rev.*, Nov. 12, 1955; *N. Y. Times*, July 20, 1941, sec. 9 (article by Olin Downes), Nov. 12, 1945 (obituary and appraisal by Deems Taylor), Nov. 13 (editorial), and Nov. 18, sec. 2 (recollections of Guy Bolton). See also *Etude*, Jan. 1946, p. 54; *Variety*, Nov. 14, 1945; Carl L. Cannon, *Am. Book Collectors and Collecting* (1941), pp. 213–15.]

HUGHSON MOONEY

KINGSBURY, ALBERT (Dec. 23, 1862–July 28, 1943), mechanical engineer, was born in Goose Lake, near Morris, Ill., the third of four children and only son of Lester Wayne and Eliza Emeline (Fosdick) Kingsbury. His father, a descendant of Joseph Kingsbury who emigrated from England around 1630 and settled at Dedham, Mass., was superintendent of a stoneware factory. The family moved to Cuyahoga Falls, Ohio, where Albert completed high school in 1880. He attended Buchtel College (later the University of Akron) for a year, then left to become an apprentice machinist.

After three years of work on heavy machinery, Kingsbury enrolled in 1884 in the freshman class of the mechanical engineering course at Ohio State University. Forced by lack of funds to withdraw near the end of his sophomore year, he worked two more years as a machinist (one of them at the Warner and Swasey shops in Cleveland) and then in 1887 entered Cornell University. There, under the direction of Robert H. Thurston [q.v.], he conducted a series of tests on Pennsylvania Railroad bearings which marked the beginning of his career in lubrication and bearing design. The tests revealed anomalies that accepted theories of friction could not explain, and Kingsbury was not then acquainted with the empirical and analytical work in lubrication which had been done in England, culminating in 1886 in the fundamental theoretical paper of Osborne Reynolds.

Following his graduation in 1889 with the degree of Mechanical Engineer, Kingsbury accepted appointment as instructor in mechanical engineering and physics at New Hampshire College (later the University of New Hampshire). He spent the year 1890–91 in Cleveland as superintendent of a cousin's machine shop but then returned as professor of mechanical engineering to New Hampshire, where he remained until 1899. For several years Kingsbury did experimental work on friction in screw threads, particularly threads used in an action similar to that of a jack screw, which exerts a large end thrust. While testing screw threads with a torsion-compression machine, he noticed quite by accident the phenomenon of air as a lubricant, but except for a minor paper in the *Journal* of the American Society of Naval Engineers (May 1897), he did not pursue this subject further. When he presented the paper, however, before the navy's Bureau of Steam Engineering in Washington, D. C., in 1896, a listener called his attention to Osborne Reynolds's work.

Reynolds's observation that the most effective lubricant for a flat bearing surface was a thin wedge of oil maintained between the fixed and moving surfaces led Kingsbury directly to the invention of his segmental end-thrust bearing. In his college laboratory in 1898 he made the initial trials of a bearing consisting of a series of flat polygonal metal tilting pads, pivoted on radial supports and arranged symmetrically about the bearing axis. They proved entirely successful: his

bearing maintained full lubrication under thrust pressure from ten to a hundred times greater than those in conventional thrust bearings. Before a patent for the Kingsbury bearing was applied for in 1907, the English engineer A. G. M. Michell had independently developed a similar bearing, also based upon Reynolds's observation, but the chronological priority of Kingsbury's early work was established (and later acknowledged by Michell) and a United States patent was issued in 1910. The names Kingsbury and Michell in America and Europe, respectively, have become generic terms for tilting-pad thrust bearings.

In 1899 Kingsbury was appointed professor of applied mechanics at Worcester (Mass.) Polytechnic Institute. Four years later he accepted a position with the Westinghouse Electric and Manufacturing Company in Pittsburgh. He was associated with Westinghouse until 1914, after 1910 as a consultant. In 1912, at Kingsbury's expense, the company built the first large commercial Kingsbury bearing for the Pennsylvania Water and Power Company's hydroelectric plant at McCall's Ferry (Holtwood) on the Susquehanna River. The success of that installation led to general acceptance of the bearing for stationary hydroelectric turbines and generators. By 1914 Kingsbury had opened an independent consulting office in Pittsburgh. The United States Navy adopted his bearing for use on propeller shafts in 1917, and it quickly superseded other types in naval applications. Kingsbury opened a shop in Philadelphia to produce the bearing, which was also manufactured to his order at ten or twelve other machine shops. After the war he expanded the Philadelphia shop and in 1924 incorporated the Kingsbury Machine Works, of which he was president until his death.

For his thrust bearing and his experimental work in lubrication, Kingsbury was awarded the Elliott Cresson Medal of the Franklin Institute (1923), the John Scott Medal (1931) of the City of Philadelphia, and the gold medal of the American Society of Mechanical Engineers (1931). In his last years he made his home in Greenwich, Conn. On July 25, 1893, at Stamford, Conn., Kingsbury had married Alison Mason, by whom he had five daughters: Margaretta Mason, Alison Mason, Elisabeth Brewster, Katharine Knox, and Theodora. Like his father before him, he was a gifted musician. He regularly attended the Presbyterian Church. He died at the Greenwich Hospital of a cerebral thrombosis at the age of eighty and was buried in Greenwood Cemetery, Brooklyn, N. Y.

[*N. Y. Times,* July 29, 1943; *Nat. Cyc. Am. Biog.,* XXXII, 38–39; *Who's Who in America,* various issues,

1903–43; information from surviving relatives; Arthur M. Kingsbury, *Kingsbury Genealogy* (1962). Albert Kingsbury's excellent article, "Development of the Kingsbury Thrust Bearing," *Mechanical Engineering,* Dec. 1950 (which includes a good reproduction of a photographic portrait), cites the pertinent published papers of Kingsbury, Reynolds, and Michell. Death record from Town of Greenwich.]

Eugene S. Ferguson

KIRCHWEY, GEORGE WASHINGTON (July 3, 1855–Mar. 3, 1942), law educator, criminologist, and penologist, was born in Detroit, Mich., the oldest of four children (two boys and two girls) of Michael and Maria Anna (Lutz) Kirchwey. His parents were both of German birth; his father, who had fled his native Prussia after taking part in the revolution of 1848, was engaged in the livestock and wholesale meat business in Detroit, and later in Chicago and Albany, N. Y. Kirchwey attended private and public schools in Chicago and Albany, graduating as class valedictorian from the Albany high school in 1875. Entering Yale College the same year, he received the B.A. degree with high honors in 1879. After studying law at Yale and the Albany Law School, he was admitted to the New York bar and practiced in Albany for about ten years. He married Dora Child Wendell of Albany, daughter of a Methodist minister, on Oct. 31, 1883. The couple had four children: Karl Wendell, Dorothy Browning, Freda, who became editor and publisher of the *Nation,* and George Washington, Jr., who died at an early age.

Kirchwey's Albany law practice thrived, but he did not find this a satisfying career. From 1887 to 1889 he served as editor of historical documents for the State of New York and then accepted the deanship of the Albany Law School, where he also taught jurisprudence and the law of contracts. He moved to New York City in 1891 to join the faculty of the Columbia Law School and became dean in 1901. During these years he published two volumes of case studies (1899–1902) and edited a book of readings on the law of real property (1900). He was a pioneer in using the case system as a pedagogical method and was regarded as the most popular member of the faculty. Again, however, he failed to find lasting fulfillment in his work. Resigning his deanship in 1910, though continuing to teach, he became increasingly involved in social welfare activities.

Kirchwey's legal work had brought him in contact with a number of welfare organizations, among them the New York Prison Association, to whose executive committee he was elected in 1907. He thus developed a broad familiarity with the treatment of criminals, both before and after conviction. In New York, as in the country at large, prison reform was in a state of flux; the use of the repressive Auburn system among adult offenders was ending, and new ideas were being applied in the handling of youthful delinquents and mature felons alike. Kirchwey was particularly impressed by the efforts of Thomas Mott Osborne [*q.v.*], who as warden at Sing Sing instituted a system of self-government among inmates similar to one he had earlier employed with juveniles in the George Junior Republic. Kirchwey's philosophy of penal reform was strongly influenced by his religious outlook as a Unitarian and by his innate compassion and optimism. Although he acknowledged some of the contributions made by Cesare Lombroso and the positivist school, he disagreed with their emphasis upon the existence of a criminal "type." He supported instead the views of British penologist Charles Goring and others, who asserted that lawbreakers must be understood as individuals whom adverse circumstances had set apart from society. An outspoken critic of the administration of justice in America, which he regarded as "the disgrace of our American civilization," Kirchwey hoped that a public made aware of archaic prison practices would force the establishment of rational, human procedures.

Kirchwey helped draft the national platform of the Progressive party in 1912 and ran unsuccessfully that year as a Progressive for judge of the New York Court of Appeals. He served on the New York State Commission on Prison Reform in 1913–14, and when Osborne temporarily stepped down at Sing Sing in 1915, pending an investigation of politically motivated charges against his conduct in office, Kirchwey was named as his replacement. He thus assured the continuation of Osborne's experiments until the latter was vindicated in the courts and reinstated the following year. In 1916, at sixty-one, Kirchwey resigned his professorship of law, and in 1917 he joined the faculty of the New York School of Philanthropy, which had been strengthening its social welfare curriculum under the leadership of Edward T. Devine. When it reorganized in 1918 and changed its name to the New York School of Social Work, Kirchwey became head of its department of criminology. In this post, which he held until his retirement in 1932, he trained a large corps of probation, welfare, and correctional workers, again using the case method. He contributed articles on criminology and related subjects to a variety of publications and spoke frequently against capital punishment; he was one of the first presidents of the American League for the Abolition of Capital

Punishment, organized in 1927. Kirchwey served on commissions investigating the penal systems of New Jersey and Pennsylvania and directed a notable survey of the operations of the Cook County Jail in Chicago. From 1922 onward he was a director of the National Society of Penal Information, which ultimately merged with the Welfare League Association to form the Osborne Association, a clearinghouse for data on prisons and other correctional institutions.

Kirchwey did not confine his energies to penal reform. An advocate of peace and international law, he was a delegate to the International Peace Congress in Geneva in 1912 and president of the American Peace Society, 1915–17. In 1918–19 he was the New York director of the United States Employment Service, which had the task of finding jobs for approximately 100,000 World War I veterans. Becoming interested in the potential of the cinema as a force for public education, he served for a number of years on the governing committee of the National Board of Review of Motion Pictures, from 1933 to 1940 as chairman. His long career brought him numerous honors, including the presidency of the American Institute of Criminal Law and Criminology (1917). He died at the age of eighty-six at his home in New York City of a cerebral hemorrhage, and was buried in Kensico Cemetery, Valhalla, N. Y. Though not an original theorist, Kirchwey played an important role in establishing the study of criminology in the United States as a scientific discipline and in fighting for methods of penal treatment based upon rehabilitative care rather than deterrence.

[Basic information on Kirchwey's life and career is contained in *Nat. Cyc. Am. Biog.*, Current Vol. B, pp. 466–67; Yale Univ., *Obituary Record of Graduates, 1941–42*; *Who Was Who in America*, vol. II (1950); and the obituary in the *N. Y. Times*, Mar. 5, 1942. Certain details were supplied by his daughter Dorothy (Mrs. LaRue) Brown. For representative articles and addresses by Kirchwey epitomizing his point of view, see "Criminology," in *Encyc. Britannica* (14th ed., 1929); "Capital Punishment," in *Encyc. of the Social Sciences* (1933); "The Death Penalty," in Am. Prison Assoc., *Proc.*, 1922, pp. 363–77; and "The Administration of Criminal Justice," *ibid.*, 1923, pp. 256–62. For details on the development of the major institutions with which Kirchwey was affiliated, see two volumes of the Bicentennial Hist. of Columbia Univ., *A Hist. of the School of Law* (1955) and Elizabeth G. Meier, *A Hist. of the N. Y. School of Social Work* (1954). A brief appreciative notice by Rustem Vambery is in the *Nation*, Mar. 14, 1942.]

W. DAVID LEWIS

KIRSTEIN, LOUIS EDWARD (July 9, 1867–Dec. 10, 1942), merchant and civic leader, was born in Rochester, N. Y. His father, Edward Kirstein, a liberal refugee of the German revolution of 1848, was a salesman who eventually owned a wholesale optical business in Rochester; he married Jeanette Leiter, and of their family two sons and two daughters grew to maturity. Having finished grammar school at thirteen, Louis attended Taylor's Business College while working as an errand boy. He had been admitted to the Rochester Free Academy but asserted his independence by running away from home at the age of sixteen; for a few years he made a living by selling dry goods and jewelry and managing a small-town baseball team. On his return, he worked as bookkeeper and salesman for his father, and also bought the franchise of the Rochester baseball club.

After his father's death in 1894, Louis and his brother, Henry, took over the management of the family business. On Jan. 23, 1896, Louis married M. Rose Stein, daughter of Nathan Stein, a Rochester clothing manufacturer. He soon acquired an interest in Andrew J. Lloyd Company, optical suppliers of Boston, and in 1907 became president of this firm. Through both the Lloyd Company and his father-in-law's firm of Stein-Bloch, which he had entered in 1901, Kirstein came to know the Boston merchants Edward A. Filene [Supp. 2] and A. Lincoln Filene, and in 1912, after lengthy negotiations, he officially joined the Filene firm, investing a quarter of a million dollars.

Filene's, a Boston women's specialty store, was then on the eve of expansion. Kirstein became a director, vice-president, and one of six managers of the firm, with responsibility for publicity and for the merchandising of men's clothing (a new department). As other managers died or retired, he was given charge of the entire merchandising operation. Holding that the retailer was a "purchasing agent for the public," he bought astutely on his many trips abroad and promoted both customer service and honest advertising. He supported the enlightened employee relations plans instituted by the Filenes and favored the right of labor to organize. Convinced of the need for cooperative efforts among large retail stores, Kirstein took an active part in the Retail Research Association, founded in 1917 to study practical problems of retailing for its members, in the Associated Merchandising Corporation (1918), which pooled buying, and later in the American Retail Federation, established in 1935 to lobby for and publicize the interests of retailers.

In 1928 Kirstein joined with two other managers of the Filene firm—Lincoln Filene and Edward Frost—to defeat Edward Filene's plans for employee participation in management. The following year the three voted to join several other large retailers in setting up the Federated

Department Stores, which thereafter held a majority of the Filene store's nonvoting stock. Edward Filene continued as president of the firm, but without real power. Lincoln Filene became chairman of the board, and Kirstein continued as vice-president until his death.

Kirstein was ever ready to put his administrative talents at the service of city, state, and country. A trustee of the Boston Public Library from 1919, he donated to the city in 1928 a branch library for businessmen. He was a member of the Massachusetts Industrial Commission (1929) and the Retail Trade Board of the Chamber of Commerce, and in 1930 became chairman of the Boston Port Authority. He served on the boards of hospitals and welfare organizations, and was president of the Associated Jewish Philanthropies of Boston (1930) and vice-president of the American Jewish Committee. During the New Deal he served the government as a member of the Industrial Advisory Board of the NRA and of the original National Labor Board. Kirstein was a member of the visiting committee of the Harvard Business School, where after his death a professorship in human relations was established in his honor.

Kirstein was a large man whose forceful manner could sometimes seem intimidating. Yet his kindness, generosity, and fairness won him many friends and gained him the familiar sobriquet of "Uncle Lou" among younger men. His colorful personality emerged in frequent speeches and articles, and newspapers published his "Kirsteinisms." Methodical and exacting, he was a merchant of the old style who thrived on competition and had a genius for merchandising and personal relations. He received an honorary master's degree from Harvard in 1933 and an honorary Doctor of Commerce degree from Boston University in 1938. Kirstein died of pneumonia at Beth Israel Hospital in Boston five months after his seventy-fifth birthday; he was buried in Mount Auburn Cemetery, Cambridge, Mass. Besides his widow, he left a daughter, Mina (Mrs. Henry T. Curtiss), and two sons, Lincoln Edward and George Garland. His will left $150,000 to Jewish charities.

[*Who's Who in America*, 1940–41; obituaries in *N. Y. Times*, Dec. 11, 1942, *Women's Wear Daily*, Dec. 10, 1942, *Bull.* of the Business Hist. Soc., June 1943, and *Am. Jewish Yearbook*, 1943–44; Gerald W. Johnson, *Liberal's Progress* (1948), a biography of Edward Filene; Mary La Dame, *The Filene Store* (1930); Louis Rittenberg, "Altruism Pays," *Am. Hebrew*, Feb. 1, 1929. Kirstein's letters, papers, and office files are in the Baker Lib., Harvard Business School. An oil portrait is in the possession of the Filene company. Some early documents give Kirstein's birth year as 1866; later accounts agree on 1867.]

ROBERT W. LOVETT

KITTREDGE

KITTREDGE, GEORGE LYMAN (Feb. 28, 1860–July 23, 1941), professor of English, was born in Boston, Mass., the elder child and only son of Edward Lyman Kittredge and his wife, the widowed Deborah (Lewis) Benson. Both parents came of old New England families, his mother's going back to the *Mayflower*. His father, born in Nelson, N. H., was a forty-niner who brought back stories rather than gold from California, and who spent the rest of his life as a respected if never overly prosperous storekeeper. That his mother had been born in Barnstable, Mass., had a profound influence on Kittredge. The family lived in Barnstable during two of his school years (1873–75, while his father farmed there), and it was his summer home all his life; this association fostered his interest in the history and lore of New England.

Kittredge prepared for college at Roxbury Latin School and entered Harvard with the class of 1882, supported in part by funds supplied by friends on Cape Cod. His concentration was in the classics, especially Greek, but his career as teacher and scholar was determined by his courses with Francis James Child [*q.v.*], Harvard's first professor of English, to whom he remained closely bound, professionally and personally, until Child's death in 1896. Although Kittredge graduated first in his class, he had also taken part in undergraduate clubs and publications, to which he contributed reviews (some of learned works), comic sketches, and light verse.

He began graduate study, but lack of money forced him to give it up after a few months, and early in 1883 he became a teacher of Latin at Phillips Exeter Academy, where he remained, except for a year of study in Europe (1886–87), until 1888. In Exeter he met and married, on June 29, 1886, Frances Gordon; their honeymoon began his year abroad. They had three children: Frances Gordon, Henry Crocker, and Dora.

Child, who already thought of Kittredge as his successor, directed his private study at Exeter, and it was doubtless by Child's advice that Kittredge spent part of his year abroad in Germany, where at the universities of Leipzig and Tübingen he extended his knowledge of the Germanic languages and made the acquaintance of numerous scholars, chief among them Eduard Sievers. He returned to Harvard in 1888 as instructor in English. On the faculty, he was one of the young conservatives who opposed President Charles W. Eliot [*q.v.*] in his modernization of the university. Each had a wary admiration for the other, and, as a contemporary remarked, though no young man debated more vigorously with Eliot than did Kittredge, none was promoted so rapidly by Eliot as was Kittredge. He became assistant professor in 1890 and professor in 1895; in 1917 he was named the first Gurney Professor of English Literature, a chair he held until his retirement in 1936.

As a teacher, Kittredge was a master of two styles. Undergraduates saw him as a classroom performer. With an impressive presence, a full beard, originally red but early becoming white, a fondness for wearing suits of a light color, one who taught while walking rather than standing, he kept the attention of even the most listless. He was witty but never clowning, moral without being oppressive. His mastery of subject enabled him to bring back almost any passage in Shakespeare from a few words quoted by a questioner and to teach the *Beowulf,* on occasion, from an unmarked text. Although in general he evoked great admiration and respect, a small minority of students regarded him as something of a martinet and even, because he emphasized the meanings of words in their historical context, a pedant. His manner in his graduate courses was altogether different. After his lectures, the class moved to his home for a series of evening meetings where the reading and discussion of the students' reports were followed by an hour or two of general talk. Here Kittredge was at his best, relaxed, informal, genial, reminiscent, never dominating the conversation and deftly bringing in the shyest among the group.

Classroom work was only a part of Kittredge's service as a teacher. Until his retirement he attended almost every oral examination given under the Division of Modern Languages, of which he was long chairman, including those for seniors who were candidates for honors in English. He was a masterly examiner, almost always on the side of the student. The dissertations which he directed, many on subjects outside his chosen fields, received meticulous attention on style and content, and he was frequently successful in arranging for publication. In retrospect it is easy to say that Kittredge slighted research for tasks which others could have done or which could have been left undone, but he would not have agreed, since for him a teacher's monument was in his students rather than in his own writings.

In this country and abroad, Kittredge for the greater part of his life was the best-known American literary scholar. The range and number of his publications can only be suggested here. His major contributions fall into broad categories. Next to Child, no one did more for the study of the English and Scottish popular ballads. Kittredge contributed comparative notes to the later sections of Child's great collection of these ballads

and after the latter's death supervised its completion. In 1904 he prepared, with the assistance of Child's daughter, a one-volume edition of Child's work, with a luminous introduction, which in time was attacked by the opponents of the so-called communal theory of ballad origins. His interest in the collection of ballads still current led directly or indirectly to the publication of half a dozen volumes of ballad versions from various parts of the United States and Canada.

His first important book, *Observations on the Language of Chaucer's Troilus* (1894), marked out another area of his scholarship. This was followed by many articles on Chaucer and by *Chaucer and His Poetry* (1915), still among the best and best written of the criticisms and interpretations of Chaucer. From his study and teaching of medieval romance came *A Study of Gawain and the Green Knight* (1916), a model of the comparative technique, modified but not impaired by the later discovery of texts which he had not known. The history of witchcraft early drew his attention, and his investigations culminated in *Witchcraft in Old and New England* (1929), where 373 pages of fascinating and horrifying exposition are bolstered by 223 pages of notes, whose learning at once encourages and intimidates any student.

For generations of Harvard students, Kittredge and Shakespeare were synonymous, and it is for his work on Shakespeare that he remains best known. His most famous course, English 2, was a year's intensive study of six of Shakespeare's plays. Throughout his career Kittredge gave many lectures, singly or in series, on Shakespeare; these, with one exception, he resolutely refused to publish, partly no doubt because of the thrifty feeling that published lectures are no longer current coin, but primarily because their form did not meet his high standards. His *Shakespeare: An Address* (1916) stands beside the *Preface* of Dr. Johnson (whom Kittredge greatly admired) in its concise, trenchant, and sensible criticism. When his *Complete Works of Shakespeare* appeared in 1936, it contained the soundest text of the plays hitherto available, and his separate editions of sixteen of them (two completed after his death by Arthur Colby Sprague), have introductions and notes seldom equaled for learning and common sense.

The history and folklore of New England engaged Kittredge's attention in books, articles, and editions ranging from the entertaining and discursive *The Old Farmer and His Almanack* (1904) to the more austere account of *Doctor Robert Child, the Remonstrant* (1919). Beginning in 1888 he was involved in the preparation of a long series of Latin grammars and texts, many of them still in use. One of his collaborators was the classicist James B. Greenough [*q.v.*], with whom he wrote *Words and Their Ways in English Speech* (1901), which, if it does not anticipate later linguistic theories, continues to fulfill its purpose of introducing the common reader to the richness and vagaries of the English language. Kittredge also helped prepare a number of English grammars and exercise books for secondary schools.

Kittredge received honorary degrees from the University of Chicago (1901), Harvard (1907), Johns Hopkins (1915), McGill (1921), Yale (1924), Brown (1925), Oxford (1932), and Union College (1936). He was a founder and fellow of the Mediaeval Academy of America and president of the Modern Language Association of America (1904–05), the American Folklore Society (1904–05), and the Colonial Society of Massachusetts (1900–07). Despite a surface austerity, which masked an unexpected shyness, Kittredge was like Dr. Johnson a clubbable man. A good talker and a good listener, fond of good food and good drink, he enjoyed the various dining and literary groups to which he belonged. He delighted in the theatre, in vaudeville and melodrama as well as Shakespeare. His wide reading included detective stories and other light literature. In political thinking he was a conservative of New England Federalist-Whig tradition and naturally at home in the Republican party. Regular church attendance was congenial to him, and he was a devout though unobtrusive Congregationalist. In 1941, five years after his retirement, he died at Barnstable from sclerosis of the coronary artery; he was buried there in the Lothrop Hill Cemetery.

[Clyde Kenneth Hyder, *George Lyman Kittredge: Teacher and Scholar* (1962); James Thorpe, comp., *A Bibliog. of the Writings of George Lyman Kittredge* (1948); Harvard Faculty Minute in *Harvard Univ. Gazette,* Apr. 25, 1942; *Who Was Who in America,* vol. I (1942); biographical introduction by Bartlett Jere Whiting in 1970 edition of Kittredge's *Chaucer and His Poetry;* Kittredge Papers in Harvard Univ. Archives: scrapbooks and extensive correspondence file, including a few copies of letters by Kittredge, who, in any event, by preference wrote short notes and postal cards.]

BARTLETT JERE WHITING

KNOX, FRANK (Jan. 1, 1874–Apr. 28, 1944), journalist, politician, and Secretary of the Navy, was born in Boston, Mass., the only son and eldest of the six surviving children of William Edwin Knox, a dealer in oysters, and Sarah Collins (Barnard) Knox. The boy was christened William Franklin, but from his youth he was known as Frank, and by about 1900 he had dropped his first name altogether. Both parents were Canadians who had come to the United States in childhood, the father, of Scottish descent, from New Brunswick, the mother, of English antecedents, from Prince Edward Island. Knox is said to have derived his generosity and sentimental nature from his father; his energy, psychological stamina, and outgoing friendliness were inspired by his mother, a pious, thrifty, vigorous woman. From his parents, his early Presbyterian training, and his public schooling, he acquired a strong sense of honesty, a dominating sense of duty, and a patriotism which for him was a matter of unquestioned belief.

When he was seven the family moved to Grand Rapids, Mich., where his father earned a modest but adequate living as a grocer. Knox left high school at the end of his junior year to become a traveling salesman, but when the depression of 1893 eliminated his job, he entered Michigan's Alma College, where he played varsity football and served for two years as a part-time instructor in physical education. Knox had nearly completed the classical curriculum when he enlisted in the Spanish-American War and fought in Cuba with Theodore Roosevelt's Rough Riders; Alma later (1912) awarded him the B.A. degree. Discharged from the service after contracting malaria, he accepted a job as a reporter for the *Grand Rapids Herald.* On Dec. 28, 1898, he married his college sweetheart, Annie Reid of Gratiot County, Mich. They had no children.

Knox's apprenticeship with the *Grand Rapids Herald* gave him experience as a reporter, city editor, and circulation manager. In 1902 he and John A. Meuhling, a printer, purchased the *Evening Journal* in Sault Ste. Marie, Mich. When, a year later, the only other newspaper in the city sold its assets to Knox and Meuhling, the partners renamed their paper the *Evening News.* It was Republican and progressive in tone, reflecting Knox's lifelong admiration for Theodore Roosevelt. Always an advocate of the strenuous life, Knox spent countless hours horseback riding and playing golf, though his stocky five-foot-nine-inch frame became a bit stout with maturity. When business was running smoothly, he often turned to politics, and from 1903 to 1912 he undertook one reform crusade after another.

In 1901 Knox had met Chase S. Osborn, a Michigan outdoorsman, newspaperman, and politician of a similar progressive bent. When Osborn ran successfully for governor in 1910, Knox was his campaign manager. His reward was the chairmanship of the Republican State Central Committee. Two years later Knox became active in Theodore Roosevelt's Bull Moose party. His political influence in Michigan reached a low point, however, when Roosevelt was defeated in the 1912 election, and soon afterward he sold the *Evening News* and moved to Manchester, N. H., on the invitation of several of that state's leading Progressives. There he and Meuhling founded a new Progressive paper, the *Manchester Leader*. Within a year, through aggressive publishing and careful business management, they took control of the major competitive paper. In the amalgamation that followed, the *Manchester Union* became a leading state newspaper, while the evening *Leader* served the city of Manchester.

When the United States entered World War I in 1917, Knox, a strong advocate of preparedness, put aside his business to volunteer for service in the army. He served in France as a major in the 78th Division, participating in the St. Mihiel and Meuse-Argonne offensives. Upon his return to New Hampshire in February 1919, he accepted a commission in the reserves and took part in organizing the American Legion. Renewing his activity in politics, this time as a conservative, Knox was a leader, at the Republican National Convention of 1920, in the unsuccessful campaign of Leonard Wood [*q.v.*] for the presidential nomination. In 1924 Knox entered the New Hampshire Republican gubernatorial primary against the liberal John G. Winant; after losing, he declared that he was through with politics.

Three years later Knox received a financially attractive offer to become publisher of the Hearst papers in Boston. He accepted, applied successfully the fundamentals of newpaper management which he had mastered, and in less than a year was promoted to the position of general manager of the Hearst system. He resigned in 1930 when, after a year of problems created by the depression, he disagreed with William Randolph Hearst's business methods. The following year Knox, with the assistance of the New England financier Theodore Ellis, bought the controlling interest in the *Chicago Daily News*. His revitalization of that great newspaper during the hardest days of the depression confirmed his reputation as a genius in the management of large newspaper properties.

Knox soon cast aside his earlier vow to avoid politics, and in 1932, at President Hoover's request, he directed a vigorous but unsuccessful campaign to bring hoarded money back into circulation. During the summer of 1933 his front page editorials in the *Chicago Daily News* sharply condemned the New Deal while defending the conservative position of Hoover. Now in demand as a political speaker, Knox believed that with Hoover's support he could win the 1936 Republican presidential nomination. He failed, however, to win Hoover's backing, and was instead given the vice-presidential nomination on a ticket headed by Alfred M. Landon. After a strenuous campaign, the Landon-Knox 1936 Republican ticket met overwhelming defeat.

Though Knox disagreed vigorously with Franklin D. Roosevelt's domestic policies, he supported the President's foreign policy and his naval preparedness program. When Roosevelt first thought of creating a bipartisan cabinet, he considered both Landon and Knox, the titular heads of the Republican party, for appointments. Landon did not wish to serve Roosevelt, and Knox, who did not want to be the only Republican in the cabinet, declined in 1939 a proffered appointment as Secretary of the Navy. Yet Knox was anxious to participate in some significant role if war came, and in July 1940, as Hitler's blitzkrieg stormed across France, he accepted the navy post at the same time that Henry L. Stimson agreed to become Secretary of War. Both Knox and Stimson were read out of the Republican party, though many Republicans approved of the appointments.

The navy secretaryship thrust Knox into an unfamiliar environment, yet he was determined to master the assignment. His newspaper training made him sensitive to efficient management practices, and he immediately initiated a series of surveys by civilian experts designed to improve departmental administration. Knox was soon surrounded by a competent corps of cooperative civilian secretaries and aides, including James V. Forrestal, Ralph Bard, and Adlai Stevenson. He did an outstanding job of coordinating the civilian secretaries and the service heads of the navy.

Though Knox had anticipated war, the Japanese attack at Pearl Harbor caught him by surprise, and he flew at once to Hawaii to survey the damage. Such a trip was only one of hundreds he made. Knox believed that by visiting the navy wherever it operated he would understand the service better and at the same time boost the morale of the men. During his four years as Secretary, he flew over 200,000 miles, from Guadalcanal in the Pacific to the coast of Italy near Salerno.

With Roosevelt's backing, Knox countered successfully most attempts by the admirals to increase military authority at the expense of civilian control. He considered support of the President's wartime policies essential, made many speeches on behalf of these policies, and frequently testified before Congressional committees in support of Roosevelt's proposals. In the early spring of 1944 his self-imposed, unrelenting pace suddenly took its toll. After contracting influenza, which he shook off with difficulty, Knox suffered a heart attack. He died four days later at his home in Washington, D. C., at the age of seventy, and was buried with full military honors in Arlington National Cemetery.

[The basic sources are the Frank Knox Papers, Lib. of Cong.; and the Correspondence File of the Secretary of the Navy, Nat. Archives. Other MS. sources include: Franklin D. Roosevelt Papers, Roosevelt Lib., Hyde Park, N. Y.; Chase S. Osborn Papers, Mich. Hist. Collections, Univ. of Mich.; Frank O. Lowden Papers, Univ. of Chicago; Charles G. Dawes Papers, Northwestern Univ.; Herbert Hoover Papers, in the Hoover Presidential Lib., West Branch, Iowa; Alfred M. Landon Papers, Kans. Hist. Soc., Topeka; and the Henry L. Stimson diary, Yale Univ. Interviews with Mrs. Knox and with Mrs. Fred Reed (Knox's last surviving sister) provided family information. Knox's *"We Planned It That Way"* (1938) is an 82-page polemic on F. D. Roosevelt's domestic policies. See also: George H. Lobdell, Jr., "A Biog. of Frank Knox" (Ph.D. dissertation, Univ. of Ill., 1954); Norman Beasley, *Frank Knox, American* (1936), a campaign biography; Donald R. McCoy, *Landon of Kansas* (1966); Robert M. Warner, "Chase S. Osborn and the Progressive Movement" (Ph.D. dissertation, Univ. of Mich., 1958); "Who Is Frank Knox?" *Fortune,* Nov. 1935; Jack Alexander, "Secretary Knox," *Life,* Mar. 10, 1941; obituary in *N. Y. Times,* Apr. 29, 1944. There are photographs of Knox in the *Chicago Daily News* Lib.]

GEORGE H. LOBDELL, JR.

KOCH, FREDERICK HENRY (Sept. 12, 1877–Aug. 16, 1944), professor of dramatics and proponent of American folk plays, was born in Covington, Ky., but grew up chiefly in Peoria, Ill., where his paternal grandfather, Heinrich Friedrich Koch, a landscape gardener, had settled after emigrating from Germany in 1858. Frederick's father, August William Koch, was an accountant and cashier for the Aetna Life Insurance Company, but in his spare time sketched and painted. Frederick's mother, Rebecca Cornelia (Julian) Koch, was the daughter of a wealthy Mississippi planter of French Huguenot descent. From his mother Koch apparently derived his gregariousness and quick wit. Growing up in a family of ten children (nine of them boys), he graduated from the Peoria high school, attended Caterals Methodist College in Cincinnati for a time, and then entered Ohio Wesleyan University, receiving the A.B. degree in 1900.

From earliest boyhood Koch had wished to become an actor. In March 1901 he enrolled at the Emerson School of Oratory in Boston, where he studied theatre arts and graduated in 1903. Perhaps because of his father's strong opposition to a theatrical career, however, he turned to teaching, becoming an instructor in English at

the University of North Dakota in 1905. There he found partial satisfaction for his theatrical urge by directing his students in dramatic productions. Feeling the need for more training, he took a leave of absence to study at Harvard, where he earned an A.M. in 1909; he was greatly influenced by Prof. George Pierce Baker [Supp. 1], who stirred his interest in developing an original American drama. At the University of North Dakota, Koch organized the Sock and Buskin Society (later called the Dakota Playmakers), a small group of faculty and students who wrote and produced one-act plays based on their own knowledge of life in the frontier state. The Playmakers traveled all through North Dakota, often carrying their dramas to communities that had never before seen a play.

Koch moved in 1918 to the University of North Carolina at Chapel Hill, at the urging of Prof. Edwin A. Greenlaw [Supp. 1], the head of the English department. There for twenty-six years he taught dramatic literature and play writing. From the start he stressed folk plays, which he described as being "concerned with folk subject matter: with the legends, superstitions, customs, environmental differences, and the vernacular of the common people." Organizing the Carolina Playmakers, modeled on his earlier group at North Dakota, he staged "Carolina Folk Plays," first in a high school auditorium and then in a small remodeled building on the university campus, and took them on tour to neighboring communities and to cities as far afield as Washington, New York, Boston, Dallas, and St. Louis. One of the students in his first class in play writing was the fledgling author Thomas Wolfe [Supp. 2]; Koch's encouragement was instrumental in Wolfe's decision to become a playwright and later to enter George Pierce Baker's 47 Workshop at Harvard. Other writers who began as Koch's students were Paul Green, Betty Smith (author of *A Tree Grows in Brooklyn*), and the newspaperman Jonathan Daniels. As Koch's fame spread, young men and women came not only from North Carolina but from other states and even from abroad to study under him.

A "Johnny Appleseed of the drama," Koch established, with the aid of the university's extension service, a Bureau of Community Drama to help school and civic groups in North Carolina develop their own dramatic programs. A traveling field secretary gave the necessary training and assistance in production. Local drama groups performed for each other at regional festivals, and once a year they gathered in Chapel Hill at a statewide dramatic festival sponsored by the Carolina Playmakers. Koch also strongly influenced the development of outdoor pageants and pageant plays based on historical themes, notable examples of which are Paul Green's *The Lost Colony,* given annually on Roanoke Island beginning in 1937, and Kermit Hunter's *Unto These Hills,* given high in the mountains at Cherokee, N. C. Three decades later, these two dramas between them were attracting more than 200,000 spectators each summer.

Koch had begun in 1918 with students as his only assistants, but he gradually added trained members to his staff, and by 1936, when the University of North Carolina established a separate department of dramatic art, he had a fairly large group of associates. To them he increasingly turned over the direction of the work, although he continued to take a lively interest in all details. In 1944, at the age of sixty-six, Koch died of a heart attack while swimming at Miami Beach, Fla., where he was vacationing with his family. A Unitarian in religion, he was buried in Chapel Hill. He was survived by his wife, Loretta Jean Hanigan, an Irish-American whom he had met in Athens while on a European tour in 1909 and had married at Denver, Colo., on Mar. 24, 1910, and by their four children: Frederick Henry, George Julian, Robert Allan, and William Julian.

Koch was not himself an outstanding artist or scholar, but his radiant and vibrant personality evoked the highest talents of students and others who worked with him. He gave a lasting stimulus to the theatre in North Carolina. The Bureau of Community Drama he had founded in North Carolina was still flourishing a quarter-century after his death.

[Samuel Selden, *Frederick Henry Koch: Pioneer Playmaker* (Univ. of N. C., *Lib. Extension Publication,* July 1954), which includes a good photograph; *Nat. Cyc. Am. Biog.,* Current Vol. A, pp. 361–62; Paul Green, "Playmakers' Progress," *Theatre Arts,* Aug. 1957; Arthur H. Quinn, *A Hist. of the Am. Drama* (2 vols., 1927). See also the various published collections of his students' plays edited by Koch, and his quarterly *Carolina Play-Book,* 1928–44. Information on Koch's enrollment from the Registrar, Emerson College, Boston.]

SAMUEL SELDEN

KOENIGSBERG, MOSES (Apr. 16, 1878– Sept. 21, 1945), journalist, was born in New Orleans, La., the youngest of the three sons and one daughter of Jewish parents, Harris Wolf and Julia (Foreman) Koenigsberg. According to family tradition, Harris Koenigsberg, born in Russia, had been given the hand of his bride, the daughter of a Polish patriot, only on condition that they escape from Czarist tyranny. Smuggled across the border, the couple emigrated to the United States shortly after the Civil War. While Moses was an infant, his father moved to San Antonio, Texas, where he prospered as a tailor.

A precocious youth, Koenigsberg made an early start in journalism. At nine, by his own account, he printed and published a monthly paper called the *Amateur.* He left school at twelve after an undeserved punishment for plagiarism and ran away from home to travel briefly with a band of Mexican revolutionaries. At thirteen he had the bulk of an adult and was able to win a job as a reporter on the *San Antonio Times,* where his exposé of corruption among prosecuting attorneys drew down on him a suit for criminal libel. (The indictment was later quashed.)

Over the bitter opposition of his father, who wished him to study medicine or law, Koenigsberg fled to Houston. He ran through two jobs there, moved on to the *New Orleans Item,* returned to San Antonio and founded a short-lived newspaper called the *Evening Star,* and then, still only sixteen, struck out again on his own. Moving from job to job, aided by his own boldness and the casual employment practices of newspapers, he worked in Kansas City, St. Louis, Chicago, Pittsburgh, and New York, returning in 1895 to St. Louis, where he stayed for three years. After brief military service in the Spanish-American War with an Alabama volunteer unit, he moved to Chicago and then to Minneapolis. In 1903 he settled in Chicago as city editor of William Randolph Hearst's *Chicago American.*

Hearst's mass journalism, with its frequent editions, huge headlines, and sensationalism, was then at its apex. On the *American,* Koenigsberg ran a news circus, achieving such coups as tracking down and engineering (by a series of telegrams from his news desk) the capture of a Boston wife-killer on a train in Colorado. He also managed a "crusade" to raise the taxes of the International Harvester Company. Although his personal contacts with the publisher were casual, Koenigsberg became embroiled in the internal politics of Hearst's retinue and in 1907 was transferred to New York. There Hearst's general manager, S. S. Carvalho [Supp. 3], signed Koenigsberg to a "personal service contract," designed to prevent the kind of raiding Hearst himself had pioneered, and sent him on to Boston to restore the *Boston American* to solvency. Without support from headquarters, he made little progress, but it was more than a year before he was allowed to return to New York. Thereafter he served as a newspaper prospector for Hearst.

As he approached the age of thirty-five, Koenigsberg decided to found his own business, a feature syndicate. After his Hearst contract expired in December 1912, he prepared an inaugural announcement but was stopped when a New York court, at Hearst's prompting, ruled that the contract remained in force unless explicitly terminated. Hearst nevertheless permitted him to found the new syndicate, to operate semi-independently within the Hearst empire, and in August 1913 the Newspaper Feature Service came into being. Thus began the fifteen-year phase of Koenigsberg's career that left an enduring mark on newspapers. Although syndicates had existed for thirty years, Koenigsberg expanded their range and volume of features and increased the size of their audience. In 1915 he founded an additional Hearst service, King Features Syndicate (the name derived from "Koenig" in Koenigsberg). Profitable almost from the first, King Features thrived especially on such comic strips as "Bringing Up Father" and proved to be highly durable, far outlasting most of the rest of the Hearst enterprises. On Apr. 1, 1919, Hearst gave Koenigsberg still another responsibility, as manager of the International News Service. INS was then on the point of failure, in debt and under order by the courts to desist from pirating news from the Associated Press. Koenigsberg gradually brought it back toward solvency and reliability. By the mid-1920's he was managing a total of eight Hearst services.

The events that led to Koenigsberg's departure from Hearst began in 1925, when he charged the Associated Press with stealing INS material. AP's directors, in retaliation, threatened to deprive Hearst newspapers of AP service. The AP thus confirmed Koenigsberg's belief that it was trying to monopolize news distribution, and when he represented INS at a League of Nations conference of press experts in 1927, he fought AP's resolution supporting private property rights in news and was instrumental in securing the adoption of a counter-resolution that read in part: "No one may acquire the right of suppressing news of public interest." For his work at the conference, the French government named Koenigsberg a chevalier of the Legion of Honor. Although Hearst had recently ordered that no one in his employ should accept a decoration from a foreign government, Koenigsberg chose to accept; he received the decoration on Feb. 19, 1928, and on the same day resigned. (He returned the award in 1933 to protest France's failure to pay her war debts.)

After leaving Hearst, Koenigsberg resumed his roving from job to job. In 1929 he worked with Eugene Greenhut, a department store magnate, in trying to build a huge newspaper chain; the stock market crash and the failure of a deal

to buy the *Denver Post* ended the plan. Later he served as executive director of the Song Writers' Protective Association and briefly helped develop a Sunday magazine at the *Philadelphia Inquirer*. He died of a heart attack in his New York City home at the age of sixty-seven and was buried in Kensico Cemetery, Valhalla, N. Y. His wife, Virginia Vivien Carter of New Haven, Conn., whom he had married on Dec. 10, 1923, and their daughter, Virginia Rose, survived him.

[The fullest source on Koenigsberg is his stilted but factual autobiography, *King News* (1941). Biographical sketches appear in *Nat. Cyc. Am. Biog.*, Current Vol. B, pp. 311–12 (a photographic portrait appears opposite p. 312); *Editor & Publisher*, Feb. 25, 1928, p. 5; *Who's Who in Am. Jewry*, 1938–39; and obituaries in the *N. Y. Times*, Sept. 22, 1945, and *N. Y. Jour.-American*, Sept. 21, 1945. There is an unflattering characterization in Emile Gauvreau, *My Last Million Readers* (1941), pp. 377–402. The League of Nations conference is discussed in Manley O. Hudson, "Internat. Protection of Property in News," *Am. Jour. of Internat. Law*, Apr. 1928. The various biographies of William Randolph Hearst contain scattered references to Koenigsberg.]

JAMES BOYLAN

KOFFKA, KURT (Mar. 18, 1886–Nov. 22, 1941), psychologist, one of the founders of Gestalt psychology, was born in Berlin, Germany, the eldest of three children of Emil Koffka, a comfortably situated lawyer, and Luise (Levy) Koffka. Though his mother was Jewish, the family attended the Evangelical Church. Koffka came of a family of lawyers, but his mother's brother, a biologist, aroused his keen interest in science and philosophy, and upon graduating in 1903 from the Wilhelms Gymnasium in Berlin, he entered the University of Berlin, planning to study philosophy. He spent the year 1904–05 at the University of Edinburgh. This experience, during which he came under the influence of several outstanding British scientists and scholars, brought him in close touch with English-speaking people and laid the foundation for the true scientific internationalism that was to be his.

After returning to Berlin, Koffka found himself "too realistically-minded to be satisfied with pure abstractions" and turned from philosophy to psychology. From his research in Wilibald Nagel's physiological laboratory came his first published paper, "Untersuchungen an einem protanomalen System," a study of his own color blindness. He received the Ph.D. degree in 1908, presenting as his dissertation "Experimental-Untersuchungen zur Lehre vom Rhythmus."

On Jan. 9, 1909, Koffka married Mira Klein. They were divorced in 1923, and on July 21 of that year he married Elisabeth Ahlgrimm, who had received her doctorate from the University of Giessen. Three years later they were divorced and Koffka remarried his first wife; but in 1928 he was again divorced and once more married Elisabeth Ahlgrimm. He had no children.

On leaving Berlin, Koffka worked with Johannes von Kries at Freiburg and with Oswald Külpe and Karl Marbe at Würzburg. The year 1910 found him as assistant to Friedrich Schumann in Frankfurt. This year was, in his own words, "of special importance in my scientific development . . . with [Wolfgang] Köhler as Schumann's other assistant and [Max] Wertheimer [Supp. 3] working on the perception of motion in the laboratory. Thus we three who knew each other slightly before were thrown into the closest contact, which resulted in lasting collaboration." From this contact developed the Gestalt theory, an approach to psychology which was in sharp contrast to the accepted frames of reference in both Europe and America at that time. The word "Gestalt," meaning form or configuration, was chosen because it emphasized a concept that the whole is more than the sum of its parts. Gestalt psychology was initially a reaction against the traditional atomistic approach to the human being where behavior was analyzed into constituent elements called sensations. Later it rejected the behavioristic psychology of J. B. Watson with its oversimplified units of stimulus and response. The Gestalt psychologist felt that these approaches denuded human life of its essential meaningfulness and were based on an unnecessarily restricted model of the physical universe. Koffka was not the most original of the great Gestaltist triumvirate, but he became in time their most influential spokesman.

In 1911 Koffka was appointed Privatdozent (lecturer) at the University of Giessen and seven years later, ausserordentlicher Professor (associate professor). He and his students at Giessen put out a steady flow of experimental studies. Eighteen articles appeared as part of the series "Beiträge zur Psychologie der Gestalt" in the *Psychologische Forschung,* the journal of the Gestalt group. During the years of World War I, Koffka worked with Prof. Robert Sommer at the Psychiatric Clinic in Giessen on patients with brain injuries and especially on aphasics. Later he was engaged on problems of sound localization, first with the army and then with the navy. In 1921 he published *Die Grundlagen der Psychischen Entwicklung,* which applied the Gestalt viewpoint to developmental psychology. Published in English as *The Growth of the Mind* (1925), the book had a considerable influence on educational theory by shifting emphasis away from rote learning and onto the significance of intuition.

Koffka's outspoken advocacy of Gestalt psychology aroused much enmity among the traditional psychologists of Germany, and it seemed unlikely that he would ever be able to rise above the provincial university of Giessen. A devoted Anglophile who spoke perfect English, he had hopes of moving to England, but conditions were academically and ideologically unsuitable. Two trips to America, as visiting professor at Cornell in 1924–25 and at Wisconsin in 1926–27, finally convinced him that opportunities lay in the United States, and in 1927 he accepted a post as William Allan Neilson Research Professor at Smith College—a five-year appointment during which no publications were demanded, no teaching required. Again the majority of experimental projects undertaken by Koffka and his students lay in the field of visual perception. These publications appeared again in *Psychologische Forschung* and were also published as *Smith College Studies in Psychology* (4 vols., 1930–33). In 1932 Koffka was given a regular teaching appointment at Smith as professor of psychology.

After joining a somewhat abortive Russian-sponsored expedition to Uzbekistan in Soviet Asia in 1932, where he contracted relapsing fever, Koffka embarked on his monumental work, *Principles of Gestalt Psychology* (1935). In it he took stock of his position, forcing himself to recognize gaps, inadequacies, and inconsistencies in Gestalt theory as he saw it, thinking through and integrating within this framework his astonishing detailed knowledge of experimental problems. With this book completed, he permitted himself, as a psychologist, to be concerned with wider problems in areas in which he had long been interested, such as art, music, and literature and general social and ethical questions. His article "Problems in the Psychology of Art," his various lectures on tolerance and on freedom, and his dialogue on "The Ontological Status of Value" all show that he had now extended the province in which he felt the psychologist had a right to participate. To all these more general topics he brought the same stringency of thought, the same careful avoidance of loose generalization, that characterized his intensive work in experimental problems.

In 1939, while spending a year as visiting professor at the University of Oxford, Koffka revived one of his old interests, working at the Nuffield Institute with patients with brain lesions and at the Military Hospital for Head Injuries, where he helped develop tests for impaired judgment and comprehension that came into general use. Despite a heart condition which had caused him to restrict his activities for several years, he continued to teach until a few days before his death. He died at his home in Northampton, Mass., of a coronary thrombosis in 1941, at the age of fifty-five. Following cremation, his ashes were scattered. His wife, who taught history at Smith College, survived him.

One of Koffka's outstanding characteristics was his genuine lack of interest in personal recognition and his ever-present appreciation of the ideas which he owed to his Gestalt colleagues. That he made major contributions of his own, his publications loudly witness; nevertheless, it remains essentially true that he will be remembered as an integral part of a movement in psychology from which he cannot and would not wish to be dissociated.

[Obituaries in *Am. Jour. of Psychology*, Apr. 1942, *Psychological Rev.*, Mar. 1942, and *N. Y. Times*, Nov. 23, 1941; Jean Matter Mandler and George Mandler, "The Diaspora of Experimental Psychology," *Perspectives in Am. Hist.*, vol. II (1968), reprinted in Bernard Bailyn and Donald Fleming, eds., *The Intellectual Migration* (1969); article on Koffka by Grace M. Heider in *Internat. Encyc. of the Social Sciences*, VIII, 435–38. See also, for discussions of the Gestalt movement, Edwin G. Boring, *A Hist. of Experimental Psychology* (1929), chap. xxii; and Robert S. Woodworth, *Contemporary Schools of Psychology* (1931), chap. iv. Information on particular points from Dr. Mira Koffka and from Koffka's death record, Mass. Registrar of Vital Statistics. Koffka's papers are in the author's possession; see "A Note on the Koffka Papers," *Jour. of Behavioral Sciences*, Apr. 1971.]

MOLLY HARROWER

KOLLER, CARL (Dec. 3, 1857–Mar. 21, 1944), ophthalmologist, known for his discovery of cocaine as a local anesthetic, was born in Schüttenhofen, Bohemia (later Susice, Czechoslovakia), the third of five children and only son of Leopold Koller, a Jewish businessman, and Wilhelmina (Rosenblum) Koller. Carl's mother died when he was a child, and the family moved to Vienna, where he received private tutoring and some instruction by Jesuit priests. After completing his studies at the Akademisches Gymnasium he studied jurisprudence for a year, but in 1876 he turned to the study of medicine at the University of Vienna.

As a medical student he was particularly interested in embryology and experimental pathology, and carried out basic research on the origin of the mesodermal layer of the chick embryo, work that gained wide recognition. He decided, however, to go into ophthalmology. His teacher in this field had pointed to the need for a local anesthetic in eye surgery. Ambitious to make an important discovery which would advance his career, Koller tried out the anesthetic properties of a number of substances in experiments on animals, but had no success and gave up the investigation. He received his M.D. degree in 1882.

While serving his internship at the Allgemeines Krankenhaus, Koller lived on the same floor with Sigmund Freud, then also an intern. Freud invited Koller to join in an investigation of the general physiological effects of cocaine, in the hope that the alkaloid might prove a possible cure for morphine addiction and an aid in treating psychiatric disorders. The ability of cocaine to numb the skin and mucous membranes had long been known. Experimenting on himself, while Freud was away on holiday, Koller pondered the drug's effect in numbing his tongue, and suddenly perceived the possibility that it might also numb the parts of the eye and thus provide the long-needed local anesthetic. He immediately tested his idea in the laboratory and found that a few drops of a cocaine solution placed in the eye of a guinea pig rendered the area insensitive to pain. After further tests on human beings, he prepared a brief paper describing his findings for the next important scientific meeting, that of the German Ophthalmology Society of Heidelberg. Poverty prevented Koller himself from attending —having become estranged from his family, he was living on his meager pay as an intern—but a friend read the paper for him on Sept. 15, 1884. It created a sensation in both Europe and the United States. A controversy over priority developed in later years, but Freud's letters written at the time clearly indicate his acceptance of Koller as the true originator of the idea.

In spite of his brilliant discovery, Koller was not offered the assistantship at the University of Vienna that he had hoped to gain, partly because of his tempestuous and undiplomatic personality, partly because of the strong anti-Semitism then prevailing in Vienna. A dispute over the treatment of a patient in the hospital clinic, in which a colleague insulted Koller as a Jew, led to a saber duel on Jan. 4, 1885, in which he severely wounded his opponent. Koller was summoned before the police, and although he later received a pardon, he became ill with worry and left Vienna, realizing that promotion was impossible. He spent two years (1885–87) as an assistant in the Utrecht Eye Hospital in Holland, went to London for several months, and in May 1888 sailed for New York.

Later that year Koller was appointed to the staff of Mount Sinai Hospital, New York City. He soon became noted as an outstanding surgeon and diagnostician and developed a highly successful clinical practice, which he continued for the next fifty-six years. He was not a prolific writer and made no further fundamental contributions, although he did publish articles dealing with tuberculous choroiditis, blepharospasm, and transient blindness resulting from the ingestion of wood alcohol.

Koller adapted readily to life in the United States. On summer holidays he took pleasure in the mountains and clear air of Maine, or fished in mountain streams of the Western states. His wide interests ranged from physics and astronomy to travel and polar exploration, and he particularly enjoyed speculating about the unsolved problems in all areas of human knowledge. On Oct. 30, 1893, Koller married Laura Blum of New York City; their two children were Hortense and Lewis Richard. Koller died in his eighty-seventh year at New York City of cancer of the prostate. He was buried in Kensico Cemetery, Valhalla, N. Y.

Koller's major discovery was as epoch-making for ophthalmic surgery as was the discovery of ether for general surgery. It brought him repeated honors in later life. In 1922 the American Ophthalmological Society made him the first recipient of its Howe Medal. Other awards were the Kussmaul Medal from the University of Heidelberg (1928), the first medal of honor given by the New York Academy of Medicine (1930), and the medal of honor of the American Academy of Ophthalmology (1934).

[Hortense Koller Becker, "Carl Koller and Cocaine," *Psychoanalytic Quart.*, July 1963, is the most comprehensive biographical source, written by his daughter on the basis of Koller's papers. See also: Milton Silverman, *Magic in a Bottle* (1941), chapter on the history of cocaine; Carl Koller, "Historical Notes on the Beginning of Local Anaesthesia," *Jour. Am. Medic. Assoc.*, May 26, 1928; and obituaries by Selina Bloom in the *Archives of Ophthalmology*, Apr. 1944, and by Percy Fridenberg in Am. Ophthalmological Soc., *Transactions*, XLII (1944), 30–32. A portrait of Dr. Koller is in the Trustees' Room of Mount Sinai Hospital, N. Y. City.]

IRVING H. LEOPOLD
ARTHUR SCHWARTZ

KRAUSE, ALLEN KRAMER (Feb. 13, 1881–May 12, 1941), physician, investigator of tuberculosis, was born in Lebanon, Pa. His parents, George Derr Krause, the proprietor of a hardware store, and Jeanie Julia (Kramer) Krause, were of Pennsylvania German Protestant stock native in the region since colonial times. Allen was one of their three children. His early education was in Lebanon public schools, with additional private instruction.

His college and professional education was rapid. He matriculated at Brown University in 1898, graduated A.B. in 1901, pursued further studies in biology at Brown and took a master's degree in 1902, began the study of medicine at Johns Hopkins University in 1903, and graduated with distinction in 1907. A special interest in

pathology led him to commence work in that field, in the academic post of instructor, under one of America's most celebrated teachers, William Henry Welch [*q.v.*]. His studies were cut short after little more than a year, however, by the development of pulmonary tuberculosis.

In his fourth year of medical school, on Oct. 10, 1906, Krause had married Clara Fletcher of Providence, R. I. She devoted her life to his needs, protecting his marginal health. They had three children: Gregory, Francis, and Fletcher. When Allen's tuberculosis was obvious, in December 1908, the Krauses moved to Saranac Lake, N. Y., then preeminent in the treatment and investigation of tuberculosis. Here Krause came under the influence of three of America's most distinguished physicians in this field, Edward L. Trudeau [*q.v.*], Edward R. Baldwin, and Lawrason Brown [Supp. 2]. He himself soon gained comparable distinction. His recovery from tuberculosis was rapid, and in the succeeding years, as assistant director (from 1909) of the Saranac Laboratory, he carried out studies on resistance and immunity to tuberculosis that made him a leading authority. An untoward episode in 1914, the development of cancer of the bowel, for which operation was necessary, proved a severe inconvenience rather than a threat to life.

In 1916 he returned to Johns Hopkins University as associate professor of medicine, director of the Kenneth Dows Tuberculosis Laboratories, and physician-in-charge of the Phipps Tuberculosis Dispensary of the Johns Hopkins Hospital. Krause's thirteen years at Hopkins were the most productive in his life. He had the laboratory and clinical facilities to test his views, and he was fortunate in association with a younger, devoted laboratory investigator, Henry Stuart Willis. Their joint researches were classics of the period. Following and greatly extending leads developed by Baldwin in Saranac Lake and by Paul Roemer of Marburg, Germany, Krause developed concepts that soon oriented this country's understanding of the pathogenesis of tuberculosis. His central concept was that the hypersensitivity (allergy) to tuberculo-protein, resulting from infection by the tubercle bacillus, fortified resistance to the disease. Extraordinarily facile in speaking and writing, Krause was prolific in publication and a remarkably effective lecturer. He became the most frequently sought author of tuberculosis chapters in the encyclopedic literature of the day.

Beginning in 1916, Krause edited the *American Review of Tuberculosis*, founded that year by the National Tuberculosis Association, a large voluntary health-promoting organization, under the inspiration of the Saranac Lake physicians. This journal developed American research on the disease enormously, and gave Krause himself a ready forum. His own extensive reading, an extraordinarily retentive memory, and meticulous attention to accuracy and style made him an outstanding editor. He held numerous correlated positions, including the editorship of an American section in the British journal *Tubercle*.

In 1929 Krause left the Johns Hopkins Medical School to venture into the field of clinical medicine, as president of the Desert Sanatorium of Tucson, Ariz., with concomitant responsibilities as clinical professor of medicine at Stanford University and the University of Southern California. He continued to edit the *American Review of Tuberculosis*. In his editorial work there was no decline, but his success was not great in the other posts. For a time his popularity was undimmed, but he deteriorated steadily in health. Slight in stature and always frail, he had apparently driven himself too hard. Newcomers in his chosen field were refuting some of his work. Gradually he drifted into mental depression. He returned to Baltimore and the Johns Hopkins Hospital in 1936, but continued to fail in health. He died in Butler Hospital, Providence, R. I., at the age of sixty, of bronchopneumonia and hypertensive heart disease. He was buried in the mausoleum of Mount Lebanon Cemetery, Lebanon, Pa.

Krause remains a legend among tuberculosis investigators, because of his imaginative research and guidance in the subject, and also because of other talents: his remarkable scholarship, his encyclopedic mind, his knowledge of history, literature, art, and music, his book collecting, and his sometimes overriding intellectual dominance among men in his professional field. He did not live to see the great progress in the treatment of tuberculosis that commenced in the 1940's and 1950's, but he left an indelible stamp on the concepts of his own time.

[Besides his book *Environment and Resistance in Tuberculosis* (1923), Krause was the author of 187 papers; for a bibliography, see *Am. Rev. of Tuberculosis,* June 1942. For biographical accounts, see Max Pinner in *ibid.,* Aug. 1941; H. S. Willis in *ibid.,* June 1942 (a memorial issue dedicated to Krause); E. R. Long in Assoc. of Am. Physicians, *Transactions,* 1942, pp. 22–23; James J. Waring in *Annals of Internal Medicine,* Oct. 1941; obituary in *Jour. Am. Medic. Assoc.,* June 7, 1941. Family information from Lebanon County Hist. Soc., Lebanon, Pa.; death record from City Registrar, Providence, R. I.]
ESMOND R. LONG

KREMERS, EDWARD (Feb. 23, 1865–July 9, 1941), pharmaceutical chemist, was born in Milwaukee, Wis., the oldest son of Gerhard and Elise (Kamper) Kremers, German immigrants who had come to the United States after the revolution of 1848. His father was secretary of the Milwaukee Gas Light Company. Kremers received his primary education in the public schools of Milwaukee, in largely German-speaking classes, and at the age of fourteen began his high school work in the "college department" of the Mission House, a German Reformed Church theological school in Sheboygan, Wis. There he studied chemistry and the natural sciences as well as Latin and Greek. When his father's illness curtailed the family finances, Kremers left school to become a pharmacist's apprentice. His preceptor, a cultured Milwaukeean who had obtained his training at the University of Munich, provided the youth with a liberal education along with a knowledge of medicinal drugs.

Kremers received his certificate at the end of two years instead of the usual three, and in the fall of 1884 entered the Philadelphia College of Pharmacy. He was dissatisfied, however, with the limited opportunity for laboratory work and after the winter term returned to enroll at the recently established college of pharmacy of the University of Wisconsin, in Madison. Working as a laboratory assistant to Frederick B. Power [*q.v.*], who had organized the department, Kremers received his diploma as a graduate in pharmacy (Ph.G.) in 1886. In the following year he published a paper on the chemistry of the volatile oils of pennyroyal ᷉and citronella for which he received the Ebert Prize of the American Pharmaceutical Association. Discovering that a degree in pharmacy commanded little respect in the academic world— an experience that helped impel his later efforts to reform pharmaceutical training—Kremers next enrolled at the university as an undergraduate and received the B.S. degree in 1888. He then went to Germany, where he studied under the chemists Otto Wallach and Friedrich Kekulé at Bonn and later with Wallach at Göttingen, receiving the Ph.D. from Göttingen in 1890 with a thesis on "The Isomerism within the Terpene Group." That fall Kremers became an instructor in pharmacy at the University of Wisconsin, and in 1892, when Powers resigned, he was made professor and director of the pharmacy program.

Kremers's experience in Germany had strengthened his resolve to reform the teaching of pharmacy, which in the United States was then largely governed by the apprentice system and by private colleges run by druggists. Few colleges of pharmacy required more than a grammar school education, and the training rarely included laboratory work. In 1892 Kremers lengthened the pharmacy course at Wisconsin from four terms to six—the equivalent of two full academic years—and limited the enrollment to high school graduates. He also offered a pioneering elective four-year program leading to a B.S. degree, the requirements including the study of botany, physics, and inorganic and organic chemistry and a graduation thesis based on original laboratory research. Kremers carried his message of reform to meetings of the American Pharmaceutical Association. Though his ideas met with some resistance, by 1896 five other state universities had followed his lead by initiating an optional four-year pharmacy course.

As Kremers's reputation spread, advanced students came to Wisconsin to work under his direction. The first M.S. degrees in the school of pharmacy were given in 1899; in 1902 the university conferred its first Ph.D. in pharmaceutical chemistry upon one of Kremers's students, Oswald Schreiner, and in 1917 the first Ph.D. in pharmacy. In time nearly sixty students earned their doctorates under Kremers and went on to become leaders in pharmaceutical research both in this country and abroad.

His own interests lay in the fields of structural organic chemistry and, particularly, phytochemistry (plant chemistry). In 1908 he began growing medicinal plants in his own garden, and a year later, in cooperation with the United States Department of Agriculture, he was able to devote an acre of university land to the project. This was the forerunner of Wisconsin's state-supported Pharmaceutical Experiment Station, established in 1913; it functioned until 1933, when the depression forced the withdrawal of state funds. Among the accomplishments of the research were the development of horsemint as a source of thymol and a new method of purifying digitalis.

Kremers served as editor (1896–1909) of the *Pharmaceutical Review* and in 1898 established the *Pharmaceutical Archives*. As early as 1902 he initiated the formation of a historical section of the American Pharmaceutical Association. The courses in the history of pharmacy and of chemistry he inaugurated at Wisconsin in 1907–08 were probably the first of their kind in any American university. Kremers's publications, which number some six hundred, include the textbook *History of Pharmacy* (1940), written with George Urdang.

Kremers married Laura Haase of Milwaukee on July 6, 1892. Their four children were Roland Edward (who became a food chemist), Elsa, Laura Ruth, and Carl Gerhard. Among the honors that came to Kremers were the Sc.D. degree from the University of Michigan (1913) and the Remington Medal of the American Pharmaceutical Association (1930). He was made honorary president of the American Pharmaceutical Association in 1933 and of the American Institute

of the History of Pharmacy in 1941. Kremers retired from teaching in 1935 and died six years later, at Madison, of a coronary occlusion. He was buried in Forest Hill Cemetery, Madison. Through his espousal of high educational and scientific standards, Kremers did much to elevate pharmacy to the level of the other academic professions.

[George Urdang, "Edward Kremers (1865–1941): Reformer of Am. Pharmaceutical Education," *Am. Jour. of Pharmaceutical Education*, Oct. 1947, is the fullest published source. See also Paul J. Jannke, "The Education of an Educator," *ibid.*, Apr. 1942; obituary by George Urdang in *Science*, Sept. 26, 1941; *Nat. Cyc. Am. Biog.*, XXX, 75–76. The Am. Inst. of the Hist. of Pharmacy, Univ. of Wis., Madison, has MS. autobiographical notes by Kremers. Death record from Wis. Dept. of Health and Social Services.]

A. H. UHL

LADD, CARL EDWIN (Feb. 25, 1888–July 23, 1943), agricultural educator, was born in McLean, Tompkins County, N. Y., at the farm of his parents, Arnold D. and Mary E. (Mineah) Ladd; he was their second son and the youngest of three children. Both parents were natives of Tompkins County; his father was descended from Daniel Ladd, who came from England to Massachusetts in 1634. Carl attended local schools and at fifteen entered the nearby Cortland (N. Y.) Normal School, from which he graduated in 1907. After a year as school principal in South Otselic, N. Y., he enrolled in the College of Agriculture at Cornell University. He received a B.S. degree in 1912 but stayed on for graduate study in the department of farm management, specializing in cost accounting under the direction of Prof. George F. Warren [Supp. 2], whose economic ideas he was to share during the agricultural crisis of the early 1930's. He received the Ph.D. in 1915.

That year Ladd became director of the New York State School of Agriculture at Delhi, one of six regional schools recently established to provide a two-year program in applied agriculture. In 1917 he assumed overall direction of the six schools as specialist in agricultural education in the State Education Department at Albany. Two years later, he became director of the State School of Agriculture at Alfred, N. Y. Ladd returned to Cornell in 1920 as extension professor of farm management. He was made director of extension work for the College of Agriculture and the College of Home Economics at Cornell in 1924.

Carl Ladd's career was built upon identification with the interests of New York agriculture. He regarded the extension service as a vehicle for transmitting the needs of the farmer to the college and as an agency for formulating research programs to meet those needs. As director of extension he worked closely with the state's Farm Bureau Federation, using its county units as local bases of operation for the College of Agriculture; through this structure extension specialists were made available to individual farmers for consultation. Under Ladd, Cornell also continued its policy of aiding farmer cooperatives such as the Dairymen's League.

In 1932 Ladd became dean of the colleges of agriculture and of home economics and director of the agricultural experiment station at Cornell. A skilled administrator and mediator, he set up meetings at the college between farmers and the businessmen who supplied their needs. Recognizing the trend toward specialization in agriculture, he altered the focus of extension work from general farming to particular commodities. He also kept Cornell in the forefront of agricultural research, concentrating on such problems as better food packaging, dehydration, and the artificial breeding of livestock. He set up a special interdepartmental research and extension project designed to expand the market for potatoes, an important state product, and encouraged the development of the frozen food industry in New York state.

Ladd's influence in agricultural matters extended beyond the campus. He had become widely known to the farming public at large through the columns of the *American Agriculturist,* edited by his close friend Edward R. Eastman. Sensitive to the techniques of public relations, he maintained contacts in Albany and Washington and with the newspaper publisher Frank Gannett. Ladd served as secretary of the State Agricultural Advisory Commission under Gov. Franklin D. Roosevelt, and later as chairman; he became chairman of the New York State Planning Council in 1936; and he was a director of the Federal Land Bank at Springfield, Mass., a major source of credit for Northeastern farmers.

Ladd's reaction to the agricultural program of the New Deal was ambivalent. He supported the Agricultural Adjustment Act as a temporary expedient and recognized the need for some government assistance, but objected to the degree of central planning envisaged by the Roosevelt administration. As new federal agencies concerned with the farmer were created, Ladd sought with considerable success to have them administered by the existing network of county agents that made up the extension service of the various land-grant colleges. The matter was formalized at a conference in 1938 between representatives of the colleges and the federal Department of

Agriculture at which a compromise (the "Mount Weather Agreement") was worked out by Ladd.

Ladd was gregarious and outgoing. He had a romantic view of America's rural past, yet it was his conviction that farms should be managed like businesses and their performance measured by business standards. He found relaxation on his own farm near Freeville, N. Y. On Mar. 9, 1912, Ladd had married Camilla Marie Cox of South Otselic, N. Y., by whom he had one daughter, Elizabeth Marie. Following the death of his first wife in 1917, he married Lucy Frances Clark of Brandford, Vt., on July 16, 1918; they had two sons, Carl Edson and Robert Daniel. In religion Ladd was a Presbyterian. While still active as dean, he died of a coronary attack at Freeville at the age of fifty-five and was buried at McLean, N. Y.

[With Edward R. Eastman, Ladd wrote a romanticized account of farm boyhood, *Growing Up in the Horse and Buggy Days* (1943). Biographical sources: Gould P. Colman, *Education & Agriculture: A Hist. of the N. Y. State College of Agriculture at Cornell Univ.* (1963); Ruby Green Smith, *The People's Colleges* (1949); *Nat. Cyc. Am. Biog.,* XXXIV, 148; *Who Was Who in America,* vol. II (1950); *N. Y. Times* obituary, July 24, 1943. Ladd's administrative files as director of extension and dean are in the Cornell Univ. Archives.]

GOULD P. COLMAN

LADD, KATE MACY (Apr. 6, 1863–Aug. 27, 1945), philanthropist, was born in New York City, the younger daughter and second of three children of Josiah Macy, Jr., and Caroline Louise (Everit) Macy. Valentine Everit Macy [*q.v.*] was her brother. Although her given name was Catherine Everit, she was known throughout her life as Kate. Her great-grandfather Josiah Macy [*q.v.*], a Quaker from Nantucket Island, had founded the New York shipping and commission house of Josiah Macy & Son. Her father, a businessman and investor, became an official of the Standard Oil Company. Her mother was the daughter of Valentine Everit, a Brooklyn leather merchant. Kate received her education from private tutors and as a young woman traveled extensively in Europe; when her father died in 1876, she inherited a sizable fortune. At twenty, on Dec. 5, 1883, she was married to Walter Graeme Ladd, a young lawyer from Brooklyn. They had no children.

Reared in the tradition of Quaker humanitarianism, Mrs. Ladd continued her family's interest in philanthropy. She made substantial donations to the Maine Seacoast Missionary Society, to the Y.W.C.A., and to various civic, educational, and relief organizations. As a friend and supporter of Martha Berry [Supp. 3], she gave generously to the Berry Schools in Georgia. She was also a friend of Lillian Wald [Supp. 2] and a contributor to the Henry Street Settlement in New York City. In 1908 Mrs. Ladd established Maple Cottage in Far Hills, N. J., a summer retreat and rest home for "professional and working women of refinement who are unable to pay for proper accommodations while convalescing from illness, recuperating from impaired health or otherwise in need of rest." For thirty-five years an average of about 300 women per year were guests there for two-week periods.

Personal misfortune determined the course of much of Mrs. Ladd's philanthropy. An invalid throughout most of her adult life, confined to her room or to a wheelchair, she was deeply influenced by two of her physicians, S. Weir Mitchell [q.v.] of Philadelphia and Ludwig Kast of New York City. These men developed in her an interest in hospital services and medical care, and much of her giving was channeled into those fields. She gave an infirmary to the New Jersey College for Women (later Douglass College), and she made numerous gifts for the support of a long list of hospitals and visiting nurse services in several states. She also supported New York City's United Hospital Fund, to provide free hospital care for the poor.

The most significant of her many contributions to philanthropy was the creation of the Josiah Macy, Jr. Foundation of New York City. When Mrs. Ladd decided to establish a memorial to her father, she asked Dr. Kast to conduct a critical study of medical research in order to determine the areas most in need of support and the most effective way for philanthropy to assist medical progress. Acting upon the findings of the study, in 1930 she established the Josiah Macy, Jr. Foundation; Kast became its first president. Mrs. Ladd directed that the initial endowment of $5,000,000 be used to support fundamental research in the areas of health and medicine, especially when the problems required study in correlated fields, "such as biology and the social sciences." She increased the endowment during her lifetime, and at her death the foundation received the bulk of her estate, bringing her total gift to about $19,000,000.

A woman of considerable personal beauty, Mrs. Ladd had a kind and gracious personality and a keen sense of the responsibility that goes with wealth. Her views on philanthropy were set forth in her letter of gift establishing the Josiah Macy, Jr. Foundation. "In an enlightened democracy," she wrote, "private organized philanthropy serves the purposes of human welfare best, not by replacing functions which rightfully should be sup-

ported by our communities, but by investigating, testing and demonstrating the value of newer organized ideas . . . from which may gradually emerge social functions which in turn should be taken over and maintained by the public." Although strongly influenced by her Quaker heritage, she became a Presbyterian after her marriage. Her health worsened with age, and during the last several years of her life she was completely bedridden. She died of arteriosclerosis at her home in Far Hills and was buried with her husband (who had died in 1933) in Woodlawn Cemetery, New York City. At her death, provisions of her husband's will became effective creating the Kate Macy Ladd Fund and leaving more than $10,000,000 for the support of various charities. Specific provision was made for the establishment of the Kate Macy Ladd Convalescence Home at the Ladds' Far Hills estate, where the work of Maple Cottage was continued.

[For her life, see: obituaries in the N. Y. Times and N. Y. Herald Tribune, Aug. 28, 1945, and in the Bernardsville (N. J.) News, Aug. 30, 1945; Kate Macy Ladd (n.d.), a booklet published by the Kate Macy Ladd Convalescence Home; Nat. Cyc. Am. Biog., Current Vol. D, p. 137, and XXXII, 48–49; and sketch by Theron F. Schlabach in Notable Am. Women. For ancestry and family, see: Silvanus J. Macy, comp., Genealogy of the Macy Family from 1635–1868 (1868); and Charles E. Fitch, Encyc. of Biog. of N. Y., V (1916), 305–07. The Josiah Macy, Jr. Foundation: A Review (1937), Twentieth Anniversary Review of the Josiah Macy, Jr. Foundation (1950), and The Josiah Macy, Jr. Foundation, 1930–1955 (1955) all contain information on the foundation. Other references: files in the N. J. Room, Newark Public Lib.; death certificate, Registrar's Office, Borough of Peapack and Gladstone, N. J. Portraits of Mrs. Ladd hang in the Kate Macy Ladd Convalescence Home.]

ROBERT J. FRIDLINGTON

LAKE, SIMON (Sept. 4, 1866–June 23, 1945), inventor, submarine pioneer, was born in Pleasantville, N. J., the only son of John Christopher and Miriam (Adams) Lake. His mother was descended from Jeremy Adams, one of the founders of Hartford, Conn.; his father from John Lake, who emigrated in 1635 from Nottinghamshire, England, to Massachusetts and later moved to Gravesend, Long Island. By Revolutionary times the Lakes had settled in Atlantic County, N. J., where later generations founded the summer resorts of Ocean City and Atlantic Highlands. Inventive ability ran in the family: Simon's paternal grandfather, two uncles, and several cousins were inventors of sorts, and his father devised a window-shade roller which he manufactured in a foundry and machine shop in Toms River, N. J. When the boy was three his mother died and his father went west for five years, leaving him in the care of a step-grandmother in Pleasantville. Thereafter Lake lived with his father, at first in Camden, N. J., then in Philadelphia, and finally in Toms River. A mischievous and quick-tempered youth, with red hair and freckles, he did not take well to classroom studies. He attended local public schools, but left at the age of fourteen to work as a molder in his father's shop. His only later formal education was a brief period at the Clinton Liberal Institute in Fort Plain, N. Y., where his father sent him to learn business methods, and a course in mechanical drawing at the Franklin Institute in Philadelphia.

By 1887 Lake had taken out a patent on an improved steering device for the high-wheel bicycle—the first of some two hundred patents granted him. The following year he modified the device for use on small boats, invented a noiseless winding gear that became popular on oyster boats in Chesapeake Bay, and moved to Baltimore, where he began manufacturing and selling these appliances. Now provided with a comfortable income, he turned his attention to designing a submarine, an interest that had begun when as a boy of ten he had read Jules Verne's *Twenty Thousand Leagues under the Sea.* He drew up plans for an even-keel submersible boat, eighty-five feet in length, with oil-burning boilers and triple-expansion steam engines, double-hull construction, a diving compartment, wheels for running on the ocean floor, and a drop keel—a design that in some ways echoed Verne's description of his imaginary craft, the *Nautilus.* Lake submitted his plans in 1893 to the United States government in a competition for a practical submarine, but the contract was awarded to the more experienced John P. Holland [*q.v.*].

Lake returned to Baltimore determined to build a modest craft that would embody the principles of his design. In 1894 he completed the *Argonaut Jr.,* a primitive fourteen-foot pine-box submersible, which he and a cousin built by hand and tested near Sandy Hook. Encouraged by the success of these tests, he organized the Lake Submarine Boat Company and contracted for the building of the *Argonaut I* with the Columbian Iron Works Dry Dock Company in Baltimore, which was also constructing Holland's *Plunger* under government contract. The rival boats were launched in August 1897. Lake's was powered by a thirty-horsepower gasoline engine, to which two tubes reaching to the surface (in anticipation of the snorkel) fed air; it was thirty-six feet long and nine feet in diameter, equipped with wheels and (another Jules Verne feature) a diver's lock and exit chamber built into the bow. Although the *Plunger* was quickly abandoned as a failure, the

Argonaut I traveled more than 2,000 miles and made the passage by open sea from Cape May to Sandy Hook, feats which prompted Verne to cable congratulations. The *Argonaut I* was sluggish in surface operations, however. Unable to attract enough capital to finance a new craft, Lake had to content himself with remodeling the old one, which he renamed *Argonaut II.* He extended her length by thirty feet and added a schooner-shaped free-flooding superstructure, both of which improved her performance on the surface.

In 1900 Lake organized the Lake Torpedo Boat Company and moved his operations to Bridgeport, Conn. There in 1902 he launched the *Protector,* and with it a whole new breed of submarines; they were equipped with hydroplanes both fore and aft to achieve his distinctive, though not original, method of submergence while maintaining an even keel. He also invented an early form of the periscope, which he called the "omniscope." Lake sought to interest the United States government in buying the *Protector,* but the navy was committed to Holland's Electric Boat Company. Lake then sold the ship to Russia, which was at war with Japan. In a cloak-and-dagger operation to evade the neutrality laws, the submarine was secretly shipped aboard a freighter to Kronstadt and, after being tested by Lake in the Baltic Sea, was transported 6,000 miles overland on the Trans-Siberian Railway to Vladivostok. In the years following, Lake delivered eleven submarines to Russia, including the *Lake X,* which he had hoped to sell to the American navy. The *Lake X* had been constructed to compete in government trials against the Electric Boat Company's *Octopus,* of which Frank T. Cable [Supp. 3] was commander, but construction delays forced her withdrawal from competition.

Lake now concentrated on the European market and for some years lived abroad. He opened offices successively in St. Petersburg, Berlin, London, and Vienna, and sold Austria its first two submarines. He also received from the Krupp Works in Germany an attractive offer of 400,000 marks a year, in addition to a percentage of its business, in return for allowing it to build and market his submarines. While he waited to have the contract approved by his board of directors, officials at Krupp, discovering that Lake had neglected to file patents in Germany, appropriated his plans and withdrew their offer. Lake suffered a nervous breakdown, and after recovery spent some time in exploring the possibilities of using submarines to salvage sunken treasure and as commercial carriers. Not until 1911 did he at last sell a submarine to the United States: the *Seal*, a 161-foot vessel which, in addition to having fixed torpedo tubes in the bow, had four torpedo tubes on deck. Lake had at last broken the Electric Boat Company's monopoly, and over the next eleven years the navy went on to buy twenty-eight more Lake submarines.

After 1923 Lake's submarine enterprises gradually collapsed. Responding to disarmament sentiment, the United States scrapped a large part of its fleet. The Lake-type *O-12* was decommissioned (renamed the *Nautilus*, she was assigned to the unsuccessful Wilkins-Ellsworth Arctic Expedition), and by 1930 most of the *Seal*-type vessels had been stricken from naval lists. Lake had meanwhile invented a concrete building block and, with others, had founded the Sunshine Homes Concrete Product Company to build inexpensive homes. The project failed, however, and Lake had to sell his Torpedo Boat Company to pay off his debts. Several subsequent ventures to salvage sunken treasure were no more successful. His fortunes steadily dwindled, and in 1937 his home in Milford, Conn., was foreclosed. With the outbreak of World War II, the aging inventor went to Washington to interest Congress in huge cargo-carrying submarines, but without success. Lake was a member of the Congregational Church. On June 9, 1890, he had married Margaret C. Vogel of Baltimore; their children were Miriam, Margaret, and Thomas Alva Edison. Lake died in Bridgeport, Conn., in 1945, at the age of seventy-eight, of arteriosclerotic heart disease. He was buried in King's Highway Cemetery, Milford, Conn.

Lake's position in the history of underwater vessels has been often debated. His most important innovations were the use of hydroplanes for level-keel submergence; the free-flooding superstructure built over the pressure hull; and the air lock and exit chamber. Later authorities have argued that the first two innovations actually delayed the appearance of the modern submarine, which Lake's competitor, Holland, more clearly strove to achieve. Nevertheless, although Lake himself often exaggerated the importance of his work, he made genuine contributions to the technology of the submarine.

[Simon Lake, *The Submarine in War and Peace* (1918), his own appraisal of his work in relation to others, is surprisingly fair, especially to his chief competitor, Holland. Less useful is Lake's autobiography, *Submarine* (1938), obviously ghost-written, though it covers the lesser-known facts of his life. (Both books reproduce photographs of Lake.) See also: Alan Burgoyne, *Submarine Navigation* (2 vols., 1903), the best available history of early submarines, which includes (I, 225–72) a valuable compilation of original Lake material on the *Argonauts* and the *Protector*; Richard K. Morris, *John P. Holland: Inventor of the Modern Submarine* (1966); Simon Lake, "Voyaging under the Sea," *McClure's,* Jan. 1899, the inventor's description of his experiences with *Argonaut I; The Submarine Versus the Submersible* (Lake Torpedo Boat Co., 1906), a useful promotional booklet reprinting articles from technical journals; *Nat. Cyc. Am. Biog.,* XV, 5–6; *N. Y. Times* obituary, June 24, 1945. The Submarine Lib., U. S. Naval Submarine Base, Groton, Conn., contains the valuable Skarrett Collection; five bound volumes of articles, documents, and pamphlets collected by a free-lance writer hired by Simon Lake. Death record from Bridgeport (Conn.) Bureau of Vital Statistics.]

RICHARD KNOWLES MORRIS

LANDIS, KENESAW MOUNTAIN (Nov. 20, 1866–Nov. 25, 1944), jurist, first commissioner of organized baseball, was born in Millville, Ohio, the fourth of five sons and sixth of seven children of Mary (Kumler) and Abraham Hoch Landis. His paternal great-grandfather had come from Switzerland to Pennsylvania in 1749. His mother was of German descent, and the family belonged to the United Brethren Church. Landis's father, while serving as a Union Army surgeon in the Civil War, lost a leg at the battle of Kennesaw Mountain in Georgia, an experience that curtailed his medical career and prompted him to name his fourth son Kenesaw Mountain (dropping an "n" in the process). Ambitious for his children, he urged them to succeed: two of his sons, Charles and Frederick, later served in Congress, and John, a physician, became health commissioner of Cincinnati.

Kenesaw, slight of build and hot-tempered, held his own with his brothers, gaining social confidence through a variety of jobs and athletic activities, including baseball and bicycling. He dropped out of high school in Logansport, Ind., where his father was then farming, but experience as a court shorthand reporter stirred his interest in the law. After attending the Y.M.C.A. Law School in Cincinnati for one year and Union College of Law in Chicago for another, he was admitted to the Illinois bar in 1891. Two years later he was appointed private secretary to President Cleveland's Secretary of State, Walter Q. Gresham [*q.v.*], his father's former commanding officer. Landis returned to Chicago following Gresham's death in 1895; there he practiced law and was befriended by Frank O. Lowden [Supp. 3], whose unsuccessful 1904 gubernatorial campaign he managed. Through Lowden's friendship with President Theodore Roosevelt, Landis was appointed in 1905 federal district judge for northern Illinois.

A courtroom showman, Landis habitually wore his hair in a long mane and made telling use of "a piercing eye, a scowl and a rasping voice." He ran a lively court, badgering witnesses, lawyers, and reporters. His decisions reflected a commitment to the general path of Rooseveltian liberalism. He gained national publicity in 1907 when he imposed a $29,240,000 fine on the Standard Oil Company of Indiana in an antitrust decision that was speedily overruled by the Supreme Court. His superpatriotic wartime decisions against William D. Haywood [*q.v.*] of the Industrial Workers of the World and Socialist Congressman Victor Berger [Supp. 1], both of whom were convicted of obstructing the country's war program, enhanced his public image, as did a theatrical attempt to summon Kaiser Wilhelm II to his court to answer for the *Lusitania* tragedy. His fame catapulted him into his second and more memorable career as commissioner of baseball.

Despite a boyhood fascination with the game and an adult reputation as a partisan of the Chicago Cubs, Landis had no contact with the baseball industry until 1915, when he presided over an antitrust suit brought against the American and National leagues by the Federal League, which sought recognition as a third major league. Landis won the friendship of the established major leagues by delaying judgment, giving them time to buy out the financially harassed Federal owners. Landis moved to the center of the baseball stage in 1920 when the club owners, as a result of the "Black Sox" scandal, a sordid affair of bribery involving eight players of the Chicago White Sox charged with throwing the World Series of 1919, decided to place the game under the control of a single administrator of national reputation. After considering Gens. John Pershing and Leonard Wood [*q.v.*], along with ex-President Taft, a delegation of owners, meeting in Chicago, offered the post to Landis, who accepted after demanding and winning full control over the conduct of the game for a seven-year term. The $50,000-a-year post he shaped in his own image, down to his personally chosen title, "commissioner."

Entrusting the details to his chosen lieutenant, Leslie M. O'Connor, Landis controlled organized baseball from 1921 until his death. (He was reappointed in 1926, 1933, and 1940.) As chief interpreter of "conduct detrimental to baseball," he struck boldly at corruption, beginning with the "Black Sox" players, whom he summarily barred from baseball for life, and going on to others involved in receiving bribes. Fraternization with fans, racetrack betting, postseason barnstorming, and prizefighting also drew threats of banishment. To protect the World Series from any repetition of the 1919 scandal, Landis watched each game himself, ruling at times on player behavior, second-guessing umpire decisions, and supervising the collection and disbursal of revenues. If his decisions were draconic, even denying players

their civil rights by holding them to a unique baseball code of law, Landis usually had the support of owners, press, and public. But sometimes he was obliged to be circumspect, as in 1927, when evidence came to light charging superstars Ty Cobb and Tris Speaker with selling games back in the late 1910's. Sensing public opposition to a banishment decree, Landis discreetly arranged to have both men transferred to different teams for 1928.

By the mid-1920's Landis was coming under frequent criticism from team owners and from the baseball journal *Sporting News* as "an erratic and irresponsible despot." His stubborn opposition to the "farm system"—a recruiting technique, once discredited but then being revived, whereby a major-league club controlled a minor-league one and used it as a feeder of talent—increasingly alienated the club owners. So, too, did his denunciations of owners and writers and his feud with President Ban Johnson of the American League that led to Johnson's exile. By 1932 a cabal of club owners stood ready to deny Landis reelection as commissioner. Although failing in this, they managed to cut his salary and forced him to conduct himself more circumspectly.

Landis's handling of two later questions helped restore the confidence of club owners. Belatedly recognizing the importance of radio, Landis in 1934 decided to make the stations pay for the privilege of broadcasting World Series games. The annual contracts he negotiated, beginning that year, for exclusive World Series broadcasts brought extra money to team owners. Of more importance was his handling of baseball during World War II. Recalling experiences in the first World War, Landis determined to prevent a repetition of charges of unpatriotic behavior. Shortly after the war's outset, with President Roosevelt's approval, he worked out railroad timetables with the Office of Defense Transportation that enabled the game to continue, although by 1944 it was necessary to alter game schedules drastically and to curtail spring training. Already in declining health, Landis died that fall of a coronary thrombosis at St. Luke's Hospital in Chicago. By his own wish his body was cremated. He was survived by his wife, Winifred Reed Landis of Ottawa, Ill., whom he had married on July 25, 1895, and their two children, Reed Gresham and Susanne.

As the man who cleaned up baseball, Landis remained widely popular with the public and inspired imitators like the film industry's "czar," Will Hays. Landis's Olympian reputation put him beyond the reach of the baseball club owners, however unhappy they were at times with his regime. Having learned their lesson, they buried commissioner autocracy with Landis. His legend, however, forced them to maintain the post of commissioner, even if its subsequent incumbents were to be relatively impotent.

[J. G. Taylor Spink, *Judge Landis and Twenty-five Years of Baseball* (1947), by the editor of *Sporting News,* is the only biography. A critical study is needed, but important primary materials, such as Landis's files as commissioner of baseball, remain uncollected and in private hands. Much valuable material of the Landis era came to light in 1951 in the testimony of Leslie M. O'Connor, Landis's former assistant, before a House subcommittee inquiring into monopoly practices in organized sports. See U.S. House of Representatives, *Organized Baseball,* Report No. 2002 to accompany H. Res. 95, 82 Cong., 2 Sess. (1952). See also: Leslie M. O'Connor, *Professional Baseball in America* (1934); files ("Former Commissioners" and "Fines") in the Office of the Commissioner of Baseball, N. Y. City; *Sporting News,* 1915–45; and *Nat. Cyc. Am. Biog.,* XXXIII, 44–45. On Landis's earlier career, see Matilda Gresham, *Life of Walter Quintin Gresham* (2 vols., 1919); William T. Hutchinson, *Lowden of Ill.* (2 vols., 1957); and Landis's decisions in: *Standard Oil Co. of Ind.* v. *U. S.,* 164 F. 376 (1908); *William D. Haywood et al.* v. *U. S.,* 268 F. 79 (1920); and *Berger et al.* v. *U. S.,* 275 F. 1021 (1921). For contemporary impressions of Landis, see *Am. Rev. of Revs.,* Oct. 1907, pp. 498–99; Harvey Brougham in *Overland Monthly,* Apr. 1921; and Henry F. Pringle, *Big Frogs* (1928).]

DAVID Q. VOIGT

LANDIS, WALTER SAVAGE (July 5, 1881–Sept. 15, 1944), chemical engineer, developer of the cyanamide process of nitrogen fixation in the United States, was born in Pottstown, Pa., the older of two children and only son of Daniel Webster Landis and Clara (Savage) Landis. His father, who operated a small business, died when Walter was three years old. After attending the Pottstown public schools and the Ulrich Preparatory School in Bethlehem, Pa., Landis entered Lehigh University, where he earned the degree of Metallurgical Engineer in 1902 and the M.S. degree in 1906. Ten years of teaching mineralogy and metallurgy at Lehigh followed, interrupted by studies in Germany at the University of Heidelberg (1904–05) and at the Technische Hochschule at Aachen (1909). On June 9, 1909, Landis married Antoinette Matilda Prince of Bethlehem, Pa. They had three children: Robert Prince, Charlotte Prince, and John Prince.

Landis left an associate professorship at Lehigh in 1912 to join Frank S. Washburn in the American Cyanamid Company, established five years earlier, which he had already had occasion to advise in connection with its electric furnace operations, a field in which he was well versed. Washburn planned to undertake the manufacture of the nitrogen compounds which are an essential ingredient of fertilizers. The natural deposits of Chile saltpeter (sodium nitrate) which had been the world's sole source were dwindling in these early years of the twentieth century, and humanity faced the problem of maintaining soil fertility on the world's farms to ensure the food supply for a growing population.

Chemically, the problem was to convert the bountiful free nitrogen of the atmosphere, unusable in that form, into a combination available to plants. Three possible approaches had been developed in Europe: Kristian Birkeland and Samuel Eyde in Norway employed a high-powered electric arc to combine the nitrogen and oxygen of the air to form nitric acid, a process that could be economical only where electric power was exceptionally cheap. Fritz Haber in Germany compressed a heated mixture of nitrogen and hydrogen over a catalyst to form ammonia, but this process required special alloys and equipment with which American technologists were unfamiliar. Albert Frank and Heinrich Caro, also in Germany, combined calcium carbide with purified atmospheric nitrogen to yield calcium cyanamide. This process, which used an electric furnace to produce the calcium carbide from lime and coke, depended on a technology well advanced in the United States and hence was chosen by Washburn, who appointed Landis as chief technologist. The American Cyanamid Company erected its first plant in Niagara Falls, Ontario; a larger plant was later operated at Muscle Shoals on the Tennessee River by the Tennessee Valley Authority.

The production of calcium cyanamide opened other possibilities besides its primary use in agricultural fertilizers, and these Landis realized and actively pursued. An early by-product was the rare gas argon, then under investigation by the General Electric Company for use in its gas-filled incandescent electric light bulbs. Argon was first produced commercially when it became concentrated in the residual gas left after the absorption of the nitrogen into the cyanamide. (The method later proved less economical than a liquid air process and was abandoned.) Further developments proved to be of more lasting value. Calcium cyanamide readily yields the organic compound cyanamide, which in turn can be converted to urea, dicyan-diamide, and melamine, each a starting point for further applications. By another route, calcium cyanamide yields ammonia. Still a different set of conditions converts cyanamide to cyanides, which are essential in metallurgy in the case hardening of steel, in the cyanide process for the recovery of gold from low-grade ores, and in electroplating, and useful also as insecticides and as starting points for further chemical syntheses. Landis played the key role in exploring each of these avenues for utilizing the basic product of his company and thus in diversifying and enlarging its operations. He obtained patents on thirty-eight of his inventions, made outstanding contributions to the production of concentrated fertilizers ("Ammo-Phos"), to metallurgy and gold mining (cyanides), and to the development of synthetic resins and numerous other organic compounds (cyanamide, urea, melamine, and their derivatives).

Landis possessed a keenly penetrating mind with an uncanny ability to get immediately to the core of any problem. His capacity for retaining facts and recalling them instantly was remarkable, and his energy and strong will were highly important qualities in his challenging field. Modest and reticent, he preferred to be known not as a trailblazing scientist or as an inventor, but as a chemical engineer who "merely found ways to use what had been discovered by others." Nonetheless, he achieved both business and professional distinction. He became a director of the American Cyanamid Company in 1922 and vice-president in 1923, offices he held for the rest of his life. He also held directorships in the American Cyanamid & Chemical Corporation, Southern Alkali Corporation, and Southern Minerals Corporation (all Cyanamid subsidiaries) and in the J. G. White Engineering Corporation. He was president of the Electrochemical Society (1920) and the American Institute of Chemical Engineers (1931). His honors included the Chemical Industry Medal (1936), the Perkin Medal of the Society of Chemical Industry (1939), and the gold medal of the American Institute of Chemists (1943).

During his later years Landis made his home in Old Greenwich, Conn. He died there of a heart attack in 1944, at the age of sixty-six, while at work in his garden clearing up debris left by a hurricane. He was buried in the cemetery of the First Congregational Church of Old Greenwich.

[Obituaries in Electrochemical Soc., *Transactions,* LXXXVI (1944), 47–49, *Chemical and Engineering News,* Sept. 25, 1944, and *N. Y. Times,* Sept. 16, 1944; *Nat. Cyc. Am. Biog.,* XXXIII, 235; various references in Williams Haynes, *Am. Chemical Industry* (6 vols., 1945–54).]

D. H. KILLEFFER

LANDSTEINER, KARL (June 14, 1868– June 26, 1943), pathologist and immunologist, was born in Vienna, Austria, the only son of Leopold Landsteiner, journalist and newspaper publisher, and his wife, Fanny Hess. The father died when the son was seven years of age. The parents (according to Peyton Rous's memoir) were Jewish, but Karl was brought up as a Roman Catholic, his mother having become a convert. Landsteiner had his secondary schooling at Gymnasiums in Vienna and Linz, where his academic grades were only moderately good. He

began medical studies at the University of Vienna in 1885, completed his military service, and took the M.D. degree in February 1891. After a brief internship in the 2nd University Medical Clinic, the young Landsteiner began an extensive period of postgraduate study and research under eminent scientists. In 1891–92 he worked at Zurich with Emil Fischer, the greatest biochemist of the time, with whom he published a joint article on a chemical topic. In 1892–93 he was at Munich with Eugen von Bamberger and Arthur Hantsch, two leading chemists. Back at Vienna he spent a year, 1894–95, in the 1st University Surgical Clinic; in 1896–97 he was an assistant in the Institute of Hygiene under Max von Gruber. He then settled down in the University Institute of Pathology, where he remained until 1907.

During these ten years the young science of immunology was advancing rapidly. The basic fact in immunology and its subdivision serology is that when a foreign substance of a certain kind —an *antigen,* usually of protein nature—gets into an animal's bloodstream, the recipient reacts by forming an opposing substance or *antibody.* If the antigen consists of blood cells of another species they will clump (agglutinate) or disintegrate; if of bacteria, they may clump or be precipitated; if of an unorganized protein, the antigen-antibody reaction may cause serious disturbances in the recipient's body. Landsteiner, working alone or with colleagues, published numerous studies on antigen-antibody reactions such as agglutination and precipitation of bacteria and red blood cells by immune sera. Out of this work came the discovery that certain basic types of human blood existed, a discovery announced in 1901 and subsequently refined by Landsteiner and his associates. Before this time, blood transfusion had been too dangerous for general use because of the harmful effects of mingling incompatible bloods. Landsteiner's discovery made it possible to avoid much of the risk by using only donor blood matched to the recipient's group. The discovery could not be widely used at first because of technical difficulties, principally clotting of the introduced blood. These problems were largely solved by the time of World War I, during which transfusion was widely used. In 1930 Landsteiner belatedly received the Nobel Prize for this discovery of the blood groups. Although he greatly appreciated the honor, he regarded his later work on the specificity of antigens as more fundamental.

Among Landsteiner's other achievements of the fruitful decade 1897–1907 were: an explanation of a peculiar blood disturbance, paroxysmal hemoglobinuria; a notable improvement of the

Wassermann test for syphilis; and introduction of the dark-field microscope for study of *Treponema pallidum*, the microorganism causing that disease. In these years also, Landsteiner advanced his studies of antigens, finding by a vast amount of research that they are highly specific and that their specificity is related to the complex chemical structure of the proteins and the consequent almost infinite variety of individual antigenic substances.

In 1908 Landsteiner was appointed prosector (pathologist) to the Wilhelmina Hospital in Vienna and in the following year was named professor extraordinarius (associate professor) on the University of Vienna faculty. At the Wilhelmina Hospital in November 1908, when making a postmortem examination of a young boy who had died of poliomyelitis, Landsteiner and the boy's physician, William Popper, inoculated two monkeys with bits of the boy's brain and spinal cord. Both animals came down with the disease. Landsteiner correctly conjectured that the infection was caused by a virus, but did not succeed in transferring it from monkey to monkey, a step taken in New York in the same year by Simon Flexner and Paul A. Lewis of the Rockefeller Institute for Medical Research. For a time the workers in Vienna and in New York ran neck and neck in experiments that established the viral nature of poliomyelitis and led others, years later, to the preparation of effective vaccines.

For many years Landsteiner studied one of the most puzzling problems of immunology. Although antigens are proteins or closely related substances, yet it was also known that antigenic reactions may be produced by nonprotein materials. Following the lead of another Viennese scientist, E. P. Pick, Landsteiner explained this by showing (1918–20) that new "synthetic" antigens may be produced when proteins are altered by chemical combination with relatively simple substances. The simpler ingredient, termed "hapten," then elicits a new and specific antibody. This discovery greatly widened the range of immunological investigation.

On Nov. 4, 1916, Landsteiner married Helene Wlasto of Vienna. They had one son, Ernest Karl, who became a surgeon in Providence, R. I. Landsteiner's intense devotion to scientific research was greatly supported by his wife's understanding of his austere temperament. After World War I, life in Vienna became very difficult for many scientists. Landsteiner's teaching duties were suspended, his facilities for research were seriously limited by the government, and in 1919 he felt it necessary to leave his native country.

He found employment at low pay as pathologist to a hospital at The Hague, Netherlands, where he did routine pathological examinations in a one-room laboratory with only a nun and manservant to assist him. He managed, however, to continue his researches in basic immunochemistry. His onetime friendly rival in poliomyelitis research, Simon Flexner, learning of this constraint of his profound investigations, offered him membership in the Rockefeller Institute. He began his work there in 1922, becoming an American citizen soon afterward.

In New York, Landsteiner lived in very simple fashion, choosing to have no telephone in his apartment and otherwise avoiding distractions. Within a small circle of intimates, however, he was a charming and stimulating friend. He had his laboratory equipped for chemical research and with a series of able associates continued to investigate the chemical nature of immunological reactions. His assistants found him an exacting leader who allowed neither himself nor them a moment of relaxation. He repeatedly tested his own findings before publication and insisted on himself making critical readings at the climax of an assistant's experiment. This perfectionism was trying at times for his associates, who, however, were thus assured of accuracy in the joint publications of his laboratory.

Among Landsteiner's earliest findings at the Rockefeller Institute was that of a new series of factors in human blood in addition to those characteristic of the four groups first known (A, B, AB, and O). These new factors, the first of which were designated M, N, and P, are not ordinarily antigenic in man, but their discovery found practical application in cases of disputed paternity. In a continuing search for new blood factors, Landsteiner with Alexander S. Wiener in 1940 found another, present in the blood of 85 percent or more of human subjects, known as the Rh factor (named for the rhesus monkey, the experimental animal used). This substance may cause serious disturbances when introduced, by blood transfusion, into an individual carrying an antibody against it. Still more seriously, as Philip Levine, a former associate of Landsteiner, discovered, an Rh-negative woman bearing a child fathered by an Rh-positive man forms antibodies to Rh that may gravely damage the infant *in utero*, causing a disease known as fetal erythroblastosis.

In the 1920's Landsteiner and his colleagues, in experiments aimed at relating the specificity of antigens to their chemical structure, succeeded by intricate chemical procedures in synthesizing chains of amino acids (the "building stones" of proteins) that were sufficiently large to serve as antigens. This investigation had a considerable influence upon eminent protein chemists of the time. With John L. Jacobs and Merrill W. Chase, Landsteiner contributed greatly to the understanding of contact dermatitis, which is often produced by relatively simple substances. They found that these nonprotein substances act as haptens, which after entering the body through the skin attach themselves to natural proteins.

Landsteiner retired from membership in the Rockefeller Institute in 1939, but went on working in his laboratory until his death from coronary occlusion, in the Institute's hospital, in 1943. His original and versatile mind remained fertile to the end of a long career often troubled by sensitivity and self-questioning unusual in a man of scientific genius, and twice interrupted by emigration from one country to another. Besides the Nobel Prize, his honors included election to the National Academy of Sciences (1932) and degrees from the University of Chicago (1927), Cambridge (1934), and Harvard (1936). It has been said of Landsteiner that he found serology a mere collection of unrelated phenomena and left it a branch of chemical science.

[Besides more than 300 journal articles, Landsteiner wrote one book, *The Specificity of Serological Reactions*, first published in German in 1933 and in English in 1936. The only full-length biography is Paul Speiser, *Karl Landsteiner, Entdecker der Blutgruppen* (Vienna, 1961), which includes portraits, documents, and a bibliography. An unfinished MS. biography by Dr. George Mackenzie is held, under temporary restrictions, by the Am. Philosophical Soc., Phila. See also Stanhope Bayne-Jones in *Science*, June 5, 1931; Merrill W. Chase (anonymously) in *Jour. of Immunology*, Jan. 1944 (portrait, definitive bibliography); Peyton Rous in Royal Soc. of London, *Obituary Notices*, May 1947 (portrait, bibliography); and George W. Corner, *A Hist. of the Rockefeller Inst., 1901–1953* (1964).]
GEORGE W. CORNER

LANE, GERTRUDE BATTLES (Dec. 21, 1874–Sept. 25, 1941), magazine editor and publishing executive, was born in Saco, Maine, the sixth child among the four daughters and three sons of Eustace and Ella (Battles) Lane. Her father, whose English ancestors had settled in Maine in the seventeenth century, was an organist and piano tuner, gentle and impractical by nature. Mrs. Lane, the strong-willed, handsome daughter of a Lowell, Mass., textile manufacturer, had grown up in the South, where her father had gone to take charge of a cotton mill. The Lanes' family life was close-knit and affectionate. Gertrude went through the public grade school in Saco before entering Thornton Academy, where she edited the literary magazine and graduated in 1892.

By her teens Gertrude had evidently decided on a literary career. She followed a course that she later held up to young women seeking business success: get some practical training, accept a modest job, and don't be impatient to leave it too soon. For a year after graduation she was tutor in a Boston family. Then, after taking a stenographic course, she became assistant editor for the American Biographical Dictionary Company in Boston. Meanwhile she contributed without pay to the *Boston Beacon,* a society weekly, and studied English at Simmons College.

In 1903 she moved to New York City to accept an assistant editorship on the *Woman's Home Companion.* Though her new job paid less than the old—only $18 a week—it proved a wise move. The Crowell Publishing Company, which had just taken over the *Companion,* was then on the eve of great expansion; Joseph Palmer Knapp bought a majority interest in 1906 and went on to acquire the *American* and *Collier's.* By 1909 Miss Lane was managing editor of the *Companion,* and even before becoming editor-in-chief in 1912, she had shaped the magazine's editorial direction. Aiming to discover and satisfy the most basic needs of the new generation of American housewives, she gave editorial attention to child care and health, menu planning and food preparation, fashions, home furnishings, and handicrafts, served with a generous helping of entertaining fiction. Although her magazine bore her firm imprint, it followed the basic pattern that Edward W. Bok [Supp. 1] had earlier cut for its archrival, the *Ladies' Home Journal.* The motto she adopted, "The Woman Makes the Home," reflected the *Companion's* emphasis on home and mother. Years later Helen Woodward, who worked with Miss Lane, noted that "among the top editors there was not one who was a mother or who had a husband." "Home" to them was a bachelor apartment, sometimes shared with another single woman. Beneath the sugar frosting, she added, the magazine had toughness.

From the start Miss Lane involved her readers. She paid them for household hints. She regularly queried them on how they spent their time and money. In 1935 she set up a corps of 1,500 reader-editors in various parts of the country who provided editorial advice on household management. An enduring feature was her Better Babies Bureau, which greatly helped in disseminating modern information on prenatal and newborn care. As an acknowledged expert on the day-to-day problems of family life, she served on the planning committee for the 1930–31 White House Conference on Child Health and Protection. Her conservatism, or perhaps her canny assessment of reader opinion, made her avoid the issue of birth control, and it was not until shortly before her death that contraception was discussed in the pages of the *Companion*.

A noteworthy feature of the *Companion* was the publication of stories by some of the best-known American writers of the time, to whom Miss Lane paid top prices. The bulk of the magazine's fiction was by perennially popular women's authors like Kathleen Norris. Though a warmly partisan Republican, Miss Lane published contributions by presidents of both parties—Taft, Wilson, Coolidge, Hoover—and, in the 1930's, a regular feature by Eleanor Roosevelt.

Like other women's magazines—for instance *Good Housekeeping* with its less than disinterested "Seal of Approval"—the *Companion* under Miss Lane easily combined the service aspect of its work for women with a quite frank exploitation of their consumer needs. The success of her promotion department in garnering advertisers was regarded as a model. Building the *Companion* into a leader in the highly competitive field of women's magazines in the 1920's and '30's, she made it the most profitable of the Crowell publications. When she died, it was the third largest magazine in the United States, with a circulation of 3,608,000 and advertising revenues of $5,935,000. Her own salary was $52,000 a year.

By hard work and quiet ability, Miss Lane became a director and in 1929 vice-president of Crowell Publishing Company, whose chairman, Joseph Knapp, called her "the best man in the business." Outwardly gentle, inwardly strong, she was of medium height and had curling brown hair, an oval face, fair skin, and gray eyes framed by a pince-nez. She made her judgments impersonally, then acted decisively. Her own interests included gourmet food, classical music, and antique collecting. In addition to her Park Avenue apartment, she had a restored country home of the federal period at Harwinton, Conn. She never married. After a decade of intermittent illness, she died in her apartment of lung cancer and was buried in Laurel Hill Cemetery, Saco. She had been a Unitarian. In the estimate of Frank Luther Mott, historian of American magazines, Gertrude Lane was "one of the greatest women editors of her generation."

[The best single biographical sketch is Betty Hannah Hoffman's in *Notable Am. Women*, II, 363–65. References to Miss Lane and her magazine appear in Helen Woodward, *The Lady Persuaders* (1960), pp. 102–23, which has an informal portrait, and Frank Luther Mott, *A Hist. of Am. Magazines*, IV (1957), 768–70. Although they deal mainly with the Crowell-Collier magazines, there are references to her in *Fortune*, Aug. 1937 (which has a portrait), and Theodore Peterson, *Magazines in the Twentieth Century* (1964), pp. 128–45. See also *Who Was Who in America*, vol. II (1950); *Current Biog.*, 1941; and

Scholastic, Nov. 19, 1938. Obituaries appeared in the *N. Y. Times*, Sept. 26, 1941, *Tide*, Oct. 15, 1941, p. 58, and *Time*, Oct. 6, 1941, p. 65, and an appreciation in the *Woman's Home Companion*, Nov. 1941.]

THEODORE PETERSON

LANGDON, HARRY PHILMORE (June 15, 1884–Dec. 22, 1944), motion picture comedian, was born in Council Bluffs, Iowa. His parents, William Wiley Langdon and Levina (Lookenbill) Langdon, were Salvation Army officers; Harry was the third of their five children, and also third of four sons. In publicity interviews during his years of fame, Langdon described an early life of poverty. Forced to quit school at ten years of age, he sold newspapers and worked at odd jobs in a theatre, occasionally getting the chance to take the place of an absent performer. When he was twelve or thirteen he left home to join a traveling medicine-show company.

Langdon spent more than twenty-five years as a vaudeville actor and comedian. He became well known on vaudeville circuits before the First World War for an act he developed around 1903, "Johnny's New Car," in which he portrayed a befuddled motorist confronting a stalled car. As he tried to start the automobile, first the tires, then the fenders, and then the doors fell off, and finally the engine exploded. He also toured in a play, *The Show Girl*. On Nov. 23, 1904, he married a fellow vaudeville performer, Rose Frances Clark, with whom he teamed for some years; their marriage ended in divorce in July 1929.

Though Langdon told interviewers he launched his motion picture career by making several comedies for the independent producer Sol Lesser, no such films were publicly released. He was, however, signed to a motion picture contract in 1923 by Principal Pictures Corporation, which thereupon sold the contract to Mack Sennett. For Sennett—who billed Langdon as "his greatest comedy 'find' since Charlie Chaplin"—he made twenty-five two-reel short films between 1924 and 1926, quickly becoming one of the most popular comedians in the great period of silent motion picture comedy.

In 1926 Langdon signed with the First National Corporation to make six feature-length comedies at a salary approaching $7,500 a week, to be produced by his own independent company. He took with him several of Sennett's most talented employees, including Harry Edwards, who directed the first Langdon feature, *Tramp, Tramp, Tramp* (1926), and Frank Capra, who directed *The Strong Man* (1926) and *Long Pants* (1927). Langdon's first three features were critically acclaimed and commercially successful, but a clash with Capra broke up his team of associates and seriously damaged Langdon's standing in the motion picture industry. Langdon himself directed the remaining three features, *Three's a Crowd* (1927), *The Chaser* (1928), and *Heart Trouble* (1928). They received a lukewarm reception, and his contract was not renewed.

Like Harold Lloyd and Buster Keaton, Langdon experienced difficulty in making the switch from silent to sound motion picture comedy—difficulty not in comic skill, but in reestablishing his place in the tightly structured organizations that manufactured motion pictures in the 1930's. His last important comedy role came in the depression musical *Hallelujah, I'm a Bum* (1933). He played in some sixty-three films from 1929 until his death, acting in several feature comedies with Stan Laurel and Oliver Hardy. He also returned to the stage for several theatrical roles during World War II.

With his boyish, innocent face and wide-open curious eyes, Langdon acted the role of a helpless child-man buffeted by a world he does not understand yet remaining always comically unharmed. In talent he belongs with Chaplin, Lloyd, and Keaton among the top silent motion picture comedians, but his passive, will-less persona provided limited scope for comic depth and development. Only when he worked with Frank Capra, who went on to become an important comedy director in the 1930's, was Langdon able to add creative elements of guile and social satire to his comic portrayals.

After the termination of his first marriage, Langdon married Helen Walton on July 27, 1929. They were divorced Feb. 10, 1934, in Mexico, and May 23, 1938, in California. He then married Mabel Watts Sheldon (on Feb. 12, 1934, in Arizona, and on June 23, 1938, in California). Langdon died of a cerebral thrombosis in Los Angeles and was buried in Grand View Memorial Park, Glendale, Calif. He was survived by his third wife and a son of their marriage, Harry Philmore, Jr., his only child.

[The best critical discussion of Langdon's comic art is Donald W. McCaffrey, *Four Great Comedians: Chaplin, Lloyd, Keaton, Langdon* (1968). *Harry Langdon* (1967), a pamphlet distributed by Audio Film Center, Inc., Mt. Vernon, N. Y., contains many photographs and film stills of Langdon, a complete listing of his 95 films, descriptions of his feature movies (many of them available for rental in 16-mm. prints), and other material. Additional information on Langdon's career is in Kevin Brownlow, *The Parade's Gone By* (1969). For Langdon interviews from the 1920's, see Madeleine Matzen in *Motion Picture Mag.*, Dec. 1926, and Dorothy Herzog in *ibid.*, Oct. 1927. Langdon wrote "The Serious Side of Comedy Making," *Theatre*, Dec. 1927. Additional information was provided by Mrs. Mabel Langdon.]

ROBERT SKLAR

LANMAN, CHARLES ROCKWELL (July 8, 1850–Feb. 20, 1941), orientalist, was born in Norwich, Conn., the seventh son and eighth of nine children of Peter and Catherine (Cook) Lanman. For a century the Lanman family had been of some importance in their small coastal town, first as importers and shippers, and then, after the War of 1812, as textile manufacturers—Peter Lanman's occupation. His son Charles was educated at the Norwich Free Academy and at Yale (B.A. 1871), where he studied Sanskrit under William Dwight Whitney [*q.v.*].

Whitney was in every way suited to excite Lanman's enthusiasm: he was (like Lanman) a lover of the outdoors, a naturalist who had explored the Colorado River, and the first American whose work could be compared with that of the new masters of Sanskrit and Indo-European philology in Germany. Accordingly, Lanman chose after graduation to continue his study of Sanskrit at Yale with Whitney. After receiving the Ph.D. in 1873, he went to Germany, where he studied at Berlin, Leipzig, and Tübingen. Working at Tübingen under Rudolf Roth, the founder of the scientific study of the Veda (who had been, a generation earlier, Whitney's teacher), Lanman began the research that led to his paper *On Noun-inflection in the Veda* (1880). Upon his return to America in 1876 he began teaching at the new Johns Hopkins University. Four years later, having been spotted there by a visiting professor, he was called to Harvard as professor of Sanskrit, a position he held until his retirement in 1926.

In Cambridge, Lanman gave up the Congregational faith of his family and became a Unitarian. To meet the needs of his students he published in 1888 a *Sanskrit Reader, with Vocabulary and Notes,* an introductory textbook that was still in use eighty years later. He gained editorial experience as secretary of the American Philological Association (1879–84) and as corresponding secretary of the American Oriental Society (1884–94), editing the *Transactions* of the first society and, as joint editor, the *Journal* of the second. On July 18, 1888, Lanman married Mary Billings Hinckley and set off with his bride for a year's sojourn in India, where he gathered Sanskrit and Prakrit manuscripts for the Harvard College Library. The marriage was to be a long and happy one. The Lanmans had six children: Faith Trumbull, Thomas Hinckley, Edith Hamilton, Jonathan Trumbull and Katharine Mary (twins), and Esther Cook.

The work for which Lanman is chiefly remembered, the editorship of the Harvard Oriental Series, began in 1891. Founded by Lanman and financed by Henry Clarke Warren [q.v.], who had been his student at Johns Hopkins, the series by 1925 had grown to thirty volumes. As a scholar Lanman may have lacked the originality and brilliance of some of his colleagues, but he possessed sound judgment, an aptitude for hard work, and a remarkable zeal for accuracy. To edit, for Lanman, meant to rewrite, to rearrange, to add, and (except when dealing with a manuscript from Whitney) to delete. It is said that he spent as much time on the editing of a manuscript as the author had spent in writing it. The volumes he produced consisted of texts, translations, and studies of works written in Sanskrit and other ancient Indian languages. He drew upon a wide range of scholars: the Americans Whitney, Warren, and Maurice Bloomfield [q.v.]; the Scotsman Arthur Berriedale Keith; the continental Europeans Sten Konow, Hendrik Kern, Johannes Hertel, and Karl Geldner; the Indian S. K. Belvalkar. Especially valuable among the volumes of the series are the basic tools of Vedic research: the Whitney-Lanman translation and annotation of the *Atharva Veda Saṃhitā* (1905), Bloomfield's *A Vedic Concordance* (1906), Keith's translations of the *Yajur Veda* (1914) and the *Rig Veda Brāhmaṇas* (1920) and his *The Religion and Philosophy of the Veda and Upanishads* (1925). Lanman did not live to see Geldner's great translation of the Rig Veda in print (1951), but it was he who did the editorial work. Other important books in the series dealt with Buddhism, among them Warren's admirable *Buddhism in Translations* (1896). An exception to the prevailing seriousness was *Rāja-çekhara's Karpūra-Mañjarī* (1901), a Prakrit comedy, to Konow's text of which Lanman added an English translation in light prose and rollicking verse. This side of his nature appeared also in his chaffing and anecdotal letters to friends and in the doggerel verse that he wrote for family occasions. Lanman's work won wide recognition both at home and abroad. He was elected to the presidency of the American Philological Association (1889–90) and twice to that of the American Oriental Society (1907–08, 1919–20) and received honorary degrees from Yale (1902) and the University of Aberdeen in Scotland (1906). Some fifteen foreign learned societies honored him with membership.

Following his retirement in 1926 Lanman lived on to a vigorous old age. He had substituted rowing for horseback riding when automobiles drove him from the public streets, and he continued his daily rowing on the Charles River, ice permitting, up to his eighty-eighth year. He died in Belmont, Mass., at the age of ninety of bronchopneumonia and was buried in Mount Auburn Cemetery, Cambridge. No other American has yet done more toward developing in the West an accurate knowledge of ancient India.

[Don Charles Stone, *The Lanman Family* (1968), traces Lanman's genealogy. There are numerous entries concerning the family in Frances M. Caulkins, *Hist. of Norwich* (1866). A number of Lanman's letters to Sanskrit scholars are preserved in the Dept. of Sanskrit and Indian Studies, Harvard Univ.; other letters are in the Harvard Univ. Archives. For obituaries see *Harvard Univ. Gazette,* May 10, 1941; *Jour. Am. Oriental Soc.,* Sept. 1941; Am. Philosophical Soc., *Year Book,* 1941; and Yale Univ., *Obituary Record of Graduates,* 1940–41. Death record from Mass. Registrar of Vital Statistics. Lanman's daughter, Mrs. Robert A. Cushman of Cambridge, Mass., provided helpful information in conversation.]

DANIEL H. H. INGALLS

LAUGHLIN, HARRY HAMILTON (Mar. 11, 1880–Jan. 6, 1943), eugenist and propagandist, was born in Oskaloosa, Iowa, the fourth of five sons and eighth of ten children of George Hamilton Laughlin and Deborah Jane (Ross) Laughlin. His father, a native of Quincy, Ill., was a schoolteacher and a minister of the Disciples of Christ. After serving as president of Oskaloosa College and then of Hiram College in Ohio (1883–87), he moved his family briefly to Kansas and in 1891 to Kirksville, Mo., where he served as minister of the local Christian church and, from 1892 until his death in 1895, taught English at the Kirksville State Normal School (later Northeast Missouri State College).

Although his four brothers became osteopaths, Harry at first followed in his father's footsteps as a small-town educator. He graduated from the Kirksville normal school in 1900 with a B.S. degree in science education and became principal of the local high school. Following his marriage on Sept. 12, 1902, to Pansy Bowen of Kirksville, he accepted a high school principalship in Centerville, Iowa, but returned to Kirksville in 1905 as superintendent of schools. Two years later he joined the faculty of the normal school, where he taught agriculture and nature study.

An interest in agricultural breeding led Laughlin to initiate a correspondence in 1907 with Charles B. Davenport [Supp. 3], director of the Carnegie Institution's Station for Experimental Evolution at Cold Spring Harbor, Long Island. Three years later, when improvement of human breeding usurped Davenport's interests, he persuaded wealthy acquaintances to found a Eugenics Record Office and chose Laughlin as its superintendent. There Laughlin remained for the rest of his career. Under his direction, the Eugenics Record Office trained field workers in collecting and analyzing human pedigrees and published many works on human heredity.

Davenport and Laughlin commanded the resources to make Cold Spring Harbor the center for major advances in the study of human genetics, but for such an undertaking Laughlin was totally unfitted by background and temperament. Although he enrolled in the graduate biology program at Princeton University in 1915, receiving an M.S. degree in 1916 and a D.Sc. in 1917, he did no important scientific work. His extreme racist beliefs and strongly hereditarian views of human nature colored all his undertakings. A humorless and dogmatic investigator, he assembled data chiefly to support eugenics programs, a goal which came increasingly to concern Davenport as well.

In 1913 a Eugenics Research Association was founded at Cold Spring Harbor, the only national organization that brought together scientists interested in human heredity; Laughlin served as its secretary-treasurer after 1917. In 1916 he and Davenport began editing *Eugenical News* as a clearing house for news of activities in this field. Soon after coming to Cold Spring Harbor, Laughlin became deeply involved in a movement to pass state laws for sexual sterilization of "hereditary defectives," in which category he included tramps, beggars, alcoholics, criminals, the feebleminded, the insane, epileptics, the physically deformed, the blind, and the deaf. (Laughlin himself had epilepsy and, although happily married, remained childless.) He served on committees that advocated sterilization and published three exhaustive reports dealing with the issue. He was also among the leaders of the American Eugenics Society, founded in the early 1920's to educate the public concerning eugenic goals. Through these many activities, Laughlin was at the center of the eugenics movement, had contacts with many leading scientists, and knew such nativist popularizers of science as Madison Grant [Supp. 2] and Lothrop Stoddard.

By the 1920's Laughlin's main interests were race and immigration restriction. In June 1920, testifying before the House Committee on Immigration and Naturalization, he expressed his concern that immigrants, especially the newer immigrants from Southern and Eastern Europe, were contributing disproportionately to the hereditary crime, insanity, and feeblemindedness that threatened the quality of American stock. The committee chairman, Albert Johnson, was impressed and appointed Laughlin the committee's expert eugenics agent. Laughlin continued his studies, including trips abroad, and appeared several times before the committee with masses of graphs and charts to demonstrate the threat posed by immigrants from inferior stock. He was, then, one of many persons with scientific credentials who lent support to the racial doctrines that underlay the immigration restriction legislation of the 1920's. His international reputation as an expounder of racist doctrines was such that in 1936 he received an honorary M.D. degree from the University of Heidelberg, then under Nazi control.

By this time, however, Laughlin had become an embarrassment to the Carnegie Institution, as well as to some of the new leaders in the eugenics movement. Davenport retired in 1934, and thereafter Laughlin's position at Cold Spring Harbor became increasingly untenable. By the end of 1939 the Eugenics Record Office had been phased out and Laughlin had been eased into early retirement. He and his wife returned to Kirksville, Mo., where at the age of sixty-two he died of a coronary thrombosis. He was buried near his parents in Highland Park Cemetery, Kirksville.

[The most important source for understanding Laughlin's career is the Charles B. Davenport Papers at the Am. Philosophical Soc. in Philadelphia, which contain some of Laughlin's correspondence, his extensive annual reports to Davenport, and the minutes and reports of the various eugenics and scientific groups to which he and Davenport belonged. The *Year Books* of the Carnegie Institution of Washington, 1910–40, summarize the activities of the Eugenics Record Office. Some of Laughlin's activities and views can be followed in publications of the Record Office and in the files of *Eugenical News*. In the campaign to pass state sterilization laws, Laughlin published a number of collections of available documents, such as *Report of the Committee to Study and Report on the Best Practical Means of Cutting off the Defective Germ-Plasm in the Am. Population* (Eugenics Record Office, Bulls. 10A & 10B, 1914), and *Eugenical Sterilization in the U. S.* (Psychopathic Laboratory of the Municipal Court of Chicago, 1922). He also assembled great masses of statistics dealing with immigration and its impact upon various social problems in America that may be found in published hearings of the House Committee on Immigration and Naturalization. Laughlin's place in the broader eugenics movement is discussed in Mark H. Haller, *Eugenics: Hereditarian Attitudes in Am. Thought* (1963). Brief biographical accounts are in *Science*, Feb. 26, 1943 (obituary by Charles B. Davenport); *Nemoscope* (alumni magazine of Northeast Mo. State College), Winter 1957; and Paul O. Selby, *One Hundred Twenty-three Biogs. of Deceased Faculty Members, Northeast Mo. State Teachers College, 1867–1962* (1963), which also includes a sketch of Laughlin's father. Dr. E. Carleton MacDowell, a geneticist associated with Laughlin for many years at Cold Spring Harbor, supplied helpful information.]

MARK H. HALLER

LAWRENCE, WILLIAM (May 30, 1850–Nov. 6, 1941), Protestant Episcopal bishop of Massachusetts, was born in Boston, the fourth of seven children and younger of two sons of Amos Adams Lawrence [*q.v.*] and Sarah Elizabeth

(Appleton) Lawrence. His ancestors were farmers. His two grandfathers, Amos Lawrence [*q.v.*] and William Appleton (1786–1862), came to Boston in their youth and became successful merchants; William's father increased his business to large proportions. William was brought up on the family estate in Longwood, Brookline, in an atmosphere of wealth, philanthropy, public concern, and deep personal religion. His father, a convert from Unitarianism to the Episcopal Church, was an admirer of John Brown [*q.v.*] and active in the effort to make Kansas a free state in the 1850's; Lawrence, Kans., was named after him. The leading men of the day were often in his home. After attending the Brookline Grammar School and a private tutoring school in Boston, William entered Harvard College. He received the A.B. degree in 1871 and stayed on for a year of graduate study in history.

Lawrence's decision to enter the ministry of the Protestant Episcopal Church reflected both the religious character of the family life and the great influence of Phillips Brooks [*q.v.*], then rector of Trinity Church, Boston. To broaden his background, Lawrence began his theological studies at a Congregational institution, the Andover (Mass.) Theological Seminary (1872–74); he continued them at the Episcopal Divinity School in Philadelphia (1874–75), with a final three months at the Episcopal Theological School in Cambridge, where he received the B.D. degree in 1875. He was ordained deacon in June of that year and priest in July 1876. Meanwhile, on May 19, 1874, he had married Julia Cunningham of Boston. Of this happy marriage were born eight children: Marian, Julia, Sarah, Rosamond (who died at an early age), Ruth, William Appleton, Elinor, and Frederic Cunningham. (The two sons became, respectively, bishop of Western Massachusetts, 1937–57, and suffragan bishop of Massachusetts, 1956–68. Sarah's husband, Charles Lewis Slattery [*q.v.*], succeeded Lawrence as bishop of Massachusetts in 1927.)

From 1876 to 1883 Lawrence served first as assistant and then as rector of Grace Church in Lawrence, Mass., a textile-mill city with which his family had been intimately connected in a business way since its founding. These years in a large industrial center gave him an understanding of the problems of wage earners and people of small means. In advance of his time he protested against child labor, and warned some of his mercantile relatives about the shortsightedness of their labor policies. In January 1884 he returned to Cambridge as professor of homiletics and pastoral care in the Episcopal Theological School. On becoming dean in 1889, Lawrence

introduced the elective system and other reforms. By taking lessons in voice culture and reading the service he "induced some of the professors to do the same and thus aroused the students to their duty in reading and preaching acceptably the Word of God." Thus he came to speak and preach effectively in direct and conversational tones.

Upon the sudden death of Phillips Brooks in 1893, Lawrence was to his surprise and consternation elected bishop of Massachusetts, a post he was to hold for thirty-four years. In the church he was regarded as a liberal, but he held with deep conviction to the central tenets of the Christian faith. Although one of the ablest administrators of his time, he also had a deep pastoral concern for the clergy and peoples of the diocese. Lawrence's belief in giving theological students large freedom of thought and action caused some conservative churchmen in the early years of his episcopate to consider that he was tainted by heresy. Throughout his long life he followed the belief that "liberty creates a sense of responsibility, and through liberty and reasonable variety the Church is led into larger fields of thought and action and appeals to a greater variety of men and women."

The need of enabling the different parts of his over-large diocese "to stand upon their own feet with self-government and self-respect" led him to propose in 1901 the creation of a separate diocese of Western Massachusetts, divided along the eastern line of Worcester County. Although the plan was opposed, Bishop Lawrence brought it about on generous terms that enabled the new diocese financially to stand upon its feet. When the diocese of Massachusetts received a bequest for the construction of a cathedral in Boston, Lawrence exercised self-restraint so far as architectural splendors were concerned. Rather than diverting large sums to building, he caused the diocese in 1912 to take over as its cathedral St. Paul's Church on Tremont Street, a church in the center of the city whose congregation had diminished, and convert this at modest cost into a vital spiritual center in the most frequented part of Boston. When the congregation of Christ Church, Salem Street (the so-called "Old North Church"), built in 1723, had lapsed into desuetude, Bishop Lawrence in 1911 took over as rector, raised the funds for the building's restoration, and persuaded various friends to transfer their allegiance to this parish. Thus before most Bostonians were concerned with historic preservation, he assured the continued survival of the oldest church building in Boston.

Lawrence's administrative talents made him a

national leader in the Episcopal Church; from 1904 to 1910 he was chairman of its House of Bishops. He was noted for his ability to raise large sums of money for worthwhile causes. Though a man of innate dignity and reserve, he genuinely enjoyed the raising of money, for he lost himself in the causes he represented and sincerely felt that he was doing a favor to donors in enlisting their support. As president of the board of trustees of Wellesley College at the time of the disastrous fire of 1914, he led in raising nearly two and a half million dollars for restoration and endowment. His greatest effort was the establishment of the Church Pension Fund to replace a variety of local funds and charities for the clergy of the Episcopal Church and their dependents. Granted leave by his diocese in 1916–17, he secured an office in New York and organized a campaign to raise five million dollars for the Fund's initial reserve—a goal that was exceeded by more than three million dollars. This carefully organized drive, which made effective use of the press, free Western Union privileges, and the talents of the public relations expert Ivy Lee [Supp. 1], rested primarily upon Lawrence's personal approaches to men with whom he felt at home and was personally congenial. The Fund was established on a secure footing in 1917, and Lawrence served as its president until 1931.

One of Lawrence's greatest interests was Harvard University. In one capacity or another he attended eighty commencements; he served the university as president of the alumni association, overseer (1894–1906, 1907–13), and, from 1913 to 1931, as a fellow of the seven-member Harvard Corporation. It was he who secured in 1924 the five-million-dollar gift from George F. Baker [Supp. 1] which built the Harvard Business School. He had the uncommon distinction of being the recipient of two Harvard honorary degrees: an S.T.D. in 1893 when he became bishop and an LL.D. in 1931 when he resigned from the Harvard Corporation. Among his other honorary degrees were doctorates from Yale, Princeton, Trinity, Hobart, Lawrence, Williams, and the Episcopal Theological School, as well as from Cambridge and Durham in England.

On political issues, Lawrence's views were close to those of his friends Theodore Roosevelt and Senator Henry Cabot Lodge [q.v.], the latter one of his Harvard classmates. He strongly favored America's intervention in World War I and with equal strength opposed American membership in the League of Nations. During his thirty-four years as bishop he found respite from his many duties in periodic visits to England, as well as in biographical writing. His autobiography, *Memories of a Happy Life* (1926), is written with the same graceful but incisive style which characterizes his biographies of his father and of Roger Wolcott, Henry Cabot Lodge, and Phillips Brooks.

Lawrence resigned as bishop of Massachusetts in 1927. His life was saddened that September by the death of his wife, but he remained active as an adviser to many people and causes. He continued until 1930 as chairman of the board of trustees of St. Mark's School, and until 1940— a full fifty-six years—as a trustee of Groton School, founded in 1884 by his friend Endicott Peabody [Supp. 3]. Lawrence won praise from liberals in 1927 for urging the governor of Massachusetts to appoint a distinguished panel to review the convictions of Nicola Sacco and Bartolomeo Vanzetti [qq.v.], but was attacked from the same quarter when he endorsed the governor's eventual refusal to commute the death sentences of the two men. With considerable success, Lawrence approached public issues with openness and tolerance. At the age of eighty-five, testifying before a Massachusetts legislative committee, he urged repeal of a state loyalty oath requirement for teachers. Characteristically, one of his last major efforts, in his ninetieth year, was a fund-raising campaign for a chapel at the Massachusetts General Hospital. He died in Milton, Mass., at the age of ninety-one of a coronary thrombosis. After services in the Cathedral Church of St. Paul in Boston, he was buried in Mount Auburn Cemetery, Cambridge.

[Lawrence's *Memories of a Happy Life* (1926) and Henry Knox Sherrill's supplementary biography, *Later Years of a Happy Life* (1943), are the basic sources. See also Lawrence's *Fifty Years* (1923) and his *Seventy-three Years of the Episcopal Theological School* (1940); *A Harvest of Happy Years: The Addresses Delivered on the Fortieth Anniversary of the Consecration of William Lawrence as Seventh Bishop of Mass.* (1933); and James A. Muller, *The Episcopal Theological School, 1867–1943* (1943). For a lively family memoir by one of Lawrence's daughters, see Marian Lawrence Peabody, *To Be Young Was Very Heaven* (1967).]

HENRY KNOX SHERRILL
WALTER MUIR WHITEHILL

LEA, LUKE (Apr. 12, 1879–Nov. 18, 1945), newspaper publisher and United States Senator, was born in Nashville, Tenn., the second son and third of four children of Ella (Cocke) and John Overton Lea. His father, whose forebears included many figures prominent in the early history of Tennessee, was a lawyer. Lea was educated in the public schools, at the University of the South (B.A. 1899, M.A. 1900), and at the Columbia University Law School (LL.B. 1903). Admitted to the bar in 1903, he established a practice in Nashville.

Lea's political career began in 1906 when, as a delegate to the Democratic state convention, he took the lead, at a critical moment of disorder, in securing the gubernatorial nomination for Malcolm R. Patterson. Soon afterward the Democratic party in Tennessee was engulfed by a long and bitter controversy over the control of alcoholic beverages, and Lea emerged as a leader of the forces that demanded statewide prohibition. In the spring of 1907 he founded a daily newspaper, the *Nashville Tennessean,* to advocate prohibition and other political reforms. He championed the cause of the prohibitionist Edward Ward Carmack [*q.v.*] against Governor Patterson's "wet" administration in the 1908 elections and, following Carmack's defeat and subsequent murder at the hands of Patterson supporters, became even more ardent in his opposition to the regular Democrats. In 1910 Lea and others led a movement of insurgent Democrats who helped elect a Republican governor, Ben W. Hooper, on a reform platform. As one of the chief organizers and strategists of this "fusion" movement, Lea in 1911 was elected by the legislature to the United States Senate.

There he quickly established a reputation as one of the most progressive Senators from the South. An early supporter of Woodrow Wilson and an influential Wilson spokesman at the Democratic national convention in 1912, he was chosen in 1913 a member of the Democratic steering committee in the upper house. He supported the President's domestic and foreign policies and became identified with the unsuccessful rebellion against the Senate seniority system. Lea's home base, however, was weak. Though he tried after 1910 to reunify the Tennessee Democratic party and in 1914 left the fusion movement and supported a Democrat, Thomas C. Rye, who defeated the incumbent Republican governor, this move cost him the support of many Tennesseans, particularly zealous fusionists. Other Democrats found his growing power oppressive, and when he ran again for the Senate, Congressman Cordell Hull, seeking to cut short the time for Lea to consolidate his machine, took the lead in arranging an early primary election in 1915, at which Lea was defeated by Kenneth D. McKellar.

When the United States entered World War I in 1917, Lea, who had served on the Senate Military Affairs Committee and was a staunch advocate of preparedness, took command of the 114th Field Artillery, a National Guard unit that he had helped organize. He participated in the Meuse-Argonne offensive, rose to the rank of colonel, and was awarded the Distinguished Service Medal. A few weeks after the armistice, the Tennessean led a small group of men in a daring but abortive attempt to capture Kaiser Wilhelm II, then living in exile in Holland. (From this adventure Lea and his accomplices escaped with a mild reprimand for indiscreet behavior.)

After leaving military service in April 1919, Lea helped organize the American Legion, on both the national and state levels, and resumed his activities as publisher of the *Nashville Tennessean.* Although he did not run again for public office and in 1929 declined appointment to a vacancy in the United States Senate, he was a powerful factor in Tennessee politics during the 1920's, being closely associated with the governorships of Austin Peay [*q.v.*] and Henry H. Horton. Lea was also involved in numerous business operations, including large-scale real estate transactions. In particular, he became linked with Rogers Caldwell, an ambitious investment banker who created a vast empire of banks, insurance companies, and other enterprises. The two purchased several large banks in Tennessee and surrounding states and in 1927 bought control of the *Memphis Commercial Appeal* and the *Knoxville Journal.* Their operations expanded rapidly, but were often based on unsound or questionable financial practices, such as securing lucrative state contracts and the deposit of state funds through Lea's political connections. By 1930, when the depression had deepened, the decline of security and property values jeopardized the future of the complex Lea-Caldwell empire, and in November of that year the whole structure collapsed. A legislative investigation and a series of criminal indictments followed. In 1931 Lea and his oldest son were convicted of conspiracy to defraud the Central Bank and Trust Company of Asheville, N. C., and after a long legal battle they were imprisoned in Raleigh, N. C., in May 1934. Sentenced to serve from six to ten years, Lea was paroled in April 1936 and given a full pardon a year later.

Having lost control of his newspapers through receivership, Lea never again wielded significant influence in public affairs. He was twice married: on Nov. 1, 1906, to Mary Louise Warner, by whom he had two children, Luke and Percy Warner; and on May 1, 1920, following the death of his first wife in 1919, to her sister, Percie Warner, by whom he had three children, Mary Louise, Laura, and Overton. Lea died in Nashville at the age of sixty-six of a chronic inflammatory condition of the stomach and was buried in Mount Olivet Cemetery in that city. He was a member of the Episcopal Church.

A man of great vitality, tall and athletic, Lea was a commanding figure. He had a driving ambition and thirst for personal power that perhaps explains his downfall in the 1920's. Yet he was connected with many civic advances in his home city, including the creation of a beautiful public park; he championed notable reforms in Tennessee politics and compiled a progressive record in the Senate; and he organized and directed an influential newspaper for a quarter of a century.

[Few personal papers of Lea are available. For biographical sketches, see *Nat. Cyc. Am. Biog.*, XV, 26–27; *Biog. Directory Am. Cong.* (1961); and obituary in *Nashville Tennessean*, Nov. 19, 1945. There are brief references to Lea in Stanley J. Folmsbee et al., *Hist. of Tenn.*, vol. II (1960). Facets of his career are illuminated in: Paul E. Isaac, *Prohibition and Politics: Turbulent Decades in Tenn., 1885–1920* (1965); Everett R. Boyce, ed., *The Unwanted Boy: The Autobiog. of Gov. Ben W. Hooper* (1963); J. Winfield Qualls, "Fusion Victory and the Tenn. Senatorship, 1910–1911," West Tenn. Hist. Soc., *Papers*, no. XV (1961), pp. 79–92; Arthur S. Link, *Wilson: The Road to the White House* (1947), pp. 396, 440–42, 445; *The Memoirs of Cordell Hull* (1948), I, 77–79, 134–35, 138; Wililam D. Miller, *Mr. Crump of Memphis* (1964); William T. Alderson, ed., "The Attempt to Capture the Kaiser," *Tenn. Hist. Quart.*, Sept. 1961; Cromwell Tidwell, "Luke Lea and the Am. Legion," *ibid.*, Spring 1969; and *N. Y. Times*, Apr. 1, 1919. John Berry McFerrin, *Caldwell and Company: A Southern Financial Empire* (1939), is indispensable for the operation and collapse of the Lea-Caldwell empire.]

DEWEY W. GRANTHAM

LEE, WILLIS AUGUSTUS (May 11, 1888–Aug. 25, 1945), naval officer, was born in Natlee, Ky., one of four children of Willis Augustus Lee, a local lawyer and judge, and Susan Ireland (Arnold) Lee. He was a direct descendant of Charles Lee, brother of Henry ("Light-Horse Harry") Lee [*qq.v.*] and Attorney General in Washington's second administration. Young Lee was reared in Owenton, Ky., and educated in the local schools. Upon graduation from high school in 1904, he received a Congressional appointment to the United States Naval Academy, from which he graduated in 1908. The nickname, "Ching," that he acquired there was later reinforced by service in China in the 1920's. At Annapolis, Lee developed an ability as a marksman that won him distinction in national shooting matches and a place on the United States Olympic team of 1920.

Lee's early years in the navy included service at Vera Cruz (1914) and World War I assignments as inspector of ordnance at a munitions plant and with the destroyer forces at Brest. His sea duty in the two postwar decades saw him as commander of three different destroyers; as navigator, then executive officer, of the battleship *Pennsylvania* (1931–33); and, after promotion to captain in 1936, as commanding officer of the light cruiser *Concord*. His last sea duty before World War II was as chief of staff to the Commander, Cruiser Divisions, Battle Force. By

1939 Lee's reputation was that of a "blue water" sailor, competent but not a stickler for regulations, an avid reader and easy mixer. He liked younger officers and among them wore his rank lightly.

On the eve of the war (June 1939–March 1942) Lee served as assistant director, then director, of fleet training. He pressed successfully to have civilian scientists incorporated into his division so that they could become intimately aware of fleet operational problems, as, for example, in the installation of radar units for gunfire direction. His principal war duty, however, was at sea. When new battleships became available in 1942, Lee received command of the first division (*Washington* and *South Dakota*) and took them into the Southwest Pacific. On Nov. 15, 1942, in one of the few battle-line engagements of the war, Lee commanded a task force off Guadalcanal that sank a Japanese battleship and destroyer and prevented the Japanese from landing extensive reinforcements on that island.

In March 1944 Lee was advanced to vice admiral, with command of a battleship squadron. Most often his new battleships, because of their speed, operated with the fast carrier task forces, providing antiaircraft gunfire cover for the carriers, a function that Admiral Lee developed to the state of an art. In the navy's "island-hopping" advance toward the shores of Japan, Lee's battleships continued to support fleet operations, often by ship-to-shore bombardment. Japanese kamikaze (suicide) aircraft attacks, however, took a heavy toll. In May 1945, after almost three years at sea and participation in every major action except the battle of Midway, Vice Admiral Lee relinquished his battleship command and returned to the United States on leave. The next month he was assigned to a special training project at Casco Bay, Maine, headed by Commodore Arleigh Burke, which was studying antikamikaze weapons and tactics. That August, while riding out to his flagship *Wyoming,* anchored in Casco Bay, Lee suffered a fatal heart attack. He was buried at Arlington National Cemetery. His wife, Mabelle Ellspeth Allen of Rock Island, Ill., whom he had married on July 14, 1919, survived him. They had no children.

[General biographical accounts: *Nat. Cyc. Am. Biog.*, XXXVI, 204–05; Keith F. Somerville and Hariotte W. B. Smith, *Ships of the U. S. Navy and Their Sponsors, 1950–1958* (1959); *N. Y. Times* obituary, Aug. 26, 1945. The most complete information on Admiral Lee's activities in World War II is found in Samuel Eliot Morison, *Hist. of U. S. Naval Operations in World War II* (15 vols., 1947–62), and in Clark G. Reynolds' scholarly study, *The Fast Carriers* (1968). Brief but significant information about Lee appears in: Julius A. Furer, *Administration of the Navy Dept. in World War II* (1959); Ken Jones and Hubert Kelley, Jr., *Admiral Arleigh (31-Knot) Burke* (1962); and Milton E. Miles, *A Different Kind of War* (1967). On Lee's marksmanship, see records in Richard Schaap, *An Illustrated Hist. of the Olympics* (1963), and James B. Trefethen, *Americans and Their Guns* (1967). Biographical information prepared by Admiral Lee and other data concerning his wartime career and death were furnished by the U. S. Naval Acad. Alumni Assoc., Annapolis, Md.]

GERARD E. WHEELER

LEHMAN, IRVING (Jan. 28, 1876–Sept. 22, 1945), jurist and Jewish community leader, chief judge of the New York Court of Appeals, the state's highest court, was born in New York City. He was the fourth of five sons (one of whom died in infancy) and seventh of the eight children of Mayer and Babette (Newgass) Lehman, both natives of Bavaria. His father was a founder of the important investment banking firm of Lehman Brothers. Irving was a brother of Arthur Lehman [Supp. 2] and of Herbert Lehman, governor of New York and United States Senator. Growing up in the affluent German-Jewish community of New York City, he attended the preparatory school of Dr. Julius Sachs [*q.v.*] and Columbia University, from which he received the degrees of A.B. (1896), A.M. (1897), and LL.B. (1898). Unlike his brothers, he never entered the family business. He served as a law clerk in the office of Marshall, Moran, Williams & McVickar and was made a member of the firm in 1901; he later became a partner in Worcester, Williams & Lehman. On June 26, 1901, he married Sissie Straus, daughter of the philanthropist Nathan Straus [*q.v.*], who herself became active in local charities. There were no children.

Lehman was elected to the Supreme Court of the State of New York in 1908, having been nominated, as a compromise candidate, on the Democratic ticket. He later attributed his selection to the influence of his father-in-law, a heavy contributor to the Democratic party and a close friend of Alfred E. Smith [Supp. 3]. Upon the expiration of his first term in 1922, he was reelected, this time with the backing of both parties. The following year, again with bipartisan support, he was elected to a fourteen-year term on the state Court of Appeals. Reelected in 1937, he served from 1940 until his death as chief judge.

In his decisions and in public addresses, Lehman maintained that the law had to accommodate itself to changes in the society it served. At the same time, he entertained a strong respect for legislative discretion, and he constantly sought a balance between scrapping outmoded precedent and preserving the continuity and stability of the state's development. Broadly interpreting the state's police power to protect the well-being of

the whole community, he insisted that the legislature could fix prices of certain commodities (*People* v. *Weller,* 237 N. Y. 316 [1924]), provide for the reorganization of mortgage guaranty companies (*In the Matter of the Application of the People of the State of New York . . . ,* 264 N. Y. 69 [1934]), and authorize the Industrial Commission to set minimum wages for women and children (*People ex rel. Tipaldo* v. *Morehead,* 270 N. Y. 233 [1936], dissent). The spirit of these decisions was antithetical to earlier United States Supreme Court precedents like *Lochner* v. *New York* (1905) and *Adkins* v. *Children's Hospital* (1923), which were revivified in the mid-1930's and reflected a restrictive view of the state's power to regulate the economy.

Lehman was similarly in advance of his times on civil liberties issues. He believed firmly that human rights are inalienable and God-given and was especially zealous in thwarting infringements of religious liberty. Thus he insisted that the state had no power to compel Jehovah's Witnesses, in opposition to their religious beliefs, to salute the American flag (*People* v. *Sandstrom,* 279 N. Y. 523 [1939], concurrence) and held a peddlers' licensing statute inapplicable to religious proselytizers who go from door to door offering Bibles and tracts for sale (*People* v. *Barber,* 289 N. Y. 378 [1944]). He condemned a contemporary New York obscenity statute as unconstitutionally vague and indefinite (*People* v. *Winters,* 294 N. Y. 595 [1945], dissent); restricted the use of labor injunctions to acts that are in themselves unlawful or involve unlawful means (*Interborough Rapid Transit Co.* v. *Lavin,* 247 N. Y. 65 [1928]), and extended the New York Civil Rights Act's ban on racial discrimination in labor organizations to a postal employees' association, despite arguments that the law could impinge on federal power over the mails (*Railway Mail Association* v. *Corsi,* 293 N. Y. 315 [1944]). He also condemned the use of third-degree tactics in police interrogations (*People* v. *Pantano,* 239 N. Y. 416 [1925]; *People* v. *Doran,* 246 N. Y. 409 [1927], dissent; *People* v. *Mummiani,* 259 N. Y. 8 [1932]).

Courteous and kindly in person, Lehman was at the same time a forceful and uncompromising presiding judge. Unlike his intimate friend and predecessor as chief judge, Benjamin Cardozo [Supp. 2], he was not a seminal thinker in the law. But he did speak for an instrumentalist juridical philosophy that was at odds with the postulates of the dominant obstructionist bloc on the United States Supreme Court in the mid-1930's. He articulated an alternative judicial position on issues of public law which could replace the dogmas of liberty of contract, dual federalism, and constitutional stasis—dogmas that had produced a proliferation of judicial vetoes on state and federal economic regulatory legislation.

Off the bench, Lehman devoted a prodigious amount of time to community activities. He served on the executive committees or boards of the American Jewish Committee, the Union of American Hebrew Congregations, the Jewish Theological Seminary, the American Friends of Hebrew University, and the Intercollegiate Menorah Association. He was president of the 92nd Street Y.M.H.A. and of Manhattan's Temple Emanu-El. Most of his free time, however, was given to the Jewish Welfare Board, whose policies he had shaped from its inception. As president from 1921 to 1940, he planned and supervised a difficult postwar transition during which the Board subordinated its wartime function as a service agency for Jews in the American armed forces to become the national coordinator of Jewish community center work.

As a distinguished jurist and public figure, Lehman was chosen to give the principal address at a New York dinner in June 1945 honoring the triumphal return of Gen. Dwight D. Eisenhower after V-E Day. In what proved to be his valedictory, he extolled two ideals that he had done so much to bring toward realization: the brotherhood of all men, and the vision of America as a land of justice and opportunity. Several months later, at the age of sixty-nine, he died of a heart ailment at his home in Port Chester, N. Y. He was buried in Salem Fields Cemetery, Brooklyn.

[Lehman's Court of Appeals decisions are in vols. 237 to 294 of the *N. Y. Reports.* His widow destroyed all of his papers in her possession at the time of his death, including his irreplaceable correspondence with Cardozo, but some of his letters survive in the Herbert H. Lehman Papers at Columbia Univ. and in the archives of the Jewish Welfare Board in N. Y. City. Lehman's principal published writings off the bench include: an address to the N. Y. County Lawyers' Assoc. in its *Year Book,* 1928; *Benjamin Nathan Cardozo: A Memorial* (1938); *The Influence of Judge Cardozo on the Common Law* (1942); "The Influence of the Universities on Judicial Decision," *Cornell Law Quart.,* Dec. 1924; "Judge Cardozo in the Court of Appeals," *Columbia Law Rev.,* Jan. 1939; "Religious Freedom as a Legal Right," *Am. Hebrew,* Sept. 23, 1927; "The Spirit of America: Tribute to General Eisenhower," *Vital Speeches,* July 1, 1945; and "Technical Rules of Evidence," *Columbia Law Rev.,* May 1926. The best evaluations of Lehman are: Edmund H. Lewis, *The Contribution of Judge Irving Lehman to the Development of the Law* (1951); Bernard L. Shientag in *Menorah Jour.,* Spring 1947; Samuel I. Rosenman in *Universal Jewish Encyc.,* VI, 595–96; Harry Schneiderman in *Am. Jewish Year Book,* 1946–47; Joseph M. Proskauer in Assoc. of the Bar of the City of N. Y., *Year Book,* 1946; "Proc. in the Court of Appeals in Reference to the Death of Honorable Irving Lehman," *N. Y. Reports,* vol. 294; obituary articles and editorial, *N. Y. Times,* Sept. 23, 24, 25, 1945. See also William M. Wiecek, "The Place of Chief Judge Irving Lehman in Am.

Constitutional Development," *Am. Jewish Hist. Quart.,* Mar. 1971; and Allan Nevins, *Herbert H. Lehman and His Era* (1963). Lehman is the subject of scattered reminiscences in the holdings of the Oral Hist. Research Office at Columbia Univ. Personal information was provided by Louis Kraft, Samuel L. Brennglass, Helen L. Buttenweiser, Raymond J. Cannon, C. S. Desmond, Joseph M. Proskauer, and Samuel I. Rosenman. An oil portrait of Lehman hangs at Temple Emanu-El, N. Y. City, and a bronze bas-relief portrait plaque at the Friedenberg Collection, Jewish Museum, N. Y. City.]

WILLIAM MICHAEL WIECEK

LEJEUNE, JOHN ARCHER (Jan. 10, 1867– Nov. 20, 1942), Marine Corps officer, was born at Old Hickory Plantation, Raccourci, Pointe Coupee Parish, La. His father, Ovide Lejeune, originally a wealthy landowner of Acadian stock, had been ruined by the Civil War and was struggling to reestablish himself. His mother, Laura Archer (Turpin) Lejeune, though born in Natchez, Miss., was of Maryland Irish-Huguenot parentage. One of her forebears, after whom the boy was named, was the Baltimore physician John Archer [q.v.]. With an elder sister, Lejeune was educated at home by his mother until, at thirteen, he was sent to school near Natchez. Two years later he entered Louisiana State University, from which, in 1884, he was appointed to Annapolis. He graduated in 1888, sixth in a class of thirty-five.

After two years of sea duty as a naval cadet, Lejeune, reasoning that his aptitude lay in handling men rather than machinery, applied for assignment to the Marine Corps. The naval authorities bluntly told him he stood too high in his class and vetoed the application. Displaying early evidence of tenacity and political adeptness, Lejeune took his case to the Secretary of the Navy and, with support from his Senator, was in July 1890 appointed second lieutenant, U.S.M.C. His early years were relatively uneventful, though he saw some action during the Spanish-American War aboard the cruiser *Cincinnati.* The postwar expansion of the Marine Corps brought him rapid promotions: captain in 1899, major in 1903. In 1903 he received command of the so-called "floating battalion" of the Atlantic Fleet. This mobile battalion, embarked aboard a naval transport, was then the most important tactical unit of the Corps. It was Lejeune's battalion that President Theodore Roosevelt sent when, in 1903, he "took Panama." In 1905 Lejeune was given command of the Marine Barracks in Washington, D. C., traditional showplace and springboard for picked officers. Then, from 1907 to 1909, he held intermittent command of the Marine brigade in the Philippines.

In 1909, promoted to lieutenant colonel, Lejeune became the first Marine officer admitted to the Army War College. He finished brilliantly and acquired as friends many army officers destined for high places in World War I. His propensity for active soldiering undoubtedly accelerated his rise in ensuing years. In 1913 he was placed in command of a new brigade, the Marine Corps Advance Base Force. When in 1914, as part of a controversy with the revolutionary government of Mexico, President Wilson ordered American occupation of the port of Vera Cruz, Lejeune's brigade, together with landing parties from the fleet, swiftly secured the city. After army garrison units arrived, Lejeune and the Marines remained at Vera Cruz for nearly a year, a fruitful tour during which he organized a Marine field artillery battalion, improvised the Corps's first motor transport unit, and directed Marine aviators in their first operational missions. In his next assignment, as Assistant to the Commandant (i.e., chief of staff) of the Marine Corps from 1915 to 1917, Lejeune's foresight, reflected in legislation in which he had a guiding hand, did much to enlarge the Corps and make it ready for World War I. Characteristically, he readily achieved harmonious relationships with members of Congress and with the Assistant Secretary of the Navy in charge of the Marine Corps, Franklin D. Roosevelt.

When America entered the war, Lejeune (promoted to brigadier general in 1916) bent every effort to get to France. Despite many obstacles, including the extreme reluctance of Gen. John J. Pershing and the army general staff to include Marine officers or units in the American Expeditionary Forces, Lejeune in 1918 obtained command of the 4th Marine Brigade, the lone Marine combat unit in France. Soon afterward, advanced to major general, he succeeded to the command of the 2d Infantry Division, generally considered the best in the A.E.F. The first Marine officer ever to command an army division, Lejeune led the 2d in a series of notable victories at St. Mihiel and Blanc Mont (which General Pétain of France called "the greatest single achievement of the 1918 campaign") and in the Meuse-Argonne.

On June 20, 1920, Lejeune was appointed Commandant of the Marine Corps. During his nine-year tenure he laid many of the foundations of the modern Corps. Besides keen administrative skill, he brought to the post leadership, foresight, and common sense, as well as shrewd political judgment. Lejeune was a modernizer, but one who respected useful traditions. He founded the Marine Corps Schools for officer education and systematized the intentionally diverse selection of future officers from many sources rather than

from any one academy. His preeminent achievement as commandant was to institute the Marines' development of amphibious warfare doctrine, tactics, and technique, and to foresee their application to future war with Japan. It was Lejeune who converted the Corps from its "Banana War" role as colonial infantry into a modern expeditionary force in readiness.

When Lejeune stepped down as commandant on Mar. 5, 1929, he was immediately chosen superintendent of the Virginia Military Institute —the first Marine officer to hold this post. He retired eight years later at the age of seventy. On Oct. 23, 1895, Lejeune had married Ellie Harrison Murdaugh of Portsmouth, Va. They had three daughters, Ellie Murdaugh, Laura Turpin, and Eugenia Dickson. Lejeune once described himself as "physically powerful and constitutionally light-hearted." In appearance he was homely, rugged, gnarled, and instantly attractive. A man of total integrity and instinctive kindness, he was also deeply religious, being an Episcopalian and, like his father, a devoted Mason. He died in 1942 at Union Memorial Hospital, Baltimore, Md., of cancer of the prostate. He was buried in Arlington National Cemetery.

[John A. Lejeune, *Reminiscences of a Marine* (1930); Charles L. Lewis, *Famous Am. Marines* (1950); Robert D. Heinl, Jr., *Soldiers of the Sea* (1962); Robert B. Asprey, "John A. Lejeune: True Soldier," *Marine Corps Gazette*, Apr. 1962; Joe Arthur Simon, "The Life and Career of Gen. John Archer Lejeune" (M.A. thesis, La. State Univ., 1967); death certificate, Baltimore City Health Dept. The Lib. of Cong. holds a collection of Lejeune's papers; additional correspondence, biographical records, and memorabilia are at the Hist. Division, Marine Corps Headquarters, Washington, D. C., and the Marine Corps Museum, Quantico, Va.]
ROBERT DEBS HEINL, JR.

LEONARD, WILLIAM ELLERY (Jan. 25, 1876–May 2, 1944), poet, translator, professor of English, was born in Plainfield, N. J., the first of two children and only son of Martha (Whitcomb) Leonard, originally of Boston, and William James Leonard, a native of Plainfield. His parents named him William Ellery Channing after the famous Boston clergyman [*q.v.*], but he later dropped the "Channing." His mother was a Unitarian. His father, after graduating from the Rochester Theological Seminary in 1865, had accepted a Baptist pastorate in Evanston, Ill., but, finding himself no longer able to accept orthodox beliefs, resigned three years later and became a journalist. At the time of his son's birth he had returned to Plainfield as editor of the *Central New Jersey Times*. Religion continued to be a strong factor in his life, however; he served for some years as a lay reader in the Episcopal Church, in 1892 helped found the Unitarian Fellowship in Plainfield, and still later became a spokesman for the New Thought movement in Boston.

Young Leonard received his early education from his mother, who had opened a small kindergarten in her home, conducted on the recently introduced Montessori principles. At the age of nine he transferred to the public school, advancing from the third to the sixth grade by the end of the year. In high school he studied the classics and began writing poetry, but left in 1893, in his junior year, when his father accepted the pastorate of the Unitarian church at Bolton, Mass. A scholarship enabled him to enter Boston University, where he developed an interest in philology and studied Sanskrit as well as Latin and Greek. After receiving the B.A. in 1898, he entered the graduate school at Harvard, where he studied English literature under George Lyman Kittredge [Supp. 3] and George Pierce Baker [Supp. 1] and metaphysics under William James [q.v.], and took an M.A. in 1899. After a year as principal of the high school in Wrentham, Mass., he traveled in Europe, studying languages and philology at the German universities of Göttingen (1900–01) and Bonn (1901–02), and then began graduate work at Columbia, where he received the Ph.D. in 1904. After two years as an editor of *Lippincott's English Dictionary,* he joined the English department at the University of Wisconsin in 1906. His publications during these years included literary criticism, several sonnets in the *Atlantic Monthly,* and a privately printed volume of poetry that was well received by the critics.

Leonard was married on June 23, 1909, to Charlotte Freeman of Madison, a gifted young woman with a history of emotional instability. Her death by suicide on May 6, 1911 (shortly after her father's death), for which her family and her friends blamed Leonard, precipitated a breakdown whose chief symptom was a paralyzing terror that for the rest of his life, with rare remissions, kept him from leaving the immediate neighborhood of his home. Many years later, through analysis and self-hypnosis, he traced this phobia to two forgotten incidents of his childhood, both independently confirmed by entries in his mother's diary. In the first, as a child of little more than two, he had been waiting with his mother at a railway station and had disobeyed her by wandering away. When the train approached he was overwhelmed by panic, for the gigantic, roaring, onrushing locomotive seemed to him the menacing face of God, bent on destroying him for having left his mother's side. The second episode occurred in his first days at the

public school when, having wet his pants, he was mocked and physically menaced by a crowd of schoolboys; in his flight, his terror was intensified by a passing train that for a time barred his way to the safety of his home. In *The Locomotive-God* (1927), the most eminently readable of his many books, Leonard describes the search for the origins of his phobia. The account reads like a detective story, but though it eventuated in his finest work of art, it did not free him from his terror, and except for a brief period (1916–17) as visiting professor at New York University, he remained for the rest of his life within a few blocks of his Madison home.

Leonard's career spans the period during which American universities, particularly as centers of graduate training, were being recreated in the image of the great German universities. Despite his German training, however, he was not the stereotypical German pedant. Scholar though he was, he emulated first of all certain German poets, especially those of the Romantic movement, men of extravagant spirit and generous commitment to life, after whose example he wrote his own verses and on whose life-style he modeled his own. Perhaps the grafting of European Romantic ideals onto a basically native Unitarian conscience explains in part the tensions in his life and thought, as well as his peculiarly American brand of internationalism.

Along with George Sylvester Viereck and Ludwig Lewisohn, his contemporaries, friends, and fellow students, Leonard translated to American soil the figure of the Romantic scholar-poet, willing to seem eccentric and to court loneliness and even social ostracism in order to live his own authentic life. His very dress, particularly his flowing "artist's" tie, usually purple, always distinguished him from his more conventional colleagues, as did his political attitudes—his opposition to America's entry into World War I, for instance, and his defense of persecuted radicals like Tom Mooney [Supp. 3]. Much of his life was lived in public, since he scorned concealment, on principle. An early defender of the right to political dissent, he was also a staunch advocate of sexual freedom for everyone on the campus, including the students; and he was merciless in his contempt for all cant, whether from self-styled "patriots" or from "moralists."

Leonard's creative work was largely autobiographical, in the best Romantic tradition. Many of his poems have political subjects; others deal with personal crises. His most noteworthy poetic work, a sonnet sequence called *Two Lives* (1925), treats the painful history of his first marriage and his wife's suicide. Redeemed by a faith in passion and a hunger for truth, it comes closest of all his work in verse to transcending the late-Victorian conventions inside of which he chose to operate. Leonard's political commitments placed him ahead of his time; his feelings and sensibility are timeless; but his style and diction were already outmoded when he used them, though he wrote in a world in which the New Poetry of T. S. Eliot and Ezra Pound had already triumphed. Nonetheless, his verse translations of *De Rerum Natura* (1916), *Beowulf* (1923), and *Gilgamesh* (1934) have authority enough to survive these limitations. He read many languages and wrote studies, scholarly and popular, on the literatures of Germany and Spain, Scotland and Ireland, Greece and Rome and ancient Israel. When his poet's ear collaborated with his scholar's eye, he was able to make his greatest contributions to knowledge, explaining, for instance, the difficult metrics of the *Cid* and *Beowulf;* but he confined himself to no one narrow field of specialization.

It is as a teacher that Leonard is and should be best remembered, for in the classroom he was everything he was out of it—translator, critic, scholar, poet, autobiographer, raconteur, philosopher, theologian, wit—plus something else: a model for the young of the way in which the stuff confided by authors long dead to the pages of books grown dusty on library shelves can again become living flesh. His knowledge was formidable, his powers of recall astonishing, his impatience with the pretentious matched only by his patience with the ignorant or confused. He taught many subjects, lectured on many authors—Beowulf and Burns, Lucretius and Chaucer—but what his students learned from him, always, was the art of teaching itself.

On Oct. 10, 1914, three years after his first wife's death, Leonard married Charlotte Charlton, who divorced him in 1934. On June 29, 1935, he married Grace Golden, who divorced him a year later. He remarried his second wife on Apr. 25, 1940. He had no children, but in the deepest sense his students, disciples, and academic colleagues were his family, and the university his home. He died in Madison of a heart attack at the age of sixty-eight and was buried there in Forest Hills Cemetery.

[Besides Leonard's autobiographical *The Locomotive-God,* see, for biographical and critical material: Ludwig Lewisohn in the *Nation,* June 6, 1923; Howard Mumford Jones in the *Double Dealer,* May 1926; Clarence E. Cason in *Va. Quart. Rev.,* July 1928; Alfred Kreymborg, *Our Singing Strength* (1929), pp. 414–18; Ernest L. Meyer in *Am. Mercury,* July 1934; Fred B. Millett, *Contemporary Am. Authors* (1940), pp. 432–36; Wilson O. Clough in *Prairie Schooner,* Spring 1946; and Clara Leiser in *Tomorrow,* May 1949. On his father, see Univ. of Rochester, *Gen. Catalogue, 1850–1928* (1928), p. 25; and *Christian Register,* Oct. 28, 1920, p. 1064.]
LESLIE A. FIEDLER

LEVERETT, FRANK (Mar. 10, 1859–Nov. 15, 1943), glacial geologist, was born in Denmark, Iowa, the oldest of at least three children of Ebenezer Turner Leverett, a farmer, and Rowena (Houston) Leverett. His father was a native of Maine, his mother of New Hampshire. After finishing his secondary education at the Denmark Academy, Leverett taught for two years and then returned to the academy (1880–83) to learn the Latin and Greek required for admission to college, serving also as an instructor in the natural sciences. With his students he collected fossils from the quarries and coal beds in the area and thus developed an interest in paleontology.

Leverett entered Colorado College at Colorado Springs in 1883. Field excursions into the mountains and assaying work in the laboratory there brought about a shift in his interests from paleontology to geology, and after a year he transferred to the Iowa State College at Ames to make up his deficiencies in physics and chemistry. He received the B.S. degree in 1885 with a thesis on an artesian well near Des Moines, Iowa. The geologist W J McGee [*q.v.*], who read it, suggested that Leverett apply for work to Thomas C. Chamberlin [*q.v.*], head of the United States Geological Survey's new Division of Glacial Geology at Madison, Wis. For the interview, Leverett walked the 250 miles from Denmark to Madison, studying the geological formations as he went; he was hired as field assistant for that summer (1886).

He continued to work for several years, on a temporary basis, under the supervision of Chamberlin, who so frequently quoted his assistant's observations that students came to refer to Leverett as "Chamberlin's eyes." In 1890 Leverett received a permanent appointment with the Geological Survey, which he held until his retirement in 1929. In 1909 he moved to the University of Michigan, where he continued until 1929 as a lecturer in geology, also conducting field trips. His exceptional knowledge outran the interests of many students but to others it was a unique asset.

Throughout his career Leverett adhered undeviatingly to the study of glacial geology. He was adept in tracing the principal features of the terrain through a welter of superficial topography, and was amazingly acute in spotting minor rises on a flat plain. In the extent of ground examined he is unequaled. He probed nearly every square mile of Illinois, Indiana, Ohio, Michigan, and Minnesota, and large parts of contiguous states and Canada. In 1908 he made a trip to Europe, where he studied the Pleistocene glacial deposits for comparison with those on the North American continent. He made most of these excursions on foot, and later calculated that during his lifetime he had walked the equivalent of four circuits of the earth.

From his maps of glacial and associated deposits throughout the upper Mississippi Valley and the Great Lakes areas, Leverett established a temporal classification which, with slight modification, remains the standard for the Pleistocene period in North America. It identifies four sheets of glacial drift from four ice advances, the duration of each advance being judged by the thickness of the drift, and the antiquity of the drift by the depth of weathering and the extent of stream dissection of its surface. Although many researchers contributed to the knowledge of Pleistocene glaciation, Leverett carried out the largest part of the studies and did much to unify them. He made the primary study of the Illinoian stage, and named it as well as the bracketing interglacial stages. His interpretation of the "gumbo" as a weathered product of ancient till was a further contribution to glacial geology. By tracing the high beaches of the Lake Erie basin to outlets and to moraines at former ice margins, he ended a long-standing controversy about the problem of glacial high water levels in the Great Lakes. His studies were intended mainly to advance knowledge, but they also produced practical benefits in helping to determine the local distribution of soils, supplies of gravel, clay, and marl, and especially ground water.

Leverett's great contribution was in the realm of observation rather than theory. Compared with contemporaries in the same field, he lacked the inductive powers of Chamberlin, the knack for elegant exposition of Israel C. Russell [q.v.], Mc-Gee's joy in the curious, and the imagination of Frank B. Taylor [Supp. 2]. More than any of these men, however, Leverett remained steadfast to his original theme. The great value of his work lies in its thoroughness and in the scrupulous accuracy and systematic recording of his observations. His professional publications total more than 5,600 pages, and include three massive government monographs that are bibles to geologists in their respective territories: *The Illinois Glacial Lobe* (1899), *Glacial Formations and Drainage Features of the Erie and Ohio Basins* (1902), and, with Frank Taylor, *The Pleistocene of Indiana and Michigan and the History of the Great Lakes* (1915). Among the honors he re-

ceived are an Sc.D. degree from the University of Michigan (1930) and election to the National Academy of Sciences (1939).

Leverett was twice married: on Dec. 22, 1887, to Frances E. Gibson, who died in 1892; and on Dec. 18, 1895, to Dorothy Christina Park, who survived him. He had no children. In religion he was a Unitarian. A familiar figure on the sidewalks of Ann Arbor, Mich., Leverett by the age of eighty was acquiring a stoop, while his walking stick was already bent from being carried horizontally behind his back, hooked by an elbow at each end. He died at his home in Ann Arbor at the age of eighty-four of myocardial failure and was cremated at Woodmere Cemetery, Detroit, Mich. Glaciers in both Greenland and Antarctica bear his name.

[The principal sources are the memorials by William H. Hobbs in Geological Soc. of America, *Proc.*, 1943, and Nat. Acad. Sci., *Biog. Memoirs*, vol. XXIII (1945), both with bibliographies of his publications. See also Stanard G. Bergquist in *Science*, Apr. 21, 1944; G. M. Stanley in Mich. Acad. Sci., 46th *Annual Report*, 1945; *Who Was Who in America*, vol. II (1950). Family data from 1870 federal census (courtesy Iowa Hist. Lib.); death record from Mich. Dept. of Public Health. A bust of Leverett by the sculptor Carleton W. Angell is at the Univ. of Mich.]

GEORGE M. STANLEY

LEVINSON, SALMON OLIVER (Dec. 29, 1865–Feb. 2, 1941), lawyer and peace advocate, was born in Noblesville, Ind., the second son and youngest of five children of Jewish parents, Newman David and Minnie (Newman) Levinson, both natives of Germany. He was originally named Solomon but later changed the spelling. His father, who had come to America in 1848, owned a general dry goods store and had a reputation as a scrupulously honest merchant. His mother was active in local charities.

After attending public school in Noblesville, Levinson applied to Yale, but was rejected for lack of Greek. He entered the University of Chicago in 1883, but after dropping out in 1886 to earn money, he again applied to Yale and was admitted as a senior. Upon graduating in 1888, he returned to Chicago. There he read law in the firm of Moses and Newman, of which his uncle Jacob Newman was a partner, and studied at the Chicago College of Law, from which he received the LL.B. degree in 1891.

Forming a legal partnership in Chicago with Benjamin V. Becker, Levinson built up a successful practice, and soon became a specialist in the financial reorganization of business corporations. In 1908 he straightened out the personal affairs of George Westinghouse [q.v.] and soon afterward those of the troubled Westinghouse companies. From his legal fees and from investments in the corporations he organized, he amassed a large fortune. Levinson did little trial work, preferring to negotiate a reasonable settlement by informal discussions out of court. He regarded a lawsuit as a miniature war, in which there was waste of every kind; it was to this conviction that he later attributed his interest in the settlement of international disputes.

That interest took shape during World War I. With the outbreak of the war, although his legal career was then at its peak, Levinson diverted his energies to the promotion of peace. At first he tried to bring together the two main bodies of neutral opinion in America, led by the pro-German financier Jacob Schiff and the pro-Allied educator Charles W. Eliot [qq.v.]; but the increasing rapacity of German submarine warfare soon ended this effort. He then turned to the idea to which he was to devote the remainder of his life. As set forth in a *New Republic* article ("The Legal Status of War," Mar. 9, 1918), this was the concept that war should be stripped of its legitimacy by making it illegal. For a time Levinson hoped that such a provision would be embodied in the peace settlement at Versailles, but when the covenant of the League of Nations failed to embody his principle, he bitterly opposed the treaty and the League, and, later, the League-affiliated World Court. To Levinson the "outlawry" of war was the basic first step to peace. Beyond that he envisaged a plan, never clearly spelled out, for the codification of international law. The third step in his peace program was the establishment of an international court, an independent institution to be modeled on the Supreme Court of the United States. Those nations which refused to recognize the "inherent and affirmative jurisdiction" of the court and resorted to war would outlaw themselves, thereby enabling the community of nations to invoke against them the inalienable right of self-defense.

Levinson supported Warren G. Harding in the presidential race of 1920, despite that candidate's reluctance to endorse his idea of the outlawry of war; and in 1921 he vainly attempted to persuade participants in the Washington Disarmament Conference to consider his proposals. That December he organized the American Committee for the Outlawry of War and launched a campaign to carry the issue to the public and the molders of opinion. Over the next few years he gained important adherents—the philosopher John Dewey, the reformer Raymond Robins, Charles Clayton Morrison, editor of the *Christian Century,* and Senator William E. Borah [Supp. 2]. Levinson wrote innumerable letters and interviewed scores of public officials; in 1923 he hired

a publicist to spread his views in Europe. His group did not always enjoy the support of other peace workers—a "harmony agreement" in 1925 with the pro-League forces led by Prof. James T. Shotwell of Columbia proved short-lived—but the outlawry advocates made up in persistence what they lacked in numbers. In April 1927 Levinson went to Europe and for the next year worked actively to effect a Franco-American agreement embodying the principle of outlawry. His efforts were finally rewarded when the Kellogg-Briand Pact was signed in 1928. This multinational treaty was ratified by the United States Senate in 1929. When President Herbert Hoover proclaimed the pact in a White House ceremony, Levinson was the only invited guest.

Levinson was twice married: on Aug. 9, 1894, to Helen Bartlett Haire, by whom he had three children, Horace Clifford, Ronald Bartlett, and Helen Winthrop; and on Jan. 10, 1914, ten years after his first wife's death, to Ruth Langworthy, by whom he had one son, John Oliver. He adhered to the Jewish religion, but in later life belonged to the Community Church in New York City as well as to Sinai Congregation in Chicago. In 1929 he donated $50,000 to the University of Idaho to establish the William Edgar Borah Outlawry of War Foundation. He was twice proposed for the Nobel Peace Prize. Levinson died at Michael Reese Hospital in Chicago of coronary sclerosis and was buried in Oak Woods Cemetery, Chicago. Outlawry of war failed in the 1930's because of the lack of machinery for enforcement, but the failure was not merely Levinson's; it was that of his generation, for after World War I many people believed that it was possible to rid the world of war through words.

[Levinson's papers—more than 40,000 letters plus some 100,000 other items—are at the Univ. of Chicago. The best single source for his career is John E. Stoner, *S. O. Levinson and the Pact of Paris* (1943). Charles Clayton Morrison, *The Outlawry of War* (1927), discusses Levinson's theory from the point of view of a supporter. A critical account of his activities appears in Robert H. Ferrell, *Peace in Their Time: The Origins of the Kellogg-Briand Pact* (1952). See also Drew Pearson and Constantine Brown, *The Am. Diplomatic Game* (1935); editorial and tributes in *Unity,* May 1941; *Nat. Cyc. Am. Biog.,* XXXI, 198–99; Yale Univ., *Obituary Record of Graduates, 1940–41.*]

ROBERT H. FERRELL

LEWIS, DEAN DE WITT (Aug. 11, 1874–Oct. 9, 1941), surgeon, was born in Kewanee, Ill., the only child of Lyman Wright Lewis, a merchant, and Virginia Winifred (Cully) Lewis. His paternal grandfather was a Baptist minister. Young Lewis attended Lake Forest (Ill.) College, graduating, A.B., in 1895. He then entered the College of Physicians and Surgeons in New York City but transferred the next year to Rush

457

Medical College in Chicago, where he received the M.D. degree in 1899.

After a year's internship at Chicago's Cook County Hospital, Lewis returned to Rush Medical College (which had become affiliated with the University of Chicago) as assistant in anatomy. There he became interested in the process of vital staining of tissues and used it to demonstrate the microscopic changes and proliferation of the chromophile cells that take place in the anterior lobe of the pituitary gland in a patient suffering from acromegaly. In 1903, after spending six months working in Leipzig with the renowned anatomist Werner Spalteholz, he was advanced to instructor.

Two years later Lewis moved to the department of surgery, where he advanced through the academic ranks to professor in 1919. In addition to giving popular courses in surgical anatomy and operative surgery, he carried on a large private practice and served as attending surgeon at the Presbyterian Hospital in Chicago. In 1917, following America's entry into World War I, Lewis was commissioned as a major in the Army Medical Corps and organized Base Hospital 13 from the staff of the Presbyterian Hospital. He took the unit to France in May 1918 and subsequently headed several evacuation hospitals that specialized in reconstructive and neurological surgery. After his discharge in 1919, with the rank of lieutenant colonel, he received the Distinguished Service Medal for his work in saving lives among the wounded combat troops.

It is said that in the five years after 1920 Dean Lewis was offered every major vacant surgical chair in the country. In January 1925 he became professor of surgery at the University of Illinois, but six months later he moved to Baltimore to fill the post formerly held by William S. Halsted [q.v.] as professor of surgery at the Johns Hopkins University School of Medicine and surgeon-in-chief of the Johns Hopkins Hospital. He retained this post until illness forced his retirement in 1939.

Lewis's publications include *A Laboratory Manual of Human Anatomy* (1904), written with Lewellys F. Barker, and a large number of papers dealing with the ductless glands, methods of transplanting nerve and bone, reconstructive surgery, acromegaly, the role of sex hormones in tumor growth, and ethylene as an anesthetic, a method he helped its discoverer, Dr. Arno B. Luckhardt, introduce into clinical use. Lewis was one of the founders and the first editor (1920–40) of the *Archives of Surgery,* a journal designed to give young surgeons a place to report their investigative work. He also edited the *Interna-*

tional Surgical Digest (1926–41) and the widely used eleven-volume set, *Practice of Surgery* (1932).

Lewis was extremely well read in both medicine and the humanities and interested in music and sports. His keen memory and broad knowledge of the medical literature made him an effective and stimulating teacher. The famous Friday noon surgical clinics for the Johns Hopkins medical students were lively, if somewhat intimidating, sessions. A warm, witty, and jovial speaker, Lewis was in great demand at medical meetings all over the country. He belonged to numerous professional societies and served as president of the American Medical Association in 1933–34.

On Nov. 26, 1903, Lewis married Pearl Miller of St. Anthony, Idaho. She died in 1926, and on Dec. 26, 1927, he married Norene Kinney of Girard, Ohio. Their three children were Julianne, Dean De Witt, and Mary Elizabeth. In 1938, on one of his many lecture trips, Lewis suffered a cerebrovascular disturbance from which he never fully recovered. He died three years later at his home in Baltimore and was buried in New Cathedral Cemetery.

[The *Archives of Surgery,* Aug. 1940, contains a brief biographical sketch of Lewis by his Chicago colleague Dr. Vernon C. David. The most useful insight into Lewis's work as teacher and surgeon may be gained from an unpublished MS., "Comments about the Surgical Chiefs at the Johns Hopkins Hospital between 1918 and 1938," kindly provided by its author, Dr. Warfield M. Firor. The most informative obituary appeared in the Baltimore *Sun,* Oct. 10, 1941. See also *Archives of Surgery,* Dec. 1941; *Jour. Am. Medic. Assoc.,* Oct. 18, 1941; *Military Surgeon,* Dec. 1941; *Who Was Who in America,* vol. I (1942); *Nat. Cyc. Am. Biog.,* XXXI, 212–13. The Johns Hopkins Univ. School of Medicine, Archives Collection, has a "Minute on the Death of Dr. Dean Lewis" by the Advisory Board of the Medical Faculty, Oct. 31, 1941. The Univ. of Chicago Lib. confirmed the dates and titles of his appointments there.]

GERT H. BRIEGER

LHÉVINNE, JOSEF (Dec. 14, 1874–Dec. 2, 1944), pianist and teacher, was born at Orel, Russia, a small town near Moscow, the son of Jewish parents, Arcadie and Fanny (Lhévinne) Lhévinne. His father was a trumpet player in the orchestra of the Bolshoi Theatre. Josef began studying piano at the age of four with Nils Chrysander, a Swedish student at the Moscow Conservatory. His talent attracted attention, and at the age of twelve, under the patronage of a banker, he entered the Moscow Conservatory as a student of Vassily Safonov, its director. Two years later, after playing for the great virtuoso Anton Rubinstein, Lhévinne was invited to make his professional debut, which took place in November 1888 at the Hall of Nobles in Moscow, with a performance of the Beethoven Piano

Concerto No. 5 (the "Emperor" Concerto) with the Moscow Symphony Orchestra under the direction of Rubinstein. He graduated from the conservatory in 1891, having won the virtuoso diploma and a gold medal award. Lhévinne spent the next few years in study with Rubinstein and in concert tours in Russia and in Central Europe. In 1895 he won the annual competition for the Rubinstein Prize, but was forced to interrupt his musical career by a year's required military service.

On June 20, 1898, Lhévinne married Rosina Bessie, daughter of a Dutch businessman, Jacques Bessie, and his Russian wife, both of whom were amateur pianists. Rosina had entered the Moscow Conservatory at the age of nine, had briefly been a pupil of Lhévinne's, and at her graduation in 1898 had received the gold medal award in piano. The Lhévinnes moved to Tiflis, where early in 1899 they made their concert debut as a two-piano team. In Tiflis Josef Lhévinne began his teaching career at the school of the Imperial Russian Music Society. He moved in 1902 to the Moscow Conservatory, where he held a professorship until the revolution of 1905 forced its closing.

Lhévinne made his American debut on Jan. 27, 1906, in Carnegie Hall, New York City, playing the Rubinstein Piano Concerto No. 5 with the Russian Symphony Orchestra under the direction of Safonov. Later that year he made a highly successful tour of the Eastern states under the auspices of the Steinway Piano Company. Returning to Europe, he settled with his family in Wannsee, a suburb of Berlin, and until the outbreak of the First World War he made concert tours throughout Europe and the United States. During the war years the Lhévinnes were interned in Germany as enemy aliens, but they continued their teaching, though forbidden to appear in public performances.

In 1919 the Lhévinnes with their two children, Constantine Don and Marianna, moved to the United States and settled in New York City. They opened a studio for piano teaching, acquired American citizenship, and in 1924 were appointed to the faculty of the newly established Juilliard Graduate School. Josef Lhévinne made yearly concert tours in the United States and Latin America, appeared as soloist with many symphony orchestras, and made European tours in 1926, 1929, and 1937. The two Lhévinnes also gave many concerts as duo-pianists.

Josef Lhévinne ranked with the greatest piano virtuosos of his day. Emotionally attuned to the Romantic composers, he was particularly famed for his performances of Chopin and Tchaikovsky,

and his few recordings include works by Liszt and Debussy. His playing was marked by flawless brilliance of technique, clarity of style, and beauty of tone, which he could control to the most refined and delicate degree. He was one of that great succession of Russian Romantic virtuosos, beginning with Anton and Nikolai Rubinstein, whose superb musicianship, technical command, and emotional projection made them masters of interpretive performance. Thus Lhévinne has been characterized as a "super-virtuoso with a poetic temperament."

Although he received great adulation from his audiences, Lhévinne remained a quiet and modest man, devoted as much to teaching as to performing. His generosity toward needy friends was unfailing. He took particular pleasure in outdoor life, and spent his summer vacations on a farm near Portage, Wis., where he could enjoy fishing and target shooting and pursue his hobby of astronomy.

Lhévinne taught at the Juilliard School until the end of his life. He gave his last public performance on July 31, 1944, at the Lewisohn Stadium in New York, where he played the Tchaikovsky Piano Concerto No. 2 with the New York Philharmonic-Symphony Orchestra. That December he died of a heart attack at his home in Kew Gardens, Queens, New York City, shortly before his seventieth birthday. He was buried in Maple Grove Cemetery, Queens. For more than a quarter of a century his wife, Rosina Lhévinne, continued her own notable teaching career at the Juilliard School.

[H. Howard Taubman, "Four Hands That Play as Two," *N. Y. Times Mag.*, Jan. 8, 1939 (on Josef and Rosina Lhévinne); obituary in *N. Y. Times*, Dec. 3, 1944; Winthrop Sargeant's profile of Rosina Lhévinne, *New Yorker*, Jan. 12, 1963; interview in *Etude*, Oct. 1923–Mar. 1924; *Who's Who in Am. Jewry*, 1938–39; *Who Was Who in America*, vol. II (1950). Useful clippings are in the files of the Music Division, N. Y. Public Lib. at Lincoln Center, and in faculty scrapbooks at the library of the Juilliard School. A biographical report prepared at the Columbia Univ. School of Library Service by Lee Johnson was helpful. An RCA Camden record, "The Art of Josef Lhévinne," collects a number of his shorter recordings.]

FRANK C. CAMPBELL

LILLIE, GORDON WILLIAM (Feb. 14, 1860–Feb. 3, 1942), frontiersman and Wild West showman, known as "Pawnee Bill," was born in Bloomingdale, Ill., the oldest of the two sons and two daughters of Susan Ann (Conant) and Newton Wesley Lillie. His mother came of a Boston family. His father, born in Quebec of Scottish parents, had established a successful flour mill in Bloomington. As a boy, Gordon attended the local school and worked in the mill in the evenings and on Saturdays. His father wished him to succeed to the business and his mother urged him to become a teacher, but visiting cousins from Kansas, with their tales of Indians, buffalo, and wild game on the Indian Territory frontier, fired him with the hope of going west to make a fortune. His dreams were further fueled by reading of the exploits of such famous plainsmen as William F. ("Buffalo Bill") Cody and James Butler ("Wild Bill") Hickock [*qq.v.*], as portrayed in Street and Smith's *New York Weekly,* Beadle and Adams's dime novels, and other favorites of the day. In 1874, while he was in high school, fire destroyed his father's mill, and the entire family moved to Kansas and resettled near the town of Wellington. There the boy helped with the chores of their primitive home, taught school for a few months, and made frequent visits to nearby Indian encampments, where he became acquainted with the Pawnees.

Still longing for adventure, Lillie left home at the age of fifteen intending to become a cowboy, but at Wichita became involved in a gunfight in which he was forced to kill his opponent. After acquittal by a coroner's jury, he rode on to visit his Pawnee friends, now removed to the Indian Territory, and stayed nearly a year, working in the Pawnee rock quarry and the government sawmill. During the next five years he led a varied existence: he spent some time in the Cherokee Outlet (later part of Oklahoma) and the Texas Panhandle, killing buffalo and other animals for their hides; held a government job as schoolteacher and interpreter at the Pawnee Agency; and worked as a cattle rancher.

His knowledge of the Pawnee language and customs led in 1883 to his introduction to show business. Buffalo Bill Cody was organizing a new version of his traveling Wild West show and wished to include a group of Pawnee Indians. The federal Indian Commissioner gave his consent if Lillie traveled with them as interpreter and protector, and for several years he toured the country with this and other shows, thus gaining his nickname of Pawnee Bill. At a performance given in Philadelphia that first summer he met May Manning, daughter of a physician; they were married on Aug. 31, 1886. Their son, born the following summer, lived only a few weeks. (A son adopted many years later died in an accident at the age of nine.) Lillie's wife learned to ride and shoot, and in 1888 when he launched his own tent show, "Pawnee Bill's Historic Wild West," she joined the company, gaining fame for her riding and marksmanship. The show failed after a few months, however, chiefly because of competition from Cody's better-known enterprise.

Returning to Wichita, Lillie took an active role in the Kansas "boomer" movement, seeking to open the unassigned lands of neighboring Indian Territory (later Oklahoma) to white settlers. At the request of the Wichita board of trade, he organized the Pawnee Bill Oklahoma Colonization Company, and when the land was officially opened on Apr. 22, 1889, he led a group of 3,200 colonists in their run to stake claims. He led a similar group at the opening of the Cherokee Outlet in 1893.

Meanwhile, in 1890, Lillie had revived his Wild West show, which now became one of the best-paying circus properties in the United States. For nearly twenty years he spent the summers touring the United States and Canada and the winters in Kansas and Oklahoma. In 1894, at the invitation of King Leopold, he took his show to the international exposition at Antwerp, Belgium, and later toured in Holland and France. After years of sometimes bitter competition from Buffalo Bill's show, Lillie agreed to a merger in 1909, but Cody was erratic in his business methods and the combination lasted only four years, after which the company was disbanded.

Lillie retired to Oklahoma, where he had acquired a 2,000-acre ranch near Pawnee, and for the rest of his life he devoted himself to the interests of the state he had helped to open. He joined the national effort to save the buffalo from extinction and maintained a large herd on his estate, helped in the establishment of an 8,000-acre tract in the Wichita Mountains as a national game preserve, bred prize swine and cattle, actively supported the local Boy Scout movement, and promoted the building of good highways across the Southwest. Still a showman, he established on his ranch an Old Town and Indian Trading Post that recaptured the romance of pioneer days and attracted many visitors. In September 1936, shortly after celebrating their fiftieth wedding anniversary, Pawnee Bill and his wife were injured in an automobile crash. She died three days later. Although Lillie survived for several years, he never fully recovered, and a few days before his eighty-second birthday he died at his ranch home. He was buried at Highland Cemetery in Pawnee.

[Glenn Shirley, *Pawnee Bill: A Biog. of Major Gordon W. Lillie* (1958), includes an extensive bibliography. See also Lillie's autobiography, *Life Story of Pawnee Bill* (1916). The Univ. of Okla. Lib. has a Gordon W. Lillie Collection. Other material is in the Pawnee Bill Archives of Mr. Allan Rock, N. Y. City, and in the author's personal collection.]

GLENN SHIRLEY

LINCOLN, JOSEPH CROSBY (Feb. 13, 1870–Mar. 10, 1944), novelist, was born in Brewster, Mass., on Cape Cod, the only child of Joseph and Emily (Crosby) Lincoln. His ancestors on both sides of the family had settled on Cape Cod in the mid-seventeenth century; his father, like his grandfather and uncles, was a sea captain. When Joseph was about a year old his father died, and the boy grew up in the home of his maternal grandmother. He was allowed to roam the Cape at will and thus acquired an intimate knowledge of its distinctive culture and became familiar with the idiom, thrifty ways, and understated humor of its people.

Joseph received his early education at the local school and when about twelve moved with his mother to Chelsea, Mass. (near Boston), where he attended high school, returning to the Cape each summer. After finishing his schooling he held various jobs, as office boy and bookkeeper in the Boston area and as clerk in a brokerage firm in Brooklyn, N. Y. For a time he studied art with the Boston illustrator Henry Sandham [q.v.], and then opened a commercial art studio in Boston. To help sell his drawings he began supplying them with humorous verses, which attracted favorable notice, and in 1896, when the fever for bicycling was at its height, he became a staff illustrator and associate editor of the *Bulletin* of the League of American Wheelmen. On May 12, 1897, he married Florence E. Sargent of Chelsea. They had one son, Joseph Freeman, who in later life became his father's collaborator on several books.

Deciding to become a writer, Lincoln returned to Brooklyn in 1899; by day he worked as an editor of a New York banking publication and at night and on weekends he wrote stories and verses. His first short story, set in Cape Cod, was accepted by the *Saturday Evening Post,* and in 1902 he published a volume of his poems, *Cape Cod Ballads,* with illustrations by the popular artist Edward W. Kemble. Lincoln's first novel, *Cap'n Eri* (1904), brought him immediate success and fame. Its hero is one of three old sea captains who, in need of a housekeeper, advertise for a wife. The humorous complications that ensue, the fresh portrayal of the Cape Cod atmosphere and characters, and passages of convincing realism in an unpretentious but well-told story made the book a best seller, and it went through many printings.

A second novel, *Partners of the Tide*, was published in 1905, and others appeared thereafter, at the rate of one or two a year, until shortly before Lincoln's death. The titles provide a kind of inventory of the harvest he drew from a lean but to him inexhaustible soil. They include *Cy Whittaker's Place* (1908), *The Depot Master* (1910), *Cap'n Warren's Wards* (1911), *Extricating*

Obadiah (1917), *The Portygee* (1920), *Galusha the Magnificent* (1921), *Great Aunt Lavinia* (1936), and, his last novel, *The Bradshaws of Harniss* (1943). Critics deplored the worn copybook morality of his plots, the repetitiousness of his tales, the lack of intellectual content, his sentimentality, and his convenient reliance on stereotypes. But the humor never flagged, and Lincoln fulfilled his aim in telling a story skillfully and projecting the character and flavor of a long-vanished Cape Cod. The author Hamlin Garland [Supp. 2], in a friendly but not undiscerning appraisal, wrote of Lincoln's "keen sense of character" and his "democracy of sentiment and fancy which never—or very seldom—loses its hold on the solid ground of experience."

Lincoln's son described him as "short, fat, laughing, and infinitely friendly," a frank sentimentalist who loved Cape Cod, people, and good food. He was an active member of the Unitarian Church. Of his more than forty novels none was a failure, and their sales ranged from 30,000 to 100,000 copies. They brought him a fortune, which enabled him to travel in Europe, to maintain a summer home at Chatham on Cape Cod as well as a winter home (first at Hackensack, N. J., and later at Villanova, Pa.), and to enjoy his chief hobbies, fishing and golf. In the last years of his life failing eyesight made writing difficult. He died of a heart ailment in his apartment at Winter Park, Fla., at the age of seventy-four and was buried at Chatham.

[*The Joseph C. Lincoln Reader* (1959), an anthology edited by his son, has an introductory memoir and tribute. Lincoln's *Cape Cod Yesterdays* (1935), non-fiction, includes much personal reminiscence. The one book about him, James W. McCue, *Joe Lincoln of Cape Cod* (1925), is inadequate. Other sources: Grant Overton, *Authors of the Day* (1922), pp. 167–88; tribute by Hamlin Garland in *Publishers' Weekly,* Apr. 17, 1920; Stanley J. Kunitz and Howard Haycraft, eds., *Twentieth Century Authors* (1942); an early biographical sketch in *Nat. Cyc. Am. Biog.,* XIV, 90–91; obituary in *N. Y. Times,* Mar. 11, 1944; information from Donald Consodine, Town Clerk, Brewster, Mass.]

HENRY BEETLE HOUGH

LINDSEY, BENJAMIN BARR (Nov. 25, 1869–Mar. 26, 1943), judge and social reformer, better known as Ben B. Lindsey, was born in Jackson, Tenn., the first of three sons and eldest of four children of Letitia Anna (Barr) and Landy Tunstall Lindsey. His father, a captain in the Confederate Army, was a native of Jackson, Miss.; according to family tradition, the first American Lindsey had migrated to pre-Revolutionary Virginia from Scotland. The boy's mother, a first-generation American of Scotch-Irish and Welsh origin, was born in Tennessee.

Ben's early childhood, spent chiefly at his maternal grandfather's home in Jackson, Tenn., was happy but not entirely free of discord. The Lindsey family's conversion to Catholicism soured relations with the Barrs, though they continued to regard their grandchildren with affection. When Ben was eleven, his father, a superintendent of telegraph operations, moved the family to Denver, Colo. He was soon persuaded, however, to enroll the boy in an elementary school attached to Notre Dame University in Indiana. That experience ended abruptly after two years when the elder Lindsey lost his job, making the family dependent upon the Barrs for support. Returning to Tennessee, Ben studied at Southwestern Baptist University—the equivalent of a preparatory school—where he participated actively in school affairs and became secretary of the debating society. Letters to his parents, who remained in Denver, were those of a happy, gregarious boy. During this period his maternal aunt's husband became a second father to him. "Uncle Bates," a follower of Henry George [q.v.] and a strong anti-Catholic, may have contributed to Lindsey's sympathy in later years for unorthodoxy in politics and economics, and perhaps influenced his decision, a few years after this Tennessee period, to leave the Catholic Church.

Shortly after Ben's return to Denver at the age of sixteen, his father, despondent over poor health and mounting debts, committed suicide. Ben and his younger brother now became the family breadwinners. Unable to finish high school, as he had hoped to do, Ben worked concurrently as a janitor, newspaper carrier, and office boy for a lawyer, with whom he began to read law. According to his own account, fatigue and despair led him to attempt suicide when he was nineteen. Out of this crisis grew a resolve to continue with the law, and in 1894, at twenty-four, he was admitted to the bar. He soon became active in Democratic politics and was rewarded in 1899 by a minor post as public guardian and administrator. In 1901 he was appointed to an unexpired term in a county judgeship, an office he continued to hold, through numerous heated elections, for the next twenty-six years. During his tenure, and largely through his efforts, his court evolved into the Juvenile and Family Court of Denver, the best-known court of its kind in the world; within a few years Lindsey had become, in the public mind, the leading representative of the burgeoning juvenile court movement.

With extraordinary energy, Lindsey drafted and effectively mobilized popular support behind every major item of children's legislation enacted in Colorado. His booklet *The Problem of the Children and How the State of Colorado Cares for Them* (1904) described the early "Lindsey Bills" and led to their adoption in a number of states, often aided by his personal appeals to legislative committees. His most important original contribution to juvenile legislation was the Colorado Adult Delinquency Act of 1903, which established the principle that adults contributing to the delinquency of a minor were legally responsible. By 1920, forty states and the District of Columbia had adopted laws based on this Colorado statute.

The Judge also won fame as a lyceum speaker. A great raconteur, he often recalled in his lectures his own conversion to the juvenile court program, with its emphasis upon probation rather than confinement. Shortly after his appointment to the county judgeship, Lindsey had sentenced a young boy to reform school for stealing some coal. The boy's mother became hysterical and had to be removed from the courtroom. The scene so unnerved the Judge that he arranged with the district attorney to place the boy on informal probation, even though there was no legal basis for the action. That evening Lindsey visited the boy's home and discovered that he had stolen the coal to heat his parents' shanty; the boy's father was unable to work and was dying of lead poisoning contracted in a mine. Under existing laws, neither the state nor the employer had any obligation to help the family. This episode invariably elicited the humanitarian sympathy of an audience and underlined the need for social legislation, which Lindsey increasingly emphasized. It also supported another major theme of Lindsey's speeches and writings, that economic injustice was the major cause of crime. A second episode, also based on fact, which became part of the Lindsey legend was his experiment in sending an "incorrigible" boy to detention school without an escort. Soon the "experiment" became a frequent practice, and the boys Lindsey trusted rarely failed him.

Lindsey's work in Denver attracted the attention of national magazines, and numerous writers visited Denver to observe his court, including Lincoln Steffens [Supp. 2], who wrote three articles for *McClure's* in 1906 on "The Just Judge." Lindsey himself described his battles with the public utilities companies of Colorado in a series of articles for *Everybody's Magazine* (1909–10), later published in book form as *The Beast* (1910). An inveterate correspondent, he formed friendships with Jacob Riis, Theodore Roosevelt, and Edward W. Scripps. He also exchanged political endorsements with Roosevelt,

Joseph W. Folk, Tom Johnson, Robert M. La Follette, and Brand Whitlock [*qq.v.*]. In the same period, he was peripherally associated with such causes as woman suffrage, prison reform, and the abolition of capital punishment. Usually a Democrat, Lindsey temporarily left his party to run unsuccessfully for governor as an independent in 1906, and again, in 1912, to aid in the formation of the Progressive party in Colorado.

In the 1920's, partly as a result of problems he encountered in his court, Lindsey became increasingly interested in, and identified with, the so-called sexual revolution. In collaboration with Wainwright Evans, he wrote *The Revolt of Modern Youth* (1925) and *The Companionate Marriage* (1927), in which he advocated compulsory education in sexual matters, including contraception, and a liberalization of divorce laws which would permit a childless couple who had failed in an honest effort to save their marriage to obtain a divorce without the cost and formality of a conventional lawsuit. Lindsey's proposals were not extremely radical, but his vehement attack on the smugness and hypocrisy of American puritans and his enthusiasm for the younger generation's growing frankness regarding sex caused the public media to portray him as chief spokesman for "flaming youth."

Lindsey's pervasive liberalism made him an inevitable target of the Ku Klux Klan, a major influence in Colorado in the 1920's. His narrow electoral victory in 1924 was reversed when the Colorado supreme court invalidated all votes in a predominantly Jewish precinct where Lindsey had run strong. In 1929 he was disbarred for receiving remuneration for legal services during his judgeship. Since the services were rendered in New York in a matter outside his jurisdiction, it was widely believed that the punishment was excessive and motivated by personal animosity.

Although the Colorado supreme court readmitted him to the bar in 1935, Lindsey spent the rest of his life in California, where he had moved in 1930. In 1934 he ran for a county judgeship in Los Angeles and won an overwhelming victory. He also drafted new proposals for children's legislation. The best known of these, adopted by the California legislature in 1939, was the Children's Court of Conciliation, a formalized effort to save marriages through counseling. Lindsey presided over the Los Angeles division of this court until his death.

On Dec. 20, 1913, Lindsey had married Henrietta Brevoort of Detroit, who was subsequently closely associated with him in his work. They had one adopted daughter, Benetta (a composite of their first names). Lindsey died of a heart attack at the Good Samaritan Hospital in Los Angeles at the age of seventy-three; his body was cremated. His ashes were strewn in the garden of the family home, except for a small portion which his widow sprinkled on the site of Lindsey's courthouse in downtown Denver.

[Charles E. Larsen, *The Good Fight: The Life and Times of Ben B. Lindsey* (1972), is a full-length biography. The Lindsey Collection in the Lib. of Cong. contains MSS. and reprints of the Judge's writings, including laws he drafted, an extensive correspondence, and newspaper scrapbooks assembled by his widow. Duplicates of a small portion of the collection, emphasizing the California years, are at the Univ. of Calif. at Los Angeles. All of Lindsey's published writings abound in personal anecdotes. His autobiography, *The Dangerous Life* (1931), provides valuable insights into his personality but is incomplete, badly organized, and occasionally inaccurate. On specific aspects of Lindsey's career see Frances A. Huber, "The Progressive Career of Ben B. Lindsey, 1900–1920" (Ph.D. dissertation, Univ. of Mich., 1963); Reuben Borough, "The Little Judge," *Colo. Quart.*, Spring 1968; Peter G. Slater, "Ben Lindsey and the Denver Juvenile Court," *Am. Quart.*, Summer 1968.]

CHARLES E. LARSEN

LITTAUER, LUCIUS NATHAN (Jan. 20, 1859–Mar. 2, 1944), glove manufacturer, Congressman, philanthropist, was born in Gloversville, N. Y., the eldest son and the second of five children of Jewish parents, Nathan and Harriet (Sporborg) Littauer. His mother was from an old, established Albany family; his father had come to the United States as a boy of sixteen from Breslau, Prussia, to which Littauer's great-grandfather had migrated from Littau, Lithuania. After peddling dry goods and opening a store in Gloversville, Nathan Littauer entered the glove business, prospered, and in 1865 moved to New York, where he established the city's first glove shop. He brought up his children in a happy home that valued work, learning, and the arts.

Lucius Littauer attended Wells Seminary in Gloversville, the Charlier Institute in New York, and Harvard College, from which he graduated in 1878. He then entered his father's Gloversville business, which on Jan. 1, 1883, was reorganized as Littauer Brothers, with the twenty-three-year-old Lucius at its head. He made it the nation's largest glove manufacturer, employing 800 to 1,000 workers, and also helped organize and served as president of the Glove Manufacturers' Association.

Although Littauer, like his father, was a Republican, he voted for Grover Cleveland in the presidential elections of 1884 and 1888. His strong support of the McKinley Tariff brought him back into the Republican fold in 1892. An effective lobbyist, he had reportedly helped William McKinley frame his prohibitive glove schedule, and in 1894 he influenced Congress to increase those duties further in the Wilson-Gorman Tariff; both acts brought prosperity and growth to the glove industry. That success, coupled with the gift of the Nathan Littauer Hospital to Gloversville, led in 1896 to Littauer's election to Congress as a Republican, though two years earlier he had failed to win the nomination.

During his five terms in Congress (1897–1907), Littauer served on the Appropriations Committee, favored government frugality, supported ship subsidies and the metric system, and facilitated migration to the United States of religious and political refugees. He became a friend of Speaker Joseph G. Cannon [q.v.], who aided Littauer's successful effort to include a high rate on gloves in the 1909 Payne-Aldrich Tariff. Despite his closeness to Cannon, however, Littauer was a progressive in New York politics and a friend and adviser of both President Theodore Roosevelt and Gov. Benjamin B. Odell [q.v.]. Publication in 1903 of the "gauntlet scandal" marred his public service. This was the revelation that during the Spanish-American War Littauer's company had made gloves for a government contractor, despite the law barring Congressmen from being even indirectly party to a federal contract. The statute of limitations made prosecution impossible, but Littauer's enemies, including Thomas C. Platt [q.v.], used the scandal in an attempt to unseat him. Littauer fought their charges and was reelected in 1904, but declined to run two years later.

For a time, he remained a strong Republican leader. In the national convention of 1912 he supported Roosevelt for the presidential nomination, but did not follow him into the Progressive party. Littauer's political career came to an end in 1914 when he and his brother William were indicted for smuggling into the country, as a present for William's wife, a diamond and pearl tiara allegedly worn by the Empress Josephine. Pleading guilty, they were each fined $1,000, but to prove that politically powerful rich men were not given preferred treatment, the court also meted out unprecedented six-month suspended prison sentences. The fact that obedience to the tariff by others had helped build his fortune compounded Littauer's humiliation.

After recovering from what he described as "a general nervous collapse" (1917 Class Report), Littauer immersed himself in business activities. A decade later, in 1924, his wife, Flora Mathilda Crawford (whom he had married on July 12, 1913), died of pneumonia, and Littauer, who was childless, began to concentrate on philanthropy. He gave $300,000 for an annex to the Littauer Hospital to be known as the Flora Littauer

Memorial, as well as other benefactions for the Gloversville area. He also gave money to hospitals in Breslau, Paris, and New York; to medical schools in New York and Albany; and for research on pneumonia, cancer, diabetes, psychiatry, and speech disorders. Proud of his heritage, he endowed in 1925 the Nathan Littauer Professorship of Jewish Literature and Philosophy at Harvard and later gave Harvard nearly 15,000 volumes of Hebrew literature. To promote "better understanding among all mankind," he established the Lucius N. Littauer Foundation, endowing it over the years with securities worth $3,800,000 and giving its directors wide latitude in disbursing funds. His greatest benefaction was the $2,250,000 he gave in 1935 and 1937 to establish Harvard's Graduate School of Public Administration; it would, he hoped, train future high-level career bureaucrats able to avoid the mistakes he felt had been made by the New Deal administration of Franklin Roosevelt.

An excellent speaker and an impressive figure, Littauer in his later years was stout and bald with a walrus moustache. Having suffered for two years from a heart ailment, he collapsed and died at the age of eighty-five at his country estate near New Rochelle, N. Y. He was buried in Salem Fields Cemetery, Brooklyn.

[Littauer destroyed virtually all of his correspondence, but three scrapbooks of newspaper clippings and some letters, as well as numerous photographs and memorabilia, are at the Lucius N. Littauer Foundation in N. Y. City. The successive *Class Reports* of his Harvard Class of 1878 include autobiographical statements (though his assertion that he was a delegate to the national Republican convention of 1884 is not confirmed by its published proceedings). An interview with Harry Starr, Littauer's friend and counsel and a director of his foundation from its inception, proved valuable. Other details of Littauer's career can be found in *N. Y. Daily Tribune*, Aug. 21, 1892, *N. Y. World*, Aug. 22, 23, 1892, and *N. Y. Times*, Aug. 23, 1892, Jan. 27, 1929, sec. 10 (see Index, 1883–1944, for other references); *Biog. Directory Am. Cong.* (1961); *Who's Who in Am. Jewry*, 1938–39; *Nat. Cyc. Am. Biog.*, XXXII, 82; editorial comment on the "gauntlet scandal" in the *Nation*, July 9, 1903; Washington Frothingham, ed., *Hist. of Fulton County* (1892); Lucius N. Littauer, ed., *Louise Littauer: Her Book* (privately printed, 1924), on the family background; brief references in Elting E. Morison et al., eds., *The Letters of Theodore Roosevelt* (8 vols., 1951–54).]

ARI HOOGENBOOM

LODGE, JOHN ELLERTON (Aug. 1, 1876–Dec. 29, 1942), art museum director, was born in Nahant, Mass., the second son and youngest of the three children of Henry Cabot Lodge [q.v.] and Anna Cabot Mills (Davis) Lodge. The poet George Cabot Lodge [q.v.] was his brother. Ellerton Lodge, as he was known, was educated by private tutors and, after 1887, when his father took his seat in Congress, at Mr.

Young's School in Washington, D. C. He entered Harvard College in the autumn of 1896 but left early in his sophomore year because of eye trouble. Although he never returned to Harvard, he lived in Boston, devoting himself to music and painting, for which he had a natural gift. He studied at the New England Conservatory in 1899–1900, and in 1907 set the choral odes and lyric scenes of Aeschylus's *Agamemnon* to music for a performance by the Harvard Greek department. When a board of trustees of the Boston Symphony Orchestra was formed in 1918, Lodge was a member; he served until 1931. On Aug. 31, 1911, he married Mary Catherine Connolly of Lourdes, Nova Scotia; there were no children.

Lodge stumbled into his true career when in May 1911 he joined the staff of the Boston Museum of Fine Arts as temporary assistant to Kakuzo Okakura, curator of Chinese and Japanese art. The museum had in the previous thirty years acquired the greatest collection of Japanese art in the Western world, and in 1905 had persuaded Okakura—a kind of Japanese William Morris—to join its staff. Lodge's three months' appointment introduced him to the art of the Far East, which became the major interest of his life. At the end of this period he was made assistant in charge of paintings and exhibitions, with responsibility for cataloguing and installing objects in the galleries. He soon devised plans for a storage-study for the safe and accessible keeping of some four thousand paintings. He was promoted to assistant curator in January 1913 and to acting curator in September of that year after Okakura's premature death.

Lodge became curator of Chinese and Japanese art in January 1916. He studied Oriental languages, reading widely in them, and built up a library in the museum on the art, religion, and philosophy of China and Japan. He attended quietly and effectively to the improvement of exhibition and conservation arrangements, and maintained the highest standards in the acquisition of objects. Of his skill in this difficult field, Kojiro Tomita, his assistant and successor, wrote: "He refused to be influenced by his own personal likes and dislikes. In selecting an object, his motto was always 'the best of its kind,' a simple phrase but one difficult to adhere to. Through his almost uncanny insight, he was able to choose the best in whatever branch of art was involved."

In December 1920 Lodge took on the added responsibility of the collection that Charles L. Freer [*q.v.*] had given to the Smithsonian Institution in Washington. At the time of Freer's death in the autumn of 1919, the Freer Gallery of Art, which was built on the Mall, had almost been completed, but it fell to Lodge to convert this great private collection into an operating public institution. Although appointed director of the Freer Gallery in 1921, he retained his Boston curatorship for a decade thereafter, dividing his time between the two institutions. The gallery in Washington was opened on May 2, 1923; it then became his responsibility to use the funds bequeathed by Freer for "the acquisition and study of Oriental Fine Arts." Upon the basis of Freer's collection, Lodge built up notable holdings of Chinese bronze, jade, sculpture, painting, and pottery; Indian sculpture and painting; Armenian, Arabic, and Persian manuscripts and painting; Islamic glass, pottery, and metal work. In these acquisitions he showed the same discriminating taste that had marked his purchases for Boston. He also stressed the importance of scholarly examination and comparison and the use of archaeological evidence, maintaining a field staff in China which worked in cooperation with the Chinese government in the investigation of ancient sites and in the study and translation of texts and inscriptions from numerous Oriental languages. The Freer Gallery thus became a valuable research center, as well as the most subtle artistic amenity in the Smithsonian complex.

Lodge resigned the Boston curatorship in the spring of 1931 but continued as director of the Freer Gallery until his death. He died in Washington in 1942 of a coronary occlusion following an operation for cancer. Although he wrote little, Lodge left an impress upon two great collections of Oriental art.

[Although Lodge consistently ignored questionnaires from his Harvard Class of 1900, the Secretary's *Tenth Report* (1945) contains a sketch of his life by his nephew, Ambassador Henry Cabot Lodge. See also obituary notices in *Ars Islamica*, IX (1942), 239–40, and *Am. Jour. of Archaeology*, May–June 1943, p. 228. There are references to Lodge in the author's *Museum of Fine Arts, Boston: A Centennial Hist.* (1970). Birth and marriage records from Mass. Registrar of Vital Statistics; death record from D. C. Dept. of Human Resources.]

WALTER MUIR WHITEHILL

LOMBARD, CAROLE (Oct. 6, 1908–Jan. 16, 1942), film actress, originally Jane Alice Peters, was born in Fort Wayne, Ind., the only daughter and youngest of three children of Frederick C. Peters, a salesman for a local manufacturing company, and Elizabeth (Knight) Peters. Her parents, natives of Indiana, were of Scottish, English, and Welsh descent. They were divorced in 1916, and Mrs. Peters took her children to Los Angeles, Calif. There, through family friends, Jane came to the attention of the veteran screen director Allan Dwan, who cast her in her first film, *The Perfect Crime,* when she was twelve. She attended the Los Angeles high school and enrolled in the Marian Nolks Dramatic School, becoming a star pupil. At sixteen she came to the notice of a scout from Fox studios, which engaged her for a leading role in *Hearts and Spurs* (1925), a Buck Jones Western. For her next film, *Marriage in Transit* (1925), Fox changed her name to Carol Lombard (the final "e" was not added until 1930), and soon gave her a five-year contract.

Her contract lapsed, however, when she was injured in an automobile accident which left a scar across the left side of her face. It was feared that this would end her film career, but plastic surgery minimized the scar, and by studying motion picture photography she worked out methods to conceal it. In 1927 she signed a contract with the Mack Sennett Company. Sennett was the master of slapstick comedy and had developed many of the screen's greatest comedians, including Charles Chaplin. At first Miss Lombard worked as one of the "Sennett Bathing Beauties," but she soon graduated to leading roles in two-reel comedies, where she developed the innate comic abilities that later made her one of the finest American movie comediennes.

Miss Lombard left the Sennett Company in 1928 and began free-lance work at various studios. Although she was given important roles, few of the films displayed more than her sleek, blond beauty. In 1930 she signed with Paramount Pictures, which also squandered her talents on indifferent films. Not until *Twentieth Century* (1934) was she given an opportunity to display her full comic talents. As the glamorous movie queen Lily Garland, she played with vivacious high spirits and managed to hold her own against her formidable co-star, John Barrymore [Supp. 3]. Other good roles followed: a gold-digging manicurist in *Hands Across the Table* (1935), and a dizzy debutante in *My Man Godfrey* (1936). Perhaps her finest performance was in *True Confession* (1937), in which she played a charming but pathological liar whose inability to tell the truth involves her in a murder trial. She found her most popular role, however, in the acerbic *Nothing Sacred* (1937), where as Hazel Flagg she becomes an instant celebrity when it is reported (incorrectly) that she is a victim of radium poisoning.

These three performances brought her career to a peak in 1937—a year in which she earned $465,000—and gave final form to the Lombard image that appealed so greatly to the audiences of the 1930's. These "screwball" comedies sharply reflected the public mood during the nation's worst economic depression—a deep loss of confidence and a delight in poking fun at conventions and values that seemed to have lost meaning. The honesty and zany breeziness she brought to her parts gained her a wide popularity. According to the critic Richard Schickel, Miss Lombard epitomized a new type of heroine, women who were realists in the company of naive, fumbling men: "They had a sharper sense of right and wrong, were better students of tactics, and were masters of the mannish wisecrack. In a movie world where women had, prior to the depression, been either innocents or exotics, they were refreshingly down-to-earth."

Noted as a practical joker, a party giver, and a ribald raconteur, off screen Miss Lombard lived up to her on-screen character as an irrepressible comedienne. Her behavior as a working actress, however, was entirely professional. She gained the respect of such directors as Ernst Lubitsch for her analytical approach to the filming of a scene and her sensitive response to direction. She also won the affection and admiration of the bit players and technicians who contribute so much to a movie's success.

Miss Lombard's first marriage, to actor William Powell on June 26, 1931, ended in divorce two years later. After a long courtship, she was married on Mar. 29, 1939, to the actor Clark Gable. Thereafter she accepted fewer film roles in order to be with Gable, whose pleasure in outdoor sports, camping, and hunting she learned to share. Their happy, sometimes boisterous, life together helped maintain her popularity. Although she never had the opportunity to repeat her earlier comic triumphs, in *They Knew What They Wanted* (1940) she displayed her versatility by her competent acting in a noncomic role.

At the outbreak of World War II, Miss Lombard was one of the first Hollywood stars to contribute to the war effort, and she made several cross-country trips selling war bonds. In January 1942, on the return flight from a trip to Indianapolis, she and her mother, along with all on board, were killed when the plane crashed into a mountain near Las Vegas, Nev. After Methodist funeral services, she was buried at Forest Lawn Memorial Park, Glendale, Calif. Her last film, *To Be or Not To Be* (1942), was released after her death.

[Homer Dickens in *Films in Rev.,* Feb. 1961; Richard Schickel, *The Stars* (1962), pp. 154–55. See also: *Life,* Oct. 17, 1938; *N. Y. Times,* Jan. 17–19, 1942; Alan S. Downer in *Notable Am. Women,* II, 425–26; Lewis Jacobs, *The Rise of the Am. Film* (1939); Pauline Kael, *Kiss Kiss Bang Bang* (1968); and Charles Samuels, *The King* (1961), a biography of Clark Gable.]

GARY CAREY

LOWDEN, FRANK ORREN (Jan. 26, 1861–Mar. 20, 1943), lawyer, governor of Illinois, presidential aspirant, agricultural leader, was born near Sunrise City, Minn., the third of eleven children of Lorenzo Orren Lowden and Nancy Elizabeth (Bregg) Lowden and the only son and second eldest among their six children who survived infancy. His mother, of English, Dutch, and French ancestry, was a schoolteacher. His father, two of whose English and Scottish forebears had emigrated in 1638 to Massachusetts, was a blacksmith-farmer, who moved in 1868 to Point Pleasant, Iowa, and later (1881) to nearby Hubbard. There he became a lawyer and acquired a reputation as a Granger, Greenbacker, and Democrat. Young Lowden attended local rural schools and taught in them for five years before entering the University of Iowa in 1881. After graduating in 1885 as valedictorian, he taught for one year at the Burlington, Iowa, high school and then went to Chicago, where he clerked for a law firm and enrolled in evening classes at the Union College of Law. He graduated in 1887 (again as valedictorian) and established a comfortable practice in Chicago. On Apr. 29, 1896, following a chance introduction on shipboard, he married Florence Pullman, elder daughter of George M. Pullman [q.v.]. They had four children: George Mortimer Pullman, Florence, Harriet Elizabeth, and Frances Orren.

His wife's devotion, as well as her wealth and social prominence, largely shaped Lowden's career. Following her father's death in 1897, Lowden managed a number of the "Car King's" enterprises and organized several large manufacturing corporations. In 1902 he moved to "Sinnissippi," an estate of 600 acres (4,400 by 1919) fronting the Rock River near Oregon, Ill., about one hundred miles west of Chicago. There, and at a summer home in the Thousand Islands, the "Squire" indulged his liking for cards, fishing, golf, and horseback riding. Although he seldom profited financially from his Sinnissippi crops, livestock, and forest, their yield in farming experience and friendships with agricultural leaders was high.

His residence at Sinnissippi, in a rock-ribbed Republican area of Illinois, turned Lowden's interest more strongly toward a political career. Long a Republican, he had helped his party for a decade in local, state, and national campaigns, and he was as favorably regarded by Roosevelt as he had been by McKinley. On his first try for elective office in 1904, Lowden narrowly missed the gubernatorial nomination. Two years later he was chosen to complete the Congressional

term of the deceased Robert R. Hitt [q.v.]. His constituency reelected him in 1908, but two years later he declined to run again because of ill health. While in Washington he centered his efforts upon bills relating to natural resources, agriculture, and tariff administration. Perhaps his most notable achievement was his successful fight to reform and upgrade the State Department's Consular Service. In 1912, the last of his eight years on the Republican National Committee, he backed Taft for renomination, even though he admired Roosevelt and thought highly of the Progressives' economic program.

Yielding to pressure from leaders of his party, Lowden sought the governorship in 1916 and defeated the Democratic incumbent, Edward F. Dunne. Although he won national acclaim by enthusiastically supporting President Wilson's measures and by making the Illinois statehood centennial celebration "a great vehicle for patriotic propaganda," Lowden's most significant achievement was administrative reform. In addition to establishing a centralized purchasing agency, a uniform accounting system, and an executive budget, he abolished or united about 125 boards, bureaus, or commissions and grouped the rest among nine departments, each under a director responsible only to the governor. By 1930 fourteen states had adopted similar measures, and the federal Bureau of the Budget, created in 1921, bore a considerable resemblance to the Illinois model.

Lowden's record at Springfield, his cooperation with Roosevelt in reuniting most of the Illinois Progressives with the Republican party, and his ability to voice the needs of both agriculture and industry made him a leading candidate for the presidential nomination in 1920. Yet Lowden had many political liabilities. His Pullman connections and his style of country living repelled many wage earners and small farmers. In addition, sharp differences with Mayor William Hale Thompson [Supp. 3] of Chicago over patronage, the reform of local governments, and the suppression of antiwar groups denied Lowden the unanimous backing of the Illinois delegation. His chief rival for the nomination was Leonard Wood [q.v.], popular with the party's progressive wing. Lowden hoped to attract the support of the Republican Old Guard, who were leaning toward Senator Warren Harding; but shortly before the start of the national convention in Chicago, a Senatorial committee accused Lowden's campaign manager of bribing two Missouri delegates. As a result, Lowden's position weakened, and when the convention deadlocked, with neither he nor Wood able to secure a majority,

Lowden released his delegates and thereby enabled Harding to win.

After the convention Lowden refused to seek a second term as governor. He also declined, over the next few years, an opportunity to run for the Senate, several important diplomatic posts, including the ambassadorship to Great Britain, and the Republican vice-presidential nomination in 1924. Instead he devoted his energies to the improvement of agriculture and the machinery of government. He worked closely with the National Institute of Public Administration and helped establish the Public Administration Clearing House. He became active in many societies concerned with rural life, and through speeches and articles he urged country folk to unite for their own betterment and city folk to recognize that their welfare was threatened by the economic ills of agriculture. Lowden's early belief that the remedy for these ills lay in federated, single-commodity marketing cooperatives, controlled by farmers, enjoyed the favor of the White House. He lost this support, however, when, from 1926 to 1933, he endorsed the "radical" McNary-Haugen bills. Hoping to underline his warnings that the rural crisis, in spite of the industrial boom, portended a general depression and thus dwarfed all other national problems, Lowden reluctantly announced his candidacy for the Republican presidential nomination in 1928. After the party's Kansas City convention upheld all of Coolidge's policies, thus implicitly labeling Lowden a "calamity howler," he abruptly withdrew his candidacy and refused to aid in Herbert Hoover's election campaign. He remained aloof, as well, from the Hoover administration, rejecting invitations to serve as Secretary of Agriculture and ambassador to Britain.

Lowden's entire political career, in both state and national politics, exemplified a basic problem of his party, its uneasy alliance between industrialists and farmers. Continuously seeking to reconcile the one wing with the other, he was misrepresented by his opponents in 1920 as an ultraconservative businessman and in 1928 as an agrarian radical. When the economic distress of the 1930's and the Democratic victory in 1932 fulfilled his predictions, Lowden became an elder statesman, the "Sage of Sinnissippi," from whom both Hoover and Franklin D. Roosevelt asked advice, and to whom Republican candidates came for a blessing. In his old age Lowden remained active. He served for a decade as one of the court-appointed trustees of the bankrupt Chicago, Rock Island, and Pacific Railway, and vigorously opposed Roosevelt's assault on the Supreme Court, his bid for a third term, and his apparent

readiness to have the United States enter World War II. The death of Lowden's wife in 1937 was a shock from which he never fully recovered. He died of cancer at Tucson, Ariz., in 1943 and was buried in Graceland Cemetery, Chicago. Convinced that country living best nurtured American ideals, he bequeathed one of his two Arkansas cotton plantations to the Farm Foundation as a site for encouraging tenants to become owners of "family-sized farms."

[The largest collection of Lowden's papers, including correspondence and MSS. of his speeches and articles, is at the Univ. of Chicago. His official papers as governor are in the Ill. State Lib., Springfield. William T. Hutchinson, *Lowden of Ill.* (2 vols., 1957), is a full-scale biography based on the papers. For accounts of Lowden's role in the 1920 Republican convention, see Robert K. Murray, *The Harding Era* (1969), and Francis Russell, *The Shadow of Blooming Grove: Warren G. Harding in His Times* (1968).]
WILLIAM T. HUTCHINSON

LOWELL, ABBOTT LAWRENCE (Dec. 13, 1856–Jan. 6, 1943), president of Harvard University, was born in Boston, Mass., the second of three sons and seven children of Augustus and Katharine Bigelow (Lawrence) Lowell. Of the five children who survived infancy, two others won distinction—the oldest, Percival, the astronomer, and the youngest, Amy, the poet [qq.v.]. The Lowells constituted a Boston-Harvard dynasty of wealth and culture, notable for judgeships, trusteeships, and entrepreneurship in manufacturing and banking. Abbott Lawrence Lowell especially admired his grandfather John Amory Lowell, for many years a member of the Harvard Corporation. He was named for his maternal grandfather, Abbott Lawrence [q.v.], one of the most conspicuous "self-made men" of his day, who won a fortune in textiles, served as ambassador to Great Britain, and founded the Lawrence Scientific School at Harvard. A. Lawrence Lowell (as he became known) was said to combine the reserve of the Lowells with the geniality of the Lawrences. From childhood, he was physically hardy, cheerful, and uncomplicated. His mother, an invalid, influenced him less than did his father, the autocratic and effective president of various banks and insurance companies, who instilled the family tradition of achievement.

Because of Mrs. Lowell's ill health, the family went abroad in 1864, and for two years the sons attended the boarding school of a Mr. Kornemann in Paris. Lawrence's ease with foreign languages stemmed from this experience. In Boston he studied at the school of W. Eliot Fette before and probably after going abroad. He pursued preparatory studies at George W. C. Noble's private classical school, entering Harvard in 1873. Five generations of Lowells had preceded him there.

He roomed in a private dwelling, first with his brother, then with his cousin and future brother-in-law, Francis Cabot Lowell. Classmates remembered him as rather uncomradely, and he later regretted having known so few of them. The long-legged, barrel-chested Lowell was noted, however, for winning several distance races in track competition.

To the distress of his father, Lowell made a mediocre academic record at Mr. Noble's and as a college freshman, but during his sophomore year he blossomed. Although he recalled favorably the teaching of Henry Adams and William James, he was especially inspired by the mathematics classes of Benjamin Peirce [qq.v.]. He took second-year honors in mathematics and graduated cum laude with highest final honors in that field. In recalling mathematics as excellent training, he claimed to have learned from it that matters are generally true or false within limits, rather than absolutely. Lowell entered the Harvard Law School in 1877 and chose the option of examinations without residence for the work of the third year. He won an LL.B. cum laude in 1880, ranking second in the class. He later described his greatest gain from law school as "a conception of the varying probative value of evidence." Lessons of relativism thus marked both his undergraduate and his professional training.

On June 19, 1879, in King's Chapel (Unitarian) in Boston, Lowell married his distant cousin Anna Parker Lowell, daughter of George Gardner Lowell, and the couple, who remained childless, established a home in the Back Bay. After apprentice work in the Boston law firm of Russell and Putnam, Lowell formed in 1880 a firm with Francis Cabot Lowell, joined in 1891 by Frederic J. Stimson [Supp. 3]. Lawrence Lowell worked chiefly in probate and investment management for charitable bodies. Although he once aspired to the United States Supreme Court, he was a self-described failure as a lawyer, apparently too impatient with the petty details of many cases.

Lowell found some outlet for his talents in managing the family trust established by his father, and in the Brahmin tradition of educational trusteeship. He followed his father as a member of the Corporation of the Massachusetts Institute of Technology in 1890 and as sole trustee of the Lowell Institute, a foundation for adult education, in 1900. In 1895 he was elected to the Boston School Committee with the backing of the Democrats; three years later he failed of reelection. The one reform in school procedure to his credit—the shift of responsibility for teacher appointment to the superintendent—identified him with the rising professionalization of the era.

Another possibility for his frustrated ambitions was scholarship. In collaboration with F. C. Lowell he published *The Transfer of Stock in Private Corporations* (1884). More suggestive of his shifting interest was his *Essays on Government* (1889), a copy of which his father proudly sent to James Bryce. Though the book drew little attention, its preference for American institutions over British contrasted sharply with Woodrow Wilson's recent defense of cabinet government. The two men began to correspond and became friends, Lowell finding Wilson's educational ideas highly attractive. Lowell turned much of his energy to the writing of *Governments and Parties in Continental Europe* (2 vols., 1896), the first comprehensive study of Continental government published by an American. It established Lowell's reputation as a scholar and brought a momentous invitation to teach at Harvard in 1897.

Lowell immediately resigned from his law firm, even though the appointment was a part-time, nonpermanent lectureship. In 1900 he accepted a professorship in government, but set the condition that he teach half time at half salary so that he could continue writing. As teacher, scholar, and institutional reformer he applied himself tirelessly and imaginatively, as if to overcome his late entry into academic life. At first he taught only a small advanced course on modern governments, but in 1898–99 he collaborated in teaching Government 1, an introductory course on constitutional government. By 1901 he had taken complete charge of the course, and its yearly enrollment soared to about four hundred. He held students' attention with an easy, nonoratorical style, spiced with anecdotes.

Lowell's scholarship flourished alongside his teaching. Two articles in the *Harvard Law Review* suggested his relativistic interpretation in matters of law. "The Judicial Use of Torture" (Nov. 25 and Dec. 25, 1897) attributed resort to torture to the requirement of complete proof. "The Status of Our New Possessions—A Third View" (November 1899), which was cited with approval by the Supreme Court in the *Insular Cases,* argued that the Constitutional guarantees of citizens' rights did not apply to residents of newly acquired lands, since many such rights "are inapplicable except among a people whose social and political evolution has been consonant with our own." Two short books, *The Government of Dependencies* (1899) and *Colonial Civil Service* (1900), applied Lowell's knowledge of comparative government to America's new colonial problems.

The Government of England, Lowell's major work, appeared in 1908. Like his study of 1896, it sought to treat government as a functioning machine, to emphasize actual workings rather than objectives or historical development. In preparing it, he frequently visited Great Britain, and he claimed to learn less from reading than from talking with the men involved. Lowell objected to suggestions that his book was "description without prophecy" and later prided himself on his prediction that the British Empire was destined to drift apart.

The appearance of this scholarly monument conveniently enhanced Lowell's candidacy for the Harvard presidency, vacated in 1909 after a forty-year tenure by the renowned Charles W. Eliot [*q.v.*]. Lowell had already made his educational views known. Though he applauded Eliot's strengthening of the professional schools at Harvard, he was displeased by tendencies in the college, notably extreme student liberty under the free elective system and emphasis on vocational motivation. An advocate of liberal culture, Lowell insisted that achievement in a special field was not an adequate outcome of a college education. He spoke in favor of the "well-rounded man" and recommended general courses that could acquaint a student with a field without the assumption that he was a future specialist in it. The college should give the student standards of judgment and develop his mental powers so that he could continue to grow intellectually. It could do this only by breaking free of utilitarianism. Only in college, Lowell reasoned, could students be made to love learning and aspire to high scholarship, for the graduate school had turned out to be merely another professional school, whose students docilely followed their specialties.

Strongly concerned for community, Lowell called on the college to provide "an intellectual and social cohesion." Lacking that, the student would have no valid standards, no recognition for his achievement, and no satisfaction in the achievement of others. Nor would he attain breadth unless he could associate with those whose special interests differed from his own. Besides intellectual gains, Lowell contended, living with other students in a democratic atmosphere of fellowship would build a strong character.

Lowell had been the driving force on the landmark Committee on Improving Instruction in Harvard College, chaired by Dean Le Baron R. Briggs [Supp. 1]. Its report in 1903, drawing on innovative questionnaires to faculty and students, criticized overspecialization, labeled the average amount of study "discreditably small," and singled out large lecture courses as lacking rigor. In the ensuing years, Lowell served on three other committees which sought to heighten intellectual ambition and achievement in the college. Of the third, appointed in 1908, he was chairman. Its report, through a provocative comparison of attitudes toward study in the college and the law school, indicated widespread undergraduate acquiescence in mediocrity. Placing principal blame on the free elective system, it recommended required concentration and distribution in each undergraduate's choice of studies. This reform passed in 1910, requiring a concentration of at least six courses in one field and the distribution among various divisions of six courses (later, to Lowell's regret, reduced to four).

Without a serious competitor, Lowell was elected president of Harvard in January 1909 and took up his duties in May. His inaugural that October concentrated on the state of the college, suggesting new institutional forms to fulfill his educational ideals. Overflowing with energy, Lowell did not seem fifty-two years old, despite a scholarly droop to his shoulders. With a handsome face and an urbane presence, he was gregarious and voluble, and his talk among friends was witty, informing, and frank. Often at a Boston luncheon club he was the last to leave the table. In more formal situations, however, he could be austere. He did not grant interviews to newspapermen. Some of his faculty complained that he was too impatient and talkative to be a good listener and that he made others feel clumsy. Disliking faculty meetings, which tended to be longwinded, he encouraged the faculty of arts and sciences to transfer considerable power to the committee on instruction, comprising all department chairmen.

To counter the view that course-taking was equivalent to education, Lowell helped establish general examinations in fields of concentration, a Harvard innovation in American education. Introduced first by the medical faculty, general examinations spread gradually to various divisions in the college. This requirement led logically to the tutorial system, under which a faculty member aided the student in correlating course material, supervised reading beyond courses, and stimulated intellectual ambition. (Both innovations drew on English models.) Out of the burden tutorials imposed on faculty members grew the "reading period"—about three weeks at the end of each semester when most teaching stopped and students studied independently. Such curricular changes heightened the intellectual quality of undergraduate life. With Lowell's encouragement, the number of students seeking degrees with distinction in their specialties gradually rose.

In his efforts to renew the sense of community, Lowell effected two dramatic changes in undergraduate residential patterns. Under a plan announced in his inaugural, freshmen were required to live together in newly constructed halls, beginning in 1914. Seeking "democratic social life," Lowell was especially concerned that boys from private preparatory schools not settle into cliques. The second residential reform, the Harvard House Plan, was an idea long in gestation; what came suddenly was the money. Edward S. Harkness [Supp. 2], finding his alma mater, Yale, dilatory in accepting his proposal to finance a residential college plan, called on Lowell in November 1928. The latter, well aware of what was in the offing, is reported by legend to have accepted Harkness's offer in ten seconds. Although at first only an honors college was planned, the scheme expanded to include enough "houses" for all members of the upper three classes. Harkness ultimately gave $13,000,000 for the undertaking. The first two units opened in 1930, five more the next year. Resembling the colleges at Oxford and Cambridge, each house had its own master, resident tutors, dining room, and library.

In the planning and construction of the freshman halls and the houses, Lowell took meticulous daily care. This visible concern for student life, his fondness for walking, and his regular chapel attendance and scripture reading made him a pervasive presence to students, even though most did not meet him. He preached the baccalaureate sermon to every class that graduated under him (collected in *Facts and Visions,* 1944). Personally devout, Lowell read the Bible nightly and often drew on religious images. He maintained his connection with King's Chapel all his life and was for a time its treasurer, but he ceased to regard himself as a Unitarian, resisting any sense of denominationalism.

Although he strove to remove professional courses from the college, Lowell was eager to see the professional schools prosper. The merger of Harvard's engineering school and the Massachusetts Institute of Technology, of which Lowell was the principal author and for which he fought tenaciously, was ended by court order in 1917. Less traumatically, a court order dissolved the union between Harvard Divinity School and Andover Theological Seminary. While still a professor, Lowell had been instrumental in founding the Graduate School of Business Administration, and he supported its expansion, insisting that business be considered a profession. His attitude toward the Graduate School of Education, established in 1920, was decidedly cooler, and it never received his wholehearted support. The medical

and law schools, thoroughly reformed under Eliot, continued their national preeminence under Lowell.

Lowell, whose creed was to choose excellent men or none—never "good" men—considered permanent appointments to the faculty his responsibility, though of course there was consultation. Sometimes accused of autocratic ways, he was nevertheless popular with his faculty, increasingly so during the course of his administration. He withdrew Harvard from forestry, leaving the field to Yale, and by acquiescing in the move of George Pierce Baker [Supp. 1] to Yale in 1924 he similarly conceded the field of playwriting and theatre production. Although there was criticism of both these economy measures, Lowell found satisfaction in budget surpluses during the 1920's which allowed him to avoid faculty salary cuts after the 1929 crash. His veto of a larger stadium was later praised by his athletics director. Although he rarely solicited gifts himself, major fund drives were launched, and during Lowell's administration Harvard's endowment rose from $22,716,000 to $128,520,000. (Lowell himself gave several million dollars to Harvard.) Foundation grants allowed major expansions, and an annual alumni appeal began in 1926.

Lowell became a leading spokesman for academic freedom during World War I and the postwar reaction. When an alumnus threatened to cancel a ten-million-dollar legacy to Harvard if it continued to tolerate the pro-German professor Hugo Münsterberg [*q.v.*], Lowell took the opportunity (notably in his *Annual Report* for 1916–17) to place the university on high ground with a classic argument for the freedom of professors, stressing their right to the constitutional liberties of all citizens. During the Boston police strike of 1919, when Lowell was urging Harvard students to replace the strikers, Harold J. Laski, then an untenured lecturer at Harvard, spoke out for the strike. Lowell resisted hints from Harvard's Board of Overseers that Laski should go, responding, "If the Overseers ask for Laski's resignation they will get mine!" Another potential confrontation with that body came in 1921 when it appointed a committee to investigate complaints against Prof. Zechariah Chafee for alleged misstatements in criticizing a prosecution under the Espionage Act of 1918. At the hearing Lowell virtually acted as Chafee's defense counsel, and the committee recommended against any action. The case won Lowell approving words in Upton Sinclair's critique of higher education in the United States, *The Goose-Step* (1923), though the author depicted Lowell as a tool of State Street where public utility interests were involved.

Lowell believed that endowed universities, by bringing students of different regions and social classes together, served a nationalizing function for which state universities were ill adapted. But in regard to ethnic variety at Harvard, he twice held stubbornly to restrictive positions which aroused strong opposition. Although residence in freshman halls was supposedly compulsory, Negro freshmen were not allowed to live there. In 1922–23 protest from both a black freshman and influential alumni drew much publicity and gave Lowell what he called a "hideous time." The Corporation formally supported Lowell, saying there would be no compulsory association between the races, but practice was modified by admitting some black freshmen to out-of-the-way college quarters. At the same time Lowell grew concerned over the proportion of Jewish students at Harvard, which had increased from 7 percent in 1900 to more than 21 percent in 1922. An assimilationist, Lowell argued that the number of Jews should be kept at a level that would foster their absorption by the larger "American" culture; he also feared a "saturation point" beyond which gentiles would withdraw. His public recommendation for an admission quota for Jewish students was blocked by the Overseers, and he concluded that he had been howled down by men who preferred hypocrisy.

Judging himself not good at detailed current administration, Lowell chose to concentrate his attention on general principles and financial balance. "I have cast the details and responsibility upon the Deans," he wrote his successor, "and I allow no one to come between me and them" (to James B. Conant, June 27, 1933, Lowell Papers). Though an effective speaker, Lowell was suspicious of publicity and believed that frequent public appearances demeaned the office of university president. He often spoke at other academic institutions, however, and developed excellent interinstitutional relations, winning acknowledgment as the leading university president of his day.

In politics Lowell called himself an independent Republican, and he voted for Cleveland in 1884 and 1892 and for Wilson at least once. His position on Progressive reforms was mixed. He favored tariff reduction, woman suffrage, and immigration restriction; he opposed recall of judges and the initiative and referendum. In 1916 he joined a group petitioning the Senate to reject the Supreme Court nomination of Louis D. Brandeis [Supp. 3] on grounds that Brandeis did not enjoy the confidence of the Massachusetts bar.

The effort to found an international peacekeeping body involved Lowell in his most strenuous political activity. He played a major part in creating and naming the League to Enforce Peace, an organization begun in 1915 by a group of Eastern internationalists. Lowell convinced others that to bring disputes between nations to arbitration, force must be authorized, and that its application should come automatically without special conferences of the powers. Former President William Howard Taft, strongly influenced by Lowell, became president of the League. As chairman of its executive committee, Lowell publicized its proposals with magazine articles and speaking tours.

Partly because its founders were chiefly Republicans, the League's relations with President Wilson were problematic. Early in 1918 Taft and Lowell presented Wilson with a draft plan for an international organization, chiefly Lowell's work, but they yielded to Wilson's request that no detailed plan be made public. When the League of Nations Covenant emerged from the Paris Peace Conference, Taft, Lowell, and others in the League to Enforce Peace campaigned in its behalf, attending specially organized regional congresses. At Lowell's suggestion, a series of articles, "The Covenanter," modeled on *The Federalist,* was published anonymously in various newspapers, with Lowell writing half of them (reprinted in World Peace Foundation, *A League of Nations,* June 1919).

Lowell was willing to have the League of Nations with or without reservations. "The question for a citizen of the United States," he wrote, "is not whether the Covenant represents his views precisely, but whether on the whole it is good or not, and whether this country had better accept it or not" (*ibid.,* pp. 165–66). In a public debate on Mar. 19, 1919, Lowell sought unsuccessfully to force Senator Henry Cabot Lodge [q.v.] to pledge himself to support the Covenant if his suggested changes were made. The League to Enforce Peace later circulated amendments suggested by Lowell and Taft, and in October 1919 Lowell conferred with Republican Senators who favored passage with mild reservations. He joined in criticism of Article 10 of the Covenant (pledging protection of the territorial integrity of member states against external aggression), arguing that this would not in fact restrain an aggressor. He placed his hopes in the sanctions provided in Article 16.

For the failure of ratification in the Senate, Lowell blamed the intransigence of both Lodge and Wilson, though he judged Wilson's responsibility greater. Concluding that Harding's election was inevitable and hoping to counteract the view that the election was a referendum on the

League of Nations, Lowell helped draft the "Statement of the Thirty-One Republicans," published Oct. 14, 1920, which argued that supporters of the League could properly vote for Harding, who would support a modified League. Some League advocates interpreted this as a betrayal, but Lowell insisted that it helped elevate internationalism above partisanship.

Another public issue in which Lowell became involved was the case of Nicola Sacco and Bartolomeo Vanzetti [qq.v.]. Early in 1927 Lowell suggested to Gov. Alvan T. Fuller of Massachusetts that, though he himself reserved judgment, many moderate and intelligent people believed there had been a miscarriage of justice in the murder convictions of the two Italian-born anarchists. In fact, the case had become a cause célèbre among intellectuals, who saw in the convictions ethnic prejudice and persecution of radicals; an article by Harvard professor Felix Frankfurter heightened the protest. On June 1, 1927, Governor Fuller announced that Lowell, Robert Grant [Supp. 2], a former Harvard Overseer, and Samuel W. Stratton [q.v.], president of the Massachusetts Institute of Technology, had agreed to serve as an advisory committee on executive clemency.

The first of the committee to be chosen, Lowell was (imprecisely) called its chairman in the press and stenographic record. The committee examined the trial transcript and ballistic evidence and questioned most of those involved in the trial, including defendants, judge, and jury. When the hearings ended, Lowell presented a draft report to his two colleagues, which in matters of substance was adopted. The formal report, dated July 27, 1927, concluded that the trial was fair, the refusals to grant a new trial justified, and the defendants guilty. It labeled the trial judge's talk about the case off the bench "a grave breach of official decorum," but denied that this had influenced the jury. Lowell's pragmatic relativism characterizes the report, notably the conclusion concerning Vanzetti. The governor in a separate investigation had reached the same conclusion as his committee, and the death sentences were carried out. So perfectly did Lowell personify Brahmin respectability that he has survived in Sacco-Vanzetti legendry more prominently than his actual role justifies; probably only the trial judge received more personal vilification. The charge against Lowell, in the relatively mild words of Laski, was that "Loyalty to his class has transcended his ideas of logic and of justice" (Felix, p. 223). On each anniversary of the execution, Lowell received abusive letters, and at Harvard's tercentenary celebration in 1936, a group of alumni circulated a pamphlet (*Walled in This Tomb*) attacking his role in the case. Lowell refused to be drawn into public discussion of the matter, writing an inquiring student, "I have done my duty as a citizen with honesty and courage" (Joughin and Morgan, p. 319).

Lowell's retirement as president of Harvard in 1933 (he was seventy-six and suffered increasing deafness) was brightened by the creation during his last year of the Society of Fellows. The new program reflected Lowell's complaints against pedantry and formalism in graduate schools. Twenty-four young college graduates were to be appointed junior fellows, to reside at Harvard with generous stipends for three years, free from academic obligations, but with access to university facilities. They were to dine weekly with senior fellows, chosen from the Harvard faculty; Lowell was one of the seven elected the first year. The Society allowed Lowell a continuing role at Harvard and brought him into close relationship with young men of promise, and they responded to his interest with confidence and affection, especially important for Lowell, whose wife had died in 1930.

Lowell's major scholarly endeavors had ceased when he assumed the presidency, but he published two series of lectures, *Public Opinion and Popular Government* (1913) and *Public Opinion in War and Peace* (1923). These books showed him unsure about the endurance of popular government, but convinced that use and control of experts would be central to the outcome. *Conflicts of Principle* (1932) reasserted his resistance to absolutes. In retirement he continued writing and public speaking. *At War with Academic Traditions in America* (1934) and *What a University President Has Learned* (1938) helped continue interest in his educational theories.

Lowell opposed most New Deal measures, which he feared would develop bitter class antagonism and undermine character. In 1935 he vainly suggested a new party of conservative Republicans and Democrats to be called the "Constitutional Party," and in 1937 he gave radio addresses attacking Roosevelt's "court-packing" plan and the proposed child labor amendment. In foreign affairs he strongly opposed appeasement, calling for sanctions against Japan in the fall of 1937 even at the risk of war. When war came to Europe, he spoke by radio in favor of arms for France and England. As to postwar peace-keeping, he argued that any plan viewed as a panacea would defeat itself.

Although he called himself "an incurable optimist," Lowell displayed growing querulousness, especially after suffering injuries in an automobile accident in 1936. He continued to take satisfaction in wood-chopping at his summer home in Cotuit, Mass., and in reading the Bible. Against his physician's advice, he marched at the head of the Harvard commencement procession in 1942. He died in Boston of a cerebral hemorrhage the following January and was buried in Mount Auburn Cemetery, Cambridge.

An academic leader of major influence, Lowell was particularly effective in the restoration of the liberal arts in American higher education. During his work for the League to Enforce Peace and afterward, he influenced Americans toward international cooperation and collective security. Contrasting with the rigidity of Woodrow Wilson, Lowell's efforts in both areas displayed a characteristic pragmatic relativism.

[The Abbott Lawrence Lowell Papers, both official and personal, are in the Harvard Univ. Archives. Henry A. Yeomans, *Abbott Lawrence Lowell, 1856–1943* (1948), is a detailed biography by a not uncritical friend and colleague. Further family context appears in Ferris Greenslet, *The Lowells and Their Seven Worlds* (1946); Delmar R. Lowell, ed., *The Historic Genealogy of the Lowells of America from 1639 to 1899* (1899); and Abbott Lawrence Lowell, *Biog. of Percival Lowell* (1935). For Lowell at Harvard, see Samuel Eliot Morison, ed., *The Development of Harvard Univ. since the Inauguration of President Eliot, 1869–1929* (1930); Morison's *Three Centuries of Harvard, 1636–1936* (1936); Crane Brinton, ed., *The Society of Fellows* (1959); and Nell Painter, "Jim Crow at Harvard: 1923," *New England Quart.,* Dec. 1971. To place Lowell in the context of the liberal culture movement, see Laurence R. Veysey, *The Emergence of the Am. Univ.* (1965). For his internationalism, see Ruhl J. Bartlett, *The League to Enforce Peace* (1944), and Warren F. Kuehl, *Seeking World Order: The U. S. and International Organization to 1920* (1969). Contrasting interpretations of Lowell's role in the Sacco-Vanzetti case appear in G. Louis Joughin and Edmund M. Morgan, *The Legacy of Sacco and Vanzetti* (1948), and David Felix, *Protest: Sacco-Vanzetti and the Intellectuals* (1965). The hearings and report of the Advisory Committee are in *The Sacco-Vanzetti Case: Transcript of the Record of the Trial of Nicola Sacco and Bartolomeo Vanzetti in the Courts of Mass. and Subsequent Proceedings,* vol. V (1929). Lowell appears conspicuously in Robert Grant, *Fourscore: An Autobiog.* (1934). For additional details, see "Abbott Lawrence Lowell, 1856–1943: Tributes by Colleagues and Friends," *Harvard Alumni Bull.,* Jan. 16, 1943; various reports of the Class of 1877 in the Harvard Univ. Archives; *N. Y. Times,* Jan. 7, 10, 14, 1943; and *Springfield Daily Republican,* Jan. 7, 1943.]

HUGH HAWKINS

LOWES, JOHN LIVINGSTON (Dec. 20, 1867–Aug. 15, 1945), literary scholar, was born in Decatur, Ind.; he was the older of two children and the only son of Abraham (or Abram) Brower Lowes and Mary Bella (Elliott) Lowes, both of Welsh, Scottish, and English descent. His father, a native of Warren County, Ohio, had graduated from Miami University in Oxford, Ohio, and Western Theological Seminary in Pittsburgh, Pa. (his studies had been interrupted by service in the Civil War). His mother was the daughter of the Rev. David Elliott, a professor at the seminary. Abraham Lowes was ordained in the Presbyterian ministry in 1867 and during his son's childhood served in Decatur, Ind. (1867–68), Tidioute, Pa. (1869–70), Mason, Ohio (1871–74), Belle Vernon, Pa. (1874–82), and, after a brief interlude as a teacher, in Washington, Pa.

John Lowes was educated at Jefferson Academy (Canonsburg, Pa.) and at Washington and Jefferson College (Washington, Pa.). He graduated at the head of his class (1888) and taught mathematics at the college until 1891, when he received his A.M. degree. Then, making a radical shift in the paternal direction, he entered Western Theological Seminary, where he graduated in 1894; although licensed, he apparently did not preach. After a year (1894–95) at the universities of Leipzig and Berlin, he became professor of ethics and Christian evidences at Hanover College in Indiana. Here he found his true vocation when his title was enlarged to include "Instructor in English" (1896–1901) and "Professor of English Language and Literature" (1901–02).

In 1902, at the age of thirty-four, Lowes went to Harvard for graduate work in English. He wrote his doctoral thesis, under the supervision of G. L. Kittredge [Supp. 3], on the prologue to Chaucer's *Legend of Good Women* and received his degree in 1905. From 1905 to 1909 he was professor of English at Swarthmore College, and from 1909 to 1918 at Washington University, St. Louis, where in 1913–14 he was also dean of the college. The crowning phase of his career began in 1918 with his appointment at Harvard, where he remained until his retirement in 1939; in 1930 he was named Francis Lee Higginson Professor. During the years 1924–26 he was chairman of the English department. (He was said to be one of the very few men in the Division of Modern Languages who would stand up to the Napoleonic Kittredge.)

When he took his Ph.D. degree, Lowes had already won his spurs; according to a famous bit of Harvard lore, his doctoral oral was "not an examination but a conference of scholars." In the early part of the century, and notably at Harvard, literary scholarship, following the German model, was preoccupied with the manifold factual data of literary history, with the tracing of themes, sources, and influences from author to author and country to country. The main field of operations was medieval literature. Such aims and methods accomplished a great deal in discovering and ordering a mass of information that more critical successors could build upon. Lowes's work in this vein was focused on Chaucer, and he contributed much to the scholarship that was establishing the chronology and literary relationships of the poems. He was distinguished from run-of-the-mill medievalists by the breadth and depth of his literary and extraliterary learning and by his active concern with the workings of poetic art—virtues that found much fuller scope in his later writings.

In 1918 he gave the Lowell Institute lectures in Boston. These became his first book, *Convention and Revolt in Poetry* (1919), which was addressed to the literary public and carried into print the qualities that made Lowes such a popular teacher. He discussed the role of traditional and original forms in English poetry, distilled some of his medieval lore and some of his later interest in Coleridge and other romantic poets, and dealt at length with the new Imagists. The book now seems old-fashioned, because its author's catholic gusto is far from the austere analytical subtlety of later critics. Yet the sophisticated reader may still feel his spirit quickened by Lowes's generous ardor, his intimate sense of the past, his insistence that poetry creates a reality beyond the merely actual, that it exists to be read by human beings and is a power in their lives. Since conceptions of art are subject to strange vagaries, notoriously in recent times, the central principles of traditional poetry are always in need of reaffirmation, and Lowes felt them vividly. His collected papers, *Essays in Appreciation* (1936), further attest his range of sympathy: they include "The Noblest Monument of English Prose" (on the King James Bible), "The Pilgrim's Progress," "The Art of Geoffrey Chaucer" (a British Academy lecture of 1930), "Two Readings of Earth" (an eloquent contrasting of Hardy and Meredith), "The Poetry of Amy Lowell," and "An Unacknowledged Imagist" (on Meredith). If Lowes's style carries an excess of literary echoes and of superlatives, these are forgivable flaws, the reflex of his passion for great writing.

Lowes's masterwork, *The Road to Xanadu* (1927), stands as the finest product of the kind of scholarship in which its author had grown up. With indefatigable labor and learned acuteness, he had followed, in one of Coleridge's notebooks, the clues to the poet's immense and heterogeneous reading, which ranged from narratives of voyages to the *Philosophical Transactions of the Royal Society,* so that he was able to find sources for almost all the descriptive details in *The Rime of the Ancient Mariner* and *Kubla Khan.* The minute and precise documentation of Coleridgean alchemy (so far, of course, as that can be described) might in other hands have been merely mechanical, but Lowes vitalized it by the imaginative insight of a critic working, as it were, within the poet's mind. Some later critics have looked down their noses at the book as "dated." An heir of nineteenth-century romanticism, Lowes regarded both poems as fantasies of "pure imagination," a view which for most modern critics has given place to more positive interpretations: the erstwhile theologian might have been expected to see more than he did in the Mariner's guilt and redemption. Yet, whatever legitimate discounts are made, *The Road to Xanadu* was an extraordinary achievement, and it remains an experience for readers of poetry.

Lowes practiced the sound principle that the scholar should try to reach the general reader, and he denied the dichotomy often made between the scholar and the teacher. A newcomer to his classroom was half prepared for the "flashing eyes" of the inspired poet described in *Kubla Khan,* but not for the voice that boomed from the small, wiry figure on the platform. At his normal best, Lowes was one of the great teachers of his day; his courses attracted and excited crowds of undergraduates and graduates. He was inspirational in the good sense of the word; he shared his own rich, discriminating experience, and at the same time he imparted, and expected to receive from students, solidly informed criticism. His zeal could stir even low-spirited writers of doctoral dissertations. He saw the advanced study of literature not as a trade but as a high calling, and he made novices feel that they were being inducted into a goodly company.

Chaucer had never been absent from Lowes's mind, and in his Swarthmore lectures of 1932 he spoke with ripe authority. He placed the poet in his medieval cosmos, in his varied everyday activities, and especially in his world of books, and illustrated his racy realism and imaginative art. But only once, perhaps, did he recognize the poet of a religious world: "In the closing lines of the *Troilus,* and in the infinite pity of his farewell to Criseyde, Chaucer, one cannot but believe, has for almost the only time revealed something of his very self." The sober comment raises a query about the speaker. Although Lowes's books seem to overflow with open-hearted spontaneity, his "very self," except as it responded to literature, remained elusive.

Lowes belonged to a generation of scholar-critics and men of letters who enjoyed more than academic repute, such as George Saintsbury and Oliver Elten, Kittredge and E. E. Stoll. Like most of his contemporaries, he did not inaugurate any radical change in the theory or practice of scholarly criticism, and he was not, like Irving

Babbitt [Supp. 1], identified with any special doctrine; but he was a strongly individual and humane embodiment of learning, taste, and discernment.

Lowes was a member of the first group of senior fellows in the Society of Fellows established at Harvard by President A. Lawrence Lowell [Supp. 3] in 1933. He served as president of the Modern Language Association of America (1933) and was elected to membership in the American Academy of Arts and Sciences, the American Philosophical Society, the National Institute of Arts and Letters, and the British Academy. His place in American literary scholarship was signalized by his being named the first incumbent of the George Eastman visiting professorship at Oxford (1930–31). Honorary degrees were bestowed upon him by Washington and Jefferson College (1924), the University of Maine (1925), Tufts (1928), Yale (1928), Oxford (1931), Brown (1932), Harvard (1932), and McGill (1936). More convivial relationships are represented by a number of clubs, including the Round Table (St. Louis), the Saturday Club and the Club of Odd Volumes (Boston), the Century (New York), and the National (London).

On June 23, 1897, Lowes had married Mary Cornett of Madison, Ind. Their last years were darkened by his failing faculties and then by her becoming blind. He died in a Boston hospital at the age of seventy-seven of a cerebral hemorrhage, and was buried in Groveland Cemetery in North Scituate, Mass., where they had long had a summer home. Mrs. Lowes, who had wished to live long enough to look after her dependent husband, died less than two months later. They left an only child, John Wilber.

[Faculty Minute in *Harvard Univ. Gazette,* Nov. 10, 1945; John S. P. Tatlock in Am. Philosophical Soc., *Year Book,* 1945; Stanley J. Kunitz and Howard Haycraft, *Twentieth Century Authors* (1942); *Nat. Cyc. Am. Biog.,* Current Vol. D, pp. 96–97; *Who Was Who in America,* vol. II (1950); information from: Mrs. John W. Lowes; D. W. Kraeuter, Reference Librarian, Washington and Jefferson College; Mayor L. J. Smith, Decatur, and D. Heller, editor of the *Decatur Daily Democrat;* Lowes's death record (Mass. Registrar of Vital Statistics); and the author's recollections. Information about his father from *Hist. of Washington Presbytery* (1899) and Western Theological Seminary, *Gen. Biog. Catalogue, 1827–1927* (courtesy of Presbyterian Hist. Soc., Phila.). For Lowes's credo one might cite his "Teaching and the Spirit of Research," *Am. Scholar,* Jan. 1933. The Houghton Lib., Harvard, has a small collection of his papers.]

DOUGLAS BUSH

LUCE, HENRY WINTERS (Sept. 24, 1868–Dec. 8, 1941), missionary educator, was born in Scranton, Pa., the second son and youngest of three children of Van Rensselaer William and Adelia (Tedrick) Luce. His father, a native of Cooperstown, N. Y., and a prosperous wholesale merchant and insurance broker, was a seventh-generation descendant of Henry Luce, an Englishman who settled on Martha's Vineyard in 1643; his mother, born in Pennsylvania, came of German and English stock. After attending local public schools, Henry prepared for college at the School of the Lackawanna, a private institution in Scranton. In his twentieth year he entered Yale, from which he graduated, B.A., in 1892.

Long an active member of the Presbyterian Church, Luce gave up his original plan for a career in law and enrolled in Union Theological Seminary in New York City in order to train for the parish ministry. There he came under the influence of the Student Volunteer Movement and decided to offer himself as a missionary to China. In 1894 he interrupted his theological education for a year of service as one of three traveling agents of the Student Volunteer Movement, visiting colleges in the South and Southwest while two fellow Yale alumni and Union classmates—Sherwood Eddy, who had volunteered for India, and Horace T. Pitkin, another China volunteer—toured the East and Middle West. At the conclusion of this mission Luce transferred to Princeton Theological Seminary with his friend Eddy for the final year of ministerial training and was granted the B.D. degree in 1896.

Accepted for the China field by the Board of Foreign Missions of the Presbyterian Church in the U.S.A., Luce delayed his departure for a year by taking the post of traveling secretary of the Inter-Seminary Missionary Alliance. On May 20, 1897, he was ordained to the ministry by his hometown pastor, and on June 1, in Palmyra, N. Y., he married Elizabeth Middleton Root, a social worker for the Scranton Y.W.C.A. That October the young couple arrived in China and established their residence at Tengchow in Shantung province, where the Presbyterian Mission operated a small college to which Henry Luce was assigned as a teacher of physics, English, and other subjects. He remained with the college, which in 1904 moved to Wei-hsien, until 1915.

Besides his teaching and his intensive study of Chinese, which resulted in the publication of a translation of a *Harmony of the Gospels* and other religious materials, Luce was active in the promotion of interdenominational cooperation in missionary education. He made two trips to the United States (1905–06, 1912–15) to raise funds for this purpose, and at the end of 1915 he accepted the vice-presidency of Shantung Christian

(Cheeloo) University, an institution which had grown out of the Presbyterian college at Weihsien but was supported jointly by American Presbyterians and English Baptists and Anglicans. Two years later, however, disagreements among the members of the teaching and administrative staff of the newly integrated university led to the resignation of the somewhat quick-tempered Luce, who moved to Shanghai as secretary of the China Christian Education Association. In 1919, after completing an extensive survey of missionary schools for the association, Luce was persuaded to return to academic administration as vice-president of Yenching University, a new interdenominational institution then being organized in Peking by American and English Congregationalists and American Methodists and Presbyterians. Along with Yenching's president, J. Leighton Stuart, Luce was chiefly responsible for securing the financial backing for this major project in higher education in China, spending all but one of the next eight years as a fund raiser in America.

In 1927 declining health and a desire to return to academic life caused him to sever his active relationship with Yenching. The next year, after an interlude of study at Columbia University and Union Theological Seminary, he was appointed to a professorship in the Chinese department of the Kennedy School of Missions of the Hartford Theological Foundation in Hartford, Conn., where he remained until retirement in 1935. His experience as an educator in both China and the United States, reinforced by an extended tour of Asia in 1935–36, had convinced him of the need to develop better understanding of the non-Western world among Americans, and in an attempt to help realize this objective, he inaugurated a series of summer "Interpreters' Institutes" for churchmen and others at Silver Bay, N. Y., beginning in 1939. Two years later, Luce, who suffered from arteriosclerosis, died in his sleep of a cerebral hemorrhage at his home in Haverford, Pa. He was seventy-three. Following cremation, his ashes were buried in Forest Hill Cemetery, Utica, N. Y.

Possessing a vigorous intellect and magnetic personality, Luce was an able administrator and highly successful fund raiser, despite his personal preference for a life of scholarship and teaching. An enduring monument to his work in inter-denominational missionary education was the United Board for Christian Higher Education in Asia, successor to the Associated Boards for Christian Colleges in China, which he helped establish in New York in 1932. He was the father of four children: Henry Robinson, Emma-

vail, Elisabeth Middleton, and Sheldon Root. The eldest, who founded and edited *Time, Life,* and *Fortune* magazines, erected two memorial buildings in China in honor of his father: a student pavilion at Yenching University in Peking and a chapel on the campus of Tunghai University in Taichung, Taiwan.

[Besides five Chinese-language studies in the New Testament, Luce was the author of "Education in Shantung, Past, Present, and Future," in Robert C. Forsyth, ed., *Shantung: The Sacred Province of China* (Shanghai, 1912). A full though rather uncritical biography is Bettis A. Garside, *One Increasing Purpose: The Life of Henry Winters Luce* (1948). Briefer accounts are found in the *N. Y. Times,* Dec. 9, 1941; *Christian Century,* Dec. 24, 1941; *Minutes* (Dec. 15, 1941) of the Board of Foreign Missions of the Presbyterian Church in the U.S.A.; Yale Univ., *Obituary Record of Graduates,* 1941–42, p. 55; *Nat. Cyc. Am. Biog.,* XXXIV, 36–37; and *Religious Leaders of America,* 1941–42. Death record from Pa. Dept. of Health. Luce's work for Yenching is mentioned in Dwight W. Edwards, *Yenching Univ.* (1959), and John Leighton Stuart, *Fifty Years in China* (1954). His missionary correspondence is available in the archives of the Presbyterian Hist. Soc. in Phila. and the United Mission Lib. in N. Y.]

CLIFTON J. PHILLIPS

LUTZ, FRANK EUGENE (Sept. 15, 1879–Nov. 27, 1943), entomologist and museum curator, was born in Bloomsburg, Pa., the younger of two children, both boys, of Martin Peter Lutz and Anna Amelia (Brockway) Lutz. His parents were of eighteenth-century Pennsylvania descent; his father was an insurance and real estate agent. As a youth Frank developed an interest in wildlife, spending his summers exploring the mountains near his home. He proved such an able student in the public schools and at the Bloomsburg State Normal School that his parents sent him to Haverford College. During his first two years there, upon his father's advice, he specialized in mathematics, planning to become an insurance actuary. Then, drawn toward a medical career, he shifted to biology.

When Lutz graduated, A.B., in 1900, his biology teacher suggested that he combine his two fields by doing graduate work in the new science of biometry, which applied statistical methods to biology. Lutz consulted Charles H. Davenport [Supp. 3] of the University of Chicago, the American leader in this field, who gave him a job waiting on tables at the summer biological laboratory in Cold Spring Harbor, Long Island, of which Davenport was director. That summer Lutz prepared his first scientific paper, "A Study of the Variations in the Number of Grooves upon the Shells of *Pecten irradians* (Lam.)" (reported in *Science,* Sept. 7, 1900), which helped win him a scholarship to the University of Chicago. There he worked under Davenport and obtained his

A.M. in 1902. A year in Europe followed, during which he studied at University College, London, with Karl Pearson and also, briefly, at Berlin. When in 1904 the Carnegie Institution established its new research laboratory, the Station for Experimental Evolution, at Cold Spring Harbor, with Davenport as director, Lutz was appointed to the staff to carry on research in entomology. For this purpose he selected the fruit fly *Drosophila*, which was just beginning to be used for the study of genetics. Meanwhile he completed his Ph.D. at Chicago (1907) with a dissertation on variation among crickets.

Lutz left the Cold Spring Harbor Station in 1909 to join a fellow researcher, the zoologist Henry E. Crampton, in the department of invertebrate zoology at the American Museum of Natural History in New York City. He remained at the museum for the rest of his life, at first as assistant curator, then as associate curator (1917), and from 1921 as curator of his own department of insects and spiders. Over the years he greatly developed the museum's collections in this field until they reached some two million specimens. He himself conducted twenty-three field expeditions to various parts of the United States and Latin America. Despite his many administrative duties, he found time for experimental work on the biology and behavior of insects. Among other studies, he recorded insect sounds and carefully analyzed the recordings through microscopical study, demonstrated that insects see ultraviolet light, and tested the ability (which proved to be great) of insects to withstand high and low air pressures and lack of oxygen. For many of his experiments he created his own equipment. A charter member of the Entomological Society of America, he was its president in 1927.

Lutz contributed greatly also to the American Museum's educational work. In the Hall of Insect Life he developed stimulating exhibits, originating the first habitat or diorama groups in this field and introducing push-button or mechanical displays and an "insect zoo" of live specimens. At Harriman State Park, where the museum had a research station on insects, he laid out in 1925 the first "nature trail," which proved an immediate success and was widely copied. Lutz was an effective writer and for many years served as editorial director of the museum's scientific publications. His own crowning achievement was the publication in 1918 of his *Field Book of Insects*, which became the standard work of reference for tens of thousands of students and amateur entomologists. (The royalties, it is said, put his four children through college.)

On Dec. 30, 1904, Lutz had married Martha Ellen Brobson of Philadelphia. Their children were Anna, Eleanor, Frank Brobson, and Laura. Lutz enjoyed his work, which he often extended into the night; he had a rich sense of humor, at times "tart and roguish." Always sympathetic with amateur naturalists, he delighted in trying to get children interested in the world of nature. Lutz was a Baptist in religious affiliation. He died at the Presbyterian Hospital in New York City in 1943, at the age of sixty-four, and was buried at Union Cemetery in Ramsey.

[Obituary articles by Harry B. Weiss in N. Y. Entomological Soc., *Jour.*, Mar. 1944, by Herbert F. Schwarz in *Entomological News*, Feb. 1944, and by Alfred E. Emerson in *Science*, Mar. 24, 1944; John C. Pallister, *In the Steps of the Great Entomologist Frank Eugene Lutz* (1966), a popular account; *Who Was Who in America*, vol. II (1950); information from Miss Anna Lutz. There are photographs of Lutz in the files of the Am. Museum of Natural Hist. For a bibliography of his writings see N. Y. Entomological Soc., *Jour.*, Mar. 1944. For his own account of the early days of his department see his "Amateur Entomologists and the Museum," *Natural Hist.*, May–June 1924.]

JOHN C. PALLISTER

McADIE, ALEXANDER GEORGE (Aug. 4, 1863–Nov. 1, 1943), meteorologist, was born in New York City, the fourth son of Scottish parents, John and Anne (Sinclair) McAdie. His father, listed in city directories as a printer, had come to the United States in 1852. Young McAdie attended New York public schools and the College of the City of New York, where he won two gold medals for excellence in English composition and studied atmospheric phenomena, such as electrical storms. He received the A.B. degree in 1881, at the age of seventeen. The Army Signal Service, which then handled weather matters for the federal government, was at that time seeking college graduates in science, and McAdie in January 1882 enlisted. After preliminary training at Fort Myer, Va., he was sent to Harvard University, where he studied under such eminent physicists as John Trowbridge and Benjamin O. Peirce and formed a friendship with Abbott Lawrence Rotch [*qq.v.*], who in 1884 established the Blue Hill Meteorological Observatory near Milton, Mass. McAdie received A.M. degrees from his alma mater in 1884 and from Harvard in 1885.

For three years (1886–89) McAdie served as an assistant in the physical laboratory of the Signal Service in Washington, D. C., a period interrupted by a winter's term (1887–88) at the weather station in St. Paul, Minn. He resigned in 1889 to teach physics and meteorology at Clark University, Worcester, Mass. Two years later he returned to Washington to join the United

States Weather Bureau, which had just been set up under civilian control, as meteorological physicist and assistant to the director. During his years there (1891–95) he also visited Rotch at the Blue Hill Observatory, where he experimented with the use of kites in obtaining meteorological data and studied the relation between atmospheric electricity and auroral phenomena.

Because of political shifts, McAdie was transferred to the San Francisco office of the Weather Bureau in 1895, and except for several months (1898–99) spent as forecast official in the New Orleans office, he remained there for eighteen years. In 1903 he was appointed professor of meteorology and director of the California section of the Bureau's climate and crop service. He soon achieved distinction as a forecaster and became an authority on the climate of California. The earthquake of 1906 stimulated his interest in seismology, and he was one of the founders, in 1907, of the Seismological Society of the Pacific, a forerunner of the Seismological Society of America, of which he was president in 1915–16. He was also president of the Astronomical Society of the Pacific (1912) and a fellow of the Royal Meteorological Society.

McAdie left the Weather Bureau in 1913 to accept appointment as professor of meteorology at Harvard and director of the Blue Hill Observatory, which had become a part of Harvard University. He held both positions until his retirement in 1931. During World War I he served as a lieutenant commander in the navy, in charge of its aerographic section.

Although McAdie made no historic contributions to meteorological science, he pioneered in the use of kites to explore the air at high altitudes, developed and patented devices to protect fruit from frost, studied the role of smoke in polluting the atmosphere, and wrote on the hazards of lightning on the ground and in the air. He also advocated standardization of the physical units employed in meteorological notation and urged the general adoption of the metric system.

McAdie's writing was notable for its style and erudition. His books include *The Climatology of California* (1903), *The Principles of Aerography* (1917), and *Cloud Formations as Hazards in Aviation* (1929). He published some four hundred papers; many of them, such as "Relativity and the Absurdities of Alice" (*Atlantic Monthly*, June 1921), were written for a lay audience and are characterized by imagination and lively humor. A man of great personal charm, he displayed in his writings his own love of life and appreciation for its natural wonders.

On Oct. 7, 1893, McAdie married Mary Ran-

dolph Browne of Edgehill, Va. They had no children. McAdie was an Episcopalian in religion. After his retirement he moved to Hampton, Va. He died of a coronary occlusion at Elizabeth City, Va., at the age of eighty. Following cremation, his ashes were buried in Charlottesville, Va.

[Mary R. B. McAdie, ed., *Alexander McAdie: Scientist and Writer* (1949), reprints many of his papers, scientific and popular, and includes a biographical sketch and a bibliography of his writings. See also *Am. Men of Sci.* (6th ed., 1938); *Nat. Cyc. Am. Biog.* XXXV, 107–08; *Who Was Who in America*, vol. II (1950); and, for background, Donald R. Whitnah, *A Hist. of the U. S. Weather Bureau* (1961). Death record from Va. Bureau of Vital Statistics.]

F. W. REICHELDERFER

McADOO, WILLIAM GIBBS (Oct. 31, 1863–Feb. 1, 1941), lawyer, Secretary of the Treasury, presidential aspirant, was born in Marietta, Ga., the second of three sons and fourth of seven children of William Gibbs McAdoo by his second wife, Mary Faith Floyd. On his father's side he came of old Tennessee stock, his great-grandfather having left western Virginia to join the settlement led by John Sevier [*q.v.*]. McAdoo's father, a graduate of East Tennessee University (later the University of Tennessee), practiced law in Knoxville and took some part in Whig politics, serving twice as attorney general for his district. At the outbreak of the Civil War he moved to Georgia, his wife's home state, to stand with the Confederacy. Both parents were Presbyterians, and McAdoo's mother was the author of several published stories and novels. Like many Southern families, the McAdoos were declassed by the war; they lost the few slaves inherited by Mrs. McAdoo and found the Floyd property in Georgia devastated and unprofitable to farm. William recalled that life in Milledgeville, Ga., where he was largely reared, was one of straitened economic circumstances. In 1877 his father accepted an adjunct professorship in English and history at the University of Tennessee, and William was able to attend the university from 1879 to 1882.

At the end of two years young McAdoo took a job as deputy clerk in the federal circuit court at Chattanooga, Tenn. He studied law at night in the office of a local lawyer and was admitted to the bar in 1885. On Nov. 18 of that year he married Sarah Houstoun Fleming. Chattanooga in the 1880's was a restless, muddy city, full of energy and sustained by an optimism that ran easily to speculation. The young lawyer skimmed $25,000 from one of the town's real estate booms and invested it in a mule-drawn streetcar line in Knoxville which he hoped to convert to electricity. Although he was able to convince Eastern bankers to back the venture, it failed for want of local technological skill, forcing McAdoo into bankruptcy. Seeking a faster way to erase his debts, he moved in 1892 to New York City.

There were no quick fortunes in New York for a young Tennessee lawyer with no connections. McAdoo sold securities to supplement his income and in time established a reasonably comfortable practice as partner in the law firm of McAdoo and McAdoo (his partner, William McAdoo, was no relation). Yet the law could not contain his restless energies or offer sufficient outlet for his imagination. A tedious ferry crossing to New Jersey in 1900 set him to thinking about a Hudson tunnel, and investigation revealed that earlier promoters had started a tunnel under the river in 1874 but were overcome by engineering and financial difficulties. McAdoo saw challenge where others saw a dangerous, slimy failure, and within a year he had brought together the capital and engineering skills for another attempt. His confidence and obvious ability brought New York's largest bankers into the effort, and by 1909 Manhattan was connected to New Jersey by four Hudson tunnels. McAdoo was now financially secure and enjoyed a reputation as a promoter endowed with acumen and drive.

In his business projects McAdoo had been drawn to jobs where he might advance the interests of the public as well as his own. It was entirely natural that he should gravitate next toward political life. In 1910 he supported Woodrow Wilson in his race for governor of New Jersey, and the following spring he joined a small group of men promoting Wilson's presidential candidacy. The informal head of this group was William F. McCombs, who became Wilson's campaign manager in 1912, and when McCombs fell ill that autumn, McAdoo assumed his duties. When Wilson cast about for a Secretary of the Treasury who had financial experience but was not too closely identified with Wall Street, McAdoo was a logical choice.

The legislative struggles of the Progressive era, combined with his own activist temperament, made McAdoo's six years as Secretary of the Treasury an incredibly busy period. Pressure for banking reform had been building since the panic of 1907, and as McAdoo took office, it was apparent that some sort of central banking system would be set up. McAdoo was among those who objected to the plans of both Senator Nelson W. Aldrich [q.v.] and Congressman Carter Glass, on the grounds that they gave too much power to bankers and too little to the public interest. He proposed a central bank operated out of the Treasury, and though his plan made little headway, it had the effect of dramatizing the importance of public control. The Federal Reserve Act (1913) was a compromise, but its centralized and public features owed as much to McAdoo as to anyone else.

By contemporary accounts, including the diaries and memoirs of cabinet members, McAdoo was the most able, energetic, and forceful of the Wilson circle. In physical appearance he was tall and straight, his long, aquiline nose, high cheekbones, and intense stare enhancing the impression of great concentration and force. On May 7, 1914, in a White House wedding, the fifty-year-old cabinet officer, a widower since 1912, married Eleanor Randolph Wilson, daughter of the President. Wilson relied upon McAdoo for political advice and used him to employ the lever of patronage during crucial legislative struggles. In cabinet and out, McAdoo's advice to Wilson was so candid, forceful, and frequently unorthodox that Wilson was occasionally irritated by it. Informed by Treasury officials in August 1914 that private shipping interests, frightened by submarine warfare, would probably fail to provide the tonnage required to maintain trade with the Allies, McAdoo suggested to Wilson the establishment of a shipping line owned and operated by the government. Throughout the submarine controversy he tended to take the firm line, and he was one of those in the fateful period after the resumption of submarine warfare who pressed the President toward war rather than acquiescence.

The war years were probably McAdoo's finest period, as they allowed the free play of his best qualities—inventiveness, organizational ability, an enormous capacity for work, and a hitherto unsuspected skill at sensing and mobilizing public opinion. He was, in addition to Secretary of the Treasury, chairman of the Federal Reserve Board, the Federal Farm Loan Board, and the War Finance Corporation, as well as director general of the railroads after their takeover by the government in 1917. McAdoo's most important job was of course the financing of the war. Wartime expenditures ultimately reached the vast sum of $24,000,000,000, exclusive of loans to Allies. Large investors were doubtful of their ability to subscribe the amounts the government had to borrow before its tax program was in operation, and economists worried that borrowing through the banking system would be disastrously inflationary. McAdoo attacked both the problem of supply and the problem of inflation by borrowing extensively from the public in four Liberty Loan drives, each accompanied by a publicity campaign designed to awaken the patriotic spirit in millions of persons unused to saving and to buying government obligations. Each loan was oversubscribed, as were the more conventional Treasury offerings to banks and prime investors.

But financing the war involved moral and political questions as well. Progressives wanted all of the expense raised by taxation of profits and wealth generally, and organizations like the Association for an Equitable Income Tax and individuals in the Congress like Claude Kitchin and Robert La Follette [qq.v.] kept up the pressure for a high tax-loan ratio and a more progressive tax system. The issue was joined early, over preparedness expenses, and McAdoo angered progressives in late 1915 by offering a tax plan that bore heavily upon the middle and lower classes with only a slight increase in surtaxes and the corporate rate. He was charged with reactionary social instincts, but the truth seems to be that, as always, he was a man with mildly progressive sentiments who easily overrode them in favor of solving the problem at hand by finding a middle way. Conservative sentiment favored consumption taxes and bond issues, with a tax-loan ratio of one to five (the suggestion of the younger J. P. Morgan [Supp. 3]). McAdoo's tax proposals, and his preference for a one-to-three tax-loan ratio in wartime financing, were thus his idea of a workable compromise. Progressives pushed through in 1916 a tax law which thrust part of the new expenses of government upon the rich, and fought with some success for similar principles in the tax laws of 1917 and 1919. In the end the Treasury raised less than $8,000,000,000 by taxation, and neither progressives nor conservatives were entirely happy. But the Treasury had mobilized America's wealth with splendid technique even if with ideological neutrality—the mark of a McAdoo performance.

His health and personal finances strained by his years in government service, McAdoo resigned from the cabinet effective January 1919 and resumed the practice of law in New York. He was widely mentioned as Wilson's likely political legatee, but the President, considering the possibility of his own renomination, refused to endorse his son-in-law, and McAdoo hesitated to seek the nomination in 1920. He made early plans, however, for 1924. In 1922 he moved to California, both because he could not hope to control the New York delegation and because he had decided to identify himself with the West-South coalition associated with William Jennings Bryan [q.v.]. In the end it was an identification fatal to his presidential hopes, and the urbane, flexible McAdoo must have been slightly uneasy as he adopted the issues and evangelical style of the provincial wing of the Democratic party. Yet in

addition to being himself of rural origin and a dry, McAdoo considered himself a progressive, and he saw the Bryan Democracy as the only progressive Democracy, with the Eastern urban machines a reactionary influence.

For a time it appeared that McAdoo might have sufficient labor support to avoid being stereotyped as a sectional candidate. His record as director general of the railroads brought him the temporary support of the Conference for Progressive Political Action after its formation in 1922. But disaster struck early in 1924 when the Senate Committee on Public Lands heard testimony from Edward L. Doheny [Supp. 1]—the man who had bribed Secretary of the Interior Albert B. Fall [Supp. 3] to secure a lease on Elk Hills reserve in California—that McAdoo had performed legal services for Doheny in oil and revenue cases before government agencies, thus linking him with the Teapot Dome scandal. Press accounts assumed that McAdoo was no longer an available candidate, and he lost much progressive support. But McAdoo chose to fight. Defending himself before the Senate committee investigating the oil scandal, and aided by such backers as Bernard Baruch, he entered a series of primary contests in the West and South. He defeated Oscar W. Underwood [q.v.] in five successive Southern primaries in early 1924 and went to the convention the leading contender. But the loss of progressive support heightened his reliance on his rural base. In the crucial primary battles he cultivated the dry vote, avoided alienating the Ku Klux Klan, and on the eve of the convention spoke of New York as an "imperial" city, "the citadel of privilege . . . reactionary, sinister, unscrupulous, mercenary, and sordid." The convention balloted 103 times, deadlocked between McAdoo and Gov. Alfred E. Smith [Supp. 3] of New York, the candidate of the other, urban half of the Democracy. Both were too clearly identified with a distinctive cultural style, and the worthless nomination went to John W. Davis.

McAdoo was sixty-one years old by the end of 1924, but though his presidential hopes were gone, his public years were not over. At the 1932 convention he announced California's switch to Franklin D. Roosevelt, returned to California to win a Senate seat that fall, and supported the New Deal loyally for six years. He was defeated in the Democratic primary of 1938 by Sheridan Downey, who was riding the crest of a Townsend-like movement for a weekly pension to all persons over fifty. While continuing the law practice he had begun in Los Angeles in 1922, McAdoo also served as chairman of the board of the government-owned American President Lines until his death early in 1941. He died in Washington, D. C., of a heart attack. After Episcopal services he was buried, as a wartime cabinet officer, in Arlington National Cemetery. He was survived by five of the six children of his first marriage: Harriet Floyd, Francis Huger, Nona Hazlehurst, William Gibbs, and Sally Fleming (the next to youngest, Robert Hazlehurst, had died in 1937); by Ellen Wilson and Mary Faith, children of his marriage to Eleanor Wilson, who had divorced him in 1934; and by his third wife, Doris I. Cross, whom he had married on Sept. 14, 1935.

McAdoo was one of the most talented men to enter public life in the twentieth century. He built his career on some of the old virtues, most notably love of hard work and an iron self-discipline. But his leading qualities were those of a modernist—flexibility, a love of technical and political innovation, an instinctive appreciation of the revolutionary effect of mass opinion upon politics and war. He inspired respect more than affection, and some observers, like Walter Lippmann, distrusted what they thought was ideological shiftiness. But the record holds strong evidence of McAdoo's liberalism: he urged Wilson to appoint a progressive Federal Reserve Board, approved of every New Freedom measure and invented one or two of his own, sided with railway labor in the wage disputes of 1918, supported equal rights for women not only at the polls but in employment, and spoke up for "radical" Judge Ben B. Lindsey [Supp. 3] when Lindsey had trouble being admitted to the California bar in the 1930's. The Klan may have found McAdoo appealing in 1924, but only because there was no other strong rural candidate; his platform that year spoke of popular government, lower tariffs, and conservation—nowhere of repression or bigotry. He was quick to sense new problems, and usually proposed new rather than familiar remedies—federal regulation and partial ownership of American shipping was his boldest idea, but he also favored federal financing of elections and the federal insurance of bank deposits. "I like movement and change," he wrote in his autobiography (p. 528), "... to reshape old forces and worn-out ideals into new and dynamic forms." Despite his association in 1924 with much that was reactionary and outdated, McAdoo in his total career was a transitional figure between two liberal reform movements. His analytical powers and organizational ability matched Wilson's, and helped restore the Democratic party's reputation as a party capable of governing; his flexibility, his problem-solving pragmatism, and his hospitality to innovation kept his talents unencum-

bered by theories, and in the days of Franklin Roosevelt, these proved the crucial and distinctive qualities of the reform mind and temperament.

[The McAdoo Papers, extensive and well organized, are in the Lib. of Cong. His autobiography, *Crowded Years* (1931), is useful, though superficial. There is no biography, although John J. Broesamle intends to expand his Ph.D. dissertation, "William Gibbs McAdoo: Businessman in Politics, 1863–1917" (Columbia Univ., 1970), into a two-volume biography. Mary Synon, *McAdoo* (1924), is a campaign eulogy. McAdoo's role in the Wilson years may be followed in the volumes of Arthur S. Link's biography of the President. There are a number of competent articles on McAdoo's presidential hopes: Wesley M. Bagby, "William Gibbs McAdoo and the 1920 Democratic Presidential Nomination," East Tenn. Hist. Soc., *Publications, 1959*; Lee N. Allen, "The McAdoo Campaign for the Presidential Nomination in 1924," *Jour. of Southern Hist.*, May 1963; J. Leonard Bates, "The Teapot Dome Scandal and the Election of 1924," *Am. Hist. Rev.*, Jan. 1955; and David H. Stratton, "Splattered with Oil: William G. McAdoo and the 1924 Democratic Presidential Nomination," *Southwestern Social Sci. Quart.*, June 1963. There is an insightful essay on McAdoo in Walter Lippmann, *Men of Destiny* (1927), and a sketch of McAdoo in the 1930's in Otis L. Graham, Jr., *An Encore for Reform: The Old Progressives and the New Deal* (1967). A perceptive study of the political forces which McAdoo sought unsuccessfully to master in the 1920's is David Burner's history of the Democratic party between Wilson and Roosevelt, *The Politics of Provincialism* (1968). On McAdoo's father and ancestry, see William S. Speer, *Sketches of Prominent Tennesseans* (1888), pp. 202–04.]

OTIS L. GRAHAM, JR.

MacCALLUM, WILLIAM GEORGE (Apr. 18, 1874–Feb. 3, 1944), pathologist, was born in Dunnville, Ontario, Canada, the older of two sons and second of four children of George Alexander MacCallum and Florence Octavia (Eakins) MacCallum, both from small Ontario towns. His father, the son of a Scottish immigrant, was a physician who maintained a busy country practice and, for a time, served as medical superintendent of two Ontario hospitals for the insane. Deeply interested in natural history, he cultivated in both his sons (the younger of whom also became a physician) a broad approach to scientific investigation. MacCallum's mother was an accomplished pianist and singer who gave her children a deep love of music.

Educated initially at home, MacCallum entered the public schools at the age of nine. He remained, however, under the tutelage of his father, to whom he was always close, accompanying him on house calls and studying with him in a makeshift home laboratory. After completing high school in 1889, he attended the University of Toronto. There he studied the classics, though he also took courses in the sciences and, through a biology professor, became interested in the trematode parasites. He received the A.B. degree in 1894 and hoped to continue the study of Greek but, at his father's insistence, agreed to shift to medicine and entered the new Johns Hopkins Medical School. Having already completed courses equivalent to the first year, MacCallum was allowed to begin at the second-year level. He graduated in 1897 at the head of the school's first graduating class, and returned home to spend the summer working in his father's woodshed laboratory. There, studying the malarial parasites in the blood of a crow, he made his first notable scientific discovery, identifying the flagellated form of the avian parasite as the agent of sexual conjugation. In later work he demonstrated that the same mechanism operated in the reproductive cycle of the human malarial parasite.

After completing his internship in 1898 at the Johns Hopkins Hospital, MacCallum stayed on as an assistant resident in pathology under William H. Welch [q.v.]. In 1900 he went to Leipzig, Germany, where he studied in Felix M. Marchand's laboratory. He returned to Baltimore in 1901, completed his training, and in 1902 was appointed associate professor of pathology. That same year he published two important papers elucidating the microscopic anatomy of the lymphatic system. In the first he demonstrated that the lymphatic vessels had complete endothelial linings and comprised a closed continuous vascular system similar to that of the arteries and veins; the second explained the mechanism by which red blood cells and other particulate matter were absorbed into this closed system. Though he had begun to study the lymphatic system in Leipzig, much of his work was carried out under the guidance of Welch, with whom he had established a warm working relationship. MacCallum also became a devoted colleague of William S. Halsted [q.v.], whose biography he later wrote. Through Halsted, MacCallum became interested in finding the cause of the complications that sometimes developed in patients who had undergone thyroidectomies, and in 1905 he undertook a series of classic experiments with the pharmacologist Carl Voegtlin. Together they distinguished the independent functions of the thyroid and parathyroid glands and defined the role of the parathyroid hormone in controlling calcium exchange in the body. They further showed that, after removal of the parathyroid glands, tetany could be prevented by injecting a solution of calcium salts. These contributions, in addition to making thyroid surgery a safe procedure, explained basic physiologic mechanisms related to many other pathologic conditions.

In 1909 MacCallum was called to New York to succeed T. Mitchell Prudden [q.v.] as professor of pathology at Columbia University and as pathologist at the Presbyterian Hospital. At Columbia he investigated the pathologic physiology of valvular heart disease and demonstrated the relationship between diabetes mellitus and the islets of Langerhans, employing an operative technique—duct ligation—that was later used by Sir Frederick Grant Banting and Charles Herbert Best to isolate insulin. In 1916 MacCallum published his *Textbook of Pathology,* a work that for the first time classified disease on the basis of etiology. Rather than giving a monotonous list of every condition that could affect each bodily organ, he discussed the general principles underlying pathological changes in the body and used all the common and important diseases to illustrate these principles; the work went through seven editions during his lifetime, and his system of presentation is still used in modern textbooks. While in New York, MacCallum also was influential in getting the old-fashioned, politically appointed city coroner replaced by a medical examiner's office headed by a trained pathologist.

MacCallum returned in 1917 to Johns Hopkins to become professor of pathology and bacteriology, succeeding Welch, who had resigned to become director of the newly established School of Hygiene and Public Health at Johns Hopkins. The most important investigation of his later years was a classic study of epidemic pneumonia among army personnel during World War I. He had a special interest in the history of medicine and served as president of the Medical History Club at Johns Hopkins, 1940–41.

Those who knew him have characterized MacCallum as a man of fastidious tastes and variable moods. An inherent shyness made him difficult to approach, and he never married. Yet he enjoyed good conversation and had a lively sense of humor that contributed to his skill as a teacher. One of his great enjoyments was travel. He received many honors, including election in 1921 to the National Academy of Sciences. In the spring of 1943 he suffered a disabling stroke. He died in Baltimore the following year at the age of sixty-nine; his ashes were buried in Greenmount Cemetery, Baltimore.

[Warfield T. Longcope in Nat. Acad. Sci., *Biog. Memoirs,* vol. XXIII (1945); Arnold R. Rich in *Archives of Pathology,* Sept. 1944 (also in Johns Hopkins Hospital, *Bull.,* Aug. 1944); Wiley D. Forbus in *Jour. of Pathology,* Oct. 1944. See also MacCallum's *William Stewart Halsted, Surgeon* (1930).]

JEFFREY A. KAHN

McCORMACK, JOHN FRANCIS (June 14, 1884–Sept. 16, 1945), lyric tenor, was born in Athlone, Ireland, the son of Andrew and Hannah (Watson) McCormack. His parents had come some years earlier from Galashiels, in the Scottish Lowlands, and three of his grandparents were Scots; but his paternal grandfather was a native of Sligo in the west of Ireland. John McCormack was the second son and the fifth—according to his own count—of eleven children. Though the father was a foreman in one of Athlone's woolen mills, the size of the family permitted few amenities. John's unusual aptitude for learning, however, gained him an education beyond the ordinary means of the family, first (1889–96) at a local school of the Marist Brothers and later (1896–1902), through scholarships, at the Diocesan College of the Immaculate Conception of Summerhill at Sligo, where upon graduation he won first prizes in languages and mathematics. Singing, and a good natural voice, came to the boy with his family heritage; but the Marists taught him to read music, his college gave him his start as an occasional soloist in public, and it was friends rather than his father (to whom singing was a private joy but unthinkable as a way of earning a living) who helped set him on the road to a musical career after he narrowly missed a scholarship to the Dublin College of Science.

That career developed quickly and smoothly, thanks in part to McCormack's natural ability but thanks also to his dogged persistence, his instinct for wise decisions, and more than a bit of luck. Early in 1903 he was accepted in the choir of Dublin's Marlborough Street Cathedral under Vincent O'Brien, who gave him his first vocal tutoring. On May 20, 1903, he won first prize in tenor solo singing at the Dublin Feis Ceóil, or Music Festival. He sang abroad for the first time in June 1904, at the Irish Village of the Louisiana Purchase Exposition in St. Louis. Later that year he made his first recordings, cylinders for Edison Bell and discs for the Gramophone Company; they were not very successful, either artistically or financially. A turning point came when friends helped send him to Milan to study with the voice coach Vincenzo Sabatini; over the next year and a half (1905–06) McCormack received the only truly professional coaching he ever had.

With Sabatini's backing, he made his operatic debut on Jan. 13, 1906, as Fritz in Mascagni's L'Amico Fritz at the Teatro Chiabrera in Savona. After additional appearances (under the name "Giovanni Foli") in Italian provincial opera houses, he returned to London, where on Mar. 1, 1907, he scored his first notable success at one of Arthur Boosey's fashionable Ballad Concerts. Other successful concert engagements followed, and then—through the intercession of Sir John Murray Scott, a friend of King Edward VII—

he was signed for the Royal Opera House at Covent Garden, making his debut on Oct. 15, 1907, as Turiddu in Mascagni's Cavalleria Rusticana. Quickly established at Covent Garden, he also toured the British provinces (once in joint recitals with Fritz Kreisler) and sang in oratorio. On Nov. 10, 1909, he made his American operatic debut in New York with the Manhattan Opera Company of Oscar Hammerstein [q.v.], as Alfredo in Verdi's La Traviata.

Although Hammerstein's venture failed, McCormack returned to the United States in 1910–11 with the Chicago-Philadelphia Opera Company and in 1912 (after a season in Australia with Nellie Melba) began the American concert career that, together with his phonograph recordings, for twenty-five years formed the major part of his public life. He sang at Covent Garden in London from 1909 through 1913, he twice more (1913 and 1920) toured in Australia and in 1926 sang in China and Japan, he appeared on a few occasions in opera at the Metropolitan Opera House; but it was Victrola records and arduous concert tours over the length and breadth of America (one involving as many as ninety-five concerts in one year) that brought McCormack the widest recognition and probably the most money of any singer of his time.

Soon after the outbreak of war in 1914 he made New York City his home, and on June 17, 1919, he became an American citizen. For thus "turning his back on England" in her time of need he was severely criticized in Britain, Canada, and Australia (where incidents shortened his tour in 1920), and he did not venture to sing again in England until 1924. His answer to the criticism was that as an Irishman and an individual he had a right to choose his own home. When the United States entered the war he took pride in raising large sums of money for war charities through benefit performances. He also gave heavily after the war to Irish and Roman Catholic charities. Paradoxically, his easy command of American dollars helped arouse bitterness toward him in other lands. His own national loyalties remained ambiguous. From 1914 to 1937 he called America his home, living first in New York and then (after making the movie Song o' My Heart in 1929) in Hollywood; but his children went to school in England, he had homes in Ireland from 1924 on, and he lived out his life there after his touring days were over. Yet in 1942 he questioned American officials as to whether he had jeopardized his American citizenship by living so long abroad.

McCormack's farewell tour in the United States ended at Buffalo on Mar. 16, 1937. His last formal concert was before a crowd of 9,000 at London's Albert Hall on Nov. 27, 1938, though he sang many times during the early years of World War II in various parts of Britain and over the BBC. At one such concert, early in 1942, he developed a chill that led eventually to the pneumonia from which he died at Booterstown, outside Dublin, where he was interred in Dean's Grange Cemetery.

Irish or American, McCormack embodied a quixotic combination of personal traits. He was brash, talkative, incurably optimistic, devoutly Catholic, extravagantly wide-ranging in his moods, so forthright that he usually blurted out his thoughts whether politic or not, so sentimental that he is alleged to have broken down once at a concert while singing "Mother Machree," yet so strong-willed that he forsook alcohol and tobacco for long periods in the interest of his singing. Tall and slender as a young man, with handsome smile and Irish blue eyes, he soon grew portly and so remained despite such athletic hobbies as tennis, golf, and swimming. He also liked race horses, expensive paintings, and the company of other public figures, whether prizefighters or movie stars. He delighted in costly gifts—especially to his wife, the former Dublin soprano Lily Foley (to whom he was married on July 2, 1906, and to whom he remained devoted), and to his children: Cyril, Gwendolyn, and Kevin, the last his wife's orphaned nephew whom he adopted. He was supremely proud of his numerous honors, chief among them the hereditary title of Papal Count, awarded by Pope Pius XI in 1928 in recognition of his services to Catholic charities.

In McCormack the singer, many of these qualities were reflected, though tempered always by a very superior sense of professionalism. Fortunate in a naturally fine tenor voice, he was fortunate also in the excellence and restraint of his limited vocal tuition. One could almost say that the mature McCormack was self-taught. It was unceasing and intelligent practice, aided by a degree of musicianship foreign to most singers, that produced the distinctive McCormack qualities: a tone richer than the ordinary "Irish tenor," not overpowerful but very clear and well focused (ideally suited to the demands of pre-1925 acoustical recording), intonation and articulation so precise that they might have come from a keyed instrument, extreme clarity of diction, a style of rhythmic delivery that was highly musical yet always sensitive to the words being sung. Fundamental to all these qualities was a remarkable control of the breath, which also made possible extraordinary feats of dynamics. Often these skills were acknowledged by critics who at the same time begrudged McCormack's devotion to the popular Irish and English ballads that endeared him to the millions; yet it is hard to find fault with an artist who could sing Mozart's "Il Mio Tesoro" and Strauss's "Allerseelen" with the same degree (though not the same kind) of expertness and sincere conviction as "Mother Machree" and "I Hear You Calling Me." Though during his early years in opera he seems to have been a tolerable actor, he seldom appeared on the operatic stage after he began his American concert career. Both he and his adoring audiences preferred that he act that one large role in which he was incomparable: John McCormack, singer.

[Seven books, none in any way definitive, have been published on McCormack, two of them written for Roman Catholic young people. Pierre V. R. Key's *John McCormack, His Own Life Story* (1918) was based on interviews but hurriedly written in a very artificial style and seems to have been withdrawn after some copies were distributed. Leonard A. G. Strong's *John McCormack* (1941) drew partly on memoirs unfinished by the singer, but lacks depth. Countess Lily McCormack's own memoirs, *I Hear You Calling Me* (1949), provide an endearing view of the man and of his personal and social life. Raymond Foxall's *John McCormack* (1963) is a short but moderately successful attempt at an all-around biography and assessment of the singer. L. F. X. McDermott Roe, *John McCormack* (1956), is a detailed discography. Two volumes of memoirs by men who worked closely with McCormack contain lengthy and interesting professional opinions: *Seeing Stars* (1940), by Charles L. Wagner, the singer's concert manager from 1912 to 1925; and *Am I Too Loud?* (1962), by his last accompanist, Gerald Moore. Innumerable magazine and newspaper articles offer little that is not in these books beyond occasional sidelights and quotations from interviews. Some of McCormack's correspondence with Wagner is in the Music Division of the Lib. of Cong.]

WILLIAM LICHTENWANGER

McCORMICK, RUTH HANNA. See SIMMS, RUTH HANNA McCORMICK.

McFARLAND, GEORGE BRADLEY (Dec. 1, 1886–May 3, 1942), physician and hospital administrator in Thailand, linguist and lexicographer, was born in Bangkok, Siam (Thailand). He was the third son and third of four children of Presbyterian missionary parents, Samuel Gamble McFarland and Jane (Hays) McFarland, both of Scotch-Irish descent and Pennsylvania birth. George was named for an uncle, George P. Hays, the first president of Washington and Jefferson College in Pennsylvania, and for Dan Beach Bradley, the pioneer American medical missionary in Thailand, in whose home he was born. The McFarlands had established the first Protestant station in the interior of Thailand in 1860 at Phetburi, a small river town. There George received his early education, chiefly from his mother, a devoted teacher who later started

a school for Thai girls. In 1878 his father resigned from the mission and accepted appointment as superintendent of a modern boys' school in Bangkok founded by King Chulalongkorn for the training of Thai youths of noble blood. George attended this school from the age of twelve, graduating with the first class in 1883 and subsequently serving as an instructor for a year and a half.

In 1885 he went to the United States to enroll in Washington and Jefferson College. After two years there he was admitted to the Western Pennsylvania Medical School (later affiliated with the University of Pennsylvania), where he received the M.D. degree in 1890. The next year he spent in Baltimore, earning a degree in surgery from the College of Physicians and Surgeons and one in dental medicine from the Chirurgical College of Dentistry.

In November 1891, after serving a three-month internship in a Baltimore hospital, Dr. McFarland returned to Bangkok to take charge of the government-sponsored Siriraj Hospital and conduct a newly organized medical school associated with it. In addition, he opened an office for the private practice of dentistry and after the death of his brother Edwin in 1895 took over the sales agency for a Siamese typewriter which Edwin had invented in 1892. George McFarland later modified and perfected this device and built a large company for the sale and repair of typewriters and other business machines in Thailand. In 1896 he brought his parents, who were in failing health, back to the United States, and in October of that year he married Marie Ina Root in Skaneateles, N. Y. Mrs. McFarland, a graduate of Wellesley College in education, worked closely with her husband in Bangkok until her death there in 1923 from tuberculosis. McFarland's second wife, whom he married in San Jose, Calif., on Feb. 16, 1925, was Bertha Blount, a teacher and later principal of Wattana Wittaya Academy, a Presbyterian mission school for girls in Bangkok. He had no children by either marriage.

A man of tremendous energy and varied talents, McFarland prepared medical textbooks and religious tracts in the Thai language and continued the linguistic work of the early missionaries by publishing *An English-Siamese Pronouncing Handbook* in 1900 and issuing in 1906 the fourth edition and first of seven revisions of *An English-Siamese Dictionary*, which his father had originally compiled and printed on a hand press in Phetburi in 1865. As a public servant of the Thai government, McFarland made his major contribution in the development of modern hospital administration and medical education. In 1903 the

institution he headed became the Royal Medical College, and 1917 it was incorporated into the newly created Chulalongkorn University. King Rama VI conferred various medals upon him and in 1915 admitted him to the third rank of the Thai nobility with the personal title of Phra Ach Vidyagama. In 1926, after the Rockefeller Foundation had assumed financial responsibility for the reorganization and further modernization of the Royal Medical College, McFarland retired from government employ.

After retirement he continued to reside in Bangkok with his wife. They both became affiliated with the Siam Mission of the Presbyterian Church as lay volunteers and played a part in the organization of the unified Church of Christ in Siam. In 1928 McFarland was chosen to edit a centennial volume entitled *Historical Sketch of Protestant Missions in Siam, 1828–1928,* which he and his wife helped to write. His chief efforts in these years, however, were spent in preparing an unabridged Thai-English dictionary, a large, encyclopedic compilation based in part upon the earlier work of Protestant missionary pioneers in Thailand. This volume, which was published in Bangkok in 1941, was reissued by the Stanford University Press in 1944 and became the standard dictionary of its kind.

When the Japanese entered Thailand in December 1941, the Thai government placed the McFarlands under arrest, though in view of the doctor's long service to the nation they were permitted to remain in their Bangkok home. A few months afterward McFarland fell ill and was transferred to Chulalongkorn Hospital, where he died in May 1942 after an unsuccessful operation for strangulated hernia. His remains were first buried in the Protestant Cemetery in Bangkok, but in May 1950 his body was disinterred and cremated and the ashes placed in one of the royal Buddhist temples in the city in recognition of his contributions to the monarchy.

[The most complete biography is Bertha Blount McFarland, *McFarland of Siam* (1958). Mrs. McFarland also recounts several episodes in her husband's life in *Our Garden Was So Fair: The Story of a Mission in Thailand* (1943). There is an obituary in the *Minutes* (May 18, 1942) of the Board of Foreign Missions of the Presbyterian Church in the U.S.A. and a short biographical account in the *Univ. of Pittsburgh Alumni Rev.,* Feb. 1938. The latter contains a photograph of the subject in his official Thai government uniform, which also appears as the frontispiece in *McFarland of Siam.* In her husband's biography Mrs. McFarland mentions a number of manuscript sources which apparently are no longer extant.]

CLIFTON J. PHILLIPS

McGRATH, MATTHEW J. (Dec. 20, 1876–Jan. 29, 1941), athlete and police officer, was born in Nenagh, Tipperary, Ireland. He was one of the eleven children (five girls and six boys) of Timothy McGrath, an impoverished tenant farmer, and his wife, Ann. Sports were popular in the towns and villages of Ireland, and young Matt won the half-mile race at Killaloe and the hundred-yard sprint and broad jump at Partree. He emigrated to the United States in 1897. During his first week in New York City he wandered into Central Park and, unexpectedly finding himself in a rural setting, kicked off his shoes, splashed in a pond, and threw rocks for exercise until a policeman mildly reprimanded him for breaking the law. The lenient Irish officer's friendliness left an imprint, and McGrath developed an ambition to wear the uniform of the metropolitan police. After working variously as a blacksmith, bartender, and salesman, he qualified for the New York Police Department in 1902.

A gregarious and high-spirited youth, McGrath also became an eager participant in amateur athletics. The sports pages of the daily and Irish press, together with a gospel of physical fitness that had caught the imagination of educators, were inspiring many young Irish-Americans to take part in track and field events sponsored by athletic clubs, colleges, playground associations, interscholastic leagues, and the Amateur Athletic Union. The broad-shouldered McGrath, six feet tall and weighing 210 pounds, began throwing weights at a time when records were falling before the onslaught of John J. Flanagan in the hammer, Martin Sheridan in the discus, and Ralph Rose in the shot-put. He joined the New York Police Athletic League when it was organized in 1906 and rapidly improved his hammer throw. In 1907 he won the United States junior championship, and the next year, despite a torn ligament, placed second to Flanagan, the three-time champion, in the London Olympics. Returning to his native Nenagh for a brief visit afterward, he set a new world record in the hammer throw.

In 1911 he set two more world records, one of 187' 4" in the hammer and another of 40' 6⅜" in the 56-pound weight throw; this last remained unsurpassed during his lifetime. The following year, at Stockholm, he set the Olympic hammer record at 179' 7⅛". Patrick J. Ryan, another of America's transplanted "Irish Whales," soon surpassed his world record, but McGrath's Olympic feat held until 1936. During World War I he competed in A.A.U. and club contests, and in 1920, at the Antwerp Olympics, placed fifth in the hammer. As the only four-time Olympic veteran in the Paris games of 1924, he had the honor of carrying the American flag. At Paris the aging athlete came in second and won the silver medal.

Meanwhile, McGrath made steady progress in his career as a policeman. The recipient of two citations for valor in the performance of his duties, he advanced successively to sergeant in 1917, lieutenant in 1918, captain in 1927, and deputy inspector in 1930. In 1936 he became police inspector, the third highest rank in the department. An expert on urban traffic problems, he was at the time of his death head of the Manhattan Traffic Division. He was married to Loretta Smith, and though the couple did not have children of their own, in 1936 they adopted an orphan of Chinese descent, Bobby Lou. McGrath died of pneumonia at St. Clare's Hospital in New York City at the age of sixty-four. Spectators by the thousands lined the streets as a mammoth funeral procession made its way to services at Our Lady of Mercy Catholic Church. He was buried in Calvary Cemetery, New York.

[Frederick A. M. Webster, *Athletics of To-day* (1929); John Kieran, *The Story of the Olympic Games* (1936); Roberto L. Quercetani, *A World Hist. of Track and Field Athletics, 1864–1964* (1964); Richard Schaap, *An Illustrated Hist. of the Olympics* (1963); *Fifth Olympiad: The Official Report of the Olympic Games of Stockholm* (1912); Amateur Athletic Union of the U. S., *Minutes of the Annual Meeting,* 1912; John B. Kennedy, "Broth of a Boy," *Collier's,* July, 2, 1932; files of *Winged Foot* and *Amateur Athlete; Irish World,* 1907-08 and Feb. 8, 1941; *Gaelic American,* Feb. 8, 1941; *N. Y. Times,* June 30, Oct. 7, 1906, May 30, 1918, Jan. 29, 30, 1941; death certificate, N. Y. City Dept. of Health.]

JOHN R. BETTS]

MACK, JULIAN WILLIAM (July 19, 1866– Sept. 5, 1943), lawyer, jurist, leader in social welfare causes and in Jewish affairs, was born in San Francisco but grew up in Cincinnati. He was the second son and second of the thirteen children of William Jacob and Rebecca (Tandler) Mack. On both sides of his family he came of pioneer German-American Jewish stock, the Macks and Tandlers being part of a significant immigration into the United States of Jews from small Bavarian towns that began in the 1830's. His mother, a native of Louisville, Ky., was the daughter of Abraham Tandler, a merchant and an early figure in American Reform Judaism, who helped found Louisville's first synagogue before moving to San Francisco during the Gold Rush. Mack's father, born in Altenkunstadt, Bavaria, had followed an older brother to Cincinnati in 1856 and had settled a year later in San Francisco, where he joined a wholesale crockery firm. In 1870, troubled by asthma, he returned with his family to Cincinnati. There he ran a small tailor shop which yielded only a modest income.

Julian was a chubby, alert, self-assured boy

with the warm and strongly outgoing manner that was to mark him as a man: "the most golden-hearted man I ever knew," Felix Frankfurter called him. He early acquired the special stamp—quite distinctive in that era—of the highly assimilated "Cincinnati Reform German Jew." From childhood on, his secure, wholly "Americanized" personality helped win him unusual acceptance among non-Jews. Though himself practically never the target of anti-Semitism, he nonetheless reacted with acute empathy when other Jews felt its cruelty. This largely explains a notable aspect of his life—the countless number of young Jewish men and women he helped in their careers, among them Frankfurter, Benjamin V. Cohen, Max Lowenthal, Maurice Raphael Cohen, Horace M. Kallen, Robert Szold, J. M. Kaplan, and Harry A. Wolfson.

After graduating from Cincinnati's Hughes High School in 1884, Mack attended the Harvard Law School, aided financially by a childless uncle, Max Jacob Mack, a prominent Reform Jew who exerted a strong influence on Julian's life. At law school, Mack was a founding editor and the first business manager of the *Harvard Law Review.* He received an LL.B. degree in 1887, graduating at the top of his class. On the recommendation of Prof. James Barr Ames [*q.v.*], Harvard awarded Mack the coveted Parker Fellowship, under which he spent the next three years in Europe studying at the universities of Berlin and Leipzig.

On his return to the United States in 1890, Mack settled in Chicago, both to be on his own and because that city had succeeded Cincinnati as the Midwest's "Queen City." There he joined the law firm of Julius Rosenthal, who was at the time the leading spokesman for Chicago Jews on public matters. As Rosenthal's protégé, Mack made an impressive speech in 1892 stressing the need to welcome and aid the rising tide of Russian Jewish immigrants, and was promptly chosen secretary of the city's Jewish Charities. Meanwhile, after a partnership with Sigmund Zeisler [*q.v.*] and Zach Hofheimer had collapsed, he became a professor of law, first at Northwestern University Law School (1895–1902) and then on the original law school faculty of the University of Chicago (1902–11). On Mar. 9, 1896, he married Jessie Fox of Cincinnati. They had one child, Ruth, who became a prominent psychoanalyst, a student and close associate of Sigmund Freud.

Mack's continuing activities in behalf of Jewish charities brought him into national prominence. He early became associated with Jane Addams [Supp. 1] and the Hull House circle, and in 1892, with their counsel and guidance, he helped establish the Maxwell Street Settlement (later merged with Hull House) to serve the immigrant residents of Chicago's west side Jewish ghetto. In 1904 he was elected president of the National Conference of Jewish Charities. Two years later he helped found and became a vice-president of the influential American Jewish Committee. As a direct result of his status in the Jewish community, Mack was named by Mayor Carter Harrison II as a city civil service commissioner in 1903, and later the same year as a Democratic candidate for the Cook County circuit court. After his election, he chose to serve on the county's juvenile court, a pioneering venture established four years earlier at the instigation of Chicago settlement house workers and women's groups. Mack had a natural sympathy for the work of this court and during his tenure greatly increased its status and effectiveness. He left the juvenile court reluctantly in 1905 to become a state appellate court justice.

Mack's enlightened and dedicated service on the juvenile court broadened his interest in social welfare work generally and deepened his already close relationship with such leaders as Jane Addams, whose approach to social problems he espoused and defended. He also collaborated with Graham Taylor [Supp. 2] of Chicago Commons, especially in support of the Chicago School of Civics and Philanthropy (which became in 1920 the University of Chicago's Graduate School of Social Service Administration) for training professional social workers. He served as president of two Chicago agencies led by settlement workers, the Juvenile Protection Association and the League for the Protection of Immigrants (later the Immigrants' Protective League); and he was one of the initiators of the first White House Conference on Children (1909), which led to the creation of the federal Children's Bureau. In 1911 Mack succeeded Jane Addams as president of the National Conference of Social Workers.

That same year he was appointed by President William Howard Taft to the newly created United States Commerce Court, established to hear final appeals from decisions of the Interstate Commerce Commission. The position carried the same rank as a judgeship on the federal Circuit Court of Appeals, the highest judicial post attained by a Jew up to that time. When the Commerce Court was abolished in 1913, Mack became an ambulatory Circuit Court judge, assigned for a time to various circuits throughout the country and after 1918 sitting mainly in New York City, where he established his residence. Serving until his retirement in 1941, he was, according to

Judge Learned Hand, "one of the most distinguished judges of his time: incisive, swift, at ease in every subtlety." His work on the bench, however, did not become widely known, in part because he wrote relatively few decisions, and those of no special literary distinction (Felix Frankfurter felt he suffered from "pen-paralysis"), but in part also because his ability to master litigation of exceptional legal and financial complexity led to his being often assigned cases which, though important, attracted little public notice.

Mack presided, however, over a number of prominent cases, including the criminal prosecution of Marcus Garvey [Supp. 2], the "Back-to-Africa" Negro leader, and of Harry M. Daugherty [Supp. 3], President Harding's Attorney General. He also adjudicated the prolonged antitrust action against the Sugar Institute, and for years after 1933 he was in charge of the long and complicated receivership of two of New York's transit systems, the Interborough Rapid Transit and the Manhattan Railway companies, which ended in transit unification and municipal control. In a 1937 government prosecution of the Electric Bond & Share Company, Mack upheld the constitutionality of the Public Utility Holding Company Act of 1935, a decision which was sustained by the Supreme Court.

Concurrently with his judicial activities, Mack was closely associated with Zionism, despite the fact that most of his close Reform Jewish friends, like the philanthropist Julius Rosenwald [q.v.], either opposed or held aloof from the movement. As the first president of the Zionist Organization of America (1918–21) and of the newly formed American Jewish Congress (1919), Mack was a member of the delegation representing American Jewry at the 1919 Paris Peace Conference. There Jewish groups from all parts of the world gathered, some seeking merely the inclusion in the peace treaty of a provision for equal rights for Jews, others urging the creation of a Jewish homeland in Palestine. To present a united front, these groups formed the Committee of Jewish Delegations, and Mack served as its first chairman. The committee successfully urged a British mandate in Palestine under which Jewish settlements would be developed in accordance with the Balfour Declaration.

In his Zionist activities, Mack was closely aligned with Justice Louis D. Brandeis [Supp. 3]. When followers of Chaim Weizmann, later the first president of Israel, repudiated the Brandeis-Mack leadership in 1921, Mack resigned as president of the Zionist Organization of America but continued to work for the development of Palestine through such organizations as Palestine Endowment Funds, Inc., and the Palestine Economic Corporation. His fund-raising activities for Jewish Palestine continued throughout the 1930's. He also served on the board of governors of the Hebrew University and Institute of Jewish Studies in Jerusalem, and aided other Zionist institutions in Palestine. The kibbutz of Ramat Hashophet (Judge's Hill) in Israel was named for Mack in recognition of his service in behalf of the restored Jewish state.

Besides his Zionist activities, Mack aided Jewish war relief during World War I, served on the federal Board of Inquiry on Conscientious Objectors, and at the same time headed the National Organization of Young Men's and Young Women's Hebrew Associations, served as a labor arbiter, and lobbied through Congress the government's landmark soldiers' insurance compensation legislation. In later years he assisted the New School for Social Research in New York City and was chairman of the Survey Associates, publishers of the leading journal in the field of social work, and a member of the National Lawyers Guild, formed in protest against the conservatism of the American Bar Association. He often deliberately lent his prestige to certain causes that ultraconservatives tended to frown upon, as for example the effort to save Nicola Sacco and Bartolomeo Vanzetti [qq.v.]. Beginning in 1919 Mack served for three terms on the Board of Overseers of Harvard University. In 1922–23 he successfully opposed the attempt of President A. Lawrence Lowell [Supp. 3] to establish a quota for the admission of Jewish students. During World War II, Mack devoted a great deal of energy to helping German Jewish refugees enter the United States.

Diabetic after 1914, Mack suffered several physical setbacks during his strenuous career, including a stroke in 1937. His health began to fail markedly after the death of his wife in 1938. On Sept. 4, 1940, he married Mrs. Cecile (Blumgart) Brunswick, the widowed mother of his son-in-law. Three years later Mack died quietly in his New York apartment at the age of seventy-seven. Rabbi Stephen S. Wise, of whose liberal Institute of Jewish Religion (later merged with Hebrew Union College of Cincinnati) Mack had been chairman, conducted the funeral service. By Mack's request, his body was cremated.

[This article is based on the author's forthcoming biography of Mack, which draws on manuscript sources, files of newspapers and specialized periodicals, interviews with relatives and friends, judicial reports, and the biographies and reminiscences of many contemporaries. Of Mack's papers, some have been in the hands of relatives and associates, such as those held by Robert Szold (mainly on Zionism). There are significant items in the Zionist Archives, N. Y. City; the Am. Jewish Archives, Hebrew Union College-Jewish Inst. of Religion, Cincinnati; the Louis D. Brandeis Papers, Univ. of Louisville; and the Rosenwald Papers, Univ. of Chicago. Of prime value on Mack's conversion to Zionism is his speech "Americanism and Zionism," *Chicago Sentinel,* July 5, 1918. Among published accounts, an important summary by a scholarly close friend is Horace M. Kallen's sketch in the *Am. Jewish Year Book,* 1944–45. Also valuable is a piece by Stephen S. Wise in his book *As I See It* (1944). See also: obituaries in *N. Y. Times,* Sept. 6, 1943, *Social Service Rev.,* Dec. 1943, and Assoc. of the Bar of the City of N. Y., *Year Book,* 1945 (by Learned Hand); Hyman L. Meites, ed., *Hist. of the Jews of Chicago* (1924); and Philip P. Bregstone, *Chicago and Its Jews* (1933).]

HARRY BARNARD

McLAREN, JOHN (Dec. 20, 1846–Jan. 12, 1943), horticulturist and landscape architect, was born on a farm near Stirling, Scotland, the son of Donald and Catherine McLaren. After serving an apprenticeship as a dairyman, he became a gardener at Bannockburn House, and continued to learn the art of horticulture by working in succession at Blairdrummond, Manderson House in Berwickshire, the Earl of Kinoul's place, the Royal Botanic Garden in Edinburgh, and the Earl of Windsor's estate at East Lothian. At the age of twenty-three he came to the United States and soon took passage for San Francisco by way of the Isthmus of Panama. His earlier success in planting sea bent grass to bind the dunes near the Firth of Forth led to his first job in California, solving a similar problem on the estate of George Howard of San Mateo County. For some years McLaren continued his gardening on various estates in the San Francisco area; a notable feat was his conversion of the wheat field of Leland Stanford [*q.v.*] into the garden of ornamental plants which later became the botanic garden of Stanford University.

In 1887 McLaren was appointed superintendent of parks of San Francisco. He thus became responsible for half a dozen downtown squares and a thousand-acre area of Sahara-like sand dunes, lying between the city and the Pacific Ocean, which in an earlier attempt at development had been named "Golden Gate Park." Only the extreme eastern end of the park, away from the ocean front, had been planted, in the early 1870's, by McLaren's predecessor, William Hammond Hall, before public opposition to the expense called a halt to what seemed a futile effort to bind the dunes.

McLaren began his conquest by planting his proven sea bent, fertilized by manure swept from San Francisco's streets and delivered daily, as he had stipulated on taking the position. Gales uprooted his grass plots repeatedly; each time the grass was stubbornly reset by hand, and with

extraordinary skill and determination McLaren gradually succeeded in establishing the sea bent. On the thin sod he then planted Monterey pines and, nearer the coast, Monterey cypresses to anchor the sands, and these were followed by oaks, eucalypts, and redwoods. He ensured the nourishment of his trees by planting each one in a large hole, often as much as six feet square and six feet deep, which he filled with straw, loam, and manure, whose decomposition produced the necessary humus. McLaren was firmly convinced that trees and shrubs grown from seed were more economical and better adapted for survival than was transplanted stock. He soon began experiments in growing plants from all parts of the world, including his favorite rhododendrons, grown from seed gathered in the Himalayas. Finding that gales and high waves frequently drenched his plantings with salt water, he determined to create a protective windbreak on the seaward side of the park. He started with a structure of laths and brush to trap the sand along the shore and, by building similar structures on top of and adjacent to the first, in the course of forty years achieved a broad barrier some twenty feet high.

McLaren strongly objected to the increasing number of statues erected among his trees and flowers, and contrived to curtain the "stookies," as he called them, with plant groupings. He defended the integrity of the parks against both political and civil authority, and when the municipality proposed to construct a streetcar line that would bisect the park, he rallied his men and defeated the plan by spending all of one night moving trees and shrubs out of the nursery into what had been an unoccupied aisle. When lack of water challenged his plan for Golden Gate Park, he drilled wells and erected two windmills to supply a thousand acres. Besides Golden Gate Park, he developed about forty-five smaller parks about the city.

International recognition came with McLaren's success in landscaping the Panama-Pacific Exposition of 1915 in San Francisco. He grew pines and eucalypts thirty feet high from seed, in record time; moved full-grown palms from the old plantings of the nurseryman George Roeding of Niles, across the Bay; and created hanging gardens by fastening flats of flowering *Mesembryanthemum*, previously grown from cuttings, onto the walls of the exhibit halls. In 1923 the Massachusetts Horticultural Society awarded him the George Robert White Medal, and in 1930 the Royal Horticultural Society made him an Associate of Honour. The University of California honored McLaren in 1931 with the Doctor of Laws degree. By 1936 he had become a legend, and June 7th that year was decreed McLaren Day in San Francisco. With Eric Walther he worked out the basic plan for the Strybing Arboretum, established in Golden Gate Park in 1937. His *Gardening in California: Landscape and Flower* (1909), the best treatise in its field, went into a third edition in 1924.

McLaren married Jane Mill in 1876; they had one son, Donald. Through the years the McLarens lived at "Park Lodge" in Golden Gate Park. McLaren enjoyed playing dominoes, and was noted for his singing of Scottish ballads. Refusing to retire at the customary age, he continued with staunch public support to superintend the city's parks until his death, of a cerebral hemorrhage, at the age of ninety-six. He died at Park Lodge and was buried in Cypress Lawn Memorial Park, Colma, Calif.

[Unfortunately, McLaren's papers in the office at Park Lodge were destroyed after his death. There are scattered references to him in the Charles F. Saunders Papers at the Henry E. Huntington Lib., San Marino, Calif., and, in the Alice Eastwood and W. H. Hall papers at the Calif. Acad. of Sci., San Francisco. For biographical accounts, see Frank J. Taylor in *Saturday Evening Post*, July 29, 1939; Roy L. Hudson in *Calif. Horticultural Jour.*, Apr. 1970; *Who's Who in Calif.*, 1928; and obituaries in *San Francisco Chronicle* and *N. Y. Times*, Jan. 13, 1943. Death certificate from Calif. Dept. of Public Health.]

JOSEPH EWAN

McLEAN, EDWARD BEALE (Jan. 31, 1886–July 27, 1941), newspaper publisher, was born in Washington, D. C., the only child of Emily (Beale) and John Roll McLean. His paternal grandfather, Washington McLean, a successful merchant and one of the founders and owners of the *Cincinnati Enquirer,* had moved to Washington in the 1880's. His father inherited the *Enquirer* and then consolidated his wealth by investing in local utility companies and by purchasing the *Washington Post;* an influential figure in the Democratic party, he was several times considered as a vice-presidential candidate. John McLean married the socially prominent daughter of Edward Fitzgerald Beale [*q.v.*], and their home, a large Renaissance structure covering half a city block, became a center for Washington's social elite. Young McLean, known as Ned, was educated at home by private tutors and, forgoing college, briefly read law with Wilton J. Lambert, attorney for the *Washington Post*. Pampered by an overprotective mother, he had little need of a formal occupation; he never practiced law, and aside from an occasional stint as a cub reporter on the *Post,* he rarely took an interest in his father's newspapers.

On July 22, 1908, Ned McLean eloped with Evalyn Walsh, daughter of Thomas F. Walsh, an Irish-born carpenter who, after striking it rich in a Colorado gold mine, had moved to Washington, D. C., where he and his wife became friends of the McLeans. Though both sets of parents objected to the elopement, each contributed $100,000 for a European honeymoon, a sum which proved insufficient when the bride, an impulsive girl who spent money as recklessly as her young husband, purchased the Star of the East diamond for $120,000. (She later paid even more for the famous Hope diamond.) At Friendship, an eighty-acre estate in Washington, the young couple maintained a household staff of thirty and entertained lavishly, once giving a reception for the Russian ambassador at the cost of $30,000. In a belated attempt to curb his son's extravagance, McLean's father limited him to an allowance of $1,000 a month, but this was generously supplemented by the Walshes. When John McLean died in 1916, his will stipulated that the family fortune, estimated at $25,000,000, be kept in trust and not be distributed until twenty years after the death of his son's youngest child. Ned McLean, who was barred from administering the estate, tried to break the will, and in a compromise settlement was given a voice in the management of the trust and control of the two newspapers. He also received the estate's net income, which amounted to more than $500,000 a year.

As a newspaper publisher, McLean left an undistinguished record. He devoted more time to the high society of Palm Beach, Newport, and Bar Harbor than to the management of the *Enquirer* and the *Post*. Nevertheless, the editorial control he exerted over two important newspapers brought him political influence, as well as the friendship of Warren G. Harding, with whom he shared a fondness for poker, golf, and liquor. Supporting Harding for the presidency, McLean changed the editorial policies of the Democratic *Enquirer* and the independent *Post* to a strong pro-Republican stand. During the Harding administration, the McLeans were close to the President's friends. When the Teapot Dome scandal exploded, a Senate committee probed the source of $100,000 that Secretary of the Interior Albert Fall [Supp. 3] had received at a time when he had leased valuable government-owned oil lands to private companies. To protect Fall, McLean at first declared, through his attorneys, that he had loaned him the money but he later admitted that he had not.

The last years of McLean's life were unhappy. His excessive drinking led to the disintegration of his marriage, and around 1928 he was permanently separated from his wife. Two years later she successfully brought suit against him for separate maintenance, charging adultery. On June 1, 1933, the *Washington Post,* suffering from years of mismanagement and neglect, was sold at a public auction to Eugene Meyer, a former governor of the Federal Reserve Board. That same year, after experiencing an apparent emotional breakdown, McLean entered the Sheppard and Enoch Pratt Hospital in Towson, Md., and in October a jury, acting on the testimony of psychiatrists, declared him insane. He remained in the hospital until his death from a heart attack in 1941. He was survived by his wife, who contined to be active in Washington society until her death in 1947, and by three of their four children: John Roll, Edward Beale, and Evalyn. The eldest, Vinson, had been killed by an automobile at the age of nine. Although McLean left no estate, his will, written ten years before his death, included a bequest of $300,000 to Rose Davies (sister of the film star Marion Davies), whom he described as "my common-law wife who has given me her association and affection."

[Obituaries in *Washington Post* and *N. Y. Times,* July 28, 1941; news items in same newspapers concerning McLean's will, July 29, 30, 1941; Evalyn Walsh McLean, *Father Struck It Rich* (1936); Mark Sullivan, *Our Times,* vol. VI (1935); Francis Russell, *The Shadow of Blooming Grove: Warren G. Harding and His Times* (1968); Robert K. Murray, *The Harding Era: Warren G. Harding and His Administration* (1969); Morris R. Werner and John Starr, *Teapot Dome* (1959). See also article on Evalyn Walsh McLean in *Notable Am. Women,* II, 471–73.]

EDWARD T. FOLLIARD

McMURTRIE, DOUGLAS CRAWFORD (July 20, 1888–Sept. 29, 1944), typographer and bibliographer, was born in Belmar, N. J., one of the two children of William McMurtrie [*q.v.*], a well-to-do industrial chemist, and Helen M. (Douglass) McMurtrie. Both parents were of Scottish ancestry; his father's forebear Joseph McMurtrie had settled in Oxford Township, N. J., about 1712. After attending private schools in New York City, Douglas McMurtrie prepared for college at the Hill School, Pottstown, Pa. A boyhood interest in printing and journalism continued at the Massachusetts Institute of Technology, which he entered in 1906, intending, at his father's insistence, to take a degree in electrical engineering. After three years, during which he designed the student yearbook, served as managing editor of the college newspaper, and acted as campus correspondent for three Boston papers, he dropped out without graduating.

McMurtrie's first job, in 1909, was as a statistician for the Pittsburgh Typhoid Fever Commission. He was soon producing its printed matter, and before long he returned to New York

as a free-lance designer and printing broker. Some of his work came to the attention of Ingalls Kimball, co-designer of the famous Cheltenham typeface, who appointed McMurtrie general manager of the Cheltenham Press. His duties there were primarily managerial; he did not become involved in the production end of the printing business until 1917, when he was made director of the Columbia University Printing Office. Two years later Columbia sold its plant equipment, and McMurtrie left to become president of the Arbor Press. Feeling strongly that high-quality printing could best be produced in the country, free from metropolitan distractions, yet close enough to a large city to provide easy access to customers and materials, he built a modern printing plant in Greenwich, Conn., in 1921. Lack of capital forced him to sell the plant to Condé Nast [Supp. 3] that same year, but McMurtrie remained for a time as manager. During this period he designed two typefaces, McMurtrie Title and Vanity Fair Capitals, and helped design the format of the *New Yorker* magazine. He was also instrumental in forming the Continental Typefounders Association, which introduced many European typefaces into the United States, and imported several on his own, among them Cochin and the original Didot.

Leaving Condé Nast Publications in 1923, McMurtrie turned again to free-lancing in New York. After three years, during which time he served (1925–26) as editor of *Ars Typographica,* he became typographic director of the Cuneo Press in Chicago, and the next year moved to the Ludlow Typograph Company. His primary responsibilities were in advertising and public relations, for which he was eminently suited, being gregarious, fluent, and an excellent copywriter. The Ludlow company also provided him with substantial support for his writing and research, an activity to which he became increasingly devoted. Among his more important books were *Modern Typography and Layout* (1929) and *The Golden Book* (1927), a history of printing which in 1938 was revised and renamed *The Book.* Like many of his publications, it leaned heavily upon the work of researchers and writers in his hire (notably Albert H. Allen), although only his name appears on the title page; this may partly explain its uneven quality. McMurtrie was nevertheless a facile and prolific writer, and his bibliography numbers over five hundred titles.

His chief importance rests upon his bibliographical work. Upon discovering in his research that little had been written about American printing since the *History of Printing in the United States* by Isaiah Thomas [*q.v.*], McMurtrie plunged into the task of filling the many historical gaps. He intended to issue his own four-volume history, but only Volume II, dealing with printing in the Middle and South Atlantic states, appeared. It was published in 1936, and that same year McMurtrie was appointed editor of a national Works Progress Administration project known as the American Imprints Inventory. Before its dissolution, it issued some thirty-five publications, and the work was continued for a time at the Newberry Library in Chicago; the unpublished cards, estimated at over fifteen million, were eventually deposited at the Library of Congress. McMurtrie also directed another WPA project, an unpublished index to printing periodicals; its thousands of index cards were later transferred to Michigan State University. While much of his work can be criticized as hasty and superficial, a solid contribution remains.

A gargantuan man, weighing usually well over three hundred pounds, with appetites to match, McMurtrie had an enormous capacity for pleasure as well as work. Something of a dandy, he was a fluent lecturer and an engaging conversationalist; his wit and generosity won many friends, though some were put off by his flamboyance. His chief outside interest was the care and education of crippled children and the rehabilitation of the crippled. From 1912 to 1919 he edited the *American Journal of Care for Cripples,* and in 1915 he became president of the Federation of Associations for Cripples. During World War I he served as director of the Red Cross Institute for Crippled and Disabled Men, whose work included physical and emotional rehabilitation, vocational training, and job placement. On Feb. 20, 1915, McMurtrie married Adele Koehler, by whom he had three children: Havelock Heydon, Helen Josephine, and Thomas Baskerville. He died suddenly of a heart attack in Evanston, Ill., at the age of fifty-six. His body was cremated at Graceland Cemetery, Chicago.

[The most complete bibliography of McMurtrie's work is Charles F. Heartman, *McMurtrie Imprints* (1942), with *Supp.* (1946). Heartman's biographical introduction, which contains some personal reminiscence, is largely based upon Frank McCaffrey, *An Informal Biog. of Douglas McMurtrie* (privately printed pamphlet, 1939). Two articles on McMurtrie by Herbert A. Kellar, containing much firsthand information although somewhat uncritical, are in the *Miss. Valley Hist. Rev.,* June 1947, and *Inter-Am. Rev. of Bibliog.,* Jan. 1955. See also obituaries in the Chicago press and the *N. Y. Times,* Sept. 30, 1944; *Wilson Lib. Bull.,* Nov. 1944 (with a portrait); *Publishers' Weekly,* Oct. 7, 1944; *Current Biog.,* 1944; and *Who Was Who in America,* vol. II (1950). Of several memorial tributes, one of the best was that of Randolph G. Adams in the *News Sheet* of the Bibliog. Soc. of America, Jan. 1, 1945. R. Hunter Middleton of the Ludlow Typograph Co. and the late Pierce Butler supplied reminiscences.]

JAMES M. WELLS

McNAIR, LESLEY JAMES (May 25, 1883–July 25, 1944), army officer, was born in Verndale, Minn., the second of four children and older of two sons of James and Clara (Manz) McNair. Both parents were Presbyterians; the father, who had emigrated with his parents from Campbelltown, Scotland, to Ohio about 1854, was a lumber merchant and operated several general stores in northwestern Minnesota. As a youth McNair hoped to become a naval officer and obtained an alternate appointment to Annapolis, but he tired of waiting and at age seventeen entered West Point by competitive examination. Sandy-haired, wiry, and of medium height, he distinguished himself at the Military Academy as a student of mathematics. He was graduated in 1904, eleventh in a class of 124, and was commissioned an artillery officer. On June 15, 1905, he married Clare Huster of New York City, whom he had met while at West Point. Their only child, Douglas Crevier McNair, later followed his father to West Point and into the artillery.

McNair spent most of the decade after his graduation with the 4th Field Artillery. In 1912, as a student at the School of Fire at Fort Sill, he made the studies, "Probabilities and the Theory of Dispersion," that provided a basis for improving gun firing techniques. In 1913 he spent eight months in France observing French artillery practice; the next summer he took part in the expedition of Gen. Frederick Funston [*q.v.*] to Vera Cruz, and in 1916–17 that of Gen. John J. Pershing into northern Mexico. During World War I, McNair's acquaintance with Pershing led to his assignment to the 1st Division, with which he went to France in June 1917. He served much of the time with Pershing's general headquarters as an artillery expert and forward observer, becoming at age thirty-five the second youngest brigadier general in the American Expeditionary Forces; for his work on the coordination of field artillery fire with infantry combat he earned the Distinguished Service Medal.

Reverting to his permanent grade of major after the war, McNair spent two years as student and instructor at the army's schools at Fort Leavenworth. After duty in Hawaii and as professor of military science at Purdue University, he attended the Army War College, from which he was graduated in 1929. For the next four years, as assistant commandant of the Field Artillery School at Fort Sill, McNair had much to do with setting and achieving high standards of training for regular officers, with developing extension courses for officers of the National Guard and Organized Reserves, and with working out new methods for coordinating artillery fire that came into use in World War II. After several intervening assignments, including duty with the Civilian Conservation Corps, McNair in 1937 was promoted once more to general officer rank and given command of the 2d Field Artillery Brigade. During this year he contributed materially in field maneuvers and studies to the streamlining and "triangularization" of the infantry division (a simplified table of organization based on units of three, from squads up to regiments) that would be carried out under his direction four years later. His next duty, as commandant of the Command and General Staff School at Fort Leavenworth, was abruptly terminated in early summer 1940 following the fall of France and the ensuing preliminary mobilization of American forces, which required the closing of the senior army schools.

Up to this point General McNair had been an obscure though highly competent officer, one of the most intellectual of American generals, and a man whom Chief of Staff George C. Marshall (whose friendship McNair had won while serving in the A.E.F.) could speak of as "the brains of the Army." Now Marshall called him to Washington to superintend the organization and training of the mobilizing ground combat forces, a task McNair performed with outstanding skill and seemingly tireless energy during the next four years. From August 1940 until March 1942 he served as chief of staff of General Headquarters, of which Marshall was nominally the commander, and thereafter until July 1944 as commanding general of the Army Ground Forces. McNair was promoted to major general in September 1940, lieutenant general in June 1941, and (posthumously) general in 1945.

In organizing American forces for action, General McNair stressed economy and simplicity. He opposed large staffs, keeping his own headquarters notably small; and he tried to strip fighting units down to their essentials in men and equipment. Though an artilleryman, he viewed the infantry as the arm of decisive action; and he opposed the proliferation of specialized units that could not be welded into a combined arms team built around the infantry. His most serious miscalculation—one that violated this principle—was his overenthusiastic backing of the mobile "tank destroyer" and of a separate antitank force built around it. In supervising the training of more than three million men, McNair aimed to develop what he called the basic soldierly qualities—"confidence in one's self, one's leaders, and one's weapons and technical equipment; self-reliance, ingenuity, and initiative; esprit and the will to do the job." He equated good training with good leadership, labeling it "plain murder" to send soldiers into combat under incompetent officers. He stressed physical fitness, "the first requisite of success in battle," and a maximum of realism in training, as by the use of live ammunition. No armchair general, he spent about a third of his time on field inspections. After Pearl Harbor he also insisted on assimilating the lessons of battle into training as promptly as possible, and obtained them by sending his own observers overseas.

In April 1943 McNair himself traveled to North Africa to observe the fighting in Tunisia. As he had done so often in World War I, he went as far forward as he could to see the results of artillery firing and was seriously wounded on his first day at the front. Five weeks after the invasion of Normandy in June 1944, the European Theater announced that McNair was in England and had been named commanding general of the 1st Army Group, an appointment designed to mislead the Germans about the planned thrust of American forces into France. Characteristically, McNair soon crossed to Normandy to get a front-line view of the action, and particularly of the planned massive aerial bombardment near St. Lô that would help break through the German defenses. On his first day at the front, July 25, 1944, he was killed when American bombs fell short of their targets. Buried in secrecy nearby, his remains were subsequently moved to the Normandy American Cemetery and Memorial overlooking "Omaha" invasion beach. McNair was the highest ranking United States officer killed in action in any American war down to that time. Twelve days after his death, his son Douglas was killed in action on Guam.

McNair was a modest man who completely immersed himself in the professional tasks of the soldier. He sought neither wealth nor honors, and received none during World War II before his death save honorary degrees from Purdue and the University of Maine. Two oak-leaf clusters were posthumously added to his Distinguished Service Medal, in recognition of his training of the ground combat forces, and in May 1945 the Army War College reservation from which he had directed that training was redesignated Fort Lesley J. McNair.

[The Lib. of Cong. has a small collection of McNair's personal papers and memorabilia; his official correspondence is in army records in the Nat. Archives and Records Service. A folder in the reference collection of the Office of the Chief of Military Hist., Dept. of the Army, records his military service. E. J. Kahn, Jr., *McNair: Educator of an Army* (1945), is the best contemporary appreciation. Two volumes in the United States Army in World War II series, *The Organization of Ground Combat Troops*, by Kent R. Greenfield et al. (1947), and *The Procurement and Training of Ground Combat Troops*, by Robert R. Palmer et al. (1948), cover McNair's official World War II activities in detail. See also: *Current Biog.*, 1942; *Nat. Cyc. Am. Biog.*, XXXIII, 6–7; *N. Y. Times*, July 28, 1944; and James B. McNair, comp., *McNair, McNear, and McNeir Genealogies*, Supp. (1955).]

STETSON CONN

McNAMEE, GRAHAM (July 10, 1888–May 9, 1942), radio announcer, was born in Washington, D. C., the only child of Annie (Liebold) and John Bernard McNamee. Both parents were natives of Ohio; his paternal great-grandfather, James Bernard McNamee, had emigrated in 1835 from Tyrone County, Ireland, to Kingston, Ontario, Canada. John McNamee, a lawyer, served during President Cleveland's first administration as legal adviser to Secretary of the Interior Lucius Q. C. Lamar [*q.v.*]. In 1894 he moved to St. Paul, Minn., where he became counsel for the Northern Pacific Railroad.

Graham McNamee received a conventional education in the St. Paul public schools. After graduating from high school, he played semiprofessional hockey and baseball and worked briefly as a clerk for the Great Northern Railroad and as a house-to-house salesman. His father wanted him to become a lawyer, but his mother, who played the piano and sang in local church choirs, favored a musical career. At her insistence he took piano and singing lessons. When his father died, about 1912, he and his mother moved first to Weehawken, N. J., and then to New York City, where McNamee studied voice under several well-known teachers. He sang in churches, appeared with light and grand opera companies, and on Nov. 22, 1920, made his debut as a concert singer at New York's Aeolian Hall.

McNamee entered the still-young radio industry in 1923 when, out of curiosity, he wandered into station WEAF in New York City. Intrigued by what he saw, he applied for a job; his clear, vibrant speaking voice impressed the program manager, and he was hired as an announcer. McNamee's coverage of sports events, such as the 1923 World's Series, early attracted attention, particularly his colorful filling-in during pauses between innings or plays. He reported not merely the game itself but the entire panorama: spectator, athlete, stadium, weather, and even the local flora. Using similar techniques, he and Phillips Carlin broadcast the proceedings of the two national political conventions in 1924, the first such broadcasts in American history. In 1927, now the best-known announcer in the industry, McNamee described the 1927 Rose Bowl football game over the first coast-to-coast hookup, and later that year he announced the arrival of Charles A. Lindbergh from Paris.

McNamee's brightest years were from 1923 to 1927, a period when commercials were only incidental to broadcasting, the sponsor usually being announced only at the beginning and end of a program. This scheme well suited McNamee's chatty style, and he became one of the first stars of radio, which like the film industry placed a high premium upon the ability of a performer to build audience loyalties. His trademarks were his salutation, "Good evening, ladies and gentlemen of the radio audience," and his sign-off, "Good night, all." But it was his air of informality and his obvious delight in describing the events before him that especially appealed to his listeners. As his stature grew, McNamee's presence on a program attracted some of the biggest sponsors. The new commercialism, however, required split-second timing of sales messages and tight program scheduling, leaving little leeway for McNamee's informal style. At about this time, also, his coverage of sports events began to be questioned, some listeners complaining of his inattention to the technical details of the game. Soon the sports specialists pushed McNamee aside.

He remained, however, a popular general announcer. During the 1930's McNamee was radio's leading "master of ceremonies" for variety and humor programs, among them the RKO Hour, the Rudy Vallee Show, and the Texaco Program, starring Ed Wynn. At the same time he was a staff announcer for the National Broadcasting Company on special events. (In 1941 he described his own 500-foot parachute jump from a training tower at Fort Benning, Ga.) He was also a regular narrator for Universal Newsreels, then a popular feature in movie houses.

A nervous, excitable man, McNamee was shy and hesitant in private conversation. His hobbies included golf and motoring. On May 3, 1921, he had married Josephine Garrett of Macomb, Ill., a soprano whom he had met on a concert program. They were divorced in February 1932, and on Jan. 20, 1934, he married Ann Lee Sims, the daughter of a planter in Rayville, La. There were no children by either marriage. McNamee died at the age of fifty-three of an embolism of the brain in St. Luke's Hospital, New York City. A Roman Catholic, he was buried in the family plot in Calvary Cemetery, Columbus, Ohio.

[McNamee's reminiscences, *You're on the Air* (with Robert G. Anderson, 1926), and his later series of articles in the *American Mag.*, Apr., May, July, Sept., Nov. 1928; interview in *Daily Princetonian*, Dec. 5, 1928; Walter Davenport in *Collier's*, Jan. 14, 1928; profile by Geoffrey T. Hellman in *New Yorker*, Aug. 9, 1930; *Nat. Cyc. Am. Biog.*, XXXI, 18–19; *N. Y. Times*, May 21, 1931, May 10, 17, 1942; *Variety*, May 13, 1942. There are useful references to McNamee in: MS. reminiscences of Phillips Carlin and

McNary

McNary

Thomas H. Cowan, Oral Hist. Collection, Columbia Univ.; William P. Banning, *Commercial Broadcasting Pioneer: The WEAF Experiment, 1922–1926* (1946); Gleason L. Archer, *Hist. of Radio to 1926* (1938); Ben Gross, *I Looked and I Listened* (1954); Sam J. Slate and Joe Cook, *It Sounds Impossible* (1963). For contemporary radio sounds, consult "Hist. of Broadcasting, 1920–1950" (Folkways Record no. 9171).]
MEYER WEINBERG

McNARY, CHARLES LINZA (June 12, 1874–Feb. 25, 1944), United States Senator, was born on his father's farm north of Salem, Oreg. He was the third son and ninth of ten children of Hugh Linza McNary, who had earlier operated a brickyard and taught school, and Mary Margaret (Claggett) McNary. His grandfather James McNary, a native of Kentucky and a grandson of Hugh McNary, a Scottish emigrant from Ulster, had moved from Missouri to Clackamas County, Oreg., in 1845. His mother's parents, of Scottish and English descent, were also from Missouri, having come to Oregon in 1852. His mother died in 1878, and after the death of his father in 1883, the nine-year-old Charles lived with three older sisters and a brother in Salem. He attended public school there and spent a year (1896–97) at Stanford University, where he earned his board by waiting on table.

Having read law in the office of his older brother John, McNary was admitted to the bar in October 1898, after which he practiced with his brother in Salem. He repurchased and expanded the family farm and in 1909 organized the Salem Fruit Union, of which he remained president until his death. He was dean of the Willamette University law school from 1908 to 1913. McNary's main career, however, was in politics. His first public offices were deputy county recorder of Marion County (1892–96); deputy district attorney (1904–11), serving under his brother John; and special counsel for the state railroad commission (1911–13). He was appointed to the state supreme court in 1913 to fill a vacancy and failed by one vote to win the Republican nomination to that post in 1914. In 1916–17 he was chairman of the Republican state central committee. Upon the death of Harry Lane in 1917, McNary was appointed to his seat in the United States Senate. Save for a few weeks in 1918, he remained in the Senate for the rest of his life.

Although McNary had been president of the Oregon Taft-Sherman Club in 1912, he called himself a progressive in 1917. Labor supported him in each of his candidacies for the Senate. During the First World War he backed the Wilson administration but joined Republican progressives on economic issues. He favored ratification of the Versailles Treaty, in 1919–20, with "mild" reservations; he voted in 1926 to join the World Court. During the 1920's he championed legislation for reclamation. In 1922 he joined George W. Norris [Supp. 3] in favoring public development of Muscle Shoals, and as chairman of the Senate Committee on Irrigation and Reclamation (1919–26) he supported development of the Tennessee, Colorado, and Columbia rivers. In the Committee on Agriculture and Forestry (of which he was chairman, 1926–33) he presided over the investigation of forest resources (1923) that led to the McNary-Clarke Act for fire protection, reforestation, forest management, and acquisition of forest lands (1924), the McNary-Woodruff Act for the purchase of lands for national forests (1928), and the McNary-Sweeney Act for forest research (1928). He was best known in the 1920's, however, as a leader of the "farm bloc" in Congress and as sponsor, with Representative Gilbert N. Haugen [Supp. 1], of the McNary-Haugen Bill, which sought to stabilize farm prices by subsidizing the sale of surplus crops abroad. This proposal (originated by George N. Peek [Supp. 3] and Hugh S. Johnson [Supp. 3]) met defeat in 1924, but enlisted growing support and was the most popular current farm relief plan. President Coolidge vetoed new versions that passed both houses in 1927 and 1928.

In much of his voting and in his personal associations in the 1920's, McNary stood with such Western progressives as Norris, Robert M. La Follette [q.v.], William E. Borah [Supp. 2], and Hiram W. Johnson [Supp. 3]. McNary was one of the nine Republican Senators who met at La Follette's call in December 1922 to plan progressive strategy; in the campaign of 1924, however, he supported Coolidge rather than La Follette. As assistant majority leader in the Senate during the years 1929–33, McNary (according to a columnist in *Collier's*) was almost the only link between the Eastern and Western factions of the party.

McNary's political skill was most striking during his service as minority leader in the Senate, 1933–44. He insisted that the party must have a forward-looking, progressive program, that it could not function as a party of negation. He opposed disciplining Republican Senators who had supported Roosevelt in 1932, and he backed most early New Deal measures. He advocated public distribution of power and supported the Tennessee Valley Authority. President Roosevelt respected his advice and often made substantial concessions to him (e.g., a high dam with electric power installations at Bonneville, on the Columbia River, rather than a low one). McNary ran for reelection in 1936 independently of the state Republican organization and gave only limited support to Alfred M. Landon, the Republican presidential candidate.

His support for the New Deal, however, was not unqualified. He was against reciprocal trade agreements except where they offered clear advantages for American producers, and he opposed the agricultural bills of 1936 and 1938 on constitutional grounds. During the Supreme Court controversy of 1937 his strategy was to keep the Republican side silent, allowing conservative Democrats to lead the opposition to Roosevelt. After that time he voted against the administration more frequently. He opposed repeal of the arms embargo in 1939, although he voted for selective service in 1940 and for lend-lease in 1941. When in 1940 the Republicans nominated Wendell Willkie [Supp. 3] for president, they picked McNary to offset Willkie's associations with big business and with Eastern internationalists. McNary had not favored Willkie's nomination, and he took occasion in his acceptance speech to endorse the TVA, which Willkie had attacked. In the campaign he emphasized reciprocal trade and agricultural issues.

McNary was nearly six feet tall, slender, sandy-haired, and blue-eyed. He spoke infrequently; his style was expository and undramatic. His great talent lay in personal relations, especially in bringing together progressive and conservative Republicans and, in his later years, in preparing a coalition with conservative Democrats. He was a skilled parliamentarian and one of the most popular members of Congress with colleagues and with the press. His first wife, Jessie Breyman, whom he had married on Nov. 19, 1902, died in 1918, and on Dec. 29, 1923, he married Cornelia Woodburn Morton. He had no children, but he and his second wife adopted a daughter, Charlotte, in 1935. McNary was a member of the Baptist Church. He died at Fort Lauderdale, Fla., in 1944, at sixty-nine, following surgery for a brain tumor, and was buried in the Odd Fellows Cemetery at Salem, Oreg.

[McNary Papers, Lib. of Cong. and Univ. of Oreg.; papers of Thomas B. Neuhausen (his campaign manager in 1918 and 1930), Univ. of Oreg.; George C. Hoffmann, "The Early Political Career of Charles McNary, 1917–1924" (Ph.D. dissertation, Univ. of Southern Calif., 1951); Howard C. Zimmerman, "A Rhetorical Criticism of the 1940 Campaign Speaking of Senator Charles Linza McNary of Oreg." (master's thesis, Univ. of Oreg., 1954); Roger T. Johnson, "Charles L. McNary and the Republican Party during Prosperity and Depression" (Ph.D. dissertation, Univ. of Wis., 1967); Howard A. De Witt, "Charles L. McNary and the 1918 Congressional Election," Oreg. Hist. Quart., June 1967; Collier's, Jan. 25, 1930, p. 40, Feb. 21, 1931, p. 53; Hugh L. Smith, The Oreg. McNary Family: Genealogy and Hist. Sketches (mimeographed, Atlanta, 1938); Edith Kerns Chambers, Genealogical Narrative: A Hist. of the Claggett-

Irvine Clans (1940); information from Mrs. Willard C. Marshall, Salem. Published data on McNary's early life are unreliable.]

EARL POMEROY

McPHERSON, AIMEE SEMPLE (Oct. 9, 1890–Sept. 27, 1944), evangelist, founder of the International Church of the Foursquare Gospel, was born near Ingersoll, Ontario, Canada. Christened Aimee Elizabeth Kennedy, she was the only child of James Morgan Kennedy, a Methodist farmer, and Minnie (Pearce) Kennedy, the foster daughter of a Salvation Army captain and herself active in Salvation Army work. Aimee was exposed throughout her early life to the Army's distinctive blend of theological conservatism, humanitarianism, and quasi-military structure. To this she added her own intuitive flair for the dramatic, which was to become characteristic of her revival work. In 1907, after a temporary "loss of faith," she underwent a conversion experience prompted by the preaching of an itinerant Pentecostal evangelist, Robert James Semple, a Scotch-Irish immigrant whom she married on Aug. 12, 1908, at the age of seventeen. Together they conducted revival meetings in Canada and the United States and in 1910 went as missionaries to Asia. They settled briefly in Hong Kong to await entry into China, but there, in August 1910, Robert Semple died of typhoid fever a month before the birth of their daughter, Roberta Star Semple.

Early in 1911 the young widow, with her infant daughter, joined her mother in New York City, where Mrs. Kennedy was working for the Salvation Army. During the following months Aimee Semple devoted herself to revival activity in New York, Chicago, and elsewhere. On Feb. 28, 1912, she married Harold Stewart McPherson, a young Providence, R. I., grocery salesman. A son, Rolf Kennedy McPherson, was born in March 1913. Mrs. McPherson soon felt called to continue revival work, and, beginning in 1916, she traveled extensively up and down the Eastern seaboard in her "gospel automobile," on which were painted evangelistic slogans. In 1917 she started a small monthly paper, the Bridal Call, and through it began to build up a following. In 1918 she and her mother and the two children, after an itinerant transcontinental gospel tour, settled in Los Angeles, Calif. From this headquarters, over the next five years, Mrs. McPherson and her mother set out on repeated cross-country tours, conducting revivals in tents, churches, and public auditoriums in most major American cities and visiting Canada and even Australia. Her husband, though for a time in favor of her evangelism, quarreled with her, and in 1921 they were divorced.

From donations received on tour, from her Los Angeles followers, and from magazine subscriptions, Aimee Semple McPherson was able to realize her dream of establishing a permanent home for what she now called the "Foursquare Gospel" movement. On Jan. 1, 1923, Angelus Temple, with a seating capacity of more than 5,000, was opened on a site adjacent to Echo Park in Los Angeles. The following year a radio station—the third in the Los Angeles area—began broadcasting from facilities in the Temple. In 1923 Mrs. McPherson (who had herself never completed high school) opened a Bible school which in 1926 became the Lighthouse of International Foursquare Evangelism and moved to its own five-story facilities adjacent to the Temple. The International Church of the Foursquare Gospel was formally incorporated in 1927. All these enterprises remained under the personal ownership and control of Mrs. McPherson and her mother.

The conservative theology of the Foursquare Gospel movement, as formulated by its founder, was built around the four roles of Jesus Christ—Savior, Baptizer, Healer, and Coming King—which Mrs. McPherson found foreshadowed in a vision of the Prophet Ezekiel. Although "speaking in tongues" was gradually deemphasized, faith healing, a part of Mrs. McPherson's work almost from the beginning, grew in importance. Many came to Angelus Temple seeking healing, their faith strengthened by a permanent display of discarded canes, crutches, and braces. Mrs. McPherson owed much of her success to her mastery of the arts of publicity and her willingness to use flamboyant techniques in a decade and a city congenial to her style. Her services included the use of orchestras and choirs, vivid portrayals of Bible stories, and elaborate costumes and pageantry. To illustrate a sermon dealing with the consequences of breaking God's laws she donned a traffic officer's uniform and rode a motorcycle down the aisle of Angelus Temple.

On May 18, 1926, Mrs. McPherson disappeared while swimming in the Pacific Ocean near Venice, Calif., not far from Los Angeles. While many of the faithful searched frantically along the coast for traces of the missing evangelist, Mrs. Kennedy sorrowfully announced at the Temple that her daughter had drowned. A month later, however, on June 23, Aimee McPherson appeared at Agua Prieta, a town on the Mexico-Arizona border, and told a story of having been kidnapped. Public interest ran high, and in the succeeding months many accounts of the disappearance were reported. Her conflicting testimony

before a grand jury investigating the occurrence resulted in a perjury charge, but early in 1927, for unstated reasons, the case was dismissed. There is some evidence to indicate that she spent at least part of the month in Carmel, Calif., with Kenneth G. Ormiston, the radio operator at Angelus Temple, who had disappeared at the same time.

This episode and the subsequent controversy resulted in serious disaffection within the top leadership at Angelus Temple, and contributed to a break between Mrs. McPherson and her mother. Despite some defections, however, it did not dampen the spirits of most of her followers. She continued to manage the affairs of the Temple and engaged in further evangelistic work in the United States, England, and France. A tour of the Holy Land in 1930 and an Asian tour in 1931 (including a pilgrimage to Robert Semple's grave in Hong Kong) helped build an international following, and Foursquare Gospel churches were established in many countries by graduates of the Bible school. In the depression-ridden 1930's, an Angelus Temple "commissary," established some years before, provided food and clothing for the needy.

A third marriage, on Sept. 13, 1931, to David Hutton, a thirty-year-old choir member at Angelus Temple, proved unhappy. Hutton filed for divorce in 1933, and the decree was awarded on Mar. 2, 1934. The years 1935–37 were marked by serious financial difficulties at the Temple and a leadership dispute which pitted Mrs. McPherson in a court struggle simultaneously against her mother, her daughter, and her associate pastor, Rheba Crawford. But with the subsidence of journalistic interest in this controversy, the era of sensationalism was largely over. Mrs. McPherson now concentrated her energies on the varied activities she once summarized as "teaching in the Bible School, giving radio talks, publishing our weekly paper, preaching on the platform, praying for the sick, and being president of about four hundred branch churches" (Thomas, *Storming Heaven*, p. 305). By the early 1940's Angelus Temple had overcome its financial difficulties and had entered a period of sustained, if less spectacular, growth. In 1944, while in Oakland, Calif., to dedicate a new Foursquare church, Aimee Semple McPherson died from what was ruled an accidental overdose of barbital sedatives complicated by a kidney ailment. After services at Angelus Temple, she was buried in Forest Lawn Memorial Park, Glendale, Calif.

In an era of colorful revivalistic preachers, Aimee Semple McPherson stands out as the most widely known female evangelist. Although she won attention largely by her unorthodox techniques and occasional notoriety, she was a woman of genuine leadership and managerial ability, boundless energy, and a fundamental sincerity of purpose. To thousands disturbed and confused by the disputes over theological "modernism" and the broader transformations of American life, she offered an appealing, updated version of Protestant fundamentalism. Hers was a gospel of love, fulfillment, and triumph. A generation after her death, under the leadership of her son and chosen successor Rolf McPherson, the denomination she had founded claimed 193,000 members in over 700 North American churches with missionary activities in twenty-seven foreign countries.

[Mrs. McPherson's most important autobiographical writings are *This Is That* (rev. ed., 1923) and *The Story of My Life* (1951), compiled from her own documents after her death. Of more limited use are her *In the Service of the King* (1927) and *Give Me My Own God* (1936). The magazines of the Foursquare Gospel, the *Bridal Call* and *Foursquare Crusader*, contain articles by Mrs. McPherson. The fullest biography (with many photographs) is Lately Thomas, *Storming Heaven* (1970); this supersedes his earlier *The Vanishing Evangelist* (1959) and Nancy Barr Mavity, *Sister Aimee* (1931), both of which concentrate on the episode of her disappearance. See also William D. Blomgren, "Aimee Semple McPherson and the Four Square Gospel, 1921–1944" (M.A. thesis, Stanford Univ., 1952); and William G. McLoughlin in *Jour. of Popular Culture*, Winter 1967, and in *Notable Am. Women*, II, 477–80.]
ROBERT L. FERM

MACRAE, JOHN (Aug. 25, 1866–Feb. 18, 1944), book publisher, was born in Richmond, Va., the third of six children and oldest of three sons of John Hampden Macrae and Sheldena A. (Beach) Macrae. His father, a railroad construction engineer, was a native of Richmond who had attended the United States Military Academy at West Point (1842–44). While serving in the Confederate Army during the Civil War, he was wounded and captured, and thus met the Union nurse from Hartford, Conn., whom he subsequently married.

Young John, after a boyhood in Greenwich, Va., and attendance at public and private schools, left home to seek his fortune. Moving gradually northward, he worked in a Baltimore factory at the age of sixteen, unsuccessfully sought a government surveyorship in Washington, D. C., and late in 1885, at the age of nineteen, went to work as an office boy at the New York publishing firm of E. P. Dutton & Company. Dutton's, founded in Boston in 1852 by Edward Dutton and Lemuel Ide, had moved to New York City in 1869 and by the mid-1880's was operating a large retail bookstore as well as publishing titles in the religious and children's fields. Edward Dutton quickly recognized Macrae's talents and

in 1886 made him manager of the religious book division and sent him on the road as a salesman. On a business trip to Europe in 1895 Macrae reached reciprocal trade agreements with British and German publishers. Moving steadily up the ladder, he became the firm's secretary in 1901, vice-president in 1905, and vice-president/treasurer in 1914. As Edward Dutton grew older, Macrae assumed an increasing share of the managerial responsibility, and with Dutton's death in 1923 he succeeded him as president, a position he was to hold until his own death.

In his years with E. P. Dutton & Company, John Macrae moved the firm to a leading position as a publisher of general trade titles, including such varied works as Vicente Blasco-Ibáñez's *The Four Horsemen of the Apocalypse* (1918); the autobiography of Samuel Gompers [*q.v.*], *Seventy Years of Life and Labor* (1925); Axel Munthe's best-selling *The Story of San Michele* (1929); and Van Wyck Brooks's *The Flowering of New England* (1936). The children's field was not forgotten, as witness such titles as *Lad: A Dog* (1919), by Albert Payson Terhune [Supp. 3], and A. A. Milne's *When We Were Very Young* (1924), *Winnie-the-Pooh* (1926), and *Now We Are Six* (1927). One of the most profitable items on the Dutton list was Everyman's Library, a collection of classics published in uniform bindings in collaboration with J. M. Dent of London. Macrae, a man of distinguished features and precisely clipped beard, clearly savored the role of urbane and cultivated bookman, establishing close personal ties with such well-known Dutton authors as William Lyon Phelps [Supp. 3] and Van Wyck Brooks. But his gifts as a salesman never deserted him, and he zestfully promoted *Eat and Grow Thin* and other works more lucrative than memorable.

Macrae's influence extended well beyond the limits of Dutton's Fifth Avenue offices; at his death *Publishers' Weekly* called him "one of the most vigorous and respected figures in American publishing." He was a leading spokesman for the industry as a whole, particularly in the years 1924–27, when he served as president of the National Association of Book Publishers. An authority on tariff, copyright, and postal matters, he kept a careful eye on developments in these fields as they affected the book business. Strong-minded and outspoken, he never hesitated to express his views, whether in Congressional testimony, speeches, magazine articles, or newspaper letters. He consistently opposed trends which seemed to threaten the small retail bookstores, which he knew intimately from his early days on the road and which he viewed as the backbone of the industry. On these grounds he attacked the price cutting of Macy's and other large department stores and bitterly opposed the rise of mail-order "book clubs" in the 1920's. When his widely circulated attack on the Book-of-the-Month Club involved him in a $200,000 lawsuit in 1929, he retracted certain specific allegations, but reasserted his general opposition and his refusal to submit Dutton titles for book club consideration.

John Macrae was married on Sept. 20, 1893, to Katharine Green of Virginia, by whom he had two sons: John (1898) and Elliott Beach (1900), both of whom joined the firm in 1922. In the early years in New York the Macraes lived on Staten Island; later they moved to Manhattan's Gracie Square. Macrae's first wife died in 1913, and on Sept. 5, 1939, he married Opal Wheeler of Beverly Hills, Calif., the director of Miss Yates's School in New York City and co-author of several children's books published by Dutton. Active to the end, Macrae died of a heart attack in 1944 at his home in New York City. After Episcopal services at New York's St. Thomas Church, he was buried in the churchyard at Greenwich, Va. In 1941 he had transferred a controlling stock interest in E. P. Dutton & Company to his son Elliott, who after his death became president, with John Macrae, Jr., as chairman of the board.

[The fullest published sources are the obituaries in *Publishers' Weekly*, Feb. 26, 1944, and the *N. Y. Times*, Feb. 20, 1944 (with portrait). See also *ibid.*, Sept. 6, 1939 (second marriage), Feb. 22, 1944 (funeral), and Aug. 29, 1929 (Book-of-the-Month-Club controversy); *Publishers' Weekly*, May 13, 1944 (reorganization of the company); *Who Was Who in America*, vols. II (1950) and IV (1968), the latter on Elliott B. Macrae; *Who's Who in America*, 1952–53, on John Macrae, Jr.; Elliott B. Macrae, "Getting Started," in Gerald Gross, ed., *Publishers on Publishing* (1961); Charles A. Madison, *Book Publishing in America* (1966), pp. 95–96, 220–25. Information about Macrae's father from Archivist, U. S. Military Acad., West Point, N. Y., and from John Macrae, Jr.]

PAUL S. BOYER

MAIN, CHARLES THOMAS (Feb. 16, 1856–Mar. 6, 1943), mechanical engineer, was born in Marblehead, Mass., the only child of Thomas and Cordelia Green (Reed) Main. Both parents came of colonial New England stock; his father was a native of Marblehead, his mother of Plymouth. Shortly after Charles's birth his mother died, and he was reared by his paternal grandparents. He received a conventional education in the Marblehead schools, but early acquired an interest in mechanical matters at a local machine shop and at the rope factory where his father, a machinist, was master mechanic and his grandfather superintendent. In 1872 Main entered the Massachusetts Institute of Technol-

ogy, from which he graduated in 1876 with an S.B. degree in mechanical engineering. He stayed on at M.I.T. for a time as an assistant instructor while doing advanced work. In 1879 he took a job as a draftsman at the textile mills in Manchester, N. H., but left at the beginning of 1881 to become an engineer with the Lower Pacific Mills in Lawrence, Mass. In this capacity he helped rebuild the company's main factory, rearranging its machinery, installing a new steam plant, and reconstructing a waterpower plant. Though promoted in 1887 to superintendent of the worsted department, which then employed 2,500 people, he left Lower Pacific Mills at the end of 1891 to become an independent engineering consultant.

After a year in Providence, R. I., Main formed a partnership in Boston with Francis Winthrop Dean, a well-known power engineer. The partnership lasted until 1907, when Main organized his own firm, incorporated in 1926 as Charles T. Main, Inc. At first Main specialized in textile mills, supervising their design and construction and handling reorganizations, valuations, tax problems, and other related matters. He planned and built numerous mills throughout New England and the Southeast, and even as far afield as Montreal and Henderson, Ky. For twenty-five years, beginning in 1899, he supervised the construction of new plants for the American Woolen Company, including the Wood Worsted Mills in Lawrence, Mass., then one of the largest single manufacturing buildings in the country. His *Notes on Mill Construction* (1886) was for some years used as a textbook at the Massachusetts Institute of Technology.

Before electricity came into widespread use, separate power plants had to be designed for each mill, and Main, who had long been interested in power problems, soon acquired a reputation as an expert on both water and steam power. In 1891 he published the first of several papers in which he outlined methods for evaluating waterpower plants, and three years later he designed and supervised the construction of a municipal lighting plant in Marblehead and a steam-electric plant for the Lynn (Mass.) Gas & Electric Company. Over the years he helped complete a number of steam and waterpower projects, including the Conowingo Dam across the Susquehanna River in Maryland and the Keokuk Dam across the Mississippi. All told, he and his firm designed nearly eighty hydroelectric plants.

On Nov. 14, 1883, Main married Elizabeth Freeto Appleton of Somerville, Mass. They had three children: Charles Reed, Alice Appleton, and Theodore. Active in professional organizations,

Main was president of the Boston Society of Civil Engineers (1912), of the Engineers Club of Boston (1914–25), of the American Institute of Consulting Engineers (1929), and of the American Society of Mechanical Engineers (1918). In 1919 he established the Charles T. Main Award, given annually to a student member of the A.S.M.E. A man of high standards, Main, while president of the Boston Society of Civil Engineers, drafted the first code of ethics adopted by any engineering society in the United States. His honors included the gold medal of the American Society of Mechanical Engineers (1935) and an honorary degree from Northeastern University (1935). Within his community he served for three years as alderman in Lawrence, Mass., and for several years as chairman of the water and sewer board in Winchester, Mass., to which he moved in 1891. He was also an active member of the Congregational Church. Main died at his home in Winchester at the age of eighty-seven of a coronary occlusion and was buried in Wildwood Cemetery, Winchester.

[William F. Uhl, *Charles T. Main (1856–1943)* (Newcomen Soc. pamphlet, 1951); Am. Soc. of Mechanical Engineers, *Transactions*, LXV (1943), RI–59–60; Am. Inst. of Consulting Engineers, *Proc.*, Jan. 1944; *Nat. Cyc. Am. Biog.*, XXXIII, 190–91; *Winchester* (Mass.) *Star*, Mar. 12, 1943; birth and marriage records from Mass. Registrar of Vital Statistics.]
CLARENCE E. DAVIES]

MALLORY, CLIFFORD DAY (May 26, 1881–Apr. 7, 1941), shipping executive, was born in Brooklyn, N. Y., the second son and third of four children of Henry Rogers Mallory and Cora Nellie (Pynchon) Mallory. His father was descended from Peter Malary, who came to Boston in 1637; his mother, from William Pynchon [q.v.], the founder of Springfield, Mass. In politics, the Mallorys had been successively Federalist, Whig, and Republican; in religion Baptist, Congregationalist, and Episcopalian. The three generations that preceded Clifford had earned economic security and social position as industrious maritime entrepreneurs. Charles (1796–1882), who settled in Mystic, Conn., in 1816, rose from a penniless apprentice sailmaker to a millionaire builder, owner, and operator of whalers, coasting sail and steam vessels, and transoceanic clippers. Charles Henry Mallory (1818–1890), who moved to Brooklyn in 1865, expanded his father's business through two closely held family firms: C. H. Mallory & Company (1866–1906), a ship-managing partnership, and the New York & Texas Steamship Company (1886–1906), a shipowning corporation. Henry Rogers Mallory (1848–1919) succeeded in turn to leadership in family and firms and made the "Mallory Line"

one of the most popular and profitable steamship lines in the American merchant marine.

This intense family tradition of maritime enterprise became the guiding force of Clifford Mallory's life. Since his older brother died in infancy, he grew up as the eldest son of his generation and as such expected to succeed his father as chief executive of the Mallory Line and to prepare his own son in turn to succeed him. He attended Brooklyn Latin and Lawrenceville schools and entered C. H. Mallory & Company as a clerk in 1900. By 1904 he was a junior partner and assistant to the superintendent of the New York & Texas Steamship Company.

In 1906, however, Henry Rogers Mallory sold the family's firms to the Consolidated Steamship Lines of Charles W. Morse [q.v.], and Clifford became the salaried secretary and assistant general manager of a Consolidated subsidiary named the Mallory Steamship Company. When Morse's businesses failed in 1907, Henry Mallory came out of retirement, reorganized Consolidated as the Atlantic, Gulf & West Indies Steamship Lines, and served as its chairman until 1915. When he retired, "A.G.W.I." had assets of $47,000,000 and was owner-operator of seventy American-flag steamships—the second largest shipping company and fifty-ninth largest corporation in the United States. At his father's request, Clifford Mallory remained an officer of A.G.W.I. and in 1915 became vice-president and director of its two largest subsidiaries, the Clyde Steamship Company and the Mallory Steamship Company. He married Rebecca Sealy, the daughter of Texas's richest banker, on Jan. 3, 1911, and continued to move in the highest social and business circles. He was a competent and respected shipping executive, but was increasingly dissatisfied with working on salary within a large corporation in whose profits he did not share. World War I gave him his chance to break free.

Upon America's entrance into the war, Mallory served on a three-man committee of shipping executives responsible for organizing and dispatching the first American troop convoy to Europe. His outstanding performance brought him the position of assistant to the director of operations of the United States Shipping Board. During 1917–19 Mallory became the government's prime specialist in the acquisition of merchant vessels, their assignment to operators, and the allocation of vessels to cargoes. He and his superior came to control 2,614 vessels deployed on government business around the world. At the close of his government service in 1919, he declined to return to A.G.W.I. and instead founded his own firm in partnership with another ex-Shipping Board official, William S. Houston. Over the next twenty-two years, C. D. Mallory & Company, in its own name and through a dozen subsidiaries, became the largest and most successful independent shipping house under the American flag.

From 1919 to 1925 Mallory specialized in the operation of government-owned tonnage on commission for the United States Shipping Board, running one line from American ports in the North Atlantic to the Mediterranean, and another to points in South Africa. In addition, he operated a number of Shipping Board vessels in various tramp (unscheduled) trades. After 1925, having lost his government contracts because of political changes, he completed a shift of emphasis he had already begun and made C. D. Mallory & Company best known thereafter as owner-operator of tankers and dry-cargo tramps and as the savior of numerous "distress companies" brought to it by creditors. From 1924 to 1941 Mallory controlled 5 percent of all American-flag tankers and dominated the independent tanker pool through his "Swiftsure," "Malston," and "Seminole" fleets. His prime customers were the large integrated oil companies, who used his vessels to supplement their own fleets. His small fleet of dry-cargo tramps specialized in contract and industrial carriage along the Atlantic and Gulf coasts. Always interested in improving marine technology, Mallory was a leading proponent of all-welded ships and diesel-electric drive and was one of the founders of Seatrain Lines, Inc., the pioneer American container-ship fleet. His ability to tailor vessel ownership or operating solutions to a wide variety of maritime problems and his expertise in all aspects of shipping were his prime business assets. His name and reputation for efficient and honest operation also frequently gave him a competitive edge. He epitomized what could be accomplished within the nonsubsidized segment of the American merchant marine.

In person, Mallory was a slender, muscular man whose moustache, rimless glasses, and impeccable clothing and manners gave him an aristocratic look. He was an avid sportsman and a premier yachtsman who began sailing competitively in 1893. He captained the American 6-meter racing team in 1923; founded and served as first president (1925–35) of the North American Yacht Racing Union; was founder and champion of the American 10-meter class (1927) and of the American 12-meter class (1928), and served as chairman for yachting of the Olympic Games in 1932.

Mallory died of a heart attack at the age of fifty-nine at Miami Beach, Fla. He was survived by his wife and their three children: Margaret Pynchon, Clifford Day, and Barbara Sealy. C. D. Mallory & Company was liquidated by its junior (and non-Mallory) partners and merged into the new and successful firm of Marine Transport Lines, Inc. Not until the 1950's was Clifford D. Mallory, Jr., able to reestablish his father's firm under its own name and to fulfill his father's wish by becoming its president.

[Mallory Family Papers, Marine Hist. Assoc., Mystic, Conn.; James P. Baughman, *The Mallorys of Mystic: Six Generations in Am. Maritime Enterprise* (1972); Carl C. Cutler in *Am. Neptune,* July 1941; obituaries in *N. Y. Herald Tribune* and *N. Y. Times,* Apr. 8, 1941, and *Greenwich* (Conn.) *Press,* Apr. 10, 1941.]

JAMES P. BAUGHMAN

MALLORY, FRANK BURR (Nov. 12, 1862–Sept. 27, 1941), pathologist, was born in Cleveland, Ohio, the older of two children and only son of George Burr Mallory and Anna (Faragher) Mallory. His father, a native of Michigan, was a sailor and later ship captain on the Great Lakes; his mother was born on the British Isle of Man. Mallory attended Cleveland public schools and then entered Harvard, where he earned his way by waiting on table in the dining room and graduated, A.B., in 1886. He received his M.D. four years later from the Hárvard Medical School.

To help support himself in medical school, Mallory worked as a technician in the histology laboratory and thereby developed a strong interest in pathology. After graduating, he spent a brief internship at the McLean Hospital, Waverley, Mass., and a few months in private practice and then, in 1891, became an assistant in the department of pathology at the Harvard Medical School and in the pathology department of the Boston City Hospital. He remained at both institutions until his retirement in 1932. In 1894, after a year of study in Prague and Freiburg, he was appointed instructor at the medical school. He subsequently advanced to assistant professor (1896), associate professor (1901), and professor of pathology (1928).

Mallory was the leader of histologic pathology and pathologic techniques in this country during the first third of the twentieth century. A superb technician, he developed, often painstakingly, many of the differential tissue stains that have become widely used, and laid the foundations for the development of histochemistry as related to pathologic states. He was a devoted photomicrographer and spent many hours in obtaining illustrations that demonstrated the lesion or cell in perfect form; a number of these photographs were used in his textbook and in his scientific articles, many more in his lectures. His two books, *Pathological Technique* (1897), which he wrote with J. Homer Wright, and *The Principles of Pathologic Histology* (1914), became the standards of excellence in their fields in America and were influential abroad.

Mallory's chief impact came through the pathologists who were trained in the Sears Laboratory at the Boston City Hospital, many of whom became professors of pathology in the decades from the 1920's through the 1940's. In contrast with the German influence in pathology, which tended toward experimentation and theoretical research, Mallory emphasized direct service to individual patients and physicians. He imbued in his house officers the ideal of prompt and effective laboratory diagnosis for the patient, rather than the time-consuming and more academic approaches then followed by many. As one effect of this precept, Mallory brought to a high state of accuracy the use of frozen tissue sections during surgery—a procedure originated by Louis B. Wilson [Supp. 3]—so that in a case of suspected cancer, for example, a surgeon could obtain an immediate diagnosis during the course of an operation.

Mallory stressed the value of detailed microscopic study of the nature of disease processes, at a time when many pathologists were content with diagnostic interpretations based on merely a gross examination that was necessarily replete with errors. His work in the classification of human cancers did much to clarify our understanding of the pathology of that disease. He felt that the best experiments were those performed by nature on man and hence had little interest in the use of experimental animals, although he did employ them in his long attempt to find the cause of alcoholic cirrhosis of the liver. He had a special interest in liver disease, in which he was for many years recognized as the outstanding authority. Because a general medical interest in tropical diseases then existed in Boston, Mallory also acquired expert knowledge in that field.

Mallory was one of the founders (1907) of the American Association for Cancer Research and of the American Association of Pathologists and Bacteriologists (president, 1910), which in 1935 awarded him the Harold C. Ernst gold-headed cane for special merit. He succeeded Ernst [q.v.] as editor of the *Journal of Medical Research*, 1923–25, and, when that became the *American Journal of Pathology*, continued as editor, 1925–40. He was awarded the George M. Kober Medal (1935) for outstanding service

in pathology. In 1933 the Boston City Hospital honored him by constructing a modern pathology laboratory and naming it the Mallory Institute of Pathology.

Mallory was impatient with theory and apt to be skeptical of the interpretations of others. His *Principles of Pathologic Histology* is one of the few textbooks based entirely on personal experience and not weighted down by references to others' work. He did not hesitate to disagree sharply with the interpretation of lesions given by other well-known pathologists, and often enlivened scientific meetings by brisk discussions of differences with such figures as William G. MacCallum [Supp. 3], James Ewing [Supp. 3], and William T. Councilman [Supp. 1].

On Aug. 31, 1893, Mallory married Persis McClain Tracy of Chautauqua, N. Y. Their two sons, Tracy Burr and George Kenneth, both became pathologists. A tall, spare man, Mallory lived a generally ascetic life. Perhaps because of poor vision in one eye, he did not enjoy most sports, but he was an ardent tennis fan and during important games, such as the Davis Cup match at the Longwood Cricket Club, the laboratory was largely deserted. He also enjoyed canoeing and was an accomplished pianist. He died at his home in Brookline, Mass., in his seventy-ninth year of bronchial pneumonia, a few days after a fall downstairs; his ashes were placed in the columbarium at Mount Auburn Cemetery, Cambridge, Mass. As a friend and admirer of many of the pioneer European pathologists and bacteriologists such as Max Askanazy, Hanns Chiari, Anton Ghon, and Louis Pasteur, Mallory served as a link between the classical pathology of Europe and the then newly developing schools of Baltimore, Boston, Chicago, Cleveland, Philadelphia, and New York.

[Memorial articles in: *New England Jour. of Medicine*, Feb. 12, 1942 (by Timothy Leary), and Dec. 21, 1944 (by William Freeman); *Jour. of Pathology and Bacteriology*, Apr. 1942 (by Samuel R. Haythorn); *Archives of Pathology*, Jan. 1942 (by Frederic Parker, Jr.); Assoc. of Am. Physicians, *Transactions*, LVII (1942), 29–31 (by S. B. Wolbach); and *Science*, Nov. 7, 1941. See also Harvard College Class of 1886, *50th Anniversary Report* (1936). Family data from census of 1870 (courtesy of Western Reserve Hist. Soc., Cleveland).]

SHIELDS WARREN

MANNING, MARIE (Jan. 22, 1873?–Nov. 28, 1945), newspaperwoman, was born in Washington, D. C., the only daughter and younger of two children of Michael Charles and Elizabeth (Barrett) Manning, both of English birth. Her mother died during Marie's early childhood, and the girl was sent to private schools in Washington, New York, and London. Her father, a War

Department employee, died when she was in her teens, after which she was reared by a guardian, Judge Martin F. Morris of Washington. Almost six feet tall, plain in appearance, indifferent to dress and formal social life, she longed to become a newspaperwoman. According to her autobiography, she found a way to realize her dream when she met Arthur Brisbane [Supp. 2], then an editor on the New York *World*, at a dinner party. Going to New York a few days later, she called on him and was given a job on the *World*, at space rates. After obtaining an interview with former President Grover Cleveland when experienced reporters had failed, she was added to the regular staff to report "the woman's angle" on news events. In 1898 she left the *World* and followed Brisbane to the *New York Journal* of William Randolph Hearst.

Miss Manning's career as a columnist began when Brisbane, then managing editor of the *Journal*, showed her three letters the paper had received from troubled women: one whose husband was a philanderer, another who had been deserted by her lover, and a third who was being bilked by a brutal son-in-law. Miss Manning suggested that the letters might form the basis for a new department, a column of advice to the lovelorn. The first column appeared July 20, 1898, under the signature "Beatrice Fairfax," a pseudonym she derived from Dante's Beata Beatrix and Fairfax County, Va., where the Manning family owned property.

The column became an almost immediate success. It was soon syndicated to 200 papers and was attracting as many as 1,400 letters a day from correspondents who wanted to discuss their perplexities and to get advice from an impartial source. Typical questions posed to Beatrice Fairfax at the turn of the century were: Should a young man go down on his knees while proposing? Should he get the consent of the girl's parents first? What should a young couple do about a chaperone when they went out on a bicycle built for two? What should a jilted girl do, especially if she were pregnant? How could a wife hold an errant husband? Miss Manning's advice was invariably commonsensical: "Dry your eyes, roll up your sleeves, and dig for a practical solution." As a national oracle on problems of love, "Beatrice Fairfax" became a byword; she was quoted in vaudeville skits and became the subject of a popular song ("Just write to Beatrice Fairfax / Whenever you are in doubt . . ."). While carrying on her column, Miss Manning, under her true name, continued to work as a journeyman reporter for the *Journal* and to write short stories, mainly for *Harper's Magazine*, as well as roman-

tic novels: *Lord Allingham, Bankrupt* (1902) and *Judith of the Plains* (1903).

On June 12, 1905, Miss Manning retired from newspaper work to marry Herman Eduard Gasch, a Washington real estate dealer. During the next twenty-five years the Beatrice Fairfax answers were composed chiefly by a series of other writers, although during World War I Mrs. Gasch interrupted the rearing of her two sons, Oliver H. and Manning, to resume the column for a short time. Severe losses in the stock market crash of 1929 obliged her again to become Beatrice Fairfax on a full-time basis. The column was still popular, being syndicated and sold to some 200 newspapers, but the problems of the lovelorn had changed. There were now more letters from men and from mature people than from the young, and a large number concerned broken homes, "the forays of the love pirate, the ennui of the restless wife and the problem of children of divorced parents." The mother confessor to Hearst readers wrote her column (which was syndicated by King Features) from Washington, where she also covered women's news for the International News Service. She died at her home in Washington of a coronary thrombosis in 1945. Although she had earlier listed herself as a Catholic, her remains were cremated and the ashes scattered on the Manning farm in Fairfax County, Va.

[Marie Manning's autobiography, *Ladies Now and Then* (1944), is the principal source. Its version of her early newspaper career is followed here, although in *Who's Who in America*, 1916–17 and later issues, she stated that she began newspaper work in London in 1897 as a special writer for the *N. Y. Herald*, joined the *Herald*'s regular staff the next year, and moved to the *Journal* in 1899. See also: Ishbel Ross, *Ladies of the Press* (1936); *Current Biog.*, 1944; *N. Y. Times* obituary, Nov. 30, 1945; *Notable Am. Women*, II, 491–92. Death record from D. C. Dept. of Public Health.]

ALDEN WHITMAN

MARLAND, ERNEST WHITWORTH (May 8, 1874–Oct. 3, 1941), oil operator, Congressman, and governor of Oklahoma, was born in Pittsburgh, Pa., the youngest of three children and only son of Alfred and Sarah (MacLeod) Marland. His mother, who also had five daughters by an earlier marriage, was a native of the Isle of Skye. His father, a grandson of Ernest Whitworth, a noted mathematician and head of Whitworth School for Boys in Manchester, was of English birth. Coming to the United States in 1862, Alfred Marland served briefly in the Confederate Army and then, after inventing an iron band for baling cotton, moved in 1864 to Pittsburgh, where he became a wealthy iron manufacturer. Known as an enlightened employer, he served in the state legislature and as a member of the Pittsburgh Select Council for twenty years. Ernest, an unathletic and pampered child, was groomed to be a "gentleman" and a future military leader or chief justice. He attended Thomas Hughes's Arnold School in Rugby, Tenn., heralded as a bit of transplanted England, and Park Institute in Pittsburgh, graduating in 1891. After failing the physical examination for West Point, he entered law school at the University of Michigan. An indifferent student, known chiefly for his poker playing, he received the LL.B. degree in 1893.

Upon his return home, finding that his father's business had failed in the depression, Marland worked in a law office, though he was still too young for admission to the bar. At twenty-one he opened his own firm and discovered the thrill and profit of land speculation as an appraiser of coal lands for the promoters James M. Guffey [q.v.] and John H. Galey. About 1900 he became general counsel for the Pittsburgh Securities and Guaranty Company, advancing to its presidency in 1903 and serving until its disintegration the following year. He married Mary Virginia Collins of Philadelphia on Nov. 5, 1903. They had no children but later adopted his wife's niece and nephew, Lydie Miller Roberts and George Roberts.

Marland's interest in coal broadened to include oil after he heard of the spectacular strike at Spindletop, Texas, in 1901. He promptly began an intensive program of self-education in geology. He was later to attribute his success to the application of science and new technologies; a contemporary based it upon a "nose for oil and the luck of the devil." Probably his greatest asset was complete self-assurance and a personality that inspired confidence. Concluding that there was coal in the panhandle of West Virginia, Marland organized, with himself as president, the Pittsburgh and West Virginia Coal Company. In 1906, while coring for coal, he struck oil, opening the Congo field. Additional wells of oil and gas quickly brought him a fortune estimated at $1,000,000, which he promptly lost in the panic of 1907. While living on borrowed money he dreamed of a new bonanza.

Hearing about the new oil fields in Oklahoma, he set out in December 1908, armed with a letter of credit for a complete drilling outfit but with only enough cash for train fare and a month's board. Shortly afterward he and George L. Miller formed the 101 Ranch Oil Company to exploit a "perfect geological dome" Marland had discovered on Miller's property near Ponca City. The first well was dry; the next seven struck

gas, for which there was little market. In 1910 Marland raised capital for another try from W. H. McFadden, a retired Carnegie Steel executive, and brought in a gusher in May 1911. The next year he opened the Blackwell field, and in subsequent years the Newkirk (1916), Petit (1919), and Burbank fields (1920); he was finally credited with the discovery of some eight fields in Oklahoma alone. By 1920 his interests extended to production in other states, and he had leases in Central America as well. He joined with Royal Dutch Shell in 1921 to create the highly successful Comar Oil Company to seek overseas production.

In 1920 his various properties were combined and incorporated in Delaware as the Marland Oil Company, with headquarters in Ponca City, Okla. At the height of its prosperity this was the largest independent oil company, controlling one-tenth of the world's supply and worth between eighty-five and one hundred million dollars. Marland made little distinction between private and corporate wealth, and his style of living attracted international attention. This short, plump, but handsome man "spent money like water." For his town he endowed schools, hospitals, churches, and playgrounds, and he gave his employees excellent salaries, insurance policies, and stock bonuses. To the State of Oklahoma he gave Bryant Baker's famous statue "The Pioneer Woman." For his family there was a sumptuously furnished mansion modeled after an English manor, a private railroad car, a luxurious yacht, a plantation in Mississippi, and two polo teams.

The expansion of his business, including a venture in manufacturing dirigibles, and his lavish mode of living strained his financial resources. In 1923 he gave stock to J. P. Morgan & Company of New York in return for a large loan. After placing Morgan men upon his board of directors, he agreed that management of the company would be vested in an executive committee, where the banking firm was also represented. This made possible continued growth, but at an unanticipated cost. As oil prices dropped in 1927 and 1928, Marland was unwilling to economize or retrench. The Morgans then took over operation of the company, making Marland virtually a pensioner as chairman of the board. He resigned in 1928, and Marland Oil, with retail sales outlets in every state and seventeen foreign countries in addition to its productive capacity, was merged with the Morgan-controlled Continental Oil Company.

In 1926—his last good year financially—Marland's wife died. Early in 1928 he had the adoption of his daughter Lydie annulled and on July

14 he married her. With the last of his fortune draining away, he attempted unsuccessfully in 1929 to organize another oil company. As an admirer of Franklin D. Roosevelt, he then turned to politics. In 1932, running as a Democrat, he was elected Congressman from the normally Republican 8th Oklahoma District in a campaign in which he successfully identified his enemies, "the wolves of Wall Street," with those of the people. In Washington he helped draft the stock exchange and securities law. In debates over the National Recovery Act he expressed his fear of corporate domination and sponsored bills to control the pipelines and "hot oil" and to assist the states in oil conservation programs. At the end of his term he announced for the governorship "because the financial and economic situation of my state is so grave and requires business leadership."

Marland promised if elected to bring the "New Deal" to Oklahoma, and using his pamphlet *My Experience with the Money Trust* as a campaign document, he won easily. Soon after his inaugural he proposed the formation of citizens' committees to study education, financial administration, public welfare, revenue and taxation, highways, natural resources, conservation, and law enforcement. He revealed that he had contracted with the Brookings Institution in Washington to furnish technical advice. He also proposed a sales tax to care for those dropped by federal relief agencies and a crude-oil tax to support a series of new boards for planning, flood control, housing, new industries, and highways. He promised to establish civil service, take the schools out of politics, give pensions to teachers, and retire the state debt.

From the Oklahoma legislature Marland secured old-age pensions, exemption of homesteads from taxation, unemployment insurance, laws regulating industrial wages and hours, an increase in the gross production tax, a highway patrol, a state planning board, and state aid for weak schools, but not the governmental reorganization he desired. He launched the Grand River hydroelectric and flood control project, and was a prime mover in creation of the Interstate Oil Compact. Approved by six states and Congress in 1935, the Compact opened its headquarters in Oklahoma City with Marland as the first chairman. But his program made enemies. His legislature was called the "spending sixteenth," and it was necessary to call out the state militia to enforce his decision to drill for oil on the capitol grounds. Despite increased taxation, the state debt mounted. By the end of his second year, eager to escape, Marland ran for the United States Senate, but he

failed to get the anticipated support from Roosevelt and lost the runoff primary to Josh Lee. In 1938 he tried again, but this time the President stumped the state for Elmer Thomas.

Marland left the governorship in January 1939 in dire personal straits. Once again he was unsuccessful in raising money for a new oil company. In 1940 he announced for Congress as a "constitutional Democrat," but illness and financial pressure prevented his campaigning and he lost the nomination. Early in 1941 he was forced to sell his mansion and move to a small house on his former estate. He died of a heart ailment that fall at his home in Ponca City, Okla., and was buried there in the Odd Fellows Cemetery.

[There is no collection of Marland papers. John J. Mathews, *Life and Death of an Oilman: The Career of E. W. Marland* (1951), is the only full-length biography. Short biographical sketches are in *Who's Who in Commerce and Industry*, 1940–41; *Nat. Cyc. Am. Biog.*, XXXIV, 115; *Who's Who in America*, various issues, 1928–42; Joseph B. Thoburn and Muriel H. Wright, *Oklahoma: A Hist. of the State and Its People* (1929), IV, 759–60 (with portrait); Rex F. Harlow, *Okla. Leaders* (1928). Useful information is found in Charles B. Glasscock, *Then Came Oil* (1938); *A Summary of the Background, Organization, Purpose, and Function of the Interstate Compact to Conserve Oil and Gas* (1947); and Burton Rascoe, "The Breeze Blew through His Whiskers," *Newsweek*, Aug. 1, 1938. A critical review of Marland as governor is found in Jerome Mason, "Oklahoma's Fuller Life Salesman," *Am. Mercury*, Jan. 1938. Obituaries are found in *Oil and Gas Jour.*, Oct. 9, 1941; *Tulsa* (Okla.) *Daily World*, Oct. 4, 1941; *Ponca City News*, Oct. 3, 1941; *N. Y. Times*, Oct. 4, 1941; Okla. City *Daily Oklahoman*, Oct. 4, 1941; and *Oil Weekly*, Oct. 6, 1941.]

JOHN S. EZELL

MARLATT, ABBY LILLIAN (Mar. 7, 1869–June 23, 1943), home economist, was born in Manhattan, Kans., the second daughter and youngest of five children of Washington and Julia Ann (Bailey) Marlatt. Her father, whose French Huguenot ancestor had come to Staten Island in 1662, was a native of Indiana; after graduating from Asbury College (later DePauw University), he had entered the Methodist ministry and settled in Manhattan, where he helped found and headed a short-lived school, Bluemont Central College. His wife, who had been his assistant at Bluemont, was of old Connecticut stock and had attended Greenwich Academy. Besides riding circuit as a minister, Marlatt prospered at farming. One of Abby's brothers, Charles Lester Marlatt, became a leading agricultural entomologist.

Abby attended the district school and at the age of fourteen entered Kansas State Agricultural College in Manhattan, receiving a B.S. degree in 1888. She stayed on to take a master's degree in chemistry (1890), and during this period worked in the kitchen laboratory of the home economics department, then headed by Mrs. Nellie (Sawyer) Kedzie (later Jones). In 1890 she was called to Logan, Utah, to establish a domestic science department at the newly founded Utah Agricultural College—one of a number of young women sent out from Kansas to organize such departments in other land-grant colleges. In 1894 she went to Providence, R. I., to start a home economics department in the Manual Training (later Technical) High School. She was a leader in the Lake Placid Conferences on Home Economics, held annually between 1899 and 1908 to explore the future of this field of study, and in connection with these conferences helped organize several joint sessions at meetings of the National Education Association to discuss the teaching of home economics. She was a charter member of the American Home Economics Association, founded in 1908 as an outgrowth of the Lake Placid Conferences, and served as its vice-president, 1912–18.

In 1909 Miss Marlatt was called to the University of Wisconsin as head of the department of home economics in the agricultural college; she remained at the university until her retirement thirty years later. When she arrived, the department had only one instructor and an assistant, forty-seven students, and twelve course offerings. Its facilities comprised a single classroom in the basement of Agricultural Hall; at the end of the first year there was one graduate. Under Miss Marlatt's leadership both the scope of the training and the size of the enrollment expanded rapidly and the shortage of space became acute. With the help of the state's women's clubs, she and her students secured an appropriation from the state legislature for a new building; they are said to have won their appeal by serving pancakes with maple syrup to the members of the finance committee.

The new home economics building opened in 1914, and in the years that followed Miss Marlatt transformed the department into one of the largest, strongest, and best known in the country. She insisted on a curriculum that was not limited to the domestic arts but also included courses in physiology and hygiene, bacteriology, English, and a foreign language. She also promoted research in problems of nutrition, the preservation of vitamins in prepared foods, and the metabolism of vitamins and proteins. By the time of her retirement the staff had grown to twenty-five, including one research assistant, and the 488 undergraduate and twenty-four graduate students could choose among eight majors and sixty-seven courses. At the June 1939 commencement, 108 B.S. and 14

M.S. degrees were granted in home economics. The first Ph.D. was awarded in 1932.

During World War I, at the request of Herbert Hoover, Miss Marlatt assisted in planning for the cooperation of the states in the food conservation program under the United States Food Administration. After spending some months in Washington on this project, she returned to Wisconsin to be secretary of the Women's Division of the Wisconsin Council of National Defense. In the influenza epidemic of 1918, she and her senior students supervised the diet of the female students among the patients. Though many male victims died, all the women recovered, and Miss Marlatt and her students received a regents' commendation.

A very large woman with a deep voice, Miss Marlatt carried a heavy walking stick, and was a dominant though warm personality. The story was often told that on an occasion when she missed a train that was to take her to a nearby town for a speaking engagement, she chartered a special train, even though the expense prevented her having a new dress that winter. She was a strong feminist, and urged the appointment of more women to faculty committees. She received honorary doctorates from her alma mater (1925) and Utah State University (1938). Miss Marlatt loved to travel and during her vacations often visited Indian villages in the Southwest or journeyed through Europe, where she studied housing conditions and pursued her two chief hobbies— watercolor painting and collecting old cookbooks. After retirement in 1939 she remained in Madison, where she died of cancer at the age of seventy-four. She was buried in Sunset Cemetery, Manhattan, Kans.

[Nellie Kedzie Jones in *Jour. of Home Economics,* Oct. 1943; W. H. Glover, *Farm and College: The College of Agriculture of the Univ. of Wis., A Hist.* (1952); "Growth and Development of Home Economics at the Univ. of Wis." (MS. in Archives of College of Agriculture); memorial resolution in Univ. of Wis. Faculty Minutes, Oct. 4, 1943; Alice Bilstein in *Wis. Country Mag.,* May 1938; *Who's Who in America, 1922–23* to *1930–31*; obituary in *Wis. State Jour.* (Madison), June 24, 1943; Julius T. Willard, *Hist. of the Kans. State College of Agriculture and Applied Science* (1940), pp. 11–15 (on her father); Lake Placid Conference, *Proc.,* 1900–08; death certificate, Wis. State Board of Health; information from Kans. State and Utah State universities and Univ. of Wis.; genealogical information from Mrs. Charles Lester Marlatt. See also Mary Tolford Wilson in *Notable Am. Women,* II, 495–97. A portrait of Abby Marlatt by Carl W. Rawson is in the Home Economics Building at the Univ. of Wis.]

EMMA SEIFRIT WEIGLEY

MARQUIS, ALBERT NELSON (Jan. 10, 1855–Dec. 21, 1943), founder and publisher of *Who's Who in America,* was born in Brown County, Ohio, the sixth of seven children and elder of two sons of Elizabeth (Redmon) Marquis, of Pennsylvania Dutch descent, and Cyrenus G. Marquis, a native of Ohio. His mother died when Albert was six and his father five years later. The boy then went to live with his maternal grandparents in nearby Hamersville, Ohio, where he attended the local schools and helped tend his grandfather's general store.

At twenty-one he left for Cincinnati, where he worked as a bookseller for a publishing house and a few years later founded his own advertising and publishing company. In 1884, believing that the rapidly expanding metropolis of Chicago offered better prospects, he moved there and established a new publishing business. His first offering, *Marquis' Hand-Book of Chicago: A Complete History, Reference Book and Guide to the City* (1885), sold well, and during the next fifteen years his firm issued a number of books, including an edition of Alfred E. Brehm's *The Animals of the World* (1895), a well-illustrated natural history translated from the German; and an "art portfolio" of contemporary stage celebrities, with biographical sketches. Most of these volumes were edited by John William Leonard, an English journalist who had emigrated to the United States in 1868 and who remained with Marquis for about two decades.

Marquis's specialty, however, was business and city directories, not only for Chicago but for other principal cities. He also prepared special editions of various newspapers which included sketches of the careers of civic leaders, and around 1894 he conceived the idea of collecting and publishing such material on a broader scale. Stimulated by the example of the British *Who's Who,* which in 1897, for the first time, presented some biographical material along with its lists of important persons, Marquis determined to issue a new type of reference book, a compilation of concise, accurate biographies of notable living Americans, who would themselves supply the facts by filling out detailed questionnaires.

Volume I of *Who's Who in America* appeared in 1899. It was so successful that new editions followed regularly at two-year intervals (save for a three-year gap between volumes III and IV). For the first four volumes John W. Leonard was listed as editor; thereafter, Marquis himself. From the beginning it was he who decided upon the persons to be listed, although he asked advice from leaders in many spheres of American life. Inclusion depended on outstanding achievement in fields such as the sciences, the arts, religion, the military, education, and government. Physical superiority alone, he believed, did not merit a listing; thus figures in the sports world were ruled out. Likewise, the emphasis upon "reputable" achievement tended to exclude important men and women of suspect political affiliations. A biographical notice in *Who's Who* was thought to confer such prestige that many persons proposed their own names as entries and some even offered bribes, but neither money nor ancestry, without accomplishment, could procure a place. Before methods of selection were standardized in the late 1930's, Marquis's own canons of morality exerted a strong influence: a divorce was a major bar to a place in *Who's Who,* and a subject convicted of a crime was automatically dropped.

Although seemingly a confirmed bachelor, Marquis on June 11, 1910, married Harriette Rosanna (Gettemy) Morgan of Monmouth, Ill., a widow. They had no children. In 1926, when he had reached the age of seventy-two, he sold control of his business, though he retained a 20 percent interest and continued as editor-in-chief until 1940. Marquis was fond of social life and enjoyed music and the opera. He was a conservative Republican in politics and a member of the Congregational Church. He strongly opposed the use of tobacco and alcohol and took an active role in the Central Howard Association, which helped find work for released prisoners. Marquis died of pneumonia at his home in Evanston, Ill., shortly before his eighty-ninth birthday and was buried at Rosehill Cemetery, Chicago.

Although of limited educational background, Marquis was a man of vision and enterprise, as well as a practical businessman. He was passionately devoted to his work. In *Who's Who in America* he created a reliable biographical dictionary of eminent Americans, chosen according to the high and impartial standards he had set.

[Marquis was reticent about his own biography; not until 1912 did he list himself in *Who's Who in America.* The fullest published account of his life and work appears in Cedric A. Larson, *Who: Sixty Years of Am. Eminence—The Story of "Who's Who in America"* (1958), which includes a bibliography. The following articles on *Who's Who* mention Marquis briefly: J. Bryan III in *Saturday Rev. of Literature,* Feb. 7, 1942; H. L. Mencken, *ibid.,* Oct. 24, 1936; Cedric Larson, *ibid.,* Aug. 18, 1956; and Henry F. Pringle in *Saturday Evening Post,* Apr. 6, 1946. See also *N. Y. Times* obituary, Dec. 22, 1943.]
                                    CEDRIC A. LARSON

MARSHALL, FRANK JAMES (Aug. 10, 1877–Nov. 9, 1944), chess player, was born in New York City, the second of seven sons of Alfred George and Sarah Ann (Graham) Marshall. His father, a flour mill salesman, was a native of London, England; his mother was of Scotch-Irish descent. When Frank was eight his family moved from New York to Montreal, where he attended public schools through high school.

At the age of ten Marshall had begun to learn chess from his father, a competent amateur, and within a year he was able to give his father a Rook and still win. He began competing at the Hope Coffee House and then joined the Montreal Chess Club. Preoccupied with chess, he studied and replayed the games of the great master Paul Charles Morphy [q.v.]. At the age of sixteen he became champion of the Montreal club and, at a simultaneous blindfold exhibition held there, won a game from Harry N. Pillsbury [q.v.], then the American champion.

In 1896 the family returned to New York, where Marshall soon established himself as a top player in the metropolitan area. In 1899, after he had captured the championship of the famous Brooklyn Chess Club, the Brooklyn and Manhattan chess clubs raised funds to send him to the London International Tournament. Much to his disappointment, he found that he was not considered eminent enough to play in the masters' division, but in a lesser group that included two well-known players Marshall won, 8½–2½. In the international tournament in Paris the following year he tied for third place, but in individual games defeated both Pillsbury and Emanuel Lasker, the world's champion. In 1904 at the international tournament held in Cambridge Springs, Pa., which was attended by the leading American and European players, he achieved perhaps his greatest triumph by finishing in first place, having won eleven games and drawn four.

Like most chess masters, Marshall supported himself by teaching, exhibitions, and prize money. During his later career he won firsts in tournaments at Monte Carlo (1904), St. Louis (1904), Scheveningen (1905), Barmen (1905), Nuremberg (1906), Düsseldorf (1908), New York (1911), Budapest (1912), Havana (1913), Lake Hopatcong (1924), and Chicago (1926). He placed second, third, or fourth at many other tournaments, and also played a large number of individual matches, although in general he performed more brilliantly when stimulated by the presence of an audience. After Pillsbury's death in 1906, Marshall was regarded as the United States champion, although he did not accept the title until 1909, when he won a match against Pillsbury's predecessor, Jackson W. Showalter. He held the championship until his retirement in 1936.

Marshall's playing style made him popular with spectators. It was attacking, combinative, open, of the Romantic school. He achieved many successes with it, but too often discovered it did not

work against positional masters. Eventually he modified it and adopted a balanced approach, although he always enjoyed taking the offensive. His most famous game, featuring a magnificent Queen sacrifice, was that against S. Lewitsky, at Breslau in 1912. His main contributions to chess theory were in the Max Lange opening, the Marshall Gambit in the Semi-Slav Defense, and the Marshall Counter Attack in the Ruy Lopez opening.

In 1915 Marshall established a Chess Divan in New York, initially at Keene's Chop House, as a meeting place for lovers of the game. This was succeeded in 1922 by the Marshall Chess Club, located eventually on West 10th Street in quarters purchased for him by admirers in 1931. Here he also made his home. *Life* magazine described Marshall in his last years as a "preoccupied old gentleman who looks like a Shakespearean actor." Well dressed, he usually wore a lavaliere tie and gray spats. A charming host, modest and kindly, he encouraged a generation of visiting players, both tyros and masters, at his various clubs. He believed that anybody could learn to play chess and that "its delights and rewards are endless," and he devoted a lifetime to the game.

On Jan. 6, 1905, Marshall married Caroline D. Kraus of Brooklyn, N. Y., who served as his business manager and as secretary of the Marshall Chess Club. Their only child was Frank J. Marshall, Jr. Marshall died of a heart attack in 1944 while visiting in Jersey City, N. J. After Presbyterian services, his ashes were buried in Cedar Grove Cemetery, Flushing, N. Y.

[Frank J. Marshall, *Chess Step by Step* (1924), *Comparative Chess* (1932), *Chess in an Hour* (1937), and *My Fifty Years of Chess* (1942); Richard Reti, *Masters of the Chessboard* (1932); Reuben Fine, *The World's Great Chess Games* (1951); P. Feenstra Kuiper, *Hundert Jahre Schach-Turniere 1851–1950* (1964); *Chess Rev.,* Dec. 1944, an issue dedicated to Marshall; *N. Y. Times,* Nov. 10, 11, 1944; information from I. A. Horowitz, Louis J. Wolff, and Harry Marshall (a brother), and from personal acquaintance. Good likenesses of Marshall are in his *My Fifty Years of Chess,* and a bust stands in the Marshall Chess Club.]

JOHN W. COLLINS

MARTEL, CHARLES (Mar. 5, 1860–May 15, 1945), librarian, was born in Zurich, Switzerland; originally named Karl David Hanke, he was the son of Franz Hanke, an antiquarian bookseller, and Maria Gertrud (Strässle) Hanke. His father, a native of Gröbnig, Silesia (now Grobniki, Poland), had settled in Zurich about 1840; his mother was from the Swiss canton of St. Gall. Karl studied at the local Gymnasium, 1872–76, spending spare hours immersed in his father's bookstore, more extensive than most libraries. With his older brother Franz Heinrich

Hanke he visited the United States in 1876 and attended the Centennial Exposition at Philadelphia.

Little is known of the next decade of his life. About March 1879, after his father's death, he left Zurich, apparently because of family financial difficulties, and came to the United States. He reportedly farmed in the North Carolina highlands for a time; when his family last heard from him, in January 1881, he was at Louisville, Ky. On Apr. 4, 1887, in the Dent County Circuit Court in Salem, Mo. (where according to one account he had been teaching school), he became a United States citizen, under the name Charles Martel. The next year found him in Iowa, where he was for some time an accountant and estate manager for a lawyer and real estate dealer in Council Bluffs.

The circumstances that drew him into library work are not known. Having moved, apparently, to Chicago, he joined the staff of the Newberry Library there in March 1892. His unusual bibliographic knowledge and linguistic skills gradually brought him recognition. During his five years at the Newberry, he received valuable professional training from Dr. William F. Poole [q.v.], the director, and others of his staff, including J. C. M. Hanson [Supp. 3]. Martel resigned in November 1897 to follow Hanson to the Library of Congress in Washington, as chief classifier.

The Library had just opened to the public in its monumental new building, and its cataloguing staff, headed by the strong-fibered Hanson, faced overwhelming problems. Martel devoted himself to constructing a modern, flexible system of book classification, capable of indefinite expansion, to apply to the vast collection that included almost every branch of learning, in both ancient and modern languages. The system then in use, originally devised by Thomas Jefferson, had already become a straitjacket. After surveying other existing systems of classification, Martel outlined a scheme which was approved in 1898. Books were assigned to main classes designated by capital letters, such as A for general works and polygraphy, J for political science, and Z for bibliography, while subclasses were expressed by numbers. Martel began the reclassification but had to suspend work for lack of staff until late in 1900, when, after Herbert Putnam had become Librarian of Congress, adequate funds were made available. Schedule E appeared in 1901, and during the next thirty years all the other schedules were completed save for K (Law), which was not developed until some years after his death.

Work on the reclassification was slowed by other demands on Martel's time. Between 1897 and 1930 he usually had his office on the main floor east of the great reading room and the public catalogue. With his vast knowledge of the collections, his command of languages, and his almost uncanny mastery of the card catalogue, as well as of bibliographies and reference works, he was often called upon to help solve difficult queries. After Hanson left the Library of Congress in 1910, Martel directed the preparation and printing of the unit catalogue cards begun by Hanson; their distribution did much to assure the excellence of card catalogues in American libraries.

On Mar. 16, 1900, at Baltimore, Md., Charles Martel married a widow, Emma (McCoy) Haas, of Woodstock, Va. They had one son, Renaud (Rennie). After his wife's death in 1906, Martel centered his interests more and more in the Library of Congress. Late in 1912 he was appointed chief of the Library's catalogue division. To this post, which he held until 1930, he brought zeal and energy, combined with extremely wide bibliographical knowledge. Early in 1928, at the invitation of the Carnegie Endowment for International Peace, Martel served with Hanson and William Warner Bishop on a commission to plan and begin a central card catalogue for the printed book collection of the Vatican Library. Martel, who spoke French and Italian perfectly, spent five months in Rome, where he contributed much toward the development of the Vatican Library catalogue rules.

Martel reached the statutory retirement age of seventy in 1930. An executive order by President Hoover specially exempted him, however, as "one of the leading authorities (perhaps the leading authority) in the highly technical work of cataloguing and classification . . . chiefly responsible for the development at the Library of Congress of the elaborate system of cataloguing, the results of which [have been] accepted by libraries generally as authoritative." That September he became a consultant in cataloguing, classification, and bibliography.

In person, Charles Martel was sturdily built, slightly below medium height, with a keenly analytical mind. Modest and self-effacing, he expressed himself precisely, usually with a tinge of humor, and wrote with copperplate regularity and clearness. He continued to work as consultant until May 1, 1945. Two weeks later he died in Washington of a cerebral thrombosis, in his eighty-sixth year. His remains were cremated.

[Personal information; communications from Stadtarchiv Zurich and from the late J. Christian Bay; obituary by Bay in *Library Jour.*, June 15, 1945; *Who*

Was Who in America, vol. II (1950); *Report* of the Librarian of Cong., 1898–1945; Lib. of Cong. records; Martel's naturalization record, Apr. 4, 1887, Dent County Circuit Court, Salem, Mo.; death record from D. C. Dept. of Public Health.]

JAMES B. CHILDS

MARTIN, EVERETT DEAN (July 5, 1880–May 10, 1941), social psychologist and adult educator, was born in Jacksonville, Ill., the oldest child of Buker E. and Mollie (Field) Martin. His father, a tobacconist, was a native of Illinois; his mother, of Iowa. Martin attended Illinois College in Jacksonville (B.A. 1904) and continued his studies at the McCormick Theological Seminary in Chicago, from which he received a diploma in 1907. Ordained that year as a Congregational minister, he held pastorates in Lombard, Ill. (1906–08), and Dixon, Ill. (1908–10), and in Des Moines, Iowa, where he was minister of the Unitarian church (1910–14). He then left the ministry to devote his time to writing on social questions.

In 1916 Martin began a long association with the People's Institute, a center for adult education in New York City founded in 1897 by Charles Sprague Smith [*q.v.*]. As its principal activity the Institute conducted an extensive series of public lectures, held at Cooper Union and known as the Cooper Union Forum. Martin, appointed initially as a lecturer in social philosophy, in 1917 was made director of the Forum and assistant director of the Institute itself (he became its director in 1922). From 1919 to 1922 he was also chairman of another Institute committee, the National Board of Review of Motion Pictures. Beginning in 1917, Martin developed still another People's Institute undertaking, a group of classes in literature, biology, psychology, and other subjects, held in libraries, settlement houses, and elsewhere, that became known as the School of Philosophy. In his own classes he was (in the words of a contemporary description) a "scholarly, witty, and genial" lecturer, who spoke "with ease and without affectation." Funds for the Institute's program, always difficult to raise, virtually vanished during the depression years, and in 1934 it went out of existence. At this time Cooper Union took over the adult lecture series, setting up for the purpose a Department of Social Philosophy with Martin as its head. He was president of the American Assocation of Adult Education in 1937.

Along with his teaching and administrative work, Martin contributed twelve books to the literature of social psychology, social philosophy, and politics. His psychological work is noteworthy as an early attempt to utilize Freudian theory in explaining the behavior of men in groups. In his first and most important book, *The Behavior of Crowds* (1920), he viewed mob action as a form of mental disorder, the product of repressed impulses of individuals which the presence of others, under certain circumstances, brought to the fore. Martin's social thought is of interest as a popular defense of liberalism and the democratic process during a period when these values were under frequent assault. In *The Meaning of a Liberal Education* (1926) he condemned what he considered the utilitarian emphasis of contemporary schooling and advocated a humanist education as the bulwark of liberal democracy, believing that it inoculated individuals against infection by the irrational behavior of crowds, behavior which paved the way for revolution. All revolutions, said Martin, were by nature antiliberal (*Farewell to Revolution*, 1935), and he insisted that viable solutions to social problems could be found only through rational and sane discussion.

Martin left Cooper Union in 1938 to become professor of social philosophy at the Claremont Graduate School in Claremont, Calif. Three years later, at the age of sixty, he died of a heart attack at Claremont. In 1907 he had married Esther W. Kirk of Jacksonville, Ill., whom he divorced in 1915. They had three children: Mary, Margaret, and Elizabeth. His second marriage, in 1915, to Persis E. Rowell, also ended in divorce; they had one son, Everett Eastman. Martin was survived by his third wife, Daphne Crane Drake, whom he had married in 1931.

[Biographical accounts of Martin, not wholly accurate, include: Stanley J. Kunitz and Howard Haycraft, eds., *Twentieth Century Authors* (1942), with photograph; *Who Was Who in America*, vol. I (1942); obituary in *N. Y. Times*, May 11, 1941. On his work at the People's Institute, see Lolla Jean Simpson, "People Who Want to Be Educated," *Harper's Monthly*, May 1929. On his contribution to social psychology, see Stanley Milgram and Hans Toch, "Collective Behavior: Crowds and Social Movements," in Gardner Lindzey and Elliot Aronson, eds., *The Handbook of Social Psychology*, vol. IV (2nd ed., 1969). Other information from: Dept. of Records, Jacksonville, Ill.; Alumni Office, McCormick Theological Seminary; records and other material about the People's Institute in the library of Cooper Union and in the N. Y. Public Lib.]

HARVEY LONDON

MARVIN, CHARLES FREDERICK (Oct. 7, 1858–June 5, 1943), meteorologist, was born at Putnam (later part of Zanesville), Ohio, the third of four children and only son of Sarah Anne (Speck) and George Frederick Adams Marvin. His father, a native of Springfield, Ohio, and a descendant of Matthew Marvin of Essex, England, who settled in Norwalk, Conn., in 1635, was a baggage master for the Railway Express Company. Young Marvin attended public schools in Columbus, Ohio, and Ohio State University, from which he received the degree of mechanical engineer in 1883.

The following year, after passing a civil service examination, Marvin was appointed junior professor of meteorology in the Army Signal Service and moved to Washington, D. C. On one of his first assignments he carried out experiments at various altitudes on Pikes Peak in Colorado; by comparing the water vapor measurements made by a dew-point apparatus and a sling psychrometer he was able to perfect the statistical tables used to calculate relative humidity. In 1888 he was made chief of the instrument division, a post he retained when in 1891 the Signal Corps weather service was transferred to civilian authority and became the United States Weather Bureau. During these years he effected improvements in the instrumentation used at the weather stations and introduced new apparatus to measure sunshine, rainfall, evaporation, and barometric pressure. He also instituted the systematic recording of earthquakes and devised modifications of the seismograph. In 1895 he began a pioneering program of kite observations to record atmospheric conditions in the upper air.

On July 29, 1913, on the recommendation of the National Academy of Sciences, Marvin was appointed chief of the Weather Bureau, a post he held until his retirement in 1934. He brought to the service both scientific insight and inventive skill, which greatly increased its usefulness. Tactful and fair as an administrator, he largely avoided the problems of rivalry and political intrigue that had caused the dismissal of his predecessor, Willis L. Moore. Under Marvin's administration the weather service expanded. When the United States entered World War I, the Bureau began supplying meteorological information to the military forces. Other innovations included the establishment of observing stations in the Caribbean and in Central America to improve the hurricane warning system; a system of river observations and flood warnings; and warnings of severe freezes that would damage crops. As civil aviation expanded during the 1920's, Marvin sought to provide special forecasts, upper-air readings, and other data essential for planning flights. For a time his efforts were hampered by inadequate appropriations, but the Air Commerce Act of 1926 led to increased funds and the opening of Weather Bureau stations at all major airports.

Marvin's chief contributions to meteorology pertained to the invention, improvement, and standardization of the instruments used. Of particular value was his work on the Robinson cup anemometer, a device for measuring wind velocity, and on the design of weather kites and the meteorograph they carried. To improve long-range forecasting he began including past frequency data, a modification which later aided the military in forecasting weather for bombing missions during World War II. Marvin was president of the American Meteorological Society in 1926 and a member of the National Advisory Committee for Aeronautics from 1915 to 1934. He was the first secretary and director of the meteorological section of the International Geophysical Union, organized at Brussels in 1919.

An opera fan and an amateur photographer, Marvin was also active in the movement for calendar reform. In 1931 he served as a delegate to a League of Nations conference on this subject held at Geneva, and he was co-author of *Moses: The Greatest of Calendar Reformers* (1927). He was a member of the Episcopal Church. Marvin was first married on June 27, 1894, to Nellie Limeburner, who died in 1905; their children were Charles Frederick, Cornelia Theresa, and Helen Elizabeth. On Nov. 8, 1911, he married Retta Mabel Bartholow, who died in 1932. He then married Sophia Augusta Beuter, on Nov. 12, 1932, who died a few months before him. Marvin was seventy-five years old at the time of his retirement. He died nine years later at Doctors Hospital in Washington, D. C., of heart failure following an operation, and was buried in Glenwood Cemetery, Washington.

[Obituaries in *Science*, July 2, 1943 (by W. J. Humphreys), and *Jour. of the Wash. Acad. of Sciences*, Apr. 15, 1944 (by F. W. Reichelderfer); Donald R. Whitnah, *A Hist. of the U. S. Weather Bureau* (1961); *Nat. Cyc. Am. Biog.*, XL, 270; biographical information gathered by Sister M. Frances Therese Meyers of the Mount Carmel Convent, New Orleans, La.; information from Mrs. Claud Livingston of Washington, D. C., a daughter.]

DONALD R. WHITNAH

MASLIANSKY, ZVI HIRSCH (May 16, 1856–Jan. 11, 1943), folk preacher of Zionism, was born in Slutzk, province of Minsk, Russia, to Chaim and Rebecca (Papok) Masliansky. He was mute until the age of five, but by the time he was seven he had become locally famous for his intellectual abilities and his tendency to orate. His father, a teacher of Hebrew and a businessman of moderate means, was an orthodox Jew untouched by contemporary currents of modernism. At the age of twelve young Masliansky left home to study at the yeshiva in Mir, and two years later went to Paritz, where he studied with the distinguished rabbi Yechiel Michael Wolfson. Following the death of his father, he helped sup-

port his mother and a younger brother by becoming a teacher in the Jewish schools of Pinsk
and nearby Karlin. He soon tired of teaching,
however, and for about five years engaged in
farming. On Mar. 3, 1875, he married Henrietta
Rubenstein, by whom he had six children: Hyman, Phillip, Bertha, Fanny, Anna, and Beatrice.

Masliansky apparently resumed his teaching career, but after the pogroms of 1881 he also became active as a public speaker in the nascent
Zionist movement, whose goal was to secure a
national home for the Jewish people in Palestine.
In 1887 he moved to Yekaterinoslav, where, in
addition to teaching, he frequently preached in
synagogues on the sabbath and other holidays.
When he spoke in Odessa in 1891, his success was
so great that, with the encouragement of local
Zionist leaders, he gave up teaching and became
a professional propagandist for the movement. He
spent the next three years as a wandering preacher in Russia and Poland; for his Zionist activities
he was deported from Odessa and Minsk and was
once arrested in Lodz. Ordered to leave Russia in
1894, Masliansky migrated to England, stopping
along the way at the major cities of Western
Europe to speak to groups of newly arrived
Russian-Jewish immigrants. He then joined the
mainstream of the Russian-Jewish emigration
and in 1895 settled in New York City. He brought
with him a reputation as the finest Yiddish orator
of his time. On the occasion of his first address,
in the Great Synagogue on the Lower East Side,
the entrance to the building was so crowded that
he had to be handed up the stairs by the police.

Masliansky adjusted quickly to his new home,
trimming his beard from its Russian fullness to
the more Americanized spade shape. In 1898 he
began weekly lectures at the Educational Alliance,
which had been established in 1889 by prominent
German Jews to facilitate the Americanization of
Eastern European immigrants. Masliansky became an interpreter of Americanism to the new
immigrants, but he was equally concerned with
implanting Jewish loyalties in their children. He
preached a deep commitment to both Jewish
tradition and Zion. His speeches were emotional
rather than analytic, studded with images drawn
from the whole range of biblical and rabbinic
literature, and often delivered in the rhythmic
singsong of Eastern European Jewish preachers.
He nevertheless emphasized the relationship of
the individual to his community rather than to a
personal God, and in so doing provided a bridge
between earlier religious pieties and the more
rational and secular interests of American Jews.

Masliansky wrote with equal ease in Hebrew
and in Yiddish, and while still in Russia had contributed several articles to Hebrew periodicals.
In 1902, with the financial backing of Louis
Marshall [q.v.] and other prominent German
Jews in New York, he became the founder, president, and co-editor of a daily Jewish newspaper,
Die Yiddishe Velt (The Jewish World), published in both Yiddish and English. The paper
was of substantial literary merit, and Masliansky
gave it a pronounced Zionist orientation. But it
also emphasized its sponsors' aims—to American-
ize the immigrants and enlist them in anti-
Tammany reform politics—in a way that the
Lower East Side readers found condescending.
Disappointed at the paper's poor reception, the
sponsors withdrew their support in 1904, and the
Jewish World ceased publication the next year,
with Masliansky losing all his personal funds. He
remained a frequent contributor to Yiddish and
Hebrew periodicals and newspapers, one of his
most important contributions being his travel diary
of a journey to Palestine in 1921 which appeared
in the Yiddish *Morgen Journal*. Three volumes of
his speeches were published in Yiddish in 1909.
His memoirs appeared in Yiddish (1924) and in
Hebrew (1929) as part of a three-volume edition
of his speeches, travel diary, and reminiscences.

Active in communal organizations, Masliansky
was vice-president from 1900 to 1910 of the Federation of American Zionists, president from 1915
to 1920 of the New York division of the Jewish
Consumptive Relief Society of Denver, and director from 1925 until his death of the Israel Matz
Foundation, engaged primarily in the support of
Hebrew writers. He also took an active part in
Jewish educational affairs, both in New York and
in Brooklyn, where after 1929 he was head of
the yeshiva of Borough Park. Though he did not
play a leading role in the political movement of
Zionism, he became on the Lower East Side of
New York a legendary figure as a folk preacher
of Jewish nationalism. Masliansky died at the age
of eighty-six at his home in Brooklyn and was
buried in Mount Carmel Cemetery, Queens, New
York City. In 1956, on the centennial of his birth,
a prize for excellence in preaching was established in his honor at the Jewish Theological
Seminary of America.

[The best biographical article is in the *Leksikon
fun der Nayer Yidisher Literatur,* V, columns 467–69
(in Yiddish) ; see also the entry in *Who's Who in Am.
Jewry,* 1938–39. The best of the many memorial ar-
ticles are Louis Lipsky, *A Gallery of Zionist Profiles*
(1956), pp. 191–97, and Max Raisin, *Great Jews I
Have Known* (1952), pp. 119–30. See also Isidor
Singer in the *Menorah,* Aug. 1901 ; and Lucy S.
Dawidowicz, "Louis Marshall's Yiddish Newspaper,
The Jewish World," *Jewish Social Studies,* Apr. 1963.
The prime source for the bulk of Masliansky's active
career, from 1881 to 1924, is his own memoirs:
Zichroines (1924), in Yiddish ; Hebrew edition, *Zich-*

ronot uMasaot (1929). A collection of his speeches in English translation, Sermons, ed. by A. J. Feldman, appeared in 1926.]

ARTHUR HERTZBERG

MATHER, WINIFRED HOLT. See HOLT, WINIFRED.

MATHEWS, SHAILER (May 26, 1863–Oct. 23, 1941), theologian, was born in Portland, Maine, the eldest of four children of Baptist parents, Jonathan Bennett Mathews and Sophia Lucinda (Shailer) Mathews. His father, a wholesale flour and tea merchant, was descended from James Mathews, who came from Gloucestershire, England, to Charlestown, Mass., in 1634. Later members of the family moved to Maine. One of his mother's forebears, Daniel Hascall, was a founder of the Baptist Education Society of the State of New York (later Colgate University), and the boy's maternal grandfather, William H. Shailer, was a prominent Baptist minister in Portland. Shailer Mathews had to drop out of high school for a time to work in his father's office when the business went into receivership in 1878, but he later attended Colby College in Waterville, Maine, and received the A.B. degree in 1884. More out of family tradition than from any strong sense of religious vocation, he then entered the Newton (Mass.) Theological Institution, a Baptist seminary, from which he graduated in 1887.

Mathews was licensed but never sought ordination or committed himself to the ministry; like many of his generation who responded to the new interest in historical and social studies, he felt better suited to nonpastoral activity. Deciding to become a teacher, he secured a position at Colby as associate professor of rhetoric. In 1889 he became professor of history and political economy, and the following spring he was granted a year's leave to study at the University of Berlin. On July 16, 1890, before sailing, he married Mary Philbrick Elden of Waterville. Three children were born to them: Robert Elden, Helen, and Mary.

In Germany, Mathews studied history, focusing on the struggle between Church and Empire from the Carolingians to the Hohenstaufens, a study that resulted in the publication of his first book, *Select Mediaeval Documents* (1892). His interest in social forces later found reflection also in his book *The French Revolution* (1901). On his return to Colby, Mathews continued to teach history and economics. In the latter field he was influenced by the social conception of economic problems set forth by Richard T. Ely [Supp. 3]. He also did some reading in the emerging field of

sociology under the guidance of a close friend and colleague at Colby, Albion W. Small [q.v.], who in 1892 left to head the sociology department at the new University of Chicago. Small planned to have Mathews join his department; but in 1894 Ernest DeWitt Burton [q.v.] invited Mathews to become associate professor of New Testament history and interpretation at Chicago, and after some hesitation over his lack of training, he accepted.

Thus Mathews returned to the religious field he thought he had left behind him and began his long tenure at the University of Chicago and its Divinity School. He became professor in 1897 and, in 1906, professor of historical and comparative theology. Two years later he was made dean of the Divinity School, an office he filled with distinction until his retirement in 1933. He caught the enthusiasm of the new university and helped shape its early development, both through personal counsel and through an active role in faculty and administrative bodies. Theologically, his efforts, in collaboration with colleagues, led to the Divinity School's becoming a center of "modernism" and to the development of a "Chicago school" of theology.

Mathews brought to his work as a theologian a sociohistorical approach derived from his earlier study and teaching. He viewed Christianity not as a body of truth but as a religious movement subject to social forces; a study of the evolution of Christian doctrine ought therefore to begin with its social background. His first statement of this view appeared as an article in the *Biblical World* in October 1915, "Theology and the Social Mind," in which he argued that Christianity in its historical development had passed through a series of doctrinal formulations, in response to the dominant cultural perspective or "social mind" of the period. Each "social mind," he held, provided analogies which facilitated the assimilation of new meaning to an inherited body of Christian understanding, to which he gave the term "generic Christianity." These doctrinal formulations, in turn, tended to become hardened with time; hence new ideas met continual resistance. As he himself observed, his view substituted a functional norm, implying relativity and efficiency in adapting to new insight and circumstances, for inspired authority which brooked no such concessions to time and change. He elaborated his thesis in subsequent articles and in four books: *The Faith of Modernism* (1924), *The Atonement and the Social Process* (1930), *The Growth of the Idea of God* (1931), and his 1933 Barrows Lectures in India, *Christianity and Social Process* (1934).

A theologian, Mathews believed, should be attuned to modern scientific thought and concerned with contemporary problems. His own commitment to the social gospel, originally stirred by the writings of Washington Gladden and Josiah Strong [qq.v.], was the stimulus to much of his activity. At the suggestion of Albion Small, then editor of the *American Journal of Sociology,* Mathews wrote a series of articles on "Christian Sociology," published in book form as *The Social Teaching of Jesus* (1897). This was acknowledged by Walter Rauschenbusch [q.v.] as the pioneer work in stating the biblical basis of the social gospel movement. Mathews's importance in this area is indicated by his election as president of the Western Economic Society (1911–19), organized by a group of socially motivated economists. Despite his gradual abandonment of many traditional Christian views, Mathews remained a staunch supporter of the church, not as an ecclesiastical power but as the one body which could and must guide the readjustment of values in modern industrialized society. In pursuing this end, he insisted, the church must develop "methods of gaining help from God." His commitment to the social role of the churches was tested but unshaken by the catastrophe of the First World War, and he defended the optimism of the social gospel against the rising criticism of postwar modes of neo-orthodoxy. Nevertheless, he shared the view emerging in that postwar era that the romance of social gospel preaching had spent itself, and that its message should now be implemented in direct efforts at social organization and action.

As a Modernist, Mathews continued to emphasize process and experience as against revelation and metaphysics, as did many liberals before him; but in doing so he adopted an increasingly scientific tone and vocabulary that caused his thought to diverge from that of evangelical liberals. While he playfully ridiculed the "Jesus" to whom appeal had been made in the theologies of the previous generation of liberals as "a mid-Victorian" who endorsed "any idealism provided it was polite," he nevertheless retained in his own theology an appeal to Jesus as the one who provided a rallying point for Christianity as a social movement, and who, in himself, exemplified a way of living that cohered both with the legacy of Christian faith and with the "way of the universe" when this is rightly and profoundly understood. In giving substance to such an appeal, he drew upon the social ideals expressed in the Sermon on the Mount, as the inspiration for Christian altruism and "the intelligent democratizing of privilege."

Under Mathews's direction, the University of Chicago Divinity School engaged in a crusade to educate the public in a critical understanding of religion and the Bible. With the endorsement of President Harper, the university gave extension courses, issued pamphlets through the American Institute of Sacred Literature, and published Bible handbooks. Mathews contributed to this public education through his addresses to clubs and organizations and through articles in popular magazines. From 1903 to 1911 he edited the *World To-day,* a Chicago journal concerned with political and social trends, and from 1913 to 1920 he was editor of the *Biblical World.* He also served for many summers as director of religious work at the Chautauqua Institution.

Because Mathews considered his sociohistorical method to be applicable and helpful to all Christians, liberal or conservative, in pointing up the appeal to the Christian witness and Christian living in the modern world, he, unlike many liberals, evangelical or modernist, sought to reach all groups within the Christian community, regardless of denominational or creedal differences. Thus his modernism was irenic rather than combative. Yet he continually provoked attack among conservative groups by the uncompromising tenor of his presentation, which seemed to be directed more toward social reform and social progress than toward the business of saving souls. Nevertheless, he worked easily with many conservatives, cooperating with them on projects of common interest, and succeeded in averting open clashes between the "modernists" and "fundamentalists" within his denomination. Mathews remained a dedicated Baptist; he praised the democratic principles by which that denomination operated, and was elected president, in 1915, of the Northern Baptist Convention—formed largely through his efforts.

Mathews was active in the interdenominational missions of Chicago-area churches, particularly as president of the Chicago Church Federation (1929–32) and as chairman, for many years, of its Inter-racial Commission. A strong ecumenist, he was president of the Federal Council of the Churches of Christ in America (1912–16) and an active participant in international church gatherings. He joined Sidney L. Gulick [Supp. 3] in a "Christian embassy" to Japan in 1915, and attended the Universal Conference on Christian Life and Work in Stockholm in 1925 and the Lausanne Conference on Faith and Order in 1927.

Mathews was a man of commanding presence, energetic and decisive. He could be abrupt and demanding, but he was commonly gracious. He smiled readily and was known for his apt, penetrating wit. His death, resulting from an embolism, occurred in Chicago in 1941. His body was cremated and the ashes interred in the crypt of the First Unitarian Church, near the University of Chicago. Mathews's enduring intellectual legacy lies in his sociohistorical method of interpreting doctrine and his popularization of "modernism" as a cultural adaptation, conserving the essence of Christianity.

[Other books by Mathews include: *The Church and the Changing Order* (1907), *The Gospel and the Modern Man* (1910), and *The Spiritual Interpretation of History* (1916). Mathews's papers (43 boxes) are in the Univ. of Chicago Archives. On Mathews's life and work, see: his autobiography, *New Faith for Old* (1936); biographical note by Robert E. Mathews and "Theology and the Social Process" by Edwin E. Aubrey in Miles H. Krumbine, ed., *The Process of Religion: Essays in Honor of Dean Shailer Mathews* (1933); Charles H. Arnold, *Near the Edge of Battle* (1966); C. T. Holman in *Christian Century*, Oct. 26, 1932; memorial tributes in *Divinity School News* (Univ. of Chicago), Nov. 1, 1941, and *Jour. of Religion*, Oct. 1942. On Mathews's broader role in the Univ. of Chicago, see Edgar J. Goodspeed, *As I Remember* (1953). Mathews's son, Robert E. Mathews, provided data about his father's background. An oil portrait of Mathews is at Swift Hall in the Univ. of Chicago Divinity School; a profile plaque is in the Hall of Christ at Chautauqua, N. Y. *The Process of Religion*, above, has a photograph of Mathews as frontispiece.]

BERNARD E. MELAND

MAURER, JAMES HUDSON (Apr. 15, 1864–Mar. 16, 1944), labor leader and socialist, was born in Reading, Pa., the third of four sons (the second of whom died in infancy) of James R. and Sarah (Lorah) Maurer. Both parents came of Pennsylvania German stock and belonged to the Lutheran Church. The father, whose forebears had emigrated from Alsace-Lorraine about 1755, was a shoemaker by trade, but worked for a time as a policeman; he died of smallpox when James was eight. His mother soon remarried, but James's stepfather proved harsh and ill-tempered. The family was poor, and at ten James went to work in a hardware plant. He could neither read nor write—his total schooling amounted to just ten months—and in his early years he spoke only the "Pennsylvania Dutch" dialect. His youth had some lighter moments. With a friend who had a skill in magic he got up a variety act and secured a few engagements. His fascination with show business later led him to stage several melodramas.

When he was nearly sixteen, Maurer became an apprentice in a local machine shop. There he was befriended by a fellow worker, Thomas King, an active member of the Knights of Labor, who taught him to read and introduced him to books on economics and the labor question. Maurer joined the local assembly of the Knights and after several months was elected "worthy foreman" (vice-president). He also joined the Greenback party and, later, a Single-Tax Club. In 1881 he left home and found work in a boilermaking plant in Pottstown, Pa. Continuing in the Knights, he became head of his local assembly and then District Master Workman for the Schuylkill Valley. He married a Pottstown girl, Mary J. Missimer, on Apr. 15, 1886. They had two children, Charles and Martha.

After working as a steamfitter in Coatesville and Royersford, Pa., Maurer returned to Reading, where in 1891 he and a brother went into business as machinists and steamfitters. The firm prospered for a time, but eventually failed, according to Maurer because his vigorous support of the Populist party had alienated prominent citizens. He next (1895) founded a short-lived Populist weekly, the *Reading Kicker*. While in the plumbing business in nearby Hamburg in 1899 he organized a local of the Socialist Labor party. That party split nationally over the question of supporting trade unions, and Maurer, ever loyal to the unions, shifted in 1901 to the newly organized Socialist party.

Working intermittently for a small machine shop in Reading, Maurer thereafter centered his activity in the socialist and labor movements. As a member of the Plumbers and Steamfitters Union, he was elected in 1901 a delegate to the Central Labor Union of Reading. He later helped organize the city's Building Trades Council. Maurer ran unsuccessfully as Socialist candidate for city controller in 1901 and for the state legislature in 1902. The following year he was elected to the party's state executive committee and in 1904 to the national executive committee. He was the Socialist candidate for governor of Pennsylvania in 1906 and polled nearly 26,000 votes. Meanwhile the Reading branch of the party was steadily building up political strength, and in 1910 Maurer became the first Socialist elected to the Pennsylvania legislature. He was defeated in 1912, but reelected in 1914 and 1916. His political effectiveness was enhanced in 1912 by his election as president of the Pennsylvania State Federation of Labor, a post he held for the next sixteen years. Attracting new members and ousting entrenched conservatives, Maurer made the Federation an important pressure group for labor legislation. No doctrinaire, he recognized that the Federation had to support legislators favorable to its program regardless of party, and he was popular both as a lobbyist and as a legislator.

Within the legislature Maurer gave effective support to a variety of labor and reform measures. He was a leader in the successful effort to obtain Pennsylvania's first workmen's compensation act, passed in 1915. He worked for industrial health legislation, regulation of child labor, and pensions for widows and orphans. He was especially active in the movement for old age pensions, and from 1917 to 1919 headed a state commission concerned with this question, for which he secured the young economist Abraham Epstein [Supp. 3] as executive secretary.

An avowed pacifist, Maurer opposed United States participation in World War I. He was one of the leaders of the People's Council of America for Democracy and Peace, organized in May 1917 to seek an early, negotiated peace, and traveled widely speaking against the war. His stand brought him into conflict with Samuel Gompers [q.v.], president of the American Federation of Labor, who countered by forming a prowar group of labor leaders and reformers, the American Alliance for Labor and Democracy. Prowar labor leaders sought to oust Maurer from the presidency of the Pennsylvania State Federation of Labor in 1918, but he was reelected by a wide margin.

During the 1920's Maurer continued his political activity. In 1927 Reading's Socialists, closely linked to the labor movement, swept the municipal elections, sending Maurer to the city council. The next year he stepped down from the presidency of the Pennsylvania Federation of Labor. He was the Socialist party's vice-presidential candidate on tickets headed by Norman Thomas in 1928 and 1932, and in 1930 its candidate, once more, for governor of Pennsylvania. He also served from 1921 to 1929 as the first president of the Workers' Education Bureau of America, which he had helped organize at the New School for Social Research in New York. Stirred by the plight of the unemployed during the depression, Maurer in 1933 helped found and served as chairman of the United Workers' Federation of Pennsylvania, an organization of the jobless. In 1934, in his last bid for elective office, he ran as a Socialist for United States Senator. When, two years later, the Socialist party advocated a united front with the Communists, whose disruptive tactics Maurer disliked, he resigned from the national organization. Living on in Reading, he died there of heart disease in 1944 at the age of seventy-nine. He was buried in West End Cemetery, Pottstown, Pa.

[Maurer's autobiography, *It Can Be Done* (1938), is the principal source. See also: Henry G. Stetler, *The Socialist Movement in Reading, Pa.* (1943); Kenneth Hendrickson, "James H. Maurer," *Hist. Rev. of Berks County*, Winter, 1969–70; *Smull's Legislative Hand Book and Manual of the State of Pa.*, 1917, p. 1140; David A. Shannon, *The Socialist Party of America* (1955); *Nat. Cyc. Am. Biog.*, Current Vol. C, pp. 259–60; *N. Y. Times* obituary, Mar. 17, 1944. Death record from Pa. Dept. of Health.]

PHILIP TAFT

MERRIAM, CLINTON HART (Dec. 5, 1855–Mar. 19, 1942), naturalist, was born in New York City, the second son and second of four children of Clinton Levi Merriam and Caroline (Hart) Merriam. The classicist Augustus Chapman Merriam [q.v.] was his uncle. His father, a merchant and stockbroker, retired from business early and built a mansion at Locust Grove in Lewis County, N. Y., where his Connecticut forebears had settled in 1800; he later served two terms as a Republican in Congress. Merriam's mother was the daughter of a Collinsville, N. Y., judge. His younger sister Florence Augusta, who married one of Merriam's close associates, the biologist Vernon Bailey, became an ornithologist and writer.

Boyhood life at Locust Grove, in the shadow of the Adirondacks, set the pattern of Merriam's career. At the age of twelve he began collecting birds and insects and soon expanded his interests to include reptiles, mammals, plants, and marine invertebrates. He received his early education from private tutors, and later studied at the Pingry Military School in Elizabeth, N. J., and Williston Seminary in Easthampton, Mass. In 1872, at the age of sixteen, through the intercession of Spencer F. Baird [q.v.] of the Smithsonian Institution, he was allowed to join the Government Survey of the Territories (popularly called the Hayden Survey) and collected a large number of birds in Utah, Idaho, and Wyoming. Two years later he entered the Sheffield Scientific School at Yale. There he developed an interest in medicine, and in 1877 he enrolled in the College of Physicians and Surgeons of Columbia University. After graduation in 1879, he practiced medicine and surgery at Locust Grove for about six years, at the same time continuing his interest in natural history.

Merriam's real career began in 1885 when, through the efforts of Baird and others, Congress voted to establish a section of "economic ornithology" under the Department of Agriculture's Division of Entomology, to carry on the survey of bird distribution in the United States begun by the American Ornithologists' Union. Merriam was put in charge of the section, which the next year was elevated to a separate division and in 1896 was given a name reflecting its broader purpose, the Division of Biological Survey. It became a bureau in 1905, and Merriam remained its head until 1910.

Under his direction, the Biological Survey actively promoted investigations of American plants and animals, organized and led biological expeditions, and built up permanent collections. Merriam revolutionized the technique of preparing specimens for study, emphasized the importance of a uniform system of measurements and the necessity of keeping detailed notes and exact geographic data, stressed the value of cranial characters in classifying mammals, and urged the combining of field and laboratory studies. About him he gathered a team of highly skilled biologists, and together they laid the foundations of the bureau's later policies. He instituted the series of North American Fauna publications in 1889. Ten years later he organized and directed a summer collecting expedition to Alaska, sponsored by the railroad financier Edward H. Harriman [q.v.], and later edited and oversaw the publication of the results, in twelve volumes (1901–14). Merriam inaugurated wildlife conservation as a federal responsibility by helping to secure the Lacey Act of 1900, which prohibited interstate commerce in illegally killed game and regulated the importation of foreign species.

Merriam was a meticulous writer who spent hours in correcting and polishing. His first major publication was *A Review of the Birds of Connecticut* (1877), which was followed by many papers on birds. After 1881, however, his interest shifted to mammals, and his publications included monographic studies of the pocket gophers, shrews, weasels, and bears. Among other noteworthy works were *The Mammals of the Adirondack Region* (1884), *Results of a Biological Survey of the San Francisco Mountain Region and Desert of the Little Colorado, Arizona* (1890) and *Results of a Biological Reconnaissance of South-Central Idaho* (1891)—two volumes in the North American Fauna series—and *Life Zones and Crop Zones of the United States* (1898). He himself wrote most of the first ten numbers of the North American Fauna, though he was not above affixing his name to the writings of subordinates. All told, Merriam described twenty-four genera and some 660 new taxa of mammals. He was basically a collector of facts rather than a theorist, but he validated through his field data the hypothesis of A. Hyatt Verrill and Joel A. Allen [q.v.] that the distribution of plants and animals was determined primarily by temperature factors. Merriam's concept of life zones was widely accepted by the scientific world, though his use of a single parameter has since been abandoned in favor of a more dynamic, complex scheme.

As the Biological Survey expanded, administrative and political pressures increased, and Merriam found his position less congenial. His friends persuaded Mrs. E. H. Harriman to establish a trust fund, to be administered through the Smithsonian Institution, that would allow him complete freedom in his research, and in 1910 he resigned from the Survey and took quarters in the Smithsonian. Instead of preparing a definitive work on North American mammals, however, as had been expected, he turned to a recently acquired new interest, the ethnology of the Indian tribes of California and Nevada, on which he published some dozen articles and two volumes of Indian folktales. His one later work on mammals, *Review of the Grizzly and Big Brown Bears of North America* (1918), was badly flawed and much criticized.

Of moderate stature and robust build, Merriam was a man of great energy and wide learning, yet without pretense. He had no use for orthodox religion. His personality evoked varying reactions. Some associates thought him dictatorial, ambitious, and perverse; others found him warmhearted, sympathetic, and charming, though intolerant of incompetence. His enthusiasm won him many friends, notably Theodore Roosevelt.

Merriam was a founder and first president (1878) of the Linnaean Society of New York, president of the American Ornithologists' Union (1900–02), the American Society of Mammalogists (1919–20), and the American Society of Naturalists (1924–25), and a founder and for many years a director of the National Geographic Society. Among his honors were election to the National Academy of Sciences (1902) and award of the Roosevelt Medal (1931).

On Oct. 15, 1886, Merriam married Virginia Elizabeth Gosnell of Martinsburg, W. Va.; they had two daughters, Dorothy and Zenaida. In 1939, two years after his wife's death, he retired from his Smithsonian post and went to live with a daughter in Berkeley, Calif. He died there of pneumonia in his eighty-seventh year. His ashes were buried at Cedar Hill Cemetery, Suitland, Md. Remembered for his contributions to mammalogy and zoogeography, Merriam was a central figure in the era of American natural history that marked the transition from the pioneer period of exploration to one of experimentation and interpretation.

[Merriam's journals, 1873–1938, are at the Lib. of Cong.; his linguistic Indian studies and a mass of ethnological notes and manuscripts are at the Smithsonian Institution; the library of the Univ. of Mich. Museum has his correspondence with Joseph Beal Steere, zoologist and explorer. The principal obituaries and memoirs are: Wilfred H. Osgood in Nat. Acad. Sci., *Biog. Memoirs*, vol. XXIV (1947), with portrait and a bibliography of Merriam's publications by Hilda W. Grinnell; Z. M. and M. W. Talbot in *Science*, May 29, 1942; T. S. Palmer in the *Auk*, Apr. 1954, with portrait; A. K. Fisher in Wash. Acad. Sci., *Jour.*, Oct. 15, 1942; and Charles L. Camp in *Calif. Hist. Soc. Quart.*, Sept. 1942. Useful information about Merriam is contained in Jenks Cameron, *The Bureau of Biological Survey: Its Hist., Activities and Organ-*

ization* (1929); and Tracy I. Storer, "Mammalogy and the Am. Soc. of Mammalogists, 1919–1969," *Jour. of Mammalogy*, Nov. 1969. For articles discussing Merriam's work on life zones, see S. Charles Kendeigh and Victor E. Shelford, both in *Wilson Bull.*, Sept. 1932; and Rexford F. Daubenmire in *Quart. Rev. of Biology*, Sept. 1938. See also: Charles H. Pope, comp., *Merriam Genealogy in England and America* (1906), pp. 322, 419–20. Personal information was supplied by Merriam's grandson, Dr. Lee M. Talbot, and by his colleagues Dr. Hartley H. T. Jackson of the Biological Survey and Dr. Waldo L. Schmitt of the Smithsonian Institution.]

RICHARD H. MANVILLE

MERRIAM, JOHN CAMPBELL (Oct. 20, 1869–Oct. 30, 1945), paleontologist, science administrator, and conservationist, was born in Hopkinton, Iowa, the oldest of three children of Charles Edward and Margaret Campbell (Kirkwood) Merriam. His only brother, Charles Edward Merriam, became a prominent political scientist at the University of Chicago. His mother, a schoolteacher, had been born in Pennsylvania but had grown up in Scotland. His father, of old American stock, had moved from Princeton, Mass., to Iowa in the 1850's. After serving in the Civil War, he became a merchant and a political leader in Hopkinton, a Presbyterian elder, and a trustee of the local Lenox College.

At Lenox, where he took the B.S. degree in 1887, John C. Merriam developed an interest in botany and geology. A family sojourn (1888–89) in Berkeley, Calif., gave him the opportunity to continue these interests at the University of California, where he studied geology with Joseph LeConte and botany with Edward L. Greene [*qq.v.*]. Like many aspiring scientists of the time, Merriam went to Germany to complete his postgraduate work, taking a doctor's degree at Munich in 1893 in the field of vertebrate paleontology. The next year, upon his return to the United States, he became an instructor at the University of California. He rose to assistant professor in 1899, associate professor in 1905, and professor in 1912.

From his university post Merriam played a key role in developing the study of paleontology on the West Coast. After the pioneer activities of the Wilkes Expedition, the Pacific Railroad surveys, and the California State Geological Survey, paleontology had entered a quarter-century of what Merriam later called "stagnation." From the early 1890's, however, investigators at both the University of California and Stanford University sent out a steady stream of field parties for the particular purpose of collecting vertebrate and invertebrate fossil remains. As a leader of this group, Merriam published papers between 1896 and 1908 on Tertiary molluscan faunas and Tertiary echinoids and on the Triassic Ichthyosauria.

In 1901 he published a classic work on the sequential stratigraphical events of the rich John Day Basin in Oregon, an area pioneered by Thomas Condon, Othniel C. Marsh, and Edward D. Cope [*qq.v.*]. Merriam's most productive period as a paleontologist was between 1900 and 1919. After the rekindling of interest in 1905 in the fossils of the Rancho La Brea tar pits at Los Angeles, he published many papers on the rich remains of Tertiary mammalian faunas of this site. He became president of the Paleontological Society of America in 1917 and of the Geological Society of America in 1919.

Gradually, however, other concerns began to intrude upon Merriam's time. As a leading West Coast scientist during the great period of institution-building in California, he necessarily became involved in efforts to promote and support research. Early in his career at Berkeley he had successfully enlisted the interest and financial backing of Annie M. Alexander, daughter of a Hawaiian sugar planter and a benefactor of the university, without whose patronage much of his research would have been difficult if not impossible to carry on. In 1912 he was appointed chairman of the newly formed department of paleontology at the university. In 1917 he became chairman of the Committee on Scientific Research of the California State Council of Defense, an agency which was interested in stimulating and coordinating research and which grew directly out of the developing network of professional scientists in California. Later, in 1919, he became chairman of the National Research Council, which was making a similar effort on a nationwide scale.

Merriam was appointed dean of the faculties at the University of California in 1920, but that same year he resigned to become the third president of the Carnegie Institution of Washington. His new position was a critical one for American science. In addition to being one of the leading patrons of research in the country, the Institution by virtue of its eminence and location in Washington, D. C., served as the unofficial scientific embassy of the nation's researchers. Merriam held this post until 1938, during which time he was a leader in the efforts to create a national climate of opinion favorable to the encouragement and support of scientific research. Elected in 1918 to the National Academy of Sciences, he was for many years chairman of its Committee on Government Relations. From 1933 to 1935 he was a member of the Science Advisory Board appointed by President Franklin D. Roosevelt to advise the government on scientific problems.

Merriam's third major career, intimately connected with those of research scientist and science administrator, was that of ardent conservationist. In 1917, along with Henry Fairfield Osborn [Supp. 1] and Madison Grant [Supp. 2], he helped establish the influential Save-the-Redwoods League, which, under his quarter-century tenure as president, acquired nearly 45,000 acres of redwood forest in northern California for park land. He was a frequent consultant to the National Park Service and a consistent champion of the need to preserve the nation's outdoor heritage for its scientific and educational, as well as its moral, usefulness. Nature was to him, in the phrase he used as a title for his last book (1943), *The Garment of God.*

After his retirement in 1938, Merriam divided his time between the University of Oregon (and work on the John Day Basin) and an office at the California Institute of Technology. His first wife, Ada Gertrude Little of Berkeley, whom he had married on Dec. 22, 1896, died in 1940, and on Feb. 20, 1941, he married Margaret Louise Webb of Pasadena. His colleagues considered him a sober and serious man, grave and distant rather than genial. He took pleasure in hunting, fishing, and working in the open. His social instincts were conventional and cautious.

Merriam died in a rest home in Oakland, Calif., of hypostatic pneumonia, following a decade of chronic myocarditis and arteriosclerosis. He was cremated. His three children survived him: Lawrence Campbell and Charles Warren, both geologists for the United States Geological Survey, and Malcolm Landers, a government economist.

[John Campbell Merriam's personal and professional papers are in the Manuscript Division of the Lib. of Cong. Biographical sketches (by Chester Stock) appear in Nat. Acad. Sci., *Biog. Memoirs,* vol. XXVI (1951); in Geological Soc. of America, *Proc.,* 1946; and in Carnegie Inst. of Wash., *Cooperation in Research* (1938). The first two memoirs include a full bibliography; each also includes a photograph of Merriam. A brief memorial appeared in the Am. Philosophical Soc., *Year Book,* 1945, and an obituary notice in the *N. Y. Times,* Oct. 1, 1945. Death record from Calif. Dept. of Public Health. On his father, see Leonard White, ed., *The Future of Government in the U. S.* (1942), pp. 3-4. For his collected writings see *Published Papers and Addresses of John Campbell Merriam* (4 vols., 1938), the fourth volume of which is devoted to his writings on subjects other than paleontology.]

CARROLL PURSELL

MICHAEL, ARTHUR (Aug. 7, 1853–Feb. 8, 1942), organic chemist, was born in Buffalo, N. Y., the younger of two sons of John and Clara (Pinner) Michael. Both parents had been brought at an early age from Germany to New York City; the father, a prosperous real estate investor, had moved to Buffalo in 1850. Arthur attended local public and private schools and worked at chemistry in a laboratory he set up at home. In 1871 the family began an extended sojourn abroad. Although he had had little formal scientific training, the boy entered the University of Heidelberg, where for two years (1872–74) he studied under the chemist Robert W. Bunsen. He then moved to the University of Berlin for further study (1875–78) with August W. von Hofmann, whose laboratory was then the world center for research in organic chemistry; during this period Michael began his own original research. Unconcerned with earning a degree, he spent a year in Paris with Charles A. Wurtz and visited Mendeleev in Russia before returning in 1880 to the United States.

In 1881 Michael accepted a professorship of chemistry at Tufts College in Medford, Mass., where he spent most of his time in research, supported largely from his own funds. He married Helen C. Abbott of Philadelphia, one of his graduate students, in June 1889, and left Tufts for an eighteen-month world tour. On his return in 1890 he became professor of chemistry at the newly established Clark University in Worcester, Mass., but resigned the following year and went to Europe. For three years he carried on research in a private laboratory he opened on the Isle of Wight. He returned to Tufts in 1894 and in 1907, at fifty-three, became professor emeritus. He continued work in his own laboratory at his home in Newton Center, Mass., and this remained the center of his work even after he was appointed professor of organic chemistry at Harvard in 1912. The appointment, which continued until his retirement in 1936, involved no lecture courses but only supervision of graduate students.

Michael's earliest research dealt with synthetic reactions. He was the first to synthesize a natural glucoside (helicin, 1879), and the method he devised became standard in synthesizing this class of compounds. He also discovered in 1887 a method involving the addition of active-hydrogen reagents to α,β-unsaturated carbonyl compounds; known as the Michael condensation, this reaction and its later modifications became valuable tools in synthesizing organic molecules by direct addition.

Michael's experimental work, however, interested him less than the basic principles underlying organic reactions. Trying to elucidate the fundamental laws and mechanisms involved, he introduced a novel general theory that interpreted organic reactions in terms of thermodynamic concepts such as free energy, bound energy, and increase in entropy. Although chemists in general did not accept his theory, he himself was able to apply it successfully in explaining and predicting organic reactions. His interpretation of addition reactions was a lasting contribution to chemical theory. Many substitution reactions involved an addition process as a preliminary stage, and he proposed the idea of an addition reaction with the formation of an intermediate "addition product," an important concept that forced chemists to recognize the existence of intermediate and mobile combinations in organic reactions.

Throughout his life Michael was a perceptive and valuable critic of current hypotheses in chemical theory. He attacked as unproven Jacobus van't Hoff's theory of geometrical isomerism and in 1895 showed experimentally that the accepted configurations of geometric isomers were wrong, and that additions to unsaturated substances did not necessarily proceed in the *cis* direction, as assumed by Johannes Wislicenus, but could proceed in the *trans* direction as well.

Michael perhaps contributed more of a fundamental character to organic chemistry than any other American of his day, though his work was more readily recognized in Europe than in the United States. The Germans regarded him as the equal of their best chemists, and during his years at Tufts many German graduate students came to study under him, thereby reversing the standard pattern of the time. When Michael retired in 1936, he had published more than 200 articles, mostly in German journals. He was elected to the National Academy of Sciences in 1889.

Michael was an eager collector of Oriental bronzes, porcelains, and landscape paintings dating back to the Chou Dynasty, and of early American silver. He enjoyed mountain climbing and took part in the first ascent of Mount Lefroy and Mount Victoria in the Canadian Rockies. Despite his cosmopolitan background, he was extremely reserved except among his few intimates, to whom he was a warm host. He was a Unitarian in religion. Michael died of arteriosclerotic heart disease in Orlando, Fla., at the age of eighty-eight. His body was cremated. Though childless himself, he liked children and bequeathed a large share of his estate to institutions for the care of Buffalo's crippled and needy children. He left his American silver to the Smithsonian Institution and the remainder of his art collection to the Albright Art Gallery in Buffalo.

[The fullest biographical accounts are the memorial minute by Edward W. Forbes, Louis F. Fieser, and Arthur B. Lamb in the *Harvard Univ. Gazette,* May 22, 1943, and a contemporary sketch by W. T. Read in *Industrial and Engineering Chemistry,* Oct. 1930. See also *Nat. Cyc. Am. Biog.,* XV, 172. Michael's ideas on organic theory are discussed in the chapter about him in Ferdinand Henrich, *Theories of Organic Chemistry* (translated by Treat B. Johnson and Dorothy A. Hahn, 1922). Two brief discussions of his

work in organic chemistry are: James R. Partington, *A Hist. of Chemistry,* IV (1964), 853–54; and Treat B. Johnson, in the chapter on organic chemistry in Charles A. Browne, ed., *A Half-Century of Chemistry in America, 1876–1926* (1926). Particular information was supplied by the Harvard Univ. Archives; by Michael's niece, Clara Michael of Derby, N. Y.; and by Michael's death record (Fla. Bureau of Vital Statistics).]

ALBERT B. COSTA

MIDGLEY, THOMAS (May 18, 1889–Nov. 2, 1944), inventor and chemist, was born at Beaver Falls, Pa., the son of Thomas and Hattie Louise (Emerson) Midgley. His mother was a daughter of James Ezekiel Emerson [*q.v.*], who invented the inserted-tooth circular and band saw. His father, born in London, England, and reared in Worcester, Mass., was also an inventor; after serving as superintendent of a steel company in Beaver Falls, he began his own wire-goods business and then, in 1896, moved to Columbus, Ohio, where he worked as factory manager of a bicycle company and afterward manufactured wire wheels and rubber tires of his own devising. Young Midgley attended the Columbus public schools and Betts Academy at Stamford, Conn., where he prepared for college. Through his chemistry course there he first became interested in the periodic table of the elements and the orderly natural relations it represented.

After graduating from Cornell University in 1911 with a degree in mechanical engineering, Midgley worked for a year as a draftsman and designer in "Inventions Department No. 3" of the National Cash Register Company at Dayton, Ohio. He then left to join his father in research to improve the composition and design of automobile tires, becoming chief engineer and superintendent of the Midgley Tires Company. The business did not prosper, and in 1916 Midgley obtained a job with the Dayton Engineering Laboratories Company (Delco), recently established by the inventor Charles F. Kettering (1876–1958). The two men formed a close scientific and personal association that lasted until Midgley's death.

Midgley's first major assignment for Kettering was to investigate the cause of "knock" in gasoline and kerosene engines, a noisy and sometimes destructive phenomenon that became worse as higher compressions were used in the cylinders and thus seriously limited the development of a more efficient engine. Working initially on the Delco-Light engine, a kerosene-powered generating unit designed to supply electric lighting to farmhouses, Midgley improvised a way of photographing the events that took place in the combustion chamber. Later he installed a quartz window in the cylinder so that he could actually see combustion taking place, and devised a high-speed indicator that enabled him to study the shape of the pressure waves produced. This work showed that the knock was not due to preignition, as had been supposed, but to a rapid increase of pressure after ignition had taken place. By accident he also discovered that the addition of iodine to kerosene (which he had used to dye the fluid red, thinking this might aid vaporization) greatly reduced the amount of knock.

With America's entry into World War I, this problem had to be put aside as Midgley concentrated on two projects: devising systems to control the direction of aerial torpedoes, and producing a gasoline that would increase the efficiency of the Liberty airplane engine. Fuel recovered from captured German planes proved to be a mixture of cyclohexane and benzene. Despite the adverse predictions of chemical experts, Midgley, working with scientists of the Bureau of Mines, found a way to produce cyclohexane by hydrogenation of benzene and developed a workable high-octane synthetic fuel, but the war ended before it or the robot bomb had gone into production.

Returning to the antiknock problem after the war, Midgley and his associates, working in Kettering's laboratory (which became in 1920 the General Motors Research Corporation), are said to have tried more than 33,000 different chemical compounds. The few that showed promise were either too expensive or had other disadvantages: tellurium and selenium compounds, for example, even in minute amounts imbued the workers with extremely repulsive garliclike odors. The experience gained during his war research had now convinced Midgley that knock was caused by the molecular structure of the fuel used. He therefore decided to abandon these hit-and-miss attempts and turned to the periodic arrangement of the elements. After long study he chose tetraethyl lead as the compound most likely to have the desired properties. Actual tests (Dec. 9, 1921) verified his prediction, and after two more years of research he found that the undesirable deposit of lead on the valves could be avoided by incorporating ethylene dibromide in the mixture. The first "Ethyl" gasoline went on sale in 1923.

There remained the problem of finding an adequate source of bromine to meet the large expected demand for the new gasoline. Midgley devised a technical procedure for extracting bromine from the ocean, which contains not more than one pound of bromine in ten tons of seawater, and the process was perfected by the Dow Chemical Company. Midgley also played a part in developing the large-scale manufacturing process

for the new gasoline additive, worked out in collaboration with the research staffs of the Du Pont Company and the Standard Oil Company of New Jersey. His discovery of an effective antiknock agent made possible the widespread use of high-compression automobile and airplane engines.

Midgley's other major contribution lay in the field of refrigerants. During the 1920's artificial refrigeration was coming into widespread use, but the gases used in refrigerating systems—ammonia, sulfur dioxide, and methyl chloride—were either toxic or flammable and hence hazardous in case of leakage or accident. At the request of the Frigidaire division of General Motors, Midgley sought to find a new chemical compound with suitable properties. Many of the compounds he tried were unstable; the inert gases would not do because their boiling points were too low. Again pondering the periodic arrangement of the elements, he concluded that an acceptable refrigerant would be found among the organic chlorofluorides, probably the substituted methanes—at first glance a strange choice, in view of the flammability of methane and the toxicity of chlorine and fluorine. He prepared dichlorodifluoromethane (1930) and found that it worked. Once on the right track, it is said, he completed the research in only three days. The product, called "Freon," quickly came into general use and greatly spurred the adoption of mechanical refrigeration and air conditioning.

Midgley also did significant research on synthetic rubbers at a time when natural rubber was in short supply. Though a drop in the price of natural rubber prevented any commercial use of his findings, which were published in nineteen research papers, they helped elucidate the structures of natural and synthetic rubber and the chemistry of vulcanization.

Midgley was an able salesman. In 1930, before a large audience, he dramatized the nontoxic and nonflammable properties of Freon vapor by inhaling a mouthful and slowly exhaling it over a lighted candle, which it extinguished. He had excellent business sense and served as vice-president of the Ethyl Corporation, organized in 1924 to prepare and market the new antiknock compound, and of Kinetic Chemicals, Inc. (which produced Freon), and as a director of the Ethyl-Dow Company, which extracted bromine from seawater. He held more than a hundred patents. A skilled if largely self-taught practical chemist, he was elected president of the American Chemical Society in 1944—the year of his death—having been chairman of its board of directors for a decade. He received honorary doctorates from the College of Wooster (1936) and Ohio State University (1944), and was elected to the National Academy of Sciences (1942). He received all the most important medals awarded for achievement in chemistry, including the Nichols (1923), Perkin (1937), Priestley (1941), and the Willard Gibbs (1942). A jovial, outgoing person, "fond of all sorts of people," he had many friends.

On Aug. 3, 1911, Midgley married Carrie May Reynolds of Worthington, Ohio; their children were Thomas Midgley III and Jane McNaughten Midgley. In the autumn of 1940 Midgley suffered an acute attack of poliomyelitis, which left him crippled. He continued for several years to direct work from his home at Worthington, near Columbus, and delivered his last speech, by telephone, to an audience in New York City only a few weeks before his death. He died at his home at the age of fifty-five, by accidentally strangling in the harness of cords and pulleys he had devised to assist him into and out of bed. He was buried in Greenlawn Cemetery, Columbus.

[The best biographical accounts are: Charles F. Kettering in Nat. Acad. Sci., *Biog. Memoirs,* vol. XXIV (1947), with photograph and a list of his publications; Thomas A. Boyd in *Jour. of the Am. Chemical Soc.,* June 24, 1953 (with list of publications); and Williams Haynes in Eduard Farber, ed., *Great Chemists* (1961), pp. 1589–97 (with photograph and bibliography). See also Robert E. Wilson's presentation address of the Perkin Medal, *Industrial and Engineering Chemistry,* Feb. 1937 (this issue also contains Midgley's Perkin Lecture, "From the Periodic Table to Production"); T. A. Boyd, *Professional Amateur: The Biog. of Charles Franklin Kettering* (1957); and, on the development of tetraethyl lead and Freon, Williams Haynes, *Am. Chemical Industry,* IV (1948), 396–405, and V (1954), 181–85.]

RALPH E. OESPER

MILLER, DAYTON CLARENCE (Mar. 13, 1866–Feb. 23, 1941), physicist, was born on his father's farm in Strongsville, Ohio. He was the oldest of the four sons and one daughter of Charles Webster Dewey Miller and Vienna (Pomeroy) Miller, both of New England descent. When he was eight, his father gave up farming and moved to Berea, Ohio, where he prospered as a hardware merchant and the organizer of a street railway. Dayton attended the public schools and the German Methodist Sunday school. His parents were both musical—his mother was a church organist and his father sang in the choir—and Dayton as a boy was strongly interested in both music and astronomy, playing the organ and flute and building his own telescopes.

After receiving the Ph.B. degree in 1886 from Baldwin College in Berea, he worked for a year in a bank owned by relatives. He disliked business and considered studying music at the Oberlin Conservatory, but chose instead to begin graduate work in astronomy under Charles A. Young [*q.v.*] at Princeton University. This study was interrupted by a year's teaching at Baldwin, where he took an M.A. degree in 1889. Returning to Princeton, he received the D.Sc. degree in 1890 with a thesis on the orbit and elements of Comet 1889V. Miller had expected to continue at Princeton as the Thaw research fellow in astronomy, but since the large glass prisms required for his research were not yet finished, he accepted a one-year appointment to teach mathematics and descriptive geometry at the Case School of Applied Science in Cleveland. There he remained for the rest of his life, transferring to the physics department in 1892. A distinguished teacher and lecturer, Miller made important innovations in physics curricula and teaching methods. His textbook, *Laboratory Physics* (1903), remained a standard work for more than thirty years. At Case, he developed one of the first programs to grant degrees for undergraduate concentration in physics, and his students included many who later became leaders in American physics.

Some of Miller's earliest physics experiments, made in 1896, dealt with the newly discovered X-rays, which he used to disclose the position of bones in a broken arm and the shape of impacted teeth—perhaps the first medical use of X-rays in the United States. His most important research, however, stemmed directly from his lifelong devotion to music. Seeking to determine how the physical characteristics of a tone were related to its musical qualities, he developed (1908) a very precise instrument, called the phonodeik ("to show sound"), to record sound waves photographically. To analyze the photographic records of tones produced by musical instruments, especially the flute, he developed harmonic analyzers and synthesizers of high precision. He used the same methods to determine the characteristics of vowel sounds, and showed for the first time that their character depends upon the resonance frequency of specific air volumes in the head and not on the pitch at which the vowel is spoken or sung, thus confirming the fixed-pitch theory of Helmholtz.

Miller also carried out research in optics in collaboration with Edward W. Morley [*q.v.*]. In 1904 they repeated the Michelson-Morley "etherdrift" experiment of 1887, which had sought to test the theory that a medium (called "ether") filled outer space and was the means by which light was transmitted. After the apparent confirmation of Einstein's general theory of relativity by the solar eclipse expeditions of 1919, Miller was encouraged to repeat the Michelson-Morley-Miller experiment at a high elevation, and in 1921, on the invitation of George E. Hale [Supp. 2], he went to the Mount Wilson Observatory. Observations were difficult in the lightweight laboratory hut, but with his superb experimental skill Miller was able to obtain a vast amount of data for many sidereal epochs during an entire year, 1925–26. His results revealed anomalous periodic shifts of the interference fringes, which he interpreted as evidence for the existence of an ether. Computer analysis of this great body of data after Miller's death proved that although the shifts were statistically significant, they were not due to an ether-drift but rather to very small temperature gradients across the interferometer which displaced the fringes. When Miller's data were reanalyzed to take account of this temperature factor, they were shown to support the postulates of the special theory of relativity.

Miller's interest in music and his friendship with Wallace C. Sabine [q.v.] led him into the science of architectural acoustics, in which he became a leading authority. He helped determine the acoustical design of a large number of buildings, including the chapels of Princeton University, the University of Chicago, and Bryn Mawr College, as well as Severance Hall, the home of the Cleveland Orchestra. Miller was himself a skilled musical performer, particularly on the flute. He was also an avid collector. Over the years he assembled nearly 1,500 flutes, together with an extensive collection of books relating to the flute; both collections were left by his will to the Music Division of the Library of Congress.

Miller married Edith C. Easton of Princeton, N. J., on June 28, 1893; they had no children. He took an active part in scientific organizations, served as president of the American Physical Society (1925–26) and the Acoustical Society of America (1931–33), and was elected to the National Academy of Sciences (1921). His books include *The Science of Musical Sounds* (1916); *Sound Waves: Their Shape and Speed* (1937); and *The Flute* (1935), an annotated bibliography of his collection. Active in his laboratory until the end of his life, he died at his Cleveland home at the age of seventy-four of a myocardial infarct. He was buried in Lake View Cemetery, Cleveland.

[Memoir by R. S. Shankland in *Am. Jour. of Physics*, Oct. 1941 (with bibliography of Miller's publications); R. S. Shankland, S. W. McCuskey, et al., "New Analysis of the Interferometer Observations of Dayton C. Miller," *Revs. of Modern Physics*, Apr. 1955. See also the brief memoir by Harvey Fletcher in Nat. Acad. Sci., *Biog. Memoirs*, vol. XXIII (1945); W. F. G. Swann in Am. Philosophical Soc., *Year*

Book, 1941; J. J. Nassau in *Case Alumnus*, May–June 1936; and William J. Maynard, "Dayton C. Miller: His Life, Work, and Contributions as a Scientist and Organologist" (M.S.L.S. thesis, Palmer Graduate Lib. School, Long Island Univ., 1971). Family data from census schedules of 1870 and 1880 (courtesy of State Lib. of Ohio); death record from Ohio Dept. of Health. A portrait of Miller by Rolf Stoll is in the Rockefeller Laboratory of Physics at Case Western Reserve Univ.]

R. S. SHANKLAND

MILLER, GLENN (Mar. 1, 1904–Dec. 15?, 1944), dance orchestra conductor of the "big band" era, was born in Clarinda, Iowa. Christened Alton Glenn Miller, he was the second of four children of Lewis Elmer Miller, a building contractor, and Mattie Lou (Cavender) Miller. Never prosperous, the family moved to North Platte, Nebr., and Grant City, Mo.; by the time Glenn reached high school they had settled in Fort Morgan, Colo. There he learned to play the trombone well enough to work for a time with a professional band. He then enrolled at the University of Colorado, but left after two years for the West Coast to join Max Fisher's band. In 1925 he moved to the dance orchestra of Ben Pollack, a talented group (one of the featured players was a young clarinetist named Benny Goodman) for which Miller wrote many arrangements. Two years later he accepted a job with the popular show orchestra of Paul Ash, which was playing in New York's Paramount Theatre. Miller married his college sweetheart, Helen Burger, on Oct. 6, 1928, and settled in New York City, where he studied arranging with Joseph Schillinger [Supp. 3].

Leaving Ash, Miller worked for a time in radio and recording studios in New York and as trombonist and arranger for Red Nichols and His Five Pennies; with this famed jazz group he also appeared in the pit of two Gershwin musical comedies of 1930, *Strike Up the Band* and *Girl Crazy*. His growing reputation led two fellow studio musicians, Tommy and Jimmy Dorsey, to ask Miller to help them organize a band in the spring of 1934. The Dorsey Brothers orchestra, playing a great many Miller arrangements and with Miller in the trombone section, became one of the most sparkling organizations during the days directly preceding the big band era. In 1935 Miller formed an American orchestra for Ray Noble, an English conductor, and wrote some of its arrangements. But Noble was also an arranger, and the two often squabbled about interpretations; late in 1936 Miller decided to organize his own band.

His first outfit, formed in March 1937, achieved little success and after ten months was disbanded. With encouragement from Tommy

Dorsey, Miller tried again in March 1938. By this time he had worked out the definite musical style so essential to the success of an orchestra. With a clarinet and a tenor saxophone doubling on the melody line, his five-man reed section produced a clear, liquid, and highly identifiable sound. Their long phrasing was somewhat in the manner of Miller's friend and fellow trombonist Tommy Dorsey, whom he greatly admired. Miller also admired the brass section of Jimmie Lunceford's band, whose "oo-wah" style (achieved by waving plastic derby hats in front of the horns) he adopted, along with some of Lunceford's showmanly visual tricks. He also took up the swinging four-beat riff-filled style of the Count Basie band, though Miller's tight, carefully rehearsed arrangements were sometimes criticized for lacking the spontaneity and warmth of jazz.

Miller's new style began to impress band bookers, and in March 1939 he received his big break: a summer engagement at the Glen Island Casino in New Rochelle, N. Y., with its frequent coast-to-coast radio broadcasts. Acclaim came almost instantly. For the next three years the band played to enthusiastic crowds in leading hotels, ballrooms, and theatres, appeared on a thrice-weekly radio show, made two motion pictures— *Sun Valley Serenade* (1941) and *Orchestra Wives* (1942)—and recorded for RCA Victor records such hits as "Moonlight Serenade" (Miller's theme song), "In the Mood," "Little Brown Jug," and "Tuxedo Junction." Vocals by Marion Hutton, Ray Eberle, Tex Beneke, and the "Modernaires" enhanced the band's romantic sound.

Less than five years after its formation, the Glenn Miller Orchestra played its last engagement on Sept. 27, 1942. Miller, though his age made him exempt from the draft, felt a moral obligation to serve his country in wartime and joined the Army Air Forces. He was assigned the job of putting together a special Air Force band. Drawing on drafted musicians—former members of leading dance orchestras, symphony string players—he assembled a band that played for marching cadets, for troop entertainments, and on a radio recruiting program. Miller's wish to perform for America's fighting forces overseas was finally granted, and in June 1944 his large entourage flew to England. After six months there the group was scheduled to fly to Paris. Miller set off from England on Dec. 15 in a small Air Force plane to make advance arrangements, but the weather was bad and the plane disappeared without trace. He was survived by his wife and their adopted son and daughter, Steven and Jonnie.

With his steel-rimmed glasses and sober, sedate appearance, Glenn Miller looked more like a schoolteacher than a showman. He was, however, a thorough musician and an able administrator who knew what he wanted to achieve and would rehearse endlessly to get it. In an age that included such popular bands as those of Benny Goodman and Tommy Dorsey, Glenn Miller had a wide and enduring following. After the war, although the era of the big bands had passed, his orchestra was twice revived, led first by Tex Beneke and later by Ray McKinley and then by Buddy De Franco. A moving picture, *The Glenn Miller Story* (1953), attested to his hold on the popular imagination, and a quarter century after his death his recordings were still being reissued.

[George T. Simon, *The Big Bands* (1967); Stephen F. Bedwell, *A Glenn Miller Discography* (rev. ed., 1956); *Metronome*, Mar. 1936, p. 17; *N. Y. Times*, Dec. 25, 1944; *Who Was Who in America*, vol. II (1950); personal acquaintance. See also: *Current Biog.*, 1942; Irving Kolodin in *Saturday Rev.*, Nov. 28, 1953, Oct. 8, 1955; obituary of Mrs. Miller in *N. Y. Times*, June 5, 1966.]

GEORGE T. SIMON

MITCHELL, ALBERT GRAEME (Feb. 21, 1889–June 1, 1941), pediatric educator, was born in Salem, Mass., the only child of Fred Albert and Maria (Graham) Mitchell. His father, a bookkeeper, was a native of Maine; his mother, of Ireland. During the boy's early childhood the family moved to Philadelphia. He attended the local public schools and after graduating from Central High School entered the medical school of the University of Pennsylvania, receiving the M.D. degree in 1910. After two years of internship and residency in the Presbyterian Hospital and the Babies Hospital of Philadelphia, he accompanied a prominent Philadelphian (George W. Childs Drexel) and his family on a long tour of Europe and the Near East, spent a few months in graduate study at the Harvard Medical School, and then opened a private practice in pediatrics in Philadelphia. When the United States became involved in World War I, he enlisted in the Army Medical Corps and saw active service in France.

After leaving the army in 1919, Mitchell resumed private practice in Philadelphia. He was also an instructor (later associate) at the University of Pennsylvania, in the department of pediatrics at the Children's Hospital. On Oct. 2, 1920, Mitchell married Adele Florence Wentz, daughter of a Philadelphia physician. They had twin daughters, Marie Graeme and Kathryn Wentz.

Mitchell had never been satisfied with his role as a private practitioner and part-time teacher. He therefore gladly accepted an invitation in

1924 to succeed Kenneth D. Blackfan [Supp. 3] as Rachford Professor and head of the department of pediatrics at the University of Cincinnati. The concept was then just beginning to emerge that teachers of clinical subjects should devote full time to their courses, and the appointment gave Mitchell a unique opportunity. With the strong support of William Cooper Proctor, then president of the board of trustees of the Children's Hospital in Cincinnati, Mitchell was able to develop a pediatric unit that by the time of his death had become preeminent.

Mitchell was responsible for the development and guidance of the Children's Hospital Research Foundation, but he himself was mainly interested in clinical problems, in teaching, and in the coordination of community health services for children. He instituted strict measures to control the spread of infection among patients in the hospital wards. His organization of the pediatric services in the Cincinnati area stands as a model for unified community health facilities established within a teaching and research framework. In addition to the centralized ambulatory and inpatient services in the contiguous units of the Children's Hospital, the General Hospital, and the Contagious Disease Hospital, this organization included district clinics (locally termed Babies' Milk Fund stations) distributed throughout the poorer sections of the city, the Children's Convalescent Home, and the hospital of the Ohio Soldiers' and Sailors' Orphans' Home at Xenia, Ohio. Each of these units provided material for research and for the training of pediatric interns and residents.

Apart from these departmental duties, Mitchell took an active role in local, state, and national medical affairs. He was a member of the Cincinnati Board of Health (1926–30), a consultant to the Ohio State Board of Health, a participant in the 1929 and 1940 White House conferences on children, and a principal consultant of the National Foundation for Infantile Paralysis. He was the first pediatrician to be appointed to the National Board of Medical Examiners and was thus able to exert wide influence on pediatric education.

Mitchell served on the editorial board of the *American Journal of Diseases of Children* and was pediatric editor of the *Cyclopedia of Medicine* (13 vols., 1934–37). Alone or with collaborators he wrote more than 150 papers, and with Echo K. Upham and Elgie M. Wallinger he published *Pediatrics and Pediatric Nursing* (1939). His most important contribution to the literature was his part in preparing the second edition of *The Diseases of Infants and Children* (2 vols., 1927),

the first edition of which (1919) had been written by J. P. Crozer Griffith, a former colleague at the University of Pennsylvania. Though subsequent revisions, including single-volume editions in 1933, 1937, and 1941 under the title *Textbook of Pediatrics*, were largely the work of Mitchell, the text continued to bear the names of both authors.

Mitchell's interests were not confined to his specialty. An amateur artist, he displayed marked craftsmanship in watercolors, etchings, and drypoint engravings. He made a notable collection of medical caricatures, drawings, and colored lithographs by such artists as Rowlandson, Daumier, and Hogarth. He was also a noted raconteur and wrote occasional essays in humorous or philosophic vein under the pseudonym "Dr. Pottlesmith." Through these means he found outlets for his restlessness and his dynamic energy. He liked people, and his ability to instill confidence in others made him a leader in pediatric affairs. Perhaps Mitchell's most important contribution was the stimulus he gave to his students, residents, and colleagues, who later regarded his years in the department as a "golden era." Mitchell was an Episcopalian and a Republican. He died at the Children's Hospital in Cincinnati of coronary disease at the age of fifty-two, and was buried in Arlington Cemetery, Drexel Hill, Pa.

[John F. Cronin and Robert A. Lyon, *Albert Graeme Mitchell* (1964); biographical sketch by W. E. Nelson in Borden S. Veeder, ed., *Pediatric Profiles* (1957); *Nat. Cyc. Am. Biog.*, XLII, 309–10. Mitchell's birth record (Mass. Registrar of Vital Statistics) gives his birth date as Feb. 21, 1889; other sources, including his death record (Ohio Dept. of Health), agree on Feb. 22.]

WALDO E. NELSON

MITCHELL, SIDNEY ZOLLICOFFER (Mar. 17, 1862–Feb. 17, 1944), public utility executive, was born in Dadeville, Ala., the youngest of the three sons of William Mandon Alexander Mitchell, a physician, and Elmira (Jordan) Mitchell. On both sides of the family he came of old Virginia stock, his forebears having moved west to the cotton kingdom of antebellum Alabama. His mother died when he was three, and Sidney and his brothers were brought up on the nearby plantation of their widowed maternal grandmother, Ann (Spivey) Jordan, a well-educated woman who came of a long line of Presbyterian ministers. Because local schools were of poor quality, he received his early education chiefly from her. At the age of seventeen, to prepare for a competitive examination for the United States Naval Academy, he spent six months at Colonel Slade's School in Columbus, Ga. He was admitted to Annapolis and, after graduating in 1883, spent two years at sea, during which time he installed a pioneer incandescent lighting system aboard the U.S.S. *Trenton*.

Upon receiving his commission in 1885, Mitchell resigned from the navy to work for Thomas A. Edison [Supp. 1], who had recently opened his Pearl Street electric generating plant in New York City. After a short but intensive management training program in which he learned every facet of the fledgling electric power industry, Mitchell went to Seattle, Wash., as Edison's sales agent for the Pacific Northwest. Since there were as yet no electric plants in this part of the country, Mitchell had to create a market for Edison products by organizing electric companies and helping them plan and install their equipment. He began with companies in Seattle and Tacoma, and in 1886 he established the Northwest Electric Supply and Construction Company, which over the next two years organized thirteen electric lighting companies in Washington, Oregon, Idaho, and British Columbia.

Responding to mounting demands for electric service and to such technological innovations as the changeover from direct to alternating current, Mitchell became increasingly absorbed in the problem of financing the expansion and modernization of existing facilities. He was among the first to recognize that because electric utilities had to attract new consumers by offering low rates, they could not, in contrast to other businesses, finance growth from retained earnings; they required from four to eight dollars of investment capital for every dollar of annual gross revenue. Mitchell's major task, therefore, was to find new sources of capital. The merger of the Edison companies in 1892 with the Thomson-Houston Company brought into being the General Electric Company, which for a time had surplus capital, but the depression of 1893 dried up this source. Capital might have been raised by forming new companies, but Mitchell was convinced that increased competition would generate losses to producers without benefiting the consumer. Indeed, he favored the consolidation of existing electric companies in order to eliminate wasteful competition, increase efficiency, and make utilities more attractive to potential investors. After handling one such consolidation, of the Tacoma Railway & Power Company, for Boston financial interests led by the engineering firm of Stone & Webster [see Charles A. Stone, Supp. 3], Mitchell left General Electric in 1902 to head the Tacoma company.

He returned to General Electric in 1905 to help set up and manage the Electric Bond & Share Company, which Charles Coffin [*q.v.*],

president of General Electric, was organizing in New York City. Its purpose was to convert unsalable securities of operating companies, received in partial payment for electrical apparatus, into marketable assets. To improve the management of these companies, most of which served small cities and towns, Mitchell assembled a group of engineers, managers, rate experts, and lawyers who for a fee gave them the advantage of advice previously available only to large concerns. Under his direction, the service staff of Bond & Share pioneered in a number of technological innovations, the most important of which was the integration of scattered systems and the use of generating plants large enough to take advantage of diversity of load conditions.

Drawing on his previous experience in the Pacific Northwest, Mitchell consolidated a number of small, contiguous operating companies, enabling them to take advantage of large, centrally located turbine generators, and then organized subholding companies under Bond & Share to manage their financial affairs. His enterprises expanded rapidly, and by 1924 the Bond & Share system controlled more than 10 percent of the nation's electric utility business. It included among its major holdings American Gas & Electric Company (1906), of which Mitchell was chairman of the board, 1906–23 and 1926–33; American Power & Light Company (1909); and National Power & Light Company (1921). Mitchell later organized the Electric Power & Light Corporation (1925), and in 1923, at the request of the State Department, he established the American & Foreign Power Company, which controlled electric utilities chiefly in Latin America. With the exception of the last, Bond & Share did not own a majority interest in any of its subholding or operating companies. This may be taken either as a sign of restraint or as an illustration of the evil of "pyramiding," which made control possible without majority ownership.

How effective holding companies were in promoting economies through common management of widely separated utilities is a matter of controversy. They were widely accused of "milking" operating companies through excessive fees; criticism of this sort persuaded General Electric in 1925 to give up its controlling interest in Bond & Share. As a device for financing further expansion, however, the holding company was a success; it attracted new investment capital through the principle of economic leverage, which greatly enhanced the potential value of its common stock. Mitchell also brought new capital into the utilities industry through such techniques as open-end mortgages, unsecured debentures that matured in a hundred years, option warrants that permitted the owner of debentures and preferred stock to purchase common stock at a later date, and campaigns to promote the sale of preferred stock to small investors. When the depression of 1929 shook the financial stability of public utilities, many of these devices were criticized as having contributed to the development of an unsound business structure, and some were later outlawed by such New Deal legislation as the Public Utility Holding Company Act (1935). As the head of the largest electric utility holding company in the country, Mitchell was especially vulnerable to such criticism, but his companies, in contrast to those of Samuel Insull [Supp. 2], were relatively free of abuses.

Mitchell retired in 1933 and devoted most of his remaining days to hunting in Alabama, a lifelong avocation. On Oct. 25, 1893, he had married Alice Pennoyer Bell of Portland, Oreg., by whom he had one son, Sidney Alexander. After the death of his first wife in 1941, he married in 1942 Neva Fenno Palmer, a widowed neighbor in Mountain Lake, Fla. A year and a half later Mitchell died of a heart attack at his Fifth Avenue home in New York City. He was buried in Portland, Oreg.

[Sidney Alexander Mitchell, *S. Z. Mitchell and the Electrical Industry* (1960); Curtis E. Calder, *"S. Z.": Sidney Z. Mitchell (1862–1944), Electrical Pioneer* (Newcomen Soc., 1950); *N. Y. Times*, Feb. 19, 1944; Sidney Z. Mitchell, *Superpower—the Name and the Facts* (1926), an address before the Bond Club of N. Y. See also J. C. Bonbright and Gardiner C. Means, *The Holding Company* (1932); Merwin H. Waterman, *Economic Implications of Public Utility Holding Company Operations* (1941); "The Curb and Its Own EBS," *Fortune*, June 1932; and Federal Trade Commission, *Utility Corporations* (96 parts, 1928–37), especially parts 23 and 24.]

JOHN ALDEN BLISS

MOFFAT, JAY PIERREPONT (July 18, 1896–Jan. 24, 1943), diplomat, was born in Rye, N. Y., the eldest of three children (two boys and a girl) of Reuben Burnham Moffat, a prosperous lawyer in New York City, and Ellen Low (Pierrepont) Moffat. His father was descended from an early eighteenth-century Scottish settler near Woodbridge, N. J.; his mother's forebears included John Jay and John Pierpont [*qq.v.*]. Having contracted tuberculosis in his early teens, young Moffat spent two years of prescribed rest in Switzerland before entering Groton School in Massachusetts. He graduated in 1913 and, following a period of recuperation in the Adirondacks, enrolled in 1915 at Harvard.

When the United States entered World War I, Moffat applied for military service but was rejected because of his poor health record. He had

earlier decided upon a career in the foreign service, and he now looked there for a place to make his wartime contribution. Leaving Harvard in 1917, he arranged, through family connections, to become private secretary to John W. Garrett, the American minister to the Netherlands. An unpaid position without official rank, it was nevertheless a useful apprenticeship. In 1919, after passing the foreign service examinations, Moffat was sent to Warsaw as third secretary of the American legation. Assignments to Japan (1921–23) and to Turkey (1923–25) followed.

Moffat's next duty was as protocol officer at the White House. He considered the assignment dull, but enjoyed the social life in Washington. There he met Lilla Cabot Grew, daughter of Under Secretary of State Joseph C. Grew. They were married on July 27, 1927, and had two children: Edith Alice Pierrepont and Peter Jay Pierrepont. A few months after his marriage Moffat went to Bern, Switzerland, where for the next four years he was first secretary of the legation. At Bern he participated in the League of Nations Preparatory Commission for the Disarmament Conference, quickly becoming expert on disarmament matters.

Moffat returned in 1931 to Washington, where he briefed officials for participation in the Geneva Disarmament Conference. In 1932 he was appointed chief of the Western European Division of the State Department, the Secretary's principal adviser on West European affairs. When the rise of militarism in Japan and Nazi Germany frustrated Moffat's hopes for disarmament, he accepted in 1935 the post of consul general in Sydney, Australia, in keeping with the rule which required all foreign service officers to spend time in the field after four consecutive years in Washington. In Sydney he worked to assuage bitterness over an unfavorable balance of trade with the United States. Moffat returned to the State Department in 1937 as chief of the newly created Division of European Affairs, an office that combined the functions of the old divisions of Eastern and Western European Affairs and part of the Near Eastern Division. He was thus one of the small group of State Department officials who guided America's response to the events leading up to World War II. A cautious internationalist who believed in limited American involvement in measures for collective security, Moffat resented such State Department activists as Ambassador William E. Dodd [Supp. 2], believing that their outspokenness complicated diplomatic relations.

Moffat accompanied Under Secretary of State Sumner Welles in 1940 on his mission to discuss with warring European nations the possibilities of a peaceful settlement. The mission was thwarted when Germany overran France. Shortly thereafter, in June 1940, Moffat was appointed American minister to Canada, a country which, after the fall of France, was increasingly important as an arsenal for Great Britain and as a possible haven for the British fleet. This was a sensitive assignment that involved coordinating the defense preparations of Canada and the United States. Moffat's career was cut short in 1943, at the age of forty-six, when he died at the legation residence in Ottawa of a coronary embolism following an operation for phlebitis. His ashes were buried in the town cemetery at Hancock, N. H.

A dependable and highly skilled adviser, Moffat had been widely regarded as one of the ablest career officers in the Foreign Service. His extensive correspondence with other diplomats and the voluminous diary in which he recorded the activities of the State Department during the 1930's constitute an important historical source.

[Moffat's papers, including correspondence, memoranda, and diplomatic journals, are in the Houghton Lib., Harvard Univ. Nancy Harrison Hooker, ed., *The Moffat Papers: Selections from the Diplomatic Journals of Jay Pierrepont Moffat, 1919–43* (1956), is drawn from the papers and includes a biographical introduction. Other information from: State Dept. Personnel File on Jay Pierrepont Moffat; *Biog. Register of the Dept. of State, 1942; Who Was Who in America,* vol. II (1950); *N. Y. Times* obituary, Jan. 25, 1943; and from Moffat's brother, Abbot Low Moffat. On his ancestry see R. Burnham Moffat, *Pierrepont Genealogies* (1913).]
JOHN D. HICKERSON

MOFFATT, JAMES (July 4, 1870–June 27, 1944), biblical scholar and church historian, was born in Glasgow, Scotland, the eldest son of George and Isabella Simpson (Morton) Moffatt. His father was a chartered accountant and an elder in the Church of Scotland. The family being of comfortable means, young Moffatt was educated at the Glasgow Academy and the University of Glasgow, from which he graduated with honors in classics in 1889. He then entered the United Free Church College in Glasgow to train for the ministry, graduating in 1894 at the head of his class. He was ordained in 1896 and called to a church in Dundonald, a fishing village on the Atlantic coast. On Sept. 29 of that year he married Mary Reith of Aberdeen; their four children were George Stuart, Eric Morton, Margaret Skelton, and James Archibald Reith. Moffatt moved to a larger church at Broughty-Ferry on the North Sea in 1907.

He had early begun the scholarly writing that was to distinguish his career. His first book, *The Historical New Testament* (1901), and his

translation of Adolf von Harnack's *The Expansion of Christianity in the First Three Centuries* (2 vols., 1904–05) reflected his two areas of interest, biblical scholarship and church history. In 1911 he published *An Introduction to the Literature of the New Testament,* which firmly established him in the scholarly world. During the next four years he served as Yates Professor of Greek and New Testament Exegesis at Mansfield College, Oxford, while continuing his ministerial duties at Broughty-Ferry. In 1915 he relinquished his parish and returned to the United Free Church College as professor of church history, a position he held for the next twelve years.

The work for which Moffatt is most widely remembered is his translation of the Bible, a monumental achievement. His initial venture in this direction grew out of his book *The Historical New Testament.* To accompany his text, he had wished to reprint passages from the English Revised Version of the New Testament (prepared by a group of English scholars and published in 1881). Finding it difficult, however, to secure the necessary permission, he resolved to make his own translation, in the hope that his fresh rendering would demonstrate to the layman the progressive changes taking place in biblical scholarship and at the same time convey something of the homely quality of the original. Defending his version against the advocates of literal translation, he commented, "If a translator's first duty is to reproduce his text as exactly as possible, his final duty is to write English."

Moffatt's translation of the complete New Testament appeared in 1913. His version of the Old Testament came out in two volumes in 1924–25, and in 1926 the two were issued together. Though critics on the whole found his work on the New Testament superior to that on the Old, their reaction was generally negative. While some tended to agree that his translation might, as he hoped, make the Old Testament "more interesting perhaps and less obscure," others charged him with overdependence on German scholarship, with transposing passages, and even with "stark vulgarity."

In 1927, hoping to divert his research toward history, Moffatt accepted an appointment as Washburn Professor of Church History at the Union Theological Seminary in New York City. Although his major critical studies dealing with the New Testament had been completed, he produced studies of selected New Testament writings after coming to the United States, together with several works in church history. As a lecturer he was in great demand. Following his official retirement from Union (1938), he continued to give lectures but devoted a major portion of his time to his work as executive secretary of the American Standard Bible Committee, which had undertaken to revise its Bible translation of 1901 in the light of recent scholarship. Moffatt's work in coordinating the efforts of this diverse group of scholars, which in 1946 produced the well-known Revised Standard Version of the Bible, was extensive, effective, and largely unacknowledged. The text of the New Testament was virtually completed before his death.

Moffatt was tall, slender, and erect in carriage, his long neck accentuated by a loose-fitting clerical collar. Through rather large spectacles his eyes had a look of "surprised innocence," with a smile "sometimes quick, yet, for the most part, breaking slowly and gradually" (Gossip, p. 14). In his later years he appeared considerably younger than his actual age. He had a capacity for warmth and affection, but his quiet and unpretentious manner tended to make him seem aloof and unemotional. Reinhold Niebuhr, his colleague at Union Theological Seminary for fifteen years, described Moffatt's prodigious capacity for work. At the same time, however, he pursued other interests, ranging from the writings of Dickens, Matthew Arnold, and J. M. Barrie to detective stories, trout fishing, and watching the New York Yankees.

Moffatt died of a heart attack in his home in New York City a few days before his seventy-fourth birthday. Funeral services were held at Union Theological Seminary, and after cremation the ashes were returned to Scotland for burial. Moffatt is remembered chiefly for his translation of the Bible, although its final influence has been limited; of greater importance is his work on the Revised Standard Version. His *Introduction to the Literature of the New Testament,* the most durable of his writings, remains a milestone in New Testament studies.

[Arthur Porritt, *More and More of Memories* (1947), pp. 146–59; Alexander Gammie, *Preachers I Have Heard* (1945), pp. 89–91; A. J. Gossip in the *Expository Times,* LVI (1944–45), 14–17; Reinhold Niebuhr in *British Weekly,* CXVI (1944), 227; Luther A. Weigle et al., *An Introduction to the Revised Standard Version of the New Testament* (1946); obituaries in London *Times,* June 29, 1944, and *N. Y. Times,* June 28, 1944; *Who Was Who in America,* vol. II (1950); sketch of Moffatt in *Dict. Nat. Biog.,* 1941–50 volume. For reviewers' comments on Moffatt's Bible translation, see *Fortnightly Rev.* (London), Feb. 1925, pp. 246–54; *Bibliotheca Sacra,* Oct. 1925, pp. 462–71; and *Current Opinion,* Feb. 1925, pp. 214–15.]
MAX GRAY ROGERS

MOISSEIFF, LEON SOLOMON (Nov. 10, 1872–Sept. 3, 1943), bridge engineer, was born in Riga, Latvia (then part of the Russian empire), the only child of Jewish parents, Solomon and Anna (Bloch) Moisseiff, whose families had been natives of the Baltic area for several generations. His father was a merchant. Leon attended the Emperor Alexander Gymnasium (1880–87) and the Baltic Polytechnic Institute (1889–91), both in Riga. In 1891 the family emigrated to the United States, having been compelled to leave their native land because of the young student's activities in liberal organizations, and settled in New York City. Leon Moisseiff enrolled in Columbia University in 1892, graduating with the degree of civil engineer in 1895, and received his citizenship in 1896.

Typical of the talented young graduate searching for his métier, Moisseiff held a variety of positions in his first professional years. He began as a draftsman with the New York Rapid Transit Railroad Commission, became a designing engineer with the Dutton Pneumatic Lock and Engineering Company in 1896, then returned to the position of draftsman with the Bronx Department of Street Improvements the following year. Less than a year later he found work more suitable to his abilities: he joined the New York Department of Bridges as chief draftsman and assistant designer, a position which he held from 1898 to 1910, and then moved up to the level of engineer of design, where he remained until 1915. During this period the three East River bridges following the Brooklyn span were constructed—the Williamsburg (opened 1903), Queensboro (1908), and Manhattan (1909)—and Moisseiff was consequently associated with their design.

The experience thus gained emboldened him to try his own hand, and in 1915 he established an independent office as a consulting engineer. This marked the beginning of a career that was to take him to the very top of his profession as the designing engineer for a number of the largest and most spectacular bridges in the world. By 1920 Moisseiff was sufficiently well known to be appointed chief designer of the Delaware River Bridge at Philadelphia, which remained the major project of his office until the span was completed in 1926. From this date until 1940 his name was associated as consulting engineer of design with many of the greatest works of the bridge-building art, among them the George Washington at New York City (1927–31); the Bayonne or Kill van Kull, between Staten Island and Bayonne, N. J. (1928–31); the Ambassador, Detroit (1928–30); the Maumee River or Anthony Wayne, Toledo (1929–32);

the Triborough, New York City (1934–36); renewal work on the older East River group (1934–37); the Bronx-Whitestone, New York City (1936–39); the Tacoma Narrows, Tacoma, Wash. (1938–40); and the Mackinac Strait Bridge Authority (1938–40). Although he did not always receive formal credit, Moisseiff was the principal designer of the George Washington, Bronx-Whitestone, Tacoma Narrows, and Mackinac bridges.

During the middle years of this period he acted as a member of the board of consulting engineers for the two huge San Francisco bridges, the Golden Gate (1929–37, construction beginning in 1933) and San Francisco-Oakland Bay (1931–37, construction also beginning in 1933). Of the various bridges with which Moisseiff was associated, all but one (the Kill van Kull arch) were suspension structures, characterized by successively longer spans. The Tacoma Narrows Bridge was destroyed by wind in November of the year it was opened as a result of the aerodynamic instability of the plate-girder stiffening structure, but neither Moisseiff nor any of the other engineers can be charged with irresponsibility in this totally unexpected failure. It led Moisseiff, however, to devote the remaining three years of his life to an investigation of aerodynamic problems and to a reexamination of the fundamental assumptions and principles underlying the design of suspension bridges. The Mackinac Strait Bridge was not built until 1954–57, and the office of David B. Steinman was placed in charge of design and construction.

Moisseiff was appointed consulting engineer to the Soviet Commissariat of Transportation in 1929, a position which he held until 1932 but which did not require his continuous presence in Russia. He acted as a consultant on structural design for the Century of Progress Exposition in Chicago in 1931–33 (the exposition was held in 1933–34) and was specifically involved in the design of the Travel and Transport Pavilion, the first building to be constructed with a cable-suspended roof. Moisseiff made a valuable contribution to engineering literature early in his career when he translated Armand Considère's *Experimental Researches on Reinforced Concrete* (1906). He was the author of numerous papers published in engineering and scientific journals on individual suspension bridges, cable wire, the action of bridges under lateral forces, the properties of high-strength steels, the theory of elastic stability, and the characteristics of aluminum bridges.

By 1930 Moisseiff's achievements in the design of long-span bridges had earned him a worldwide reputation, and in the following decade his adopted country offered him a steady flow of honors and prizes. Among them were the Lewis E. Levy Medal of the Franklin Institute (1933), for his paper "The Design, Materials and Erection of the Kill van Kull Arch," which had been published in its *Journal* the previous year; the George H. Norman Medal (1934) and the James Laurie Prize (1939) of the American Society of Civil Engineers; Columbia University's Egleston Medal (1933) for distinguished achievement in engineering; and the Modern Pioneer Award (1940) of the National Association of Manufacturers.

On Jan. 5, 1893, while a student at Columbia, Moisseiff had married Ida Assinofsky. They had three children, two daughters, Liberty and Grace, and a son, Siegfried. In his private life Moisseiff was known for his wide learning and cultivated taste in music, the graphic arts, and the literatures of many languages, indications of a curiosity and sensitivity on the personal scale that paralleled the combination of daring imagination and great accuracy of detail in his engineering designs. His immensely productive life ended at the age of seventy with a heart attack suffered at his summer home in Belmar, N. J. He was buried in Cedar Grove Cemetery, Flushing, N. Y.

[Memoir in Am. Soc. of Civil Engineers, *Transactions*, CXI (1946), 1509–12; obituaries in *Civil Engineering*, Oct. 1943, and *Engineering News-Record*, Sept. 9, 23, 1943; *Who's Who in Am. Jewry*, 1938–39; *Who Was Who in America*, vol. II (1950). See also, on Moisseiff's engineering work, Carl W. Condit, *Am. Building Art: The Twentieth Century* (1961); Wilbur J. Watson, *A Decade of Bridges* (1937); and William Ratigan, *Highways over Broad Waters* (1954).]

CARL W. CONDIT

MOONEY, THOMAS JOSEPH (Dec. 8, 1882–Mar. 6, 1942), labor radical, was born in Chicago, Ill., the eldest of three surviving children of Bryan—called Bernard—and Mary (Hefferon, or Heffernan) Mooney. His father, born of Irish parents in a railroad construction camp in Indiana, was a coal miner, and Tom and his brother and sister grew up around the mines of Washington, Ind. His mother, a native of County Mayo, Ireland, had lived in Holyoke, Mass., before her marriage. After her husband died in 1892, she returned with her children to Holyoke, where she took a job sorting rags in a paper mill.

Young Tom attended a Catholic parochial school for a short time, but after being flogged for lying, transferred to public school. At the age of fourteen he went to work in a local factory; the following year he was apprenticed as an iron molder. He soon joined the molder's union, but found work in his trade only sporadically. On a trip to Europe in 1907 he became converted to socialism. Back in the United States, he hawked Socialist literature from the campaign train of Eugene Debs [*q.v.*] during the 1908 presidential race, and two years later he attended the International Socialist Congress at Copenhagen.

On July 3, 1911, in Stockton, Calif., Mooney married Rena Ellen (Brink) Hermann, a divorced music teacher; they had no children. Settling in San Francisco, he affiliated with various radical and labor groups, including the Industrial Workers of the World and the left-wing faction of the San Francisco Socialists, whose newspaper, *Revolt,* he helped publish. In 1910 he ran as the Socialist candidate for superior court judge and in 1911 for sheriff. Dedicated to left-wing unity, he organized molders for William Z. Foster's Syndicalist League of North America and joined the International Workers Defense League, an organization formed to provide legal aid to radicals.

In 1913 Mooney and a young drifter from New York, Warren Knox Billings, joined a prolonged, violent strike of electrical workers against the Pacific Gas and Electric Company. During the turmoil Billings was arrested by a dogged company detective, Martin Swanson, for carrying dynamite, and he was later imprisoned. Fearing that Swanson would try to implicate him as well, Mooney went into hiding, but was arrested near Richmond, Calif., and charged with illegal possession of high explosives. After two trials resulting in hung juries, he was acquitted in 1914. Two years later he attempted unsuccessfully to provoke a wildcat strike by streetcar men in San Francisco.

During the San Francisco Preparedness Day parade (July 22, 1916), one of the many held throughout the United States to demonstrate for military readiness, a bomb exploded on Steuart Street, killing ten persons and wounding forty. Because radicals of every type, as well as organized labor, had opposed the parade, the press depicted the crime as an act of anarchist terrorism. Beyond a few fragments of shrapnel, little physical evidence was discovered; but District Attorney Charles M. Fickert theorized that a time bomb had been carried to the scene in a suitcase. Acting on information supplied by Mooney's nemesis, Swanson, Fickert arrested Tom and Rena Mooney, Warren Billings, and several others, charging them with the crime.

Billings was tried in September 1916 and sentenced to life imprisonment. Mooney, defended by Maxwell McNutt and Bourke Cockran [*q.v.*], was tried in January 1917 before Judge Franklin

A. Griffin. The prosecution's star witness, not called at the Billings trial, was Frank C. Oxman, a wealthy cattleman, who claimed to have seen Mooney and Billings in the Steuart Street area carrying a suitcase. Although Oxman's testimony conflicted with that of another prosecution witness, Mooney was convicted of first-degree murder and sentenced to hang. Later, after a motion for a retrial was denied, it was revealed that Oxman had perjured himself in his affidavit to the district attorney; the defense also discovered that Oxman had a history of fraudulent activities, and that he had probably not even arrived in San Francisco until four hours after the crime. Despite this evidence, Fickert, pressured by the Hearst press and the Chamber of Commerce "Law and Order Committee," opposed a retrial. Rena Mooney was tried without Oxman's testimony in the summer of 1917 and was acquitted.

During Mooney's trial his support had come primarily from labor radicals, led by the anarchist Robert Minor, who reactivated the dormant International Workers Defense League to publicize the cause; from the militantly progressive wing of the trade-union movement, particularly the Chicago Federation of Labor; and from a small group of concerned attorneys headed by Bourke Cockran. After his conviction, however, more orthodox groups, including the previously recalcitrant San Francisco Labor Council, joined in seeking a commutation of his sentence. In the protracted legal battle that ensued, Mooney was aided by many prominent citizens, including Roger Baldwin of the American Civil Liberties Union; Frank P. Walsh [Supp. 2], his chief defense attorney from 1923 to 1939; Fremont Older [Supp. 1], editor of the *San Francisco Bulletin;* and Samuel Gompers [*q.v.*] of the A. F. of L. His case soon became an international cause célèbre. When mobs protesting his conviction marched on the American embassy in Petrograd in 1917, threatening the success of an American mission to Russia, President Wilson urged California's governor to order Mooney to be retried. That summer a Federal Mediation Commission appointed to investigate I.W.W. strikes against the copper and lumber industries was persuaded by Col. Edward M. House [Supp. 2] to look into the case; its report questioned the justice of the verdict. In November 1918 Gov. William D. Stephens commuted Mooney's sentence to life imprisonment.

With Mooney saved from hanging, public interest in the case slackened. For two decades his supporters continued their efforts to win his freedom, either through executive clemency or through legal action; but a succession of cautious Republican governors, a partisan state supreme court, and procedural deficiencies in the criminal code and state constitution all served to keep Mooney in San Quentin and Billings in Folsom prison. Unlike Bartolomeo Vanzetti [*q.v.*], Mooney was unattractive in character. Vain, preoccupied with the burdens of his injustice, determined to run his own defense movement from prison, he alienated those who served him best. During the New Deal years sentiment began to stir in his favor. Upton Sinclair, in his unsuccessful campaign for governor in 1934, pledged to free Mooney if elected. An appeal to the United States Supreme Court on the ground that due process had been violated when Mooney was imprisoned as a result of perjured testimony brought a decision (*Mooney* v. *Holohan,* 1935) expanding the federal role in habeas corpus proceedings, but did not change Mooney's status. He was finally pardoned by a Democratic governor, Culbert L. Olson, on Jan. 7, 1939. Billings, whose cause had never received the same attention, was freed by commutation of sentence that October; he was officially pardoned in 1961.

After his release, Mooney went on tour under labor auspices but soon faded from view. The years in prison had left him in poor health, $20,000 in debt, and estranged from his wife. He spent most of his last two years at St. Luke's Hospital, San Francisco, suffering from bleeding ulcers. He died there and was buried in Cypress Lawn Cemetery, Colma, Calif.

[The Bancroft Lib. of the Univ. of Calif., Berkeley, has a large collection of Mooney correspondence, pamphlets, legal documents, and photographs. Other important papers are those of Bourke Cockran, Frank P. Walsh, and the Am. Civil Liberties Union (on microfilm) at the N. Y. Public Lib.; the Dept. of Justice files, Nat. Archives; and the Governor's Office records at the Calif. State Archives, Sacramento. The fullest study, with an extensive bibliography, is Richard H. Frost, *The Mooney Case* (1968). Earlier books are: Henry T. Hunt, *The Case of Thomas J. Mooney and Warren K. Billings* (1929), a detailed brief by an Am. Civil Liberties Union attorney; Ernest J. Hopkins, *What Happened in the Mooney Case* (1932); *The Mooney-Billings Report* (1932), prepared for the federal Wickersham Commission on Law Observance and Enforcement; and Curt Gentry, *Frame-up: The Incredible Case of Tom Mooney and Warren Billings* (1967). See also James McGurrin, *Bourke Cockran* (1948). Birth, marriage, and death certificates are available from vital statistics offices in Chicago and Sacramento.]

RICHARD H. FROST

MOORE, CHARLES (Oct. 20, 1855–Sept. 25, 1942), journalist and city planner, was born in Ypsilanti, Mich., the youngest of three children and only son of Charles Moore, a successful merchant, and Adeline (MacAllaster) Moore. His parents had moved to Michigan from their native New Hampshire in 1834. Young Charles was orphaned at the age of fourteen, but a brother-in-law became his guardian and a substantial inheritance enabled him to continue his education. He attended the Kenmore School in Pennsylvania, Phillips Andover Academy, and Harvard College, where he studied history, political science, and philosophy and acquired from Charles Eliot Norton [*q.v.*] a lifelong interest in Renaissance architecture.

While in college Moore was editor of the *Harvard Crimson,* the student newspaper, and Boston correspondent for the *Detroit Post* and the *Detroit Tribune.* He graduated in 1878, and shortly afterward, on June 27, married Alice Williams Merriam of Middleton, Mass.; they had two sons, MacAllaster and James Merriam. Returning to Ypsilanti, he leased the *Ypsilanti Commercial,* and two years later he purchased *Every Saturday,* a Detroit newspaper which he operated for about a year. In 1883 he invested his entire inheritance in the *Detroit Times,* and the following year lost everything in a fire that destroyed the newspaper's plant. For the next five years Moore worked as a reporter for the *Detroit Journal* and the *Detroit Sunday News,* making occasional contributions to New York dailies.

While covering the elections of 1888 he met James McMillan [*q.v.*], who the next year, after his election to the United States Senate, appointed Moore as his political secretary. In this capacity Moore soon became involved in city planning problems. McMillan had long been interested in such problems, having served from 1881 to 1883 on the Detroit Park Commission; in Washington he became chairman of the Senate Committee on the District of Columbia. Moore, as clerk of the committee, compiled and edited reports advocating improved hospitals, schools, charities, and parks in Washington. At Moore's suggestion, and at the urging of the American Institute of Architects, McMillan secured in 1901 the establishment of a Senate Park Commission to plan the future development of Washington. Its members were the architects Daniel H. Burnham and Charles F. McKim, the sculptor Augustus Saint-Gaudens [*qq.v.*], and the younger Frederick Law Olmsted (1870–1957), landscape architect. Moore, as secretary, accompanied members of the commission on a summer tour of several European capitals. Upon returning to the United States in the fall of 1901, he helped Olmsted prepare a report which called for a return to the baroque design motifs of Pierre L'Enfant [*q.v.*], the original planner of Washington, and in particular the creation of the formal mall L'Enfant had envisaged stretching westward from the Capitol to the Potomac River. To bring the mall into being required relocation of the Pennsylvania Railroad tracks and station. Moore, acting as strategist, publicist, and go-between for the Park Commission, helped prepare the necessary legislation, including provisions for the construction of the new Union Station, and after McMillan's death in 1902 he remained in Washington to see the legislation passed.

Returning to Michigan in 1903, Moore accepted a position as private secretary to Francis H. Clergue, who operated a complex of steel, railroad, and power enterprises at Sault Sainte Marie, Mich. When Clergue's company failed in 1904, Moore became secretary of the Union Trust Company of Detroit, the receiver of the bankrupt enterprise. He then moved in 1906 to Boston, where he was chairman of the Submarine Signal Company. Two years later he returned to Detroit as vice-president of the Security Trust Company.

Following the death of his wife in 1914, Moore retired from business and, among other things, turned to writing. He had long been interested in the study of history, and while serving as secretary to Senator McMillan had written *The Northwest under Three Flags, 1635–1796* (1900) and completed the degrees of M.A. (1899) and Ph.D. (1900) at Columbian College (later George Washington University). He was treasurer of the American Historical Association, 1917–30. He went on to write biographies of Daniel Burnham (1921) and Charles F. McKim (1929), which between them provide a history of the City Beautiful movement and the development of the classical revival style of architecture. Moore was appointed adviser and acting chief of the Manuscript Division of the Library of Congress in 1918 and helped build a number of important collections, among them the First World War Collection, the Richard Todd Lincoln Collection, and the Willam Howard Taft Papers.

Meanwhile, Moore continued to be active in the city planning movement. He edited the *Plan of Chicago* (1909) which had been prepared by Daniel Burnham and Edward H. Bennett, and from 1912 to 1919 he was president of the Detroit City Plan and Improvement Commission. In 1910 Moore was appointed by President Taft to the new federal Fine Arts Commission, established by Congress to judge the artistic suitability and appropriate location of all proposed monuments, statues, and public buildings in Washington, D. C. (except those on the grounds of the Capitol). As its chairman from 1915 to 1937, he served as an intermediary between the architects of the City Beautiful movement and those powerful in business and government who could carry out their plans. The commission, under his leadership, zealously defended the Senate Park Commission plan of 1901, upholding its proposal for the location and design of the Lincoln Memorial and encouraging the construction of the Arlington Memorial Bridge in 1924. Moore was skilled at getting things done through gentlemanly compromises which never jeopardized the essence of his scheme.

Moore's work won recognition in the award of the New York Architectural League Medal of Honor (1927), the Carnegie Corporation Award for service to the arts in America (1937), and honorary degrees from George Washington University (1923), Miami University (1930), and Harvard (1937). After retiring from the federal Fine Arts Commission in 1937, he lived with his son MacAllaster in Gig Harbor, Wash., and it was there that he died at the age of eighty-six of a blood clot on the brain. He was buried in Middleton, Mass.

[The basic source is Moore's papers (6,000 items) in the Lib. of Cong., including a MS. autobiography and the MS. of his projected book, "Makers of Washington," which was helpful on the 1920's and '30's. Other useful material is in the files of the Fine Arts Commission (in the Nat. Archives) and of the Olmsted Associates Office in Brookline, Mass. Moore's *Park Improvement Papers* (1903), which were written with Frederick Law Olmsted, Jr., comprise the report of the Senate Park Commission. His historical writings include *The Hist. of Mich.* (4 vols., 1915), consisting of one volume of history and three volumes of biographical sketches. The most helpful published biographical sources are the shrewd appraisal by Gilmore D. Clarke in *Landscape Architecture*, Jan. 1943; H. P. Caemmerer, "Charles Moore and the Plan of Washington," U. S. Commission of Fine Arts, *Fourteenth Report*, 1940–44; the sketch in Moore's *Hist. of Mich.*, IV, 2296–97; Harvard College Class of 1878, *Fiftieth Anniversary Report* (1928); and the article on Moore in the *Am. Soc. Legion of Honor Mag.*, Autumn 1945. Interviews with Col. James Merriam Moore, Constance McLaughlin Green, and David C. Mearns were helpful. A portrait of Moore by Eugene Savage (1935) is in the Fine Arts Commission's office in Washington.]

CHARLES CAPEN MCLAUGHLIN

MOORE, FREDERICK RANDOLPH (June 16, 1857–Mar. 1, 1943), Negro journalist, was born in Prince William County, Va., the son of Evelyne (or Evelina) Moore, an enslaved house servant, and a white father, listed on the son's death certificate as Eugene Moore and sometimes said to have been related to the Virginia Randolphs. Fred Moore was brought to the District of Columbia at an early age and was educated in the public schools. Like many enterprising blacks in the nation's capital, he spent his youth on the street selling newspapers. At eighteen he became a messenger in the Treasury Department, a position he retained from the Grant administration through the first presidential term of Cleveland; he is said to have served Secretary of the Treasury Daniel Manning [q.v.] as a confidential aide. Leaving the Treasury Department at about the same time as Manning, Moore became a clerk in the Western National Bank, of which Manning was president. In April 1879 he married Ida Lawrence, sister of Mattie Lawrence of the original Fisk Jubilee Singers, who bore him eighteen children, of whom six lived to adulthood: two sons, Eugene and Gilbert, and four daughters, Ida, Marion, Gladys, and Marjorie.

In 1904 Moore moved to New York City, where he immediately entered the most powerful class in Negro society, a small, often light-skinned elite. Booker T. Washington [q.v.], the nationally influential Alabama-based Negro educator, chose him to serve as a traveling organizer for the National Negro Business League, which sought to encourage black economic development. Moore urged Negroes to "learn to value money." "Jews support Jews," he told the league's convention in 1904, "Germans support Germans . . . and Negroes should now begin to support Negroes." He himself became an investor and an officer in the Afro-American Realty Company, a short-lived firm (1904–08) which was instrumental in opening up the new community of Harlem to Negro residents. He also became active in Republican politics in Brooklyn, serving as a district captain and, for five months in 1904, as Deputy Collector of Internal Revenue, and running for the state assembly in 1905; though defeated, he made a good showing.

At the request of Booker T. Washington, Moore in 1904 also assumed the editorship of the Boston *Colored American Magazine,* which he promptly moved to New York. In 1907, when Washington secured financial control of the New York *Age,* the country's leading Negro newspaper, Moore became its editor and part owner. Even though he supported Washington's goals of race pride, economic nationalism, and self-help, Moore frequently challenged the Tuskegee leader's facade of moderation by attacking lynching and the lukewarm racial policy of the Republican party, and by supporting Northern black radical groups such as the Niagara Movement. As his influence in journalism grew, Moore remained active in the Republican party, attending several national conventions as a delegate or an alternate and receiving an appointment in 1912 as United States minister to Liberia. He did not actually assume this office, however, either because the incoming administration of Woodrow Wilson was expected to make the customary patronage changes or because of the press of business activities.

During his years in New York, Moore developed a strong loyalty to the Harlem community. As Negroes moved northward from midtown, he moved the location of his newspaper office with them. He was active in the National League for the Protection of Negro Women, the Katy Ferguson Home, the Committee for the Improving of Industrial Conditions of Negroes in New York, and the National Urban League. In 1915 he was in the forefront of the black protests against the motion picture *The Birth of a Nation.* With other black leaders, he held discussions with the American Federation of Labor in 1918 in fruitless attempts to expand wartime job opportunities for Negro labor.

Like many prominent Negroes of his day, Moore maintained a keen interest in the urban, progressive, interracial social service organizations active in New York City. But he also retained his early faith in Washington's ideal of a thriving black capitalist economy and society, and served on the board of the city's Dunbar National Bank. He was instrumental in bringing national Negro leaders such as Congressman Oscar DePriest of Chicago and Bishop Reverdy Ransom to New York to campaign for black candidates. He himself was elected to two terms as a New York alderman, in 1927 and 1929, and in the latter year he helped carry the Harlem district in the New York state assembly for a black ticket.

By World War II Moore's political career had come to an end. The New York *Amsterdam News* was cutting into the readership of the *Age,* and new social forces and movements had emerged in Harlem to reshape and replace the ideas of Moore's generation. He died of pneumonia in Harlem in 1943, at the age of eighty-five. His wife had died four years earlier. He was buried in Flushing Cemetery, Flushing, N.Y.

[Moore letters in Booker T. Washington Papers, Lib. of Cong.; vertical file, A. A. Schomburg Collection, N. Y. Public Lib.; files of the N. Y. *Age*; obituaries in *Jour. of Negro Hist.,* Apr. 1943, N. Y. *Age,* Mar. 6, 1943, and *N. Y. Times,* Mar. 3, 1943; death certificate, N. Y. City Dept. of Health; August Meier, "Booker T. Washington and the Negro Press: With Special Reference to the *Colored American Mag.*" *Jour. of Negro Hist.,* Jan. 1953; Richard Bardolph, *The Negro Vanguard* (1959); Gilbert Osofsky, *Harlem: The Making of a Ghetto, Negro N. Y., 1890–1930* (1966); Seth M. Scheiner, *Negro Mecca: A Hist. of the Negro in N. Y. City, 1865–1920* (1965); August Meier, *Negro Thought in America, 1880–1915* (1963).]

THOMAS R. CRIPPS

MORGAN, HELEN (Aug. 2, 1900–Oct. 8, 1941), popular singer and actress, was born in Danville, Ill., the only child of Frank Riggins of Danville and Lulu (Lang) Riggins, a teacher from Iowa. While Helen was still a small child, her mother divorced Riggins and married Thomas Morgan. They separated a few years later, and Mrs. Morgan eventually moved to Chicago. There Helen left Crane Technical High School around 1918 to take a job packing crackers and then as a manicurist. Investing her wages in singing and dancing lessons, she began performing in Chicago speakeasies and was recruited by a talent scout for the chorus of a Broadway musical, *Sally* (1920), produced by Florenz Ziegfeld [*q.v.*]. She then returned for another stint in small Chicago night clubs.

Accounts of the next few years vary. Making her way again to New York, reportedly on the basis of winning a beauty contest at a winter carnival in Montreal, she secured a small singing part in *George White's Scandals* of 1925. She also sang that year at Billy Rose's Backstage Club, in a room so small and crowded she had to sit on the piano, a perch which became her trademark. Undoubtedly influenced by Fanny Brice, Dorothy Jardon, and Marion Harris, but quite unique, her small, throbbing, high contralto was ideally suited to the new "torch song" and crooning styles she did much to develop and popularize. With a subtle suggestion of Negro urban blues, she conveyed the bitter frustration of the city girl keyed up to the potential of romance, then let down. She was becoming a star for the times; the public was wearying of stentorian vaudeville singers, rowdy or grandiloquent but always loud. Her artless crooning suited the new milieu of electrical recording: talkies, radio, the intimate revue (the 1926 revue, *Americana,* was her next step to stardom), and above all, the speakeasy. Over the next decade, her plaintive voice wafted gently through the indulgent alcoholic haze of "the clubs" which were her natural habitat.

But she had much wider appeal. She triumphed as the mulatto Julie LaVerne in Jerome Kern's *Show Boat* (1927–28), where her greatest number, "Bill" (lyrics by P. G. Wodehouse), was a theme song for the "emancipated" but lonely city girl who desperately needed a man. She immortalized the Gershwins' "The Man I Love" ("Someday he'll come along"). Her hit songs in the Kern-Hammerstein musical of 1929, *Sweet Adeline,* in which she starred—"Don't Ever Leave Me" and "Why Was I Born?"—reiterated her theme of alienation and isolation. So did the Victor Young–Ned Washington "Give Me a Heart to Sing To" from her 1935 film *Frankie and Johnny.*

Petite, with the rather somber allure of lambent dark eyes, "the brooding bitterness of a mouth that had found life an empty glass" (Charles Darnton), a heavy drinker, with a pale complexion to match her wan, intensely forlorn voice, she had the night-pallor charisma of the then fashionable "shopworn angel." She was married twice. Her first marriage, on May 15, 1933, to Maurice Maschke of Cleveland, law student son of the city's Republican leader, floundered during her constant engagements in New York, London, and Paris. Her second marriage, on July 27, 1941, was to Lloyd Johnson, a Los Angeles auto dealer. On the surface her lifestyle like her singing suggested the "sophistication" of the interwar years. She read Hemingway, Joyce, D. H. Lawrence, dismissed her 1935 divorce with the comment, "Bud's a nice boy, it was all a mistake—no more marriage for me, I'll just live in sin" (*New York Post,* Oct. 24, 1935; *New York Times,* Oct. 9, 1941). But beneath the surface was a naively trusting, warmly emotional, extravagant—and extravagantly generous—woman who could spend an entire yearly income of $177,000 on impulsive gifts, charities, and $600 dresses. She sometimes relinquished her proceeds to supporting casts caught by an early closing, and despite her large earnings she died in financial difficulties.

Her name was a household word into the 1930's. She followed her 1929 film debut in *Applause* with half a dozen other movies, including the film version of *Show Boat* (1936), and also appeared on Broadway (*Ziegfeld Follies* of 1931 and *George White's Scandals* of 1936) and on radio. Until moving to Hollywood in 1935 she continued to work in Manhattan night clubs she partly owned.

By the late 1930's, with swingy, nonchalant band vocalists crowding older individual song stylists, her career was passing its zenith. However, her soft delivery was now in the mainstream of popular singing, and she was still a headliner on tour in Chicago at the time of her death there, from cirrhosis of the liver and hepatitis, at the age of forty-one. A Roman Catholic convert in her last illness, she was buried at Holy Sepulchre Cemetery, Worth, Ill. In 1957 a film, *The Helen Morgan Story,* dramatized her life.

Helen Morgan's influential "refined" white blues style was admired by an era which similarly admired Paul Whiteman's orchestral blending of jazz and the classics. Her "morning after" feeling empathized with, and enraptured, a public disillusioned with the tinsel lure of early twentieth-century hedonism. In short, her talent fit her time. But beyond this timeliness, she is timeless in taste, sensitivity, finesse.

[Information was obtained through the County Clerk of Vermilion County, Ill.; from the Prothonotary and Clerk of Courts, New Castle, Pa. (first marriage); from Miss Morgan's mother (who supplied her birth date); from an aunt, Mrs. Ruby Hembrey; and from clippings in the Theatre Collection of the N. Y. Public Lib. at Lincoln Center. The Rodgers and Hammerstein Room at Lincoln Center contains several recordings from the 1930's. Record albums commercially available at the time of writing include Victor LPV 561, "Fanny Brice and Helen Morgan" (with biographical liner notes); Epic 2-6072, "Encores from the 1930's"; and Columbia C 3L 35, "The Original Sound of the Twenties," containing one Morgan track, a booklet by Rogers Whitaker with some firsthand data on Miss Morgan's lifestyle (see comments on Record III, side one), and a superb late 1920's portrait. Miss Morgan's film career is partially illustrated in Daniel Blum, ed., *A Pictorial Hist. of the Talkies* (1958). Written material on Helen ·Morgan is largely ephemeral, but Irving Hoffman's article in the *N. Y. American*, Feb. 2, 1936, Michel Mok's interview in the *N. Y. Post*, Oct. 24, 1935, and Charles Darnton's review of *Sweet Adeline*, *N. Y. Evening World*, Sept. 4, 1929, are valuable, as are obituaries in the *Danville* (Ill.) *Commercial-News*, Oct. 9, 1941, *N. Y. Times*, Oct. 9, 10, 12, 1941 (good on her later life but inaccurate on her childhood), and *Variety*, Oct. 15, 1941. See also Robert J. Dierlam in *Notable Am. Women*, II, 579–80.]

HUGHSON MOONEY

MORGAN, JOHN PIERPONT (Sept. 7, 1867–Mar. 13, 1943), investment banker, was born in Irvington, N. Y., the second of four children and only son of John Pierpont Morgan [*q.v.*], founder of J. P. Morgan & Company, and Frances Louisa (Tracy) Morgan. He was educated at St. Paul's School in Concord, N. H., and at Harvard, from which he graduated with the A.B. degree in 1889. On Dec. 11, 1890, he married Jane Norton Grew of Boston. The couple had four children: Junius Spencer, Jane Norton, Frances Tracy, and Henry Sturgis.

After a brief association with the Boston banking house of Jacob C. Roberts, Morgan in 1892 became a partner in his father's firm. A short apprenticeship in New York followed, after which he went to London to study banking in the firm of J. S. Morgan & Company, founded by his grandfather Junius Spencer Morgan [*q.v.*]. His eight years in London (1893–1901) gave him not only a knowledge of banking but also an affection for England that he retained for the rest of his life. On the death of his father in 1913, he became the head of J. P. Morgan & Company.

"Jack" Morgan—a nickname used to distinguish him from the elder J. P.—thus presided over the banking house during World War I. The firm's London and Paris connections made it a logical financial agent for the Allied governments. Through Morgan's initiative, it became the sole purchasing agent in America for the British and French; from early 1915 until the United States entered the war in 1917, J. P. Morgan & Company handled orders for more than \$3,000,000,000 worth of war supplies at a commission of 1 percent. When President Wilson lifted the government's restriction on loans to belligerents in 1915, Morgan, without compensation to his company, organized a syndicate of 2,200 banks to underwrite a loan of unprecedented size: \$500,000,000 of 5-percent bonds jointly guaranteed by Great Britain and France. Subsequent issues over the next two years raised the total to \$1,550,000,000. Morgan's association with the Allied cause brought an attempt on his life: in July 1915, at his estate in Glen Cove, Long Island, he was shot by a German sympathizer but escaped serious injury.

The postwar years found the firm's situation substantially changed. The war marked a shift in the financial headquarters of the world from Europe to the United States, the great creditor nation of the war. Thus the Morgan company's London connections were no longer as important as they had been. Moreover, the rapid growth of the postwar American economy, the increased needs of domestic and foreign borrowers, and the emergence of a mass public market for securities offerings created unparalleled opportunities for investment bankers. Other financial intermediaries soon entered the investment field, and as a result J. P. Morgan & Company under Jack Morgan did not enjoy the preeminent position it had under his father. Yet the house remained the acknowledged leader of American banking. Its power was based not on its resources, for it was not the largest bank on Wall Street, but on the quality of its clients, its reputation for fair and honest service, and the financial skill of the Morgan partners.

In the postwar period the firm carried on important work in foreign government finance, and Morgan gained a reputation for recapitalizing national debts much like his father's for recapitalizing railroad debts. Between 1917 and 1926 J. P. Morgan & Company floated bond issues for Great Britain, France, Belgium, Italy, Austria, Switzerland, Japan, Argentina, Australia, Cuba, Canada, and Germany, totaling about \$1,700,000,-000. Morgan served at Paris in 1922 on a committee of bankers that sought to adjust German reparations, an important preliminary to the Dawes committee of 1924. He was an American delegate to the reparations conference headed by Owen D. Young in 1929 which created the plan for the Bank of International Settlements. J. P. Morgan & Company became that institution's American representative and floated its American shares; the firm also headed the syndicate that handled the American portion of the Young Plan loan, amounting to \$98,250,000.

The Morgan bank sold about $4,000,000,000 in stocks and bonds for American companies during the 1920's. About half of this amount consisted of railroad bonds, and another $1,000,000,000 were the issues of public utility companies and public utility holding companies. Although by this time American companies had come to favor stock issues to bonds, only a little more than 3 percent of all the domestic securities the Morgan bank handled were common stocks. Morgan was abroad at the time the Wall Street panic marked the end of the economic boom of the 1920's, but his firm became a natural rallying point for the financial forces of the country. On Oct. 24, 1929, representatives of five other banking institutions met in the Morgan offices with Thomas W. Lamont and formed a pool, estimated at from $20,000,000 to $30,000,000, with which they made an unsuccessful attempt to stem the panic.

During the 1930's both Morgan and his firm were subjected to close governmental and public scrutiny. The United States Senate in 1933 investigated stock exchange abuses which contributed to and followed the crash. Questioning revealed that the Morgan firm and partners, though not guilty of the glaring abuses of many banking houses, had offered new stocks to selected persons at lower than market prices, and that Morgan and his twenty partners, taking advantage of legal loopholes, had avoided paying any income taxes for the depression years of 1931 and 1932. In 1936 Morgan was called before Senator Gerald P. Nye's committee looking into the role of munitions makers in international relations. Nye maintained, without substantiation, that the United States had entered World War I to save the banker's loans and credits to Great Britain and France. Meanwhile, the Banking Act of 1933 had ordered a separation of investment and deposit banking, and the following year J. P. Morgan & Company withdrew from the investment banking field to become a private commercial bank. Although a number of the partners left and formed a new investment bank, Morgan, Stanley & Company, Jack Morgan remained as head of the commercial bank.

Tall and well-proportioned, Morgan in later years came to resemble his father, although he was spared the bulbous nose and forbidding scowl. He was, according to one observer, "reserved to the point of brusqueness," and he liked to pursue his hobbies—yachting, gardening, and the management of his American and British estates—far from the public eye. Those who knew Morgan well—and they were few—described him as generous and likable, a man of exceedingly high standards. An elitist, he maintained that any tampering with the free capitalist system and the leisure class which it supported would "destroy civilization." Yet he had a strong sense of philanthropic duty. He donated large sums to the Episcopal Church, in which he was an active layman. During World War I he gave $2,000,000 to the Red Cross, and he was known for his annual subsidy to the New York Lying-In Hospital. Like his father, he was a well-known collector of rare books and manuscripts. He continued to build the holdings of the Morgan Library in New York, begun by his father, and in 1923 transformed it from a personal collection into a permanent, endowed institution. Knowledgeable in art and literature, he donated art objects to the Metropolitan Museum of Art and the Wadsworth Atheneum in Hartford, Conn. He served on the boards of several academic institutions and received honorary doctorates from half a dozen.

By the mid-1930's Morgan was devoting much time to his avocations, leaving the direction of the Morgan bank increasingly to other partners; it was incorporated in 1940. While on a fishing holiday in 1943, Morgan died of a cerebral stroke at Boca Grande, Fla., at the age of seventy-five. His ashes were interred in the family plot at Cedar Hill Cemetery, Hartford, where his wife had been buried in 1925.

[Harvard College Class of 1889, *Anniversary Reports*: 25th (1914), 30th (1919), and 50th (1939); *Who Was Who in America*, vol. II (1950); Lewis Corey, *The House of Morgan* (1930); Herbert L. Satterlee, *J. Pierpont Morgan: An Intimate Portrait* (1939); Edwin P. Hoyt, Jr., *The House of Morgan* (1966); Vincent P. Carosso, *Investment Banking in America: A Hist.* (1970); Ferdinand Pecora, *Wall Street under Oath* (1939); Thomas W. Lamont, *Across World Frontiers* (1951); U. S. Senate, 73 Cong., 1 Sess., *Hearings before the Committee on Banking and Currency, Stock Exchange Practices*, parts 1 and 2 (1933), and 74 Cong., 2 Sess., *Hearings before the Special Committee Investigating the Munitions Industry*, parts 25–29 (1936). For a contemporary analysis, see John K. Winkler, "Mighty Dealer in Dollars," *New Yorker*, Feb. 2, 9, 1929. The most useful obituaries are in the *N. Y. Times*, Mar. 13, 1943, and Business Hist. Soc., *Bull.*, Nov. 1943. Morgan did not grant interviews or write any articles or books. No MS. collection, if one exists, has been made public.]

ERLING A. ERICKSON

MORGAN, THOMAS HUNT (Sept. 25, 1866–Dec. 4, 1945), zoologist and geneticist, was born in Lexington, Ky., the first of three children and elder son of Charlton Hunt Morgan and Ellen Key (Howard) Morgan. His mother belonged to an old Baltimore family, her two grandfathers being Col. John Eager Howard of the Revolutionary army and Francis Scott Key [qq.v.]. Thomas's father was a descendant of James Morgan, who with his brother Miles had come to Boston, Mass., from Wales in 1636. From Miles derives the line of the banker John Pierpont Morgan [*q.v.*]. Hence, as Prof. Alfred H. Sturtevant has noted, the male-determining Y chromosomes of T. H. Morgan and J. P. Morgan, each distinguished in his own way, had a common origin six generations back. From New England, Thomas's forebears had moved to Tennessee and thence to Huntsville, Ala. His father, a graduate of Transylvania University who served in his youth as American consul in Messina and was a friend of the Italian patriot Garibaldi, fought during the Civil War in the Confederate Army with Morgan's Raiders under the command of his brother, Gen. John Hunt Morgan [*q.v.*]. After the war he became steward of the Eastern Lunatic Asylum in Lexington, Ky.

As a boy Morgan displayed a keen interest in natural history and science, collecting birds and fossils on summer vacations in western Maryland. Somewhat later he found summer employment in geological and biological field surveys in the mountains of Kentucky. After receiving the B.S. degree in 1886 from the State College (later University) of Kentucky, he went to the Johns Hopkins University for graduate work, spending the intervening summer at the marine laboratory at Annisquam, Mass., predecessor of the Marine Biological Laboratory at Woods Hole, Mass., with which he was to be long associated. At Johns Hopkins, Morgan was much influenced by the zoologist William Keith Brooks [*q.v.*] and by the physiologists H. Newell Martin [*q.v.*] and William H. Howell [Supp. 3], as well as by his fellow students Edwin G. Conklin and Ross G. Harrison, who became his lifelong friends. Morgan carried out research on the regeneration of earthworms and in 1890 received the Ph.D. degree with a thesis on the embryology of sea spiders. A Bruce fellowship enabled him to spend a year studying in the Caribbean, and in 1894–95 he did joint research with the German biologist Hans Driesch at the zoological station at Naples. Meanwhile, in 1891, Morgan had become associate professor of biology at Bryn Mawr College, where he was a colleague of Ross Harrison and Jacques Loeb [*q.v.*]. Among his students at Bryn Mawr who later made important contributions to biology were Nettie M. Stevens, cytologist, and Lilian Vaughan Sampson, embryologist and geneticist. He and Miss Sampson were married on June 6, 1904. They had four children: Howard Key, Edith Sampson, Lilian Vaughan, and Isabel Merrick.

In 1904 Morgan was appointed professor of experimental zoology at Columbia University, where he was to remain for the next twenty-four years. At Columbia he was a close scientific associate of Edmund B. Wilson [Supp. 2], noted embryologist and cytologist. The two were unlike in temperament, Wilson striving for an orderly, exhaustively complete command of his subject, while Morgan was impatient with details, concerned with broad generalizations, and eager to attack the next exciting idea. Nevertheless, they remained lifelong friends and exercised strong reciprocal influences in their thinking and in their work.

For half a dozen years at Columbia, Morgan continued to work in experimental embryology—regeneration, self-sterility in *Ciona,* gynandromorphism, differentiation and sex determination in aphids and phylloxerans. His laboratory studies of regeneration led to an interest in the mechanism of evolution. He rejected Lamarckism but for some time saw no empirical reason to accept the Darwinian concept that species were created by natural selection, acting on minute heritable variations. The experiments of the Dutch botanist Hugo de Vries and the rediscovery (1900) of Mendel's work stirred his interest in the newly developing field of genetics. Like many of his contemporaries schooled in classical biology, Morgan was skeptical of the "easy" explanations of Mendelian genetics. As he commented in a paper read before the American Breeders Association in 1908, ". . . the results are often so excellently 'explained' because the explanation was invented to explain them. We work backwards from the facts to the [Mendelian] factors, and then, presto! explain the facts by the very factors that we invented to account for them." He sought an alternative to Mendelism and Darwinism in the theory of de Vries, which accounted for speciation through discrete, large-scale mutations. In 1908 and 1909 Morgan began genetic studies, first on mice and rats and then on the tiny fruit fly, *Drosophila melanogaster,* which he and his associates were to transform into the reigning queen of the new biology. In 1909–10 Morgan found a white-eyed mutant of *Drosophila* to be a sex-linked recessive. Within the next two years he discovered many additional mutant traits, such as eye colors, body colors, and wing variations, and worked out their modes of inheritance. Since these patterns accorded with the Mendelian theory, he abandoned his initial skepticism toward chromosomal inheritance and embraced Darwinism as well.

The resulting excitement in Morgan's laboratory was transmitted to colleagues and students. Among the latter were Alfred H. Sturtevant and Calvin B. Bridges [Supp. 2], who as undergraduates were invited to work in his laboratory, which soon became widely known as "the fly room." Perhaps never in the history of biology has so much knowledge originated in so small a space and at so little cost. Only sixteen by twenty-three feet, the fly room contained eight desks and was always occupied by five or more researchers. The American and foreign postdoctoral students who occupied desks or worked closely with the group at one time or another included a major fraction of the most brilliant geneticists of the period—men such as Otto L. Mohr, Curt Stern, Theodosius Dobzhansky, and Hermann J. Muller. In the early days flies were grown in milk bottles, some of them retrieved from trash cans, and the standard fly food consisted of slightly overripe bananas, purchased at discount from nearby grocery and fruit shops, crushed, and seeded with yeast. Sturtevant has recorded that "This group worked as a unit. Each carried on his own experiments, but each knew what the others were doing, and each new result was freely discussed. There was little attention paid to priority or the source of new ideas or new interpretations. What mattered was to get ahead with the work. . . . This was due in large part to Morgan's own attitude, compounded of enthusiasm combined with a strong critical sense, generosity, open-mindedness, and humor. No small part of the success of the undertaking was due also to Wilson's unfailing support and appreciation of the work . . . [as] head of the department" (National Academy of Sciences, *Biographical Memoirs,* XXXIII, 295).

Among the many significant advances in the new science of genetics that came out of the fly room were a clear understanding of sex-linkage, final and convincing proof of the chromosome theory of inheritance, establishment of the linear arrangement of genes in the chromosome, the demonstration of interference in crossing-over, the fact that such genetic recombination occurs in the four-strand stage, and the discovery of chromosomal inversions. With Sturtevant, Muller, and Bridges, Morgan in 1915 published *The Mechanism of Mendelian Heredity,* which marked a high point in the development of genetics. Although by about 1925 Morgan had begun to devote an increasing share of his time and energy to the embryological problems that he had never wholly abandoned, he always retained his deep interest in the work of his associates in genetics.

In 1928 Morgan moved to the California Institute of Technology in Pasadena to help create a new division of biology, the first phase of which was known as the William G. Kerckhoff Laboratories of the Biological Sciences. Several former students and associates moved with him:

Sturtevant, Bridges, Ernest G. Anderson, Dobzhansky, Albert Tyler, and Jack Schultz. He quickly recruited additional faculty members who were outstanding in the fields of animal physiology, plant physiology, biochemistry, and related areas. In a setting in which the mathematical, physical, and chemical sciences were exceptionally strong, "Caltech" became a mecca for experimental biologists. Early work on the genetics of the red bread mold *Neurospora* was carried out there by Carl C. Lindegren. Modern bacteriophage biology and genetics were begun by Emory Ellis and Max Delbrück. The spirit, as well as the simplicity and economy, of the fly room was transplanted to the new laboratory. Morgan declined the directorship, however, saying that he was willing to be chairman of a division but that he did not want to be a part of a laboratory in which investigators were to be "directed."

A small marine laboratory was also established at Corona del Mar, about an hour's drive from Pasadena, where Morgan returned wholeheartedly to his first love, the embryology of marine and amphibian organisms, and studied the role of temperature, gravity, and various chemicals in producing abnormal forms. Whenever possible, he returned to the Woods Hole laboratories for the summer, as he had done throughout his life. In his last book, *Embryology and Genetics* (1934), he embodied his views on the two fields in which he made his chief scientific contributions.

As a person, Morgan was simple and unpretentious in dress, manner, and mode of life. In this his wife was fully sympathetic. She never gave up her interest in genetics and about 1925 returned to laboratory research, discovering attached-X and ring-X chromosomes in *Drosophila,* both of which proved to be important tools in sophisticated studies of genetic recombination. Morgan was warmhearted, with a well-developed sense of humor not infrequently mischievous. He was generous in so modest a way that many of his closest associates were unaware of specific acts of intervention, or that fellowships received by some of his needy and deserving students were often made possible through his personal financing.

Morgan carried out an enormous amount of research and published some 400 papers and fifteen or more books. The importance of his work was recognized by the many honorary degrees he received, including those from the universities of Kentucky, McGill, Edinburgh, California (Berkeley), Michigan, Heidelberg, Zurich, and Paris. Other awards include the Darwin Medal (1924) and the Copley Medal

(1939) of the Royal Society, of which he was elected a foreign member. He served as president of the American Morphological Society (1900), American Society of Naturalists (1909), and Society for Experimental Biology and Medicine (1910–12), as well as of the National Academy of Sciences (1927–31) and the American Association for the Advancement of Science (1930). In 1933 he received the Nobel Prize in physiology or medicine.

The true influence of a scholar in science is measured only in part by his personal accomplishments in research, his publication record, and the honors bestowed upon him. Equally important, sometimes more so, is his influence on others—colleagues, students, and those who read his writings or hear his presentations at scientific meetings. By any one of these criteria Morgan's influence on the development of genetic science was great indeed.

Morgan died in Pasadena, Calif., at the age of seventy-nine, of a ruptured stomach artery. His body was cremated at Mountain View Crematorium, Pasadena.

[Memoir by Alfred H. Sturtevant in *Nat. Acad. Sci., Biog. Memoirs*, vol. XXXIII (1959); obituaries in *Science*, May 3, 1946 (by H. J. Muller), *Biological Bull.*, Aug. 1947 (by E. G. Conklin), and *Obituary Notices of Fellows of the Royal Soc.*, V (1947), 451–66 (by R. A. Fisher and G. R. de Beer); Garland E. Allen, "Thomas Hunt Morgan and the Problem of Natural Selection," *Jour. of the Hist. of Biology*, Spring 1968; A. H. Sturtevant, *A Hist. of Genetics* (1965). On Morgan's father, see Robert Peter, *Hist. of Fayette County, Ky.* (1882), p. 661.]
GEORGE W. BEADLE

MORTON, FERDINAND JOSEPH (Sept. 20, 1885?–July 10, 1941), jazz musician and composer, known as "Jelly Roll" Morton, was born in New Orleans, La., and christened Ferdinand Joseph La Menthe. Both his mother, Louise Monette, and his father, F. P. (Ed) La Menthe, a carpenter and an able trombonist, were apparently descended from free colored Creole families long settled in Louisiana. His parents separated, and he eventually adopted the name of his stepfather, Willie Morton. Growing up in the polyglot culture of New Orleans, Ferdinand acquired a deep sense of Creole exclusiveness and an antipathy toward darker-skinned Negroes that was to influence his personal relationships and his evaluations of fellow musicians.

In later years Morton tended to romanticize the facts of his boyhood, and many details remain obscure or contradictory. He attended a local grammar school, but his chief interest was music, and he often heard performances at the French Opera House, where he became familiar with European musical forms. By his own account, he took up the harmonica at the age of five and the Jew's harp two years later. In the next few years he became a skilled guitarist and began playing blues and ragtime with small street bands. He started the piano at about ten, studying for a time with a teacher at St. Joseph's University in New Orleans. After his mother's death, when he was about fourteen, he and his two half sisters were left in the care of their great-grandmother, though Ferdinand lived chiefly with his godmother, who encouraged his piano study.

When Morton was about seventeen he began working as a piano player in the brothels of Storyville, the red-light district of New Orleans. His stern, respectable great-grandmother then barred him from the family, a hurt he never forgot. Morton soon gained fame as one of the best pianists in Storyville. His chief rival was Tony Jackson, a ragtime pianist for whom he always had a high regard. Morton cultivated a "barrelhouse" style which he considered different from ragtime, and by 1902 or 1903 he had begun composing. Some of his most popular works of the period were "New Orleans Blues," "King Porter Stomp," "Wolverine Blues," and "Jelly Roll Blues."

By 1904 he had begun to travel in other parts of the South, playing the piano in sporting houses and organizing small bands in which he sometimes played trombone or drums. Before long he had left New Orleans for good. For a decade before 1917 he wandered through the Midwest and Southwest, working in minstrel shows and in vaudeville, and supplementing his earnings as a piano player with winnings as a pool shark and gambler, together with profits from assorted small enterprises in Memphis, St. Louis, Chicago, and Kansas City. He also began making written arrangements of his compositions; his "Jelly Roll Blues," published in 1915, was probably the first jazz orchestration ever printed. With increasing prosperity, and with growing recognition as a jazz musician, he fully indulged his fondness for striking dress and had a diamond inserted in a front tooth.

In 1917 Morton moved to California, where he remained for five years, playing in Los Angeles night clubs and establishing one of his own. He then returned to Chicago, which had become the new center of jazz, and entered the most successful phase of his career. A Chicago company, Melrose Brothers, began publishing his music. In 1923 he made his first recordings, a series of piano solos and ensembles with the New Orleans Rhythm Kings, for Gennett Studios at Richmond, Ind., where most of his major compositions were first recorded. Significant as these were, his subsequent sides made for Victor, mainly in New York and Chicago between 1926 and 1930, were even more important. For these he recruited such top New Orleans jazz musicians as Omer Simeon, Kid Ory, Johnny St. Cyr, and Johnny and Warren "Baby" Dodds to form the small band known as the Red Hot Peppers; they recorded some of his most original compositions, including "Black Bottom Stomp" and "Grandpa's Spells." Although at times difficult to get along with, Morton showed considerable tact and judgment in his dealings with these men. He rehearsed each number approximately three hours, providing the basic ideas but letting the individual musicians build upon them and improvise their solos. The results proved to be some of the best jazz records made.

Morton took his Red Hot Peppers (with lesser-known personnel) on successful tours of white hotels and colleges throughout the Midwest, New England, and Canada. These successes made the last half of the 1920's prosperous for him, but his popularity declined in the 1930's. He spent much of that decade in New York City, which had displaced Chicago as the jazz capital. In the era of big swing bands, Morton's music seemed old-fashioned; for nearly ten years he made no recordings and fell upon hard times. He continued to compose, however, creating and arranging almost continuously when he was not eking out a living in successively lower jobs. He took his misfortunes bitterly, believing that both publishers and booking agents were cheating him and even that a West Indian partner had cast a voodoo spell upon him. For a time he ran a night club in Washington, but it was not successful. He now had a small but loyal following among enthusiasts of jazz, one of whom, the folklorist Alan Lomax, had him tell his life story, with many examples of his playing, on a series of documentary records made for the Library of Congress.

In 1917, during his first stay in California, Morton began living with Anita Gonzales (Johnson?), also from New Orleans. In November 1928 he married Mabel Bertrand, a night-club entertainer and daughter of a New Orleans doctor. Late in 1940, after he had developed hypertensive heart disease, Morton returned to California and reestablished a home with Anita. He died the next year in the Los Angeles County General Hospital of cardiac decompensation. Reared as a Catholic, he was buried with the last rites of the Church in Calvary Cemetery in Los Angeles.

Although he was a gentle, generous, and reasonably modest friend to those whom he trusted,

Morton was known to the public as an unbridled egotist with a flair for colorful behavior. His flamboyant dress contributed to his reputation as a showman and ladies' man. Many regarded him as an incorrigible braggart and embroiderer of fact, as in his claim that he had "invented" jazz in 1902. He carried on several bitter feuds, including one with W. C. Handy, known as "The Father of the Blues."

Whatever his shortcomings, Morton was an important figure in the development of American music. Although somewhat limited in technique in comparison with some of the other well-known pianists of his day, he brought to his best solos a unique touch and warmth. As a bandleader and arranger he made several important records. But it was as a composer that he made his greatest contribution. He was the first jazz composer, one who wrote not merely tunes but carefully structured orchestrations. Many of his compositions—including "Milneburg Joys," "The Pearls," "Shoe Shiners Drag," "Wild Man Blues," and "Kansas City Stomps"—became standards in the jazz repertory. Jazz was not the creation of any one man, but Jelly Roll Morton's compositions, in which the formalistic and generally rigid structure of ragtime is suffused with the emotional intensity and improvisational freedom of the blues, are among the earliest embodiments of true jazz.

[The fullest biography is Alan Lomax, *Mister Jelly Roll* (1950), which combines the subject's reminiscences from the 1938 Lib. of Cong. records with Lomax's own research. Gunther Schuller, *Early Jazz* (1968), pp. 134–74, provides the most thorough discussion of Morton's music yet to appear. Other useful sources are: Martin Williams, *Jelly Roll Morton* (1963) and the chapter on Morton in Williams's *Jazz Masters of New Orleans* (1967); Orrin Keepnews, "Jelly Roll Morton," in Nat Shapiro and Nat Hentoff, eds., *The Jazz Makers* (1957); Leonard Feather, *The Encyc. of Jazz* (2nd ed., 1960); and Rudi Blesh, *Shining Trumpets* (rev. ed., 1958). Death record from Calif. Dept. of Public Health.]

NEIL LEONARD

MORTON, JELLY ROLL. See MORTON, FERDINAND JOSEPH.

MOSES, GEORGE HIGGINS (Feb. 9, 1869–Dec. 20, 1944), New Hampshire politician, was born in Lubec, Maine, the fifth son and youngest of six children of Thomas Gannett Moses, a minister of the Christian Church, and Ruth Sprague (Smith) Moses. His father, whose ancestors, of Scottish origin, had long inhabited northern New England, held pastorates in several towns including Eastport, Maine, and Franklin, N. H. George attended public schools in both these towns. Thereafter, stretching a lean family budget by odd jobs and scholarship loans, he grad-

uated from Phillips Exeter Academy in 1887 and
Dartmouth College (A.B. 1890, A.M. 1893).
As his schooling ended, he attached himself to the
ruling politicians of New Hampshire's Republican organization, serving as secretary to Gov.
David H. Goodell in 1889–90, as a reporter and
news editor on the *Concord Evening Monitor* of
Senator William E. Chandler [*q.v.*] beginning
in 1890, and as secretary of the state forestry
commission from 1893 to 1906.

Chandler's tutelage was particularly crucial to
his progress. In 1898 Moses became chief editor
of the *Monitor,* sharing its control with Chandler's son and operating as the Senator's main
political lookout in New Hampshire. He was a
tireless and aggressive partisan, and acquired
a sure feel for the forces which defined the terms
of Republican dominion in the state—White
Mountain timber interests, the mammoth Amoskeag textile mills in Manchester, and, above all,
the Boston & Maine Railroad. Men like Lucius
Tuttle of the Boston & Maine, Thomas J. Coolidge [*q.v.*] of the Amoskeag, and Massachusetts
Senator Henry Cabot Lodge [*q.v.*], all Bostonians, confirmed his respect for the reach of
power and his deference to its agents.

A shrewd provincial, pugnacious and tart,
Moses was more artful at the editorial desk and
in dealing with statehouse politicians than he was
before a popular crowd. The defeat of his mentor
Senator Chandler, a longtime critic of the Boston
& Maine, in 1901, and after that the stir of Progressive insurgency, jarred his political calcula-
tions and honed his instinct for party regularity.
He regarded the reformism of New Hampshire's
Winston Churchill as little more than the "gospel
of gush" (Moses to Chandler, Nov. 30, 1906,
Moses Papers). Failing to win election to the
legislature in 1904 and 1906, Moses sought polit-
ical and financial safety in a foreign mission.
Theodore Roosevelt refused him, but in 1909
Senator Lodge's intercession with President Taft
won him the post he coveted, the ministry to
Greece and Montenegro.

In Athens, Moses pursued tactics friendly to
the new Venizelos regime, worked on plans for
a Balkan federation, and glumly eyed the Balkan
drift toward war. In 1912 he resigned, stripped
of diplomatic illusions. Back home, he organized
a syndicate to promote trade with Greece, worked
for the Republican Publicity Association in Washington, and tried to patch up an accommodation
of regulars and insurgents among New Hampshire Republicans. He yearned for a seat in the
United States Senate, and when Jacob H. Gallin-
ger [*q.v.*] died in 1918, Moses won the election
for his place.

He joined the inner circle of the Republican
Senatorial establishment with uncommon speed,
and gloried in its ways of power. His diplomatic
experience and friendship with former Secretary
of State Philander C. Knox [*q.v.*] won him
prompt appointment to the Senate Foreign Relations Committee. An irreconcilable foe of the
League of Nations on grounds of nationalist real-
politik, he was a vociferous ally in Lodge's campaign against Wilsonian internationalism, and
later fought American participation in the World
Court. In 1924 he chaired a noisy investigation
into the innocuous Peace Plan of Edward Bok
[Supp. 1]. The patterns in his domestic conservatism were granitic. He opposed woman suffrage,
favored restraints on organized labor, and lauded
government economy—though backing higher
postal rates and larger allotments for the diplomatic corps. He proudly claimed to be Calvin
Coolidge's earliest supporter for the Republican
nomination in 1924. As president pro tempore of
the Senate after March 1925, he spiked efforts
by Vice-President Charles G. Dawes to speed
up Senate business by reforming rules of debate.

A contemporary description of Moses as "that
humorous and independent mossback" *(New York
Times,* Oct. 22, 1923) seems apt, if a shade indulgent. He kept track of New Hampshire's interests as he understood them, and his zest for
combat in their defense was unguarded. He fought
efforts to bar the importation of dyestuffs used
by textile makers, and waged a running feud with
the farm bloc over its neglect of apples, hay,
and tariff protection for Eastern manufacturers.
In 1929 his labeling of Midwestern agrarian Senators as "sons of the wild jackass" *(ibid.,* Nov.
10, 1929) ignited a furor which almost cost him
his chairmanship of the Republican Senatorial
campaign committee.

Meanwhile Moses battled doggedly with the
liberal wing of the New Hampshire Republican
party led by Gov. John G. Winant. He survived
liberal challenges to his reelection in 1920 and
1926, but the depression undid him, and he lost
his seat to a Democrat in 1932. Over the next
year he wrote a syndicated column for his old
friend Frank Knox [Supp. 3], publisher of the
Chicago Daily News, on affairs under the New
Deal, which he regarded as "undiluted sovietism"
(Moses to Herbert Hoover, Apr. 18, 1933, Moses
Papers). In 1936 he helped promote Knox's
abortive presidential ambitions, and in the New
Hampshire primaries suffered the defeat of his
own hope to return to the Senate. His last major
public service was to preside at the New Hampshire state constitutional convention in 1938. He
died of a coronary thrombosis at his home in Con-

cord, where he had long been a member of the South Congregational Church. He was survived by his wife, Florence Abby Gordon, whom he had married Oct. 3, 1893, and his son, Gordon. He was buried in the Franklin (N. H.) Cemetery. His career was a monument to the concept of the Old Guard.

[The Moses Papers (about 1,800 items) in the N. H. Hist. Soc., Concord, N. H., are valuable for his early career in state politics and journalism, but sketchy on the Senatorial years, which may be followed in the *Cong. Record* and *N. Y. Times*. See also Merrill A. Symonds, "George Higgins Moses of N. H.—The Man and the Era" (Ph.D. dissertation, Clark Univ., 1955); Ezra S. Stearns, ed., *Genealogical and Family Hist. of the State of N. H.* (1908), IV, 1868–69 (on Moses and his father); Leon B. Richardson, *William E. Chandler, Republican* (1940); and Bernard Bellush, *He Walked Alone: A Biog. of John Gilbert Winant* (1968). There is a biographical summary in the *Nat. Cyc. Am. Biog.,* Current Vol. C, pp. 71–72, and obituaries in the *Concord Daily Monitor* and *N. Y. Times,* Dec. 21, 1944.]
GEOFFREY BLODGETT

MURDOCK, VICTOR (Mar. 18, 1871–July 8, 1945), Kansas journalist, Congressman, and Progressive, was born at Burlingame, Osage County, Kans., to Victoria (Mayberry) and Marshall Mortimer Murdock. His father, who came of a Scotch-Irish West Virginia family, had moved to Kansas from southern Ohio in 1856. During the next half century Marshall Murdock served at various times as a state senator and as postmaster of Wichita, but his principal activity was as a newspaper publisher, first in Burlingame and then, from 1872, in Wichita. Victor was the second of eight children, but only four, of whom he was the oldest, survived childhood. He was educated in Wichita common schools and at Lewis Academy. On May 21, 1890, he married Mary Pearl Allen of Wichita. They had two daughters, Marcia and Katherine Allen.

Murdock had early learned the printer's trade, and at fifteen he became a reporter on his father's *Wichita Daily Eagle*. A facile writer, he covered the 1890 Congressional race in his district, in the course of which he dubbed Jerry Simpson [q.v.], the Populist candidate, with the famous "Sockless" epithet. Murdock moved to Chicago in 1891 to become a reporter on the *Inter Ocean,* where he introduced baseball slang to sports reporting. But in 1894, at a time of business depression, he returned to Wichita to serve as managing editor of his father's paper.

In 1903 the Republican convention of the "Big Seventh" Congressional district, Simpson's old bailiwick, nominated Murdock to replace Chester I. Long, whom the Kansas legislature had just sent to the United States Senate. Murdock cap-tured two-thirds of the vote in the general election; he was reelected regularly thereafter through 1912. When he first entered Congress, Murdock was in the conservative mainstream of Kansas Republicanism, but he gradually began to move leftward. In his first term he championed irrigation, an issue important to his constituents and also acceptable to G.O.P. leaders. But he was effectively silenced by the House leadership when he complained of excessive expenditures in the Post Office Department—the first of his several confrontations with the prevailing House rules. In 1904 his uncle Thomas Benton ("Bent") Murdock, editor of the *El Dorado Republican,* worked actively with Edward W. Hoch and Walter R. Stubbs [Supp. 1] against the established Republican leadership in Kansas, and by 1906 Victor was aligned with Stubbs and other reformers.

In those years, Murdock supported several regulatory measures. In 1905–06 he backed the Townsend and Hepburn bills for railroad rate regulation, though he considered the latter measure insufficiently stern. As a member of the Committee on Post Offices and Post Roads, he fought for a downward revision of the weighing formula by which the government paid railroads for carrying mail. He was, however, ruled out of order, and his reform was subsequently achieved by executive rather than Congressional action. His legislative positions and his alignment with reform elements made him unpopular with the powerful railroad interests in Kansas, and though he bid for a Senate seat in 1906, the legislature chose the more conservative Charles Curtis [Supp. 2].

With his solid figure, angular features, and wiry reddish hair, Murdock looked the part of a reformer. As George W. Norris [Supp. 3] recalled, he was honest, courageous, and well informed. Impatient to correct wrongs, he "did not care much for technicalities." Murdock revealed his pugnacity as a leader, with Norris, of the "Insurgents" who waged the successful fight of 1910 against Speaker Joseph G. Cannon [q.v.] and the autocratic House rules.

Murdock bolted the Republican party to support Theodore Roosevelt in 1912, and was reelected to Congress in that year as a Progressive. Two years later, with Senators now popularly elected, he ran as Progressive candidate for Senator. In his campaign he found, in the words of a contemporary, "almost as many" things wrong in Washington as "the Populists of twenty years ago, and they are largely of the same character" (*Atchison Globe,* Oct. 7, 1914); but a split in the reform ranks assured the reelection of Curtis. Murdock became Progressive national chairman in February 1915, and Bainbridge Colby unsuccessfully proposed him as the third party's presidential candidate in June 1916, after Roosevelt declined. In the campaign of that year Murdock and the *Wichita Eagle* supported Woodrow Wilson's reelection. Wilson appointed the Kansan to the Federal Trade Commission in 1917 and again to a full seven-year term in 1918, during part of which he served as chairman; he resigned in 1924.

Murdock returned to Wichita as editor-in-chief of the *Eagle*. Until the end of his life he continued to be a "booster" of the Plains region, supporting highway development and the growth of the oil, natural gas, and aviation industries which were rapidly becoming key parts of the regional economy. He oversaw the transformation of the *Eagle* into a modern newspaper, survived intense local competition, and wrote over three and a half million words in editorials and in a historical and human interest column. He enjoyed music and traveling and in 1920 published a volume of his letters from China. Murdock died in a Wichita hospital in 1945 of chronic myocarditis and nephritis. He was buried in Old Mission Mausoleum near his wife, who had died five years earlier. With his passing, following soon after the deaths of William Allen White [Supp. 3] and Joseph L. Bristow [Supp. 3], the era of Kansas progressive editors came to a close.

[No scholarly biography of Murdock exists, but three master's theses have been written at the Univ. of Kans. under the supervision of Prof. James C. Malin: Anna Marie Edwards, "The Congressional Career of Victor Murdock, 1903–09" (1947, the best of the three); Lillian Tuttle, "The Congressional Career of Victor Murdock, 1909–1911" (1948); and Lenis Boswell, "The Political Career of Victor Murdock, 1911–1917" (1949). A long obituary, with photograph, appeared in the *Wichita Eagle*, July 9, 1945. No MSS. are available, but a substantial collection of clippings and printed material is at the Kans. State Hist. Soc., Topeka. Death record from Kans. State Dept. of Health. On Murdock's role in the Cannon fight, see George E. Mowry, *Theodore Roosevelt and the Progressive Movement* (1946), and George W. Norris, *Fighting Liberal* (1945); on his father, see William E. Connelley, *A Standard Hist. of Kans. and Kansans*, III (1918), 1223–24.]
W. T. K. NUGENT

MYERS, GUSTAVUS (Mar. 20, 1872–Dec. 7, 1942), historian and reformer, was born in Trenton, N. J., one of the youngest of five children (four boys and a girl) of Jewish parents, Abram and Julia (Hillman) Myers; he was a younger brother of the painter Jerome Myers [Supp. 2]. His mother was a native of Baltimore, his father the son of a French soldier who had settled in Virginia after the Napoleonic wars. Abram Myers was a wanderer who did little to support his wife and children; they moved north from Virginia to New Jersey, and thence to Philadelphia and New York City. Gustavus was reared in poverty and saw little of either parent, having been "shunted off" to three public institutions during his childhood. At fourteen he was put to work in a factory, where he developed a keen sympathy for the underprivileged.

His education was "ordinary," but he early became a persistent reader, attended lectures, and was earnestly concerned about public issues. He began newspaper work on the *Philadelphia Record* when he was nineteen years old, then moved to New York to write for newspapers and magazines. Myers developed a clear journalistic style, serious and without graces. His social partialities turned from Populism to socialism, and in 1907 he joined the Socialist party. Meanwhile he had developed his lifelong habits of research which, though untutored, resulted in formidable accumulations of original materials.

His first targets, inspired by his associations in New York's Social Reform Club, were corruption in the dispensing of public franchises and Tammany Hall. His "History of the Public Franchises in New York City," published in the reform periodical *Municipal Affairs* (March 1900), foreshadowed the muckraking era, though because of its provocative tone it met little public response. His *History of Tammany Hall* (1901) also failed to impress; it was too radical in its approach, and too unaware of the sources of Tammany's durability. Only a limited edition was issued (Myers published it himself), and rumor had it that copies were being mysteriously bought up to withdraw them from the market.

On Dec. 23, 1904, Myers married Genevieve Whitney of Springfield, Mass.; they had two children, Theobald Kirkhoven and Marcella Kirkhoven. A slight, sober man of intellectual mien, Myers settled into a routine of library research, articles for magazines, and concern for the future of socialism, as in his contributions to *The New Encyclopedia of Social Reform* (1908 edition) of William D. P. Bliss [*q.v.*]. During much of the first decade of the twentieth century he worked without encouragement on what would become his best-known study, his *History of the Great American Fortunes*. Living within limited means, he was scornful of his muckraking contemporaries, who gained audiences and profit from what seemed to him shallow investigations. Although his own investigations were rigorous, they were circumscribed by socialistic premises which did not take into account differences in human psychology or traditions. His manuscript was rejected by a variety of publishers, but was finally issued (1909–

10) in three volumes by the Chicago socialist publisher Charles H. Kerr. Taking to task historians' uncritical treatment of America's men of wealth, Myers sought to show that their fortunes had been accumulated, not through the mythical virtues of industry and honesty, but rather by preemption and plunder. The book brought him his first substantial newspaper and magazine reviews, but these did not help his cause. The *American Historical Review* (July 1910), in a notice by Emerson D. Fite, acknowledged Myers's research, but saw the text as "a socialistic tract," and "so interlarded with rant as to be disappointing." The book gradually won a following, however, and by the depression year of 1936 was considered enough of a classic to be reissued in the Modern Library series.

Myers pressed on to publish, in similar vein (and also through Kerr and Company), his *History of the Supreme Court* (1912) and *History of Canadian Wealth* (1914). *Beyond the Borderline of Life* (1910) collected articles he had written on psychic phenomena. Meanwhile his outlook was changing. He left the Socialist party in 1912, critical of what he deemed its materialism and anti-individualism. (See his "Why Idealists Quit the Socialist Party," *Nation*, Feb. 15, 1917.) He also discovered a fresh identity with his homeland. A new edition of his *History of Tammany Hall* (1917) was more respectfully published (by Boni and Liveright), if not better received. Following American entry into World War I, Myers served with conviction on the Creel Committee on Public Information, which sought to bolster the war effort by patriotic and anti-German literature. His own *The German Myth: The Falsity of Germany's "Social Progress" Claims* (1918) found him on the side of dominant American opinion.

A new concern for bigotry set him on a fresh track of investigation. His *Ye Olden Blue Laws* (1921), which traced sumptuary legislation in America from colonial times onward, was cordially received. Myers now wrote with some regularity for the *New York Times,* the *Century,* and other publications. In 1925 his *History of American Idealism,* reversing his earlier attitudes, portrayed America as progressively correcting its social inequities. He welcomed Franklin Roosevelt's New Deal as evidence of intrinsic American nobility. Myers became sensitive to foreign criticism of America, and in *America Strikes Back* (1935), his one best seller, he defended his country at length from foreign "baiting."

Continuing to develop his new positive approach, Myers in 1939 published *The Ending of Hereditary American Fortunes,* in which he ar-gued that the redistribution of wealth in America was nearly complete. It was a book, as a *Time* reviewer wryly observed, from which "leftists [were] not likely to crib" (Nov. 27, 1939). In 1941 he received a Guggenheim Fellowship to enable him to continue his researches on bigotry. He suffered a collapse while completing his work and died at his home in the Bronx section of New York City of a cerebral hemorrhage. He was buried in New York's Woodlawn Cemetery. His *History of Bigotry in the United States* was published posthumously in 1943.

[Myers's place on the periphery of his times resulted in relatively few traces being left of his career and personality. Stanley J. Kunitz and Howard Haycraft, *Twentieth Century Authors* (1942), includes a brief biography by Myers himself. See also *Nat. Cyc. Am. Biog.,* XXXI, 443; *Who's Who in Am. Jewry,* 1938–39; and obituary in *N. Y. Times,* Dec. 9, 1942. Death record from N. Y. City Dept. of Health. On his family background, see Jerome Myers, *Artist in Manhattan* (1940). Two books that discuss his work are John Chamberlain, *Farewell to Reform* (1931), and Louis Filler, *Crusaders for Am. Liberalism* (1939); the latter seeks to distinguish him from the muckrakers. Myers's methods as pursued in his *Hist. of the Great Am. Fortunes* are seriously impugned in an essay in historiography, R. Gordon Wasson, *The Hall Carbine Affair: A Study in Contemporary Folklore* (1941; rev. ed. 1948).]
                                        LOUIS FILLER

NAST, CONDÉ MONTROSE (Mar. 26, 1873–Sept. 19, 1942), magazine publisher, was born in New York City, the third of four children and younger son of William Frederick Nast and Esther Ariadne (Benoist) Nast. His paternal grandfather, William Nast [*q.v.*], a founder of German Methodism in the United States, had come from Württemberg in 1828. His father, born in Cincinnati, was an unsuccessful speculator-inventor. His mother's family was originally French and presumably Roman Catholic, since Nast was reared in that faith. He is said to have been named for a maternal forebear, André Auguste Condé, a military surgeon who had come to St. Louis in 1760.

Condé Nast attended public schools in St. Louis—his mother's birthplace, to which the family moved in his early childhood. At the age of seventeen he enrolled in Georgetown University in Washington, D. C., where he earned an A.B. degree in 1894 and a master's degree in 1895. He then entered the St. Louis Law School at Washington University and graduated in 1897.

Nast did not remain long in St. Louis or the law. A Georgetown friend, Robert J. Collier, son of the publisher Peter Fenelon Collier [*q.v.*], was given the editorship of the ailing *Collier's Weekly* in 1898 and persuaded Nast to come to New York as the magazine's advertising manager at $12 a week. Nast raised the advertising revenue from a level of $5,500 a year when he arrived to more than $1,000,000 by 1905. His salary meanwhile reached $40,000 a year. Two years later, in 1907, he left to develop his own enterprises.

As early as 1904 Nast had been a co-founder of the Home Pattern Company, which manufactured and sold dress patterns. In 1909 he bought a small New York society magazine called *Vogue,* which had been founded in 1892. Believing that advertisers would be attracted to a "class" magazine that could guarantee a selective, high-income readership, he resisted the temptation to dilute circulation by adding popular features. He determined that *Vogue* would offer one service: it would help well-to-do women dress fashionably.

Nast was fortunate in choosing his editorial partners. In 1914 he promoted Mrs. Edna Woolman Chase, a *Vogue* staff member, to editor. Together they built *Vogue* into the country's most prestigious fashion magazine, in fact creating a new culture of women's fashions. They were innovators in display and illustration and were successful in harnessing a variety of diverse and unruly talents. Nast's other great colleague was Frank Crowninshield, whom he asked to edit his second magazine acquisition, *Dress & Vanity Fair.* Crowninshield shortened the title to *Vanity Fair* and created a sophisticated monthly that covered "the things people talk about at parties"— entertainment, literature, society.

Nast continually expanded his operations. In 1914 he set up the Vogue Pattern Company; a year later he gained sole ownership of *House and Garden.* In 1916 he established the first overseas edition of *Vogue* in Britain, partly because the war had hampered distribution from New York. A French *Vogue* was started in 1920 and, a year later, a more popular French magazine, *Jardin des Modes.* In that same year he purchased from Douglas C. McMurtrie [Supp. 3] a printing plant in Greenwich, Conn., which he subsequently enlarged into the Condé Nast Press. Nast's various holdings were consolidated in 1922 as Condé Nast Publications, Inc. He also became president of a Manhattan real estate concern.

Nast had invested in the stock market, and the crash of 1929 hit him hard, leaving him in debt and with his personal holdings in Condé Nast Publications threatened. Then the depression cut the company's revenues from more than $10,000,000 in 1930 to only $5,558,000 in 1933, and substantial profits became a loss of more than $500,000. At the point of yielding control to creditors, Nast was rescued by Lord Camrose, an English press magnate, who bought an interest in the company and left Nast in charge. For the rest of his life Nast worked relentlessly to reestablish the com-

pany's prosperity. In 1936 he merged the money-losing *Vanity Fair* into *Vogue,* relegating Crowninshield to an advisory post. In 1939 Nast brought out a new magazine, *Glamour,* aimed at a relatively wide circulation among career girls. Meanwhile he poured out a stream of fault-finding memoranda that almost forced even Mrs. Chase to break with him.

Nast's personal life also had been troubled. He had established over the years a public reputation as a suave entertainer; his gatherings at 1040 Park Avenue were widely publicized for their rich assortments of the notable. Meanwhile, however, his marriages had failed. His first wife, Jeanne Clarisse Coudert, whom he had married on Aug. 20, 1902, divorced him in 1925. Their two children were Charles Coudert and Margarita Natica. On Dec. 28, 1928, he married a young *Vogue* employee, Leslie Foster, and this marriage ended within five years. He was visiting the daughter of his second marriage, Leslie, at a camp when he suffered the most severe of a series of heart seizures. Two weeks later he died in New York at his penthouse apartment. His funeral was held at the Roman Catholic Church of St. Ignatius Loyola in that city; interment was at the Gate of Heaven Cemetery, Hawthorne, N. Y. *Time* called Nast a "superlative technician of the publishing world." His single-mindedness in pursuing his concept of the class magazine was vindicated in the prosperity of his magazines after World War II.

[Edna Woolman Chase and Ilka Chase, *Always in Vogue* (1954); Phyllis Lee Levin, *The Wheels of Fashion* (1965); Frank L. Mott, *A Hist. of Am. Magazines,* vol. IV (1957); Theodore Peterson, *Magazines in the Twentieth Century* (2nd ed., 1964); unpublished biographical report compiled by Doris B. Morrison, La. State Univ. Lib. School; obituaries in *N. Y. Times* and *N. Y. Herald Tribune,* Sept. 20, 1942; *Time,* Sept. 28, 1942, pp. 50–52. A photographic portrait of Nast appears in *Vogue,* Oct. 15, 1942, p. 26. Nast's birth year, sometimes given as 1874, is confirmed by family sources.]

JAMES BOYLAN

NAZIMOVA, ALLA (June 4, 1878–July 13, 1945), stage and screen actress, was born in Yalta, Russia, on the Crimean coast. According to family sources, she was the second daughter and youngest of three children of Jacob Leventon, a pharmacist, and Sophia (Harvit) Leventon. During her lifetime her family name was generally given as "Nazimoff"; the *National Cyclopaedia of American Biography* lists her parents as Jacob and Sophie (Leventon) Nazimoff. A further element of uncertainty is that Nazimova (as she came to style herself when she began playing in English) used the patronymic "Alexandrovna" while appearing on the Russian stage. Both parents came of Jewish stock but had joined the Russian Orthodox Church.

As a small child, Alla was taken to Switzerland to be educated with her brother and sister. There they lived a Spartan existence in the care of a peasant family near Zurich. Returning to Russia when she was twelve, Alla enrolled at a high school in Odessa and seriously considered a career as a violinist. Her interest turned, however, to the theatre, and at seventeen she entered the dramatic school of the Philharmonic Society of Moscow, where she received three years of training under the leadership of the influential director and playwright Vladimir Nemirovich-Danchenko. Upon graduating in 1898, Alla and most of her classmates were taken into the Moscow Art Theatre, newly founded by Nemirovich-Danchenko and Konstantin Stanislavski. Here she studied Stanislavski's techniques of training the actor to build a character internally as well as externally. At twenty (according to family sources) she was married to a fellow student, Sergei Golovin, but they soon separated.

To gain experience in leading roles and to enlarge her repertoire, Alla left the Moscow Art Theatre to spend several rigorous seasons with provincial troupes in Kislovodsk, Kostroma, and Vilna. In 1903–04 she acted at a "theatre for working people" in St. Petersburg, where she appeared with the actor-director Paul Orlenev in a performance of Ibsen's *Ghosts.* Orlenev had somehow been able to obtain the censor's approval for the Ibsen production but found himself unable to gain permission to do a pro-Jewish play, *The Chosen People,* by Evgeni Chirikov. He decided to offer the play outside Russia, and organized a company which included Nazimova in one of the leading roles. They appeared in Berlin, London, and finally New York.

The Chosen People (played in Russian) opened at the Herald Square Theatre on Mar. 23, 1905. The critics were favorable despite the language barrier, and they particularly praised Nazimova. Since the improvident Orlenev had made no long-term arrangements for a theatre, financial difficulties ensued, and the group was forced to move to a small, wretched building on the Lower East Side which also housed a dance hall and a barroom. There he offered a repertoire of plays seldom or never seen in New York: plays by Chekhov, Strindberg, Hauptmann, and Ibsen. Nazimova put all her theatrical resources to work, sewing costumes, translating scripts, composing incidental music, and directing many of the productions. The intensity of her dedication to her art was unusual in the American theatre of that time. Though the company's audiences were composed mainly of Russian immigrant Jews, New York theatrical, literary, and even society figures also found their way to this theatre in the ghetto. When the venture failed, Orlenev returned to Russia, but Nazimova remained in New York and was signed by the Shuberts to make her English-speaking debut.

After learning English over the summer, she appeared as Hedda in Ibsen's *Hedda Gabler* at the Princess Theatre on Nov. 13, 1906. The actor-producer Henry Miller [*q.v.*] was nominally in charge, but the diminutive actress, with shining black hair and luminous blue eyes, directed her own debut. The critics were enthusiastic, but it was not until two months later, when she played Nora in Ibsen's *A Doll's House,* that the full impact of Nazimova's particular kind of acting became evident. Here was an actress who did not possess a fixed and immutable stage personality, but who could, by free and expressive use of her body, portray the unique inner motivations of different individuals. The *New York Times* wrote (Jan. 20, 1907): "Her Nora . . . is astonishing in its revelation of what might be termed a new personality—one as distinct and as far removed as possible from that which we knew in her Hedda Gabler," and concluded, "The Russian woman is a genius."

Although the Shuberts gave her other Ibsen roles—Hilda Wangel in *The Master Builder* (September 1907) and Rita Allmers in *Little Eyolf* (April 1910)—these were combined with inconsequential box-office plays; she had become a theatrical "property." She signed next with Charles Frohman [*q.v.*], but he did nothing more than provide her with a popular but third-rate vehicle called *Bella Donna* (1912), casting her as a "bizarre, temperamental, exotic" woman. Identification with this type of character dogged much of her later career. In 1913 she was reported to have married the actor Charles Bryant; in fact they never married, and they separated in 1925.

In 1915 Nazimova, for lack of better opportunities, toured the vaudeville circuit in the short pacifist play *War Brides.* The film version the next year, altered to become a piece of anti-German propaganda, served to launch her as a screen star, and she appeared in such silent classics as *Revelation* (1918) and *Salomé* (1922), the latter an "artistic" film with mise-en-scène inspired by Aubrey Beardsley drawings. Again the exotic was stressed, making Nazimova a prototype for the strange, passionate women who added a foreign allure to the more common "vamp" of the silent screen. For several years, aided by an intensive publicity campaign, she had a wide popular following, and her salary reached $13,000 a week. But her popularity presently declined, and her insistence upon quality in the production of her films made them so expensive that she was forced to finance them herself. She lost what money she had made, and in 1925 she left Hollywood, to remain away for almost two decades.

Nazimova had not deserted the stage completely during the years in California: in 1918 she played a series of Ibsen dramas for the producer Arthur Hopkins, and in 1923 the title role in *Dagmar*. She joined Eva Le Gallienne's Civic Repertory Theatre in New York in 1928—the year after she became an American citizen—and that October gave a memorable performance as Madame Ranevsky in Chekhov's *The Cherry Orchard*.

In 1930 Nazimova joined the Theatre Guild. She won acclaim as Natalia Petrovna in Turgenev's *A Month in the Country* and particularly as Christine Mannon, the counterpart of Clytemnestra, in Eugene O'Neill's *Mourning Becomes Electra* (October 1931). "Alla Nazimova's Christine," wrote John Mason Brown, "is superbly sinister, possessed of an insidious and electric malevolence, and brilliant with an incandescent fire" (Brown, p. 57); the playwright Gerhart Hauptmann called her "the greatest actress I have seen since Duse." Continuing her work with the Theatre Guild, she played the leading role of a Chinese peasant in the dramatization of Pearl Buck's *The Good Earth* (1932) and appeared as the priestess in Bernard Shaw's *The Simpleton of the Unexpected Isles* (1935). She earned enthusiastic praise once again in her final significant stage performance, as Mrs. Alving in Ibsen's *Ghosts* (1935). Nazimova then returned to Hollywood, playing character roles in such films as *Escape* (1940), *Blood and Sand* (1941), *The Bridge of San Luis Rey* (1944), and *Since You Went Away* (1944). She died of a heart attack in 1945 in the Good Samaritan Hospital in Hollywood. Her ashes were placed in Forest Lawn Memorial Park, Glendale, Calif.

Nazimova's enduring fame rests with her more than forty-year career on the American stage. In the early 1900's, when theatre in the United States had become more and more a matter of "giving the public what it wants," she convinced audiences that there was more to acting than posturing and declamation. Her dedication may have wavered in the face of the money, luxury, and stardom which were thrust upon her, but she was never completely false to the ideals and aims of her younger days. She was not a technical actress. In an age when many actors took pride

in their unvarying performances, she said that she never really knew how a particular character would behave on a particular night until she had spoken the first line. Companies would watch from backstage, fascinated by the ever-changing nuances with which she imbued her scenes. Although she did little teaching, Nazimova's influence upon the art of acting was considerable. At the time of her death one admirer wrote, "I think of all actors she was, certainly to my generation of apprentices, the most intensely studied and admired."

[Any study of Nazimova must be based on a wide variety of sources. Clippings and other materials are found in the Theatre Collection of the N. Y. Public Lib. at Lincoln Center, the Harvard Theatre Collection, the library of the Acad. of Motion Picture Arts and Sciences in Los Angeles, the Samuel Stark Collection at Stanford Univ., and the Baxrushin State Theatrical Museum in the U.S.S.R. For Nazimova's own account of her childhood, see her "My Yesterdays," *Bohemian*, June 1907 (clipping at N. Y. Public Lib.). Her conception of acting is set forth in Morton Eustis, *Players at Work* (1937). Useful references to her are found in: Frank P. Morse, *Backstage with Henry Miller* (1938); Pavel N. Orlenev, *Zhizn' i Tvorchestvo Russkogo Aktera Pavla Orleneva* (1931); Emma Goldman, *Living My Life* (1931); Eva Le Gallienne, *With a Quiet Heart* (1935); William A. Brady, *Showman* (1937); and, for comments on particular roles, John Mason Brown, *Dramatis Personae* (1963), and Howard Taubman, *The Making of the Am. Theatre* (1965). An account of her English-speaking debut will be found in Clifford Ashby, "Alla Nazimova and the Advent of the New Acting in America," *Quart. Jour. of Speech*, Apr. 1959. See also *Nat. Cyc. Am. Biog.*, XXXVI, 415; and the sketch by John Gassner in *Notable Am. Women*, II, 611–13, which includes material supplied by her sister, Mrs. Nina Lewton.]

CLIFFORD ASHBY

NEWBERRY, TRUMAN HANDY (Nov. 5, 1864–Oct. 3, 1945), businessman, public official, United States Senator, was born in Detroit, Mich., the eldest of three children (two boys and a girl) of John Stoughton Newberry [*q.v.*] by his second wife, Helen Parmelee Handy; there was one older son by the first marriage. A wealthy manufacturer of railroad cars and a partner of James McMillan [*q.v.*], afterward a Republican Senator from Michigan, John S. Newberry was in 1878 elected to a single term in Congress.

Truman Newberry attended Michigan Military Academy at Orchard Lake, Charlier Institute in New York City, and Reed's School at Lakeville, Conn., before entering the Sheffield Scientific School at Yale. In 1885 he graduated, Ph.B., and started his business career on the staff of the Detroit, Bay City, and Alpena Railroad. Because of his father's failing health, the son had to assume the major responsibility for managing the family's business enterprises, taking complete control at his father's death in 1887. On Feb. 7, 1888, he married Harriet Josephine Barnes of New York City. They had three children: a daughter, Carol, and twin sons, Barnes and Phelps.

Newberry shrewdly managed the fortune he had inherited and became a multimillionaire. Together with such families as the Algers, Buhls, and McMillans, the Newberrys ranked as leaders of that Michigan society of established wealth, position, and orthodox Republicanism that had its business headquarters in Detroit and its social center in Grosse Pointe. He was a director of several firms, among them the Union Guardian Trust Company, Parke Davis & Company, and the Michigan Bell Telephone Company, all in Detroit, and the Cleveland-Cliffs Iron Company. He was one of a group of Detroit investors, including Henry B. Joy [Supp. 2], who brought the Packard Company from Warren, Ohio, to Detroit just after the turn of the century, thus helping to make Detroit the center of the automotive industry; he became a director of the Packard Motor Car Company in 1903.

An ardent yachtsman, Newberry in 1893 organized a naval militia unit, known after 1894 as the Michigan State Naval Brigade. During the Spanish-American War he served on the cruiser *Yosemite* and saw action off the Cuban coast. President Theodore Roosevelt appointed him Assistant Secretary of the Navy in 1905, and three years later Newberry became Secretary of the Navy, a position he held for the last three months of the Roosevelt administration. In this capacity he attempted to overhaul the administrative system of the navy; but his plan was criticized by Adm. William S. Sims [Supp. 2], President Roosevelt's naval aide, and was not adopted.

When the United States entered the First World War, Newberry was a lieutenant commander in the naval reserve; that July he was appointed assistant to the commandant of the Third Naval District, with headquarters in New York City. In June 1918 President Wilson induced Henry Ford to run for the Senate from Michigan as a Democrat and an administration supporter; and the state Republican organization chose Newberry to oppose him. Since the Michigan open primary law permitted the nominally Republican Ford to be entered in the primaries of both parties, the G.O.P. regulars feared that cross-filing might work to the advantage of the popular auto maker and deprive them of a candidate in the November race. Primed with money from Newberry's wealthy friends, his campaign committee spent some $176,000 on advertising and publicity, despite federal and state laws which limited a Senatorial candidate to contributions or expenses of $3,750. Newberry's aides, fired by wartime passions, made harsh attacks on Ford for his pacifism, and insinuated that Ford's son Edsel [Supp. 3], who had been deferred from military service, was a draft dodger. In the primary, held in August, Ford won the Democratic nomination, but lost the Republican contest to Newberry by 43,163 votes.

Throughout the primary and general election campaigns, Newberry remained at his naval post in New York. He won the November election by a slim margin of 7,567 votes out of 432,541. Since the state was normally strongly Republican, this was hardly an impressive showing. Nevertheless, it was generally assumed that the wealthy Newberry had purchased his election, and the still lively progressive antagonism toward plutocracy worked against him. In the Senate in 1919, Newberry signed the Lodge Resolution opposing the covenant of the League of Nations.

Newberry's Senate career, however, was soon put in jeopardy when Henry Ford, still rankling from the campaign attacks on his son and himself, petitioned the Senate to look into Newberry's primary expenditures; an investigation was voted in December 1919. Meanwhile, in November, a federal grand jury had indicted Newberry and 134 others on a charge of criminal conspiracy to violate the Corrupt Practices Act. At the trial, much of the evidence was amassed by lawyers and a corps of field agents whose undercover operations across the state were subsidized by Ford. In March 1920 Newberry was found guilty and was given the maximum sentence of two years in prison and a $10,000 fine; sixteen of his co-defendants were also convicted. The convictions, however, were overturned by the Supreme Court in May 1921 by a 5-to-4 decision (*Newberry* v. *United States*, 256 U.S. 232). In January 1922 the Senate, after debating the findings of its investigation for two months, voted 46 to 41 to adopt a resolution declaring Newberry entitled to his seat but expressing grave disapproval of the sum spent to obtain his election as "harmful to the honor and dignity of the Senate." The Corrupt Practices Act of 1925 was a direct consequence of the Newberry case.

In November 1922, when a new move was launched to unseat him, Newberry resigned from the Senate. Retiring from politics, he devoted the rest of his life to business affairs. In religion he was a Presbyterian. Newberry died at his home in Grosse Pointe Farms, Mich., in 1945, of myocardial failure, complicated by severe arteriosclerosis and diabetes, and was buried in Elmwood Cemetery, Detroit.

[The Truman H. Newberry Papers, consisting of MS. materials and clippings covering the years 1879–1936, are in the Burton Hist. Collection, Detroit Public Lib. Additional materials pertinent to his career are in the George Dewey Papers, Lib. of Cong., and in the papers of Roy D. Chapin, Edwin Denby, and Henry B. Joy, all at the Mich. Hist. Collections, Univ. of Mich. Spencer Ervin, *Henry Ford vs. Truman H. Newberry* (1935), a legalistic defense of Newberry, draws heavily on the trial record. Elting E. Morison, *Admiral Sims and the Modern Am. Navy* (1942), touches on his career in the Navy Dept. See also Arthur Pound, *Detroit: Dynamic City* (1940); Keith Sward, *The Legend of Henry Ford* (1948); Allan Nevins and Frank Ernest Hill, *Ford: Expansion and Challenge, 1915–1933* (1957); Seward W. Livermore, *Politics Is Adjourned: Woodrow Wilson and the War Congress, 1916–1918* (1966); *N. Y. Times*, Oct. 4, 1945.]

WILLIAM GREENLEAF

NEWELL, EDWARD THEODORE (Jan. 15, 1886–Feb. 18, 1941), numismatist, was born in Kenosha, Wis., one of two children and the only son of Frederick Seth Newell and Frances Cecelia (Bain) Newell. His father, an executive of the Bain Wagon Company of Kenosha, was of English descent and had moved to Wisconsin from New Haven, Conn.; his mother had come to Kenosha from New York. The family was well-to-do. Newell was prepared for college at the Harvard School in Chicago and by a private tutor. He received the B.A. degree from Yale in 1907, spent the following year traveling in Europe and Egypt, and then returned to the Yale graduate school to improve his knowledge of languages, receiving the M.A. degree in 1909. On Apr. 22, 1909, he married Adra Nelson Marshall of Jersey City, N. J.; they had no children.

As an undergraduate Newell had developed a serious interest in coins, particularly those of ancient Greece, and had joined the American Numismatic Society. He had the enthusiasm, the taste, and the financial means to acquire coins as objets d'art, and his wife encouraged and assisted the growth of his collection. His regard for her role is indicated by the provision in his will which allowed her to choose a thousand items for herself, the remainder going to the Numismatic Society. Her selections made a breathtaking exhibition when after her death in 1967 they also came to the Society. The whole body is too large ever to be displayed at one time, containing some 60,000 Greek, 23,000 Roman, and 2,000 Byzantine pieces. Although by the standards of American collectors the wealth expended had not been vast, Newell had been persistent, expert, and single-minded in assembling his treasure.

Newell never lost his skill in selecting choice specimens of Greek art, but he was primarily a scholar and gave his chief attention to the study of coins as historical documents. His first major work, "Reattribution of Certain Tetradrachms of Alexander the Great," published in the *American Journal of Numismatics*, April 1911, was an approach to a difficult problem of great importance: the proper assignment of the coins of Alexander to their respective mints and dates of issue. There had been no general treatment of the Alexander coinage since Ludvig Müller's *Numismatique d'Alexandre le Grand*, published in Copenhagen in 1855, and that work, although of considerable value, was largely based on the false assumption that subsidiary symbols were signs of different mints. Working with the contents of a hoard of some 10,000 large silver pieces (tetradrachms) found in Egypt in 1905, Newell was able to prove by the use of identical dies on different issues that the symbols were in fact the marks of moneyers and not of mints. This finding greatly diminished the number of places of issue and laid the foundation for a scientific treatment of all the currency of Alexander and his successors, who had continued to use Alexander's types. Newell discussed the question in a series of important books: *The Coinages of Demetrius Poliorcetes* (1927), *The Coinage of the Eastern Seleucid Mints* (1938), *The Coinage of the Western Seleucid Mints* (1941), and an unfinished work on Lysimachus. His other publications include more than fifty titles. Newell was an authority also on Islamic and Indian coinages, collected Greek and Roman glass, and acquired more than 1,500 Babylonian and Assyrian cuneiform tablets, which he presented to Yale in 1938. His knowledge of numismatics was profound, and he eagerly shared it with others, giving particular encouragement to beginners.

During World War I, Newell worked with the military intelligence department of the army in Washington, D. C. He was a trustee of the American Schools of Oriental Research (1922–41) and a member of many learned societies in the United States and in Europe. As president (1916–41) of the American Numismatic Society, he was largely influential in transforming it from a collectors' club to a scholarly body whose accomplishments ranked with those of its European counterparts. In 1918 he was awarded its Archer M. Huntington Medal; he also received the medals of the Société Royale de Numismatique de Belgique (1922) and the Royal Numismatic Society (1925), the Prix Allier d'Hauteroche (1929) of the Académie des Inscriptions et Belles-Lettres, and the medal of the Société Française de Numismatique et d'Archéologie (1936).

Newell was a Republican and a member of the Congregational Church. He died of a heart attack in New York City at the age of fifty-five and was buried in the Cold Spring (N. Y.) Memorial Cemetery. In his honor the Edward T. Newell Memorial Award was established in 1952, to be given annually to a member of the American Numismatic Association for contributions to Greek and Roman numismatics.

[Yale Univ., *Obituary Record of Graduates*, 1940–41; obituary in *Numismatist*, Apr. 1941, with bibliography of Newell's writings and a photograph; Howard L. Adelson, *The Am. Numismatic Soc., 1858–1958* (1958); *Nat. Cyc. Am. Biog.*, XLI, 62–63; personal recollection.]

ALFRED L. BELLINGER

NEWLON, JESSE HOMER (July 16, 1882–Sept. 1, 1941), educator, was born in Salem, Ind., the oldest of eight children of Richard Rosecrans Newlon, a farmer of Irish Quaker descent, and Arra Belle (Cauble) Newlon. After earlier schooling, he entered Indiana University, where he majored in history, but lack of money forced him to interrupt his education for two years, during one of which (1905–06) he was principal of the Charlestown (Ind.) high school. He completed the A.B. degree in 1907. After a year as teacher of history and mathematics at the New Albany (Ind.) high school, Newlon moved in 1908 to the high school in Decatur, Ill., where he taught history and civics and then was principal (1912–16). He obtained an A.M. degree from Teachers College, Columbia University, in 1914. Moving to Lincoln, Nebr., as high school principal in 1916, he accepted the next year the position of superintendent of schools.

Sympathetic with the progressive education movement of the period, Newlon agreed with other influential educators that the traditional "classical" course taught in the average high school was an inadequate preparation for life in the modern industrial age. School curricula, he believed, should be determined not by school boards, whose members usually belonged to a privileged economic class, but by the teaching profession itself, which should be responsive to the needs of students in a democracy that included diverse social classes and racial groups. Newlon had little chance to develop his ideas until he became superintendent of schools in Denver, Colo., in 1920. Three years later, with the support of the Denver school board, he appointed committees of teachers from the city's elementary and secondary schools to study their particular fields and propose revised curricula that would be relevant to the needs of their pupils and to the changing times—one of the first such programs in the United States. The committees, working under the guidance of nationally known educators, produced revised courses of study and research monographs that had a

wide sale and exercised a strong influence on school curricula throughout the country.

In the fall of 1927 Newlon moved to Teachers College at Columbia as professor of education and director of the Lincoln School, an experimental progressive school founded in 1917 to assist in improving the education of pupils in elementary and secondary schools throughout the United States. To promote unity in the Lincoln School, which was then beset with conflicts, Newlon held regular staff meetings, encouraged pupil participation in the selection and organization of school activities, and arranged seminars and discussion groups for parents. He also served as chairman of the division of instruction at Teachers College (1934–38) and, after the retirement of William H. Kilpatrick, became director of the division of foundations in education (1938–41). In this role he was a strong leader in promoting the concept that education should not be directed to the teaching of facts in separate areas such as history, sociology, languages, and the sciences, but should be a single process leading the individual child to maturity within a particular social environment. The methods of the classroom teacher, he believed, were a key factor in this process.

A Deweyan in philosophy and a humanist in psychology, Newlon was deeply concerned by the ideological conflicts of his day, both in this country and in Europe. A visit to Russia in 1937 convinced him that the outlook for democracy there was a gloomy one, and he feared the dangers of fascism. At home, he regarded the loyalty oaths that some states were requiring of teachers as an attempt to control thought. He firmly believed in the values of democracy even in an increasingly complex society. He regarded sound education as essential to the preservation of freedom, and believed that the educator should not promulgate doctrines but should teach the student to think for himself. In his writings he stressed his conviction that "a school whose procedures are authoritarian will only condition youth, and teachers, too, to acceptance of authority." His books include *Junior-Senior High School Administration* (1922, with Charles H. Johnston and Frank G. Pickell), *Educational Administration as Social Policy* (1934), and *Education for Democracy in Our Time* (1939).

Newlon served as president of the National Education Association in 1924–25. He was a member of the American Historical Association's Commission on Social Studies (1929–33) and of the Progressive Education Association's Commission on the Relation of Schools and Colleges (1932–41), and he took an active part in the committee for academic freedom of the American

Civil Liberties Union. On Dec. 29, 1909, Newlon married Letha Hiestand of Martinsburg, Ind.; they had no children. Discouraged by the war and by the rising opposition to the progressive movement in education, Newlon died of a coronary thrombosis at his summer home in New Hope, Pa., in 1941, at the age of fifty-nine. He was buried in Crown Hill Cemetery in his hometown of Salem, Ind.

[Jesse Newlon Papers, Univ. of Denver Lib.; Gary L. Peltier, "Jesse L. Newlon as Superintendent of the Denver Public Schools, 1920–1927" (doctoral dissertation, Univ. of Denver, 1965), and Peltier's article, "Teacher Participation in Curriculum Revision: An Historical Case Study," Hist. of Education Quart., Summer 1967; obituaries in Teachers College Record, Oct. 1941 (by George S. Counts), Jour. of the Nat. Education Assoc., Oct. 1941, and N. Y. Times, Sept. 2, 1941; Nat. Cyc. Am. Biog., XXXII, 358–59; Who Was Who in America, vol. I (1942). See also: Laurence A. Cremin, David A. Shannon, and Mary E. Townsend, A Hist. of Teachers College, Columbia Univ. (1954); and Cremin, The Transformation of the School: Progressivism in Am. Education, 1876–1957 (1961).]

L. THOMAS HOPKINS

NIELSEN, ALICE (June 7, 1870?–Mar. 8, 1943), operatic soprano and concert singer, was born in Nashville, Tenn. Her father, Erasmus Ivarius Nielsen, was Danish; her mother, Sarah (Kilroy) Nielsen, was an American of Irish extraction. Reports of Alice's childhood are vague and conflicting. Her father is said to have been a soldier in the Union Army and to have died when Alice was still a small child. The family, which included several other children, lived for a time in Warrensburg, Mo., but after the father's death moved to Kansas City, Mo., where Mrs. Nielsen opened a boardinghouse. According to her own account, Alice, who reportedly inherited her musical talent from her father, began singing in the streets for pennies and small coins when she was about eight. She attended St. Teresa's Academy and joined the choir of St. Patrick's Catholic Church. Her first stage experience came about 1885 when she sang the role of Nanki-Poo in a juvenile production of The Mikado that toured small Missouri towns for some seven weeks. On May 7, 1889, in Kansas City, she married Benjamin Nentwig, organist of St. Patrick's, who helped her develop her voice; she also took lessons from a local music teacher, Max Decsi. Although the couple had a son, Benjamin, they soon separated and were divorced in 1898.

Alice Nielsen left Kansas City in 1892 as a member of a concert company that was eminently unsuccessful. Struggling through Omaha, Denver, and Salt Lake City, she arrived in Oakland, Calif., where in 1893 she sang Yum-Yum in The

Mikado as presented by the Burton Stanley Opera Company. In San Francisco, her goal of the moment, she sang at the Wigwam, a carefree music hall, and then at the Tivoli (for two years), where she found a voice teacher of considerable ability, Ida Valerga. When the Bostonians, the best and most famous light opera troupe in America, came to San Francisco, she determined to join them. Successful in her drive to the top, she quickly became one of the company's leading ladies and toured with it for two seasons, ultimately singing the part of Maid Marian in the operetta Robin Hood by Reginald De Koven [q.v.]. The wife of another composer, Victor Herbert [q.v.], after hearing Alice Nielsen sing, insisted that she be the heroine of her husband's The Serenade. Opening in Cleveland on Feb. 17, 1897, and in New York on Mar. 16, 1897, this proved immensely popular. Herbert, delighted with Miss Nielsen's charm, spirit, and ability, then wrote for her one of his operetta masterpieces, The Fortune Teller (Toronto, Sept. 14, 1898; New York, Sept. 26, 1898). By this time she headed her own opera company, managed by Frank L. Perley. She appeared in one more Herbert operetta the following year, The Singing Girl (Montreal, Oct. 2, 1899; New York, Oct. 23, 1899). Of Herbert's various prima donnas, Alice Nielsen proved the best.

Taking The Fortune Teller to London in 1901, where it ran for about three months, she was heard by the well-known teacher and impresario Henry Russell, who advised her to study for grand opera in Italy. This she did, a wealthy patroness of the arts, Mrs. Lionel Phillips, financing her studies in Rome. Miss Nielsen made a successful debut as Marguerite (in Faust) in Naples at the Teatro Bellini on Dec. 6, 1903. The following month she sang at the famous San Carlo in Naples, then returned to London, singing the roles of Zerlina, Susanna, and Mimi at Covent Garden. When Henry Russell became manager of the New Waldorf Theatre in London, he engaged Miss Nielsen as prima donna. During this period she twice returned to the United States on tour: in 1905–06, when she made her American grand opera debut in Don Pasquale (Casino Theatre, New York, Nov. 10, 1905), and in 1907–08 with the San Carlo Opera Company.

In 1909 Alice Nielsen joined the Boston Opera Company, with which, on Mar. 3, 1911, she created the role of Chonita in the opera The Sacrifice, by Frederick S. Converse [Supp. 2]. At the same time she was a member of the Metropolitan Opera Company (1909–13), singing Mimi, Norina (Don Pasquale), and Nedda. With this company, however, her appearances were rather infrequent. In 1917 she briefly returned to light opera, singing in *Kitty Darlin'*, a musical version of a play by David Belasco [*q.v.*], *Sweet Kitty Bellairs,* with music by Rudolf Friml. This was not successful and was abandoned after a few weeks at the Casino in New York. The final years of her professional career were devoted chiefly to concert appearances; her last public performance was in Symphony Hall, Boston, in 1923.

Alice Nielsen was vivacious, zestful, intelligent, and sometimes temperamental. Her greatest success was in Victor Herbert's operettas. Attempts at domestic life were discouraging; a later marriage, on Dec. 21, 1917, to LeRoy R. Stoddard, a New York surgeon, also ended in divorce. The last twenty years of her life were spent in relative seclusion in New York City, where she died in 1943. She was buried in St. Mary's Cemetery, Lawrence, N. Y.

[Alice Nielsen's autobiographical articles, "Born to Sing," *Collier's,* June 11, 18, 25, July 2, 9, 1932, have a ghost-written and publicity-conscious air. See also her "I Owe What I Am to Women," *Delineator,* Sept. 1926. Differing versions of her childhood and family background appear in interviews she gave at various times (clippings in Harvard Theatre Collection). Other sources: Lewis C. Strang, *Prima Donnas and Soubrettes* (1900); *Who Was Who in America,* vol. II (1950); obituaries in the *N. Y. Times,* Mar. 9, 1943, *Musical Courier,* Mar. 20, 1943, and *Musical America,* Mar. 25, 1943; E. N. Waters, *Victor Herbert* (1955); Henry Russell, *The Passing Show* (1926); Quaintance Eaton, *The Boston Opera Company* (1965). See also *Notable Am. Women,* II, 631–33. Alice Nielsen's marriage license application of May 1889 (Recorder of Deeds, Jackson County, Mo.) gives her age as 18; this would make her birth year 1870. In later life she commonly gave the year as 1876. A still earlier birth year is suggested by her death certificate (N. Y. City Dept. of Health), which gives her age as 74, but the certificate contains many inaccuracies in personal data.]

EDWARD N. WATERS

NOCK, ALBERT JAY (Oct. 13, 1870–Aug. 19, 1945), author and editor, was the only child (an elder sister having died in infancy) of Emma Sheldon (Jay) and Joseph Albert Nock. He was born in Scranton, Pa., the home of his mother's parents, but lived until the age of ten in the quiet suburb of Brooklyn, N. Y., where his father, an Episcopal minister, had a parish. The family then moved to Alpena, Mich., a lumbering town settled by New Englanders. Albert grew up in a home lacking all frills yet filled with books, where respect for learning and religion were quietly inculcated. This instilled in him a hatred for superfluous possessions and a disdain for materialism that influenced him throughout his life and permeated his social ideas. His ancestry was English Methodist on his father's side and French Protestant on his mother's; this heritage of dis-

sidence, despite the mediation of his father's Episcopalianism, vigorously colored Nock's later ideas. He regarded his mother and her relatives as the chief influences on his youthful character, especially the "suave irony, characteristically French" and the "gentle and persuasive scepticism" which induced his early agnostic bent.

Until he was fourteen Nock was kept at home, his education "wholly self-directed," thus permitting him ample time for outdoor sports and rambling. He then went to a boarding school in Illinois and in 1887 entered St. Stephen's (later Bard) College, where he took his B.A. in 1892. Over the next few years he apparently attended graduate school erratically, including a year (1895–96) at Berkeley Divinity School, then in Middletown, Conn. He may also have played semiprofessional baseball. Nock never earned an advanced degree, but instead, at his mother's urging, entered the Episcopal ministry in 1897. Until 1909 he led the quiet life of a minister, with parishes successively in Titusville, Pa., Blacksburg, Va., and Detroit, Mich. On Apr. 25, 1900, he married Agnes Grumbine of Titusville; they had two children, Samuel A. and Francis Jay.

The circumscribed parish life soon palled. Nock gave up the ministry late in 1909, left his wife and family, and turned to a career in journalism and scholarship. He wrote first for the muckraking *American Magazine,* where as a staff member (1910–14) he was associated with Lincoln Steffens [Supp. 2], Ida Tarbell [Supp. 3], and John Reed [*q.v.*]; his most lasting achievement during this period was to cajole Brand Whitlock [*q.v.*], the progressive mayor of Toledo, into writing his autobiography. An ardent pacifist, Nock worked for Woodrow Wilson's election in 1916, but Wilson's subsequent course so infuriated him that he became an almost purebred philosophical anarchist and scarcely ever said a good word about a living politician afterward. He worked briefly for Oswald Garrison Villard's *Nation* in 1919, and then started his own magazine, the *Freeman,* in 1920, editing it with Francis Neilson, a British liberal and single-taxer whose wife, a Swift heiress, subsidized the venture. Nock quickly earned a reputation as an excellent editor, capable of getting the best from his writers; his austere formality often chilled more vibrant men, but his total devotion to intellectual freedom, Western culture, and the English language soon produced a magazine admired even by those who were exasperated by its politics. The mounting deficit and his own ill health led to his resignation in 1924. Thereafter he devoted himself to the writing of books and articles, receiving substantial financial support from a succession of admirers, and living in New York City and at various rural retreats in New England, with frequent sojourns abroad, especially in Brussels.

Nock's essays, dealing chiefly with education, feminism, morals, and other social topics, have been collected in part in three books: *On Doing the Right Thing* (1928), *Free Speech and Plain Language* (1937), and *Snoring as a Fine Art* (1958). Of his books, *Jefferson* (1926) is still read as an excellent introduction to Thomas Jefferson's character and intellectual life. His *Francis Rabelais: The Man and His Work* (with Catherine R. Wilson, 1929), which reflects his warm admiration for Rabelais's gaiety and detachment, remains a useful tool for students. His long essay, *Henry George* (1939), surveys the life of one of Nock's chief intellectual mentors. His greatest book is his *Memoirs of a Superfluous Man* (1943), an autobiography that seems likely to have a permanent place in American letters. Two years after its publication, Nock died of lymphatic leukemia at the home of a friend, Ruth Robinson, in Wakefield, R. I. He was buried in Riverside Cemetery in Wakefield.

Nock was one of those figures who achieves minor importance in so many areas that he tends to be passed over by those who study his ideas as part of a single discipline. In culture and criticism he was a disciple of Matthew Arnold, whose plea for an "interesting civilization" and whose argument for an elite "remnant" of humanity Nock adopted wholeheartedly. He attacked American materialism with epithets about its "economism" and its faith in "Fordismus," the capitalistic mystique of Henry Ford. In political science Nock was influenced chiefly by Herbert Spencer; he defended free trade and the notion of a self-regulating Nature even after he decided that progress was a myth. In history he was a Jeffersonian, yearning after rural peace even as he lived most of his life in New York, hating big government and centralization with great passion and wit, and arguing for Jefferson's elitist plan of education. Although he endorsed Henry George's single tax idea early in his career, he was not a social reformer except in the sense of wanting to civilize society. From the anthropologist Franz Oppenheimer, Nock derived his view of the state as the organization of one class to exploit the rest. He was also a historical revisionist, whose first book attacked the idea that Germany was solely guilty for starting World War I, and an isolationist, whose cosmopolitanism belied the stereotype of the isolationists as Midwestern primitives or sour progressives. He insisted that women should be regarded as persons

in their own right, argued for their full equality before the law and for a single sexual standard, and upheld their right to vote, even while ridiculing suffrage as a social panacea and deploring the vulgarization of life inherent in the rise of "the New Woman of Anglo-American feminism." Finally, in *The Theory of Education in the United States* (1932) he wrote one of the first critiques of John Dewey's educational ideas as applied to colleges, thus joining Abraham Flexner, Robert Maynard Hutchins, and others in trying to reinvigorate classical, "useless" learning.

Nock retains a firm if minor place in American intellectual history. He was not a seminal thinker, and his affection for Jeffersonian agrarianism and the single tax lingered far longer than they should have. He was all but immune to criticism, no matter how perceptive, and the more his ideas differed from American, "democratic" norms, the more stubbornly he clung to them. He had some influence on modern education and on the radical right after World War II. In his attacks on the centralized state and the growing impersonality and materialism of modern life, he had much in common with the New Left of the 1960's and 1970's. But his real place is in the select gallery of American nonconformists, whose legacy is their ability to irritate men into thought, to encourage the flouting of conventional wisdom, and to maintain certain standards of value in an age of flux.

[The chief primary sources are Nock's own *Memoirs of a Superfluous Man;* Van Wyck Brooks, *Days of the Phoenix* (1957); Francis Neilson, *My Life in Two Worlds* (2 vols., 1952–53), on the *Freeman* years; and Frank Chodorov, *Out of Step* (1962), on the later years. See also Ruth Robinson's "Memories of Albert Jay Nock," in Francis J. Nock, ed., *Selected Letters of Albert Jay Nock* (1962). Secondary material includes Susan J. Turner, *A Hist. of the Freeman* (1963); and Robert M. Crunden, *The Mind and Art of Albert Jay Nock* (1964). The chief Nock papers are at Yale; lesser collections are the Nock and Brand Whitlock papers in the Lib. of Cong., and the Oswald Garrison Villard papers at Harvard. There is a good likeness printed in the original edition of the *Memoirs*. The Crunden study contains the fullest bibliography to date, and includes identification of many of Nock's unsigned articles.]

ROBERT M. CRUNDEN

NORRIS, CHARLES GILMAN SMITH (Apr. 23, 1881–July 25, 1945), novelist, was born in Chicago, Ill., to Benjamin Franklin Norris, a well-to-do jeweler, and Gertrude Glorvina (Doggett) Norris. He was the youngest of their five children, but only he and his brother Frank [*q.v.*], later the celebrated naturalistic novelist, survived early childhood. His mother named him after her obstetrician, having little interest in the baby who "had cost her so much during her struggle to bring him to birth" (Kathleen Norris, *Family Gathering,* p. 74) ; Norris early dropped the "Smith."

Although eleven years younger than his brother, Charles shared most of Frank's youthful experiences, in a family environment where the cultural ambitions of their mother, a former actress, clashed with the drive for material success of their father, an ardent follower of the evangelist Dwight L. Moody [*q.v.*]. The Norrises moved to Oakland, Calif., in 1884, and the following year to San Francisco. In 1887 they spent a year in London and Paris, where Frank concocted medieval stories around Charles's toy soldiers, thus inspiring Charles's first writing, a historical romance about Louis XIV composed at age ten. Back in California, the boys' father abandoned his family in 1892, to be divorced by his wife five years later. Turning her primary attention to Frank, Gertrude Norris in 1894 took her sons to Cambridge, Mass., for a year, so that Frank could study at Harvard. Charles completed his education in California, graduating from the University of California with the Ph.B. degree in 1903.

He then went to New York City to serve as an assistant editor of the magazine *Country Life in America*. Tiring, however, of rural assignments, he returned to San Francisco in 1905 to become the circulation manager of *Sunset* magazine, then issued by the Southern Pacific Railroad. It was in *Sunset* that his first published fiction appeared: a sentimental story reminiscent of Bret Harte [*q.v.*] ("An Audience of One," December 1906) ; and it was during this period that he met a young San Francisco newspaperwoman, Kathleen Thompson, who became his wife on Apr. 30, 1909. They were married in New York City, where Norris had moved the year before to become art editor of the *American Magazine*. Three children were born to the Norrises: a son, Frank, who became a physician, and twin daughters who died in infancy; some years later, in 1918, they adopted another son, William Rice Norris. Charles Norris remained on the reform-conscious *American* staff until 1913, serving briefly also as assistant editor of the *Christian Herald* in 1912. He then resigned all regular employment, for the rapidly increasing income from his wife's fiction made it possible for both to become full-time writers.

Norris's first novel, *The Amateur* (1916), was followed by *Salt, or The Education of Griffith Adams,* published in 1918. Enlisting that year in the R.O.T.C., Norris served until the Armistice as an infantry officer. In 1919 he and his wife lived in Rio de Janeiro, where Norris wrote his third novel, *Brass* (1921), but the death of his mother brought them back to California, where they finally settled on a ranch in Saratoga. Their guests there and at their winter home in Palo Alto included many of the most prominent people of the stage, the screen, publishing, and politics, among them Frank Doubleday, Sinclair Lewis, Edna Ferber, Harold Ross, Gertrude Lawrence, Somerset Maugham, Noel Coward, Herbert Hoover, Charles Lindbergh, and Theodore Roosevelt, Jr. [Supp. 3].

Charles Gilman Norris was a sensitive, generous man, although he was frequently in polar disagreement with his wife on basic ideologies: he was Episcopalian, she an ardent Roman Catholic; he an antiprohibitionist, she an active member of the W.C.T.U.; he was a vocal interventionist even before Pearl Harbor, while she was one of the organizers of the America First movement. Kathleen Norris wrote with ease; Charles Norris wrote slowly and carefully, doing detailed research for each of his novels, all of which dealt with controversial social and ethical problems. Despite his apparently uneventful career, his novels contain numerous semiautobiographical passages which reflect some of the deepest concerns of his life. *The Amateur* is partly patterned after the life of Frank Norris; *Salt* details the systems of graft in railroad promotional magazines; *Bread* (1923) deals with problems of the married career woman; and most of his novels deal with marriage, divorce, and families in reduced circumstances, as in *Brass, Zelda Marsh* (1927), *Zest* (1933), *Hands* (1935), and *Bricks without Straw* (1938). There is considerable overlapping of thematic material in all his work, but *Salt* is particularly concerned with the American educational system, *Pig Iron* (1925) with business ethics, *Seed* (1930) with birth control, and *Flint* (1944) with labor strife. Norris's novels were generally well received, and though they never earned the critical acclaim awarded his brother's works, or approached the total ten million sales of his wife's fiction, *Seed* sold more than 70,000 copies in its first edition and *Brass,* another best seller, was made into a motion picture (1923). Moreover, Norris avoided the romanticism of his brother's writing and the sentimentality of Kathleen Norris.

On one occasion (*Bookman,* December 1925, p. 410), Norris named as his favorite fictional character Hurstwood, in Dreiser's *Sister Carrie,* a novel which Frank Norris had "discovered" as a reader for Doubleday. The choice exemplifies Charles Gilman Norris's place as an heir to both Frank Norris and Theodore Dreiser [Supp. 3], whom he resembled in the scrupulous honesty of his characterization and plot motivation and the cool precision of his sociological description. In the judgment of F. Scott Fitzgerald [Supp. 2], Norris wrote "intelligently and painstakingly— but without passion and without pain." Clearly, his work lacks the flair and effusiveness of Frank Norris and the overwhelming impact of Dreiser, but he shared with both the cosmic sense of conflicting natural forces and the truthful approach to a morally neutral environment which distinguished American naturalism.

Aside from his novels, Norris wrote a few short stories and some poetic dramas for the Bohemian Club of San Francisco. He edited the manuscript of his brother's *Vandover and the Brute,* published in 1914 after Frank Norris's death, adding about five thousand words of his own, and wrote a brief sketch of his brother for Doubleday, Page and Company. He died in Palo Alto of a heart ailment and was buried there at Alta Mesa Cemetery.

[The Bancroft Lib. of the Univ. of Calif., Berkeley, has an extensive collection of C. G. Norris papers. Kathleen Norris's two autobiographies, *Noon* (1925) and *Family Gathering* (1959), contain many details of her husband's life, and the latter has numerous photographs of Norris and his friends. Some biographical material is included in Franklin Walker's *Frank Norris* (1932); in Charles Norris's introduction to his wife's novel *Mother* in *Golden Book,* Nov. 1924, p. 50; and in an interview with Arnold Patrick in *Bookman,* July 1925, pp. 563–66. Of interest, too, is Kenneth S. Lynn's chapter on Frank Norris in *The Dream of Success* (1955). A good critical study is Arnold L. Goldsmith, "Charles and Frank Norris," *Western Am. Literature,* Spring 1967. Factual sources include *Who Was Who in America,* vol. II (1950); Stanley J. Kunitz and Howard Haycraft, eds., *Twentieth Century Authors* (1942); and obituary in *N. Y. Times,* July 26, 1945.]

FRED E. H. SCHROEDER

NORRIS, GEORGE WILLIAM (July 11, 1861–Sept. 2, 1944), Congressman and Senator from Nebraska, was born on a farm in Sandusky County, Ohio, the eleventh child and second son of Chauncey and Mary Magdalene (Mook) Norris. Of the twelve children in the family, ten reached maturity. Norris's father, born in Connecticut of Scotch-Irish descent, and his mother, of Pennsylvania Dutch background, had both settled in upstate New York, where they were married in 1838; both were uneducated and wrote their names with difficulty. In 1846 they set out by wagon for Ohio, where the family prospered and grew. At the time of George's birth his father was fifty-four years old, his mother forty-three, and his two eldest sisters already married. When "Willie" was only three his father died of pneumonia and his only brother, a soldier

in General Sherman's army, died of wounds received at Resaca, Ga. The mother assumed management of the eighty-acre farm. Although unable to provide intellectual or cultural stimulation, she taught her children a concern for the poor and a belief in the absolute goodness and righteousness of the Lord. She was, however, not a church member, and her son never joined a church.

While a pupil at the local district school, Norris spent the summers working on the family farm or for neighboring farmers. He attended Baldwin University (later Baldwin-Wallace College) in Ohio in 1877–78 and, after teaching school for a year to earn money, entered Northern Indiana Normal School and Business Institute (later Valparaiso University), where he studied law, excelled in rhetoric and debate, and received the LL.B. degree in 1883. Although admitted to the Indiana bar the same year, he spent the next two years teaching school in Ohio and Washington state. In 1885 he moved to Nebraska and opened a law office, at first in Beatrice and then in Beaver City.

Nebraska was prosperous in these years, and Norris quickly established himself as a rising young man. In conjunction with his law practice he engaged in the milling and mortgage-loan businesses and was local attorney for the Burlington & Missouri Railroad (later the Chicago, Burlington & Quincy). On June 1, 1889, he married Pluma Lashley, daughter of Beaver City's most prominent businessman and banker. They had three daughters: Hazel, Marian, and Gertrude.

Nebraska's prosperity gave way in the 1890's to drought and depression, and Norris's business ventures suffered severely. Although he was a Republican in a heavily Populist area, he decided to seek a livelihood in public office. He secured appointment to two unexpired terms as prosecuting attorney of Furnas County and then was elected in his own right in 1892. Three years later, narrowly defeating the Populist incumbent, he won the first of two four-year terms as judge of Nebraska's fourteenth judicial district. Norris moved in 1900 from Beaver City to McCook, Nebr., which became his permanent home. A heavy personal blow came the next year when his wife died shortly after the birth of their third daughter. Despite his agreement with much of the Populist program, Norris remained a loyal Republican, and in 1902, seeking a larger stage for his talents, he won the party's Congressional nomination in his district. In the November election he defeated the Democratic incumbent by 181 votes. On July 8, 1903, he married a McCook schoolteacher, Ellie Leonard, at the home of her parents in San Jose, Calif. Their only children died at birth.

As a freshman Congressman, Norris displayed neither marked ability nor marked liberal tendencies. He sympathized with Theodore Roosevelt's domestic policies, but he was indebted to the party organization and to railroad officials for help in his campaign. Joseph G. Cannon [q.v.], the conservative Republican leader in the House with whom he was later to cross swords, even spoke in his district when Norris ran for reelection in 1904. Yet Norris was sensitive to the political mood of his constituents. He approved the legislation being enacted in Nebraska to curb the railroads and the brewers and to make government more efficient and more representative. By supporting the federal administration's railroad bills, and by quietly returning his free railroad pass in 1906, Norris broke his ties with the Chicago, Burlington & Quincy. In May 1908, furthermore, he openly cast his lot with the House insurgents, who introduced an abortive resolution that would have sharply curtailed the power of Speaker Cannon by ending his control of the powerful Committee on Rules. Norris soon learned the price of insurgency. Although he backed the presidential candidacy of William Howard Taft in 1908, he received little help from either the state or the national Republican organization in his own reelection campaign. He won by a mere twenty-two votes; the experience convinced him that he should not tie his political fortunes too firmly to those of the Republican party.

With Taft in the White House, animosity between the Old Guard and the insurgents became more pronounced, heightened by the sympathetic coverage the insurgents received in the press. Taft withdrew patronage from the rebels and sought support for his legislative program from Speaker Cannon, leading to insurgent charges that he had abandoned the principles of Roosevelt. House Democrats, for their part, encouraged the renewed efforts of insurgent Republicans to curb the power of a now thoroughly aroused and angered Speaker. Norris, whose role in the 1908 revolt had cost him desirable committee assignments, precipitated the dramatic revolution on Mar. 17, 1910, with a request for permission to present a matter privileged by the Constitution. When Cannon unsuspectingly acceded, Norris called for an elected Rules Committee on which the Speaker would not be eligible to sit. Cannon initially declared the resolution out of order but eventually had to give way. After an emotional thirty-six-hour fight, Norris's resolution was adopted by a vote of 191 to 156. While pleased by this fundamental procedural reform, possibly the most important in the history of the House of Representatives, Norris recognized that it was only an initial step toward achieving progressive social and economic legislation.

Now a national political figure, George Norris won easy election to a fifth term in 1910 and figured prominently in the rapidly coalescing progressive movement. He was chosen first vice-president of the National Progressive Republican League when it was formed in January 1911. He endorsed Robert M. La Follette [q.v.] for the 1912 Republican presidential nomination, switching his support to Theodore Roosevelt only when convinced that La Follette could not win the nomination. He stayed out of Roosevelt's third-party campaign of that year, not wishing to relinquish Nebraska's Republican organization to the "stand-pat" elements and thus jeopardize his own ambitions to rise to the Senate. His strategy succeeded; he defeated the incumbent Senator Norris Brown, a Taft supporter, in the Republican primary of April 1912, and in a bitter, hard-fought campaign that autumn emerged as the only major Republican victor in a Democratic landslide in Nebraska.

Entering the Senate on Mar. 4, 1913, at the age of fifty-one, Norris was to serve in that body continuously for the next thirty years. In these three decades of political and social upheaval, he steadily gained in stature, preserving his independence yet never becoming a mere obstructionist. During the Woodrow Wilson era Norris supported many of the administration's key measures, including the Federal Reserve and anti-monopoly bills, and in 1916 he was one of three non-Democratic Senators to vote for the Supreme Court nomination of Louis D. Brandeis [Supp. 3]. But he objected to Democratic efforts to assure total support of Wilson's program through caucus control, contending that it prevented the addition of worthwhile amendments and represented a continuation of "Cannonism" under Democratic auspices. On foreign affairs, Norris was highly critical of Wilson's Mexican policy and particularly of the American occupation of Vera Cruz in 1914. Three years later he was one of the "little group of willful men"—in Wilson's phrase—who opposed a resolution authorizing the arming of merchant ships traversing the Atlantic war zone. Believing that the United States was being led into the European hostilities by the nation's financial and commercial interests, he was also one of six Senators who voted against the American declaration of war in April 1917.

Norris nevertheless unstintingly supported the

administration in the prosecution of the war, while endorsing such antiprofiteering measures as heavier taxation and, where possible, direct government operation of industries. Rejected because of his age when he volunteered for military service, he was easily elected to a second Senate term in 1918 by Nebraskans dissatisfied with wartime agricultural restrictions and the monopolistic practices of meat packers. Although an advocate of international cooperation to ensure a permanent peace, Norris felt the Versailles Treaty contained serious inequities; he especially denounced the secret diplomacy by which Shantung was transferred to Japanese control and the sanctioning of continued British domination of colonial peoples. As a result, he joined the Senate "Irreconcilables" in opposition to the treaty.

During the Republican ascendancy of the 1920's, Norris served as chairman of the Senate's Agriculture and Forestry and Judiciary committees; but his views were out of harmony with those of the dominant groups in his party. He was one of those labeled "sons of the wild jackass" by Senator George Moses [Supp. 3] of New Hampshire for their unrelenting criticism of the complacency and business domination of the Harding, Coolidge, and Hoover administrations. Norris's disillusionment with his party stemmed in part from the low caliber of Republicans appointed or elected to public office, many of whom, he believed, were too intimately connected with corporate wealth or corrupt interests. On these grounds he opposed Senate confirmation of the nominations of Charles Evans Hughes and John J. Parker to the Supreme Court, of Charles B. Warren as Attorney General, and of Thomas F. Woodlock to the Interstate Commerce Commission, as well as the seating in the Senate of Truman H. Newberry [Supp. 3], Frank L. Smith, and William S. Vare [q.v.]. Of these, only Hughes and Newberry were approved, and the latter soon resigned his Senate seat. Norris's foreign policy views in the 1920's were similarly unorthodox. He early favored recognition of the Soviet Union, opposed the activities of American corporations and United States Marines in Nicaragua, and sympathized with the aspirations of the Mexican revolution.

Even in the hostile political environment of the 1920's, however, Norris's role was never merely one of opposition. Emerging as the leader of the Congressional liberals after the death of Robert La Follette in 1925, he became an outspoken advocate of farm relief, the rights of labor, more efficient use of the nation's natural resources, and the direct election of presidents. An early participant in the so-called farm bloc, in 1924 he introduced the Norris-Sinclair Bill, a predecessor of the McNary-Haugen plan for government purchase and sale abroad of farm surpluses. He was the author of the Norris–La Guardia Anti-Injunction Act of 1932, which curbed the use of injunctions in labor disputes, barred the enforcement of "yellow-dog" (antiunion) contracts, and asserted the right of labor to organize and bargain collectively. He was also responsible for the Twentieth Amendment to the Constitution (the "Lame Duck" amendment), shifting the date of presidential inaugurations from March to January and eliminating the holdover ("lame-duck") session of the outgoing Congress formerly held between the election and the presidential inauguration. This amendment, the only one enacted almost entirely through the efforts of one man, was proposed to the legislatures of the several states in March 1932 and ratified the following February.

Braving the wrath of utility-company spokesmen, Norris in the 1920's became the leading figure in political life favoring the public production, transmission, and distribution of hydroelectric power. The most important battle he engaged in during the decade was his almost single-handed fight to save from private exploitation the valuable hydroelectric facilities partially developed by the government as a wartime measure at Muscle Shoals, Ala. First he had to stave off measures calling for the sale of these properties to private bidders, among them Henry Ford and private utility companies, at figures far below their actual value. By 1928 he had won many colleagues to his position, and his bill calling for government ownership and development of Muscle Shoals was enacted by Congress. President Coolidge vetoed the measure, however, as did Herbert Hoover when it was reenacted in 1931.

Norris's loose ties to the Republican party continued to weaken during the 1920's. He favored Hiram Johnson [Supp. 3] for the presidency in 1920, and in 1924 he supported Robert La Follette's third-party bid—though not publicly, since he was himself seeking election to a third Senate term. In 1928 he denounced his party's platform planks on agriculture and hydroelectric power and opposed the candidacy of Herbert Hoover. He campaigned that year for progressive Senators of both parties, and shortly before the election he publicly endorsed Alfred E. Smith [Supp. 3], the Democratic candidate. With the economic collapse after 1929, Norris's disaffection with his party intensified. The Hoover administration's depression policies he regarded as either unrealistic and unworkable or overly helpful to those who least needed help: the banks and large corporations. In 1930 Republican regulars, plotting his defeat in the Nebraska primary, endorsed another George W. Norris, a grocery clerk, but the scheme was frustrated by the courts and the "grocer Norris" later served a prison sentence for his part in the plot.

Norris endorsed the presidential candidacy of Franklin D. Roosevelt in 1932 and was a staunch supporter of most New Deal measures. He was largely responsible for the passage of the Norris-Rayburn Rural Electrification Act of 1936, which made permanent the Rural Electrification Administration, and the Norris-Doxey Farm Forestry Act of 1937. Still deeply committed to the public development of natural resources, he was the chief author of the act in May 1933 which created the Tennessee Valley Authority (TVA) to supervise the multipurpose development of the Tennessee River. Though broader in scope, the TVA was clearly rooted in the Norris bills earlier vetoed by Presidents Coolidge and Hoover. In recognition of his sponsorship of the immense project, the first dam built by the TVA was called Norris Dam, and his name was also given to the model community developed nearby. He was responsible, too, for the construction of a "little TVA" in Nebraska which helped make it, like Tennessee, an all-public-power state. His advocacy of the multiple-purpose public development of other river valleys, however, was unsuccessful.

Senator Norris was closer to Franklin Roosevelt, politically and personally, than to any other president under whom he served. He openly supported F.D.R. in all four of his presidential races and actively campaigned for him in 1932 and 1940, playing a particularly effective role in Western states, where public power was an important issue. In 1936, when Norris successfully ran as an independent for a fifth Senate term, the President strongly endorsed him, and the Democratic party in Nebraska reluctantly followed suit.

Even in the New Deal years, however, Norris remained his own man. A critic of Roosevelt's 1937 court-packing plan, he proposed his own measure to limit all federal judges to one nine-year term and to require a two-thirds vote of the Supreme Court to invalidate acts of Congress. Norris was, furthermore, relentless in his criticism of partisanship and of the patronage policies of James A. Farley, Postmaster General and chairman of the Democratic National Committee. He insisted on writing into the TVA and Rural Electrification acts the provision that all appointments and promotions should be entirely on a merit basis. In his home state he played a major

role in the adoption, in 1934, of a constitutional amendment establishing a unicameral legislature to be chosen in nonpartisan elections.

With the advent of the Second World War, Norris reluctantly concluded that totalitarian aggression could be met only by force or the threat of force. Though he opposed the establishment of compulsory military service in 1940, he did support a revision of the neutrality law to allow the Allies to buy American arms on a "cash and carry" basis; and in 1941 he endorsed the Lend-Lease Bill. As early as 1938 he called for a consumer boycott of Japanese silk, and after Pearl Harbor he voted for the declaration of war on Japan. Always sensitive to civil liberties issues, he criticized the Justice Department and the Federal Bureau of Investigation for their wartime treatment of aliens and other suspect persons. One of his last legislative concerns was the drive to repeal the poll tax in national elections.

Early in 1942 Norris announced his intention of retiring, but when the campaign was well under way he changed his mind and ran for a sixth Senatorial term. Wartime duties kept him in Washington until the weekend before the election, while his opponents directly appealed to Nebraska voters increasingly disillusioned with the Roosevelt administration. Despite endorsements of Norris by the President and by numerous Senate colleagues of both parties, the Democratic party in Nebraska stood by its own candidate, and Norris, running again as an independent, was defeated by a Republican, Kenneth S. Wherry.

Returning to his hometown of McCook, Norris retained his keen interest in the issues of public power and resource utilization and developed a new concern over global matters and the nature of the postwar world. His autobiography, *Fighting Liberal* (written with the help of James E. Lawrence, a Nebraska newspaper editor and political associate), was completed in August 1944, several weeks before he was stricken with a cerebral hemorrhage. He died in McCook at the age of eighty-three and was buried in the town's Memorial Park Cemetery.

The remarkable political success of George Norris was rooted in part in his personal style. He was a fearless speaker whose integrity could never be doubted. Yet he always spoke in a conversational fashion, devoid of oratorical effects. His manner was amiable and mild, and he willingly conceded that he could be mistaken. Normally slow to anger, he became aroused whenever he detected the involvement of private privilege or partisan politics in public issues. Though not lacking in wit and humor, he could hardly be described as jovial, and he was prone to occasional periods of depression. He was a phenomenally hard worker, and few surpassed him in parliamentary skill.

In the popular mind Norris was widely regarded as an idealist who would fight for his beliefs to the bitter end regardless of person or party—an impression heightened by the sternness of his visage and the steadiness of his gaze. In fact he was neither unrealistic nor rigid politically, and the prospect of compromise did not alarm him, provided he could thereby gain at least a part of what he sought. Though firmly rooted in rural America, Norris clearly understood the impact of an increasingly industrialized and integrated national economy upon the lives of farmers and city dwellers alike, and did not hesitate to call for extensions of federal power to curb privilege or promote the general welfare.

Norris is usually grouped politically with other progressive Republicans like La Follette and William E. Borah [Supp. 2] of Idaho, but he differed from them in significant respects. Unlike La Follette, whose views were perhaps closest to his own, he never stressed the necessity of organization and discipline among progressives. He and Borah were both "loners" in politics, but Borah's unpredictability, bombastic style, and love 'of publicity—as well as his emphasis on states' rights—were all uncharacteristic of Norris. With La Follette, Norris understood that patient attention to legislative detail and committee routine were integral parts of a Senator's job.

Norris's career, unlike that of many politicians, ended on a note of fulfillment rather than of decline. After his years in the political wilderness, power and recognition flowed to him in the 1930's. With the lone exception of the 1910 insurgency fight against Speaker Cannon, his major achievements—the Anti-Injunction Law, the "Lame Duck" amendment, TVA, the Rural Electrification Act, the unicameral legislature in Nebraska—all came after he had passed the age of seventy. In his last years he was widely regarded as one of the outstanding legislators in American political history, and perhaps that history's most distinguished independent. "He stands forth," said Franklin Roosevelt of Norris during the 1932 campaign, "as the very perfect, gentle knight of American progressive ideals."

[Norris's papers are in the Lib. of Cong.; a small collection is in the Nebr. State Hist. Soc. His autobiography, *Fighting Liberal*, gives insight into his personality but is uncritical of most men and many measures that concerned him during his career. Richard Lowitt, *George W. Norris*, is a full-scale scholarly biography, of which two volumes have been published (1963, 1971). Norman L. Zucker, *George W. Norris: Gentle Knight of Democracy* (1966), is a topical study of Norris's political career. Earlier biographies are Alfred Lief, *Democracy's Norris* (1939); and Richard L. Neuberger and Stephen B. Kahn, *Integrity: The Life of George W. Norris* (1937). Interpretive essays are Arthur M. Schlesinger, Jr.'s introduction to the Collier Books edition (1961) of Norris's autobiography; and David Fellman, "The Liberalism of Senator Norris," *Am. Political Sci. Rev.*, Feb. 1946. See also Charles A. Madison's chapter on Norris in his *Leaders and Liberals in 20th Century America* (1961); and Claudius O. Johnson in John T. Salter, ed., *The Am. Politician* (1938). The June 1961 issue of *Nebr. Hist.* was devoted to Norris. Useful material on aspects of Norris's career is found in Kenneth W. Hechler, *Insurgency: Personalities and Politics of the Taft Era* (1940); *The Journals of David E. Lilienthal*, vol. I (1964); Judson King, *The Conservation Fight, from Theodore Roosevelt to the Tennessee Valley Authority* (1959); and Preston J. Hubbard, *Origins of the TVA: The Muscle Shoals Controversy, 1920–1932* (1961). For conditions in Norris's state throughout the years he served in Congress, see James C. Olson's *Hist. of Nebr.* (1955).]

RICHARD LOWITT

NORTON, CHARLES HOTCHKISS (Nov. 23, 1851–Oct. 27, 1942), mechanical engineer and machine tool designer, was born in Plainville, Conn. (then part of the town of Farmington), the first of three children, all sons, of John Calvin and Harriet (Hotchkiss) Norton. He was a descendant of John Norton [*q.v.*], a Puritan clergyman who emigrated to Massachusetts in 1635, and of Samuel Hotchkiss, who settled in New Haven, Conn., about 1641. Norton's father, born in Boston, was a cabinetmaker who worked in the Whiting and Royce clock dial factory in Plainville; his mother was employed by the same firm as a painter of dials.

After attending the public schools of Plainville and Thomaston, Conn., Norton went to work in 1866 as a chore boy for the Seth Thomas Clock Company in Thomaston. His aptitude and resourcefulness in machine building soon led to his promotion to machinist and then to foreman, superintendent of machinery, and manager of the department making tower clocks. During his years with Seth Thomas he designed many public clocks, and through practical experience became familiar with the mass production methods of interchangeable manufacture which Connecticut clockmakers working in the tradition of Chauncey Jerome [*q.v.*] were refining and extending in the years after the Civil War.

In 1886 Norton took a position as assistant engineer with the Brown & Sharpe Manufacturing Company at Providence, R. I., later becoming its designer and engineer for cylindrical grinding machinery. When he came to Providence the grinding machine, as pioneered by Jacob R. Brown and others between 1864 and 1876, was in a state of rapid transition; no longer employed merely for sharpening tools and finishing surfaces, it was being used in the manufacture of small metal parts and was potentially a metal-cutting device capable of both high precision and volume production. The universal grinding machine exhibited by Brown & Sharpe at the Paris Exposition of 1876 had been one of the peak achievements of this early period. In 1887 Norton redesigned this machine to give it greater rigidity, and within the next two years perfected a spindle that made internal grinding commercially feasible. By 1890 the major elements and standard types of precision grinding machines were familiar in progressive factories and shops, and had been greatly improved by automatic power and a variety of controls. Nevertheless, precision grinding was for the most part still confined to light manufacturing.

Norton left Brown & Sharpe in 1890 to become a partner in the newly established Detroit firm of Leland, Faulconer & Norton Company. Henry Martyn Leland, a former machinist and department head at Brown & Sharpe who later became one of the pioneers of the automotive industry, was vice-president and general manager; Robert C. Faulconer, who had put up $40,000 for the venture, was president; and Norton was brought in as a designer of new machinery and given a small stock interest. The firm quickly prospered, and its diversified business gave Norton broader experience in the design and building of production machine tools. He withdrew from the firm in 1895 (it later merged with the Cadillac Automobile Company) and, after working briefly as a mechanical engineer in Bridgeport, Conn., returned the next year to Brown & Sharpe.

During his second sojourn with the Providence firm Norton formulated the principles of precision grinding that marked his most creative contribution to the American machine tool industry, then entering upon a highly innovative era with the emergence of the newer mass production industries, notably automobile manufacture. His use of a larger and wider grinding wheel made it unnecessary to traverse the workpiece, thereby making possible the construction of a machine operating on the feed principle. This fast, flexible, and economical technique, later known as plunge grinding, involved greater power, higher speed, heavier cuts, and more rigid construction. Additional improvements made it possible to turn out highly accurate contoured work on a commercial volume basis. With these ideas Norton developed the precision grinding machine from a light production tool of limited capability to a heavy special-purpose machine integral to modern industrial technology.

Norton's revolutionary approach encountered considerable opposition at Brown & Sharpe, and in 1900 he left to found the Norton Grinding Company in Worcester, Mass. Individual members of the Norton Emery Wheel Company in Worcester (known after 1900 as the Norton Company), to whose founders he was not related, gave him financial backing, and he became chief engineer of his new firm. The two companies were completely independent until 1919, when the Norton Company acquired the grinding firm by merger; thereafter Charles H. Norton served as chief engineer of the machinery division until 1934, when, now in his eighties, he became consulting engineer.

After forming his own company Norton promptly built his first heavy-production cylindrical grinding machine, patenting it in 1904. It weighed more than 15,000 pounds, had a metal-cutting capacity of one cubic inch of steel per minute, and from rough stock turned out work of extremely fine dimensional accuracy and high surface finish. (This first machine, built in 1900, was sold to R. Hoe & Company, printing press manufacturers, and is now in the Henry Ford Museum at Dearborn, Mich.) By 1903 Norton had also produced a special crankshaft-grinding machine which performed in fifteen minutes a series of operations that had formerly required five hours. It was adopted by automobile manufacturers, among them Henry Ford, who ordered thirty-five for making the Model T at his new Highland Park plant. A camshaft-grinding machine invented by Norton also proved of great value to the automotive industry. During the First World War the Norton firm made important contributions to the output of aircraft engines, field artillery, and munitions. Well after his sixty-fifth year, Norton continued to introduce new types of cylindrical grinding machines that progressively reduced the cost of precision-ground work. He held more than a hundred patents and was the author of *Principles of Cylindrical Grinding* (1917). In 1925 he received the John Scott Medal from the City of Philadelphia for his invention of accurate high-gear grinding machinery.

Norton was married three times. His first wife, whom he married on Jan. 7, 1873, was Julia Eliza Bishop of Thomaston, Conn., by whom he had two daughters, Ida and Fannie. On June 16, 1896, following a divorce, he married Mary E. Tomlinson of Plainville. After her death in 1915 he married Mrs. Grace (Drake) Harding of Spencer, Mass., on Jan. 7, 1917. Norton was a Congregationalist. Shortly after selling his company in 1919 he made Plainville his permanent residence. He died there at the age of ninety of chronic myocarditis and was buried in Plainville's West Cemetery.

[Robert S. Woodbury, *Hist. of the Grinding Machine* (1959); Lionel T. C. Rolt, *A Short Hist. of Machine Tools* (1965); Joseph W. Roe, *English and Am. Tool Builders* (1916); *Nat. Cyc. Am. Biog.,* XXXI, 10–11 (with excellent likeness of Norton opposite p. 10); Charles Nutt, *Hist. of Worcester and Its People* (1919), III, 413–14; obituaries in *Worcester* (Mass.) *Evening Gazette,* Oct. 27, 1942, and *N. Y. Times,* Oct. 28, 1942; *Who Was Who in America,* vol. III (1960); information and death certificate from Town Clerk, Plainville, Conn. See also: Ottilie M. Leland and Minnie D. Millbrook, *Master of Precision: Henry M. Leland* (1966); Allan Nevins and Frank Ernest Hill, *Ford: The Times, the Man, the Company* (1954); and Mildred M. Tymeson, *The Norton Story* (1953). Between 1900 and 1925 numerous articles on Norton's work appeared in the *American Machinist, Machinery,* and *Abrasive Industry.* Some of his manuscripts are in the files of the Norton Co., which provided information about his parents.]

WILLIAM GREENLEAF

NORTON, WILLIAM WARDER (Sept. 17, 1891–Nov. 7, 1945), book publisher, was born in Springfield, Ohio. He was the only child of Percy Norton, a patent lawyer, and Emily (Warder) Norton. His father's family, of English descent, had moved to Springfield from Jericho, Vt. His mother, who died when the boy was two, came of a family that had moved west from Philadelphia around 1800 to escape yellow fever. John Aston Warder [q.v.], Ohio physician, horticulturist, and forester, was his great-uncle.

Brought up as an Episcopalian, Norton attended St. Paul's School in Concord, N. H., and Ohio State University, where he studied mechanical engineering. Vigorous, restless, and questing, he left college after three years, in 1912, to become foreign sales manager of Kilbourne & Jacobs Manufacturing Company of Columbus, Ohio. Subsequently he joined Harrisons & Crossfield, Ltd., an English trading firm in Philadelphia, traveled widely for them, and in 1916 opened their export office in New York. When the United States entered World War I he became a supply officer in the Naval Overseas Transport Service.

Though he reentered the export business after the war, Norton's interests gradually shifted. He worked at Greenwich House, a New York settlement, and in 1921 became treasurer of the American Association of Social Workers. He took courses at the New School for Social Research and was one of the organizers and chairman (1920–22) of the New School Association, the student group supporting the school. Membership on the board of trustees of the People's Institute further strengthened his interest in adult education. On June 6, 1922, he married Mary Dows Herter, daughter of the physician Christian A. Herter [q.v.]. They had one daughter, Anne Aston Warder Norton.

For a time Norton toyed with the idea of starting a short-story magazine to include foreign stories (in translation) as well as American material, old and new. Though this scheme did not work out, the idea of publishing had taken root in his mind, and in the summer of 1923 he and his wife composed a letter to Everett Dean Martin [Supp. 3], director of the People's Institute, proposing publication of the lecture courses given by the Institute at the Cooper Union Forum. Martin's reply was a telegram asking the Nortons to come to Nantucket to discuss the project, which that fall took form as the People's Institute Publishing Company.

Martin's own *Psychology* was the first publication; others were Harry A. Overstreet's *Influencing Human Behavior* and John B. Watson's *Behaviorism.* The lectures were taken down and transcribed by a stenographer each week, edited in the evening by the Nortons, and printed in separate pamphlets that were distributed week by week to subscribers and collected into slipcases for sale in bookstores. This format, however, proved awkward, and in 1926 Norton took the plunge and became a full-time publisher, changing the name of his firm to W. W. Norton & Company, Inc., changing his publications to regularly bound books, and spreading his editorial net far beyond the halls of the People's Institute. The total paid-in capital of his firm was $7,500. Influenced by his reading of the English biologist T. H. Huxley, Norton from the start followed the principle that leaders of thought should wherever possible give their own accounts of work in their fields and not leave informing the public to popularizers. He was able to impress upon many the validity of that notion, with the result that early Norton authors included Walter B. Cannon [Supp. 3], Edith Hamilton, Malvina Hoffman, Lancelot Hogben, H. S. Jennings, Thomas Hunt Morgan [Supp. 3], Gustave Reese, and Bertrand Russell.

The firm was modestly successful and grew steadily. The original publications in the field of psychology led to the special field of psychiatry and to Freud, Karen Horney, Otto Fenichel, and many others later. Mrs. Norton's interest in music resulted ultimately in perhaps the most extensive list of books on music in the English-speaking world. The firm branched out into fiction (Henry Handel Richardson) and poetry (Rainer Maria Rilke, translated by Mrs. Norton). The expanding list of serious nonfiction led to the starting of a college department.

Warder Norton (as he was known to his friends) was a man of quick enthusiasm and firm loyalty. He expended himself unreservedly in any cause he undertook. He maintained his interest in adult education, served as treasurer of the American Friends of Spanish Democracy, was at various times chairman of the Joint Board of Publishers and Booksellers, president of the National Association of Book Publishers (1934), and president of the Publishers Lunch Club. For two and a half years, until November 1944, when ill health forced him to give up the work, he was chairman of the Council on Books in Wartime, a joint industry endeavor that resulted in a tremendous outpouring of paperback books distributed to the men and women in the armed services—some 1,180 different titles in a total of 123 million books. Norton died in the Doctors Hospital in New York City in 1945, at the age of fifty-four.

[The files of W. W. Norton & Co., Inc., through 1945 have been deposited in the Columbia Univ. Lib. Included is a short manuscript history of the firm by H. P. Wilson, its treasurer during most of the period of Norton's presidency. The obituary notice in the *N. Y. Times* (Nov. 9, 1945) contains minor errors of fact and emphasis. More helpful are the sketches in the *Ohio State Monthly,* Oct. 1938, and *Publishers' Weekly,* Dec. 2, 1944; see also Charles A. Madison, *Book Publishing in America* (1966), pp. 354–56. Robert O. Ballou, *A Hist. of the Council on Books in Wartime* (1946), and John Jamieson, *Editions for the Armed Services, Inc.: A Hist.* (1948), contain useful information on their special subjects. The present notice is largely based on the minutes of directors' and stockholders' meetings (not yet deposited with Columbia) and on the personal recollections of Mrs. Norton and of other friends and associates, including the author.]

GEORGE P. BROCKWAY

NOYES, ALEXANDER DANA (Dec. 14, 1862–Apr. 22, 1945), financial journalist, was born in Montclair, N. J., the second of four sons and third of six children of Charles Horace Noyes and Jane Radcliffe (Dana) Noyes. Both parents were of New England stock, the mother a descendant of Richard Dana, who settled in Cambridge, Mass., in 1640, the father a descendant of the Rev. James Noyes, who emigrated from England in 1634 and was a co-founder with his cousin Thomas Parker [*q.v.*] of Newbury, Mass. Charles Noyes, a Congregationalist, had invested in several Montclair stores and a bank. The family lived in "easy circumstances" and there was "abundant good reading" in the home.

As a boy Noyes dreamed of a literary career. At Amherst College, where he graduated, A.B., in 1883, he was editor of the college weekly, and he completed his education with several months of European travel. Meanwhile his father had died, leaving each of the children a substantial legacy. After a year as a space reporter for the *New York Tribune,* Noyes joined the *New York Commercial Advertiser* as an editorial writer in 1884. Though he had dropped his one economics course at Amherst and had to learn finance on Wall Street and by spare-time reading, in 1891 he became financial editor of the prestigious New York *Evening Post.*

Noyes first won widespread attention in 1896, when public demand for free coinage of silver reached its height in the presidential campaign of William J. Bryan [*q.v.*]. To counter the influential free-silver tract by William H. ("Coin") Harvey [Supp. 2], *Coin's Financial School,* Noyes wrote *The Evening Post's Free Coinage Catechism,* a popular and effective question-and-answer reply. Two million copies of his pamphlet were printed, many for distribution by campaign supporters of McKinley. During the 1890's, while continuing on the *Evening Post,* he contributed many articles to the *Political Science Quarterly* and the *Nation,* and later to other magazines. His first book, *Thirty Years of American Finance . . . 1865–1896* (1898), described financial events rather than investigating motives, but was well received; he brought out an extended version, *Forty Years of American Finance . . . 1865–1907,* in 1909. His brief *History of the National-Bank Currency* (1910), prepared for the National Monetary Commission, showed why bond-backed national bank notes did not expand or contract with the needs of business and was influential in promoting the Federal Reserve System's more elastic type of notes.

Noyes wrote his *Financial Chapters of the War* (1916) to explain war financing to the public. From 1915 to 1930 he frequently contributed a financial column to *Scribner's* magazine. By now he was increasingly troubled by the liberal policies of the *Evening Post's* owners, and in 1920 he accepted a long-standing offer to become the financial editor of the *New York Times.* Another book appeared in 1926, *The War Period of American Finance, 1908–25,* a sequel to *Forty Years.* The third of an informal trilogy was *The Market Place: Reminiscences of a Financial Editor* (1938); although autobiographical, it also brought his financial history down to 1933.

Long before 1929 Noyes warned the public in his *New York Times* and *Scribner's* articles of the likelihood, judging by financial history, that America would have further depressions. Yet he included enough qualifications to protect himself (see *Scribner's,* November 1926, April, September 1927). He told a Senate committee in 1933 that his pessimistic views had made him "the most unpopular man in the community" at the time. But when events bore him out, he became a hero and a prophet. In 1933 and 1934 Noyes said that relief measures produce only transitory recovery, expressed fear of inflation, and opposed devaluation of the dollar.

Noyes was a methodical individual, decided in his opinions and short on humor, but he could be most charming. His hobbies were horseback riding in Central Park, walking, the theatre, and membership, after 1898, in the Century Club, of which he was secretary for twenty years (1918–37). From about 1900 on, Noyes shared a New York apartment with his sister Jane, who provided a home atmosphere for her bachelor brother and entertained his friends. She also encouraged him to take vacations, especially business-pleasure trips to Europe. She died in 1939. From the mid-1930's Noyes confined his work on the *New York Times* to his Monday column and general supervision of foreign financial news. Since Adolph Ochs [*q.v.*], publisher of the *Times,* had specified that no editor should be retired against his will, Noyes hung on to the end. He died in 1945, at the age of eighty-two, of arteriosclerosis leading to heart failure. After Episcopal services, he was buried in Mount Pleasant Cemetery, Newark, N. J.

Noyes's views reflect the sounder financial thinking of his day. His eye was generally on the longer trends because he believed that "even financial history repeats itself" (*Market Place,* p. 49); his writings are full of historical analogies. In the judgment of the *New York Herald Tribune,* Noyes "did more than any other American of his time to raise and maintain standards of financial journalism."

[Henry E. and Harriette E. Noyes, *Genealogical Record of Some of the Noyes Descendants,* vol. II (1904); Elizabeth E. Dana, *The Dana Family in America* (1956); Noyes's autobiography, *The Market Place; Amherst College Biog. Record,* 1951; *Who Was Who in America,* vol. II (1950); U. S. Senate, "Investigation of Economic Problems," Hearings before Committee on Finance, pursuant to S. Res. 315, 72 Cong., 2 Sess. (1933), part 7, pp. 809–18; *N. Y. Times,* Apr. 23, 25, May 2, 1945; *N. Y. Herald Tribune,* Apr. 23, 24, 1945; information from R. Dana Noyes, a nephew. For contemporary comment on Noyes, see *Annals of Am. Acad. of Political and Social Sci.,* Sept. 1898, pp. 111–14; *Bookman,* Apr. 1904, pp. 140–41; *Time,* Jan. 13, 1936, pp. 51–52. For his columns, see "Financial Markets," *N. Y. Times,* 1920–45, and "The Financial Situation," *Scribner's,* Aug. 1915–Apr. 1930.]

DONALD L. KEMMERER

NOYES, WILLIAM ALBERT (Nov. 6, 1857–Oct. 24, 1941), chemist, was born on a farm near Independence, Iowa, the youngest of four children (two boys and two girls) of Spencer Williams and Mary (Packard) Noyes, and a distant cousin of Arthur Amos Noyes [Supp. 2]. On both sides his forebears were early English settlers in Massachusetts. His father, who had attended Phillips Academy at Andover, Mass., had been a cobbler in Abington, Mass., but in 1855 he moved his family to Iowa and took out a homestead. Both parents had a great respect for learning and encouraged their children to go on to college.

After attending country schools, Noyes entered Iowa (later Grinnell) College in 1875 and enrolled in the classical course. He excelled in languages, becoming expert in Greek, Latin, French, and German. He also took the few chemistry courses offered by the college and completed qualitative and quantitative analysis on his own. After graduating in 1879 with both the B.A. and B.S. degrees, he stayed on for a year to teach Greek and chemistry, received the M.A. in 1880, and then took temporary charge of the chemistry department for one term. In January 1881 he began graduate work at Johns Hopkins University under the distinguished chemist Ira Remsen [*q.v.*]. Permitted by Remsen to begin his thesis work promptly, Noyes received the Ph.D. in June 1882.

Over the next two decades Noyes held academic positions at the University of Minnesota (1882–83), the University of Tennessee (1883–86), and Rose Polytechnic Institute in Terre Haute, Ind. (1886–1903). He took a one-year leave from Rose Polytechnic to study under the organic chemist Adolf von Baeyer at the University of Munich, from which he received a second Ph.D. in 1889. In 1903 Noyes became the first chief chemist of the newly created United States Bureau of Standards, and established his reputation as a chemist by developing standard methods of analysis and standard specifications for chemicals. He left the bureau in 1907 to become chairman of the chemistry department at the University of Illinois, where he was commissioned to develop a strong graduate program. During the nineteen years of his tenure, the teaching staff more than doubled, the number of graduate students increased from seventeen to more than a hundred, and the chemistry department at Illinois became one of the most productive in the nation. His interest in chemical education was reflected in the eight textbooks he wrote, several of which were widely used in colleges.

Noyes's specialty was organic chemistry, and his research, often carried out in collaboration with students, included studies of the oxidation of benzene derivatives, the structure of camphor, molecular rearrangements in the camphor series, and the electronic theory of valence. He also introduced new analytic methods for detecting and estimating the amounts of benzene in illuminating gas, strychnine in the exhumed human body, and phosphorus, sulfur, and manganese in steel and iron. His work in inorganic chemistry included more accurate determinations of the atomic weights of oxygen and chlorine.

Long active in the American Chemical Society, Noyes served as secretary (1903–07) and president (1920). His most important service to the society was in guiding the expansion and quality of its publications. From 1902 to 1917 he was the editor of its principal periodical, the *Journal of the American Chemical Society*. He was the first editor as well (1907–10) of its important new publication *Chemical Abstracts,* a difficult task that involved collaboration among hundreds of chemists in all fields and many countries. Noyes was also the initial editor of *Scientific Monographs* (1919–41), a series of original books covering single areas of chemistry, and of *Chemical Reviews* (1924–26), a quarterly journal presenting comprehensive reviews of recent research.

On Dec. 24, 1884, Noyes married Flora Elizabeth Collier, a former student at Grinnell College. They had three children: two daughters who died in early childhood, Helen Mary and Ethel, and a son, William Albert, who followed his father's career as chemist and editor. After the death of his first wife in 1900, Noyes married on June 18, 1902, Mattie Laura Elwell, who died in 1914; their only child was Charles Edmund. His third marriage, on Nov. 25, 1915, was to Katharine Haworth Macy, an English teacher at Grinnell and a daughter of Jesse Macy [*q.v.*]. They had two sons: Richard Macy (who became a physical chemist) and Henry Pierre (who became a theoretical physicist).

Noyes received many honors, including the Priestley Medal (1935), the highest award of the American Chemical Society, and election to the National Academy of Sciences (1910). For many years he served as deacon of the First Congregational Church of Champaign-Urbana, Ill. He was deeply interested in world affairs and became increasingly devoted to the cause of world peace and disarmament, on which he wrote a series of pamphlets. At the age of eighty-three Noyes suffered a heart attack and died five days later, at his home in Urbana, Ill. He was cremated, and his ashes were buried in the Macy family plot at Grinnell, Iowa.

[The two most complete accounts of Noyes's life and career are those by B. S. Hopkins in *Jour. Am. Chemical Soc.,* July 1944, and by Roger Adams in Nat. Acad. Sci., *Biog. Memoirs,* vol. XXVII (1952); both include a list of Noyes's scientific publications and a portrait. Briefer accounts are in *Science,* Nov. 21, 1941 (by Austin M. Patterson), and in *Nat. Cyc. Am. Biog.,* XLIV, 258–59. Noyes's activities for the Am. Chemical Soc. are well documented in Charles A. Browne and Mary Elvira Weeks, *A Hist. of the Am. Chemical Soc.* (1952).]

ALBERT B. COSTA

NUTTING, WALLACE (Nov. 17, 1861– July 18, 1941), Congregational minister, antiquarian, landscape photographer, was born in Rockbottom village in the town of Marlborough, Mass., the younger of two children and only son of Albion and Elisa Sanborn (Fifield) Nutting. His father was from Augusta, Maine; his mother came of a New Hampshire family of "good buildings, broad acres, and family pride." Albion Nutting had been a farmer, but when his wife grew dissatisfied with farm life, he entered manufacturing in Boston. Believing, however, that "no proper child could be reared in a city," he made his home in Marlborough. He died of illness while serving in the Union Army, and in 1865 the family moved back to Maine.

Wallace Nutting spent an unhappy boyhood on the farm of an uncle near Manchester, Maine. When he was about twelve he entered the high school in Augusta, but left in 1876 because of poor health and in the next four years held a succession of jobs. His mother wished him to become a minister, and by 1880 he had saved enough money to enter Phillips Exeter Academy. After graduating in 1883, he entered Harvard College but left in 1886 before taking a degree, presumably because of failing health and dwindling financial resources. He next attended the Hartford Theological Seminary (1886–87) and then Union Theological Seminary in New York; in 1888 he was ordained a minister of the Congregational Church. On June 5 of that year he married Mrs. Mariet (Griswold) Caswell of Colrain, Mass.; they had no children. Over the next sixteen years Nutting was pastor of Congregational churches in Newark, N. J. (1888–89), St. Paul, Minn. (1889–91), Seattle, Wash. (1891–94), and Providence, R. I. (1894–1904). He resigned from the ministry in 1904 on the advice of physicians after suffering an attack of typhoid fever, a disturbance of the inner ear, and what he termed a nervous breakdown.

Several years earlier Nutting had begun taking scenic photographs as a hobby. Now, when his doctor prescribed an outdoor life, he began to make "camera journeys" into the Vermont countryside. His hobby soon turned into a business. Traveling by bicycle and train, he photographed rural New England scenes—country lanes, apple trees in blossom, white birches, cottage gardens, and, later on, colonial house interiors. He placed some of his photographs in art shops, and they began to sell. In 1905 he bought a pre-Revolutionary house in Southbury, Conn., where he established a studio and workshops. Nutting had a refined eye for composition, and he mastered the technical skill of printing fine-grain platinum prints with good contrast. He enhanced the appeal of his pictures by having them hand tinted, using a force of young women employees that at times numbered over a hundred. His success in marketing his photographs, as in his later ventures, may be attributed to his ability to supply a product that satisfied a pervasive nostalgia for America's past. For a generation suffering from cultural homesickness, Nutting recreated the familiar scenes of life on the farm and in the small town. He traveled widely in search of subjects, taking many exposures, from which he made a careful selection. Shortly before World War I the business grossed as much as a thousand dollars a day, and toward the end of his life he estimated that more than ten million of his framed prints decorated the walls of American homes.

Nutting moved his headquarters in 1912 to Framingham Center, Mass. At about this time he purchased and restored four historic structures: the Wentworth-Gardner House in Portsmouth, N. H., the Hazen Garrison House in Haverhill, Mass., the Cutler-Bartlet House in Newburyport, Mass., and the Webb-Welles-Washington House in Wethersfield, Conn. These he used for his photographs of colonial interiors. To fill them with authentic period pieces, he began to collect American antiques, in massive quantities. In 1917 he opened a shop to reproduce early American furniture and thus initiated another phase of his career, that of supplying ersatz antiques. He had bought the property of the seventeenth-century ironworks at Saugus, Mass., in 1916. There he restored the forge and the ironmaster's house and began to manufacture reproductions of early hardware. In 1919 he bought a large studio in Ashland, Mass., to consolidate his picture and furniture business. Three years later, however, he sold all his business interests, as well as his historic houses and their contents, and retired, planning to devote himself to his personal collection of American antique furniture, particularly of the seventeenth century.

His retirement, however, was brief. In 1923, becoming dissatisfied with the way in which the business, still under his name, was being handled, he sold his collection of antiques for $90,000 to the younger J. P. Morgan [Supp. 3]—who in turn donated it to the Wadsworth Atheneum in Hartford—and thus was able to repurchase his company. He next bought a large building in Framingham, Mass., and spent substantial sums equipping it to reproduce colonial furniture, including more than "six hundred types" of early cabinetwork.

Nutting had begun writing about American furniture as early as 1917, when he issued *A Windsor Handbook*, illustrating and describing Windsor chairs and other furniture in that style. This was followed by *Furniture of the Pilgrim Century, 1620–1720* (1921) and—his most durable work—the three-volume *Furniture Treasury* (1928–33). The first two volumes of the *Treasury* contained more than 5,000 illustrations; the third was largely text, illustrated with line drawings by Ernest John Donnelly. Assembling photographs from collectors, museums, and dealers, and using a large number of his own, Nutting compiled a comprehensive photographic archive of American furniture. Although later research has revealed many errors, the *Furniture Treasury* remains an indispensable reference for the collector.

More popular were a series of "States Beautiful" books combining Nutting's photographs with an anecdotal text. Published by his own Old America Company, these began with *Vermont Beautiful* (1922) and continued with similarly titled volumes on Connecticut, Massachusetts, and New Hampshire (all in 1923), Maine and Pennsylvania (1924), New York (1927), and Virginia (1930), with volumes also on Ireland (1925) and England (1928). Most went into second editions, and some sold as many as 30,000 copies.

Nutting published the final edition of his catalogue of furniture reproductions in 1937. He died at his Framingham home four years later, at seventy-nine, of heart disease. He was buried in Mount Pleasant Cemetery, Augusta, Maine. The former minister had proved himself a remarkably able entrepreneur, well attuned to popular taste.

[*Wallace Nutting's Biog.* (1936)—actually his autobiography—which is stronger on anecdote and personal philosophy than on concrete fact; Marion T. Colley, "I Never Learned to Live until I Was Fifty," *American Mag.*, Jan. 1927, an interview, which presents a much harsher picture of his childhood than the autobiography; obituary sketch in Harvard College Class of 1887, *50th Anniversary Report* (1937), pp. 313–20; *Nat. Cyc. Am. Biog.*, XXX, 329–30; obituaries in *Framingham News*, July 19, 1941, and *N. Y. Times*, July 20, 1941; Reminiscences of Israel Sack (MS., 1953), Oral Hist. Section, Ford Motor Co. Archives; Helen Comstock, "Wallace Nutting and the *Furniture Treasury* in Retrospect," *Antiques*, Nov. 1961; birth record from City Clerk, Marlborough, Mass.; marriage and death records from Mass. Registrar of Vital Statistics.]

WENDELL D. GARRETT

O'CONNELL, WILLIAM HENRY (Dec. 8, 1859–Apr. 22, 1944), Roman Catholic archbishop, was the son of John and Bridget (Farley) O'Connell. His parents were married in County Cavan, Ireland, emigrated in 1848 by way of Montreal, Canada, to upper New York state, and settled finally in Lowell, Mass., in 1853. There William was born, the youngest of eleven children, seven of them boys. His father, a laborer in a textile mill, died in 1865, and William then became deeply devoted to his mother, who earnestly desired that he should enter the religious life. His education in the Protestant-dominated public schools of Lowell, so he later recalled with some bitterness, sharpened his identity as an Irish Catholic.

After graduating from high school in 1876, O'Connell studied at St. Charles College near Baltimore. Illness, however, forced his return after two years, and he enrolled in the Jesuit-sponsored Boston College, graduating in 1881. Determined to become a priest, he approached Archbishop John Joseph Williams [q.v.] of Boston, who accepted him as a student and sent him for theological studies to the North American College in Rome. This marked a crucial point in O'Connell's life, for he became and remained for the rest of his days a fervent admirer of Roman life and culture and a dedicated ultramontane.

Ordained on June 7, 1884, O'Connell intended to continue work for the Doctorate in Divinity, but again illness intervened, and he returned to Boston in December of that year. He was appointed assistant pastor in Medford, Mass., and later served St. Joseph's Church in the teeming West End of Boston. During these years he attained fame as an orator, widely in demand on public occasions for speeches dealing with Ireland and advocating personal temperance. He was offered several teaching posts and in 1895 attracted a great deal of attention when he gave a series of lectures on church history at the Catholic Summer School at Plattsburgh, N. Y.

In that same year, serious conflicts within the American Catholic Church led to the removal of Denis O'Connell as rector of the North American College in Rome. Denis O'Connell was a close associate of Archbishop John Ireland [q.v.] and other members of the hierarchy who were seeking to adapt the American Catholic Church to the needs of American society. Their efforts were frequently misunderstood by Roman officials and caused divisions within the American hierarchy. Wishing to remove the North American College from any association with these factional disputes, Archbishop Francesco Satolli, apostolic

delegate to the United States, urged the appointment of William O'Connell, whom he had known as one of his students in Rome, as its new head. O'Connell was uninvolved with the internal controversies in the American church and hence was ideally suited to restore the college's position. He served as rector with distinction, improved the facilities of the college, and made further contacts within the Roman curia and in the American colony in Rome. In particular he was instrumental in securing the donation to the college of the Haywood Library of 8,000 rare books. His services were recognized by commendations from Pope Leo XIII, by his appointment as a domestic prelate in June 1897, and, finally, by his nomination as bishop of Portland, Maine, in 1901, a nomination made by Rome in disregard of the wishes of the New England hierarchy and the Maine clergy.

In Portland, O'Connell reorganized diocesan administration, expanded the number of churches and priests, and fostered the growth of laymen's associations, while at the same time consciously seeking to improve relations between Catholics and Protestants. In 1905—again recommended by one of his Roman friends, this time Cardinal Merry del Val, Papal Secretary of State—O'Connell was chosen by Pope Pius X to serve as special legate to the Japanese court to explore the possibility of Japanese-Vatican diplomatic relations and to report on the state of Catholicism in Japan. He spent several weeks in Japan and at the conclusion of his trip recommended changes in church policy there, including modification of French domination of missionary efforts and establishment of a Catholic university. These suggestions were followed, although diplomatic exchange was delayed by Japanese preoccupation with the aftermath of the Russo-Japanese war.

Rome was highly pleased with O'Connell's mission, and upon its completion he was named titular archbishop of Constantia and coadjutor to the archbishop of Boston with right of succession. Once again, O'Connell owed his elevation to his influence in Rome, and many priests in the diocese were displeased. Nevertheless, he was very close to the aging archbishop, John Williams, and he easily established his authority. When he formally assumed the leadership of the diocese after Williams's death in 1907, O'Connell was only forty-eight years old; he was destined to dominate the church in New England for almost forty years.

As archbishop of Boston he set out to modernize diocesan administration, and he soon made his diocese a model for others in the United States. The major feature of his work was the centralization of control in the hands of the archbishop, who operated through a diocesan curia which retained day-to-day supervision of the finances and operation of all diocesan institutions and imposed clear guidelines upon parish administration. Although during the first four years of O'Connell's tenure over thirty new church buildings were constructed, each was required to possess a large proportion of its cost before construction began. Many hitherto weak charitable foundations were reorganized in order to bring the scope of their work in line with the funds available. A Diocesan Charitable Bureau centralized and coordinated charitable activities, while a Diocesan House at Brighton became the focal point for all diocesan activities. Although some flexibility was lost by these changes, the efficiency of the church's work was undoubtedly enhanced.

Similarly, Archbishop O'Connell's efforts to expand education in the diocese were linked to sound and responsible financing and administrative centralization. Boston College received considerable diocesan support to build its new campus at Chestnut Hill and to extend its program to that of a full-fledged university. Other colleges and academies were enlarged and new ones begun, including Regis College for women, founded in 1927. Parish schools were expanded and educational administration was reorganized to provide for a regular system of curriculum, examinations, health services, and inspection. The expanded educational system required the services of increased numbers of teachers, so that during O'Connell's years as archbishop the number of religious in the diocese more than trebled. The most important of the diocesan schools was the seminary at Brighton. Here again, the Archbishop centralized control by removing the Sulpician Order and placing the seminary under his immediate supervision and providing it with a staff of diocesan priests.

Another of O'Connell's interests was lay organization. He insisted that branches of the Holy Name Society be set up in all parishes and fostered numerous professional guilds for Catholic men. He promoted the growth of lay retreats in the diocese and encouraged the foundation and work of the Catholic Women's League, which concentrated on charitable and educational work, occasionally becoming involved in public issues. In 1908 he purchased the Boston *Pilot,* which had originally been a diocesan organ but had been under private management for many years. The *Pilot* became an agency for communication within the diocese and a vehicle through which O'Connell could express his views on issues both within the church and within American society. O'Connell also made the Boston archdiocese the center of support for foreign missions. He aided one of his priests, James Anthony Walsh [Supp. 2], in the formation of the Catholic Foreign Mission Society of America (Maryknoll) in 1911 and thereafter worked hard to secure financial support for the missions from the people of the diocese. Boston's contributions reached over $750,000 annually in the last years of O'Connell's term of office.

Under the Archbishop's firm control and supervision the work of his archdiocese expanded dramatically. Its Catholic population rose from 750,000 to more than 1,000,000, making it the nation's third largest; the number of parishes increased from 194 to 322, and the number of secular priests more than doubled. By the start of World War II the diocese had 158 parish schools, sixty-seven high schools, seven Catholic hospitals, and ten orphanages, plus a wide range of social and charitable institutions. In his insistence on efficient administration, O'Connell did not hesitate to remove persons he felt were not doing their jobs well, a fact that may have contributed to his reputation for having a somewhat cold personality.

His domination of the church in Boston extended beyond the organizational centralization which marked his administration and reflected the more sophisticated approach to diocesan management which was to replace the flexible response of the earlier generation to the huge waves of immigration in the nineteenth century. Once composed of outcasts from Ireland and Europe, the Catholic population during O'Connell's reign came to dominate the political life of Massachusetts. O'Connell's powerful oratory and overwhelming personality reflected the new self-confidence of the Catholic people. He believed that the time had come for the church and its members to come to the fore and take a proud and unapologetic stance in relation to their fellow citizens. A refined and cultured man, O'Connell was frequently disdainful of Irish-American mores and critical of Catholic politicians like James Michael Curley. From his contacts with the American colony in Rome he had come to appreciate the cultural sophistication of New England Protestants, particularly Episcopalians and Unitarians, and he moved easily among them back home. Still, he was alert for any sign of revival of anti-Catholic bigotry and was unafraid to speak out on public issues which threatened Catholic interests or challenged Catholic morality. He frequently issued pastoral letters on moral questions which touched upon the politics of the state. In addition, he occasionally took a direct part in opposing movements which he considered harmful to the interests of the church and to the welfare of the commonwealth. For example, in 1935 he played a crucial role in defeating a bill to establish a state lottery, and both in the 1920's and in the early 1930's he intervened to combat the proposed child labor amendment to the federal Constitution. O'Connell believed that the amendment could be used as a wedge to gain control of education by the federal government, a step he thought contained great potential harm for Catholic schools. His stand was successful in Massachusetts, where the amendment was twice overwhelmingly defeated, but it brought him into conflict with others in the American church.

In national ecclesiastical affairs O'Connell was a staunch proponent of Roman authority and fought any move that would compromise papal authority or lessen the autonomy of individual bishops. He was made a cardinal in 1911, and after the death of James Gibbons [*q.v.*] of Baltimore in 1921, O'Connell was the dean of the American hierarchy. He joined actively in the cooperative efforts of Catholic officials during World War I and in the formation of the National Catholic Welfare Conference after the war. Nevertheless, O'Connell fought hard to ensure that the N.C.W.C. remained a voluntary and advisory meeting of bishops whose decisions were not binding upon the individual prelate within his diocese. This position, together with his preoccupation with diocesan affairs, prevented him from becoming the kind of national leader that Gibbons had been or that Francis Cardinal Spellman of New York would be in later years. During the depression of the 1930's O'Connell defended the rights of organized labor but at the same time damaged his own popularity by vigorously attacking Father Charles E. Coughlin, the radio orator. In later years he frequently pointed to the growing influence of Communist ideas in American society and encouraged lay efforts within his diocese to combat these developments.

A large man of impressive bearing, O'Connell was constantly in demand as a speaker at meetings of Catholic and Irish groups around the country, and his published addresses eventually reached eleven volumes. In addition, he translated an Italian work on the life of Christ (*The Passion of Our Lord*, by Gaetano Cardinal De Lai, 1923) and wrote his autobiography, *Recollections of Seventy Years* (1934). He was deeply interested in religious music, strongly supported the reform of church music undertaken by Pope Pius X, and himself composed a number of hymns. Although sparing in his commitments to outside activities, he served as a trustee of the Boston Public Library (1932–36) and occasionally joined other prominent citizens in organizations aimed at civic improvement. He vacationed regularly in Europe or at his home in Nassau in the Bahamas and daily took long walks which helped preserve his generally robust health. With the aid of Richard J. Cushing, who became his auxiliary bishop in 1939, he continued to administer the diocese until the spring of 1944. He died that April, at the age of eighty-four, of a cerebral hemorrhage followed by pneumonia. According to his wishes, he was buried in the Chapel of the Blessed Virgin which he had had built on the grounds of St. John's Seminary in Brighton.

Cardinal O'Connell of Boston represented in American Catholicism the victory of those who felt that the future of the church would be best ensured by emphasizing its unity, its centralized control and direction, and its loyalty to Rome, a position which contrasted with the proposals of the liberals of the late nineteenth century. His generally conservative stance on social issues, together with his authoritarian conduct of diocesan business, made many Catholics think of him as a somewhat reactionary figure. O'Connell devoted himself to winning respectability for the church in the eyes of the dominant Protestant leadership of New England society—the honorary degree Harvard awarded him in 1937 is perhaps one measure of his success—but his methods of bringing this about, which centered upon impressing the nation with the power and the strength of the church and its leaders, frequently resulted in damaging the image of Catholicism in the minds of more liberal Americans. Within the church, the combination of diocesan centralization and national decentralization, together with the emphasis upon administrative efficiency and organizational strength, which were the characteristics of O'Connell's tenure as archbishop of Boston were typical of the development of American Catholicism in the twentieth century.

[The major source for the life of William Cardinal O'Connell is the collection of his papers in the archives of the Archdiocese of Boston. His autobiography, *Recollections of Seventy Years*, is a valuable and colorful account of his life before 1933. Dorothy G. Wayman has written a biography, *Cardinal O'Connell of Boston* (1955), and her papers, located at Catholic Univ. of America, contain accounts of interviews with leading Boston churchmen. The third volume (1944) of the excellent *Hist. of the Archdiocese of Boston* by Robert H. Lord, John E. Sexton, and Edward T. Harrington is also invaluable. The collected *Sermons and Addresses of Cardinal O'Connell* (11 vols., 1922–38) bring together his major writings on a wide range of topics.]

DAVID J. O'BRIEN

OLDFATHER, WILLIAM ABBOTT (Oct. 23, 1880–May 27, 1945), classicist, was born at Urumiah in what was then Persia, where his parents for many years were Presbyterian missionaries. He was the second son and fourth of five children of Jeremiah M. and Felicia Narcissa (Rice) Oldfather. The family name had been translated by his paternal great-grandfather from the original Austrian "Altvater"; on his mother's side he was descended from Daniel Boone [*q.v.*]. A sister, Helen, married August Karl Reischauer, a Presbyterian missionary to Japan, founded the Deaf Oral School in Tokyo, and became the mother of Edwin O. Reischauer, distinguished scholar in Japanese studies and United States ambassador to Japan; William's younger brother, Charles Henry, became a specialist in ancient history and dean of the graduate school of the University of Nebraska.

When Oldfather was a boy his family returned from the mission field and settled in Hanover, Ind. After graduating from the local Hanover College (A.B. 1899), he went on to Harvard, where he took a second A.B. (1901) and an A.M. (1902). On Sept. 22, 1902, he married Margaret Agnes Giboney; they had two daughters, Margaret and Helen. Oldfather now planned a scholarly career. While serving as an instructor in classics at Northwestern University (1903–06) he prepared himself, by reading great quantities of German, for matriculation at one of the universities that were then the indispensable training ground for a classical scholar. At the University of Munich, where he received a Ph.D. in 1908, he studied under the most eminent scholars of the day, from whom he learned an approach to classical culture as a whole that remained his lifelong ideal. He returned to Northwestern in 1908 as assistant professor of Latin, but in the following year moved to the University of Illinois as associate professor and later professor of classics (1915–45).

Oldfather brought zest, enthusiasm, and tireless energy to the study and interpretation of Graeco-Roman civilization in all its aspects, from Homer to Jerome and beyond. His students at all levels knew him as an absorbing lecturer in the classroom, as an overwhelmingly learned guide of broad views in the seminar, and as a demanding but generous mentor. To them he was a whole man, who exemplified the humanist ideal of Terence ("homo sum, humani nil a me alienum puto") not only in his teaching but in his life. Although he might abash them with his abrupt and magisterial manner in an academic context (he was referred to surreptitiously as "der Herr"), on the tennis court (where he was

a master), on the baseball diamond, on a hike, or in his home he was a warm and genial friend. To his colleagues and associates he was a man to be admired, respected, feared, or even hated, but never to be disregarded. His vigorously liberal views on all matters made him a champion of the underdog and an enemy of sham and pretense. He was also a deeply religious man, but not in the terms of any sect, as he made clear in a lecture entitled "Is Religion Essential to Every Adequate Philosophy of Living?" (published by the University of California Y.M.C.A., 1934).

Oldfather's scholarly studies began with his dissertation, *Lokrika* (1908), and Locris and its people continued to be one of his principal concerns. In later years he made repeated visits to Greece to explore this ancient territory and expounded his findings in many of the more than 500 articles he contributed to the *Realenzyklopädie der klassischen Altertumswissenschaft*. He also devoted much attention to textual criticism and the transmission of texts, and made significant contributions on the texts of Avianus, Epictetus, and St. Jerome. As a translator he produced versions of Epictetus, the Greek Tacticians, and Terence, and also of Leonard Euler's treatise on elastic curves and Samuel Pufendorf's legal writings. Seeking to provide useful tools for the study of the classics, he enlisted the cooperation of large numbers of his students and colleagues in preparing indexes to the vocabularies of Seneca's tragedies, Apuleius, and Cicero's letters. In the same category belongs his too-modestly titled "Contributions toward a Bibliography of Epictetus" (*University of Illinois Bulletin*, 1927). In the field of history, his thought is represented principally by a joint study with Howard V. Canter, *The Defeat of Varus and the German Frontier Policy of Augustus* (1915). He had undertaken a major study of the causes of the decline of civilization but did not live to complete the work.

As head of his department at Illinois (1926–45), Oldfather was a vital force in the development of the university, but his influence extended far beyond the campus through his teaching in various summer schools and as visiting professor at the University of California (1943), the American School of Classical Studies in Athens (1937), and Columbia University (1938). He was an effective force in the professional societies to which he belonged, including the American Philological Association (president, 1937–38), the Linguistic Society of America, and the National Research Council. He was also a member of the American Committee for Democracy and

Intellectual Freedom and a charter member and active spirit in the American Association of University Professors.

At sixty-four, still at the height of his powers, although saddened and disillusioned by the course of events attendant upon the Second World War, Oldfather met his end among friends in the enjoyment of an old and favorite sport. While he was canoeing on the flooded Salt Fork at Homer Park, Ill., not far from Urbana, the canoe capsized, and as he tried to rescue it he was drawn under by an eddy and drowned. He was buried in Roselawn Cemetery in Urbana.

[For a listing of Oldfather's publications, see the annual *Proc.* of the Am. Philological Assoc., 1908–44. On his life, see obituary notices by Clarence A. Forbes in *Classical Jour.*, Oct. 1945 (with portrait), and Arthur S. Pease in Am. Philological Assoc., *Proc.*, 1945, pp. xxiv–xxvi. Two poems have been published in his memory: by Richmond Lattimore in *New Republic*, Nov. 13, 1961, p. 15; and by Levi R. Lind in his *Epitaph for Poets* (1966). An oil portrait of Oldfather is in the Classics Seminar of the Univ. of Ill. Lib.]

LLOYD W. DALY

OLMSTEAD, ALBERT TEN EYCK (Mar. 23, 1880–Apr. 11, 1945), orientalist and ancient historian, was born in Troy, N. Y., the eldest of three children of Charles and Ella (Blanchard) Olmstead. He spent his early childhood in the village of Sand Lake, not far from Troy, where his father owned a small truck farm and later a store; after the store was destroyed in a flash flood, the family moved to Troy. There Albert was able to obtain an excellent schooling in the classical languages, Hebrew, and history. He won a scholarship to Cornell University, where he earned his A.B. (1902), A.M. (1903), and, in 1906, a Ph.D. in ancient oriental history under the guidance of Nathaniel Schmidt [Supp. 2]. At Cornell, Olmstead received the training in historical method and political science which, combined with his knowledge of classical and oriental languages, was to win him renown as a historian of the pre-Islamic civilizations of the Near East. His doctoral dissertation, *Western Asia in the Days of Sargon of Assyria, 722–705 B.C.*, distinguished for its critical acumen, was published in 1908.

Even before he finished his doctoral studies, Olmstead had completed the first of several extended sojourns in the Near East. In 1904–05, as fellow of the American Schools of Oriental Research in Jerusalem, he toured numerous sites in Syria and Palestine. In 1906–07 he was a fellow of the American School of Classical Studies in Athens, broadening his already extensive knowledge of the classical world. In 1907–08 he served as director of the Cornell University Expedition to Asia Minor and the Assyro-Babylonian Orient and tramped through many remote areas in Anatolia and Mesopotamia. These trips, reinforced by a later tour of duty as annual professor for the American Schools of Oriental Research in Baghdad in 1936–37, gave him invaluable firsthand experience of the terrain about which he wrote and lent peculiar vividness to his description of past events in that remote world.

Olmstead's academic career began with a year as instructor in Greek and Latin at the Princeton (N. J.) Preparatory School (1908–09), followed by several years of teaching ancient history at the University of Missouri (1909–17). During this period he published *Travels and Studies in the Nearer East* (1911) and *Assyrian Historiography* (1916). The latter, though only a small monograph, became a classic in the fields of Assyriology and ancient history by establishing the principles of source interpretation for the vast literature of the Assyrian royal annals. Before Olmstead's book, these annals, unabashedly propagandistic, had sometimes been taken at face value, with little or no attempt at either textual or historical criticism. Olmstead stressed the need to sift the various versions of the annals in order to arrive at the original text and then, by systematic collecting and comparison of ancient sources, to test their relation to reality.

In 1917 Olmstead moved to the University of Illinois, where he served as professor of history and as curator of the Oriental Museum until 1929. He was president of the American Oriental Society in 1922–23, a signal accolade for so young a scholar. (He later, 1941–42, was president of the Society for Biblical Research.) His mammoth and definitive *History of Assyria* appeared in 1923; and he contributed to scholarly journals and anthologies a series of analytical articles on the history of Babylonia and Assyria and numerous essays on politics, geography, anthropology, and ancient art.

In 1929 Olmstead was appointed Oriental Institute Professor of Oriental History at the University of Chicago, a post he held until his death. While producing major books in new areas such as his *History of Palestine and Syria* (1931) and *Jesus in the Light of History* (1942), Olmstead trained in his seminars a significant number of young historians of the ancient Near East and inculcated in them a methodical accuracy and insistence on comprehension and sensitive interpretation of the original sources. His final work, *History of the Persian Empire*, appeared posthumously in 1948.

Olmstead married Cleta Ermine Payne of Shelbina, Mo., on June 25, 1913; they had three daughters: Cleta Margaret, Ella Mary, and Ruth Carol. Olmstead's religious affiliation, in his early years at least, was with the Methodist Church. An arduous career of research and teaching prematurely weakened his strength. Shortly before his scheduled retirement, he died at Billings Hospital, Chicago, of a cerebral thrombosis following an operation for a fractured hip. His remains were cremated.

Olmstead was practically unique among historians of his day in trying to cover almost all of the pre-Islamic Near East. The only other comparable scholar, the German historian Eduard Meyer, wrote broad syntheses dealing with periods of history across several countries, whereas Olmstead preferred to write of one country at a time in great detail. His pioneering and highly interpretative work, although since superseded by later scholarship, will long be remembered, especially for its principles of source utilization.

[Obituaries by John A. Wilson in *Bull. of the Am. Schools of Oriental Research*, July 1945, and in the Olmstead Memorial Issue of the *Jour. of Near Eastern Studies*, Jan. 1946 (both with portraits); *N. Y. Times*, Apr. 12, 1945; *Who Was Who in America*, vol. II (1950); information from Mrs. Olmstead and from death record.]

JOHN A. BRINKMAN

O'NEILL, ROSE CECIL (June 25, 1874–Apr. 6, 1944), illustrator and author, creator of the Kewpie doll, was born in Wilkes-Barre, Pa., the second of seven children and oldest daughter of William Patrick and Asenath Cecelia (Smith) O'Neill. Both parents were natives of Pennsylvania; the father was of Irish descent. More interested in the arts than in a steady livelihood, he operated a bookstore in Wilkes-Barre, but during the depression year of 1878 moved his family to a Nebraska homestead and later to Omaha, where he made an uncertain living as a salesman.

Rose was reared a Catholic and educated in parochial schools. She taught herself to draw, and at the age of fourteen produced a pen-and-ink sketch ("Temptation Leading down into an Abyss") which won a prize of five dollars offered by the *Omaha World-Herald* for the best drawing by a pupil in the local schools. After a brief attempt at an acting career, she began selling illustrations to magazines in Denver and Chicago. To secure further training, she went at about seventeen to New York City, where she lived under the care of a Catholic sisterhood on Riverside Drive and sold illustrations to magazines like *Truth* and *Puck*. Two years later she rejoined her family, now settled on a three-hundred-acre claim, "Bonniebrook," in Taney County, Mo. Having acquainted editors with her work and established

a market, she was able to execute her commissions by mail from this Ozark fastness, much to the benefit of the family's finances.

Back in New York in 1896, she was married to Gray Latham, a handsome but indolent Virginian then engaged in trying to develop a successful motion picture projector in the industry's infancy. His high-handed appropriation of her growing earnings helped wreck their marriage, which ended in divorce in 1901. Her second marriage (June 7, 1902)—childless like the first—was to Harry Leon Wilson [Supp. 2], a former editor of *Puck*, whose novels *The Spenders* (1902) and *The Lions of the Lord* (1903) she illustrated. They were a discordant pair, she ebullient and communicative, he a dour humorist, given to sardonic silences and frequent hangovers; and after their return from two years abroad on the island of Capri and in Paris, they separated permanently in September 1907. Yet in spite of their inability to get on together, there remained much sympathy and affection between them.

The fairies endowed Rose O'Neill with dazzling gifts. She had wit, beauty, goodness, and an almost bottomless purse. Riches began to come to her soon after sketches of her Kewpies—her diminutive for cupids—first appeared in the December 1909 issue of the *Ladies' Home Journal*. She had frequently drawn similar cherubs as tailpieces for magazine stories, but now, at the suggestion of the *Journal*'s editor, Edward Bok [Supp. 1], she devoted a full page to their adventures, along with her commentary in verse. Almost immediately rival editors began to vie for her favor, and for nearly a quarter of a century her jolly little elves disported themselves on the pages of various women's magazines. On Mar. 4, 1913, she patented the Kewpie doll, from which she is estimated to have made more than a million dollars. Royalties came also from Kewpies used as decorations on nursery china, wallpaper and stationery, from figurines for radiator caps and inkwells, and from her many Kewpie books.

In her prosperity she was almost pathologically generous. She sent money to Charles Caryl Coleman [q.v.], an elderly and needy American painter whom she had met during her visit to Capri, who gratefully turned over to her his villa there. From 1912 to the early 1920's many protégés enjoyed the hospitality of her Greenwich Village apartment, and almost anyone who called himself an artist could charge a meal to her account at the Hotel Brevoort. In 1922 she bought an eleven-room house near Westport, Conn., which she named Carabas Castle after the marquis in the fairy tale "Puss in Boots." Living there with her mother, her sister Callista, and her brother Clarence ("Clink"), she fed and gave encouragement to dozens of obscure poets, artists, and musicians. Her ability to help the frustrated and incomplete was closely related to her deep understanding of the child mind.

Rose O'Neill also produced drawings and paintings of serious intent. Her "secret" art revealed the vein of terror and grotesquerie that lay beneath her public character as an invincibly merry prattler. These pen-and-ink drawings portrayed demonic and titanic figures—their mass built up of minute traceries—in towering or tender juxtaposition to tiny, naked humans. Acclaimed at the time by French and American critics, they were exhibited at the Paris Salon in 1906 (when she was made a member of the Société des Beaux Arts), at the Devambez Galleries in Paris in 1921, and at the Wildenstein Gallery in New York in 1922.

Rose O'Neill published four novels, none of them greatly successful either artistically or commercially. *The Loves of Edwy* (1904), though too sentimental for present-day taste, is of autobiographical interest, since the hero is an illustrator and the heroine's father is a recognizable portrait of William P. O'Neill. *The Lady in the White Veil* (1909) is a mystery involving the disappearance of a painting by Titian. *Garda* (1929) turns upon the quasi-mystical rapport between a brother and his twin sister. The influence of Hawthorne is plain in *The Goblin Woman* (1930), a Gothic tale in which one character, after murdering his brother by shoving him over a cliff, marries the brother's twelve-year-old daughter, with whom he furtively lives abroad for many years; finally, he attempts to atone for his sins by wearing sackcloth and inflicting upon himself two terrible scars. Rose also published *The Master-Mistress* (1922), a volume of poems, probably the best of which are those to her mother and sister.

During the Great Depression, after the vogue of the Kewpies had passed, Rose's carelessness about money overtook her, and, almost penniless, she had to give up the Connecticut property and retire to Bonniebrook. Ever hopeful, she invented a new doll, a Buddha-like creature called Ho-Ho, but it never caught the public fancy. She died of a paralytic stroke at Springfield, Mo., in 1944 and by her own wish was buried without religious ceremony in the family cemetery at Bonniebrook.

[Ralph Alan McCanse, *Titans and Kewpies: The Life and Art of Rose O'Neill* (1968), is the fullest biographical account; it contains photographs of Rose at different stages in her career. See also a sketch by Carlin T. Kindilien in *Notable Am. Women*, II, 650–51 (which lists additional references); George Kummer, *Harry Leon Wilson* (1963); and Terry Ramsaye, *A Million and One Nights* (1926). For an appreciative chapter on Rose's poetry, see Clement Wood, *Poets of America* (1925). For sidelights on her character, see Van Wyck Brooks, *Days of the Phoenix* (1957); Orrick Johns, *Time of Our Lives* (1937); and Vance Randolph, *Ozark Superstitions* (1947). Paul E. O'Neill, a nephew, furnished valuable information about the family. Landmarks in Kewpie history are discussed in Janet Pagter Johl, *The Fascinating Story of Dolls* (1941), and Mary Hillier, *Dolls and Doll-Makers* (1968). There are collections of Kewpies and other O'Neill memorabilia in the Shepherd of the Hills Memorial Museum in Branson, Mo., and in the School of the Ozarks at Hollister.]

GEORGE KUMMER

OSGOOD, WILLIAM FOGG (Mar. 10, 1864–July 22, 1943), mathematician, was born in Boston, Mass., the son of William and Mary Rogers (Gannett) Osgood, natives, respectively, of Kensington, N. H., and Cohasset, Mass. His father, a Harvard graduate and a Unitarian, was the fourth in a direct line of general practitioners of medicine in New England and was known for his concern for the poor of the community. Except for twin sons who died in infancy, William was an only child. He prepared for college at the Boston Latin School, entered Harvard in 1882, and was graduated with the A.B. degree in 1886, summa cum laude.

As an undergraduate, Osgood had devoted his first two years largely to the classics, in which he received second-year honors. Influenced, however, by the mathematical physicist Benjamin Osgood Peirce [q.v.]—one of his favorite teachers—and by Frank Nelson Cole [q.v.], who began lecturing at Harvard in Osgood's senior year, his interests turned to mathematics. He remained at Harvard for one year of graduate work in that field, receiving the degree of A.M. in 1887, before going on for further study at the University of Göttingen in Germany with Felix Klein, under whom Cole had recently studied.

Two schools of thought were rivals in the stimulating mathematical atmosphere of Europe at that time. One, as represented by Bernhard Riemann, employed intuition and arguments borrowed from the physical sciences; the other, as represented by Karl Weierstrass, stressed strict, rigorous proof. Osgood throughout his career chose the best from the two schools, using intuition in its proper place to suggest results and their proofs, but relying ultimately on rigorous logical demonstrations. The influence of Klein on the "arithmetizing of mathematics" remained with Osgood throughout his later life. After two years at Göttingen he went to Erlangen, where he received his Ph.D. degree in 1890. His dissertation was a study of Abelian integrals of the first, second, and third kinds based on previous work by Klein and Max Noether. The subject was part of the theory of functions, to which

Osgood was to devote so much of his career. On July 17, 1890, before his return from Germany, he married Therese Anna Amalie Elise Ruprecht of Göttingen. They had three children: William Ruprecht, Frieda Bertha, and Rudolf Ruprecht. During the early years of the marriage German was normally spoken in the household, and much of Osgood's scientific writing was done in that language.

Upon his return from Germany in 1890, Osgood joined the department of mathematics at Harvard, where he remained for the rest of his life, becoming assistant professor in 1893 and professor in 1903. Like other young Americans of his generation who had studied in Germany, he was ambitious to raise the scientific level of mathematics in the United States. There was no spirit of research at Harvard then except Osgood's own, but a year later Maxime Bôcher [*q.v.*] was appointed to the department, and the two were close friends both personally and scientifically until Bôcher's death in 1918.

Osgood's scientific articles were of impressively high quality from the start. In 1897 he published a paper on uniform convergence of sequences of real continuous functions; this strongly influenced the later development of the subject. The next year he brought out a paper on the solutions of the differential equation $y' = f(x,y)$ that is now known as a classic. In 1900 Osgood established, by methods derived from Henri Poincaré and others, the Riemann mapping theorem, namely that an arbitrary, simply connected region with at least two boundary points can be mapped uniformly and conformally onto the interior of a circle. This is a theorem of great importance, long conjectured to be true, but until then without a satisfactory proof. Osgood always did his research on problems that were both intrinsically important and classical in origin—"problems with a pedigree," as he used to say. Felix Klein, as one of the editors, invited Osgood to contribute to the *Encyklopädie der Mathematischen Wissenschaften,* and Osgood's article "Allgemeine Theorie der analytischen Funktionen a) einer und b) mehreren komplexen Grössen" appeared in 1901. This was a deep, scholarly historical report on mathematical analysis; the writing of it gave Osgood an unparalleled familiarity with the literature of the field.

Osgood loved to teach at all levels. His exposition, though not always thoroughly transparent, was accurate, rigorous, and stimulating, invariably with emphasis on classical problems and results. Ranking with his teaching were his numerous books, notably his great *Lehrbuch der*

Funktionentheorie (vol. I, 1906–07, and five later editions; vol. II, 1924–32). Its purpose was to present systematically and thoroughly the fundamental methods and results of analysis, with applications to the theory of functions of a real and of a complex variable. More systematic and more rigorous than French *traités d'analyse,* a monument to the care, orderliness, rigor, and didactic skill of its author, the book became a standard work wherever higher mathematics was studied. Osgood's text on the differential and integral calculus (1907) showed deep originality, especially in weaving the material into a single whole by anticipating at any stage more advanced material.

Osgood's influence throughout the mathematical world was very great through the soundness and depth of his *Funktionentheorie,* through the results of his research, through his stimulating yet painstaking teaching of both undergraduate and graduate students (though he did not direct many Ph.D. theses), and through his scholarly textbooks. He was elected to the National Academy of Sciences in 1904 and was president of the American Mathematical Society in 1904–05.

Tall, spare, alert, and keen-eyed, Osgood during his middle years wore a square black beard. His favorite recreations were occasional boating, golf, tennis, and touring by motorcar. He owned a summer cottage at Silver Lake, N. H., and ordinarily spent his summers there. Although to outsiders he seemed reserved and somewhat formal, his friends found him warm and tender. Osgood's first marriage ended in divorce; on Aug. 19, 1932, he married Mrs. Céleste Phelps Morse. Osgood retired from Harvard in 1933 and for the next two years taught in China at the National University of Peking. He died in 1943, at the age of seventy-nine, at his home in Belmont, Mass., of acute pyelonephritis. Cremation followed at Forest Hills Cemetery, Boston.

[Personal recollections; *Class Reports* of Harvard College Class of 1886; clippings in Harvard Univ. Archives; *Who Was Who in America,* vol. II (1950); birth and death records in office of Mass. Registrar of Vital Statistics. Published accounts of Osgood include: Raymond C. Archibald, *Semicentennial Hist. of the Am. Mathematical Soc.* (1938), which contains a biographical sketch and a bibliography of his publications; and the Harvard faculty memorial minute in *Science,* Nov. 5, 1943.]

J. L. WALSH

O'SULLIVAN, MARY KENNEY (Jan. 8, 1864–Jan. 18, 1943), labor organizer and reformer, was born in Hannibal, Mo., the second daughter and third of four children of Michael and Mary (Kelly) Kenney. Her parents, both Catholics, had emigrated from Ireland in the early 1850's. They were married in New Hampshire, and soon afterward went west to work on a railroad construction gang, with Kenney as foreman and his wife cooking and serving meals. When their children were born, Kenney got a job in the Burlington Railroad's machine shop in Hannibal.

The hardworking Kenneys lived comfortably and enjoyed close ties with their neighbors. The parents were strict but warmly affectionate, and Mary, something of a tomboy, was very close to her father. She attended a convent school until she "struck" against its arbitrary discipline and transferred to a public school. As was common then, she was apprenticed at an early age to a dressmaker and never completed grammar school. With the death of her father in 1878, she took a job as bookbinder and after four years became a forewoman. When her employer moved to Keokuk, Iowa, she relocated with her now invalid mother. There she saw firsthand the protracted Burlington Railroad strike of 1888, which instilled in her an undying faith in unions.

The Keokuk bindery's failure forced Mary Kenney to go to Chicago in search of work, which she quickly found. She was appalled by the squalor of urban life, "the tragedies of meagerly-paid workers, the haunting faces of undernourished children, the filth, the everlasting struggle, and then the whole thing over again . . ." (Autobiography, p. 75). In response to such conditions, she organized the Chicago Women's Bindery Workers' Union, an offshoot of Ladies' Federal Labor Union No. 2703 (A.F. of L.). She was then elected to the Chicago Trades and Labor Assembly, where she assumed an active position of leadership. She became a lifelong friend of Jane Addams [Supp. 1] after Hull House was opened to union meetings. There Florence Kelley [Supp. 1], in conjunction with Mary Kenney, the Chicago Trades Assembly, and others, investigated Chicago's sweatshops, prepared a shocking and widely read report on labor conditions, and, by effectively lobbying in the Illinois legislature, secured the establishment of a Factory Inspection Department in 1893. Mary Kenney then became one of ten inspectors under Florence Kelley.

Meanwhile, in April 1892, Samuel Gompers [q.v.], president of the American Federation of Labor, had appointed Miss Kenney as the Federation's first national woman organizer. She spent June and July organizing women workers in New York City, traveled upstate, and then went to Massachusetts. Despite her commendable efforts, the A.F. of L. executive council terminated her position in 1893. While visiting Boston, she met John F. O'Sullivan, a fellow A.F. of

L. organizer, a former seaman and streetcar driver, and a widower. They were married on Oct. 10, 1894, in New York City, with Gompers as a witness to the civil ceremony. They made their home in Boston, where O'Sullivan was labor editor of the *Boston Globe*. The couple had four children: Kenney, Mortimer, Roger, and Mary Elizabeth.

While bearing and rearing her children, Mary O'Sullivan continued to speak and organize. As a member of the board of directors of the Women's Educational and Industrial Union of Boston and as executive secretary of the Union for Industrial Progress, she helped bridge the gap between wealthy women and working women. British trade unionists, American labor leaders, and public figures like Louis D. Brandeis [Supp. 3] were visitors in the O'Sullivan home; Mary later recalled that it "was like the cradle of a new-born movement. And our life there expressed the joy of youth finding comrades in ideals . . ." (*ibid.*, p. 158). Although her mother and oldest child died and the house burned down, her enthusiasm was undaunted as the O'Sullivans took quarters in nearby Denison House, a social settlement.

Her efforts in founding the National Women's Trade Union League represented a culmination of her work in bringing together settlement-house workers and union organizers. During the 1903 convention of the A.F. of L. in Boston, Mary O'Sullivan and William English Walling [Supp. 2] drafted the essential structure of the League; she became its first secretary and later first vice-president. The League was a significant agency for reform during the Progressive period.

In 1900 the O'Sullivans moved to suburban Beachmont, "where the children could stretch their legs and play in the sun." Two years later John O'Sullivan was killed by a train. Although friends, including Charles H. Taylor [q.v.] of the *Boston Globe,* found jobs in real estate management that enabled Mary O'Sullivan to support the children and continue her reform efforts, she suffered a breakdown in 1904 and briefly entered a sanitarium (*Woman's Journal,* June 8, 1907). But she was never one to be down long; in 1909 she was able to buy land and build a house for her family in nearby West Medford.

Her enthusiasm and fighting spirit were revitalized during the Lawrence (Mass.) textile strike of 1912. Already familiar with conditions there, Mary O'Sullivan returned to investigate, endorsed and aided the I.W.W. leadership, and worked to gain support for the strike. At one point she met personally with the intransigent president of the American Woolen Company. Responding partly to conditions at Lawrence, the state of Massachusetts in 1914 created a Division of Industrial Safety (from 1919 part of the Department of Labor and Industries), and from November 1914 until her retirement on Jan. 7, 1934, Mrs. O'Sullivan served as a factory inspector.

She never lost her commitment to reform. She vigorously opposed World War I and personally went to New York City to prevent her son from enlisting; subsequently she became a member of the Women's International League for Peace and Freedom. A stout supporter of woman suffrage, she was a delegate in 1922 to the national conference of the League of Women Voters. In 1924 she campaigned actively for Robert La Follette [q.v.] when he ran for president as a Progressive. She died in West Medford of arteriosclerotic heart disease at the age of seventy-nine. After a solemn high requiem mass, she was buried in St. Joseph Cemetery, West Roxbury, Mass.

[MS. autobiography and clippings in Schlesinger Lib., Radcliffe College; obituary in *Boston Globe*, Jan. 19, 1943; sketch by Eleanor Flexner and Janet Wilson James in *Notable Am. Women*, II, 655–56. See also Allen F. Davis, *Spearheads for Reform* (1967), pp. 138–47; Philip Foner, *Hist. of the Labor Movement in the U. S.*, II (1955), 189–95; Samuel Gompers, *Seventy Years of Life and Labor*, I (1925), 483–86; and Alice Henry, *Women and the Labor Movement* (1923), pp. 107–10.]

CHARLES SHIVELY

PARK, ROBERT EZRA (Feb. 14, 1864–Feb. 7, 1944), sociologist, was born in Harveyville, Luzerne County, Pa., the elder of two surviving sons of Theodosia (Warner) and Hiram Asa Park, both natives of Pennsylvania. When he was very young the family moved to Red Wing, Minn., where his father, a Civil War veteran, operated a wholesale grocery and supply business. After graduating from the local high school, Park entered the University of Minnesota but transferred after a year to the University of Michigan. There, under the influence of the Goethe scholar Calvin Thomas [q.v.] and the young philosopher John Dewey, he developed an interest in the study of human behavior. Upon graduating in 1887 with a Ph.B. degree, he became a newspaper reporter. He spent the next decade working on papers in Minneapolis, Detroit, Denver, and New York City, gathering experience and insight on the varieties of human behavior in the modern city. On June 11, 1894, he married Clara Cahill of Lansing, Mich., a portrait artist and daughter of a justice of the Michigan supreme court. They had four children: Edward Cahill, Theodosia Warner, Margaret Lucy, and Robert Hiram.

In 1891 and 1892 Park collaborated with John Dewey and Franklin Ford, a New York journalist, in an unsuccessful effort to establish a new type of newspaper, to be called *"Thought News,"* which would help form an enlightened public opinion by offering an interpretation-in-depth of current events in terms of the broad pattern of social evolution. This interest in the relation between social change and "news"—the increasing volume and variety of information available to the public—impelled Park to abandon journalism and resume his formal education. In 1898 he began graduate work at Harvard, where he studied philosophy with Josiah Royce and William James and psychology with Hugo Münsterberg [qq.v.]. James in particular left a lasting imprint upon Park, who never tired of citing James's essay "On a Certain Blindness in Human Beings" to students of sociology who he felt lacked empathy with the people they were studying. Park received the M.A. in 1899 and went to Germany, remaining there for the next four years. At the University of Berlin he heard lectures by Georg Simmel, philosopher and sociologist, and at Strassburg he studied under Wilhelm Windelband, whom he later followed to Heidelberg, where he received the Ph.D. in 1904. Park had returned to Cambridge, Mass., in 1903, and while polishing his thesis, published in 1904 as *Masse und Publikum* ("Crowd and Public") (a résumé of classical and contemporary writings in the field which Park would later rename "collective behavior"), he taught philosophy as an assistant at Harvard.

Weary of academic life once again, Park in 1904 became secretary of the Congo Reform Association, an organization dedicated to exposing Belgian atrocities in the Congo. In the course of this work he met Booker T. Washington [q.v.], who awakened his interest in Negro Americans and persuaded him to tour the South and accept a salary from Tuskegee Institute. As press agent, ghost writer, and general assistant to Washington, Park spent the next seven winters at Tuskegee and traveling through the South on Institute business, attempting to understand the folkways of blacks and the intricate system of social "etiquette" which defined their relations with whites. In 1912 he organized a conference on race relations at Tuskegee at which he met William I. Thomas, the University of Chicago sociologist who became his patron and a major influence on his social theory. A year later, at the age of forty-nine, Park accepted an invitation to join the department of sociology at Chicago as a part-time lecturer. He had had an independent income since the death of his father and hence was able to devote far more time to his teaching than his peripheral position required. In 1923 he was promoted to professor; he retired in 1929 but remained an influence on the Chicago department, through personal contact and the presence of his students on the faculty, until his death in 1944.

Soon after his arrival in Chicago, Park published a seminal essay entitled "The City: Suggestions for the Investigation of Human Behavior in the City Environment" (*American Journal of Sociology*, March 1915). He saw the modern city as an ideal laboratory for explaining the effects of evolutionary change on human nature and social organization. As a young reporter in New York he had gained a conception of the city as a social organism rather than a mere geographical entity. From his small-town background and from European theorists like Ferdinand Tönnies and Georg Simmel, Park, like many of his contemporaries, had acquired an acute awareness of the city's rapid tempo of change and unique heterogeneity. Park was especially impressed by the city's fragmentation into differing milieus or subcultures, which in their variety produced an unintended tolerance and made it possible for every human impulse to find expression. With the city as the crucial locale and his own experience of a simpler society ever present for contrast, Park searched for the key variables, such as the intensity and forms of human communication, which distinguished types of society and personality. He directed detailed investigation by his students of Chicago's subcommunities or "natural areas"—its slums, ghettos, and suburbs, its downtown and other specialized zones. In areas like the slum, where the rate of change was highest, the dissolution of such older forms of social control as the family and the neighborhood was most apparent, as was their partial replacement by substitute forms of community like the juvenile gang. With a passion for accuracy and understanding rooted in his experience as a reporter, and given theoretical support by the teaching of William James and the German *Verstehensoziologie,* he urged that investigations of such areas be carried out with both detachment and empathy, emphasizing that generalization must arise from empirical research in a limited area. The result was a stream of ground-breaking monographs, including Nels Anderson's *The Hobo* (1923), Frederic M. Thrasher's *The Gang* (1927), Louis Wirth's *The Ghetto* (1928), and Harvey W. Zorbaugh's *The Gold Coast and the Slum* (1929).

Using such empirical studies, Park hoped to construct a set of hypotheses which could be applied to other aspects of society. Yet he never produced a systematic treatise of sociology. Instead he drew upon his wide knowledge of sociological theory, especially of the work of Simmel, to provide a set of categories within which empirical data might be classified. In the *Introduction to the Science of Sociology* (1921), which he wrote with Ernest W. Burgess, he emphasized processes of social interaction rather than institutions such as the family, bureaucracy, etc., as most later American sociologists would do. Organized around such processes, the book introduced a number of related concepts in each section, and then presented a variety of relevant theoretical statements from other writers, as well as historical, literary, and scientific documents which illustrated some aspect of the process under discussion. It was here that Park first adumbrated his system of human ecology, which rested upon the notion that society could be analyzed in terms of two orders: the "ecological" or "biotic," and the "social" or "moral." The biotic order was drawn from the naturalist's description of the balanced web of relationships produced in an ecological community by Darwinian competition among plants and animals. In parallel fashion, the biotic order of society was governed by competition among men and groups for possession of scarce resources—resources both material and social—which brought about an unstable state of equilibrium and determined more specific social processes like social mobility and the arrangement of ecological subgroups in geographic and social space. This approach stimulated the use of quantification to measure social processes. Park's concept of "social distance," for example, suggested that ethnic prejudice (the degree of hostility between identifiably distinct peoples) might be measured in terms of a metaphor of spatial distance. At Park's suggestion, Emory S. Bogardus developed his social distance scale, one of the first efforts to measure the intensity of social attitudes.

The biotic order, in Park's view, was a substructure of impersonal, utilitarian forces, interacting constantly with a superstructure of cultural attitudes and values—the "social" or "moral" order, consisting of customs, beliefs, and laws, together with a corresponding body of artifacts. Variations in the "social" order were governed largely by the process of communication, which affected the degree of consensus and collective action present in a society at any given time and could be measured by such crystallizations of consensus as folkways, mores, and formal laws. Park conceived of society as a collection of potentially antagonistic elements held together in a temporary equilibrium constantly upset by changes in the biotic and social orders. The study of "collective behavior," which was one of Park's lasting contributions to the fields of sociology, concerned itself with the processes by which social consensus was disrupted and then rebuilt into new patterns. These processes followed a three-stage sequence, proceeding from social unrest to mass movements to the formation or modification of institutions to provide a new equilibrium. The stages involved three different types of social control: spontaneous (the crowd, ceremony, prestige, and taboo); explicit (gossip, rumor, news, and public opinion); and formal (law, dogma, religious and political institutions). Park was from the first fascinated by the role of communications media as methods of social control, and in several essays he discussed the manner in which newspapers facilitated the emergence of a collective will after a period of disruption and conflict.

As his typology of process would suggest, Park's sociology was concerned with the problem of change over time. According to his "natural history" model of social change, the disruption of a temporarily stabilized state of society intensified competition, setting in motion an interaction cycle which proceeded through a series of states: competition (continuous, individual, and impersonal interaction); conflict (intermittent, personal, and conscious interaction); accommodation (the cessation of overt conflict when groups reach a state of symbiosis); and assimilation (the absorption of conflicting groups or individuals into a new consensus).

From his notion that a capacity for collective action characterized the social order, Park concluded that the individual must have a capacity for conscious participation in a collective purpose, and therefore a capacity for conscious role playing and self-conception. Through his acquaintance with the interactional psychology of "social selves" offered by James, Charles Horton Cooley, and George Herbert Mead [q.v.], he developed this conception into the field of social psychology later known as role theory. His statement in 1921 —"We come into the world as individuals. We acquire status and become persons. Status means position in society. The individual inevitably has some status in every social group of which he is a member"—became a classic definition. A key example of role playing is the "marginal man," a person whose roles and concept of self are confused because he has been socialized into more than one separate culture, like the American mulatto, the European Jew, the Eurasian, the *assimilado*. He is unable to feel wholly at ease

in any one social group, yet this very separation produces a special sensitivity. The conception of the marginal man contributed both to the development of reference group behavior and to a deeper understanding of the social origins of intelligence.

Park's ecological concepts were developed as an effort to systematize his insights into human behavior. Many later students have concluded that his special theories in more limited areas, notably those on ethnic and cultural contacts which he developed in the 1910's and 1920's, may have more permanent value than his rather hasty general system. He ranks with Franz Boas [Supp. 3] and William I. Thomas as one of the pioneers of the modern study of race and ethnic relations. Incorporating and elaborating some of Thomas's earlier insights, Park explained racial antagonism as the result of one stage in the interaction cycle described above. His theory marked a long step beyond the biological or "instinct" theories previously current, and its suggestions are still being explored by students of the field. Park, however, was not a liberal optimist. He believed that visible ethnic differences would remain a more or less permanent barrier to full understanding and sympathy among peoples, and he retained a residue of belief in distinct racial "temperaments." In addition, he had a strong dislike of meddling elitist reformers, and a marked reverence for the complexity and persistence of the social processes he studied. He exhibited a certain fatalism, a tendency to hypostatize the existing etiquette of race relations, and a deep-seated skepticism about engineering social change. These attitudes brought Park under attack from younger scholars like Oliver C. Cox and Gunnar Myrdal in the 1940's.

Though Park's corpus of writings was not extensive, it was suggestive and wide-ranging, and had great influence on the development of American sociology. At Chicago in the 1920's he was perhaps the central figure in the most vigorous sociology department in the United States. Much of Park's influence came from his remarkable power as a teacher of advanced students. His blunt, informal, outspoken personality, his willingness to give his time generously, and his intense concern for understanding the subjective worlds of exotic peoples left a lasting impression on a generation of graduate students. He helped develop methods of instruction which made research an integral part of sociological training. The Park and Burgess textbook was very widely used. His principal influence was not that of the field worker or the meticulous researcher, nor that of the closely articulated conceptual theorist; it was that of the guide who, surveying an unknown land, defines boundaries and points out methods of exploration and tentative categories of interpretation.

Park served as president of the American Sociological Society in 1925–26 and received an honorary degree in 1937 from the University of Michigan. He was a Republican and a member of the congregation of the Disciples of Christ, whose pastor, Edward Scribner Ames, was his colleague at Chicago. After retiring in 1929, Park spent a year traveling and lecturing in the Orient, taught at the University of Hawaii (1931–32) and Yenching University (1932), and in 1933 lectured in India, Africa, and South America. An appointment as visiting professor (1935–37) at Fisk University took him to Nashville, Tenn., where he remained the rest of his life. He died of a cerebral thrombosis at his home in Nashville a week before his eightieth birthday; he was buried at Freeport, Ill., the home of a married daughter.

[Park's other publications include *The Principles of Human Behavior* (1915); *Old World Traits Transplanted* (with Herbert A. Miller, 1921); *The Immigrant Press and Its Control* (1922); and three volumes of *Collected Papers* (1950–55)—*Race and Culture, Human Communities,* and *Society*—edited after his death by Everett C. Hughes and others, which include most of his sociological essays written between 1913 and 1943. *Race and Culture* contains (pp. v–ix) a brief autobiographical note. See also: Robert E. Park, *On Social Control and Collective Behavior* (1967), a selection of papers edited by Ralph H. Turner with an introductory essay and a bibliography of Park's writings; Edna Cooper, "Bibliog. of Robert E. Park," *Phylon,* Fourth Quarter 1945; obituaries by Ellsworth Faris in *Am. Sociological Rev.,* June 1944, by Charles S. Johnson in *Sociology and Social Research,* May–June 1944, by Erle F. Young, *ibid.,* July–Aug. 1944, and by Ernest W. Burgess, *ibid.,* Mar.–Apr. 1945; Helen MacGill Hughes in *Internat. Encyc. of the Social Sciences,* XI, 416–17; Robert E. L. Faris, *Chicago Sociology 1920–32* (1967); Morton and Lucia White, *The Intellectual versus the City* (1962); Maurice R. Stein, *The Eclipse of Community* (1960); Park D. Goist, "City and 'Community': The Urban Theory of Robert Park," *Am. Quart.,* Spring 1971; Barbara Klose Bowdery, "The Sociology of Robert E. Park" (Ph.D. dissertation, Columbia Univ., 1951); Fred H. Matthews, "Robert Ezra Park and the Development of Am. Sociology" (Ph.D. dissertation, Harvard Univ., 1972). The main body of Park's papers is at the Univ. of Chicago. A portrait of Park by his daughter Theodosia Park Breed is in the Social Science Building at the Univ. of Chicago.]

PHILIP M. HOSAY
FRED H. MATTHEWS

PARKER, THEODORE BISSELL (Aug. 20, 1889–Apr. 27, 1944), civil engineer, chiefly known for his association with the Tennessee Valley Authority, was born in the Roxbury section of Boston, Mass., the only child of Franklin Wells Parker and Sarah (Bissell) Parker. His father was a native of Roxbury, his mother of

Wilmington, Vt. Franklin Parker, listed as a clerk at the time of his son's birth, later derived his livelihood from the rental of tenements built on the site of the family homestead. Theodore attended public schools in Roxbury and Wellesley, Mass., and the Massachusetts Institute of Technology, from which he received the degree of Bachelor of Science in Civil Engineering in 1911. He spent the following year in graduate study aided by an assistantship that included some teaching in M.I.T.'s civil engineering department. On May 10, 1913, he married Estelle Peabody of Wellesley, Mass. They had two children, Franklin Peabody and Nancy.

Meanwhile, in 1912, a few months after leaving M.I.T., Parker had entered into his lifelong specialty of waterway and hydroelectric engineering when he joined the Utah Power and Light Company at Salt Lake City as a hydraulic engineer. He left in 1917 for wartime service with the Army Corps of Engineers, during which he commanded a company in the American Expeditionary Forces in Europe. After a brief period (April 1919–October 1920) as a hydraulic engineer with the Electric Bond and Share Company of New York, he returned to the Corps of Engineers and spent a year of study at the Army Engineering School at Fort Humphreys, Va. Although he remained active in the reserve and in 1933 attended the army's Command and General Staff School, Parker resumed civilian employment in 1922 and for the next eleven years found congenial activity as a hydroelectic engineer with the Stone & Webster Engineering Corporation of Boston [see Charles A. Stone, Supp. 3].

The depression and the New Deal administration of President Franklin Roosevelt precipitated Theodore Parker into a career with governmental agencies that was to bring him national and eventually international prominence. His experience with the Corps of Engineers and with Stone & Webster had revealed administrative as well as engineering ability, and in 1933 he was appointed state engineer and acting director for Massachusetts of the Federal Emergency Administration of Public Works (later Public Works Administration). Two years later President Roosevelt named Parker chief engineer of construction of the Tennessee Valley Authority, and in 1938 chief engineer, a position which he held until 1943. The first organization of its kind in the world, TVA was an integrated multipurpose agency concerned with the balanced conservation and development of water, forest, soil, and mineral resources within the Tennessee Valley region. Parker's appointment grew out of his continuing association with the Corps of Engineers, since the corps had made the original hydrographic survey and had drawn up a preliminary plan for flood control and power generation on the Tennessee River and its tributaries which was substantially adopted by the TVA. Serving as he did throughout the period of most extensive construction, Parker played a major role in creating the program and the physical plant of the TVA, in association with the remarkably creative team that included the first two directors, Arthur E. Morgan and David E. Lilienthal, the agronomist and board member Harcourt A. Morgan, and the chief architect, Roland Anthony Wank.

For the design and construction of the controlling installations, the staff of the TVA relied extensively on the experience of the Bureau of Reclamation gained through the construction of dams and hydroelectric facilities in the West. Many innovations had to be introduced, however, to adapt the bureau's principles to navigational requirements in the Tennessee River and to balance flood-control needs against hydroelectric demand over a vast integrated system in a region of high rainfall. Parker's designing talent and administrative skills are attested by the great river-control projects completed by the TVA under his tenure—Wheeler (1936), Pickwick Landing (1938), Guntersville (1939), Chickamauga (1940), Watts Bar (1942), and Fort Loudoun (1943) in the main river; Norris (1936), Hiwassee (1940), Cherokee (1942), Apalachia (1943), and Douglas (1943) among the high-head tributary structures. In addition to these, Kentucky Dam (1938–44), the largest main-river facility, and Fontana Dam (1942–45), the most impressive of all the TVA installations, were designed and placed under construction during his engineering administration.

Parker served the government also as a member of the Water Resources Committee of the National Resources Planning Board. His published writings include contributions to the *Technical Reports* of TVA and a number of articles that appeared in engineering journals, chief among them "TVA River Engineering" (Boston Society of Civil Engineers, *Journal*, January 1944).

With the major phase of construction completed, Parker resigned from the Tennessee Valley Authority staff to accept an appointment as professor of civil engineering and chairman of the department at his alma mater, but he served less than an academic year before his early and unexpected death. In April 1944, at the age of fifty-four, he died of abdominal cancer at his home in Wellesley, Mass. He was buried in Woodlawn Cemetery in Wellesley.

[Memoir in Am. Soc. of Civil Engineers, *Transactions*, CX (1945), 1786–90; *Who Was Who in America*, vol. II (1950); obituaries in *Civil Engineering*, June 1944, and *Technology Rev.* (M.I.T.), June 1944; on TVA, Carl W. Condit, *Am. Building Art: The Twentieth Century* (1961), and John H. Kyle, *The Building of TVA* (1958); letters from Franklin P. Parker; birth and death records from Mass. Registrar of Vital Statistics.]

CARL W. CONDIT

PARSONS, ELSIE WORTHINGTON CLEWS (Nov. 27, 1875–Dec. 19, 1941), sociologist and anthropologist, was born in New York City, the eldest of three children and only daughter of Henry Clews [*q.v.*], a prominent investment banker of English birth, and Lucy Madison (Worthington) Clews of Kentucky, a grandniece of President James Madison. Instead of following the pattern of social life which the status of her family indicated, Elsie Clews entered Barnard College, from which she was graduated in 1896. She continued her studies at Columbia University under the inspiration of the distinguished sociologist Franklin H. Giddings [Supp. 1], receiving the A.M. degree in 1897 and the Ph.D. in 1899. Under Giddings's supervision she served as Hartley House Fellow at Barnard College from 1899 to 1902 and as lecturer in sociology there from 1902 to 1905. She did not hold a permanent academic post after 1905 but chose to carry on independent research. On Sept. 1, 1900, she married Herbert Parsons, a New York attorney who served in Congress (as a Republican) from 1905 to 1911. Two of their six children died shortly after birth; the four who survived were Elsie, John Edward, Herbert, and Henry McIlvaine.

Mrs. Parsons was a prolific writer. Her first publication appeared in 1898, and with the exception of a few years, notably between 1907 and 1912, she produced books and articles every year until her death. Her early writings were much concerned with the role of women in society. Focusing on the social, rather than political, disabilities of her sex, she maintained that excessive distinction between the sexes and the cult of chivalry were both stale customs, inherited from an earlier age and no longer relevant. The modern woman would make a suitable wife or mother only if she enjoyed wider opportunities to realize her own potential. But Elsie Parsons's concern for freedom extended beyond women to all individuals who endure constraint from nonrational conventions. In her books *The Family* (1906), *The Old-Fashioned Woman* (1913), and *Fear and Conventionality* (1914), she upheld the claims of personality and self-expression against the overbearing power of conformity. In keeping with these views, she herself shunned convention and artifice in demeanor and dress, usually appearing in rough outdoor clothes. Her husband sympathized with her independence. When their children passed through an adolescent phase of disapproving her iconoclasm, she accepted this with good humor. In all her personal relations she was candid, but gentle and generous. An English reviewer of *The Family* thought that its frankness with regard to sexual and familial relations was not suitable for "youths and maidens from the ages of seventeen to twenty-one"; and her preceptor, Giddings, shared this view. To avoid notoriety, she published her study of *Religious Chastity* (1913) under a pseudonym: "John Main."

Mrs. Parsons's early major publications bore a marked ethnological imprint. She called *The Family* "an ethnographical and historical outline"; *Religious Chastity* was subtitled "an ethnological study." Her other early books were cross-cultural in point of view. Between 1910 and 1915 she made a few trips to New Mexico, where she became interested in the Pueblo Indians; she made some use of her ethnographic observations in *The Old-Fashioned Woman* and *Fear and Conventionality*. About 1915 she decided to devote herself to field research in ethnology. She had previously made the acquaintance of the eminent anthropologist Franz Boas [Supp. 3] at Columbia University and of Pliny Earle Goddard [*q.v.*] of the American Museum of Natural History. Under their influence, her intellectual posture shifted dramatically from the deductive sociology and weighty generalization of her early writings to a new concern for the smallest empirical detail of particular cultures. For the rest of her life she devoted herself diligently to field work among the American Indians, primarily the Pueblo Indians of the Southwest, but extended her researches to Plains tribes and to cultures in Mexico and Ecuador. Besides scores of articles and monographs, the finest fruits of this meticulous research were *Mitla, Town of the Souls* (1936), which explored the subtle mingling of Spanish and native cultures, and *Pueblo Indian Religion* (2 vols., 1939), in which Elsie Parsons's final conclusions about cultural change were supported by a massive marshaling of data.

Side by side with her ethnological researches, she devoted herself to the collection of folktales, recorded by dictation from informants, among them American Negroes, American Indians, and peoples of the West Indies. *Folk-Lore of the Antilles, French and English* (3 vols., 1933–43) is outstanding in this area of research. Mrs. Parsons was active in several learned societies—as president (1919–20) of the American Folklore Society and for many years associate editor of its

journal; as treasurer (1916–22) and president (1923–25) of the American Ethnological Society; and as the first woman to be elected president of the American Anthropological Association (1940). She also helped found the New School for Social Research and lectured at its first session in 1919.

Elsie Clews Parsons was a woman of great integrity and high ideals. Modest and unassuming, she sought no recognition for herself. Her life was one of devotion to the work and values she prized greatly: freedom for personal development and expression in the earlier years, ethnological science in the later years, and enlightenment always. She was in a position to render financial assistance to science and scholarship. For a number of years the American Folklore Society owed its solvency to her generosity, and behind the facade of "The Southwest Society" she financed field trips and publications for young anthropologists. In 1941, just eight days before she was to officiate as president at the annual meeting of the American Anthropological Association, she died in New York City following an appendectomy. Her remains were cremated.

[In addition to her own writings, Elsie Clews Parsons translated Gabriel Tarde's *Les Lois de l'Imitation* (1903) and meticulously edited the magnificent *Hopi Jour. of Alexander M. Stephen* (2 vols., 1936), as well as two other lesser Pueblo journals. For material about her, see the memorial number of the *Jour. of Am. Folklore*, Jan. 1943, which contains, in addition to articles pertinent to her work, an obituary by Gladys A. Reichard, a bibliography of Mrs. Parsons's writings, and a photograph of her. Obituaries by Leslie Spier and A. L. Kroeber, both colleagues and friends of Mrs. Parsons, appear in the *Am. Anthropologist*, Apr. 1943. See also the sketch in *Notable Am. Women*, II, 20–22. Her papers are at the Am. Philosophical Soc., Philadelphia.]

LESLIE A. WHITE

PATCH, ALEXANDER McCARRELL (Nov. 23, 1889–Nov. 21, 1945), army officer, was born at Fort Huachuca, Arizona Territory, where his father, a West Point graduate, was on duty. He was the second son and second of three children of Alexander McCarrell Patch and Annie (Moore) Patch, both of whom had grown up in Washington, Pa. The family soon returned to Pennsylvania, for his father, having lost a leg in an accident incurred while chasing horse thieves, was retired for disability in 1890. Settling in Lebanon County, he became an executive of the Cornwall Railroad. Young Patch, after earlier schooling and a year at Lehigh University, followed his father to West Point. He graduated in 1913, having excelled in field and track, and was assigned to the 18th Infantry in Texas. While on leave in Washington, D. C., on Nov. 20, 1915, he married Julia Adrienne Littell, daughter of

Gen. Isaac William Littell. They had two children, Alexander and Julia Ann.

When the United States entered World War I, Patch accompanied the 18th Infantry to France, where in June 1917 it became a part of the new 1st Division. Machine guns were new to the division, and Patch was among the first Americans to be schooled by the British in their use; for several months in 1918 he directed the A.E.F. Machine Gun School. During the Meuse-Argonne campaign he commanded his regiment's second battalion. In 1918 he was a victim of the influenza epidemic, which left him chronically susceptible to pneumonia whenever overtaxed.

During the next two decades Patch alternated between regimental duty and assignments as a military student and instructor. He had three tours of duty on the faculty of the Staunton (Va.) Military Academy, and the Shenandoah Valley became his permanent home. In 1924 he attended the Command and General Staff School, and in 1931 he entered the Army War College. At that time the army was moving toward greater mechanization, seeking newer automatic weapons, and developing a slimmer division. Major Patch's term paper dealt with a mechanized division of only three regiments. A classmate, Major George S. Patton, Jr. [Supp. 3], who likewise proposed a mechanized division, was greatly impressed with Patch's concepts. For three years (1936–39) Patch, now a lieutenant colonel, served on the Infantry Board. The three-regiment or "triangular" division was then being formed and field-tested, and Patch made many improvements in it, placing automatic weapons and antitank guns in the combat units. In August 1940 he became commander of the 47th Infantry.

Six weeks after Pearl Harbor, Gen. George C. Marshall selected Patch, whom he had watched since World War I, to command the task force destined to defend New Caledonia, a strategic island astride sea lanes to Australia. Raw American units, arriving in piecemeal fashion, had to be deployed quickly, but by late May 1942 Patch (now a major general) had assembled them into a fighting team, the Americal Division. That December he was placed in command of American ground operations in the Guadalcanal-Tulagi zone. He immediately organized two army divisions and one Marine division into one of America's first separate corps, the XIV. On Jan. 10, 1943, he launched a well-planned and brilliantly executed attack which crushed the enemy's resistance. Tired and needing rest, Patch was ordered home at mid-March personally by Marshall, who wanted an experienced commander to form a new IV corps for European duty.

On Mar. 1, 1944, Patch was given command of the U. S. Seventh Army, which was scheduled to invade southern France in concert with an Allied advance from a northern beachhead in Normandy. Within a few months he had assembled his assault forces, which included a full-sized French army. That August he was given the temporary rank of lieutenant general. On Napoleon's birthday, Aug. 15, he began his landings along the Riviera, an operation so perfectly executed that it remains a model in the annals of amphibious warfare. By the end of August his Allied columns held Marseilles and Toulon and were advancing up the Rhone Valley; on Sept. 11, they joined Gen. George Patton's Third Army near Epinal, having trapped sizable German formations. Despite his men's exhausted condition, and hobbled by a 450-mile supply line, Patch gambled on forcing the Burgundy gateway and descending the rift of the Rhine. At mid-September the guns of Belfort barred his way, and there Patch met his first and only tactical draw. Fleshed out with new divisions, Patch's army moved on the Saverne Gap with the objective of seizing Strasbourg; during the fighting that October his son, Capt. Alexander Patch III, was killed in action.

With Marseilles as a port and a smooth-working supply line, Patch enjoyed a logistical advantage over all other Allied commanders. On Nov. 13 he struck along the Marne-Rhine canal. His infantry advanced well, and he held his armor patiently, timing the very moment when it should break through the enemy's lines. In ten days, Patch was the first American commander to reach the Rhine, and on his fifty-fifth birthday he occupied Strasbourg. Well in front of Patton on his left, Patch hastened his army into Alsace, preparatory to jumping the Rhine; but his American superiors, after an all-day debate, directed him to advance west of the Rhine and, when Patton was ready, to join him in enveloping the Saar. Though bitterly disappointed, Patch reoriented his advance, and within three weeks was through the Wissembourg Gap into the Palatinate. During January 1945 he met and repelled Hitler's last major offensive on the western front. When Germany collapsed, Patch's army controlled Brenner Pass, 900 miles from the Riviera.

Marshall ordered Patch home in June to ready the Fourth Army for Pacific duty. When Japan capitulated, Patch headed a board to study the army's postwar structure and spent a month in Europe collecting data. That November, exhausted and realizing his need for medical attention, he entered Brooke General Hospital in San Antonio, Texas; he died six days later of pneumonia. His remains were buried at West Point.

Patch's services were recognized by many governments, but he was so modest a man that he often objected to receiving the decorations. He was an able professional officer with high standards of conduct. Because of his reddish, close-cropped hair and light blue eyes intimate friends addressed him as "Sandy"; they remembered him for his deadpan wit. Tall, lean, and erect, he enjoyed hunting and riding. Rudyard Kipling's works were his hobby, and he owned some valuable first editions. He was an Episcopalian. His devotion in life centered around his family, his countryside in the Shenandoah Valley, and his classmates at West Point. Posthumously, in 1954, he became a general in the Army of the United States.

[MS. Diary of the Seventh Army, 1944–45, in Nat. Archives, Washington, D. C.; Patch's "Some Thoughts on Leadership," *Military Rev.*, Dec. 1943, and his class paper at the Army War College, "What Should Be the Organization and Equipment of the War Strength Infantry Division?" (AWC 387–51, Carlisle Barracks, Pa.); Francis D. Cronin, *Under the Southern Cross: The Saga of the Americal Division* (1951); John Miller, *Guadalcanal: The First Offensive* (1949); obituary in *Assembly* (West Point alumni magazine), July 1946, and additional information from the U. S. Military Academy; *Nat. Cyc. Am. Biog.*, XXXVIII, 13–14; *Current Biog.*, 1943; *N. Y. Times*, Nov. 22, 23 (editorial), 24, and 26, 1945.]
CHARLES F. ROMANUS, SR.

PATRICK, MASON MATHEWS (Dec. 13, 1863–Jan. 29, 1942), army officer and aviator, was born in Lewisburg, W. Va., to Alfred Spicer Patrick and his wife, Virginia Mathews. His father, a descendant of Mathew Patrick, who came from Ireland to Massachusetts about 1720, was a surgeon in the Confederate Army. Mason Patrick attended both public and private schools at Lewisburg and himself taught school for some two years before winning an appointment to the United States Military Academy in 1882. At West Point he proved an excellent student, graduating second out of seventy-seven in the class of 1886.

On graduating, Patrick was commissioned a second lieutenant in the Corps of Engineers, and over the next three decades he performed a wide variety of duties. For three years he was stationed at Willetts Point (later Fort Totten), Long Island, serving as company commander and completing the postgraduate course for engineering officers. In 1889 he rendered yeoman service in aiding the survivors of the Johnstown, Pa., flood. He twice served three-year tours of duty (1892–95, 1903–06) teaching military engineering at West Point. In 1901 he was made assistant to the Chief of Engineers in Washington. In the fall of 1906 Patrick went to Cuba as commander of

the 2nd Battalion of Engineers, a part of the Army of Pacification. He became chief engineer of this army a few months later and was assigned to the staff of the commanding general in Cuba. While on this assignment Patrick was responsible for mapping the entire island and for building many miles of hard-surface roads. From 1909 to 1916 he was in charge of river and harbor work, first in Virginia and then in Michigan. In mid-1916 Patrick organized and commanded the 1st Regiment of Engineers at San Antonio, Texas, serving with it on the Mexican border during the crisis arising out of Pancho Villa's raid into New Mexico.

When the United States entered the First World War, Patrick (then a colonel) went to France as commanding officer of the 1st Engineers. He was promoted to the temporary rank of brigadier general shortly after his arrival and became chief engineer and then commanding general of the lines of communication. In his next post, as director of construction and forestry operations, he had charge of all engineering construction of the American Expeditionary Forces in France.

In May 1918 the tough, crusty, moustachioed Patrick, now a major general, was handed the most important assignment of his career when his West Point classmate Gen. John J. Pershing asked him to take command of all Air Service units in the A.E.F. Internal jealousies and organizational confusion had plagued America's infant air arm for months. It was apparent that what was needed was a "square-jawed will and a strong hand able to apply discipline and see that the several units cooperated according to a given plan, on a given date, in a given way and no other way" (Hudson, p. 56). General Pershing reasoned that Patrick would be able to stand above the ambitious young air officers, almost all of whom—including William ("Billy") Mitchell [Supp. 2] and Benjamin D. Foulois—were under forty. The appointment of Patrick, a nonflying officer, to head the Air Service may have dampened strategic air thinking, but it did bring order out of confusion. Largely because of his managerial skill, the American Air Service provided effective observation, pursuit, and tactical bombing support for Pershing's land forces in the St. Mihiel and Meuse-Argonne campaigns. By the end of the war American air strength in the A.E.F. had increased to 45 combat squadrons and 23 balloon companies manned by approximately 60,000 officers and men.

Patrick returned to the United States in July 1919 and took up duties with the Corps of Engineers, but two years later, in October 1921, he was appointed chief of the army's Air Service. Realizing the need for greater rapport with the young aviators under his command, Patrick, although nearly sixty years old, learned to fly. In his six-year tenure he sought both to advertise air power to the American people and to improve the status of the air arm within the armed forces. In addition to reorganizing the experimental flight program at Wright Field, Ohio, and establishing the Air Corps Training Center at San Antonio, Texas, he promoted such newsworthy events as the first flight around the world by army pilots in 1924 and goodwill flights to the various Central and South American capitals.

Patrick's chief assistant from 1921 to 1926 was the irrepressible Billy Mitchell, who had already begun to agitate publicly for an independent air force. Unlike the impatient Mitchell (on whose court-martial board he served in 1925), General Patrick, although convinced of the importance of air power, chose the moderate approach to gaining a degree of autonomy for the Air Service. In his testimony before the various investigation boards in 1924 and 1925 he urged the creation of an Air Corps directly responsible to the Secretary of War; as he put it, he wanted a "status in the Army similar to that of the Marine Corps in the Navy Department." The Air Corps Act of 1926 incorporated some of his recommendations but fell far short of setting up the semiautonomous force the aviators desired.

Patrick retired from the army in December 1927 but continued to lead an active life. His book *The United States in the Air* was published in 1928, and over the next few years he wrote several articles and gave many lectures on problems of air traffic. Although Patrick was a Democrat, President Hoover appointed him public utilities commissioner for the District of Columbia in 1929, a post he held for four years. On Nov. 11, 1902, Patrick had married Grace Webster Cooley of Plainfield, N. J.; they had an adopted son, Bream Cooley. In religion Patrick was an unaffiliated Protestant. He died at Walter Reed General Hospital in Washington, D. C., early in 1942 of arteriosclerotic heart disease and cancer, and was buried in Arlington National Cemetery.

[Patrick's writings include: *Final Report of Chief of Air Service, A.E.F.* (1921); *Notes on Road Building in Cuba* (1910); "Military Aircraft and Their Use in Warfare," *Jour. of the Franklin Inst.*, Jan. 1925; and many articles in aviation and other magazines. Typical examples of his expert testimony can be found in President's Aircraft Board [Morrow Board], "Aircraft," *Hearings* (4 vols., 1925), and House Select Committee of Inquiry into Operations of U.S. Air Services [Lampert Committee], 68 Cong., 2 Sess., *Hearings* (6 vols., 1925). For Patrick's World War I career, see James J. Hudson, *Hostile Skies: A Combat Hist. of the Am. Air Service in World War I*

(1968); for his role in the 1920's, see Alfred Goldberg, ed., *A Hist. of the U. S. Air Force, 1907–1957* (1957), and Wesley Frank Craven and James Lea Cate, eds., *The Army Air Forces in World War II* (1948). For general summaries of Patrick's life, see Flint DuPre, *U. S. Air Force Biog. Dict.* (1965); *Nat. Cyc. Am. Biog.*, XLIV, 266; and *Who Was Who in America*, vol. I (1942). Death record from D. C. Dept. of Human Resources. Patrick's Flight Log Books and a few letters are in the U. S. Air Force Museum, Wright-Patterson Air Base, Ohio; his World War I diaries and a photo album are at the Air Academy; several photographs of Patrick are at the U.S.A.F. Hist. Division Archives, Maxwell Air Force Base, Ala. Other papers are in the Sallie Bennett Maxwell Collection at the Univ. of W. Va. Lib. The Gorrell Air Service Histories in the Nat. Archives, Washington, D.C., contain much material on Patrick.]

JAMES J. HUDSON

PATTEN, GILBERT (Oct. 25, 1866–Jan. 16, 1945), dime novelist, creator of the ninth-inning hero Frank Merriwell, was born in Corinna, Maine. Christened George William Patten, he was the younger of two children and only son of Cordelia (Simpson) and William Clark Patten; since his sister died in 1867, he grew up as an only child. His father was a moderately prosperous carpenter of Scotch-Irish descent, and both parents were Seventh-Day Adventists. Resisting his father's desire that he follow the carpentry trade and his mother's hope that he would study for the ministry, Patten seasoned his undistinguished school record with a midnight diet of forbidden dime novels and the creation of stories based on his reading. Increasing conflict with his parents caused him to run away, at sixteen, to Biddeford, Maine, where he worked for six months in a machine shop. He returned home determined to make his way in the world, preferably as an author, and soon afterward sold two short stories to the dime-novel publishing firm of Beadle and Adams [see Erastus F. Beadle, Supp. 1].

Patten now planned to enter college, and at Corinna Union Academy discovered Poe, Hawthorne, Stevenson, and Dickens, whose works seemed "a hundred times more gripping and stirring than any dime novel possibly could be." To help pay for his education he worked for two summers as a reporter on newspapers in nearby towns, and at nineteen, despite his expanding horizons, he began to turn out dime novels. A revised early work, *The Diamond Sport,* brought fifty dollars from Beadle and Adams, and he was soon earning as much as $150 a novel. But marriage on Oct. 25, 1886, to Alice Clair Gardner, a Corinna classmate, brought new responsibilities, and after his father was disabled in an accident Patten had his parents to support as well. Abandoning his dream of college, he committed his total energies to writing cheap thrillers for a mass audience. His wife recopied his hastily written manuscripts, corrected his spelling, and improved his casual grammar.

Seeking wider fields, Patten moved in 1891 to New York City. There he produced a series of Westerns for Beadle and Adams under the pseudonym "William West Wilder—Wyoming Will," only to discover that the Wild West story was giving ground to the urban detective mystery and that the dime novel itself was being replaced by five-cent pulp weeklies. Decreasing fees and increasing expenses—a son, Harvan Barr, was born in 1892—led Patten to leave Beadle and Adams. After a short stint with the six-cent juvenile weekly *Golden Hours,* he approached the publishing firm of Street and Smith, with whom he served a two-year apprenticeship in miscellaneous juvenile fiction before receiving a commission to create a new series concerning a schoolboy athlete. Patten invented a pseudonym for himself, "Burt L. Standish," and a name for his hero, "Frank Merriwell," and in four days wrote a 20,000-word episode. The first number—"Frank Merriwell: or, First Days at Fardale" —appeared in *Tip Top Weekly* ("An Ideal Publication for the American Youth—Price, Five Cents") on Apr. 18, 1896, and Frank was launched on his immediately successful and remarkably long-lived career.

The alter ego for a shy, clumsy, unathletic, success-hungry Maine boy who never made it to college, Frank Merriwell was devastatingly strong and handsome, impossibly proficient, and stiffly moral. He touched neither alcohol nor tobacco (Patten enjoyed both). Frank's manly contempt for cheap, ungentlemanly cads and overdressed Harvard bullies, his "double-shoot" baseball curve which broke both ways, and his inevitable last-minute triumph to win the game for Fardale or Yale over seemingly insurmountable odds pushed the weekly circulation of *Tip Top* to over 135,000 and a prosperity which the author only partially shared. Employed on a piecework basis, Patten wrote a Merriwell story each week for fifty dollars (gradually increased to $150 per week)—an arrangement that lasted for seventeen years and produced more than 800 Merriwell stories.

Even Frank Merriwell began to grow stale after seventeen years. Patten's desperate manipulations of plot—including the invention of a younger brother Dick who followed Frank to Fardale and Yale, and a son, Frank, Jr.—failed to sustain reader interest, and in 1913 he abandoned the series, though other hands carried it on until 1916. Meanwhile Patten (who by this time

was calling himself Gilbert Patten) had turned to the College Life Series and the Big League Series for Street and Smith's new adult sports fiction magazine *Top Notch,* to juvenile fiction such as the Rex Kingdon Series and the Oakdale Series, and to Western love stories.

Patten had been divorced from his first wife in 1898, and in 1900 he married Mary Nunn of Baltimore. This marriage, too, ended in divorce, and on June 27, 1918, he wed Carol Kramer of New York City. In his later years, Patten spent increasingly long periods at "Overocks," his summer home in Camden, Maine. Gradually he turned away from hack writing. He supervised the revival of Frank Merriwell in a comic strip and a radio program, and worked on a serious novel, an autobiography, and a final, unsuccessful tribute to his hero—*Mr. Frank Merriwell* (1941). Income from his writing had sharply declined, and after his wife's death in 1938 he suffered a serious breakdown. He moved to California in 1941 to regain his health and to be near his son. Patten died of heart disease at his son's home in Vista, Calif., at the age of seventy-eight. His ashes were placed with those of his wife Carol in New York.

In his sixty-year career as an author, under his own name and a dozen pseudonyms, Patten produced at least 1,500 works of fiction—all of them undistinguished—for a remarkable total of 40,000,000 published words. Failing to find the time or the ability for the serious writing he had always intended to do, he developed increasing admiration for the character whose life story was his chief work. At first he had called the Merriwell stories "a joke," but he began to take his work seriously "when it got so that a half million kids were reading him every week. . . . Yes, I loved [Frank Merriwell]. And I loved him most because no boy, if he followed in his tracks, ever did anything that he need be ashamed of" (Cutler, p. 110). No dime novelist ever placed a character more firmly or apparently more permanently in the mythology of American adolescence.

[Patten sketches his life in "Dime-Novel Days," *Saturday Evening Post,* Feb. 28 and Mar. 7, 1931; and in *Frank Merriwell's "Father"* (1964), an autobiography discovered in his papers. The only comprehensive study is John L. Cutler, *Gilbert Patten and His Frank Merriwell Saga* (Univ. of Maine Studies, 1934), which contains a partial bibliography of Patten's work. Also useful are James M. Cain, "The Man Merriwell," *Saturday Evening Post,* June 11, 1927; Irving Wallace, "The Return of Frank Merriwell," *Esquire,* Aug. 1952; Stewart H. Holbrook, "Frank Merriwell at Yale Again—and Again and Again," *Am. Heritage,* June 1961. For background see Edmund Pearson, *Dime Novels* (1929); Merle Curti, "Dime Novels and the Am. Tradition," *Yale Rev.,* Summer 1937; and Albert Johannsen, *The House of Beadle and Adams* (3 vols., 1950–62). Death certificate (under William Gilbert Patten) from Calif. Dept. of Public Health.]

HAROLD H. KOLB, JR.

PATTERSON, RUFUS LENOIR (June 11, 1872–Apr. 11, 1943), inventor and developer of tobacco manufacturing machinery, was born in Salem, N. C., the fourth of six children, all sons, of Rufus Lenoir Patterson, a merchant, and his second wife, Mary Elizabeth, daughter of Francis Fries [q.v.], pioneer Southern industrialist. The Patterson forebears were Scotch-Irish; the Fries, German. The elder Patterson, maintaining the family code of leadership, served as mayor of Salem and as a member of various statewide public bodies. As a child young Rufus was exposed to the distinctive customs and beliefs of the Unitas Fratrum or Moravian Church, in whose councils his mother's family had been prominent for generations and which his father eventually joined. The lad attended the Moravian Boys' School, completed the Winston graded schools, worked for a season with camping and survey parties of the Roanoke and Southern Railroad, and then in 1889 enrolled in the University of North Carolina. After about a year he ended his formal education for a "fine opening" in the bleachery of a textile firm in Concord, N. C. By the spring of 1891 he was working closely with one of the managers, William H. Kerr, inventor of a machine which made muslin bags of various sizes, including the small sacks used in the packaging of granulated smoking tobacco.

Wearied by his twelve-hour workday, the usually gay youth in 1892 eagerly accepted an opportunity to accompany the Kerr machines to England, where they were offered to British manufacturers. He squeezed his way into Westminster Abbey for Tennyson's funeral, which was "simply grand," visited art galleries, attended theatres and musical gardens, and acquired lifelong friends. At the same time he thoughtfully observed British machine design, agonized over his own future, and made solemn resolve. to be a success in business. Soon after his return in 1893, he settled in Durham, N. C., to work with the man who had subsidized Kerr's invention, Julian S. Carr, master of the Blackwell factory, where famed Bull Durham tobacco was produced. In the winter of 1894-95 Carr and Patterson negotiated with Kerr for the creation of a new machine, one which would weigh, pack, stamp, and label smoking tobacco. The contract acknowledged that such a device had been "mentally conceived" by Kerr, who engaged himself to construct the machine, which would then be promoted by Carr and Patterson. Kerr drowned in June 1895, and the dismayed Patterson of necessity had to complete what Kerr had begun. The patent for the machine which became known as the Patterson Packer was issued Mar. 23, 1897, and assigned to the Automatic Packing and Labeling Company, Durham, of which Patterson was president. Despite business pressures, he found time for a lively round of social activities and effected a notable alliance when, on Nov. 21, 1895, he married Margaret Morehead, granddaughter of Gov. John Motley Morehead [q.v.].

Before the end of 1897 James B. Duke [q.v.], creator of the powerful American Tobacco Company, visited the Patterson operations, commended the youthful engineer, and in 1898 hired two-thirds of his time for $7,500 per year. Patterson, a man of personal charm as well as mechanical ingenuity, was accepted as Duke's close ally and received rapid promotions, becoming a vice-president of the American Tobacco Company in 1901. His energies were soon absorbed in the operation of subsidiary corporations, the most important being the American Machine and Foundry Company, of which he was principal founder and president. These companies designed and manufactured cheroot-rolling machines, mechanical tobacco stemmers, cigarette-manufacturing machines, variations of the Patterson Packer, and other equipment for the tobacco trade. Patterson remained high in the councils of the combination, and had the uncomfortable distinction of being named, along with Duke, as one of the twenty-nine individual defendants in the epochal antitrust case, *United States* v. *American Tobacco Company* (221 U.S. 106). In the unscrambling of the industry which followed the verdict of 1911, the American Machine and Foundry Company, which Patterson still headed, became independent of the old alliances and achieved a conspicuous prosperity.

Patterson was probably more responsible for the mechanization of the tobacco industry than any other individual. His greatest engineering triumph was the perfection, about 1918, of a machine which produced high-quality long-filler cigars, previously the product of hand labor. Under his guidance the American Machine and Foundry Company and its subsidiaries became the world's largest suppliers of equipment for the tobacco industry, and expanded into baking, apparel manufacturing, and other fields. He served as president of the parent company continuously from 1900, the time of its incorporation, to 1941; then as chairman of the board until his death. By 1935 he was among the eight highest-paid executives in the United States, reportedly earning $197,000 per year.

With affluence Patterson enjoyed a clubman's

life in New York City and established a notable home, Lenoir, in Southampton, Long Island. His hobbies included horticulture (especially orchids), horses, Republican politics, and a continuing interest in the University of North Carolina, which in 1935 awarded him the honorary LL.D. degree. High blood pressure and a fractured hip plagued Patterson's last years. He died at his home in New York City and was buried in the family plot at Southampton Cemetery. Surviving him were his wife and their two children: a son, (Eugene) Morehead Patterson, who had succeeded to the presidency of the American Machine and Foundry Company in 1941, and a daughter, Lucy Lathrop (Patterson) de Rham.

[Patterson Papers, N. C. Dept. of Archives and Hist., Raleigh; letters, including copy of Kerr contract, in family papers held by Mrs. Casimir de Rham, Tuxedo Park, N. Y.; B. N. Duke Papers, Duke Univ. Lib., Durham, N. C.; various collections of clippings and administrative correspondence, Univ. of N. C. Lib., Chapel Hill; N. Y. Times obituary, Apr. 12, 1943; Who Was Who in America, vol. II (1950); Official Gazette of the U. S. Patent Office, vols. 78 (1897) and 99 (1902); Gustave Anjou, comp., "Hist. of the Patterson Family of Scotland, Ireland and the New World" (1907), typescript owned by Dr. John L. Patterson, Jr., Richmond, Va.; Samuel A. Ashe, ed., Biog. Hist. of N. C., vol. II (1905); Nannie May Tilley, The Bright-Tobacco Industry, 1860–1929 (1948); William K. Boyd, The Story of Durham: City of the New South (1925); John K. Winkler, Tobacco Tycoon: The Story of James Buchanan Duke (1942); "Rufus Lenoir Patterson's Cigar Machine," Fortune, June 1930; brochures and press releases from Am. Machine & Foundry Co.; conversations with Patterson's daughter, Mrs. Casimir de Rham, his niece Mrs. John Page Williams, his nephew Dr. Howard A. Patterson, and his business associate Clarence J. Johnson. An oil portrait, painted in 1920 by Sir William Orpen, hangs in the reception room of the Rufus L. Patterson World Tobacco Engineering Center in Richmond, Va.]

JOSEPH C. ROBERT

PATTON, GEORGE SMITH (Nov. 11, 1885–Dec. 21, 1945), army officer, was born at San Gabriel, near Pasadena, Calif., the elder of two children and only son of George Smith Patton (the second of that name) and Ruth (Wilson) Patton. His paternal ancestor in America was Robert Patton, a Scotsman who emigrated to Virginia in the 1770's and married the daughter of another Scottish immigrant, Hugh Mercer [q.v.], physician and Revolutionary War general. John Mercer Patton [q.v.], Virginia lawyer and Congressman, was General Patton's great-grandfather. His grandfather, the first George Smith Patton, was a graduate of the Virginia Military Institute who, as a Confederate colonel, commanded the 22nd Virginia Infantry and died in 1864 of wounds received at the battle of Winchester. The widow moved with her chil-

dren to Los Angeles after the war, and there married her husband's cousin. Her son, George Smith Patton, after graduating from V.M.I., practiced law with his stepfather and was prominent in local and state politics.

The third George Patton's early years were spent riding, hunting, and fishing on the San Gabriel ranch which had been part of the extensive land holdings of his maternal grandfather, Benjamin Davis Wilson, a prominent California rancher and politician of the Mexican and early statehood periods. Leading an active outdoor life, the boy did not go to school until he was twelve years old; as a result, his spelling was always erratic. Yet he was an omnivorous reader, particularly of military adventure stories, for he gloried in the martial exploits of his ancestors. In September 1903, after six years of study at Dr. Stephen Cutter Clark's Classical School for Boys in Pasadena, he entered the Virginia Military Institute. The following year he transferred to the United States Military Academy at West Point. Over six feet in height and solidly built, he was an outstanding student leader and athlete. But he had difficulty with mathematics and took five years to complete the West Point course. Upon graduation in 1909, standing forty-sixth in a class of 103, he was commissioned a second lieutenant of cavalry.

Patton married Beatrice Ayer, daughter of Frederick Ayer, a wealthy Boston textile magnate, on May 26, 1910, at St. John's Episcopal Church in Beverly Farms, Mass. They had three children: Beatrice, Ruth Ellen, and George Smith Patton IV. Two events of Patton's early military career took him abroad. In 1912 he represented his country in the Stockholm Olympic Games, where he placed fifth in the military pentathlon, an event consisting of steeplechase riding, pistol shooting, fencing, swimming, and a 5,000-meter foot race. The next year he spent the summer at Saumur, France, studying instructional methods for the cavalry saber, and, incidentally, became familiar with the bocage country where he would achieve fame thirty years later.

As an unofficial aide to Gen. John J. Pershing, Patton participated in the punitive expedition into Mexico in 1916. His leading of a motorized patrol—said to have been the first combat use of the automobile by the United States Army—and his killing of three of Pancho Villa's bodyguards in a gunfight attracted considerable notice. In May 1917, now a captain and still on Pershing's staff, he sailed for France. Detailed to the Tank Corps, he attended courses at the French tank school and observed British training methods. As a major, he organized and directed the American Tank

Center at Langres, France (later at Bourg), and formed the 304th Brigade of the Tank Corps, which he commanded (as lieutenant colonel) in the St. Mihiel offensive, Sept. 12–14, 1918. He participated in the Meuse-Argonne offensive with his brigade, but wounds on the first day of the attack (Sept. 26) put him in the hospital and took him out of action for the duration of the war. Ending the war as a colonel, Patton was awarded the Distinguished Service Medal for his contributions to tank warfare and the Distinguished Service Cross for "conspicuous courage, coolness, energy and intelligence in directing the advance of his brigade . . . under heavy machine-gun and artillery fire," even after being painfully wounded.

From March 1919 to September 1920, Patton commanded the 304th Tank Brigade at Camp Meade, Md., but when he recognized that little immediate attention was to be given to tanks and armored warfare, he rejoined the cavalry and commanded a squadron at Fort Myer until November 1922. He graduated from the Cavalry School at Fort Riley (1923), the Command and General Staff College (1924), and, after intervening duty in Boston, Hawaii, and the office of Chief of Cavalry in Washington, D. C., from the Army War College (1932). In that same year he participated, under Gen. Douglas MacArthur, in the forcible ejection from Washington of the "Bonus Army"—veterans who had encamped near the Capitol to demand economic relief in the Great Depression. Resuming the round of peacetime assignments to various army posts, Patton expended his restless energy at polo and sailing and in horse show and hunt club competition. A close student of military history, he also wrote frequent articles and reviews on weapons, tactics, and doctrine for service journals in the 1920's and 1930's.

After the Germans demonstrated their use of tanks in blitzkrieg operations in Poland and France, the United States at last began to organize an armored force, and in July 1940 Patton took command of a brigade of the 2nd Armored Division at Fort Benning, Ga. In April 1941, as a major general, he became the division commander, and on Jan. 19, 1942, commanding general of the I Armored Corps. That October, in command of the Western Task Force—the equivalent of four divisions built under his I Armored Corps headquarters—Patton sailed from Norfolk, Va. He directed the amphibious operations near Casablanca, French Morocco (Nov. 8), which, together with simultaneous landings in Algeria, comprised the Allied invasion of northwest Africa under Gen. Dwight D. Eisenhower. French resistance soon came to an end, but

Patton became widely known for his hard-driving aggressiveness in combat.

In March 1943, after the Germans inflicted a severe defeat on American units at Kasserine Pass in Tunisia, Patton was appointed commanding general of the II Corps. He rebuilt morale, training, and pride among the troops and led the corps in a series of successful operations. Near the end of the Tunisian campaign he turned over his command to Gen. Omar N. Bradley and began to prepare for operations in Sicily. On July 11, 1943, with Patton (now lieutenant general) in command of the U. S. Seventh Army and Bernard L. Montgomery heading the British Eighth Army, the Allies invaded Sicily. Patton's forces came ashore at Licata, Gela, and Scoglitti, then swept across the western part of the island to take Palermo, and finally turned eastward and captured the climactic objective, Messina. The island was conquered in a lightning campaign of thirty-eight days, and under Patton's leadership American combat performance was brought to maturity. Away from the battlefield, however, his impulsiveness and overweening self-assurance—assets in combat situations—embroiled him in controversy. On Aug. 10, 1943, while touring military hospitals in Sicily, he impetuously slapped and verbally abused two soldiers suffering from combat exhaustion. He later claimed that he deliberately tried to shock the soldiers out of their battle fatigue, but the incident incurred the wrath of his superiors and, when it was widely publicized in November, nearly ended his career. Eisenhower nevertheless refused to send him home because of his skill as a combat leader.

In March 1944, assigned to the European theatre of operations and transferred to England, Patton trained the U. S. Third Army for its role as the major American follow-up force after the cross-channel invasion of Normandy. His army moved to France in the weeks following D-Day (June 6, 1944), and on Aug. 1, in the midst of a breakthrough of the German defenses achieved by General Bradley near St. Lô, Patton took operational command of his force. The Third Army moved from the base of the Cotentin peninsula near the town of Avranches in three directions—westward into Brittany, southward toward the Loire River, and eastward toward Le Mans. His western forces reached Brest and Lorient after spectacularly rapid movements, but were unable at once to capture the port cities. His southern forces reached the Loire at Angers, then turned eastward and rolled to the Paris-Orleans gap. His units driving eastward encircled the German Fifth Panzer and Seventh armies in Normandy and by a sudden northward thrust to Argentan trapped and demoralized them. In a campaign marked by boldness and ruthless drive, Patton demonstrated the long-range thrust, mobility, firepower, and shock action that were possible when armor, infantry, artillery and support aircraft worked in close combination. He reached and crossed the Seine River on Aug. 21, then swept eastward toward Metz. The breakout that had turned into a pursuit came to a halt at the end of August, however, when the logistical machinery was unable to bring forward supplies, particularly gasoline, swiftly enough. By the time these deficiencies were remedied, the Germans had stabilized their defenses, and a static period ensued during the autumn and winter months along the western approaches to Germany.

When the Germans launched their Ardennes counteroffensive in December—the "Battle of the Bulge"—Patton, in one of the most remarkable movements in military history, took only a few days to turn his army from an eastward to a northward orientation and bring it into position to shore up the southern shoulder of the Bulge. When his troops linked up with the encircled defenders of Bastogne, the failure of the German offensive was sealed. The Third Army crossed the Rhine in March 1945 at Mainz and Oppenheim, and against crumbling and spotty opposition that occasionally braced for brief and bitter fights, drove through the heart of Germany. After meeting First Army elements at Giessen and Kassel to achieve the encirclement of the Ruhr, Patton swung his army to the southeast and headed for Czechoslovakia and Austria. The discovery of Ohrdruf, the first of the Nazi concentration camps to be liberated, filled him with the deepest revulsion. In accordance with the decision to stop the Allied forces along the line of the Elbe, Mulde, Moldau, and Enns rivers, Patton's forces took Carlsbad, Pilsen, and Budejovice in Czechoslovakia, and Linz, Austria, as the war came to an end. He was by then a four-star general, having been promoted in April.

In the brief time remaining to him, Patton grew obsessed by what he considered the looming menace of Russian expansion and a Communist take-over of Europe. In several private and semi-official conversations he urged a continuation of the war, now in collaboration with the Germans, to drive the Russian forces back within their national boundary. In charge of the "denazification" program in Bavaria, he was upset by the wholesale dismissal of former Nazis from governmental positions, believing this would pave the way for a Communist coup. At a news conference on Sept. 22, 1945, he urged the employment of "more former members of the Nazi party in ad-

ministrative jobs and as skilled workmen," and agreed with a reporter's suggestion that most Nazis had joined the party "in about the same way that Americans become Republicans or Democrats." For expressing these opinions he was removed from command of the Third Army and given command of the Fifteenth Army, a largely paper force. On Dec. 9, while on a hunting trip, Patton suffered a broken neck in an automobile accident. Hospitalized at Seventh Army headquarters in Heidelberg, he died twelve days later of a pulmonary embolism. He was buried in the United States Military Cemetery at Hamm, Luxembourg.

Deeply religious yet often violently profane in his language, irascible yet given to mawkish sentimentality, identified by the ivory-handled pistols that became his trademark, "Blood and Guts" Patton was first and foremost a professional soldier who consciously cultivated toughness as the proper image for a fighting man. He has been compared to J. E. B. Stuart and Nathan Bedford Forrest [qq.v.] in his mastery of military principles, but is probably most like William T. Sherman [q.v.], who understood and practiced total war. He was an innovator as well, for he shaped the development of tank warfare and made this form of combat peculiarly his own. Audacity tempered by meticulous attention to staff work, the ability to drive himself and his subordinates beyond the limits of reasonable effort, the gift of instilling pride and confidence in his troops, and an intuitive sense of how and where to strike in order to keep his adversary off balance were the attributes which made General Patton the outstanding American field commander of the Second World War.

[Patton Papers, Lib. of Cong.; Patton's autobiographical *War as I Knew It* (1947); biographies of Patton: Robert S. Allen, *Lucky Forward* (1947), Harry H. Semmes, *Portrait of Patton* (1955), Fred Ayer, Jr., *Before the Colors Fade* (1964), and especially Ladislas Farago, *Patton: Ordeal and Triumph* (1963); Martin Blumenson, *The Patton Papers*, vol. I, 1885–1940 (1972). For other views of Patton, see Brenton G. Wallace, *Patton and His Third Army* (1946); Charles R. Codman, *Drive* (1957); and Stephen E. and Judith D. Ambrose, "George Patton," *Am. Hist. Illustrated*, July 1966. On the military operations in which he was involved, see: George F. Howe, *Northwest Africa: Seizing the Initiative in the West* (1957); Martin Blumenson, *Kasserine Pass* (1967); Albert N. Garland and Howard M. Smyth, *Sicily and the Surrender of Italy* (1965); Martin Blumenson, *Breakout and Pursuit* (1961) and *The Duel for France* (1963); Hugh M. Cole, *The Lorraine Campaign* (1950) and *The Ardennes: Battle of the Bulge* (1965). See also: Forrest C. Pogue, *The Supreme Command* (1954); Lucian K. Truscott, Jr., *Command Decisions* (1959); Dwight D. Eisenhower, *Crusade in Europe* (1948); Omar N. Bradley, *A Soldier's Story* (1951); Stephen E. Ambrose, *The Supreme Commander: The War Years of Gen. Dwight D. Eisenhower* (1970).]

MARTIN BLUMENSON

PAWNEE BILL. See LILLIE, GORDON WILLIAM.

PEABODY, ENDICOTT (May 30, 1857–Nov. 17, 1944), educator, was born in Salem, Mass., the third of the five children and four sons of Samuel Endicott Peabody and Marianne Cabot (Lee) Peabody. Descended from or related to many of the prominent early families of Massachusetts, he was born and reared a patrician. His great-grandfather was Joseph Peabody [q.v.], master of a fleet of merchant ships and the wealthiest man in early nineteenth-century Salem.

Living in Salem until he was thirteen, Endicott attended the Hacker School and early acquired his lifelong devotion to sailing, horseback riding, and physical fitness. In 1870 the family moved to London, where his father was a partner in Peabody and Morgan, a banking firm established by a distant relative, George Peabody [q.v.] of Baltimore. In England, Endicott Peabody attended Cheltenham School for five years and then Trinity College, Cambridge, where he graduated in 1878 with a first class in the lower tripos. On his return to the United States, he entered Lee, Higginson, and Company, a Boston brokerage firm, but although he gave promise as a businessman, he was not content. His English experiences and friendships had profoundly affected his outlook. Influenced by Phillips Brooks [q.v.] and others, in 1881 he enrolled in the Episcopal Theological School in Cambridge, Mass., despite the family tradition of Unitarianism. While still a divinity student he accepted a call to Arizona's first Episcopal church, in Tombstone, where he served from January to June 1882. Returning to Massachusetts, he was ordained in 1884.

For some time he had been interested in starting an Episcopal school for boys. A gift of land by the Lawrence family in Groton, Mass., thirty-four miles from Boston, made the dream a fact. With the backing of an impressive board of trustees, including Phillips Brooks and the elder J. P. Morgan [q.v.], Peabody opened Groton School on Oct. 18, 1884, with twenty-seven boys and two masters besides himself. With his future now more definitely settled, he was married on June 18, 1885, to a first cousin, Fannie Peabody of Danvers, Mass. This happy union produced six children: Malcolm Endicott, Helen, Rose Saltonstall, Elizabeth Rogers, Margery, and Dorothy.

From the beginning, Groton School attracted an elite clientele. The boys were mostly drawn from social-register families of Boston and New York City, and many of them went on—by way of Harvard, Yale, and Princeton—to distinguished careers. In addition to President Franklin D. Roosevelt, the alumni roll includes three cabinet members, seventeen ambassadors and ministers, three Senators, five Congressmen, and many prominent figures in education, literature, publishing, the military, and philanthropy. This record is the more noteworthy considering the deliberately small enrollment, which in Peabody's time never exceeded two hundred. A gifted fund raiser, Peabody used Groton's substantial endowment ($3,600,000 by 1939) to give the school a faculty salary scale far in advance of other preparatory schools and many colleges.

But Peabody never strove to make Groton a "social" school in the conventional sense; indeed, he was highly skeptical of "society" as exemplified by the ostentation of Fifth Avenue and Newport. Nor was he an educational innovator; mistrusting fads, he made few original contributions to pedagogical practice. The quality of his mind was not remarkable, and his literary tastes were conventional: Dickens, Tennyson, Thackeray. Yet by common agreement Groton School under Peabody was a remarkable place, and its distinctiveness lay in the character of its founder and headmaster.

Endicott Peabody was, in some respects, a contradictory person. A strikingly attractive man—very large, blond, outgoing, with a keen sense of humor—"Cotty" loved human companionship and could display great charm in such encounters. Yet, like his friend Theodore Roosevelt, he inhabited a moral universe of absolute right and wrong, adhering to a code of behavior as stern as it was simplistic. When he felt that that code had been broken, he could be blunt and harsh in his judgments. He applied his rigid standards to himself no less than to others, and in letters to intimates often expressed a nagging sense of inadequacy and failure. He believed that the decline of virile moral leadership was one of America's gravest problems in the post-Civil War generation, and in founding Groton he deliberately set out to train a patrician class which would reassert that leadership. If he had a model, it was probably Thomas Arnold, to whose headmastership at Rugby, portrayed in *Tom Brown's School Days*, he often admiringly referred. Like Arnold, he emphasized hard work and hard play, discipline, and character. Yet he was no uncritical imitator of the English public school system. He was, for example, repelled by the system of "fagging," whereby older boys tyrannized the younger, and he did what he could to prevent its taking root at Groton.

The accommodations at the school were spartan. Athletics, especially football, loomed large.

"He made a sacrament of exercise," a friend once remarked of Peabody. Deeply religious, he always saw himself as a priest first and a schoolmaster second. Though not an outstanding preacher, he was forceful and moving in his short, extemporaneous talks in Groton's compulsory daily chapel services. Social responsibility was tirelessly stressed. Masters and students were urged to participate in the Groton School Camp operated in the summers at Squam Lake, N. H., for underprivileged boys, and Peabody himself set an example of civic consciousness by maintaining active membership in more than thirty committees and organizations, ranging from the Audubon Society to the Birth Control League of Massachusetts.

As headmaster, Peabody knew every boy in the school intimately, and his efforts to mold character did not end with graduation day. In their college years and beyond, he kept a watchful and dubious eye upon former students, and did not hestitate to write stern letters when word of some misstep reached him. This close supervision extended to the masters and staff of the school as well. By the 1920's such paternalism had come to seem somewhat anachronistic, and during Peabody's final decade as headmaster the turnover of masters was high and student dissatisfaction more vocal. Inevitably a personality as strong and as self-assured as Peabody's aroused strong feelings in others, and he had both his fierce partisans and his bitter detractors. The former praised his emphasis on character formation; the latter charged that his moral rigidity encouraged mindless conformity and choked off individuality.

Nevertheless, Peabody's retirement in 1940, after fifty-six years as active headmaster, produced an outpouring of affectionate tributes from Groton alumni and others. The praise also extended to Mrs. Peabody, who, although sharing her husband's fundamental values, had through her graciousness somewhat tempered his sternness. Peabody continued to live in Groton until his sudden death from a heart attack in 1944, at the age of eighty-seven. He and Mrs. Peabody, who died in 1946, are buried in the cemetery in the town of Groton.

[Frank D. Ashburn, *Peabody of Groton* (1944) and *Fifty Years On: Groton School, 1884–1934* (1935); William Amory Gardner, *Groton Myths and Memories* (privately printed, 1928). For other impressions of the man and the school see George Biddle in *Harper's,* Aug. 1939; George W. Martin, *ibid.,* Jan. 1944; and Cleveland Amory in *Saturday Evening Post,* Sept. 14, 1940. About 60 volumes of letters to and from Peabody are in the files of the Groton School at the Houghton Lib., Harvard, which also has the Atwood Papers, a voluminous correspondence between Pea-

body and his close friend Bishop Julius Atwood. Peabody's date of birth was supplied by the City Clerk, Salem, Mass.]

FRANK D. ASHBURN

PEARSON, THOMAS GILBERT (Nov. 10, 1873–Sept. 3, 1943), ornithologist and wildlife conservationist, was born in Tuscola, Ill., the younger son among the five children of Thomas Barnard Pearson and Mary (Eliott) Pearson. His father claimed descent from a Pearson who came to America and settled with William Penn. A nomadic farm family, the Pearsons moved to Indiana and in 1882 to Archer, Fla., to join other Quakers in citrus farming. There young Gilbert (as he was known) learned to shoot birds and collect eggs, activities which produced his first published work (in the *Oologist* for January 1888) and paid for his first two years of board and tuition at Guilford College in North Carolina, given in exchange for his collection of eggs and mounted birds. Entering in 1891 at the preparatory level, Pearson studied for six years at Guilford, where he continued his work in natural history and developed a marked talent for public speaking and promoting his own professional interests. By 1894 he was styling himself "Field Ornithologist and Oologist," and in 1895 he composed and distributed a thousand copies of a leaflet against "wearing birds and feathers on hats."

Patronage resulting from a statewide Republican victory in 1896 afforded Pearson upon graduation a job in the office of the North Carolina state geologist, with duties that encouraged both political involvement and further nature study, and a salary that permitted enrollment at the University of North Carolina, where he took a B.S. degree in 1899. Then for two years he taught biology at Guilford and, from 1901 to 1904, biology and geology at the State Normal and Industrial College for Women, Greensboro, N. C. On June 17, 1902, he married Elsie Weatherly of Greensboro, by whom he had three children: Elizabeth, Thomas Gilbert, and William Gillespie.

Pearson's first book, *Stories of Bird Life* (1901), prompted William Dutcher, first president of the National Association of Audubon Societies, to ask Pearson to organize the North Carolina Audubon Society, which was formed in 1902. Here began the major phase of Pearson's career, his work with the Audubon movement. The North Carolina society was given authority to enforce the state's pioneer bird-protection law passed in 1903, again involving Pearson in politics. In January 1905 he helped incorporate the

National Association of Audubon Societies, acting first as secretary, receiving executive responsibility following Dutcher's paralytic seizure in 1910, and serving as president from the latter's death in 1920 until retirement in 1934. After 1911 he made his home in New York City.

Although Pearson continued both his field study and his professional writing, he devoted these National Audubon years mainly to public activities, educational, organizational, and political. Bird protection had effectively begun late in the nineteenth century, but great obstacles remained. Many states had no laws protecting songbirds; others enforced such laws poorly. Game-bird laws were lacking or inadequate, permitting widespread market hunting and unchecked international trade. Commerce in millinery plumes and bird skins persisted, often without effective opposition, state or national. There were few wildlife sanctuaries, and many natural refuges were threatened by exploitation or by serious environmental changes. Building on his North Carolina experience, Pearson worked for protective measures and game-warden systems elsewhere in the South, addressing the legislatures of Tennessee and Arkansas and lecturing and lobbying in other states.

In New York, then the citadel of the millinery plume trade, Pearson for the first time registered as an avowed lobbyist, supporting the Audubon Plumage Bill. This notable measure was passed, and in other states various protective laws were obtained; but Pearson early learned that in politics, resurgent opposition forces often turned an apparent conservation victory into defeat. Furthermore, domestic laws varied widely—and they were also partly nullified by uncontrolled trade from abroad. The Federal Migratory Bird Law of 1913, passed with much Audubon help, largely remedied the first problem, but meanwhile Pearson had begun his campaign for international control by visiting President Diaz of Mexico in 1909, with only brief success. Later negotiations with Canada, in which Pearson joined, resulted in the important Migratory Bird Treaty of 1916. In 1922 Pearson visited Europe and at a London meeting founded the International Committee for Bird Preservation, serving as president until 1938 and as chairman of the United States section (and later the Pan-American section) until his death.

The effort to establish refuges and maintain a favorable environment for birds and other wildlife in the United States was another aspect of Pearson's forty years of work with the Audubon movement, and affords a good paradigm of his professional life. As in other areas, there were the

governmental agencies and the politicians to be supported or enlisted or opposed, the influential private persons and pressure groups to be brought into alliance if possible or fought if necessary, the affected citizens to be persuaded by lecture or pamphlet or publicity campaign. To such struggles Pearson brought the moral rectitude of his Quaker background, the political skills and forensic zest of his Southern upbringing, the factual resources of a lifetime devoted to the study of nature, the organizational talents and abundant energy and self-confidence of a natural leader—plus a shrewd sense of human frailty and the limitations of human endeavor, however righteous. Such were the qualities that made T. Gilbert Pearson, in the words of his colleague Frank M. Chapman [Supp. 3], "the leading bird conserver of his generation."

Pearson died in New York City in his seventieth year. Following Presbyterian services, his remains were cremated at Ferncliff Crematory.

[Pearson's autobiography, *Adventures in Bird Protection* (1937), is the major primary source; see also his "Fifty Years of Bird Protection in the U. S.," in *Fifty Years' Progress of Am. Ornithology* (Am. Ornithologists Union, 1933). Dr. Dean Amadon, Chairman, Dept. of Ornithology, Am. Museum of Natural History, has kindly provided useful Pearson-Chapman correspondence. No complete bibliography of Pearson's writing is known. He was editor of *Portraits and Habits of Our Birds* (1920); senior editor of *Birds of America* (3 vols., 1917); co-author of *The Birds of N. C.* (1919); and co-editor of *The Book of Birds* (1937). His books for children were *Stories of Bird Life* (1901), *The Bird Study Book* (1917), and *Tales from Birdland* (1918). He also contributed notes, articles, reports, editorials, etc., to *Bird-Lore*, 1905–40, *Audubon Mag.*, 1941–42, and *Nat. Geographic Mag.*, 1933–39. Other sources: short review of Pearson's career in *Bird-Lore*, Nov.–Dec. 1934 (with portrait); "Appreciation" in *Audubon Mag.*, Jan.–Feb. 1943 (portrait); obituary notices, *ibid.*, Sept.–Oct. and Nov.–Dec. 1943, and in the *Auk*, Apr. 1947. See also *Who's Who in America*, 1912 and later years; *Am. Men of Sci.* (3rd through 6th eds.); *Nat. Cyc. Am. Biog.*, Current Vol. D, p. 334, and XXXIII, 339; *N. Y. Times*, Sept. 5, 1943.]

ROBERT H. WELKER

PEEK, GEORGE NELSON (Nov. 19, 1873– Dec. 17, 1943), businessman and farm leader, first administrator of the Agricultural Adjustment Administration, was born at Polo, Ill., the second son and third of four children of Henry Clay Peek, a seventh generation member of a New England family (the name was originally spelled Peake), and Adeline (Chase) Peek, whose family were New York Quakers. Henry Peek engaged in the livestock business in Polo, served as sheriff of Ogle County, and in 1885 moved to a farm near Oregon, Ill. He provided an average living for his family, but farming did not appeal to young George. After graduating from the Oregon high school in 1891, he attended Northwestern University in Evanston for one school year (1891–92). In January 1893 he obtained a job in Minneapolis with Deere and Webber, a branch of the John Deere Plow Company.

Six feet tall and weighing 180 pounds, Peek was an energetic, self-confident, and forceful person who rose rapidly in the farm machine business. In 1901 he was named general manager of the John Deere Plow Company in Omaha, and a decade later he moved to the company's home office in Moline, Ill., as vice-president in charge of sales at a salary of $12,000 a year. Meanwhile, on Dec. 22, 1903, he had married Georgia Lindsey of Omaha, the daughter of Zachary T. Lindsey, president of the Interstate Rubber Company. The Peeks had no children.

Peek first achieved national attention in 1917 when he was appointed industrial representative on the War Industries Board. He became the board's commissioner of finished products in March 1918, working closely with the new chairman, Bernard M. Baruch. In February 1919, after the W.I.B. had finished its work, Peek was appointed chairman of the ill-fated Industrial Board in the Department of Commerce. Without real power to influence the economy during the period of reconversion, he and his fellow board members resigned in disgust in April.

Shortly after leaving government service, Peek accepted the presidency of the Moline Plow Company. (He had resigned from Deere & Company when he became chairman of the Industrial Board.) He had scarcely settled in his new $100,000-a-year job when the postwar depression hit agriculture with special fury and the sale of farm machinery dropped sharply. It was the farm depression which started Peek and his vice-president, Hugh S. Johnson [Supp. 3], on the search for a program which would restore agricultural prosperity. In 1922 they came up with a plan of "Equality for Agriculture" which called for federal help in removing price-depressing surpluses from the domestic market. This was to be done through a special government corporation which would buy up farm surpluses and dispose of them abroad; any losses thus incurred were to be recouped from a tax (or "equalization fee") on each unit of a commodity sold by the farmer. Resigning his business post in 1924, Peek thereafter devoted all his time and effort to organizing support for his farm relief plan.

Peek's ideas were incorporated in the successive McNary-Haugen bills (see Charles L. McNary [Supp. 3] and Gilbert N. Haugen [Supp. 1]), which were before Congress almost constantly between 1924 and 1928. As lobbyist

he coordinated the efforts of farm organizations supporting the bills, lined up testimony before Congressional hearings, and himself talked to Congressmen and federal officials. Twice, in 1927 and 1928, a McNary-Haugen bill passed both houses, only to be killed by presidential veto. In the party conventions of 1928, Peek sought, without success, to get the Republicans to endorse the McNary-Haugen plan. When the Democrats incorporated its essence in their platform, Peek left the Republican party to campaign in the farm belt for the Democratic candidate, Alfred E. Smith [Supp. 3]. Though his program failed of enactment, Peek had organized supporters of farm legislation more effectively than at any previous time in American history. He pointed up the special nature of farm problems, promoted the concept of "farm parity," and convinced a growing number of people that the federal government had a responsibility to assist agriculture.

During the 1932 presidential campaign, Peek acted as an adviser on farm problems to Franklin D. Roosevelt. When Congress created the Agricultural Adjustment Administration in May 1933, Peek was named as its head—despite the opposition of New Deal "intellectuals"—to ensure the support of farmers and businessmen. Almost immediately, however, he found himself in sharp disagreement with Secretary of Agriculture Henry A. Wallace. Peek opposed acreage restriction as a permanent policy and favored expanded sales through marketing agreements as a means of reducing surpluses; a prickly subordinate, he also worked to make the AAA an independent agency. His differences with Wallace became so severe that in December 1933 President Roosevelt shifted Peek to a post as special adviser on foreign trade. But on Nov. 26, 1935, he angrily resigned following a conflict with the administration over its reciprocal trade policies, which he opposed as "internationalist" and as "unilateral economic disarmament."

Peek now became a bitter and vocal critic of the New Deal. In 1936 he campaigned for the Republican presidential candidate, Alfred M. Landon. Increasingly isolationist, he worked vigorously in 1940 for the America First Committee. Peek was not a churchgoer and had no religious affiliation. He died of a cerebral hemorrhage in 1943 at his home at Rancho Santa Fe near San Diego, Calif., where he had lived since 1937, and was buried in the family plot in the Moline (Ill.) Cemetery.

[Gilbert C. Fite, *George N. Peek and the Fight for Farm Parity* (1954); George N. Peek and Samuel Crowther, *Why Quit Our Own* (1936), which voices his anti-New Deal views. See also Richard S.

Kirkendall, *Social Scientists and Farm Politics in the Age of Roosevelt* (1966) ; and Rexford G. Tugwell's unfriendly description of Peek's role in 1932 in *The Brains Trust* (1968). Peek's personal and farm relief papers are in the Western Hist. Manuscripts Collection, Univ. of Mo., Columbia.]

GILBERT C. FITE

PELHAM, ROBERT A. (Jan. 4, 1859–June 12, 1943), politician, journalist, and government official, was born on a farm near Petersburg, Va., the second son and fifth of seven children of free black parents, Robert A. and Frances (Butcher) Pelham. Soon after his birth, the family left the South and, after living briefly in Columbus, Ohio, and Philadelphia, settled around 1862 in Detroit, Mich. There Pelham's father worked as a plasterer, mason, and independent contractor. After 1870, when Negroes were enfranchised, he became active in Republican politics, serving regularly in city, county, and state conventions. He was also a trustee of the Bethel African Methodist Episcopal Church in Detroit.

Young Pelham attended the public schools of Detroit, which were segregated until 1872. While still in school, he began work in 1871 as a newsboy for the *Detroit Post,* the city's leading Republican daily newspaper. Following his graduation from high school in 1877, he joined the paper full time, and eventually ran its subscription department. From 1884 to 1891 he and a younger brother, Benjamin, who later became a distinguished civil servant in Michigan, distributed the *Post* as independent contractors. They also published and edited two black weeklies: the *Venture* (1879), a short-lived amateur newspaper, and, in association with others, the *Plaindealer* (1883–93). The latter, which Robert Pelham managed for eight years, soon became the leading Negro newspaper in the Midwest and made Pelham, while still in his twenties, nationally prominent as an editor and race leader. In 1884 he represented Detroit at the National Colored Men's Convention in Pittsburgh, and in 1888 he served as temporary chairman of a similar statewide convention. He was also a founder in 1889 of the Afro-American League, of which the militant *Plaindealer* became the Michigan organ.

Pelham, like his father before him, was active in Republican politics. He was a founder in 1884 of the nearly all-white political-social Michigan Club, and a member of the Young Men's League, which he represented at the National League of Republican Clubs. In 1884 he clerked in the office of the Collector of Internal Revenue for Detroit, and in 1887 he was appointed state deputy oil inspector for Detroit. A delegate to the 1888 Republican National Convention in Chicago, Pelham lobbied among blacks for the nomination of Michigan's favorite-son candidate, Gen. Russell A. Alger [*q.v.*]. At the 1896 convention, Pelham, having declined nomination as a delegate, served with his older brother Joseph as a sergeant-at-arms. Later that year he was a member of the Afro-American bureau of the Republican National Committee. As the leading Negro Republican in Michigan in the 1880's and '90's, he helped weld the black community to the G.O.P.

Pelham left the *Plaindealer* in 1891 to serve as special agent of the United States General Land Office, a position that took him to northern Michigan and Minnesota. Returning to Detroit in 1893, he became an inspector for the Detroit Water Department. Then, with the return of the Republicans to the White House, he was named again in 1898 a special agent of the Land Office. Two years later he was appointed a clerk in the Census Bureau and moved to Washington, D. C., his home for the rest of his life.

At the Census Bureau, where he served until his retirement in 1937, Pelham made significant contributions as an inventor and statistician. In 1905 he devised the first tabulating machines used in the census of manufactures and, in 1913, a tallying machine used in the population division. Pelham worked in the agricultural division of the Census Bureau and on Negro statistics; he compiled the "mortality" and "home ownership" sections of the Bureau's monumental demographic volume, *Negro Population, 1790–1915* (1918). While working for the Census Bureau, he also attended Howard University, and in 1904 was awarded the LL.B. degree.

After retiring from public service at the age of seventy-eight, Pelham headed a Negro news service and edited the *Washington Tribune,* a Negro newspaper. On Apr. 5, 1893, he had married Gabrielle S. Lewis of Adrian, Mich., by whom he had four children: Dorothy, Sarah, Benjamin, and Frederick. Mrs. Pelham, an accomplished pianist and a graduate of Adrian College, served on the executive committee of the Michigan State Music Teachers' Association, was director of music at Howard University (1905–06), and later operated a school of music. Contemporaries remembered Pelham as a dynamic and hardworking editor and politician. He was a handsome man and, like other members of his family, had light skin and deep-set eyes with dark eyebrows. As a young man he grew a moustache, possibly to deemphasize his political precociousness, and in his later years, as his moustache whitened and his closely cropped hair grayed at the temples, he had a distinguished appearance.

Pelham died at his home in Washington at the age of eighty-four of a coronary occlusion, and was buried in Washington's Lincoln Memorial Cemetery. His career reflected the style of life and achievements of the upper-class Negro elite around the turn of the century, a well-educated group that lived as much in the white world as in the black.

[William J. Simmons, *Men of Mark* (1887), devotes a chapter to Pelham; and I. Garland Penn, *The Afro-Am. Press and Its Editors* (1891), has a biographical sketch and a discussion of the *Plaindealer*. Francis H. Warren, comp., *Mich. Manual of Freedmen's Progress* (1915), records the careers of both Pelham and his wife and includes demographic chapters contributed by Pelham. Information on all of the Pelhams can be found in Aris A. Mallas, Jr., Rea McCain, and Margaret K. Hedden, *Forty Years in Politics: The Story of Ben Pelham* (1957), a revised master's thesis written from insufficient sources. Pelham's political and editorial careers can be traced through the Midwestern black weeklies the *Plaindealer* (Detroit), the *Freeman* (Indianapolis), and the *Cleveland Gazette*, as well as in the white *Detroit Post* and its successor, the *Tribune*; see especially the sketches of Pelham in the *Freeman*, Apr. 17, 1897, and the *Sunday News-Tribune* (Detroit), Apr. 10, 1898. There is an obituary in Florence Murray, ed., *The Negro Handbook*, 1944, p. 236. Pelham's views on a large variety of issues can be found in the *Plaindealer*. He occasionally contributed to other periodicals; see, e.g., his "Negro Journals," *Freeman*, Dec. 29, 1900, and "The Negro in the West," *A.M.E. Zion Quart. Rev.*, Apr. 1901. Death record from D. C. Health Dept. The Simmons book, above, contains a portrait of Pelham as a young man; the Warren book one of Pelham in middle age.]
DAVID M. KATZMAN

PENDERGAST, THOMAS JOSEPH (July 22, 1872–Jan. 26, 1945), political boss, was born in St. Joseph, Mo., the fourth of nine children in a devoutly Roman Catholic family. His parents, Michael and Mary Elizabeth (Reidy) Pendergast, had migrated in the mid-nineteenth century from Ireland to the United States, where the father found work as an unskilled laborer, first in Gallipolis, Ohio, and then in St. Joseph.

Thomas was educated in the St. Joseph public schools and Christian Brothers' College (a parochial secondary school), but it was from his older brother James Pendergast that he learned the art of politics. James had moved in 1876 to Kansas City, Mo., where he eventually purchased a saloon in the city's West Bottoms and another in the North End, both heterogeneous neighborhoods inhabited by low-income Irish, Italian, German, Negro, and native white laborers. At that time neither Republicans nor Democrats had organizations in Kansas City, and neither party dominated local politics. James Pendergast stepped into this political void and organized the first permanent Democratic club, which soon had control of the wards in which his saloons were located. He was elected to the city council for nine consecutive terms, from 1892 until his retirement in 1910. Popular among the working class, he provided cash relief, food, fuel, and clothing for the poor and dispensed local patronage to his followers.

In 1890 James invited his brothers to Kansas City, one of whom, Michael, became an organizer of ward clubs. Tom, who came to work as a bookkeeper in James's saloons, also became active in politics, and in 1896 was appointed deputy county marshal. In 1900, when James was at the height of his political power, Tom Pendergast was appointed to the patronage-rich office of city superintendent of streets, and two years later he was elected county marshal (1902–04). From 1910 to 1914 he served on the city council, the last elective position he was to hold.

When his older brother retired from politics in 1910 because of illness, Tom Pendergast inherited the Democratic leadership of the North End and West Bottoms. Driven by a desire for power and money, he now attempted to win control of the city and county party machinery. Besides its working-class elements, Kansas City had a heavy population of native-born white Protestants, and these shared many of the values of the rural population of Jackson County, of which Kansas City was a part. While James Pendergast had been concentrating on organizing working-class ethnic voters, his longtime Democratic rival, Joseph B. Shannon, had actively built support in the county, and the two men had therefore shared elective and patronage decisions. Tom Pendergast, while keeping a tight rein on the working-class wards, undertook to extend his influence to middle-class residential areas by establishing political clubs, which also provided such social activities as dances, picnics, bridge parties, and teas. He won friends by awarding city and county construction contracts to favored contractors, and franchises and tax deductions to cooperative businessmen. Money from business interests supported the services that Pendergast supplied to the middle and working classes, and generously supplemented his personal fortune derived from a wholesale liquor business, a concrete factory, and a third-rate hotel which was also a thriving center of prostitution. Through a series of maneuvers, including alliances with former Shannon supporters and the successful endorsement of his protégé Harry S. Truman for county judge in 1922, Pendergast undercut Shannon's power and emerged by the mid-1920's as the boss of the Democratic party in Kansas City and Jackson County.

Pendergast was the only Democrat in Missouri with the power to deliver a massive block of votes. He used this leverage to influence state patronage and to protect Kansas City's liquor interests. But the greatest boon to his power on the state level came with the New Deal. Indebted to Pendergast for support in the 1932 Democratic convention, President Roosevelt the next year gave the Missouri boss control over many local federal appointments under the Civil Works Administration and, after 1935, the Works Progress Administration. Pendergast demonstrated his muscle in state politics when in 1934 he succeeded in having Truman elected to the United States Senate. Through WPA projects and patronage, Pendergast became one of the strongest political bosses in the nation.

Where persuasion had its limitations, Pendergast elected candidates by stuffing ballot boxes, bribing business interests, and offering police protection to criminals, who intimidated voters and rival candidates. Yet his opponents were unable to break the Pendergast machine, in part because it effectively provided jobs for the unemployed during the depression. It took a federal investigation of illegal voting practices and of Pendergast's income to destroy his power. The investigation was initiated by Maurice M. Milligan, a federal district attorney who was bitter over Pendergast's opposition to the candidacy of his brother Jacob L. Milligan in the 1934 Democratic Senatorial primary. Revelations of corruption and sensational newspaper headlines moved Gov. Lloyd C. Stark to turn against Pendergast, and in 1938 Stark successfully supported an antimachine candidate for the state supreme court in the Democratic primary. On the basis of this defeat and the findings of the Milligan investigation, the Roosevelt administration deserted Pendergast for Stark. In 1939 Pendergast was convicted of income tax evasion and sentenced to fifteen months in federal prison at Leavenworth, Kans.

With the master broker disparaged and in prison, the organization collapsed. Six years later, at seventy-two, Pendergast died of a heart ailment at Menorah Hospital in Kansas City. He was buried in the city's Calvary Cemetery. He left his widow, the former Carrie E. Snyder, whom he had married on Jan. 25, 1911, and three adopted children: Marceline, Eileen, and Thomas. Never since has any man been able to unite the state in such a powerful organization.

[There is no single collection of Pendergast papers. Some of his letters and many referring to him can be found in the Western Hist. Manuscripts Collection at the Univ. of Mo., and in the correspondence of the Democratic Nat. Committee at the Franklin D. Roosevelt Lib., Hyde Park, N. Y. Lyle W. Dorsett, *The Pendergast Machine* (1968), is a scholarly study of the life cycle of the machine. William M. Reddig, *Tom's Town* (1947), is a good social history of Kansas City during the Pendergast era. A. Theodore Brown, *The Politics of Reform* (1958), is excellent on the last fifteen years that the machine was in power. Other useful sources are: Franklin D. Mitchell, *Embattled Democracy: Mo. Democratic Politics, 1919–1932* (1968); and Darrell Garwood, *Crossroads of America: The Story of Kansas City* (1948). Maurice M. Milligan, *The Inside Story of the Pendergast Machine* (1948), a study by the man who prosecuted Pendergast, is one-sided, but gives details of the events which led up to Pendergast's trial and conviction. Marriage record from County Clerk, St. Clair County, Ill.; death record from Mo. Division of Health.]

LYLE W. DORSETT

PERCY, WILLIAM ALEXANDER (May 14, 1885–Jan. 21, 1942), Southern author, was born in Greenville, Miss., to Camille (Bourges) and LeRoy Pratt Percy. He had a younger brother who died in childhood. Percy's maternal grandparents, Roman Catholics of French descent, had moved from New Orleans to the Delta country of Mississippi after the Civil War. His father was descended from Charles B. Percy, who came, probably from England, to Wilkinson County, Miss., in the 1770's. LeRoy Percy, an Episcopalian and the son of a Confederate officer, was a prominent and prosperous lawyer and planter who served in the United States Senate from 1910 to 1913, having defeated James K. Vardaman [*q.v.*] in a closely contested race that exacerbated the class cleavages in Mississippi politics.

Reared as a Catholic, William Percy was initially educated at a convent school and by tutors in Greenville. In 1900 he entered his father's alma mater, the University of the South at Sewanee, Tenn., where he gave up formal religious connections. Graduating, A.B., in 1904, he went on to the Harvard Law School and received the LL.B. in 1908. He then returned to Greenville, where he practiced law with his father and other partners.

The outbreak of war in 1914 found Percy traveling in Europe. He returned briefly to Mississippi but was soon back in Europe for Herbert Hoover's relief commission, because "men were fighting for what I believed in." He stayed with the commission until the United States entered the war, when he became an army officer. Although a small, frail man, he fought in France, rose to captain of infantry, and was awarded the Croix de Guerre with a gold and silver star.

After the war he went back to Greenville to make his home, though he continued to travel—to Europe, the South Seas, and Japan. He resumed the practice of law, and after his father's death in 1929 he added the management of the Percy plantation, Trail Lake. He never married, but adopted three young cousins—Walker, LeRoy, and Phinizy Percy—and reared them in his home.

Percy began writing poetry after his return from

Harvard and in 1915 published his first volume, *Sappho in Levkas and Other Poems*. He took his poetry seriously; it was, he said, "more essentially myself than anything I did or said." He published three more volumes—*In April Once* (1920), *Enzio's Kingdom and Other Poems* (1924), *Selected Poems* (1930)—and served as editor of the Yale Series of Younger Poets from 1925 to 1932. Shunning the sheer intellectuality of Ezra Pound and other modern giants, Percy (in the words of Willard Thorp) "deliberately stood aside from the poetic movements of his time" (*New York Times Book Review*, Sept. 5, 1943, p. 4). His artistic and moral values were intimately and inextricably connected with his personal and family tradition, though his chief theme, man's duty to himself, is an age-old one. His verse reflects, as did his entire life, the stoic values of his college teachers and of his father. Percy thought himself a good, but not great, poet, "stranded by uncongenial tides."

Percy is best known for his autobiography, *Lanterns on the Levee: Recollections of a Planter's Son*, published in 1941. It was widely praised. The *New York Times* commended Percy's "candor and completeness" in revealing "the Southern aristocrats' point of view" (*ibid.*, Mar. 23, 1941, p. 5); and the attitudes traditionally associated with the Southern landed gentry—gentility, family pride, and intense localism but an absence of provincialism—do indeed pervade this quiet and sensitive book. Percy celebrated a way of life he knew was passing, and sought, in recalling the practicality and piquancy of his female relatives and the heroism of his father, to discern "the pattern that gave them strength and direction . . . that permitted them to be at once Puritans and Cavaliers." His father's simple code of conduct— one of earnestness in seeking justice, tempered by humility and a humane regard for individuals— seemed all the more necessary in an age where demagoguery and fascism could destroy democracy, in itself a system whose rightness and superiority Percy sometimes questioned. It is a mellow book, sober in its recognition of the author's estrangement from contemporary life, but never conceding futility.

Discussion of the race question permeates *Lanterns*, and there, stating his beliefs eloquently, Percy held nothing back. As a traditional Southern paternalist, he believed that the moral and intellectual development of the Negro had to precede social and political equality because, in his view, the race was immature, irresponsible, and amiably weak-natured, a people "who thieve like children and murder ungrudgingly as small boys fight." But he also believed passionately that the Negro should be treated humanely. Education, he argued,

would at once elevate blacks and inculcate in ignorant whites an attitude of decency and forbearance toward the Negroes they feared and exploited. Percy did more than talk. Like his father, he risked his own safety to defend Negroes against the Ku Klux Klan. Even though he felt that the mass of Negroes should be kept in a subordinate position for an undetermined time, he accepted the gifted Negro with respect (see, e.g., Langston Hughes, *I Wonder as I Wander*, 1956, p. 52). For his beliefs, liberals and rabid racists alike excoriated him.

A mild, generous man, Percy enjoyed company and had deep friendships, yet remained lonely. He died in Greenville in 1942 of cardiovascular disease and was buried in the Greenville Cemetery.

[*Lanterns on the Levee* is the most important biographical source. Full obituaries can be found in the Jan. 22, 1942, issues of the *New Orleans Times-Picayune* and the *Memphis Commercial Appeal*. Correspondence with Walker Percy clarified several matters. Percy's published poetry was brought together posthumously in *The Collected Poems of William Alexander Percy* (1943). Louis D. Rubin, Jr., ed., *A Bibliog. Guide to the Study of Southern Literature* (1969), p. 258, lists personal reminiscences and critical essays.]

WILLIAM J. COOPER, JR.

PERKINS, DWIGHT HEALD (Mar. 26, 1867–Nov. 2, 1941), architect, was born in Memphis, Tenn., the only child of Marland Leslie Perkins, a lawyer, and Marion (Heald) Perkins. His father, whose ancestors were among the early seventeenth-century settlers of Massachusetts Bay Colony, brought the family to Chicago during his son's early childhood, and all of the boy's education up to college occurred in the public schools of that city. In 1885 Dwight Perkins enrolled in the school of architecture of the Massachusetts Institute of Technology; he had completed two years when his precocity led to his appointment as instructor in architecture. He held the position for a single academic year, returning to Chicago in 1888 to join the architectural firm of Burnham and Root. His maturity and sense of responsibility quickly impressed Daniel Burnham [*q.v.*], who placed him in charge of the big and expanding office during Burnham's tenure (1891–93) as chief of construction of the World's Columbian Exposition.

This schooling in one of the leading architectural firms in the nation led Perkins to establish his own office in 1894. Chicago by that date was well launched into the brilliant period of building art known as the Chicago school, and Perkins was soon to play a leading role in the movement. Among his early commissions, the major works are Steinway Hall (1896) and the Abraham Lincoln Center (1902–05), a Chicago settlement house founded by the Rev. Jenkins Lloyd Jones [*q.v.*]. The latter building placed its designer in the new Prairie group of architects emerging around the turn of the century under the influence of Louis Sullivan [*q.v.*]. The full measure of Perkins's talent suddenly burst forth with his appointment in 1905 as architect to the Chicago Board of Education during the reform administration of Mayor Edward F. Dunne. Within five years he created modern scholastic architecture by bringing to bear on the problems of school construction the Chicago principles of functionalism and organic design. These he expressed through formal elements and a system of ornament which, though recognizable as belonging to the Prairie school, bear the stamp of Perkins's own originality.

The chief works in his five-year career with the Board of Education are Lane Technical High School (1909), Carl Schurz High School (1910; his masterpiece), Bowen High School (1910), Trumbull Elementary School (1910), and Cleveland Elementary School (1911). Most remarkable of the designs that Perkins prepared in this period was a project for a commercial high school to be erected in the urban core (1908–09). Conceived as a fifteen-story building, it would have been the first skyscraper school planned for the commercial center of the city. Among Perkins's schools built outside Chicago at this time is the Lincolnwood School in Evanston (1909), described as the first multiclassroom one-story school designed for the urban environment.

Perkins was dismissed from the staff of the Board of Education in 1910, after a spectacular public controversy in which the school administration charged him with incompetence, inefficiency, and insubordination. These charges represent such grotesque distortions of the truth that no biographer can take them seriously. The true reason for the dismissal was that the conservative members of the board and of other municipal agencies were aghast at Perkins's radical school designs, as is suggested by the fact that his successor, A. F. Hussander, immediately returned to a lifeless classical respectability for Chicago schools.

The troubles with the Chicago board in no way damaged Perkins's reputation among his colleagues and his potential clients outside the city's educational establishment. He had designed forty-three new buildings and additions for Chicago and had reached a level of creative imagination that he was rarely to achieve again, but he was to receive over 160 additional commissions before his retirement. He established the firm of Perkins, Fellows, and Hamilton in 1911, which became

Perkins, Chatten, and Hammond in 1927 and dissolved in 1933, three years before he withdrew finally from active practice. Among the many buildings designed by these offices are elementary schools in the Chicago suburbs of Evanston, Skokie, and Wilmette; the campus plan, gymnasium, and auditorium of the original New Trier Township High School in the suburb of Winnetka; and, the most impressive of all, Evanston Township High School (1924). Other buildings include the refectory in Lincoln Park, Chicago, known as Cafe Brauer, and the Lion House of the Lincoln Park Zoological Garden, one of several works for which he received the gold medal of the American Institute of Architects in 1912 and was subsequently elected an honorary fellow.

A passionate conservationist, Perkins helped found in 1904 the Prairie Club, which under his leadership played a major role in securing the legislation of 1913 which established the Forest Preserve District of Chicago and Cook County. Numerous civic offices attest to his concern with community recreation: he was chairman of the Special Committee on Playgrounds and Small Parks, Chicago Park Commission, 1899–1909; chairman of the planning committee of the Forest Preserve District, 1916–22; president, Northwest Park District Commission, Evanston, 1911–16; honorary president, Regional Planning Association of Chicago, following its establishment in 1925. The forest preserve area in Evanston was named Dwight H. Perkins Forest in honor of his long service to the cause of conservation.

On Aug. 18, 1891, Perkins married Lucy A. Fitch of Hopkinton, Mass., who became a writer of children's books, well known for her "Twins" series. They had two children, Eleanor Ellis and Lawrence Bradford; the son followed his father's profession. Dwight Perkins was a man of the most exacting professional standards and was almost puritanical in his personal moral character, but he was described by associates and family members as possessing great personal charm and an engaging sense of humor. He was a Unitarian by religious conviction and an amateur painter whose work was several times exhibited in the Art Center of Evanston, Ill., where the family made their home. He was as fond of travel in foreign lands as he was of exploring the trails of Cook County forests. Surviving his wife by three years, he died of a cerebral hemorrhage at Lordsburg, N. Mex., in 1941, while en route to his winter home at Pasadena, Calif. He was buried in Graceland Cemetery, Chicago.

[H. Allen Brooks, "The Early Work of the Prairie Architects," *Jour. of the Soc. of Architectural His-*

torians, Mar. 1960; Chicago Board of Education, *Annual Reports,* 1905–06 to 1910–11; Carl W. Condit, *The Chicago School of Architecture* (1964); obituaries in *Chicago Tribune,* Nov. 3, 1941, and *Evanston Rev.,* Nov. 6, 1941; Frank A. Randall, *Hist. of the Development of Building Construction in Chicago* (1949); Peter B. Wright in *Architectural Record,* June 1910; *Who's Who in Chicago and Vicinity,* 1936, 1941; Eleanor Ellis Perkins, *Perkins of Chicago* (privately printed, 1966) and *Eve among the Puritans* (1956), a biography of Lucy Fitch Perkins; papers of the Lawrence B. Perkins family; miscellaneous clippings on Dwight H. Perkins, Evanston Public Lib.]

CARL W. CONDIT

PERRY, CLARENCE ARTHUR (Mar. 4, 1872–Sept. 5, 1944), social worker, was born in Truxton, Cortland County, N. Y., the older of two children and only son of Duane Oliver Perry and Hattie (Hart) Perry. Both parents were natives of New York state and descendants of early English immigrants to New England. Perry's father worked as a farmer and teamster, and once tried acting as a member of a touring stock company. Memories of childhood poverty, of having to sell newspapers while other children played, always remained with Perry and probably stimulated his professional interest in recreational opportunities for the young.

Presumably lack of funds delayed his college education, for he was in his twenties when he entered Stanford University. After two years (1893–94, 1896–97) he transferred to Cornell, from which he received the B.S. degree in 1899. His early career was in teaching and included two years in the Philippines. After a summer of study at Columbia's Teachers College (1904), he went to Ponce, Puerto Rico, as a high school principal (1904–05). There he met Leonard P. Ayres, general superintendent of schools in Puerto Rico and secretary of the Russell Sage Foundation's investigation of backward children. In 1907 the Foundation established a Committee on Playground Extension, which two years later became the Division of Recreation in the Department of Child Hygiene and in 1913 a separate Department of Recreation. Upon Ayres's recommendation, Perry, then employed as a special agent of the United States Immigration Commission, was in 1909 appointed to the Foundation staff. He advanced to associate director of the Department of Recreation in 1913 and remained in that position, save for two years' service in the army Quartermaster Corps during World War I, until his retirement in 1937.

Believing that the public school, even more than the social settlement, could serve as a stimulus to neighborhood social cohesion and regeneration, Perry became active in the community center movement. Its goal was to widen the after-hours use of the public school plant for recreational, social, civic, and educational purposes. The community center principle had diverse roots. Settlement workers had long sought to link the school to the neighborhood and to the life experience of children; social workers and progressive educators had worked to adapt the school curriculum to the needs and interests of individual children and to make the school an agency of Americanization; the organized recreation movement had viewed the public school as a significant experimental laboratory; and individual social reformers like Jacob Riis [*q.v.*] had regarded the public school as a nuclear instrument for neighborhood regeneration in a pluralistic society. In the most direct sense, the community center movement evolved from earlier limited experiments in the "socialization of school property." These included, in New York City, the public lecture program developed by Henry Leipziger [*q.v.*] and the efforts of Evangeline E. Whitney to open the schools as evening recreation centers for youths of working age. The movement was officially launched in October 1911, when the first National Conference on Civic and Neighborhood Center Development was held in Madison, Wis. In Perry's words, "we came away from Madison in a state of religious exaltation—like missionaries going forth to read a new gospel."

Over the next decade the gospel was promulgated by Perry and his Division of Recreation at the Russell Sage Foundation, along with the extension division of the University of Wisconsin and the National Community Center Association, which had evolved out of the Madison conference. In seeking to redefine the school's function, Perry was particularly concerned with supervised group recreation, in which he saw opportunities for character building, moral uplift, and citizenship training. Yet Perry's major contribution to the community center movement lay not in the realm of theory but in his talent for interpretation and promotion. Under his direction the Division of Recreation published three books and twenty pamphlets which publicized the progress of the movement and introduced new techniques for establishing social centers. Perry's interest in recreation embraced motion pictures—for many years, beginning in 1911, he served on the general committee of the National Board of Review of Motion Pictures, a private and unofficial censorship group—and the community or "little" theatre movement, which he was active in promoting during the 1920's. Perry also helped organize the New York Training School for Community Workers in 1915–16, and was active during the 1920's in the development of the Playground and Recreation

Association's Training School for Recreation Workers.

In the fall of 1921 Perry wrote a historical review of the community center movement. He concluded that, despite wide acceptance of after-hours use of the school plant, neighborhood organization of civic, cultural, and recreational activities had nowhere been fully established. Having acknowledged that the community center ideal was a failure, he now turned to housing and planning, where he became identified with the neighborhood unit concept. The objective remained the same—creation of an institutional basis for socialization and cooperative citizenship on the neighborhood level—but the means shifted from the public school to the planning of the physical environment. Perry's notion of neighborhood unity derived in part from his experience of living in Forest Hills Gardens, Long Island, a model middle-income garden suburb planned in 1909 under the auspices of the Russell Sage Foundation. He was influenced also by the sociologist Charles H. Cooley, who held that face-to-face or primary group relationships engendered cooperation.

Perry conceived of the neighborhood unit as a kind of village cell, transcending the depersonalization of urban society. Essentially it was a scheme to arrange the physical environment of urban neighborhoods so as to encourage primary group association and a vigorous, organized community life. The interior roads were designed to discourage all but local traffic, and wide arterial streets along the periphery defined the unit's boundaries. At its core lay the public school, a nucleus for social and civic activities. Substantial land was allotted for park, playground, and recreational purposes, and each unit was to have its own shopping center. To enhance the environmental stimulus to voluntary group association, Perry advocated fairly homogeneous population groupings. He set the ideal population at from 4,800 to 9,000, and believed the scheme applicable to both undeveloped tracts and blighted areas. Implementation of the neighborhood unit required large-scale tract development, which Perry hoped would lead to the mechanization and rationalization of the home-building industry and to enlarged powers for municipal housing and planning authorities. Although he had developed the essentials of his plan as early as 1923, its impact upon contemporary planning was greatest after 1929 when, as a member of the social division of the Russell Sage Foundation's Regional Plan of New York and Its Environs, he published *The Neighborhood Unit: A Scheme of Arrangement for the Family Community*. Perry later participated in the President's Conference on Home Building

and Home Ownership (1931), was a member of the Committee on Slum Clearance of the New York City Tenement House Department, and served on the Community Action Committee of the New York City Housing Authority.

Hardworking, serious, and modest, Perry found relaxation in tinkering with electrical equipment. On Apr. 27, 1901, he had married Julia St. John Wygant, a physician, by whom he had one daughter, Sara Janet. Perry was a member of the Congregational Church. Suffering from arteriosclerosis, he died at the age of seventy-two of a cerebral hemorrhage in New Rochelle, N. Y. His body was cremated and his ashes buried in Hillside Cemetery, Peekskill, N. Y.

[For Perry's views on recreation and community center development, see his *Wider Use of the School Plant* (1910); "A Survey of the Social-Center Movement," *Elementary School Teacher*, Nov. 1912; "Why Recreation in the Schoolhouse?" and "The School as a Factor in Neighborhood Development," Nat. Conference of Charities and Correction, *Proc.*, 1914; "The High School as a Social Centre," in Charles H. Johnston, ed., *The Modern High School* (1914); *The Extension of Public Education: A Study in the Wider Use of School Buildings* (U. S. Bureau of Education, *Bull.*, no. 28, 1915); *Educational Extension* (Survey Committee of the Cleveland Foundation, 1916); "The Quicksands of Wider Use," *Playground*, Sept. 1916; and, with Marguerita P. Williams, *N. Y. School Centers and Their Community Policy* (1931). Clarence A. Perry and Lee F. Hanmer, *Recreation in Springfield, Ill.: A Section of the Springfield Survey* (Russell Sage Foundation, 1914), is a pioneer community survey. Perry deals with the movies and theatre in *The Attitude of High School Students toward Motion Pictures* (1923) and *The Work of the Little Theatres* (1933). His writings on housing, planning, and the Neighborhood Unit include: *The Rebuilding of Blighted Areas* (Regional Plan Assoc., 1933); and *Housing for the Machine Age* (1939). See also Roy Lubove, "New Cities for Old: The Urban Reconstruction Program of the 1930's," *Social Studies*, Nov. 1962. James Dahir, *The Neighborhood Unit: Its Spread and Acceptance* (1947), is an annotated bibliography. Considerable information on Perry's career can be found in John M. Glenn, Lilian Brandt, and F. Emerson Andrews, *Russell Sage Foundation, 1907–1946* (2 vols., 1947). See also obituaries in *N. Y. Herald Tribune* and *N. Y. Times*, Sept. 7, 1944; *Who Was Who in America*, vol. II (1950). Perry's daughter, Mrs. Sara Janet Fairhurst, provided a great deal of information. Death certificate from N. Y. State Dept. of Health.]

ROY LUBOVE

PHELPS, WILLIAM LYON (Jan. 2, 1865–Aug. 21, 1943), teacher of English, literary critic, and lecturer, was the fifth and youngest child (the third son to attain maturity) of the Rev. Sylvanus Dryden Phelps and his wife, Sophia Emilia Lyon Linsley. Born in New Haven, Conn., he received the name of his mother's grandfather, who had been a colonel during the American Revolution. His father, a direct descendant of William Phelps, who settled in Windsor, Conn., in 1636, was a graduate of Brown University. In 1876 Sylvanus Phelps exchanged the pastorate of the First (later Calvary) Baptist Church, New Haven, for that of the Jefferson Street Baptist Church, Providence, R. I., and in 1878 left the active ministry to become editor and proprietor of the *Christian Secretary,* a Baptist weekly published in Hartford, Conn. He had long been interested in printing and publishing, and his wife wrote regularly for a religious weekly. "Billy" Phelps, as nearly everyone styled him (his parents called him "Willie" and he himself preferred "Bil"), received most of his early education in the public schools of New Haven, Providence, and Hartford. In adolescence he began to read voraciously. He was active in all kinds of athletic sports and did well in all subjects except mathematics, which he always spoke of as the bane of an otherwise happy childhood and youth.

Phelps entered Yale in 1883, was a member of the second baseball nine, played tennis, and won a championship in the cross-country run. He was elected to the board of the *Yale Literary Magazine* and to Phi Beta Kappa and graduated with special honors in English and philosophy. During 1887–88 he continued at Yale as general secretary of the Y.M.C.A. and part-time graduate student. The year following he taught English and coached athletics at the Westminster School, Dobbs Ferry, N. Y., returning to Yale, 1889–90, for full-time graduate work. An eye affection resembling conjunctivitis, which prevented his reading for more than ten minutes at a time, so interfered with his studies that the faculty did not renew his scholarship. After spending a happy summer in a cycling tour of England and the Continent (during which the malady vanished), he entered the Harvard graduate school with a scholarship in the autumn of 1890 and received the A.M. degree from Harvard and the Ph.D. from Yale on the same day, in June 1891. After a year as instructor in English at Harvard, he returned to Yale as instructor in the autumn of 1892. On Dec. 21 of that year he was married to Annabel Hubbard of Huron City, Mich., who had been in school with him in Hartford. Her parents' house in Huron City became henceforth his summer home. There were no children.

Phelps remained on the Yale faculty for forty-one years, teaching an average of four hundred students a year. From the beginning he broke with tradition. He treated his pupils with friendly informality, inaugurated the first course in literature open to Yale freshmen (refusing to teach them composition), scandalized the press by offering upperclassmen a course in the modern novel (1895–96), and later instituted a course in modern drama. His innovations roused alarm and hostility in the faculty, but he was made professor in 1901. Though he taught all literature with delight, he accepted the philosophy of Browning as his own and was best known at Yale for his course in Tennyson and Browning ("T & B").

After publishing his dissertation, *The Beginnings of the English Romantic Movement* (1893) —a remarkably good dissertation for its day and his one extended work of research scholarship— he invested his writing time for several years in editing authors from Shakespeare to Ibsen. With *Essays on Modern Novelists* (1910) he found the mode that gave him greatest satisfaction. Having begun his career as a public lecturer in 1895, he soon found himself the most sought-after speaker on literature in the country, not only giving many single discourses, but also conducting annual courses of lectures in New Haven, New York, Brooklyn, and Philadelphia. Favorite subjects were the modern novel, the modern theatre, and the King James Version of the Bible. His books were generally collections of magazine essays, which in turn had originated as public lectures.

Five feet eight and a half inches tall, with blue-gray eyes and abundant black hair that in middle life turned iron-gray and later white, Phelps continued to play hockey till he was thirty-seven, baseball till he was forty-five, and tennis doubles till he was seventy. His graceful but masculine platform style reflected his athleticism. He loved travel and made frequent trips to Europe. A gregarious man of warm hospitality, he built a handsome Georgian house on Whitney Avenue in New Haven, which during his lifetime had under its roof a multitude of famous writers, artists, actors, and musicians. He made the acquaintance of practically every author of distinction in Great Britain and America, and persuaded most of them to speak at Yale. For some thirty-five years he served as president of the Little Theater Guild of New Haven, and from 1912 to 1935 was president of the New Haven Symphony Orchestra. Having been a licensed occasional preacher since 1887, he assumed complete summer charge, beginning in 1922, of the Methodist church in Huron City, Mich. On Dec. 16, 1928, he was ordained honorary pastor of Calvary Baptist Church, New Haven, of which he had long been a deacon, and after that occasionally officiated at weddings and funerals.

World War I made Phelps again a center of controversy. His unqualified pacifism and particularly his sponsorship, just before America's entrance into the war, of an antiwar address at Yale by David Starr Jordan [*q.v.*], roused deep alumni resentment. This, however, subsided when he later supported the war effort. In 1922 he began his favorite piece of writing, the monthly series of *causeries* in *Scribner's Magazine* called "As I Like It," in which he joyfully dispensed opinions on any subject that interested him and judgments on English usage for the large un-academic audience who wanted rules, not schol-arly discussions. In 1924, while in Paris on sabbatical, Phelps suffered a severe depression and nervous breakdown and spent four months convalescing in Augusta, Ga. Whatever the cause of this illness, his recovery seemed complete. He began a syndicated weekly newspaper column in 1927. He gained his greatest newspaper publicity in 1928 by bringing his friend James Joseph ("Gene") Tunney, the prizefighter, to lecture on Shakespeare to his class at Yale. Insomnia had been a lifelong burden, and in 1929 he began to be bothered by asthma, suffering increasingly from shortness of breath.

On retiring from teaching (July 1, 1933), Phelps began a series of radio addresses (and a column on books for the *Rotarian*) and stepped up his syndicated newspaper column from a weekly to a daily. At the Yale commencement of 1934, while he was presenting the candidates for honorary degrees in his long-held office of public orator, he was himself to his complete surprise presented for the LL.D. All told, he re-ceived honorary degrees from nineteen colleges or universities, beginning with Brown and Col-gate in 1921 and including New York University (1927) and Columbia (1933). He was elected to the National Institute of Arts and Letters (1910, president 1929–31) and its inner group, the American Academy of Arts and Letters (1931, secretary 1937–43), the American Acad-emy of Arts and Sciences (1921), and the American Philosophical Society (1927), whose Franklin Medal he received in 1937. Mrs. Phelps's death in March 1939 broke the pattern of his life, but he continued his accustomed social routine with outward serenity. He died four years later, of pneumonia following a cere-bral hemorrhage, at his home in New Haven and was buried in the Grove Street Cemetery, New Haven.

Phelps once said that on graduation from col-lege he was uncertain whether to be a teacher, a preacher, or a journalist, and that he ended by becoming all three. His written style did not rise above superior journalism. His approach to litera-ture was that of an unashamed popularizer. He paid little attention to the formal elements of prose or verse, but looked to literature for nice observations of human nature and human be-havior. Like his contemporaries Shaw and Ches-terton, he was fond of the seeming paradox. His

criticisms of novelists and playwrights, once very useful to general readers, now have little circula-tion. Of his critical studies, the *Robert Browning* (1915, new enlarged edition 1932) stands the best chance of survival, though perhaps less for its critical judgments than for its sensible expli-cation of obscurities.

No writing of Phelps, however, can transmit the full scope and appeal of his personality. To meet Phelps face to face was to be made over. His lectures, book reviews, and popular essays championed the joys of reading and thus made an impact, however diffuse, on contemporary cul-ture. As a teacher Phelps led the revolution for informality and geniality in the classroom and for the inclusion of contemporary literature in the curriculum. He did much to establish the primacy of literature over language in graduate study. He pioneered in making Russian fiction known in America. His fondness for old books infected many of his pupils with a fruitful pas-sion for collecting. He had enormous zest for life and a Boswellian faculty for enjoying enjoy-ment. He delighted in literature and he strove to rouse that delight in other people—people in quantity.

[Masses of Phelps's correspondence are preserved in the Memorabilia Room at Yale, and there are exten-sive collections of pamphlets, offprints, clippings, etc., there and in the general collection of the Sterling Memorial Lib., in the Beinecke Rare Book and Manu-script Lib., and especially in Alumni Records at Yale. Phelps's diaries are in a large collection of memorabilia which the William Lyon Phelps Foundation maintains at his former home in Huron City, Mich. His *Auto-biog. with Letters* (1939) contains a vast amount of precise information, desultorily presented and sketchily indexed. Other sources include: the *Class Book* and eight succeeding *Records* of the Yale Class of 1887; the Yale *Obituary Record of Graduates,* 1943–44, pp. 37–40; *Nat. Cyc. Am. Biog.,* XXXII, 444–45; *New Haven Evening Register,* Aug. 21, 23, 1943; tributes by three pupils: Henry Seidel Canby in *Saturday Rev. of Literature,* Sept. 4, 1943 (editorial), Sinclair Lewis, *ibid.,* Apr. 1, 1939, and Chauncey B. Tinker in Am. Acad. of Arts and Letters, *Com-memorative Tributes, 1942–1951* (1951); Florence H. Barber, *Fellow of Infinite Jest* (1949); long personal acquaintance. The most complete checklist of Phelps's very numerous publications is a typescript in Folder 8 of the Alumni Records collection, Yale. The *Auto-biog.* reproduces several photographs of him, and there is a fine series in *Life,* Dec. 5, 1938.]

FREDERICK A. POTTLE

PINCHOT, AMOS RICHARDS ENO (Dec. 6, 1873–Feb. 18, 1944), lawyer, political publicist and reformer, was born in Paris, France, while his parents were traveling abroad. He was the second son and youngest of three children of James Wallace Pinchot and Mary Jane (Eno) Pinchot and the brother of Gifford Pinchot, forester and conservationist. His paternal grandfather, Cyril Constantine Désiré Pinchot, a captain in Napoleon's army, had emigrated in 1816 to Milford, Pa., where he opened a general store. His maternal grandfather, Amos Richards Eno, was a well-known real estate speculator and banker in New York City; William Phelps Eno [Supp. 3] was the boy's uncle. His father achieved sufficient success in the wallpaper business to retire at the age of forty-four and devote the rest of his life to philanthropy and conservation. The family lived at 2 Gramercy Park in New York City.

Amos Pinchot attended Westminster School (Dobbs Ferry, N. Y.), Saint George's School (Newport, R. I.), Yale (B.A., 1897), and the Columbia Law School. He left Columbia before the end of his first year, however, to serve with the New York Volunteer Cavalry in Puerto Rico during the Spanish-American War, after which he attended the New York Law School. He was admitted to the bar in 1900, and soon afterward accepted a position as deputy assistant district attorney of New York City. The following year he resigned to devote full time to managing the family estate—the role marked out for Amos from his youth so as to free his older brother, Gifford, for the distinguished political career that, by general family conviction, lay in store for him.

Amos Pinchot first became active in politics in 1908 when his brother, then chief of the United States Forest Service, accused Secretary of Interior Richard A. Ballinger [q.v.] of favoring corporate interests at the expense of the government's conservation program. President Taft sided with Ballinger and ordered Gifford's removal from office, precipitating a famous controversy. Amos, who had served his brother as an unofficial adviser and liaison man, emerged from this experience determined to break the hold that he believed industrial monopolies had on government policy. He supported the presidential aspirations of Robert M. La Follette [q.v.] and in 1911 helped found the National Progressive Republican League. He backed La Follette until January 1912 when, with his brother and other insurgent Republicans, he switched to Roosevelt and helped organize the Progressive party. That same year, seeking to publicize the new party, he ran for Congress in New York.

Within the Progressive party, Pinchot aligned himself with the "radical nucleus," a small group that favored public ownership of waterpower, forests, utilities, and other sources of energy, and the breaking up of private monopolies. His unsuccessful efforts to have these reforms incorporated into the platform left him disenchanted with what he regarded as the opportunism of the party

leaders. He then launched a vigorous attack on George W. Perkins [q.v.], chairman of the Progressive national executive committee and a prominent banker, whom he accused of favoring the protection of private monopoly and of tying the party to business interests. Their quarrel came to a head in 1914 when a letter that Pinchot had sent to leading Progressives urging Perkins's resignation was leaked to the press and widely publicized. Roosevelt publicly repudiated his suggestion, and embarrassed party officials, who regarded Pinchot as unrealistic, intractable, and dogmatic, suggested that he leave the party.

Though at first reluctant to break with his brother's party, Pinchot soon faded from the Progressive group. In 1916 he assumed the chairmanship of the Wilson Volunteers of New York, a move that temporarily alienated his brother. Pinchot disagreed with Wilson on many domestic issues but admired him for his peace stand. Fearful that American involvement in World War I would destroy hard-won economic and social gains, he became an ardent antimilitarist. He was chairman of the Committee on Real Preparedness (1916), served on the executive committee of the American Union against Militarism (1916–17), and was treasurer (1917–18) of the defense committee set up to support *Masses,* which had been excluded from the mails under the Espionage Act of 1917. Such infringements on the activities of people opposed to the war had awakened in Pinchot a deep interest in civil rights, and in 1917 he helped found the National Civil Liberties Bureau, predecessor of the American Civil Liberties Union, of whose executive committee he was a member until his death.

When the war ended Pinchot helped organize the "Committee of Forty-Eight," initially set up as an independent pressure group to influence the selection of candidates by the two established political parties. In 1920 it sought to form a new third party in the progressive tradition, but the effort proved abortive, and Pinchot, disheartened, withdrew from politics. During this period he wrote, but did not finish, his *History of the Progressive Party,* published posthumously in 1958.

Pinchot returned to the political arena in 1932 as an enthusiastic supporter of Franklin D. Roosevelt, but broke with him the following year over the question of monetary policy. Objecting strenuously to the growth of federal power, he increasingly viewed the New Deal as an incipient political dictatorship. His opposition to big government was consistent with his early views on business monopolies; he regarded all aggregations of power as a threat to the individual. In radio speeches and pamphlets Pinchot attacked the administration's labor policies, the "court-packing" bill, the executive reorganization plan, and Roosevelt's bid for a third term. He joined a number of anti-New Deal organizations, among them the Sound Money League, the Committee for the Nation, and the National Committee to Uphold Constitutional Government. Convinced that the President was leading the country toward war, he also helped found the America First Committee (1940) and later served on its national committee.

Fastidious in dress, tall and muscular, Pinchot had the look of a cultivated and athletic gentleman. He played squash, was an enthusiastic fisherman, and took great pleasure in following tennis and baseball. On Nov. 14, 1900, he had married Gertrude Minturn of New York City; they had two children, Gifford and Rosamond. This first marriage ended in divorce in 1919, and on Aug. 9 of that year Pinchot married Ruth Pickering of Elmira, N. Y., by whom he had two daughters, Mary Eno and Antoinette Eno. Illness, a series of financial setbacks, and the suicide of his daughter Rosamond in 1938 contributed to a sense of discouragement and disintegration, and in 1942 Pinchot himself attempted suicide. He died two years later of bronchial pneumonia at the West Hill Sanitarium in the Bronx, New York City. After Presbyterian services, he was buried in Milford, Pa.

[Amos Pinchot Papers and Gifford Pinchot Papers, Lib. of Cong.; papers of other Progressives and of Woodrow Wilson; interviews with family, friends, and associates of Pinchot. Published sources: the author's biographical introduction to Pinchot's *Hist. of the Progressive Party* (1958); Yale College Class of 1897, *Half Century Record* (1948); Yale Univ., *Obituary Record of Graduates*, 1943–44; *Nat. Cyc. Am. Biog.*, XXXII, 379–80; *N. Y. Times*, Nov. 15, 1900 (on his first marriage), Aug. 7–9, 1942, Feb. 19, 1944. See also: M. Nelson McGeary, *Gifford Pinchot* (1960); Martin L. Fausold, *Gifford Pinchot* (1961); Robert M. La Follette, *La Follette's Autobiog.* (1913); Belle Case and Fola La Follette, *Robert M. La Follette* (1953); Otis L. Graham, *An Encore for Reform: The Old Progressives and the New Deal* (1967). The best collection of portraits and photographs is in the possession of Mrs. Amos Pinchot.]

HELENE MAXWELL BREWER

POLK, FRANK LYON (Sept. 13, 1871– Feb. 7, 1943), lawyer, municipal reformer, and diplomat, was born in New York City, the son of Dr. William Mecklenburg Polk [*q.v.*] and Ida Ashe (Lyon) Polk. Though his career was to be intimately connected with the urban Northeast, he came of a family steeped in the culture of the antebellum South. Leonidas Polk [*q.v.*], Episcopal bishop and Confederate general, was his grandfather; the North Carolina Revolutionary officer Col. William Polk [*q.v.*] was his great-

grandfather, and President James K. Polk a kinsman. His mother was from Demopolis, Ala. Frank was one of five children, three of whom died in infancy and a fourth, a younger brother, soon after completing medical school. The family's bereavement was all the more startling in view of the father's preeminence as a medical educator and gynecologist, which allowed for an affluent and genteel standard of living. Frank's formal education began at the Cutler School, and he graduated in turn from Groton School (1890), Yale (B.A. 1894), and the Columbia University Law School (LL.B. 1897).

Upon graduation from law school, Polk joined the prestigious legal firm of Evarts, Choate, and Beaman in New York. Within the year, however, the Spanish-American War caused him to enlist in the New York National Guard (May 1898); he rose quickly from private to captain and served under Gen. Oswald Ernst [*q.v.*] during the campaign in Puerto Rico. Soon after resuming his legal practice, in 1900, he decided to form a new partnership known as Alexander, Watriss, and Polk. As the legal work prospered, he accepted a succession of civic and political responsibilities that included membership on the New York Board of Education (1906–07) and the presidency of the Municipal Civil Service Commission (1908–09). At this time he became seriously interested in political reform at the municipal level, seeking to replace administrative corruption with an effective merit system. By his calm, deliberate style, he promoted many salutary reforms affecting the police, teachers, and other civil servants in New York. As an independent Democrat, Polk actively engaged in organizing opposition to the Tammany machine and in 1914 was a staunch champion of the reform candidacy of John Purroy Mitchel [*q.v.*] for mayor. Mayor Mitchel appointed him corporation counsel, a position he found so satisfying that he declined other opportunities for political office. On Apr. 17, 1914, Polk was injured when a deranged blacksmith, Michael Mahoney, fired on Mitchel, with whom Polk was seated in an automobile; the bullet struck Polk instead, penetrating his jaw and severing two teeth.

In national politics, Polk supported Woodrow Wilson for president in 1912, and thereafter found himself increasingly sympathetic with the goals of the New Freedom. When, in 1915, William Jennings Bryan [*q.v.*] resigned as Secretary of State, Wilson selected Robert Lansing [*q.v.*] to succeed Bryan and appointed Polk to serve in Lansing's place as Counselor (second ranking officer) in the State Department. At the time it appeared that Polk lacked sufficient technical training and experience in international affairs, but he had for some years read extensively on many facets of contemporary world politics, and he quickly impressed his associates, Congressmen, and members of the press with his grasp of diplomatic policy and procedures.

It was the Mexican crisis of 1915–16 that afforded him his first sizable responsibility at the State Department. He handled the diplomatic ramifications created by Gen. John J. Pershing's punitive expedition in pursuit of Pancho Villa and then arranged to have the ensuing differences with Mexico submitted to a Joint High Commission. As chief legal officer, he also advised the Wilson administration on the problems of neutral rights which arose from the European war, including complicated international property settlements and responses to U-boat attacks, Allied interception and searching of American mail, and the British blacklist of American companies trading with Germany. He was deeply involved in the difficult transition from neutral to belligerent status that occurred after April 1917. Polk became coordinator for the several governmental investigatory agencies which were created in 1917–18 for purposes of gathering useful intelligence data abroad. In 1918 he announced the government's decision to dispatch American troops to Siberia. From December 1918 to mid-July 1919, while Secretary Lansing was in Paris serving as plenipotentiary at the Peace Conference, Polk remained in Washington as Acting Secretary of State. With Lansing's return, Polk proceeded to Paris to direct the American peace delegation until it was dissolved in December 1919. Because his services so clearly exceeded the responsibilities associated with the office of Counselor or even Assistant Secretary, Congress in June 1919 adopted a recommendation from the administration and created the new position of Under Secretary, of which Polk became the first occupant. He remained until Lansing's successor, Bainbridge Colby, could be properly oriented before he resigned, effective June 15, 1920.

Polk then returned to New York and formed a legal partnership (Davis, Polk, Wardwell, Gardiner, and Reed) headed by John W. Davis, recently American ambassador to England. Polk also accepted directorships of several banks and corporations, including the Northern Pacific Railway, the Bowery Savings Bank, and the Mutual Life Insurance Company of New York. In state politics he was an early supporter of Alfred E. Smith [Supp. 3] for governor, and he subsequently assisted Franklin D. Roosevelt and Herbert H. Lehman to that office. In 1924 he was John W. Davis's manager in the preconvention

campaign for the presidency and his floor manager at the Democratic convention. At the municipal level, Polk headed a citizens' committee supporting the reelection of Mayor Fiorello La Guardia on a fusionist ticket in 1941. While generally favoring the New Deal program of President Franklin D. Roosevelt, Polk, like many prominent leaders of the bar, vigorously opposed Roosevelt's attempt to "pack" the Supreme Court in 1937. Although Polk's interest in foreign affairs did not falter, leading him to participate in conferences sponsored by the Institute of Pacific Relations and other groups, his chief intellectual concern in the 1920's and 1930's was to defend the reputation of Woodrow Wilson against revisionists and isolationists. During World War II he lent his prestige to chairing the American Friends of Yugoslavia (1941–43) and, in 1940–41, supported the Committee to Defend America by Aiding the Allies.

Frank Polk was married on Jan. 27, 1908, to Elizabeth Sturgis Potter of Philadelphia. They had five children: John Metcalf, Elizabeth Sturgis, Frank Lyon, James Potter, and Alice Potter. He belonged to several clubs, including the Century in New York and the Metropolitan in Washington. In religion he was an active Episcopalian. Polk died at his Fifth Avenue home in New York in 1943 of a coronary occlusion and was buried in Woodlawn Cemetery, New York City.

[The Frank Polk Papers, Yale Univ., include correspondence, memoranda, diaries, and an extensive clippings file. There are useful references to Polk in Arthur Link's *Wilson,* vols. II–V (1956–65), particularly to his activities in the State Dept. See also memorial by John W. Davis in Assoc. of the Bar of the City of N. Y., *Year Book,* 1944; and Yale Univ., *Obituary Record of Graduates,* 1942–43.]

LAWRENCE E. GELFAND

PORTER, EDWIN STANTON (Apr. 21, 1870–Apr. 30, 1941), pioneer motion picture director, was born in Connellsville, Pa., to Thomas Richard Porter, a merchant, and Mary Jane (Clark) Porter; he had three brothers and one sister. After attending public schools in Connellsville and Pittsburgh, Porter worked, among other odd jobs, as an exhibition skater, a sign painter, and a telegraph operator. He was employed for a time in the electrical department of William Cramp & Sons, a Philadelphia ship and engine building company, and in 1893 enlisted in the navy as an electrician. During his three years' service he showed aptitude as an inventor of electrical devices to improve communications.

Porter entered motion picture work in 1896, the first year movies were commercially projected on large screens in the United States. He was briefly employed in New York City by Raff & Gammon, agents for the films and viewing equipment made by Thomas A. Edison [Supp. 1], and then left to become a touring projectionist with a competing machine, Kuhn & Webster's Projectorscope. He traveled through the West Indies and South America, showing films at fairgrounds and in open fields, and later made a second tour through Canada and the United States. Returning to New York, he worked as a projectionist and attempted, unsuccessfully, to set up a manufacturing concern for motion picture cameras and projectors.

In 1899 Porter joined the Edison Company. Soon afterward he took charge of motion picture production at Edison's New York studios, operating the camera, directing the actors, and assembling the final print. During the next decade he became the most influential filmmaker in the United States. From his experience as a touring projectionist Porter knew what pleased crowds, and he began by making trick films and comedies for Edison. One of his early films was *Terrible Teddy, the Grizzly King,* a satire made in February 1901 about the then vice-president-elect, Theodore Roosevelt. Like all early filmmakers, he took ideas from others, but rather than simply copying films he tried to improve on what he borrowed. In his *Jack and the Beanstalk* (1902) and *Life of an American Fireman* (1903) he followed earlier films by Georges Méliès of France and James Williamson of Great Britain. Instead of using abrupt splices or cuts between shots, however, Porter created dissolves, gradual transitions from one image to another. In *Life of an American Fireman* particularly, the technique helped audiences follow complex outdoor movement.

In his next and most important film, *The Great Train Robbery* (1903), Porter took the archetypal American Western story, already familiar to audiences from dime novels and stage melodrama, and made it an entirely new visual experience. The one-reel film, with a running time of about ten minutes, was assembled in twenty separate shots, along with a startling close-up of a bandit firing at the camera. It used as many as ten different indoor and outdoor locations. No earlier film had created such swift movement or variety of scene. *The Great Train Robbery* was enormously popular. For several years it toured throughout the United States, and in 1905 it was the premier attraction at the first store-front nickel theatre. Its success firmly established motion pictures as commercial entertainment in the United States.

After *The Great Train Robbery* Porter continued to try out new techniques. He presented two parallel stories in *The Kleptomaniac* (1905), a film of social commentary like his technically more conventional film of 1904, *The Ex-Convict*. In *The Seven Ages* (1905) he used side lighting, close-ups, and changed shots within a scene, one of the earliest examples of a filmmaker departing from the theatrical analogy of a single shot for each scene. Between 1903 and 1905 he successfully demonstrated most of the techniques that were to become the basic modes of visual communication through film. Yet he seemed to regard them only as separate experiments and never brought them together in a unified filmmaking style.

In 1909 Porter left Edison and joined with others in organizing an independent motion picture company, Rex. He also took part in launching a company to manufacture Simplex motion picture projectors. After three years with Rex, he accepted an offer from Adolph Zukor to become chief director of the new Famous Players Film Company, the first American company regularly to produce feature-length films. Porter directed the stage actor James K. Hackett [*q.v.*] in the first five-reel American film, *The Prisoner of Zenda* (1913), and also directed Mary Pickford and John Barrymore [Supp. 3] in feature films. But his directorial skills had not kept pace with rapid changes in motion picture art, and he left Famous Players during a reorganization in 1916.

From 1917 to 1925 Porter served as president of the Precision Machine Company, manufacturers of the Simplex projectors. After his retirement in 1925 he continued to work on his own as an inventor and designer, securing several patents for still cameras and projector devices. During the 1930's he was employed by an appliance corporation. He died at the Hotel Taft in New York City at the age of seventy-one and was buried in Kensico Cemetery, Valhalla, N. Y. He was survived by his wife, Caroline Ridinger, whom he had married on June 5, 1893; they had no children.

Porter remains an enigmatic figure in motion picture history. Though his significance as director of *The Great Train Robbery* and other unusual early films is undeniable, he rarely repeated an innovation after he had used it successfully, never developed a consistent directorial style, and in later years never protested when others rediscovered his techniques and claimed them as their own. He was a modest, quiet, cautious man who felt uncomfortable working with the famous stars he directed between 1912 and 1916. Perhaps Zukor was right when he said of Porter that he was more an artistic mechanic than a dramatic artist, a man who liked to deal with machines better than with people.

[The most reliable information about Porter's life appears in the *Nat. Cyc. Am. Biog.*, XXX, 407–08. Standard critical discussions of his films are in Albert R. Fulton, *Motion Pictures* (1960), pp. 44–57; Lewis Jacobs, *The Rise of the Am. Film* (1939), pp. 35–51; and Kenneth Macgowan, *Behind the Screen* (1965), pp. 111–17. Much new information about Porter's early films is presented in Kemp R. Niver's *The First Twenty Years* (1968). Arthur Miller describes working for Porter at the Rex studios in 1910–11 in Fred J. Balshofer and Arthur C. Miller, *One Reel a Week* (1967); Adolph Zukor discusses his relations with Porter in *The Public Is Never Wrong* (1953). Porter wrote an article, "Evolution of the Motion Picture," in *Moving Picture World,* July 11, 1914. A photograph of Porter appears in Terry Ramsaye's *A Million and One Nights* (1926), facing p. 416.]

ROBERT SKLAR

PRATT, JAMES BISSETT (June 22, 1875– Jan. 15, 1944), philosopher, was born in Elmira, N. Y., the only child of Daniel Ransom Pratt by his second wife, Katherine Murdoch; there were three sons and a daughter by the first marriage. James's father, born in Elmira of Connecticut ancestry, was a banker and a trustee of the local Presbyterian church. His mother, to whom he was close in temperament and interests, was the daughter of a Presbyterian minister who had emigrated from Scotland to Canada and in 1850 to Elmira. He was much influenced also by an uncle (after whom he was named), James Bissett Murdoch, dean of the medical school of the University of Pittsburgh. After graduating in 1893 from the Elmira Free Academy, Pratt went to Williams College, with which he was to be associated for the remainder of his life.

His teacher of philosophy at Williams, Prof. John E. Russell, urged Pratt to devote himself to philosophical studies, and after graduating from Williams in 1898, he went on to Harvard. There the realist trend in his philosophical thinking at Williams was challenged by the impressive idealist teaching of G. H. Palmer and Josiah Royce, who in turn were being challenged by the pragmatism of William James [*qq.v.*]. So confused was Pratt at the end of his first year of graduate work that he decided to abandon philosophy, and, following his father's wish, he entered the law school at Columbia. A year there, however, convinced him that he preferred the "confusion" of philosophy to the "boredom" of the law. Determining to study at the University of Berlin, he taught Latin for two years in Elmira and thus financed a year abroad (1902–03). At Berlin he found little inspiration except in Prof. Otto Pfleiderer, who stimulated his interest in the philosophy of religion.

Returning to Harvard, Pratt became engrossed

in the psychology of religious consciousness. William James had just published his *Varieties of Religious Experience* (1902), and with James as director, Pratt pursued research in this field for his Ph.D. degree (1905) and devoted his first book to it: *The Psychology of Religious Belief* (1907). There followed in rapid succession a large number of critical articles and reviews on the psychology of religion. This subject, during the two decades after the appearance of James's book, was one of the most extensively debated fields of research and interpretation among psychologists and philosophers. Pratt's intense, critical participation in this movement culminated in his most noted work: *The Religious Consciousness: A Psychological Study* (1920). Meanwhile he had returned, after completing his Ph.D., to Williams, where he advanced from instructor (1905) to Mark Hopkins Professor of Intellectual and Moral Philosophy (1917).

Drawn by his deep religious convictions toward the idealism of Royce and Palmer, yet influenced by his association with James, Pratt for a time found himself unable to accept either idealism or pragmatism. Nor could he share the position of the so-called New Realists, whose vigorous campaign against idealism, beginning in 1910, finally provoked him to commit himself philosophically, in his article "The Confessions of an Old Realist" (*Journal of Philosophy,* Dec. 7, 1916). He had already questioned the validity of pragmatism in *What Is Pragmatism?* (1909). The new realism with its "neutral monism" seemed to him to be no adequate reply to either pragmatism or idealism. In 1916, as the epistemological controversy grew, Pratt worked out his own "dualistic realism" and that year joined the evolving group that came to be known as the Critical Realists. Besides contributing to their *Essays in Critical Realism* (1920), he also published his own interpretation of this type of realism in his book *Matter and Spirit* (1922).

The chief work of Pratt's later years was in the field of Oriental religions. This growing interest was shared by his wife, Catherine Mariotti, whom he married in Milan, Italy, on Aug. 5, 1911. The daughter of an American mother and an Italian father and the sister-in-law of a Williams classmate of Pratt's, she retained her Catholic faith as he retained a nondenominational Protestant one; they sent their two children, David Mariotti and Edith Cornell, to the local Episcopal church. Together with his wife, Pratt used his sabbatical leaves from Williams (1913–14, 1923–24) to study religions in India, Ceylon, Burma, Siam, Indo-China, and Java, as well as in China and Japan. From these journeys came his *India and Its Faiths* (1915) and *The Pilgrimage of Buddhism* (1928). These contributions to the history and understanding of Oriental religions, along with his growing courses and other work in the appreciation and history of religions, became Pratt's major lifework and constitute what is generally regarded as his most enduring achievement.

Pratt was a visiting professor at the Chinese Christian University in 1923–24 and at Rabindranath Tagore's school in Santiniketan, India, in 1931–32, and he lectured at several American universities. In 1934 he was elected president of the American Theological Society and in 1935 of the Eastern Division of the American Philosophical Association. He spent much of his leisure time hiking in the hills and mountains surrounding Williamstown, until a blood clot resulted in the amputation of a leg in 1938. Pratt retired from teaching in 1943. The following year he died of a cerebral hemorrhage at his home in Williamstown, Mass. He was buried in the Williams College Cemetery.

[Other major publications by Pratt are: *Adventures in Philosophy and Religion* (1931), *Personal Realism* (1937), *Naturalism* (1939), *Can We Keep the Faith?* (1941), and the posthumous *Reason in the Art of Living* (1949), a textbook of ethics. See also his autobiographical statement in George P. Adams and William P. Montague, eds., *Contemporary Am. Philosophy* (1930), II, 213–19. A full bibliography of his writings is in Gerald E. Myers, ed., *Self, Religion, and Metaphysics: Essays in Memory of James Bissett Pratt* (1961), which also includes a biographical sketch by Myers and reminiscences of Pratt by William Ernest Hocking.]

HERBERT W. SCHNEIDER

PRICE, GEORGE MOSES (May 21, 1864–July 30, 1942), physician and public health worker, was born in Poltava, Russia, to Alexander and Leah (Schwartz) Price. He was educated at the Real Gymnasium in Poltava before joining the exodus of Russian Jews to the United States in 1882. On July 22, 1891, he married Anna Kopkin. They had two children, Lucy Ella and Leo.

Nothing is known of Price's first years in New York City, but by 1885, when he became a city sanitary inspector for the Tenth Ward, he had begun his lifelong effort to improve the industrial health conditions of his fellow immigrants in the ghetto garment shops and tenements of the Lower East Side. In 1894 he was appointed an inspector for the Tenement Commission. His earnings from these positions enabled him to attend the University Medical College (New York University), from which he received the M.D. degree in 1895. For the next two decades Price combined a career in the private practice

of medicine with one in public health, until 1904, as an inspector for the New York City Health Department.

Price's major accomplishments came as an outgrowth of his association with the International Ladies' Garment Workers Union, beginning in 1910. The cloakmakers' strike of that year ended with the signing of the "Protocol of Peace," a long-term agreement devised by Louis D. Brandeis [Supp. 3], one feature of which was the establishment of a Joint Board of Sanitary Control with responsibility for health and sanitation in the garment industry. Price was designated director of the board and remained in that capacity until its demise in 1925.

The board's first report, an investigation of working conditions in 1,243 coat and suit shops in the city, appeared shortly before the tragic Triangle Waist Company fire of March 1911, which took the lives of 142 young women operatives. The report had warned of fire hazards in the garment industry, and when public outrage forced the state legislature to create a State Factory Commission in August, Price was made director of investigation. With Price heading its inspection of manufacturing establishments, the commission issued two reports: the first, in 1912, recommended legislation to correct the most flagrant abuses in sanitation and fire safety; the second, in 1913, was an inquiry into wage rates in the different industries of the state.

Meanwhile, under Price's leadership, the Joint Board of Sanitary Control had undertaken to improve health conditions in the garment industry through the introduction of a sanitary label, certifying that the item of clothing had been produced under adequate health standards. The board also eliminated the common drinking cup and the roller towel as health hazards, sought to improve the quality of light and air in the factories, and prodded the industry into eliminating the worst sanitary and health abuses which remained as a legacy from sweatshop days. Price's inspired dedication to industrial health and safety enabled the Joint Board of Sanitary Control to survive the end of the Protocol in 1916 and to continue its pioneering joint union-management efforts to create healthful work environments in the industry. These efforts, combined with a gradual shift of the consumer garment market in New York City, led to the migration of the industry from lower Manhattan to the more spacious and sanitary midtown garment center.

In 1913, after the Joint Board's findings revealed that garment workers suffered from a high incidence of tuberculosis and other industry-related diseases, and that medical care for the immigrant labor force was virtually nonexistent, Price founded the Union Health Center, to which he thereafter devoted his full time. This was the first attempt by a trade union to provide medical services for its members and became a model for later union clinics developed during and after the New Deal period. Starting in a single room at union headquarters, it grew into a modern health facility, staffed by dozens of physicians and incorporating the latest medical techniques. The center stressed preventive medicine and undertook massive health education programs for the union's members. Price also persuaded the I.L.G.W.U. to establish an insurance scheme whereby a member incapable of working would receive a weekly stipend during his illness.

Price wrote several books on industrial hygiene and public health, one of which, *The Modern Factory: Safety, Sanitation and Welfare* (1914), was translated into many languages and helped spur factory reforms in a number of industrial countries. He died at his home in Manhattan at the age of seventy-eight, of cerebral thrombosis and general arteriosclerosis. His work as director of the Union Health Center was continued by his son, Dr. Leo Price.

[Julius Henry Cohen, *Law and Order in Industry* (1916), pp. 43–60, and *They Builded Better Than They Knew* (1946), pp. 238–44; Lewis L. Lorwin, *The Women's Garment Workers* (1924), pp. 466–81; "The Common Welfare," *Survey,* Feb. 1, 1913, pp. 557–59; N. Y. State Factory Commission, *First Report* (1912) and *Second Report* (1913); obituaries in *N. Y. Times,* July 31, 1942, and *Jour. Am. Medic. Assoc.,* Aug. 29, 1942.]

HYMAN BERMAN

PRYOR, ARTHUR W. (Sept. 22, 1870–June 18, 1942), trombonist, bandmaster, composer, and recording artist, was born in St. Joseph, Mo., to Samuel Daniel Pryor and Mary A. or Mollie (Coker) Pryor. His father was a popular Missouri bandmaster, his mother a pianist. Arthur was one of three brothers, all of whom followed musical careers. A child prodigy, he studied piano, violin, bass viol, cornet, and alto horn, and by the age of eleven had become an accomplished performer on the valve trombone. He then taught himself to play the slide trombone. His desire to master the instrument became an obsession, and he is said to have practiced ten hours daily during his teens.

In 1889 Pryor became soloist with the touring band of Signor Alessandro Liberati. He declined, however, a similar opportunity the next year with the band of Patrick Gilmore [*q.v.*] in order to become conductor of the Stanley Opera Company in Denver. Pryor's rise to national fame began in 1892 when he was selected for the newly formed band of John Philip Sousa [*q.v.*] in Chicago. After several months he became featured trombone soloist, and about 1895, assistant conductor. The association with Sousa was an inspiration to Pryor, and in concerts throughout the United States and Europe his playing brought him international renown.

Determined not to be surpassed on his instrument, Pryor developed his technique to such a degree that he was called the "Paganini of the trombone." He employed many artificial slide positions and tricks, such as three-note chords, and was outstanding in his production of both high notes and pedal tones. To exhibit his virtuosity, he composed several solos for himself that required the use of these and other devices. His wizardry as a trombonist was acknowledged by Sousa, who stated many times that Pryor was without equal and that he had explored the possibilities of the trombone to a greater degree than any other man, a judgment shared by band musicians who heard him in his prime. He was also known, however, for his lyric playing of simple songs. He had a distinctive rapid natural vibrato which his brother Walter attributed to a partial facial paralysis resulting from a boyhood farm accident.

In the summer of 1903, after having performed more than ten thousand solos with Sousa, Pryor formed his own band by reorganizing a group his father had established before his death. Known for a short time as the American Band, and thereafter as Pryor's Band, it rivaled Sousa's in excellence and made six coast-to-coast tours between 1903 and 1909. Thereafter the Pryor band performed chiefly at expositions and amusement parks, and in later years made several series of radio broadcasts. Among regular summer engagements were those at Asbury Park, N. J. (seventeen seasons), Willow Grove Park near Philadelphia (ten seasons), Royal Palm Park, Miami (ten seasons), Coney Island, New York City, and Atlantic City, N. J. As a conductor Pryor was known for his brief but violent outbursts of temper over inaccurate playing during performances. These were disconcerting to new players, but his ire immediately subsided and was promptly forgotten, and he was otherwise kindly and democratic in his relations with his men.

Pryor made approximately one thousand phonograph recordings over a period of nearly thirty years, principally for the Victor Talking Machine Company and nearly all by the acoustic process, before the days of the microphone. Most were with his own band or as director of a studio band, but more than sixty were trombone solos. He was one of the first to create special band arrangements for recording. Records made by Pryor's Band far outnumbered those of any other American concert band.

As a composer, Pryor had some three hundred musical works to his credit. His most popular was a novelty tune, "The Whistler and His Dog." Although most of his compositions were very short, he wrote three operettas: *Uncle Tom's Cabin, On the Eve of Her Wedding Day,* and *Jingaboo.* He had a flair for producing cakewalk and ragtime tunes, such as "Little Nell," and for marches, such as "On Jersey Shore." Among his more popular trombone solos were "Love Thoughts," "The Patriot," and variations on "Blue Bells of Scotland." He was a charter member (1914) of the American Society of Composers, Authors and Publishers (ASCAP) and of the American Bandmasters Association (1929).

Pryor was married on Feb. 19, 1895, to Maud Russell of Salt Lake City. Their two children also became active in the entertainment field, Roger as a movie actor and radio announcer and Arthur, Jr., as a radio producer and advertising executive. Pryor was an Episcopalian by faith. With his wife, he retired in 1933 to a farm at West Long Branch, N. J., where he taught music at his leisure. He died there of a cerebral hemorrhage and was buried in the local Glenwood Cemetery.

[Glenn Bridges, *Pioneers in Brass* (1965); Harry W. Schwartz, *Bands of America* (1957); Kenneth Berger, *Band Encyc.* (1960); John Philip Sousa, *Marching Along* (1928); Nolbert Hunt Quayle, "Stars and Stripes Forever," *Instrumentalist,* Oct. 1954; obituary in *N. Y. Times,* June 19, 1942; interview, "Sousa and His Mission," *Music,* July 1899; personal interviews with Louis Morris, Donald Bassett, Harold Stambaugh, and Fred Pfaff, former members of Pryor's Band; death certificate; correspondence with the St. Joseph Public Lib.]

PAUL E. BIERLEY

PURDY, CORYDON TYLER (May 17, 1859–Dec. 26, 1944), structural engineer, closely associated with the early development of the steel-framed skyscraper, was born in Grand Rapids, Wis. (later Wisconsin Rapids), the first son and first of three children of Samuel Jones Purdy, a carpenter and joiner, and Emma Jane (Tyler) Purdy. His parents, whose English forebears had come to America in the early eighteenth century, had moved to Wisconsin from New York state. Corydon Purdy was educated in the local public schools and at the University of Wisconsin. Entering in 1881, he left after his freshman year to join the Chicago, Milwaukee & St. Paul Railroad as a draftsman associated with the construction

of the new line between Chicago and Evanston, Ill., but returned in 1883, completed his undergraduate study in 1885 with a degree of Bachelor of Science in Civil Engineering, and added a year's graduate study to earn the degree of Civil Engineer in 1886. During his graduate year and the year following he also held the position of city engineer of Eau Claire, Wis. Purdy worked as an engineer for the Keystone Bridge Company in 1888 and 1889, and in the latter year he established a partnership in Chicago with Charles G. Wade. Although the firm specialized in the design of steel bridges before its dissolution in 1891, it was also responsible for the structural system of the Rand McNally Building in Chicago, which involved the first all-steel skeleton ever used.

An architectural revolution was in the making, its major phase then occurring in Chicago, and Purdy was quick to see the possibilities of steel framing for high-building construction. He turned completely from bridge to building design, and after a short-lived partnership with J. N. Phillips (1891–92), he founded a new firm with Lightner Henderson in 1893, which was to continue as a corporation after the latter's death in 1916. Purdy's rise to prominence was spectacular, a consequence not only of his own energy but also of the rapidity with which building techniques were evolving in Chicago during the heroic decade of the 1890's. He was concerned with the construction of high buildings as early as 1891, when he designed the iron frames of two that fell in the skyscraper class at the time, the twelve-story Boyce Building and the fourteen-story Ellsworth Building, both completed in 1892. The skeleton of the Old Colony Building (1894) was the first from Purdy's hand in which steel was used extensively, and probably the first in which portal arches were adopted for wind bracing. The famous Marquette Building in Chicago, a skyscraper classic also completed in 1894, is the first of his works with a frame constructed entirely of steel.

Purdy and Henderson opened a New York office in that year, and shortly after the turn of the century they opened branch offices in Boston, Montreal, Seattle, Vancouver, and Havana. The best known of the firm's New York skyscrapers are the Fuller (commonly known as the Flatiron) Building (1903), unique because of its narrow triangular plan, and the Metropolitan Tower (1909), the highest building in the world at the time it was completed. In 1896 George A. Fuller, one of the leading building contractors of Chicago, asked Purdy to establish a New York office for him and persuaded the busy engineer to manage it for one year. In 1898 the office of

Purdy and Henderson added to their designing activities the role of structural consultants to the United States Realty and Construction Company. The engineers received international attention in 1900 when they accepted an invitation from the United States government to prepare an exhibit on steel-frame construction for the Paris Exposition of that year. After the disastrous Baltimore fire of 1904, Mayor E. Clay Timanus engaged Purdy as the consulting engineer for the revision of the city's building code, a long overdue step that greatly stimulated local progress in both steel and reinforced-concrete construction.

Purdy's mastery of the structural design of large and complex buildings—among them hotels, banks, department stores, newspaper headquarters, many office towers, and the Union Station in Toronto (1927)—inevitably led to invitations to lecture before engineering societies and at colleges. His paper on the New York Times Building, which was concerned with the problem of vibration in tall structures, was read before a meeting of the Institute of Engineers of Great Britain and brought its author the award of the Institute's Telford Premium in 1909. Purdy retired as president of his firm in 1917 but continued his association as chairman of the board of directors until his death. In later years he devoted increasing time to the management of a farm near Monroe, N. Y., which had been a family property since 1734. The one nonprofessional office he held was membership on the board of directors of the National Child Welfare Association. In religion he was a Congregationalist. He was twice married: to Eugenia Cushing of Turner, Maine, in 1889 and, following her death, to Rose Evelyn Morse of Livermore, Maine, on Mar. 19, 1892. By his second wife he had one child, Corydon Phillips. In his last years Purdy made his home in Melbourne, Fla., and it was there that he died, of a coronary thrombosis, at the age of eighty-five.

[Memoir of Purdy by P. J. Reidy in Am. Soc. of Civil Engineers, *Transactions,* CX (1945), 1797-1800; obituary in *Civil Engineering,* Feb. 1945; *Who Was Who in America,* vol. II (1950); death record from Fla. Bureau of Vital Statistics; father's occupation from 1860 and 1870 census schedules (courtesy of State Hist. Soc. of Wis.). For Purdy's Chicago buildings see: *Lakeside Annual Directory of the City of Chicago,* 1891-94; Carl W. Condit, *The Chicago School of Architecture* (1964); and Frank A. Randall, *Hist. of the Development of Building Construction in Chicago* (1949).]

CARL W. CONDIT

PYLE, ERNEST TAYLOR (Aug. 3, 1900– Apr. 18, 1945), newspaper columnist and war correspondent, popularly known as Ernie Pyle, was born on a farm southwest of Dana, Ind., the only child of William Clyde Pyle and Maria (Taylor) Pyle. The forebears of both parents were mostly Scottish and English. His father, a tenant farmer, was a native of Dana; his mother came from Illinois. The slight, shy, red-haired boy grew up a Methodist. After graduating from high school in 1918, he joined the navy but was still in training when the war ended. He then enrolled in journalism at Indiana University. A restless youth, he dropped out of school in his senior year, in 1923, and served for a short time as a reporter on the *La Porte* (Ind.) *Herald Argus* before taking a job on the copy desk of the Scripps-Howard *Daily News* in Washington, D. C. In 1926 he moved to New York City, where he was a copy editor on the *Evening World* and the *Evening Post.* Rejoining the Washington *Daily News* at the end of 1927, he soon advanced from telegraph editor to aviation editor, and then, in 1932, to managing editor.

Ernie Pyle's career as a syndicated columnist began in 1935. That year, to shake off the lingering effects of an influenza attack, he took a three-month sick leave and toured the country in an automobile, accompanied by his wife, Geraldine Elizabeth Siebolds, a native of Langdon, Minn., whom he had married on July 7, 1925. Upon returning to Washington, he wrote up their travel experiences for syndication as a fill-in for the vacationing columnist Heywood Broun [Supp. 2]. Pyle's informal, chatty columns were popular with newspaper readers, many of whom were beginning to make automobile tours, and the Scripps-Howard management created the post of roving correspondent for him. Thereafter he and "that girl who rides with me"—the Pyles had no children—crossed the continent thirty-five times and traveled in Mexico, South America, and Hawaii, gathering material for hundreds of columns on subjects ranging from the Dionne quintuplets to the lepers of Molokai.

With the outbreak of World War II, Pyle went overseas. His coverage of the Nazi bombing of London in 1940 was so graphic that his dispatches were cabled back for British readers. As he accompanied the military forces to the successive fronts, his daily war reports, written in folksy style and including the names and hometowns of countless "G.I. Joes," made many readers feel that he was writing them personal letters. During the North African campaign he developed deep affection for the combat infantryman. The rugged invasion of Sicily in July 1943 exhausted "the little guy"—he weighed only 110 pounds—and he flew home to Albuquerque, N. Mex., for rest and to patch up his homelife. His wife, to whom he was devoted, had for some years suffered from an emotional disorder that involved periodic depression, compulsive drinking, and more than one suicide attempt. With the concurrence of her doctors he had divorced her in 1942, in a futile attempt to stimulate her efforts toward mental health, but had remarried her by proxy on Mar. 10, 1943. She died late in 1945.

A home-front celebrity at the age of forty-three, Pyle was showered with lecture and radio invitations, virtually all of which he rejected, though he did authorize a motion picture based on his war career, *The Story of G.I. Joe* (1945), with Burgess Meredith as Pyle. Returning to the Italian front, he wrote his most famous column, on the death of Capt. Henry T. Waskow of Belton, Texas, to which the Washington *Daily News* devoted its entire front page (Jan. 10, 1944). Although ill with anemia, Pyle covered the Anzio beachhead, where he narrowly escaped death. In April 1944 he went to England and, while awaiting the invasion of Normandy, received the Pulitzer Prize for his war correspondence. After covering the liberation of Paris, Pyle, who had been overseas twenty-nine months and had written 700,000 words on the war, again returned home for a rest, though condemning himself as a "deserter." In the United States he received honorary degrees from Indiana University and the University of New Mexico. His column now appeared in more than 200 papers, with a combined circulation of 14,000,000, and a collection of his war columns published as *Brave Men* (1944) brought his personal earnings to more than half a million dollars.

Though fearful that his "chances" were "used up," Pyle, half bald and gray, with a thin, gentle face, chose to return to the battlefront, this time with the navy in the Pacific. There on Apr. 17, 1945, he landed with the 77th Infantry Division on Ie Shima in the Ryukyus. After passing the night under fire in a former Japanese dugout, he started for the front the next morning in a jeep and was caught in a machine gun ambush. Taking refuge in a ditch, he was killed instantly a few minutes later when he raised his head. Buried where he fell, his body was later moved to Okinawa and then to the National Memorial Cemetery of the Pacific, Punchbowl Crater, near Honolulu. Ernie Pyle's sensitive understanding of the average soldier and his feelings had made him one of the most widely admired of all war correspondents.

[Pyle's other books are *Ernie Pyle in England* (1941), *Here Is Your War* (1947), *Last Chapter* (1946), and *Home Country* (1947), the last a post-humous collection of his prewar travel pieces. Pyle's friend and co-worker, Lee G. Miller, wrote and compiled the two fullest biographical sources, *An Ernie Pyle Album: Indiana to Ie Shima* (1946) and *The Story of Ernie Pyle* (1950). See also: *Who Was Who in America*, vol. II (1950); *N. Y. Times*, Apr. 19, 1945; *Current Biog.*, 1941; Stanley J. Kunitz, ed., *Twentieth Century Authors*, First Supp. (1955); John E. Drewry, ed., *More Post Biogs.* (1947); Rafer Brent, ed., *Great War Stories* (1957); John Mason Brown, *Seeing Things* (1946); Charles Fisher, *The Columnists* (1944); Mildred and Milton Lewis, *Famous Modern Newspaper Writers* (1962); Warren Price, *The Literature of Journalism* (1959); Lincoln K. Barnett, *Writing on Life: Sixteen Close-ups* (1951). An excellent bust was produced by the sculptor Jo Davidson in 1944. A portrait of Pyle by Dean Cornwell, painted for *True* magazine, is at Indiana Univ., Bloomington.]

IRVING DILLIARD

QUEZON, MANUEL LUIS (Aug. 19, 1878– Aug. 1, 1944), first president of the Commonwealth of the Philippines, was born in Baler, Tayabas (now Quezon) Province, on the island of Luzon. He was the elder of two sons of Lucio Quezon and his wife, Maria Dolores Molina, who also had a son by a previous marriage. Both parents were *mestizos* (of part Spanish, part Filipino descent). Although they were poor, their position as schoolteachers was prestigious, and they owned a small rice paddy; they were the only Filipinos in the town who spoke Spanish. Manuel was educated by his parents and the parish priest until the age of eleven, when his parents sent him to Manila for secondary schooling at the "college" of San Juan de Letrán. After graduating in 1893, he entered the University of Santo Tomás and began to study law. When revolution broke out against Spain in 1896, Quezon, attracted to the islands' Spanish culture and mindful of his family's obligations to the Spanish clergy of Baler, declined to participate. The United States, however, had no claims upon him; and after fighting had begun between Filipino and American forces in February 1899, he joined the insurrection and served as an officer in Emilio Aguinaldo's army. He surrendered in 1901 and, after an embittering period in prison, resumed his legal studies.

Quezon received the LL.B. degree in 1903 and entered practice in Manila. Later that year he moved to Tayabas Province. There he came to the attention of American officials and through them secured the patronage of Trinidad H. Pardo de Tavera, leader of the pro-American Federalista party. In 1906, running on a platform advocating immediate independence, Quezon was elected governor of Tayabas; and in 1907 his province elected him to the first Philippine Assembly, where he became floor leader of the majority party, the Nacionalista. In 1909 the Assembly chose him as one of the two Philippine resident commissioners to the United States, a position he held until 1916.

Quezon's attitude toward his people's future relations with the United States was ambiguous. A dramatic orator, reputedly the most stirring in the islands, he was all fire and passion in his public advocacy of early independence. In a famous speech he exclaimed, "I would prefer a government run like hell by Filipinos to one run like heaven by Americans . . ." (Kalaw, p. 209). Nevertheless, he valued modernization, prosperity, and civil liberties more than independence, and recognized that they were likely to be realized more fully if independence were at least postponed. For this reason, he cooperated with the United States in many matters that otherwise might have become issues between the two peoples. He supported the introduction of the English language and defended increases in taxation made necessary by programs for the improvement of transportation and communications, the reform of the courts and the currency system, the provision of health, sanitation, and agricultural services, and the extension of education. Privately, within the Nacionalista party, he fought his colleagues' desire to replace Americans in high technical and professional offices in the government with unproven Filipinos. When, in 1908, Speaker Sergio Osmeña questioned confirming a franchise to English and American railroad developers because it perpetually alienated the patrimony of the Filipino people, Quezon, at the request of American officials, engineered its acceptance by the Assembly.

Independence, however, was the most popular and emotional issue in Philippine politics; and by becoming resident commissioner in Washington, Quezon associated his political future with advocacy of the national cause. In 1911 he cooperated with William Atkinson Jones, anti-imperialist chairman of the House Committee on Insular Affairs, in preparing a bill to give the islands early independence, and he played a leading role two years later in Wilson's selection of the strongly anti-imperialist Francis Burton Harrison to be governor general. Personally, however, Quezon considered Harrison naive, and in the winter of 1913–14 he secretly urged the Wilson administration to propose a new bill designed to give Filipinos not independence, but greater autonomy and the right to choose independence after economic growth and the spread of literacy had been achieved. When no such action was taken, he turned again to Jones and helped draft the second Jones Bill, which provided for an elective senate and other steps toward autonomy, but deferred independence until a stable government had been established. For this bill he lobbied strenuously and adeptly. After its passage in slightly modified form in 1916, he returned to the Philippines a national hero.

Elected president of the new Philippine Senate, Quezon shared leadership of the government with Speaker Osmeña and Governor Harrison from 1917 to 1921. He and Osmeña presided over the Filipinization of the government and certain newly nationalized industries, filling many positions with political allies and, in effect, rearing two power blocs in preparation for a showdown between themselves. Quezon personally became president of the Manila Railway.

Harding's election in 1920 and his appointment of Gen. Leonard Wood [q.v.] to replace Harrison made further Filipinization impossible. Quezon used the period of retrenchment to consolidate his position. In 1922–23 he challenged and defeated Osmeña for control of the Philippine legislature and the Nacionalista party, then precipitated a government crisis which led to the resignation of Wood's Filipino cabinet. By these two moves, he established himself as the symbol of opposition to colonial status and as the leader of his people. Normal working relations were restored between the executive and the legislature after Wood's death.

The Great Depression cooled American interest in imperial responsibilities, and in 1932–33 a special mission headed by Osmeña and Assembly Speaker Manuel Roxas obtained from Congress the Hare-Hawes-Cutting Act, which provided for Philippine independence after ten years. To have independence won by his political rivals, however, was intolerable to Quezon. He launched a bitter fight against the act, concentrating on its provisions regarding future Philippine-American trade relations and retention of Philippine bases by the United States army and navy. First deposing Osmeña and Roxas from their offices and then securing rejection of the act by the legislature, Quezon himself took a new mission to the United States and obtained from Congress the Tydings-McDuffie Act (1934). Although it differed little except in removing American army bases after independence, it was unanimously ratified by the Philippine legislature.

In 1935, after forming a new coalition with Osmeña and his followers, Quezon was overwhelmingly elected president of the Commonwealth, the transitional government prior to full independence. He dedicated his administration to achieving military preparedness, economic stability, and "social justice." These goals proved elusive, however; and agrarian and labor discontent grew to be major problems. In response, Quezon began to speak of a new "Distributive State" and secured the passage of social legislation setting minimum wages, establishing an eight-hour workday, and defining the conditions of agricultural tenancy. The laws, however, were minimal and poorly enforced. Simultaneously, he steadily centralized power in his own hands. By 1940 he was openly calling for the abolition of political parties. That year the National Assembly voted him extensive emergency powers over the economy and amended the constitution to allow him two four-year terms instead of one term of six years. In 1941 he was reelected by a margin of approximately seven to one.

At the outbreak of war, Quezon retreated first to Corregidor and then to the United States, where with Osmeña he maintained a war cabinet. In 1943, at his own insistence, the United States Congress extended his tenure of office. He died at Saranac Lake, N. Y., in 1944 of a long-standing case of pulmonary tuberculosis. He left his wife, Aurora Aragon Quezon (his first cousin, whom he had married in Hong Kong on Dec. 14, 1918), and three children, Maria Aurora, Maria Zeneida, and Manuel Luis. A fourth child, Luisa Corazon Paz, had died in infancy. Born a Catholic, but for more than twenty years a Freemason, Quezon had returned to Catholicism in the 1930's; a Catholic ceremony preceded his burial in the family plot in Manila North Cemetery.

Quezon was a mercurial and charismatic figure. His politics were opportunistic and his personal life often scandalous, but an intensely dramatic personality and an unusually acute mind gave him ascendancy over his rivals. In private he was by turns charming, impulsive, and menacing; in public he seemed the embodiment of Philippine nationalism. He loved the Philippines, but also admired America. His legacy to his people, apart from a cult of personality and the centralization of political power in the presidency, is the reconciliation of two once hostile nations.

[Quezon's personal and official papers are housed in the Nat. Library, Manila (available in part on microfilm at the Univ. of Mich.). It is essential to compare them with relevant materials in: the records of the U. S. Bureau of Insular Affairs, especially file 4325, in the Nat. Archives, Washington; the Journal of W. Cameron Forbes (Lib. of Cong. and Houghton Lib., Harvard Univ.) and Forbes's letter files and scrapbooks (Houghton Lib.); the papers of Woodrow Wilson, Francis Burton Harrison, and Leonard Wood (Lib. of Cong.), Henry L. Stimson (Yale Univ.), Frank Murphy (Univ. of Mich.), and Franklin D. Roosevelt (Hyde Park, N. Y.). Quezon's memoirs, *The Good Fight* (1946), were written during the war when he was separated from his papers. There are two admiring biographies, Sol H. Gwekoh, *Manuel L. Quezon: His Life and Career* (1948), and Carlos Quirino, *Quezon: Man of Destiny* (1935), but no recent scholarly work. For his public career, see

Teodoro A. Agoncillo, *A Short Hist. of the Philippines* (1969); Roy W. Curry, *Woodrow Wilson and Far Eastern Policy, 1913–1921* (1957); Michael P. Onorato, "Manuel L. Quezon, Governor General Leonard Wood, and the Cabinet Crisis of July 17, 1923" and "Independence Rejected: The Philippines, 1924," in his *A Brief Rev. of Am. Interest in Philippine Development and Other Essays* (1968); Theodore Friend, *Between Two Empires: The Ordeal of the Philippines, 1929–1946* (1965); and Charles O. Houston, "The Philippine Commonwealth, 1934–1946," *Univ. of Manila Jour. of East Asiatic Studies,* July 1953. For personal recollections, see Teodoro M. Kalaw, *Aide-de-Camp to Freedom,* translated by Maria Kalaw Katigbak (1965); and Claude A. Buss, "Charismatic Leadership in Southeast Asia: Manuel Luis Quezon," *Solidarity,* July–Sept. 1966. See also obituary in *N. Y. Times,* Aug. 2, 1944.]

PETER W. STANLEY

RACHMANINOFF, SERGEI VASILYE-VICH (Apr. 2, 1873–Mar. 28, 1943), composer, pianist, and conductor, was born on his parents' estate of Oneg, near Novgorod, Russia. His father, Vasili Arkadyevich Rachmaninoff, a well-born army officer, was wealthy, kind, and profligate; his mother, Lubov Petrovna (Butakova) Rachmaninoff, brought more wealth to the family, which her husband soon squandered. After he had lost the several estates he had acquired, the family, its social position lowered, moved in 1882 to a crowded flat in St. Petersburg. Soon afterward the father, by agreement, departed from the family circle.

Both parents played the piano, the father's side of the family being especially musical, and Sergei, the second son and third of six children, showed musical talent at an early age. He attended the St. Petersburg Conservatory (1882–85), where he excelled in music and piano but, idle and lazy, was unsuccessful in his other studies. On the advice of his cousin, the distinguished pianist-conductor Alexander Siloti [Supp. 3], he was sent to the Moscow Conservatory to study with Nikolai Zverev (1885–88), a strict disciplinarian. In 1886 he entered Anton Arensky's harmony class, then studied composition with Sergei Taneyev and piano with Siloti. He composed a scherzo for orchestra in 1887 and wrote numerous piano pieces and songs. He also wrote sketches for an opera, *Esmeralda* (based on Hugo's *Notre Dame de Paris*), in 1888, but did not complete it. That same year he met his first cousin Natalia Satina, also a gifted pianist, and they were married on Apr. 29, 1902. They had two daughters, Irina and Tatiana.

Rachmaninoff graduated from the Moscow Conservatory as a pianist in 1891 and as a composer in 1892, on the latter occasion receiving the gold medal for his one-act opera *Aleko*. This was the year, too, in which he composed his famous Prelude in C-sharp Minor, one of the most popular piano pieces ever written. He now earned his living as a piano teacher (an occupation he did not enjoy—he never taught after 1918) and continued to compose. His First Symphony, in D Minor, performed in St. Petersburg on Mar. 15, 1897, was badly played, and its poor reception deeply discouraged him. In 1900 a period of intense depression was cured by Dr. Nikolai Dahl, a Moscow neurologist, to whom Rachmaninoff the following year dedicated his Second Piano Concerto, probably the most popular work of its kind in the twentieth century.

Rachmaninoff next turned to conducting, and in two years at the Bolshoi Theatre in Moscow (1904–06) proved to be outstanding. The desire for more time to compose took him to Dresden, Germany, where he chiefly lived from 1906 to 1909. In the fall of the latter year he made his first trip to the United States. His American debut was in a recital at Smith College, Northampton, Mass., on Nov. 4, 1909; on Nov. 28 he was soloist in the world premiere of his splendid Third Piano Concerto in New York City, with Walter Damrosch conducting. While in America, Rachmaninoff was offered the conductorship of the Boston Symphony Orchestra, which he declined, as he did when it was offered a second time in 1918. He returned to Moscow and lived there from 1910 to 1917 (some of that time conducting the Moscow Philharmonic Society Orchestra). The Bolshevik revolution drove him out of his country, and he never saw it again.

He now deliberately set out on a career as virtuoso pianist, becoming one of the finest in the history of music. Always a great artist, he retrained and redisciplined himself to an incredible degree of perfection, and his musical sensibility guaranteed interpretations of startling but convincing originality. Long and exhausting tours took him all over America and Europe, where his individualistic playing—both reflective and demoniac—combined with his striking, dour-visaged appearance to make an unforgettable impression. His phonograph recordings, too, both solo and with orchestra, were epoch-making; those unable to hear him in person could (and can) still be amazed by his art. While he pursued this arduous career, his composing was curtailed but never discontinued. Several large and important works were produced during his self-imposed exile from Russia: the Fourth Piano Concerto (1926), "Variations on a Theme by Corelli" (piano solo, 1931), "Rhapsody on a Theme by Paganini" (piano and orchestra, 1934), Third Symphony (1936), and "Symphonic Dances" (in two versions, for orchestra and for two pianos, 1940).

Rachmaninoff was one of the most important composers of the twentieth century, and he achieved this eminence in spite of the fact that he was not progressive in the usual sense of the term. He could not abide modernity as practiced by the musical revolutionaries who were his contemporaries and successors, and he took no pains to conceal his antipathies. Joseph Yasser (in *Tempo,* Winter 1951–52) quotes him as saying, in substance: "I am organically incapable of understanding modern music, therefore I cannot possibly like it; just as I cannot like a language, let us say, whose meaning and structure are absolutely foreign to me." Disciples of the musical vanguard had little use for Rachmaninoff's music, characterizing it as passé, old-fashioned, cloying, the last vestige of a Russian romanticism already dead. They prophesied its early extinction; but nearly three decades after his death his work was still part of the standard concert repertoire. It has the staying power of great art, derived from the composer's artistic integrity and his ability to realize fully his creative capacity.

Rachmaninoff's compositional technic was enormous; he was eminently sincere in his utterance and persuasively lyrical in his musical thinking. His music, though not deliberately nationalistic, is unmistakably Slavic both in texture and tone color. He has been compared, not unfairly, with Tchaikovsky, but his manner and style are his own. Although his accomplishments in the field of orchestra, choral music, and song are notable, his writing for piano demands special comment. An absolute master of the keyboard, he created large works (the concertos and the *Paganini Rhapsody*) and small (especially the Preludes and the "Études Tableaux") that exploit every resource of the instrument, often with highly original figuration, in moods that are lyrical, reflective, dramatic, melancholy, and triumphant. Though not advanced in the contemporary sense, his harmony is thoroughly adequate for the message he conveys.

Rachmaninoff was a prolific composer who wrote for a variety of mediums. To his three published operas (*Aleko, The Miserly Knight, Francesca da Rimini*) must be added the unfinished *Monna Vanna*. His orchestral works include three symphonies and two symphonic poems. His chamber music is comparatively scanty, but it includes a fine cello sonata, two piano trios, and two short pieces for string quartet. His choral works, headed by *The Bells* (really a secular oratorio, based on Poe's poem), contain some remarkably impressive contributions to music of the Russian Orthodox Church, in which he had been reared. He wrote more than seventy songs, many of them truly eloquent, and nearly a hundred piano pieces, including two sonatas, two notable sets of variations, and two suites for two pianos.

Although Rachmaninoff found a warm welcome in the United States, he considered himself a loyal subject of the Czar and for years refused to become an American citizen. His dislike of the Soviet regime remained steadfast until 1941, when the German invasion of Russia impelled him to change his position to the extent of supporting Russian relief. In 1942 he and his wife settled in California, eventually acquiring a home in Beverly Hills. Here, on Feb. 1, 1943, they both became American citizens, at last officially embraced by a country that had long appreciated the musical wealth they brought to it. Active to the end, Rachmaninoff died at home only a few weeks later, having succumbed to melanoma, a rapid form of cancer. He was buried in Kensico Cemetery, Valhalla, N. Y.

[Though Rachmaninoff had to leave behind most manuscripts of his early work when he departed from Russia, an extensive family archive covering his career since 1917, systematically organized by his sister-in-law Sophie Satina (herself a noted geneticist) and augmented by his daughter Irina R. Wolkonsky, is in the Lib. of Cong. A brief description of the original gift will be found in the Library's *Quart. Jour. of Current Acquisitions*, Nov. 1951. Sergei Bertensson and Jay Leyda, *Sergei Rachmaninoff: A Lifetime in Music* (1956), is the best biography. See also Sergei Rachmaninoff, *Rachmaninoff's Recollections* (1934); Lyle Watson, *Rachmaninoff: A Biog.* (1939); John Culshaw, *Sergei Rachmaninoff* (1949); the Rachmaninoff number of *Tempo*, Winter 1951–52; and Sophie Satina in *Jour. of the Am. Musicological Soc.*, Spring 1968, pp. 120–21.]

EDWARD N. WATERS

RAND, EDWARD KENNARD (Dec. 20, 1871–Oct. 28, 1945), classicist and medievalist, was born in South Boston, Mass., the second of five children and only son of Edward Augustus and Mary Frances (Abbott) Rand. Both parents were descended from seventeenth-century English settlers in New England; Rand's father was a native of Portsmouth, N. H., his mother of Thomaston, Maine. The elder Rand, a graduate of Bowdoin College, was a Congregational minister who in 1880 entered the Episcopal ministry. He augmented his income by publishing more than fifty books, most of them juveniles, and was thus enabled to meet both the family expenses and those imposed by his calling, including the erection of church buildings in three successive parishes in the Boston vicinity.

Young Rand attended schools in Boston and Watertown, Mass., and graduated from Harvard summa cum laude in 1894, with honors in classics. He then enrolled for a year at the Harvard Divinity School, where he studied Dante with Charles Eliot Norton [*q.v.*] and scholastic phi-losophy with George Santayana. After two years of teaching Latin literature at the University of Chicago, he returned to Cambridge to prepare for the ministry and spent the academic year 1897–98 as a student at the Episcopal Theological School. Going back to Chicago for the summer, he took a course with the New Testament scholar Caspar René Gregory [*q.v.*], who opened up to Rand the new world of paleography. The call to holy orders apparently stilled, in the autumn of 1898 Rand went to Europe to continue his philological studies; in this first of his many visits to France he found in Tours "the heart of France and of all beauty." He matriculated at the University of Munich and, after beginning his studies under Eduard Wölfflin, entered upon a fruitful association with Ludwig Traube, who, he wrote, came to be his "master in Latin palaeography and all things mediaeval and much else." Rand received the Ph.D. in philology in 1900—again summa cum laude—and with Traube's backing published in the eminent *Jahrbücher für classische Philologie* his dissertation on the *De Fide Catholica* attributed to Boethius.

Rand returned to Harvard as instructor in Latin in 1901, was made professor in 1909, and held the Pope Professorship of Latin from 1931 until his retirement in 1942. In his teaching, whether at the seminar table, in a college classroom, or in a public lecture hall, he combined a mastery of his material and an often daring freshness of approach with clear exposition and engaging wit, qualities that were also evident in his writings. As a scholar, he never wearied of his research in philology and paleography as means to illuminate our knowledge of Roman and medieval cultures. His Lowell Institute lectures of 1928 discussed the merging of the Roman culture with that of the early Church fathers and the subsequent rise of medieval civilization. These lectures formed the basis of what was probably his most influential book, *Founders of the Middle Ages* (1928). In 1942 he delivered a second series of Lowell Lectures; these were published as *The Building of Eternal Rome* (1943). His other publications include several books—among them *Ovid and His Influence* (1925) and *The Magical Art of Virgil* (1931)—as well as more than a hundred scholarly articles and innumerable reviews. In addition to writings concerned with literary themes, he produced largely technical works in Latin paleography and textual criticism, notably his monumental *Studies in the Script of Tours* (2 vols., 1929–34) and an as yet unpublished critical text of the *Opuscula sacra* of Boethius. He also directed work on the Harvard edition of the Servian commentaries on Virgil and saw the first volume to completion just before his death. Rand was devoted to the poetry of both Horace and Virgil, himself spoke Latin fluently, and produced many facile compositions in Latin, notably his Harvard Tercentenary *Salutatio* and the goliardic Phi Beta Kappa poem of June 1935.

Rand was one of the founders (1925) and first president of the Mediaeval Academy of America, and editor for the first fourteen numbers of its quarterly journal, *Speculum*. He had earlier been president of the American Philological Association (1922–23). With his devotion to his subject and his genius for friendship, he maintained many close acquaintanceships on both sides of the Atlantic. In recognition of his high qualities as scholar, teacher, and friend he was presented in 1938 with a *Festschrift*. Among his honors were: life membership in the American Academy in Rome (of which he had been trustee); election to the British Academy and other learned societies abroad; and honorary doctorates from Manchester (1926), Western Reserve (1931), Trinity College, Dublin (1932), Glasgow (1936), Harvard (1941), Pennsylvania (1942), and Paris (1945, posthumous).

On June 20, 1901, Rand married Belle Brent Palmer of Louisville, Ky. They had no children. He remained an active member of the Episcopal Church throughout his life. Among the concerns of his last years was wartime aid to France and Great Britain, on behalf of which he wrote frequent letters to the press in 1940–41. He died of a heart attack in Cambridge, Mass., in his seventy-fourth year and was buried there in Mount Auburn Cemetery.

[Extensive materials (MS. and other) on Rand are in the Harvard Univ. Archives. Among printed materials, the most useful is the largely autobiographical record found in the successive *Reports* of the Harvard Class of 1894. See also: memorial minute of Harvard Faculty of Arts and Sciences, *Harvard Univ. Gazette*, Jan. 19, 1946; memoirs in *Speculum*, July 1946, and Am. Philological Assoc., *Proc.*, 1945; and the appreciations of Ludwig Bieler, in *Wiener Studien*, vol. LXIII (1948), and B. M. Peebles, in *Scriptorium*, vol. I, no. 1 (1946–47). Death record from Mass. Registrar of Vital Statistics. On Rand's father, see *Who Was Who in America*, vol. I (1942). Recordings of Rand in both English and Latin are kept in the Harvard Vocarium (Lamont Lib.). An oil portrait by E. Piutti-Barth (1929) is in the Harvard Portrait Collection.]
BERNARD M. PEEBLES

RAND, JAMES HENRY (May 29, 1859– Sept. 15, 1944), inventor and businessman, was born in Tonawanda, N. Y., the second son and third of nine children of Calvin Gordon Rand, a schoolteacher and farmer, and Almira Hershe (Long) Rand. His father, a descendant of John Rand, one of the founders of Charlestown, Mass.,

was a native of Batavia, N. Y.; he died when James was twelve. His mother was a great-grandchild of the first white child born on the Niagara frontier.

Rand attended a country school near Tonawanda and then a business school in nearby Brockport. At eighteen he took his first job, as a railroad telegraph operator. Three years later he became a cashier in a Tonawanda bank. There his natural curiosity and passion for detail served him well. Bank activity was increasing rapidly in the United States, and as the number of accounts grew, together with the number of bank services offered, the rising volume of paper work was becoming a serious problem. Rand noticed, while working at the Tonawanda bank, that bank clerks and bookkeepers spent an excessive amount of time searching for records in what were then "blind" card files, letter files, and ledgers, that is, files without dividers or indexes. He created what became known as a "visible" index system of dividers, colored signal strips, and tabs. Rand's system substantially increased the speed and efficiency of bank personnel, and he saw great commercial possibilities for the general use of his system in business offices and warehouses, in fact everywhere that information had to be filed and quickly found.

At first, however, Rand concentrated his attention on timesaving devices for banks. He formed his own firm, the Rand Ledger Company. His older brother, Benjamin Long Rand, served as vice-president and took charge of production, while Rand himself spent most of his time traveling to introduce potential users to his products and to solicit orders. The company's line of products was steadily supplemented by Rand's new inventions. These included index files for bank deposit tickets and checks, a stop-payment register, sorters, and similar devices. As sales increased, his firm acquired a nationwide reputation and opened sales offices in several major American cities.

On Jan. 8, 1884, Rand married Mary Jameson Scribner. They had five children: Adelaide Almira, James Henry, Mary Scribner, Mabel, and Philip. The older son, James Henry Rand, Jr. (1886–1968), entered the family business after his graduation from Harvard in 1908 and ran the company from 1910 to 1914 during his father's illness. Their views differed, however, on how best to further the growth of the firm. The younger Rand urged that a million dollars be spent on a nationwide advertising campaign. When his father, who preferred less spectacular and expensive methods of promotion, vetoed the proposal, young Rand left the firm and, with

$10,000 of borrowed money, started his own business, the American Kardex Company, in 1915.

The rivalry between father and son was always friendly; the latter wanted to prove to himself and to his father that he could prosper independently. Within five years, his new company's gross sales had exceeded a million dollars, and he yielded to his mother's suggestion that father and son resume their business association. In 1925 the two firms were combined as the Rand-Kardex Company, with the senior Rand as chairman and his son as president and general manager. Separately, the firms had been the nation's two largest manufacturers of record-keeping supplies; as merged, their holdings included factories in Canada and Germany, as well as 210 United States and foreign patents. The combined firms produced more than 4,000 separate products and operated the world's largest distribution network: 4,500 field representatives in 219 branch offices in the United States and 115 agencies in foreign countries. Rand-Kardex's primary customers were banks, insurance companies, libraries, and government agencies, for all of whom accurate record keeping was essential.

After their business reunion, the Rands began a vigorous program of mergers and acquisitions. These additions included the Library Bureau (which had originated the first vertical filing system in 1882) and the Safe-Cabinet Company (which pioneered fireproof record-keeping equipment). The younger Rand's efforts led to the merger in 1927 of Rand-Kardex with the Remington Typewriter Company (which had introduced the first noiseless typewriter in 1909 and the first electric typewriter in 1925). The resulting firm, the Remington-Rand Company, including all subsidiaries, had assets of $73,000,000 and earned a net profit of $2,800,000 during its first year of combined operations.

After 1927, when he became sixty-eight, James Rand, Sr., played a less active role in business, limiting his function at Remington-Rand to that of a director. He was a Republican and a Methodist, but with no particular interest in politics or organized religion. He enjoyed his family life, his privacy, and his unblemished business reputation. For some years Rand had maintained a home at North Falmouth, Mass., and it was there that he died, at the age of eighty-five, of bronchopneumonia and arteriosclerosis. Burial was in Oak Grove Cemetery, Falmouth.

[Rand shunned publicity and guarded his privacy so closely that personal material is scant. See Keene Sumner, "They Were Father and Son at Home but Rivals in Business," *American Mag.*, Feb. 1926; and the obituary in the *N. Y. Times*, Sept. 17, 1944. On his business dealings see: *ibid.*, Mar. 27, 1925, May 24, 1935, June 4, 1968; M. David Gould, "Remington-Rand," *Mag. of Wall Street*, Mar. 12, 1927; *Commercial & Financial Chronicle* (N. Y.), Feb. 12 and 19, 1927; *Barron's*, July 9, 1934; *Library Assoc. Record*, Jan.–Feb. 1915, pp. 18–23, Apr. 1921, pp. 116–222; Remington-Rand Co. annual reports; *Sperryscope*, vol. XVII, no. 2 (1968). For family data see Florence O. Rand, *A Genealogy of the Rand Family in the U. S.* (1898); other information from City of Tonawanda Public Lib. Death record from Mass. Registrar of Vital Statistics.]

ROBERT HESSEN

RANSON, STEPHEN WALTER (Aug. 28, 1880–Aug. 30, 1942), neurologist and anatomist, was born in Dodge Center, Minn., the youngest of three boys and three girls. His parents, Stephen William Ranson, a physician, and Mary Elizabeth (Foster) Ranson, were of English and Welsh lineage, natives, respectively, of Ottawa, Canada, and Vermont. They encouraged higher education for their children; three became physicians and two gained the Ph.D. degree.

Stephen Ranson graduated from the local high school, entered the University of Minnesota, and, following the example of one of his sisters, planned to become a psychologist. As his study progressed, however, his interest shifted to the physical structure of the nervous system, and during summer vacations at home he carried out animal experiments in a makeshift laboratory. His reading of the influential monograph by Henry H. Donaldson [Supp. 2], *The Growth of the Brain*, led him to transfer to the University of Chicago to concentrate on neurology. His credits there enabled him to receive the A.B. degree from Minnesota in 1902, after which he continued study at Chicago under Donaldson. He received the Ph.D. degree in 1905 with a thesis on "Retrograde Degeneration in Spinal Nerves." He next enrolled at Rush Medical College in Chicago, which granted him the M.D. degree in 1907, and after a year's internship at the Cook County Hospital he opened an office for the part-time practice of medicine. At the same time he became an assistant in anatomy at Northwestern University Medical School.

In 1910 Ranson was made associate professor of anatomy at Northwestern and abandoned his clinical career for one of teaching and research. He spent a year (1910–11) studying with Robert E. E. Wiedersheim at the University of Freiburg, and then returned to Northwestern as professor and chairman of the department of anatomy, a post he held for the next thirteen years. Ranson was a conscientious and able teacher, although he was less effective in classroom lectures than in the laboratory, where his enthusiasm for his field, his high standards of workmanship, and his insistence on logical thinking were a strong stimulus to individual students. He also exerted a wide influence through his textbook, *Anatomy of the Nervous System* (1920), which was the first full and adequate presentation of the subject; before his death he had prepared the seventh edition.

Ranson's interest in research, however, outweighed his concern for teaching. Hoping to find greater freedom for his own work, in 1924 he accepted an appointment as professor and head of the department of neuroanatomy and histology at the Washington University Medical School in St. Louis. Four years later he returned to Northwestern as professor of neurology to organize and direct the research of the newly founded Institute of Neurology, where he remained for the rest of his life. Ranson was an unusually able administrator and director of research at the Institute, whose laboratories issued some thirteen volumes of papers during his fourteen years as its head. His own bibliography contains about 200 titles, more than half deriving from work by him and his collaborators during this same period. Among other research, he investigated the processes of degeneration and regeneration of nerve fibers, the structure of the vagus nerve, vasomotor pathways, and the functional role of spinal ganglia; he also developed a pyridine silver stain that could differentiate the various components of nerve tissue. Perhaps his most significant contributions were his experimental studies of the function of the hypothalamus, through its influence on the pituitary gland and the autonomic nervous system, as the control center for the sympathetic nervous system, temperature regulation and water exchange in the body, emotional response, and sexual function.

In 1940 the Association for Research in Nervous and Mental Diseases published a volume of research papers on the hypothalamus dedicated to Ranson. Other honors that came to him included the presidency of the American Association of Anatomists (1938–40), membership on the editorial board of the *Archives of Neurology and Psychiatry,* and election to the National Academy of Sciences (1940).

Ranson was by nature dignified, yet unassuming and approachable. He was indifferent to formal social activities and spent his evenings largely in the quiet enjoyment of his family: his wife, Tessie Grier Rowland of Oak Park, Ill., whom he had married on Aug. 18, 1909, and their children, Stephen William (who became a physician), Margaret Jane, and Mary Elizabeth. His religious affiliation was Presbyterian. A gastric ulcer, which was particularly troublesome in his later years, further curtailed his activities outside the labora-

tory. In 1941 Ranson suffered a coronary thrombosis. He made a fairly good recovery, but a recurrence the next year, just after his sixty-second birthday, brought death almost instantly, at his home in Chicago. His remains were cremated at Chicago's Graceland Cemetery.

[Obituary articles (with photograph) in: *Anatomical Record,* Aug. 1943 (by Leslie B. Arey), *Archives of Neurology and Pathology,* Mar. 1943 (by Joseph C. Hinsey), and Northwestern Univ. Medic. School, *Quart. Bull.,* Winter 1942 (by Horace W. Magoun), with bibliography of Ranson's publications; Florence R. Sabin in Nat. Acad. Sci., *Biog. Memoirs,* vol. XXIII (1945), with photograph and bibliography; Horace W. Magoun in Webb Haymaker, *Founders of Neurology* (1953), pp. 77–80; Leslie B. Arey in *Northwestern Univ. Medic. School, 1859–1959* (1959), pp. 394–99; death record from Ill. Dept. of Public Health.]

LESLIE B. AREY

RECORD, SAMUEL JAMES (Mar. 10, 1881–Feb. 3, 1945), forester, was born in Crawfordsville, Ind., the son of Mary Minerva (Hutton) and James Knox Polk Records. (He later dropped the "s" from the family name.) Both parents were of English stock long resident in the United States. His father, a descendant of John Records who emigrated around 1732 to Sussex County, Del., was a farmer and schoolteacher.

After attending local schools, Sam Record entered Wabash College in Crawfordsville, graduating in 1903 with the B.A. degree. He then enrolled at the Yale University School of Forestry, but left after one year to become an assistant in the Division of Forestry (later the Forest Service) of the United States Department of Agriculture. In 1906 he took a leave of absence to serve for one semester as instructor in botany and forestry at Wabash College, from which he also received an M.A. that year. Upon returning to the Forest Service, Record made a reconnaissance of the public domain in the Ozarks which later served as a basis for establishing the Arkansas National Forest. Promoted in 1907 to chief of reconnaissance in forest management, he had charge of investigations in the Pacific Northwest and also directed work in Arizona and New Mexico. Later that year he was made supervisor of the combined Arkansas and Ozark National Forests, and when these were reorganized a few years later as separate units, he retained administrative control of the Arkansas (later the Ouachita) Forest, then an area of nearly two million acres.

Record returned to Yale in 1910 to lecture on Forest Service administration. Later that year he was awarded the Master of Forestry degree (as of 1905) and was appointed instructor in forestry.

He remained at Yale until his death, being promoted in 1917 to professor and in 1939 to dean of the School of Forestry. Record early became interested in study of the systematic anatomy of the woods of the world; he developed new techniques for identifying woods, based on the distinctive qualities of the various species, such as structure, weight, grain, intrinsic strength, durability, and color. In 1912 he published *Identification of the Economic Woods in the United States* and, two years later, *The Mechanical Properties of Wood,* both of which long served as standard textbooks in the nation's forestry schools.

When Yale in 1916 established a department of tropical forestry, Record's interests shifted to tropical woods, and, in collaboration with Clayton D. Mell, he wrote *Timbers of Tropical America* (1924). To promote research in wood anatomy, especially of tropical trees, he founded in 1925 *Tropical Woods,* a quarterly journal which he edited until his death. After 1925 he devoted much of his time to building a collection of wood specimens on a selective basis, working with collaborators—mostly botanists—in various parts of the world and especially in the American tropics. At the time of his death the Yale Collection of Woods of the World comprised over 41,000 specimens, representing almost 12,000 identified species of trees. The collection served as a stimulus for studies of wood structure, identification methods, and wood descriptions. The most important studies were compiled in *Timbers of the New World* (with Robert W. Hess, 1943).

On Apr. 1, 1906, Record married Mary Elizabeth Strauss of Topeka, Kans., by whom he had four children: Harold Clayton, who died in infancy, Mary Elizabeth and Mason Thomas (twins), and Alice Louise. Active in professional organizations, Record helped found in 1931 the International Association of Wood Anatomists, and from 1932 to 1938 served as its secretary-treasurer. For many years he was closely associated with the Field Museum of Natural History in Chicago, having been appointed research associate there in 1928. In the course of his research and field work in Central America, he discovered five new species of trees which bear his name; several species and two genera (*Recordoxylon* and *Recordia*) discovered by others were also named in his honor. Record died at the age of sixty-three of myocardial infarction at the New Haven (Conn.) Hospital. His ashes were buried in Hutton Cemetery near Crawfordsville.

[Memoirs by Henry S. Graves and Paul C. Standley, with a bibliography of Record's writings, in *Tropical Woods,* June 1, 1945. See also obituary articles in *Yale Forest School News,* Apr. 1945, *Am.*

Forest, Mar. 1945, *Jour. of Forestry,* Mar. 1945, and *Science,* Mar. 23, 1945 (by Paul C. Standley); Tom Gill, "Men Who Made Yale Foresters," in *The First Thirty Years of the Yale School of Forestry* (1930); *Nat. Cyc. Am. Biog.,* XXXIII, 459–60; *Who Was Who in America,* vol. II (1950); *Am. Men of Sci.* (7th ed., 1944); Yale Univ., *Obituary Record of Graduates,* 1944–45.]

GEORGE A. GARRATT

REED, JAMES ALEXANDER (Nov. 9, 1861–Sept. 8, 1944), Senator from Missouri, came of Scotch-Irish Presbyterian forebears who had settled in Pennsylvania before the American Revolution. He was born in Richland County, Ohio, near Mansfield, the second among five children and second of three sons of John A. Reed, a farmer, and Nancy (Crawford) Reed. His parents moved in 1864 to Linn County, Iowa, where the boy worked on the family stock farm and attended district school during winters. When he was eight his father died. Reed graduated from the Cedar Rapids high school in 1880. After a "special course" at Coe College in Cedar Rapids, he read law at night and was admitted to the bar in 1885. He married Lura Mansfield Olmsted, daughter of a Cedar Rapids physician, on Aug. 1, 1887, and that year moved to Kansas City, Mo., which remained his home thereafter. In Iowa, Reed had been chairman of the county Democratic committee at the age of eighteen. Courageous and eloquent, he entered Missouri political life with a forthright attack on the anti-Catholic American Protective Association.

For ten years Reed combined a rapidly growing law practice with energetic work in Democratic politics, the latter bringing him into close association with the political organization headed by Thomas J. Pendergast [Supp. 3] and his brothers. Reed's first public post was city counselor (1897–98), followed by election as prosecuting attorney of Jackson County, which included Kansas City. In two years he tried 287 cases and obtained convictions in all but two. With this remarkable record, he swept into the mayor's chair in 1900 as a reform candidate. Leading a consumers' war on street railway, electric, and telephone utilities, he won reelection in 1902. He was a delegate to his first national Democratic convention in 1908, and at the 1912 convention he placed House Speaker Champ Clark [q.v.] in nomination against Woodrow Wilson. Although in 1904 he had unsuccessfully opposed the popular Joseph W. Folk [q.v.] for the Democratic nomination for governor, Jim Reed, as he was invariably called, was elected to the United States Senate in 1910 over David R. Francis [q.v.]. The last Missouri Senator to be chosen by the legislature, he was reelected by statewide vote, with increasing majorities, in 1916 and 1922.

In the Senate, Reed generally supported the Wilson administration's New Freedom legislation and its foreign policies, including the declaration of war against Germany in 1917. But he soon turned against wartime measures, especially economic controls. When Herbert Hoover was appointed Food Administrator, Reed attacked the Lever Food Act as "vicious and unconstitutional," denounced its enforcer, Hoover, as the "arch gambler of this day," and sent his constituents a letter so bitterly critical of food controls that Wilson described it as "perfectly outrageous" (Baker, pp. 166, 234). Condemning the dispatch of conscripted troops to Europe, Reed protested the 1917 draft act and proposed as a substitute a volunteer defense system.

Reed's criticism of the conduct of the war, however, paled beside his utterly uncompromising stand against the Versailles peace treaty and in particular against the covenant of the League of Nations, which he labeled "the product of British statesmanship." He not only came out flatly against ratification but joined Republican Senators Hiram W. Johnson [Supp. 3], William E. Borah [Supp. 2], and Medill McCormick [q.v.] in trailing Wilson with counterarguments during the President's speaking tour of September 1919 to present the treaty directly to the voters. "I decline," Reed said on Sept. 22, "to help set up any government greater than that established by the fathers, greater than that baptized in the blood of patriots from the lanes of Lexington to the forests of the Argonne. . . ." The determination and passion of Reed and his colleagues caused them to be known as "irreconcilables" and "bitter-enders." Reed put through a Congressional resolution for the early recall of American soldiers from garrisons in Germany, and nearly a decade after the armistice he continued to inveigh against the World Court. He likewise opposed the war's debt settlements and the four-power treaty proposed by the Washington Conference on arms limitation in 1921.

Reed's course caused a grave breach in the Democratic party. When the Senator sought to justify his position before the Missouri legislature in 1919, Wilson supporters first walked out and later passed a censure resolution. The next year the state Democratic convention repudiated Reed's stand and denied him a delegate's seat at the national convention in San Francisco. After seeking unsuccessfully to get James M. Cox, the Democratic presidential nominee, to back his anti-League position, Reed declined to endorse the national ticket. Two years later, when Reed ran for a third Senatorial term, Woodrow Wilson, then one year out of the White House, called

him "my implacable opponent in everything that is honorable and enlightened" and "a discredit to the party to which he pretends to belong" (Mitchell, p. 47). Reed countered by declaring that the conflict arose from Wilson's mistaken insistence on "personal allegiance," and maintained that each Senator was an "independent legislator," to be tested not in terms of the British plan of "responsible party government" but by votes "in accordance with sound public policy."

At the outset of the 1922 campaign, Reed seemed to face certain defeat. The press scored him harder than ever. Wilson Democrats organized "Rid-us-of-Reed" clubs and staged a mock funeral. The cigar-chewing, tobacco-spitting Senator, however, waged an intense battle and achieved a double triumph. He won the primary race by 6,000 votes over a fervent Wilsonian, former Assistant Secretary of State Breckinridge Long, and then gained reelection by 44,000, his largest lead. Aided by popular dislike for federal prohibition, which he condemned as unconstitutional, Reed garnered the ballots of thousands of wet Republicans, in addition to urban, anti-League Irish and German groups. It was a stunning personal victory for one virtually read out of his party only two years earlier.

During his last Senate term Reed was a bitter critic of the successive Republican administrations and of such leaders as Hoover and Andrew W. Mellon [Supp. 2]. His long tenure in the Senate had brought him memberships on both the Foreign Relations and Judiciary committees. No aspect of Senatorial service was more to his liking than the investigative function. In his first term he had opposed shipping company practices and exposed the operations of Washington lobbyists. In 1926 he headed a committee investigating illegal campaign expenditures; as a result of its work the Senate refused to seat Frank L. Smith of Illinois and William S. Vare [q.v.] of Pennsylvania. Reed also helped probe the Anti-Saloon League's political activities, as well as the sugar industry's connections with Charles B. Warren, who was rejected by the Senate for Attorney General. Not all of Reed's positions appeared to square. Thus while 'he opposed the protective tariff and economic monopoly, he objected to most government regulation. Similarly, though he espoused individual liberty and heaped scorn on the Ku Klux Klan and anti-Semites, he rejected woman suffrage and the proposed child labor amendment.

Reed made a serious bid for the Democratic presidential nomination in 1928, and consequently did not run for reelection to the Senate.

Upon leaving Washington, he resumed his law practice in Kansas City. Increasingly opposed to government "paternalism" and "socialist or regulatory schemes," he became a foe of the New Deal and of President Franklin D. Roosevelt. In 1936 he organized the National Jeffersonian Democrats and stumped for Alfred M. Landon; four years later he again supported the Republican nominee, Wendell L. Willkie [Supp. 3]. Reed's first wife died Aug. 12, 1932, and on Dec. 13, 1933, he married Mrs. Nell (Quinlan) Donnelly; there were no children by either marriage. A tall, straight figure of a man, with flashing eyes and ruddy complexion, Reed had what was described as a Grecian face, set off in later life by white hair. He died in his eighty-third year, of myocarditis and bronchopneumonia, at his summer estate near Fairview, Mich., and was buried in Mount Washington Cemetery, Kansas City.

The journalist Oswald Garrison Villard, who found in Reed a resemblance to Andrew Jackson, called him the Senate's "roughest and hardest hitter," capable of "profound public service." Another seasoned observer, William Hard, credited Reed with rising to "heights of sublimity which it is difficult to believe have ever been surpassed in parliamentary history" (Villard, pp. 89, 93, 98). But Mark Sullivan said that "in debate, he is violent, vituperative, and . . . unfair" (*World's Work*, August 1922). The *New Republic* called him "an actor" who "always dramatized every struggle in which he was engaged" (Dec. 15, 1926), and *Collier's* went so far as to say that he was "never really dedicated to any cause except the cause of Jim Reed" (Sept. 15, 1928, p. 42). Though other judgments might differ, the *St. Louis Globe-Democrat* spoke well when it said that in more than forty years of public life, Reed "never dodged a fight or asked for odds" (Sept. 9, 1944). Few men so fiercely independent have ever sat in the United States Senate.

[Lee Meriwether, *Jim Reed, "Senatorial Immortal"* (1948); Franklin D. Mitchell, *Embattled Democracy: Mo. Democratic Politics, 1919–1932* (1968); *Biog. Directory Am. Cong.* (1961); *Who Was Who in America*, vol. II (1950); *Current Biog.*, 1944; *Nat. Cyc. Am. Biog.*, XV, 99–100, and XXXIV, 9–11; *Who's Who in the Nation's Capital*, 1927; Lyle W. Dorsett, *The Pendergast Machine* (1968); Edwin C. McReynolds, *Missouri: A Hist. of the Crossroads State* (1962); David D. March, *The Hist. of Mo.* (4 vols., 1967); Louis G. Geiger, *Joseph W. Folk of Mo.* (1953); Oswald Garrison Villard, *Prophets, True and False* (1928); Mark Sullivan, *Our Times*, vol. V (1933); Ray Stannard Baker, *Woodrow Wilson*, vol. VII (1939); Carroll H. Wooddy, *The Case of Frank L. Smith* (1931). Representative magazine articles: Charles G. Ross, "Reed of Mo.," *Scribner's*, Feb. 1928; Frederick H. Brennan, "The Presidency in 1924?: James A. Reed," *Forum*, Nov. 1923; Paul Y. Anderson, "'Jim' Reed: Himself," *North Am. Rev.*, Apr. 1928. See also newspapers through Reed's career, especially those of Washington, Kansas City, St. Louis, and N. Y. at the time of his death. Reed's "The Pestilence of Fanaticism," *Am. Mercury*, May 1925, is a good summary of his political philosophy. Other information from a useful biobibliography compiled at the Univ. of Wis. Lib. School by Hildegard Adler, 1965; and from personal recollection.]

IRVING DILLIARD

REED, MARY (Dec. 4, 1854–Apr. 8, 1943), missionary to lepers, was born in Lowell, Washington County, Ohio. She was the eldest daughter and second of the eleven children (three of whom died in infancy) of Wesley W. Reed, whose parents had come to Ohio from New Jersey and Virginia, and Sarah Ann (Henderson) Reed, of Virginia descent. Her father is listed in the 1860 census as a saddler, and the family moved about the area, residing in turn at Crooked Tree, Noble County, again at Lowell, and finally at nearby Beckett's Post Office. The great event of Mary's adolescence was religious conversion at sixteen. She graduated from the Malta (Ohio) high school and in 1878 from the Ohio State Normal School at Worthington. For five years she taught school, the last appointment being at Kenton in north central Ohio.

Moved by reports on the plight of women in the zenanas of India, Miss Reed applied for service to the Cincinnati branch of the Woman's Foreign Missionary Society of the Methodist Episcopal Church, and was sent to India in 1884. She was assigned to zenana work at Cawnpore, but when her health broke she was sent for rest to Pithoragarh in the Himalayas near Almora in Kumaon district close to the border of Nepal. There she became acquainted with the ministry to lepers carried on by the London-based interdenominational Mission to Lepers, founded by Wellesley Cosby Bailey in 1874. Her next assignment was that of headmistress of a girls' high school at Gonda. But again her health failed, and she went home on furlough in 1890. In Cincinnati and New York, physicians tentatively agreed with her premonition that she had leprosy, a diagnosis that was subsequently affirmed by specialists in London and Bombay. Mary Reed understood this affliction to be a special call of God to minister to the lepers whom she had met in the Himalayas. Upon the request of the Methodist bishop in India, James Mills Thoburn [*q.v.*], the Mission to Lepers in 1891 appointed Miss Reed as superintendent of the leper asylum at Chandag Heights near Almora; henceforth she was a staff member of both the Methodist Mission and the Mission to Lepers. Leprosy was then considered incurable, and Mary Reed's plight and example, when known, made her at once a heroine.

Chandag Heights is located on a high ridge of the Himalayas above the Shor valley, five days by foot or pony over mountain paths from Almora. There Mary Reed ministered to the lepers from 1891 to her death in 1943. Because of the public's horror of the disease, she avoided direct contact with well persons. She wore long gloves, ate alone while her guests lodged and dined in a separate bungalow, and during this period of more than fifty years came down from her mountain retreat only three times. In 1899, at the insistence of fellow missionaries, she attended the Methodist Annual Conference at Lucknow. An eighteen months' furlough in 1904–05 took her to Palestine, and she made a final visit home to the United States for six months in 1906. Her disease had been declared cured in 1896. This caused great controversy, some doubting whether she had ever had leprosy. It did become active again in 1932–33, but by that time the disease could be arrested and even cured, and injections checked it.

At Chandag, Miss Reed kept in touch with other missionaries in the region. Until too aged, she did some traveling in the leper work, being allowed to cross the Nepal border at will; and in 1905 she relieved Dr. Albert Leroy Shelton [q.v.] at Bhot on the Tibet border while he was absent. Numerous visitors found their way to Chandag. Miss Reed kept in touch with the outside world by reading newspapers, magazines, and books; the walls of her "Sunny Crest Cottage" were covered with clippings about persons and events. She found much enjoyment in playing the organ and singing hymns, of which she had made a large collection.

Miss Reed increased the mission land at Chandag from sixty-six to about a hundred acres. Over the years the population under her care varied from around sixty to more than a hundred. There were separate homes for men and women, each with cottages and land for gardening and grazing cattle. When villagers refused the lepers access to the nearest well, she brought water from government land a mile distant by ditches and pipes. She erected a hospital, a dispensary, which served a larger clientele, and a chapel, Bethel, the spiritual center of the colony. School was maintained for leper children, and uncontaminated children were sent to the mission at Pithoragarh. Chandag was a haven of mercy, hope, and eventually of healing.

The King's Birthday Honors List of 1917 announced the award to Mary Reed of the Kaisar-I-Hind Medal. With advancing age she grew enfeebled and increasingly blind, and in 1938 the burden of administration was taken over by Miss Kate Ogilvie. During the last days of 1942 Miss

Reed fell on her cottage steps and was severely injured. She died the following April, and was buried on the mountain slope before the chapel.

[John Jackson, *Mary Reed: Missionary to the Lepers* (1900); Lee S. Huizenga, *Mary Reed of Chandag* (1939); *The Story of Mary Reed, Missionary to the Lepers,* a leaflet issued in various reprints by the Mission to Lepers and the Woman's Foreign Missionary Society of the Methodist Episcopal Church beginning about 1908; E. Mackerchar, *Mary Reed of Chandag* (1943). See also sketches in: Mrs. B. R. Cowen, *Hist. of the Cincinnati Branch, W.F.M.S., 1869–1894* (1895), pp. 125–27; Edwin C. Dawson, *Heroines of Missionary Adventure* (1909), pp. 61–65; Annie Ryder Gracey (Mrs. J. T.), ed., *Eminent Missionary Women* (1898); and W. X. Ninde, *The Picket Line of Missions* (1897), pp. 245 ff. Contemporary articles about Miss Reed appeared in the *Christian Advocate, Classmate, Methodist Woman,* and *Without the Camp.* Obituaries: *Indian Witness,* Apr. 15, 1943; *Methodist Woman,* July 1943 (also in 1943 *Annual Report* of the W.F.M.S.); N. Y. *Sun,* May 21, 1943; and elsewhere. On the family: Martin B. Andrews, ed., *Hist. of Marietta and Washington County, Ohio* (1902), pp. 1340–41; and 1860 census schedule for Jackson Township, Noble County, Ohio. The United Missionary Lib. (Methodist and Presbyterian), N. Y. City, has a biographical file.]

R. PIERCE BEAVER

REGAN, AGNES GERTRUDE (Mar. 26, 1869–Sept. 30, 1943), Catholic educator and social reformer, was born in San Francisco, Calif. She was the third daughter and fourth child in a family of nine; two of her sisters became nuns. Her father, of Irish and English parentage, was born in Valparaiso, Chile, but in 1849 migrated to San Francisco, at which time he changed his name from Santiago del Carmen O'Regan to James Regan. After working briefly in the gold fields, he served for ten years as private secretary to Joseph S. Alemany [q.v.], the first Catholic archbishop of San Francisco. He then became associated with a brother-in-law, Richard Tobin, in the law firm of Tobin & Tobin and in the Hibernian Bank, of which he was a director. In 1863 he married Mary Ann Morrison, whose family had emigrated in 1847 from Ireland.

Agnes Regan was reared in a large home in a section of San Francisco later known as the Western Addition. She was educated at St. Rose Academy and at the San Francisco Normal School. Upon graduating in 1887, she began an active career in the San Francisco public school system, serving successively as elementary teacher (1887–1900) and principal (1900–14), and then as a member of the board of education (1914–19).

Miss Regan had long been interested in social reform—she served on the city playground commission (1912–19) and helped secure California's first teachers' pension act—and in 1920 she accepted appointment as the representative of the San Francisco diocese to the organizational meeting of the National Council of Catholic Women in Washington, D. C. There she was elected second vice-president and a member of the board of directors. When a few months later she was appointed executive secretary, she moved to Washington. A successor to the women's committee of the National Catholic War Council, the National Council of Catholic Women was conceived as a federation of women's organizations, national, diocesan, and local, and reflected the deepening involvement of the American Catholic hierarchy in matters of social welfare. Operating as a central coordinating agency, it disseminated information about impending social legislation, stimulated and supported research on social problems, directed the deployment of Catholic social agencies, and won for Catholic women representation on committees and governmental agencies dealing with social issues of interest to them.

In her position as executive secretary Miss Regan encouraged the development of new local organizations and mobilized the strength of Catholic women on such questions as birth control, divorce, urban housing, religious education, recreational facilities, community life in rural areas, and immigration and Americanization. Meeting with groups around the country, Agnes Regan helped organize community centers, training programs for immigrants, and welfare services. She encouraged women to support child labor laws and the proposed Sheppard-Towner Act (passed in 1921), which provided maternity aid to indigent mothers.

Miss Regan also played an important part in social work education. As new organizations became affiliated with the National Council of Catholic Women, and as the scope of its services broadened, the need for trained social workers became pressing, and in 1921 the Council assumed control of "Clifton," a temporary school for this purpose that had been established in 1918 by the National Catholic War Council under the leadership of Bishop John J. Burke [Supp. 2]. The school was immediately reorganized as the National Catholic Service School for Women (later the National Catholic School of Social Service), and its training program was extended from six months to two years; at the completion of the course of study a certificate, or in the case of college graduates, a master's degree, was conferred by the Catholic University of America. Miss Regan, now an authority in the field of social legislation, was in 1922 appointed instructor in community organization at the school. In 1925 she became assistant director, and she remained in that position until her death, serving for two of those years (1935–37) as acting director. Her relationship with the students was always warm

and motherly, and she was especially active in publicizing the work of the school and in raising funds.

At the same time she continued her work with the National Council of Catholic Women, after 1927 on a half-time basis. In that capacity she testified before Congressional committees and was a member of the White House Conference on Children in a Democracy (1939–40). She also served on the advisory committee of the federal Women's Bureau and on the board of directors of the National Travelers' Aid Society and participated in the American Federation of Housing Authorities and the Catholic Association for International Peace. Miss Regan received many honors, including the papal decoration Pro Ecclesia et Pontifice (1933). She died in Washington of a heart attack at the age of seventy-four. Following a solemn requiem mass in the San Francisco Cathedral, she was buried at Holy Cross Cemetery, Daly City, Calif.

[Loretto R. Lawler, *Full Circle: The Story of the Nat. Catholic School of Social Service* (1951); files of the *Nat. Catholic War (Welfare) Council Bull.*, later *Catholic Action*, 1919–43; obituary by Margaret T. Lynch, *ibid.*, Oct. 1943; Dorothy A. Mohler in *New Catholic Encyc.*, XII, 199–200, and in *Notable Am. Women*, III, 128–30.]

PAUL HANLY FURFEY

REID, MONT ROGERS (Apr. 7, 1889–May 11, 1943), surgeon, was born on a farm near the village of Oriskany, Va., one of seven children, six of them boys, of Harriet Pendleton (Lemon) and Benjamin Watson Reid. Mont Reid's childhood and adolescence, spent in a remote mountain community, instilled an imperturbable poise and simplicity that he retained all his life, along with a love for the unsophisticated neighbors of his boyhood. He received his early education from his father, a schoolteacher as well as a farmer. In 1902 he entered the normal school at Daleville, Va., and in 1904 enrolled at Roanoke College at Salem, Va., receiving the A.B. degree in 1908. Four years later he graduated from the Johns Hopkins University School of Medicine. His class standing gained him the internship of his choice, a year's surgical clerkship at the Johns Hopkins Hospital under William S. Halsted [*q.v.*], who exercised a strong influence on Reid's entire career. He also took a year of work in pathology under Joseph C. Bloodgood [Supp. 1], after which he returned to the surgical service, becoming chief resident in 1918.

In 1922, now one of Halsted's more eminent disciples, Reid moved, with another Johns Hopkins surgeon, George J. Heuer, to the University of Cincinnati, where as an associate professor in the medical school's newly organized department of surgery he contributed largely to its successful development. He succeeded Heuer as chairman of the department in 1931 and held the post for the rest of his life. During his tenure Reid secured funds not only for his own department, but also for the remodeling of the Cincinnati General Hospital, which served as the base for clinical instruction of medical students. With a strong interest in civic affairs, he made friends in many fields and in his quiet and persuasive way awakened the citizens of Cincinnati to their obligations in support of their university and medical school. Under his leadership the standards of surgical care rose and the department became one of the great training centers in the United States for residents in surgery. Reid was the first surgeon to recognize the importance of placing veterans' hospitals near medical schools. On his initiative, the American Surgical Association endorsed this policy, which was later carried out after World War II.

Reid's chief contribution to his science centered in his experimental and clinical studies of surgery of the thyroid gland and of the large blood vessels. Some eighty-five papers, published over a period of thirty years, reflect his work in these fields, as well as in the surgical treatment of other medical conditions, such as angina pectoris, pigmented moles, and cancer. In 1934 he was awarded the Rudolph Matas Medal for his work in vascular surgery. Probably his most enduring accomplishment is to be found in the many young surgeons he trained in the total care of the patient. For Reid, this meant a painstaking personal history, a complete physical examination, an unhurried and meticulous operation, and vigilant postoperative care.

Reid spent a year (1925–26) as visiting professor of surgery in the Union Medical College of Peking in China, followed by participation in one of the Mongolian expeditions of Roy Chapman Andrews. Malaria contracted in China weakened his health for a time. He married Elizabeth Harmon Cassatt on Jan. 26, 1929; they had one son, Alfred Cassatt. In religion Reid was a Presbyterian. He died at his home in Cincinnati at the age of fifty-four of a myocardial infarction.

[Obituaries in: *Science*, June 25, 1943 (by George J. Heuer), *Annals of Surgery*, Apr. 1944 (by B. N. Carter), *Jour. Am. Medic. Assoc.*, May 22, 1943, and *Surgery*, Oct. 1943; *Who Was Who in America*, vol. II (1950); *Nat. Cyc. Am. Biog.*, XXXIV, 172–73.]
WARFIELD M. FIROR

REISNER, GEORGE ANDREW (Nov. 5, 1867–June 6, 1942), Egyptologist, was born in Indianapolis, Ind., the oldest of several children of George Andrew and Mary Elizabeth (Mason) Reisner, natives, respectively, of Virginia and Indiana. His paternal grandfather, John Jacob Reisner, a Napoleonic soldier, had emigrated from Alsace; his father was a clerk and later partner in a shoe store. George Reisner graduated from the Indianapolis Classical High School in 1885, at the top of his class, and in 1889 (A.B. summa cum laude) from Harvard College. A year spent working in Indianapolis in a law office, as athletic director of the Y.M.C.A., and as a census taker enabled him to earn enough to return to Harvard for graduate work in Semitic languages and history. On Nov. 23, 1892, he married Mary Putnam Bronson of Indianapolis; they had one child, Mary Bronson, born in 1903.

After taking a Ph.D. in 1893, Reisner went to Germany for further study. Originally an Assyriologist, he continued his early interest at Göttingen, but as a second subject studied Egyptology with Kurt Sethe and Adolf Erman, an association which was to determine his future career. Under Erman's aegis, Reisner was in 1894 appointed a scientific assistant in the Egyptian department of the Berlin Museum. He returned to Harvard in 1896–97 as an instructor in the Semitic department.

In 1897 Reisner went to Egypt as American member of an international commission designated to catalogue the Khedivial Museum in Cairo. While engaged in that task he met the wealthy Mrs. Phoebe Apperson Hearst [q.v.], then traveling in Egypt, who engaged him as director of an expedition that she planned to finance under the auspices of the University of California, of which she was a regent. Reisner began excavating in 1898 at Quft in Upper Egypt, where he assembled a team of workmen that was to remain with him for more than forty years. He was a pioneer among American archaeologists, the first to develop a system of scientific excavation, setting a pattern of thorough recording which has served as a model to both American and foreign scholars.

In 1903, when the Egyptian Department of Antiquities unexpectedly granted concessions to excavate the valley temples and tombs near the great pyramids at Giza, Reisner began work in a singularly fruitful area that contained the great royal cemetery laid out by Cheops and his architects when the First Pyramid was built. He had scarcely begun to explore this magnificent site when Mrs. Hearst notified him that she could no longer afford to support the expedition. As it would have been unthinkable to abandon this superlative concession and break up his efficient organization, he sought another sponsor. Albert M. Lythgoe, curator of Egyptian art at the Boston Museum of Fine Arts, who was in Egypt at the time, saw the crisis as a providential opportunity for the museum to sponsor excavations directly. Thus in 1905 a Harvard University–Boston Museum of Fine Arts Egyptian Expedition was created, of which Reisner was director until his death in 1942. Although he left Egypt only infrequently, Reisner was a member of the Harvard faculty, as assistant professor of Semitic archaeology, 1905–10, assistant professor of Egyptology, 1910–14, and professor of Egyptology, 1914–42. From 1910 to 1942 he was also curator of the department of Egyptian art of the Boston Museum of Fine Arts, whose collections were constantly enriched by the results of his excavations.

Reisner's activities ranged geographically over a wide area. During the years 1908–10 he was director of Harvard's Palestinian Expedition; his excavation of the palace of Mori, Ahab, and Jeroboam II and other buildings in Samaria was a brilliant example of the handling of a complex stratified site. Meanwhile his work in Egypt continued. At Giza he excavated progressively from 1899 to 1938 large portions of the cemetery west of the Great Pyramid; the entire royal family cemetery to the east, including the intact tomb of Queen Hetep-heres, mother of Cheops, an outstanding example of archaeological dissecting which resulted in the recovery of the only household furniture of the 4th Dynasty; and the temples of the Third Pyramid of Mycerinus, which yielded some of the most distinguished royal sculpture of the Old Kingdom. The whole Giza area provided new evidence on the family relationships of the 4th Dynasty and on the development of funerary architecture in the Old Kingdom.

Farther south, at Deir el Bersheh, Reisner worked on Middle Kingdom tombs of provincial nobles, discovering the finest wooden painted coffin and funerary equipment of the period. His excavations in the Girga district of provincial cemeteries at Naga-ed-Der, Mesheikh, Mesaeed, and Sheikh Farag, ranging from early Predynastic down to Roman times, threw new light on the evolution of burial customs and funerary architecture. In 1907–09, during construction to raise the height of the Aswan Dam, Reisner was in charge of the Egyptian government's archaeological survey in Lower Nubia of the area soon to be flooded between the First Cataract and the Sudan border. These survey excavations uncovered burials of all periods from Predynastic to Meroitic.

Reisner also worked extensively in the Sudan. The forts which he uncovered at Semna, Uronarti, Shalfak, and Mirgissa, in the Second Cataract region, added to the knowledge of Egyptian military architecture. At Kerma he excavated an Egyptian frontier post of Middle Kingdom and First Intermediate date, whose fortified buildings and cemeteries revealed the hitherto unknown impact of Egyptian culture on native Sudanese civilization of the period. In the Napatan district, his excavation of temples and cemeteries at Gebel Barkal and pyramids at Barkal, Kurru, and Nuri brought to light tombs of the 25th Dynasty kings of Egypt, their ancestors, and their descendants. Reisner's work on three cemeteries at Meroë explored pyramid tombs of the kings and queens of the Meroitic Kingdom of Kush, and private and princely tombs of the inhabitants of Meroë from 700 B.C. to 300 A.D. All told, his Sudanese investigations from Kerma to Meroë made possible the reconstruction of the ancient history of Kush-Ethiopia from the Middle Kingdom to the fall of Meroë and the recovery of the names and chronology of the Kushite royal family from 700 B.C. to 300 A.D.

The results of George Reisner's labors have appeared in definitive book form in only fourteen titles (19 volumes), although he published a host of pioneering articles in the form of preliminary reports and special studies in many scholarly journals throughout his active career. He has sometimes been criticized for not publishing more definitive works, but it was Reisner's belief that, owing to political conditions, active field work by foreign expeditions in Egypt would not be possible for long; that the scientific results, if adequately recorded and preserved, would constitute a mine of source material for future scholars; and that, as long as the opportunity for active field work continued, the excavator was not justified in delaying operations unduly in order to write and publish. Time has shown much merit in this view.

In the opinion of the Egyptologist Herbert E. Winlock, director of the Metropolitan Museum of Art, "George Andrew Reisner was without any doubt the greatest excavator and archaeologist the United States has ever produced in any field." His outstanding characteristics were two: his amazing energy and capacity for continuous hard work, and his utter devotion to scholarship, for which he made many sacrifices, both of his own comfort and that of his family and associates. He was as indifferent to the amenities of life as he was to its financial rewards; to him money was simply a necessary means to furthering the work of the Expedition. He was a great teacher, but he could not abide incompetence or any lack of complete integrity. Hospitable and helpful to many colleagues, he had a gift for friendship for those he respected. His affection for his Egyptian workmen was deep, and his understanding of their mentality and customs profound.

Reisner suffered from increasing blindness in the final years, but struggled to continue his work despite this calamitous handicap. His last visit to the United States was in 1939, when he returned for the fiftieth reunion of his Harvard class; at this time Harvard awarded him the honorary degree of Doctor of Letters. He had continued his excavations relentlessly through the first World War; in the second, he remained in his camp at Giza, working on excavation reports, even though, out of concession to air raids, he placed his records in a subterranean rock-cut tomb and rigged offices and sleeping quarters for his staff in other underground chambers. Although his wife and daughter were persuaded to return to the United States in the summer of 1940, he remained at Giza. Blind, bedridden, and speechless at the end, he was taken to a Cairo hospital, but he insisted on being carried back, and in June 1942, aged seventy-four, he died at his home camp behind the Great Pyramid in Egypt. He was buried in the European Cemetery in Cairo.

[In chronological sequence, Reisner's larger works were: *The Hearst Medical Papyrus* (1905), *The Archaeological Survey of Nubia* (1907–08), *The Early Dynastic Cemeteries of Naga-ed-Dêr* (1908), *Excavations at Kerma* (1923), *Harvard Excavations at Samaria, 1908–10* (1924), *Mycerinus: The Temples of the Third Pyramid at Giza* (1931), *A Provincial Cemetery of the Pyramid Age: Naga-ed-Dêr* (1932), *The Development of the Egyptian Tomb down to the Accession of Cheops* (1936), and *A Hist. Of the Giza Necropolis* (1942). Tributes to Reisner include: Alan H. Gardiner in *Nature*, July 18, 1942; George Steindorff in *Bull. of the Museum of Fine Arts*, Oct. 1942; Dows Dunham in *Am. Jour. of Archaeology*, July–Sept. 1942; and Herbert E. Winlock in Am. Philosophical Soc., *Year Book*, 1942. Family data from 1870 and 1880 census schedules and Indianapolis city directories (courtesy of Ind. State Lib.). See also: Harvard College Class of 1889, *Fiftieth Anniversary Report* (1939); Theodate Geoffrey in *World's Work*, July 1925 (a contemporary sketch); Dows Dunham, *The Egyptian Dept. and Its Excavations* (1958); and Walter Muir Whitehill, *Museum of Fine Arts, Boston: A Centennial Hist.* (2 vols., 1970), chap. viii. The full record of Reisner's work, published and in manuscript, is in the Dept. of Egyptian Art, Museum of Fine Arts, Boston.]

DOWS DUNHAM

RICE, ALICE CALDWELL HEGAN (Jan. 11, 1870–Feb. 10, 1942), author, was born in Shelbyville, Ky., at the homestead of her maternal grandfather, Judge James Caldwell. She was the older of two children and only daughter of Samuel Watson Hegan, an art dealer of Irish descent, and Sallie (Caldwell) Hegan, whose family had come to Kentucky from Virginia in 1800. Alice was reared in the Campbellite faith and because of delicate health received her early education at home. She enjoyed making up stories and plays to entertain her young cousins, and when at the age of ten she entered Miss Hampton's private school for girls in Louisville, she wrote sketches for the school paper. When she was fifteen the *Louisville Courier-Journal* printed a humorous article she had submitted anonymously.

At sixteen Alice Hegan began assisting in a mission Sunday school in a Louisville slum known as the Cabbage Patch. There she was impressed with the way the poor "met their problems and triumphed over their difficulties. . . . Looking for the nobility that lay hidden in the most unpromising personality became for me a spiritual treasure hunt" (*The Inky Way*, p. 39). With Louise Marshall, she later (1910) founded the Cabbage Patch Settlement House, which by the time of her death had grown to include a paid staff and more than a hundred volunteer workers.

After finishing school Miss Hegan made her debut into Louisville society. She continued to engage in charitable work and became a member of the Authors Club of Louisville, a group of young women who aspired to become writers. With their encouragement, she wrote her first novel, *Mrs. Wiggs of the Cabbage Patch,* a story built around an old woman she knew who often came begging for food but displayed courage and a sense of humor in the face of poverty. Submitted to the publisher S. S. McClure, the novel was accepted at once and on its publication (1901) became a best seller. In the next forty years it sold more than 500,000 copies, was translated into a number of foreign languages, and became a success as a stage play and as a movie.

On Dec. 18, 1902, Miss Hegan was married to Cale Young Rice, a Harvard graduate and an instructor at Cumberland University, whose first volume of poetry had recently been published. Going to New York for their honeymoon, they were invited to join McClure and his party on a trip to Europe, where Alice met and formed a lasting friendship with the writer Ida Tarbell [Supp. 3]. The Rices had no children. Although they established their permanent home in Louisville and often spent their summers in Maine, they made many long trips to Europe and the Orient, their travels providing material for some of Mrs. Rice's fiction and her husband's poetry.

Although remembered only as a "period" writer, Alice Hegan Rice was one of the most famous authors of her day. She published twenty novels and numerous short stories, some of the latter written in collaboration with her husband. Of her novels, *Lovey Mary* (1903) was a sequel to *Mrs. Wiggs*. *Sandy* (1905), which the *Century* magazine serialized, was a fictional account of S. S. Mc-Clure, based on his reminiscences of his youth. *Captain June* (1907) depicted child life in Japan. Perhaps her most serious novel was *Mr. Opp* (1909), which portrayed a man who, though a failure in a worldly sense, maintained self-respect by caring for his mentally incompetent sister and choosing to regard his life as a success. Mrs. Rice's own favorite among her novels was *Mr. Pete & Co.* (1933), the story of a junk dealer whom she met along the Louisville waterfront. In her autobiography, *The Inky Way* (1940), she attributed the wide appeal of her books to the "exaggerated sensibility that made things appear . . . a bit funnier or a bit more pathetic [to her] than to the average person." Though she romanticized the poor and their problems in her tales, she had a genuine concern for them and was not content merely to make people laugh or cry about their miseries; *Calvary Alley* (1917) was a strong plea to alleviate intolerable housing conditions.

During a long period of ill health in the 1920's Mrs. Rice produced very little, but when the onset of the depression brought financial problems she resumed writing. She received honorary degrees from Rollins College (1928, with her husband) and the University of Louisville (1937). She died of a coronary occlusion at her Louisville home shortly after her seventy-second birthday, and was buried in Cave Hill Cemetery in Louisville. Her husband, desolate without her, committed suicide little more than a year later.

[Mrs. Rice's autobiography, *The Inky Way*, provides the fullest account of her life. There are brief references to her in Cale Young Rice's autobiography, *Bridging the Years* (1939), and in several articles in the *Filson Club Hist. Quart.*: Mariam S. Houchens, "Amazing Best Sellers by Ky. Women Writers" (Oct. 1967); Abby M. Roach, "The Authors Club of Louisville" (Jan. 1957); and Laban L. Rice, "Alice Hegan Rice—Home Maker" (July 1954). See also: Stanley J. Kunitz, *Authors Today and Yesterday* (1933); *Who Was Who in America*, vol. I (1942); and *N. Y. Times* obituary, Feb. 11, 1942. Death record from Ky. State Dept. of Health. Good photographs are in *The Inky Way* and the *Times* obituary.]
WILLIAM T. McCUE

RICHARDS, LAURA ELIZABETH HOWE (Feb. 27, 1850–Jan. 14, 1943), author, was born in Boston, Mass., the third daughter and fourth child among the four daughters and two sons of Julia (Ward) and Samuel Gridley Howe

[*qq.v.*]. Her mother gained renown as the author of the "Battle Hymn of the Republic" and was later active in the suffrage and woman's club movements; her father was a physician who fought in the Greek war of independence and then, returning to Boston, for many years headed the Perkins Institution for the Blind. Young Laura, named for her father's most famous pupil, the blind deaf-mute Laura Bridgman [*q.v.*], grew up in a well-to-do, fun-loving family of broad intellectual interests and philanthropic concerns. Reading, music, and her mother's singing of folk songs and ballads were an integral part of her childhood. She was educated at home by her parents and tutors and at private schools in Boston, and at the age of seventeen traveled in Europe with her parents. On June 17, 1871, she was married to the architect Henry Richards, a Harvard classmate of her brother Henry. They had seven children: Alice Maud, Rosalind, Henry Howe, Julia Ward, Maud (who died in infancy), John, and Laura Elizabeth. During the depression of 1876 her husband gave up his Boston architectural practice and settled in Gardiner, Maine (the town of his birth), where he helped manage the family paper mill. Gardiner remained the Richardses' home for the rest of their lives.

Mrs. Richards had been writing since childhood, but her professional career began only after the birth of her first child, when she started composing jingles and nonsense rhymes, many of them as nursery songs. Beginning in 1873, *St. Nicholas* magazine published a number of these, such as the tale of "The Owl, the Eel, and the Warming Pan," who joyfully turned a meeting-house upside down, and "Little John Bottlejohn," who married a mermaid. In these verses, some of which are reminiscent of Edward Lear and Lewis Carroll, talking animals and eccentric human beings disport themselves amid delightful nonsense words and impeccable rhythms. These and other poems, including "The Seven Little Tigers and the Aged Cook," appeared in Mrs. Richards's *Sketches & Scraps* (1881), illustrated by her husband. The first book of nonsense verse to be written by an American and published in the United States, it brought fame to its author, whose earnings were a welcome supplement to her husband's income. Later collections included *In My Nursery* (1890), *The Hurdy-Gurdy* (1902), and *The Piccolo* (1906).

As her children emerged from infancy, Mrs. Richards began to make up stories to suit their developing needs. In her first published collection, *Five Mice in a Mouse-Trap* (1881), the Man in the Moon tells a series of stories whose characters are children of various lands and personified animals who often get into ludicrous predicaments. The tales were written in strong, simple English with a marked sense of humor; many were illustrated by the English artist Kate Greenaway. Among the books of this period were *The Joyous Story of Toto* (1885) and *Toto's Merry Winter* (1887), tales of a small boy who lives with his grandmother at the edge of a forest. With *Queen Hildegarde* (1889), Mrs. Richards produced the first of her books for young girls. Sequels made up a Hildegarde series, and *Three Margarets* (1897) also had its successors. Perhaps her most popular book for girls was *Captain January* (1890), the story of a Maine lighthouse keeper who rescues an infant girl from a shipwreck and brings her up. A best seller, the book was twice made into a movie.

Once her children were grown, Mrs. Richards broadened the scope of her writing, publishing juvenile biographies of Florence Nightingale (1909), Abigail Adams (1917), and others. Several New England novels, such as *Mrs. Tree* (1902) and *The Wooing of Calvin Parks* (1908), reveal her appreciation of the quirks of Yankee character and idiom.

Probably her most enduring works, aside from the nonsense verse, are the books relating to her parents. She spent many years in editing her father's papers, published in the two-volume *Letters and Journals of Samuel Gridley Howe* (1906–09). *Two Noble Lives* (1911) portrayed both her parents; and she collaborated with her sister Maud Howe Elliott on *Julia Ward Howe* (1915), which won a Pulitzer Prize. Mrs. Richards also published two books of fables "for young and old," *The Golden Windows* (1903) and *The Silver Crown* (1906), which she regarded as her best work. She was deeply religious in the nonsectarian tradition of the Unitarian Church, and these tales exemplify the ethical convictions that underlay all her work.

During a writing career that produced more than seventy books Laura Richards found time to take an active part in the civic and philanthropic activities of Gardiner. She helped establish the town library, organized children's reading clubs, supported public health projects, and served as president of the Maine Consumers' League (1905–11). In 1900 she and her husband founded Camp Merryweather, one of the first summer camps for boys. She befriended and encouraged the young poet Edwin Arlington Robinson [Supp. 1] and in her later years enjoyed an extensive literary correspondence with Alexander Woollcott [Supp. 3] and other noted writers of the day.

Mrs. Richards never stopped writing, and her joy in life remained undiminished. *Tirra Lirra* (1932), which appeared when she was eighty-two, collected many of her best published verses along with some freshly composed pieces that were as lighthearted and amusing as any of her earliest. The previous year she published *Stepping Westward,* a warm evocation of memories of her childhood and of her own domestic life. She died of pneumonia at her home in her ninety-third year, and was buried in Christ Church Yard in Gardiner.

[The principal biographical sources are Mrs. Richards's informal autobiography, *Stepping Westward* (1931), and her recollections of her childhood, *When I Was Your Age* (1894). The best critical estimate is by Anne T. Eaton in *Horn Book*, July–Aug. 1941. See also Ruth Hill Viguers, *ibid.*, Apr., June, Oct., Dec. 1956; and E. D. H. Johnson in *Notable Am. Women*, III, 146–48.]

LYLE G. BOYD

RICHARDS, ROBERT HALLOWELL (Aug. 26, 1844–Mar. 27, 1945), mining engineer, was born in Gardiner, Maine, the fifth son and sixth of seven children of Francis and Anne Hallowell (Gardiner) Richards. His birthplace was named after his mother's great-grandfather, Dr. Silvester Gardiner [*q.v.*]; her father, Robert Hallowell Gardiner [*q.v.*], founded the Gardiner Lyceum in 1821, a pioneering venture in American technical education. Francis Richards, a businessman, took his family to England in 1857 for the sake of his sons' education and soon thereafter drowned. Tutors and a private school in Gardiner had not inoculated Robert with a fever for learning. Neither did the ensuing five years of English private schooling. A private school and tutoring in Boston, after his widowed mother brought her children there in 1862, did not get him into Harvard in 1863, nor did Phillips Exeter Academy, which he attended for the two following years, reconcile him to "learning dead languages by heart." "Up to twenty-one years of age," he later wrote, "I was the dunce of every school I attended, but . . . my mind was active in observing and studying nature."

In February 1865 his perceptive mother suggested that the Massachusetts Institute of Technology, just about to open, might suit him better than Harvard. Richards quit Exeter at once and became the seventh student to register. One of the new school's two temporary rooms was a laboratory in which Richards "learned from experiment and experience what might be expected to happen if a given collection of material were put together, or if a given set of forces started to act. . . . The interest which began in those days captured me, body and soul." Some credit was also due Tech's extraordinary faculty. A summer job with the United States Coast Survey in 1867 gave him new assurance and purpose, and another in 1868 with the Calumet & Hecla copper mine in Michigan initiated his lifelong interest in ore dressing.

When he graduated, B.S., in 1868, the elements of his career had been determined. Appointed a chemistry instructor at M.I.T., he soon found his greatest strength to be in laboratory instruction, in the visual and tangible rather than the abstract and verbal. Lack of laboratory equipment brought out his talent for improvising. In 1871 his enthusiasm and energy led president John D. Runkle [q.v.] to put him in charge of organizing the mining and metallurgical laboratories at the Institute. Without much consciousness of historic innovation, simply doing his youthful best in the pioneering spirit which pervaded the new school, Richards worked out a laboratory program and equipment which for the first time anywhere made possible ore dressing and smelting on a scale large enough to illustrate and test actual mill operations, yet not too large for the finances of the school or the strength of the boys. Richards emphasized ore dressing or concentrating—the elimination of unwanted materials by mechanical processes—more than he did the chemical processes of smelting. As professor of mining engineering and head of the department from 1873 to 1914, Richards at one time or another taught mineralogy, metallurgy, and mining engineering as well as ore dressing, and directed the mining and metallurgical laboratories. His lectures were painstakingly prepared; his explanations were simple, clear, and patient; his goal was to instill good habits of thought and work and to teach those underlying principles which would be most useful in practice. In 1886 he was elected president of the American Institute of Mining Engineers.

The needs of his laboratory and the problems of consulting work led Richards to invent or improve a number of machines for ore dressing: separators, pulsators, jigs, and classifiers, the most significant being his "hindered-settling" classifier, devised for the lab in 1874 and adapted to industry in 1894. Although he did occasional consulting work for mining companies during more than half a century, especially for Calumet & Hecla, 1878–88, his suggestions for mechanical improvement were often developed commercially by others without royalties to him; he found that only close, prolonged, and sympathetic supervision in the mill ensured the proper introduction of a new device, and teaching kept him from that. His published papers numbered more than a hundred, mostly brief and technical. Beginning in 1893, he collected, collated, and analyzed data on the tech-

niques and machinery of nearly a hundred American mills for a four-volume work of more than 2,000 pages, *Ore Dressing* (1903–09), the only such study in English. Though it made him a recognized authority in the industry, the first two volumes were soon outmoded in part by the appearance of the Wilfley table, and the second two by the equally prompt introduction of ore flotation. He did not recover the $20,000 of his own money he had spent on the research. His one-volume *A Textbook of Ore Dressing* (1909) was much used, however, and revised as late as 1940. In the end, his most significant contributions to technology were probably in helping to strengthen M.I.T., setting a pattern for the education of mining engineers, and training some 700 of them, many of whom won high distinction in later life.

On June 4, 1875, Richards had married one of his students, Ellen Henrietta Swallow, the first woman admitted to M.I.T. Mrs. Richards [q.v.] shared her husband's interests fully (their honeymoon consisted of a field trip with his entire mechanical engineering class) and taught chemistry at M.I.T. until her death in 1911. On June 8, 1912, he married Lillian Jameson, who died in 1924. Both marriages were childless, but Richards's Jamaica Plain home during seventy years usually included one or more boarding students.

Richards retired, with some reluctance, in 1914, at the age of seventy. Thereafter he busied himself with consulting work, traveling often and keeping up a Boston office; with the affairs of the Protestant Episcopal congregation in which he had always been active; with tolerantly received advice to successive M.I.T. presidents; and with keeping fit by regular exercise, sensible diet, and abstinence from smoking. Tall, erect, naturally strong, with an aristocratic face and a full moustache, he lost no dignity in the long spinning out of his years. At eighty-five he toured Japan, where one of his former students, Baron Takuma Dan, was a leading industrialist. In 1936, now M.I.T.'s oldest living graduate, he published his memoirs, *Robert Hallowell Richards: His Mark,* pleasantly and interestingly discursive, full of simplehearted good nature. At ninety-six he had to give up archery, but on the eve of his hundredth birthday he was quoted as saying, "I've had a wonderful time" (*Boston Herald,* July 9, 1944). He died of hypostatic pneumonia at a nursing home in Natick, Mass., in his 101st year and was buried in Forest Hills Cemetery, Boston. He was survived by his brother Henry, who died at 100 four years later.

[Richards's autobiography, above, is the principal source; except as noted, the quotations are taken from it. The M.I.T. Archives has a collection of clippings and institutional correspondence relating to Richards (see especially President's Office File No. 354), some small memorandum books with brief notes made by him during the early 1870's, and some of his published writings. See also articles about him in M.I.T.'s *Technology Rev.*, July 1908 (with a full bibliography of his publications through 1907), July 1914, July 1922, and May 1945; the first two references include portraits. For a description of his home life with his first wife, see Caroline L. Hunt, *The Life of Ellen H. Richards* (1912), especially chap. vii. Death record from Mass. Registrar of Vital Statistics.]

ROBERT V. BRUCE

RIPLEY, WILLIAM ZEBINA (Oct. 13, 1867–Aug. 16, 1941), economist, was born in Medford, Mass., the only child of Nathaniel L. and Estimate (Baldwin) Ripley. His father, a descendant of William Ripley, who had come from England to Hingham, Mass., about 1638, was a manufacturer of jewelry in Boston. After attending public school in Newton, Mass., young Ripley enrolled at the Massachusetts Institute of Technology. The unusual breadth of his interests was early evident. He graduated in 1890 with the S.B. degree in civil engineering, but remained for an additional year of graduate work in economics. He then went to Columbia University, where in 1893 he was awarded the Ph.D. in political economy. His dissertation, *The Financial History of Virginia, 1609–1776,* was published that year. Ripley's academic career began simultaneously at M.I.T. and Columbia. At the first, he taught in the department of political science (1893–95) and then in sociology and economics, rising from instructor to professor (1901). At Columbia he was "Prize Lecturer" in physical geography and anthropology (or ethnology), 1893–99, and thereafter, until December 1901, in sociology. (For one year, 1901–02, he added a third appointment, as lecturer in economics at Harvard.) On Feb. 20, 1893, Ripley married Ida Sabine Davis, daughter of Charles S. Davis, a Boston piano manufacturer; their four children were Ruth, Davis Nichols, William Putnam, and Bettina.

The most influential of Ripley's early writings were in the field of anthropology. *The Races of Europe: A Sociological Study,* published in 1899 together with a slim companion volume entitled *A Selected Bibliography of the Anthropology and Ethnology of Europe,* grew out of a series of lectures he had delivered at Columbia and at the Lowell Institute in Boston. In this study, essentially a synthesis of the findings of European physical anthropologists between 1860 and 1895, Ripley divided the population of Europe into three white races: the Teutonic in the north and the Mediterranean in the south, both of old European stock, and, in between, the Alpine, migrants from Asia who had brought agriculture and the Neo-

lithic economy to central Europe. Onto the polygenism of European physical anthropology he grafted an environmentalist approach, attributing various physiological changes to social and geographical conditions, but at the same time holding that the essence of each racial type was impervious to environmental forces.

At a time when few people made any distinction between race, language, and culture, Ripley's book served to clarify the concept of race for American social scientists. Its most significant impact, however, was upon nativists, who quickly incorporated Ripley's concept of static racial types into their arguments and then attributed to each type a set of psychological characteristics: to their preferred race, the Teutonic (or "Nordic"), an aptitude for leadership in government; to the Alpine, a plodding but virtuous character; and to the Mediterranean, an artistic and licentious bent. After the turn of the century Ripley devoted most of his time to economics, but he still occasionally wrote or lectured on anthropology. One such lecture, in which he suggested that the consequence of racial intermixture might be reversion to a primitive type, greatly influenced a well-known advocate of immigration restriction, Madison Grant [Supp. 2].

In 1902 Ripley accepted appointment as professor of political economy at Harvard, where he remained until his retirement in 1933. He had meanwhile undertaken the first of many public service assignments. As expert agent on transportation for the United States Industrial Commission (1900–01), he investigated the relations of the railroads with the anthracite coal industry. In the years following, Ripley served as general editor of Selections and Documents in Economics, a ten-volume series devoted to making technical material on economic questions more accessible to students and the interested public; he personally edited two of the volumes, *Trusts, Pools and Corporations* (1905) and *Railway Problems* (1907).

Ripley's most important writings are the two companion volumes *Railroads: Rates and Regulation* (1912) and *Railroads: Finance & Organization* (1915). These reveal a man dedicated to the attainment of adequate service at reasonable rates from a vital industry. The battle to subject common carriers to public control had been won, but wise exercise of public authority remained to be achieved. To this end, he called for an informed public, a less corrupt and more enlightened railroad management, and broader vision on the part of federal and state governments. Ripley urged the country to give proper encouragement to private capital; otherwise he believed the federal government must take over ownership of the railroads—he called a mixed proprietorship "unthinkable." He based his conclusions on a voluminous mass of raw material, which he classified and realigned, finally formulating the governing economic principles.

Because of his expert knowledge of transportation and labor economics, Ripley was frequently called into government service. In 1916, as part of an investigation by the United States Eight-Hour Commission into the operation of the Adamson Act, he traveled widely to examine the working and living conditions of railway employees and prepared a special report on their wage schedules. During World War I he served the War Department as administrator of labor standards for army clothing (1918). He was chairman of the National Adjustment Commission of the United States Shipping Board, 1919–20.

When the Transportation Act of 1920, which returned the railroads to private ownership after the war, authorized voluntary consolidation of existing roads, Ripley, as a special examiner for the Interstate Commerce Commission, submitted a plan (1921) for grouping all the nation's railways into twenty systems. With minor modifications, his report was adopted by the Commission as its program, and Ripley worked hard behind the scenes to reconcile differences among the railroads that stood in the way. To his bitter disappointment, legislative approval did not come until 1932, by which time the crippling effect of the depression on the railroads prevented implementation of the plan. In accordance with his urge to improve railroad management, Ripley served as a director of the Chicago, Rock Island & Pacific Railway Company from 1917 to 1933.

During the 1920's Ripley returned to his earlier interest in corporation finance. His last book, *Main Street and Wall Street*, was published in 1927. A unified collection of essays, it focused on a number of disturbing developments in corporate practices and offered constructive remedial suggestions. By general agreement, it was one of the most provocative and controversial economic studies of the period. The title essay, originally published in the *Atlantic Monthly* in January 1926 as "From Main Street to Wall Street," dealt with the growing separation between corporate ownership and control through such devices as the establishment of holding companies and the issuance of nonvoting common stock. Public reaction to the article swamped the offices of the *Atlantic Monthly* with letters and provoked a decision by the board of governors of the New York Stock Exchange to consider in future refusing to add to its trading list the securities of companies with nonvoting common stock. The article won Ripley a Harmon Foundation award and gold medal in 1927.

A rugged-looking man with an outdoor complexion, Ripley was at ease not only with his scholarly peers but also with mill and railroad workers and with country farmers. In religion he was a Unitarian. He served as president of the American Economic Association (1933) and was awarded honorary degrees by Columbia (1929), Wisconsin (1930), the University of Rochester (1931), and Bucknell University (1931). He was also the first American to receive the Huxley Memorial Medal of the Royal Anthropological Institute of Great Britain and Ireland (1908), and was a corresponding member of the anthropological societies of Paris and Rome and of the Society of Natural Sciences, Cherbourg, France. In 1927 Ripley sustained a serious injury in a taxicab accident in New York City, from which he never fully recovered. He died at the age of seventy-three at Boothbay, Maine, near his summer home in East Edgecomb; the cause of his death is recorded as suicide by drowning. He was buried in the Boothbay Cemetery.

[*N. Y. Times* references to Ripley, particularly Sept. 26, 1926 (a biographical article in the magazine section), Jan. 20, 22, June 27, Sept. 25, 1927, May 1, 1932 (sec. 5), Dec. 31, 1932, Feb. 10, 1933, and obituary, Aug. 17, 1941; memoir in *Harvard Univ. Gazette*, Apr. 25, 1942; *Nat. Cyc. Am. Biog.*, XXXII, 65–66; *Who Was Who in America*, vol. I (1942); information supplied by surviving sons, Davis and William Ripley, and from official records of M.I.T., Columbia, Harvard, and the Am. Economic Assoc.; death record from Town Clerk, Boothbay, Maine. On Ripley's anthropological writings and their influence, see Carleton S. Coon, *The Races of Europe* (1939); George W. Stocking, Jr., *Race, Culture, and Evolution* (1968); and John Higham, *Strangers in the Land* (1955). A photograph and a biographical sketch of Ripley appear in the *Am. Economic Rev.*, Sept. 1952; an oil portrait and a collection of his papers are at Harvard.]

RITCHEY, GEORGE WILLIS (Dec. 31, 1864–Nov. 4, 1945), optical expert and astronomer, was born at Tuppers Plains, Meigs County, Ohio, the second of five sons of James and Eliza (Gould) Ritchey. His father, a native of Ireland, had migrated to the United States during the potato famine of 1846. A cabinetmaker by trade, he was also an amateur astronomer, owner of an 8½-inch reflecting telescope made by John A. Brashear [*q.v.*]. Thus George Ritchey was inspired early with a love of astronomy. He also possessed a manual dexterity and an inventive ability that later proved invaluable in his grinding of telescope mirrors and design of mountings. Ritchey attended public school near Pomeroy, a mining community in southeastern Ohio, until, in 1880, the family moved to Cincinnati. There he took courses (1883–84, 1886–87) at the University of Cincinnati; from 1886 to 1887 he was also an assistant at the Cincinnati observatory and made a 9-inch reflector. On Apr. 8, 1886, he married Lillie M. Gray of Cincinnati, by whom he had two children, Willis and Elfreda.

After moving to Chicago in 1888, Ritchey became head of the woodworking department at the Chicago Manual Training School. There, while working on the construction of a 2-foot telescope mirror, he met the young astronomer George Ellery Hale [Supp. 2]. In 1896 Hale, now director of the University of Chicago's Yerkes Observatory, brought Ritchey to its staff, at first as head of the optical laboratory and later as superintendent of instrument construction. Ritchey also taught practical astronomy at the University of Chicago (1901–04).

The 40-inch refracting telescope at Yerkes, the largest in the world, had originally been designed for visual observation only. By means of a color screen and isochromatic plate Ritchey turned it into a camera, and with it he took sharp, detailed photographs of the moon, planets, and planetary nebulae that have rarely been equaled in quality. At Yerkes also, his 24-inch reflector, with a skeleton tube and a design notable for its efficiency, was mounted; with it he took plates that helped prove the superiority of the reflector in the photography of faint stars, star clusters, and nebulae. There, too, he ground the mirror for a 60-inch reflector, for which Hale's father, William Hale, had donated the funds.

On the design of a telescope, the grinding of a mirror, the taking and developing of a plate, Ritchey would spend endless hours, never satisfied until the result was as near perfection as possible. Yet many of his plates, while beautiful, are limited in scientific value because he failed to record the date and time of observation or scribbled them on the dome door, where an irate carpenter later planed them off and painted them over. With the soul of an artist, he had, as a colleague put it, "the temperament of a thousand prima donnas."

In 1904, when the Mount Wilson Observatory was founded near Pasadena, Calif., under Hale's direction, Ritchey joined the staff as superintendent of construction (until 1909), then took charge of the optical shop. He worked first with Hale on the auxiliary instruments and design of the Snow horizontal reflecting telescope. He continued work on the 60-inch reflector, already ground and partly polished at Yerkes, and perfected a method of parabolizing that eliminated the need for any hand work. The telescope, with a fork-type mounting and "mechanical flotation" support system of his design, was set up on Mount Wilson in 1908 and was soon proving its superiority over any reflector yet built. In 1917 Ritchey's chance discovery of a nova in the galaxy NGC 6946, on a plate made with the 60-inch reflector, followed by the discovery of similar objects by other astronomers, played a key role in the interpretation of the nature of galaxies and measurement of their distances.

In 1908 the disc for a 100-inch telescope, ordered by Hale, arrived from the Saint Gobain company in France. It contained numerous bubbles: Ritchey was sure it was a failure. When it was finally accepted, he undertook with deep pessimism the slow, tedious process of grinding that, with the help of two able assistants, led to its completion in 1917. He worked also on the initial design of the mounting, later greatly modified. He was, however, convinced that the future of large telescopes lay in cellular mirrors and in a form of mounting which later, as the Ritchey-Chrétien aplanatic system (with a tube length considerably less than the focal length), was applied to various telescopes, including one at the Pic du Midi in the French Pyrenees and a 40-inch reflector at the United States Naval Observatory in Flagstaff, Ariz. When these and other ideas were not adopted at Mount Wilson, Ritchey's sense of isolation and persecution grew. In 1919, because of personality problems, accentuated by epileptic attacks, he was asked to resign.

For the next several years he carried on work in his private laboratory. In 1924—the year he was elected an associate member of the Royal Astronomical Society—Ritchey became director of the Dina Optical Laboratory of the Paris Observatory. His experiments there included the design of a series of "super" tower telescopes with interchangeable mirrors, all of the cellular type. "As cathedrals and churches, as universities and schools are dedicated to God," he wrote, "so these super-telescopes will be dedicated and soon." Unfortunately his dream proved impractical at the time. After leaving the Paris Observatory, he moved in 1931 to the Naval Observatory in Washington, D. C., where for the next five years he continued his research in astronomical photography. In 1936 he retired to his citrus ranch in Azusa, Calif., where he died in his eighty-first year of chronic myocarditis. Cremation followed at Rose Hills Crematory, Covina, Calif.

[Of Ritchey's published articles, some were based on his own outstanding work; in certain instances, however, he claimed credit for the plans and ideas of others. Some recent authors, relying too heavily on Ritchey's writings, have presented a distorted picture of his contribution to the growth of large telescopes and the development of celestial photography.

His articles include: "On the Modern Reflecting Telescope and the Making and Testing of Optical Mirrors," *Smithsonian Contributions to Knowledge,* vol. XXXIV (1904); a series of articles on "The Modern Photographic Telescope and the New Astronomical Photography" in the *Jour.* of the Royal Astronomical Soc. of Canada, May through Nov. 1928 and Jan., Apr. 1929; "L'évolution de l'astrographie et les grands télescopes de l'avenir," with a biographical introduction by L. Delloye, published by the Société Astronomique de France (1929). Manuscript sources include the Hale Papers at the Hale Observatories and the Calif. Inst. of Technology; and the Elihu Thomson Papers at the Am. Philosophical Soc., Philadelphia. Biographical articles include: F. J. Hargreaves in *Royal Astronomical Soc., Monthly Notices,* vol. CVII, no. 1 (1947); Deborah J. Mills in *Am. Scientist,* Mar. 1966. See also *Am. Men of Sci.* (7th ed., 1944); and *Who Was Who in America,* vol. IV (1968). Accounts of different aspects of Ritchey's work appear in G. Edward Pendray, *Men, Mirrors and Stars* (1935); Henry C. King, *The Hist. of the Astronomy of the 20th Century* (1962); and Helen Wright, *Explorer of the Universe* (1966), a biography of George E. Hale.]

HELEN WRIGHT

RITTER, WILLIAM EMERSON (Nov. 19, 1856–Jan. 10, 1944), naturalist and science administrator, was born on his father's farm near Hampden, Wis., the first son and third of five children of Horatio and Leonora (Eason) Ritter, both natives of New York state. In later life he spoke of the influence which his rural boyhood, with its close communion with nature, had had upon his philosophical predilections and choice of career. He graduated in 1884 from the State Normal School at Oshkosh and taught in the public schools of both Wisconsin and California before enrolling at the University of California during the year 1886–87 to study with Joseph Le Conte [*q.v.*], some of whose writings he had read. After receiving the B.S. degree in 1888, he went on to graduate study in natural history at Harvard, where he took an A.M. degree in 1891 and the Ph.D. in 1893, at the age of thirty-six.

Upon receipt of his master's degree Ritter had returned to the University of California, where he was appointed an instructor in biology and organized the university's first laboratory instruction in that subject. At this same time (June 23, 1891) he married Dr. Mary E. Bennett, who, after some years of private practice as a physician in Berkeley, joined the university as a lecturer on hygiene and then as medical examiner of women students; they had no children. In 1893 Ritter was raised to the rank of assistant professor. He spent the academic year 1894–95 abroad, at the Zoological Station at Naples and at the University of Berlin. He became associate professor in 1898 and professor in 1902.

Until about 1910 Ritter's major scientific interests lay in the fields of morphology and taxonomy. His doctoral dissertation, "On the Eyes, the

Integumentary Sense Papillae, and the Integument of the San Diego Blind Fish (*Typhlogobius californiensis, Steindachner*)," affirmed his interest in marine life, an interest that was broadened by his participation in 1899 in the Harriman Alaska Expedition. In connection with his teaching, Ritter conducted a series of informal summer laboratories at various places along the southern California coast. As early as 1901 he had begun to think of a permanent marine biology station where "detailed, comprehensive, continuous and long-continued observation and experiment" would be possible.

Like other scientists in these years before the existence of philanthropic foundations and government subvention, Ritter was forced to raise money among interested individuals to finance his summer excursions. His wife testified that he was one "who could never ask anyone directly for a dollar," but he had the talent of inspiring prospective donors with something of his own interest in research. Through the aid of Dr. Fred Baker, a San Diego physician and amateur naturalist, the Marine Biological Association of San Diego was incorporated in 1903 to support Ritter's summer laboratory, which at that time was moved to the San Diego area, at La Jolla. The association began raising funds; among those contributing were the newspaper publisher E. W. Scripps and his sister Ellen Browning Scripps [*qq.v.*].

Scripps had a deserved reputation for being difficult to know, but something, perhaps their common rural background, brought him close to Ritter. Indeed, it has been said that the latter was "the only person with whom he ever developed a genuine and close personal friendship." Together, the philanthropist and the scientist were to establish three important institutions: the Scripps Institution of Oceanography at La Jolla, the Foundation for Population Research at Miami University in Ohio, and Science Service in Washington, D. C.

The biological station at La Jolla gradually evolved, between 1903 and 1909, from a summer teaching operation into the ongoing research center which Ritter had envisioned. In 1909 he moved to La Jolla as its full-time head, a position he held until 1923, at which time he became professor emeritus at the University of California. Named the Scripps Institution for Biological Research when the university took it over in 1912, the station became the Scripps Institution of Oceanography in 1925. Ritter and Scripps worked closely together during its early years, though it was clear that their perceptions of its fundamental purpose diverged somewhat. Although Ritter was not without his own philosophical quirks, he was thinking in terms of a fairly straightforward biological (later oceanographic) research center. Scripps, for his part, had always been attracted to the problem of man's true nature, and during his association with Ritter he came to believe that biology was, in fact, the parent of the social sciences.

When the expansion of the Institution's program to include man as well as marine species appeared clearly to conflict with University of California policy, Ritter and Scripps turned to other agencies to carry on this broader work. The Foundation for Population Research was established in 1922, with Scripps providing the endowment and the sociologist Warren S. Thompson as director. Its work reflected the concern of Scripps over the growth, distribution, and support of world population, especially the apparent migration from rural to urban areas.

Science Service, a news agency, sought to bring accurate scientific information to the public by preparing material for newspapers and by its own weekly *Science News-Letter*. Founded in 1921, with trustees nominated by both scientific and newspaper groups, the Service encountered early difficulties, for, as Ritter discovered, many of his colleagues regarded "newspaper science" with some abhorrence. At the suggestion of Scripps, Ritter gave up his directorship at La Jolla in 1923 and moved to Washington, D. C., to give Science Service his personal attention.

Ritter returned to Berkeley in 1927 and spent most of the rest of his life dealing with those philosophical questions which he had long considered to be implicit in his biological work. A Unitarian in religion, he had been influenced by Le Conte, by Josiah Royce [*q.v.*] at Harvard, and by a faculty colleague in the philosophy department at Berkeley, George Holmes Howison [*q.v.*], who considered himself a subjective idealist. Increasingly, after 1910, Ritter—no doubt under the prodding of Scripps—concentrated his attention on the problem of finding in nature a justification for the moral principles which he already cherished. He published many articles on the subject, and such books as *War, Science and Civilization* (1915), *The Higher Usefulness of Science* (1918), and *The Unity of the Organism* (1919). The two major works to appear after his retirement were *The Natural History of Our Conduct* (1927) and *The California Woodpecker and I* (1938), both of which sought to examine human conduct in the light of the behavior of non-human animals. After his death another collection of his biological-philosophical papers was published under the title *Charles Darwin and the Golden Rule* (1954).

Ritter continued his mental activity even during the last few months of his life when his health was far from robust. He made his home at the Hotel Claremont in Berkeley and died of a heart attack in that city in 1944, at the age of eighty-seven. He was buried in the Sunset Mausoleum in Berkeley.

[Ritter's personal papers and MSS. were left to Edna Watson Bailey of Berkeley, who had collaborated on some of his books, as literary executor. Some of these papers, together with a photograph, a biographical sketch, and a complete bibliography of his writings, appear in *Charles Darwin and the Golden Rule*. Obituary notices and biographical sketches also appear in *Sci. Monthly*, Mar. 1927; *Science*, Apr. 28, 1944 (by Francis B. Sumner); *Science News-Letter*, Jan. 22, 1944; *Auk*, Oct. 1947; *N. Y. Times*, Jan. 11, 1944; and Univ. of Calif., *In Memoriam, 1943-45*, pp. 75-77. See also *Who Was Who in America*, vol. II (1950); *Nat. Cyc. Am. Biog.*, XVI, 43-44. Information about Ritter's family from federal census returns of 1860 and 1870 (courtesy of State Hist. Soc. of Wis.). Aspects of his career as an administrator are covered by Ritter himself in the pamphlet *Science Service as One Expression of E. W. Scripps's Philosophy of Life* (1926) and in the booklet, *The Marine Biological Station of San Diego: Its Hist., Present Conditions, Achievements, and Aims* (1912). For a discussion of Ritter's relationship with Scripps and their joint projects, see Oliver Knight, ed., *I Protest: Selected Disquisitions of E. W. Scripps* (1966), pp. 725-29.]

CARROLL PURSELL

ROBERTS, ELIZABETH MADOX (Oct. 30, 1881–Mar. 13, 1941), author, was born at Perryville, Ky., the first daughter and second child in a family of six boys and two girls. Her forebears had come from Wales, Ireland, and Germany to Virginia and North Carolina in the eighteenth century. Her father, Simpson Roberts, traced his descent from Abram Roberts, who had migrated over Boone's Trace to the Kentucky wilderness, and her mother, Mary Elizabeth (Brent) Roberts, was also descended from Kentucky pioneers. Both families had taken the Confederate side in the Civil War. Elizabeth's parents had been schoolteachers, but when she was about three the family moved to Springfield, Ky., where her father opened a grocery store and worked as a surveyor and engineer. He had lost his library in a fire and was not prosperous, but his love for telling his children Greek and Roman myths and recounting his Civil War adventures early stimulated Elizabeth's imagination. She wrote her first story when she was eight and her first poem when she was eleven, but she had little confidence in her abilities and little formal training, and received scant encouragement.

Springfield had no public schools, but Elizabeth attended Covington Institute, a private school in the town. In 1896 she went to high school in Covington, Ky., where she lived with her mother's relatives and graduated in 1900. Soon afterward she became a member of the Springfield Christian Church. Although she had been admitted to the University of Kentucky, poor health or lack of money frustrated her wish to go to college.

In the years 1900–10 Miss Roberts conducted private classes at home and then taught in the new Springfield public school and at schools in the surrounding countryside. In this way she absorbed a knowledge of rural Kentucky and its people, their idiom and folklore. Suffering from respiratory ailments including incipient tuberculosis, she spent much time after 1910 in Colorado with her brother Charles and her sister, Llewellyn. There she began serious attempts to write. Verses which she composed to accompany photographs of mountain flowers by Kenneth Hartley appeared in a booklet issued in Colorado Springs for the tourist trade: *In the Great Steep's Garden* (1915). These first published poems revealed her characteristic precision of observation and pantheistic view of nature.

In 1917, at the age of thirty-six, Elizabeth Roberts enrolled at the University of Chicago, helping to support herself by giving music lessons to children. She became a protégée of Prof. Robert Morss Lovett and also studied under the medievalist Edith Rickert [Supp. 2]. The literary and cultural renaissance then flourishing in Chicago exercised a liberating influence, and her studies in literature and philosophy strengthened her determination to become a writer. Although very reserved in manner and jealous of her privacy, she formed strong friendships among a group of students who later achieved literary recognition, including Glenway Wescott, Yvor Winters, Janet L. Lewis, Monroe Wheeler, and Vincent Sheean. She was an active member of the University Poetry Club, and Harriet Monroe [Supp. 2], the editor of *Poetry* magazine, encouraged her. Miss Roberts was elected to Phi Beta Kappa and in 1921 received the Ph.B. degree in English, with honors. The fruits of her college literary activity were published in *Under the Tree* (1922; enlarged edition, 1930), a volume of poems based on her childhood experiences.

After graduation Miss Roberts returned to Springfield and, drawing upon the Kentucky life that she had known closely since childhood, began her work as a writer of fiction. Because of continued ill health and severe headaches she spent the winter of 1923–24 in treatment at the Austen Riggs Foundation in Stockbridge, Mass. Her first novel, *The Time of Man* (1926), won international acclaim. In this story Miss Roberts juxtaposed the rich experience of Ellen Chesser's inner life, from youth through middle age, with the harsh circumstances of her outer life as a tobacco farmer's daughter and then as a farmer's wife. The epical struggle which men of the soil must always wage with the elements informs the "poetic realism" underlying the book. In *My Heart and My Flesh* (1927), which added to her reputation, she charted the progression of Theodosia Bell, a self-centered girl born to all worldly advantages, through deprivation and suffering to a womanhood of poised serenity. *Jingling in the Wind* (1928), which merged fantasy and satire to comment upon the materialism of American life, is her least controlled and significant book.

Miss Roberts's second major success was *The Great Meadow* (1930), a re-creation of pioneer life in Kentucky during the period of the Revolutionary War and a novel which powerfully evokes her own ancestral past. Based partly on family records and memories, the book centers upon Diony Jarvis, who advances through physical hardship and the deepening of sensibility to spiritual strength. Her inner growth is seen as the necessary counterpart to the heroic struggles of her husband, Berk Jarvis, in the world of action. The feminine as well as the masculine attributes were indispensable in civilizing the wilderness. The novel is notable for its fusion of historical fact, Berkeleyan philosophy, psychological insight, and lyric intensity. In *A Buried Treasure* (1931) the virtues of the Kentucky pioneers, surviving into the present, influence the maturing of Ben Shepherd. This book, Miss Roberts's most vivid excursion into the life of the Kentucky folk, also traces the disintegrative effects of cupidity upon Philly Blair and her husband. They eventually recognize that their treasure is the land, rather than the money which they discover and are soon robbed of.

Miss Roberts continued to live with her parents in Springfield (eventually in an addition to their house which she built), while making long visits to her sister in California and to New York. During the years 1931–35 her health was much improved. Those who knew her well testify to her integrity as an artist, her aloofness and self-possession, and her charm.

In 1932 she published her first collection of short stories, *The Haunted Mirror,* impressionistic in style and psychologically oriented. Her next novel, *He Sent Forth a Raven* (1935), was an allegorical work that received little praise or understanding. Its theme was the spiritual triumph of Jocelle Drake, with her "needs of a heart," over the forces of materialism, skepticism, and alienation, represented by other characters and a world at war. Miss Roberts used the same theme in a more restricted setting and area of experience in *Black Is My Truelove's Hair* (1938). In this book she recounts the spiritual awakening of Dena Janes after a traumatic sexual betrayal and her subsequent escape from the death-bringing influence of her seducer.

From the mid-1930's Miss Roberts's reputation with the general public declined sharply, and with it the income from her books. She had begun to suffer from chronic anemia and a persistent skin infection. Now spending her winters in Florida, she commenced work on a novel dealing with the great Louisville flood of 1937 and started an epic poem about Daniel Boone, neither of which she lived to complete. A second volume of poems, *Song in the Meadow,* appeared in 1940, and a second volume of short stories, *Not by Strange Gods,* in 1941, shortly after her death. Although in her last years she received a number of honors, including election to the National Institute of Arts and Letters in 1940, she withdrew increasingly from personal contacts and apparently retreated deep into the self. In 1941 her illness was diagnosed as Hodgkin's disease. She died at Orlando, Fla., in her sixtieth year, and was buried on Cemetery Hill in Springfield, Ky.

Although Miss Roberts's novels are graphic portrayals of Kentucky life, they are most impressive for their timeless qualities. Her strongest characters have an authentic life on the soil, and her work is memorable for its depiction of the intimate relationships that exist between man and nature. Her characters are also convincing when they are part of the bizarre world of nightmare, neurotic suffering, and tragic defeat; to some degree, her novels are all parables that illustrate the themes of psychic death and psychic restoration. In her awareness of the complexities of the inner life, she probed more deeply into the psychic realm than did any Southern novelist before the generation of Thomas Wolfe [Supp. 2], William Faulkner, Katherine Anne Porter, Eudora Welty, and Caroline Gordon. She was a conscious stylist who skillfully employed the devices of language to secure her precise and subtle effects, and she was able to combine structural firmness with the luminous rendition of the minds of her central characters.

[The Elizabeth Madox Roberts Papers are in the Lib. of Cong. Books on her life and work are: Harry M. Campbell and Ruel E. Foster, *Elizabeth Madox Roberts: Am. Novelist* (1956), informative but uncritical; Earl H. Rovit, *Herald to Chaos: The Novels of Elizabeth Madox Roberts* (1960), an incisive study of the novels as literary art; and Frederick P. W. McDowell, *Elizabeth Madox Roberts* (1963), in which the biographical details were checked with Ivor S. Roberts, Miss Roberts's brother and literary executor.

Woodridge Spears, "Elizabeth Madox Roberts: A Biog. and Critical Study" (Ph.D. dissertation, Univ. of Ky., 1953), contains many interesting details but lacks focus. The bibliographies of the Rovit and McDowell books, above, list the principal periodical articles and critical essays on Miss Roberts. See also: Mary E. Brent Roberts, "Memories of Life on a Farm in Hart County, Ky., in the Early Sixties" (with preface by Elizabeth M. Roberts), *Filson Club Hist. Quart.,* July 1940; obituaries in *Louisville Courier-Jour.,* Mar. 14, 15, 1941; John M. Bradbury, *Renaissance in the South: A Critical Hist. of the Literature, 1920–1960* (1963); Robert Penn Warren's introduction to Compass Books edition of *The Time of Man* (1963); and Herman E. Spivey, "The Mind and Creative Habits of Elizabeth Madox Roberts," in Robert A. Bryan et al., eds., *All These to Teach: Essays in Honor of C. A. Robertson* (1965).]

FREDERICK P. W. McDOWELL

ROBINS, MARGARET DREIER (Sept. 6, 1868–Feb. 21, 1945), social reformer and labor leader, was born in Brooklyn, N. Y., the first of five children of German parents, Theodor and Dorothea Adelheid (Dreier) Dreier. Her father had migrated to America in 1849 from Bremen, where for generations the Dreiers had been merchants and civic leaders. Finding employment in the New York branch of an English iron firm, he launched a successful career in the metal trade. On a visit to Germany in 1864, he married a cousin, the daughter of a country parson in the German Evangelical Church. Settling in Brooklyn, the Dreiers rose to local prominence. Margaret had a sunny childhood, growing up as she did in most comfortable circumstances amid a large, affectionate family. She attended small private schools in Brooklyn but did not go to college because her parents considered cultural pursuits more fitting. Her father, himself an active civic leader, also instilled in her a spirit of service and idealism. Quickly wearying of the conventional round of social activities, she undertook as a young woman a private course of study in history and philosophy and increasingly moved in a highminded circle of Brooklyn educators, ministers, and doctors. From the age of nineteen, too, she served as secretary-treasurer of the women's auxiliary of the Brooklyn Hospital. In its wards she was first exposed in a direct way to the plight of the poor.

In her early thirties, as the momentum of social reform mounted in New York, Margaret Dreier found her vocation. Invited in 1902 to join the State Charities Aid Association's city visiting committee for the state insane asylums, she became a strong advocate of improved treatment of the insane. She also helped transform the Women's Municipal League, originally founded to aid the candidacy of Seth Low [*q.v.*] for mayor of New York City in 1901, into a continuing organization for mobilizing women in support of social legislation. As chairman of the League's legislative committee, she led the strenuous campaign of 1903–04 that resulted in a pioneering state law regulating private employment agencies in New York. These activities drew Miss Dreier under the tutelage of such notable reformers as Homer Folks. She had discovered her calling, but not yet her distinctive place.

The National Women's Trade Union League had been formed in 1903 during the annual convention of the American Federation of Labor. Although the initiative had come primarily from outside the labor movement—William English Walling [Supp. 2] was a prime mover—and membership was not restricted to wage workers, the League held closely to the trade union objectives of organizing female workers and improving their conditions through collective bargaining. In early 1904 Margaret and her sister Mary were enlisted into the League's struggling New York branch, and Margaret quickly became its president. Thenceforth organized labor was the primary interest of the Dreier sisters. They gave it priority over legislation and social welfare for working women. It was not only a matter of wages and hours, Margaret argued. "Beyond these is the incentive for initiative and social leadership. . . . The union shop calls up the moral and reasoning faculties, the sense of fellowship, independence and group strength. In every workshop there is unknown wealth of intellectual and moral resources" (*New York Times,* Feb. 22, 1945). To release these energies among America's depressed laboring women, Margaret Dreier committed herself to the Women's Trade Union League, and became thereby one of the handful of Progressives—and the most notable among them—who channeled their efforts primarily into trade unionism.

On June 21, 1905, she married Raymond Robins, head of the Northwestern University Settlement in Chicago, and transferred her activities to that city. Although both were independently wealthy, they moved into a cold-water flat in a tenement in Chicago's slum-ridden West Side and resided there through most of their active careers. (They had no children.) In 1907 Mrs. Robins became president of the National Women's Trade Union League, as well as president of the Chicago branch. She played a leading part in the great strikes of garment workers during the years 1909–11. In Philadelphia she mobilized the middle-class women who raised money, acted as watchers on picket lines to prevent police brutality, and publicized the plight of the striking girls. In Chicago she served on the strike committee and helped organize the commissary that

fed thousands of strikers and their families. At her instigation, the N.W.T.U.L. in 1914 established a school to train working women for trade union leadership—a pioneering effort in the American labor movement. After World War I, Mrs. Robins's labor interests became international. She called the first International Congress of Working Women, which convened in Washington, D. C., in 1919, and served as its president until 1923. Until her retirement as N.W.T.U.L. president in 1922, she did yeoman service for the League, helping to edit its journal, *Life and Labor,* raising funds (including her own) for its activities, and through her vibrant and sympathetic personality giving it strong leadership. "More than any other single person," in the judgment of a recent historian, "she was responsible for making the League an effective and efficient force for the organization and protection of women wage earners" (Davis, *Spearheads for Reform,* p. 146).

Mrs. Robins engaged in a wide range of other activities, often along with her husband. She participated in the woman suffrage movement and aided the work of her husband for municipal reform. An active member of the Progressive party in 1912, she served on its state executive committee. After 1916 she supported the Republican party, and in 1919 and 1920 was a member of the women's division of the Republican National Committee. In the 1930's, however, she became an enthusiastic supporter of the New Deal.

In 1925 Mrs. Robins and her husband moved permanently to their estate, Chinsegut Hill, in Hernando County, Fla., where they had vacationed ever since their marriage. Suffering from pernicious anemia and rheumatic heart disease, she died there in 1945 and was buried on the estate.

[The only biography, Mary E. Dreier, *Margaret Dreier Robins* (1950), is an adulatory account but includes generous portions of her speeches and correspondence as well as a good portrait. The *N. Y. Times,* Feb. 22, 1945, contains an obituary, and the sketch in the *Nat. Cyc. Am. Biog.,* XXXIII, 584, details her various offices and affiliations. See also sketch by Allen F. Davis in *Notable Am. Women,* III, 179–81, and Davis's *Spearheads for Reform* (1967). Mrs. Robins's papers are deposited at the Univ. of Fla. at Gainesville, her husband's at the Wis. State Hist. Soc. The Nat. Women's Trade Union League Papers are in the Lib. of Cong. The Mary Anderson Papers and the Leonora O'Reilly Papers, both in the Schlesinger Lib., Radcliffe College, also contain letters of Mrs. Robins.]

DAVID BRODY

ROBSON, MAY (Apr. 19, 1858–Oct. 20, 1942), actress, was born Mary Jeanette Robison at Wagga Wagga near the Murrumbidgee River in New South Wales, Australia, the daughter of

English parents, Henry and Julia Robison. Her father, a former sea captain, had retired and migrated with his family to the Australian bush in an effort to regain failing health; he died three months after Mary's birth. Mrs. Robison took her baby and the older children—two boys and a girl—to St. Kilda, Victoria, a suburb of Melbourne, and, when Mary was seven, moved to England.

In London, Mary studied at the Convent of the Sacred Heart at Highgate. There she learned to sew; a passion for needlework remained with her throughout her life. Her education proceeded at the Pension Semboiselle in Brussels and the Pension Passy in Paris. While home on vacation, she met and quickly married Charles Levison Gore. In 1877 they sailed for America and settled in Fort Worth, Texas, where their three children were born. After several years, Gore lost his capital in an unsuccessful venture in livestock and moved his family to New York City. He died soon afterward, and two of the children also died at about this time.

Left penniless in New York with a son, Edward, to support, Mary tried painting china and menu cards for Tiffany's, and taught painting. Her earnings were meager, however, and she turned on impulse to the stage. She had had no previous theatre experience, but in her debut on Sept. 17, 1883, at the Grand Opera House, Brooklyn, she played Tilly, a kitchen slavey, in *Hoop of Gold* so successfully that the manager enlarged the role. Through a printer's error, her name appeared on the program as May Robson, a form which she retained for luck.

Her first role served in important respects as a prototype for most of the eighty-odd characterizations which she evolved for the stage. The auburn-haired beauty delighted in playing eccentrics, usually elderly or unhandsome. She diverted her painting skills to greasepaint, gaining renown as a makeup expert. Although adept at eliciting tears from her audiences, she excelled in comedy. She displayed her capacities now in melodrama or realistic plays and again in vaudeville, musical comedy, or burlesque.

Between 1884 and 1901 May Robson played in the stock companies of three famous managers: A. M. Palmer [*q.v.*] of the Madison Square Theatre, Daniel Frohman [Supp. 2] of the Lyceum, and Charles Frohman [*q.v.*] of the Empire. She also taught character acting at the schools connected with the Frohman theatres and, later, at the American Academy of Dramatic Art. On May 29, 1889, she was married to Dr. Augustus Homer Brown, police surgeon for New York City. She had no children by this marriage, which lasted until Brown's death in 1920.

After leaving Charles Frohman's management in 1901, May Robson searched for a script that would capitalize on her peculiar talents, all the while continuing to play featured roles such as Mrs. Meade in *Cousin Billy* (1905) and Mrs. Sibsey in *The Mountain Climber* (1906), both with Francis Wilson. *The Rejuvenation of Aunt Mary* launched her as a star at Scranton, Pa., on Oct. 8, 1907. Although New York rejected the piece, she toured the whole of the United States and Canada in it for most of a decade, transporting it in August 1910 to England for an interim stand. From time to time she tried, with indifferent success, to wean her audiences away to other plays—notably *The Three Lights,* renamed *A Night Out,* which she co-authored with Charles T. Dazey.

She made a movie of *The Rejuvenation of Aunt Mary* for Cecil B. DeMille, released in 1927. Her film experience, however, dated back to work with Vitagraph in 1911 and continued on through the late 1920's and '30's, when she supported some of the era's biggest stars. Although she appeared in such important films as *Strange Interlude* (1932), *Reunion in Vienna* (1933), and *Dinner at Eight* (1933), her greatest single success came in 1933 as Apple Annie in Frank Capra's *Lady for a Day.* Her consistently high-quality performances won her many honors, including the American Institute of Cinematography's Award of Achievement. A beloved member of the motion picture colony, she was a trouper to the last, continuing to play film roles, despite failing eyesight, until a few months before her death of cancer at the age of eighty-four. She died at her home in Beverly Hills, Calif., survived by her son, a grandson, and two great-grandchildren. Following cremation, her ashes were buried in Flushing, N. Y., beside those of Dr. Brown.

[May Robson's papers in the Lib. of Cong.—scrapbooks, letters, photographs, autographs, mementos—comprise the best biographical source. Second in value is the Robinson Locke Collection of Scrapbooks in the Theatre Collection, N. Y. Public Lib. at Lincoln Center. See also: May Robson, "My Beginnings," *Theatre,* Nov. 1907; Lewis C. Strang, *Famous Actresses of the Day in America* (1899), chap. xxxi; Frank Condon in *Collier's,* Jan. 26, 1935; George C. D. Odell, *Annals of the N. Y. Stage,* vols. XII–XV (1940–49); John Parker, ed., *Who's Who in the Theatre* (8th ed., 1936, and 9th ed., 1939); *The Am. Movies Reference Book: The Sound Era* (1969); *N. Y. Times,* Oct. 21, 24, 1942; death record (from Calif. Dept. of Public Health). On her birthplace and early life, see *British Australasian,* Sept. 8, 1910; Burns Mantle, "How Mary Robison Became May Robson" (unidentified clipping, May Robson Papers); and *Fort Worth* (Texas) *Record,* Apr. 2, 1911.]

CLARA M. BEHRINGER

ROOSEVELT, FRANKLIN DELANO (Jan. 30, 1882–Apr. 12, 1945), thirty-second president of the United States, was born on an estate at Hyde Park, N. Y. For generations his ancestors on both sides had been men of affairs who enjoyed high social standing. Roosevelt took pride in their exploits, which helped give him an immediate, personal view of the nation's history; in college he boasted of the "democratic spirit" of his Dutch ancestors, who felt that "there was no excuse for them if they did not do their duty by the community." On his father's side he traced his lineage to Claes Martenzen van Rosenvelt, who emigrated from Holland to New Amsterdam in the seventeenth century—the common ancestor of Franklin D. Roosevelt and his fifth cousin, Theodore Roosevelt.

For several generations the Roosevelts were merchants and sugar refiners in New York City. Franklin's great-grandfather bought an estate on the Hudson River near Poughkeepsie, and his branch of the family became country gentlemen. Franklin D. Roosevelt four times took his oath of office as president on the family's old Dutch Bible, but in fact he had little Dutch blood; most of his ancestors had originally come from England. The forebear of his mother's family, the Delanos, was Philippe de la Noye of Luxembourg. who had come to Plymouth with the English Pilgrims in 1621. His mother's father, Warren Delano, made a fortune in the China trade and Appalachian coal properties and lived on an estate across the Hudson near Newburgh. Roosevelt's mother, Sara Delano, a handsome, strongminded woman, at twenty-six married James Roosevelt, a widower twice her age who had a grown son. The vice-president of the Delaware & Hudson Railroad, James Roosevelt led a leisurely life managing his investments and acting like a benign English squire toward the villagers in Hyde Park.

Franklin, their only child, received a rather unusual upbringing for an American boy. He was taught at home by a Swiss governess and accompanied his parents to various European watering places several months each year. His one experience in a public school was six weeks at a Volksschule at Bad Nauheim. It was a sheltered childhood, but a happy one. Roosevelt learned to speak both French and German, developed pleasant manners and charm, and became as much at ease on one side of the Atlantic as on the other. His father taught him outdoor sports. At home, his playmates were almost entirely relatives or children from neighboring estates. He read omnivorously and retained what he read with remarkable ease. He was, however, active rather than contemplative, and a collector of stamps, birds, and naval prints as well as books. The troubles of America in the 1880's and 1890's scarcely impinged upon his consciousness. Although high-spirited and gregarious as a youth, Roosevelt learned early to cope with the highly structured existence his parents imposed upon him by keeping some of his thoughts and actions to himself. He thus prevented clashes with his dominant mother, and avoided alarming his elderly and ill father. It was a trait he developed to the point of stoicism. Once on a train with them a steel bar fell and gashed his forehead. Yet he hid the mishap from his parents all day to protect his father from distress.

In 1896, at fourteen, Roosevelt was plunged into the Spartan rigors of Groton School, Groton, Mass., where Rector Endicott Peabody [Supp. 3] sought to educate the sons of the elite and indoctrinate them in their Christian responsibilities to society. Roosevelt stoically accepted the customary hazing from his classmates, managed to stay out of trouble, and lastingly bore the impress of Peabody's strenuous social ethic. Peabody reinforced Roosevelt's rather uncomplicated Episcopalian faith. Though Roosevelt never demonstrated much interest in theology, he was for years senior warden of St. James' Church in Hyde Park, and his Book of Common Prayer was well thumbed.

From Groton, Roosevelt went on to Harvard. His grades were acceptable, but it is less certain that he learned much from the famous professors, including Frederick Jackson Turner [q.v.], with whom he studied than that he maintained an active extracurricular life. In his senior year he was president (editor) of the *Harvard Crimson* and was elected permanent chairman of the class committee of the Class of 1904. (Completing the requirements in three years, he had actually received his A.B. in 1903.) Roosevelt next entered the Columbia Law School. His work was fairly good, but after passing his bar examinations in the spring of the third year, he did not bother to finish his courses and take his LL.B. degree.

In his final year at Harvard, Roosevelt had become engaged to Anna Eleanor Roosevelt, a distant cousin and the niece of Theodore Roosevelt. She was a willowy young woman of earnestness and energy combined with high ideals. It was a noble courtship, carried on against the initial opposition of Roosevelt's mother. In time Sara Delano Roosevelt capitulated, but then sought to dominate her son's bride. On Mar. 17, 1905, President Theodore Roosevelt came to New York City to review a St. Patrick's Day parade and to give away his niece at her wedding. At the reception, the bride and groom found themselves deserted, and joined the throng around the president. Franklin had long admired Theodore Roosevelt and, although his branch of the family were Democrats, had voted for him in 1904. It was to a considerable extent the example of Theodore Roosevelt that impelled him toward politics and public service.

In his first years out of law school, Roosevelt seemed little more than another pleasant young New York socialite and law clerk. He spent three indifferent years with Carter, Ledyard, and Milburn, a Wall Street firm. Small claims cases that brought him into contact with ordinary people in the municipal courts aroused his greatest interest; he later said that it was through social service while at Harvard and his work in these courts that he came to know the way of thinking of "people having a desperately hard time making a living." His wife, Eleanor, who had worked for the Consumers' League and at the Rivington Street Settlement, also helped make him aware of the poverty of slum dwellers.

Yet Roosevelt during his early political career was to be a spokesman for farmers rather than for the urban underprivileged. His entrance into politics came in 1910 when Democratic leaders in heavily Republican Dutchess County, where Hyde Park is located, invited him to run for the state senate. Despite the odds against him, Roosevelt campaigned with verve, driving up and down the farm roads in a red Maxwell touring car, an unusual sight. He spoke out against political bosses of both parties. The New York Republicans split that year between conservatives and progressives, and in the Democratic landslide, Roosevelt was elected.

In the New York senate Roosevelt, just turning twenty-nine, almost immediately made himself one of the most publicized figures in state politics. He assumed leadership of Democratic insurgents blocking the election in the legislature of the Tammany Hall candidate for United States Senator, William F. Sheehan, a traction and utilities magnate. For three months they held out before compromising and accepting another candidate of the New York City Democratic organization, James A. O'Gorman. Roosevelt, firmly established as a progressive on the basis of his opposition to Tammany, went on to champion the interests of the upstate farmers, conservationists, and advocates of good government. Again and again he sparred with the Tammany legislators, particularly over such reforms as the direct primary, which he supported. Ironically, however, it was the Tammany men who in the aftermath of the Triangle shirtwaist factory fire of 1911 did most to enact factory safety legislation and other welfare laws, many of which Roosevelt favored. He also backed a workmen's compensation bill that the State Federation of Labor sought. As his following grew, Roosevelt began to rid himself of his aristocratic mode of dress and a habit of holding his head high which made him appear a rather toplofty young patrician. When he ran for reelection in 1912, typhoid fever kept him from campaigning. At this point, a shrewd, wizened newspaperman from Saratoga, Louis McHenry Howe [Supp. 2], went to work for him so effectively that Roosevelt not only won but ran ahead of the Democratic candidates for president and governor. Howe for the rest of his life continued working for Roosevelt, as secretary, press agent, and alter ego.

Early in 1912 Roosevelt projected himself into presidential politics as a spokesman for New York progressive anti-Tammany Democrats who favored Woodrow Wilson, and he continued his strong advocacy both before and after the Democratic convention. His reward was an appointment, in March 1913, as Assistant Secretary of the Navy, the office he most coveted in Washington. At thirty-one, he assumed his duties amidst unusual publicity, since it was from this position that Theodore Roosevelt had catapulted himself to national fame and the White House. Franklin Roosevelt during his seven years' service was closely supervised by his firm superior, Secretary of the Navy Josephus Daniels. He was often impatient with Daniels and sometimes tried to undercut his authority, but in the end learned much from him, including how to get along with Congressional leaders. Roosevelt also gained firsthand experience in labor relations dealing with the workers in navy yards, and developed administrative skills. Later, as president, he was to act at times as though he were his own Secretary of the Navy, appointing to responsible commands officers whose worth he had gauged as young men.

Roosevelt was soon established in Washington as one of a handful of promising young progressive Democrats. He was an enthusiastic admirer of President Wilson and knew and respected Justice Louis D. Brandeis [Supp. 3], but he knew more about the men than about the policies of the New Freedom. Thanks to Eleanor Roosevelt, he also saw much of Theodore Roosevelt's old friends, Henry Cabot Lodge, Henry Adams [qq.v.], Justice Oliver Wendell Holmes [Supp. 1], and the British ambassador, Sir Cecil Spring-Rice. His preoccupation, however, was with the navy, and with New York politics. From his Washington base, he tried, and failed, to outmaneuver Tammany. He gained a small share of New York patronage for the upstate progressive Democrats, but Wilson, needing votes for New Freedom measures, gave the important appointments to the conservative Tammany Senator, O'Gorman. In 1914, when Roosevelt campaigned for the nomination for United States Senator in the New York Democratic primary, Tammany easily defeated him. He learned his lesson. Thereafter, he and the Tammany leaders kept an uneasy peace; each needed the votes the other could command if the Democrats were to be successful. In 1917 Roosevelt delivered the Fourth of July address at Tammany Hall, an indication of future working relationships.

The outbreak of war in Europe in 1914 plunged the United States into a difficult neutrality. Roosevelt within a few months became an ardent advocate of preparedness, sympathizing with Theodore Roosevelt, Leonard Wood [q.v.], and Lodge rather than with the more cautious President Wilson and Secretary Daniels. Although he was often close to insubordination, he managed to survive as Assistant Secretary and did much to help prepare the navy for war. During World War I, Roosevelt achieved a reputation as one of the most capable young administrators in the capital. " 'See young Roosevelt about it' . . ." had been a "by-word in Washington," reported *Time* (May 28, 1923). (On the other hand, his detractors considered him charming but shallow. They suggested that "F. D." stood for "feather-duster.") Roosevelt was largely responsible for the building of numbers of small coastal patrol boats, of dubious worth, and the laying of a mine barrage to contain German submarines in the North Sea, which was becoming effective as the war ended. In the summer of 1918 he made an extensive inspection of navy installations in Europe and visited the front in France. Upon his return he sought to resign as Assistant Secretary to take a commission in the navy, but the war was almost at an end. He again visited Europe in the winter of 1918–19 to supervise the disposal of navy property. In Paris he was able to observe the peace conference, and he returned on the *George Washington* with President Wilson, who transformed him into an ardent public supporter of the League of Nations.

Late in 1918 the Roosevelts underwent a serious family crisis. Eleanor Roosevelt discovered that her husband was romantically involved with her social secretary, Lucy Mercer. She offered him a divorce. He refused and, according to one account, told her not to be foolish. (Miss Mercer subsequently married; as a widow in the 1940's she again saw Roosevelt from time to time and

was at Warm Springs, Ga., when he died there.) But though the Roosevelts remained married, their relationship was altered. Mrs. Roosevelt, deeply and permanently hurt, accelerated the process, already begun, of developing a public and personal life of her own.

In 1920 Roosevelt, now thirty-eight, received the Democratic nomination for vice-president as the running mate of Gov. James M. Cox of Ohio. Cox chose him presumably to balance the ticket and mollify Wilsonian progressives. Roosevelt campaigned energetically throughout the United States against the tide of Republicanism and on behalf of American entrance into the League and a continuation of progressivism. His one mishap came in a campaign speech, when he ad-libbed that he had written the constitution of Haiti, which was then under Marine administration. The aside, both untrue and unfortunate, brought a retort from the Republican presidential candidate, Warren G. Harding, and long thereafter plagued Roosevelt. Otherwise, Roosevelt made a favorable impression, besides gaining invaluable experience and making political acquaintances throughout the country, many of whom subsequently became supporters. The Harding landslide in November 1920 was not a personal defeat for Roosevelt.

As the Republicans inaugurated the New Era in Washington, Roosevelt in 1921 became a vice-president in New York City for a surety bonding concern, the Fidelity and Deposit Company of Maryland. He also entered into a law partnership in which he was not very active; in 1924 he left it to form a new partnership with Basil O'Connor. Meanwhile he engaged in numerous social and charitable activities, and especially in Democratic politics. He was still youthful in appearance, tall, handsome, and physically active. Walter Camp, the Yale coach, while in Washington to supervise a wartime physical fitness program, had written, "Mr. Roosevelt is a beautifully built man, with the long muscles of the athlete. . . . His spirit is resilient, and . . . he imparts [to others] some of his own vitality." A promising future seemed to stretch ahead. Then suddenly, in August 1921, personal disaster struck. While vacationing at his summer home at Campobello Island, New Brunswick, Roosevelt fell ill with poliomyelitis. It was a severe attack which left him never again able to walk without braces and a cane. Throughout the months-long painful ordeal and emotional shock, as Roosevelt struggled to recover, he retained his cheerful optimism; within a few days he had resumed his political correspondence.

There followed grim years in which Roosevelt

doggedly worked at trying to regain the use of his legs and to remain a national political figure. Despite treatment by leading specialists, he made only limited improvement. He spent several winters on a houseboat in Florida, swimming when the weather was warm. More substantial recuperation began when he discovered the warm, buoyant mineral waters at Warm Springs, a run-down resort in Georgia which he first visited in the fall of 1924. Three years later he formed the Georgia Warm Springs Foundation, which took over the property and developed it into a therapeutic center for the treatment of polio. Each year he spent part of his time at Warm Springs, gradually rebuilding muscles until in 1928 he could with difficulty walk with leg braces and two canes. Later, as president, he gave the appearance of walking by grasping a cane in one hand, the arm of one of his tall sons with the other, and swinging his powerful hips to thrust forward his legs locked in braces. Few people realized that during these years his ordinary means of locomotion was a wheelchair.

Both Roosevelt and his family had to make serious readjustments to his new condition. He had to give up permanently the physical mobility which had led him to dash from place to place and participate energetically in golf and a variety of other activities. Fortunately he could still enjoy swimming, sailing, fishing, and a number of hobbies. So far as possible, he refused to give in to immobility. Seated at his desk or in a chair, he could not easily get rid of callers if they brought up subjects he did not wish to discuss. Consequently, he developed the habit of taking command of the conversation, with charm and a flow of anecdotes keeping his visitors from talking. On the other hand, he was dependent upon these visitors as a main source of knowledge; though he read more than before his illness, he picked the brains of countless persons, many of whom Mrs. Roosevelt brought to see him as a means of educating him on important topics. Roosevelt's cheerfulness in the face of his adversity, his patience, and his sympathy for the unfortunate all became manifest. The impression of those around him was that his illness had deepened and matured him.

For Eleanor Roosevelt, a shy woman, Roosevelt's illness completed the transition she had already begun toward public activity. Into the war years she had been largely preoccupied with bringing up a family of five children: Anna Eleanor, James, Elliott, Franklin Delano, and John Aspinwall (another Franklin Delano had died while a baby). First war work, then bitterness over her husband's romance with Lucy

Mercer, led her toward greater independence. Whatever her personal feelings may have been, she remained intensely loyal to Roosevelt. When polio immobilized him, in order to keep him active in politics and thus bolster his morale she began to act as his substitute at meetings. Under the tutelage of Louis Howe she managed to overcome her shyness, become an effective public speaker, and in countless ways serve as eyes and ears for her husband. Soon she was a significant political figure in her own right.

With the aid of Mrs. Roosevelt and Howe, Roosevelt succeeded in continuing without a break as a significant Democratic figure in both state and national politics. Indeed, during the years of Republican ascendancy he actually turned his affliction into an asset. As early as 1922 he was suggested as a candidate for either United States Senator or governor, and from then on he could decline all such suggestions by insisting that he would not again run for office until he had regained use of his legs. He was thus able to operate above many of the factional quarrels racking the Democrats and assume the role of youthful "elder statesman" seeking national party unity. Roosevelt engaged in extensive political correspondence throughout the nation, and from time to time issued public manifestos to promote candidates or establish Democratic policies. Behind the scenes, Howe planned these moves and helped to carry on the correspondence.

In New York, Roosevelt tied himself to the popular Alfred E. Smith [Supp. 3], who had risen from the ranks of Tammany to become an outstanding governor. In July 1922 Roosevelt wrote the state Democratic conference urging it to renominate Smith, thereby reaping headlines and earning Smith's gratitude. When Smith became a contender for the Democratic presidential nomination of 1924, he asked Roosevelt to manage his campaign. Smith regarded Roosevelt as attractive but ineffectual and wanted no more than his name and national contacts. Nor did Roosevelt, then or later, have much influence upon Smith. He did work vigorously, if unsuccessfully, to mitigate the growing bitterness between the urban, wet, Catholic supporters of Smith and the rural, dry, Protestant backers of William Gibbs McAdoo [Supp. 3]. At the Democratic national convention in New York City, Roosevelt as Smith's floor leader won acclaim for his eloquent nominating speech, but though he retained the admiration of many McAdoo delegates, he could not break the deadlock between Smith and McAdoo. After 103 ballots, the delegates settled on John W. Davis as a compromise candidate. Almost the only person who had gained from the convention was Roosevelt, who had throughout appeared gallant and statesmanlike.

At the 1928 convention, Roosevelt again made the speech nominating Smith, the "Happy Warrior," and this time his candidate was chosen on the first ballot. Both before and after the nomination, Roosevelt peppered Smith with suggestions which were ignored. Roosevelt felt out of the campaign, and in Sepember 1928 was at Warm Springs, trying to strengthen his leg muscles. It seemed again a good year not to be running for office, since there was strong prejudice against Smith throughout Protestant America, and his opponent, Herbert Hoover, was popular. Repeatedly Roosevelt had declined suggestions that he run for governor that year to strengthen Smith in New York, but during the state convention he unexpectedly gave in to Smith's pleas over the telephone. Mrs. Roosevelt and Howe were dumbfounded.

In high spirits Roosevelt undertook a four-week campaign for governor of New York. Campaigning was his favorite occupation. He denounced bigotry against Smith and outlined a positive liberal state program. Republican newspapers warned that Roosevelt was a cripple, physically unable to serve as governor, but his energetic appearance belied the warnings. Smith remarked, "A Governor does not have to be an acrobat." Samuel I. Rosenman, a Smith worker assigned to write speeches for Roosevelt, found the candidate quite different from his preconceptions: "I had heard stories of his being something of a playboy and idler, of his weakness and ineffectiveness. That was the kind of man I had expected to meet. But the broad jaw and upthrust chin, the piercing, flashing eyes, the firm hands—they did not fit the description" (*Working with Roosevelt*, p. 16). While Smith was losing New York by 100,000 votes, Roosevelt carried it by the narrow margin of 25,000 votes out of four and a quarter million. Even before he took office, he was being discussed as a likely Democratic nominee for president in 1932.

Roosevelt undertook to become an outstanding governor in his own right. Cautiously he moved out from the shadow of Al Smith, who had been one of the most creative and popular governors of the twentieth century. Building upon Smith's foundation of issues and personnel, he developed his own program and organization. He took over many of Smith's administrators, including Frances Perkins, whom he made industrial commissioner, but refused to appoint as his secretary Mrs. Belle Moskowitz [Supp. 1], who was brilliant, forceful, but totally loyal to Smith. In his inaugural address Roosevelt paid tribute to Smith's remarkable achievements, with their urban emphasis, then in following days focused upon issues appealing to upstate middle-class and rural voters of Republican and progressive sympathies. He maintained an uneasy truce with Tammany in New York City and concentrated upon building an effective upstate Democratic organization. It was Roosevelt's conviction that "a good affirmative liberal program and a good party organization" were closely interconnected and both essential to success at the polls. They were the key to his success in New York State and to his winning of a national following.

In his first two-year term as governor, Roosevelt established himself as a moderate progressive, an effective administrator, and an extraordinarily able political leader. From Smith's program he singled out electric power development to emphasize and embellish. In the 1920's this was the issue that perhaps more than any other appealed nationally to middle-class progressives. Smith had favored public development and private exploitation of hydroelectric power from the Niagara and St. Lawrence rivers. Roosevelt, accepting much of the program of Senator George W. Norris [Supp. 3] and his coterie of power specialists, went further and favored both public development and firm regulation of rates to consumers. He persuaded the Republican legislature to establish a Power Authority, to which he appointed experts who recommended the development of cheap power. Roosevelt also fought what he labeled as unfair telephone and utility rates, and insisted that the state regulatory body, the Public Service Commission, should act vigorously on behalf of consumers. He developed a state farm program that appealed nationally to farmers and progressives, primarily by shifting the tax burden away from the farm. Yet Roosevelt did not have to commit himself on the critical national question of controlling the surpluses in basic commodities, since New York farmers grew little wheat or corn. Other parts of the Roosevelt program, such as judicial reform, improvement of prisons, and the creation of a new parole system, were scarcely controversial.

In the drafting of his proposals, Roosevelt drew upon the knowledge of specialists, many of them academic men such as Raymond Moley of Columbia, an expert on crime and penology. Roosevelt demonstrated his political skill in obtaining support for his programs. Time and again he outmaneuvered the unimaginative Republican majority leaders in the legislature, and beginning in the winter of 1930 he met regularly with the Democratic minority leaders to plan their tactics.

A press bureau sent small upstate papers frequent reports on locally popular programs, but since most newspapers were Republican, Roosevelt early began to circumvent them with monthly statewide radio broadcasts.

Republicans were successful in counterpressuring Roosevelt in only one area—corruption in New York City. As revelations of graft within the Tammany organization became increasingly sensational, both Republican and reform leaders insisted that the Governor should step in. Roosevelt, who could not afford the loss of Tammany's political support, alternated between vigor and falling back upon legalistic protests that he could not constitutionally intervene. One of his moves was to appoint Judge Samuel Seabury to head an investigation of New York City's magistrates' courts, but Seabury, a zealous reform Democrat, became one of Roosevelt's most prominent critics. It was the Tammany issue that caused many liberals, both within and without the state, to look upon Roosevelt as a weak, vacillating governor. He finally resolved it in 1932, after his nomination for president, by personally presiding over a careful hearing into charges against Mayor James J. Walker of New York City. After several days of Roosevelt's questioning, Walker resigned on Sept. 1, 1932.

By this time, however, the Great Depression, which had steadily become more and more disastrous in the years after the stock market crash of 1929, had transformed both state and national politics. In response to it, Roosevelt gradually changed from a cautious progressive whose policies were scarcely distinguishable from those of President Herbert Hoover into a daring innovator, the prime challenger of the President. The transformation was slow and not always consistent. At the national Governors' Conference in the summer of 1930, for example, he criticized the Hoover administration for departing from laissez-faire and pouring money into public works, yet the same year, in advance of every other major political figure, he also advocated unemployment insurance. A year later, at the 1931 Governors' Conference, he asserted, "More and more, those who are victims of dislocations and defects of our social and economic life are beginning to ask . . . why government can not and should not act to protect its citizens from disaster" (*Public Papers of Franklin D. Roosevelt, . . . Governor*, 1931, p. 734).

As governor, Roosevelt mobilized the resources of his state to provide at least minimum security for those in distress. Several of his proposals and agencies foreshadowed the New Deal. In August 1931 he obtained legislation establishing a Temporary Emergency Relief Administration, which under Harry Hopkins provided aid to 10 percent of the state's families. Bank crashes led Roosevelt to seek remedial legislation to protect small depositors, but he could not get the Republican legislature to act. As the depression deepened, Roosevelt's political fortunes soared. Economic distress neutralized the prohibition issue which had split the Democratic party in the 1920's. At the beginning of the 1930 gubernatorial campaign, Roosevelt announced he favored state and local option on liquor, and was unhurt. Nationally he aligned himself with Southern and Western Democratic leaders against Smith forces in the Democratic National Committee who continued to want to make prohibition repeal the prime issue. November saw Roosevelt's reelection as governor by a spectacular margin. Republicans tried to defeat him on the Tammany issue, but only succeeded in forcing Tammany reluctantly to turn out the vote for Roosevelt. Upstate voters were more concerned over economic distress than city corruption. Although three of Hoover's cabinet members came to New York to campaign against Roosevelt, he won reelection by an unprecedented plurality of 725,000 votes. Immediately the state Democratic chairman, James A. Farley, proclaimed that Roosevelt would be the next presidential nominee of his party.

As the obvious front-runner for the 1932 Democratic presidential nomination, Roosevelt had to stay so far ahead that none of the coalitions formed to stop him could succeed. This was no easy task since under the traditional Democratic two-thirds rule designed to protect the South, one-third plus one of the delegates at the 1932 convention could block him. While Roosevelt went through the political ritual of protesting that he was not a candidate, his personal organization worked at top speed. From New York City, Howe supervised an enormous national correspondence. Farley and others sounded out state and local leaders and sought pledges of delegates. Roosevelt's greatest strength was outside the urban areas, especially in the South, where he was accepted as the candidate most likely to defeat the Smith forces. By this time the rift between Roosevelt and Smith had become open; in the Massachusetts primary, Smith defeated Roosevelt. One other strong candidate appeared, Speaker of the House John Nance Garner of Texas, who won the California primary. Roosevelt, however, made an impressive showing in other states. At the convention, a "stop Roosevelt" movement almost succeeded, as the combination of urban Smith followers and rural Garner supporters, together with the delegates of "favorite sons," controlled more than one-third of the votes through three ballots. At that point Garner, realizing that continued deadlock would aid the urban forces rather than bring his own nomination, released his delegates, and Roosevelt was nominated on the fourth ballot. Since the Texas delegates would switch to Roosevelt only if Garner were chosen for vice-president, that became part of the arrangement.

In the depression year 1932, Roosevelt was an appealing, even spectacular campaigner. He instantly shattered precedent upon being nominated. Instead of waiting for weeks until an official delegation notified him of his nomination, he flew immediately to Chicago to deliver his acceptance address before the delegates. In his peroration he declared, "I pledge you, I pledge myself, to a new deal for the American people" (*Public Papers and Addresses,* 1928–32, p. 659). A cartoonist picked up the words "New Deal" and lettered them on a drawing of the airplane carrying Roosevelt. The term caught on, and Roosevelt's national program thus acquired its name.

Roosevelt campaigned cautiously in 1932 in order not to alienate any of the numerous groups of voters disillusioned with Hoover. His effectiveness came from the geniality of his personality in contrast to the bleak solemnity of Hoover. In dealing with the issues, Roosevelt concentrated upon optimistic generalities, making such contradictory statements concerning the tariff that Hoover likened him to a chameleon on plaid. While Roosevelt's speeches offended some intellectuals, they offered hope to millions of voters, and through the texts, if one knew where to look, ran the threads of the forthcoming New Deal program. Early in 1932 Roosevelt had assembled a group of campaign advisers and speech writers, for the most part Columbia University professors, under the supervision of Raymond Moley. They prepared proposal after proposal for the receptive Roosevelt, and incorporated many of their ideas in vague form in his speeches. Newspapermen labeled this group the "brain trust." In these speeches, Roosevelt not only assailed Hoover for deficit spending, but proposed familiar progressive solutions for recovery and reform. Several also contained proposals for economic planning. In the most important of these addresses, delivered in San Francisco, Roosevelt asserted that the economy had expanded perhaps as far as it could. The task of the government now must be to regulate the economy for the common good in order to guarantee to every man his right to make a comfortable living. "Our Government formal and informal, political and economic, owes to everyone an avenue to possess himself of a portion of that plenty sufficient for his needs, through his own work" (*ibid.,* p. 754). In the election of 1932, Roosevelt defeated Hoover, winning 22,809,638 popular votes (57.4 percent) to Hoover's 15,758,901 (39.7 percent). The electoral vote, 472 to 59, was even more decisive. Democrats also elected such substantial majorities to each house of Congress that Roosevelt could expect ready enactment of his recovery program.

Carefully, Roosevelt set about planning administrative appointments and recovery and reform measures. The appointments he announced shortly before taking office were of political leaders for the most part little known, representative of various parts of the nation and of the political coalition that had elected him. A leading Southern supporter, Senator Cordell Hull of Tennessee, an advocate of lower tariffs, became Secretary of State, and James A. Farley, who had managed the 1932 campaign, became Postmaster General. Three appointees had earlier been Republicans: Secretary of Agriculture Henry A. Wallace, Secretary of the Interior Harold L. Ickes, and Secretary of the Treasury William Woodin. (Soon Woodin fell mortally ill, and within a year Henry Morgenthau, Jr., Roosevelt's longtime friend and Dutchess County neighbor, replaced him.) Roosevelt for the first time appointed a woman to cabinet rank, Frances Perkins, who became Secretary of Labor. Subsequently, under some pressure from Mrs. Roosevelt and other Democratic women leaders, he chose several women for lesser administrative positions. He also appointed more Negroes than his predecessors. A number of brain trusters, like Moley and Rexford G. Tugwell, became close presidential advisers, and Louis Howe, for so long Roosevelt's political strategist, became White House secretary.

During the months before he took office, Roosevelt gave little hint of the specifics of his forthcoming program. An exception was his dramatic announcement during a visit with Senator George Norris to Muscle Shoals that he would seek legislation to develop public power in the Tennessee Valley, as Norris had long advocated. (Congress was to respond in May 1933 with the act creating the Tennessee Valley Authority, which came to encompass power production and regional planning.) By thus making few advance announcements, Roosevelt protected his program from serious and prolonged criticism before he could marshal his powers as president to bring its enactment. On the other hand, he gave suffering Americans little concrete reason for hope.

Four months of acute depression intervened before the new president could take office; the

Norris "lame duck" amendment had not yet gone into effect, and Roosevelt was not to be inaugurated until Mar. 4. It was a time of bewilderment and despair. Industrial production was far below levels of the 1920's, a quarter of the wage earners were unemployed, and a quarter of the farmers had lost their land. President Hoover had been resourceful, drawing cautiously upon precedents of World War I, but his innovations had not sufficed. Senate hearings in February 1933 brought the old standard advice from business and political leaders alike—cut government spending, raise taxes, and balance the budget. It was deflationary advice when the nation was suffering above all from acute deflation. Conservative Democratic leaders in Congress intended that Roosevelt should follow this course, as indeed he had promised throughout his campaign. He seemed to bring to the presidency little new except a jaunty optimism in place of President Hoover's gloom.

President Hoover's view of President-elect Roosevelt was quite different. There had been a brief upturn during the summer of 1932, but the economy plummeted during the winter months. Hoover blamed the drop on business fear of Roosevelt's future policies (a prognosis hard to substantiate), and in several letters sought to persuade Roosevelt to abandon these policies. Especially he wished Roosevelt to pledge that he would keep the nation on the gold standard. Roosevelt, intent upon developing a program of economic nationalism, was noncommittal. Negotiations on foreign economic policy deepened Hoover's distrust of his successor. In late November, Roosevelt met with Hoover to discuss European war debts owed to the United States and, as a related side issue, the planning for the forthcoming International Economic and Monetary Conference. Hoover hoped through concessions on debts to persuade European nations to return to the gold standard, but Roosevelt would make no pledges. In January, however, the President-elect met with the outgoing Secretary of State, Henry L. Stimson, and endorsed the "Stimson doctrine" of nonrecognition of Japanese conquests in Manchuria. Thereafter, through Stimson's arrangements, Roosevelt became involved in discussion of debt questions and in planning for the London Economic Conference.

While he was preparing to take office, tragedy almost intervened. In Miami on the night of Feb. 15, 1933, Roosevelt barely missed being shot by a would-be assassin, Joseph Zangara. A woman grappling with Zangara deflected the bullets, but Mayor Anton J. Cermak [Supp. 1] of Chicago, standing near Roosevelt, was mortally wounded.

Roosevelt's response was sympathetic concern for those who had been hit, and personal stoicism. "Roosevelt was simply himself," Moley observed, "—easy, confident, poised, to all appearances unmoved" (*After Seven Years*, p. 139). Roosevelt's relaxed confidence carried him through not only the near assassination that month but also the hysteria of a national banking crisis.

The banking crisis became more acute from day to day through the latter part of February 1933. Runs on depression-weakened banks led to the closing, by governor's proclamation, of all banks in Michigan on Feb. 14, and in succeeding days in several other states. A rapid flight of gold from the country added to the strain on banks. President Hoover sent Roosevelt a lengthy longhand letter blaming the crisis on "steadily degenerating confidence" and calling upon him to pledge that he would retain the gold standard, refrain from heavy borrowing, and balance the budget. Since Roosevelt refused to act, and indeed did not answer Hoover's letter for eleven days, Hoover and his followers subsequently charged that the New Dealers deliberately wished conditions to worsen so that they could start anew from the bottom. In actual fact, Roosevelt at first did not take the banking crisis seriously, and subsequently he refused to take responsibility for dealing with it until he had authority as president. By inauguration day, all banking in the country was either restricted or suspended, and the nation was in a state of shock.

The effect of Roosevelt's powerful, positive inaugural address on Mar. 4, 1933, was in consequence electric. Speaking solemnly and forcefully, he sought to reassure the American people. "This great Nation will endure as it has endured, will revive and prosper," he declared. "So, first of all, let me assert my firm belief that the only thing we have to fear is fear itself" (*Public Papers and Addresses*, 1933, p. 11). Throughout his address there was also a note of moral, almost religious, fervor foreshadowing the reform component of the New Deal. This speech brought to Roosevelt for a few weeks the enthusiastic, uncritical backing of an overwhelming majority of the people, the press, and Congress. For the time being, conservatives both in the Capitol and the country were almost silent. With few restraints upon him, Roosevelt asserted energetic leadership, and the nation was in a mood to follow. His overall plan was basically twofold. He hoped through a series of emergency measures to bring rapid recovery. Next, through reforms he wished to eliminate the shortcomings and evils in the American economy that might bring future depressions. Thus he had promised Miss Perkins before she became Secretary of Labor that he would support a social security program.

The banking crisis forced Roosevelt to act even more speedily than he had planned. He issued a proclamation on Mar. 6, 1933, closing all banks and stopping gold transactions until Congress could meet in special session. Just three days later Congress enacted a conservative emergency banking bill, drafted by Hoover's treasury officials. This permitted only the stronger banks to reopen —and kept the weaker ones closed. Controls over gold continued; on Apr. 19, 1933, Roosevelt officially took the nation off the gold standard. This limited legislation sufficed to bring the runs on banks to an end. Roosevelt capped it by making a brief national radio broadcast on Mar. 12, the first of his "fireside chats." Talking simply, as he had earlier as governor of New York, he urged people to return their money to banks. "I can assure you," he said, "that it is safer to keep your money in a reopened bank than under the mattress" (ibid., p. 64). Within a month hoarders redeposited a billion dollars in gold and currency. Bankers shared the general enthusiasm over Roosevelt's action; confidence was for the time being restored. The stock market rose 15 percent. One momentous change grew out of the conservative banking measure. Roosevelt in his first press conference, on Mar. 8, explained off the record that thereafter the United States would have a system of managed currency.

Economy had been a major theme of Roosevelt's campaign for election, and during his first few weeks in office he further gladdened conservatives with his insistence upon cutting governmental expenses. In fact, he came to resort to deficit spending only reluctantly and out of the humane necessity to provide federal money for relief. The economy bill he sent Congress in the wake of the banking legislation demonstrated his hope for a balanced budget. It reduced the salaries of government employees and the pensions of veterans as much as 15 percent. Over Roosevelt's veto, Congress soon restored some of the funds to veterans, but the President reduced federal services and employees throughout the executive departments. The cuts in scientific and statistical services were especially serious. Thereafter he maintained two budgets, the regular budget covering departments and older government agencies, which he took pride in keeping balanced, and an emergency budget which carried heavy deficits. One other Roosevelt bill, hailed at the time as a recovery measure, was the legalization of beer of 3.2 percent alcoholic content, pending the ratification by the end of 1933 of an amendment repealing prohibition.

In this fashion, during his first two weeks in office, Roosevelt reassured businessmen and financiers, conservative journalists and Congressional leaders. Only in restrictions upon gold had he departed from the prevalent orthodoxy. Yet behind him was a national consensus, reflected in the stock market's rise. He had planned to delay his legislative program for some weeks, but he now decided to take advantage of the national enthusiasm, keep Congress in session, and send it bill after bill. His decision was in keeping with his belief that the nation could expect normally to be under conservative political control, with only intermittent liberal innovation. It was important to act quickly while the conservatives were in disarray.

In framing his legislation Roosevelt drew elements from the varying proposals of the advisers and political supporters, of many differing views, whom he had rallied around him. There were planners like Tugwell, together with opponents of bigness and centralization like Justice Louis D. Brandeis [Supp. 3] and Felix Frankfurter, and even more conservative monetary theorists, like Prof. George F. Warren [Supp. 2]. Roosevelt enlisted them all into the New Deal, at the same time that he continued in private to consult partners of the Morgan bank and to depend upon old-fashioned Democratic Congressional leaders to obtain enactment of his program. One of Roosevelt's most remarkable skills was his ability to capture the imagination of men of quite diverse outlooks and to weave something of their ideas into the overall pattern of the New Deal. "The President has utilized the thinking and expert service of many schools of thought, shaping them all into a single pattern," wrote Raymond Moley in 1934. "Those who have been close to the making of this policy have profound admiration for the skill with which the President has created a new synthesis out of many old strands" (Today, Apr. 14, 1934, p. 23).

As one who had closely observed both Theodore Roosevelt's and Wilson's executive leadership and who as governor of New York had himself mastered some of their techniques, Roosevelt with rare skill stimulated national excitement and brought it to bear upon the normally conservative, slow-moving, and independent Congress. He transformed the presidential press conferences from the dry answering of presubmitted questions into a lively give-and-take, largely valuable for the off-the-record background information he gave reporters. Nor did he allow himself to be directly quoted without permission. On occasion he delivered brief, simple, direct radio talks— "fireside chats." In his use of both devices he seemed, in contrast to his predecessors, warm and exciting as he discoursed with self-assuredness and authority. Roosevelt believed that though public interest could be stimulated to a high point from time to time, it could not long be kept at a peak. In consequence he was careful not to resort too often to the radio or public pronouncements for fear he might dull his effectiveness.

While Roosevelt was rallying public opinion in the spring of 1933, he was also utilizing familiar techniques to persuade powerful Congressional leaders of basically nineteenth-century views to accept his recovery and relief programs. Behind these leaders were heavy majorities of Democratic members in each house, many of them elected for the first time and ready to vote for the administration. He also courted Republican progressives in the Senate, especially Norris, the younger Robert M. La Follette, and Hiram Johnson [Supp. 3]. Republicans like these were important to Roosevelt not only for their votes in Congress but also for their following throughout the country. Roosevelt flattered Congressional leaders by soliciting their views from time to time and by entertaining them at the White House and on the presidential yacht. He also kept them in line by whetting but as yet not gratifying their expectations of rewards. He would not grant patronage until his program was enacted, although that spring every Congressman was being hounded by his constituents for jobs and government projects. Many a Congressional leader assented to measures which he did not understand, or of which he did not approve, because of Roosevelt's personal charm, out of party loyalty, and because of varieties of pressures from his constituency. Into 1937, this formula was basically to work for Roosevelt, even as more and more of the Congressional leaders, especially from the South, longed to return to their old ways of voting. This is not to say that the Congress of the spring of 1933 was, as Roosevelt's opponents later charged, a rubber-stamp body. Although it acted with unprecedented speed, it did much to shape and modify the President's legislative proposals, such as the agricultural program, and was responsible for some innovations, most notably bank deposit insurance through the establishment of the Federal Deposit Insurance Corporation.

So it was that between March and May of 1933 Roosevelt sent to Congress in rapid succession a number of messages and draft bills. By June 16 Congress had enacted every one of these measures. In total they made up the program which he had planned and for which he had laid much of the political groundwork during the months before he took office; there remained only certain reform bills which would take long-range research and preparation of Congress and the public. In July 1933 the President assured the electorate that "all of the proposals and all of the legislation since the fourth day of March have not been just a collection of haphazard schemes, but rather the orderly component parts of a connected and logical whole" (*Public Papers and Addresses,* 1933, p. 295). The logic was more political than economic: to each of the distressed interest groups in the nation Roosevelt was giving some positive benefits; from each he was trying to obtain some requisite responsibilities. Whatever the measures may have lacked in economic consistency, they did indeed represent the collective thinking of those groups whose votes would be essential to the continuation of the New Deal.

The legislation of Roosevelt's "first hundred days" emphasized recovery and relief. In the recovery program, the key measures were the farm recovery bill Roosevelt submitted to Congress on Mar. 16, leading to the Agricultural Adjustment Administration, and the industrial recovery bill of May 17, proposing the National Recovery Administration and the Public Works Administration. Both were omnibus measures. Their purpose was to benefit a wide array of interests within agriculture and business and to foster recovery without adding materially to the cost of the federal government. They were bootstrap recovery devices. Like the economy act, they made good on Roosevelt's campaign promises to keep government expenses low. Roosevelt backed farm and business leaders in their quest for recovery through limiting output and raising prices, stipulating only that there must be advantages for workers and protection for consumers. It was expected that when prosperity returned these restrictions could disappear and there would be an abundance for everyone. The two programs, together with the Tennessee Valley Authority, marked the direct, positive, peacetime intervention of the federal government in the economy in an unprecedented fashion and on an unparalleled scale. In proposing them, Roosevelt was following the spirit of Theodore Roosevelt's New Nationalism rather than the negative tradition of Wilson's New Freedom.

As he signed the National Industrial Recovery Act in June 1933, Roosevelt called it "the most important and far-reaching legislation ever enacted by the American Congress." It created the National Recovery Administration, rather analogous to the War Industries Board of World War I but the reverse in its regulatory thrust, since its machinery sought to bring prosperity through limiting rather than raising production, and through placing a floor rather than a ceiling on prices. It enabled industries and businesses to draw up codes of fair practices similar to earlier private trade association agreements, codes which would have behind them the power of federal enforcement. In return, the industries were to guarantee workers minimum wages, maximum hours, and the right to bargain collectively. In his fireside chat of July 1933, Roosevelt explained the theory behind the NRA: "If all employers in each competitive group agree to pay their workers the same wages—reasonable wages—and require the same hours—reasonable hours—then higher wages and shorter hours will hurt no employer. Moreover, such action is better for the employer than unemployment and low wages, because it makes more buyers for his product. That is the simple idea which is the very heart of the Industrial Recovery Act" (*ibid.*, pp. 298–99).

The NRA scheme, as Roosevelt pointed out at the time, would not work if men were to "thwart this great common purpose by seeking selfish advantage." That, however, was just what happened. Industries sought to build inventories of relatively low-cost goods before restrictions on wages and hours went into effect. The result was an NRA "boomlet" in the summer of 1933, as factory production shot up from the March index figure of 56 to 101 in July. Then, because there had been no comparable rise in purchasing power, a collapse threatened. Roosevelt hurriedly proclaimed a blanket code for the American economy to protect all wages and hours, and slowly, into early 1934, the code-making negotiations under the NRA administrator, Gen. Hugh S. Johnson [Supp. 3], went on until Roosevelt had approved 557 basic codes and 208 supplementary codes.

Congress had sought to create the additional purchasing power essential to the NRA program through providing in the enabling act for $3,300,000,000 of public works construction—a staggering sum for that time. Roosevelt, still firmly of the view that his program must be so far as possible self-sustaining, wished the projects to be labor-creating and quick-acting but stipulated that they also should be substantial and pay for themselves. He entrusted the program to Secretary of the Interior Ickes, who ran the Public Works Administration so cautiously that the program was not in peak operation for several years. It took time to develop sound proposals. Roosevelt approved of Ickes's deliberate policies, and focused so little upon public works as a stimulant to the economy that at one point he considered acquiring the buildings of foundered banks to avoid constructing new post offices.

The NRA floundered during the first two years of the New Deal, suffering from the lack of purchasing power, the unwillingness of desperate businessmen to give up competitive undercutting, and the basic unenforceability of a multiplicity of code regulations. Businessmen objected to the concessions to workers and began to nurture resentment toward Roosevelt. Before the end of the summer of 1933, a few publishers and political leaders were beginning to denounce the New Deal in general and the NRA in particular.

NRA labor policies, irritating as they were to businessmen, were disappointing to workers. Few received pay increases through the NRA. An organizing drive began under the guarantee in Section 7-a of the National Industrial Recovery Act that workers should have the right to bargain collectively through unions of their own choice. (Organizers modified this into the slogan, "President Roosevelt wants you to join a union.") Strikers sought without much success to break down employers' resistance to unions and to secure wage increases. Roosevelt tried to quell labor strife by establishing a National Labor Board. This set another precedent: that in peacetime, too, the federal government would intervene in the process of industry-wide collective bargaining. When the first board failed, Roosevelt in the summer of 1934 replaced it with a slightly stronger one, the National Labor Relations Board. He preferred paternalistic federal action on behalf of labor through wages and hours regulation and prohibition of child labor, and he failed to throw his weight behind labor unions in their struggles with management. Yet the tentative steps that he took led employers to distrust him and workers to feel that the President was on their side. It was the beginning of a strong political alliance between the New Deal and organized labor.

Roosevelt's achievement was more substantial through the Agricultural Adjustment Administration, which put into effect the crop restriction program that the Farm Bureau Federation had favored. A plan most benefiting the larger commercial farmers, it paid producers of basic commodities to reduce their acreage (or pork production). The subsidies came through the levying of a processing tax on the commodities, which the legislation specified should not be passed on to the consumer. The theory behind the Triple-A, as Roosevelt frequently explained, was that the nation could not be prosperous unless farmers enjoyed good incomes; it was impossible to continue as in the 1920's "half boom and half broke." City dwellers would also be beneficiaries of higher farm prices, he pointed out: "It is obvious that if we can greatly increase the purchasing power of the tens of millions of our people who make a living from farming and the distribution of farm crops, we shall greatly increase the consumption of those goods which are turned out by industry" (*ibid.*, p. 298).

Farm income did rise about 20 percent in the first year of the AAA; in subsequent years it improved still further, although drought did more than government programs to cut production of wheat, corn, and hogs. Republican critics of Roosevelt thereafter referred incessantly to the emergency reduction of the summer of 1933, the ploughing under of every fourth row of cotton and the slaughter of millions of little pigs. Critics to the left pointed out that the farm program worked to the disadvantage of marginal farmers, especially Southern sharecroppers. Roosevelt sanctioned programs for these poorest of farmers, but Congress never funded them on a large scale. Economists have suggested that in the first four years the agricultural program overall made little contribution to recovery, since subsidies totaled only $1,500,000,000 and, despite the stipulation of the law, diminished the buying power of consumers by that amount. But Roosevelt won the loyalty of millions of farmers, both substantial and poor, who, together with the workers, came to form an integral part of the New Deal political coalition. Further, he had introduced federal planning and subsidies into agriculture, where they continued indefinitely.

Roosevelt succeeded in bringing a modicum of quick relief to millions who were hungry and in danger of losing their homes and farms. He backed mortgage programs that refinanced loans on a fifth of the nation's farms and a sixth of the homes. In March 1933 he rushed to Congress a proposal to establish nationally, with federal funds behind it, the type of relief program he had innovated in New York. Congress in May created the Federal Emergency Relief Administration. Roosevelt appointed Harry Hopkins, who had been New York administrator, to head it; and Hopkins quickly funneled an initial half-billion dollars into state relief administrations. Roosevelt backed Hopkins in his early insistence that state relief programs meet professional standards and not operate as Democratic patronage machines. In the late New Deal there were complaints against the relief program, but in the spending of all the billions of dollars that came to be appropriated, there was relatively little scandal.

Human erosion and loss of moral values among the unemployed worried Roosevelt. As firmly as the most conservative of his opponents he believed in the work ethic, and he was sympathetic as Hopkins, the relief administrator, sought to put the unemployed to work through work-relief programs. At the outset of the New Deal, Roosevelt persuaded Congress to establish the Civilian Conservation Corps to enlist unemployed men, mostly youths, in projects for reforestation and flood control. This program was popular and continued through the New Deal.

The bursting of the NRA boomlet in the summer of 1933 led Roosevelt to try a monetary expedient as a recovery device. George F. Warren of Cornell, agricultural economist and advocate of the "commodity dollar," showed Roosevelt charts intended to prove that if the price of gold were pushed upward, prices of all other commodities would follow. Through the fall of 1933, Roosevelt experimented with reducing the gold content of the dollar, thus raising the price of gold. The devaluation of the dollar may have helped foreign trade; major competing nations had already devalued their currencies. It achieved little within the United States, and in January 1934 Roosevelt ended currency manipulation, setting the gold content of the dollar at 59.06 percent of its earlier level.

By the fall of 1933 Roosevelt's honeymoon with the American electorate was over. Many Congressmen, including conservative Democrats, were in a disgruntled mood; the program had gone much further than they had wished, and they were beginning to hear criticisms from their hometown businessmen and bankers. The facts were that Roosevelt had not brought the rapid recovery for which he had been aiming and that he had begun to unsettle many American assumptions and institutions. He continued during the next two years to make overtures to American businessmen and bankers, seeking still to be president to all groups within the American economy. Nevertheless, polarization was already under way. Roosevelt still commanded the support and goodwill of farmers, working people, and a large part of those who were suffering economic distress. But the farm subsidies, the billions of dollars being given out in aid, and the labor disorders which accompanied unionization drives under New Deal protection alarmed those who had faith in the old verities and who feared the New Deal would bring personal and national economic ruin. The shrillness of their opposition, and the fact that their program, so far as one could judge from the expressed opinions of Republican political leaders and some Democratic conservatives, involved nothing more than a return to pre-Roosevelt days, did much to strengthen Roosevelt's appeal to the have-nots. Their lot might as yet not be much better under Roosevelt, but his opponents promised them only greater privation.

The distress of the needy as winter approached in 1933 was too great for Roosevelt to ignore. In response to the pleas of the federal relief administrator, Harry Hopkins, he turned temporarily to the expedient of a large-scale work relief program. But the Civil Works Administration was so costly and the make-work nature of some of its projects aroused so much criticism that when spring came Roosevelt abandoned it, although extreme need still existed. CWA had, in its brief duration, employed four and a quarter million persons, achieved a number of useful improvements, and poured a billion dollars into the economy.

The rise and fall of the CWA illustrate the way in which Roosevelt responded to varying pressures. Hopkins had appealed to his humanitarian side; Henry Morgenthau, Jr., who had become Secretary of the Treasury, had appealed to his frugality. On the one hand, in November 1933 when Roosevelt met with CWA administrators, he said to them: "Speed is an essential. I am very confident that the mere fact of giving real wages to 4,000,000 Americans who are today not getting wages is going to do more to relieve suffering and to lift the morale of the Nation than anything that has ever been undertaken before" (*ibid.,* p. 471). On the other hand, he lamented to the National Emergency Council in January 1934, "You know, we are getting requests practically to finance the entire United States. . . . There is a general feeling that it is up to the government to take care of everybody, financially and otherwise. . . . One very simple illustration is CWA. . . . If we continue CWA through the summer . . . it will become a habit with the country. . . . We must not take the position that we are going to have permanent depression in this country . . ." (*New Deal Mosaic,* pp. 75–76). Through his first two terms in office, Roosevelt sought to reconcile these two rather contradictory aims, to alleviate suffering and stimulate the economy through large-scale spending, and to prevent the federal deficit from soaring to dangerous heights.

Of the two conflicting pressures upon Roosevelt, that from the dispossessed was the greater and the more sustained. Roosevelt responded to it with continued but cautious spending. Toward the organizing drives and strikes of the labor unions he was also cautious. Left-wing intellectuals became sharply critical of Roosevelt and his programs, especially the NRA and the AAA, claiming that they helped the well-to-do more than the poverty-stricken, the workers, and the

consumers. Further, several popular leaders began to challenge Roosevelt in their appeals to the common man. There was Dr. Francis E. Townsend of California, urging pensions for the aged; Father Charles E. Coughlin, a Detroit priest with millions of radio followers, as yet more populist than fascist in his ideology; and above all, Senator Huey P. Long [Supp. 1] of Louisiana, who was proposing a "Share Our Wealth" program. Long, effectively appealing to voters far beyond the bounds of Louisiana, and popular with many onetime Populists and Progressives, was the most serious threat to Roosevelt. The President responded vigorously, especially to Long. By 1935 he was telling his administrators in private, "Don't put anybody in and don't keep anybody that is working for Huey Long or his crowd! . . . Anybody working for Huey Long is not working for us" (*ibid.,* p. 437).

It was not until 1935 that Roosevelt came into direct political conflict with these left-wing groups. In the Congressional elections of 1934 the groups had few candidates on the ballot, so that in many contests the voters' only choice was between Republicans critical of Roosevelt for having gone too far and Democrats pledging themselves to be 100 percent behind the President's programs. In the 1920's, midterm elections had swung toward the party out of power, but in 1934 they augmented the Democratic majority. Moreover, most of the newly elected Democrats were enthusiastic New Dealers. Consequently Roosevelt had behind him overwhelming majorities in Congress as he looked forward to 1936, when the growing left-wing discontent might threaten his reelection. If Long and his cohorts formed a third party, so the chairman of the Democratic National Committee, James A. Farley, warned, they might take sufficient votes away from Roosevelt to give the election to the Republicans. Indeed, this was Long's plan.

Roosevelt was under critical attack from both the left and the right in the early months of 1935. Not only was Long making headlines, but conservatives within Roosevelt's own party formed the American Liberty League and brought to Washington as their keynote speaker Al Smith, who warned of radicalism in the administration. The Republican view was that recovery was well advanced and that only New Deal tampering with business was preventing the return of full-scale prosperity. Some political observers consequently were predicting that Roosevelt, caught between left and right, would lose in 1936. Yet he remained relatively quiet while his critics commanded headlines and prime radio time. When supporters expressed alarm over his inaction, he calmly explained that it was a matter of political timing: "The public psychology," he wrote Ray Stannard Baker in March 1935, ". . . cannot . . . be attuned for long periods of time to a constant repetition of the highest note on the scale. . . . For example, if since last November I had tried to keep up the pace of 1933 and 1934, the inevitable histrionics of the new actors, Long and Coughlin and [Hugh] Johnson [now a right-wing critic], would have turned the eyes of the audience away from the main drama itself! I am inclined to think . . . that the time is soon at hand for a new stimulation of united American action" (*Personal Letters,* pp. 466–67).

The new action was the great burst of reform legislation, some of it in the planning since Roosevelt took office, some newly fabricated in 1935, which historians often refer to as "the second New Deal." Probably Roosevelt undertook it for a multiplicity of reasons, as was his habit. It was partly a response to political pressures, partly a substitute for collapsing programs like the NRA code system, which the Supreme Court invalidated in May 1935. In part it rose from the strong moral, humanitarian base of Roosevelt's thinking. To one supporter during these months he wrote, "Things are not as well economically and socially as they appear on the surface—on the other hand, they are better politically" (*ibid.,* p. 486).

The reforms of 1935 began when Roosevelt in his annual message to Congress in January asserted, "We have not weeded out the over-privileged, and we have not effectively lifted up the underprivileged" (*Public Papers and Addresses,* 1935, p. 16). He suggested measures to reinforce "the security of the men, women, and children of the nation." Of the concrete programs that followed, the most significant was the Social Security Act, one of the momentous achievements of Roosevelt's presidency, and one in which he took considerable pride. Of immediate, but less lasting, consequence was Roosevelt's insistence that the nation establish a work relief program, the Works Progress Administration, rather than continue the less expensive policy of giving relief checks, as conservatives favored. "We have here a human as well as an economic problem," Roosevelt told the Congress. "Continued dependence upon relief induces a spiritual and moral disintegration fundamentally destructive to the national fibre. . . . Work must be found for able-bodied but destitute workers" (*ibid.,* pp. 19–20). Over the next six years the WPA, under the direction of Harry Hopkins, had a monthly average enrollment of more than 2,000,000 workers, four-fifths of them in public works and conservation projects, but many also engaged in the fields

of art, music, the theatre, and writing. Roosevelt was less successful in his proposals for slum clearance and federal construction of housing; the programs which slowly evolved were relatively small, and significant mainly for the precedents they created.

The breakdown of Roosevelt's first economic recovery program by late spring of 1935 was forcing him into major readjustments. The NRA had not worked well, so in some respects the adverse Supreme Court decision was a mercy killing. But while conservatives rejoiced, Roosevelt fumed, declaring to reporters that the Supreme Court was taking a horse-and-buggy view of the power of the government to regulate the economy. Yet what was most viable in the NRA program continued. Just before the court's decision, Roosevelt had finally accepted Senator Robert F. Wagner's bill establishing strong federal protection for collective bargaining, and in July this became the National Labor Relations Act.

Much of the failure of the earlier recovery program resulted, Roosevelt believed, from bad business practices and from the refusal of business to cooperate with the government. Increasingly he sought to reform business, in part as a means of achieving recovery. The Securities Exchange Act of 1934 had placed the stock market under federal regulation. In March 1935 Roosevelt proposed to Congress legislation prohibiting the pyramiding of public utility holding companies, and in June he recommended restructuring federal taxes to increase substantially the levies on wealthy individuals and corporations. Both proposals created a furor; hostile newspapers termed them the "holding company death sentence" and the "soak-the-rich tax." In the outcome Roosevelt obtained modified holding company legislation and an income tax measure which, in sharp contrast to those of the 1920's, set individual rates of up to 75 percent for the highest incomes and imposed a 15 percent corporate income tax. The outcry against the holding company and tax bills further helped convince the underprivileged that Roosevelt was their champion.

Altogether the 1935 program did much to meet the challenge from the left. Huey Long was assassinated in September, but his political position had already been undercut by Roosevelt. On the other hand, conservative resentment against Roosevelt had grown into anger. Well-to-do people attacked him as a traitor to his class. Roosevelt still tried to be conciliatory, and in response to a plea from the newspaper publisher Roy Howard, assured him at the end of the 1935

Congressional session that indeed the time had come for a breathing spell for business.

Nonetheless, national politics continued to be polarized sharply for and against Roosevelt. He was the lone issue in the 1936 campaign. The Republicans nominated a onetime Bull Mooser, Gov. Alfred M. Landon of Kansas, who made constructive criticisms of the New Deal. But the alarmist right wing among both Republicans and Democrats denounced Roosevelt in cataclysmic terms, and it was to them that the President responded. In his acceptance address he attacked them as "economic royalists," and at the conclusion of the campaign he asserted: "Never before in all our history have these forces been so united against one candidate as they stand today. They are unanimous in their hate for me—and I welcome their hatred" (*ibid.*, 1936, p. 568).

The result was a sweeping victory for Roosevelt, who received the electoral votes of every state except Maine and Vermont. He also carried additional Democrats into both houses of Congress. Roosevelt accepted his reelection as a national mandate for further reform. His second inaugural address in January 1937 was a plea on behalf of the underprivileged: "I see a great nation, upon a great continent, blessed with a great wealth of natural resources. . . . But here is a challenge to our democracy: . . . I see one-third of a nation ill-housed, ill-clad, ill-nourished" (*ibid.*, 1937, p. 5).

A single conservative bulwark seemed to stand between Roosevelt and his reform objectives—the Supreme Court. The court had invalidated his initial industrial and agricultural recovery programs and several other New Deal measures. Many employers were flouting both the social security and collective bargaining legislation in the expectation that the court would also declare them unconstitutional. Roosevelt had made no secret of his dissatisfaction with the Supreme Court's decisions, and had taken the view that what was at fault was not the New Deal measures, but rather the court's interpretation of them. During the 1936 campaign he had refused to allow Landon to draw him into a discussion of the Supreme Court. After the election he carefully laid his plans, so secretly that he did not even take Congressional leaders into his confidence. Without warning, in February 1937, he suddenly proposed to Congress an overhauling of the federal judiciary, purportedly to help the courts keep up with their growing dockets. At the heart of Roosevelt's bill was the proposal that he be empowered to name as many as six new Supreme Court justices.

Roosevelt's court plan shocked Congress and alarmed a large number of those who had voted for him in 1936. To most Americans the Supreme Court seemed more a bulwark of democratic institutions than a protector of privilege. What Roosevelt was promising, especially since he was not candid stating his objectives, seemed dangerously parallel to the way in which European dictators had seized power. Even many of his supporters feared that while Roosevelt himself clearly had no such ambitions, he was creating dangerous precedents. For the first time the minority of conservatives in Congress were able to win a strong popular following. A number of Democrats in both houses who because of political pressure had previously supported Roosevelt were able upon this occasion to join in the opposition. The Supreme Court itself affected the political battle when, by 5-to-4 decisions, it upheld both the National Labor Relations Act and the Social Security Act. There seemed no longer to be any need for Roosevelt's proposal, and in the end it was defeated.

In one respect the court fight had been a victory for Roosevelt and the New Deal, since henceforth the court allowed almost unlimited economic regulation on the part of the federal government. On the other hand, Roosevelt had suffered a humiliating political defeat at the very time when he had seemed at the height of his popularity. A resurgence of conservatism had taken place in Congress, and though the group remained a minority, it was able thereafter seriously to harass and occasionally to block Roosevelt's measures. The conservatives were by no means in control. Roosevelt failed to obtain enactment of a government reorganization bill, but his failure came about mainly because of bitter fights among conflicting government agencies that would be affected and because of the strength of lobbies behind these interests. Indeed, Roosevelt was able to obtain a good deal of substantial, though not spectacular, legislation, pointing toward lasting changes in the function of the presidency and the federal role within the economy. Under the authority of the Reorganization Act of 1939, Roosevelt established the Executive Office of the President, placing within it the Bureau of the Budget and the National Resources Planning Board, and also providing for an office for emergency management, to be set up in the event of a national crisis. He was further empowered to appoint administrative assistants.

Numerous pieces of legislation aided one or another group of Americans. For workers, there was the Fair Labor Standards Act of 1938, which made a start toward establishing minimum wages (only twenty-five cents an hour at first) and maximum hours, and prohibited child labor. Agriculture received subsidies based now upon soil conservation (withdrawal of land from the growing of soil-depleting crops), and for the poorest of farmers a number of relief measures were passed. For city people there was a beginning of slum clearance and public housing, and extensive erection of public buildings through the Public Works Administration.

Some of the federal benefits—more than at any time since Reconstruction—reached blacks. Although subsequently Roosevelt did little directly to further the incipient civil rights revolution, and though local administrators often deprived poor Negroes of aid, both the President and Mrs. Roosevelt were acclaimed as friends of the black people. Roosevelt did indeed follow an equivocal course on antilynching legislation, not wishing to jeopardize economic measures which depended upon Southern leaders for passage through Congress. On the other hand, programs designed for the needy did bring at least limited help to Negroes, who came to occupy almost a third of the newly constructed public housing and were enrolled in large numbers on WPA projects. By 1934 Negro voters had massively switched their allegiance from the party of Lincoln to that of Roosevelt, and with Roosevelt they remained.

In 1937 the New Deal seemed to be bringing such a substantial degree of recovery that Roosevelt feared a dangerous, unhealthy boom would result. Upon the advice of Secretary of the Treasury Morgenthau, he drastically cut back government spending, furloughing large numbers of WPA workers. His goal as always was to balance the budget, and it seemed to him the time had come. Economists subsequently have felt that Roosevelt's fears about the boom were needless and that his action was precipitate, plunging the nation into a sharp recession. Business leaders blamed the recession upon the President; what caused the economy to plummet, they asserted, was their uncertainty over what Roosevelt might undertake in the future. Roosevelt for his part was ready to blame the recession upon the selfishness of businessmen, seeking too large a share of profits for themselves rather than raising the wages of labor and thus contributing to consumer buying power. To discipline business, he seemed inclined to resort to antitrust techniques, appointing Thurman Arnold to head a revived program in the Department of Justice, and recommending to Congress the creation of an investigatory Temporary National Economic Commission. Even faced with the recession, he had not become committed to heavy government spending as a means of pulling the nation out of the depression.

It was during this new economic crisis, however, that many of the younger economists in the New Deal, who had previously been strong advocates of one or another approach to recovery, began to coalesce in support of the ideas of the British economist John Maynard Keynes. What began to take shape was not so much Keynesianism as an American program of countercyclical government intervention in the economy. Roosevelt himself was well aware of Keynes's ideas, and at one point even had a rather disappointing meeting with Keynes, but never became a convert. He did in October 1937 obtain an appropriation of $5,000,000,000 for relief and public works from Congress, meeting in special session, and by the summer of 1938 recovery was again under way. Roosevelt, in his trial-and-error fashion, seemed to have developed a means of restoring recovery even before defense spending hastened the process. But his opponents viewed him as having brought the nation to the brink of bankruptcy, as the national debt soared from $19,000,000,000 in 1932 to $40,000,000,000 in 1939.

Defenders of the status quo were alarmed not only by the increase in the national deficit, but also by the growing labor strife, as the rival C.I.O. and A.F. of L., under the protection of the Wagner Act, sought to organize mass production industries. The sit-down strikes of 1937, which many middle-class people regarded as labor preemption of employers' property, were especially frightening. Opponents placed the blame upon Roosevelt. It was indeed true that Roosevelt had signed the Wagner Act and had welded a vital alliance between the Democratic party and organized labor, which had already borne fruit in the election of 1936. On the other hand, Roosevelt's interest in workers had remained rather paternalistic, reflecting a preference for wages and hours legislation and unemployment insurance. He had always disliked strikes, lockouts, and violence in industrial relations, whether the fault of workers or employers. Throughout the New Deal his role was considerably more neutral than conservatives suspected. It was undoubtedly with much sincerity that he commented concerning a struggle between the C.I.O. and one of the steel companies, "A plague on both your houses." John L. Lewis of the C.I.O. retorted, "It ill behooves one who has supped at labor's table and who has been sheltered in labor's house to curse with equal fervor and fine impartiality both labor and its adversaries when they become locked in deadly embrace" (*Vital Speeches*, September 1937, p. 733). Lewis returned to the Republican party, taking few workers with him. On the other hand, Lewis's anger did little to convince middle-class Americans that Roosevelt shared their fears.

In the Congressional election of 1938, for the first time since 1932, the Republicans gained a number of seats in both houses of Congress. The election seemed to be another serious political setback for Roosevelt. Contrary to his earlier policy, he had openly intervened in several Democratic primaries in opposition to conservatives. Newspapers accused him of attempting a "purge," and noted that in almost every instance the well-entrenched incumbents, like Senators Walter George of Georgia and Millard Tydings of Maryland, had won over the lesser-known challengers that he supported. Actually, the number of interventions was small, and the election was far from a rout. The Democrats still were in a majority in both houses of Congress, and although conservatives among them could join with Republicans to thwart domestic measures, Roosevelt by dint of much persuasion could command a majority on bills involving foreign policy. By this time, 1939, Europe was on the brink of war, and increasingly Roosevelt was turning his attention toward foreign dangers and American defense.

Foreign affairs always interested Roosevelt, and even during the domestic crisis of the first month of his administration he had given a good bit of attention to them. He enjoyed being head of state and liked to engage in personal diplomacy, feeling that somehow, meeting face to face with the leader of a foreign country, he could bring about accommodation, just as he could through his negotiations with rival political leaders. He looked upon his ambassadors, quite correctly, as his personal envoys. Although he respected Cordell Hull, the prestigious Jeffersonian figure whom he placed in charge of the State Department, he often bypassed Hull in negotiations and did not keep him informed. On the other hand, Roosevelt himself much of the time did not seem to be aware of the extent to which policy was continually and rather automatically formulated by the powerful men who headed the various desks within the State Department, even though, as in the case of Far Eastern affairs, the day-by-day decisions of these men were ultimately to have momentous effects. The Senate was another tempering influence on Roosevelt's control, and he himself, though always giving the appearance of being a bold innovator, was personally cautious. It is hard to say to what extent foreign policy was shaped by forces outside the White House and to what extent by the Chief Executive, but there is no indication that Roosevelt was seriously thwarted in formulating his overall policies.

Roosevelt's initial major decision in the realm of foreign affairs was a fundamental economic one: that the United States should seek recovery through a nationalistic program rather than one involving international economic cooperation. This was implicit in the early New Deal measures, but for several months, as so often was the case, Roosevelt tried to move in another direction simultaneously. He proceeded with plans for the London Economic Conference scheduled for the early summer of 1933, asserting that world cooperation was necessary to "establish order in place of the present chaos." Then at the last minute he changed his mind and cabled a "bombshell message" asserting that the United States would not participate in international currency stabilization. The conference probably would have collapsed anyway, but its dissolution was blamed upon Roosevelt's bumbling action.

As a means of aiding the American economy and, secondarily, to help other nations, the United States did enter into numerous arrangements in the next several years. Before the end of 1933 Roosevelt recognized the Soviet Union, primarily in the hope of stimulating foreign trade, and in 1934 he gave his backing to Hull's cherished reciprocal trade program. These actions did little to breach the high economic walls around the United States, but they constituted a gesture toward freer trade.

Throughout the Western Hemisphere, Roosevelt projected himself as a smiling, benign "good neighbor." He and Secretary Hull dramatically pledged to Latin American nations that the United States would not intervene with armed force, and they held to the new policy even in 1938 when Mexico expropriated American oil holdings. Gradually, as military threats became more serious in both Europe and East Asia, Roosevelt began to change the Good Neighbor program into a mutual security arrangement foreshadowing the post-World War II Pan-American pacts.

Toward Japan's expansionism in East Asia, Roosevelt brought some of the views he had acquired during his years in President Wilson's Navy Department. At one of his first cabinet meetings he discussed the possibility of war with Japan, and within several months he was channeling some of the public works funds into naval construction. In 1934 he obtained passage of a measure which began the rebuilding of the United States fleet. On the other hand, he conducted for some years a conciliatory diplomacy toward Japan in the hope that less bellicose elements would come to dominate the Japanese cabinet. Roosevelt's policies toward Japan aroused little controversy; it was an area toward which the nationalist so-called isolationists in Congress were ready to permit a firm policy.

Europe was another matter. There Roosevelt proceeded cautiously, and with good reason, since he could easily arouse acute criticism in Congress and among the electorate. Mussolini seemed to Roosevelt to have been a stabilizing force in Italy, and for several years the President looked upon him with favor. It was different with Hitler. He came into power a few months before Roosevelt, who in private immediately spoke of him as a menace. In May 1933 Roosevelt sent an encouraging message to the Geneva Disarmament Conference, but he was so afraid of alarming isolationists in Congress that it was not until early 1935 that he even sought to obtain American entrance into the World Court. As in the past, isolationists in the Senate blocked the move.

While the European dictatorships and Japan strengthened their armies and fleets and threatened weaker nations, Roosevelt long kept the nation on a neutral course. Like most of the American people, he deplored the aggression, and the Nazi mistreatment of Jews, but did not want to see the United States again become involved in war. It was an era of reaction against American participation in the First World War, and Senate hearings bolstered a widespread view that selfish bankers and munitions makers had duped the United States into involvement. In the fall of 1934 Roosevelt lamented to Josephus Daniels that the pacifist William Jennings Bryan [q.v.] had resigned as Secretary of State in the Wilson administration. In 1935, as he saw Mussolini preparing to conquer Ethiopia, he signed a Neutrality Act imposing restrictions of the sort Bryan would have favored for the United States in World War I: when the President proclaimed that a state of war existed, it became illegal for Americans to sell munitions to belligerents on either side, and Americans could travel on the vessels of belligerents only at their own risk. During the gathering crisis in Europe, Congress enacted, and Roosevelt signed, further neutrality measures. In these, the President sought to obtain discretion whether or not to act—the sort of discretion which would make it possible for him to favor victims over aggressors. He obtained little of this power from Congress; what bit he did gain made it possible for him to begin the move toward collective security.

Isolationists warned that collective security could bring involvement in war, but to Roosevelt it was a possible way to stay out, and the ultimate failure of his policies is no proof, as some critics have asserted, that he was a secret warmonger.

Rather, it seems to have been in all sincerity that, in what he considered a major campaign address in 1936, he asserted "I hate war," detailing the horrors he had seen in France in 1918. "I have passed unnumbered hours," he declared, "I shall pass unnumbered hours, thinking and planning how war may be kept from this Nation" (*Public Papers and Addresses,* 1936, p. 289).

In the fall of 1937, as the Japanese armies advanced into north China, Roosevelt made a first tentative proposal looking toward collective security, stating at Chicago that peace-loving nations should act in concert to quarantine war as they would a contagion. Although Roosevelt did not seem to have in mind anything more drastic than a collective breaking off of diplomatic relations, there was such a frightened reaction throughout the country that the President backtracked. Public sentiment was so opposed to a strong stand against Japan that at the end of 1937 when Japanese aviators sank a United States gunboat, the *Panay,* in Chinese waters, Roosevelt quickly accepted Japanese offers of apology and indemnity. Throughout the Spanish Civil War he pursued a neutral course. Toward Hitler he shared with the leaders of France and England feelings of apprehension. When Hitler threatened war in 1938 over Czechoslovakia, Roosevelt urged him to accept a peaceful solution, but the President's message was not a factor of any significance in the Munich settlement. Apprehension turned to alarm during the next few months as Hitler began to put pressure upon Poland. If war came, as seemed likely, Roosevelt hoped the United States could stay out, but he was not ready to keep the nation at peace if the price were intolerable. During the Munich negotiations he wrote privately, "If we get the idea that the future of our form of government is threatened by a coalition of European dictators, we might wade in with everything we have to give" (*Personal Letters,* p. 810).

At once Roosevelt began to develop the policy that he followed until December 1941, one of trying to deter Hitler through developing the potentially enormous American military production. By building war plants to produce quantities of armaments, and by then making these armaments available to victims of the aggressor nations, he hoped to avoid direct involvement of American forces. Repeatedly in ordering this program Roosevelt overrode his military advisers, who sought rather the balanced development of American forces with which to meet the potential foes. As several military historians have pointed out, Roosevelt's primary aim was less to prepare for combat than to provide an alternative to American involvement in war. Especially he emphasized a program he thought would impress the Nazis. In November 1938, against the protest of the military leaders, he ordered a spectacular increase in aircraft production to 10,000 combat airplanes a year; at that time the Air Corps possessed fewer than 900 first-line planes.

When war broke out in Europe in 1939, Roosevelt in his neutrality proclamation declared, "This nation will remain a neutral nation, but I cannot ask that every American remain neutral in thought as well" (*Public Papers and Addresses,* 1939, p. 463). He called Congress into special session and obtained modification of the Neutrality Act to allow belligerents to purchase arms on a "cash and carry" basis, an arrangement favoring the British and French. During the first few months of the war he secured only small increases in army and navy appropriations, but he helped the French contract for aircraft plants which, by the time they were built, became essential to American wartime production. During the Nazi blitz of Western Europe in May 1940, Roosevelt upped his production quota to 50,000 planes a year, again against the advice of the military. A large portion of the American planes produced in the next few months went to the British.

Hitler's triumphs in 1940 led Roosevelt to enlist the full backing of the United States, short of armed intervention, for the beleaguered British. With strong popular support, he moved the United States from neutrality to an active nonbelligerency. On June 10, 1940, as France was about to fall before Hitler's onslaught, Mussolini declared war on the French. Speaking that evening, Roosevelt bluntly declared, "The hand that held the dagger has struck it into the back of its neighbor" (*ibid.,* 1940, p. 263). After the fall of France he bolstered the British fleet with fifty reconditioned American destroyers, given in return for long-term leases on bases in British colonies in the Western Hemisphere, from British Guiana to Newfoundland.

Although public opinion polls indicated that 60 percent of the American people favored aid to Britain even at the risk of American involvement, aid to the Allies was the chief issue in the election of 1940. There had been indications before the war crisis became intense that Roosevelt intended to retire at the end of his second term, in keeping with American tradition. Like a canny politician, he had not closed out his options, and in the national emergency following the fall of France he accepted the Democratic nomination for a third term. Without difficulty he parried conservative Democratic forces rallying around James A.

Farley and Vice-President John Nance Garner. Roosevelt, despite the repugnance of many Democratic politicians, insisted upon the nomination for vice-president of Henry A. Wallace, who had been Secretary of Agriculture.

The Republicans had responded to the national emergency by nominating the personable Wendell L. Willkie [Supp. 3], who as the president of an electric power company had fought Roosevelt over the issue of TVA and publicly produced power. Willkie, who won the support of the liberal, internationalist wing of the Republican party, was a formidable candidate, whose views on aid to Britain did not differ markedly from Roosevelt's. Both men, seeking to win the isolationist vote, repeatedly avowed their intentions of avoiding direct military intervention if at all possible. In a speech in Boston, Roosevelt declared, "I have said this before, but I shall say it again and again and again: your boys are not going to be sent into any foreign wars" (*ibid.,* p. 517). Nevertheless, many of those who had broken with Roosevelt over domestic policies now returned to his support in the expectation that he would follow a strong course against Hitler, while those opposing outright belligerency under any circumstances turned to Willkie. It was a relatively close election, Roosevelt winning by 27,000,000 to 22,000,000.

In the year between his reelection and Pearl Harbor, Roosevelt followed a complex and difficult course. He established defense organizations, stimulated the building of plants to produce enormous quantities of the matériel of war, gave massive aid to Britain, and tightened economic pressure upon Japan. Early in 1941, since the British were reaching the end of funds with which to buy munitions, Roosevelt pushed through Congress a new measure of aid, the Lend-Lease Act. This was a means of circumventing existing legislation prohibiting cash loans to nations which had not paid their World War I debts. Roosevelt proposed lending goods instead of money, and explained that the goods could be returned after the war. "Suppose my neighbor's home catches fire, and I have a length of garden hose," suggested Roosevelt in a simple analogy. "If he can take my garden hose . . . I may help him to put out his fire" (*ibid.,* p. 607). In Roosevelt's words, the nation was to become the "arsenal of democracy." By the end of World War II the United States had provided foes of the Axis, through lend-lease, with goods and services worth more than $48,000,000,000.

In order to ensure the arrival of lend-lease goods in England, Roosevelt established naval patrols, and subsequently convoys against Nazi submarines. He met with Prime Minister Winston Churchill of England in the summer of 1941 and issued with him a statement of idealistic war aims, the Atlantic Charter. By the fall of 1941 Roosevelt was extending lend-lease to the Soviet Union, against which Hitler had launched an attack in June, and was engaged in open warfare on the Atlantic against German submarines. After an attack upon the American destroyer *Greer,* he ordered the navy to "shoot on sight."

Step by step Roosevelt had moved toward war against Germany, but like the American public, which according to opinion polls seemed to favor these steps, he refrained from the ultimate decision, to ask the Congress for a declaration of war. In part the vehemence of isolationist attacks upon him within Congress and throughout the nation may have been a factor. In part it may have been his unwillingness to take the responsibility for sending untold numbers of young Americans to their death. He recalled in 1939 how President Wilson had explained similar restraint to him in 1917. He quoted Wilson as having declared, "I don't want to do anything . . . that would allow the definitive historian in later days to say that the United States had committed an unfriendly act against the central powers" (*ibid.,* 1939, p. 117).

When an attack came it was from Japan, not Germany. Roosevelt after the fall of France had tried to restrain the Japanese advance into the power vacuum in Southeast Asia by denying Japan warmaking supplies. After Germany attacked Russia, Japan, no longer fearing a thrust from Siberia, determined to occupy southern Indochina and Thailand, even at the risk of war with the United States. Roosevelt did not want war with Japan in the fall of 1941 and seemed to think that through firmness he could cause Japan to moderate her demands. He was wrong. As negotiations dragged on, the Japanese planned and then on Dec. 7 launched their attack upon Pearl Harbor. Roosevelt and his advisers can be charged with having miscalculated, but accusations that they sought the attack on Pearl Harbor as a means of getting the nation into war against Germany are baseless.

It was an angry president addressing a united Congress and nation who called on Dec. 8 for a declaration of war against Japan. Three days later Germany and Italy declared war on the United States. With the country fully involved in global war, Roosevelt assumed the role of Commander-in-Chief of the American nation. It was a role he relished, as he concentrated upon broad strategy and, like Wilson, upon moral objectives. As president of the United States he

sought to head the coalition of nations arrayed against the Axis. Roosevelt had already set forth the nation's peace aims in his annual message to Congress in January 1941. "In the future days, which we seek to make secure," he had declared, "we look forward to a world founded upon four essential human freedoms": freedom of speech and expression, freedom of every person to worship God in his own way, freedom from want, and "freedom from fear—which, translated into world terms, means a world-wide reduction of armaments to such a point and in such a thorough fashion that no nation will be in a position to commit an act of physical aggression against any neighbor—anywhere in the world" (*ibid.,* 1940, p. 672). As the war proceeded, Roosevelt also became increasingly the foe of colonialism and the advocate of a new world organization, the United Nations.

The United States and its allies were to suffer one acute setback after another in the Pacific during the first months after Pearl Harbor. Yet even before hostilities began, the nation was well on its way toward winning the battle of production. In munitions, aircraft, and ships, the United States by the time of Pearl Harbor was already outproducing the Axis. Roosevelt had indeed helped make the United States the "arsenal of democracy."

To mobilize the country's resources, Roosevelt set up a variety of war agencies. He was not entirely satisfied with them and reshuffled them several times. He had first established rather weak defense agencies after the fall of France in 1940, acting under authority dating from 1916 so as to avoid debate in Congress. In 1941 he added the Office of Price Administration under Leon Henderson, which set price ceilings and handled a rationing program for scarce commodities, and in January 1942, the War Production Board under Donald M. Nelson. At times there was confusion and almost always there was debate among some of the agencies. Minor clashes growing out of overlapping authority sometimes brought, through healthy competition, a greater efficiency. Some of the major interagency quarrels, as well as acute disputes with John L. Lewis and other labor leaders, required Roosevelt's direct intervention and exhausted him. In October 1942 he succeeded in delegating much of the regulation of the economy to Justice James F. Byrnes, who resigned from the Supreme Court to become head of the Office of Economic Stabilization (after May 1943 the Office of War Mobilization). Despite some sensational squabbles, the war agencies succeeded in coordinating unprecedented production.

Like President Wilson, Roosevelt tried to adjourn politics during the war. He was more successful than Wilson in avoiding the semblance of partisanship, but he came under bitter and continuing conservative attack from Congress. Congress voted the war measures Roosevelt wished, but he had to pay the price of acquiescing in the dismantling of several New Deal agencies, including the National Resources Planning Board, which had offended by proposing postwar increases in social security. The electorate, now more prosperous and more conservative, in the 1942 election still further reduced the Democratic majorities in both houses. Roosevelt dealt with Congress in a rather preoccupied way, failing to give its members close attention as in past years. Even had he done so, there is no indication that he would have been much more successful. His occasional clashes with Congress came over his efforts to raise taxes still higher, and to counter the inflationary pressures which the Congressmen's constituents and lobbyists were bringing to bear upon them.

At one press conference Roosevelt remarked that in place of "Dr. New Deal" he had brought in "Dr. Win-the-War," but it soon became apparent that with victory Roosevelt would bring back "Dr. New Deal." He continued to advocate long-range humane goals, even though during the war neither he nor Congress did much to implement them. In his annual message to Congress in January 1944 he called for enactment of a second, economic Bill of Rights, "under which a new basis of security and prosperity can be established for all—regardless of station, race, or creed" (*ibid.*, 1944–45, p. 41). He outlined the components of security in earning a living, and added the rights to a decent home, to adequate medical care, and to protection from economic fears of old age, sickness, accident, and unemployment, and, finally, the right to a good education. For returning veterans, Congress did provide financing for further education, for a start in business or farming, or for the purchase of a house, through the Servicemen's Readjustment Act of 1944, popularly called the "G.I. Bill of Rights." When he signed the measure, Roosevelt congratulated Congress upon carrying out his recommendations concerning veterans, urged consideration of related problems of reconversion, and emphasized, "A sound postwar economy is a major present responsibility."

In wartime policies toward minorities, Roosevelt's actions fell short of his ideals. He shared the national fears regarding Japanese-Americans after Pearl Harbor, and signed an order evacuating 112,000 persons, two-thirds of them United States citizens, from their homes on the West Coast to concentration camps. Toward Jews facing Nazi persecution in the 1930's and then during the war the "final solution" of the gas chamber, he repeatedly expressed his sympathetic concern and approved cautious aid. He refused, however, to seek bargains with Hitler to obtain their release, insisting that the best way to help the Jews was to win the war quickly. Public opinion opposed large-scale admission of Jewish refugees; the State Department interposed technicalities to keep the trickle of those admitted below quota levels. Roosevelt did not intervene with all his power, and to that degree shares national and international responsibility for the failure to act more effectively.

For Negroes, that loyal component of his political coalition, Roosevelt obtained small gains. In June 1941, in response to threats of a march on Washington, he established the Fair Employment Practices Committee. It possessed little power, but was of some help in breaking down barriers against employment of minorities. He sought greater opportunities for blacks in the armed forces, but did not interfere with the segregation in the army and the failure of the navy to enlist more than a few Negroes, most of whom served as mess attendants. When a spokesman for Negro publishers told him in February 1944 that it was his responsibility to obtain better treatment for blacks in the armed forces, he granted there was discrimination. "The trouble lies fundamentally in the attitude of certain white people," he said. "And we are up against it, absolutely up against it" (*ibid.*, pp. 66–67).

While the war continued, most of the slight glimpses Americans caught of Roosevelt were in his role as Commander-in-Chief, somewhat aging and a little tired, but still imposing and authoritative. As Commander-in-Chief, Roosevelt's idealistic long-term objective was to achieve a world order in keeping with the Four Freedoms. Yet his immediate concern was to secure the speediest possible end to the war at the smallest cost in American lives. Realities and the necessity to compromise led him into deviations from his long-range plan, just as in domestic policies. The extent to which his wartime actions fell short of his long-range goals is a measure less of ambivalence than of his skill in achieving a consensus, first among his own military commanders, then among the United States and its allies.

In exercising his powers as Commander-in-Chief, Roosevelt operated at the apex of the total warmaking, production, and diplomatic structures of the nation. His was the ultimate power and his were the ultimate decisions. By his Military

Order of 1939 he placed military procurement and production under civilian control and strategic questions under the military. Their basic coordination depended upon him. He also had to effect accommodation between military and foreign policy, and between the United States and its allies. As always he had to take into account pressures from Congress and the public. To these multifaceted accommodations Roosevelt brought the skills he had perfected as a peacetime president. The Commander-in-Chief varied from the President in little except that he was able to cloak many of his moves in wartime secrecy. He depended heavily upon his military commanders, especially Gen. George C. Marshall, Chief of Staff of the Army, and Adm. Ernest J. King, Chief of Naval Operations. On the whole, Roosevelt's choices of top personnel were wise and effective. He almost never clashed directly with them and during the war seldom overrode them except to reach consensus with the British.

Although Roosevelt's initial hope that the United States could contribute to defeat of the Axis solely through production of war matériel had gradually evaporated before Pearl Harbor, he continued to feel that the United States must build a preponderance of armed might through which to crush the enemies with a minimum loss of American lives. When in January 1941 he had authorized the military to engage in secret planning with the British for joint action in case the United States became involved in war, he set as their guidelines: "Our military course must be very conservative until our strength [has] developed"; and "We must be ready to act with what is available" (Greenfield, p. 75). After the United States entered the war, Roosevelt accepted the basic policy that although Japan had launched the attack, the United States must give priority to the defeat of Germany, the more dangerous enemy. Yet he permitted sufficient allocation of men and resources to the Pacific war so that the defeat of Japan swiftly followed that of Germany.

At a series of summit meetings to determine grand strategy, Roosevelt demonstrated his skill as a compromiser, making concessions first to the British and later to the Russians in order to hold together the alliance until final victory. At the same time, Roosevelt guarded what he conceived to be the vital interests of the United States. For the first two years of the American involvement, most of the negotiations were with the British, who with their greater weight of armaments and experience were for a time dominant in strategic planning. Gradually, as the Americans grew in arms power and experience, they took the lead.

Roosevelt's role in this process focused for the initial two and a half years of the war around the question of an invasion across the English Channel into France. The Russians urged Roosevelt to invade as early as possible so as to relieve the Nazi pressure on the Russian front. Churchill, visiting Washington when the Germans seemed about to take over Egypt, fought for an invasion of North Africa instead. Roosevelt subsequently agreed to the invasion of North Africa and the postponement of the cross-Channel thrust. In mid-January 1943 he and Churchill met, without Stalin, at Casablanca, Morocco, to plan the next stage in the war. Churchill again was persuasive, this time on behalf of an invasion of Sicily, even though it would again delay the move into France.

Roosevelt's own efforts at Casablanca were spectacular, with rather debatable results. He tried to bring about amity and cooperation between two rival French leaders, Gen. Henri H. Giraud and Gen. Charles de Gaulle. They reluctantly shook hands before Roosevelt, but in the months that followed, De Gaulle successfully undercut Giraud, whom the President had been backing. Even more startling was Roosevelt's unexpected announcement at a press conference that the Allied policy toward the Axis would be one of unconditional surrender. (Roosevelt had earlier broached the topic with Churchill.) Roosevelt's aim was to avoid the sort of misunderstandings that had clouded the German armistice of 1918, misunderstandings which had given Hitler so much opportunity to make false propaganda charges. Opponents of Roosevelt's policy at the time, and some historians since, have claimed that the unconditional surrender policy discouraged German groups unfavorable to Hitler, gave the Nazis an additional propaganda weapon, and helped contribute to diehard fighting at the end of the war. There is no evidence, however, to indicate that Roosevelt's statement lengthened the war, and considerable reason to believe that Nazi leaders would have fought to the bitter end anyway, since they knew that they would be tried for war crimes, including the liquidation of millions of Jews.

By 1943 the balance of armed power had shifted perceptibly from Churchill to Roosevelt. At a conference in Washington they agreed upon May 1, 1944, as a tentative date for a cross-Channel invasion. Churchill later tried to develop an alternative move into the Balkans, but Roosevelt and his commanders held Churchill and the British firmly to the direct thrust into Europe. Roosevelt and Churchill regarded each other with high esteem, but there was considerable friction between them since Roosevelt insisted that the war must bring an end to the old type of colonialism. Roosevelt meant no more than that there should be no establishment of mandates and similar paternalistic systems, but Churchill declared publicly in November 1942 that he had not become the King's first minister to preside over the liquidation of the British Empire. De Gaulle felt similarly about the French colonies.

The key to postwar peace, Roosevelt believed, would be American-Russian amity. He long sought a face-to-face meeting with Marshal Stalin, hopeful that he could persuade him to cooperate effectively both during the war and thereafter. The first such meeting came when Churchill, Stalin, and Roosevelt conferred at Teheran, Iran, in November 1943. Roosevelt tried to win over Stalin, and returned from the conference feeling that indeed he had done so. The 1944 invasion of France (on June 6) was a success, and when Stalin, Churchill, and Roosevelt met for a second time at Yalta, in the Crimea, early in 1945, the war was close to an end. In subsequent years Roosevelt has been harshly criticized for the agreements he made there with the Russians. Agreements concerning Poland and other parts of liberated or defeated Europe provided for interim governments of democratic leaders to be followed by free elections—vague terms which the Russians interpreted quite differently from the Americans. A secret agreement, intended to bring Russia into the war against Japan, made concessions to Russia in East Asia contrary to the Atlantic Charter. When Roosevelt returned with the Yalta agreements, those parts which were made public led to general rejoicing, since there was expectation that future relations with Russia would be fair and fruitful. Instead, difficulties rapidly compounded as Russian troops fought their way westward in the closing days of the European war. By March 1945 Stalin was accusing the United States of treachery concerning Nazi surrender negotiations in Italy. Roosevelt replied to Stalin, "It would be one of the great tragedies of history if at the very moment of the victory, now within our grasp, such distrust, such lack of faith should prejudice the entire undertaking after the colossal losses of life, matériel and treasure involved" (*Foreign Relations of the United States*, 1945, III, 746).

Roosevelt did not live to face the bitter charges against him in the United States growing out of the failure of Yalta. Some of these charges were exaggerated, since the Russian arrangements in Poland and in other parts of Eastern Europe occupied by the Red Armies could scarcely have

been altered by anything short of armed force. The concessions to Russia in East Asia, it has been argued, were acceptable to the Chinese Nationalist government. But there is no refuting the charge that Roosevelt was overoptimistic and willing to accept vague and ambiguous arrangements. He had come by 1945 to pin his hopes upon the United Nations, and felt that cooperation of the United States with Russia in that body would make possible whatever rectification might become necessary. Even before his own death, his hopes were proving false, and the United States and Russia were moving rapidly toward cold war.

In his thinking about the postwar world, Roosevelt from early in the war felt strongly that the only way to avoid the impotency of the League of Nations was to vest responsibility for maintenance of the peace in the major powers. The basic postwar problem, he thought, would be to prevent the resurgence of Germany and Japan—and to police Japan he visualized the buildup of Nationalist China as a major power. So it was that the peace-keepers were to be the United States, Great Britain, the Soviet Union, and China, to which he sometimes referred in private as the "four policemen."

Slowly Roosevelt came to accept the concept of a United Nations as an international peacekeeping organization. Its Assembly would embody all nations, big and small, each with a vote, but there would be little real power in the Assembly. Rather, the effective body was to be the Security Council, with eleven seats, four of which were to go permanently to the major powers (a fifth, France, was subsequently added). To protect the interests of the United States, Roosevelt insisted that each member of the Security Council be given veto power. Stalin opposed the veto, and demanded that each of the sixteen constituent Soviet republics be given a vote in the Assembly. At Yalta, Roosevelt secured the veto power, and in return agreed that the Soviet Union could have two additional seats in the Assembly. When there was a protest in the United States over the seats, Roosevelt remarked to reporters, "It is not really of any great importance. It is an investigatory body only" (Divine [1969], p. 70). His hope was that within the framework of the United Nations, the Americans and the Russians could cooperate to maintain world order. At the time of his death he was preparing to go to San Francisco to address the opening session of the conference that would found the United Nations.

Even though the war was rapidly drawing to a close in Europe and Roosevelt was thinking seriously about peacekeeping, Japan was continuing its stubborn resistance. Roosevelt, accepting the conservative estimates of his military advisers, warned in March 1944, "We must be prepared for a long and costly struggle in the Pacific." An imponderable element in the estimates was a new secret weapon upon which Roosevelt had long since authorized work: the atomic bomb. All through the war, American scientists raced to try to develop an atomic bomb in advance of the Germans. In the summer of 1939 Albert Einstein had sent a letter to Roosevelt warning him that German physicists had achieved atomic fission with uranium and might succeed in constructing such a device. After further warnings, Roosevelt authorized a small research program which in time became the mammoth Manhattan Project. By 1945 it was apparent that the Germans were not even close to producing a bomb, but that the United States might soon have a workable one. The question was whether it should be used against Japan. Roosevelt was ready to postpone that decision until the bomb was tested.

Despite deteriorating health, Roosevelt in 1944 ran for a fourth term as president and was re-elected. Because of his physical condition, Democratic aspirants maneuvered energetically, seeking the vice-presidential nomination. Many party leaders, especially in the South, objected to Vice-President Henry A. Wallace, who was advancing liberal postwar aims both for the United States and for underdeveloped parts of the world. Roosevelt compromised with conservative and Southern party leaders and accepted Senator Harry S. Truman of Missouri as his running mate. Roosevelt's Republican opponent was the youthful governor of New York, Thomas E. Dewey, who charged that the Roosevelt administration had "grown tired, old, and quarrelsome in office." But Dewey had trouble campaigning against the Commander-in-Chief, although Roosevelt did indeed appear old and exhausted in some newspaper photographs. At the end of September, Roosevelt threw himself into the campaign with his earlier zest, ending it by riding all day in an open car through New York City in a pelting rain. He promised voters security at home and abroad, and by a popular vote of 25,600,000 to 22,000,000 won the election. It was almost the last display of the Roosevelt dynamism.

In the months after the 1944 election, Roosevelt's health continued to decline. He was suffering from high blood pressure with attendant complications, and did not take as much rest as his doctors suggested. He was in full command of his mental faculties, but at times his characteristic joviality gave way to testiness. After his return from the Yalta conference he was so tired that he addressed Congress sitting down rather than undergo the ordeal of standing with his braces locked. He went to Warm Springs, Ga., for a vacation. It was there, on Apr. 12, 1945, that he died of a massive cerebral hemorrhage.

Roosevelt's death was mourned throughout the nation and the world. Prime Minister Churchill requested the House of Commons to adjourn in memory of the President, "whose friendship for the cause of freedom and for the causes of the weak and poor have won him immortal renown." He was buried, as he had wished, under a simple headstone in the rose garden of the estate at Hyde Park. Eleanor Roosevelt, after her death in 1962, was buried next to him.

Many contemporaries and some later writers have considered Roosevelt an enigmatic, contradictory figure. He polarized American society; as with Theodore Roosevelt, few people were neutral in their opinions about him. Both ardent admirers and vehement haters were united in their feeling that they could not always understand him. Outwardly he was jovial, warm, and capable of seeming most indiscreet in his candor when he was not being indiscreet at all, and sometimes far from candid. He effectively communicated his friendly solicitude and emphatic self-assurance in his public appearances and radio talks; they convinced millions of people that he was a friend, indeed a mainstay. Yet toward the public and even toward those with whom he was most intimate, including his immediate family, there was an inner reserve. He seldom talked about his thinking or his plans until he had firmly made up his mind. "I am a pig-headed Dutchman," he once told Adm. William Leahy during World War II. ". . . We are going ahead with [this] and you can't change my mind" (Leahy, p. 136). On the other hand, as Edward Flynn has pointed out, "Roosevelt would adopt ideas only if he agreed with them. If he disagreed, he simply did nothing" (Flynn, p. 214). In not sharing his thought processes, he helped build an aura of mystery and authority, and he kept power firmly to himself. Effective though these traits were when he was president, their origins lay far back in his early life. Eleanor Roosevelt wrote to one of her sons, "His was an innate kind of reticence that may have been developed by the fact that he had an older father and a very strong-willed mother, who constantly tried to exercise control over him in the early years. Consequently, he may have fallen into the habit of keeping his own counsel, and it became part of his nature not to talk to anyone of intimate matters" (Lash, p. 344).

Roosevelt's merits as an administrator have

also been frequently debated. On the surface he was haphazard in his handling of affairs, and often hazy or contradictory in instructions. Sometimes the effect was chaos or bitter internecine struggle, and sometimes greater effectiveness. As Eliot Janeway has written, "Roosevelt's normal way of organizing a Department was to split it right down the middle" (*The Struggle for Survival*, 1951, p. 51). He liked to draw elaborate organization charts, but they seldom counted for much. His real interest was less in agencies than in men who could be loyal to him and effective. From Raymond Moley in 1933 to Admiral Leahy in World War II, these men frequently received nebulous assignments. Roosevelt expected them to make the most of their authorization, even when they found themselves competing with someone else with similar authority. They must keep out of the headlines, take the blame for what went wrong, and leave the president the credit for achievements. Some, like Moley, found themselves ultimately in an impossible situation and ideologically at odds with Roosevelt. The surprising thing is how many administrators of widely varying views and talents, with little in common except their willingness to work for Roosevelt, continued over the years to render important service. Measured by these public servants and their contributions, Roosevelt ranks well as an administrator.

At the time of his death, Roosevelt was eulogized as one of the greatest figures of modern times. In the next few years, as conservatives in Congress sought to obliterate New Deal domestic programs and blamed the travail of the cold war upon Roosevelt's mistaken policies, his reputation declined. Isolationist historians in the 1940's, and "New Left" historians a generation later, found little to praise. Many other historians and biographers have been cautious both in their praise and criticism. Yet Roosevelt's popular reputation throughout the world has been little diminished. Despite adverse judgments concerning some of his policies and actions, he remains a major figure in modern history. His twelve years as president brought basic, lasting changes in both domestic and foreign policy. The government came to assume responsibility for the economic security of the American people and to be concerned with the security of peoples throughout the world. Roosevelt's "four freedoms" became a national, and to some extent an international, goal. Although his inner reserve often baffled those closest to him, his basic character was not much different from that of a large part of the American people: a soaring idealism tempered by realism. He wrote in 1942

to Jan Smuts, "I dream dreams but am, at the same time, an intensely practical person" (*Personal Letters*, p. 1372). He has been honored for having sought noble goals, and criticized for having fallen short of them. Others fell short, too, but few had the vision of Roosevelt, who, the day before his death, worked on the draft of a speech ending, "The only limit to our realization of tomorrow will be our doubts of today." Roosevelt added in his own hand, "Let us move forward with strong and active faith."

[The voluminous papers of Franklin D. Roosevelt are in the Franklin D. Roosevelt Lib., Hyde Park, N. Y. They cover his family background, personal life from early childhood, and public career. The library also contains the papers of Eleanor Roosevelt and of a number of those associated with Roosevelt, including Harry Hopkins and Henry Morgenthau, Jr. There is much material concerning Roosevelt and some by him in numerous manuscript collections throughout the United States, such as the Raymond Moley Papers, Hoover Inst., Stanford, Calif. Roosevelt's official papers as governor of New York are on indefinite loan from the state to the Roosevelt Lib. A few of his official papers as president, and earlier as Assistant Secretary of the Navy, are in the Nat. Archives. There are thousands of references to Roosevelt in the transcripts of interviews in the Oral Hist. Collection, Columbia Univ.; additional interviews concerning Roosevelt are at Hyde Park at the Roosevelt Lib., and concerning Roosevelt at Warm Springs, at the Franklin D. Roosevelt Warm Springs Memorial Commission. The Roosevelt Lib. also houses extensive collections of books and articles, still and motion pictures, recordings and memorabilia. The Roosevelt home at Hyde Park, the Little White House at Warm Springs, Ga., and the summer home at Campobello Island, New Brunswick, are all open to the public.

The Public Papers and Addresses of Franklin D. Roosevelt, ed. by Samuel I. Rosenman (13 vols., 1938–50), contains speeches, proclamations, and orders, a few official letters, portions of press conference transcripts, and useful, often detailed, explanatory notes. The *Complete Presidential Press Conferences of Franklin D. Roosevelt* (12 vols., 1972) supplies the full unedited transcripts. For official materials on Roosevelt's foreign policies, see the volumes of *Foreign Relations of the U. S.* covering the years 1933–45. Supplementing these and containing much of an informal character is the multivolume *Franklin D. Roosevelt and Foreign Affairs*, ed. by Edgar B. Nixon (1969–). Nixon has also edited comparable volumes on conservation policies: *Franklin D. Roosevelt & Conservation, 1911–1945* (2 vols., 1957). *New Deal Mosaic: Roosevelt Confers with His Nat. Emergency Council, 1933–1936*, ed. by Lester G. Seligman and Elmer E. Cornwell, Jr. (1965), contains transcripts of meetings. On Roosevelt's years as governor of New York, see *Public Papers of Franklin D. Roosevelt, Forty-eighth Governor of the State of N. Y.* (4 vols., 1930–39). *F.D.R.: His Personal Letters*, ed. by Elliott Roosevelt (4 vols., 1947–50), contains a selection covering his lifetime. Some of Roosevelt's speeches and statements, with editorial comments, appear in Roosevelt's *Looking Forward* (1933) and *On Our Way* (1934).

The standard modern biography of Roosevelt is the two volumes by James MacGregor Burns, *Roosevelt: The Lion and the Fox* (1956), covering up to Pearl Harbor, and *Roosevelt: The Soldier of Freedom* (1970). Arthur M. Schlesinger, Jr., *The Age of Roosevelt* (1957–), contains brilliant interpretive sections on Roosevelt within the panoramic setting of the era. Frank Freidel, *Franklin D. Roosevelt*

(1952–), is a multivolume study. William E. Leuchtenberg, *Franklin D. Roosevelt and the New Deal, 1932–1940* (1963), a history rather than a biography, is concise and authoritative. Rexford G. Tugwell, *The Democratic Roosevelt* (1957), contains remarkable insights into Roosevelt before 1937. John Gunther, *Roosevelt in Retrospect* (1950), is a breezy account, inaccurate in detail but luminous as a sketch of Roosevelt's personality. Most of the numerous contemporary biographies are no longer useful, with the exception of Ernest K. Lindley's perceptive *Franklin D. Roosevelt: A Career in Progressive Democracy* (1931), a classic among campaign biographies. Joseph P. Lash, *Eleanor and Franklin: The Story of Their Relationship, Based on Eleanor Roosevelt's Private Papers* (1971), is indispensable on Roosevelt's personal life and marriage. Alfred B. Rollins, Jr., *Roosevelt and Howe* (1962), effectively delineates Howe's role in forwarding Roosevelt's career. Paul K. Conkin, *FDR and the Origins of the Welfare State* (1967), is a significant critical essay. Edgar E. Robinson, *The Roosevelt Leadership, 1933–1945* (1955), is an outstanding conservative critique. Two carefully reasoned "New Left" interpretations are the introduction to Howard Zinn, ed., *New Deal Thought* (1966), and Barton J. Bernstein's essay in Bernstein, ed., *Towards a New Past* (1968).

Numerous memoirs and published diaries contain useful views and information, but they must be used with caution, as they sometimes reflect the author better than they do Roosevelt and are not always accurate. The most important, indeed indispensable, diaries are John M. Blum, *From the Morgenthau Diaries* (3 vols., 1959–67), which Blum has brilliantly synthesized and analyzed, and Harold L. Ickes, *The Secret Diary of Harold L. Ickes* (3 vols., 1953–54). William D. Hassett, *Off the Record with F.D.R., 1942–1945* (1958), is an intimate wartime diary. Eleanor Roosevelt's memoirs, *This Is My Story* (1937) and *This I Remember* (1949), contain much of significance on her husband. Among other memoirs, diaries, and collections of letters are: Francis B. Biddle, *In Brief Authority* (1962); James F. Byrnes, *All in One Lifetime* (1958); James A. Farley, *Behind the Ballots* (1938) and *Jim Farley's Story* (1948); Herbert Feis, *1933: Characters in Crisis* (1966); Felix Frankfurter, *Felix Frankfurter Reminisces*, ed. by Harlan B. Phillips (1960), and *Roosevelt and Frankfurter: Their Correspondence, 1928–1945* (1967), annotated by Max Freedman; Edward J. Flynn, *You're the Boss* (1947); James Forrestal, *The Forrestal Diaries* (1951), ed. by Walter Millis; Cordell Hull, *The Memoirs of Cordell Hull* (2 vols., 1948); Jesse H. Jones and Edward Angly, *Fifty Billion Dollars: My Thirteen Years with the RFC, 1932–1945* (1951); Ernest J. King and Walter M. Whitehill, *Fleet Admiral King: A Naval Record* (1952); Arthur Krock, *Memoirs* (1968); William D. Leahy, *I Was There* (1950); Raymond Moley, *After Seven Years* (1939) and (with Elliot A. Rosen) *The First New Deal* (1966); Frances Perkins, *The Roosevelt I Knew* (1946); William M. Rigdon (with James Derieux), *White House Sailor* (1962); Elliott Roosevelt, *As He Saw It* (1946); James · Roosevelt and Sidney Shalett, *Affectionately, F.D.R.* (1959); Sara Delano Roosevelt, as told to Isabel Leighton and Gabrielle Forbush, *My Boy Franklin* (1933); Samuel I. Rosenman, *Working with Roosevelt* (1952); Robert E. Sherwood, *Roosevelt and Hopkins* (1948); Edward R. Stettinius, Jr., *Roosevelt and the Russians*, ed. by Walter Johnson (1949); Joseph W. Stilwell, *The Stilwell Papers*, ed. by Theodore H. White (1948); Henry L. Stimson and McGeorge Bundy, *On Active Service in Peace and War* (1948); Rexford G. Tugwell, *The Brains Trust* (1968); Grace G. Tully, *F.D.R., My Boss* (1949); Arthur H. Vandenberg, *The Private Papers of Senator Vandenberg*, ed. by Arthur H. Vandenberg, Jr. (1952); and Louis B. Wehle, *Hidden Threads of History: Wilson through Roosevelt* (1953).

Specialized books and articles cover Roosevelt's family background and a number of aspects of his personal life. On the Roosevelt family, see Alvin P. Johnson, *Franklin D. Roosevelt's Colonial Ancestors* (1933), and Karl Schriftgiesser, *The Amazing Roosevelt Family, 1613–1942* (1942). The life at Hyde Park is covered in Olin Dows, *Franklin Roosevelt at Hyde Park* (1949), and Clara and Hardy Steeholm, *The House at Hyde Park* (1950); the polio attack and Roosevelt's struggle to recover in Jean Gould, *A Good Fight: The Story of F.D.R.'s Conquest of Polio* (1960), and Turnley Walker, *Roosevelt and the Warm Springs Story* (1953). Jonathan Daniels presents many details of Roosevelt's Washington social life and his romance with Lucy Mercer in *The End of Innocence* (1954) and *Washington Quadrille* (1968). Dr. Ross T. McIntire's account of Roosevelt's health as president in *White House Physician* (1946) has been modified by Dr. Howard G. Bruenn, "Clinical Notes on the Illness and Death of President Franklin D. Roosevelt," *Annals of Internal Medicine*, Apr. 1970.

A topical analysis of Roosevelt's ideology is Thomas H. Greer, *What Roosevelt Thought* (1958). On special aspects, see Torbjørn Sirevåg, *Franklin D. Roosevelt and the Use of History* (1968); Willard Range, *Franklin D. Roosevelt's World Order* (1959); and Daniel R. Fusfeld, *The Economic Thought of Franklin D. Roosevelt and the Origins of the New Deal* (1956). On political techniques, see Harold F. Gosnell, *Champion Campaigner: Franklin D. Roosevelt* (1952). On overseas views, see the compendious Nicholas Halasz, *Roosevelt through Foreign Eyes* (1961), and a Russian interpretation, Nicolai N. Yakovlev, *Franklin Roosevelt—chilovek i politik* (1965). On Catholic views of Roosevelt, see George Q. Flynn, *Am. Catholics & the Roosevelt Presidency, 1932–1936* (1968); and David J. O'Brien, *Am. Catholics and Social Reform: The New Deal Years* (1968). On criticism, George Wolfskill and John A. Hudson, *All but the People: Franklin D. Roosevelt and His Critics, 1933–1939* (1969). Other studies of aspects of Roosevelt's career include: Bernard Bellush, *Roosevelt as Governor of N. Y.* (1955); Frank Freidel, *F.D.R. and the South* (1965); and A. J. Wann, *The President as Chief Administrator: A Study of Franklin D. Roosevelt* (1968). On the relationship of Negroes to Roosevelt, the New Deal, and the war administration, see the essays in Bernard Sternsher, ed., *The Negro in Depression and War* (1969), and Louis Ruchames, *Race, Jobs, & Politics: The Story of FEPC* (1953).

Among the many volumes on Roosevelt's foreign policy to 1941, see especially Bryce Wood, *The Making of the Good Neighbor Policy* (1961); Francisco Cuevas Cancino, *Roosevelt y la Buena Vecindad* (1954); Lloyd C. Gardner, *Economic Aspects of New Deal Diplomacy* (1964), an economic determinist interpretation; Robert A. Divine, *The Illusion of Neutrality* (1962); Dorothy Borg, *The U. S. and the Far Eastern Crisis of 1933–1938* (1964). Detailed factual accounts of Roosevelt and the European crisis up to American entrance into World War II are William L. Langer and S. E. Gleason, *The Challenge to Isolation, 1937–1940* (1952) and *Undeclared War* (1953), and Donald F. Drummond, *The Passing of Am. Neutrality* (1955). On special topics, see Arnold A. Offner, *Am. Appeasement: U. S. Foreign Policy and Germany, 1933–1938* (1969); Richard P. Traina, *Am. Diplomacy and the Spanish Civil War, 1936–1939* (1968); Saul Friedländer, *Prelude to Downfall: Hitler and the U. S., 1939–1941* (1967); John M. Haight, Jr., *Am. Aid to France, 1938–1940* (1970); Theodore A. Wilson, *The First Summit: Roosevelt and Churchill at Placentia Bay, 1941* (1969); Warren F. Kimball, *The Most Unsordid Act: Lend-Lease, 1939–1941* (1969). On the election of 1940, see Bernard F. Donahoe, *Private Plans and Public Dangers: The Story of FDR's Third Nomination* (1965), and Warren Moscow, *Roosevelt and Willkie* (1968). On the crisis with Japan, see Herbert Feis, *The Road to Pearl Harbor* (1950), and Roberta

Wohlstetter, *Pearl Harbor: Warning and Decision* (1962). Vigorous criticism of Roosevelt's policies is in Charles A. Beard, *Am. Foreign Policy in the Making, 1932–1940* (1946) and *President Roosevelt and the Coming of the War, 1941* (1948). An equally strong rebuttal is Basil Rauch, *Roosevelt: From Munich to Pearl Harbor* (1950).

There is little on Roosevelt and domestic problems in World War II. Allen Drury, *A Senate Jour., 1943–1945* (1963), records the growing animus of many Senators. Davis R. B. Ross, *Preparing for Ulysses: Politics and Veterans during World War II* (1969), analyzes the shaping of the G.I. Bill of Rights. On Japanese-Americans, see Jacobus tenBroek et al., *Prejudice, War and the Constitution* (1954), and Audrie Girdner and Anne Loftis, *The Great Betrayal: The Evacuation of the Japanese-Americans during World War II* (1969). On the failure to rescue victims of Nazi persecution, see David S. Wyman, *Paper Walls: America and the Refugee Crisis, 1938–1941* (1968), and Henry L. Feingold, *The Politics of Rescue: The Roosevelt Administration and the Holocaust, 1938–1945* (1970).

Brief interpretive introductions to Roosevelt's role in diplomacy and strategy during World War II are Robert A. Divine, *Roosevelt and World War II* (1969); Kent R. Greenfield, *Am. Strategy in World War II: A Reconsideration* (1963); Samuel Eliot Morison, *Strategy and Compromise* (1958); Gaddis Smith, *Am. Diplomacy during the Second World War, 1941–1945* (1965); John L. Snell, *Illusion and Necessity: The Diplomacy of Global War, 1939–1945* (1963); and William L. Neumann, *After Victory: Churchill, Roosevelt, Stalin and the Making of the Peace* (1967). A lengthy, authoritative account of wartime diplomacy is Herbert Feis, *Churchill, Roosevelt, Stalin* (1957). Gabriel Kolko, *The Politics of War: The World and U. S. Foreign Policy, 1943–1945* (1968), is a "New Left" view. On the formation of the United Nations, see Robert A. Divine, *Second Chance: The Triumph of Internationalism in America during World War II* (1967). Anne Armstrong, *Unconditional Surrender* (1961), is critical of Roosevelt. On the death and funeral of Roosevelt, see Bernard Asbell, *When F.D.R. Died* (1961).

A bibliography (which does not include books) is William J. Stewart, comp., *The Era of Franklin D. Roosevelt: A Selected Bibliog. of Periodical and Dissertation Literature, 1945–1966* (1967).]

FRANK FREIDEL

ROOSEVELT, KERMIT (Oct. 10, 1889– June 4, 1943), explorer, army officer, shipping official, was born at Oyster Bay, Long Island, N. Y., the second son and second of the five children of President Theodore Roosevelt and Edith Kermit (Carow) Roosevelt; his older brother was Theodore Roosevelt, Jr. [Supp. 3]. Kermit was a quiet, dreamy, rather detached child for that bustling family. Politics would never appeal to him, but his romantic nature responded to other parental interests. Under careful tutelage at home and at the Groton School (1902–08), he found pleasure in language and literature. On Western outings with his father's friends he discovered delight also in hunting and rough adventure. In 1909, while at Harvard, he accompanied his father on an expedition to East Africa, serving as photographer. As his father noted with delight, "the rather timid boy of four years ago has turned out a perfectly cool and daring fellow" (*Letters*, VII, 10).

The ten-month journey fulfilled all his schoolboy imaginings, and inclined him further away from any routine career. Though he returned to Harvard and received the A.B. degree in 1912, he spent the summer of 1911 in Arizona hunting mountain sheep. Upon graduation, he passed up an opening in New York to go into engineering with the Brazil Railroad Company. There, late in 1913, he joined his father on an expedition into the Brazilian wilderness to trace the uncharted River of Doubt, a harrowing exploration that almost cost his father's life. On June 11, 1914, in Madrid, Kermit married Belle Wyatt Willard, daughter of the United States ambassador to Spain. They had four children: Kermit, Joseph Willard, Belle Wyatt, and Dirck. The young couple settled in Buenos Aires, Argentina, where Roosevelt assumed the position of assistant manager in the newly opened branch of the National City Bank.

America's entry into war in 1917 found him as eager as his three brothers to get into combat. Aided by his father, who recognized that "Kermit's whole training fits him for work in the open, in such a campaign as that in Mesopotamia" (*Letters*, VIII, 1202), he quickly obtained an honorary commission with the British forces opposing the Turks in the Tigris-Euphrates valley. For his gallant actions in light-armored Rolls Royces, recounted modestly in his first book, *War in the Garden of Eden* (1919), he was awarded the British Military Cross in June 1918. He was then transferred to the 1st Division of the American army as a field artillery captain on the Western Front.

Returning to the United States in 1919, Kermit finally found his business career in shipping. He began as an executive of the Kerr Line and in 1920 formed the Roosevelt Steamship Company to operate the American-Indian line for the United States Shipping Board. When his firm was merged into the International Mercantile Marine Company in 1931, Roosevelt became vice-president of the parent concern. But even so glamorous a pursuit could not satisfy his longing for high adventure in faraway places. In 1922–23 he hunted tigers in Korea and India. In 1925 he and his brother Theodore organized, for Chicago's Field Museum, an expedition to collect animals and birds in Eastern Turkestan. On that epic journey, recorded in their *East of the Sun and West of the Moon* (1926), they bagged the legendary *Ovis poli*, a rare mountain sheep, and an ibex with horns of record size. A second expedition for the museum in 1928–29 took them into Yünnan and Szechuan provinces of China, from which they brought back the first golden snub-nosed monkey and giant panda to be seen in America.

When the German threat again emerged, Roosevelt resigned his shipping post in 1938 and in September 1939 sailed for England. Becoming a British citizen, he was commissioned a major with the Middlesex regiment. He saw action in Norway, at Narvik in 1940, but persistent illness following a dysentery attack while serving in Egypt brought him back to America for treatment the next year. By April 1942 he had sufficiently recovered to enlist in the United States Army as a major. Assigned to intelligence duty in Alaska, he died there at the age of fifty-three. He was buried in the military cemetery at Fort Richardson, Anchorage.

[Kermit Roosevelt's papers are in the Harvard College Lib. and the Lib. of Cong. Many of Theodore Roosevelt's letters to and about Kermit are in Elting E. Morison and John M. Blum, eds., *The Letters of Theodore Roosevelt* (8 vols., 1951–54); see also Will Irwin, ed., *Letters to Kermit from Theodore Roosevelt, 1902–1908* (1946), and Joseph B. Bishop, ed., *Theodore Roosevelt's Letters to His Children* (1919). For the African and Brazilian expeditions, see his father's *African Game Trails* (1910) and *Through the Brazilian Wilderness* (1914), both with Kermit's photographs. Other books by Kermit include *The Happy Hunting-Grounds* (1920), a collection of his articles; and, with Theodore Roosevelt, Jr., *Trailing the Giant Panda* (1929). For family insights, see his brother Theodore's *All in the Family* (1929) and Hermann Hagedorn, *The Roosevelt Family of Sagamore Hill* (1954). The *N. Y. Times* gave good coverage to his activities; see also its obituary, June 6, 1943.]

G. WALLACE CHESSMAN

ROOSEVELT, THEODORE (Sept. 13, 1887–July 12, 1944), businessman, public official, army officer, was the oldest of the five children of President Theodore Roosevelt by his second wife, Edith Kermit (Carow) Roosevelt; he had an older half sister, Alice (later Mrs. Nicholas Longworth). Born at Sagamore Hill, the family's residence in Oyster Bay, N. Y., he attended grade schools in Oyster Bay, Albany, and Washington, as his father moved into state and national politics, and then spent four years (1900–04) at the Groton School in Massachusetts. A quiet and reticent youth, who like his father was plagued by poor eyesight and headaches, he nevertheless participated vigorously in sports, especially boxing and football. After a year of tutoring at Sagamore Hill, he entered Harvard in 1905. There, as the son of the President, he received considerable publicity and, to the embarrassment of his father, was twice placed on academic probation, but he completed his degree requirements in less than four years and received the A.B. in 1908.

After college, Roosevelt entered business, taking a job as a wool sorter at the Hartford Carpet Company in Thompsonville, Conn. He married Eleanor Butler Alexander, daughter of a prominent New York City lawyer, on June 20, 1910, at the Fifth Avenue Presbyterian Church. They had four children: Grace Green, Theodore, Cornelius Van Schaack, and Quentin. Immediately after their marriage, the couple moved to San Francisco, where Roosevelt became manager of the Hartford company's Pacific Coast branch. He returned to New York in the winter of 1912 as a bond salesman for a brokerage house. Two years later he became a partner in the Philadelphia banking firm of Montgomery, Clothier and Tyler, and was named manager of its New York office.

Although business absorbed most of his energy, Roosevelt, like his father, was an early advocate of military preparedness. In 1915, after the sinking of the *Lusitania*, he helped organize a summer camp at Plattsburgh, N. Y., to train civilians as reserve officers. When the United States entered World War I, he joined the regular army as a captain in the 1st Division. He was among the first of the American troops to arrive in France, where he fought in the front lines and was twice wounded, at Cantigny in March 1918 and at Soissons in July. He received numerous decorations, including the Distinguished Service Medal and the French Croix de Guerre. Following his discharge, he remained in the army reserve with the rank of colonel. On his return to the United States he helped organize the American Legion.

Roosevelt made his initial venture into politics in 1919, winning the first of two annual terms in the New York legislature as an assemblyman from Nassau County. Except for his opposition to the expulsion of Socialists from the assembly, however, his stay in Albany—in contrast to that of his father—did not attract wide attention. In the presidential year of 1920, he supported Gen. Leonard Wood [*q.v.*] for the Republican nomination, but after the convention campaigned for Warren G. Harding. He was rewarded the next year by appointment as Assistant Secretary of the Navy, again a position his father had held. Roosevelt was one of four men who drafted the famous "stop-now" speech delivered by Secretary of State Charles Evans Hughes in opening the Washington Conference on limiting armaments. During the conference he served as Hughes's chief technical adviser and was instrumental in negotiating the capital-ship ratios with Great Britain, France, and Japan.

Roosevelt resigned from the Navy Department in 1924 to run as the Republican candidate for governor of New York. Here the parallel with his father ended. Alfred E. Smith [Supp. 3], a popular governor running for a third term, defeated Roosevelt by more than 100,000 votes, even though Calvin Coolidge swept the state by a margin of 800,000. Contributing to Roosevelt's defeat was the Teapot Dome scandal; he had been a stockholder of the Sinclair Oil Company, the principal lessee of the federal naval oil reserve lands, and his brother Archibald was a vice-president of the company.

During the next few years Roosevelt and his brother Kermit [Supp. 3] led two zoological expeditions into central and southeast Asia, collecting numerous specimens of mammals, birds, and reptiles. Theodore returned to public life in 1929 when President Hoover appointed him governor of Puerto Rico. An able administrator, he subdivided public lands, making them available to small farmers; he also succeeded in getting federal aid for education, which enabled him to triple the number of students in rural high schools, to institute a teacher training program, and to improve facilities for vocational education. In January 1932 he resigned to become governor general of the Philippine Islands, where he initiated similar educational and land reforms and greatly improved health care, especially in the areas of child health and the control of tuberculosis and leprosy.

An "out-of-season" Roosevelt after his kinsman Franklin was elected to the presidency, Roosevelt resigned his post in the Philippines in 1933. In 1934 he became chairman of the board of the American Express Company, and the following year an editor (and later vice-president) of the publishing firm of Doubleday, Doran. He also devoted much time to service organizations: as a vice-president in 1935 of the National Council of Boy Scouts, of which he had been a member since 1919; as national chairman, 1930–40, of the United Council for Civilian Relief in China; and as a member of the board of directors of the National Association for the Advancement of Colored People. Still in the public eye, he vigorously opposed the lavish spending programs of the New Deal and the centralization of power in Washington. He nevertheless supported the President in his foreign policy, endorsing the Neutrality Acts and later the Lend-Lease Act.

In April 1941 the army reactivated Roosevelt, placing him in charge of his old unit. Promoted to brigadier general that same year, he participated in the Tunisian and Italian campaigns. On June 6, 1944, when the invasion of Normandy was launched, Roosevelt was the only general to land with the first wave of troops, leading the 4th Division on Utah Beach. The next month, while serving as military governor of Cherbourg,

France, he died of a heart attack at the age of fifty-six. He was buried in the American Military Cemetery, St. Laurent, France. Roosevelt had achieved his greatest success in the military sphere. With the posthumous award of the Medal of Honor, he had won, in the course of two major wars, every combat decoration of the United States Army ground forces.

[The papers of Theodore Roosevelt, Jr., are in the Lib. of Cong. His writings include: *Average Americans* (1919), *Rank and File: True Stories of the Great War* (1928), *All in the Family* (1929), *Colonial Policies of the U. S.* (1937), *Three Kingdoms of Indo-China* (with Harold J. Coolidge, Jr., 1933), and, with his brother Kermit, *East of the Sun and West of the Moon* (1926) and *Trailing the Giant Panda* (1929). The only extended biographical study is Lawrence H. Madaras, "The Public Career of Theodore Roosevelt, Jr." (Ph.D. dissertation, N. Y. Univ., 1964). See also: 25th and 40th anniversary *Reports* of Harvard College Class of 1909; Eleanor Butler Roosevelt, *Day before Yesterday: The Reminiscences of Mrs. Theodore Roosevelt, Jr.* (1959); and obituary in *N. Y. Times*, July 14, 1944.]

LAWRENCE H. MADARAS

ROPER, DANIEL CALHOUN (Apr. 1, 1867–Apr. 11, 1943), cabinet officer, was born in Marlboro County, S. C., a descendant of John Roper, who had been a vestryman of Blisland Parish, Va., in 1678. His father, John Wesley Roper, a Confederate veteran, was a farmer; a native of adjacent Richmond County, N. C., he had bought the ancestral plantation of his wife, Henrietta Virginia McLaurin, upon their marriage in 1866. Daniel was an only child, his mother dying less than three years after his birth, but he had two half brothers and two half sisters by his father's remarriage in 1874. After attending a one-room elementary school and the high school in Laurinburg, N. C., he entered Wofford College, Spartanburg, S. C., but transferred at the end of his sophomore year, in 1886, to Trinity College (later Duke University) in Durham, N. C., from which he received the B.A. degree in 1888. On Dec. 25, 1889, he married Lou McKenzie of Gibson, N. C., a teacher and the daughter of an architect. They had seven children: Margaret May, James Hunter, Daniel Calhoun, Grace Henrietta, John Wesley, Harry McKenzie, and Richard Frederick.

After leaving college, Roper briefly taught school (1889–90), farmed, and sold life insurance. In 1890, during the agrarian upheaval in South Carolina led by Ben Tillman [*q.v.*], he joined the Farmers' Alliance. Although a Populist at heart, he chose, like Tillman, to remain within the Democratic fold. He was elected in 1892 to the South Carolina house of representatives, where he promptly introduced a prohibition bill. The next year, his party loyalty won him an appointment as clerk to the United States Senate's Interstate Commerce Committee. After a brief term as an office manager in New York City (1896–98), Roper returned to Washington in 1898 as a life insurance agent. A new federal appointment, in 1900, took him to the Bureau of the Census as an enumerator of cotton gins, and over the next eleven years he developed an expert knowledge of the foreign and domestic cotton trade. During this period, in 1901, he earned a law degree from National University. In 1911, with the help of Congressman Albert S. Burleson [Supp. 2], Roper became clerk of the House Ways and Means Committee. Well known by now in Democratic party circles for his familiarity with the economics of cotton and his support of tariff revision, he had substantial influence among the Southern delegations.

Roper's major opportunity came when he joined the movement to make Woodrow Wilson the Democratic presidential nominee in 1912. For his role, he was rewarded with the post of First Assistant Postmaster General, responsible for filling the 60,000 postmasterships made available by the defeat of the Republicans. He worked closely with another member of the Wilson administration, Franklin D. Roosevelt, to rebuild the Northeastern wing of the party in Wilson's image. Roper left the Post Office Department in August 1916 to serve in Wilson's campaign for reelection. In March 1917 he became vice-chairman of the United States Tariff Commission, and in September of that year, Commissioner of Internal Revenue. He administered the narcotics and wartime prohibition laws, created an intelligence unit to investigate tax frauds, and was popularly credited with the improvement of both the administration and the collection of the income tax. After leaving office, Roper served for a year in New York as president of a manufacturing firm, the Marlin Rockwell Corporation, while it was undergoing reorganization and then returned to Washington to practice law. At the Democratic convention of 1924 he was closely associated with the bid of William Gibbs McAdoo [Supp. 3] for the presidential nomination, and at the 1932 convention he played a significant role in swinging McAdoo's votes to Franklin D. Roosevelt.

Roosevelt named Roper to his cabinet in 1933 as Secretary of Commerce. Despite his earlier Wilsonian liberalism, the South Carolinian became a conservative influence within the administration. During the economy mood of 1933, he cut his department's budget and its domestic and foreign programs, and he set up a Business Advisory Council to funnel business attitudes to both Congress and the President. Although chairman of the cabinet committee set up to oversee the National Recovery Administration, he was generally overshadowed by its head, Hugh Johnson [Supp. 3], and he often found himself ranged against more advanced New Dealers on social and fiscal issues. His integrity was widely respected, and he was an important link with the Southern leaders in Congress, but his own leadership was no longer dynamic. Once appraised as a "crisp administrator," he was, in the New Deal, largely a harmonizer and balancer, skilled at smoothing ruffled feathers.

Roper eventually came to believe that the administration had placed too much blame for the depression on big business, and when F.D.R.'s reorganization plan divested the Commerce Department of several of its units, he resigned in December 1938. The next year he returned briefly to government service as United States minister to Canada, having been appointed to serve during the visit of King George to North America. Roper was an active member of the Methodist Church. He died of leukemia in Washington in 1943 and was buried in Washington's Rock Creek Cemetery.

[Roper's autobiography, *Fifty Years of Public Life* (1941), written in collaboration with Frank H. Lovette, is the basic source. His other writings include: *The U. S. Post Office* (1917); "Basis for Reform of Federal Taxation," *Annals of the Am. Acad. of Political and Social Sci.*, May 1921; "Long-Range Planning," Acad. of Political Sci., *Proc.*, Jan. 1934; and "The Constitution and the New Deal," *Vital Speeches*, Nov. 5, 1934. See also Arthur S. Link, *Wilson: The New Freedom* (1956); Arthur M. Schlesinger, Jr., *The Crisis of the Old Order* (1957) and *The Politics of Upheaval* (1960); Raymond Moley, *After Seven Years* (1939); Alfred B. Rollins, Jr., *Roosevelt and Howe* (1962); and the sketch of Roper in *Nat. Cyc. Am. Biog.*, XXXI, 5–6.]
ALFRED B. ROLLINS, JR.

ROSE, MARY DAVIES SWARTZ (Oct. 31, 1874–Feb. 1, 1941), nutritionist, was born in Newark, Ohio, the oldest of the three daughters and two sons of Martha Jane (Davies) Swartz, a teacher, whose parents had emigrated from Wales in 1840, and Hiram Buel Swartz, whose mother and father were natives of Ohio and Pennsylvania respectively. A graduate of the University of Michigan, Swartz was a lawyer who served two terms as mayor of Wooster, Ohio, and later was elected probate judge of Wayne County.

Mary Swartz graduated as valedictorian of her class in the Wooster high school in 1892. For the next nine years she alternated study at Shepardson College (later part of Denison University) and the College of Wooster with teaching at the Wooster high school. She received a Litt.B. degree from Shepardson in 1901 and the next year earned a diploma in domestic science from the Mechanics' Institute in Rochester, N. Y. She then taught high school home economics for three years in Fond du Lac, Wis. In 1905 she entered Teachers College, Columbia University, receiving a B.S. degree in 1906. After assisting at Teachers College for one year, she went to Yale for graduate study in physiological chemistry under Prof. Lafayette B. Mendel [Supp. 1]. There she was elected to Sigma Xi, the first woman so honored at Yale.

Upon receiving her Ph.D. in 1909, with a thesis on the carbohydrates of lichens and algae, Mary Swartz returned to Teachers College to become its first full-time instructor in nutrition and dietetics. On Sept. 15, 1910, she was married to Anton Richard Rose, who had been a fellow graduate student at Yale; he later became chief chemist for the Prudential Insurance Company. Their only child, Richard Collin Rose, was born in 1915. Rising through the academic ranks, Mrs. Rose was appointed in 1923 to a professorship of nutrition, possibly the first such post in an American university.

At Columbia she worked closely with the nutritional chemist Henry C. Sherman, and her department became an outstanding center for teaching the scientific principles of nutrition and dietetics and for training future teachers of the subject. Her own research included work on the body's utilization of food materials, the relation of diet to the health and growth of children in institutions, the nutritional role of certain trace elements, the influence of nutrients on anemia, comparison of the proteins from milk and meat, hemoglobin regeneration in rats, and the vitamin content of foods. Long active on the editorial board of the *Journal of Nutrition,* she contributed frequently to it, as well as to the *Journal of Biological Chemistry, Journal of Home Economics, Journal of the American Dietetic Association,* and others.

Mrs. Rose's *A Laboratory Hand-book for Dietetics,* which proved of value to countless laboratory students, first appeared in 1912. She also wrote several books in which she applied the findings of the nutrition laboratory to people's everyday lives. In *Feeding the Family* (1916), considered by many to be a classic in its field, she recalculated tables of food composition to fit ordinary recipes and foods as eaten, putting the chemical aspects of nutrition in terms a homemaker could understand and use. The fourth edition was completed the year before her death. *Everyday Foods in War Time* was published in 1918. *The Foundations of Nutrition,* a well-

known text and reference book, appeared in 1927, with revisions in 1933 and 1938; former colleagues have since produced three more editions, the latest in 1966. Results of studies which Mrs. Rose and some of her advanced students conducted on nutrition education in the elementary grades were published in *Teaching Nutrition to Boys and Girls* (1932). She also wrote many Teachers College bulletins.

During 1918–19 Mary Swartz Rose served as deputy director for New York City of the wartime Bureau of Food Conservation, set up under state and federal auspices. From 1933 until her death she was a member of the Council on Foods and Nutrition of the American Medical Association. She was a member of the nutrition committee set up by the Health Organization of the League of Nations in 1935. The many scientific organizations to which she belonged included the American Society of Biological Chemists, the American Public Health Association, and the American Physiological Society. She was made a fellow of the American Association for the Advancement of Science and an honorary member of the American Dietetic Association. A founder of the American Institute of Nutrition, she served as its president in 1937–38. Since 1949 the Mary Swartz Rose Fellowship, financed by the Nutrition Foundation and administered by the American Dietetic Association, has been granted annually for graduate study in nutrition and allied fields.

A small woman, about five feet tall and weighing barely one hundred pounds, Mary Rose made many of her clothes and trimmed her own hats. A colleague recalled that she "loved those things which added to the gaiety of living"—flowers, music, parties, something new for her home. Mrs. Rose retired from active service at Columbia on July 1, 1940; she died of cancer at her Edgewater, N. J., home seven months later. A lifelong Baptist, she had attended Riverside Church in New York City, where memorial services were held. She was buried in Maple Grove Cemetery, Granville, Ohio.

[Clyde Beatrice Schuman, "Mary Swartz Rose, Scientist and Educator" (Ph.D. dissertation, N. Y. Univ., 1945); obituaries in *Jour. of Home Economics,* Apr. 1941 (by Grace MacLeod), *Jour. Am. Dietetic Assoc.,* Mar. 1941, *Jour. of Nutrition,* Mar. 1941 (by Henry C. Sherman), and *Jour. Am. Medic. Assoc.,* May 24, 1941; Clara Mae Taylor, "Recollections of Mary Swartz Rose," *Jour. Am. Dietetic Assoc.,* July 1963; Mary I. Barber, ed., *Hist. of the Am. Dietetic Assoc., 1917–1959* (1959); *Am. Men of Sci.* (6th ed., 1938); *Who Was Who in America,* vol. I (1942); *N. Y. Times* and *N. Y. Herald Tribune,* Feb. 2, 1941; E. Neige Todhunter, "Some Classics of Nutrition and Dietetics," *Jour. Am. Dietetic Assoc.,* Feb. 1964; J. H. Beers, *A Biog. Record of Wayne County, Ohio*

(1889); B. F. Bowen, *Hist. of Wayne County* (1910); death certificate, N. J. Dept. of Health; information from Denison Univ. Alumni Soc. and from Dr. Clara Mae Taylor. A portrait of Mrs. Rose by Ivan Olinsky is in Dodge Hall at Teachers College.]

EMMA SEIFRIT WEIGLEY

ROURKE, CONSTANCE MAYFIELD

(Nov. 14, 1885–Mar. 23, 1941), cultural historian and folklorist, was born in Cleveland, Ohio, the only child of Henry Button Rourke and Constance Elizabeth (Davis) Rourke. Their ancestry was mixed Irish, English, Welsh, and French, of Southern pioneer stock. The father, a lawyer, died when his daughter was about seven, and Mrs. Rourke moved to Grand Rapids, Mich., where she taught school and Constance attended the public schools. Trained as a kindergarten teacher, Mrs. Rourke was also a skilled amateur painter, with talents in handicrafts, the love of which she transmitted to her daughter. Theirs was an unusually affectionate and sympathetic relationship. Going to Vassar College, Constance took her A.B. in 1907 and then spent a year at the Sorbonne; from 1908 to 1910 she was a research reader at the Bibliothèque Nationale and the British Museum. For the next five years she taught English at Vassar, resigning in 1915 to return to Grand Rapids, where she lived with her mother and devoted herself to research and writing in the field of American culture.

How she came to concentrate in this field is not known. At Vassar her interest had been aesthetics and literary criticism. Probably it was in her own background that she discovered the richness of folklore and social history. Though her parents made little of their ancestry, Constance had grown up with some sense of her heritage among the "plain people" of the South like her maternal grandfather, a Methodist minister. One of her ancestors, George Mayfield, had been stolen by the Creeks and reared as an Indian, had known Davy Crockett [q.v.], and had been Jackson's interpreter in the Creek War; his story exemplified for her the varicolored fabric of the American past. Beginning with an article on "Vaudeville" in the *New Republic* (Aug. 27, 1919), she spent the rest of her life exploring and interpreting this past. She had instinctive tact and charm, and her buoyancy and infectious enthusiasm enabled her to move easily among "old timers round about the country," who opened to her their stores of reminiscence, folk sayings, and songs, which she collected, compared, and knitted together as the basis for her articles and books. Like these people, she had a profound sense of rootedness in her own community, and all her writings are imbued with this feeling for particularity and locality.

The biographical studies of great popular figures in her first book, *Trumpets of Jubilee* (1927), reflect this interest in regional character. With an uncertain grasp of religious history, she could produce only a superficial analysis of New England theology in the thought of Lyman Beecher [q.v.], or even in the broader life of his children. The whole book, in fact, is marred by a dwelling on the brash and bizarre. She was more successful in her treatment of Horace Greeley, of whom she drew a sympathetic portrait, and of P. T. Barnum [qq.v.]. In dealing with Harriet Beecher Stowe [q.v.] she argued for a just literary evaluation of *Uncle Tom's Cabin*, and in a later essay on Mrs. Stowe (in the *Encyclopedia of the Social Sciences*), she demonstrated that author's fruitful use of a long tradition of Yankee and Negro characterization. Miss Rourke's contention that the novel was "folk drama" became the theme of much of her work, and led to her most suggestive critical concept: that the forms and artifacts of folk culture are not mere deposits within more serious art, but its vitalizing element.

Her *American Humor* (1931), a study of native American comic types and forms and their influence upon literature, is still fresh and significant. Its definition of the comic tradition in terms of masquerade and minstrelsy underlined her conviction that American consciousness and character were essentially projected through drama, that even Calvinistic religion had the aspect of theatre. She was at her best in delineating the three great comic figures of the Yankee, the backwoodsman, and the Negro, and in demonstrating the borrowings and transmutations that marked the evolution of these types. Her racy, zestful style made *American Humor* a classic of historical portraiture, and her massive investigations produced an abundance of detail and local incident and a deft, rounded expression of the dominant strain in American humor. Less successful were the essays on the major figures of American literature in which she attempted to demonstrate their uses of this heritage, though she did point up the importance of humor in their writings, especially the humor of the grotesque, of braggadocio, and of comic inflation.

Her most fully realized critical study was *Charles Sheeler* (1938), an examination and appraisal of the folk roots of his painting. A book of genuine insight, it was equally an empathic one, for she found in Sheeler's vision of painting the same love of craftsmanship and the same appreciation of the artistic possibilities of plasticity, texture, and architectural form that she herself had discerned. Drawing on Sheeler's observations on the Shaker aesthetic, with its economy of means and unerring sense of proportion, she captured the excitement of his discovery that (in the words of a Shaker saying) "Every force has its form." In placing Sheeler within an authentically American tradition, she argued that the thoughtful study of "essentially democratic arts" could provide an "anatomy of our creative powers" in the past, and that the "human expressive values" discoverable in them could be appropriated for a broad enrichment of American art.

Miss Rourke died before writing her projected history of American culture, in which she might have developed more completely and convincingly her insights into the relationship between folk tradition and formal art. Six fragments from her manuscripts, edited by Van Wyck Brooks, were published as *The Roots of American Culture* (1942), an inferior book, but one that demonstrates the breadth of her interests and her commitment to making accessible to "the precarious, strange, and tragic present" a dense, variegated body of native tradition. In spite of the liveliness of her writing and the suggestive hints her studies contain, today's reader notices in her work as a whole her failure to appreciate fully the uses of the comparative approach and her tendency to celebrate folk tradition and popular culture at the expense of analysis and generalization. Equipped with a perceptive yet modest critical apparatus, she left even her best studies in a state of incompleteness, and ultimately they have limited explanatory power. These, however, were the shortcomings of a pioneer who gave great stimulus to the field of American literary history.

Constance Rourke never married. She died at the age of fifty-five in Grand Rapids, Mich., from a thrombosis after a fall, and was buried in the Woodlawn Cemetery there.

[Miss Rourke's other books are: *Troupers of the Gold Coast* (1928), on the early California stage; *Davy Crockett* (1934); and *Audubon* (1936). Her personal papers are in the possession of Mrs. Carl Shoaff, Carbondale, Ill. For biographical and critical material, see: Stanley Edgar Hyman, *The Armed Vision* (1948), pp. 127–41; Alfred Kazin, "The Irreducible Element," *New Republic*, Aug. 31, 1942; Kenneth S. Lynn's introduction to the paperback edition (1963) of Miss Rourke's *Trumpets of Jubilee* and his article in *Notable Am. Women*, III, 199–200; Van Wyck Brooks's preface to her *Roots of Am. Culture*; Margaret Marshall in *Nation*, June 21, 1941; Stanley J. Kunitz and Howard Haycraft, eds., *Twentieth Century Authors* (1942); *Nat. Cyc. Am. Biog.*, XXXII, 100. The last reproduces a photograph as do the *Mag. of Art*, Apr. 1937, and *Time*, Aug. 10, 1942, p. 91.]

MARIE CASKEY

RUCKSTULL, FREDERICK WELLINGTON (May 22, 1853–May 26, 1942), sculptor, was born at Breitenbach, Alsace, France, one of four children of John and Jeanette (Steeb) Ruckstuhl. (During World War I he changed the spelling to Ruckstull.) The family emigrated to America in 1855 and settled in St. Louis, Mo., where during the Civil War the elder Ruckstuhl, a machinist, was chief engineer of the machine shop of the St. Louis arsenal. Frederick's mother died when he was six. The boy attended public schools and showed an early interest in carving, but his father, who wanted him to become a missionary, sent him to the Rochester Theological Seminary (Baptist). Ruckstull left after a year, a confirmed religious skeptic. A period of aimlessness followed, during which he worked at a variety of jobs in many parts of the country and grew so depressed that he reportedly contemplated suicide. The way out of his despondency came when a chance visit to an art exhibit in St. Louis revived his interest in sculpture.

Ruckstull's first formal instruction in art began at the age of twenty-two, when he enrolled in night classes at the Washington University Art School in St. Louis. He soon gave up other work to devote his full time to art. When, in 1882, the model he had submitted in a competition for a statue of Gen. Francis P. Blair [*q.v.*] was first accepted but then rejected because of his inexperience, he decided to go to Europe for a year's study. The works he saw at the annual Paris Salon of 1883 disappointed him, and, with characteristic self-confidence, he decided that with three years of study he could do better himself; he therefore returned to St. Louis and worked as salesman in a toy store to save the necessary funds.

Back in Paris in 1885, Ruckstull entered the Académie Julian, where he studied with Gustave Boulanger and Camille Lefèvre. According to his own statement, he also received instruction from Jean Dampt and Antoine Mercié and could have become a pupil of Auguste Rodin had the latter's work not repelled him. His first major effort, in 1887—a full-length figure personifying "Evening"—received an honorable mention the following year at the annual Salon. His next ideal piece, "Mercury Teasing the Eagle of Jupiter," clearly revealed Ruckstull's dedication to the neo-Baroque classicism then advocated at the École des Beaux Arts and other academies in Paris. After three years he returned to St. Louis, but by 1892 he had established a studio in New York City, where he quickly became part of that community's sizable circle of sculptors. His work won national attention at the World's Columbian Exposition of 1893, where his "Evening" received the grand medal for sculpture. His first major commission was an equestrian statue of Gen. John F. Hartranft [q.v.] for the Pennsylvania State Capitol at Harrisburg; it was completed in 1897.

Ruckstull was instrumental in founding, in 1893, the National Sculpture Society, which did much to promote the art of sculpture in the United States; he was its first secretary. His abilities as an organizer are seen in his role as general manager of the Dewey Arch project—the plaster triumphal arch erected in New York in 1899 to honor the famous naval hero when he visited the city—in which numerous sculptors collaborated under Ruckstull's guidance. Soon afterward Ruckstull was selected as coordinator of the statuary for the new Appellate Court Building in New York; he produced two heroic figures ("Wisdom" and "Force") and assigned other subjects to fellow members of the Sculpture Society. Ruckstull was placed in charge of sculptural projects for the St. Louis exposition of 1904, but bickering among the sculptors and architects soon brought his resignation, and he was replaced by Karl Bitter [q.v.]. There followed a considerable succession of war memorials, ideal figures, and portrait statues, among which the most notable are the "Phoenicia" (New York Custom House), an equestrian statue of Gen. Wade Hampton [q.v.] and a monument to Confederate women (both at Columbia, S. C.), marble statues of John C. Calhoun and the Arkansas jurist Uriah M. Rose [qq.v.] (Statuary Hall, United States Capitol), the Confederate Monument (Baltimore), and the "Defense of the Flag," another Confederate monument (Little Rock, Ark.).

A successful sculptor in the academic style of the day, Ruckstull was also one of the most vocal defenders of the old regime in art, beginning with the early advances of the modern movement shortly before World War I. In his lectures and in articles, especially for the *Art World*, he ridiculed "this intellectual pest called Modernism" as the outrageous production of lunatics. After the war Ruckstull continued to operate his studio but undertook increasingly fewer commissions. On Mar. 28, 1896, he had married Adelaide (Adele) Pohlman, by whom he had one son, Myron Jackson. Living on to the age of eighty-nine, he died at his home in New York City. His remains were cremated.

[Ruckstull's autobiography, in his *Great Works of Art and What Makes Them Great* (1925); articles about him by Elizabeth Graham in *Metropolitan Mag.*, Nov. 1899, and Richard Ladegast in *New England Mag.*, Jan. 1902; Lorado Taft, *Hist. of Am. Sculpture* (rev. ed., 1924); Wayne Craven, *Sculpture in America* (1968), pp. 477–81; *Who Was Who in America*, vol. II (1950); *Nat. Cyc. Am. Biog.*, XXXII, 348–49; obituaries in *N. Y. Times*, May 27, 1942, and *Art Digest*, June 1942.]
WAYNE CRAVEN

RUSSELL, CHARLES EDWARD (Sept. 25, 1860–Apr. 23, 1941), journalist, author, reformer, socialist, was born in Davenport, Iowa, one of at least four children (three of them girls) of Edward and Lydia (Rutledge) Russell. Both of his grandfathers were natives of England, where William Russell had worked as a clerk in a distillery and then become a temperance lecturer; William Rutledge, also a temperance reformer, was a Baptist clergyman. Both had emigrated to the United States in the 1840's and eventually settled in Iowa. Charles's father, after working in his youth as a carpenter and builder, became the editor of the *Davenport Gazette*. An ardent abolitionist in the face of threats from the town's strong proslavery element, he was later a steadfast Republican. After the Civil War he defended the small farmer and attacked the corrupt practices of Western railroads, until one of them bought a controlling interest in the *Gazette* and forced him out of his job. Charles recalled his mother as "a modest, . . . sensitive woman whose interests in life were her family, her church and her music."

Despite the family's reform tradition, Charles Russell arrived at his mature social views gradually, drawing from his own reading and observations. When he showed little aptitude for the business side of journalism, his father sent him to the St. Johnsbury (Vt.) Academy for a proper Eastern education. The cultural shock administered by the pious village and its semifeudal social structure (St. Johnsbury was dominated by the Fairbanks Scale family and factory) sent him searching for a philosophy of social reconstruction. He read Henry George and Wendell Phillips [qq.v.] and discussed social problems with a literate local mechanic. Soon he came to see free trade as the panacea he sought, and upon his return to Iowa after graduation (1881) he founded the Iowa Free Trade League. In 1884 he married Abby Osborn Rust of St. Johnsbury. They had one child, John Edward.

For the next twenty years Russell combined journalism and reform. He held a succession of jobs as reporter or editor in Davenport, Minneapolis, Detroit, and New York City (through the 1880's and early '90's) and then as city editor of the New York *World* (1894–97), managing editor of the *New York American* (1897–1900), and publisher of William Randolph Hearst's *Chicago American* (1900–02). In off hours he lectured on free trade or worked for the Populists.

Although these were busy years, with frequent moves and a postgraduate education on the police beat in New York's slums, they could hardly have been entirely satisfying, for Russell had deep urges to participate in the cause of human betterment and creative drives for which reportorial writing was scant outlet. His wife died in 1901, and when his own health broke the following year, he settled down to write a book on American music, a lifetime interest. He abandoned this project in 1905 when Erman J. Ridgway of *Everybody's* magazine recruited him for an apparently routine article on Chicago meat-packing. Russell produced an electrifying series of articles on the "Beef Trust"; his talents and his social views meshed, and he became a leading muckraker. He wrote for *Everybody's,* *Hampton's* and *Cosmopolitan,* on themes such as railroad accidents and financing, child labor, electoral fraud, and great fortunes. Industrious, eclectic in interest, a lucid writer with a popular touch, he became, along with men like Ray Stannard Baker, Upton Sinclair, and Lincoln Steffens [Supp. 2], one of the best-known journalists of exposure. He widened his audience with frequent books (twenty-seven in all), among them *The Greatest Trust in the World* (1905), *The Uprising of the Many* (1907), and *Lawless Wealth* (1908). Like the best of the muckrakers, Russell mastered difficult subjects, such as railroading and banking, and learned to communicate the abstruse with clarity and controlled passion.

Just as muckraking began to wane, Russell started a long career as a Socialist, joining the party in 1908 and writing *Why I Am a Socialist* in 1910. He was a welcome convert, not only because of his reputation but also because of a rare and transparent sincerity that gave him access to men of divergent views and cast him often in the role of peacemaker. Although more interested in ideas than in politics, Russell ran as the Socialist candidate for governor of New York in 1910 and 1912, for mayor of New York City in 1913, and for United States Senator in 1914. He was advanced by New York Socialists as a presidential candidate at the party's convention in 1912, where he ran third behind Eugene V. Debs [*q.v.*]. The presidential nomination of 1916 apparently could have been his had he not previously antagonized party opinion by advocating military preparedness. When the United States entered World War I in April 1917, Russell was an enthusiastic supporter, and over this issue he broke with the movement, along with other right-wing Socialists like William English Walling [Supp. 2], John Spargo, William J. Ghent [Supp. 3], Upton Sinclair, and Robert Hunter [Supp. 3]. The loss of these former progressives, men who were able to influence native, middle-class Americans, was a stunning blow to the Socialist party. Russell was formally expelled

from the party in 1917 when he accepted President Wilson's invitation to join the mission to Russia headed by Elihu Root [Supp. 2]. In 1919 he became commissioner to Great Britain and Ireland for the wartime Committee on Public Information, and later the same year he was named a member of the President's Industrial Commission.

Unlike Spargo and Hunter, however, Russell remained a socialist, just as he remained a reformer: for him they had always been the same thing. Although most reform journalists had dropped social problems by 1912, Russell wrote a series of articles in *Pearson's* magazine in 1914 explaining how advertiser pressure had put an end to muckraking. In 1915 he moved to North Dakota and joined the Non-Partisan League as editor of its *Leader.* Although less active after 1920, he lent his support to countless campaigns for the underdog: the Negro (he was one of five founders of the National Association for the Advancement of Colored People in 1909), the Irish and Philippine independence movements, penal reform, an end to capital punishment, and civil liberties. As he took up the cause of the Jews in Germany in the late 1930's, he had few peers in length of service on behalf of those who suffered.

Russell's enthusiasm sometimes carried him to questionable positions. During World War I he reportedly used the word "traitor" in describing the antiwar socialists from whom he had separated; and his sympathy with the cause of Ireland—abetted, perhaps, by his old ties with the Hearst press in Chicago—induced him to lend his support in 1928 to the shoddy campaign of Mayor William Hale Thompson [Supp. 3] against a "pro-British" school superintendent. It is true, too, that Russell was prone to panaceas, embracing in turn (and always uncritically) the single tax, free trade, and socialism. Lincoln Steffens condemned this trait as a religious style of thought, and reported that Russell confessed to him: "I had to have something to believe" (Steffens, *Autobiography,* 1931, II, 632). Yet Russell did not follow other reformers into the comfortable extremes of left or right. He kept working at the small things, declined to hate capitalist or communist even as he condemned their systems (in *Why I Am a Socialist,* 1910, and *Bolshevism and the United States,* 1919), admitted the evils of the world without letting the existence of evil poison his humanism or his faith in progress.

In his final years Russell turned to poetry and biography, writing *The American Orchestra and Theodore Thomas* (1927, a Pulitzer Prize winner) and biographies of Julia Marlowe, Charlemagne, and Haym Salomon [*q.v.*], along with a number of poems and travel books. His autobiography, *Bare Hands and Stone Walls* (1933), brought together the recollections of an eyewitness to fifty years of American and international reform. Russell died of a coronary occlusion at his home in Washington, D. C., in 1941; his remains were cremated. He was survived by his son and by his second wife, Theresa Hirschl of Chicago, whom he had married on July 5, 1909.

Charles Edward Russell was not and never pretended to be an original or profound thinker. He was a reporter, and his strengths were a wide-ranging curiosity, a passion for facts, and an unflagging optimism. He reached a large audience and exercised an undetermined but surely not inconsiderable influence upon his generation. In some cases that influence is clear. The State of Georgia instituted penal reforms after his articles on her convict camps, and Trinity Church in New York went out of the business of tenement management in large part because of another exposure series. All who knew Russell reported him the most genial and sincere reformer in that idealistic, contentious collection of individualists. In a parochial era he was a cosmopolitan, widely traveled and acutely aware of the importance to America of worldwide events. Yet he was always a man of the American plains, egalitarian, preferring facts to theory, holding to gradualism through disappointments that turned other men to despair or to advocacy of violence.

[The Charles Edward Russell Papers are in the Lib. of Cong. His own writings, especially his autobiography, are a basic source. The best account of his family background is in his sketch of his father, *A Pioneer Editor in Early Iowa* (1941). See also Lloyd Morris, *Postscript to Yesterday* (1947); David M. Chalmers, *The Social and Political Ideas of the Muckrakers* (1964); and Louis Filler, *Crusaders for Am. Liberalism* (1939). Russell's role in American Socialism may be followed in Donald D. Egbert and Stow Persons, eds., *Socialism and Am. Life* (2 vols., 1952), especially in Daniel Bell's essay, "The Development of Marxian Socialism in America"; and in Ira Kipnis, *The Am. Socialist Movement, 1897–1912* (1952), and David A. Shannon, *The Socialist Party of America* (1955). For his activities with the Non-Partisan League, see Theodore Saloutos and John D. Hicks, *Agricultural Discontent in the Middle West, 1900–1939* (1951); for the founding of the N.A.A.C.P., see Charles F. Kellogg, *The Nat. Assoc. for the Advancement of Colored People, 1909–1920* (1967). I am grateful to Michael Heskett for permission to read his unpublished seminar paper on Russell.]

OTIS L. GRAHAM, JR.

RUSSELL, JAMES EARL (July 1, 1864–Nov. 4, 1945), educator, was born on his father's farm near Hamden, Delaware County, N. Y., the only son and the eldest of nine children of Charles and Sarah (McFarlane) Russell. His father's parents had come to the United States from Falkirk, Scotland, about 1818; his mother had grown up in the vicinity of Hamden. Russell received his early education in the local rural schools and at Delaware Academy in nearby Delhi. In 1883 he won a New York State Regents' scholarship to Cornell University, where in his senior year he concentrated in classical philology and philosophy under the tutelage of Benjamin Ide Wheeler [*q.v.*] and Jacob Gould Schurman [Supp. 3]. He received the A.B. degree in 1887 with first honors in philosophy. Deciding on a teaching career, Russell taught Latin and Greek for three years in private preparatory schools and in 1890 became headmaster of the Cascadilla School in Ithaca, N. Y. While in Ithaca he also served as review editor of the *School Review,* an educational journal established by Schurman, for which he systematically reviewed educational literature from throughout the world.

Dissatisfied with the rigid formalism prevailing in American secondary schools, Russell determined to study the systems used in other countries, and in 1893 he resigned his headmastership and went to Germany. He studied pedagogy at Jena under Wilhelm Rein and then, in May 1894, went to Leipzig, where he worked with Johannes Volkelt (philosophy), Friedrich Ratzel (geography), and Wilhelm Wundt (psychology) and received the Ph.D. degree in 1894. He also visited secondary schools in France and England.

Although he fundamentally disliked the authoritarian and antidemocratic characteristics of the German empire, Russell was favorably impressed by the training given to German teachers and by the way the German educational system prepared individuals for their roles in society. He wrote several articles on German education which received wide attention in the United States and were collected as *German Higher Schools* (1899); Abraham Flexner later (1940) called the book one of the best studies ever made of German education. Russell left Germany convinced that the subjects taught and the methods used in public education should reflect the underlying philosophy and the pragmatic needs of a country; that in a democracy education should assist all citizens to realize their highest intellectual and occupational capacities; that a high degree of professional training was necessary and desirable for teachers; and that education itself was a subject worthy of study and research at the university level.

Returning to the United States in 1895, Russell accepted an appointment as professor of philosophy and pedagogy at the University of Colorado at Boulder. During his two-year stay, he successfully reorganized and expanded the university's program for the training of teachers. He also began to achieve a national reputation through his publications and through his increasing activity in state and national educational associations.

In September 1897 Russell accepted an invitation to become head of the department of psychology at Teachers College in New York City, then a struggling normal school affiliated with Columbia University and primarily concerned with training kindergarten, domestic science, and manual training teachers. The affiliation with Columbia was in danger of being terminated because of philosophical and jurisdictional disputes between an influential group of Teachers College trustees and representatives of Columbia headed by President Seth Low [q.v.] and Prof. Nicholas Murray Butler. Russell was able to win the confidence of all parties to the controversy and proposed a new administrative arrangement by which Teachers College became a professional school and an integral part of the university structure. Within three months after his arrival in New York, he was named dean.

Over the next few years Russell developed a concept and a curriculum for a professional school of education of university caliber. He early began bringing to the faculty outstanding young men and women who shared his educational vision. He helped them see the possibilities for teaching and research in their fields, and then left them free to build their own programs; thus, while he gained wide respect within his profession, he never achieved so great a popular reputation as did some of his faculty. Russell possessed a remarkable ability to recognize talent. Among the new faculty members he recruited, at a time when they were still relatively unknown, were Edward L. Thorndike in experimental psychology, David Snedden in educational sociology, David Eugene Smith [Supp. 3] in mathematics, Mary Swartz Rose [Supp. 3] in nutritional chemistry, Thomas D. Wood in physical education and hygiene, Paul Monroe in the history of education, George D. Strayer in educational administration, and William H. Kilpatrick in educational theory and philosophy. John Dewey, the Columbia philosopher, also lectured at Teachers College. His presence helped focus and intensify the spirit of educational liberalism and social concern found in Russell's own philosophy, with the result that Teachers College became the "intellectual crossroads" of the progressive education movement in the United States.

Russell's strong belief in the importance of research in education led to the establishment by Teachers College of the experimental Speyer School in 1902 and the Lincoln School in 1917, as well as the Institute of Educational Research (1921), the International Institute (financed in 1923 by a $1,000,000 grant from the International Education Board), and the Institute of Child Welfare Research (1924). His belief that trained educators were needed in many areas outside the traditional academically oriented schools led him to encourage the establishment at Teachers College of programs for such fields as nursing, rural education, scouting, citizenship education, adult education, and vocational education.

Throughout his career at Teachers College, Russell received strong support from an influential and devoted group of trustees headed by Grace H. Dodge and V. Everit Macy [qq.v.], who not only admired his professional vision but also respected his efficient management of the College's resources. Under Russell, the College's enrollment grew from 169 students in 1897 to nearly 5,000 in 1927, its budget expanded from $250,000 to $2,500,000, its physical plant from two buildings to seventeen, and its endowment from nothing to nearly $3,000,000. In three decades it had become perhaps the largest and most influential university school of education in the world.

Russell married Agnes Fletcher in Delhi, N. Y., on June 19, 1899. They had four sons: William Fletcher, Charles, James Earl, and John McFarlane. After his first wife's death in 1927, Russell married Alice Forman Wyckoff on Jan. 24, 1929. When he retired from the deanship of Teachers College in 1927, the trustees chose as his successor his son William, himself an educator of note.

In retirement James Russell devoted his time to other educational activities. He had helped organize the American Association of Adult Education and served as its first president, 1926–30, and thereafter as chairman and then honorary chairman until his death. He was a member of the National Council on Radio in Education, and worked in a variety of capacities with the Boy Scouts, Girl Scouts, and 4-H Club organizations. Russell was also known in agricultural circles for his scientific breeding of dairy cattle. His Glenburnie Farm herds of Guernsey cattle, maintained first near Peekskill, N. Y., and later near Lawrenceville, N. J., were famous for their bloodlines and for their milk production records. He served on the New Jersey Milk Control Board and, from 1932 to 1940, as a member of the New Jersey State Board of Health. He died of cancer at his home in Trenton, N. J., in 1945, at the age of eighty-one; his ashes were placed in the family plot in the cemetery at Lawrenceville, N. J.

[Primary sources: Russell Family Papers (including a fragmentary MS. autobiography dealing with Russell's early life and his career before coming to Teachers College), in the possession of John M. Russell; the President's Files of Teachers College; the Teachers Collegiana Collection of the Teachers College Lib.; and the President's Files of Columbia Univ. Also of value are Frank D. Fackenthal, ed., *Columbia Univ. and Teachers College: Documents and Correspondence* (1915); Russell's volume of reminiscences, *Founding Teachers College* (1937); and his annual *Report of the Dean* of Teachers College, 1898–1927. Secondary sources: Kenneth H. Toepfer, "James Earl Russell and the Rise of Teachers College, 1897–1915" (Ph.D. dissertation, Teachers College, Columbia Univ., 1966); Lawrence A. Cremin, David A. Shannon, and Mary Evelyn Townsend, *A Hist. of Teachers College, Columbia Univ.* (1954); Lawrence A. Cremin, *The Transformation of the School: Progressivism in Am. Education, 1876–1957* (1961); extensive tributes to Russell by Teachers College trustees, faculty, and alumni in *Teachers College Record,* May 1923; Maurice A. Bigelow, "Thirty Years of Practical Arts in Teachers College under the Administration of James E. Russell," *ibid.,* Apr. 1927; and transcription of memorial service, *ibid.,* Feb. 1946. Two of the more informative obituaries are those in the *N. Y. Times,* Nov. 5, 1945, and the *Adult Education Jour.,* Jan. 1946.]

KENNETH H. TOEPFER

RUTHERFORD, JOSEPH FRANKLIN (Nov. 8, 1869–Jan. 8, 1942), second president of Jehovah's Witnesses, was born in Morgan County, Mo., near the town of Boonville, the son of James Calvin and Leonora (Strickland) Rutherford. Although little information is available about his personal life, it is known that his parents were Baptists and farmers. Showing early an interest in law, he won their consent to the necessary study by contributing to the wages of a hired hand to replace him on the farm. Rutherford financed his education at a local academy by learning shorthand and becoming a court stenographer. After two years of tutoring by a local judge, he was admitted to the Missouri bar at the age of twenty-two and started practice with a Boonville law firm. Later he was for four years a public prosecutor and for a time a special judge.

Rutherford's first introduction to the teachings of Charles Taze Russell [*q.v.*], founder of the religious group that became known as Jehovah's Witnesses, is said to have come when a member of the group visited his office in 1894; he first met "Pastor" Russell around the turn of the century. He apparently joined the Watch Tower Bible and Tract Society (then the group's official name) in 1906 and was soon sharing the public platform with Russell. At a time when both the society and Russell himself were becoming involved in litigation, Rutherford proved invaluable as perhaps the only lawyer in the society and a skilled courtroom defender. In 1909 he negotiated the move of the group's headquarters from Pittsburgh, Pa., to Brooklyn, N. Y. Although its legal center remained the Watch Tower Bible and Tract Society of Pennsylvania, Rutherford at the time of the move incorporated the society in New York under the name "People's Pulpit Association" (later, "Watchtower Bible and Tract Society, Inc.")—a complicated move that helped him gain full control of the organization after Russell's death in 1916. In January 1917 Rutherford was elected president of the society by the three directors (of whom he was one) and, with virtual unanimity, by the members.

The new president faced a difficult situation. America was entering a period of wartime hysteria, yet according to the thought of the Russellites (as the group was then generally known), the millennial rule of Christ had begun in 1914 and war was unchristian. "Neutralists" rather than pacifists, they saw Satan as the ruler of nations, and thus believed that to fight for any nation was equivalent to warring for Satan against God. Publications expounding this belief were judged seditious, and on June 21, 1918, Rutherford and seven other Russellites were convicted of violating the Espionage Act and sentenced to twenty years in the federal penitentiary at Atlanta. In prison, Rutherford organized Bible study classes among the inmates and began writing weekly letters to his followers. These later became a journal, at first called the *Golden Age,* which eventually evolved into *Awake.* In March 1919 the defendants were admitted to bail, the case having been appealed. A new trial was ordered in May, but by then the war hysteria had died down and the government dropped the case. Now regarded as a martyr, Rutherford commanded even greater loyalty from the society, and his influence increased. Having refused the title "Pastor" in preference to that of "Counselor" when he succeeded Russell, Rutherford focused on matters of organization and warned against any tendency to a cult of personality. In his writings he stressed the central and all-sufficient importance of the Bible.

An expert organizer, "Judge" Rutherford (as he was called by his followers) led the group to use modern methods of advertising, beginning in 1921; the billboard slogan "Millions now living will never die" proved especially effective. He produced large quantities of literature himself, writing a score of books and many pamphlets. He gave talks over the society's radio station, WBBR (begun in 1924), and made imaginative use of the phonograph; in 1937 the group's house-to-house visitors began carrying portable phonographs which played four-minute sermons recorded by Rutherford. He emphasized the importance of making each individual Witness a minister—a move that made every member an active carrier of the group's message and at the same time attempted to solve the problem of military service in time of war, since members could then claim clerical exemption. Rutherford also settled on an official title for the group. At the Columbus, Ohio, convention of 1931, he explicitly chose the name "Jehovah's Witnesses"—based on Isaiah 43:9 among other biblical citations. (Officially, the name is spelled with a small "w," a reflection of the group's belief that all institutionalized religions are agents of the devil.) Of the litigations in which Jehovah's Witnesses have been involved, most of the major Supreme Court decisions were handed down after Rutherford's death; but it was he who set the pattern of court appeal which led officials of the American Civil Liberties Union to state that no group had done more to advance the cause of civil liberties than the Witnesses.

Under Rutherford's leadership the membership of the organization grew, despite some defections. From less than 1,000 in the United States and some 3,000 abroad in 1918, it had increased to 30,000 American Witnesses and a worldwide membership of more than 50,000 by the time of his death (cf. Cole, pp. 220–28); this growth has continued.

Dignified and self-confident in appearance, Rutherford in his prime looked "more like a Senator than most Senators." Perhaps sensing that he lacked the personal warmth of Russell, he made few public appearances. During the last twelve years of his life he remained increasingly aloof from his followers, spending long periods of time at Beth-Sarim ("House of the Princes"), a mansion in San Diego, Calif., which the society had built in 1929 for the purpose of housing Abraham and the prophets upon their return to earth, which was believed imminent. Although Jehovah's Witnesses later were to assert that Rutherford was a bachelor, he is known to have married. Neither his wife, Mary, nor their son, Malcolm G., took part in his public activities. Rutherford died of uremia at Beth-Sarim at the age of seventy-two, a few weeks after an operation for cancer. Burial there, which had been his wish, was not permitted under local ordinances, and five months later he was interred in Rossville, Staten Island, N. Y.

[The two best sources of official information, although biased, are: *Jehovah's Witnesses in the Divine Purpose* (1959) and files of the *Watchtower*, the denomination's semimonthly journal; see also Marley Cole, *Jehovah's Witnesses* (1955). Studies of the movement by outsiders include Herbert Stroup, *The Jehovah's Witnesses* (1945); and Milton S. Czatt, *The Internat. Bible Students: Jehovah's Witnesses* (1933). Charles S. Braden, *These Also Believe* (1949), pp. 358–84, offers the most succinct doctrinal summary. Death record from Calif. Dept. of Public Health.]

HERBERT STROUP

RYAN, JOHN AUGUSTINE (May 25, 1869–Sept. 16, 1945), pioneer Catholic spokesman for social reform, grew up in an atmosphere richly Irish and Catholic. His father, William Ryan, born in County Tipperary, went to Minneapolis after an unsuccessful fling in the California gold rush and there married Maria Elizabeth Luby, a refugee from the Irish potato famine. The couple farmed 160 (later 393) acres in Vermillion, a township eight miles south of St. Paul that was a colony of Irish "exiles." There, without much cash, they reared their family of six boys and four girls. Two of the boys became priests, two of the girls nuns. John—christened Michael John—was the eldest child. After attending a local ungraded school until he was sixteen, he went on for two years (1885–87) to the Cretin School, run by the Christian Brothers in St. Paul. Sensing that he had a vocation to the priesthood, he then switched to St. Thomas Seminary (called after 1893 St. Paul Seminary), taking first a five-year "classical" course, from which he graduated as valedictorian in 1892, and then the "clerical" course, two years of philosophy and four years of theology, plus a generous slice of economics, sociology, English, German, and laboratory sciences. He was ordained to the priesthood on June 4, 1898.

That fall Ryan began graduate work in theology at the Catholic University of America in Washington, D. C., working primarily with Father Thomas J. Bouquillon [q.v.], an exacting teacher and theologian already noted for his liberal social ideas and for his empirical rather than deductive approach to ethical questions. At the end of one year, Ryan received his degree as S.T.B. (bachelor in sacred theology); at the end of two (1900), he won his licentiate in sacred theology (S.T.L.)—a canonical license to teach sacred sciences in Catholic institutions—maxima cum laude. He stayed on in Washington for two more years to work on his doctorate, then returned to St. Paul Seminary—now separated from St. Thomas College—to teach moral theology. He received his doctorate in sacred theology (S.T.D.) from Catholic University in 1906. His thesis, *A Living Wage: Its Ethical and Economic Aspects,* was published that same year by the Macmillan Company, with an introduction by the economist Richard T. Ely [Supp. 3].

A Living Wage contained the central economic and moral ideas in Ryan's public career: that every man, "endowed by nature, or rather, by God, with the rights that are requisite to a reasonable development of his personality," has a right to share in the bounty of the earth's products; that this right, in an industrial society, takes the form of a living wage, enough to provide a "decent livelihood" worthy of a man's dignity; that the state has "both the right and the duty to compel" employers, if necessary, to pay a fair wage. Ryan drew on traditional theological manuals and, more proximately, on *Rerum novarum* (1891), Pope Leo XIII's social encyclical. Though Leo stressed the inviolability of private property and the dangers of socialism, he also spoke unequivocally of the laborer's right to "reasonable and frugal comfort," and he applauded public intervention to protect the weak. Ryan also drew heavily on the "underconsumption theory" of the English economist John A. Hobson, who argued that a nation prospered only when workers received enough wages to purchase as consumers the goods that the economy produced.

For thirteen years (1902–15), Father Ryan taught at St. Paul Seminary. In class he was an intense no-nonsense monologist, speaking hurriedly with a sense of urgency, and students, even those who were enthusiastic about his ideas, found him a dull teacher. Like his mother, he hated shams, and he punctured pomposity with a sharp wit. He was just under medium height, and he grew stocky whenever he did not watch his eating and keep up his exercise. His rumpled clothes were something of a legend among his acquaintances, and his earthy wit was a delight to his male friends.

During vacations, Ryan lectured elsewhere in the country to any group of laymen or priests that would invite him. At a time when raucous denunciations of socialism generally served as a total social philosophy for American Catholics, Ryan's criticism of Catholic inaction ran the danger of stirring up nests of hornets, both lay and clerical, especially since his progressivism was very much in the outspoken tradition of Henry Demarest Lloyd [q.v.]. In 1909 he put together (and published in the *Catholic World*) a full program of reform: a legal minimum wage; the eight-hour working day; protective laws for women and children; protection of peaceful picketing and boycotting; employment bureaus; insurance against unemployment, accidents, illness, and old age; municipal housing; public ownership of public utilities and of mines and forests; control of monopolies; progressive income and inheritance taxes; taxation on the future increase in land values (an idea he owed to Henry George [q.v.]); an end to speculation on the stock and commodity exchanges. Working with the National Consumers' League, he helped lobby minimum-wage bills for women and children through the legislatures of Wisconsin and Minnesota in 1913.

Many felt that Ryan's activities flirted with socialism; yet Ryan blandly insisted that he was merely applying orthodox Catholic theology to the needs of an industrial society. Dealing with his critics, Ryan armed himself with prudence; he never went looking for an abrasive confrontation with anyone. He allied himself with other individuals and groups doing the same kind of work—groups like the National Conference of Catholic Charities within the Church and the National Conference of Charities and Correction outside. And he exploited ecclesiastical support fully: the fortuitous support of Archbishop John Ireland [q.v.] and his successors, who, though conservative themselves, never interfered with Ryan's public stands; and the unassailable support of Rome itself speaking through Leo XIII's *Rerum novarum*.

Ryan transferred in 1915 to Catholic University, at first as associate professor of political science, then successively as associate professor of theology (1916), professor of theology (1917), and dean of the School of Sacred Sciences (1919), the last a position he held at irregular intervals during the next fifteen years. Just after his arrival in Washington he published *Distributive Justice: The Right and Wrong of Our Present Distribution of Wealth* (1916), a closely reasoned study of the relative claims of landowner, capitalist, entrepreneur, and worker to the finished products of industry. This book was Ryan's last substantial scholarly contribution to the field shared by ethics and economics. Soon after his arrival at Catholic University he began teaching economics and political science at neighboring Trinity College, and later he lectured regularly at the National Catholic School of Social Service. In 1917 he founded the *Catholic Charities Review,* and for five years served as its editor, business manager, and principal contributor.

In Washington, Ryan became more a public figure than a productive scholar. In 1919 the four-member Administrative Committee of the National Catholic War Council, an assembly of the American bishops, issued the "Bishops' Program of Social Reconstruction," the most forward-looking document issued by the Church in

America up to that time (see John Joseph Burke [Supp. 2]). It was, in fact, a memorandum hastily written by Ryan out of his stock of familiar ideas. When the bishops set up the National Catholic Welfare Council (later Conference) in 1919, Ryan was the obvious man to serve as the Washington director of its Social Action Department, created in 1920. Continuing at Catholic University and at all his other teaching posts, Ryan now divided his time between the classroom and the public forum. With an official podium to speak from, he found that his fame and his impact grew even in the conservative decade of the 1920's. He worked with Roger Baldwin in the American Civil Liberties Union as a member of its national board, with Senator Thomas J. Walsh [*q.v.*] in support of the proposed federal child labor amendment, with Felix Frankfurter on a minimum-wage law for the District of Columbia, with Sidney L. Gulick [Supp. 3] of the Federal Council of Churches on a gamut of social projects, with Senator George Norris [Supp. 3] on public power, with Carlton J. H. Hayes and James T. Shotwell on international peace. He came to oppose prohibition as unenforceable and undesirable, delighting even H. L. Mencken with the tone and force of his attack.

Working with people of other faiths or of no religious faith, Ryan always tried to concentrate on conditions in need of reform rather than on differences in ideas. He was not always successful, and on some issues—artificial contraception, for one example, and the Mexican government's attack on the Catholic Church for another—he and his liberal allies simply agreed to disagree, sometimes quite acridly. On one issue, the relation between church and state, Ryan achieved an unwanted fame. In 1922, as co-author of the book *The State and the Church,* he published an extended commentary on Leo XIII's encyclical letter of 1885, *Immortale Dei,* on the political order and constitution of states. Ryan, as orthodox in interpreting this encyclical as he had been with *Rerum novarum,* propounded as Catholic teaching that the state had an obligation to recognize the Catholic religion as the religion of the commonwealth. In a completely Catholic state, Ryan said, constitutions could be changed; "non-Catholic sects may decline to such a point that the political proscription of them may become feasible and expedient." Although Ryan believed that this teaching, however sound in theory, had no relation to the United States, which was not a Catholic state and would probably never become one, his statement was nevertheless used in the election campaign of 1928 to challenge the presidential candidacy of Alfred E. Smith. Ryan bitterly resented the misunderstanding of his argument and, indeed, the whole anti-Catholic mood revealed in the campaign. Nevertheless, when he published the revised edition of *The State and the Church* under a new title, *Catholic Principles of Politics* (1940), the offending passage remained essentially unchanged.

Hardly a warm partisan of Herbert Hoover, especially after the bitterness of the 1928 campaign, Ryan welcomed the New Deal as the triumphant realization of his lifetime struggle for social justice. The National Industrial Recovery Act impressed him as an imaginative fulfillment of Pope Pius XI's plan for industrial reorganization expressed in *Quadragesimo anno* (1931), and Ryan—now Monsignor Ryan after Pope Pius named him a domestic prelate in 1933—was happy to serve on the Industrial Appeals Board of the National Recovery Administration (July 1934–May 1935) and to advise various other New Deal agencies. He defended President Franklin D. Roosevelt against the radio attacks of Father Charles E. Coughlin in 1936; as a token of appreciation, Roosevelt named him to give the benediction at the inauguration in 1937. Ryan never regretted his open support of Roosevelt, for he believed that the Social Security Act, the National Labor Relations Act, and the Fair Labor Standards Act "have done more to promote social justice than all the other federal legislation enacted since the adoption of the Constitution."

Just before his seventieth birthday the Catholic University trustees made seventy the mandatory retirement age, and although Ryan hoped for a suspension of the rule in his case, no exception was made. He left the university with some bitterness in 1939 but stayed on at the National Catholic Welfare Council until his death. As the war approached America, he actively supported American aid to Britain and France, at the same time resenting the foot-dragging that he detected among his fellow Irish-Americans. He hoped for a major reconstruction of the American economy in the postwar years, but deteriorating health prevented his making any real contribution to planning for the future. In 1945 he again gave the benediction at Roosevelt's inaugural. Later that year he died of a lingering urological infection at St. Joseph's Hospital, St. Paul, Minn. He was buried in Calvary Cemetery in St. Paul.

Monsignor Ryan's special role was to show Catholic America how to reinterpret traditional Catholic principles of social justice in an industrial American society. He was the peerless leader of progressive Catholic social thinkers who drew the Church away from the individualist's fear of the state as the agent of encroaching socialism and toward confidence in the state as the agent of social justice for the whole people. By his close cooperation with Protestant, Jewish, and secular reformers, he brought Catholic social thought into the mainstream of American reform.

[The prime sources on Ryan are his collected papers at the Catholic Univ. of America, quite complete for the period 1925–45, thinner for the earlier years, and his published books and articles. Theodora E. McGill, "A Bio-Bibliog. of Monsignor John A. Ryan" (M.A. dissertation, Catholic Univ., 1952), contains an accurate summary of his published work. Ryan's autobiography, *Social Doctrine in Action* (1941), is half extracts from articles and speeches, half mild reminiscent commentary on his forty-year struggle for social justice. Collections of his articles in book form, notably *The Church and Socialism* (1919), *Declining Liberty* (1927), *Questions of the Day* (1931), and *Seven Troubled Years, 1930–1936* (1937), are especially revealing. Francis L. Broderick, *Right Reverend New Dealer* (1963), is a well-disposed biography, and Patrick W. Gearty, *The Economic Thought of Monsignor John A. Ryan* (1953), is knowledgeable on both economics and theology. See also Richard J. Purcell in *Studies* (Dublin), June 1946. George G. Higgins, "The Underconsumption Theory in the Writings of Monsignor John A. Ryan" (M.A. dissertation, Catholic Univ., 1942), deals authoritatively with one of Ryan's central economic ideas.]
FRANCIS L. BRODERICK

SACHS, BERNARD (Jan. 2, 1858–Feb. 8, 1944), neurologist, was born in Baltimore, Md., to German Jewish parents, Joseph and Sophia (Baer) Sachs. Called Barney, after the son of a family friend, he adopted the name Bernard only when he began the study of medicine. He and his twin brother (who died of scarlet fever at the age of five) were the youngest in a family that included three older brothers and a sister. His parents had eloped from Würzburg, Bavaria, and migrated to America in 1847 in the advance wave of young intellectuals who fled from Germany during the uprisings of 1848. His father, who had trained as a teacher, found employment successively in the schools of Philadelphia, Baltimore, and Boston, and in 1859 established a prosperous boarding and day school in New York City, a tradition followed by his scholarly eldest son, Julius Sachs [*q.v.*].

After attending New York public schools and preparing for college under his brother's tutelage, Barney Sachs entered Harvard. Although planning a scientific or medical career, he concentrated on the classics and English literature and graduated with honors in 1878. He was greatly influenced by his study of psychology under William James [*q.v.*], to which he attributed his later interest in mental and nervous diseases. Since American medical schools were then inferior to those of Europe, Sachs chose to enter the University of Strassburg, where he

studied under such giants as Friedrich von Recklinghausen in pathology, Adolf Kussmaul in medicine, and Friedrich Goltz in physiology. He also spent a semester in Berlin, where he profited from the teaching of Rudolf Virchow in pathology and Carl Westphal in neuropsychiatry. After receiving the M.D. degree in 1882, he moved on to Vienna (where he was a fellow student with Freud) for graduate work in cerebral anatomy and neuropsychiatry under Theodor Meynert, whose book *Der Psychiatrie* he later translated (1885). The next year was spent with Jean Charcot and Pierre Marie in Paris and with Hughlings Jackson in London.

Sachs returned to New York in 1884 and, after three years of general practice as assistant to Dr. Isaac Adler, established his own office for the treatment of neurologic and psychiatric illness. In 1885 he was made an instructor at the New York Polyclinic Hospital, where from 1888 to 1905 he served as professor of mental and nervous diseases. He was later professor of clinical neurology at the College of Physicians and Surgeons of Columbia University. Sachs was appointed consulting neurologist at Mount Sinai Hospital in 1893. There he was instrumental in establishing (1900) an independent neurological bed service, the first such division created in a general hospital in New York. A leading influence on the medical staff of Mount Sinai, he served as president of its medical board from 1920 to 1923.

In the developing field of organic neurology Sachs was a major figure. He published some two hundred articles and books, one of the most important of which was *Nervous Diseases of Childhood* (1895). From 1886 to 1911 he was editor of the *Journal of Nervous and Mental Disease*. He was particularly interested in the neurological disorders of children, and in 1887 made one of his most important contributions, a comprehensive description of the disease entity he called "amaurotic family idiocy," a genetically caused arrest of cerebral development, associated with blindness. Since the ocular and certain other characteristics of the illness had been independently observed by the British ophthalmologist Warren Tay, the condition became known as Tay-Sachs disease. Sachs later served as director of the Division of Child Neurology at the New York Neurological Institute, of which he was a trustee (1932-42), and as director of the Child Neurology Research Fund established by the Friedsam Foundation in 1936. Throughout his career Sachs adhered to his belief in neuropsychiatry as a single practice, rather than separate practices of neurology and psychiatry.

He looked upon the Freudians with tolerance but viewed their uncritical generalizations (as he saw them) with skepticism. He was especially critical of Freudians who had not had basic training and experience in organic neuropathology, neurophysiology, and clinical medicine.

Sachs was elected president of the American Neurological Association in 1894 and again in 1932. He played a major role in establishing international collaboration in the field of neurology and helped organize the first International Neurological Congress, held in Bern, Switzerland, in 1931. He was president of the New York Academy of Medicine (1933-35), and a founder and onetime president of the Charaka Club, a group of distinguished medical scholars who met several times a year to enjoy each other's company and exchange conversation, exclusively non-medical, about their varied intellectual and cultural interests.

Erect, handsome, and soft-spoken, Sachs was the model of a cultured gentleman. His warm personality, his basic optimism, and his scholarship attracted the friendship of leaders in his field throughout the world. On Dec. 18, 1887, Sachs married Bettina R. Stein of Frankfurt am Main, Germany, by whom he had two daughters, Alice and Helen. His wife died in 1940, and in 1941 he married Mrs. Rosetta Kaskel. Barney Sachs died at his home in a New York hotel at the age of eighty-six and was buried at Salem Fields Cemetery, Brooklyn.

[*Barney Sachs, 1858–1944* (privately printed, 1949) —autobiographical notes, with a list of Sachs's publications; special edition of the *Jour. of Mount Sinai Hospital,* Dec. 1942, dedicated to Sachs, including articles about him by Henry A. Riley and Alfred Wiener and a bibliography of his medical writings; obituary by Louis Hausman in *Archives of Neurology and Psychiatry,* May 1944 (also in *Jour. of Nervous and Mental Disease,* June 1944). See also obituary in *N. Y. Times,* Feb. 9, 1944. An excellent portrait of Sachs is in the President's Gallery of the N. Y. Acad. of Medicine.]

GEORGE BAEHR

SANDERSON, EZRA DWIGHT (Sept. 25, 1878–Sept. 27, 1944), entomologist and rural sociologist, was born in Clio, Mich., the eldest of the three sons of John Phillip Sanderson, a Congregational minister, and Alice Gertrude (Wright) Sanderson. His father, a descendant of Thomas Sanderson, who had come from England to Pennsylvania before the American Revolution, was a native of Philadelphia; his mother, of Springfield, Ohio. Dwight, as he was known, grew up in a series of Michigan towns where his father held pastorates. After attending public schools in Detroit and Lansing, he entered the Michigan Agricultural College, from which he

graduated, B.S., in 1897. He then enrolled at Cornell University, where he studied entomology and in 1898 received a second B.S. degree. On Sept. 19, 1899, he married Anna Cecilia Blandford, a schoolteacher from Brandywine, Md.; they had a daughter, Alice Cecilia.

For the next two decades Sanderson worked in the field of economic entomology. He served successively as assistant state entomologist of Maryland (1898); entomologist at the Delaware Agricultural Experiment Station and professor of zoology at Delaware College (1898-1902); state entomologist of Texas and professor of entomology at the Texas Agricultural and Mechanical College (1902-04); state entomologist of New Hampshire and professor of zoology at New Hampshire College (1904-10). Beginning in 1907, he was also director of the New Hampshire Agricultural Experiment Station. From 1910 to 1915 Sanderson served as dean of the college of agriculture of West Virginia University and, from 1912, as director of its Agricultural Experiment Station. During these decades he published four books and fifty articles on various aspects of entomology, and especially on methods for the control of insect pests. He also took part in a movement to standardize and ensure proper labeling of insecticides which culminated in the passage of the Federal Insecticide Act (1910). Recognized as an authority in his field, Sanderson in 1910 was elected president of the American Association of Economic Entomologists.

In his work as an administrator, particularly in West Virginia, Sanderson served the entire agricultural population of the state and came to feel an increasing concern with the broader economic and social problems of the farmer. A gift subscription to the *American Journal of Sociology* sparked an interest in that discipline, and he took a correspondence course in sociology from the University of Chicago. In 1916, at the age of thirty-eight, he formally enrolled there as a graduate student in sociology; he received the Ph.D. in 1921. While at Chicago he met Albert R. Mann, who upon being appointed dean of the college of agriculture at Cornell University invited Sanderson to become head of Cornell's department of rural social organization (later renamed the department of rural sociology). Sanderson accepted the position in 1918 and remained until his retirement in 1943.

At Cornell, drawing upon his knowledge of entomological taxonomy, he developed techniques for classifying and describing the spatial organization of rural society. He was especially interested in neighborhood and community units, which he termed locality groups. In a long series of studies of rural towns and counties in New York state, culminating in his book *The Rural Community: A Natural History of a Sociological Group* (1932), Sanderson and his students endeavored to identify the community patterns of rural regions. Sanderson rejected the idea that shared locality alone constituted a neighborhood, and proposed as the two necessary criteria a sense of "neighborliness" and the ability of residents to function as a group. In delineating various types of locality groups, he employed five descriptive categories of inquiry: identity; composition; intergroup relationships; intragroup relationships; structure and mechanism. Although his interests focused almost entirely upon communities, he later applied this method of analysis to the rural family, developing an outline for observing, analyzing, and classifying different types of families in a systematic way.

Believing, as he once said, that "research without action is sterile," Sanderson worked consistently to translate his sociological findings into programs to advance the welfare of rural people. He helped state school administrators locate new schools in the center of developing communities so that they could serve as integrating forces. He further promoted community use of the school plant, advocated the establishment of vocational training programs and health services in local schools, and, at Cornell, took part in developing an active university extension service. His *Leadership for Rural Life* (1940) provided systematic guidance for community leaders. Sanderson was one of the founders (1919) of the American Country Life Association and its president in 1938. In 1933–34 he headed the rural research unit of the Division of Research and Statistics of the Federal Emergency Relief Administration, where he supervised a survey of rural families on relief. Sanderson was also active in his own community, as a board member of several Ithaca charities and, for many years, as director of the Social Services League, which operated two settlement houses.

Although somewhat lacking in humor, Dwight Sanderson maintained a warm and friendly working relationship with his students and colleagues. He helped found the Rural Sociological Society, serving as its first president in 1938, and in 1942 was elected president of the American Sociological Society. Just two days after his sixty-sixth birthday, he died in Ithaca of arteriosclerosis. He was buried in Lake View Cemetery, Ithaca.

Sanderson's other writings include *The Farmer and His Community* (1922); "Scientific Research in Rural Sociology," *Am. Jour. of Sociology*, Sept. 1927; *Rural Community Organization* (1939), with Robert A. Pol-

son; and *Rural Sociology and Rural Social Organization* (1942), a textbook. Sanderson's papers are in the Collection of Regional Hist. and Univ. Archives, Cornell Univ. Biographical sources: memorial articles on Sanderson in *Rural Sociology*, Mar. 1946 (also obituary in issue of Dec. 1944); Lowry Nelson, *Rural Sociology: Its Origin and Growth in the U. S.* (1969); Gould P. Colman, *Education and Agriculture: A Hist. of the N. Y. State College of Agriculture at Cornell Univ.* (1963). See also obituaries in *Jour. of Economic Entomology*, Dec. 1944, and *Am. Sociological Rev.*, Dec. 1944; *Nat. Cyc. Am. Biog.*, XXXIV, 196; *Who Was Who in America*, vol. II (1950). Death record from N. Y. State Dept. of Health.]

PHILIP M. HOSAY

SARG, TONY (Apr. 24, 1880–Mar. 7, 1942), puppeteer, illustrator, and author, was born at Coban, Guatemala. Christened Anthony Frederick, he was one of two sons and three daughters of Francis Charles Sarg, a German coffee and sugar planter, and his English wife, Mary Elizabeth Parker. Growing up in an English-speaking household, he spent his early years on the family plantation and received a musical education from his father, a strict disciplinarian. At the age of seven he was sent to school in Darmstadt, Germany, and at fourteen to the Prussian military academy at Lichterfelde, near Berlin; upon graduating, in 1899, he was commissioned a lieutenant in the German army.

Sarg resigned his commission in 1905 and went to England, where he later became a naturalized citizen. He had always enjoyed drawing, although he had no formal artistic training, and he saw humor in everything around him. Putting his natural talent to use, he first obtained a job making sketches for an advertising agency, then began selling jokes with illustrations to humor magazines. He also became a theatrical artist for the *Sketch*. On one of his assignments for this magazine he encountered the marionette show of Thomas Holden, then the largest and most famous in Europe. Sarg was fascinated by the puppets, read all he could find on the subject in the British Museum, and repeatedly watched Holden's performances until he had mastered the mechanics involved. He then began to design his own marionettes. For a studio he rented an old building reputed to be the "Old Curiosity Shop" Dickens had made famous, fitted out one room as "Little Nell's bedroom," complete with a four-poster bed and a collection of antique toys, and charged admission. The fees helped pay the rent, and the studio was the scene of his first marionette performances.

On Jan. 20, 1909, Sarg married Bertha Eleanor McGowan of Cincinnati, Ohio, whom he had first met when he was an officer and she a tourist in Germany. They had one child, Mary Eleanor Norcliffe. With the outbreak of World War I,

Sarg as a former officer in the German army found his position in England uncomfortable, and in 1915 he moved with his family to New York City. He became an American citizen in 1921. He easily found work as a cartoonist, his first assignment being to illustrate a *Saturday Evening Post* series by Irvin S. Cobb [Supp. 3], later published as *"Speaking of Operations—"* (1915). Sarg also drew humorous illustrations for other magazines such as *Collier's, Cosmopolitan,* and *Red Book;* his fine draftsmanship and distinctive, lively style won him an appreciative audience.

In his studio on the top floor of the Flatiron Building, one of New York's first skyscrapers, Sarg also made marionettes, and he and two fellow illustrators, Frank Godwin and Charles E. Searle, began giving performances for their friends. His creations attracted the notice of the theatrical producer Winthrop Ames [Supp. 2], who was planning a marionette show for his children's matinees. He commissioned Sarg to stage three playlets: Franz von Pocci's *The Three Wishes* and *The Green Suit* and Hamilton Williamson's *A Stolen Beauty and the Great Jewel.* The Ames production in 1916 was an artistic success, but the expense of mounting it—the three-foot-tall marionettes required special operators, and actors were hired to speak the lines—made it a financial failure.

In an expanded studio and workshop, occupying two floors of a small Greenwich Village apartment building, Sarg now began to make smaller puppets whose lines would be spoken by their operators. A short road tour proved this method workable, and in 1920 he formed the Tony Sarg Company to give marionette shows in New York and on tour. He employed able creative talent to write and compose for his marionettes, and over the next decade his shows attained great popularity. Among the plays he presented were *Rip Van Winkle* (which toured the United States for two eight-month runs, playing two shows a day, six days a week), *Don Quixote, Ali Baba and the Forty Thieves, Treasure Island, Alice in Wonderland,* and Thackeray's *The Rose and the Ring,* all of which played two full seasons, while *The Mikado, Uncle Remus, Robinson Crusoe,* and others continued to be given for years. Besides his theatrical presentations, Sarg created marionette shows for night clubs, such as the Club Bal Tabarin at Chicago's Sherman Hotel and his own Tony Sarg's Bohemia in New York. His industrial show for the A & P food-store chain at the Chicago World's Fair of 1933 played to millions of persons, and thousands more saw his special shows at New York's Roxy Theatre and elsewhere. The puppeteers Sue Hastings, Rufus

and Margo Rose, and Bil Baird were among those who began their professional careers in the ranks of Sarg's performers.

A man of boundless energy who loved to keep busy, Sarg meanwhile continued his work as a designer and illustrator. His double-page spreads in the *Saturday Evening Post* and *Time* magazine drew top prices. Besides illustrating books for others, he wrote and illustrated nearly a dozen of his own, including *Tony Sarg's Book for Children—from Six to Sixty* (1924) and *Tony Sarg's New York* (1926). He produced animated films and designed Christmas window displays for department stores. One of his most memorable creations, for Macy's department store in New York, was the collection of giant animal balloons that for years was a feature of its Thanksgiving Day parades. He also painted murals for cocktail lounges and restaurants, whose walls came alive with dozens of tipsy giraffes, hippopotami, pigs, and chickens, or with a historic city landscape. He took an active role in such organizations as the Dutch Treat Club and the Salmagundi Club in New York, the Illustrators Society, and the yacht club at Nantucket, Mass., his summer home. Stocky and muscular of build, he was a gay, animated host at parties in his New York studios.

During the depression years Sarg's marionette shows were less successful on tour, and the use of photography diminished the demand for his drawing talent. He went bankrupt in 1939 and was forced to sell most of his marionettes and their equipment, although he continued to write and illustrate books for children. He died in New York's Manhattan General Hospital shortly before his sixty-second birthday, of peritonitis following a ruptured appendix. Though Sarg's illustrations were widely enjoyed, his most important influence was on puppetry. Breaking with the "little people" style of marionettes he had encountered in Europe, he developed three-dimensional caricature and made artful use of animal characters. His style set the direction of American puppetry for half a century.

[Tony Sarg, "The Revival of Puppet-Play in America," *Theatre Arts Monthly,* July 1928; autobiographical sketch in *Saturday Evening Post,* Apr. 7, 1928, pp. 47-48; Anne Stoddard in *Mentor,* May 1928; Clayton M. Hamilton, *Seen on the Stage* (1920); Walt Reed, ed., *The Illustrator in America* (1966), p. 103; *Nat. Cyc. Am. Biog.,* XXXIII, 99; *N. Y. Times* obituary, Mar. 8, 1942; personal acquaintance. Marriage record from Probate Court, Hamilton County, Ohio (which gives his age in Jan. 1909 as 28).]

BIL BAIRD

SAXTON, EUGENE FRANCIS (Aug. 11, 1884–June 26, 1943), editor and publisher, was born at Baltimore, Md., the youngest of nine children of Alexander and Rose (White) Saxton. His father, a physician, was of English descent. The family was Roman Catholic, and Saxton was educated at Loyola College in Baltimore, beginning as a junior in its high school department in 1898. He received the A.B. degree in 1904.

After graduation, he began the study of law at Georgetown University, but left after a year to work briefly as editor of the *Baltimore Mirror*, a weekly newspaper. He moved to New York City in 1906, to assist in preparing the first edition of the *Catholic Encyclopedia*. In 1910 he entered the field of general book publishing, first with Doubleday, Page & Company, next (1917) with George H. Doran Company, where his duties as editor-in-chief for a time included editing the *Bookman*, and finally, in 1925, with Harper & Brothers. There he served until his death as head of the book editorial department, and in later years also as secretary and vice-president of the firm, working closely with the president, Cass Canfield.

A man of broad interests, Saxton was credited with reviving the house of Harper by expanding the scope of its trade publications and emphasizing the quality of its fiction list. Though he seemed a leisurely worker, he dealt with an impressive number of new manuscripts every week, as well as a large correspondence. His desk was usually piled high with scripts of fiction read but not acted upon. When an associate asked him why he did not clear them away with letters of either acceptance or refusal, he replied that he liked to delay a decision to see whether the characters would remain sharply in his mind. Once a book had been accepted, he rarely proposed editorial changes, preferring to trust the writer's judgment in creative matters. This sense of his sustaining belief in them brought his authors to their best achievement; they were confident that he would recognize what they were about in each book and regard it as part of the development of an artist's career, not merely as a salable product.

Saxton presided over the publication of works of Aldous Huxley, Joseph Conrad, H. M. Tomlinson, Edna St. Vincent Millay, O. E. Rolvaag, John Dos Passos, Thornton Wilder, and Amy Lowell. Among American authors whose initial books he guided into print were Ann Parrish, Glenway Wescott, Paul Horgan (all three of whom won the Harper Prize under his editorship), E. B. White, Richard Wright, and James Thurber. Saxton was often classed with Maxwell Perkins of Charles Scribner's Sons as one of the two great book editors of his day, though their methods and temperaments were quite different.

Saxton was a man of medium height and rather stocky build, whose light blue eyes could express sympathy, merriment, or compassion. His manner was calm, his speech deliberate, and his courtesy exquisite. His sense of humor could be lightly derisive, or affectionately reassuring. If he made editorial misjudgments, they erred on the side of generosity to literary novices. As an officer of the house, he strongly defended the policy of *Harper's Magazine* against those who at times advised a less controversial editorial stand than that of Lee Hartman, the magazine's editor.

On Nov. 14, 1912, at the church of St. Paul the Apostle in New York, Saxton was married to Martha Plaisted of Springfield, Ohio. Their sons were Mark, who became a novelist and editor, and Alexander Plaisted, who became a novelist and historian. Martha Saxton carried on a professional career, first as an editor of the periodical the *World's Work* and later as head of the English department of the Nightingale-Bamford School in New York City. Saxton died in New York City at the age of fifty-eight after a long struggle with heart disease and was buried in Mill River, Mass., in the Berkshires, his summer home. In his memory the house of Harper established the Eugene F. Saxton literary fellowship, to award occasional financial aid to young authors engaged in creative writing.

[*In Memoriam: Eugene F. Saxton* (1943), a privately printed memorial resolution by the Board of Directors of Harper & Brothers (which reproduces an excellent photograph); obituaries in *Publishers' Weekly*, July 3, 1943, and *N. Y. Times*, June 27, 1943; records of Loyola College, Baltimore; files and archives of Harper and Row, Inc.; information from Mark and Alexander Saxton; recollections of Cass Canfield, Sr.; personal acquaintance.]

PAUL HORGAN

SCARBOROUGH, LEE RUTLAND (July 4, 1870–Apr. 10, 1945), Southern Baptist clergyman and educator, was born in Colfax, La., the fifth son and eighth of nine children of George Washington and Martha Elizabeth (Rutland) Scarborough. His father, a native of Mississippi, had fought for the Confederacy; a yeoman farmer, he moved in 1874 to McLennan County, Texas, where he became a Baptist preacher, and then in 1878 to Jones County in West Texas. One of the first settlers there, he lived in a dugout and supported himself by farming and ranching while he evangelized and organized churches throughout the area. His wife had been a devout Baptist since her girlhood in Tennessee.

As a boy Lee sporadically attended schools at Anson and Merkel, Texas, supplementing this instruction with home tutoring by his cousin, Emma

Scarborough, the first teacher in Jones County. At the age of eight he was picking cotton and herding cattle; but after witnessing a murder trial at age twelve he determined to seek a career in law. At eighteen he enrolled in Baylor University, the *summa schola* of Texas Baptists, in Waco, where he boarded with an uncle, Judge J. B. Scarborough, a lawyer and a Baylor trustee. Every Sunday at First Baptist Church in Waco he heard Benajah Harvey Carroll, "colossus of Texas Baptists," and by his father's command sent home written reports on the sermons. Earning a B.A. in 1892, Scarborough taught in the preparatory department at Baylor, 1892–94, then served for a year as principal of the high school at nearby Mexia while continuing law studies with Judge Scarborough. In 1895 he entered the pre-law program at Yale, where the next year he received a second bachelor's degree and was elected to Phi Beta Kappa. At this point, however, he yielded to a conviction which had grown too strong to resist further: he felt a divine call to the ministry.

Scarborough's religious development had followed the classic outlines of evangelical pietism in nineteenth-century America. He had professed conversion at age fourteen and had been baptized (by immersion) at Anson, Texas. Three years later he came under such powerful religious impressions as to regard this experience as his real conversion, and in 1889 he was rebaptized at Waco by B. H. Carroll. Upon his return from Yale to Texas in 1896 he was licensed to preach and became pastor of the Baptist church at Cameron, Texas, where he was ordained later that same year. Save for a leave in 1899–1900, when he attended the Southern Baptist Theological Seminary at Louisville, Ky.—his last formal schooling—he remained at Cameron until 1901. From then until 1908 he was pastor of the First Baptist Church in Abilene, Texas. During the twelve years of his two pastorates he more than doubled the membership of both churches and conducted more than a hundred revival meetings, preaching an average of five hundred sermons each year and earning a reputation as "possibly the greatest pastor-evangelist in the Baptist denomination of that day" (Dana, p. 81). But his most significant ministry still lay ahead.

B. H. Carroll had resigned his pastorate at Waco and had become the head of a new seminary growing out of the theological department of Baylor University. With large designs for the future, Carroll persuaded Scarborough in 1908 to join his faculty as professor of evangelism—purportedly the first such post in the history of theological education. It quickly became evident that Scarborough's fund-raising efforts were as persuasive as his preaching. With the seminary in search of a permanent home, he collected $100,000 from the Baptists of Fort Worth, purchased land south of the city, and began a large building. The school moved to Fort Worth in 1910 and was chartered as Southwestern Baptist Theological Seminary. Carroll died in 1914, bequeathing his mantle to his protégé, who was installed as president the next year. Scarborough served until his retirement in 1942, all the while continuing as professor of evangelism—a post which became popularly known as "The Chair of Fire."

Southern Baptists turned frequently to President Scarborough for denominational leadership. When they conceived the "Seventy-Five Million Campaign" in 1919 as a five-year program of missionary advance, he was made the general director; within a year he had secured pledges for nearly $93,000,000, although because of the postwar depression only $58,000,000 was actually collected. He was president of the Baptist General Convention of Texas, 1929–32; vice-president of the Southern Baptist Convention, 1934–35, and president, 1939–40; president of the convention's Relief and Annuity Board, 1941; vice-president of the Baptist World Alliance, 1940–42; and sometime member of numerous denominational boards and committees. In 1936 he undertook a 25,000-mile evangelistic tour of South America for the Foreign Mission Board, and in 1939 he led (with Roland Q. Leavell) a South-wide revival which won for Southern Baptist churches 266,000 new members. Intensely loyal to his denomination, he defended its principle of the freedom of individual church institutions against the attacks of J. Frank Norris, fundamentalist pastor of the large and wealthy First Baptist Church in Fort Worth. Scarborough himself was "soundly fundamental, but never rabidly fundamentalist (*ibid.*, p. 130); in 1926 he joined with Edgar Young Mullins, president of Southern Baptist Theological Seminary, in ignoring a Southern Baptist Convention resolution which required all denominational boards and institutions to disavow evolutionary theories. During Scarborough's presidency Southwestern Seminary erected buildings costing more than a million dollars and, with its three schools of theology, religious education, and sacred music, became one of the largest theological seminaries in the world, though it was never completely a graduate institution until several years after his death.

While attending literally thousands of Baptist meetings—he missed only one national convention between 1896 and 1942—and traveling countless miles preaching and raising funds, Scarborough found time to write sixteen books. In the spirit of John R. Mott and the Student Volunteer Movement (though lacking their broad ecumenical temper), *Recruits for World Conquest* (1914) promoted the idea of "calling out the called"—a campaign which climaxed with the dedication of 15,000 young missionary volunteers in 1919. Recalling that B. H. Carroll had urged him to create a new literature for kindling "the holy fires of evangelism," Scarborough next produced his most durable book, *With Christ after the Lost: A Search for Souls* (1919), a methods manual of 352 pages "meant for preachers to read and to teach to soul-winning bands in their churches, and in study courses in their Sunday schools, young people's organizations and mission bands, for classes in personal work and evangelism in Theological Seminaries, Missionary Training Schools, and Bible Departments in Christian Schools." Revised in 1953 by Eldred Douglas Head, Scarborough's successor at Southwestern Seminary, this widely used textbook has convinced thousands of young preachers that the primary—if not sole—task of a Christian is to convert wayward souls. Being himself an outstanding exemplar of the way in which his denomination has wedded the evangelistic fervor of the frontier preacher to the academic respectability of a trained minister, Scarborough became a chief architect of the Southern Baptist program of popular theological education.

On Feb. 4, 1900, Scarborough married Mary Parker ("Neppie") Warren of Abilene, Texas. It was a long and happy union, enriched with six children whom they saw educated and launched on successful careers: George Warren, Euna Lee, Lawrence Rutland, Neppie, Ada Beth, and William Byron. In May 1941 Scarborough suffered a light stroke, which forced him to retire the next year.

With his wife he moved to Edinburg, Texas, where his son Lawrence operated a citrus farm. After a second stroke in the summer of 1944 he was taken to the Amarillo home of his daughter Euna Lee (Mrs. A. D.) Foreman. The next year he died at North West Texas Hospital in Amarillo of cerebral apoplexy complicated by arteriosclerosis. His body was buried in the Rose Hill Cemetery east of Fort Worth; in 1955 it was reinterred in a newly purchased family plot in Fort Worth's Greenwood Cemetery. Scarborough's major monument is unquestionably the seminary which he built and served for a third of a century, and he is memorialized there in Scarborough Hall, built to house the School of Theology in 1949.

[Among fourteen other books by Scarborough are *Marvels of Divine Leadership* (1920), on the purpose and program of the Seventy-Five Million Campaign; and *A Modern School of the Prophets* (1939), a history of the first thirty years of Southwestern Baptist Seminary. Scarborough's papers are at Southwestern Seminary; they include documents in the official files of the school, sermon outlines, and private correspondence. Published biographical accounts are mainly appreciations by admiring friends. There are two book-length treatments: Harvey E. Dana, *Lee Rutland Scarborough: A Life of Service* (1942), and Leroy Benefield, "Lee Rutland Scarborough and His Preaching" (Th.D. dissertation, Southwestern Baptist Seminary, 1970). John M. Price, *Ten Men from Baylor* (1945) and *Southwestern Men and Their Messages* (1948), contain chapters on Scarborough. See also William W. Barnes, *The Southern Baptist Convention, 1845–1953* (1954); and Norman F. Furniss, *The Fundamentalist Controversy, 1918–1931* (1954), p. 125. The Seminary possesses two oil paintings of Scarborough, one by Cornelius Hankins (1926), the other by Mrs. L. M. Rice of Austin, Texas (1942); the latter hangs in the rotunda of Scarborough Hall.]

C. C. GOEN

SCHELLING, FELIX EMANUEL (Sept. 3, 1858–Dec. 15, 1945), professor of English, was born in New Albany, Ind. His family background was cosmopolitan. His father, Felix Schelling, had left the Canton of St. Gallen, Switzerland, where he was born, and the profession of medicine, to which he had been trained, to become a teacher of music. Coming to America after the revolutions of 1848, he married in Louisville, Ky., Rose, the daughter of George Busby White of Cambridge, England. Ultimately, after some years in the East and in Europe, he became director of the St. Louis Conservatory of Music. He wished both his sons to become musicians, and the younger, Ernest Henry Schelling [Supp. 2], achieved international renown as a concert pianist, composer, and conductor. Felix, the elder son, studied music with Henry C. Timm [*q.v.*] and became a gifted pianist, but decided against becoming a professional performer. Owing to frail health and the mobility of the family, he had received his early schooling from tutors and from his mother. He entered the University of Pennsylvania as a sophomore, received his A.B. degree in 1881, and continued in the graduate and law schools, receiving an LL.B. in 1883 and an A.M. in 1884. He began a law practice but abandoned it in 1886 to become an instructor in English at the university; he remained there for the rest of his career.

The University of Pennsylvania had had notable professors of rhetoric, but Schelling was the real creator of a department of English language and literature in the modern sense. The task of reorganization was entrusted to him in 1888. Among his startling innovations was a course in modern novelists (at that time Scott, Thackeray, Dickens,

Austen, Eliot, and Hawthorne) and, somewhat later, the appointment of a specialist in American literature. Under his direction the department became large and powerful, assuming in the humanities the dominance formerly held by the classics department. Although at heart a belletrist, suspicious of the German influence upon American graduate studies, Schelling introduced a Ph.D. program, complete with the Germanic seminar, and set an example in creative scholarship by becoming the first American student of English Renaissance literature and drama to be taken seriously in England.

From 1889 until his retirement in 1934 a steady procession of learned books and articles issued from his hand, not to mention familiar essays, treatises on education, and poems circulated privately to his friends. Among the books was an inspired anthology, *A Book of Elizabethan Lyrics* (1895), and a graceful study, *The English Lyric* (1913); among the articles, one that changed the contours of seventeenth-century literary history: "Ben Jonson and the Classical School" (*Publications of the Modern Language Association of America*, vol. XIII, 1898). His interest in typological and generic studies in the drama was indicated by his *The English Chronicle Play* (1902). The interest bore fruit in his best-known work, *Elizabethan Drama, 1558–1642* (2 vols., 1908). This study now seems too densely schematic, but it was a landmark of comprehensiveness in 1908; no earlier literary history had made such full use of scattered secondary as well as primary materials. A more charming book, and more indicative of his gifts as a writer, is *English Literature during the Lifetime of Shakespeare* (1910). He produced several anthologies and editions, including the Everyman *Complete Plays of Ben Jonson* (2 vols., 1910) and *Typical Elizabethan Plays* (1926).

Schelling was tall and lean, with aristocratic mien and deportment. The diversity of his talents and interests, and the intensity of his devotion to arts and letters, were formidable. There was a Renaissance ruthlessness as well as courtliness about his manners, and association with him could be abrasive. A graduate student who had written the ingratiating type of scholarly report once asked in bewilderment the meaning of his comment, "Too closely calculated to the meridian of your instructor," not realizing that he had been stabbed. On the other hand, Schelling personally read all the papers of his students, and read them line by line; the process may have contributed to his near-blindness in later years. A flood of papers was required in the department he founded; students complained that one dared not read a weather report without producing a critique. Although he was honored with doctorates from several universities and with membership in various learned societies, including the National Institute of Arts and Letters (1911), his chief reward was local veneration. In 1923, after thirty years of tenure of the John Welsh Centennial Professorship of History and English Literature, twenty of his former students issued the *Schelling Anniversary Papers*. Later he held a professorship established in his name, and in 1935 an appreciation and bibliography was issued by the University of Pennsylvania Press.

On Mar. 7, 1886, Schelling married Caroline, the daughter of James Alexander Derbyshire, a Quaker of Bucks County, Pa. A daughter, Dorothea Derbyshire, was born in 1890, a son, Felix, in 1895. The daughter became the wife of Prof. Joseph Seronde of Yale, the son an artist and art teacher. Schelling's wife died in 1935. His last years were spent as an invalid in Mount Vernon, N. Y., where he was cared for by the artist Gertrude Bueb, who in 1939 became his wife. He died at Mount Vernon at the age of eighty-seven of myocarditis and was buried in Mount Moriah Cemetery, Philadelphia.

[Biographical sketch by Arthur H. Quinn in *Schelling Anniversary Papers* (1923); *Felix E. Schelling* (Univ. of Pa. Press, 1935), which includes a bibliography of his writings; Arthur H. Quinn in Am. Philosophical Soc., *Year Book*, 1945; *Who Was Who in America*, vol. II (1950); *N. Y. Times*, Dec. 16, 1945.]
ALFRED HARBAGE

SCHILLINGER, JOSEPH (Sept. 1, 1895–Mar. 23, 1943), composer and musical theorist, was born Iosif Moiseyevich Schillinger in Kharkov, Russia, the only child of Moses and Anna (Gielgur) Schillinger. His father was a prosperous businessman of Jewish descent. Receiving his early education from tutors, Joseph displayed a strong interest in art and music and wrote his first composition at the age of ten. He began his formal education at the Classical College in St. Petersburg, where he studied mathematics, physics, and languages; he also developed an interest in philosophy. In 1914 he entered the Imperial Conservatory of Music at St. Petersburg. He studied composition under Vasily Kalafati and Joseph Vitols, and conducting with Nicolai Cherepnin, obtaining a gold medal for composition, and graduated in 1918. For the next four years Schillinger taught at the State Academy of Music in Kharkov, becoming dean; he also conducted the student orchestra and, in 1920–21, the Ukraine Symphony. Thereafter, he lectured at various institutions in Leningrad.

Schillinger began his composing career in

Leningrad, where he was associated with modernist circles. His works of this period include a symphonic suite, "March of the Orient" (1924), and a Sonata-Rhapsody (1925) for piano. His Symphonic Rhapsody (1927) won a competition for the best work composed during the first ten years of the Soviet regime. In that same year he took part in an ethnomusicological expedition sent to the Caucasus to record the folk music of some of the Georgian tribes and organized and directed the first "jazz" orchestra in Russia. In November 1928, at the invitation of the American Society for Cultural Relations with Russia, Schillinger came to the United States. Settling in New York City, he lectured on composition at the New School for Social Research (1932–33) and on "Rhythmic Design" in the fine arts department of Teachers College, Columbia University (1934–36); he became an American citizen in 1936.

Even before coming to the United States, Schillinger had been devoting much of his time to studying and elucidating principles of modern music. Under the influence of Alexander Scriabin, whose mystical notions he rejected while retaining the interest in a universal art, he began exploring alternatives to the tempered scale, which he regarded as insufficient. As early as 1918 he urged the construction of electric instruments to produce scientifically correct intervals. In America, during the years 1928–31, he collaborated with Leo Theremin in the development of the electronic instrument bearing the latter's name and composed for it the "First Airphonic Suite," first performed by the Cleveland Symphony on Nov. 28, 1929. Schillinger predicted that electronic instruments would eventually displace conventional ones, as part of the evolutionary process through which music would become completely abstracted from the obsolescent forms of the past.

Schillinger's radical theories found their most characteristic expression in his application of strict mathematical principles and formulae to musical composition. His method was fully developed in two posthumous books, *The Schillinger System of Musical Composition* (2 vols., 1946) and *The Mathematical Basis of the Arts* (1948). These expounded his view that composition should be freed from dependency on intuitive invention and "inspiration," and that unplanned or unconscious mathematical patterns underlying much of the creative process ought to be made explicit and logically elaborated. Schillinger's system of composition, which he taught in private classes, was founded on the concept of rhythm as a pattern from which stemmed the development of melody and harmony. A musical

phrase of a given length, for example, could be developed by treating each element (rhythm, pitch, tonal interval) as an algebraic quantity and applying algebraic and geometric operations to yield permutations and combinations of these elements. The resulting new relationships could then be converted into musical terms. The same principles, he maintained, could be applied to the elements of painting and architecture. He himself did some painting; several of his art works were placed in the permanent collections of American museums.

The "Schillinger system" attracted wide attention and evoked some skepticism. Several popular composers became his students, including the clarinetist Benny Goodman, the pianist Oscar Levant, and the band leader Glenn Miller [Supp. 3], who wrote "Moonlight Serenade" as a Schillinger exercise. Schillinger's most famous student was George Gershwin [Supp. 2], who found in the Schillinger system the technical orchestration techniques (as reflected partly in *Porgy and Bess*) that he needed to give disciplined form to his ever-flowing musical ideas.

Schillinger's first marriage, on May 22, 1930, to a Russian actress, Olga Mikhailovna Goldberg, ended in divorce; he was married for the second time, on Nov. 12, 1938, in New York, to Frances Rosenfeld Singer, who survived him. There were no children. Schillinger died of cancer at his home in New York City in his forty-eighth year. Several Schillinger Societies and college seminars were formed to teach his system of composition.

[Other writings by Schillinger include: "Electricity, a Musical Liberator," *Modern Music*, Mar.–Apr. 1931; "The Destiny of the Tonal Art," *Music Teachers' Nat. Assoc.*, *Proc.*, 1937; and *Kaleidophone* (1940), in which he tabulated scales and chords according to statistical data without regard to their traditional functions. On Schillinger and his work, see: Frances Schillinger, *Joseph Schillinger: A Memoir by His Wife* (1949); four articles about him in *Music News*, Mar. 1947; Vernon Duke, "Gershwin, Schillinger, and Dukelsky," *Music Quart.*, Jan. 1947; David Ewen, *George Gershwin* (1970); Horace M. Kallen, *Art and Freedom* (2 vols., 1942); "Music by Slide Rule," *Newsweek*, Sept. 25, 1944; *Baker's Biog. Dict. of Musicians* (ed. by Nicolas Slonimsky, 1958); N. Slonimsky in Friedrich Blume, ed., *Die Musik in Geschichte und Gegenwart*, vol. XI (1963); Alexandria Vodarsky-Shiraeff, comp., *Russian Composers and Musicians* (1940); information from Mrs. Schillinger; personal acquaintance. The Joseph Schillinger Papers are in the Music Division, N. Y. Public Lib. at Lincoln Center; other source materials are at the Museum of Modern Art and Columbia Univ.]

NICOLAS SLONIMSKY

SCHINZ, ALBERT (Mar. 9, 1870–Dec. 19, 1943), professor of French, Rousseau scholar, was born in Neuchâtel, Switzerland, the son of Charles Émile Schinz, a well-to-do merchant, and

Ida (Diethelm) Schinz. He received a bachelor's degree in letters at the University of Neuchâtel in 1888, a licentiate in letters in 1889, and a licentiate in theology in 1892. He then studied for a year at the University of Berlin and in 1894 obtained the Ph.D. in philosophy at Tübingen. After further study at the University of Paris (1894–96), he returned to the University of Neuchâtel, where he served for a year as an instructor in philosophy. In 1897 he emigrated to the United States, seeking a teaching post in philosophy or in French or German literature.

Following a year as a fellow at Clark University and a year as instructor of French at the University of Minnesota (1898–99), Schinz taught at Bryn Mawr College (1899–1913) and at Smith College (1913–28). His leadership earned the French department at Smith a distinguished reputation among American institutions of higher learning. In 1928 he accepted a professorship at the University of Pennsylvania, where he taught until his retirement in 1941.

An energetic though not a robust man, who once spoke of "the harassing duties of a professorial career in the United States," Schinz produced a formidable array of articles, books, reviews, anthologies of French literature, and editions of French texts. His scholarly concerns ranged from bibliographical work on medieval French literature to a study of accents in French writing, from Dadaism and a philosophical treatise, *Anti-Pragmatism* (1909), to an investigation which resulted in his book *French Literature of the Great War* (1920). But his overriding passion and interest centered on Jean-Jacques Rousseau. Schinz labored arduously and unremittingly to explain the life and writings of his fellow countryman to the world. Among his many published studies are *La Question du "Contrat Social"* (1913); *Vie et Œuvres de J.-J. Rousseau* (1921), a book for the particular use of students; *La Pensée religieuse de Rousseau et ses récents interprètes* (1927); *La Pensée de Jean-Jacques Rousseau* (1929)—his most important work, summing up many of his previous articles; and *État présent des travaux sur J.-J. Rousseau* (1941), an indispensable (if occasionally inaccurate) bibliographical tool.

Schinz had a tendency to assume that Rousseau could do no wrong. Not all reviewers accepted his logic or all his conclusions, or his thesis of a Rousseau who oscillated in his writings between the opposite poles of Roman or Calvinistic austerity and discipline and Romantic freedom and unrestraint. Daniel Mornet, while considering Schinz an excellent literary historian and an even better philosopher, reproached him for "a sort of imperious dogmatism . . . which tended to make him present pure hypotheses as unshakable certainties" (*Revue d'histoire littéraire de la France,* April–June 1930). Schinz did battle with the Rousseauphobes of the world—with Pierre Lasserre and Ernest Seillière in France, and with the New Humanists in America, led by Irving Babbitt [Supp. 1] of Harvard and Paul Elmer More [Supp. 2] of Princeton. Babbitt's book *Rousseau and Romanticism* (1919), particularly, was anathema to Schinz, and their ideological feud was bitter.

Small of stature, with a distinctive goatee, Schinz was kind and courteous by nature, free of professional jealousy, generous with his time and knowledge when called upon by colleagues and students, yet capable of trenchant criticism. He was recognized as an authority on Rousseau on both sides of the Atlantic. His wife, Angelica de Beyersdorff, whom he had married before coming to the United States, was hospitalized for long periods and died before him. Schinz served as visiting professor in a number of American universities. In 1943, while at the State University of Iowa, he died of lobar pneumonia at the University Hospital in Iowa City. His body was cremated and the ashes buried at Oakland Cemetery, Iowa City.

[Obituary articles by Alexis François in *Annales Jean-Jacques Rousseau,* XXX (1943–45), 183–86, André Morize in *French Rev.,* Jan. 1944, and Osmond T. Robert in *Smith Alumnae Quart.,* Feb. 1944; *A Critical Bibliog. of French Literature,* vol. IV (1951); *Who Was Who in America,* vol. II (1950); information from records of Clark Univ. (letter of Schinz to G. Stanley Hall, Feb.[?] 8, 1896) and the Univ. of Pa., from Prof. Marine Leland of Smith College, and from Prof. Richard O'Gorman of the Univ. of Iowa.]

PAUL M. SPURLIN

SCHLESINGER, FRANK (May 11, 1871–July 10, 1943), astronomer, was born in New York City, the youngest of seven children of William Joseph and Mary (Wagner) Schlesinger. Both parents were natives of the German province of Silesia who had met and married in New York. When Frank was about nine his father died, leaving the family in financial difficulties. Frank attended New York public schools and the College of the City of New York, where he displayed unusual mathematical ability and graduated, B.S., in 1890. Unable, for lack of money, to continue his studies, he worked as a surveyor for six years, during the last two of which he was also enrolled as an astronomy student in the graduate school of Columbia University. He received the M.A. degree in 1897 and the Ph.D. in 1898. That summer he spent at the Yerkes Observatory in Wisconsin as a voluntary assistant to the director, George Ellery Hale [Supp. 2]. For four years (1899–1903) he was observer-in-charge at the New International Latitude Station at Ukiah, Calif.

From the beginning of his work in astronomy, Schlesinger's principal contributions lay in the field of photographic astrometry—the measurement of precise star positions by photographic means. He became the acknowledged master and leader in this field. For his doctoral dissertation, using the photographic plates of star fields made by Lewis M. Rutherfurd [q.v.], he measured the precise positions of stars in the Praesepe cluster. His first major astronomical contribution, which came during a two-year period (1903–05) on a research grant at the Yerkes Observatory, was the development of a photographic technique for measuring stellar parallax. Using photographs made with the observatory's long-focus 40-inch refractor—the largest instrument of its kind in the world—Schlesinger worked out procedures to obtain the positions of the "parallax" star relative to a small number of reference stars. He also devised new methods of measuring and reducing the photographic plates. The methods and the results he published in a series of papers in the *Astrophysical Journal* (1910–11) which are still required reading for anyone concerned with photographic astrometry. An elegant, concise summary is the "Photographic Determination of Stellar Parallaxes" in the festschrift volume *Probleme der Astronomie* (1924). In later years only minor improvements have been made in Schlesinger's technique, which was widely used by astronomers of other observatories.

In 1905 Schlesinger became director of the Allegheny Observatory at the University of Pittsburgh. He effected a reorganization of the institution and moved its instruments to a better site. He also acquired a powerful telescope designed specifically for photographic observations, the 30-inch Thaw refractor. With this, about 1914, he initiated a program that greatly increased the knowledge of parallaxes of stars in the northern celestial hemisphere. In addition, he and his colleagues carried out excellent spectroscopic work and determined the orbits of many double stars that could not be resolved visually.

Schlesinger moved to Yale in 1920 as director of its observatory, a position he held until his retirement in 1941. He at once began planning the establishment of an observing station in the southern hemisphere. He designed the instrument, a 26-inch photographic refractor of long focus, which was ground by the Brashear Company; the mechanical parts and mounting were built in the Yale workshop. The site he chose for the station

was in South Africa, on the grounds of the University of Witwatersrand in Johannesburg. The observational program began there in 1925 under the direction of Harold L. Alden; the results have done much to rectify the previous imbalance between knowledge of stellar distances in the northern and southern hemispheres.

Schlesinger next took up problems of determining stellar positions and motions. Instead of depending on visual observations, as in the past, he developed a photographic method for determining the positions of stars as faint as the ninth magnitude, with the aid of a wide-angle camera designed by Frank E. Ross. Each plate measured 17 x 17 inches and covered an area of about 120 square degrees. These investigations, carried out with the collaboration of Ida Barney, eventually yielded precise positions and proper motions of more than 100,000 stars, which were published in some fifteen volumes of the *Transactions* of the Yale Observatory. Other major contributions were Schlesinger's *Catalogue of Bright Stars* (1930) and *General Catalogue of Stellar Parallaxes* (1935), which became standard astronomical reference books.

In his younger years Schlesinger was ambitious and single-minded in the pursuit of his work and exacting of his fellow workers. He had few interests other than astronomy. In his later years he found more time for sociability and delighted in conversation with small groups; his rich memory included stories of most of the American astronomers of his day. He was a central figure in the "Neighbors," an informal association of Eastern astronomers that often met at Yale, and although a nonsmoker and nondrinker, he always offered his guests cigars and good wine. In the 1920's and '30's Schlesinger was a striking figure at astronomical meetings, and in two lectures given during the Tercentenary Summer School of Astronomy at Harvard University (July 1936) he lucidly summarized the problems of classical astrometry, such as distortion of the photographic film, the effects of atmospheric dispersion, the sensitivity of emulsions, and optical distortion. He was president of the American Astronomical Society, 1919–22, and of the International Astronomical Union, 1932–35—only the second American to be so honored. He was elected to the National Academy of Sciences (1916), the American Philosophical Society, and the American Academy of Arts and Sciences.

On June 19, 1900, Schlesinger married Eva Hirsch. Their only child, Frank Wagner Schlesinger, later became director of the Fels Planetarium in Philadelphia and, in 1945, of the Adler Planetarium in Chicago. Schlesinger's first wife died in 1928, and on July 1, 1929, he married Mrs. Katherine Bell (Rawling) Wilcox. Although he was apparently of Jewish ancestry, he had no religious affiliation. After five years of failing health, Schlesinger died of a heart attack at his summer home at Old Lyme, Conn., in 1943; following cremation, his ashes were scattered in the woods nearby.

[Dirk Brouwer in Nat. Acad. Sci., *Biog. Memoirs*, vol. XXIV (1947); Henry Norris Russell in Am. Philosophical Soc., *Year Book*, 1943; S. A. Mitchell in Astronomical Soc. of the Pacific, *Publications*, Oct. 1943; Frederick Slocum in *Astrophysical Jour.*, Nov. 1943; Frank Schlesinger, "From an Astronomer's Diary, 1925," *Popular Astronomy*, Nov. 1926. See also *Nat. Cyc. Am. Biog.*, XXXII, 198; *Universal Jewish Encyc.*, X, 408.]

PETER VAN DE KAMP

SCHOENHEIMER, RUDOLF (May 10, 1898–Sept. 11, 1941), biochemist, was born in Berlin, Germany, the son of Hugo and Gertrud (Edel) Schoenheimer. His father was a physician who specialized in gynecology. Rudolf received his early education in local schools and graduated from the Realgymnasium in 1916. Drafted into the German army, he spent the next two years at the Western Front. He then began the study of medicine at the University of Berlin, receiving his degree in 1922. For a year he was resident pathologist at the Moabit Hospital in Berlin, carrying out studies on the production of atherosclerosis in animals by administration of cholesterol. Recognizing his deficiency in biochemical knowledge, he then studied at the University of Leipzig under a Rockefeller Foundation fellowship for three years. While working there in the laboratory of Karl Thomas, he continued his earlier work on the role of cholesterol and in 1926 published a unique procedure for the synthesis of peptides.

In that same year, Schoenheimer became a docent (assistant professor) at the University of Freiburg, where he was on the staff of Ludwig Aschoff in the Pathological Institute. He spent the year 1930–31 in the United States as Douglas Smith Fellow in the department of surgery at the University of Chicago and was then made head of the department of pathological chemistry in Freiburg. Here he continued his work on sterols, investigating the occurrence and transformation of these compounds in both plants and animals, and establishing the fact that cholesterol undergoes continuous synthesis and degradation in mammals. On Oct. 27, 1932, he married Salome Gluecksohn, a zoologist who had just completed her Ph.D. at Freiburg; she continued an active scientific career after the Schoenheimers came to the United States. They had no children.

An edict of the new Nazi government in April 1933 ordered the dismissal of all Jewish faculty members in German universities. Prof. Hans T. Clarke, chairman of the biochemistry department at Columbia University's College of Physicians and Surgeons, immediately offered Schoenheimer an assistant professorship, which he accepted. At Columbia, Schoenheimer continued his work on sterols and, in association with Warren M. Sperry, developed a procedure for determining traces of free and bound cholesterol in blood serum and plasma.

His most significant research began in 1934, after Harold Urey had successfully concentrated the heavy hydrogen isotope, deuterium. Seeking to use deuterium as an isotopic tracer, Schoenheimer, in conjunction with David Rittenberg, who had worked on deuterium in Urey's laboratory, developed methods of synthesizing isotopically labeled compounds (such as linseed oil hydrogenated with deuterium) and studying their fate in the bodies of experimental animals (mice and rats). It had formerly been believed that animals used the fats from freshly ingested food for their energy sources, drawing on their fat depots only in times of inadequate food intake. Schoenheimer's feeding experiments showed that, on the contrary, labeled fatty acids were laid down in fat depots even during times of starvation. He also fed heavy water (deuterium oxide, D_2O) to animals; when heavy hydrogen showed up in various compounds, it revealed active use of the water in metabolic processes.

After the nitrogen-15 isotope was concentrated in Urey's laboratory in the form of heavy ammonia, Schoenheimer and his colleagues turned to the problem of protein metabolism. They prepared various compounds, particularly amino acids, labeled with nitrogen–15 or doubly labeled with deuterium and nitrogen–15. When such compounds were fed to animals, various nitrogenous metabolic products were recovered, showing that body constituents are in a highly dynamic rather than a static state, as had generally been assumed. From Schoenheimer's experiments emerged the concept of a "metabolic pool," with body tissues continually drawing chemical substances from it and releasing others to it.

Schoenheimer's career came to a sudden close on Sept. 11, 1941, when he committed suicide by taking poison at his home in Yonkers, N. Y. For some time he had been in state of severe mental depression associated with the successes of the German armies in Europe, with Nazi treatment of the Jews, and with personal problems. His remains were cremated. Besides his specific findings, Schoenheimer developed the methodology connected with the use of isotopic tracers in a period before radioactive isotopes were abundantly available, as they would be in the decade following his death.

[The circumstances of Schoenheimer's life were unfavorable to the preservation of personal papers. His early published work appeared principally in the *Zeitschrift für physiologische Chemie,* his later work principally in the *Jour. of Biological Chemistry.* There is no bibliography of his publications except for the partial listings in Johann Poggendorff, *Handworterbuch zur Geschichte der exacten Wissenschaften,* vol. 7a (1960), p. 224, and the cumulative Author Indexes of *Chemical Abstracts.* Extensive accounts of his work are found in Schoenheimer's "Chemistry of Steroids," *Annual Rev. of Biochemistry,* 1937; "Metabolism of Proteins and Amino Acids," *ibid.,* 1941; "The Study of the Intermediary Metabolism of Animals with the Aid of Isotopes," *Physiological Rev.,* Apr. 1940; and "The Investigation of Intermediary Metabolism with the Aid of Heavy Nitrogen," *The Harvey Lectures, 1936–1937* (1937). His Dunham Lectures (delivered by H. T. Clarke from manuscripts prepared before his death) are published as *The Dynamic State of Body Constituents* (1942). There are no biographies of Schoenheimer except for the obituaries by H. T. Clarke in *Science,* Dec. 12, 1941, and J. H. Quastel in *Nature,* Jan. 3, 1942.]

                                        AARON J. IHDE

SCHREMBS, JOSEPH (Mar. 12, 1866–Nov. 2, 1945), Roman Catholic prelate, was born in Wurzelhofen near Regensburg (Ratisbon), Bavaria, Germany, the fifteenth of sixteen children of George Schrembs, a blacksmith, and his second wife, Mary (Gess) Schrembs. The boy attended elementary school in Regensburg until 1877, when, at the invitation of Bishop Rupert Seidenbisch of Minnesota, who had visited the Schrembs household, he came to America and entered the Benedictine Scholasticate at St. Vincent's Archabbey in Latrobe, Pa., where an older brother was a priest. He left St. Vincent's in 1882 and, after teaching for two years at St. Martin's parish in Louisville, Ky., where some of his family had located, decided to enter the priesthood. Accepted by the diocese of Grand Rapids, Mich., he was sent to the Grand Séminaire in Montreal, Canada. He was ordained on June 29, 1889.

Beginning as curate at St. Mary's parish in Saginaw, Mich., Schrembs soon moved to St. Mary's in nearby Bay City, and then in 1900 to Grand Rapids, where he quickly rose from pastor of St. Mary's, a German parish, to vicar general of the diocese and, in 1911, auxiliary bishop. Later that year he was appointed the first bishop of Toledo, Ohio. In organizing the new diocese, he established thirteen new parishes and thirty-three new schools, expanded Catholic hospital services, and founded a Catholic Charities Bureau, besides developing social and religious services for such special groups as deaf-mutes.

On the national level, Schrembs was one of four bishops who during World War I administered the National Catholic War Council, organized in 1917 to coordinate Catholic wartime efforts, from fund raising to supplying chaplains. When the war ended the Council was continued, largely through the efforts of Bishop Thomas Joseph Shahan [*q.v.*] and Father John Joseph Burke [Supp. 2], as the National Catholic Welfare Council. As one of seven bishops on a permanent committee in charge of the N.C.W.C., Schrembs directed its department of lay organization, establishing in 1920 the National Council of Catholic Men and the National Council of Catholic Women. He was instrumental in saving the N.C.W.C. itself, in 1922. Pope Benedict XV, fearing that the American organization would develop into a national church, had drawn up a decree of dissolution shortly before his death. Delegated by the American bishops, Schrembs went to Rome, interceded with the new pope, Pius XI, and persuaded him to reverse the decree. In 1923, in deference to those who worried about possible encroachment on the authority of local bishops, the name was changed to the National Catholic Welfare Conference. When Schrembs retired in 1934 from the administrative board of the Conference, its lay organizations had grown to nearly 4,000 units, engaged in promoting cooperation between laity and clergy, channeling information from the N.C.W.C. to local dioceses, and stimulating the application of Catholic principles to education and to social, economic, and political affairs. Schrembs was also active in national liturgical observances, especially the Eucharistic Congresses.

Meanwhile, in 1921, he had become bishop of Cleveland, Ohio, a post he held for the rest of his life (from 1939 with the personal title of archbishop). Faced with a heterogeneous flock composed mainly of second-generation Germans and Irish, but also of Bohemian, Hungarian, Slovak, Polish, Slovenian, and Italian immigrants, he worked to minimize differences in religious custom rooted in the heritage of each national group. Though his own background made him sympathetic to the desire of new immigrants to maintain ancestral ties, he nevertheless insisted that they adapt to their American environment. At times he found it necessary to act forcefully in settling disputes in parochial administration that hinged on nationality conflicts. Schrembs maintained good relations with Cleveland's immigrants by acquiring at least a minimal knowledge of several languages, encouraging the participation of immigrant associations in community affairs, and recommending that the curriculum of parochial schools include courses in the language and culture of the countries from which the city's newcomers had recently emigrated. At the same time he required that English be used in schools and churches.

An able administrator, Bishop Schrembs established seventeen new parishes in what would become the diocese of Youngstown, which then lay in his jurisdiction, and forty-two new parishes in the diocese of Cleveland. The majority of these were territorial rather than nationality parishes. He built more than ninety elementary schools, appointed a central school board in 1922, and in 1928 centralized the training of teachers at the newly established Sisters' College. He also founded two local Catholic colleges for women, expanded a third, and built a new seminary.

Schrembs had a rugged constitution and great energy, but during his later years he suffered from diabetes. He was hospitalized for the last six years of his life, and died in Cleveland at the age of seventy-nine. He was buried in the crypt of St. John Cathedral, but his body was later transferred to the mortuary chapel of the newly reconstructed Cathedral.

[Manuscript sources include the diocesan archives of Grand Rapids, Toledo, and Cleveland and the archives of the Nat. Catholic Welfare Conference. Information may also be found in files of the Cleveland *Universe Bull.*, the diocesan newspaper. The most valuable secondary work is Michael J. Hynes, *The Hist. of the Diocese of Cleveland* (1953), which includes a good likeness of Schrembs. See also: *Nat. Cyc. Am. Biog.,* Current Vol. E, pp. 419–20; obituary in *Catholic World,* Dec. 1945; and *New Catholic Encyc.,* XII, 1178–79.]

DONALD P. GAVIN

SCHUCHERT, CHARLES (July 3, 1858–Nov. 20, 1942), paleontologist, was born in Cincinnati, Ohio, the eldest of the four sons and two daughters of Philip and Agatha (Müller) Schuchert. The father, born in Kranlucken, Saxony, was a cabinetmaker who had made his way to "free America" as a stowaway. Settling in the German community at Cincinnati, he established a furniture factory and married a native of Reussendorf, Bavaria, who had been working as a domestic and as a seamstress in a sweatshop. Schuchert later described his father as "industrious and studious," his mother as "religious, poetic, animated."

Charles (originally Karl) attended a German Catholic school for six and a half years, but at twelve was sent to the Gundry Mercantile School to learn bookkeeping so as to enter the family business. As his father's employee, he worked long hours for low pay. He managed, however, to take drawing courses at the Ohio Mechanics' Institute, and with his father's encouragement also pursued a precocious interest in science, particularly in fossils, which abound in the Cincinnati area. He taught himself how to prepare and describe specimens and mastered the art of lithography. Becoming acquainted with some of the city's enthusiastic amateur fossil collectors, Schuchert in 1878 began attending meetings of the Cincinnati Society of Natural History, where he formed a close friendship with Edward O. Ulrich [Supp. 3], then curator of the society's paleontology collections.

Fire burned out the Schuchert factory in 1877, and Charles's father, bankrupt and buffeted by the business depression, fell victim to intemperance, leaving to nineteen-year-old Charles the responsibility for both family and factory. For a time Charles revived the firm, but a second fire in 1884 destroyed the plant and forced him to become a foreman in another furniture factory. Disliking this role, he was glad to exchange it for a job as Ulrich's assistant (1885–88) in preparing lithographs for the Illinois and Minnesota geological surveys. He also began exchanging specimens with other geologists in this country and abroad and started amassing a collection of fossil brachiopods. By 1888 this was large enough to draw the attention of James Hall [q.v.], director of the New York geological survey, who came to Cincinnati to examine Schuchert's specimens and hired him as an assistant. Schuchert's two years at Albany he later called the most educational of his life. Although Hall did not encourage him to publish scientific papers (and, in fact, used his work without acknowledgment), Schuchert had the use of Hall's great library and found close comrades in two fellow assistants, John M. Clarke and Charles Emerson Beecher [qq.v.]. In the summer of 1891 he was able to join Newton H. Winchell [q.v.], state geologist of Minnesota, in studies of Minnesota brachiopods, at double his old salary and with joint authorship. Subsequently, in 1892, Beecher brought Schuchert to the Peabody Museum at Yale as a preparator, and in June 1893 he was hired by the United States Geological Survey, becoming assistant curator of invertebrate paleontology at the National Museum a year later. For the next decade he undertook research, prepared collections, and did summer field work, including an 1897 expedition to Greenland with Robert Peary [q.v.]. In 1903 he represented the United States government at the International Geological Congress in Vienna, making extensive purchases and exchanges of fossils on the way.

Beecher died in 1903, and the following year Schuchert succeeded him at Yale as curator of geological collections at the Peabody Museum and professor of historical geology. He was chairman of the geology department, 1909–21, acting dean of the graduate school, 1914–16, and administrative head of the museum, 1912–23. He retired from teaching in 1925 but remained at the museum for the rest of his life, notably enriching its collections. Although never very successful with undergraduates, Schuchert proved a great teacher and "foster-father" of graduate students. During his three decades there, Yale became the preeminent training ground for invertebrate paleontology and stratigraphy.

Schuchert's own writings—234 titles in all— fall chiefly into these two fields. His first major publication was *A Synopsis of American Fossil Brachiopoda* (1897), and he later produced other important summaries of the brachiopods. Many of his writings are concerned with stratigraphy, the study of rock strata and their changes throughout geologic time. To assist his students in stratigraphy, Schuchert plotted the outcrops on outline maps, the beginning of an interest that led to his pioneering *Paleogeography of North America* (1910). He continued to revise his maps and planned to complete and publish them, along with an extensive text synthesizing the stratigraphic data on which they were based, in his *Historical Geology of North America.* Two of the projected three volumes appeared: *Historical Geology of the Antillean-Caribbean Region* (1935) and *Stratigraphy of the Eastern and Central United States* (1943). Left unfinished by his death was a volume which would have summed up the work he and his students had undertaken in Newfoundland and the Maritime Provinces of Canada, an area where Schuchert did particularly noteworthy field work.

Schuchert's influence in geology was felt through both his graduate students at Yale, who in turn became university teachers, and his college texts. His textbook of historical geology (originally published in 1915, together with a companion section on physical geology by Louis V. Pirsson, under the title *A Text-book of Geology*) went through four editions (the two later ones in collaboration with Carl O. Dunbar) and between the two World Wars was used by almost all undergraduate geology students in North America.

Schuchert was a bachelor wedded to his science; his only romantic attachment had ended unhappily. Though reared as a Roman Catholic, he became a skeptic in his teens and left the church at twenty-three, forming no other religious affiliation. His accomplishments earned him election to twenty-five learned societies, including the National Academy of Sciences

(1910), and honorary doctorates from Yale and Harvard. He died in New Haven of cancer at the age of eighty-four and was buried in the Grove Street Cemetery on the Yale campus. He left most of his estate to Yale.

[The Charles Schuchert Papers, Yale Univ., which include a MS. autobiography and an "Abridged Record of Family Traits"; memoirs by Carl O. Dunbar in Geological Soc. of America, *Proc.*, 1942, and by Adolph Knopf in Nat. Acad. Sci., *Biog. Memoirs*, vol. XXVII (1952), both with photograph and list of publications; conversations with R. S. Bassler, G. A. Cooper, and C. O. Dunbar; death record from Conn. Dept. of Health. A portrait of Schuchert by Deane Keller is in the Peabody Museum at Yale.]

ELLIS L. YOCHELSON

SCHURMAN, JACOB GOULD (May 22, 1854–Aug. 13, 1942), philosopher, college president, diplomat, was born in Freetown, Prince Edward Island, Canada, the third of eight children of Robert and Lydia (Gouldrup) Schurman. His family were New Yorkers of Dutch descent who had moved to Canada during the American Revolution because of Loyalist sympathies. Though his great-grandfather had been a leading figure in New Rochelle, N. Y., family fortunes gradually declined in Canada. The Schurmans were Baptists, and Jacob joined the church as a young boy.

Dislike of heavy labor on his father's farm was the consciously remembered cause of the boy's initial desire to seek a higher education. At thirteen he left the farm to clerk in a store and in three years saved enough money to attend grammar school for one year. He then won the first of a series of scholarships which were to support him for the next eight years. After a year (1872–73) at the local Prince of Wales College and two years at Acadia College in Nova Scotia, he went abroad to the University of London, where he received a B.A. degree in 1877 from University College, with first-class honors in mental and moral science. In the absence of a strong philosophy faculty at London, Schurman had attended James Martineau's lectures on mental and moral philosophy and religion at Manchester New College, and he credited Martineau with helping him resolve some of his doubts about the conflict between natural science and religion. He next studied philosophy for a year at Edinburgh, while simultaneously studying for an M.A. at London, and earned a D.Sc. with distinction in 1878. At Edinburgh he formed a lasting friendship with Andrew Seth (later Pringle-Pattison), who was to become an eminent philosopher. Refusing a teaching post at Acadia, in part because its Baptist traditions now seemed too narrow, he decided to spend two years in Germany.

His first year he studied at the University of Heidelberg, particularly savoring the lectures of Kuno Fischer in the history of philosophy. The second year he divided between Berlin, where he came to admire Eduard Zeller, and Göttingen. In Berlin he boldly called on Andrew Dickson White [q.v.], the American minister to Germany and president of Cornell University, to announce his availability for a professorship at that school. Though White was favorably impressed, no appointment materialized, and Schurman was forced to return to Acadia as professor of English literature in 1880. In 1882 he became professor of English literature and rhetoric at Dalhousie University in New Brunswick, and professor of metaphysics in 1884. He continued to travel and to do research in the United States. On Oct. 1, 1884, he married Barbara Forrest Munro, daughter of George Munro [q.v.], the New York publisher. They had seven children: Catherine Munro, Robert, George Munro, Helen, Jacob Gould, Barbara Rose, and Dorothy Anna Maria.

Partly on the strength of his philosophical writing, and with the backing of White, Schurman went to Cornell in 1886 as the hand-picked candidate of Henry W. Sage [q.v.], the lumber magnate and trustee, for the professorship of Christian ethics and mental philosophy recently endowed by Sage. Toward Sage, who was then the most powerful policy-making figure in the university, Schurman always remained obsequiously respectful, and a very close relationship developed. In 1890 Sage endowed a School of Philosophy at Cornell, with Schurman as its dean.

Schurman had already established himself as a philosopher of some distinction with *Kantian Ethics and the Ethics of Evolution* (1881), his first book, and the first English-language critique of Kant's ethical system. It was both a sympathetic exposition and a critique of Kantian ethics, together with an assault on the materialistic ethics of Charles Darwin and Herbert Spencer. Schurman argued that Kant had been correct in asserting the absolutely unconditioned nature of the moral law, but that he had ultimately failed of his ethical purpose. The Kantian theory of the free will involved a determinism of which Kant himself was dimly aware but had failed to reconcile with his overall system; yet without autonomy of the will, there was no escape from the hedonistic egoism Kant had tried to supplant. Schurman held that Kant's distinction between the sensible sphere of phenomena and the transcendental sphere of noumena was destructive of moral obligation. The categorical imperative was merely formal, and subjective in the extreme. Far from liberating ethics from egoism, Kant had made the ego constitutive of the laws of the known world and left the grounds of duty undefined save in a self-given law of reason. The true system of ethics was still to be found in Aristotelian theory, which would balance the one-sidedness of Kant.

Schurman especially criticized Kant for ignoring and even excluding the development of individual objective consciousness through heritage and through interaction with the social environment, an objection he also raised against Spencerian ethics. Although Schurman took pains to state that he had no quarrel with Darwinism as a biological hypothesis, he ridiculed Spencer's *The Data of Ethics* (1879) for attempting to deduce a science of ethics from the laws of evolution while denying the freedom of the will, without which moral responsibility is nullified. Spencer's proposal that an ethical system could be developed which would measure human actions against an evolutionary scale of life-nurturing versus life-destroying conduct. Schurman dismissed as a sort of "hygienic almanac." In the end, while accepting evolutionism's stress on the gradual development of moral conceptions, he insisted that it neither explained the process nor provided philosophical validation for the end results. These points he developed in detail in *The Ethical Import of Darwinism* (1888) and in two books comprising his popular lectures, *Belief in God* (1890) and *Agnosticism and Religion* (1896). He moved in a more liberal direction by the 1890's, though tardily in comparison with many around him. He had never highly valued intellectual originality. By 1896 he praised "the Vague" over "the Definite" in such a way as to suggest that he had abandoned a search for final philosophical answers altogether. After 1898 he wrote nothing further in these abstract realms.

The objective idealism espoused by Schurman, who emphasized the totality of human experience in its social, historical, and institutional aspects, held sway at the Sage School of Philosophy. There James Edwin Creighton, formerly a student of Schurman's at Dalhousie, Ernest F. Albee [qq.v.], Frank Thilly [Supp. 1], and William A. Hammond, all distinguished teachers and philosophers, trained a remarkable number of teachers of philosophy. The "Cornell school" was highly influential for over a generation. During the several years when Schurman gave nearly all the philosophy instruction at Cornell he gained a reputation as a brilliant lecturer, maintaining a uniform pitch of eloquent clarity. Early in 1891 he began to urge the creation of an association of philosophers which would meet annually, like the groups recently founded in other disciplines. In

1892 the first general scholarly journal devoted to philosophy in America, the *Philosophical Review*, began publication at Cornell under his editorship.

But now Schurman was suddenly lifted onto a new and still larger stage. President Charles Kendall Adams [*q.v.*] of Cornell, successor to White, had made many enemies on the faculty, and factional warfare had demoralized the campus. Though the faculty probably preferred Benjamin Ide Wheeler [*q.v.*] as a replacement, the all-powerful Sage favored Schurman, and he became president in 1892. Sage's death in 1897 created a vacuum which Schurman easily filled; thereafter his was the dominant voice at Cornell. The trustees might occasionally balk, as they did over hiring a woman on the faculty in 1898, but they were a large, unwieldy body, made still larger when, in 1909, Schurman permitted the addition of five members appointed by the State of New York, in return for assured state support of agricultural and medical education.

Likewise Schurman dominated the faculty; he did so by upholding views which were so congenial to most of them that they considered him their genuine spokesman. He was almost unique among the younger university presidents of the 1890's for the way in which he practiced academic freedom. The faculty were allowed to nominate deans, unlike the prevailing situation elsewhere. Schurman even succeeded in adding nonvoting faculty representation to the board of trustees, an almost unprecedented step. Thus, despite his aggressiveness and the manner in which he had been elevated, Schurman was rightfully considered the faculty's own kind of president. His dedication to certain liberal ideals was undeniably sincere; in contrast to the narrower prejudices of A. Lawrence Lowell [*q.v.*] of Harvard, Schurman sternly rebuked undergraduates who petitioned against allowing black students to live in the dormitories.

Because of the persistently poor financial condition of the university, Schurman did not gain many concrete benefits for the faculty (other than a pension system). Indeed, except in his relations with the Sage family, he was not a very successful fund raiser; higher education in these years was not a widely fashionable philanthropy. Schurman would have liked to expand the university in every conceivable direction, but again the budgetary situation prevented him. During his twenty-eight-year regime, however, the enrollment increased from 1,538 to 5,765, and the campus grew from 200 to 1,465 acres. He created a Veterinary College, a College of Agriculture (headed by the equally aggressive Liberty Hyde Bailey, whom Schurman only pretended to ad-

mire), a Medical College, and an ill-fated College of Forestry. He succeeded, as early as 1892, in boldly begging funds from the state legislature, and under his presidency Cornell changed from a privately endowed to a mixed public and private institution.

Schurman had inherited an institution which bore strong traces both of the eccentric radicalism of Andrew D. White and the eccentric conservatism of Henry W. Sage. Lacking any single consuming passion of his own, Schurman worked to standardize the university, to make it more like other leading institutions in the range of instruction and services it offered. For instance, following a nationwide fashion, it moved away from an extreme version of the elective system into a conventional program of disciplinary majors and distributional requirements. As a result, by 1920 Cornell was much better balanced, though not so often talked about.

As an executive, Schurman was hard-headed, with a rather ruthless streak. His great physical and mental vigor impressed everyone and awed some. He could overwhelm people with his speed, thoroughness, and steadfast attention to all the major and minor duties of his office. He said little that was truly remarkable; his educational philosophy amounted to a hodgepodge undeserving of notice. Yet he compared favorably with other university presidents of his generation, avoiding the arrogance and autocracy of men like Nicholas Murray Butler and Benjamin Ide Wheeler and the weakness of Arthur T. Hadley [*q.v.*].

Meanwhile, as early as 1899 Schurman had intermittently begun a career of public service, into which he fully stepped after his retirement from Cornell in 1920. He was furthered in this career not only by his reputation for fair-minded intelligence but by his obedient identification with the orthodox wing of the Republican party. Still, within the limits of these loyalties Schurman was as liberal-minded as one could be. He was an anti-imperialist in 1898; he spoke out against the "Red" raids of A. Mitchell Palmer [Supp. 2] in 1920, calling them the Bolshevization of America; and he opposed retreat into isolationism during the 1920's. Toward the League of Nations treaty he was a mild reservationist. Further, he rendered important nonpartisan service as first vice-president of the New York State Constitutional Convention of 1915 and as a member of the New York State Food Commission of 1917–18. In the spring of 1920 he went on a private mission to Japan in the cause of world peace, speaking against militarism. Schurman's political outlook can be called middle-of-the-road. His rhetoric was slightly to the left of center, but his practical ties were a good distance to the right. It is especially interesting, in view of his career, that in 1920 he attacked "balance of power" diplomacy and appeared to accept the Wilsonian assumption that a fundamentally new and more principled basis for the conduct of international relations was on the horizon. Eight years later, Schurman greeted the Kellogg peace pacts with enthusiasm.

Yet in his several official posts it was his seemingly hard-hitting realism which drew praise from his contemporaries. In the recently conquered Philippines (1899), Schurman, as chairman of a government commission to investigate local conditions, gathered testimony from local inhabitants and tried to avert the growing insurrection against American rule by promising a large measure of self-government. The commission's *Report* to McKinley (1900) reveals his probing mind and immense labor. His experience on the islands convinced him that his anti-imperialist views had been correct. By January 1902 he was publicly arguing (in his lecture and book, *Philippine Affairs*) that "any decent kind of government of Filipinos by Filipinos is better than the best possible government of Filipinos by Americans," and two years later he signed a manifesto calling for Philippine independence as soon as practicable. He also served as minister to Greece and Montenegro (1912–13).

Schurman's most important diplomatic post was as minister to China (June 1921 to May 1925). It was a period of almost constant civil war, marked by struggles among rival warlords. The United States might conceivably have won friends and influenced events if it had followed the lead of Germany and the Soviet Union in renouncing extraterritorial privileges for its citizens, but a powerful business lobby wanted no change. Schurman temporized, speaking for an eventual end to extraterritoriality and proposing meanwhile a compromise of mixed foreign-Chinese tribunals. He carried out the directives of the Harding administration in threatening the Chinese government after the murder of an American businessman by Chinese soldiers in 1922. The American community in China sometimes urged him to be even firmer, but for the most part they heartily applauded him for his energetic tours of American consulates and his demand for internal political stability above every other consideration. The judgment of historians is less kind. Schurman did nothing to combat the tendency toward drift in America's China policy, nor did he understand the real forces at work there. "Communism," he wrote to Coolidge, "is wholly alien to Chinese life and sentiment and institutions."

In Germany, where he served as ambassador from June 1925 to January 1930, Schurman was even more of a helpless bystander. His appointment was initially greeted by hostility inside Germany because of his vigorous support of World War I. But Schurman spoke German well, and after the war he had been a leading spirit in raising $500,000 for the University of Heidelberg and had urged that Germany be admitted to the League of Nations. During his ambassadorship he became genuinely popular with the centrist political elements which, however, were rapidly losing ground inside Germany. Foreseeing the downfall of Weimar, Schurman nonetheless hoped for the best from Hitler.

Schurman was still a vigorous man when he retired from his diplomatic career at the age of seventy-six. He spent the following year, 1931–32, lecturing on international relations at the California Institute of Technology. Thereafter he traveled frequently all over the globe, maintaining a residence in Bedford Hills, N. Y. After a period of failing health, he died of a heart attack in Memorial Hospital, New York City. He was buried in the cemetery of St. Matthew's Church, Bedford, N. Y.

[There is no biography or autobiography of Schurman except for a Ph.D. thesis by Eugene Hotchkiss 3rd, "Jacob Gould Schurman and the Cornell Tradition" (Cornell, 1960), which throws some light on his early life. Good obituaries are in the *N. Y. Times*, Aug. 13, 1942, and (by Carl Becker) in the Am. Philosophical Soc. *Year Book*, 1942. The invaluable, central source on Schurman's Cornell period and his academic personality is Morris Bishop, *A Hist. of Cornell* (1962). Schurman's papers are at Cornell; other letters by him are scattered through a number of university archives. Andrew D. White, *Autobiog.* (1905), I, 440–41, and Waterman T. Hewett, *Cornell Univ.: A Hist.* (1905), II, 68–69, 74–75, contain important facts and impressions about Schurman. Schurman's *A Generation of Cornell, 1868–1898* (1898), is an especially dependable guide concerning events not involving his own rise to the presidency. His later writings on the critical philosophy are: "Kant's Critical Problem," *Philosophical Rev.*, Mar. 1893, and "The Genesis of the Critical Philosophy," *ibid.*, Jan., Mar., May 1898. On his contribution to the evolutionary debate, see William F. Quillian, Jr., "Evolution and Moral Theory in America," in Stow Persons, ed., *Evolutionary Thought in America* (1950). On Schurman and the Cornell school of idealism, see Herbert W. Schneider, *A Hist. of Am. Philosophy* (1946), pp. 469–71. For background on Schurman's diplomatic career, see W. Cameron Forbes, *The Philippine Islands* (1928), I, 118–22; Akira Iriye, *After Imperialism* (1965), especially pp. 29, 48, and Iriye's *Across the Pacific* (1967), especially p. 149; and Charles Dailey, "Dr. Schurman's Departure," *China Weekly Rev.*, Aug. 2, 1924.]

LAURENCE VEYSEY

SCOTT, JAMES BROWN (June 3, 1866– June 25, 1943), international lawyer and foundation executive, was born in Kincardine, Bruce County, Ontario, Canada, the last of five children and second son of John and Jeannette (Brown) Scott. Both parents had emigrated from Scotland to New York in the 1840's, moving to Canada in 1854, a year after their marriage. Scott's father, a stonecutter, was a devout Presbyterian and a harsh disciplinarian; his mother, however, encouraged a spirit of independence in her children. In 1876 the family settled in Philadelphia, where James graduated from the Central High School (1887). He then entered Harvard, from which he received the A.B. degree, summa cum laude, in 1890 and an A.M. in 1891. After studying international law at Harvard and at the universities of Berlin, Heidelberg, and Paris, he earned the degree of Doctor of Civil and Canon Laws from Heidelberg in 1894.

Scott's health had suffered in Europe, and in 1894, attracted by the California climate, he opened a law office in Los Angeles. Two years later he organized the Los Angeles Law School (later incorporated into the University of Southern California) and served as its dean until 1899. In that year he was called to the University of Illinois as dean of its College of Law, and in 1903 he became professor of law at Columbia University. His *Cases on International Law* (1902 and many subsequent editions) firmly established his reputation in this field.

Late in 1905, learning that the Solicitor (the chief legal officer) of the State Department had resigned, the twenty-nine-year-old Scott wrote to Secretary of State Elihu Root [Supp. 2] applying for the post. He was hired the next year after a single interview. Scott accompanied the American delegation to the Second Hague Peace Conference and subsequently prepared a massive two-volume text and documents, *The Hague Peace Conferences of 1899 and 1907* (1909). He also participated in discussions which resulted in the formation in 1906 of the American Society of International Law, of which Root was the first president. Dedicated to the idea of an international legal system, Scott devoted considerable energy to the society, serving as its secretary (1906–24), as founder and editor of its publication, the *American Journal of International Law* (1907–24), and as president (1929–39). He and Root were also associated in the establishment of the Carnegie Endowment for International Peace in 1910. Scott resigned his State Department post in March 1911 to become the Endowment's permanent secretary and the director of its Division of International Law, positions he held until 1940. Under his direction the division sought to develop international law through a vast program of publications, including collections of documents and of the writings of early legal scholars. Scott

edited and wrote many of these, and as secretary he recommended that the Endowment make grants to societies engaged in similar activities throughout the world.

Scott's theories of international law were influenced by the sixteenth-century Spanish theological jurist Francisco de Vitoria, who emphasized morality in international relations, and by the seventeenth-century Dutch jurist Hugo Grotius, who argued that nations like men are governed by natural law, and that a general code acceptable to most governments can be drafted. As a result of his studies Scott developed an almost mystical belief that warfare should give way to legal principles and practices. No Utopian, he realized that international law could only function when governments were ready to accept its rules, and he thus placed his faith in education. He endorsed the principle of conferences to achieve agreements and understandings among governments and served as a delegate or technical adviser to ten such meetings, including the Paris Peace Conference of 1919, the Washington Conference of 1921–22, and the Sixth Pan-American Conference in 1928. An advocate of arbitration and conciliation, he served on eight official commissions between 1928 and 1937 to conciliate disputes between nations.

Scott's special ideal, however, was an international court of justice. Until the outbreak of the First World War, he sought to bring into being the tribunal proposed at the Second Hague Conference, and afterward he prepared various proposals for a world organization centered around a flexible court to resolve controversies. He did not respond warmly to the Covenant of the League of Nations, feeling that it subordinated principles of justice, reflected a belief that wars should be stopped only after they began, and called for decisions after political rather than legal hearing. He did, however, welcome the provision in the Versailles Treaty for the creation of a judicial body, and he attended, as a legal adviser, the meeting at The Hague in 1920 where a committee of jurists drafted plans for the Permanent Court of International Justice.

Many other facets of Scott's life reflected his singular attachment to international law. He became deeply involved in the work of the European-based Institute of International Law, serving as its president in 1925–27 and 1928–29. He was a founder (1915) and the first president of the American Institute of International Law, modeled after its European counterpart. He was a co-founder (1923) and supporter of the Academy of International Law at The Hague. In a related area, he worked successfully to obtain an international convention in 1933 which recognized that the rights of women were equal to those of men in questions of nationality. Fluent in French, German, and Spanish, Scott lectured widely in Europe and Latin America, as well as in the United States. Over the years he continued to hold academic posts: professor of law and international law at George Washington University (1906–11), lecturer at Johns Hopkins University (1909–16), professor of international law and international relations at the Georgetown University School of Foreign Service (1921–40), and professor of international law, jurisprudence, and Roman law at the Georgetown University Law School (1933–40). He also wrote several scholarly works, but it was as a publicist and an institutional founder and administrator that he was best known.

Scott married Adele Cooper Reed on Sept. 1, 1901, in Champaign, Ill. They had no children. He enjoyed music and the arts, and once (1899) prepared an edition of Edward FitzGerald's *Rubaiyat of Omar Khayyam*. His qualities of refinement and sensitivity were apparent only to his family and close friends; others thought of him as cold and impersonal. Scott's work was widely recognized, as witness the seventeen honorary degrees he received from United States,. Canadian, Latin American, English, and European universities and ten decorations from foreign governments. In 1940 he relinquished most of his posts and retired to Anne Arundel County, Md., near Annapolis. He died of a heart attack at his home in Wardour, Md., at the age of seventy-seven. Having served in the infantry during the Spanish-American War and in the army's legal branch in World War I, he was buried in Arlington National Cemetery, Washington, D. C.

[Scott's personal papers are at Georgetown Univ.; there is much Scott correspondence also in the papers of the Carnegie Endowment for Internat. Peace at Columbia Univ. Information on his family can be found in Doris Stevens, *Paintings & Drawings of Jeannette Scott, 1864–1937* (privately printed, 1940), a volume on his sister. Details of his work are in the memorial sketches in the *Am. Jour. of Internat. Law,* Apr. 1944 (by George A. Finch) and Oct. 1943 (by Frederic R. Coudert), and in the *Am. Philosophical Soc., Year Book,* 1943 (by Philip C. Jessup). A wide variety of biographical directories yield information, notably the *Nat. Cyc. Am. Biog.,* Current Vol. C, pp. 69–70 (which contains a photograph). Also useful is the *N. Y. Times* obituary, June 27, 1943. Scott's books include: *An Internat. Court of Justice* (1916), *Peace through Justice* (1917), *James Madison's Notes of Debates in the Federal Convention of 1787 and Their Relation to a More Perfect Society of Nations* (1918), *The United States of America: A Study in Internat. Organization* (1920), *Robert Bacon, Life and Letters* (1923), *The Spanish Origin of Internat. Law: Francisco de Vitoria and His Law of*

Nations (1934), and *Law, the State, and the Internat. Community* (2 vols., 1939).]

WARREN F. KUEHL

SEARS, RICHARD DUDLEY (Oct. 26, 1861–Apr. 8, 1943), first national amateur tennis champion of the United States, was born in Boston, Mass., the eldest of three sons and second of four children of Frederick Richard Sears and Albertina Homer (Shelton) Sears, both of old New England stock. He was a direct descendant of Richard Sears, who emigrated to Plymouth, Mass., sometime before 1633. The family included a son and daughter by his father's first marriage, and it was his half brother, Frederick R. Sears, Jr., who initially interested him in tennis. In Nahant, where the family spent its summers, young Richard practiced by hitting the ball against a barn door. His mother sewed pieces of old flannel shirts around rubber balls to make tennis balls, but according to family lore he did not get to use them until Frederick had finished with them. He later recalled that his half brother, together with Dr. James Dwight—sometimes known as the "father of American tennis"—introduced the game of lawn tennis to America in 1874, though this has been disputed by historians of the sport.

Sears was educated at the private school of J. P. Hopkinson in Boston and at Harvard, from which he graduated in 1883. While still in college, in 1880, he won the first tennis challenge cup, and the following year, at Newport, R. I., he captured the first United States national championship. He also played in England, Ireland, and France, but with less success than in his own country. Here he went on to win six more singles championships (1881–87)—a feat subsequently equaled only by William A. Larned [*q.v.*] and William Tilden—and six doubles championships (1882–87), five with Dwight as his partner and one with Joseph S. Clark of Boston. Considered "brilliant but erratic players" by A. Wallis Meyers, the British tennis authority, Sears and Dwight are thought by many to have been the first to follow service to the net, though others have made this claim for earlier English players. Contemporaries said of Sears that he hit with keen accuracy and fair severity.

In 1888 Sears retired from active competition in lawn tennis because of a neck injury, thought to have been sustained when he was struck by a partner's service. A few years later he turned to court tennis, an ancient game played in a large indoor court, complete with sloping roof and flying buttresses, and in 1892, at New York City, he won the first national championship. He originated the "railroad" service, an overhead twist shot, which has since been in the repertoire of leading players of court tennis. Sears was also a prominent Boston player of squash racquets, but according to some authorities he lacked the severity to reach the top of the game.

On Nov. 24, 1891, Sears married Eleanor M. Cochrane. They had two children, Miriam and Richard Dudley. Sears edited Solomon C. F. Peille's *Lawn Tennis as a Game of Skill* (1885) and was a founder of the Tennis and Racquet Club in Boston and the Myopia Hunt Club in Wenham, Mass. In business he followed the typical upper-class Boston occupation of trustee, with offices on State Street. He died of a cerebral hemorrhage at the Massachusetts General Hospital in Boston at the age of eighty-one. His ashes were buried at Christ Church (Episcopal), in the Longwood section of Brookline, Mass. The noted Boston sportswoman Eleonora Sears was his niece.

[Samuel P. May, *The Descendants of Richard Sares (Sears) of Yarmouth, Mass., 1638–1888* (1890); Harvard College Class of 1883, *Fiftieth Anniversary Report* (1933); *N. Y. Times* obituary, Apr. 10, 1943; obituary of his wife in *Boston Herald*, Apr. 12, 1954; E. H. Brann, *Sketches of Nahant* (1911); Frank G. Mencke, *The Encyc. of Sports* (1963); John M. and C. G. Heathcote et al., "Tennis" and "Lawn Tennis" in *The Badminton Lib. of Sports and Pastimes*, vol. XVIII (1890); A. Wallis Meyers, *Lawn Tennis at Home and Abroad* (1903); Allison Danzig, *The Racquet Game* (1930).]

HAROLD KAESE

SEIBOLD, LOUIS (Oct. 10, 1863–May 10, 1945), journalist, was born in Washington, D. C., the eldest of five children (four sons and a daughter) of Louis Philip Seibold and Josephine Burrows (Dawson) Seibold. His mother was a Virginian of Scotch-Irish and English descent; his father, born in Maryland, came of a German Roman Catholic family. A Union officer during the Civil War, he afterward served for many years on the District of Columbia police force and in 1896 founded a customhouse brokerage firm.

After attending Washington public schools, young Seibold embarked on a newspaper career. He began on the *Washington Post* as an office boy and was made a reporter in 1886. Three years later he went west to cover the Ute Indian war in Colorado and stayed to work on newspapers in Denver, St. Louis, Chicago, San Francisco, and Pendleton, Oreg. About 1894 he joined the New York *World* of Joseph Pulitzer [*q.v.*], where he was to spend most of his working life. The *World* sent him to cover the fighting in Cuba during the Spanish-American War. In May 1902

he was the first reporter to reach Martinique after the great eruption of Mount Pelée.

Seibold evidently left the *World* briefly in 1902, but by 1905 was back as the newspaper's statehouse correspondent in Albany. That year he scored a celebrated coup when the state attorney general slipped him, over the weekend, a still secret official report confirming many muckraking charges of corrupt practices in the insurance industry. By setting stenographers to work around the clock, Seibold was able to copy it and get it back by 6 a.m. Monday morning; the *World* printed it on July 11, 1905. Pulitzer, who had been following a mild editorial policy on the insurance question, reacted by firing Seibold, but soon relented and sent him back to Albany, where, one of the publisher's aides observed, he stood "head and shoulders above the other correspondents . . . keen, clear, accurate."

Seibold also covered national politics, attending every national party convention from 1896 to 1920 and gaining exclusive interviews with two presidents, Taft and Wilson. After war broke out in Europe in 1914, he briefly displayed his old skill as a war correspondent. When, the following year, the American government chose to leak the "Albert papers," inadvertently left on a New York elevated train by a German diplomat, Seibold was the chosen recipient. The resulting revelations of German intrigue, published on Aug. 15, 1915, led to the recall of the German ambassador.

Seibold was close to President Wilson, and gained a reputation as a launcher of the President's trial balloons. After heading the *World*'s Washington bureau in 1916 and 1917, he accompanied Wilson on his tour of Europe at the end of World War I. He was with Wilson at Versailles and on the cross-country campaign for the League of Nations during which the President collapsed. In June 1920 Wilson's secretary, Joseph P. Tumulty, and Mrs. Wilson chose Seibold to conduct an interview designed to show that Wilson had recovered. Although the interview won Seibold a Pulitzer Prize, it was clear by the end of the 1920 campaign either that Seibold had exaggerated the President's recovery or that Wilson's health had subsequently deteriorated sharply.

Among Seibold's postwar topics were the workings of national prohibition and the rise of the Non-Partisan League in the agrarian Midwest; he wrote series on both subjects that were collected in book form. In the spring of 1921 Seibold moved from the *World* to the *New York Herald,* for which he wrote extensively on Japan, and later to the New York *Evening Post.* In his last active years he apparently did free-lance work. Like other newspapermen who remained reporters throughout their careers, Seibold made little attempt to enhance or preserve his reputation. Of his personal traits, not much is remembered beyond the fact that he never learned to use a typewriter, preferring to dictate his stories while puffing on a cigarette. His wife, Jennie L. Hopkins of Illinois, whom he had married on Apr. 6, 1891, died before 1930; their only child, Martin, met an accidental death in 1918. Louis Seibold died of congestive heart failure at the age of eighty-one at the home of his brother George in Washington, D. C. A Baptist minister conducted his funeral services, and he was buried in Washington's Rock Creek Cemetery.

[Material on Seibold is thin and scattered. The fullest biographical listing is in the *Nat. Cyc. Am. Biog.*, Current Vol. B, p. 120. For obituaries see *N. Y. Times, N. Y. Herald Tribune,* and *Washington Post,* May 11, 1945; see also N. Y. *World,* May 30, 1921. Two letters to Seibold from Wilson appear in Ray Stannard Baker, *Woodrow Wilson: Life and Letters,* vol. VII (1935). Anecdotes can be found in James W. Barrett, *Joseph Pulitzer and His World* (1941); Mark Sullivan, *Our Times,* vol. VI (1935); and Samuel Hopkins Adams, *Incredible Era* (1939). See also Charles H. Brown, *The Correspondents' War* (1967); James E. Pollard, *The Presidents and the Press* (1947); and W. A. Swanberg, *Pulitzer* (1967). Death record from D. C. Dept. of Public Health. The author is indebted to Louis M. Starr for notes from the Joseph Pulitzer collection, Columbia Univ.; to Richard Dorsey for preliminary research; and to Sue Shivers of the D. C. Public Lib. and to Seibold's nephews, Louis Seibold and Louis Brown, for information on his family.]

JAMES BOYLAN

SETCHELL, WILLIAM ALBERT (Apr. 15, 1864–Apr. 5, 1943), botanist, authority on marine algae, was born in Norwich, Conn., the second child and first son among the ten children of George Case Setchell, at first a coffee and spice mill worker and later a manufacturer, and Mary Ann (Davis) Setchell. His father's ancestors had emigrated from England in the late eighteenth century; his mother had come to the United States as a child with her English-Welsh parents.

Setchell early showed a strong interest in natural history, especially botany. The gift of a copy of *Familiar Lectures on Botany,* by Almira Hart Lincoln Phelps [*q.v.*], helped him determine the names of many of the local plants. This experience at identification foreshadowed his later work in systematics, a branch of botany in which he made great contributions. A botany course he took while attending the Norwich Free Academy further stirred his interest. With another local plant enthusiast, George R. Case, he published his first paper (privately printed) in 1883, a twelve-page catalogue of the wild plants growing

in Norwich and vicinity. Around 1880 he also made the first of a series of visits to the seashore in eastern Connecticut to collect seaweeds, the field of his later major research.

At Yale, which Setchell entered in 1883, there was as yet little instruction in botany, particularly for someone taking, as he did, the classical course. His discovery, however, of the fern *Asplenium montanum* growing in Connecticut, far east of its usual habitat, had attracted the notice of Prof. Daniel Cady Eaton [*q.v.*] of Yale, an authority on ferns, who offered Setchell a study table in his home and the use of his library and herbarium. Eaton sent him on, after he took his B.A. in 1887, to Prof. William G. Farlow [*q.v.*] at Harvard, where Setchell received the Ph.D. in 1890 with a thesis on the New England kelp *Saccorhiza dermatodea.* Acquaintance with other enthusiastic students of seaweed, notably Isaac Holden and Frank S. Collins [*q.v.*], intensified Setchell's interest in marine algae, and in 1895 the three issued the first group of a series of mounted and named specimens, the *Phycotheca Boreali-Americana,* that ultimately (1919) reached fifty-one fascicles of thirty-five to fifty numbers each, distributed to subscribers throughout the world.

Setchell returned to Yale as assistant (1891) and instructor (1892–95) in biology. For five years (1890–95) he spent his summers at Woods Hole, Mass., as supervisor of the work in marine botany at the Marine Biological Laboratory. In 1895 he was called to the University of California at Berkeley as professor of botany and chairman of the department, a position he held until his retirement in 1934.

At the time when Setchell arrived in California, the rich marine algal flora of the Pacific Coast remained virtually unexplored. This became the major subject of his research for more than four decades, during much of the time in collaboration with Nathaniel L. Gardner. He summed up his findings in *The Marine Algae of the Pacific Coast of North America,* of which three parts—on the blue-green, green, and brown algae—had been published (with Gardner as co-author, 1919–25) before his death. These long remained basic guides to the classification and characterization of orders, families, genera, and species. Setchell's interests, however, went beyond orderly classification to include the causes of geographic distribution of algae, particularly as affected by temperature. He established the critical temperature intervals governing the zone of distribution of various algae species, and made similar studies, as well, of aquatic seed plants, especially eelgrass, and land plants.

A visit to the Samoan Islands in 1920 under

the auspices of the Carnegie Institution of Washington initiated one of Setchell's most significant investigations, into the role of algae in the formation of coral reefs. Charles Darwin and many of his followers had credited the formation of reefs to the corals themselves. J. Stanley Gardiner, around the turn of the century, took the novel position that certain kinds of coralline algae, the nullipores, were necessary for coral-reef formation, since corals of themselves have no powers of coherence or adherence sufficient to form an enduring framework. To Setchell must go the credit for bringing together the facts, many supplied from his own investigations, in support of Gardiner's concept, which is generally accepted today.

Broad in his interests, Setchell as a sideline at Harvard had studied the smut fungus genus *Doassansia*. He later published two important papers on this genus and directed the work of several students in mycology. Setchell also initiated the important work on the cytogenetics and taxonomy of the tobacco plant, *Nicotiana,* which was carried on for a long time at the University of California by his former students Thomas H. Goodspeed and Roy E. Clausen and their assistants.

Setchell was largely responsible for building his department at Berkeley into one of the world's major botanical centers. He also served as director of the university's Botanical Garden and, for many years, as botanist of the California Agricultural Experiment Station. He gave particular attention to the development of the University Herbarium, purchased and gave to the university many rare books, and left it his own outstanding collection of algological books and pamphlets. Setchell contributed, as well, to the broader development of the University of California during the early presidency of Benjamin Ide Wheeler [*q.v.*]. Through service on administrative and faculty committees, he was (in the words of Goodspeed) "one of those who interpreted the academic atmosphere and traditions of Harvard and Yale in terms of Western ideals and aspirations," and he helped formulate the university's pioneering system of student self-government.

A large man of distinguished appearance, Setchell loved people and good conversation. He was for many years an active member of the Bohemian Club of San Francisco. He was especially happy when surrounded by the young, to whom he enjoyed acting as adviser and host. A generous man, he often gave timely financial help to needy students or young colleagues.

On Dec. 15, 1920, Setchell married Mrs. Clara Ball (Pearson) Caldwell, of Edgewood, R. I.

They had no children, and during the next twelve years Mrs. Setchell accompanied her husband on his scientific journeys, principally in the Pacific region, and helped him in his research in the laboratory. She died in 1934. Setchell had no religious affiliation. For some years he had suffered from myocarditis; he died of internal hemorrhages at his apartment in Berkeley a few days before his seventy-ninth birthday. His ashes were buried in Swan Point Cemetery, Providence, R. I. Among his honors were election to the American Philosophical Society and the National Academy of Sciences (both in 1919) and to several distinguished societies abroad.

[Notebooks of autobiographical data in Univ. of Calif. Herbarium; biography by T. H. Goodspeed in *Essays in Geobotany in Honor of William Albert Setchell* (1936); obituary articles and memoirs by: Charles B. Lipman in *Science,* May 21, 1943; Herbert L. Mason in *Madroño,* July 1943 (an excellent statement of Setchell's personal qualities); Lincoln Constance in Wash. Acad. of Sci., *Jour.,* Sept. 15, 1943; Francis Drouet in *Am. Midland Naturalist,* Nov. 1943; Roy E. Clausen, Lee Bonar, and H. M. Evans in Univ. of Calif., *In Memoriam,* 1943; W. J. V. Osterhout in Am. Philosophical Soc., *Year Book,* 1943; Douglas H. Campbell in Nat. Acad. Sci., *Biog. Memoirs,* vol. XXIII (1943). Other sources: Yale Univ., *Obituary Record of Graduates,* 1942–43; C. R. Ball, "Dr. Setchell and Alaska Willows," *Madroño,* July 1940; death record (Calif. Dept. of Public Health); information from friends and colleagues; personal recollections. A charcoal sketch of Setchell which hangs in the Faculty Club at Berkeley is reproduced in the references by Goodspeed and Campbell cited above, each of which also includes a list of his publications.]

GEORGE F. PAPENFUSS

SHEAR, THEODORE LESLIE (Aug. 11, 1880–July 3, 1945), classical archaeologist, was born in New London, N. H., his parents' summer home. He was the youngest of three sons and third of four children of Theodore R. Shear, a lawyer, and Mary Louise (Quackenbos) Shear, natives, respectively, of Albany and New York City. Growing up in New York, Shear attended the Halsey Collegiate School and New York University, from which he received an A.B. degree in 1900 and an A.M. degree in 1903. Meanwhile, in 1901, he had begun graduate work at the Johns Hopkins University, where he wrote a doctoral dissertation under the direction of Prof. Basil L. Gildersleeve [*q.v.*]—published in 1906 as *The Influence of Plato on St. Basil*—and received the Ph.D. degree in 1904. He next spent a year as a member of the American School of Classical Studies at Athens and, in order to round out his training, a year at the University of Bonn, where he studied chiefly under Prof. Georg Loeschcke.

On his return in 1906 Shear was appointed an instructor in Greek and Latin at Barnard

College. In 1910 he moved to Columbia University as associate in classical philology and thereafter spent much of his time in archaeological excavation. In 1920 he was appointed lecturer in the department of art and archaeology at Princeton, becoming professor of classical archaeology in 1928; from 1927 onward he served also as curator of classical art in the university's art museum.

Shear is especially remembered for his direction of large-scale excavations on various sites in ancient Greece. During the years 1911–13 he was engaged in the reconnaissance of southwestern Anatolia, with particular emphasis on ancient Cnidus and Loryma, where he made discoveries of sculpture and inscriptions. In 1914 he joined a Princeton expedition directed by Howard Crosby Butler [q.v.] to Sardis, the capital of ancient Lydia and the seat of King Croesus. The work of the expedition was interrupted by World War I and was eventually terminated by the Graeco-Turkish War of 1922–23. From Butler, Shear learned how to organize and conduct a major excavation; after Butler's death in 1922, he assumed charge of the operation. Their most impressive work was the clearance of the huge Temple of Artemis, previously known only from two protruding columns. Extensive excavations were also carried out in the ancient cemeteries. Subsequently Shear published detailed studies of a hoard of thirty gold staters (coins), the marble head of a horse, a series of gaily painted architectural terracottas, and a Roman chamber tomb.

His next site was Corinth, where he worked intensively from 1925 to 1931. Four campaigns were devoted to the clearance of the theatre, one of the largest and most interesting in Greece. The building had been discovered in 1896 and had been partially explored in subsequent soundings, but earlier excavators had been deterred by the cost of moving vast quantities of earth. This was done by Shear at his own expense. He then took up the exploration of the North Cemetery in the plain below ancient Corinth. Here again determination, breadth of vision, and the liberal use of private means enabled him to carry to completion a project that had been begun by others long before. Some 530 graves were systematically examined, ranging in date from the Middle Bronze Age into the Roman period. The wealth of finds, combined with meticulous observation on the part of the excavators, have shed much light on Greek burial customs and on the history of Greek ceramics. Shear also carried out a salvage operation on a villa of the Roman period on the outskirts of ancient Corinth. This rambling structure was distinguished by mosaic floors with mythological and idyllic scenes, one of the best-preserved and artistically most pleasing series of mosaics known from Greece.

His proven competence in the conduct of large excavations made Shear the logical choice as field director for the exploration of the Agora, the marketplace or civic center of ancient Athens, that was begun in 1931 by the American School of Classical Studies with financial support from John D. Rockefeller, Jr., and the Rockefeller Foundation. The first step in this undertaking was the acquisition of over 350 pieces of property occupied by some 5,000 persons in the middle of the modern capital. Then followed the removal of an overburden of earth and rubble ranging in depth from five to thirty-five feet. This operation brought to light the principal civic buildings that had served the ancient city-state, greatly enriching our knowledge of Athenian life from the Neolithic period to the Turkish. Shear directed the excavations through ten annual campaigns until work was interrupted by World War II in 1940. His death in 1945 prevented him from seeing the completion of the enterprise in the postwar years, but its success was assured by the warm relations he had established with the Greek people and authorities, by his genius for the organization and recording of field work, and by his ability to assemble a team of devoted assistants.

Although Shear left scholarly publication of his archaeological findings for the most part to others, he brought his work to wide attention through popular articles and lectures. These are marked by a fresh and lucid style; they glow with a buoyant and infectious enthusiasm for the classical world. His treatment of archaeological subjects was invariably enriched by a full and sensitive acquaintance with the ancient authors. Modern Greece and its people were as dear to him as the ancients, and the last years of his life were devoted to efforts to ameliorate conditions brought about by Nazi occupation of the country during World War II.

Shear was elected to membership in the American Philosophical Society and the American Academy of Arts and Sciences. In religion he was an Episcopalian. He married Nora Cornelia Jenkins, daughter of an American dentist in Dresden, Germany, on June 29, 1907. She accompanied him on his archaeological expeditions and illustrated his publications with watercolors. Following her death in 1927, he married, on Feb. 12, 1931, Josephine Platner, a trained classical scholar who worked closely with him in his excavations at Corinth and Athens. Shear had a daughter, Chloe Louise, by his first marriage and a son, Theodore Leslie, by his second. He died of a coronary thrombosis in 1945 at his summer home in Newbury, N. H., on Lake Sunapee, and was buried in the Old Cemetery at Princeton, N. J. Theodore Leslie Shear, Jr., followed his father's career in classical archaeology and assumed direction of excavations in the Athenian Agora in 1968.

[A complete bibliography of Shear's publications is given in a commemorative volume of the journal *Hesperia* (Supp. VIII, 1949, pp. vii–xi) ; a photograph of Shear appears as the frontispiece. For his work at Corinth, see two volumes in the reports of the Corinth excavations: Richard Stillwell, *The Theatre* (1952), and Carl W. Blegen, Hazel Palmer, and Rodney S. Young, *The North Cemetery* (1964). The results of the excavations in the Athenian Agora are in process of publication by the Am. School of Classical Studies at Athens ; for a brief comprehensive account see Homer A. Thompson et al., *The Athenian Agora: A Guide to the Excavation and Museum* (1962). Information on certain points was supplied by relatives of Shear, by the registrars of Columbia and Princeton, and by the N. H. Dept. of Health and Welfare. See also: memoir by Edward Capps in Am. Philosophical Soc., *Year Book,* 1945 ; *Who Was Who in America,* vol. II (1950) ; and *Nat. Cyc. Am. Biog.,* XLII, 208–09.]

HOMER A. THOMPSON

SHEPPARD, JOHN MORRIS (May 28, 1875–Apr. 9, 1941), Congressman and Senator from Texas, was born near Wheatville, Texas, the eldest of seven children of Margaret Alice (Eddins) and John Levi Sheppard, and a descendant of Robert Sheppard, who emigrated in the 1640's from England to Surrey County, Va. His father, a native of Alabama, was a lawyer who served in Texas as a state judge (1888–96) and as Congressman from 1899 to his death in 1902; he was a progressive Democrat and a supporter of Gov. James S. Hogg [*q.v.*]. Young Sheppard, after attending public schools in several Texas cities, worked as a night watchman to help pay his way through the University of Texas, from which he received the degrees of B.A. in 1895 and LL.B. in 1897. He took a Master of Laws degree at Yale University in 1898, and then practiced for one year in Pittsburg, Texas, before moving to Texarkana, his home for the rest of his life. On Dec. 1, 1909, he married Lucile Sanderson of Texarkana, by whom he had three daughters, Janet, Susan, and Lucile.

In 1902, at the age of twenty-seven, Morris Sheppard was elected to fill his father's unexpired Congressional term, the beginning of a long Congressional career. Sheppard became known for his oratorical ability and his sharp criticism of the Republican party. As a Congressman he favored federal insurance of bank deposits and a federal income tax. He also introduced legislation which would have empowered the Interstate Commerce Commission to fix railway rates on its own initiative, and a bill prohibiting the issuance of federal liquor licenses in local option communities. In 1913, when Joseph Weldon Bailey [Supp. 1] stepped down from his seat in the United States Senate, Sheppard was chosen by the Texas legislature to succeed him. He remained in the Senate until his death.

In the Senate, Sheppard, an ardent Wilsonian, espoused a broad range of progressive measures including woman suffrage, child labor laws, improved antitrust legislation, and tariff reform. He became best known as the author of the Eighteenth Amendment, the "father of national prohibition." An active Methodist and an unswerving teetotaler, he viewed prohibition as a moral necessity and continued to preach its virtues long after it had been repealed. Sheppard also supported President Wilson's foreign policies. During the Mexican civil war he urged greater protection of the Texas border, but on the question of intervention in Mexico he backed Wilson's policy of "watchful waiting." An advocate of preparedness, he early spoke in favor of the development of military aviation. After World War I, he became a committed and consistent champion of the League of Nations. Although he usually remained aloof from Texas politics, Sheppard's endorsement of prohibition, woman suffrage, and Wilson's moderate Mexican policies won him the enmity of conservative state leaders like Bailey, Gov. James E. Ferguson [Supp. 3], and former governor O. B. Colquitt. Yet with dry support, Sheppard never had difficulty winning reelection.

During the postwar decades Sheppard continued to favor "humanizing" legislation. He was the Senate sponsor of the Sheppard-Towner Act, passed in 1921, which provided federal aid to the states for maternal and infant health care. As an original member of the "farm bloc," he introduced a bill in 1922 authorizing a study of the practicability of federal crop insurance. He often aligned himself with progressives like Robert M. La Follette[*q.v.*], George W. Norris [Supp. 3], and William E. Borah [Supp. 2], but he remained a loyal Democrat, even supporting the presidential candidacy of Alfred E. Smith [Supp. 3] in 1928, an act which threatened his position among prohibition forces. In the 1930's Sheppard backed most of the economic and social measures of President Franklin D. Roosevelt. He himself sponsored the Federal Credit Union Act of 1934 which gave workers access to low-interest credit. A firm believer in economic individualism and the deconcentration of industrial power, Sheppard lauded the New Deal's efforts to aid small businessmen, farmers, and homeowners. He was critical of the Supreme Court for invalidating important New Deal legislation and endorsed Roosevelt's "court-packing" proposal of 1937. His only significant difference with the administration came when he chaired a special Senate Investigating Committee on Campaign Expenditures which discovered political interference by the Works Progress Administration in the 1938 elections. The committee's report led to passage of the Hatch Act of 1939 severely restricting such activity.

With the outbreak of war in Europe in 1939, Sheppard as chairman of the Senate Committee on Military Affairs worked to strengthen American military preparedness. In 1941, shortly after leading the floor fight in the Senate for passage of the Burke-Wadsworth Selective Service Act, the nation's first peacetime compulsory military training law, Sheppard suffered a cerebral hemorrhage and died at Walter Reed Hospital in Washington, D. C. He was buried in Hillcrest Cemetery, Texarkana. Besides his Methodist affiliations, Sheppard was active in fraternal organizations, including the Elks, Knights of Pythias, Red Men, Odd Fellows, and Masons; for almost a half century he was national treasurer of the Woodmen of the World Life Insurance Society.

[Sheppard Papers, Univ. of Texas Lib.; Escal F. Duke, "Political Career of Morris Sheppard, 1875–1941" (Ph.D. dissertation, Univ. of Texas, 1958); Lucile Sheppard Keyes, "Morris Sheppard" (1950), typescript in Archives, Univ. of Texas Lib.; *Memorial Services Held in the House of Representatives and Senate . . . in Eulogy of Morris Sheppard* (77 Cong., 1 Sess., 1943). See also J. Stanley Lemons, "The Sheppard-Towner Act: Progressivism in the 1920's," *Jour. Am. Hist.*, Mar. 1969.]

ESCAL F. DUKE

SILOTI, ALEXANDER ILYITCH (Oct. 10, 1863–Dec. 8, 1945), pianist and conductor, was born on his father's estate near Kharkov, Russia, the fourth in a family of five sons and two daughters. His father, Ilya Matvey Siloti, a member of the nobility, traced his surname to an early Italian immigrant to Russia. His mother, Vera (Rachmaninoff) Siloti, was an aunt of the composer Sergei Rachmaninoff [Supp. 3]. Both parents were musically gifted. Siloti's maternal grandfather, Arkadi Rachmaninoff, a competent pianist, had studied with the Irish composer-pianist John Field, who lived in Russia for many years.

Siloti revealed a musical aptitude at an early age and was enrolled in the Moscow Conservatory in 1876. He studied piano with Nikolai Rubinstein, the founder of the conservatory, whose method of teaching and sympathetic spirit deeply impressed Siloti, and with Nikolai Zverev, who was also Siloti's guardian. The composer Tchaikovsky taught him theory and composition. The musical circle in Moscow at the time included Alexander Borodin, Cesar Cui, Anton Rubinstein, Mily Balakirev, Anton Arensky and Ferruccio Busoni, all of whom had some influence on Siloti, who met them at Zverev's home. He graduated in 1881 as a gold medal winner.

While still a student in the conservatory, Siloti had made his first appearance as soloist with an orchestra, in Moscow in 1880. After graduating, he went to Germany, where a concert he gave in Leipzig in 1883 brought him considerable acclaim. From 1883 to 1886 he studied at Weimar with Franz Liszt. This was the formative experience of Siloti's life, for not only did he regard Liszt as an incomparably great pianist—as far above Anton Rubinstein as the latter was above others —but he came to have a close personal relationship with Liszt, who gave him private lessons; he was regarded as one of Liszt's finest pupils. Throughout his career Siloti sought to perpetuate the spirit of Liszt's playing. Siloti returned to Russia in 1887 to teach at the Moscow Conservatory, where he helped guide the musical training of his cousin Sergei Rachmaninoff. A disagreement with the new director of the conservatory led Siloti to resign in 1890 and turn to a concert career.

He quickly gained renown as one of the great virtuosos in the era of the grand manner of piano playing. Tall, slender, and animated, he had immense hands which sometimes enabled him to employ unusual fingering. His piano style has been described as "a combination of vitality and refinement, backed by a big technique" (Schonberg, p. 306). He toured England and America in 1898–99, receiving critical acclaim. His programs often featured Rachmaninoff's works, especially the Prelude in C-sharp Minor.

Siloti also gained a reputation as a conductor. He led the Moscow Philharmonic Orchestra, 1901–02, and from 1903 to 1917 he conducted and organized in St. Petersburg what came to be called the Siloti Concerts. These became immensely popular and soon eclipsed the academicism of the Imperial Russian Musical Society. Siloti was remarkably cordial to contemporary music and musicians. Among the composers he invited to perform or to introduce their newest works were Rimsky-Korsakov, Glazunov, Scriabin, Sibelius, and Schoenberg. He also gave first performances of new works by Stravinsky, Prokofieff, Debussy, Ravel, Richard Strauss, Elgar, Delius, de Falla, and Enesco.

In 1919, during the political upheaval following the Russian Revolution, Siloti left his post as director of the Marinsky Opera in St. Petersburg and fled the country. After living in England and Belgium, he came to the United States in 1922. Two years later he became a member of the faculty of the Juilliard Graduate School of Music in New York City, and from then until his retirement in 1942 he devoted his principal energies to teaching and to music editing. His arrangements include Bach's Concerto in D for piano, violin, flute, and strings; Vivaldi's Concerto in D Minor for small orchestra; and special editions of piano pieces. Siloti continued to make concert appearances, performing over the years with the nation's most prominent symphony orchestras. In 1929, at the age of sixty-six, he gave a memorable performance in Carnegie Hall, playing three major works—Tchaikovsky's Concerto in B-flat Minor, Beethoven's *Emperor* Concerto, and Liszt's *Totentanz* or *Danse Macabre*—with a virtuosity and youthful spirit that evoked critical praise.

On Feb. 6, 1887, Siloti had married Vera Tretyakova, wealthy daughter of Pavel Tretyakov, art collector and founder of the famous Tretyakov Gallery in Moscow. They had five children: Alexander, Levko, Vera, Oxana, and Kyriena. Siloti in his later years was a genial, kindly man who handled his pupils with sympathy and insight. He was a member of the Greek Orthodox Church. He died at his New York City apartment, after a long illness, at the age of eighty-two.

[Siloti's *My Memories of Liszt* (n.d.) is an important source on his early training. There are useful references to Siloti in Harold C. Schonberg, *The Great Pianists* (1963); in the biographies of Rachmaninoff by John Culshaw (1949) and Sergei Bertensson and Jay Leyda (1956); and in Nicolas Slonimsky, *Music Since 1900* (3rd ed., 1949). See also articles by Siloti in *Etude*, July, Aug. 1920, and May 1922; and articles about him, *ibid.*, Apr. 1922 (p. 239) and July 1946 (by Sergei Bertensson). Biographical sketches appear in Oscar Thompson, ed., *The Internat. Cyc. of Music and Musicians* (4th ed., 1946); and Eric Blom, ed., *Grove's Dict. of Music and Musicians* (5th ed., 1954). The archives of the Juilliard School contain unclassified materials. The *N. Y. Times* published reviews of his recitals from 1922 to 1929 and an obituary, Dec. 10, 1945. No phonograph records of Siloti's playing are known to exist.]

OLGA LLANO KUEHL

SIMMONS, WILLIAM JOSEPH (May 6, 1880–May 18, 1945), founder of the twentieth-century Ku Klux Klan, was born at Harpersville in Shelby County, Ala., one of eight children of Calvin Henry Simmons and Lavonia (David) Simmons. His father was a physician, farm owner, and sometime mill operator in Shelby and Talladega counties. Simmons's aspirations for a medical career were disrupted in his early teens by his father's death. In 1898, after brief and uneventful service in an Alabama volunteer regiment during the Spanish-American War, he enrolled in Southern University at Birmingham, but after a few months decided to enter the ministry in the Methodist Episcopal Church, South. Licensed to preach at the age of nineteen, he spent the next thirteen years riding the circuit in rural districts in Alabama and northern Florida. In 1912, when he was assigned to another "backwoods" district instead of the church of his own he had demanded, he quarreled with his bishop, and the Alabama Methodist Conference suspended his ministerial license.

Simmons then moved to Atlanta, Ga., where he became a representative for various fraternal orders, particularly the Woodmen of the World, in which he quickly rose to the rank of colonel (district manager). This was a boom era for adult fraternal orders in America, and he was soon earning a handsome personal income. In 1915, while hospitalized in Atlanta as a result of an automobile accident, he sketched plans for his most ambitious fraternal project—a new order to be called the Knights of the Ku Klux Klan. His father had been an officer in the original Ku Klux Klan in Alabama during the years after the Civil War. Like many other Southern children, Simmons had heard ghostly tales of this secret society, whose acts of terrorism and intimidation were credited with defeating the Radical Republican scheme for black dominance of the South, and the romantic image seems to have taken a special hold on his imagination. In the fall of 1915, with thirty-three Atlanta acquaintances he had enlisted, he formally "revived" the Klan in ceremonies atop nearby Stone Mountain on Thanksgiving night. Shrewdly timing his publicity to coincide with the Atlanta opening of *The Birth of a Nation*, D. W. Griffith's overtly racist and pro-Klan motion picture, Simmons soon signed up more than a hundred members. In the summer of 1916 the state of Georgia granted a permanent corporate charter for the "Invisible Empire, Knights of the Ku Klux Klan, Inc.," officially described as a "patriotic, military, benevolent, ritualistic, social and fraternal order."

Simmons was likable and well meaning, and he made an impressive personal appearance. A two-hundred-pound six-footer who wore pince-nez spectacles, he had gray eyes, light red hair, a prominent nose, square chin, and a powerful speaking voice with which he indulged his penchant for florid oratory. But despite his earlier success as a fraternal organizer, he evidently had little notion of what his new Klan's purpose should be. By 1920 it numbered no more than 6,000 members concentrated in Atlanta, Birmingham, Mobile, and a few other cities of the Deep South.

In June of that year Simmons secured the sales talent his Klan had been lacking when he formed a contract with the Atlanta-based Southern Publicity Association, run by Edward Young Clarke and Elizabeth Tyler, two talented, if unscrupulous, promoters. Realizing the opportunities inherent in the tense political and social climate of the post-World War I years, Clarke and Tyler transformed the rather nebulous principles of Simmons's Klan into a militant creed of "100 percent Americanism." The Klan thus became a secret superpatriotic society, an intractable foe of Roman Catholics, Jews, political radicals, "uppity" Negroes, and foreign immigrants, as well as of dishonest politicians, bootleggers, libertines, and modernist theologians. It quickly spread through the South and into every part of the nation, enrolling several hundred thousand members in a period of eight or nine months and committing numerous acts of terrorism. This violence prompted a Congressional investigation in October 1921, but the hearings were rambling and inconclusive. Simmons, as "Imperial Wizard," testified at length, eloquently and sometimes tearfully maintaining that the Klan was a law-abiding organization which worked in behalf of patriotism, Protestant religion, and racial harmony.

Thereafter, while the Klan continued to grow at an astonishing rate and ultimately enrolled more than two million members, Simmons's power and influence within it dwindled steadily. While accumulating a sizable personal fortune from the Klan, mainly from the two dollars he received of each ten-dollar initiation fee, he relinquished more and more executive authority to the money-hungry Clarke. In the fall of 1922 Simmons and Clarke faced a revolt led by national secretary Hiram W. Evans of Texas, David C. Stephenson of Indiana, and several other state leaders who wanted to make the Klan a well-organized, well-financed national political organization. Yielding to their pressure, at the Klan's first national convention, held that year in Atlanta, Simmons handed over the Imperial Wizardship to Evans and assumed the essentially powerless title of "Emperor."

The new regime soon severed all ties with Clarke and the Southern Publicity Association, and thereby effectively isolated Simmons, who tried to fight back by creating first a women's counterpart to the Klan and then a second degree for Klansmen who would owe allegiance only to him. Evans and his associates blocked both moves by court action and by forming the Women of the Ku Klux Klan. Simmons countered with suits of his own. The resulting legal tangle and power struggle were not resolved until early 1924, when the Klan settled with Simmons for $90,000 in cash plus the deed to the "Imperial Palace," a large residence on Peachtree Road in Atlanta owned by the Klan and occupied by Simmons. In exchange Simmons resigned from the organization and gave up all copyrights on Klan literature and paraphernalia.

Simmons subsequently tried to organize two new patriotic and white-supremacy orders, first the Knights of the Flaming Sword and then the Caucasian Crusade. Neither project succeeded, but the hapless Simmons at least had the satisfaction of seeing the Ku Klux Klan fall apart. Wracked by internal disorders and scandals, and thwarted by public hostility, it ended the decade with fewer than 100,000 members.

Little is known of Simmons's life after the 1920's. He continued to reside in Atlanta, supporting himself and his family on the remainder of his Klan settlement plus occasional lecture fees. Much of the time he seems to have been in poor health. In the spring of 1941, now almost forgotten, he entered the Veterans Administration Hospital in Atlanta, where he died four years later of heart disease. He was survived by his wife, Bessie, and one son, Kirk. The man who had brought into existence the mightiest secret society in American history was buried in simple ceremonies at Luverne, Ala.

[There is no adequate biographical study of Simmons, nor is there likely to be in view of the absence of personal papers and of substantial information on his life after he left the Klan. The obituary notices in the *Atlanta Constitution* and *Atlanta Jour.*, May 21, 1945, are of some use. For his career to the time he left the Klan, the most reliable information is in three articles by William G. Shepherd, written after extensive interviews with Simmons, in *Collier's*, July 14, 21, and 28, 1928. Also helpful is Charles O. Jackson, "William J. Simmons: A Career in Ku Kluxism," *Ga. Hist. Quart.*, Dec. 1966. Some additional data can be gleaned from the *Literary Digest*, Feb. 5, 1921, pp. 40–46, Mar. 8, 1924, pp. 36–40; and Robert L. Duffus in *World's Work*, May 1923. All of the above magazine articles include good photographic likenesses of Simmons. See also his extended testimony in U. S. House of Representatives, "The Ku Klux Klan," *Hearings* before the Committee on Rules, 67 Cong., 1 Sess. (1921). Simmons's *The Klan Unmasked* (1924) gives his own interpretation of the Klan and its mission, and throws some light on the development of his ideas. For the history of the twentieth-century Klan, see David M. Chalmers, *Hooded Americanism* (1965); Kenneth T. Jackson, *The Ku Klux Klan in the City, 1915–1930* (1967); Charles C. Alexander, *The Ku Klux Klan in the Southwest* (1965); and Arnold S. Rice, *The Ku Klux Klan in Am. Politics* (1962). Simmons's death record (Ga. Dept. of Public Health) supplied his date of birth and the names of his parents.]

CHARLES C. ALEXANDER

SIMMS, RUTH HANNA McCORMICK (Mar. 27, 1880–Dec. 31, 1944), Congresswoman from Illinois, was born in Cleveland, Ohio, the second daughter and youngest of three children of Marcus Alonzo Hanna [q.v.], Ohio business and political entrepreneur, and Charlotte Augusta (Rhodes) Hanna. Her mother, a sister of the historian James Ford Rhodes [q.v.], was a daughter of Daniel Pomeroy Rhodes, a wealthy coal and iron merchant who had come to Ohio from Vermont. Ruth Hanna attended the Hathaway-Brown School in Cleveland, the Masters School in Dobbs Ferry, N. Y., and Miss Porter's School, Farmington, Conn. Through her father she was early exposed to politics, but her active involvement followed her marriage, on June 10, 1903, to Joseph Medill McCormick [q.v.] of Chicago, who was to serve briefly as publisher of the *Chicago Tribune* before entering a political career. The presence at the wedding of President Theodore Roosevelt, two weeks after his endorsement by the Ohio Republican convention had dashed Mark Hanna's purported presidential ambitions, attracted additional attention to the elaborate event. The McCormicks had three children: Katherine (Katrina) Augusta (born 1913), John Medill (1916), and Ruth Elizabeth (1921).

Both Mrs. McCormick and her husband actively supported Roosevelt's bid for the presidency in 1912, and Medill McCormick, running as a Progressive, was elected that year to the first of two terms in the Illinois legislature. Ruth McCormick now became a lobbyist before the legislature for a number of causes, among them the child labor law sought by the Consumers' League in 1915 and minimum-wage legislation sponsored by the Women's Trade Union League. Her greatest success came during the legislative session of 1913, in which the Progressive bloc held the balance of power, when she worked successfully for the passage of the Illinois Equal Suffrage Act, extending to women the right to vote in municipal and presidential elections. After this victory, she served for two years (1913–15) as chairman of the Congressional Committee of the National American Woman Suffrage Association, the major body lobbying for a federal suffrage amendment. In appearance Mrs. McCormick was tall and slender with prominent dark eyes. Unbridled as a youth, in political appearances she affected a rather severe air in dress and mien, dramatically offset by her vivacity and sharp repartee in conference or on the platform.

Despite her early association with the Progressive party and later with Midwestern agrarian liberalism (she was an active floor leader for Frank O. Lowden [Supp. 3] at the 1920 and 1928 Republican conventions and a supporter of the McNary-Haugen farm bills), Mrs. McCormick was essentially a highly partisan Republican regular. Her husband, who had followed a similar political course, was elected to Congress in 1916 and to the Senate in 1918. Mrs. McCormick advocated military preparedness before America's entry into World War I and later bitterly opposed both the League of Nations and the World Court. When the Republican party in December 1918 created a Women's National Executive Committee, she was appointed its first chairman. In 1920 she was placed on the party's regular National Executive Committee. During her tenure she consistently argued against separation of the sexes in political affairs, even opposing the League of Women Voters as "a political fifth wheel." In 1924, when the Republican National Committee was reorganized to include one committeeman and one committeewoman from each state, she was unanimously elected to represent Illinois.

Medill McCormick was defeated for reelection in the Republican primary in 1924, the year before he died. Convinced that his defeat was partly the result of a low level of political activity by Republican women, Ruth Hanna McCormick over the next four years organized effective women's Republican clubs in 90 of Illinois's 102 counties. In so doing she created for herself a potent statewide political "machine." Refusing in 1928 to join the drive to overthrow the dominant Republican faction led by Mayor William Hale Thompson [Supp. 3] of Chicago, she skillfully avoided the pitfalls and blandishments of factional politics by becoming a candidate for one of the state's two at-large Congressional seats, on a platform of "no promises and no bunk." Now a professional politician in her own right, she topped a slate of eight candidates in the April primary and led the Republican ticket in the general election, garnering 1,700,000 votes. She thus became the first woman in the United States to win a statewide election. Announcing her candidacy for the Senate shortly after this election, she swamped the incumbent Senator, Charles S. Deneen (who had defeated her husband in 1924), in the 1930 primary, only to be defeated in November by former Senator J. Hamilton Lewis [Supp. 2], whom Medill McCormick had unseated in 1918. Lewis in his campaign made an issue of her previously strong support of prohibition, as well as the Republican party's economic failures.

During the 1930's Mrs. McCormick devoted herself largely to her personal affairs. Three Rockford, Ill., newspapers that she had purchased in the late 1920's were merged in 1930 into the Rockford Consolidated Newspapers, Inc., which also acquired a radio station. On Mar. 9, 1932, she married Albert Gallatin Simms, a New Mexico banker and former Congressional colleague, in Colorado Springs. Mrs. Simms owned a ranch in the Jackson Hole country of Wyoming, which she had used as a summer retreat. After her second marriage, she moved to a ranch near Albuquerque, N. Mex., and her activities increasingly became centered in the Mountain States. Since 1912 she had also owned Rock River Farm in Byron, Ill., which she had helped develop into a model in the production of certified milk, the raising of Holstein dairy cattle, and the growing of alfalfa. She sold this property in 1937 and acquired the 250,000-acre cattle- and sheep-raising Trinchera Ranch near Fort Garland, Colo. In 1934 Mrs. Simms founded the Sandia School for Girls at Albuquerque, which she ran until 1942. As a memorial to her son, killed in a mountain-climbing accident in 1938, she also endowed the Fountain Valley School in Colorado.

A bitter opponent of New Deal domestic and foreign policies, Mrs. Simms reemerged on the national political scene in 1939 as co-chairman of the Dewey for President Committee. In 1941 she identified herself with the principles of "America First." She rejoined the Republican National Committee in 1944 as committeewoman from New Mexico, and served the same year as leader of the Mountain States division of the Draft Dewey Committee.

In October 1944 Mrs. Simms fractured her right shoulder in a fall from a horse and entered Billings Hospital in Chicago. On Dec. 4, three days after her release, she returned to Billings and underwent emergency surgery for acute hemorrhagic pancreatitis. She died there on Dec. 31 and was buried in Fairview Cemetery, Albuquerque. Ruth Hanna McCormick Simms had made a unique reputation in the arena of practical politics. Throughout her career, despite frequent charges of "bossism" and opportunism, she delighted in her self-described role as the "first woman ward politician."

[Mrs. Simms's papers, preponderantly correspondence of the 1927–30 and 1942–44 periods, constitute 125 of the 136 boxes of the Hanna-McCormick Family Papers in the Lib. of Cong. Her suffrage activities are well documented in the Nat. Am. Woman Suffrage Assoc. Papers, in the same lib. The most recent biographical account is that of Ralph A. Stone in *Notable Am. Women*, III, 293–95. Earlier sketches are in the *Nat. Cyc. Am. Biog.*, XXXIV, 162–63; Mabel W. Cameron, comp., *Biog. Cyc. Am. Women*, I (1924), 188–89; and *Biog. Directory Am. Cong.*, (1961). The most useful contemporary treatments are: (on her political career) Mildred Adams in the

Nation, Oct. 26, 1927; Duff Gilfond in *Am. Mercury*, Oct. 1929, and in the *New Republic*, Mar. 12, 1930; William Hard in *Rev. of Revs.*, Mar. 1930; S. J. Woolf in *N. Y. Times Mag.*, Feb. 18, 1940; (on her women's role) Emily Newell Blair, "Women at the Convention," *Current Hist.*, Oct. 1920; Ida Clyde Clarke in *Century*, Mar. 1927; (on her farming) Mildred Adams in *Woman Citizen*, Feb. 1926; Charles W. Holman in *Farmer's Wife*, Feb. 1928. For a scathing attack on her 1930 campaign, see editorials in the *Christian Century*, Mar. 12–May 14, Sept. 3–Nov. 19, 1930, *passim*. Major obituaries are in the *Rockford* (Ill.) *Register–Republic, Chicago Daily Tribune*, and *N. Y. Times* of Jan. 1, 1945. Of secondary accounts, William T. Hutchinson, *Lowden of Ill.* (2 vols., 1957), is an invaluable primer of Illinois politics and of her associations with Lowden; Harold L. Ickes, *The Autobiog. of a Curmudgeon* (1943), is critical; and Alice Roosevelt Longworth, *Crowded Hours* (1933), adulatory. For her work in behalf of woman suffrage see Ida H. Harper, ed., *Hist. of Woman Suffrage*, vols. V and VI (1922).]

JAMES P. LOUIS

SINGER, ISRAEL JOSHUA (Nov. 30, 1893–Feb. 10, 1944), Yiddish novelist, was born in Bilgoray, Poland (then part of the Russian empire), the eldest son and second of the four surviving children of Pinhos-Mendel Singer, a Hasidic rabbi, and Bathsheba (Silberman) Singer, daughter of the licensed rabbi of Bilgoray and a woman of learning in her own right. The visionary, impractical father made a poor living and the family suffered privation. When Joshua was three, they moved to Leoncin, a small town near Warsaw, and in 1908, after a brief stay at nearby Radzymin, to Warsaw. Joshua was educated from childhood for the rabbinate, but he felt a strong thirst for life and early rebelled against his parents' otherworldliness. Though reading was forbidden in orthodox homes, he secretly read Hebrew, Yiddish, Russian, and Polish books on secular topics and came in time to reject his religious upbringing altogether. He changed his Hasidic dress to Western clothes, cut his earlocks, and at the age of eighteen left home "in quest of enlightenment and worldly knowledge" ("Autobiographical Sketch," p. 300).

Living in Warsaw without money or a trade, the young rebel barely kept himself alive by doing odd jobs. He devoted most of his time to the study of languages, mathematics, and science and sought expression in painting and in writing. His earliest stories, set in the Hasidic world against which he had rebelled, sought to give meaning to his past. During the First World War he spent brief periods as a conscript in the Russian army and at forced labor during the German occupation of Poland in 1915.

Ignited, like so many of his contemporaries, by the promise of the Russian Revolution, Singer emigrated in 1917 to the Russian city of Kiev. There, in 1918, he married Genia Kupfershtock, a native of Poland; according to his own account, they "faced want, actual starvation, murder raids and pogroms which came in the wake of the civil war." He worked as a proofreader on a small Jewish newspaper, published short stories in the Kiev daily *Naie Zeit*, and completed a story, "Pearls," and two dramas, *Three* and *Earth Woes*, which dealt with wars and pogroms. In these early works the major themes of his fiction began to unfold: alienation of "little people" who, uprooted from their traditions, were defeated by the brutal world around them, and the tragedy of heroes condemned to loneliness and suffering. Three years in Russia, however, brought Singer his second major rejection of belief. Disillusioned with the Bolshevik experiment, he returned in 1921 to Warsaw, where his sons, Jacob and Joseph, were born.

Singer now entered vigorously into the literary movements of Warsaw, at a time when Poland was the world center of Yiddish culture. He helped found two literary magazines (*Ringen* and the *Haliastre*), contributed to others, was an editor of the *Literarishe Bletter*, and served as a correspondent for two major Warsaw Yiddish dailies. His story "Pearls," first published in Warsaw in 1921, attracted the attention of Abraham Cahan, editor of the *Jewish Daily Forward* in New York City, who in 1923 invited Singer to become a regular contributor.

Renewed contact with the Soviet Union in 1926, as a special correspondent of the *Daily Forward*, led to his book *Nai Russland* (1928), in which he expressed concern for the fate of the Russian Jews and the survival of Yiddish culture. His disillusionment was given artistic expression in his novel *Steel and Iron* (*Shtol un Eisen*, 1927, first published in English as *Blood Harvest*, 1935) and in *Savinkov* (1932), a drama based on the life of the revolutionary terrorist who became a murderous antirevolutionary. As an alternative to the Soviet ideal, Singer made an impassioned plea for a literary world conference that would bring Jewish writers closer together and "create a tie between us and the world." This call, which was otherwise unheeded, provoked bitter attacks by leftist critics and newspapers. Embittered, Singer for a time gave up writing. In 1931, however, with the encouragement of Abraham Cahan, he began *Yoshe Kalb*, a realistic novel about a mystic, set in the rabbinical courts of nineteenth-century Galicia. Nahum, an ascetic son of a rabbi, commits adultery with his young mother-in-law, exiles himself, and spends the rest of his life waiting for redemption that never comes.

Yoshe Kalb, after appearing serially in the *Daily Forward*, was published in Yiddish and English (as *The Sinner*) in 1933. Now identifying his career with the Jewish literary world of New York, Singer moved there with his family in 1934. In his new home, freed from the quarrels and failures of Warsaw, he wrote in rapid succession many of his most impressive works. In *The Brothers Ashkenazi* (1936) he depicted the rise and fall of the textile city of Lodz, Poland, and the fate of the Jews whose lives were woven into its history. This was followed by two volumes of short stories and by *East of Eden* (1939), a novel in which an idealistic worker is crushed by the forces of human corruption in Poland and the Soviet Union. He then wrote *In die Berg* (1942), a novel set in America, and *The Family Carnovsky* (1943)—perhaps his most successful novel artistically—the story of a family of orthodox Jews who emigrate from Poland and begin an odyssey that spans three generations, always searching for meaning and adjustment. The first and only volume of his unfinished memoirs, ironically entitled *Of a World That Is No More*, appeared posthumously in 1946 (English translation, 1970). In it the author recalls his childhood without bitterness, and the book, perhaps because it reveals that Singer had come to accept his past, is one of his finest. Singer died of a heart attack in New York City in 1944, at the age of fifty. He was buried in the Workmen's Circle Mount Carmel Cemetery, New York.

I. J. Singer was basically a disillusioned man unable to resign himself to accepting human limitations. He could find redemption neither for himself nor for his characters. He asked questions, but discarded the answers; he fought for sustaining values, yet denied them. Singer created a body of work that gives artistic expression to the struggles he observed and underwent. He was not always successful, but he chose as subjects the most difficult and complex crises of his time. His later novels, written in New York, explain the conflicts of the Old World to the New. At least one of these, *The Brothers Ashkenazi*, published in English translation by Alfred A. Knopf in 1936, found a readership outside the Jewish community. But it remained for Singer's younger brother Isaac Bashevis, nearly a generation later, to bring the Yiddish tradition fully into the mainstream of American letters.

[Singer's "Autobiog. Sketch," *Wilson Lib. Bull.*, Jan. 1937, and his *Of a World That Is No More* are the principal English sources; see also, on the family background, Isaac Bashevis Singer's autobiographical *In My Father's Court* (1966) and *A Day of Pleasure* (1969). Knopf also published English translations of I. J. Singer's *East of Eden* (1939) and a volume of his short stories, *The River Breaks Up* (1938); *The Family Carnovsky* was not published in English until 1969 (Vanguard Press). A useful introduction to Yiddish stories in general and I. J. Singer in particular is Irving Howe and Eliezer Greenberg, eds., *A Treasury of Yiddish Stories* (1954). Singer is touched on also in Abraham A. Roback, *The Story of Yiddish Literature* (1940), and Charles A. Madison, *Yiddish Literature: Its Scope and Major Writers* (1968). A lengthy biographical article (in Yiddish) by Zainvill Diamond is in Z. Reizen, *Lexicon fun der Naier Yiddisher Literatur* (1960), XXXIV, 640–46; it includes a bibliography of Singer's Yiddish publications and translations and the major critical writings about him, mostly in Yiddish. The *N. Y. Times Book Rev.*, July 25, 1971, reproduces a photograph of Singer by Carl Van Vechten.]

LIBBY OKUN COHEN

SKINNER, OTIS (June 28, 1858–Jan. 4, 1942), actor, was born in Cambridge, Mass., the second of three sons of the Rev. Charles Augustus Skinner, a Universalist minister, and Cornelia (Bartholomew) Skinner. His father traced his descent from Thomas Skinner, a mid-seventeenth-century English settler in Massachusetts; the family's Puritan ancestors included doctors, jurists, and clergymen. In later years Otis marveled that he and his brothers (Charles, a poet and writer, and William, a painter) could have stemmed from such solid, unartistic forebears.

As a small boy in Cambridge, Otis frequently crossed the Charles River with his parents to view the "educational" stage entertainments at the Boston Museum. When he was nine or ten, his father was called to Hartford, Conn. Otis attended the local high school, but though he had a fine, inquiring mind and later became an avid reader as well as a graceful prose stylist, he disliked school and left before graduating. While he worked as an insurance clerk, a shipping clerk, and later as Hartford correspondent for the New York *Dramatic News* and editor of the *Hartford Clarion,* his thoughts constantly reverted to the theatre. On a visit to his brother Charles in New York City he witnessed a gaslit performance of *The Hunchback of Notre Dame,* and his early ambition to become an actor was strengthened. He read plays assiduously, developed the characters in his spare moments, and gave amateur performances as an "elocutionist and impersonator."

In 1877 a letter of recommendation from the showman P. T. Barnum [*q.v.*], an acquaintance of his father, helped the youthful Skinner obtain a position as "utility" actor with the poverty-stricken stock company of William Davidge, Jr., at the Philadelphia Museum. During his first season he played ninety-two roles ranging from villains to black servants to frowsy old women in dozens of now-forgotten plays. He spent the next season (1878–79) with the more prosperous Walnut Street Theatre stock company in Phila-

delphia, a group which rehearsed long hours to support such visiting luminaries as Rose Eytinge, Fanny Janauschek, John McCullough, Frank Chanfrau [*qq.v.*], and Mary Anderson [Supp. 2]. In the spring of 1880 he played minor roles for ten weeks with a company formed around Edwin Booth [*q.v.*], who became his revered friend and teacher.

From 1881 to 1884 Skinner acted with Lawrence Barrett [*q.v.*], gradually acquiring such prized roles as Mark Antony in *Julius Caesar.* He finally left Barrett's troupe because he felt he "had begun to lose the emotion of acting" (*Footlights and Spotlights,* p. 123) and was taking on Barrett's peculiar mannerisms, defects which he remedied by laboring on the technical facets of his art for five seasons with the celebrated comedy company of Augustin Daly [*q.v.*]. Supporting there such renowned performers as Mrs. G. H. Gilbert [Anne Hartley Gilbert, *q.v.*], May Irwin [Supp. 2], Ada Rehan, and John Drew [*qq.v.*], Skinner grew in popularity and dramatic stature.

Barrett, as Booth's business manager, engaged Skinner for second leads in the combined tour (1889–90) of Booth and the Polish tragedienne Helena Modjeska [*q.v.*]. He thus had the opportunity to increase his breadth with roles of dramatic substance, playing Bassanio and Macduff to Booth's Shylock and Macbeth. In 1892, as the climax to his apprenticeship, he became Modjeska's leading man for over two years, himself playing Shylock and Macbeth, his first starring Shakespearean roles.

Skinner was now prepared to manage his own company. His first two seasons on the road, beginning in September 1894, increased his reputation as a star in his own right who could play romantic heroes and character roles with equal facility. Over the next few years he enjoyed many successes in new vehicles as well as in Shakespearean plays and nineteenth-century favorites. His most noteworthy appearances during this period were in *His Grace de Grammont* (1894), a comedy by Clyde Fitch [*q.v.*] set in Restoration England; *Villon the Vagabond* (1895), written by Skinner and his brother Charles; *Hamlet* (1895); Sheridan's *The Rivals* (1899), on tour with Joseph Jefferson [*q.v.*]; a dramatization of Robert Louis Stevenson's *Prince Otto* (1900), Skinner's first New York success as a star; a revival of *Francesca da Rimini,* an old Barrett favorite (1901); a season of classic comedies with Ada Rehan (1903); and a poetic French drama, *The Harvester* (adapted by Charles Skinner, 1904).

By 1904 Skinner was an established star on

Broadway and in "the provinces." That year he went under the management of the producer Charles Frohman [*q.v.*], who presented him in Henri Lavedan's *The Duel* (1906) and in a dramatization of Balzac's *La Rabouilleuse* called *The Honor of the Family* (1907)—part comedy, part melodrama—in which Skinner scored one of his biggest hits as the villain, Col. Philippe Bridau. At a revival of this play in 1926, the critic John Mason Brown sat enthralled at Skinner's technical virtuosity. "It is a veteran's method, sure in its devices. . . . It is character acting enlarged beyond the ordinary; bold, romantic, mellow but high-tensioned. It admits no moments of loafing and is never more active than when some one else is speaking" (*Upstage*, pp. 100–01).

After appearing as a hammy old actor in *Your Humble Servant* (1910), Skinner went on to his greatest triumph as Hajj, the beggar who becomes a king and a beggar again in a single day, in Edward Knoblauch's Arabian fantasy, *Kismet* (1911). He played *Kismet* for three years (in New York and on tour) and made two films of the play, a silent version in 1916 and one with sound in 1930. Skinner continued his stardom as a deaf philanthropist in Jules Eckert Goodman's *The Silent Voice* (1914), as a lovable Italian organ-grinder in his friend Booth Tarkington's *Mister Antonio* (1916), as a bullfighter in *Blood and Sand* (1921), as Sancho Panza in the play of that name (1923), and as Falstaff in The Players club's revival of *Henry IV* (1926) and in the 1927 production of *The Merry Wives of Windsor* by Minnie Maddern Fiske [*q.v.*]. In the 1930's Skinner went on tour with Maude Adams, playing Shylock to her Portia, and appeared in several classic revivals presented by The Players, of whom he was a prominent member and sometime vice-president. In 1938 he was elected president of the Episcopal Actors' Guild. He retired from the stage in 1940.

Otis Skinner was, as Burns Mantle put it, "our most respected link with three generations of the American theatre" (New York *Daily News*, June 28, 1938). He received his training when that theatre was dominated by the actors, such luminaries as Booth and Joseph Jefferson, who "trouped" throughout the length of the country. When he ended his career, the playwright and director had become the dominant figures, Americans such as Eugene O'Neill and Maxwell Anderson had written plays of high artistic quality, and the theatre was centralized in New York and a few other large cities. Skinner never appeared in an American play of lasting value, and he won most of his twentieth-century successes in old-fashioned romantic costume dramas. Nonetheless,

his hard-earned craft survived a severe change in acting styles, a change which saw the technical theatricality of the nineteenth century, with its classical use of voice and body, replaced by a more subtle, internally motivated, naturalistic approach.

On Apr. 21, 1895, Skinner had married his leading lady, Maud Durbin, whom he met when they were both with Modjeska; she died in 1936. Their only child, Cornelia Otis (born in 1902), became a well-known author and actress. Otis Skinner died of uremic poisoning at his New York City apartment at the age of eighty-three and was buried beside his wife in River Street Cemetery, Woodstock, Vt., near his summer home.

[A large collection of the papers of Otis and Cornelia Otis Skinner (letters, contracts, photographs, prompt books) is located in the Harvard Theatre Collection. The most helpful published source is Skinner's autobiography, *Footlights and Spotlights* (1924). His other published works, in addition to a score of magazine articles, include *The Last Tragedian* (1939), containing some of Edwin Booth's letters; *Mad Folk of the Theatre* (1928); and *One Man in His Time* (1938), the diary of Harry Watkins, actor, which Skinner edited with his wife, Maud. See also Cornelia Otis Skinner, *Family Circle* (1948). For well-rounded appraisals of his acting, see: John Mason Brown, *Upstage* (1930), and Garff B. Wilson, *A Hist. of Am. Acting* (1966). See also *N. Y. Times*, Jan. 5, 12, 1942; *Nat. Cyc. Am. Biog.*, XXXII, 91–92.]

GEORGE PHILIP BIRNBAUM

SLEMP, CAMPBELL BASCOM (Sept. 4, 1870–Aug. 7, 1943), Congressman and presidential secretary, was born in Turkey Cove, Lee County, Va., the second son and fourth of seven children of Campbell and Nannie B. (Cawood) Slemp. His father's forebears, originally German, had lived in Virginia for several generations; his mother was a native of Oswald County, Ky. Slemp grew up in a prosperous Methodist family. His father, who had served as a colonel in the Confederate Army, dealt in livestock and owned extensive coal and timber lands. He became a leading politician in southwestern Virginia, serving in the state legislature (1879–83) and, having turned Republican in 1884 over the tariff issue, as presidential elector (1888, 1892) and Congressman (1903–07).

Young Slemp, after attending local public schools, graduated in 1891 from the Virginia Military Institute. He studied law in 1892 at the University of Virginia. For the next few years the family business interests were probably his principal concern, although he taught mathematics for one year (1900–01) at V.M.I. Admitted to the bar in 1901, he established a law practice in Big Stone Gap, Va.

C. Bascom Slemp, as he called himself, shared his father's interest in politics. In 1905 he became chairman of the Republican state committee, the youngest man in the nation at that time to hold such a position. When the father died in October 1907, the son was chosen to complete his unexpired Congressional term and went on to win reelection to seven consecutive terms. Representing a constituency traditionally hostile to Virginia's eastern Democratic leadership, Slemp consistently voted with the Republican "Old Guard." He supported the Payne-Aldrich Tariff of 1909, backed Speaker of the House Joseph G. Cannon [q.v.] in his fight against progressive insurgents who sought to curb the Speaker's power, and opposed a series of antilynching bills. By 1922, when he decided not to run again, he was one of the most influential Southerners in the Republican party.

His party position commended him to President Calvin Coolidge, who in 1923 appointed Slemp presidential secretary. The appointment was widely interpreted to mean that Coolidge intended to win the presidential nomination in 1924, using Slemp as his bridge to the Southern delegates. By all accounts the Virginian was a loyal, hardworking aide. He acted as the administration's liaison man with Congress and with the Republican National Committee, of which he was a member. He also exercised a voice in patronage matters, and carefully insulated his chief from much of the daily tedium that accrues to the presidency. When anyone wanted to accomplish anything at the White House, he was usually told to "see Slemp."

The Teapot Dome scandals, which erupted in January 1924, posed a threat to Coolidge by revealing corruption in the Harding administration, of which he had been a part. Slemp personally came under attack when circumstantial evidence made it appear that he had acted as an intermediary between the White House and two of the accused men, Albert B. Fall [Supp. 3] and Edward B. McLean [Supp. 3], prior to their appearances before a Senate investigating committee. Called upon to testify, he denied having acted in any such capacity, though he admitted having met with both men. In the end, Coolidge emerged from the Teapot Dome affair with his political position strengthened. Slemp and other Coolidge lieutenants virtually ran the Republican convention in June and contributed to the President's easy victory in November.

Slemp resigned as presidential secretary in March 1925, possibly out of disappointment over having been denied a cabinet post in the new administration. He nevertheless retained a lifelong admiration for Coolidge. After his resignation he represented a Chicago law firm in Washington, where his acute knowledge of those who could get things done was his most important asset. Tall, slender, and gray-haired, the courtly Southerner was, according to the editor William Allen White [Supp. 3], a "fluent and delightful conversationalist" (White, p. 276). Though Slemp remained on the Republican National Committee until 1932, he never again sought public office. He helped found the Institute of Public Affairs at the University of Virginia in 1927; a year later, after initially urging the renomination of Coolidge, he worked to swing Southern delegates behind Herbert Hoover. After 1932 Slemp, a lifelong bachelor, devoted most of his time to business affairs. While returning from a vacation in Florida in 1943, he was stricken with a heart ailment and was taken to St. Mary's Hospital in Knoxville, Tenn., where he died ten days later. He was buried in the family cemetery at his birthplace.

[Calvin Coolidge Papers, Lib. of Cong., Slemp file; Guy B. Hathorn, "The Political Career of C. Bascom Slemp" (Ph.D. dissertation, Duke Univ., 1950); J. Frederick Essary, ed., *Selected Addresses of C. Bascom Slemp* (1938); *Literary Digest*, Jan. 5, 1924, pp. 38–42; *Current Opinion*, Oct. 1923, pp. 413–15; *N. Y. Times* and *Washington Post*, Aug. 8, 1943; William Allen White, *A Puritan in Babylon* (1938); Donald R. McCoy, *Calvin Coolidge: The Quiet President* (1967); Lyon G. Tyler, *Men of Mark in Va.*, II (1907), 349–50, on his father; *Biog. Directory Am. Cong.* (1961), on Slemp and his father; *Who Was Who in America*, vol. II (1950); information from Campbell Edmonds, Big Stone Gap, Va.]

ROBERT JAMES MADDOX

SLOAN, MATTHEW SCOTT (Sept. 5, 1881–June 14, 1945), public utilities executive, was born in Mobile, Ala., the son of Matthew Scott Sloan, chief of the Mobile fire department, and Mary Elizabeth (Scott) Sloan. He entered Alabama Polytechnic Institute in Auburn at fourteen and took a B.S. degree in electrical engineering in 1901 and an M.S. in 1902. After brief stints with a small-town light plant in Alabama and a street railway in Memphis, he worked for the General Electric Company in Schenectady, N. Y., where he advanced to supervisor of turbine installations. In 1906 he began an eleven-year career with G. E.'s subsidiary, the Electric Bond and Share Company, which operated utilities in various parts of the nation. Eight of those years were spent in Birmingham, three in New Orleans; in the latter city he was vice-president and general manager of the local electric railway and light company.

In 1917 Sloan was transferred to New York City, where the most interesting part of his career unfolded. Consolidated Gas Company, which controlled electric power distribution in the city through four subsidiaries, was notoriously inefficient, in part because it was ridden with politics. Using the leverage of the city's franchise power, political leaders had evolved a system whereby public utility jobs were treated as part of the political patronage, and contracts for buildings, coal, and the like went to political favorites. In his first two years with the system Sloan was assistant to the president of the New York Edison Company (one of the Consolidated Gas subsidiaries) and hence powerless to effect reform. But in 1919 he became president of Brooklyn Edison and launched a modernization program. Despite his education he lacked technical skill, but he had a keen eye for talent and was an excellent administrator, and he was thus able to direct Brooklyn Edison on a course of modernization based upon the pattern being set by such utility pioneers as Samuel Insull [Supp. 2] in Chicago and Alex Dow [Supp. 3] in Detroit. His company installed huge generating plants, adopted uniform 60-cycle alternating current, simplified and rationalized its operations, repeatedly cut its rates and expanded its service, and far surpassed its sister companies in the Consolidated Gas system.

In 1928 the several companies in and around New York were combined (they were later reorganized as Consolidated Edison), and Sloan became president and operating head of the various constituent organizations. For four years he made a valiant effort to do for the entire system what he had done in Brooklyn, but the obstacles were enormous. For one thing, the system was a technological mess: New York Edison, for example, used partly 25-cycle alternating current and partly 3-wire direct current in Manhattan, and 4-phase alternating current in the Bronx; United Electric Light and Power (operating in Manhattan and the Bronx) used a variety of phases of a.c. at the same frequency as Brooklyn but at different voltage. Through his skill at internal politics and on the plea that uniformity was necessary as a means of supplying power to the subway system the city was just then building, Sloan was able to make considerable headway against the technical problems; but then other problems arose. Most important, at first, was the Great Depression, for after 1930 sales fell off and capital became extremely difficult to raise. Labor problems compounded the economic problems, but the final blow was political.

Sloan had made many political enemies by insisting upon rationality and efficiency instead of the "spoils system" that had earlier characterized the utilities' management, and late in 1931 his

political enemies overcame him. So strained were his relations with Tammany Hall that, it was said, he was unable for six months to obtain from the city fathers a permit even to open a manhole cover. That made his situation hopeless, and early in 1932 the directors demanded his resignation. With his departure also departed from New York the likelihood that the city would ever obtain electric service of a quality and at a price that were normal in most of urban America.

The rest of Sloan's career was anticlimactic, though distinguished: from 1934 until 1945 he served as president and chairman of the board of the Missouri-Kansas-Texas Railroad and about a dozen related lines. An Episcopalian and a Republican, Sloan was active in many civic and business groups, such as the Brooklyn Academy of Music (vice-president), Long Island University (trustee and treasurer), the National Electric Light Association (president, 1930), and the United States Chamber of Commerce (a director). He died in New York City in 1945 and was buried in Auburn, Ala. He was survived by his widow, Lottie Everard Lane, whom he had married on Feb. 23, 1911, and by a daughter, Liddie Lane (Mrs. Andrew M. McBurney, Jr.).

[*Electrical World*, Feb. 13, 1932; *Who Was Who in America*, vol. II (1950); *Nat. Cyc. Am. Biog.*, XXXIV, 151–52; *N. Y. Times*, Jan. 29, 1932 (career portrait), and June 15, 1945 (obituary); U. S. Federal Trade Commission, *Utility Corporations* (96 parts, 1928–37); Frederick L. Collins, *Consolidated Gas of N. Y.: A Hist.* (1934).]

FORREST MCDONALD

SMITH, ALFRED EMANUEL (Dec. 30, 1873–Oct. 4, 1944), four-term governor of New York, progressive reformer, and the first Roman Catholic nominated for the presidency of the United States by a major party, was born on New York City's Lower East Side to Alfred Emanuel Smith and his young second wife, Catherine Mulvehill. His father, an East Side native and a Civil War veteran, was the son of a German mother and an Italian father. His mother, born in the same neighborhood, was the offspring of Irish parents: a Catholic tailor, and a Protestant of English stock who had converted to Catholicism upon her marriage. At the time of his son's birth, the elder Smith owned a small trucking business. As the Smiths had only one other child, Mary, born two years after Alfred, their five-room flat was uncrowded, and the Lower East Side was not yet the slum it would become by the end of the century.

Al's early childhood, passed amid the bustle and variety of the East River waterfront, was happy and relatively secure. He served as an altar boy at St. James Roman Catholic Church and attended the local parish school. An average student, he excelled in oratory, winning a citywide contest when only eleven years old with an oration on the death of Robespierre.

When Al was twelve his father died, leaving the family very poor. At fourteen, a month before completing the eighth grade, he dropped out of school to work as an errand boy for a trucking firm, the first of a succession of odd jobs. At eighteen he became general clerk for Feeney and Company, a wholesale commission house in the Fulton Fish Market area. For two years he sold fish to merchants and restaurants, earning $12 a week—good wages for the time. He changed jobs again at twenty, this time working in a boiler manufacturing plant in Brooklyn. Active in the social life of his community, he often appeared in lead roles in productions of the St. James Dramatic Society, a church-sponsored amateur group, and occasionally worked as an extra on the stage of a local professional theatre. He married Catherine Dunn, an Irish girl from the Bronx, on May 6, 1900, after five years of courtship. They had five children: Alfred Emanuel, Emily, Catherine, Arthur, and Walter.

Smith's entry into politics was somewhat fortuitous. At the local saloon where he frequently dropped in for a glass of beer and conversation, he was befriended by the owner, Tom Foley, who was Democratic precinct leader and a Tammany Hall man. In 1894, after several years of running political errands for Foley, Smith followed him in opposing the man chosen by Tammany boss Richard Croker [q.v.] as the 4th District's Congressional nominee. The insurgents failed to elect their man but helped defeat the Tammany candidate, and the vote in their district also helped elect as mayor a Republican reform candidate, William L. Strong [q.v.]. Early in 1895, consequently, Smith was appointed process server for the commissioner of jurors at the comfortable salary of $800 a year. In 1903 Foley (now reconciled to Tammany and a district leader) chose Smith as the Democratic nominee for state assemblyman. Nomination was equivalent to election, but Smith conducted an energetic campaign.

Untrained in the law or in parliamentary procedure, the new assemblyman was at first ignored by both the Republican majority and the Tammany leaders, who instructed him how to vote but did not take him into their counsel. But slowly he learned assembly politics and state government, partly from his early roommate, Robert Wagner, a young lawyer who had also experienced poverty in his youth. Smith was appointed to the insurance committee in 1906, a year of insurance company

scandals, but he attracted little notice in the assembly until 1907, when, as a member of a special committee to revise the New York City charter, he emerged as one of the best-informed and most articulate Democratic debaters on the floor, heatedly defending home rule and the rights of the city's "plain people." Through informal weekly dinners the Lower East Side politician became acquainted with many upstate men, and soon his spirit and wit, as well as his reputation for honesty, were well known in Albany. In 1911, after a Democratic election sweep, Smith was selected by Charles F. Murphy [q.v.], the head of Tammany, as majority leader of the assembly and chairman of the ways and means committee. He became speaker of the assembly in 1913.

In these years of his political emergence, Smith's energies were directed both to protecting the interests of Tammany and to achieving a variety of progressive reforms. He opposed a series of antimachine measures backed by the Republican governor, Charles Evans Hughes, in 1910. As majority leader he was deeply involved in patronage matters, in issues of interest to the machine such as racetrack gambling and public franchises, and in opposition to direct-primary and local-option measures. On weekly trips to New York City he usually conferred with Murphy. Yet at the same time he supported home rule for New York City (a favorite progressive issue), a state conservation department, and improvements in workmen's compensation. Indeed, the last issue would preoccupy Smith during most of his political career. Notwithstanding his Tammany connections, Smith won at least sporadic endorsement from the Citizens' Union, a New York City reform group. For Smith, there was nothing incongruous in the dual nature of his politics. Tammany had little use for the theoretical abstractions of progressivism, but practical humanitarian and reform measures which had wide popular appeal were acceptable to a political organization whose main objective was to gain and hold power.

Perhaps the most important single event in Smith's development as a reformer was the 1911 Triangle Waist Company fire, a New York City disaster which took 146 lives, most of them working girls and women. As a man of conscience, Smith was deeply moved by the tragedy; as a politician, he recognized its political potential. His bill to establish a factory investigating commission quickly passed the assembly, and the commission launched a statewide series of surveys and on-the-spot investigations of factory conditions. As its vice-chairman (Robert Wagner was chairman), Smith was thrown into a close working relationship with a remarkable group of independent and sometimes brilliant social workers and reformers —an association that broadened his intellectual and social horizons, challenged his ingrained ideas on many subjects (including woman suffrage), modified the reformers' prejudice against Smith's machine background, and increased his stature in the eyes of Tammany colleagues. The commission's work continued until 1915, and Smith sponsored much of the social legislation it recommended: sanitary, health, and fire laws; wage and hour regulations for women and children; and improved workmen's compensation laws. These reforms, some enacted over the opposition of business and industrial interests, perhaps constitute Al Smith's greatest political achievement.

At the New York constitutional convention of 1915, Smith's intimate knowledge of state government and his adroit efforts on behalf of budgetary reform and home rule for New York City impressed both the newspapers and the predominantly Republican delegates, including such notables as Elihu Root [Supp. 2] and Henry L. Stimson. The acclaim spurred his ambition, and that autumn he was elected to a two-year term as sheriff of New York City, a position worth more than $60,000 a year in fees and thus a welcome change for an underpaid assemblyman with a growing family. He was boomed for mayor in 1917, but Murphy, paying off other political debts, backed John F. Hylan [Supp. 2] of Brooklyn. Smith, however, won easy election as president of the board of aldermen.

By 1918 the most popular man in the New York Democratic party, supported by Tammany, upstate politicians, and independent reform groups, Smith was the logical Democratic candidate for governor. To help broaden Smith's support and to prevent a break with the publisher William Randolph Hearst (who also wanted to be governor), Murphy allowed upstate Democrats to take the lead in putting Smith forward. After winning the nomination, Smith mapped out his own gubernatorial campaign. An independent "Citizens' Committee for Smith," composed of reformers and professional people, including associates from the factory investigation days, was established. Women and minority group members were appointed to the campaign staff: Belle Moskowitz [Supp. 1], Frances Perkins, and Joseph M. Proskauer—all of whom (with Robert Moses, who joined Smith somewhat later) were to become longtime advisers. Smith in his campaign urged a broad reorganization of the state government, economy measures, and social legislation, especially the regulation of hours and wages for women and children. When a fatal crash occurred

on the Brooklyn-Manhattan subway line four days before the election, Smith attacked his opponent, Gov. Charles S. Whitman, for allowing laxity in the Public Service Commission, the agency responsible for subway regulation. The disaster produced a large Smith vote in Brooklyn, and the flu epidemic curtailed upstate voting, but 1918 was a Republican year, and Smith won by only 15,000 votes.

The 1919–21 gubernatorial term set the pattern for Smith's later incumbencies. Most jobs went to deserving Democrats, but a few major appointments demonstrated the new governor's independence: a well-qualified Republican became the patronage-rich highway commissioner, and Frances Perkins, an independent, was appointed to the State Industrial Commission. Applying himself to crisis situations in city housing and milk distribution, two issues basic to tenement dwellers, Smith supported the temporary extension of wartime rent controls, tax incentives for the construction of low-cost housing, and price-fixing of milk by a state commission. But though he brought his formidable political skills to bear on the Republican majority in the legislature, that body killed his milk bill and passed a housing bill lacking the key rent-control provision. When the legislature refused appropriations for a commission to reorganize the structure of state government, Smith found private benefactors who underwrote the expenses of a research staff. Normally prolabor, Smith utilized the State Industrial Commission to mediate labor differences, as in the Rome, N. Y., copper strike of 1919, when Frances Perkins initiated public hearings which led to negotiations and eventual recognition of the union. He was prepared, however, to call out the state militia when labor disputes led to violence, and indeed did so on one occasion.

In a time of political reaction, Governor Smith vetoed several antisedition bills which would have severely curtailed the civil liberties of Socialists and others. When the assembly expelled five duly elected Socialists, Smith declared that "to discard the methods of representative government leads to misdeeds of the very extremists we denounce." In 1923, during his second term, he pardoned an Irish revolutionary, Jim Larkin, imprisoned under the state sedition law, arguing that the "public assertion of an erroneous doctrine" was insufficient grounds for punishment. He granted clemency to the Communist Benjamin Gitlow on the Holmesian grounds that Gitlow's actions posed no "clear and present danger" to New York. He apparently saw such a threat, however, in the Ku Klux Klan, for in that same year Smith signed a bill virtually outlawing the organization in the state. He supported the League of Nations; Wilsonianism evidently awakened in him an interest in international affairs that persisted into the 1920's. Before his first term was completed, the *New Republic* called him "one of the ablest governors New York has ever had."

In 1920, with an anti-Democratic current running nationally, Smith lost his bid for reelection by 75,000 votes. The result was a moral victory, however, for the national Democratic ticket lost New York in the same election by 1,200,000 votes. During the next two years, while serving as board chairman of the United States Trucking Corporation (headed by his close friend James J. Riordan), Smith kept in close touch with politics. He was renominated in 1922 despite a bitter challenge from Hearst, and in his campaign he again emphasized such welfare and reform issues as a forty-eight-hour week, governmental reorganization, conservation, and the creation of a public hydroelectric power authority. Smith's personal popularity, the continued support of his heterogeneous coalition, and a national business depression identified with the Republicans gave him a record 388,000 plurality over the incumbent governor, Nathan L. Miller. Two more successful gubernatorial campaigns followed in 1924 and 1926.

After Murphy's death in 1924, Smith was himself the most important Democratic leader in the state, and was thus freed from dependence upon bosses and machines. He supported James J. ("Jimmy") Walker for mayor of New York in 1925, but he did not reward Tammany heavily with the spoils of politics. When faced by legislative opposition in the 1920's, Smith, with his acute sense of timing, responded with persuasion, compromise proposals, and the use of referenda and radio appeals to the voters. By such means, he compiled a record of significant achievement. In the area of administrative reorganization, he reduced 152 competing, often overlapping, agencies to a comparatively few cabinet-level positions. His welfare program included state support for low-cost housing projects, bond issues to develop an extensive park and recreation system, more funds for state education, and support for the State Labor Department in enforcing safety requirements and administering workmen's compensation. At the same time, through economies, long-term funding, and the introduction of a modern system of budgeting, taxes were reduced. Although unsuccessful in achieving the public development of New York's waterpower resources, Smith did in 1922 and 1927 block the legislative transfer of several prime power sites to private interests. In short, in a decade little

known for reform politics, Governor Smith played an almost classic progressive role.

Smith's position, and his record, almost automatically made him a serious presidential contender. Early in his second term Charles Murphy and Belle Moskowitz (his publicity director and most influential political lieutenant) had quietly sounded other parts of the country and learned that Smith had strong support in the states with the largest electoral votes. But the 1924 Democratic convention was torn apart by a conflict between the rural-dry-Protestant forces, centered in the South and West, and the urban-wet-Catholic representatives of the Northeast. Urban strategists almost forced through a platform plank condemning the Ku Klux Klan, but in so doing they crippled Smith's chances of gaining the two-thirds majority needed for nomination. After nearly two weeks of deadlock, both William Gibbs McAdoo [Supp. 3], representing the rural wing, and Smith—the "Happy Warrior" of Franklin Roosevelt's nominating speech—finally withdrew. Smith's obstinacy in prolonging the deadlock has been attributed to his anger at the anti-Catholicism manifested during the floor fight over the Klan and his conviction that his opponents represented the forces of bigotry.

By 1928 McAdoo was out of the running and William Jennings Bryan [*q.v.*] was dead, leaving the rural Democrats with no leader of national stature. Moreover, no one in the party wanted a second deadlocked convention. The religious issue, however, could not be stilled. In April 1927 the *Atlantic Monthly* published an article by Charles C. Marshall, a prominent Episcopal layman, suggesting a basic conflict between Smith's loyalty to the Roman Catholic Church and his allegiance to the Constitution of the United States. The Governor's immediate reaction to Marshall's largely legalistic argument was, "I know nothing whatsoever about papal bulls and encyclicals." Replying more formally in the May *Atlantic,* Smith emphasized that his Catholicism was not theologically oriented, that he believed in the total separation of church and state, and that he could foresee no conflict between the duties of a president and those of a Catholic. (As early as 1925 he had told an emissary from Cardinal William O'Connell [Supp. 3] of Boston, who was urging him to oppose a child labor bill then before the state legislature, that he would accept the Church's authority on matters of faith and morals, but not on economic, social, or political issues.) His advisers counseled minimizing his religion and his urban background, but privately Smith vowed, "I'll be myself, come what may!" He continued to dress nattily and to speak at Tammany rallies, and when a papal legate visited New York City in 1926, Smith, kneeling, kissed the bishop's ring. Religion, however, was only one facet of the image Smith projected. Others emerged during the coming presidential campaign.

By 1928 Smith's candidacy could not be denied, and on the first ballot the Houston convention nominated him for the presidency. The campaign which followed has usually been interpreted as a victory for bigotry and narrow-minded rural prohibitionism. Unquestionably, fears of "demon rum," the big city, and the Catholic Church did play a part. In Oklahoma and Montana, crosses blazed along the railroad tracks as Smith's campaign train passed. Scurrilous literature and a whispering campaign against the candidate and his wife spread across large sections of the country. Yet with Republican prosperity then reaching its zenith the Democratic cause was all but hopeless. Often forgotten, too, is the ineptness of Smith's campaign. No serious effort was made to broaden his regional appeal. The Governor appointed a fellow Catholic, John J. Raskob, a General Motors executive, as Democratic national chairman. Smith believed that he needed the financial support of big business to win, but the choice of Raskob also reflected a growing personal conservatism. His closest friends and supporters were businessmen like Raskob, Riordan, William Kenny, and James Hoey. Smith's progressivism had always been rooted less in ideology than in his direct exposure to economic hardship and the plight of urban workers, and by the mid-1920's, with these earlier experiences far behind him, the conservatism which lay deep in the background of this self-made man of humble origins had reemerged.

Raskob's Catholicism, his outspoken opposition to prohibition, his close connections with big business, and his political inexperience hampered Smith's campaign from the outset. While ignoring the South out of overconfidence, Raskob poured large sums into hopelessly Republican Pennsylvania. As for the economically depressed farm belt, the Democratic platform did implicitly support the McNary-Haugen farm relief bill, and the influential farm leader George N. Peek [Supp. 3] campaigned for Smith, but these factors were insufficient to overcome the New Yorker's image as a big-city politician, a Catholic, and a wet. Smith and his running mate, Senator Joseph T. Robinson [Supp. 2] of Arkansas, received only 15,000,000 votes to Herbert Hoover's 21,400,000; the electoral count was 444 to 87. Hoover carried several Southern states, and even won Smith's home state of New York. But in losing, Smith polled more votes than any

former Democratic presidential candidate, and he broke into areas of traditional Republican strength. He won the nation's two most urbanized (and Catholic) states, Massachusetts and Rhode Island; carried the nation's twelve largest cities; and compiled significant pluralities among most immigrant groups.

The bigotry of the campaign shook Smith's vision of America and left him, for the first time in a third of a century, without immediate political prospects. His hoped-for return to influence in Albany following Franklin D. Roosevelt's somewhat unexpected gubernatorial victory in 1928 was thwarted by Roosevelt's desire for independence. Instead, Smith entered business as president of the Empire State Building Corporation (of which Raskob was a director) at a yearly salary of $50,000; he also served as chairman of a trust company. As he settled in a Fifth Avenue apartment and was lionized by New York's social and business circles, his conservatism hardened, and he drifted into an acrimonious feud with Roosevelt. Believing that he had built Roosevelt's political career, he was irked by the latter's indifference, particularly in matters of patronage and prestige. Although himself critical of Hoover's handling of the depression—in January 1932 he called for a federal bond issue to pay for unemployment relief—Smith was even more disturbed by Roosevelt's emergence as the prime Democratic presidential contender. Late in 1931, probably in an attempt to forestall Roosevelt, he launched an ill-organized campaign for the presidential nomination. He labeled "demagogic" Roosevelt's plea in April 1932 for the "forgotten man at the bottom of the economic pyramid," and throughout the next two years he expressed similar views in a monthly column of political opinion in the *New Outlook,* which he also served as editor. In the mid-1930's his close association with the privileged classes and his genuine alarm at the New Deal led Smith to an active role in the right-wing, anti-Roosevelt American Liberty League. In a broadcast speech before this group early in 1936, the former progressive told the nation that Roosevelt's administration was socialistic and was concentrating too much power in the federal bureaucracy. The attack drew cheers from his immediate audience and the anti-Roosevelt press, but many of his old supporters were puzzled and saddened.

Smith's opposition to the Democratic ticket in 1936 (and again in 1940) was largely ineffectual. Although he never voluntarily abandoned politics, "political power and influence slowly ebbed from him" (Josephson, p. 422). In contrast to his political frustrations after 1928, his personal life was somewhat happier. Knighted by the Pope and active in many church charities, he became the best-known Catholic layman of his time. His autobiography, *Up to Now,* appeared in 1929, and in the 1930's he wrote articles for the *Saturday Evening Post.* But even in the private realm tranquility was not to be his. The stock-market crash left two of his sons, a nephew, and several close friends deeply in debt, and Smith assumed heavy obligations on their behalf. The Empire State Building, completed in 1931, remained largely unoccupied, and only extreme efforts prevented bankruptcy. (Smith even made a trip to the White House to ask Roosevelt to rent federal office space in the building.) The approach of World War II partially mended the breach between Smith and Roosevelt. Smith supported the President's 1939 Neutrality Act amendments and actively backed the lend-lease program. Soon the two men were exchanging pleasantries, and Smith twice visited informally at the White House. The death of his wife in May 1944 was a loss from which he never recovered. His own death, of lung congestion and heart trouble, occurred later that year in Rockefeller Institute Hospital in New York City; his age was seventy. After a requiem mass at Saint Patrick's Cathedral, where his body had lain in state (Smith was the second layman accorded that honor, the pianist Paderewski being the first), he was buried in Calvary Cemetery, Long Island City, N. Y.

[The best recent study is Matthew and Hannah Josephson, *Al Smith: Hero of the Cities* (1969). Earlier books include the admiring *Gov. Al Smith* (1959), by James A. Farley and James C. G. Conniff; the straightforward *Al Smith, American* (1945), by Frank Graham; Henry F. Pringle, *Alfred E. Smith: A Critical Study* (1927); Oscar Handlin's warm appreciation, *Al Smith and His America* (1958); Norman Hapgood and Henry Moskowitz's useful *Up from the City Streets: Alfred E. Smith* (1927); Smith's own *Up to Now;* Charles C. Marshall's strenuously subjective *Gov. Smith's Am. Catholicism* (1928); Edmund A. Moore's scholarly study, *A Catholic Runs for President* (1956); Robert Moses's adulatory *A Tribute to Gov. Smith* (1962); and *The Happy Warrior* (1956), by Emily Warner, Smith's daughter, in collaboration with Hawthorne Daniel. Other books with sections on Smith include William Allen White's *Masks in a Pageant* (1928); Michael Williams's fascinating *The Shadow of the Pope* (1932); Frank Freidel, *Franklin D. Roosevelt,* vols. II and III (1954–56); and David Burner, *The Politics of Provincialism: The Democratic Party in Transition, 1918–1932* (1968). Scholarly articles include: Samuel B. Hand, "Al Smith, Franklin D. Roosevelt, and the New Deal," *Historian,* May 1965; and Jordan A. Schwarz, "Al Smith in the Thirties," *N. Y. Hist.,* Oct. 1964. A small collection of Smith letters is in the State Lib., Albany, N. Y. Four volumes of his *Public Papers* were published between 1919 and 1938. See also *Progressive Democracy: Addresses and State Papers of Gov. Alfred E. Smith, Democratic Candidate for President* (1928); and his *Addresses . . . Delivered at the Meetings of the Soc. of the Friendly Sons of Saint Patrick, 1922–1944* (1945).]

DAVID BURNER

SMITH, DAVID EUGENE (Jan. 21, 1860–July 29, 1944), mathematical educator and historian of science, was born in Cortland, N. Y., the second of four children and younger of two sons of Abram P. Smith, lawyer and county judge, and Mary Elizabeth (Bronson) Smith. His father was descended from Henri Schmidt, who immigrated to the United States about 1770, probably from Alsace, and settled in Cortland; his mother was the daughter of a cultivated country physician. David learned Greek and Latin from his mother, who died when he was twelve. He attended the newly founded State Normal School in Cortland and went on to Syracuse University, where he studied art and classical languages, including Hebrew. Graduating with a Ph.B. degree in 1881, he followed his father's wishes and took up the law, but after being admitted to the bar in 1884 he abandoned the legal profession to accept an appointment as teacher of mathematics in the State Normal School at Cortland. While there he received the degrees of Ph.M. (1884) and Ph.D. (1887) from Syracuse, the latter in art history.

From the beginning, Smith's mathematical interests lay in teaching and history rather than in original research. In 1891 he became professor of mathematics at the State Normal College at Ypsilanti, Mich. He published his first textbook, *Plane and Solid Geometry* (written with Wooster W. Beman), in 1895; his *History of Modern Mathematics* appeared the following year. In 1898 (having taken the degree of Master of Pedagogy at Ypsilanti) Smith was made principal of the State Normal School at Brockport, N. Y. Three years later he became professor of mathematics at Teachers College, Columbia University, where he remained until his retirement in 1926. From this position he wielded a great and lasting influence on mathematical instruction in the United States. The textbooks he wrote, sometimes with collaborators, for use in elementary and secondary schools numbered at least 150; they were widely adopted throughout the United States and were used in translation in other countries as well. Through everyday examples and other means, they brought a new liveliness and variety to the subject.

Smith's proficiency in languages, combined with his love of travel, early brought him in touch with mathematicians abroad. An appointment to the International Commission on the Teaching of Mathematics, headed by Prof. Felix Klein of Göttingen, placed him in a position of international influence. He served as vice-president of this group, 1908–20, as president, 1928–32, and as honorary president thereafter. His foreign affiliations included membership in the Deutsche Mathematiker Vereinigung, the Circolo Matematico di Palermo, the Comité de Patronage de l'Enseignement Mathématique, and the British Mathematical Association (honorary).

Of even greater importance were his many activities in the mathematical organizations of the United States, through which he came into close contact with the then current trends in the work of American mathematicians. His correspondence reveals the extent to which his professional advice was sought. He was an early member of the New York Mathematical Society (1893), and after it became the American Mathematical Society, he was appointed librarian and an associate editor of its *Bulletin*. During his long tenure in both offices (1902–20), Smith expanded the society's book collection into a noteworthy library. He was vice-president of the society in 1922. He rendered equally important service to the Mathematical Association of America, becoming an associate editor of the *American Mathematical Monthly* in 1916 and president of the association during the term 1920–21. Several other publications owe much to Smith's active interest and promotion. He was among those who encouraged Otto Neugebauer to set up the *Mathematical Reviews,* the American equivalent of the *Zentralblatt für Mathematik*. He supported Herbert E. Slaught in establishing the Carus Monograph series, and played a primary role in the founding of *Scripta Mathematica* at Yeshiva College in New York City (1932).

Smith's greatest contribution was to the history of mathematics. He was instrumental in the founding of the History of Science Society in 1924, served as its first president in 1927, and strongly supported the compilation and translation of historical material by established scholars such as Thomas L. Heath, Raymond C. Archibald, George Bruce Halsted [q.v.], Eric T. Bell, Julian L. Coolidge, and Leonard E. Dickson. An avid collector, Smith traveled to all parts of the world, buying rare books, manuscripts, and mathematical and astronomical instruments. He worked closely with a fellow collector, the publisher George A. Plimpton [Supp. 2], and advised him on many purchases. The nearly 11,000 books Smith himself assembled covered with great comprehensiveness the writings of mathematicians before 1900, but he concentrated particularly on objects from India and the Far East and on medieval material from Europe and the Islamic countries. To his efforts can be ascribed the awakening of interest in the mathematics of the medieval Orient and the Middle East. His collection, which he donated to Columbia in 1931,

has become part of the Plimpton-Smith-Dale Library there. Smith's range may be gauged by his election as a fellow of both the Mediaeval Academy of America and the American Association for the Advancement of Science.

Smith was a prolific writer. His best-known historical works are the *Rara Arithmetica* (1908), *Number Stories of Long Ago* (1919), and his *History of Mathematics* (2 vols., 1923–25). He also produced valuable works in collaboration with others, notably the translation with Marcia L. Latham of René Descartes's *La Géométrie* (1925); *Hindu-Arabic Numerals* (1911), with Louis C. Karpinski; *A History of Japanese Mathematics* (1914), with Y. Mikami; and a *History of Mathematics in America before 1900* (1934), with Jekuthiel Ginsburg.

Smith's joy in his collecting experiences greatly enhanced his skill as a raconteur, whether on the lecture platform or in his home, where he entertained extensively. He was twice married: on Jan. 19, 1887, to Fanny Taylor of Cortland, N. Y., who died in 1928; and, late in his life (Nov. 5, 1940), to Eva May Luse, with whom he had collaborated earlier on textbooks. He was a member of the Methodist Episcopal Church. Smith died at the age of eighty-four at his home in New York City and was buried in the Rural Cemetery at Cortland.

[David Eugene Smith Papers (professional and personal correspondence), Butler Lib., Columbia Univ.; vol. I (1936) of the periodical *Osiris*, which was dedicated to Smith and includes a bibliography of his writings by Bertha M. Frick and an account of the David Eugene Smith Mathematical Lib. of Columbia Univ.; the May 1926 issue of the *Mathematics Teacher*, which contains a series of articles about Smith and reproduces the portrait by Leo Mielziner at Teachers College; William David Reeve in *Scripta Mathematica,* Sept.–Dec. 1945 (also in *Mathematics Teacher,* Oct. 1944); W. Benjamin Fite in *Am. Mathematical Monthly,* May 1945; Lao Genevra Simons in Am. Mathematical Soc., *Bull.,* Jan. 1945; Frederick E. Brasch and Lavada Hudgens, "The Hist. of Science Soc. and the David Eugene Smith Festschrift," *Science,* May 8, 1936; *Scripta Mathematica,* April 1936, pp. 182–84; *Am. Men of Sci.,* 1st through 7th editions; *Who Was Who in America,* vol. II (1950). See also Smith's "The David Eugene Smith Gift of Historical-Mathematical Instruments to Columbia Univ.," *Science,* Jan. 24, 1936; and, for an excellent account of the Internat. Commission on the Teaching of Mathematics, *Mathematics Teacher,* Dec. 1909. Family information from a niece, Mrs. Helen Jewett McAleer, courtesy of Cortland (N. Y.) Free Lib.]

CAROLYN EISELE
LYLE G. BOYD

SMITH, ELLISON DuRANT (Aug. 1, 1864–Nov. 17, 1944), Senator from South Carolina, known as "Cotton Ed" Smith, was born at Tanglewood, the 2,000-acre plantation near Lynchburg, S. C., which had been in family hands since his English forebears settled there in 1747.

He was one of five children and the youngest of the three sons of William Hawkins Smith, a Methodist minister, and Mary Isabella (McLeod) Smith; his brother Alexander Coke Smith became a prominent Methodist bishop. His mother was a native of the Scottish Isle of Skye. The boy received his early education at schools in Lynchburg and Charleston, S. C. He entered South Carolina College in 1885, but the following year transferred to Wofford College, where he was graduated in 1889. On May 26, 1892, he married Martha Cornelia Moorer of St. George, S. C., who died the following year; their only child, Martius Ellison, was killed in 1912 in a hunting accident. On Oct. 31, 1906, Smith married Annie Brunson Farley of Spartanburg, S. C., by whom he had four children: Anna Brunson, Isobel McLeod, Ellison DuRant, and Charles Saxon Farley.

Smith first entered politics in 1890, the year in which Benjamin R. Tillman led the agrarian masses in a political revolt against Wade Hampton [qq.v.] and the aristocrats. When, that October, a convention of die-hard conservatives met and nominated Alexander C. Haskell as an independent candidate against Tillman, Smith was listed as a delegate, although he later denied being present. Despite his early Bourbon affiliations, Smith was deeply affected by the ideology of the agrarian protest, and in his subsequent political career he waged a continuous battle against such old Populist enemies as the tariff, Wall Street, hard money, and big business. He represented Sumter County in the state legislature from 1897 to 1900 and made an unsuccessful bid for election to Congress in 1901.

Himself a cotton farmer at Lynchburg, Smith became active during the next few years in a movement to organize Southern cotton growers. He attended growers' conventions in Louisiana in 1904 and 1905, where his forensic efforts attracted wide attention and earned him the nickname "Cotton Ed," which he thereafter cherished. In 1905 he became a field agent for the Southern Cotton Association, which sought to raise cotton prices; the statewide contacts he established strengthened his political base. As a candidate for the United States Senate in 1908, "Cotton Ed" unveiled the pageantry that was to become his trademark. Perched on two cotton bales in a wagon drawn by lint-plastered mules, with a cotton boll in his lapel, he stumped the state proclaiming his devotion to "my sweetheart, Miss Cotton." Smith won the election over several formidable opponents, the beginning of a long Senate career.

In Washington the new Senator joined the

Democratic and Progressive onslaught upon the Taft Republicans, and with the Democratic triumph in 1912 he became an adherent of Woodrow Wilson and the New Freedom. Like other Southern agrarians, Smith lent enthusiastic support to Wilson's farm program, the Federal Reserve Act, the Underwood Tariff, and the Federal Highways Act. He voted with less enthusiasm for the Clayton Act, the Adamson Act, and the Federal Trade Commission Act; and he opposed child labor legislation and woman suffrage. A reliable Wilson supporter during and after World War I, Smith sponsored the bill creating the Wilson Dam at Muscle Shoals for the production of nitrates. After the Harding landslide of 1920, he reverted to his earlier role as Senatorial critic of the Republican administration, opposing the Fordney-McCumber Tariff, the fiscal policies of Secretary of the Treasury Andrew Mellon [Supp. 2], and the Smoot-Hawley Tariff, but voting for restrictive immigration laws and the soldiers' bonus. Smith helped form the Senate's farm bloc in 1921. He opposed the McNary-Haugen bills in 1924 and 1926, but did support later versions of the McNary-Haugen plan. He also supported the World Court, a stand that, together with the opposition of Coleman L. Blease [Supp. 3] and the Ku Klux Klan, almost cost him the election of 1926, when his opponent (Edgar A. Brown) claimed that the Court had three Negro judges. In the 1932 election, however, Smith had little difficulty in defeating Blease himself, as he had previously in 1914.

An early supporter of Franklin D. Roosevelt, Smith had looked forward to a position in the new administration that would enable him to "make that crowd that is in eat out of a Southern spoon" (Columbia State, June 15, 1932). Although he became chairman of the Senate Agriculture Committee, Smith had little influence in shaping the New Deal farm program. He thought the Agricultural Adjustment Administration too complicated, and though he favored price supports, he opposed crop controls. The severity of the depression and Roosevelt's initial popularity caused him to vote for most of the early New Deal legislation, but he had little enthusiasm for the WPA, the NRA, and other agencies that threatened to interfere with the South's social and economic structure.

After 1935 Smith became more openly hostile to the administration. He also became more demagogic. Whereas previously it was not Smith but his opponents (such as Blease) who had injected race-baiting into the political campaigns, Smith now unleashed a barrage of vitriolic tirades in the Senate against Negroes and against the proposed antilynching law. He vigorously opposed the regulation of wages and hours and, with appeals to the sanctity of states' rights, fought against the judiciary and executive reorganization bills of 1937. Roosevelt attempted to "purge" Smith in the 1938 elections, but the strategy backfired and the Senator went on to win the greatest political triumph of his career. The mainstay of his campaign was the "Philadelphia Story," a masterpiece of Southern political demagoguery in which he regaled his audiences with an account of his well-publicized walkout from that year's Democratic National Convention following an invocation by a Negro minister.

Smith's last term was an anticlimax. The prosperity that accompanied World War II obscured the domestic issues he had hoped to raise, and his opposition to selective service, lend-lease, and other wartime policies irritated a constituency that ardently supported the war effort. These factors, together with the effects of old age (he was now eighty), brought about his defeat in 1944 by Gov. Olin D. Johnston. "Cotton Ed" died at Tanglewood of a coronary thrombosis just a few weeks before his term expired. He was buried in the cemetery of St. Luke's Methodist Church near Lynchburg. At the time of his death his tenure of almost thirty-six years was the longest in Senate history.

Ellison D. Smith committed the cardinal sin of remaining in office too long. The race-baiting histrionics of his last years, attributable partly to political frustration and to the decline of his faculties, obscured the respectable, though modest, accomplishments of his earlier career.

[The author knows of no collection of Smith papers. The most comprehensive study of Smith is Selden K. Smith, "Ellison DuRant Smith: A Southern Progressive, 1909–1929" (Ph.D. dissertation, Univ. of S. C., 1970). There is a good photograph of Smith, along with a biographical sketch, in David D. Wallace, *The Hist. of S. C.,* vol. IV (1934). Smith's speeches and voting record can be traced in the *Cong. Record,* 1909–44. Various aspects of his career are discussed in Robert McCormick, "He's for Cotton," *Collier's,* Apr. 23, 1938, and Beverly Smith, "F.D.R. Here I Come," *American Mag.,* Jan. 1939. See also John A. Rice, *I Came Out of the Eighteenth Century* (1942); Ernest M. Lander, Jr., *A Hist. of S. C., 1865–1960* (1960); Frank E. Jordan, *The Primary State: A Hist. of the Democratic Party in S. C., 1876–1962* (1967); Harry S. Ashmore, *An Epitaph for Dixie* (1957); Daniel W. Hollis, " 'Cotton Ed Smith'—Showman or Statesman?" *S. C. Hist. Mag.,* Oct. 1970.]

DANIEL WALKER HOLLIS

SMITH, GEORGE OTIS (Feb. 22, 1871–Jan. 10, 1944), geologist and public administrator, was born in Hodgdon, Maine, the older of two children and only son of Joseph Otis Smith by his second wife, Emma Mayo; he had one older half sister. His father was a descendant of John Smith, who settled in Barnstable, Mass., in

1630. Joseph Smith in 1878 founded a newspaper in Skowhegan, Maine, and edited it for many years, save for a brief period (1881–84) when he served as Maine's secretary of state.

George Smith at first leaned toward journalism, but at Colby College, where he graduated, A.B., in 1893, he developed an interest in geology. Going on to Johns Hopkins University, he earned his Ph.D. in 1896 and promptly joined the United States Geological Survey. In the next ten years of field work he published thirty-five papers, mostly in the Survey's *Bulletin,* and distinguished himself as an energetic if not especially original worker in petrographic geology. By 1906 he had become the head of the Survey's petrographic section. At that time the Keep Committee was studying the workings of the federal government for President Theodore Roosevelt, and Smith was asked to chair a special subcommittee to study the business methods of the Survey. The task won him attention in the government outside his own bureau, especially among the small circle of advisers who had the presidential ear on resource and conservation issues. When Charles D. Walcott [*q.v.*] resigned as head of the Geological Survey to become secretary of the Smithsonian Institution in 1907, Secretary of the Interior James R. Garfield reached down the seniority ladder to appoint the thirty-seven-year-old Smith as the new director.

The Geological Survey had an illustrious scientific past, but had suffered grave political wounds shortly before Smith joined it in 1896. In the 1880's John Wesley Powell [*q.v.*] had worked to create ties with a constituency of outside groups while cultivating important Congressmen, all in the classic style of agency politics. He had, however, stretched the mission of the Geological Survey to its limits, even to producing a blueprint for national economic development based on the findings of science, and in the end had very nearly shattered the coalition of supporting groups and Congressmen. It had fallen to Walcott to pull in the overextended boundaries. Although Walcott made an effort to nurture the tradition of original work in science begun under Powell, the energies of the Survey were increasingly devoted to the inventory and classification of natural resources, such as coal, oil, gas, phosphates, potash, and waterpower sites.

When Smith became director in 1907, this work continued as the Survey's chief concern and developed into its principal contribution to the coordinated policies known as the conservation movement. Smith's standing with the Roosevelt conservationists declined precipitously when he sided with Richard Ballinger [*q.v.*] in the

Pinchot-Ballinger controversy which exploded in the Taft years, but his conception of the Survey as a politically neutral "fact finder" kept him from going under entirely. In truth, his limitations reflected the bureau's role in changing America. At a time when the economic and political life of the nation was being organized along bureaucratic lines, Smith played the modern agency head's game of arbitrating between the "public" and "private" sectors of the new corporate social order.

The new direction of the Geological Survey was given impetus by President Woodrow Wilson's preparedness program. When the Council of National Defense asked if the nation could support itself if foreign mineral supplies were cut off, Smith launched an inventory of minerals in the United States. Later, for President Wilson's "Inquiry"—a group of experts to advise the President on the peace—he prepared a tour de force among inventories, *The World Atlas of Commercial Geology: Part I, Distribution of Mineral Production of the World* and *Part 2, Water Powers of the World.* Both were ready in time to be used by the Peace Commission.

The *Atlas*, with its emphasis on power, diverted Smith's career in new directions. In 1920, with a Congressional appropriation of $125,000 and $26,000 contributed by thirty-six corporations, he and his bureau conducted the Superpower Survey, "a special investigation and report on the power supply for the Boston-Washington industrial region," which laid the foundation for the interconnection of power plants later characteristic of this seaboard area. For the rest of Smith's public career questions of power resources predominated. By the end of the 1920's he was the nation's power authority most congenial to industry and engineering groups. With an engineer in the White House, Smith was offered the chairmanship of the new Federal Power Commission in 1930. His acceptance proved his undoing. Because he favored regulated private power, he was viewed with suspicion from the beginning by advocates of public power, and he found himself in the center of a storm of indignation when the commission discharged two officials who stood for public development. The Senate withdrew its approval of his appointment, and although President Herbert Hoover stood firm, it ultimately took a Supreme Court decision to establish Smith's right to the position. In 1933 President Franklin Roosevelt "suggested" to Smith (as one of his biographers delicately put it) "that he submit his resignation so that the post would be available for someone with closer affiliations to those in power" (Smith, p. 321).

A Baptist and a Republican, Smith was a member of the Cosmos Club in Washington and served as president of the American Institute of Mining and Metallurgical Engineers (1928), president of the District of Columbia Y.M.C.A., and chairman of the board of trustees of his alma mater, Colby. On Nov. 18, 1896, he had married Grace M. Coburn of a Maine lumbering family, who died in 1931; their children were Charles Coburn, Joseph Coburn, Helen Coburn, Elizabeth Coburn (who died in infancy), and Louise Coburn. Returning after his retirement to Skowhegan, Maine, Smith died eight years later of a heart attack in Augusta, Maine, where he was attending a meeting of the board of directors of the Central Maine Power Company. He was buried in Northside Cemetery, Skowhegan.

[Thomas G. Manning, *Government in Science: The U. S. Geological Survey, 1867–1894* (1967); J. C. and M. C. Rabbitt, "The U. S. Geological Survey: 75 Years of Service to the Nation, 1879–1954," *Science,* May 28, 1954; Samuel P. Hays, *Conservation and the Gospel of Efficiency: The Progressive Conservation Movement, 1890–1920* (1959); Donald C. Swain, *Federal Conservation Policy, 1921–1933* (1963). Biographical material is scanty, but see the memorial article by Philip S. Smith in Geological Soc. of America, *Proc.,* 1944; *Who Was Who in America,* vol. II (1950); and *Nat. Cyc. Am. Biog.,* XXXV, 385–86. On his father, see Louise H. Coburn, *Skowhegan on the Kennebec,* II (1941), 500.]

JAMES PENICK, JR.

SMITH, PRESERVED (July 22, 1880–May 15, 1941), historian, son of the Rev. Henry Preserved Smith [*q.v.*] and Anna (Macneale) Smith, and nephew of Richmond Mayo-Smith [*q.v.*], was born in Cincinnati, Ohio, the first son and second of four children, of whom the two youngest died in childhood. His sister, Winifred, became a professor of English at Vassar College and founder of its drama department. His father, a professor at Lane Theological Seminary and a pioneer in introducing the higher criticism of the Bible into the United States, was tried for heresy and suspended from the Presbyterian ministry in 1892. He then resigned his professorship and left Cincinnati.

After traveling abroad with his father for more than a year, young Smith entered Lawrenceville School in New Jersey and, later, Amherst College, from which he graduated, B.A., in 1901. He then began graduate work in history at Columbia University, taking the M.A. degree in 1902. At this point his study was interrupted by an attack of tuberculosis, from which, however, he recovered sufficiently to resume graduate work and to take an instructorship at Williams College, 1904–06. He obtained the Ph.D. degree at Columbia in 1907, his thesis being a critical study of Luther's *Table Talk*. The years at Columbia under the influence of James Harvey Robinson [Supp. 2] were of crucial importance, reinforcing Smith's native tendency toward a liberal humanitarianism and rationalism and furnishing the presuppositions on which his later interpretation of history was based.

After leaving Columbia he was granted a seven-year fellowship from Amherst, which enabled him to spend the next three years studying in Berlin and Paris. He returned briefly to marry Helen Idella Kendall of Walpole, Mass., on Apr. 28, 1909; his only child, Priscilla, was born the following year in Paris. The years of his fellowship, which he later recalled as the happiest of his life, ended in the winter of 1913 with the death of his wife and a second attack of tuberculosis. For the next five years Smith lived in enforced retirement with his sister at Vassar, gradually recovering from his illness. On June 20, 1918, he married Lucy Henderson Humphrey of New York City and moved to Cambridge, Mass. He lectured for a semester at Harvard and another at Wellesley College before receiving a permanent appointment as professor of history at Cornell University in 1922, a post he held until his death.

Preserved Smith had already acquired a solid scholarly reputation by the publication of several distinguished books and innumerable articles and reviews. His interest continued for many years to be focused on Luther and the Reformation. His *Life and Letters of Martin Luther* (1911) won immediate acclaim and was followed by a collection of *Luther's Correspondence and Other Contemporary Letters* (2 vols., 1913–18) which he edited and translated (the second volume in association with Charles M. Jacobs). While critical of Luther's dogmatism and violence, the *Life and Letters* was warmly appreciative of the elements of greatness in the Reformer's character. As a by-product of his study of Luther's doctrine of the Eucharist, Smith also published *A Short History of Christian Theophagy* (1922). Although he had lost faith in revealed religion, Smith regarded the Reformation as a crucial turning point in history, which by breaking the universal authority of the Catholic Church opened the way for divergence of opinion and the rise of rationalism. In *The Age of the Reformation* (1920)— still, fifty years later, the most comprehensive one-volume treatment of the sixteenth century in English—he placed the Reformation in relation to the economic, social, political, and intellectual currents of the age.

Smith next turned to the study of Erasmus, the champion of "undogmatic Christianity," who, he felt, typified the contact between Renaissance and Reformation. *Erasmus: A Study of His Life, Ideals and Place in History* (1923) and the brief monograph *A Key to the Colloquies of Erasmus* (1927) were works of sound scholarship, warmed by intuitive insights into a personality for which Smith felt a particular affinity. Further study convinced him that it was the rise of modern science and rationalism rather than either the Renaissance or the Reformation which marked the beginning of the modern era. His *History of Modern Culture* (2 vols., 1930–34), covering the years 1543–1776, was written to fill the need for a comprehensive synthesis of modern intellectual history. Two more volumes were planned and partly written, but failing energy forced him to leave the work uncompleted. Despite inevitable errors, it has not yet been superseded.

More than most scholars, Smith lived in a world of books and ideas, somewhat inhibited from social intercourse by frail health and an inherent shyness. His personality was most fully expressed in his writing, which was characterized by lucidity, emotional warmth, and a fine turn of wit. Those students and friends who were admitted to intimacy knew him as a gentle, affectionate man, always generous in giving aid and encouragement and in acknowledging his scholarly debts. His final illness, a recurrence of tuberculosis, began in September 1940 while he was visiting his daughter in her home near Louisville, Ky. He died in the Jewish Hospital in Louisville the next year and was buried in Ithaca, N. Y.

[William Gilbert, "The Work of Preserved Smith," *Jour. of Modern Hist.*, Dec. 1951; John A. Garraty, "Preserved Smith, Ralph Volney Harlow, and Psychology," *Jour. of the Hist. of Ideas*, June 1954; *Who Was Who in America*, vol. I (1942); obituaries in *Am. Hist. Rev.*, July 1941, pp. 1016–17, Am. Philosophical Soc., *Year Book*, 1942 (by Robert L. Schuyler), and *N. Y. Times*, May 16, 1941.]

WALLACE K. FERGUSON

SMOOT, REED OWEN (Jan. 10, 1862–Feb. 9, 1941), businessman, churchman, and Senator from Utah, was born in Salt Lake City into a leading Mormon family. His father, Abraham Owen Smoot, of Scottish and English ancestry, had become a convert to Mormonism in his native Kentucky in 1835 and had led a division of settlers to Utah in the exodus of 1847. He served as mayor of Salt Lake City (1856–66) and later of Provo, Utah (1868–80). Reed's mother, Anne Kirstine Morrison (originally Mauritzen), a Mormon convert from Norway, was one of Abraham Smoot's several wives by plural marriage; of her seven children, Reed was the third. He attended church schools and entered

Brigham Young Academy (later University) in the first class in 1877. After his graduation in 1879, he joined his father in the extensive business enterprises the latter had begun after moving to Provo. Reed was manager of the Provo Co-op Institution, a general store, at eighteen, and of the Provo Woolen Mills, an important local industry founded by his father, at twenty-three. He established a drug firm, bought and sold livestock, organized a coal and lumber company, built a business block, and was a founder and the first president of the Provo Commercial and Savings Bank. He also invested in mining, railroads, insurance, agriculture, and electric power enterprises, and by thirty-five had amassed a considerable fortune.

Smoot was not especially religious in his youth, but in 1895, having progressed through all the formal ranks of the Mormon priesthood, he was named a counselor in the presidency of the Utah stake, a geographical subdivision of the church. In 1900 he was ordained as one of the Quorum of Twelve Apostles of the Church of Jesus Christ of Latter-day Saints, a position second only to the presidency of the church. As an apostle until his death, eventually as the senior member of the quorum, he gave absolute loyalty to the two presidents under whom he served, Joseph F. Smith and Heber J. Grant. Although himself the son of a polygamous marriage, he accepted as a direct revelation of God the church's manifesto of 1890 (issued as part of Utah's efforts to achieve statehood) which called for an end to polygamy, and was a powerful force in assuring its acceptance.

Until the 1890's, Utah politics had been of a parochial character, divided between the church-based People's party and the non-Mormon Liberal party. Smoot, as an ardent believer in the high protective tariff, was one of the earliest in Utah to become a Republican. He had, however, held no significant political office when, in 1902, he was nominated by his party for the United States Senate; his election to that office by the Utah legislature followed in January 1903. Because of his high position in the church, he faced strong non-Mormon opposition in this first campaign and again in 1908 and 1914, but he was consistently reelected, serving in Washington until 1933.

Anti-Mormon hostility shadowed Smoot's first Senate term. His right to a seat was challenged on the ground that he was a leader in a church which still harbored polygamists and which disregarded the Constitutional separation between church and state. Personal innuendo figured in the anti-Smoot campaign as well, and for more than two years (January 1904 to June 1906) the Senate's Committee on Privileges and Elections considered his case in an atmosphere often charged with intolerance. The committee issued an adverse report, but this was overruled in February 1907 by the Senate, voting strictly along party lines, with pressure by President Theodore Roosevelt contributing to the outcome.

This vindication strengthened Smoot's already great devotion to the Republican party. In his early years in politics he supported such Roosevelt reforms as conservation and the national parks movement, but his fundamental conservatism was recognized by Senator Nelson W. Aldrich [q.v.], who in 1909 gave him a place on the Senate Finance Committee. With this new status and the departure of Roosevelt, Smoot's conservatism blossomed, and he became a leading member of the standpat Republicans, exerting wide influence through numerous committee positions both in the Senate and in the national party organization.

Smoot had a passion for economy which membership on the Finance Committee and, after 1911, the Appropriations Committee provided ample opportunity to gratify. He consistently fought for lower taxes and governmental efficiency and during the 1920's was known as the watchdog of the Treasury. A strong nationalist, he was suspicious of the League of Nations, and although not considered an "Irreconcilable" in the Senate fight over America's entry into the League, he was a prominent member of the "Reservationists" led by Senator Henry Cabot Lodge [q.v.]; he also worked energetically to secure repayment of America's war debt. A rigid moralist, Smoot vigorously opposed the effort of some Senators, in 1929–30, to limit the censorship power of federal customs officials over the importation of books.

No subject stirred Smoot's interest more than tariff protection, particularly for the woolen and beet-sugar industries, two of his many business interests. It was, therefore, a fitting climax to his career when he achieved the chairmanship of the Finance Committee in 1923 and thus gave his name, along with that of Congressman Willis C. Hawley [Supp. 3], to the highly protectionist Smoot-Hawley Tariff Act of 1930.

Smoot had married Alpha Mae Eldredge of Salt Lake City on Sept. 17, 1884. They had six children: Harold Reed, Chloe, Harlow Eldredge, Anna Kirstine, Zella Esther, and Ernest Winder. Mrs. Smoot died in 1928 after a long illness, and on July 2, 1930, Smoot married Mrs. Alice (Taylor) Sheets, the widowed daughter of a Yorkshire banker.

Brusque and sometimes abrasive in manner, Smoot was an indefatigable worker. His Senate power stemmed from a monumental grasp of facts and figures. When the Democratic landslide of 1932 at last brought political defeat, he returned to Utah and gave his full time to church affairs. He regarded the New Deal with something akin to horror and regretted that he was not in a position to oppose it in the Senate. His final years were also darkened by a serious decline in his personal fortune caused by the depression. He died in 1941, of heart and kidney disease, while vacationing in St. Petersburg, Fla., and was buried in Provo Burial Park, Provo, Utah.

[The Reed Smoot Papers, at Brigham Young Univ.; Milton R. Merrill, "Reed Smoot, Apostle in Politics" (Ph.D. dissertation, Columbia Univ., 1950); Merrill's article of the same title in *Western Humanities Rev.*, Winter 1954–55; and *Reed Smoot, Utah Politician* (Utah State Agricultural College monograph series, 1953). For accounts of Smoot and Mormonism, see Brigham H. Roberts, *A Comprehensive Hist. of the Church of Jesus Christ of Latter-day Saints*, vol. VI (1930); and Wallace Turner, *The Mormon Establishment* (1966). See also: Reed Smoot, "Why I Am a Mormon," *Forum*, Oct. 1926, and "Utah in Politics," *Independent*, Oct. 17, 1907; Nels Anderson, "Pontifex Babbitt," *Am. Mercury*, Oct. 1926; J. Cecil Alter, *Utah: The Storied Domain*, II (1932), 4–6; *Nat. Cyc. Am. Biog.*, XXXV, 63–64; and *N. Y. Times* obituary, Feb. 10, 1941. Death record from Fla. Bureau of Vital Statistics. On Smoot's father, see Orson F. Whitney, *Hist. of Utah*, IV (1904), 98–102.]

MILTON R. MERRILL

SPEYER, JAMES JOSEPH (July 22, 1861– Oct. 31, 1941), financier and philanthropist, was born in New York City to German Jewish parents, one of three children and the older of two sons. His father, Gustavus Speyer, a member of one of Germany's most powerful banking houses, had come in 1845 from Frankfurt am Main to New York City to join the American branch of the firm, Philip Speyer & Company, which a brother had established in 1837. Gustavus married Sophie Rubino in 1860 and four years later returned with her to Frankfurt.

James Speyer grew up in Frankfurt and attended public schools there. He entered the family bank at the age of twenty-one, spent two years of training at the London and Paris branches, and in 1885 joined the New York branch. By this time the American firm, now known as Speyer & Company, had shifted its business from dealing in foreign exchange and imports to underwriting and distributing railroad securities and foreign government bonds. Speyer became senior partner in 1899. Though genial and gregarious, he was also domineering. His proud individuality won him the hostility of several powerful men; J. P. Morgan [q.v.], for example, refused to sit on any corporate board with him, and Edward H. Harriman [q.v.], after purchasing the Southern Pacific in 1901, immediately ousted the Speyer interests.

Through his family, however, Speyer was one of a small group of American bankers able to mobilize large amounts of foreign capital. Speyer & Company was widely regarded in the early 1900's as one of the great international banking houses of the time, along with Morgan and Kuhn, Loeb in New York and Kidder, Peabody and Lee, Higginson in Boston. The Speyer firm acted as financial agent for the railroad interests of Collis P. Huntington [q.v.], floated millions of dollars of securities for the Pennsylvania Railroad, and handled the reorganization of the Lake Shore & Rock Island and the Baltimore & Ohio railroads (1896). In 1905, together with several New York and German bankers, Speyer reorganized and financed the consolidation of the Mexican railroad system, and in 1906 he helped finance the construction of the Philippine Railway. He later distributed British securities for the construction of the London subway system. He also took the lead in financing several projects in Bolivia and Ecuador and in distributing $35,000,000 of bonds to establish the credit of the newly established Republic of Cuba. Other concerns for which he acted as financial adviser included Corn Products Refining, Pittsburgh Steel, Victor Talking Machine, and the Radio Corporation of America.

With the outbreak of World War I, the prestige and power of Speyer & Company began to decline rapidly. Speyer himself was decidedly pro-German; indeed, he spent every summer in Germany and was a frequent guest of Kaiser Wilhelm. Early in the war, he and Count Johann von Bernstorff, the German ambassador to the United States, made a futile attempt to enlist support for a peace drive. Speyer & Company was placed on the British blacklist in 1916, and shortly afterward Sir Edgar Speyer, James's brother, was forced to close the family's London branch. A postwar decline in railroad stocks further weakened the company. So, too, did the rapid postwar expansion of American investment capital, as the United States shifted from a debtor to a creditor nation, thus reducing the importance of foreign capital. By 1930, having grossed less than $400,000,000 in the previous four years, Speyer & Company was no longer among the first fifty private banking houses. The final blow came with the rise of Nazi anti-Semitism, which forced the closing in 1934 of the Speyer banks in Berlin and Frankfurt. James Speyer formally retired in 1938, and the American firm was liquidated in 1939.

But the eclipse of the House of Speyer was not the result of external factors alone; Speyer's temperament and business methods were also to blame. He ran essentially a one-man company and made no real attempt to train a successor. At the same time, his interests were too varied to permit him to devote to the banking business the effort required to perpetuate the Speyer firm. He had long participated actively in New York social, philanthropic, and civic affairs. His marriage, on Nov. 11, 1897, to Ellin Leslie (Prince) Lowery, a widow of colonial ancestry and eminent social standing, accorded him a place in New York society. The couple, who were childless, entertained lavishly, with all the appurtenances of Old World elegance, both at their Fifth Avenue town house and at their one-hundred-acre estate, Waldheim, at Scarborough-on-Hudson. Speyer, who always dressed in the height of fashion, belonged to numerous social clubs and was the only Jewish member of the exclusive Racquet Club.

An active philanthropist, Speyer was one of the founders of the University Settlement Society (1891), of which he was an early treasurer and president, 1921–24; he was also a founder (1894) and, at various times, treasurer and president of the Provident Loan Society, for which he helped raise $100,000. He and his wife in 1902 gave the funds for the Speyer School of Columbia University's Teachers College, an experimental school closely linked with settlement work. Speyer was one of the founders in 1913 of the American Society for the Control of Cancer. He established in 1905 the Theodore Roosevelt Exchange Professorship between the University of Berlin and Columbia; he also donated to various Jewish charities. A founder in 1923 and a trustee of the Museum of the City of New York, which is devoted to the history of the city, he contributed a number of paintings and over $250,000, and was chairman of its finance committee. In political affairs, Speyer was a supporter of Grover Cleveland in 1892. He was also a vice-president and treasurer of the progressive German-American Reform Union, and a member of the executive committee of the Committee of Seventy, which spearheaded the election of reform mayor William L. Strong [q.v.] in 1894. During the 1920's he was an active opponent of prohibition.

Speyer died at the age of eighty at his home in New York City. After funeral services conducted by both a rabbi and an Episcopal minister, he was buried in Sleepy Hollow Cemetery, Tarrytown, N. Y. He left his home on Fifth Avenue to the Museum of the City of New York.

[Bertie C. Forbes, *Men Who Are Making America* (1917), pp. 360–67; Lyman H. Weeks, ed., *Prominent Families of N. Y.* (1897), p. 517; *Nat. Cyc. Am. Biog.*, XXXVI, 56–57; *Who Was Who in America*, vol. I (1942); "The Banking House of Speyer & Co.," *Independent*, Apr. 2, 1903; "The New Generation in Wall St.," *ibid.*, Dec. 26, 1912; references to Speyer in *World's Work*, Oct. 1905, Feb. 1907, and Feb. 1913; interview in *Mag. of Wall Street*, Feb. 7, 1920; *Fortune*, Aug. 1931, pp. 79–82; *Time*, June 13, 1938, pp. 64, 66, June 26, 1939, p. 73; various newspaper references, especially *N. Y. Times*, May 2, 1937 (sec. 2), June 4, 1938, June 13, 1939, Nov. 1, 4, 7, 1941. See also Dixon Wecter, *The Saga of Am. Society* (1937), pp. 154–55; and sketch of Ellin Speyer in *Notable Am. Women*.]

HERMAN E. KROOSS

STANDISH, BURT L. See PATTEN, GILBERT.

STEAGALL, HENRY BASCOM (May 19, 1873–Nov. 22, 1943), Congressman from Alabama, was born in Clopton, Ala., the second son and fourth of ten children of Mary Jane (Peacock) and William Collinsworth Steagall. His mother was the daughter of a local farmer. His father, a native of Georgia and the son of a Methodist minister, was a prosperous physician, trained at the New York Medical College; he was also active in local Democratic politics and served two terms in the state senate. Henry Steagall attended private schools, the Southeast Alabama Agricultural School in Abbeville, from which he graduated in 1892, and the University of Alabama, where he received the LL.B. degree in 1893. He then returned to his native Dale County and established a law practice in Ozark, the county seat. A friendly extrovert, he was active in the Methodist Church and joined the Masons, the Woodmen of the World, and the Knights of Pythias. On Dec. 27, 1900, he married Sallie Mae Thompson of Tuskegee, Ala., who died in 1908. They had five children: Margaret Thompson, Mabelle Massey, Myra Mitchell, Porter Collinsworth, and Sallie Mae.

Although Steagall sympathized with the aims of the Populist movement of the 1890's, he embarked upon a political career in the Democratic party. He gained a reputation for eloquence and in 1898 was appointed county solicitor. Popular and ambitious, he won election in 1906 to the state house of representatives. There he supported the reform program of Gov. Braxton Bragg Comer [q.v.] and was rewarded for his loyalty with the post of solicitor (district attorney) of the third judicial circuit, to which he was appointed in 1907; he was elected to a full term in 1910. In 1914 he unsuccessfully challenged the incumbent Congressman from his district, Henry D. Clayton [Supp. 1]. Later that year, however, Clayton was appointed to the federal bench, and Steagall was victorious in a special primary to complete his unexpired term. He was never seriously challenged for reelection and served continuously until his death.

In Congress, Steagall devoted himself to his major committee assignment, the Banking and Currency Committee, which considered legislation affecting farmers as well as the financial community. He was a loyal but relatively unimportant supporter of the Wilson administration, making a minor contribution to the creation of the Federal Land Bank System. As a member of a small and often querulous Democratic minority during the 1920's, he joined the bipartisan farm bloc and frequently attacked Republican claims of prosperity on the ground that farmers were not sharing in the general affluence. He supported the McNary-Haugen farm bills, attacked the growth of branch banking—which, he contended, favored great Eastern institutions at the expense of the South and West—and proposed federal insurance of bank deposits. At the same time he extended his influence in the Democratic party by speaking in behalf of candidates in New York, New England, and the Midwest, and by supporting Alfred E. Smith [Supp. 3], albeit reluctantly, in the 1928 presidential campaign. When the Democrats won control of Congress in 1930, Steagall became chairman of the Banking and Currency Committee. Aware of the gravity of the depression, he sought to cooperate with President Hoover in efforts to revive the economy. The Glass-Steagall Act of 1932, which he sponsored, broadened the acceptability of commercial paper for rediscount by the Federal Reserve System. He warmly endorsed Franklin D. Roosevelt in 1932 and campaigned for him.

Steagall's position as chairman of one of the most powerful House committees gave him an important role in shaping the economic programs of the New Deal. For the most part, he translated the ideas of others into legislation. An exception, however, was the provision for federal deposit insurance that, with assistance from Senator Arthur Vandenberg of Michigan, he managed to include in the Glass-Steagall Act of 1933, overcoming the combined opposition of the Roosevelt administration, Senator Carter Glass of Virginia, chairman of the Senate Banking Committee, and the powerful American Bankers' Association. Steagall prevented Glass and his allies from forcing state banks into the Federal Reserve System in order to maintain membership in the Federal Deposit Insurance Corporation, and he helped push through Congress the Banking Act of 1935, which gave the board of governors of the Federal Reserve greater authority over rediscount rates and reserve requirements of member banks. An advocate of free silver, he and other inflationists also forced upon an unwilling President the Silver Purchase Act of 1934.

Steagall supported most New Deal measures and co-sponsored the Wagner-Steagall National Housing Act of 1937, which created the United States Housing Authority to subsidize local construction of public housing. His rural bias, however, made him increasingly skeptical of legislation benefiting labor and the urban poor, and in the latter years of his career he concentrated on agricultural issues. He gave enthusiastic support to the Bankhead-Jones Farm Tenant Act of 1937, but during World War II used his power to aid the so-called "substantial" farmers. Agreeing with the Farm Bureau Federation that farmers should share wartime prosperity, he extended the number of "basic" crops to be subsidized (the "Steagall commodities") and forced Roosevelt to accept a bill providing that no price ceiling of less than 110 percent of parity would be placed on farm products. He also vehemently fought the administration policy of controlling food prices by granting subsidies to consumers. Ignoring his physician's warning that his heart could not endure the strain, Steagall launched an impassioned attack on the subsidy policy in the fall of 1943. In the midst of the debate, he collapsed in the House cloakroom of a heart attack. He died a few days later in the George Washington Hospital, Washington, D. C., and was buried in the City Cemetery in Ozark, Ala.

[Steagall's papers, numbering several thousand items, are in the possession of his daughter, Mrs. Myra Steagall Law, Ozark, Ala. There is no full-length biography, but there is a sketch in Thomas McA. Owen, *Hist. of Ala. and Dict. of Ala. Biog.,* IV (1921), 1616. Other sources are "Ala.'s Steagall," *Time,* June 20, 1932; Jack Brien Key, "Henry B. Steagall: The Conservative as a Reformer," *Ala. Rev.,* July 1964; and the same writer's "The Congressional Career of Henry B. Steagall of Ala." (M.A. thesis, Vanderbilt Univ., 1952).]

J. B. KEY

STEARNS, HAROLD EDMUND (May 7, 1891–Aug. 13, 1943), journalist and social critic, was born in Barre, Mass. His birth record lists him as Harold Edmund Doyle and his mother as Sarah E. Doyle. He later took the name of Stearns (as did his older brother, Clyde M. Doyle), identifying his parents in *Who's Who. in America* as Frank and Sarah Ella (Doyle) Stearns. His father had died, he reports in his autobiography, before he was born, and his mother had gone to a Barre sanatorium to recover from the shock. She was a trained nurse with little sense of financial responsibility, who during his childhood led a "polite gypsy . . . life" in a half-dozen towns in the Boston area, thus contributing to her son's sense of rootlessness. Stearns found a source of direction in his talents as a writer and a student. By age sixteen he was a theatre critic for the *Boston Transcript*. Success at the Attleboro and Malden high schools led to admission to Harvard's Class of 1913. Within three years he had completed all requirements for an A.B. degree, cum laude, in philosophy and had won the respect of George Santayana.

During what would have been his senior year he established a career in New York City as an editorial writer on the *Sun* and then as a theatre critic, first for the *Dramatic Mirror* and soon after for the *Press*. Following a gloomy trip to Europe just as the war was breaking, he began a bohemian life in Greenwich Village, supported by a small salary from the *New Republic* and free-lance reviewing of books and plays. American participation in the European war transformed him into a social critic. He hated the war, yet believed that a lasting peace could result from it. As editor of *Dial* magazine in Chicago during 1918 he found a forum for his views on reconstruction. His first book, *Liberalism in America* (1919), distinguished between the policies of discredited Wilsonian idealism and those of pragmatic liberalism, whose common-sense approach to peace would, he argued, find support in the common man's postwar distrust of moralistic cant.

Stearns's faith in a new America was undermined by the "Red Scare" and the prohibition campaign. In his second book, *America and the Young Intellectual* (1921), he spoke less of the liberal's responsibility to his society than of American society's oppression of its free spirits. The book launched him as a public figure. Its message was underscored by the publication of a symposium on *Civilization in the United States* (1922) edited by Stearns, in which thirty-three intellectuals measured the extent of American provincialism, materialism, and conformity. Stearns lent the indictment added impact by leaving America on July 4, 1921, after completing his introduction to the book. His expatriation, understood as a public act, seemed the natural result of his social views; but his autobiography suggests that the death of his wife, Alice Macdougal, a mere eleven months after their marriage on Feb. 11, 1919, was the decisive factor. Her death in childbirth destroyed Stearns's hopes for stability in his personal life and resigned him to drift and loneliness.

For a while his life abroad, as a foreign correspondent for the Baltimore *Sun* and for *Town and Country* magazine and as a reporter on the *New York Herald*'s Paris edition, went well. In December 1922 Stearns quit the *Herald* to have time for serious writing. In fact, he wrote less. His energies went instead to exploring the open life of an American in France. A brief trip to California to meet his son, Philip Stearns Macdougal, adopted by Alice's parents, heightened his sense of aimlessness. Although he promised his publisher a book on America, Paris eroded his resolve. When the opportunity came in 1926 to gratify his love of horseracing as "Peter Pickem," the racing handicapper of the *Chicago Tribune*'s Paris edition, he accepted gladly. He preferred the company of the *Tribune* crowd to that of the Montparnasse aesthetes, whose "artiness" and love of illogic offended him.

Late in 1929 Stearns entered a dark period. A shift to the London *Daily Mail*'s Paris edition deprived him of the American society he needed. Then the years of too little food and too much drink finally caught up with him. Poisoning from his decaying teeth threatened blindness and led to dismissal from the paper. His sight remained, but he was alone and jobless. After months of drift, he accepted the American Aid Society's offer to pay his way back to America.

Soon after his arrival he published an article in *Scribner's Magazine* (May 1932) entitled "A Prodigal American Returns." He was the prodigal again in *Rediscovering America* (1934); in *The Street I Know* (1935), his autobiography; and in *America: A Re-Appraisal* (1937). Anger against the oppressiveness of America had become a confession of personal weakness. "A lot of people," he wrote in *The Street I Know* (p. 299), "need no encouragement to talk about the evils of oppressive stupidity and intolerance, when all they really want is the freedom to be irresponsible. (I know; I have done it myself....)" Stearns's books were received as the testament of a foolish generation. "He needed," commented Carl Van Doren, "thirteen years and a long exile to become aware of the obvious America."

His next book, a symposium on *America Now* (1938), was his last. One he planned on the "foibles" of America was never written. Marriage to Elizabeth Chalifoux Chapin in August 1937 had given him the home he had always wanted, and he lived with her in Locust Valley, Long Island, N. Y., out of the public eye, until his death. He died in Meadowbrook Hospital, Hempstead, Long Island, at the age of fifty-two, of peritonitis following an operation for cancer. The *New York Times* obituary called him "America's foremost expatriate."

[Of the few articles which Stearns wrote during the prewar years and during his exile in Paris, the most significant are "Confessions of a Harvard Man," *Forum*, Dec. 1913 and Jan. 1914; and "Apologia of an Expatriate," *Scribner's*, Mar. 1929. See also his autobiography, *The Street I Know*. Contemporary response to his career can be seen in: *Current Opinion*, Mar. 1922 (with photograph); Louis Bromfield, "Montparnasse Is Dead," *Saturday Rev. of Literature*, May 5, 1934; *N. Y. Times*, Nov. 24, 1935, sec. 6; and *Time*, Oct. 24, 1938, p. 69. Obituaries were published by the *N. Y. Times*, Aug. 14, 1943 (with photograph), *N. Y. Herald Tribune*, Aug. 14, 1943, and *Time*, Aug. 23, 1943. See also Stanley J. Kunitz and Howard Haycraft, *Twentieth Century Authors* (1942) and First Supp. (1955); Harvard Class of 1913, *Fortieth Anniversary Report* (1953); and *Who Was Who in America*, vol. II (1950). Birth record from Town Clerk, Barre, Mass.; death record from N. Y. State Dept. of Health.]

MARC PACHTER

STEJNEGER, LEONHARD HESS (Oct. 30, 1851–Feb. 28, 1943), zoologist, was born in Bergen, Norway, the first of seven children of Peter Stamer Steineger, a prosperous merchant of German ancestry, and Ingeborg Catharina (Hess) Steineger. Young Stejneger, who at the age of eighteen adopted the Norwegian form of the name, received his early education at private schools in Bergen and from tutors in the southern Tyrol (then part of Austria), where the family wintered because of his mother's poor health. Entering the University of Kristiania, he received degrees in arts (1870), philosophy (1872), and, after an interval of medical study in Berlin, in law (1875). He spent some five years in his father's business, but when financial reverses in 1880 brought it into bankruptcy, he decided to follow his real interests and adopt a career in natural science. Since openings in Europe were few, he embarked for the United States.

From boyhood Stejneger had been deeply interested in natural history, with special attention to birds. During his years at the university he had published several short papers on Tyrolean birds (1871–72), a manual for field study of Norwegian birds (1873), and a similar manual on Norwegian mammals (1874). He had also established a correspondence with naturalists in other countries, including Spencer Fullerton Baird [*q.v.*], secretary of the Smithsonian Institution. Arriving in Washington in October 1881, Stejneger called on Baird, who found him a place in the division of birds of the Smithsonian Institution's National Museum.

The following March, after preparing several papers on American birds for publication in the museum's *Proceedings*, Stejneger left on his first field trip, to the Commander Islands and other islands in the Bering Sea that had been leased by the Russians to an Alaskan company. Under the joint sponsorship of the United States Signal Service and the Smithsonian Institution, he spent more than a year in the islands, establishing

meteorological stations, studying the fur seal rookeries, and collecting natural history material, which included some 700 bird specimens as well as skeletal remains of the extinct Steller's sea cow and the recently extinct Pallas's cormorant. These collections formed the basis of several major reports. Shortly after his return to the United States in October 1883, he applied for United States citizenship; he received his final papers in February 1887.

On Dec. 1, 1884, Stejneger was appointed assistant curator in the division of birds. He occupied that post until March 1889 when, after the head of the division of reptiles and amphibians had resigned, Stejneger was persuaded to take his place. He plunged into the new assignment with enormous enthusiasm, although he continued to publish ornithological papers for several more years.

In the autumn of 1889, weakened by a bronchial ailment and overwork, Stejneger was sent for a rest to join a Smithsonian field party making a biological survey in Arizona. After a period of recuperation, he regained his health and was able to collect reptiles and amphibians of the Southwest before returning to Washington. In 1894 he collected in the Badlands of South Dakota, and in 1900 in Puerto Rico. Stejneger's familiarity with the Bering Sea islands led to his being sent for three successive years (1895–97) to investigate the fur seals in the Commander and Pribilof islands in connection with an international controversy over the control of sealing operations in that area.

In 1911 Stejneger became head curator of the department of biology in the National Museum. Though more of his time thereafter was taken up with administrative work, he continued to publish new papers of his own, particularly in herpetology. Of the nearly 400 titles in his bibliography, the major works include: *The Poisonous Snakes of North America* (1895), *Herpetology of Porto Rico* (1904), *Herpetology of Japan and Adjacent Territory* (1907), *A Check List of North American Amphibians and Reptiles*, written with Thomas Barbour (1917), and *Georg Wilhelm Steller* (1936), a biography of the pioneer student of Alaskan natural history, in whom he had become interested during his first trip to the Commander Islands. Both in the extent of his researches and in their quality, Stejneger made substantial contributions to knowledge of the taxonomy and geographic distribution of birds, reptiles, and amphibians.

His command of classical and modern languages made Stejneger a valuable representative of the Smithsonian Institution at international scientific meetings and congresses, which he regularly attended. In 1898 he was elected to the International Commission on Zoological Nomenclature. Stejneger belonged to a large number of scientific societies, both here and abroad, and was president of the American Society of Ichthyologists and Herpetologists in 1919. He was elected to the National Academy of Sciences in 1923, and was made a Knight First Class of the Royal Norwegian Order of St. Olav in 1906 and Commander in 1939.

Stejneger was warmly regarded and genuinely respected by his friends and colleagues. He was kindly and helpful to other researchers and enjoyed entertaining visitors at his home. Stejneger was first married, on Oct. 30, 1876, to Anna Normann of Bergen, Norway. The marriage proved incompatible and ended in divorce shortly after he left for the United States. On Mar. 22, 1892, in Washington, D. C., he married Helene Maria Reiners of Crefeld, Germany. He had no children by either marriage, but he and his second wife adopted an infant daughter, Inga, in 1907.

Spare and slender, Stejneger retained for much of his life a youthful vigor. At the age of eighty he was still regularly walking the several miles back and forth from his home to his office. Although a law enacted in 1932 made retirement mandatory for all government employees at the age of seventy, he was one of the few persons specially exempted from the requirement by executive order, and he was still actively working at the museum until a few days before his death, at the age of ninety-one, following an operation for cancer in a Washington hospital. He was buried in Fort Lincoln Cemetery, Washington.

[Alexander Wetmore in Nat. Acad. Sci., *Biog. Memoirs*, vol. XXIV (1947)—the fullest account, with a bibliography of Stejneger's publications; Albert K. Fisher in *Copeia*, Oct. 30, 1931; Paul Bartsch in *Science*, July 16, 1943; Doris M. Cochran in Wash. Acad. of Sci., *Jour.*, Mar. 15, 1944. See also Karl P. Schmidt, "Herpetology," in *A Century of Progress in the Natural Sciences, 1853–1953* (Calif. Acad. of Sci., 1955); sketch by Waldo L. Schmitt in *Systematic Zoology*, Dec. 1964; and *Nat. Cyc. Am. Biog.*, XIV, 130–31. Death record from D. C. Dept. of Human Resources. An oil portrait of Stejneger by Bjorn Egeli is in the library of the Division of Reptiles and Amphibians of the Nat. Museum, Washington, D. C.]

JAMES A. PETERS

STELZLE, CHARLES (June 4, 1869–Feb. 27, 1941), Presbyterian minister, intermediary between the church and the workingman, was born in New York City, the only son and oldest of the five children of John and Dora (Uhlendorf) Stelzle. Both parents had come from Germany as children. His father, who owned a small brewery, died when Charles was a boy, and his mother maintained the family in a precarious tenement-house existence on Manhattan's Lower East Side by taking in sewing and washing. Charles took his first part-time job at the age of eight, stripping tobacco leaves in a sweatshop. He attended and became a member of Hope Chapel, a Presbyterian mission. When he was eleven he dropped out of public school and worked as a cutter in an artificial-flower shop. Later he went to work for R. Hoe & Company, printing press manufacturers, where at the age of sixteen he was enrolled as a machinist's apprentice. He attended night school during the five-year apprenticeship period, earned the title "superior workman," and became a member of the union of his craft, the International Association of Machinists.

Deeply immersed in church activities from his youth and a Presbyterian elder from the age of twenty-one, Stelzle was distressed at the gap between the church and the workingman. In 1890 he undertook a program of self-study and private tutoring to prepare for religious work in this field; in further preparation, he gave up his job as a machinist in 1893 and enrolled for ten months at the Moody Bible Institute in Chicago. Stelzle began his church service in 1895 as a lay worker in Hope Chapel, Minneapolis, Minn., a downtown mission of the sort that was then being all but abandoned by many churches as their parishioners moved out from the center city. In this chapel, characteristically located in a low-income working-class area, he sought particularly to reach boys, such as newsboys and bootblacks. In 1897 Stelzle moved to his own boyhood church, Hope Chapel in New York. Frustrated there by the undemocratic control of a conservative board, he moved on to the Soulard Market Mission— soon to become Markham Memorial Church—in St. Louis, where he served from 1899 to 1903. He was ordained as a Presbyterian minister in 1900.

Convinced that the alienation of workingmen from the church was deepening, Stelzle appealed to the Board of Home Missions of the Presbyterian Church in the U. S. A., which in 1903 gave him a "special mission to workingmen." By 1906 his mission had grown into the Board's Department of the Church and Labor, with Stelzle as superintendent—the first official church agency to pursue an aggressive social gospel campaign through the efforts of a paid secretary. Through much traveling, speaking, preaching, and writing he formally and informally fulfilled his chosen special role, that of interpreter of the labor movement to the church and of the churches to working people. He encouraged the exchange of fraternal delegates between city central labor unions and ministerial associations; at its peak, the practice was observed in some 150 cities. In 1905 he addressed the convention of the American Federation of Labor, and for a decade thereafter he served as fraternal delegate to this organization, representing at first his Department and after 1909 the fledgling Federal Council of the Churches of Christ in America, of whose new Commission on the Church and Social Service he became an officer. He encouraged the observance of Labor Sunday (the day before Labor Day) in the churches, supplying program materials and urging union cooperation; the idea was widely adopted beginning in 1904.

Stelzle wrote many articles for religious periodicals, seeking to acquaint middle- and upperclass churchgoers with the conditions of working people. His first book, *Workingmen and Social Problems* (1903), was largely a collection of such articles. His second, *Boys of the Street: How to Win Them* (1904), was an outgrowth of his own experiences. In *The Church and Labor* (1910) Stelzle contributed greatly to the growing popularity of the use of sociological survey methods in church work. His *American Social and Religious Conditions* (1912) employed charts and graphs to call attention to the unhappy situation of many of America's immigrant and minority groups. Stelzle also began writing a weekly column syndicated to some 250 weekly and monthly labor periodicals, a practice he continued for the rest of his life. Several later books were essentially compilations of these articles. Much of his writing grew out of his public speaking and retained a direct, anecdotal style. His messages to workingmen were brief, common-sense pieces often focused around his central theme of the need for cooperation between church and labor.

Stelzle's work contributed significantly to the spread of the social gospel movement, then making a considerable impact on American Protestantism. Unlike most social gospel leaders, he was broadly conservative in theology, but he was not a theoretician like Walter Rauschenbusch [*q.v.*]; instead, he focused on the practical application of the gospel to social situations. His perception of the central importance of the burgeoning industrial city and his dedication to recalling the church to its urban role are manifest in his most important contribution to social Christian literature, *Christianity's Storm Center: A Study of the Modern City* (1907). In it he not only decried the churches' retreat from the city, but also, stressing that workers are naturally religious, called for a program of "aggressive evangelism"

expressed in social service measures through the institutional church.

Stelzle put his ideas into practice with the founding in 1910 of Labor Temple, located in a building on New York's Second Avenue, at Fourteenth Street, which he had persuaded Presbyterian authorities to purchase. Here, in the manner of a social settlement, he directed for two years a widely publicized program designed to appeal to workingmen through a network of meetings and open forums. He further advocated such methods across the nation in 1911–12 as dean of the Social Service Department of the Men and Religion Forward Movement, which conducted eight-day educational and inspirational campaigns in sixty American cities.

From 1912, as religious views polarized toward what would emerge in the 1920's as the Fundamentalist-Modernist doctrinal controversy, and as the Presbyterian Church in the U. S. A. reexamined its social stand in an effort to effect consolidation with the more conservative Southern, United, and Reformed Presbyterian churches, Stelzle found his ministry facing mounting criticism and finally, in 1913, a steep budget cut. Committed more to his work than to any single institution, Stelzle resigned his post and undertook a third career, in the field of public relations. He developed his own office and staff to undertake survey, publicity, and promotional services in behalf of social and religious causes. He had long been interested in promotion; an earlier book had outlined *Principles of Successful Church Advertising* (1908). During this period he was a member of several editorial staffs, served as relief director of New York City during the 1914–15 unemployment crisis, and undertook a study of the liquor problem in Europe and America. His book *Why Prohibition!* (1918) brought together the results of his investigations on behalf of temperance. This work was financed by William F. Cochran, Baltimore philanthropist, who also paid for Stelzle's services as field secretary (1916–18) of the Federal Council of the Churches of Christ in America, in which post he sought to make effective in program and action the "social creed of the churches." During the First World War, Stelzle took charge of publicity for the American Red Cross in Washington in the field of industry and the church.

At the peak of his ministerial career, Stelzle was described as being below average height, with a broad, bald head, wide-set eyes, prominent nose, and strong chin. His speaking was quiet and without rhetorical flashes, but forceful in its sincerity. He was quick in retort and resourceful in illustration, "a tireless human kaleidoscope."

On Nov. 28, 1889, Stelzle had married Louise Rothmayer; they had one son, Robert Clarence. On Sept. 11, 1890, following his first wife's death, he married Louise Ingersoll, by whom he had two daughters, Hope Ingersoll and Frances.

In the postwar years, now no longer a prominent public figure, Stelzle directed many promotional campaigns for religious, patriotic, and community organizations. In 1936–39 he was executive director of the Good Neighbor League, giving special attention to the celebration of a century and a quarter of peace on the Canadian-American boundary and to opposing totalitarian philosophy. He died of uremia in New York City in 1941 after a long illness and was buried in Mount Hope Cemetery, Hastings-on-Hudson, N.Y.

[Charles Stelzle's autobiography, *A Son of the Bowery* (1926); William T. Ellis, "A Union Preacher," *Outlook*, Aug. 13, 1910; obituary in *N. Y. Times*, Feb. 28, 1941; interviews and correspondence with Miss Hope Stelzle. See also George H. Nash, III, "Charles Stelzle: Apostle to Labor," *Labor Hist.*, Spring 1970; and C. Howard Hopkins, *The Rise of the Social Gospel in Am. Protestantism, 1865–1915* (1940). The Charles Stelzle Papers at Columbia Univ. (14 boxes) contain miscellaneous correspondence, articles, clippings, pamphlets, and MSS., with materials for a revision and continuation of his autobiography.]

ROBERT T. HANDY

STEVENS, JOHN FRANK (Apr. 25, 1853–June 2, 1943), civil engineer and railroad executive, was born on his father's farm near West Gardiner, Maine, the son of Harriet Leslie (French) and John Smith Stevens and a direct descendant of Henry Stevens, who emigrated in 1635 from Cambridge, England, to Boston. He attended local schools and the State Normal School in Farmington, Maine, graduating in 1872. After several months of schoolteaching, however, he decided to become an engineer and found work on a field crew in Lewiston, Maine, making surveys for mills and industrial canals. In 1873 he went to Minneapolis, Minn., where an uncle, himself an engineer, helped him get a job as a rodman for the city engineer. By studying assiduously at night, he advanced in 1874 to assistant city engineer.

In 1875 Stevens decided to seek his fortune in railroading. After two years as a junior engineer on various railways in Minnesota, he moved to northern Texas, where he made several surveys for the Sabine Pass & Northwestern Railroad. He was promoted to chief engineer, but when the company failed in 1878 he had to accept employment as a trackhand. He soon worked himself up to roadmaster, and in 1879 became assistant engineer for location and construction of the New Mexico and Durango extensions of the Denver & Rio Grande Railroad. Similar positions followed with the Chicago, Milwaukee & St. Paul Railroad (1881–82 and 1885–86), working chiefly in Iowa; with the Canadian Pacific Railroad (1882–84), in Manitoba and British Columbia; and, beginning in 1886, with the Duluth, South Shore & Atlantic Railroad. On this last, given complete charge of a project for the first time, he conducted the initial surveys and line location and supervised the construction of a road stretching almost four hundred miles from Sault Ste. Marie to Duluth through the dense forests and swamps of the Upper Peninsula of Michigan.

Stevens next worked briefly as assistant engineer of the Spokane Falls & Northern Railway, where he gained valuable knowledge of the Pacific Northwest, and then began an important association with the Great Northern Railway and its president, James J. Hill [q.v.]. Hill was building an unsubsidized transcontinental railroad through the northernmost tier of states, and one of Stevens' first assignments was to explore the route west from Havre, Mont. Over a period of weeks and in the bitterest winter cold, he established the feasibility of the now famous Marias Pass, which provided the key passage across the Continental Divide. Sent next to Washington to explore the Columbia River and the Cascades for the final route down the western slopes of the Divide, he located another important pass, later named Stevens Pass, near Lake Wenatchee. He then worked on the western part of the Great Northern's "Pacific Extension," from Stevens Pass to Everett, Wash., laying out at the summit of the Cascades a switchback route that could be used temporarily until a tunnel was completed. His work attracted the personal attention of Hill.

When the Pacific Extension was completed in 1893, Stevens became assistant chief engineer on the regular staff of the Great Northern. He was dropped the following year, chiefly because of the depression, but was rehired in 1895 as chief engineer and, except for a brief absence in 1898–99, remained with the railroad until 1903, from 1902 as general manager. During these years he supervised the planning and construction of more than a thousand miles of new track, much of it in Minnesota, where he built a line serving the iron-bearing Mesabi Range with a lower maximum grade than any other railroad in the area. Another of his major projects was the completion of the first Cascade Tunnel, a 2.6-mile rock bore built between 1897 and 1900. He also modernized existing facilities and lowered operating costs by widening embankments, laying heavier steel rails, reducing curves and grades, rebuilding bridges, installing masonry culverts, and improving alignments.

Stevens left the Great Northern in 1903 to become chief engineer (in 1904, second vice-president) of the Chicago, Rock Island & Pacific Railway. The following year he was named to the federal Philippine Commission, to head its railroad building program. Before he could serve, however, Secretary of War William Howard Taft named Stevens, on Hill's suggestion, as chief engineer of the Isthmian Canal Commission. His appointment came just after the commission had been reorganized, giving the chief engineer control over both the construction and engineering phases of the Panama Canal.

When Stevens arrived at the Canal Zone in the early part of 1906, he found conditions chaotic. Equipment, largely inherited from the French, was antiquated, housing and food were inadequate, and the labor force of about 17,000 was demoralized by frequent outbreaks of yellow fever and malaria. Drawing on his years of railroad experience, Stevens immediately set about reorganizing the work force and engineering staff. He developed supply lines to bring food into the area, constructed commissaries and mess halls to deliver it at reasonable cost, and rebuilt existing housing. Recognizing that progress on the canal depended upon efficient transportation, he gave most of his time to organizing and building an extensive system of railroads to carry out the soil and rock from the Culebra (now Gaillard) Cut at the interoceanic divide. He also accepted the theory of the mosquito as the vector for yellow fever and malaria and aided Col. William C. Gorgas [q.v.], head of the sanitation department, in implementing adequate sanitary and health measures. Although Stevens had at first favored a sea-level canal, his own investigations soon convinced him that only a locked canal was feasible. In the *Report of the Board of Consulting Engineers for the Panama Canal* (1906), he therefore concurred with the minority opinion in opposing a sea-level canal, and he was instrumental in persuading President Theodore Roosevelt to accept this view. To facilitate construction, Stevens successfully sought a reorganization of the Canal Commission giving the chief engineer, in the absence of the chairman (who was usually resident in Washington), complete control over the Canal Zone. By the end of 1906 construction was under way; but Stevens—frustrated by political maneuvering in Washington, including the award of the principal contract to a firm he considered of questionable reliability, and eager to return to a less strenuous position—resigned a few months later. His successor, George W.

Goethals [q.v.], later said of Stevens, "The Canal is his monument."

Upon returning to the United States, Stevens became vice-president of the New York, New Haven & Hartford Railroad. He made a systematic valuation of the company's steam railroad properties and, as part of a modernization program, electrified the trackage from Woodlawn, N. Y., to Stamford, Conn. But the railroad was in poor financial condition, principally because of excessive investments in outside properties, and in 1909 he accepted an offer to rejoin Hill in a new project. This was the building of a southward extension of the Hill lines from the Columbia River through central Oregon, the first step toward a connection with San Francisco. The plan was sharply challenged, both in the courts and through the construction of a competing line, by the Union Pacific and Southern Pacific interests of Edward H. Harriman [q.v.], but Stevens, as president of the Oregon Trunk Railway Company, successfully completed the new line in 1911. He then moved to New York City, where for several years he was a private consultant.

In 1917, following the collapse of the Czarist regime in Russia during World War I, Stevens was appointed by President Wilson as chairman of an advisory commission of American railway experts to study the Russian railway system. The United States was interested in ensuring the continued participation of Russia in the war, and the commission was charged with the task of keeping railroad and supply lines open. Having completed his study, Stevens went to Siberia, later in 1917, as head of a second American commission, the Russian Railway Service Corps, and, with a force of about two hundred engineers, began reorganizing the Trans-Siberian and Chinese Eastern railways. In 1919 he was named president of the Technical Board of the Inter-Allied Railway Commission, an international body set up to supervise railways in those parts of Siberia and Manchuria where Allied troops were stationed. He also improved the operation of the railways by such steps as installing a telephone system on the main line from Vladivostok to Omsk, introducing the more efficient American system of train dispatching, and reorganizing the railway repair shops.

After American troops were withdrawn from Siberia in 1921, Stevens stayed on with a small staff in an advisory capacity. Upon his return to the United States in 1923, he became a member of the board of directors of the Baltimore & Ohio Railroad and made his home in Baltimore. Though he had turned seventy, he continued to be active as an engineering consultant until 1931. His last major project was a feasibility study for a new, longer tunnel at the Stevens Pass. The report was completed in 1925, and the new Cascade Tunnel, with its 7.8-mile bore, was constructed between 1926 and 1928.

Stevens served in 1927 as president of the American Society of Civil Engineers. An extremely able engineer, with a gift for organization, he was nevertheless regarded by some acquaintances as authoritarian and temperamental. Among his many honors were degrees from Bates College, the universities of North Carolina and Michigan, and the Polytechnic Institute of Brooklyn, and decorations from the United States, France, China, Japan, and Czechoslovakia. In 1925 a statue of Stevens was erected at Marias Pass. On Jan. 6, 1876, he had married Harriet O'Brien of Boston. They had five children: Frank and Abby, both of whom died in infancy, Donald French, John Frank, and Eugene Chapin. Stevens spent his last years in Southern Pines, N. C., where he died at the age of ninety of pulmonary infarction. He was buried near his wife in Mount Hope Cemetery, Boston, Mass.

[John F. Stevens, *An Engineer's Recollections* (1936), originally serialized in the *Engineering News-Record*; memoir by Ralph Budd in Am. Soc. of Civil Engineers, *Transactions*, CIX (1944), 1440–47; *Nat. Cyc. Am. Biog.*, XXXII, 326–27; information from records of Am. Soc. of Civil Engineers; Ralph W. and Muriel E. Hidy, "John Frank Stevens: Great Northern Engineer," *Minn. Hist.*, Winter 1969; Miles P. DuVal, Jr., *And the Mountains Will Move* (1947), a history of the building of the Panama Canal; Jacqueline D. St. John, "John F. Stevens: Am. Assistance to Russian and Siberian Railroads, 1917–1922" (Ph.D. dissertation, Univ. of Okla., 1969); C. H. Heffelfinger, "John F. Stevens," *Wash. Hist. Quart.*, Jan. 1935; William H. Galvanni, "Recollections of J. F. Stevens and Senator Mitchell," *Oreg. Hist. Quart.*, Sept. 1943; Tom Inkster, "John Frank Stevens," *Pacific Northwest Quart.*, Apr. 1965; death record, N. C. State Board of Health.]

NEAL FITZSIMONS

STILES, CHARLES WARDELL (May 15, 1867–Jan. 24, 1941), medical zoologist and public health expert, was born in Spring Valley, N. Y., the younger of two children and only son of the Rev. Samuel Martin Stiles and Elizabeth (White) Stiles. Both parents were of early New England descent; Stiles's father was a native of Pittsfield, Mass., his mother, of Whiting, Vt. A Methodist minister, Samuel Stiles supplemented his income by work as a stenographer. In 1878 the family moved to Hartford, Conn. While in high school there, Charles demonstrated an aptitude for languages, an interest in natural science and medicine, a fascination with military drill which proved lifelong, and skill in baseball and football. In 1885 he

enrolled at Wesleyan University, his father's alma mater, but eye trouble caused him to drop out during his sophomore year. He then obtained family permission to continue his studies of languages and science in Europe.

After a few months at the Sorbonne, the Collège de France, and the University of Göttingen, Stiles studied science intensively for two years at the University of Berlin under such professors as Hermann von Helmholtz in physics, Emil du Bois-Reymond in physiology, and the zoologists Friedrich E. Schultze and Wilhelm Waldeyer. Instead of then going on into medicine, he moved to the University of Leipzig to concentrate on zoology with the great parasitologist Rudolph Leuckart. He received his Ph.D. degree in 1890. After an additional year spent at Robert Koch's laboratory in Berlin, at the Austrian Zoological Station in Trieste, at the Collège de France, and at the Pasteur Institute, Stiles returned to the United States in 1891 to begin work in Washington as principal zoologist in the Bureau of Animal Industry of the Department of Agriculture. On June 23, 1897, he married Virginia Baker; they had two children, Virginia Ruth Fordyce and Elizabeth.

At the Bureau, Stiles was a productive researcher and writer. He was not a speculative thinker; his strength lay rather in observation. Meticulous and objective, he reported new species of parasitic worms, analyzed old ones, and worked for order in his field. To this end, he urged zoologists to cling uncompromisingly to established rules of zoological classification and particularly to observe the law of priority in naming new species. His leadership in this work was recognized by his peers as early as 1895 when he was chosen a member of the five-man International Commission on Zoological Nomenclature, of which he subsequently served as secretary for nearly forty years, 1898–1936. As a vigorous participant in this and many other professional bodies, European and American, he became a distinguished successor to Joseph Leidy [*q.v.*] in the development of systematic zoology in the United States.

Much of Stiles's work at the Bureau of Animal Industry was of direct economic importance to American agriculture. In 1895 and 1896 he investigated livestock disease caused by filth-ridden slaughterhouses in country towns. Stiles also became the focal point of the Bureau's concern with trichinosis in pork. This concern came to a climax in 1898, when he was detailed as science attaché to the American embassy in Berlin in connection with long-standing German restrictions on American pork. During a two-year assignment he investigated and refuted German charges that American inspection of exported meat was inadequate and that American pork had caused trichinosis in Germany. At the same time, his criticism of the cumbersome German system of microscopic inspection of pork prevented its adoption in the United States. Stiles also helped analyze, in 1898, the internal parasites of the fur seal. In 1900 and 1901, at the request of Congressman Rudolph Kleberg, he went to Texas to investigate losses of cattle, sheep, and goats owing to parasitic worms.

In 1902 Stiles transferred to the Hygienic Laboratory of the United States Public Health and Marine Hospital Service, where, for the next thirty years, he was chief of the Division of Zoology. He was also professor of medical zoology at Georgetown University from 1892 to 1906, special lecturer in the subject at the Johns Hopkins University between 1897 and 1937, and lecturer at the army and navy medical schools for shorter periods. In these posts he did much to educate American physicians as to the importance of zoology in medicine.

Stiles's most dramatic and far-reaching contributions to public health were in connection with hookworm disease. In 1902 he discovered a variety of hookworm indigenous to the Western Hemisphere which he named *Uncinaria americana*, or *Necator americana*. That same year he confirmed that unrecognized hookworm disease was endemic among poor whites of the South, and showed it to be a major cause of the depressed condition of the region. The popular press picked up his report, and Stiles's discovery of the "germ of laziness" gave rise to numerous jokes, verses, and cartoons. Meanwhile political action against hookworm disease lagged. During the next few years Stiles traveled extensively to gather statistical data and educate physicians, health officers, and laymen about the hookworm. In 1908 and 1909, as an expert on President Roosevelt's Country Life Commission, he was able to interest Walter Hines Page, Wallace Buttrick, and Frederick T. Gates [qq.v.] in the problem. The result was the formation in 1909 of the Rockefeller Sanitary Commission, financed by John D. Rockefeller [Supp. 2], which went on to conduct an extensive and highly successful campaign against hookworm disease through rural sanitation and education. Stiles, who crisscrossed the South many times as the commission's part-time medical director, lectured and distributed educational material, assisted local boards of health, designed privies, made field studies of schoolchildren and other groups, and conducted extensive laboratory research in connection with

the campaign. As a consequence of this work his contemporaries recognized that few if any other individuals had accomplished so much for rural health in the United States.

Stiles also investigated the health of cotton mill workers, mine sanitation, and other public health problems. During World War I he examined new recruits and worked with state health boards of several Southern states on the control of epidemic diseases. Following the war, he directed experiments on soil pollution which demonstrated how fecal matter and bacteria were spread by ground water. An even larger project was his publication, with Albert Hassall, of the *Index-Catalog of Medical and Veterinary Zoology*. Their preparation of the first four volumes (1902–20) of this work, together with a series of supplemental *Key Catalogs* (of insects, parasites, protozoa, crustacea, and arachnoids), was a continuing task from the 1890's until the mid-1930's. It was a scientific and bibliographic accomplishment comparable in magnitude and importance to the *Index-Catalogue* of the Surgeon General's Library prepared by John Shaw Billings [q.v.].

For this and his other contributions, Stiles received a number of honors, including degrees from the University of North Carolina (1912) and Yale (1915) and the gold medal of the National Academy of Sciences. After his formal retirement in October 1931, he continued some helminthological work at the Smithsonian Institution and taught zoology at Rollins College in Florida for several winters. In October 1940 he was admitted to the Marine Hospital, Baltimore, Md., where he died a few months later of myocarditis. His father's home in later years had been in New Jersey, and Stiles was buried in Rosedale Cemetery, Orange, N. J.

[No substantial collection of personal papers has been discovered, though MS. material on particular phases of Stiles's career is available in the archives of the Smithsonian Institution and in the U. S. Nat. Archives. Most of Stiles's research papers can be found in official publications of the Bureau of Animal Industry and the Public Health Service. Some significant exceptions are his chapters on parasitic disease in the first volume (1907) of William Osler's *Modern Medicine* (in vol. II in later editions) and his contributions to the *Annual Reports* of the Rockefeller Sanitary Commission, 1910–14. Stiles wrote one autobiographical article, "Early History, in Part Esoteric, of the Hookworm (Uncinariasis) Campaign in Our Southern U. S.," *Jour. of Parasitology*, Aug. 1939. For biographical accounts see: Benjamin Schwartz, "A Brief Resumé of Dr. Stiles's Contributions to Parasitology," *ibid.*, June 1933; F. G. Brooks in *Bios*, Oct. 1947; Mark Sullivan, *Our Times*, III (1930), 290–332; *Nat. Cyc. Am. Biog.*, Current Vol. D, pp. 62–63; *Who Was Who in America*, vol. I (1942); obituaries in *Jour. of Parasitology*, June 1941, and *N. Y. Herald Tribune*, *N. Y. Times*, and *Washington Evening Star*, Jan. 25, 1941; James H. Cassedy, "The 'Germ of Laziness' in the South, 1900–1915," *Bull. of the Hist. of Medicine*, Mar.–Apr. 1971, and "Applied

Microscopy and Am. Pork Diplomacy," *Isis,* Spring 1971. See also Frederick A. Virkus, *The Abridged Compendium of Am. Genealogy,* II (1926), 380–81; Ralph C. Williams, *The U. S. Public Health Service, 1798–1950* (1951); and Daniel E. Salmon, *The U. S. Bureau of Animal Industry at the Close of the Nineteenth Century* (1901); and, on Stiles's father, *Alumni Record of Wesleyan Univ., 1831–1911* (1911). Additional information was obtained in personal interviews with Mrs. Livingston Merchant (daughter), Dr. James Leake, and Dr. Wilbur Wright.]

JAMES H. CASSEDY

STIMSON, FREDERIC JESUP (July 20, 1855–Nov. 19, 1943), lawyer, diplomat, and author, sought throughout a long life to maintain, in an industrialized and heterogeneous nation, the values and perspectives of an aristocrat reared in the "true democracy" of the New England town. Although it is usually stated that he was born in Dedham, Mass., that town's vital records do not list him, and the movements of his family in the 1850's suggest that his birthplace may have been either New York City or Dubuque, Iowa. His roots, however, were in Dedham, where his paternal grandfather, a physician and banker, had settled in 1804; and the Stimson line in Massachusetts extends back at least to 1670.

The only child of Edward and Sarah Tufts (Richardson) Stimson, Frederic led a distinctly privileged life, traveling widely. His father, a graduate of Harvard and its medical school, practiced in New York City for a time and then, moving west because of his wife's poor health (she died in 1858), entered the banking business in Dubuque with Frederic S. Jesup of New York City and became president of the Dubuque and Pacific Railroad. Frederic thus passed his early boyhood in Iowa. In the mid-1860's Edward Stimson sold the railroad, was married again (to his cousin Charlotte Godfrey Leland of Philadelphia, by whom he had a daughter, Elsie) and "retired" to Dedham, where Frederic attended public schools. After a year at a boarding school in Lausanne, Switzerland, Frederic entered Harvard. He received his A.B. in 1876 and, after two years in the Harvard Law School, the LL.B. degree.

He then established a practice in Boston, specializing in railroad law. He was an incorporator, vice-president, and general counsel of the State Street Trust Company of Boston and sat on many corporation boards. For a time (1891–97) he operated in partnership with Francis Cabot Lowell and A. Lawrence Lowell [Supp. 3]. During these years Stimson began to consider social problems. He fought to give full legal rights to the American Indian and protested against American imperialism. In particular, he sought to reconcile his reformer's desire to control trusts and to ensure justice for the laboring man

with his fear (which proved dominant) of government interference with individual liberty and property rights.

Stimson's interest in labor law found expression in his article "The Modern Use of Injunctions" (*Political Science Quarterly,* June 1895), an early attack on the use of the Sherman Anti-Trust Act against labor combinations. In his *Labor in Its Relations to Law* (1895) he supported labor's aspirations but argued strongly that it should seek justice not through the closed shop but through noncoercive "collective bargaining." A year later Stimson's useful *Handbook to the Labor Law of the United States* appeared. In 1897 he was appointed advisory counsel to the United States Industrial Commission, a post he held for the next four years, during which compiled two volumes on American and European labor legislation.

Meanwhile Stimson had in 1891 been appointed to a Massachusetts state commission supporting the American Bar Association's effort to promote uniform legislation throughout the United States. He shared the Association's fear that if the states did not voluntarily reduce interstate legal conflict, the federal government would coerce them and disturb the delicately balanced federal system. As secretary of the national conference of state commissioners from 1891 to 1902 and, by the end of this period, chairman of the Massachusetts commission, Stimson was specially interested in unifying state commercial law, reforming divorce law, and making Southern laws regulating child labor and factory hours as strong as Northern ones.

While serving on the Massachusetts Commission on Corporation Laws in 1902–03, Stimson wrote, with Charles Washburn, the 1903 law which significantly relaxed that state's stringent control over corporate financing. He had returned in 1902 to law practice in Boston, at the same time accepting a part-time position in the history and government department at Harvard, first as lecturer on "Tendencies of American Legislation" and, from 1904 to 1915, as professor of comparative legislation. Out of his lectures at Harvard and at the Lowell Institute came *The American Constitution* (1908), *The Law of the Federal and State Constitutions of the United States* (1908), *Popular Law-Making* (1910), *The American Constitution as It Protects Private Rights* (1923), and *The Western Way: The Accomplishment and Future of Modern Democracy* (1929). These volumes exalted the traditional Anglo-Saxon constitutional protection of individual rights and attempted to reverse the trend toward centralization that Stimson detected in Progressivism. His compilations and digests, the fruit of prodigious labor, were first-rate; his scholarship—especially his adherence to the Teutonic theory of legal history—was thin and outdated.

Stimson's political career had begun soon after his graduation from college, as one of Dedham's regular delegates to the Republican state convention and financial manager for Congressman Theodore Lyman (1833–1897) [q.v.]. In 1884 the Republican governor of Massachusetts, George Robinson, named Stimson assistant attorney general. He resigned, however, upon the nomination of James G. Blaine [q.v.], helped initiate the "Mugwump" movement in Boston and New York City, and became a Democrat, an affiliation he retained until the New Deal. He supported the Gold Democrats rather than Bryan in 1896 and 1900, and played a role in reknitting the divided Massachusetts Democratic party after 1900. In 1914 President Wilson appointed Stimson ambassador to Argentina. He served until 1921 and was credited with helping induce the neutral Argentines to sell large quantities of wheat to the allies during World War I.

Throughout his life Stimson had a "second career" as an author. Between 1882 and 1922 he published (in the '80's under the pen name "J. S. of Dale") seven novels, four collections of short stories and novellas, and several lesser works. His short stories appeared in popular magazines well into the 1930's. His first novels—including the very successful romance of Harvard undergraduate life, *Guerndale* (1882)—identified him as one of a school of upper-class Boston novelists that included his friends Russell Sullivan, Arlo Bates [q.v.], Robert Grant [Supp. 2], and John T. Wheelwright. Another friend, John Boyle O'Reilly [q.v.], helped Stimson plot perhaps his best work, *King Noanett* (1896), a historical romance which Carl Van Doren (in the *Cambridge History of American Literature*, vol. III, 1921, p. 91) considered one of the best books in "the remarkable outburst of historical romance just preceding the Spanish War." Most of Stimson's fiction, like his legal writing, celebrated the values of an earlier America. Whatever artistic reputation he earned in his lifetime quickly faded. His literary virtues—his broad experience and his whimsical and sometimes satirical humor—are preserved in his fine autobiographical survey of America, *My United States* (1931). The "chief pleasure in life," he concluded (p. 126), is "to be an all-round man."

Stimson was married on June 2, 1881, to Elizabeth Bradlee Abbot, daughter of a Boston merchant. She died in 1896. On Nov. 12, 1902,

he married Mabel Ashhurst of Philadelphia. His three children, all by the first marriage, were Mildred, Elizabeth Bradlee (who died in infancy), and Margaret Ashton. Stimson was a member of the Episcopal Church. He died in Dedham at the age of eighty-eight of bronchopneumonia and was buried there in the Old Village Cemetery.

[Although not a formal autobiography, Stimson's *My United States* records the basic facts of his life. Other sources: obituaries in *N. Y. Times*, Nov. 21, 1943, and *Boston Herald*, Nov. 23, 1943; Charles Warren in Mass. Hist. Soc., *Proc.*, LXVIII (1944–47), 470–71; Harvard College Class of 1876, *Tenth Report* (1926); Stimson Papers at the Mass. Hist. Soc., relating primarily to his diplomatic service; *Nat. Cyc. Am. Biog.*, X, 361, XLIV, 84–85; *Boston Herald*, Oct. 8, 1902; *Boston Record*, Nov. 3, 1902; *Boston Jour.*, Nov. 13, 1902; death record from Mass. Registrar of Vital Statistics. On Stimson's father, see unidentified obituary clippings, Harvard Univ. Archives; Frederick A. Virkus, *The Abridged Compendium of Am. Genealogy*, I (1925), 213; and, on his association with Frederic Jesup, Henry G. Jesup, *Edward Jessup of West Farms . . . and His Descendants* (1887), pp. 179–80. A photographic portrait of Stimson is in the *Bookman*, June 1896, p. 295.]

ROBERT L. CHURCH

STOCK, FREDERICK AUGUST (Nov. 11, 1872–Oct. 20, 1942), orchestra conductor, was born in Jülich, near Cologne, Germany, the only child of Friedrich Karl and Louise (Leiner) Stock. His father, a bandmaster in the Prussian army, gave the boy his first music lessons. At fourteen, young Stock entered the Cologne Conservatory as a violin pupil of Georg Japha, studying theory and composition with Engelbert Humperdinck and Gustav Jensen. He joined the violin section of the Cologne Municipal Orchestra (also known as the Gürzenich Orchestra) in 1891. Theodore Thomas [q.v.], the conductor of the Chicago Orchestra, heard him there and engaged him. When Stock arrived in Chicago in October 1895, however, there was no vacancy in the violin section, and he was assigned to the violas.

In 1899 Thomas, in his sixties and wishing to ease his burdens, chose Stock as assistant conductor. Although he continued to play viola, Stock began to conduct occasional rehearsals and to direct accompaniments for soloists, especially on tour. He thus obtained matchless training under one of the world's great conductors. Some critics grumbled about entrusting the orchestra to so young and unknown a musician, but Thomas had confidence in his protégé. Stock's growing gifts as a composer were recognized when Thomas conducted his "Symphonic Variations" in 1903. When Thomas died on Jan. 4, 1905, three weeks after the opening of Orchestra Hall, the orchestra's first permanent home, Stock was asked to serve until a new permanent conductor could be found. Unsuccessful negotiations with several eminent Europeans followed, after which, in April 1905, the trustees elected Stock conductor. He was not yet thirty-three and relatively unknown outside Chicago, but the local press warmly approved.

Continuing and broadening the policies that Thomas had developed, Stock gave careful attention to the construction of his programs, introduced works by contemporary composers, encouraged young performers, and took the orchestra on tours throughout the Middle West and South, greatly extending its sphere of influence. He also made significant innovations. Thomas had conducted occasional popular and children's concerts, but Stock expanded these into regular series: the popular concerts, for which low-priced tickets were distributed through civic organizations, in 1914 and the children's concerts in 1919.

The steady growth in influence of the Chicago Symphony Orchestra under Stock's direction was disrupted by anti-German prejudice during World War I. Although Stock had applied for United States citizenship on his first day in Chicago, he had neglected taking out his second papers within the allotted time, and in 1914 he was not an American citizen. With the declaration of war in Europe, he announced to the orchestra that henceforth rehearsals would be conducted in English rather than in German, as they had been since the orchestra's inception. Feeling against Germans increased with America's entry into the war, and on Aug. 17, 1918, believing that his presence was damaging the orchestra, Stock resigned as conductor. The trustees regretfully acquiesced and appointed Eric DeLamarter, a local organist and composer, as assistant conductor to fill what they hoped would be a temporary interregnum. During the season of 1918–19 Stock observed the orchestras in such cities as Boston, New York, and Philadelphia. On Feb. 7, 1919, he filed his application for second papers; on Feb. 19 the orchestra's trustees invited him to resume conducting; and on Feb. 28 he appeared on the stage for the first time since the close of the preceding season, receiving an ovation. He became a citizen on May 22.

The dislocations of the war had made evident the shortcomings of the United States as a training ground for orchestral performers. In a far-seeing plan, Stock suggested to the trustees of the Chicago Symphony the formation of a training orchestra designed to teach the orchestral repertoire and the necessary routine in ensemble work. The formation of the Civic Orchestra was announced on Dec. 4, 1919, with Stock as direc-

tor; he conducted its first concert on Mar. 29, 1920. He also gave much attention to encouraging musical education in the public schools and sometimes conducted concerts by high school orchestras.

Besides his regular conducting in Chicago, Stock participated in numerous music festivals and served as guest conductor for the New York Philharmonic (1926, 1927) and Philadelphia orchestras. Conductors of his generation had no prejudice against altering or cutting the works of the masters, and he did not hestitate to amplify or change orchestrations, even of Beethoven symphonies. His own compositions included two symphonies, three overtures, a violin concerto, his "March and Hymn to Democracy" (1919), and other orchestral works, as well as numerous orchestral arrangements, chamber works, and songs.

Stock was not a spectacular or particularly graceful conductor; of only medium height, somewhat round-shouldered, with a ruddy complexion and prominent blue eyes, he was not physically impressive. Yet his daring conceptions, supported by solid musicianship and common sense, enabled him to draw from the orchestra precisely the effects he wanted. He made the orchestra an integral part of the community by striving to serve the musical needs of broad sectors of the population through well-planned special programs. Under Stock, the Chicago Symphony Orchestra dominated the musical life of the Middle West by its brilliant performances and by a repertory more extensive and catholic than that of any other American orchestra of his day. He conducted a Mahler Festival in 1917 and performed works by other major composers, such as Stravinsky's *Rite of Spring*, years before they were heard in New York. When Howard Hanson in 1938 made a survey of American performances of works by American composers over the previous twenty years, he reported that the Chicago Symphony Orchestra headed the list, having played 272 compositions by eighty-five composers. Yet Stock, while hospitable to new music, was at his best conducting the late romantics, the music of his youth.

Stock received honorary degrees from several universities including Northwestern (1915), Michigan (1924), and Chicago (1925); he was made a chevalier of the Legion of Honor (France) in 1925. He married Elizabeth (Elsa) Muskulus in Milwaukee, Wis., on May 25, 1896; they had one child, Vera Fredericka. Stock died at his Chicago home of a coronary thrombosis in 1942, shortly before his seventieth birthday. His ashes were placed in Rosehill Cemetery, Chicago.

[Obituaries and articles in *Chicago Daily News*, Oct. 20, 1942, *Chicago Tribune*, Oct. 21, 25, Nov. 1, 8, 15, 1942, *N. Y. Times*, Nov. 3, 21, 1940, Oct. 21, 1942; Philo A. Otis, *The Chicago Symphony Orchestra . . . 1891–1924* (1924); David Ewen, *Dictators of the Baton* (1943); Howard Hanson, "Report of Committee on Am. Music," Music Teachers Nat. Assoc., *Proc.*, 1938; Chicago Symphony Orchestra programs, 1940–43; Rose F. Thomas, *Memoirs of Theodore Thomas* (1911); *Nat. Cyc. Am. Biog.*, Current Vol. A, pp. 519–20; *Die Musik in Geschichte und Gegenwart* (1949); Deems Taylor, *Music to My Ears* (1949); Frederick Stock and Horace A. Oakley papers, Newberry Lib., Chicago; death record from Ill. Dept. of Public Health.]

DENA J. EPSTEIN

STOESSEL, ALBERT FREDERIC (Oct. 11, 1894–May 12, 1943), conductor, violinist, and composer, was born in St. Louis, Mo., the eldest of the two sons and one daughter of Albert John and Alfreda (Wiedmann) Stoessel. Both parents were first-generation Americans, their families having come, respectively, from Switzerland and the German province of Swabia. Stoessel's father, a professional violinist and leader of a theatre orchestra in St. Louis, began teaching his son the violin at a very early age, and by the age of twelve Albert had begun composing. He attended local public schools through the eighth grade and continued his violin study with St. Louis teachers. In 1910, at the age of fifteen, with money earned chiefly from the sale of two published compositions, he went to Berlin to study at the Hochschule für Musik with such masters as Emanuel Wirth, Willy Hess, and August Hermann Kretzschmar.

After completing his studies in 1913, Stoessel began his professional career, touring Europe as second violinist with the Hess Quartet. He made his debut as solo violinist in November 1914 with the Blüthner Orchestra in Berlin, and followed this appearance with others in London and Paris. He returned to the United States in the summer of 1915, established a home at Auburndale, Mass., and made his American debut with the St. Louis Symphony on Nov. 19. On June 27, 1917, at Auburndale, Stoessel married Julia Pickard, who had been a pupil of his in Berlin. Their children were Albert Frederick, who died in childhood, Edward Pickard, and Frederick. Reared in the Evangelical Lutheran Church, Stoessel after his marriage became a Christian Scientist, like his wife, but later joined the Episcopal Church.

After America's entry into World War I, Stoessel was drafted into the army and later commissioned a second lieutenant as bandmaster of the American Expeditionary Forces' 301st Infantry Band, which reached France in July 1918. At the close of the war he was appointed director of the newly founded A.E.F. Bandmaster's School in Chaumont, France, where he met the conductor Walter Damrosch, one of the school's sponsors. Stoessel returned to the United States in 1919 and the next year accepted Damrosch's invitation to serve under him as assistant director of the New York Oratorio Society. He also continued his composing and undertook a heavy schedule of concert tours, beginning with a performance of the Brahms Violin Concerto with the Boston Symphony Orchestra under Pierre Monteux on Apr. 1, 1920. In 1921 he traveled as assisting artist to Enrico Caruso [*q.v.*] on the tenor's last tour of the United States.

Starting in 1921, Stoessel gradually shifted the emphasis of his career from the violin to the podium. In that year he succeeded Walter Damrosch as director of the New York Oratorio Society and became an orchestral conductor at the annual Chautauqua (N. Y.) Music Festival. He later (1928) became musical director at Chautauqua, where he organized a permanent opera company. From 1925 he also served as director of the Worcester (Mass.) Music Festival, where each October he presented a week's concerts of symphonic music, choral works, and opera, with performers recruited from local groups and professional musicians from New York. He retained all three directorships until his death.

Stoessel's educational activities date from 1923, when he was asked to organize and direct the first music department of New York University. He resigned in 1930 to give full time to the duties at the Juilliard Graduate School in New York that he had assumed in 1927. There, as head of the orchestra and opera departments, he directed the training of student conductors, orchestra members, and young singers, and conducted the school's opera performances. Many of his students later made successful careers as conductors, section leaders and first-chair players in orchestras, and members of opera companies.

Stoessel continued to appear as guest conductor with leading symphony orchestras, including those of St. Louis, Cleveland, New York, and Boston. In his concerts he presented many new works by composers such as Werner Josten, Robert Russell Bennett, George Antheil, and Gian Francesco Malipiero, as well as his own orchestral compositions. He was responsible for the first New York production of Richard Strauss's *Ariadne auf Naxos* (1934), and for the first uncut performances given in New York of Bach's two great choral works, the Mass in B Minor and the *St. Matthew Passion*.

As a conductor Stoessel commanded the affection and respect of his musicians. More than six feet tall and sturdy in build, he possessed innate dignity and kindliness and carried his points on the podium by careful instructions, a clear beat, and unfailing courtesy. Always even-tempered, he yet conducted with fire and brilliance. As a composer, he was thoroughly trained, painstaking, and somewhat conservative. His works won acceptance with both audiences and critics, who commended their lyricism and melodic interest as well as their disciplined craftsmanship. Best known among his works, perhaps, are his opera *Garrick* (1936), with libretto by Robert A. Simon; his Concerto Grosso for Piano and String Orchestra (1936); his *Suite Antique* for two violins and chamber orchestra (1922); and his symphonic portrait, *Cyrano de Bergerac* (1922). He also composed several works for chorus and orchestra, a sonata for violin and piano, and other symphonic and chamber works. He was the author of an instruction manual, *Technique of the Baton* (1919).

Early in 1943 Stoessel, now forty-eight, was disappointed in his hope of being made director of the Cleveland Symphony. He showed some signs of heart disease and was warned to take a year's rest, but agreed to give a final concert conducting members of the New York Philharmonic at the annual award ceremonies of the American Academy of Arts and Letters in New York City. As the orchestra played the closing chord of the premier performance of Robert Nathan and Walter Damrosch's narrative cantata, *Dunkirk*, he collapsed on the podium and died immediately of a heart attack. He was buried in the Stoessel family plot at the Rural Cemetery in New Bedford, Mass.

[Charles D. McNaughton, "Albert Stoessel, Am. Musician" (Ph.D. dissertation, N. Y. Univ., 1958), is the fullest source. See also: Nicolas Slonimsky, ed., *Baker's Biog. Dict. of Musicians* (5th ed., 1958); Eric Blom, ed., *Grove's Dict. of Music and Musicians* (5th ed., 1954); John Tasker Howard, *Our Am. Music* (1946 ed.); John Erskine, *My Life in Music* (1950); *N. Y. Times*, Feb. 21, 1937 (interview), Feb. 25, 1937 (review of *Garrick*), May 13, 1943 (obituary); and obituary in *N. Y. Herald Tribune*, May 13, 1943.]

SHEILA KEATS

STOKES, ISAAC NEWTON PHELPS (Apr. 11, 1867–Dec. 18, 1944), architect and housing reformer, was born in New York City, the eldest of nine children (four boys and five girls) of Anson Phelps Stokes [*q.v.*], banker and philanthropist, and Helen Louisa (Phelps) Stokes. Both parents were descended from George Phelps, who emigrated from Gloucestershire, England, to Dorchester, Mass., about 1630. Reared in an atmosphere of gracious luxury and devout Episcopalian faith, Stokes inherited a strong tradition of public service and benev-

olence. Besides his father, other philanthropists of note in the family were his grandfather James Boulter Stokes, one of the founders of the New York Association for Improving the Condition of the Poor, and his aunts Caroline and Olivia Phelps Stokes [*qq.v.*]. After attending the Berkeley School in New York City and St. Paul's School in Concord, N. H., where the homesick lad often became ill and never remained for the full year, Stokes entered Harvard in 1887. College was more of a social than an intellectual experience for him, and his record at Harvard was little better than the conventional "gentleman's C."

Following his graduation in 1891, Stokes acceded to his father's demand that he enter the banking business. But after two years he decided to study architecture, enrolling first at Columbia University, where he specialized in economic planning, and then in 1894 at the École des Beaux Arts in Paris. He returned to the United States in 1897, and that year, with John Mead Howells, son of the novelist William Dean Howells [*q.v.*], submitted the winning design for the University Settlement building. Encouraged by this success, the pair opened an architectural office in Manhattan, a partnership which lasted until 1917. Among their more noteworthy designs were the Baltimore Stock Exchange, the headquarters for the American Geographical Society in New York, the Bonwit Teller department store in New York, St. Paul's Chapel at Columbia University, the Dudley Memorial Gate and the Music Building (later Paine Hall) at Harvard, and Woodbridge Hall at Yale.

Stokes's decision to enter the field of architecture, as he later recalled, was based in part on discussions with such reform leaders as Josephine Shaw Lowell [*q.v.*] and Robert W. de Forest [Supp. 1], who convinced him "that better housing for the poor, and particularly for the working classes, was one of the crying needs of the day, and that the designing and promotion of better housing . . . furnished as good an opportunity for useful service as any other profession" (*Random Selections*, p. 91). While studying in Europe Stokes had met Samuel Barnett, an English housing reformer, and in 1896 he submitted a design in a competition for a model tenement house sponsored by New York's Improved Housing Council.

Upon returning to New York, Stokes helped organize in 1898 the Charity Organization Society's Tenement House Committee. He was chiefly responsible for the preparation of the committee's tenement architecture competition and exhibition, which led in 1900 to the establishment by Gov. Theodore Roosevelt of the New York State Tenement House Commission. Appointed to the commission in 1901, Stokes focused on the city's ubiquitous dumbbell tenements. The dumbbell design, conforming to the city's traditional deep and narrow lot (and, ironically, the winner of an earlier architectural competition), had contributed to the development of tenement districts which were regarded by many as the most unsanitary and congested in the world. Determined that new housing for the poor . should be more healthful, Stokes showed that, by planning a whole city block and transcending the standard 25-by-100-foot lot, the same number of people could be housed at the same cost per unit in new apartments with adequate light, air, and open space. He incorporated some of these ideas in the design of the Tuskegee Houses, a six-story tenement for Negroes built in 1901 by Caroline and Olivia Stokes. Linking apartment construction to slum clearance, Stokes proposed that the city purchase the worst tenement blocks, demolish the old buildings, and, after converting the center of a block into a park and playground area, sell the strips along the perimeter to private developers for the construction of low-cost housing. He hoped in this way to reserve sufficient open space for local residents, while freeing builders from the restrictive dimensions of the standard city lot.

Though Stokes helped write the New York Tenement House Law of 1901, which set minimum standards for air, light, and sanitation, he soon lost faith in this type of legislation. He was especially annoyed when his Dudley model tenements, which were built in 1910, had to wait three years for approval from the Tenement House Department. Convinced that detailed codes, as advocated by such reformers as Lawrence Veiller, inhibited the architectural experimentation necessary for the development of low-cost housing, Stokes resigned in 1912 from the Charity Organization Society's Tenement House Committee because of its emphasis on restrictive legislation. He now believed that the solution to the housing problem lay entirely in the development of more economical designs; thereafter, as president (1911–24) and secretary (1924–37) of the Phelps-Stokes Fund, which had been established by Caroline Phelps Stokes in 1911, he concentrated on technical problems to lower the cost of construction. His approach to the housing problem was realistic, but narrowly conceived. An officer in several family real estate ventures, he never questioned the sanctity of speculative real estate practices; indeed, he thought the key to the housing problem was to make good hous-

ing profitable enough to attract speculators, and during the 1930's he vigorously objected to the federal government's public housing program as utopian and impractical.

Tall, with a formal black beard, I. N. Phelps Stokes was a dignified man whose desire to serve society sprang from a feeling akin to noblesse oblige. He lamented the sacrifice of harmony and stability to what he considered the rampant selfishness and egalitarianism of the twentieth century, and hoped for a religious revival to restore social order. Late in his life, he admitted that he was both an "idealist" and a "conservative."

Beginning in 1908, when his historical imagination was fired by the Hudson-Fulton Celebration in New York, Stokes collected prints of old Manhattan as a hobby. Eventually his collection took the form of the monumental published compilation, *The Iconography of Manhattan Island, 1498–1909* (6 vols., 1915–28), a full record of the physical evolution of the island.

On Aug. 21, 1895, he had married Edith Minturn, daughter of a New York merchant and granddaughter of Robert Bowne Minturn [q.v.]. They had no children of their own but adopted a young English girl, Helen Bicknell. Stokes died of a cerebral hemorrhage at the age of seventy-seven at the home of a sister in Charleston, S. C. His body was cremated, and his ashes were placed beside those of his wife in the wall of St. Paul's Chapel, Columbia University.

[Stokes's autobiography, *Random Reflections of a Happy Life* (rev. ed., mimeographed for private distribution, 1941), is a fascinating record of a late-nineteenth-century childhood spent in a world he thought "better in most respects" than the period of his mature life. The voluminous Isaac Newton Phelps Stokes Papers in the N.-Y. Hist. Soc. contain extensive personal and professional correspondence. For his contribution to architecture and housing reform, see Robert W. de Forest and Lawrence Veiller, *The Tenement House Problem* (2 vols., 1903); James Ford et al., *Slums and Housing, with Special Reference to N. Y. City* (2 vols., 1936); and Roy Lubove, "I. N. Phelps Stokes: Tenement Architect, Economist, Planner," *Jour. of the Soc. of Architectural Historians*, May 1964. See also obituaries in N.-Y. Hist. Soc., *Quart. Bull.*, Jan. 1945 (by R. W. G. Vail), *N. Y. Hist.*, Apr. 1945, and *N. Y. Herald Tribune*, Dec. 19, 1944. Death record from S. C. State Board of Health. For his genealogy, see A. T. Servin, *The Phelps Family of America* (1899).]

MARVIN E. GETTLEMAN

STONE, CHARLES AUGUSTUS (Jan. 16, 1867–Feb. 25, 1941), and **EDWIN SIBLEY WEBSTER** (Aug. 26, 1867–May 10, 1950), electrical engineers, were closely associated throughout their professional lives as founders of the firm of Stone & Webster, which became active in the financing, construction, and management of electric power plants and public utility corporations. Both men came of old New England stock long resident in the Boston area. Stone was born in Newton, Mass., the younger of two sons of Charles Hobart Stone, a wholesale butter merchant, and Mary Augusta (Greene) Stone. Webster was born in Roxbury, Mass. (later part of Boston), the second of three children of Frank G. and Mary Fidelia (Messenger) Webster. His father became a member of the Boston banking firm of Kidder, Peabody & Company in 1888 and was later a senior partner. Charles Stone and Edwin Webster first met in 1884 when taking the entrance examinations for the Massachusetts Institute of Technology. Electing the recently inaugurated course of study in electrical engineering and seated together, they became such close friends that their classmates knew them even then as "Stone and Webster." Later, they prepared a common senior thesis pertaining to the efficiency of a Westinghouse alternating-current generator. Upon graduating in 1888, they planned to go into partnership as electrical engineers, at that time a new profession offering great opportunity.

Their plan was discouraged, however, by Charles R. Cross, professor of physics and head of electrical engineering at M.I.T., who doubted that there would be enough demand in Boston for two consulting electrical engineers. Stone, therefore, worked first as an assistant to Elihu Thomson [Supp. 2] at the Thomson Electric Welding Company of Lynn, Mass., and then as the agent for the C & C Motor Company in Boston. Webster spent several months touring Europe observing business and engineering developments there, and then worked at Kidder, Peabody & Company. Yet their idea persisted, and in November 1889, with $2,600 borrowed from their parents, Stone and Webster launched a consulting engineering company in Boston. Since neither gave up his regular job, they employed a recent M.I.T. graduate to manage the office. Slowly, in their spare time, the partners proceeded to organize the company further and to find clients. Webster began full-time work with the company in January 1890, and Stone a few months later. Their firm, at first called the Massachusetts Electrical Engineering Company, listed among its references Gen. Francis A. Walker [q.v.], president of M.I.T., Prof. Charles Cross, and Webster's father. The ties with M.I.T. engineering and Boston finance were—and would remain—close.

Stone and Webster's concept of the company, expressed in its early literature, suggests the state of electrical technology and helps define the function of the consultant at that time. Noting in 1890 that the development of "electrical inven-

tion" in the past few years had been marvelously rapid, the partners believed that the business community needed advice before "taking pecuniary interest in electrical matters brought before them." Stone, Webster, and their experts therefore offered to design, estimate, and superintend construction of electric light and power plants; they were also prepared to test and calibrate equipment.

Their first major project provided New England with one of its earliest high-voltage power transmission facilities. On the recommendation of President Walker and Professor Cross, S. D. Warren & Company in 1890 commissioned the young consulting firm to design and construct a 400-horsepower hydroelectric plant on the Presumpscot River at Saccarappa, Maine, where excess waterpower was available, to supply electricity for its Cumberland paper mill, a mile distant. Stone and Webster used 1,000-volt direct current for the transmission system. There was little engineering precedent for the work, and they drew confidence from its success. During the next few years they built small electric light plants, reported on the operations of existing facilities, and gained support for their laboratory by testing electrical materials for the Underwriters Union, which did not establish its own laboratory until 1895.

The depression of 1893 greatly affected the careers of Stone and Webster. Electrical manufacturers such as General Electric and Westinghouse had taken the securities of operating light and power companies in partial payment for equipment when the investment market would not come forward fast enough with the needed capital. During the panic of 1893, banks demanded reduction on loans to manufacturers, and General Electric had to turn the unseasoned and unsalable securities over to a syndicate, the Street Railway and Illuminating Properties Trustees. Unable to evaluate the properties, the syndicate engaged the firm of Stone & Webster to examine and report upon them.

With a combined background in engineering and finance, Charles Stone and Edwin Webster were well suited for the assignment; they also learned greatly from the experience. From examination of the various properties in many parts of the country they became familiar with the problems of financing, operating, and managing electrical plants. On the advice of the elder J. P. Morgan [q.v.], they invested in one of the most promising of the properties, the Nashville (Tenn.) Electric Light and Power Company, thus entering what Stone called "the entrepreneur business," which he defined as the "business of conceiving, creating, developing, and operating any important enterprise." They later gained a controlling interest in the Nashville company, extended and developed it, and within a few years sold it for a staggering profit. "The way was paved," Stone later wrote, "for investing in various power, lighting, and railroad interests throughout the United States."

In the decade before World War I, the organizational genius of the two partners allowed the company, like the electrical industry itself, to grow rapidly. To distinguish, however, between their respective contributions is impossible. They maintained desks side by side; they even signed correspondence as "Stone & Webster." Until 1905 they were the only partners and were known as the "firm," but then Russell Robb, an M.I.T. classmate, was taken in, and others followed, until by 1912 there were seven. Earlier, Stone and Webster together had managed all the company affairs; now department heads assumed increased responsibility for engineering, construction, reporting, managing, and banking. By 1912 Stone & Webster had about 600 officials and employees and occupied an eight-story building. Of the 283 college men in the organization, ninety-four were M.I.T. graduates and fifty were from Harvard.

Stone and Webster had begun the executive management of public utilities in October 1895, when they agreed to supervise the Edison Illuminating Company of Brockton, Mass., for $250 per month. By 1912 their firm managed thirty-five utilities, primarily electric and railway. For a fee, they provided specialized managerial and engineering consultants, as well as a local manager and treasurer; but the utility's board of directors, legal staff, operating organization, and bank account remained local and independent. This remained the policy until 1925, when the Engineers Public Service Company, organized by Stone & Webster, acquired control of companies the firm had managed.

Meanwhile, the need for capital to improve and extend the utilities they managed had led the partners to establish, in 1902, a securities department in their firm which acted as fiscal agent in floating securities for the utility companies under their management. By World War I, Stone & Webster was handling as large a volume of utility securities as passed over the counters of the leading investment bankers. To inform officers, directors, stockholders, and potential stockholders of the financial condition of Stone & Webster-managed public utilities, they also began publication, in 1902, of an annual "black book."

Although the finance and management functions of Stone & Webster grew in importance, engineering did not languish. At first the partners made engineering designs but sublet construction. Gradually, however, they added construction men to their staff, and in 1906 they formed the Engineering Corporation to systematize design and construction and to relate these to management and finance. Clients were not confined to the managed utilities; the Massachusetts Institute of Technology had these two graduates of the Class of 1888 build the monumental neoclassic limestone-faced buildings of its new campus (1913–15) on the Charles River esplanade.

Other Stone & Webster engineering achievements were notable. The Big Creek transmission system extending 241 miles from Big Creek to Los Angeles, Calif., with 150,000-volt lines, was, in 1913, the highest voltage over the longest distance yet attempted. In 1913 the company also completed construction of the Keokuk hydroelectric station at Des Moines Rapids on the Mississippi River, which had the highest capacity—120,000 horsepower—of any high-voltage transmission system in the world. The firm arranged the financing of the $25,000,000 enterprise, and Stone negotiated the sale of half the power to St. Louis, Mo., 144 miles distant.

World War I in Europe and an industrial boom in the United States brought a slump in electric utilities; according to Webster, the firm "had about as quiet a time as we ever had." During the war Stone moved his offices to New York City to facilitate discharging his additional responsibility as president of the American International Corporation, formed in 1915 to promote American industry and trade abroad. The move also brought him nearer the Hog Island Shipyard in Philadelphia, a mammoth undertaking constructed in 1917–18 by his firm.

The utility business recovered sharply in the 1920's. By 1930 the partners could survey some notable achievements. In about a quarter of a century, their company had completed more than $1,000,000,000 of construction, examined and reported on properties worth over $7,000,000,000, participated in new security issues totaling much more than $1,000,000,000, and built steam and hydroelectric plants developing one-tenth of the nation's central-station power. The firm could justly claim a prominent role in ushering in the age of electricity.

Various structural changes had come during the postwar decade. In 1920 the partnership was incorporated in Massachusetts as Stone & Webster, Inc., with Webster as president and Stone as chairman of the board. Webster became vice-chairman in 1930 and succeeded to the chairmanship after Stone's death in 1941. Subsidiary firms were set up to manage the company's various functions: in 1927, Stone, Webster & Blodget, Inc. (later Stone & Webster Securities Corporation), to handle securities sales; in 1928, Stone & Webster Engineering Corporation, to assume the engineering and construction work; and in 1929 the Stone & Webster Service Corporation, to take over the development and operation of public utility properties.

Until 1925 Stone and Webster had not used the holding company as a financing device, despite the precedent of such American super-holding companies as Electric Bond & Share Company, headed by Sidney Z. Mitchell [Supp. 3]. In 1925, however, they helped form, and later controlled, the Engineers Public Service Corporation, which acquired several utilities receiving management services from Stone & Webster. A new corporation, Stone & Webster, Inc., of Delaware, formed in 1929, became the top holding company in the corporate structure, and in 1930 it acquired 90 percent of Engineers Public Service Corporation, which by 1933 had invested $95,116,675 in six major groups of light, power, and street railway companies located in fourteen states. Stone & Webster, Inc., also controlled the Sierra Pacific Electric Company. In aggregate, the Stone & Webster group consisted of forty-three companies, not including outside companies it managed; the total securities investment of Stone & Webster, Inc., in 1932 was $66,601,913. Two years after the passage of the Public Utility Holding Company Act of 1935, Stone & Webster divested itself of Engineers Public Service Corporation and relinquished controlling interest in public utilities.

Despite these changes in organization, Charles Stone and Edwin Webster in their later years saw their company continue to provide services along the lines they had established. Though their offices were separate, they preserved the tradition of desks side by side, two in New York and two in Boston. Both served on the executive committee of M.I.T. for many years and were directors of numerous organizations. Stone also raised thoroughbred horses on his farms, including the Thomas Jefferson estate in Albemarle County, Va.; Webster was president of the Massachusetts Horticultural Society and of the board of trustees of the American School of Classical Studies in Athens. Stone had married Mary Adams Leonard of Hingham, Mass., on June 3, 1902; their children were Charles Augustus, Margaret, Whitney, and Janet Elizabeth. Webster had married Jane de Peyster Hovey of Brookline, Mass., on June 1, 1893; their children were Frances, Mabel, Edwin Sibley, and Mary

Messenger. Charles Stone died of pneumonia in New York City in 1941, and Edwin Webster of a cerebral hemorrhage in Newton, Mass., in 1950. Stone was buried in the Locust Valley (Long Island) Cemetery, Webster in Mount Auburn Cemetery, Cambridge, Mass.

[Unpublished materials in the files of Stone & Webster, Inc., N. Y. City; *Stone & Webster Public Service Jour.*, 1907–32; Stone & Webster, *Black Book*, 1902–29; *Stone & Webster: The Firm, Engineering Corporation, Management Assoc., Securities Dept.* (pamphlet, 1912, reprinted from *Electrical World*); "Stone & Webster Organization and the Properties It Manages," *Street Railway Jour.*, July 7, 1906; Stone & Webster, Inc., *Stone & Webster* (1932) and *Hist. of Stone & Webster, 1889–1966* (undated 30-page booklet); "Stone & Webster," *Fortune*, Nov. 1930; "Electric-Power Industry: Control of Power Companies," 69 Cong., 2 Sess., *Senate Document No. 213* (1927); Federal Trade Commission, *Utility Corporations*, part 66 (1934); *Nat. Cyc. Am. Biog.*, XXXVIII, 582–83 (on Webster); obituaries in *N. Y. Times*, Feb. 26, 1941, May 11, 1950, and *Technology Rev.* (M.I.T.), Apr. 1941, July 1950; birth and marriage records and death record of Webster from Mass. Registrar of Vital Statistics.]

THOMAS PARKE HUGHES

STONE, JOHN STONE (Sept. 24, 1869–May 20, 1943), telephone and radio engineer, was born at Dover, Va., one of at least three children and the only son of Gen. Charles Pomeroy Stone [*q.v.*] and his second wife, Annie Jeannie (Stone) Stone, from whom he derived his double name. General Stone, a native of Massachusetts and a graduate of West Point, had served as a Union officer in the Civil War, during which he met and married a Louisiana girl descended from a Maryland family of the same surname. His career was blighted, however, by charges of incompetence after the defeat at Ball's Bluff. Leaving the army, he became superintendent of a mining company in Virginia, but in 1870 accepted an appointment as chief of staff of the Egyptian army.

John Stone thus grew up in the luxury of a foreign court. He was educated by private tutors and, upon the family's return to the United States in 1883, at the Columbia Grammar School in New York City. He began his college training at Columbia University's School of Mines (1886–88), where he studied mathematics, physics, chemistry, and electricity, and completed it at Johns Hopkins University (1888–90), where he worked with the great physicist Henry A. Rowland [*q.v.*] but did not take a degree. In 1890 Stone entered the research laboratory of the American Bell Telephone Company in Boston. There he experimented with radiotelephony and proposed carrier telephony over wire circuits, though both ideas were in advance of the times. In 1892 he received the first two patents (relating to the development and distribution of electric current in a telephone cable) of the more than 120 he received during his lifetime.

Stone left the telephone company in 1899 to become a consulting engineer, with his own office in Boston. Continuing his work on radio, or "wireless telegraphy," he was among the first to see the need for sharper tuning and greater frequency selectivity in both the transmitter and the receiver. To meet this need he developed and patented (1902) a system comprising a pair of loosely coupled resonant circuits to be used in each; his invention anticipated by several months a similar one of Marconi, who obtained his famed "four-tuned-circuits" patent in 1903. (A few weeks after Stone's death, his priority was established by a ruling of the United States Supreme Court.) In 1902 Stone incorporated the Stone Telegraph and Telephone Company to manufacture and market his inventions, which were widely adopted in early radio apparatus. The company made contributions to the development of carefully calibrated meters, early antenna measurements, and marine direction finding, but it did not achieve commercial success and failed in 1910. In the following year Stone moved to New York City, where he resumed consulting work and established himself as an expert witness in patent litigations. He was one of the first to appreciate the importance of Lee de Forest's grid Audion tube (triode) as an amplifier for transcontinental telephony.

Stone's health was never robust, and in 1919 he moved to the milder climate of San Diego, Calif. There he continued his scientific investigations as associate engineer at large for the American Telephone and Telegraph Company, a position he held from 1920 until his retirement in 1934. His later work centered on short-wave and ultrashort-wave radio, including an antenna design which foreshadowed later high-frequency long-distance beam transmission.

Of most lasting significance among Stone's publications is the paper "The Practical Aspects of the Propagation of High-Frequency Electric Waves along Wires" (*Journal of the Franklin Institute,* October 1912), for which he received the Franklin Institute's Longstreth Medal in 1913. In 1907 Stone founded in Boston the Society of Wireless Telegraph Engineers, which in 1912 merged with a similar New York group, the Wireless Institute, to become the Institute of Radio Engineers, one of the predecessors of the Institute of Electrical and Electronics Engineers. Stone served as the I.R.E.'s president in 1914–15 and in 1923 was awarded its Medal of Honor.

On Nov. 28, 1918, Stone married Sibyl Wilbur of Elmira, N. Y., a journalist. They had no children, and the marriage ended in divorce. Stone was a member of the Episcopal Church and of various clubs and scientific societies, and was devoted to the arts, particularly painting and music. After retirement he lived very quietly. He died at his home in San Diego at the age of seventy-three, of heart disease due to arteriosclerosis. His remains were cremated.

John Stone Stone was one of the few theoreticians among early radio engineers. In a day when the experimentalist was king, he relied almost wholly on mathematical analysis, rather than laboratory work, to test the validity of his concepts. He is recognized as one of the pioneers both in radio and in high-frequency wire transmission. Had his practical abilities matched his theoretical ones, he would rank with Marconi, Michael Pupin [Supp. 1], Nikola Tesla [Supp. 3], and the other great names in electrical communications.

[George H. Clark, *The Life of John Stone Stone* (privately printed, 1946), by a close friend and admirer, is the fullest account. See also obituaries in Inst. of Radio Engineers, *Proc.,* Sept. 1943, pp. 463, 521–23; *N. Y. Times,* May 21, 1943; and *Nat. Cyc. Am. Biog.,* XXIV, 336–37. Death record from Calif. Dept. of Public Health.]

CHARLES SÜSSKIND

STRAUS, PERCY SELDEN (June 27, 1876–Apr. 6, 1944), department store executive, was born in New York City, the second son and second of seven children of Isidor Straus [*q.v.*] and Ida (Blun) Straus. Like his older brother, Jesse Isidor Straus [Supp. 2], Percy was educated at the Collegiate Institute of Dr. Julius Sachs [*q.v.*] in New York City and at Harvard (A.B. 1897). Having inherited his father's scholarly interests and analytical mind, he thoroughly enjoyed academic life and would have preferred to devote himself to teaching and scholarship. His father, however, had other ideas. Isidor and Nathan Straus [*q.v.*] had in 1896 acquired complete ownership of the R. H. Macy department store in New York. Isidor had already planned to bring his two older sons into the business and intended them to work as a team. Jesse was to learn "soft goods," sales promotion, and the financial aspects of the business; Percy was to familiarize himself with furniture, furnishings, groceries, and other "hard" merchandise and to specialize in systems and operations, including personnel, maintenance and delivery.

Like his brother, Percy Straus accepted the paternal plan with good grace; he began work in Macy's in September 1897, and almost from the outset his role was a major one. He and Jesse persuaded their father and uncle to move the store from its original location on 14th Street to 34th Street; they were thus in the vanguard of the uptown movement of retail trade. In turn, the two sons were given responsibility for carrying out the complex move, from the acquisition of the real estate to the completion of the new store facilities. Because Jesse fell ill during the early stages, Percy had to bear a disproportionate share of the task, which was finally completed in November 1902.

After the death of Isidor Straus, along with his wife, in the *Titanic* disaster of 1912, his share of the store was inherited by his three surviving sons (Herbert had entered the business in 1903); and at the end of 1913, as a result of differences between them and their uncle, they became the sole owners. With the incorporation of R. H. Macy & Company in 1919, Percy Straus became vice-president of what was by then the world's largest department store; he subsequently also held offices in the department stores in Toledo, Atlanta, and Newark which Macy's acquired between 1923 and 1929. Although for many years Jesse was the recognized leader of the team, devising most of the firm's policies on merchandising, advertising, and finance, Percy took the lead in implementing management plans. After Jesse, an ardent supporter of Franklin D. Roosevelt, was appointed ambassador to France in 1933, Percy succeeded him as president; and the death of his brother Herbert shortly thereafter left him with the heavy task of leading the organization alone, a role he filled until 1939.

During Straus's half-century career, Macy's experienced several major transitions, including the establishment of a management hierarchy in place of direct supervision by the partners, an expansion in business volume and an upgrading of Macy's line of merchandise, and intensified competition in the retail trade. Straus matured in the era of scientific management; it appealed to his way of thinking. He was one of the first in industry to use objective testing devices in connection with the hiring and placing of employees, and he was a leader in the introduction of formal training programs, first for the lower ranks and later (1919) for executives. Likewise, he was one of the first to push for standardization of systems and procedures and the use of labor-saving and automatic devices in retail operations. On the technical aspects of store management he was probably the best-informed man in the world.

A prodigious worker, Straus also bore his share in wider business, civic, and educational activities. He was one of the founders and a director of the National Retail Foundation and a director of the National Dry Goods Association. During World War I he served on the staff of the Council of National Defense. He was a member of the Committee of Fourteen formed in New York City in 1918 to investigate organized prostitution, and of the mayor's committee on city planning (1934–38). He was a member (1920) and vice-president (1928) of the finance committee of the Democratic National Committee. Early in his career he sought to help Jewish immigrants find employment through the Jewish Agricultural and Industrial Aid Society, in due course becoming its president. He likewise became treasurer and eventually chairman of the board of the Federation for Support of Jewish Philanthropic Societies of New York. With his brothers he established the Isidor Straus Professorship of Business History at Harvard (1924) and contributed $300,000 for the construction of Harvard's Straus Hall (1925). A member of the council of New York University, he organized the drive to raise $47,750,000 for its Centennial Fund in 1926, himself giving an unrestricted endowment of $1,000,000.

Straus disliked ostentation and the limelight. Tall, slender, somewhat formal and reserved in his manner, he was a calm, patient, and courteous man, who reportedly never lost his temper. The weekends which he regularly devoted to horticulture and horseback riding seem to have helped him withstand the tremendous pressures of his responsibilities. He suffered a heart attack in 1939, after which he filled the position of chairman and elder statesman in the Macy firm. He died in New York City in 1944, at the age of sixty-seven. He was survived by his wife, Edith (Abraham) Straus, whom he had married on Nov. 27, 1902, and their three sons, Ralph Isidor, Percy Selden, and Donald Blun. Burial was in Woodlawn Cemetery, New York City.

[Ralph M. Hower, *Hist. of Macy's of N. Y., 1858–1919* (1943); *N. Y. Times*, Apr. 8, 20, 1944; *Nat. Cyc. Am. Biog.*, XL, 51–52; *Who Was Who in America*, vol. II (1950); Harvard College Class of 1897, *Reports* for the 25th, 40th, and 50th anniversaries; personal conversations with Percy Straus, 1940–42.]

RALPH M. HOWER

STUART, ELBRIDGE AMOS (Sept. 10, 1856–Jan. 14, 1944), businessman, was born in Guilford County, N. C., near Greensboro, the seventh of eight sons and twelfth of thirteen children of Amos and Matilda (Hadley) Stuart. He was christened Amos Elbridge, but around the age of ten persuaded his parents to reverse the names. His mother was of Irish Quaker background. His father, a farmer, was a great-grandson of Alexander Stewart, who came from Scotland to Pennsylvania about 1697. When Elbridge was five, Amos Stuart took his family to Indiana, where he continued to farm, first as a tenant, then on his own place in Henry County. The boy attended nearby Spiceland Academy, attaining the equivalent of the eighth grade.

In 1871 Elbridge and an older brother, Addison, set up a small produce commission house in Indianapolis. The business failed the following year, and for a few months in 1873 Elbridge drove a team and wagon for the United States Express Company in Richmond, Ind. Troubled with rheumatic fever, he went that fall to live with his brother Jehu, a physician in Lawrence, Kans. There he attended high school for a year and considered a medical career, but the witnessing of a postmortem caused him to change his mind. The next winter he worked as a day laborer, then went to western Kansas as a bookkeeper for a railroad contractor. He was back in Lawrence in 1876, clerking in a dry goods store, and remained there until 1880, when he worked briefly in New Mexico as a line grader for the Santa Fe Railroad and as timekeeper and commissary manager for a grading company.

In January 1881 Stuart, now twenty-four, joined with a partner to open a general store in El Paso, Texas. Originally Stuart & Sutherland, then Stuart & McNair, and, finally, E. A. Stuart & Company, the enterprise evolved into a wholesale and retail grocery firm. On Nov. 13, 1884, Stuart married Mary Jane Horner, a schoolteacher and a native of Rutland, Vt. They had two children, Elbridge Hadley and Katherine Moore.

In search of a climate beneficial to his wife's health, Stuart transferred his interests in 1894 to Los Angeles. There he became a member of the firm of Craig, Stuart & Company, wholesale grocers, but he left the concern in the spring of 1899 because of lack of harmony with his partners. Not finding another opportunity to his liking in the grocery business, in August of that year he reluctantly joined Thomas E. Yerxa in purchasing an abandoned condensed milk plant in Kent, Wash., near Seattle. The concern was chartered as the Pacific Coast Condensed Milk Company in 1900. In 1916 it became the Carnation Milk Products Company, and in 1929 the Carnation Company.

As president, Stuart was largely responsible for the company's success. He assembled a group of loyal suppliers, chose the brand name "Carnation," and personally persuaded retailers to stock his company's product. Demand for "Carnation

Cream" in the Alaska gold fields boosted sales. Stuart bought out his partner Yerxa in 1901 and the following year opened a second plant in Forest Grove, Oreg. By 1906, when a Chicago advertising agency suggested the slogan "Milk from contented cows," Stuart's firm had five plants. During World War I the firm's sales quadrupled and Stuart extended his operations into Canada. In 1919 Carnation took a controlling interest in the American Milk Products Company (later the General Milk Company, Inc.), established to sell canned milk in foreign markets. When Stuart resigned the presidency of the Carnation Company in 1932, the firm had plants in eighteen states and Carnation was the largest selling brand of evaporated milk in the world. Moreover, the company had extended into fresh milk and ice cream processing and distributing and, through purchase of the Albers Milling Company in 1929, into the processing and distribution of cereals and feeds. Stuart continued as chairman of the board and of the executive committee of the Carnation Company until his death.

Perhaps Stuart's most important accomplishment was the improvement of dairy herds in the United States and abroad. As early as 1910 he established Carnation Farms in Washington's Snoqualmie Valley for the purpose of breeding cows that would give high milk flows. In 1920 a Carnation cow, the first of many Carnation champions, established a new world record for milk production. By the 1930's animals of the Carnation strain were enriching herds throughout the United States and in many foreign countries. Stuart's hobby in his later years was the training of gaited horses. He was a member of the Holstein-Friesian Association of America and the American Hackney Horse Society and, from about 1922 to 1926, served as president of the Pacific International Live Stock Exposition.

A stern businessman, Stuart drove himself hard and demanded a high level of performance from his employees. He had been reared a Quaker but in Seattle and Los Angeles was a member of Congregational churches. He became a 32nd degree Mason. Stuart made his home in Seattle from 1899 to 1930, when he moved back to Los Angeles. He died of pneumonia in that city in his eighty-eighth year and was buried in Forest Lawn Memorial Park, Glendale, Calif.

[James Marshall, *Elbridge A. Stuart* (1949), is based on Stuart's dictated recollections; it includes photographs of Stuart. See also Bertie C. Forbes, *Men Who Are Making the West* (1923), pp. 76–96; *Nat. Cyc. Am. Biog.*, XXXII, 58–59; and obituary articles in *Los Angeles Times*, *Seattle Times*, and *N. Y. Times*, Jan. 15, 1944.]

IRENE D. NEU

SULZER, WILLIAM (Mar. 18, 1863–Nov. 6, 1941), Congressman and governor of New York, was born in Elizabeth, N. J., the second son among the seven children (five sons and two daughters) of Thomas and Lydia (Jelleme) Sulzer. Two brothers died in the Spanish-American War, and a third, Charles August Sulzer, was a territorial delegate to Congress from Alaska at the time of his death in 1919. Their mother, of Scotch-Irish and Dutch ancestry, came from Passaic, N. J.; their father, a German patriot who was imprisoned during the revolution of 1848, had escaped to Switzerland and emigrated to New York in 1851.

William Sulzer grew up on his father's farm in Wheatsheaf, N. J., a suburb of Elizabeth, where he attended a country school. As a boy he worked on a brig sailing to South America. His family moved to New York City's Lower East Side when he was fourteen, and he took a job clerking in a wholesale grocery house while attending night classes at Cooper Union. His Presbyterian parents hoped that he would enter the ministry, but he turned instead to politics and the law. After attending lectures at Columbia Law School and reading law in the offices of Parrish and Pendleton, Sulzer was admitted to the New York bar in 1884, whereupon he opened an office in Manhattan. At the same time he began his political career as a member of the general committee of Tammany Hall and as a campaign speaker for the Democratic National Committee.

Sulzer represented an East Side district in the state assembly from 1890 to 1894, serving as speaker in 1893 and minority leader the following year. In 1894 he was one of only five Democrats elected to the 54th Congress from districts north of the Mason-Dixon line. During nine terms in the House, Sulzer compiled a creditable record of support for progressive measures, including the graduated income tax and direct election of United States Senators. He initiated legislation creating a cabinet-level Labor Department and a Bureau of Corporations to enforce antitrust laws, increasing salaries of letter carriers, and providing pensions for widows and orphans of Union Army soldiers. As chairman of the House Foreign Affairs Committee after 1910, he opposed American intervention in Mexico and was responsible for the resolution abrogating the 1832 treaty of commerce with Russia because that country refused to honor passports of American Jews. He advocated Cuban independence and supported the Boers' struggle in South Africa. Sulzer's spellbinding oratory (partisans considered him an eloquent champion of the common people; critics accused him of demagogu-

ery), his tall, ungainly figure, and his rugged features were reminiscent of Henry Clay, and he deliberately cultivated the Kentuckian's gestures, dress, and unruly shock of hair.

Although a product of Tammany Hall, Sulzer was a reformer independent enough to be opposed by the machine in one of his Congressional races. When Tammany boss Charles F. Murphy [*q.v.*] finally accepted him as the organization's choice for governor in 1912 (the politically ambitious Sulzer had openly sought the nomination since 1896), he campaigned as the "unbossed" candidate; after he won he promised that he would be "his own" governor, "the people's governor." As governor, Sulzer irritated Murphy by denying patronage to Tammany and by ordering investigations which revealed vast corruption, inefficiency, and maladministration in state departments. When the Tammany-dominated state legislature twice refused to approve his bill replacing party nominating conventions with statewide direct primaries, Sulzer's break with the machine became irrevocable. Resentful legislators seeking to discredit him uncovered evidence that he had diverted unreported campaign contributions to speculation in the stock market. Impeachment proceedings began, and on Oct. 17, 1913, in his tenth month as governor, Sulzer was found guilty on three of eight charges: falsification of campaign receipts and disbursements, perjury in the financial statement he had filed, and suppression of evidence sought by the legislative investigating committee. Popular opinion held that Sulzer was removed from office because he refused to be subservient to Tammany Hall. His misdeeds were not grievous enough to have attracted attention had he not provoked Murphy; but regardless of Tammany's motives for initiating charges against him, he was validly impeached for actual violations of the law.

The Sulzer impeachment became the main issue in New York's mayoralty election in the fall of 1913 and was considered the major reason for Tammany's defeat by Fusionist John Purroy Mitchel [*q.v.*]. Sulzer himself was again elected to the state assembly, this time for one term on the Progressive ticket. Defeated in the Progressive gubernatorial primary in 1914, he ran unsuccessfully as the American-Prohibition candidate. His political career ended ingloriously in 1916 when the Prohibitionists refused to make him their presidential candidate and he declined the American party nomination.

Sulzer devoted his post-political years to his Manhattan law practice and Alaskan gold-mining interests. He died at his Greenwich Village home in 1941, after several years of ill health. Following Masonic funeral services, he was buried in Evergreen Cemetery, Hillside, N. J. His wife, Clara Rodelheim of Philadelphia, a nurse before their marriage on Jan. 7, 1908, survived him; they had no children.

[In addition to the main body of Sulzer Papers deposited in the Cornell Univ. Lib., there are Sulzer MSS. in the N.-Y. Hist. Soc., the N. Y. Public Lib., the State Hist. Soc. of Wis., and the libraries of Emory and Indiana universities. His political career is documented in *Life and Speeches of William Sulzer* (2 vols., 1897–1916, both with photographs), *Public Papers of William Sulzer, Governor* (1914), and George W. Blake, *Sulzer's Short Speeches* (1912), all of which include short biographical sketches. Jacob A. Friedman, *The Impeachment of Gov. William Sulzer* (1939), can be supplemented by the proceedings of the Court for the Trial of Impeachments, *The People of the State of N. Y. by the Assembly Thereof against William Sulzer, as Governor* (2 vols., 1913). See also: articles about Sulzer in *Cosmopolitan,* July 1912, pp. 248–49, *Independent,* Jan. 2, 1913, pp. 45–46, *Outlook,* Oct. 18, 1913, pp. 356–61, and *Rev. of Revs.,* Sept. 1913, pp. 259–72; *Nat. Cyc. Am. Biog.,* III, 369; *Who Was Who in America,* vol. I (1942); *N. Y. Times,* especially May 17, Oct. 1, 4, 9, 25, Dec. 5, 1914, July 22, 1916, Apr. 17, 1919, Nov. 7, 9, Dec. 13, 1941; New York *Sun, Post,* and *World Telegram,* Nov. 6, 1941; *N. Y. Herald Tribune,* Nov. 7, 1941. Mrs. Charlotte S. Wilbert of Newton Highlands, Mass., a cousin of Governor Sulzer, supplied personal information.]

NANCY J. WEISS

SUMNER, FRANCIS BERTODY (Aug. 1, 1874–Sept. 6, 1945), zoologist, was born in Pomfret, Conn., the second son and second of three children of Arthur and Mary Augusta (Upton) Sumner. Both parents, nominally Unitarians, were of old New England stock, chiefly of English descent. Francis's paternal grandfather, Bradford Sumner, was a Boston lawyer of some prominence. His father after the Civil War had been principal of a school for freed Negroes in Charleston, S. C., where his mother also taught.

When Francis was a few months old the family moved to a small farm near Oakland, Calif., where they lived a somewhat austere and isolated existence, supported by a small inheritance and gifts from more prosperous relatives. Arthur Sumner, a man of scholarly tastes but impractical and moody, was a stern disciplinarian. His wife, though energetic and generous, was governed by her emotions and had few intellectual interests. The clash of temperaments generated domestic friction, and Francis grew up largely alienated from his parents. Until he was ten he was taught by his father and, lacking companionship, immersed himself in collecting and studying insect and reptile specimens.

In 1884 the family moved to Colorado Springs, Colo., where Sumner for the first time went to school, and three years later to Minneapolis, Minn., where he attended a private academy and, at the age of sixteen, entered the University of Minnesota. At first attracted to philosophy and psychology, he came under the influence of the zoologist Henry F. Nachtrieb, who crystallized his already strong inclinations toward natural history. After receiving the B.S. degree in 1894, he took a year off and journeyed by ocean to South America in the hope of improving his somewhat frail health. He entered the graduate school at Columbia University in 1895; there he studied zoology under Edmund B. Wilson [Supp. 2], Henry Fairfield Osborn [Supp. 1], and Bashford Dean [*q.v.*] and psychology under James McKeen Cattell [Supp. 3]. In 1899 Sumner went to the Egyptian Sudan on an expedition, sponsored by Columbia, which hoped to secure material for embryological studies on an archaic fish, *Polypterus.* He later spent some time at the Zoological Station at Naples, Italy. He received the Ph.D. from Columbia in 1901, with a thesis on "Kupffer's Vesicle and Its Relation to Gastrulation and Concrescence," which involved pioneering experimentation to elucidate some aspects of embryo formation in fishes.

From 1899 to 1906 (except for a two-year leave of absence) Sumner taught undergraduate biology at the College of the City of New York. He found this position stifling to his research interests and welcomed the opportunity to continue his zoological investigations in the summer, beginning in 1903, as director of the laboratory of the United States Fish Commission at Woods Hole, Mass., close to the Marine Biological Laboratory. In 1906 he quit teaching to devote full time to this work; aided by associates, he conducted an extensive survey of marine life and its environment. He next became naturalist (1911–13) on the Bureau of Fisheries' pioneering marine research ship, *Albatross,* and surveyed in detail the physical and biological parameters of San Francisco Bay.

That survey brought Sumner to the attention of William Emerson Ritter [Supp. 3], who was then developing at La Jolla, Calif., the Scripps Institution for Biological Research. Recognizing Sumner's competence both as field naturalist and as experimental biologist, Ritter in 1913 offered him a position as assistant professor in that institution, where he spent the remainder of his career, advancing to professor of biology in 1926. At La Jolla, Sumner turned his attention to a study of speciation in field mice of the genus *Peromyscus,* particularly the relation between coat color and differing physical environments. From a long series of breeding experiments he demonstrated that the accumulation of minor adaptive characteristics was a major factor in the evolution of the various geographic races. This study in the interrelationships between heredity and environment is regarded as his most important contribution.

When the Scripps Institution for Biological Research was transformed in 1925 into the Scripps Institution of Oceanography, Sumner returned to the biology of fishes. It was his habit to concentrate on one research problem at a time in order to penetrate deeply into its fundamental aspects. He has been largely credited with determining the mechanisms of protective coloration in flatfish; the ability of other fish species to become acclimatized to changes in salt concentration or in water temperature; and—his last major work—the quantitative biochemical changes that take place in the white and black pigments of fish in response to varying degrees of lightness or darkness in their backgrounds.

Sumner's researches were acclaimed for originality, precision, and significance, and brought him wide recognition. In 1938, as vice-president of the American Association for the Advancement of Science, he headed the American Society of Zoologists. He was elected to the National Academy of Sciences (1937) and the American Philosophical Society.

Sumner's interests extended far beyond the laboratory. A strong individualist and a man of complete intellectual integrity, he was deeply concerned with the problems of human society, although not optimistic regarding the chance of effecting solutions. He supported the work of the American Civil Liberties Union, participated in groups seeking to preserve wildlife and scenic beauty, and was a vigorous proponent of birth control as a means of halting overpopulation. In La Jolla he was a leading member of a "town and gown" discussion group.

Sumner died in La Jolla at the age of seventy-one of an enlarged heart condition. Following cremation, his ashes were scattered. He was survived by his wife, Margaret Elizabeth Clark of Salisbury, Conn., whom he had married on Sept. 10, 1903, and by their three children: Florence Anne, Elizabeth Caroline, and Herbert Clark.

[Sumner's candid and philosophical autobiography, *The Life Hist. of an Am. Naturalist* (1945), includes his childhood background and nontechnical details of his varied researches. Charles Manning Child in Nat. Acad. Sci., *Biog. Memoirs*, vol. XXV (1949), summarizes Sumner's life and work, reproduces a photograph of him, and includes a complete bibliography of his publications. Short memorials by Carl L. Hubbs appeared in *Copeia*, Dec. 31, 1945, and the *Anatomical Record*, July 1946, and by Denis L. Fox in Am. Philosophical Soc., *Year Book*, 1945. Dr. Fox also provided personal reminiscences for this account. On Sumner's ancestry, see William Sumner Appleton, *Record of the Descendants of William Sumner* (1879).]

CARL L. HUBBS

SUTHERLAND, GEORGE (Mar. 25, 1862–July 18, 1942), Senator from Utah, justice of the United States Supreme Court, was born at Stony Stratford, Buckinghamshire, England, the oldest of the five sons and one daughter of Alexander George and Frances (Slater) Sutherland. Named after his father, he later dropped the Alexander to avoid confusion. The elder Sutherland, of Scottish lineage, became a Mormon convert and in 1863 immigrated to Springville, Utah Territory. He soon left the Mormon fold and prospected in Montana, but by 1869 had returned to Utah, settling first in Silver City and then in Provo. In succession he was a mining recorder, justice of the peace, postmaster, and lawyer.

Young George left school at the age of twelve to work as a clothing store clerk in Salt Lake City and then as a Wells Fargo agent. In 1879 he entered the new Brigham Young Academy in Provo, where he came under the influence of a disciple of Herbert Spencer, Karl G. Maeser, who believed the United States Constitution to be a "divinely inspired instrument." Sutherland left the academy in 1881 to take a job as forwarding agent for the contractors building the Denver & Rio Grande Western Railroad, but the next year enrolled as a law student at the University of Michigan. Studying under such teachers as Thomas M. Cooley and James V. Campbell [*qq.v.*], he became convinced that government power, especially in the economic sphere, must be limited in order to preserve individual liberty. Within a year he was admitted to the Michigan bar and also to that of Utah, to which he returned to practice and to marry, on June 18, 1883, Rosamond Lee of Beaver, Utah, whom he had met at Brigham Young Academy. They had three children: Emma, Philip, who died in boyhood, and Edith.

For three years Sutherland practiced law in Provo with his father; he then entered a partnership with other young attorneys. Although an Episcopalian, he acted as counsel for the Mormon Church in litigation arising from Congressional prohibition of polygamy. In politics he first joined the non-Mormon Liberal party and was its candidate for mayor of Provo in 1890; but by 1892, when he ran unsuccessfully for territorial delegate to Congress, he had become a Republican. Although he supported William Jennings Bryan [*q.v.*] on the silver issue in 1896, he served as a delegate to every Republican national convention from 1900 to 1916. Ambition led Sutherland to move in 1893 to Salt Lake City, where he joined a leading law firm and rose rapidly through railroad and other corporate cases. With the admission of Utah to the Union in 1896, he was elected to the first state senate (1897–1901), and in 1900 to Utah's sole Congressional seat. In Congress Sutherland helped write the Reclamation Act, sponsored a bill allowing settlement on the Uintah Indian reservation, and, in the interests of Utah's sugar-beet growers, opposed tariff reciprocity with Cuba on sugar. He was to remain a strong protectionist. He did not seek reelection, but returned to Utah in 1903 and, by speaking at patriotic and civic gatherings, began to muster support for a seat in the United States Senate. In January 1905 he won the first of two consecutive Senate terms.

Despite his basic conservatism, Sutherland as Senator yielded to the progressive sentiments of the day and supported much of Theodore Roosevelt's reform program, including the Pure Food and Drug Act, the Postal Savings Act, the establishment of the Children's Bureau, the Employers' Liability Act, and the Hepburn Act for railroad regulation. He was, however, a leader in opposing the proposed income tax amendment. For three years (1906–09) Sutherland performed a major share of the work of a landmark joint Congressional committee revising and codifying federal statutes. He pioneered with a proposal to authorize the Supreme Court to set rules of procedure for lower federal courts, and he sought to raise judicial salaries. As a Spencerian, Sutherland saw no basic virtue in majority rule; in 1911 he spoke out against admitting Arizona and New Mexico to the Union because their constitutions included provision for the initiative, referendum, and recall, devices that he believed made possible the "tyranny" of the majority over the minority.

When the Republicans split over Progressivism, Sutherland kept Utah in line for William Howard Taft at the 1912 convention and in the presidential election, when only Vermont cast its electoral vote with Utah's. During Woodrow Wilson's administration Sutherland was notably less favorable to reform. He especially opposed such measures as the Federal Reserve Act and the Federal Trade Commission Act, which he regarded as government meddling. He was a foremost critic in the long campaign against the confirmation of Louis D. Brandeis [Supp. 3], whom Wilson appointed to the Supreme Court. Sutherland did, however, introduce a constitutional amendment in 1915 calling for woman suffrage, and he was generally receptive to remedial legislation sought by labor, notably in his support of the Seamen's Act of 1915.

Defeated for reelection in the Democratic year of 1916, Sutherland took up law practice in Washington, D. C. He was president of the American Bar Association in 1916–17. He op-

posed the League of Nations—although he supported the World Court—and during the presidential campaign of 1920 he was a prominent adviser to his friend and former Senate colleague Warren G. Harding. Sometimes called the "Colonel House of the Harding Administration," Sutherland served as chairman of the advisory committee for the Washington Arms Conference (1921).

On Sept. 5, 1922, after the resignation of Associate Justice John H. Clarke [Supp. 3], Harding appointed Sutherland to the Supreme Court. Over the next sixteen years Sutherland produced more than 300 opinions, including many that spoke for the Court. His judicial handiwork has resisted simple characterization. He was often aligned with the Court's other conservative justices—Pierce Butler [Supp. 2], Willis Van Devanter [Supp. 3], and James C. McReynolds—in effective opposition to federal and state regulatory legislation and appeals under the Bill of Rights. Yet he occasionally took positions that were surprising for their liberality.

During the 1920's many of Sutherland's opinions reflected his commitment to the limitation of political authority, as well as to the survival of "dual federalism," the balance between state and federal power. In *Adkins* v. *Children's Hospital* (261 U.S. 525 [1923]), for example, he resurrected the largely discarded precedent of *Lochner* v. *New York* to support his view that the establishment by Congress of minimum wages for women in the District of Columbia violated the principle of freedom of contract. His majority opinion in *Bedford Cut Stone Company* v. *Journeymen Stone Cutters' Association* (274 U.S. 37 [1927]) declared that a peaceful work stoppage by a trade union was in restraint of interstate trade. In a number of dissents, he defended the rights of the states against federal encroachments; but in the merged cases of *Massachusetts* v. *Mellon* and *Frothingham* v. *Mellon* (262 U.S. 447 [1923]) he spoke for the Court's majority in sustaining federal grants, under the national spending power, against both state and private suits. Furthermore, in *Village of Euclid* v. *Ambler Realty Company* (272 U.S. 365 [1926]) he upheld a local zoning ordinance on the ground that such a law strengthened rather than infringed upon property rights; this decision gave the judicial basis for thousands of municipal enactments.

During the 1930's Sutherland contended that the depression could be overcome only by "self-denial and painful effort" and not by government intervention, as in state postponement of mortgage payments (*Home Building & Loan Association*

v. *Blaisdell*, 290 U.S. 398 [1934]). He led the majority that found unconstitutional much of the legislation of Franklin D. Roosevelt's New Deal, or curtailed the activities of New Deal agencies. It was his opinion, for example, that held invalid the Guffey Coal Act of 1936 (*Carter* v. *Carter Coal Company*, 298 U.S. 238 [1936]); and the decision he rendered in *Jones* v. *Securities and Exchange Commission* (298 U.S. 1 [1936]) was a strong defense of individual liberty against "a general, roving, offensive, inquisitorial, compulsory investigation" by government bodies. In *Humphrey's Executor* v. *United States* (295 U.S. 602 [1935]), Sutherland spoke for a unanimous Court in a major decision that severely limited the power of the president to remove members of independent federal agencies. In cases involving foreign relations, however, Sutherland sought to enlarge rather than restrict the concept of national authority. He believed that the federal government's power in this area did not derive solely from the Constitution but was also inherent in the membership of the United States in the "family of nations"; and his opinions afforded Congress and the president the widest possible latitude in controlling foreign commerce and safeguarding the national security (e.g., *United States* v. *Curtiss-Wright Export Corporation*, 299 U.S. 304 [1936], and *United States* v. *Belmont*, 301 U.S. 324 [1937]).

Sutherland's opinions dealing with civil liberties formed a diverse pattern. After having opposed the free press decision in *Near* v. *Minnesota* (283 U.S. 697 [1931]), he delivered the eloquent and scholarly ruling (actually written by Justice Benjamin N. Cardozo [Supp. 2]) in *Grosjean* v. *American Press Company* (297 U.S. 233 [1936]) that voided the Louisiana newspaper tax of Huey Long [Supp. 1]. In one case in 1935, his opinion ordered a new trial for a defendant found unfairly treated by the prosecutor (*Berger* v. *United States*, 295 U.S. 78); but in another the same year he rejected a criminal appeal on a technicality (*Herndon* v. *Georgia*, 295 U.S. 441). In 1931 he delivered the decisions barring citizenship to two Canadian conscientious objectors (*United States* v. *Macintosh*, 283 U.S. 605, and *United States* v. *Bland*, 283 U.S. 636) —much criticized rulings that were expressly reversed fifteen years later (*Girouard* v. *United States*, 328 U.S. 61). Yet Sutherland's most memorable opinion came in a civil liberties case. In *Powell* v. *Alabama* (287 U.S. 45 [1932]), the first of the "Scottsboro" cases, he rendered a landmark decision by which the Supreme Court for the first time applied the Sixth Amendment's guarantee of counsel to defendants in state courts.

On Jan. 6, 1938, some six months after the defeat of President Roosevelt's plan to enlarge the Supreme Court, Sutherland announced his retirement. He continued to live in Washington. Long afflicted with high blood pressure, he died of a coronary thrombosis in 1942, at the age of eighty, while vacationing in Stockbridge, Mass. He was buried in the Abbey Mausoleum, Arlington, Va., but his remains were subsequently moved to Cedar Hill Cemetery, Washington.

In the judgment of one student of the Court, Sutherland was "the ablest and hardest-working" of the anti-New Deal phalanx, and "a master at the lawyerly use of precedent and logic to paint a smooth-surfaced verisimilitude of unanswerable argument in defense of decisions actually arrived at for less lofty and more mortal reasons" (Rodell, p. 219). A successor justice, Robert H. Jackson, wrote that "nowhere can one find the philosophy of conservatism and opposition to the [Roosevelt] Administration's policy more intelligently or earnestly expressed than in the opinions of Justices Sutherland and Butler" (Jackson, p. 312). Chief Justice Harlan F. Stone noted Sutherland's "respectful tolerance for the views of colleagues who differed with him" (memorial proceedings, 323 U.S. xxi). Temperate and optimistic, the amiable, trim-bearded legal scholar was the only man who had served as president of the national bar, in both chambers of Congress, and on the nation's highest tribunal.

[Joel Francis Paschal's *Mr. Justice Sutherland: A Man against the State* (1951) is a model of integrity and fairness. It contains references to additional sources, as do David Burner's sketch of Sutherland in Leon Friedman and Fred L. Israel, eds., *The Justices of the U. S. Supreme Court*, vol. III (1969); and Paschal's chapter in Allison Dunham and Philip B. Kurland, eds., *Mr. Justice* (1956). See also Alpheus T. Mason, "The Conservative World of Mr. Justice Sutherland, 1883–1910," *Am. Political Sci. Rev.*, June 1938; James G. Rogers, *Am. Bar Leaders, 1878–1928* (1932); *Biog. Directory Am. Cong.* (1961); Frank Esshom, *Pioneers and Prominent Men of Utah* (1913), p. 1196, on Sutherland and his father; *Who Was Who in America*, vol. II (1950); newspapers generally at the time of appointment to the Supreme Court and at death. There are useful references to Sutherland and his judicial work in: Charles Warren, *The Supreme Court in U. S. Hist.* (rev. ed., 1937); Robert H. Jackson, *The Struggle for Judicial Supremacy* (1941); Fred Rodell, *Nine Men* (1955); Alpheus T. Mason, *The Supreme Court from Taft to Warren* (1958); Percival E. Jackson, *Dissent in the Supreme Court* (1969); William F. Swindler, *Court and Constitution in the Twentieth Century: The Old Legality, 1889–1932* (1969); Irving Brant, *The Bill of Rights* (1965); Henry F. Pringle, *The Life and Times of William Howard Taft* (1939); Merlo J. Pusey, *Charles Evans Hughes* (1951); Samuel J. Konefsky, *The Legacy of Holmes and Brandeis* (1956); Alpheus T. Mason, *William Howard Taft: Chief Justice* (1964); and Daniel S. McHargue, "Appointments to the Supreme Court of the U. S." (doctoral dissertation, Univ. of Calif., Los Angeles, 1949). Certain information from Mrs. Martha R.

Stewart, Utah State Hist. Soc. An oil portrait by Nicholas R. Brewer hangs in the Supreme Court, one by Stanley M. Perkins in the Univ. of Utah Law School; the Paschal biography reproduces an excellent Harris and Ewing photograph. Sutherland destroyed a large part of his papers, but there is a collection in the Lib. of Cong.]

IRVING DILLIARD

SZOLD, HENRIETTA (Dec. 21, 1860–Feb. 13, 1945), Zionist leader, was born in Baltimore, Md., the eldest of the eight daughters of Rabbi Benjamin Szold [*q.v.*] and Sophia (Schaar) Szold, recently arrived from Europe. Her father had been called to Baltimore in 1859 by Oheb Shalom, a moderately liberal congregation. Henrietta was reared in a comfortable, highly cultivated home, where she and her four surviving sisters seem to have formed an unusually close-knit circle. Graduating from Western Female High School in Baltimore at the age of sixteen, she was thereafter to receive very little formal education, but her father, a distinguished Hebraist and Talmudist, instructed her in Hebrew and French (as well as German, the language of the Szold household), Bible studies, history, and philosophy. From her mother, it appears, she imbibed a strong sense of duty, order, and domesticity. For fifteen years after her graduation she taught modern languages, algebra, botany, and other subjects at the Misses Adams' School in Baltimore, as well as children's and adult classes at her father's congregational school. She also aided her father in his research and writing, and was active in an immigrant-founded Jewish literary society. She was not yet twenty when she became Baltimore correspondent for the *Jewish Messenger,* a New York weekly.

When the large influx of East European Jews began in the 1880's, Miss Szold helped found (1889), under the sponsorship of the literary society, an evening school to teach the immigrants subjects like English, American history, bookkeeping, and dressmaking—one of the first such schools in the United States. She served both as a teacher and as superintendent and raised funds for the school's support. In her work with immigrants she discovered for the first time the seriousness of European anti-Semitism and became aware of the Zionist hopes that sustained many of the refugees. In 1893, four years before the publication of Theodor Herzl's *Judenstaat* and two years before her own public espousal of Zionism, she helped a Baltimore immigrant group establish Hebras Zion, one of the country's first Zionist societies.

That year she became editor of the Jewish Publication Society of America, one of whose founders was Cyrus Adler [Supp. 2], a family friend. This

was an important educational agency whose purpose Miss Szold saw as the preservation and revitalization of the Jewish heritage. Retaining the editorship for twenty-three years, she produced translations of such major works as Moritz Lazarus's *Ethics of Judaism,* the first two volumes of Louis Ginzberg's *Legends of the Jews,* and Nahum Slouschz's *Renascence of Hebrew Literature.* Among her most notable achievements was a painstaking revision of the five-volume English version of Heinrich Graetz's monumental *History of the Jews,* for which she also compiled an index volume. From 1904 to 1908 she undertook sole editorial responsibility for the *American Jewish Year Book.* Another beneficiary of her culture and enthusiasm was the Federation of American Zionists, organized in 1897. By 1899 she was a member of its executive council and was soon writing and translating articles for its monthly *Maccabaean,* in addition to editing a number of its pamphlets. She also wrote articles for the *Jewish Encyclopaedia* (1901–06).

The retirement of her father placed greater responsibilities on Henrietta Szold, who helped nurse him through a protracted illness and also supervised the education of her sisters. While the sisters went on to college and marriage, Henrietta remained at home, and despite her conviction that the proper role of woman was that of wife and mother, she continued to discourage suitors and labored at her domestic and editorial tasks. Her father's death in 1902 led Miss Szold, with her mother, to leave Baltimore the next year for New York City. Feeling herself insufficiently learned to edit Rabbi Szold's unpublished manuscripts, she enrolled at the Jewish Theological Seminary of America, the only woman student at that time. There she studied Talmud under Louis Ginzberg, whom she assisted as translator and editor. Though thirteen years his senior, she fell in love with Ginzberg, but he married another woman in 1909.

That year Henrietta Szold went to Europe with the hope of reordering her life. A brief exposure to the filth and desolation of Ottoman Palestine made her realize that Zionism was a more difficult goal than she had imagined, but her visit also instilled in her an even greater commitment to the fitness and necessity of a Jewish national refuge there. Returning to New York, she became increasingly involved in Zionist work. In 1910 she began serving as secretary of the American-sponsored Jewish agricultural experiment station established in Palestine by Aaron Aaronsohn, and organized women's study groups (called Hadassah) to publicize and help finance the cause. Although she still dreamed of a career for herself as a writer, she soon abandoned this idea and accepted election as the unpaid secretary to the Federation of American Zionists, then a disputatious, nearly bankrupt organization. Her extraordinary executive and speaking abilities were soon apparent to such leading Zionists as Louis D. Brandeis [Supp. 3] and Julian W. Mack [Supp. 3], who subsequently (1916) established a fund which made Miss Szold financially independent, enabling her to carry on her Zionist work full time.

In 1912 Miss Szold founded and assumed the presidency of the national Hadassah Women's Zionist Organization. The new group was soon enabled by Nathan Straus [q.v.] to dispatch two public health nurses to Jerusalem, and in 1918 Hadassah, with support from the American Jewish Joint Distribution Committee, sent to Palestine the American Zionist Medical Unit, made up of forty-four doctors, nurses, and other health specialists; this was later (1922) renamed the Hadassah Medical Organization. Hadassah itself, beginning with forty members, would in time, through its founder's efforts, become a large and effective organization with an unsurpassed record of service to the medical needs of Palestine and, after 1948, of the State of Israel. Miss Szold remained president of Hadassah until 1926 and honorary president thereafter until her death.

With the outbreak of World War I in 1914, she became a member of the Provisional Executive Committee for General World Zionist Affairs established in neutral America with Brandeis as chairman. Her pacifism, however, and her unwillingness to see the Medical Unit attached to the British army in Palestine brought her into conflict with Brandeis. The Federation of American Zionists was reorganized in 1918 as the Zionist Organization of America, with Miss Szold as director of its education department, but she soon resumed her activity on behalf of the Medical Unit and in 1920, at the age of fifty-nine, left for Palestine to help Dr. Isaac M. Rubinow [Supp. 2] in the unit's administration. That year she also founded and became the first president of the Histadrut Nashim Ivriot (Jewish Women's Organization) in Jerusalem. Although she had not planned to settle in Palestine, through her work she came to spend most of her remaining twenty-five years there.

Holding various administrative posts for the Hadassah Medical Organization and seeking support for it from American Jewish leaders, Miss Szold shuttled between Palestine and the United States. In 1927, at Basel, she was elected one of the three members of the Palestine Zionist Executive of the World Zionist Organization, and two years later, at Zurich, a member of the newly formed Jewish Agency Executive in Jerusalem. These appointments imposed on her until 1930 responsibility for the education and health portfolios in what constituted, in effect, the government of Jewish Palestine. Elected in 1931 to the Vaad Leumi or national council of the General Assembly of the Knesset Israel (the political community of Jewish Palestine sanctioned by the British mandatory government), she was given responsibility for the education and health programs transferred to that body by the Jewish Agency and was charged with the establishment of a social service department. She left her Vaad Leumi seat in 1933 but remained director of the social service department until 1939. It was under her administration that a modern system of social service was created for Palestinian Jewry and that a school for social workers was organized in Jerusalem.

In 1933 Miss Szold was appointed director of the Jewish Agency's Youth Aliya Bureau (for which Hadassah accepted sponsorship in 1935) and as such took a leading role in efforts to settle German Jewish children in Palestine. She made three trips to Nazi Germany to organize the rescue operations. Sixteen years before, she had admitted to a feeling that she "should have had . . . many children" (Lowenthal, p. 99); now in a way that wish was gratified. By the end of World War II, Youth Aliya had rescued 13,000 children from Germany and Poland. On Miss Szold's seventy-fifth birthday, Kfar Szold, a kibbutz of Youth Aliya "graduates," was founded in the Negev (it was later moved to Upper Galilee). She also in subsequent years organized a boys' village and a home for girls. In 1941 she guided Hadassah in the establishment of Jerusalem's Alice Seligsberg Vocational School for Girls and also created for the Vaad Leumi an agency to coordinate child and youth welfare activity in Palestine.

Her relations with Zionist officialdom were not always smooth. Her insistence that Youth Aliya realistically estimate how much responsibility it could undertake led the Jewish Agency to attack her as a "minimalist." Her strictures against what she saw as a developing theocracy in Palestine displeased the Orthodox, and her pacifism, too, provoked controversy. In 1942 she joined Judah L. Magnes in Ichud, a group advocating Arab-Jewish binationalism in Palestine. For her, Zionism meant no "necessary antagonism between the hopes of the Jews and the rights of the Arabs" (Zeitlin, p. 139).

Long afflicted with cardiovascular disease, Henrietta Szold died at the Hadassah Hospital in Jerusalem in 1945 at the age of eighty-four. She was buried in the Jewish cemetery on the Mount of Olives.

[Irving Fineman, *Woman of Valor* (1961), is the best biography; others are Marvin Lowenthal, *Henrietta Szold: Life and Letters* (1942), and Rose Zeitlin, *Henrietta Szold* (1952). See also: Alexandra L. Levin, *The Szolds of Lombard Street* (1960); Louis Lipsky, *A Gallery of Zionist Profiles* (1956); Sulamith Schwartz in *Hadassah Newsletter,* Dec. 1940–Jan. 1941; Lotta Levensohn in *Am. Jewish Year Book,* 1945–46, pp. 51–70; obituary in *N. Y. Times,* Feb. 14, 1945; and Henrietta Szold, "Recent Jewish Progress in Palestine," *Am. Jewish Year Book,* 1915–16, pp. 27–158. S. U. Nahon, ed., *Henrietta Szold, 1860–1945: Twenty-five Years after Her Death* (Executive of World Zionist Organization, 1970) reproduces a good photograph. Manuscript sources include Henrietta Szold Papers, Central Zionist Archives, Jerusalem, Israel; and a smaller collection in the Am. Jewish Archives, Cincinnati, Ohio. Other papers are at Hadassah headquarters in N. Y. City and in family possession.]
STANLEY F. CHYET

TAFT, HENRY WATERS (May 27, 1859–Aug. 11, 1945), lawyer, was born in Cincinnati, Ohio, the second son and second of four surviving children of Alphonso Taft [*q.v.*], lawyer, judge, and member of President Grant's cabinet, by his second wife, Louisa Maria Torrey of Millbury, Mass. Henry's older brother was William Howard Taft [*q.v.*]. He had one younger brother, Horace Dutton Taft, who founded the Taft School for boys in Watertown, Conn., and a younger sister. Charles Phelps Taft [*q.v.*] was one of his two older half brothers. Taft was reared in a warm and closely knit family which nevertheless provided a highly competitive environment in which intellectual skills received heavy stress. He attended Cincinnati public schools and, like his father and brothers, went on to Yale. There he followed family tradition by combining academic achievement with vigorous participation in sports and other undergraduate activities. After receiving his B.A. in 1880, he returned home and taught high school for a year while taking classes at the Cincinnati Law School. Then he read law in the New York firm of Chamberlain, Carter & Hornblower while studying law at Columbia (1881–82). He was admitted to the New York bar in 1882 and entered the law office of Thomas Thacher.

The young Ohioan at first had doubts of his ability to succeed in the law, in part at least shared by his family, who considered him moody and nervous. He enjoyed New York, however, and ultimately was to have a most successful career there. After practicing alone and with a partner, Taft in 1899 received a partnership in the firm of Strong & Cadwalader. He remained in the firm, which in 1914 became Cadwalader, Wickersham & Taft, for the rest of his life.

Taft developed a widely diversified law prac-

tice involving frequent appearances in both regular and appellate courts. Although best known to the public as counsel for the New York, New Haven & Hartford Railroad, he handled such matters as contested wills, railroad reorganizations, and antitrust cases. As special assistant to the federal Attorney General, 1905–07, he helped prosecute the tobacco and licorice trusts; he later defended corporate clients in several other antitrust actions. Respected in his profession, Taft served as president of the New York state (1919–20), county (1930–32), and city (1923–25) bar associations.

Taft early took an interest in civic affairs. He was one of the leaders in a hard-fought battle for educational reform which in 1896 secured legislation creating a central board of education for New York City in place of the previous system of ward trustees. That fall Mayor William L. Strong [*q.v.*] appointed him to the new board. During his four years of service Taft played an important part in establishing the city's high school system and Manhattan's first free training school for teachers, and he served on several subsequent committees dealing with school matters. In 1921 he headed the Coalition Campaign Committee that unsuccessfully opposed the reelection of Mayor John F. Hylan [Supp. 2]. Other persistent interests were the Salvation Army, of whose advisory board for New York City he was chairman, 1920–40, and the League for Political Education (later Town Hall, Inc.), of which he was president, 1919–35. He was a trustee of the New York Public Library, 1908–19, and president of the University Settlement Society, 1917–20.

Early in his career Taft showed some interest in public office. In 1882 he unsuccessfully sought the Republican nomination for a seat in the state assembly. The Republicans nominated him for a justiceship on the state supreme court in 1898, but he was defeated. When, however, Gov. Theodore Roosevelt offered him an appointment to a vacancy on the same court in 1900 (the year after he joined Strong & Cadwalader), Taft refused, and thereafter he declined all such offers, including an opportunity for the Republican gubernatorial nomination in 1904. He was active, however, in the efforts to advance his brother William to the presidency, beginning as early as 1903. Always a loyal Republican, he served as a delegate to the party's national conventions of 1920 and 1924.

Widely traveled and well read in foreign affairs, Taft firmly supported the League of Nations and the World Court. In the 1920's he was unsympathetic to the Soviet experiment but treated Fascist Italy more gently. Between the wars he worked diligently for improved United States-Japanese relations and served as president of the Japan Society of New York (1923–28, 1934–41). On Mar. 28, 1883, in Troy, N. Y., Taft had married Julia Walbridge Smith. They had four children: Walbridge Smith, Marion Jennings (who died in infancy), William Howard, and Louise Witherbee. Although his wife, who died in 1942, became a Catholic convert, Taft remained a Unitarian. He died· at the age of eighty-six in St. Luke's Hospital, New York City, as a result of a hip injury suffered in a fall and was buried beside his wife in Gate of Heaven Cemetery, Hawthorne, N. Y. Best remembered, perhaps, as the brother of a president, Henry Taft was representative of a select group of New Yorkers who combined a successful legal practice with dedicated public service.

[The Family Papers Series in the William Howard Taft Collection, Lib. of Cong., is a rich source of information on Henry Taft. The best biographical sketch is the memorial by Frederic R. Coudert in the 1946 *Year Book* of the Assoc. of the Bar of the City of N. Y. See also: Yale Univ., *Obit. Record of Graduates,* 1945–46; *Nat. Cyc. Am. Biog.,* XXXIV, 318–19; *Who Was Who in America,* vol. II (1950); and obituary in *N. Y. Times,* Aug. 12, 1945. Ishbel Ross's *An Am. Family: The Tafts* (1964) contains some helpful information, as does Henry F. Pringle, *The Life and Times of William Howard Taft* (2 vols., 1939). Taft published ten books, including two on Japan and one on law reform.]

STANLEY D. SOLVICK

TALBOT, ARTHUR NEWELL (Oct. 21, 1857–Apr. 3, 1942), civil engineer and engineering educator, was born in Cortland, Ill., a frontier community fifty-five miles west of Chicago. He was the oldest of four children of Charles A. Talbot, a farmer of modest means, and Harriet (Newell) Talbot. Both parents had come to Illinois in their youth: his father from London, England; his mother from Brockville, Ontario, Canada. After earlier education in Cortland and the high school in nearby Sycamore, Talbot taught country school for two years. He then entered Illinois Industrial University (the later University of Illinois) at Urbana, where he majored in civil engineering and achieved a reputation for both scholastic excellence and leadership in extracurricular activities. After graduating, B.S., in 1881, he worked in railroad location, construction, and maintenance in Colorado, New Mexico, Kansas, and Idaho. Four years later he returned to the University of Illinois as assistant professor of engineering and mathematics. He was promoted in 1890 to professor of municipal and sanitary engineering and held this position until his retirement in 1926.

Although Talbot considered teaching his most important role, his work as a pioneer in applied scientific research established his reputation nationally. Two of his earliest contributions were formulas for computing the rates of maximum rainfall and the size of waterways for bridge and culvert design. In 1899 he published *The Railway Transition Spiral,* which went through numerous editions and became a basic treatise for laying out easement curves. His interest in practical municipal problems such as the design of septic tanks and the standardization of paving brick led to the establishment of a center for laboratory research and the consequent founding (1903) and administration of the Engineering Experiment Station at the University of Illinois.

Talbot was one of the most distinguished members of the Joint Committee on Concrete and Reinforced Concrete of the American Society of Civil Engineers and the American Society for Testing Materials, to which he was appointed in 1904 (and whose subcommittee on design he headed until 1909). The committee's twelve-year investigation into the properties of reinforced concrete and its use in beams, slabs, columns, footings, pipes, frames, and buildings has formed one of the major foundations of the modern construction industry.

Talbot also made extensive studies of the construction, mode of action, and resistances of railroad rails, ties, ballast, and roadbed under different loads traveling at varying speeds. Begun in 1914 under the sponsorship of the American Society of Civil Engineers and the American Railway Engineering Association, these studies continued for nearly three decades. Talbot's report (American Railway Engineering Association, *Bulletin,* August 1933) helped modify the design of rolling stock and right-of-way construction and is considered one of the earliest reliable contributions to the scientific understanding of safe, high-speed transportation.

A believer in professional association as a "powerful engine in technical affairs," Talbot served in administrative capacities in many engineering societies. He was president (1890–91) of the Illinois Society of Engineers (which he had helped found four years earlier), of the Society for the Promotion of Engineering Education (1910–11), of the American Society for Testing Materials (1913–14), and of the American Society of Civil Engineers (1918), and vice-president of the American Association for the Advancement of Science (1928). His coworkers in research found him precise and often argumentative; his professional colleagues enjoyed his wry sense of humor.

Among the honors that came to Talbot were the George Henderson Medal of the Franklin Institute (1924), for his innovations in railway engineering, the Henry C. Turner Medal of the American Concrete Institute (1928), for his work on reinforced concrete, the Benjamin Garver Lamme Medal of the Society for the Promotion of Engineering Education (1932), for his achievements in engineering education, and the John Fritz Medal of the United Engineering Societies (1937), the highest annual award to an engineer. He also received honorary doctorates from the universities of Pennsylvania (1915), Michigan (1916), and Illinois (1931). In 1938 the University of Illinois named a laboratory building for him, the first time a living individual had been so honored.

On June 7, 1886, Talbot married Virginia Mann Hammet, a classmate at the University of Illinois. They had four children: Kenneth Hammet, who became a civil engineer; Mildred Virginia, who married Herbert James Gilkey, an engineering professor; Rachel Harriet, who married Harald M. Westergaard, another notable engineering educator; and Dorothy Newell. Mrs. Talbot died in 1919. Talbot's religious affiliation was with the Congregational Church. In 1942 he suffered a heart attack while attending a convention of the American Railway Engineering Association in Chicago and died in a Chicago hospital at the age of eighty-four. He was buried in Mount Hope Cemetery, Urbana.

[Memoir in Am. Soc. of Civil Engineers, *Transactions*, 1943, pp. 1530–37; *John Fritz Medal: Biog. of Arthur Newell Talbot* (1937); *A Tribute to Arthur Newell Talbot* (Univ. of Ill., 1938), a 64-page bulletin including a biographical sketch, a bibliography of Talbot's technical papers and discussions, and four pictures of him; *Who Was Who in America*, vol. II (1950); obituaries in *Engineering News-Record*, Apr. 9, 1942, *Civil Engineering*, May 1942, *N. Y. Times*, Apr. 4, 1942, and *Ill. Alumni News*, May 1, 1942.]

RAYMOND HARLAND MERRITT

TAMARKIN, JACOB DAVID (July 11, 1888–Nov. 18, 1945), mathematician, was born in Chernigov in the Russian Ukraine, the only child of David and Sophy (Krassilschikoff) Tamarkin. His father was a physician; his mother belonged to the landed gentry. The family later moved to St. Petersburg, where the father had a flourishing practice. J. D. (as he was known to his many friends) graduated from the Gymnasium of Emperor Alexander I in St. Petersburg in 1906. Among his classmates was the future physicist Alexander Alexandrovich Friedmann, who became Tamarkin's first collaborator and closest friend. Their early interest in number theory led to a joint paper on quadratic congruences and Bernoulli numbers (1906), for which the school awarded them gold medals.

Tamarkin and Friedmann continued working on number theory at the University of St. Petersburg, which they entered in 1906. After 1908 they came under the influence of the famous mathematician V. A. Steklov, who awakened their interest in mathematical physics; Tamarkin turned to boundary value problems, Friedmann to fluid mechanics. Following his graduation from the University of St. Petersburg in 1910, Tamarkin accepted an academic position there and at a second institution, the School of Communications, while he carried out work for the Magister degree in applied mathematics. Although he seems to have passed his examination in 1912, his dissertation, on problems in the theory of ordinary linear differential equations, was delayed by the First World War and was not published until 1917. Probably because of his bad eyesight, Tamarkin did not serve in the war. In 1913 he had added to his other teaching posts an instructorship at the Electro-Technical School, and in 1917 he became a professor at all three institutions. After a brief interlude (1920–22) at the University of Perm, he returned to his professorships in what was then Petrograd and accepted a fourth, at the Naval Academy, probably because each position included a set of ration cards, an important consideration in these early years after the Russian Revolution.

Tamarkin had been a wealthy man before the revolution and had not only a large mathematical library but also a musical library and a collection of instruments sufficient for a small orchestra. (At one of his weekly musicales the young Shostakovich in 1924 played part of his first symphony.) Both his background and his Menshevik views made Tamarkin suspect to the Bolshevik regime, and in 1924 he fled Russia, reaching the United States the next year. After two years as a visiting lecturer at Dartmouth College, he was appointed to the faculty of Brown University (in 1927–28 as assistant professor, thereafter as professor), where his many-sided talents found full scope, bringing the university's mathematics department into a front-rank position. Tamarkin was an excellent lecturer—his lecture notes were mimeographed and widely circulated and quoted —and more than twenty students received their doctorates under his direction. His influence soon extended far beyond the Brown campus. In the 1930's he played a prominent role in improving the quality of American mathematical periodicals, and his counsel was frequently sought in the affairs of the American Mathematical Society. He was also active in finding positions for German refugees.

Tamarkin was one of the early contributors to the theory of functional analysis and did much to make the new theory appreciated. He also worked on general theory of summability, summability of Fourier series, moment problems, Fourier and Laplace transforms, differential equations, boundary value problems, Green's functions, integral equations, mathematical physics, approximations, and abstract spaces. He read widely and was always willing to help students and friends with constructive criticism of their work. His warm hospitality was extended to mathematicians and musicians alike; his booming voice and contagious laughter enlivened many a scholarly gathering. He wrote a total of seventy-one papers, alone or with collaborators, and was co-author of some five books (the exact number of his early Russian works is uncertain).

In America Tamarkin remained a member of the Greek Orthodox Church. He was married in Petrograd on Nov. 14, 1919, to Helen Weichardt. They had one child, Paul, who became a physicist. The death of Tamarkin's wife in June 1934 was a severe blow and virtually put an end to his scientific activities; he published only three papers after 1935. He retired from Brown after a heart attack in February 1945 and died the following November in the Georgetown University Hospital in Washington, D. C., of congestive heart failure. He was buried in Swan Point Cemetery, Providence, R. I.

[There is biographical and bibliographical material on Tamarkin in the Brown Univ. Lib. The memoir by E. Hille in the *Bull.* of the Am. Mathematical Soc., May 1947, includes a bibliography of his publications. See also: *Am. Men of Sci.* (7th ed., 1944); and *Who Was Who in America*, vol. II (1950). Death record from D. C. Dept. of Public Health. A biography in Russian by I. I. Markush is believed to be in course of publication.]

EINAR HILLE

TARBELL, IDA MINERVA (Nov. 5, 1857–Jan. 6, 1944), writer, was born in a log farmhouse in Hatch Hollow, four miles south of Wattsburg in Erie County, Pa. Her parents, Franklin Sumner Tarbell and Esther Ann (McCullough) Tarbell, both of whose families had settled in northwestern Pennsylvania, were of English and Scottish stock. Her father was a carpenter restless for new opportunities; her mother had taught school before marriage. Ida was the eldest of four children, one of whom died in infancy. While she was yet a baby, plans for family migration to Iowa were laid aside in the excitement of oil strikes in Erie County, and Ida's father launched a brisk business making wooden oil tanks. The prospering family moved first to Rouseville, Pa., and then in 1870 to Titusville. There Ida attended high school and developed an early scientific curiosity. Her parents, originally Presbyterian, became ardent Methodists while she was growing up. Her youthful efforts to reconcile inherited religious beliefs with the revelations of science produced a crisis of doubt from which she emerged (like so many American girls of her generation) stripped of dogma, grasping for ethical certainties, and yearning for a function beyond the confines of the home.

Fascinated by microscopes, she first thought to pierce life's puzzles through biology. In 1876 she entered Allegheny College, a coeducational Methodist school in nearby Meadville. Although college confirmed an implacable desire to pursue a "career," she discovered that science offered no such opportunity for a woman, and after graduation in 1880 she took a post as preceptress at a seminary in Poland, Ohio. She found her teaching burdens oppressive and left at the end of two years. Returning to Meadville, she went to work in the editorial offices of the *Chautauquan,* a monthly magazine serving the needs of a large adult audience searching for self-culture. The Chautauqua idea, like oil, excited the region, and Ida found her calling as a journalist in an environment heady with aspirations to improvement.

A diffuse impulse to social reform now competed with her older desire to observe and understand. Her work with the *Chautauquan* was pleasant but confining; after eight years of it she wanted emancipation. In 1891 she gathered her savings and boldly departed for Paris. There she lived with friends in the Latin Quarter, dividing her time between lectures at the Sorbonne, research at the Bibliothèque Nationale on the role of women in the French Revolution, and writing topical columns for a group of Midwestern American newspapers. The editor S. S. McClure found her in Paris in 1892. Her article on Louis Pasteur a year later in *McClure's Magazine* established a connection with that journal that would last over the next dozen years.

On her return to the United States in 1894 McClure hired Ida Tarbell to write a serial biography of Napoleon Bonaparte based on a private portrait collection in Washington, D. C., where she pursued her work at the Library of Congress. The success of the Napoleon series led her next to Abraham Lincoln, a subject she revered and one to which she would return repeatedly over the next forty years. Her Lincoln writings were voluminous and readable, but she was correct in minimizing, as she did in her autobiography, their durable importance.

By the turn of the century Miss Tarbell had become a valued member of the *McClure's* staff, as the magazine turned increasingly to the probing of public abuses that came to be called muckraking. In 1901, spurred on by the creative enthusiasm of McClure, she set to work on the most important assignment of her career, her famous inquiry into the oil interests of John D. Rockefeller [Supp. 2]. The project lasted five years, ran to nineteen articles in *McClure's,* and appeared as a two-volume history in 1904. It revealed her at her most characteristic: scrupulous, thorough, attentive to human detail, earnest for balanced truth, moderately reformist. What began as a careful exposure of the oil trust as a national economic fact ended as a studied ethical indictment of corporate arrogance, dishonesty, and secret privilege. Clearly her perspective as a daughter of the oil region on which Rockefeller had imposed his will against the interest of independent oilmen like her father and brother lent an air of indignation to her conclusions. Yet business historians of a later generation would acknowledge the general accuracy of her narrative. The age of muckraking journalism produced no document more substantial than *The History of the Standard Oil Company.*

Ida Tarbell had become, somewhat to her dismay, a public figure. In 1905 she went to Kansas and Oklahoma to report the controversies touched off by oil strikes in those states and was quickly drawn into local quarrels as a reluctant champion of the antimonopoly cause. As she later described it, she found herself, "fifty, fagged, wanting to be let alone while I collected trustworthy information for my articles" (*All in the Day's Work,* p. 247), being paraded through the streets of Tulsa as the "Joan of Arc of the oil industry," followed by a brass band. By the time the federal government launched its antitrust suit against Standard Oil in 1907, she had largely exhausted her interest in the issue.

In 1906 the staff at *McClure's* blew apart in controversy over S. S. McClure's ambitious managerial policies and erratic personal behavior. Miss Tarbell was intimately involved in the struggle against him. The dispute ended in her resignation and departure, along with John S. Phillips, Ray Stannard Baker, and Lincoln Steffens [Supp. 2]. This group, soon joined by Finley Peter Dunne [Supp. 2] and William Allen White [Supp. 3], promptly acquired control of the *American Magazine.* By the end of 1906 Miss Tarbell had launched her next major series, on the tariff, in its pages. Her animus against high protection was apparent in every paragraph, but she was troubled by her inability to master the

political and technical complexities of the tariff issue and reduce them to moral categories. Again her interest slowly faded. Captivated by Woodrow Wilson as she had been by no politician since Grover Cleveland, she nevertheless took little interest in Wilsonian tariff reform, and in 1916 she refused a place on the newly created federal Tariff Commission.

The limits of her reformist zeal were also revealed in her journalistic inquiry into the status of women. As one who had herself shunned marriage for a career, Miss Tarbell was oddly put off by the assertive restlessness of those caught up in the drive for women's rights and bewailed their inattention to the values of home and family. Sensitive to criticism of her failure to support the suffrage cause, she privately characterized the movement as "part of what seems to me the most dangerous fallacy of our times—and that is that we can be saved morally, economically, socially by laws and systems" (to J. S. Phillips, undated letter in Tarbell Papers, Smith College Library). The judgment reflected her growing distrust of politics and group militance as ways to human progress. To her mind the suffragists shared with the urban boss and the trade union leader a mistaken reliance on coercion to get what they wanted. She was more sympathetic with the settlement house work and peace activities of Jane Addams [Supp. 1] and others, but found herself unwilling to join in such dramatic gestures as the Ford Peace Ship.

Henry Ford helped convert her to a fresh dream, however—that of welfare capitalism, or what she called "the Golden Rule in Industry." From 1912 to 1915 she traveled widely to examine factory conditions, and was awestruck by Ford's mass-production methods, his wage policy, and his "sociological" treatment of his work force. Similarly, she came to place great confidence in the scientific management plans of Frederick W. Taylor [*q.v.*] as an antidote for industrial strife and inefficiency. Once more her conclusions startled some who had tagged her as a radical muckraker and who felt her newfound faith in corporate "fair play" was platitudinous.

Though nearing sixty and settled comfortably in her Connecticut farm home when she ended her connection with the *American Magazine* in 1915, Miss Tarbell remained a prolific free-lance magazine writer and lecturer over the next two decades. Participation in government conferences on industrial problems and two trips abroad, one in 1919 to report on war-torn France and the other in 1926 to examine Mussolini's Italy, kept her busy. Depressed by the postwar public atmosphere, she turned to biography, her old love.

Great men had always attracted her; now they seemed society's most hopeful resource. Her adulatory biography of the steel magnate Elbert H. Gary [*q.v.*] in 1925, while inspiring talk of the "taming of Ida Tarbell," merely confirmed her prewar admiration for ethical capitalists, as did her 1932 study of the career of Owen D. Young. She sensed a growing need for national industrial planning and praised Young and Mussolini alike on this count. In the 1930's, her hopes for the politics of democracy reviving, she heartily supported President Franklin Roosevelt's National Recovery Administration and social security programs, though she bewailed the New Deal's bent toward hasty improvisation.

Ida Tarbell died of pneumonia in Bridgeport, Conn., in her eighty-seventh year and was buried in Woodlawn Cemetery, Titusville, Pa. Tall, grave, sturdy, and alert, she had retained into old age the brisk and open-minded habits of her early years. Never a profound political analyst, but a remarkably sensitive reporter to an early twentieth-century audience eager for ethical instruction, she ranked high among the secular clergy of that age.

[The large collection of Miss Tarbell's papers in the Reis Lib., Allegheny College, is the main source; the collection includes a comprehensive checklist of writings by and about her from 1893 to 1944. A smaller MS. collection is in the Smith College Lib. Papers relating to her history of the oil industry are in the Drake Museum, Titusville, Pa. Her autobiography, *All in the Day's Work* (1939), is bland but generally reliable. Other major writings unmentioned above include *Madame Roland* (1896); *The Life of Abraham Lincoln* (1900); *The Tariff in Our Times* (1911); *The Business of Being a Woman* (1912); *New Ideals in Business* (1916); *The Rising of the Tide* (1919), an unsuccessful novel; and *The Nationalizing of Business, 1878–1898* (1936), in the History of American Life series. Among secondary works, Louis Filler, *Crusaders for Am. Liberalism* (1939), Peter Lyon, *Success Story: The Life and Times of S. S. McClure* (1963), and Harold S. Wilson, *"McClure's Magazine" and the Muckrakers* (1970), are useful. The *N. Y. Times,* Jan. 7, 1944, carries a long obituary.]

GEOFFREY BLODGETT

TAUSSIG, FREDERICK JOSEPH (Oct. 26, 1872–Aug. 21, 1943), gynecologist, was born in Brooklyn, N. Y., the younger of two children of Mary L. (Cuno) Taussig and Joseph S. Taussig, a banker who had emigrated from Prague, Bohemia. His brother, Albert Ernest, born in St. Louis, Mo., also became a physician. When Frederick was still an infant the family returned to St. Louis. Taussig attended Smith Academy there, followed his brother to Harvard, where he received the A.B. degree in 1893, and then entered the Washington University Medical School in St. Louis, from which he graduated in 1898. After a two-year internship at the St. Louis

City Hospital for Women, where he also served as assistant superintendent, Taussig went to Europe for further gynecologic training in Berlin and Vienna. He established a private practice upon his return to St. Louis in 1902 and joined the medical faculty of his alma mater; in 1911 he achieved the rank of professor of clinical obstetrics and gynecology, a post he held for the rest of his life. He also served on the staffs of several St. Louis hospitals.

Taussig early became interested in the problem of abortion in both its medical and social aspects and in 1910 published a pioneering monograph, *The Prevention and Treatment of Abortion.* State laws at the time recognized few reasons for therapeutic abortion, but Taussig's clinical experience convinced him that it was a vital factor in preventive medicine and maternal health. In 1930 he visited the Soviet Union and studied existing procedures in hospitals in Moscow and Kiev. In his exhaustive treatise, *Abortion, Spontaneous and Induced: Medical and Social Aspects* (1936), he cited statistics of fifteen states showing that 25 percent of the puerperal deaths resulted from abortion, predominantly induced, under improper auspices. Listing many medical reasons for interruption of pregnancy, Taussig added social and eugenic ones as well, including rape. "As physicians," he pleaded, "we are justified and obligated in trying to persuade our fellow-citizens to consider this problem from the broader aspects of preventive medicine, and ask them to take such steps, legal and otherwise, as will make it possible for the conscientious physician to do an abortion under such circumstances to preserve the health of the mother and the integrity and well being of the family" (*Abortion,* p. 321). Taussig also suggested, as the most important measure for the control of abortion, the widespread establishment of clinics for the dissemination of contraceptive materials among the poor.

Taussig's second major interest was the prevention and proper treatment of cancer of the vulva. In journal articles, chapters in surgical textbooks, and his monograph *Diseases of the Vulva* (1923), he stressed his belief that untreated leucoplakia of the vulva inevitably leads to cancer, a view that has been sharply modified by later students of the subject. Because of the poor results with radiotherapy in the treatment of vulvar cancer, he became a staunch advocate of surgical excision.

Taussig served as president of the American Gynecological Society (1936–37), vice-chairman of the American Medical Association's Section on Obstetrics and Diseases of Women (1910–11)

and its renamed Section on Obstetrics, Gynecology, and Abdominal Surgery (1923–24), and chairman of the Missouri State Cancer Commission. He was a director of the American Society for the Control of Cancer (1938) and one of the founders of the American College of Surgeons.

On May 4, 1907, Taussig married Florence Gottschalk. They had two children, Mary Bolland and Frederick. Taussig, who had no formal religious affiliation, was a member of the Ethical Society of St. Louis. He died of pneumonia at the age of seventy while on vacation at Bar Harbor, Maine. His ashes were buried in Bellefontaine Cemetery, St. Louis.

[Obituaries in *Am. Jour. of Obstetrics and Gynecology*, Nov. 1943 (by H. S. Crossen), *Jour. Am. Medic. Assoc.*, Sept. 4, 1943, and *Science*, Nov. 26, 1943; *Am. Men of Sci.* (6th ed., 1938); *Who Was Who in America*, vol. II (1950); family information from Taussig's Harvard Class Reports.]

HAROLD SPEERT

TAYLOR, CHARLES ALONZO (Jan. 20, 1864–Mar. 20, 1942), writer and producer of the popular theatre, known at the turn of the century as "The Master of Melodrama," was born in Greenfield, Mass., the eldest child and only son of Dwight Bixby Taylor and Nellie E. (Farr) Taylor. His father, who became a photographer after serving in the Union Army, moved his family to Oakland, Calif., in 1869 because of the failing health of his wife, who died when Charles was thirteen. During adolescence, the boy spent much of his time in the Oakland railroad yards. At first performing menial errands for the yardmen, he rapidly became an assistant fireman. In 1883, while serving on the trains that were hauling Chinese laborers in boxcars into the desert, where they were to build the track from Mojave to Needles, he acquired, by his own admission, his taste for high adventure. While still in his teens, he became a conductor on the run between Oakland and Tulare. Here, legend has it, he pulled the brake on a runaway Pullman car, thus saving the lives of Gov. Leland Stanford and Senator George Hearst [*qq.v.*], the father of William Randolph Hearst. As Taylor was to remember the incident, the Senator gave him a hundred dollars and said, "If you ever need a job, go see my son, Billy, in San Francisco." Taylor, whose interest in railroad work was diminishing as it became more prosaic, soon secured a position as a reporter on the younger Hearst's newspaper, the *San Francisco Examiner*.

His newspaper career was a brief one, for his editors discouraged the imaginative touches he added to his reporting. Attracted to the theatre in childhood, Taylor had performed in skits and minstrel shows of his own devising while working for the railroad, and he now turned to writing for the stage. His first effort, *The Brother's Crime*, enjoyed a short run in San Francisco in 1891. His second, based upon a tour of Yosemite Valley, was staged during the same season and became immediately popular, first as *The Devil's Punch Bowl* and later simply as *Yosemite*. This, like all of his works, contained a sweet, virtuous heroine, a handsome and courageous hero, and a corrupt figure of wealth and influence determined to destroy the sanctity of American womanhood. To this well-established formula Taylor added a couple of touches of his own. One was a liking for exotic settings—San Francisco's Chinatown, a Turkish harem, or the teahouses of Japan. Another was a yen for spectacular effects. Mechanical devices fascinated him, and often a troupe of acrobats would travel with the company, so that standing on each other's shoulders they might rescue heroines from burning buildings and the like. To such effects he was willing to sacrifice characterization, in a medium already noted for stereotyped characters, and even plausibility. While still in railroad work, on June 3, 1888, Taylor had married Emma McNeill, who died in December 1890 following the birth of their son, Charles Edward. A second marriage, to Nellie Follis in 1891, proved unsuccessful.

Traveling soon after his second marriage to New York City, Taylor found there a ready market for his talents as author and showman. He began with *The Derby Mascot* (1894), a slightly altered version of *The Brother's Crime*, and then wrote, for Al Woods, *The Queen of the White Slaves*. During the following decade he was to turn out twenty of these melodramas; in 1898 he reportedly had five playing at one time in the ten-twenty-thirty-cent theatres of New York, besides several companies on tour. Best among his "blood-and-thunder" dramas were *The King of the Opium Ring, The Queen of the Highway, The Female Detective, Through Fire and Water, The White Tigress of Japan,* and *The Child Wife* (subsequently titled *Daughter of the Diamond King*).

In 1901 Taylor discovered an actress who personified the dewy-eyed virginity which his scripts attributed to his heroines. Her name was Loretta Cooney, and she was appearing at that time at the Athenaeum in Boston under the billing "La Belle Laurette." Taylor, a tall, nattily dressed ladies' man, was attracted to this girl twenty years his junior and, after taking her on tour for one season, swept her into marriage (on May 1, 1901) and into the title role of *The Child Wife*.

Laurette Taylor's first successful vehicle, however, was a widely popular melodrama that Taylor wrote for her in 1903 titled *From Rags to Riches*. She continued to appear in his melodramas over the next few years, in road companies which toured the country and as the star of a stock-company venture of Taylor's in Seattle. They separated, however, late in 1907, he to tour the gold camps of Alaska with a dramatic company and she to begin the Broadway career that won her fame. The marriage, which ended bitterly in divorce in September 1910, produced two children: Dwight (who became a motion picture scenarist) and Marguerite.

Ever the impresario, Taylor wrote himself into a life drama in which it is difficult to separate fact from fiction. It is clear, however, that his fortunes and prestige declined as rapidly as Laurette's grew. He traveled constantly around the United States until settling in retirement at Glendale, Calif. He had a lifelong fondness for pets and was habitually buying small farms where he could surround himself with animals. His fourth marriage, about which little is known, was to a woman from Virginia, "Dixie" Cameron, and took place in Chicago in 1912. His hearing, impaired in a railroad accident in his youth, grew steadily worse in later life. In 1930 he was afflicted with heart disease; he died twelve years later, at Glendale, of acute dilatation of the heart. Following cremation, his ashes were returned to the family plot in South Hadley, Mass.

[Marguerite Courtney's biography of her mother, *Laurette* (1968), devotes thirty pages to an informed discussion of Taylor's early life and his marriage to Laurette Taylor. Dwight Taylor's *Blood-and-Thunder* (1962), on his father, consists largely of anecdotal material. Obituaries, not always accurate, may be found in the *Glendale* (Calif.) *News Press*, Mar. 21, 1942, and the *N. Y. Times*, Mar. 22, 1942. Information on particular points from Mrs. Courtney and the Los Angeles Bureau of Records.]
ALBERT F. McLEAN, JR.

TAYLOR, HENRY OSBORN (Dec. 5, 1856–Apr. 13, 1941), historian, was born in New York City, the third of four sons and fourth of five children of Henry Augustus Taylor, a New York merchant, and Catharine Augusta (Osborn) Taylor. His father was descended from William Taylor, who came to Massachusetts in 1635 and settled in Wethersfield, Conn. Taylor grew up in New York City and at his family's summer home in rural Connecticut. He was a thoughtful child of bookish tastes, deeply attached to his parents. Privately tutored, he expected to follow a business career and at the age of fourteen worked briefly in a shipbroker's office. During part of his seventeenth year he was bookkeeper

of a mining company in Austin, Nev., of which his father was president. In this uncongenial Western environment, history and literature attracted him more than ever, and he decided to go to college.

Taylor entered Harvard in 1874 and studied American history under Henry Adams [*q.v.*], who taught him research methods. On graduating, he entered Columbia Law School (he received an LL.B. in 1881). His studies there, which he did not enjoy, were interrupted by a year at the University of Leipzig, where he studied Roman law. Stimulated by his German training, his interests turned toward legal theory. He was admitted to the New York bar in 1884, but his practice dwindled while he composed his *Treatise on the Law of Private Corporations* (1884), which became a standard law school text.

Taylor had experienced considerable tension in choosing between an active life and a contemplative one, but finally an inheritance gave him a modest financial independence which enabled him to devote himself to scholarship. The motivating force behind his early work was the desire to follow the evolution of human ideals. His first historical study, *Ancient Ideals: A Study of Intellectual and Spiritual Growth from Early Times to the Establishment of Christianity* (2 vols., 1896), was a product of youthful enthusiasm and has been replaced by later research. His next book, however—*The Classical Heritage of the Middle Ages* (1901)—became a minor classic. Taylor's most objective work, it was a pioneering study of the transition from ancient to medieval culture; its chief shortcoming, neglect of Byzantine influences, is excusable considering the state of Byzantine studies in 1901. His masterpiece was *The Mediaeval Mind* (2 vols., 1911), an impressive synthesis of intellectual development from the Latin Fathers to Dante, based on extensive reading in the original sources. Perhaps its most original feature was its recognition of emotion as an element in intellectual progress. For Taylor, the important contribution of the Middle Ages was not the rational structure of scholastic philosophy but the emotional humanizing of patristic Christianity. The book is primarily a history of medieval sensibility, particularly religious sensibility. Its critics pointed out Taylor's failure to relate the history of ideas to social, political, and economic developments, and noted that his "medieval mind" excluded the mentality of the merchant, the peasant, and the practical statesman. Taylor was a generalist in the age of the monograph, and his exaltation of emotion was out of harmony with scientific historiography. The book, however, met with a warm response from students and the general public and eventually became a standard college text. Taylor's *Thought and Expression in the Sixteenth Century* (2 vols., 1920), a less successful work, embodies a medievalist's revolt against the Burckhardtian concept of the "Renaissance" (a term Taylor rejected); it concludes a series which collectively forms an intellectual history of Western civilization in premodern times.

On Oct. 21, 1905, Taylor married Julia Isham, daughter of William Bradley Isham, a New York banker. They had no children. The marriage was singularly happy, contributing to the serenity and productivity of Taylor's later years. The couple lived in New York City and maintained a summer home in Portland, Conn.

Taylor's life was in the tradition of the nineteenth-century patrician historian. He lectured for two years at Columbia in the late 1890's, but gave this up because it interfered with his research and writing and never held any other academic post. He did, however, belong to a medieval club in New York composed of distinguished scholars; and his circle of friends included the historian James Harvey Robinson [Supp. 2], the theologian Arthur Cushman McGiffert [Supp. 1], and the philosopher Alfred North Whitehead. Taylor received honorary doctorates from Harvard (1912), Wesleyan University (1921), and Columbia (1926). He was elected to the National Institute of Arts and Letters in 1915 and in 1940 to its inner circle, the American Academy. He was president of the American Historical Association in 1927.

In his later years Taylor turned increasingly to philosophy, and in three books sought to sum up the knowledge and insight gained in a lifetime of research and reflection: *Freedom of the Mind in History* (1923), *Human Values and Verities* (1928), and *Fact, the Romance of the Mind* (1932). By formal affiliation he was an Episcopalian, but his religious views gradually evolved into a kind of mystical theism. He died of pneumonia at his New York home at the age of eighty-four. By his will he left more than a quarter of a million dollars to Harvard College to maintain professors' salaries. Although the tremendous increase in historical knowledge since Taylor's death has diminished the value of his books as repositories of learning, they continue to hold an honored place in historical literature, and *The Mediaeval Mind* remains a classic of intellectual history.

[The most important source is Taylor's autobiography, apparently written as a personal counterpart to his *Human Values and Verities* and hence, some-

what confusingly, titled *Human Values and Verities, Part I* (privately printed, 1929); a frank and intimate account of his personal development stressing his early years, it contains six photographs of the author at various ages. See also *Who Was Who in America,* vol. I (1942); Harvard College Class of 1878, *Fiftieth Anniversary Report* (1928); obituaries in *N. Y. Times,* Apr. 14, 1941, *Am. Hist. Rev.,* July 1941, *Speculum,* July 1942; and Am. Acad. of Arts and Letters, *Commemorative Tributes, 1905–41* (1942), pp. 418–26. For a recent evaluation of Taylor's work, see Kenneth M. Setton's introduction to the Harper Torchbook edition (1963) of Taylor's *The Classical Heritage of the Middle Ages.* Family data from Sherman W. Adams, *The Hist. of Ancient Wethersfield, Conn.,* II (1904), 700, and from Mr. Murray Taylor of N. Y. City, a nephew.]

CATHERINE E. BOYD

TERHUNE, ALBERT PAYSON (Dec. 21, 1872–Feb. 18, 1942), author, was born in Newark, N. J., the second son and youngest of six children of Edward Payson Terhune, a Presbyterian minister of French Huguenot ancestry, and Mary Virginia (Hawes) Terhune [*q.v.*]. His mother was a successful popular author under the name "Marion Harland," and all three of the children who reached adulthood—Albert and two of his sisters—became writers. After a family sojourn in Europe (1876–78) for the sake of his mother's health, Albert grew up chiefly in Springfield, Mass., and, after 1884, in Brooklyn, N. Y., where his father held successive pastorates. His summers he spent at Sunnybank, his parents' country home in Pompton Lakes, N. J. His love for Sunnybank with its horses and dogs became the dominant theme in his life.

Terhune had wanted to go to Yale, but because his mother wished to keep her last child closer to home, he was sent to Columbia. He was an undistinguished student and derived little from his college experience except from the literature courses given by Brander Matthews and George E. Woodberry [*qq.v.*], which "enthralled" him. He also enjoyed his extracurricular lessons in boxing, wrestling, and fencing. After graduating with the A.B. degree in 1893, Terhune went to Europe and then with his mother to the Near East, where he helped her collect material for a book on the Holy Land. During this adventurous year he visited a leper house in disguise, traveled throughout Syria on horseback, lived for a time with a Bedouin tribe, and collected Arabic folktales, experiences that he recounted in his first book, *Syria from the Saddle* (1896), and later used in some of his stories. He returned to the United States in 1894 and became a reporter for the New York *Evening World,* a post he disliked but held for more than twenty years. On Jan. 10, 1898, he married Lorraine Marguerite Bryson, who died in the same year, shortly after giving birth to Terhune's only child, Lorraine. He was married again, on Sept. 2, 1901, to Anice Morris Stockton, a concert pianist, composer (*Songs of Sunnybank*), and writer.

In his newspaper post, Terhune wrote news stories and book reviews and ghost-wrote personal accounts by celebrities in the theatre and sports worlds. For one assignment, he described his experiences in fighting six specially arranged bouts with leading heavyweight boxers of the time, including James J. Corbett [Supp. 1]. Terhune, a handsome, husky man over six feet two inches tall and in middle life weighing some 220 pounds, lost two teeth and broke his hand, but was not knocked down. He added to his income by free-lance work, producing joke columns, serial sketches such as "Fifty Blackguards of History," and novelized versions of popular plays.

Terhune had hoped to become a serious writer and in collaboration with his mother had produced a novel, *Dr. Dale: A Story without a Moral* (1900), but his sporadic efforts at other fiction at first met with little success. Since boyhood he had also dreamed of becoming financially independent so that he could settle at Sunnybank, and in 1905 he began a sustained effort to earn the necessary money by writing. By 1912 he was able to buy Sunnybank and by 1916, when he retired from the *Evening World,* he had increased his annual income to some $30,000 by producing each year twenty short stories and five or more 60,000-word serials, besides novelizing motion picture serials for the Pathé Company. Among his better works of the period were a series of stories about a philosopher-crook for *Smart Set* (1913–15) and several novels: *The Fighter* (1909), which he considered his best; *Caleb Conover, Railroader* (1907), for which a fellow newspaperman, Irvin S. Cobb [Supp. 3], unofficially supplied two chapters; and *Dad* (1914), to which Sinclair Lewis similarly contributed. Terhune's three collections of essays are superficial homilies; his more than 150 short stories are virtually indistinguishable from one another.

Terhune had long wanted to write tales based on his experiences with his beloved collies, but editors had discouraged him, and not until 1915 did he publish "His Mate," in *Red Book* magazine, the earliest of his many dog stories. First collected in *Lad, A Dog* (1919), these finally brought him fame. Their popularity was long-lived; more than half a century after the first appearance of *Lad,* eighteen of his dog books were still in print. Terhune had not intended his stories for children, but young people quickly identified the adventures of their own pets with those of the collies in his brief, lively episodes and became his chief audience. Terhune attributed an almost psychic sense to some of his dogs, but remembering the strictures of Professor Matthews, he avoided sentimentality and the pathetic fallacy, remarking that he never knew a dog with sense enough to unwind its own tangled chain. It is this "blend of super-and-sub-intelligence" which probably explains the continuing appeal of the Sunnybank stories.

With the success of his dog stories Terhune abandoned all attempts at serious literature. He came to recognize that he lacked creative talent and as he reached middle age believed that he had never discovered his true vocation. His greatest pleasures were life at Sunnybank, his friends, and travel. In 1928, while taking an evening walk, Terhune was hit by a car and suffered injuries from which he never fully recovered. He did little more writing, save for a highly readable autobiography, *To the Best of My Memory* (1930); a life of Jesus, *The Son of God* (1932)—Terhune was a staunch Presbyterian and deeply religious—and *The Book of Sunnybank* (1934). Having developed cancer and heart trouble, he died of a heart attack at Sunnybank in his seventieth year. He was buried in the Dutch Reformed Cemetery at Pompton Lakes, N. J.

[The most extensive and reliable source for Terhune's life is his own autobiography. Other autobiographical statements appear in *Saturday Evening Post,* Mar. 28, 1925, p. 185; in Stanley J. Kunitz and Howard Haycraft, eds., *Twentieth Century Authors* (1942); and in portions of Terhune's *Now That I'm Fifty* (1924). Anice Terhune's *The Bert Terhune I Knew* (1943) and *Across the Line* (1945) are eulogistic but illuminating. *Marion Harland's Autobiog.* (1910), by Terhune's mother, has peripheral information about his youth. See also: *Nat. Cyc. Am. Biog.,* XXXIV, 102–03; *Who Was Who in America,* vol. II (1950); *N. Y. Times* obituary, Feb. 19, 1942; and Robert H. Boyle, "Kind and Canny Canines," *Sports Illustrated,* Jan. 15, 1968, which includes critical judgments. There are a few Terhune letters at Columbia Univ., and others at the Lib. of Cong., which also has MSS. of some of his novels.]

FRED E. H. SCHROEDER

TESLA, NIKOLA (July 9, 1856–Jan. 7, 1943), inventor and electrical engineer, was born in Smiljan in the Lika province of Croatia (then part of Austria-Hungary). He was the second of two sons and fourth of five children of Milutin Tesla, a Serbian Orthodox clergyman, and his wife, Djouka (Georgina) Mandich. Nikola's mother, although she could neither read nor write, showed an inventive skill in developing household devices. Both parents came of families whose men traditionally made careers in the army or the church. Nikola attended the village school and in 1863, when the family moved to the small city of Gospic, entered the normal school there, graduating from the Real Gymnasium at fourteen and three years later from the Higher Real Gymnasium at Karlovac (Carlstadt) in Croatia. He was intended for the church, but strongly opposed the idea and early in life gave up all religious beliefs.

As a child Tesla had shown a precocious talent for mental arithmetic and a fascination with mechanical problems, and at last he persuaded his father to let him study engineering. He entered the Joanneum, a polytechnic college at Graz in Austria, at the age of nineteen, and during the next four years acquired a sound knowledge of mathematics, physics, and mechanics—as well as a brief fondness for gambling, billiards, and chess. In 1879 he enrolled in the philosophical faculty of the University of Prague, but his father's death required him to become self-supporting and he left without a degree. Over the next three years he held a variety of jobs, as a draftsman for the Central Telegraph Office of Hungary, as chief electrician in a newly formed telephone company in Budapest, and then as junior engineer with the Continental Edison Company in Paris.

While at Graz, Tesla had become preoccupied with the problem of eliminating the useless sparks produced at the commutators and brushes of early direct-current electric motors. During his year in Budapest he conceived the idea of the spatially rotating electric field to make possible the efficient use of alternating-current electricity, a principle that underlies the design of all· later polyphase induction motors. His attempts to exploit his invention in Europe proved unsuccessful, and in 1884 he sailed to New York, armed with a letter of introduction to Thomas A. Edison [Supp. 1]. Edison, committed to the use of direct rather than alternating current, rejected Tesla's ideas but gave him a job designing direct-current components. Tesla resigned, however, in the spring of 1885 after a disagreement over the compensation due him. With a group of promoters he then formed a company to develop an arc lamp for the lighting of streets and factories, but when his work proved successful and manufacture began, he was eased out of the company.

A period of poverty ensued, during which Tesla earned his living by day labor, including digging ditches. By the spring of 1887, however, with the support of officers of the Western Union Telegraph Company, he had formed the Tesla Electric Company and had set up a laboratory to develop his idea for an alternating-current motor.

During the next two years Tesla took out the first twelve of the basic patents that covered the principles involved in his electrical systems. A lecture he gave before the American Institute of Electrical Engineers in May 1888 firmly established his reputation and led to the sale of his patents for a polyphase induction motor to George Westinghouse [q.v.]. Tesla joined the staff of the Westinghouse Company in Pittsburgh, but resigned after a year, both because of conflicts with the company's engineers and because he realized that for creative work he required complete independence. He became an American citizen in 1889.

The next few years, a period of great affluence for Tesla, witnessed an extraordinary outburst of creative activity and epoch-making discoveries that were to be unmatched by any achievements of his middle and later life. His work on arc lights, which produced an objectionable hum at low frequencies, led him to become interested in the generation of high-frequency currents. Working in his New York laboratory, he constructed machines with output frequencies up to 25,000 cycles per second. Although similar machines were to play a part in the development of radio-telegraphy, he foresaw their limitations and turned his attention to other high-frequency circuits and components, of which the Tesla coil, a resonant air-core transformer, is the best known. He also designed or conceived apparatus for the high-frequency heating of dielectrics, which anticipated diathermy and induction heating. In May 1891 he demonstrated his high-frequency devices before a meeting of the American Institute of Electrical Engineers and created a sensation. His lecture brought him worldwide scientific fame and made him a social celebrity. An attractive man, more than six feet tall and very thin, always well dressed, he enjoyed being lionized and became a noted host, fascinating his friends with laboratory demonstrations of his inventions. In February 1892 he visited Europe and exhibited his devices before large audiences in London and Paris.

Tesla's lectures were interrupted by the news that his mother, whom he idolized as the source of his creative genius, was gravely ill. He returned to Gospic, arriving only a few hours before her death, and then himself became very ill. During his weeks as an invalid he resolved to withdraw from social life and to concentrate on what he believed to be his true destiny, the discovery of new scientific principles, and on his return to New York he adopted the increasingly solitary and eccentric pattern of living that characterized the rest of his career. One of his few lasting friendships, begun at about this time, was with Robert Underwood Johnson [Supp. 2], editor of the *Century* magazine.

Tesla exhibited some of his recent inventions at the Chicago World's Fair of 1893—whose buildings and grounds were illuminated by means of his polyphase alternating-current system—and the following year he received honorary doctorates from Columbia and Yale. Fire destroyed his laboratory (which was not insured), with all his notes and apparatus, in the spring of 1895, but with financial aid from the banker J. P. Morgan [*q.v.*] he was able to open a new one. The next year saw one phase of his work come to impressive fruition with the completion of the Niagara Falls project: the world's first hydroelectric generating plant and a network for transmitting and distributing the electric power, both in Niagara Falls and in Buffalo, twenty-two miles away. The project used Tesla's polyphase alternating-current system; the conception of this system, the prototype of all large-scale electric networks, was his greatest achievement. He also devised important ancillary inventions, including the use of oil immersion to prevent sparking in high-voltage transformers; phosphor-coated vacuum and gas-filled tubes, which anticipated fluorescent and neon lights; the special many-stranded wire later developed for efficient transmission of high-frequency currents ("Litz" wire); and electric clocks. Tesla did not hesitate to let his mind range outside his chosen specialty of electrical engineering: a decade before the first flight of the Wright brothers, he stated that the future of aviation depended on the use of aluminum, then a scarce and expensive metal whose reduction from ore became economical only after cheap electric power had become available.

In 1892, five years after Heinrich Hertz had demonstrated electromagnetic-wave propagation but before radiotelegraphy had become a reality, Tesla had forecast the possibility of transmitting electricity without wires, not merely for communication but as a means of sending large amounts of power from one place to another. In 1897 he successfully demonstrated his wireless communications system over a distance of twenty-five miles. The methods he proposed were not well conceived, and radio ultimately developed along quite different lines, but he correctly foresaw that elements such as elevated antennas and tuned resonant circuits would be needed. At the same time—two decades before the start of commercial broadcasting—he predicted that radio would "prove very efficient in enlightening the masses, particularly in still uncivilized countries and less accessible regions," and that it would

involve "the employment of a number of plants, all of which are capable of transmitting individualized signals to the uttermost confines of the earth."

In 1898 Tesla patented and then built a model of a radio-controlled ship, the ancestor of all remotely guided craft. The next year, working in Colorado Springs, he built and successfully tested a high-voltage transmission system and experimented with the production of artificial lightning. The following year, with the financial support of J. P. Morgan, he began construction of Wardencliff, a huge plant on Long Island intended to implement his "World System" for wireless communication and power transmission, but lack of money forced him to abandon the project, unfinished, in 1905.

In the last four decades of his life Tesla experienced increasing poverty and produced few realizable ideas, although he continued to conceive startling new devices. In spite of his genius, his personality imposed severe handicaps. He was out of sympathy with the developments of modern physics and atomic theory. He displayed little tact in dealing with the industrial engineers whose cooperation was essential to his success. Although developing and testing his inventions required enormous sums of money, Tesla showed no practical understanding of the problem, did little to profit from the sale of his own inventions, and refused to accept the aid of a business manager. In 1912, despite his need for funds, he refused to be co-recipient with Edison of the Nobel Prize in physics, perhaps because he regarded himself as a creative scientist and Edison as a mere inventor. He was, however, persuaded to accept the Edison Medal of the American Institute of Electrical Engineers in 1917. Because others had consistently exploited his work, Tesla increasingly concealed the details of his new concepts and insisted on working in complete independence. As he gradually withdrew from human society he developed a fondness for pigeons, which he fed in the New York parks and harbored in his hotel room.

Tesla nevertheless remained in the public eye for many years and made several predictions of remarkable prescience. Besides his earlier forecast of radio, a prediction he made in 1917 described several features of pulsed radar nearly twenty years before it was realized, although Tesla suggested electromagnetic propagation through water, not through air. He envisaged shooting out a concentrated stream of electric charges at a very high frequency. If, he said, one could "intercept this ray, after it has been reflected from a submarine hull for example, and cause this intercepted ray to illuminate a fluorescent screen . . . then our problem of locating the hidden submarine will have been solved." Tesla's predictions were not invariably fulfilled; a careful study of his later writings would doubtless reveal more bad guesses than good. On his seventy-eighth birthday, he announced that he had invented a powerful "death ray," but the claim was never substantiated.

Throughout his life Tesla worked long hours and required very little sleep. His inventive genius was aided by his extraordinary ability to visualize the subjects of his thinking and mentally to manipulate the components of a motor, for example, as though they were solid objects. Because of his encyclopedic, photographic memory, he kept few written records of his experiments; this further limited the value of his later work. Tesla was a man of strong will and commanding presence, with habits that were unusual to the point of eccentricity and with a strong dash of mysticism—a Faustian figure. In an autobiographical sketch published in 1915, he characteristically recalled that the idea for the rotating electric field came to him "like a lightning flash" as he was reciting a passage from Goethe's *Faust.* Although he rejected theories of spiritualism and the supernatural, he had supersensory experiences at various stages of his life.

Tesla was granted more than a hundred patents, but his fame rests almost entirely on the discoveries he made before he was thirty-six. In Yugoslavia, which now includes his birthplace, he is considered a national hero. In Czechoslovakia the principal state-owned electronics firm is named after him. Tesla never married. He became a complete recluse in his later years, adhered to a vegetarian diet, led an ascetic existence, and was almost wholly dependent on a yearly gift of $7,200 from the Yugoslavian government. At the age of eighty-six he died in his sleep of "natural causes incident to senility" in his room in the New Yorker Hotel in New York City. His remains were cremated at Ferncliff Cemetery, Ardsley, N. Y.

[Tesla's papers are in the Tesla Museum in Belgrade; some letters to and from him are in the Lib. of Cong., the N. Y. Public Lib., and (mainly copies) at Columbia Univ. Leland I. Anderson has edited a bibliography of his works (2nd ed., 1956). A book of source materials (in English), *Nikola Tesla, 1856–1943: Lectures, Patents, Articles*, including an autobiographical sketch, was published by the Tesla Museum on the occasion of the centenary of his birth in 1956; see also a commemorative volume containing the speeches at the celebration, *Tribute to Nikola Tesla: Presented in Articles, Letters, Documents* (1961). John J. O'Neill, *Prodigal Genius* (1944), is a full-scale biography. The best shorter accounts are: Kenneth M. Swezey in *Science*, May 16, 1958, and in *Electrical Engineering*, Sept. 1956; and Haraden

Pratt in Inst. of Radio Engineers, *Proc.*, Sept. 1956. Obituaries appeared in *ibid.*, May 1943, and *N. Y. Times*, Jan. 8, 1943.]

CHARLES SÜSSKIND

THOMPSON, OSCAR LEE (Oct. 10, 1887–July 3, 1945), music critic, was born in Crawfordsville, Ind., the third son and youngest of four children of Will Henry and Ida (Lee) Thompson. His mother was the daughter of a Crawfordsville railroad president, John Lee. His father, a Confederate veteran, born in Georgia of Scotch-Irish and German descent, had moved in 1868 to Indiana with his brother James Maurice Thompson [*q.v.*], later a prominent author. Both worked for a time as civil engineers but turned to the practice of law, a calling in which Will Thompson continued for the rest of his life, although his poem, "The High Tide at Gettysburg" (*Century Magazine*, July 1888), attracted some attention. In 1889 he moved his family and his practice to Seattle, Wash.

Oscar Thompson attended Seattle public schools and studied music from childhood with private teachers. Though he later made some public appearances as a singer, he chose journalism for a career. At sixteen he was a reporter on the *Seattle Times,* and by 1909, at twenty-one or twenty-two, he was assistant editor of the *Seattle Star.* He then moved to Tacoma, Wash., where he worked as telegraph editor of the *News* (1909–13) and then as managing editor of the *Ledger* (1913–17). On the *Ledger,* along with his editorial duties, he wrote music, drama, and book criticism. He served in the army during World War I and then returned to Tacoma as city editor of the *News Tribune.*

Music, however, had remained a strong interest, and late in 1919 Thompson moved to New York City to become a critic on the staff of the magazine *Musical America.* He subsequently became associate editor and, from 1936 to 1943, editor. Concurrently he served as music critic of a succession of New York newspapers: the *Evening Post* (1928–34), the *Times* (1935), and the *Sun,* where he became first critic in 1937, succeeding William J. Henderson [Supp. 2]. This post Thompson held until his death.

Thompson is best remembered for his books. His first, *Practical Music Criticism* (1934), was an able treatment of the art of reviewing music for newspapers. His deep interest in singing led to *The American Singer* (1937), which traced the history of a century of opera singing in the United States through its principal participants. Perhaps his most significant work was *The International Cyclopedia of Music and Musicians* (1939), a one-volume compendium of information with feature articles by many eminent authorities, which became a standard reference in the field. His other books include *How to Understand Music* (1935) and *Debussy, Man and Artist* (1937), a biography. He also taught in the department of music of the extension division at Columbia University from 1939 to 1945.

Thompson was a characteristic example of a genus fast becoming extinct on the American scene—the journalist-critic, well schooled in the trade of newspaper work, but essentially lacking in comprehensive technical knowledge of the art with which he dealt in the daily press. Informed, conscientious, and enthusiastic about his work, he considered it his responsibility to give his audience an objective account of what took place at a particular performance, while furnishing the layman some understanding of the language of music. As a writer, he favored exactness rather than the purple prose characteristic of more flamboyant critics of the day such as Henry T. Finck, James G. Huneker [*qq.v.*], and Paul Rosenfeld. His reporting was characterized by care and accuracy, qualities that stood him in good stead in his lexicographical labors with the *International Cyclopedia*.

Thompson married Janviere Maybin of Tacoma on Apr. 14, 1914; their four children were Keith, Hugh (who attained some prominence as a baritone and as a stage director for the Metropolitan Opera Company), Letitia, and Janet. Mrs. Thompson died in 1923. Oscar Thompson died in New York City of hypertensive heart disease in his fifty-eighth year and was cremated at Fresh Pond Crematory.

[Published biographical material is scant: obituaries in the *N. Y. Times* and *Seattle Times,* July 4, 1945; *Who Was Who in America,* vol. II (1950); and entries in Thompson's own *Internat. Cyc. of Music and Musicians* (5th ed., revised by Nicolas Slonimsky, 1949) and *Baker's Biog. Dict. of Musicians* (5th ed., also revised by Slonimsky, 1958). Other information from newspaper clippings, private correspondence, and the preliminary research of A. P. Van Veckhoven of the La. State Univ. Lib. School, including correspondence with Charles B. Welch and Katharine Hunt of the *Tacoma* (Wash.) *News Tribune.* On Thompson's father, see Dorothy R. Russo and Thelma L. Sullivan, *Bibliog. Studies of Seven Authors of Crawfordsville, Ind.* (1952); Richard E. Banta, comp., *Ind. Authors and Their Books* (1949); and Harvey K. Hines, *An Illustrated Hist. of the State of Wash.* (1893), pp. 619–20.]

IRVING LOWENS

THOMPSON, WILLIAM HALE (May 14, 1867–Mar. 19, 1944), mayor of Chicago, was born in Boston, Mass., the first son and second of four children of William Hale and Medora (Gale) Thompson. On the paternal side he was descended from Robert Thompson, an English-

man who emigrated to New England around 1700. His father was a wealthy Boston merchant with extensive inherited landholdings in New Hampshire; while serving as a staff officer under Adm. David G. Farragut [*q.v.*] during the Civil War, he married a Chicago girl, the daughter of one of the city's original incorporators, and in 1868 moved to Chicago, where he prospered in real estate and was elected as a Republican to the state legislature (1877–81).

Young Bill attended the select Charles Fessenden Preparatory School in Chicago, but at the age of fourteen rebelled and won permission to strike out for himself in the West. Big for his age, he caught on as a ranch hand and for the next six years spent nine months a year on the Wyoming range and, under parental compulsion, the three winter months in Chicago at the Metropolitan Business College. In 1888 his father bought him a 3,800-acre ranch at Ewing, Nebr., which he managed well, showing a profit of $30,000 at the end of three years. The death of his father in November 1891 brought him back to Chicago. With few responsibilities (family real estate holdings, valued at more than $2,000,000, were ably managed by others), Thompson spent most of his time at the Chicago Athletic Club, where he became expert at water polo, played baseball well, excelled at football, and mastered the difficult sport of yachting.

In 1899 a wealthy friend persuaded him to run for alderman of the second ward, and Thompson won his first political contest. Labeled a reformer, he hardly lived up to his billing. He took little part in the activities of the city council and declined to run for reelection at the end of his two-year term. Nevertheless, his proven ability to win votes in both the silk-stocking and the boarding-house districts of the second ward attracted the attention of the powerful Republican manipulator William Lorimer [Supp. 1]. Under Lorimer's sponsorship Thompson was elected to the Cook County Board of Commissioners. After serving without distinction from 1902 to 1904, Thompson dropped politics and again devoted himself to athletics, even organizing a new club, the Illinois Athletic, of which he was immediately elected president. His victories in yacht racing brought considerable newspaper publicity, and to Fred Lundin, the rising, ambitious boss who succeeded Lorimer, Thompson looked like a certain winner. Lundin quietly built an effective Republican organization which in 1915 elected Thompson mayor by the largest plurality ever given to a Republican in Chicago.

Once in office Thompson paid scant attention to his campaign promises to clean up the police department, appoint a woman to the school board, and make the municipal government economical and efficient. Lundin, pulling the strings behind the scenes, manipulated the police and wrecked the civil service. The Thompson administration did begin implementing the Chicago Plan of Daniel H. Burnham [*q.v.*] to beautify the city, but many a citizen noted what appeared to be exorbitant fees of real estate appraisers and the fat profits of contractors. With Lundin's encouragement, Thompson in 1918 entered the Republican primary for the United States Senate. Having already gained national notoriety through his outspoken opposition to United States participation in World War I, he now proposed to conscript excess war profits and keep the country free of all foreign alliances. Although his position on foreign affairs drew a favorable response from Chicago's large German population, it alienated downstate voters and contributed to Thompson's overwhelming defeat in the primary by Medill McCormick [*q.v.*].

Unabashed, Thompson announced that he would run again for mayor in 1919. Reelected by only 21,000 votes, he immediately spurred on a program of public works: street widening, bigger sewers, new viaducts, the long-planned Michigan Avenue bridge across the Chicago River, all regardless of cost. Criticism was met by a booster slogan: "Throw away your hammer! Get a horn and blow loud for Chicago!" Other events, however, cut seriously into his popularity. In the summer of 1919 he was criticized for allowing a race riot to get out of hand before calling on the governor for the National Guard. That same year the courts overruled his board of education's ouster of a capable school superintendent, Charles E. Chadsey, and fined Thompson's supporters on the board for contempt. The *Chicago Tribune,* bitterly hostile, pointed up extravagance in municipal spending by suing Thompson and two associates for conspiracy to defraud the city of over $2,000,000 in "expert's" fees. Never one to discount his appeal to the voter, Thompson was still confident of a third term when a grand jury in 1922 produced sufficient evidence to indict Lundin and twenty-two other members of the Thompson organization for robbing the school treasury of over $1,000,000 through fake contracts, false bids, and exorbitant prices for school supplies. Holding Lundin responsible for ruining his reelection plans, Thompson broke with his mentor and withdrew as a candidate for mayor.

Thompson spent the next four years courting newspaper publicity by getting up an abortive "expedition" to hunt tree-climbing fish in the South Seas and denouncing the World Court and the King of England. By 1927 he was ready for a comeback. Running again for mayor, he attacked prohibition, the League of Nations, and William McAndrew [Supp. 2], Chicago's superintendent of schools, whose rigid regime had won the enmity of the city's teachers and organized labor. With state and federal patronage controlled by Lundin and by Thompson's longtime enemy Senator Charles S. Deneen, "Big Bill" drew on the financial support of underworld leader Al Capone and won by a margin of 32,000 over the combined votes of his opponents.

Once in office, Thompson moved promptly against the man he had labeled a "stool pigeon for King George." The Thompson-dominated school board suspended Superintendent McAndrew, charging that he had introduced pro-British history textbooks into the public schools. The ensuing trial, at which a succession of "experts" traced the insidious ways of British propaganda, together with Thompson's abortive attempt to purge the bookshelves of the Chicago Public Library, brought nationwide ridicule. The gangland-style bombing of the homes of two Thompson opponents during the Republican primary of 1928 further turned sentiment against him, and his candidates went down to defeat. Though he himself won renomination in 1931, Thompson lost decisively to his Democratic opponent, Anton J. Cermak [Supp. 1]. This defeat marked the end of Thompson's political career, although he made two more bids for office. In 1936, running for governor on the Union party ticket of William F. Lemke, he came in a poor third. Three years later he entered the Republican primary for mayor but was badly beaten by Dwight H. Green.

After 1939 Thompson rarely appeared in public. He had been married, on Dec. 7, 1901, to Mary Walker Wyse (they had no children), but in 1931 he left his wife to live in hotels, with a young woman, Ethabelle Green, established nearby as secretary and companion. In the last years of his life he became fat, flabby, and lethargic. He died in Chicago in 1944 of arteriosclerotic heart disease. After funeral services in the Thoburn Methodist Church, which he had joined in 1932, he was buried in Oak Woods Cemetery, Chicago.

Remembered as the mayor who had threatened to "bust King George in the snoot," Thompson was perhaps the most famous of America's urban demagogues. As a campaigner he had the common touch and put on a good show. Save for Anglophobia and an America First isolationism, his political policies showed little pattern or consistency. Even among Chicago's ethnic groups he regularly cultivated support (by public appearances and patronage) only from the Negro wards. Thompson's administrations were marked by extensive public improvements, but critics questioned whether they were worth the price, in money and civic reputation. Suits charging corruption were filed against him and his associates, but only two came to conclusive ends; in one, decided in 1937, he was required to pay to the American Red Cross $73,000, approximately half of the amount he had raised for flood relief ten years earlier and never remitted. He left a total estate of $2,103,024, over half of it in bills of large denominations stuffed into the several safe deposit boxes that stood in his name.

[Lloyd Wendt and Herman Kogan, *Big Bill of Chicago* (1953), is the only complete biography. William H. Stuart, *The Twenty Incredible Years* (1935), an impassioned and uncritical defense of Thompson by a Hearst editor, is a handy source of detailed information about his three administrations. *Tribune Co.* v. *Thompson et al.*, Printed Briefs and Abstract of Record, filed in Ill. Supreme Court, Oct. term, 1929, is indispensable. See also obituary and account of funeral in *Chicago Tribune*, Mar. 20, 21, 1944; Charles E. Merriam, *Chicago: A More Intimate View of Urban Politics* (1929), by a reformer and bitter foe of Thompson; and references to him in Fletcher Dobyns, *The Underworld of Am. Politics* (1932), Alex Gottfried, *Boss Cermak of Chicago* (1962), and William T. Hutchinson, *Lowden of Ill.* (2 vols., 1957).]

PAUL M. ANGLE

TRAIN, ARTHUR CHENEY (Sept. 6, 1875– Dec. 22, 1945), lawyer and author, was born in Boston, Mass., the only child of Charles Russell Train and his second wife, Sarah Maria Cheney. His father, who was fifty-seven when Arthur was born, was a lawyer who served as a Republican Congressman during the Civil War and later as attorney general of Massachusetts. Both parents came of old colonial stock, and Arthur grew up in a comfortable Back Bay home; but he suffered in his youth from a sense of social inferiority. He also found oppressive his strict and undemonstrative upbringing—Puritan in spirit, though his father was an Episcopalian and his mother a Unitarian. He attended Boston public schools, and at the age of twelve was sent to St. Paul's School in Concord, N. H. Entering Harvard in 1892, he concentrated in English and in 1896 received the A.B. degree cum laude. On Apr. 20, 1897, he married Ethel Kissam of New York City. Their four children were Margaret, Lucy, Arthur Kissam, and Helen.

Train later claimed that he had wanted to become a writer from early boyhood. That career, however, was an unacceptable choice for a young Bostonian, and he entered the Harvard Law School, receiving the LL.B. degree in 1899.

After several months as a member of a Boston law firm, he moved to New York City early in 1900 and in January 1901 became an assistant district attorney of New York County. The election of the crusading William Travers Jerome [Supp. 1] to the position of district attorney later in 1901 turned the office into a center of reform action. Train became a skillful prosecutor and courtroom lawyer, but in 1908 left to engage in private practice, without notable success. In 1910 he served a short-lived appointment as a special deputy attorney general for the State of New York, charged with cleaning up political corruption in Queens County, and in the fall of 1913 once again became an assistant district attorney for New York County. The next year he prosecuted his most famous case, securing the conviction of the banker Henry Siegel for crimes involved in the collapse of his mercantile ventures. In 1915, his final year in public office, Train served as chief of staff to the new district attorney, Charles A. Perkins, his longtime personal friend and subsequent law partner (1916–23).

Early in his career as a public prosecutor Train had begun to fashion stories based on his courtroom experiences and his encounters with persons embroiled with the law. The first to be published, a fictional account of a case involving stolen diamonds, appeared in *Leslie's Monthly* in July 1904. In the following twelve months he published seven more, in *Scribner's, McClure's,* and the *Saturday Evening Post;* these were collected in 1905 as *McAllister and His Double.* Thereafter writing became Train's major passion, and in the next two decades his short stories and serialized novels appeared regularly in magazines. As an established professional writer, he also became interested in the legal rights pertaining to authorship and in 1912 was instrumental in founding the Authors' League of America, an organization that did much to secure reforms in the copyright law and more equitable publishing contracts. Train continued his legal practice, in spite of his increasing disenchantment with the profession, until 1922, when *Cosmopolitan Magazine* offered him a profitable contract. Thereafter he devoted full time to his writing.

Train's stories usually opened with the arrest of an accused person and then related the events that led to his acquittal or conviction and sentencing—he called them court stories, as opposed to those of crime and detection. His best-known character was Ephraim Tutt, an ideal lawyer embodying the virtues of Robin Hood, Lincoln, Puck, and Uncle Sam. Mr. Tutt made his first appearance in the *Saturday Evening Post* in

June 1919, and in the next twenty-five years served as the hero of at least eighty short stories. Train's purpose was to portray the inherent difference between law and justice, and Ephraim Tutt, with his passionate efforts to secure justice despite the limitations of the law, became one of the best-loved characters in American fiction. Train's close identification with Tutt was most clearly apparent in the fictional *Yankee Lawyer: The Autobiography of Ephraim Tutt* (1943). Train's name did not appear on the title page, and many of his readers refused to believe that Tutt was not an actual person; *Who's Who* invited Tutt to supply a biographical sketch, and only the intervention of Train's publishers kept him from complying.

Train wrote a number of novels, now largely forgotten, dealing with the society and manners of his generation. Of these the best in his own opinion was *Ambition* (1928), which treated the growing disillusionment and ultimate redemption of a young Wall Street lawyer. He also wrote several nonfiction works based on his personal experiences, including *True Stories of Crime* (1908) and *From the District Attorney's Office* (1939), as well as *Puritan's Progress* (1931), an entertaining history of New England manners.

Train had great initiative and a disciplined approach to the art of writing. Agreeable and urbane, he enjoyed travel, hiking, and fishing and belonged to several of New York's leading clubs. He had no formal religious affiliation. He was elected to the National Institute of Arts and Letters in 1924 and served as its president, 1941–45. His first wife died in 1923, and on Jan. 6, 1926, he married Mrs. Helen (Coster) Gerard; they had one son, John. Train died of cancer at the age of seventy in Memorial Hospital, New York City. His ashes ware scattered on the cliff of his summer home at Bar Harbor, Maine, where he had done much of his writing.

One of the most successful authors of his generation—he left an estate of more than a million dollars—Train was a shrewd and civilized observer of the human scene, especially in upper-class society. Those of his writings based on his legal experiences provide valuable insight into the functioning of the system of criminal justice in his era.

[Arthur Train's autobiography, *My Day in Court* (1939), and his *Puritan's Progress* (1931), esp. pp. 326–42, 347–62; *Mr. Tutt Finds a Way* (1945), pp. 1–17, 228–41; *Mr. Tutt at His Best* (1961), with an introduction by Judge Harold Medina; obituary notices in *N. Y. Herald Tribune* and *N. Y. Times*, Dec. 23, 1945; Grant Overton, *Am. Nights Entertainment* (1923), pp. 91–101; Dorothea Lawrance Mann, *Arthur Train, Man of Letters and Man of Laws* (pamphlet,

Scribner's, 1924?); Robert Van Gelder, *Writers and Writing* (1946), pp. 169–72; Stanley J. Kunitz and Howard Haycraft, eds., *Twentieth Century Authors* (1942) and First Supp. (1955); *Who Was Who in America,* vol. II (1950); *Biog. Directory Am. Cong.* (1961), on his father; correspondence with Arthur Train, Jr. (nom de plume of Arthur Kissam Train).]
DAVID HARRIS FLAHERTY

TRASK, JAMES DOWLING (Aug. 21, 1890–May 24, 1942), pediatrician and medical researcher, was born in Astoria, Long Island, N. Y., the second of the three sons of James Dowling Trask, a native of White Plains, N. Y., and Julia Norton (Hartshorne) Trask. Both his father and his paternal grandfather were physicians; their ancestors had emigrated from England to Massachusetts in the seventeenth century. His maternal grandfather, originally from Highlands, N. J., had sailed around Cape Horn and settled in San Francisco during the gold rush of 1849. When young Trask's father retired from practice the family moved to Highlands.

As a boy Trask attended Craigie School in New York City and the Lawrenceville (N. J.) School and spent much of his vacations sailing with his father and brothers in the adjacent coastal waters of New Jersey and New York. He entered the Sheffield Scientific School at Yale in 1908, where he studied civil engineering, but in his senior year an operation for appendicitis forced him to drop out for a time and turned his interests toward medicine. On his return to Yale, he shifted to biology, entering as a junior, and graduated with a Ph.B. degree in 1913. He then enrolled at Cornell Medical College and received the M.D. degree in 1917. Since the country was engaged in World War I, he had an abbreviated internship at Bellevue Hospital in New York City (1917–18) and then served until the close of the war as a lieutenant in the Army Medical Corps, stationed at Camp Wadsworth, Spartanburg, S. C.

Having decided against entering private practice, Trask applied for a research post at the hospital of the Rockefeller Institute for Medical Research. In 1919 he was appointed assistant resident physician and joined the brilliant group of bacteriologists, immunologists, organic chemists, and clinicians that included Oswald T. Avery, A. Raymond Dochez, Donald D. Van Slyke, and Francis G. Blake. Under Blake's direction, Trask embarked on an ambitious project to determine whether measles was caused by a specific virus or, as some workers believed, by a streptococcus. The two demonstrated that measles was indeed a virus disease. This early success encouraged Trask to continue in medical research, and in 1921, when Blake was appointed the first full-time professor of medicine at Yale, Trask joined him in the move to New Haven, as instructor in medicine.

In the next few years, with Blake and others, he made important studies of scarlet fever and the use of antistreptococcal sera. Seeking a greater opportunity to study infectious diseases, he decided to specialize in pediatrics, and in 1927 he was made associate professor in that specialty at Yale. He thus came under the immediate direction of Edwards A. Park and Grover F. Powers and carried out significant studies on pneumonia, scarlet fever, and streptococcal infections. When in 1931 an epidemic of infantile paralysis swept New Haven, Trask served on the Yale Poliomyelitis Commission and thereafter made intensive studies of the disease and its mode of transmission in association with John R. Paul and others. Trask's interests went beyond his immediate teaching and clinical responsibilities. He was concerned not only with the individual patient but also with the patient's family and with the circumstances under which the patient had become ill. This concept of family epidemiology led to his appointment in 1939 to the New Haven Board of Health.

On June 4, 1921, Trask married Phyllis Hayden Randall of Fort Wayne, Ind., a former nurse. They had one daughter, Phyllis Randall. Trask was active in the Episcopal Church and belonged to a large number of professional groups, including the American Association of Immunologists, the Society of American Bacteriologists, and the Society for Pediatric Research. Although his duties included teaching, the practice of hospital medicine, the direction of a large research unit, and the writing of the resulting papers, he also found time for duck hunting, trout fishing, and sailing. His love of the outdoors was only one of the many personal qualities, including cheerful good humor, enthusiasm, wit, and generosity, that won him friends in every walk of life.

In 1941 Trask was appointed to two commissions of the army's epidemiological board, one on neurotropic virus diseases and the other on hemolytic streptococcal infections. In the spring of 1942, while investigating an outbreak of streptococcal disease at Chanute Field, Ill., he contracted an acute colon bacillus infection and died forty-eight hours later, of septicemia and peritonitis, at Billings Hospital, Chicago, at the age of fifty-one. He was buried at the White Plains (N. Y.) Rural Cemetery.

[Memoirs of Trask in *Yale Jour. of Biology and Medicine*, July 1942 and May 1944, and in *Am. Jour. of Diseases of Children*, Aug. 1942; Yale Univ., *Obituary Record of Graduates*, 1941-42; sketch in *Semi-Centennial Vol. of the Am. Pediatric Soc.* (1938), p. 259; *Nat. Cyc. Am. Biog.*, XXXI, 468-70.]
JOHN R. PAUL

TRELEASE, WILLIAM (Feb. 22, 1857–Jan. 1, 1945), botanist, was born in Mount Vernon, N. Y., the son of Samuel Ritter Trelease and Mary Elizabeth (Gandall) Trelease, of Cornish and Dutch ancestry. He was reared as a Methodist. His father was a pattern cutter in metals; his mother's family on both sides were millwrights and builders; and Trelease himself served an apprenticeship in a machine shop before deciding to pursue his interest in the natural sciences. After attending high school in Branford, Conn., and night classes in Brooklyn, N. Y., he entered Cornell University in 1877. There he studied under the botanist A. N. Prentiss and the entomologist John H. Comstock [Supp. 1]. Melding his interests in plants and insects, Trelease while still an undergraduate published four papers on pollination in the *American Naturalist* and the *Bulletin* of the Torrey Botanical Club. He also worked part-time in his junior year as an entomologist for the United States Department of Agriculture, for which he made field studies of cotton insects in Alabama. He received the B.S. degree in 1880 and then began graduate work at Harvard, studying fungi under William G. Farlow [q.v.]. There he also came under the influence of Asa Gray, Sereno Watson, George L. Goodale, and Samuel H. Scudder [qq.v.].

In 1881 Trelease was appointed instructor in botany at the University of Wisconsin. There, in addition to classes in systematic botany, horticulture, forestry, and economic entomology, he offered the university's first course in bacteriology, then a relatively new subject in the United States. In 1883 he was made professor of botany and head of the department. He received the S.D. degree from Harvard the next year, with a thesis on "Zoogloeae and Related Forms."

Trelease moved from Wisconsin in 1885 to St. Louis, Mo., to become Engelmann Professor of Botany and head of the newly established Shaw School of Botany at Washington University. The donor of the school, Henry Shaw [q.v.], had chosen him for the post on Asa Gray's strong recommendation. Shaw had also founded in St. Louis, with the assistance of the botanist George Engelmann [q.v.], the Missouri Botanical Garden—the first such institution in the United States both instructional and open to the public—and upon Shaw's death in 1889 Trelease was given the additional appointment of director of the Garden. Over the next two decades he improved or constructed stone walls, roads, and walks; assembled a library of some 70,000 books (including the Sturtevant pre-Linnaean library, acquired in 1892); and added new plants, until there were 12,000 species under cultivation and 700,000 specimens in the herbarium. In 1904 the Garden was awarded two grand prizes at the St. Louis World's Fair, one for beauty and one for efficiency. In his encouragement of students and his development of the Garden in accordance with Shaw's wishes, Trelease successfully pursued the dual goals, never easy to balance, of producing scientific work of value to botanists and of displaying flower beds for the public.

Trelease resigned as director of the Missouri Botanical Garden in 1912 when the time he devoted to research and travel came under criticism. After a year in Europe, he returned to become professor of botany and head of the department at the University of Illinois, a post he retained until his retirement in 1926.

Trelease published some three hundred papers and books. They included, chronologically: *The Botanical Works of the Late George Engelmann* (1887), edited in collaboration with Asa Gray; translations of German and Danish technical works; articles for inclusion in Liberty Hyde Bailey's influential *Cyclopedia of American Horticulture* (4 vols., 1900–02); and extensive monographs such as *Agave in the West Indies* (1913), *The Genus Phoradendron* (1916), and *The American Oaks* (1924). During his later years he devoted much time to research on the neotropical Piperaceae, studies that were completed and published in 1950 by Truman G. Yuncker. All of Trelease's taxonomic studies were marked by unusual bibliographic thoroughness, with attention to early and foreign literature. He described about 2,500 species and varieties of plants. His successors who have turned to population sampling and cytogenetics will find a solid reference base on which to build their recensions.

Trelease's lifelong interest in organizations ranged from the local to the international, from entomology to botany. He was president of the Cambridge (Mass.) Entomological Club in 1889; first president (1894–95) of the Botanical Society of America, and, after its reorganization, president again in 1918; and president (1903) of the American Society of Naturalists. He was elected to the National Academy of Sciences in 1902 and to the American Philosophical Society the following year. He received honorary degrees from the University of Wisconsin (1902), the University of Missouri (1903), and Washington University (1907).

Trelease married Julia M. Johnson at Madison, Wis., on July 19, 1882. Their five children were Frank Johnson, Marjorie, Sam Farlow (who became a plant physiologist), Sidney Briggs, and William. Trelease continued active work until a few weeks before his death. He died of pneumonia in Urbana, Ill., at the age of eighty-seven and was buried in Bellefontaine Cemetery, St. Louis. Three genera of plants memorialize him, and in 1933 the National Geographic Board gave his name to a mountain peak above Loveland Pass in Colorado, not far from peaks commemorating Gray and Torrey.

[Four "Scrapbooks" of letters, clippings, and memorabilia collected over Trelease's lifetime are preserved at the Mo. Botanical Garden. The most detailed biographical account is that of Louis O. Kunkel in Nat. Acad. Sci., *Biog. Memoirs*, XXXV (1961), 307–32 (with portrait). Two other sketches (which tell much of their authors' personalities) are by L. H. Bailey, in Am. Philosophical Soc., *Year Book*, 1945; and by J. M. Greenman, in *Mo. Botanical Garden Bull.*, Apr. 1945 (with portrait). For briefer entries see *Who Was Who in America*, vol. II (1950); and *Am. Men of Sci.* (7th ed., 1944). Louis H. Pammel privately published a florilegium of 77 letters from Trelease's students and associates on the occasion of his retirement: *Prominent Men I Have Met*, no. III (Ames, Iowa, 1927); included is a bibliography of his writings to 1927 arranged by subjects. T. G. Yuncker provided a bibliography covering Trelease's entire life for the Kunkel memoir, above. J. Christian Bay, *William Trelease, 1857–1945, Personal Reminiscences* (12 pp., Chicago, 1945), is a fragrant bouquet. On the naming of Mount Trelease, see *Delta Upsilon Quart.*, Jan. 1934.]

JOSEPH EWAN

TRESCA, CARLO (Mar. 9, 1879–Jan. 11, 1943), Italian-American labor leader and radical journalist, was born in Sulmona, Abruzzi, Italy, the third son and fourth of eight children of Filippo and Filomena (Faciano) Tresca. Both parents came from established wealthy families. When Carlo was still young, however, his father, who managed the family estate and engaged in business ventures and local politics, lost the ancestral lands and home through speculative investments. Now unable to attend a university, Tresca was frustrated in his ambition to become a lawyer and disillusioned with the capitalist system and bourgeois society. His mother, a devout Catholic, wanted him to become a priest, but he refused, having imbibed at an early age his father's anticlericalism. He attended a commercial high school, but the prospect of becoming a petty bureaucrat repelled him. An unruly and pugnacious youth, he later attributed his lifelong rebellion against authority to his father's domineering character.

The social unrest of the 1890's reached the provincial town of Sulmona when a group of militant railroad workers formed a socialist club, which Tresca soon joined. He was bored by Marxist theory, but talk of class struggle appealed to his combative nature. While earning a meager salary as branch secretary of a railroad workers' union, he threw himself into a local campaign to organize the peasants. The response to his first speech told him that he had discovered his vocation as "a man of command, of action." As editor and founder of the socialist weekly *Il Germe,* he wrote scathing attacks on the clerical and secular establishment of Sulmona which led to his conviction for libel in 1904. Faced with the harsh sentence of a year's imprisonment plus six months of solitary confinement, he chose to go into exile and, at twenty-five, fled to the United States. His wife, Helga Guerra, whom he had married on Sept. 20, 1903, joined him sometime later.

Going to Philadelphia, where readers of *Il Germe* had collected money for his emigration, Tresca joined the Italian Socialist Federation and became editor of its newspaper, *Il Proletario.* He left the group, however, after two years, having grown weary of internal bickering over fine points of socialist doctrine, and, attracted to the communist anarchism of Enrico Malatesta, began his own weekly, *La Plebe.* Convicted in 1908 of libeling the Italian consul of Philadelphia, Tresca moved his paper to Pittsburgh, where he became involved in a number of labor disputes. In 1909 he was again convicted of libel, this time for alleging that a local Roman Catholic priest was having an affair with his maid, and soon afterward the Post Office Department revoked the mailing privileges of *La Plebe:* Tresca then went to New Kensington, Pa., where a friend helped him found another newspaper, *L'Avvenire.*

Through his attacks on labor agents, bankers, consular officials, and priests, all of whom he felt exploited the Italian immigrant, Tresca emerged as a spokesman for the Italian worker. He gradually broadened his appeal to workers of other nationalities by becoming active in the Industrial Workers of the World, helping to lead their strikes and free-speech fights in Lawrence, Mass. (1912), Paterson, N. J. (1913), and elsewhere. At this time, as earlier, he was the target of several assassination attempts, one of which left an ugly scar on the left side of his face. During the 1915 I.W.W. strike at the iron mines in the Mesabi Range in Minnesota, Tresca was arrested as an accessory to the murder of a sheriff's deputy, but the charge was later dropped. The strenuous pace of these tempestuous years, together with several amorous interludes, was more than his marriage could stand, and in 1914 his wife sued for divorce, naming Elizabeth Gurley Flynn, the "girl rebel" of the I.W.W., as

corespondent. By World War I, Tresca had acquired a reputation as "one of the most rabid of the I.W.W. trouble makers" (*New York Times,* Oct. 1, 1917), although he had actually broken with the group two years earlier. He was arrested in September 1917, along with other present and former Wobbly leaders, on a charge of conspiracy to violate the Espionage Act, and though he was never tried, his newspaper, *L'Avvenire,* was banned from the mails. Tresca then purchased another paper, *Il Martello,* and transformed it into a champion of radical causes, though, with uncharacteristic discretion, he tempered his statements against American pariicipation in the war.

When, after the war, Tresca again turned to labor agitation, he experienced a cold reception from most union leaders, who considered him too radical, an impression reinforced by his willingness to associate with Communists. Gradually, however, Tresca became alienated from the Stalinists by their repressive tactics in the Soviet Union and abroad, particularly the party purges of the 1930's. In 1937 he joined a commission headed by John Dewey to investigate Soviet charges against Leon Trotsky. Thereafter he wrote exposés of the Stalinists, denouncing the Moscow treason trials as a sham and assailing the Communist "liquidation" of anarchists and other non-Communist Loyalists during the Spanish Civil War. By the 1930's he had become a hero of the non-Communist American left; Max Eastman considered him, after Eugene Debs, "the most universally esteemed and respected man in the revolutionary movement" (*New Yorker,* Sept. 15, 1934, p. 31).

Meanwhile Tresca had been from the beginning an implacable foe of the Fascist regime in Italy. His strong attacks in *Il Martello* on the Fascisti in Italy and the United States prompted the Italian ambassador to request that Tresca be silenced. In response, the federal government in 1923 brought Tresca to trial on a charge of sending obscene material through the mails. The charge stemmed from a four-line advertisement in *Il Martello* for a book on birth control; he was convicted and sentenced to a year in prison. When the political nature of his conviction came to light, public protests persuaded President Coolidge to commute his term to four months. Tresca immediately resumed his battle against the Fascists both in the meeting halls and on the streets of America's "Little Italy," where his followers frequently clashed with the "Blackshirts."

During World War II, Tresca cooperated with the Office of War Information in organizing the

Italian-American Victory Council, a body intended to shape United States policy toward a liberated Italy. He joined the Mazzini Society, newly organized by anti-Fascist exiles from Italy. In both groups he took an uncompromising stand against the admission of Communists and ex-Fascists, thus embarrassing those who were seeking to live down past associations. A contentious figure with many enemies, Tresca was shot and killed one January night in 1943 as he left his office in New York City. His death stirred considerable controversy; some thought the Communists responsible, others the Fascists, and yet others, the underworld. A memorial committee headed by the Socialist leader Norman Thomas kept the investigation into his death alive for more than a decade, but the murder was never solved. Tresca's body was cremated at Fresh Pond Crematory, Maspeth, Long Island. He was survived by his second wife, Margaret De Silver, and her two children by a previous marriage, Burnham and Harry, as well as by his daughter by his first marriage, Beatrice.

Tresca was an anachronism in twentieth-century America, a European romantic revolutionary of nineteenth-century vintage. Ruggedly handsome, with neatly trimmed beard and glasses, he wore a large black hat and flowing cloak. When not in the midst of a fight, he was reported to be genial and charming. Tresca's politics flowed from his passionate temperament rather than his intellect. No theoretician, he was the revolutionary activist par excellence. His impact was limited to the sphere of his personal influence; but within that sphere he rallied many a man to struggle for a better life. Though attacked for his unorthodoxy, unlike many of his erstwhile comrades he embraced neither the totalitarianism of the right nor that of the left.

[Tresca's unpublished autobiography, Carlo Tresca Memorial Committee Papers, N. Y. Public Lib., is the best source for his youth in Italy and early years in America; the papers also contain correspondence, clippings, and other material relating to Tresca's career and murder. An unpublished biography by Max Nomad, "Romantic Rebel" (Istituto di Studi Americani, Univ. of Florence), is based largely on the autobiography but is supplemented by material from *Il Martello*. Published biographical sources include: memorial issue of *Il Martello*, Mar. 28, 1943; Tresca Memorial Committee, *Who Killed Carlo Tresca?* (1945); profile by Max Eastman in the *New Yorker*, Sept. 15, 22, 1934; and obituaries of Jan. 12, 1943, in the *N. Y. Times* and *PM*. Other useful sources are: Ezio Taddei, *The Tresca Case* (1943); Am. Civil Liberties Union, *Foreign Dictators of Am. Rights: The Tresca and Karolyi Cases* (1925). Two articles deal briefly with Tresca's career: Mario de Ciampis, "Storia del Movimento Socialista Rivoluzionario Italiano," *La Parola del Popolo*, Dec. 1958–Jan. 1959; and John P. Diggins, "The Italo-Am. Anti-Fascist Opposition," *Jour. Am. Hist.*, Dec. 1967. See also references to him in two histories of the I.W.W.: Melvyn Dubofsky, *We Shall Be All* (1969), and

Joseph R. Conlin, *Bread and Roses Too* (1969). Interviews with the following were helpful: Vanni Montana, A. J. Muste, Max Nomad, Max Schachtman, and Norman Thomas.]

RUDOLPH J. VECOLI

TRUETT, GEORGE WASHINGTON (May 6, 1867–July 7, 1944), Southern Baptist clergyman, was born on a farm two miles west of Hayesville in Clay County, N. C., a remote mountain region in the southwestern part of the state. He was the sixth son and seventh of eight children of Charles Levi and Mary Rebecca (Kimsey) Truett. His forebears, of English and Scotch-Irish descent, had early migrated from the Southern seaboard into the Appalachian region of North Carolina and Georgia. Both his maternal grandfather and a great-uncle, Elijah Kimsey, were Baptist preachers well known in this area. His father's 250-acre mountain farm provided an austere living for the family. After attending Hayesville Academy from 1875 to 1885, George Truett taught in a one-room school in nearby Towns County, Ga. He had since childhood attended the Baptist church in Hayesville, and in 1886, during a series of evangelistic meetings, he experienced conversion. His first plan was to become a lawyer, and to earn money for college he opened a subscription school at Hiawassee, Ga., in 1887, which after two years had grown to include 300 students and three teachers. He gave up his school, however, in 1889 when the family moved to Whitewright, Texas.

That fall Truett enrolled at Grayson Junior College in Whitewright. His activity in the local church attracted attention, and in the following year the members persuaded him, with some difficulty, that it was his duty to give up the law for the ministry. Ordained in 1890, at the age of twenty-three, he was chosen as financial secretary of the Baptist-affiliated Baylor University in Waco, Texas, and was given the awesome task of clearing its debt of $92,000. His success, during twenty-three months of traveling and preaching throughout the state, marked him as a man of unusual ability. In the fall of 1893 he enrolled as a freshman at Baylor; earning his way by serving as pastor of the East Waco Baptist Church, he received his bachelor's degree in 1897. That same year he was called to the pastorate of the First Baptist Church of Dallas, where he remained until his death. On June 28, 1894, while in college, Truett had married a fellow student, Josephine Jenkins. Their three daughters were Jessie Jenkins, Mary, and Annie Sallee.

Truett quickly gained recognition as a great preacher in the evangelical tradition, and under his vigorous leadership the Dallas church throve.

During his forty-seven years as pastor the membership increased from 715 to 7,804. The church auditorium was enlarged to attain a seating capacity of four thousand, but it was not uncommon for a thousand more to be turned away on occasion. Armed with his conviction that money and power were stewardships to be used for the benefit of others, Truett continued to be an able fund raiser for church causes. One of his earliest projects was promoting the establishment of the Texas Baptist Memorial Sanitarium in Dallas, later the Baylor Hospital and Medical Center, for which he obtained large gifts and which he served as a trustee. Early in his Dallas pastorate he was urged to accept the presidency of Baylor University, but chose to continue his ministry. In 1902 he began holding summer camp meetings for cowboys in the Davis Mountains of West Texas, a practice he continued for the next thirty-six years.

Truett's remarkable ability to reach the emotions of his listeners soon spread his fame beyond Texas, and he accepted invitations to conduct revival meetings in most of the major cities of the United States. By 1918 he had gained a national reputation, and President Woodrow Wilson designated him one of twenty men sent to Europe through the Y.M.C.A. to preach to American troops. At a Washington meeting of the Southern Baptist Convention on May 16, 1920, Truett spoke from the steps of the Capitol to 15,000 persons. He served as president of the Southern Baptist Convention from 1927 through 1929. A summer preaching tour of South America in 1930 drew large crowds, and in 1934 he was unanimously chosen for a five-year term as president of the Baptist World Alliance, for which he made a tour of Baptist missions in 1935–36. He died in Dallas at the age of seventy-seven of Paget's disease and cardiorespiratory complications and was buried in Hillcrest Cemetery in that city.

In his prime George W. Truett was nearly six feet tall and weighed about 200 pounds, with unusually broad shoulders and erect carriage. Solemn in appearance, he was black-haired, with blue-gray eyes and a wide, sensitive mouth. His remarkable voice made him audible to large crowds without the aid of an amplifying system. He was orthodox in theology, and his oratory, which led him to be compared with William Jennings Bryan [q.v.], was characterized by directness and conviction; it earned him a place as one of the great preachers of his day.

[Truett's published works, compiled and edited by others, include ten volumes of sermons, two of addresses, and two of Christmas messages. Powhatan W. James, *George W. Truett* (1935), a biography by his son-in-law, is the only extended treatment; a revised edition (1945) adds a chapter on his final years and death. The best short biographical sketches are: Wayne Gard in Walter P. Webb, ed., *The Handbook of Texas* (1952), II, 805; Powhatan W. James in *Encyc. of Southern Baptists* (1958), II, 1429–30; and *Who Was Who in America*, vol. II (1950). George W. Gray, "Out of the Mountains Came the Preacher of the Plains," *American Mag.*, Nov. 1925, is the most useful magazine article. Dallas newspapers (1897–1944) provide full coverage of his career. Personal information was furnished by Truett's grandson, Dr. George Truett James of Dallas. There is no formal collection of Truett papers.]

JOHN S. EZELL

TUFTS, JAMES HAYDEN (July 9, 1862– Aug. 5, 1942), philosopher, was born in Monson, Mass., the only child of James and Mary Elizabeth (Warren) Tufts. His mother's forebears had come to Massachusetts in the 1630's. His father, born in Vermont and descended from a Scotch-Irish immigrant of about 1728, was a graduate of Yale and the Andover Theological Seminary; he had planned on a ministerial career but after difficulties with his voice turned instead to teaching.

Young Tufts was educated at the Monson Academy, where his parents were teachers, and was privately prepared for college by his father. For two years before entering Amherst College he taught district school, and after graduating in 1884, he spent a year as principal of a high school and two years as instructor in mathematics at Amherst. He then entered the Yale Divinity School, where he received the B.D. degree in 1889. At Amherst, however, his Calvinist heritage had been challenged by the evolution controversy then being agitated by the writings of Herbert Spencer. Tufts had planned to enter the ministry, but President Julius Seelye and Prof. Charles E. Garman [qq.v.] of Amherst advised him to teach philosophy, and, with both possibilities in mind, he took not only theology courses at Yale but also philosophy and anthropology. He was particularly influenced by William Graham Sumner, who gave him a lifelong concern with the diversity of moral codes, and by William Rainey Harper [qq.v.]. An invitation in 1889 from President James B. Angell [q.v.] to teach philosophy at the University of Michigan tipped the balance in favor of an academic career.

Tufts had been at Michigan for two years when Harper, now organizing the new University of Chicago, sought out his former student and persuaded him to go to Berlin and Freiburg for postgraduate study in preparation for a teaching assignment at Chicago. Tufts received the Ph.D. at Freiburg in 1892 and that fall joined the philosophy department at Chicago. He became chair-

man of the department in 1905, a post he held
until his retirement in 1930. An important figure
in the early development of the University of
Chicago, he served as dean of the senior college
(1899–1904, 1907–08), dean of faculties (1923–
26), vice-president (1924–26), and, during the
interregnum of 1925–26, acting president.

While at Freiburg, Tufts had adopted, to some
extent, the Hegelian approach to the history of
philosophy, writing his doctoral dissertation
(under Prof. Alois Riehl) on Kant's teleology.
During his first year at Chicago he translated
Wilhelm Windelband's *History of Philosophy*; in
the preface he explained that the study of philosophical history enabled one to make a critical
examination of one's own assumptions. At Michigan, Tufts had made personal contacts that
deepened his awareness of the conflict between
past and present. One of his colleagues there was
John Dewey, who had begun to break away from
German philosophy, as earlier he had broken with
British empiricism; Dewey was called to Chicago
from Michigan on Tufts's recommendation. Another Michigan colleague, George Herbert Mead
[Supp. 1], also came to Chicago. The inadequacies
of classical philosophy and theology were the
theme of many others at the University, among
them Albion Small [*q.v.*] and W. I. Thomas in
sociology, Charles Merriam in political science,
Jacques Loeb [*q.v.*] in physiology, and Thorstein
Veblen [*q.v.*] in economics. Tufts thus became
part of the vigorous, antitraditional group that
gave rise to the "Chicago School of Instrumentalist Philosophy" and spread its influence to a variety of disciplines.

The impact of the Chicago experience upon
Tufts's classical learning is partially revealed in
Ethics (1908), the textbook he co-authored with
Dewey. This influential book departed from nineteenth-century treatises, with their emphasis on
duty to God, country, and self, to shift the focus
to moral problem-solving and the development of
intelligent purposes, without falling into the calculating, hedonistic point of view of the British
Utilitarians. Tufts's thinking on ethics was further
shaped by his work in civic reform, where he fell
in with the progressive ideas of such nonacademic
reformers as Jane Addams [Supp. 1], Earl Dean
Howard, vice-president of the clothing manufacturing firm of Hart, Schaffner & Marx, and Sidney Hillman of the Amalgamated Clothing Workers Union. Tufts became a spokesman for Chicago
social workers when they sought new legislation;
he was a member of Illinois's first state housing
commission; and he served as chairman (1919–
21) of two boards of arbitration which helped
establish a new pattern of labor relations in the

clothing industry. He regarded this experience as
crucial to his own intellectual growth, for it
taught him that ethical problems could not be
understood by purely conceptual analysis. His
studies of anthropology, history, and social psychology had impressed him with the social and
class origins of moral values, and of the evolution
of those values. He concluded that "the great
ethical question of to-day" was the need to restrain the "naked principle of capitalism" and
lawless pressure groups. Many of his books reflect these views, such as *Our Democracy* (1917),
The Real Business of Living (1918), and *Education and Training for Social Work* (1923).

Although he was editor of the *International
Journal of Ethics* (1914–34), Tufts in his own
lifetime ranked below Dewey and others of the
Chicago School as an innovating philosopher,
partly because his writings were sociological in
orientation. He is now best remembered for his
contributions to pragmatic moral theory and his
examination of contemporary moral problems, as
in *America's Social Morality* (1933). All of his
writing gives evidence of historical erudition and
profound respect for much of the philosophical inheritance of the past, but there is sometimes a
lackluster quality arising from his judicious habit
of trying to conserve what was of value in traditional forms while presenting the claims of a
new generation. His thought on religion reflects
this approach. Retaining his membership in the
Congregational Church, Tufts held that religion
had a key role in modern society, which had "seen
the passing of systems of thought which had
reigned since Augustine." Yet he never treated
religion systematically or indicated the ways in
which the church would have to change to provide values for society. These hesitant and ambivalent qualities enhanced his effectiveness as a
teacher, and successive generations of students
thanked him for making them come to grips with
opposing points of view.

Tufts was president of the American Philosophical Association in 1914. Tall and large-
boned, he was still vigorous and alert when he
retired from Chicago. Moving to California, he
taught briefly (1931–33) at the University of
California at Los Angeles, gave occasional lectures elsewhere, and continued his work as a
productive scholar until shortly before his death.
He was twice married. His first marriage (Aug.
25, 1891) was to Cynthia Hobart Whitaker of
Leverett, Mass., by whom he had two children,
Irene and James Warren. Cynthia Tufts died in
1920, and on June 18, 1923, Tufts married
Matilde Castro (Ph.D., University of Chicago,
1907), who had taught at Bryn Mawr. He died

in Berkeley, Calif., of a heart ailment at the age of eighty and was buried in Monson, Mass.

[James Hayden Tufts, "What I Believe," in George P. Adams and William P. Montague, eds., *Contemporary Am. Philosophy*, vol. II (1930); memorial by John Dewey in Am. Philosophical Assoc., *Proc. and Addresses*, 1942; *James Hayden Tufts* (1942?), a 68-page booklet containing memorial addresses given at the Univ. of Chicago; Darnell Rucker, *The Chicago Pragmatists* (1969); *Amherst College Biog. Record*, 1951, p. 36. A collection of Tufts's correspondence and papers, *c.* 1911–20, relating to his teaching and some of his civic interests, is in Special Collections, Univ. of Chicago Lib.; smaller collections are at the libraries of Amherst College and Southern Ill. Univ.]

WAYNE A. R. LEYS

TYTUS, JOHN BUTLER (Dec. 6, 1875–June 2, 1944), inventor and steel mill superintendent, was born in Middletown, Ohio, where his grandfather, Francis Jefferson Tytus, a native of Virginia who had come to Ohio in 1827, and his father, John Butler Tytus, operated a paper mill. His mother, Minnesota (Ewing) Tytus, was from Fort Wayne, Ind. John was the oldest of four brothers. After local schooling and preparation at the Westminster School, Dobbs Ferry, N. Y., he entered Yale, which his father had attended, and received a B.A. degree in English literature in 1897. He then returned to Middletown and began work in the shipping department of the family paper mill. Since boyhood he had been interested in the mill's machinery; as he later recalled, he was particularly fascinated by the way in which the Fourdrinier machines converted wood pulp into a continuous sheet of paper.

After his father's death and the subsequent sale of the family's interest in the paper mill, Tytus went to work for a bridge builder in Dayton, Ohio. His employer, noting his ability to comprehend engineering problems, set him to work on blueprints. Becoming interested in steelmaking, Tytus in 1904 took a job as a laborer with the American Rolling Mill Company (Armco), which in 1901 had begun operations in his hometown of Middletown, fabricating "black" and galvanized steel sheets. As a "spare hand," one who took the place of any member of the crew who might be absent, he learned steelmaking firsthand and observed the time-consuming process by which sheets of steel were passed by hand through a succession of wringerlike rolls until they had reached the desired degree of thinness. Remembering the Fourdrinier machines that produced an unending sheet of paper, Tytus began to study the possibility of designing machinery that would dispense with these separate manual operations and would produce a continuous and uniform sheet of steel. The idea

of a continuous-strip rolling process was not new. In the eighteenth and nineteenth centuries a number of English and American steel men had attempted to design a practical continuous mill, but all had failed. The principal problems were determining the exact contours of the successive rolls through which the steel sheets passed and overcoming the tendency of sheets to buckle during the rolling process.

Tytus took on increasing responsibilities in the operation of Armco, which before World War I was beginning various expansion programs. In 1906 he became superintendent of the company's new plant in Zanesville, Ohio; and in 1909, as operations chief at Middletown, he planned a new mill in that city. Meanwhile, he continued to work at designing a continuous process, aided by the addition of new research facilities at Armco. Progress in the development of electric motors powerful enough to drive the giant rolls envisioned by Tytus, and the increasing demand for steel, especially by the automobile industry, made him confident of eventual success. The coming of World War I and the immediate postwar demand for steel forced Armco to postpone innovative capital projects, but its acquisition in 1921 of blast furnaces and open hearth furnaces from a financially distressed company in Ashland, Ky., gave Tytus his opportunity. He persuaded George M. Verity [Supp. 3] and Armco's board of directors to authorize the construction of a mill at the Kentucky site to test his ideas for a continuous sheet process.

Designed by Tytus, with the backing of Charles R. Hook, then general superintendent of Armco, the revolutionary plant began operation in January 1924, its mills linked together in a giant moving line. After some early breakdowns and repeated testing, the plant began to turn out sheet steel at a rate many times greater than that achieved by the old process, and within three years it was producing 40,000 tons a month, a figure far in excess of the estimated 18,000 tons needed to justify the capital investment. The continuous mill won almost immediate acceptance within the steel industry. Nearly all large companies, under licensing granted by Armco, began to employ Tytus's invention. By 1940 at least twenty-six continuous mills had been constructed in the United States, at a cost of more than $500,000,000. As one consequence, national production of steel rose, consumption increased, and costs fell. For his contribution to steel production Tytus in 1935 received the Gary Medal of the American Iron and Steel Institute.

Tytus's invention of the continuous mill was a landmark in the history of technology, and it contributed significantly to the growth of the steel industry. But it would be a mistake to attribute to its inventor the rank of genius. Rather, he was a man of singular determination who had at his command the services of money and science; and, like other inventors, he owed much to men who had labored in the field before him. He and his invention were characteristic emanations of an industrial age attuned to science, technology, and expanding markets.

Tytus was a tall and rather handsome man. Although his father had been a Baptist, he became an Episcopalian. On June 27, 1907, he married Marjorie Denny; they had a daughter, Elizabeth, and twin sons, Francis Jefferson and John Butler. Tytus died in Cincinnati, Ohio, of a coronary thrombosis and was buried in Woodside Cemetery, Middletown, Ohio.

[George C. Crout and Wilfred D. Vorhis, "John Butler Tytus: Inventor of the Continuous Steel Mill," *Ohio Hist.*, Summer 1967, is the fullest account, citing published and unpublished sources. Christy Borth, *True Steel: The Story of George Matthew Verity and His Associates* (1941), though uncritical, describes in detail Tytus's activities at Armco. For his own analysis of the technical problems involved in designing a continuous mill, see John B. Tytus, "Sheet and Jobbing Mills," Armco *Bull.*, Mar. 1916. See also Yale Univ., *Biog. Record of the Class of Seventy* (1904), on his father, and *Obituary Record of Graduates,* 1943–44.]

CARL M. BECKER

ULRICH, EDWARD OSCAR (Feb. 1, 1857–Feb. 22, 1944), geologist and paleontologist, was born in Cincinnati, Ohio, the eldest of the four sons and one daughter of Charles Ulrich and his first wife, Julia Schnell. Edward's parents were both natives of Alsace. The elder Ulrich had come to the United States in 1840 and settled in Cincinnati, where he engaged in carpentry and furniture making. In 1867 the family moved across the Ohio River to Covington, Ky., where they belonged to the Immanuel German Methodist Episcopal Church. Ulrich's mother died in 1874, and his father married again and had two more daughters and another son.

Edward Ulrich's interest in paleontology began in boyhood when he expressed curiosity about a collection of rocks discarded by a neighbor and was informed that they were "ancient animals turned to stone." A frail child, he attended the local schools irregularly and did not finish grammar school until he was fifteen. Instead of entering high school, he got a job with a group of surveyors working on excavations for a reservoir at Cincinnati, an area rich in fossils, and was thus able to continue his study, aided by works on geology discovered in a secondhand bookstore. At the age of seventeen he was admitted to Ger-

man Wallace (later Baldwin-Wallace) College in Berea, Ohio, which emphasized training for the Methodist ministry, but dropped out after his second year. For two winters he attended the Pulte and Ohio medical colleges at Cincinnati, but in 1877 he abandoned medicine to return to the study of fossils and joined the Cincinnati Society of Natural History. The following year was a decisive one: he was appointed honorary curator of the society's fossil collection; its newly established journal published his first scientific paper, "Observations on Fossil Annelids, and Description of Some New Forms"; and he began a friendship with young Charles Schuchert [Supp. 3], who shared his passion for the study of fossils and went on to a similar career.

Ulrich, now a powerful man more than six feet tall, added to his geological knowledge during two years spent near Boulder, Colo., as superintendent of a silver mine. He then returned to Cincinnati, where he supported himself by working as a carpenter. Devoting all his spare time to research, he was soon recognized as an authority on the stony Bryozoa and other fossils. His publications attracted the attention of the Illinois and Minnesota geological surveys, which contracted with him to describe and prepare lithograph illustrations of their Bryozoa and other fossil groups. His work on these surveys and the reputation established during these years as a free-lance geologist brought him in 1900 a permanent appointment with the United States Geological Survey in Washington, D. C.

He was soon recognized as the leading stratigrapher in the Geological Survey and became the master authority on the early Paleozoic formations and fossils in the eastern United States. He was a brilliant, forceful man, argumentative and aggressive, and with a phenomenal memory for the characteristics of particular geological formations and the details of fossil species. Though genial and approachable, he was not easy to dissuade from an idea. By temperament he was a rebel and an innovator, often dissatisfied with current beliefs. His theory that tilting continental shorelines permitted marine embayments alternately from opposite directions was useful in the Midcontinent region but failed to explain the geological events of the more complicated Appalachian region. His "Revision of the Paleozoic Systems" (Geological Society of America, *Bulletin*, Aug. 31, 1911), in which he proposed the existence of Ozarkian and Canadian systems between the Cambrian and Ordovician, failed of general acceptance because a paleontological base for these periods was not established.

Ulrich made fundamental contributions in

thirteen major animal groups and was largely responsible for developing the classification of fossil Bryozoa, Ostracoda, and conodonts. In collaboration with Ray S. Bassler, his former student and assistant in Cincinnati days, he popularized these fossils and made them useful in stratigraphy. He pioneered in the study of ancient Bivalvia and Gastropoda and contributed to our knowledge of crinoids, cystoids, sponges, and trilobites. In his last years, with the help of younger men, he described the brachiopods and cephalopods from the rocks of his moot Ozarkian and Canadian systems.

Ulrich was elected to the National Academy of Sciences in 1917 and in 1931 received its Mary Clarke Thompson Medal for distinction in paleontology and stratigraphy. This was followed in 1932 by the Penrose Medal, highest honor of the Geological Society of America. In 1892 Baldwin-Wallace College had given him an honorary Sc.D. degree. Ulrich married Albertina Zuest, a teacher in the Cincinnati public schools, on June 29, 1886. She became seriously ill with diabetes in 1922 and died in 1932. They had no children. On June 20, 1933, Ulrich married Lydia Sennhauser of Adorf, Germany, who had been his wife's nurse. Although officially retired from the Geological Survey in 1932, he never stopped work. He died of cancer of the esophagus at his home in Washington, D. C., shortly after his eighty-seventh birthday, and was buried at Fort Lincoln Cemetery in Washington.

[Ray S. Bassler's memoir in the Geological Soc. of America, *Proc.*, 1944, is the basic source. See also Rudolf Ruedemann in Nat. Acad. Sci., *Biog. Memoirs,* vol. XXIV (1947). Information about the Ulrich family from Cincinnati and Covington city directories (courtesy of Cincinnati Hist. Soc.), from census listings of 1870 and 1880, and from records of Immanuel Church (courtesy of Mrs. James W. Wolcott, Covington, Ky.). Death record from D. C. Dept. of Public Health.]

G. Arthur Cooper

UNDERWOOD, FREDERICK DOUGLAS (Feb. 1, 1849–Feb. 18, 1942), railroad executive, was born in Wauwatosa, Wis., the older of two sons and third of the five children of Enoch Downs Underwood, a farmer and Baptist clergyman, and Harriet Flint (Denny) Underwood. His father, an opponent of slavery, had moved west from his native Virginia by way of Illinois, settling on the Wisconsin frontier in 1836. Young Underwood was educated at public schools and at the Wayland Academy, Beaver Dam, Wis.

At the age of eighteen he went to work for the Chicago, Milwaukee & St. Paul Railroad, in whose service he remained for the next eighteen years, advancing through the ranks from brakeman to division superintendent. In 1886 he accepted the position of general superintendent of the Minneapolis & Pacific Railway. Before the year was up he had become general superintendent of construction with its successor, the Minneapolis, St. Paul & Sault Ste. Marie Railway (the Soo Line). Promoted soon afterward to general manager, he supervised the construction of nearly 1,300 miles of line. This great extension of the Soo brought it into bitter rivalry with the St. Paul, Minneapolis & Manitoba Railway, which was then being vigorously promoted by James J. Hill [*q.v.*]. The two railroad leaders finally worked out a compromise, and when Hill, who had come to respect Underwood's ability, became a major stockholder of the Baltimore & Ohio Railroad, he saw to it that Underwood in 1899 was made general manager and vice-president. During his two years with the road, Underwood gave characteristic attention to the physical rehabilitation of the property.

In 1901, mainly because control of the Baltimore & Ohio by the Pennsylvania Railroad was in the offing, Underwood accepted an offer from J. Pierpont Morgan [*q.v.*] to become president of the Erie Railroad. The Erie had a checkered history, marked by frequent financial distress and continuing physical inadequacies. A reorganization by Morgan in 1895 had brought the interest on the bonded debt within normal earning power, but the Erie had then undergone a period of economic retrenchment. When Underwood assumed his duties the property was physically decrepit, financially weak, and low in public esteem.

His great accomplishment was the rebuilding of the Erie into a first-class railroad. Extensive double tracking, grade reduction, and the construction of three low-grade freight cutoffs on the eastern section gave the line favorable grades second only to those of the New York Central, despite the mountainous terrain traversed. Line improvements were complemented by the extension of major terminals, the consolidation and rebuilding of shops, and the acquisition of heavier locomotives. An able administrator, Underwood made good use of limited financial resources to build a sound base for the cultivation of traffic and earning power. He made the Erie one of the superior freight-service routes between New York and Chicago, a worthy competitor of the larger Eastern trunk lines and one that surpassed most others in traffic growth. Although freight-train mileage increased only slightly, the amount of freight carried by the road more than doubled. Under his leadership the Erie also served as a prime training ground for railroad executives.

Underwood had a lifelong facility for recognizing and advancing promising men, including several who later became leaders in the industry, notably Daniel Willard [Supp. 3] and Edward Eugene Loomis.

When Underwood retired in 1926, *Railway Age* commented that "it may properly be said that he represents the last of a preceding generation of railroad leaders." Although a hard taskmaster on the job, he was a warm and generous person who enjoyed a wide circle of friends. In 1875 he had married Sara Virginia Smith, by whom he had two sons, Enoch William and Russell Sage. They were divorced in 1886, and in 1893 Underwood married Alice Stafford Robbins. A licensed captain and early automobile fancier, he owned three yachts in succession and always maintained a stable of cars. He also had two farms, one in Wauwatosa and the other in Farmington, Minn., where he raised blooded cattle and spent his summers. Underwood died of pneumonia at the age of ninety-three at his home in New York City.

[Edward Hungerford, *Men of Erie* (1946); *Railway Age*, Dec. 25, 1926, Feb. 28, 1942; Lucien M. Underwood, comp., *The Underwood Families of America*, vol. II (1913); *N. Y. Times*, Feb. 20. 1942.]
                                ERNEST W. WILLIAMS, JR.

UPDIKE, DANIEL BERKELEY (Feb. 24, 1860–Dec. 29, 1941), scholar-printer, was born in Providence, R. I., the only child of Caesar Augustus Updike, a lawyer, and Elisabeth Bigelow (Adams) Updike. His first American ancestor, Gysbert op Dyck, was a native of Westphalia who came to New Amsterdam in the 1630's and married a daughter of Richard Smith, the first English settler of the Narragansett country. Through this marriage Smith's lands around what became Wickford, R. I., passed to the Updike family, which stayed on or close to them for more than two centuries. Daniel Updike's incomplete formal education was acquired in private schools in Providence, where he was unhappy. He was a slight, physically frail, shy boy with protruding ears, and was dominated by his mother, a woman of remarkable intellectual powers who was intimately acquainted with English and French literature and instilled in her son the feeling that his origins placed him on a higher level than most of his contemporaries. The sudden death of his father in 1877 raised the unpleasant necessity of making his own way in the world, a task for which he was poorly fitted. For financial reasons, college was out of the question.

After a winter as an assistant in the Providence Athenaeum, Updike went to Boston in the spring of 1880 to the publishing firm of Houghton, Mifflin & Company. He began as an errand boy, carrying proof between its Boston office and the Riverside Press in Cambridge, then moved on to preparing copy for advertisements. Although bored and unhappy, he learned much about bookmaking and became known for his taste in typographical arrangement. He found consolation in the Episcopal Church, and his first published work (except for a few anonymous articles in the *Atlantic Monthly*) was a somewhat precious piece of antiquarian ecclesiology, *On the Dedications of American Churches* (1891), in which he collaborated with a fellow Anglo-Catholic, Harold Brown, younger son of the Providence collector John Carter Brown [*q.v.*]. The next year Updike collaborated with Bertram Grosvenor Goodhue [*q.v.*] in designing and decorating an edition of the Book of Common Prayer that was printed by Theodore L. De Vinne [*q.v.*].

Although the book was highly praised, Updike was mortified by its appearance, and realized that he could never fulfill his desire to "do things well" until he became his own master. As Harold Brown stood ready to finance the production of an Altar Book for use in the Episcopal Church, Updike left Houghton, Mifflin in 1893 and launched out for himself in Boston as a "typographic adviser." This was the beginning of the Merrymount Press, a name adopted in 1896. His original intention was merely to design books that would be composed and printed by other firms, for, unlike most great printers, he derived no pleasure from the feel of type or the smell of ink. Finding the appropriate typographical dress for a text was for Updike an intellectual exercise in bringing order out of chaos.

For the Altar Book, which in its style reflected the products of William Morris's Kelmscott Press, Goodhue designed decorated borders and a heavy Roman typeface called Merrymount. By the time the volume appeared in 1896, Updike had designed nineteen other books, as well as various smaller bits of printing. He soon found that adding his design fees to the normal costs of printing done by others produced unacceptably high prices. To reduce costs, he reluctantly invested in a small amount of type and ornaments, and thus became a printer, with John Bianchi, formerly of the Riverside Press, in charge of the composing room (in 1915 he was made a partner). The Merrymount Press became an indispensable Boston institution that never compromised with quality.

Unlike the Kelmscott, Doves, and Ashendene presses in England, which established a style based on a specially cut typeface, Updike chiefly employed a variety of historic types of the seventeenth, eighteenth, and nineteenth centuries. He soon moved beyond the heavy neomedievalism of the Kelmscott Press and found more acceptable inspiration in the Renaissance and the eighteenth century. In 1904 Herbert P. Horne designed for him the Montallegro font, a lighter Roman modeled on an early Florentine face, that was intended to be a good "reading type." This was first used in Horne's translation of Ascanio Condivi's *The Life of Michelagnolo Buonarroti,* published by the Merrymount Press in 1904, and subsequently in the eight volumes of The Humanist's Library, edited by Lewis Einstein, that the press published between 1906 and 1914. This handsome series of translations of Renaissance texts had title pages designed not only by Horne but also by William Addison Dwiggins and Thomas Maitland Cleland, who often worked with Updike on other projects. The Montallegro face was only occasionally used thereafter.

Although the press had three black-letter faces useful in ecclesiastical work, most of its printing was done in historic roman and italic faces that Updike rediscovered and appreciated earlier than most of his contemporaries. Having begun with Caslon and Scotch, he added in 1903 fonts designed by the seventeenth-century Dutch founder Anton Janson and the eighteenth-century Englishman John Bell. In 1906 he acquired Oxford, a type originally developed by John Binny and James Ronaldson, the first successful typefounders in America. These simple and versatile faces were long Updike's chief stock in trade. In 1925 he added Poliphilus and the related Blado italic, in 1927 Lutetia, and in 1930 Bodoni, but in comparison with the number of faces available at the average printing office of his time, the variety was restricted. What was significant was the full and imaginative use he made of what he had.

The Merrymount Press seldom acted as a publisher. Updike's belief that "the modern printer's problem is to produce books mechanically well-made, tasteful without pretension, beautiful without eccentricity or sacrifice of legibility" is exemplified in the many books that he printed for trade publishers in the early years of the press, and in the considerable amount of learned and institutional printing that he constantly produced. The Merrymount Press was prepared to print a billhead, a penny postcard, or a label for a catsup bottle, but even these workaday pieces of job printing had the distinction and appropriateness that invariably characterized Updike's work. The variety and ingenuity of his designs is best seen in the many books that he privately printed for his Boston friends, and in the work that he did for his fellow members of the Club of Odd Volumes and the Grolier Club, or for the Limited Editions Club. In some of these he commissioned illustrations by the wood engraver Rudolph Ruzicka. Updike was always especially felicitous when dealing with Rhode Island books or anything connected with the Episcopal Church. His masterpiece is the folio edition of the 1928 revision of the Book of Common Prayer that he completed in 1930 for J. Pierpont Morgan [Supp. 3]. Unlike the Altar Book of 1896, it is without decoration; here Updike relied solely upon the simplicity of Janson type, meticulously printed in black and red upon handmade paper.

During the years 1911–16 Updike gave a course at the Harvard Business School on the technique of printing which he eventually recast into the two scholarly volumes of *Printing Types, Their History, Forms, and Use* (1922), published by the Harvard University Press and printed at the Merrymount Press. The Harvard Press also published Updike's autobiographical *Notes on the Merrymount Press & Its Work* (1934), which embodies the essence of his principles and is the proof of his belief that "a trade can be practised in the spirit of a profession."

Updike never married. Although a reserved man, without natural bonhomie, he had a dry wit and made a distinct place for himself in the social life of Boston. Under the disguise of an elegant dilettante he effectively concealed from the casual observer the vast amount of plain hard work that he put into the creation of the Merrymount Press and the maintenance of its standards. Updike was a founder of the Boston Society of Printers (1905) and its president in 1912–14, as well as a gold medalist and honorary member of the American Institute of Graphic Arts. He received honorary M.A. degrees from Brown University (1910) and Harvard (1929). He died of pneumonia at his home in Boston at the age of eighty-one and was buried in St. Paul's Cemetery, Wickford, R. I. Through the Merrymount Press, Updike had exerted great influence in improving the graphic arts in the United States during the first third of the twentieth century.

[Updike's volumes of essays, *In the Day's Work* (1924) and *Some Aspects of Printing, Old and New* (1941), although brief, are important. He also wrote and published (1937) a monograph on his ancestor Richard Smith. Beyond his own writing, the most useful sources are: George Parker Winship, *The Merrymount Press of Boston* (1929) and *Daniel Berkeley Updike and the Merrymount Press* (1947); Huntington Lib., *The Work of the Merrymount Press and Its Founder Daniel Berkeley Updike* (1942); Am. Inst. of Graphic Arts, *Updike: Am. Printer and His Merrymount Press* (1947); Ray Nash, *Printing as an Art* (1955); and Daniel B. Bianchi, *D. B. Updike and John Bianchi: A Note on Their Association* (1965). Updike's printing collection, correspondence, and documents accumulated through five generations of his

family are in the Providence Public Lib. The file copies of Merrymount Press books are in the Henry E. Huntington Lib., San Marino, Calif.; the job tickets of the press with samples of ephemeral printing are in the Boston Athenaeum. All three libraries have in addition numerous examples of his work.]
WALTER MUIR WHITEHILL

VAILLANT, GEORGE CLAPP (Apr. 5, 1901–May 13, 1945), archaeologist, student of pre-Columbian Mexico, was born in Boston, Mass., the only son and second of the three children of George Wightman Vaillant and Alice Vanlora (Clapp) Vaillant. His father, at that time in the foundry business and later a stockbroker, was a native of Cleveland, Ohio; his mother, of Rockland, Mass. Forebears on both sides of the family had been early settlers in New England; his paternal great-grandparents were French royalists who had emigrated to the United States after the revolution of 1848. A Unitarian in religion, George attended Phillips Academy at Andover, Mass., and in 1918 entered Harvard, where his interests centered in literature and history.

In the summer of 1919 he accompanied a college friend to Maine on a field expedition headed by the friend's father, the archaeologist Warren K. Moorehead. While helping excavate an Indian burial site near Waterville, Vaillant unearthed a set of slate spear-points, and on his return to Harvard he began to concentrate in anthropology and archaeology. Graduating cum laude in 1922, he continued his studies at Harvard. During his years as an undergraduate and graduate student Vaillant did archaeological field work with Samuel J. Guernsey and Alfred V. Kidder at Indian sites in Arizona and New Mexico, observing at first hand the initial attempts at detailed stratigraphic excavations in the Americas. He also spent one field season with George A. Reisner [Supp. 3] in Egypt and the Sudan and another with the Carnegie Institution group at Chichen Itza in Yucatan. It was the Mexican research that most attracted him, and as a student of Prof. Alfred M. Tozzer at Harvard he wrote his doctoral dissertation on "The Chronological Significance of Maya Ceramics," receiving the Ph.D. degree in 1927. His dissertation, a highly original piece of work, drew together, from both the literature and the museums, the scattered information produced by a half century of exploration, and constructed the first relative chronological framework proposed for the Maya area. In it he demonstrated not only his devotion to scholarship but also his extraordinary feeling for cultural style and his perceptiveness as an archaeologist.

In 1927 Vaillant was appointed an assistant curator at the American Museum of Natural History in New York. From this post he set out to apply the stratigraphic methods which he had learned from Kidder, using pottery and figurines to determine the sequence of pre-Columbian cultures in the Valley of Mexico. Over the next three years he made a series of excavations—at Zacatenco, Ticoman, El Arbolillo, and Gualupita —which placed Mexican archaeology on a firm scientific footing. His work established that the Archaic or preclassic period, which had first been defined by Manuel Gamio of Mexico and Franz Boas [Supp. 3], extended much further back in time and could be subdivided into a series of sequent phases. Within this sequence he demonstrated that an evolution could be traced from one cultural phase to another, ranging from the village farmers of the Archaic period to the urban dwellers of the Teotihuacan civilization. Mindful of his earlier studies of Maya ceramics, Vaillant also saw the development of the Valley of Mexico as but one part of a larger network of cultural relationships that spread throughout the whole of Middle America. His last excavations in Central Mexico were concerned with the post-Teotihuacan periods and with the Toltecs; in these studies he was able to unite archaeology with history in revealing the story of pre-Columbian Mexico.

Vaillant became associate curator of Mexican archaeology at the American Museum of Natural History in 1930 and for the next decade was largely occupied in New York with his curatorial duties, the completion of his Mexican monographs, the preparation of numerous new articles, and part-time teaching duties at Columbia, Yale, and New York universities. He was president of the American Ethnological Society, 1936–39. His major work, *The Aztecs of Mexico,* was published in 1941 and was the summation of his research career.

On Mar. 10, 1930, Vaillant married Mary Suzannah Beck, the daughter of an American banker living in Mexico City. They had three children: Joanna Beck, George Eman, and Henry Winchester. Vaillant was a man of consummate charm with a captivating, mercurial intelligence; he was always able to see the old in a new way, stripping away stale concepts and classifications and presenting the conventional in a fresh light. There was little of formality about him and he had a pleasant naiveté of manner, yet he was a very complex individual.

In 1941 he became director of the University Museum of the University of Pennsylvania in Philadelphia and moved with his family to Devon, Pa. He was an able director, but his first love was research—the study, he once said, "of the countless permutations of the things made by human hands" and the meaning of these permutations. When the United States entered World War II Vaillant tried to obtain military duty but was refused because of his age. He served as senior cultural relations officer in the American embassy in Lima, Peru, in 1943–44. Upon his return the State Department asked him to take a similar post in Spain. He was preparing to leave for this assignment when, for reasons unknown and seemingly without premeditation, he took his own life, at his home in Devon, at the age of forty-four.

[Obituary by A. V. Kidder in *Am. Anthropologist*, Oct.–Dec. 1945, which includes a photograph and a full bibliography; Vaillant's writings; information about his parents from his birth record (Mass. Registrar of Vital Statistics) and from Boston city directories; personal acquaintance, 1938–45. See also *Nat. Cyc. Am. Biog.*, XXXIV, 194–95.]

GORDON R. WILLEY

VAN ANDA, CARR VATTEL (Dec. 2, 1864–Jan. 28, 1945), journalist, was born in Georgetown, Brown County, Ohio, the only child of Frederick C. and Mariah E. (Davis) Van Anda. Both parents were natives of Virginia. His mother, listed in the 1870 census as an invalid, evidently died soon afterward, for by 1880 his father had remarried and was living, with his son and his new wife, in Wapakoneta, Auglaize County, Ohio. A lawyer, he was serving in that year as prosecuting attorney.

Young Van Anda early evinced a passion for newspapers by producing his own paste-up version at the age of six. When he was ten he built a makeshift printing press. He soon acquired a regular small press and began doing job printing, spending the profits on materials for experiments in chemistry and physics. At sixteen he entered Ohio University at Athens, filled with ambition to excel in mathematics and physics. But after two years, deciding he had had enough "formal" education, he returned to Wapakoneta as printing foreman for one of the three village weeklies, the *Auglaize Republican.* He retained, however, throughout his life a strong and perceptive interest in science and mathematics.

After a year with the village weekly, Van Anda in 1883 joined the *Cleveland Herald,* graduating from printer to reporter to telegraph editor. When his paper was merged with the *Plain Dealer,* he moved to the *Evening Argus,* but it failed in 1886. Traveling east, he applied at the office of one of the leading newspapers of the country, the Baltimore *Sun,* and at twenty-two was offered the important position of night editor, with final responsibility for the selection of news and production of the paper's editions through the late night and early morning hours.

He left Baltimore in 1888 to become a reporter and copyreader for the New York *Sun,* published by Charles A. Dana [*q.v.*] and generally regarded as the top-ranking training ground for newspapermen. There, from 1893 to 1904, he served as night editor. While in Cleveland, on Dec. 16, 1885, Van Anda had married Harriet L. Tupper; she died after the birth of their daughter, Julia Blanche, in December 1887. On Apr. 11, 1898, he married Louise Shipman Drane of Frankfort, Ky., by whom he had a son, Paul Drane.

Van Anda's work at the New York *Sun* had come to the attention of another former Midwesterner who also had dropped out of school to become a printer—Adolph S. Ochs [*q.v.*] of the *New York Times,* who in February 1904 hired Van Anda as his managing editor. During the next two decades, under Ochs's direction, Van Anda joined with editor Charles R. Miller [*q.v.*] and business manager Louis Wiley to develop a newspaper of outstanding stature. Van Anda's province was the newsroom, and it was his skill and leadership that stamped the *Times* by the 1920's as the foremost news operation in the country. Both historians of the *Times* agree that it was Van Anda who was "most directly concerned with the extraordinary development of the news department" (Davis, p. 274) and who "had an extraordinary flair for extending news-gathering techniques into fields previously held too deep for the reading masses" (Berger, p. 160). But Ochs also wanted top-quality news gathering, spent the money for it, and insisted that Van Anda's news be put into the paper before space was allocated to advertising, and not vice versa.

Much of Van Anda's almost legendary fame is owing to his intuitive sense of news values, his enormous capacity for long hours of work, his keenly analytical intellect, and his educated curiosity about all manner of subjects. He loved to handle a major story, matching speed and wits against a deadline. He also loved to exploit an important but underdeveloped story and give it painstaking coverage and significant play. But he never lost sight of the importance of conscientious and intelligent handling of the bulk of the news, and he transmitted this spirit to his staff, which found him a reserved, modest, and sympathetic chief.

Van Anda is credited with an important role in the early use of trans-Atlantic wireless news by the *Times,* in its development of a network of staff correspondents in the United States and abroad, in its introduction of rotogravure printing in 1914, in the development of the concept of the *Times* as a "newspaper of record," which began with its exhaustive coverage of World War I, and in the founding of the famed *New York Times Index*. It was Van Anda who produced the tremendous editions of the *Times* reporting the sinking of the *Titanic* in 1912; who focused attention on Einstein's theory of relativity in 1919 and later years; who obtained exclusive *Times* coverage of stories of adventure and science, ranging from the opening of the tomb of Tut-ankh-amen to the flights of Adm. Richard E. Byrd over the poles and of Auguste and Jean Piccard in the stratosphere; who saw the *Times* win a Pulitzer Prize in 1918 for its documented war coverage; and who gloried in one of his final news beats, won by tying up the only telephone line into the remote Vermont village where Calvin Coolidge was taking a midnight oath of office as president of the United States.

When Van Anda became too ill and exhausted in 1925, at age sixty, to continue his twelve-hour daily pace, he retired, but retained the title of managing editor until 1932. He held stock in the *Times,* and his son, a lawyer, became a company director. His second wife died in 1942. On Jan. 28, 1945, his daughter, Blanche, died; a few hours later Carr Van Anda died of a heart attack in his New York apartment. Episcopalian rites were conducted for both father and daughter, and their ashes were buried at Frankfort, Ky. Obituaries made clear that the man who had insisted upon virtually complete anonymity during his working life was recognized by his peers as "a giant of the press."

[Barnett Fine, *A Giant of the Press: Carr Van Anda* (1933); Meyer Berger, *The Story of the N. Y. Times* (1951); Elmer Davis, *Hist. of the N. Y. Times* (1921); Edwin Emery, *The Press and America* (3rd ed., 1972); Gerald W. Johnson, *An Honorable Titan: A Biog. Study of Adolph S. Ochs* (1946); profile of Van Anda by Alva Johnston in the *New Yorker,* Sept. 7, 1935; obituaries in *N. Y. Times,* Jan. 29–Feb. 1, 1945, and in *Time* and *Newsweek,* Feb. 5, 1945; family data from census schedules of 1870 and 1880.]

                                    EDWIN EMERY

VAN DEVANTER, WILLIS (Apr. 17, 1859–Feb. 8, 1941), lawyer and judge, justice of the United States Supreme Court, was born in Marion, Ind., the first of eight children (of whom two died in infancy) of Isaac and Violetta Maria (Spencer) Van Devanter. Both parents had been born in Ohio of pre-Revolutionary stock; his father had moved as a young man to Marion and became a prominent lawyer there. Young Willis attended Indiana Asbury (later DePauw) University, 1875–78, spending the first two years in its Academy, and the Cincinnati Law School, where he obtained an LL.B. degree in 1881. He

then practiced law in his father's office in Marion for three years. On Oct. 10, 1883, he married Dollie Paige Burhans of Ionia, Mich., by whom he had two sons, Isaac Burhans and Winslow Burhans. In July 1884 Van Devanter and his wife moved to Cheyenne, Wyo., where a brother-in-law and later partner, John W. Lacey, had been appointed territorial chief justice.

Cheyenne, as Van Devanter himself described it in 1885, was "a lively, busy and substantial" pioneer community "with a population something in excess of 8,000" and a property valuation of seven million dollars. Able, well-trained professionals were at a premium, and Van Devanter soon had a thriving law practice. He was also drawn into public service and Republican politics. He served in turn as commissioner to revise the Wyoming statutes (1886), as Cheyenne's city attorney (1887–88), as a member of the territorial legislature and chairman of its judiciary committee (1888), and as chief justice of Wyoming (1889–90). Thereafter his political involvement was chiefly as a party manager. He had in 1885 formed an alliance with Wyoming's territorial governor and later United States Senator, Francis E. Warren [*q.v.*], and he soon became Warren's most trusted adviser. As Republican state chairman (1892–96) and national committeeman (1896–1903), Van Devanter raised funds, organized campaigns, kept in touch with local party officials, and fought election challenges through the courts.

Although Wyoming went for William Jennings Bryan [*q.v.*] in 1896, Van Devanter fought hard for William McKinley and was able to prevent a widespread Silverite defection from party ranks in his state. His efforts were brought by Senator Warren to the attention of Mark Hanna [*q.v.*], and with McKinley's accession to the presidency, Van Devanter entered federal office, never again to leave it. In 1897 he became Assistant Attorney General in charge of Indian and public lands cases in the Department of the Interior. It was from this post that President Theodore Roosevelt raised him in 1903 to a judgeship on the federal circuit court of appeals for the 8th Circuit. Here he served until President Taft made him associate justice of the Supreme Court of the United States. Taking his seat on Jan. 3, 1911, he held it for twenty-six years.

Van Devanter's outlook was formed on the last frontier. He believed in property rights, in "economic freedom," and in the philosophy that that government governs best which governs least. Some of his colleagues on the Supreme Court spoke more often and more loudly for doctrines of constitutional law proceeding from this phil-

osophy. But Van Devanter, a consummate lawyer and subtle negotiator, wielded an important influence. He wrote slowly and with difficulty. But he spoke decisively and lucidly in conference, and he labored indefatigably. These qualities made him, in the opinion of Chief Justice William Howard Taft [*q.v.*], "far and away the most valuable man in our Court" (to James R. Angell, Dec. 2, 1926, Taft Papers, Library of Congress). Van Devanter was also the chief draftsman of the Judiciary Act of 1925 and of the revised Rules of Court which implemented it. He was chairman, in the mid-1920's, of a committee of justices to supervise a receivership of valuable lands on the Oklahoma-Texas border, growing out of a boundary dispute between those two states which the Court had adjudicated.

Among Van Devanter's opinions, a number, such as *Evans* v. *Gore* (253 U.S. 245 [1920]) and *Indian Motorcycle Company* v. *United States* (283 U.S. 570 [1931]), which carved out certain immunities from federal and state taxation, have been overridden by a later judicial philosophy. But such an important judgment as that upholding the Federal Employers' Liability Act (223 U.S. 1 [1912]) speaks in more modern tones. Other notable opinions include: *National Prohibition Cases* (253 U.S. 350 [1920]), sustaining the constitutionality of the Eighteenth Amendment; *Pennsylvania* v. *West Virginia* (262 U.S. 553 [1923]), applying the commerce clause of the Constitution to prevent a state from reserving its natural resources for use exclusively in its internal commerce; *McGrain* v. *Daugherty* (273 U.S. 135 [1927]), affirming the Congressional power to investigate; and *New York ex. rel. Bryant* v. *Zimmerman et al.* (278 U.S. 63 [1928]), upholding a state statute under which the Ku Klux Klan was required to disclose its membership. An opinion displaying Van Devanter's mastery of the law affecting the Supreme Court's jurisdiction is *Dahnke-Walker Milling Company* v. *Bondurant* (257 U.S. 282 [1921]). One of his rare dissents, in *Herndon* v. *Lowry* (301 U.S. 242, 264 [1937]), argued the validity under the Fourteenth Amendment of a conviction of a Negro Communist organizer for violating a Georgia anti-insurrection statute.

Van Devanter's final years on the Court found his economic philosophy at odds with that of President Franklin D. Roosevelt. He was a firm member of the group of five justices who declared key New Deal measures unconstitutional. Roosevelt, frustrated by such decisions, proposed in 1937 to enlarge the Court. Van Devanter had contemplated retiring since his wife's death three years before. He announced his retirement at a time—on May 18, 1937—when the Senate Judiciary Committee was voting on the "court packing" bill. Thus his retirement probably contributed to the bill's defeat.

Judicious in speech and action, dignified and reserved in manner, with unfailing courtesy and consideration for others, Van Devanter was universally respected. The grand Wyoming outdoors had made him an inveterate hunter and camper. His religious affiliation, though not formal in later years, was with the Methodist Church. Following his retirement, and despite his advanced years, he accepted assignment to sit as trial judge in a number of criminal cases in the federal district court in New York in January and February 1938 and received much public acclaim for the masterful fashion in which he discharged these duties. Thereafter he lived on his 788-acre farm near Ellicott City, Md. He died of a coronary occlusion in Washington, D. C., at the age of eighty-one, and was buried in Rock Creek Cemetery there.

[Van Devanter Papers, Lib. of Cong.; "Proc. in Memory of Mr. Justice Van Devanter," 316 U.S. v (1942); Lewis L. Gould, "Willis Van Devanter in Wyo. Politics, 1884–1897" (Ph.D. thesis, Yale Univ., 1966) and *Wyoming: A Political Hist., 1868–1896* (1968). See also sketch of Van Devanter in *Fortune,* May 1936; *N. Y. Times* obituary, Feb. 9, 1941; *Who Was Who in America,* vol. I (1942). A biographical sketch by David Burner, with excerpts from several of Van Devanter's decisions, appears in Leon Friedman and Fred L. Israel, eds., *The Justices of the U. S. Supreme Court,* vol. III (1969).]

ALEXANDER M. BICKEL

VAN LOON, HENDRIK WILLEM (Jan. 14, 1882–Mar. 11, 1944), popular historian and illustrator, was born in Rotterdam, the Netherlands, the second of two children and only son of Hendrik Willem van Loon, a well-to-do jeweler's son, and Elisabeth Johanna (Hanken) van Loon. A moody, sensitive boy, he suffered, as did his mother and sister, from the "uncertain temper" of his paranoid father. When the latter broke with his own father and moved his family to The Hague, van Loon, at age nine, came under the protection of his maternal uncle, Jan Hanken, a surgeon, art connoisseur, and amateur musician, whose American wife, Sarah Parker, had been a music teacher. Dr. Hanken saw to it that the boy was sent to nearby boarding schools, with weekends spent largely at the Hanken home, which was frequented by fledgling art dealers and young musicians. Encouraged by his uncle, van Loon developed his interests in history, art, and music, his instrument being the violin. His mother's death, in 1900, and his father's precipitate remarriage to an unpleasant, much younger woman led van Loon to accompany his

uncle in 1902 to the United States, where he entered Cornell. He spent the year 1903–04 at Harvard but returned to Cornell, where he received his A.B. degree in 1905. On June 18, 1906, he married Eliza Ingersoll Bowditch, daughter of Henry Pickering Bowditch [q.v.], former dean of the Harvard Medical School; they had two sons, Henry Bowditch and Gerard Willem.

Espousing journalism, van Loon worked for the Associated Press in Washington, D. C., and in 1906 was sent to St. Petersburg, Moscow, and Warsaw to report on the aftermath of the 1905 revolution. Aspiring to an academic career, he quit newspaper work in 1907 to enroll at the University of Munich, where he received a doctorate in history in 1911. He returned to the United States that same year and settled in Washington, where he vainly attempted to gain a foothold in the academic world. He fared better as an itinerant lecturer on modern European history, soon giving up the accustomed magic-lantern slides in favor of self-drawn maps and sketches made, as he talked, on large sheets of paper. Aided by his American wife, he turned his doctoral thesis into his first book, *The Fall of the Dutch Republic* (1913).

Neither this nor *The Rise of the Dutch Kingdom* (1915) made a significant impression. Van Loon taught briefly at the University of Wisconsin in the summer of 1914. With the outbreak of World War I, he went to Holland as a free-lance reporter. He returned to lecture at Cornell (1915–16) and published *The Golden Book of the Dutch Navigators* (1916) and *History with a Match* (1917), an account of the voyages of discovery to North America—illustrated with a match dipped in india ink—which hinted at his later style. Van Loon became an American citizen on Jan. 14, 1919, and for a brief, rather undistinguished period did publicity work in New York City, where he established contact with the American literary world centered in Greenwich Village.

Ancient Man (1920) was projected as the first of a series of juvenile history books, but with the appearance of H. G. Wells's *Outline of History*, van Loon's publisher, Horace Liveright [Supp. 1], conceived the revolutionary notion of his turning out a similar work aimed at the juvenile market. In 1921 *The Story of Mankind* established van Loon as a best-selling author and won the first John Newbery Medal of the American Library Association. Not anticipating his success, van Loon had joined the faculty of the small experimental Antioch College in Ohio in 1922, but he left after a year to join H. L.

Mencken briefly on the editorial staff of the Baltimore *Sun*. At Liveright's suggestion, he wrote *The Story of the Bible* (1923), which did not do well. Fundamentalists took issue with van Loon's depiction of Christ as a historical figure, with no mention of the virgin birth or the resurrection. Almost in rebuttal, his next book, *Tolerance* (1925), was largely a history of bigotry and religious intolerance through the ages, voicing his admiration for such figures as Erasmus.

Van Loon's anecdotal style, his personal reflections upon great men and nations, and the profuse, curiously individual drawings with which he illustrated his books brought him a popularity and prestige which he took more seriously than his often flippant comments might have indicated. He professed indifference to academic critics who quarreled with his "slips of the pen" and slapdash generalizations. In *America* (1927), *Life and Times of Pieter Stuyvesant* (1928), and *Man the Miracle Maker* (1928), van Loon continued to cement his reputation as a "juvenile" author. This irked him. Seeking to break the mold, he produced in *R.v.R.* (1930) a largely autobiographical novel depicting the painter Rembrandt and his world. Its lack of success caused van Loon to quit Liveright. Switching to Simon & Schuster, he soon had another best seller in *Van Loon's Geography* (1932). This was followed by *The Arts* (1937), which, being self-illustrated, dismayed art historians but delighted van Loon's loyal public. Yet another best seller was *Van Loon's Lives* (1942), in which he somewhat sentimentally cast himself as genial host to the great figures of history.

Van Loon was divorced by his first wife in 1920, and on Aug. 3 of that year married Eliza Helen ("Jimmie") Criswell, a graduate of Bryn Mawr. They were divorced in 1927. On Oct. 10, 1927, he married Frances Goodrich, actress and future playwright. This marriage, too, ended in divorce in 1929, van Loon having returned to his second wife (although they never remarried). Six feet, two-and-a-half inches tall and weighing close to 300 pounds, van Loon was an imposing figure on the lecture platform and a sought-after toastmaster. In 1935 he attracted a new audience through his radio talks over the National Broadcasting System, which were collected that year in *Air-Storming*.

The rise of fascism in Europe stirred van Loon to write *Our Battle* (1938), his answer to Adolf Hitler's *Mein Kampf*, and with the outbreak of World War II he conducted a Dutch shortwave radio program over WRUL in Boston beamed at his Nazi-occupied homeland. Van Loon's anxieties over the war, his overweight, and per-

petual neurasthenia, against which, as he said, "work is my only drug," served to aggravate a heart condition which had been in evidence for many years. He died in 1944 at his home in Old Greenwich, Conn., and was buried in the Old Greenwich Cemetery.

[*Report to St. Peter* (1947), an uncompleted autobiography, gives van Loon's reflections upon his childhood. Clifton Fadiman, ed., *I Believe* (1939), cites van Loon's religious skepticism. Stanley J. Kunitz and Howard Haycraft, eds., *Twentieth Century Authors* (1942), offers a sketch of his life unreliably composed by himself; there are additional details in "Dilly Tante" [Stanley J. Kunitz], ed., *Living Authors* (1931). Gerard Willem van Loon, *The Story of Hendrik Willem van Loon* (1972), is a candid biography based on thorough research. Van Wyck Brooks, in his *Days of the Phoenix* (1957), devotes a chapter, "A Humanist," to van Loon, his erstwhile Westport, Conn., neighbor and lifelong friend. Two *New Yorker* profiles, by Waldo Frank (June 19, 1926) and Richard O. Boyer (Mar. 20, 27, Apr. 3, 1943), are informative. See also Frank Case, *Tales of a Wayward Inn* (1938); Margaret Widdemer, *Golden Friends I Had* (1964); Waldo Frank, *Time Exposures* (1926); and obituary in *N. Y. Times*, Mar. 12, 1944.]

LOUIS FILLER

VAN VLECK, EDWARD BURR (June 7, 1863–June 2, 1943), mathematician, was born in Middletown, Conn., of Dutch, English, and French Huguenot descent, the third of four children and only son of Ellen Maria (Burr) and John Monroe Van Vleck. His mother was from Middletown. His father, born in Stone Ridge, N. Y., in the Hudson Valley, was a descendant of Tielman Van Vleck, who had come in 1658 from Maastricht, Netherlands, to Nieuw Amsterdam in America. From 1858 to 1904 John Van Vleck was professor of mathematics and astronomy at Wesleyan University in Middletown. The family were Methodists.

Edward's first education was in the local schools and at Wilbraham (Mass.) Academy. He then studied, like his father before him, at Wesleyan, from which he received the A.B. degree in 1884. Though drawn also to the classics, he chose to follow his father's field. From 1885 to 1887 he pursued graduate work at Johns Hopkins; from 1887 to 1890 he was back at Wesleyan as a tutor in mathematics. Like other young mathematicians of that time, he then went to the University of Göttingen, where he studied under the guidance of Felix Klein and received his Ph.D. in 1893. His dissertation, dealing with the expansion of hyperelliptic and related integrals into continued fractions, was published in the *American Journal of Mathematics* for January 1894. After two years (1893–95) as an instructor at the University of Wisconsin, Van Vleck returned to Wesleyan, wher he was associate professor (1895–98) and then professor of mathematics. The University of Wisconsin called him back in 1906, and he re-

mained as professor of mathematics until his retirement in 1929. For many years he was chairman of the department.

Van Vleck's mathematical work, especially in his earlier period, showed the profound influence of Klein. This was typified by a broad approach to the problems, using both analytical and geometrical methods, together with a keen sense for the relationship between different fields—differential equations, divergent series, continued fractions, group theory, the geometry of the complex domain, and, later, the theory of point sets. This broad approach is revealed not only in many of his papers, but in particular in the addresses he gave from time to time, which were widely read and appreciated. Among these were: "Selected Topics in the Theory of Divergent Series and of Continued Fractions" (*American Mathematical Society Colloquium Lectures,* Boston, 1905); "The Influence of Fourier's Series upon the Development of Mathematics" (*Science,* Jan. 23, 1914); "Role of the Point-Set Theory in Geometry and Dynamics" (*Bulletin* of the American Mathematical Society, April 1915); and "Current Tendencies of Mathematical Research" (*ibid.,* October 1916). The last address deals with integral equations, Lebesgue integrals, and the General Analysis of Eliakim H. Moore [Supp 1].

As a teacher Van Vleck was conscientious, clear, and meticulous in his presentation. As one of the editors of the *Transactions* of the American Mathematical Society in its early years (1906–10), he set a tradition of precision and elegance of expression. Van Vleck was president of the Society, 1913–15. He was elected to the National Academy of Sciences in 1911 and was a member of the National Research Council, 1921–24. He received honorary degrees from Clark University (1909), Groningen (1914), the University of Chicago (1916), and his alma mater (1925).

On July 3, 1893, Van Vleck married Hester Laurence Raymond of North Lyme, Conn. Their only child, John Hasbrouck, became professor of mathematical physics at Harvard. Edward Van Vleck and his wife shared a love of art and travel; they had a distinguished collection of Japanese prints, to which they added on a trip around the world following his retirement. Van Vleck died in Madison, Wis., shortly before his eightieth birthday, of arteriosclerosis. He was buried in Madison. A hall at the University of Wisconsin was named for him in 1963. Although there had been isolated creative figures before his time, Van Vleck belonged to that generation of mathematicians in the United States which laid the foundations for the continuous growth of mathematical research and teaching.

[Rudolph E. Langer and Mark H. Ingraham in Nat. Acad. Sci., *Biog. Memoirs*, vol. XXX (1957); Program of Univ. of Wis. Dedication Dinner for E. B. Van Vleck Hall, May 1963, with addresses by M. H. Ingraham and Warren Weaver; obituary by George D. Birkhoff in Am. Math. Soc., *Bull.*, Jan. 1944; B. H. Camp, *Science at Wesleyan, 1831–1942* (1967); R. A. Rosenbaum in *Wesleyan Univ. Alumnus*, Nov. 1956.]

D. J. STRUIK

VERITY, GEORGE MATTHEW (Apr. 22, 1865–Nov. 6, 1942), steel manufacturer, was born in East Liberty, Ohio, the younger of two children and only son of Jonathan and Mary Ann (Deaton) Verity. His father's family, of French Huguenot origin, had emigrated from Yorkshire, England, to Ohio in 1831; his mother was of colonial Virginia descent. She died when her son was two, and for the next two years, until their father's remarriage, the children lived with their maternal grandparents. Jonathan Verity was a poorly paid Methodist minister whose assignments kept him moving from one part of Ohio to another, and George, with little opportunity to make lasting friendships, had a lonely, impoverished childhood. He attended various schools, finally graduating from the high school in Georgetown, Ohio, in 1883. When his father moved to a new pastorate in Cincinnati, George attended Woodward High School for a few months and then took an eight-month course at Nelson's Business College. He began his business career in 1884 as manager of the W. C. Standish Grocery Company in Cincinnati. By 1887 he had become convinced that a competing company posed a serious threat to the firm's existence and persuaded the widowed Mrs. Standish to sell out. On Oct. 19 of that year he married her daughter, Jennie M. Standish; they had three children, Calvin, Leah, and Sara.

Verity next secured a position with the Sagendorph Iron Roofing and Corrugating Company of Cincinnati, and in 1888 became its manager. The firm, which manufactured sheet metal roofing, was in receivership, but Verity introduced new bookkeeping methods and, through careful supervision of production and a vigorous sales campaign, nursed it back to financial health. After a fire nearly destroyed the company's plant, he took the lead in reorganizing it in 1891 as the American Steel Roofing Company, becoming its vice-president and general manager. During the 1890's, a decade of cannibalism among industrial competitors, he was active in forming an association of producers of sheet metal building materials and nearly effected a corporate merger of twenty-five of them in 1899. Shortly thereafter, he became involved in a plan to organize a company to construct a sheet-steel

rolling mill. Ordinarily such mills bought steel bar from Pittsburgh and rolled it into sheets, but Verity and William Simpson, a former tin plate manufacturer, decided to become self-sufficient by erecting their own open-hearth furnace for making steel. After much difficulty, the two men were able to raise $500,000 to construct facilities in Middletown, Ohio.

Incorporated in 1899 as the American Rolling Mill Company (Armco), with Verity as president, the company experienced early financial and production crises, but soon won some repute for bringing together an open-hearth furnace, bar mill, sheet mill, and galvanizing shop to provide a continuous chain of production. With a rising demand for steel, the company prospered; by 1904 its capitalization had risen from $500,000 to $1,400,000 and the number of employees from 350 to 1,000.

What role Verity played in the initial and subsequent success of Armco is difficult to assess. Though a resolute and industrious man, he was not a financial, marketing, or mechanical genius, but he had the ability to select line and staff men from whom he could elicit a full measure of effort. Some impressive innovations took place under his presidency. In cooperation with the Westinghouse Electric and Manufacturing Company before World War I, Armco developed steel with magnetic permeability for use with dynamos, motors, generators, and transformers. During the same period the company successfully experimented with "ingot iron," which resisted corrosion and was therefore especially useful for making culverts and wire fencing. In the early 1920's Verity helped commit his company to the construction of a revolutionary continuous steel mill invented by John Butler Tytus [Supp. 3]; the mill was the prototype of many others that increased production of steel nationally. Through such ventures, Verity's company found an array of specialized markets. Armco was never one of the giants in the steel industry, but under Verity's leadership it became one of the leading middle-size steel producers in the nation.

Verity was a pioneer in welfare capitalism, introducing the eight-hour day and a variety of recreational and safety programs to Armco plants. He was also active in many projects involving the health, education, and recreation of the entire community. He won praise as a beneficent employer and civic leader, though he was occasionally accused of paternalism in his relations with employees and the community. As an industrialist, he exemplified the traditional rags-to-riches story of the businessman who, without special advantages or abilities, achieved success

by pluck and diligence. He died at his home in Middletown, Ohio, in 1942, shortly after suffering a stroke, and was buried there in Woodside Cemetery.

[Manuscript materials relating to Verity are held by his family. Christy Borth's *True Steel: The Story of George Matthew Verity and His Associates* (1941), though reverential and uncritical, is a basic source. Of some value is a typed manuscript, "Biog. of Geo. M. Verity," in the files of the Public Relations Dept. of Armco. George C. Crout and Wilfred D. Vorhis, "John Butler Tytus," *Ohio Hist.*, Summer 1967, provides in its notes a bibliography of sources relating to Verity and the development of Armco. Verity wrote several articles on Armco; these and his addresses that were published in pamphlet form may be found in the General Office of the company and in the Middletown (Ohio) Public Library. Portraits of him may be seen in several of the principal offices of Armco.]

CARL M. BECKER

VINCENT, GEORGE EDGAR (Mar. 21, 1864–Feb. 1, 1941), adult educator, sociologist, university and foundation president, was born in Rockford, Ill., the only child of the Rev. John Heyl Vincent [*q.v.*] and Elizabeth (Dusenbury) Vincent. His father, of Pennsylvania background, went on from his Methodist pastorate in Rockford to become executive head of the denomination's Sunday School Union in New York City (1866–88), bishop of Buffalo, and co-founder of the Chautauqua Institution. George Vincent attended the public schools of Plainfield, N. J., prepared for college at the Pingry School in Elizabeth, and graduated from Yale, B.A., in 1885. Much of his education, however, resulted from association with his father in the Chautauqua Institution, which gave him extensive contacts with eminent persons in public life, scholarship, and organized religion.

Unlike some of its traveling namesakes, Bishop Vincent's Chautauqua was a serious attempt to bring together adults seeking knowledge with academic experts and public figures who would give them lectures and lessons. Following his graduation from college, the son was brought into all aspects of the work. His first post (1886) was as literary editor of the Chautauqua Press. In 1888 he became vice-principal of instruction, with responsibility for the educational program. Pursuing his work with Chautauqua along with the academic career he began in 1892, Vincent advanced to principal of instruction in 1898 and to president of the Chautauqua Institution in 1907, a position he held until his demanding duties at the University of Minnesota necessitated his resignation in 1915. Thereafter he continued to serve on the board of trustees and spent a part of nearly every summer at Chautauqua. In the Chautauqua program Vincent deemphasized in-dividual moral improvement and stressed contemporary social relations and conditions. He himself was an unusually able, poised, and witty lecturer, and his addresses on such topics as "What Is the Public Mind?" "The Theory of Crowds and Mobs," and "Public Opinion and Democracy" were among the most exhilarating delivered in the Chautauqua amphitheater. Lecture series which he organized on social problems featured addresses by Jane Addams [Supp. 1], Florence Kelley [Supp. 1], and other authorities.

At Chautauqua, Vincent became acquainted with William Rainey Harper [*q.v.*], the energetic president of the University of Chicago, who persuaded him to enroll there in the graduate department of sociology—the first such department in America—when the university opened in 1892. In 1894 Vincent joined with Prof. Albion W. Small [*q.v.*], the head of the department, in writing *An Introduction to the Study of Society,* an early text for use in college courses. He received the doctorate two years later; his dissertation was published as *The Social Mind and Education* (1897). Appointed an instructor at Chicago in 1895, he advanced through the academic ranks to professor in 1904. His scholarly interests centered in the new field of collective psychology, especially in the application of its findings to educational theory and practice. The fragmentation of education which had resulted from specialization could be counteracted, he believed, by the creation of courses of study built on the insights of social psychology. He was a charter member of the American Sociological Society, served as its president in 1916–17, and was associate editor of the *American Journal of Sociology* from 1895, when it began publication, until 1915.

Always interested in educational problems, Vincent was drawn into administration at the University of Chicago in 1900, when he became dean of the junior colleges, which were responsible for instructing and advising students in their first two years. Vincent encouraged greater flexibility, successfully urging the abolition of Latin as a requirement for the S.B. and Ph.B. degrees and a less restrictive distribution system. Perhaps influenced by his happy undergraduate experience at Yale, he was eager to create opportunities for students to form friendships. The heterogeneous character of the student body, especially among the men, had worked against the development of the cohesive student life Vincent valued, and he supported the foundation of clubs and residential houses. In 1907 he became dean of the faculties of arts, literature, and science, a position which put him in closer touch with the teaching and scholarly activities of the academic departments.

Vincent's successful performance in administration led naturally to his being considered for a university presidency, and in 1911 he left Chicago to become the third president of the University of Minnesota. Although he remained there only six years, his vigorous and constructive leadership left a lasting mark. The effects were most pronounced in the long-neglected professional schools. Several of these had relied upon part-time teachers instead of a regularly appointed, full-time faculty. Owing to retirements and resignations, Vincent was able to appoint new deans in nearly all the schools, choosing men like Guy Stanton Ford as dean of the graduate school and Lotus D. Coffman [Supp. 2] as dean of the college of education, both of whom were among his successors in the Minnesota presidency. Major struggles between the president and recalcitrant faculties occurred in the medical school and the college of engineering. Over the opposition of the medical faculty, Vincent forged a mutually profitable connection with the Mayo Clinic to provide advanced medical training. Graduate study in arts and sciences received unprecedented support from the president's office, with the result that Minnesota became a major Midwestern institution for graduate work. Other schools, from agriculture to law, felt Vincent's invigorating impulse. Always, the new men he brought in and those on the faculty whom he supported were, like himself, forceful leaders with definite and constructive plans.

At Minnesota Vincent also enlarged and systematized financial support and procedure. He enjoyed good relations with the state legislature, whose appropriations for instructional expenses increased 80 percent during his tenure. A modern system of accounting was introduced, including the first budget in the university's history. The president, however, had no intention of being, as he put it, a "construction engineer," and expenditures for capital improvements dropped sharply. The Chautauqua influence may be seen in the support Vincent gave at Minnesota to popular education. There was a marked increase in campus events of a mixed social, educational, and cultural character, open to the public. The extension service was developed. A touring exhibition of lectures, plays, recitals, and readings, called "University Week," visited the cities and towns of the state to extend and sell the university and its benefits to the people. In sum, Vincent arrived at Minnesota at a critical moment in its history when it stood poised between college and university, ready to respond to a firm

guiding hand. In the view of Dean Ford, Vincent's presidency, brief as it was, marked a "second founding."

George Vincent resigned from the University of Minnesota in 1917 in order to become president of the Rockefeller Foundation, succeeding John D. Rockefeller, Jr. Already familiar with the Rockefeller philanthropies through his association with the University of Chicago and his membership, after 1914, on the General Education Board, Vincent used his powers of witty, lucid, and dramatic expression to explain the foundation's objectives to a large American and international audience. The intentions of the Rockefeller Foundation had been challenged in Congress and the press when a federal charter was unsuccessfully sought between 1910 and 1913, and again in 1915 following a controversial excursion by the foundation into problems of industrial relations. Vincent's principal achievement was to convince the public of the foundation's integrity and its disinterested dedication to public service, a task made possible by the fact that he manifestly possessed the same qualities. Important activities undertaken during his term included international medical and health relief during the First World War, disease control, support for schools of public health, and grants for improvements in medical education. Just before his retirement in 1929, a reorganization was carried through, consolidating the Laura Spelman Rockefeller Memorial with the Rockefeller Foundation and giving the foundation new programs in the natural and social sciences and the humanities to complement the activities of its International Health Division and Division of the Medical Sciences.

Vincent had married Louise Mary Palmer, daughter of Henry Wilbur Palmer, formerly attorney general of Pennsylvania, in Wilkes-Barre on Jan. 8, 1890. They had three children: Isabel Darlington, John Henry, and Elizabeth. In retirement Vincent continued to take an active part in public affairs, lecturing frequently. In 1931 he served on President Hoover's Public Works Commission to reduce unemployment, and from 1935 to 1937 was chairman of a survey of New York City hospitals which recommended procedural reforms and additional public hospital facilities for the poor. He died of pneumonia in New York City in 1941, in his seventy-seventh year, and was buried at Portville, N. Y., the home of his mother's family.

[Jesse L. Hurlbut, *The Story of Chautauqua* (1921); Rebecca Richmond, *Chautauqua* (1943); Joseph E. Gould, *The Chautauqua Movement* (1961); Richard J. Storr, *Harper's University: The Beginnings* (1966); *The Idea and Practice of General Edu-*

cation: *An Account of the College of the Univ. of Chicago* (1950); James Gray, *The Univ. of Minnesota, 1851–1951* (1951) and *Open Wide the Door* (1958); Rockefeller Foundation, *Annual Reports, 1917–29*; Raymond B. Fosdick, *The Story of the Rockefeller Foundation* (1952); Robert Shaplen, *Toward the Well-Being of Mankind: Fifty Years of the Rockefeller Foundation* (1964); obituaries in *Am. Jour. of Sociology*, Mar. 1941 (by E. W. Burgess), *Am. Sociological Rev.*, Apr. 1941, and Yale Univ., *Obituary Record of Graduates*, 1940–41.]

JOHN BARNARD

WAITE, HENRY MATSON (May 15, 1869–Sept. 1, 1944), civil engineer and public administrator, was born in Toledo, Ohio, the second son and second child of Henry Selden Waite and Ione (Brown) Waite. His maternal grandfather, Joseph W. Brown, was a brother of Jacob W. Brown [q.v.] and a prominent figure in the early history of Michigan, serving as territorial chief justice and as major general of the state militia. His paternal grandfather, Morrison R. Waite [q.v.], was Chief Justice of the United States. Waite's father, who had been born in Connecticut, moved west to Ohio around 1850, served for a time as assistant city engineer of Maumee, and then settled at nearby Toledo, where he went into business.

Henry Waite was educated in the public schools of Toledo and at the Massachusetts Institute of Technology. Following his graduation in 1890 with a B.S. degree in civil engineering, he found work as a transitman with a surveying crew on the Cleveland, Cincinnati, Chicago & St. Louis Railway, and in 1892 advanced to engineer of maintenance of way. The following year he took a position with the Cincinnati, New Orleans & Texas Pacific Railway, serving first as division engineer (1893–99), then successively as bridge engineer, roadmaster, and superintendent of the railway's Cincinnati division (1899–1905), and finally as superintendent of its Chattanooga division (1905–07). From 1907 to 1909 he was general superintendent of the Seaboard Air Line Railway. He then left the railroad industry to become vice-president and chief engineer of the Clinchfield Coal Corporation in Dante, Va.

Waite entered public service in 1912 as chief engineer of the City of Cincinnati. Two years later, when Dayton, Ohio, adopted the city manager form of municipal government, Waite was appointed city manager there. Dayton was still recovering from the disastrous Ohio Valley floods of 1913, and Waite immediately initiated a flood-control program that eventually put an end to the annual destruction wrought by the Ohio River and its tributaries. An able and public-spirited administrator, he reorganized the

city government, employing experts where needed, and energetically promoted a more efficient system of food inspection, a correctional farm for workhouse prisoners, free legal aid and employment bureaus, and new recreational centers. He left this position in 1918, following America's entry into World War I, in order to serve in Europe as a colonel in the Army Corps of Engineers.

On his return to civilian life in 1919, Waite became vice-president and chief engineer of the Lord Construction Company of New York City, and the following year president of its subsidiary, the Lord Dry Dock Corporation. He soon resigned, however, to establish an independent consulting practice in New York, which he maintained until 1927. In that year he was appointed chief engineer of the newly organized Cincinnati Union Terminal Company, with responsibility for the planning and construction of a new union station in Cincinnati. Begun in 1929, this proved to be the last of the great metropolitan railway terminals. Since its track and approach system required the unification of rail lines previously disposed in the most disorganized pattern of any American city, it embodied many novel structural features. It was also the first big station to be designed (by the achitectural firm of Fellheimer and Wagner) in the modern style.

After completion of the Cincinnati Union Terminal in 1933, Waite went to Washington, D. C., to help in the planning of one of the emergency relief agencies of President Franklin D. Roosevelt, the Public Works Administration. Together with Col. George R. Spalding of the Army Corps of Engineers, he organized a tentative staff, and when the PWA came into being in June, Secretary of the Interior Harold L. Ickes appointed Waite as its deputy administrator, a post which carried the responsibility of deciding the merits of the hundreds of projects submitted for federal aid. Waite's plan for a decentralized organization, however, was opposed by Ickes, who felt it jeopardized his role as administrator. Waite resigned in September 1934, but remained on friendly terms with Ickes, who privately described him as a man of "imagination and character" (*Secret Diary*, I, 193).

Waite next became the director (1934–37) of the Regional Department of Economic Security, a nongovernmental agency at Cincinnati, where he supervised an unemployment survey. He returned to federal service as technical adviser to the National Youth Administration and consultant to the National Resources Committee (later the National Resources Planning Board) from 1937 to 1940. Meanwhile, in 1937, he had established a consulting office in Cincinnati. At the request of Ickes, he also served as chairman of the transportation committee of the Chicago Subway Commission, under whose auspices the city's first subway was built (1938–43). From 1940 until his death he was director of the War Projects Unit of the federal Bureau of the Budget.

For his public achievements at Dayton and Cincinnati, Waite received honorary degrees from Miami University at Oxford, Ohio, and the University of Cincinnati. His versatility in professional life was matched in private life by a lively interest in music, literature, painting, and the theatre. On Apr. 15, 1914, he married Mary Mason Brown of Lexington, Ky. They had no children. Waite's government service in World War II took him again to Washington, D. C., and it was there that he died, at the age of seventy-five, of bronchial asthma. He was buried in Spring Grove Cemetery, Cincinnati.

[Memoir of Waite in Am. Soc. of Civil Engineers, *Transactions,* CX (1945), 1631–35; obituaries in *Civil Engineering,* Oct. 1944, p. 447, and *Technology Rev.,* Dec. 1944, p. viii; *Nat. Cyc. Am. Biog.,* Current Vol. D, pp. 30–31; *Who Was Who in America,* vol. II (1950); Chester E. Rightor, *City Manager in Dayton* (1919). See also Harold L. Ickes, *Back to Work: The Story of PWA* (1935) and *The Secret Diary of Harold L. Ickes* (2 vols., 1953–54); and J. Kerwin Williams, *Grants-in-Aid under the Public Works Administration* (1939). On the Cincinnati Union Terminal, see Carl W. Condit, *Am. Building Art: The Twentieth Century* (1961). On Waite's maternal grandfather, see W. B. Hartzog, "Gen. Joseph Brown," *Mich. Hist. Mag.,* July–Oct. 1921.]
CARL W. CONDIT

WALKER, STUART ARMSTRONG (Mar. 4, 1880–Mar. 13, 1941), playwright, theatrical producer, and film director, was born in Augusta, Ky., the only son of Cliff Stuart Walker and Matilda Taliaferro (Armstrong) Walker. His father, who had come from North Carolina, was in 1880 a clerk on the Ohio River steamer *Bonanza* and afterward a railroad freight agent until he acquired business interests in Louisiana. The family lived in Covington, Ky., across the river from Cincinnati, Ohio. Stuart attended Woodward High School in Cincinnati and received a bachelor's degree from the University of Cincinnati's College of Engineering in 1903.

A toy theatre, given to him by his father during a childhood bout with measles, began his lifelong fascination with the theatre, which always remained to him a place of wonder and mystery. At the University of Cincinnati he was one of the founders of the Comedy Club, writing and acting in some original playlets. Upon graduation he went to work as a shipping clerk at the Southern Creosoting Company of Slidell, La.,

but soon found the lumber trade dreary and uninspiring. In 1908 he enrolled in the American Academy of Dramatic Arts in New York.

The following year Walker met David Belasco [q.v.] and appeared in a minor role in Belasco's production of *Is Matrimony a Failure?* Thereafter he served the producer for several years as play reader, actor, and director. From this exposure to the lavish, flamboyant, often vulgar realism of Belasco's productions Walker emerged with the integrity of his theatrical vision intact; his slim, boyish good looks and wire-rimmed spectacles belied a fierce individuality. In 1914 he became a director for Jessie Bonstelle [Supp. 1] at her theatres in Buffalo and Detroit.

After approximately a year with Miss Bonstelle, Walker struck out on his own, utilizing his engineering training and his theatrical experience to create what he called his Portmanteau Theatre. Billed as "The Theatre That Comes to You," this was a completely self-contained mobile unit. Scenery, lighting equipment, and properties traveled in cartons which were overturned to form the stage floor, and the stage could be erected within an hour. Stagecraft and decor were simple, but Walker's innovative and dramatic lighting techniques produced effects of beauty (he introduced the "X-ray" system of stage lighting in 1915 and, in 1918, the independent spotlight system, which became standard theatrical practice). His ideal was to make imaginative drama of high quality available to large numbers of Americans in every part of the nation.

Walker was a writer of talent, as well as a gifted director and technician, and when the Portmanteau Theatre first opened at the Christodora Settlement House in New York City on July 14, 1915, its repertory contained two of his original plays, *The Trimplet* and *Six Who Pass While the Lentils Boil.* Both contained strong elements of fantasy, which was Walker's forte, and demanded an imaginative response from the audience, as did the best of his later plays, *The Lady of the Weeping Willow Tree* and *Jonathan Makes a Wish.* Two volumes of his work, *Portmanteau Plays* and *More Portmanteau Plays,* appeared in 1917 and 1919, respectively, and in 1921 Walker published *Portmanteau Adaptations,* which included his version of *Gammer Gurton's Needle,* one of the earliest English farces. He also adapted *The Book of Job* and Booth Tarkington's *Seventeen,* and later toured successfully with both.

With its repertory of fourteen plays (for which Walker drew heavily on the works of the Irish dramatist Lord Dunsany, whose mystical parables suited his taste and the Portmanteau's limitations), the Portmanteau played at two theatres in New York and then traveled through the Midwest. Walker regarded the repertory system as the best way to ensure the artistic development of individual actors and the entire company, and he was one of the first to introduce the "apprentice system" for training young actors. There were no "stars" in his company, only talented young apprentices who were capable of exchanging roles within the repertory; they were devoted to Walker, and several later became stars, including Spring Byington, Kay Francis, Lillian Ross, and Blanche Yurka. In his Portmanteau, Walker caught the essence of the "little theatre" movement, which, originating in the art theatres of Europe, was being imported to the United States as an antidote to the commercial mediocrity of the American stage. In his noncommercialism (he originally funded the project himself), his advocacy of the poetic in dramatic literature, his championing of theatre for everyone, his willingness to experiment, and his desire to foster the growth of young talent, Walker emerges as an unassuming and often overlooked hero of the movement.

In 1917 he abandoned his portable stage and became resident director of the Indianapolis Repertory Company, a position he held until 1923. From 1922 to 1931 he directed the Cincinnati Repertory Company (after 1929 called the Stuart Walker Repertory Company); for two years of this period (1926–28) he concurrently directed the Indianapolis company again. Though he received less attention than he had with his unique Portmanteau, Walker established an impressive record of experimentation, putting on several hundred plays—among them a sizable number of premieres of plays by foreign and native authors —continuing his work with the repertory idea and the training of young actors, and achieving surprising financial success.

In 1930 Walker grew restless and turned to motion pictures. Originally engaged by Paramount as a screen writer and acting coach, he soon was directing his own films. At first these were conventional studio products (*Tonight Is Ours, The Eagle and the Hawk, Evenings for Sale*), but during an interim (1934–35) with Universal Pictures he made *Great Expectations* and *The Mystery of Edwin Drood*. He returned to Paramount in 1936 as an associate producer and as such supervised the screen version of *Seventeen* (1940) and a succession of "Bulldog Drummond" features.

Walker never married, although in 1926 he adopted a son, Arthur Helm, whom he had met

through a Kentucky relative and who took his name. He died of a heart attack at the age of sixty-one in Beverly Hills, Calif., and after an Episcopal funeral service was buried next to his parents in Spring Grove Cemetery, Cincinnati. Though Stuart Walker was creatively engaged until his death, his noteworthy contribution was to the theatre during the years 1915–30. Impelled by a vision of fine and exciting drama becoming part of the American experience, he brought people who would never see the lights of Broadway into the mainstream of American theatrical life.

[Biographical sources: *Nat. Cyc. Am. Biog.,* XXXVIII, 305-06; *Who Was Who in America,* vol. I (1942); *Who's Who in the Theatre* (9th ed., 1939); obituaries in the *N. Y. Times, Cincinnati Enquirer, Louisville Courier-Jour.,* and *Indianapolis Star,* Mar. 14, 1941; and, on his father, Cincinnati city directories, 1879–1913 (courtesy of Cincinnati Hist. Soc.). For an understanding of the theatrical period and Walker's place in the little theatre movement, see Vandervoort Sloan in *Drama,* Feb. 1918; Montrose J. Moses, "The Season's Plays," *Rev. of Revs.,* Jan. 1925; Kenneth Macgowan, *Footlights across America* (1929); and, especially, Constance D'Arcy Mackay, *The Little Theatre in the U. S.* (1917). There are two useful articles in the *Theatre* magazine: Stuart Walker's "The Spirit of Youth Behind the Footlights" (Feb. 1918) and Kate Milner Rabb's "Stuart Walker Delights Indianapolis" (Nov. 1921). Edward Hale Bierstadt's introductory remarks to each volume in Walker's Portmanteau series present an uneven but valuable history of Stuart Walker's theatre. The Theatre Collection of the N. Y. Public Lib. at Lincoln Center has extensive materials on Walker, including some letters, photographs of the Portmanteau Theatre, photos and programs of his activities at Cincinnati, and his own collection of scrapbooks about the stage and cinema. A photograph of Walker with a working model of his Portmanteau Theatre appears in *More Portmanteau Plays.*]

RICHARD MOODY

WALLER, FATS. See WALLER, THOMAS WRIGHT.

WALLER, THOMAS WRIGHT (May 21, 1904–Dec. 15, 1943), jazz pianist, composer, and entertainer, known as "Fats" Waller, was born in New York City, the youngest son and seventh in a family of twelve children, six of whom died in infancy. His parents, Edward Martin Waller and Adeline (Lockett) Waller, had moved from Virginia sometime in the 1880's, settling first in Manhattan's Negro community in Greenwich Village and later moving uptown to Harlem. Both parents were deeply religious; his father, who had his own trucking business, was a deacon of Harlem's Abyssinian Baptist Church. The family also had a musical tradition: Thomas's mother played the piano and the organ, and his paternal grandfather, Adolph Waller, had toured the South as a violinist shortly after the Civil War.

Young Waller began learning the piano before

he was six, with his mother as teacher, and soon progressed to the organ. His musical interests became so all-absorbing that he dropped out of New York's DeWitt Clinton High School at the age of fourteen. The next year he won a local piano contest and was hired as organist at the Lincoln Theatre in Harlem, providing background music for silent films. The death of his mother in 1920 left him disconsolate, and the following year, at seventeen, he married a childhood friend, Edith Hatchett. They had a son, Thomas Wright, but the marriage was short-lived, and in 1926 Waller married Anita Priscilla Rutherford, by whom he had two more sons, Maurice and Ronald.

While still in his teens, Waller attracted the attention of established Harlem jazz musicians, including the brilliant pianist-composer James P. Johnson. Johnson offered the youngster personal instruction and a basic grounding in the music business of the period, then dominated by publishers of sheet music and firms producing rolls for player-pianos. Waller was quickly accepted into the fraternity of older ragtime-based composer-pianists that included, besides Johnson, Willie "The Lion" Smith, Luckey Roberts, Eubie Blake, and Clarence Williams. By 1922 Waller had cut his first piano roll, had turned out several phonograph recordings for the Okeh label, and had become a composer by reworking an old piece called "Boy in the Boat" into a new number, "Squeeze Me."

He composed with remarkable ease and swiftness, often conceiving and completing a song in less than half an hour. This gift led him naturally to writing scores for musical shows, particularly the elaborate revues staged by Harlem nightclubs for white audiences. The first of these, *Keep Shufflin'* (1928), produced his song "Willow Tree." The songs for another 1928 show, called *Load of Coal* (most of these productions included stereotyped, often offensive, roles for black performers, and even artists of Waller's rank had to live with the facts of bigotry), included "Honeysuckle Rose," "Zonky," and "My Fate Is in Your Hands." His first big success in popular song writing was "Ain't Misbehavin'," which he and his lyricist, Andy Razaf, wrote in 1929 for *Connie's Hot Chocolates*. Other successful songs, tossed off with Waller's usual facility, were "I've Got a Feeling I'm Falling," "Blue, Turning Grey over You," "Keepin' out of Mischief Now," and "I'm Crazy about My Baby."

More important musically are Waller's many excellent piano solos. "Clothes Line Ballet," "Viper's Drag," "African Ripples," "Handful of Keys," "London Suite," "Jitterbug Waltz," and "The Rusty Pail" are of permanent interest for both form and content. The last was performed on the pipe organ; Waller was the only jazz organist of consequence during his lifetime. A deeply committed jazz musician, he continually developed his art, studying composition with Carl Bohm at the Juilliard School of Music and, during a Chicago engagement, Bach with Leopold Godowsky [Supp. 2].

Waller had a warm, easy personality and an irrepressible sense of humor that made him a natural entertainer. By 1925 he was touring in cabaret and vaudeville appearances. In 1931, for the first time, he made a set of recordings on which he sang as well as played. His vocals—sometimes facetious, sometimes raucous—made an immediate hit, and thereafter the entertainer came to obscure the creative pianist. His boisterous singing and lilting playing were ideally suited to radio; he was a pioneer performer on the air, starting at a small Newark station in 1923, and by the early 1930's had his own program on the Columbia network. He made the first of several trips abroad in 1932, and after 1934 spent most of his professional time on the road. His energy and conviviality seemed limitless as he clowned his way over the United States, around the British Isles, and across Europe. As a youth he had earned the nickname "Fats." In maturity nearly six feet tall, with large hands that easily played octaves and spanned even thirteenths without difficulty, he grew larger in girth, weighing close to 300 pounds. His reputation for consuming vast amounts of liquor encouraged fans and acquaintances to challenge the big man to ever greater excesses.

By 1943 he had reached an apex of popularity and commanded a large income at a time when most jazz musicians were struggling to subsist. Ignoring his failing health, during that year Waller appeared in the film *Stormy Weather*, turned out the score for another show (*Early to Bed*), made tours to entertain the armed forces, and still maintained a crushing schedule of one-night stands and theatre performances. Early in December, while in Hollywood to play an engagement, he suffered an attack of influenza but started back to New York by train to spend the holidays with his family in St. Albans, Long Island. He was found dead in his Pullman compartment when the train stopped at Kansas City, Mo.; an autopsy established the immediate cause of death as bronchial pneumonia. After funeral services at the Abyssinian Baptist Church, he was cremated at the Fresh Pond Crematory, Middle Village, N. Y.

From the start "Fats" Waller's life was filled

with paradoxes. His youth had encompassed both a middle-class churchgoing home and New York's speakeasy subculture. A loving family man and a generous friend, he was careless about money and could never remember to support his firstborn child; on at least one occasion he spent time in jail for nonsupport. A dominating, life-of-the-party figure who on occasion improvised at the piano for stag films, he periodically retreated to an organ loft to play spirituals, Bach, or extemporized sonatas. He scorned elaborate arrangements or even minimal planning for his recording sessions, but his best formal compositions were meticulously developed, and in them he explored the expressive potential of both piano and organ with the care and precision of a Chopin or a Liszt. Perhaps the best measure of Waller's musical contribution is to be found in the stature of those pianists who regard him as a major influence in their development. They include men older than Waller, such as Duke Ellington; contemporaries such as Count Basie, Joe Sullivan, Mary Lou Williams, and Art Tatum; and younger players like Erroll Garner, Ralph Sutton, Dick Wellstood, and Don Ewell.

[Ed Kirkeby, ed., *Ain't Misbehavin'* (1966), an informal narrative of Waller's life by his personal manager (with excellent discography); Charles Fox, *Fats Waller* (1961), a good paperback summary of Waller's life and music; John R. T. Davies, *The Music of Thomas "Fats" Waller* (1953), a careful discography, with reprinted essays on Waller; Richard Hadlock, *Jazz Masters of the Twenties* (1965), chapter on Waller and James P. Johnson; Gunther Schuller, *Early Jazz: Its Roots and Musical Development* (1968), a musicological study, which includes a chapter on Harlem pianists, including Waller; André Hodeir, *Jazz: Its Evolution and Essence* (1956), which includes a short but valuable musical analysis of Waller as composer and improviser. See also: Samuel B. Charters and Leonard Kunstadt, *Jazz: A Hist. of the N. Y. Scene* (1962), chapter on Waller; Nat Shapiro and Nat Hentoff, eds., *Hear Me Talkin' to Ya* (1955), collected comments of jazz musicians; Willie ("The Lion") Smith and George Hoefer, *Music on My Mind* (1964); Mezz Mezzrow and Bernard Wolfe, *Really the Blues* (1946).]

RICHARD B. HADLOCK

WALLER, WILLARD WALTER (July 30, 1899–July 26, 1945), sociologist, was born in Murphysboro, Ill., the older of the two surviving sons of Elbert and Margaret Dora (Clendenin) Waller. His mother was the daughter of a physician of Scots ancestry; orphaned at an early age, she had been reared by an aunt as a Catholic. His father, the son of a prosperous pioneer farmer of the Baptist faith, was a schoolteacher who farmed in the summers; upon losing his farm to creditors, he became a full-time school superintendent in successive small Illinois towns. A reform-minded moralist, he combined intellectual pursuits with a faculty for alienating people which cost him

friends and jobs, thus bringing him into unending conflict with his conventional wife, who decried his failures and ridiculed his high-mindedness. Their son was later to look back on this quarrelsome, insecure life as providing significant insights into family sociology.

After completing high school at Albion, Ill., in 1915, young Waller entered McKendree College at Lebanon, Ill. Two years later he transferred to the University of Illinois, where he studied sociology under Edward C. Hayes [Supp. 1]. A tour of duty in the navy in 1918 delayed his graduation by one semester. He received the B.A. in 1920 and, following a short stint as a reporter on the *Evansville* (Ind.) *Courier,* took a job near Chicago, Ill., at the Morgan Park Military Academy, where for the next six years he taught Latin and French. On Jan. 3, 1922, he married Thelma A. Jones of Evansville.

Although Waller loved teaching, he found the high school atmosphere intellectually stultifying and began taking courses in 1921 on a part-time basis at the University of Chicago, at first in education, then in law, and finally in sociology under Chicago's distinguished faculty. He completed the M.A. degree in 1925. Having separated from his wife, he transferred to the University of Pennsylvania, where he was both instructor and graduate student. A roommate acquainted Waller with psychoanalytic techniques, which he later used in giving lay therapy and in analyzing case studies. Though formerly a Methodist, he now became antireligious, cultivated a cynical manner, and prided himself on the tough-minded iconoclasm which was to become the hallmark of his sociological investigations. He received the Ph.D. in 1929 with a study of divorce, *The Old Love and the New* (1930), in which he analyzed the process by which married people become alienated from each other and provided original insights into the nature of marital dissolution and readjustment. It became a pattern for Waller, whose first marriage had ended in divorce, to rework his personal experience into his scholarly writing. On Aug. 13, 1929, he married Josephine Wilkins of Philadelphia; their children were Peter, Bruce, and Suzanne.

In the fall of 1929 Waller went to the University of Nebraska as an assistant professor of sociology. He quickly established himself as a popular teacher. Students responded enthusiastically to his unorthodox views, and he, in turn, took on the role of lay therapist and mentor. He fostered an unblinking social realism in his students, had them provide personal life histories and diaries as research data, and even urged them to write candid introspective studies of their own families.

Parents and fellow instructors complained about Waller's procedures, and when a university official discovered in February 1931 that his unmarried and pregnant daughter had been confidentially counseled by Waller, the young professor was immediately dismissed. Paid the balance of his salary, Waller moved to Chicago, where he completed his second book, *The Sociology of Teaching* (1932). This study depicted the school in terms of symbolic social interaction, where a nexus of small group relationships involved continual bargaining and conflict over the distribution of power within a precarious social order verging on collapse. To maintain the authority structure, he pointed out, thus required immense energy and constant attention.

Waller next (May 1931) joined the faculty of Pennsylvania State College (later University) as associate professor of sociology; he was promoted to professor in 1933. Here he continued to unmask the realities that he felt lay behind polite social fictions and sacrosanct institutions. He published two important studies in the *American Sociological Review,* "Social Problems and the Mores" (December 1936) and "The Rating and Dating Complex" (October 1937). In the first he contended that social problems are actually perpetuated by so-called respectable social institutions. In the second he analyzed student dating patterns and ratings of self and others, material which appeared also in his textbook, *The Family* (1938), which drew on his parents' marriage for illustration. This study of middle-class families as closed units of interacting personalities emphasized the conflicts and tensions that so frequently underlie the seeming stability of domestic life. In contrast to the bland, even squeamish, textbooks that preceded his, Waller's book used acerb epigrams, pointed literary allusions, and paradoxes to puncture the static, abstract, and idealized conception of the family. Written in a graceful style, it caught on outside academic circles, and Waller was soon giving advice to troubled married couples.

In 1937 he accepted the chairmanship of the sociology department at Wayne University in Detroit, but then negotiated his release to take an associate professorship at Barnard College, Columbia University. He utilized his location in New York City to broaden his activities. Partly because he was never promoted and partly because of his desire to implement constructively his iconoclastic views, he turned to publishing ventures, popular articles, and radio speeches on social policy, and his scholarly output declined sharply. The outbreak of war found him an isolationist, but he eventually accepted American participation in the conflict. Concerned about the long-term effects of the organization of American society into a war-making machine, he wrote *The Veteran Comes Back* (1944), a plea for a humane, planned demobilization of returning veterans. The average American, once made a soldier, he argued, would be so converted to military values that he would be unfitted for civilian life and in his confusion might turn to insurrection. The book was oversimplified, repetitious, unsophisticated, and non-sociological, but it sold well. Rejected for military service on physical grounds, Waller threw himself into touring the country to publicize the need for government programs to ease the adjustment of veterans. He died of a heart attack in the subway station near Columbia a few days before his forty-sixth birthday. His body was cremated.

Despite his early death, Waller made significant contributions to the social psychology of marriage and the family. He correctly foresaw that there was no necessary conflict between the "artistic" method he espoused and the quantitative, and his skilled use of the case study and of disciplined introspection added to the understanding of social interaction.

[Willard W. Waller, *On the Family, Education, and War* (1970), a selection of Waller's writings edited by William J. Goode, Frank F. Furstenberg, Jr., and Larry R. Mitchell, includes a list of his works and an extended biography by the editors. See also obituaries in *Am. Sociological Rev.,* Oct. 1945, and *N. Y. Times,* July 28, 1945; and the essay on Waller by Reuben L. Hill in the *Internat. Encyc. of the Social Sciences,* XVI, 443–45.]

LARRY R. MITCHELL

WALTER, EUGENE (Nov. 27, 1874–Sept. 26, 1941), playwright, was born in Cleveland, Ohio, the second son and second of at least two children of George Andrew Walter and his wife, Jennie (or June) King. His father was born in Pennsylvania of Connecticut parents; his mother was a native of London, England. George Walter, a bookkeeper, was active in amateur opera companies and musical programs as a singer and director, and his wife appeared in at least one amateur theatrical performance in Cleveland, in 1873.

Eugene's formal education was limited to public school in Cleveland. When he was "still in knickerbockers" his family moved to a logging camp in northern Michigan. At twelve, he worked his way back to Cleveland as a sailor on a Great Lakes schooner and afterward found a job as an office boy on the *Cleveland Press.* He soon rose to political reporter and assistant editor, but shortly thereafter was dismissed for insubordination. This pattern of rapid promotion followed by dismissal recurred in a series of newspaper jobs, reportedly because of his lack of objectivity on social and political issues. Nonetheless, at the *Plain Dealer* in Cleveland, the *News* in Detroit, the *Star* in Seattle, and the *Sun* and *Globe* in New York, Walter earned the reputation of being able to cover a big story effectively in less time than any other reporter.

Further experience broadened his background. At age fifteen he had briefly joined Troop H of the Sixth Cavalry, stationed at Fort Assiniboine in northern Montana. In April 1898, on the day war was declared against Spain, he enlisted in the 1st Ohio Volunteer Cavalry as a saddler, but his company did not leave the continental United States. Not long afterward, during one period of unemployment in the early 1900's, he went to Alaska in search of gold, returning in mid-winter by dog team through Canada.

Walter drew on his cavalry experience for his first play, *Sergeant James,* which was produced in Boston in 1902 but failed to reach Broadway. At this point the dark, stocky, energetic young man decided to serve a practical theatre apprenticeship and became an "advance man," crisscrossing the country to publicize "coming attractions" which ranged from Shakespearean productions to burlesque. Meanwhile he continued to write intermittently. Two lifelong friends, the producers Edgar and Arch Selwyn, finally persuaded him to stay with them and give full time to his scripts, and in 1905 he wrote *The Flag Station* and *Undertow.* Arch Selwyn, acting as his agent, failed to get a New York contract for *Undertow,* but arranged for fourteen simultaneous productions in stock, opening Apr. 15, 1907, in Los Angeles. These were a phenomenal success—unheard of for a play which had never appeared on Broadway—and with $8,000 from the first week's proceeds Walter retired for further play writing, living with the Selwyns in Southold, Long Island. *Paid in Full,* after failing in tryouts, reached Broadway in 1908 and enjoyed a lengthy success, and was followed later that year by *The Wolf,* which he wrote in a week. On Dec. 1, 1908, Walter married Charlotte Walker, a popular actress; many of his later plays were written with his wife in mind for the leading female role.

Walter now came into his most creative and successful period. He had learned and perfected the techniques of writing melodrama, the tricks of structure, characterization, and dialogue which produced the most popular fare on the American stage in the early years of the century. He was, as the critic Brooks Atkinson later called him, a "play carpenter" rather than a dramatist or artist, but he skillfully applied his craft to contemporary social situations which fascinated his audience. He wrote about the "middle class," which he defined as "those who are neither wealthy nor poor; neither dependent nor independent; but who exist through their years of life in constant apprehension of a curtailment of income, and without a trade which gives them the opportunity for quick re-employment, provided they are suddenly deprived of work." His main character was usually a woman, often motivated by a desire for security.

In 1909 David Belasco [Supp. 1] produced Walter's *The Easiest Way,* the story of an actress, formerly a rich man's mistress, who tries to clean up her life to win the love of a virtuous newspaperman but finds that sin is an "easier way" than starving. The play was an overwhelming critical and financial success. Walter's use of the novel device of an unhappy ending in which vice is triumphant caused him to be hailed as a great realist, the American Ibsen, the American Pinero. This extravagant acclaim colored the appraisal of all his later work; every subsequent play was compared unfavorably with *The Easiest Way.* Walter himself judged *Fine Feathers* (1911) a better play, but he had difficulty getting it produced.

Among his more notable works in the following years were *Just a Wife* (1910), *The Trail of the Lonesome Pine* (1911), and *The Little Shepherd of Kingdom Come* (1916), the last two adapted from popular novels by John William Fox [*q.v.*]. By 1918 Walter was participating in financing his own plays. *The Heritage* (1918) and *The Challenge* (1919), in which the central figures were men rather than women, reduced him to bankruptcy, but his plays continued to be produced in the 1920's, the most successful and best being *A Man's Name* (in collaboration with Marjorie Chase, 1921) and *Jealousy* (1928), adapted from a French drama by Louis Verneuil, which was his last play.

In the meantime Walter had begun a profitable connection with moving pictures. By 1917, film rights to a successful Broadway play would sell for a minimum of $10,000, and most of Walter's plays were made into popular films: *The Wolf* (1914), *Fine Feathers* (1915), *The Trail of the Lonesome Pine* (1916), in which Charlotte Walker made her first film appearance, and, of course, *The Easiest Way* (1917). (Sound versions of the last two appeared in the 1930's.) In later years, besides his authorship of the original play, Walter was sometimes credited with the screenplay or dialogue. He remained in New York City, where many of the feature silent films were made, until he was signed by

Radio pictures in 1929 and moved to Hollywood. From this time until his death he was almost always under contract to a movie studio. As contract writers usually did not receive screen credit, it is impossible to know exactly how much work he did.

Walter divorced Charlotte Walker on Apr. 3, 1930, charging her with desertion, and on Apr. 26 in Mexicali, Mexico, secretly married Mary Kissel, an artist's model. After a second divorce he married Mary Dorne, a stage actress, in 1941. He died of cancer that year in his Hollywood apartment and was buried in the Veterans Administration Cemetery in Los Angeles. A survivor from a more innocent era in the American theatre, when good craft was as warmly appreciated as good art, he never lost his ability to tell a dramatic and theatrical story with strong audience appeal.

[James J. Gilmore, "The Contributions of Eugene Walter to Am. Drama" (M.A. thesis, Univ. of Wash., 1939); John Parker, ed., *Who's Who in the Theatre* (9th ed., 1939); *Who Was Who in America*, vol. I (1942); obituary in *N. Y. Times*, Sept. 27, 1941; information about Walter's family from Cleveland city directories and the *Annals of Cleveland* (courtesy of Miss Ethel L. Robinson, Cleveland Public Lib.) and from the census of 1880 (courtesy of Mrs. Carl Main, Western Reserve Hist. Soc., Cleveland). The Nat. Archives and Record Service provided data on Walter's army career; death record from Calif. Dept. of Public Health. For estimates of Eugene Walter's place in the history of the American theatre, the following are useful: Walter Prichard Eaton, *The Am. Stage of Today* (1909) and *At the New Theatre and Others* (1910); Montrose J. Moses, *The Am. Dramatist* (1925); Arthur H. Quinn, *A Hist. of Am. Drama*, vol. II (1927); George Jean Nathan, *Art of the Night* (1928); and Brooks Atkinson, *Broadway* (1970). Montrose J. Moses, *Representative Plays by Am. Dramatists*, vol. III (1921), contains the text of *The Easiest Way* and valuable information on the playwright and the writing of his greatest success. Walter's *How to Write a Play* (1925) affords a revealing look at his dramatic technique and contains parts of three of his other plays: *Paid in Full*, *The Wolf*, and *Fine Feathers*. A portrait of Walter appears in *Arts & Decoration*, Dec. 14, 1920.]

GEORGE SAVAGE

WARD, HENRY BALDWIN (Mar. 4, 1865– Nov. 30, 1945), zoologist and parasitologist, was born in Troy, N. Y., one of four children and the older of the two sons of Richard Halsted Ward [*q.v.*], physician and microscopist, and Charlotte Allen (Baldwin) Ward. Both parents were natives of Bloomfield, N. J. Henry B. Ward attended the public schools of Troy and Williams College (his father's alma mater), from which he graduated, A.B., in 1885. After three years of teaching science in the Troy high school, he went to Europe in 1888 for graduate study in zoology, and for two years attended the universities of Göttingen, Freiburg, and Leipzig,

spending the vacation periods at the marine laboratories of Naples, Ville-Franche-sur-Mer, and Helgoland. He was particularly influenced by Prof. Rudolph Leuckart of Leipzig, an authority on the invertebrates and founder of the celebrated laboratory of parasitology. At Leipzig, Ward conceived the ambition to found a similar laboratory in the United States. Upon his return in 1890, he entered the graduate school of Harvard University, where he received the Ph.D. degree in 1892 with a dissertation on the marine nematomorph *Nectonema agile* Verrill, a species he had observed at Naples.

Ward was appointed instructor in zoology at the University of Michigan in 1892 but moved after a year to the University of Nebraska, at first as associate professor, from 1896 as professor. While at Nebraska he published a series of papers on parasites of man and discovered the presence in the United States of the human lung fluke, *Paragonimus*. He played a major role in developing a two-year premedical course and in 1902 became the first dean of the University of Nebraska College of Medicine, newly established at Lincoln in affiliation with the Omaha Medical College. In 1909, however, plans were made to move the Lincoln unit to the Omaha campus. When it became clear that, because of rivalries between the two medical faculties, Ward would not be retained as dean after the move, he resigned.

That fall he went to the University of Illinois as head of the department of zoology, a position he was to occupy with distinction until his retirement in 1933. In addition to teaching zoology at the undergraduate level, he established one of the first research laboratories in the United States to offer graduate work in parasitology. The large number of students who received the Ph.D. under his supervision later made significant contributions to the growth of this science. To provide an outlet for publishing the results of such research, he inaugurated in 1914, with the assistance of his colleagues Stephen A. Forbes [*q.v.*] and William Trelease [Supp. 3], the series of Illinois Biological Monographs. That same year he also founded the *Journal of Parasitology*, the first American publication devoted to the field; he continued to edit the journal until 1932, when he presented it to the American Society of Parasitologists to become its official organ.

Ward's research reflected in part his love of the outdoors. He early began biological research on the Great Lakes, at first for the Michigan Fish Commission, afterward for the United States Fish Commission. For many years, beginning in 1906, he conducted summer field investigations of the Alaska and Pacific salmon. Besides his papers on parasites, which dealt with such subjects as parasites of the human eye, the relations of animal parasites to disease, and the spread of fish tapeworm, he was the co-author, with George Chandler Whipple, of *Fresh-Water Biology* (1918), long a standard work. An active member of the Izaak Walton League of America, of which he was president, 1928–30, and of the National Wild Life Federation, Ward was deeply concerned with national problems of wildlife conservation and the pollution of streams.

Ward belonged to a large number of scientific societies and was a leader of many, including the American Microscopical Society (president, 1905), the American Society of Zoologists (president, 1912–14), and the American Society of Parasitologists, of which he was the first president when it was founded in 1925. He contributed significantly to the development of the American Association for the Advancement of Science, as secretary of Section F (zoology) in 1900, general secretary (1902), vice-president (1905), and permanent secretary (1933–37); and of the scientific honor society, Sigma Xi, as secretary (1904–21) and president (1922–23). Ward was influential also in university affairs. At Illinois he worked closely with President Edmund J. James [*q.v.*]; articulate and well-spoken, he was particularly effective on faculty committees. He received honorary doctorates from the universities of Cincinnati (1920), Oregon (1932), and Nebraska (1945) and from Williams College (1921).

Ward was a handsome, vigorous man, somewhat above average height. Aristocratic, autocratic, ambitious, and enthusiastic, he demanded excellence of himself and of others. On Sept. 11, 1894, he married Harriet Cecilia Blair of Chicago, who was teaching at the music school of the University of Nebraska. They had two daughters, Cecilia Blair and Charlotte Baldwin. Ward was a member of the Presbyterian Church. He died in Urbana, Ill., of a heart attack in his eighty-first year, and was buried there in Mount Hope Cemetery. Sometimes called the "father of American parasitology," he was to America what Leuckart had been to Germany.

[W. W. Cort, "Prof. Henry Baldwin Ward and the Jour. of Parasitology," *Jour. of Parasitology*, Dec. 1932; obituaries in *Science*, Dec. 28, 1945 (by W. W. Cort), and Am. Microscopical Soc., *Transactions*, Apr. 1946 (by James E. Ackert); *Am. Men of Sci.* (7th ed., 1944); *Nat. Cyc. Am. Biog.*, XXXV, 174–75; *Who Was Who in America*, vol. II (1950); tribute by C. E. McClung in Henry B. Ward and Edward Ellery, *Sigma Xi Half Century Record and Hist.* (1936); J. Jay Keegan, "An Inside Story of the Univ. of Nebr. College of Medicine from 1902 to 1929," *Nebr. State*

Medic. Jour., Mar. 1964; Eloise B. Cram, "Stepping Stones in the Hist. of the Am. Soc. of Parasitologists," *Jour. of Parasitology*, Oct. 1956; Joseph C. Kiger, "The Am. Soc. of Parasitologists: A Short Hist.," *ibid.*, Oct. 1962; information from Joseph G. Svoboda, Univ. of Nebr. Archivist; biographic notes compiled by Ward's daughter, Charlotte Baldwin Ward.]

HORACE W. STUNKARD

WEBER, JOSEPH MORRIS (Aug. 11, 1867–May 10, 1942), and **LEWIS MAURICE FIELDS** (Jan. 1, 1867–July 20, 1941), dialect and burlesque comedians, theatrical producers, were both born in the Bowery section of New York City. Joe Weber was one of the youngest of at least seventeen children of Abraham Weber, a kosher butcher, and Gertrude (Enoch) Weber; the family had emigrated in the 1860's from Poland to the impoverished Jewish enclave on the Lower East Side. In the same neighborhood, having also migrated from Poland, lived Solomon (or Samuel) Schanfield, a tailor, and his wife, Rachel (or Sarah) Franks. Their son Lewis—who later took the stage name Fields—was one of the younger sons in a family of at least eight children. Weber and Fields became friends at the Allen Street School in the Bowery, from which, according to tradition, they were expelled at the age of eleven for practicing handstands in the corridors and performing Lancashire clogs in the classrooms. The poverty of their families had forced them to work by the age of nine, Fields as a soda jerk and Weber in a cigarette factory, but lack of money did not keep them from attending the cheap variety shows and theatres of the Bowery, and both became fascinated by the stage.

Their first performance as a team occurred in 1876. Billing themselves as a blackface acrobatic song-and-dance act, they were hired at the Elks Serenaders Social Club at Turn Hall on East Fourth Street, but were discharged after a single performance. Not easily daunted, the nine-year-olds secured a four-week engagement at the newly opened Chatham Square Museum and in the following year played at the Globe Museum, where for the first time they developed their "Dutch" act. Writing their own scripts and music, the youngsters would dress in oversized clothes, Weber padding himself heavily through the middle and Fields adding inches to his height with built-up shoes. After their entrance singing their theme, "Here we are, a jolly pair," they would pummel each other in the best slapstick tradition, all the while conducting a comic dialogue in what was supposedly the stage German dialect of the time but which owed more than a little to the Yiddish spoken in their homes and to the faulty English of their Polish neighborhood. With this act, as well as Irish and blackface song-and-dance routines, they served a long apprenticeship in the nickel museums, amusement parks, and ten-cent theatres of New York and New Jersey. Gradually they acquired the experience and reputation to secure bookings at the better houses, like Keith and Batchelder's Museum in Boston, where in 1883 they received forty dollars a week.

Over the years that followed, Weber and Fields traveled widely around the country, first with circuses and road shows and then, in 1890, with their own company. By 1891 they were earning $400 weekly apiece in skits in which the stubby and rotund Weber played the innocent, as the comic foil for the lanky and superior Fields. In "The Pool Room," a refinement of their Dutch act, Weber would goggle upward and say, "I am delightfulness to meet you," whereupon Fields would reply, "Der disgust is all mine." Fields would introduce Weber to the fundamentals of pool, bilk his gullible partner by a free interpretation of the rules of the game, and, when Weber sputtered his outraged protest, chase him around the table, beating him mercilessly with a pool cue.

By the 1890's, however, the public appetite for dialect humor was diminishing, as ethnic groups became increasingly sensitive about their cultural backgrounds. Weber and Fields, sensing the trend, began to focus their comic ingenuity in another direction, that of the legitimate theatre. The start of their career in true burlesque, as Fields would later tell it, was an engagement at Hammerstein's Olympia Theatre during which they found themselves outclassed by the preceding performer, a quick-change artist who gave a one-act drama with all six parts played by himself. In desperation they counterattacked with a burlesque of the drama and of the quick-change art. They soon formed a company for this sort of burlesque and leased the Imperial Theatre on Broadway, renaming it Weber and Fields' Music Hall.

Thus on Sept. 5, 1896, Weber and Fields began the seven-year zenith of their career with a variety show featuring the famous pool-table skit and a burlesque, "The Art of Maryland," a travesty on *The Heart of Maryland* in which Mrs. Leslie Carter [Caroline Carter, Supp. 2] was then starring for David Belasco [Supp. 1]. The second season opened Sept. 2, 1897, with *The Glad Hand*, containing "Secret Servants," their comic version of the play *Secret Service* by William Gillette [Supp. 2]. This was replaced in December by "Pousse Cafe, or the Worst Born," burlesquing Anna Held in *La Poupée* and Belasco's *The First Born*—the earliest of many Weber and Fields burlesques written by Edgar Smith and put to music by John Stromberg. In their own stage roles, Weber at this period affected the loud checked suits which accentuated his artificial padding, and

both men mimicked the city "sport" of the day with bushy chin whiskers and shallow derbies.

So successful were Weber and Fields that they could attract top talent, and it was in the nature of an accolade for a Broadway production to be parodied by them. Richard Mansfield [q.v.] allowed them to watch a dress rehearsal of *Cyrano de Bergerac*, which they then presented at the Music Hall as "Cyranose de Bricabrac" (November 1898). Annie Russell [Supp. 2] and her company attended the opening night (Jan. 19, 1899) of the burlesque of her play *Catherine* in which Fay Templeton assumed the title role, with David Warfield as the father. Miss Russell asserted "they never again were able to give a completely serious performance of the original for recollection of the counterfeit" (Isman, p. 248). *Helter Skelter* followed in April 1899, and then *Whirl-i-gig* (September 1899), the first of several productions in which Lillian Russell [q.v.] joined the group. DeWolf Hopper [Supp. 1] appeared in *Fiddle-dee-dee* (1900) and *Hoity Toity* (1901). The eighth and final season opened with *Whoop-dee-doo* on Sept. 24, 1903, in which Louis Mann [q.v.] scored a hit. On Dec. 30 of that year the disastrous Iroquois Theatre fire in Chicago impelled New York to radical changes in its fire laws, changes which would have meant rebuilding or abandoning the Music Hall, and the theatre closed Jan. 30, 1904.

The "Weberfields," as they were affectionately known, parted company with the final performance of *Whoop-dee-doo* at the New Amsterdam Theatre on May 29, 1904. According to Weber, they separated for "purely business reasons," although their biographer, Felix Isman, contends that Weber's jealousy of Fields played a part. Weber bought out his partner and during the eight years of the Weber and Fields schism maintained control of the New Amsterdam Theatre. In the fall of 1904 he opened with *Higgledy-Piggledy* and a cast that included Marie Dressler [Supp. 1] and Anna Held. Fields, with two partners, launched his own theatre on Broadway with a light opera by Victor Herbert [q.v.], *It Happened in Nordland* (December 1904). This was followed by a travesty of a current stage hit, *The Music Master*, and a succession of musical shows.

Following a reconciliation which supposedly took place at the funeral of Fields's father, Weber and Fields joined forces once again in *Hokey Pokey* (February 1912). The following November they opened their New Music Hall on 44th Street with *Roly Poly*. Time, however, had wrought changes in the popular mood, and burlesque was not to regain its former glory. After a single season their theatre closed, and the partners diverted their talents to musical comedy, vaudeville, and later to motion pictures. Fields continued to act in musicals and in 1914 made a rare appearance in a straight dramatic play, *The High Cost of Loving.* Just before the opening of *The Wild Rose* in 1926, however, he was taken ill, and except for a small part in the motion picture *The Story of Vernon and Irene Castle* (1939), he gave up acting. He did produce musical and comic shows during his later years: *Peggy Ann* (1926), *A Connecticut Yankee* (1927), and, at the Lew Fields Mansfield Theatre, *Present Arms* (1928). Weber was also active as a producer. In 1918 he and Fields had collaborated in *Back Again,* and in 1925 they made a motion picture version of *Friendly Enemies.*

Both men retired in 1930 and moved with their families to Beverly Hills, Calif. Lew Fields had been married on Jan. 1, 1893, to Rose Harris. They had four children—Joseph, Herbert, Dorothy, and Frances; two of the children became prominent in the fields of popular music and musical comedy, Herbert as a composer and Dorothy as a lyricist. Joe Weber had married Lillian Friedman on Jan. 3, 1897; they are not known to have had any children. Even in retirement, Weber and Fields appeared in two motion pictures, *Blossoms on Broadway* (1937) and *Lillian Russell* (1940), and they made a short comeback in vaudeville at the Palace Theatre in New York in 1932. In September of that year their Golden Jubilee Dinner at the Astor Hotel was a sentimental gathering for a generation of show business folk. Lew Fields died in Los Angeles of pneumonia in 1941 at the age of seventy-four. His burial place was kept secret. Weber died in Los Angeles ten months later, after six weeks of hospitalization for arteriosclerosis, and was cremated at the Hollywood Cemetery. In their heyday, an era of increasingly large theatres and audiences, their company had played to an intimate clientele, sophisticated enough to enjoy satire of the popular theatre but hungry for the broad comedy that was the Weber and Fields stock-in-trade.

[Felix Isman, *Weber and Fields* (1924), a laudatory biography by an associate, is the most comprehensive work on the two men and contains numerous photographs. See also their obituaries in the *N. Y. Times,* July 22, 1941, and May 11, 1942, and a feature article by Karl Schriftgiesser on Jan. 17, 1943; *Nat. Cyc. Am. Biog.,* XIV, 317 (on Fields); and *Who's Who in Am. Jewry,* 1928. Joe Weber contributed "My Beginnings" to the *Theatre Mag.,* Mar. 1907. Vital statistics information was secured from the County Recorder, Los Angeles.]

ALBERT F. McLEAN

WEBSTER, EDWIN SIBLEY. See STONE, CHARLES AUGUSTUS.

WEISS, SOMA (Jan. 27, 1899–Jan. 31, 1942), professor of medicine, researcher in pharmacology and physiology, was born in the town of Bestercze, Hungary, the elder of two sons of Jewish parents, Ignač and Leah (Kahan) Weiss. His father, an architect and engineer, was decorated by Emperor Franz Josef for his achievements in constructing bridges and roads in Hungary. Soma's brother, Oscar, became a geophysicist in England and South Africa. In 1916 Soma Weiss entered the Royal Hungarian University in Budapest, where he studied physiology and biochemistry under Paul Hari and served (1918–20) as demonstrator and instructor in biochemistry. In 1919 he published a paper on respiratory metabolism that attracted favorable attention in the United States.

Since the political climate prevailing in Hungary after the end of World War I was not favorable to research, Weiss came to the United States in 1920. A letter of introduction he brought with him led to his meeting the Cornell physiologist Eugene F. DuBois, with whom he formed a lasting friendship. Weiss enrolled at Columbia University, receiving the A.B. degree in 1921, and then entered the Cornell University Medical School. To support himself, he served as assistant in the pharmacological laboratory and carried out basic research, with Robert A. Hatcher [Supp. 3], on the emetic action of digitalis and other drugs; an interest in pharmacology and pharmacotherapy persisted throughout his professional life. After receiving the M.D. degree in 1923, Weiss spent two years as an intern at the Bellevue Hospital in New York, where he continued his research in pharmacology and became outstanding for the accuracy of his diagnoses. In 1925 he moved to Boston, as a research fellow in medicine at the Harvard Medical School and assistant at the Thorndike Memorial Laboratory of the Boston City Hospital; he was appointed director of the second and fourth medical services at the City Hospital in 1932.

In his fourteen years at the Thorndike Laboratory, Weiss and his associates published some 150 papers. With Herrman L. Blumgart he pioneered in the biological use of radioactive tracers and published classic papers on the velocity of blood flow in human beings. With Frederick Parker he wrote the definitive description of the changes in the pulmonary vessels caused by mitral stenosis and the changes in renal vessels caused by pyelonephritis. He contributed greatly to knowledge of the pathophysiology of left ventricular failure and acute pulmonary edema. He was interested in the autonomic nervous system and, in a series of papers with James P. Baker, Eugene

B. Ferris, Jr., and Richard B. Capps, described a number of clinical syndromes that are produced by abnormalities in portions of the autonomic nervous system. His work on the hypersensitive carotid sinus syndrome led him to an increased concern for the causes of syncope, shock, and sudden death, and he made major contributions to their pathophysiology. In 1936, with Robert W. Wilkins, he wrote the definitive paper on the relation between cardiovascular disturbances and vitamin deficiencies, and showed that heart failure in patients suffering from beri-beri was caused by a deficiency of thiamine and hence could be quickly relieved. In collaboration with Lewis Dexter, he also published a monograph reporting an elaborate investigation into toxemia of pregnancy.

At the Harvard Medical School, Weiss meanwhile had gained rapid academic advancement, becoming instructor (1927–29), assistant professor (1929–32), and associate professor of medicine (1932–39). In 1939 he was appointed Hersey Professor of the Theory and Practice of Physic, and in the same year he left the Thorndike to become physician-in-chief of the Peter Bent Brigham Hospital in Boston. Thus in nineteen years he had risen from an unknown immigrant applying for his first citizenship papers to the holder of the senior chair of medicine in a leading university. At the Brigham, Weiss gave new life to its medical research and encouraged basic work in biochemistry and pharmacology. He implemented a plan of cooperation among the personnel of hospital clinics, the pharmacologists of the Harvard Medical School, and the organic chemists at Harvard University to advance the treatment of disease. This group introduced into clinical medicine the effective use of chemotherapy for thyrotoxicosis. During his three years at the Brigham, Weiss published some thirty papers, which included the first description of scleroderma heart disease.

Weiss served on the committee for the revision of the United States Pharmacopoeia, and on the Council on Pharmacy and Chemistry of the American Medical Association. He was also a member of the American Society for Clinical Investigation and the American Heart Association, and was a fellow of the American College of Physicians. His intellectual and scientific gifts earned the respect of his colleagues, and his extraordinary charm won their affection and that of his patients.

On Oct. 6, 1928, Weiss married Elizabeth Sachs, daughter of Paul J. Sachs, professor of fine arts at Harvard. They had three children: Paul Sachs, Robert Hatcher, and Louise. Weiss died at his home in Cambridge, Mass., a few days after his forty-third birthday from the rupture of a congenital intracranial aneurysm and was buried in Mount Auburn Cemetery, Cambridge.

[*In Memoriam: Soma Weiss* (39-page pamphlet, Peter Bent Brigham Hospital, 1942); death record from Mass. Registrar of Vital Statistics; information from Weiss's widow, Mrs. Elizabeth Weiss Jones; personal acquaintance. See also: obituaries in Assoc. of Am. Physicians, *Transactions*, LVII (1942), 36–38, *Science*, Feb. 27, 1942, *Jour. Am. Medic. Assoc.,* Apr. 18, 1942, p. 1369, and *Lancet,* May 9, 1942; memorial resolution in *Harvard Univ. Gazette,* Mar. 7, 1942 (reprinted in *Annals of Internal Medicine,* Apr. 1942); Solomon R. Kagan, *Jewish Contributions to Medicine in America* (2nd ed., 1939).]

EUGENE A. STEAD, JR.

WELLS, HARRY GIDEON (July 21, 1875–Apr. 26, 1943), pathologist, known as H. Gideon Wells, was born in Fair Haven, Conn., the second child and first son of Romanta Wells, a pharmacist and wholesale druggist, and Emma Townsend (Tuttle) Wells, daughter of a local farmer. Through his father he was descended from Thomas Welles, second governor of the Hartford Colony. The boy attended public schools in both Fair Haven and New Haven (into which Fair Haven was absorbed), including New Haven's Hillhouse High School. During his high school years his family moved to a new residence near Yale University where their neighbors included the distinguished chemists Lafayette B. Mendel [Supp. 1], Thomas B. Osborne, and Samuel W. Johnson [*qq.v.*]. Wells's contact with these men may have influenced his choice of a career. In 1892 he entered the Sheffield Scientific School at Yale with an interest in paleontology, but by his third year he had turned to biochemistry. Working under Mendel and Russell H. Chittenden [Supp. 3], he graduated with the Ph.B. degree in 1895.

Family contacts also played a part in the next stage in his career. The failure of his father's drug business had led the family, impressed by the wonders of the Chicago World's Fair of 1893, to move to that city, where the elder Wells bought a drugstore close to Rush Medical College. The store also housed the office of a noted surgeon, Edward W. Lee, who was associated in practice with John B. Murphy [*q.v.*] of Rush. Wells's acquaintance with these two men decided him on a medical career, and he enrolled at Rush, receiving the M.D. degree in 1898.

Although Wells served a year's internship at the Cook County Hospital, his interests lay in research rather than in medical practice, and he next obtained a fellowship to begin graduate study in pathology at the University of Chicago and to work as assistant to Ludvig Hektoen, one of his professors at Rush. At the university Wells took work in chemistry under Julius Stieglitz [Supp. 2] and carried out research on tetanus, the role of iodine in the functioning of the thyroid gland, and blastomycetic dermatitis. He received the Ph.D. in pathology in 1903 for his study of fat necrosis. He had been appointed to the medical faculty of the University of Chicago in 1901 as an associate in pathology; he was made an instructor in 1903 and assistant professor in 1904, after which he went abroad for a year's postgraduate study at the University of Berlin. There he worked with such men as Ernst Salkowski, the outstanding chemical pathologist of the era, and Emil Fischer, the great biochemist.

Wells returned to Chicago in 1905 to begin a productive period of research; within a decade he had become the leading authority in the United States on the chemical aspects of pathology and immunology. His early work on fat necrosis was followed by research on tissue staining, enzyme action, degenerative processes, and pathologic calcification. He also continued his affiliation with the medical school, becoming associate professor (1909) and professor (1913) of pathology, a position he held until 1940.

In 1911 Wells took on additional responsibility as the first director of the Otho S. A. Sprague Memorial Institute, established in Chicago for the study of disease and the relief of human suffering. In this position, which he also retained until 1940, he stimulated and supported research in many fields, including the chemotherapy of tuberculosis and the role of heredity in cancer. The latter investigation involved him in much debate because of the controversial theories of his associate in the work, Maud Slye.

In 1917, during World War I, Wells joined an American Red Cross mission to Romania to investigate epidemics of cholera, typhoid, and typhus. The mission's work was cut short, but after the armistice Wells returned to Romania, where, under the auspices of the Red Cross and the United States Food Administration, he had responsibility for the relief of a large population and supervised the distribution of supplies from Red Cross ships. He proved an able administrator and received the Order of the Star of Romania from the royal family.

Wells returned to Chicago in 1919 to resume his research. Although his major interests were in chemotherapy and immunology, he was also an outstanding tissue pathologist, and he conducted autopsy conferences at the County Hospital and at the University of Chicago. His work included studies of adrenal gland atrophy, muscle degeneration, and postoperative embolism. These investigations often kept him in the laboratory far into the night, but he found relaxation in going to late movies and in slipping into the baseball park located near the County Hospital whenever the opportunity presented itself.

Wells's most notable contribution to medicine was his classic book, *Chemical Pathology*. First published in 1907, it remained the most authoritative work on the subject for many years, the fifth and last edition appearing in 1925. His second book, *The Chemistry of Tuberculosis* (1923), was written in collaboration with Lydia De Witt and Esmond R. Long. His work on protein sensitivity and anaphylaxis, in collaboration with Thomas B. Osborne, was also of great importance and culminated in *The Chemical Aspects of Immunity* (1924). Wells was also author or co-author of approximately 250 papers, the first, on congenital syphilis, published in 1897, the last, on seminoma, shortly before his death. He was much interested in the pathology of the liver and did considerable research on experimental cirrhosis, primary carcinoma of the liver, acute yellow atrophy, and chloroform necrosis of the liver. He also worked on fat and lipoid changes in malignant tumors of the kidney. He produced papers on the chemistry of autolysis and immunity, the chemical composition of the tubercle bacillus, purine metabolism, calcification, ossification, the chemistry of proteins, anaphylaxis, and cancer in mice, the latter work being done with collaborators.

Wells was an effective teacher of both medical undergraduates and postgraduates. Witty, sarcastic, and enthusiastic, he made pathology a vital subject and assembled an outstanding museum of specimens designed for teaching. He served as secretary (1908–09) and chairman (1909–10) of the section on pathology and physiology of the American Medical Association. He was president of the American Association of Pathologists and Bacteriologists (1919), of the American Association of Immunologists (1923), and of the American Association for Cancer Research (1915–16, 1919–20), and a member of various other societies, including the American Society of Biological Chemists and the American Society for Experimental Pathology. He was elected to the National Academy of Sciences in 1925.

Wells's chief hobby was fishing; a major inducement in persuading him to lecture out of town was proximity to a fishing area. He was also an excellent trap shooter, though less successful as a golfer. In religion he was an Episcopalian. On Apr. 2, 1902, Wells married Bertha

Robbins of Newington, Conn. Their only child was Gideon Robbins, who became a physician. In the early 1930's Wells became aware of a serious cardiac condition, and though for several years he tried to continue his academic activities as head of the department of pathology, his bad health forced him to retire in 1940. He died at the age of sixty-seven at the Billings Hospital in Chicago, following surgery for carcinoma of the colon.

[Esmond R. Long's memoir in Nat. Acad. Sci., *Biog. Memoirs,* vol. XXVI (1951), is the fullest account. See also Paul R. Cannon in *Archives of Pathology,* Sept. 1943, and in Assoc. of Am. Physicians, *Transactions,* LVIII (1944), 40–42; and *Nat. Cyc. Am. Biog.,* XXXVII, 110–11. The Circulation and Records Dept. of the Am. Medic. Assoc. provided information. The Sept.–Oct. 1941 issue of the *Am. Jour. of Pathology* was devoted to Wells. A portrait of him was presented to the Univ. of Chicago in 1939 by his students and friends.]

MILTON B. ROSENBLATT

WERTHEIMER, MAX (Apr. 15, 1880–Oct. 12, 1943), psychologist, founder of the Gestalt movement, was born in Prague, Bohemia, the younger of two children of Wilhelm and Rosa (Zwicker) Wertheimer. Though his parents were Jewish, he himself was not affiliated with any religious group during his adult life. Wertheimer's family background contributed to the rich and varied interests that were reflected in his lifework. From his mother he received training in music that might have led to a career as a composer; his maternal grandfather introduced him to philosophy; and the companions of his youth included men like Max Brod and Franz Werfel who later became important figures in the world of literature. His father, who had devised new methods of teaching commercial subjects and finally established a school of his own in Prague, directed the son's interest to problems of thinking and teaching, and to the field of mathematics.

Wertheimer began his university career in Prague with the study of law at the Charles University, but finding himself interested more in the philosophical meaning of legal problems and in methods of determining the truth of testimony than in legal practice, he left for the University of Berlin to study psychology with Carl Stumpf and Friedrich Schumann. He went on to Würzburg, where he studied with Oswald Külpe and received his doctorate in 1904, summa cum laude. His dissertation dealt with the psychology of legal testimony and involved a pioneering effort in the use of word association for the detection of lies. During the next few years, as he pursued a wide variety of problems in Prague, Berlin, and Vienna, his thinking began to move toward the theoretical position for which he would finally be known, but it was not until 1910 that he came to grips with a problem in the field of perception that enabled him to formulate this position in clear-cut terms. This work was done at Frankfurt am Main, where he formed his lifelong association with two younger men who had recently taken their degrees at Berlin, Kurt Koffka [Supp. 3] and Wolfgang Köhler; and it was from Frankfurt in 1912 that he published the paper on the perception of movement that marks the official beginning of Gestalt psychology.

The dominant approach of psychology at that time treated the experience of everyday life, the perception of objects, of people, of movement, of sound, as constructs that could best be understood by analyzing them into elements of sensation, imagery, and affect from which they were supposed to have been built up through associative processes in the course of the individual's life. Wertheimer's paper reversed this emphasis, beginning with the assumption that everyday experience must be studied in its own right, and that analysis of conditions affecting it must make use of units that are relevant to the quality of the experience itself. This is what he attempted in his paper on the perception of movement. In the discussion of his results he introduced a physiological model for possible neural processes underlying perception, insisting that any theory of these processes must be in harmony with the nature of the experience being studied. This model, based on the concept of an isomorphism between experience and underlying bodily processes, has led to widespread discussion of theories in this area, and the paper itself stimulated more than a hundred studies of apparent movement over a period of thirty years.

Wertheimer's work during World War I on localization of sound gave him further evidence of the validity of Gestalt assumptions. He was at Berlin from 1916 until 1929 as privatdozent and then as "ausserordentlicher Professor," and during that period he joined with Koffka, Köhler, and others to establish the *Psychologische Forschung,* a multilanguage journal which served as the special organ of the group from 1921 on. Among the best known of his Berlin students were Wolfgang Metzger, afterward professor at Münster, Rudolph Arnheim, who later emigrated to America, and Karl Duncker, who later taught at Swarthmore. In 1929 Wertheimer moved to Frankfurt as professor, remaining there until Hitler came to power in 1933, when he went with his family to Czechoslovakia. He came to New York City in September 1933 at the invitation of Prof. Alvin Johnson to join the faculty of the New School for Social Research. Ten years later he died of a coronary thrombosis in New Rochelle, N. Y., where he had made his home, and was buried in Beechwoods Cemetery of that city. His marriage, in 1923, to Anni Caro had ended in divorce in 1942. Four children survived: Valentin, Michael, Lise, and Peter.

During his decade in America, Wertheimer played an active part in the development of the New School for Social Research and was a memorable teacher in its adult education and graduate programs. The topics of his seminars ranged from experimental and social psychology to logic and the psychology of music and art. He gave his students a fresh approach to research, his own eager curiosity leading to new problems in his discussions with them. Among those who were influenced by him during this period were Solomon Asch, George Katona, Abraham S. Luchins, Abraham H. Maslow, David Rapaport, Martin Scheerer, and Herman Witkin. He was also deeply involved in the application of Gestalt principles to the crucial ethical and political issues of the day. He had left Germany before the danger of remaining under Nazi rule became fully evident because he did not want his children to grow up in a country where a man like Hitler could come to power. In the country of his adoption—he proudly became an American citizen in 1939—he wrote a series of articles expressing his strong feelings about truth and the nature of democracy and his fears of the kind of erosion of freedom that he had watched in Germany. He considered as particularly dangerous the ethical relativism then current in sociology and anthropology.

His research, at this time as earlier, touched a wide range of topics. Of these, the most significant was his search for a creative and structural method of learning, a search which clearly foreshadowed the subsequent revolution in the teaching of arithmetic. As before, however, the rich flow of his ideas made him reluctant to commit them to the finality of print. His papers and a posthumous book, *Productive Thinking*, first published in 1945 and later in an enlarged form by his son Michael in 1959, make up the list of his printed works. Still more than his writings, it is the impact of the Gestalt movement, the many papers written by others to develop his ideas, and the continuing work of his students that are the measure of Max Wertheimer's influence on the course of psychology in this century. In the words of Luchins, "His greatness lay in his ability to fire the imagination and creativeness of two generations of psychologists in America and abroad."

[Biographical details were found in the *N. Y. Times* obituary, Oct. 13, 1943, and *Wer Ist's*, vol. X (1935); further information was supplied by Wertheimer's two sons. The best general references are the article on Wertheimer by A. S. Luchins in the *Internat. Encyc. of the Social Sciences*, XVI, 522–27; and obituaries by Wolfgang Köhler in *Psychological Rev.*, May 1944, and E. B. Newman in *Am. Jour. of Psychology*, July 1944. See also Jean Matter Mandler and George Mandler, "The Diaspora of Experimental Psychology," *Perspectives in Am. Hist.*, vol. II (1968), reprinted in Bernard Bailyn and Donald Fleming, eds., *The Intellectual Migration* (1969). Edwin G. Boring, *Sensation and Perception in the Hist. of Experimental Psychology* (1942), gives a good evaluation of Wertheimer's paper on apparent movement. For Wertheimer's writings on broader social themes, see "On Truth," *Social Research*, May 1934; "Some Problems in the Theory of Ethics," *ibid.*, Aug. 1935; and "On the Concept of Democracy," in Max Ascoli and Fritz Lehmann, eds., *Political and Economic Democracy* (1937). Wertheimer's papers are in the N. Y. Public Lib.]

GRACE M. HEIDER

WEST, ANDREW FLEMING (May 17, 1853—Dec. 27, 1943), classicist and graduate dean at Princeton, was born in Allegheny, Pa., probably the only son of the Rev. Nathaniel West, a graduate of the University of Michigan, and Mary Tassey (Fleming) West, both Scotch-Irish Presbyterians. The family moved afterward to Cincinnati, then to Brooklyn and to Philadelphia, where West attended a private school. He entered the College of New Jersey (Princeton) in January 1870 but soon withdrew in poor health and for two years attended Centre College in Danville, Ky., where his family was then living. Returning to Princeton, he received his A.B. in 1874. He taught Latin in Ohio high schools for seven years, traveled abroad, and in 1881 became principal of Morris Academy, Morristown, N. J. President James McCosh [*q.v.*] of Princeton, who greatly admired West, secured his appointment in 1883 as Giger Professor of Latin; earlier that year the trustees had awarded him an honorary Ph.D. Despite his eventual commitment to graduate education, he appears never to have undertaken formal graduate study.

West remained at Princeton the rest of his life. He produced some scholarly work—editions of Terence and the *Philobiblion* of Richard de Bury and a readable short book, *Alcuin and the Rise of the Christian Schools* (1892)—although much of it was criticized for imprecision and errors of judgment. He served as president of the American Philological Association (1901–02) and as one of the vice-presidents of the Archaeological Institute of America (1913–27). A trustee of the American Academy at Rome, he was for many years chairman of the American School of Classical Studies there.

West's role, however, increasingly became that of an administrator and an educational controversialist. For fifty years he defended the classics without compromise. Militantly he attacked the unrestricted elective system of studies (or, as he called it, "the educational lunch counter") and the bestowal of academic credit in utilitarian subjects. Some of his most hard-hitting essays were collected in *Short Papers on American Liberal Education* (1907). In 1917 he helped organize the American Classical League, which tried to show by taking surveys that the classics were not really dying out.

West believed the aim of education was to discipline the mental faculties and to develop moral character. Though he eagerly helped Princeton expand, his outlook remained tied to the nineteenth-century college. Rejecting the increasingly influential Germanic tradition of scholarship, he regarded instruction as a civilizing process. Outside the classroom he valued gentlemanly sociability and esprit de corps. Especially after visiting Oxford in 1902, he sought almost slavishly to imitate the English pattern of higher education, including its architecture. He lacked sympathy for, and probably any real comprehension of, the modern freewheeling style of intellectual life. He opposed hiring the historian Frederick Jackson Turner [q.v.] because Turner was a Unitarian.

As a man, West had great presence. His large frame, straight gaze, booming voice, and firm stride conveyed an air of dignity and command. He was regarded as an inspiring teacher. At dinner he was witty, expansive, and sometimes light-hearted. He wrote clever limericks and elegantly flattering appreciations. Supremely capable of ingratiating himself with the prominent (he persuaded ex-President Grover Cleveland to live in Princeton), West was a talented fund raiser who basked in the social contacts this activity gave him. Ceremonialism, elegant living, academic politics, and a paternal fondness for some of his students helped fill a void in his personal life. His wife (Lucy Marshall Fitz Randolph, whom he had married on May 9, 1889) lost her sanity while bearing their only child, Randolph, and was for thirty-nine years institutionalized and unable to recognize him.

West is mainly remembered as Woodrow Wilson's antagonist in a long struggle for control of policy at Princeton. Under President Francis Landey Patton [q.v.], West became a major power behind the throne. In 1901 a formal, autonomous graduate school was opened, with West as its head. He supported Wilson for president of Princeton in 1902, despite whatever jealousies he may have harbored. Thereafter his major aim was to build a residential college for graduate students, the first such institution in the United States. Wilson supported the project but gave it low priority. Both men fundamentally agreed on educational philosophy, although Wilson was intellectually somewhat more modern and in the end more rhetorically democratic. At bottom, on both sides the dispute was a struggle for personal power. Even so, its memory divided Princeton families forty years afterward.

West grew impatient. In 1906 he was offered the presidency of the Massachusetts Institute of Technology, despite his extreme antipathy to science and practicality. Thereupon the Princeton trustees promised rapid support for the graduate college, and West's sense of power rose noticeably. He began to insist that the college should be built some distance from the main campus, doubtless believing he would be more his own master in such an environment. Wilson, however, threatened to deprive the graduate college of attention and resources by his own scheme to curb the socially exclusive eating clubs through the creation of undergraduate houses. West's enmity now became open and bitter. It was further heightened when Wilson moved to reduce West's authority over graduate academic affairs, strongly supported by the younger faculty, who feared that West's autocracy and archaism would cripple graduate education at Princeton.

Wilson appeared to be winning the battle over the site of the graduate college when in May 1909 the first of two gifts with terms supporting West was announced. The soap manufacturer William Cooper Procter [Supp. 1], an old acquaintance of West, donated half a million dollars. The Princeton community now became deeply split, with most of the alumni firmly behind West and the faculty equally committed to Wilson. The controversy was finally ended by a second gift, this from the estate of Isaac C. Wyman. West, who was one of the executors, perhaps honestly publicized it as totaling at least $2,500,000, though the amount actually received was about $660,000. Soon afterward the trustees voted to accept the more distant site for the graduate college, and Wilson, having conceded defeat, resigned from Princeton in order to enter politics.

The dedication of the graduate college on Oct. 22, 1913, was the crowning moment in West's life. That same year his extensive powers as dean were decisively curtailed when, for reasons of administrative efficiency, the graduate school was stripped of its autonomous position and placed directly under the president and board of trustees. Dean West retired in 1928, solemnly witnessing the dedication of a life-size seated statue of himself in the college courtyard. After a protracted, lonely, and sometimes ill-tempered old age, he gradually lost strength and died in his home on the graduate college grounds in 1943. He was buried in the Princeton Cemetery.

[The Andrew Fleming West Papers, Princeton Univ. Archives, include much of his correspondence as dean of the graduate school, along with a few personal letters and considerable memorabilia. West's published writings include a long article, "The Am. College," in Nicholas Murray Butler, ed., *Education in the U. S.* (1900). Extremely revealing is the recorded discussion by West and interchange with other educational leaders in the *Proc. of the Internat. Cong. of Education* (Nat. Education Assoc., 1894), pp. 150–56. Many of his revealing magazine articles, too numerous to note here, are listed in the *Readers' Guide to Periodical Literature*, especially between 1893 and 1925. Published material about West: Henry W. Bragdon, *Woodrow Wilson: The Academic Years* (1967); Ray Stannard Baker, *Woodrow Wilson: Life and Letters* (1927); Arthur Walworth, *Woodrow Wilson* (1958), especially I, 84–85; Hardin Craig, *Woodrow Wilson at Princeton* (1960); Arthur S. Link, *Woodrow Wilson: The Road to the White House* (1947); Thomas J. Wertenbaker, *Princeton, 1746–1896* (1946); biographical account of West in the *Nation*, Oct. 25, 1906; critical review of West's *A Latin Grammar for Schools* (1902) in *Educational Rev.*, Dec. 1902; *Nat. Cyc. Am. Biog.*, XII, 209; *Daily Princetonian*, Feb. 22, 1928; *N. Y. Times*, Dec. 28, 1943; *Princeton Bull.*, Dec. 29, 1943; *Princeton Alumni Weekly*, Feb. 18, 1944, pp. 7–9, Jan. 15, 1960, pp. 11–14. Other sources: interviews and correspondence with Mrs. Foulk, West's secretary in his last years; with Prof. Willard Thorp of Princeton, who knew West and is writing a history of the Princeton Graduate School; and with M. Halsey Thomas, Princeton archivist.]
                                    LAURENCE R. VEYSEY

WESTLEY, HELEN (Mar. 28, 1875–Dec. 12, 1942), actress, christened Henrietta Remsen Meserole Manney, was born in Brooklyn, N. Y., the only daughter and younger of two children of Charles Palmer Manney, owner of a pharmacy, and Henrietta (Meserole) Manney. One of her maternal forebears was Jean Mesurolle, a native of Picardy who came to the New World in 1663; his descendants intermarried with Brooklyn Dutch families. Her father was of French Huguenot ancestry. Her brother, Charles Fonteyn Manney, became a music editor and composer. After attending school in Brooklyn, Henrietta received her stage training at the Academy of Dramatic Arts, New York, and at the Emerson School of Oratory, Boston. Her early dramatic career was mainly on the road, including one-night stands with an Ohio River troupe, and in vaudeville. Her first New York appearance was in the role of Angelina McKeagey in *The Captain of the Nonsuch* (Sept. 13, 1897). On Oct. 31, 1900, in a Dutch Reformed Church ceremony, she was married to the actor John Wesley Wilson Conroy—known professionally as John Westley—after which she retired from the stage for several years. Her only child, Ethel Meserole Westley, was born

in 1907. The marriage ended in divorce about 1912.

Helen Westley had become a resident of Greenwich Village in New York City during its early bohemian and avant-garde period. Here, at the Liberal Club, she became acquainted with the international patent attorney and playwright Lawrence Langner, a founder of the Washington Square Players, the crusading little theatre that brought together such talented individuals as Philip Moeller, Lee Simonson, Roland Young, and Katharine Cornell. Langner wrote a stirring manifesto for the Players, who rented the Bandbox Theatre on East 57th Street and opened on Feb. 19, 1915, with a bill of one-act plays. In one of these, *Another Interior* (a parody of Maeterlinck's *Interior*), a metabolistic pantomime representing a human stomach beset by gastric juices, Helen Westley, clothed in gray, impersonated an oyster. She remained with the group at the Bandbox and later at the Comedy Theatre until their demise in 1918, performing in a wide variety of plays, from *Neighbors,* by Zona Gale [Supp. 2], to Chekhov's *Sea Gull.*

Several professional engagements followed, including one in 1918 as Nastasia Ivanovna in Arthur Hopkins's famous revival of Tolstoi's *Redemption,* starring John Barrymore [Supp. 3]. In December 1918, at the invitation of Lawrence Langner, Helen Westley helped found America's most vital and enduring theatre, the Theatre Guild, and was a member of its original board of managers. In the Guild's opening play, Jacinto Benavente's *Bonds of Interest* (Apr. 19, 1919), she took the role of Doña Sirena, and until her departure in 1936 she was the organization's most constant and durable performer, acting in over forty-five productions and finding no part too small where the good of the Guild was concerned. The following are only a handful of her many notable performances: Mrs. Clegg in *Jane Clegg* (1920), Mrs. Muskat in *Liliom* (1921), Zinida in *He Who Gets Slapped* (1922), Mrs. Zero in *The Adding Machine* (1923), Mamma in *The Guardsman* (1924), Aunt Ella in *Green Grow the Lilacs* (1931), and the unforgettable cigar-smoking Frau Lucher in *Reunion in Vienna* (1931). When Shaw and O'Neill became the Guild's standbys, Miss Westley found ample opportunity in their plays for her wide range of character interpretations: Ftatateeta in *Caesar and Cleopatra* (1925), Mrs. Amos Evans in *Strange Interlude* (1928, in which her daughter, Ethel Westley, also appeared), and many more.

In 1934 and 1935 Helen Westley made several ventures in motion pictures, and in 1936, after much solicitation from Hollywood, she left the

Guild—though remaining for a time on its board—for another highly successful acting career. Among the many films in which she played character roles were *Moulin Rouge* (1934), *Death Takes a Holiday* (1934), *The House of Rothschild* (1934), *Roberta* (1935), *Show Boat* (1936), and *Rebecca of Sunnybrook Farm* (1938). She returned to Broadway as Grandma in *The Primrose Path* in 1939, but at the onset of her final illness she was completing a picture, *My Favorite Spy* (1942). Though a longtime devotee of Buddhism and Yoga, which led to the practice of a regime of spiritual and bodily health (Langner, p. 220), she became incapacitated by arteriosclerosis and after a long and painful illness died from a coronary thrombosis in Franklin Township, N. J., late in 1942. Her body was cremated at the Rosehill Crematory, Linden, N. J.

Her friends and theatrical associates agree in describing Miss Westley as a striking and unforgettable woman. Lawrence Langner was immediately attracted to her vivid, dark beauty. Theresa Helburn, later the Guild's executive director, found her, at their first meeting, "individual, striking, and Bohemian," and confessed to being scared to death of her. Her unusual and exotic dress off-stage aroused inevitable notice. The critic George Jean Nathan, who admired her, depicted her as "begauded . . . like the gypsy queen in an 1890 comic opera." Her forte as a character actress lay in the vivid performance of roles calling for violent, unconventional behavior. She herself blamed her casting in a long line of hags and harridans on her acceptance of the part of Matryona, accomplice in the killing of a baby, in *Power of Darkness* (1920). With this reputation in mind Roland Young, an associate in the Washington Square Players, caricatured her amusingly in a volume of sketches as the Theatre Guild's Private Medusa.

Helen Westley's service to the Theatre Guild extended far beyond the impersonation of harridans or otherwise. As a member of the board she shared the arduous task of selecting playscripts for production; the other members were always impressed and influenced by her originality, her sincerity, her vehement and trenchant criticism, and her genuine love of the theatre. In her own words, "The popular play presents the actor; the actor of the art theatre presents a play" (Eaton, p. 181). For her, the play was truly the thing. In one of her few errors of judgment, she rejected *Green Pastures* because God was portrayed as smoking a cigar, but this slip may be forgiven in view of the superior Guild repertoire over the years. In her choice of plays and in her acting she splendidly represented the great age of imaginative realism in the American theatre.

[Helen Westley's death certificate (under the name Henrietta Manney Conroy) verifies the year of birth as 1875, not 1879 as usually given. Facts about her family background have been supplied by the Long Island Hist. Soc., especially by Miss Sandra Shoiock, Research Assistant, and by Miss Westley's daughter, Mrs. Kenneth M. Hjul of San Francisco. For stage appearances and other theatrical information, see John Parker, ed., *Who's Who in the Theatre* (9th ed., 1939); Walter Pritchard Eaton, *The Theatre Guild: The First Ten Years* (1929); Lawrence Langner, *The Magic Curtain* (1951); Theresa Helburn, *A Wayward Quest* (1960); and Norman Nadel, *A Pictorial Hist. of the Theatre Guild* (1969). Eaton's book contains an article by Miss Westley, "The Actor's Relation to the Art Theatre and Vice Versa," pp. 179–83. Roland Young's caricature appears in *Actors and Others* (1925). Besides clippings in the Harvard Theatre Collection, one should consult Helen Westley's obituary in the *N. Y. Times*, Dec. 13, 1942.]

EDMOND M. GAGEY

WEYERHAEUSER, FREDERICK EDWARD (Nov. 4, 1872–Oct. 18, 1945), lumberman and financier, was born in Rock Island, Ill., the fourth son and youngest of seven children of Frederick Weyerhaeuser (1834–1914) and Elizabeth Sarah (Bloedel) Weyerhaeuser. Both parents were born in Niedersaulheim, Germany (fourteen miles southwest of Mainz); the father had come to the United States in 1852 and settled in North East, Pa., before moving to Rock Island in 1856 and marrying a year later. In 1860 he formed a partnership with his brother-in-law Frederick C. A. Denkmann and bought a sawmill in Rock Island at a foreclosure sale. From operation of this enterprise the two families extended their activities to timberland and saw mill ownership as well as log driving on the Chippewa, St. Croix, upper Mississippi, and St. Louis rivers. On all these streams the elder Weyerhaeuser initiated and became the key figure in extensive joint endeavors with a score of families and partnerships, acting occasionally as chief executive officer of such firms as the Mississippi River Logging Company, Chippewa Logging Company, Chippewa Lumber & Boom Company, Cloquet Lumber Company, Pine Tree Manufacturing Company, Mississippi River Lumber Company, and numerous other land, manufacturing, dam, and boom enterprises. He moved to St. Paul, Minn., in 1891, where he bought a home adjoining that of James J. Hill [*q.v.*], president of the Great Northern Railway Company. In that city, after 1898, he led numerous family groups in investing in timberlands and sawmills located in Louisiana, Arkansas, Idaho, Oregon, and Washington. These ventures were soon represented by such corporations as the Southern Lumber Company, Boise Payette Lumber Company, Potlatch Lumber Company, and Weyerhaeuser Timber Company, their well-known successors being Boise Cascade Corporation, Potlatch Forests, Inc., and the Weyerhaeuser Company.

Into this nexus of joint, often competitive enterprises, coordinated only through the family financial office, Frederick E. Weyerhaeuser moved at age twenty-four. He had attended public schools in Rock Island, Phillips Academy at Andover, Mass., and Yale University, where he won a B.A. degree (1896) and election to Phi Beta Kappa, Skull and Bones, and Delta Kappa Epsilon. After spending four years learning the various functions of the lumber business through performing them, the budding executive in 1900 became president of Southern Lumber Company, Warren, Ark. There he and others built saw mills, a railroad, and other facilities for manufacturing and marketing lumber. Having had a baptism of practical experience in the field, in 1903 he entered his father's office in St. Paul. He gradually assumed responsibility for the coordination of family investments, as well as the financial supervision of the numerous lumber firms in which the family held an interest, taking complete charge after his father's death in 1914. His brothers—John Philip, Rudolph Michael, and Charles Augustus—played active roles in various manufacturing enterprises.

While managing the family office and its associated functions, F. E. Weyerhaeuser engaged in a variety of other activities. Early in his career he instituted an auditing system which resulted in standardized financial reporting and more effective comparative analysis of the performance of the numerous companies with which he was concerned. His most original achievement was the development of the Weyerhaeuser Sales Company. Noting that many of the family's associated mills competed with each other in the same markets and utilized a variety of wholesaling outlets, he suggested that the wholesaling function be performed by a new, common agency. Beginning informally in 1916, the Weyerhaeuser Sales Company was incorporated three years later. After near destruction by the extreme individualism of mill managers, the corporation became a nationwide wholesaler and remained active until its operations and properties were absorbed by the Weyerhaeuser Company in the 1960's. At various times Weyerhaeuser Sales handled the sawmill products of a score of associated firms in Minnesota, Idaho, Arkansas, and Washington; it contributed to improved marketing of forest products throughout the United States.

F. E. Weyerhaeuser participated not only in lumber enterprises but in several other types of business. He held directorships in the Edward Hines Lumber Company, Boise Payette Lumber Company, Northwest Paper Company, Virginia and Rainy Lake Lumber Company, and Weyerhaeuser Timber Company, as well as in the Great Northern Railway Company, the Merchants National and First National banks of St. Paul, and the Illinois Bank and Trust and Continental Illinois National Bank and Trust companies of Chicago. He served as treasurer of the Weyerhaeuser Timber Company, the most important single firm among the Weyerhaeuser associated enterprises, from 1906 to 1928 and as president from 1934 until his death.

Civic, charitable, and religious activities also engaged his attention. He was strongly interested in Macalester College for a number of years and headed the St. Paul Community Chest in 1922. He served for twenty-four years on the board of directors of the St. Paul Young Men's Christian Association and for a time as a member of the International Committee of the Y.M.C.A. An elder of the House of Hope Presbyterian Church in St. Paul, he was for a number of years president and a vigorous supporter of the Union Gospel Mission.

Weyerhaeuser had married Harriette Louise Davis, daughter of a prominent lumberman of Saginaw, Mich., on Dec. 3, 1902; they had three children: Virginia, Frederick, and Charles Davis. He died in St. Paul of leukemia at the age of seventy-two, and was buried there in Oakland Cemetery.

[Ralph W. Hidy, Frank E. Hill, and Allan Nevins, *Timber and Men: The Weyerhaeuser Story* (1963), and references cited; *St. Paul Pioneer Press*, Oct. 18, 1945; *Who Was Who in America*, vol. II (1950).]

RALPH W. HIDY

WEYMOUTH, FRANK ELWIN (June 2, 1874–July 22, 1941), hydraulic engineer, was born in Medford, Maine, the third son and sixth of at least seven children of Andrew Jackson Weymouth, a farmer, and Charlotte Prudence (Powers) Weymouth. He received his education at the public schools of Medford and nearby Fort Fairfield and at the University of Maine, from which he graduated with the B.S. degree in civil engineering in 1896.

Weymouth's first professional positions, with the City of Malden, Mass., near Boston, and with the Metropolitan Water District for the Boston area, took him into the field of water-supply planning and construction that was to occupy most of his life. In 1899, after several months as assistant city engineer in Winnipeg, Manitoba, he joined the engineering staff of the Isthmian Canal Commission, to survey proposed routes in Panama and Nicaragua. One of his associates there was Arthur Powell Davis [Supp.

1], and when, in 1903, Davis became a supervising engineer of the newly established United States Reclamation Service, Weymouth joined him.

Weymouth's early activities in the Reclamation Service centered on irrigation projects in Montana, North Dakota, and Idaho. In 1908 he became supervising engineer for the Idaho district and directed, among other projects, the construction of Arrowrock Dam on the Boise River, 349 feet high and at that time the highest dam in the world. In 1916 Weymouth was named chief of construction for the Reclamation Service, and in 1920, chief engineer. It was a period of remarkable engineering accomplishment, notably in dam design and construction, as best exemplified by the multipurpose Hoover Dam in Boulder Canyon on the Colorado River. Weymouth's feasibility report provided the basis for its construction, but neither Weymouth nor his chief, Davis, saw the project to completion. In 1923 Secretary of the Interior Hubert Work [Supp. 3] reorganized the Reclamation Service and brought in a new head, and Weymouth resigned the next year.

For two years he conducted his own engineering firm, Brock and Weymouth, in Philadelphia. He then went to Mexico for the John G. White Engineering Corporation, in charge of irrigation and reclamation projects on behalf of the Mexican government. Congressional passage in late 1928 of the Swing-Johnson Bill, authorizing construction of the Boulder Canyon dam, opened the way for Weymouth's last major work, the Colorado River Aqueduct.

The City of Los Angeles, needing a new supply of water for its rapidly growing population, had looked to the proposed dam as a possible source and in 1929 appointed Weymouth to study the feasibility of an aqueduct from the Colorado. Later that year a group of thirteen cities organized the Metropolitan Water District of Southern California to carry out the project. Weymouth was named chief engineer and, in 1931, general manager. The undertaking involved complex problems of planning, finance, and construction. Weymouth's estimates of practicability convinced the area's electorate, which in 1931 accepted a proposed $220,000,000 bond issue—one of the largest ever passed—by a margin of 5 to 1. When completed, the system comprised 242 miles of main aqueduct and 150 miles of laterals, with over 100 miles of the total length in tunnel. There were four important dam structures, five pumping stations to lift the water 1,600 feet, and 237 miles of high-voltage transmission lines from Hoover Dam to provide power for the pumps. The construction was undertaken across a desert whose geological and topographical conditions were largely unknown. All told, the Colorado River Aqueduct was one of the most impressive engineering accomplishments of its time.

The project was completed June 18, 1941. A month later, at the age of sixty-seven, Weymouth died of a heart attack at his home in San Marino, Calif. A Catholic, he was buried in Calvary Cemetery, Los Angeles. Weymouth was known to his associates as a single-minded man, with no hobbies and few outside interests. He was married twice: on Dec. 3, 1900, to Mary Maude Lane, who died in January 1937; and on Nov. 10, 1938, to Barbara Turner, who survived him. There were no children by either marriage.

[The chief source of biographical information is the memoir by Julian Hinds in Am. Soc. of Civil Engineers, *Transactions,* vol. CVII (1942). See also obituaries in *N. Y. Times* and *Los Angeles Times,* July 23, 1941; and *Who's Who in Engineering,* 1941. Weymouth's several contributions to technical periodicals are best located in *Engineering Index,* but see especially "Major Engineering Problems: Colo. River Development," *Annals of Am. Acad. of Political and Social Sci.,* Mar. 1930, Supp. See also Metropolitan Water District of Southern Calif., *Hist. and First Annual Report* (1939); and "The Proposed Colo. River Aqueduct and Metropolitan Water District," Am. Soc. of Civil Engineers, *Proc.,* LVI (1930), 1283–89, and discussion, 1289–91. Weymouth's work in Mexico is described in "Compuertas Automaticas de la Presa Don Martin-Sistema de Riego, No. 4," *Irrigacion en Mexico,* Oct. 1930. Family data from 1880 census, courtesy of Maine Hist. Soc., Portland.]
BRUCE SINCLAIR

WHETZEL, HERBERT HICE (Sept. 5, 1877–Nov. 30, 1944), phytopathologist and mycologist, was born on his father's farm near Avilla, Ind., the oldest of six children (three boys and three girls) of Joseph Conrad Whetzel and Gertrude (Eckles) Whetzel. His father, of German ancestry and a native of Pennsylvania, was descended from John Wetzel, a brother of Lewis Wetzel [*q.v.*], the famous eighteenth-century scout and Indian fighter. Herbert's mother, of Scotch-Irish and Dutch descent, was a native of Ohio. He was reared as a Presbyterian.

Whetzel received his early education at a rural school and at the Avilla high school. After teaching in a country school for two years, he entered Wabash College, where he majored in botany and graduated in 1902. He then began graduate work at Cornell University under the mycologist George F. Atkinson [*q.v.*]. In 1906, before he could complete his work for the doctorate, Dean Liberty Hyde Bailey of Cornell's College of Agriculture appointed Whetzel assistant professor and head of the new department of agricultural botany, the name of which was changed the following year to department of plant pathology. In accepting the appointment Whetzel became ineligible for a degree at Cornell, and hence never received a Ph.D.; he was nevertheless promoted in 1909 to professor. As department chairman, Whetzel gave considerable time to organizational and procedural matters. He resigned the post in 1922 in order to give younger men in the department an opportunity to advance, and thereafter devoted himself to teaching and research.

Whetzel was a dynamic and innovative teacher. In 1909 he developed an industrial fellowship plan under which commercial and growers' organizations provided direct financial assistance to graduate students, who conducted experiments under actual field conditions on plant disease problems affecting agriculture in New York. He also devised a new method of instruction in his elementary course in plant pathology. Though a stimulating lecturer, he became dissatisfied with conventional teaching methods and instead had each student choose from a group of plant diseases one in which he was especially interested. No time limit was set, but at the conclusion of his investigation the student was required, in an individual conference, to demonstrate his knowledge of the specific disease and its relationship to general principles of plant pathology. Whetzel also sought to serve his students by organizing the subject matter of phytopathology and developing more precise terminology.

In research, Whetzel's early efforts were chiefly devoted to practical problems. He wrote numerous papers on plant disease control, and as a member of Cornell's extension staff he counseled farmers throughout the state on the use and advantages of various new fungicides. By temperament, however, he was a naturalist, and he devoted an increasing amount of time to mycology (the study of fungi), collecting specimens on field trips to various parts of North and South America. He soon acquired an extensive collection, which in later years formed the nucleus of the plant pathology herbarium at Cornell. He early became interested in sclerotium-producing fungi, especially those in the genera *Botrytis* and *Sclerotinia*. On the latter, beginning in 1926, he published a series of taxonomic papers in which he described the condial, spermatial, and sclerotial stages, as well as the pathogenicity and life history of different species. Though he did not live long enough to complete the general monograph he had planned, his researches on the family *Sclerotiniaceae,* to which he devoted the last twenty-five years of his life, represent a major contribution to the field of plant pathology.

Active in professional organizations, Whetzel was president of the American Phytopathological Society (1915) and of the Mycological Society

of America (1939), and from 1911 to 1913 was an editor of *Phytopathology*. He received honorary degrees from Wabash College (1931) and the University of Puerto Rico (1926). On May 17, 1904, he had married Lucy Ethel Baker of Avilla, Ind., by whom he had two children, Lucy Gertrude and Joseph Conrad. Two years after the death of his first wife, he married, on June 10, 1914, Bertha A. Baker, also of Avilla. He died of cancer at his home in Ithaca, N. Y., and was buried there in Lake View Cemetery.

[Obituary articles by H. M. Fitzpatrick in *Mycologia,* July–Aug. 1945, and by M. F. Barrus and E. C. Stakman in *Phytopathology,* Sept. 1945 (with a list of Whetzel's publications); Gould P. Colman, *Education and Agriculture: A Hist. of the N. Y. State College of Agriculture at Cornell Univ.* (1963); files of the Dept. of Plant Pathology, Cornell Univ.; death record from N. Y. State Dept. of Health.]

G. C. Kent

WHITE, WILLIAM ALLEN (Feb. 10, 1868– Jan. 29, 1944), newspaper editor and author, was born in Emporia, Kans., which in the course of his lifetime he saw pass from the frontier into the modern age. Save for a younger brother who died in infancy, he was an only child. His father, Allen White, traced his descent from Nicholas White, an English emigrant who settled in Massachusetts in 1639. Born near Norwalk, Ohio, Allen White had gone west in 1859 to Kansas, where he practiced medicine and ran a general store, and later a drugstore. His first, childless marriage ended in divorce. His second wife, Mary Ann Hatton, had been born in the wilderness of Quebec to Irish Catholic parents who soon afterward moved to Oswego, N. Y. Orphaned at sixteen, she was taken by Congregational foster parents to Galesburg, Ill., where she attended Knox College in the late 1850's and became an evangelical Protestant and an ardent abolitionist. Following the Civil War, she went to Kansas to teach school. Will's father was an easygoing freethinker and a loyal Democrat, his mother stern, humorless, and a radical Republican, yet they agreed in favoring woman suffrage and prohibition.

Freckle-faced, red-haired "Willie" grew up in Eldorado, Kans., to which Dr. White moved his family in 1869. The eager, curious youth heard public issues debated at home and so learned a lifelong rule of tolerance for contrary views. Taught to revere the Puritan conscience, he attended Sunday schools and camp meetings as part of family life. However, he was an adult before he joined the Congregational Church. His father's death came in the midst of financial reverses when Will was in high school. To send him to the College of Emporia for two years (1884–86) his mother conducted a boardinghouse. Alternating between newspaper printshops and classes, he attended the University of Kansas, 1886–90, and absorbed laissez-faire economics, but did not graduate.

White's first job after college was running the *Eldorado Republican.* Over the next five years he worked for newspapers in Topeka, Kans., and Kansas City, Mo. For three valuable, shaping years (1892–95) he wrote editorials on the *Kansas City Star,* advancing the community causes of publisher William R. Nelson [*q.v.*]. Then White borrowed $3,000 and, on June 1, 1895, bought the daily *Emporia Gazette.* With fewer than 500 subscribers, it was not a promising venture. He had married, on Apr. 27, 1893, Sallie Lindsay, a schoolteacher in Kansas City, Kans., who from the outset was a major help in his many-sided and overly full career. They had two children, William Lindsay, who became a well-known war correspondent, editor, and author, and Mary Katherine, who died at seventeen after a horse-back-riding accident. White's moving editorial tribute to her (May 17, 1921) was widely reprinted.

At first Emporians did not take the affable, boyish editor seriously, and some even ridiculed his efforts at local betterment. But his lively, conversational editorial style soon made him the most celebrated person in town. On Aug. 15, 1896, the stubby, rotund publisher printed an impulsive, furiously bitter attack on the Populist movement, entitled "What's the Matter with Kansas?" The editorial, which mirrored White's unadulterated straight-line Republicanism, made him famous. Republican editors in Chicago and New York reprinted it, and in the heat of the campaign against William Jennings Bryan [*q.v.*] and free silver, the Republican national chairman, Marcus A. Hanna [*q.v.*], distributed more than a million copies over the country.

White later was ashamed of the editorial's narrowness and intemperance, though at the time it helped him launch his first book of fiction, *The Real Issue* (1896), a collection of stories of Kansas life inspired by James Whitcomb Riley [*q.v.*]. The book was well reviewed, and Eastern magazines began soliciting his work. For *McClure's* he wrote a series of boyhood stories later collected as *The Court of Boyville* (1899). A group of fictionalized articles on politics for *Scribner's Magazine,* published in 1901 as *Stratagems and Spoils,* reflected his Republican conservatism.

Yet by 1901 his political outlook had begun to change. On his first trip east, in 1897, he met Theodore Roosevelt, and the two took to each other at once. Under the influence of Roosevelt,

who quickly became his political hero, White began to see a need for government regulation of business and such reforms as the direct primary. He also met the editor S. S. McClure and formed friendships with two of McClure's writers, Lincoln Steffens [Supp. 2] and Ray Stannard Baker. Although White did not join these two in the periodical literature of exposure known as muckraking, the sketches he wrote for *McClure's* of such politicians as Senator Thomas C. Platt [*q.v.*], the New York boss, had a similar political realism. When in 1906 Steffens, Baker, Ida M. Tarbell [Supp. 3], and others took over the *American* magazine, White joined them as an Emporia-based editorial associate. His articles for the *American* and *Collier's* now expounded progressive ideas. In Kansas he worked to build up a reform-minded antirailroad wing of the Republican party. He embodied his new faith in a popular novel, *A Certain Rich Man* (1909), the story of a "malefactor of great wealth." White helped found the National Progressive Republican League in 1911 and was an early supporter of Robert M. La Follette [*q.v.*] for president. The next year he followed Roosevelt into the Progressive party.

After the Progressive spell broke, White returned, disheartened, to the Republican fold. He found courage and wisdom but also arrogance in Woodrow Wilson. He praised Wilson's progressivism in 1913, and during the war years he backed the government's control of prices, wages, and the railroads and vigorously supported the League of Nations. A mission to inspect Red Cross services took him overseas in 1917, and in 1919 he reported the Paris Peace Conference.

The materialism of the 1920's tested White's optimism. As a member of the platform committee of the Republican national conventions of 1920 and 1928 he sought, with little success, to commit the party to more progressive policies. He admired Hoover and worked for his nomination as early as 1920, when he reluctantly accepted Harding. Coolidge intrigued him as an authentic product of small-town America, but he looked with disfavor on the Vermonter's subservience to business values. White supported the unions in the 1922 railroad strike, during which he was briefly under arrest for displaying a prounion poster in the window of the *Gazette* office. His editorial during the controversy, "To an Anxious Friend" (July 22, 1922), received a Pulitzer Prize. He was an uncompromising foe of the Ku Klux Klan. When in 1924 he could not persuade either candidate for governor of Kansas to oppose the Klan, he ran as an independent, delighting in the opportunity to speak out against intolerance.

White shared a small-town dislike of the cities and their way of life that, together with his strong prohibitionism, led him to attack Alfred E. Smith [Supp. 3], in the campaign of 1928, with a severity that distressed even members of his family.

White's attitude toward the New Deal was ambivalent. He did not wholly trust Franklin D. Roosevelt and criticized many of his specific proposals. Still, he could write of the program as a whole, in June 1934: "Much of it is necessary. All of it is human. And most of it is past due." There was considerable truth in Roosevelt's statement in 1936 that he had White's support "for three and a half years out of every four." White's efforts to liberalize the Republican platform in 1936 were again unsuccessful, and his backing of his fellow Kansan Alfred M. Landon was less than enthusiastic. White was most consistent in his endorsement of Roosevelt's foreign policies, including the reciprocal trade agreement program and the Good Neighbor approach toward Latin America. The latter interest developed from a study of conditions in Haiti he had made for Hoover in 1930. After the outbreak of World War II he became a leading advocate of supplying Britain and France with arms and war materials. His chairmanship of the Committee to Defend America by Aiding the Allies, organized in 1940, lent special prestige to the cause, since it came from so respected a figure of the traditionally noninterventionist Middle West. He was, nevertheless, "strictly a 'short-of-war' man" (W. L. White, p. 17), and when influential members of the Committee moved beyond this position, White was in effect eased out (Jan. 2, 1941).

For years the Sage of Emporia had enjoyed a rich and rewarding mixture of grass roots journalism, state and national politics, literary pursuits, and intimate association with high and low, plus no little travel and public speaking. He produced most of the *Gazette*'s editorials and contributed each year a score or more of articles and reviews to magazines. His books after World War I were nonfiction; among the best was his penetrating biography of Coolidge, *A Puritan in Babylon* (1938). A classic example of White's terse, unmistakable editorial comment was his appraisal, on Dec. 23, 1925, of Frank A. Munsey [*q.v.*]. In its entirety, it read: "Frank Munsey, the great publisher, is dead. Frank Munsey contributed to the journalism of his day the talent of a meat packer, the morals of a money changer and the manners of an undertaker. He and his kind have about succeeded in transforming a once-noble profession into an eight per cent security. May he rest in trust!"

As he turned down Eastern editorships, White

also resisted the appeal of public office. He did serve as a regent of the University of Kansas (1903–13) and as a trustee of the Rockefeller and Woodrow Wilson foundations. Beginning in 1926, he was one of the judges of the Book-of-the-Month Club, a responsibility he took seriously because of its implications for large masses of readers. Many honors came to him, including degrees from eight colleges and universities and the presidency in 1938 of the American Society of Newspaper Editors.

With his round, cherubic face and puckish humor, White was sometimes called the "Peter Pan of the Prairies." His modest home in Emporia was visited by noted people over the years, and this was true also of his rustic summer abode in the Colorado Rockies, where he did as much writing as he could. In October 1943, while hard at work on his *Autobiography*, which when published in 1946 would earn him a second, posthumous Pulitzer Prize, White became ill with inoperable cancer. He died at his Emporia home shortly before reaching the age of seventy-six. He was buried in Maplewood Cemetery, Emporia. President Roosevelt expressed the opinion of many when he said that Will White "as a writer of . . . forcible and vigorous prose . . . was unsurpassed." Two decades earlier Silas Bent [Supp. 3] had called him "the most distinguished figure in the American daily press." For nearly a half-century William Allen White had been nationally recognized as a spokesman and interpreter of rank-and-file, first-name, commonsense, God-fearing, good-neighbor, small-town, Main Street America.

[White's other books include: two volumes of short stories, *In Our Town* (1906) and *God's Puppets* (1916); a second progressive novel, *In the Heart of a Fool* (1918); *Woodrow Wilson* (1924), a biography; *Masks in a Pageant* (1928), sketches of politicians; *The Changing West* (1939), a series of lectures at Harvard; and two volumes of his collected editorials, *The Editor and His People* (1924) and *Forty Years on Main Street* (1937). For listings of his voluminous writings, see Walter Johnson and Alberta Pantle in *Kans. Hist. Quart.*, Feb. 1947; and *A Bibliog. of William Allen White* (Kans. State Teachers College, Emporia, 2 vols., 1969), compiled by Gary Mason and others. Collections of White's letters are Walter Johnson, ed., *Selected Letters of William Allen White, 1899–1943* (1947), and Gil Wilson, ed., *Letters of William Allen White and a Young Man* (1948). The principal biographies are Everett Rich, *William Allen White* (1941); Frank C. Clough, *William Allen White of Emporia* (1941); David Hinshaw, *A Man from Kans.* (1945); and Walter Johnson's comprehensive *William Allen White's America* (1947). White's *Autobiog.* left off in the 1920's, but his son added a final chapter, "The Last Two Decades." W. L. White also gave a centennial speech at the Univ. of Kans., *The Sage of Emporia* (1968). Useful references to White can be found in: Frank L. Mott, *Am. Journalism* (1941); Edwin Emery, *The Press and America* (1962); Silas Bent, *Ballyhoo* (1927); Oswald Garrison Villard, *Fighting Years* (1939); Peter Lyon, *Success Story: The Life and Times of S. S. McClure* (1963); Harold S. Wilson, *McClure's Mag. and the Muckrakers* (1970); Richard Hofstadter, *The Age of Reform* (1955); Otis L. Graham, Jr., *An Encore for Reform: The Old Progressives and the New Deal* (1967). Lewis Copeland, ed., *The World's Great Speeches* (1942), contains an example of White's oratory. Much of the Feb. 3, 1944, issue of the *Emporia Weekly Gazette* was devoted to an extensive obituary, funeral report, and tributes. See also newspapers generally then and at the time of White's centennial. Other information through the assistance of Edward P. Bassett, Lawrence, Kans., Nyle H. Miller, Kans. State Hist. Soc., Topeka, and Mary Mewes, St. Louis, Mo., and from personal acquaintance. An oil portrait of White by Joseph Hirsch is at the William Allen White School of Journalism, Univ. of Kans.]

IRVING DILLIARD

WHITNEY, GERTRUDE VANDERBILT (Jan. 9, 1875–Apr. 18, 1942), sculptor and art patron, was born in New York City, the second of three daughters and fourth of seven children of the younger Cornelius Vanderbilt [*q.v.*], financier and philanthropist, and Alice Claypoole (Gwynne) Vanderbilt. Her father presided over the railroad empire founded by his grandfather, "Commodore" Cornelius Vanderbilt [*q.v.*].

Gertrude Vanderbilt was educated by private tutors and at the Brearley School in New York. On Aug. 25, 1896, she married Harry Payne Whitney [*q.v.*], financier and sportsman. The couple had three children: Cornelius Vanderbilt, Flora Payne, and Barbara. Mrs. Whitney had early been attracted to the fine arts, and after her marriage she became seriously committed to a career in sculpture. About 1900 she began study in New York with Hendrik Christian Andersen and then with James Earle Fraser, and at the Art Students' League. For several years before 1914 she was a pupil of Andrew O'Connor in Paris; she also received guidance from Auguste Rodin, whose influence may be noted in the firmness of her handling of materials and in her interest in the formal structure of figures. Mrs. Whitney, however, proved capable of developing her own style. As early as 1901 she exhibited her first work, "Aspiration," at the Pan-American Exposition in Buffalo. Six years later she opened a studio in Greenwich Village, and in 1908 she won her first award, for her figure "Pan," in a competition held by the New York Architectural League.

During these years in Greenwich Village, Mrs. Whitney came to understand the problems of the young artists engaged in a movement to liberate American art from academic restrictions and open the way for new viewpoints. When in 1908 "The Eight," led by Robert Henri [*q.v.*] and including John Sloan, William Glackens [Supp. 2], Arthur B. Davies [*q.v.*], and George Luks [*q.v.*], held their own exhibition at the Macbeth Gallery in protest against the refusal of the National Academy of Design to show their realistic paintings, Mrs. Whitney purchased four of the seven paintings sold. Soon she was providing exhibit space in her studio to the dissidents and contributing to their organizations. In 1914 she bought the house adjoining her studio, converted it into galleries, and, with the help of Mrs. Juliana Force, opened the Whitney Studio to artists who might otherwise have found the doors of private galleries and established societies closed to them. Through further organizations—the Friends of Young Artists (1915), the Whitney Studio Club (1918), and finally the Whitney Studio Galleries (1928)— she helped exhibit and sell the work of dozens of American artists, including Sloan, Glackens, Ernest Lawson [Supp. 2], Charles Sheeler, Edward Hopper, Stuart Davis, Joseph Stella, Reginald Marsh, and John Steuart Curry.

In 1929, believing that museums and galleries had become more hospitable to the modernists, Mrs. Whitney decided to close her gallery and donate her entire collection of almost five hundred contemporary American works to the Metropolitan Museum of Art. When her offer was flatly refused by the conservative director of the Metropolitan, she organized her own institution, with Mrs. Force as its director. The Whitney Museum of American Art opened in November 1931. It grew rapidly in prestige and influence, moving in 1954 from its original quarters on 8th Street in Greenwich Village to a larger building on West 54th Street. To a great extent, its success derived from its receptivity to the new and experimental and from its policy of purchasing only the works of living American artists.

Throughout these years, Mrs. Whitney continued her own work. Most significant among her commissions were the "Aztec Fountain" (1912) for the Pan American Building, Washington, D. C.; the "Titanic Memorial" (1914–31) at Potomac Park in Washington; and the "El Dorado Fountain," which won her the bronze medal for sculpture at the 1915 Panama-Pacific International Exposition at San Francisco. After the outbreak of World War I, Mrs. Whitney equipped and maintained the American Field Hospital in the war zone at Juilly, France. The war also had an impact upon her sculpture, affecting not so much her technique, which was always realistic, as her subject matter. Her earlier works had been decorative in intent and function and tended to the formally heroic or sentimental. Her war sculpture was far more simple and direct, as in the panels for the "Victory Arch" (1918–20) and the "Washington

Whitney

Heights War Memorial" (1921), both in New York City, and the "St. Nazaire Monument" (1924) in France. Mrs. Whitney's unsentimental figures express the meaning of the conflict and the heroism of the solitary soldier. The same simplicity distinguishes her later commissions, such as the "Spirit of the Daughters of the American Revolution" (1917) on the grounds of Constitution Hall in Washington; the equestrian statue of William F. ("Buffalo Bill") Cody [*q.v.*] (1922) in Cody, Wyo.; the "Columbus Memorial" (1928–33) at Palos, Spain; and the "Peter Stuyvesant Monument" (1936–39) at Stuyvesant Square in New York. Her last work, "The Spirit of Flight" (1939–40), designed for the New York World's Fair, contains a lyrical note not otherwise present in her work. Mrs. Whitney's "Caryatid" (1913) and "Spanish Peasant" (1912) are in the Metropolitan Museum of Art; "Wherefore," a seated figure bowed as though overwhelmed by the burden of life, was purchased by the Art Institute of Chicago in 1910.

Mrs. Whitney's greatest contribution to art, however, was as a patron. For almost thirty-five years she utilized the immense Vanderbilt and Whitney wealth to promote American art and aid artists less fortunate than herself. The Society of Independent Artists, formed in 1917, was supported for fifteen years by her contributions, as was *The Arts,* the leading liberal art magazine of the 1920's, edited by Forbes Watson. The Whitney Museum of American Art represented the culmination of her many efforts to encourage art in the United States.

Gertrude Whitney was a woman of modest disposition who carried on her public activities quietly. She was elected an Associate of the National Academy of Design in 1940 and received honorary degrees from New York University (1922), Tufts (1924), Rutgers (1934), and Russell Sage College (1940). She was also a patron of the opera and donated funds for the Whitney Wing of the American Museum of Natural History in New York. She died in New York City of heart disease and was buried, after Episcopal services, at Woodlawn Cemetery in the Bronx. The Whitney Museum, supported by her bequest, moved in 1966 to a new building on Madison Avenue at 75th Street.

[Manuscript sources, correspondence, newspaper clippings, magazine articles, and photographs are on file at the Whitney Museum Research Lib., with microfilmed copies at the Archives of Am. Art in the Smithsonian Institution, Washington, D. C. Printed material includes: three publications of the Whitney Museum, *Memorial Exhibition: Gertrude Vanderbilt Whitney* (1943), *Juliana Force and Am. Art* (1949), and *The Whitney Museum and Its Collection* (1954);

Whorf

Guy Pène du Bois, "Mrs. Whitney's Journey in Art," *Internat. Studio,* Jan. 1923; Margaret Breuning, "Gertrude Vanderbilt Whitney's Sculpture," *Mag. of Art,* Feb. 1943; Forbes Watson, "The Growth of the Whitney Museum," *ibid.,* Oct. 1939; Juliana Force, "The Whitney Museum of Am. Art," *Creative Art,* Nov. 1931; Lloyd Goodrich, "The Whitney's Battle for U. S. Art," *Art News,* Nov. 1954; *Nat. Cyc. Am. Biog.,* XVII, 149; *N. Y. Times,* Apr. 18, 21, 1942; *Art Digest,* Apr. 1, 1936, Oct. 1, 1939, May 1, 15, 1942, Feb. 1, 1943; *Art News,* Jan. 11, 1930, Mar. 12, 1932, Mar. 28, 1936, Feb. 1, 1943; and the sketch in *Notable Am. Women,* III, 601–03, by Stuart Preston, who is at work on a biography. A sculptured bust of Mrs. Whitney by her friend Jo Davidson is at the Nat. Portrait Gallery, Smithsonian Institution, Washington, D. C.]

LILLIAN B. MILLER

WHORF, BENJAMIN LEE (Apr. 24, 1897–July 26, 1941), chemical engineer and anthropological linguist, was born in Winthrop, Mass., the eldest of three sons of Harry Church Whorf and Sarah Edna (Lee) Whorf, both of early New England descent. The father was by profession a commercial artist, but avocationally a dramatist, stage designer, and popular lecturer. Whorf's brothers both had successful careers, John as an artist known for his watercolors and Richard as an actor, playwright, and director in New York and Hollywood. Benjamin Whorf graduated from the Winthrop high school in 1914 and entered Massachusetts Institute of Technology, where he obtained a B.S. degree in chemical engineering in 1918. He then joined a training program in fire prevention engineering at the Hartford Fire Insurance Company, in whose employ he remained for the rest of his life, becoming widely respected as an expert in industrial fire prevention.

His enduring renown, however, rests on his avocational work in linguistic theory. Early in his career Whorf developed the habit of self-directed reading and inquiry in his off hours and during his frequent business trips. An interest in religious problems, set off by the seeming conflict between his Methodist upbringing and his scientific training, led him to study Hebrew and the works of A. Fabre d'Olivet, an early nineteenth-century French mystic who believed that the phonetic elements of the letters of the Hebrew alphabet were a key to their primitive, God-given meanings. Whorf sought parallels for this concept in such American Indian languages as Aztec and Maya, and in so doing became interested in problems of comparative linguistics, as well as in the problem of deciphering Maya hieroglyphic writing. About 1927 he started to correspond with scholars in Mexican archaeology and linguistics, notably Herbert J. Spinden and Alfred M. Tozzer. On their advice he sought and obtained a grant from the Social Science Research Council to make field studies in Mexico. During a very

819

few weeks spent in Mexico in 1930, Whorf amassed data that became the basis for several important studies, for example his sketch of the Milpa Alta dialect of Nahuatl, published posthumously in Harry Hoijer's *Linguistic Structures of Native America* (1946).

When Edward Sapir [Supp. 2], the most prominent American linguist of the period, came to take the chair of anthropology and linguistics at Yale in 1931, Whorf became a part-time graduate student there (1931–32). Sapir put before him theories, techniques, and problems of contemporary interest in American Indian linguistics and in linguistics generally; his ideas concerning the relations of language, thought, and meaning were especially appealing to Whorf. With Sapir's encouragement, Whorf made intensive studies of the Hopi language, partly in the field, in Arizona, and partly with the help of a native informant who lived in New York City. It was chiefly from this work that Whorf's theory of linguistic relativity—the notion that the structure of the particular language a person speaks influences his patterns of thought and action—emerged. He presented his ideas in a number of technical articles in *Language* and other professional journals, but they came to wide notice through three semipopular essays originally published in M.I.T.'s *Technology Review* in 1940–41: "Science and Linguistics," "Linguistics as an Exact Science," and "Languages and Logic." These and other works were reprinted in 1956 in a collection entitled *Language, Thought, and Reality*.

During the last ten years of his life, Whorf was a prominent and highly respected linguistic scientist, even in his "amateur" status. He told his friends that the emoluments and conditions of his regular employment actually made it easier for him to pursue scholarly work than if he were in academic life. Only once, in 1937–38, did he hold a teaching appointment, as lecturer in anthropology at Yale, on leave from his insurance position. A tall but rather frail person, he moved and talked deftly and gracefully. Without seeming to have great energy, he nevertheless accomplished a prodigious amount of work with impressive efficiency. On Nov. 6, 1920, Whorf married Celia Inez Peckham of Old Lyme, Conn.; they had three children, Raymond Ben, Robert Peckham, and Celia Lee. Whorf died of cancer at his home in Wethersfield, Conn., at the age of forty-four; his ashes were placed in the cemetery in Winthrop, Mass.

Whorf's work touched on many problems in linguistic theory and comparative linguistics, mainly (but not always) in American Indian languages. He is credited with major contribu-

tions to the classification of these languages. He is most remembered, however, for his concept of linguistic relativity—often referred to as the "Whorfian hypothesis"—a concept that, though still controversial, has continued to claim the attention of linguists, anthropologists, and psychologists.

[A more extended biographical essay, a bibliography, and a photograph are in J. B. Carroll, ed., *Language, Thought, and Reality: Selected Writings of Benjamin Lee Whorf* (1956). See also George L. Trager in *Language*, Oct. 1942, and in *Internat. Encyc. of the Social Sciences*, XVI, 536–38; and *Nat. Cyc. Am. Biog.*, XXX, 464. Other information from Whorf's colleagues, from members of the family, and from personal acquaintance. Manuscripts of certain unpublished writings are available in microfilm form in the Middle American collections of the Univ. of Chicago Lib.]

JOHN B. CARROLL

WIGMORE, JOHN HENRY (Mar. 4, 1863–Apr. 20, 1943), legal scholar and educator, was born in San Francisco, the first of six children of John Wigmore and his second wife, Harriet (Joyner) Wigmore; he had a half brother by his father's first marriage. Wigmore's father, a native of Youghal, County Cork, Ireland, had immigrated to the United States and settled in San Francisco, where he became a furniture manufacturer and later a lumber merchant. Wigmore's mother, born in Warwickshire, England, had moved to San Francisco with her family as a young girl. Young Wigmore was reared in a strongly Episcopalian household. He was educated at the private Urban Academy in San Francisco and at Harvard, where he received the A.B. degree in 1883 and the A.M. and the LL.B. in 1887. On Sept. 16, 1889, having practiced law in Boston for two years, he married Emma Hunt Vogl of Cambridge, Mass. That same year Wigmore accepted an appointment as professor of Anglo-American law at Keio University in Tokyo, Japan. In 1893, the year after his return to the United States, he became professor of law at Northwestern University. He was made dean of the law shool in 1901, a position he retained until his retirement in 1929.

At Northwestern, which before his arrival was a law school of uncertain reputation and future, Wigmore championed the "case method" of legal teaching, developed originally at Harvard. Under his leadership, Northwestern played an important role in the movement to update and systematize legal education in the United States. Stimulated by competition from the new University of Chicago Law School, Wigmore was adept at raising funds to expand the facilities and staff of his school. During his long tenure as dean, Northwestern was noted for the variety of its course offerings and for instituting in 1919—well ahead of most American law schools—an entrance requirement of a college bachelor's degree (or three years of college for students entering an enlarged four-year law program). Though Wigmore was an early proponent of clinical experience as a supplement to the formal law school curriculum, believing that legal aid work in Chicago would provide Northwestern students with an understanding of "the law in operation," his principal concern was to make the school a center of legal learning. Scholarship, he felt, should be the "prime requisite" for service on his faculty, which he was pleased to commend as "the most prolific" in the country.

Wigmore himself set an example of scholarly productivity that few could even attempt to emulate. While at law school he had been one of four students who founded the *Harvard Law Review;* in the next twenty-five years he firmly established himself, as Oliver Wendell Holmes, Jr. [Supp. 1] put it in 1911, as "the first law writer in the country" (*Northwestern University Law Review,* September-October 1963, p. 457). His only rival for that distinction was Roscoe Pound, whose career at Harvard had been preceded by a brief term on Wigmore's faculty at Northwestern. In all, Wigmore wrote or edited more than one hundred volumes dealing with such diverse subjects as torts, comparative law, criminal law and criminology, and legal history. Most celebrated was his massive *A Treatise on the System of Evidence in Trials at Common Law,* first published in four volumes in 1904–05, but expanded to ten volumes and more than 7,000 pages by 1940, when the third edition appeared. It was, according to Felix Frankfurter, "unrivaled as the greatest treatise on any single subject of the law" (*ibid.,* p. 443). Despite Wigmore's fondness for replacing traditional legal terminology with his own (e.g., "real evidence" became "autoptic proference"), the *Treatise on Evidence* was widely cited and admired. It sought to impose system on an "apparently warring mass of judicial precedents" and provided guidelines for a generation of procedural reformers. Along with his other works in the field, especially *The Principles of Judicial Proof* (1913), it reflected Wigmore's larger purpose of creating a "science" out of his subject, "a *novum organum* for the study of Judicial Evidence." Characteristic of his innovative temperament was his campaign to make modern technical analysis of handwriting and other documents admissible in court.

Always concerned to lay a "scientific" foundation for American law, Wigmore drew with profit on his unusually wide-ranging familiarity with the legal literature of other cultures. Originally he had planned to specialize in comparative law; while a young man teaching law in Japan, he had edited two books on the legal history of that country. Probably his most influential contributions to the study of comparative law were several multivolume publication projects that he planned, among them the Modern Legal Philosophy Series (1911–22), Continental Legal History Series (1912–28), and Evolution of Law Series (1915–18). Most notable for its impact was his Modern Criminal Science Series (1911–17), an outgrowth of the National Conference on Criminal Law and Criminology which met in Chicago in 1909. Having been the principal architect of that conference, Wigmore became the first president of the newly organized American Institute of Criminal Law and Criminology. "In 1909," he later recalled, "we knew and cared nothing about Criminology—the very name was unknown" (Millar, p. 8). Through the Institute's *Journal* as well as its Criminal Science Series, Wigmore labored to introduce Americans to leading European schools of criminology and thus establish the field on a sound basis in his own country.

Skilled in many languages, Wigmore was an internationalist within his profession and without In 1928 he published the three-volume *A Panorama of the World's Legal Systems,* to edify lawyers and laymen alike by taking them on "a temporary flight above the earth." So global a perspective was deeply appealing to Wigmore, who had been a supporter of both the League of Nations and the International Court of Justice— for which his name was advanced as a candidate. A founder of the Inter-American Bar Association, he attempted in the 1930's to promote "some sort of affiliation between the organized Bars of all nations," noting with regret that law was the only profession without "formal means of mutual acquaintance" that crossed national boundaries.

Broad as his interests and understanding were, Wigmore did not hesitate to proclaim his lack of sympathy with much that he saw in the world and in his own society. In his *Panorama* he brusquely dismissed the elaborate legal codes of the Soviet Union as the work of "ferocious political lunatics." At home, having taken a leave of absence from Northwestern during World War I to serve on the staff of the Judge Advocate General (1917–19), where he attained the rank of colonel, Wigmore grew alarmed by what he regarded as radical threats to national security. Critical of those "tender champions of free speech" who showed "obtuse indifference to the vital issues at stake" during the war (*Illinois*

Law Review, March 1920, pp. 558, 545), he was generally approving of the subsequent crusade of Attorney General A. Mitchell Palmer [Supp. 2] against domestic dissent. In 1927, responding to Felix Frankfurter's caustic analysis of the Sacco-Vanzetti trial, Wigmore rushed into print in Boston's *Evening Transcript* to defend the integrity of the Massachusetts court system. Denouncing Frankfurter as a "past master of evasion and insinuation," he charged that agitation for the two condemned men had commenced "among various alien Communist circles." Even President A. Lawrence Lowell [Supp. 3] of Harvard, no friend to Sacco and Vanzetti, expressed displeasure in private at Wigmore's hyperbolic performance.

Like many of his generation, Wigmore espoused a brand of reformism that upheld traditional moral and social values. Believing the deterrence theory to be "the kingpin of the criminal law," he was impatient with the defense arguments of Clarence Darrow [Supp. 2] in the Loeb-Leopold murder trial of 1924. In his view, determinism had no place in a court of law, since "Society's right to eliminate its human weeds is not affected by the predetermined character of the weeds." Much as he appreciated the educational opportunities offered by Northwestern's location in a great city, he was not a man who found the political complexities of American urban life agreeable. As early as 1889, when he published *The Australian Ballot System,* he had expressed concern over the nature of political practices in "our largest cities," arguing for a secret ballot system that would eliminate corruption and "coercive influences" in municipal elections. Long a key member of the American Judicature Society, he tried but failed in the early 1920's to persuade the voters of Cook County to remodel their court system following principles of efficiency. He could mobilize lawyers to support the cause of judicial reform, but other interest groups were not with him.

Though in his early years he had been irritated by what he would later remember as the "universal complacent torpidity" of the organized American bar, Wigmore eventually became a revered and often reverent member of that community. At Northwestern he sponsored a course entitled "The Profession of the Bar," to expose students (with the help of lantern slides) to the deeds and words of "professional heroes" and thereby awaken "the deep sense of becoming a member of a great professional fraternity." Not everyone should be permitted to enter the fraternity, Wigmore was sure. To require college education before law school, he told the American Bar Association in 1915, would exclude from the profession only and precisely those "poor young men" who lacked the motivation and stamina to make their way to and through college. Nothing would be lost in that event, since in his view the bar was already overcrowded with "shiftless, ill-fitted lawyers" who threatened to overwhelm quality with a "spawning mass of promiscuous semi-intelligence." Only by maintaining standards of exclusivity did Wigmore feel the American bar could regain "its prestige of leadership in public thought." As he told the A.B.A. in 1931, a year before he became the fourth recipient of its gold medal for "conspicuous service," the legal profession in America had "latent national power." Wigmore wanted to wield that power in part because it was his belief that every effective legal system in history depended upon the strength of "a highly trained professional class."

According to a close colleague, Wigmore was "the last Mid-Victorian." Without becoming obsolescent, he retained ideals and even manners that derived from an earlier age. Tall and elegant, he moved about Northwestern carrying a green cloth bag that contained among other items pocket editions of Shakespeare and the Bible. Childless, he was in the habit of referring to law students as "his boys," commanding respect but not inviting intimacy. Never having owned a car, he died in Chicago at the age of eighty of injuries received in a taxicab accident; he was buried in Arlington National Cemetery. In the years after his retirement as dean, he had continued to work full time on a variety of characteristic projects, including study in the emerging fields of radio and aeronautics law. If he had not become fully a man of the twentieth century, he had not lost his appetite for inquiry and experimentation. In the end his immense professional reputation rested above all, as one admirer put it, on his diverse contributions as a "roving scholar."

[For an extended discussion of Wigmore's career, with useful bibliography, see William R. Roalfe, "John Henry Wigmore—Scholar and Reformer," *Jour. of Criminal Law, Criminology, and Police Sci.,* Sept. 1962. Also helpful are the multiple appraisals of Wigmore in *Jour. of Criminal Law and Criminology,* XXXII (1941–42). 261–96, and *Northwestern Univ. Law Rev.,* Sept.–Oct. 1963. On Wigmore's role at Northwestern, see James A. Rahl and Kurt Schwerin, "Northwestern Univ. School of Law: A Short Hist.," *ibid.,* May–June 1960. See also Sir William S. Holdsworth, "Wigmore as a Legal Historian," *Ill. Law Rev.,* Dec. 1934; Robert W. Millar in *Jour. of Criminal Law, Criminology, and Police Sci.,* May–June 1955; Albert Kocourek in *Jour. Am. Judicature Soc.,* Dec. 1943; and G. Louis Joughin and Edmund M. Morgan, *The Legacy of Sacco and Vanzetti* (1948), pp. 260–62. An unpublished manuscript, "Recollections of a Great Scholar and Superb Gentleman, A Symposium," ed. by Albert Kocourek, is in the Northwestern Univ. Law School Lib., which also has an extensive collection of Wigmore's papers. A full bibliography of his publications by Kurt Schwerin is in preparation, as is a book-length biography by William R. Roalfe.]

STEPHEN BOTEIN

WILLARD, DANIEL (Jan. 28, 1861–July 6, 1942), railroad executive, was born in North Hartland, Vt., one of three children and the only son of Mary Anna (Daniels) and Daniel Spaulding Willard, and a descendant of Simon Willard, 1605–1676 [q.v.], one of the founders of Concord, Mass. When the boy was five, his mother died, and for a short while he lived with his grandparents. His father (who later remarried and had several sons by his second wife) was a farmer, and Daniel, though never a robust youth, soon learned the chores that were part of running a 250-acre farm. He received his early education at local country schools. While still in school he was superintendent of the Sunday school of the local Methodist church, of which his father was a member, and he taught briefly in the Hartland Hill district school. Following his graduation in 1878 from the Windsor (Vt.) high school, he hoped to enter nearby Dartmouth College, but because his father could not afford to send him there, he enrolled instead at the Massachusetts State Agricultural College in Amherst, which then offered New Englanders free tuition. Forced to withdraw from college a few months later by eye trouble, later diagnosed as astigmatism, he returned home.

Willard had little enthusiasm for a farmer's life, and he was fascinated by the Vermont Central Railroad, which cut across the family acres. When in 1879 a friend offered him a job on a Vermont Central section gang at a dollar a day, he eagerly accepted. Shortly afterward he became a fireman on the Connecticut and Passumpsic Railroad, and before he was twenty he was promoted to locomotive engineer. Moving west to Indiana in 1883 for higher wages, Willard became an engineer on the Lake Shore and Michigan Southern Railway. A business depression in the spring of 1884 brought temporary unemployment, but he soon found work as a brakeman on a construction train of the Minneapolis, St. Paul & Sault Ste. Marie Railway (Soo Line), which was then building a new road in northern Wisconsin. He remained with the Soo for the next fourteen years, during which time he steadily advanced in position, serving as conductor, operator, agent, fireman, engineer, roundhouse foreman, trainmaster, assistant superintendent, and division superintendent. He gained invaluable experience in railway operation and management, and was soon helping prepare

specifications and memoranda for the purchase of new equipment.

When Frederick D. Underwood [Supp. 3], the Soo's general manager, was appointed general manager and vice-president of the Baltimore & Ohio Railroad in 1899, he took Willard with him as assistant general manager. Given direct supervision over major purchases on the road, Willard acquired an intimate knowledge of its personnel and physical character. In 1901, when Underwood became president of the Erie Railroad, Willard declined an offer to succeed him as general manager of the Baltimore & Ohio and instead accepted the position of first vice-president and general manager of the Erie. Three years later, when James J. Hill [q.v.], who had a substantial interest in the Erie, acquired the Chicago, Burlington & Quincy, he asked Willard to become the road's operating vice-president. Willard, distrustful of Hill and desirous of remaining with Underwood, was finally persuaded to accept when the salary was raised to $50,000 a year. Over the next six years, by purchasing new locomotives and by improving the track, he brought the Burlington to a high level of operating excellence. A former member of the Brotherhood of Locomotive Engineers, he also helped improve the morale of company personnel by substituting a demerit system for the previous practice of suspension as a means of enforcing work discipline.

Willard returned to the Baltimore & Ohio in 1910 as president, turning down Hill's counteroffer of the presidency of the Burlington. The Baltimore & Ohio was a historic line with a good reputation, but after coming under the administrative control of its chief competitor, the Pennsylvania Railroad, it had suffered from a decade of neglect and was in poor physical shape. Willard carried out an ambitious rebuilding program, spending tens of millons of dollars for new locomotives and cars, improved bridges and track facilities, and a general upgrading of the entire physical plant. He was adept in his negotiations with Wall Street bankers, and during his first year raised more than $60,000,000 in investment capital. A major portion of his time was spent personally inspecting the line. Quick to appreciate new opportunities, he not only weathered the Ohio River flood of 1913, which washed out embankments, bridges, and large sections of track, but turned the situation to advantage by improving the northerly Pittsburgh line, which had been least affected by the disaster, and making it into the main line between Baltimore and Chicago.

Willard fully cooperated with the federal government in its defense preparations for World War I. He was a member and chairman of the advisory commission of the Council of National Defense, and in 1917 was instrumental in avoiding a nationwide railroad strike over the issue of the eight-hour day and the delayed implementation of the Adamson Act. When the United States entered the war, he played a major role in the creation of the Railroad War Board, and later for a brief period was chairman of the important War Industries Board. After the war Willard was active in industry-wide efforts to ease the return of the railroads to private management, and at the same time was active in the leadership of both the American Railway Association and the Association of Railway Executives.

In the 1920's, largely because of Willard's earlier investment in plant, the Baltimore & Ohio enjoyed a major increase in traffic and revenues. During these years he continued to make improvements, especially in the area of passenger service. He introduced the first mechanically air-conditioned passenger equipment, and also took an early interest in both lightweight streamlined equipment and Diesel-electric locomotives. But with the onset of the depression at the end of the decade, his program of expansion came to an end, and the Baltimore & Ohio, like all American railroads, underwent a period of retrenchment. In 1932 Willard almost single-handedly obtained from the nation's railroad unions an agreement to reduce all wages by 10 percent. As the depression continued, he had his own salary reduced from $150,000 to $60,000 a year. His successful efforts at economy clearly saved the Baltimore & Ohio from receivership. From his seventieth birthday onward, Willard repeatedly offered his resignation to the board of directors, but it was not accepted until June 1, 1941, when he was elected chairman of the board, a position he retained until his death.

Few railroad executives had better working relationships with both management and labor. Having risen through the ranks from a common laborer on a section gang, Willard was always sympathetic to the grievances of the worker. At the same time he retained a reserve and natural dignity, and though he rarely gave a direct order, his subordinates realized that he expected his suggestions to be carried out. His passion for exact and factual information helped give substance to the cool-headed persuasiveness which served him so well in business negotiations. He received honorary degrees from thirteen universities and colleges, but the honor he cherished most was the newly created "degree," Doctor of the Humani-

ties, awarded him in January 1930 by the combined labor organizations of the Baltimore & Ohio Railroad. Active in civic affairs in the city of Baltimore, he was a member (1914–42) and president (1926–41) of the board of trustees of Johns Hopkins University. He was a Republican in politics and a Unitarian in religion. On Mar. 2, 1885, Willard had married Bertha Leone Elkins of North Troy, Vt.; they had two children, Harold Nelson and Daniel. After a prolonged illness, Willard died of heart disease at the age of eighty-one in the Union Memorial Hospital, Baltimore. He was buried in the family plot at Hartland, Vt.

[Edward Hungerford, *Daniel Willard Rides the Line* (1938); Edward Hungerford, *The Story of the Baltimore & Ohio Railroad* (1928); *Nat. Cyc. Am. Biog.*, XXX, 532–34; *Baltimore and Ohio Mag.*, Aug. 1942; *Who Was Who in America*, vol. II (1950); *N. Y. Times*, July 7, 1942; *Railway Age*, May 3, 1941, and July 11, 1942.]

JOHN F. STOVER

WILLETT, HERBERT LOCKWOOD (May 5, 1864–Mar. 28, 1944), Disciples of Christ clergyman, biblical scholar, was born in Ionia, Mich., the first of four children (all boys) of Gordon Arthur and Mary Elizabeth (Yates) Willett. The families of both parents had moved to Michigan from the Finger Lakes section of upstate New York. During the Civil War, Gordon Willett served with the United States Sanitary Commission and had charge of the hospital ship *S. R. Spaulding,* on which his wife helped care for the sick and wounded. After the war he joined with his father-in-law to found a farm machinery store in Ionia, which soon prospered.

Herbert Willett never attended public school, but studied at home under the direction of his mother, meanwhile clerking part-time in his father's store. After teaching for two winters in country schools near Ionia, he entered Bethany College in West Virginia, founded by Alexander Campbell [*q.v.*] of the Christian Church (Disciples of Christ); he graduated three years later, in 1886, with the B.A. degree. Having decided in his senior year to become a minister of the Disciples, he accepted a call to a church in North Eaton, Ohio, then moved in 1887 to another in Dayton; he was ordained in 1890. On Jan. 4, 1888, he married Emma Augusta Price of Kenton, Ohio; they had three children: Herbert Lockwood (originally named Floyd), Robert Leslie, and Paul Yates.

Determined to begin graduate study as soon as circumstances would permit, Willett received a leave from his congregation to enter Yale Divinity School in the fall of 1890. He had planned to take the regular theological course, but Prof. William Rainey Harper [*q.v.*] persuaded him instead to concentrate on Hebrew. When Harper left after a year to become president of the University of Chicago, Willett returned to his Dayton pastorate, but, convinced that his true vocation was teaching, he resigned two years later to resume graduate study with Harper at Chicago. A man of extraordinary energy, Willett became involved in several important projects. He interrupted his studies to teach for six months at the University of Michigan in a new extracurricular "Bible Chair" founded by the Disciples to provide biblical instruction for undergraduates. He helped organize (1894) the Hyde Park (later University) Church of the Disciples in Chicago and served as its pastor until 1897. When in 1894 his denomination established Disciples Divinity House in conjunction with the divinity school of the University of Chicago, Willett was selected as acting dean and then dean (1896), a position he held for the next quarter of a century. In spite of varied responsibilities, he received his Ph.D. at the University of Chicago in 1896, writing a doctoral thesis on "The Development of the Doctrine of Immortality among the Hebrews." He later spent a year of study at the University of Berlin (1898–99).

Upon the completion of his graduate work, Willett received a teaching appointment in the department of Semitics at the University of Chicago. He remained on the faculty, while continuing at times to hold pastorates, until his retirement in 1929, becoming assistant professor in 1900, associate professor in 1909, and professor of Oriental languages and literature in 1915. An authority on the Old Testament, he applied the methods of historical criticism to the Bible, which he regarded as an inspired work, not in the sense of supernatural dictation, but in the sense that the spirit of God had motivated the sacred authors and the lives of the people about whom they wrote.

Willett's major importance was as a popularizer of liberal biblical scholarship, both within his own denomination, where he assisted and strengthened its liberal wing, and beyond it. He wrote many expository articles for denominational weeklies and served for some years as associate editor of the *Christian Century*. He was perhaps most widely known as a lecturer. A speaker of quiet eloquence and power, he addressed interdenominational groups across the country. To Willett, no task was more important than that of interpreting the Bible to the Christian layman.

Convinced of the folly of denominationalism, Willett supported the cause of Christian unity at every level. During his ministry with the First Christian Church in Chicago (beginning in 1905), he led the congregation to unite with a nearby Baptist church and continued as minister of the united congregation until 1920. A founder of the Chicago Federation of Churches and its president from 1916 to 1920, he served for five years as executive secretary of the Western Section of the Federal Council of Churches of Christ in America. He represented his denomination at the first assembly of the Federal Council in 1908 and was a delegate to the 1937 ecumenical conferences in Oxford and Edinburgh.

The Union Church in Kenilworth, Ill., a Chicago suburb, called Willett as pastor in 1926, three years prior to his retirement at the University of Chicago. Although for some years a heart ailment had slowed his pace, he continued active even after 1940, when he resigned his Kenilworth pastorate in order to spend the winters in a warmer climate. For many years he had spent his summers in a cottage overlooking Lake Michigan near Pentwater, Mich., where a group of Disciples had purchased a tract of land. He died of a coronary thrombosis in Winter Park, Fla., in 1944, in his eightieth year.

[Some Willett papers, consisting mainly of correspondence and memorabilia, are in the archives of the Disciples of Christ Hist. Soc., Nashville, Tenn. Herbert L. Willett III compiled and added material to his grandfather's autobiography, *The Corridor of Years* (reproduced from a typed original, 1967; copy at Disciples Divinity House, Univ. of Chicago). For additional information, see Robert L. Lemon, "Herbert Lockwood Willett: Modern Disciple" (unpublished B.D. thesis, Disciples Divinity House, 1952); obituary article in *N. Y. Times*, Mar. 29, 1944; editorial tribute in *Christian Century*, Apr. 12, 1944; and *Who Was Who in America*, vol. II (1950). Winfred E. Garrison and Alfred T. DeGroot, *The Disciples of Christ—A Hist.* (1948), places his work in denominational context. Among Willett's more important books are *The Moral Leaders of Israel* (1916), *Our Bible* (1917), *The Bible through the Centuries* (1929), and *The Jew through the Centuries* (1932). For a bibliography of his writings, see Claude E. Spencer, *An Author Catalog of Disciples of Christ and Related Religious Groups* (1946). A portrait of Willett by Charles W. Hawthorne hangs in the library of Disciples Divinity House.]

WILLIAM E. TUCKER

WILLIAMS, EDWARD THOMAS (Oct. 17, 1854–Jan. 27, 1944), missionary and diplomat in China, professor of Oriental languages and literature, was born at Columbus, Ohio. He was the eldest son and the second of eight children of William Williams, a plasterer who also built and sold houses, and Dinah Louisa (Hughes) Williams, both natives of Wales. Young Williams attended high school in Columbus, graduating as valedictorian in 1872. Although reared as a Baptist, he entered Bethany College in West Virginia, founded by Alexander

Campbell [*q.v.*] of the Disciples of Christ, to prepare for the ministry in that denomination.

After graduating in 1875, Williams was ordained and accepted his first pastorate, at the Christian church in Springfield, Ill. In the years that followed he held pastorates in Denver (1877–78), Brooklyn, N. Y. (1878–81), and Cincinnati, Ohio (1881–87). In 1887 he offered his services to the board of the Foreign Christian Missionary Society and for the next nine years served as a missionary in China. Settling in Nanking in a small Buddhist monastery in October 1887, he began an intensive study of the Chinese language and within six months was able to begin preaching. During the next few years, however, his studies of astronomy, geology, and especially evolution, as well as of comparative religions, produced a change in his religious views, and in 1896 he left the ministry. That summer he obtained an appointment as translator at the American consulate general in Shanghai.

Williams spent the next twenty-five years in the service of the American and the Chinese governments. His sympathy and affection for the Chinese people, his interest in their culture and literature, and his command of the language made him unusually valuable. In 1897 he was appointed vice-consul general at Shanghai. He left the American consular service temporarily (1898–1901) to serve the Chinese government as a translator at the Shanghai Arsenal, working on textbooks for use in the schools. In 1901 he was appointed Chinese secretary at the American legation at Peking. Among his duties were interpreting at the Manchu court, working on the "Boxer Protocol," a revision of the commercial treaty between the United States and China, and preparing reports for the State Department on such topics as extraterritoriality and currency. His compilation, *Recent Chinese Legislation* (1904), included various decrees relative to reform in China. During the year 1908–09 he served as consul general at Tientsin.

In 1909 Williams was transferred to Washington as assistant chief of the Division of Far Eastern Affairs in the State Department, and for the next two years he was involved, with some reluctance on his part, in the "dollar diplomacy" of Chinese railroad loans. At this time he also became a member of the All Souls Unitarian Church. In 1911 he returned to China for the last time. As first secretary at the American legation in Peking (1911–13) he twice served as chargé d'affaires. An early advocate of American recognition of the Chinese republican government headed by Yüan Shih-k'ai,

Williams represented President Wilson at the formal recognition ceremonies in May 1913. He felt strongly that the stability of China depended on the continuance of the Yüan regime; and, believing Yüan to be capable of crushing a rebellion led by Sun Yat-sen in the summer of 1913, he successfully urged the American government not to intervene.

Williams became chief of the Far Eastern Division in the State Department in 1914, a post he held for four years. When Japan, in 1915, issued her "Twenty-one Demands" concerning her rights in China, Williams at first denounced them; but later, noting Japan's "special interests" in Manchuria and Inner Mongolia, he urged the State Department to consider the demands on a quid pro quo basis by which Japan would agree not to interfere with American commercial interests in China. Williams also felt that China could absorb Japan's excess population and thus reduce Japanese immigration to the United States and the resulting tensions. His concept of Japan's "special interests" was later incorporated into the Lansing-Ishii Notes of 1917. During the Paris Peace Conference, Williams was technical adviser on Far Eastern affairs to the American delegation. Despite his personal recommendation to President Wilson, however, the "Big Three" decided that former German rights in Shantung should go to Japan. Williams then advised the Chinese delegation to refuse to sign the Versailles Treaty, and in the summer of 1919, after his return to Washington, he criticized the Shantung decision before the Senate Foreign Relations Committee.

Williams left the State Department in 1918 to accept an appointment at the University of California at Berkeley as Agassiz Professor of Oriental Languages and Literature, a chair he held until his retirement in 1927. He had for some years belonged to a number of scholarly associations, both in China and in the United States, and had published *The State Religion of China under the Manchus* (1913) as well as several articles. Williams interrupted his teaching in 1921 to serve as an expert assistant to the American delegation at the Washington Conference on arms limitation and the Far East. During his academic years he published his two best-known books, *China Yesterday and To-day* (1923) and *A Short History of China* (1928).

A scholar by temperament, Williams had, in the judgment of Cordell Hull, "a quiet sense of humor and an extraordinary capacity for making friends." He was three times decorated by the Chinese government. Williams was first married on Aug. 12, 1884, to Caroline Dorothy Loos, professor of French and German in the Christian College for Women at Columbia, Mo., and the daughter of Charles L. Loos, a Disciples of Christ minister and professor of ancient languages at Bethany College. Their two sons were Edward Thrasher and Charles Louis Loos. His wife died in China in 1892, and on Jan. 8, 1894, at Chinkiang, Williams married Rose Sickler, an American teacher at a mission school in China. They had two children, Alice Sickler and Gwladys Louise. Williams died of pneumonia at Berkeley General Hospital in his ninetieth year and was buried in Mountain View Cemetery, Oakland, Calif.

[The E. T. Williams Papers at the Bancroft Lib., Univ. of Calif. at Berkeley, include correspondence, journals, and his 360-page MS. "Recollections." (For a description of the papers, see *Bancroftiana,* July 1965, p. 8.) For useful references to Williams's diplomatic career, see: Tien-yi Li, *Woodrow Wilson's China Policy, 1913–1917* (1952); Roy Watson Curry, *Woodrow Wilson and Far Eastern Policy* (1957); and Russell H. Fifield, *Woodrow Wilson and the Far East: The Diplomacy of the Shantung Question* (1952). Writings about Williams include: William T. Ellis, "The American on Guard in China," *Am. Rev. of Revs.,* Dec. 1911; Esson M. Gale's memorial sketch in *Far Eastern Quart.,* Aug. 1944; and F. D. Lessing, P. A. Boodberg, and N. W. Mah in Univ. of Calif., *In Memoriam,* 1944. See also *Nat. Cyc. Am. Biog.,* XVIII, 238. Kenneth S. Latourette's review of *China Yesterday and To-day* and *A Short Hist. of China* in the *Am. Hist. Rev.,* July 1929, pp. 846–48, reveals the limitations of Williams's scholarship. There is brief mention of his years at Nanking in Archibald McLean, *Hist. of the Foreign Christian Missionary Soc.* (1919).]

WOODBRIDGE BINGHAM

WILLIAMS, FANNIE BARRIER (Feb. 12, 1855–Mar. 4, 1944), Afro-American lecturer and civic leader, was born in Brockport, N. Y., the youngest of the three children of Anthony J. and Harriet (Prince) Barrier. Her parents and grandparents had been born free, and her father, a native of Philadelphia, had lived in Brockport since childhood. A modestly successful small businessman and an active leader in the Baptist church, he provided a comfortable and secure life for his children. The Barriers were one of the few black families in Brockport and associated freely with whites. Fannie graduated from the State Normal School in Brockport in 1870 and, like many educated Northern black women of the Reconstruction era, then went south to teach the freedmen. There she encountered discrimination for the first time and, in her words, "began life as a colored person, in all that that term implies" ("A Northern Negro's Autobiography," p. 91). After several years, she returned north to study at the New England Conservatory of Music in Boston and then at the School of Fine Arts in Washington, D. C. In Washington she met S.

Laing Williams, a recent graduate of the University of Michigan and of Washington's Columbian College of Law, and they were married in 1887. They had no children. The couple moved to Chicago, where Williams established a law practice. They quickly found a niche in the city's small, closely knit black community, and joined the Unitarian All Souls Church of Jenkin Lloyd Jones [*q.v.*].

Fannie Williams made her debut as a public figure in 1893 at the World's Columbian Exposition in Chicago, where she gave a widely acclaimed address on "The Intellectual Progress of the Colored Women of the United States" before the World's Congress of Representative Women. An impassioned and forceful speaker, she excoriated white America for denying equal opportunity to blacks and "thus attempting to repress the yearnings of common humanity." Widely hailed in the press and by prominent black leaders, Mrs. Williams was soon in demand as a lecturer and writer. She gave a second successful address during the Exposition, this time before the World's Parliament of Religions, and for the next decade she traveled extensively, speaking to women's clubs and church groups on various aspects of Afro-American life. She also wrote for several newspapers, including the *Chicago Record-Herald* and the *New York Age.*

In 1894 Mrs. Williams was nominated for membership in the Chicago Woman's Club. She was admitted only after fourteen months of bitter wrangling which attracted wide publicity; for thirty years she was the club's only black member. At the same time, she worked to develop an organizational and institutional life in the black community. She was a leader in the National Association of Colored Women; a director of the Frederick Douglass Center, a social settlement on Chicago's South Side; a member of the board of the Phyllis Wheatley Home for Girls; and an active supporter of Provident Hospital, one of the first black-controlled medical centers in the country.

In her early lectures and writings, Mrs. Williams voiced the militant protest ideology of Frederick Douglass [*q.v.*], arguing that nothing less than the eradication of segregation and discrimination would solve the American racial problem. But after 1900 she began to drift toward the more conciliatory philosophy of Booker T. Washington [*q.v.*]. She urged black Americans to stop complaining about white hostility and instead to help themselves, to acquire property, and "to cultivate strength against adversity and wrong-doing" (*Chicago Record-Herald,* Oct. 9, 1904). Fulsome in her praise of Washington's cautious leadership, she supported him in his dispute with the more militant W. E. B. DuBois. Many other black leaders at the turn of the century retreated in the face of mounting social discrimination, but Mrs. Williams also had a personal motivation. Her husband was seeking a federal appointment which he could secure only through Washington's influence; when Laing Williams was appointed Assistant United States Attorney in 1908, his wife was widely credited with his success.

After 1908 Mrs. Williams wrote and lectured less often. She and her husband continued to endorse Washington's self-help philosophy, but by 1912, with the Washington-DuBois controversy ebbing, they were working with the more militant National Association for the Advancement of Colored People as well. Mrs. Williams also participated in the woman suffrage movement, urging black women to play a leading role in the struggle for the rights of all women. After her husband's death in 1921, she curtailed many of her activities, but did accept an appointment to the city's Library Board in 1924, the first woman and the first Afro-American to serve on that body. Two years later, in declining health, she resigned and moved back to Brockport, where she spent the rest of her life with her unmarried sister. She died of arteriosclerosis in Brockport at the age of eighty-nine and was buried in the Barrier family plot at the High Street Cemetery.

Fannie Williams was a pioneer in the effort to make black women a potent social and political force. Contemporaries described her as a charming and attractive woman who spoke with eloquence and wit. Middle-class in background and outlook, she had little real knowledge of—or rapport with—the black masses, even while she worked for their uplift. She spoke instead for an educated black elite, attempting to formulate viable tactics and goals in the midst of an increasingly hostile white world.

[The outline of Fannie Williams's life can be found in Charlotte Elizabeth Martin, *The Story of Brockport for One Hundred Years* (1929?), pp. 86–87; Elizabeth Lindsay Davis, *Lifting as They Climb* (1933), pp. 266–67; and in obituaries in the *Chicago Defender*, Mar. 11, 1944, *Chicago Tribune*, Mar. 8, 1944, and *Brockport Republic Democrat*, Mar. 9, 1944. Further information on the Barrier family can be obtained from Brockport tax rolls and from the lot book of the Brockport cemetery. In her own account of her early life, "A Northern Negro's Autobiog.," *Independent*, July 14, 1904, Mrs. Williams writes revealingly of the events that shaped her outlook and attitudes. For her many civic activities in Chicago, see the local press, particularly the *Broad Ax*, 1899–1924, which is usually critical of her, and the more sympathetic *Defender*, 1909–24. The best approach to her racial thought is through her own articles, including: "The Intellectual Progress of the Colored Women of the U. S. since the Emancipation Procla-

mation," in May Wright Sewall, ed., *The World's Cong. of Representative Women* (1894), II, 696–711; "Religious Duty to the Negro," in John W. Hanson, ed., *The World's Congress of Religions* (1894), pp. 893–97; "The Club Movement among Colored Women in America," in J. E. MacBrady, ed., *A New Negro for a New Century* (1900), pp. 409–21; "Opportunities and Responsibilities of Colored Women," in James T. Haley, comp., *Afro-Am. Encyc.* (1895), pp. 146–61; and "Social Bonds in the 'Black Belt' of Chicago," *Charities*, Oct. 7, 1905.]

ALLAN H. SPEAR

WILLKIE, WENDELL LEWIS (Feb. 18, 1892–Oct. 8, 1944), lawyer, public utility executive, presidential candidate, was born in Elwood, Ind. Originally named Lewis Wendell, he was the third son and fourth of six children of Herman Francis and Henrietta (Trisch) Willkie. All four of his grandparents had emigrated from Germany, mainly to escape repressive political conditions. His parents, both of whom had earlier taught school, were energetic and public-spirited lawyers, practicing together; Herman Willkie was active in church affairs as a Methodist and then as a Presbyterian.

After attending Elwood public schools, Wendell Willkie entered Indiana University, from which he received the B.A. degree in 1913. To earn money for law school, he next taught history at the Coffeyville (Kans.) high school but in November 1914 resigned (to the deep regret of the student body) to take a more remunerative job as a chemist in a Puerto Rican sugar factory. He entered the Indiana University law school in 1915 and a year later received his LL.B. Later stories of his having been a "campus radical" were exaggerated, but he certainly incurred official disfavor, as class orator at his law school graduation, by his spirited advocacy of extending Woodrow Wilson's New Freedom program to Indiana. After graduation he joined his parents' law firm; but on the outbreak of World War I in the spring of 1917, he volunteered for military duty and gained a commission as first lieutenant in the 325th Artillery. The regiment got to France but to Willkie's intense disappointment never engaged in combat. On Jan. 14, 1918, he married Edith Wilk of Rushville, Ind.; they had one child, Philip Herman.

After his discharge from the army early in 1919, Willkie joined the legal staff of the Firestone Tire and Rubber Company in Akron, Ohio. He resigned at the end of 1920 to enter a private law firm in Akron and soon earned a reputation as a brilliant and aggressive courtroom lawyer. During these years he also became a popular after-dinner speaker and a crusader for the League of Nations and against the Ku Klux Klan. Willkie's firm was counsel for the Northern Ohio Power and Light Company, which in 1929 became (as Ohio Edison) a subsidiary of the Commonwealth & Southern Corporation, a giant public utility holding company organized in that year by Bernard C. Cobb. Cobb offered Willkie the job of counsel for the new corporation, and after some hesitation he accepted and moved to New York City. In 1933 he succeeded Cobb as president and chief executive officer, and supplied the company with effective leadership during the Great Depression. He also gained national attention as the most articulate opponent of two New Deal projects: the Public Utility Holding Company Act and the Tennessee Valley Authority. Though acknowledging severe abuses in the past management of privately owned utilities, Willkie nevertheless opposed not only public ownership but also what he regarded as an excessive measure of federal control. The Holding Company Act was eventually sustained by the United States Supreme Court, as was TVA, but Willkie was generally credited with a victory when in 1939 he sold the Tennessee Electric Power Company (a subsidiary of Commonwealth & Southern) to TVA and local municipalities for $78,600,000.

Willkie's winning of the Republican presidential nomination at Philadelphia in 1940 was an event unparalleled in American history. A liberal Democrat in early life, he had largely withdrawn from politics after serving as a delegate to the party's disastrous national convention in 1924, and his change of party affiliation in 1939, inspired by his distaste for Roosevelt and his policies, was hardly known even to his friends. Moreover, he did not seriously consider trying for the nomination until early in 1940, and did not fully commit himself until May, too late for most primaries. He was, however, well known to the business community; he had also written articles for the *Atlantic,* the *Saturday Evening Post,* and *Reader's Digest,* as well as for *Fortune,* whose managing editor, Russell Davenport, helped him gain the support of the publishers Henry Luce and John and Gardner Cowles; and he was aided by several key Republicans. But above all, it was his personal warmth and magnetism, along with his forthright stand for aid to Britain after the shock of Hitler's easy conquest of western Europe, that created the wave of popular enthusiasm on which he was swept to a sixth-ballot victory over Thomas E. Dewey and Robert A. Taft. With his nomination, he resigned the presidency of Commonwealth & Southern.

In the contest with Franklin Roosevelt, who was seeking a third presidential term, Willkie

waged a vigorous campaign. He alienated many Republicans by supporting the Selective Service Act and Roosevelt's policy of aid to Britain. At the same time, he accused the President of deliberately leading the country toward war and, on the domestic front, attacked Roosevelt's seeming acceptance of the idea of a closed economy rather than an expanding one, though the issues were sometimes obscured by reckless campaigning invective on both sides. Willkie polled a larger popular vote than any other Republican candidate before Eisenhower but lost in the electoral college by a wide margin. Roosevelt retained the loyalty of lower income groups, who felt that during the depression he had responded to their needs, as Republicans in general had not; and he drew the support of many internationalists who were appalled by the isolationist record of the principal Republican leaders, especially in Congress.

During the next year Willkie devoted himself to unifying the country behind a policy of increasing military aid to Britain, to which country he paid a dramatic visit during the intense German bombings early in 1941. Again he earned the enmity of conservative Republicans by his unqualified support of Roosevelt's Lend-Lease proposal, as well as by his continued crusade against isolationism. After the Japanese attack on Pearl Harbor, Willkie turned to two concerns that dominated the closing years of his life: the creation of an international organization to preserve world peace, and the defense of civil liberties, with an increasing emphasis on Negro rights. The first of these concerns led him to accept eagerly Roosevelt's invitation, in August 1942, to visit the Middle East—and eventually the Soviet Union and China—as a sort of goodwill ambassador. This mission he carried out brilliantly, although he incurred criticism in some quarters by a statement (from Russia) urging an early Allied second front in western Europe and another (from China) advocating, and predicting, the end of colonialism. On his return in October he summed up his observations and conclusions in a radio "Report to the People" (estimated to have had a larger audience than any previous radio broadcast except Roosevelt's following the Pearl Harbor attack) and later in his book *One World* (1943), which sold millions of copies in a few months. His main theme was the desire of the awakening colonial peoples to join the West in a global partnership based on economic, political, and racial justice.

A related notion, the urgent need for postwar harmony between the United States and the Soviet Union, was in part responsible for his unsparing attacks on the State Department's complacent reliance on fascist leaders in areas freed from Nazi control, such as Admiral Jean Darlan in French North Africa and Marshal Pietro Badoglio in Italy. These views once more infuriated conservatives in both parties, who were further enraged when Willkie successfully defended before the Supreme Court a naturalized citizen, William Schneiderman, whose citizenship the Justice Department was trying to revoke because he was an admitted Communist.

Late in 1943 Willkie embarked on a strenuous campaign to win the 1944 Republican presidential nomination. His hopes were crushed in the Wisconsin primary in April 1944 when, after an all-out campaign in which he asked rank-and-file Republicans to repudiate the "narrow nationalism," "economic Toryism," and "pathological" mentality of the Old Guard, he finished fourth behind Thomas E. Dewey, Harold Stassen, and Gen. Douglas MacArthur, none of whom had actively campaigned. He immediately withdrew from the race. Excluded by Dewey from an active role at the convention, Willkie sought to influence the proceedings by a series of short newspaper articles, entitled a "Proposed Platform," in which he attacked as outworn the concept of states' rights; urged federal anti–poll tax and antilynching laws; called for extension of social security (including the guarantee to every child in America of "the basic necessities of good food, adequate clothing, medical care, and a decent home"); recognized industrial workers' "need to control for themselves the circumstances which dictate their working lives"; declared that "the day of economic imperialism is over"; and demanded a world organization in which small states would have a genuine voice. This "platform," together with two articles written for *Collier's* magazine following the convention, was published a few days after Willkie's death as *An American Program*.

During the campaign, Dewey's alliance with former isolationists strengthened Willkie's previous distrust of the candidate, and although under intense pressure from many quarters, he withheld his support. He also refused to support Roosevelt—though he was receptive to the President's proposal that the two of them work together after the election to bring about a realignment of American political parties, with a clear division between liberals and conservatives.

Willkie's prolonged expenditure of energy in public affairs apparently took its toll. In October 1944, after a series of heart attacks over a period of a month, he died of a coronary thrombosis at Lenox Hill Hospital in New York City at the age

of fifty-two. He was buried in East Hill Cemetery, Rushville, Ind., where he owned the farm that in later years he had come to think of as "home," though he lived there only during brief vacations.

Although magnanimous in personal relations, Willkie in his last years was too outspoken and uncompromising to be successful in politics. Nevertheless, it may be plausibly argued that he played a greater part than any other single person in unifying the country before its entry into World War II and in turning the Republican party away from its long-standing isolationism. Perhaps not less significant, in a struggle whose outcome is still clouded, was his unflagging crusade for civil liberties and racial equality.

[The most important collection of Willkie MSS. available to scholars is at the Franklin D. Roosevelt Lib., Hyde Park, N. Y. Other collections are at Indiana University at Bloomington and at Rushville. Two good general biographies are Joseph Barnes, *Willkie* (1952), and Ellsworth Barnard, *Wendell Willkie* (1966); the latter is fully documented. Donald B. Johnson's *The Republican Party and Wendell Willkie* (1960) is a thorough and scholarly study of Willkie's political career. Other works which are based more or less on original sources include: Herman O. Makey, *Wendell Willkie of Elwood* (1940); Alden Hatch, *Young Willkie* (1944); Mary Earhart Dillon, *Wendell Willkie* (1952); Muriel Rukeyser, *One Life* (1957); and Warren Moscow, *Roosevelt and Willkie* (1968).]

ELLSWORTH BARNARD

WILLOUGHBY, WESTEL WOODBURY (July 20, 1867–Mar. 26, 1945), political scientist, adviser to the Chinese government, was born in Alexandria, Va., one of the twin sons of Westel and Jennie Rebecca (Woodbury) Willoughby. His father, a native of New York state, was descended from John Willoughby, who emigrated from England in the early eighteenth century and settled in Connecticut; after the Civil War, in which he was severely wounded at the battle of Chancellorsville, he moved to Alexandria and practiced law there and in Washington, D. C. Young Westel, along with his twin brother, William Franklin (who also became a noted political scientist and later an economist with the Brookings Institution), attended St. John's Military Academy (1879–82), the Washington high school (1882–85), and Johns Hopkins University (A.B. 1888). Westel returned to Johns Hopkins to do graduate work, receiving his Ph.D. in 1891. His doctoral dissertation, *The Supreme Court of the United States* (1890), written under the direction of Herbert Baxter Adams [*q.v.*], was a rather uncritical treatment. Having been admitted to the bar in 1891, Willoughby practiced law for a time with his father, but found the law not to his liking and in 1895 accepted a teaching position at Johns

Hopkins. He continued there until his retirement in 1933.

Willoughby was one of the founders of academic political science in the United States. His small department of political science (a one-man department for most of the years he served) produced seventy Ph.D.'s during his tenure, most of whom became eminent professors. He was a leader in organizing the American Political Science Association, formed in 1903 by members drawn from the American Historical Association and the American Economic Association. He was secretary-treasurer of the organization from its founding until 1912 and president for the year 1913. As the first editor (1906–16) of the *American Political Science Review,* he was able to exert substantial influence on the establishment and early growth of the discipline. A number of his books—*An Examination of the Nature of the State* (1896), *The Constitutional Law of the United States* (1910), and *The Fundamental Concepts of Public Law* (1924)—were widely used as college texts.

Willoughby was best known for his writings in the areas of political theory and jurisprudence. In a generation of American academicians greatly influenced by European idealistic thought and analytical jurisprudence, he saw political theory as divisible into "ethical" and "juristic" aspects; in the former he subscribed to the doctrines of Thomas Hill Green and the Oxford School, and in the latter to the theories of John Austin. Willoughby viewed the state in formal rather than descriptive terms, ascribing to it "sovereignty" and "personality" as an organic entity with its own history and evolution. Thus he and his generation of political scientists largely abandoned the traditional American theories of social contract, natural rights, popular sovereignty, and divided sovereignty. With "political behavior," the central interest of many later political scientists, he was largely unconcerned.

During World War I, Willoughby served in Peking—succeeding his brother—as constitutional adviser to the young Chinese republic (1916), and following the war he turned his attention largely to international affairs, principally in the Far East. He served the Chinese government again on later occasions: in 1921–22 as technical expert at the Washington Conference on arms reduction; in 1923 as counselor and adviser at two international opium conferences; and in 1931 as counselor at the League of Nations Conference on Narcotic Drugs and as legal adviser in the League's debate on the Manchuria crisis. Several books grew from these experiences, including *Foreign Rights and Interests in China* (1920). A prolific writer,

Willoughby published a number of other books, of which the most influential in the field of political theory are: *The Ethical Basis of Political Authority* (1930), which enlarged on and refined his earlier *Nature of the State* (1896); *Social Justice* (1900), a treatise on ethics and its relationship to political science and economics; and *Political Theories of the Ancient World* (1903).

On June 27, 1893, Willoughby married Grace Robinson of Dubuque, Iowa, who died in 1907. They had two children, Westel Robinson and Laura Robinson. After his retirement in 1933, Willoughby moved to Washington, D. C. He died there twelve years later, at the age of seventy-seven, of a heart attack. Although his political and juristic theories have been largely abandoned by political scientists, his works on American constitutional law and his many volumes on the Far East are still useful sources.

[John M. Mathews and James Hart, eds., *Essays in Political Science in Honor of Westel Woodbury Willoughby* (1937), includes an evaluation of his contribution by James W. Garner and a bibliography of his writings; it also reproduces a portrait by George Bernhard Meyer that hangs in Gilman Hall at Johns Hopkins Univ. See also obituary by James Hart in *Am. Political Sci. Rev.,* June 1945; *Nat. Cyc. Am. Biog.,* XIII, 435; and *Who Was Who in America,* vol. II (1950). There is a small collection of Willoughby's papers at the Johns Hopkins Univ. Lib. Additional information on his life and career, along with a complete bibliography, can be found in William H. Hatcher, "The Political and Legal Theories of Westel Woodbury Willoughby" (doctoral dissertation, Duke Univ., 1961).]

WILLIAM H. HATCHER

WILSON, LOUIS BLANCHARD (Dec. 22, 1866–Oct. 5, 1943), pathologist and medical educator, was born in Pittsburgh, Pa., to Henry Harrison Wilson and his wife, Susan E. Harbach (or Harbaugh). His father was of Scottish descent, his mother seven-eighths Scottish and one-eighth German. Mrs. Wilson died when Louis was born, and since his father was on military duty in the regular army, the boy was reared by his maternal grandparents on their farm near Pittsburgh. His grandfather died when Louis was six, and his youth was filled with fifteen-hour days of work and little play. An uncle, however, taught him to make things and to shoot. His grandfather had taught him to read before he began school, and the family's resources included a rather unusual library. Little is known of Louis's relationship with his father (who remarried), but Henry Wilson did supply his son with books and a microscope.

Teaching was a family tradition, and at sixteen Louis entered the State Normal School at California, Pa. After graduating in 1886, he stayed on for a year to teach and then went west to Des Moines, Iowa, as principal of a grade school. In

1888 he moved to St. Paul, Minn., as a teacher in the Central High School. While there, he also became a part-time medical student at the University of Minnesota. Teaching biology and physics in the high school enabled him to have a laboratory, which the army physician Walter Reed [q.v.] used when he was stationed in St. Paul in 1893. This association stimulated Wilson's interest in bacteriology, an interest which was greatly furthered by Frank Wesbrook [q.v.], director of the laboratory of the state board of health and professor of bacteriology and pathology at the University of Minnesota. After receiving his M.D. degree in 1896, Wilson became Wesbrook's assistant. A short period of study followed at Harvard, chiefly under Frank Burr Mallory [Supp. 3]. For two summers, beginning in 1902, Wilson was sent to Montana with Dr. William Chowning to conduct the first field and laboratory studies on the causes of Rocky Mountain spotted fever. Their findings helped lay the groundwork for the conclusive research of Howard T. Ricketts [Supp. 1] on the disease.

In 1905, at the invitation of Dr. W. J. Mayo [Supp. 2], Wilson joined the staff of the Mayo Clinic in Rochester, Minn., to establish laboratories for pathologic and bacteriologic studies. Freed now of the necessity of supplementing his small salary by general practice, he devoted his entire time to developing improved methods in the laboratory and to extensive studies in pathology, both of tissue removed during surgery and of tissue obtained at autopsy. Microscopic examination of tissue was, at the time, a slow process. Wilson recognized that the surgeon needed information about the pathology of the tissue immediately after it was removed. His frozen-tissue method for rapid but accurate histologic diagnosis, first described in a publication of 1905, enabled him to give the needed information within minutes; modified only slightly, the method has since been in constant use. Of his other studies in pathology, the most extensive and important were those bearing on the relation between gastric cancer and ulcer and those concerning the various disease states of the thyroid gland. The latter were carried out with the clinical collaboration of Henry S. Plummer [Supp. 2] and the chemical collaboration of Edward C. Kendall. They provided a classification of thyroid disease that has aided greatly in subsequent investigations.

Wilson's interest in teaching led to his appointment as the first director (1915–37) of the Mayo Foundation for Medical Education and Research, later the Mayo Graduate School of Medicine. Under his guidance it became one of the leading institutions of its kind, with some 300 physicians and scientists enrolled at the time of his retirement in 1937. During this period Wilson was president of the Association of American Medical Colleges (1931–33). Of his published papers (numbering about 150), many dealt with graduate medical education; it was in this area that he made his most enduring contributions. Wilson was an original member (1915–24) of the National Board of Medical Examiners, president of the Advisory Board of Medical Specialties (1934–37), chairman of the medical section of the American Association for the Advancement of Science (1931–32), and president of the scientific honorary society, Sigma Xi (1932–34).

For fifteen months during World War I, Wilson served in the army as assistant director of the Laboratory Division of the American Expeditionary Forces in France, a service for which he won the Distinguished Service Medal. From his youth he had been interested in firearms, and during the war and in a later series of experiments (1928–34) for the army's Surgeon General he studied the wound-producing effects of various types of ballistics. His research resulted in a number of fundamental observations on bullet action in tissues.

To his many lay friends, Wilson's outstanding characteristic was his widespread knowledge. He was interested in everything around him: botany, horticulture, photography, including early use of Lumière plates, and the breeding and training of hunting dogs. His interest in photography led to the formation of a section of photography at the Mayo Clinic. The organizations of which he was a member included the National Rifle Association, the Minnesota Horticultural Society, and the Unitarian Church. His younger friends remember him for his willingness to discuss their problems and his seemingly effortless help in getting them jobs or in giving whatever assistance they needed.

On Aug. 26, 1891, Wilson married Mary Elizabeth Stapleton of St. Paul, Minn. They had two children: Alice Mary and Carroll Louis. On Aug. 23, 1924, four years after his first wife's death, Wilson married Mrs. Annie Maud Headline Mellish, director of the editorial section of the Mayo Clinic. She died in 1933, and on Jan. 2, 1935, he married her close friend, Grace Greenwood McCormick. Six years after his retirement, Wilson died in Rochester, Minn., of amyotrophic lateral sclerosis. He was buried in Oakwood Cemetery, Rochester.

[Personal papers and miscellaneous correspondence of Louis B. Wilson, Mayo Clinic/Foundation Archives; collected reprints of Wilson, Mayo Clinic/ Foundation Lib., particularly his response at a dinner given by the Mayo Foundation Chapter of Sigma Xi in his honor on Nov. 8, 1941; Physicians of the Mayo

Clinic and the Mayo Foundation (1937), pp. 1485–91; exhibit on Wilson by Clark W. Nelson, in the Mayo Building, Rochester, Minn.; personal acquaintance. A portrait of Wilson is in the Mayo Clinic. See also obituaries in Jour. Am. Medic. Assoc., Oct. 16, 1943, and the Diplomate, Dec. 1943.]

SAMUEL F. HAINES
CLARK W. NELSON

WITMARK, ISIDORE (June 15, 1869–Apr. 9, 1941), music publisher and composer, was born in New York City, the eldest of six children (five sons and one daughter) of Marcus and Henrietta (Peyser) Witmark. Both parents were of Jewish descent and natives of Prussia. The father had immigrated in 1853 to Fort Gaines, Ga., where he worked as a peddler and, with the zest and drive that later characterized his children, soon accumulated enough money to buy a store and acquire a few slaves. He served as a captain in the Confederate Army during the Civil War. Returning home to find his business ruined, he moved to New York City and, after several unsuccessful ventures, eventually prospered in the liquor business.

The family publishing house, of which Isidore was the head, grew out of a toy printing press that one of his brothers won as a school arithmetic prize. Their father, noting the interest of Isidore, Julius Peyser (1870–1929), and Jay (1872–1950), bought them a real press in 1883. Family ties were always close, and Isidore and his brothers dropped their education short of high school and turned to commercial printing to supplement their father's still precarious income. Musical talent, although without formal training, ran in the family: Isidore composed, Julius ("Julie") as a boy soprano had begun a successful career as a singer, and the two youngest brothers, Frank and Adolph ("Ed"), later followed suit. In 1886 the three older brothers organized the music printing and publishing firm known from that time on as "M. Witmark & Sons," although the father never directed the business. Isidore Witmark was president, his brother Jay business manager.

As their own printers, the Witmarks had for some time a competitive advantage over other music publishers. Deriving much of their initial capital from sales of Isidore's timely "President Cleveland's Wedding March" (1886), they soon purchased the first of the ten publishing houses they eventually absorbed. Julie, touring coast to coast as a member of leading minstrel companies, promoted Witmark material; in those days before radio or much mechanical reproduction, touring companies were the stellar medium of exploitation. Julie and his singer friends, deluged by composers wishing to get material performed and published, steered the best to Witmark, on terms mutually advantageous to writer and publisher. Julie himself was a shrewd businessman and had a performer's unerring ear for hits.

Before others had sensed the value of building a catalogue of popular numbers for sale throughout the country, the Witmarks recognized that the biggest market for sheet music lay outside New York, in smaller communities where people stayed home more. They tapped this market speedily by aggressive nationwide promotion among vaudeville circuits. The time was ripe. Telegraph and telephone stood ready to rush orders, and fast coast-to-coast railway postal service to deliver sheet music and advertisements. Because they were genuinely absorbed in music, the Witmarks had special rapport with composers, performers, and public. They hired good orchestral arrangers, whose scores they distributed gratis to pit bands, and Julie, a pioneer in "song plugging," gave free copies of songs to important entertainers.

The Witmarks knew their public's tastes. In the late 1880's and early 1890's their catalogue stressed genteel Victorian ballads of romantic love and motherhood, with some voguish Irish comedy numbers. They proudly announced (and continued to announce) that they never published a "dirty song," although their first fortune was made by a Charles Graham ballad—"The Picture That Is Turned toward the Wall" (1891), lamenting a wayward daughter disowned by her parents—whose oblique treatment of sex fascinated the prurient tastes of that era. More conventional were "The Sunshine of Paradise Alley" (1895) and "My Wild Irish Rose" (1899), by Chauncey Olcott [q.v.], two of a multitude of waltz ballads, and Harry Armstrong's "Sweet Adeline" (1903). Frequently maudlin, such music salved the rawness of life for newcomers to the cities.

The Witmark firm built a strong catalogue of "high class" numbers, including works by Ernest R. Ball ("Mother Machree") and Caro Roma, and operettas by Gustav Luders (Prince of Pilsen, 1902), Karl Hoschna (Madame Sherry, 1910), Sigmund Romberg (The Desert Song, 1926; New Moon, 1928), and Victor Herbert [q.v.], the dean of American (actually European-style) light opera. To these the Witmarks added their own works. Frank composed the popular "Zenda Waltzes" (1890) for the Graustarkian historical romance Prisoner of Zenda. Isidore wrote the score for Austerlitz (1889) and many ephemeral songs for his own sometimes bathetic lyrics (including "A Mother's a Mother After All," 1885, and "Little Woman of the West," 1908). The Witmarks capitalized on this old-world kitsch without condescension: it was their own taste. Isidore, who collected verse of Ella Wheeler Wilcox [*q.v.*], published L. F. Gottschalk's musical setting to her "Laugh and the world laughs with you; Weep, and you weep alone" (1899). The Witmarks' own world was sentimentally familial; in 1900 the thriving brothers bought their parents an expensive, floridly furnished home east of Central Park.

Despite their "refined" romanticism, the Witmarks were enthralled by ragtime and, doubtless through Julie's minstrel show experience, appreciated its commercial potential. In 1896 three big hits—Ernest Hogan's "All Coons Look Alike to Me" and two songs by Ben Harney [Supp. 2], "Mister Johnson, Turn Me Loose" and "You've Been a Good Old Wagon but You Done Broke Down"—put them among the first big publishers successfully to exploit the new vogue. In 1897 they issued the first piano ragtime instruction manual; later, in the vanguard of the so-called jazz age, they published the first scoring for saxophone.

By 1900 the Witmark firm had branches in Chicago, San Francisco, London, Paris, and Melbourne; its growth epitomized the dominance of New York City in world music publishing. Called "the Tiffany of the music world" by producer Sam Shubert, the firm originated the lucrative publishing of folios and of completely scored amateur minstrel shows. It also took the lead in promoting the copyright laws which after 1908 protected publishers and writers, and Jay Witmark was among the founders in 1914 of the American Society of Composers, Authors, and Publishers (ASCAP), formed to protect the performing rights of copyrighted works.

After 1920 the Witmark fortunes, contingent primarily on sheet music sales and only secondarily on royalties from phonograph records and player piano rolls, began to decline. The firm was hurt by radio, from which publishers could then derive little remuneration, by musical films, which eliminated theatre musicians, and by the automobile and movies in general, which lured people away from the parlor piano, neighborhood vaudeville, and amateur musicals. Sales were temporarily bolstered by the continuing popularity of Victor Herbert and Sigmund Romberg—the latter in his affection for Isidore refused a more favorable contract from a rival—and by the "symphonic" arrangements of Ferde Grofé, Louis Katzmann, and Archie Bleyer for the growing dance band trade. In 1928 Witmark sold the company to Warner Brothers film studios, which sought to avoid copyright infringements by owning a large music catalogue. Isidore

stayed on as an executive in the Warner-absorbed firm, which retained the Witmark name.

Typical of later nineteenth-century businessmen in their drive and initiative, the Witmarks pioneered in modern mass promotional methods. True, their contribution to popular culture was limited by a frequently indiscriminating preference for the ephemeral. Isidore, a bibliophile who requested autographed first editions from scores of the most popular authors of his day, willed to Columbia University a hodgepodge of Hamlin Garland and Elinor Glyn, John Hay and James Whitcomb Riley. This miscellany suggests the Witmark music catalogue, especially in the earlier decades. Without uniform quality, it had only one common denominator: timely sales appeal. Nevertheless, through their sincere interest in black artists—Isidore collected the verse of Paul Laurence Dunbar [*q.v.*] before it was widely known—the Witmarks invigorated popular culture. They foreshadowed the Harlem Renaissance by publishing the "serious" ragtime operetta Dunbar wrote with Will Marion Cook [Supp. 3], *Clorindy: The Origin of the Cakewalk* (1898). However banal their "sweet" arrangements now seem, they developed among popular musicians and public a greater expertise and sophistication. They built a catalogue notable for good, sometimes brilliant, music as well as much trivia.

Of the Witmark brothers, Isidore was especially esteemed among the firm's clients and employees, as among business and civic leaders. He had married, in January 1909, Viola Cahn of Omaha; they had two daughters, Marian and Carolyn. Witmark died of pneumonia in his seventy-second year at the Polyclinic Hospital in New York City and was buried in Westchester Hills Cemetery, Hastings-on-Hudson, N. Y.

[Isidore Witmark's anecdotal autobiography, *From Ragtime to Swingtime* (1939), written with Isaac Goldberg, contains photographs and a complete list of Witmark music. Dates of birth and other personal information were provided by a nephew, Mr. Julius P. Witmark, and by an old employee of the firm. A good brief account is in David Ewen, *Panorama of Am. Popular Music* (1957). Ewen's *The Life and Death of Tin Pan Alley* (1964), p. 70, assesses the long-range significance of the firm; its place in the history of ragtime is shown in Rudi Blesh and Harriet Janis, *They All Played Ragtime* (1950). See also obituaries in *N. Y. Times*, Apr. 10, 1941 (Isidore), and Feb. 18, 1950 (Jay), and *Variety*, June 19, 1929 (Julius), Apr. 16, 1941 (Isidore), and Feb. 22, 1950 (Jay). The Witmark Collection at Columbia Univ. includes Isidore's books, clippings, a file of letters he received, and a few manuscript scores. A number of original printed Witmark scores are in the Music Division of the N. Y. Public Lib. at Lincoln Center.]

HUGHSON MOONEY

WOOD, CASEY ALBERT (Nov. 21, 1856–Jan. 26, 1942), ophthalmologist, ophthalmic ornithologist, and bibliophile, was born in Wellington, Ontario, Canada, the third of four children of Orrin Cottier Wood and Rosa Sophia (Leggo) Wood. His father, a physician, was a native of Jefferson County, N. Y., and a descendant of a seventeenth-century New England settler from Yorkshire. His mother, the daughter of a Crown official in Canada, was of French descent, the family name having originally been Legault. Wood attended private French and English schools and in 1874 graduated from the Ottawa (Ontario) Collegiate Institute. He then entered the medical school of the University of Bishop's College (the school, located in Montreal, was later merged with the medical school of McGill University); he received the degrees of Master of Surgery and Doctor of Medicine in 1877. While a student he attended the lectures of Dr. William Osler [q.v.] at McGill, and the two became lifelong friends. Atfer completing his training, Wood practiced general medicine for several years in Montreal, where he served as professor of pathology and chemistry at Bishop's and attending physician to the Western Hospital. On Oct. 28, 1886, he married Emma Shearer of Montreal, who shared his interest in natural history and his pleasure in an outdoor life. They had no children.

Becoming interested in diseases of the eye, Wood in 1886 began a course of training at the New York Eye and Ear Infirmary and the Post-Graduate Medical School. He then went to Europe, where he studied at eye clinics in Berlin, Vienna, and Paris and spent the years 1888–89 as clinical assistant at the Royal London Ophthalmic Hospital (Moorfields). Returning to the United States in 1890, he settled in Chicago. There he served on the staffs of several hospitals and was professor of clinical ophthalmology at the Chicago Post-Graduate Medical School (1890) and the medical schools of the University of Illinois (1899–1906, 1913–17) and Northwestern University (1906–08). He was a popular teacher, and his kindly manner and ability as a clinician and surgeon attracted a large private practice.

During these years Wood produced many scientific papers and several books, including *Lessons in the Diagnosis and Treatment of Eye Diseases* (1891), *The Commoner Diseases of the Eye* (1904), *A System of Ophthalmic Therapeutics* (1909), and *A System of Ophthalmic Operations* (2 vols., 1911). He also edited *The American Encyclopedia and Dictionary of Ophthalmology* (18 vols., 1913–21) and served as editor of the *Annals of Ophthalmology* (1896–98) and the *Ophthalmic Record* (1897–1918).

In recognition of his professional standing, Wood was elected chairman of the section on ophthalmology of the American Medical Association in 1898 and president of the American Academy of Ophthalmology and Otolaryngology in 1906. He was a founder member of the American College of Surgeons (1913).

Wood had been a member of the Army Medical Corps reserve since 1908, and when war was declared in 1917 he entered active service. After hospital duty in Ohio, he was assigned to Washington, D. C., where he worked with the Red Cross on the training and rehabilitation of blinded soldiers and then helped prepare a history of army hospitals during the war. Wood had long had a strong interest in medical history and in book collecting. In Washington he formed a close friendship with another medical historian and bibliophile, Fielding H. Garrison [Supp. 1]; the two collaborated in preparing *A Physician's Anthology of English and American Poetry* (1920). In 1918 Wood was appointed to the editorial board of the newly established *Annals of Medical History*.

After retiring from his army post in 1920 with the rank of colonel, Wood, now sixty-three, moved to Palo Alto, Calif., and devoted the final two decades of his life to what had been his avocations. Among these was a strong interest in birds, particularly in their mechanism of seeing, as evidenced by his book *Fundus Oculi of Birds* (1917). In the fall of 1920 he joined the famous zoologist William Beebe in a trip to British Guiana to study the eyes of birds and reptiles of that tropical area. He spent two years there, interrupted by brief visits to California, and collected more than two thousand specimens for research. His ornithological interests brought him election to the American and British ornithological unions and appointment (1931) as honorary collaborator in the Division of Birds of the Smithsonian Institution. In later years, often accompanied by his wife, Wood carried out similar studies in many parts of the world. He made long sojourns in India and Ceylon, spent more than a year traveling throughout the islands of the South Pacific, and often visited Europe. During these trips he also searched for medieval books and manuscripts relating to the history of ophthalmology, and in 1929 he brought out a translation of *De Oculis,* a fifteenth-century treatise by Benevenutus Grassus of Jerusalem. Two years later he published *An Introduction to the Literature of Vertebrate Zoology,* the result of many years' research.

Thereafter Wood spent most of his time in Rome, where he was given free access to the treasures of the Vatican Library. With the help of scouts and dealers throughout Europe, he assembled a large personal collection of rare books, particularly in the field of ophthalmology, and enlisted the aid of scholars in the translations. The works included the "Memorandum Book" of Ali ibn Isa, a tenth-century oculist of Baghdad. Wood learned enough Arabic to translate the book, with the assistance of Dr. Max Weyerhof of Cairo, and it was published in 1936. His final publication, *The Art of Falconry* (1943), was a translation of a thirteenth-century work, *De Arte Venandi cum Avibis,* by Frederick II of Hohenstaufen, made by Wood and his niece and close companion, F. Marjorie Fyfe. With the outbreak of World War II, Wood reluctantly left Rome and returned to California. He died at the age of eighty-five at the Scripps Metabolic Clinic in La Jolla, Calif., eight weeks after a cerebral hemorrhage. His ashes are buried in the Mount Royal Cemetery, Montreal.

Throughout his life Wood was devoted to McGill University, which gave him the honorary degrees of Doctor of Medicine (1906) and Doctor of Laws (1921). Through the Casey A. Wood Foundation at McGill, which he had endowed in 1912, he established the Wood Gold Medal for the best examination in clinical subjects. At his death he left all of his books, papers, and museum specimens to the university.

[Obituaries in: *Archives of Ophthalmology,* Apr. 1942 (by Frank Brawley); *Am. Jour. of Ophthalmology,* May 1942 (by Burton Chance), and editorial in issue of Apr. 1942; *Canadian Medic. Assoc. Jour.,* Mar. 1942; *Jour. Am. Medic. Assoc.,* Mar. 21, 1942; *Military Surgeon,* May 1942; *New Eng. Jour. of Medicine,* June 25, 1942; and, on Wood's ornithological work, the *Auk,* Oct. 1942. See also *Who Was Who in America,* vol. II (1950). The dates of Wood's appointments at the Univ. of Ill. College of Medicine were supplied by Dr. Alexander M. Cain of the Lib. of Medic. Sci., Univ. of Ill. at the Medic. Center, Chicago. Other information from Mrs. Margaret Farmer of the Medic. Lib. and Miss Ellen B. Wells of the Osler Lib. at McGill Univ.]

DERRICK T. VAIL

WOOD, CHARLES ERSKINE SCOTT (Feb. 20, 1852–Jan. 22, 1944), army officer, lawyer, author, was born in Erie, Pa., the second of seven children—all boys but the youngest—of Rose (Carson) and William Maxwell Wood. His mother, born in Mercersburg, Pa., was of Scots ancestry; his father, a native of Baltimore, Md., was of English descent. A physician who served in the navy during the Civil War and later became surgeon general, William Wood ruled his sons through military discipline, which he considered character building, but which Erskine (as he was called), who had literary inclinations, detested.

After the war the family moved from Erie to a farm at Owings Mills, Md., not far from Baltimore, where Erskine attended the Baltimore City College, really only a high school.

In 1870 his father secured the youth's appointment to the United States Military Academy at West Point. Wood made a mediocre showing and often threatened to leave, but graduated in 1874 and was assigned to the 21st Infantry as a second lieutenant. After service at Fort Bidwell, Calif., and Fort Vancouver, Washington Territory, he became aide-de-camp in 1877 to Gen. O. O. Howard [*q.v.*]. This was during the campaign against the Nez Percé tribe led by Chief Joseph [*q.v.*], whose moving surrender speech Wood personally took down. The following year he served with Howard in the campaign against the rampaging Bannocks and Paiutes. By his later account, he became "bitterly opposed to the corruption of the Indian Ring in Washington." It "stole the appropriations made for the Indians and when we were ordered out to fight them, I felt I was supporting an unworthy cause" (MS. vita, Wood Papers). He was sent to Washington with a special report, and while there, on Nov. 26, 1878, married Nannie Moale Smith. Their five children who lived to maturity were Erskine, Berwick, Nan, William Maxwell, and Lisa. Wood brought his bride to Fort Vancouver, where he remained the aide of General Howard, who commanded the Department of the Columbia. When Howard was transferred to West Point, Wood accompanied him and served as adjutant of the Military Academy. Once again he was restive, and in 1881 he enrolled at Columbia University. The next year he secured a leave to attend classes full time; he earned the degrees of Ph.B. (1882) and LL.B. (1883).

In 1884 Wood resigned from the army and settled in Portland, Oreg., where he established himself in the practice of law. Through intense application he made a substantial success as an expert in maritime and corporation law and sometimes practiced before the United States Supreme Court. He also became a crusader for justice, working tirelessly for such causes as those of Tom Mooney [Supp. 3] and Nicola Sacco and Bartolomeo Vanzetti [*qq.v.*], and becoming known as a philosophical anarchist. "I have ridden, in the course of my campaigns," he wrote (*ibid.*), "over this country from the Rockies to the Pacific . . . and I have seen that vast domain . . . taken by the few with the aid of Congress and secured to their heirs and assigns forever by that relic of the Middle Ages—the fee simple deed. There is not a place for the common man in the covered wagon." In short, he believed that the United States needed a new economic system. His philosophy brought him into contact with muckrakers like Lincoln Steffens [Supp. 2] and reformers like Emma Goldman [Supp. 2].

While practicing law Wood continued the creative work he had begun during his military days. He wrote sporadically, contributing poems, articles, and stories to *Century Magazine* and the *Pacific Monthly,* sometimes under a pseudonym. His chief recreation was painting in oil, watercolor, and pastel; his works were exhibited in New York, Philadelphia, Chicago, and San Francisco. At sixty-six he retired from law practice and was succeeded in the firm by his oldest son, Erskine.

Wood then went to San Francisco, where, having separated from his wife, who refused to grant him a divorce, he began living with Sara Bard Field, a poet thirty years his junior, who had divorced her husband in order to marry Wood. (After Mrs. Wood's death, they were married on Jan. 20, 1938.) Wood now entered the most creative period of his life, constantly writing both prose and poetry, often with no idea of publication. Of his published works, the best known are *The Poet in the Desert* (1915, with later versions in 1918 and 1929) and *Heavenly Discourse* (1927), the latter having undergone more than forty reprintings. Other works include *A Book of Tales: Being Some Myths of the North American Indians* (1901), *A Masque of Love* (1904), *Maia,* a sonnet sequence (1918), *Poems from the Ranges* (1929), *Too Much Government,* in which he set forth his anarchistic political thought (1931), and *Earthly Discourse* (1937).

Wood considered the 1918 version of *The Poet in the Desert,* a long poem in splendid free verse, his finest work; of it, a fellow author, Zoe Akins, wrote: "I know nothing like it for sheer splendor of speech." Deep in the desert, the Poet, in an extended dialogue with Truth, asks how a sick society can be healed and learns that its cure lies in man's ultimate acceptance of Nature's law: "growth through freedom." In *Heavenly Discourse,* which has come to be regarded as a modern classic, the dialogues occur between God and numerous thinkers of venerated reputation, and in their tangy speeches is to be found some of the finest satire in American literature. The book will score its points as long as war, oppression, exploitation, bigotry, and discrimination exist. Wood's reputation as a minor but enduring American author rests mainly on these two works.

Wood was tall, with curling brown hair and beard that turned gray in later years. His eyes were large and luminous, and he made a dramatic appearance in the long military cape that he habitually wore. In 1937 he suffered a coronary thrombosis and was never again in good health. He died at the age of ninety-one at his home near Los Gatos, Calif.; his remains were cremated and the ashes scattered over his estate.

[Wood's papers, which include an unfinished autobiography, are at the Huntington Lib., San Marino, Calif. Helena Kay has written an M.A. thesis, "Charles Erskine Scott Wood: His Life and Works" (Univ. of Texas, 1937). Biographical details appear in the foreword by Sara Bard Field and the introduction by William Rose Benét to Wood's *Collected Poems* (1949). See also Wood's journals for 1878 and 1879, as printed in *Oreg. Hist. Quart.,* Mar., June 1969; Edwin R. Bingham, "Oregon's Romantic Rebels: John Reed and Charles Erskine Scott Wood," *Pacific Northwest Quart.,* July 1959; obituaries in *Assembly* (West Point alumni magazine), Oct. 1944 (by Sara Bard Field), *San Francisco Chronicle,* Jan. 23, 1944, and *San Jose Mercury Herald-News,* Jan. 23, 1944; Sara Bard Field in *Saturday Rev. of Literature,* Mar. 24, 1945; and, on the sales of *Heavenly Discourse, Publishers' Weekly,* July 13, 1940, pp. 113–14.]
                                    THURMAN WILKINS

WOOD, EDITH ELMER (Sept. 24, 1871–Apr. 29, 1945), housing reformer, was born in Portsmouth, N. H., the elder of two children and only daughter of Horace Elmer, a naval officer and graduate of Annapolis, and Adele (Wiley) Elmer. Both parents were natives of New Jersey and descendants of English colonists. Edith led a peripatetic childhood as her father's duties took the family to various points at home and abroad. She received her early education from tutors and in 1886 entered Smith College, from which she graduated four years later with a B.L. degree. On June 24, 1893, she married Albert Norton Wood, a career naval officer. They had four children: Horace Elmer, who died in childhood, Thurston Elmer, a second Horace Elmer, and Albert Elmer.

During her early married years Mrs. Wood took to writing short stories and books of travel and romantic fiction. In 1906, however, while her husband was stationed in Puerto Rico, the illness of a servant girl, who had contracted tuberculosis, roused her interest in social problems. Discovering the high incidence of this disease in the island, she launched a public health campaign and founded the Anti-Tuberculosis League of Porto Rico, serving as its president until 1910, when she returned to the mainland. Further experience in Washington, D. C., convinced her that tuberculosis was closely related to slum conditions and poor housing. In 1913 she helped draft a bill to allow the District of Columbia to issue low-interest loans to limited-dividend companies for the purpose of improved housing. Although the bill was defeated, government support for housing became the main theme of her life's work.

Her husband's retirement made it possible for the family to move to New York City, and in 1915, to better prepare herself for social work, Mrs. Wood entered the New York School of Philanthropy (later the New York School of Social Work). Two years later she received her diploma, and at the same time a master's degree from Columbia University, where she had enrolled. In 1919, after writing a thesis—published the same year as *The Housing of the Unskilled Worker*—she received a Columbia Ph.D.

An acute shortage of dwellings after World War I brought the housing problem to national attention, and Mrs. Wood became one of the leading spokesmen for a new approach to housing reform. Earlier legislation had emphasized restrictive measures, which set minimum standards for light, air, sanitation, and fire protection. These were later supplemented by zoning laws, which attempted to stabilize patterns of land use by preventing industrial and commercial encroachment on residential neighborhoods. With a small group of architects and housing experts, Mrs. Wood argued that, although such measures eliminated bad housing, they did little to generate the construction of good housing. Indeed, building and zoning codes, by establishing high standards, actually increased the cost of housing and thus exacerbated the shortage for the poor. Such codes, she was convinced, needed to be supplemented by a constructive program under which the government would encourage the building of homes for those who otherwise could not afford them.

Through numerous articles, pamphlets, and books, through the courses she taught in the extension division of Columbia University, and through her chairmanship of the American Association of University Women's national committee on housing (1917–29), Edith Wood expounded her analysis of the housing problem and its solution. Dividing the population into three groups according to income, she maintained that real estate subdividers and speculative builders had failed to provide adequate homes for families of middle and lower income. For those in the middle group, she proposed that the government grant low-interest loans, tax exemptions, and subsidies to encourage limited-dividend and cooperative housing ventures, both of which would hold down housing costs. She further advocated that low-interest loans be given directly to workers who wished to construct their own homes. A national housing fund, financed by the issuance of government bonds, would constitute the primary source for such government aid. Although she believed such projects would indirectly aid the poor, as middle-income families vacated older housing, Mrs. Wood for the immediate future urged the federal government to lend money to cities and towns for slum clearance and the construction of government-owned housing projects. She envisioned a national housing agency to administer the joint program of low-interest loans and public housing. Through its control over federal funds the agency would be able to enforce minimum housing standards throughout the country; it would also serve as a clearinghouse for information on housing and town planning.

Although government support for housing was common in a number of European countries, many Americans in the 1920's regarded the idea as radical and even socialistic. Mrs. Wood sought to allay such concern by arguing that the government should receive a limited but reasonable return on its investment, and by pointing out the incalculable public saving that would result from reducing the costs of the social ills she attributed to slum housing. When a movement for community and regional planning developed in the 1920's, Mrs. Wood became an officer of the Regional Planning Association of America; but she remained essentially a housing reformer, little interested in subordinating housing programs to broader social and economic planning.

The economic depression of the 1930's generated new interest in government housing programs, both for their own sake and as a means of providing employment in the construction industry. In 1932 Mrs. Wood became vice-president of the National Public Housing Conference, founded under the leadership of Mary K. Simkovitch. Composed primarily of social workers, this well-organized lobby was of considerable assistance to Senator Robert F. Wagner in mobilizing support for the Wagner-Steagall National Housing Act, passed in 1937. The act marked the beginning of federal support for public housing, a goal for which Mrs. Wood had long fought. She served as a consultant to the United States Housing Authority, set up under the act, as she had earlier to the Housing Division of the Public Works Administration. She was a commissioner of the New Jersey State Housing Authority in 1934–35.

After 1919 the Woods lived in Cape May Court House, N. J. Surviving her husband by twelve years, Edith Wood died of a cerebral hemorrhage in the state hospital at Greystone Park, N. J., at the age of seventy-three. She was buried in the Naval Academy Cemetery at Annapolis.

[For biographical details, see Durward Howes, ed., *Am. Women*, 1939–40; *Who Was Who in America*, vol. II (1950); *N. Y. Times* obituary, May 1, 1945; and Roy Lubove in *Notable Am. Women*, III, 644–45. Mrs. Wood's ideas of the 1920's on housing reform are set forth in her *Housing Progress in Western Europe* (1923) and *Recent Trends in Am. Housing* (1931). The best histories of housing reform are Roy Lubove's *The Progressives and the Slums* (1963) and *Community Planning in the 1920's* (1964). For the activity which led to the passage of housing legislation under the New Deal, see Timothy L. McDonnell, *The Wagner Housing Act* (1957). A debate between John J. Murphy, Frederick L. Ackerman, and Mrs. Wood, published as *The Housing Famine* (1920), and a comparison of Mrs. Wood's *Recent Trends in Am. Housing* with Catherine Bauer's *Modern Housing* (1934) offer interesting contrasts between Mrs. Wood's relatively limited approach to housing and the views of those interested in integrating housing reform into broader programs of social planning. Her papers are at Columbia Univ.]

STANLEY BUDER

WOOD, FREDERICK HILL (Jan. 2, 1877– Dec. 28, 1943), lawyer, was born in Lebanon, Maine, the only child of Frederick Ansel Wood and Mary Calista (Hill) Wood. His father, a Union Army veteran and a staunch Republican, was a schoolteacher; he moved in 1886 to Kansas, where he continued to teach, and later became a real estate dealer in Kansas City, Mo. Young Frederick attended Kansas City public schools and the University of Kansas in Lawrence, receiving the A.B. degree in 1897 and the LL.B. in 1899. Upon graduation he was admitted to the bar in Kansas and Missouri and opened a practice in Lawrence; for two years he was an assistant professor in the university's law school. He next joined a law firm in Kansas City, Mo., but in 1905 embarked upon a career as a railroad lawyer. He was general attorney of the St. Louis & San Francisco Railroad (1905–10) and general solicitor and commerce counsel of the Kansas City Southern Railway (1910–13), after which he moved to New York City as general attorney and commerce counsel of the Southern Pacific Railway, a position he held until 1924. On July 14, 1914, he married Margery Pearson; they had one daughter, Patricia.

With an opportunity to argue important railroad cases before the Interstate Commerce Commission and the United States Supreme Court, Wood quickly acquired a reputation as a forceful and lucid advocate. He served the railroads faithfully, defending them in public as well as in the courts. In 1924, at the invitation of Paul D. Cravath [Supp. 2], Wood joined the prestigious New York law firm of Cravath, Henderson, and de Gersdorff, which in 1928 was reorganized as Cravath, de Gersdorff, Swaine, and Wood. He continued to represent the railroads, winning substantial rate increases in the Railway Mail Pay case (279 U.S. 73 [1929]) and acceptance of a more favorable method of rate valuation in *St.*

Louis & O'Fallon Railway Company v. *United States* (279 U.S. 461 [1929]). He also served other large corporate clients, such as Bethlehem Steel and Westinghouse Electric.

During the 1930's Wood entered the most important phase of his career, during which he established himself as a leading constitutional authority and as one of the most successful anti-New Deal lawyers in the country. Claiming that the policies of the Roosevelt administration would lead to "an autocracy or dictatorship" and were in principle "totalitarian," he questioned the constitutionality of such measures as the National Industrial Recovery Act, the Agricultural Adjustment Act, the Banking Act of 1933, and the Securities Exchange Act. When the Cravath firm, on behalf of its steel clients, offered its services in the major court test of the National Industrial Recovery Act, Wood won the landmark Supreme Court decision of 1935 declaring the act unconstitutional (*A.L.A. Schechter Poultry Corporation* v. *United States*, 295 U.S. 495). The following year he won a similar decision invalidating the Guffey Coal Act (*Carter* v. *Carter Coal Company*, 298 U.S. 238).

In other New Deal cases Wood successfully sought to impose procedural restrictions on government agencies. In *Morgan et al.* v. *United States* (304 U.S. 1 [1938]), he persuaded the Supreme Court to void an order, issued by the Secretary of Agriculture under the Packers and Stockyards Act of 1921, fixing the rates of marketmen selling livestock at public stockyards; the Court held that the Secretary's improper hearing procedures had denied the marketmen the "rudimentary requirements of fair play." The decision had far-reaching implications for other government agencies as well. In subsequent litigation, for example, in which Wood represented the Ford Motor Company, the National Labor Relations Board was compelled to adopt more formal procedures, including the furnishing of preliminary reports to companies under investigation. A conspicuous exception to Wood's general opposition to the New Deal was his support of Roosevelt's demonetization of gold. Taking action on behalf of several Cravath clients who would otherwise have gone bankrupt, Wood won favorable decisions in the Gold Clause cases (294 U.S. 240 [1935]), in which the Supreme Court sustained the power of Congress to invalidate gold clauses in private contracts.

A short man of somewhat slight build, Wood "tempered his relentless logic with good humor" and had many friends, even among his professional opponents. In court he was a shrewd cross-examiner. He worked hard at his job, continuing even after severe heart attacks in 1938 and 1940, despite the warnings of his doctors. Indeed, he expanded his public interests during the early years of World War II, becoming chairman of the board of trustees of Town Hall, Inc., in New York, national chairman of United China Relief, and an active participant in the National War Fund drive. In 1942 he won substantial judgments for the Bethlehem Steel Company against the United States Shipping Board Emergency Fleet Corporation. He died suddenly the next year in his New York office at the age of sixty-six.

[Wood's writings include "The Small Investor and Railroad Ownership and Management," Acad. of Political Sci. in the City of N. Y., *Proc.*, XI (1924–26), 433–41; and "Some Constitutional Aspects of the Nat. Recovery Program," *Am. Bar Assoc. Jour.*, May 1934; see also *N. Y. Times*, May 29, 1935, p. 11, May 15, 1938, sec. 4, and May 26, 1938, p. 10. Biographical sources: Robert T. Swaine, *The Cravath Firm and Its Predecessors, 1819–1948*, vol. II (1948); memoir in Assoc. of the Bar of the City of N. Y., *Year Book*, 1944; obituaries in *N. Y. Times* and *Kans. City Times*, Dec. 29, 1943.]

EDWARD A. PURCELL, JR.

WOOD, GRANT (Feb. 13, 1892–Feb. 12, 1942), painter, christened Grant De Volsen Wood, was born on his father's farm near Anamosa, Iowa. He was the second son and second of four children of Francis Maryville Wood and Hattie De Ette (Weaver) Wood. His father, a descendant of Quaker settlers of Pennsylvania, was from Winchester, Va.; his mother's parents had come to Iowa from New York state. Maryville ("Murvill") Wood, a serious man of Presbyterian convictions, enjoined his household from reading *Grimm's Fairy Tales* and directed them toward the more secure reality of Cooper's *Leatherstocking Tales* and Dickens's *Child's History of England*. Upon his death in 1901, Mrs. Wood, who had supplemented the family's modest income by teaching school, sold the farm and moved her family to Cedar Rapids, where she lived in genteel poverty for the next two decades.

In Cedar Rapids, Grant Wood combined formal education in the public schools with a variety of odd jobs. Washington High School, from which he graduated in 1910, offered no courses in art, but he did well in manual training, took a mail-order course in design, and was active in art projects for both the school and the Cedar Rapids Art Association. In 1911–12 he taught in a country school near Cedar Rapids. He studied design and metalwork for two summers under Ernest Batchelder at the Minneapolis School of Design and Handicraft and for a few months one winter attended life classes at the evening school of the University of Iowa.

During these formative years Wood developed a wide range of skills and character traits indicative of his ripening potential as a serious artist. Metalwork and carpentry came to him easily, and his sense of color and design led him into interior decoration, which he practiced in Cedar Rapids. His equanimity in personal relationships helped bring him acceptance and patronage. By aiding in the support of his mother and sister during these early years, he seems also to have developed the sense of local roots which would assert itself in his painting and personal life after a period of broadening and travel.

After an unsuccessful attempt to establish himself as a silversmith in Chicago, during which time he took evening courses at the Art Institute, Wood in 1917 was inducted into the army and assigned to camouflage work in Washington. At the end of the war he took up a life of teaching art in the public schools in Cedar Rapids, interspersed with frequent travel to Europe. In 1923 he studied at the Académie Julian in Paris, where he quickly adapted to the expatriate bohemian life-style by assuming a beard and beret and reading H. L. Mencken. His paintings took on the delicate coloration of a derivative Impressionism and, while conforming to a type, also reflected a personal delight in the visual charms of the Old World. He traveled for fourteen months in Europe, living for extended periods in Paris, Munich, and Sorrento. From his own account, his development as a painter owed much more to his almost daily visits to galleries and museums than it did to whatever studio instruction he received. Critics have made much of his enchantment with the late medieval primitives of Germany and Flanders, whose works are well represented in the museums of Munich. In 1928 he returned to Munich to oversee personally the manufacture of a stained glass window commissioned by the war memorial committee of Cedar Rapids. Once more he had the opportunity to absorb from the primitives their style of straightforward, unemotional portraiture and their technique of applying multiple overlays of glazing to obtain an effect of solid color without loss of brilliance.

Both the style and the technique of the primitives were evident in his portrait of "John B. Turner—Pioneer" (1929), in whose Cedar Rapids mortuary Wood was to hold his first exhibition. This was the first of several portraits in which the artist captured the stern and intense character of his native Iowa. "Woman with Plants" (1929), a painting of his mother, reveals in detailed and meticulous fashion both her personal qualities and the regional type, suggesting beneath the careworn, expressionless face the internal dynamics of faith and hard work. In 1930, prompted by a chance glimpse of a Gothic-arched window incongruously situated in the gable of a white-clapboard farmhouse, he posed his sister and the local druggist in rural dress for his most famous painting, "American Gothic." This work, considered in intellectual circles as a piece of debunking in the vein of Mencken and Sinclair Lewis, won the Harris prize at the Chicago Art Institute that year and was purchased for the museum's permanent collection; three years later it was a highlight of the museum's Century of Progress exhibit. Wood's neighbors and the Cedar Rapids press, with considerable justification, considered the painting an admirably authentic piece of local color realism and refused to interpret Wood's whimsy as anything approaching satire.

In spite of the popularity of "American Gothic," Wood allowed himself only one other painting which even suggested the darker side of his humor. This was the portrait of three sere and astringent matrons posed, teacups in hand, before the famous painting by Emanuel Leutze [q.v.], "Washington Crossing the Delaware." Wood had been personally abused by representatives of the Cedar Rapids Daughters of the American Revolution for having the work on the war memorial window done in a nation only recently engaged in war against this country. "Daughters of Revolution" (1932), which slyly used the style of the German primitives and took as background a symbol of American heroism wrought by a German painter, was the only rebuttal Wood was ever to make to such misdirected patriotism.

Previous to the national recognition of his work occasioned by "American Gothic," Wood had been selling his paintings to acquaintances and neighbors for small amounts, barely sufficient to cover the cost of materials, but during the decade of his mature work he was able to ask prices upward of $1,000. Because of his time-consuming technique of glazing, however, it often took him months to complete a painting, and he found it necessary to supplement his income by yearly lecture tours throughout the country. He was generous with both his time and money to aspiring artists, often entertained at home, and for two summers operated the Stone City Art Colony, a small tent city near Cedar Rapids which brought together artists of many schools. In 1934 he was appointed state chairman of the federal Public Works of Art Project, and himself contributed to post office murals in Washington, D. C. Some of the murals effected under his supervision were criticized for their supposed glorification of the labor movement, but for the most part Iowans appeared to accept them as faithful depictions of regional activities and scenes.

As an established figure of national prominence, Wood was appointed in 1934 an associate professor of art at the University of Iowa. He took a keen interest in the work of promising students, but was impatient with academic practices and openly contemptuous of contemporary methods of teaching art. Rather than lecture to his students on theory and history, he preferred to set them immediately at work in the studio to develop their own styles through experimentation. He was subsequently appointed chairman of the department, but faculty in-fighting cut short his tenure, and though he was eventually (1941) promoted to full professor, he was allowed to conduct what was, in essence, a studio in the European tradition of teaching, outside the formal academic program.

During the 1930's Wood capitalized on his growing reputation as a painter of regional subjects, producing not only a sizable number of paintings but also book illustrations, most notably a series of portraits in pen and ink for a collectors' edition of Sinclair Lewis's *Main Street,* and inexpensive lithographs. His landscape paintings, among them "Young Corn" (1931) and "Arbor Day" (1932), though regional in basic subject matter, were cast in a mold more decorative than realistic and were characterized by stereometric shapes which owed at least something to the cubist movement. Among his best-known works are the "Midnight Ride of Paul Revere" (1931), "Birthplace of Herbert Hoover" (1931), "Dinner for Threshers" (1934), "Death on Ridge Road" (1934), and "Parson Weems' Fable" (1939).

A movement toward "Regionalism" in the arts formed during the 1930's around Wood and two of his contemporaries, Thomas Hart Benton and John Steuart Curry. Together they spoke for the indigenous values and subject matter of the Midwest as embodying the peculiarly American character and spirit, and rejected the following of European trends which they saw as characteristic of art circles in American cities. Although much publicized, "Regionalism" proved to be a passing phase of a more generalized reaction against the social and political dislocations of the time and had few important followers.

On Mar. 2, 1935, Wood married Mrs. Sara (Sherman) Maxon, a widowed music teacher in Cedar Rapids. The marriage was childless and ended in divorce in 1939. Wood died of cancer in Iowa City just short of his fiftieth birthday. He was buried in Riverside Cemetery, Anamosa, Iowa.

[The only biography of Grant Wood is Darrell Garwood, *Artist in Iowa* (1944). Further information is available in *Current Biog.*, 1940, and the *Nat. Cyc. Am. Biog.*, XXXV, 522–23. An essay on the man and his work by Park Rinard and Arnold Pyle prefaces the *Catalogue of a Loan Exhibition of Drawings and Paintings by Grant Wood* (Lakeside Press Galleries, Chicago, 1935). Full color reproductions of his best-known paintings may be found in *Life,* Jan. 18, 1943. Critical essays of interest are Thomas Craven in *Scribner's Mag.*, June 1937; Matthew Baigell, "Grant Wood Revisited," *Art Jour.*, Winter 1966; and H. W. Janson, "The Internat. Aspects of Regionalism," *College Art Jour.*, May 1943. Wood's booklet, *Revolt Against the City* (1935), articulates the ideas of the Regionalist movement but perhaps reflects more faithfully the views of its editor, Frank Luther Mott, than of Wood himself. Most sources, including his death certificate, give Wood's birth year as 1892; according to Garwood he was actually born in 1891.]

ALBERT F. McLEAN, JR.

WOOLLCOTT, ALEXANDER HUMPHREYS (Jan. 19, 1887–Jan. 23, 1943), author, dramatic critic, and radio commentator, was the fifth and youngest child of Walter and Frances Grey (Bucklin) Woollcott. He was born at the "Phalanstery," an eighty-five-room house on a large farm near Red Bank, N. J., the site of a Fourierist community founded in 1843 and presided over by his maternal grandfather, John S. Bucklin. Though the communal order had long since lapsed, much of its intellectual, nonconformist spirit still lingered on among the fifty or sixty persons who lived there, most of them related by blood or marriage. The boy was named for Alexander Humphreys [q.v.], a wealthy engineer whose wife was Mrs. Woollcott's closest friend.

Aleck's father, an Englishman, roamed casually from job to job with indifferent success. For six years (1889–95) the family lived in Kansas City, Mo., where Walter Woollcott was secretary of the local Light & Coke Company, but Aleck grew up chiefly at the "Phalanstery" and in Philadelphia, where he was sent to finish grammar school and to attend the Central High School, boarding with local families. An avid reader, of somewhat girlish habits and a misfit among his schoolmates, he grew more self-oriented under this solitary regimen, which strengthened his peculiarities. In his summers at home he enjoyed a rich intellectual life which included music, art, and reading aloud by his father, particularly from the novels of Dickens and Thackeray. In 1905, helped by a scholarship and a loan of $3,000 from Humphreys, he entered Hamilton College at Clinton, N. Y., where he found an outlet for his talents and capitalized on his idiosyncrasies. The humanistic curriculum broadened both his mind and his knowledge, and the college became his spiritual home, to which he remained forever loyal. Before

he graduated, Ph.B., in 1909, he had edited the college literary magazine, won election to Phi Beta Kappa, founded a dramatic club, and formed several lifelong friendships.

Armed with a diploma, Woollcott set off for New York City determined to work for a newspaper. He was unsuccessful in his first application to the *New York Times* and became a bank messenger at $15 a week. In midsummer he came down with a severe attack of mumps, which permanently reduced his sexual powers. He won a job on the *Times* in September. At first he covered the criminal courts, but his talent and ambition soon promoted him to front-page news, and after various assignments he was made dramatic critic in 1914.

His new salary of $60 a week gave him a taste of affluence, but the real wealth lay in the theatrical world for which he had had a passion since childhood and to which he now had entree. His theatre column, "Second Thoughts on First Nights," quickly became popular, as much because of his graceful style as because of his delight in the subject. In the spring of 1915, when the Shubert brothers objected to his unfavorable review of one of their productions and barred him from their theatres, the *Times* fought back and Woollcott became a celebrity; his column doubled in length and his salary jumped to $100 a week. When the United States joined the war in 1917, he enlisted in the army and went to France, where he served as an orderly at Base Hospital No. 8 at Savenay. He was presently transferred to Paris to write for the weekly *Stars and Stripes,* a newspaper for enlisted men edited by Harold Ross, the later founder of the *New Yorker*. A chubby, owlish sergeant wandering myopically through the war zone, Woollcott left a memorable impression.

Returning from France in the summer of 1919, he resumed his place on the *Times*. His vitality was enormous. He reviewed plays, wrote his column, ground out magazine pieces, corresponded widely, made and broke reputations. In his flowing cape, opera hat, and cane, he turned heads at first nights. His biting wit at the Hotel Algonquin Round Table helped win that luncheon gathering its name as the "Vicious Circle." He also frequented the "Thanatopsis Literary and Inside Straight Club" (so christened by Franklin P. Adams), a weekly poker game limited chiefly to the male members of the Round Table. An inveterate gambler, Woollcott played any game passionately, often for high stakes, and enjoyed winning.

In October 1922 he moved to the *New York Herald* at the unheard-of salary of $2,000 a month for the eight months of the theatrical season. In

the summer of 1924, with half a dozen friends, he established an island retreat at Lake Bomoseen, Vt. He ruled the place autocratically and eventually came to spend the greater part of his time there. When the *Herald* merged with the *Tribune,* Woollcott briefly wrote for the New York *Sun,* but, disliking the anticlimax of an evening paper, he signed a three-year contract to begin in August 1925 with the *World.* Here he joined Franklin P. Adams, Heywood Broun [Supp. 2], Laurence Stallings, friends from his days on *Stars and Stripes,* and other brilliant journalists who made this New York's most influential newspaper.

When his contract with the *World* neared its end, Woollcott turned to free-lance writing for the leading magazines. He began a column for the *New Yorker,* "Shouts and Murmurs," in February 1929. That September he made his radio debut on station WOR of Newark. Awkward and uncomfortable at first, he soon became expert in the new medium, and his book reviews, storytelling, and showmanship became familiar features on the Mutual network. He switched in 1930 to the Columbia Broadcasting System and in 1937 became known to millions from coast to coast as "The Town Crier."

He was less successful at writing plays. *The Channel Road,* an adaptation of a story by De Maupassant on which he collaborated with George S. Kaufman in 1929, closed after fifty performances. Four years later a mystery play called *The Dark Tower* fared no better. He was more successful as an actor. In two S. N. Behrman plays, *Brief Moment* (1931) and *Wine of Choice* (1938), he played roles obviously modeled on himself. When in their play *The Man Who Came to Dinner* (1939) his friends George Kaufman and Moss Hart portrayed a caricature of an acidulous critic, Woollcott gave his blessing and toured triumphantly in the part with the Pacific Coast company.

Fat, self-indulgent, hardworking, and capricious, Woollcott suffered a heart attack in April 1940. Recuperating at Lake Bomoseen, he rested and shed weight in order to resume an active life, but his health constantly worried him. He returned to the air in the fall of 1940 to campaign for Franklin Roosevelt and to attack the isolationist sentiments of the America First Committee. In the fall of 1941 a British warship took him to London, where he broadcast over the BBC to promote understanding between the two English-speaking nations. On his return he contracted with the *Reader's Digest* for a series of articles at $24,000 a year. He planned new broadcasts, but a heart attack canceled them. After under-

going gall bladder surgery in June 1942, he attempted to resume his busy career, but in January 1943, while participating in a radio program, "The People's Forum," he suffered a fatal heart attack at the CBS studios in New York City. His ashes were buried in the cemetery of Hamilton College.

As a critic Woollcott became a national figure, yet his critical standards were lax, subjective, and arbitrary. Given to romantic sentimentality, he often praised the ordinary. His unusual command of language and his immense knowledge, however, enabled him to write reviews that touched the widest range of readers. A gifted phrasemaker, he could also damn with a phrase. Always eager to dominate an occasion or a scene, he cultivated idiosyncrasies and never hesitated to strike an air or a pose. On social occasions he was a compulsive talker. He trampled on friendship for the sake of celebrity. These habits tended to hide his better qualities; his generosity, his loyalty, his industry, his patriotism were known to only a few intimates. His writing was like his character, more manner than substance. But he helped make dramatic criticism a vital element in the American theatre, and his urbanity struck a note of style that was widely emulated.

[Woollcott's books are chiefly collections of his articles and reviews, of which the most successful was *While Rome Burns* (1934). Samuel Hopkins Adams, *A. Woollcott* (1945), is a lively biography by a fellow journalist who saw his subject lucidly, described him dispassionately, and understood him thoroughly. Less satisfactory is Edwin P. Hoyt, *Alexander Woollcott* (1968), which attempts to offset some of the uncomplimentary statements and implications of the Adams biography. See also *The Letters of Alexander Woollcott,* ed. by Joseph Hennessey and Beatrice Kaufman (1944); and Margaret Case Harriman, *The Vicious Circle* (1951).]

H. L. KLEINFIELD

WOOLSEY, JOHN MUNRO (Jan. 3, 1877– May 4, 1945), jurist, was born in Aiken, S. C., the oldest of four children (three sons and a daughter) of William Walton Woolsey and Katherine Buckingham (Convers) Woolsey. For reasons of health his father, a civil engineer, had taken up cotton planting in the South, but the family's roots lay in the North. The American progenitor, George Woolsey, had come to New Amsterdam from England in the mid-seventeenth century; John Woolsey's grandfather was president of the Merchants' Exchange of New York City, and a great-uncle, Theodore Dwight Woolsey [*q.v.*], was president of Yale.

After attending private school in Englewood, N. J., and Phillips Academy in Andover, Mass., John Woolsey entered Yale, where he was elected to Phi Beta Kappa and graduated in

1898. In his college years he considered becoming a historian, but the prospect of joining the Manhattan law firm of a maternal uncle, Ebenezer Convers, proved more appealing. At the Columbia Law School, from which he received the LL.B. degree in 1901, he was a founder (1901) and first secretary of the *Columbia Law Review.* He was admitted to the New York bar in 1901 and joined his uncle's firm, Convers & Kirlin (later Kirlin, Woolsey, Campbell, Hickox & Keating), with which he was associated for twenty-eight years. The firm specialized in admiralty law, and as an authority in this field, Woolsey argued several cases before the Supreme Court of the United States, including one in which a significant new application of the ancient writ *scire facias* was established. From 1922 to 1929 he was an associate editor of the *Revue de Droit Maritime Comparé* of Paris.

In 1929 Woolsey was appointed by President Hoover to the United States District Court for the Southern District of New York. "From the time I began to study law I always wanted to be a Federal Judge," he later recalled. "In no other position is a man so well placed to see the pageant of American life pass before his eyes" (*New York Times,* Mar. 11, 1934). As a federal judge in the depression and New Deal years, Woolsey heard many cases involving the bankruptcy, receivership, or reorganization of elaborate business combinations—"corporate omelets," he called them—formed in the expansive 1920's. In a case of November 1933 (*Campbell* v. *Chase National Bank,* 5 F. Supp. 156) he upheld the constitutionality of the anti-gold-hoarding provisions of the Emergency Banking Act of March 1933, an important piece of New Deal fiscal legislation. Whatever the complexity of the issues, his rulings were marked by a perceptive grasp of detail and a terse economy of expression.

It was through his decisions in the realm of censorship and freedom of the press that Judge Woolsey became known to a broader public. Coming to the bench at the close of a decade of increasing permissiveness in sexual matters, Woolsey in several notable cases gave his judicial imprimatur to this trend. He found the drift away from governmental censorship personally congenial, having acquired from William Graham Sumner [*q.v.*] at Yale a belief in the virtue of unfettered competition in the realm of ideas as in the marketplace. In July 1931 he reversed a federal ban on the importation of the works of Dr. Marie C. Stopes, the British birth control advocate, and on Dec. 6, 1933, in his most famous ruling, he similarly cleared the way

for the free circulation of James Joyce's *Ulysses,* a novel which the government had for years stigmatized as obscene. In a decision which has often been reprinted (*United States* v. *One Book Called "Ulysses,"* 5 F. Supp. 182), Woolsey wrote: "Joyce has attempted—it seems to me, with astonishing success—to show how the screen of consciousness with its ever-shifting kaleidoscopic impressions carries, as it were on a plastic palimpsest, not only what is in the focus of each man's observation of the actual things about him, but also in a penumbral zone residua of past impressions, some recent and some drawn up by association from the domain of the subconscious." The shocking words in *Ulysses,* he noted, "are old Saxon words known to almost all men and, I venture, to many women, and are such words as would be naturally and habitually used, I believe, by the types of folk whose life, physical and mental, Joyce is seeking to describe." In one of the epigrams for which he was noted, Woolsey added that in evaluating the prevalent sexuality in *Ulysses* "it must always be remembered that his locale was Celtic and his season spring."

A Republican in politics and an Episcopalian in religion, Woolsey displayed in his private life the same cultivated sensibility which marked many of his judicial utterances. Antique furniture, paintings, old books, and prints filled his East 66th Street duplex, and his summer estate in Petersham, Mass., included a restored colonial town hall which he used as his library and occasionally as his judicial chamber. In appearance he was full-faced and bald, with prominent forehead and heavily lidded eyes. A pipe, gold-framed octagonal glasses, and comfortable but well-tailored clothes completed an image many found reminiscent of an English country gentleman.

Intensely loyal to his various alma maters, Woolsey served in the 1930's as president of the alumni associations of both Phillips Andover Academy and the Columbia Law School. He was a member of many social clubs and organizations, including the Century of New York and the Union Club of Boston. Woolsey was married on Nov. 14, 1911, in Athol, Mass., to Alice Bradford Bacon, the daughter of a New London, Conn., clergyman. They had one son, John Munro.

A sufferer from chronic cardiovascular disease, John Woolsey retired from the federal bench in December 1943 and died of a heart attack at his home sixteen months later. His age was sixty-eight. After funeral services at St. George's Church in New York City, he was buried in the Woolsey family cemetery near Glen Cove, Long Island, N. Y.

[There is no published biography. Sketches and summaries of Woolsey's career may be found in the *Quarter Century Record* (1925) and *Fifty-Year Report* (1949) of the Class of 1898, Yale College; Yale Univ., *Obituary Record of Graduates,* 1944–45; *Who Was Who in America,* vol. II (1950); and *Nat. Cyc. Am. Biog.,* Current Vol. C, p. 311 (with photograph), useful for his career as an attorney. See also *N. Y. Times,* Dec. 4, 1943, p. 12, an editorial appraisal of his career upon his retirement; and S. J. Woolf, "A Judge Who Scans the Drama of Life," *N. Y. Times Mag.,* Mar. 11, 1934, a personal profile with a pencil sketch by the author. The principal obituaries are in the *N. Y. Times* and the *N. Y. Herald Tribune,* May 5, 1945. John M. Woolsey, Jr., provided family information and bibliographical assistance. The *Ulysses* decision is reprinted in the Modern Lib. edition of *Ulysses* (1934) and is discussed in: Ben Ray Redman, "Obscenity and Censorship," *Scribner's,* May 1934; James C. N. Paul and Murray L. Schwartz, *Federal Censorship: Obscenity in the Mails* (1961); and Paul S. Boyer, *Purity in Print* (1968). Morris L. Ernst, *The Best Is Yet* (1945), the autobiography of the attorney who defended *Ulysses* before Judge Woolsey, contains interesting personal sidelights. A collection of Woolsey's briefs, opinions, and other documents of his legal career is at Yale.]

PAUL S. BOYER

WORK, HUBERT (July 3, 1860–Dec. 14, 1942), physician and cabinet officer, was born in Marion Center, Pa., the sixth of seven children and only son of Moses Thompson Work, a farmer, and his second wife, Tabitha Logan (Van Horn) Work. On both sides of the family he was descended from a long line of Pennsylvania pioneers. After attending local schools and the Indiana (Pa.) State Normal School, Work began medical training at the University of Michigan (1882–84) and completed it at the University of Pennsylvania, where he received his M.D. in 1885. He then went west to seek his fortune and settled in Colorado, where he began practice in Greeley, removed to Fort Morgan, and in 1896 founded the Woodcroft Hospital for mental and nervous diseases in Pueblo.

Work was a Republican and early took part in local politics. In 1908 he chaired the Republican state convention and was sent as a delegate to the national convention. He became chairman of the state Republican committee and from 1913 to 1919 was a member of the party's national committee. Meanwhile he continued to be active in his profession, acquiring a reputation as a competent clinician and psychiatrist. He served on the State Board of Medical Examiners and the State Board of Health and was elected president of the Colorado State Medical Society in 1896, the American Medico-Psychological Society in 1911, and the American Medical Association in 1921. When the United States entered the First World War he joined the Army Medical Corps, where he supervised medical aspects of the draft.

In 1920, now a figure of some prominence, Work was called upon by Will Hays, the Republican national chairman, to aid the presidential campaign by organizing farmers in support of the Harding-Coolidge ticket. After the election, when Hays took over the Post Office Department, Work accepted appointment as First Assistant Postmaster General. Hays resigned in January 1922, and after two months as acting Postmaster General, Work succeeded to the post on Mar. 4, 1922. He held office for little more than a year, but left a mark on the department. Particularly concerned with businesslike efficiency in government operations, he won support from the Treasury Department to have the government own, rather than lease, post-office buildings.

After the resignation of Albert B. Fall [Supp. 3] in March 1923, President Harding appointed Work Secretary of the Interior. He inherited a department beset by internal conflict and attacked from the outside as corrupt and inefficient and as an enemy of conservation. These feelings were heightened with the gradual disclosure of the Teapot Dome scandal. Work believed that much of the reputation of the Interior Department was undeserved and set out to revamp its public relations. As in the Post Office Department, he stressed efficiency and "business" methods. He brought in new employees from the business world, established a central personnel office for the department as part of the Secretary's office, and brought all the Washington bureaus of the department together in a single location. On policy matters, he affirmed his support of conservation of natural resources. Noting that mineral deposits, timber supplies, streams, soils, and even grazing ranges were being exhausted, he warned that the period of exploitation, so far as the government was concerned, had passed. He also called for legislation to stop unauthorized and unrestricted grazing, which was destroying the public domain.

The Reclamation Service posed a particular problem. It had been set up as a self-financing system, its funds to be replenished by fees paid by water users, but in the agricultural depression of the early 1920's many hard-pressed settlers defaulted on their payments. Concerned over this unbusinesslike situation, Work reorganized the Service in 1923 as the Reclamation Bureau, removed its director, Arthur Powell Davis [Supp. 1], an engineer little attuned to social and economic considerations, and appointed a "Fact Finders" committee to review federal reclamation policy. Many of the committee's findings were adopted, and in 1924 Work appointed one of its members, the able Elwood Mead [Supp. 2], to head the Bureau. Finally, Work made a number of improvements in the Bureau of Indian Affairs, stressing benefits to the Indians, expanding health activities, initiating a survey of the irrigation and reclamation of Indian lands, and requesting that a private concern—the Institute for Government Research—recommend changes in Indian policy.

Work left the Interior Department in July 1928 to become chairman of the Republican National Committee, in which capacity he directed the election campaign of Herbert Hoover. This was his final public service; now sixty-eight, he retired to Colorado and made his home in Denver. On Aug. 31, 1887, Work had married Laura M. Arbuckle of Madison, Ind. They had five children: Philip, Frances Mary, Hubert, Dorcas, and Robert, of whom the second and third died in infancy. His wife died in 1924, and on Dec. 8, 1933, he married Mrs. Ethel Reed Gano, the widow of George W. Gano, a Denver merchant. Work was a Presbyterian in religion. He died of a coronary thrombosis at St. Joseph's Hospital in Denver in 1942, at the age of eighty-two, and was buried in Arlington National Cemetery.

[Work Papers, Colo. State Archives, Denver; Work's Postmaster General Files and his Speech and Office Files in the Dept. of Interior Records, both in the Nat. Archives, Washington; Harding Papers, State Hist. Soc., Columbus, Ohio; Coolidge Papers, Lib. of Cong.; Hoover Papers, Hoover Lib., West Branch, Iowa; Von Gayle Hamilton, *Work Family Hist.* (1969); *Nat. Cyc. Am. Biog.*, Current Vol. A, p. 14; Eugene P. Trani, "Hubert Work and the Dept. of the Interior, 1923–28," *Pacific Northwest Quart.*, Jan. 1970; Donald C. Swain, *Federal Conservation Policy, 1921–1933* (1963); obituaries in *N. Y. Times,* Dec. 15, 1942, *Jour. of Nervous and Mental Disease,* Mar. 1943, and *Jour. Am. Medic. Assoc.,* Dec. 19, 1942; information from Colo. State Archives and from librarian, Indiana (Pa.) Univ.]

EUGENE P. TRANI

WRIGHT, HAROLD BELL (May 4, 1872– May 24, 1944), novelist, was born on a farm near Rome, N. Y., the second of the four sons of Alma T. (Watson) and William A. Wright. His father's forebears had come from Essex, England, in 1640 and had settled at Wethersfield, Conn.; later descendants moved to Oneida County, N. Y., where in 1800 they established the county's first church, in Rome. William Wright, after serving in the Civil War, failed to adapt to civilian life, became addicted to drink, and as an itinerant carpenter shifted his family from town to town, finally settling in Sennett, N. Y., where they lived in extreme poverty.

Harold was sent to the local primary school, regularly attended the Presbyterian Sunday school

and church, and from his mother learned something of art and literature. She died of tuberculosis when he was eleven, the family broke up, and for the next ten years he was essentially homeless. Sent to work for neighboring farmers, he later lived with various relatives, held a succession of odd jobs in Ohio (where he had briefly joined his father), and one winter worked in a bookstore, where he was allowed to read freely. After completing his apprenticeship with a house painter, he began to regret his scanty education and employed a tutor, with whom he studied at night.

A chance encounter with an evangelist reawakened his early religious convictions, and he joined the Disciples of Christ. To educate himself for the ministry, he enrolled in 1894 in the junior preparatory department of the denomination's Hiram College in Ohio, where he spent two years before wandering on for lack of money. He worked for a while at a stone quarry, suffered a nearly fatal attack of pneumonia, and began painting landscapes to earn a living. A stubborn eye infection ended this venture, as well as his hopes of returning to college. To regain his health, he made a canoe trip down the Ohio River and then joined relatives in the Ozarks, near Notch, Mo. There he regularly attended church and first began preaching. Though without formal training, for the next ten years he served as a minister of the Christian Church: at Pierce City, Mo. (1897–98), Pittsburg, Kans. (1898–1903), Kansas City, Mo. (1903–05), Lebanon, Mo. (1905–07), and Redlands, Calif. (1907–08). He then left the ministry to devote full time to writing novels, hoping to carry his message to a larger audience than he could reach through the pulpit.

Although Wright had done some writing while a student at Hiram College, he made his first serious attempt at fiction during his years in Kansas when he wrote *That Printer of Udell's* (1903). Originally entitled *Practical Christianity* and largely autobiographical in its material, it embodied his conviction that most churches had forgotten the true teachings of Christ and had failed in their social responsibilities to the poor. Although rejected by Eastern publishers, the work was accepted by the Book Supply Company of Chicago, a mail-order house, and, well advertised, sold 450,000 copies. Wright next wrote *The Shepherd of the Hills* (1907), set in his beloved Ozark mountains, which became an immediate best seller, and *The Calling of Dan Matthews* (1909), a fictional critique of current religious practices. *The Winning of Barbara Worth* (1911), perhaps Wright's best novel, sold more than a million and a half copies. Set in the Imperial Valley of California, where Wright was then living, it dealt with the reclamation project that had turned that desert waste into a place of homes and fertile fields. Other novels followed in steady succession, usually at intervals of two years, until 1932, with a final novel in 1942. D. Appleton & Company became his publisher in 1921.

Although Wright's novels were phenomenal best sellers and made him a wealthy man, they had little merit as literature, and their popularity bewildered the critics, one of whom declared: "He writes badly, he is blatantly, even grotesquely false to life, his technique is something to weep over, but somehow or other, he does make the reader see" (Frederic Taber Cooper in *Bookman*, January 1915, p. 500). Wright's style and technique were in fact better than many people unfamiliar with his work could easily believe, and he wrote out of deep conviction. He created his melodramatic plots and stereotyped characters solely to illustrate his chosen themes: that true religion should be a part of daily life, not merely a Sunday ritual; that simple country folk living close to nature are morally superior to wealthy urbanites; and that the evils of the American social structure could be corrected by true men and true women who lived according to Christian principles. He had a wide readership among plain people of rural and small-town America. Though his popularity declined somewhat after the First World War, the nineteen books produced during his lifetime sold more than ten million copies, one of the records of popular culture.

All his life Wright was subject to respiratory infections, and in the 1920's he developed tuberculosis, which he successfully treated by an open-air existence in Arizona and California. He was normally a robust man, more than six feet tall, who loved fine horses and the outdoors. While living in the Imperial Valley, he had raised blooded horses; and later he grazed cattle on the Cross Anchor ranch near Tucson, Ariz. In 1934 he established a farm near Escondido, Calif., which produced many kinds of fruit and vegetables.

On July 18, 1899, Wright had married Frances Elizabeth Long of Buffalo, N. Y.; their three sons were Gilbert Munger (1901), Paul William (1902), and Norman Hall (1910). He was divorced from his first wife in 1920, and on Aug. 5 of that year married Mrs. Winifred Mary (Potter) Duncan of Los Angeles. Wright died of bronchial pneumonia at the age of seventy-two at La Jolla, Calif. His ashes are held at Greenwood Memorial Park, San Diego, Calif., in a book-shaped copper urn imbedded in sand from the

Imperial Valley, the scene of his most successful novel.

[The fullest account of Wright's life is his autobiography, *To My Sons* (1934), which is supplemented by his article "Why I Did Not Die," *American Mag.*, June 1924. The following include brief treatments of Wright's career: James D. Hart, *The Popular Book* (1950); Frank L. Mott, *Golden Multitudes* (1947); Edward Wagenknecht, *Cavalcade of the Am. Novel* (1952); and, on *The Winning of Barbara Worth*, Franklin Walker, *A Literary Hist. of Southern Calif.* (1950). See also articles about Wright and his work in *Bookman*, Jan. 1915, Jan. 1917, July 1918, Feb. 1923, *Literary Digest*, Aug. 21, 1920, and *Harper's*, Oct. 1947; and obituaries in *N. Y. Times* and *San Diego* (Calif.) *Union*, May 25, 1944. Hiram College verified the dates of his enrollment.]

THURMAN WILKINS

WYETH, NEWELL CONVERS (Oct. 22, 1882–Oct. 19, 1945), painter and illustrator, was born in rural Needham, Mass., the eldest of four sons of Andrew Newell Wyeth and Henriette (Zirngiebel) Wyeth. Both parents were natives of Cambridge, Mass. His father, a grain dealer, came from an old New England family; his mother was the daughter of a Swiss florist whose family included several artists. In his early boyhood Convers (as he was called in the family) began to draw the scenes and activities of the countryside in which he grew up. He attended the Needham high school, but left after two years, with the warm support of his mother and the reluctant consent of his father, to study art at the Mechanic Art High School in Boston. He continued his education at the Massachusetts Normal Art School and the Eric Pape School of Art in Boston, and also studied with Charles W. Reed.

In 1902, at the age of twenty, Wyeth went to Wilmington, Del., to join the small art school conducted by the famous illustrator Howard Pyle [*q.v.*]. The group included roughly a dozen talented young men and women, who paid no tuition, carried out necessary chores, and shared the costs of heating, equipment, and modeling fees. Winters were spent in the Wilmington studio, summers at nearby Chadds Ford, Pa., in the Brandywine Valley, the scene of many notable events in colonial history and the Revolutionary War. The curriculum included drawing from plaster casts and figures, weekly compositions submitted to the whole class for criticism, eloquent informal talks by Pyle on a variety of subjects, and many sketching excursions into the countryside. In this setting Wyeth's talent developed quickly and steadily.

Many artists of his time were attracted to the romance of the frontier, and Wyeth, as a descendant of the trader Nathaniel Jarvis Wyeth [*q.v.*], an early explorer of Oregon, had a special interest in Western themes. Pyle constantly exhorted his pupils to live their paintings, to immerse themselves in firsthand knowledge and experience of their subjects, and in 1904 Wyeth took his small savings and journeyed to a Colorado ranch, where he sketched cowboys, cattle, and the new landscape. When his money was stolen, he got a job as a government mail rider and traveled south to New Mexico, where he visited the Navajo reservation and absorbed the activities and colors of Indian life. The trip was a great experience. He returned east with a large number of drawings and ideas and immediately sold several Western pictures to magazines. Soon he began to receive commissions from publishing houses for book illustrations, the first of which were published in 1906.

On Apr. 16, 1906, Wyeth married Carolyn Brenneman Bockius of Wilmington. The couple settled in Chadds Ford. Of their five children, three became artists: Henriette Zirngiebel (born in 1907), Carolyn Brenneman (1909), and Andrew (1917). Nathaniel Convers (1911) became an inventor, and Ann (1915) a musician and composer. The family spent many summers near Port Clyde, Maine, in the Penobscot region, and both the coast and the people became subjects for Wyeth's imagination. The death of a fisherman friend inspired his famous "Island Funeral," and his illustrations for Kenneth Roberts's *Trending into Maine* (1938) were based on a rich store of experience. Though Wyeth was never the teacher Pyle had been, he attracted young artists who sought advice and criticism. Three stayed on to study and paint: Paul Horgan, who later chose writing as a career; the watercolorist John McCoy, who married Wyeth's daughter Ann; and the painter Peter Hurd, who married Henriette.

The career as an illustrator that Wyeth had launched on his return from the West continued for more than four decades. Many well-known magazines published his work, including the *Saturday Evening Post, Harper's, Scribner's, Collier's,* and the *Ladies' Home Journal.* Of his book illustrations, his work for children reached the widest audience. Beginning in 1911 with Robert Louis Stevenson's *Treasure Island,* he illustrated eighteen volumes in Scribner's Illustrated Classics series, among them Stevenson's *Kidnapped* (1913), *The Black Arrow* (1916), and *David Balfour* (1924), Jules Verne's *Mysterious Island* (1918), Charles Kingsley's *Westward Ho!* (1920), and James Fenimore Cooper's *The Last of the Mohicans* (1919) and *The Deerslayer* (1925). The format—a squarish book with a

four-color illustration on the dust jacket repeated and pasted on the book's dark cover, two-color end papers, and full-page four-color illustrations in the text—was quickly imitated by other publishers.

Apart from those published by Scribner's, Wyeth illustrated a number of other books, for adults as well as children. These usually had historical or romantic themes: Mary Johnston's *The Long Roll* (1911) and *Cease Firing* (1912), Longfellow's *The Courtship of Miles Standish* (1920) and *The Song of Hiawatha* (1920), Defoe's *Robinson Crusoe* (1920), Irving's *Rip Van Winkle* (1921), Rafael Sabatini's *Captain Blood* (1922), James Boyd's *Drums* (1928), Hervey Allen's *Anthony Adverse* (1934), Marjorie Kinnan Rawlings's *The Yearling* (1939), and C. S. Forester's *Captain Horatio Hornblower* (1939). A great admirer of Henry Thoreau, Wyeth illustrated a volume of selections from his journals published as *Men of Concord* (1936).

Wyeth was a large man, more than six feet tall, with a rough, great-hearted manner and a New England accent which he never lost. He was usually up early and at work during all the daylight hours. From him his children learned the discipline and basic knowledge so necessary to the professional artist; they also learned to enjoy life. Wyeth would seize any excuse to drag out the costume trunk. He yearly dressed as Santa Claus and once stomped around the roof on Christmas Eve with almost disastrous results. He outfitted family and friends to act as models, used actual scenes for backgrounds, and often completed a painting in two or three days. To dramatize the action he frequently employed camera techniques, including close-ups and angle shots. After 1911 he illustrated, on the average, nearly a book a year, producing some three thousand illustrations in all.

Wyeth did his book illustrations in oil for the most part. He preferred to work on a large canvas, and after accepting an initial invitation to paint a mural for a hotel in Utica, N. Y., he went on to paint many others in various parts of the United States. The list includes five large murals representing maritime commerce for the First National Bank of Boston (1924; later removed to the Boston Public Library); two historic panels in the Federal Reserve Bank in Boston; a large mural for the Franklin Savings Bank in New York City, one for the Penn Mutual Life Insurance Company building in Philadelphia, and a group for the Metropolitan Life Insurance Company in New York; and two Civil War battle scenes in the Missouri State Capitol in Jefferson City. He also painted a triptych for the Chapel of the Holy Spirit in the National Episcopal Cathedral in Washington, D. C.

Only during the last two decades of his life did Wyeth find the time to turn to easel painting of his own. His several hundred still lifes, portraits, studies, and landscapes were not well known until after his death. From his son-in-law Peter Hurd he learned to work in egg tempera, and he spent increasing amounts of time with this medium.

Although he moved little in conventional artistic circles, Wyeth was a member of the National Academy of Design and the Society of Illustrators. Among the prizes he received were the gold medal at the Panama-Pacific Exposition in San Francisco in 1915 and the W. A. Clarke Prize of the Corcoran Gallery in Washington, D. C. (1932), for his painting "In a Dream I Met General Washington." In 1945 he received an honorary A.M. degree from Bowdoin College. Later that year, a few days before his sixty-third birthday, he was killed when his car was struck by a train near his home in Chadds Ford. Wyeth is remembered for his illustrations, which for a generation of children breathed life and romance into a group of literary classics, and, in the 1970's, as the father and teacher of a famous artist son.

[Henry C. Pitz, *The Brandywine Tradition* (1969); Ernest W. Watson, "Giant on a Hilltop," *Am. Artist,* Jan. 1945; *N. Y. Times* obituary, Oct. 20, 1945; *Who Was Who in America,* vol. II (1950); exhibition catalogue, Wilmington Soc. of the Fine Arts, Jan. 1946 (with foreword by Paul Horgan); Dudley Lunt in *Horn Book,* Sept.–Oct. 1946; Stimson Wyeth, *ibid.,* Feb. 1969; Wyeth Collection, Needham Public Lib., Needham, Mass.; birth record, from Mass. Registrar of Vital Statistics. See also: Theodore Bolton, *Am. Book Illustrators* (1938), for a checklist of his books; Stanley J. Kunitz and Howard Haycraft, eds., *Junior Book of Authors* (2nd rev. ed., 1951); and feature story in *Life,* June 17, 1946. Collections of Wyeth's work may be found in the Farnsworth Museum, Rockland, Maine, which also collects the work of other members of the family, and in the Wilmington (Del.) Soc. of the Fine Arts. Several Western oils are in the Southern Ariz. Bank and Trust Co., Tucson, Ariz. Possibly the largest collection is owned by the Wyeth Foundation at Chadds Ford. The Brandywine River Museum in Chadds Ford is the chief center of study of Howard Pyle and the Wyeth family of painters. *The Wyeths: The Letters of N. C. Wyeth, 1901–1945,* ed. by Betsy James Wyeth (1971), includes reproductions of his work, as does Henry Pitz's article on Wyeth in *Am. Heritage,* Oct. 1965.]

CATHERINE HITCHINGS
SINCLAIR HITCHINGS

YON, PIETRO ALESSANDRO (Aug. 8, 1886–Nov. 22, 1943), organist and composer, was born at Settimo Vittone, Italy, near Turin. He was the second son and sixth of eight children of Antonio and Margherita (Piazza) Yon. (Two other boys died in infancy.) The parents were modest people, the father being a watchmaker, photographer, and storekeeper. At the age of six Pietro began to study the organ with Angelo Burbatti, cathedral organist in nearby Ivrea. His subsequent musical training included work with Polibio Fumagalli at the Milan Conservatory, with Franco Da Venezia, Roberto Remondi, and Giovanni Bolzoni at the Turin Conservatory (1901–04), and, finally, at the Liceo di S. Cecilia in Rome, where his teachers were Remigio Renzi for organ, Alessandro Bustini and Giovanni Sgambati for piano, and Cesare De Sanctis for composition. He was graduated with honors in 1905 and became Renzi's assistant as organist at St. Peter's Basilica in Rome.

Yon soon began to play recitals in various cities in Europe and the United States. In 1907, following the example of his elder brother, S. Constantino Yon—also an organist—he emigrated to New York City. For the next two decades—save for an interlude (1919–21) back in Rome as assistant organist at the Cappella Giulia in St. Peter's—Yon was organist and choir director of the (Roman Catholic) Church of St. Francis Xavier in New York. He became a United States citizen in 1921. Six years later he was appointed organist at St. Patrick's Cathedral on Fifth Avenue (*American Organist,* May 1927). He later succeeded Jacques C. Ungerer as choir director as well, and remained there until his death.

Pietro Yon was not only a church musician but also a concert organist, composer, conductor, and teacher. He was well known on both sides of the Atlantic as a virtuoso player, and is credited with having introduced the paid-admission organ recital and the completely memorized program to New York (T. Scott Buhrman, *ibid.,* March 1928). His fame naturally brought him talented pupils. To them he was able, in Robert Elmore's words, "to pass on . . . something of his own intense and passionate devotion to every note of music he played." He and his brother, who was organist at the Church of St. Vincent Ferrer, taught in a Carnegie Hall studio. Yon's long list of compositions includes vocal works, among them *The Triumph of St. Patrick* (an oratorio with text by Armando Romano), twenty-one masses, and various motets; a *Concerto Gregoriano* for organ and orchestra; chamber music; many organ pieces; piano pieces; and songs, most with English texts. An instruction book, *Organ Pedal Technic,* was published posthumously in 1944.

Yon's mature career centered around St. Patrick's Cathedral, where he was credited with greatly advancing the cause of music. But his works were also performed elsewhere. *The Triumph of St. Patrick* had its world premiere at Carnegie Hall on Apr. 29, 1934, in a performance attended by Mayor Fiorello La Guardia, former governor Alfred E. Smith [Supp. 3], and the conductor Arturo Toscanini; and Yon played under Walter Damrosch and other secular virtuosi. He was consulted in the design not only of the great Kilgen organ at the cathedral but also of the instrument installed at Carnegie Hall in 1929.

On May 21, 1919, Yon married Francesca Pessagno, who died in 1929. They had one son, Mario Charles. Yon suffered a cerebral stroke in April 1943. He died the following November at the Huntington, Long Island, home of his son's father-in-law. His body, placed in a vault at Gate of Heaven Cemetery, Mount Pleasant, N. Y., for burial in Italy after World War II, remained there a quarter-century later. The war was a personal tragedy for Pietro Yon since the two countries he loved—Italy and the United States—were on opposite sides.

Pietro Yon has been called "strong and aristocratic." Certainly he was a force in his day. Conservative like the church he served all his life, he was not in the Italian avant-garde of composers but allied himself with those who continued to breathe new life into old traditions. He was by virtue of his position and talents the informal dean of Catholic church music for many years. His influence in the United States, however, was doubtless limited by the slow development of musical standards in the Roman Catholic Church and overshadowed by the predominance of Protestant church musicians in the professional world of music. Pietro Yon is remembered, if at all, for a pretty little Christmas song, "Gesù Bambino" (1917), in which he combines his own siciliano tune with a fragment of "Adeste Fideles" ("O Come All Ye Faithful"); the song has been published in many vocal and instrumental arrangements. "Natale in Sicilia" ("Christmas in Sicily," 1912), an organ piece, has also had a more than parochial circulation.

[*N. Y. Times*, Nov. 23, 24, 27, 1943; Sergio Martinotti in *Musik in Geschichte und Gegenwart*, vol. XIV (1968); *Baker's Biog. Dict. of Music and Musicians* (5th ed., 1958); *Enciclopedia della Musica* (1964); Carlo Schmidl, *Dizionario Universale dei Musicisti* (1929); *Who Was Who in America*, vol. II (1950); files of the *Am. Organist* and the *Diapason* (especially tribute by Robert Elmore, Feb. 1, 1944); letters from Edward J. Rivetti, chancel organist at St. Patrick's Cathedral, and from Mrs. S. Constantino Yon, N. Y. City. Vera B. Hammann and Mario C. Yon, *The Heavens Heard Him* (1963), a novel based on the life of Pietro Yon, contains many authentic anecdotes. The *Times* obituary includes a photograph of Yon taken by James Abresch in 1936.]

VERNON GOTWALS

YOST, CASPER SALATHIEL (July 1, 1864–May 30, 1941), newspaper editor, was born in Sedalia, Mo., to George Casper Yost, a saddler and native of Gallatin County, Ill., and Sarah Elizabeth (Morris) Yost of Saugerties, N. Y. He was the seventh of their eight children and fourth among five sons. His mother's family came from Wales. The paternal line went back to Germany, its early emigrants, who arrived about 1725, having become farmers in eastern Pennsylvania. Casper's grandfather, Henry Yost, was a Maryland tanner who developed scruples against slaveholding, freed his bondsmen, and moved to Franklin County, Ill.

Schooled in Lebanon and Richland in rural Missouri, Casper Yost early became a printer's devil and while still a boy was put to setting type at the *Laclede County Leader* in Lebanon. In 1881, at seventeen, he worked briefly as a reporter on the *St. Louis Chronicle*. Intending to become a railroad man, he returned to Richland and learned telegraphy. On May 2, 1883, he married Anna Augusta Parrott; they had three sons: Alfred Clarence, Robert George, and Casper Salathiel II. Yost returned to St. Louis and journalism in 1885 as a reporter for the *Missouri Republican*. Four years later he joined the staff of the *St. Louis Globe-Democrat* and thus began an association of more than a half century.

After news and feature assignments for the daily and Sunday issues, including an assistantship under Joseph B. McCullagh [q.v.], Yost became editor of the editorial page in 1915. His Republican principles were staunchly conservative, and he generally opposed innovative programs such as the New Deal. Yet he could rise above partisanship, as in supporting Wilson's international policies and Franklin D. Roosevelt's proposals to aid Great Britain early in World War II. He viewed liberty as responsibility, not as license. A member of the Christian (Disciples) Church, he was, like his mother before him, deeply religious, a characteristic reflected in his editorship to such an extent that for a time the *Globe-Democrat* called itself "the great religious daily." Yost's front-page editorials for Christmas, Easter, and Thanksgiving were models of their kind, and his 1938 series, "The American Way," was widely distributed in booklet form.

A pioneer in concern for professional standards among newspapermen, Yost led in founding the American Society of Newspaper Editors. An article by Moorfield Storey [q.v.] in the January 1922 *Atlantic Monthly* that was highly critical of the daily press stirred him to carry out an idea he had already entertained. Yost drew up a constitution and then, on Apr. 25 of that year, assembled a nucleus of metropolitan editors to whom he presented the case for a national organization "for the consideration of their common problems and the promotion of their professional ideals." Agreeing readily, his colleagues elected him the society's first president. He was reelected annually until 1926, when he called for a new president, but remained a director. He presided over the drafting of the A.S.N.E.'s first "Code of Ethics" and sought further to develop the professional status of editors by writing *The Principles of Journalism* (1924). A historian of the press (Emery, p. 716) described Yost's book as a "constructive discussion" that "counter-balanced" the press exposés of the day.

The new organization in 1924 became involved in a bitter dispute over whether to expel Frederick G. Bonfils [Supp. 1], editor of the *Denver Post,* for evident blackmail in connection with the Teapot Dome oil scandals. Although Willis J. Abbot [Supp. 1] and others favored expulsion, Yost took a strong stand against turning the society into an enforcement agency. As he put the issue some years later: "Without exception we condemn censorship in any form. How then can we consistently endeavor to set up a censorship of our own?" On another matter, he anticipated a need as well as a later development when he appeared before the American Bar Association in 1924 to ask for cooperation between the press and the courts in the administration of justice.

A prolific writer, Yost produced several books that reflected his varied interests: *The Making of a Successful Husband* (1907), *The World War* (1919), *The Quest of God: A Journalist's View of the Bases of Religious Faith* (1929), *The Religious Motive in the Colonization of America* (1935), and *The Carpenter of Nazareth: A Study of Jesus in the Light of His Environment and Background* (1938). In *Patience Worth: A Psychic Mystery* (1916) Yost gave his support to Mrs. John H. (Pearl Lenore Pollard) Curran of St. Louis, who had issued a stream of novels, plays, poems, and allegories which she said came to her by spirit communication via the Ouija board from a seventeenth-century English girl named Patience Worth. Undisturbed by a long controversy as to authenticity, Yost helped prepare Patience Worth materials for publication and, to verify the transmitted description, even visited the English town in which Mrs. Curran claimed the girl had lived. William Marion Reedy [*q.v.*], editor of the St. Louis weekly *Reedy's Mirror,* though at first denunciatory, joined Yost in sympathetic attention. Sixty years later the riddle was still unsolved.

Yost was slight, slender, soft-spoken, and scholarly looking, with a close-clipped moustache that grew white. He was amused when dubbed "Lavender and Old Lace." As others took up the typewriter, he continued his flow of copy in pen-and-ink longhand. Golf was his recreational sport. He was active in civic and literary groups and served in state and national offices of the Sons of the American Revolution. Survived by his wife and two sons, he died of a coronary thrombosis in St. Louis and was buried in Oak Grove Cemetery. Four colleges had granted him honorary degrees, and in 1932 the University of Missouri awarded him its medal for "distinguished service to journalism."

[*Who Was Who in America*, vol. I (1942); Jim A. Hart, *A Hist. of the St. Louis Globe-Democrat* (1961); Charles C. Clayton, *Little Mack* (1969); Frank L. Mott, *Am. Journalism* (1941); Edwin Emery, *The Press and America* (2nd ed., 1962); *Centennial Hist. of Mo.*, vol. V (1921); Irving Litvak, *Singer in the Shadows: The Strange Story of Patience Worth* (1972); Am. Soc. of Newspaper Editors, *Bull.,* June 4, 1941, Supp., and July 1968; *Editor & Publisher,* June 7, 1941; newspapers generally at time of death, especially *St. Louis Globe-Democrat* and *St. Louis Post-Dispatch,* and on the occasion of Yost's fiftieth anniversary at the *Globe-Democrat;* John S. Knight, "An Editor's Notebook," *Phila. Inquirer* and other Knight newspapers, Apr. 23, 1972; personal recollection. The assistance of Robert Yost, George A. Killenberg, and Roy T. King of St. Louis and Richard K. Rein of Princeton, N. J., is gratefully acknowledged.]

IRVING DILLIARD

YOUNG, ART (Jan. 14, 1866–Dec. 29, 1943), cartoonist, author, and socialist, was registered as Henry Arthur in the family Bible, recorded Arthur Henry elsewhere, but called Art throughout life. He was born in Stephenson County, Ill., near Orangeville, on a farm that had been the birthplace of his father, Daniel Stephen Young, a storekeeper. The Youngs, of English ancestry, had come from northern New York; Art's Pennsylvania Dutch mother, Amanda Wagner, was a descendant of German Lutheran emigrants from the Palatinate. She was a Methodist, his father something of a freethinker. Art was third among four children and second of three boys. When he was a year old, the family moved to nearby Monroe, Wis., where he grew up on the homestead farm, at the district school, in the Young general store, and around the courthouse square, whose leading lights he caricatured in schoolboy sketches. While working as a photographer's helper, he sold to *Judge* for $7 a comic boy-and-dog drawing that poked fun at "literary Bostonese."

Emboldened by this success, at the age of eighteen he went to Chicago, enrolled in the Academy of Design, and began to support himself as a free-lance illustrator. He published his first cartoon in 1884 in a grocers' magazine, the *Nimble Nickel*. That year he commenced a series of connections as staff artist with Chicago newspapers. After short hitches on the *Evening Mail*, the *Daily News*, and the *Tribune*, during which his coverage ranged from disasters to celebrities, he moved on to New York City in 1888 to enroll at the Art Students League. The next year he tackled Paris and the Académie Julian, only to be stricken in six months by pleurisy and an operation that nearly cost his life. Following a long convalescence in Monroe, in 1892 he signed up to draw daily political cartoons on the *Chicago Inter Ocean* for $50 a week.

"A Republican without knowing why," Young pictured the "dangers" in low tariffs and drew cartoons violently critical of Gov. John P. Altgeld [*q.v.*], for which he was thoroughly ashamed later. With the friendly encouragement of Thomas Nast [*q.v.*], then briefly connected with the paper, he also participated in the *Inter Ocean's* colored Sunday supplement launched in 1892. Young was married on Jan. 1, 1895, to a "hometown girl," Elizabeth North. They had two sons, North and Donald Minot, and separated after eight years. "I am an artist," Young explained, "and the duties and courtesies of married life are too much for me." In 1896 he served briefly as cartoonist for the *Times* in Denver, but it was long enough for him to begin questioning the quality of economic justice, thanks largely to the sermons of a Denver minister and Christian Socialist, Myron Reed, and lectures by the British labor leader Keir Hardie.

Foreseeing his future in New York, Young moved to Washington Square and prepared comic drawings for *Judge, Life,* and *Puck*. At the invitation of Arthur Brisbane [Supp. 2], he drew cartoon illustrations for editorials in Hearst's *Evening Journal* and *Sunday American*. He volunteered his talents in 1902 for the reelection campaign of Gov. Robert M. La Follette of Wisconsin [*q.v.*]. As he approached forty, Young undertook serious debate of public issues at Cooper Union, came under the influence of the muckraking journalists, and steeped himself in radical literature. His new turn was illustrated by a double-page drawing for *Life* in 1907, "This World of Creepers," wherein a cringing horde crawled under a forbidding sky, "afraid to stand up and call their souls their own."

Young now refused to draw cartoons whose ideas he did not support and by 1910 concluded that he belonged in the socialist "war on capitalism." He was a frequent contributor to the *Masses,* beginning with its first issue in January 1911. Exulting in his new freedom, Young militantly hurled "pictorial shafts" at the "symbols of the system—financiers, politicians, editors." The most poignant of his *Masses* drawings depicted two slum children gazing into the night sky, the boy saying: "Chee, Annie, look at de stars—thick as bed-bugs!" For much of this period, Young was also Washington correspondent (1912–17) for *Metropolitan* magazine, on whose behalf he interviewed and drew caricatures of notables. These *Metropolitan* assignments also included illustrating articles by Walter Lippmann. His political cartoons in the election year of 1916 were syndicated by the Newspaper Enterprise Association to more than 200 dailies.

Young strove for a clear, uncluttered style, stripped of nonessentials. A foremost critic (Murrell, pp. 172–73), reviewing his "concise, richly expressive drawings in both . . . political and homely satire," also credited him with "great ability in a purely humorous vein." Dealing with the simple foibles of the American folk, Young delineated them "at home and in the Big Town; never overdrawn, never grotesque, but always with a kindly sympathetic humor."

His *Masses* cartoons were twice involved in prosecutions brought by institutions he lampooned. In November 1913 he was indicted, along with Max Eastman, editor of the *Masses,* on a charge of criminal libel filed by the Associated Press. The offending cartoon, "Poisoned at the Source," showed a man personifying the Associated Press pouring into a reservoir labeled "The News" the dark contents of bottles of "Lies, Suppressed Facts, Prejudice, Slander, and Hatred of Labor Organizations." The case was dropped after a year. In April 1918 Young, with several colleagues, was charged with "conspiracy to obstruct enlistment." A cited cartoon, "Having Their Fling," presented an editor, capitalist, politician, and minister doing a wild dance before a war-munitions orchestra led by Satan. In the widely reported testimony, Young was asked for his motive in drawing antiwar cartoons. "For the public good," he replied. The defendants were tried twice and released because the juries disagreed.

When the *Masses* was suppressed in 1918, Young joined in establishing the *Liberator*, to which he contributed steadily. Representative of his *Liberator* cartoons was one that burlesqued the judicial invalidation of the 1918 Child Labor Act by showing an overstuffed, cigar-smoking boss leading a crowd of juvenile workers in a factory yard: "Now, children, all together, three cheers for the Supreme Court." From 1919 to

1921 he enjoyed the tribulations as well as satisfactions of publishing his own *Good Morning*, a weekly of art and comment. During the early 1930's he contributed occasional cartoons and some prose to the *New Yorker*.

Writing came harder than drawing, yet Young wrote with grace, spirit, humor, and seeming ease. His first book, *Hades up to Date* (1892), self-illustrated as were all the others, appeared in Chicago when he was twenty-six. Other titles were: *Author's Readings* (1897), *Through Hell with Hiprah Hunt* (1901), *Trees at Night* (1927), and *Thomas Rowlandson* (1938). *Art Young's Inferno* (1934) climaxed a long fascination with portrayals by Doré and others of the Hades of "Homer, Virgil, Dante, Milton and the Hell-fire preachers." In *On My Way* (1928), a "rambling record" in diary form, he looked with mixed serenity and uneasiness toward the age of sixty. John N. Beffel edited the autobiographical *Art Young: His Life and Times* (1939), a delightful melange of recollections, opinions, and protests. A harvest of his drawings, *The Best of Art Young*, appeared in 1936.

Foe of sweatshops and firetrap tenements, Young also opposed racial segregation and discrimination against women. When reforms came too slowly he tried running for office, as Socialist candidate for the New York assembly in 1913 and for the state senate in 1918. His finances were frequently precarious, and at times friends came to his aid. Rotund and rumpled, with wispy hair, a "light comedy" nose, and a walking stick, he was a familiar figure in Greenwich Village, his home for twenty years. He also had a studio-gallery on Chestnut Ridge outside Bethel, Conn., where a stream of visitors enjoyed his warm hospitality. Young died of a heart attack in his apartment at the Irving Hotel on Gramercy Park, Manhattan, as he neared the age of seventy-eight. A memorial service was conducted by the Rev. John Haynes Holmes at the Community Church. As he had requested, he was cremated and the ashes deposited in the "good earth" at Bethel. Reflecting his interest in the Russian Revolution, half of the donated memorial fund was assigned for Soviet artists.

The *New York Times* (Dec. 31, 1943), saluting Art Young as "a lovable soul," found a paradox in his participation in mass movements since he was "as individualistic as a Vermont hill farmer." Floyd Dell, a *Masses* colleague, attributed Young's greatness to the fact that "his love of humanity is given enough scope to balance his scorn for our failures and follies." In the judgment of a historian, Young demonstrated that "social satire can be mordant without becoming either sour or cantankerous" (Aaron, p. 104). Frank Jewett Mather, Jr., professor of art at Princeton, spoke for many when he called Art Young "easily our greatest caricaturist."

[In addition to the autobiographical writings cited above, see: *Who Was Who in America*, vol. II (1950); *Current Biog.*, 1940; William Murrell, *A Hist. of Am. Graphic Humor, 1865–1938* (1938); Stephen Hess and Milton Kaplan, *The Ungentlemanly Art: A Hist. of Am. Political Cartoons* (1968); Gil Wilson, ed., *Letters of William Allen White and a Young Man* (1948); Willis Birchman, "Art Young," *Faces and Facts* (1937); Daniel Aaron, "Good Morning and Art Young: An Introduction and Appraisal," *Labor Hist.*, Winter 1969; *Art Digest*, Jan. 15, 1934; *New Republic*, Jan. 9, 1929; *New Yorker*, Mar. 2, 1935; *Time*, Dec. 11, 1939; "Art Young Gives His Credo," *Daily Worker* (N. Y.), June 18, 1942; *New Masses*, Feb. 1, 1944 (memorial issue); newspapers and magazines generally at the time of death, especially *N. Y. Times* and *N. Y. Herald Tribune*. The valuable assistance of Walt Partymiller, York, Pa., is gratefully acknowledged. Collections of Young's original cartoons and drawings are at the N. Y. Public Lib., Phila. Free Lib., and the Argosy Gallery, N. Y. City. *The Best of Art Young* has as its frontispiece an excellent photograph of Young in his later years by Frederick Hier. A caricature portrait by José Clemente Orozco is reproduced in *Art Young's Inferno*.]

IRVING DILLIARD

YOUNG, HUGH HAMPTON (Sept. 18, 1870–Aug. 23, 1945), urologist, was born in San Antonio, Texas, the only child of William Hugh Young, a lawyer and real estate developer, and Frances Michie (Kemper) Young. His parents were descended from colonial families of Virginia, his father's forebear, Hugh Young, having come there from Ulster, Ireland, in 1741. Young's father and his paternal grandfather, Hugh Franklin Young, who had settled in Texas, fought with the Confederacy during the Civil War, both rising to the rank of brigadier general.

Hugh Hampton Young attended public schools and, beginning at the age of fifteen, a succession of private schools: San Antonio Academy, the Aspinhill School, and Staunton Academy in Virginia. After a summer's work as surveyor with a group of engineers, he entered, in 1890, the University of Virginia, where he received both the A.B. and A.M. degrees in 1893 and the M.D. degree in 1894. He spent a year in graduate study at the Johns Hopkins Hospital and a summer as pathologist and bacteriologist at the Thomas Wilson Sanitarium and then became an intern on the surgical staff of the Johns Hopkins Hospital, under William S. Halsted [*q.v.*]. Young had planned a career in general surgery, but Halsted determined his future by securing his appointment in 1897 as head of the genito-urinary dispensary at the hospital. The following year he became instructor in genito-urinary diseases and surgery at the Johns Hopkins Medical School. Successive promotions brought him in 1914 to the post of clinical professor of urology, and he was professor of urology from 1932 until his retirement in 1942. Beginning in 1898, he also carried on a private practice in Baltimore.

Young was an eminent pioneer in the development of modern urology, particularly in the diagnosis and surgical treatment of prostatic hypertrophy. In 1903 he devised a radical operation for total removal of the cancerous prostate gland. He had remarkable mechanical ingenuity, designed improved versions of the cystoscope and other instruments, and invented a number of new instruments and novel surgical procedures for treating urogenital diseases. One of the most important of his devices was an instrument known as the Young Punch; used to excise the prostate gland in cases of urinary obstruction, it was the prototype of instruments that have come into general use. He also made pioneer studies in the diagnosis and treatment of hermaphroditism.

Young was a brilliant teacher who demanded work of the highest quality from his interns and residents, took a warm interest in furthering their careers, and, when necessary, gave them financial aid. He trained large numbers of gifted young surgeons who themselves contributed to the field of urology. His skill as a surgeon brought him patients from throughout the United States, including many prominent persons. In 1912 he performed a successful operation on the celebrated James Buchanan ("Diamond Jim") Brady, who in gratitude donated funds for the establishment of the James Buchanan Brady Urological Institute at the Johns Hopkins Hospital. With Young as director, it accepted its first patients in January 1915.

In 1917, when the United States entered World War I, Young went to France with the Army Medical Corps to organize a urological service, which under his direction significantly lowered the incidence of venereal disease among the troops. His war experiences interested him in the use of various dye compounds as antiseptic agents, and after his discharge in 1919, with the rank of colonel, he returned to the Brady Institute, where he and his associates developed the drug they named "mercurochrome," which he used as an intravenous antiseptic. Young also pioneered in the use of sulfanilamide and other modern drugs in the treatment of venereal disease. Possessing abundant energy, powers of concentration, and organizing skill, Young managed to combine a teaching career and a busy private practice with extensive publication. He founded the *Journal of Urology* in 1917 and served as its editor until his death. He published more than 350 technical

papers, and his book, *Young's Practice of Urology* (2 vols., 1926), written with collaborators, became a classic. He was a member of many professional organizations, including the American Association of Genito-Urinary Surgeons (president, 1909), the American Urological Association (president, 1909), and the International Association of Urology (president, 1927).

Young was a man of great personal charm, with an audacious wit. He took an active role in state and civic affairs. In 1903, working through an influential politician who had been his patient, he secured passage by the Maryland legislature of laws for the control of tuberculosis that set a precedent followed by other states. He served as chairman of the Maryland State Lunacy Commission (later the Board of Mental Hygiene) from its formation in 1908. An enthusiastic flyer, he was appointed chairman of the Maryland State Aviation Commission in 1929 by Gov. Albert C. Ritchie. Young was a close friend of Ritchie and an active Democrat, and at the party's 1932 convention he was a leader in the movement to win Ritchie the presidential nomination. In his home city, Young served as vice-president of the Baltimore Museum of Art and president of the Baltimore Opera Club and of the Lyric Theatre. He was an Episcopalian in religion.

On June 4, 1901, Young married Bessy Mason Colston of Catonsville, Md. Their four children were Frances Kemper, Frederick Colston, Helen Hampton, and Elizabeth Campbell. Young died of a coronary occlusion in the Brady Institute of the Johns Hopkins Hospital shortly before his seventy-fifth birthday. He was buried in Druid Ridge Cemetery, Pikesville, Md.

[The best source on Young is his own *Hugh Young: A Surgeon's Autobiog.* (1940). See also "The Clinic of Dr. Hugh Hampton Young," *British Jour. of Surgery*, IX (1921), 272–80; and obituaries or memoirs in: *Jour. of Urology*, Feb. 1947; Alexander Blain Hospital (Detroit), *Bull.*, Feb. 1948; *Science*, Oct. 26, 1945; and *Jour. Am. Medic. Assoc.*, Sept. 1, 1945. Death record from Baltimore City Health Dept. One of the best portraits of Young is in the Baltimore Museum of Art.]

WILLARD E. GOODWIN

YOUNG, KARL (Nov. 2, 1879–Nov. 17, 1943), medievalist and professor of English, was born in Clinton, Iowa, the third son and last of four children of George Billings Young and Frances Eliza (Hinman) Young. His parents were of New England descent. His paternal grandfather, George Drummond Young, a graduate of Princeton Theological Seminary, had served as a Presbyterian minister in Maryland, Ohio, and Iowa. His father, a graduate of Oberlin College, became a lawyer and later a county and then a circuit court judge. After the father's death in 1893, Young was taken by his mother to her former home, Ypsilanti, Mich., where he attended the local high school and received excellent training in the classics. Christened Carl Hinman Young, he changed the spelling of his first name before entering the University of Michigan, in 1897, and later dropped his middle name.

Early in life Young had been attracted to literature and had determined on a scholarly career. His mother's death, in his freshman year, left him without family obligations, and after receiving the A.B. in 1901 he began graduate work in English at Harvard. There his courses with George Pierce Baker [Supp. 1] first stimulated his interest in the drama of the medieval church. After receiving the A.M. in 1902, he spent two years as instructor in English at the United States Naval Academy. Himself a Presbyterian, while in Annapolis he continued his research by studying the liturgy and the Roman Rite under the guidance of a Catholic priest of the Redemptorist Order, Father James Barron. Each summer he went abroad to consult medieval material in the European libraries, and he spent some time in liturgical studies with French Benedictine monks on the Isle of Wight.

Returning to Harvard for work with George Lyman Kittredge [Supp. 3], Young received his Ph.D. in 1907 with a thesis on the literary origins of Chaucer's *Troilus,* published in England (1908) by the Chaucer Society as *The Origin and Development of the Story of Troilus and Criseyde.* He spent the year 1907–08 on a traveling fellowship in such manuscript centers as Paris, Rome, and Montecassino, and then returned to become assistant professor of English at the University of Wisconsin. On Aug. 10, 1911, he married Frances Campbell Berkeley of Morgantown, W. Va., an instructor in the same department. Their two sons were George Berkeley and Karl.

Young left Wisconsin in 1923 to become professor of English, and later (1938) Sterling Professor, at Yale University. His long work on medieval drama was now nearing fruition: he had searched out liturgical manuscripts in most of the countries of Western Europe, and had written some twenty monographs on the subject, presenting many new texts. In 1927–28 he went on leave to London with all his materials and there proceeded to assemble a definitive corpus of the texts, with accompanying exposition, interpretation, and evaluation. Young had intended to pay the printing costs from his own pocket, but through the intervention of John M. Manly

[Supp. 2] the Clarendon Press undertook to publish the resulting two-volume work, *The Drama of the Medieval Church* (1933), which for the first time made possible broad, intelligent study in this field.

Young next returned to his early interest in Chaucer, particularly a study of his literary sources as a measure of the extent of Chaucer's learning. During visits to England, Young examined and took notes on hundreds of manuscripts to which Chaucer had or might have had access: dictionaries, schoolbooks, classical and medieval texts. Many of these he had photocopied. Finding that common fourteenth-century schoolbooks, such as the *Liber Catonianus,* contained selections from the works of many Latin authors, Young concluded that Chaucer probably used such compilations and was not himself a scholar. Similarly, a collection of antifeminist tracts by Walter Map, Theophrastus, and St. Jerome, which seems to have been in common circulation at such universities as Oxford, could have provided the material Chaucer used in the Wife of Bath's Prologue. A number of articles by Young and dissertations by his students were based on these materials he collected, and their use has continued.

Young would bend over his microfilm reader into the small hours. As director of graduate studies in English at Yale he was tireless in urging and helping students to excel, always stressing the importance of their knowing other languages, particularly Latin and Greek. Where teaching and scholarly administration were concerned, as his fellow medievalist John S. P. Tatlock has written, Young always "stood out for the essentials. . . . He set his face like a flint against watering down, and held others to the same exactingness." Yet "his candor, his brilliance, his spontaneous wit, his valuing of the distinguished, so combined with his social gifts and ability to handle things lightly that they did not clash with his tolerance, his enduring loyalties, and his generous appreciations." His chief recreation was music, and his friends knew him as a skilled pianist.

Young received honorary degrees from the University of Wisconsin (1934) and the University of Michigan (1937). He served as president of the Modern Language Association of America (1940–41), was a fellow of the Mediaeval Academy of America (latterly president of the fellows) and of the Royal Society of Literature, and in 1941 received the Gollancz Memorial Prize from the British Academy. He died in New Haven, Conn., of a heart attack, a few days after his sixty-fourth birthday, and was buried in the family plot in Springdale Cemetery, Clinton, Iowa.

[*A Memoir of Karl Young* (privately printed, 1946) includes essays by J. S. P. Tatlock, Frances Berkeley Young, Frank Sullivan, and Robert A. Pratt, and a bibliography of Young's publications. See also George Sherburn in Am. Council of Learned Societies, *Bull.*, Dec. 1944. On Young's father, see *The Hist. of Clinton County, Iowa* (1879) and P. B. Wolfe, ed., *Wolfe's Hist. of Clinton County, Iowa* (2 vols., 1911).]

Robert A. Pratt

INDEX GUIDE
TO THE SUPPLEMENTS

INDEX GUIDE

TO THE SUPPLEMENTS

Index Guide to the Supplements

Index Guide to the Supplements

Index Guide to the Supplements

Index Guide to the Supplements

Index Guide to the Supplements

Index Guide to the Supplements

Index Guide to the Supplements

Index Guide to the Supplements

Index Guide to the Supplements

Index Guide to the Supplements

Index Guide to the Supplements

Index Guide to the Supplements

Index Guide to the Supplements

Index Guide to the Supplements

Index Guide to the Supplements

Index Guide to the Supplements

Index Guide to the Supplements

Index Guide to the Supplements

Index Guide to the Supplements

Index Guide to the Supplements